# CAMPERSTOP EUROPE 2019

## motorhome stopovers in

| | |
|---|---|
| Albania | Luxembourg |
| Austria | Montenegro |
| Belgium | Netherlands |
| Bosnia-Herzegovina | Norway |
| Croatia | Poland |
| Czech Republic | Portugal |
| Denmark | Romania |
| Finland | Slovakia |
| France | Slovenia |
| Germany | Spain |
| Greece | Sweden |
| Hungary | Switzerland |
| Ireland | United Kingdom |
| Italy | |

Publisher - Herausgeber - Éditeur - Editore

Facile Media

### Reliable information

*Every summer, 50 teams of Facile Media drive all across Europe to inspect the motorhome stopovers. The inspections take place according to predefined guidelines. The inspections by these specially trained motorhome enthusiasts have made it possible to make the information in the guide as up-to-date as possible. More than 10,750 motorhome stopovers and 8,311 illustrative photos are the result.*

### Unique way to find the motorhome sites

*The motorhome stopovers can be easily located on the 39 maps. Below each map, you'll find a location name index with map referral and a page number where the location can be found in the guide. In addition, the type of motorhome stopover is indicated. In a glance, you'll be able to see whether it is the type of stopover you had in mind. In order to provide you with additional information, the location is described extensively on the relevant page, usually with a picture.*

### GPS-data sets on your navigation system

*In addition to this guide, you can order datasets online, which you can download. The sets can be uploaded to the most common navigation systems. This allows you to drive to the motorhome stopovers listed in this guide without any effort. More information about this is available on page 7.*

**Follow us on Facebook for the latest news:**
**facebook.com/CamperstopEurope**

For more information: camperstop.com/app

# Preface

COLOPHON

A publication of:

Facile Media b.v., Tilburg
Kraaivenstraat 25-49A
NL-5048 AB Tilburg
Tel: +31 13 20 45 091
E-mail: info@camperstop.com
Internet: camperstop.com

Chief editors
Anne van den Dobbelsteen
Elise van den Dobbelsteen

The draft of this version is saved
in October 2018

Comments or suggestions can
be sent to the publisher:

Facile Media
Kraaivenstraat 25-49A
NL-5048 AB Tilburg
E-mail: info@camperstop.com
Tel.: +31 13 20 45 091

ISBN 978-90-76080-58-1

Copyright 2018 Facile Media

When I compiled the very first motorhome guide in 1996, I couldn't have imagined that in 2018 the number of motorhome stopovers would have increased so explosively. As a result, that little 'guide' has become a full-fledged comprehensive guide with simple camperstops to luxury motorhome parks throughout Europe.

In the early years the camperstops were described as: 'behind the church', 'at the cemetery', 'in the village second street to the left'. They also weren't real motorhome stopovers like the ones we know nowadays. We didn't know GPS coordinates yet, let alone a mobile app to navigate you to the right place with a few clicks. A lot has changed, but in my opinion in a positive way for us motorhome owners.

After all these years it is time to pass on the baton. My daughter Elise will be the driving force behind Facile Media from this year. She will be the editor of the motorhome guides and the Camperstop-App. Elise will monitor the quality of the data and give a new twist to a number of issues.

In the coming years I will still stay closely involved with the company, but hope to have more time for my passion: motorhoming!

I would like to hand you over to Elise:
Thank you, I will introduce myself briefly. I have worked within the company for several years, first during my studies and afterwards as a full-time employee. I have come to know the entire company from the background. From now on I will be happy to take over the editing and guarantee the quality that you are used to from us.

With parents like mine, I naturally have been motorhoming from an early age, whether I wanted to or not. Since a few years I myself own a motorhome and in my little spare time I like to go out and explore the beautiful places in Europe with my partner.

This year our big trip went to Denmark, a country with a lot of history and certainly a up-and-coming motorhoming country. In three weeks we toured through Jutland. Where in the past you used to be mainly restricted to camp sites, you are now welcome at many marinas. So as not to miss anything in Denmark, we largely followed the Marguerite route, in order to drive past all tourist attractions.

From large cities to small picturesque villages in the countryside, Denmark is a versatile country with something for everyone. It has many historic sites, we visited the Koldinghus, the Spøttrup Borg and the Lindholm Høje. And for children there is plenty to do like Legoland, Fårup Sommerland and the Viking center in Ribe. And don't forget, miles of long beaches and many nature reserves. The highlight is the northernmost point, Grenen in Skagen. A special place where the North Sea and the Baltic come together and that is well worth a visit.

I hope that this guide will provide you with inspiration for beautiful motorhome trips. Nearby or far away, short or long, it does not matter as long as you enjoy the freedom.

*Anne & Elise
van den Dobbelsteen
Chief editors*

# Table of content

### Maps

On pages 12-13 the countries are divided into sections. The number in each box is the number of the map. On the map the red dots indicate the location of the town. Next to each map an index is published with the places on maps. The index shows the name, type of stopover, map code and page number of each location. This way the description of the motorhome stopover can be found quickly and easy.

### Type of camperstop

**MOTORHOME PARK**
This symbol indicates a motorhome park, a park designed for motorhomes with a range of facilities.

**OFFICIAL MOTORHOME STOPOVER**
This symbol indicates an area suitable for overnight parking.

**OVERNIGHT PARKING TOLERATED**
In some countries tolerated places are mentioned. This means that it is officially prohibited but is being tolerated by local authorities. Therefore the local or national situation may change at any time. Nevertheless these places are listed because they were frequently being used by motorhomes at the time of writing.

**OVERNIGHT STAY IN HARBOUR/MARINA**
Motorhome stopover in or near harbour or marina, often with a beautiful view.

**OVERNIGHT STAY AT FARM/VINEYARD**
Farms and vineyards that welcome motorhomes, you may be encouraged to sample and buy their fare.

**OVERNIGHT STAY AT RESTAURANT**
Motorhomes are allowed to stopover on the car park of a hotel, restaurant or bar. You should expect to dine or drink in the bar. Some restaurants insist on you having dinner. Sometimes a nominal charge is asked for the overnight stay.

**OVERNIGHT STAY AT SPA**
A growing number of spas and thermal baths offer stopovers to motorhomes.

**OVERNIGHT STAY AT ZOO/MUSEUM/ AMUSEMENT PARK**
Motorhomes are allowed to stopover on the car park of a zoo, museum or amusement park. Entrance is not always obligated.

**OVERNIGHT STAY AT COMPANY/ENTERPRISE**
Overnight stay, mostly inside the gates, at companies/enterprises.

**OVERNIGHT STAY OUTSIDE THE CAMPSITE**
Motorhomes are allowed to stopover on the parking place outside the gate of a campsite.

**MOTORHOME PITCHES ON CAMPSITE**
Campsite with special pitches for motorhomes.

**CAMPSITE**
Overnight stay on a campsite.

**CAR-PARK**
Motorhome parking bays, suitable for daytime use only. Often in large cities and/or tourist towns, charges may apply.

### Searching in a region

In the table of contents, at the beginning of the guide, one can search a region in preferred country. On the page of the region a map indicates the different departments/provinces with a reference to the pages.

### Searching for a town

Places identified in this guide can be found under the name of the local town in the alphabetical index at the back. Use the index like a dictionary to look for specific towns, the facilities offered, map references and relevant page numbers.

### Country specific rules

When travelling you have to take into account that each country has its own rules and regulations. These rules are written on the first page of each countries section.

### Advise

It is recommended not to wait to long to look for an overnight stop. It could be that chosen motorhome stopover is already full and you have to go looking for an alternative.

### Blue bar

**Type of camperstop**
**Name of town** with particularities like :

town worth visiting ⛲ touristic town 🛒 shopping town
**Map code**: 36B1, map 36 (page 80) grid B1

### Contact information Camperstop

**Name - Address** of the camperstop
**GPS coordinates** indicated in decimal degrees

⬆ Signposted on the spot

➡ Signposted in town

✗ No signs to indicate the motorhome stopover

### Payment

Collector parking fee

Parking meter

Reception/office on the spot

Payment only with a credit/debit card

Payment with cash and credit/debit card

### Description of the Camperstop

Camperstop 'Reisemobilstellplatz Wien', with 167 pitches on grass and gravel, is situated in an urban area and is open all year round. The camperstop is situated 12 kilometers from the city centre; 4 kilometers from the motorway; at 30 meters there is a restaurant and shops; the bus and metro stops are 50-150 meters; 100 meters distance to a cycle route.

**167 € 19 :** 167 pitches, the price is € 19 per night, all year.

**included :** all service included except electricity.

**(167x)€ 2/24h :** 167 power connections, € 2 per 24 hours.

### Motorhome service facilities

| | | | |
|---|---|---|---|
| 🚰 | drinking water | WC | toilets |
| | grey water dump | | showers |
| Ch | chemical toilet disposal point | | washing machine/ dryer (price/price) on the spot |
| | charging battery | | |
| | power connection available | | wifi access point |
| | | | animals not allowed |

# GPS-convenience

### Downloading GPS-coordinates

Downloads of the gps-coordinates for the motorhome stopovers listed in this guide are available from www.camperstop.com. The files are suitable for most navigation systems. The data that appears on the screen gives the town name and page number in this guide so you can look up the details of the facilities very easily.

The downloadable files list the stopovers and most of the other facilities mentioned in the guide. Therefore it could be a stopover with or without service facilities, a place with service facilities only, but also a tourist information office or a campsite.

You can easily check for your nearest stopover, the navigation system will list the stopovers by distance. Use the guide to see what facilities are available. Once a choice has been made you can navigate to there without a problem.

The costs for downloading are € 3.25 per country/dataset. The Netherlands/Belgium/Luxembourg are sold as one country, also Austria/Switzerland and Spain/Portugal are treated the same.

Full downloading instructions are found on at camperstop.com. There are different downloads of several navigation systems.

# Handy information

### Database camperstops from 1996
For more than 22 years the data of motorhome stopovers have been accurately recorded in the database for motorhome stopovers. This is updated every day; adjustments, pictures, new camperstops and places that have unfortunately been closed. Would you like to help keeping the data as up-to-date as possible, please send us your information: info@camperstop.com.

### This guide in 5 languages
Did you know that this guide is available for European motorhomers in 5 languages, namely: German, Italian, Dutch, French and English.

### Inspection camperstops
Facile Media trains people to inspect motorhome stopovers. Every year about 50 couples travel through Europa to inspect the camperstops.

### Camperstop app
The latest available data of the camperstops can be found in the Camperstop-App. The app can be downloaded from the Android and Apple stores. The full version of the app, selling price € 5,49/± £4.79, is free with the code in this guide (page 9) and is valid for 12 months. For more information see: camperstop.com/app.

### Always informed
Register yourself for our newsletter and receive, among others, exclusive benefits, inspiration for your next motorhome trip and much more: camperstop.com/newsletter. You can also follow us on facebook: facebook.com/camperstopeurope.

# Camperstop-App

The Camperstop-App contains all motorhome stopovers from this guide, over 10,750, spread througout the 27 European countries. After purchasing the most up-to-date edition, you can use all functionalities and the complete database of the Camperstop-App for free for one year.

The Camperstop-App (Android and iOs) is suitable for both smartphone and tablet and is very easy to use. With the help of the steps below your next camperstop can quickly be found.

## Clear

Easily search for camperstops near your current location or destination on the handy overview maps or with the search & filter function.

## Detailed information

Based on the detailed information you can easily assess whether the camperstop meets your needs & requirements. All camperstops are shown with the current local weather forecast.

## Reviews

Rate a camperstop on the basis of reviews from other motorhome owners. Have you visited a camperstop? Easily share your experiences with others by writing reviews.

## Offline use

All maps can easily be downloaded per country for offline use. So you don't need internet to use the Camperstop-App.

## Smartphone & Tablet

The Camperstop-App can be fully used on smartphones and tablets! On both Android and iOS devices. The app is made to function correctly on the tablet so lying down and not standing.

# Driving regulations in Europe

Each country has different driving rules. For motorhomes sometimes there are different regulations. Here below an overview with maximum speed limits for motorhomes.

Per country there are also different rules as for warning triangles, security vests or driving with daily lights. Here below this information at a glance.

| | within towns | single carriageway <3,5T | single carriageway >3,5T | expressway <3,5T | expressway >3,5T | motorway <3,5T | motorway >3,5T | compulsory in your vehicle |
|---|---|---|---|---|---|---|---|---|
| **AL** Albania | 40 | 80 | 70 | 90 | 70 | 110 | 80 | triangle, first aid |
| **A** Austria | 50 | 100 | 70 | | | 130 | 80 | triangle, vest, first aid — A10-A12-A13-en A14 : 22-05h max. 110km/h. |
| **B** Belgium | 50 | 70 (Flanders) | 90 (Wallonia) | | | 120 | 90 | triangle, vest, fire extinguisher, first aid |
| **BIH** Bosnia and Herzegovina | 50 | 80 | | 100 | 80 | 130 | 80 | triangle, vest, fire extinguisher, first aid, spare bulbs |
| **CH** Switzerland | 50 | 80 | | 100 | | 120 | 100 | triangle, vest, spare bulbs |
| **CZ** Czech Republic | 50 | 90 | 80 | 90 | 80 | 130 | 80 | triangle, vest, first aid, spare bulbs |
| **D** Germany | 50 | 100 | 80 | 130 | 100 | 130 | 100 | triangle, vest, first aid, spare bulbs — 130km/h is a recommended speed limit. |
| **DK** Denmark | 50 | 80 | 70 | 110 | 80 | 130 | 80 | triangle, vest, fire extinguisher, spare bulbs |
| **ES** Spain | 50 | 80 | | 90 | 80 | 100 | 90 | triangle, vest |
| **FIN** Finland | 50 | 80 | | 100 | 80 | 100 | 80 | triangle, vest, spare bulbs |
| **F** France | 50 | 90 | 80 | 110 | 100 | 130 | 110 | triangle, vest — Speed limits on a dry road. Safety vest also for bicycles. |
| **GB** Great Britain | 30 | 60 | 50 | 70 | 60 | 70 | | 30mph=48km 50mph=80km 60mph=96km 70mph=112km Speed limits in mph. |
| **GR** Greece | 50 | 90 | | 110 | 90 | 130 | 90 | triangle, fire extinguisher, first aid |
| **HR** Croatia | 50 | 90 | 80 | 110 | 80 | 130 | 90 | triangle, vest, first aid, spare bulbs — Set of spare bulbs. |
| **HU** Hungary | 50 | 90 | 70 | 110 | 70 | 130 | 80 | triangle, vest, fire extinguisher, first aid, spare bulbs |

| | within towns | single carriageway | | expressway | | motorway | | compulsory in your vehicle: |
|---|---|---|---|---|---|---|---|---|
| | | <3,5T | >3,5T | <3,5T | >3,5T | <3,5T | >3,5T | |
| (IRL) Ireland | 50 | 80 | | 100 | 80 | 120 | 80 | |
| (I) Italy | 50 | 90 | 80 | 110 | 80 | 130 | 100 | Speed limits on a dry road. * Suburban. |
| (L) Luxemburg | 50 | 90 | 75 | | | 130 | 90 | Speed limits on a dry road. |
| (MNE) Montenegro | 50 | 80 | | 100 | 80 | 100 | 80 | |
| (NL) The Netherlands | 50 | 80 | | 100 | 80 | 130 | 80 | >3,5 ton = motorhome on truck basis. |
| (N) Norway | 50 | 80 | | 90 | 80 | 100 | 80 | |
| (PL) Poland | 50 | 90 | 70 | 120 | 80 | 140 | 80 | |
| (P) Portugal | 50 | 90 | 70 | 100 | 80 | 120 | 100 | |
| (RO) Romania | 50 | 80 | | 90 | 80 | 120 | 110 | |
| (S) Sweden | 50 | 70 | | 100 | 70 | 120 | 80 | |
| (SK) Slovakia | 60 | 90 | | 90 | 80 | 130 | 90 | Set of spare bulbs. |
| (SLO) Slovenia | 50 | 90 | 80 | 100 | 80 | 130 | 80 | |

warning triangle

security vest

fire extinguisher

first aid kit

daily lights

recommended

Information is based on information available in November 2018.

# Overview map

| | | | |
|---|---|---|---|
| Portglenone (UK) | ⚓🅂 | 1C1 | 769 |
| Portrush (UK) | �🅂 | 1C1 | 769 |
| Portumna (IE) | ⚓🅂 | 1B2 | 594 |
| Praa Sands (UK) | 🚢 | 1E3 | 777 |
| Presteigne (UK) | 🚢🅂 | 1F2 | 775 |
| Rake (UK) | 🍴🅂 | 1G3 | 777 |
| Rathdrum (IE) | 🚢 | 1C2 | 594 |
| Rye (UK) | 🍴 | 1H3 | 777 |
| Roosky (IE) | 🚢🅂 | 1C2 | 594 |
| Scarborough (UK) | 👑🅂 | 1G1 | 777 |
| Settle (UK) | 🚢🍴 | 1F1 | 777 |
| Sewerby (UK) | 🍴🅂 | 1G1 | 777 |
| Shrewsbury (UK) | 🍴🅂 | 1F2 | 777 |
| Skipton (UK) | 🚢 | 1G1 | 777 |
| Sneem (IE) | 🚢🍴🅂 | 1B3 | 595 |
| Southampton (UK) | 🚢 | 1G3 | 778 |
| St Austell (UK) | 🚢🅂 | 1E3 | 778 |
| St Ives (UK) | 🍴🅂 | 1G2 | 778 |
| Staple Fitzpaine (UK) | 🚢🅂 | 1F3 | 778 |
| Stoke St Gregory (UK) | 🍴🅂 | 1F3 | 778 |
| Stratford-upon-Avon (UK) | 🚢🍴🅂 | 1G2 | 778 |
| Tallington (UK) | 🍴 | 1G2 | 778 |
| Tarrington (UK) | 🍴🅂 | 1F2 | 778 |
| Templeboy (IE) | 🍴🅂 | 1B1 | 594 |
| Tenby (UK) | 🚢🅂 | 1D3 | 775 |
| Thaxted (UK) | 🚢🅂 | 1G2 | 778 |
| Tintagel (UK) | 🚢🅂 | 1E3 | 778 |
| Torrington (UK) | 🚢 | 1E3 | 778 |
| Welshpool (UK) | 🚢🅂 | 1F2 | 775 |
| Westward Ho! (UK) | 🚢 | 1E3 | 778 |
| Whaplode St Catherines (UK) | 🍴🅂 | 1G2 | 779 |

| | | | |
|---|---|---|---|
| Whitehead (UK) | 🚢🅂 | 1D1 | 769 |
| Winchester (UK) | 🚢 | 1G3 | 779 |
| Yeovil (UK) | 🚢🅂 | 1F3 | 779 |
| York (UK) | 👑🅂 | 1G1 | 779 |

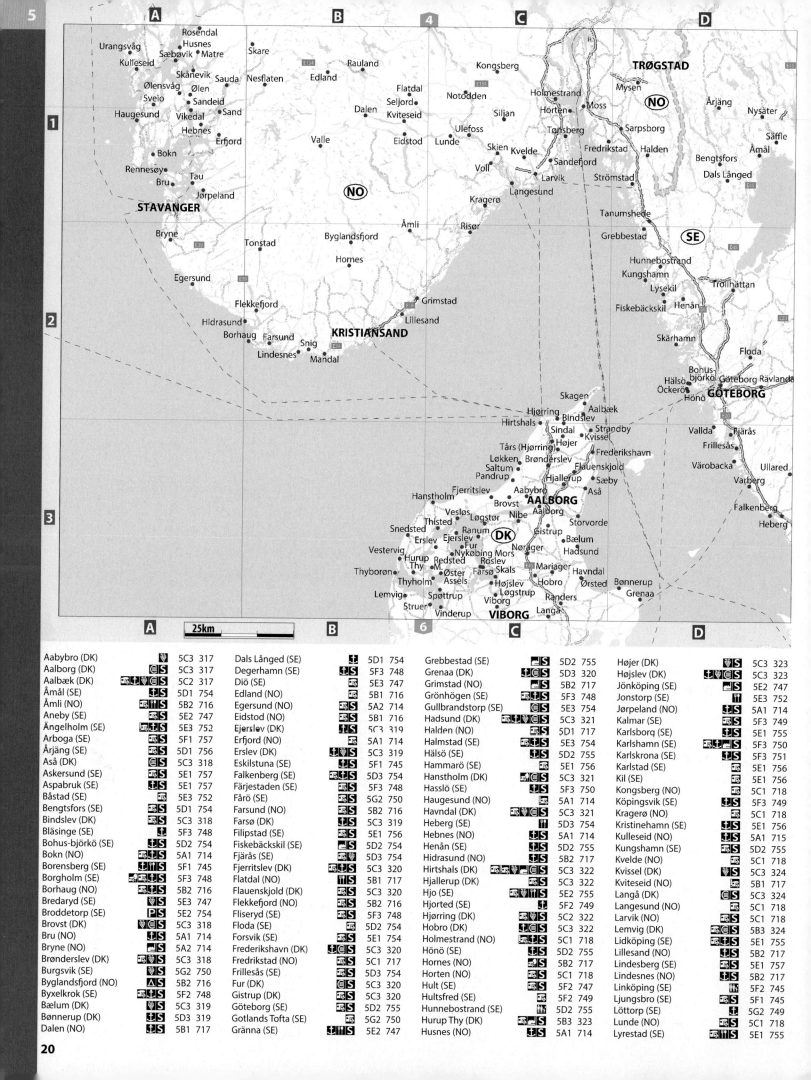

| Place | Grid | Page |
|---|---|---|
| Aabybro (DK) | 5C3 | 317 |
| Aalborg (DK) | 5C3 | 317 |
| Aalbæk (DK) | 5C2 | 317 |
| Åmål (SE) | 5D1 | 754 |
| Åmli (NO) | 5B2 | 716 |
| Aneby (SE) | 5E2 | 747 |
| Ängelholm (SE) | 5E3 | 752 |
| Arboga (SE) | 5F1 | 757 |
| Årjäng (SE) | 5D1 | 756 |
| Aså (DK) | 5C3 | 318 |
| Askersund (SE) | 5E1 | 757 |
| Aspabruk (SE) | 5E1 | 757 |
| Båstad (SE) | 5E3 | 752 |
| Bengtsfors (SE) | 5D1 | 754 |
| Bindslev (DK) | 5C3 | 318 |
| Bläsinge (SE) | 5F3 | 748 |
| Bohus-björkö (SE) | 5D2 | 754 |
| Bokn (NO) | 5A1 | 714 |
| Borensberg (SE) | 5F1 | 745 |
| Borgholm (SE) | 5F3 | 748 |
| Borhaug (NO) | 5B2 | 716 |
| Bredaryd (SE) | 5E3 | 747 |
| Broddetorp (SE) | 5E2 | 754 |
| Brovst (DK) | 5C3 | 318 |
| Bru (NO) | 5A1 | 714 |
| Bryne (NO) | 5A2 | 714 |
| Brønderslev (DK) | 5C3 | 318 |
| Burgsvik (SE) | 5G2 | 750 |
| Byglandsfjord (NO) | 5B2 | 716 |
| Byxelkrok (SE) | 5F2 | 748 |
| Bælum (DK) | 5C3 | 319 |
| Bønnerup (DK) | 5D3 | 319 |
| Dalen (NO) | 5B1 | 717 |
| Dals Långed (SE) | 5D1 | 754 |
| Degerhamn (SE) | 5F3 | 748 |
| Diö (SE) | 5E3 | 747 |
| Edland (NO) | 5B1 | 716 |
| Egersund (NO) | 5A2 | 714 |
| Eidstod (NO) | 5B1 | 716 |
| Ejerslev (DK) | 5C3 | 319 |
| Erfjord (NO) | 5A1 | 714 |
| Erslev (DK) | 5C3 | 319 |
| Eskilstuna (SE) | 5F1 | 745 |
| Falkenberg (SE) | 5D3 | 754 |
| Färjestaden (SE) | 5F3 | 748 |
| Farö (SE) | 5G2 | 750 |
| Farsund (NO) | 5B2 | 716 |
| Farsø (DK) | 5C3 | 319 |
| Filipstad (SE) | 5E1 | 756 |
| Fiskebäckskil (SE) | 5D2 | 754 |
| Fjärås (SE) | 5D3 | 754 |
| Fjerritslev (DK) | 5C3 | 320 |
| Flatdal (NO) | 5B1 | 717 |
| Flauenskjold (DK) | 5C3 | 320 |
| Flekkefjord (NO) | 5B2 | 716 |
| Fliseryd (SE) | 5F3 | 748 |
| Floda (SE) | 5E1 | 754 |
| Forsvik (SE) | 5E1 | 754 |
| Frederikshavn (DK) | 5C3 | 320 |
| Fredrikstad (NO) | 5C1 | 717 |
| Frillesås (SE) | 5D3 | 754 |
| Fur (DK) | 5C3 | 320 |
| Gistrup (DK) | 5C3 | 320 |
| Göteborg (SE) | 5D2 | 755 |
| Gotlands Tofta (SE) | 5G2 | 750 |
| Gränna (SE) | 5E2 | 747 |
| Grebbestad (SE) | 5D2 | 755 |
| Grenaa (DK) | 5D3 | 320 |
| Grimstad (NO) | 5B2 | 717 |
| Grönhögen (SE) | 5F3 | 748 |
| Gullbrandstorp (SE) | 5E3 | 754 |
| Hadsund (DK) | 5C3 | 321 |
| Halden (NO) | 5D1 | 717 |
| Halmstad (SE) | 5E3 | 754 |
| Hälsö (SE) | 5D2 | 755 |
| Hammarö (SE) | 5E1 | 756 |
| Hanstholm (DK) | 5C3 | 321 |
| Hasslö (SE) | 5F3 | 750 |
| Haugesund (NO) | 5A1 | 714 |
| Havndal (DK) | 5C3 | 321 |
| Heberg (SE) | 5D3 | 754 |
| Hebnes (NO) | 5A1 | 714 |
| Henån (SE) | 5D2 | 755 |
| Hidrasund (NO) | 5B2 | 717 |
| Hirtshals (DK) | 5C3 | 322 |
| Hjallerup (DK) | 5C3 | 322 |
| Hjo (SE) | 5E2 | 755 |
| Hobro (DK) | 5C3 | 322 |
| Holmestrand (NO) | 5C1 | 718 |
| Hönö (SE) | 5D2 | 755 |
| Hornes (NO) | 5B2 | 717 |
| Horten (NO) | 5C1 | 718 |
| Hult (SE) | 5F2 | 747 |
| Hultsfred (SE) | 5F2 | 749 |
| Hunnebostrand (SE) | 5D2 | 755 |
| Hurup Thy (DK) | 5B3 | 323 |
| Husnes (NO) | 5A1 | 714 |
| Højer (DK) | 5C3 | 323 |
| Højslev (DK) | 5C3 | 323 |
| Jönköping (SE) | 5E2 | 747 |
| Jonstorp (SE) | 5E3 | 752 |
| Jørpeland (NO) | 5A1 | 714 |
| Kalmar (SE) | 5F3 | 749 |
| Karlsborg (SE) | 5E1 | 755 |
| Karlshamn (SE) | 5F3 | 750 |
| Karlskrona (SE) | 5F3 | 751 |
| Karlstad (SE) | 5E1 | 756 |
| Kil (SE) | 5E1 | 756 |
| Kongsberg (NO) | 5C1 | 718 |
| Köpingsvik (SE) | 5F3 | 749 |
| Kragerø (NO) | 5C1 | 718 |
| Kristinehamn (SE) | 5E1 | 756 |
| Kulleseid (NO) | 5A1 | 715 |
| Kungshamn (SE) | 5D2 | 755 |
| Kvelde (NO) | 5C1 | 718 |
| Kvissel (DK) | 5C3 | 322 |
| Kviteseid (NO) | 5B1 | 717 |
| Langå (DK) | 5C3 | 324 |
| Langesund (NO) | 5C1 | 718 |
| Larvik (NO) | 5C1 | 718 |
| Lemvig (DK) | 5B3 | 324 |
| Lidköping (SE) | 5E1 | 755 |
| Lillesand (NO) | 5B2 | 717 |
| Lindesberg (SE) | 5E1 | 757 |
| Lindesnes (NO) | 5B2 | 717 |
| Linköping (SE) | 5F2 | 745 |
| Ljungsbro (SE) | 5F1 | 745 |
| Löttorp (SE) | 5G2 | 749 |
| Lunde (NO) | 5C1 | 718 |
| Lyrestad (SE) | 5E1 | 755 |

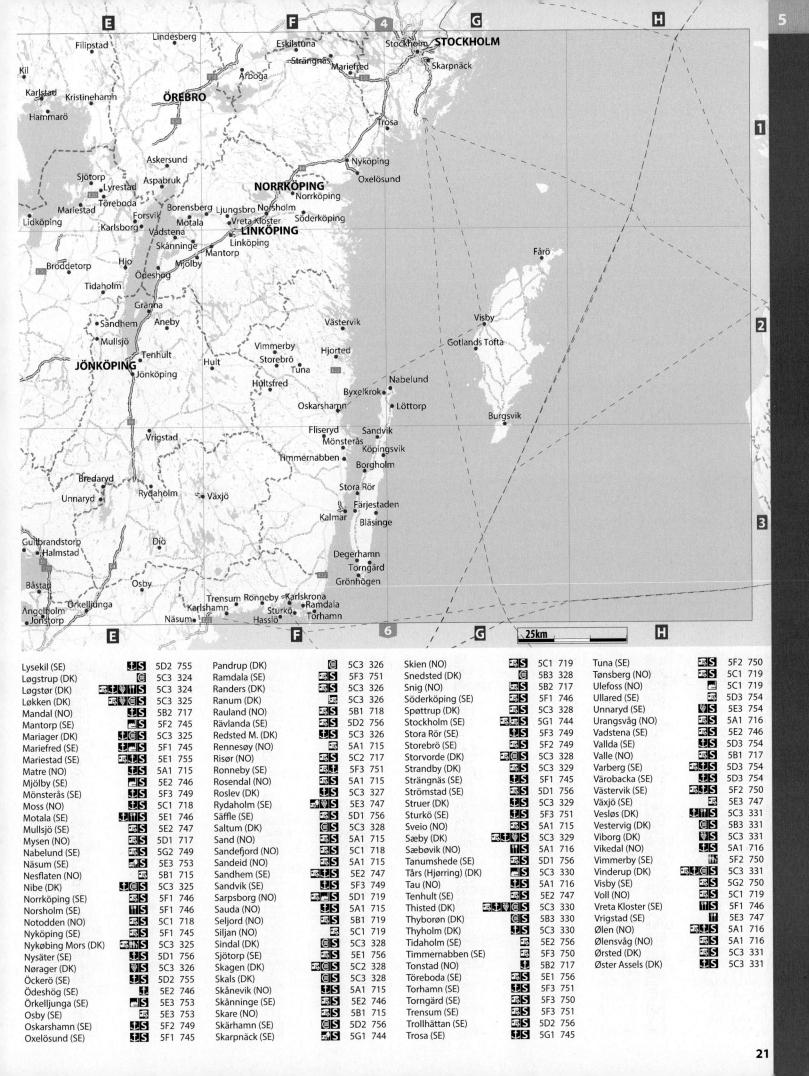

Map: Southern Sweden / Gotland region (grid E–H, 1–6). 25km scale.

Place names on map: Filipstad, Lindesberg, Eskilstuna, Strängnäs, Mariefred, Stockholm, STOCKHOLM, Skarpnäck, Kil, Karlstad, Kristinehamn, Arboga, Hammarö, ÖREBRO, Trosa, Askersund, Nyköping, Sjötorp, Aspabruk, NORRKÖPING, Norrköping, Oxelösund, Lyrestad, Töreboda, Borensberg, Ljungsbro, Norsholm, Mariestad, Forsvik, Motala, Vreta Kloster, Söderköping, Lidköping, Karlsborg, Vadstena, LINKÖPING, Skänninge, Linköping, Broddetorp, Hjo, Mjölby, Mantorp, Fårö, Ödeshög, Tidaholm, Gränna, Västervik, Visby, Sandhem, Aneby, Gotlands Tofta, Mullsjö, Vimmerby, Hjorted, JÖNKÖPING, Tenhult, Hult, Storebrö, Tuna, Jönköping, Hultsfred, Nabelund, Byxelkrok, Löttorp, Oskarshamn, Burgsvik, Fliseryd, Sandvik, Mönsterås, Köpingsvik, Vrigstad, Timmernabben, Borgholm, Bredaryd, Stora Rör, Unnaryd, Rydaholm, Växjö, Färjestaden, Kalmar, Bläsinge, Gullbrandstorp, Halmstad, Diö, Degerhamn, Torngärd, Grönhögen, Båstad, Osby, Trensum, Ronneby, Karlskrona, Ängelholm, Örkelljunga, Karlshamn, Ramdala, Jonstorp, Näsum, Sturkö, Torhamn, Hasslö.

| Place | Grid | Page |
|---|---|---|
| Lysekil (SE) | 5D2 | 755 |
| Løgstrup (DK) | 5C3 | 324 |
| Løgstør (DK) | 5C3 | 324 |
| Løkken (DK) | 5C3 | 325 |
| Mandal (NO) | 5B2 | 717 |
| Mantorp (SE) | 5F2 | 745 |
| Mariager (DK) | 5C3 | 325 |
| Mariefred (SE) | 5F1 | 744 |
| Mariestad (SE) | 5E1 | 755 |
| Matre (NO) | 5A1 | 715 |
| Mjölby (SE) | 5E2 | 746 |
| Mönsterås (SE) | 5F3 | 749 |
| Moss (NO) | 5C1 | 718 |
| Motala (SE) | 5E1 | 746 |
| Mullsjö (SE) | 5E2 | 747 |
| Mysen (NO) | 5D1 | 717 |
| Nabelund (SE) | 5G2 | 749 |
| Näsum (SE) | 5E3 | 753 |
| Nesflaten (NO) | 5B1 | 715 |
| Nibe (DK) | 5C3 | 325 |
| Norrköping (SE) | 5F1 | 746 |
| Norsholm (SE) | 5F1 | 746 |
| Notodden (NO) | 5C1 | 718 |
| Nyköping (SE) | 5F1 | 745 |
| Nyköbing Mors (DK) | 5C3 | 325 |
| Nysäter (SE) | 5D1 | 756 |
| Nørager (DK) | 5C3 | 326 |
| Öckerö (SE) | 5D2 | 755 |
| Ödeshög (SE) | 5E2 | 746 |
| Örkelljunga (SE) | 5E3 | 753 |
| Osby (SE) | 5E3 | 753 |
| Oskarshamn (SE) | 5F2 | 749 |
| Oxelösund (SE) | 5F1 | 745 |
| Pandrup (DK) | 5C3 | 326 |
| Ramdala (SE) | 5F3 | 751 |
| Randers (DK) | 5C3 | 326 |
| Ranum (DK) | 5C3 | 326 |
| Rauland (NO) | 5B1 | 718 |
| Rävlanda (SE) | 5D2 | 756 |
| Redsted M. (DK) | 5C3 | 326 |
| Rennesøy (NO) | 5A1 | 715 |
| Risør (NO) | 5C2 | 717 |
| Ronneby (SE) | 5F3 | 751 |
| Rosendal (NO) | 5A1 | 715 |
| Roslev (DK) | 5C3 | 327 |
| Rydaholm (SE) | 5E3 | 747 |
| Säffle (SE) | 5D1 | 756 |
| Saltum (DK) | 5C3 | 328 |
| Sand (NO) | 5A1 | 715 |
| Sandefjord (NO) | 5C1 | 718 |
| Sandeid (NO) | 5A1 | 715 |
| Sandhem (SE) | 5E2 | 747 |
| Sandvik (SE) | 5F3 | 749 |
| Sarpsborg (NO) | 5D1 | 719 |
| Sauda (NO) | 5A1 | 715 |
| Seljord (NO) | 5B1 | 719 |
| Siljan (NO) | 5C1 | 719 |
| Sindal (DK) | 5C3 | 328 |
| Sjötorp (SE) | 5E1 | 756 |
| Skagen (DK) | 5C2 | 328 |
| Skals (DK) | 5C3 | 328 |
| Skånevik (NO) | 5A1 | 715 |
| Skånninge (SE) | 5E2 | 746 |
| Skare (NO) | 5B1 | 715 |
| Skärhamn (SE) | 5D2 | 756 |
| Skarpnäck (SE) | 5G1 | 744 |
| Skien (NO) | 5C1 | 719 |
| Snedsted (DK) | 5B3 | 328 |
| Snig (NO) | 5B2 | 717 |
| Söderköping (SE) | 5F1 | 746 |
| Spøttrup (DK) | 5C3 | 328 |
| Stockholm (SE) | 5G1 | 744 |
| Stora Rör (SE) | 5F3 | 749 |
| Storebrö (SE) | 5F2 | 749 |
| Storvorde (DK) | 5C3 | 328 |
| Strandby (DK) | 5C3 | 329 |
| Strängnäs (SE) | 5F1 | 745 |
| Strömstad (SE) | 5D1 | 756 |
| Struer (DK) | 5C3 | 329 |
| Sturkö (SE) | 5F3 | 751 |
| Sveio (NO) | 5A1 | 715 |
| Sæby (DK) | 5C3 | 329 |
| Sæbøvik (NO) | 5A1 | 716 |
| Tanumshede (SE) | 5D1 | 756 |
| Tårs (Hjørring) (DK) | 5C3 | 330 |
| Tau (NO) | 5A1 | 716 |
| Tenhult (SE) | 5E2 | 747 |
| Thisted (DK) | 5C3 | 330 |
| Thyborøn (DK) | 5B3 | 330 |
| Thyholm (DK) | 5C3 | 330 |
| Tidaholm (SE) | 5E2 | 746 |
| Timmernabben (SE) | 5F3 | 750 |
| Tonstad (NO) | 5B2 | 717 |
| Töreboda (SE) | 5E1 | 756 |
| Torhamn (SE) | 5F3 | 751 |
| Torngärd (SE) | 5F3 | 750 |
| Trensum (SE) | 5F3 | 751 |
| Trollhättan (SE) | 5D2 | 756 |
| Trosa (SE) | 5G1 | 745 |
| Tuna (SE) | 5F2 | 750 |
| Tønsberg (NO) | 5C1 | 719 |
| Ulefoss (NO) | 5C1 | 719 |
| Ullared (SE) | 5D3 | 754 |
| Unnaryd (SE) | 5E3 | 754 |
| Urangsvåg (NO) | 5A1 | 716 |
| Vadstena (SE) | 5E2 | 746 |
| Vallda (SE) | 5D3 | 754 |
| Valle (NO) | 5B1 | 717 |
| Varberg (SE) | 5D3 | 754 |
| Värobacka (SE) | 5D3 | 754 |
| Västervik (SE) | 5F2 | 750 |
| Växjö (SE) | 5E3 | 747 |
| Vesløs (DK) | 5C3 | 331 |
| Vestervig (DK) | 5B3 | 331 |
| Viborg (DK) | 5C3 | 331 |
| Vikedal (NO) | 5A1 | 716 |
| Vimmerby (SE) | 5F2 | 750 |
| Vinderup (DK) | 5C3 | 331 |
| Visby (SE) | 5G2 | 750 |
| Voll (NO) | 5C1 | 719 |
| Vreta Kloster (SE) | 5F1 | 746 |
| Vrigstad (SE) | 5E3 | 747 |
| Ølen (NO) | 5A1 | 716 |
| Ølensvåg (NO) | 5A1 | 716 |
| Ørsted (DK) | 5C3 | 331 |
| Øster Assels (DK) | 5C3 | 331 |

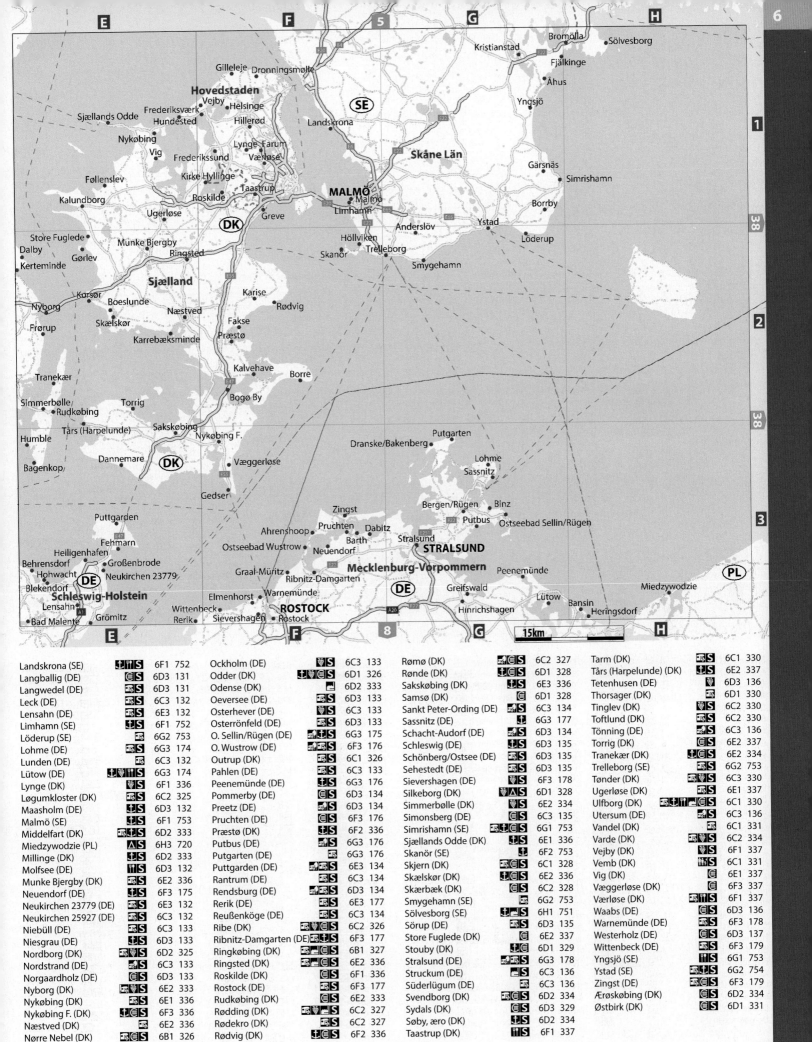

| | | | | | | | | | |
|---|---|---|---|---|---|---|---|---|---|
| Landskrona (SE) | 6F1 752 | Ockholm (DE) | 6C3 133 | Rømø (DK) | 6C2 327 | Tarm (DK) | 6C1 330 |
| Langballig (DE) | 6D3 131 | Odder (DK) | 6D1 326 | Rønde (DK) | 6D1 328 | Tårs (Harpelunde) (DK) | 6E2 337 |
| Langwedel (DE) | 6D3 131 | Odense (DK) | 6D2 333 | Sakskøbing (DK) | 6E3 336 | Tetenhusen (DE) | 6D3 136 |
| Leck (DE) | 6C3 132 | Oeversee (DE) | 6D3 133 | Samsø (DK) | 6D1 328 | Thorsager (DK) | 6D1 330 |
| Lensahn (DE) | 6E3 132 | Osterhever (DE) | 6C3 133 | Sankt Peter-Ording (DE) | 6C3 134 | Tinglev (DK) | 6C2 330 |
| Limhamn (SE) | 6F1 752 | Osterrönfeld (DE) | 6D3 133 | Sassnitz (DE) | 6G3 177 | Toftlund (DK) | 6C2 330 |
| Löderup (SE) | 6G2 753 | O. Sellin/Rügen (DE) | 6G3 175 | Schacht-Audorf (DE) | 6D3 134 | Tönning (DK) | 6C3 136 |
| Lohme (DE) | 6G3 174 | O. Wustrow (DE) | 6F3 176 | Schleswig (DE) | 6D3 135 | Torrig (DK) | 6E2 337 |
| Lunden (DE) | 6C3 132 | Outrup (DK) | 6C1 326 | Schönberg/Ostsee (DE) | 6D3 135 | Tranekær (DK) | 6E2 334 |
| Lütow (DE) | 6G3 174 | Pahlen (DE) | 6D3 133 | Sehestedt (DE) | 6D3 135 | Trelleborg (SE) | 6G2 753 |
| Lynge (DK) | 6F1 336 | Peenemünde (DE) | 6G3 176 | Sievershagen (DE) | 6F3 178 | Tønder (DK) | 6C3 330 |
| Løgumkloster (DK) | 6C2 325 | Pommerby (DE) | 6D3 134 | Silkeborg (DK) | 6D1 328 | Ugerløse (DK) | 6E1 337 |
| Maasholm (DE) | 6D3 132 | Preetz (DE) | 6D3 134 | Simmerbølle (DK) | 6E2 334 | Ulfborg (DK) | 6C1 330 |
| Malmö (SE) | 6F1 753 | Pruchten (DE) | 6F3 176 | Simonsberg (DE) | 6C3 136 | Utersum (DE) | 6C3 136 |
| Middelfart (DK) | 6D2 333 | Præstø (DK) | 6F2 336 | Simrishamn (SE) | 6G1 753 | Vandel (DK) | 6C1 331 |
| Miedzywodzie (PL) | 6H3 720 | Putbus (DE) | 6G3 176 | Sjællands Odde (DK) | 6E1 336 | Varde (DK) | 6C2 334 |
| Millinge (DK) | 6D2 333 | Putgarten (DE) | 6G3 176 | Skanör (SE) | 6F2 753 | Vejby (DK) | 6F1 337 |
| Molfsee (DE) | 6D3 132 | Puttgarden (DE) | 6E3 134 | Skjern (DK) | 6C1 328 | Vemb (DK) | 6C1 331 |
| Munke Bjergby (DK) | 6E2 336 | Rantrum (DE) | 6C3 134 | Skælskør (DK) | 6E2 336 | Vig (DK) | 6E1 337 |
| Neuendorf (DE) | 6F3 175 | Rendsburg (DE) | 6D3 134 | Skærbæk (DK) | 6C2 328 | Væggerløse (DK) | 6F3 337 |
| Neukirchen 23779 (DE) | 6E3 132 | Rerik (DE) | 6E3 177 | Smygehamn (SE) | 6H1 751 | Værløse (DK) | 6F1 337 |
| Neukirchen 25927 (DE) | 6C3 132 | Reußenköge (DE) | 6C2 134 | Sölvesborg (SE) | 6G3 135 | Waabs (DE) | 6D3 136 |
| Niebüll (DE) | 6D3 133 | Ribe (DK) | 6C2 326 | Store Fuglede (DK) | 6E2 337 | Warnemünde (DE) | 6F3 178 |
| Niesgrau (DE) | 6D3 133 | Ribnitz-Damgarten (DE) | 6F3 177 | Stouby (DK) | 6D1 329 | Westerholz (DE) | 6D3 137 |
| Nordborg (DK) | 6D2 325 | Ringkøbing (DK) | 6B1 327 | Stralsund (DE) | 6G3 178 | Wittenbeck (DE) | 6F3 179 |
| Nordstrand (DE) | 6C3 133 | Ringsted (DK) | 6E2 336 | Struckum (DE) | 6C3 136 | Yngsjö (SE) | 6G1 753 |
| Norgaardholz (DE) | 6D3 133 | Roskilde (DK) | 6F1 336 | Süderlügum (DE) | 6D2 334 | Ystad (SE) | 6G2 754 |
| Nyborg (DK) | 6E2 333 | Rostock (DE) | 6F3 177 | Svendborg (DK) | 6D2 334 | Zingst (DE) | 6F3 179 |
| Nykøbing (DK) | 6E1 336 | Rudkøbing (DK) | 6E2 333 | Sydals (DK) | 6D3 329 | Ærøskøbing (DK) | 6D2 334 |
| Nykøbing F. (DK) | 6F3 336 | Rødby (DK) | 6C2 327 | Søby, æro (DK) | 6D2 334 | Østbirk (DK) | 6D1 331 |
| Næstved (DK) | 6E2 336 | Rødding (DK) | 6C2 327 | Taastrup (DK) | 6F1 337 | | |
| Nørre Nebel (DK) | 6B1 326 | Rødekro (DK) | 6C2 327 | | | | |
| | | Rødvig (DK) | 6F2 336 | | | | |

| Place | Grid | Page |
|---|---|---|
| Akkrum (NL) | 7D3 | 676 |
| Anjum (NL) | 7E2 | 676 |
| Apen (DE) | 7G3 | 138 |
| Appelscha (NL) | 7E3 | 677 |
| Appingedam (NL) | 7F2 | 681 |
| Assen (NL) | 7E3 | 684 |
| Aurich (DE) | 7G2 | 138 |
| Bad Zwischenahn (DE) | 7G3 | 139 |
| Balk (NL) | 7D3 | 677 |
| Barßel (DE) | 7G3 | 140 |
| Bergum (NL) | 7E3 | 677 |
| Berne (DE) | 7H3 | 140 |
| Blauwestad (NL) | 7F3 | 681 |
| Blesdijke (NL) | 7E3 | 677 |
| Blijham (NL) | 7F3 | 681 |
| Blomberg (DE) | 7G2 | 141 |
| Bockhorn (DE) | 7G2 | 141 |
| Bolsward (NL) | 7D3 | 677 |
| Borger (NL) | 7F3 | 684 |
| Brake (DE) | 7H2 | 142 |
| Brantgum (NL) | 7E2 | 677 |
| Bremen (DE) | 7H3 | 143 |
| Bremerhaven (DE) | 7H2 | 143 |
| Bunde (DE) | 7G3 | 144 |
| Burdaard (NL) | 7E3 | 677 |
| Büsum (DE) | 7H1 | 127 |
| Butjadingen (DE) | 7H2 | 144 |
| Cloppenburg (DE) | 7G3 | 145 |
| Cuxhaven (DE) | 7H1 | 145 |
| Damwoude (NL) | 7D3 | 677 |
| Dangast (DE) | 7G2 | 146 |
| De Westereen (NL) | 7E3 | 677 |
| Delfzijl (NL) | 7F2 | 682 |
| Delmenhorst (DE) | 7H3 | 146 |
| Den Helder (NL) | 7C3 | 675 |
| Den Oever (NL) | 7C3 | 675 |
| Detern (DE) | 7G3 | 146 |
| Ditzum (DE) | 7F2 | 146 |
| Doezum (NL) | 7E3 | 682 |
| Dokkum (NL) | 7E2 | 677 |
| Dornum (DE) | 7G2 | 147 |
| Dörpen (DE) | 7F3 | 147 |
| Dorum (DE) | 7H2 | 147 |
| Drachten (NL) | 7E3 | 677 |
| Earnewâld (NL) | 7E3 | 677 |
| Edewecht (DE) | 7G3 | 148 |
| Eext (NL) | 7F3 | 684 |
| Eggestedt (DE) | 7H3 | 148 |
| Elsfleth (DE) | 7H3 | 148 |
| Elsloo (NL) | 7E3 | 678 |
| Emden (DE) | 7F2 | 148 |
| Esens (DE) | 7G2 | 148 |
| Esterwegen (DE) | 7G3 | 149 |
| Finsterwolde (NL) | 7F3 | 682 |
| Friedeburg (DE) | 7G2 | 149 |
| Friedrichskoog (DE) | 7H1 | 128 |
| Friesoythe (DE) | 7G3 | 149 |
| Groningen (NL) | 7E3 | 682 |
| Großefehn (DE) | 7G2 | 150 |
| Großenkneten (DE) | 7H3 | 150 |
| Großheide (DE) | 7F2 | 151 |
| Hage (DE) | 7F2 | 151 |
| Hambergen (DE) | 7H2 | 151 |
| Haren (NL) | 7E3 | 682 |
| Harlingen (NL) | 7D3 | 678 |
| Harpstedt (DE) | 7H3 | 152 |
| Heerenveen (NL) | 7E3 | 678 |
| Hesel (DE) | 7G2 | 153 |
| Hogebeintum (NL) | 7D2 | 678 |
| Hoogersmilde (NL) | 7E3 | 685 |
| Hude (DE) | 7H3 | 154 |
| Ihlienworth (DE) | 7H1 | 154 |
| Ihlow (DE) | 7G2 | 154 |
| IJlst (NL) | 7D3 | 678 |
| Jade (DE) | 7H2 | 154 |
| Jelsum (NL) | 7D3 | 678 |
| Jever (DE) | 7G2 | 154 |
| Joure (NL) | 7D3 | 678 |
| Kollum (NL) | 7E3 | 678 |
| Koudum (NL) | 7D3 | 678 |
| Krummhörn (DE) | 7F2 | 155 |
| Langweer (NL) | 7D3 | 678 |
| Lauwersoog (NL) | 7E2 | 682 |
| Leek (NL) | 7E3 | 682 |
| Leens (NL) | 7E2 | 682 |
| Leer (DE) | 7G3 | 155 |
| Leeuwarden (NL) | 7D3 | 679 |
| Lekkum (NL) | 7D3 | 679 |
| Lemmer (NL) | 7D3 | 679 |
| Lemwerder (DE) | 7H3 | 156 |
| Lollum (NL) | 7D3 | 679 |
| Lorup (DE) | 7G3 | 156 |
| Losdorp (NL) | 7F2 | 682 |
| Loxstedt (DE) | 7H2 | 156 |
| Lutjegast (NL) | 7E3 | 682 |

10km

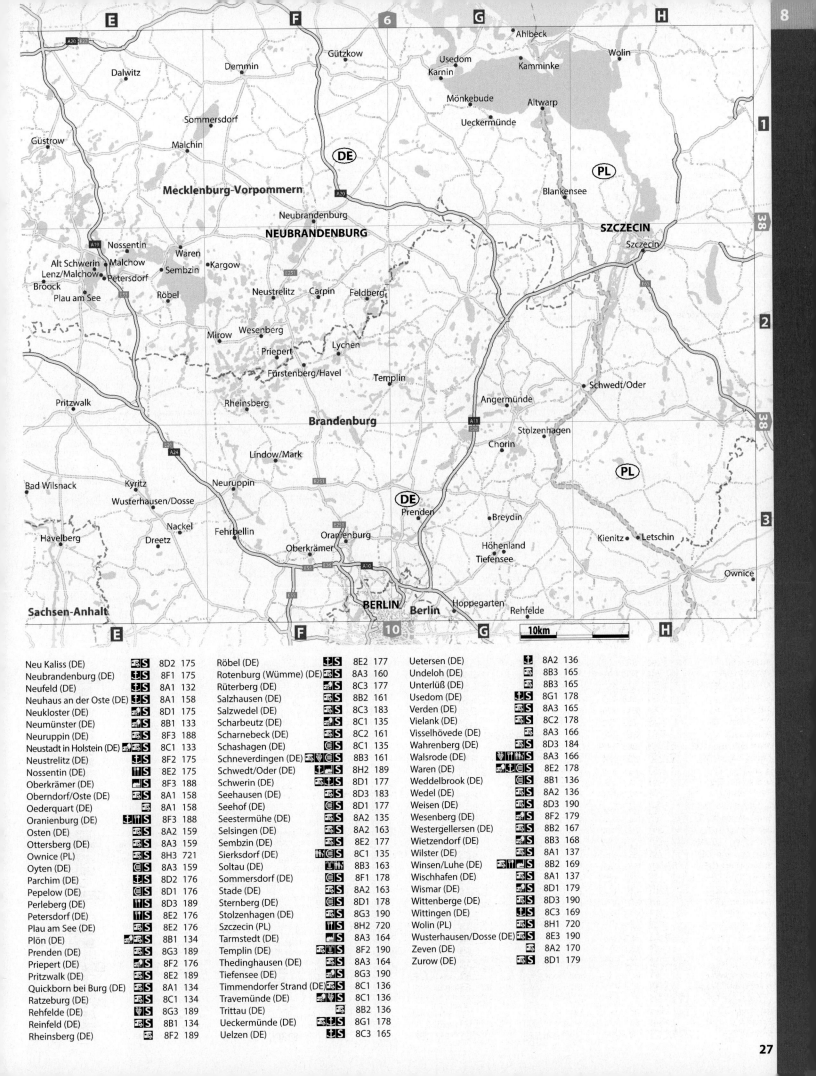

Map labels:

Dalwitz, Demmin, Gützkow, Ahlbeck, Wolin, Usedom, Kamminke, Karnin, Mönkebude, Altwarp, Ueckermünde, Sommersdorf, Güstrow, Malchin, DE, PL, Blankensee, Mecklenburg-Vorpommern, Neubrandenburg, NEUBRANDENBURG, SZCZECIN, Szczecin, Nossentin, Waren, Kargow, Alt Schwerin, Malchow, Sembzin, Lenz/Malchow, Petersdorf, Broock, Röbel, Plau am See, Neustrelitz, Carpin, Feldberg, Mirow, Wesenberg, Lychen, Priepert, Fürstenberg/Havel, Templin, Schwedt/Oder, Pritzwalk, Rheinsberg, Angermünde, Brandenburg, Stolzenhagen, Chorin, PL, Lindow/Mark, Bad Wilsnack, Kyritz, Neuruppin, Wusterhausen/Dosse, DE, Prenden, Breydin, Nackel, Fehrbellin, Oranienburg, Höhenland, Kienitz, Letschin, Havelberg, Dreetz, Oberkrämer, Tiefensee, Sachsen-Anhalt, BERLIN, Berlin, Hoppegarten, Rehfelde, Ownice, 10km

10km

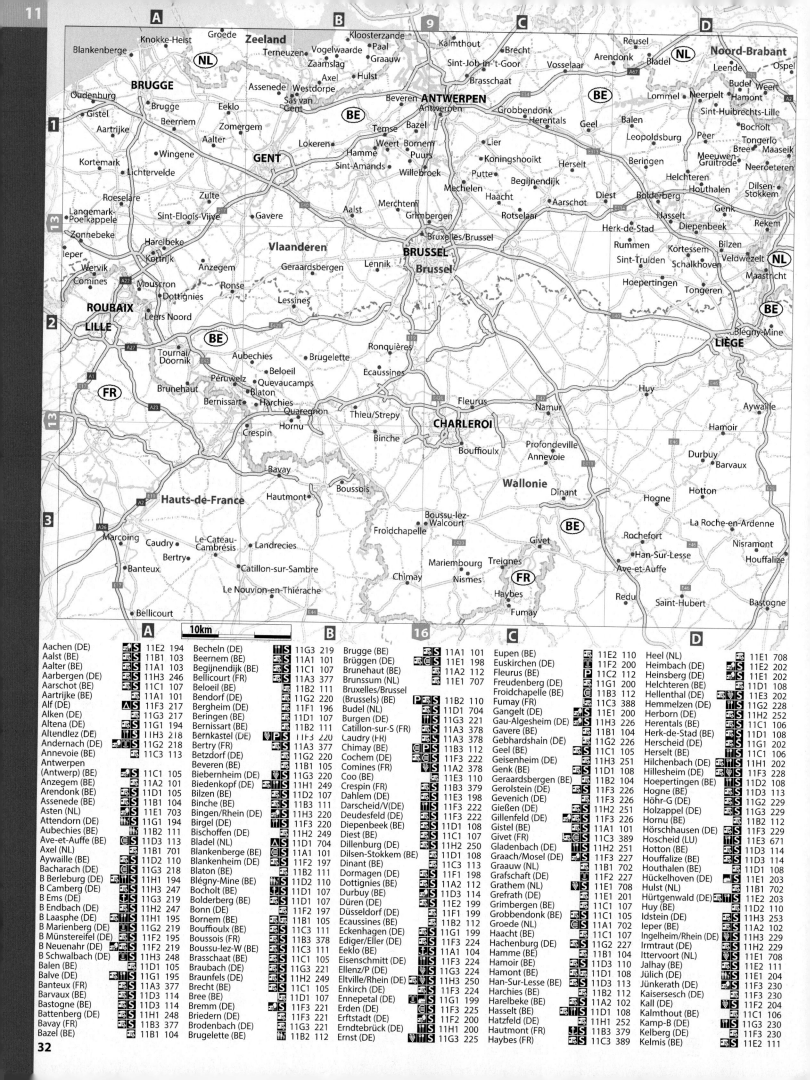

Map of the Belgium / Netherlands / Germany / France border region (Brugge, Gent, Antwerpen, Brussel, Liège, Charleroi, Lille, Roubaix, Aachen area). Scale: 10km.

Index (columns A–D):

**A**

| Place | Grid | Page |
|---|---|---|
| Aachen (DE) | 11E2 | 194 |
| Aalst (BE) | 11B1 | 103 |
| Aalter (BE) | 11A1 | 103 |
| Aarbergen (DE) | 11H3 | 246 |
| Aarschot (BE) | 11C1 | 107 |
| Aartrijke (BE) | 11A1 | 101 |
| Alf (DE) | 11F3 | 217 |
| Alken (DE) | 11G3 | 217 |
| Altena (DE) | 11G1 | 194 |
| Altendlez (DE) | 11H3 | 218 |
| Andernach (DE) | 11F3 | 217 |
| Annevoie (BE) | 11C3 | 113 |
| Antwerpen (Antwerp) (BE) | 11C1 | 105 |
| Anzegem (BE) | 11A2 | 101 |
| Arendonk (BE) | 11D1 | 105 |
| Assenede (BE) | 11B1 | 104 |
| Asten (NL) | 11E1 | 703 |
| Attendorn (DE) | 11G1 | 194 |
| Aubechies (BE) | 11B2 | 111 |
| Ave-et-Auffe (BE) | 11D3 | 113 |
| Axel (NL) | 11B1 | 701 |
| Aywaille (BE) | 11D2 | 110 |
| Bacharach (DE) | 11G3 | 218 |
| B Berleburg (DE) | 11H1 | 194 |
| B Camberg (DE) | 11H3 | 247 |
| B Ems (DE) | 11G3 | 219 |
| B Endbach (DE) | 11H2 | 247 |
| B Laasphe (DE) | 11H1 | 195 |
| B Marienberg (DE) | 11H2 | 219 |
| B Münstereifel (DE) | 11F2 | 195 |
| B Neuenahr (DE) | 11F2 | 219 |
| B Schwalbach (DE) | 11F2 | 219 |
| Balen (BE) | 11D1 | 105 |
| Balve (DE) | 11G1 | 195 |
| Banteux (FR) | 11A3 | 377 |
| Barvaux (BE) | 11D3 | 114 |
| Bastogne (BE) | 11D3 | 114 |
| Battenberg (DE) | 11H1 | 248 |
| Bavay (FR) | 11B3 | 377 |
| Bazel (BE) | 11B1 | 104 |

**B**

| Place | Grid | Page |
|---|---|---|
| Becheln (DE) | 11G3 | 219 |
| Beernem (BE) | 11A1 | 101 |
| Begijnendijk (BE) | 11C1 | 107 |
| Bellicourt (FR) | 11A3 | 377 |
| Beloeil (BE) | 11B2 | 111 |
| Bendorf (DE) | 11G2 | 220 |
| Bergheim (DE) | 11F1 | 196 |
| Beringen (BE) | 11G3 | 217 |
| Bernissart (BE) | 11B2 | 111 |
| Bernkastel (DE) | 11F3 | 220 |
| Bertry (FR) | 11A3 | 377 |
| Betzdorf (DE) | 11G2 | 220 |
| Beveren (BE) | 11B1 | 105 |
| Biebernheim (DE) | 11G3 | 219 |
| Biedenkopf (DE) | 11H1 | 249 |
| Bilzen (BE) | 11D2 | 107 |
| Binche (BE) | 11B3 | 111 |
| Bingen/Rhein (DE) | 11H3 | 220 |
| Birgel (DE) | 11F3 | 220 |
| Bischoffen (DE) | 11H2 | 249 |
| Bladel (NL) | 11D1 | 704 |
| Blankenberge (BE) | 11A1 | 101 |
| Blankenheim (DE) | 11F2 | 197 |
| Blaton (BE) | 11B2 | 111 |
| Blégny-Mine (BE) | 11D2 | 110 |
| Bocholt (BE) | 11D1 | 107 |
| Bolderberg (BE) | 11D1 | 107 |
| Bonn (DE) | 11F2 | 197 |
| Bornem (BE) | 11B1 | 105 |
| Bouffioulx (BE) | 11C3 | 111 |
| Boussois (FR) | 11C3 | 378 |
| Boussu-lez-W (BE) | 11C3 | 111 |
| Brasschaat (BE) | 11C1 | 105 |
| Braubach (DE) | 11G3 | 221 |
| Braunfels (DE) | 11H2 | 249 |
| Brecht (BE) | 11C1 | 105 |
| Bree (BE) | 11D1 | 107 |
| Bremm (DE) | 11F3 | 221 |
| Briedern (DE) | 11F3 | 221 |
| Brodenbach (DE) | 11G3 | 221 |
| Brugelette (BE) | 11B2 | 112 |
| Brugge (BE) | 11A1 | 101 |
| Brüggen (DE) | 11E1 | 198 |
| Brunehaut (BE) | 11A2 | 112 |
| Brunssum (NL) | 11E1 | 707 |
| Bruxelles/Brussel (Brussels) (BE) | 11B2 | 110 |
| Budel (NL) | 11D1 | 704 |
| Burgen (DE) | 11G3 | 221 |
| Catillon-sur-S (FR) | 11A3 | 378 |
| Caudry (FR) | 11A3 | 378 |
| Chimay (BE) | 11B3 | 112 |
| Cochem (DE) | 11F3 | 222 |
| Comines (FR) | 11A2 | 378 |
| Coo (BE) | 11E3 | 110 |
| Crespin (FR) | 11B3 | 379 |
| Dahlem (DE) | 11E3 | 198 |
| Darscheid/V(DE) | 11F3 | 222 |
| Deudesfeld (DE) | 11F3 | 222 |
| Diepenbeek (BE) | 11D1 | 108 |
| Diest (BE) | 11C1 | 107 |
| Dillenburg (DE) | 11H2 | 250 |
| Dilsen-Stokkem (BE) | 11D1 | 108 |
| Dinant (BE) | 11C3 | 113 |
| Dormagen (DE) | 11F1 | 198 |
| Dottignies (BE) | 11A2 | 112 |
| Durbuy (BE) | 11D3 | 114 |
| Düren (DE) | 11E2 | 199 |
| Düsseldorf (DE) | 11F1 | 199 |
| Ecaussines (BE) | 11B2 | 112 |
| Eckenhagen (DE) | 11G1 | 199 |
| Ediger/Eller (D) | 11F3 | 224 |
| Eeklo (BE) | 11A1 | 104 |
| Eisenschmitt (DE) | 11F3 | 224 |
| Ellenz/P (DE) | 11F3 | 224 |
| Eltville/Rhein (DE) | 11H3 | 250 |
| Enkirch (DE) | 11F3 | 224 |
| Ennepetal (DE) | 11G1 | 199 |
| Erden (DE) | 11F3 | 225 |
| Erftstadt (DE) | 11F2 | 200 |
| Erndtebrück (DE) | 11H1 | 200 |
| Ernst (DE) | 11G3 | 225 |

**C**

| Place | Grid | Page |
|---|---|---|
| Eupen (BE) | 11E2 | 110 |
| Euskirchen (DE) | 11F2 | 200 |
| Fleurus (BE) | 11C2 | 112 |
| Freudenberg (DE) | 11G1 | 200 |
| Froidchapelle (BE) | 11B3 | 112 |
| Fumay (FR) | 11C3 | 388 |
| Gangelt (DE) | 11E1 | 200 |
| Gau-Algesheim (DE) | 11H3 | 226 |
| Gavere (BE) | 11B1 | 104 |
| Gebhardshain (DE) | 11G2 | 226 |
| Geel (BE) | 11C1 | 105 |
| Geisenheim (DE) | 11H3 | 251 |
| Genk (BE) | 11D1 | 108 |
| Geraardsbergen (BE) | 11B2 | 104 |
| Gerolstein (DE) | 11F3 | 226 |
| Gevenich (DE) | 11F3 | 226 |
| Gießen (DE) | 11H2 | 251 |
| Gillenfeld (DE) | 11F3 | 226 |
| Gistel (BE) | 11A1 | 101 |
| Givet (FR) | 11C3 | 389 |
| Gladenbach (DE) | 11H2 | 251 |
| Graach/Mosel (DE) | 11F3 | 226 |
| Graauw (NL) | 11B1 | 702 |
| Grafschaft (DE) | 11F2 | 227 |
| Grathem (NL) | 11E1 | 708 |
| Grefrath (DE) | 11E1 | 201 |
| Grimbergen (BE) | 11C1 | 107 |
| Grobbendonk (BE) | 11C1 | 105 |
| Groede (NL) | 11A1 | 702 |
| Haacht (BE) | 11C1 | 107 |
| Hachenburg (DE) | 11G2 | 227 |
| Hamme (BE) | 11B1 | 104 |
| Hamoir (BE) | 11D3 | 110 |
| Hamont (BE) | 11D1 | 108 |
| Han-Sur-Lesse (BE) | 11D3 | 113 |
| Harchies (BE) | 11B2 | 112 |
| Harelbeke (BE) | 11A2 | 102 |
| Hasselt (BE) | 11D1 | 108 |
| Hatzfeld (DE) | 11H1 | 252 |
| Hautmont (FR) | 11B3 | 379 |
| Haybes (FR) | 11C3 | 389 |

**D**

| Place | Grid | Page |
|---|---|---|
| Heel (NL) | 11E1 | 708 |
| Heimbach (DE) | 11E2 | 202 |
| Heinsberg (DE) | 11E1 | 202 |
| Helchteren (BE) | 11D1 | 108 |
| Hellenthal (DE) | 11E3 | 202 |
| Hemmelzen (DE) | 11G2 | 228 |
| Herborn (DE) | 11H2 | 252 |
| Herentals (BE) | 11C1 | 106 |
| Herk-de-Stad (BE) | 11D1 | 108 |
| Herscheid (DE) | 11G1 | 202 |
| Herselt (BE) | 11C1 | 106 |
| Hilchenbach (DE) | 11H1 | 202 |
| Hillesheim (DE) | 11F3 | 228 |
| Hoepertingen (BE) | 11D2 | 108 |
| Hogne (BE) | 11D3 | 113 |
| Höhr-G (DE) | 11G2 | 228 |
| Holzappel (DE) | 11G3 | 229 |
| Hornu (BE) | 11B2 | 112 |
| Hörschhausen (DE) | 11E3 | 229 |
| Hoscheid (LU) | 11E3 | 671 |
| Hotton (BE) | 11D3 | 114 |
| Houffalize (BE) | 11D3 | 114 |
| Houthalen (BE) | 11D1 | 108 |
| Hückelhoven (DE) | 11E1 | 203 |
| Hulst (BE) | 11B1 | 702 |
| Hürtgenwald (DE) | 11E1 | 203 |
| Huy (BE) | 11D2 | 110 |
| Idstein (DE) | 11H3 | 253 |
| Ieper (BE) | 11A2 | 102 |
| Ingelheim/Rhein (DE) | 11H3 | 229 |
| Irmtraut (DE) | 11H2 | 229 |
| Ittervoort (NL) | 11E1 | 708 |
| Jalhay (BE) | 11E2 | 111 |
| Jülich (DE) | 11E1 | 204 |
| Jünkerath (DE) | 11F3 | 230 |
| Kaisersesch (DE) | 11F3 | 230 |
| Kall (DE) | 11F2 | 204 |
| Kalmthout (BE) | 11C1 | 106 |
| Kamp-B (DE) | 11G3 | 230 |
| Kelberg (DE) | 11F3 | 230 |
| Kelmis (BE) | 11E2 | 111 |

10km

**Map region labels (Hessen / Thüringen / Bayern):**

Korbach · Kassel · Kaufungen · Asbach/Sickenberg · Bad Sooden-Allendorf · Bad Bibra · Meineringhausen · Bad Emstal · Baunatal · Helsa · Groß-almerode · Berkatal · Wanfried · Waldeck · Niedenstein · Edermünde · Hessisch Lichtenau · Eschwege · Bad Tennstedt · Vöhl · Edertal · Melsungen · Treffurt · Bad Langensalza · ERFURT · Bad Wildungen · Fritzlar · Waldkappel · Mihla · Weimar · Bad Zwesten · Sontra · Ringgau · Eisenach · Frankenberg/Eder · Borken · Homberg/Efze · Rotenburg a/d Fulda · Gotha · Erfurt · Bad Berka · JENA · Rosenthal · Neuental · Friedendorf · Hessen · Bebra · Gilserberg · Schwalmstadt · Bad Hersfeld · Tabarz · Ichtershausen · Neukirchen · Oberaula · Dorndorf · Tiefenort · Bad Liebenstein · Brotterode · Rudolstadt · MARBURG · Kirchheim · Vacha · Bad Salzungen · Tambach-Dietharz · Marburg · Amöneburg · Ottrau · Stadtlengsfeld · Breitungen · Schmalkalden · Oberhof · Alsfeld · Grebenau · Rasdorf · Homberg/Ohm · Burghaun · Thüringen · Zella-Mehlis · Ilmenau · Sitzendorf · Saalfeld · Schwalmtal · Schlitz · Hünfeld · Tann/Rhön · Kühndorf · Schmiedefeld · Lauterbach · Bad Salzschlirf · Meiningen · Grünberg · Ulrichstein · Hilders · Themar · Lauscha · Laubach · Herbstein · Fulda · Steinheid · Lich · Grebenhain · FULDA · Poppenhausen · Ostheim · Münzenberg · Hungen · Oberelsbach · Mellrichstadt · Eisfeld · Rothenkirchen · Hirzenhain · Bischofsheim an der Rhön · Bad Rodach · Bad Nauheim · Friedberg · Schlüchtern · Steinau/Strasse · Bad Brückenau · Bad Bocklet · Bad Neustadt · Bad Königshofen · Bad Colberg/Heldburg · Coburg · Kronach · Büdingen · Bad Soden-Salmünster · Mernes · Sinntal · Münnerstadt · Ahorn · Bayern · Bad Kissingen · Burgkunstadt · Kulmbach · Gelnhausen · Bad Orb · Oberthulba · Hofheim in Unterfranken · Ebern · Bad Staffelstein · Weismain · Flörsbachtal-Lohrhaupten · Hammelburg · Ramsthal · Dittelbrunn · Königsberg · FRANKFURT AM MAIN · Schöllkrippen · Gräfendorf · Niederwerrn · Schweinfurt · Hassfurt · Zeil am Main · Baunach · Rodgau · Lohr/Main · Arnstein · Garstadt · Röthlein · Grafenrheinfeld · Eltmann am Main · Memmelsdorf · Mistelgau · Rothenbuch · Wipfeld · Gerolzhofen · Bamberg · Litzendorf · Aufseß · Aschaffenburg · Eisenheim · Ebrach · Zellingen · Eisenheim · Strüllendorf · Thüngersheim · Escherndorf · Volkach · Ebrach · Hirschaid · Wiesenttal · Nordheim am Main

Scale: 10km

**Index**

| Place | Grid | Page |
|---|---|---|
| Adorf (DE) | 12E2 | 191 |
| Ahorn (DE) | 12D3 | 287 |
| Alsfeld (DE) | 12A2 | 246 |
| Amöneburg (DE) | 12A2 | 246 |
| Arnstein (DE) | 12B3 | 288 |
| Arzberg (DE) | 12E3 | 288 |
| Aš (CZ) | 12E2 | 122 |
| Asbach/Sickenberg (DE) | 12B1 | 259 |
| Aschaffenburg (DE) | 12A3 | 288 |
| Aufseß (DE) | 12D3 | 288 |
| Bad Alexandersbad (DE) | 12E3 | 289 |
| Bad Berka (DE) | 12D1 | 259 |
| Bad Berneck (DE) | 12E3 | 289 |
| Bad Bibra (DE) | 12D1 | 180 |
| Bad Bocklet (DE) | 12B3 | 289 |
| Bad Brückenau (DE) | 12B3 | 289 |
| Bad Colberg/Heldburg (DE) | 12C3 | 259 |
| Bad Elster (DE) | 12E2 | 191 |
| Bad Emstal (DE) | 12A1 | 247 |
| Bad Hersfeld (DE) | 12B1 | 247 |
| Bad Kissingen (DE) | 12B3 | 290 |
| Bad Klosterlausnitz (DE) | 12E1 | 259 |
| Bad Königshofen (DE) | 12C3 | 290 |
| Bad Kösen (DE) | 12E1 | 180 |
| Bad Langensalza (DE) | 12C1 | 259 |
| Bad Lausick (DE) | 12F1 | 191 |
| Bad Liebenstein (DE) | 12C1 | 259 |
| Bad Lobenstein (DE) | 12E2 | 259 |
| Bad Nauheim (DE) | 12A3 | 247 |
| Bad Neustadt (DE) | 12C2 | 290 |
| Bad Orb (DE) | 12A3 | 247 |
| Bad Rodach (DE) | 12C2 | 290 |
| Bad Salzschlirf (DE) | 12B2 | 248 |
| Bad Salzungen (DE) | 12C1 | 259 |
| Bad Soden-Sr (DE) | 12A3 | 248 |
| Bad Sooden-Allendorf (DE) | 12B1 | 248 |
| Bad Staffelstein (DE) | 12D3 | 290 |
| Bad Steben (DE) | 12E2 | 290 |
| Bad Tennstedt (DE) | 12C1 | 259 |
| Bad Wildungen (DE) | 12A1 | 248 |
| Bad Zwesten (DE) | 12A1 | 248 |
| Bamberg (DE) | 12D3 | 291 |
| Bärnau (DE) | 12F3 | 291 |
| Baunach (DE) | 12D3 | 291 |
| Baunatal (DE) | 12A1 | 248 |
| Bayreuth (DE) | 12E3 | 291 |
| Bebra (DE) | 12B1 | 248 |
| Berkatal (DE) | 12B1 | 249 |
| Bischofsgrün (DE) | 12E3 | 292 |
| Bischofsheim/Rhön (DE) | 12B2 | 292 |
| Borken (DE) | 12A1 | 249 |
| Breitenbrunn (DE) | 12F2 | 191 |
| Breitungen (DE) | 12C2 | 259 |
| Brotterode (DE) | 12C1 | 259 |
| Büdingen (DE) | 12A3 | 249 |
| Burghaun (DE) | 12B2 | 250 |
| Burgkunstadt (DE) | 12D3 | 293 |
| Cheb (CZ) | 12F3 | 122 |
| Coburg (DE) | 12D3 | 294 |
| Dennheritz (DE) | 12F1 | 191 |
| Dittelbrunn (DE) | 12C3 | 294 |
| Dorndorf (DE) | 12B1 | 259 |
| Dresden (DE) | 12G1 | 191 |
| Ebern (DE) | 12C3 | 295 |
| Ebrach (DE) | 12C3 | 295 |
| Edermünde (DE) | 12A1 | 250 |
| Edertal (DE) | 12A1 | 250 |
| Eisenach (DE) | 12C1 | 259 |
| Eisenheim (DE) | 12C3 | 295 |
| Eisfeld (DE) | 12D2 | 260 |
| Eltmann am Main (DE) | 12C3 | 295 |
| Erbendorf (DE) | 12E3 | 296 |
| Erfurt (DE) | 12D1 | 260 |
| Escherndorf (DE) | 12C3 | 296 |
| Eschwege (DE) | 12B1 | 250 |
| Fichtelberg (DE) | 12E3 | 296 |
| Flörsbachtal-L (DE) | 12B3 | 250 |
| Frankenberg/Eder (DE) | 12A1 | 251 |
| Freiberg (DE) | 12G1 | 192 |
| Friedberg (DE) | 12A3 | 251 |
| Friedenfels (DE) | 12E3 | 296 |
| Frielendorf (DE) | 12A1 | 251 |
| Fritzlar (DE) | 12A1 | 251 |
| Fulda (DE) | 12B2 | 251 |
| Garstadt (DE) | 12C3 | 297 |
| Gelnhausen (DE) | 12A3 | 251 |
| Gerolzhofen (DE) | 12C3 | 297 |
| Gilserberg (DE) | 12A1 | 251 |
| Goldkronach (DE) | 12E3 | 297 |
| Gotha (DE) | 12C1 | 260 |
| Gräfendorf (DE) | 12B3 | 298 |
| Grafenrheinfeld (DE) | 12C3 | 298 |
| Grebenau (DE) | 12B2 | 251 |
| Grebenhain (DE) | 12A2 | 251 |
| Großalmerode (DE) | 12B1 | 251 |
| Grünberg (DE) | 12A2 | 251 |
| Grünhain (DE) | 12F2 | 192 |
| Hammelburg (DE) | 12B3 | 299 |
| Hassfurt (DE) | 12C3 | 299 |
| Helsa (DE) | 12B1 | 252 |
| Herbstein (DE) | 12A2 | 252 |
| Hermsdorf (DE) | 12G1 | 192 |
| Hessisch Lichtenau (DE) | 12B1 | 252 |
| Hilders (DE) | 12B2 | 252 |
| Hirschaid (DE) | 12D3 | 299 |
| Hirzenhain (DE) | 12A2 | 252 |
| Hof/Saale (DE) | 12E2 | 299 |
| Hofheim in Unterfranken (DE) | 12C3 | 300 |
| Hohenberg/Eger (DE) | 12E3 | 300 |
| Homberg/Efze (DE) | 12A1 | 253 |
| Homberg/Ohm (DE) | 12A2 | 253 |
| Hořin (CZ) | 12H2 | 122 |
| Hünfeld (DE) | 12B2 | 253 |
| Hungen (DE) | 12A2 | 253 |
| Ichtershausen (DE) | 12D1 | 260 |
| Ilmenau (DE) | 12D2 | 261 |
| Jáchymov (CZ) | 12F2 | 122 |
| Karlovy Vary (CZ) | 12F2 | 122 |
| Kassel (DE) | 12A1 | 253 |
| Kaufungen (DE) | 12B1 | 253 |
| Kemnath (DE) | 12E3 | 301 |
| Kirchenlamitz (DE) | 12E3 | 301 |
| Kirchheim (DE) | 12B2 | 253 |
| Königsberg (DE) | 12C3 | 301 |

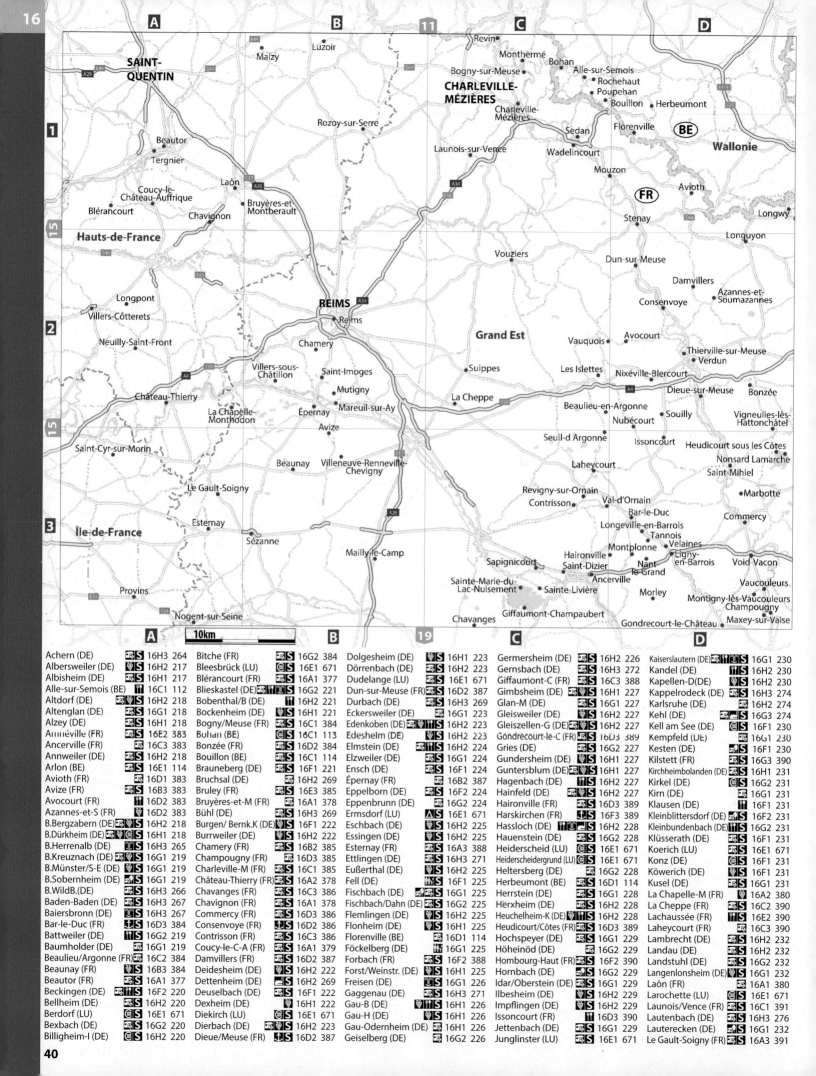

**SAINT-QUENTIN** · Malzy · Luzoir · Revin · Monthermé · Bohan · Alle-sur-Semois · Rochehaut · Poupehan · Bouillon · Herbeumont · Bogny-sur-Meuse · **CHARLEVILLE-MÉZIÈRES** · Charleville-Mézières · Florenville · (BE) **Wallonie** · Beautor · Tergnier · Rozoy-sur-Serre · Launois-sur-Vence · Sedan · Wadelincourt · Mouzon · (FR) · Avioth · Coucy-le-Château-Auffrique · Laôn · Stenay · Longwy · Blérancourt · Chavignon · Bruyères-et-Montberault · Longuyon · **Hauts-de-France** · Vouziers · Dun-sur-Meuse · Longpont · Damvillers · Azannes-et-Soumazannes · Villers-Côtterets · Consenvoye · Neuilly-Saint-Front · **Grand Est** · Vauquois · Avocourt · Thierville-sur-Meuse · Verdun · Chamery · Suippes · Les Islettes · Nixéville-Blercourt · Villers-sous-Châtillon · Saint-Imoges · La Cheppe · Dieue-sur-Meuse · Bonzée · Château-Thierry · Mutigny · Beaulieu-en-Argonne · Nubécourt · Souilly · Vigneulles-lès-Hattonchâtel · La Chapelle-Monthodon · Épernay · Mareuil-sur-Ay · Seuil-d'Argonne · Issoncourt · Heudicourt sous les Côtes · Avize · Saint-Cyr-sur-Morin · Laheycourt · Nonsard Lamarche · Beaunay · Villeneuve-Renneville-Chevigny · Saint-Mihiel · Le Gault-Soigny · Revigny-sur-Ornain · Val-d'Ornain · Marbotte · Contrisson · Bar-le-Duc · Commercy · **Île-de-France** · Esternay · Longeville-en-Barrois · Tannois · Sézanne · Montplonne · Velaines · Provins · Mailly-le-Camp · Hironville · Ligny-en-Barrois · Void-Vacon · Sapignicourt · Saint-Dizier · Nant-le-Grand · Vaucouleurs · Sainte-Marie-du-Lac-Nuisement · Ancerville · Morley · Montigny-lès-Vaucouleurs · Champougny · Nogent-sur-Seine · Sainte-Livière · Chavanges · Giffaumont-Champaubert · Gondrecourt-le-Château · Maxey-sur-Vaise

**10km**

| Place | Grid | Page |
|---|---|---|
| Achern (DE) | 16H3 | 264 |
| Albersweiler (DE) | 16H2 | 217 |
| Albisheim (DE) | 16H1 | 217 |
| Alle-sur-Semois (BE) | 16C1 | 112 |
| Altdorf (DE) | 16G1 | 218 |
| Altenglan (DE) | 16G1 | 218 |
| Alzey (DE) | 16H1 | 218 |
| Amnéville (FR) | 16E2 | 383 |
| Ancerville (FR) | 16C3 | 383 |
| Annweiler (DE) | 16H2 | 218 |
| Arlon (BE) | 16E1 | 114 |
| Avioth (FR) | 16D1 | 383 |
| Avize (FR) | 16B3 | 383 |
| Avocourt (FR) | 16D2 | 383 |
| Azannes-et-S (FR) | 16D2 | 383 |
| B.Bergzabern (DE) | 16H2 | 218 |
| B.Dürkheim (DE) | 16H1 | 218 |
| B.Herrenalb (DE) | 16H3 | 265 |
| B.Kreuznach (DE) | 16G1 | 219 |
| B.Münster/S-E (DE) | 16G1 | 219 |
| B.Sobernheim (DE) | 16G1 | 219 |
| B.WildB.(DE) | 16H3 | 266 |
| Baden-Baden (DE) | 16H3 | 267 |
| Baiersbronn (DE) | 16H3 | 267 |
| Bar-le-Duc (FR) | 16D3 | 384 |
| Battweiler (DE) | 16G2 | 219 |
| Baumholder (DE) | 16G1 | 219 |
| Beaulieu/Argonne (FR) | 16C2 | 384 |
| Beaunay (FR) | 16B3 | 384 |
| Beautor (FR) | 16A1 | 377 |
| Beckingen (DE) | 16F2 | 220 |
| Bellheim (DE) | 16H2 | 220 |
| Berdorf (LU) | 16E1 | 671 |
| Bexbach (DE) | 16G2 | 220 |
| Billigheim-I (DE) | 16H2 | 220 |
| Bitche (FR) | 16G2 | 384 |
| Bleesbrück (LU) | 16E1 | 671 |
| Blérancourt (FR) | 16A1 | 377 |
| Blieskastel (DE) | 16G2 | 221 |
| Bobenthal/B (DE) | 16H2 | 221 |
| Bockenheim (DE) | 16H1 | 221 |
| Bogny/Meuse (FR) | 16C1 | 384 |
| Bohan (BE) | 16C1 | 113 |
| Bonzée (FR) | 16D2 | 384 |
| Bouillon (BE) | 16C1 | 114 |
| Brauneberg (DE) | 16F1 | 221 |
| Bruchsal (DE) | 16H2 | 269 |
| Bruley (FR) | 16E3 | 385 |
| Bruyères-et-M (FR) | 16A1 | 378 |
| Bühl (DE) | 16H3 | 269 |
| Burgen/ Bernk.K (DE) | 16F1 | 222 |
| Burrweiler (DE) | 16H2 | 222 |
| Chamery (FR) | 16B2 | 385 |
| Champougny (FR) | 16D3 | 385 |
| Charleville-M (FR) | 16C1 | 385 |
| Château-Thierry (FR) | 16A2 | 378 |
| Chavanges (FR) | 16C3 | 386 |
| Chavignon (FR) | 16A1 | 378 |
| Commercy (FR) | 16D3 | 386 |
| Consenvoye (FR) | 16D3 | 386 |
| Contrisson (FR) | 16C3 | 386 |
| Coucy-le-C-A (FR) | 16A1 | 379 |
| Damvillers (FR) | 16D2 | 387 |
| Deidesheim (DE) | 16H2 | 222 |
| Dettenheim (DE) | 16H2 | 269 |
| Deuselbach (DE) | 16F1 | 222 |
| Dexheim (DE) | 16H1 | 222 |
| Diekirch (LU) | 16E1 | 671 |
| Dierbach (DE) | 16H2 | 223 |
| Dieue/Meuse (FR) | 16D2 | 387 |
| Dolgesheim (DE) | 16H1 | 223 |
| Dörrenbach (DE) | 16H2 | 223 |
| Dudelange (LU) | 16E1 | 671 |
| Dun-sur-Meuse (FR) | 16D2 | 387 |
| Durbach (DE) | 16H3 | 269 |
| Eckersweiler (DE) | 16G1 | 223 |
| Edenkoben (DE) | 16H2 | 223 |
| Edesheim (DE) | 16H2 | 223 |
| Elmstein (DE) | 16H2 | 224 |
| Elzweiler (DE) | 16G1 | 224 |
| Ensch (DE) | 16F1 | 224 |
| Épernay (FR) | 16B2 | 387 |
| Eppelborn (DE) | 16F2 | 224 |
| Eppenbrunn (DE) | 16G2 | 224 |
| Ermsdorf (LU) | 16E1 | 671 |
| Eschbach (DE) | 16H2 | 225 |
| Essingen (DE) | 16H2 | 225 |
| Esternay (FR) | 16A3 | 388 |
| Ettlingen (DE) | 16H3 | 271 |
| Eußerthal (DE) | 16H2 | 225 |
| Fell (DE) | 16F1 | 225 |
| Fischbach (DE) | 16G1 | 225 |
| Fischbach/Dahn (DE) | 16G2 | 225 |
| Flemlingen (DE) | 16H2 | 225 |
| Flonheim (DE) | 16H1 | 225 |
| Florenville (BE) | 16D1 | 114 |
| Föckelberg (DE) | 16G1 | 225 |
| Forbach (FR) | 16F2 | 388 |
| Forst/Weinstr. (DE) | 16H1 | 225 |
| Freisen (DE) | 16G1 | 226 |
| Gaggenau (DE) | 16H3 | 271 |
| Gau-B (DE) | 16H1 | 226 |
| Gau-H (DE) | 16H1 | 226 |
| Gau-Odernheim (DE) | 16H1 | 226 |
| Geiselberg (DE) | 16G2 | 226 |
| Germersheim (DE) | 16H2 | 226 |
| Gernsbach (DE) | 16H3 | 272 |
| Giffaumont-C (FR) | 16C3 | 388 |
| Gimbsheim (DE) | 16H1 | 227 |
| Glan-M (DE) | 16G1 | 227 |
| Gleisweiler (DE) | 16H2 | 227 |
| Gleiszellen-G (DE) | 16H2 | 227 |
| Gondrecourt-le-C (FR) | 16D3 | 389 |
| Gries (FR) | 16G2 | 227 |
| Gundersheim (DE) | 16H1 | 227 |
| Guntersblum (DE) | 16H1 | 227 |
| Hagenbach (DE) | 16H2 | 227 |
| Hainfeld (DE) | 16H2 | 227 |
| Haironville (FR) | 16D3 | 389 |
| Harskirchen (FR) | 16F3 | 389 |
| Hassloch (DE) | 16H2 | 228 |
| Hauenstein (DE) | 16G2 | 228 |
| Heiderscheid (LU) | 16E1 | 671 |
| Heiderscheidergrund (LU) | 16E1 | 671 |
| Heltersberg (DE) | 16G2 | 228 |
| Herbeumont (BE) | 16D1 | 114 |
| Herrstein (DE) | 16G1 | 228 |
| Herxheim (DE) | 16H2 | 228 |
| Heuchelheim-K (DE) | 16H2 | 228 |
| Heudicourt/Côtes (FR) | 16D3 | 389 |
| Hochspeyer (DE) | 16G1 | 228 |
| Höheinöd (DE) | 16G2 | 229 |
| Hombourg-Haut (FR) | 16F2 | 390 |
| Hornbach (DE) | 16G2 | 229 |
| Idar/Oberstein (DE) | 16G1 | 229 |
| Ilbesheim (DE) | 16H2 | 229 |
| Impflingen (DE) | 16H2 | 229 |
| Issoncourt (FR) | 16D3 | 390 |
| Jettenbach (DE) | 16G1 | 229 |
| Junglinster (LU) | 16E1 | 671 |
| Kaiserslautern (DE) | 16G1 | 230 |
| Kandel (DE) | 16H2 | 230 |
| Kapellen-D(DE) | 16H2 | 230 |
| Kappelrodeck (DE) | 16H3 | 274 |
| Karlsruhe (DE) | 16H2 | 274 |
| Kehl (DE) | 16G3 | 274 |
| Kell am See (DE) | 16F1 | 230 |
| Kempfeld (DE) | 16G1 | 230 |
| Kesten (DE) | 16F1 | 230 |
| Kilstett (FR) | 16G3 | 390 |
| Kirchheimbolanden (DE) | 16H1 | 231 |
| Kirkel (DE) | 16G2 | 231 |
| Kirn (DE) | 16G1 | 231 |
| Klausen (DE) | 16F1 | 231 |
| Kleinblittersdorf (DE) | 16F2 | 231 |
| Kleinbundenbach (DE) | 16G2 | 231 |
| Klüsserath (DE) | 16F1 | 231 |
| Koerich (LU) | 16E1 | 671 |
| Konz (DE) | 16F1 | 231 |
| Köwerich (DE) | 16F1 | 231 |
| Kusel (DE) | 16G1 | 231 |
| La Chapelle-M (FR) | 16A2 | 380 |
| La Cheppe (FR) | 16C2 | 390 |
| Lachaussée (FR) | 16E2 | 390 |
| Laheycourt (FR) | 16C3 | 390 |
| Lambrecht (DE) | 16H2 | 232 |
| Landau (DE) | 16H2 | 232 |
| Landstuhl (DE) | 16G2 | 232 |
| Langenlonsheim (DE) | 16G1 | 232 |
| Laôn (FR) | 16A1 | 380 |
| Larochette (LU) | 16E1 | 671 |
| Launois/Vence (FR) | 16C1 | 391 |
| Lautenbach (DE) | 16H3 | 276 |
| Lauterecken (DE) | 16G1 | 232 |
| Le Gault-Soigny (FR) | 16A3 | 391 |

10km

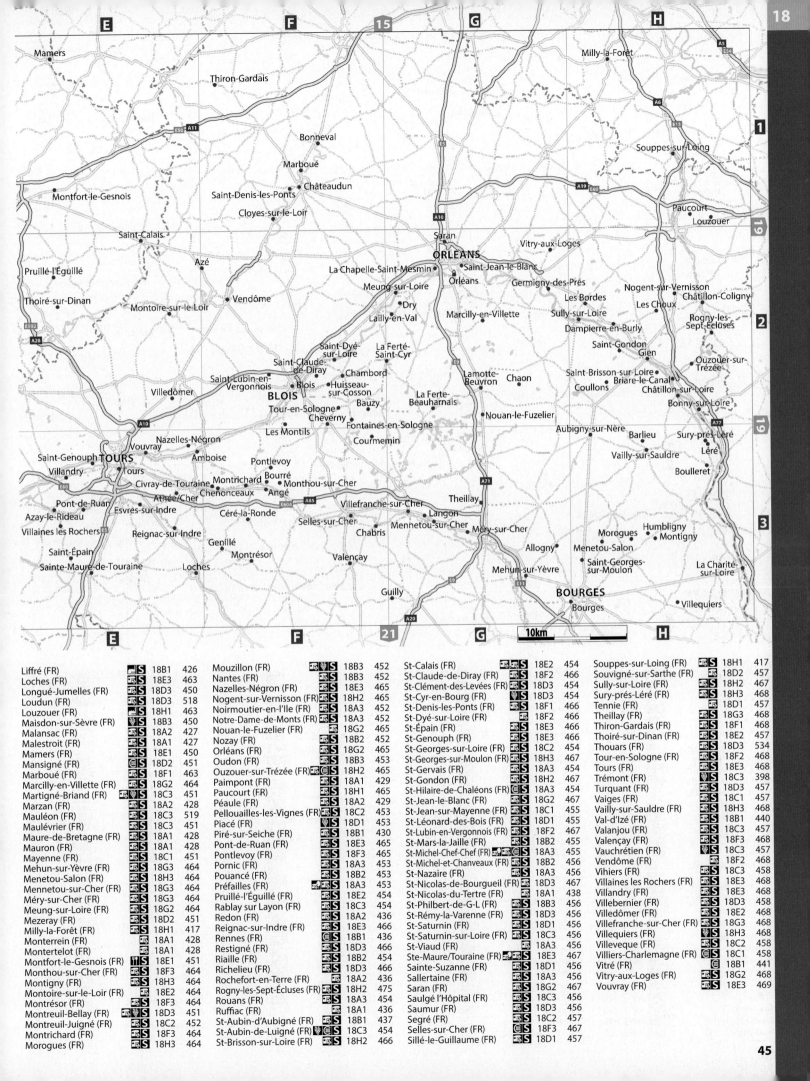

10km

**A** — **B** — 16 — **C** — **D**

**1** · **18** · **2** · **18** · **3**

Île-de-France

Bray-sur-Seine

TROYES
Piney
Montier-en-Der  Wassy
Brienne-le-Château
Dienville
Lusigny-sur-Barse
Mesnil-Saint-Père
Dolancourt
Bar-sur-Aube
Colombey-les-deux-Eglises
Joinville
Donjeux
Froncles
Viéville
Maxey-sur-Meuse
Rollainville
Rebeuville
Certilleux  Tilleul
Pompierre
Goncourt

Vendeuvre-sur-Barse
Aix-en-Othe
Sens
Gron
Javernant
Juzennecourt
Rennepont
Chaumont

Grand Est

Saint-Julien-du-Sault
Chaource
Essoyes
Les Riceys
Arc-en-Barrois

Grand Est
Champigny-lès-Langres
Peigney
Langres
Corgirnon

Gurgy
Pontigny
Beine
Auxerre
Chablis
Laignes

Saint-Fargeau
Mailly-le-Château
Treigny

Bourgogne-Franche-Comté
Montbard
Bussy-le-Grand
Semur-en-Auxois
Champlitte
Savoyeux
Fontaine-Française
Gray

Rouvray
Marigny-le-Cahouët
Savigny-le-Sec

Quarre-les-Tombes
DIJON
Dijon
Heuilley-sur-Saône

Chaumot
Marsannay-la-Côte
Broindon

Pougues-les-Eaux
Château-Chinon  Anost
Arnay-le-Duc
Nuits-Saint-Georges
Dôle

**A** — **B** — 22 — **C** — **D**

10km

**Baden-Württemberg** · **Bayern** · **Tirol** · **Vorarlberg**

10km

10km

| E | F | 22 | G | H | 25 |

**CHAMBÉRY** — Bourgneuf, Chambéry, Aiguebelle, Mâcot-la-Plagne, Val d'Isère, Céresole Reale, Valsavarenche, Rhêmes-Notre-Dame, **Valle D'Aosta**, Biella, Ponderano, Candelo, Mongrando, Donato, Chiaverano, Vidracco, Ivrea, Saint-Bon-Tarentaise, La Tania, Les Menuires, La Chambre, Le Cheylas, Allevard, Vialfrè, Romano Canavese, Aglié, Cuceglio, Maglione, Saint-Jean-de-Maurienne, **Auvergne-Rhône-Alpes**, Locana, Pont Canavese, **GRENOBLE**, Prapoutel-les-Sept-Laux, Les Karellis, Vaujany, Valloire, Chamrousse, Susa, Chianocco, Chiusa di San Michele, Druento, Venaria Reale, Chivasso, **TORINO**, Alpe d'Huez, Villar Focchiardo, Sant Antonino di Susa, Rosta, Collegno, Torino, Montiglio Monferrato, Les Deux-Alpes, Usseaux, Avigliana, Chieri, Névache, Fenestrelle, Giaveno, Saint-Théoffrey, Pragelato, Sestriere, Le Monêtier-les-Bains, La Salle-les-Alpes, Montgenèvre, Cesana Torinese, Prali, Pinerolo, **Piemonte**, Asti, La Mure, Briançon, Prarostino, San Damiano d'Asti, Puy-Saint-Vincent, Villar Pellice, Castiglione Tinella, Bibiana, Cavour, Sommariva Perno, Neive, Canelli, Orcières-Merlette, Saint-Crépin, Saint-Véran, Crissolo, Alba, Grinzane Cavour, Saint-Jean-Saint-Nicolas, Barge, Sanfront, Saluzzo, Cherasco, Castiglione Falletto, Cortemilia, **Provence-Alpes-Côte d'Azur**, Pontechianale, Genola, Vars, Venasca, Melle, La Roche-des-Arnauds, Chorges, Crots, Niella Belbo, Gap, Marsaglia, Mombarcaro, Veynes, Aspres-sur-Buëch, Savines-le-Lac, Accéglio, Castelletto Stura, Niella Tanaro, Cengio, La Bréole, Le Lauzet-Ubay, Jausiers, Pietraporzio, Cuneo, Mondovì, Saint-Pons, Barcelonnette, Selonnet, Pra-Loup, Battifollo, **Liguria**, Laragne-Montéglin, Seyne, Vinadio, Borgo San Dalmazzo, Roaschia, Chiusa di Pesio, Prato Nevoso, Frabosa Soprana, Mison, Allos, Valdieri, Vernante, Garessio, Sisteron, Colmars-les-Alpes, Isola, Entracque, Ormea, Loano

**10km**

| E | F | 28 | G | H |

---

Mâcot-la-Plagne (FR) 25F1 489
Maglione (IT) 25H1 602
Malaucène (FR) 25D3 570
Marsaglia (IT) 25H3 602
Marsanne (FR) 25C3 489
Marvéjols (FR) 25A3 552
Massiac (FR) 25A1 489
Melle (IT) 25G3 602
Mende (FR) 25A3 552
Mévouillon (FR) 25D3 489
Meyras (FR) 25B2 489
Mirabel-aux-B (FR) 25D3 490
Mison (FR) 25E3 570
Mombarcaro (IT) 25H3 602
Mondovì (IT) 25H3 602
Mongrando (IT) 25H1 602
Montbrison/Lez (FR) 25C3 490
Montélimar (FR) 25C3 490
Montgenèvre (FR) 25F2 570
Montiglio Monferrato (IT) 25H2 602
Neive (IT) 25H2 602
Névache (FR) 25F2 571
Niella Belbo (IT) 25H3 602
Niella Tanaro (IT) 25H3 602
Nyons (FR) 25D3 491
Orcières-Merlette (FR) 25E2 571
Orgnac l'Aven (FR) 25B3 492
Ormea (IT) 25H3 603
Pietraporzio (IT) 25G3 603
Pinerolo (IT) 25G2 603
Piolenc (FR) 25C3 571

Planfoy (FR) 25C1 492
Ponderano (IT) 25H1 604
Pont Canavese (IT) 25G1 604
Pontechianale (IT) 25G3 604
Pra-Loup (FR) 25F3 571
Pradelles (FR) 25B2 492
Pragelato (IT) 25F2 604
Prali (IT) 25G2 604
Prapoutel-les-SL (FR) 25E1 493
Prarostino (IT) 25G2 604
Prato Nevoso (IT) 25H3 604
Puy-St-Martin (FR) 25C3 493
Puy-St-Vincent (FR) 25F2 571
Raucoules (FR) 25B1 493
Retournac (FR) 25B1 493
Reventin-Vaugris (FR) 25C1 493
Rhêmes-N-Dame (IT) 25G1 597
Rieutort-de-R (FR) 25A3 557
Roaschia (IT) 25G3 604
Romano Canavese (IT) 25H1 604
Romans-sur-Isère (FR) 25C2 493
Rosans (FR) 25D3 572
Rosta (IT) 25G2 605
Ruoms (FR) 25B3 493
Ruynes-en-M (FR) 25A2 493
Sablet (FR) 25C3 572
Sagnes-et-G (FR) 25B2 493
Saillans (FR) 25D2 493
St-Agrève (FR) 25B2 494
St-Alban-A (FR) 25B3 494
St-André-de-C (FR) 25B1 494

St-Bon-Tarentaise (FR) 25F1 494
St-Bonnet-le-Château (FR) 25B1 494
St-Bonnet-le-Froid (FR) 25C1 494
St-Chély-d'Apcher (FR) 25A2 558
St-Christophe/D (FR) 25B2 494
St-Crépin (FR) 25F2 572
St-Désirat (FR) 25C1 494
St-Donat-sur-l'H (FR) 25C2 494
St-Félicien (FR) 25C2 495
St-Ferréol-T-Pas (FR) 25D3 495
St-Genest-de-B (FR) 25B3 495
St-Georges (FR) 25A2 495
St-Georges-d'Esp. (FR) 25C1 495
St-Jean-de-Bournay (FR) 25D1 495
St-Jean-de-M (FR) 25E1 496
St-Jean-en-Royans (FR) 25D2 496
St-Jean-St-Nicolas (FR) 25E2 572
St-Julien-Chapteuil (FR) 25B2 496
St-Just (FR) 25A2 496
St-Just-d'Ardèche (FR) 25C3 496
St-Laurent-de-C (FR) 25C3 559
St-Paul-le-Jeune (FR) 25B3 496
St-Paul-Trois-C (FR) 25C3 496
St-Pons (FR) 25F3 573
St-Rémèze (FR) 25C3 497
St-Restitut (FR) 25C3 497
St-Romain-d'Ay (FR) 25C1 497
St-Romain-de-L (FR) 25C2 497
St-Romain-Lachalm (FR) 25C1 497
St-Théoffrey (FR) 25E2 497
St-Thomé (FR) 25C3 497

St-Véran (FR) 25F2 573
St-Victor/Loire (FR) 25B1 497
Saluzzo (IT) 25G2 605
Sanfront (IT) 25G2 605
S Damiano d'Asti (IT) 25H2 605
S'Antonino di S (IT) 25G2 605
Sassenage (FR) 25D1 498
Saugues (FR) 25A2 498
Savines-le-Lac (FR) 25F3 574
Selonnet (FR) 25E3 574
Sestriere (IT) 25F2 605
Seyne (FR) 25F3 574
Siaugues-Ste-M (FR) 25A2 498
Sisteron (FR) 25E3 574
Solignac/Loire (FR) 25B2 498
Solignat (FR) 25A1 499
Sommariva Perno (IT) 25H2 605
St Anthème (FR) 25B1 499
Susa (IT) 25G1 605
Suze-la-Rousse (FR) 25C3 499
Tence (FR) 25B2 499
Thueyts (FR) 25B2 499
Tiranges (FR) 25B1 499
Torino (Turin) (IT) 25H2 605
Tournon/Rhône (FR) 25C2 499
Tourzel-Ronzières (FR) 25A1 500
Treffort (FR) 25D2 500
Usseaux (IT) 25G2 606
Vaison-la-Romaine (FR) 25D3 575
Val d'Isère (FR) 25F1 500
Valdieri (IT) 25G3 606

Valloire (FR) 25F1 500
Vallon-Pont-d'Arc (FR) 25B3 500
Valréas (FR) 25C3 575
Valsavarenche (IT) 25G1 597
Vars (FR) 25F3 575
Vassieux-en-Vercors (FR) 25D2 500
Vaujany (FR) 25E1 500
Védrines-St-Loup (FR) 25A2 501
Venaria Reale (IT) 25H2 606
Venasca (IT) 25G3 606
Verclause (FR) 25D3 501
Vernante (IT) 25G3 606
Vernosc-lès-Annonay (FR) 25C1 501
Veynes (FR) 25E3 575
Vialfrè (IT) 25H1 607
Vidracco (IT) 25H1 607
Vieille-Brioude (FR) 25A1 501
Vienne (FR) 25C1 501
Villar Focchiardo (IT) 25G2 607
Villar Pellice (IT) 25G2 607
Villards-de-Lans (FR) 25D2 501
Vinadio (IT) 25G3 607
Virieu (FR) 25D1 502
Visan (FR) 25C3 575
Viverols (FR) 25B1 502
Vogüé (FR) 25B3 502
Vorey/Arzon (FR) 25B1 502

10km

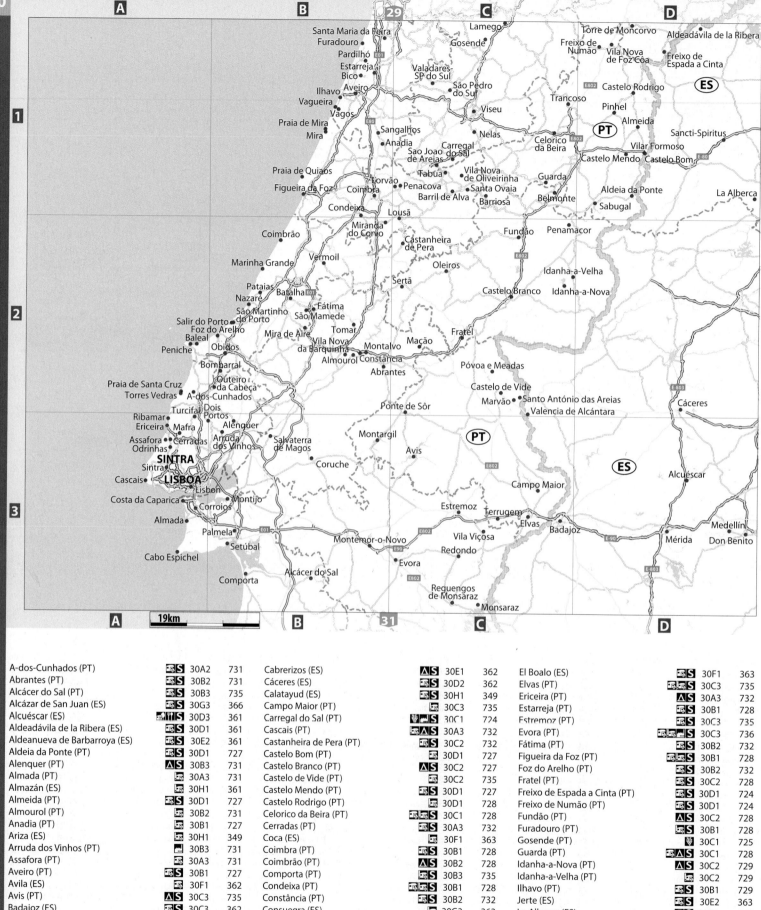

A | B | C | D

**19km**

A   B   30   C   D

Melides
Vila Nova de Santo André
Grândola
Alvito
Luz
Villanueva del Fresno
Zafra
Santiago do Cacém
Lousal
Ferreira do Alentejo
Estrela
Jerez de los Caballeros
Pedrogão do Alentejo
Fuente de Cantos
Porto Covo
Beja
Cumbres Mayores
Messejana
PT
Almograve
Cavaleiro
São Martinho das Amoreiras
Mina de São Domingos
ES
El Real de la Jara
Alanís
Odeceixe
Santa Clara-e-Velha
Mértola
Aljezur
Carrapateira
Alferce
Silves
Ameixial
Pereiro
Sanlúcar de Guadiana
Valverde del Camino
Las Pajanosas
Vila do Bispo
Caldas de Monchique
São Bartolomeu de Messines
Alcoutim
Odeleite
Cabo de São Vicente
Lagos Alvor
Algoz
Paderne
Castro Marim
Ayamonte
Isla Cristina
SEVILLA
Sevilla
Budens
Pêra
Consiguinte
Altura
Manta Rota
Vila Real de Sto António
Gelves
Almensilla
Alcalá de Guadaíra
Sagres
Carvoeiro
Albufeira
Moncarapacho
Tavira
Huelva
Quarteira
Faro
Fuseta
HUELVA
Dos Hermanas
Sanlúcar de Barrameda
Chipiona
Jerez de la Frontera
Arcos de la Frontera
El Bosque
El Puerto de Santa Maria
JEREZ DE LA FRONTERA
Algar
Ubrique
Sancti Petrí La Barrosa
Conil de la Frontera
Vejer de la Frontera
Barbate
GIBRALTAR
Tarifa
La Línea de Concepción

A   19km   B   C   D

| Place | Grid | Page |
|---|---|---|
| Abla (ES) | 31G2 | 366 |
| Águilas (ES) | 31H2 | 350 |
| Alanís (ES) | 31D1 | 366 |
| Albufeira (PT) | 31B2 | 738 |
| Alcalá de Guadaíra (ES) | 31D2 | 366 |
| Alcoutim (PT) | 31C2 | 738 |
| Alferce (PT) | 31B2 | 738 |
| Algar (ES) | 31D3 | 366 |
| Algoz (PT) | 31B2 | 738 |
| Alicún de las Torres (ES) | 31G2 | 366 |
| Aljezur (PT) | 31A1 | 738 |
| Almayate (ES) | 31F3 | 366 |
| Almensilla (ES) | 31D2 | 366 |
| Almerimar (ES) | 31G3 | 366 |
| Almograve (PT) | 31B1 | 735 |
| Altura (PT) | 31C2 | 738 |
| Alvito (PT) | 31B1 | 735 |
| Alvor (PT) | 31B2 | 738 |
| Ameixial (PT) | 31B2 | 738 |
| Antequera (ES) | 31E2 | 366 |
| Archena (ES) | 31H1 | 351 |
| Archidona (ES) | 31E2 | 366 |
| Arcos de la Frontera (ES) | 31D3 | 366 |
| Ayamonte (ES) | 31C2 | 366 |
| Baena (ES) | 31F2 | 366 |
| Baeza (ES) | 31F1 | 366 |
| Barbate (ES) | 31D3 | 367 |
| Beja (PT) | 31B1 | 735 |
| Benarrabá (ES) | 31E3 | 367 |
| Budens (PT) | 31A2 | 738 |
| Cabo de Gata (ES) | 31H3 | 367 |
| Cabo de São Vicente (PT) | 31A2 | 738 |
| Cabra (ES) | 31F2 | 367 |
| Cala de Mijas (ES) | 31E3 | 367 |
| Caldas de Monchique (PT) | 31B2 | 738 |
| Caleta de Vélez (ES) | 31F3 | 367 |
| Calnegre (ES) | 31H2 | 353 |
| Canjáyar (ES) | 31G3 | 367 |
| Carboneras (ES) | 31H3 | 367 |
| Carrapateira (PT) | 31A2 | 738 |
| Carvoeiro (PT) | 31B2 | 739 |
| Casares (ES) | 31E3 | 367 |
| Castell de Ferro (ES) | 31F3 | 367 |
| Castro Marim (PT) | 31C2 | 739 |
| Cavaleiro (PT) | 31B1 | 735 |
| Ceutí (ES) | 31H2 | 354 |
| Chipiona (ES) | 31D2 | 367 |
| Conil de la Frontera (ES) | 31D3 | 367 |
| Consiguinte (PT) | 31B2 | 739 |
| Córdoba (ES) | 31E1 | 367 |
| Cuevas de San Marcos (ES) | 31F2 | 367 |
| Cuevas del Almanzora (ES) | 31H2 | 367 |
| Cullar (ES) | 31G2 | 367 |
| Cumbres Mayores (ES) | 31D1 | 363 |
| Dólar (ES) | 31G2 | 367 |
| Doña Mencía (ES) | 31F2 | 368 |
| Dos Hermanas (ES) | 31D2 | 368 |
| El Bosque (ES) | 31D3 | 368 |
| El Higuerón (ES) | 31E1 | 368 |
| El Puerto de Santa Maria (ES) | 31D3 | 368 |
| El Real de la Jara (ES) | 31D1 | 368 |
| Estrela (PT) | 31C1 | 735 |
| Faro (PT) | 31B2 | 739 |
| Ferreira do Alentejo (PT) | 31B1 | 736 |
| Frailes (ES) | 31F2 | 368 |
| Fuengirola (ES) | 31E3 | 368 |
| Fuente de Cantos (ES) | 31D1 | 363 |
| Fuseta (PT) | 31B2 | 739 |
| Gelves (ES) | 31D2 | 368 |
| Granada (ES) | 31F2 | 368 |
| Grândola (PT) | 31B1 | 736 |
| Grazalema (ES) | 31E3 | 368 |
| Hornachuelos (ES) | 31E1 | 343 |
| Huelva (ES) | 31C2 | 368 |
| Huércal-Overa (ES) | 31H2 | 368 |
| Isla Cristina (ES) | 31C2 | 368 |
| Jerez de la Frontera (ES) | 31D3 | 369 |
| Jerez de los Caballeros (ES) | 31D1 | 363 |
| Júzcar (ES) | 31E3 | 369 |
| La Isleta (ES) | 31H3 | 369 |
| La Línea de Concepción (ES) | 31D3 | 369 |
| Lagos (PT) | 31B2 | 739 |
| Las Pajanosas (ES) | 31D2 | 369 |
| Lora del Río (ES) | 31E2 | 369 |
| Lorca (ES) | 31H2 | 356 |
| Lorquí (ES) | 31H2 | 356 |
| Los Albaricoques (ES) | 31H3 | 369 |
| Lousal (PT) | 31B1 | 736 |
| Luz (PT) | 31C1 | 736 |
| Málaga (ES) | 31F3 | 369 |

A    B    27    C    D

Olite, Jaca, Sabiñánigo, Aínsa, Arguedas, Alquézar, Tudela, Fontellas, Aragón, La Joyosa, Peñaflor, ZARAGOZA, Zaragoza, Catalunya, Carinena, LLEIDA, Lleida, Bovera, La Vilella Baixa, Ascó

10km

A    B    33    C    D

Map labels:

A — B — C — D

Albalate del Arzobispo  Alcañiz
Andorra
Calaceite  El Masroig  El Catllar  Creixell
El Grao de  Cambrils  Altafulla
Tortosa
Mas de Barberans
Morella  Deltebre
La Sénia  Amposta  Els Muntells
San Rafael del Río  Ulldecona
Albarracín  La Salzadella
Teruel  Peñíscola
San Agustín  Alcossebre
Montanejos
El Grao de  CASTELLÓN DE
Castellón  LA PLANA
Benagéber  Segorbe  Nules
Moncófar
VALENCIA
Turis  Valencia  PALMA DE
MALLORCA  Felanitx
Jalance
Bicorp
Ayora  Tavernes de la Valldigna
Carcaixent  Simat de la Valldigna
L'Olleria  Daimús  L'Alqueria de la Comtessa
El Palomar  Oliva
Yecla
Ibi  Callosa d'en Sarrià
Moraira
Calpe
Altea
El Campello
La Romana  Alicante
ALICANTE
Orihuela  Dolores  Sta.Pola
Bigastro  La Marina
Murcia  San Fulgencio
MURCIA
Balsicas  San Javier
Los Alcázares
Cartagena
La Azohia

25km

## Map

A · B · 38 · C · D
Grid rows: 1 · 17 · 2 · 20 · 3 · 39

Scale: 19km

Hluboká nad Vltavou · Nová Bystřice · Třebon · Znojmo · Břeclav · Banka
CESKÉ BUDEJOVICE · Karlstein an der Thaya · Schrems · Retz · Bernhardsthal · Hohenau/March
Ceský Krumlov · CZ · Pernegg · Pulkau · Wilfersdorf · NITRA
Horní Planá · Weitra · Horn · Eggenburg · Gars am Kamp · SK
Hurka · Zwettl · Schönberg · Göllersdorf
Lipno nad Vltavou · Langschlag-Mitterschlag · Schiltern/Langenlois · Langenlois · Stockerau · Pillichsdorf
Haslach · Arbesbach · Armschlag · Rossatzbach · Klosterneuburg · Bratislava
Kefermarkt · Königswiesen · Ottenschlag · Laimbach/Ostrong · Aggsbach Markt · Bad Deutsch-Altenburg · Hainburg/Donau
Aschach/Donau · Aggsbach Dorf · WIEN · Šamorín · Dunajská Streda
Eferding · Gallneukirchen · Waldhausen/Strudengau · Wien · Orth/Donau · Deutsch Jahrndorf · SK
LINZ · Naarn · Ardagger · Erlauf · Gumpoldskirchen · Halászi · Nagysáp
Kronstorf · Aschbach Markt · Sankt Martin am Ybbsfelde · Altenmarkt/Triesting · Jois · Podersdorf · Andau · HU
Kremsmünster · Weistrach · Gaming · Oslip · Illmitz · GYOR · Gyor · Budapest
Schlierbach · Mitterbach · Wiener Neustadt · HU · BUDAPEST
Scharnstein · Hollenstein/Ybbs · Reichenau/Rax
Sankt Pankraz · Hieflau · Veitsch · Horitschon
Liezen · Vordernberg · Pápa
Gaishorn am See · Bad Tatzmannsdorf · Bozsok
Pichl-Kainisch · Passail · Kaindorf · Cserszegtomaj
Großlobming · Deutschfeistritz · Bad Waltersdorf · Moschendorf · Gyenesdiás
Judenburg · HU · Balatonkeresztúr
Stadl an der Mur · Unterlamm · Koppányszántó
Bad Sankt Leonhard im Lavanttal · Greisdorf · Riegersburg · Sankt Stefan im Rosental · Kisbárapáti
Bad Gams · Wildon · GRAZ · Jagerberg · Deutsch Goritz · Somogyvár
Deutschlandsberg · Stainz · Deutsch Cankova · Goritz · Moravske Toplice · Dobrovnik · Lenti
Schwanberg · Oberrakitsch · Murfeld · Gosdorf
Pölfing-Brunn · Gamlitz · Apače · Bad Radkersburg · Murska Sobota
Soboth · Mureck · Lendava
KLAGENFURT AM WÖRTHERSEE · Leutschach · Pesnica · Ljutomer
Wernberg · Kamnica · Maribor · Mala Nedelja · Ivanjkovci · Sormás · Magyaregregy
Rosegg · Klagenfurt · Ferlach · SLO · Rogla · Zrece · Ptuj · Cirkulane · Ormož · HU
Ledenitzen · Slovenj Gradec · Tepanje · Patosfa
Zgornje Jezersko · Solčava · Recica/Savinji · SLO · PÉCS
Kranjska Gora · Rateče · Mojstrana · Tržič · Stahovica · Braslovce · Rogaška Slatina · Koprivnica
Bled · Kovor · Kamniška Bistrica · Žalec · Celje · HR

## Index

| Place | Grid | Page |
|---|---|---|
| Aggsbach Dorf (AT) | 36B1 | 87 |
| Aggsbach Markt (AT) | 36B1 | 87 |
| Altenmarkt/Triesting (AT) | 36B2 | 87 |
| Andau (AT) | 36C2 | 98 |
| Apače (SI) | 36B3 | 763 |
| Arbesbach (AT) | 36A1 | 87 |
| Ardagger (AT) | 36A1 | 87 |
| Armschlag (AT) | 36A1 | 87 |
| Aschach/Donau (AT) | 36A1 | 86 |
| Aschbach Markt (AT) | 36A2 | 87 |
| Bad Deutsch-A (AT) | 36C1 | 98 |
| Bad Gams (AT) | 36B3 | 94 |
| Bad Großpertholz (AT) | 36A1 | 88 |
| Bad Radkersburg (AT) | 36B3 | 94 |
| B.Skt Leonhard/L (AT) | 36A3 | 97 |
| Bad Tatzmannsdorf (AT) | 36B2 | 98 |
| Bad Waltersdorf (AT) | 36B2 | 94 |
| Balatonkeresztúr (HU) | 36C3 | 592 |
| Banka (SK) | 36C1 | 759 |
| Bernhardsthal (AT) | 36C1 | 88 |
| Bled (SI) | 36A3 | 760 |
| Bleiburg (AT) | 36A3 | 97 |
| Bozsok (HU) | 36C2 | 593 |
| Braslovče (SI) | 36B3 | 763 |
| Bratislava (SK) | 36C1 | 759 |
| Břeclav (CZ) | 36C1 | 123 |
| Cankova (SI) | 36B3 | 763 |
| Celje (SI) | 36B3 | 763 |
| Český Krumlov (CZ) | 36A1 | 122 |
| Cirkulane (SI) | 36B3 | 763 |
| Cserszegtomaj (HU) | 36C3 | 592 |
| Deutsch Goritz (AT) | 36B3 | 94 |
| Deutsch Jahrndorf (AT) | 36C1 | 98 |
| Deutschfeistritz (AT) | 36B2 | 94 |
| Deutschlandsberg (AT) | 36B3 | 94 |
| Dobrovnik (SI) | 36C3 | 764 |
| Dunajská Streda (SK) | 36C1 | 759 |
| Eferding (AT) | 36A1 | 86 |
| Eggenburg (AT) | 36B1 | 88 |
| Erlauf (AT) | 36A1 | 88 |
| Ferlach (AT) | 36A3 | 97 |
| Gaishorn/See (AT) | 36A2 | 94 |
| Gallneukirchen (AT) | 36A1 | 86 |
| Gaming (AT) | 36A2 | 88 |
| Gamlitz (AT) | 36B3 | 94 |
| Gars am Kamp (AT) | 36B1 | 88 |
| Göllersdorf (AT) | 36B1 | 88 |
| Gosdorf (AT) | 36B3 | 95 |
| Graz (AT) | 36B3 | 95 |
| Greisdorf (AT) | 36B3 | 95 |
| Großlobming (AT) | 36A3 | 95 |
| Gumpoldskirchen (AT) | 36B1 | 88 |
| Gyenesdiás (HU) | 36C3 | 592 |
| Győr (HU) | 36C2 | 593 |
| Hainburg/Donau (AT) | 36C1 | 88 |
| Halászi (HU) | 36C2 | 593 |
| Haslach (AT) | 36A1 | 86 |
| Hieflau (AT) | 36A2 | 88 |
| Hluboká nad Vltavou (CZ) | 36A1 | 122 |
| Hohenau/March (AT) | 36C1 | 88 |
| Hollenstein/Ybbs (AT) | 36A2 | 88 |
| Horitschon (AT) | 36C2 | 98 |
| Horn (AT) | 36B1 | 88 |
| Horní Planá (CZ) | 36A1 | 122 |
| Hůrka (CZ) | 36A1 | 122 |
| Illmitz (AT) | 36C2 | 98 |
| Ivanjkovci (SI) | 36B3 | 764 |
| Jagerberg (AT) | 36B3 | 95 |
| Jois (AT) | 36C2 | 98 |
| Judenburg (AT) | 36A3 | 95 |
| Kaindorf (AT) | 36B2 | 95 |
| Kamnica (SI) | 36B3 | 764 |
| Kamniška Bistrica (SI) | 36A3 | 761 |
| Karlstein/Thaya (AT) | 36A1 | 88 |
| Kefermarkt (AT) | 36A1 | 86 |
| Kishárapáti (HU) | 36D3 | 592 |
| Klagenfurt (AT) | 36A3 | 97 |
| Klosterneuburg (AT) | 36B1 | 88 |
| Königswiesen (AT) | 36A1 | 86 |
| Koppányszántó (HU) | 36D3 | 593 |
| Koprivnica (HR) | 36C3 | 591 |
| Kovor (AT) | 36A3 | 764 |
| Kranjska Gora (SI) | 36A3 | 761 |
| Kremsmünster (AT) | 36A2 | 86 |
| Kronstorf (AT) | 36A2 | 86 |
| Laimbach/Ostrong (AT) | 36A1 | 88 |
| Langenlois (AT) | 36B1 | 88 |
| Langschlag-Mitterschlag (AT) | 36A1 | 89 |
| Ledenitzen (AT) | 36A3 | 98 |
| Lendava (SI) | 36C3 | 764 |
| Lenti (HU) | 36C3 | 593 |
| Leutschach (AT) | 36B3 | 95 |
| Liezen (AT) | 36A2 | 95 |
| Lipno nad Vltavou (CZ) | 36A1 | 122 |
| Luče (SI) | 36A3 | 762 |
| Magyaregregy (HU) | 36D3 | 593 |
| Mala Nedelja (SI) | 36B3 | 765 |
| Maribor (SI) | 36B3 | 765 |
| Mitterbach (AT) | 36B2 | 89 |
| Mojstrana (SI) | 36A3 | 762 |
| Moravske Toplice (SI) | 36B3 | 765 |
| Moschendorf (AT) | 36C3 | 98 |
| Mosonmagyaróvár (HU) | 36C2 | 593 |
| Mureck (AT) | 36B3 | 96 |
| Murfeld (AT) | 36B3 | 96 |
| Murska Sobota (SI) | 36B3 | 765 |
| Naarn (AT) | 36A1 | 87 |
| Nagysáp (HU) | 36D2 | 593 |
| Nová Bystřice (CZ) | 36A1 | 123 |
| Oberrakitsch (AT) | 36B3 | 96 |
| Ormož (SI) | 36B3 | 766 |
| Orth/Donau (AT) | 36C1 | 89 |
| Oslip (AT) | 36C2 | 99 |
| Ottenschlag (AT) | 36A1 | 89 |
| Pápa (HU) | 36C2 | 593 |
| Passail (AT) | 36B2 | 96 |
| Patosfa (HU) | 36D3 | 593 |
| Pécs (HU) | 36D3 | 592 |
| Pernegg (AT) | 36B1 | 89 |
| Pesnica pri Mariboru (SI) | 36B3 | 766 |
| Pichl-Kainisch (AT) | 36A2 | 96 |
| Pillichsdorf (AT) | 36B1 | 89 |
| Podersdorf (AT) | 36C2 | 99 |
| Pölfing-Brunn (AT) | 36B3 | 96 |
| Ptuj (SI) | 36B3 | 766 |
| Pulkau (AT) | 36B1 | 89 |
| Rateče (SI) | 36A3 | 762 |
| Rečica ob Savinji (SI) | 36B3 | 766 |
| Reichenau/Rax (AT) | 36B2 | 89 |
| Retz (AT) | 36B1 | 89 |
| Riegersburg (AT) | 36B3 | 96 |
| Rogaška Slatina (SI) | 36B3 | 767 |
| Rogla (SI) | 36B3 | 767 |
| Rosegg (AT) | 36A3 | 98 |
| Rossatzbach (AT) | 36B1 | 89 |
| Šamorín (SK) | 36C1 | 759 |
| Sankt Martin/ Y/ (AT) | 36A1 | 89 |
| Sankt Pankraz (AT) | 36A2 | 87 |
| Sankt Stefan/Rosental (AT) | 36B3 | |
| Scharnstein (AT) | 36A2 | 87 |
| Schiltern/Langenlois (AT) | 36B1 | 89 |
| Schlierbach (AT) | 36A2 | 87 |
| Schönberg (AT) | 36B1 | 89 |
| Schrems (AT) | 36A1 | 89 |
| Schwanberg (AT) | 36B3 | 97 |
| Slovenj Gradec (SI) | 36B3 | 767 |
| Soboth (AT) | 36B3 | 97 |
| Solcava (SI) | 36A3 | 762 |
| Somogyvár (HU) | 36D3 | 593 |
| Sormás (HU) | 36C3 | 593 |
| Stadl an der Mur (AT) | 36A3 | 97 |
| Stahovica (SI) | 36A3 | 767 |
| Stainz (AT) | 36B3 | 97 |
| Stockerau (AT) | 36B1 | 90 |
| Tepanje (SI) | 36B3 | 767 |
| Třeboň (CZ) | 36A1 | 123 |
| Tržič (SI) | 36A3 | 763 |
| Unterlamm (AT) | 36B3 | 97 |
| Veitsch (AT) | 36B2 | 97 |
| Vordernberg (AT) | 36A2 | 97 |
| Waldhausen/Str. (AT) | 36A1 | 87 |
| Weistrach (AT) | 36A2 | 90 |
| Weitra (AT) | 36A1 | 90 |
| Wernberg (AT) | 36A3 | 98 |
| Wien (Vienna) (AT) | 36B1 | 90 |
| Wiener Neustadt (AT) | 36B2 | 90 |
| Wildon (AT) | 36B3 | 93 |
| Wilfersdorf (AT) | 36B1 | 90 |
| Žalec (SI) | 36B3 | 767 |
| Zgornje Jezersko (SI) | 36A3 | 768 |
| Zreče (SI) | 36B3 | 768 |
| Zwettl (AT) | 36A1 | 90 |

| | | |
|---|---|---|
| Adršpach (CZ) | 38A3 | 122 |
| Bad Muskau (DE) | 38A3 | 191 |
| Białystok (PL) | 38D1 | 721 |
| Biskupice (PL) | 38A2 | 721 |
| Bystrice nad Pernstejnem (CZ) | 38A4 | 124 |
| Červená Řečice (CZ) | 38A4 | 124 |
| Czaplinek (PL) | 38A1 | 720 |
| Częstochowa (PL) | 38B3 | 722 |
| Dobre Miasto (PL) | 38B1 | 721 |
| Ebersbach/Sachsen (DE) | 38A3 | 192 |
| Gaj (PL) | 38C4 | 722 |
| Gdańsk (PL) | 38B1 | 720 |
| Gierloz (PL) | 38C1 | 721 |
| Golčův Jeníkov (CZ) | 38A4 | 122 |
| Gora Swietej Anny (PL) | 38B3 | 722 |
| Görlitz (DE) | 38A3 | 192 |
| Haligovce (SK) | 38C4 | 759 |
| Janské Lázně (CZ) | 38A3 | 122 |
| Karpacz (PL) | 38A3 | 722 |
| Kraków (PL) | 38C4 | 722 |
| Kutná Hora (CZ) | 38A4 | 122 |
| Lipce Reymontowskie (PL) | 38C2 | 722 |
| Liptovský Ján (SK) | 38C4 | 759 |
| Löbau (DE) | 38A3 | 192 |
| Malbork (PL) | 38B1 | 720 |
| Mikolajki (PL) | 38C1 | 721 |
| Milolyn (PL) | 38B1 | 721 |
| Miroslawiec (PL) | 38A2 | 720 |
| Mrągowo (PL) | 38C1 | 721 |
| Naklo (PL) | 38B3 | 722 |
| Nové Město pod Smrkem (CZ) | 38A3 | 123 |
| Oderwitz (DE) | 38A3 | 193 |
| Oswiecim (PL) | 38B4 | 722 |
| Parchowo (PL) | 38A1 | 721 |
| Paslek (PL) | 38B1 | 721 |
| Piecki (PL) | 38C1 | 721 |
| Pieniezno (PL) | 38B1 | 721 |
| Poznań (PL) | 38A2 | 721 |
| Prague (CZ) | 38A4 | 123 |
| Řásná (CZ) | 38A4 | 124 |
| Rokytnice nad Jizerou (CZ) | 38A3 | 123 |
| Sękowa (PL) | 38C4 | 722 |
| Snina (SK) | 38D4 | 759 |
| Sorkwity (PL) | 38C1 | 721 |
| Svitavy (CZ) | 38A4 | 123 |
| Svoboda nad Úpou (CZ) | 38A3 | 123 |
| Tolkmicko (PL) | 38B1 | 721 |
| Toruń (PL) | 38B2 | 721 |
| Uciechów (PL) | 38A3 | 722 |
| Uherský Brod (CZ) | 38B4 | 124 |
| Varín (SK) | 38B4 | 759 |
| Velká Jesenice (CZ) | 38A4 | 123 |
| Veverská Bítýška (CZ) | 38A4 | 124 |
| Vyšný Medzev (SK) | 38C4 | 759 |
| Vysoké Tatry (SK) | 38C4 | 759 |
| Warszawa (Warsaw) (PL) | 38C2 | 722 |
| Wetlina (PL) | 38D4 | 722 |
| Wieliczka (PL) | 38C4 | 722 |
| Wierzbna (PL) | 38A2 | 721 |
| Zagaje (PL) | 38A1 | 721 |
| Žďár nad Sázavou (CZ) | 38A4 | 124 |
| Zittau (DE) | 38A3 | 193 |
| Łukta (PL) | 38B1 | 721 |

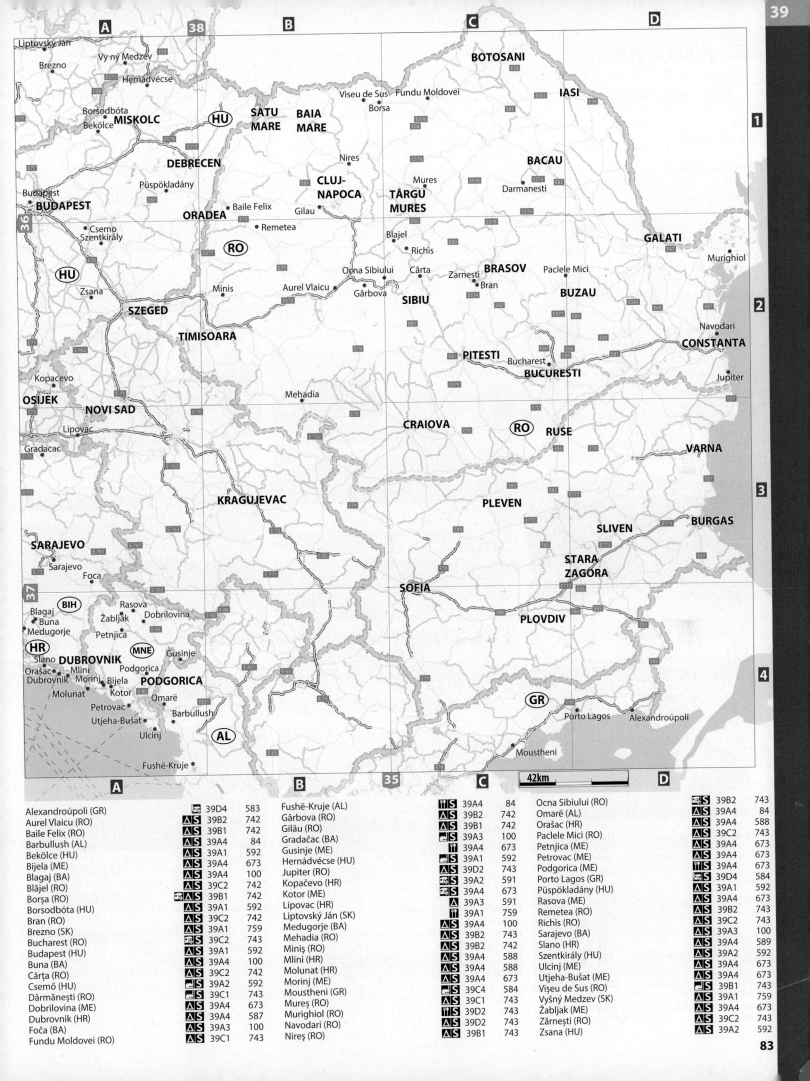

42km

# Albania

Capital: Tirana
Government: parliamentarian republic
Official Language: Albanian
Population: 3,047,987 (2017)
Area: 28.748 km²

## General information
Dialling code: 0355
General emergency: 112
Currency: Lek (ALL) € 1 = 125 ALL, 100 ALL = € 0,80
£1 = 143 ALL, 100 ALL = £0.70 (October 2018)
Credit cards are accepted in the main cities.

## Regulations for overnight stays
Wild camping is allowed with permission from
land owner/manager or local government.

### Additional public holidays 2019
March 14 Dita e Verës (Summer Day)
March 21 Nowruz (Iranian New Year)
April 19 Good Friday
October 19 Mother Teresa Day
November 28 Independence Day
November 29 Liberation Day

### Time Zone
Winter (Standard Time) GMT+1
Summer (DST) GMT+2

AL

---

### △S Barbullush — 39A5
**Gardenland Resort**, Shkodër. **GPS:** n41,93853 e19,54487.
30 🏕 € 2 + € 4-6,50/pp ⚡ Ch 🚿 2 WC 📶 included.
**Location:** Comfortable, isolated, quiet. **Surface:** grassy.
🗓 01/01-31/12.
**Distance:** 🏖 2km ⊗ on the spot.
**Remarks:** Swimming pool.

### 🅿 Benjé-Novoselë — 35E1
**Rruga e Benjes. GPS:** n40,24362 e20,43115.
10 🏕 free. **Location:** Rural, simple, isolated, quiet.
**Surface:** grassy/gravel. 🗓 01/01-31/12.
**Distance:** 🏊 on the spot.

### 🅲🆂 Berat — 35E1
**Berat Caravan Camping**, Ura Vajgurore. **GPS:** n40,77914 e19,85848.

30 🏕 € 17 ⚡ Ch 🚿 WC 📶 included. 🏠 **Location:** Rural,
comfortable, isolated. **Surface:** grassy. 🗓 01/01-31/12.
**Distance:** 🏙 city centre Berat 18km ⊗ on the spot 🚐 on the spot.

### 🍴 Divjakë Plazh — 35E1
**Bar/Rest/Hotel Adrian Satka. GPS:** n40,97156 e19,48036.

🏕 🗓 01/01-31/12.

### 🅷🆂 Fushë-Kruje — 39A5
**Hotel Nordpark**, Rruga Nacionale. **GPS:** n41,47078 e19,69875. ⬆

25 🏕 € 19 ⚡ Ch 🚿 WC 📶 included. 🏠 🏄
**Location:** Rural, comfortable, isolated, noisy. **Surface:** metalled.
🗓 01/01-31/12.

---

**Distance:** 🏖 2km ⊗ on the spot.
**Remarks:** Incl. access swimming pool. 🍽

### 🅿 Gjirokaster 🌿 🍲 — 35E1
**Viroi**, SH4. **GPS:** n40,10308 e20,12289.

2 🏕 free. 🗓 01/01-31/12.
**Distance:** 🏖 3km ⊗ on the spot.

### △S Himarë 🏖 — 35E1
**Camping Kranea**, Livadh Beach. **GPS:** n40,10734 e19,72739.

🏕 € 14 🚿 2 🔌 3. 🗓 01/01-31/12.

### △S Himarë 🏖 — 35E1
**Camping Moskato**, Livadh Road. **GPS:** n40,10986 e19,72280.

25 🏕 € 13 ⚡ Ch 🚿 WC 📶 included 🔌 € 2/time. 🗓 01/01-31/12.

### △S Hudënisht 🏖 — 35E1
**Peshku**, SH3. **GPS:** n40,96725 e20,64274.
30 🏕 € 5-12 ⚡ Ch 🚿 WC 📶 included 🔌 € 2.
**Location:** Rural, simple, quiet. **Surface:** grassy.
🗓 01/01-31/12.
**Distance:** 🏊 on the spot ⊗ on the spot 🍺 100m.
**Remarks:** Lake Ohrid, free use of sun beds and beach chairs.

### 🅿🆂 Kavajë — 35E1
**Camp Pa Emer**, Rrakull-Karpen. **GPS:** n41,18138 e19,47750. ⬆

---

34 🏕 € 17-19 ⚡ Ch 🚿 WC 📶 included. 🏠
**Location:** Rural. **Surface:** grassy/gravel. 🗓 01/04-01/11.
**Distance:** 🏖 1km ⊗ on the spot ⊗ on the spot.

### 🅿🆂 Ksamil 🏖 — 35E1
**Sunset**, SH81. **GPS:** n39,77908 e20,00831. ⬆

20 🏕 € 10 ⚡ Ch 🚿 WC 📶 included. 🏠
**Location:** Rural, simple, quiet. **Surface:** metalled. 🗓 01/04-30/09.
**Distance:** 🏖 Sarandë 10km ⊗ on the spot ⊗ on the spot 🍺 1km.

### 🌿🆂 Leskovik 🌿 🍴 — 35E1
**Farma Sotira**, SH75, Leskovik > Ersekë 15km.
**GPS:** n40,21477 e20,64611. ⬆

20 🏕 € 15 ⚡ Ch 🚿 WC 📶 included.
**Location:** Rural, isolated. **Surface:** grassy. 🗓 01/04-01/11.
**Distance:** 🏄 on the spot ⊗ on the spot 🐾 on the spot 🥾 on the spot.

### △ Llogara 🏔 🍴 — 35E1
**Hotel Hamiti**, SH8. **GPS:** n40,21035 e19,57924.
🏕 € 5. 🗓 01/01-31/12.

### △S Omarë — 39A5
**Lake Shkodra Resort**, Rruga E Liqenit.
**GPS:** n42,13836 e19,46562. ⬆ ➡
🏕 € 12, Jul/Aug € 14 ⚡ Ch 🚿 2 WC 🔌 3,95 📶 included.
**Location:** Simple, isolated. **Surface:** grassy. 🗓 01/04-15/11.
**Distance:** 🏖 Skodër 10km 🏊 lake with sandy beach 🥾 on the spot
⊗ on the spot.
**Remarks:** Free use of sun beds and beach chairs, canoe and bicycle
rental.

**Orikum** 35E1

**Camping Dion**. **GPS**: n40,34407 e19,48280.

12 🛏 € 10 ⚡🍴 Ch 💧 📶 included.
**Surface:** metalled. 📷 01/01-31/12.
**Distance:** 🚶500m ⛱on the spot ⊗on the spot.
**Remarks:** S 148.

**Radhimë** 35E1

**Rezidenca Cekodhima**, SH8. **GPS**: n40,37706 e19,47872.⬆.

20 🛏 € 20 ⚡🍴 Ch 💧 WC 📶.
**Location:** Rural, comfortable, quiet. **Surface:** gravel. 📷 01/01-31/12.
**Distance:** ⛱pebbled beach ⊗on the spot.

**Sarandë** 35E1

**Hotel Mediterrane**, Rruga Skënderbeu. **GPS**: n39,87041 e20,01854.⬆.

10 🛏 € 15 ⚡💧included WC 📶. **Location:** Urban, central, noisy.
**Surface:** asphalted. 📷 01/01-31/12.
**Distance:** 🚶city centre 1km ⛱600m ⊗on the spot.

**Tirana** 35E1

**Hotel Baron**, Rruga e Elbasanit. **GPS**: n41,29947 e19,85012.⬆.

6 🛏 € 15 ⚡Ch 💧 WC 📶 included. **Location:** Urban, comfortable.
**Surface:** metalled. 📷 01/01-31/12.
**Distance:** 🚶centre 4km ⊗on the spot.

AL

# Austria

Capital: Vienna
Government: federal, parliamentarian, democratic republic
Official Language: German
Population: 8,754,413 (2017)
Area: 83,871 km²

### General information
Dialling code: 0043
General emergency: 112
Currency: Euro

### Regulations for overnight stays
In general overnight parking is allowed, except: Tyrol, Vienna, nature reserves and in areas where locally prohibited. No "camping" activities allowed and disposal wastewater must be at official places.

### Additional public holidays 2019
January 6 Epiphany
May 1 Labor Day
June 20 Corpus Christi
August 15 Assumption of the Virgin Mary
October 26 National Holiday
November 1 All Saints' Day
December 8 Immaculate Conception

### Time Zone
Winter (Standard Time) GMT+1
Summer (DST) GMT+2

Lower Austria pages: 87-90

Vienna Vienna page: 90

Upper Austria pages: 86-87

Salzburg

Burgenland pages: 98-99

Styria pages: 94-97

Vorarlberg page: 90

Innsbruck

Salzburg pages: 92-93

Tyrol pages: 90-92

Carinthia pages: 97-98

Klagenfurt

AT

## Upper Austria

### Aschach an der Donau — 36A1
Schopperplatz 6. **GPS:** n48,37417 e14,02824.

4 🚐 € 12/24h ⚡ € 3/80liter Ch 🚰 WC. 🚐 **Location:** Rural, isolated, quiet. **Surface:** grassy/gravel. 🔲 01/01-31/12.
**Distance:** 🚶1,5km ⊗1km 🚲 on the spot.
**Remarks:** At Danube cycle route, water closed during wintertime.

### Ebensee — 20H1
**Am Traunsee**, Trauneck. **GPS:** n47,81283 e13,77730. ⬆.

10 🚐 € 12/24h ⚡ € 0,50/50liter 🔌Ch 🚰(12x)€ 3 WC.
**Location:** Rural, simple, quiet. **Surface:** asphalted.
🔲 01/01-31/12.
**Distance:** 🚶500m ⚓on the spot ⊗300m.
**Remarks:** At lake, max. 3 days.

### Ebensee — 20H1
**Freizeitanlage Rindbach**, Strandbadstraße.
**GPS:** n47,80934 e13,79002. ⬆.

### Haslach — 36A1
**Gasthof Furtmühle**, Schwackerreith 20, St.Oswald.
**GPS:** n48,60497 e14,01967.
15 🚐free 🚰 🚿against payment. 🔲 01/01-31/12 ◉ Tue.
**Distance:** ⊗on the spot.

### Kefermarkt — 36A1
**Schloßbrauerei Weinberg**, Weinberg 2. **GPS:** n48,44856 e14,53957. ⬆.

5 🚐guests free. **Location:** Rural, simple. **Surface:** asphalted.
🔲 01/01-31/12.
**Distance:** 🚶800m ⊗on the spot.

### Königswiesen — 36A1
**Freibad**, Badgasse 4. **GPS:** n48,40450 e14,84080. ⬆ ➡.

3 🚐 € 2 + € 2/pp ⚡ Ch 🚰 WCincluded. **Location:** Rural, simple, quiet. **Surface:** asphalted. 🔲 01/04-31/10.
**Distance:** 🚶500m ⊗10m Freibadbuffet 🍴300m.
**Remarks:** Parking swimming pool.

### Kremsmünster — 36A2
**Parkplatz Benediktiner Stift**, Fuxjägerstraße.
**GPS:** n48,05407 e14,12607.
🚐. 🔲 01/01-31/12.
**Distance:** 🚶500m ⊗500m.

### Kronstorf — 36A2
**Stellplatz Metzenhof**, Dörfling 2. **GPS:** n48,12828 e14,43432. ⬆.

---

### Eferding — 36A1
Brandstatt, Pupping. **GPS:** n48,33503 e14,02698.
🚐. 🔲 01/01-31/12.
**Remarks:** On the Danube river.

### Gallneukirchen — 36A1
**Freizeitcentrum**, Veitsdorfer Weg 10. **GPS:** n48,36045 e14,40797. ⬆.

10 🚐free. **Location:** Rural, simple. **Surface:** asphalted.
🔲 01/01-31/12.
**Distance:** 🚶1km ⊗on the spot 🍴1km.

### Gosau — 20H2
**Gasthaus Echo**, Echoweg 9. **GPS:** n47,55171 e13,51345.
10 🚐free ⚡ € 5 📶. **Location:** Rural, simple, isolated, quiet.
**Surface:** asphalted. 🔲 01/05-31/10.
**Distance:** ⚓400m ⊗on the spot.

### Gosau — 20H2
**Hotel Gosauschmied**, Gosau 57. **GPS:** n47,55072 e13,51607.
10 🚐 € 10 ⚡Ch 🚰on demand. **Surface:** asphalted.
🔲 01/01-31/12.
**Distance:** 🚶3km ⊗on the spot 🍴3km 🚌on the spot 🎿500m ⛷ on the spot.

Above the middle column (Haslach section top):
### Haslach — 36A1

10 ⌷ € 18, 2 pers.incl 🚰🔧Ch🔌WC📶included.
**Location:** Rural, comfortable, isolated, quiet.
**Surface:** gravel/metalled. 🗓 01/03-30/11.
**Distance:** 🏊on the spot 🛒on the spot.
**Remarks:** At golf court, bread-service, swimming pool.

## Naarn 36A1

**Bauernhof Mostschenke**, Dirnwagram 1.
**GPS:** n48,21750 e14,61972.⬆

5 ⌷ € 10 🔧Ch🔌€ 2/day WCincluded. **Location:** Rural, simple.
**Surface:** asphalted. 🗓 01/01-31/12.
**Distance:** 🚶2km 🛒on the spot 🛒2km.
**Remarks:** Arrival <19.30h, max. 4 days.

## Naarn 36A1

**Gasthof zur Post**, Marktplatz 1. **GPS:** n48,22579 e14,60662.

5 ⌷ € 6, 2 pers.incl. **Location:** Simple, noisy. **Surface:** asphalted.
🗓 01/01-31/12 🔴 Thu.
**Distance:** 🚶on the spot 🛒on the spot.

## Ranshofen 17G3

**Gasthof Putscher**, Scheuhub 2. **GPS:** n48,23228 e12,99893.
5 ⌷ € 15, 2 pers.incl 🚰🔧Ch🔌€ 2. **Surface:** grassy.
🗓 01/01-31/12.
**Distance:** 🚶2km 🛒on the spot 🛒2km 🛒2km.

## Sankt Pankraz 36A2

**Parkplatz Klauser Stausee**, Klaus an der Pyhrnbahn.
**GPS:** n47,82733 e14,15703.
⌷. 🗓 01/01-31/12.
**Remarks:** Along river.

## Scharnstein 36A2

**Camping Schatzlmühle**, Viechtwang 1A.
**GPS:** n47,91578 e13,97353.➡

5 ⌷ € 17 🚰🔧Chincluded 🔌€ 3 ⌷€ 2 🔴€ 2. **Location:** Rural, quiet.
**Surface:** grassy/gravel. 🗓 01/05-31/10.
**Distance:** 🚶2km 🛒on the spot 🛒600m 🛒on the spot 🚲on the spot
🚶on the spot ⛷on the spot ⛵on the spot.
**Remarks:** Bread-service.

## Schlierbach 36A2

**Bauernhof Eisterer**, Föhrenweg 7. **GPS:** n47,95083 e14,08639.⬆
3 ⌷ € 6,50 + € 4/pp 🔧Ch🔌€ 2,50/day ⌷. **Location:** Rural,
comfortable. **Surface:** grassy. 🗓 01/01-31/12.

## Straß im Attergau 20H1

**Landgasthof Rosslwirt**, Halt 4. **GPS:** n47,90488 e13,44677.➡

6 ⌷guests free 🚰🔧🔌4Amp WCfree. **Location:** Rural, simple,
quiet. **Surface:** grassy/gravel. 🗓 01/01-31/12.
**Distance:** 🛒on the spot 🛒5km.
**Remarks:** Near sports fields, breakfest-service, playground.

## Suben 17H3

**Hotel Suben**, Etzelshofen 125. **GPS:** n48,40149 e13,42582.⬆
40 ⌷ € 10 🚰🔧Ch🔌included. **Location:** Motorway, simple, noisy.
🗓 01/01-31/12.
**Distance:** 🚶on the spot 🛒on the spot.

## Vöcklabruck 20H1

**Hallenbad am Freizeitgelände**, Hausruckstraße.
**GPS:** n48,01107 e13,65299.⬆

6 ⌷free 🚰🔧Ch🔌. **Location:** Rural, simple.
**Surface:** metalled. 🗓 01/01-31/12.
**Distance:** 🚶500m 🛒on the spot 🛒450m 🛒200m.
**Remarks:** At swimming pool, max. 48h.

## Waldhausen im Strudengau 36A1

**Badesee**, Schloßberg. **GPS:** n48,28420 e14,95883.➡

6 ⌷voluntary contribution 🚰€ 1/10minutes ⌷Ch🔌€ 1/8h,10Amp.
**Location:** Rural, isolated, quiet. **Surface:** gravel.
🗓 01/04-31/10.
**Distance:** 🚶2km 🏊on the spot 🛒on the spot 🛒2km 🛒2km.
**Remarks:** E-bike rental.

# Lower Austria

## Aggsbach Dorf 36B1

**Gasthof Pension zur Kartause**, Aggsbach-Dorf 38.
**GPS:** n48,29638 e15,42604.⬆
10 ⌷free 🚰free. **Location:** Rural, isolated, quiet. **Surface:** grassy.
🗓 01/01-31/12.
**Distance:** 🏊Danube river 1,5km 🛒on the spot 🛒190m.

## Aggsbach Markt 36B1

**Badestrand**, Donau Bundesstrasse. **GPS:** n48,29814 e15,40497.⬆

26 ⌷ € 13 🚰🔧Ch🔌€ 1/24h WC⌷. **Location:** Rural,
comfortable, isolated, quiet. **Surface:** gravel. 🗓 01/03-31/10.
**Distance:** 🚶500m 🛒50m Donaustüberl 🛒500m.
**Remarks:** On the Danube river.

## Altenmarkt an der Triesting 36B2

**Gasthof Zum Kleinen Semmering**, Hafnerberg 15.
**GPS:** n48,01762 e16,01383.⬆

10 ⌷free 🚰WC. **Location:** Rural, simple. **Surface:** gravel.
🗓 01/01-31/12.
**Distance:** 🚶2,3km 🛒on the spot 🛒2,3km.

## Arbesbach 36A1

**Am Ganser. GPS:** n48,49123 e14,95683.⬆

15 ⌷ € 5 🚰🔧Ch🔌included. **Location:** Rural, simple.
**Surface:** gravel. 🗓 01/01-31/12.
**Distance:** 🚶500m 🏊on the spot 🛒500m 🛒500m 🛒500m.
**Remarks:** Check in at town hall.

## Ardagger 36A1

**Stellplatz am Donauwellenpark**, Markt 39.
**GPS:** n48,17981 e14,82579.⬆

10 ⌷free 🚰€ 2 ⌷Ch🔌(6x)€ 1/kWh WC.
**Location:** Rural, simple. **Surface:** gravel. 🗓 01/01-31/12.
**Distance:** 🚶100m 🚲7km 🛒100m 🛒100m 🚴on the spot.
**Remarks:** At Danube cycle route.

## Armschlag 36A1

**Mohndorf. GPS:** n48,45222 e15,21944.⬆

5 ⌷ € 7, 2 pers.incl. 🚰🔧Ch🔌included.
**Location:** Rural, simple. **Surface:** asphalted. 🗓 01/01-31/12.
**Distance:** 🚶on the spot 🛒on the spot 🛒2km 🚶Mohnstrudelwan-
dernetz.

## Aschbach Markt 36A2

**Fam. Edtbauer**, Auckental 1 u. 2. **GPS:** n48,10682 e14,69988.⬆

8 ⌷free 🚰🔧🔌€ 2. **Location:** Rural, quiet. **Surface:** grassy.
🗓 15/04-30/10.

AT

**Distance:** 🚶7km 🚲3km 🚏7km.

| 🏕️ | **Bad Deutsch-Altenburg** 🌳 | 36C1 |

**Parking Donaupromenade**, Donaupromenade.
**GPS:** n48,14110 e16,90090. 🔼.

🗑️.
**Location:** Rural, simple. **Surface:** asphalted. 🅿️ 01/01-31/12.
**Distance:** 🚶500m 🏊on the spot ⊗1km 🚏1km.

| 🏕️ | **Bad Großpertholz** | 36A1 |

**Busparkplatz Naturpark Nordwald**, Scheiben.
**GPS:** n48,61765 e14,81548.
🗑️. **Location:** Rural. **Surface:** asphalted. 🅿️ 01/01-31/12.

| 🏕️ | **Bernhardsthal** | 36C1 |

**Am Bernhardsthaler Teich**, Schulstrasse.
**GPS:** n48,69402 e16,87481. 🔼➡️.

5 🗑️free.
**Surface:** grassy. 🅿️ 01/01-31/12.
**Distance:** 🚶500m 🏊on the spot �’on the spot ⊗weekends only.

| 🏕️ S | **Eggenburg** ⚓🏛️ | 36B1 |

**Stellplatz an der Stadtmauer**, Erzherzog-Karl-Ring 19.
**GPS:** n48,64513 e15,81745. 🔼➡️.
8 🗑️€4 �’€ 1/10minutes 🔌Ch. 🔑(8x)€ 1/8h.
**Location:** Rural, comfortable. **Surface:** gravel. 🅿️ 01/04-31/10.
**Distance:** 🚶on the spot 🚲4km 🏊creek ⊗300m 🚏200m 🏪500m
🏊‍♂️on the spot 🧗300m.

| 🏨 S | **Erlauf** | 36A1 |

**Plaikawirt**, Plaika 1, Bergland. **GPS:** n48,16866 e15,16436. 🔼.

10 🗑️guests free 🔌€ 2/100liter 🔑€ 2/24h. **Location:** Rural, quiet.
**Surface:** asphalted. 🅿️ 01/01-31/12 🅿️ Mo.
**Distance:** 🚶2km ⊗on the spot 🚏on the spot.

| 🏕️ | **Gaming** | 36A2 |

**Kartause. GPS:** n47,92463 e15,08223.
🗑️. 🅿️ 01/01-31/12.

| 🏕️ S | **Gars am Kamp** | 36B1 |

**Sport- und Erlebnisbad**, Gföhler Strasse/Strandgasse, Thunau am
Kamp. **GPS:** n48,59300 e15,65723. 🔼.

5 🗑️€ 16 🔌🔌Ch. 🔑WCincluded. **Location:** Comfortable.
**Surface:** gravel. 🅿️ 01/01-31/12.
**Distance:** 🚶200m ⊗on the spot 🚏200m.
**Remarks:** At swimming pool.

| 🏕️ | **Göllersdorf** 🍽️ | 36B1 |

**Parkplatz Barbara Heuriger**, Spitalgasse 467.
**GPS:** n48,49667 e16,11171. 🔼.

10 🗑️free.
**Location:** Rural, simple. **Surface:** gravel. 🅿️ 01/01-31/12.
**Distance:** 🚶500m 🚲1km ⊗on the spot 🚏1km.

| 🏕️ | **Gumpoldskirchen** | 36B1 |

Brunngasse. **GPS:** n48,04212 e16,27820. 🔼.

10 🗑️free. **Location:** Rural, simple. **Surface:** asphalted.
🅿️ 01/01-31/12.
**Distance:** 🚶500m ⊗500m.
**Remarks:** Max. 8M.

| S | **Gumpoldskirchen** | 36B1 |

Neustiftgasse. **GPS:** n48,04423 e16,27552.
🔌Ch. 🅿️ 01/01-31/12.

| **Hainburg/Donau** | 36C1 |

**Parkplatz an der Donau**, Donaulande 4.
**GPS:** n48,15110 e16,94440. 🔼.

🗑️. **Location:** Rural, simple. **Surface:** asphalted.
🅿️ 01/01-31/12.
**Distance:** 🚶500m 🏊on the spot ⊗on the spot 🚏500m.

| **Hohenau/March** | 36C1 |

**Freizeitzentrum**, Kindergartenstrasse. **GPS:** n48,61095 e16,91010.

🗑️free. **Surface:** asphalted. 🅿️ 01/01-31/12.
**Remarks:** Swimming pool 200m.

| 🏕️ S | **Hollenstein/Ybbs** | 36A2 |

**Der Wentsteinhammer**, Wenten 1. **GPS:** n47,76884 e14,77270.
3 🗑️€5 🔌🔌Ch. 🔑. **Location:** Rural, isolated, quiet.
🅿️ 01/01-31/12.
**Distance:** 🚶4km.

| 🏨 S | **Hollenstein/Ybbs** | 36A2 |

**Gasthof Staudach**, Walcherbauer 5. **GPS:** n47,80703 e14,76687. 🔼.
8 🗑️€ 13-18, 4 pers.incl 🔌🔑WCincluded.
**Location:** Rural, simple, quiet. **Surface:** grassy. 🅿️ 01/04-31/10.
**Distance:** 🚶200m ⊗10m 🚏200m 🏊‍♂️on the spot.

| 🏕️ S | **Horn** | 36B1 |

**Wohnmobil-Stellplatz Horn**, Höhe Spitalgasse 49.
**GPS:** n48,67246 e15,66108.

4 🗑️free, tourist tax € 1,60/pp 🔌€ 1/50liter 🔌Ch. 🔑€ 1/8h.
**Surface:** gravel/sand. 🅿️ 01/01-31/12.
**Distance:** 🚶1km ⊗500m 🚏500m.
**Remarks:** Max. 5 nights.

| 🏕️ | **Karlstein an der Thaya** | 36A1 |

Sieghartser Straße. **GPS:** n48,88186 e15,40442. 🔼.
🗑️. **Surface:** grassy. 🅿️ 01/01-31/12.
**Distance:** 🚶200m 🚏200m.
**Remarks:** At tennis-court.

| 🏕️ S | **Klosterneuburg** | 36B1 |

**Euromobil Campers**, Bahnhofplatz 16, Kritzendorf.
**GPS:** n48,33582 e16,29863. 🔼➡️.

4 🗑️free 🔌🔌Ch. **Location:** Simple. **Surface:** asphalted.
🅿️ 01/01-31/12.
**Distance:** 🚲12,5km ⊗300m 🚏500m.
**Remarks:** Lock-up parking, guarded.

| 🏕️ S | **Laimbach am Ostrong** | 36A1 |

**Bauernhof Stoiber**, Wagmühle 34. **GPS:** n48,31711 e15,12565. 🔼.

5 🗑️€ 12 🔌🔌Ch. 🔑included. **Location:** Rural, simple.
**Surface:** grassy. 🅿️ 01/01-31/12.
**Distance:** 🚶300m ⊗300m 🚏300m.

| 🏕️ S | **Langenlois** 🍽️ | 36B1 |

**Reisemobilstellplatz Langenlois**, Krumpöckallee 21.
**GPS:** n48,47063 e15,69782. 🔼.

AT

7 🛏 € 8 + € 1,50/pp 🔌 € 1/10minutes 🗑Ch 💧(7x) € 1/8h.
**Location:** Rural, simple, quiet. **Surface:** metalled.
◻ 01/01-31/12.
**Distance:** 🚶1,5km 🚲1km 🛒1km.

| 🏕S | **Langschlag-Mitterschlag** | 36A1 |

**Freizeitanlage Frauenwieserteich**, Böhmerwald-Bundesstraße.
**GPS:** n48,58038 e14,83507. ⬆.

10 🛏free.
**Location:** Rural, simple, isolated, quiet. **Surface:** grassy/gravel.
◻ 01/01-31/12.
**Distance:** 🚶5km 🏊on the spot 🛒on the spot 🗑on the spot 🛒5km.

| 🏕S | **Mitterbach** | 36B2 |

**Biobauernhof Sepplbauer**, Bergstraße 11. **GPS:** n47,83216 e15,30648.
10 🛏 € 6 💧 € 2. **Location:** Rural, isolated, quiet. **Surface:** grassy.
◻ 01/05-30/09.
**Distance:** 🚶4km.

| 🏕 | **Orth/Donau** | 36C1 |

**P2**, Am Rosenhügel. **GPS:** n48,14523 e16,70383. ⬆.

4 🛏free. **Location:** Urban, simple. **Surface:** grasstiles.
◻ 01/01-31/12.
**Distance:** 🚶on the spot 🏊3km 🗑250m 🛒1,2km.

| 🏕S | **Ottenschlag** | 36A1 |

Florianigasse. **GPS:** n48,42361 e15,22750. ⬆.

8-10 🛏 € 5 🔌 € 1/10minutes 🗑Ch 💧 € 1/8h. **Location:** Rural,
simple. **Surface:** gravel. ◻ 01/01-31/12.
**Distance:** 🚶500m 🗑Gaststätte 🛒500m.

| 🏕S | **Pernegg** | 36B1 |

**Freizeitanlage Gallien**, Gallien 1. **GPS:** n48,71333 e15,66139. ⬆➡.
20 🛏 € 15 + € 5/pp 🔌🗑Ch 💧 WC included. 🧺
**Location:** Rural, comfortable. **Surface:** grassy/gravel.
◻ 01/01-31/12.
**Distance:** 🛒on the spot 🗑on the spot.

| 🏕S | **Pillichsdorf** | 36B1 |

**Am Tennisclub**, Bahnstraße 8A. **GPS:** n48,36167 e16,53750. ⬆➡.

6 🛏 € 15, 2 pers.incl, extra pers € 5 🔌🗑Ch 💧 WC included.
**Location:** Urban, simple, noisy. **Surface:** gravel.
◻ 15/04-15/10.
**Distance:** 🚶500m, Vienna 15km 🗑300m 🛒500m 🚌on the spot.
**Remarks:** Playground.

| 🏕S | **Pulkau** | 36B1 |

Rat-Cumfe Straße. **GPS:** n48,70430 e15,86637. ⬆➡.

8 🛏 € 5 🔌 € 1/10minutes 🗑Ch 💧 € 1/6h. **Location:** Urban, simple.
**Surface:** gravel. ◻ 01/01-31/12.
**Distance:** 🚶500m 🗑300m 🛒on the spot 🚌on the spot.

| 🏕 | **Reichenau/Rax** | 36B2 |

**Kaiserbrunn**, Bundesstraße Höllental 27. **GPS:** n47,73480 e15,79188.

🛏free. **Surface:** metalled. ◻ 01/01-31/12.

| 🏕S | **Reichenau/Rax** | 36B2 |

**Gasthof Flackl Wirt**, Hinterleiten 12. **GPS:** n47,69056 e15,82778.

5 🛏 € 14/pp breakfest incl 🔌🔌according consumption WC at
restaurant. **Location:** Rural. **Surface:** grassy/gravel. ◻ 01/01-31/12.
**Distance:** 🚶1,5km 🗑on the spot.

| 🏕S | **Retz** | 36B1 |

**Parkplatz Alter Sportplatz**, Jahnstraße. **GPS:** n48,75382 e15,95105.

2 🛏 € 3 🔌 € 1/10minutes 🗑Ch 💧 € 1/8h. **Location:** Simple.
**Surface:** asphalted. ◻ 01/04-31/10 ◻ last weekend of Sep.
**Distance:** 🚶500m 🗑300m 🛒500m 🚌250m.

| 🏕S | **Rossatzbach** 🏰 | 36B1 |

**Wohnmobilplatz Artner**, Aggsteiner-Bundesstraße.
**GPS:** n48,38750 e15,51722. ⬆➡.

12 🛏 € 12 🔌🗑Ch 💧(12x) WC included.
**Location:** Rural, comfortable. **Surface:** gravel. ◻ 01/01-31/12.
**Distance:** 🚶300m 🏊on the spot 🗑100m 🛒1,5km.
**Remarks:** Vinotheek 300m.

| 🏕S | **Sankt Martin am Ybbsfelde** 🌱 | 36A1 |

**Gemeindeparkplatz**, St. Martin. **GPS:** n48,16465 e15,01995. ⬆.

5 🛏free 🔌 € 5/day 🗑Ch 💧(2x) € 5/day.
**Location:** Rural, simple, quiet. **Surface:** grasstiles. ◻ 01/01-31/12.
**Distance:** 🚶on the spot 🗑on the spot 🚌200m 🚶on the spot.
**Remarks:** Parking in front of church.

| 🏕 | **Schiltern bei Langenlois** | 36B1 |

**Erlebnisgärtner Kittenberger**, Laabergstraße 15.
**GPS:** n48,51180 e15,63277. ⬆.

3 🛏free. **Location:** Rural, simple, isolated. **Surface:** metalled.
◻ 01/01-31/12.
**Distance:** 🚶500m 🗑on the spot.

| 🏕S | **Schönberg** 🍇 | 36B1 |

**Freizeitzentrum**, Badgasse. **GPS:** n48,52063 e15,69377. ⬆.

5 🛏 € 5, first night free WC. **Location:** Rural, simple.
**Surface:** asphalted. ◻ 15/05-31/08.
**Distance:** 🚶200m 🗑300m 🛒200m 🚲 Kamptalradweg.
**Remarks:** Along river, use sanitary only during opening hours swimming pool.

| 🏕 | **Schrems** | 36A1 |

**Parkplatz Stadthalle**, Doktor-Karl-Renner-Straße.
**GPS:** n48,79167 e15,07120. ⬆.

3 🛏free. **Location:** Urban, simple, central. **Surface:** asphalted.
◻ 01/01-31/12.
**Distance:** 🚶on the spot 🗑on the spot 🛒100m.

AT

### Stockerau | 36B1

**Hallenbad Wellness Oase**, Pestalozzigasse.
**GPS:** n48,39385 e16,21912.

6 ⚡free ⚡€ 2 ⚡€ 2 Ch€ 2 WC sanitary in swimming pool.
**Location:** Urban, comfortable. **Surface:** gravel. ☀ 01/01-31/12.
**Distance:** 1,5km ⚡500m ⊗50m 🛒600m 🚌400m.

### Stockerau | 36B1

**Alte Au**, Zum Spitzgarten. **GPS:** n48,38366 e16,20394.

3 ⚡free. **Location:** Urban, simple. **Surface:** asphalted.
☀ 01/01-31/12.
**Distance:** 1km ⊗50m 🛒1km.
**Remarks:** At sports centre.

### Weistrach | 36A2

**Parkplatz Sportplatz. GPS:** n48,05475 e14,58167.

10 ⚡free. **Location:** Rural, simple. **Surface:** asphalted.
☀ 01/01-31/12.
**Distance:** 200m ⊗on the spot 🛒200m.
**Remarks:** Near sports fields.

### Weitra | 36A1

**Freizeitzentrum Hausschachen**, Promenade.
**GPS:** n48,70414 e14,89343.

10 ⚡free. **Location:** Simple, quiet. **Surface:** gravel.
☀ 01/01-31/12.
**Distance:** 600m ⊗600m 🛒300m.
**Remarks:** Max. 1 night.

### Wiener Neustadt | 36B2

**Parkplatz Stadion**, Stadionstrasse. **GPS:** n47,82156 e16,25629.

20 ⚡. **Location:** Urban. **Surface:** asphalted. ☀ 01/01-31/12.
**Distance:** 500m ⚡on the spot.

### Wilfersdorf | 36B1

**Schloss Wilfersdorf**, Parkplatz am Schloss.
**GPS:** n48,58600 e16,64514.

3 ⚡4 ⚡💬(2x) WC. ☀ 01/01-31/12.
**Distance:** 100m ⊗300m ⚡on the spot.
**Remarks:** Check in at Schloss, 10-16h tue/su.

### Zwettl | 36A1

**Wirtshaus zur Minidampfbahn**, 47, Teichhäuser bei Zwettl.
**GPS:** n48,66278 e15,15444.

10 ⚡€ 7 ⚡💬Ch⚡€ 3 WCincluded. **Location:** Rural, simple, quiet.
**Surface:** grassy. ☀ 01/03-31/10.
**Distance:** 2km ⚡200m ⊗on the spot 🛒2,5km.

## Vienna

### Wien 🌺🛝🍎 | 36B1

**Reisemobilstellplatz Wien**, Perfektastraße 49-53, Vienna (Wien).
**GPS:** n48,13698 e16,31582.

167 ⚡€ 19 ⚡💬Ch⚡(167x)€ 2/24h WC 📶included 🍽️👤
☀ 01/01-31/12.
**Distance:** city centre 12km ⚡4km ⊗30m 🛒30m 🚇metro 150m,
bus 50m 🚲100m.

### Wien 🌺🛝🍎 | 36B1

**Kurpark Oberlaa**, Filmteichstrasse 5, Vienna (Wien).
**GPS:** n48,15215 e16,40363.

⚡free. **Location:** Urban, simple. **Surface:** grasstiles. ☀ 01/01-31/12.
**Distance:** 🚌centre > bus 68A Reumannplatz > tram U1 Stefansdom.
**Remarks:** No camping activities.

**Tourist information Vienna (Wien):**
ℹ️ Overnight parking prohibited.
ℹ️ Tourist-Info, Albertinaplatz 1, info.wien.at/. Imperial city, many
curiosities, capital of the classic music.
ℹ️ Wien-Karte. Card gives 72h entrance to public transport and
discounts on museums, curiosities. Available at Tourist-Info and hotels.
🎫 € 24,90.
👁 Spanische Hofreitschule, Michaelerplatz 1. Spanish Riding School,
morning-training can be visited without reservation.
10-12.
Ⓜ Kunsthistorisches Museum, Maria Theresien-Platz. Important painting collection. ☀ Tue-Su 10-18h, Thu 10-21h. 🎫 € 15.

Wurstelprater. Amusement park.
☀ 15/03-15/10 10-24h.

## Vorarlberg

### Dornbirn | 20B3

**Stellplatz Mathis**, Obere Härte 27. **GPS:** n47,40577 e9,72492.

3 (7-8-10m) ⚡€ 17 + € 1,10/pp tourist tax ⚡💬Ch⚡📶included.
**Location:** Comfortable. **Surface:** grasstiles.
☀ 01/01-31/12.
**Distance:** ⚡on the spot ⚡2km 🚴on the spot 🚶on the spot.

## Tyrol

### Achenkirch 🏔️🎿❄️ | 20E2

**Wohnmobilhafen Achensee**, Achenkirch 17.
**GPS:** n47,49947 e11,70655.

10 ⚡from € 14 + € 1,50/pp tourist tax, € 1 Umwelttaxe ⚡💬
Ch⚡€ 3,50/24h WCincluded. **Location:** Rural, comfortable, quiet.
**Surface:** grasstiles/metalled. ☀ 01/01-31/12.
**Distance:** ⚡on the spot 🚐on the spot.
**Remarks:** Max. 1 night, dog € 4,50, extra pers € 11,50, child € 7,
electricity winter € 0,70/kWh.

### Biberwier 🏔️🎿❄️ | 20D3

**Wohnmobilhafen Arienberg**, Marienbergstrasse 15.
**GPS:** n47,37472 e10,89223.

18 ⚡€ 18, 2 pers.incl, tourist tax € 2/pp ⚡💬Ch⚡€ 1,50/24h
📶included. **Location:** Rural, comfortable. **Surface:** grassy/gravel.
☀ 01/01-31/12.
**Distance:** ⚡on the spot 🛒2km 🚴on the spot 🎿on the spot.

### Bichlbach | 20D2

**Almkopfbahn. GPS:** n47,42367 e10,78116.

15 ⚡free. ☀ 01/01-31/12.
**Distance:** 5km ⊗on the spot 🚐on the spot 🎿on the spot.

### Breitenwang | 20D2

**Seespitze. GPS:** n47,47438 e10,78515.
⚡€ 22,50-31, 2 pers.incl ⚡💬Ch⚡WC📶. ☀ 01/01-31/12.

### Breitenwang | 20D2

**Sennalpe. GPS:** n47,48639 e10,83972.
⚡€ 14. ☀ 15/12-15/10.

**AT**

AT

### Feichten/Kaunertal — 20D3
**Kaunertal. GPS:** n47,05333 e10,75056.
60 € 26,80 Ch WC 01/05-30/09.

### Galtür — 20C3
**Bergbahnen**, Silvretta-Bundesstraße, B188, Wirl.
**GPS:** n46,96570 e10,16390.

€ 20, summer free Ch.
**Location:** Rural. **Surface:** gravel. winter.
**Distance:** 100m on the spot on the spot on the spot.
**Remarks:** Free skibus to Ischgl.

### Galtür — 20C3
**Zeinissee**, Zeinisjochstrasse. **GPS:** n46,97824 e10,12738.

30 € 23-25,50 incl. 2 pers, dog € 3 € 0,70/kWh
WC included against payment.
**Location:** Rural. **Surface:** grassy/gravel.
Whitsuntide-05/10.
**Distance:** Galtür 8,5km on the spot.
**Remarks:** Breakfast-service, Silvrettacard incl., one night stay + € 5.

### Gerlos — 20F3
**Bauernhof Schönachhof**, Schönachtal 242.
**GPS:** n47,22639 e12,05476.

24 € 25, winter € 35 + tourist tax, dog € 4 Ch € 0,80/kWh
WC. **Location:** Rural, isolated, quiet. **Surface:** grassy.
01/01-31/12.
**Distance:** 1km 900m 1km 1km.

**Tourist information Gerlos:**
Activ Wellness. Free wellness program. 01/07-30/09.

### Gries am Brenner — 20E3
**Gasthof Humler-Hof**, Nößlach 483. **GPS:** n47,06660 e11,47187.
50 € 10 WC included. 01/01-31/12.
**Distance:** Gries 5km 1km on the spot.

### Hall in Tirol — 20E3
**Wohnmobilpark**, Scheidensteinstraße 24.
**GPS:** n47,28444 e11,49665.

10 € 10, 01/05-30/09 € 15-20, 2 pers.incl, extra pers € 2,50
included. **Location:** Urban. **Surface:** metalled.
01/01-31/12.
**Distance:** 400m 200m Gaststätte 300m.

**Remarks:** Max. 1 night, swimming pool.

### Heiterwang — 20D2
**Ferienhof Sunnawirt**, Mühle 4. **GPS:** n47,44951 e10,74812.

30 € 7 + tourist tax € 2/pp Ch € 3.
**Surface:** grassy/gravel. 01/01-31/12.
**Distance:** 200m Heiterwanger See 1,6km on the spot 3km
on the spot 3km on the spot.
**Remarks:** Bread-service.

### Ischgl — 20C3
Mathoner Straße 5, Ischgl-Mathon. **GPS:** n46,98967 e10,24751.

8 € 15 + € 2,20/pp tourist tax Ch (8x).
**Location:** Rural, simple. **Surface:** gravel. 01/01-31/12.
**Distance:** 1km 100m on the spot.
**Remarks:** Free skibus to Ischgl and Galtür.

### Jenbach — 20E2
**Gasthof Rieder**, Fischl 3. **GPS:** n47,40131 e11,77500.

3 🛏free 🚰. **Location:** Rural, simple, isolated. **Surface:** asphalted.
🅾 01/01-31/12.
**Remarks:** Guests only.

### Kramsach 20F2
**Camping & Appartements Seehof**, Moosen 42.
**GPS:** n47,46206 e11,90733.
10 🛏 € 25-39, 2 pers. incl., dog € 3-3,50 🚰🔌Ch✏
(10x)4kWh,16Amp WC☐included 🔲€ 4/4 📶€ 3/day 🧺
**Location:** Rural. **Surface:** asphalted.
**Distance:** 🚶3km 🏊4km ⛵Reintalersee ⟶on the spot ⊗on the spot 🍴on the spot ⟶free 🚲on the spot 🧍on the spot 🎿on the spot.
**Remarks:** Tariff on presentation of the most recent guide or
Camperstop-App.

### Matrei 20F3
**Matreier Tauernhaus**, Nähe Tauer 22. **GPS:** n47,11833 e12,49778.
20 🛏 € 10/24h. **Surface:** gravel. 🅾 25/05-15/10.
**Distance:** ⊗on the spot 🧍on the spot.

### Nassereith 20D3
**Roßbach**, Roßbach 325. **GPS:** n47,31046 e10,85524.

🛏 € 21-22 🚰🔌Ch✏€ 2,50 WC☐. **Surface:** grassy.
🅾 01/01-31/12.
**Distance:** 🍴500m.

### Obsteig 20D3
**Gasthof zum Lenz**, Gschwent 282. **GPS:** n47,30930 e10,94482.⬆

6 🛏 € 15 🚰🔌Ch✏included. **Location:** Rural, simple, isolated.
**Surface:** grassy/gravel. 🅾 01/01-31/12.
**Distance:** 🧍on the spot 🎿on the spot.

### Pettneu am Arlberg 20C3
**Camping Arlberg**, Pettneu am Arlberg 235. **GPS:** n47,14506 e10,33816.

54 🛏 € 15, winter € 23 + tourist tax, dog € 3 🚰🔌Ch included
✏€ 1/2kWh 📶. **Location:** Luxurious. **Surface:** grassy/metalled.
🅾 01/01-31/12.
**Distance:** 🚶1km 🏊250m ⟶on the spot.
**Remarks:** Bread-service, winter: skibus, summer: hiking bus.

### Pfunds 20D3
**Wohnmobilplatz Via Claudiasee**, Rauth 714.
**GPS:** n46,95429 e10,51171.⬆

---

10 🛏 € 10 + € 1,50/pp tourist tax, dog € 1,50 🚰€ 1/80liter 🔌Ch
✏€ 0,60/kWh WC☐sanitary € 3/pp 📶from € 0,50.
**Location:** Rural, comfortable.
**Surface:** grassy/metalled.
🅾 01/01-31/12.
**Distance:** 🚶2km ⟶on the spot ⊗200m 🚲on the spot 🧍on the spot.
**Remarks:** Bread-service.

### Schwaz 20E2
**Wohnmobilstellplatz Königfeld**, Königfeldweg.
**GPS:** n47,34655 e11,70436.⬆

10 🛏 € 6 🚰€ 1 🔌Ch. **Location:** Urban, simple, central.
**Surface:** asphalted. 🅾 01/01-31/12.
**Distance:** 🚶500m 🏊1,9km ⊗Gaststätte 50m 🍴50m.
**Remarks:** Max. 3 nights.
**Tourist information Schwaz:**
👁 Schwazer Silberbergwerk. 🅾 01/05-30/09 9-17, 01/10-30/04
10-16h.

### Steinach am Brenner 20E3
**Gasthaus Wolf**, Brennerstraße 36. **GPS:** n47,06704 e11,48574.
5 🛏guests free 🚰. **Surface:** asphalted. 🅾 01/01-31/12.
**Distance:** 🚶2km ⟶on the spot.

### Stumm 20F3
**Gasthof Rißbacher Hof**, Ahrnbachstraße 37.
**GPS:** n47,27951 e11,89347.⬆

3 🛏 € 15 WC📶. **Location:** Rural, simple. **Surface:** asphalted.
🅾 01/01-31/12 🔘 Wed.

### Wenns/Piller 20D3
**Gasthof Sonne**, Piller 41. **GPS:** n47,13581 e10,69390.⬆

3 🛏 € 5, guests free 🚰. **Location:** Rural, simple, isolated.
**Surface:** gravel. 🅾 01/01-31/12.
**Distance:** ⊗on the spot 🍴50m 🎿on the spot.
**Remarks:** Altitude 1350m.

### Wiesing 20E2
**Inntal**, Dorf 100. **GPS:** n47,40585 e11,80536.

---

🛏 € 20-24,50 🚰🔌Ch✏WC☐📶. 🅾 01/01-31/12.

# Salzburg

### Altenmarkt im Pongau 20H2
**Stellplatz Kellerbauer**, Kellerdörfl 18. **GPS:** n47,37043 e13,42903.⬆

10 🛏 € 12 🚰🔌Ch(15x)✏ 3/24h,16Amp WC☐€ 1/1 📶included.
**Location:** Comfortable, isolated, quiet. **Surface:** grassy/gravel.
🅾 01/01-31/12.
**Distance:** 🚶1,2km 🏊4km ⛵2km ⊗1,2km 🍴1,2km 🧍on the spot
🚴1km.

### Embach Lend 20G2
**Biobauernhof Unteregg**, Heuberg 6. **GPS:** n47,29749 e13,03055.
6 🛏 € 18 🚰included 🔌Ch✏🔲. **Location:** Rural, comfortable,
isolated, quiet. 🅾 01/01-31/12.
**Distance:** ⟶on the spot.

### Golling 20G2
**Wohnmobil-Park Aqua Salza**, Mösslstraße 199.
**GPS:** n47,59543 e13,17222.⬆

15 🛏 € 9,90 + € 1/pp tourist tax 🚰€ 1/80liter 🔌Ch✏€ 0,50/kWh.
**Location:** Rural, quiet. **Surface:** asphalted.
🅾 01/01-31/12.
**Distance:** 🚶500m ⊗300m 🍴300m ⟶200m.
**Remarks:** Max. 5 days, check in on arrival, coins available at pay-desk
of theTherme.

### Hüttschlag 20H3
**Bauernhof Stockham-Camping**, See 5. **GPS:** n47,14775 e13,28947.⬆
5 🛏 € 15,60, 2 pers.incl 🚰€ 1 🔌Ch✏€ 2,50 WC☐€ 1.🏠
**Location:** Rural, simple, quiet. **Surface:** grassy/gravel.
🅾 01/04-31/10.
**Distance:** 🚶6km ⊗150m 🍴6km.

### Krimml 20F3
**Hotel Krimmlerfälle**, Wasserfallstraße 42.
**GPS:** n47,21827 e12,17543.⬆➡

10 🛏 € 20, dog € 4 🚰🔌Ch included ✏(4x).
**Location:** Rural, simple. **Surface:** grassy/gravel. 🅾 15/05-25/10.
**Distance:** 🚶500m ⊗on the spot.

### Leogang 20G2
**Leoganger Bergbahnen**, Hütten 39. **GPS:** n47,43963 e12,72040.⬆

---

AT

50 ⬚€ 18 + € 2/pp tourist tax ⟲⬚Ch⬚(50x)€ 2,50/24h WC.
**Location:** Rural, comfortable, quiet. **Surface:** grassy/gravel.
◻ 01/04-31/10.
**Distance:** 🚶3,5km ⊗on the spot.

| ⬚⬚S | Maria Alm | 20G2 |

**Wohnmobilstellplatz Stegerbauer**, Stegen 16.
**GPS:** n47,39765 e12,90350.

10 ⬚€ 12-14 + € 1,50/pp tourist tax ⟲⬚Ch⬚(10x)€ 2.
**Surface:** gravel. ◻ 01/01-31/12.
**Distance:** 🚶1km ⇤on the spot ⊗500m ⬚1km ⬚200m 🚶on the spot ⬚1km ⬚on the spot.
**Remarks:** Bread-service.

| ⬚⬚S | Neukirchen 🌳 | 20F3 |

**Panoramastellplatz**, Scheffau 96. **GPS:** n47,23862 e12,24083.

17 ⬚€ 8, discount for clients ⟲⬚Ch⬚€ 3/24h WC⬚.
**Location:** Rural, isolated, quiet. **Surface:** gravel.
◻ 01/01-31/12.
**Distance:** 🚶4km ⊗on the spot ⬚Tauernradweg 🚶on the spot ⬚on the spot ⬚on the spot.
**Remarks:** Bread-service.

| ⬚⬚S | Salzburg 🌿⚓⬚⛰ | 20G1 |

**Reisemobil - Stellplatz Salzburg**, Carl-Zuckmayer-Straße 26.
**GPS:** n47,83586 e13,05997. ⬆→.

106 ⬚€ 19-26 ⟲⬚Ch⬚(106x),6Amp WC⬚included ⬚€ 2.⬚
**Location:** Rural, comfortable, luxurious, quiet. **Surface:** grassy.
◻ 01/01-31/12.
**Distance:** 🚶on the spot 🏊1,5km ⊗10m ⬚150m ⬚on the spot ⬚50m.

**Tourist information Salzburg:**
ℹ Salzburg Card, Tourismus Information. Card gives entrance to museums, public transport etc.
ℹ Tourismus Salzburg, Altstadt, Mozartplatz; Hauptbahnhof, Bahnsteig 2a; Autobahn A10, Abfahrt Süd, www.salzburg.info. City, UNESCO's List of World Heritage, also Mozart city.

Ⓜ✠ Festung Hohensalzburg, Mönchsberg 34. High fortress. ◻ 15/6-14/9 9-18, 15/9-14/6 9.30-17h.
Ⓜ Mozart-Wohnhaus, Makartplatz 8. Former dwellinghouse of the Mozart family. ◻ 9-18h, 01/07-31/08 9-19h.
Ⓜ Mozarts Geburtshaus, Getreidegasse 9. Life and work of Mozart. ◻ 9-18h, 01/07-31/08 9-19h.
Ⓜ Salzburger Trachten, Griesgasse 23. History of the costumes. ◻ Tue-Fri 10-12h, 14-16h.
✠ Schloß Hellbrunn. Italian villa with park.
✠ Schloß Mirabell.
✝ Nonnberg. Convent.

| ⬚⬚S | Tweng | 20H3 |

**Landhotel Postgut**, Tweng 2. **GPS:** n47,19058 e13,60210.

10 ⬚€ 20 ⬚included. **Surface:** metalled. ◻ 01/01-31/12.
**Distance:** 🚶on the spot ⊗on the spot 🚶on the spot ⬚on the spot.
**Remarks:** Breakfast-service, sauna incl..

| ⬚⬚S | Wildon | 36B3 |

**Stellplatz Wildon**, Wurzingerstraße. **GPS:** n46,88793 e15,51923.
32 ⬚€ 9 ⟲⬚Ch⬚€ 3/1day,16Amp ⬚included.
**Location:** Urban, comfortable. **Surface:** grassy. ◻ 01/04-30/09.
**Distance:** ⬚on the spot ⊗180m ⬚400m.

AT

**200 m to the bus**

in 20 minutes in the centre

**3,5 km from highway to the Motorhome - Stopover**

**24 hours a day & Open all year**

## 1. REISEMOBIL-Stellplatz Graz

**A-8054 Graz, Martinhofstraße 3**
GPS: 47°01'29" N   15°23'49" E

🚐+🚐 **Perfect services, next to swimming pool**

🚐+🚐 **2 Sanitary facilities for Man & Women**

🚐+🚐 **Plots from 10 bis 20 m length**

🚐+🚐 **9 Supply/waste disposal facilities**

☎: 0043 (0) 676 3785 102, Fax.: 0043 1 863 11 12
Email: office@reisemobilstellplatz-graz.at

**www.reisemobilstellplatz-graz.at**

AT

# Styria

### Bad Gams  36B3

**Freizeitzentrums GamsBad**, Bad Gams 2.
**GPS:** n46,86730 e15,22743.⬆.

6 ⛺ € 5 ⛽🚰Ch. **Surface:** grasstiles/metalled. 🅿 01/01 31/12.
**Distance:** 🚶200m ⛱on the spot ⊗200m 🏊100m 🚌200m.
**Remarks:** Check in at Gamsbad.

### Bad Radkersburg  36B3

**Camping Alt-Weindörfl**, Altneudörfl 144. **GPS:** n46,69444 e15,98991.
25 ⛺ € 5 + € 3/pp 🚽WCincluded. **Surface:** gravel.
🅿 01/03-31/10.
**Distance:** 🚶750m ⊗on the spot 🍺750m.

### Bad Waltersdorf  36B2

**Gasthof Erhardt**, Am Waltersdorfberg 99.
**GPS:** n47,16687 e15,98921.⬆.

4 ⛺ € 8, guests free. **Location:** Rural, simple. **Surface:** grasstiles.
🅿 01/01-31/12.
**Distance:** 🚶1,8km 🏊3,2km ⊗on the spot.

### Bad Waltersdorf  36B2

**Thermenland Camping**, Campingplatzweg 316.
**GPS:** n47,16246 e16,02296.

10 ⛺Mondscheinplätze € 10/18-9h, 2 pers. incl. + tourist tax.
🅿 01/01-31/12.
**Distance:** 🚶1,6km 🏊3km ⊗Stüberl.

### Deutsch Goritz  36B3

**Pechmann's Alte Ölmühle**, Ratschendorf 188.
**GPS:** n46,75072 e15,81337.⬆.
15 ⛺customers free 🚰 🛒according consumption.
**Surface:** metalled. 🅿 01/01-31/12.
**Distance:** 🚶850m ⊗on the spot.

### Deutschfeistritz  36B2

**Union Camping Deutschfeistritz**, Am Quellengrund 11.
**GPS:** n47,20116 e15,32710.⬆.

20 ⛺ € 16 ⛽Ch. 🚰€ 3 WC included ⬛. **Location:** Simple, quiet.
**Surface:** gravel/metalled. 🅿 01/04-31/10.
**Distance:** 🚶500m ⊗500m 🐎on the spot 🚶on the spot.
**Remarks:** At manege, check in on arrival, bread-service.

### Deutschlandsberg  36B3

**Koralmhalle**, Höhe Frauentalerstraße 51.
**GPS:** n46,81783 e15,22248.⬆.

2 ⛺free. **Surface:** asphalted. 🅿 01/01-31/12.
**Distance:** 🚶200m ⊗on the spot 🍺100m 🚌on the spot.
**Remarks:** Max. 3 days.

### Gaishorn am See  36A2

**Sportzentrum**, Sieberer Weg, B113. **GPS:** n47,48583 e14,54803.⬆.
10 ⛺ € 10 + € 1,20/pp ⛽🚰Ch. 🛁(6x)€ 1 WC included. 🚿
**Location:** Rural, comfortable, noisy. **Surface:** gravel.
🅿 15/04-30/09.
**Distance:** 🚶500m 🏊4,6km ⛵Gaishorner See 100m ⊗150m
🍺500m.

### Gamlitz  36B3

**Wohnmobilstellplatz Gamlitz**, Untere Hauptstraße 455.
**GPS:** n46,72028 e15,56833.⬆⬆➡.

30 ⛺ € 20 ⛽€ 1/100liter 🚰Ch. 🔌€ 1/2kWh WC.🚰
**Location:** Rural, comfortable. **Surface:** gravel.
🅿 01/04-31/10.

**Distance:** 1km 5km on the spot on the spot on the spot.
**Remarks:** Parking at Motorikpark.

### Gamlitz — 36B3
**Buschenschank Loar-Moar**, Untere Hauptstraße 21.
**GPS:** n46,72196 e15,56495.

8 € 22 Ch WC included.
**Location:** Rural. **Surface:** grassy. 01/05-31/10.
**Distance:** 900m 5,5km.
**Remarks:** Bread-service.

### Gosdorf — 36B3
**Hof Schönwetter**, Haus 5. **GPS:** n46,72630 e15,79652.
6 € 10 . **Surface:** grassy. 01/01-31/12.
**Distance:** 500m 2km.

### Graz — 36B3
**Reisemobil Stellplatz Graz**, Martinhofstraße 3.
**GPS:** n47,02472 e15,39694.

160 € 19-26 Ch (160x) WC included € 2/2 € 2/day.
**Location:** Urban. **Surface:** grassy/gravel. 01/01-31/12.
**Distance:** on the spot 3,5km on the spot on the spot
200m 250m 200m on the spot on the spot.
**Remarks:** Video surveillance.

### Graz — 36B3
**Stellplatz Wölfl**, Steinfeldgasse 47. **GPS:** n47,06527 e15,42046.
5 € 12 € 2/day. **Location:** Simple. **Surface:** asphalted.
01/01-31/12 Sa-Su. **Distance:** 1,5km 3,7km.
**Remarks:** At motorhome dealer, check in during opening hours.

**Tourist information Graz:**
M Freilichtmuseum, Stübing. Open air museum. 18/03-31/10.
Schloß Eggenberg, Eggenberger Allee 90. 01/04-31/10 Tue-Su
10-17h. T € 11,50.
 Schlossbergbahn, Kaiser-Franz-Josef-Kai. Mountain railway,
gradient 61%.

### Greisdorf — 36B3
Greisdorf, St. Stefan ob Stainz. **GPS:** n46,92734 e15,21589.

10 € 15 Ch included (4x)€ 1/2kWh,10Amp.
**Location:** Rural. **Surface:** gravel. 23/04-04/11.
**Distance:** 550m 7km 550m 6km 100m.

### Großlobming — 36A3
**Murinsel**, Teichweg 1. **GPS:** n47,19326 e14,80422.
16 € 9/18-10h 2 pers.incl, 1 hour € 1 Ch included.
**Surface:** grassy. 01/01-31/12.
**Remarks:** Reservation in winter peak season.

### Hieflau — 36A2
**Gasthaus zum Harmonika Wald**, Wandau 9.
**GPS:** n47,62255 e14,75411.
5 guests free included. **Surface:** asphalted.
01/01-31/12 Wed.
**Distance:** 1,8km on the spot.

### Jagerberg — 36B3
Am Freibad. **GPS:** n46,85152 e15,74655.

6 free € 0,50/60liter Ch. **Location:** Rural, simple.
**Surface:** asphalted/gravel. 01/01-31/12.
**Distance:** 500m 500m 500m.

### Jagerberg — 36B3
**Kindergarten Vorplatz**, Jagerberg 98.
**GPS:** n46,85692 e15,74292.

15 free Ch (1x). **Location:** Rural, simple. **Surface:** gravel.
01/01-31/12.
**Distance:** 400m 400m 400m 400m.

### Judenburg — 36A3
**Erlebnisbad**, Fichtenhainstraße. **GPS:** n47,16407 e14,65308.

5 € 8 Ch WC included.
**Surface:** gravel. 01/01-31/12.
**Distance:** 500m 200m 200m.
**Remarks:** Check in at swimming pool.

### Kaindorf — 36B2
**Buschenschank Schleiss**, Obertiefenbach 42.
**GPS:** n47,23839 e15,84498.

4 € 6, guests free Ch. **Location:** Rural, simple.
**Surface:** asphalted. 01/03-15/12.
**Distance:** on the spot.

### Leutschach — 36B3
**Weinbau Peter Grill**, Kranach 48. **GPS:** n46,68478 e15,47191.
4 free free € 3. **Surface:** grassy. Easter-01/11.
**Distance:** 4,5km.

### Leutschach — 36B3
**Weingut oberGuess**, Schloßberg 9. **GPS:** n46,63898 e15,45872.
10 guests free Ch . 08/04-12/11.
**Distance:** 6km.

### Liezen — 36A2
**Sportzentrum**, Friedau. **GPS:** n47,56500 e14,23333.

3 free € 1 € 1. **Surface:** gravel. 01/01-31/12.
**Distance:** 1km 5,3km 300m 1km on the spot.

**AT**

Relaxation · Rest

**Directly on the forest's edge**
**200m to the city centre**

**9,5 km from highway to**
**the Motorhome - Stopover**

**Open from 1 April till 31 October**

## 1. REISEMOBIL-Stellplatz Mureck

**A-8480 Mureck, Austraße 9**
GPS: 46°42'15.826" N   15°46'22.912" E

🚐+🚗 **Perfect services, next to swimming pool**

🚐+🚗 **Sanitary facilities for Man & Women**

🚐+🚗 **Plots from 10 bis 20 m length**

🚐+🚗 **Supply/waste disposal facilities**

☎: 0043 (0) 676 911 4011, Fax.: 0043 1 863 11 12
Email: office@reisemobilstellplatz-mureck.at

**www.reisemobilstellplatz-mureck.at**

---

AT

### Mureck 36B3

**Reisemobil - Stellplatz Mureck**, Austraße 9.
**GPS:** n46,70489 e15,77240.

82 € 19-26 Ch (82x),6Amp WC included € 2/2 € 2.
**Location:** Rural, comfortable, luxurious, quiet.
**Surface:** grassy. 19/03-31/10.
**Distance:** on the spot 9,5km 150m 150m 250m on the spot 150m on the spot on the spot.

### Mureck 36B3

**Ölmühle Sixt**, Oberrakitsch 53. **GPS:** n46,73818 e15,74574.

10 € 13 Ch included WC. **Location:** Rural, comfortable, quiet. **Surface:** gravel. 01/03-31/10.
**Distance:** 600m 5km.
**Remarks:** Bread-service.

### Murfeld 36B3

**Gasthof Dorfheuriger Rom Thomas**, Dorfstrasse 1, Unterschwarza.
**GPS:** n46,71557 e15,67624.

---

40 € 15 Ch WC included. **Location:** Rural, comfortable. **Surface:** grassy. 01/01-31/12.
**Distance:** 200m 2,5km on the spot.
**Remarks:** Check in at restaurant, bread-service, wifi code: Camping01, entrance code: camp1.

### Oberrakitsch 36B3

**Ölmühle Sixt**, Oberrakitsch 115. **GPS:** n46,73863 e15,74605.

10 € 10 Ch WC included. **Location:** Rural, simple. **Surface:** gravel. 01/01-31/12.
**Distance:** 1km on the spot 1km 3km 4km.
**Remarks:** Bread-service.

### Passail 36B2

**Almenland Stellplatz**, Auen 61. **GPS:** n47,28217 e15,55711.

---

4 free € 0,50/60liter Ch € 0,50/kWh. **Location:** Rural, comfortable. **Surface:** asphalted. 01/01-31/12.
**Distance:** Passail 3,5km.

### Pichl-Kainisch 36A2

**Sportstüberl Andrea**, Pichl 57. **GPS:** n47,56711 e13,85207.
3 guests free. **Surface:** metalled. 01/01-31/12 Wed.

### Pölfing-Brunn 36B3

**Kipferlbad**, Badstraße 13. **GPS:** n46,72422 e15,29268.

10 free.
**Location:** Rural, simple. **Surface:** grassy. 01/01-31/12.
**Distance:** 1km on the spot on the spot 1km 1km.

### Riegersburg 36B3

**P Seebad**. **GPS:** n46,99677 e15,94107.

10 🛏free. **Location:** Rural, simple. **Surface:** asphalted.
🅿 01/01-31/12.
**Distance:** 🚰500m 🏊on the spot 🚽500m.
**Remarks:** Swimming pool available.

**Sankt Stefan im Rosental**  36B3
Schichenauerstraße 6. **GPS:** n46,90634 e15,71431.

15 🛏free 🚰€ 1/100liter 🔌Ch ⚡(6x)€ 0,50/kWh WC.
**Location:** Rural, comfortable. **Surface:** gravel. 🅿 01/01-31/12.
**Distance:** 🚰200m ✕200m 🚽200m.

**Schwanberg**  36B3
**Freibad**, Badstraße. **GPS:** n46,76361 e15,20639.

4 🛏free, 16/05-14/09 € 6 🚰🔌Ch⚡included.
**Surface:** gravel. 🅿 01/01-31/12 🔵 service: 15/09-15/05.
**Distance:** 🚰500m 🏊on the spot ✕on the spot 🚽500m 🚌500m.

**Soboth**  36B3
**Parkplatz Soboth-Stausee. GPS:** n46,68142 e15,03805.

12 🛏€ 10 + € 1,20/pp tourist tax 🚰Chincluded.
**Location:** Rural, simple, quiet.
**Surface:** asphalted.
🅿 01/01-31/12.
**Distance:** 🚰5km 🏊on the spot ✕200m on the spot 🚶on the spot.
**Remarks:** Parking at artificial lake.

**Stadl an der Mur**  36A3
**Da' Bräuhauser**, Steindorf 23. **GPS:** n47,08885 e13,98824.
15 🛏€ 16-19 + € 1,20/pp tourist tax, dog € 1,50 🚰Chincluded
⚡€ 0,60/kWh 🅿.
**Surface:** grassy. 🅿 01/01-31/12.
**Distance:** 🚰500m.
**Remarks:** Breakfast-service.

**Stainz**  36B3
Ettendorfer Straße 3. **GPS:** n46,89377 e15,26823.

---

10 🛏free. **Surface:** metalled. 🅿 01/01-31/12.
**Distance:** 🚰100m ✕100m 🚽100m.

**Stainz**  36B3
TSV Stelzl, Bad-Gamser-Straße 21. **GPS:** n46,88498 e15,25471.
10 🛏. **Location:** Rural, isolated, quiet. 🅿 01/01-31/12.
**Distance:** 🚰1,2km ⚓on the spot.
**Remarks:** At fish lake.

**Tourist information Stainz:**
ℹ Region Süd-Weststeiermark, Hauptplatz 34, www.stainz.at. Das
Land des Schilcher, country of the Austrian rosé wine.
🚂 Der Stainzer Flascherlzug. Narrow-gauge steam train.
👁 01/05-31/10 Sa/Su/holidays 15h.
     Ren(nt)a Traktor, Anton Nettwall, Sommereben 95, St. Stefan ob
Stainz. With a tractor through Schilcherland.
🎫 € 58 1/2 day.

**Unterlamm**  36B3
**Sieglhof**, Magland 44. **GPS:** n46,98152 e16,09172.

10 🛏€ 5 🚰on demand. **Location:** Rural, simple.
**Surface:** grassy/gravel. 🅿 01/01-31/12 🔵 Tue + Wed.
**Distance:** 🚰4km ✕on the spot 🚽1,5km 🚌on the spot.

**Veitsch**  36B2
**Marktgemeindeamt**, Obere Hauptstraße 18.
**GPS:** n47,57896 e15,48961.

2 🛏free. **Surface:** asphalted. 🅿 01/01-31/12.
**Distance:** 🚰300m ✕100m 🚽100m 🚌100m.

**Vordernberg**  36A2
Hauptplatz 2. **GPS:** n47,48617 e14,99202.

6 🛏free 🚰€ 1/10minutes 🔌Ch ⚡€ 1/8h.
**Surface:** gravel. 🅿 01/04-31/10.
**Distance:** 🚰500m ✕500m 🚽500m 🚌on the spot.

# Carinthia

**Bad Sankt Leonhard im Lavanttal**  36A3
**Bachwegbrücke. GPS:** n46,96037 e14,79358.

---

8 🛏€ 4 🚰Chincluded. 🅿 01/01-31/12.
**Remarks:** Parking behind Spar-supermarket.

**Bleiburg**  36A3
Grabenstraße. **GPS:** n46,59095 e14,79550.

4 🛏free. **Surface:** grasstiles. 🅿 01/01-31/12.
**Distance:** ✕100m 🚽on the spot 🚌200m.

**Ferlach**  36A3
**Messeparkplatz Schloß Ferlach**, Messeplatz 5.
**GPS:** n46,52633 e14,29750.

30 🛏€ 4/24h 🚰€ 1/10minutes 🔌Ch ⚡(10x)€ 1/8h. 🅿
**Location:** Urban, simple. **Surface:** metalled. 🅿 01/01-31/12.
**Distance:** 🚰500m 🏊on the spot ✕300m 🚽300m 🚌300m.
**Remarks:** Max. 24h, no camping activities.

**Heiligenblut**  20G3
**Möllfluss-Camping**, Pockhorn 25. **GPS:** n47,02371 e12,86180.
🛏€ 19,90 + tourist tax.
**Surface:** asphalted. 🅿 15/06-01/09.

**Hermagor**  23H1
**Schluga**, Vellach 15. **GPS:** n46,63147 e13,39532.

6 🛏€ 14 2 pers.incl, dog € 3,10 🚰🔌Ch ⚡(6x)€ 2,72 WC included
💧€ 0,80. **Location:** Urban, simple. **Surface:** gravel.
🅿 01/01-31/12.
**Distance:** 🚰2,5km ✕on the spot 🚽2km 🚌winter free shuttle to
piste 🚶on the spot 🚶on the spot.
**Remarks:** Peak season max. 3 days, max. 7 days, bicycle rental.

**Tourist information Hermagor:**
🚶 Presseggersee. Nature reserve, no motor boats allowed.

**Klagenfurt**  36A3
**Messeparkplatz**, St. Ruprechter Straße. **GPS:** n46,61828 e14,30566.

AT

4 🛏 € 5/24h 🚰 € 0,10/10liter ⚡Ch. ⚡€ 0,62/kWh. 🚰
**Location:** Simple, central. **Surface:** asphalted.
⬛ 01/01-31/12.
**Distance:** 🚶700m ⊗700m.
**Tourist information Klagenfurt:**
ℹ️ Klagenfurt Tourismus, Neuer Platz 1. Capital Carinthia on the
Wörther lake.
👁 Altstadt. Historical centre.

### Kötschach–Mauthen 23G1

**Gasthof Gailberghöhe**, Gailberg 3. **GPS:** n46,71525 e12,96753.

70 🛏 € 14,50, 2 pers.incl. 🚰⚡Ch. ⚡WCincluded.
**Surface:** asphalted/gravel. ⬛ 01/05-15/11, 15/12-15/03.
**Distance:** 🚶7km ⊗on the spot ⚡7km 🚌on the spot 🚴on the spot
🚶on the spot 🚲2km 🚆7km.
**Remarks:** Breakfast-service, use of sauna against payment.

### Ledenitzen 36A3

**Familien-Camping Ferien am Walde**, Sportplatzweg 1.
**GPS:** n46,57000 e13,95242.
220 🛏 € 13-18 🚰⚡Ch. ⚡WC📷💡. ⬛ 01/05-01/10.

### Mörtschach 20G3

**Gasthaus Schwaiger**, Mörtschach 35. **GPS:** n46,92287 e12,91348.

4 🛏 guests free 🚰⚡📶. **Surface:** grassy. ⬛ 01/05-31/10.
**Distance:** ⊗on the spot.

### Rosegg 36A3

**Gasthof Roseggerhof**, Schulweg 4. **GPS:** n46,59026 e14,02037.

30 🛏 € 10,50-12 + € 1,20/pp tourist tax 🚰⚡📷€ 2 📶included.
**Location:** Rural, simple. **Surface:** grassy.
⬛ 01/04-31/10.
**Distance:** ⚡8km ⊗on the spot ⚡bakery 150m.

### Sachsenburg 20H3

**Restaurant Auszeit**, Obergottesfeld 79. **GPS:** n46,79959 e13,35137.

---

10 🛏 guests free.
**Location:** Rural, simple. **Surface:** gravel.
⬛ 01/01-31/12 💡 week after Easter, week after All Saints' Day.
**Distance:** ⚡9km ⊗on the spot.

### Wernberg 36A3

**Landgasthof Fruhmann**, Triester Straße 1.
**GPS:** n46,62501 e13,92933.

5 🛏 guests free. **Location:** Rural, simple. **Surface:** gravel.
⬛ 01/01-31/12.
**Distance:** 🚶Villach 6,5km ⚡1,2km ⊗on the spot ⚡bakery +
butcher.

### Zlan 20H3

**Nagelerhof**, Ziebl 4. **GPS:** n46,74042 e13,57707.

8 🛏 € 17,20 + € 1,50/pp tourist tax 🚰⚡Ch. ⚡€ 1,50 WC📷included.
**Location:** Simple. **Surface:** grassy.
⬛ 01/03-31/10.
**Distance:** ⚡8km.
**Remarks:** Not suitable for motorhomes +7m.

# Burgenland

### Andau 36C2

**Pusztasee. GPS:** n47,77426 e17,01307.
150 🛏 € 19-23 🚰⚡Ch. 📷💡. ⬛ 15/04-15/10.

### Bad Tatzmannsdorf 36B2

**Thermencamping**, Am Campingplatz 1, Oberschützen.
**GPS:** n47,33912 e16,21892.

15 🛏 € 13-20,20 + € 1,50/pp tourist tax 🚰⚡Ch. ⚡€ 0,52/kWh
WC📷included 💡. **Location:** Rural, comfortable. **Surface:** gravel.
⬛ 01/01-31/12.
**Distance:** 🚶1,5km ⊗500m ⚡450m.

### Deutsch Jahrndorf 36C1

**Deutsch Jahrndorf**, Söldnergasse 19. **GPS:** n48,00777 e17,11073.

---

17 🛏 voluntary contribution 🚰⚡Ch. 🔋
**Location:** Rural, simple. **Surface:** grassy. ⬛ 01/04-31/10.
**Distance:** 🚶500m ⊗500m ⚡500m.
**Remarks:** Max. 3 nights.

### Horitschon 36C2

**Weingut Duschanek**, Hauptstraße 104. **GPS:** n47,59162 e16,53493.

10 🛏 € 5, guests free 🚰included ⚡€ 3/24h WC. 🔋
**Location:** Simple. **Surface:** metalled. ⬛ 01/01-31/12.
**Distance:** 🚶600m ⊗on the spot ⚡600m 🚌on the spot.

### Illmitz 36C2

**Wohnmobilstellplatz Pustablick**, Ufergasse 42.
**GPS:** n47,75851 e16,79606.

5 🛏 voluntary contribution 🚰⚡€ 2. **Location:** Rural, simple.
**Surface:** grassy. ⬛ 01/04-01/11.
**Distance:** 🚶900m ⊗900m ⚡bakery 500m.

### Jois 36C2

**Bioweingut Edelhof**, Hauptplatz 6. **GPS:** n47,95922 e16,79012.

3 🛏 € 15 🚰⚡Ch. ⚡included.
**Location:** Rural, simple. **Surface:** grassy/gravel.
⬛ 01/03-31/10.
**Distance:** 🚶on the spot ⊗50m ⚡800m 🚴on the spot 🚶on the spot.
**Remarks:** In the courtyard of a medieval farmstead.

### Moschendorf 36C3

**P Weinmuseum-Kulturverein Moschendorf**, Moschendorf 95.
**GPS:** n47,05784 e16,47713.

🛏 free. **Location:** Urban, simple. **Surface:** asphalted.
⬛ 01/01-31/12.
**Distance:** 🚶on the spot.

**⌂⊓S** Oslip 36C2

**Kulturzentrum Gasthof Cselly Mühle**, Sachsenweg 63.
**GPS:** n47,84119 e16,62510. ⬆.

10 ⌐free ⌐⚡. **Location:** Rural, simple, isolated. **Surface:** grassy.
◻ 01/01-31/12.
**Distance:** 🚲1,2km ⊗on the spot.
**Remarks:** Check in on arrival.

**⌂⊓S** Podersdorf 🌳 36C2

**Weingut Schaller**, Frauenkirchnerstraße 20.
**GPS:** n47,85032 e16,83934. ⬆.

8 ⌐€ 8 ⌐⚡Chincluded ⚡€ 2/24h. **Location:** Rural, simple.
**Surface:** grassy. ◻ 01/04-30/11.
**Distance:** 🚲300m.
**Remarks:** When buying wine 1 night free.

**⌂⊓S** Podersdorf 🌳 36C2

**Weingut Sloboda**, Alte Satz 1. **GPS:** n47,85020 e16,83091. ⬆.

11 ⌐€ 12 + € 1,50/pp tourist tax ⌐⚡Ch ⚡WCincluded.
**Location:** Rural, comfortable, quiet. **Surface:** grassy.
◻ 01/03-31/10.
**Distance:** 🚲500m ⚡ 13,5km ⚓500m Neusiedler See ⊗on the spot
⚑1km.
**Remarks:** Max. 3 nights, when buying wine 1 night free.

AT

# Bosnia and Herzegovina

Capital: Sarajevo
Government: Federation
Official Language: Bosnien, Croatien and Serbian
Population: 3,856,181 (2017)
Area: 51,209 km²

### General information
Dialling code: 0387
General emergency: 112
Currency: convertible Mark (BAM) also the Euro is accepted as currency.
Credit cards are accepted in the main cities.

### Regulations for overnight stays
Wild camping is not allowed.

### Additional public holidays 2019
March 1 Independence Day
May 1 Labour Day
May 9 Victory Day
November 25 Statehood Day

### Time Zone
Winter (Standard Time) GMT+1
Summer (DST)  GMT+2

Bosnia and Herzegovina
page: 100

Sarajevo

---

**BA**

## △S Banja Luka 37D2
**Kamp Olimp. GPS:** n44,71114 e17,16642.
10 € 15 Ch included. **Location:** Rural, simple, isolated, quiet. **Surface:** grassy. 01/01-31/12.
**Distance:** 8km on the spot on the spot.

## △S Bihać 37C2
**Kamp Orljani. GPS:** n44,80145 e15,90643.
120 € 18,50 Ch included. **Location:** Rural, simple, isolated. **Surface:** grassy/gravel. 01/05-01/11.
**Distance:** 3,5km on the spot 100m.

## △S Bihać 37C2
**Una Kiro Rafting**, Golubić. **GPS:** n44,78250 e15,92472.
9 € 17 Ch included. **Location:** Rural, simple, quiet. **Surface:** grassy. 01/04-01/11.
**Distance:** 5km on the spot on the spot on the spot.

## ⫪S Bila 37D2
**Motel Carousel. GPS:** n44,17886 e17,75475.

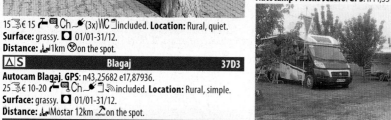

15 € 15 Ch (3x) WC included. **Location:** Rural, quiet. **Surface:** grassy. 01/01-31/12.
**Distance:** 1km on the spot.

## △S Blagaj 37D3
**Autocam Blagaj. GPS:** n43,25682 e17,87936.
25 € 10-20 Ch included. **Location:** Rural, simple. **Surface:** grassy. 01/01-31/12.
**Distance:** Mostar 12km on the spot.

## △S Blagaj 37D3
**Mail Wimbledon. GPS:** n43,26317 e17,87799.
60 € 11-14 Ch € 3 included. **Location:** Rural, simple. **Surface:** grassy/gravel. 01/01-31/12.
**Distance:** Mostar 10km 150m 100m.
**Remarks:** Dog € 2/day.

## △S Blagaj 37D3
**River Camp Aganovac. GPS:** n43,25724 e17,88774.
8 € 18 Ch included. **Location:** Urban, simple. **Surface:** grassy/sand. 01/01-31/12.
**Distance:** on the spot on the spot 200m 150m.

## △S Bosanska Krupa 37C2
**Una Camping. GPS:** n44,91484 e16,15696.
€ 16 Ch included. **Location:** Rural, simple, isolated. **Surface:** grassy. 01/04-01/10.
**Distance:** on the spot on the spot.

## △S Buna 37D3
**River Camp Half Island. GPS:** n43,24166 e17,83861.

20 € 17 Ch € 3 included. **Location:** Rural, comfortable, quiet. **Surface:** grassy. 01/04-01/10.
**Distance:** on the spot on the spot 500m 500m.
**Remarks:** Only cash payment.

## △S Foča 39A4
**Auto Camp Drina. GPS:** n43,52948 e18,78254.
15 € 17 Ch included. **Location:** Rural, comfortable, isolated, quiet. **Surface:** grassy. 01/05-15/09.
**Distance:** 3km on the spot on the spot on the spot.

## S Gradačac 37D2
**Hipodrom Vuković. GPS:** n44,91860 e18,41893.
€ 20 Ch included. **Location:** Rural. **Surface:** grassy/sand. 01/04-01/11.
**Distance:** on the spot.

## △S Jajec 37D2
**Autocamp Plivsko Jezero. GPS:** n44,35103 e17,22682.

40 € 21 Ch included. **Surface:** grassy. 15/04-31/10.
**Distance:** 5km 100m 100m on the spot.

## △S Krupa na Vrbasu 37D2
**Camp Krupa. GPS:** n44,61616 e17,14837.
80 € 12 Ch included. **Location:** Rural, simple, isolated. **Surface:** grassy. 01/05-01/10.
**Distance:** on the spot on the spot 200m on the spot.

## △S Kulen Vakuf 37C2
**RC Discover Bihac. GPS:** n44,56909 e16,08338.

25 € 5 + € 5/pp Ch WC included. **Location:** Rural. **Surface:** grassy/gravel. 01/04-30/10.
**Distance:** on the spot on the spot on the spot on the spot.

## △S Medugorje 37D3
**Camp Zemo. GPS:** n43,19432 e17,67612.
45 € 10 Ch included WC. **Location:** Urban, simple. **Surface:** gravel. 01/01-31/12.
**Distance:** 100m 100m.

## △S Sarajevo 39A4
**Oaza Resort. GPS:** n43,82799 e18,29659.

350 € 20,90 Ch included € 2,60. **Surface:** grassy. 01/01-31/12.
**Distance:** 10km 100m 800m.

## ⫪S Ščit 37D3
**Konoba Gaj. GPS:** n43,80230 e17,52560.
5 € 10 Ch included. **Location:** Rural. **Surface:** grassy/gravel. 01/01-31/12.
**Distance:** on the spot on the spot on the spot.

# Belgium

Capital: Brussels
Government: Constitutional monarchy
Official Language: Dutch/Flemish, French and German
Population: 11,491,346 (2017)
Area: 30,528 km²

## General information
Dialling code: 0032
General emergency: 112
Currency: Euro

## Regulations for overnight stays
Wild camping is forbidden.

## Additional public holidays 2019
May 1 Labour Day
July 11 Feast Flemish Community
July 21 National Day
August 15 Assumption Day
September 27 Feast of the Walloon Region
November 1 All Saints' Day
November 11 Armistice Day 1918

## Time Zone
Winter (Standard Time) GMT+1
Summer (DST) GMT+2

*Map of Belgium showing regions:*
Antwerp pages: 105-106
East Flanders pages: 103-105
West Flanders pages: 101-103
Limburg pages: 107-110
Flemish Brabant page: 107
Brussels page: 110
Hainaut pages: 111-112
Liège pages: 110-111
Namur pages: 112-113
Luxembourg pages: 114-115

**BE**

---

# West Flanders

### Aartrijke 11A1
Sint-Aarnoutstraat. **GPS:** n51,11341 e3,08983.⬆️.

3 🅿️free. **Surface:** asphalted. 🕐 01/01-31/12.
**Distance:** 🚶400m ⊗80m 🚉50m.

### Anzegem 11A2
**Vital Moreelsplein**, Tiegemberg. **GPS:** n50,81712 e3,46666.⬆️.
3 🅿️free. **Surface:** unpaved. 🕐 01/01-31/12.
**Distance:** 🚶Anzegem 3km ⊗200m.

### Beernem 11A1
**Kanaaloever Beernem**, Oude Vaartstraat.
**GPS:** n51,13482 e3,33427.⬆️.

6 🅿️€ 10/24h 🔌🚰Ch🚿(4x)WCincluded 🗑️€ 1,sanitary at harbour building.🏠 **Location:** Rural. **Surface:** metalled.
🕐 01/01-31/12.
**Distance:** 🚤1,9km.

---

**Remarks:** Max. 72h, only exact change.

### Blankenberge 11A1
**Kampeerautoterrein De Wielen**, Zeebruggelaan 135.
**GPS:** n51,31106 e3,15154.⬆️.
26 🅿️€ 20-23 🔌🚰Ch🚿included 🗑️€ 0,50 🚿€ 4/3.
**Surface:** grassy/metalled. 🕐 01/01-31/12.
**Distance:** 🚶2km 🏖️2km.

**Tourist information Blankenberge:**
ℹ️ Dienst Toerisme, Koning Leopold III-plein. Lively bathing resort.
Sea Life Centre, Koning Albert I Laan 116. Underwaterworld.
🕐 10-18h.
Serpentarium, Zeedijk 147. World of the reptiles. 🕐 Easter-Oct 10-18h, 01/07-31/08 10-21h.

### Brugge 11A1
Bargeweg. **GPS:** n51,19633 e3,22544.⬆️➡️.

59 🅿️€ 19, 01/04-30/09 € 25 🔌€ 0,50 🚰Ch🚿included.🗑️🚿
**Location:** Urban, simple, central. **Surface:** metalled.
🕐 01/01-31/12.
**Distance:** 🚶within walking distance 🚌on the spot.
**Remarks:** Arrival <22h, max 3,5t, monitored parking.

**Tourist information Brugge:**
ℹ️ Brugge City Card gives for free entrance on among other things 27 museums, boat trips and many discounts on purchases. 🎫 € 47.
ℹ️ Toerisme Brugge, 't Zand 34, www.brugge.be. City with medieval character, hiking itinerary available at Tourist office.
👁️ Brouwerij Halve Maan, Walplein 26. Town brewery. 🕐 11-16u. 🎫 € 8,50.
👁️ Lamme Goedzak, Noorweegsekaai 31. Boat excursion from Bruges

---

to Damme with the `Lamme Goedzak', departure Noorweegse Kaai.
🕐 01/04-30/09 10-16.
🅼 Diamantmuseum, Katelijnestraat 43. Diamond museum. 🕐 10.30-17.30h.
Boudewijn Seapark, Alfons De Baeckerstraat 12, Sint-Michiels.
Attractions park with dolphinarium, seal island etc., in winter large skating rink covered. 🕐 01/07-31/08 10-18h.

### Diksmuide 13D2
**'t Nesthof**, Zijdelingstraat 2a. **GPS:** n51,07178 e2,86422.⬆️.

14 🅿️€ 9/night 🔌€ 1 🚰Ch🚿€ 2/24h. 🚲 **Location:** Rural, isolated, quiet. **Surface:** grassy. 🕐 01/04-01/10.
**Distance:** 🚶5km 🚲on the spot 🚶on the spot.
**Remarks:** Bread-service.

### Gistel 11A1
Sportstraat. **GPS:** n51,16112 e2,96495.⬆️.

2 🅿️free 🔌🚰Chfree. **Surface:** metalled. 🕐 01/01-31/12.
**Distance:** 🚶1km 🚲3,3km 🚌on the spot 🚶on the spot.

**Remarks:** Parking behind swimming pool, max. 1 night, key service at swimming pool, many walking and bicycle area.

### ⚏S 🚿 Harelbeke 11A2

**Kampeerautoterrein De Dageraad**, Stasegemsesteenweg 21. **GPS:** n50,84396 e3,31057.

8 ⚏ € 5/24h 🚰🔌Ch🔧included WC⚏ € 1,25 📶free. 🚐
**Location:** Urban, comfortable, quiet. **Surface:** metalled. 📅 01/01-31/12.
**Distance:** 🚶1,6km 🚲4,5km ⚓700m 🚌100m.
**Remarks:** Parking next to midget golf, service during opening hours: 8-20h.

### ⚏S 🚿 Ieper ⚜ 11A2

**Kampeerautoterrein Zillebekevijver**, Zillebekevijverdreef. **GPS:** n50,83578 e2,90504.

17⚏ € 8/24h 🚰€ 1/100liter ⚏Ch🔧included. 🚐⚏
**Location:** Rural, comfortable. **Surface:** grasstiles/metalled.
📅 01/01-31/12.
**Distance:** 🚶2,5km ⊗500m ⚓1,5km 🚌1km 🚲on the spot 🚶on the spot.
**Remarks:** Max. 48h.

### △S 🚿 Knokke-Heist 11A1

**Holiday**, Natiënlaan 72. **GPS:** n51,33612 e3,28866.
10⚏ € 18-24 🚰⚏Ch🔧WC⚏📶free.
**Surface:** metalled. 📅 01/01-31/12.
**Distance:** 🚶1km ⚓on the spot ⚓100m.

### ⚏S 🚿 Kortemark 11A1

**Sporthal Kortemark**, Ichtegemstraat 2a. **GPS:** n51,03201 e3,04168.⬆

2 ⚏free 🚰€ 2 ⚏€ 2 Ch. **Surface:** metalled. 📅 01/01-31/12.
**Distance:** 🚶500m 🚌on the spot.
**Remarks:** Max. 48h.

### ⚏S 🚿 Kortrijk ⚜ 11A2

**Kampeerautoterrein Broeltorens**, Damkaai.
**GPS:** n50,83120 e3,26818.⬆

8 ⚏ € 10/24h 🚰⚏Ch🔧📶included. 🚐⚏
**Location:** Urban. **Surface:** metalled. 📅 01/01-31/12.
**Distance:** 🚶centre 400m ⊗100m.

**Tourist information Kortrijk:**
ℹ Dienst Toerisme, Begijnhofpark, www.kortrijk.be. Historical little town with Beguine convent.

### ⚏S Langemark- Poelkappele 11A1

Boezingestraat 51a. **GPS:** n50,90944 e2,91763.⬆

8 ⚏ € 12/24h 🚰⚏Ch🔧(4x)included ⚏ € 1. 🚐
**Location:** Urban, simple. **Surface:** grasstiles.
📅 01/01-31/12.
**Distance:** ⊗on the spot 🚶on the spot.
**Remarks:** Max. 72h, check in at reception sports centre.

### ⚏ Lichtervelde 11A1

**O.C. De Schouw**, Twee Lindenstraat. **GPS:** n51,02389 e3,13493.⬆

2 ⚏free. **Surface:** metalled. 📅 01/01-31/12.
**Distance:** 🚶600m ⊗600m ⚓300m on the spot 🚲on the spot 🚶on the spot.
**Remarks:** Max. 48h.

### ⚏ Mesen 13D2

Kerkstraat. **GPS:** n50,76391 e2,89825.⬆

3 ⚏free. **Surface:** metalled. 📅 01/01-31/12.
**Distance:** 🚶on the spot ⊗frituur 200m ⚓100m.
**Remarks:** In front of church, max. 24h.

### ⚏S Middelkerke 13D1

**Camperpark Zeester**, Oostendelaan 193. **GPS:** n51,19071 e2,83327.⬆

15⚏ € 12,50-25 🚰⚏Ch🔧(16x)WC⚏📶included ⚓🚐⚏
**Location:** Urban, comfortable. **Surface:** metalled.
📅 01/01-31/12.
**Distance:** 🚶1km ⚓500m ⚓500m 🚌100m 🚲100m 🚶100m.

### P Middelkerke 13D1

Koning Ridderdijk. **GPS:** n51,16684 e2,78246.⬆
6 ⚏ € 15. **Location:** Simple. 📅 01/01-31/12, 9-19h.
**Distance:** ⚓on the spot.
**Remarks:** Beach parking.

### ⚏S Nieuwpoort ⚜ 13D1

**De Zwerver**, Brugsesteenweg 29, N367. **GPS:** n51,12988 e2,76576.⬆

28 ⚏ € 18/24h, then € 0,50/h 🚰€ 0,50/50liter ⚏Ch🔧
included,10Amp WC⚏ € 1,20 ⚏€ 5/3 📶. 🚐 **Location:** Urban, comfortable, quiet. **Surface:** grassy. 📅 01/01-31/12.
**Distance:** 🚶800m ⚓3,3km ⚓4km ⊗800m ⚓800m 🚌50m
🚲100m 🚶100m.

### ⚏S Oudenburg 11A1

**Carpool**, Stationsstraat. **GPS:** n51,19387 e3,00567.

⚏free 🚰€ 2 ⚏€ 2 Ch. **Surface:** metalled. 📅 01/01-31/12.
**Distance:** 🚶800m.
**Remarks:** P service max. 30 min.

**Tourist information Oudenburg:**
🚹 📅 Wed-afternoon.

### ⚏ Poperinge ⚜ 13D2

Oudstrijdersplein. **GPS:** n50,85333 e2,72332.

⚏. 📅 01/01-31/12 ⚪ Fri.
**Distance:** 🚶500m 🚶50m.

### ⚏ Roeselare 11A1

O.L. Vrouwenmarkt. **GPS:** n50,94786 e3,13450.⬆

1 ⚏free. **Surface:** metalled. 📅 18-9h, 01/01-31/12h.
**Distance:** 🚶200m 🚌on the spot.
**Remarks:** Max. 1 night.

### ⚏ Roeselare 11A1

Trakelweg. **GPS:** n50,94438 e3,13320.⬆

10 ⚏free. **Location:** Urban. **Surface:** asphalted. 📅 01/01-31/12.
**Distance:** 🚶1km 🚲on the spot 🚶on the spot.
**Remarks:** No camping activities.

## Sint-Eloois-Vijve — 11A1

**Kampeerautoterrein Leiekamper**, Leiesas 15.
**GPS:** n50,90879 e3,40468. ⬆.

8 ⬡ € 5 ⬡ € 1/100liter ⬡ included,16Amp. 🚐 ⬡ 01/01-31/12.
**Distance:** 🚶400m ⊗400m ⬡1km 🚲 on the spot 🏃 on the spot.
**Remarks:** Max. 72h.

## Stavele — 13D2

**Hof van Commerce**, IJzerstraat 16. **GPS:** n50,94313 e2,67206. ⬆.
⬡ guests free. **Surface:** gravel.
⬡ 01/01-31/12 ⬡ 15/08-14/09.
**Distance:** ⬡ on the spot ⬡ on the spot ⊗ on the spot.

## Wervik — 11A2

**Kampeerautoterrein De Balokken**, De Balokken.
**GPS:** n50,77456 e3,03705. ⬆.

8 ⬡ € 10/72h ⬡ € 1/100liter ⬡ Ch ⬡ included.
**Surface:** grasstiles. ⬡ 01/01-31/12.
**Distance:** 🚶1km ⬡ on the spot ⬡ on the spot ⊗cafetaria ⬡700m bakery 🚲 on the spot 🏃 on the spot.
**Remarks:** On leisure island, max. 72h.

## Westende — 13D1

**Camperpark Westende**, Heidestraat 18. **GPS:** n51,15597 e2,76623.

30 ⬡ € 20-23, 2 pers.incl ⬡ ⬡ Ch ⬡ 10Amp WC included ⬡. ⬡ 🚐
**Location:** Urban, luxurious, quiet. **Surface:** grassy/metalled.
⬡ 01/01-31/12.
**Distance:** 🚶on the spot ⬡1km ⊗300m ⬡400m.
**Remarks:** Discount longer stays, swimming pool (summer).

## Westende — 13D1

**Kompas Camperpark**, Strandjuttersdreef. **GPS:** n51,15594 e2,76019. ⬆.

35 ⬡20h € 12,50-19, 44h € 21-30 ⬡ ⬡ Ch ⬡ included ⬡. ⬡ 🚐
**Surface:** grasstiles/metalled. ⬡ 01/01-31/12.
**Distance:** 🚶on the spot ⬡1km ⊗Taverne, Frituur ⬡ on the spot.

## Westende — 13D1

**Poldervallei**, Westendelaan 178. **GPS:** n51,16675 e2,78242. ⬆.

---

15 ⬡ € 16-23 ⬡ ⬡ Ch ⬡ included. ⬡ 🚐
**Surface:** asphalted. ⬡ 01/01-31/12.
**Distance:** ⬡1km ⬡500m.
**Remarks:** Nearby camp site.

## Westvleteren — 13D2

**Camperpunt Sixtusbos**, Nachtegaalstraat 2. **GPS:** n50,89844 e2,71033.

18 ⬡ € 10 ⬡ Ch included ⬡ ⬡ 2. ⬡ **Location:** Rural.
**Surface:** grassy/gravel. ⬡ 01/01-31/12.
**Distance:** 🚶5km ⊗950m 🚲 on the spot.
**Remarks:** Bread-service, narrow entrance.

## Wingene — 11A1

**Smart - ijs**, Noordakkerstraat 1a. **GPS:** n51,07377 e3,26515. ⬆.

6 ⬡ € 8, discount for clients ⬡ ⬡ Ch ⬡,10Amp ⬡ included. ⬡ 🚐
**Location:** Rural. **Surface:** gravel. ⬡ 01/01-31/12.
**Distance:** 🚶2km ⬡1,5km bike junction 🏃 on the spot.
**Remarks:** Max. 72h.

## Zonnebeke — 11A2

**Café De Dreve**, Lange Dreef 16. **GPS:** n50,85410 e2,97924.

⬡free. **Surface:** gravel. ⬡ 01/01-31/12.
**Distance:** 🚶Zonnebeke 2,7km ⬡ 3,5km A19 ⊗snacks 🚲 on the spot 🏃 on the spot.
**Remarks:** Passendalemuseum-Zonnebeke.

# East Flanders

## Aalst — 11B1

Zwembadlaan 2. **GPS:** n50,93825 e4,05829.

2 ⬡free ⬡ € 5,50 ⬡ Ch ⬡ € 5,50/1h.
**Surface:** metalled.
⬡ 01/01-31/12.

---

**Distance:** 🚶city centre ± 1km ⬡ 3,8km ⬡on the spot 🚲 on the spot 🏃 on the spot.
**Remarks:** Only 2 plots indicated, more plots permitted.

**Tourist information Aalst:**
🚶 ⬡ Thu-morning.

## Aalter — 11A1

Vaart-Zuid, Bellem. **GPS:** n51,09821 e3,49365. ⬆.

25 ⬡free. **Location:** Rural, simple, quiet. **Surface:** asphalted.
⬡ 01/01-31/12.
**Distance:** ⬡Canal.

## Aalter — 11A1

Vaart-Noord, Bellem. **GPS:** n51,09875 e3,49468. ⬆.

25 ⬡free. **Surface:** asphalted. ⬡ 01/01-31/12.
**Distance:** ⬡600m 🚲500m.

## Aalter — 11A1

Bellemdorpweg, Bellem. **GPS:** n51,09323 e3,48308. ⬆.

2 ⬡free. **Surface:** asphalted. ⬡ 01/01-31/12.
**Distance:** 🚶500m.
**Remarks:** At football ground.

## Aalter — 11A1

Wingenestraat, Maria Aalter. **GPS:** n51,09915 e3,37141. ⬆.

2 ⬡free ⬡ € 1 ⬡ € 1. **Location:** Simple, quiet. **Surface:** grasstiles.
⬡ 01/01-31/12.
**Distance:** 🚶on the spot ⊗100m ⬡4km 🚐 on the spot 🚲 on the spot 🏃 on the spot.
**Remarks:** Near church.

## Aalter — 11A1

**Domein Hooggoed**, Stratem. **GPS:** n51,08835 e3,39870. ⬆.

**BE**

2 free. **Location:** Rural, simple, isolated, quiet. **Surface:** gravel. 01/01-31/12.
**Distance:** 4,2km on the spot on the spot.
**Tourist information Aalter:**
Kasteel Poeke, Kasteelstraat 26, Poeke. weekend, holidays, 01/04-31/10 Su 14-17h.
Wed-morning.

### Assenede 11B1

**Sporthal Assenede**, Kapelledreef 4. **GPS:** n51,23067 e3,74891.

6 € 10 € 1/60liter € 1.
**Location:** Urban, comfortable, quiet. **Surface:** grassy.
01/01-31/12 Service: winter.
**Distance:** 500m 600m on the spot on the spot.
**Remarks:** Behind gymnasium, max. 72h, payment only with coins, sanitary during opening hours gymnasium.

### Bazel 11B1

**Sporthal De Dulpop**, Beekdam 1. **GPS:** n51,14778 e4,30583.

10 free. **Location:** Rural, simple. **Surface:** asphalted.
01/01-31/12.
**Distance:** 200m 6km 3km 500m 500m on the spot on the spot.
**Remarks:** Barn-museum 200m.

### Eeklo 11A1

**Jachthaven Eeklo**, Jachthaven 1. **GPS:** n51,17884 e3,54959.

12 € 10/24h € 0,50/130liter Ch € 5/24h,6Amp WC € 1.
**Location:** Urban, comfortable, quiet. **Surface:** grasstiles/metalled.
01/01-31/12.
**Distance:** 1,5km on the spot 1,5km 800m on the spot on the spot.
**Remarks:** Max. 72h, check in at harbourmaster, use sanitary only during opening hours.
**Tourist information Eeklo:**
Provinciaal Domein "Het Leen", Gentsesteenweg 80. Nature reserve.
9-12h, 13-17h Mo.

### Gavere 11B1

Sportdreef. **GPS:** n50,92823 e3,65810.

12 free. **Surface:** asphalted. 01/01-31/12.
**Distance:** on the spot.
**Remarks:** Behind sports complex.

### Geraardsbergen 11B2

**Jeugdherberg 't Schipken**, Kampstraat 59.
**GPS:** n50,79500 e3,90412.

4 free. **Surface:** grassy. 01/01-31/12.
**Distance:** Geraardsbergen 3,7km on the spot.
**Remarks:** Max. 1 night.
**Tourist information Geraardsbergen:**
Provinciaal Domein "de Gavers", Onkelzelestraat 280. Recreation area; swimming, watersports, fishing, boat trips and tennis.Free entrance, payment per attraction.

### Hamme 11B1

**Camperplaats Mirabrug**, Hamveer. **GPS:** n51,10418 e4,14246.

2 free. **Location:** Rural, simple, quiet. **Surface:** metalled.
01/01-31/12.
**Distance:** 1km 400m 500m on the spot on the spot.
**Remarks:** Max. 48h.

### Lokeren 11B1

Veerstraat. **GPS:** n51,11013 e3,97163.

5 free. **Location:** Urban, noisy. **Surface:** metalled.
01/01-31/12.
**Distance:** 1,5km, bakery 500m.
**Remarks:** Parking in front of church, max. 48h.

### Lokeren 11B1

**Verloren Bos**, Aardeken. **GPS:** n51,10981 e3,99525.

2 free. **Location:** Rural, simple. **Surface:** gravel.
01/01-31/12.
**Distance:** 800m 50m 800m 800m 800m.
**Tourist information Lokeren:**
Stationsplein. Flea market. Su 7-12h.
Molsbroek. Protected European Nature Reserve, 80ha marsh area with many birds, asphalted hiking trail. Su 14-17h, 01/07-31/08 Wed-Su 14-17h.

### Ronse 11A2

Engelsenlaan/Boulevard des Anglais. **GPS:** n50,74447 e3,58794.

4 free free. **Surface:** asphalted. 01/01-31/12.
**Distance:** 1km 200m on the spot. **Remarks:** Behind swimming pool, entrance code available at swimming pool.

### Temse 11B1

**De Zaat**, Nagelheetmakerslaan 1. **GPS:** n51,12466 e4,21007.

20 € 2 € 2/10minutes € 4.
**Location:** Urban. **Surface:** grasstiles/metalled. 01/01-31/12.
**Distance:** 400m 250m.
**Remarks:** Behind police station, temporary stopover.

### Temse 11B1

**Camperbedrijf Alpha Motorhomes**, Kapelanielaan 13a, N16.
**GPS:** n51,13699 e4,18017.

4 free Chfree. **Location:** Urban, simple, noisy.
**Surface:** gravel/metalled. 01/01-31/12.
**Distance:** city centre 3km.
**Tourist information Temse:**
Grote Markt. Fri-morning.

### Vosselaar 11C1

**Sportcentrum Diepvenneke**, Diepvenneke 43.
**GPS:** n51,30142 e4,89418.

4 free. **Location:** Rural, simple. **Surface:** metalled.
01/01-31/12.
**Distance:** city centre 1,5km on the spot on the spot.

### Zomergem 11A1

**'t Hof bij Steven**, Bekestraat 12. **GPS:** n51,13140 e3,60052.

5 € 10 € 2/24h WC € 1/time included.
**Location:** Rural, simple, isolated, quiet. **Surface:** grassy.
01/01-31/12.
**Distance:** 4km 300m 4km on the spot on the spot.

BE

**Remarks:** Free shuttle to station.

### 🅂 Zulte � 11A1
Leihoekstraat, Machelen. **GPS:** n50,96103 e3,48352. ⬆.

8 🅿 € 8/72h ⚡ € 1 🅲h ⚡ included. **Surface:** metalled. 🅞 01/01-31/12.
**Distance:** 🚶150m ⊗50m 🚰150m on the spot.
**Remarks:** Max. 72h.

# Antwerp

### 🅂 Antwerpen 🌿🏕🍺 11C1
**Vogelzang,** Vogelzanglaan 7-9, Antwerp (Antwerpen). **GPS:** n51,18983 e4,40074. ⬆.

115 🅿 € 10, Jul/Aug € 15 ⚡ € 1 🅲h ⚡ (30x)€ 1/kWh.
**Location:** Simple. **Surface:** grassy/metalled.
🅞 04/01-22/12.
**Distance:** 🚶city centre 3km 🚲1km 🏊3km ⊗500m 🚰1km ⊙3km 🚌150m.
**Remarks:** Outside environmental zone.

**Tourist information Antwerp (Antwerpen):**
ℹ Antwerp City Card. Antwerp City Card gives free City tour, entrance to museums, churches and many discounts on purchases. 🎫 from € 27.
ℹ Toerisme Antwerpen, Grote Markt, 13, www.visitantwerpen.be. Large port city, worth seeing is the city centre.
🎪 Dageraadsplaats. 🅞 Thu 8-13h.
🎪 Lijnwaadmarkt. Antiques market. 🅞 Easter-Oct Sa 9-17h.
🎪 St. Andriesplaats. 🅞 Tue 8-13h.
🎪 St. Jansplein. 🅞 Wed, Fri 8-13h.
🎪 St. Jansvliet. Bric-a-brac market. 🅞 Su 9-17h.
🎪 Theaterplein. Exotic market. 🅞 Sa.
🎪 Vogelenmarkt, Theaterplein. Famous flea market. 🅞 Su-morning.

### 🅂 Arendonk 11D1
De Vloed. **GPS:** n51,32253 e5,08610. ⬆.

10 🅿 free. **Location:** Urban, simple, quiet. **Surface:** metalled.
🅞 01/01-31/12.
**Distance:** 🚶400m ⊗on the spot 🚰400m ⊙400m 🚌100m 🏃on the spot 🚶on the spot.
**Remarks:** Parking in front of swimming pool, water during opening-hours swimming pool.

### Balen 11D1
**Vrijetijdscentrum De Kruierie,** Berg. **GPS:** n51,17043 e5,16255. ⬆.

2 🅿 free. **Location:** Urban, simple, central. **Surface:** asphalted.

🅞 01/01-31/12.
**Distance:** 🚶400m ⊗200m 🚰500m 🚲2km 🏃2km.
**Remarks:** Max. 24h.

### Beveren 11B1
**De Meerminnen,** Klapperstraat. **GPS:** n51,21201 e4,24377. ⬆.

2 🅿 free. **Location:** Urban, simple, quiet. **Surface:** asphalted.
🅞 01/01-31/12.
**Distance:** 🚶200m 🚰300m.
**Remarks:** At sports park.

### Bornem 11B1
**Abdij Bornem,** Kloosterstraat. **GPS:** n51,09441 e4,22650. ⬆.

4 🅿 free. **Location:** Urban, simple, central, quiet.
**Surface:** metalled.
🅞 01/01-31/12.
**Distance:** 🚶on the spot ⊗500m 🚰1km 🚌on the spot 🏃on the spot.
**Remarks:** Max. 48h, sale of wines.

### Bornem 11B1
**Kasteel d'Ursel,** Koningin Astridlaan. **GPS:** n51,10294 e4,27261. ⬆.

5 🅿 free. **Location:** Rural. **Surface:** unpaved.
🅞 01/01-31/12.
**Remarks:** Parking next to castle, open 8-21h.

### 🅂 Brasschaat 11C1
**P5b,** Elshoutbaan 17. **GPS:** n51,28555 e4,50325. ⬆.

15 🅿 free ⚡ € 1/100liter 🅲h ⚡ € 0,50/kWh.
**Location:** Rural. **Surface:** forest soil. 🅞 01/01-31/12.
**Distance:** 🚶1,7km 🚲6km ⊗500m 🚰500m 🏃on the spot 🚶on the spot.
**Remarks:** Parking sports and recreation centre, max. 72h.

**Tourist information Brasschaat:**
🎪 Armand Reusensplein. 🅞 Mo 8-13h.

### 🅂 Brecht 11C1
Mudeausstraat. **GPS:** n51,34790 e4,64130. ⬆.

2 🅿 free 📶 at townhall. **Location:** Urban, central. **Surface:** metalled.
🅞 01/01-31/12.
**Distance:** 🚶on the spot 🚲1,2km ⊗150m 🚰150m 🚌on the spot 🏃on the spot.
**Remarks:** Max. 48h.

### 🅒 Brecht 11C1
Schoolstraat. **GPS:** n51,34992 e4,64577.

10 🅿 free. **Surface:** grassy/metalled. 🅞 01/01-31/12.
**Distance:** 🚶800m 🚲1,5km.

### 🅒🅂 Essen 🌿 9C3
Kerkeneind, N133. **GPS:** n51,47086 e4,46401. ⬆.

2 🅿 free ⚡🅲h free. **Location:** Urban, simple, central, quiet.
**Surface:** metalled. 🅞 01/01-31/12.
**Distance:** 🚶500m 🚰150m 🚌on the spot 🏃on the spot.
**Remarks:** Max. 24h.

### 🅒 Essen 🌿 9C3
**Parking Kiekenhoeve,** Moerkantsebaan 48. **GPS:** n51,45805 e4,44230.
10 🅿 free. **Location:** Urban, simple. **Surface:** metalled.
🅞 01/01-31/12.
**Distance:** ⊗on the spot 🚰500m.

### 🅒🅂 Geel 🍺 11C1
**Parking Pas,** Fehrenbachstraat 26. **GPS:** n51,15828 e4,99158. ⬆.

7 🅿 € 5 ⚡ € 0,50/100liter 🅲h ⚡ € 1/kWh. 🏪
**Location:** Simple, quiet. **Surface:** gravel/sand. 🅞 01/01-31/12.
**Distance:** 🚶city centre 200m ⊗400m 🚰400m 🚌on the spot 🏃on the spot.
**Remarks:** At swimming pool, service 100m, tuesday morning market.

### 🅒🅂 Grobbendonk 👫 11C1
Vaartkom. **GPS:** n51,18954 e4,73638. ⬆.

6 free €1/5minutes Ch€1 (6x)€1. **Location:** Simple, central. **Surface:** metalled. 01/01-31/12. **Distance:** 200m 3,6km frituur 200m on the spot on the spot.

### Herentals 11C1
Herenhoutseweg. **GPS:** n51,16586 e4,82664.

13 free free. **Location:** Simple, noisy. **Surface:** metalled. 01/01-31/12.
**Distance:** 1,5km 2,8km 200m bakery 200m on the spot on the spot.
**Remarks:** Parking multipurpose area, next to footballstadium VC Herentals.

### Herentals 11C1
Jachthaven, Noordervaart 45. **GPS:** n51,17666 e4,85694.

4 €10 €0,50/kWh WC included. **Location:** Simple, noisy. **Surface:** metalled. 01/01-31/12.
**Distance:** 3,9km on the spot on the spot 2km on the spot on the spot.
**Tourist information Herentals:**
Augustijnenlaan. Su-morning.
Grote Markt. Fri-morning.

### Herselt 11C1
**Taverne Herberg Mie Maan**, Diestsebaan 28. **GPS:** n51,06025 e4,92897.

6 free . **Surface:** gravel. 01/01-31/12.
**Distance:** 3km on the spot 3km.
**Remarks:** Restaurant visit appreciated, intersection hiking and biking trails.

### Kalmthout 11C1
Kalmthoutse Heide, Heibloemlaan. **GPS:** n51,37688 e4,44911.

2 free. **Location:** Rural, simple, isolated, quiet. **Surface:** grasstiles. 01/01-31/12.
**Distance:** city centre 2km 50m on the spot on the spot.
**Remarks:** Parking nature reserve, max. 24h.

### Koningshooikt 11C1
Donderheide. **GPS:** n51,08439 e4,56541.

4 free. **Location:** Rural, simple, isolated. **Surface:** grassy/sand. 01/01-31/12.
**Remarks:** In front of 'Het Fort'.

### Lier 11C1
**Parking Mol Poort**, Aarschotsesteenweg 2. **GPS:** n51,12525 e4,57332.

2 free €1 Ch. **Surface:** asphalted. 01/01-31/12.
**Distance:** 1km 1km 1km on the spot on the spot on the spot.
**Tourist information Lier:**
Dienst Toerisme, Grote Markt 57. City with old centre worth a visit.
City walls, prison tower and Zimmertoren. 10-12h, 14-17/18h.
Grote Markt/Eikelstraat. Sa 8-13h.
Kerststallentocht. Dec.

### Mechelen 11C1
Douaneplein. **GPS:** n51,02667 e4,50058.

5 free. **Location:** Urban, simple, noisy. **Surface:** gravel/sand. 01/01-31/12.
**Distance:** centre 1,2km 200m 200m on the spot on the spot. **Remarks:** Nearby sports park, max. 24h.
**Tourist information Mechelen:**
Dienst Toerisme Stad Mechelen, Hallestraat 2-4, www.mechelen.be/. Historical city, city of carillons.
Brouwerijmuseum Het Anker. Old brewery, 1369. 01/04 30/09 14-18h, guided tour 15h. €3,30.
De Nekker. Sports and recreation area with ponds, sports grounds etc.
Dierenpark Planckendael. Zoo. 10-18h.
Technopolis. Interactively "discover" museum.
Caroluswandeling. City walk along historical bldg. And breweries, information Dienst Toerisme.

### Putte 11C1
Ixenheuvel, Heuvel. **GPS:** n51,04678 e4,62564.

2 free Chfree. **Location:** Rural, simple. **Surface:** asphalted. 01/01-31/12.
**Distance:** 1,5km 1,5km 1,5km.
**Remarks:** Max. 48h.

### Puurs 11B1
Eeuwfeeststraat/Kerkhofstraat. **GPS:** n51,07476 e4,28337.

2 free Chfree. **Location:** Urban, simple. **Surface:** metalled. 01/01-31/12 water: 15/10-01/04.
**Distance:** 200m 5,3km on the spot on the spot.
**Remarks:** Max. 48h, intersection hiking and biking trails.

### Sint-Amands 11B1
**Parking Noord**, Emile Verhaerenstraat. **GPS:** n51,05906 e4,20206.

2 free Ch free. **Location:** Urban, simple, quiet. **Surface:** metalled. 01/01-31/12.
**Distance:** 200m on the spot 200m 200m 300m on the spot on the spot.
**Remarks:** Max. 48h.

### Sint-Job-in-'t-Goor 11C1
**Parking Vaartlaan**, Vaartlaan. **GPS:** n51,30151 e4,56888.

2 free. **Location:** Urban, simple, central, noisy. **Surface:** metalled. 01/01-31/12.
**Distance:** 50m 50m 50m on the spot on the spot.
**Remarks:** Max. 48h.

### Weert 11B1
**Camperplaats Sint Annakerk**, Appeldijkstraat 2. **GPS:** n51,10120 e4,19210.

5 free. **Location:** Rural, simple, quiet. **Surface:** grassy/sand. 01/01-31/12.
**Distance:** 200m 200m 100m on the spot on the spot.
**Remarks:** Max. 48h, bicycle rental.

### Willebroek 11B1
Dijlelaan. **GPS:** n51,06028 e4,34472.

3 free €1 €1 Ch. **Location:** Urban, simple.

**Surface:** metalled. ⏻ 01/01-31/12.
**Distance:** 🚶2km 🚲300m.
**Remarks:** Max. 2 nights.

# Flemish Brabant

| 🏕S | Aarschot 🌿 | 11C1 |
|---|---|---|

Demervallei. **GPS:** n50,98483 e4,84031. ⬆.

8 🏕free 🅒Ch🚿free. **Location:** Rural, simple, noisy.
**Surface:** grassy/sand. ⏻ 01/01-31/12.
**Distance:** 🚶500m ⊗on the spot 🚲on the spot.
**Remarks:** Max. 48h.

| 🏕S | Begijnendijk | 11C1 |
|---|---|---|

Vissendijk. **GPS:** n51,01725 e4,78197. ⬆.

2 🏕free 🚰€ 0,50/100liter 🅒€ 0,50 Ch€ 0,50 WC.
**Location:** Urban, simple, central, noisy. **Surface:** metalled.
⏻ 01/01-31/12.
**Distance:** 🚶200m ⊗200m 🛒200m.

| 🏕S | Diest 🌿 | 11C1 |
|---|---|---|

De Halve Maan, Omer Vanaudenhovelaan 48.
**GPS:** n50,98607 e5,06373. ⬆ ⬆.

4 🏕€ 15 🚰 🅒Ch🚿(4x)included WC 🍴 🚽 ♻ **Location:** Rural,
comfortable, quiet. **Surface:** grassy/gravel. ⏻ 01/03-31/10.
**Distance:** 🚶1,2km, beguine convent 350m 🛒20m ⊗200m 🚲100m
🚶100m.
**Remarks:** Check in at pay desk recreation centre, max. 3 nights.
**Tourist information Diest:**
👁 Begijnhof. Beguine convent. Art studios open: sa/so afternoon and
in july/aug each afternoon. ⏻ Beguine convent daily, Angel convent
Sa/Su 14.30-17h, church Easter-Oct Su 14-17h.

| 🏕S | Grimbergen 🌿 | 11C1 |
|---|---|---|

**K.S.C. Grimbergen**, Brusselsesteenweg. **GPS:** n50,92787 e4,36610. ⬆.

10 🏕free. **Location:** Simple. **Surface:** asphalted.
⏻ 01/01-31/12.
**Distance:** 🚶1km 🚲1km 🚌> Brussels.
**Tourist information Grimbergen:**
ℹ Gemeentelijke Dienst voor Toerisme, Prinsenstraat 22. Well-known
for the Abbey beer, info at the beer museum.
👁 Abdijkerk. Abbey-church. ⏻ 10-12h, 13-17h.
🎪 Jaarmarkt. Village festival with among other things fair, cattle

market. ⏻ 1st weekend Sep.

| 🏕S | Haacht 🎵 | 11C1 |
|---|---|---|

Lombaardenlaan. **GPS:** n50,97796 e4,64055. ⬆🚫➡.

2 🏕free. **Location:** Urban, simple, central. **Surface:** asphalted.
⏻ 01/01-31/12.
**Distance:** 🚶200m ⊗200m 🛒200m 🚲on the spot.
**Remarks:** Check in on arrival, max. 72h.

| 🏕S | Lennik | 11B2 |
|---|---|---|

**Sporthal Jo Baetens**, Alfred Algoetstraat. **GPS:** n50,80756 e4,16346. ⬆.

4 🏕free 🚰 🅒Ch free. **Location:** Simple, central. **Surface:** asphalted.
⏻ 01/01-31/12.
**Distance:** 🚶650m ⊗650m 🛒650m.
**Remarks:** Behind gymnasium.

| 🏕S | Merchtem | 11B1 |
|---|---|---|

Brusselsesteenweg. **GPS:** n50,95553 e4,24011. ⬆.

4 🏕free 🚿.
**Surface:** metalled. ⏻ 01/01-31/12.
**Distance:** 🚶300m 🚌Good bus connection for Brussels.
**Remarks:** Next to cemetery and sports fields, no camping activities.

| 🏕S | Rotselaar 🍴 | 11C1 |
|---|---|---|

**Recreatiedomein Sportoase Ter Heide**, Vakenstraat 18.
**GPS:** n50,96217 e4,72288. ⬆.

4 🏕free 🚰€ 1/100liter 🅒Ch🚿€ 1/kWh WC 🍴. **Location:** Urban,
simple, comfortable, quiet. **Surface:** gravel. ⏻ 01/01-31/12.
**Distance:** 🚶2km 🏊100m 🚌100m 🛒500m 🚲2km 🚶200m
🚲on the spot 🚶on the spot.
**Remarks:** Key service at reception.

# Limburg

| 🏕 | Beringen | 11D1 |
|---|---|---|

**P Koolmijnmuseum**, Koolmijnlaan. **GPS:** n51,07048 e5,22097. ⬆.
2 🏕free. **Surface:** metalled. ⏻ 01/01-31/12 ⏻ events.
**Distance:** 🚶2,3km.
**Remarks:** Temporarily closed, max. 24h.

| 🏕S | Bilzen 🏰 | 11D2 |
|---|---|---|

**Parking Lanakerdij**, Lanakerdij. **GPS:** n50,86985 e5,52215. ⬆.

2 🏕free 🚰€ 2/4minutes 🅒Ch🚿(5x)€ 2/12h.
**Surface:** asphalted. ⏻ 01/01-31/12.
**Distance:** 🚶300m 🚲3km ⊗300m 🛒300m 🚲on the spot 🚶on the
spot.
**Remarks:** Max. 24h.
**Tourist information Bilzen:**
👁 Alden Biesen, Kasteelstraat 6. ⏻ Tue-Su 10-17h. 🎫 € 3.
👁 Zuivelhoeve 't Wanthof. Dairy farm. ⏻ Tue-Fri 10-22h, Sa-Su
9-23h.
🎪 Markt. ⏻ Wed.

| ⚓S | Bocholt ⛵ | 11D1 |
|---|---|---|

**Heuvelzicht-VVW Bocholt vzw
Bocholt**

- Located near marina
- Sanitary facilities
- Ideal base for walking and cycling

www.vvw-bocholt.be
info@vvw-bocholt.be

**Heuvelzicht**, Schipperstraat 1. **GPS:** n51,17722 e5,58500. ⬆.
10 🏕€ 10/24h 🚰€ 0,50/10minutes 🅒Ch🚿WCincluded
🍴€ 0,50/10minutes. 🚲 ♻
**Location:** Urban, comfortable, central. **Surface:** grassy/metalled.
⏻ 01/01-31/12.
**Distance:** 🚶200m ⊗50m 🛒100m 🚲200m.
**Remarks:** Parking marina at Zuidwillemsvaart, max. 48h.

| 🏕S | Bolderberg | 11D1 |
|---|---|---|

**Domein Bovy**, Galgeneinde. **GPS:** n50,98690 e5,27048. ⬆.

3 🏕free 🚰€ 2 Ch🍴€ 2/1h.
**Location:** Rural. **Surface:** metalled.
⏻ 01/01-31/12.
**Distance:** 🚶500m 🏊150m 🛒500m 🚲on the spot 🚶on the spot.
**Remarks:** Estate with i.e. restaurant, bar, brasserie, marked hiking
trails, herb garden, petting zoo, old tools.

| 🏕 | Bree 🌿 | 11D1 |
|---|---|---|

N721, Opitter. **GPS:** n51,11788 e5,64524. ⬆.

5 🏕free. **Surface:** metalled. ⏻ 01/01-31/12.
**Distance:** 🚶on the spot ⊗on the spot.

**Remarks:** Parking next to church, in front of petrol station, max. 48h.

**Tourist information Bree:**
Vrijthof. ❑ Fri.
Sint-Antoniuskapel, Opitter.

### Diepenbeek 11D1
**Demerstrand**, Stationsstraat 27. **GPS**: n50,91323 e5,42189.⬆.

4 ⛺ € 8 ⛽ € 2/100liter ⛱ ⛲ € 2/8h.
**Surface:** asphalted. ❑ 01/01-31/12.
**Distance:** 🚶500m 🚲250m 🚉1km 🚌on the spot 🧍on the spot.
**Remarks:** At gymnasium, max. 48h, video surveillance.

### Dilsen-Stokkem 11D1
**De Wissen**, Maaspark 3. **GPS**: n51,02361 e5,74945.⬆.

3 ⛺free. **Location:** Rural. **Surface:** gravel. ❑ 01/01-31/12.
**Distance:** 🚶500m 🚣on the spot 🛵on the spot ⊗Taverne Maascentrum 🚉500m 🚌on the spot 🚲on the spot 🧍on the spot.
**Remarks:** Parking at tourist office De Wissen, starting point of cycle routes.

### Genk 11D1
**Parking Kattevennen**, Kattevennen. **GPS**: n50,95728 e5,53337.⬆.

7 ⛺ € 5 ⛽ Ch ✎included.
**Surface:** asphalted. ❑ 01/01-31/12.
**Distance:** 🚶3km ⊗taverne 🚌on the spot 🚲on the spot 🧍on the spot.
**Remarks:** Max. 24h, mountainbike and hiking trails, national park Hoge Kempen.

**Tourist information Genk:**
Zondagsmarkten. Flea market. ❑ 01/06-31/08 9-13h.

### Hamont 11D1
**Deken Dolsstraat. GPS**: n51,25423 e5,54371.⬆.

4 ⛺free. **Location:** Simple, quiet. **Surface:** grasstiles.
❑ 01/01-31/12.
**Distance:** 🚶400m ⊗400m 🚉250m 🚲on the spot.
**Remarks:** Next to cemetery.

### Hamont 11D1
Michielsplein, Achel. **GPS**: n51,25421 e5,48128.

4 ⛺free. **Location:** Urban. **Surface:** metalled. ❑ 01/01-31/12.
**Distance:** 🚶on the spot ⊗on the spot 🚉on the spot.
**Remarks:** At bicycle trail Limburgse Kempen, behind church of Achel, max. 24h, market Tuesday 8-13h.

### Hamont 11D1
Kerkplein. **GPS**: n51,25152 e5,54612.⬆.

5 ⛺free. **Location:** Urban. **Surface:** metalled. ❑ 01/01-31/12.
**Distance:** 🚶on the spot ⊗50m 🚉50m 🚌50m 🚲on the spot.
**Remarks:** Behind church, max. 24h.

### Hamont 11D1
Stadpark. **GPS**: n51,25085 e5,55200.⬆.

5 ⛺free.
**Location:** Rural. **Surface:** grasstiles/grassy.
❑ 01/01-31/12.
**Distance:** 🚶200m.
**Remarks:** Large parking in the centre behind tennis-courts, max. 24h.

**Tourist information Hamont:**
VVV, Generaal Dempseylaan 1, www.hamontachel.com. Historical little town. ❑ Mo-Fri 9-12h, 13-16h, Sa 9-12h.

### Hasselt 11D1
**Sporthal Alverberg**, Herkenrodesingel. **GPS**: n50,93871 e5,32081.⬆.

>5 ⛺free ⛽ € 2 ⛱ Ch. **Surface:** asphalted. ❑ 01/01-31/12.
**Distance:** 🚶city centre 3km 🚉Carrefour 🚌on the spot.

### Hasselt 11D1
Bakkerslaan. **GPS**: n50,92141 e5,32562.⬆.

3 ⛺free. **Location:** Urban, simple. **Surface:** grasstiles/grassy.
❑ 01/01-31/12.
**Distance:** 🚶2km 🚲600m ⊗500m 🚉500m 🚌on the spot.

### Hasselt 11D1
**Restaurant Aan het Water**, Overdemerstraat 20, Kuringen.
**GPS**: n50,94663 e5,30877.⬆.

8 ⛺guests free. **Surface:** grassy. ❑ 01/01-31/12 ◉ Tue, Wed, 26/09-06/10.
**Distance:** ⊗on the spot 🚉bakery 50m.

### Helchteren 11D1
**Parking de Dool**, Sportstraat. **GPS**: n51,06087 e5,38650.⬆.

10 ⛺free. **Surface:** asphalted. ❑ 01/01-31/12.
**Distance:** 🚶1km ⊗500m 🚌500m.
**Remarks:** Next to castle.

### Herk-de-Stad 11D1
**Park Olmenhof**, Pikkeleerstraat 14. **GPS**: n50,93361 e5,16654.⬆.

6 ⛺free ⛽ € 1/100liter ⛱Ch ✎ € 0,60/kWh WC.
**Location:** Rural, simple. **Surface:** asphalted. ❑ 01/01-31/12.
**Distance:** 🚶400m 🚴7km ⊗50m 🚉300m 🚲on the spot.
**Remarks:** At football ground, max. 48h.

### Hoepertingen 11D2

**De Verborgen Parel**, Hoenshovenstraat 5. **GPS**: n50,80224 e5,29073.
20 ⛺ € 10 ⛽ Ch ✎included. 🔌
**Location:** Simple. **Surface:** grassy. ❑ 01/01-31/12.
**Distance:** 🚶1,5km ⊗on the spot 🚉1,5km 🚲on the spot 🧍on the spot.
**Remarks:** Bread-service, use of sauna against payment.

### Houthalen 11D1
**Parking Kelchterhoef**, Kelchterhoefstraat.
**GPS**: n51,03015 e5,44063.⬆.

BE

4 ⛺free. **Location:** Rural. **Surface:** grasstiles/metalled.
◯ 01/01-31/12.
**Distance:** 🚲6km 🛒on the spot ⊗on the spot 🚴 on the spot.
**Remarks:** In front of abbey farm.

### Kortessem 🌿 | 11D2

Kapittelstraat. **GPS:** n50,85724 e5,39126. ⬆️

5 ⛺free 🔌(10x). **Surface:** asphalted. ◯ 01/01-31/12.
**Distance:** 🚲200m 🏊200m 🛒bakery 200m 🚴 on the spot.
**Remarks:** At gymnasium, max. 2 nights.

**Tourist information Kortessem:**
✘ 't Rood Kasteel, Guigoven. Former medieval water castle.

### Leopoldsburg 🌿🏛️🌳 | 11D1

**Jachthaven**, Antwerpsesteenweg 129. **GPS:** n51,12892 e5,25028. ⬆️

22 ⛺€ 10 🔌🚿included WC 🚽€ 1. **Location:** Urban, comfortable.
**Surface:** asphalted. ◯ 01/01-31/12.
**Distance:** 🚲2km 🏊on the spot ⊗on the spot 🛒2km.
**Remarks:** Check in at harbourmaster.

### Lommel 🏛️🌿 | 11D1

**Taverne Haven de Meerpaal**, Boskantstraat 60.
**GPS:** n51,24266 e5,36891. ⬆️

10 ⛺€ 10 🔌€ 0,50 🚿Ch 🚿(6x)€ 1 WC 🚽€ 1 🚽€ 5. 🏠
**Location:** Urban, comfortable, quiet. **Surface:** asphalted.
◯ 01/01-31/12.
**Distance:** 🚲500m ⊗on the spot 🚴 on the spot 🚶 on the spot.
**Remarks:** Near marina.

### Maaseik 🌿 | 11D1

Sportlaan P4. **GPS:** n51,10108 e5,78964. ⬆️

20 ⛺free. **Surface:** asphalted. ◯ 01/01-31/12.
**Distance:** 🚲historical centre 200m.

**Tourist information Maaseik:**
🏛️ Marktplein. ◯ Wed 9-12h.

### Meeuwen-Gruitrode | 11D1

**CC Gruitrode**, Royerplein 1, Gruitrode. **GPS:** n51,08939 e5,58949. ⬆️⬆️

8 ⛺free. **Surface:** metalled. ◯ 01/01-31/12.
**Distance:** 🚲200m ⊗on the spot 🛒200m 🚴 200m 🚴 on the spot.
**Remarks:** Max. 24h.

### Meeuwen-Gruitrode | 11D1

**Totale Rust en Stilte**, Ophovenstraat. **GPS:** n51,06404 e5,56442. ⬆️

16 ⛺€ 10 🔌🚿Ch 🚿included. 🏠
**Location:** Rural, isolated, quiet. **Surface:** metalled. ◯ 29/03-31/12.
**Distance:** 🚲4km 🥖1km 🏊800m ⊗2km 🛒3km 🍽️4km 🚴2km
🚴 on the spot 🚶 on the spot.

### Neeroeteren | 11D1

**Den Aftrap**, Komweg. **GPS:** n51,08375 e5,70284. ⬆️

6 ⛺€ 7 🔌€ 1/150liter 🚿€ 1 Ch€ 1 🚿€ 1/3h WCincluded 🚽€ 1,80.
🏠 **Surface:** metalled. ◯ 01/01-31/12.
**Distance:** 🚲100m 🥖7km 🛒100m ⊗50m 🍽️1km 🚴200m.
**Remarks:** At football ground.

### Neerpelt | 11D1

**De Welvaart**, Jaak Tassetstraat. **GPS:** n51,23333 e5,43164. ⬆️

8 ⛺€ 6/24h 🔌🚿Ch 🚿included. 🏠
**Location:** Simple, quiet. **Surface:** metalled. ◯ 01/01-31/12.
**Distance:** 🚲500m.
**Remarks:** At the canal, parking marina, max. 48h, checked, coin waste dump € 1.

### Peer | 11D1

**P1 Aan den Boogaard**. **GPS:** n51,13193 e5,45741.
⛺free. ◯ 01/01-31/12.
**Distance:** 🚲100m.
**Remarks:** Max. 24h.

### Peer | 11D1

**P2 Noordervest**. **GPS:** n51,13422 e5,45511.
⛺free. ◯ 01/01-31/12.
**Distance:** 🚲150m.
**Remarks:** Max. 24h.

### Rekem | 11D1

Kanaalstraat. **GPS:** n50,92177 e5,70493. ⬆️

10 ⛺free. **Location:** Rural. **Surface:** gravel. ◯ 01/01-31/12.
**Distance:** 🚲1km 🏊on the spot 🛒on the spot ⊗500m 🛒1km
🚴100m 🚴 on the spot 🚶 on the spot.
**Remarks:** Max. 48h, walking and bicycle area.

**Tourist information Rekem:**
ℹ️ Oud-Rekem with museum-church, city walls and castle, marked walking route 2km.

### Rummen | 11D2

Ketelstraat. **GPS:** n50,89285 e5,16037. ⬆️

4 ⛺free. **Surface:** gravel. ◯ 01/01-31/12.
**Distance:** 🚲on the spot ⊗300m 🛒250m 🚴 on the spot 🚶 on the spot.
**Remarks:** At gymnasium.

### Schalkhoven | 11D2

**Nollekes Winning**, Schalkhovenstraat 79. **GPS:** n50,84531 e5,44687. ⬆️

9 ⛺€ 12,50 🔌🚿Ch 🚿WC 🚽🚿included. 🏠 **Location:** Rural, comfortable, quiet. **Surface:** grasstiles/metalled. ◯ 01/01-31/12.
**Distance:** 🚲200m ⊗on the spot.
**Remarks:** Sale of wines.

### Sint-Huibrechts-Lille 🍴 | 11D1

**De Bosuil**, Bosuilstraat 4. **GPS:** n51,22371 e5,49502. ⬆️

32 ⛺€ 6 🔌🚿Ch 🚿included. 🏠 **Location:** Rural, quiet.
**Surface:** grassy. ◯ 01/01-31/12.
**Distance:** 🚲1,5km ⊗on the spot 🚴 on the spot 🚶 on the spot.
**Remarks:** Check in on arrival.

### Sint-Truiden 🌿 | 11D2

**Domein Terbiest**, Hasseltsesteenweg. **GPS:** n50,82946 e5,20547. ⬆️

30 ⛺free 🔌🚿Chfree. **Location:** Urban, simple. **Surface:** metalled.
◯ 01/04-31/05, 01/09-30/09.

**Distance:** 🚲city centre 2km ⊗2km 🚱2km 🏍on the spot 🚶on the spot ⚓on the spot.
**Remarks:** Check in at tourist office.
**Tourist information Sint-Truiden:**
ℹ️ Toerisme Sint-Truiden, Stadhuis, Grote Markt, www.sint-truiden.be. Abbey-town.
🎪 Grote Markt, Groenmarkt, Trudoplein, Minderbroedersplein. ⬛ Sa 7.30-13h.
🎪 Veemarkt, Speelhoflaan. Antiques and flea market. ⬛ Sa 6-12h.

🅿️Ⓢ **Tongeren** 11D2
**Pliniuspark**, Fonteindreef 8. **GPS:** n50,78626 e5,45256. ⬆️➡️.

25 🛏€ 10/24h 🚰€ 0,50/100liter 🚽Ch 🔌€ 0,50/kWh.🚐🗑
**Location:** Rural. **Surface:** grasstiles/metalled. ⬛ 01/01-31/12.
**Distance:** 🚲1km 🏍on the spot 🚶on the spot.
**Remarks:** At swimming pool, max. 24h.
**Tourist information Tongeren:**
ℹ️ Dienst Toerisme, Stadhuisplein 9, www.tongeren.be. Oldest city of Belgium with numerous historico-cultural heritage.
🎪 Maastrichterstraat, Schiervelstraat, Clarissenstraat. Biggest antique market in the Benelux, also all antique stores open. ⬛ Su 6-13h.

🅿️Ⓢ **Tongerlo** 11D1
**De Kieper**, Keyartstraat. **GPS:** n51,12397 e5,65449. ⬆️.

4 🛏free 🚰€ 1/100liter 🔌€ 1. **Location:** Rural. **Surface:** metalled. ⬛ 01/01-31/12.
**Distance:** 🚲10 min walking 🚌on the spot ⊗on the spot 🏍on the spot 🚶on the spot.

🅿️ **Veldwezelt** 🌱 11D2
**Omstraat 20. GPS:** n50,86195 e5,62696. ⬆️.

5 🛏free. **Surface:** metalled. ⬛ 01/01-31/12.
**Distance:** 🚲800m ⊗200m 🚱500m.
**Remarks:** Parking gymnasium.

# Brussels

🅿️ **Bruxelles/Brussel** 🌱🎪🥗 11B2
**Bruparck**, Wemmel/Heizel, Brussels (Bruxelles/Brussel).
**GPS:** n50,89745 e4,33826.
🛏. ⬛ 01/01-31/12.
**Remarks:** Max. 24h. Ring road Brussels exit 8.

🅿️Ⓢ **Bruxelles/Brussel** 🌱🎪🥗 11B2
**Auberge de Jeunesse Génération Europe**, Rue de l'Eléphant 4, Brussels (Bruxelles/Brussel). **GPS:** n50,85317 e4,33479. ⬆️.

5 🛏€ 30 🚰🚽Ch 🔌WC 🚿 📶included. 🚐🗑
**Location:** Urban, comfortable, central, quiet. **Surface:** asphalted.
⬛ 01/01-31/12.
**Distance:** 🚲city centre 1,5km ⊗on the spot 🚱on the spot 🚃600m metro > Brussel.
**Remarks:** Check in at reception, breakfeast (max. 4p) included.

🅿️ **Bruxelles/Brussel** 🌱🎪🥗 11B2
**Heizel/Heysel Metro**, Brussels (Bruxelles/Brussel).
**GPS:** n50,89736 e4,33827.
🛏. ⬛ 01/01-31/12.
**Remarks:** Nearby Bruparck.

**Tourist information Brussels (Bruxelles/Brussel):**
ℹ️ Brussels City Card gives for free entrance on public transport and museums and many discounts on purchases. 🎟 € 22.
ℹ️ Bureau van Toerisme, Office de Tourisme, Grote Markt 1, Grand Place, visit.brussels. Capital of Belgium, with a history of more than 1000 years. A lot of buildings worth seeing and historical places.
👁 Koninklijke Serres van Laken, Les serres royales à Laeken. Park, garden, nature area.
Ⓜ✝ Basiliek van Koekelberg, basilique de Koekelberg. The fifth largest church of the world. ⬛ Wed, Thu, Sa, Su 14-16h. 🎟 € 5.
Ⓜ Autoworld, Jubelpark 11, Parc du Cinquantenaire. Motorcar history from 1886 up to 1970s. ⬛ 01/04-30/09 10-18, 01/10-31/03 10-17.
Ⓜ Museum van de stad Brussel Broodhuis, Musée de la ville Bruxelles, Grote Markt 44, Grand Place. History of the city. ⬛ Tue-Su 10-17h.
🎪 Grote Zavel, Place du Grand Sablon. Antiques and book market.
⬛ Sa 9-17h, Su 9-14h.
🎪 Vossenplein. Flea market. ⬛ 6-14h.
🎪 Grote Markt, Grand place. Flowers and plant market.
⬛ 8-18h.
🎪 Kunstmarkt, marché d'art, Boterstraat, rue au Beurre. Painters and portraitists. ⬛ 11-18h.
Atomium, Bruparck, Boulevard du Centenaire, Laeken. Built for the occasion of the 1958 Brussels World Fair, symbolising a crystallised iron molecule to the scale of its atoms enlarged 160 thousand million times. ⬛ 10-18h.
Bruparck, Boulevard du Centenaire 20, Laeken. Family park with among other things Mini-Europe, paradise pool and The Village with restaurants, cafés and shops. ⬛ 01/01-31/12.
Mini-Europe, Bruparck, Boulevard du Centenaire, Laeken. Europe in miniature, 350 monuments.
Oceade, Bruparck, Boulevard du Centenaire, Laeken. Subtropical leisure pool park. ⬛ holidays, Sa-Su 10-22h.

# Liège

🅿️Ⓢ **Aywaille** 🎪🥗 11D2
**Esplanade du Fair-Play**, Rue de la Heid. **GPS:** n50,47583 e5,67809. ⬆️➡️.

8 🛏€ 8/48h, incl. 1 coin (water or 2h electricity) 🚰€ 3 🚽Ch 🔌
(4x)€ 3/2h. **Surface:** metalled. ⬛ 01/01-31/12.
**Distance:** 🚲300m 🚱200m 🏍on the spot 🚶on the spot.
**Remarks:** At recreation area, coins at swimming pool.

🅿️Ⓢ **Blégny-Mine** 11D2
**Domaine de Blégny-Mine**, Rue Lambert Marlet.
**GPS:** n50,68617 e5,72367. ⬆️.

8 🛏free 🚰Chfree 🔌(8x)€ 2/12h. **Location:** Rural, comfortable, isolated, quiet. **Surface:** gravel. ⬛ 01/01-31/12.
**Distance:** 🚲4,6km ⊗on the spot 🏍on the spot 🚶on the spot.
**Remarks:** At former coalmine, UNESCO World Heritage, access € 12,50, 1 day all inclusive € 29,50, coins electricity at reception park.

🅿️ **Coo** 11E3
**Parking**, Petit Coo. **GPS:** n50,39222 e5,87531. ⬆️.

+10 🛏9-18h € 5. 🚐 **Location:** Simple. **Surface:** asphalted.
⬛ 01/01-31/12.
**Distance:** 🚲150m ⊗150m 🏍on the spot 🚶on the spot.
**Remarks:** Water falls Coo 250m.

🅿️ **Eupen** 🌱 11E2
**Langesthal 164. GPS:** n50,62180 e6,09148.

🛏free. **Surface:** asphalted. ⬛ 18-10h.
**Distance:** 🚲Eupen 4km ⊗150m Taverne.
**Remarks:** At weir, isolated.

**Tourist information Eupen:**
🎪 Benedenstad. ⬛ Wed 7-12.30h.
🎪 Eupen/Keltenis. Flea market. ⬛ Su 7-16h.

🅿️Ⓢ **Hamoir** 🏰🌳🎪🚣 11D3
**Complexe Sportif**, Quai du Batty. **GPS:** n50,42463 e5,53522. ➡️.

10 🛏€ 8/24h 🚰🚽Chincluded. 🚐🗑 **Location:** Urban, comfortable. **Surface:** grassy/gravel. ⬛ 01/01-31/12.
**Distance:** 🚲200m ⚓on the spot 🚌on the spot ⊗200m 🚱200m.
**Remarks:** Along the Ourthe river, max. 24h.

🅿️ **Huy** 🌱 11D2
**Avenue Godin Parnajon. GPS:** n50,52379 e5,24310. ⬆️.

2 🛏free. **Location:** Urban, central, noisy. **Surface:** asphalted.
⬛ 01/01-31/12.

BE

**Distance:** 500m on the spot 500m.
**Remarks:** Parking in front of restaurant Quick.

### 🅿 Huy 🔆 | 11D2
Quai de Namur. **GPS:** n50,51673 e5,23453. ⬆.

2 free. **Location:** Urban, central, noisy. **Surface:** asphalted.
◻ 01/01-31/12.
**Distance:** 500m on the spot on the spot 500m.
**Remarks:** Under the citadel, along the Meuse River, in front of Hôtel du Fort to the right to the quay.
**Tourist information Huy:**
ℹ Office du Tourisme, Quai de Namur,1, www.huy.be. Tourist town, citadel above the city.
Ⓜ Fort en museum. ◻ Easter-Sep 10-17/18/19h.

### 🅿 S Jalhay | 11E2
**Baraque de La Gileppe**, Route de la Gileppe.
**GPS:** n50,58759 e5,96980. ⬆.

4 free (4x)free. **Location:** Quiet. **Surface:** asphalted.
◻ 01/01-31/12.
**Distance:** 3,5km on the spot on the spot on the spot.
**Remarks:** At artificial lake.

### 🅿 S Kelmis | 11E2
Schützenstraße. **GPS:** n50,71558 e6,00962. ⬆.

8 free Ch. **Location:** Urban, simple, central.
**Surface:** asphalted. ◻ 01/01-31/12.
**Distance:** Aachen 8km 300m 300m.

### 🅿 S Malmedy 🔆 ❄ | 11E3
Avenue de la Gare, N62. **GPS:** n50,42282 e6,03080. ⬆ ➡.

30 € 5/24h Ch (8x).
**Surface:** gravel/metalled. ◻ 01/01-31/12.
**Distance:** 300m 300m bakery 100m, supermarket 800m on the spot on the spot on the spot Waimes 5km.
**Remarks:** At cycle route (former railroad).
**Tourist information Malmedy:**
Place St. Géréon. ◻ Fri 7-13h.
Hautes Fagnes. Nature reserve Hautes Fagnes.

### 🅿 S Sankt Vith | 11E3
**An den Weyern**, Rodter Strasse 9a. **GPS:** n50,28091 e6,12240. ⬆ ➡.

20 free € 1/4minutes. **Location:** Urban, simple.
**Surface:** asphalted. ◻ 01/01-31/12.
**Distance:** 500m on the spot on the spot.
**Remarks:** At sports centre.

### 🅿 Sourbrodt 👫 ❄ | 11E2
**Signal de Botrange**, Rue de Botrange. **GPS:** n50,50148 e6,09312. ⬆.

20 free. **Location:** Rural, simple, noisy. **Surface:** gravel.
◻ 01/01-31/12.
**Distance:** on the spot on the spot on the spot.

### 🅿 S Stavelot 🔆 | 11E2
**Circuit de Spa - Francorchamps**, Route du Circuit 55, Francorchamps.
**GPS:** n50,44388 e5,97208. ⬆.

76 € 15 Ch WCincluded.
**Surface:** gravel. ◻ 01/01-31/12.

### 👫 S Waimes 👫 | 11E3
**La Faitafondue**, Rue de Merkem 4. **GPS:** n50,39532 e6,07024. ⬆.

10 € 9, free with a meal WC. **Location:** Rural, comfortable. **Surface:** gravel. ◻ 01/01-31/12 ◉ Wed.
**Distance:** 4km 6km on the spot on the spot 200m.

# Hainaut

### 🅿 Aubechies | 11B2
**Parking Archéosite**, Rue de l'Abbaye 1Y. **GPS:** n50,57419 e3,67546.
2 free. **Surface:** gravel. ◻ 01/01-31/12.
**Remarks:** At museum.
**Tourist information Aubechies:**
ℹ Archéosite d'Aubechies. Archeological open air museum. ◻ Mo-Fri 9-17h, 01/04-31/10 9-18h.

### 🅿 Beloeil 🔆 | 11B2
**Château Beloeil**, Rue de la Hunelle. **GPS:** n50,55128 e3,73280.
free. **Surface:** unpaved. ◻ 01/01-31/12.
**Remarks:** Parking castle.
**Tourist information Beloeil:**
Château de Beloeil, www.beloeil.be/. ◻ 01/06-30/09 10-19h, 01/04-31/05 Sa/Su/holidays 10-19h.

### 🅿 Bernissart 🔆 | 11B2
**Musée de l'Iguanodon**, Ruelle des Médecins. **GPS:** n50,47530 e3,64958.

free. ◻ 01/01-31/12.
**Distance:** 6km.
**Remarks:** Parking 100m of dinosaur museum.

### 🅿 S Binche 🔆 | 11B3
**Pastures**, Rue des Pastures. **GPS:** n50,41413 e4,17070.

50 free Ch (2x). **Surface:** asphalted. ◻ 01/01-31/12.
**Distance:** on the spot.
**Remarks:** Parking just outside centre.
**Tourist information Binche:**
ℹ Office du Tourisme, Parc communal, rue des Promenades, 2, www. binche.be. Medieval city with ramparts.

### 🅿 S Blaton | 11B2
Place de Feignies. **GPS:** n50,50179 e3,66135.

free. ◻ 01/01-31/12.
**Distance:** 200m.
**Remarks:** Nearby Romanesque church.

### 🅿 S Bouffioulx | 11C3
**Maison de la Poterie**, Rue du Général Jacques.
**GPS:** n50,39024 e4,51406. ⬆.

3 free € 0,50/10minutes Ch € 0,50/60minutes.
**Location:** Urban, simple, noisy. **Surface:** metalled.
◻ 01/01-31/12.
**Distance:** on the spot 100m 100m.
**Remarks:** Next to Centre d'Interprétation de la Poterie, coins at Maison de la Poterie.

### 🅿 S Boussu-lez-Walcourt | 11C3
**Les Lacs de l'Eau d'Heure**, Route de la Plate Taille.
**GPS:** n50,19265 e4,37958. ⬆.

20 € 10 Chfree. **Surface:** asphalted. ◻ 01/01-31/12.

BE

**Distance:** 🏊on the spot 🚰on the spot ⊗on the spot 🚶on the spot.

| 🏕 | Brugelette | 11B2 |

**Pairi Daiza**, Domaine de Cambron. **GPS:** n50,58892 e3,88670.

🗑€ 7. **Surface:** gravel/sand. ◻ 01/04-31/10.
**Remarks:** Max. 1 night.

**Tourist information Brugelette:**
Parc Paradisio, Domaine de Cambron. Park with bird paradise and monkey island. ◻ 26/03-06/11 10-18.

| 🏕 | Brunehaut | 11A2 |

Quai de l'Escaut. **GPS:** n50,51697 e3,42150.⬆.
20 🗑free. **Location:** Simple. **Surface:** metalled.
◻ 01/01-31/12.
**Distance:** 🚂900m 🏊on the spot.

| ⊞S | Chimay | 11B3 |

**Communal de Chimay**, Allée des Princes 1.
**GPS:** n50,04557 e4,30956.➡.

7🗑€5 🚰€5 Ch🚿included 📷🛒♻ **Location:** Urban,
comfortable, quiet. **Surface:** grassy/metalled. ◻ 01/01-31/12.
**Distance:** ⊗300m 🚊800m 🚌200m.

| P | Chimay | 11B3 |

Place Froissart. **GPS:** n50,04728 e4,31307.
🗑. ◻ 01/01-31/12.

| P | Chimay | 11B3 |

Place Léopold. **GPS:** n50,04747 e4,31784.
🗑. ◻ 01/01-31/12 📷 Fri.

| ⊞S | Dottignies | 11A2 |

Rue des Écoles. **GPS:** n50,72821 e3,30011.⬆.

4🗑free 🚰🗑free. **Surface:** asphalted. ◻ 01/01-31/12.
**Distance:** 🚂500m ⛵1,3km.
**Remarks:** Square behind fire-station.

| 🏕 | Ecaussines | 11B2 |

**Eglise Sainte Aldegonde**, Rue Jacquemart Boulle 28, Ecaussines-Lalaing. **GPS:** n50,57085 e4,18107.
🗑free. **Location:** Urban, simple, noisy. **Surface:** asphalted.
◻ 01/01-31/12.
**Distance:** 🚂500m.

| P | Fleurus | 11C2 |

**Parking Gare**, Avenue de la Gare. **GPS:** n50,48215 e4,54433.⬆.
3🗑free. **Location:** Urban, simple. **Surface:** asphalted.
◻ 01/01-31/12.

| P | Fleurus | 11C2 |

**Stade Communal**, Rue de Fleurjoux. **GPS:** n50,47852 e4,55237.⬆.

🗑free. **Location:** Rural, simple. **Surface:** asphalted.
◻ 01/01-31/12.
**Distance:** 🚂on the spot.

| ⊞ | Froidchapelle | 11B3 |

Rue de l'Ecureuil. **GPS:** n50,19280 e4,34972.⬆.

30🗑€5 🚰🗑Ch.🚿 **Location:** Rural, comfortable, isolated, quiet.
**Surface:** grassy. ◻ 01/01-31/12.
**Distance:** 🚰75m ⊗200m 🚌on the spot 🚶on the spot.
**Remarks:** Max. 48h.

| 🏕 | Harchies | 11B2 |

Place du Rivage. **GPS:** n50,47106 e3,69619.
🗑. ◻ 01/01-31/12.

| 🏕 | Hornu | 11B2 |

**Le Site du Grand Hornu**, Rue Sainte-Louise 82.
**GPS:** n50,43488 e3,83707.⬆.

🗑free.
◻ 01/01-31/12.
**Distance:** 🚂1km.

**Tourist information Hornu:**
👁 Grand-Hornu. Old industrial mining complex, a remarkable reminder of the Industrial Revolution. ◻ Tue-Fri 10-18h. 🎫 € 8.

| ⊞S | Leers Noord | 11A2 |

**La Maison du Canal**, Rue du Canal 6. **GPS:** n50,69089 e3,25728.➡.

3🗑free 🚰🗑Chfree. **Location:** Rural, quiet. **Surface:** gravel.
◻ 01/01-31/12.
**Distance:** 🚰on the spot ⊗on the spot 🚌on the spot 🚶on the spot.
**Remarks:** Tarerne closed on Monday.

| 🏕 | Lessines | 11B2 |

Rue des 4 fils Aymon. **GPS:** n50,71280 e3,83403.
🗑free. **Location:** Quiet. **Surface:** unpaved. ◻ 01/01-31/12.
**Distance:** 🚂400m 🚌on the spot 🚶on the spot.

| 🏕 | Mouscron | 11A2 |

**Musée du Folklore**, Rue des Brasseurs, 3. **GPS:** n50,74217 e3,21795.
🗑free.
◻ 01/01-31/12.
**Remarks:** Possibility make a reservation tel 02.56.33.23.36.

| ⚓S | Péruwelz | 11A2 |

**Port de plaisance**, Rue de la Boitérie. **GPS:** n50,51864 e3,60904.

10🗑€6 🚰🗑WC🗑€1,80 📷 🏠 **Location:** Urban, simple, noisy.
**Surface:** asphalted/gravel. ◻ 01/02-30/11.
**Distance:** 🚂1,5km 🚊1km.

| 🏕 | Quaregnon | 11B2 |

La Grand Place. **GPS:** n50,44369 e3,86428.
2🗑. ◻ 01/01-31/12.

| 🏕 | Quevaucamps | 11B2 |

**Musée de la Bonneterie**, Rue Paul Pastur.
**GPS:** n50,52671 e3,68776.⬆➡.

2🗑free. ◻ 01/01-31/12.
**Remarks:** Parking in front of museum, via N527.

| 🏕 | Ronquières ✳ | 11B2 |

**Grande tour et promenade en Bateau Mouche**, Rue Rosemont.
**GPS:** n50,60636 e4,22249.⬆.

20🗑free. **Location:** Rural, simple, quiet. **Surface:** gravel.
◻ 01/01-31/12.
**Distance:** 🚰on the spot 🚌on the spot.

| 🏕 | Thieu/Strepy | 11B2 |

Rue Saint-Géry. **GPS:** n50,47156 e4,09069.⬆.
+10🗑free. **Surface:** metalled. ◻ 01/01-31/12.
**Distance:** 🏊on the spot 🚰on the spot 🚌on the spot.

| 🏕S | Tournai/Doornik ✳ | 11A2 |

**Maison de la Culture**, Avenue des Frères Rimbaud, Tournai (Tournai/Doornik). **GPS:** n50,60432 e3,38199.⬆.

15🗑free 🚰🗑Chfree. **Surface:** metalled. ◻ 01/01-31/12.
**Distance:** 🚂5 min walking ⊗5 min walking 🚊5 min walking 🚌on the spot.

# Namur

| 🏕 | Alle-sur-Semois ✳⛵🎪🌾 | 16C1 |

**Recreatiecentrum Recreale, restaurant les Pierres du Diable**, Rue Léon Henrard 16. **GPS:** n49,84648 e4,97579.⬆.

10🗑free. **Location:** Rural, simple. **Surface:** unpaved.
◻ 01/01-31/12.
**Distance:** 🚂700m 🏊on the spot 🚰fishing permit obligatory ⊗on the spot 🚊700m.

**Tourist information Alle-sur-Semois:**
Recrealle. Canoe rent; departures for canoe and kayaks, fishing and swimming possibilities, bowling, tennis, play ground, restaurant.

BE

### Annevoie 11C3

**Les Jardins d'Annevoie**, Rue des Jardins d'Annevoie.
**GPS**: n50,34659 e4,84496.

10 € 1,25. **Surface**: gravel. 01/01-31/12.
**Distance**: 750m 800m on the spot.
**Remarks**: Max. 1 night, only for guest, beautiful view.

### Ave-et-Auffe 11D3

**Le Roptai**, Rue du Roptai 34. **GPS**: n50,11144 e5,13373.

10 € 15-20 Ch (10x)€ 3/24h WCincluded € 1 € 4
€ 1/3h. **Location**: Rural, comfortable, quiet. **Surface**: grassy/gravel.
08/01-31/12.
**Distance**: 4km 2km 1km 5km 1km on the spot.
**Remarks**: Bread-service, Han 5km.

### Bohan 16C1

**Camping des Bouleaux**, Rue de Monts les Champs 208C.
**GPS**: n49,86918 e4,88628.

4 € 14,15, 2 pers.incl Ch included against payment.
**Location**: Rural, simple, quiet. **Surface**: metalled.
01/01-31/12 Service: winter.
**Distance**: 600m 600m 600m.

### Dinant 11C3

**La Citadelle de Dinant**, Rue du Fort. **GPS**: n50,26117 e4,91675.

20 free. **Location**: Urban, simple, quiet. **Surface**: gravel.
01/01-31/12.
**Distance**: 200m 1km 1km 1,5km.

### Han-Sur-Lesse 11D3

Rue de la Lesse. **GPS**: n50,12751 e5,18819.

40 € 7,50-12 Ch WCincluded. **Location**: Urban.
**Surface**: asphalted. 01/01-31/12.

**Distance**: 300m 200m 200m on the spot.
**Remarks**: Parking nearby caves and centre.
**Tourist information Han-Sur-Lesse**:
Tourist centre around the caves.
Grottes de Han. Caves, son-et-lumière and boat trip on underground
river. 01/04-31/10 10-16/18h, 01/11-31/03 11.30-16h.
Réserve d'Animaux. European animals alive today and those which lived
previously in this area. 01/03-31/12 10-17h, 01/07-31/08 9.30-18h.

### Hogne 11D3

**Aire del Foy**, 60 rue de Serinchamps. **GPS**: n50,24981 e5,27933.

25 € 10 € 0,50/100liter Ch (25x)€ 1/2kWh,16Amp
WC included € 4/time . **Location**: Rural, comfortable, quiet.
**Surface**: grassy/metalled. 01/03-31/10.
**Distance**: 7km on the spot on the spot.
**Remarks**: Bread-service.

### Mariembourg 11C3

**Brasserie des Fagnes**, 26, route de Nismes.
**GPS**: n50,08403 e4,52377.

20 guests free. **Location**: Rural, simple, quiet.
**Surface**: grassy/gravel. 01/01-31/12.
**Distance**: 3km on the spot.

### Namur 11C2

**Tabora**, Place André Ryckmans.
**GPS**: n50,46770 e4,85056.

8 free Service € 7,50 Ch. **Location**: Urban, simple.
**Surface**: asphalted. 01/01-31/12.
**Distance**: 1km 500m 1km 200m.
**Remarks**: Behind gymnasium.

### Nismes 11C3

Rue Longue. **GPS**: n50,07387 e4,54863.

± 8 € 5 € 2/100liter Ch € 2/h.
**Surface**: asphalted. 01/01-31/12.
**Distance**: on the spot 100m bakery 100m on the spot on
the spot.
**Remarks**: Coins at tourist info.

### Profondeville 11C3

Chaussée de Namur. **GPS**: n50,37644 e4,87106.

4 free. **Surface**: asphalted. 01/01-31/12.
**Distance**: 50m 150m 50m.
**Remarks**: Max. 24h.

### Rochefort 11D3

Route de Marche. **GPS**: n50,15800 e5,22639.

10 free. **Location**: Urban, simple. **Surface**: metalled.
01/01-31/12.
**Distance**: 200m 200m 200m.

### Saint-Hubert 11D3

**Fourneau Saint Michel**, Rue Saint Hubert.
**GPS**: n50,08480 e5,33902.

10 free Chfree (4x)€ 1/h. **Location**: Rural, simple.
**Surface**: asphalted/grassy. 01/01-31/12.
**Distance**: St Hubert 9km 200m on the spot.
**Remarks**: At open air museum from Fourneau Saint-Michel.

### Saint-Hubert 11D3

Rue du Parc. **GPS**: n50,02689 e5,38088.

3 free free. **Location**: Urban, simple. **Surface**: gravel.
01/01-31/12.
**Distance**: 500m 500m 500m on the spot on the spot.
**Remarks**: Max. 48h, 10 parking places tolerated, European campital
of hunting, events: 1st weekend September and November 1st Saint
Hubert.

### Treignes 11C3

Rue de la Gare. **GPS**: n50,09085 e4,68182.

3 free € 2 Ch € 2. **Surface**: gravel. 01/01-31/12.
**Distance**: 900m.
**Remarks**: At former station, coins at tourist info Nismes, steam train
museum.

**BE**

# Luxembourg

## Arlon 16E1

**Casserne Callemeyn**, Drève des Espagnols, N882.
**GPS**: n49,68990 e5,81929.

5 free free. **Location**: Urban, simple. **Surface**: asphalted. 01/01-31/12.
**Distance**: 600m 5,8km.
**Remarks**: At fire-station.

**Tourist information Arlon:**
Parc Archéologique, Rue des Thermes. Archeological site. 9-12h, 14-17h.
Flea market. 01/03-31/10 1st Su of the month 7-19h.

## Barvaux 11D3

Petit Barvaux. **GPS**: n50,35223 e5,49501.

15 €10/24h €2 Ch €2.
**Surface**: grasstiles.
01/01-31/12.
**Distance**: 300m Delhaize 50m Ravel-route on the spot.
**Remarks**: Along the Ourthe river, max. 24h, coins at tourist info.

**Tourist information Barvaux:**
Labyrinthus, Rue Basse Commene. Labyrinth park. Jul/Aug 10-19h, Sep 11-17h.
Domaine de Hottemme. Nature reserve with visitor centre.
10.30-17h, summer 10.30-18h. €2.

## Bastogne 11D3

Avenue Albert I. **GPS**: n49,99825 e5,71526.

10 free free. **Location**: Urban, simple, central. **Surface**: asphalted. 01/01-31/12.
**Distance**: 300m 3km 300m 300m.

## Bouillon 16C1

**Parking du stade**, Rue de la Poulie. **GPS**: n49,79106 e5,05767.

10 free Ch €1/kWh.
**Surface**: gravel. 01/01-31/12.
**Distance**: 1,3km 1,3km 1,5km.
**Remarks**: Max. 24h, coins at tourist info.

## Durbuy 11D3

**P Mobilhome Le Vedeur**, Rue Fond de Vedeur 1.
**GPS**: n50,35780 e5,45672.

50 €21, 2 pers.incl Ch WC included.
**Location**: Comfortable. **Surface**: gravel. 01/01-31/12.
**Distance**: 750m on the spot fishing permit obligatory 750m 750m on the spot.
**Remarks**: Monitored parking 24/24.

**Tourist information Durbuy:**
Confiturerie Saint Amour, Rue St Amour 13. Production of traditional products. 10-18h 01/10-31/03 Mo. free.
Diamour, Rue de la Prevoté 2. Centre of diamonds and goldsmithing. 10.30-19.30h Tue-Wed. free.
Parc des Topiaires, Rue Haie Himbe. Model garden. 10-18h 01/01-31/01. €4,50.
Antiques and flea market. 01/03-30/09, 9-17h, 2nd Sa of the month.

## Florenville 16D1

**Muno**, Rue des Vieilles-Voies. **GPS**: n49,71223 e5,16950.

15 free. **Location**: Rural, simple, isolated, quiet. **Surface**: asphalted. 01/01-31/12.
**Distance**: 1km 1km 1km.

## Herbeumont 16D1

Avenue de Combattants. **GPS**: n49,77729 e5,23700.

50 free Ch free.
**Location**: Rural. **Surface**: asphalted/grassy. 01/01-31/12.
**Distance**: 500m 500m.
**Remarks**: Parking of old station.

**Tourist information Herbeumont:**
Royal Syndicat d'Initiative, Avenue des Combattants, 7, www.herbeumont.be. Beautiful position in the Ardennes landscape. Ruins of medieval castle, free entry.
Au cœur de l'Ardoise, Rue du Babinay 1, Bertrix. Slate mine. sa-su 10-18h, wed 14h. €9,50.

## Hotton 11D3

Haie Notre Dame. **GPS**: n50,26937 e5,45738.

6 €10 Ch Location: Rural, simple, quiet.
**Surface**: asphalted. 01/01-31/12.
**Distance**: 1km 800m 800m RAVeL.

## Hotton 11D3

Rue du Batty. **GPS**: n50,26828 e5,44416.

4 €10 Ch included.
**Location**: Urban, simple. **Surface**: asphalted. 01/01-31/12.
**Distance**: 300m 50m 200m 500m.

**Tourist information Hotton:**
Grottes de Hotton, Chemin du spéléoclub 1. Caves. 01/04-31/10 10-17h, 01/07-31/08 10-18h.

## Houffalize 11D3

Cour de l'Abbaye. **GPS**: n50,13210 e5,78800.

8 €12 Ch included WC.
**Location**: Urban. **Surface**: asphalted. 01/01-31/12.
**Distance**: 150m 300m on the spot.

## La Roche-en-Ardenne 11D3

Mâboge. **GPS**: n50,16749 e5,62597.

50 free. **Surface**: grassy. 01/01-31/12.
**Distance**: on the spot on the spot.
**Remarks**: Along river, max. 24h.

## La Roche-en-Ardenne 11D3

Rue du Harzé. **GPS**: n50,19075 e5,57432.

5 free. **Location**: Urban, simple. **Surface**: asphalted.
01/01-31/12. **Distance**: 500m 500m 500m on the spot.
**Remarks**: Parking at sports park.

**Tourist information La Roche-en-Ardenne:**
Syndicat d'Initiative, Place du Marché, 15, www.la-roche-tourisme.com. Small town totally destroyed during the battle of the Ardennes, 1944/45.
Medieval citadel. 10-12h, 14-17h, 01/07-31/08 10-19h, winter Sa-Su frost.

## Nisramont 11D3

**Barrage de Nisramont**, Rue de barrage. **GPS**: n50,14089 e5,67118.

BE

10 ⌁free. **Location:** Simple, isolated, quiet. **Surface:** metalled.
◻ 01/01-31/12.
**Distance:** ⌁3,7km ⋆15km ⌁on the spot ⌁on the spot ⊗on the spot ⌁on the spot.
**Remarks:** At artificial lake.

| ⌁⌁S | **Poupehan** ⌁⌁⌁⌁⌁ | 16C1 |

Rue du Pont. **GPS:** n49,80886 e5,00418. ⤊.

20 ⌁free ⌁⌁Chfree. **Location:** Rural, simple, quiet.
**Surface:** gravel. ◻ 01/01-31/12.
**Distance:** ⌁on the spot ⌁on the spot ⊗200m ⌁300m ⌁on the spot ⌁on the spot.
**Remarks:** Along the Semois river, next to sports fields, max. 24h, canoe rental.

| ⌁⌁ | **Redu** | 11D3 |

Rue de Saint Hubert. **GPS:** n50,00877 e5,16348. ⤊.

10 ⌁free. **Location:** Rural, simple. **Surface:** gravel.
◻ 01/01-31/12.
**Distance:** ⌁on the spot.

| ⌁⌁S | **Rochehaut** | 16C1 |

**Le Palis**, Le Routi 25. **GPS:** n49,84156 e5,01073.

39 ⌁€ 12-15 ⌁⌁Ch ⌁(39x)included. **Location:** Rural.
**Surface:** grassy/metalled. ◻ 01/01-31/12.
**Distance:** ⌁100m ⌁500m ⊗100m ⌁100m ⌁300m ⌁on the spot ⌁on the spot.
**Remarks:** Video surveillance.

# 🇨🇭 Switzerland

Capital: Bern
Government: Direct democracy, Federal republic
Official Language: German, French, Italian, Romansh
Population: 8,236,000 (2017)
Area: 41,284 km²

## General information
Dialling code: 0041
General emergency: 112
Currency: Swiss franc (CHF)
CHF 1 = € 0,85, € 1 = CHF 1,16
CHF 1 = £0.76, £1 = CHF 1,31 (October 2018)

## Regulations for overnight stays
Overnight parking is allowed, max 15 hours.

## Additional public holidays 2019
April 19 Good Friday
April 22 Easter Monday
June 20 Corpus Christi
August 1 National Day

## Time Zone
Winter (Standard Time) GMT+1
Summer (DST) GMT+2

North page: 118
Basel
Bern
West pages: 116-118
East pages: 118-119
Genève
South pages: 119-121

CH

## Switzerland West

### Aeschi 22G1
**Panorama**, Scheidgasse 272. **GPS:** n46,65399 e7,70070.
50 CHF 22,40-31,20 Ch CHF 3 WC 15/05-15/10.

### Avenches 22F1
**Camping-Port-Plage. GPS:** n46,90351 e7,04918.
300 CHF 36,60, 01/07-15/08 CHF 44,60 Ch WC.
30/03-30/09.

### Boltigen 22G1
**Jaunpass. GPS:** n46,59208 e7,33758.
117 Ch WC. 01/01-31/12.

### Böningen 22H1
**TCS Camping Bönigen**, Campingstrasse 14.
**GPS:** n46,68987 e7,89398.
CHF 25, 2 pers. incl. included.
**Location:** Central, quiet.
**Remarks:** Quick-Stop: >18h - <9h.

### Brienz 22H1
**Aaregg. GPS:** n46,74859 e8,04957.
180 CHF 15-26 Ch WC.
**Location:** Rural.
**Surface:** asphalted.
24/03-31/10.
**Distance:** 500m on the spot on the spot.

**Tourist information Brienz:**
Alpen Region Brienz-Meiringen-Hasliberg, Bahnhofstrasse 22, Meiringen, www.alpenregion.ch. Village of wood-cutters.
during school hours 01/07-31/08.
Brienz Rothorn Bahn. Steam rack-railway. 01/06-31/10 8.45h.
CHF 57-88.
Freilichtmuseum Ballenberg. Open air museum. 15/04-31/10 10-17h.

### Bullet 22F1
**Restaurant Les Cluds**, Les Cluds. **GPS:** n46,84248 e6,55991.

4 CHF 10 Ch (4x)included.
**Location:** Rural, simple, isolated, quiet. **Surface:** asphalted.
01/01-31/12 Restaurant: Mo.
**Distance:** on the spot on the spot on the spot.
**Remarks:** Max. 2 nights, pay at restaurant.

### Burgdorf 19G3
**Camping Waldegg. GPS:** n47,05407 e7,62895.
CHF 28-31,50 Ch CHF 4 WC. 13/04-15/10.

### Château-d'Oex 22G2
**Le Berceau**, Route des Mosses 16. **GPS:** n46,46673 e7,12529.
57 CHF 38,50 Ch WC. 01/01-31/12.

### Dürrenroth 19G3
**Reisemobilstellplatz Blueberry Hill**, Brunnen 54.
**GPS:** n47,06563 e7,76553.

5 CHF 10 CHF 2. **Location:** Rural, comfortable, quiet.
**Surface:** gravel. 01/01-31/12.
**Distance:** Dürrenroth 3,5km on the spot on the spot.
**Remarks:** Panoramic view.

### Echallens 22F1
Chemin du Pont. **GPS:** n46,63945 e6,64096.

5 free Ch free. **Location:** Rural, simple. **Surface:** asphalted.
01/01-31/12.
**Distance:** 700m 300m 700m.
**Remarks:** Max. 1 night.

### Estavayer-le-Lac 22F1
**Nouvelle-Plage. GPS:** n46,85602 e6,84801.
30 CHF 37-46,60 Ch WC. 30/03-21/10.

### Frutigen 22G1
**Camping Grassi**, Grassiweg 60. **GPS:** n46,58178 e7,64213.
68 CHF 29-31 Ch. 01/01-31/12.

### Gampelen 22F1
**TCS Camping Gampelen**, Seestrasse 50. **GPS:** n47,00154 e7,03957.
CHF 25, 2 pers. incl. included. 24/03-09/10.
**Remarks:** Quick-Stop: >18h - <9h.

### Gerlafingen 19G3
Derendingenstrasse. **GPS:** n47,17870 e7,58187.
12 CHF 20 Ch included. **Location:** Urban, comfortable.
**Surface:** gravel/metalled. 01/04-15/10.
**Distance:** 700m 600m 600m.

### Grandson 22F1
**Le Pécos**, Chemin du Pécos 3. **GPS:** n46,80371 e6,63575.
15 CHF 38 Ch WC. **Location:** Rural, simple, quiet.
**Surface:** metalled. 01/04-01/10.
**Distance:** 800m 100m on the spot.
**Remarks:** Next to campsite.

### Grindelwald 22H1
**Camping Eigernordwand**, Bodenstrasse 4. **GPS:** n46,62135 e8,01683.
CHF 37 Ch.
01/01-31/12.
**Distance:** on the spot on the spot.

**Tourist information Grindelwald:**
Jungfraubahn. Train journey to the highest train station of Europe

### Gryon 22G2
Place de la Barboleuse. **GPS:** n46,28222 e7,07028.

4 CHF 2,80/pp, Summer CHF 5,30/pp Ch (4x)CHF 5.
**Location:** Rural, simple, quiet. **Surface:** asphalted.
01/01-31/12.
**Distance:** 200m 3,5km on the spot 100m.
**Remarks:** To be paid at office de tourisme.

### Gstaad 22G2
**Camping Bellerive**, Bellerivestrasse 38. **GPS:** n46,48106 e7,27328.
CHF 27,50-30 Ch. 01/01-31/12.

### Gwatt-Thun 22G1
**TCS Camping Thunersee**, Gwattstrasse 103a. **GPS:** n46,72749 e7,62760.
CHF 25 included. 29/03-14/10.
**Remarks:** Quick-Stop: >18h - <9h.

### Häusernmoos 19G3
**Restaurant Koi-Gartenteich**, Huttwilstrasse 22.
**GPS:** n47,07890 e7,74935.
4 CHF 10, overnight stay free Ch CHF 4 included, at restaurant. 01/01-31/12 Restaurant: Mo-Tue.
**Distance:** on the spot 2km.

### Hinterkappelen 22G1
**Kappelenbrucke**, Wohlenstrasse 62. **GPS:** n46,96433 e7,38361.
70 Ch WC. 01/01-31/12.

### Huttwil 19H3
**FLYER Stellplatz**, Schwende 1. **GPS:** n47,11527 e7,86795.

16 free Ch free.
**Location:** Rural. **Surface:** gravel. 01/01-31/12.
**Distance:** 500m.
**Remarks:** E-bike factory, guided tour Tuesdays 14.30h.

### Interlaken 22H1
**Camping Lazy Rancho**, Lehnweg 6. **GPS:** n46,68583 e7,83095.
6 CHF 33-52 Ch WC CHF 4,50 WC.
27/04-21/10.

### Interlaken 22H1
**Camping Hobby**, Lehnweg 16. **GPS:** n46,68424 e7,83022.
80 CHF 29,40-40 Ch WC. 01/04-30/09.

**Tourist information Interlaken:**
Heimwehfluhbahn. Telpher carrier from 1906. 24/03-23/10 10-17.

JungfrauPark. Attractions and themepark. ☐ 01/05-23/10 11-18u.

### ▲S La Brévine ❄ 22F1
Les Varodes. **GPS:** n46,97195 e6,58860. ⬆.

10 💲free ⛽🔌Ch 💧(2x)WCfree. **Location:** Rural, simple, isolated, quiet. **Surface:** asphalted. ☐ 01/01-31/12.
**Distance:** 🚶3km ⛵on the spot ⊗1,5km 🚴on the spot 🎿on the spot on the spot.
**Remarks:** Parking at Lac des Tailleres.

### ▲S La Chaux-de-Fonds ❄ 19F3
Bois du Couvent. **GPS:** n47,09334 e6,83593. ⬆.

2 💲free ⛽🔌Ch 💧(4x)free. **Location:** Rural, simple.
**Surface:** gravel. ☐ 01/05-30/09.
**Distance:** 🚶1,3km ⊗350m 🚉700m 🎿on the spot.
**Remarks:** In front of campsite du Bois du Couvent.
**Tourist information La Chaux-de-Fonds:**
🛈 Tourisme neuchâtelois - Montagnes, Espacité 1, Place Le Corbusier. Capital of the clock industry.
Ⓜ Musée International d'Horlogerie, Rue des Musée 29. Watch museum. ☐ 10-17h ⊙ Mo, 25/12-01/01.
Ⓜ Musée paysan et artisanal, Rue des Crêtets 148. The farmers' life and old crafts industry. ☐ 01/04-31/10 14-17h, 01/11-28/02 Wed, Sa, Su 14-17h ⊙ Mo, 01/03-31/03.

### S Langenthal 19G3
Lexa-Wohnmobile, Bern-Zürichstrasse 49b.
**GPS:** n47,22461 e7,77944. ⬆.

5 💲free ⛽🔌Ch 💧free. **Surface:** asphalted. ☐ 01/01-31/12.
**Distance:** 🚶2km.
**Remarks:** At motorhome dealer.

### ▲S Lausanne 🌿☕🍴 22F2
Vidy, Chemin du Camping 3. **GPS:** n46,51734 e6,59777. ⬆➡.

10 💲CHF 23,60 or € 20 ⛽🔌Ch 💧WC included 📶CHF 4,35/4h 🔥📷.
**Location:** Urban, simple, central. **Surface:** grassy/metalled.
☐ 01/01-31/12.
**Distance:** ⛵on the spot ⊗on the spot.
**Remarks:** Next to campsite the Vidy, pay at reception, service passerby CHF 3, free bus to centre.
**Tourist information Lausanne:**
🛈 Lausanne Tourisme, Avenue de Rhodanie 2, www.lausanne-tourisme.ch. Parking at the port, rack-railway to city centre.

---

Ⓜ Musée Olympique, Quai d'Ouchy 1. All about the Olympic games.
☐ 01/05-14/10 9-18h, 14/10-30/04 10-18h ⊙ Mo, 01/10-30/04.

### ▲S Lauterbrunnen ❄ 22H1
Camping Jungfrau. **GPS:** n46,58834 e7,90882.
💲CHF 48,40 ⛽🔌Ch 💧WC 📶. ☐ 01/01-31/12.

### ▲S Lauterbrunnen ❄ 22H1
Schützenbach. **GPS:** n46,59047 e7,91194.
💲⛽🔌Ch 💧WC
☐ 01/01-31/12.
**Tourist information Lauterbrunnen:**
👁 Jungfraubahn, Grindelwald. Train journey to the highest train station of Europe.
👁 Klöppelstube, Altes Schulhaus. Making of bobbin lace. ☐ Fri 13.30-16.30h. 🎟 free.
👁 Trümmelbachfälle, Lauterbrunnen dir Stechelberg. Underground waterfalls. ☐ 01/04-30/11 9-17h.

### ▲S Le Landeron 19F3
Camping des Pêches, Rue du Port 6. **GPS:** n47,05257 e7,06993.
💲⛽🔌Ch 💧WC 📶. ☐ 01/04-15/10.
**Tourist information Le Landeron:**
⊗ Restaurant Le Carnotzet, Rue de la Gare 22. Restaurant with regional specialities. ☐ Tue-Sa 11-14h, 17-23h ⊙ Mo, Su.

### ▲S Les Ponts-de-Martel 22F1
Rue du Bugnon. **GPS:** n46,99644 e6,73065. ⬆➡.

3 💲free ⛽🔌Ch 💧(2x)free. **Location:** Rural, simple.
**Surface:** asphalted. ☐ 01/01-31/12.
**Distance:** 🚶600m 🚉700m.
**Remarks:** At community centre.

### 🏨S Malvilliers 22F1
Hotel-Restaurant La Croisée, Route de Neuchâtel.
**GPS:** n47,03200 e6,86779. ⬆➡.

5 💲CHF 5 🔌Ch 💧(4x)included. **Location:** Simple, noisy.
**Surface:** asphalted. ☐ 01/01-31/12.
**Distance:** 🚶100m ⊗on the spot.

### ⛺S Meiringen 🏔 22H1
Alpencamping, Brüningstrasse 46. **GPS:** n46,73448 e8,17122. ⬆.

8 💲CHF 29,90 ⛽🔌Ch 💧WC 📶included. 🔥.
**Location:** Rural, comfortable, quiet. **Surface:** grassy.
☐ 01/01-31/12.
**Distance:** 🚶1km ⊗1km.
**Remarks:** Max. 3 nights.

### ⛺S Morges 22F2
TCS Camping Morges, Promenade du Petit-Bois 15.
**GPS:** n46,50446 e6,48894.
170 💲CHF 25 📶included. ☐ 29/03-14/10.
**Remarks:** Quick-Stop: >18h - <9h.

### ▲S Moutier 19G3
Chemin de la Piscine. **GPS:** n47,27365 e7,37923. ⬆➡.

---

5 💲free ⛽🔌Chfree. **Location:** Urban, simple, quiet.
**Surface:** asphalted. ☐ 01/01-31/12.
**Distance:** 🚶1km.
**Remarks:** At swimming pool.

### ▲S Murten 🌿☕🍴 22G1
Lac de Morat, Ryf. **GPS:** n46,93240 e7,11967. ⬆.

30 💲CHF 1/h, overnight stay free. 🏧 **Location:** Urban, simple, central.
**Surface:** grasstiles. ☐ 01/01-31/12.
**Distance:** 🚶on the spot ⛵on the spot ⊗on the spot.

### ▲S Neuchâtel 🌿☕🍴 22F1
Route des Falaises. **GPS:** n47,00145 e6,95735. ⬆.

8 💲free ⛽🔌Ch 💧(4x)free.
**Location:** Simple, noisy. **Surface:** grasstiles.
☐ 01/01-31/12.
**Distance:** 🚶city centre 2km ⛵300m 🚂100m.
**Remarks:** Max. 2 days, max. 7m.
**Tourist information Neuchâtel:**
🌿 Le Creux-du-Van, Val-de-Travers. Nature reserve. ☐ 01/01-31/12.

### 🏨S Oberburg 19G3
Reisemobilstellplätze Kürbishof, Krauchthalstrasse 40.
**GPS:** n47,03807 e7,62079. ⬆.
5 💲CHF 13 or € 9 ⛽🔌Ch 💧CHF 4,50 WC against payment. 🏠
**Location:** Urban, simple, quiet. **Surface:** grassy.
☐ 01/01-31/12.
**Distance:** 🚶600m ⊗300m.
**Remarks:** Payment also in euros.

### ⛺S Payerne 🍴 22F1
Place des Tireurs à la Cible. **GPS:** n46,82376 e6,94343. ⬆.

2 💲free ⛽🔌Ch 💧(2x)free. **Location:** Urban, simple, central, noisy. **Surface:** asphalted. ☐ 01/01-31/12.
**Distance:** 🚶on the spot ⊗on the spot ⛵on the spot.

### ▲S Portalban 🌿☕🍴 22F1
Route du Port. **GPS:** n46,92131 e6,95614. ⬆.

25 �CHF 24, 2 pers. incl. ⌂🔌Ch✎(30x)WC⌐included. 🚐
**Location:** Rural, simple. **Surface:** grasstiles.
🔲 01/01-31/12.
**Distance:** 🚶on the spot ⚓200m ⊗on the spot ⚌on the spot.
**Remarks:** In harbour, near campsite, check in at reception.

| 🅰️Ⓢ | Prêles | 19G3 |

**Prêles**, Route de la Neuveville 61. **GPS:** n47,08569 e7,11714.
⌐CHF 37,50 ⌂🔌Ch✎WC⌐ 🔲 01/04-15/10.

| 🅲Ⓢ | Rolle | 22E2 |

**Camping de Rolle Aux Vernes**, Chemin de la Plage.
**GPS:** n46,46191 e6,34630.
5⌐CHF 18-30 + CHF 8,50-10/pp tourist tax ✎CHF 3.
**Surface:** asphalted. 🔲 01/03-01/10.
**Distance:** 🚶500m.
**Remarks:** Max. 48h.

| 🅴Ⓢ | Romont 🌿⛲ | 22F1 |

Promenade des Avoines. **GPS:** n46,69753 e6,91774. ⬆️➡️

2⌐CHF 2,15/pp tourist tax ⌂🔌Ch✎(4x)free.
**Location:** Rural, simple, noisy. **Surface:** grasstiles.
🔲 01/01-31/12.
**Distance:** 🚶on the spot ⊗100m ⚌700m.
**Remarks:** Max. 24h.

| 🅴Ⓢ | Saignelégier | 19F3 |

Chemin de la Tuilerie. **GPS:** n47,25223 e7,00347. ⬆️

10⌐free ⌂🔌Ch🚐free. **Location:** Rural, simple, noisy.
**Surface:** grasstiles. 🔲 01/01-31/12.
**Distance:** 🚶700m ⊗on the spot ⚌200m.

| 🅴Ⓢ | Saint Blaise 🏖 | 22F1 |

Chemin des Pêcheurs. **GPS:** n47,01139 e6,98778. ⬆️➡️

12⌐CHF 16/24h ⌂🔌Ch✎(4x)WC⌐📶included. 🚐📷
**Location:** Urban, simple, central, noisy. **Surface:** asphalted.
🔲 01/01-31/12.
**Distance:** 🚶Neuchâtel 5km 🏖300m ⚓250m ⚌500m 🛒600m.

| 🅴Ⓢ | Saint-Aubin 🏖 | 22F1 |

Port de St-Aubin-Sauges. **GPS:** n46,89181 e6,77427. ⬆️➡️

---

10⌐CHF 20 ⌂🔌Ch✎(6x)WC⌐included. 🚐 **Location:** Urban,
simple, quiet. **Surface:** asphalted. 🔲 01/01-31/12.
**Distance:** 🚶600m ⚓on the spot 🚤on the spot ⊗400m ⚌400m.
**Remarks:** Parking port, nearby the capitainerie.

| 🅴Ⓢ | Sainte-Croix ❄❄ | 22F1 |

**Grand-Rue**, L'Auberson. **GPS:** n46,82019 e6,47230. ⬆️

4⌐free ⌂🔌Ch✎(4x)free. **Location:** Rural, simple.
**Surface:** asphalted. 🔲 01/01-31/12.
**Distance:** 🚶2km ⊗on the spot ⚌3km.

| 🅰️Ⓢ | Satigny | 22E2 |

**Bois de Bay**, Route du Bois-de-Bay 19. **GPS:** n46,20087 e6,06619.
🔌Ch✎WC. 🔲 01/01-31/12.

| 🅰️Ⓢ | Vesenaz | 22E2 |

**Pointe a la Bise**, Chemin de la Bise 19. **GPS:** n46,24517 e6,19331.
105⌐CHF 62 ⌂🔌Ch✎WC⌐🔲📶. 🔲 28/03-05/10.

| 🅰️Ⓢ | Zweisimmen | 22G1 |

**Camping Vermeille**, Ey-Gässli 2. **GPS:** n46,56265 e7,37766.
25⌐CHF 24,80-30,30 ⌂🔌Ch✎. 🔲 01/01-31/12.

# Switzerland North

| 🚰Ⓢ | Altikon 🍴 | 20A2 |

**Stellplatz auf dem Bauernhof**, Feldstrasse 18.
**GPS:** n47,57337 e8,78391.
3⌐CHF 10 ⌂🔌Ch 1 ✎CHF 4 ⌐CHF 2. 🚐
**Surface:** metalled. 🔲 01/01-31/12.
**Distance:** ⊗200m ⚌200m.
**Remarks:** Max. 48h.

| 🅰️Ⓢ | Brunnen | 23A1 |

**Hopfraeben**. **GPS:** n46,99700 e8,59300.
40⌐CHF 23-42 ⌂🔌Ch✎WC⌐🔲📶. 🔲 01/05-01/10.

| 🅰️Ⓢ | Engelberg | 22H1 |

**Sporthotel Eienwäldli**, Wasserfallstrasse 108.
**GPS:** n46,81009 e8,42243.
71⌐CHF 28-36 ⌂🔌Ch✎WC📶. 🔲 01/01-31/12.
**Distance:** ⊗on the spot 🚋on the spot.

| 🅰️Ⓢ | Giswil | 22H1 |

**Stellplatz an der Kirche**, Panoramastrasse. **GPS:** n46,83230 e8,17900.
3⌐free. **Surface:** asphalted. 🔲 01/01-31/12.
**Distance:** 🚶on the spot ⊗on the spot ⚌on the spot.
**Remarks:** Max. 1 night.

| 🚰Ⓢ | Hemmiken | 19H3 |

**Stellplatz Bauernhof**, Asphof 50. **GPS:** n47,49682 e7,88749.
3⌐CHF 20 ⌂🔌Ch✎⌐. **Location:** Isolated, quiet.
**Surface:** unpaved. 🔲 01/01-31/12.
**Distance:** 🚶1,4km.

| 🅲Ⓢ | Horw | 22H1 |

**TCS Camping Luzern**, Seefeldstrasse. **GPS:** n47,01100 e8,31100.
⌐CHF 25 ✎included. 🔲 29/03-14/10.
**Remarks:** Quick-Stop: >18h - <9h.

| 🅰️Ⓢ | Reinach | 19G3 |

**Waldhort**, Heideweg 16. **GPS:** n47,49923 e7,60296.
⌐CHF 36 ⌂🔌Ch✎WC⌐🔲. 🔲 04/03-28/10.

| 🚰Ⓢ | Weggis 🌿⛲🏠❄ | 19H3 |

**Bauernhof Gerberweid**, Eichistrasse 2. **GPS:** n47,03888 e8,41446. ⬆️

---

15⌐CHF 6-10 + CHF 6/pp + CHF 2,70/pp tourist tax ⌂CHF 1
🔌Ch⌐CHF 3 ⌐CHF 2. 🚐 **Location:** Rural, isolated, quiet.
**Surface:** grassy. 🔲 01/04-15/10.
**Distance:** 🚶2km ⊗1km ⚌1km 🛒500m 🏕on the spot.

| 🅴Ⓢ | Willisau | 19H3 |

Bisangmatt. **GPS:** n47,11937 e7,99829. ⬆️

4⌐CHF 5 ⌂🔌Ch✎(4x)included.
**Surface:** metalled. 🔲 01/01-31/12.
**Distance:** 🚶800m ⊗800m ⚌800m.
**Remarks:** At fire-station, max. 24h.

| 🅰️Ⓢ | Zug | 20A3 |

**TCS Camping Zug**, Chamer Fussweg 36. **GPS:** n47,17758 e8,49358.
⌐CHF 25 Ch✎📶included. 🚐
🔲 29/03-14/10.
**Remarks:** Max. ^3.17m, Quick-Stop: >18h - <9h.

# Switzerland East

| 🍴Ⓢ | Altstätten 🏔 | 20B3 |

**Gasthausziel**, Trogenerstrasse 99. **GPS:** n47,38892 e9,53457.
6⌐CHF 10, guests free ⌂🔌Ch✎CHF 5/day. 🚐
🔲 01/01-31/12 🔴 Wed.-Thu.
**Distance:** 🚶3km ⊗on the spot.

| 🅰️Ⓢ | Andeer | 23B1 |

**Camping Andeer**, Sut Baselgia 120 c. **GPS:** n46,60651 e9,42630.
⌐CHF 30 ⌂🔌Ch✎WC⌐🔲. 🔲 01/01-31/12.

| 🍴Ⓢ | Appenzell 🌿⛲🏔❄ | 20B3 |

**Restaurant Eggli**, Egglistrasse. **GPS:** n47,32104 e9,46565.
10⌐guests free ⌂🔌Ch.
**Surface:** asphalted. 🔲 01/01-31/12.
**Remarks:** The most beautiful panorama of Appenzell.

| 🅴Ⓢ | Bivio ⛲❄❄ | 23B2 |

**Wohnmobil-Stellplatz Tua**. **GPS:** n46,46304 e9,65597.

20⌐CHF 10-15 + CHF 2,50/pp tourist tax ⌂🔌Ch✎CHF 7/day.
**Location:** Isolated, quiet. **Surface:** grasstiles.
🔲 01/01-31/12.
**Distance:** 🚶Savognin 18km ⊗on the spot ⚌18km 🎿on the spot.
**Remarks:** Parking ski-lifts.

| 🅴Ⓢ | Breil/Brigels ⛲🏔❄ | 23A1 |

**Wohnmobil-Stellplatz Brigels**. **GPS:** n46,77104 e9,06770. ⬆️

20 CHF 25 CHF 2/50liter Ch. CHF 3/day.
**Surface:** metalled. 01/01-31/12.
**Distance:** 600m on the spot Imbiss on the spot, restaurants
600m 600m on the spot on the spot nearby.
**Remarks:** At Brigeler See.

### Chur — 23B1
**Stellplätze Camp Au**, Felsenaustrasse. 61. GPS: n46,86187 e9,50756.
5 CHF 15 + CHF 1,20/pp tourist tax ChWC.
**Location:** Urban, comfortable, noisy. **Surface:** asphalted.
01/01-31/12.
**Distance:** 3km 2km on the spot on the spot.
**Remarks:** Max. 1 night, oldest city of Switzerland.

### Churwalden — 23B1
**Pradafenz**, Girabodawag 34. GPS: n46,77690 e9,54121.
50 CHF 34 Ch. CHF 0,50/kWh WC. 01/01-31/12.

### Davos — 23C1
**Rinerlodge Talstation**, Landwasserstrasse.
**GPS:** n46,74390 e9,77929.
10 CHF 26-42 Ch. CHF 2.
01/01-31/12.
**Distance:** 1km on the spot on the spot on the spot
on the spot.
**Remarks:** Max. 24h.
**Tourist information Davos:**
Davos Alpengarten. Botanical garden.
01/05-30/09 9-17h.
Berghaus Stafelalp, Frauenkirch. 250 Year old inn where they still
cook on a wood oven and shimmer paraffin lamps are lit.

### Elm — 23B1
**Sportbahnen Elm**, Schiessblock. GPS: n46,91332 e9,16228.
50 free. **Surface:** metalled. 01/03-30/11.
**Distance:** 650m 650m on the spot on the spot.

### Kreuzlingen — 20B2
**Fischerhaus**, Promenadestraße 52. GPS: n47,64745 e9,19898.
CHF 41-51 Ch. WC. 28/03-21/10.

### Neuhausen — 20A2
**Parkplatz Fischacker**, Nohlstrasse. GPS: n47,67373 e8,60866.

50 first hour CHF 5, than CHF 2/h ChWC.
**Location:** Urban, comfortable. **Surface:** grassy/metalled.
01/01-31/12.
**Distance:** 200m on the spot 200m 1km.
**Tourist information Neuhausen:**
Der Rheinfall. Water falls.

### Pontresina — 23C2
**Plauns.** GPS: n46,46200 e9,93400.
Ch. 01/06-15/10, 15/12-15/04.

### Samnaun — 20C3
**Wohnmobilstellplatz Samnaun-Ravaisch**, Sportplatzweg 13.
**GPS:** n46,94906 e10,36705.

30 CHF 13-38/day, CHF 6/pp Ch. WC included.
**Location:** Rural, comfortable, quiet. **Surface:** grassy/gravel.
01/01-31/12.
**Distance:** 1km 750m 200m on the spot.
**Remarks:** At football ground, bread-service.

### Sankt Gallen — 20B3
**Paul-Grüninger-Stadion**, Grütlistrasse. GPS: n47,43361 e9,40464.
2 CHF 2/9-19h, CHF 1/19-8h CHF 1/100liter CHF 0,50/kWh.
**Surface:** asphalted. 01/01-31/12.
**Distance:** 2km 300m.

**Remarks:** Next to sports fields.

### Sankt Moritz — 23C1
**TCS Camping St. Moritz**, Via San Gian 55. GPS: n46,47800 e9,82600.
CHF 25 included. 18/05-23/09.
**Remarks:** Quick-Stop: >18h - <9h.
**Tourist information Sankt Moritz:**
Clean Energy Tour. Hiking trail, nature, energy, climate and weather
adventure. Sign up at Kur- und Verkehrsverein St. Moritz.
15/06-01/10 Wed 13.45h duration 2,5 hours.

### Santa Maria Val Müstair — 23D1
**Hotel Stelvio**, Via Veglia 107. GPS: n46,60123 e10,42226.
10 € 20 Ch.
**Location:** Rural. **Surface:** metalled. 01/01-31/12.
**Distance:** on the spot on the spot on the spot on the spot
on the spot.
**Remarks:** Max. 3 nights.

### Savognin — 23B1
Veia Sandeilas. **GPS:** n46,59660 e9,59226.
15 CHF 15 + CHF 8/pp CHF 1 Ch. CHF 2,50.
**Surface:** gravel. 01/01-31/12.
**Distance:** 500m.
**Remarks:** Near the chair-lift, summer: parking at campsite Julia.

### Schiers — 20B3
**Restaurant Prättiguaerhof**, Flurystrasse 19. GPS: n46,97034 e9,68752.
2 free, use of a meal obligated .
**Surface:** metalled. 01/01-31/12 Sa + Su.
**Distance:** 300m on the spot 100m.

### Sent — 23C1
**Camping Sur En. GPS:** n46,81852 e10,36596.
10 CHF 15 + CHF 2,50/pp tourist tax CHF 3.
**Surface:** grassy/gravel. 01/01-31/12.
**Distance:** on the spot.
**Remarks:** Max. 1 night, 17-10h.

### Splügen — 23B1
**Camping Splügen**, Campingstrasse 18. GPS: n46,54922 e9,31399.
CHF 40-45 Ch. WC. 01/01-31/12.

### Steckborn — 20A2
**Wohnmobilplatz Steckborn**, Schützengraben.
**GPS:** n47,66813 e8,98462.

8 CHF 12/24h Ch. (8x)included. 01/01-31/12.
**Location:** Urban. **Surface:** gravel. 01/01-31/12.
**Distance:** 400m 200m 400m 300m.

### Tinizong-Rona — 23B1
**Stellplatz Restaurant dalla Punt**, Julierstrasse.
**GPS:** n46,56124 e9,62396.
20 CHF 20 Ch. WC included . **Location:** Rural,
comfortable, noisy. **Surface:** gravel. 01/01-31/12.
**Distance:** on the spot on the spot on the spot on the spot
on the spot.

### Unterwasser — 20B3
**Hotel Restaurant Post**, Dorfstrasse 16. GPS: n47,19673 e9,30949.

8 CHF 15 + CHF 2,60/pp tourist tax, guests free Ch. (6x).
**Surface:** asphalted. 01/01-31/12.
**Distance:** 300m on the spot 300m on the spot.

### Vaduz/Liechtenstein — 20B3
**Rheinparkstadion**, Rheindamm. GPS: n47,14022 e9,50945.

10 CHF 0,50/h, 19-7h free ChWCfree.
**Surface:** asphalted. 01/01-31/12.
**Distance:** 1,8km on the spot.
**Remarks:** Along the Rhine river, parking near stadium, max. 24h.
**Tourist information Vaduz/Liechtenstein:**
Liechtenstein Tourismus, Städtle 37, www.vaduz.li. Monarchy on the
Austrian-Swiss border.
Kunstmuseum Lichtenstein, Städtle 32. Tue-Su 10-17h.
Erlebniswelt Neuguthof, Neugutweg 30. Maize labyrinth with wild-
west city. 15/06-30/09 Wed 13-18h, Sa-Su 10-20h, holidays Mo-Fri
10-20h, Sa-Su 10-22h.

### Vals — 23B1
**Stellplatz Vals**, Vallée. GPS: n46,60891 e9,17438.

9 CHF 17 + CHF 3,40/pp tourist tax WCincluded.
**Surface:** metalled. summer.
**Distance:** 300m on the spot 300m 300m on the spot.
**Remarks:** Parking funicular railway.

### Zizers — 23B1
**K. Lüthi**, Rappagugg. GPS: n46,91937 e9,56270.
5 free Ch. **Surface:** metalled. 01/01-31/12.
**Distance:** 1,6km on the spot.
**Remarks:** At motorhome dealer.

### Zürich — 20A3
**Camping Zürich**, Seestrasse 559. GPS: n47,33641 e8,53960.
. 01/01-31/12.
**Tourist information Zürich:**
Zürich Tourismus, Im Hauptbahnhof, www.zuerich.com. Historical
city with large pedestrian area.

# Switzerland South

### Avegno — 23A2
**Piccolo Paradiso**, Via Cantonale 13. GPS: n46,20100 e8,74300.
280 CHF 59,40-75,40 Ch. WC. 23/03-31/10.

### Bellinzona — 23A2
**Centro Sportivo**, Viale Giuseppe Motta. GPS: n46,20116 e9,01729.

7 CHF 20 CHF 1/20liter Ch.
**Location:** Noisy. **Surface:** asphalted. 01/01-31/12.
**Distance:** 1,5km 4km.
**Remarks:** Max. 48h.
**Tourist information Bellinzona:**
Castelgrande, Via Salita Castelgrande 18. 11-16h, Apr/Jun/Sep/
Oct 10-18h, Jul/Aug 10-19h.
Castello di Montebello, Via Artore 4. 01/03-30/11 10-18h.
Castello di Sasso Corbaro. 01/04-30/11 10-18h.
Palestra di Roccia San Paolo, Palazo Civico. Climbing garden for
beginners and experienced, 30.000²m, 23 climbing trails.

### Bouveret — 22F2
**Rive Bleue. GPS:** n46,38645 e6,86041.
CHF 29,20-37,20 Ch. WC. 30/03-30/09.

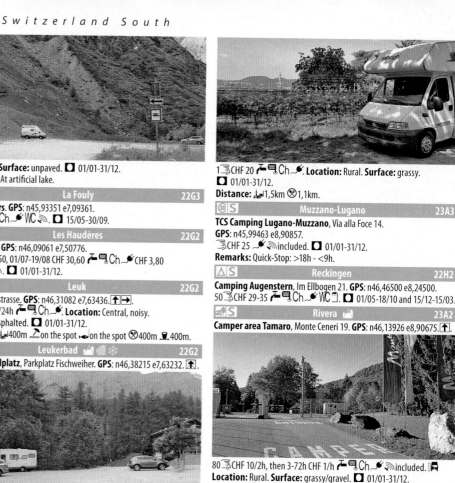

## △S Brig — 22H2
**Brigerbad**. GPS: n46,30209 e7,93102.
400 🏕CHF 31-35 ⟵🔧Ch ⚡ WC 🚿 🔲. 🔲 30/04-02/11.

## ⊞S Bürchen 🏔🌲 — 22H2
**Zengerbern**. GPS: n46,27726 e7,81499.⬆.
15 🏕CHF 18 ⚡. 
**Location:** Rural, simple, isolated. 🔲 01/01-31/12.
**Distance:** 🚂400m 🚶on the spot 🚡on the spot.

## △S Champéry 🏔❄ — 22F2
**Route de la Fin**. GPS: n46,17592 e6,87076.⬆.

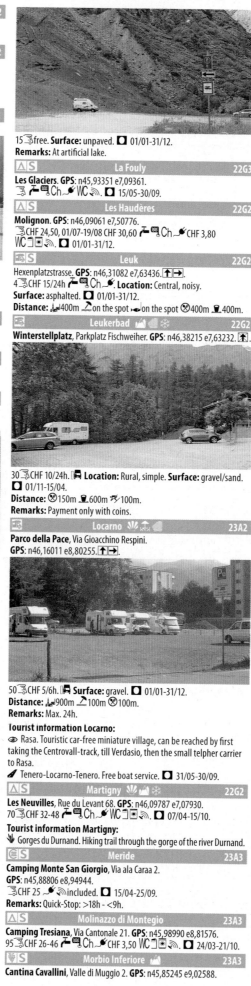

6 🏕CHF 18 + CHF 2,20/pp ⟵🔧Ch ⚡(4x)included.
**Location:** Rural, simple. **Surface:** asphalted. 🔲 01/01-31/12.
**Distance:** ⊗100m 🚂on the spot 🚌200m 🚡200m.
**Remarks:** Parking supermarket, nearby the téléphérique.

## △S Evolène — 22G2
**Camping d'Evolène**, Route de Lannaz. GPS: n46,11075 e7,49654.
🏕CHF 29-31 ⟵🔧Ch ⚡ WC 🔲🚿. 🔲 01/01-31/12.

## △S Gordevio — 23A2
**Bella Riva**. GPS: n46,22159 e8,74194.
🏕🔧Ch ⚡ WC. 🔲 01/04-01/10.

## ⊞S Grimentz 🌿🏔🌲❄ — 22G2
**Aire camping-car l'Îlôt Bosquet**, Route de Moiry.
GPS: n46,17432 e7,57271.⬆➡.

20 🏕CHF 15 ⟵🔧Ch ⚡included. 🚐♻.
**Location:** Rural, simple, quiet. **Surface:** unpaved. 🔲 01/01-31/12.
**Distance:** 🚂on the spot ⊗on the spot 🚂on the spot 🚌on the spot
🚡nearby 🎿nearby.
**Remarks:** Pay and coins at tourist office, public transport, free entrance swimming pool (summer).

**Tourist information Grimentz:**
🛈 Grimentz/St.Jean Tourisme, www.grimentz.ch. Many signposted cycle and hiking routes.
👁 La Maison bourgeoisiale. Life of the citizens of Grimentz. 🔲 guided tour Mo. 🎫 free.

## ⊞S Grimselpas 🏔🌲 — 22H1
**Berghotel Grimselblick**, Grimselpasshöhe.
GPS: n46,56115 c8,33673.⬆.

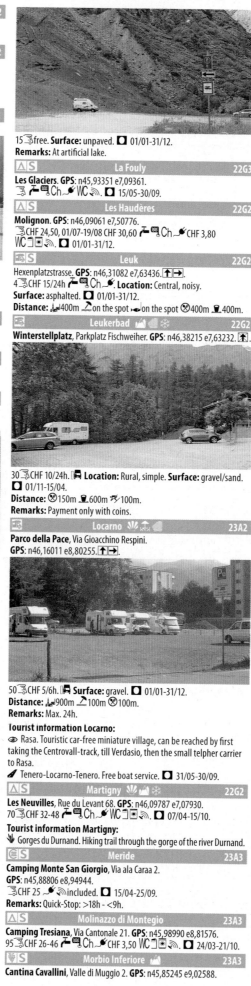

20 🏕CHF 20 ⟵⚡. **Location:** Rural. **Surface:** asphalted.
🔲 14/06-31/10.
**Distance:** 🚂on the spot 🚶on the spot.
**Remarks:** Service at hotel.

## Hérémence — 22G2
**Val des Hérémence, Parking B,C,D en E**, Le Chargeur.
GPS: n46,08882 e7,40362.

15 🏕free. **Surface:** unpaved. 🔲 01/01-31/12.
**Remarks:** At artificial lake.

## △S La Fouly — 22G3
**Les Glaciers**. GPS: n45,93351 e7,09361.
🏕🔧Ch ⚡ WC 🚿. 🔲 15/05-30/09.

## △S Les Haudères — 22G2
**Molignon**. GPS: n46,09061 e7,50776.
🏕CHF 24,50, 01/07-19/08 CHF 30,60 ⟵🔧Ch ⚡CHF 3,80
WC🔲🚿🔲. 🔲 01/01-31/12.

## ⊞S Leuk — 22G2
**Hexenplatzstrasse**. GPS: n46,31082 e7,63436.⬆➡.
4 🏕CHF 15/24h ⟵🔧Ch ⚡. **Location:** Central, noisy.
**Surface:** asphalted. 🔲 01/01-31/12.
**Distance:** 🚂400m 🚶on the spot 🚌on the spot ⊗400m 🚂400m.

## ⊞S Leukerbad 🏔🌲❄ — 22G2
**Winterstellplatz**, Parkplatz Fischweiher. GPS: n46,38215 e7,63232.⬆.

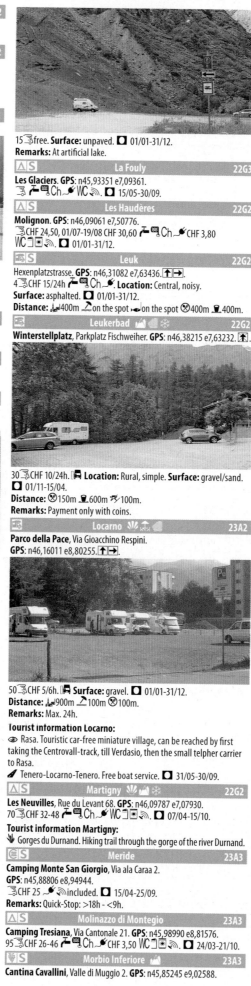

30 🏕CHF 10/24h. 🚐 **Location:** Rural, simple. **Surface:** gravel/sand.
🔲 01/11-15/04.
**Distance:** ⊗150m 🚂600m 🚡100m.
**Remarks:** Payment only with coins.

## ⊞S Locarno 🌿🏔🌲 — 23A2
**Parco della Pace**, Via Gioacchino Respini.
GPS: n46,16011 e8,80255.⬆➡.

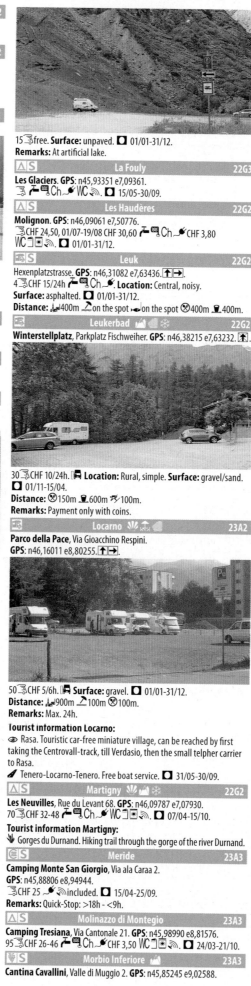

50 🏕CHF 5/6h. 🚐 **Surface:** gravel. 🔲 01/01-31/12.
**Distance:** 🚂900m 🚣100m ⊗100m.
**Remarks:** Max. 24h.

**Tourist information Locarno:**
👁 Rasa. Touristic car-free miniature village, can be reached by first taking the Centrovall-track, till Verdasio, then the small telpher carrier to Rasa.
🚢 Tenero-Locarno-Tenero. Free boat service. 🔲 31/05-30/09.

## △S Martigny 🌿🏔❄ — 22G2
**Les Neuvilles**, Rue du Levant 68. GPS: n46,09787 e7,07930.
70 🏕CHF 32-48 ⟵🔧Ch ⚡ WC 🔲🔲🚿. 🔲 07/04-15/10.

**Tourist information Martigny:**
🚶 Gorges du Durnand. Hiking trail through the gorge of the river Durnand.

## ⊞S Meride — 23A3
**Camping Monte San Giorgio**, Via ala Caraa 2.
GPS: n45,88806 e8,94944.
🏕CHF 25 ⚡🚿included. 🔲 15/04-25/09.
**Remarks:** Quick-Stop: >18h - <9h.

## △S Molinazzo di Montegio — 23A3
**Camping Tresiana**, Via Cantonale 21. GPS: n45,98990 e8,81576.
95 🏕CHF 26-46 ⟵🔧Ch ⚡CHF 3,50 WC🔲🚿🔲. 🔲 24/03-21/10.

## ⊞S Morbio Inferiore 🌲 — 23A3
**Cantina Cavallini**, Valle di Muggio 2. GPS: n45,85245 e9,02588.

1 🏕CHF 20 ⟵🔧Ch ⚡. **Location:** Rural. **Surface:** grassy.
🔲 01/01-31/12.
**Distance:** 🚂1,5km 🚡1,1km.

## ⊞S Muzzano-Lugano — 23A3
**TCS Camping Lugano-Muzzano**, Via alla Foce 14.
GPS: n45,99463 e8,90857.
🏕CHF 25 ⚡🚿included. 🔲 01/01-31/12.
**Remarks:** Quick-Stop: >18h - <9h.

## △S Reckingen — 22H2
**Camping Augenstern**, Im Ellbogen 21. GPS: n46,46500 e8,24500.
50 🏕CHF 29-35 ⟵🔧Ch ⚡ WC 🔲. 🔲 01/05-18/10 and 15/12-15/03.

## ⊞S Rivera 🏔 — 23A2
**Camper area Tamaro**, Monte Ceneri 19. GPS: n46,13926 e8,90675.⬆.

80 🏕CHF 10/2h, then 3-72h CHF 1/h ⟵🔧Ch ⚡🚿included. 🚐
**Location:** Rural. **Surface:** grassy/gravel. 🔲 01/01-31/12.
**Distance:** ⊗on the spot.
**Remarks:** Video surveillance.

## ⊞S Saas Fee 🏔🌲❄ — 22H2
**Parkplatz P4**. GPS: n46,11090 e7,93208.⬆.

50 🏕CHF 26/24h ⟵🔧Chincluded ⚡CHF 2 WC🚐.
**Location:** Rural, simple, isolated, quiet. **Surface:** grassy/gravel.
🔲 01/01-31/12 🔲 Service: winter.
**Distance:** 🚂100m ⊗200m 🚂900m 🚡200m.

## Saillon — 22G2
**Bains de Saillon**, Route du Centre Thermal 16. GPS: n46,17353 e7,19372.
12 🏕free. **Surface:** grassy.
🔲 01/01-31/12.
**Distance:** 🚶4km.
**Remarks:** Max. 48h.

**Tourist information Saillon:**
🚶 Sentier des Vitraux. Hiking trail, 45 minutes, through wine region.

## ⊞S Saint-Léonard — 22G2
**Place du Lac Souterrain**. GPS: n46,25564 e7,42600.⬆➡.

15 🏕CHF 10/night ⟵🔧Ch ⚡(4x)WCincluded.
**Location:** Rural, simple, central, quiet. **Surface:** asphalted/grassy.
🔲 01/01-31/12 🔲 service: 01/11-19/03.
**Distance:** 🚶5,5km ⊗300m.
**Remarks:** Pay in at kiosk.

**CH**

**⚏S** | Simplon 🏔 | 22H2
**Col du Simplon**, Simplonstrasse. **GPS:** n46,24944 e8,03056. ⬆.

18 ⬚free 🚰🚽ChWCfree. **Location:** Rural, simple, isolated.
**Surface:** asphalted. ⬛ 01/01-31/12.
**Distance:** ⊗200m.

**⚏S** | Sonogno | 23A2
**Camper Area Sonogno**, Cioss. **GPS:** n46,35058 e8,78846. ⬆➡.
15 ⬚€ 16/night 🚰🚽Chincluded. 🚐 **Location:** Rural, isolated,
quiet. **Surface:** grassy. ⬛ 01/01-31/12.
**Distance:** �︎200m ⊗200m 🍸200m.

**⚏S** | Stampa | 23B2
**Tankstelle Esso**, Strada Principale. **GPS:** n46,34593 e9,59660. ⬆.
8 ⬚ChCHF 8 🚰CHF 3 🚽Ch ⚡CHF 3.
**Surface:** grassy. ⬛ 01/01-31/12.
**Distance:** 🍸on the spot.
**Remarks:** Max. 24h.

**△S** | Tenero 🏔🏞 | 23A2
**Camping Tamaro**, Via Mappo 32. **GPS:** n46,17525 e8,84779.
⬚CHF 37-67 🚰🚽Ch ⚡WC 📶. ⬛ 17/03-04/11.

**△S** | Tenero 🏔🏞 | 23A2
**Lido Mappo**, Via Mappo. **GPS:** n46,17692 e8,84433.
⬚CHF 36-95 🚰🚽Ch ⚡ 📶. ⬛ 18/03-23/10.

**⚏S** | Trient 🏔 | 22F3
**Place de Repos Du Peuty**, Le Peuty. **GPS:** n46,04645 e6,99499. ⬆.

6 ⬚CHF 3/pp 🚰🚽free. **Location:** Rural, simple, isolated, quiet.
**Surface:** grassy. ⬛ 01/01-31/12.
**Distance:** ⊗1,5km 🚶on the spot.

CH

# Czech Republic

Capital: Prague
Government: parliamentary constitutional republic
Official Language: Czech
Population: 10,674,723 (2017)
Area: 78,866 km²

## General information
Dialling code: 00420
General emergency: 112
Currency: Koruna(CZK)
€ 1 = 26 CZK, 1 CZK = € 0,04
£1 = 29 CZK, 10 CZK = £0.34 (October 2018)
Credit cards are accepted almost everywhere.

### Regulations for overnight stays
Wild camping is not allowed.

### Additional public holidays 2019
May 1 Labour Day
May 8 Liberation Day
July 5 St. Cyril & St. Methodius Day
July 6 Jan Hus Day
September 28 St. Wenceslas Day
October 28 Independent Czechoslavak State Day
November 17 Freedom and Democracy Day

### Time Zone
Winter (Standard Time) GMT+1
Summer (DST)  GMT+2

Prague
Bohemia
pages: 122-123
Moravia
pages: 123-124

CZ

## Bohemia

### Adršpach  38A3
GPS: n50,61717 e16,12212.
20 CZK 400 WC. Location: Rural, isolated, quiet.
Surface: asphalted. 01/01-31/12.
Distance: on the spot on the spot.

### Aš  12E2
Camping Pod Rozhlednou, U Rozhledny. GPS: n50,23027 e12,20388.

50 € 7, 2 pers.incl. Chincluded € 2 WC. grassy.
Location: Rural. Surface: grassy. 01/01-31/12.
Distance: on the spot on the spot 200m.

### Ceský Krumlov  36A1
Camper - Ceský Krumlov, Chvalšinská 227. GPS: n48,81606 e14,30916.

15 € 15. Location: Urban, noisy. Surface: grassy/sand.
01/01-31/12.
Distance: 100m on the spot on the spot on the spot.

### Cheb  12F3
Camping Briza, Bříza 19. GPS: n50,09124 e12,28210.
40 € 13,90 (24x) € 4,20 WC. Surface: grassy.
02/04-31/10.
Distance: on the spot on the spot on the spot on the spot.

### Golčův Jeníkov  38A4
Mamolina, Římovice 9. GPS: n49,80428 e15,44581.
20 € 7,50 Chincluded € 2. Location: Rural, isolated.
Surface: unpaved. 01/01-31/12.
Distance: on the spot on the spot.

### Hluboká nad Vltavou  36A1
Camping Kostelec, Kostelec 8. GPS: n49,13863 e14,47408.

25 € 12,11, 01/07-27/08 € 24,85 Ch € 4/day WCincluded
€ 0,50 € 5,50. Surface: grassy. 29/04-07/09.
Distance: 200m on the spot on the spot on the spot on the spot.
Remarks: Bread-service.

### Hořin  12H2
Zoopark Zelčín, Zelin 1. GPS: n50,32659 e14,43623.

15 CZK 200 Ch CZK 70.
Location: Rural. Surface: grassy. 01/01-31/12.
Distance: on the spot on the spot on the spot.
Remarks: Possibility for reservation.

### Horní Planá  36A1
Jezerní penzion Lipno, Hůrka 52. GPS: n48,74140 e14,08847.
15 € 10-20 Ch WC. Location: Rural, isolated, quiet.
Surface: grassy. 01/01-31/12.
Distance: on the spot on the spot on the spot.

### Horní Planá  36A1
Caravan Camping Horní Planá, Jiráskova. GPS: n48,76086 e14,02588.
160 € 15-18 Ch WC included.
Surface: asphalted/grassy. 15/04-29/10.
Distance: on the spot on the spot on the spot 500m
600m on the spot on the spot.

### Hůrka  36A1
Jezerní penzion, Hurka 52. GPS: n48,74239 e14,08705.

30 Ch WC. Surface: grassy.
Distance: on the spot on the spot on the spot on the spot.

### Jáchymov  12F2
Loučná pod Klínovcem. GPS: n50,40686 e12,98456.
5 CZK 150 WC. Location: Rural. Surface: asphalted.
01/01-31/12.
Distance: 400m.

### Janovice N.U  17G1
Camping U Dvou Orechu, Splz 13- Strzov. GPS: n49,28137 e13,24008.

10 € 19/22 Ch WC included.
Surface: grassy/metalled. 01/05-15/09.
Distance: 3km 3km 500m on the spot on the spot.

### Janské Lázně  38A3
Parking U Lesního Domu, Krkonošská. GPS: n50,63377 e15,78522.
CZK 70 CZK 100 WC. Location: Rural, central, quiet.
Surface: asphalted. 01/01-31/12.
Distance: on the spot on the spot on the spot on the spot.
Remarks: At ski-lift.

### Karlovy Vary  12F2
U. Podjezdu 1616/5. GPS: n50,21992 e12,83688.
10 Chincluded € 2,50. Location: Urban, central.
Surface: grassy. 01/03-01/11.
Distance: 400m 1km.

### Kutná Hora  38A4
Autocamp Transit, K Malínskému Mostu 35. GPS: n49,96467 e15,30273.

40 € 10-11 WC. Location: Rural. Surface: grassy.
01/04-30/09.
Distance: 3km on the spot.
Remarks: Max. 2 nights.

### Lipno nad Vltavou  36A1
Camping Hotel Panorama, Lipno nad Vltavou 22.
GPS: n48,63869 e14,22484.

40 🛏 € 10,50-25 ⚡🔌 Ch 🚿 WC 🚽🖥 📶 included. **Location:** Rural.
**Surface:** grassy/metalled. ☐ 01/04-01/10.
**Distance:** 🏊 on the spot ⊗100m 🛒 on the spot 🚶 on the spot.
**Remarks:** Bread-service.

| 🔺S | **Loděnice** | 12H3 |
|---|---|---|

**Camp Valek**, Chrustenice 155. **GPS:** n50,01065 e14,14889.
100 🛏 € 13,80-16,48 ⚡🔌 Ch 🚿 WC 📶 included.
**Location:** Rural. **Surface:** grassy. ☐ 01/05-30/08.
**Distance:** 🏊 on the spot 🛒 on the spot 🚲 on the spot 🚶 on the spot.
**Remarks:** Bread-service.

| 🅿 | **Mariánské Lázně** | 12F3 |
|---|---|---|

Kollárova 94/26. **GPS:** n49,95800 e12,70155.⬆
20 🛏 € 0,80/h, € 12/24h. 🏠 ⚡ **Location:** Rural, quiet.
**Surface:** asphalted. ☐ 01/01-31/12.
**Distance:** 🏊 1km ⊗1km 🛒 1,2km.
**Remarks:** Monitored parking.

| 🔺S | **Mariánské Lázně** | 12F3 |
|---|---|---|

**Camping Stanowitz**, Stanoviště 9. **GPS:** n49,94404 e12,72811.

25 🛏 € 15 ⚡🔌 Ch 🚿 € 3,80 WC 🚽 included 🖥 📶.
**Location:** Rural. **Surface:** grassy. ☐ 01/04-31/10.
**Distance:** 🏊 3km ⊗on the spot 🚲 on the spot 🚶 on the spot.

| ⚓S | **Nelahozeves** | 12H2 |
|---|---|---|

**Marina Vltava**, Dvořákova stezka. **GPS:** n50,25898 e14,30230.
15 🛏 € 6 ⚡ € 2/100liter 🚿 € 2 🚽 € 2 📶. 🚿 **Surface:** grasstiles.
☐ 01/01-31/12.
**Distance:** 🏊 on the spot ⊗on the spot 🛒300m 🚲 on the spot 🚶 on the spot.

| ☘ | **Nová Bystřice** | 36A1 |
|---|---|---|

**Farma Alpaka**, Dobrá Voda čp 20. **GPS:** n49,06400 e15,10481.
10 🛏 € 8 🚿 € 4 Ch 🚿 **Location:** Rural. **Surface:** gravel.
☐ 01/01-31/12.
**Distance:** 🏊 6km 🚲 on the spot 🚶 on the spot.
**Remarks:** Bread-service.

| ☘S | **Nové Město pod Smrkem** | 38A3 |
|---|---|---|

**Ludvikov Horses&Holiday**, Ludvikov pod Smrkem 9.
**GPS:** n50,91579 e15,20486.⬆
15 🛏 CZK 400, 2 pers. incl ⚡🔌 Ch 🚿 included WC 🚽 CZK 100/50
📶. **Location:** Rural. **Surface:** grassy. ☐ 01/01-31/12.
**Distance:** 🏊 on the spot 🚶 on the spot 🏇10km.
**Remarks:** Dutch owners, breakfast-service.

| 🅿S | **Prague** 🌅⛴🍲 | 38A4 |
|---|---|---|

**AutoCamp Trojská**, Trojská 375/157.
**GPS:** n50,11718 e14,42765.

8 🛏 € 17-20 ⚡🔌 Ch 🚿 € 4 WC 🚽🖥 📶. **Location:** Rural.
**Surface:** grassy. ☐ 01/01-31/12.
**Distance:** 🏊 centre 4km 🚲 on the spot.

| ⬛S | **Prague** 🌅⛴🍲 | 38A4 |
|---|---|---|

**Nonstop Parking Praha**, Izraelská 6.
**GPS:** n50,07942 e14,48245.⬆.

50 🛏 € 18 ⚡ € 1/day 🚿 € 6 🚿 € 5/day WC 📶 included. 🚌
**Location:** Urban. **Surface:** grassy/gravel. ☐ 01/01-31/12.
**Distance:** 🏊 100m 🚲 5km 🛒 150m 🛒1,2km 🚲 100m.
**Remarks:** 24/24 surveillance.

| 🔺S | **Prague** 🌅⛴🍲 | 38A4 |
|---|---|---|

**Camp Drusus**, K Řeporyjím 4.
**GPS:** n50,04357 e14,28455.
70 🛏 € 16-20 ⚡🔌 Ch 🚿 WC 🚽🖥 📶 included.
**Location:** Rural. **Surface:** grassy. ☐ 01/04-05/10.
**Distance:** 🚲 100m 🚲 on the spot 🚶 on the spot.
**Remarks:** Bread-service.

| 🔺S | **Prague** 🌅⛴🍲 | 38A4 |
|---|---|---|

**Camp Herzog**, Trojská 602/161. **GPS:** n50,11719 e14,42717.
20 🛏 € 14 ⚡🔌 Ch 🚿 € 3,50 WC 🚽🖥 📶 included.
**Location:** Urban. **Surface:** grassy.
☐ 01/01-31/12.
**Distance:** 🚲 4,2km 🚲 500m.

| 🔺S | **Prague** 🌅⛴🍲 | 38A4 |
|---|---|---|

**Caravan Camping Císařská Louka**, Císařská louka 16.
**GPS:** n50,05584 e14,41336.⬆
40 🛏 € 16,50 ⚡🔌 Ch 🚿 WC € 3,50 🖥 included. **Location:** Urban,
noisy. **Surface:** grassy. ☐ 01/01-31/12.
**Distance:** 🚲 4km 🚲 750m on the spot.
**Remarks:** Bread-service.

| 🔺S | **Prague** 🌅⛴🍲 | 38A4 |
|---|---|---|

**Dana Troja**, Trojská 357/129. **GPS:** n50,11716 e14,43176.⬆
15 🛏 € 19 ⚡🔌 Ch 🚿 € 3 WC 🚽🖥 € 2,50 📶 included.
**Location:** Urban, comfortable. **Surface:** grassy.
☐ 01/01-31/12.
**Distance:** 🚲 4km 🚲 200m.

| 🔺S | **Protivín** | 17H1 |
|---|---|---|

**Camping U Serifa**, Chelčického 889/2. **GPS:** n49,19046 e14,22004.

38 🛏 € 9 ⚡ € 3 WC 🚽. **Location:** Rural, quiet. **Surface:** grassy.
☐ 01/04-15/09.
**Distance:** 🚲 300m 🏊 on the spot 🚲 on the spot 🛒 400m
🚲 on the spot 🚶 on the spot.

| 🅿 | **Rokytnice nad Jizerou** 🏔❄ | 38A3 |
|---|---|---|

**P1**, Horní Rokytnice. **GPS:** n50,73686 e15,47618.⬆
🛏. **Location:** Central, quiet. **Surface:** gravel.
☐ 01/01-31/12.
**Distance:** 🚲 on the spot ⊗on the spot 🏇on the spot 🎿 on the spot.
**Remarks:** At ski-lift.

| 🅿S | **Sněžník** | 12H1 |
|---|---|---|

**Stellplatz Sněžník**, Jílové. **GPS:** n50,79647 e14,08425.⬆

15 🛏 € 5/5h, then € 0,60/h ⚡ € 0,10/10liter 🚿 Ch 🚿 € 0,60/kWh.
**Location:** Rural, comfortable, quiet. **Surface:** gravel.

☐ 01/01-31/12.
**Distance:** ⊗50m 🚲 on the spot 🚶 on the spot.

| 🅿S | **Svitavy** | 38A4 |
|---|---|---|

**U Stadion**, U stadion 17/937. **GPS:** n49,75146 e16,46521.⬆.
6 🛏 free ⚡🔌 Ch free 🚿 € 0,25/kWh. **Location:** Urban.
**Surface:** metalled. ☐ 01/01-31/12.
**Distance:** 🚲 1km ⊗on the spot.
**Remarks:** At stadium.

| 🏨S | **Svoboda nad Úpou** 🏔❄ | 38A3 |
|---|---|---|

**Pension Riegel**, Maršovská 12. **GPS:** n50,63765 e15,81264.⬆
4 🛏 € 10 ⚡🔌 Ch 🚿. **Location:** Noisy. ☐ 01/01-31/12.

| 🔺S | **Třeboň** | 36A1 |
|---|---|---|

**Autocamp Třeboň**, Domanín 285. **GPS:** n48,99287 e14,76675.

100 🛏 € 13,20 🚿 WC 🚽 📶. **Location:** Rural. **Surface:** grassy.
☐ 28/04-01/10.
**Distance:** 🚲 200m 🏊 on the spot 🚣 on the spot ⊗on the spot 🚲 on
the spot 🚶 on the spot.

| 🅿S | **Velemín** | 12H2 |
|---|---|---|

**Finaso**, Velemin 198. **GPS:** n50,53639 e13,97333.⬆.

6 🛏 free ⚡🔌 Ch free 🚿 € 0,50/kWh. **Location:** Simple, noisy.
**Surface:** metalled. ☐ 01/01-31/12.
**Remarks:** At motorhome dealer.

| 🅿S | **Velká Jesenice** | 38A4 |
|---|---|---|

**Stellplatz Rozkoš**, Vodní nádrž Rozkoš . **GPS:** n50,36444 e16,05944.⬆.

16 🛏 € 11 ⚡🔌 Ch 🚿 📶 included. 🏠 **Location:** Rural.
**Surface:** grassy. ☐ 01/01-31/12.
**Distance:** 🏊 on the spot 🚣 on the spot.

| ☘S | **Velké Přílepy** | 12H2 |
|---|---|---|

**The Dragon Valley**, Okoř 3. **GPS:** n50,16132 e14,25834.⬆.
6 🛏 € 15 ⚡🔌 Ch 🚿 WC 🚽 included. **Location:** Rural.
**Surface:** grassy. ☐ 01/01-31/12.
**Distance:** 🚲 Prague 20km ⊗on the spot 🚲 on the spot 🚲 on the spot
🚶 on the spot.
**Remarks:** Bread-service, video surveillance.

# Moravia

| 🔺S | **Břeclav** | 36C1 |
|---|---|---|

**Autokemp Apollo**, Slovácká 722/4. **GPS:** n48,78583 e16,82620.

70 🛏 € 15 🚿 WC 🚽 📶 included. **Location:** Rural. **Surface:** grassy.

CZ

**◻** 01/05-30/09.

**Distance:** ⟋on the spot ⤙on the spot ⊗on the spot 🏍on the spot 🚶on the spot.

**Remarks:** Bread-service.

---

**△S** **Bystrice nad Pernstejnem** 🏔 | 38A4

**Autocamp Na Kopci. GPS:** n49,54522 e16,29192.⬆.
🛏CZK 130-180 + CZK 95/pp ⛽🗑Ch ✎WC🗑🔌🖥.🏠
**Location:** Isolated, quiet. **Surface:** grassy. **◻** 01/01-31/12.
**Distance:** 🏍on the spot 🚶on the spot.
**Remarks:** Dutch owners, possibility for reservation.

---

**△S** **Červená Řečice** | 38A4

**Camping Kovarna**, Červená Řečice 63. **GPS:** n49,51922 e15,15661.⬆.
39 🛏CZK 270, 01/07-31/08 CZK 345 ⛽🗑Ch ✎€ 3,75
WC🗑🖥included. **Location:** Rural, simple, isolated. **Surface:** grassy.
**◻** 01/06-26/08.
**Distance:** ⟋on the spot ⊗5km 🎣2km 🚲on the spot 🚶on the spot.
**Remarks:** Bread-service.

---

**△S** **Řásná** | 38A4

**Camp Velkopařezitý**, Řásná 10. **GPS:** n49,22792 e15,38426.
🛏€ 9,70 ✎€ 3 WC🗑€ 1/5minutes.
**Location:** Rural. **Surface:** grassy.
**Distance:** 🎣1km ⟋200m ⟋200m ⊗100m 🚲on the spot
🚶on the spot.

---

**△** **Uherský Brod** | 38B4

**Aquapark Delfin**, Slovácké náměstí 2377.
**GPS:** n49,01960 e17,64828.⬆.
2 🛏free. **Location:** Urban. **Surface:** metalled. **◻** 01/01-31/12.
**Distance:** ⊗100m 🎣150m.

---

**△S** **Veverská Bítýška** | 38A4

**Hana Camping**, Dlouhá 135. **GPS:** n49,27593 e16,45353.⬆.
55 🛏CZK 220 + CZK 90/pp ✎WC🗑🔌🖥.🏠 **Surface:** grassy.
**◻** 30/04-30/09.
**Distance:** 🎣1km.

---

**△S** **Žďár nad Sázavou** | 38A4

**Autokempink Pilák. GPS:** n49,59077 e15,92072.

🛏€ 10 ✎WC🗑€ 0,80. **Location:** Rural, quiet. **Surface:** grassy.
**◻** 01/05-30/09.
**Distance:** ⟋on the spot ⤙on the spot ⊗on the spot 🏍on the spot
🚶on the spot.

CZ

# Germany

Capital: Berlin
Government: Federal republic
Official Language: Germany
Population: 82,800,000 (2017)
Area: 357,121 km²

## General information
Dialling code: 0049
General emergency: 112
Currency: Euro

## Regulations for overnight stays
Overnight stays on the public highway are
allowed, if there is no local prohibition, but no
"camping" activities are allowed.

## Additional public holidays 2019
January 6 Epiphany
April 19 Good Friday
April 22 Easter Monday
May 1 Labor Day
June 10 White Monday
June 20 Corpus Christi
August 15 Assumption of the Virgin Mary
October 3 Day of German Unity
November 1 All Saints' Day

## Time Zone
Winter (Standard Time) GMT+1
Summer (DST) GMT+2

Schleswig-Holstein/
Hamburg
pages: 125-137

Hamburg

Mecklenburg-Western Pomerania
pages: 170-179

Bremen

Lower Saxony/Bremen
pages: 137-170

Brandenburg/Berlin
pages: 184-190

Berlin

Saxony Anhalt
pages: 179-184

North Rhine Westphalia
pages: 194-217

Cologne

Hesse
pages:
246-258

Thuringia
pages:
259-263

Saxony
pages:
191-193

Dresden

Rhineland-Palatinate/
Saarland
pages: 217-246

Frankfurt

Nürnberg

Bavaria
pages: 287-316

Stuttgart

Baden Württemberg
pages: 264-287

Munich

DE

---

# Schleswig-Holstein/
# Hamburg

### Achtrup — 6C3

**Landgasthof Achtruper Stuben**, Ladelunderstrasse 24.
**GPS:** n54,79337 e9,02676.

3 🚐 free 🔌💧 free. **Location:** Simple.
📅 01/01-31/12 Mo-Tue.
**Distance:** 🛒5km ⊗on the spot 🍴5km on the spot 🚶on the spot.
**Remarks:** Along through road, max. 72h, free, use of a meal obligated.

### Albersdorf — 8A1

**Freitzeitbad Albersdorf**, Weg zur Badeanstalt 18.
**GPS:** n54,15135 e9,28055. ⬆➡.

6 🚐 € 15 swimming pool incl 🔌💧Ch 🚿(6x)⤵included.
**Location:** Rural, simple, isolated, quiet. **Surface:** grassy.
📅 01/05-31/08.
**Distance:** 🛒1km ⊗100m 🍴300m 🛁on the spot 🚶on the spot.

---

**Remarks:** Parking at swimming pool, max. 3 days.

### Altenhof — 6D3

**Wohnmobilpark Ostsee 'Grüner Jäger'**, Grünen Jäger.
**GPS:** n54,44392 e9,90526. ⬆➡.

80 🚐 € 10 💧🔌Chincluded 🚿(40x)€ 4/24h WC⤵€ 1 🧺.
**Location:** Rural, simple, isolated, quiet. **Surface:** grassy.
📅 01/01-31/12.
**Distance:** 🛒Eckernförde 6km ⛱2km ⊗50m 🍴6km 🚌200m
busstop -> Kiel 🛁on the spot 🚶on the spot.
**Remarks:** Check in at restaurant Grüner, bread-service.

### Aukrug — 8B1

**Parkplatz am Freibad**, Zum Sportplatz 1.
**GPS:** n54,07441 e9,79160. ⬆➡.

10 🚐 € 8 🔌💧Ch 🚿(10x)WC⤵included. **Location:** Rural.
**Surface:** grassy/metalled. 📅 01/01-31/12.
**Distance:** 🛒1km ⊗800m 🍴1km 🛁on the spot 🚶on the spot.
**Remarks:** Max. 5 days, check in and key service at pay-desk of

---

swimming pool.

### Aventoft — 6C3

**Wohnmobillstellplatz Zu den Fuchswiesen**, Revtoftweg 1.
**GPS:** n54,87661 e8,84562. ⬆.

15 🚐 € 5 🔌💧Chincluded 🚿€ 1,50/24h. 🛁
**Location:** Rural, simple, isolated, quiet. **Surface:** asphalted/grassy.
📅 01/01-31/12.
**Distance:** 🛒3km ⊗3km 🍴3km 🛁on the spot.
**Remarks:** Bread-service.

### Bad Bramstedt — 8B1

**Parkplatz P7, Am Bahnhof**, König Christian Strasse.
**GPS:** n53,92167 e9,88967. ⬆➡.

5 🚐 free. **Location:** Urban, simple, central, noisy. **Surface:** metalled.
📅 01/01-31/12.
**Distance:** 🛒centre 500m ⊗100m 🍴500m 🚌on the spot.
**Remarks:** At station, max. 1 night, service at camping Roland,
Kielerstrasse.

## Bad Malente 6E3

**Parkplatz Krützen**, Sebastian-Kneipp-Straße.
**GPS**: n54,17198 e10,54919. ⬆.

4 🛏 € 5 + € 2/pp tourist tax 🚰 € 1 ⚡ € 1 Ch. 🚽
**Location**: Rural, simple, quiet. **Surface**: metalled.
◻ 01/01-31/12.
**Distance**: 🛒 on the spot ⊗ 500m 🚉 1km.
**Remarks**: Max. 24h.

## Bad Oldesloe 8B1

**Wohnmobilplatz Exer**, Am Bürgerpark.
**GPS**: n53,81101 e10,36915. ⬆➡.

8 🛏 free 🚰 € 1/10minutes ⚡Ch 🔧 (8x)€ 2/10h WC 🚽.
**Location**: Urban, simple, quiet. **Surface**: metalled.
◻ 01/01-31/12.
**Distance**: 🛒 on the spot 🚲 3km ⊗ on the spot 🚉 400m.
**Remarks**: Max. 3 nights, bread-service.

## Bad Schwartau 8C1

**Landschaftsschutzgebiet Riesebusch. GPS**: n53,92405 e10,69795.
15 🛏 € 5/24h, tourist tax € 1,65/pp 🚰 € 1/90liter ⚡Ch 🔧 € 1/8h. 🚽
**Location**: Urban, simple. **Surface**: asphalted.
◻ 01/01-31/12.
**Distance**: 🛒 1,5km ⊗ 1,5km.
**Remarks**: Max. 72h.

## Bad Segeberg 8B1

**Kalkbergblick**, Kastanienweg 1b. **GPS**: n53,93872 e10,31423. ⬆➡.

25 🛏 € 8 🚰 ⚡Ch included 🔧 (15x)€ 2/12h,6Amp. 🚽
**Location**: Rural, comfortable, isolated, quiet. **Surface**: gravel.
◻ 01/01-31/12.
**Distance**: 🛒 500m 🚲 A7 3km ⛱ 600m Segerberger See 🚏 600m
⊗ 500m 🚉 500m 🛒 on the spot 🚶 on the spot.
**Remarks**: Jun/Aug Karl May Spiele, open air theater.

## Barkenholm 6C3

**Gaststätte Jägerstuben**, Dorfstraße 28. **GPS**: n54,23497 e9,17484. ⬆.

6 🛏 € 5, free with a meal 🚰 free 🔧 € 1/day. 🚽
**Location**: Rural, simple, isolated, quiet. **Surface**: grasstiles.
◻ 01/01-31/12 ⬤ Wed.
**Distance**: 🛒 8km ⊗ on the spot.
**Remarks**: Wifi at restaurant.

## Barmstedt 8B1

**Parkplatz am Rondeel**, Platz Roissy-en-Brie.
**GPS**: n53,78640 e9,76420. ⬆.

5 🛏 € 5 🚰 ⚡Ch 🔧 WC 🚽 included.
**Location**: Urban, simple. **Surface**: metalled. ◻ 01/01-31/12.
**Distance**: 🛒 on the spot ⊗ 50m 🚉 500m 🚏 on the spot
🚲 on the spot.
**Remarks**: To be paid at swimming pool, key electricity at pool.

## Behrensdorf 6E3

**Campingpark Waldesruh**, Neuland. **GPS**: n54,35754 e10,60216. ⬆.

23 🛏 € 11-13, 2 pers. incl., dog € 1,50 🚰 ⚡Ch 🔧 € 0,40/kWh
WC 🚽. **Location**: Rural, comfortable, isolated. **Surface**: grassy.
◻ 01/04-31/10.
**Distance**: 🛒 2km ⛱ 300m 🚏 on the spot ⊗ on the spot
🛒 on the spot.
**Remarks**: Dog € 1,50/night.

## Blekendorf 6E3

**Am Sehlendorfer Strand**, Strandstrasse 24.
**GPS**: n54,30571 e10,69358. ⬆.

42 🛏 € 10,50-16,50 🚰 € 1 ⚡ € 1 Ch € 1 WC included 🚽 € 1 📷 🚗 📷
**Location**: Rural, comfortable, isolated. **Surface**: grassy.
◻ 01/04-31/10.
**Distance**: 🛒 1km ⛱ on the spot 🚏 on the spot ⊗ on the spot 🚉 5km
🛒 on the spot.
**Remarks**: At the beach.

## Bordesholm 8B1

**Festplatz**, Kielerstrasse. **GPS**: n54,18389 e10,02667. ⬆.

6 🛏 free. **Location**: Rural, simple, quiet. **Surface**: grassy/sand.
◻ 01/01-31/12.
**Distance**: 🛒 1,5km 🚲 4km ⊗ 1,2km 🚉 700m.
**Remarks**: Max. 18h, service at petrol station.

## Bordesholm 8B1

**Shell tankstelle**, Bahnofstrasse 78. **GPS**: n54,17343 e10,03497.
🚰 ⚡Ch 🔧. ◻ 01/01-31/12.

## Borgdorf-Seedorf 6D3

**Seecampingplatz BUM**, Hauptstrasse 99.
**GPS**: n54,18256 e9,88422. ⬆.

12 🛏 € 13,50 🚰 ⚡Ch 🔧 € 3,50. **Surface**: grassy. ◻ 01/01-31/12.
**Distance**: 🛒 3km ⛱ on the spot 🚏 on the spot.

## Bosau 8B1

**Dat Gröne Huus**, Stadtbeker Strasse 97. **GPS**: n54,09198 e10,42886. ⬆.

3 🛏 € 5 🔧 € 3,50 WC 🚽. 🚽 **Location**: Rural, simple, quiet.
**Surface**: gravel. ◻ 01/04-30/11.
**Distance**: 🛒 100m ⛱ Großer Plöner See 🚏 on the spot ⊗ on the spot
🚉 1km 🚲 on the spot.
**Remarks**: Bread-service.

## Bösdorf 8B1

**Wohnmobilcamp Augustfelde**, Vierer See, Augustfelde.
**GPS**: n54,12898 e10,45506. ⬆➡.

16 🛏 € 11,50-13,50 🚰 ⚡Ch 🔧 (16x)WC included 🚽 € 0,75. 🚽
**Location**: Rural. **Surface**: grassy. ◻ 01/04-25/10.
**Distance**: ⛱ on the spot 🚏 on the spot ⊗ 50m 🚉 on the spot.

## Bösdorf 8B1

**Landhaus zur Tenne**, Hörn 6. **GPS**: n54,12792 e10,50194.
10 🛏 € 6 🚰 ⚡Ch included 🔧 € 2/day. **Surface**: grassy/gravel.
◻ 01/01-31/12.
**Distance**: 🚲 on the spot 🚶 on the spot.

## Bösdorf 8B1

**Campingpark Gut Ruhleben**, Missionsweg 2, Ruhleben.
**GPS**: n54,14308 e10,45021.

10 🛏 € 11-13 🚰 ⚡Ch 🔧 € 2,50 🚽 included. 🚽
**Location**: Rural, simple. **Surface**: grassy/gravel. ◻ 01/04-30/09.
**Distance**: ⛱ on the spot 🚉 1,2km 🚲 on the spot 🚶 on the spot.
**Remarks**: At lake, max. 3 nights.

## Bredstedt 6C3

**Süderstraße. GPS**: n54,61307 e8,97082. ⬆➡.

15 free. **Location:** Rural, simple, quiet. **Surface:** asphalted.

01/01-31/12.

**Distance:** 900m 800m Aldi 650m 1,2km.

**Remarks:** Nearby sports complex, nearby swimming pool.

## Brodersby 6D3

**Ferienhof Lassen**, Gross Brodersbyer Weg 5.
**GPS:** n54,53850 e9,71402.

2 € 10 Ch (1x),16Amp included.
**Location:** Rural, simple, quiet. **Surface:** grassy. 01/01-31/12.
**Distance:** 500m 2km 500m.

## Brokdorf 8A1

**Stellplatz Brokdorf**, Dorfstrasse 53. **GPS:** n53,86417 e9,31667.

30 € 5, 01/03-31/10 € 10 € 1/70liter € 1 Ch (30x)€ 0,50/kWh WCincluded € 1. **Location:** Rural, comfortable.
**Surface:** metalled. 01/01-31/12.
**Distance:** 800m 400m on the spot 500m on the spot on the spot.
**Remarks:** Max. 3 days.

## Brunsbüttel 8A1

**An der Braake**, Am Freizeitbad. **GPS:** n53,89832 e9,13138.

12 € 8 € 2 Ch € 1/kWh € 2,50.
**Location:** Rural, comfortable, central, quiet. **Surface:** grassy/metalled.
01/01-31/12.
**Distance:** 500m 500m 500m on the spot.
**Remarks:** To pay at swimming pool.

## Büdelsdorf 6D3

**Hermann-Ehlers-Platz**, Agnes Miegel Strasse.
**GPS:** n54,31583 e9,69306.

10 free. **Location:** Urban, simple, central. **Surface:** metalled.
01/01-31/12.
**Distance:** on the spot 1km 1,5km.
**Remarks:** Max. 1 night.

## Busdorf 6D3

**Autohof Wikingerland**, Wittgenstein 2. **GPS:** n54,47736 e9,54454.

---

6 free € 1/80liter € 1/time Ch € 1/time (6x) WC.
**Location:** Rural, simple, noisy. **Surface:** asphalted.
01/01-31/12.
**Distance:** on the spot on the spot.
**Remarks:** At petrol station, special part for motor homes.

## Büsum 7H1

**Wohnmobilstellplatz Nordsee**, Dr. Martin Bahr Strasse.
**GPS:** n54,12889 e8,86889.

100 € 13, 01/03-31/10 € 15 € 0,50/50liter Ch (100x) included WC € 0,50 € 1/4minutes € 0,50/day.
**Location:** Rural, comfortable, isolated, quiet. **Surface:** grassy.
01/01-31/12.
**Distance:** 1km 500m 300m on the spot on the spot.
**Remarks:** Key shower at Imbiss.

## Damp 6D3

**Wohnmobilpark Damp**, Parkstrasse 2.
**GPS:** n54,57742 e10,01572.

80 € 13 + € 1/pp tourist tax € 0,10/10liter Ch (60x)€ 0,60/kWh,6Amp WC € 1/4minutes included.
**Location:** Rural, comfortable, quiet. **Surface:** grassy/gravel.
01/01-31/12.
**Distance:** 600m 500m 500m 500m 150m on the spot.

## Drelsdorf 6C3

**Drelsdörper Krog**, Dorfstrasse 23. **GPS:** n54,60555 e9,03555.

10 € 7, guests free € 2 WC.
**Location:** Rural, simple, isolated, central, quiet, noisy. **Surface:** grassy.
01/01-31/12.
**Distance:** 200m on the spot 2km.
**Remarks:** Along through road.

## Eckernförde 6D3

**Wohnmobilstellplatz am Noor**, Kakabellenweg.
**GPS:** n54,46443 e9,83402.

---

49 € 14 excl. tourist tax € 1/100liter Ch € 0,50/kWh WC € 2/2 included. **Location:** Urban, comfortable, central, quiet. **Surface:** grassy. 01/01-31/12.
**Distance:** 1km on the spot on the spot 500m on the spot on the spot on the spot.

## Elmshorn 8A1

**Stellplatz Elmshorn**, Nordufer. **GPS:** n53,75157 e9,65268.

4 free € 1/80liter ChWC.
**Location:** Urban, simple, central, quiet. **Surface:** metalled.
01/01-31/12 last week of Aug.
**Distance:** 800m on the spot on the spot on the spot.

## Emmelsbüll-Horsbüll 6C3

**Stellplatz am Badedeich**, Südwesthörner Strasse.
**GPS:** n54,79686 e8,66075.

3 free € 1. **Location:** Rural, simple, isolated, quiet.
**Surface:** grassy/gravel. 01/01-31/12.
**Distance:** on the spot on the spot.
**Remarks:** Max. 5 days.

## Eutin 8C1

**Reisemobilpark Eutiner See**, Oldenburger Landstraße 21.
**GPS:** n54,13378 e10,62919.

24 € 16 € 1/100liter Ch € 0,50/kWh WC € 1 included. **Location:** Rural. 01/01-31/12.
**Distance:** 1km 1km 250m on the spot on the spot.
**Remarks:** Max 3,5t.

## Eutin 8C1

Elisabethstrasse. **GPS:** n54,13507 e10,60935.

3 free. **Location:** Urban, simple. **Surface:** asphalted.
01/01-31/12.
**Distance:** on the spot 300m.
**Remarks:** Parking at station.

## Eutin 8C1

**Forsthaus am Ukleisee**, Zum Ukleisee 23, Sielbeck.
**GPS:** n54,18181 e10,64137.
€ 5. **Surface:** grassy/gravel. 01/01-31/12.

## Fehmarn 6E3

**Wohnmobilpark Wulfener Hals**, Wulfener-Hals-Weg 16, Wulfen.
**GPS:** n54,40687 e11,17489.

100 ⏚from € 12,90-49 ⛽⛽Chincluded ⚡€ 4,20 WC⛽€ 0,90 ⊡⛽🏠 **Location:** Rural, luxurious. **Surface:** grassy.
⬛ 01/01-31/12.
**Distance:** ⛱on the spot ⊗on the spot.
**Remarks:** Pay at reception, bike/car rental, golf court.

**Hintz-Heizungsbau**, Landkirchenerweg 1b, Burg.
**GPS:** n54,44228 e11,18967.⬆.

16 ⏚€ 10 ⛽€ 1 ⛽Ch ⚡(16x)€ 5. **Location:** Simple, quiet.
**Surface:** metalled. ⬛ 01/01-31/12.
**Distance:** ⛽on the spot.

**Parkplatz Ost**, Osterstrasse, Burg. **GPS:** n54,43754 e11,19990.⬆.

30 ⏚€ 8 (21-8h). 🏠 **Location:** Urban, simple. **Surface:** metalled.
⬛ 01/01-31/12.
**Distance:** ⛽100m.

**Kommunal- und Yachthafen Burgstaaken**, Burgstaaken/Am Binnensee. **GPS:** n54,42028 e11,19224.⬆.

15 ⏚€ 10 21-08h. 🏠 **Location:** Rural, simple. **Surface:** metalled.
⬛ 01/01-31/12.
**Distance:** ⊗100m ⛱100m.

**Ferienhof Wachtelberg. GPS:** n54,44653 e11,26039.
4 ⏚€ 13, 2 pers.incl, extra pers € 5 ⛽⚡WC⛽included.
**Location:** Rural, simple, isolated, quiet. **Surface:** grassy.
⬛ 01/01-31/12.
**Distance:** ⛱1km.

**Camping Strukkamphuk**, Strukkamp. **GPS:** n54,41239 e11,10223.⬆.

---

21 ⏚€ 14,50-31 ⛽⛽Ch ⚡WC⛽included. ⛽
**Location:** Rural, simple. **Surface:** grassy. ⬛ 01/01-31/12.
**Distance:** ⊗10m.

Am Industriehafen, dir Flensburg Mürwick.
**GPS:** n54,80430 e9,44334.⬆⬆⬅.

12 ⏚free. **Location:** Urban, simple, isolated, quiet. **Surface:** gravel.
⬛ 01/01-31/12.
**Distance:** ⛽1,5km ⛱on the spot ⛽on the spot.
**Remarks:** Max. 1 night.

**Am Freibad**, Grosse Rheie 17a. **GPS:** n54,30187 e9,60456.⬆.

3 ⏚free ⛽Chfree WC⛽. **Location:** Rural, simple, isolated, quiet.
**Surface:** grassy/gravel. ⬛ 01/04-31/10.
**Distance:** ⛽800m ⊗800m ⛱800m ⛽on the spot ⛷on the spot.
**Remarks:** Parking swimming pool, max. 24h.

**P2**, Nordseestrasse. **GPS:** n54,03272 e8,84833.⬆➡.

40 ⏚€ 10/24h ⛽⛽Chincluded. 🏠
**Location:** Rural, comfortable, isolated, quiet.
**Surface:** asphalted/grassy. ⬛ 01/03-31/10.
**Distance:** ⛽1km ⛱550m ⊗800m ⛷on the spot.
**Remarks:** Bread-service.

**Friedrichstädter Wohnmobilstellplatz**, Halbmond 5.
**GPS:** n54,37256 e9,08868.⬆.

65 ⏚€ 13 ⛽€ 0,10/10liter ⛽Ch ⚡€ 0,60/kWh WCfree ⛽€ 1
⊡€ 3,50/3,50 ⛽included. 🏠 **Location:** Rural, luxurious.
**Surface:** grassy/gravel. ⬛ 01/01-31/12.

---

**Distance:** ⛽300m ⛽on the spot ⊗300m.

**Alter Schiffsanleger 777**, Elbuferstrasse.
**GPS:** n53,42574 e10,37907.⬆.

8 ⏚€ 7 ⛽€ 1/100liter ⛽Ch ⚡(12x)€ 0,50/kWh. ⛽
**Location:** Rural, simple. **Surface:** grasstiles/metalled.
⬛ 01/01-31/12.
**Distance:** ⛽1,5km ⛱on the spot ⛽on the spot ⊗1,5km ⛽2km
⛽on the spot ⛷on the spot ⛽on the spot.
**Remarks:** Along the river Elbe, max. 3 days.

**Yachthafen Gelting-Wackerballig**, Strandweg, Wackerballig.
**GPS:** n54,75564 e9,87842.⬆.

12 ⏚€ 8 ⛽€ 0,10/10liter ⛽Ch ⚡€ 1,50/night WC⛽€ 0,50. 🏠
**Location:** Rural, simple, quiet. **Surface:** grassy/gravel.
⬛ 01/04-31/10.
**Distance:** ⛽1,5km ⛽on the spot ⊗on the spot ⛽2km
⛷on the spot.
**Remarks:** Key sanitary building/waste dump at harbour master, caution € 20.

**Park & Ride platz**, Pentzstrasse. **GPS:** n53,78776 e9,43145. ⬆⬆.

10 ⏚free. **Location:** Urban, simple. **Surface:** asphalted.
⬛ 01/01-31/12.
**Distance:** ⛽900m ⛽200m ⛷on the spot ⛷on the spot.

**Am Außenhafen**, Am Hafen. **GPS:** n53,78560 e9,41088.⬆➡.

16 ⏚€ 10. **Location:** Rural, comfortable. **Surface:** metalled.
⬛ 01/01-31/12 ⬛ high water.
**Distance:** ⛽1km ⛱on the spot ⛽on the spot ⊗on the spot
⛷on the spot ⛷on the spot.
**Remarks:** Along the river Elbe, money in envelope in mail box.

**WSG Arin/Grödersby**, Friedenshöher Straße 21.
**GPS:** n54,63444 e9,92944.⬆.

20 🛏 € 15 🚐⚡Ch🚿WC🚽💧€ 3/2 📶included. 🚲
**Location:** Rural, simple, quiet. **Surface:** gravel/metalled.
📅 01/05-30/09.
**Distance:** 🚂200m 🛒on the spot 🍴on the spot ⊗200m 🏊on the spot 🚌on the spot.
**Remarks:** Bicycle rental.

🏕️S | **Grömitz** | 6E3
**Großraumparkplatz**, Gildestraße 14. **GPS:** n54,14490 e10,95262.⬆️➡️

60 🛏 € 15, 01/11-14/03 € 6 🚐€ 0,50 Ch🚿(20x)€ 1/kWh. 💧
**Location:** Rural, simple. **Surface:** metalled.
📅 01/01-31/12 💧 water disconnected in winter.
**Distance:** 🏊200m 🛒on the spot ⊗200m 🚌500m.

🏕️S | **Grömitz** | 6E3
**Wohnmobilstellplatz am Lensterstrand**, Blankwasserweg.
**GPS:** n54,15650 e10,99134.⬆️

50 🛏free, 15/03-31/10 € 10 WC. 💧 **Location:** Rural. **Surface:** grassy.
📅 01/01-31/12 💧 water disconnected in winter.
**Distance:** 🏊on the spot 🍴on the spot.
**Remarks:** Max. 24h.

🏵️S | **Grömitz** | 6E3
**Wohnmobilplatz Kattenberg**, Kattenberg 8, Cismar.
**GPS:** n54,18637 e10,96541.

5 🛏 € 8 🚐Ch🚿(5x)€ 2 WCincluded. **Surface:** grassy.
📅 01/04-31/10.
**Distance:** 🚂2km 🚲7km 🏊5km 🍴5km ⊗5km 🚌6km 🏊on the spot 🍴on the spot.

🏰 | **Großenaspe** 🌳 | 8B1
**Wildpark Eekholt**, Eekhol 1. **GPS:** n53,94819 e10,02916.⬆️

10 🛏free. **Location:** Rural, simple, isolated, quiet.

---

**Surface:** grassy/sand. 📅 01/01-31/12.
**Distance:** 🚲4km Grossenaspe ⊗Kiek ut Stuben, Game preserve 🚌> Wildpark.

🏕️S | **Großenbrode** | 6E3
**Wassersportzentrum**, Am Kai 29. **GPS:** n54,35583 e11,07798.⬆️➡️

50 🛏 € 10-12 🚐€ 0,50/100liter Ch🚿€ 1/kWh WC🚽€ 0,50 📶.
🚲 **Location:** Rural. **Surface:** grassy/metalled. 📅 01/01-31/12.
**Distance:** 🏊300m 🍴on the spot 🚌2km.

⚓S | **Großenbrode** | 6E3
**Wohnmobilhafen Reise**, Südstrand 1.
**GPS:** n54,36170 e11,08567.⬆️➡️

46 🛏 € 12-16 🚐€ 0,50/150liter Ch🚿(46x),6Amp WC🚽included 💧€ 3/2 📶€ 0,50/day 💳. **Location:** Rural, comfortable.
**Surface:** grassy/gravel. 📅 01/01-31/12.
**Distance:** 🚲1,8km 🏊300m 🛒300m ⊗100m 🚌30m 🚌100m 🏊on the spot 🍴on the spot.
**Remarks:** Bread-service.

🏕️S | **Großsolt** 🍴 | 6D3
**Stellplatz Mühlenbrück**, Flensburger strasse, Mühlenbrück.
**GPS:** n54,70853 e9,52243.⬆️

13 🛏 € 10 🚐⚡Ch🚿(13x)€ 2/day WC🚽€ 0,50. 🚲
**Location:** Rural, comfortable, quiet. **Surface:** gravel.
📅 01/03-01/10.
**Distance:** 🚌200m.

🏕️S | **Hamburg** 🌊⚓🍴📶 | 8B2
**Elbepark-Bunthaus**, Moorwerder Hauptdeich 33.
**GPS:** n53,46194 e10,06265.⬆️

80 🛏 € 13-18, 2 pers.incl 🚐⚡Ch🚿(70x)WCincluded 💧€ 0,50/5minutes 💧€ 1 📶. 🚲
**Location:** Rural, comfortable, quiet. **Surface:** asphalted.
📅 15/03-05/10.
**Distance:** 🚲15km 🚌on the spot 🏊on the spot.
**Remarks:** Several locations, bread-service, possibility for reservation.

🏕️S | **Hamburg** 🌊⚓🍴📶 | 8B2
**Wohnmobilhafen Hamburg**, Grüner Deich 8, Hammerbrook.
**GPS:** n53,54360 e10,02570.⬆️➡️

---

60 🛏 € 19 🚐⚡Ch🚿,6Amp WC🚽included. 🚲
**Location:** Urban, simple, central, noisy. **Surface:** gravel.
📅 01/01-31/12.
**Distance:** 🚲4km 🚌200m.

🏕️S | **Hamburg** 🌊⚓🍴📶 | 8B2
**Heiligengeistfeld**. **GPS:** n53,55523 e9,97361.⬆️

30 🛏 € 18 🚐€ 5/day 🚿€ 5/day 📶included. 🚲
**Location:** Urban, simple. **Surface:** gravel/sand.
📅 01/01-31/12 💧 during event.
**Distance:** 🚲on the spot ⊗300m 🚌300m.
**Remarks:** Accessible via entrance C, max. 3 nights, possibility for reservation, special part for motor homes.

🏕️ | **Hamburg** 🌊⚓🍴📶 | 8B2
**Am Strand Pauli**, St. Pauli Hafenstraße. **GPS:** n53,54598 e9,96099.
20 🛏 € 12,50-19,50.
**Location:** Urban, simple.
**Surface:** asphalted.
📅 01/01-31/12.
**Distance:** 🚲Hamburg Altstadt 2,4km 🏊on the spot ⊗many restaurant 100m 🚌600m.

**Tourist information Hamburg:**
ℹ️ Hamburg-card. Card offers free entrance to public transport and museums, discounts on boat trips, zoo etc. Available at Tourist Information. 🎫 € 9,90 1 day, € 25,50/3 days, 1 adult max. 3 childeren.
👁️ Sankt Pauli. City district with well-known Reeperbahn.
🎭 Flohschanze, Rinderschlachthalle St Pauli. Antiques and flea market.
📅 Sa 8-16h.
Tierpark Hagenbeck, Stellingen. Zoo.
🏛️ Antikpassage, Klosterwall 9-21. Arcade with 39 antique stores.
📅 Tue-Fri 12-18h, Sa 10-16h.

🏕️S | **Handewitt** | 6C3
**Scandinavian Park**, Scandinavian-Park. **GPS:** n54,77857 e9,33528.⬆️

40 🛏 € 10 🚐€ 1 Ch€ 1 WC€ 0,50/time 💧💧.
**Location:** Urban, simple, central, quiet. **Surface:** asphalted.
📅 01/01-31/12.
**Distance:** 🚲2km ⊗on the spot 🚌on the spot.
**Remarks:** At shopping centre, service at petrol station.

🏵️S | **Hanerau-Hademarschen** 🍴 | 8A1
**Ferienhof Sievers**, Wilhelmsburg. **GPS:** n54,12360 e9,38627.⬆️

DE

5 ⬛€ 10 ⌁🕳Ch⌁(6x)WC⬚included. 🚐 **Location**: Rural, comfortable, isolated, quiet. **Surface**: grasstiles/grassy. 🅿 01/01-31/12.
**Distance**: 🚶2km �500m 🚲on the spot 👤on the spot.

| 🚿S | Hasloh | 8B2 |

**Stellplatz Tante Henni**, Garstedter Weg 36a.
**GPS**: n53,69251 e9,92608. ⬆.

21 ⬛€ 17 ⌁🕳Ch⌁(21x)€ 0,50/kWh WC⬚🧺€ 1/5minutes 🚿included. **Location**: Rural, comfortable, quiet. **Surface**: grassy.
🅿 01/01-31/12.
**Distance**: 🚶on the spot 🏊on the spot 🚴4km ⊗1,5km 🍺1,5km �800m 🚲on the spot 👤on the spot.
**Remarks**: Check in on arrival, discount longer stays.

| 🚿S | Hasselberg | 6D3 |

**Ostseecamping Gut Oehe**, Drecht 6. **GPS**: n54,71590 e9,99030. ⬆➡.

10 ⬛€ 11 WC⬚included. 🚐 **Location**: Rural, simple, quiet.
**Surface**: grassy. 🅿 01/04-30/09.
**Distance**: 🚶3km 🏊on the spot ⊗on the spot 🚲on the spot.

| 🚿S | Heide 🛒 | 8A1 |

**Wohnmobilplatz Heide**, Langvogt-Johannsen-strasse.
**GPS**: n54,20181 e9,11319. ⬆.

16 ⬛€ 7 ⌁€ 1/100liter 🕳€ 1 Ch⌁€ 1/2kWh 🚿🛢🎥
**Location**: Urban, comfortable, central, noisy.
**Surface**: grasstiles/metalled. 🅿 01/01-31/12.
**Distance**: 🚶800m 🚤5,5km ⊗100m 🍺300m.
**Remarks**: At swimming pool, use of sauna against payment.

| 🚿S | Heiligenhafen ⛵🚤 | 6E3 |

**Reisemobilstellplatz Heiligenhafen**, Eichholzweg 26.
**GPS**: n54,37721 e10,95548. ⬆.

99 ⬛€ 13-16 + € 3/pp tourist tax ⌁€ 1/100liter 🕳Ch⌁€ 0,50/kWh, + € 0,50 WC⬚🧺€ 2/2 🚿included. 🛢
**Location**: Urban. **Surface**: metalled. 🅿 01/01-31/12.
**Distance**: 🚶1km 🏊on the spot 🍺2,5km.
**Remarks**: At sea.

| 🚿S | Hohenfelde | 6D3 |

**Campingpark Ostseestrand**, Strandstraße.
**GPS**: n54,38588 e10,49152. ⬆➡.

---

25 ⬛€ 14,50-17, dog € 2 ⌁🕳Ch⌁WC⬚included 📷.
**Location**: Rural, luxurious. **Surface**: grassy. 🅿 01/04-15/10.
**Distance**: 🚶1km 🏖beach 150m 🚤150m ⊗on the spot 🍺on the spot.

| 🍴S | Hohenfelde | 6D3 |

**Wohnmobilplatz Radeland**, Strandstraße 18.
**GPS**: n54,38278 e10,49295. ⬆➡.

20 ⬛€ 9,50-14,50, dog € 2 ⌁included 🕳Ch⌁€ 2,50 WC⬚🧺€ 0,20/1minutes. **Location**: Rural. **Surface**: grassy/sand.
🅿 01/04-30/09.
**Distance**: 🏊300m.

| 🍴S | Hohn | 6D3 |

**Rosenhof Hohn**, Westende 12. **GPS**: n54,29944 e9,49622. ⬆.

5 ⬛€ 10 ⌁🕳Ch⌁🚐 **Location**: Rural, simple, isolated, quiet.
**Surface**: grassy. 🅿 01/04-31/10.
**Distance**: 🚶800m ⊗on the spot 🍺1km 🚲on the spot.

| 🚿S | Hohwacht | 6E3 |

**Parkplatz Alt-Hohwacht**, Strandstrasse.
**GPS**: n54,31902 e10,67529. ⬆➡.

19 ⬛€ 10 ⌁€ 1/80liter 🕳€ 1 Ch⌁(20x)€ 1/kWh. 🛢
**Location**: Urban. **Surface**: metalled. 🅿 01/01-31/12.
**Distance**: 🏊on the spot 🚤on the spot.

| 🚿S | Hörnum | 6C3 |

Zeltplatz. **GPS**: n54,76385 e8,28335.
30 ⬛€ 18 ⌁€ 0,50 🕳€ 0,50 Ch⌁€ 0,45/kWh WC⬚🚿.
**Location**: Rural, comfortable, isolated, quiet. **Surface**: sand.
🅿 01/01-31/12.
**Distance**: 🏊on the spot 🚤on the spot ⊗750m.

| 🚿S | Hörsten ⛵🚤 | 6D3 |

**Reisemobilstellplatz NOK**, Schachtholm 1.
**GPS**: n54,22499 e9,60243. ⬆.

---

49 ⬛€ 10 ⌁€ 1/75liter 🕳€ 1/time Ch⌁€ 1/time ⌁(48x)€ 0,50/kWh, 16Amp WC⬚included. 🚐 **Location**: Rural, comfortable, isolated, quiet. **Surface**: grassy. 🅿 16/03-15/11 and 30/12-02/01.
**Distance**: 🏊on the spot ⊗700m 🚲on the spot 👤on the spot.
**Remarks**: At the canal, bread-service.

| 🚿S | Husum 🌿🛫🐚 | 6C3 |

**Loof's Wohnmobilhafen**, Dockkoogstrasse 7.
**GPS**: n54,47451 e9,04249. ⬆.

30 ⬛€ 12 ⌁€ 1 🕳€ 2 Ch€ 2 ⌁(30x)€ 3 WCincluded 🧺€ 0,50. 🚐
**Location**: Urban, simple, central, quiet. **Surface**: gravel.
🅿 01/01-31/12.
**Distance**: 🚶200m 🏊200m 🚤200m ⊗200m 🍺200m 🚲on the spot 👤on the spot.

| 🚿S | Husum 🌿🛫🐚 | 6C3 |

**Wohnmobilplatz Am Dockkoog**, Dockoogstrasse 17.
**GPS**: n54,47888 e9,01138. ⬆.

25 ⬛€ 13 ⌁🕳ChWCincluded 🧺. 🚐
**Location**: Rural, simple, quiet. **Surface**: grassy. 🅿 Easter-15/10.
**Distance**: 🚶500m 🏊200m 🚤200m 🍺on the spot 🚲on the spot 👤on the spot.
**Remarks**: Max. 3 nights, sanitary at campsite.

| 🚿S | Itzehoe | 8A1 |

**Malzmüllerwiesen**, Schuhmacherallee.
**GPS**: n53,91970 e9,51815. ⬆➡.

5 ⬛free ⌁(4x)€ 0,50/kWh.
**Location**: Rural, simple, central, quiet. **Surface**: metalled/sand.
🅿 01/01-31/12 📷 during event.
**Distance**: 🚶600m 🚤20m 🚲on the spot 👤on the spot.

| 🚿S | Jagel | 6D3 |

**Wohnmobilhafen Jagel**, Bundesstrasse 13.
**GPS**: n54,45448 e9,53654. ⬆.

31 ⌺ 10 ⛽ Ch ⚡€2/night WC ♨ **Location:** Rural, comfortable, quiet. **Surface:** grassy. ◻ 01/01-31/12. **Distance:** 🏊250m ⛵4,5km 🚉400m.

## ⚓S Kaltenkirchen ♨ 8B1
**Reisemobilstellplatz Holstentherme**, Norderstrasse 8. **GPS:** n53,84056 e9,94650. ⬆➡.

20 ⌺free ⛽€1/80liter 🔌€1 Ch€1 ⚡€0,50/kWh. **Location:** Urban, quiet. **Surface:** grassy/gravel. ◻ 01/01-31/12. **Distance:** 🏊1,5km ⛵1km ⊗on the spot 🚉1,5km 🚌on the spot. **Remarks:** Coins available at pay-desk of theTherme.

## ⚓S Kappeln ⛵ 6D3
**Aral-Tankstelle**, Eckernförder Strasse 9/B. **GPS:** n54,65688 e9,94480.

10 ⌺ 5 ⛽€0,50/80liter 🔌€0,50/time Ch€0,50/time ⚡€5/night ♨ 🚗 **Location:** Urban, simple, quiet. **Surface:** metalled. ◻ 01/01-31/12. **Distance:** 🏊300m ⛵2km ⊗on the spot 🚉500m. **Remarks:** At petrol station, caution key electricity € 25.

## ⚓S Kappeln ⛵ 6D3
**Anker Yachting**, Am Hafen 23A. **GPS:** n54,66612 e9,93698. ⬆.

50 ⌺ 12 ⛽🔌Ch ⚡€2/4kWh WC 🔌€1 📶 🚗 **Location:** Rural, comfortable, central, quiet. **Surface:** gravel. ◻ 15/02-15/11. **Distance:** 🏊1km ⛵1km ⊗300m 🚌on the spot. **Remarks:** Near marina, caution key electricity € 5.

## ⚓S Kellinghusen ♨ 8A1
**Am Freibad**, Jacob-Fleischer-Strasse 6. **GPS:** n53,94715 e9,71035. ⬆➡.

6 ⌺free ⛽€0,50/100liter 🔌€0,50 Ch€0,50 ⚡(4x)€1,6Amp WC 🚽use sanitary facilities at swimming pool. **Location:** Rural, simple, quiet. **Surface:** gravel. ◻ 01/01-31/12.

**Distance:** 🏊centre 500m ⊗500m 🚉500m 🚲on the spot. **Remarks:** Check in at swimming pool.

## ⚓S Kiel ♨🚂 6D3
**Wohnmobilstellplatz Kiel, Förde und Kanalblick**, Mecklenburg-strasse 58. Kiel-Wik. **GPS:** n54,36907 e10,14641. ⬆➡.

48 ⌺ 12-15 ⛽Ch ⚡(25x)€3,50/24h WC included 🔌€1/5minutes 🚿€3,50/3,50. **Location:** Urban, simple, central, noisy. **Surface:** metalled. ◻ 01/01-31/12. **Distance:** 🏊7km ⛵on the spot ⊗1km 🚉1km 🚲on the spot 🚶1km. **Remarks:** Check in and pay at reception, bread-service.

## ⚓S Kiel ♨🚂⛵ 6D3
**Olympiahafen Schilksee**, Soling 26. **GPS:** n54,43033 e10,16634. ⬆.

20 ⌺ 10 ⛽€0,50/3minutes 🔌€1 Ch ⚡WC. **Location:** Rural. **Surface:** metalled. ◻ 01/01-31/12 ● last 2 weeks of Jun. **Distance:** 🏊13km ⛵400m 🚉400m. **Remarks:** Check in and coins service at harbourmaster.

### Tourist information Kiel:
Ⓜ Schleswig-Holsteinisches Freilichtmuseum, Hamburger Landstraße 97, Molfsee. Open air museum. ◻ 01/04-31/10 daily 9-18h, 01/11-31/03 Su/holidays 11-16h. ⓣ € 8, family card € 17.

## 🍴S Krempe 8A1
**Am Schul- und Sportzentrum**, Am Freibad. **GPS:** n53,83356 e9,49447. ⬆➡.

3 ⌺free. **Location:** Rural, simple, quiet. **Surface:** gravel. ◻ 01/01/2019-31/12/2019. **Distance:** 🏊200m.

## 🍴S Kropp 6D3
**Hotel Wikingerhof**, Tetenhusener Chaussee 1. **GPS:** n54,40837 e9,51042. ⬆.

12 ⌺free ⚡WC 📶. **Location:** Urban, simple, central, quiet. **Surface:** metalled. ◻ 01/04-31/10. **Distance:** 🏊300m ⊗on the spot 🚉300m.

## Kropp 6D3
**Garage Audi-VW Thomsen**, Werkstrasse 2. **GPS:** n54,41381 e9,52878. ⬆.

4 ⌺ 5 ⛽€0,50/80liter 🔌€0,50/time Ch€0,50/time ⚡🚗 **Location:** Urban, simple, quiet. **Surface:** metalled. ◻ 01/01-31/12. **Distance:** 🏊300m ⛵300m 🚉300m. **Remarks:** Max. 3 days, service at petrol station.

## ⚓S Laboe 6D3
**Ostseebad Laboe Ehrenmal**, Steinerweg/Prof. Munzerring. **GPS:** n54,41029 e10,23289. ⬆.

18 ⌺ 12 ⛽€1/100liter 🔌€1 Ch. 🚗 **Location:** Urban, simple. **Surface:** grassy. ◻ 01/01-31/12. **Distance:** 🏊1km ⛵400m 🚴400m ⊗on the spot 🚉1km.

## ⚓S Ladelund 🚂 6C3
**Am Naturbad**, Stato. **GPS:** n54,84919 e9,03629. ⬆.

5 ⌺ 10 ⛽🔌Ch ⚡WC included ♨ **Location:** Rural, comfortable, isolated, quiet. **Surface:** grassy. ◻ 01/01-31/12. **Distance:** 🏊1km ⊗on the spot.

## ⚓S Langballig 🚂⛵ 6D3
**Campingplatz Langballigau**, Strandweg 3, Langballigau. **GPS:** n54,82234 e9,65969. ⬆.

50 ⌺ 11, dog €1 🔌Ch included ⚡€2,50/night WC 🔌€1 🔌€1. ♨ **Location:** Rural, simple. **Surface:** grassy/gravel. ◻ 01/01-31/12. **Distance:** ⛵100m ⊗on the spot.

## ⚓S Langwedel ♨⛵ 6D3
**Caravanpark am Brahmsee**, Mühlenstraße 30a. **GPS:** n54,21462 e9,91943. ⬆➡.

20 ⌺ 15 ⛽€1/80liter 🔌Ch ⚡€2,50/24h,6Amp WC sanitary at campsite. **Location:** Rural, comfortable, quiet. **Surface:** grassy/gravel. ◻ 01/01-31/12.

DE

**Distance:** 600m 3km Brahmsee 500m 500m 7km.
**Remarks:** Check in at reception campsite, bread-service.

| ⚓S | Lauenburg/Elbe 🌊🏄🛶 | 8C2 |

**Marina Lauenburg/Yachthafen,** Hafenstrasse 14.
**GPS:** n53,37156 e10,56527.⬆

20 € 10 € 1/100liter (8x)€ 1/kWh WC € 0,50 1 4/4.
**Location:** Rural, comfortable.
**Surface:** metalled.
01/01-31/12.
**Distance:** 10 min walking on the spot 10 min walking.

| ⊞S | Leck | 6C3 |

**Reisemobilhafen Leck,** Am Stadion 3. **GPS:** n54,76704 e8,98123.⬆

20 € 5 € 1/80liter (20x)€ 0,50/kWh WC 2.
**Location:** Urban, comfortable, central, quiet. **Surface:** grassy/gravel.
01/01-31/12.
**Distance:** 1km 2km 100m 1km on the spot on the spot.
**Remarks:** At swimming pool, to be paid at swimming pool.

| ⊞S | Lensahn | 6E3 |

**Reisemobilplatz Lensahn,** Dr. Julius-Stinde strasse.
**GPS:** n54,21446 e10,87745.⬆➡

15 € 8 € 1/80liter 1 Ch (4x)€ 2. **Location:** Rural,
simple. **Surface:** grasstiles. 01/01-31/12.
**Distance:** 1,5km on the spot 200m 2,5km.

| ⚓S | Lübeck 🌊🏄🛶 | 8C1 |

**Wohnmobil Treff Lübeck,** An der Hülshorst 11.
**GPS:** n53,89510 e10,71088.⬆

45 € 11/day Ch WC € 1/5minutes included.
**Location:** Urban, luxurious, quiet. **Surface:** gravel. 02/01-31/10.
**Distance:** 4,5km 5km 100m 50m.

| ⊞ | Lübeck 🌊🏄🛶 | 8C1 |

**Media Docks,** Willy-Brandt-Allee. **GPS:** n53,87307 e10,68189.
39 € 2/h, € 10/24h. **Location:** Central. **Surface:** metalled.
01/01-31/12.
**Distance:** 200m 200m.
**Remarks:** Max. 24h.

| ⚓S | Lübeck 🌊🏄🛶 | 8C1 |

**Wohnmobilstellplatz Lübeck Marienbrücke P4,** Lastadie.
**GPS:** n53,87163 e10,67915.⬆➡

---

16 € 2/h, € 10/24h.
**Location:** Urban, simple. **Surface:** asphalted.
01/01-31/12.
**Distance:** 500m 2km on the spot on the spot.
**Remarks:** Max. 24h.

**Tourist information Lübeck:**
Ⓜ Museum Holstentor, Holstentorplatz. Historical museum. 10-16/17h. € 7, family card € 15.
Ⓜ Niederegger Einkaufserlebnis, Café und Marzipan-Museum, Breite strasse 89. Marzipan, Lübecker speciality, museum, café and shop.

| ⊞ | Lunden 🛶 | 6C3 |

Wollersumer Straße. **GPS:** n54,33280 e8,99697.⬆

10 free. **Location:** Rural, simple. **Surface:** grassy/gravel.
01/01-31/12 high water.
**Distance:** 1,7km on the spot.

| ⚓S | Maasholm 🌊🏄🛶 | 6D3 |

**Stellplatz am Yachthafen,** Uleweg 31. **GPS:** n54,68334 e9,99436.⬆

40 € 12 Ch € 2/night WC € 0,50 2 .
**Location:** Rural, comfortable, central, quiet. **Surface:** grassy/gravel.
01/01-31/12.
**Distance:** 100m 5km on the spot on the spot 100m 300m.
**Remarks:** Parking marina.

| ⊞S | Meldorf | 7H1 |

**Reisemobil-Stellplatz am Deich,** Deichstraße 2.
**GPS:** n54,09409 e8,95070.⬆

80 € 8 (18x)€ 3 WC € 2.
**Location:** Rural, comfortable, isolated, quiet.
**Surface:** grassy/metalled. Easter-31/10.
**Distance:** 7km on the spot Imbiss 10-18 uur on the spot on the spot.

| ⊞S | Molfsee 🌊 | 6D3 |

**Freilichtmuseum/Restaurant Drathenhof,** Hamburger Landstrasse 99. **GPS:** n54,27411 e10,07571.⬆

---

20 free, use of a meal desired WC at restaurant.
**Location:** Simple, central. **Surface:** gravel.
01/01-31/12.
**Distance:** on the spot on the spot on the spot on the spot on the spot.
**Remarks:** At open air museum.

| ⊞S | Mölln | 8C2 |

Alt Möllner strasse. **GPS:** n53,62564 e10,68314.⬆

24 € 7 (20x)included.
**Location:** Rural. **Surface:** gravel. 01/01-31/12.
**Distance:** 1km 250m 300m.
**Remarks:** Service: Vorkamp 19, GPS N53,62024, E10,67701.

| ⚓S | Neufeld | 8A1 |

**SBC Neufeld,** An'n Hoven. **GPS:** n53,90677 e9,02042.⬆

20 € 10 (20x)€ 2/day WC included. **Location:** Rural,
comfortable, quiet. **Surface:** grasstiles/grassy. 01/04-31/10.
**Distance:** on the spot on the spot on the spot.
**Remarks:** Dog € 2/day.

| ⊞S | Neukirchen 23779 | 6E3 |

**Wohnmobilhafen Seepark Sütel,** Sütel.
**GPS:** n54,33359 e11,06620.⬆

30 € 12-14, 2 pers. incl included.
**Surface:** grassy. 01/01-31/12.
**Distance:** 500m 750m on the spot on the spot.
**Remarks:** Bread-service in summer period.

| ⊞S | Neukirchen 25927 | 6C3 |

**Sportzentrum,** Kirchenweg 2. **GPS:** n54,86602 e8,73304.⬆

4 free . **Location:** Rural, simple, quiet. **Surface:** concrete.
01/01-31/12.

DE

**Distance:** 500m 500m 350m.
**Remarks:** Max. 4 days.

### Neumünster 8B1

**Bad am Stadtwald**, Hansaring 177. **GPS:** n54,08078 e9,96064.

22 € 13 € 0,50/100liter € 0,50 Ch (22x)€ 0,50/kWh
WC 1 included. **Location:** Rural, comfortable, central, quiet.
**Surface:** grassy/gravel. 01/01-31/12.
**Distance:** 2km A7 1 km on the spot 300m on the spot.
**Remarks:** Check in at swimming pool.

### Neustadt in Holstein 8C1

**Wohnmobilstellplatz Ostsee**, Auf der Pelzer Wiese 45, Pelzerhaken.
**GPS:** n54,08889 e10,87250.

90 € 14 + tourist tax (summer) € 1/100liter € 1 Ch
(90x)€ 1/2kWh WC 2. **Location:** Rural, luxurious, noisy.
**Surface:** grassy. 01/03-31/12.
**Distance:** 900m 150m 900m 400m on the spot.

### Neustadt in Holstein 8C1

**P5**, Am Binnenwasser. **GPS:** n54,11096 e10,81496.

10 Mo-Fr € 5/24h, Sa-Su free (2x)€ 0,50/kWh.
**Location:** Urban, simple. **Surface:** metalled. 01/01-31/12.
**Distance:** on the spot.

### Niebüll 6C3

**Parkplatz**, Lornsenstrasse 19. **GPS:** n54,78901 e8,82546.

25 € 5 € 1/70liter € 1 Ch (12x)€ 1/8h included.
**Location:** Urban, simple, central, quiet. **Surface:** grassy.
01/01-31/12 1st week in June.
**Distance:** on the spot 200m 300m.
**Remarks:** Parking swimming pool, max. 24h.

### Niesgrau 6D3

**Wohnmobilstellplatz Gelting-Mole**, Gelting-Mole 1.
**GPS:** n54,75194 e9,86242.

23 € 15 Ch WC included .
**Location:** Rural. **Surface:** metalled. 01/01-31/12.
**Distance:** on the spot on the spot 100m.
**Remarks:** Check in at harbourmaster.

### Nordstrand 6C3

**Wohnmobilplatz Margarethenruh**, Süderhafen 8.
**GPS:** n54,46944 e8,91000.

16 € 22,80-27,50, 2 pers.incl Ch € 3,20/24h WC included
€ 3/3. **Location:** Rural, comfortable, central, quiet.
**Surface:** grassy/gravel. 01/01-31/12.
**Distance:** 3km 300m 150m 3km.
**Remarks:** Bread-service.

### Nordstrand 6C3

**Womoland**, Norderquerweg 2. **GPS:** n54,51736 e8,93012.

44 € 7 + € 4,50/pp Ch € 0,60/kWh,16Amp WC included.
**Location:** Rural, comfortable, isolated, quiet.
**Surface:** grassy/gravel.
15/03-31/10.
**Distance:** 10km 6km on the spot on the spot 6km.
**Remarks:** Bread-service.

**Tourist information Nordstrand:**
Former Wadden island.

### Norgaardholz 6D3

**Campingplatz Nordstern**, Nordstern 1. **GPS:** n54,78528 e9,79889.

10 € 8 Ch (10x)€ 2/night WC € 1,use sanitary € 4/night
€ 3 € 2/24h. **Location:** Rural, simple, isolated, quiet.
**Surface:** gravel/metalled. 01/04-30/09.
**Distance:** on the spot on the spot on the spot on the spot
on the spot.

### Ockholm 6C3

**Wohnmobilstellplätze Altes Pastorat**, Baderstrasse 5/6.
**GPS:** n54,66517 e8,82940.

5 € 9, 2 pers. incl Ch (5x)€ 2/24h WC included € 5/5.
**Location:** Rural, simple, isolated, quiet. **Surface:** grassy/gravel.
01/01-31/12.
**Distance:** 100m on the spot.
**Remarks:** Along through road, bread-service.

### Oeversee 6D3

**Wohnmobilstellplatz Schnell**, Frörupsand 2.
**GPS:** n54,69253 e9,43252.

20 € 6 Ch € 1/night WC free. **Location:** Rural,
simple, quiet. **Surface:** grassy. 01/01-31/12.
**Distance:** 400m 500m 400m.

### Osterhever 6C3

**Stellplatz Norderheverkoog**, Norderheverkoogstraße 12, Norderheverkoog. **GPS:** n54,39656 e8,76163.

10 € 10 Ch (10x)WC included € 1. **Location:** Rural,
isolated, quiet. **Surface:** grassy. 01/04-31/10.
**Distance:** 1km 2km 1km on the spot on the spot.
**Remarks:** Bread-service, bicycle rental.

### Osterrönfeld 6D3

**Wohnmobilhafen am Kanal-Café NOK**, Am Kamp-Kanal 1.
**GPS:** n54,28955 e9,66959.

33 € 16 € 1/100liter Ch € 0,60/kWh WC € 1 .
**Location:** Urban, comfortable. **Surface:** metalled.
01/01-31/12.
**Distance:** on the spot 100m.
**Remarks:** Along river.

### Pahlen 6C3

Fischerstrasse 17. **GPS:** n54,27101 e9,30015.

4 € 6 + € 1/pp (12x)WC included. **Location:** Rural,

DE

comfortable, quiet. **Surface:** grassy. ◻ 01/01-31/12.
**Distance:** 🚶200m 🏊50m ➤50m ⊗200m 🛒200m.

### Plön 8B1

**Wohnmobilhafen Plön**, Ascheberger straße 76.
**GPS:** n54,14709 e10,39841. ⬆️➡️

14 🛏€ 17, dog € 3 🚰♨️Ch. 🚿WC 📶included. **Location:** Urban,
comfortable, noisy. **Surface:** grassy/gravel. ◻ 01/04-15/12.
**Distance:** 🚶1,5km ⊗on the spot 🚊200m.
**Remarks:** Max. 4 nights.

### Plön 8B1

**Womo-Stop Kleinen Plöner See**, Hamburgerstrasse/Aschenberg
strasse, B430. **GPS:** n54,15278 e10,40417. ⬆️➡️.

11 🛏€ 5 🚰€ 1 ♨️€ 0,50 Ch. 🏠 **Location:** Simple.
**Surface:** asphalted. ◻ 01/01-31/12.
**Distance:** ⊗on the spot.
**Remarks:** In front of passage to beach, max. 24h.

### Pommerby 6D3

**Wohnmobilhafen Ostseesonne**, Gammeldam 6.
**GPS:** n54,76335 e9,97097. ⬆️.
30 🛏€ 10-12 🚰♨️Ch. 🚿€ 3/night. 🏠 **Location:** Rural, simple,
quiet. **Surface:** grassy. ◻ 01/04-31/10.
**Distance:** ⚓on the spot ➤on the spot ⊗on the spot 🚴on the spot.

### Preetz 6D3

**Wohnmobilpark Preetz**, Kahlbrook 25a.
**GPS:** n54,22811 e10,28616. ⬆️➡️.

11 🛏€ 16,50 🚰♨️🚿WC 📶included. 💧
**Location:** Urban, comfortable, quiet. **Surface:** gravel.
◻ 01/01-31/12 service 01/11-31/03.
**Distance:** 🚶1km ⚓on the spot ⊗on the spot.
**Remarks:** Bread-service, canoe and bicycle rental.

### Puttgarden 6E3

**Wohnmobilplatz Johannisberg**, Johannisbergstrasse.
**GPS:** n54,50054 e11,17938. ⬆️➡️.

50 🛏€ 10-15 🚰€ 0,10/10liter ♨️€ 2 Ch. ♨️€ 0,50/kWh WC 🚿€ 1
🚿€ 3,50/2. 💧
**Location:** Rural, simple, quiet. **Surface:** grassy/metalled.
◻ 01/01-31/12.
**Distance:** 🚶2,5km ⚓800m ➤800m ⊗on the spot.
**Remarks:** In nature reserve Am Grüner Brink, bread-service.

### Puttgarden 6E3

**Bade- und Surfstrand Grüner Brink**, Krögenweg.
**GPS:** n54,51174 e11,18285.
30 🛏€ 9 🚰€ 2,50 ♨️Ch. **Surface:** gravel. ◻ 01/01-31/12.
**Distance:** ⚓on the spot.

### Quickborn bei Burg 8A1

**Am Helmschen-Bach**, Hauptstraße 2. **GPS:** n54,01165 e9,21648. ⬆️➡️.

5 🛏€ 6 🚰included. ♨️€ 0,60/kWh. 💧 **Location:** Rural, comfortable,
quiet. **Surface:** grassy. ◻ 01/04-30/09.
**Distance:** 🚶300m 🚴on the spot.

### Rantrum 6C3

**Reisemobilhafen Rantrum**, Bannony. **GPS:** n54,43369 e9,12743. ⬆️.

13 🛏€ 10 🚰♨️Ch. ♨️(12x)WC 📶included. **Location:** Rural,
simple, isolated, quiet. **Surface:** gravel. ◻ 01/01-31/12.
**Distance:** 🚶8km ⚓30km 🚊300m.
**Remarks:** At swimming pool.

### Ratzeburg 8C1

**Hallenbad Aqua Siwa**, Fischerstrasse 43.
**GPS:** n53,69567 e10,77598. ⬆️➡️.

12 🛏€ 8/24h 🚰€ 1/80liter ♨️Ch. ♨️€ 0,50/kWh. 🏠
**Location:** Urban, simple, central, noisy. **Surface:** gravel.
◻ 01/01-31/12.
**Distance:** 🚶500m ⚓on the spot ➤on the spot ⊗on the spot.

### Reinfeld 8B1

**Am Herrenteich**, Karpfenplatz. **GPS:** n53,83024 e10,48362. ⬆️.

5 🛏free 🚰€ 0,50/70liter ♨️€ 0,50 Ch. ♨️€ 0,50/kWh.
**Location:** Urban, simple, quiet. **Surface:** metalled.
◻ 01/01-31/12.
**Distance:** 🚶500m ⊗200m 🚊400m on the spot 🛶on the spot.

### Rendsburg 6D3

**Wohnmobil-Hafen Eiderblick**, An der Untereider 9.
**GPS:** n54,30406 e9,65610. ⬆️➡️.

40 🛏€ 15 🚰€ 1/75liter ♨️Ch. ♨️(45x)€ 0,50/kWh WC included.
📶against payment. 🏠 **Location:** Urban, luxurious, central, quiet.
**Surface:** gravel. ◻ 01/01-31/12.
**Distance:** 🚶800m ⚓on the spot 🚊800m ➤on the spot
🚴on the spot 🛶on the spot.
**Remarks:** Bread-service, internetcafé.

### Rendsburg 6D3

**Wohnmobilhafen am Kreishafen NOK**, Am Kreishafen 30-3.
**GPS:** n54,29434 e9,68170. ⬆️.

35 🛏€ 12 🚰€ 1/100liter ♨️Ch. ♨️€ 0,60/kWh WC 🚿€ 1 📶. 🚗
**Surface:** asphalted. ◻ 01/01-31/12.
**Distance:** 🚶500m ⚓on the spot 🚊300m 🛶on the spot.

**Tourist information Rendsburg:**
👁 Eiserne Lady. Train-bridge North Sea-Baltic Canal, 42m high.
🚲 Blue Line. City walk 3 km.
🍺 Hausbrauerei Niewarker, Paradeplatz. Guided tour and tastery.

### Reußenköge 6C3

**Amsinck Haus**, Sönke Nissenkoog 36a. **GPS:** n54,61666 e8,87027. ⬆️➡️.

11 🛏€ 7 🚰♨️(6x)€ 2/24h WC included. 🚗€ 3.
**Location:** Rural, comfortable, isolated, quiet. **Surface:** asphalted.
◻ 01/04-31/10.
**Distance:** 🚶4km ⚓4km 🚴on the spot.
**Remarks:** Bicycle rental.

### Sankt Peter-Ording 6C3

**Reisemobilhafen St.Peter-Ording**, Am Ketelskoog.
**GPS:** n54,30881 e8,63522. ⬆️➡️.

70 🛏€ 16 + tourist tax 🚰€ 1/50liter ♨️Ch. ♨️(70x)€ 0,60/kWh,6Amp
WC€ 0,20 🚿€ 1,50 📶€ 1/h. 💧 **Location:** Rural, comfortable.
**Surface:** gravel. ◻ 01/01-31/12 ◻ 01/11-15/12.
**Distance:** 🚶300m ⚓1km ⊗300m 🚊300m.
**Remarks:** Arrival <22h, market Wednesday.

**Tourist information Sankt Peter-Ording:**
Westküstenpark, Wohldweg 6. Animal park. ◻ summer 9.30-18h,
winter 11h-sunset.

### Schacht-Audorf 6D3

**WohnmobilPark Schacht-Audorf**, K76. **GPS:** n54,30611 e9,71250. ⬆️.

41 🛏€ 12,50 🚰€ 0,50/100liter 🚽Ch.🔌(33x)€ 0,60/kWh WC€ 1
🚿€ 1/6minutes 📶.🛒.
**Location:** Rural, comfortable, quiet. **Surface:** gravel.
🅿 01/01-31/12.
**Distance:** 🚶700m 🛣 A7 2km ⊗800m 🛒1km 🚰on the spot
🚲on the spot.
**Remarks:** At the canal, max. 3 nights, payment only with coins.

### Scharbeutz 8C1
**Womohafen Scharbeutzer Strand**, Hamburger Ring 6-8.
**GPS:** n54,03112 e10,75242.⬆.

90 🛏€ 10,40 + € 2,80/pp tourist taks, beach tax incl 🚰€ 1/100liter
Ch.🔌(2x)€ 1/2kWh 🚽€ 2 🛒.
**Location:** Rural, simple. 🅿 01/01-31/12.
**Distance:** 🚶300m 🏊300m, dog friendly beach 1km ⊗400m.

### Schashagen 8C1
**Ostsee-Campingplatz Kagelbusch**, Strandweg/Kagelbusch.
**GPS:** n54,12570 e10,92789.

🛏€ 12 🚰€ 1. 🅿 01/01-31/12.
**Distance:** 🏊500m.

### Schashagen 8C1
**Wohnmobilpark Ostseeblick**, Biesdorf.
**GPS:** n54,11934 e10,92108.⬆➡.

30 🛏€ 7, 01/04-30/09 € 14,50-16,50, 2 pers. incl., dog € 2,50-3,50
🚰€ 1/80liter 🚽Ch.🔌€ 0,50/kWh 🛒.
**Location:** Rural, comfortable, quiet. **Surface:** grasstiles.
🅿 01/01-31/12 🅿 Service: winter.
**Distance:** 🏊300m.

### Schleswig 6D3
**Am Schleswig Stadthafen**, Am Hafen 5. **GPS:** n54,51203 e9,56802.⬆.

45 🛏€ 12, 01/03-30/11 € 18 🚰🚽Ch.🔌(30x),10Amp
WC🚽🛒€ 2,50/2,50 📶included.🛒.
**Location:** Urban, comfortable, central. **Surface:** gravel/metalled.
🅿 01/01-31/12 🅿 Service: winter.
**Distance:** 🚶150m 🛣 5km 🏊on the spot 🚰on the spot ⊗50m
🛒500m 🚰nearby 🚐50m.
**Remarks:** Max. 48h, check in at harbourmaster, caution key € 20.

### ⚓🅂 Schleswig 6D3
**Wiking-Yachthafen**, Wikingeck 11. **GPS:** n54,50670 e9,54733.⬆.

8 🛏€ 12 🚰€ 1 🚽€ 1 Ch.🔌€ 0,40/kWh WC🚽€ 2 🛒.🚲.
**Location:** Urban, simple, quiet.
**Surface:** metalled.
🅿 01/05-30/09.
**Distance:** 🚶2km 🏊on the spot 🚰on the spot ⊗on the spot
🛒on the spot 🚲on the spot.
**Remarks:** Check in at harbourmaster.
**Tourist information Schleswig:**
ℹ Tourist Information Schleswig, Plessenstrasse 7. Historical city,
founded by the Vikings, Haithabu.
🅼🍴 Schloß Gottorf. Regional museum, archeological museum and
museum for art and culture.
🅼 Museum am Danewerk, Ochsenweg 5, Dannewerk.
Fortifications, 650-1200.
🅿 winter 10-16h, 01/04-31/10 Tue-Fri 9-17h, Sa-Su 10-18h.
🅼 Wikinger Museum Haithabu, Haddeby-Busdorf. All about the life of
the Vikings.
🅿 01/04-31/10 9-17h, 01/11-31/03 Tue-Su 10-16h.

### 🅂 Schönberg/Ostsee 6D3
**Parkplatz Brasilien**, Seesternweg. **GPS:** n54,42408 e10,39116.⬆➡.

40 🛏€ 9, 15/05-15/09 € 11 🚰🚽Ch.🔌included.🚲.
**Location:** Rural, simple. **Surface:** grassy. 🅿 01/01-31/12.
**Distance:** 🏊200m 🚶200m.

### 🅂 Schönberg/Ostsee 6D3
**Stellplatz Mittelstrand**, Mittelstrand.
**GPS:** n54,42233 e10,39573.⬆➡.

50 🛏€ 10, 01/05-30/09 € 13, 2 pers.incl 🚰🚽Ch.🔌€ 2 WCincluded.
🚲 **Location:** Rural. **Surface:** grassy. 🅿 01/01-31/12.
**Distance:** 🏊200m 🚶200m ⊗on the spot.
**Remarks:** Bread-service in summer period.

### 🅂 Seestermühe 8A2
Achtern Diek 5. **GPS:** n53,70333 e9,56232.⬆➡.

4 🛏€ 2 🚰€ 2 🚽€ 2 Ch.🔌€ 2 🚽€ 2/day 🚰€ 1,50.
**Location:** Rural. **Surface:** metalled. 🅿 01/01-31/12.
**Distance:** ⊗200m.
**Remarks:** Check in on arrival.

### 🅂 Sehestedt 6D3
**Wohnmobilstellplatz Sehestedt**, Fährstrasse 1.
**GPS:** n54,36466 e9,81973.⬆➡.

13 🛏€ 8/24h 🚰€ 0,50/80liter 🚽Ch.🚲.
🅿 01/01-31/12.
**Surface:** gravel.
**Distance:** 🚶750m 🛣 A7 13km ⊗on the spot 🛒200m.
**Remarks:** Directly at North Sea-Baltic canal.

### Sierksdorf 8C1
**Hansa-Park**, Am Fahrenkrog 1. **GPS:** n54,07417 e10,77522.

100 🛏€ 6/24h. **Surface:** asphalted. 🅿 01/04-15/10.
**Distance:** 🏊1km 🚰on the spot ⊗750m 🛒800m 🚐on the spot.

### 🅲🅂 Sierksdorf 8C1
**Wohnmobilstellplatz Hof Sierksdorf**, Altonaer Straße.
**GPS:** n54,06013 e10,75737.⬆.
15 🛏€ 11 excl. tourist tax 🚰€ 1 🚽€ 1 Ch.🔌€ 0,50/kWh WC🛒.
**Location:** Rural, simple, quiet. **Surface:** gravel.
🅿 01/04-30/09.
**Distance:** 🏊beach 100m.

### 🅲🅂 Simonsberg 6C3
**Nordsee Camping Zum Seehund**, Lundenbergweg 4.
**GPS:** n54,45515 e8,96958.⬆➡.

15 🛏€ 15-21 🚰🚽Ch.🔌WC included 🛒€ 3 📶free.🚲.
**Location:** Rural, comfortable, isolated, quiet. **Surface:** gravel.
🅿 Easter-31/10.
**Distance:** 🚶3km 🏊500m ⊗on the spot 🛒on the spot 🛒on camp
site 🚲on the spot 🎿on the spot.
**Remarks:** Use steam bath, sauna, fitness-studio incl.

### 🅂 Sörup 6D3
**Südensee**, Seeblick. **GPS:** n54,71086 e9,66511.⬆➡.

DE

5 ⌂€ 4 🚰🅂Ch 🔌€ 2/night WC. 🚿
**Location:** Rural, simple, quiet. **Surface:** gravel. 🅾 01/04-31/10.
**Distance:** 🚶500m 🏊on the spot 🍴on the spot ⊗kiosk 🚴on the spot 🎣on the spot.
**Remarks:** Parking at small lake.

### 🏞🅂 Struckum ✈ 6C3
**Marschblick**, Kennedy Weg 3. GPS: n54,58597 e8,99117. ⬆➡.

30 ⌂€ 10 🚰🅂Ch 🔌WC included 🅾€ 3.
**Location:** Rural, simple, quiet. **Surface:** asphalted.
🅾 01/01-31/12.
**Distance:** 🚶100m 🏊8km ⊗750m 🚉1,5km 🚌100m 🚴on the spot.
**Remarks:** Money in envelope in mail box.

### 🏕 Süderlügum 6C3
**Wohnmobilplatz Mehrzweckhalle**, Jahnstrasse.
GPS: n54,87472 e8,90306. ⬆.

5 ⌂free. **Location:** Rural, simple, central, quiet. **Surface:** metalled.
🅾 01/01-31/12.
**Distance:** 🚶500m 🚉300m.
**Remarks:** Max. 7m.

### Tetenhusen 6D3
**Heuherberge Tetenhusen**, Sein 10. GPS: n54,34795 e9,50330. ⬆.

6 ⌂€ 12 🚰🔌 included WC € 2. 🚿 **Location:** Rural, simple,
isolated, quiet. **Surface:** grassy. 🅾 01/01-31/12.
**Distance:** 🚶300m 🏊on the spot 🚉250m 🚴on the spot.
**Remarks:** Breakfast-service, canoe rental.

### 🏕🅂 Timmendorfer Strand 8C1
**Am Vogelpark, P4**, Bäderrandstraße, B76.
GPS: n53,99136 e10,81439. ⬆➡.

50 ⌂€ 10 + € 3/pp tourist tax 🔌€ 0,50/120liter 🅂Ch 🔌€ 1/3kWh.

---

🏕 **Location:** Rural, simple. **Surface:** grassy/sand.
🅾 01/01-31/12.
**Distance:** ⊗180m.
**Remarks:** Max. 1 night.

### 🏕🅂 Tönning 🌊 6C3
**Wohnmobilhafen Kapitänshaus**, Am Eiderdeich.
GPS: n54,31109 e8,94114. ⬆.
53 ⌂€ 12 2p incl. + tourist tax 🔌€ 2 🅂Ch 🔌€ 0,60/kWh
WC 🅾 4/3 🔌€ 2,50/5h. 🚐
**Location:** Rural. **Surface:** grassy. 🅾 01/01-31/12.
**Distance:** 🏊on the spot ⊗on the spot.
**Remarks:** Along the Eider river.

### 🏕🅂 Tönning 🌊 6C3
**Wohnmobilplatz Eiderblick**, Am Strandweg.
GPS: n54,30920 e8,93684. ⬆.

33 ⌂€ 12 2p incl. + tourist tax 🔌€ 1/100liter 🅂Ch 🔌€ 0,60/kWh
🔌included 🅾 4/3 🔌€ 1/2h. 🚐
**Location:** Rural, luxurious, isolated, quiet. **Surface:** grassy.
🅾 01/01-31/12.
**Distance:** 🚶500m 🏊on the spot 🚴on the spot 🎣on the spot.
**Remarks:** Along the Eider river, swimming pool 200m.

### 🏕🅂 Travemünde 🌊✈🍴 8C1
**Wohnmobilparkplatz Kowitzberg**, Kowitzberg.
GPS: n53,97598 e10,87830. ⬆➡.

49 ⌂€ 12, 15/09-14/05 € 8 🔌€ 1/100liter 🅂Ch 🔌(48x)€ 1/5kWh.
**Location:** Rural, simple. **Surface:** grassy. 🅾 01/01-31/12.
**Distance:** 🚶2,5km 🏊800m 🍴800m ⊗300m 🚉250m 🚌50m.

### 🚐🅂 Travemünde 🌊✈🍴 8C1
**Evershof**, Kowitzberg 3. GPS: n53,97514 e10,87070. ⬆.
3 ⌂€ 12-14 + € 1,40/pp tourist tax 🔌€ 3 WC € 2 🔌. **Location:** Rural.
**Surface:** grassy. 🅾 01/04-31/10.
**Remarks:** Dog € 2/day.

### 🚐 Trittau 8B2
Zum Schützenplatz. GPS: n53,61063 e10,40843. ⬆.

5 ⌂free WC. **Location:** Urban, simple, central, quiet.
**Surface:** asphalted. 🅾 01/01-31/12.
**Distance:** 🚶500m ⊗500m 🚉500m 🚌50m.
**Remarks:** Next to swimming pool.

### ⚓ Uetersen 8A2
Am Stichhafen, Ziegelei. GPS: n53,67977 e9,66861. ⬆.

---

4 ⌂free. **Location:** Urban, simple. **Surface:** metalled.
🅾 01/01-31/12.
**Distance:** 🚶400m 🚲7,4km ⊗300m.

### 🏕🅂 Utersum 6C3
**Wohnmobilstellplatz Föhr**, Strunwai 14. GPS: n54,71593 e8,40117. ⬆.

30 ⌂€ 20 🔌€ 0,50/100liter 🅂Ch 🔌 WC 🔌€ 0,50 🔌included.
**Location:** Rural, comfortable, quiet. **Surface:** grassy.
🅾 15/03-15/11.
**Distance:** 🚶400m 🏊400m.

### 🏕🅂 Waabs 🚤 6D3
Gut Ludwigsburg. GPS: n54,50350 e9,95767. ⬆.

18 ⌂€ 15 🚰🅂Ch 🔌,16Amp WC 🔌included 🅾 🔌€ 4/24h. 🚐
**Location:** Rural, simple, isolated, quiet. **Surface:** grassy.
🅾 01/04-30/09.
**Distance:** 🏊on the spot ⊗on the spot 🍴on the spot 🚴on the spot.

### 🏕🅂 Weddelbrook 🎡 8B1
**Campingplatz Vogelzange**, Schulstraße 19.
GPS: n53,89995 e9,82657. ⬆.

6 ⌂€ 10 🚰🅂Ch included 🔌€ 3 WC 🔌€ 1/4minutes.
**Location:** Rural, simple, quiet. **Surface:** grassy.
🅾 01/01-31/12.
**Distance:** ⊗300m 🚴on the spot.
**Remarks:** At lake, check-in and key at reception.

### 🏕🅂 Wedel 8A2
Am Freibad. GPS: n53,57860 e9,69520. ⬆.

20 ⌂€ 10 🔌€ 1/10minutes 🅂Ch 🔌(14x)€ 1/8h WC 🔌.
**Location:** Rural, simple, quiet. **Surface:** grassy/metalled.
🅾 01/01-31/12 🅾 during event.
**Distance:** 🚶800m.

**Remarks:** Max. 3 days, to be paid at swimming pool.

**[C][S] Westerholz 6D3**
**Campingplatz Fördeblick**, Kummle 1. **GPS:** n54,81944 e9,66666.⬆️

35 🚐 € 10 🚰 € 1/40liter 🧺Ch 💧€ 3/24h,6Amp WC 🚽€ 1 📷against payment 📶included 🧺 🏠 **Location:** Rural, simple, quiet.
**Surface:** grassy/gravel. ⭕ 01/04-30/09.
**Distance:** 🏊600m 🌊200m ⊗800m 🛒2,5km 🍴on the spot.
**Remarks:** At Flensborg Fjord, max. 24h.

**[S] Wilster 8A1**
**Colosseumplatz**, Etatsrätin-Doos-Straße 14-17.
**GPS:** n53,92419 e9,37449.⬆️➡️

15 🚐free 🚰€ 1/5minutes 🧺Ch € 1 💧(4x)€ 0,50/kWh.
**Location:** Urban, simple, central, quiet. **Surface:** grassy/gravel.
⭕ 01/01-31/12 📷 fair.
**Distance:** 🏊200m 🛒100m 🚌on the spot 🚲on the spot.

**[S] Wischhafen 8A1**
**Alter Hafen**, Hafenstraße 10. **GPS:** n53,77278 e9,32278.⬆️➡️

8 🚐free 💧(6x)€ 1/kWh. **Location:** Rural, simple.
**Surface:** grassy/gravel. ⭕ 01/01-31/12.
**Distance:** ⊗500m 🛒1km.

**[S] Wischhafen 8A1**
Ziegelstraße, Gewerbegebiet Wischhafen.
**GPS:** n53,76417 e9,32111.⬆️➡️

3 🚐free 🚰🧺Chfree. **Location:** Rural, simple. **Surface:** gravel.
⭕ 01/01-31/12.
**Distance:** 🏊1km 🌊200m.

**[S] Wischhafen 8A1**
**Süder-Elbe**, Glückstädter Straße. **GPS:** n53,78678 e9,34017.⬆️➡️

15 🚐free. **Location:** Rural, simple, isolated. **Surface:** gravel.

---

⭕ 01/01-31/12.
**Distance:** 🏊3km 🌊150m.
**Remarks:** Parking at ferry-boat.

**[S] Wischhafen 8A1**
Unterm Deich 7. **GPS:** n53,77528 e9,32111.⬆️➡️

6 🚐free. **Location:** Rural, simple. **Surface:** grassy.
⭕ 01/01-31/12.
**Distance:** 🏊300m ⊗on the spot 🛒1km.

# Lower Saxony/Bremen

**[S] Adendorf 8C2**
**Stellplatz am Freibad**, Scharnebecker Weg 12.
**GPS:** n53,28859 e10,45570.⬆️

30 🚐€ 10 🚰🧺Ch💧included. 📶 **Location:** Rural, simple, quiet.
**Surface:** metalled. ⭕ 01/01-31/12.
**Distance:** 🏊500m 🚴3km ⊗100m 🛒1km 🚌100m.

**[S] Aerzen 10A2**
**Restaurant Waldquelle**, Waldquelle 1.
**GPS:** n52,05952 e9,26146.⬆️➡️

5 🚐€ 5 🚰💧(1x)€ 2/day. **Location:** Rural, isolated. **Surface:** gravel.
⭕ 01/01-31/12 📷 Tue.
**Distance:** 🏊2km 🛒1km 🚌500m 🍴on the spot.
**Remarks:** Check in at hotel, bread-service and breakfast buffet.

**[S] Ahlerstedt 8A2**
**Ahlerstedt Ottendorf**, Rickstücken 2. **GPS:** n53,39261 e9,41422.⬆️➡️

10 🚐€ 10 🚰🧺Ch💧(44x)included. 🐾 **Location:** Rural, simple, isolated, quiet. **Surface:** metalled. ⭕ 01/01-31/12.
**Distance:** 🏊3km 🛒3km.

**[S] Alfeld/Leine 10B2**
Bornstrasse. **GPS:** n51,98586 e9,82769.⬆️

---

4 🚐free 💧. **Location:** Urban, simple. **Surface:** metalled.
⭕ 01/01-31/12.
**Distance:** 🏊on the spot ⊗80m 🛒200m.
**Remarks:** Parking in city centre behind the evangelical church.

**[S] Altenau 10C2**

**Alter Bahnhof Altenau**, Rothenberger Strasse 52.
**GPS:** n51,80124 e10,43396.⬆️➡️
40 🚐€ 11 excl. tourist tax 🚰€ 1/70liter 🧺Ch💧(20x)€ 0,60/kWh, 6Amp WC 🚽€ 2 📷€ 2,50/2,50 📶included. 🏠 🧺
**Location:** Rural, comfortable, quiet. **Surface:** gravel.
⭕ 01/01-31/12.
**Distance:** 🏊900m 🚴450m 🚲2,9km 🚌600m 🛒1,5km 🚌1,5km 🍴on the spot 🚶on the spot 🚴1,7km 🎿on the spot.
**Remarks:** Bread-service, e-bike rental, shuttle bus.

**[S] Altenau 10C2**
**Kristall-Saunatherme Heißer Brocken**, Karl-Reinecke-Weg 35.
**GPS:** n51,79836 e10,44408.⬆️

20 🚐€ 10 + € 2/pp tourist tax 🚰€ 0,50/40liter 🧺Ch💧€ 0,50/kWh 🚽€ 1,50. **Location:** Rural, quiet. **Surface:** metalled.
⭕ 01/01-31/12.
**Distance:** 🏊1,5km ⊗on the spot 🛒on the spot 🚌on the spot.
**Remarks:** Pay at pay-desk of theTherme.

**[S] Amelinghausen 8B3**
**Kronsbergheide**, Hochseilgarten. **GPS:** n53,13500 e10,23389.⬆️➡️

40 🚐€ 3,50-5 💧. **Location:** Rural, simple, isolated, quiet.
**Surface:** metalled/sand. ⭕ 01/01-31/12.
**Distance:** 🏊1km 🚴500m 🛒on the spot ⊗1km 🛒1km 🚴on the spot 🚶on the spot.
**Remarks:** Ticket available at petrol stations, kiosk Lopausee, pay-desk Waldbad and tourist office.

DE

### Amelinghausen 8B3
**Lopausee**, Auf der Kalten Hude. **GPS:** n53,13324 e10,23441.

50 € 5, 1/9-1/7 € 3,50 Ch included.
**Location:** Rural, simple, isolated, quiet. **Surface:** gravel/sand.
01/01-31/12.
**Distance:** 1km 100m 100m 1km 1km on the spot on the spot.
**Remarks:** Bread-service in summer period, ticket available at petrol stations, kiosk Lopausee, pay-desk Waldbad and tourist office.

### Amelinghausen 8B3
**Waldbad**, Zum Lopautal. **GPS:** n53,12402 e10,23018.

40 € 5-8 Ch included € 0,50.
**Location:** Comfortable. 01/01-31/12.
**Distance:** 1km 500m 1km 1km on the spot on the spot.
**Remarks:** Bread-service in summer period, incl. access swimming pool.

### Amelinghausen 8B3
**Schwindbeckerheide**, Steinbeckerstrasse, Soderstorf.
**GPS:** n53,12247 e10,09934.

15 € 3,50-5. **Location:** Rural, simple, isolated.
**Surface:** grassy/gravel. 01/01-31/12.
**Distance:** 4km 6km 6km on the spot on the spot.
**Remarks:** Ticket available at petrol stations, kiosk Lopausee, pay-desk Waldbad and tourist office.

### Amelinghausen 8B3
**Landgasthaus Eichenkrug**, Unter den Eichen 10, Dehnsen.
**GPS:** n53,12804 e10,16817.

4 € 6 € 6/1day included.
**Location:** Simple, isolated. **Surface:** metalled. 01/01-31/12.
**Distance:** 4km on the spot 4km on the spot on the spot.
**Remarks:** Max. 3 nights.

### Amelinghausen 8B3
**Schenck's Hotel & Gasthaus**, Lüneburgerstrasse 48.
**GPS:** n53,12568 e10,21426.

15 € 10 € 0,80/kWh,+ € 1,50 WC included.
**Location:** Simple, central. **Surface:** metalled.
01/01-31/12.
**Distance:** on the spot on the spot on the spot on the spot on the spot.

**Tourist information Amelinghausen:**
Oldendorfer Totenstatt. Hunnebed cineraria from the ice-age.
guided tour 01/05-30/09.

### Apen 7G3
**Am Freibad**, Hauptstraße, Hengstforde. **GPS:** n53,21795 e7,78706.

10 free. **Location:** Rural, simple. **Surface:** metalled.
01/05-15/09.
**Distance:** 5,8km 50m on the spot.
**Remarks:** Along railwayline, max. 3 days, swimming pool Hengstforde.

### Apen 7G3
**Viehmarktplatz**, Hauptstraße. **GPS:** n53,21820 e7,80221.

10 free. **Location:** Urban, simple. **Surface:** metalled.
01/01-31/12.
**Distance:** 100m 5km 50m 200m.
**Remarks:** Max. 2 days.

### Artlenburg 8C2
**Am Sportboothafen**, Am Deich 9. **GPS:** n53,37680 e10,48550.

30 € 10-15 Ch WC. **Location:** Rural, comfortable, quiet.
**Surface:** grassy. 15/04-15/10.
**Distance:** 500m on the spot on the spot 500m 500m.
**Remarks:** Along the river Elbe.

### Auetal 10A2
**Am Freibad**, Horstsiek. **GPS:** n52,23552 e9,14805.

4 free € 1/100liter € 1/2kWh. **Location:** Simple, quiet.
**Surface:** gravel. 01/01-31/12.
**Distance:** 800m 950m.
**Remarks:** At fire-station, at swimming pool.

### Aurich 7G2
**Familienbad De Baalje**, Tannenbergstraße.
**GPS:** n53,46540 e7,47568.

20 free € 10 € 1/100liter Ch € 1/time (24x)€ 1/kWh € 1.
**Location:** Urban, comfortable, quiet. **Surface:** metalled.
01/01-31/12.
**Distance:** 500m 100m.
**Remarks:** Check in and pay at pay desk swimming pool.

### Aurich 7G2
**An den Kiesgruben**, Tannenhausen. **GPS:** n53,52173 e7,47834.

5 free. **Surface:** unpaved. 01/01-31/12.
**Distance:** 1km 10m on the spot.
**Remarks:** At the lake of Tannenhausen.

### Aurich 7G2
**Landgasthof Alte Post**, Essenerstrasse. **GPS:** n53,54573 e7,60736.

6 € 6, guests € 3 € 1 Ch WC. **Location:** Rural, isolated,
quiet. **Surface:** metalled. 01/01-31/12.
**Distance:** on the spot on the spot.
**Remarks:** Caution key electricity € 10.

### Bad Bentheim 9F2
**Am Mühlenberg**, Mühlenberg. **GPS:** n52,29360 e7,10095.

10 € 8 € 1/80liter Ch € 0,50/kWh WC.
**Location:** Rural, simple, central. **Surface:** metalled. 01/01-31/12.
**Distance:** 200m 50m 200m on the spot on the spot.
**Remarks:** Max. 3 days.

### Bad Bentheim 9F2
**Am Schloßpark**, Funkenstiege. **GPS:** n52,30328 e7,15448.

35 ⬛€ 9/24h ⬛€ 1/80liter ⬛Ch ⬛(36x)€ 0,50/kWh WC ⬛.⬛
**Surface:** metalled. ⬛ 01/01-31/12.
**Distance:** ⬛200m ⬛100m.

### Bad Bevensen 8C3
Am Waagekai. **GPS:** n53,07417 e10,60139.⬛⬛.

30 ⬛€ 5,40 + € 3/pp tourist tax ⬛⬛Chincluded ⬛€ 0,50/2kWh.
⬛ **Location:** Rural, simple, quiet. **Surface:** gravel/sand.
⬛ 01/01-31/12.
**Distance:** ⬛1km ⬛on the spot ⬛1km ⬛600m ⬛500m ⬛on the spot ⬛on the spot.
**Remarks:** Along river.

### Bad Essen 9H1
**Wohnmobilstellplatz Falkenburg**, Falkenburg 3.
**GPS:** n52,32352 e8,36384.⬛.

50 ⬛€ 7 ⬛€ 1/100liter ⬛Ch ⬛€ 2/4kWh WC ⬛€ 0,50 ⬛⬛.⬛
**Location:** Rural, comfortable, quiet. **Surface:** grassy/metalled.
⬛ 01/03-30/10.
**Distance:** ⬛1,2km ⬛900m ⬛300m.
**Remarks:** At the Mittelland canal, near marina, bread-service (weekend).

### Bad Gandersheim ⬛ 10B2
**Wohnmobil-Stellplatz Rio Gande**, An der Wiek.
**GPS:** n51,87191 e10,01881.⬛⬛.

24 ⬛€ 7/24h, tourist tax incl ⬛€ 1/100liter ⬛Ch ⬛(14x)€ 0,50/kWh
⬛ 01/01-31/12.
**Location:** Rural, simple. **Surface:** gravel.
**Distance:** ⬛400m ⬛100m ⬛200m ⬛on the spot ⬛on the spot.
**Remarks:** Max. 3 nights, bread-service only in summer.

### Bad Lauterberg ⬛⬛ 10C3
**Erlebnisbad Vitamar**, Mast Tal 1. **GPS:** n51,63358 e10,48661.⬛.

---

5 ⬛free ⬛€ 1 ⬛€ 1 Ch€ 1. **Location:** Rural, simple, quiet.
**Surface:** metalled. ⬛ 01/01-31/12.
**Distance:** ⬛1,5km ⬛30km ⬛on the spot ⬛1,5km ⬛on the spot.

### Bad Lauterberg ⬛⬛ 10C3
**Wiesenbeker Teich**, Wiesenbek 75. **GPS:** n51,61719 e10,49074.⬛⬛.

4 ⬛€ 13 ⬛Ch ⬛included.
**Location:** Isolated, quiet. **Surface:** gravel.
⬛ 01/01-31/12.
**Distance:** ⬛2km ⬛30km ⬛on the spot ⬛on the spot ⬛on the spot ⬛2km ⬛2km ⬛on the spot.
**Remarks:** Check in and pay at reception campsite, max. 1 night.

### Bad Münder 10A2
**Rhomelbad**, Lindenallee. **GPS:** n52,19305 e9,47111.⬛.

5 ⬛free ⬛Ch. **Location:** Simple. **Surface:** metalled.
⬛ 01/01-31/12.
**Distance:** ⬛400m ⬛on the spot ⬛400m ⬛200m.

### Bad Nenndorf 10A1
**Wohnmobilstellplatz am Schulzentrum**, Bahnhofstrasse 77.
**GPS:** n52,34294 e9,37666.⬛.

20 ⬛free ⬛€ 2/45liter ⬛Ch ⬛(8x)€ 1/6h WC ⬛.
**Location:** Rural, simple, quiet. **Surface:** gravel/metalled.
⬛ 01/01-31/12.
**Distance:** ⬛700m ⬛3,4km ⬛on the spot ⬛on the spot on the spot.
**Remarks:** At sports centre, use sanitary only during opening hours swimming pool.

### Bad Pyrmont ⬛⬛ 10A2
**Reisemobilhafen in den Emmerauen**, Hauptmann Boelke-Weg.
**GPS:** n51,98092 e9,25108.⬛⬛.

---

65 ⬛€ 11 + € 2,30-3,20/pp tourist tax ⬛€ 0,10/10liter ⬛Ch ⬛
(60x)€ 0,50/kWh WC ⬛⬛included. ⬛
**Location:** Urban, central. **Surface:** grassy/gravel.
⬛ 01/01-31/12.
**Distance:** ⬛historical centre 400m ⬛200m ⬛400m ⬛100m
⬛on the spot ⬛on the spot.
**Remarks:** Bread-service, e-bike rental, free shuttle to spa resort, free entrance swimming pool.
**Tourist information Bad Pyrmont:**
⬛ Bad Pyrmont Tourismus GmbH, Europa-Platz 1, www.badpyrmont.de. Health resort.

### ⬛ Bad Sachsa ⬛⬛⬛⬛⬛ 10C3
**Harzer Schnitzelhaus & Waffelbäckerei**, Schützenstrasse 13.
**GPS:** n51,59778 e10,55056.⬛.

2 ⬛guests free. **Location:** Urban, simple, central. **Surface:** asphalted.
⬛ 01/01-31/12.
**Distance:** ⬛on the spot ⬛on the spot ⬛100m.
**Remarks:** Max. 2 days.

### Bad Salzdetfurth ⬛ 10B2
**Am Solebad**, Solebadstraße, Detfurth.
**GPS:** n52,07193 e10,01859.⬛⬛.

10 ⬛€ 5/24h ⬛€ 1/50liter ⬛Ch ⬛€ 1/6h WC ⬛€ 3.⬛
**Location:** Rural. **Surface:** asphalted.
⬛ 01/01-31/12.
**Distance:** ⬛2km ⬛Bistro 50m ⬛100m ⬛on the spot ⬛on the spot.
**Remarks:** Use sanitary only during opening hours swimming pool, market Friday-morning.

### Bad Zwischenahn ⬛⬛⬛ 7G3
**Park der Gärten**, Elmendorfer Straße 40. **GPS:** n53,19963 e7,99182.⬛.

12 ⬛tourist tax € 2,30/pp ⬛€ 0,50/100liter ⬛€ 1/2kWh. ⬛
**Location:** Urban, simple. **Surface:** grassy/sand.
⬛ 01/01-31/12.
**Distance:** ⬛1,5km ⬛3km ⬛on the spot ⬛on the spot.

### Bad Zwischenahn ⬛⬛⬛ 7G3
**Wohnmobilstellplatz Am Badepark**, Am Badepark 1.
**GPS:** n53,18722 e8,00021.⬛⬛.

50 ⬛€ 14 tourist tax incl ⬛€ 0,50/100liter ⬛Ch ⬛(35x)€ 0,60/kWh
WC ⬛(spa resort) ⬛included. ⬛
**Location:** Urban, simple. **Surface:** metalled. ⬛ 01/01-31/12.
**Distance:** ⬛350m ⬛6,8km ⬛on the spot ⬛on the spot ⬛100m

**DE**

500m ⇌ on the spot.

**⚓S Balge 🏖 10A1**

**Stellplatz Marina Mehlbergen**, Werderstraße.
**GPS**: n52,68788 e9,17779.⬆.

20 🏷€ 10 ⛽🔌Ch ⚡(16x)€ 0,50/kWh WC included ▣€ 3/time.
🚿 **Location:** Rural, comfortable, isolated, quiet. **Surface:** metalled.
⏱ 01/04-31/10.
**Distance:** 🏊2km ⛵on the spot ⤵on the spot ⊗2km 🛒2km ⇌1km
🚲on the spot 🚶on the spot.
**Remarks:** Check in on arrival.

**🏛 Balje 8A1**

**Am Natureum**, Neuenhof 8, Neuhaus. **GPS**: n53,81958 e9,03867.⬆.

6 🏷free. **Location:** Rural, simple, isolated. **Surface:** grassy.
⏱ 01/01-31/12.
**Distance:** 🏊4km ⛵on the spot ⊗4km 🛒4km.
**Remarks:** Along river.

**⚓S Barnstorf 9H1**

**Wohnmobilstellplatz Midden int Dörp**, Rathausweg/Brinkstraße.
**GPS**: n52,71170 e8,50780.⬆➡.

3 🏷free ⛽€ 1/100liter 🍽Ch ⚡(3x)€ 1/6h.
**Location:** Rural, simple, central, quiet. **Surface:** metalled.
⏱ 01/01-31/12.
**Distance:** 🏊on the spot ⊗100m 🛒300m.

**⚓S Barßel 🏖🚤 7G3**

**Am Bootshafen**, Deichstrasse. **GPS**: n53,16754 e7,73441.⬆➡.

18 🏷€ 6 ⛽🔌Ch ⚡(34x)€ 2/24h WC🚰€ 1 🚿included.🚽
**Location:** Rural, simple. **Surface:** grasstiles.
⏱ 01/01-31/12.
**Distance:** 🏊500m ⤵on the spot ⊗on the spot 🛒500m
🚲on the spot.

**⚓S Barsinghausen 🌿 10A1**

**Wohnmobilstellplatz am Besucherbergwerk Klosterstollen**,
Conrad-Bühreweg. **GPS**: n52,29858 e9,46943.⬆➡.

5 🏷€ 6,50 ⛽🔌 ⚡(5x)included. 🚽 **Location:** Rural, simple.
**Surface:** gravel. ⏱ 01/01-31/12.
**Distance:** 🏊300m ⊗nearby 🛒300m.
**Remarks:** Max. 3 days, visit coalmine possible.

**⚓S Berge 9G1**

**Stift Börstel**, Börstel 5. **GPS**: n52,64957 e7,69438.⬆.

2 🏷€ 5 ⛽€ 2/time ⚡€ 2/2kWh WC🚰.
**Location:** Rural, simple, isolated, quiet. **Surface:** metalled.
⏱ 01/01-31/12.
**Distance:** 🏊city centre Haselünne 7km ⊗3km 🛒7km ⇌150m.
**Remarks:** Near abbey, max. 2 nights, money in envelope in mail box.

**⚓S Bergen 8B3**

**Stellplatz am Ziegeleiweg**, Ziegeleiweg. **GPS**: n52,81273 e9,96457.⬆.

6 🏷€ 3,50 ⛽€ 1 🍽Ch⚡included.
**Surface:** gravel.
⏱ 01/01-31/12.
**Distance:** 🏊nearby ⊗300m 🛒450m ⇌250m.
**Remarks:** Caution key € 20 at town hall.

**Tourist information Bergen:**
 Wildpark Lüneburger Heide, Nindorf. Game preserve. ⏱ 01/03-
31/10 8-19h, 01/11-28/02 9.30-16.30h.

**⚓S Berne 🏖 7H3**

**Fähranleger Motzen**, Motzener Strasse. **GPS**: n53,17972 e8,55778.⬆.

4 🏷free ⛽€ 1/60liter 🍽Ch ⚡(4x)€ 1/6h.
**Location:** Urban, simple, noisy. **Surface:** gravel/sand.
⏱ 01/01-31/12.
**Distance:** 🏊3,5km ⤵on the spot ⊗1km 🛒100m ⇌200m 🚲100m.
**Remarks:** Parking at ferry-boat at river Weser.

**⚓ Bevern 10A2**

**Schwimm- und Freizeitzentrum**, Jahnstrasse.
**GPS**: n51,85750 e9,50805.➡.

5 🏷free. **Location:** Rural, simple. **Surface:** asphalted.
⏱ 01/01-31/12.
**Distance:** 🏊1,2km 🛒500m ⇌500m.
**Remarks:** At swimming pool.

**⚓S Bienenbüttel 🏖 8C3**

**Wohnmobilstellplatz Ilmenauwiese**, Niendorfer strasse, K42.
**GPS**: n53,14514 e10,49051.⬆.

12 🏷€ 6/24h ⛽€ 1/10minutes 🍽Ch ⚡(14x)€ 1/8h WCfree 🚰€ 0,50.
🚽 **Location:** Rural, comfortable, quiet.
**Surface:** metalled. ⏱ 01/01-31/12.
**Distance:** 🏊500m ⤵on the spot ⊗on the spot 🛒500m ⇌500m
🚶special sculpture route.

**⚓ Bippen 🌲🏡 9G1**

**Dorfteich**, Hauptstrasse. **GPS**: n52,58209 e7,73887.⬆.

2 🏷free. **Location:** Rural, simple, quiet. **Surface:** concrete.
⏱ 01/01-31/12.
**Distance:** 🛒1km 🚶on the spot.

**🍇S Bippen 🌲🏡 9G1**

**Ferienhof Nyenhuis**, Hallweg 8. **GPS**: n52,59360 e7,73005.➡.

20 🏷€ 13 ⛽🔌Ch ⚡WC🚰€ 2,50. 🚽 **Location:** Rural, simple,
isolated, quiet. **Surface:** grassy. ⏱ 01/01-31/12.
**Distance:** 🏊1km ⇌100m.

**⚓S Bispingen 🌲 8B3**

**Parkplatz Oberhaverbeck**, Oberhaverbeck. **GPS**: n53,14281 e9,91998.

30 🏷€ 3/day, € 6/night ⛽€ 1/10minutes 🍽Ch ⚡(8x)€ 1/10h. 🚐
**Location:** Rural, simple, isolated, quiet. **Surface:** grassy/gravel.
⏱ 01/01-31/12 ▣ Service: winter.
**Distance:** 🏊6km ⊗350m 🛒6km ⇌100m 🚲on the spot
🚶on the spot.

**Remarks:** In nature reserve the the Lüneburg Heide (heath).

### Bispingen 8B3

**Parking Rathaus**, Borsteler Straße 4-6. **GPS:** n53,08499 e9,99789.

5 free. **Location:** Rural, simple, central. **Surface:** metalled. 01/01-31/12. **Distance:** on the spot 1km 100m 100m on the spot on the spot.

### Bispingen 8B3

**Parkplatz Luhetalbad**, Trift 19. **GPS:** n53,09074 e10,00582.

20 free. **Location:** Rural, simple. **Surface:** metalled. 01/01-31/12. **Distance:** 1km 3km. **Remarks:** Parking at swimming pool.

### Bispingen 8B3

**Reiter- und Ferienhof Cohrs**, Volkwardingen 1, Moorweg. **GPS:** n53,13409 e10,00047.

10 € 16 Ch included WC € 3. **Location:** Rural, comfortable, isolated, quiet. **Surface:** grassy. 01/01-31/12. **Distance:** 3km 5,5km 500m 5km 350m on the spot. **Remarks:** Bread-service.

### Bissendorf 9H2

**Reisemobil-Center Veregge & Welz**, Gewerbepark 14, A30 Abfahrt Bissendorf. **GPS:** n52,24026 e8,13977.

6 free € 1/5minutes Ch (4x) € 1/6h. **Location:** Urban, simple, quiet. **Surface:** metalled. 01/01-31/12. **Distance:** 1km 650m 800m 800m.

### Bleckede 8C2

**Campingpark Elbtalaue**, Am Waldbad 23. **GPS:** n53,25948 e10,80526.

5 € 10/night € 1/80liter Ch € 0,70/kWh WC sanitary € 3,50/pp € 3,50/3 € 4/day. **Location:** Rural, luxurious, isolated, quiet. **Surface:** grassy. 01/03-31/10. **Distance:** 2km 300m 800m 6km 50m on the spot on the spot. **Remarks:** Bread-service, dog € 3,50, possibility for reservation, free entrance swimming pool.

### Bleckede 8C2

**Parking Bleckede**, Schützenweg. **GPS:** n53,29520 e10,73309.

10 free. **Location:** Rural, simple. **Surface:** grassy/metalled. 01/01-31/12. **Distance:** 500m 500m 900m on the spot on the spot.

### Blomberg 7G2

**Dorfplatz Blomberg**, Hauptstrasse. **GPS:** n53,57718 e7,55815.

20 free € 1 Ch € 1 (12x) € 1/kWh WC. **Location:** Rural, comfortable, quiet. **Surface:** grassy/metalled. 01/01-31/12 service 01/11-31/03. **Distance:** on the spot 200m 200m 50m.

### Bockenem 10B2

**Freibad**, In den Reesen. **GPS:** n52,00787 e10,13610.

5 free. **Location:** Rural, simple, quiet. **Surface:** gravel. 01/01-31/12. **Distance:** 800m 200m 300m 260m.

### Bockenem 10B2

**Hotel Sauer**, Allensteiner strasse 7. **GPS:** n52,00224 e10,13379.

10 guests free € 1,50 Ch (8x) € 2,50 WC € 1,50. **Location:** Rural, simple. **Surface:** metalled. 01/01-31/12. **Distance:** 300m on the spot 500m.

### Bockhorn 7G2

**Erlebnisbad**, Urwaldstrasse 35a. **GPS:** n53,39876 e7,99410.

5 free. **Location:** Rural, simple. **Surface:** gravel. 01/01-31/12. **Distance:** on the spot. **Remarks:** Parking swimming pool, max. 1 day.

### Bockhorn 7G2

**Gaststätte Altdeutsche Diele**, Landesstrasse 11, Steinhausen. **GPS:** n53,41404 e8,03466.

3 free (3x)against payment WC. **Location:** Simple. **Surface:** metalled. 01/01-31/12.

### Bockhorn 7G2

**Reisemobilplatz Germer**, Am Geeschendamm 1. **GPS:** n53,38575 e8,00857.

30 € 7 € 1,50 Ch (15x) € 0,75/kWh WC € 2. **Location:** Rural, comfortable. **Surface:** grassy. 01/01-31/12. **Distance:** 400m 700m on the spot on the spot.

### Bodenwerder 10A2

**Wohnmobilstellplatz Bodenwerder**, Am Mühlentor. **GPS:** n51,98037 e9,51795.

25 € 6, tourist tax € 1/pp € 2/10minutes Ch € 2,50/day WC € 1,50. **Location:** Urban, simple. **Surface:** grassy. 01/01-31/12. **Distance:** 200m Weser 200m 200m 500m 200m. **Remarks:** Along river, max. 1 day, check in and pay at kiosk.

### Bohmte 9H1

**Golfclub Arenshorst**, Arenshorster Kirchweg 2. **GPS:** n52,35651 e8,28450.

3 guests free. **Location:** Rural, simple. **Surface:** grassy/metalled.

DE

## WASSERWELT

## Reisemobil-Stellplatz

### Equipment motorhome stopover

➤ 17 paved motorhome pitches, 5x10 meters
➤ Electricity and fresh water supply
➤ Free Wi-Fi
➤ 10% discount on day tickets in Freizeitbad
➤ Dogs are also welcome!

Am Schützenplatz 1 | 38114 Braunschweig | www.wasserwelt-bs.de

**DE**

📅 01/01-31/12.
**Distance:** 🚶3km ⊗on the spot 🚊3km.

| 🏴 S | **Bohmte** | 9H1 |

**Landgasthaus Gieseke-Asshorn**, Bremer strasse 55.
**GPS:** n52,36674 e8,31261.

4 🏕guests free 🚰free 📶. **Location:** Urban, simple, quiet.
**Surface:** metalled. 📅 01/01-31/12.
**Distance:** 🚶50m ⊗100m 🚊200m 🚌400m.

| 🏴 S | **Brake** 🌊🌳🍦 | 7H2 |

**City-Parkplatz**, Breite Strasse. **GPS:** n53,32534 e8,47982. ⬆➡.

2 🏕free 🅿€3 WC🚽. **Location:** Urban, simple, central, noisy.
**Surface:** metalled. 📅 01/01-31/12.
**Distance:** 🚶on the spot ⊗on the spot 🚊200m 🚌200m
🚲 on the spot.
**Remarks:** Key at aparthotel Panorama (50m).

| 🏴 S | **Brake** 🌊🌳🍦 | 7H2 |

**Am Binnenhafen**, Hafenstrasse. **GPS:** n53,32802 e8,48296. ⬆.

4 🏕free 🅿€ 1/10minutes 🍴Ch 🅿(4x)€ 1/6h.
**Location:** Urban, simple, central, noisy. **Surface:** grasstiles.
📅 01/01-31/12.
**Distance:** 🚶on the spot 🚊1km 🚾100m 🚊200m 🚌200m
🚲 on the spot.

| 🏴 S | **Bramsche** | 9G1 |

**Wohnmobilstellplatz Waldwinkel**, Zum Dreschhaus 4.
**GPS:** n52,39591 e8,10244. ⬆➡.

60 🏕€7 🅿€ 0,10/10liter 🍴Ch 🅿(80x)€2 WC🚽€ 1.
**Location:** Rural, comfortable, isolated, quiet. **Surface:** grassy.
📅 01/01-31/12.
**Distance:** 🚶3,5km 🚾100m 🚊3,5km 🚌100m 🚲 on the spot
🏃 on the spot.
**Remarks:** Next to campsite Waldwinkel.

| 🏴 | **Bramsche** | 9G1 |

**Hasebad**, Malgartener strasse 49. **GPS:** n52,41493 e7,99423. ⬆.

6 🏕free. **Location:** Urban, simple, quiet. **Surface:** metalled.
📅 01/01-31/12.
**Distance:** 🚶500m ⊗200m 🚊on the spot 🚌100m.

| 🏴 S | **Bramsche** | 9G1 |

**Reisemobile Lewandowsky**, Am Kanal 1b.
**GPS:** n52,38524 e7,92958. ⬆➡.

2 🏕free 🅿🍴Chfree 🅿€ 2/day. **Location:** Rural, simple.
**Surface:** gravel. 📅 01/01-31/12.
**Distance:** 🚶1km ⊗1km 🚊1km 🚌1,2km.
**Remarks:** Also repairs possible, service during opening hours, walking
and bicycle area.

## Braunschweig — 10C1

**Freizeitbad Wasserwelt**, Am Schützenplatz 1.
**GPS:** n52,28589 e10,51871.

17 € 10 Ch WC. **Location:** Urban, simple, central.
**Surface:** metalled. 01/01-31/12.
**Distance:** on the spot 300m 200m on the spot on the spot.
**Remarks:** Max. 5 days.

## Braunschweig — 10C1

**Theodor-Heuss-Straße. GPS:** n52,24964 e10,51835.

16 free € 1/10minutes Ch (16x)€ 1/8h.
01/01-31/12.
**Location:** Urban, simple, noisy. **Surface:** asphalted.
**Distance:** 2km 400m 200m 50m.
**Remarks:** Max. 2 nights.

## Bremen — 7H3

**Wohnmobil Oase Bremen**, Schoster born, via Emil von Behringstrasse.
**GPS:** n53,06778 e8,86333.

8 € 15 + tourist tax € 1/pp € 2 Ch WC included
€ 1,50, use luxurious bathroom € 5, sauna € 5 € 6.
**Location:** Urban, comfortable, central. **Surface:** gravel.
01/01-31/12.
**Distance:** 4km on the spot 50m Tram on the spot.
**Remarks:** Motorhome < 7m, outside environmental zone.

## Bremen — 7H3

**Am Kuhhirten**, Kurhirtenweg. **GPS:** n53,06500 e8,81871.

70 € 15 € 1/100liter Ch (70x)€ 0,50/kWh WC € 1
€ 1/5minutes. **Location:** Urban, comfortable, central.
**Surface:** gravel. 01/01-31/12.
**Distance:** Old city centre 1,3km 500m on the spot 800m
Tram 700m on the spot.
**Remarks:** Bread-service, outside environmental zone.

## Bremen — 7H3

**Bremer Schweiz**, Im Pohl, Lesum. **GPS:** n53,16765 e8,69560.

---

7 € 5/24h € 1/10minutes Ch (8x)€ 1/8h.
**Location:** Urban, comfortable, quiet. **Surface:** gravel.
01/01-31/12.
**Distance:** on the spot 2,4km on the spot 300m on the spot on the spot.
**Remarks:** Outside environmental zone.

## Bremen — 7H3

**Maritime Meile**, Schulkenstrasse. **GPS:** n53,17298 e8,60906.

5 € 5 + tourist tax € 1/80liter Ch (4x)€ 1/8h.
**Location:** Urban, comfortable, central, quiet.
**Surface:** asphalted.
01/01-31/12.
**Distance:** Bremen 20km 100m 100m 200m on the spot.
**Remarks:** Outside environmental zone.

**Tourist information Bremen:**

Tourist Information, Obernstrasse en Hauptbahnhof,
www.bremen-tourism.de. Hanseatic city and second harbour of
Germany.
Böttcherstrasse. Pedestrian passage.
Weserpromenade Schlachte. Antiques and flea market. Sa
8-14h.

## Bremerhaven — 7H2

**Reisemobil-Parkplatz Doppelschleuse**, An der Neuen Schleuse.
**GPS:** n53,53230 e8,57607.

63 € 10 € 1/80liter Ch (40x)€ 0,50/kWh WC € 0,50
€ 0,50. **Location:** Urban, comfortable, central, quiet.
**Surface:** asphalted. 01/01-31/12.
**Distance:** 1km 8km 1km 1,5km 1,2km on the spot.
**Remarks:** Bread-service.

## Bremerhaven — 7H2

**Reisemobil-Parkplatz Fischereihafen**, Hoebelstrasse, Fischereihafen
1. **GPS:** n53,52634 e8,57610.

47 € 10, tourist tax incl € 1/100liter Ch (36x)€ 0,50/kWh
WC included € 0,50. **Location:** Urban, luxurious, central, quiet.
**Surface:** asphalted/metalled. 01/01-31/12.
**Distance:** 4km on the spot on the spot 500m 500m
200m 200m.
**Remarks:** At harbour, caution key sanitary € 5.

---

## Bremerhaven — 7H2

**Havenhostel Bremerhaven**, Bürgermeister-Smidt-Straße 209.
**GPS:** n53,55932 e8,56793.

23 € 15 Ch WC € 2/2 included.
**Location:** Urban, simple, central. **Surface:** grassy. 01/01-31/12.
**Distance:** 1,4km on the spot 1km 100m 100m
on the spot.
**Remarks:** Check in at reception, breakfast-service.

## Bremervörde — 8A2

**Wohnmobilstation Bremervörde**, Kiebitzweg 1.
**GPS:** n53,49453 e9,15576.
40 € 9,50, 01/11-28/02 € 6,50 Ch (21x)€ 3/day,10Amp
WC € 1 included. **Location:** Rural, comfortable, quiet.
**Surface:** metalled. 01/01-31/12.
**Distance:** 1,5km 100m 100m 300m 1km 1,5km
on the spot on the spot.

## Brietlingen — 8B2

**Reihersee**, Grosse strabe. **GPS:** n53,34344 e10,45844.

50 € 8 € 2,50. **Location:** Rural, simple, isolated.
**Surface:** grassy. 01/03-31/10.
**Distance:** on the spot.

## Brietlingen — 8B2

**Landhotel Franck**, Bundesstrasse 31b. **GPS:** n53,32951 e10,44491.

5 guests free (1x)€ 5/night. **Location:** Rural, simple, quiet.
01/01-31/12.
**Distance:** on the spot on the spot 500m.

## Bruchhausen-Vilsen — 8A3

**Reisemobilstellplatz Bruchhausen-Vilsen**, Bollenstrasse.
**GPS:** n52,82671 e8,99536.

DE

40 🚐 6 ⛽ € 1/100liter 🚻Ch ⚡(24x)WCincluded 📶.
**Location:** Urban, simple. **Surface:** grassy/gravel.
⭕ 01/01-31/12.
**Distance:** 🚶200m ⊗200m 🗑200m.
**Remarks:** Max. 3 days.

### Buchholz/Nordheide 8B2
**Campingplatz Nordheide**, Weg zum Badeteich 20.
**GPS:** n53,28202 e9,87495.⬆️

12 🚐 12-15 ⛽🚻Ch ⚡(6x)€ 2 WCincluded 🍴.♻️
**Location:** Rural, comfortable. **Surface:** metalled/sand.
⭕ 01/01-31/12.
**Distance:** 🚶200m 🏖on the spot ⊗800m 🗑200m 🚌250m.

### Bückeburg 10A2
**Am Schloss**, Georgstrasse/Liebesallee. **GPS:** n52,25777 e9,04583.⬆️➡️

20 🚐 7/24h ⛽€ 1/8minutes 🚻Ch ⚡(24x)€ 1/12h. 🚐
**Location:** Urban, quiet. **Surface:** gravel/metalled.
⭕ 01/01-31/12.
**Distance:** 🚶500m ⊗500m 🗑500m 🚌200m 🚶on the spot.

### Bückeburg 10A2
**Neumarktplatz**, Unterwallweg 5c. **GPS:** n52,26326 e9,05040.⬆️

10 🚐 free ⛽€ 1/80liter 🚻Ch ⚡(6x)€ 0,50/kWh. **Location:** Urban, simple. **Surface:** gravel. ⭕ 01/01-31/12.
**Distance:** 🚶250m ⊗250m 🗑250m 🚶on the spot.

### Büddenstedt 10C2
**Am Sportplatz. GPS:** n52,17567 e11,01843.⬆️

3 🚐 free. **Location:** Rural, simple, quiet.
**Surface:** asphalted. ⭕ 01/01-31/12.
**Distance:** 🚶1km ⊗on the spot 🗑2km.
**Remarks:** Parking swimming pool.

### Büddenstedt 10C2
**Parking K22**, Barneberger Straße, Offleben.
**GPS:** n52,13738 e11,04409.⬆️

---

2 🚐 free. **Location:** Rural, simple. **Surface:** asphalted.
⭕ 01/01-31/12.
**Distance:** 🚶500m ⊗500m 🗑500m.

### Büren 10B3
**Alter Festplatz**, Im Teich. **GPS:** n51,48378 e9,67451.⬆️➡️

20 🚐 2 ⛽€ 2 🚻Ch. ♻️ **Location:** Rural, isolated.
**Surface:** grassy. ⭕ 01/01-31/12.
**Distance:** 🚶700m 🗑5km 🚶on the spot 🏃on the spot.

### Bunde 7F3
**Am Friedhofsweg. GPS:** n53,18500 e7,26639.⬆️➡️

15 🚐 5 ⛽€ 1 🚻1 Ch ⚡€ 1/10h. **Location:** Central.
**Surface:** grasstiles. ⭕ 01/01-31/12.
**Distance:** 🚶100m 🚲2,3km ⊗350m 🗑200m 🚌100m.
**Remarks:** At townhall, max. 3 days.

### Bunde 7F3
**Freizeitgelände**, Denkmalstrasse 11, Ditzumerverlaat.
**GPS:** n53,26028 e7,26861.⬆️➡️

10 🚐 3/24h ⛽€ 0,50 🚻Ch ⚡(8x)€ 1/8h.
**Location:** Rural, comfortable, quiet. **Surface:** metalled.
⭕ 01/01-31/12 ⭕ during event.
**Distance:** 🚶250m 🏖on the spot 🚶on the spot ⊗350m 🗑250m.
**Remarks:** Max. 3 days.

### Bunde 7F3
**Möhlenlandbad**, Kellingwold 25. **GPS:** n53,18683 e7,27418.⬆️

10 🚐 € 3. ♻️ **Location:** Simple, quiet. **Surface:** metalled.
⭕ 01/01-31/12.
**Distance:** 🚶500m 🚲3km ⊗600m 🗑1,5km.
**Remarks:** At swimming pool.

---

### Butjadingen 7H2
**Henken's Stellplatz**, Am Hafen 6, Fedderwardersiel.
**GPS:** n53,59581 e8,35669.⬆️➡️

80 🚐 6 + tourist tax € 0,95-2,30/pp ⛽€ 0,01/1liter 🚻Ch€ 1/24h ⚡(48x)€ 2,50/day. ♻️ **Location:** Rural, comfortable, central, quiet.
**Surface:** grassy. ⭕ 01/03-31/10.
**Distance:** 🚶500m 🏖on the spot 🚶on the spot ⊗on the spot 🗑on the spot 🚲500m 🏃on the spot.
**Remarks:** Bread-service.

### Butjadingen 7H2
**Freizeithafen Fedderwardersiel**, Sielstraße.
**GPS:** n53,59518 e8,35700.⬆️

45 🚐 12, 2 pers.incl. tourist tax € 2,3/0pp, dog € 0,50 ⛽€ 1,50 🚻Ch€ 1,50 ⚡(20x)€ 2,50/day WC 🍴€ 0,50/3minutes 🔲€ 6. ♻️
**Location:** Rural, comfortable, isolated, quiet. **Surface:** grassy.
⭕ 01/04-31/10.
**Distance:** 🚶800m 🏖on the spot 🚶on the spot ⊗800m 🗑800m 🚌on the spot 🚲on the spot 🏃on the spot.

### Butjadingen 7H2
**Hof Iggewarden**, Iggewarden 1. **GPS:** n53,58622 e8,32653.⬆️➡️

20 🚐 8 ⛽€ 1/100liter 🚻Ch ⚡(2x)included WC. ♻️
**Location:** Rural, comfortable, isolated, quiet. **Surface:** gravel.
⭕ 01/05-30/09.
**Distance:** 🚶2km 🏖2km ⊗on the spot 🚶on the spot 🗑300m 🚲on the spot 🏃on the spot.

### Butjadingen 7H2
**Knaus Campingpark Burhave**, An der Nordseelagune 1.
**GPS:** n53,58306 e8,37000.⬆️➡️

125 🚐 14,50 + € 2,30/pp tourist tax ⛽€ 1/70liter 🚻Ch ⚡€ 0,70/kWh WC 🍴€ 3,50,sanitary € 3,50/pp 📶€ 4/day. 🚐
**Location:** Rural, comfortable, quiet. **Surface:** grassy.
⭕ 15/04-15/10.
**Distance:** 🚶1km 🏖on the spot ⊗200m 🗑1km.

### Buxtehude 8A2
**Pfingstmarktplatz**, Cuxhavenerstrasse, Neukloster, B73.
**GPS:** n53,47974 e9,63528.⬆️

40 ⊠free ⌁€ 1/100liter ⊞ChWC⊟€ 2.
**Location:** Rural, simple. **Surface:** asphalted.
◻ 01/01-31/12 ⊡ week before/after Whitsuntide.
**Distance:** ⚓3km ⊗Imbiss ⚑bakery 200m 🚌150m.
**Remarks:** Key shower at Imbiss.

---

### ⊞S Buxtehude 🌿🍴🏖 8A2

**Stellplatz am Schützenplatz**, Genslerweg.
**GPS:** n53,47139 e9,69528.⬆➡.

30 ⊠€5 ⌁€ 1/100liter ⊞Ch ⚡(18x)€ 1/kWh.
**Location:** Urban, simple, central, noisy. **Surface:** gravel/sand.
◻ 01/01-31/12.
**Distance:** ⚓nearby Old city centre ⊗50m ⚑bakery 50m 🚲on the spot 🅿on the spot.

---

### ⊞S Buxtehude 🌿🍴🏖 8A2

**Wassersportverein Hansa**, Am Hafen 5. **GPS:** n53,47871 e9,70359.⬆.

5 ⊠€10 ⌁Ch ⚡WC 📶included.🚿
**Location:** Urban, simple, central. **Surface:** grassy/metalled.
◻ 01/05-30/09.
**Distance:** ⚓1km ⊗350m ⚑500m 🚌200m.
**Tourist information Buxtehude:**
👁 Das Fleth. Old inland-port.

---

### ⊞S Cadenberge 8A1

**Reisemobilvermietung Hennig**, Alter Postweg 1.
**GPS:** n53,76686 e9,05681.⬆.

4 ⊠€5 ⌁€ 0,50/100liter ⚡€ 1,50/24h.🚿 **Location:** Rural, simple.
**Surface:** grassy. ◻ 01/01-31/12.
**Distance:** ⚓50m ⊗on the spot ⚑50m 🚌300m.

---

### ⊞S Celle 10B1

**Schützenplatz**, Hafenstraße. **GPS:** n52,62794 e10,07348.⬆.

---

5 ⊠free ⌁€ 1/100liter ⊞ChWC. **Surface:** grassy/metalled.
◻ 01/01-31/12.
**Distance:** ⚓150m ⊗100m ⚑1km.

---

### ⊞S Celle 10B1

**Am Badeland**, Langensalzaplatz. **GPS:** n52,61842 e10,08052.➡.

3 ⊠free. **Surface:** metalled. ◻ 01/01-31/12.
**Distance:** ⚓on the spot ⊗700m ⚑700m.

---

### ⊞S Clausthal-Zellerfeld 🌿🌳 10C2

**Busbahnhof**, Bahnhofstraß2 5. **GPS:** n51,81360 e10,33602.⬆.

4 ⊠tourist tax € 1,50 WC. **Location:** Rural, simple. **Surface:** metalled.
◻ 01/01-31/12.
**Distance:** ⚓on the spot ⊗200m ⚑600m 🚌on the spot 🅿on the spot.
**Remarks:** Pay at tourist office.

---

### 🌿S Clenze 🌳 8C3

**Regenbogen-Hof**, Mützen. **GPS:** n52,94079 e10,93899.⬆➡.

5 ⊠€ 7/pp ⌁⊞Ch ⚡WC⊟included. **Location:** Rural, simple, isolated, quiet. **Surface:** grassy. ◻ 01/01-31/12.
**Distance:** ⚓3km ⊗on the spot ⚑3km 🚌on the spot.
**Remarks:** Arrival <22h.

---

### ⊞S Cloppenburg 7G3

**Am Stadtpark**, Hagenweg. **GPS:** n52,84649 e8,04687.⬆.

8 ⊠€ 5, tourist tax incl ⌁€ 1/80liter ⊞Chfree ⚡€ 0,50/kWh.
**Location:** Urban, simple. **Surface:** metalled.
◻ 01/01-31/12.
**Distance:** ⚓100m 🚲2km ⊗100m ⚑300m.
**Remarks:** Max. 3 days.

---

### ⊞S Cloppenburg 7G3

**Museumsdorf Cloppenburg**, Bether Straße.
**GPS:** n52,85197 e8,05335.⬆.

20 ⊠free WC. **Location:** Rural, simple, quiet. **Surface:** metalled.
◻ 01/01-31/12.
**Distance:** ⚓900m ⚑1km ⊗1km ⚑bakery 200m 🚌400m.
**Remarks:** Parking in front of museum village, max. 24h.

---

### ⊞S Coppenbrügge 🌳 10A2

**Parkplatz am Frei- und Hallenbad**, Felsenkellerweg.
**GPS:** n52,11613 e9,53676.⬆➡.

11 ⊠€ 3,50 ⌁€ 2,50 ⊞Ch ⚡(12x)€ 1 WC⊟included.
**Location:** Rural, simple. **Surface:** grassy/gravel.
**Distance:** ⚓1,5km ⊗500m ⚑500m 🚲on the spot 🅿on the spot.
**Remarks:** Check in at campsite, use sanitary only during opening hours swimming pool.

---

### ⊞S Cuxhaven ⚓🏖 7H1

**Duhner Allee**, Duhnen. **GPS:** n53,88284 e8,64814.⬆.

60 ⊠€ 8, peak season € 10 ⌁⊞Chincluded ⚡€ 2/day WC€ 0,50 ⊟€ 1.🚿 **Location:** Rural, simple, quiet. **Surface:** asphalted.
◻ 01/01-31/12.
**Distance:** ⚓1km ⊗1km ⚑1km.
**Remarks:** Beach parking, in front of campsite am Bäderring.

---

### ⊞S Cuxhaven ⚓🏖 7H1

**Elbe-Ferry**, Am Fährhafen. **GPS:** n53,87508 e8,70315.⬆➡.

100 ⊠€ 10-13, tourist tax incl ⌁€ 1/80liter ⊞Ch ⚡(100x)€ 1/kWh.
🚿 **Location:** Urban, simple. **Surface:** asphalted.
◻ 01/01-31/12.
**Distance:** ⚓1km ⊗500m ⚑900m.
**Remarks:** Bread-service.

---

### ⊞S Cuxhaven ⚓🏖 7H1

**Privatparkplatz Kugelbake Halle**, Nordfeldstraße.
**GPS:** n53,89033 e8,67703.⬆.

DE

80 ⌂ € 8 ⛽ Ch WC included. 🏪 **Location:** Urban, simple.
**Surface:** metalled. 🗓 01/01-31/12.
**Distance:** ⚓200m ⊗100m.

**Cuxhaven** ⚓ 7H1

**Wohnmobilparkplatz zur Schleuse**, Präsident-Herwig-Straße 21.
**GPS:** n53,86678 e8,71007.⬆.

18 ⌂ € 15 ⛽ 🔌 included. 🏪 **Location:** Urban, simple.
**Surface:** metalled. 🗓 01/01-31/12.
**Distance:** 🚶1,4km ⊗400m 🍺400m.

**Cuxhaven** ⚓ 7H1

**Campingplatz Finck**, Am Sahlenburger Strand 25.
**GPS:** n53,86039 e8,59167.⬆➡.

16 ⌂ € 17, tourist tax incl ⛽ Ch 🔌(16x)included WC ⌐ € 0,50 ⚬.
♨ 🚿 **Location:** Rural, comfortable. **Surface:** metalled.
🗓 15/03-31/10.
**Distance:** 🚶3km ⚓on the spot ⊗50m 🔲on camp site 🚌100m.
**Remarks:** Sanitary at campsite.

**Damme** 9H1

**Stellplatz am Flugplatz**, Am Flugplatz 8.
**GPS:** n52,49055 e8,17925.⬆➡.

12 ⌂ € 10 ⛽ € 0,50/80liter Ch 🔌(12x) € 0,50/kWh WC ⌐ € 1. 🚰
**Location:** Rural, luxurious. **Surface:** grassy/gravel. 🗓 01/01-31/12.
**Distance:** 🚶1,4km ⊗on the spot 🚌100m.
**Remarks:** Parking airport Damme.

**Damme** 9H1

**Olgahafen**, Dümmerstrasse, Dümmerlohausen.
**GPS:** n52,52917 e8,31098.⬆.

12 ⌂ free ⛽ € 1 Ch 🔌(12x) € 1/kWh.
**Location:** Rural, simple, quiet. **Surface:** gravel.

---

🗓 01/01-31/12.
**Distance:** ⚓100m 🚣100m ⊗on the spot 🍺bakery 🚲on the spot.
**Remarks:** At lake Dümmer, max. 3 days.

**Dangast** 7G2

Sielstrasse 30. **GPS:** n53,44539 e8,10979.⬆.

40 ⌂ € 9, tourist tax excl 🚰 🔌(14x)included. 🏪 **Location:** Simple.
**Surface:** grassy. 🗓 15/04-15/10.
**Distance:** ⚓on the spot 🚣on the spot ⊗on the spot.

**Dannenberg** 8C3

Bäckergrund 32. **GPS:** n53,10062 e11,10903.
4 ⌂ Ch. 🗓 01/04-30/09.
**Distance:** ⚓300m 🍺850m.

**Dassel** 10B2

Am Badesee in der Ortschaft, Lauenberg.
**GPS:** n51,75750 e9,76389.⬆➡.

8 ⌂ free, 01/05-01/10 € 5 ⛽ € 1/80liter Ch 🔌 € 1/8h
⌐included,01/05-30/09. 🏪 **Location:** Rural, isolated, quiet.
**Surface:** asphalted. 🗓 01/01-31/12.
**Distance:** 🚶8,5km ⚓on the spot ⊗300m 🍺300m 🚌300m
🚲on the spot 🚶on the spot.

**Dassel** 10B2

**Am Sollingbad**, An der Badeanstalt. **GPS:** n51,80722 e9,68917.⬆➡.

5 ⌂ free WC ⌐. **Location:** Rural, simple, isolated. **Surface:** asphalted.
🗓 01/05-01/10.
**Distance:** 🚶Old city centre 500m ⊗500m 🍺1km 🚲on the spot
🚶on the spot.
**Remarks:** Use sanitary only during opening hours swimming pool.

**Deinste** 8A2

**Gut Deinster Mühle**, Im Mühlenfeld 30. **GPS:** n53,53132 e9,43301.⬆.
15 ⌂ free. **Location:** Rural. **Surface:** grassy. 🗓 01/01-31/12.
**Distance:** 🚣on the spot ⊗on the spot 🍺400m bakery 🚌on the spot
🚲on the spot 🚶on the spot.
**Remarks:** Golf court.

**Delmenhorst** 7H3

**Reisemobilhafen Delmenhorst**, An den Graften.
**GPS:** n53,04722 e8,62278.⬆➡.

8 ⌂ free ⛽ Ch free 🔌(4x) € 1/kWh.
**Location:** Urban, simple, central, quiet. **Surface:** gravel/sand.
🗓 01/01-31/12 🔲 during event.

---

**Distance:** 🚶on the spot 🚴2,8km ⊗on the spot 🍺200m.
**Remarks:** Max. 7 days.

**Detern** 7G3

**Reisemobilhafen Detern**, Alte Heerstrasse 6, Stickhausen.
**GPS:** n53,21560 e7,64743.⬆➡.

40 ⌂ € 8 ⛽ € 1/100liter Ch 🔌(44x) € 2/24h WC ⌐ € 1/6minutes
🔲 € 2 ⚬ € 1/24h. 🏪 **Location:** Urban, luxurious.
**Surface:** asphalted/gravel. 🗓 01/01-31/12.
**Distance:** 🚶on the spot 🚴6km 🚣on the spot 🚣on the spot
⊗on the spot 🚲on the spot 🚶on the spot.
**Remarks:** Behind tourist info, bread-service.

**Diepenau** 9H1

**Stellplatz am Bahnhof**, Am Bahnhof. **GPS:** n52,42470 e8,74106.⬆.

5 ⌂ free ⛽ € 1 Ch 🔌(5x) € 1/8h. **Location:** Rural, simple.
**Surface:** metalled. 🗓 01/01-31/12.
**Distance:** 🚶500m ⊗500m 🍺500m 🚌200m.

**Diepenau** 9H1

**Wohnmobilstellplatz Am Tor zum Moor**, Steinbrinkerstrasse 8.
**GPS:** n52,47664 e8,74016.

30 ⌂ € 8 ⛽ Ch 🔌 included. **Location:** Rural, simple, isolated,
quiet. **Surface:** grassy/metalled. 🗓 01/04-31/10.
**Distance:** 🚶on the spot ⊗on the spot 🍺1km 🚌100m.

**Diepholz** 9H1

**Parkplatz Am Heldenhain**, Am Heldenhaim (B69).
**GPS:** n52,61250 e8,37056.⬆➡.

20 ⌂ free ⛽ € 1/80liter Ch 🔌(20x) € 0,50/kWh ⚬ free.
**Location:** Urban. **Surface:** grassy. 🗓 01/01-31/12.
**Distance:** 🚶500m ⊗500m 🍺500m.
**Remarks:** Max. 3 days.

**Ditzum** 7F2

**Ankerplatz Blank**, Pogumer Straße. **GPS:** n53,31489 e7,27619.⬆.

15 ⬛€ 9/24h 🚰€ 1/100liter ⬛Ch ⚡(10x)€ 1/2kWh WC⬛€ 0,50/3minutes ⬛📶. **Location:** Rural, comfortable, quiet. **Surface:** metalled. ⬛ 01/01-31/12. **Distance:** 🚶100m ⚓300m ⛵300m ⊗100m ⛽300m 🚐100m.

### Ditzum  7F2
**Reisemobilstellplatz Ditzum**, Am Deich. **GPS:** n53,31555 e7,28666. ⬆️.

45 ⬛€ 9/night 🚰€ 1/100liter ⬛Ch ⚡(45x)€ 1/2kWh. **Location:** Rural, simple, quiet. **Surface:** metalled. ⬛ 01/01-31/12. **Distance:** 🚶100m ⚓100m ⛵100m ⊗100m ⛽300m 🚐200m. **Remarks:** Bread-service, waste dump € 1, shower € 1.

### Dornum  7G2
Schöpfwerkstraße, Dornumersiel. **GPS:** n53,67272 e7,48092. ⬆️.

30 ⬛€ 9, Nordsee-ServiceCard incl ⚡(12x)€ 1/8h. ⬛ **Location:** Rural, simple, quiet. **Surface:** metalled. ⬛ 01/01-31/12. **Distance:** ⚓500m ⊗100m ⛵100m.

### Dornum  7G2
Schützenplatz. **GPS:** n53,64829 e7,42367. ⬆️.

30 ⬛€ 9, Nordsee-ServiceCard incl 🚰€ 1/65liter ⬛Ch ⚡€ 1/8h. ⬛ **Location:** Urban, simple, quiet. **Surface:** grassy. ⬛ 01/01-31/12. **Distance:** ⚓on the spot ⊗300m ⛵50m. **Remarks:** Max. 1 night.

### Dornum  7G2
**Wohnmobilstellplatz Nordseeblick. GPS:** n53,67912 e7,47767. ⬆️➡️.

38 ⬛€ 13 Nordsee-ServiceCard incl 🚰€ 2/100liter ⬛Ch ⚡€ 1/kWh

---

WC⬛. ⬛ **Location:** Rural, comfortable, quiet. **Surface:** grasstiles. ⬛ 24/03-03/10. **Distance:** 🚶900m ⚓200m ⛵200m ⊗500m ⛵500m. **Remarks:** Swimming pool.

### Dörpen 🍴  7F3
**Festplatz**, Veeneweg. **GPS:** n52,97115 e7,33425. ⬆️➡️.

5 ⬛free. **Location:** Rural, simple, quiet. **Surface:** grassy/metalled. ⬛ 01/01-31/12 ⬛ 1st week in June: fair. **Distance:** 🚶500m ⊗900m ⛵500m ⛽800m 🧍on the spot. **Remarks:** Max. 4 nights.

### Dorum 🌊  7H2
**Wohnmobilhafen Grube-Petrat**, Am Neuen Deich 2. **GPS:** n53,73838 e8,51966. ⬆️➡️.

20 ⬛€ 14 + € 2-3,40 tourist tax 🚰 ⬛Ch ⚡included WC⬛€ 1 📶 ⬛⚡ **Location:** Rural, simple. **Surface:** metalled. ⬛ 01/01-31/12. **Distance:** ⚓on the spot ⛵on the spot ⊗on the spot 🚐300m. **Remarks:** Check in at Deichhotel, bread-service, discount longer stays.

### Dörverden 🌿🏕️🌳  8A3
In der Worth. **GPS:** n52,84529 e9,22568. ⬆️➡️.

5 ⬛free 🚰€ 1/80liter ⚡(5x)€ 1/8h. **Location:** Urban, simple, quiet. **Surface:** gravel. ⬛ 01/01-31/12. **Distance:** 🚶200m ⊗200m ⛵200m 🚐Bremen/Hanover 🚲100m 🧍1km. **Remarks:** Behind town hall, max. 3 nights.

### Dörverden 🌿🏕️🌳  8A3
**Wolfcenter**, Kasernenstraße, Barme. **GPS:** n52,82635 e9,21417. ⬆️.

10 ⬛free WC. **Location:** Rural, simple, isolated. **Surface:** concrete. ⬛ 01/01-31/12. **Distance:** 🚶Dörverden 3km ⊗on the spot ⛵3km. **Remarks:** Parking wolf park, service during opening hours.

### Drage/Elbe 🌊  8B2
**Reisemobilplatz Stover Strand**, Stover Strand 10. **GPS:** n53,42467 e10,29213. ⬆️.

---

100 ⬛€ 14, dog € 2 🚰€ 1/80liter ⬛Ch ⚡(100x) 0,50/kWh WC⬛€ 0,50/4minutes ⬛€ 4/4 📶€ 2/h. **Location:** Rural, comfortable. **Surface:** grassy. ⬛ 01/01-31/12. **Distance:** ⚓on the spot ⛵on the spot ⊗on the spot ⛽on the spot 🚐500m 🧍on the spot. **Remarks:** Next to campsite.

### Drochtersen ⚓  8A2
**Wohnmobilstellplatz Krautsand**, Hinterm Elbdeich, Krautsand. **GPS:** n53,75167 e9,39028. ⬆️➡️.

10 ⬛€ 10 ⚡WCincluded. ⬛ **Location:** Rural, simple. **Surface:** grassy/metalled. ⬛ 15/04-03/10. **Distance:** ⚓Elbestrand ⊗150m ⛵300m 🚐250m.

### Drochtersen ⚓  8A2
**Hallenbad Drochtersen**, Am Sportplatz. **GPS:** n53,70548 e9,38215. ⬆️.

3 ⬛free. **Location:** Rural, simple. **Surface:** metalled. ⬛ 01/01-31/12. **Distance:** 🚶1km ⊗650m ⛵600m 🚐500m. **Remarks:** Parking at swimming pool.

### Drochtersen ⚓  8A2
**Am Alten Hafen**, Asseler Sand. **GPS:** n53,69418 e9,43928. ⬆️.

6 ⬛free. **Location:** Rural, simple, quiet. **Surface:** gravel. ⬛ 01/01-31/12. **Distance:** ⊗500m ⛵1km 🚐500m.

### Duderstadt 🌿🏕️  10C3
**P&R Parkplatz**, Adenauerring. **GPS:** n51,51043 e10,27278. ⬆️➡️.

20 ⬛free 🚰€ 1/120liter ⬛€ 1 Ch€ 1 ⚡(4x)€ 0,50/kWh. **Location:** Rural, quiet. **Surface:** gravel. ⬛ 01/01-31/12. **Distance:** 🚶800m 🚲17km ⊗800m ⛵200m 🚐100m. **Remarks:** Coins available at the shop.

DE

## Duderstadt 10C3

**Eichsfeldhalle**, August Werner Allee. **GPS:** n51,50662 e10,25890.

5 free. **Location:** Rural, simple. **Surface:** gravel.
01/01-31/12.
**Distance:** 900m 17km 900m 900m 700m.
**Remarks:** Max. 1 night.

## Duderstadt 10C3

**Hotel Rosenthaler Hof**, Rosenthaler Str. 31. **GPS:** n51,51556 e10,21194.
35 € 15, 2 pers.incl Ch (50x) included .
**Surface:** metalled.
01/01-31/12.
**Distance:** 5km on the spot.
**Tourist information Duderstadt:**
Gästeinformation der Stadt Duderstadt, Marktstrasse 66, www.
duderstadt.de. Old part of town with half-timbered houses.

## Edewecht 7G3

**Am Marktplatz**, Rathhausstrasse. **GPS:** n53,12834 e7,98201.

5 € 5/24h € 1/80liter Ch (8x) € 1/6h.
**Location:** Urban, simple. **Surface:** grassy. 01/01-31/12.
**Distance:** on the spot 400m Aldi 50m.

## Egestorf 8B3

**Naturerlebnisbad Acquadies**, Ahornweg 5.
**GPS:** n53,19796 e10,05455.

30 € 8 € 1 Ch (20x) € 2/10h WC 2.
**Location:** Rural, simple, quiet. **Surface:** gravel/metalled.
01/01-31/12.
**Distance:** 1km 2,2km on the spot 700m 1km.
**Remarks:** At swimming pool, shower during opening hours.

## Eggermühlen 9G1

**Reiterhotel Vox**, OT Bockraden 1. **GPS:** n52,57278 e7,79553.

8 € 25, clients € 7,50 Ch WC included.
**Location:** Rural. **Surface:** grassy. 01/01-31/12.
**Distance:** 3km 3km.

## Eggestedt 7H3

**Eggestedt**, Betonstrasse/Habichthorsterweg.
**GPS:** n53,22819 e8,63902.

8 free. **Location:** Rural, simple, isolated, noisy.
**Surface:** metalled/sand. 01/01-31/12.
**Distance:** 4km 400m.

## Einbeck 10B2

**Am Schwimmbad**, Ochsenhofweg. **GPS:** n51,82433 e9,86464.

30 € 5 € 1/60liter € 1 Ch (18x) € 0,50/kWh.
**Location:** Simple. **Surface:** gravel. 01/01-31/12.
**Distance:** 800m 500m 500m on the spot on the spot.
**Remarks:** Parking at swimming pool, free entrance swimming pool.
**Tourist information Einbeck:**
Alte Marktplatz. Wed + Sa morning.

## Elsfleth 7H3

**Im Hafen**, An der Kaje. **GPS:** n53,23771 e8,46545.

28 € 8/24h € 1/80liter Ch (16x) € 1/12h WC 2.
**Location:** Urban, comfortable, central, noisy. **Surface:** concrete.
01/01-31/12.
**Distance:** 150m 900m on the spot 100m 500m on
the spot on the spot.

## Emden 7F2

**Alter Binnenhafen**, Am Eisenbahndock. **GPS:** n53,36306 e7,20778.

29 € 9 € 0,50/100liter € 0,50 Ch (36x) € 0,50/kWh
WC € 0,50 € 1 € 3/1. **Location:** Urban, comfortable, central.
**Surface:** metalled. 01/01-31/12.
**Distance:** 500m 500m 500m.
**Remarks:** Pay at harbourmaster, charging point for electric bicycles.

## Emden 7F2

**Wohnmobilstellplatz Knock**, Jannes Ohling Strasse 39.
**GPS:** n53,35559 e7,00367.

20 € 6,50/night. **Location:** Rural, simple, quiet. **Surface:** metalled.

01/01-31/12.
**Distance:** 13km on the spot 500m 13km.
**Remarks:** Beautiful view.

## Emden 7F2

**Außenhafen Emden**, An der Nesserlanderschleuse.
**GPS:** n53,33798 e7,18395.
10 5. **Surface:** asphalted. 01/01-31/12.
**Distance:** 3,5km on the spot on the spot.

## Emden 7F2

**Friesen Therme**, Theaterstraße 2. **GPS:** n53,37530 e7,20203.

4 free (4x) € 0,50/kWh. **Location:** Urban, simple.
**Surface:** metalled. 01/01-31/12.
**Distance:** 1,5km 400m.

## Emmerthal 10A2

**Gronhnder Fahrhaus**, Grohnder Fähre 1. **GPS:** n52,01940 e9,42610.

40 € 12 Ch included (40x) € 0,50/kWh € 2/5minutes
€ 3/time. **Location:** Rural, quiet. **Surface:** grassy/gravel.
01/01-31/12.
**Distance:** on the spot on the spot 700m on the spot.

## Eschershausen 10B2

**Reisemobil-Stellplatz am Angerplatz**, Angerweg.
**GPS:** n51,92965 e9,62806.

10 free € 1/100liter € 1 Ch (6x) € 0,50/kWh.
**Surface:** metalled. 01/01-31/12.
**Distance:** 1km 350m 1km.

## Esens 7G2

**Wohnmobil-Stellplatz Esens**, Schutzenplatz.
**GPS:** n53,63921 e7,61077.

20 € 2 + € 2,80/pp tourist tax Ch included.
**Location:** Rural, comfortable, quiet. **Surface:** grassy.
01/01-31/12.
**Distance:** 500m 50m 200m.
**Remarks:** Max. 2 nights.

## Essel 10B1

**Hotel Heide-Kröpke**, Esseler Damm 1. **GPS:** n52,73240 e9,69419.

5 ⓢfree ⚡🚿(3x) 📶. **Surface:** grassy.
🔌 01/01-31/12.
**Distance:** ⊗on the spot 🚉9km.
**Remarks:** Use of a meal desired, bird reserve Ostenholzer-Moor.

## Esterwegen 7G3

**Am Erikasee. GPS:** n52,99366 e7,66768.⬆️.

10 ⓢfree ⚡€ 1/100liter 🗑Ch🚿(8x)€ 1/2kWh WC🚽.
**Location:** Rural, simple, isolated. **Surface:** gravel/metalled.
🔌 01/01-31/12.
**Distance:** 🚤2km 🏖100m ⊗Imbiss 80m.
**Remarks:** Walking and bicycle area.

## Estorf 8A2

**Wohnmobilstellplatz Gräpel - An der Prahmfähre,** Zum Hafen 21.
**GPS:** n53,56596 e9,17315.➡️.

3 ⓢfree. **Location:** Rural, simple. **Surface:** gravel.
🔌 01/01-31/12.
**Distance:** 🚤on the spot ⊗on the spot 🚴on the spot 🚶on the spot.
**Remarks:** Along the Oste river.

## Eystrup 8A3

Bahnhofstrasse 21. **GPS:** n52,78004 e9,21840.⬆️➡️.

5 ⓢfree. **Surface:** grassy. 🔌 01/01-31/12.
**Distance:** 🚉100m.
**Remarks:** Max. 5 days.

## Faßberg 8B3

**Am Schützenplatz,** Moorweg. **GPS:** n52,90518 e10,16991.⬆️.

50 ⓢ€2 ⚡€ 1 🗑ChWC. **Surface:** grassy.
🔌 01/01-31/12 🔲 marksmen's festival end of September.
**Distance:** 🚤700m ⊗700m 🚉700m.

---

## Faßberg 8B3

**Parkplatz Heidesee,** Unterlüßerstraße, L280, Müden.
**GPS:** n52,87889 e10,12472.⬆️.

30 ⓢ€ 2 ⚡€ 1 🗑Ch🚿€ 1. **Surface:** grassy.
🔌 01/01-31/12 🔲 end Sep.
**Distance:** ⊗500m 🚉1km.

## Faßberg 8B3

**Parkplatz am Wildpark,** Willinghäuser Kirchweg, Müden.
**GPS:** n52,87222 e10,10861.⬆️.

15 ⓢ€ 2/night. **Surface:** grassy. 🔌 01/01-31/12.
**Distance:** 🚤1km ⊗1km 🚴on the spot.

## Fredenbeck 8A2

**Restaurant Niedersachsenschänke,** Schwingestraße 33.
**GPS:** n53,52646 e9,39314.⬆️.

5 ⓢfree. **Location:** Rural, simple. **Surface:** grassy.
🔌 01/01-31/12 🔲 Tue, Wed.
**Distance:** 🚤800m ⊗on the spot 🚉800m ➡on the spot 🚴on the spot 🚶on the spot.

## Freiburg/Elbe 8A1

**Stellplatz am Freizeitcentrum,** Am Bassin 25.
**GPS:** n53,82285 e9,29305.⬆️➡️.

30 ⓢ€8 ⚡🗑Ch🚿WCincluded 🗑€ 1.🚿
**Location:** Rural, simple. **Surface:** metalled.
🔌 01/01-31/12.
**Distance:** 🚤200m ➡50m ⊗300m 🚉400m.
**Remarks:** Find more possibilities on the city plan.

## Freistatt 9H1

**Freistätter Feldbahn,** Badeweg. **GPS:** n52,62613 e8,65147.⬆️➡️.

6 ⓢ€7 ⚡🗑Ch🚿included. **Location:** Rural, quiet.

---

**Surface:** metalled. 🔌 01/01-31/12.
**Distance:** ⊗1km 🚉400m.

## Friedeburg 7G2

**Schützenplatz. GPS:** n53,45488 e7,83349.⬆️.

20 ⓢ€ 5 ⚡🗑Ch🚿(6x)€ 1/8h WCincluded 🗑according consumption. **Location:** Urban, simple. **Surface:** grassy.
🔌 01/01-31/12.
**Distance:** 🏊15/05-15/09 🚉400m. **Remarks:** Service 500m.

## Friedeburg 7G2

**Gasthaus Wilken am See,** Friedeburger Straße 19.
**GPS:** n53,45794 e7,88265.⬆️.

10 ⓢ€ 5 ⚡🚿📶included. **Location:** Rural, simple, quiet.
**Surface:** grassy. 🔌 01/01-31/12.
**Distance:** ➡on the spot ⊗on the spot.
**Remarks:** At lake.

## Friesoythe 7G3

**Am Aquaferrum,** Thüler Straße 28A. **GPS:** n53,01149 e7,86152.

5 ⓢfree ⚡€ 1/100liter 🗑Ch🚿 3 🚿(8x)€ 6/24h. **Location:** Simple.
**Surface:** metalled. 🔌 01/01-31/12.
**Distance:** 🚤900m 🚉900m ➡800m.
**Remarks:** At swimming pool.

## Fürstenau 9G1

**Schlossinsel Fürstenau,** Schlossplatz 1. **GPS:** n52,51638 e7,67333.⬆️.

2 ⓢfree ⚡€ 3 🗑Ch🚿€ 2/day WC. **Location:** Quiet.
**Surface:** metalled. 🔌 01/01-31/12.
**Distance:** 🚤100m ⊗100m 🚉100m 🚴on the spot 🚶on the spot.
**Remarks:** Next to castle.

## Gartow 8D3

**Imbiss am See,** Springstraße 88. **GPS:** n53,02944 e11,44944.⬆️.

DE

20 🛏€5 ⛽included20liter WC. **Surface:** gravel/metalled. 🅿 01/03-30/10.
**Distance:** 🚶1km ⛴on the spot ⚓on the spot ⊗on the spot.
**Remarks:** Imbiss 11-21h.

| 🚐S | Geeste | 9F1 |
|---|---|---|

**Am Speicherbecken**, Biener Straße 13. **GPS:** n52,59407 e7,27417. ⬆

50 🛏free WCfree. **Location:** Quiet. **Surface:** grassy/metalled.
🅿 01/01-31/12.
**Distance:** 🚶2km ⚓200m ⊗100m 🍺4km 🚲on the spot 🚶on the spot.
**Remarks:** Max. 1 night.

| 🚐 | Geeste | 9F1 |
|---|---|---|

**P Biotop/Ausblick**, Osterbrocker Strasse. **GPS:** n52,59840 e7,29279. ⬆

4 🛏free. **Surface:** metalled. 🅿 01/01-31/12.
**Distance:** 🚶1,5km 🍺1,5km on the spot 🚶on the spot.
**Remarks:** Max. 1 night, hiking area.

| 🚐S | Gehrden | 10B1 |
|---|---|---|

**An den Sporthallen**, Lange Feldstraße 12.
**GPS:** n52,31197 e9,60971. ⬆

2 🛏free ⚡(2x)€ 0,50/kWh. **Location:** Simple. **Surface:** metalled.
🅿 01/01-31/12.
**Distance:** 🚶centre 700m ⚓200m.

| 🚐S | Gifhorn 🌾 | 10C1 |
|---|---|---|

**Frei- und Hallenbad Allerwelle**, Konrad Adenauerstrasse.
**GPS:** n52,48437 e10,55407. ⬆➡
12 🛏€5/24h ⛽€1/90liter 🚽Ch⚡(12x)€1/8h WC.
**Location:** Rural, comfortable, quiet. **Surface:** grasstiles.
🅿 01/01-31/12.
**Distance:** 🚶200m ⚓100m ⊗250m 🍺200m ⛴200m on the
spot 🚶on the spot.
**Remarks:** Max. 3 days.

| 🚐S | Gifhorn 🌾 | 10C1 |
|---|---|---|

**Fischer Camping + Gas**, Schmiedeweg 4, Wische.
**GPS:** n52,50863 e10,48462. ⬆

3 🛏free ⛽€ 0,50/50liter 🚽Ch⚡(8x). **Location:** Rural, simple,
isolated. **Surface:** grassy. 🅿 01/01-31/12.
**Distance:** 🚶3km ⊗500m 🍺3km.
**Remarks:** Max. 1 night, accessory shop.

| 🚐S | Gnarrenburg | 8A2 |
|---|---|---|

**Parkplatz Brillit**, Alte Strasse, Brillit. **GPS:** n53,41390 e9,00007. ⬆➡

15 🛏free ⛽🚽Chfree. **Location:** Rural, simple. **Surface:** gravel.
🅿 01/01-31/12.
**Distance:** 🚶1km ⊗3km 🍺1km on the spot 🚶on the spot.
**Remarks:** At community centre.

| 🚐S | Gnarrenburg | 8A2 |
|---|---|---|

**Schulzentrum**, Brilliterweg. **GPS:** n53,39000 e9,00028. ⬆➡

20 🛏free ⛽🚽Chfree. **Location:** Urban, simple. **Surface:** metalled.
🅿 01/01-31/12.
**Distance:** ⊗1km 🍺500m.
**Remarks:** Sports centre.

| 🚐 | Goldenstedt ⚓ | 9H1 |
|---|---|---|

**Haus im Moor**, Arkeburger Straße 22. **GPS:** n52,72777 e8,39120. ⬆
6 🛏free. **Location:** Rural, simple. **Surface:** grassy/sand.
🅿 01/01-31/12.
**Distance:** 🚶8,5km.

| ⚓S | Gorleben ⛵ | 8D3 |
|---|---|---|

**Am Sportboothafen**, Ringstraße. **GPS:** n53,04972 e11,35111. ⬆

5 🛏€ 7,50 ⛽€ 1/10minutes ⚡(4x)€ 1/10h WC🍴€ 1,50.
**Location:** Rural, comfortable, quiet. **Surface:** grasstiles.
🅿 01/05-30/09.
**Distance:** ⛴on the spot ⚓on the spot ⊗500m.
**Remarks:** Bakery 500m.

| 🚐 | Goslar | 10C2 |
|---|---|---|

Bertha von Suttner Straße. **GPS:** n51,91003 e10,41785. ⬆
10 🛏free. **Location:** Urban. **Surface:** metalled.
🅿 01/01-31/12.
**Distance:** 🚶1,5km 🚲on the spot 🚶on the spot.

| 🚐S | Göttingen 🚉🍴 | 10B3 |
|---|---|---|

**Reisemobilhafen Eiswiese**, Windausweg 6.
**GPS:** n51,52320 e9,92965. ⬆➡

28 🛏€ 9 ⛽€ 1/100liter 🚽Ch⚡(24x)€ 0,50/kWh WC🚿€ 1/15h.
**Location:** Urban, comfortable. **Surface:** gravel. 🅿 01/01-31/12.
**Distance:** 🚶500m 🚴5,2km ⚓100m ⛴20-400m ⊗100m 🍺500m
🚲100m.
**Remarks:** Max. 3 nights.

| 🚐S | Grasberg | 8A3 |
|---|---|---|

**P&R**, Wörpedorfer Straße. **GPS:** n53,18411 e8,98433. ⬆

10 🛏free ⛽€ 1/15liter 🚽Ch⚡(8x)€ 1/6h. **Location:** Urban, simple.
**Surface:** gravel. 🅿 01/01-31/12.
**Distance:** 🚶on the spot 🍺on the spot ⛴> Bremen.

| 🚐S | Gronau/Leine | 10B2 |
|---|---|---|

**Kuhmasch. GPS:** n52,08265 e9,77034. ⬆➡

4 🛏€5 🚰⚡WCincluded. **Location:** Rural, simple. **Surface:** grassy.
🅿 01/01-31/12.
**Distance:** 🚶200m ⊗300m 🍺300m on the spot.
**Remarks:** Check in at swimming pool, caution key electricity € 10.

| 🍴S | Großefehn | 7G2 |
|---|---|---|

**Ostfriesen-Bräu Bagband**, Voerstad 8, Badband.
**GPS:** n53,35034 e7,61060. ⬆

4 🛏€ 7 ⛽🚽⚡16Amp WC. **Location:** Simple, quiet.
**Surface:** metalled. 🅿 01/01-31/12.
**Distance:** 🚶10km ⊗on the spot 🍺3km.

| 🚐S | Großenkneten | 7H3 |
|---|---|---|

**Dorfplatz**, Bahnhofstrasse, Huntlosen. **GPS:** n52,99145 e8,28658. ⬆

6 🛏free ⛽€ 1/80liter ⚡€ 1/kWh. **Location:** Rural, simple.
**Surface:** grasstiles. 🅿 01/01-31/12.
**Distance:** 🚶on the spot ⊗50m 🍺1km.

| 🚐S | Großenkneten | 7H3 |
|---|---|---|

**Wilhelm-Wellman-Platz**, Ahlhorner Strasse/markt.
**GPS:** n52,94274 e8,25751. ⬆

6 🛏free ⛽€ 1/80liter 🚽Ch⚡€ 1/kWh. **Location:** Rural, simple.
**Surface:** grasstiles. 🅿 01/01-31/12.
**Distance:** 🚶200m ⊗200m 🍺on the spot.

| 🚐S | Großenwieden ⚓ | 10A2 |
|---|---|---|

**Am Steinbrink**, Hessisch Oldendorf. **GPS:** n52,17191 e9,18982. ⬆➡

4 ⌘free. **Location:** Rural, simple. **Surface:** gravel.
◻ 01/01-31/12.
**Distance:** 🚲3,8km ⊗Gasthaus/Biergarten 300m 🚲 Weserradweg
🚶 on the spot.

### Großenwörden 8A2

Deichstraße 21. **GPS:** n53,67757 e9,25769. ⬆.

3 ⌘€ 5 🚿€ 2 🚿€ 2/stay WCfree. 💦 **Location:** Rural, simple,
isolated. **Surface:** grasstiles. ◻ 01/01-31/12.
**Distance:** ⊗200m.
**Remarks:** Along the Oste river.

### Großheide 7F2

**Moormuseum**, Kirchweg, Berumerfehn.
**GPS:** n53,56040 e7,34713. ⬆➡.

6 ⌘free. **Location:** Urban, simple, quiet. **Surface:** metalled.
◻ 01/01-31/12.
**Distance:** 🚲on the spot⊗on the spot 🍽2km.
**Remarks:** Max. 2 nights.

### Großheide 7F2

**P Freizeitanlage Am Kiessee**, Doornkaatsweg.
**GPS:** n53,58718 e7,36560. ⬆⬆➡.

15 ⌘free. **Location:** Rural, simple, quiet. **Surface:** gravel.
◻ 01/01-31/12.
**Distance:** ⊿on the spot.

### Großheide 7F2

**AC Dehne**, Dorfstraße 86. **GPS:** n53,56254 e7,36077. ⬆.

20 ⌘€ 4 🚿Ch🚿(9x)€ 1 ⬚€ 1. **Location:** Rural, comfortable,
quiet. **Surface:** grassy. ◻ 01/01-31/12.
**Distance:** 🚲on the spot.

---

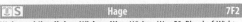
### Hage 7F2

**Wohnmobilstellplatz Wichter Weg**, Wichter Weg 58, Blandorf-Wichte.
**GPS:** n53,60501 e7,31950. ⬆➡.

12 ⌘€ 9, 15/03-31/10 € 12,60 🚿€ 0,50/80liter 🚿Ch🚿
(12x)€ 1/2kWh,16Amp 📶included. 🚰 **Location:** Rural, comfortable,
quiet. **Surface:** metalled. ◻ 01/01-31/12.
**Distance:** 🚲2,5km ⊿on the spot ⊗on the spot 🍽2,2km 🚲on the
spot 🚶 on the spot.

### Hagenburg 10A1

**Grillplatz**, Steinhuder-Meer-Straße. **GPS:** n52,43684 e9,32388. ⬆.

8 ⌘free 🚿(8x)€ 1/6h. **Location:** Rural, isolated. **Surface:** gravel.
◻ 01/01-31/12.
**Distance:** 🚲500m ⊿Lake Steinhude 1,1km 🍽200m.
**Remarks:** At sports park.

### Hahnenklee ❄ 10C2

Am Bocksberg. **GPS:** n51,85757 e10,34176. ⬆.
⌘free 🚿€ 2/60liter 🚿Ch. **Location:** Rural, comfortable, quiet.
**Surface:** concrete. ◻ 01/01-31/12.
**Distance:** 🚲500m 🍽1km 🚌500m 🚲on the spot 🚶 on the spot
🚠on the spot.

### Hambergen 7H2

**Festplatz**, Kirchweg/Am Langenend. **GPS:** n53,31050 e8,82389. ⬆➡.

20 ⌘€ 3,50 🚿Ch🚿(6x)included. **Location:** Urban, simple.
**Surface:** gravel/sand. ◻ 01/01-31/12.
**Distance:** 🚲on the spot ⊗50m 🍽50m 🚌1km 🚲on the spot
🚶 on the spot.
**Remarks:** Caution key service € 25.

### Hameln 10A2

**Wohnmobilstellplatz Hameln**, Ruthenstrasse 14.
**GPS:** n52,09623 e9,35853. ⬆➡.

27 ⌘€ 8/24h 🚿€ 1/100liter 🚿Ch🚿(27x)€ 1/8h. 🚰
**Location:** Urban, simple. **Surface:** metalled. ◻ 01/01-31/12.
**Distance:** 🚲1km ⊗600m 🍽600m 🚲800m 🚲 Weser-Radweg.

### Hameln 10A2

**Campingplatz Hameln**, Uferstraße 80.
**GPS:** n52,10932 e9,34768. ⬆➡.

---

30 ⌘€ 12 🚿€ 1/100liter 🚿Ch. 🚲 **Location:** Rural.
**Surface:** gravel/metalled. ◻ 01/01-31/12.
**Distance:** 🚲2km ⊗800m 🚲on the spot.

### Hankensbüttel 8C3

**Parkplatz Am Boldhamm**, Wiesenweg.
**GPS:** n52,73111 e10,61417. ⬆➡.

10 ⌘€ 6 🚿Chincluded. 💦
**Location:** Rural. **Surface:** grassy.
◻ 01/04-30/09.
**Distance:** 🚲900m ⊗1km 🍽1km.
**Remarks:** Service: Mo/Fr 6-12h, Sa/Su 8-10h.

**Tourist information Hankensbüttel:**
 Otter-Zentrum. Zoo. ◻ 15/03-31/10 9.30-18h, 01/11-14/03 9.30-
17h ◻ 15/12-15/01.

### Hannover 10B1

Carl-Neuberg-Strasse. **GPS:** n52,38761 e9,80746. ⬆.

5 ⌘€ 10 🚿(5x)included. 🚰 **Location:** Urban, noisy.
**Surface:** metalled. ◻ 01/01-31/12.
**Distance:** 🚲on the spot ⊗900m 🍽900m.

**Tourist information Hanover (Hannover):**
ℹ Hannover Tourismus Service, Ernst-August-Platz 2,
www.hannover.de.
 Zoo, Adenaueralle 3. Zoo. ◻ 01/03-31/10 9-18h, 01/11-28/02
10-16h.

### Hannoversch Münden 10B3

**Am Weserstein**, Tanzwerder. **GPS:** n51,42000 e9,64888. ⬆➡.

30 ⌘€ 6/24h 🚿€ 1 🚿Ch🚿(16x)€ 1/8h. 🚰
**Location:** Central. **Surface:** metalled.
◻ 01/01-31/12 ◻ Easter Market, service: 01/11-31/03.
**Distance:** 🚲900m 🍽100m 🚲on the spot 🚶 on the spot.
**Remarks:** 01/11/- 31/03 no service.

### Hannoversch Münden 10B3

**Am Hochbad**, Rattwerder. **GPS:** n51,40595 e9,64643. ⬆.

15 �⃝free. **Location:** Rural. **Surface:** asphalted. ◻ 01/01-31/12.
**Distance:** 1,7km 1km on the spot.
**Remarks:** At swimming pool.

### Hannoversch Münden 10B3
**Am Werraweg**, Werraweg. **GPS:** n51,41701 e9,66176.

10 ⌝free. **Location:** Simple. **Surface:** gravel. ◻ 01/01-31/12.
**Distance:** 700m 600m 600m on the spot.
**Remarks:** Along the Werra river.

### Hannoversch Münden 10B3
**Grüne Insel Tanzwerder**, Tanzwerder 1. **GPS:** n51,41694 e9,64751.

DE

20 ⌝€ 6 + € 4,50/pp, dog € 2 ⌁ Ch included (6x)€ 0,60/kWh,+
€ 2 WC € 3/h.
**Location:** Urban, simple. **Surface:** grassy.
◻ 01/01-31/12.
**Distance:** 100m 150m 150m 200m on the spot
on the spot.
**Remarks:** Max. 3t.

#### Tourist information Hannoversch Münden:
ℹ Touristik Naturpark Münden e.V, Rathaus, www.hann-muenden.
net/spontan. Old city centre with 430 half-timbered houses.

### Hardegsen 10B3
**Wohnmobilhafen Steinbreite**, Alte Uslarer Straße 1.
**GPS:** n51,65093 e9,82267.

15 ⌝€ 6 ⌁€ 1/100liter Ch (16x)€ 1/8h WC€ 2/day
€ 2 €2,50/day. **Location:** Rural, comfortable, quiet.
**Surface:** grasstiles. ◻ 01/01-31/12.
**Distance:** 500m 500m 800m on the spot on the spot.

### Haren/Ems 9F1
**Am Schloss Danken**, Am Tiergarten. **GPS:** n52,79724 e7,20530.

22 ⌝€ 12/24h Ch (18x)WC included € 1.
**Location:** Rural, simple. **Surface:** grassy/gravel.
◻ 21/03-25/10.
**Distance:** 1km 2,8km on the spot on the spot on the
spot on the spot.

### Haren/Ems 9F1
**Stellplatz an der Ems**, Schleusenstraße. **GPS:** n52,78890 e7,24744.

20 ⌝free. **Location:** Rural, simple, quiet. **Surface:** grasstiles.
◻ 01/01-31/12.
**Distance:** 500m 550m.

### Harpstedt 7H3
**Tielingskamp**. **GPS:** n52,90799 e8,59406.

4 ⌝free ⌁€ 0,50/100liter Ch (4x)€ 0,50/kWh. **Location:** Rural.
**Surface:** grassy/gravel. ◻ 01/01-31/12.
**Distance:** 500m on the spot.

### Harsefeld 8A2
**Klosterpark**, Kirchenstrasse. **GPS:** n53,45384 e9,50344.

5 ⌝free ⌁ (10x). **Location:** Rural, simple. **Surface:** gravel.
◻ 01/01-31/12.
**Distance:** 100m 100m 100m 100m on the spot
on the spot.
**Remarks:** Caution key electricity € 10 at hotel, parking park of monastery, max. 5 days.

### Haselünne 9G1
**Erholungsgebiet am See**. **GPS:** n52,67060 e7,49907.

8 ⌝free ⌁€ 1/100liter Ch. **Location:** Rural, quiet.
**Surface:** metalled. ◻ 01/01-31/12.
**Distance:** centre 1,2km on the spot on the spot 1,2km.

### Haselünne 9G1
**Sportzentrum**, Lingener Strasse 28. **GPS:** n52,66778 e7,48222.

4 ⌝free ⌁ Ch. **Location:** Simple, quiet. **Surface:** metalled.
◻ 01/01-31/12.
**Distance:** 400m 400m 400m 100m on the spot.
**Remarks:** Parking swimming pool.

### Haselünne 9G1
**Dröge-Polle**, Poller Straße 19. **GPS:** n52,65123 e7,49849.

3 ⌝€ 11 ⌁ WC included. **Location:** Rural, quiet.
**Surface:** grassy. ◻ 01/01-31/12.
**Remarks:** Check in at restaurant.

### Helmstedt 10C1
**Am Maschweg**, Maschweg. **GPS:** n52,23535 e11,01128.

25 ⌝free ⌁€ 1/3minutes €1/4h. **Location:** Rural, simple.
**Surface:** metalled. ◻ 01/01-31/12.
**Distance:** 500m 800m 50m 200m on the spot on the spot.
**Remarks:** Other parking in case of festivities.

### Helmstedt 10C1
**Brunnentheater**, Brunnenweg 6A, Bad Helmstedt.
**GPS:** n52,23676 e11,06411.

5 ⌝free. **Location:** Rural, simple, isolated, quiet. **Surface:** asphalted.
◻ 01/01-31/12.
**Distance:** 4km 500m 4km on the spot on the spot.

### Hermannsburg 8B3
**Parkplatz Waldschwimmbad**, Lotharstrasse 66.
**GPS:** n52,82718 e10,10807.

3 ⌝free ⌁€ 1 €1 Ch. **Surface:** metalled. ◻ 01/01-31/12.
**Distance:** 500m 100m.
**Remarks:** Parking at swimming pool.

## Hermannsburg 8B3

**Schützenplatz**, Lotharstraße 75. **GPS:** n52,82787 e10,10963. ⬆.

40 🚐 € 2 ⚡🔌Ch. **Surface:** grassy. 🅾 01/01-31/12.
**Distance:** 🚲500m ⊗on the spot.
**Remarks:** Max. 1 night, service at Waldbad (50m).

## Hermannsburg 8B3

**Grillplatz Bonstorf**, Schulstrasse. **GPS:** n52,86492 e10,05134. ⬆.

4 🚐free. **Surface:** grassy. 🅾 01/01-31/12.
**Distance:** 🚲5km ⊗5km ⛽5km.
**Remarks:** Parking sports park.

## Hermannsburg 8B3

**Parkplatz am Feuerwehrhaus**, Weesenerstrasse, Weesen.
**GPS:** n52,83645 e10,13692. ⬆.

3 🚐free. **Surface:** grassy. 🅾 01/01-31/12.
**Distance:** 🚲500m ⛽50m.
**Remarks:** Parking fire-station.

## Hermannsburg 8B3

**Parkplatz Örtzetal-Halle**, Lutterweg. **GPS:** n52,83363 e10,09579. ⬆.

3 🚐free. **Surface:** metalled. 🅾 01/01-31/12.
**Distance:** 🚲1km ⊗600m ⛽100m.

## Hermannsburg 8B3

**Lutter Hof**, Waldstrasse, Lutter. **GPS:** n52,84188 e10,09894. ⬆.

5 🚐€ 5 ⚡🔌according consumption ⬜included. **Surface:** grassy.
🅾 01/01-31/12.
**Distance:** 🚲2km ⊗2km ⛽2km.

## Herzlake 9G1

**Hasetal**, Im Mersch. **GPS:** n52,68211 e7,60780. ⬆.

30 🚐free ⚡🔌ChWCfree. **Surface:** grassy. 🅾 15/03-15/11.
**Distance:** ⊗700m ⛽200m.
**Remarks:** Parking sports centre.

## Hesel 7G2

**Dorfplatz**, Kirchstrasse. **GPS:** n53,30497 e7,59174. ⬆➡.

12 🚐€ 4 ⚡🔌Chincluded ⚡€ 1/8h. **Location:** Rural, simple, quiet.
**Surface:** metalled. 🅾 01/01-31/12.
**Distance:** 🚲on the spot ⚡on the spot ⛽1km 🚴on the spot 🚶on
the spot.
**Remarks:** Pay at tourist office.

## Hessisch Oldendorf 10A2

**Südwall P1**, Weserstraße. **GPS:** n52,16693 e9,25049. ⬆➡.

4 🚐free ⚡€ 0,50/5minutes 🔌€ 0,50 Ch€ 0,50. **Location:** Rural,
simple. **Surface:** grassy/gravel. 🅾 01/01-31/12.
**Distance:** 🚲400m ⊗500m ⛽500m 🚴 Weserradweg 1km.
**Remarks:** Max. 5 days.

## Hessisch Oldendorf 10A2

**Steinbrink**, Am Steinbrink. **GPS:** n52,17222 e9,19056. ⬆.

4 🚐free. **Location:** Rural, simple, quiet. **Surface:** gravel.
🅾 01/01-31/12.
**Distance:** 🚲200m ⊗200m ⛽200m.

## Hitzacker 8C3

**Bleichwiesen**, K36, Elbufferstrasse. **GPS:** n53,15074 e11,04941. ⬆.

60 🚐free ⚡€ 2/80liter 🔌Ch (17x)€ 2/6h WC.
**Location:** Rural, comfortable. **Surface:** metalled.
🅾 01/01-31/12.
**Distance:** 🚲200m ⊗450m.
**Remarks:** Max. 1 night.

## Hohne 10C1

**Am Waldbad**, Am Schwimmbad 23. **GPS:** n52,59340 e10,37398. ⬆.

4 🚐€ 5 ⚡🔌Ch ⚡(4x)WC⬜included. **Location:** Rural, comfortable,
quiet. **Surface:** gravel. 🅾 01/01-31/12.
**Distance:** 🚲1km ⊗50m ⛽200m.
**Remarks:** Max. 7 days, caution key € 50, use sanitary only during opening hours swimming pool.

## Hohnstorf/Elbe 8C2

**Wohnmobilstellplatz Hohnstorf**, Schulstraße 1.
**GPS:** n53,36234 e10,56223. ⬆.

9 🚐€ 8/24h ⚡€ 1/100liter 🔌Ch ⚡(3x)€ 1/10h. 🚐
**Location:** Comfortable. **Surface:** metalled. 🅾 01/01-31/12.
**Distance:** ⚡on the spot ⊗500m ⛽500m.
**Remarks:** Along the river Elbe.

## Holdorf 9H1

**Zeltplatz Heidesee**, Zum Heidesee 53. **GPS:** n52,57788 e8,11424. ⬆➡.

60 🚐€ 10 ⚡🔌Chincluded ⚡€ 3 🚿against payment.
**Location:** Comfortable. **Surface:** grasstiles.
🅾 01/03-15/10.
**Distance:** 🚲1,5km 🚴3,4km 🏖Sandy beach ⊗on the spot ⛽1,5km.
**Remarks:** At tennis-courts, bread-service.

## Hollern 8A2

**Am Deich**, Twielenfleth. **GPS:** n53,60417 e9,55917. ⬆➡.

15 🚐€ 5/24h. 🚐 **Location:** Rural, simple. **Surface:** metalled.
🅾 01/01-31/12.
**Distance:** 🚲200m ⊗Imbiss 300m.
**Remarks:** Along the river Elbe.

## Holzminden 10A2

**Mobilcamping Holzminden**, Stahler Ufer 16.
**GPS:** n51,82681 e9,43909. ⬆➡.

145 ⌷€ 5-8,50 ⚹€ 1/100liter ⛏Ch⚡(150x)€ 0,60/kWh WC⚡€ 0,50/4minutes ⛶. **Location:** Urban, comfortable. **Surface:** grassy. ⬤ 01/01-31/12.
**Distance:** ⚓550m ⚓100m ⊗100m ⚓100m ⚌200m ♨on the spot ⚹on the spot.
**Remarks:** At swimming pool, bread-service.

| 🍴S | Hornburg 〰〰 | 10C2 |

**Iberg-Gaststätte**, Schützenallee 1. **GPS:** n52,03133 e10,59677. ⬆➡.

20 ⌷€ 2 ⚡(6x)€ 1/night. **Location:** Rural, simple, quiet.
**Surface:** grassy/metalled. ⬤ 01/01-31/12.
**Distance:** ⚓600m ⚹5km ⊗on the spot ⚹1km ♨on the spot.

| 🚐S | Hoya/Weser | 8A3 |

**Reisemobilstellplatz Weserblick**, Stettiner Straße.
**GPS:** n52,80106 e9,13987. ⬆➡.

10 ⌷voluntary contribution ⚹€ 1/150liter ⛏Ch.
**Surface:** grassy/gravel. ⬤ 01/01-31/12.
**Distance:** ⚓500m ⚓100m ⊗500m ⚹700m.

| 🚐S | Hude 〰〰 | 7H3 |

**Wohnmobilstellplatz Hude**, Schützenstrasse.
**GPS:** n53,10758 e8,45867. ⬆➡.

10 ⌷€ 5 ⚹€ 1 ⛏Ch⚡(12x)€ 0,50/kWh. ⛶.
**Location:** Urban, quiet. **Surface:** gravel. ⬤ 01/01-31/12.
**Distance:** ⚓on the spot ⊗on the spot ⚹400m ⚌on the spot ♨on the spot ⚹1km.

| 🚐S | Hüde (49448) | 9H1 |

**Freizeitarena Dümmer See**, Rohrdommelweg 33.
**GPS:** n52,50176 e8,35425. ⬆.

**Distance:** ⚓150m ⊗150m ⚓bakery 300m ♨on the spot.

| 🍴S | Ihlienworth 〰 | 7H1 |

**Auf der Schöpfwerkinsel**, Hauptstrasse 40.
**GPS:** n53,74539 e8,91831. ⬆.

50 ⌷€ 10 ⚹€ 3/day WC⚡included. **Location:** Rural, quiet.
**Surface:** grassy. ⬤ 15/04-01/11.

9 ⌷€ 5 ⚹€ 0,10/10liter ⛏free Ch€ 1 ⚡€ 1/kWh.⛶
**Location:** Rural, simple. **Surface:** grassy/metalled.
⬤ 15/03-15/11.
**Distance:** ⚓on the spot ⚓on the spot ⊗500m.

| 🚐S | Ihlow | 7G2 |

**Straub's Bürgerstuben**, 1.Kompanieweg 3, Ihlowerfehn.
**GPS:** n53,41153 e7,44013. ⬆➡.

6 ⌷free ⚹€ 1/5minutes ⛏Ch€ 1/time ⚡(4x)€ 0,50/kWh.
**Location:** Rural, simple, quiet. **Surface:** metalled.
⬤ 01/01-31/12 ⬤ Wed.
**Distance:** ⚓on the spot ⚓on the spot ⊗on the spot.

| 🚐S | Isterberg 〰 | 9F1 |

**Am Isterberger Waldhaus**, Lehmstrasse.
**GPS:** n52,35167 e7,14906. ⬆➡.

15 ⌷€ 7 ⚹€ 2/10minutes ⛏Ch⚡€ 1/6h. **Location:** Rural,
comfortable, quiet. **Surface:** grassy/gravel. ⬤ 01/04-30/09.
**Distance:** ⊗on the spot ⚌100m ♨on the spot ⚹on the spot.

| 🚐S | Jade 〰〰 | 7H2 |

**Bäderstraße**, Sehestedt. **GPS:** n53,43605 e8,29553. ⬆.

10 ⌷€ 10 ⛏Chincluded ⚡(8x)€ 2/night WC⚡.⛶
**Location:** Rural. **Surface:** grassy/gravel. ⬤ 01/05-30/09.
**Distance:** ⊗100m ♨on the spot.

| 🚐S | Jade 〰〰 | 7H2 |

**Quittenweg**, Süderschweiburg. **GPS:** n53,39139 e8,26639. ⬆.

8 ⌷free ⚹€ 1 ⛏Ch⚡(8x)€ 1/8h. **Location:** Rural, comfortable,

isolated. **Surface:** gravel/metalled. ⬤ 01/01-31/12.
**Distance:** ⚓800m ⚓500m ⊗1km ⚹800m ♨on the spot ⚹on the spot.

| ℹS | Jade 〰〰 | 7H2 |

**Drei Eichen**, Kreuzmoorstrasse 28. **GPS:** n53,31531 e8,23084. ⬆.

10 ⌷€ 10 ⚹⛏Ch⚡(3x)€ 2 WCincluded ⛏€ 1.⛶
**Location:** Rural, simple, quiet. **Surface:** grassy/gravel.
⬤ 01/01-31/12.
**Distance:** ⚹4km.
**Remarks:** At manege.

| 🍴S | Jade 〰〰 | 7H2 |

**Schützenhof**, Am Schützenplatz, Vareler Strasse.
**GPS:** n53,34111 e8,18667. ⬆.

10 ⌷guests free ⚹on demand ⚡(3x)€ 2/night.⛶
**Location:** Simple. **Surface:** metalled. ⬤ 01/01-31/12.
**Distance:** ⚓on the spot ⊗on the spot ⚹on the spot.
**Remarks:** Parking of Shooting Club.

| ℹ | Jade 〰〰 | 7H2 |

**Jaderpark**, Tiergartenstrasse 69, Jaderberg.
**GPS:** n53,32679 e8,18521. ⬆.

20 ⌷free. **Location:** Simple. **Surface:** gravel.
⬤ 01/01-31/12.
**Distance:** ⚓on the spot ⊗on the spot.
**Remarks:** Parking Jarderpark, zoo and adventure park, max. 1 night.

| 🚐S | Jever 〰 | 7G2 |

**Jahnstrasse. GPS:** n53,57733 e7,89074. ⬆➡.

20 ⌷€ 8 ⚹⛏Ch⚡(20x)included. **Location:** Urban, simple.
**Surface:** metalled. ⬤ 01/01-31/12.
**Distance:** ⚓Old city centre 750m ⚹100m.
**Remarks:** Sports centre, max. 3 days, coins at petrol station Henn.
**Tourist information Jever:**
M⛏ Schloßmuseum. Castle, English gardens and museum. ⬤ Tue-Su 10-18h, 01/07-31/08 Mo-Su 10-18h.
M Friesisches Brauhaus. Brewery with museum. Guided tour 2 hours, 2 drinks included. ⬤ Mo-Fri 9.30-16.30h, Sa 9.30-12.30h.

| 🚐S | Jork 〰 | 8A2 |

**Festplatz**, Schützenhofstrasse/Festplatzweg.
**GPS:** n53,53100 e9,68336. ⬆➡.

80 🛏️€ 7 ⛽€ 1/100liter 🚿Ch WC 🚽€ 0,50. 🚐 **Location:** Rural, simple. **Surface:** metalled. ⊙ 01/01-31/12.
**Distance:** 🚲200m ⊗200m 🚶200m.
**Remarks:** Parking event ground, max. 24h.

### Jork 8A2

**Stellplatz Lühe-Anleger**, Fährstraße, Grünendeich.
**GPS:** n53,57271 e9,63129. ⬆️.

10 🛏️€ 10/24h WC€ 0,50/time. 🚐 **Location:** Urban, simple.
**Surface:** grassy/metalled. ⊙ 01/01-31/12.
**Distance:** ⊗on the spot 🚢2km.

### Jork 8A2

**Am Yachthafen**, Neuenschleuse. **GPS:** n53,55375 e9,66858. ⬆️➡️.

18 🛏️€ 7 ⛽€ 1/90liter 🚿Ch 🔌(18x)€ 0,50/kWh WC 🚽€ 2. 🚐
**Location:** Urban, simple. **Surface:** unpaved.
⊙ 01/01-31/12.
**Distance:** 🚲Jork 3km ⊗on the spot 🚴on the spot 🚶on the spot.
**Remarks:** Along the river Elbe.

### Jork 8A2

**Stubbe's Gasthaus**, Lühe 46. **GPS:** n53,56861 e9,63333. ⬆️.

14 🛏️€ 10 🔌€ 2 📶. **Location:** Rural, comfortable. **Surface:** grassy.
⊙ 01/01-31/12.
**Distance:** ⊗on the spot.
**Remarks:** Bread-service, picnic area Am Gartenteich.

### Königslutter am Elm 10C1

**P1 Niedernhof**, Amtsgarten. **GPS:** n52,25009 e10,81996. ⬆️➡️.

5 🛏️free ⛽€ 1/5minutes 🚿€ 1 🔌(4x)€ 1/8h.
**Location:** Urban, comfortable, central, noisy. **Surface:** asphalted.
⊙ 01/01-31/12.
**Distance:** 🚲500m 🚴7km ⊗100m 🚢100m 🚌100m 🚴900m

---

🚶900m.

### Kranenburg 8A2

**Fährverein Brobergen**, Fährstraße, 21726. **GPS:** n53,59708 e9,17080.
5 🛏️€ 10 ⛽🚽 WC🚽included. **Location:** Rural, simple, isolated, quiet. **Surface:** gravel/metalled. ⊙ 01/05-30/09.
**Distance:** 🚲1km 🚴on the spot 🚶on the spot.

### Krummendeich 8A1

**Stellplatz Krummendeich**, Osterwechtern.
**GPS:** n53,83145 e9,20231. ⬆️➡️.

6 🛏️free WC€ 0,50 🚽€ 0,50. **Location:** Rural, simple. **Surface:** gravel.
⊙ 01/01-31/12.
**Distance:** 🏊100m 🚶300m.

### Krummhörn 7F2

**Reisemobilhafen Greetsiel**, Mühlenstrasse 3, Greetsiel.
**GPS:** n53,49711 e7,10181. ⬆️.

55 🛏️€ 11, 2 pers.incl ⛽€ 2/90liter 🚿Ch 🔌(40x)€ 1/8h. 🚐
**Location:** Rural, comfortable, quiet. **Surface:** gravel.
⊙ 01/01-31/12.
**Distance:** 🚲250m 🚶250m.

### Kutenholz 8A2

**Festhalle**, Bürgermeister-Schmetjen-Platz.
**GPS:** n53,48163 e9,31486. ➡️.

10 🛏️free. **Location:** Rural, simple. **Surface:** metalled.
⊙ 01/01-31/12.
**Distance:** ⊗800m 🚢500m 🚴on the spot 🚶on the spot.

### Laar 9F1

**Wohnmobilstellplatz an der Mühle**, Hauptstraße.
**GPS:** n52,61415 e6,74320. ⬆️➡️.

8 🛏️€ 5 ⛽€ 1/80liter 🚿Ch 🔌(8x)€ 1/2kWh.
**Location:** Simple, quiet. **Surface:** metalled. ⊙ 01/01-31/12.
**Distance:** 🚲900m 🚢200m ⊗500m 🚴on the spot 🚶on the spot.

### Lamspringe 10B2

**Am Bahnhof**. **GPS:** n51,95404 e10,00656. ⬆️➡️.

---

3 🛏️free. **Location:** Rural, isolated. **Surface:** gravel.
⊙ 01/01-31/12.
**Distance:** 🚲750m ⊗1km 🚢400m 🚶250m 🚴Radweg zur Kunst 🚶on the spot.
**Remarks:** Max. 3 days.

### Lauenau 10A1

**Brauhaus Felsenkeller**, Feggendorfer Straße 10.
**GPS:** n52,27914 e9,36906.

5 🛏️free ⛽🔌📶free. **Location:** Rural, simple. **Surface:** gravel.
⊙ 01/01-31/12.
**Distance:** 🚲500m 🚴2,4km ⊗on the spot 🚌on the spot.
**Remarks:** Check in at restaurant.

### Lauenförde 10A3

**Yachthafen Dreiländereck**, Würgasser Straße.
**GPS:** n51,65045 e9,37983. ⬆️➡️.

50 🛏️€ 11,50 ⛽🚿Chincluded 🔌(35x)€ 2,20/day WC🚽€ 0,50 🔥€ 2,50 💧€ 4,95. **Location:** Rural, comfortable. **Surface:** gravel.
⊙ 01/04-01/11.
**Distance:** 🚲3km 🏊on the spot 🚢3km 🚴on the spot 🚶on the spot.
**Remarks:** Bread-service.

### Lautenthal 10C2

**Kaspar Bitter Strasse 7b**. **GPS:** n51,87020 e10,28729. ⬆️.

25 🛏️€ 4 + 🚶€ 1,50/pp tourist tax ⛽€ 1/60liter 🚿€ 2 Ch€ 2 🔌(8x)€ 1/6h. **Location:** Rural, comfortable, quiet. **Surface:** gravel.
⊙ 01/01-31/12.
**Distance:** 🚲300m ⊗300m 🚢500m 🚌50m.

### Leer 7G3

**P9**, Große Bleiche. **GPS:** n53,22577 e7,44686. ⬆️.

6 🛏️free ⛽€ 1/100liter 🚿€ 1 Ch 🔌(6x)€ 1/24h WC🚽€ 0,50 🚽€ 1.

**Location:** Urban, simple. **Surface:** metalled.
01/01-31/12.
**Distance:** 200m on the spot 2km on the spot on the spot.
**Remarks:** Max. 3 nights, caution key sanitary € 30, sanitary at offices Bruchbrücke.

| | Leer | 7G3 |

**Am Hafen**, Nessestrasse. **GPS:** n53,22527 e7,45472.

10 free WC € 0,50 € 1. **Location:** Urban, simple.
**Surface:** asphalted/gravel. 01/01-31/12.
**Distance:** 500m 300m 2km.
**Remarks:** Max. 3 nights, caution key sanitary € 30, sanitary at offices Bruchbrücke.

| | Leer | 7G3 |

**Segelnverein**, Segelerweg 3. **GPS:** n53,21907 e7,44793.

3 € 8 Ch included € 0,30/kWh WC € 1.
**Location:** Urban, simple, quiet. **Surface:** metalled.
01/01-31/12.
**Distance:** 1,8km 150m.

| | Leer | 7G3 |

**Landgaststätte zur Jümme-Fähre**, Amdorfer Straße 101.
**GPS:** n53,22429 e7,52593.

guests free € 2/24h. **Location:** Rural, quiet. **Surface:** grassy.
01/01-31/12.
**Distance:** 3km on the spot on the spot on the spot 3km on the spot on the spot.
**Remarks:** Along river.

| | Leer | 7G3 |

**Windmühlenhof Eiklenborg**, Logabirumer Straße, Logabirum.
**GPS:** n53,24745 e7,51582.

5 € 12 Ch WC € 2,50. **Location:** Urban, comfortable, quiet. **Surface:** grassy/metalled. 01/01-31/12.
**Distance:** on the spot.
**Remarks:** Near old Dutch windmill.

| | Leese | 10A1 |

**Wohnmobilhafen Leeser See**, Mühlenberg.
**GPS:** n52,50616 e9,10360.

8 free € 1/10minutes Ch (7x) € 1/6h.
**Location:** Rural, simple, quiet. **Surface:** grasstiles.
01/03-31/10.
**Distance:** on the spot bakery 500m on the spot.

| | Leese | 10A1 |

**Loccumer Straße. GPS:** n52,50272 e9,11733.

4 free. **Surface:** metalled. 01/01-31/12.
**Distance:** 200m on the spot 200m.

| | Leese | 10A1 |

**Rasthaus Leeser Tanger**, Bahlweg. **GPS:** n52,49372 e9,12055.

8 € 15, discount for clients included. **Location:** Simple.
**Surface:** metalled. 01/01-31/12.
**Distance:** 800m on the spot.

| | Lembruch | 9H1 |

**Stellplatz Dümmer-See Lembruch**, Seestraße.
**GPS:** n52,52439 e8,36703.

10 free. **Location:** Rural. **Surface:** grassy. 01/01-31/12.
**Distance:** 300m 100m.

| | Lembruch | 9H1 |

**Campingplatz Seeblick**, Birkenallee. **GPS:** n52,52583 e8,36056.

20 € 9 Ch on camp site € 5,50. **Location:** Rural, simple.
**Surface:** grassy. 01/01-31/12.
**Distance:** 50m 50m.
**Remarks:** Max. 1 night.

| | Lemwerder | 7H3 |

**Reisemobilhafen Peter-Baxmann-Platz**, Schulstrasse 44.
**GPS:** n53,15784 e8,61783.

50 € 3/24h Ch included (40x) € 1/8h.
**Location:** Urban, comfortable, isolated, quiet. **Surface:** gravel.
01/01-31/12.
**Distance:** on the spot 200m 500m 500m 300m.
**Remarks:** Nearby swimming pool.

| | Lemwerder | 7H3 |

**Vulkanparkplatz an der Weser**, Uferweg.
**GPS:** n53,17000 e8,60028.

5 free. **Location:** Urban, simple, quiet. **Surface:** asphalted/metalled.
01/01-31/12.
**Distance:** 2km on the spot 2km 2km on the spot on the spot.

| | Letschin | 8H3 |

**Gasthof Zum Hafen**, Deichweg 20. **GPS:** n52,67458 e14,44256.
15 € 16 WC free. **Location:** Rural. **Surface:** grassy.
01/01-31/12.
**Distance:** on the spot 300m.

| | Lingen/Ems | 9F1 |

**Linus Bad**, Teichstrasse. **GPS:** n52,51863 e7,30606.

30 € 5 € 1 Ch (16x) € 0,50/kWh. **Location:** Rural.
**Surface:** gravel. 01/01-31/12.
**Distance:** 1km 600m 600m on the spot on the spot.
**Remarks:** At swimming pool, max. 3 days.

| | Lorup | 7G3 |

**Rastdorferstrasse. GPS:** n52,92501 e7,64540.

5 free free. **Surface:** metalled. 01/01-31/12.
**Distance:** on the spot 600m bakery 100m.
**Remarks:** Key service at town hall.

| | Loxstedt | 7H2 |

**Stotel**, Alte Schulstraße 75. **GPS:** n53,44067 e8,59356.

DE

4 ⛺free. **Location:** Urban, simple, quiet. **Surface:** grassy.
⏲ 01/01-31/12.
**Distance:** 🚶600m 🚲1km ⛱Stoteler See ⊗100m ⛽on the spot.

### 🛏S Loxstedt 🚻 | 7H2

**Am Bootshafen**, Fährstrasse. **GPS:** n53,44438 e8,49942.⬆.

5 ⛺€ 5 ⚡(6x)€ 0,50/kWh. **Location:** Rural, simple.
**Surface:** gravel/sand. ⏲ 01/04-15/10.
**Distance:** 🚶300m ⛱on the spot ⊗on the spot 🚲on the spot.
**Remarks:** Along the Weser river.

### 🛏 Lüchow | 8C3

Parkstraße. **GPS:** n52,96983 e11,14594.⬆.

2 ⛺free. **Location:** Urban, simple. **Surface:** asphalted/metalled.
⏲ 01/01-31/12.
**Distance:** 🚶900m 🚲900m 🚊1,7km.
**Remarks:** Max. 3 nights.

### 🛏S Lüdersfeld | 10A1

**Heinrichs'Reisemobil Stellplatz**, Am Hülsebrink 10+11.
**GPS:** n52,35972 e9,25512.⬆.

45 ⛺€ 6 🚰 ♻Ch ⚡(8x)included. **Location:** Rural, simple.
**Surface:** gravel. ⏲ 01/01-31/12.
**Distance:** 🚶500m ⊗on the spot.
**Remarks:** Check in at hotel, bread-service.

### 🛏S Lüneburg | 8B2

**Am Sülzwiesen**, Pieperweg. **GPS:** n53,24556 e10,39694.⬆.

53 ⛺€ 13 🚰€ 1/10minutes ♻Ch ⚡(40x),01/10-30/04 € 2/8h.🚐.
**Location:** Rural, comfortable, isolated, quiet. **Surface:** metalled.
⏲ 01/01-31/12.
**Distance:** 🚶1km 🚊300m.
**Remarks:** Max. 1 night.

### 🛏S Mardorf | 10A1

**Wohnmobilstellplatz Steinhuder Meer**, Rote-Kreuz-Strasse 16.
**GPS:** n52,48704 e9,30065.⬆➡.

60 ⛺€ 9 🚰€ 1/100liter ♻Ch ⚡(60x)€ 3.
**Location:** Comfortable. **Surface:** grassy. ⏲ 01/01-31/12.
**Distance:** 🚶1km ⛱300m 🚲1km.
**Remarks:** Bread-service.

### 🛏S Marienhafe | 7F2

**Rechtsupweg**, Poststrasse. **GPS:** n53,52658 e7,32550.⬆➡.

20 ⛺free ⚡against payment. **Location:** Rural, simple, quiet.
**Surface:** gravel. ⏲ 01/01-31/12.
**Distance:** 🚶150m ⊗150m 🚊150m.

### 🛏S Marienhafe | 7F2

**Tjücher Moortun**. **GPS:** n53,52835 e7,28168.⬆➡.

5 ⛺€ 5 🚰€ 1/100liter ♻Ch ⚡(5x)€ 1/24h.🚐
**Location:** Rural, comfortable, quiet. **Surface:** gravel.
⏲ 01/01-31/12.
**Distance:** 🚶400m ⊗on the spot 🚊Lidl 400m.

### 🛏 Marienhafe | 7F2

**Dorfplatz Leezdorf**, Sträkweg. **GPS:** n53,54802 e7,29354.⬆.

4 ⛺free. **Location:** Urban, simple, quiet. **Surface:** metalled.
⏲ 01/01-31/12.
**Distance:** 🚶on the spot ⊗150m 🚊on the spot.

### 🛏 Melle | 9H2

Am Wellenbad 43. **GPS:** n52,20497 e8,32368.⬆.

10 ⛺free. **Location:** Simple, quiet. **Surface:** metalled.
⏲ 01/01-31/12.
**Distance:** 🚶on the spot 🚲1,2km ⊗nearby 🚊300m.
**Remarks:** Parking swimming pool.

### 🛏S Meppen | 9F1

**Reisemobilplatz am Hallenbad**, An der Bleiche.
**GPS:** n52,69107 e7,28399.⬆.

10 ⛺€ 8, swimming pool incl. 1 pers 🚰€ 2/100liter ♻Ch
⚡(4x)€ 2/24h. **Location:** Urban, simple. **Surface:** metalled.
⏲ 01/01-31/12.
**Distance:** 🚶200m ⊗on the spot 🚊300m.
**Remarks:** Parking swimming pool, max. 2 nights.
**Tourist information Meppen:**
🛈 ⏲ Tue-Sa morning.

### 🛏 Moormerland | 7G2

**Am Rathaus**, Theodor Heussstrasse 12, Warsingsfehn.
**GPS:** n53,30826 e7,48613.⬆➡.

4 ⛺free. **Location:** Urban, simple. **Surface:** metalled.
⏲ 01/01-31/12.
**Distance:** 🚶50m ⊗50m 🚐50m.
**Remarks:** Parking townhall, max. 3 nights.

### 🛏S Moormerland | 7G2

**Bei Cassi**, Deichlandstraße 10, Rorinchem.
**GPS:** n53,32010 e7,35473.⬆➡.

15 ⛺€ 5, free with a meal 🚰€ 1 ♻Ch ⚡€ 2 WC € 1 📶included.
**Location:** Rural. **Surface:** gravel/metalled.
⏲ 01/04-31/10. 🍴 Restaurant: Mo.
**Distance:** ⊗on the spot.

### 🛏 Moringen | 10B3

**Domänenhof**, Amtsfreiheit. **GPS:** n51,69833 e9,86861.⬆➡.

3 ⛺free. **Location:** Rural, simple. **Surface:** gravel.
⏲ 01/01-31/12.
**Distance:** 🚶on the spot 🚲5,5km ⊗300m.
**Remarks:** At city park.

### 🛏 Nessmersiel | 7F2

Strandstrasse. **GPS:** n53,68369 e7,35963.⬆.

DE

25 🛏€ 10. 🅿️ **Location:** Rural, simple. **Surface:** grassy/gravel.
🗓 01/01-31/12.
**Distance:** 🚉2km ⚓on the spot.

### 🅿️S Neuharlingersiel ⛱🌊 7G2

**Wohnmobilstellplatz am Ostanleger**, Am Hafen Ost.
**GPS:** n53,70173 e7,70741. ⬆️.

23 🛏€ 12 + € 1-2,50/pp tourist tax 🚰€ 1/100liter 💧included WC.
🅿️ **Location:** Rural, comfortable, quiet. **Surface:** metalled.
🗓 01/01-31/12.
**Distance:** 🚉500m ⚓800m ⊗on the spot 🍴1km.
**Remarks:** Max. 3 nights.

### ♨️S Neuhaus an der Oste 🌊 8A1

**Am Yachthafen. GPS:** n53,80348 e9,04013. ⬆️➡️.

13 🛏€ 9 🚰💧Chincluded 💧€ 2/day WC ⛟€ 3/time ⚡€ 7,50/time.
♨️ **Location:** Rural, simple. **Surface:** grasstiles/metalled.
🗓 01/03-30/10.
**Distance:** ⚓on the spot ⛽on the spot 🚲on the spot.

### 🅿️S Nienburg 10A1

**Reisemobilstellplatz Nienburg/Weser**, Oyler Straße.
**GPS:** n52,64094 e9,20137. ⬆️➡️.

25 🛏€ 5 🚰€ 1/120liter 💧Ch💧(16x)€ 1/8h. **Surface:** gravel.
🗓 01/01-31/12.
**Distance:** 🚉600m ⚓on the spot ⛽on the spot ⊗300m 🍴500m.
**Remarks:** Along the river Weser.

### 🅿️S Norddeich 🌿⛱🌊 7F2

**Wohnmobilhafen Norddeich**, Itzendorferstrasse.
**GPS:** n53,61014 e7,15777. ⬆️➡️.

100 🛏€ 11/24h, 2 pers. + tourist tax, incl. 30% discount Erlebnisbad
Ocean Wave 🚰💧Chincluded 💧(96x)€ 1/2kWh WC ⛟€ 1. 🅿️

**Location:** Rural, comfortable, quiet. **Surface:** metalled.
🗓 01/01-31/12.
**Distance:** 🚉100m ⚓100m ⊗100m 🍴500m ⛽100m.

### ♨️S Norddeich 🌿⛱🌊 7F2

**Womo Park Norddeich**, Deichstraße 24. **GPS:** n53,60166 e7,13527. ⬆️.

60 🛏€ 13, tourist tax excl., dog € 3 🚰€ 1/100liter 💧Ch💧€ 1/kWh
WC ⛟€ 1 ⚡€ 3/1,50 📶. 🅿️ **Location:** Rural, comfortable, quiet.
**Surface:** gravel. 🗓 01/01-31/12.
**Distance:** 🚉2km ⚓beach 1,5km, beach (dog allowed) 1km ⊗on the
spot 🍴500m ⛽100m.
**Remarks:** Bread-service.

### 🅿️S Nordenham 🌿 7H2

**Freizeitbad Störtebeker**, Atenser Allee.
**GPS:** n53,49478 e8,47368. ⬆️➡️.

15 🛏€ 6 🚰€ 1/liter 💧Ch💧(16x)€ 0,50/kWh ⛟€ 2,at sauna. 🅿️
**Location:** Urban, comfortable, noisy. **Surface:** grasstiles.
🗓 01/01-31/12.
**Distance:** 🚉1km 🚤2km ⊗on the spot 🍴400m ⛽on the spot
🚲on the spot.
**Remarks:** Max. 3 days, bread-service.

### 🌿S Nordenham 🌿 7H2

**Volkers**, Deichstrasse 158. **GPS:** n53,54003 e8,50905. ⬆️.

6 🛏€ 8 🚰€ 1/100liter 💧Ch💧(16x)€ 0,50/kWh WC ⛟€ 1/4minutes
⚡📶on demand. 🚲 **Location:** Rural, comfortable, quiet.
**Surface:** gravel. 🗓 01/01-31/12.
**Distance:** 🚉2km ⚓100m ⛽500m 🚲on the spot.
**Remarks:** Grill and picknic area.

### 🅿️S Nordholz 7H1

Wuster Strasse 12, Spieka. **GPS:** n53,75772 e8,59409. ⬆️.

5 🛏€ 5 + tourist tax 🚰€ 1/100liter 💧€ 1 Ch 💧(5x)€ 1/2kWh.
**Location:** Rural, simple. **Surface:** metalled.
🗓 01/01-31/12.
**Distance:** 🚉on the spot ⊗100m.

### 🅿️S Nordhorn 🍞 9F1

**Vechtesee**, Heseperweg. **GPS:** n52,43683 e7,08190. ⬆️.

35 🛏€ 5 🚰€ 1/80liter 💧€ 1/5h. 🅿️ **Location:** Rural.
**Surface:** grassy/metalled. 🗓 01/01-31/12.
**Distance:** 🚉400m ⊗300m 🍴300m 🚲on the spot 🏃on the spot.

### 🅿️S Northeim 10B3

**Grosser Freizeitsee**, Am Nordhafen. **GPS:** n51,72920 e9,96286. ⬆️.

10 🛏€ 6 🚰€ 0,50/50liter 💧Ch💧(8x)€ 1/kWh. 🅿️
**Location:** Rural, simple, noisy. **Surface:** gravel.
🗓 01/01-31/12.
**Distance:** 🚉5km 🚤3km ⊗on the spot 🍴2km.

### 🅿️S Oberndorf/Oste 8A1

**Wohnmobilplatz Bentwisch**, Hoffmann-von-Fallersleben-Straße 10.
**GPS:** n53,75398 e9,15054. ⬆️➡️.

8 🛏€ 5 🚰€ 2/100liter 💧Ch💧(6x)€ 2/8h WC ⛟€ 0,50 ⚡€ 0,50. 🚲
**Location:** Rural, comfortable. **Surface:** grassy/gravel.
🗓 01/01-31/12.
**Distance:** 🚉2km ⚓100m ⛽100m 🚲on the spot.

### 🅿️S Oederquart 8A1

Am Sportplatz. **GPS:** n53,80411 e9,24485. ➡️.

6 🛏free. **Location:** Rural, simple, isolated. **Surface:** metalled.
🗓 01/01-31/12.
**Distance:** ⊗300m.
**Remarks:** At sports centre.

### 🅿️S Oldenburg ⛱🍞🌊 7H3

**Am Küstenkanal**, Westfalendamm. **GPS:** n53,12927 e8,21465. ⬆️➡️.

3 🛏voluntary contribution. **Location:** Rural, simple. **Surface:** gravel.
🗓 01/01-31/12.
**Distance:** 🚉on the spot 🚤1km ⚓on the spot ⊗100m 🍴400m.
**Remarks:** Alternative: in front of campsite Am Flötenteich, 53,166944
8,235, 2 pitches free.

**S** Oldenburg 7H3
**Hymer Zentrum Fassbender**, Sieben Berge.
GPS: n53,19144 e8,22603.

4 € free Ch free € 0,50/kWh. **Location:** Urban, simple, noisy. **Surface:** metalled. 01/01-31/12.
**Distance:** 6km 50m 900m.

**S** Osnabrück 9G2
**Wohnmobilplatz Nettebad**, Im Haseesch 6.
GPS: n52,30194 e8,05031.

5 € 10 € 1/100liter Ch € 1/6h. **Location:** Urban, simple, quiet. **Surface:** grassy/metalled. 01/01-31/12.
**Distance:** on the spot on the spot.
**Remarks:** At swimming pool, max. 24h, outside environmental zone.

**S** Osten 8A2
**Festhalle**, Altendorf 13. GPS: n53,69602 e9,18813.

10 € 8 Ch (2x)included. **Location:** Rural, simple.
**Surface:** metalled. 01/01-31/12.
**Distance:** on the spot on the spot 500m.
**Remarks:** Pay at Hotel Fährkrug.

**S** Osterholz-Scharmbeck 7H3
**August-Schlüter-Turnhalle**, Lange Strasse 28.
GPS: n53,22562 e8,79000.

4 € free € 1/100liter . **Location:** Urban, simple, central.
**Surface:** metalled. 01/01-31/12.
**Distance:** on the spot on the spot on the spot.

**S** Osterode 10C3
**Aloha-Aqualand**, Schwimmbadstraße.
GPS: n51,72263 e10,24998.

7 € 8-12 € 1/75liter € 1 Ch (11x)€ 1,50/8h.

Location: Rural, noisy. **Surface:** metalled. 01/01-31/12.
**Distance:** 1km 200m 500m.
**Remarks:** Max. 2 nights, discount at swimming pool.

**S** Osterode 10C3
**Campingplatz Eulenburg**, Scheerenberger Straße 100.
GPS: n51,72766 e10,28347.

13 € 10, 2 pers.incl € 1/100liter Ch (12x)€ 1/kWh
WC € 0,70/4minutes € 4/day. **Location:** Rural, comfortable, quiet.
**Surface:** gravel. 01/01-31/12.
**Distance:** 2km on the spot 2,5km on the spot on the spot on the spot on the spot.
**Remarks:** Bread-service, swimming pool incl.

**S** Ostrhauderfehn 7G3
**Reisemobilhafen Ostrhauderfehn**, Hauptstrasse 115.
GPS: n53,13872 e7,62318.

32 € 7 Ch (12x)€ 1/2kWh WC € 0,50 € 2 included. **Location:** Urban, comfortable, quiet. **Surface:** grassy/metalled. 01/01-31/12 during fair in June.
**Distance:** 100m 100m 100m 200m on the spot.
**Remarks:** Caution key € 10, sanitary at bar.

Otterndorf 7H1
**Schützenplatz**, Fröbelweg. GPS: n53,80861 e8,89444.

8 free. **Location:** Rural, simple. **Surface:** metalled.
01/01-31/12.
**Distance:** on the spot 200m.

**S** Otterndorf 7H1
**Seglertreff**, Schleuse 5. GPS: n53,82250 e8,89472.

12 € 12, 2 pers.incl Ch € 0,60/kWh WC € 1,50.
**Location:** Rural, comfortable. **Surface:** grassy/gravel.
01/01-31/12.
**Distance:** 2km 50m on the spot on the spot 2km on the spot on the spot.

**S** Ottersberg 8A3
**Am Sportzentrum**, Fährwisch. GPS: n53,10721 e9,13558.

8 free € 1 Ch € 1/8h. **Location:** Simple.
**Surface:** gravel/sand. 01/01-31/12.
**Distance:** 500m 200m.

**S** Ovelgönne 7H2
**Burgdorf Ovelgönne**, Am Sportplatz. GPS: n53,34333 e8,42750.

5 free € 1/100liter Ch free. **Location:** Urban, simple, isolated, quiet. **Surface:** gravel. 01/01-31/12.
**Distance:** 700m 700m 700m on the spot.

**S** Oyten 8A3
**KNAUS Reisemobilpark**, Oyter See 1. GPS: n53,04645 e9,00396.

28 € 22 Ch € 3,50 WC included € 1 .
**Location:** Rural, comfortable. **Surface:** metalled.
01/03-01/11.
**Distance:** 2,5km 3km Oyter See 150m.
**Remarks:** Caution key € 5, service passerby € 4.

Papenburg 7G3
**Roten Kreuz**, Rathausstraße. GPS: n53,07646 e7,39266.

50 free. **Location:** Urban, simple. **Surface:** grassy/sand.
01/01-31/12.
**Distance:** on the spot 300m.
**Remarks:** Nearby hospital.

**S** Papenburg 7G3
**Hotel-Restaurant Hilling**, Mittelkanal links 94.
GPS: n53,07879 e7,43894.

22 € 8 € 1 € 1 Ch € 0,50/kWh WC € 2,50/time included. **Location:** Rural, comfortable, quiet.
**Surface:** grasstiles/grassy. 01/01-31/12.
**Distance:** on the spot 500m on the spot on the spot.

**DE**

### Papenburg 7G3

**Poggenpoel**, Zum Poggenpoel. **GPS**: n53,06526 e7,42630. ↑→.

20 ⌂ € 10 🚰 € 3/100liter 🗑 € 3 Ch ⚡(8x)€ 2,50/24h WC 🗑 € 2. ♨
**Location:** Rural, simple. **Surface:** gravel. ☐ 01/01-31/12.
**Distance:** 🚶3,5km ⚓Badesee 🛒500m.
**Remarks:** At lake, max. 3 nights.

### Rastede 7H3

Mühlenstraße. **GPS**: n53,24806 e8,20944. ↑.

4 ⌂ free. **Location:** Urban, simple. **Surface:** metalled.
☐ 01/01-31/12.
**Distance:** 🚶1km 🏊2,7km ⊗1km 🛒2km.
**Remarks:** Use sanitary only during opening hours swimming pool.

### Rehburg-Loccum 10A1

**Wohnmobilstellplatz Rehburg**, Auf der Bleiche 14.
**GPS**: n52,47370 e9,23227. ↑→.

8 ⌂ € 5 🚰 € 1/100liter 🗑 Ch ⚡ € 1/12h.
**Location:** Rural. **Surface:** gravel. ☐ 01/01-31/12.
**Distance:** 🚶500m 🏊4km 🛒500m 🚌400m 🚲on the spot 🚶on the spot.

**Tourist information Rehburg-Loccum:**
Dinosaurierpark Münchehagen. Attractions park around the dinosaur. ☐ 12/03-30/10 9-18.

### Rhauderfehn 7G3

**Paddel- und Pedalstation**, Am Siel 8. **GPS**: n53,13878 e7,58689. ↑→.

16 ⌂ € 8 🚰 € 1/100liter 🗑 Ch ⚡(16x)€ 1/8h WC 🗑 € 1,50
🛜included. 📠**Location:** Rural, luxurious, quiet. **Surface:** grassy.
☐ 01/01-31/12.
**Distance:** 🚶500m 🏊on the spot 🚣on the spot ⊗50m 🚲on the spot 🚶on the spot.
**Remarks:** Caution key sanitary € 10, canoe and bicycle rental.

### Rhede/Ems 7F3

**Emspark**, Am Sportplatz 6. **GPS**: n53,05853 e7,27621. ↑.

5 ⌂ free. **Location:** Simple. **Surface:** metalled.
☐ 01/01-31/12.
**Distance:** 🚶500m ⊗500m 🛒500m.
**Remarks:** Parking in front of sports park.

### Rhede/Ems 7F3

**Gasthof Prangen**, Kirchstraße 25. **GPS**: n53,05943 e7,26923. ↑.

10 ⌂ guests free 🛜free. **Location:** Urban, simple, quiet.
**Surface:** grassy/gravel. ☐ 01/01-31/12.
**Distance:** 🚶on the spot ⊗on the spot 🛒100m 🚲on the spot.

### Rieste 9G1

**Reisemobilhafen am Alfsee Center**, Westerfeldstraße 76.
**GPS**: n52,49309 e7,98953. ↑.

30 ⌂ € 8-15 🚰 € 1/100liter 🗑 € 1/time ⚡(20x)€ 0,50/kWh. 🗑
**Location:** Rural, quiet. **Surface:** metalled. ☐ 01/01-31/12.
**Distance:** 🚲on the spot 🚶on the spot.

### Rieste 9G1

**Wohnmobilstellplätze-Alfsee**, Bootshafenstraße 4.
**GPS**: n52,47824 e7,98961. ↑.

10 ⌂ € 12, dog € 1,50 🚰 € 1/100liter 🗑 Ch ⚡ € 0,50/kWh WC 🗑.
**Location:** Rural, isolated, quiet. **Surface:** grassy/gravel.
☐ 01/01-31/12.
**Distance:** 🚶2km ⊗on the spot.
**Remarks:** Caution key sanitary € 10.

### Rinteln 10A2

**Reisemobilplatz am Weseranger**, Dankerser strasse.
**GPS**: n52,19226 e9,07842. ↑→.

40 ⌂ free 🚰 € 4/100liter 🗑 € 4 Ch € 2 ⚡(36x)€ 1/kWh,16Amp.
**Location:** Rural, simple. **Surface:** grassy/gravel.
☐ 01/01-31/12.

**Distance:** 🚶600m 🏊on the spot 🚣on the spot ⊗100m 🛒400m
🚌400m 🚲Weserradweg 🚶on the spot.
**Remarks:** Max. 3 days.

### Rodenberg 10A1

**Rikes Wohnmobilstellplatz am Deister**, Gottlieb Daimler Straße 11.
**GPS**: n52,30690 e9,36757. ↑.

8 ⌂ € 6 🚰 € 1/100liter 🗑 Ch ⚡ € 0,50/kWh.
**Surface:** gravel. ☐ 01/01-31/12.
**Distance:** 🚶centre 1,2km.
**Remarks:** Bread-service.

### Rodewald 10A1

**Am Freibad**, Im Zentrum. **GPS**: n52,66369 e9,48020. ↑.

6 ⌂ voluntary contribution 🚰 € 0,50/100liter 🗑 ⚡(10x)€ 0,50/kWh.
**Surface:** grasstiles. ☐ 01/01-31/12.
**Distance:** 🛒200m 🚲on the spot 🚲on the spot.

### Rotenburg (Wümme) 8A3

**Am Weichelsee**, Bremer Straße. **GPS**: n53,11960 e9,38230. ↑→.

20 ⌂ € 8 🚰 🗑 Ch ⚡(20x)€ 3 🗑 € 2. ♨ **Location:** Rural, simple.
**Surface:** metalled. ☐ 01/01-31/12.
**Distance:** 🚶2km 🏊on the spot ⊗Strandhouse 🛒bakery 200m
🚌2km 🚲on the spot.
**Remarks:** Check in at StrandHouse.

### Salzgitter 10B2

**Reisemobilstellplatz am Salzgittersee**, Zum Salzgittersee.
**GPS**: n52,15222 e10,31306. ↑→.

18 ⌂ free 🚰 € 2/100liter 🗑 Ch ⚡(14x)€ 1/6h.
**Location:** Rural, comfortable. **Surface:** grassy/metalled.
☐ 01/01-31/12.
**Distance:** 🚶1km 🏊on the spot ⊗500m 🛒1km 🚌on the spot
🚲on the spot 🚶on the spot.
**Remarks:** Max. 4 days, boat rental.

### Salzgitter 10B2

**Thermalsolebad**, Parkallee 3, Salzgitter-Bad.
**GPS**: n52,03724 e10,38351. ↑→.

6 ⛺free. **Location:** Rural, simple, quiet. **Surface:** metalled.
◯ 01/01-31/12.
**Distance:** 1,5km ⚑on the spot 🏊1,5km 🚌on the spot 👣on the spot.
**Remarks:** Max. 4 days, use sanitary only during opening hours swimming pool, against payment, no camping activities.

### Salzhausen 8B2

**Am Waldbad**, Schwienbrink. **GPS:** n53,22199 e10,17841.⬆.

6 ⛺free 🚰€ 1/10minutes 💧Ch 💦(4x)€ 1/12h.
**Location:** Rural, simple. **Surface:** gravel. ◯ 01/01-31/12.
**Distance:** 1km 🏊500m.

### Salzhemmendorf ♨ 10B2

**Ith-Sole-Therme**, In der Saale-Aue. **GPS:** n52,07093 e9,58564.⬆.

20 ⛺€ 7,50 🚰€ 0,20/20liter 💧€ 1 Ch 💦(20x)€ 1/kWh ⬛included.
**Location:** Rural, quiet. **Surface:** grassy/gravel. ◯ 01/01-31/12.
**Distance:** 400m 🏊300m 🚌on the spot.
**Remarks:** Check in at pay-desk of the Therme.

### Salzhemmendorf ♨ 10B2

**Rasti-land**, Quanthofer strasse 9. **GPS:** n52,09706 e9,66451.⬆.

5 ⛺free. **Location:** Isolated. **Surface:** gravel/sand.
◯ 01/01-31/12.
**Distance:** 1km.
**Remarks:** Bus parking amusement park.
**Tourist information Salzhemmendorf:**
Rasti-Land, Quanthofer strasse 9. Amusement park. ◯ 01/04-31/10 10-17/18h, Apr, Sep: Sa, Su.

### Sande (Nieder-Sachsen) 7G2

**Paddel- und Pedalstation**, Alt-Marienhausen.
**GPS:** n53,51174 e8,01076.⬆.

12 ⛺€ 6/24h 🚰€ 1/100liter 💧Ch 💦€ 0,50/kWh. 🚐
**Location:** Rural, simple, quiet. **Surface:** gravel/sand.
◯ 01/01-31/12.
**Distance:** 1km 🏊Sander See 50m 🚌on the spot 👣on the spot.

### Sande (Nieder-Sachsen) 7G2

**Am Markt. GPS:** n53,50251 e8,01113.⬆.

4 ⛺free. **Location:** Urban, simple. **Surface:** metalled.
◯ 01/01-31/12.
**Distance:** 100m ⊗100m 🏊100m.

### Sande (Nieder-Sachsen) 7G2

**Jade Weser Airport**, Mariensielerstrasse. **GPS:** n53,50788 e8,05245.⬆.

2 ⛺free. **Location:** Rural, simple. **Surface:** grassy/metalled.
◯ 01/01-31/12.
**Distance:** 3km ⊗on the spot.

### Sande (Nieder-Sachsen) 7G2

**Sander See**, Loppelter Weg. **GPS:** n53,51162 e8,00206.⬆.

4 ⛺free. **Location:** Rural, simple, noisy. **Surface:** gravel/sand.
◯ 01/01-31/12.
**Distance:** 2km 🏊on the spot.

### Sande (Nieder-Sachsen) 7G2

**Freizeitmobile von der Kammer**, Huntestraße 1.
**GPS:** n53,49076 e8,02292.⬆.
🚰💧Ch 💦on demand. ◯ 01/03-31/10.

### Sandstedt 7H2

## Wohnmobilstellplatz Sandstedt Sandstedt

- **Paved and flat motorhome pitches**
- **Rural location**
- **Located near marina**

**www.hagen-cux.de**
**touristik@hagen-cux.de**

**Wohnmobilstellplatz Sandstedt**, Am Radarturm 5.
**GPS:** n53,36317 e8,51231.⬆.➡.
10 ⛺€ 5 🚰€ 1/100liter 💧€ 1 Ch€ 1 💦(9x)€ 1.
**Location:** Rural, comfortable, isolated, quiet. **Surface:** metalled.
◯ 01/04-30/09.
**Distance:** 500m 🚲5km 🏊100m 🚤950m ⊗3km 🚌500m 🚶on the spot 👣on the spot.

### Sankt Andreasberg 🏔 ❄ 10C3

**Silbererzgrube Samson**, Am Samson 4. **GPS:** n51,71398 e10,51625.⬆.

20 ⛺€ 15 🚰💧Ch 💦(20x)included. 🚐 **Location:** Rural, simple, quiet. **Surface:** gravel. ◯ 01/01-31/12.
**Distance:** 1km ⊗400m 🏊1km 👣on the spot.
**Remarks:** At Historical Mine of Silver Ores.

### Saterland 🍽 🌳 7G3

**Reisemobilhafen am Maiglöckchensee**, Am Sportplatz, Scharrel.
**GPS:** n53,07060 e7,70116.⬆.➡.

25 ⛺€ 5 🚰€ 1/100liter 💧€ 1 Ch€ 1 💦(28x)€ 2/24h WC ⬛€ 0,50 🚿€ 2. 🛁 **Location:** Rural, luxurious, quiet. **Surface:** grassy.
◯ 01/01-31/12.
**Distance:** 300m 🚲50m ⊗50m 🏊1km 🚤500m 🚌500m 🚶on the spot 👣on the spot.
**Remarks:** Barbecue place.

### Saterland 🍽 🌳 7G3

**B&B Seelter Venture**, Koloniestrasse 83, Sedelsberg.
**GPS:** n53,05378 e7,77245.⬆.

5 ⛺€ 9/pp 💦🚿WC 📶included. 🛁 **Location:** Rural, comfortable, isolated, quiet. **Surface:** grassy. ◯ 01/01-31/12.
**Distance:** 8km ⊗2,4km.

### Scharnebeck 🌿🌾 8C2

**Wohnmobilstellplatz Am Schiffshebewerk**, Adendorfer Straße 40.
**GPS:** n53,29196 e10,49320.⬆.

15 ⛺€ 6/24h, park € 2 🚰€ 1/10minutes 💧Ch 💦(8x)€ 1/8h. 🚐
**Location:** Rural, comfortable, isolated, quiet. **Surface:** metalled.
◯ 01/01-31/12.
**Distance:** 1km ⊗200m 🏊Aldi 400m.
**Remarks:** Climbing wall 100m, boat lift Scharnebeck.

### Schneverdingen 8B3

**Wohnmobil-Park Lüneburger Heide**, Badeweg 3, Heber.
**GPS:** n53,07104 e9,86481.⬆.

DE

44 🛏️ € 16 🚐 € 1/80liter 🔧Ch 🚿(40x),10Amp WC ⌷included
📶🏠 **Location:** Rural, comfortable. **Surface:** grassy/metalled.
◻ 01/04-31/10.
**Distance:** 🚶7km 🚲5km 🏊on the spot ⊗on the spot 🍽on camp site 🚴on the spot 🏃on the spot.
**Remarks:** Use sanitary facilities at campsite, car rental, shuttle bus.

| 🚰S | Schneverdingen ⛱🚣 | 8B3 |

**Am Quellenbad**, Inseler Straße. **GPS:** n53,13110 e9,77280.⬆➡

10 🛏️free 🚐 € 2 🔧ChWC⌷ € 1. **Location:** Urban, simple.
**Surface:** grassy. ◻ 01/01-31/12.
**Distance:** 🚶2km 🏊on the spot 🚴on the spot 🏃on the spot.
**Remarks:** Max. 2 nights, use sanitary only during opening hours swimming pool.

| 🏕️ | Schneverdingen ⛱🚣 | 8B3 |

**Parkplatz Festhalle**, Im Osterwald. **GPS:** n53,11893 e9,80681.⬆

10 🛏️free. **Location:** Simple. **Surface:** metalled.
◻ 01/01-31/12.
**Distance:** 🚶2km 🏊2km.
**Remarks:** Max. 2 nights, entrance via Festhalle.

| 🚐 | Schneverdingen ⛱🚣 | 8B3 |

**Walter-Peters-Park**, Verdener Straße. **GPS:** n53,11307 e9,78799.⬆

2 🛏️free. **Location:** Urban, simple. **Surface:** metalled.
◻ 01/01-31/12.
**Distance:** 🚶500m ⊗100m 🏊500m.
**Remarks:** Nearby police station.

| 🚱S | Schneverdingen ⛱🚣 | 8B3 |

**Mariechen´s Hoff**, Voßbarg 15, Reinsehlen.
**GPS:** n53,17122 e9,83316.⬆➡

8 🛏️ € 8 🚐Ch 🚿(8x)included. **Location:** Rural, simple,

isolated, quiet. **Surface:** grassy. ◻ 01/01-31/12.
**Distance:** 🚶7km 🚲15km ⊗3km 🍽4km 🚴on the spot 🏃on the spot.

| 🚰S | Schneverdingen ⛱🚣 | 8B3 |

**Reisemobilhafen Lüneburgerheide**, Badeweg 3, Heber.
**GPS:** n53,07108 e9,86464.⬆.

5 🛏️ € 12 🚐🔧Ch 🚿(5x)included WC⌷ € 2,50.🏠🚿
**Location:** Rural, luxurious, quiet. **Surface:** grasstiles/metalled.
◻ 01/04-31/10.
**Distance:** 🚶5km 🏊on camp site 🚴on the spot 🏃on the spot.
**Remarks:** Sanitary at campsite.

| 🚐 | Schöppenstedt | 10C2 |

**Elm-Asse-Platz**, Schützenplatz am Berge.
**GPS:** n52,14756 e10,77737.⬆

15 🛏️free. **Location:** Rural, simple, noisy. **Surface:** asphalted.
◻ 01/01-31/12.
**Distance:** 🚶600m ⊗1km 🏊1km.
**Remarks:** Next to sports fields.

**Tourist information Schöppenstedt:**
ℹ The region of Till Eulenspiegel. Tills-Tauf-Tour: cycle and hiking routesin the country of Jester Till, start at the Till Eulenspiegel museum.
◻ Tue-Fri 14-17h, Sa/Su/holidays 11-17h.
Ⓜ Till Eulenspiegelmuseum, Nordstrasse 4a. ◻ Tue-Fri 14-17h, Sa/Su/holidays 11-17h ⦿ Mo.

| 🚐 | Schortens | 7G2 |

**Aqua-toll**, Beethovenstrasse. **GPS:** n53,53961 e7,93780.

2 🛏️free. **Surface:** metalled. ◻ 01/01-31/12.
**Distance:** 🏊200m 🚌25m.
**Remarks:** Parking swimming pool, max. 6,5m.

| 🍴 | Schortens | 7G2 |

**Reisemobilstellplatz Fair-Cafe**, Birkenstraße.
**GPS:** n53,55281 e7,97650.

6 🛏️guests free. **Surface:** unpaved. ◻ 01/01-31/12.
**Distance:** 🚶3km 🏊100m.

| 🚱S | Schulenberg 🌿❄ | 10C2 |

Wiesenbergstrasse. **GPS:** n51,83535 e10,43464.⬆

20 🛏️ € 5 + € 1,50/pp tourist tax 🚐 € 1/80liter 🔧Ch 🚿(6x) € 0,50/kWh WC. 🚿 **Location:** Rural, comfortable, quiet. **Surface:** gravel.
◻ 01/01-31/12.
**Distance:** 🚶on the spot ⊗on the spot 🏊6km 🚌on the spot 🏃on the spot.
**Remarks:** Check in at tourist office, view at Okerstausee.

| 🚐S | Schüttorf | 9F2 |

**Am Kuhmplatz**, Graf-Egbert-Straße. **GPS:** n52,32123 e7,22642.⬆

10 🛏️free 🚐🔧Chfree. **Location:** Rural, simple. **Surface:** gravel.
◻ 01/01-31/12.
**Distance:** 🚲2,4km 🏊100m.
**Remarks:** Parking swimming pool.

| 🚐 | Schwanewede | 7H3 |

**Am Markt**, Am Markt. **GPS:** n53,22412 e8,59644.⬆

3 🛏️free. **Location:** Simple, central. **Surface:** metalled.
◻ 01/01-31/12.
**Distance:** 🚶on the spot ⊗on the spot 🏊on the spot.

| 🚐 | Schwanewede | 7H3 |

**Brücke zu Harriersand**, Inselstraße. **GPS:** n53,26489 e8,49762.⬆

5 🛏️free. **Location:** Rural, simple, isolated. **Surface:** grassy.
◻ 01/01-31/12.
**Distance:** 🚶7km.

| 🚐 | Schwanewede | 7H3 |

**Löhnhorst**, Hammersbeckerweg/Am Fosshall.
**GPS:** n53,20355 e8,62453.⬆

2 🛏️free. **Location:** Rural, simple, isolated, quiet. **Surface:** metalled.
◻ 01/01-31/12.
**Distance:** 🚶6km ⊗6km 🏊6km.

DE

## Schwanewede — 7H3

**Wohnmobilstellplatz**, Klint, Neuenkirchen. **GPS**: n53,23670 e8,50919. ⬆

5 ⌷free. **Location**: Rural, simple, quiet. **Surface**: unpaved.
◎ 01/01-31/12.
**Distance**: 🚶500m.
**Remarks**: Dead end street.

## Seelze — 10A1

**Marina Rasche Werft**, Werftstraße 10. **GPS**: n52,39560 e9,56435. ⬆

13 ⌷€ 6,50 ⛽included ⚿(13x)€ 3 WC 🚿€ 2 ◉. **Location**: Rural,
simple, noisy. **Surface**: gravel/metalled. ◎ 01/04-15/10.
**Distance**: 🚶2km ⛵4,5km ⊗on the spot.
**Remarks**: Bread-service, boat rental.

## Selsingen — 8A2

**Wohnmobilstation**, Im Sick. **GPS**: n53,37573 e9,20681. ⬆➡

25 ⌷free ⛽Chfree. **Location**: Rural, simple. **Surface**: metalled.
◎ 01/01-31/12.
**Distance**: 🚶500m ⊗500m 🍴100m.

## Soltau — 8B3

**Soltau Therme**, Stubbendorffweg. **GPS**: n52,99301 e9,84443.

10 ⌷free. **Location**: Simple, central, quiet. **Surface**: metalled.
◎ 01/01-31/12.
**Distance**: 🚶1km ⊗on the spot 🚴on the spot 🚶on the spot.
**Remarks**: Max. 1 night.

## Soltau — 8B3

**Heidepark**. **GPS**: n53,02166 e9,87370.

100 ⌷€ 6. 🛁
**Location**: Rural, simple, isolated. **Surface**: grasstiles.
◎ 19/03-30/10.

---

**Remarks**: Parking amusement park.
**Tourist information Soltau:**
Heidepark. Amusement park. ◎ 01/03-31/10 9-18h, 01/07-15/08
Sa 9-21h.

## Springe — 10A2

**Alter Museumshof**, Auf dem Burghof. **GPS**: n52,20765 e9,55717. ⬆

5 ⌷free. **Location**: Simple. **Surface**: asphalted. ◎ 01/01-31/12.
**Distance**: 🚶Old city centre 200m ⊗300m 🍴800m.

## Stade — 8A2

**Wohnmobilstellplatz Am Schiffertor**, Schiffertorsstrasse 21.
**GPS**: n53,60278 e9,46667. ⬆➡

79 ⌷€ 9,50/24h ⛽€ 1/80liter 🚿Ch ⚿€ 0,50/kWh WC 🚿.📷
**Location**: Urban, central. **Surface**: gravel.
◎ 01/01-31/12.
**Distance**: 🚶500m ⊗700m 🚴on the spot.

## Stadland — 7H2

**Am Sportplatz**, Hauptstrasse, Seefeld. **GPS**: n53,45639 e8,35778. ⬆

5 ⌷free ⛽€ 1/10minutes ⚿(4x)€ 1/8h. **Location**: Urban, simple,
quiet. **Surface**: asphalted. ◎ 01/01-31/12.
**Distance**: 🚶on the spot ⊗on the spot 🍴on the spot 🚶on the spot
🚴on the spot.
**Remarks**: Next to sports fields.

## Stadland — 7H2

**Deichparkplatz**, Fährstrasse, Kleinensiel. **GPS**: n53,44250 e8,47833. ⬆

5 ⌷free ⛽€ 1/100liter ⚿(4x)€ 1. **Location**: Rural, simple, isolated,
quiet. **Surface**: gravel. ◎ 01/01-31/12.
**Distance**: 🚶500m ⛱200m Weserstrand 🍴300m 🚴on the spot.

## Stadland — 7H2

**Rathausplatz**, Am Markt, Rodenkirchen. **GPS**: n53,39944 e8,45444. ⬆

---

10 ⌷free ⛽€ 1/10minutes 🚿Ch ⚿(4x)€ 1/8h.
**Location**: Urban, simple, central, quiet.
**Surface**: grasstiles/metalled.
◎ 01/01-31/12 ⊚ Thu 5-13h market.
**Distance**: 🚶on the spot ⊗500m 🍴500m 🚴on the spot 🚶on the
spot.

## Stadland — 7H2

**Birkenweg**, Kleinsiel. **GPS**: n53,44194 e8,47444.
🚿Chfree. **Location**: Urban. ◎ 01/01-31/12.

## Stadthagen — 10A1

**Reisemobilplatz am Tropicana**, Jahnstraße 2.
**GPS**: n52,32236 e9,18896. ⬆

15 ⌷free ⛽€ 1/100liter 🚿Ch ⚿(4x)€ 1/2kWh WC 🚿🔌.
**Location**: Rural, quiet. **Surface**: gravel. ◎ 01/01-31/12.
**Distance**: 🚶2km ⊗1km 🍴500km 🚴on the spot 🚶on the spot.
**Remarks**: Max. 3 days, service at Tropicana.

## Stadtoldendorf — 10B2

**Mobilcamping unter den Homburg**, Linnenkämper Strasse 33.
**GPS**: n51,87777 e9,63500. ⬆➡

30 ⌷€ 5/day ⛽€ 1 🚿€ 1 Ch ⚿(25x)€ 2/day. 🛁 **Location**: Simple.
**Surface**: grassy. ◎ 01/01-31/12.
**Distance**: 🚶1km ⊗on the spot 🍴800m 🚍800m.
**Remarks**: Check in at restaurant.

## Steimbke — 10A1

**Klostergarten**. **GPS**: n52,65989 e9,38707. ⬆➡

8 ⌷voluntary contribution ⛽80liter 🚿⚿(8x)€ 0,50/kWh.
**Location**: Rural, simple, quiet. **Surface**: metalled.
◎ 01/01-31/12.
**Distance**: ⊗400m 🚴on the spot.
**Remarks**: At swimming pool.

## Steinfeld — 9H1

**Zur Schemder Bergmark**, Dammer Strasse.
**GPS**: n52,58308 e8,21476. ⬆➡

10 ⌷free ⛽€ 1/100liter 🚿€ 0,50 Ch€ 0,50.
**Location**: Rural, quiet. **Surface**: metalled. ◎ 01/01-31/12.
**Distance**: 🚶500m 🍴500m.
**Remarks**: Parking swimming pool, max. 3 days.

DE

## Steinhude — 10A1

**Wohnmobilstellplatz Steinhude**, Am Bruchdamm.
**GPS:** n52,44874 e9,35478. ↑.

168 € 11 € 1 € 1 Ch (168x)€ 0,60/kWh WC € 1/5minutes € 2,50/2,50.
**Location:** Rural, comfortable. **Surface:** grassy.
01/01-31/12.
**Distance:** 500m 500m 500m 500m.
**Remarks:** Max. 3 nights, bread-service.
**Tourist information Steinhude:**
ℹ Marina on lake of the same name.

## Steyerberg — 10A1

**Wohnmobilstellplatz Steyerberg**, Kleine Straße 7.
**GPS:** n52,56655 e9,02505. ↑ →.

4 free € 1 Ch € 1 (8x)€ 1/8h. **Location:** Rural, simple, quiet.
**Surface:** gravel. 01/01-31/12.
**Distance:** on the spot.
**Remarks:** Nearby bus station.

## Stolzenau — 10A1

**Reisemobilstellplatz Stolzenau**, Weserstrasse.
**GPS:** n52,51021 e9,08104. ↑ →.

24 € 4 € 1/60liter Ch (24x)€ 2/12h. **Surface:** grasstiles.
01/01-31/12 service 01/11-31/03.
**Distance:** 250m on the spot on the spot 300m 300m.
**Remarks:** Along the Weser river.

## Strücklingen — 7G3

**Reisemobilpark Sagter Ems**, Haupstrasse.
**GPS:** n53,12166 e7,66761. ↑ →.

55 € 7 € 1/100liter Ch € 0,50/kWh € 1/10minutes € 3 included. **Location:** Rural, comfortable. **Surface:** grassy/gravel.
01/01-31/12.
**Distance:** on the spot on the spot 500m on the spot on the spot.

## Strücklingen — 7G3

**Reisemobilplatz Am Bootshafen**, Hauptstrasse 640.
**GPS:** n53,12819 e7,66762. ↑.

---

15 € 5 € 1/100liter € 1 Ch € 1 € 2/24h WC € 1 € 1.
**Location:** Rural, simple, quiet. **Surface:** grassy/gravel.
01/01-31/12.
**Distance:** 100m on the spot on the spot on the spot on the spot 100m.
**Remarks:** Canoe and bicycle rental.

## Südbrookmerland — 7F2

**Grosses Meer**, Langerweg. **GPS:** n53,44454 e7,30808. ↑ →.

30 € 9 € 0,50/100liter € 0,50 Ch € 0,50 € 1/2kWh WC included. **Location:** Rural, comfortable, quiet.
**Surface:** metalled. 01/01-31/12.
**Distance:** on the spot on the spot.
**Remarks:** Caution key sanitary € 50.

## Sulingen — 9H1

**Am Stadtsee**, Kornstraße. **GPS:** n52,67653 e8,80127. ↑.

20 free € 1/5minutes € 1 Ch € 1 against payment.
**Surface:** metalled. 01/01-31/12.
**Distance:** 600m 300m.

## Surwold — 7G3

**Privatplatz Klapper**, Papenburgerstrasse 57.
**GPS:** n53,01774 e7,48470. ↑.

10 € 10 Ch (4x)€ 2/24h WC € 2.
**Location:** Rural, simple. **Surface:** grassy. 01/01-31/12.
**Distance:** 1km 1,5km 1km 1km.
**Remarks:** Swimming pool and picnic area available.

## Surwold — 7G3

**Erholungsgebiet Surwolds Wald**, Waldstrasse 26.
**GPS:** n52,96743 e7,51535. ↑.

20 € 20, 2 pers.incl € 1/100liter Ch € 3 WC € 2.

---

**Location:** Rural, comfortable. **Surface:** grassy. 01/01-31/12.
**Distance:** 800m 250m.

## Tarmstedt — 8A3

**Landtechniek Grabau**, Bahnhofstraße.
**GPS:** n53,22421 e9,08728. ↑ →.

15 € 6 Ch included according consumption.
**Location:** Simple. **Surface:** metalled. 01/01-31/12.
**Distance:** on the spot 500m on the spot.

## Thedinghausen — 8A3

**Reisemobilstellplatz Erbhof**, Braunschweiger Straße 45.
**GPS:** n52,96188 e9,03020. ↑.

8 € 5 € 1/10minutes Ch (8x)€ 1/6h WC.
**Surface:** grasstiles. 01/01-31/12.
**Distance:** 500m on the spot on the spot.

## Timmel — 7G2

**Ferienhof Welsch**, Ulbagrgerstrasse 17. **GPS:** n53,36492 e7,52840. ↑.

8 € 6 € 1/100liter Ch € 0,50/kWh € 2,50 free.
**Location:** Comfortable, quiet. **Surface:** grassy. 01/01-31/12.
**Distance:** 500m 250m 500m 200m 200m.

## Twist — 9F1

**Am Hallenbad**. **GPS:** n52,64719 e7,08918. ↑.

6 free € 1/100liter Ch (8x)€ 1/2kWh.
**Surface:** metalled. 01/01-31/12.
**Distance:** on the spot on the spot.
**Remarks:** Barefoot path.

## Uchte — 10A1

**Balkenkamp**. **GPS:** n52,49761 e8,90618. ↑.

3 free € 1 Ch € 1/8h,10-16Amp.
**Surface:** metalled. 01/01-31/12.

**Distance:** 🚶100m ⊗500m 🛒100m.

| 🚐🅂 | **Uchte** 🌳 | 10A1 |
|---|---|---|

Kirchstraße 7. **GPS:** n52,49653 e8,90555. ⬆️➡️.

2 🚐free 🚰€ 1 🔌€ 1 Ch 💧(4x)€ 3/6h. **Location:** Urban, central, quiet. **Surface:** metalled. 🅾️ 01/01-31/12.
**Distance:** 🚶on the spot ⊗75m 🛒300m.

| 🚐🅂 | **Uelsen** 🎡 | 9F1 |
|---|---|---|

**Am Waldbad**, Am Waldbad 6. **GPS:** n52,48690 e6,88460. ⬆️➡️.

13 🚐€ 5 🚰€ 1/100liter 🔌€ 1 💧€ 0,50/kWh 📶included. 🚌 🧺
**Location:** Rural, simple, quiet. **Surface:** grassy/metalled.
🅾️ 01/01-31/12.
**Distance:** 🚶1km ⊗1,5km 🛒1km 🚲on the spot 🚶on the spot.
**Remarks:** At swimming pool.

| 🛳️🅂 | **Uelzen** 🌳 | 8C3 |
|---|---|---|

**Im Sportboothafen**, Riedweg 7. **GPS:** n52,95722 e10,59444. ⬆️.

6 🚐€ 8 + 🚰€ 1/pp 🚰€ 1/70liter 🔌€ 1 Ch 💧(8x)€ 1/6h,16Amp
WC included 🚿€ 2,50/2,50. **Location:** Rural, simple, quiet.
**Surface:** metalled. 🅾️ 01/01-31/12.
**Distance:** 🚶2,5km 🅿️on the spot ⊗on the spot
🛒2km 🚲on the spot 🚶on the spot.
**Remarks:** Max. 3 nights, free bicycles available, playground.

| 🚐 | **Undeloh** 🌳🎡 | 8B3 |
|---|---|---|

**Am Naturschutzpark**, Wilseder Straße. **GPS:** n53,19253 e9,97709.

30 🚐€ 3/day, € 6/night. 🚌 **Location:** Rural, simple.
**Surface:** unpaved. 🅾️ 01/01-31/12.
**Distance:** 🚶500m 🛒100m 🚶on the spot.
**Remarks:** In nature reserve the the Lüneburg Heide (heath).

| 🚐 | **Unterlüß** | 8B3 |
|---|---|---|

**Dr. August Biermann Stadion**, Am Hochwald 1.
**GPS:** n52,84578 e10,28251.
5 🚐free. **Location:** Urban, simple. **Surface:** grassy.
🅾️ 01/01-31/12.
**Distance:** ⊗on the spot.
**Remarks:** Max. 72h.

| 🚐🅂 | **Uplengen** 🌳 | 7G2 |
|---|---|---|

**Remelser Paddel- & Pedalstation**, Uferstrasse.
**GPS:** n53,30123 e7,75151. ⬆️.

5 🚐€ 5 🚰🔌Ch 💧(4x)€ 1/12h. **Surface:** metalled.
🅾️ 01/01-31/12.
**Distance:** 🚶500m 🏊50m 🛒500m.
**Remarks:** Max. 3 days, canoe and bicycle rental.

| 🚐🅂 | **Uplengen** | 7G2 |
|---|---|---|

**Schützenplatz**, Schützenstraße. **GPS:** n53,30719 e7,74708. ⬆️➡️.

10 🚐€ 5 🚰🔌Chincluded 💧€ 1/12h. **Location:** Urban, simple.
**Surface:** grasstiles. 🅾️ 01/01-31/12 🌙 10/06-25/06.
**Distance:** 🚶500m ⊗500m 🛒600m 🚏600m.
**Remarks:** Max. 3 nights.

| 🍴🅂 | **Uplengen** | 7G2 |
|---|---|---|

**Zum grünen Jäger**, Hollener Straße 36. **GPS:** n53,27825 e7,75244. ➡️.

10 🚐free 🚰free 💧€ 5. **Location:** Rural, quiet. **Surface:** metalled.
🅾️ 01/01-31/12.
**Distance:** 🚶4km 🗡️3km ⊗on the spot 🛒4km 🚲on the spot
🚶on the spot.
**Remarks:** Restaurant closed on Monday.

| 🚐🅂 | **Uslar** 🛳️ | 10B3 |
|---|---|---|

**Reisemobilpark am Badeland**, Zur Schwarzen Erde.
**GPS:** n51,66753 e9,62831. ⬆️➡️.

20 🚐€ 6 + reduction swimming pool 🚰€ 1/10minutes 🔌Ch
💧€ 1/6h WC € 0,50. **Location:** Quiet. **Surface:** grasstiles.
🅾️ 01/01-31/12.
**Distance:** 🚶1km ⊗on the spot 🛒500m 🚏on the spot.

| 🍇🅂 | **Uslar** 🛳️ | 10B3 |
|---|---|---|

**Am Lindenhof**, Lindenhof 1. **GPS:** n51,67213 e9,62952. ⬆️➡️.

5 🚐first night € 8, € 2 each additional night 🚰🔌Chincluded
💧€ 0,50/kWh. 🧺
**Location:** Rural, simple. **Surface:** grassy/gravel.

🅾️ 01/01-31/12.
**Distance:** 🚶2,5km ⊗2,5km 🛒2,5km 🚲on the spot.

**Tourist information Uslar:**
🏛️ Market, city centre. 🕐 Fri 9-13h.
Alaris Schmetterlingspark. Butterfly park in tropical rain forest.
🅾️ 18/03-01/10 9.30-17.30, 02/10-01/11 9.30-16.30.
Uslarer Badeland. Swimming pool complex. 🕐 Sa 13-19h, Su
10-18h, Tue-Fri 15-20h.

| 🚐 | **Vechta** | 9H1 |
|---|---|---|

**Am Hallenwellen- und Freibad**, Dornbusch.
**GPS:** n52,74000 e8,29639. ⬆️.

10 🚐free. **Location:** Urban, simple. **Surface:** grassy/metalled.
🅾️ 01/01-31/12.
**Distance:** 🚶1km ⊗1km 🛒1km.
**Remarks:** Parking swimming pool, max. 3 days, service Bokenerd-
damm 40.

| 🚐🅂 | **Vechta** | 9H1 |
|---|---|---|

Oldenburgerstraße. **GPS:** n52,73245 e8,28833. ⬆️.

5 🚐free. **Location:** Urban, simple. **Surface:** metalled.
🅾️ 01/01-31/12.
**Distance:** 🚶on the spot ⊗on the spot 🛒on the spot.

| 🚐🅂 | **Verden** 🎡🌳 | 8A3 |
|---|---|---|

Conrad-Wode-Straße. **GPS:** n52,92572 e9,22738. ⬆️➡️.

14 🚐€ 6/24h 🚰€ 1/90liter 🔌Ch 💧(18x)€ 1/8h. 🚌
**Location:** Urban, comfortable, central.
**Surface:** grassy.
🅾️ 01/01-31/12.
**Distance:** 🚶350m 🗡️4km ⊗300m 🛒300m 🚲300m.

**Tourist information Verden:**
🏇 Reiterstadt, horse city of international reputation.
🏛️ Deutsches Pferdemuseum, Holzmarkt 9 . Horse museum. 🕐 Tue-Su
10-17h.
🏛️ Verdener Bauernmarkt. 🕐 Sa 8-13h.

| 🚐 | **Vienenburg** 🎡🌳 | 10C2 |
|---|---|---|

Schacht I. **GPS:** n51,95705 e10,56772. ⬆️➡️.

4 🚐free. **Location:** Rural, simple, quiet. **Surface:** metalled.
🅾️ 01/01-31/12.
**Distance:** 🚶700m ⊗700m 🛒600m 🚲on the spot 🚶on the spot.
**Remarks:** At Vienenburg Lake, max. 24h.

**DE**

## Visselhövede — 8A3

**Neuen Marktplatz**, Waldweg 1. **GPS**: n52,98758 e9,57963.
free. **Location**: Urban. **Surface**: asphalted. 01/01-31/12.
**Distance**: 100m 400m.

## Visselhövede — 8A3

**Zu den Visselwiesen**, Wüstenhof 1. **GPS**: n52,98530 e9,57772.

8 free. **Location**: Urban, simple. **Surface**: metalled.
01/01-31/12.
**Distance**: on the spot 100m 200m.

## Vrees — 7G3

**Herzog-Arenberg-Straße 5. GPS**: n52,88972 e7,77488.

6 free € 1/100liter Ch € 1/2kWh. **Location**: Quiet.
01/01-31/12.
**Distance**: on the spot 350m.

## Wagenfeld — 9H1

**Hallen-Freibad**, Schulstraße 12. **GPS**: n52,54531 e8,59634.

6 € 7 Ch included. **Location**: Rural, quiet.
**Surface**: grassy. 01/01-31/12.
**Distance**: 300m 300m.
**Remarks**: Check in at swimming pool.

## Wagenfeld — 9H1

**Ströher Lokschuppen**, Bahnhofstraße 29, Ströhen.
**GPS**: n52,53954 e8,68465.

25 € 4 € 1,50/100liter € 1,50 Ch € 1/2kWh € 3
included. **Location**: Rural, quiet. **Surface**: grassy.
01/01-31/12.
**Distance**: on the spot bakery on the spot.

## Walchum — 7F3

**Marinapark Emstal**, Steinbilder Straße. **GPS**: n52,92680 e7,29624.

10 € 10 Ch (6x) WC € 1,50.
**Location**: Rural. **Surface**: grassy. 01/01-31/12.
**Distance**: fishing permit obligatory 300m on the spot
on the spot on the spot.

## Walsrode — 8A3

**Ferienhof Wiechers**, Klein Eilstorf 6. **GPS**: n52,81462 e9,47898.

3 € 10 + € 1/pp Ch € 2/night WC € 1.
**Location**: Rural, simple, isolated, quiet. **Surface**: grassy.
01/01-31/12.
**Distance**: 11km 4km 11km.

## Walsrode — 8A3

**Forellenhof**, Hünzingen 3. **GPS**: n52,89855 e9,59122.

10 € 15 (2x) included.
**Location**: Rural, simple, isolated, quiet. **Surface**: grasstiles/grassy.
01/01-31/12.
**Distance**: 3km on the spot 3km.
**Remarks**: Free with a meal.

## Walsrode — 8A3

**Weltvogelpark**, Am Vogelpark. **GPS**: n52,88425 e9,59720.

20 free Ch (12x)€ 1/8h. **Location**: Rural, simple, central.
**Surface**: grassy. 01/01-31/12.
**Distance**: 2,5km on the spot 2,5km. **Remarks**: Max. 1 night.
**Tourist information Walsrode**:
Weltvogelpark. Bird park and botanical garden. 01/03-31/10
10-17h.

## Wangerland — 7G2

**Am Hallenwellenbad**, Hooksiel. **GPS**: n53,63435 e8,03532.

18 € 10, dog € 3 € 1/100liter Ch (12x)€ 0,50/kWh
included. **Location**: Rural, simple, quiet. **Surface**: metalled.

01/01-31/12.
**Distance**: 1km 100m.
**Remarks**: To be paid at swimming pool.

## Wangerland — 7G2

**An der Ostdüne**, Bäderstrasse, Hooksiel.
**GPS**: n53,64103 e8,03514.

75 € 17 + € 2,90/pp tourist tax, dog € 3,10 Ch WC
included. **Location**: Rural, comfortable, quiet.
**Surface**: grassy/gravel. 01/04-30/10.
**Distance**: 1,7km beach ±250m on the spot.

## Wangerland — 7G2

**Bismarckstraße 30. GPS**: n53,66497 e7,92751.

12 € 3/pp tourist tax € 1/80liter Ch (12x)€ 0,50/kWh.
**Location**: Rural, comfortable, quiet. **Surface**: gravel.
01/01-31/12.
**Distance**: 750m on the spot 750m 1km.
**Remarks**: Max. 2 nights.

## Wangerland — 7G2

**Nordsee-Camping-Schillig**, Jadestraße, Schillig.
**GPS**: n53,69986 e8,02338.

80 € 13 + € 2,90/pp tourist tax, dog € 3,10 Ch
(80x)WC included. **Location**: Rural, comfortable, quiet.
**Surface**: grassy. 01/04-15/10.
**Distance**: 200m on the spot on the spot on the spot.

## Wangerland — 7G2

**Wangermeer**, Jelliestede. **GPS**: n53,66962 e7,90975.

10 free (4x)€ 0,50/kWh. **Location**: Rural, simple, quiet.
**Surface**: grassy/sand. 01/01-31/12.
**Distance**: 800m on the spot 100m.
**Remarks**: Max. 2 days.

## Wangerland — 7G2

**Am Yachthafen**, Zum Hafen, Horumersiel.
**GPS**: n53,68293 e8,02091.

22 ⌁ € 12 ⌁ € 1 ⌁Ch ⌁WC⌁included. ⌁
**Location:** Rural, comfortable, central, quiet. **Surface:** concrete.
⌁ 01/04-30/10.
**Distance:** ⌁600m ⌁on the spot ⌁on the spot.

### Wardenburg 7H3
Keilstrasse, Astrup. **GPS:** n53,04770 e8,21197.⌁

5 ⌁free ⌁(3x). **Location:** Urban, simple. **Surface:** grassy.
⌁ 01/01-31/12.
**Distance:** ⌁2,5km.

### Wardenburg 7H3
**Marktplatz**, Huntestraße. **GPS:** n53,06401 e8,19832.⌁⌁

3 ⌁free. **Location:** Urban, simple. **Surface:** metalled.
⌁ 01/01-31/12.
**Distance:** ⌁on the spot ⌁3,6km.

### Weener 7F3
**Am Alten Hafen**, Panneborgstrasse. **GPS:** n53,16953 e7,36167.⌁

45 ⌁€ 7,50/24h ⌁€ 1/100liter ⌁Ch ⌁(45x)€ 2,50/24h WC⌁€ 1.
⌁ **Location:** Urban, comfortable. **Surface:** asphalted.
⌁ 01/01-31/12 ⌁ during harbor festival 3rd week of June.
**Distance:** ⌁on the spot ⌁on the spot ⌁on the spot ⌁on the spot.
**Remarks:** Max. 3 days.

### Weener 7F3
**Am Yachthafen**, Am Marina-Park. **GPS:** n53,16570 e7,36480.⌁⌁

24 ⌁€ 7,50 ⌁€ 1/24h ⌁Ch ⌁€ 2,50 WC⌁€ 1.⌁
**Location:** Urban, simple, quiet. **Surface:** metalled.
⌁ 01/04-30/09.
**Distance:** ⌁centre 1,2km ⌁50m.

### Werdum 7G2
Raiffeisenplatz. **GPS:** n53,65823 e7,71515.⌁

15 ⌁€ 10 ⌁€ 0,50 ⌁Ch ⌁(6x)€ 0,50/kWh.
**Location:** Rural, simple, quiet. **Surface:** gravel. ⌁ 01/01-31/12.
**Distance:** ⌁on the spot ⌁on the spot.
**Remarks:** Pay at tourist office.

### Werlte 7G3
**Kreutzmanns Mühle**, Kirchstraße 28. **GPS:** n52,85463 e7,68155.⌁

6 ⌁free ⌁€ 1/100liter ⌁Ch ⌁(8x)€ 1/2kWh. **Location:** Urban,
comfortable. **Surface:** metalled. ⌁ 01/01-31/12.
**Distance:** ⌁200m ⌁200m ⌁200m.

### Westergellersen 8B2
**Turniergelände Luhmühlen**, Westergellerser Heide.
**GPS:** n53,23306 e10,21623.⌁⌁

35 ⌁€ 8 ⌁€ 1 ⌁Ch ⌁(35x)€ 1/8h WC⌁. ⌁ **Location:** Rural,
comfortable, isolated, quiet. **Surface:** grassy. ⌁ 01/01-31/12.
**Distance:** ⌁4km ⌁1,5km ⌁4km ⌁4km ⌁2km.
**Remarks:** Key sanitary building at Autohaus.

### Westerholt 7G2
**Schützenplatz**, Nordener Straße. **GPS:** n53,58918 e7,45327.⌁

6 ⌁free ⌁€ 1/5minutes ⌁€ 1/time Ch€ 1/time ⌁(12x)€ 1/2kWh.
**Location:** Rural, comfortable, quiet. **Surface:** metalled.
⌁ 01/01-31/12.
**Distance:** ⌁400m ⌁400m ⌁on the spot ⌁on the spot.
**Remarks:** Max. 3 days.

### Westerholt 7G2
**Sportzentrum**. **GPS:** n53,59120 e7,44852.⌁

10 ⌁free ⌁Ch. **Location:** Rural, simple, quiet. **Surface:** metalled.
⌁ 01/01-31/12.
**Distance:** ⌁500m ⌁750m ⌁800m.

### Westerstede 7G3
**Albert-Post-Platz**, Auf der Lohe. **GPS:** n53,25883 e7,92685.⌁

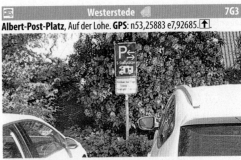

5 ⌁free. **Location:** Urban, simple. **Surface:** metalled.
⌁ 01/01-31/12.
**Distance:** ⌁100m ⌁2km ⌁250m.
**Remarks:** Max. 3 days.

### Westerstede 7G3
**Badesee Karlshof**, Bekassinenweg. **GPS:** n53,18811 e7,86954.⌁

5 ⌁free. **Location:** Rural, simple, isolated. **Surface:** gravel.
⌁ 01/01-31/12.
**Distance:** ⌁Badesee.
**Remarks:** Max. 3 days.

### Westerstede 7G3
**Hössensportanlage**, Jahnallee. **GPS:** n53,25369 e7,91229.⌁

5 ⌁free. **Surface:** grasstiles. ⌁ 01/01-31/12.
**Distance:** ⌁1km ⌁500m ⌁500m.
**Remarks:** At swimming pool, max. 3 days.

### Westerstede 7G3
**Am Hobbie Rhododendronpark**, Zum Hullen 3.
**GPS:** n53,28727 e8,00885.⌁

50 ⌁free. **Location:** Rural, simple, isolated. **Surface:** grassy.
⌁ 01/01-31/12.

### Westerstede 7G3
**Wohnmobilhafen Westerstede**, Süderstraße 2.
**GPS:** n53,24968 e7,93438.⌁

50 ⌁€ 12 ⌁⌁Ch ⌁WC⌁included. ⌁ **Location:** Urban,
comfortable, quiet. **Surface:** grassy/gravel. ⌁ 01/01-31/12.
**Distance:** ⌁800m ⌁1,4km ⌁McDonalds 200m.

DE

## Westoverledingen 7G3

**Reisemobilhafen zur Mühle**, Mühlenstrasse 214, Steenfelderfehn.
**GPS**: n53,12944 e7,44051. ↑ →.

30 ⌷ € 6 ⟍ Ch ⟋ (18x) WC included. ⚑ **Location**: Rural, simple.
**Surface**: grassy/metalled. ◻ 01/01-31/12.
**Distance**: ⊗ on the spot ⛲ 1km ⚓ on the spot ⚿ on the spot.

## Westoverledingen 7G3

**Schützenplatz Flachsmeer**, Papenburger strasse 74, Flachsmeer.
**GPS**: n53,12700 e7,46367. ↑ →.

10 ⌷ € 6 ⟍ Ch ⟋ (10x) included. ⚑ **Location**: Rural, simple.
**Surface**: grassy. ◻ 01/01-31/12.
**Distance**: ⊗ on the spot ⛲ on the spot ⟍ 100m.

## Wiefelstede 7G3

**Wohnmobilstellplatz am Bernsteinsee**, Dorfstrasse 11, Conneforde.
**GPS**: n53,32657 e8,06362. ↑ →.

30 ⌷ € 9 ⟍ € 1 ⟍ € 2 Ch ⟋ (25x) € 0,50/kWh WC ⊐ € 0,50 ⊡ on camp site. 🚐
**Location**: Rural, comfortable. **Surface**: grassy. ◻ 01/01-31/12.
**Distance**: ⚓ on the spot ⊗ on the spot.
**Remarks**: In front of campsite, caution sepkey € 5.

## Wiefelstede 7G3

**Am Schützenplatz**, Gristeder Strasse 8. **GPS**: n53,25239 e8,10965. ↑.

6 ⌷ free. **Location**: Rural. **Surface**: grassy. ◻ 01/01-31/12.
**Distance**: ⚓ 700m ⊗ 50m ⛲ 550m 🚌 on the spot.

## Wiefelstede 7G3

**Freibad Wiefelstede**, Alter Damm 11. **GPS**: n53,26146 e8,10713. ↑.

10 ⌷ free. **Location**: Rural, simple, quiet. **Surface**: metalled.
◻ 01/01-31/12.
**Distance**: ⚓ 500m ⊗ on the spot ⛲ 1,5km.

---

## Wiesmoor 7G2

Auf dem Marktplatz. **GPS**: n53,41351 e7,73511. ↑ →.

5 ⌷ € 7 ⟋ (4x) included. **Location**: Urban, simple, quiet.
**Surface**: metalled. ◻ 01/01-31/12.
**Distance**: ⚓ on the spot ⊗ 100m ⛲ 800m.
**Remarks**: Pay in at kiosk.

## Wiesmoor 7G2

**Bootshafen Ottermeer**, Am Stadion. **GPS**: n53,40951 e7,71841. ↑ →.

14 ⌷ € 5,50 ⟍ Ch ⟋ included. **Surface**: grassy/metalled.
◻ 01/01-31/12.
**Distance**: ⚓ 1,5km.
**Remarks**: Key service at Gaststätte (12-19h).

## Wiesmoor 7G2

**Campingplatz Ottermeer**, Am Ottermeer 52. **GPS**: n53,41570 e7,70930.

4 ⌷ € 15, dog € 2 ⟍ Ch ⟋ € 2,50 WC ⊐ € 3 ⚡ included.
**Location**: Rural, simple, isolated, quiet. **Surface**: grasstiles.
◻ 01/01-31/12.
**Distance**: ⚓ 1,5km ⛲ 8km.

## Wietzendorf 8B3

**Südsee Camp**, Südsee camp 1, K41. **GPS**: n52,93120 e9,96474. ↑.

40 ⌷ € 16 ⟍ € 1/100liter Ch ⟋ € 0,50/kWh WC ⊐.
**Location**: Rural, comfortable. **Surface**: metalled.
◻ 01/01-31/12.
**Distance**: ⚓ 2km ⚓ 100m ⛲ on the spot.
**Remarks**: Max. 3 nights, caution key service € 3.

## Wildemann 10B2

**Stellplatz am Wanderheim**, Im Schwarzewald 21.
**GPS**: n51,81964 e10,27438.
15 ⌷ € 2,50 + € 2/pp tourist tax ⟍ ⟍ ⟋ € 0,40/kWh, +
€ 1,50 WC ⊐ included. **Location**: Rural, simple, isolated, quiet.
**Surface**: grassy. ◻ 01/01-31/12.
**Distance**: ⚓ 1,5km ⊗ on the spot.

## Wildemann 10B2

**Bergpension Haus Vogelsang**, Am Sanickel 22.
**GPS**: n51,83365 e10,28760.
5 ⌷ € 12-15 ⟋ WC included ⊐ against payment. **Location**: Rural,
simple, isolated, quiet. **Surface**: grassy. ◻ 01/01-31/12.
**Distance**: ⊗ 450m.
**Remarks**: Bread-service, possibility for reservation.

---

## Wildeshausen 7H3

**Am Krandel**, Krandelstrasse. **GPS**: n52,90042 e8,42728. ↑ →.

19 ⌷ € 5/24h ⟍ € 0,50/80liter Ch ⟋ (20x) included ⊐ € 2. 🚐
**Location**: Rural, simple, quiet. **Surface**: grassy/metalled.
◻ 01/01-31/12.
**Distance**: ⚓ 500m ⟍ 4,4km ⊗ 400m ⛲ 700m.
**Remarks**: Parking at swimming pool.

## Wilhelmshaven 7G2

**Wohnmobilhafen Nautimo**, Friedenstrasse 99.
**GPS**: n53,53546 e8,10104. ↑ →.

26 ⌷ € 9 ⟍ € 1/100liter Ch ⟋ (26x) € 0,60/kWh, 10Amp WC ⊐ € 1
⚡ € 2/h. 🚐 **Location**: Rural, comfortable, quiet. **Surface**: metalled.
**Distance**: ⚓ 2km ⟍ 3km ⛲ 4km ⚓ 1,5km ⊗ on the spot ⛲ 200m
⚓ 1,5km 🚌 100m ⚿ on the spot ⚿ on the spot.
**Remarks**: Max. 7 days.

## Wilhelmshaven 7G2

**Wohnmobilstellplatz Schleuseninsel**, Schleussenstrasse 37.
**GPS**: n53,51478 e8,15218. ↑.

30 ⌷ € 10, trailer € 5 ⟍ € 1/100liter Ch ⟋ (28x) € 3/24h WC € 1,50
⊐ € 1,50/day ⚡. **Location**: Rural, comfortable, quiet. **Surface**: gravel.
◻ 01/01-31/12.
**Distance**: ⚓ 2,5km ⛲ on the spot ⊗ 250m ⛲ Jadebus.
**Remarks**: Along river.

## Wilhelmshaven 7G2

**Am Freibad Nord**, Möwenstraße 30. **GPS**: n53,57032 e8,10368. ↑ →.

6 ⌷ € 6, free with use of swimming pool ⟋ (6x) € 1/6h WC ⊐ € 1. 🚐
**Location**: Rural, simple, quiet. **Surface**: gravel.
◻ 01/05-31/08.
**Distance**: ⚓ 1,5km.
**Remarks**: Use sanitary only during opening hours swimming pool.

## Wilhelmshaven 7G2

**Reisemobilstellplatz Wilhelmshaven Südstadt**, Banterweg 12.
**GPS**: n53,51559 e8,09072. ↑.

16 🛏 € 10 🚰 Ch 💧 (16x)included 📶. **Location:** Urban, simple, noisy. **Surface:** gravel. 🅿 01/01-31/12. **Remarks:** Motorhome washing place.

### Wilhelmshaven 🏖 7G2
**Fliegerdeich West**, Fliegerdeich. **GPS:** n53,50996 e8,12718. ⬆➡.

40 🛏 € 0,75/h, € 12/day. 🚐 **Location:** Rural, simple, quiet. **Surface:** metalled. 🅿 01/01-31/12. **Distance:** 🚶2,5km 🏖sea ⊗nearby. **Remarks:** No camping activities.

### Wilhelmshaven 🏖 7G2
**Wohnmobilstellplatz Jade**, Bunsenstraße 10. **GPS:** n53,51047 e8,08879. ⬆.

10 🛏 € 10 🚰 💧 (10x)WC included. 🚿 **Location:** Rural, comfortable, noisy. **Surface:** gravel. 🅿 01/01-31/12 💧 water: 01/11-31/03. **Distance:** 🚶5km 🏖1km ⊗2km.

**Tourist information Wilhelmshaven:**
👁 Aquarium Wilhelmshaven, Südstrand 123. Sea aquarium. 🅿 10-18h.

### Winsen/Luhe 🏖 8B2
Bannetzer Str. 34. **GPS:** n52,68000 e9,89610.
5 🛏free. **Location:** Urban. **Surface:** metalled. 🅿 01/01-31/12. **Distance:** 🚶850m 850m 🍺850m.

### Winsen/Luhe 🏖 8B2
**Festplatz Bleiche**, Tönnhäuserweg. **GPS:** n53,36452 e10,21228. ⬆.

10 🛏free. **Location:** Simple, central. **Surface:** asphalted. 🅿 01/01-31/12. **Distance:** 🚶100m ⊗100m 🍺100m.

### Winsen/Luhe 🏖 8B2
**GreenEagle Golf Courses**, Radbrucher Straße 200. **GPS:** n53,32278 e10,22778. ⬆.

---

5 🛏free, playing golf obligatory WC 🚰. **Location:** Rural, simple, quiet. **Surface:** gravel. 🅿 01/01-31/12. **Distance:** 🚶6km 🚲2,2km ⊗on the spot 🚴4km 🚴on the spot. **Remarks:** Service only during opening hours.

### Winsen/Luhe 🏖 8B2
**Grube's Fischerhütte**, Hoopter Elbdeich 32. **GPS:** n53,39474 e10,17159. ⬆.

5 🛏free. **Location:** Urban, simple. **Surface:** asphalted/metalled. 🅿 01/01-31/12. **Distance:** 🚶4,5km ⊗on the spot 🍺300m 🚴400m. **Remarks:** Max. 1 night, restaurant closed on Monday.

### Winsen/Luhe 🏖 8B2
**Freizeit Center Albrecht**, Porchestrasse 15, Gewerbegebiet Lühdorf. **GPS:** n53,33750 e10,21947. ⬆.

10 🛏free 🚰 € 1 🚿 € 2 Ch (11x) WC. **Location:** Rural, simple. **Surface:** metalled. 🅿 01/01-31/12. **Distance:** 🚶4,5km 🚴on the spot.

### Wittingen 🏖 8C3
**Wittinger Sporthafen**, Am Sporthafen 1. **GPS:** n52,72706 e10,66187. ⬆➡.

20 🛏€ 10 + € 0,50/pp 🚰 Ch 💧 (20x)WC included 🔌 € 2,50/2,50. **Location:** Rural, comfortable. **Surface:** grassy. 🅿 01/04-01/10. **Distance:** 🚶4km 🏖on the spot 🚴on the spot ⊗on the spot 🍺4km 🚴200m 🚴on the spot. **Remarks:** Near marina.

### Wittmund 🏖 7G2
**Am Gulfhof**, Funnixer Riege 11. **GPS:** n53,64202 e7,78566. ⬆.

8 🛏€ 9 🚰 Ch included. 🚿 **Location:** Rural, simple, quiet. **Surface:** grassy. 🅿 01/01-31/12.

---

### Wittmund 🏖 7G2
**Schützenplatz**, Auricherstrasse. **GPS:** n53,57357 e7,77071. ⬆.

+10 🛏free 📶free. **Surface:** grassy. 🅿 01/01-31/12. **Distance:** 🚶800m 🍞bakery 200m.

### Wittmund 🏖 7G2
**Wohnmobilstellplatz an der Mole**, Am Harlesiel 20. **GPS:** n53,70941 e7,80839. ⬆➡.

54 🛏€ 13 + € 2,50/pp tourist tax, dog € 2 🚰 Ch 💧 (18x)€ 3 WC 🚰. **Location:** Rural, comfortable, quiet. **Surface:** metalled. 🅿 15/03-31/10. **Distance:** 🏖on the spot 🚴on the spot ⊗on the spot. **Remarks:** Caution key electricity € 10.

### Wittmund 🏖 7G2
**Campingplatz Harlesiel**, Am Harlesiel, Carolinensiel-Harlesiel. **GPS:** n53,70797 e7,80649. ⬆.

50 🛏€ 13 + € 2,50/pp tourist tax, dog € 2 🚰 Ch 💧 (40x)€ 3 WC 🚰. **Location:** Rural, comfortable, quiet. **Surface:** asphalted. 🅿 15/03-31/10. **Distance:** 🚶500m 🏖100m 🚴100m ⊗on the spot.

### Wolfenbüttel 🏖 10C2
**Sporthalleninsel**, Vor dem Wehre. **GPS:** n52,16168 e10,52646. ⬆➡.

2 🛏free 🚰 € 1/80liter 💧 (4x)€ 1/8h. **Location:** Urban, central, noisy. **Surface:** metalled. 🅿 01/01-31/12. **Distance:** 🚶250m ⊗500m 🍺500m 🚴200m. **Remarks:** Along railwayline.

### Wolfenbüttel 🏖 10C2
**Wohnmobilpark Stadtbad Okeraue**, Harztorwall 21. **GPS:** n52,15680 e10,54024. ⬆.
44 🛏€ 12, 2 pers.incl 🚰 Ch 💧 (44x)WC free included. **Location:** Urban, comfortable. **Surface:** grassy. 🅿 01/01-31/12. **Distance:** 🚶1km ⊗500m. **Remarks:** Next to swimming pool.

### Wolfsburg 🏖 10C1
**Autostadt P2**, Berliner Brücke. **GPS:** n52,43485 e10,79716. ⬆.

DE

9 ⬛€ 3/day, € 6/24h 🚐✎included. 🛢
**Location:** Urban, noisy. **Surface:** asphalted. ⬜ 01/01-31/12.
**Distance:** 🚶2km ⊗on the spot 🚊2km.
**Remarks:** Caution key € 50.

**Tourist information Wolfsburg:**
  Autostadt. Of the Volkswagen-concern; with pavilion of several car makes, car tower of 20 floors, test driving. ⬜ 9-20h.

| 🅢 | Zetel 🎣👥 | 7G2 |
|---|---|---|

**Johann Quathamer**, Fuhrenkampstrasse 60.
**GPS:** n53,40084 e7,91893.⬆.

15 ⬛€ 8 🚐€ 1/100liter 🚰Ch✎(15x)WCincluded 🚽€ 1.♨
**Location:** Rural, comfortable, quiet. **Surface:** grassy.
⬜ 01/01-31/12.
**Distance:** 🚶4km ⊗3km 🚊3km.

| 🅢 | Zetel 🎣🌲 | 7G2 |
|---|---|---|

Markthamm, Neuenburger Strasse. **GPS:** n53,41706 e7,97000.⬆.

40 ⬛free 🚐🚰Chfree ✎(6x)€ 1/kWh.
**Location:** Urban, simple, central. **Surface:** grasstiles.
⬜ 01/01-31/12.
**Distance:** 🚶on the spot ⊗Imbiss.
**Remarks:** Parking centre, max. 2 days, service Kläranlage open: Mo/Tue 11-23h, Thu/Sa 11-23h, Su 16-23h.

| 🅢 | Zetel 🎣👥 | 7G2 |
|---|---|---|

Driefeler Esch. **GPS:** n53,41835 e7,98445.⬆.

10 ⬛free. **Location:** Simple. **Surface:** gravel. ⬜ 01/01-31/12.
**Remarks:** Parking swimming pool, max. 48h.

| 🅢 | Zetel 🎣👥 | 7G2 |
|---|---|---|

**Schulmuseum Bohlenbergerfeld**, Wehdestrasse.
**GPS:** n53,41322 e7,92143.⬆.

---

10 ⬛free. **Location:** Rural, simple, isolated. **Surface:** grassy/gravel.
⬜ 01/01-31/12.
**Distance:** 🚶2,5km.
**Remarks:** At museum.

| | Zetel 🎣👥 | 7G2 |
|---|---|---|

**Urwald**, Urwaldstrasse, Neuenburg. **GPS:** n53,39293 e7,96547.⬆⬆.

20 ⬛free. **Location:** Rural, simple, quiet. **Surface:** unpaved.
⬜ 01/01-31/12.
**Remarks:** Max. 1 day.

| | Zetel 🎣👥 | 7G2 |
|---|---|---|

**Kläranlage**, Moorstraße. **GPS:** n53,42302 e7,97937.
🚰Chfree. ⬜ 01/01-31/12.
**Remarks:** Mo/Thu 7-16h, Fri 7-13h, Sa/Su 9-9.30h.

| | Zeven | 8A2 |
|---|---|---|

**Viehmarktplatz**, Meyerstrasse/Godenstedterstrasse.
**GPS:** n53,29764 e9,27514.⬆⬆.

4 ⬛free. **Location:** Simple. **Surface:** metalled.
⬜ 01/01-31/12.
**Distance:** 🚶500m.

| 🅒🅢 | Zorge 🌲 | 10C3 |
|---|---|---|

**Campingplatz im Waldwinkel**, Kunzental 2.
**GPS:** n51,64188 e10,64881.⬆➡.

30 ⬛€ 9,50, 2 pers.incl 🚐€ 0,20/10liter 🚰Ch✎(15x)€ 2/day
WC€ 1/pp. **Location:** Rural, simple, quiet. **Surface:** grassy/gravel.
⬜ 01/01-31/12.
**Distance:** 🚶1,5km ⊗on the spot 🚊6km 🚌300m 🚶on the spot
🏊on the spot.
**Remarks:** Max. 2 nights.

# Mecklenburg-Western Pomerania

| 🅢 | Ahlbeck 🌾🎣☂ | 8G1 |
|---|---|---|

**Caravanplatz Am Wiesenrand**, Gothenweg 5a.
**GPS:** n53,94100 e14,17600.⬆➡.

27 ⬛€ 11-13 🚐🚰Ch€ 0,60/kWh WCincluded 🚽€ 1 📷€ 3/2
💧€ 3,50/3h. **Location:** Rural, comfortable, quiet. **Surface:** grassy.
⬜ 01/03-31/10.
**Distance:** 🚶10min 🏊10min ⊗500m 🚊200m.
**Remarks:** Bread-service, possibility for reservation.

---

| 🅢 | Ahlbeck 🌾🎣☂ | 8G1 |
|---|---|---|

**Wohnmobilstellplatz Rauthe**, Waldstrasse 7.
**GPS:** n53,93660 e14,18660.⬆➡.

30 ⬛€ 16 🚐€ 2/1day 🚰Ch✎(30x)WCincluded 🚽€ 2 📷€ 4.♨
**Location:** Urban, central, noisy. **Surface:** grassy.
⬜ 01/01-31/12.
**Distance:** 🚶on the spot 🏊5 min ⊗200m 🚊200m.

| | Ahlbeck 🌾🎣👥 | 8G1 |
|---|---|---|

**Parkplatz an der Grenze**, Swinemünder Chaussee 16.
**GPS:** n53,92380 e14,21280.⬆.

30 ⬛€ 6 + € 2,50/pp.♨ **Location:** Urban, simple, isolated.
**Surface:** metalled. ⬜ 01/01-31/12.
**Distance:** 🚶3km ⊗200m 🚌on the spot.
**Remarks:** Max. 24h.

| | Ahrenshoop 🎣🌊 | 6F3 |
|---|---|---|

**An der Helios-Klinik**, Dorfstraße. **GPS:** n54,39155 e12,43914.⬆.

10 ⬛€ 6/day, € 25/night. 🛢 **Location:** Rural, simple, isolated, noisy.
**Surface:** gravel. ⬜ 01/01-31/12.
**Distance:** 🚶2km 🏊beach 50m.
**Remarks:** Max. 1 day.

| 🅒🅢 | Alt Schwerin 👥🌊 | 8E2 |
|---|---|---|

**Insel Camping Werder**, Wendorf 8. **GPS:** n53,38384 e12,32443.➡.

13 ⬛€ 15,80 🚐€ 0,50/40liter 🚰Ch✎€ 2 WC🚽€ 1 📷€ 3/3
💧included. **Location:** Rural, luxurious, quiet. **Surface:** grassy.
⬜ 01/01-31/12.
**Distance:** 🚶4km 🏊on the spot 🚶on the spot ⊗1km 🚊3,5km.
**Remarks:** Max. 9m, dog € 2/day.

| 🅢 | Altwarp 🌊 | 8G1 |
|---|---|---|

**Hafen**, Seestrasse. **GPS:** n53,73905 e14,27147.⬆➡.

DE

40 ⏚ € 9,50, dog € 2 🔌 Ch ⚡ € 2/24h WC included ⟦ 1 ⟧ € 2/1.
**Location:** Rural, luxurious, quiet. **Surface:** grassy/metalled.
☐ 01/01-31/12.
**Distance:** 500m 300m on the spot ⊗300m 🍺400m 🚌300m
🚲 on the spot 🚶 on the spot.
**Remarks:** At tourist office.

### Bansin 6H3

**Waldparkplatz Bansin**, Am Heuberg 1. **GPS:** n53,98834 e14,11291. ➡

100 ⏚ € 5-6 + € 3-3,50/pp, dog € 1,50 🔌 Ch ⚡ € 2,70/24h
WC included ⟦ 1 ⟧ € 4,50/3. **Location:** Rural, comfortable, isolated,
quiet. **Surface:** grassy/metalled. ☐ 25/04-25/09.
**Distance:** 3km 400m 🍺 on the spot.

### Barth 6F3

**Segelverein**, Am Westhafen. **GPS:** n54,37130 e12,72510.

20 ⏚ € 16 🔌 € 1/100liter Ch ⚡ € 2 WC ⟦ 1. **Location:** Urban,
comfortable, quiet. **Surface:** grassy. ☐ 01/05-01/10.
**Distance:** on the spot on the spot on the spot ⊗100m
🍺900m.
**Remarks:** Caution key sanitary € 20.

### Barth 6F3

**Wohnmobilparkplatz Barth**, Am Osthafen.
**GPS:** n54,36965 e12,73251. ⬆

10 ⏚ € 7 ⚡ (8x)€ 0,50/kWh. 🅿 **Location:** Urban, simple, noisy.
**Surface:** metalled. ☐ 01/01-31/12.
**Distance:** 300m ⊗300m 🍺300m 🚲 on the spot 🚶 on the spot.

### Beckerwitz 8D1

**Ostseecamping Beckerwitzer Strand**, Ostseestrasse 10.
**GPS:** n53,94137 e11,31682. ⬆➡

12 ⏚ € 8-10 🔌 € 1 Ch ⚡ € 2,60/night WC ⟦ € 0,50 ⏚ € 3,50/3,50.
**Location:** Rural, comfortable. **Surface:** grassy. ☐ 01/04-10/10.
**Distance:** on the spot on the spot ⊗ on the spot 🍺4km
🚲 on the spot 🚶 on the spot.
**Remarks:** Max. 24h.

---

### Bergen/Rügen 6G3

**Wohnmobilstellplatz Rügen**, Tilzower Weg 32a.
**GPS:** n54,40281 e13,42781. ⬆➡
20 ⏚ € 14, 2 pers.incl 🔌 € 1/90liter Ch ⚡ (16x)€ 2/24h,25Amp
WC € 2/6minutes 💡 € 4/4 📶 included. **Location:** Rural, comfortable.
**Surface:** metalled. ☐ 01/01-31/12.
**Distance:** 1km ⊗400m 🍺500m, bakery 300m 🚌100m 🚲 on the
spot.
**Remarks:** Car rental.

### Binz 6G3

**Wohnmobil-Oase Rügen**, Proraer Chaussee 60.
**GPS:** n54,44819 e13,56181. ⬆➡

150 ⏚ € 13-18 🔌 € 1/50liter Ch € 0,50 ⚡ € 1/kWh WC ⟦ € 0,50/
minutes 💡 € 4/4 📶 free. **Location:** Rural, luxurious, isolated, quiet.
**Surface:** grassy/gravel. ☐ 15/04-31/10.
**Distance:** Binz 6km 1km ⊗ on the spot 🍺6km 🚌 on the spot.
**Remarks:** Bread-service.

### Binz 6G3

**Parkplatz Zentrum**, Proraer Chaussee 5.
**GPS:** n54,40278 e13,60194. ⬆

60 ⏚ € 17/24h.
**Location:** Urban, simple. **Surface:** grassy/metalled.
☐ 01/01-31/12.
**Distance:** on the spot on the spot ⊗50m 🍺50m 🚌 on the spot.
**Remarks:** Next to petrol station.

### Blankensee 8G1

**Reisemobilplatz Lühn**, Am Achterfeld 1.
**GPS:** n53,51787 e14,31844. ⬆
4 ⏚ € 4 🔌 € 2 Ch ⚡ € 0,50/kWh WC. **Location:** Quiet.
**Surface:** grassy. ☐ 01/01-31/12.
**Distance:** 800m 600m 🍺5km.

### Boiensdorf 8D1

**Am Strand**, Bungalowsiedlung. **GPS:** n54,02412 e11,54744. ⬆➡

---

35 ⏚ € 8/24h 🔌 € 0,20/10liter Ch ⚡ € 2/day WC € 0,50. 🅿
**Location:** Rural, comfortable, quiet. **Surface:** grassy.
☐ Easter-31/10.
**Distance:** on the spot 🚌 on the spot ⊗50m 🚲 on the spot
🚶 on the spot.

### Boizenburg/Elbe 8C2

Hafenplatz 2. **GPS:** n53,37623 e10,71509. ⬆
4 ⏚ free ⚡ (4x)€ 0,50/kWh WC € 0,50. **Location:** Simple, central,
quiet. **Surface:** metalled. ☐ 01/01-31/12.
**Distance:** 400m on the spot ⊗100m 🚲 on the spot 🚶 on the
spot.

### Boltenhagen 8C1

**Krämer's Wohnmobilhafen**, Ostsee-allee 58b.
**GPS:** n53,98122 e11,21908. ⬆

45 ⏚ € 12-14, 2 pers. incl 🔌 € 0,20/20liter Ch ⚡ € 2,50/day
WC ⟦ € 0,50. 🅿 **Location:** Urban, comfortable, central, noisy.
**Surface:** grassy/gravel. ☐ 01/01-31/12.
**Distance:** 800m 200m 🚌200m ⊗100m 🍺700m 🚌 on the
spot 🚲 on the spot 🚶 on the spot.
**Remarks:** Bread-service in summer period, bicycle rental.

### Boltenhagen 8C1

**Wohnmobilpark Boltenhagen**, Ostsee-allee 58.
**GPS:** n53,98133 e11,21854. ⬆

50 ⏚ € 10-14 + € 2,10/pp tourist tax, dog € 1,50 🔌 € 2
Ch ⚡ € 2,50/day WC ⟦ € 1,50 💡 € 5 📶. 🅿 **Location:** Urban, simple,
noisy. **Surface:** grassy. ☐ 01/01-31/12.
**Distance:** 700m 200m ⊗ on the spot 🍺700m
🚲 on the spot 🚶 on the spot.
**Remarks:** Playground.

### Boltenhagen 8C1

**Swin Golf Boltenhagen**, Ausbau 15, Redewisch.
**GPS:** n54,00851 e11,17180. ⬆

10 ⏚ € 15 🔌 € 2/day ⚡ WC 📶 € 2/day. 🅿 **Location:** Rural,
comfortable, quiet. **Surface:** grassy. ☐ 01/04-31/10.
**Distance:** on the spot 🚶 on the spot 🏌 on the spot.
**Remarks:** At golf course.

### Boltenhagen 8C1

**Regenbogen Boltenhagen**, Ostseeallee 54.
**GPS:** n53,98196 e11,21714. ⬆

DE

20 🛏€ 20-25 🚐🔧Ch🚿WC⬛included ⬛€ 4/3 📶€ 1/h. **Location:** Urban, comfortable, central, noisy.
**Surface:** grassy/metalled. 📅 01/01-31/12.
**Distance:** 🚶600m 🏊200m ⛵200m 🎣on the spot 🛒100m 🚌on the spot 🚲on the spot 🏕on the spot.
**Remarks:** Max. 1 night, check in at reception.

### 🍴 S — Brenz — 8D2

**Landhaus Böttcher**, Parchimer strasse 11.
**GPS:** n53,38688 e11,67103.⬆️

5 🛏€ 10, guests free 🚐🔧€ 1,50 🚿(4x)€ 2/day WCincluded.
**Location:** Rural, simple. **Surface:** grassy/metalled.
📅 01/01-31/12.
**Distance:** 🚶on the spot 🚣3km 🎣on the spot 🛒5km 🚌200m.

### 🍴 S — Broock — 8E2

**Hotel-Restaurant Am Worns-Berg**, Am Worns-Berg 1.
**GPS:** n53,46734 e12,10698.⬆️

6 🛏€ 5, free with a meal 🚐🔧Ch🚿€ 2 WC⬛€ 1,50.
**Location:** Rural, noisy.
**Surface:** grassy/gravel.
📅 01/01-31/12.
**Distance:** 🚶5km 🏊1,5km ⛵1,5km 🎣on the spot 🛒5km 🚌500m.

### 🍴 S — Carpin — 8F2

**Landgasthof Am Schlesersee**, Hauptstrasse 25.
**GPS:** n53,35424 e13,24028.⬆️

10 🛏€ 5, free with a meal 🚐🔧🚿€ 5 WCincluded 📶.
**Surface:** metalled. 📅 01/01-31/12.
**Distance:** 🚶500m 🏊on the spot 🎣on the spot 🎣on the spot 🛒4km.
**Remarks:** Max. 1 night.

### ⚓ S — Dabitz — 6F3

**Hafen Dabitz**, Boddenstraße. **GPS:** n54,36217 e12,80610.⬆️➡️

5 🛏€ 10/night 🚐🔧Ch🚿🎣 **Location:** Rural, simple, quiet.
**Surface:** concrete. 📅 01/01-31/12.
**Distance:** 🚶500m 🏊on the spot 🎣on the spot 🚲on the spot 🏕on the spot.

### 🍴 S — Dalwitz — 8E1

**Ferien Gut Dalwitz**, Dalwitz 46. **GPS:** n53,93484 e12,53830.⬆️

2 🛏€ 10 🚐€ 1 🚿WC⬛⬛€ 3/3 📶. **Location:** Rural.
**Surface:** grassy. 📅 01/01-31/12.
**Distance:** 🚶15km 🎣on the spot 🛒on the spot.
**Remarks:** Parking estate.

### 🍴 S — Dassow — 8C1

**Reisemobilplatz Ostseestrand**, Straße des Friedens 14, Rosenhagen.
**GPS:** n53,96040 e10,94430.⬆️

10 🛏€ 10 🚐🔧Ch🚿€ 3 WCincluded ⬛€ 3. 🐕 **Location:** Rural,
comfortable, quiet. **Surface:** grassy. 📅 01/01-31/12.
**Distance:** 🏊1km 🎣500m.
**Remarks:** At Café Strandgut.

### ⚓ S — Demmin — 8F1

**Kanuhaus Demmin**, Meyenkrebs 15. **GPS:** n53,91806 e13,02833.⬆️

2 🛏€ 6-8,40 🚐🚿WCincluded ⬛€ 1/3minutes. 🐕
**Location:** Rural, simple. **Surface:** grassy. 📅 01/04-31/10.
**Distance:** 🚶1km 🏊on the spot 🎣400m 🛒500m.

### ⚓ S — Dömitz — 8D3

**WasserWanderZentrum Dömitz**, An der Schleuse 1.
**GPS:** n53,14078 e11,25908.⬆️

30 🛏€ 13, 2 pers.incl 🚐€ 1,50/100liter 🔧Ch🚿€ 0,50/kWh
WC⬛€ 1. **Location:** Rural, comfortable, quiet. **Surface:** grassy.
📅 01/01-31/12.
**Distance:** 🚶400m 🏊on the spot 🚲on the spot 🎣100m 🛒800m ⛵200m.

### ⚓ S — Dömitz — 8D3

**Dömitzer Hafen**, Hafenplatz 3. **GPS:** n53,13724 e11,26034.⬆️

22 🛏€ 8 🚐€ 1/50liter 🔧🚿(10x)€ 3/day WC⬛€ 1.
**Location:** Rural, comfortable, quiet. **Surface:** grassy.
📅 01/01-31/12.
**Distance:** 🚶1km 🏊10m 🎣10m 🛒200m ⛵500m 🚌300m.
**Remarks:** Bread-service.

### ⚓ S — Dranske/Bakenberg — 6G3

**MC Burgstaedt Wohnmobilstellplatz**, Nonnevitz 23a.
**GPS:** n54,67139 e13,29278.⬆️➡️

12 🛏€ 19-25 🚿€ 3/day WC⬛included. **Location:** Rural, simple,
isolated, quiet. **Surface:** grassy. 📅 15/05-31/10.
**Distance:** 🚶6km 🏊100m 🎣300m 🛒300m.
**Remarks:** Dog € 2/day, possibility for reservation.

### 🚐 S — Dranske/Bakenberg — 6G3

**Küstencamp**, Nonnevitz 23. **GPS:** n54,66288 e13,26929.⬆️➡️

15 🛏€ 13,50-15 🚐🔧Ch🚿€ 3,20/day WCincluded ⬛€ 1/2minutes
⬛€ 3/3. **Location:** Rural, comfortable, isolated, quiet.
**Surface:** metalled. 📅 01/01-31/12.
**Distance:** 🚶7km 🏊400m 🎣400m 🛒500m.
**Remarks:** Bread-service, car rental.

### 🚐 S — Eldena — 8D2

**Bootshafen und Campingplatz Eldena**, Am Bootshafen 1.
**GPS:** n53,23163 e11,42422.

12 🛏€ 10,50 🚐🔧Ch🚿€ 0,60 WCincluded ⬛€ 1,10 ⬛€ 3,50/3,50.
🏠 **Location:** Rural, comfortable, quiet. **Surface:** grassy.
📅 01/04-31/10.
**Distance:** 🚶400m 🏊10m 🚲10m 🎣50m 🛒400m 🚌on the spot.

### ⚓ S — Elmenhorst — 6F3

**Stellplatz Elmenhorst**, Gewerbeallee 3a.
**GPS:** n54,15250 e12,01667.⬆️➡️

24 🛏 € 12 ⛽ € 1/100liter 🔌 Ch 💧 € 0,50/kWh WC 🚽 € 2 🚿 free. 🛁
**Location:** Urban, quiet. **Surface:** metalled. ⬛ 01/01-31/12.
**Distance:** 🚶 300m.
**Remarks:** Discount longer stays.

**Firma Stuhr**, Haupstrasse 47. **GPS:** n54,15882 e12,00464. ⬆️.

40 🛏 € 10 ⛽ € 1 🔌 Ch included 💧 (38x) € 2/day,16Amp WC € 2,50
🚽 € 2,50. **Location:** Rural, simple, quiet. **Surface:** grassy.
⬛ 01/01-31/12.
**Distance:** 🚶 1km 🏊 1,3km 🛒 1km ⊗ 1km 🛒 800m 🍴 3km
🚉 300m 🚴 on the spot 🚶 on the spot.
**Remarks:** Use sanitary € 2/pp per day.

Weidendamm 1. **GPS:** n53,33583 e13,44176. ⬆️.

10 🛏 € 10 + € 1,50/pp tourist tax. **Location:** Urban, simple.
**Surface:** grassy/metalled. ⬛ 01/01-31/12.
**Distance:** 🏊 on the spot ⊗ 150m 🍴 400m.

**Wohnmobilhafen an der Edle**, Eldeufer 1.
**GPS:** n53,26355 e11,54243. ⬆️.

23 🛏 € 10 ⛽ 🔌 Ch included 💧 € 2/day WC 🚽 € 1/pp. 🛁
**Location:** Rural, comfortable, isolated, quiet. **Surface:** grassy.
⬛ 01/01-31/12.
**Distance:** 🏊 on the spot 🚶 on the spot ⊗ 2km 🍴 2km 🚴 on the spot
🚶 on the spot.

**Strandmitte**, Buchenkampweg. **GPS:** n54,25663 e12,25005. ⬆️➡️.

20 🛏 € 15/24h, tourist tax € 2/pp ⛽ € 1/100liter 🔌 🚐
**Location:** Rural, simple, quiet. **Surface:** grassy/metalled.

---

⬛ 01/01-31/12.
**Distance:** 🚶 500m 🏊 on the spot 🛒 on the spot ⊗ 500m 🍴 500m
🚴 on the spot 🚶 on the spot.
**Remarks:** Max. 3 days.

**Stadthafen**, Canalstrasse. **GPS:** n53,27738 e11,55949. ⬆️.

18 🛏 € 5 ⛽ € 0,50/125liter 🔌 € 0,50 Ch 💧 € 2 WC € 0,50 🚽 € 1.
⬛ 01/01-31/12, service: 8 9.30h and 18.30-20h.
**Distance:** 🚶 200m 🏊 on the spot 🛒 on the spot ⊗ 100m 🍴 50m.

**Am Museumhafen**, Marienstraße 10. **GPS:** n54,09887 e13,38945. ⬆️.

20 🛏 € 15 ⛽ € 2/100liter 🔌 Ch 💧 WC 🚽 € 4 🔌 € 4/4 🚿 included.
**Location:** Urban, comfortable.
**Surface:** metalled.
⬛ 01/03-30/11.
**Distance:** 🚶 300m 🍴 300m 🛒 1km.
**Tourist information Greifswald:**
👁 Fischerdorf Greifswald-Wieck. Fishermen's village worth seeing.

**Gleviner Platz**. **GPS:** n53,79117 e12,18054. ⬆️.

3 🛏 free ⛽ 🚽. **Location:** Urban. **Surface:** asphalted.
⬛ 01/01-31/12.
**Distance:** 🚶 400m 🏊 5km 🛒 5km 🍴 100m 🛒 100m.

**Hotel Am Tierpark**, Verbindungschaussee 7.
**GPS:** n53,79159 e12,21577. ⬆️.
30 🛏 € 15 + € 2,50/pp ⛽ Ch 💧 (30x) included WC 🚽 use sanitary
€ 2,50/pp 🚿.
**Location:** Rural. **Surface:** grassy. ⬛ 01/01-31/12.
**Distance:** 🚶 5km 🏊 on the spot 🍴 5km 🚉 station 2km.
**Remarks:** Bread-service + breakfast-service, discount on access sauna/
wellness.

**Rittergut Schloss Pentin**, Zum Bollwerk 11.
**GPS:** n53,91824 e13,46763. ➡️.

10 🛏 € 10 ⛽ € 0,50/80liter 🔌 Ch 💧 € 0,50/kWh 🚽 € 1. 🛁
**Location:** Rural, simple. **Surface:** grassy/gravel.
⬛ 01/01-31/12.

---

**Distance:** ⊗ 1km 🍴 400m.
**Remarks:** Bread-service, nature reserve.

**Blasendorff**, Labahnstrasse 10. **GPS:** n53,95940 e14,15680. ⬆️.

3 🛏 € 10 + € 2,50/pp tourist tax ⛽ € 0,50/40liter 🔌 € 1,50 💧 € 0,65/
kWh. 🛁 **Location:** Urban, simple. **Surface:** grassy.
⬛ 01/03-30/11.
**Distance:** 🚶 10min 🏊 300m ⊗ 300m 🍴 300m.

**Korbwerk**, Waldbühnenweg 2, Heringsdorf Seebad.
**GPS:** n53,95056 e14,16611.

15 🛏 € 15 ⛽ 🔌 Ch 💧 WC 🚽 included. **Location:** Urban, comfortable,
noisy. **Surface:** gravel. ⬛ 01/01-31/12.
**Distance:** 🚶 500m 🏊 600m ⊗ 200m 🛒 200m.

**Reisemobilstellplatz Wöller**, Chausseestraße 12.
**GPS:** n54,07450 e13,35230. ⬆️.

50 🛏 € 10 ⛽ 🔌 Ch 💧 included WC 🚽. **Location:** Rural, comfortable,
quiet. **Surface:** grassy/gravel. ⬛ 01/01-31/12.
**Distance:** 🚶 3,5km 🏊 1,8km 🍴 800m.
**Remarks:** Use sanitary € 5/motorhome, in winter limited services,
service passerby € 5.

**Gartencenter Offermann**, Dorfstraße 1. **GPS:** n53,89473 e11,54159. ⬆️.

20 🛏 € 10 ⛽ 🔌 Ch 💧 included. **Location:** Rural, simple, noisy.
**Surface:** concrete. ⬛ 01/01-31/12.
**Distance:** 🍴 900m.

**Strandparkplatz Timmendorf**, Tau n Lüchttorm.
**GPS:** n53,99287 e11,38058. ⬆️.

**DE**

60 🛏€ 5/day, € 4/night + € 2/pp tourist tax 🚰 € 0,50/80liter 🚽
Ch🚻 ♨(64x)€ 2/2kWh ☕€ 1.🚮 **Location:** Rural, simple, quiet.
**Surface:** grassy. 🗓 01/01-31/12.
**Distance:** 🚿150m 🏊500m ⊗200m 🛒 300m 🚲 on the spot
🚶 on the spot.
**Remarks:** Check in at kosk, caution key sanitary € 10.

---

**⛱🅂 Insel Poel ⚓🏖 8D1**

**Poeler Forellenhof**, Niendorf 13. **GPS:** n53,99454 e11,44714. ⬆➡

16 🛏€ 13, 2 pers.incl 🚰 € 2/100liter 🚽Ch♨WC☕included
🔌€ 2,60/2,60.🚮 **Location:** Rural, simple. **Surface:** concrete.
🗓 01/01-31/12. **Distance:** 🚿1,5km 🏊on the spot 🚣on the spot
⊗on the spot 🛒1,5km 🚲on the spot 🚶on the spot.
**Remarks:** Check in at restaurant, steam bath and sauna, fish smoke-
house.

---

**Kamminke 8G1**

Ortstraße. **GPS:** n53,86750 e14,20480.⬆

15 🛏€ 8.🚮 **Surface:** grassy. 🗓 01/01-31/12.
**Distance:** 🚿on the spot ⊗on the spot.

---

**🌾🅂 Karenz 🌳 8D2**

**Reiterhof am Steinberg**, Grebserstrasse 1. **GPS:** n53,23638 e11,34836.

3 🛏€ 10 🚰 € 1 🚽Ch♨€ 1,50 WC☕. **Location:** Rural, simple,
isolated. **Surface:** grassy. 🗓 01/01-31/12.
**Distance:** 🚿1km ⊗1km 🛒300m.
**Remarks:** Parking at manege.

---

**⛱🅂 Kargow 🌳 8F2**

**Reisemobilstellplatz Ziegenwiese**, Schwarzenhof 7.
**GPS:** n53,46433 e12,79925.⬆

10 🛏€ 9 🚰 € 3 🚽Ch♨€ 1,50. **Location:** Rural, quiet.
**Surface:** grassy. 🗓 01/01-31/12.

---

**Distance:** 🚿1km 🚣1km ⊗200m 🛒4km.

**⚓🅂 Karnin 🐟 8G1**

**Hafen**, Karnin 14a. **GPS:** n53,84450 e13,85860.⬆

3 🛏€ 10 🚰 € 0,50/100liter 🚽Ch☕ 1 ♨€ 0,50/kWh WC☕ 1 🔌€ 4.
🚤 **Location:** Rural, quiet. **Surface:** metalled. 🗓 01/01-31/12.
**Distance:** 🚿6km 🏊500m 🛒6km 🚲on the spot 🚶on the spot.
**Remarks:** Intersection hiking and biking trails.

---

**⛱🅂 Langen Brütz 👥 8D1**

**Landhaus Bondzio**, Hauptstrasse 21a. **GPS:** n53,65722 e11,55737.⬆

4 🛏€ 12 🚰 ♨WCincluded ☕€ 2. 🚤 **Location:** Rural, simple.
**Surface:** asphalted/grassy. 🗓 01/01-31/12 🍽 Restaurant: Mo.
**Distance:** 🚿150m ⊗on the spot 🛒on the spot 🚐50m.
**Remarks:** Bread-service.

---

**⛱🅂 Lenz über Malchow 🏖 8E2**

**Lenzer Hafen**, Zum Hafen 1. **GPS:** n53,46793 e12,34929.⬆

25 🛏€ 13,30-16,30 🚰 🚽€ 2 Ch♨0,50 ♨€ 1/2kWh WC☕€ 1,50
🔌€ 3 📶included.
**Location:** Rural, quiet. **Surface:** grasstiles.
🗓 01/03-31/10.
**Distance:** 🚿5km 🏊on the spot 🚣on the spot ⊗on the spot 🛒5km.
**Remarks:** Parking eastern bank Plauersee, bread-service, possibility
for reservation.

---

**⛱🅂 Lohme ⚓🏖 6G3**

**Wohnmobilstellplatz Dorfladen**, Arkonastrasse 4.
**GPS:** n54,58300 e13,61150.➡

35 🛏€ 14-17 🚰 € 1/90liter 🚽Ch♨€ 1 ♨€ 1/2kWh WC☕€ 2/5minutes
🔌€ 3/3 📶included. **Location:** Rural, comfortable.
**Surface:** grassy/metalled.
🗓 01/01-31/12.
**Distance:** 🚿on the spot 🏊200m ⊗on the spot 🛒on the spot
🚐on the spot.
**Remarks:** Dog € 1,50/night, breakfast-service, discount longer stays.

---

**⛱🅂 Lohme ⚓🏖 6G3**

**Zum Königsstuhl**, Stubbenkammerstraße 57, Hagen.
**GPS:** n54,56220 e13,62590.⬆

---

40 🛏€ 10,50 + € 1/pp tourist tax 🚰 € 1/100liter 🚽Ch♨€ 2,50/24h
WC€ 0,50 ☕€ 1/4minutes.🚮 **Location:** Rural, comfortable.
**Surface:** grassy/metalled. 🗓 01/01-31/12.
**Distance:** ⊗on the spot 🛒600m 🚐on the spot.

---

**⛱🅂 Ludwigslust 🌾🏖 8D2**

**Am Schloss**, Friedrich-Naumann-Allee. **GPS:** n53,32735 e11,49080.⬆

20 🛏€ 7/24h 🚰 € 1/100liter 🚽€ 1 Ch♨€ 1 ♨€ 1/2kWh WC.🚮
**Location:** Rural, simple, quiet. **Surface:** gravel/sand.
🗓 01/01-31/12.
**Distance:** 🚿600m ⊗500m 🛒600m.
**Remarks:** Coins at the shops.

---

**⛱🅂 Lütow 🏖 6G3**

**Yachtlieger Achterwasser**, Netzelkow. **GPS:** n54,02690 e13,90950.➡

22 🛏€ 5-10 + € 1/pp 🚐 🚽Chincluded ♨(20x)€ 0,25/kWh WC☕ 2.
**Location:** Rural, comfortable, isolated, quiet. **Surface:** grassy.
🗓 01/01-31/12.
**Distance:** 🏊on the spot 🚣on the spot ⊗on the spot.
**Remarks:** Bread-service, bike/car rental.

---

**🌾🅂 Lütow 🏖 6G3**

**Köster's Hof**, Zum Möwenort 12. **GPS:** n54,01089 e13,87609.
3 🛏€ 10, 2 pers. incl. 🚰 🚽Ch♨€ 3/day WC☕ 2 📶included.
**Location:** Rural. **Surface:** grassy. 🗓 01/04-30/09.
**Distance:** 🏊on the spot 🚣on the spot ⊗700m 🚐450m 🚲on the
spot 🚶on the spot.

---

**⛱🅂 Lütow 🏖 6G3**

**Pommi's Traumoase**, Neuendorfer Weg 7. **GPS:** n54,01352 e13,87947.
10 🛏€ 12-22, dog € 3,20 🚰 Ch♨♨€ 0,65/kWh WC☕included
📶€ 2/day. **Location:** Rural. **Surface:** grassy. 🗓 01/04-31/10.
**Distance:** 🏊350m ⊗300m 🚐on the spot.
**Remarks:** Bread-service, breakfast-service, bicycle rental.

---

**Malchin 🏖 8E1**

**Malchiner Kanu-club**, Am Kanal 2. **GPS:** n53,74417 e12,76611.⬆

8 🛏€ 10 🚰 Ch♨€ 1 WCincluded ☕€ 0,50 🔌€ 3/2.
**Location:** Urban, comfortable, quiet. **Surface:** grassy.
🗓 01/05-30/09.
**Distance:** 🚿500m 🏊on the spot 🚣on the spot ⊗500m 🛒500m.
**Remarks:** Dog € 4.

---

**⛱🅂 Malchow 🏖 8E2**

**Marina Malchow**, Ziegeleiweg 5. **GPS:** n53,46432 e12,42417.⬆

**DE**

20 🍴€ 10-20 excl. tourist tax 🚰🗑Ch 🚿€ 2,50 WC included 🚽€ 2,50. **Location:** Rural, comfortable, quiet. **Surface:** grassy. 🅿 01/05-30/09.
**Distance:** 🚶2km 🏄4km 🏊on the spot 🛒on the spot ⊗2km 🍺4km 🚌250m.
**Remarks:** Bread-service.

### Malchow 8E2
**Wohnmobilstellplatz Am Plauer See**, Zum Plauer See 1.
**GPS:** n53,49192 e12,37268.

5 🍴€ 10-12, 2 pers.incl 🚰🗑Ch 🚿(5x)€ 3,30 WC 🔌📶included.
**Location:** Rural, quiet. **Surface:** grassy. 🅿 01/01-31/12.
**Distance:** 🚶5km 🏊on the spot 🛒on the spot ⊗on the spot 🍺on the spot.
**Remarks:** Use sanitary € 2/pp per day.

### Mirow 8F2
Schloßstraße 1A. **GPS:** n53,27623 e12,81348.

8 🍴free 🚰€ 1 🗑€ 1 Ch€ 1 🚿(8x) WC€ 0,50. **Location:** Simple.
**Surface:** grasstiles/metalled. 🅿 01/01-31/12.
**Distance:** 🚶400m 🏊200m ⊗400m.

### Mönkebude 8G1
**Stettinger Haff**, Am Hafen. **GPS:** n53,77174 e13,96868.

25+15 🍴€ 8,50-10 + € 1/pp tourist tax, dog € 2 🚰€ 0,50/100liter 🗑Ch€ 2/24h WC€ 1 🔌€ 3,50/3 📶€ 4/4h.
**Location:** Rural, comfortable. **Surface:** grassy. 🅿 01/01-31/12.
**Distance:** 🚶50m 🏊on the spot ⊗on the spot 🍺50m.
**Remarks:** Peak season: sanitary installation, nov/apr service only on demand.

### Mönkebude 8G1
**Gastätte Kregelin's Bistro**, Hauptstrasse.
**GPS:** n53,76663 e13,97614.

---

4 🍴guests free. **Surface:** metalled. 🅿 01/01-31/12.
**Distance:** ⊗on the spot.

### Muess 8D2
**Feriendorf Muess**, Alte Crivitzer Landstrasse 6.
**GPS:** n53,59995 e11,47940.

15 🍴🗑 10, 01/03-30/09 € 20, dog € 1 🚰🗑Ch 🚿WC 🔌included, winter fee no shower 📶€ 2/1,70.
**Location:** Rural, comfortable. **Surface:** grassy. 🅿 01/01-31/12.
**Distance:** 🚶100m 🏊100m 🍺100m 🚌100m 🚲100m on the spot.
**Remarks:** At open air museum, check in at reception, breakfest-service, bicycle rental.

### Neu Kaliss 8D2
**Find's hier**, An der Elde 2. **GPS:** n53,17810 e11,29720.

16 🍴🗑 10 🚰🗑Ch included 🚿€ 2/night WC 🔌€ 1.
**Location:** Rural, simple, isolated, quiet. **Surface:** grassy. 🅿 01/01-31/12.
**Distance:** 🏊on the spot 🛒on the spot ⊗on the spot 🍺400m 🚌400m.

### Neubrandenburg 8F1
**Wassersportzentrum Tollensesee**, Augustastrasse 7.
**GPS:** n53,53861 e13,25665.

30 🍴🗑 10 🚰€ 1 Ch€ 1 🚿€ 0,50/kWh WC 🔌€ 1 📶€ 2/day.
**Location:** Urban, comfortable, quiet. **Surface:** grassy/metalled. 🅿 15/03-31/10.
**Distance:** 🚶2km 🏊on the spot 🛒on the spot ⊗200m 🍺500m.
**Remarks:** Water sports centre.

### Neuendorf 6F3
**Wohnmobilstellplatz Saal Neuendorf**, Am Hafen.
**GPS:** n54,33516 e12,52812.

---

36 🍴🗑 10 🚰🗑Ch included WC€ 0,20 🔌€ 1 📶on demand.
**Location:** Rural, simple, quiet. **Surface:** grassy. 🅿 01/04-31/10.
**Distance:** 🚶100m 🏊on the spot 🛒on the spot ⊗Imbiss 🍺kiosk 🚌400m on the spot 🚲on the spot.
**Remarks:** Bread-service.

### Neuenkirchen 9G1
**Sawiko**, Ringstraße. **GPS:** n52,49676 e8,07583.
5 🍴free 🚿free. **Location:** Urban. **Surface:** grassy. 🅿 01/01-31/12.
**Distance:** 🚶on the spot.

### Neukloster 8D1
**Wohnmobilpark Neuklostersee**, Alte Gärtnerei 3.
**GPS:** n53,86121 e11,69536.

69 🍴€ 12 🚰🗑Ch included 🚿€ 1/2kWh WC 🔌€ 2 📶€ 4/2.
**Location:** Rural, comfortable, quiet. **Surface:** gravel. 🅿 16/03-31/10.
**Distance:** 🚶500m 🏊on the spot 🛒50m ⊗500m 🍺1,2km 🚌500m 🚲on the spot 🚲on the spot.

### Neustrelitz 8F2
**Parkplatz Am Stadthafen**, Zierker Nebenstrasse 6.
**GPS:** n53,36568 e13,05551.

25 🍴🗑 8 🚰€ 0,50/80liter 🗑€ 0,50 Ch€ 0,50 🚿€ 0,50/kWh WC€ 0,20 🔌€ 0,50 📶€ 2.
**Location:** Urban, comfortable, quiet. **Surface:** metalled. 🅿 01/01-31/12.
**Distance:** 🚶on the spot 🏊100m, swimming 1km 🛒200m ⊗100m 🍺200m 🚌200m 🚲on the spot 🚲on the spot.
**Remarks:** Coins at harbourmaster (200m), historical centre.

### Nossentin 8E2
**Am Fleesensee**, Am Park 33. **GPS:** n53,51866 e12,46766.

5 🍴🗑 8 🚰🗑Ch 🚿WC included 🔌. **Location:** Rural, comfortable, isolated, quiet. **Surface:** grassy. 🅿 01/04-31/10.
**Distance:** 🚶5km 🏊100m 🛒100m ⊗on the spot 🍺5km.

### Ostseebad Sellin/Rügen 6G3
**Reisemobilhafen Sellin**, Kiefernweg 4b. **GPS:** n54,37170 e13,70165.

DE

50 ⌁€ 13-15 ☇€ 0,50/60liter ⌁Ch ⚡(50x)€ 0,50/kWh WCincluded
⌁€ 0,50/2minutes. **Location:** Urban, comfortable, central.
**Surface:** grassy/metalled. ◻ 15/03-15/11.
**Distance:** ⌁300m ⌁1km ⌁1km ⊗200m ⌁300m ⌁300m.

### ⚓S Ostseebad Sellin/Rügen 〰⌁⌁⌁ 6G3

**Hafen Seedorf**, Seedorf 8. **GPS:** n54,35410 e13,65359.⬆.

5 ⌁€ 15 + € 2,80/pp tourist tax ☇€ 1/100liter ⚡€ 0,50/kWh
⌁€ 0,50/2minutes. 🏠 **Location:** Rural, simple, quiet.
**Surface:** metalled. ◻ 01/03-31/10.
**Distance:** ⌁250m ⊗250m ⌁250m.
**Remarks:** Pay at harbourmaster.

### ⌁S Ostseebad Wustrow ⌁⌁ 6F3

**Surfcenter Wustrow**, An der Nebelstation 2.
**GPS:** n54,34080 e12,38040.⬆➡.

30 ⌁€ 19-24 + € 5/pp tourist tax, dog € 2,50-5 ☇⌁Ch ⚡€ 3/day
WC⌁€ 2/2minutes ⌁included.🏄
**Location:** Rural, simple, quiet. **Surface:** asphalted.
◻ 01/04-31/10.
**Distance:** ⌁1km ⌁50m ⌁on the spot ⊗1,5km ⌁1,5km ⌁on the
spot ⌁ on the spot.

### ⌁ Ostseebad Wustrow ⌁⌁ 6F3

Hafenstraße. **GPS:** n54,34363 e12,40053.⬆.

30 ⌁€ 4/day, € 10/night. ⌁ **Location:** Rural, simple, quiet.
**Surface:** grassy/sand. ◻ 01/01-31/12.
**Distance:** ⌁400m ⌁1,5km ⌁on the spot ⊗on the spot ⌁on the
spot ⌁ on the spot.
**Remarks:** Max. 1 night.

### ⌁S Parchim 8D2

**Yachthafen**, Am Fischerdamm. **GPS:** n53,42594 e11,84494.⬆.

---

10 ⌁€ 6 ☇€ 0,50/50liter ⌁Ch€ 0,50 ⚡€ 0,50/kWh WC€ 0,50
⌁€ 0,50. **Location:** Urban, comfortable, central. **Surface:** metalled.
◻ 01/01-31/12.
**Distance:** ⌁100m ⌁on the spot ⌁on the spot ⊗100m ⌁100m.

### ⚓S Peenemünde 6G3

Fährstrasse 9. **GPS:** n54,13611 e13,76252.➡.
80 ⌁€ 8-10 ☇€ 1 ⌁€ 1 Ch€ 1 ⚡€ 2 WC⌁€ 2 ⌁€ 3/3h.
**Location:** Rural. **Surface:** grassy.
◻ 01/01-31/12 🔲 15/06-19/06.
**Distance:** ⌁1km ⌁1km ⌁100m ⊗100m ⌁800m ⌁on the spot
⌁ on the spot.

### ⌁S Pepelow ⌁ 8D1

**Wohnmobilpark Am Salzhaff**, Seeweg 1.
**GPS:** n54,03805 e11,58441.⬆.

39 ⌁€ 10-15, 2 pers.incl ☇⌁Ch ⚡€ 3,30/night WC⌁€ 2,50/pp
🔲€ 3/3 ⌁included. ◻ 01/01-31/12.
**Surface:** grassy. **Location:** Rural, luxurious, quiet.
**Distance:** ⌁700m ⌁on the spot ⌁on the spot ⊗on the spot
⌁on the spot ⌁on the spot ⌁ on the spot.

### ⌁⌁S Petersdorf 8E2

**Hotel Haus Waldesruh**, Lenzerstrasse 19.
**GPS:** n53,45892 e12,36060.⬆.

10 ⌁€ 7,50 ☇€ 1 ⌁Ch ⚡€ 2 WC⌁€ 1,50 🔲€ 1,50/1,50.
⌁included. **Location:** Rural. **Surface:** grassy. ◻ 01/01-31/12.
**Distance:** ⌁7km ⌁600m ⌁600m ⊗on the spot ⌁7km.
**Remarks:** Bowling, use of sauna against payment.

### ⌁S Plau am See ⌁⌁ 8E2

Eichbaumallee. **GPS:** n53,43060 e12,27386.⬆.
5 ⌁€ 7,50 ☇included. **Location:** Rural, simple, quiet. **Surface:** gravel.
◻ 01/01-31/12.
**Distance:** ⌁on the spot ⌁on the spot ⊗1,5km.

### ⌁⌁S Priepert 8F2

**Wohnmobilpark Am Großen Priepertsee**, An der Freiheit 8.
**GPS:** n53,22043 e13,04201.⬆.

30 ⌁€ 7 ☇⌁Chincluded ⚡€ 2,25 WC€ 3/day ⌁€ 1 🔲€ 5.🏠
**Location:** Rural, comfortable, quiet. **Surface:** grassy.
◻ 01/01-31/12.
**Distance:** ⌁on the spot ⌁70m ⌁70m ⊗500m ⌁12km.

---

**NATURCAMP Pruchten ★★★★**, Am Campingplatz 1.
**GPS:** n54,37947 e12,66131.⬆. 
70 ⌁€ 18, 01/06-31/08 € 25 ☇⌁Ch ⚡(70x)€ 2,90/4kWh
WC⌁€ 4/4 ⌁included. 🏠⌁
**Location:** Rural, luxurious, quiet. **Surface:** grassy. ◻ 01/04-31/10.
**Distance:** ⌁800m ⌁600m ⌁600m ⊗on the spot ⌁on the spot
⌁on the spot ⌁ on the spot.
**Remarks:** Bicycle rental.

### ⌁S Putbus 〰 6G3

**Im-Jaich OHG**, Am Yachthafen 1, Lauterbach.
**GPS:** n54,34278 e13,50167.⬆.

20 ⌁€ 19-21 ☇€ 0,50/50liter ⌁Ch ⚡WC⌁€ 1 🔲€ 4/3
⌁included. **Location:** Rural, luxurious. **Surface:** grassy/gravel.
◻ 01/01-31/12.
**Distance:** ⌁500m ⌁on the spot ⌁on the spot ⊗on the spot
⌁800m.
**Remarks:** Bread kiosk, seaview.

### ⌁S Putbus 〰 6G3

**Wohnmobilstellplatz Lauterbach**, Chausseestrasse 14.
**GPS:** n54,34639 e13,49889.⬆.

26 ⌁€ 13, 15/06-15/09 € 15, 2 pers.incl ☇€ 0,60/50liter ⌁Ch
⚡€ 0,70/kWh WC€ 0,30 ⌁€ 2/5minutes 🔲€ 4/4 ⌁€ 1/day.
**Location:** Rural, luxurious, quiet. **Surface:** grassy/metalled.
◻ 12/04-15/10.
**Distance:** ⌁1km ⌁400m ⌁400m ⌁100m.
**Remarks:** Max. 8M.

### ⌁ Putgarten ⌁ 6G3

**Kap Arkona**, Varnkevitzer Weg. **GPS:** n54,67190 e13,40800.⬆.

30 ⌁€ 5, ^3,10m € 15. **Location:** Simple. **Surface:** asphalted.

---

⊙ 01/01-31/12.
**Distance:** 100m Imbiss 6km.
**Remarks:** Max. 24h.

### Rerik 6E3
**Wohnmobilhafen Ostseebad Rerik**, Straße am Zeltplatz 8.
**GPS:** n54,11332 e11,63037. ↑ →.

35 € 14, Jul-Aug € 23 Ch WC € 0,30 € 3/3
included. **Location:** Rural, comfortable, quiet. **Surface:** grassy.
⊙ 01/01-31/12.
**Distance:** sandy beach 600m on the spot on the spot on the
spot on the spot on the spot.
**Remarks:** Check in at reception.

### Ribnitz-Damgarten 6F3
**Gänsewiese**, Am See 50. **GPS:** n54,24513 e12,42265. ↑ →.

25 free, night € 8 € 1/100liter Ch € 0,50/12h WC.
**Location:** Rural, simple, quiet. **Surface:** grasstiles/grassy.
⊙ 01/01-31/12.
**Distance:** 500m on the spot on the spot 500m 500m
on the spot on the spot.

### Ribnitz-Damgarten 6F3
**Hafen Ribnitz**, Am See 44. **GPS:** n54,24536 e12,42921. ↑.

10 free, night € 10 WC € 1/3minutes.
**Location:** Urban, simple, quiet. **Surface:** concrete.
⊙ 01/01-31/12.
**Distance:** 100m on the spot on the spot on the spot
200m on the spot on the spot.

### Röbel 8E2
**Am Seglerhafen**, Müritzpromenade 20. **GPS:** n53,38734 e12,61755. ↑.

30 € 15, 01/07-01/09 € 18 € 1/100liter Ch € 2
WC included € 1 free. **Location:** Rural, comfortable, quiet.
**Surface:** grasstiles/metalled. ⊙ 01/04-31/10.
**Distance:** 2km on the spot on the spot 300m 1km.

### Rostock 6F3
Mühlendamm. **GPS:** n54,08444 e12,15361.
24 € 12/24h Ch (24x)included. **Surface:** metalled.
⊙ 01/01-31/12.
**Distance:** 1km 1,5km 450m on the spot.

### Rostock 6F3
**Am Stadthafen**, Warnowuffer. **GPS:** n54,09297 e12,12878. ↑.

25 € 12. **Location:** Urban, simple. **Surface:** asphalted/metalled.
⊙ 01/01-31/12.
**Distance:** on the spot on the spot on the spot.
**Tourist information Rostock:**
ℹ️ www.rostock.de. Hanseatic city with historical centre.

### Rüterberg 8C3
**Wohmobilparkplatz Dorfrepublik Rüterberg**, Ringstraße 2.
**GPS:** n53,15294 e11,18511. ↑.

10 € 5/24h+ € 1/pp € 1/50liter € 1 Ch € 1 € 2/24h
WC € 1. **Location:** Rural, simple, central, quiet. **Surface:** grassy.
⊙ 01/01-31/12.
**Distance:** 10m 50m.
**Remarks:** Bread-service.

### Sassnitz 6G3
Hafenstraße. **GPS:** n54,51436 e13,64568. ↑.
15 € 20. **Location:** Urban. **Surface:** metalled.
⊙ 01/01-31/12.
**Distance:** on the spot on the spot 100m 100m.

### Schwerin 8D1
**Am Hauptbahnhof**, Wismarsche Straße. **GPS:** n53,63692 e11,40893. ↑.

4 € 8/24h € 1/80liter Ch (4x)€ 1/2kWh.
**Location:** Urban, simple, central, noisy. **Surface:** metalled.
⊙ 01/01-31/12.
**Distance:** on the spot on the spot on the spot on the spot.

### Schwerin 8D1
**Am Stadthafen**, Schliemannstraße. **GPS:** n53,62977 e11,41966. ↑.

10 € 16/24h (8x)€ 0,50/kWh.
**Location:** Urban, simple, central, noisy. **Surface:** metalled.
⊙ 01/01-31/12.
**Distance:** on the spot 8km on the spot on the spot
on the spot on the spot on the spot.
**Remarks:** No camping activities.

### Schwerin 8D1
**Marina-Nord Schwerin**, Buchenweg 19.
**GPS:** n53,64584 e11,43264. ↑ ↑.

16 € 10 + € 1/pp Ch (14x)€ 0,50/kWh WC € 1,50
€ 1/24h. **Location:** Rural, comfortable, quiet. **Surface:** grassy.
⊙ 15/04-15/10.
**Distance:** 4km 5km on the spot on the spot on the spot
1km 100m on the spot on the spot.
**Remarks:** Check in at reception, bread-service.

### Schwerin 8D1
**Parkplatz Jägerweg**, Jägerweg/Am Schlossgarten.
**GPS:** n53,61989 e11,41195. ↑.

10 € 8/day. **Location:** Urban, simple, noisy. **Surface:** asphalted.
⊙ 01/01-31/12.
**Distance:** 1km.

### Schwerin 8D1
**Hangar 19**, Bornhövedstraße 95-97. **GPS:** n53,63746 e11,43308. ↑.
20 € 20-25 (20x),16Amp WC included.
**Location:** Urban, comfortable, luxurious. **Surface:** grassy/gravel.
⊙ 01/01-31/12.
**Distance:** 1,5km 20m 500m 800m 100m.

### Schwerin 8D1
**Sportbootzentrum Ziegelsee**, Güstrower Straße 88.
**GPS:** n53,64823 e11,43004. ↑.

16 € 15/24h € 0,50/70liter Ch (20x),16Amp WC included
€ 1/6minutes € 5/5 . **Location:** Rural, comfortable, quiet.
**Surface:** concrete. ⊙ 01/04-30/10.
**Distance:** 3,5km 5km on the spot on the spot 300m
300m 50m 200m.

### Seehof 8D1
**Campingplatz Seehof**, Am Zeltplatz 1. **GPS:** n53,69676 e11,43658. ↑.

10 € 15, 2 pers.incl € 5 Ch € 5 WC € 1/5minutes
€ 3,50/3,50. **Location:** Rural, comfortable. **Surface:** grassy.
⊙ 01/03-31/10.
**Distance:** 1,2km on the spot on the spot on the spot
on the spot on the spot on the spot.
**Remarks:** Bread-service, bike/boat rental.

### Sembzin 8E2
**Rasthof Sembzin**, Dorfstrasse 2. **GPS:** n53,46445 e12,60386. ↑.

16 🛏 € 8 🚰 🍴 Ch 💧 included WC 🗑 € 1/24h. **Location:** Rural, noisy. **Surface:** grassy/gravel. 📅 01/04-31/10.
**Distance:** 🚲 8km ⊗ on the spot 🛒 1,5km.
**Remarks:** € 8 voucher restaurant, use sanitary € 2/pp per day, swimming pool incl.

### Sievershagen 6F3

**Ferienhof Dubberke**, Alt Sievershagen 16.
**GPS:** n54,11480 e12,03481. ⬆

7 🛏 € 10 🚰 🍴 Ch 💧 WC included 🗑 € 1. 🛝 **Location:** Rural, comfortable, quiet. **Surface:** grassy. 📅 01/04-31/10.
**Distance:** 🚲 500m, Rostock 5km 🏊 2km ⊗ 800m 🛒 800m 🚴 on the spot 🎣 on the spot.

### Sommersdorf 8F1

**Wohnmobilpark Sommersdorf**, Am Kummerower See.
**GPS:** n53,79824 e12,87576.

28 🛏 € 6-12, 2 pers. incl 🚰 🍴 Ch 💧 € 3/day WC 🗑 € 2/day 🖥 🌊 included. **Location:** Rural, comfortable, isolated, quiet.
**Surface:** grassy. 📅 01/01-31/12.
**Distance:** 🚲 1km 🏊 on the spot 🎣 on the spot ⊗ 1km.
**Remarks:** Use sanitary € 2/pp per day.

### Sternberg 8D1

**Camping Sternberger Seenland**, Maikamp 11.
**GPS:** n53,71318 e11,81236. ⬆

15 🛏 € 14-18 🚰 🍴 Ch 💧 € 3/day WC 🗑 included 🌊 € 2.
**Location:** Rural. **Surface:** grassy. 📅 01/04-31/10.
**Distance:** 🚲 1km 🏊 on the spot 🎣 on the spot ⊗ on the spot 🛒 500m.

### Stralsund 6G3

**An der Rügenbrücke**, Werftstraße 9a. **GPS:** n54,30222 e13,09889. ⬆

40 🛏 € 15, 2 pers.incl 🚰 € 1/50liter 🔌 € 1 Ch € 1 🗑 (40x)€ 0,50/kWh WC included 🚿 € 1/4minutes 🖥 € 3/3 🚿 🛝 **Location:** Urban, comfortable, noisy. **Surface:** grassy/gravel. 📅 01/01-31/12.
**Distance:** 🚲 1,8km 🏊 1,8km 🛒 200m 🚴 on the spot.
**Remarks:** Bread-service.

### Stralsund 6G3

**Wohnmobilstellplatz-Stralsund**, Boddenweg 3.
**GPS:** n54,27605 e13,10822. ⬆

18 🛏 € 15, 2 pers.incl 🚰 € 1/100liter 🔌 Ch 💧 € 0,50/kWh WC 🗑 included 🚿. 🚲 **Location:** Urban, luxurious, quiet.
**Surface:** gravel. 📅 01/01-31/12.
**Distance:** 🚲 city centre 5km 🏊 200m.
**Remarks:** Bread-service, bicycle rental.

### Ueckermünde 8G1

**An der Uecker**, Ueckerstrasse 125. **GPS:** n53,73470 e14,04930. ⬆

13 🛏 € 10 excl. tourist tax 🚰 🍴 Ch 💧 included.
**Location:** Urban, simple. **Surface:** grassy/metalled.
📅 01/01-31/12.
**Distance:** 🚲 Old city centre 200m ⊗ 200m 🛒 100m.

### Ueckermünde 8G1

**See Sport**, Grabenstrasse. **GPS:** n53,73917 e14,04944. ⬆
5 🛏 € 6 🚰 € 0,50/100liter 💧 € 0,50/kWh WC 🗑 € 0,50/2minutes. 🚲
**Location:** Urban, central, quiet. **Surface:** grassy.
📅 01-01/31/12.
**Distance:** 🚲 200m 🎣 on the spot ⊗ 200m 🛒 500m.

### Usedom 8G1

**Am Hafen Usedom**, Peenestraße. **GPS:** n53,87099 e13,92679. ⬆ ⬆

20 🛏 € 10 🚰 € 0,50/50liter 🔌 Ch 💧 € 0,50/kWh WC € 0,50 🗑 € 2. 🚲
**Location:** Rural, simple. **Surface:** metalled.
📅 01/01-31/12.
**Distance:** 🚲 600m 🏊 on the spot ⊗ on the spot 🛒 1,3km.
**Remarks:** At former fishing-port.

### Vielank 8C2

**Vielanker Brauhaus**, Lindenplatz 1. **GPS:** n53,23443 e11,14023. ⬆

12 🛏 free 💧 € 3 WC. **Location:** Rural, simple, quiet. **Surface:** grassy.
📅 01/01-31/12.
**Distance:** 🚲 20m ⊗ on the spot.
**Remarks:** Check in at reception.

### Waren 8E2

**Blumen und Parken**, Mecklenburgerstrasse.
**GPS:** n53,51363 e12,69431. ⬆

40 🛏 € 10 + € 2/pp tourist tax 🚰 🍴 Ch 💧 € 0,50/kWh WC included 🗑 € 1/5minutes. 🖥 **Location:** Urban, simple. **Surface:** grassy/gravel.
📅 01/01-31/12.
**Distance:** 🚲 100m 🏊 1km 🎣 1km ⊗ 1km 🛒 1km 🚴 on the spot.

### Waren 8E2

**Wohnmobilpark Kamerun**, Zur Stillen Bucht 3, Müritz.
**GPS:** n53,51175 e12,65174. ⬆

65 🛏 € 13-18 + tourist tax 🚰 🔌 Ch 💧 € 3,30 WC 🗑 🖥 € 0,75 🚿 included. **Location:** Rural, comfortable, quiet. **Surface:** grassy.
📅 01/01-31/12.
**Distance:** 🚲 3km 🏊 on the spot 🎣 on the spot ⊗ on the spot 🛒 on the spot 🚴 500m.
**Remarks:** Use sanitary € 2/pp per day.

### Waren 8E2

**Parkplatz Am Hafen**, Strandstrasse 3. **GPS:** n53,51194 e12,68583. ⬆

20 🛏 € 15 🚰 🍴 Ch 💧 🚿 included. **Location:** Urban.
**Surface:** metalled. 📅 01/01-31/12.
**Distance:** 🚲 on the spot 🏊 on the spot 🎣 on the spot ⊗ on the spot 🛒 on the spot.

### Waren 8E2

**Campingplatz Ecktannen**, Fontanestraße 66.
**GPS:** n53,49944 e12,66361. ⬆ ➡

17 🛏 € 15-20, 2 pers.incl 🚰 🍴 Ch 💧 WC 🗑 🖥 € 2,60/2,60 🚿 included.
**Location:** Rural, comfortable, quiet. **Surface:** grasstiles/metalled.
📅 01/01-31/12.
**Distance:** 🚲 3,5km 🏊 500m 🎣 500m ⊗ Bistro 🛒 3km 🚴 on the spot.

### Warnemünde 6F3

Am Bahnhof. **GPS:** n54,17762 e12,09002. ⬆

100 🅿 € 6/3h, € 12/12h, € 17,50/24h ⛽ € 0,50/100liter. 🏪
**Location:** Urban, simple, central, noisy. **Surface:** grassy/metalled.
🗓 01/01-31/12.
**Distance:** 🛒 on the spot 🏖 on the spot 🍽 on the spot ⊗ on the spot 🚆 on the spot 🚌 on the spot 🚶 on the spot.

| 🅿 S | Warnemünde 🌿♨⛲🗑⛵ | 6F3 |

**Parkplatz Strand-Mitte**, Parkstrasse 46. **GPS:** n54,17643 e12,05765.⬆

100 🅿 € 10/24h + tourist tax € 2,25/pp WC. 🏪
**Location:** Urban, simple, noisy. **Surface:** metalled.
🗓 01/01-31/12.
**Distance:** 🛒 2,5km 🏖 100m ⊗ 400m 🚆 2km 🚌 on the spot 🚴 on the spot 🚶 on the spot.

| 🅿 S | Wesenberg | 8F2 |

**Stellplatz Marina Wesenberg**, Ahrensberger Weg 11.
**GPS:** n53,27666 e12,98694.⬆

34 🅿 € 17, 2 pers. incl ⛽📷Ch🚿 WC🗑 included. **Location:** Rural,
comfortable, quiet. **Surface:** grassy. 🗓 01/04-01/10.
**Distance:** 🛒 1km 🏖 on the spot 🍽 on the spot ⊗ 1,5km 🚆 2,5km
🚌 1km.
**Remarks:** Bread-service, boat rental.

| 🅿 S | Wismar 🌿♨⛲🗑 | 8D1 |

**Wohnmobilpark Westhafen Wismar**, Schiffbauerdamm 12.
**GPS:** n53,89430 e11,45151.⬆

65 🅿 € 7/12h, € 10/24h ⛽ € 1/100liter 📷Ch🚿 € 1/8h WC included
🗑 € 1 📶. 🏪 **Location:** Urban, simple, central, noisy.
**Surface:** asphalted/gravel. 🗓 01/01-31/12.
**Distance:** 🛒 800m 🏖 500m ⊗ 300m, Burger King 400m 🚆 300m
🖥 800m 🚌 100m.
**Remarks:** Caution key sanitary € 10, service passerby € 3.

| 🅿 S | Wittenbeck ⛵ | 6F3 |

**Sanddornstrand**, Bäderweg. **GPS:** n54,14513 e11,79277.⬆

---

150 🅿 € 12-15 ⛽📷Ch🚿(40x)€ 3/24h WC € 0,50 🗑included. 💧
**Location:** Rural, simple, quiet. **Surface:** grassy/metalled.
🗓 01/03-31/10.
**Distance:** 🛒 1km 🏖 on the spot 🍽 on the spot ⊗ on the spot 🚆 5km
🚴 on the spot 🚶 on the spot.
**Remarks:** Bread-service.

| 🅿 S | Zingst ♨⛵🏖 | 6F3 |

**Strandübergang 6**, Straminke. **GPS:** n54,44070 e12,70750.⬆

40 🅿 € 10-15 + € 2,80/pp + tourist tax ⛽ € 1/100liter 🚿 € 3/day
WC 🗑 € 1. 💧 **Location:** Rural, simple, quiet. **Surface:** grassy.
🗓 01/04-31/10.
**Distance:** 🛒 500m 🏖 on the spot ⊗ 500m 🚆 500m 🖥 1km 🚌 1km
🚴 on the spot 🚶 on the spot.

| © S | Zingst 🌿⛵🏖 | 6F3 |

**Wohnmobilhafen Am Freesenbruch**, Am Bahndamm 1.
**GPS:** n54,44060 e12,66058.⬆

40 🅿 € 8-12 + € 10/pp, dog € 5 ⛽📷Ch🚿 € 2,30/day WC🗑 € 3/3
📶included. 💧 **Location:** Rural, comfortable, noisy. **Surface:** grassy.
🗓 01/01-31/12.
**Distance:** 🛒 1,5km 🏖 50m 🍽 50m ⊗ on the spot 🚆 on the spot
🚴 on the spot 🚶 on the spot.
**Remarks:** Bread-service.

| 🅿 S | Zurow 🗑 | 8D1 |

**Urlaub am Schloss**, Kastanienallee 56, Krassow.
**GPS:** n53,87379 e11,56618.⬆➡

10 🅿 € 5 ⛽ € 1 📷Ch🚿 € 2/day WC🗑 € 2 📶. 💧
**Location:** Rural, simple, quiet. **Surface:** grassy/metalled.
🗓 01/01-31/12.
**Distance:** 🛒 1,5km ⊗ 1km 🚆 3km 🚌 100m 🚴 on the spot 🚶 on the spot.
**Remarks:** Caution key sanitary € 10.

# Saxony Anhalt

| 🍴 S | Ahlum | 8C3 |

**Fischerhütte Ahlumer See**, Am Mühlenberg 63.
**GPS:** n52,69541 e11,00583.⬆

---

100 🅿 € 10, 2 pers.incl ⛽📷Ch🚿 € 0,50 WC 🗑included.
**Location:** Rural, simple, quiet. **Surface:** grassy.
🗓 01/01-31/12.
**Distance:** 🏖 on the spot 🍽 on the spot ⊗ 50m.
**Remarks:** Bread-service.

| 🍴 S | Allrode | 10C3 |

**Hotel Harzer Land**, Teichstraße 28. **GPS:** n51,67774 e10,96478.⬆

25 🅿 € 15,50 ⛽📷Ch🚿 WC🗑included. 🚐📶 **Location:** Urban,
comfortable, central. **Surface:** grassy. 🗓 01/01-31/12.
**Distance:** 🛒 on the spot ⊗ on the spot.
**Remarks:** Breakfest-service, swimming pool and sauna on site.

| 🅿 | Altenbrak 🌿🏖 | 10C2 |

**Bodewiese**, Am Bielstein. **GPS:** n51,72569 e10,94196.⬆

8 🅿 € 3, overnight stay free. 🏪 **Location:** Rural, simple, isolated.
**Surface:** metalled. 🗓 01/01-31/12.
**Distance:** 🛒 100m 🍽 on the spot ⊗ 100m 🚌 200m 🚶 on the spot.
**Remarks:** Along river.

| 🍴 S | Altenbrak 🌿🏖 | 10C2 |

**Hotel Zur Talsperre**, Oberbecken 1, Wendefurth.
**GPS:** n51,73434 e10,90690.⬆

20 🅿 € 10 excl. tourist tax ⛽🚿(20x)€ 0,50/kWh WC🗑included. 💧
**Location:** Rural, simple, isolated. **Surface:** asphalted/grassy.
🗓 01/01-31/12.
**Distance:** ⊗ on the spot.
**Remarks:** At lake.

| © S | Arendsee | 8D3 |

**Im kleinen Elsebusch**, Lüchower strasse 6a.
**GPS:** n52,87656 e11,46121.⬆➡

10 🅿 € 11 ⛽📷 € 1,50 Ch € 1,50 🚿 € 1/5minutes. **Location:** Rural.

---

**Surface:** grassy. ☐ 01/01-31/12.
**Distance:** 🚶2,5km ⊗on the spot 🍺2,5km.
**Remarks:** Dog € 2/day.

### ⌖S Aschersleben �803⚓ 10D2

**Sport- und Freizeitzentrum Ballhaus**, Seegraben.
**GPS:** n51,76101 e11,45760.⬆.

8 🅿free ⚡€ 1/15minutes 🔌€ 2 Ch€ 2 ⚡(12x)€ 1/6h.
**Location:** Urban, comfortable, central, quiet. **Surface:** asphalted.
☐ 01/01-31/12.
**Distance:** 🚶1km ⊗200m 🍺200m ⊙on the spot 🚲on the spot
🚶on the spot.
**Remarks:** Caution key € 15, key at reception desk BallHaus.

### ⌖ Bad Bibra ⚓ 12D1

**Parkplatz am Schwimmbad**, B 176. **GPS:** n51,21214 e11,60002.⬆.

20 🅿€ 3.🚐 **Location:** Rural, simple, isolated, quiet.
**Surface:** gravel/metalled. ☐ 01/01-31/12.
**Distance:** 🚶1,5km ⊗200m 🍺1,5km.
**Remarks:** At swimming pool.

### ⌖ Bad Bibra ⚓ 12D1

**Parkplatz Bürgergarten**, Haus des Gastes.
**GPS:** n51,20526 e11,57929.⬆.

10 🅿€ 3.🚐 **Location:** Urban, simple, central, quiet.
**Surface:** gravel/metalled. ☐ 01/01-31/12 ⊙ Acsension.
**Distance:** 🚶200m ⊗250m 🍺500m.

### ⌖S Bad Kösen 🌲 12E1

**Am Saalebogen**, Stendorf 14. **GPS:** n51,11356 e11,69609.⬆➡.

15 🅿€ 8 ⚡🔌Ch⚡(15x)€ 2/day WCincluded 🚿€ 1.🚐
**Location:** Rural, comfortable, quiet. **Surface:** grasstiles/metalled.
☐ 01/01-31/12.
**Distance:** 🚶3km ⊗200m 🍺bakery 200m 🚍on the spot 🚲on the
spot.

### ⌖S Bad Suderode 🌲🌿 10D2

**Restaurant Am Kurpark**, Jägerstrasse 7. **GPS:** n51,72685 e11,12078.⬆.

---

4 🅿€ 10, € 13 service incl ⚡🔌Ch⚡🍳€ 5/day.🚐
**Location:** Urban, comfortable, central, quiet.
**Surface:** grasstiles/grassy. ☐ 01/01-31/12.
**Distance:** 🚶100m ⊗on the spot 🍺200m 🚍200m 🚲on the spot
🚶on the spot.

### ⌖S Ballenstedt 🌿 10D2

**Verkehrslandeplatz Ballenstedt/Quedlinburg**, Asmusstedt 13.
**GPS:** n51,74190 e11,23427.⬆.

32 🅿€ 9 ⚡🔌Ch⚡(16x)WC🚿📶included.🚐
**Location:** Rural, simple, isolated, quiet. **Surface:** grasstiles/metalled.
☐ 01/01-31/12.
**Distance:** 🚶2km ⊗50m 🍺2km 🚍200m.

### ⌖S Bergwitz 🏖 10F2

**Camping Bergwitzsee**, Strandweg. **GPS:** n51,79439 e12,57773.⬆.

20 🅿€ 6 ⚡€ 3 🔌Ch.🚐 **Location:** Rural, simple, isolated, quiet.
**Surface:** grassy/sand. ☐ 01/01-31/12.
**Distance:** 🚶1km ⚡50m 🍺50m ⊗300m 🍺1,5km.
**Remarks:** Check in at reception campsite, service on campsite.

### ⌖S Berssel 10C2

**Gasthof Zum Schloß**, Am Schloß 1. **GPS:** n51,95266 e10,76027.⬆.

5 🅿free ⚡on demand. **Location:** Rural, simple, quiet.
**Surface:** metalled. ☐ 01/01-31/12.
**Distance:** 🚶200m ⊗on the spot 🚲on the spot 🚶on the spot.

### ⌖S Bertingen 10D1

**Hotel La Porte**, Im Wald 2. **GPS:** n52,35994 e11,82264.⬆➡.

P Wohnmobile

30 🅿€ 8,50 ⚡🔌Ch⚡included. **Location:** Rural. **Surface:** grassy.
☐ 01/01-31/12.
**Distance:** ⊗on the spot 🍺5km.
**Remarks:** Bread-service, barbecue place.

---

### ⌖S Bitterfeld 10E2

**Spaßbad Woliday**, Reudener Straße, Bitterfeld-Wolfen.
**GPS:** n51,67102 e12,24842.⬆.

10 🅿€ 13 ⚡WC🚿included. 🚐 **Location:** Rural.
**Surface:** grasstiles. ☐ 01/01-31/12.
**Distance:** 🚶1,2km ⊗on the spot 🍺900m.
**Remarks:** Incl. access swimming pool.

### ⌖S Blankenburg 🌿 10C2

**Am Schnappelberg**, Schnappelberg 2. **GPS:** n51,78862 e10,96036.⬆.

4 🅿€ 6 ⚡€ 1 ⚡€ 2/night WC.🚐 **Location:** Urban, simple, central,
quiet. **Surface:** asphalted. ☐ 01/01-31/12.
**Distance:** 🚶500m ⊗300m 🍺on the spot.

### ⌖S Blankenburg 🌿 10C2

**Busparkplatz**, Am Schnappelberg. **GPS:** n51,78884 e10,96076.⬆.

6 🅿€ 4/24h ⚡(6x)€ 1/kWh. 🚐 **Location:** Urban, simple, quiet.
**Surface:** metalled. ☐ 01/01-31/12.
**Distance:** 🚶400m ⊗300m 🍺200m 🚍on the spot 🚶on the spot.

### ⌖S Blankenburg 🌿 10C2

**Teichwirtschaft**, Harzstraße 31a, Timmenrode.
**GPS:** n51,76874 e10,99134.⬆.

10 🅿€ 9, 2 pers. incl ⚡€ 1 🔌Ch⚡€ 1 🚿€ 1.🚐 **Location:** Rural,
simple, quiet. **Surface:** grassy/metalled. ☐ 01/01-31/12.
**Distance:** 🚶Blankenburg 5km 🚍on the spot ⊗on the spot.
**Remarks:** Fishpond, playground.

### ⌖S Brachwitz 🏖 10E3

**Marina Saale-Ufer**, An der Fähre. **GPS:** n51,53388 e11,87055.⬆➡.

30 🅿€ 5 ⚡(4x)€ 0,50/kWh WC€ 2.🚐 **Location:** Rural, comfortable,
quiet. **Surface:** grassy. ☐ 01/01-31/12.
**Distance:** 🚶500m 🚍on the spot ⊗500m.

**⌂S** **Braunsbedra** 10E3

**Mobilpark am Geiseltalsee**, Schortauer Weg.
**GPS**: n51,29421 e11,85346. ⬆.

25 🛏 € 10 🚰🔌Ch 💧 € 1/kWh WCincluded 🗑 € 3 📷
against payment. 🚿 **Location:** Urban, comfortable, quiet.
**Surface:** grassy/metalled. ⬜ 01/01-31/12.
**Distance:** 🏊700m ⊗ on the spot 🛒 500m.
**Remarks:** Bread-service + breakfast-service, bike and e-bike rental.

**⛷S** **Breitenstein** 👭 10C3

Hauptstrasse, L236. **GPS**: n51,61756 e10,94957. ⬆.

8 🛏free 🚰 € 1 🔌Ch 💧 (4x) € 1/8h. **Location:** Rural, simple, quiet.
**Surface:** gravel. ⬜ 01/01-31/12.
**Distance:** 🏊400m ⊗Sportgaststätte.
**Remarks:** Next to sports fields.

**⛵S** **Burg bei Magdeburg** 〰 10E1

**Wassersportfreunde Burg**, Am Kanal 20a.
**GPS**: n52,28329 e11,84808. ⬆.

6 🛏 € 18 🚰 € 1/100liter 💧 WC🗑included. **Location:** Rural, simple,
quiet. **Surface:** grassy. ⬜ 01/05-30/09.
**Distance:** 🏊1km ⛵ on the spot.

**⛵S** **Coswig/Anhalt** 10E2

**Marina Coswig**, Post Elbstrasse 22. **GPS**: n51,88071 e12,43552. ⬆➡.

40 🛏 € 14,50, dog € 1,50 🚰 € 1/100liter 🔌Ch 💧 € 0,60/kWh
WC 🗑 € 1/4minutes. **Location:** Comfortable, quiet. **Surface:** gravel.
⬜ 01/01-31/12.
**Distance:** 🏊750m ⛵on the spot ⊗ on the spot 🛒 150m 🚌on the
spot.
**Remarks:** Breakfest-service.

**⌂S** **Coswig/Anhalt** 10E2

**Hotel Zur Fichtenbreite**, Fichtenbreite 5.
**GPS**: n51,88723 e12,40749. ⬆➡.

---

15 🛏 € 5 🚰🔌Chincluded 💧 (4x) € 2,50/day 🗑 € 3,50 📷📷
**Location:** Rural, simple, noisy. **Surface:** grassy.
⬜ 01/01-31/12 📷 24/12.
**Distance:** 🏊2km 💧 500m ⊗on the spot 🛒2km.
**Remarks:** Bread-service, bicycle rental.

**⎙S** **Dankerode** 👭 10D3

**Campingplatz Panoramablick**, Hinterdorf 79.
**GPS**: n51,58832 e11,14189. ⬆➡.

12 🛏 € 10 excl. tourist tax 🚰 € 1 🗑 € 1 Ch💧 1 (6x) € 2,50
WC 🗑 € 1 💧 € 0,50. 🚿 **Location:** Rural, simple, isolated, quiet.
**Surface:** grassy. ⬜ 01/04-30/10.
**Distance:** 🏊500m ⊗on the spot 🛒 500m 🏍 on the spot 🚶on the
spot.

**⛷S** **Darlingerode** 🏰 10C2

**Wohnmobilpark Harzblick**, Hinter den Gärten 11.
**GPS**: n51,85278 e10,73667. ⬆➡.

25 🛏 € 8 🚰 € 1/80liter 🔌Ch 💧 (12x) € 0,60/kWh 🗑 € 1/day. 🚿
**Location:** Rural, comfortable, quiet. **Surface:** grassy/gravel.
⬜ 01/01-31/12.
**Distance:** 🏊600m ⊗500m 🛒 500m 🚌500m 🏍 on the spot
🚶on the spot.

**⎙S** **Dessau-Roßlau** 10E2

**Flugplatz Hugo Junkers**, Alte Landesbahn 27.
**GPS**: n51,83447 e12,18289. ⬆.

8 🛏 € 11 🚰🔌Ch 💧 WC🗑included 🗑 🚿
**Location:** Rural, comfortable, isolated, quiet.
**Surface:** grassy/metalled. ⬜ 01/01-31/12.
**Distance:** 🏊5km ⊗1km 🛒 1km.
**Remarks:** Arrival < 19h, max. 8M, bicycle rental.

**⛵S** **Dessau-Roßlau** 10E2

**Seesport Dessau**, Leopoldshafen 4. **GPS**: n51,85648 e12,21992.
10 🛏 € 12, 2 pers.incl 🚰🔌Ch 💧 € 1 🗑 1. **Surface:** grassy.
⬜ 01/01-31/12.
**Distance:** 🏊5km 💧 500m 🛒 500m.

**⌂S** **Dessau-Roßlau** 10E2

**Bowling Treff**, Hermann-Wäschke-Weg 17. **GPS**: n51,89889 e12,25667.

---

50 🛏 € 10 🚰 € 1/80liter 🔌Ch 💧 € 2/24h. 🗑
**Surface:** grassy/gravel. ⬜ 01/01-31/12.
**Distance:** 🏊2,5km ⊗1km 🛒 800m 🚌300m.
**Remarks:** At bowling centre.

**⌂S** **Dessau-Roßlau** 10E2

**Hotel Garni Kochstedt**, Königendorfer Str. 36.
**GPS**: n51,79621 e12,17666.
5 🛏 € 20, 2 pers.incl 🚰🔌Ch 💧 WC 🗑 🗑included.
**Location:** Comfortable, isolated, quiet. **Surface:** grassy.
⬜ 01/01-31/12.
**Distance:** 🏊5km ⊗4,5km 🛒 1,5km.
**Remarks:** Breakfast-service.

**⌂S** **Drübeck/Harz** 👭 10C2

**Zur Waldschänke**, Tänntalstraße 6. **GPS**: n51,84564 e10,71415. 🧗.

8 🛏first day € 10, then € 5 🚰🔌Ch 💧included. 🚿
**Location:** Rural, simple, quiet. **Surface:** grassy/gravel.
⬜ 01/01-31/12 📷 Restaurant: Mo-Tue.
**Distance:** 🏊1,5km ⊗on the spot 🛒 2km.
**Remarks:** Breakfast-service.

**⎙S** **Elend** 🏰🌲❄ 10C2

**Waldbad Schenke**, Am Waldbad 1. **GPS**: n51,74612 e10,69531. ⬆.

10 🛏 € 5 + € 2,50/pp tourist tax 💧 (5x) € 1. 🚿
**Location:** Rural, simple, quiet. **Surface:** grassy/metalled.
⬜ 01/01-31/12.
**Distance:** 🏊600m ⊗on the spot 🚌500m 🏍 on the spot 🚶on the
spot.

**⌂S** **Freyburg/Unstrut** 🏰〰 10E3

**Stellplatz Schleusenblick**, Wasserstraße 22.
**GPS**: n51,21049 e11,76979. ⬆.

8 🛏 € 19, 2 pers.incl, tourist tax € 1,50/pp 🚰🔌Ch 💧 WCincluded
🗑 € 2/day. 🚿 **Location:** Urban, comfortable, central, quiet.
**Surface:** metalled. ⬜ 01/01-31/12.
**Distance:** 🏊100m ⊗50m 🛒 300m.
**Remarks:** Along the Unstrut river, barbecue place.

**⎙S** **Gernrode** 🏰👭 10D2

**Osterteich**, Osterallee. **GPS**: n51,72449 e11,16007. ⬆.

20 free. **Location:** Rural, simple, isolated, quiet. **Surface:** metalled. 01/01-31/12.
**Distance:** 1,5km 300m 1,5km on the spot.
**Remarks:** Next to train stop Selketalbahn.

### Haldensleben 10D1

**Am Stendaler Turm**, Bornsche Strasse. **GPS:** n52,29291 e11,41342.

10 free. **Surface:** concrete. 01/01-31/12.
**Distance:** 200m 250m 150m Aldi.

### Haldensleben 10D1

**Am Sportboothafen**, Kronesruhe. **GPS:** n52,27933 e11,40240.

15 € 10 € 1/100liter € 1 Ch. € 0,50/kWh WC € 1/4minutes
. **Location:** Rural. **Surface:** grassy. 15/04-31/10.
**Distance:** 2km 14km on the spot on the spot 200m.
**Remarks:** Bread-service.

### Halle/Saale 10E3

**Parkplatz**, Fährstraße. **GPS:** n51,50210 e11,95397.

3 € 4,50 € 1/80liter Ch. € 1/8h WC against payment.
**Location:** Urban, simple, central, noisy. **Surface:** metalled.
01/01-31/12.
**Distance:** 2km 7km 200m 500m on the spot.
**Remarks:** Max. 5 days, green zone: environmental badge obligatory.

### Halle/Saale 10E3

**P25**, An der Stadtschleuse. **GPS:** n51,48065 e11,96183.

10 free. **Location:** Urban, simple, central, noisy. **Surface:** metalled.
01/01-31/12.
**Distance:** Old city centre 500m 12km on the spot 600m
on the spot.
**Remarks:** Along railwayline, outside environmental zone.

### Harzgerode 10D3

**Parkplatz Wallgarten**, Wallstrasse. **GPS:** n51,64210 e11,13983.

4 free. **Location:** Urban, simple, quiet. **Surface:** metalled.
01/01-31/12.
**Distance:** 100m 1km 3km 100m 100m 100m
1km.
**Remarks:** Max. 1 night.

### Hasselfelde 10C3

**P Pullman City/Westernstadt**, Im Rosentale.
**GPS:** n51,70179 e10,86604.

10 € 5. **Location:** Rural, simple, quiet. **Surface:** gravel.
15/04-31/10.
**Distance:** 1km on the spot 900m.

### Havelberg 8E3

**Campinginsel**, Spülinsel 6. **GPS:** n52,82830 e12,06853.

24 € 6 € 1 € 3 Ch. (24x) 1/kWh.
**Location:** Rural. **Surface:** metalled. 01/01-31/12.
**Distance:** 1km 700m.
**Remarks:** Bread-service in summer period.

### Kelbra 10D3

**Seecamping Südharz**, L1040, Lange Straße 150.
**GPS:** n51,42583 e11,00287.

15 € 10-12 2 pers.incl, dog € 2 Ch. (16x)included against
payment. **Location:** Rural. **Surface:** gravel.
01/01-31/12.
**Distance:** 2,5km on the spot on the spot on the spot.
**Remarks:** Boat rental.

### Lutherstadt Wittenberg 10F2

**Platz der Jugend**. **GPS:** n51,86712 e12,63120.

5 free. **Location:** Urban, simple, noisy. **Surface:** metalled.
01/01-31/12.
**Distance:** centre 500m 150m 150m.
**Remarks:** Max. 8h, overnight stay allowed.

### Magdeburg 10D2

**Stellplatz Petriförde**, Petriförder 1. **GPS:** n52,13289 e11,64714.

50 € 8 € 1 € 1 Ch. **Location:** Urban. **Surface:** metalled.
01/01-31/12.
**Distance:** on the spot 850m 700m 850m.
**Remarks:** Along the river Elbe, outside environmental zone, bar.

### Merseburg 10E3

**Am Saaleufer**, Brühl. **GPS:** n51,35491 e12,00234.

3 free. **Location:** Urban, simple. **Surface:** metalled.
01/01-31/12.
**Distance:** 500m 350m 500m Saale-Rad-Wanderweg
on the spot.

### Merseburg 10E3

**Luftfahrt und Technik-museum Merseburg**, Kastanienpromenade
50. **GPS:** n51,36004 e11,97044.

6 € 8, guests free € 3 Ch. **Location:** Rural, simple, quiet.
**Surface:** gravel/metalled. 01/01-31/12.
**Distance:** 1km 1,5km.

### Naumburg/Saale 12E1

**Altstadtparkplatz Vogelwiese**, Luisenstraße.
**GPS:** n51,14861 e11,81391.

15 € 10 € 0,50/80liter Ch. (6x)€ 0,50/kWh WC.
**Location:** Rural. **Surface:** gravel. 01/01-31/12.
**Distance:** 500m 50m 500m 50m.
**Remarks:** Max. 3 days.

### Oranienbaum-Wörlitz 10E2

**Jugendverkehrsschule Oranienbaum**, Dessauer Strasse 47.
**GPS:** n51,80279 e12,39023.

6 🚐 € 7,50 ⚡ Ch ✈ (6x) WC included 🗑 € 1/day. ♿
**Location:** Rural, comfortable, quiet. **Surface:** gravel/metalled.
⏱ 01/01-31/12.
**Distance:** 🛒 1km.

### ⛟ S Prettin 10F2
**Bade- und Angelsee**, Hinterfährstraße. **GPS:** n51,66485 e12,90551.

5 🚐 € 6 + € 2,80/pp ⚡ Ch included ✈ € 0,30/kWh.
**Surface:** gravel. ⏱ 01/04-31/10.
**Distance:** 🛒 1,5km 🏊 on the spot ⊗ 1km 🍴 1km.

### ⛟ S Quedlinburg 🚶 ⚓ 10D2
**An den Fischteichen. GPS:** n51,79308 e11,14863. ⬆ ➡

20 🚐 € 10 + € 2,50/pp tourist tax ⚡ € 1/80liter 🔌 ✈ (8x) € 1/6h.
**Location:** Urban, comfortable, central, quiet.
**Surface:** grasstiles/metalled. ⏱ 01/01-31/12.
**Distance:** 🛒 350m ⊗ 300m 🍴 250m 🚌 150m.

### ⛟ S Quedlinburg 🚶 ⚓ 10D2
**Marschlinger Hof. GPS:** n51,79138 e11,13965. ⬆ ➡

6 🚐 € 15/24h ⚡ € 1/80liter 🔌 Ch ✈ (4x) € 1/6h WC. 🛁
**Location:** Urban, comfortable, central, quiet. **Surface:** metalled.
⏱ 01/01-31/12.
**Distance:** 🛒 100m ⊗ 50m 🍴 400m 🚌 200m.
**Remarks:** Max. 7m.

### ⛟ S Quedlinburg 🚶 ⚓ 10D2
**Schloßparkplatz**, Schenkgasse. **GPS:** n51,78755 e11,13507. ⬆ ➡

6 🚐 € 10/24h + tourist tax € 2,50/pp ⚡ € 1/80liter 🔌 Ch ✈
(4x) € 2/8h 🛁. **Location:** Urban, comfortable, quiet.
**Surface:** metalled. ⏱ 01/01-31/12.
**Distance:** 🛒 on the spot ⊗ 100m.
**Remarks:** At bowling centre.

### ⛟ S Quedlinburg 🚶 ⚓ 10D2
**Wohnmobilparkplatz Am Lehof**, Feldmark links der Bode 17.
**GPS:** n51,80387 e11,16803. ⬆ ➡

10 🚐 € 13 ⚡ ✈ € 2/day WC included 🗑 🛁 ♿ **Location:** Rural, simple,
quiet. **Surface:** concrete. ⏱ 01/01-31/12.
**Distance:** 🛒 2,5km ⊗ 650m.
**Remarks:** Barbecue place, use of sauna against payment.

### ⛟ S Salzwedel 8C3
**Stellplatz der Hansestadt Salzwedel**, Dämmchenweg 41.
**GPS:** n52,85049 e11,13911. ⬆

6 🚐 € 3 ⚡ Ch ✈ € 2 WC 🗑 € 2,sanitary € 2.
**Location:** Urban. **Surface:** metalled. ⏱ 01/01-31/12.
**Distance:** 🛒 historical centre 1km ⊗ 100m.
**Remarks:** Caution € 10.

### ⛟ Sangerhausen 10D3
**An der Walkmühle**, Taubenberg. **GPS:** n51,49056 e11,31127. ⬆

50 🚐 free. **Surface:** sand. ⏱ 01/01-31/12.
**Distance:** 🛒 2km ⊗ on the spot 🍴 1,5km.

### ⛟ Sangerhausen 10D3
**P7**, An der Probstmühle. **GPS:** n51,47707 e11,30798. ⬆

20 🚐 free. **Location:** Rural. **Surface:** grassy/gravel.
⏱ 01/01-31/12.
**Distance:** 🛒 500m ⊗ 200m 🚌 100m.

### 🍴 Sangerhausen 10D3
**Markl's Pferdestall**, Walkberg 1. **GPS:** n51,49417 e11,31361.
3 🚐 free ✈ on demand. **Location:** Rural. **Surface:** gravel.
⏱ 01/01-31/12 🔴 Mo.
**Distance:** 🛒 1,5km ⊗ on the spot 🍴 2km.

### S Sangerhausen 10D3
**Rosarium**, Sotterhäuser Weg. **GPS:** n51,47245 e11,31798. ⬆
⚡ € 5 🔌 Ch. **Surface:** metalled. ⏱ 15/04-15/10.
**Remarks:** Check in at shop.

### ⛟ S Schierke ⚓ ❄ 10C2
**Campingplatz Am Schierker Stern**, Hagenstrasse.
**GPS:** n51,75696 e10,68398. ⬆

6 🚐 € 10 excl. tourist tax ⚡ Ch included ✈ (6x) WC 🗑 against
payment. ♿ **Location:** Rural, simple, quiet. **Surface:** gravel/metalled.
⏱ 01/01-31/12.
**Distance:** 🛒 1km ⊗ on the spot 🍞 on the spot 🚌 on the spot 🚶 on the
spot 🍴 on the spot.

### ⛟ S Seehausen 8D3
**Stellplatz Seehausen**, Arendseer Str. 6. **GPS:** n52,89068 e11,75119. ⬆

12 🚐 € 5 ⚡ € 2 🔌 Ch ✈ (3x) € 2. **Location:** Rural. **Surface:** metalled.
⏱ 01/01-31/12.
**Distance:** 🛒 100m ⊗ 300m 🍴 200m.
**Remarks:** Check in at tourist office.

### ⛟ S Stendal 10D1
**Nordwall-Schützenplatz. GPS:** n52,61116 e11,86121. ⬆

20 🚐 free ⚡ € 1/80liter 🔌 Ch. **Surface:** grassy/metalled.
⏱ 01/01-31/12.
**Distance:** 🛒 on the spot ⊗ 500m 🍴 bakery 50m 🚌 200m.

### ⛟ Stolberg/Harz 🚶 ⚓ 🏰 🌲 10C3
**Am Bahnhof. GPS:** n51,56727 e10,95696. ⬆

5 🚐 free, tourist tax € 2/pp. **Location:** Rural, simple, quiet.
**Surface:** asphalted. ⏱ 01/01-31/12.
**Distance:** 🛒 centre 800m ⊗ 750m 🍴 350m.
**Remarks:** Max. 2 days, pay at tourist office.

### ⛟ Stolberg/Harz 🚶 ⚓ 🏰 🌲 10C3
**Am Rittertor**, Rittergasse. **GPS:** n51,57655 e10,94539. ⬆

5 🚐 free, tourist tax € 2/pp. **Location:** Rural, simple, quiet.
**Surface:** asphalted. ⏱ 01/01-31/12.
**Distance:** 🛒 1km ⊗ on the spot 🍴 2km.
**Remarks:** Max. 2 days, pay at tourist office.

DE

## Stolberg/Harz 10C3

**Freizeitbad Thyragrotte**, Thyratal 5. **GPS**: n51,56378 e10,95796.

3 free. **Location**: Rural, simple. **Surface**: asphalted.
01/01-31/12.
**Distance**: city centre 1km 1km 200m on the spot.
**Remarks**: Max. 2 days, pay at tourist office, swimming pool.

## Tangermünde 10E1

**Tangerplatz**, Klosterberg. **GPS**: n52,53774 e11,96803.

30 € 8/24h, € 14/48h Ch included.
**Surface**: metalled. 01/01-31/12.
**Distance**: 700m 150m 700m 550m.
**Remarks**: Max. 2 days.

## Wahrenberg 8D3

**Stellplatz Storchenwiese**, Eichenwinkel 34.
**GPS**: n52,98342 e11,67362.

8 € 5 € 1/100liter Ch 2 (6x)€ 2,50,16Amp.
**Location**: Rural. **Surface**: grassy. 01/01-31/12.
**Distance**: Elbe 600m on the spot on the spot.

## Weissenfels 10E3

**Caravan- und Freizeitmarkt Gerth**, Drei Wege 5.
**GPS**: n51,19822 e11,99875.

7 free € 1/80liter Ch (4x)€ 1/stay. **Location**: Urban,
simple, noisy. **Surface**: asphalted. 01/01-31/12.
**Distance**: 4km on the spot on the spot Saale–Radwander-
weg on the spot.

## Wernigerode 10C2

**Am Katzenteich**, Schlachthofstraße. **GPS**: n51,83882 e10,78168.

20 € 5/stay € 1/40liter Ch (20x)€ 1/kWh WC € 0,50.
**Location**: Comfortable, quiet. **Surface**: metalled. 01/01-31/12.

**Distance**: 500m 200m 500m on the spot on the spot
on the spot.

## Wernigerode 10C2

**Schlossparkplatz am Anger**, Halberstädler strasse 1.
**GPS**: n51,83807 e10,79535.

24 € 5 + € 2,50 tourist tax, overnight stay free € 2 Ch
WC 0,50. **Location**: Urban, simple, central, quiet.
**Surface**: metalled. 01/01-31/12, service 9-18h.
**Distance**: 300m 200m 600m on the spot on the spot.

## Wienrode 10C2

**Unterm Tappenstieg**, Harzstraße L93. **GPS**: n51,75860 e10,97998.
1 € 8 € 1 Ch € 2. **Location**: Rural. **Surface**: grassy.
01/01-31/12.
**Distance**: 900m.

## Wörlitz 10E2

**Seeparke**, Seespitze, K2376. **GPS**: n51,84899 e12,41296.

24 € 5 day/€ 5 night free (24x)€ 3 WC € 0,50 € 0,50.
**Location**: Rural, comfortable, quiet. **Surface**: metalled.
01/01-31/12.
**Distance**: 800m 500m 800m 800m on the spot on
the spot.
**Remarks**: Parking at the edge the Wörlitzer park, pay in at kiosk, max.
24h, caution key sanitary € 15.

## Wörlitz 10E2

**Hotel Coswiger Elbterrasse**, Elbterrasse 1.
**GPS**: n51,87750 e12,45097.

10 € 5, guests free **Location**: Rural, simple, quiet.
**Surface**: grassy. 01/01-31/12.
**Distance**: 1,5km on the spot on the spot 4km.
**Remarks**: Along the river Elbe, check in at hotel, guests free.

## Zeitz 12E1

**Obsthof Martin**, Kloster Posa 1. **GPS**: n51,05836 e12,15797.

20 € 5 Ch included (4x)€ 3/day.
**Location**: Rural, comfortable, quiet. **Surface**: grassy.
01/01-31/12.
**Distance**: 1,5km 200m 1km.
**Remarks**: Regional products.

# Brandenburg/Berlin

## Alt-Zeschdorf 10H1

**Reiterhof Blumrich**, Falkenhagerweg 11.
**GPS**: n52,42649 e14,42328.

30 € 10 Ch included. **Location**: Rural, simple, quiet.
**Surface**: grassy. 01/01-31/12 winter Mo.
**Distance**: 1,5km 800m.
**Remarks**: At manege, bread-service.

## Altdöbern 10H2

**Q1 Rasthof Altdöbern**, Senftenberger strasse 11.
**GPS**: n51,64523 e14,03544.

20 € 10 Ch WC included. **Location**: Rural.
**Surface**: metalled. 01/01-31/12.
**Distance**: 500m 500m.
**Remarks**: Bread kiosk.

## Angermünde 8G2

**Parkplatz Am Oberwall**, Oberwall 5. **GPS**: n53,01501 e14,00371.

5 free € 1/100liter (8x)€ 1/2kWh. **Location**: Urban, simple,
central. **Surface**: metalled. 01/04-31/10.
**Distance**: on the spot on the spot on the spot Historische
Stadtkerne Märkischer Landweg.
**Remarks**: Near city wall.

## Angermünde 8G2

**NABU-Erlebniszentrum Blumberger Mühle**, Blumberger Mühle 2.
**GPS**: n53,03572 e13,96806.

5 free. **Location**: Rural, simple, isolated, quiet.
**Surface**: grassy/metalled. 01/01-31/12.
**Distance**: 4km near fish pond on the spot on the spot
on the spot on the spot.
**Remarks**: At biosphere reserve.

## Bad Belzig 10F1

**An der SteinTherme**, Am Kurpark 15. **GPS**: n52,15153 e12,59742.

12 ⌁€ 9 + € 1,50/pp tourist tax ⌁€ 1/100liter Ch ⌁€ 1/6h.
**Location:** Rural, simple, quiet. **Surface:** metalled.
01/01-31/12.
**Distance:** 2,5km ⊗500m on the spot on the spot.

### Bad Saarow — 10G1
**Parkplatz Strolin**, Silberbergerstrasse. **GPS:** n52,28726 e14,03895.

4 ⌁free. **Location:** Rural, simple, quiet. **Surface:** metalled.
01/01-31/12.
**Distance:** 1km ⌁100m ⊗100m on the spot.
**Remarks:** Max. 24h.

### Bad Saarow — 10G1
**Saarow-Therme**, Ringstrasse. **GPS:** n52,29399 e14,06243.

6 ⌁free. **Location:** Rural, simple, quiet. **Surface:** metalled.
01/01-31/12.
**Distance:** on the spot ⊗300m 400m 200m.

### Bad Wilsnack — 8E3
**Bauernhof Nickel**, An der Kirche 8. **GPS:** n52,96523 e11,85283.

2 ⌁€ 15/night, 2 pers. incl ⌁ included. **Location:** Rural, simple, quiet. **Surface:** grassy. 01/01-31/12.
**Distance:** 250m.

## WohnmobilPark Berlin

- Paved and flat motorhome pitches
- Sanitary facilities
- Comfortable motorhome stopover
- Reservations possible
- Outside environmental zone
- Point of interest
- Old town
- Located in a quiet area
- Open all year

---

**Remarks:** Barbecue place.

### Bad Wilsnack — 8E3
**Kur- und Gradier-Therme Bad Wilsnack**, Am Kähling.
**GPS:** n52,96316 e11,95007.

80 ⌁€ 13,50 + € 1/pp tourist tax ⌁Ch (32x)WC included.
01/01-31/12 24/12.
**Distance:** 500m ⊗200m 500m.
**Remarks:** Check in at pay-desk of the Therme, bread-service, discount on access sauna/wellness.

### Baruth — 10G2
**Spruch's Alter Landgasthof**, Dornswalder Straße 1.
**GPS:** n52,04484 e13,59732.

20 ⌁€ 8 ⌁liter Ch included. **Location:** Rural, simple, isolated, quiet. **Surface:** metalled. 01/01-31/12.
**Distance:** ⊗on the spot 10km.
**Remarks:** Max. 24h, free with a meal.

### Beeskow — 10H1
**An der Marina**, Spreeinsel 5. **GPS:** n52,17017 e14,25313.

30 ⌁€ 12 ⌁€ 2/100liter ⌁€ 2/time Ch € 1/10minutes.
**Location:** Rural, simple, quiet. **Surface:** grassy/gravel.
01/01-31/12.
**Distance:** 500m ⊗200m.

### Berlin — 10F1
**Historisches Fährhaus Berlin**, Muggelbergallee 1, Berlin-Köpenick.
**GPS:** n52,41851 e13,58734.

---

15 ⌁€ 19-23 incl. 2 pers, dog € 3 ⌁Ch (15x)€ 4/24h WC included € 1/5minutes € 5/stay. **Location:** Urban, luxurious, quiet. **Surface:** grassy/gravel. 01/01-31/12.
**Distance:** on the spot 8km on the spot on the spot ⊗on the spot 100m, supermarket 750m 1km tram 100m.
**Remarks:** Along river, outside environmental zone, possibility for reservation, sauna € 5.

### Berlin — 10F1
**Reisemobilhafen Berlin Spandau**, Askanierring 70.
**GPS:** n52,55309 e13,20050.

180 ⌁€ 16 2p incl. + tourist tax € 1, dog € 2 ⌁€ 0,10/10liter Ch WC included € 1/5minutes € 2/24h.
**Location:** Urban, simple, central, noisy. **Surface:** grassy/gravel.
01/01-31/12.
**Distance:** on the spot ⊗100m 900m on the spot 300m.
**Remarks:** Near approach route of airport, 23-5h quiet, check in at kosk, outside environmental zone. In area of the former English barracks 'Alexander Barracks', A10 exit Berlin-Spandau, follow road till cross roads Heerstraße/Gatowerstraße, here to the left, at Flakenseerplatz straight on, Neuendorferstraße, before Hohenzollernring to the left.

### Berlin — 10F1
**Köpenicker Hof**, Stellingdamm 15, Berlin-Köpenick.
**GPS:** n52,45929 e13,58532.

40 ⌁€ 12-18 2 pers. Incl., dog € 3 ⌁€ 1/80liter Ch € 0,50/kWh WC included. **Location:** Urban, simple, quiet.
**Surface:** grassy/metalled. 01/01-31/12.
**Distance:** on the spot ⊗on the spot Tram (centre 300m).
**Remarks:** Caution key sanitary building € 20, bread-service, dog € 1,50/night, outside environmental zone.

### Berlin — 10F1
**WohnmobilPark Berlin**, Waidmannsluster Damm 12-14.
**GPS:** n52,59559 e13,28910.

90 ⌁€ 10-24, 2 pers.incl, tourist tax € 1/pp, dog € 2 € 1/100liter Ch € 4/24h,3Amp WC sanitary € 5/day € 4/4. **Location:** Urban, comfortable, central, quiet.
**Surface:** grassy/metalled. 01/01-31/12.
**Distance:** centre Berlin 16km 600m ⊗on the spot on the spot metro 1km.
**Remarks:** Key sanitary building € 4/day, outside environmental zone, hotline-Nr.: 0176 – 99 55 25 00.

## Berlin 10F1
**Wohnmobil-Oase-Berlin**, Hochstraße 4.
**GPS**: n52,54884 e13,38384.

100 € 23-32 + € 1/pp tourist tax, dog € 2,50 € 1/100liter Ch included WC sanitary € 2/day
**Location**: Urban, simple, central, quiet.
**Surface**: asphalted.
01/01-31/12.
**Distance**: on the spot 600m 300m on the spot.
**Remarks**: Bread-service, barbecue place..

## Berlin 10F1
**Marina Lanke Berlin**, Scharfe Lanke 109-131.
**GPS**: n52,50344 e13,18801.

20 € 12-16, dog € 2 Ch WC included € 3/2.
**Location**: Urban, comfortable. **Surface**: asphalted.
01/05-15/10.
**Distance**: centre Berlin 16km on the spot on the spot 1km on the spot.
**Remarks**: Check in at harbourmaster, outside environmental zone.

## Berlin 10F1
**Marina Wendenschloss**, Wendenschlossstrasse 350-354.
**GPS**: n52,42558 e13,58384.

10 € 15-20 Ch WC included € 1/5minutes.
**Location**: Urban, simple, quiet. **Surface**: grassy/metalled.
01/04-31/10.
**Distance**: 18km city centre on the spot on the spot 100m Tram 200m.
**Remarks**: Outside environmental zone, barbecue place, boat rental.

## Berlin 10F1
**Sunset Marina**, Siemenswerderweg 42.
**GPS**: n52,50646 e13,20206.

12 € 30 Ch night WC € 1/time included.
**Location**: Rural, comfortable, quiet.
**Surface**: grassy.
01/03-31/10.
**Distance**: 8km 600m 500m.

**Tourist information Berlin:**
Berlin Card gives for free entrance on public transport and museums and many discounts on purchases. from € 42.
Tourist Info, Europacenter, Eingang Budapester strasse 3; Branden-

burgertor, Südflügel; Fernsehturm, Alexanderplatz, http://www.visitberlin.de/. Documentation available, via Internet.
Haus am Checkpoint Charly, Friedrichstrasse 44. At the former border crossing. History of the Wall is told with photographs. 9-22h.
Zeughaus. German historical museum.
Alexanderplatz. The old historical centre of Berlin.
Brandenburger Tor. Built in 1791 as a triumphal arch after the construction of the Berlin Wall the arch remained as a symbol of the German separation. free.
Schloß Charlottenburg, Spandauer Damm 10-22. Summer residence of the Prussian kings.
Tue-Su 10-18h 01/11-31/03.
€ 10.
Arkonaplatz. Flea market. Su 10-16h.
Ostbahnhof. Antiques and flea market. Su 9-17h.
Strasse des 17. Juni. Arts and fleamarket. Sa-Su 10-17h.
Zoologischer Garten, Hardenbergplatz 8. City-zoo. 01/04-30/09 9-18.30h, 01/10-31/10 9-18h, 01/11-28/02 9-17h.

## Brandenburg 10E1
**Am Brandenburger Dom**, Grillendamm.
**GPS**: n52,41724 e12,56576.

60 € 10 € 1/100liter Ch (26x) € 1/kWh WC € 1/4minutes.
**Location**: Urban, simple, noisy. **Surface**: asphalted.
01/01-31/12.
**Distance**: Neustadt 15min, Altstadt 15min on the spot Imbiss 50m on the spot on the spot.
**Remarks**: Next to sports fields.

## Brandenburg 10E1
**Wassersportzentrum Alte Feuerwache**, Franz Zieglerstrasse 27.
**GPS**: n52,40485 e12,54868.

30 € 12 Ch € 1/day WC € 1 included.
**Location**: Urban, simple, central, noisy. **Surface**: grassy/metalled.
01/01-31/12.
**Distance**: 500m on the spot 500m 1,2km 300m on the spot on the spot.
**Remarks**: Bread-service, boat rental, bike and e-bike rental.

## Brandenburg 10E1
**Stadtmarina**, Am Hafen 7. **GPS**: n52,42483 e12,55363.

25 € 12, 01/05-30/09 € 16 € 1/100liter Ch € 0,50/kWh € 2/pppd € 4/4 included. **Location**: Urban, comfortable.
**Surface**: asphalted/metalled. 01/01-31/12.
**Distance**: 1,5km 500m 500m on the spot on the spot.

## Breydin 8G3
**Landhotel Trampe**, Am Landhotel 1. **GPS**: n52,76898 e13,84030.

6 € 12 included. **Location**: Rural, simple.
**Surface**: gravel/metalled. 01/01-31/12.
**Distance**: 500m on the spot.
**Remarks**: Check in at restaurant.

## Burg/Spreewald 10H2
**Landgasthof zur Wildbahn**, Wildbahnweg 20.
**GPS**: n51,85104 e14,09384.

9 € 20, 2 pers. incl., dog € 2 WC included.
**Location**: Rural, comfortable, isolated, quiet. **Surface**: grassy.
01/03-30/10.
**Distance**: on the spot 1km 1km.
**Remarks**: Water closed during wintertime.

## Chorin 8G3
**Auf dem Ökohof Engler**, Serwester Dorfstraße 72.
**GPS**: n52,92910 e13,92502.

3 € 10 € 2,50/24h Ch included € 2,50/24h WC € 5/time. **Location**: Rural, simple, isolated, quiet. **Surface**: grassy.
01/01-31/12.
**Distance**: 300m 2km 5km.

## Dollenchen 10G2
**Gasthaus Stuckatz**, Hauptstrasse 29. **GPS**: n51,60745 e13,86226.

20 € 10, 2 pers. incl. Ch WC included.
**Location**: Rural, simple, quiet. **Surface**: grassy. 01/01-31/12.
**Distance**: on the spot on the spot 3km on the spot.
**Remarks**: Check in at restaurant, barbecue place, bike and e-bike rental, charging point for electric bicycles.

## Dreetz 8E3
**Reiterhof Müller**, Schulstrasse 61. **GPS**: n52,79796 e12,46874.

10 € 14 Ch included WC. **Location**: Rural, simple,

isolated, quiet. **Surface:** grassy. ◻ 01/01-31/12.
**Distance:** 🚶800m 🏊300m ⚓500m 🚌200m.

---

### ⚐S Fehrbellin — 8F3

**FF Freizeitmobile**, Gewerbepark 29. **GPS:** n52,79770 e12,78624. ⬆️➡️.

10 ⚐€ 7,50 🚐🔌Ch included ⚡€ 2,50/day WC 💧free. 🚿
**Location:** Urban, simple, quiet.
**Surface:** grassy.
◻ 01/01-31/12.
**Distance:** 🚶1km 🏊2km ⊗1km ⚓1km 🚲on the spot 🚶on the spot.
**Remarks:** Accessory shop.

---

### ⚑S Felixsee — 10H2

**Wohnmobil-Stellplatz Minipony-Ranch**, Ohmixstraße 4.
**GPS:** n51,60601 e14,51249.

22 ⚐€ 11 🚐🔌Ch ⚡€ 2/day WC 💧included. **Location:** Rural,
comfortable, quiet. **Surface:** grassy/gravel. ◻ 01/04-15/10.
**Distance:** 🚶100m 🏊15km ⊗400m ⚓300m 🚲50m 🚶50m.
**Remarks:** Bike and e-bike rental.

---

### ⚑S Finsterwalde — 10G2

Karl-Marx-Straße 5. **GPS:** n51,63295 e13,71033. ⬆️.

4 ⚐free ⚡€ 1/100liter 🔌Ch ⚡(4x)€ 1/2kWh.
**Location:** Urban, simple, central. **Surface:** metalled.
◻ 01/01-31/12 💧 water: 01/10-31/03.
**Distance:** 🚶200m ⊗on the spot.

---

### ⚑⚑S Frankfurt (Oder) — 10H1

**Marina Winterhafen**, Hafenstrasse 2. **GPS:** n52,35497 e14,55021. ⬆️➡️.

7 ⚐€ 15, 2 pers.incl 🚐🔌Ch ⚡€ 0,50/kWh WC 💧included.
**Location:** Urban, comfortable, central, quiet. **Surface:** grassy.
◻ 01/01-31/12.
**Distance:** 🚶1km 🏊on the spot 🛶on the spot ⊗400m ⚓on the spot 🚲on the spot 🚶on the spot.
**Remarks:** Arrival 15.30><18h.

---

### ⚑⚑S Fürstenberg/Havel — 8F2

**Marina Fürstenberg**, Ravensbrücker Dorfstrasse 26.
**GPS:** n53,19489 e13,14895. ⬆️➡️.

---

50 ⚐€ 12-14 🚐€ 1,50/100liter 🔌Ch ⚡€ 0,60/kWh WC 💧€ 0,50
💧. 🚿 **Location:** Rural, comfortable, quiet. **Surface:** grassy.
◻ 29/03-31/10.
**Distance:** 🚶1km 🏊on the spot 🛶on the spot ⊗on the spot ⚓1km 🚲on the spot 🚶on the spot.
**Remarks:** Wifi code at harbour master, boat rental, near the former women's concentration camp Ravensbrück.

---

### ⚑⚑S Havelsee — 10E1

**Havel-Oase**, Vor dem Kietz 8a. **GPS:** n52,49667 e12,45150. ⬆️.

20 ⚐€ 10-15 🚐🔌Ch ⚡€ 1/kWh WC included 💧 1,50/5minutes
💧 1,50/324h. 🚿🚿 **Location:** Rural, luxurious, quiet.
**Surface:** grassy. ◻ 01/04-30/10.
**Distance:** 🚶300m ⚓200m.

---

### ⚑⚑S Höhenland — 8G3

**Das Forsthaus**, Bahnhofstraße 13. **GPS:** n52,68433 e13,88171. ⬆️➡️.

8 ⚐€ 11 🚐🔌Ch ⚡ WC 💧included 💧€ 5/day. 🚿
**Location:** Rural, comfortable, quiet. **Surface:** grasstiles.
◻ 01/01-31/12.
**Distance:** 🚶3km ⊗on the spot 🚲on the spot 🚶on the spot.
**Remarks:** Bread-service.

---

### ⚑⚑S Hoppegarten — 8G3

Schwarzer Weg 2. **GPS:** n52,55665 e13,64815. ⬆️.

4 ⚐€ 15 🚐🔌Ch ⚡€ 1 💧. **Location:** Rural, simple, isolated, quiet.
**Surface:** grassy. ◻ 01/01-31/12.
**Distance:** ⊗2km ⚓2km.
**Remarks:** Max. 7 days.

---

### ⚑⚑S Kienitz — 8H3

**Ferienhaus Marth**, Kienitzeroderstrasse 20.
**GPS:** n52,67616 e14,39890. ⬆️.

---

8 ⚐€ 10 🚐🔌Ch ⚡€ 1,50 WC included 💧 1,50.
**Location:** Rural, simple, quiet. **Surface:** grassy. ◻ 01/04-30/09.
**Distance:** 🚶3km 🏊3km 🚌100m.

---

### ⚑⚑S Kloster Lehnin — 10F1

**Hotel Seehof**, Am See 51. **GPS:** n52,34924 e12,70374. ⬆️.

15 ⚐€ 10, guests free 🚐🔌Ch ⚡€ 2/day WC included 💧€ 2. 🚿🚿
**Location:** Rural, comfortable. **Surface:** grassy/metalled.
◻ 01/01-31/12.
**Distance:** 🚲1,8km 🏊on the spot ⊗on the spot 🚲on the spot 🚶on the spot.
**Remarks:** Check in at hotel.

---

### ⚑S Kolkwitz — 10H2

**Bauernhof Korreng**, Papitzerstrasse 48. **GPS:** n51,76676 e14,22410. ⬆️.

3 ⚐€ 12 🚐🔌Ch ⚡ WC included. **Location:** Rural, quiet.
**Surface:** grassy. ◻ 01/03-31/10.
**Distance:** 🚶2,5km 🚌400m.

---

### ⚑⚑S Kyritz — 8E3

**Parkplatz Wässering**, Graf-von-der-Schulenburg-Straße.
**GPS:** n52,94044 e12,40053. ⬆️.

15 ⚐free ⚡€ 1/100liter 🔌Ch ⚡€ 1/8h WC€ 0,50 💧€ 1.
**Location:** Urban, comfortable, noisy. **Surface:** grasstiles.
◻ 01/01-31/12.
**Distance:** 🚶city centre 100m 🏊on the spot ⊗250m ⚓250m 🚲on the spot 🚶on the spot.

---

### ⚑S Lauchhammer — 10G3

**Grünewalder Lauch**, Lauchstraße 101.
**GPS:** n51,50751 e13,66849. ⬆️➡️.

54 ⚐€ 18 🚐🔌Ch ⚡(54x)€ 0,60/16kWh WC 💧included. 🚍
**Location:** Rural, comfortable. **Surface:** gravel. ◻ 01/04-01/11.
**Distance:** 🏊on the spot 🛶on the spot 🚲on the spot 🚶on the spot.
**Remarks:** Bread-service, monitored parking.

---

### S Lindow/Mark — 8F3

Am Wutzsee. **GPS:** n52,97205 e12,98924. ⬆️.

3 ⌁ free, tourist tax € 0,50/pp. 🚿 **Location:** Urban, simple, noisy.
**Surface:** metalled. ⬛ 01/01-31/12.
**Distance:** 🚰 on the spot ⚓ on the spot ⊗150m 🚮150m 🚲 on the spot 🚶 on the spot.
**Remarks:** Max. 1 night, pay at tourist office.

| 🅿️ 🆂 | **Lübbenau** | 10G2 |

**Autocamping Käppler**, Chausseestrasse 17a, Lübbenau-Zerkwitz.
**GPS:** n51,86559 e13,93324. ⬆️ ➡️.

6 ⌁ € 16/24h + € 1,50/pp tourist tax, dog € 1 🚰 🔌 Ch 🔧 WC
⬛ included. **Location:** Urban, comfortable, quiet.
**Surface:** grasstiles/grassy. ⬛ Easter-31/10.
**Distance:** ⚓2,5km ⊗1,5km 🚮500m 🚲 on the spot 🚶 on the spot.

| 🅿️ 🆂 | **Lübbenau** | 10G2 |

**Spreewald Wohnmobilpark**, Dammstraße 62.
**GPS:** n51,86219 e13,97090. ⬆️ ➡️.

30 ⌁ € 17-19, 2 pers. incl, tourist tax € 2/pp 🚰 🔌 Ch 🔧 € 0,50/kWh
⬛ € 1/3minutes ⬛ € 3/time 📶 included.
**Location:** Rural. **Surface:** grassy. ⬛ Easter-15/10.
**Distance:** 🚰 on the spot ⚓100m 🚮 on the spot 🚉 station 1km.

| 🅿️ 🆂 | **Lübbenau** | 10G2 |

**Am Bahnhof**, Bahnhofstraße (B115). **GPS:** n51,86139 e13,96361.

10 ⌁ € 8 🚰 € 1/80liter 🔌 Ch 🔧 (10x) € 0,50/kWh. 🚮
**Location:** Urban, noisy. **Surface:** asphalted. ⬛ 01/01-31/12.
**Distance:** 🚰800m ⚓3,3km ⊗350m 🚮50m 🚉 on the spot.
**Remarks:** Along railwayline, max. 2 days.

| 🅿️ 🆂 | **Luckau** | 10G2 |

Südpromenade 11. **GPS:** n51,85026 e13,71305. ⬆️.

15 ⌁ € 6 🚰 🔌 Ch included WC € 1/time. 🚮 **Location:** Rural, simple,

quiet. **Surface:** grasstiles/metalled. ⬛ 01/01-31/12.
**Distance:** 🚰500m ⊗300m.

| 🚤 🆂 | **Lychen** 🏘️ 🏖️ | 8F2 |

**Marina-Yachthafen Lychensee**, Schlüssstrasse 7.
**GPS:** n53,21187 e13,29686. 🚶.

6 ⌁ € 10 🚰 🔌 Ch 🔧 € 2,50/day WC ⬛ € 1. 🚿 **Location:** Rural,
simple, quiet. **Surface:** grassy. ⬛ 15/04-15/10.
**Distance:** 🚰700m 🚮650m.
**Remarks:** Check in at harbourmaster, boat rental.

| 🅿️ 🆂 | **Märkische Heide** | 10G1 |

**Mobilhafen Halbinsel Raatsch**, Halbinsel Raatsch 1.
**GPS:** n52,11550 e13,92784.
15 ⌁ € 10 🚰 🔌 Ch 🔧. **Location:** Rural, simple, isolated.
**Surface:** grassy. ⬛ 01/01-31/12.
**Distance:** 🚲 on the spot 🚶 on the spot.

| 🚤 🆂 | **Muggerkuhl** | 8D2 |

Dorfstraße 8. **GPS:** n53,26223 e11,90419. ⬆️ ➡️.

3 ⌁ € 5 🚰 € 1/100liter 🔌 Ch 🔧 € 1. **Location:** Rural, isolated, quiet.
**Surface:** metalled. ⬛ 01/01-31/12.
**Distance:** 🚰3km 🚮3,5km 🚲 on the spot.

| 🍴 🆂 | **Nackel** | 8E3 |

**Gaststätte Birkenhof**, Segeletzerstrasse 2.
**GPS:** n52,82503 e12,56528. ⬆️.

3 ⌁ € 3 🚰 € 3 🔌 Ch 🔧 WC included. 🚿
**Location:** Rural, simple, isolated, quiet. **Surface:** metalled.
⬛ 01/01-31/12 ⬛ Tue.
**Distance:** 🚰5km ⊗ on the spot 🚲 on the spot 🚶 on the spot.

| 🅿️ 🆂 | **Neuruppin** 🌿 🏖️ 🏘️ 🏖️ | 8F3 |

**Sportcenter Neuruppin**, Trenckmannstrasse 14.
**GPS:** n52,91573 e12,80365. ⬆️.

30 ⌁ € 6 WC ⬛ € 2,50 📶. 🚿 **Location:** Urban, simple, quiet.
**Surface:** grasstiles. ⬛ 01/01-31/12.
**Distance:** 🚰 on the spot ⚓Neuruppiner See 500m ⊗ on the spot
🚮200m, bakery 400m 🚲 on the spot 🚶 on the spot.
**Remarks:** Check in at sport centre.

| 🅿️ 🆂 | **Oberkrämer** 🌿 🏖️ | 8F3 |

**Bäckerei Plentz**, Dorfstraße 43. **GPS:** n52,73643 e13,08540. ⬆️ ➡️.

4 ⌁ € 8 🚰 🔌 Ch 🔧 WC included. 🚿 **Location:** Rural, simple, quiet.
**Surface:** metalled. ⬛ 01/01-31/12.
**Distance:** 🚰 on the spot 🚏1km ⊗700m 🚮500m 🚉train 500m
🚲 on the spot 🚶 on the spot.
**Remarks:** Along railwayline, in front of bakery, max. 48h.

| 🚤 🆂 | **Oranienburg** 🏖️ | 8F3 |

**Am Schlosshafen**, Rungestrasse 47. **GPS:** n52,75760 e13,23879. ⬆️.

36 ⌁ € 15, dog € 2 🚰 € 1,50/80liter 🔌 Ch 🔧 (16x) € 1/kWh WC € 0,50
⬛ € 1/5minutes ⬛ € 5. 🚮
**Location:** Rural, comfortable, central, quiet. **Surface:** metalled.
⬛ 01/01-31/12.
**Distance:** 🚰600m ⚓ on the spot ⊗600m 🚮600m 🚲 on the spot
🚶 on the spot.
**Remarks:** Tallycard: service, electricity, sanitary building, caution € 10.

| 🍴 🆂 | **Oranienburg** 🏖️ | 8F3 |

**Motel Havelidyll**, Havelhausener Brücke 1, Havelhausen.
**GPS:** n52,72161 e13,25047. 🚶.

5 ⌁ € 15, 2 pers.incl, dog € 2,50 🚰 🔌 Ch 🔧 WC ⬛ 📶 included. 🚿
**Location:** Rural, simple, isolated, quiet. **Surface:** grassy.
⬛ 01/04-15/11.
**Distance:** 🚰10km ⚓4km ⚓ on the spot ⊗ on the spot 🚮900m
🚉900m.

| 🅿️ 🆂 | **Ortrand** 🏘️ | 10G3 |

**Erlebniscamping Lausitz**, Am Bad 1. **GPS:** n51,37272 e13,77947. ⬆️ ➡️.
6 ⌁ € 9, dog € 1,50 🚰 € 2,50 🔌 Ch € 2,50 🔧 € 0,50/kWh WC ⬛
⬛ € 2,50/2,50. 🚮 🚲
**Location:** Rural, quiet. **Surface:** grassy/metalled. ⬛ 01/01-31/12.
**Distance:** 🚰2km ⚓3km 🚏 on the spot 🚮2km 🚲2km 🚲 on the spot
🚶 on the spot.
**Remarks:** Use sanitary € 2,50/pp per day.

DE

## Perleberg 8D3

Neue Mühle 3. **GPS:** n53,09125 e11,87066.

18 € 10 Ⓒincluded € 2 € 1/3minutes.
**Location:** Rural, simple, isolated, quiet. **Surface:** grassy.
01/01-31/12.
**Distance:** 2km on the spot 1,5km.

## Potsdam 10F1

Am Krongut, Potsdamer Straße 196. **GPS:** n52,41332 e13,02905.

11 € 10/24h. **Location:** Urban, simple. **Surface:** concrete.
01/01-31/12.
**Distance:** city centre 2km 100m 500m Tram 300m.

## Potsdam 10F1

Historische Mühle von Sanssouci, Maulbeerallee 5.
**GPS:** n52,40562 e13,03453.

5 € 2/h, max. € 20/24h. **Location:** Urban, simple.
**Surface:** metalled. 01/01-31/12.
**Distance:** 2km on the spot 500m.

## Potsdam 10F1

Zum Alten Krug, Hauptstraße 2. **GPS:** n52,45606 e12,96616.

8 € 10 Ch € 2,50/day included. **Location:** Rural,
simple, noisy. **Surface:** gravel. 01/01-31/12 Mo.
**Distance:** on the spot on the spot on the spot on the spot
on the spot.
**Remarks:** Playground.

**Tourist information Potsdam:**
Filmpark Babelsberg, Großbeerenstrasse 200. Attractions park
concerning the film. 23/03-31/10 10-18.

## Prenden 8G3

Ützdorfer Straße 3. **GPS:** n52,79131 e13,54553.

---

7 free € 1 (7x)€ 1/4h. **Location:** Rural, simple, quiet.
**Surface:** metalled/sand. 01/01-31/12.
**Distance:** 400m 1,5km.
**Remarks:** Max. 72h.

## Pritzwalk 8E2

Dömnitzinsel, Gartenstrasse/Meyenburger Tor.
**GPS:** n53,15196 e12,17746.

6 € 10 € 1/10minutes Ch (8x)€ 1/8h. **Location:** Urban,
simple, quiet. **Surface:** asphalted/metalled. 01/01-31/12.
**Distance:** 400m 100m on the spot on the spot.

## Pritzwalk 8E2

Hainholz, Hainholzweg. **GPS:** n53,16883 e12,19338.

4 free (4x)€ 1/2kWh. **Location:** Rural, simple, isolated, quiet.
**Surface:** grasstiles/metalled. 01/01-31/12.
**Distance:** 3km 2,5km.
**Remarks:** At swimming pool, shady.

## Rathenow 10E1

Baustraße 11. **GPS:** n52,60786 e12,33618.

5 free € 1/80liter Ch (4x)€ 1/2kWh. **Location:** Urban,
simple, noisy. **Surface:** metalled. 01/01-31/12.
**Distance:** 500m 400m on the spot on the spot.

## Rehfelde 8G3

Campershof, Alt Werder 8. **GPS:** n52,52012 e13,94646.

12 € 7,50 Ⓒincluded € 1,50/day WC € 2,50.
**Location:** Rural, comfortable, quiet. **Surface:** grassy.
01/01-31/12.
**Distance:** 2km 2km 2km on the spot on the spot.
**Remarks:** Bread-service.

## Rheinsberg 8F2

Friedrichszentrum 1. **GPS:** n53,10415 e12,89484.

---

4 free. **Location:** Urban, simple. **Surface:** metalled.
01/01-31/12.
**Distance:** 500m on the spot.

## Schmergow 10F1

Zum fröhlichen Landmann, Ziegeleiweg 17.
**GPS:** n52,45416 e12,80553.

30 € 7,50 Ch € 1/2kWh included.
**Location:** Rural, simple, isolated. **Surface:** grassy.
01/04-31/10.
**Distance:** 500m on the spot 500m 400m.

## Schmerkendorf 10G3

Stellplatz Schmerkendorf, Hauptstraße 45.
**GPS:** n51,56633 e13,25277.

10 € 5 € 1/80liter € 2/24h WC € 3/24h.
**Location:** Rural, comfortable, isolated, quiet. **Surface:** grassy.
01/01-31/12.
**Distance:** 2,5km 3km 2km 2km.
**Remarks:** Bread-service (weekend), sauna € 5.

## Schwedt/Oder 8H2

Wassersportzentrum Schwedt, Regattastrasse 3.
**GPS:** n53,05759 e14,29861.

30 € 5 + € 5/pp, dog € 1 Ch WC € 1,50/time
included.
**Location:** Urban. **Surface:** grassy.
01/01-31/12 Mo.
**Distance:** 1km on the spot on the spot 500m on the spot
on the spot.
**Remarks:** Check in at harbourmaster or bar, breakfast-service.

## Schwedt/Oder 8H2

Uckermark-Wohnmobile, Am Wasserplatz 4.
**GPS:** n53,05813 e14,29788.
8 € 10-15 Ch 4kWh WCincluded € 2.
**Location:** Urban, comfortable, central, quiet. **Surface:** grassy.
01/01-31/12.
**Distance:** on the spot 300m 300m.
**Remarks:** At motorhome dealer, barbecue place, bicycle rental.

## Senftenberg 10H3

Wohnmobilstellplatz Buchwalde, Buchwalder Straße 52.
**GPS:** n51,51256 e14,02278.

12 ⃞€ 15 ⛽🚰Ch🚿€ 2/24h WCincluded ⛽€ 0,50/3minutes.
**Location:** Rural. **Surface:** gravel. 🅾 01/04-01/11.
**Distance:** 🚲2km 🏊Senftenberger See ⊗on the spot 🚐on the spot
🚶on the spot.
**Remarks:** Max. 4 nights, caution key sanitary € 20, barbecue place, playground.

🄲🅂 **Senftenberg** 10H3

**Reimann-Mobile**, Brieske Dorf 27. **GPS:** n51,49069 e13,94885.➡️.

20 ⃞€ 7 ⛽🚰Chincluded 🚿(12x)€ 2 WC. **Location:** Rural, simple,
quiet. **Surface:** grassy. 🅾 01/01-31/12.
**Distance:** 🚲4km ⊗on the spot 🛒2km 🏍on the spot.
**Remarks:** Bread-service, playground.

🄲🅂 **Senftenberg** 10H3

**Familienpark Senftenberger See**, Straße zur Südsee 1.
**GPS:** n51,49206 e14,04650.⬆️.

5 ⃞€ 15-19 ⛽🚰Ch🚿included 🍴€ 0,50 🅿€ 2/time.🛒
**Location:** Rural, simple. **Surface:** grassy/gravel.
🅾 01/01-31/12.
**Distance:** 🚲8km 🏊on the spot ⊗300m 🚐on the spot 🏍on the spot.
**Remarks:** Max. 1 night.

🄲🅂 **Stolzenhagen** 8G3

**Am Kietz**, Kietz 9. **GPS:** n52,94916 e14,10833.⬆️➡️.

20 ⃞€ 7,50 ⛽🚰Ch🚿(10x)€ 2,50/day WCincluded 🍴€ 2,50/pp.🛒
**Location:** Rural, comfortable, quiet. **Surface:** grassy/metalled.
🅾 01/01-31/12.
**Distance:** 🏊on the spot ⊗Imbiss 🚐600m 🚴Oder-Neiße-Radweg
🚶on the spot.
**Remarks:** Directly on the canal, check in at Imbiss, bread-service.

🄲🅂 **Storkow/Mark** 10G1

**An der Schleuse**, Kirchstrasse. **GPS:** n52,25792 e13,93178.⬆️➡️.

---

5 ⃞€ 10 🚰🚿 included. **Location:** Rural. **Surface:** grasstiles.
🅾 01/01-31/12.
**Distance:** 🚲200m ⊗300m 🛒500m.
**Remarks:** At the Storkower Canal, max. 36h.

🄲🅂 **Templin** 8F2

Alter Knehdenerstrasse. **GPS:** n53,12359 e13,49423.⬆️➡️.

40 ⃞free ⛽€ 1/60liter 🚿Ch. **Location:** Urban, simple, quiet.
**Surface:** asphalted/metalled. 🅾 01/01-31/12.
**Distance:** 🚲300m ⊗300m 🛒300m 🚐on the spot 🚶on the spot.

🄶🅂 **Templin** 8F2

**Wohnmobilstellplatz an der NaturTherme**, Dargersdorfer Straße 121.
**GPS:** n53,10201 e13,52762.⬆️.

50 ⃞€ 15 ⛽€ 1/100liter 🚰€ 2/time Ch€ 2 🚿(50x)€ 0,50/kWh
WC€ 2/30minutes 🅿€ 2/2 🔌included.🛒
**Location:** Rural, luxurious, quiet. **Surface:** asphalted/grassy.
🅾 01/01-31/12.
**Distance:** 🚲on the spot 🏊1km 🛶1km ⊗100m 🛒1,8km 🚐200m
🏍on the spot 🚶on the spot.
**Remarks:** Bread-service, barbecue place, discount on access terme.

🄲🅂 **Tiefensee** 8G3

**Reisemobilplatz, Country Camping Tiefensee**, Schmiedeweg 1.
**GPS:** n52,68302 e13,84292.⬆️➡️.

64 ⃞€ 16,50 incl. 2 pers, dog € 1,50 ⛽🚰Ch🚿(51x)WCincluded
🍴€ 0,50 🅿€ 2,50.🛒 **Location:** Rural, comfortable, quiet.
**Surface:** grassy. 🅾 01/01-31/12.
**Distance:** 🚲on the spot 🏊on the spot 🛶on the spot ⊗on the spot
🛒on the spot 🚐on the spot 🏍on the spot 🚶on the spot.
**Remarks:** Check in at reception campsite.

🄲🅂 **Weisen** 8D3

**Wohnmobilstellplatz Am Biotop**, Heinrich-Heine-Strasse 4.
**GPS:** n53,01983 e11,78134.⬆️.

---

8 ⃞€ 5 ⛽🚰Chincluded. **Location:** Rural, simple. **Surface:** gravel.
🅾 01/04-30/09.
**Distance:** 🚲300m ⊗200m 🛒300m.

🄲🅂 **Werder/Havel** 🌿🏕🚣 10F1

Unter den Linden. **GPS:** n52,37807 e12,93704.⬆️.

25 ⃞€ 7 + € 1,50/pp tourist tax 🚰€ 0,50/80liter 🚿Ch🚿(8x)€ 0,50/
kWh WC€ 0,50.🛒 **Location:** Urban, simple. **Surface:** gravel.
🅾 01/01-31/12.
**Distance:** 🚲on the spot 🏊on the spot ⊗on the spot 🛒on the spot
🚐100m 🏍on the spot.
**Remarks:** Check in at harbourmaster.

🄲🅂 **Wittenberge** 🚣 8D3

**Nedwiganger**, Elbstraße 65. **GPS:** n52,99069 e11,74531.⬆️➡️.

30 ⃞€ 10,50 🚰€ 0,70 🚿€ 1 Ch🚿€ 0,70 🍴€ 2.🛒
**Location:** Rural, comfortable, quiet. **Surface:** grassy/metalled.
🅾 01/01-31/12.
**Distance:** 🚲1km ⊗500m.
**Remarks:** Along the river Elbe, closed when high water.

🄲🅂 **Wittenberge** 🚣 8D3

**Wassersportverein**, Dorfstrasse 12. **GPS:** n52,98249 e11,77477.⬆️.

7 ⃞€ 20, 2 pers.incl 🚿€ 2 WC included. **Location:** Rural, simple,
noisy. **Surface:** grassy. 🅾 01/01-31/12.
**Distance:** 🚲Wittenberge 6km ⊗on the spot.

🄲🅂 **Wusterhausen/Dosse** 🌿🏕 8E3

**Dossehalle**, Zur Dossehalle 6. **GPS:** n52,89337 e12,46537.⬆️.

3 ⃞free ⛽€ 1/25liter 🚿Ch🚿€ 1/8h. **Location:** Urban, simple,
quiet. **Surface:** asphalted. 🅾 01/01-31/12.
**Distance:** 🚲centre 500m 🛒450m.

# Saxony

## Adorf 12E2

**Waldbad**, Waldbadstrasse 5. **GPS:** n50,30778 e12,25056.

3 free. **Surface:** metalled. 01/03-30/11.
**Distance:** 1km 500m.
**Remarks:** Max. 24h.

**Tourist information Adorf:**
TouristInfo, Freiberger Str. 8.

## Bad Düben 10F3

**Im Kurgebiet**, Parkstraße 1. **GPS:** n51,60139 e12,58247.

4 free, tourist tax € 1,50/pp € 1/80liter €1 Ch€ 1 WC.
**Location:** Rural, simple, isolated. **Surface:** metalled.
01/01-31/12.
**Distance:** 750m 1,4km 1,4km.

## Bad Elster 12E2

**Albertbad**, Austus-Klingner Straße. **GPS:** n50,28545 e12,24034.
5 € 8 + € 2,20/pp tourist tax € 1/100liter included.
**Location:** Rural. **Surface:** metalled. 01/01-31/12.
**Distance:** 1km 250m.
**Remarks:** Check in at pay desk swimming pool, caution € 20, swimming pool and sauna on site.

## Bad Lausick 12F1

**Freizetbad Am Riff**, Am Riff 3. **GPS:** n51,14321 e12,65383.

10 free. **Location:** Rural, simple, central, quiet. **Surface:** grasstiles.
01/01-31/12.
**Distance:** 100m 100m on the spot on the spot.
**Remarks:** At swimming pool.

## Bad Muskau 38A3

**Am Fürst-Pückler-Park**, Bautzener Straße 39.
**GPS:** n51,53382 e14,71838.

25 € 8, € 12 service incl. + € 1,25/pp tourist tax Ch (25x)
WC. **Location:** Urban, comfortable, central, quiet.
**Surface:** grasstiles/metalled. 01/01-28/12.
**Distance:** 400m 4km 2km on the spot on the spot.
**Remarks:** Bread-service.

## Bautzen 10H3

Schliebenstraße. **GPS:** n51,18168 e14,41482.

4 free € 1 €1 (4x)€ 0,50/kWh WC.
**Location:** Urban. **Surface:** metalled. 01/01-31/12.
**Distance:** 1,2km 800m on the spot on the spot.
**Remarks:** Max. 2 nights.

## Breitenbrunn 12F2

**Sportpark Rabenberg**, Rabenbergweg. **GPS:** n50,45556 e12,74417.

15 € 8,50 + € 8,50/pp Chincluded € 2/day WC €1.
**Location:** Rural, isolated. **Surface:** metalled. 01/01-31/12.
**Distance:** 5km 3km 5km 3km.
**Remarks:** Arrival <22h, dog € 2/day.

## Dennheritz 12F1

**Caravan Service Bressler**, Zwickauerstrasse 78.
**GPS:** n50,80889 e12,48667.

6 € 5/night € 1 Ch (4x)€ 0,50/kWh.
**Surface:** metalled. 01/01-31/12.
**Distance:** 2km 800m 3km.
**Remarks:** At motorhome dealer.

## Diera-Zehren 10G3

**Zum Zuessenhaus**, Elbstraße 10. **GPS:** n51,19500 e13,41917.

10 € 5. **Location:** Rural, simple. **Surface:** grassy/metalled.
01/01-31/12.
**Distance:** 900m 270m.

## Diesbar-Seusslitz 10G3

**Parkplatz Am Schloss**, An der Weinstraße.
**GPS:** n51,24111 e13,41575.

6 € 4 (9-19h), overnight stay free (6x)€ 1/6h.
**Location:** Rural, simple, quiet. **Surface:** metalled.
01/01-31/12.
**Distance:** 100m 200m on the spot on the spot.

## Dresden 12G1

**Parkplatz Grosse Meissner**, Wiesentor Strasse.
**GPS:** n51,05639 e13,74306.

60 € 18/24h € 2/100liter Ch€ 2 (14x)€ 5/day WC.
**Location:** Urban, simple, central. **Surface:** asphalted.
01/01-31/12.
**Distance:** 100m 100m on the spot on the spot on the
spot 150m on the spot.

## Dresden 12G1

**Sachsenplatz Dresden**, Käthe-Kollwitz-Ufer 4.
**GPS:** n51,05700 e13,75990.

150 € 10 (25x)€ 5/24h. **Location:** Urban, central.
**Surface:** metalled/sand. 01/01-31/12.
**Distance:** Old city centre 2,2km on the spot 300m Aldi
700m 500m.

## Dresden 12G1

**Werner Knopf**, B6, Meissner Landstrasse.
**GPS:** n51,08131 e13,65563.

7 € 5 € 2 (8x)€ 2/night € 1,50. **Location:** Urban, simple,
quiet. **Surface:** grasstiles. 01/03-30/10.
**Distance:** 6km 500m 500m on the spot.
**Remarks:** Gate closes at 22h.

## Dresden 12G1

**Wohnmobilstellplatz am Blüherpark**, Zinzendorfstraße 7.
**GPS:** n51,04426 e13,74371.

50 € 15 € 1 €1 Ch€ 1 € 4/night,16Amp €2/pppd
included. **Location:** Urban, comfortable, central.
**Surface:** grassy/metalled. 01/01-31/12.
**Distance:** 1km 5km 500m 450m.
**Remarks:** Check in at Cityherberge, Lingnerallee 3, 24/24.

## Dresden 12G1

**Wohnmobilstellplatz Dresden**, Kesselsdorfer Straße 153.
**GPS:** n51,03988 e13,66949.

DE

5 ⌗ € 12 ⌐ ▤ Ch ◢ (5x) € 2,50/night ⌐ € 2/pppd. ▨
**Location:** Urban, comfortable, central. **Surface:** gravel/metalled.
◻ 01/01-31/12.
**Distance:** ⌐centre Dresden 4km ◢ 4km ⊗ on the spot ⚏ 200m
⚍ 800m.
**Remarks:** At Wellnesshotel Landlust, breakfast-service.

### Dresden ⚘ ♨ 🏛 ▥ 　12G1

**CaravaningPark Schaffer**, Kötzschenbroderstrasse 125.
**GPS:** n51,08639 e13,68222. ⬆.

100 ⌗ € 15 ⌐ € 0,50/60liter ▤ € 0,50 Ch € 0,50 ◢ (100x) € 0,50/kWh
WC ⌐ € 0,50 ⚋.
**Location:** Urban, comfortable.
**Surface:** grassy.
◻ 01/01-31/12.
**Distance:** ⌐Dresden 5km ⚓ 2km ⊗ 200m ⚏ 500m ⚍ 200m
⚲ 500m.
**Remarks:** Bread-service, repair possibilities motorhome, access
<19h.

**Tourist information Dresden:**
ℹ Dresden-City-Card. Card gives among other things for free public
transport, entrance to many museums, discounts on boat trips, restaurants etc. ◻ 01/01-31/12. ⊤ € 35/48h.
ℹ Tourist Information, Prager strasse;
Schinkelwache/Theaterplatz, www.dresden.de. Former residence city
with many curiosities.
❋ Striezelmarkt, Altstadt. Christmas fair. ◻ advent season.

### Ebersbach/Sachsen ⚘　38A3

**Fest- und Parkplatz am Freibad**, Kottmarsdorfer Strasse 1.
**GPS:** n51,00972 e14,59806. ⬆.

7 ⌗ € 5, € 10 service incl ⌐ ▤ Ch ◢ WC ⌐. **Location:** Rural, simple,
isolated, quiet. **Surface:** metalled. ◻ 01/01-31/12.
**Distance:** ⌐1km ⊗ 500m ⚏ 1km ⚲ on the spot.
**Remarks:** Use sanitary only during opening hours swimming pool.

### Elsterheide　10H3

**Wohnmobilstellplatz Lothar Meusel**, Am Hochwald 27, Tätzschwitz.
**GPS:** n51,48304 e14,10750. ⬆➡.

14 ⌗ € 8,50 ⌐ € 1 ▤ Ch ◢ included WC ⌐ € 2,50/day ⌐ ▨
**Location:** Rural, comfortable, isolated, quiet.
**Surface:** grasstiles/grassy. ◻ Easter-31/10.
**Distance:** ⊗ 3km ⚏ 8-10km ⚲ on the spot.

---

### Freiberg ⚒　12G1

**Am Johannisbad**, Lessingstraße. **GPS:** n50,91461 e13,33368. ⬆.

10 ⌗first night € 10, € 7,50 second night ⌐ € 1/80liter ▤ € 1 Ch € 1
◢ (10x) € 0,50/kWh WC ⌐. ▨
**Location:** Urban, simple, central, quiet. **Surface:** metalled.
◻ 01/01-31/12.
**Distance:** ⌐Altstadt 900m ⚏ 150m ⚏ Kaufland 500m ⚲ on the spot.

### Geierswalde ▥　10H3

**Ferien- und Freizeitpark Geierswalde See**, Promenadeweg 1-3.
**GPS:** n51,49372 e14,13481. ⬆.

100+ ⌗ € 6 ⌐ € 2/day ▤ Ch ◢ € 3 WC ⌐. ▨ **Location:** Rural,
simple, isolated, quiet. **Surface:** grassy. ◻ 01/01-31/12.
**Distance:** ⌐500m ⚏ Geierswaldesee 300m ⊗ 1km ⚏ 5km
⚲ on the spot.

### Görlitz　38A3

**Reisemobil & Caravans Hoke**, Zittauer Strasse 62.
**GPS:** n51,13907 e14,97947.
4 ⌗ € 8/24h ⌐ ▤ Ch ◢ included.
**Location:** Urban. **Surface:** metalled. ◻ 01/01-31/12.
**Distance:** ⌐2km ⊗ 400m ⚏ 500m ⚍ 50m.
**Remarks:** At motorhome dealer.

### Großenhain　10G3

Carl-Maria-von-Weber-Allee. **GPS:** n51,29032 e13,53584. ⬆.
5 ⌗ € 5, 15/09-15/05 free ⌐ € 1/70liter ▤ € 1 Ch € 1 ◢ € 1/4h.
**Surface:** metalled. ◻ 01/04-30/09.
**Distance:** ⌐500m ⊗ 100m ⚏ 400m.
**Remarks:** To pay at swimming pool.

### Grünhain　12F2

**Freizeitpark**, Auer Strasse 82, Haus des Gastes, Grünhain-Beierfeld.
**GPS:** n50,58139 e12,79167.

6 ⌗ € 10 ⌐ € 1 ▤ € 1,customers free Ch ◢ € 1,50/day WC ⌐ € 1.
**Location:** Rural, simple, quiet. **Surface:** metalled.
◻ 01/01-31/12.
**Distance:** ⌐1km ⊗ 100m ⚏ 3km.

### Hermsdorf ❄　12G1

**Ski- & Sporthotel SWF**, Bahnhofstraße 7.
**GPS:** n50,73241 e13,66400. ⬆.

8 ⌗ € 5 + € 1/pp tourist tax ⌐ € 2 ▤ € 2 Ch ◢ € 0,50/kWh ⌐ € 1. ▨
**Location:** Rural, simple, isolated, quiet. **Surface:** gravel/metalled.

---

◻ 01/01-31/12.
**Distance:** ⊗ on the spot ⚲ on the spot ⚽ on the spot ⚓ on the spot.
**Remarks:** Use of sauna against payment.

### Königsfeld-Stollsdorf　12F1

**Spreer's Ferienhaus**, Hauptstrasse 28. **GPS:** n51,04861 e12,74500.

5 ⌗ € 8 ⌐ ▤ Ch ◢ € 2. ◻ 01/01-31/12.
**Distance:** ⌐4km ⚏ 4km.

### Königstein ⚒　12H1

**Panoramhotel Lilienstein**, Ebenheit 7. **GPS:** n50,92505 e14,07546. ⬆.

10 ⌗ € 22 ⌐ ▤ ◢ included ⌐ € 5. ▨ **Location:** Rural, simple,
isolated, quiet. **Surface:** grassy/gravel. ◻ Easter-15/11.
**Distance:** ⌐1,5km ⊗ on the spot ⚍ on the spot ⚲ on the spot
⚽ on the spot.
**Remarks:** Bread-service and breakfast buffet.

### Leipzig ⚘ ♨ 🏛　10E3

**Stellplatz Melinenburg**, Stöhrerstraße 3.
**GPS:** n51,36648 e12,42717. ⬆.

30 ⌗ € 12, 2 pers.incl, extra pers € 1, dog € 1 ⌐ € 1 ▤ € 1 Ch € 1 ◢
(8x) € 2/day ⚋. ▨ **Location:** Urban, comfortable, central, quiet.
**Surface:** concrete. ◻ 01/01-31/12.
**Distance:** ⌐4,5km ⊗ on the spot ⚏ 1,2km ⚍ 200m.
**Remarks:** Bread-service, outside environmental zone.

### Löbau ⚒　38A3

**Am Löbauer Berg**, Beethovenstraße. **GPS:** n51,09508 e14,68088. ⬆.

3 ⌗free ◢ (3x) € 3/day. **Location:** Rural, simple, isolated, quiet.
**Surface:** grasstiles/metalled. ◻ 01/01-31/12.
**Distance:** ⌐1km ⊗ 1,5km ⚏ 900m.

### Lohsa ▥　10H3

**Dreiweibern See**, Am strand Weißkollm 1.
**GPS:** n51,40782 e14,40008. ⬆➡.

14 🛏 € 12,50 ⛽ € 1/80liter 💧Ch 🚿(14x)WC included. 🚐
**Location:** Rural, comfortable, isolated, quiet.
**Surface:** grasstiles/grassy. 📅 01/04-31/10.
**Distance:** 🚰1,5km 🛒 on the spot ⊗Imbiss 🍽 on the spot.
**Remarks:** Bread-service.

### Lommatzsch 10G3
**Sportstätte**, Scheerau. **GPS:** n51,20350 e13,30560.
5 🛏 free. **Location:** Rural. 📅 01/01-31/12.
**Distance:** 🚰1km ⊗800m 🚌800m.

### Marienberg 12G2
Ratseite-Wiesenweg, Pobershau. **GPS:** n50,63250 e13,20896. 🔼
10 🛏 € 3 + € 1/pp tourist tax ⛽€ 1 🚿€ 1. 📅 01/04-31/10.
**Distance:** 🚰Marienberg 5km ⊗200m.

### Marienberg 12G2
**Tourismuszentrum Rätzteich**, Gelobtland 27c.
**GPS:** n50,62417 e13,17861.

4 🛏 € 3 ⛽€ 1 💧€ 1 Ch€ 1 🚿€ 1. **Location:** Comfortable.
**Surface:** metalled. 📅 01/01-31/12.
**Distance:** 🚰5km ⊗on the spot ⊗500m 🚌5km 🚲on the spot 🚶on the spot 🚴3km 🏊on the spot.
**Remarks:** Recreation area.

### Marienberg 12G2
**Drei Brüder Höhe**, Drei Brüder Höhe 1. **GPS:** n50,65660 e13,12437. 🔼
10 🛏 € 6/pp ⛽ 🚿WC included. **Location:** Rural, simple, isolated.
**Surface:** grassy/gravel. 📅 01/04-31/10.
**Distance:** 🚰3,5km ⊗on the spot 🚌3km.

### Meissen 10G3
**Wellenspiel**, Berghausstraße 2. **GPS:** n51,17444 e13,49861. 🔼➡
19 🛏 € 9, dog € 2 ⛽💧Ch included 🚿€ 2/day 🚌€ 1,50. 🚐
**Location:** Rural, simple, quiet. **Surface:** grassy/metalled.
📅 01/04-31/10.
**Distance:** 🚰900m ⊗600m 🚌2km 🚲on the spot.
**Remarks:** At swimming pool, caution key € 20.

### Meissen 10G3
**An der Elbe**, Hochuferstraße. **GPS:** n51,16806 e13,47361. 🔼

20 🛏 € 5. 🚾 **Location:** Urban, simple, central. **Surface:** metalled.
📅 01/01-31/12.
**Distance:** 🚰800m ⊗on the spot ⊗800m 🚌2km 🚗300m 🚲on the spot.

### Neustadt in Sachsen 12H1
**Mariba**, Götzingerstraße 12. **GPS:** n51,02465 e14,20893. 🔼
3 🛏 free 🚿€ 5. **Location:** Urban. **Surface:** concrete.
📅 01/01-31/12.
**Distance:** 🚰on the spot ⊗300m 🚌600m 🚲on the spot.
**Remarks:** At paradise pool, max. 2 days.

### Neustadt in Sachsen 12H1
**Waldbad Polenz**, Flämmigtweg 3. **GPS:** n51,01964 e14,17960. 🔼

---

10 🛏 € 7,50/night ⛽€ 2 🚿€ 2 💧included. **Location:** Rural.
**Surface:** grassy. 📅 01/01-31/12.
**Distance:** 🚰800m.
**Remarks:** Check in and pay at kiosk, swimming pool.

### Oberwiesenthal 12F2
**OTG Tennishalle**, Vierenstrasse 11a. **GPS:** n50,42722 e12,96944.

20 🛏 € 18, 01/11-31/03 € 25, tourist tax excl ⛽💧Ch 🚿WC included 💧€ 1. **Location:** Urban. **Surface:** metalled.
📅 01/01-31/12.
**Distance:** 🚰1km ⊗on the spot 🚌1,5km 🚴250m.
**Remarks:** At sports centre, check in at reception tennishall < 22h, bread-service.

### Oderwitz 38A3
**Rodelpark Oberoderwitz**, Spitzbergstraße 4a.
**GPS:** n50,96528 e14,70111. 🔼

5 🛏 free. **Location:** Rural, simple, isolated, quiet.
**Surface:** gravel/metalled. 📅 01/01-31/12.
**Distance:** 🚰600m ⊗on the spot 🚌850m.

### Pirna 12H1
**Schloßpark Pirna**, Schloßpark 13a. **GPS:** n50,95998 e13,95232. 🔼

8 🛏 € 12 ⛽💧Ch included 🚿€ 1/kWh. **Location:** Quiet.
**Surface:** metalled. 📅 01/01-31/12.
**Distance:** 🚰2,5km 🚌500m.

### Pirna 12H1
**Elbeparkplatz**, Hauptplatz 14. **GPS:** n50,96654 e13,93775. 🔼

15 🛏 free. **Surface:** asphalted. 📅 01/01-31/12.
**Distance:** 🚰650m 🚲on the spot ⊗350m 🚲on the spot.
**Remarks:** Along the river Elbe, max. 24h.

---

DE

### Seiffen 12G1
**Berghof**, Kurhausstrasse 36. **GPS:** n50,64605 e13,48114.

20 🛏 guests free ⛽💧Ch 🚿against payment 💧free.
**Location:** Rural. **Surface:** asphalted. 📅 01/03-30/11.
**Distance:** 🚰2,5km ⊗on the spot 🚌300m.
**Remarks:** Bread-service.

### Seiffen 12G1
**Waldgasthof Bad Einsiedel**, Badstraße 1. **GPS:** n50,64669 e13,48651.
20 🛏 € 10, 2 pers.incl. + tourist tax € 2 ⛽💧Ch 🚿included.
**Location:** Rural. **Surface:** grassy. 📅 01/01-31/12 ⊙ Tue.
**Distance:** 🚰2,5km ⊗on the spot.

### Struppen 12H1
**Camping-Stellplatz Struppen**, Kirchberg 20.
**GPS:** n50,93814 e14,01307. 🔼

30 🛏 € 10, 18/03-05/11 € 13 + tourist tax € 0,75/pp ⛽€ 1/100liter 💧Ch 🚿(30x)€ 0,60/kWh 💧€ 1 🚿€ 3/3. **Location:** Rural, luxurious.
**Surface:** grassy/metalled. 📅 01/01-31/12.
**Distance:** 🚰500m 🚌500m.

### Weißwasser 10H2
**Am Tierpark**, Teichstraße 56. **GPS:** n51,51205 e14,63665. 🔼

10 🛏 free. **Location:** Urban, simple, central. **Surface:** metalled.
📅 01/01-31/12.
**Distance:** 🚰500m ⊗on the spot ⊗500m 🚌500m 🚲on the spot.

### Zittau 38A3
**Zittau Am Dreiländereck**, Brückenstrasse 23.
**GPS:** n50,89457 e14,82143. 🔼➡

100 🛏 € 7 ⛽€ 1/10minutes 💧Ch 🚿(32x)€ 1/6h WC. 🚾
**Location:** Urban, comfortable, central, quiet. **Surface:** grassy.
📅 01/01-31/12.
**Distance:** 🚰1,5km 🚌200m ⊙100m 🚲on the spot.
**Remarks:** Three Countries' Corner Germany-Czech Republic-Poland, grill and picknic area.

### Zwota 12F2
**Natur Camping Platz**, Merkneukirchner Strasse 79.
**GPS:** n50,35111 e12,38111. 🔼

40 ⌁€ 15 ⌁€ 1,50 ⌁€ 1 Ch ✎(16x)WC included.
**Location:** Rural. **Surface:** grassy. ◯ 01/01-31/12.
**Distance:** Klingenthal 6km 🏊6km.

# North Rhine Westphalia

| 📷S | Aachen 🌿♨️☕♀ | 11E2 |
|---|---|---|

**Stellplatz Bad Aachen**, Branderhofer Weg 11.
**GPS:** n50,76111 e6,10306. ⬆️➡️.

46 ⌁€ 17 ⌁Ch ✎ WC ⌁€ 1/5minutes 📶included. 🚐
**Location:** Urban, luxurious, central, quiet. **Surface:** metalled.
◯ 01/01-31/12. **Distance:** 2,3km ⊗800m 🏊800m 🚃300m.
**Remarks:** Baker 8.30-09.00, green zone: environmental badge obligatory.

| 📷S | Ahaus ♀ | 9F2 |
|---|---|---|

**Am Aquahaus**, Vredener Dyk. **GPS:** n52,07778 e6,98361. ⬆️➡️.

7 ⌁free ⌁€ 0,50/40liter ⌁Ch ✎(8x)€ 0,50/kWh,16Amp WC ⌁.
**Location:** Rural, simple, isolated. **Surface:** metalled.
◯ 01/01-31/12.
**Distance:** 2km ⊗1,5km 🏊on the spot.
**Remarks:** Max. 3 nights.

| 📷S | Ahaus ♀ | 9F2 |
|---|---|---|

**Kirmesplatz**, Schlossstrasse. **GPS:** n52,07450 e7,00299. ⬆️➡️.

10 ⌁free ⌁€ 0,50/80liter ⌁Ch ✎(6x)€ 0,50,16Amp WC ⌁.
**Location:** Rural, simple, isolated. **Surface:** metalled. ◯ 01/01-31/12
◉ during event.
**Distance:** on the spot ⊗600m 🏊600m.
**Remarks:** Parking centre, max. 3 nights.

| 📷S | Ahlen ♀ | 9G3 |
|---|---|---|

**Parkbad Ahlen**, Dolbergerstrasse 66. **GPS:** n51,75559 e7,89694. ⬆️.

---

4 ⌁€ 8/24h 🔌⌁Ch ✎included. **Location:** Rural, comfortable,
quiet. **Surface:** metalled. ◯ 01/01-31/12.
**Distance:** centre 300m ⊗100m 🏊300m on the spot 🚶on the spot.
**Remarks:** Max. 3 nights, caution key service € 10, 50% discount at
swimming pool.

| 📷S | Alpen | 9E3 |
|---|---|---|

**Reisemobilstellplatz An der Motte**, Burgstrasse 66.
**GPS:** n51,57985 e6,51846. ⬆️➡️.

11 ⌁€ 7,50 🔌⌁Ch ✎📶included. **Location:** Rural, comfortable.
**Surface:** gravel. ◯ 01/01-31/12.
**Distance:** 500m ⚓2,5km ⊗700m 🏊500m.
**Remarks:** At tennis-courts, service passerby € 3.

| | Altena ♀ | 11G1 |
|---|---|---|

**Sauerlandhalle Pragpaul**, Hermann Vossstrasse 14.
**GPS:** n51,30861 e7,66056. ⬆️➡️.

8 ⌁free 🔌€ 1 ⌁€ 1 Ch ✎(6x)€ 1/2kWh. **Location:** Rural, simple,
quiet. **Surface:** asphalted/gravel. ◯ 01/01-31/12.
**Distance:** 2km ⚓10km ⊗nearby 🏊2km on the spot 🚶on the
spot.
**Remarks:** Along river, next to sports fields.

| ♀S | Altenbeken 🌳♀ | 10A3 |
|---|---|---|

**Landhaus Friedenstal**, Hüttenstrasse 42. **GPS:** n51,75992 e8,95111. ⬆️.

5 ⌁€ 5 ✎(5x)€ 2,50/24h WC on demand,at restaurant. 🚐🛁
**Location:** Rural, simple, central. **Surface:** grassy/gravel.
◯ 01/01-31/12.
**Distance:** 200m ⊗100m 🏊200m.

| 📷S | Altenberge ♀ | 9G2 |
|---|---|---|

**Sportpark Grosseberg**, Sportzentrum. **GPS:** n52,05528 e7,47056. ⬆️.

15 ⌁free 🔌€ 0,50/60liter ⌁Ch ✎📶.
**Location:** Rural, isolated, quiet. **Surface:** metalled.
◯ 01/01-31/12 ◉ water disconnected in winter.
**Distance:** 1,6km ⊗on the spot 🏊1,5km.
**Remarks:** Parking sports centre.

| | Arnsberg | 9H3 |
|---|---|---|

An der Schlacht. **GPS:** n51,40174 e8,06574. ⬆️.
4 ⌁free. **Location:** Simple. **Surface:** gravel. ◯ 01/01-31/12.
**Distance:** ⚓3,3km 🏊Lidl 50m.

---

| ♀ | Arnsberg | 9H3 |
|---|---|---|

**Wohnmobilstandort Neheim Jahnallee**, Jahnallee 38, Neheim.
**GPS:** n51,44855 e7,95105.
⌁free. ◯ 01/01-31/12.
**Distance:** city centre 1km ⊗on the spot 🏊3km.

| | Ascheberg | 9G3 |
|---|---|---|

**Appelhof**, Appelhofstraße. **GPS:** n51,79003 e7,61902. ⬆️➡️.

4 ⌁free. **Location:** Rural, simple, central, quiet. **Surface:** metalled.
◯ 01/01-31/12.
**Distance:** on the spot ⊗on the spot 🏊on the spot.

| 📷S | Ascheberg | 9G3 |
|---|---|---|

**Gasthaus Eickholt**, Frieport 22, Davensberg. **GPS:** n51,82619 e7,59391.

6 ⌁€ 5, free with a meal 🔌€ 3/day ✎€ 3/day WC 📶free.
**Location:** Simple. **Surface:** grassy. ◯ 01/01-31/12 ◉ Mo.
**Distance:** 800m ⚓1km ⊗on the spot 🏊1km 🚃800m 🚌on the
spot.
**Remarks:** Swingolf.

| ♀S | Attendorn | 11G1 |
|---|---|---|

**Atta Höhle**, Finnentroper Straße 39. **GPS:** n51,12489 e7,91421. ⬆️.
6 ⌁€ 7,50 ⌁Ch ✎included. **Surface:** metalled.
◯ 01/01-31/12.
**Distance:** 500m ⊗600m 🏊Lidl 400m 🚃600m.
**Remarks:** Parking at the caves.

| 📷S | Bad Berleburg ♀❄ | 11H1 |
|---|---|---|

Bismarckstraße 8. **GPS:** n51,04986 e8,39406. ⬆️.
3 ⌁free 🔌€ 2/80liter ⌁Ch ✎€ 1/6h. **Location:** Urban.
**Surface:** metalled. ◯ 01/01-31/12.
**Distance:** 500m ⊗500m 🏊500m 🚃400m.

| ♀S | Bad Berleburg ♀❄ | 11H1 |
|---|---|---|

**Hotel-Restaurant Erholung - Laibach**, Auf dem Laibach 1.
**GPS:** n51,06776 e8,44527.

5 ⌁free with a meal 🔌✎(1x)€ 5/day WC. **Location:** Comfortable,
isolated. **Surface:** asphalted. ◯ 01/01-31/12.
**Distance:** 5km ⊗on the spot 🏊5km 🚃on the spot 🚌on the spot
🚶on the spot 🚲1,5km.

| ♀S | Bad Berleburg ♀❄ | 11H1 |
|---|---|---|

**Landgasthof Wittgensteiner Schweiz**, Teiche 2.
**GPS:** n51,06838 e8,47995.
3 ⌁€ 5 ✎included. **Location:** Rural, isolated, quiet.
**Surface:** metalled. ◯ 01/01-31/12.
**Distance:** ⊗on the spot 🚌on the spot 🚶on the spot.

| ♀S | Bad Berleburg ♀❄ | 11H1 |
|---|---|---|

**Pension-Bauernladen Schmelzhütte**, K52 Hoheleye.
**GPS:** n51,13874 e8,45742.

6 🛏 € 10 🚰 € 2,50 ⚡Ch 🚿 € 2. **Location:** Rural, isolated, quiet.
**Surface:** asphalted. 🗓 01/01-31/12 🅿 Mo.
**Distance:** 🛒1km ⊗on the spot 🚉1km.
**Remarks:** Bread-service.

| 🅿 | **Bad Driburg** 🍴 🌳 | 10A3 |

**Sachsenklause**, Westenfeldmark 6. **GPS:** n51,73118 e9,00646.
5 🛏 free. **Location:** Rural. **Surface:** metalled. 🗓 01/01-31/12.
**Distance:** 🛒6km ⊗on the spot 🚉6km.

| ♨ S | **Bad Driburg** 🍴 🌳 | 10A3 |

**P Driburg Therme**, Georg-Nave-Strasse 24.
**GPS:** n51,74194 e9,02542. ⬆.

15 🛏 € 7 + tourist tax € 2,60/pp ⚡Ch 🚿(10x) € 3/24h WC. 🚽
**Location:** Rural, simple, quiet. **Surface:** asphalted.
🗓 01/01-31/12.
**Distance:** 🛒1km ⊗on the spot 🚉1km 🚌on the spot 🚶on the spot 🚶on the spot.
**Remarks:** Max. 7m, caution € 10, key electricity at pay-desk, discount on access terme.

| ♨ S | **Bad Laasphe** 🍴 | 11H1 |

**Mühlenstrasse. GPS:** n50,92412 e8,41146. ⬆➡.

7 🛏 € 9/24h 🚰 € 0,50/80liter ⚡Ch 🚿(6x) € 0,50/kWh. 🚐
**Location:** Simple. **Surface:** asphalted. 🗓 01/01-31/12.
**Distance:** 🛒500m ⊗500m 🚉500m.
**Remarks:** Parking at town hall.

| 🛏♨S | **Bad Laasphe** 🍴 | 11H1 |

**Hotel Jagdhof Glashütte**, Glashütterstrasse 20, Volkholz.
**GPS:** n50,92008 e8,28070.

6 🛏 € 13,80, guests free 🚿 WC 📶. **Location:** Rural, isolated, quiet.
**Surface:** grassy. 🗓 01/01-31/12 🅿 23-24/12.
**Distance:** 🛒4km 🍴on the spot ⊗on the spot 🚉4km 🚌1,5km.

| | **Bad Laasphe** 🍴 | 11H1 |

**Restaurant-Café Marburger**, Hesselbacher Straße 21.
**GPS:** n50,88558 e8,36338.
6 🛏 guests free. 🗓 01/01-31/12 🅿 Mo.
**Distance:** ⊗on the spot.

| ♨ S | **Bad Lippspringe** | 10A3 |

**Arminiuspark**, Burgstraße 10. **GPS:** n51,78124 e8,82447.

11 🛏 € 6,50 🚰 € 1/100liter ⚡Ch 🚿 € 1/8h. **Location:** Urban, simple,
quiet. **Surface:** metalled. 🗓 01/01-31/12.
**Distance:** 🛒300m ⊗350m 🚌on the spot 🚶on the spot.
**Remarks:** Pay at tourist office.

| 🛏♨S | **Bad Münstereifel** | 11F2 |

**Wohnmobilpark Bad Münstereifel**, Dr.-Greve-Straße 16.
**GPS:** n50,54600 e6,76514. ⬆➡.

26 🛏 € 7, tourist tax € 1/pp 🚰 € 1/100liter 🚰 € 1 Ch 🚿(30x)included
WC 🚽 € 1,80. 🚽
**Location:** Rural, comfortable, quiet. **Surface:** grassy/metalled.
🗓 01/01-31/12.
**Distance:** 🛒350m ⊗on the spot 🚉100m.
**Remarks:** Pay and coins at swimming pool, 20% discount pool.

| 🛏♨S | **Bad Oeynhausen** 🌳 | 9H2 |

Südbahnstraße/Detmolder Straße. **GPS:** n52,19680 e8,80038. ⬆⬆.
3 🛏 free. **Location:** Urban, simple, noisy. **Surface:** asphalted.
🗓 01/01-31/12.
**Distance:** ⊗150m 🚌on the spot.
**Remarks:** Max. 2 days.

| 🍴 | **Bad Oeynhausen** 🌳 | 9H2 |

**Siekmeiers Hof**, Volmerdingsener strasse 111.
**GPS:** n52,24679 e8,78394.

10 🛏 guests free. **Location:** Urban, quiet. **Surface:** gravel.
🗓 01/01-31/12 🅿 Mon, Tue.
**Distance:** 🛒on the spot ⊗on the spot 🚉1km.

| 🛏♨S | **Bad Salzuflen** | 9H2 |

**Wohnmobilpark Flachsheide**, Forsthausweg 1.
**GPS:** n52,09868 e8,74569. ⬆.

66 🛏 € 7 + € 2,90-3,20/pp tourist tax 🚰⚡Ch 🚿 € 0,50/kWh
WC included 🚰 € 2,80/30minutes 📶. 🚽 **Location:** Rural, simple,
quiet. **Surface:** grassy. 🗓 01/01-31/12.
**Distance:** 🛒1,5km 🎣5,5km 🍴on the spot ⊗500m 🚉1,5km
🚌free.

| ♨ S | **Bad Sassendorf** 🌳 | 9H3 |

**Kurcamping Rumkerhof**, Weslarnerstrasse 30.
**GPS:** n51,59581 e8,17909. ⬆➡.

90 🛏 € 9, tourist tax excl 🚰⚡Ch 🚿(93x) € 0,50/kWh 📶included.
**Location:** Rural, isolated, quiet. **Surface:** gravel.
🗓 01/01-31/12.
**Distance:** 🛒1,3km ⊗1,3km.
**Remarks:** Waste dump € 0,50, bread-service.

| 🛏♨S | **Bad Waldliesborn** | 9H3 |

**Wohnmobilpoint**, Quellenstraße. **GPS:** n51,71759 e8,33587. ⬆.

10 🛏 € 4,40 + € 7,55/pp 🚰 € 2/100liter ⚡Ch 🚿(8x) € 2/24h.
**Location:** Rural, quiet. **Surface:** gravel. 🗓 01/01-31/12.
**Distance:** 🛒400m ⊗200m 🚉400m 🚌400m.
**Remarks:** Discount on access terme.

| 🛏♨S | **Bad Westernkotten** | 9H3 |

**Wohnmobilplatz An den Sole-Thermen**, Mühlenweg 1.
**GPS:** n51,63126 e8,35195. ⬆.

46 🛏 € 8, tourist tax € 2/pp 🚰 € 1/100liter ⚡Ch 🚿 € 0,50/kWh. 🚐
**Surface:** grassy. 🗓 01/01-31/12.
**Distance:** 🛒600m ⊗800m 🚉bakery 300m.
**Remarks:** Bread-service.

| 🛏♨S | **Bad Wünnenberg** 🍴 | 9H3 |

**Wohnmobilhafen**, In den Erlen. **GPS:** n51,52058 e8,70133. ⬆➡.

12 🛏 € 6 🚰 € 1/100liter ⚡Ch 🚿(12x) € 1/24h. 🚽
**Location:** Urban, central. **Surface:** gravel.
🗓 01/01-31/12.
**Distance:** 🛒100m 🚌400m ⊗100m 🚉400m 🚌on the spot
🚶on the spot.

| 🛏♨S | **Balve** 🍴🍴 | 11G1 |

**Am Hallenbad**, In der Murmke 9. **GPS:** n51,32729 e7,86920. ⬆➡.

3 🛏 free 🚰 € 1/80liter ⚡Ch 🚿 € 1/kWh. **Location:** Urban, simple.
**Surface:** metalled. 🗓 01/01-31/12.

**Distance:** 📍600m ⊗600m 🛒600m 🚲on the spot 🚶on the spot.

### 🏨🅂 Balve ⛲🍴 11G1

**Haus Recke Hönnetal**, Binolen 1. GPS: n51,37037 e7,86108.⬆️
3 🚐 € 10, guests free 🚰🔌Ch. ▫️ 01/01-31/12.
**Distance:** ⊗on the spot 🚲on the spot.

### 🅂 Barntrup 10A2

**Freibad Barntrup**, Badeanstaltsweg. GPS: n51,98790 e9,10990.⬆️➡️

5 🚐 € 6 🚰 € 1/100liter 🔌Ch 🔌 € 1/kWh 📶. **Location:** Rural,
simple. **Surface:** asphalted. ▫️ 01/01-31/12.
**Distance:** 📍450m ⊗450m 🛒450m 🚰450m.
**Remarks:** To be paid at campsite Teutoburger Wald.

### 🅂 Barntrup 10A2

**Ferienpark Teutoburger Wald**, Badeanstaltsweg 4.
GPS: n51,98768 e9,11027.⬆️

9 🚐 € 15, tourist tax € 1/pp, dog € 2,25 🚰🔌Ch 🔌WC 📶🔌 € 5/5
📶included. **Location:** Rural, luxurious, quiet.
**Surface:** grassy/metalled. ▫️ 01/04-31/10.
**Distance:** 📍450m ⊗450m 🛒450m 📍450m 🚲on the spot 🚶on
the spot.

### 🅂 Beckum 9G3

**Am Hallenbad**, Paterweg 4. GPS: n51,75129 e8,03585.⬆️➡️

3 🚐free 🚰 € 0,50/100liter 🔌Ch 🔌(2x)€ 0,50/kWh.
**Location:** Urban, simple, noisy. **Surface:** metalled.
▫️ 01/01-31/12.
**Distance:** 📍1km 🚲4km ⊗1km 🛒1km.
**Remarks:** Max. 3 nights.

### 🅂 Bedburg-Hau 🍴 9E3

**Womo-Moyland**, Moyländer Allee 3a, Moyland.
GPS: n51,75562 e6,24381.⬆️➡️

45 🚐 € 8,50 🚰 € 0,50/50liter 🔌Ch 🔌(40x)€ 1,50/24h 📶included.
📶 ▫️ 01/01-31/12.
**Location:** Rural, comfortable, isolated, quiet. **Surface:** grassy.
**Distance:** 📍Kleve 8km 🚲2,5km ⊗300m 🚲on the spot.
**Remarks:** Golf court 500m, Schloss Moyland 300m.

**Tourist information Bedburg-Hau:**
Ⓜ️✖️ Schloß Moyland, Am Schloss 4. Castle. ▫️ Tue-Fri 11-18h, Sa-Su
10-18h, 01/04-30/09 Tue-Su 11-17h ▫️ Mon.

---

### Bergheim 11F1

**Stellplatz Paffendorf**, Königsstrasse/Kastanienallee.
GPS: n50,96389 e6,61194.⬆️➡️

8 🚐free. **Location:** Rural, simple, quiet. **Surface:** asphalted.
▫️ 01/01-31/12.
**Distance:** 📍Bergheim 2km 🚲2,3km ⊗300m 🛒500m 🚲on the spot
🚶on the spot.
**Remarks:** Max. 3 days, castle Paffendorf 100m.

### Bergkamen 🍴 9G3

**Wohnmobilhafen Marina Rünthe**, Hafenweg, Rünthe.
GPS: n51,64106 e7,64309.⬆️➡️

18 🚐 € 8/24h 🚰 € 1/80liter 🔌Ch 🔌(18x)€ 0,50/kWh. 🚽
**Location:** Rural, quiet. **Surface:** grassy/gravel. ▫️ 01/01-31/12.
**Distance:** 📍500m 🚲3,8km ⊗1km.
**Remarks:** Max. 3 days, only exact change.

### Bergkamen 🍴 9G3

**Freizeitzentrum Im Häupen**, Häupenweg 29.
GPS: n51,61300 e7,63075.⬆️➡️

5 🚐free. **Location:** Rural, simple, central. **Surface:** asphalted.
▫️ 01/01-31/12.
**Distance:** 📍500m 🚲3,4km ⊗500m 🛒500m.
**Remarks:** Max. 72h.

### Bestwig 9H3

**Besucherbergwerk**, Ziegelwiese, Ramsbeck.
GPS: n51,31821 e8,40318.⬆️

10 🚐free. **Location:** Rural, simple. **Surface:** metalled.
▫️ 01/01-31/12.
**Distance:** ⊗800m 🛒800m.

### Bestwig 9H3

Ludwigstrasse. GPS: n51,36064 e8,40165.⬆️

---

4 🚐free. **Location:** Simple. **Surface:** metalled.
▫️ 01/01-31/12.
**Distance:** 📍on the spot ⊗300m 🛒200m.

### 🅿️🅂 Bestwig 9H3

Rathausplatz 1. GPS: n51,36093 e8,40151.
4 🚐free 🚾. **Location:** Urban, simple, central. **Surface:** metalled.
▫️ 01/01-31/12.
**Distance:** ⊗100m 🛒100m 🚰200m.

### 🅂 Beverungen 🧁🌳🪵 10A3

**Wohnmobilhafen Weser**, Am Hakel. GPS: n51,66167 e9,37639.⬆️➡️

10 🚐free 🚰 € 1/100liter 🔌Ch € 1 🔌(12x)€ 1/6h.
**Location:** Urban, simple. **Surface:** grassy/metalled.
▫️ 01/01-31/12 🔌 service: 01/11-01/03.
**Distance:** 📍on the spot 🚲on the spot 🚴on the spot ⊗250m
🛒on the spot 🚐50m.
**Remarks:** Closed because of renovation during 2018 and 2019, next to
Festplatz.

### Beverungen 🧁🌳🪵 10A3

Schützenstrasse. GPS: n51,66201 e9,37548.⬆️
10 🚐free. **Surface:** metalled. ▫️ 01/01-31/12.
**Distance:** 📍on the spot ⊗200m 🛒600m 🚐on the spot.
**Remarks:** Closed because of renovation during 2018 and 2019, along
river, max. 72h.

### 🏨🅂 Beverungen ⛲🍴🪵 10A3

**Alte Linde**, Würrigser Straße 4. GPS: n51,64530 e9,41734.
8 🚐 € 10 🚰included 🔌 € 2/24h. **Surface:** grassy.
▫️ 01/01-31/12.
**Distance:** 📍5km ⊗on the spot 🚲 Weserradweg R 99 200m.
**Remarks:** Discount at restaurant.

### 🅂 Bielefeld 🌿🍴 9H2

**Am Johannisberg**, Dornbergerstrasse 53.
GPS: n52,02270 e8,51155.⬆️➡️

10 🚐 € 5/24h 🚰 € 0,50/40liter 🔌Ch 🔌(10x)€ 1/2kWh. 🚽
**Location:** Rural, comfortable, quiet. **Surface:** metalled.
▫️ 01/01-31/12.
**Distance:** 📍2km 🍴Imbiss 🛒2km 🚐300m.
**Remarks:** Max. 5 days.

### 🅂 Billerbeck 🍞 9F2

**Am Freibad**, Osterwickerstrasse. GPS: n51,97928 e7,28190.⬆️➡️

11 ⌁ 8 ⛽ € 1/100liter ⬛Ch⬛ ✦(8x)€ 1/2kWh,16Amp WC⬛. 🐕‍🦺
**Location:** Urban, simple. **Surface:** gravel. ⬛ 01/01-31/12.
**Distance:** 🚶500m ⊗300m ⬛500m.
**Remarks:** At swimming pool, max. 4 nights, use sanitary only during opening hours swimming pool.

### ⬛S | Blankenheim | 11F2

**An der Weiherhalle**, Koblenzer Straße. **GPS:** n50,43499 e6,65439.⬆

15 ⌁ € 8/24h ⛽ € 1/80liter ⬛Ch€ 1 ✦(12x)€ 2/6h.⬛
**Location:** Rural, simple, quiet. **Surface:** metalled.
⬛ 01/01-31/12.
**Distance:** 🚶150m ⛹on the spot 🧍on the spot.
**Remarks:** Max. 8M.

### ⬛S | Bocholt 🍴 | 9F3

**WoMo Park am Aasee**, Uhlandstraße 39.
**GPS:** n51,83496 e6,63146.⬆⬆

50 ⌁ € 7,50 ⛽ € 0,50/50liter ⬛Ch€ 0,50 ✦(48x)€ 0,50/kWh
WC€ 0,50 ⬛€ 1 ⬛€ 3,50/2,50 ⬛€ 1/24h. 🚿 **Location:** Rural, comfortable, noisy. **Surface:** metalled. ⬛ 01/01-31/12.
**Distance:** 🚶800m ⛵300m ⊗300m ⬛300m ⬛300m ⬛200m 🚲on the spot 🧍on the spot.
**Remarks:** Service passerby € 2.

### ⬛ | Bocholt 🍴 | 9F3

**Euregio-Gymnasium**, Unter den Eichen, Blücherstrasse.
**GPS:** n51,84884 e6,63700.

3 ⌁free. **Location:** Urban, simple, noisy. **Surface:** metalled.
⬛ 01/01-31/12.
**Distance:** 🚶1km ⊗700m 🚲on the spot.
**Remarks:** Parking 'Stadtswald', max. 3 nights.

### ⬛S | Bocholt 🍴 | 9F3

**Inselbad Bahia**, Hemdenerweg 169. **GPS:** n51,86265 e6,61002.⬆➡

10 ⌁free ⛽€ 1 ⬛€ 1 Ch€ 1.
**Location:** Rural, simple, quiet. **Surface:** grasstiles.
⬛ 01/01-31/12.
**Distance:** 🚶2,5km ⛵450m ⬛1km ⊗on the spot.
**Remarks:** Max. 72h, coins at swimming pool, first coin € 3, next € 0,50.
**Tourist information Bocholt:**
🧍 Rathaus - Gasthausplatz. ⬛ Thu-evening.

### ⬛ | Bonn | 11F2

**An der Rheinaue**, Ludwig-Erhard-Allee. **GPS:** n50,70981 e7,13904.⬆

---

18 ⌁free. **Surface:** asphalted. ⬛ 01/01-31/12. ⬛ 06/05-07/05.
**Distance:** 🚶centre 4km 🚗A565 4,6km ⊗300m ⬛300m line 66 > Bonn centre.
**Remarks:** Outside environmental zone.

### ⬛S | Borken 🌿🍴🧁🌳🍺 | 9F3

**Reisemobilstellplatz am Aquarius-Freizeitbad**, Parkstraße.
**GPS:** n51,83618 e6,86074.⬆➡

15 ⌁ € 5/night ⛽included ⬛Ch ✦€ 1/24h.⬛
**Location:** Rural, simple. **Surface:** grasstiles.
⬛ 01/01-31/12.
**Distance:** 🚶1km 🚣4km ⬛1km ⊗800m ⬛500m 🚲on the spot 🧍on the spot.
**Remarks:** Parking swimming pool, max. 72h.

### ⬛ | Borken 🌿🍴🧁🌳🍺 | 9F3

**Festplatz Weseke**, Borkenwirther strasse, Weseke.
**GPS:** n51,90529 e6,85210.⬆

10 ⌁free. **Location:** Rural, simple. **Surface:** metalled.
⬛ 01/01-31/12.
**Distance:** 🚶500m ⊗500m ⬛500m.
**Remarks:** Max. 3 nights.

### ⬛ | Borken 🌿🍴🧁🌳🍺 | 9F3

**Schlossklinik Pröbsting**, Pröbstinger Allee.
**GPS:** n51,83861 e6,80556.⬆

10 ⌁free. **Location:** Rural, noisy. **Surface:** metalled.
⬛ 01/01-31/12.
**Distance:** ⛵Badesee 150m ⊗300m 🚲on the spot 🚲on the spot 🧍on the spot.
**Remarks:** Max. 3 days.

### ⬛ | Borken 🌿🍴🧁🌳🍺 | 9F3

**Wasserburg Gemen**, Coesfelderstrasse, Gemen.
**GPS:** n51,86172 e6,86909.⬆➡

5 ⌁free. **Location:** Rural, simple. **Surface:** metalled.
⬛ 01/01-31/12.
**Distance:** 🚶1km ⛵500m 🎣500m ⊗1km ⬛1km.
**Remarks:** Parking sports park, max. 3 nights.

### ⬛S | Borken 🌿🍴🧁🌳🍺 | 9F3

**Gestüt Forellenhof Wolter**, Zum Homborn 9.
**GPS:** n51,86245 e6,89797.⬆

---

15 ⌁ € 10 ⛽Chincluded ✦(7x)€ 0,50/kWh.
**Location:** Rural. **Surface:** gravel. ⬛ 01/01-31/12.
**Distance:** 🚶Borken 3,5km 🎣fish pond ⊗on the spot.
**Remarks:** Check in at Gaststätte, € 5 euro discount coupon.

### ⬛ | Bottrop | 9F3

**Hans-Böckler-Straße 165. GPS:** n51,52966 e6,90404.

5 ⌁free. **Location:** Rural, simple, quiet. **Surface:** metalled.
⬛ 01/01-31/12.
**Distance:** 🚶2km ⊗1km ⬛3km ⬛400m.
**Remarks:** At cemetery, outside environmental zone.

### ⬛ | Bottrop | 9F3

**Movie Park**, Kirchhellen, Warner Allee 1.
**GPS:** n51,62400 e6,97096.⬆➡

50 ⌁ € 6/night. **Location:** Rural. **Surface:** metalled.
⬛ 01/04-31/10.
**Distance:** 🚶2,7km ⊗100m ⬛2,7km.
**Remarks:** Outside environmental zone.
**Tourist information Bottrop:**
Alpincenter, Prosperstrasse. Indoor ski centre. ⬛ 9-24h. ⬛ day ticket from € 49, <18h € 25.
Warner Bros Movie World, Kirchhellen. Attractions park concerning the film.

### ⬛S | Brakel/Bellersen 🚲🏞🍴 | 10A3

**Wohnmobilhafen Mühlengrund**, Meinolfussstrasse 6.
**GPS:** n51,77217 e9,18804.⬆

23 ⌁ € 9,50 ⛽ ⬛€ 0,50 Ch ✦(23x)included. 🚿 **Location:** Rural, comfortable, isolated. **Surface:** grasstiles. ⬛ 01/01-31/12.
**Distance:** 🚶800m ⊗400m ⬛800m ⬛800m 🚲on the spot 🧍on the spot.

### ⬛ | Brakel/Bellersen 🏞🍴 | 10A3

**P9**, Bredenweg. **GPS:** n51,71927 e9,18395.
3 ⌁free. **Surface:** gravel/metalled. ⬛ 01/01-31/12.
**Distance:** 🚶400m ⊗300m ⬛800m.

### ⬛ | Bruchhausen | 10A3

Bruchhäuserstrasse. **GPS:** n51,70714 e9,29192.⬆

4 ⌕free. **Location:** Rural, simple. **Surface:** grassy/gravel.
🅾 01/01-31/12.
**Distance:** 🛒200m ⊗200m 🚰200m 🚃1,2km.

🚏S **Brüggen** 11E1
**Wohnmobilhafen Brüggen**, Bornerstraße 48.
**GPS:** n51,24264 e6,18955. ⬆️➡️.

40 ⌕€ 5 🚐🗑️Chincluded 🚿€ 2/24h. **Surface:** gravel.
🅾 01/01-31/12.
**Distance:** 🛒500m ⊗100m 🚰50m 🚃50m.
**Remarks:** Behind Aldi-süd.

🚏S **Brüggen** 11E1
**Freizeitplatz Brachter Wald**, St.-Barbara-Straße 40–42, Bracht.
**GPS:** n51,25713 e6,17022.

14 ⌕€ 9, 2 pers.incl 🚐🗑️Ch 🚿€ 2,50/day WCincluded 🗑️ 1.
**Location:** Rural, comfortable, quiet. **Surface:** grasstiles.
🅾 01/01-31/12.
**Distance:** 🛒2km ⊗on the spot 🚰on the spot.

🚏 **Bünde** 9H2
**Stadthallen**, Steinmeisterstrasse. **GPS:** n52,19869 e8,58986. ⬆️.

5 ⌕free. **Location:** Urban, simple, quiet. **Surface:** metalled.
🅾 01/01-31/12.
**Distance:** 🛒50m ⊗50m 🚰50m.
**Remarks:** Max. 72h.

🚏S **Büren** 9H3
**Wohnmobilparkplatz Netz - Bürener Land**, Fürstenberger Strasse.
**GPS:** n51,54969 e8,56356. ⬆️.

8 ⌕free 🚐€ 1/10minutes 🗑️Ch 🚿€ 1/8h 📶free.
**Location:** Urban, simple, central. **Surface:** asphalted.
🅾 01/01-31/12.

**Distance:** 🛒on the spot ⊗500m 🚰200m.
**Remarks:** Parking nearby swimming pool, coins at petrol station.

🚏 **Büren** 9H3
**Dorfhalle**, Niederhagen, Wewelsburg. **GPS:** n51,60947 e8,65544. ⬆️.
⌕free. 🅾 01/01-31/12.
**Distance:** 🚰600m.

🚏 **Büren** 9H3
**Ringelsteiner Wald**, Eichenweg, Ringelstein.
**GPS:** n51,50097 e8,56999. ⬆️.
⌕free. **Location:** Rural, simple, isolated. **Surface:** metalled.
🅾 01/01-31/12.
**Distance:** 🛒1km ⊗1km 🚰1km 🧍on the spot.

🚏S **Coesfeld** 9F2
**Konzert Theater Coesfeld**, Osterwicker Straße 39.
**GPS:** n51,95322 e7,17390. ⬆️.

12 ⌕€ 8 🚐€ 1/100liter 🗑️Ch 🚿(12x)€ 1/2kWh 🗑️ 1.
**Location:** Rural, simple. **Surface:** gravel/metalled.
🅾 01/01-31/12.
**Distance:** 🛒800m ⊗800m 🚰100m 🚲on the spot.
**Remarks:** Natural swimming pool, max. 4 days.

🚏S **Coesfeld** 9F2
**Brauhaus Stephanus**, Overhagenweg 1. **GPS:** n51,93719 e7,15617. ⬆️.

4 ⌕guests free 🚐🚿📶. **Location:** Urban, simple, noisy.
**Surface:** metalled. 🅾 01/01-31/12.
**Distance:** ⊗on the spot 🚰100m 🚃on the spot.
**Remarks:** Breakfast-service.

🚏S **Dahlem** 11E3
**Flugplatz Dahlemer Binz**, Dahlemer Binz.
**GPS:** n50,40663 e6,53700. ⬆️.

3 ⌕free 🚐€ 1/80liter 🗑️Ch. **Location:** Rural, simple, isolated.
**Surface:** asphalted. 🅾 01/01-31/12.
**Distance:** ⊗on the spot 🚃100m.
**Remarks:** Airport Dahlemer Binz.

🚏S **Dahlem** 11E3
**Wohnmobilstellplatz Kronenburger See**, Seeuferstrasse 6.
**GPS:** n50,35785 e6,46989. ⬆️➡️.

12 ⌕€ 10/24h 🚐€ 1/120liter 🗑️Ch 🚿(12x)included. 📟
**Location:** Rural, simple, quiet. **Surface:** grassy.
🅾 01/01-31/12.

**Remarks:** At artificial lake.

🚏 **Dinslaken** 9F3
**Am Rotbachsee**, Am Freibad. **GPS:** n51,56707 e6,77807. ⬆️➡️.

10 ⌕free. **Location:** Rural, simple. **Surface:** sand.
🅾 01/01-31/12.
**Distance:** 🛒100m ⊗100m 🚰100m 🚲on the spot 🧍on the spot.
**Remarks:** Outside environmental zone.

🚏S **Dormagen** 11F1
**Parkplatz Flügeldeich**, Herrenweg, Feste Zons.
**GPS:** n51,12553 e6,85001. ⬆️.

3 ⌕€ 5 🚿€ 0,50/kWh. **Location:** Simple, quiet. **Surface:** metalled.
🅾 01/01-31/12.
**Distance:** 🛒400m ⚓on the spot 🚣on the spot ⊗100m 🚰500m.
**Remarks:** Near the Rhine river, max. 3 days.

🚏S **Dorsten** 9F3
**Reisemobilhafen An der Lippe**, Zur Lippe.
**GPS:** n51,66550 e6,96744. ⬆️➡️.

38 ⌕€ 8/24h 🚐🗑️Chincluded 🚿(34x)€ 1/8h 🗑️ 2. 📟
**Location:** Urban, central, quiet. **Surface:** metalled/sand.
🅾 01/01-31/12.
**Distance:** 🛒300m ⊗300m 🚰300m.
**Remarks:** Bread-service in summer period, charging point for electric bicycles.

**Tourist information Dorsten:**
🏵 Marler Str.. Flea market. 🅾 2nd Su of the month, 11-18h.

🚏S **Dortmund** 🌿🏕️🍺🌳〰️ 9G3
**Mobil-Camp Wischlingen**, Wischlinger Weg 50-61, Wischlingen.
**GPS:** n51,52001 e7,39868. ⬆️➡️.

50 ⌕€ 8, 2 pers.incl 🚐€ 0,10/10liter 🗑️Ch 🚿(30x)€ 0,50/kWh
WC🗑️ 1. 📟 **Location:** Rural. **Surface:** asphalted. 🅾 01/01-31/12.
**Distance:** 🛒1km ⊗100m 🚃Rewe 1km 🚰200m.
**Remarks:** Former tennis-court in recreation area, green zone: environmental badge obligatory.

🚏S **Drensteinfurt** 9G3
**Am Erlbad**, Im Erlfeld 2. **GPS:** n51,78972 e7,74778. ⬆️.

3 �[sym]free [sym] Ch. [sym]€ 3/24h WC included [sym]€ 3.
**Location:** Rural, simple, noisy. **Surface:** asphalted/metalled.
[sym] 01/01-31/12 [sym] service: 01/09-30/04.
**Distance:** [sym]800m [sym]9km [sym]800m.
**Remarks:** Max. 3 nights, max. 8M, check in at swimming pool, swimming pool incl.

| | Duisburg | 9F3 |
|---|---|---|

**Landschaftspark Duisburg-Nord**, Emscherstraße 71, Meiderich.
**GPS:** n51,48163 e6,78490.[sym]

5 �[sym]free [sym]€ 1/100liter [sym]Ch€ 0,50/time. **Location:** Urban, simple.
**Surface:** asphalted. [sym] 01/01-31/12.
**Distance:** [sym]1,6km [sym]on the spot [sym]on the spot.
**Remarks:** Green zone: environmental badge obligatory.

| | Dülmen | 9F3 |
|---|---|---|

**Reisemobilstellplatz Hüttendyk**, Ecke Halterner Strasse.
**GPS:** n51,82606 e7,27228.[sym][sym]

8 ⌐[sym]free [sym]€ 1/80liter [sym]Ch [sym](8x)€ 2/8h. **Location:** Rural, simple.
**Surface:** metalled. [sym] 01/01-31/12.
**Distance:** [sym]500m [sym]200m [sym]100m.
**Remarks:** Max. 72h.

| | Dülmen | 9F3 |
|---|---|---|

**Reisemobilstellplatz Kapellenweg**, Kapellenweg.
**GPS:** n51,82331 e7,27945.[sym]

7 ⌐[sym]free [sym][sym]Ch. **Location:** Rural, simple. **Surface:** metalled.
[sym] 01/01-31/12.
**Distance:** [sym]500m [sym]650m [sym]600m [sym]on the spot [sym]on the spot.
**Remarks:** Max. 72h.

| | Dülmen | 9F3 |
|---|---|---|

**Reisemobilstellplatz Düb**, Nordlandwehr 99.
**GPS:** n51,84408 e7,27300.[sym][sym]

7 ⌐[sym]free. **Location:** Rural, simple. **Surface:** grasstiles/metalled.
[sym] 01/01-31/12.
**Distance:** [sym]2km [sym]1km.
**Remarks:** Max. 72h.

| | Dülmen | 9F3 |
|---|---|---|

**Reisemobilstellplatz Hausdulmen**, Sandstrasse.
**GPS:** n51,80707 e7,24746.[sym][sym]

20 ⌐[sym]free. **Location:** Rural, simple, quiet. **Surface:** grassy.
[sym] 01/01-31/12.
**Distance:** [sym]2,5km [sym]500m [sym]400m [sym]on the spot [sym]on the spot.
[sym]on the spot.
**Remarks:** Max. 72h.

| | Düren | 11E2 |
|---|---|---|

**IG Reisemobilhafen Düren**, Rurstrasse 188. **GPS:** n50,80861 e6,46556.

20 ⌐[sym]€ 7 [sym][sym]Ch included [sym](18x)€ 2. [sym] **Location:** Rural, simple,
quiet. **Surface:** gravel. [sym] 01/01-31/12.
**Distance:** [sym]900m [sym]Bistro 100m [sym]Lidl 500m [sym]on the spot.
**Remarks:** Service passerby € 2.

| | Düsseldorf | 11F1 |
|---|---|---|

**P Rheinterasse/Tonhalle**, Robert-Lehr-Ufer.
**GPS:** n51,23710 e6,77029.[sym]

30 ⌐[sym]€ 2,20/h, max. € 12/24h. **Surface:** metalled.
[sym] 01/01-31/12 [sym] spring fair.
**Distance:** [sym]Old city centre 1km [sym]50m [sym]1,3km.
**Remarks:** Green zone: environmental badge obligatory.

**Tourist information Düsseldorf:**
[sym] Tourist Info, Immermannstrasse, Gegenüber Station; Kö-Galerie/
Finanzhaus, Berliner Alee; Burgplatz, Berliner Alee; www.duesseldorf-tourismus.de. Historical centre, important city of fashion, all large marks established in the Königsallee, Umweltzone: the green environmental badge is required.
[sym] During the Caravan Salon (by the end of August/beginning September) there is a large area for motorhomes available. Free shuttlebus to the exhibition and Old city centre. Also several events on the exhibition grounds.

| | Eckenhagen | 11G1 |
|---|---|---|

**Rodener Festplatz**, Rodener Platz. **GPS:** n50,98667 e7,69361.[sym]

5 ⌐[sym]free [sym]Ch. **Location:** Urban, simple, quiet.
**Surface:** asphalted/gravel. [sym] 01/01-31/12.
**Distance:** [sym]200m [sym]4km [sym]300m [sym]300m [sym]on the spot [sym]on the spot.
**Remarks:** Key service at Kurverwaltung.

| | Emmerich | 9E3 |
|---|---|---|

**Auf dem Eltenberg Hoch Elten**, Luitgardisstraße.
**GPS:** n51,86559 e6,17265.[sym][sym]

25 ⌐[sym]free. **Location:** Rural, simple. **Surface:** grassy/gravel.
[sym] 01/01-31/12.
**Distance:** [sym]1km [sym]100m [sym]1km [sym]on the spot.
**Remarks:** Service at marina.

| | Emmerich | 9E3 |
|---|---|---|

**P6**, Kleiner Wall, Rheinpromenade. **GPS:** n51,83229 e6,23594.[sym][sym]

6 ⌐[sym]free. **Location:** Urban, simple, central, noisy. **Surface:** gravel.
[sym] 15/03-01/11.
**Distance:** [sym]on the spot [sym]on the spot [sym]on the spot [sym]on the spot.

| | Emmerich | 9E3 |
|---|---|---|

**Yachthafen Emmerich**, Fackeldey 15 - 65.
**GPS:** n51,83693 e6,21948.[sym]

50 ⌐[sym]€ 12 [sym][sym]Ch [sym](50x)WC [sym]€ 0,50 [sym]included. [sym]
**Location:** Rural, luxurious, isolated, noisy. **Surface:** grassy/metalled.
[sym] 15/03-31/10.
**Distance:** [sym]2,5km [sym]on the spot [sym]on the spot [sym]1,5km [sym]on the
spot [sym]on the spot.
**Remarks:** Arrival <22h.

| | Ennepetal | 11G1 |
|---|---|---|

**Am Platsch**, Mittelstraße 108. **GPS:** n51,29295 e7,37668.[sym]

4 ⌐[sym]€ 3 [sym]included. [sym] **Surface:** gravel. [sym] 01/01-31/12.

**Distance:** ⚓ 10,8km ⊗5km ⚡5km ⚓on the spot ♻on the spot ⚓routes for nordic walking. **Remarks:** Check in at pay-desk of swimming pool, use sanitary only during opening hours swimming pool, on the spot: bistro, pool, sauna and golf court.

**Ennepetal** 11G1

**Firma Möller-Elektronic**, Königstrasse 17, Oelkinghausen. **GPS:** n51,29086 e7,32050.

5 free ⬛Ch ⚡3. **Location:** Urban, simple, quiet. **Surface:** metalled. ☐ 01/01-31/12. **Distance:** ⚓2km ⊗1km ⚡200m ♻on the spot ⚓on the spot.

**Ennigerloh** 9G3

Am Freibad 3. **GPS:** n51,83304 e8,01629. ⬆➡.

2 free ⬛€ 0,50/50liter ⬛Ch ⚡(2x)€ 0,50/kWh,16Amp. **Location:** Rural, simple, noisy. **Surface:** metalled. ☐ 01/01-31/12. **Distance:** ⚓600m ⊗600m ⚡600m ♻on the spot ⚓on the spot.

**Erftstadt** 11F2

**Mobilcamp am Ville-Express**, Carl-Schurz-strasse 1a, Liblar. **GPS:** n50,81781 e6,81986. ⬆➡.

8 €6 ⬛€ 1/80liter ⬛Ch ⚡(11x)€ 0,50/kWh. 🚐 **Location:** Urban, comfortable. **Surface:** metalled. ☐ 01/01-31/12. **Distance:** ⚓1km ⚓4,4km ⚓500m ⊗200m ⚡1km.

**Erndtebrück** 11H1

**Pension Hofius**, Hilchenbachterweg 2, Zinse. **GPS:** n51,00599 e8,21224. ➡.

3 €6/24h ⬛Ch ⚡included. 🚐 ☐ 01/01-31/12. **Distance:** ⚓5km ♻on the spot ⚓on the spot. **Remarks:** Max. 8M.

**Euskirchen** 11F2

**Badewelt**, Stresemannstraße 1. **GPS:** n50,66827 e6,80333. 50 guests free. **Surface:** gravel. ☐ 01/01-31/12. **Distance:** ⚓3km ⊗1km ⚡1km ⚡3,5km.

**Everswinkel** 9G2

**Vitus-Bad**, Alverkirchenerstrasse 29. **GPS:** n51,92309 e7,83776. ⬆.

3 free ⬛€ 0,50/50liter ⬛Ch ⚡€ 0,50/kWh. **Location:** Rural, simple, noisy. **Surface:** metalled. ☐ 01/01-31/12. **Distance:** ⚓500m ⊗on the spot ⚡100m ⚡on the spot ♻100-Schlösser-Route ⚓on the spot. **Remarks:** Parking swimming pool.

**Freudenberg (NRW)** 11G1

P5, Lohmühle. **GPS:** n50,89625 e7,87636. ⬆.

3 free. **Location:** Quiet. **Surface:** metalled. ☐ 01/01-31/12. **Distance:** ⚓on the spot ⊗100m ⚡200m. **Remarks:** Max. 3 days.

**Freudenberg (NRW)** 11G1

**Parkplatz am Freibad**, Gambachsweg. **GPS:** n50,90484 e7,87615. ⬆. 3 free. **Location:** Isolated, quiet. **Surface:** grassy/gravel. ☐ 01/01-31/12. **Distance:** ⚓1km ⊗1km ⚓on the spot. **Remarks:** At swimming pool, max. 3 days.

**Gangelt** 11E1

**Rodebachtal**, Am Freibad 13. **GPS:** n50,98583 e5,99806. ⬆➡.

40 €10 ⬛Ch ⚡€ 0,40/kWh WC ⬛€ 0,60/4minutes ⬛€ 2,40. **Location:** Rural, luxurious, quiet. **Surface:** metalled. ☐ 01/01-31/12. **Distance:** ⚓on the spot ⚓on the spot ⊗on the spot ⚡1,5km ♻on the spot ⚓on the spot. **Remarks:** Arrival <18h, caution key € 10.

**Geldern** 9E3

**Am Holländer See**, Am Holländer See 19. **GPS:** n51,51131 e6,32867. ⬆➡.

45 € 8/24h, 3 days € 19 ⬛€ 1/90liter ⬛Ch ⚡(44x)€ 0,50/kWh. **Location:** Comfortable, quiet. **Surface:** grassy/metalled. ☐ 01/01-31/12. **Distance:** ⚓1km ⊗1km ⚡1km ⚓on the spot. **Remarks:** Parking centre, bread-service (weekend).

**Geldern** 9E3

**Reisemobilhafen Am Freibad**, Am Freibad 16, Walbeck. **GPS:** n51,49461 e6,22666. ⬆➡.

50 € 8/24h ⬛€ 1/80liter ⬛Ch ⚡(36x)€ 0,50/kWh. **Surface:** grassy/sand. ☐ 01/01-31/12. **Distance:** ⚓city centre Walbeck 1km, city centre Geldern 6km ⊗1km ⚡1km. **Remarks:** At swimming pool.

**Geldern** 9E3

**Reisemobilstellplatz Am Sportplatz**, Hülspassweg 20, Veert. **GPS:** n51,52960 e6,30347. ⬆➡.

30 free. **Surface:** gravel. ☐ 01/01-31/12. **Distance:** ⚓city centre Veert 200m, city centre Geldern 2km ⚡500m. **Remarks:** Parking at sports park.

**Geldern** 9E3

**Freizeit-Store Diepers**, Liebligstrasse 33. **GPS:** n51,52971 e6,35456. ⬛€ 1 ⬛€ 1 Ch. ☐ 01/01-31/12, during opening hours.

**Tourist information Geldern:**
✳ Internationaler Wettbewerb der strassenmaler und strassenmusi-kanten und -theatergruppen, Centrum. International street painting competition, street musicians and theater groups. ☐ beginning Sep.
✳ Internationales Reisemobilfest. International festival for motorcara-vanners with vast tourist program. Not necessary to book in advance,. ☐ last weekend April. ⬛ free.

**Gelsenkirchen** 9F3

**Stellplatz Nienhausen**, Feldmarkstraße 201. **GPS:** n51,50167 e7,06333. ⬆.

20 € 7, 2 pers.incl. ⬛€ 1/90liter ⬛Ch ⚡€ 1/2kWh ⬛3. 🚿 **Location:** Rural, central. **Surface:** metalled. ☐ 01/01-31/12. **Distance:** ⚓2,8km ⚓3,2km ⊗100m ⚡2km ⚡Tram 700m. **Remarks:** Bread-service, green zone: environmental badge obligatory.

**Gladbeck** 9F3

**Freizeitstätte Wittringer Wald**, Bohmertstrasse 277. **GPS:** n51,55912 e6,98403. ⬆➡.

25 free ⬛voluntary contribution ⬛Ch. **Location:** Rural, simple, quiet. **Surface:** grasstiles/grassy. ☐ 01/01-31/12. **Distance:** ⚓2km ⚓1km ⊗200m ⚡1km. **Remarks:** Green zone: environmental badge obligatory, Wasserschloß Wittringen 450m.

**Goch** 9E3

**Friedensplatz**, Thielenstrasse. **GPS:** n51,67556 e6,16639. ⬆➡.

DE

70 �\€ 5/24h ⌐€ 1/100liter ⌸Ch ⌁(60x)€ 0,50/kWh. ⌺
**Location:** Urban, comfortable, quiet. **Surface:** grassy.
◯ 01/01-31/12.
**Distance:** ⌐700m ⌐on the spot ⌧700m ⌐700m ⌐100m.
**Remarks:** Along the Niers river.

| 🛈 | **Goch** | 9E3 |

**Reisemobilstellplatz GochNess**, Kranenburger Strasse 20, Kessel.
**GPS**: n51,70291 e6,08915. ⬆.

10 ⌐free.
**Location:** Rural, simple, isolated, quiet.
**Surface:** grassy.
◯ 01/01-31/12.
**Distance:** ⌐1km ⌐1km ⌐1km.
**Remarks:** At swimming pool.
**Tourist information Goch:**
⌇ Pilgrimage for motorhomes. ◯ last weekend Jun.
⌇ Museumscafé Edison, Museum Goch. Collection of gramophones.
◯ Su 15-17h.
⌁ Herrensitz-Route. Cycle route along the Meuse and the Niers, available at Kultourbühne Goch. 🎫 € 7,90.

| 🛈 | **Grefrath** | 11E1 |

**Eissportzentrum Grefrath**, Stadionstrasse. **GPS:** n51,34889 e6,33972.

50 ⌐free. **Surface:** grasstiles.
◯ 01/01-31/12.
**Distance:** ⌐2km ⌐500m ⌧300m ⌐2km.
**Remarks:** Niederrheinisches Freilichtmuseum, Open air museum 650m.

| 🛈S | **Greven** | 9G2 |

**Reisemobilhafen Camp Marina**, Fuestruperstrasse 37, Fuestrup.
**GPS:** n52,04449 e7,68328. ⬆➡.

90 ⌐€ 12,50 ⌐€ 0,50/50liter ⌸Ch ⌁€ 2,50/day WC ⌐€ 1 ⌐€ 3/2,50 ⌒included.
**Location:** Rural, comfortable, isolated, quiet. **Surface:** grassy.
◯ 01/01-31/12.
**Distance:** ⌐on the spot ⌧Restaurant/Biergarten ⌐3km ⌐on the spot ⌐on the spot.
**Remarks:** Marina at canal, bread-service, shopping service.

| 🛈S | **Gronau** | 9F2 |

**Erholungsgebiet Dreiländersee**, Brechterweg.
**GPS:** n52,23716 e7,08006. ⬆➡.

---

100 ⌐€ 8/24, only exact change ⌐€ 0,50/60liter ⌸Ch ⌁(32x)€ 0,50/kWh WC ⌐€ 1,50. **Location:** Rural, simple, isolated.
**Surface:** grassy/metalled. ◯ 01/01-31/12.
**Distance:** ⌐3km ⌐100m ⌐on the spot ⌧200m ⌐50m (camping) ⌐on the spot.
**Remarks:** Near the lake, max. 48h.

| 🛈S | **Haltern am See** ⌇ | 9F3 |

**Wohnmobilpark Haltern am See**, Hullerner Straße 45-49.
**GPS:** n51,74186 e7,20179. ⬆➡.

30 ⌐€ 10/night ⌐€ 1/100liter ⌸Ch ⌁(30x)€ 0,50/kWh,16Amp WC ⌐€ 1,50 ⌒included ⌐. **Location:** Rural, comfortable, central.
**Surface:** grasstiles. ◯ 01/01-31/12.
**Distance:** ⌐1km ⌐3km ⌐300m ⌐1km ⌐1km ⌐200m ⌐200m ⌐200m.
**Remarks:** At swimming pool, use sanitary only during opening hours swimming pool, discount at swimming pool.

| 🛈S | **Haltern am See** ⌇ | 9F3 |

**RMS ReisemobileSpezialist**, Hellweg 252.
**GPS:** n51,75589 e7,20127. ⬆.

4 ⌐€ 10, 2 pers. incl. ⌐€ 1/100liter ⌸Chincluded ⌁(4x)€ 3/12h,16Amp. ⌺
**Location:** Rural, simple, isolated. **Surface:** grassy/gravel.
◯ 01/01-31/12.
**Distance:** ⌐2km ⌐4km ⌐800m ⌧800m ⌐1,2km ⌐50m ⌐50m.
**Remarks:** Video surveillance.

| 👥 | **Hamm** | 9G3 |

**Freizeitpark Maximilian Park**, Alter Grenzweg 2.
**GPS:** n51,68392 e7,88395. ⬆.

10 ⌐free. **Location:** Rural, simple. **Surface:** grassy.
◯ 01/01-31/12.
**Distance:** ⌐300m ⌧300m ⌐300m ⌐200m ⌐on the spot ⌐on the spot.

| 🛈 | **Harsewinkel** | 9H2 |

**Frei- und Hallenbad**, Prozessionsweg 8. **GPS:** n51,96556 e8,21935.

---

6 ⌐free. **Location:** Rural, simple, quiet. **Surface:** grassy.
◯ 01/01-31/12.
**Distance:** ⌐200m ⌧100m ⌐200m ⌐200m ⌐on the spot.
**Remarks:** Parking next to swimming pool, max. 48h.

| 🛈S | **Hattingen** ⌇ | 9F3 |

**Roonstrasse. GPS:** n51,40124 e7,18389. ⬆➡.

2 ⌐€ 4 ⌐€ 1/80liter ⌐. ⌺ **Location:** Urban, simple, quiet.
**Surface:** asphalted/metalled. ◯ 01/01-31/12.
**Distance:** ⌐300m ⌐5km ⌧300m ⌐300m.

| 🛈S | **Hattingen** ⌇ | 9F3 |

**Wohnmobilstellplatz Ruhrtal**, Ruhrdeich 24.
**GPS:** n51,40839 e7,18091. ⬆➡.

16 ⌐€ 10/night ⌐€ 1/90liter ⌸Ch ⌁(18x)€ 1/2kWh ⌐€ 1/4minutes ⌒free. **Location:** Rural, comfortable, quiet.
**Surface:** gravel. ◯ 01/01-31/12.
**Distance:** ⌐2,5km ⌐5km ⌐on the spot ⌐on the spot ⌧500m ⌐1km.
**Remarks:** Along the Ruhr river, next to midget golf.

| 🛈 | **Hattingen** ⌇ | 9F3 |

**August-Bebel strasse. GPS:** n51,39833 e7,18028. ⬆.

2 ⌐€ 3. ⌺ **Location:** Urban, simple, central, noisy. **Surface:** metalled.
◯ 01/01-31/12.
**Distance:** ⌐on the spot ⌐5km ⌧on the spot ⌐on the spot ⌐on the spot.
**Remarks:** At shopping centre Carré.

| 🛈 | **Hattingen** ⌇ | 9F3 |

**Ruhrgasse**, Bahnhofstrasse. **GPS:** n51,40083 e7,17676. ⬆➡.

3 ⌐free. **Location:** Urban, simple, quiet. **Surface:** gravel.
◯ 01/01-31/12.

**Distance:** 🚶500m 🚲5km ⊗500m 🚉500m.
**Remarks:** Parking behind the Amtshäusern, only on Sa and Su.

| 📷 | **Hattingen** 🏛️ 🍴 | **9F3** |

**Wanderparkplatz**, Isenbergstrasse. **GPS:** n51,38969 e7,15340. ⬆️

3 🏕️free. **Location:** Rural, simple. **Surface:** gravel.
⬛ Mo-Fri, 01/01-31/12.
**Distance:** 🚶2km 🚲5km ⊗300m 🚉1km 🚌on the spot 🚲on the spot 🧍on the spot.
**Remarks:** Parking along the Ruhr, max. 2 days.

| 📷 S | **Havixbeck** 🌿 | **9G2** |

**Am Freibad**, Kardinal-von-Hartmann-Straße.
**GPS:** n51,97507 e7,42092. ⬆️➡️

8 🏕️free 🚰€ 1/80liter 🔌Ch 🧹(8x)€ 0,50/kWh WC.
**Location:** Simple, quiet. **Surface:** metalled. ⬛ 01/01-31/12.
**Distance:** 🚶1km 🚲1km ⊗800m 🚉800m 🚲on the spot.
**Remarks:** Parking at swimming pool, small pitches.

| 🍴 S | **Havixbeck** 🌿 | **9G2** |

**Klute's Historischem Brauhaus**, Poppenbeck 28.
**GPS:** n51,98938 e7,39291. ⬆️

15 🏕️guests free 🚰🧹(8x)€ 5 📶♨️. **Location:** Rural, simple,
isolated. **Surface:** metalled. ⬛ 01/01-31/12.
**Distance:** 🚶2km ⊗on the spot 🚉2km 🚲on the spot 🧍on the spot.
**Remarks:** Max. 1 night.

| 📷 S | **Heimbach** 🍴 | **11E2** |

**Wohnmobilhafen am Nationalpark-Tor**, An der Laag 4.
**GPS:** n50,63683 e6,47265. ⬆️

19 🏕️€ 7,50/24h, € 0,45/pp tourist tax 🚰€ 1/100liter 🔌Ch 🧹
(20x)€ 0,50/kWh 🍽️ 1. **Location:** Rural, simple, noisy. **Surface:** gravel.
⬛ 01/01-31/12.
**Distance:** 🚶200m ⊗100m 🚌on the spot.
**Remarks:** Nearby Regioshuttle Rurtallbahn.

| 📷 S | **Heinsberg** | **11E1** |

**Heinsberg am Lago**, Fritz-Bauer-Strasse 3.
**GPS:** n51,07333 e6,09278. ⬆️➡️

43 🏕️P1 € 10/day, P2 € 10/2 days 🚰€ 1/100liter 🔌Ch 🧹(43x)€ 0,50/
kWh,16Amp. 🏠 **Location:** Rural, luxurious, quiet. **Surface:** grasstiles.
⬛ 01/01-31/12.
**Distance:** 🚶800m 🚲3,5km 🛥️Bagger See 🚉300m 🚉10m 🚉800m
🚌30m 🚲10m 🧍500m.

| 📷 | **Hellenthal** 🏛️🌲❄️ | **11E3** |

**Europa-Wohnmobilhafen**, Am Weissen Stein, Udenbreth, B265.
**GPS:** n50,40896 e6,37220. ⬆️➡️➡️

28 🏕️€ 10 🚰€ 2 🔌Ch 🧹(28x)included. 🏠
**Location:** Rural, simple. **Surface:** metalled.
⬛ 01/01-31/12.
**Distance:** 🚲on the spot 🚉on the spot.
**Remarks:** Service on campsite, winter sports area Hellenthal am Wald.

| 📷 | **Hellenthal** 🏛️🍴❄️ | **11E3** |

**Grenzlandhalle Hellenthal**, Aachenerstrasse.
**GPS:** n50,49251 e6,43651. ⬆️

15 🏕️free. **Location:** Rural, simple. **Surface:** grasstiles.
⬛ 01/01-31/12.
**Distance:** 🚶500m ⊗on the spot 🚉200m.
**Remarks:** Service on campsite.

| 🌿 S | **Hellenthal** 🏛️🍴❄️ | **11E3** |

**Breuerhof**, Zum Wilsamtal 39, Udenbreth.
**GPS:** n50,41081 e6,38992. ⬆️

2 🏕️€ 10 🚰🔌Ch 🧹(2x). ♨️ **Location:** Rural, comfortable, quiet.
**Surface:** metalled. ⬛ 01/01-31/12.
**Distance:** 🚲2km 🚉on the spot.
**Remarks:** Check in at nr. 35.

**Tourist information Hellenthal:**
👁️ Greifvogelstation, Wildfreigehege 1. Predatory bird station.
⬛ 01/11-31/03 10-17h, 01/04-31/10 9-18h.

| 🌿 | **Hemer** 🍴 | **9G3** |

**Wohnmobilstellplatz Hemer**, Hönnetalstraße.
**GPS:** n51,37841 e7,77151. ⬆️

20 🏕️€ 2/8-20h 🚰€ 1/80liter 🔌Ch 1 🧹(12x)€ 0,50/kWh.
**Location:** Urban, comfortable, quiet. **Surface:** asphalted/grassy.
⬛ 01/01-31/12.
**Distance:** 🚶1km 🚲6km ⊗300m 🚉bakery 500m 🧍on the spot.
**Remarks:** Max. 3 nights.

| 📷 S | **Herford** | **9H2** |

**H20**, Wiessenstrasse 90. **GPS:** n52,10750 e8,68534. ⬆️➡️

22 🏕️€ 5 🚰€ 1/100liter 🔌Ch 🧹1 WC 🍽️1 📶included. 🏠
**Location:** Rural, comfortable. **Surface:** metalled.
⬛ 01/01-31/12.
**Distance:** 🚶on the spot 🚲2km ⊗200m.
**Remarks:** At swimming pool.

| 📷 S | **Herford** | **9H2** |

**Am Stadion**, Dennewitzstrasse 15. **GPS:** n52,10474 e8,68931. ⬆️➡️

10 🏕️free. **Location:** Rural, simple. **Surface:** asphalted.
⬛ 01/01-31/12.
**Distance:** 🚶2,5km 🚲3km ⊗350m 🚉350m.

| 📷 S | **Herscheid** 🍴 | **11G1** |

**Am Warmwasserfreibad**, Unterdorfstraße.
**GPS:** n51,17567 e7,74368. ⬆️

3 🏕️free 🚰€ 1/10minutes 🔌Ch 🧹(4x)€ 1/8h.
**Location:** Rural, comfortable, quiet. **Surface:** gravel.
⬛ 01/01-31/12.
**Distance:** 🚶1,2km 🚲10km ⊗400m 🚉650m 🧍on the spot.

| 📷 S | **Hilchenbach** 🏛️🍴 | **11H1** |

**Hallenbad Dahlbruch**, Bernhard-Weiss-Platz, Dahlbruch.
**GPS:** n50,97792 e8,05343. ⬆️

3 🏕️free 🚰€ 1/10minutes 🔌. **Surface:** asphalted/metalled.
⬛ 01/01-31/12.

**Distance:** 🚶400m ⊗300m 🛒400m.
**Remarks:** Parking behind swimming pool, max. 48h, use sanitary only during opening hours swimming pool, against payment.

| 🏕️S | Hilchenbach 🍴💧 | 11H1 |

**Parkplatz P4**, Rothenberger strasse, L728.
**GPS:** n50,99702 e8,11103. ⬆️➡️.

3 🛏️free WC.
**Surface:** metalled. ◻️ 01/01-31/12.
**Distance:** 🚶100m ⊗200m 🛒100m.
**Remarks:** Parking in front of shopping centre Gerberpark, max. 48h.

| 🏕️ | Hilchenbach 🍴💧 | 11H1 |

**Bürgerhaus**, Merklinghäuser weg, Müsen.
**GPS:** n50,99267 e8,04497. ⬆️.

3 🛏️free. **Surface:** asphalted. ◻️ 01/01-31/12.
**Distance:** 🚶8km ⊗800m 🛒600m.
**Remarks:** Max. 48h.

| 🏕️ | Hilchenbach 🍴💧 | 11H1 |

**Gillerberg**, Gillerbergstraße 28. **GPS:** n50,97175 e8,16130.
3 🛏️free. ◻️ 01/01-31/12.
**Distance:** 🚶9km 🎿on the spot.

| 🏨S | Hilchenbach 🍴💧 | 11H1 |

**Landhotel Steubers Siebelnhof**, Siebelnhoferstrasse, Vormwald.
**GPS:** n50,98658 e8,13173. ⬆️.
6 🛏️€ 20,50, use sanitary facilities/swimming pool sauna incl WC☐included. **Location:** Rural, simple, isolated, quiet.
**Surface:** asphalted/metalled. ◻️ 01/01-31/12.
**Distance:** 🚶2km ⊗on the spot 🛒2km.

| 🏕️S | Hopsten | 9G1 |

**Dreifachturnhalle**, Rüschendorfer strasse 4.
**GPS:** n52,38544 e7,60490. ⬆️.

6 🛏️free 🚰🔌Ch💧free. **Location:** Rural, simple.
**Surface:** grassy/metalled. ◻️ 01/01-31/12.
**Distance:** 🚶100m ⊗100m 🛒100m 🎿on the spot.
**Remarks:** Parking at gymnasium, max. 3 days.

| 🏕️S | Horn 🍴 | 10A2 |

**Wohnmobilhafen am Bad Meinberger Badehaus**, Wällenweg, Bad Meinberg. **GPS:** n51,89818 e8,99249. ⬆️➡️.

24 🛏️€ 7,50 + € 1,60/pp tourist tax 🚰€ 1/100liter 🔌€ 0,50
Ch💧€ 0,50/kWh WC☐€ 2,50.

---

**Location:** Rural, quiet. **Surface:** grassy/metalled.
◻️ 01/01-31/12.
**Distance:** 🚶200m ⊗on the spot 🛒200m 🛍️100m.
**Remarks:** Behind spa, bread-service, discount at swimming pool.

| 🏕️S | Hörstel 🍴 | 9G2 |

**Wohnmobilhafen Riesenbeck**, Postdamm-Lazarusbrücke.
**GPS:** n52,25574 e7,63387. ⬆️.

18 🛏️€ 5/24h 🔌€ 1/2kWh. **Location:** Rural, comfortable, central, noisy. **Surface:** grassy/gravel. ◻️ 01/01-31/12.
**Distance:** 🚶700m ⛵on the spot 🚣on the spot 🛒300m 🚌on the spot 🚲 100-Schlösser-Route 🚶on the spot.
**Remarks:** Max. 3 nights.

| 🏕️S | Hövelhof 💧 | 9H2 |

**P Bahnhof**, Westfalenstrasse. **GPS:** n51,82417 e8,66099. ⬆️.

6 🛏️free 🚰free 💧(6x)€ 1/2kWh. **Location:** Urban, simple.
**Surface:** gravel. ◻️ 01/01-31/12.
**Distance:** 🚶500m 🚂4,2km ⊗500m 🛒700m 🚌50m 🚲on the spot 🚶on the spot.

| 🏕️S | Hövelhof 💧 | 9H2 |

**Wohnmobil-stellplatz Apelhof**, Paderborner Straße 172.
**GPS:** n51,80166 e8,67697. ⬆️.
8 🛏️€ 8 🚰. **Surface:** grassy. ◻️ 01/01-31/12.
**Distance:** 🚶3km ⊗250m 🛒3km.

| 🏕️S | Höxter 🌿🏖️🍴💧🌾 | 10A3 |

**Freizeitanlage Höxter-Godelheim**, Godelheimer Strasse.
**GPS:** n51,75787 e9,37557. ⬆️➡️.

50 🛏️€ 8/24h 🚰Ch WC☐included. 🚐
**Location:** Rural, comfortable, quiet. **Surface:** grasstiles.
◻️ 01/01-31/12 ⊙ service: 01/10-01/04.
**Distance:** 🚶800m ⛵on the spot ⊗50m 🛒1,2km 🚲on the spot 🚶on the spot.
**Remarks:** Bread-service, recreation area.

| 🏕️S | Höxter 🌿🏖️🍴💧🌾 | 10A3 |

**Wohnmobilhafen Floßplatz**, Milchweg.
**GPS:** n51,77325 e9,38781. ⬆️➡️.

70 🛏️€ 7/24h 🚰€ 1/100liter 🔌Ch💧(40x)€ 1/2kWh. 🚐
**Location:** Rural, comfortable, central, quiet.
**Surface:** grassy/gravel.
◻️ 01/01-31/12.

---

**Distance:** 🚶300m ⛵on the spot 🎣fishing permit available ⊗100m 🛒500m 🚐500m on camp site 🚌200m 🚲on the spot.
**Remarks:** Parking beside river Weser, bread-service in summer period.

| 🏞️S | Hückelhoven | 11E1 |

**Hückelhovener Ruraue**, Rheinstraße 4b. **GPS:** n51,05146 e6,21208. ⬆️.

6 🛏️€ 4,50 🚰€ 0,50/100liter 🔌Ch💧€ 0,50/kWh. 🚲
**Location:** Rural, simple, isolated, quiet. **Surface:** metalled.
◻️ 01/01-31/12 ⊙ With snow.
**Distance:** 🚶1,5km.

| 🏕️ | Hürtgenwald 💧 | 11E2 |

**Einmündung Kall-Rur**, Zerkall. **GPS:** n50,69156 e6,45212. ⬆️.

10 🛏️free. **Location:** Rural, simple. **Surface:** gravel.
◻️ 01/01-31/12.
**Distance:** 🚶100m ⛵on the spot 🚣on the spot 🚌200m.
**Remarks:** Along the river Kall/Rur.

| 🏕️ | Hürtgenwald 💧 | 11E2 |

**Parkplatz Burgstrasse**, Burgstrasse, Bergstein.
**GPS:** n50,69582 e6,43848. ⬆️.

5 🛏️free. **Location:** Simple. **Surface:** metalled.
◻️ 01/01-31/12.
**Distance:** ⛵700m 🛒1km.

| 🏕️ | Hürtgenwald 💧 | 11E2 |

**Soldatenfriedhof**, Höhenstrasse, Hürtgen.
**GPS:** n50,70552 e6,36063. ⬆️.

9 🛏️free. **Location:** Rural, simple, noisy. **Surface:** asphalted.
◻️ 01/01-31/12.
**Distance:** ⊗1,2km.

| 🏨S | Hürtgenwald 💧 | 11E2 |

**Landhotel Kallbach**, Kallweg 24, Simonskall. **GPS:** n50,66716 e6,35395.

5 ⚡€ 12 🚰🔌Ch. **Location:** Rural, comfortable, quiet.
**Surface:** metalled. 🗓 01/01-31/12.
**Distance:** 🚶200m ⊗on the spot.
**Remarks:** Discount at restaurant.

| 📷 | **Hüsten** | **9G3** |
|---|---|---|

**Parkplatz Große Wiese. GPS:** n51,43151 e8,00475.⬆.
4 ⚡free. **Surface:** asphalted. 🗓 01/01-31/12.
**Distance:** 🚲2km 🛶on the spot 🚴on the spot.
**Remarks:** Next to the Sole-Bad.

| 📷 | **Ibbenbüren** | **9G2** |
|---|---|---|

**Aseebad**, An der Umfluth 99. **GPS:** n52,26181 e7,73171.➡.

30 ⚡€ 3. **Location:** Comfortable, central, quiet. **Surface:** grassy.
🗓 01/01-31/12.
**Distance:** 🚲2,3km.
**Remarks:** Parking next to swimming pool, max. 4 nights.

| 📷 S | **Iserlohn** 🌳 | **9G3** |
|---|---|---|

**Parkplatz Seilerblick**, Friesenstraße. **GPS:** n51,38456 e7,71128.⬆➡.

5 ⚡free 🚰€ 1 🔌€ 1 Ch 1 ✂(4x)€ 0,50. **Location:** Urban, simple,
noisy. **Surface:** asphalted. 🗓 01/01-31/12.
**Distance:** 🚶2km 🚲2,5km 🚴on the spot 🏃on the spot.
**Remarks:** Next to tennis-court.

| 📷 S | **Isselburg** 🌳 | **9E3** |
|---|---|---|

**Stellplatz am Stadtturm**, Münsterdeich. **GPS:** n51,83452 e6,46477.⬆.

6 ⚡€ 5 🚰€ 1/100liter 🔌Ch ✂(6x)€ 1/day.🚐 **Location:** Rural,
simple, quiet. **Surface:** grassy. 🗓 01/01-31/12.
**Distance:** 🚶on the spot 🛶on the spot ⊗300m 🚰100m.
**Remarks:** At the Issel, parking centre, max. 72h.

| 📷 | **Isselburg** 🌳 | **9E3** |
|---|---|---|

**Hotel Restaurant Brüggenhütte**, Hahnerfeld 23, Anholt.
**GPS:** n51,85301 e6,47187.⬆.

5 ⚡free.
**Location:** Rural, simple, noisy. **Surface:** grassy.
🗓 01/01-31/12.
**Distance:** 200m ⊗on the spot 🚰2km 🚴on the spot.
**Remarks:** Along through road, behind restaurant, max. 3 days.

| 🍴 | **Isselburg** 🌳 | **9E3** |
|---|---|---|

**Bürgerhaus**, Anholter strasse, Vehlingen. **GPS:** n51,83089 e6,42297.⬆.

5 ⚡free. **Location:** Rural, simple. **Surface:** gravel.
🗓 01/01-31/12.
**Distance:** 🚶1km ⊗on the spot.
**Remarks:** Max. 2 nights.

| 📷 S | **Isselburg** 🌳 | **9E3** |
|---|---|---|

**Biotopwildpark Anholter Schweiz**, Pferdehorster Str. 1.
**GPS:** n51,83225 e6,43013.⬆➡.

6 ⚡€ 7 ✂(6x)included. **Location:** Rural, simple.
**Surface:** gravel/metalled. 🗓 15/03-25/10.
**Distance:** 🚶1km.
**Remarks:** Max. 3 nights, check in at pay-desk, caution key electricity
€ 20.

| 📷 | **Isselburg** 🌳 | **9E3** |
|---|---|---|

**Ponyhof Leiting**, Alte Bundesstrasse 3, Werth.
**GPS:** n51,81332 e6,49258.⬆➡.

10 ⚡free. **Location:** Rural, simple, quiet. **Surface:** grassy.
🗓 01/01-31/12.
**Distance:** ⊗on the spot.
**Remarks:** Max. 72h.

| 📷 S | **Issum-Sevelen** | **9E3** |
|---|---|---|

**Wohnmobilpark Hexenland-Sevelen**, Koetherdyck 18.
**GPS:** n51,49926 e6,43676.⬆➡.

20 ⚡€ 9 🚰🔌Ch ✂€ 3/24h WC€ 1/10minutes 🔌included.
**Location:** Rural, comfortable, quiet. **Surface:** gravel.
🗓 01/01-31/12.
**Distance:** 🚶Sevelen 1km 🛶200m ⊗100m 🚰1km.

| 📷 S | **Jülich** | **11E1** |
|---|---|---|

**Brückenkopf-Park**, Rurauenstrasse 11. **GPS:** n50,92345 e6,34029.⬆.

22 ⚡€ 9,50 🚰€ 1/100liter 🔌Ch ✂WC€ 1.

**Location:** Urban, simple, central, noisy. **Surface:** grassy.
🗓 01/01-31/12 🔲 sanitary building: 01/11-31/03.
**Remarks:** Parking at the Rur.
**Tourist information Jülich:**
ℹ Old fortress city.

| 📷 S | **Kalkar** | **9E3** |
|---|---|---|

**Reisemobilstellplatz Kalkar**, Waysche strasse.
**GPS:** n51,74008 e6,30101.⬆➡.

35 ⚡€ 7,50 🚰€ 1/30liter 🔌€ 1 Ch ✂(24x)€ 1/2kWh 🔌included.
🚐 **Location:** Rural, comfortable, central. **Surface:** grassy/gravel.
🗓 01/01-31/12.
**Distance:** 🚶500m 🛶400m 🚰700m 🚴on the spot.
**Remarks:** Max. 3 nights.
**Tourist information Kalkar:**
KernWasser Wunderland. Amusement park.

| 📷 S | **Kall** | **11F2** |
|---|---|---|

**Im Kallbachtal**, Kapellenstrasse 25, Golbach.
**GPS:** n50,52784 e6,53681.⬆➡.

10 ⚡€ 6 🚰€ 1 🔌Ch ✂(8x)€ 0,50/kWh. **Location:** Rural, simple,
quiet. **Surface:** gravel. 🗓 01/01-31/12.

| 📷 | **Kamp-Lintfort** | **9E3** |
|---|---|---|

**Pappelsee**, Berthastraße 74. **GPS:** n51,50026 e6,53861.⬆➡.

20 ⚡free. **Location:** Simple. **Surface:** asphalted.
🗓 01/01-31/12.
**Distance:** 🚶1,5km ⊗1km 🚰1,5km.
**Remarks:** Caution € 2,50 to pay-desk of the park.
**Tourist information Kamp-Lintfort:**
🏛 Marktplatz, Eberstrasse. 🗓 Thu, Sa.
🏛 Rathausplatz. 🗓 Tue 7.30-13h.
☀ Mittelalterlicher Markt, Abteiplatz. Medieval market. 🗓 3rd
weekend Sep.

| 📷 S | **Kempen** | **11E1** |
|---|---|---|

**Reisemobilpark Kempen am Aqua-sol**, Berliner Allee.
**GPS:** n51,36719 e6,40910.⬆.

29 ⚡€ 8/24h 🚰€ 1/100liter 🔌Ch ✂€ 0,50/kWh,16Amp.
**Location:** Urban, simple. **Surface:** metalled. 🗓 01/01-31/12.
**Distance:** 🚶1,5km ⊗on the spot 🚰1,5km.

## Kerken — 9E3

**Wohnmobilpark Aldekerker Platte**, Kempener Straße 9, Aldekerk.
**GPS**: n51,43551 e6,41902.

30 € 7 Ch included (30x) € 3. **Location**: Rural, simple, quiet. **Surface**: grassy/gravel. 01/01-31/12.
**Distance**: 400m 2,5km 2km 2km 400m 500m 300m on the spot on the spot.

## Kevelaer — 9E3

**Den Heyberg**, Im Auwelt 45, Twisteden. **GPS**: n51,56345 e6,19418.

150 € 9 Ch (150x)included. **Location**: Comfortable.
**Surface**: asphalted/metalled. 01/01-31/12.
**Distance**: 2km 100m 2km 100m.
**Remarks**: Bread-service (weekend), barbecue place.

## Kevelaer — 9E3

**Sporthotel Schravelsche Heide**, Grotendonkerstrasse 56-58.
**GPS**: n51,59556 e6,25306.

100 € 9,50 € 1 Ch WC € 0,50 included.
**Location**: Rural, comfortable, quiet. **Surface**: grassy.
01/01-31/12.
**Distance**: 1,5km 100m 1km on the spot on the spot.

## Kevelaer — 9E3

**Europaplatz**, Bahnhof/Geldernstrasse, B9.
**GPS**: n51,57904 e6,25192.

3 free. **Surface**: asphalted. 01/01-31/12.
**Distance**: 500m 500m on the spot.

**Tourist information Kevelaer:**
Fr 14-18h.

## Kirchhundem — 11H1

**Restaurant Rhein-Weser-Turm**, Rhein-Weser-Turm 2.
**GPS**: n51,07109 e8,19791.

10 € 10 Ch included. **Location**: Rural. **Surface**: gravel.
01/01-31/12.
**Distance**: on the spot.

## Kirchhundem — 11H1

**Restaurant Zur Hahnenquelle**, Rhein-Weser-Turm.
**GPS**: n51,07198 e8,19792.
10 € 10 Ch included. **Location**: Simple. 01/01-31/12.
**Distance**: on the spot.

## Kirchhundem — 11H1

**PanoramaPark Sauerland Wildpark**, Rinsecker Straße 100.
**GPS**: n51,06972 e8,17417.
10 € 2. **Location**: Rural, simple. 01/01-31/12.

## Kleve — 9E3

**Stellplatz van-den-Bergh-Straße**, Van-den-Bergh-Straße.
**GPS**: n51,78917 e6,14836.

60 € 5 Ch free (30x) € 0,50/kWh. **Location**: Urban, simple, noisy. **Surface**: metalled. 01/01-31/12.
**Distance**: 500m 400m 200m.
**Remarks**: Behind railway station, max. 72h.

## Kleve — 9E3

**Reisemobilpark Kleve**, Landwehr/Spyckstraße.
**GPS**: n51,80083 e6,13222.

75 € 8,50 € 1 Ch (45x) € 3,50 WC € 0,50 € 1.
**Location**: Urban, comfortable. **Surface**: grassy/metalled.
01/01-31/12.
**Distance**: Kleve-zentrum 1,5km 300m 400m.
**Remarks**: 4th night free.

## Kleve — 9E3

**Am Willisee**, Zyfflicherstrasse 33, Keeken.
**GPS**: n51,84013 e6,08307.

25 € 10 Ch (25x) € 2/day WC included.
**Location**: Rural, luxurious, isolated, quiet. **Surface**: grassy/gravel.
01/01-31/12.
**Distance**: 900m, Kleve city centre 7km on the spot on the spot 400m 4,2km 150m on the spot on the spot.
**Remarks**: Fishing permit available.

## Kleve — 9E3

**Parkplatz Sporthalle Kleve-Kellen**, Postdeich, Kellen.
**GPS**: n51,80463 e6,16378.

20 free. **Location**: Rural, simple, quiet. **Surface**: metalled.
01/01-31/12.
**Distance**: 2,5km Steakhaus 350m 300m on the spot.

## Kleve — 9E3

**Schenkenschanz**. **GPS**: n51,83526 e6,11205.

5 free. **Location**: Rural, simple, isolated, quiet. **Surface**: gravel.
01/01-31/12.
**Distance**: Kleve 6,5km 1km 2,5km.

## Kleve — 9E3

**Stellplatz Reichswalde**, Dorfanger, Reichswalde.
**GPS**: n51,75985 e6,10243.

10 free. **Location**: Urban, simple, quiet. **Surface**: asphalted.
01/01-31/12.
**Distance**: Kleve 3km 200m 500m on the spot on the spot on the spot.

## Kleve — 9E3

**Stellplatz Rindern**, Drususdeich, Rindern.
**GPS**: n51,81212 e6,12884.

5 free. **Location**: Rural, simple, quiet. **Surface**: metalled.
01/01-31/12.
**Distance**: Kleve-zentrum 2,3km 450m 400m on the spot on the spot.
**Remarks**: Behind church.

## Kleve — 9E3

**Tiergarten**, Tiergartenstrasse, B9 dir Nijmegen.
**GPS**: n51,79784 e6,12059.

5 free. **Location**: Motorway, simple. **Surface**: metalled.
01/01-31/12.
**Distance**: 800m 250m.

## Kleve 9E3

Wehrpöhl, Griethausen. **GPS**: n51,82476 e6,16448. ⬆.

5 ⓈⒻfree. **Location**: Rural, simple, quiet. **Surface**: asphalted.
🅾 01/01-31/12.
**Distance**: 2,5km ⊗300m 🚊300m 🚲on the spot.
**Remarks**: Access via Brienen.
**Tourist information Kleve**:
🎆 Lichterfest. City celebration. 🅾 2nd Sa of the month.
Tiergarten Kleve, Tiergartenstrasse. Animal park.

## Köln 11F1

**Reisemobilhafen Köln**, An der Schanz, Cologne (Köln).
**GPS**: n50,96256 e6,98601. ⬆➡.

65 ⓈⒻ€ 12/24h ⌕€ 1 Ch (30x)€ 0,50/kWh. 🚐
**Location**: Urban, comfortable, quiet. **Surface**: asphalted.
🅾 01/01-31/12.
**Distance**: on the spot 5km ⊗600m 🚊800m 🚈metro 10 min
walking 🚲on the spot 🚶on the spot. **Remarks**: Along the Rhine river,
green zone: environmental badge obligatory.

## Königswinter 11F2

Hauptstrasse, Niederdollendorf. **GPS**: n50,69697 e7,17641. ⬆.

30 ⓈⒻfree. **Location**: Urban, simple. **Surface**: asphalted/metalled.
🅾 01/01-31/12.
**Distance**: 400m 9km 🚈800m 🚲on the spot 🚶on the spot.

## Kranenburg 9E3

**Am Sportzentrum**, Großen Haag, 47599.
**GPS**: n51,79242 e6,01033. ⬆➡.

30 ⓈⒻ€ 4/24h ⌕€ 0,20/liter €1 Ch (12x)€ 0,50/kWh.🚐
**Location**: Rural, simple. **Surface**: grassy. 🅾 01/01-31/12.
**Distance**: 500m 1km 1km ⊗500m 🚊500m 🚲on the spot
🚶on the spot.
**Remarks**: Service 500m.

## Krefeld 11F1

**Reisemobilstellplatz Linn**, Alte Rheinbabenstraße.
**GPS**: n51,33570 e6,62974.
8 ⓈⒻfree. **Location**: Urban. **Surface**: metalled. 🅾 01/01-31/12.
**Distance**: 6km ⊗600m 🚊500m 🚈250m 🚲on the spot
🚶on the spot.
**Remarks**: Max. 48h, outside environmental zone.

## Kreuztal 11G1

Heugraben. **GPS**: n50,95778 e7,99167. ⬆.

3 ⓈⒻfree ⌕€ 1/100liter Ch (4x)€ 1/2kWh.
**Surface**: metalled. 🅾 01/01-31/12.
**Distance**: 300m 7,5km ⊗300m 🚊300m 🚈station 100m.
**Remarks**: Max. 3 days.

## Kürten 11G1

**Wohnmobilpark am Splash**, Broch 8. **GPS**: n51,05586 e7,28943. ⬆.

20 ⓈⒻ€ 8 ⌕€ 2 Ch €2 WC.
**Location**: Rural, simple, quiet. **Surface**: gravel.
🅾 01/01-31/12.
**Distance**: 2km 17km ⊗on the spot 🚲on the spot 🚶on the spot.
**Remarks**: Behind Sauna-/Badeland Splash.

## Ladbergen 9G2

**Rathauspark**, Jahnstrasse. **GPS**: n52,13652 e7,74009.

8 ⓈⒻfree. **Location**: Rural, simple, quiet. **Surface**: grassy.
🅾 01/01-31/12.
**Distance**: 200m ⊗200m 🚊300m 🚈200m 🚲on the spot.
**Remarks**: Parking behind town hall.

## Lennestadt 11H1

**Naturerlebnisbad**, Fasanenweg 10. **GPS**: n51,11814 e8,16990.
3 ⓈⒻfree . **Location**: Urban, simple. **Surface**: metalled.
🅾 01/01-31/12.
**Distance**: 300m ⊗300m.
**Remarks**: At swimming pool.

## Lennestadt 11H1

**Parkplatz P4**, An der Sauerlandhalle. **GPS**: n51,10557 e8,08017. ⬆.

4 ⓈⒻfree (4x)€ 0,50/4h. **Location**: Simple. **Surface**: asphalted.
🅾 01/01-31/12.
**Distance**: 700m ⊗700m 🚊100m.

## Leverkusen 11F1

**Camping-Caravaning Meier**, Adolf-Kaschny-Straße 9, Küppersteg.
**GPS**: n51,05211 e7,00003. ⬆.

10 ⓈⒻfree ⌕€ 0,50/50liter Ch€ 0,50.
**Location**: Urban, simple. **Surface**: gravel. 🅾 01/01-31/12.
**Distance**: 3,2km.
**Remarks**: Motorhome dealer, accessory shop, repairs.

## Lienen 9G2

**Hallenfreibad**, Holperdorperstrasse 37/39.
**GPS**: n52,15575 e7,97392. ⬆➡.

3 ⓈⒻfree ⌕€ 5 Ch WC €3. **Location**: Rural, simple, quiet.
**Surface**: metalled. 🅾 01/01-31/12.
**Distance**: 1km ⊗100m 🚊2km 🚲on the spot 🚶on the spot.
**Remarks**: Parking in front of swimming pool, max. 3 nights, service to
be paid at swimming pool.

## Lindlar 11G1

**Am Freizeitpark**, Brionner Straße 1. **GPS**: n51,01550 e7,36645. ⬆➡.

2 ⓈⒻfree ⌕€ 1/10minutes Ch (4x)€ 1/6h. **Location**: Urban,
simple. **Surface**: metalled. 🅾 01/01-31/12.
**Distance**: 1km 16km ⊗1km 🚊1km 🚲on the spot 🚶on the
spot.

## Lippstadt 9H3

Bückeburger Straße. **GPS**: n51,67348 e8,33336.

11 ⓈⒻfree ⌕€ 1/100liter Chfree €1/4h.
**Location**: Urban, comfortable, quiet. **Surface**: metalled.
🅾 01/01-31/12.
**Distance**: 1,2km ⊗500m 🚊600m 🚲on the spot 🚶on the spot.
**Remarks**: At swimming pool, max. 4 days.

## Lippstadt 9H3

**Camping Lippstadt**, Seeuferstraße 16. **GPS**: n51,70194 e8,40789.
18 ⓈⒻ€ 11, 2 pers. incl., dog € 2,50 ⌕€ 0,50/50liter
Ch €0,50/kWh WC. **Location**: Rural, simple, isolated, quiet.
**Surface**: grassy/gravel. 🅾 01/03-31/10.
**Distance**: 200m 200m.

## Lippstadt 9H3

**Campingoase Lange**, Dorfstraße 47, Benninghausen.
**GPS**: n51,66103 e8,24435.

15 ⌁€ 10, 2 pers.incl ⌁⌁Ch ⌁included ⌁€ 1. **Location:** Rural, simple. **Surface:** metalled. ⬚ 01/01-31/12. **Distance:** ⌁300m ⌁on the spot.

| 🅢 | **Löhne** | 9H2 |

**Reisemobilstellplatz**, Albert-Schweitzer-strasse 12. **GPS:** n52,20399 e8,71892. ⬆➡.

18 ⌁€ 8 ⌁⌁Chincluded ⌁(18x)€ 1/2kWh. **Location:** Rural, quiet. **Surface:** metalled. ⬚ 01/01-31/12. **Distance:** ⌁500m ⌁1km ⌁100m ⌁500m ⌁500m.

| 🅢 | **Lotte** 🐑 | 9G2 |

**Fam. Arendröwer**, Am Nordberg 4. **GPS:** n52,26306 e7,89833. ⬆.

4 ⌁€ 5 ⌁€ 2 ⌁Ch ⌁€ 2/24 ⌁included. **Location:** Simple, isolated, noisy. **Surface:** grassy/metalled. ⬚ 01/03-01/10. **Distance:** ⌁3km ⌁500m ⌁3km.

| 🅢 | **Lotte** 🐑 | 9G2 |

**Tennishalle Lotte**, Kornweg 3. **GPS:** n52,27192 e7,92275. ⬆.

10 ⌁free. **Location:** Simple, quiet. **Surface:** gravel/metalled. ⬚ 01/01-31/12. **Distance:** ⌁900m ⌁3,5km ⌁1km ⌁300m.

| 🅢 | **Lübbecke** | 9H1 |

**Stellplatz Lübbecke**, Rahdener Straße. **GPS:** n52,31019 e8,61839.

4 ⌁€ 6 ⌁€ 3 ⌁Ch ⌁€ 3. ⌁ **Location:** Urban, central. **Surface:** metalled. ⬚ 01/01-31/12. **Distance:** ⌁600m ⌁700m ⌁500m ⌁on the spot ⌁on the spot. **Remarks:** Max. 3 days.

| 🅢🅢 | **Lüdenscheid** 🐑 | 11G1 |

**Familienbades Nattenberg**, Talstraße 59. **GPS:** n51,21042 e7,61803. ⬆➡.

---

4 ⌁free ⌁€ 1/200liter ⌁Ch ⌁(4x)€ 1/6h. **Location:** Urban, simple. **Surface:** metalled. ⬚ 01/01-31/12. **Distance:** ⌁city centre 1,6km ⌁4km ⌁Burger King 450m ⌁Aldi 900m ⌁on the spot.

| 🅢 | **Lüdinghausen** 🐑 | 9G3 |

**Parkplatz Rosengarten**, Am Rosengarten, Seppenrade. **GPS:** n51,76407 e7,39728. ⬆.

2 ⌁free ⌁. **Location:** Urban, simple, quiet. **Surface:** asphalted. ⬚ 01/01-31/12. **Distance:** ⌁200m ⌁200m ⌁800m.

| 🅢 | **Lüdinghausen** 🐑 | 9G3 |

**Parkplatz Aqua-See**, Rohrkamp 23. **GPS:** n51,77229 e7,42731. ⬆.

5 ⌁free. **Location:** Rural, simple, quiet. **Surface:** metalled. ⬚ 01/01-31/12. **Distance:** ⌁1,5km ⌁500m ⌁1km ⌁on the spot. **Remarks:** Parking swimming pool.

| 🅢🅢 | **Lüdinghausen** 🐑 | 9G3 |

**Am Gasthaus Peters**, Ondrup 18. **GPS:** n51,77750 e7,40972. 10 ⌁€ 5, 2 pers.incl ⌁⌁Chincluded ⌁€ 2/day WC⌁⌁⌁. **Location:** Rural, comfortable, isolated, quiet. **Surface:** gravel. ⬚ 01/01-31/12. **Distance:** ⌁3,5km ⌁on the spot ⌁on the spot ⌁on the spot. **Remarks:** Bread-service.

| 🅢🅢 | **Marsberg** 🐑 | 10A3 |

**Wohnmobilhafen**, Am Sportplatz. **GPS:** n51,45974 e8,84864. ⬆➡.

4 ⌁€ 5/24h ⌁⌁Ch ⌁(4x)included. ⌁ **Location:** Urban, simple. **Surface:** asphalted. ⬚ 01/01-31/12. **Distance:** ⌁100m ⌁200m ⌁200m. **Remarks:** Max. 5 days, caution key € 20 (pay-desk of theTherme).

| 🅢🅢 | **Mechernich** | 11F2 |

**Mühlental**, Elisabethhütte, B477. **GPS:** n50,59686 e6,63207. ⬆.

---

20 ⌁free. **Location:** Rural, simple, noisy. **Surface:** asphalted. ⬚ 01/01-31/12. **Distance:** ⌁500m.

| 🅢🅢 | **Mechernich** | 11F2 |

**Parkplatz Essensgasse**, Am Kirchberg, Kommern. **GPS:** n50,61376 e6,64479.

8 ⌁free. **Location:** Rural, simple, noisy. **Surface:** metalled. ⬚ 01/01-31/12. **Distance:** ⌁historical centre 200m. **Remarks:** Via B266.

| 🅢🅢 | **Meinerzhagen** | 11G1 |

**An der Musikschule**, Schulplatz. **GPS:** n51,10865 e7,64329. ⬆.

3 ⌁free ⌁(4x)€ 0,50/kWh. **Location:** Urban, simple, quiet. **Surface:** asphalted. ⬚ 01/01-31/12. **Distance:** ⌁400m ⌁3km ⌁400m ⌁400m ⌁on the spot ⌁on the spot.

| 🅢🅢 | **Meschede** 🐑🐑 | 11H1 |

**Am Wofibad**, Im Ohl 13, Freienohl. **GPS:** n51,37574 e8,17664. ⬆.

3 ⌁free ⌁against payment. **Location:** Simple. **Surface:** metalled. ⬚ 01/01-31/12.

| 🅢 | **Meschede** 🐑🐑 | 11H1 |

**An der Ruhr**, Arnsberger Strasse. **GPS:** n51,34897 e8,27356. ⬆➡.

10 ⌁free. **Location:** Simple. **Surface:** metalled. ⬚ 18.30-9.30h. **Distance:** ⌁500m ⌁on the spot ⌁on the spot ⌁500m ⌁500m. **Remarks:** At swimming pool.

| 🅒🅢 | **Meschede** 🐑🐑 | 11H1 |

**Knaus Campingpark Hennesee**, Mielinghausen 7. **GPS:** n51,29846 e8,26366. ⬆.

DE

17 � € 8-10 🚰 € 1/60liter ⚡€ 0,50 Ch € 0,50 💧(16x) € 0,70/kWh WC 🚿sanitary € 2,30-3,50 📶. **Location:** Rural, comfortable, isolated, quiet. **Surface:** grassy/metalled. 🅿 01/01-31/12.
**Distance:** �5km 🏊100m 🚃100m ⊗on the spot 🍴on the spot 🚲on the spot 🚶on the spot.

### Mettingen · 9G2
**Hallenbad**, Bahnhofstrasse 18-20. **GPS:** n52,31738 e7,78312.⬆.

2 ⌐free 🚰 ⚡ 🚿 WC. **Location:** Simple. **Surface:** metalled. 🅿 01/01-31/12.
**Distance:** 🚶on the spot ⊗200m 🍴200m 🚃on the spot 🚲on the spot 🚶on the spot.
**Remarks:** Parking swimming pool, service: Kläranlage, Neuenkirchenerstrasse 208, bicycle rental.

### Minden · 10A2
**Reisemobilstellplatz Kanzlers Weide**, Hausbergerstrasse. **GPS:** n52,28750 e8,92551.⬆.

100 ⌐€ 5 ⚡€ 1/100liter 🚿Ch 💧(18x) € 0,50/kWh,6Amp.
**Location:** Urban, simple, quiet. **Surface:** metalled. 🅿 01/01-31/12.
**Distance:** 🚶200m 🏊50m 🚃50m ⊗200m 🍴200m 🚃200m.
**Remarks:** Max. 3 nights, not during big events.

### Moers · 9F3
**Am Aktivbad Solimare**, Filder Straße 144. **GPS:** n51,43897 e6,62004.

11 ⌐free 🚰 🚿Ch 💧. **Location:** Urban. **Surface:** asphalted. 🅿 01/01-31/12.
**Distance:** 🚶1km ⊗on the spot 🚶on the spot.
**Remarks:** At sports grounds.

### Moers · 9F3
**Freizeitpark Schoßpark**, Krefelder straße. **GPS:** n51,44659 e6,61642.⬆➡.

4 ⌐free. **Location:** Rural. **Surface:** grasstiles. 🅿 01/01-31/12.
**Distance:** 🚶700m ⊗700m 🍴500m.

### Möhnesee · 9H3
**Freizeitanlage Möhnesee-Körbecke**, Börnigeweg. **GPS:** n51,49160 e8,12555.⬆.

20 ⌐€ 6/24h 💧(8x) € 2/24h. 📶 **Location:** Simple. **Surface:** metalled. 🅿 01/01-31/12.
**Distance:** 🚶1km 🏊on the spot ⊗on the spot 🍴1km 🚲on the spot 🚶on the spot.
**Remarks:** Max. 24h.

### Möhnesee · 9H3
**Stockumer Eichen**, Stockumer Eichen 1. **GPS:** n51,48668 e8,14981.
20 ⌐€ 10/24h Ch 💧(12x) WC 🚿included. 📶 **Location:** Rural, comfortable, isolated, quiet. **Surface:** metalled. 🅿 01/03-01/11.
**Distance:** 🚶2km 🏊Möhnesee 🚃on the spot ⊗300m on the spot 🚶on the spot.

### Möhnesee · 9H3
**Strandbad**, Linkstraße 20, Delecke. **GPS:** n51,49177 e8,08255.⬆.
50 ⌐€ 15, Jul/Aug € 20 🚰 Ch 💧(32x) WC 🚿included. 📶 💳
**Location:** Rural, comfortable, quiet. **Surface:** gravel.
🅿 01/03-01/11.
**Distance:** 🚶Möhnesee 3,5km 🛫7km A44 🏊Möhnesee ⊗750m.
**Remarks:** Bread-service.

### Möhnesee · 9H3
**Wildpark/Freizeitanlage**, Alte Feld. **GPS:** n51,47360 e8,19831.⬆➡.

10 ⌐free. **Surface:** grassy/gravel. 🅿 01/01-31/12.
**Distance:** 🏊1,5km ⊗300m 🚶on the spot.
**Remarks:** Playground.

### Möhnesee · 9H3
**ADAC campingplatz**, Brückenstraße 23. **GPS:** n51,49065 e8,12197.
10 ⌐€ 15 ⚡€ 0,50/kWh 🚿included. **Surface:** gravel/sand.
🅿 01/01-31/12.
**Distance:** 🏊on the spot 🚃on the spot ⊗100m 🍴1km.

### Mönchengladbach · 11E1
**Schloß Wickrath**, Neukircherweg, Wickrath. **GPS:** n51,12889 e6,42258.⬆.

10 ⌐free. **Surface:** asphalted. 🅿 01/01-31/12.
**Distance:** 🚶2km ⊗2km 🍴500m.

**Remarks:** Parking behind castle (500m), max. 2 days, outside environmental zone.

### Mönchengladbach · 11E1
**Camping-Center Krings**, Monschauerstrasse 10/32. **GPS:** n51,19454 e6,40884.⬆➡.

15 ⌐free 🚰 🚿Chfree. **Surface:** metalled. 🅿 01/01-31/12.
**Distance:** 🚶3km ⊗1km 🍴500m.
**Remarks:** Max. 2 nights, service during opening hours, green zone: environmental badge obligatory.

### Monschau · 11E2
**Biesweg**, B258. **GPS:** n50,55389 e6,23194.⬆➡.

4 ⌐€ 12/24h 🚰€ 5/7minutes Ch 💧(4x) € 5/10h. 📶
**Location:** Simple, noisy. **Surface:** asphalted. 🅿 01/01-31/12.
**Distance:** 🚶600m ⊗600m 🍴600m.
**Remarks:** Max. 1 night.

### Monschau · 11E2
**Haus Vennblick**, Hauptstrasse 24, Höfen. **GPS:** n50,53934 e6,25292.⬆.

8 ⌐€ 10, guests free. **Location:** Rural, simple, noisy. **Surface:** gravel.
🅿 01/01-31/12 ⊙ Wed.
**Distance:** 🚶300m ⊗on the spot 🚲4km 🚶on the spot 🛒4km.

### Mülheim/Ruhr · 9F3
**Mintarder Straße 45**. **GPS:** n51,41462 e6,86934.⬆.

6 ⌐free. **Location:** Rural, simple. **Surface:** metalled.
🅿 01/01-31/12.
**Distance:** 🚶2,7km ⊗50m 🍴100m 🚲on the spot 🚶on the spot.
**Remarks:** Max. 72h, green zone: environmental badge obligatory.

### Mülheim/Ruhr · 9F3
**Bauwagenhotel & Kanu**, Mintarder Straße 139. **GPS:** n51,39615 e6,89152.
5 ⌐free. **Surface:** gravel. 🅿 01/01-31/12.
**Distance:** 🚶4km ⊗on the spot.
**Remarks:** Outside environmental zone, restaurant closed on Tuesday.

### Mülheim/Ruhr · 9F3
**Hymer Zentrum**, Kölner Strasse 35-37. **GPS:** n51,39985 e6,87700.
🚰€ 0,50/80liter 🚿Ch. 🅿 01/01-31/12.
**Remarks:** At motorhome dealer, outside environmental zone.

### Münster · 9G2
**Am Ostbad**, Mauritz-Lindenweg. **GPS:** n51,95922 e7,65879.⬆.

6 🛒free. **Location:** Urban, simple. **Surface:** metalled.
🕐 01/01-31/12.
**Distance:** 🚲2,5km 🚏100m ⊗300m 🛒300m 🚰on the spot.
**Remarks:** At swimming pool, max. 8M.

### Münster 9G2

Hafenstraße/Albersloher Weg. **GPS:** n51,95199 e7,63600.

6 🛒€ 2/h, overnight stay free. **Location:** Urban, simple, central, noisy.
**Surface:** asphalted. 🕐 01/01-31/12.
**Distance:** 🚲Old city centre 1km ⊗on the spot 🛒on the spot
🚰on the spot.
**Remarks:** Along railwayline, outside environmental zone.

### Münster 9G2

**Campingplatz Münster**, Laerer Werseufer.
**GPS:** n51,94583 e7,69082.

24 🛒€ 15 2 pers.incl, dog € 3,50 🚰€ 0,50 🛒€ 0,50 Ch€ 0,50 ⚡
WCincluded 🚿€ 0,50/3 ≋€ 3/day. **Location:** Rural, simple.
**Surface:** gravel. 🕐 01/01-31/12.
**Distance:** 🚲Münster 4,5km ⊗100m 🛒on the spot 🚰100m
🚲on the spot 🚶on the spot.
**Remarks:** Pay at reception campsite, outside environmental zone.

### Netphen 11H1

**Freizeitpark Netphen, P3**, Brauersdorferstrasse.
**GPS:** n50,91250 e8,12567.

3 🛒€ 3,50/day 🚰€ 1/70liter 🛒Ch. **Surface:** metalled.
🕐 01/01-31/12.
**Distance:** 🚲2km 🛒2km.
**Remarks:** Max. 3 nights, coins at swimming pool.

### Nettersheim 11F2

# Wohnmobilhafen Nettersheim
# Nettersheim

■ **Rural location**
■ **BBQ area**
■ **Open all year**

# www.wohnmobilstellplatz.de
# naturzentrum@nettersheim.de

**Wohnmobilhafen Nettersheim**, Urftstraße.
**GPS:** n50,48606 e6,62627.
25 🛒€ 8,50/24h 🚰€ 1 🛒Ch ⚡(25x)included. 🚐
**Location:** Rural, simple, quiet. **Surface:** metalled.
🕐 01/01-31/12.
**Distance:** 🚲500m ⛵7,5km 🚏on the spot ⊗500m 🛒1,5km
🚰700m 🚲on the spot 🚶on the spot 🛶on the spot.
**Remarks:** Bread-service.

### Nettetal 11E1

**Am Nettebruch**, Flothender straße/Flothend.
**GPS:** n51,30188 e6,26715.

5 🛒free. **Surface:** grassy/gravel. 🕐 01/01-31/12.
**Distance:** 🚲1km 🚲on the spot ⊗on the spot 🛒1km.

### Nettetal 11E1

**Am Krickenbeck See**, Krickenbecker Allee 38. **GPS:** n51,34460 e6,25793.

10 🛒free, use of a meal desired. **Location:** Simple, noisy.
**Surface:** asphalted. 🕐 01/01-31/12.
**Distance:** 🚲2km ⊗on the spot 🛒2km.

### Neukirchen-Vluyn 9F3

**Wohnmobilstellplatz Niederrhein**, Krefeld Straße 9.
**GPS:** n51,44484 e6,57701.
15 🛒€ 8 🚰€ 1/80liter 🛒Ch 🛒€ 0,60/h WC 🚿€ 0,50/10minutes
⚡€ 2/2 ≋included. **Location:** Rural, quiet. **Surface:** grassy.
🕐 01/01-31/12.
**Distance:** 🚲400m ⊗50m 🚲on the spot 🚶on the spot.
**Remarks:** Video surveillance, bicycle rental.

### Neuss 11F1

**Allrounder Winterworld/Skihalle**, An der Skihalle 1.
**GPS:** n51,17316 e6,64862.

30 🛒free. **Surface:** metalled. 🕐 01/01-31/12.
**Distance:** ⊗on the spot 🎿indoor ski.
**Remarks:** Outside environmental zone.

### Nideggen 11E2

**Parkplatz Danzley**, Bahnhofstrasse. **GPS:** n50,69247 e6,47952.

14 🛒free. **Location:** Rural, simple. **Surface:** metalled.
🕐 01/01-31/12.
**Distance:** 🚲500m 🛒500m.

### Nordkirchen 9G3

**Wohnmobilstellplatz Nordkirchen**, Am Gorbach 10a.
**GPS:** n51,74004 e7,53418.
23 🛒€ 10 🚰€ 1/100liter 🛒Ch ⚡€ 0,55/kWh ≋included. 🚐
**Location:** Rural, central, quiet. **Surface:** grassy/gravel.
🕐 01/01-31/12.
**Distance:** 🚲600m ⊗450m 🛒600m 🚲on the spot 🚶on the spot.
**Remarks:** Castle 500m.

### Nordkirchen 9G3

**Bikertreff**, Berger 25. **GPS:** n51,72484 e7,50726.
20 🛒free 🚰🛒Ch ⚡. **Surface:** gravel/metalled.
🕐 01/03-31/12.
**Distance:** 🚲2km ⊗on the spot.

### Nordkirchen 9G3

**Hotel Plettenberger Hof**, Schlossstrasse 28.
**GPS:** n51,73659 e7,52819.

2 🛒guests free 🚰⚡≋. **Surface:** asphalted.
🕐 01/01-31/12.
**Distance:** 🚲200m ⊗on the spot 🛒200m.
**Remarks:** Breakfast-service, restaurant closed on Monday.

### Nottuln 9G2

**Wellenfreibad/Hallenbad**, Rudolf-Harbigstrasse.
**GPS:** n51,92410 e7,34514.

10 🛒free. **Location:** Rural, simple. **Surface:** metalled.
🕐 01/01-31/12.
**Distance:** 🚲1,5km 🛒bakery 800m 🚰on the spot.
**Remarks:** Parking swimming pool.

### Oberhausen 9F3

**Stellplatz Kaisergaten**, Am Kaisergarten 28.
**GPS:** n51,48743 e6,85519.

60 🅪€ 7 ⛽€ 1/100liter 🗑Ch⚡(24x)€ 0,50/2h. 🏧
**Location:** Urban, noisy. **Surface:** grassy. 🕐 01/01-31/12.
**Distance:** 🚶Oberhausen City 30 min walking 🚆1,6km ⊗1,7km 🚰1,7km 🚌400m.
**Remarks:** Green zone: environmental badge obligatory.

### 🅿S Oberhausen 🍴💧 9F3
**Stellplatz Marina**, Heinz-Schleußer-Straße 1.
**GPS:** n51,49444 e6,88417. ⬆➡.

18 🅪€ 15 ⛽€ 0,50/100liter 🗑Ch⚡WCincluded 🚿€ 1/4minutes ◉€ 1.🏧 **Location:** Urban, simple. **Surface:** gravel/metalled.
🕐 01/01-31/12.
**Distance:** 🚶1km ⛴200m 🚌on the spot ⊗250m 🚰800m.
**Remarks:** Green zone: environmental badge obligatory.

### 🅿 Oberhausen 💧🍴 9F3
**Parking 10 - CentrO**, Arenastraße. **GPS:** n51,48930 e6,87063. ⬆➡.

40 🅪free. **Surface:** metalled. 🕐 01/01-31/12.
**Distance:** 🚶100m ⊗on the spot 🚰on the spot.
**Remarks:** At CentrO, green zone: environmental badge obligatory.

**Tourist information Oberhausen:**
🛈 CentrO. Large shopping centre, 250 shops, 100 restaurants/bars and a market. 🕐 10-20h restaurants till 22h, thu 10-21h.

### 🅿 Oedt 11E1
**Wohnmobile-Stellplatz Niers-Perle-Oedt**, Mühlengasse.
**GPS:** n51,32327 e6,37650. ⬆.

7 🅪free. **Surface:** asphalted. 🕐 01/01-31/12.
**Distance:** 🚶800m ⊗500m 🚰500m.

### 🅿S Oelde 💧 9H3
**Pott's Brau und Backhaus**, In der Geist 120.
**GPS:** n51,81192 e8,13103. ⬆➡.

---

6 🅪€ 5 ⛽€ 1/60liter 🗑Ch⚡included. **Location:** Simple, noisy.
**Surface:** grassy/metalled. 🕐 02/01-23/12.
**Distance:** 🚆500m ⊗on the spot.
**Remarks:** Caution key € 35, bicycle rental.

### 🅿S Olpe 11G1
**Freizeitbad Olpe**, Seeweg 5. **GPS:** n51,03242 e7,84163. ⬆➡.

10 🅪€ 8/24h ⛽€ 0,20/liter 🗑Ch⚡(4x)€ 1/2kWh WC included, at swimming pool 7-22h. 🏧 **Location:** Urban. **Surface:** asphalted.
🕐 01/01-31/12.
**Distance:** 🚶500m 🚆2km ⊗250m.
**Remarks:** On the banks of the Biggesee, max. 3 days, to be paid at swimming pool.

### 🅿S Olsberg 9H3
**Wohnmobilplatz am AquaOlsberg**, Zur Sauerlandtherme 1.
**GPS:** n51,35637 e8,48487. ⬆.
10 🅪€ 8,50/24h, tourist tax € 1,50/pp ⛽€ 1/80liter 🚿⚡€ 1/8h.
**Surface:** grassy. 🕐 01/01-31/12.
**Distance:** 🚶on the spot ⊗250m 🚰250m.
**Remarks:** Discount at swimming pool.

### 🅿S Ostbevern 9G2
**Bever Bad**, Am Hanfgarten 22. **GPS:** n52,03673 e7,84392. ⬆.

6+10 🅪€ 10, overnight stay only 20-9h free ⛽🗑Ch⚡WCincluded.
**Location:** Luxurious, quiet. **Surface:** grassy.
🕐 01/01-31/12.
**Distance:** 🚶400m ⊗300m 🚰300m 🚌300m.
**Remarks:** Parking swimming pool, caution key service € 10, incl. access swimming pool.

### 🅿S Overhetfeld 11E1
**Camp Graskamp**, Graskamp 19. **GPS:** n51,22259 e6,13977. ⬆.

5 🅪€ 8 ⛽🗑Ch⚡WCincluded. **Location:** Rural, comfortable, quiet. **Surface:** grassy. 🕐 01/01-31/12.
**Distance:** 🚶200m ⊗200m 🚰on the spot.

### 🅿S Paderborn 🌿💧🍴 9H3
**Maspernplatz, P4**, Hathumarstrasse 22.
**GPS:** n51,72278 e8,75417. ⬆➡.

7 🅪day € 6, Sunday free ⚡(4x)€ 0,50/h. **Location:** Urban, central, noisy. **Surface:** metalled. 🕐 01/01-31/12.
**Distance:** 🚶500m 🚆4km ⊗100m 🚰500m 🚌on the spot.

---

### 🅿S Paderborn 🌿💧🍴 9H3
**Rolandsbad**, Fürstenweg 36. **GPS:** n51,72825 e8,74509.

16 🅪€ 5/24h ⛽€ 0,50/60liter 🗑Ch⚡(16x)€ 0,50/kWh.
**Surface:** asphalted. 🕐 01/01-31/12.
**Distance:** 🚶centre 700m ⊗on the spot 🚌on the spot 🏍on the spot 🚶on the spot.
**Remarks:** Max. 72h.

### 🅿S Paderborn 🌿💧🍴 9H3
**Lippesee-Nordufer**, Sennelagerstraße 62, Sande.
**GPS:** n51,76087 e8,67756. ⬆.

10 🅪free. **Location:** Rural, simple. **Surface:** grassy.
🕐 01/01-31/12.
**Distance:** 🚶city centre Paderborn 9km ⛴150m 🚌150m ⊗1km 🚰500m 🏍on the spot.

### 🏛 Paderborn 🌿💧🍴 9H3
**Heinz Nixdorf MuseumsForum**, Fürstenallee 7.
**GPS:** n51,73193 e8,73592. ⬆.
3 🅪guests free. **Surface:** metalled. 🕐 01/01-31/12.
**Distance:** 🚶centre 2,5km ⊗on the spot.
**Remarks:** At museum.

### 🅿S Petershagen 10A1
**Am Sportplatz**, Hohoffstraße 15. **GPS:** n52,37532 e8,96875. ⬆➡.

10 🅪free ⛽€ 1/90liter ⚡(8x)€ 1/kWh. **Location:** Urban, quiet.
**Surface:** metalled. 🕐 01/01-31/12.
**Distance:** 🚶100m ⊗100m 🏍on the spot.
**Remarks:** Nearby football ground, max. 3 days, check in at tourist office.

### 🅿S Plettenberg 💧 11G1
**Aqua Magis**, Albert Schweizerstrasse, Böddinghausen.
**GPS:** n51,23220 e7,85308. ⬆➡.

12 🅪free ⛽€ 1/40liter 🗑Ch⚡(8x)€ 0,50 WC.
**Location:** Rural, comfortable, quiet. **Surface:** metalled.
🕐 01/01-31/12.
**Distance:** 🚶on the spot 🚆11km ⊗on the spot 🚰200m 🏍on the spot 🚶on the spot.
**Remarks:** At paradise pool, max. 48h.

### 🅿S Porta Westfalica 10A2
**Porta-Bad**, Sprengelweg 10. **GPS:** n52,22780 e8,93400.
8 🅪free 🚿. **Surface:** metalled. 🕐 01/01-31/12.

**DE**

**Distance:** 🚶1,5km.
**Remarks:** Max. 3 days.

| 🚐 S | **Pulheim** | 11F1 |

**Aquarena**, In den Benden. **GPS:** n51,01481 e6,75055.
6 🚐free 🚰€ 1/100liter ⚡€ 1/2kWh. **Location:** Urban.
**Surface:** asphalted. 🅾 01/01-31/12.
**Distance:** 🚶900m ⊗500m 🚉1,4km.
**Remarks:** Service only during opening hours.

| 🚐 S | **Raesfeld** 🌾 | 9F3 |

**Wohnmobilstellplatz Graf Alexander**, Südring.
**GPS:** n51,76523 e6,83035. ⬆➡.

8 🚐€ 8 🚰€ 1/8minutes 🗑Ch ⚡(8x)€ 1/12h WC included. 🚿
**Location:** Rural, simple, quiet. **Surface:** gravel.
🅾 01/01-31/12.
**Distance:** 🚶1km ⊗150m 🚴on the spot 🚶on the spot.
**Remarks:** At historic moated castle, max. 2 nights.

| ⚓ S | **Recke** | 9G1 |

**Yackthafen Marina Recke**, Auf der Haar 23.
**GPS:** n52,35082 e7,71174. ⬆.

40 🚐€ 13 🚰🗑Ch⚡(10x)€ 1,50 WC 🚿€ 1,50 🚽 🚿
**Location:** Rural, comfortable, quiet. **Surface:** grassy/metalled.
🅾 01/01-31/12.
**Distance:** 🚶1km, Recke 3,5km ⛵on the spot ⛴on the spot ⊗on the spot 🚉900m ⛽400m 🚴on the spot 🚶on the spot.
**Remarks:** At the Mittelland canal, check in at harbourmaster.

| 🚐 S | **Rees** | 9E3 |

**Stellplatz Rees am Niederrhein**, Ebentalstrasse.
**GPS:** n51,76428 e6,38829. ⬆➡.

46 🚐€ 8/day 🚰🗑Ch€ 2 🚿included. 🚿 **Location:** Urban,
comfortable, central. **Surface:** gravel. 🅾 01/01-31/12.
**Distance:** 🚶400m.
**Remarks:** Behind swimming pool, bread-service.

| 🚐 S | **Reken** 🐑 | 9F3 |

**Wohnmobilstellplatz Reken**, Berge 2a.
**GPS:** n51,82864 e7,05895. ⬆➡.

20 🚐€ 6 🚰€ 1/200liter 🗑Ch⚡(20x)€ 0,50/kWh. 🚿
**Location:** Rural, comfortable, quiet. **Surface:** grassy.
🅾 01/01-31/12.
**Distance:** 🚶1km ⊗1km 🚉1km 🚴on the spot 🚶on the spot.

---

**Remarks:** Max. 3 days, friday market.

| 🚐 | **Remscheid** | 11F1 |

**Brückenpark Müngsten**, Müngstener Brückenweg.
**GPS:** n51,16833 e7,13750. ⬆.

4 🚐free. **Location:** Rural, simple, quiet. **Surface:** gravel.
🅾 01/01-31/12.
**Distance:** 🚶5km 🚲4km ⛵100m ⛴100m 🚶on the spot.
**Remarks:** Max. 1 night, outside environmental zone.

| 🚐 | **Remscheid** | 11F1 |

**Dörperhöhe**, Bei Haus nr. 15, Lennep. **GPS:** n51,17986 e7,30205.
4 🚐free. **Surface:** asphalted. 🅾 01/01-31/12.
**Remarks:** Max. 1 night, outside environmental zone.

| 🚐 S | **Remscheid** | 11F1 |

**Garage Pauli GmbH**, Lenneperstrasse 152. **GPS:** n51,18020 e7,22591.
3 🚐free 🚰🗑Chfree. **Surface:** grasstiles. 🅾 01/01-31/12.
**Remarks:** At motorhome dealer, max. 1 night, outside environmental zone.

| 🚐 S | **Rheda-Wiedenbrück** | 9H2 |

**Am Werl**, Gütersloherstrasse. **GPS:** n51,85456 e8,29768.

4 🚐free 🚰🗑Ch⚡ WC. **Location:** Urban. **Surface:** metalled.
🅾 01/01-31/12.
**Distance:** 🚶300m 🚉300m.
**Remarks:** Max. 3 days.

| 🚐 | **Rheda-Wiedenbrück** | 9H2 |

**P Hallenbad**, Ostring/Am Hallenbad, Wiederbrück.
**GPS:** n51,83188 e8,32350. ⬆➡.

4 🚐free. **Location:** Urban, quiet. **Surface:** metalled.
🅾 01/01-31/12.
**Distance:** 🚶1km ⊗200m 🚉bakery 200m 🚴on the spot 🚶on the spot.
**Remarks:** Parking swimming pool.

| 🚐 S | **Rhede** | 9F3 |

**Reisemobilstellplatz Kettelerplatz**, Kettelerstrasse 9.
**GPS:** n51,83677 e6,69346. ⬆.

15 🚐free 🚰€ 1/3minutes 🗑Ch⚡(6x)€ 1/stay.
**Location:** Urban, simple, quiet. **Surface:** grassy.
🅾 01/01-31/12.
**Distance:** 🚶750m ⊗750m 🚉500m.
**Remarks:** At fire-station.

---

| 🚐 | **Rhede** | 9F3 |

**Hallen- und Freibad**, Heideweg 59. **GPS:** n51,83164 e6,68635. ⬆.

2 🚐free. **Location:** Urban, simple, quiet. **Surface:** metalled.
🅾 01/01-31/12.
**Distance:** 🚶1,5km ⊗600m 🚉1,2km.
**Remarks:** Parking swimming pool, max. 3 days.

| 🚐 | **Rheinbach** | 11F2 |

**Freizeitpark Monte Mare**, Münstereifelerstraße 69.
**GPS:** n50,61883 e6,93262. ⬆➡.

4 🚐free. **Location:** Rural, simple. **Surface:** metalled.
🅾 01/01-31/12.
**Distance:** 🚶1,5km ⊗on the spot 🚉1,5km.
**Remarks:** Max. 3 days.

| 🚐 | **Rheine** | 9G2 |

**Im Stadtpark**, Kopernikusstrasse. **GPS:** n52,28137 e7,45478. ⬆.

2 🚐free. **Location:** Urban, simple. **Surface:** metalled.
🅾 01/01-31/12.
**Distance:** 🚶500m ⊗on the spot 🚉500m 🚉300m 🚴on the spot 🚶on the spot.

| 🚐 | **Rheine** | 9G2 |

**Am Naturzoo**, Weihbishof-Dalhaus-strasse.
**GPS:** n52,29526 e7,41645. ⬆.

10 🚐free. **Location:** Rural, simple. **Surface:** grasstiles.
🅾 01/01-31/12.
**Distance:** 🚶1,5km 🚲5km ⛴on the spot 🚴100m.

| 🚐 S | **Rheurdt** | 9E3 |

**Wohnmobilhafen Ökodorf**, St. Nikolausweg 15.
**GPS:** n51,46302 e6,46780. ⬆➡.

21 🚐€ 7 🚰🗑Ch⚡included WC. **Surface:** metalled.

🚐 01/01-31/12.
**Distance:** 🚶500m ⊗500m 🍴500m 🚴 on the spot 🚶 on the spot.

### 🏕️S Rietberg 🌿 9H3
Jakobistrasse, Mastholte. **GPS:** n51,75667 e8,39111.⬆️.

6 🚐free 🚰 € 0,50/80liter 🚽Ch. **Location:** Rural, central.
**Surface:** asphalted. 🚐 01/01-31/12.
**Distance:** 🚶100m ⊗100m 🍴100m.

### 🏕️S Rietberg 🌿 9H3
**Parkplatz Rottwiese**, Jerusalemer Straße.
**GPS:** n51,80999 e8,41203.⬆️.
🚐free 🚰🚽Ch. **Surface:** gravel. 🚐 01/01-31/12.
**Distance:** 🚶centre 1,2km.
**Remarks:** At museum.

### 🏕️S Rietberg 🌿 9H3
**Am Heimathaus**, Langenberger Strasse, Mastholte.
**GPS:** n51,75765 e8,38945.⬆️.

2 🚐free. **Location:** Urban. **Surface:** asphalted. 🚐 01/01-31/12.
**Distance:** 🚶100m ⊗100m 🍴100m.

### 🏕️S Roetgen 11E2
**Am Bahnhof**, Bahnhofstrasse. **GPS:** n50,64868 e6,18506.

15 🚐free. **Location:** Rural, simple, noisy. **Surface:** gravel/metalled.
🚐 01/01-31/12.
**Distance:** 🚶300m 🍴300m.

### 🏕️S Rosendahl 🌳🐑 9F2
**Wohnmobilplatz Darfeld**, Sudetenstrasse, Darfeld.
**GPS:** n52,02696 e7,26501.⬆️➡️.

20 🚐free 🚰 € 1/100liter 🚽Ch. 🚿(12x) € 1/6h.
**Location:** Rural, simple. **Surface:** grassy/metalled.
🚐 01/01-31/12.
**Distance:** 🚶500m ⊗on the spot 🍴500m 🚶1km.
**Remarks:** At sports park.

### 🏕️S Rüthen 9H3
**Auf dem Kamp**, Auf dem Kamp 1. **GPS:** n51,49523 e8,43293.

12 🚐€5 🚰 € 1 🚽Ch. 🚿€ 1/8h. **Surface:** asphalted.
🚐 01/01-31/12.
**Distance:** 🚶on the spot 🍴200m.

### 🏕️S Sassenberg 🧁 9H2
**Parkplatz Feldmark**, Feldmark. **GPS:** n52,00370 e8,06528.⬆️.

3 🚐free 🚰 € 1/80liter 🚽Ch. **Location:** Rural, simple.
**Surface:** metalled. 🚐 01/01-31/12.
**Distance:** 🚶2,5km 🏊100m ⊗on the spot 🍴on the spot 🚴on the spot 🚶on the spot.

### 🏕️S Schieder 🌳🏡🟨 10A2
**Freizeitzentrum Schiedersee**, Kronenbruch.
**GPS:** n51,92073 e9,16471.⬆️➡️.

300 🚐€ 10 🚰 € 1/100liter 🚽Ch. 🚿€ 0,50/kWh
WC🚽 € 0,50/5minutes ⚡€ 2 🔌. **Location:** Rural, comfortable, quiet.
**Surface:** grassy/metalled. 🚐 01/01-31/12.
**Distance:** 🚶1,3km 🏊50m 🎣50m ⊗on the spot 🍴on the spot 🚴on the spot 🚶on the spot.
**Remarks:** Bread-service.

### 🏕️S Schleiden 🏡🟨 11E2
**Wohnmobil Hafen am Nationalpark Eifel**, Pfarrer-Kneipp-Straße,
Gemünd. **GPS:** n50,57855 e6,49107.⬆️➡️.

55 🚐€ 10 + € 1/pp tourist tax 🚰🚽Ch. 🚿included 🔌€ 1.🚽
**Location:** Rural, comfortable, quiet. **Surface:** gravel/metalled.
🚐 01/01-31/12.
**Distance:** 🚶within walking distance ⊗500m 🍴500m 🚴on the spot 🚶on the spot.
**Remarks:** Bread-service.

### 🏕️S Schleiden 🏡🟨 11E2
**Erlebnisfreibad**, Im Wiesengrund. **GPS:** n50,52993 e6,47022.⬆️.

3 🚐free. **Location:** Rural, simple, quiet. **Surface:** asphalted.
🚐 01/01-31/12.
**Remarks:** Max. 24h.

### 🏕️S Schloss Holte/Stukenbrock 9H2
**American Store Niebel**, Hauptstraße 65. **GPS:** n51,90722 e8,66444.
25 🚐€ 12 + € 2/pp, dog € 1 🚰🚽Ch. 🚿included.
**Surface:** grassy/metalled. 🚐 01/01-31/12.
**Distance:** 🚶1km 🚲3km ⊗200m 🍴1km.

### 🏕️S Schloss Holte/Stukenbrock 9H2
**Reisemobilstellplatz Am Sennebach**, Liemkerstrasse 27, Liemke.
**GPS:** n51,86979 e8,61531.⬆️.

15 🚐€5 🚰🚽Ch € 2 🚿(18x) € 2. **Location:** Rural, isolated, quiet.
**Surface:** grasstiles. 🚐 01/01-31/12 ⭕ service: sa/su.
**Distance:** 🚶5km ⊗1km 🍴1km.
**Remarks:** Behind Froli Kunstoffwerk Fromme, max. 3 days.

### 🏕️S Schmallenberg 🏡🟨 11H1
**Im Sorpetal**, Zum Sorpetal 4. **GPS:** n51,16083 e8,34056.➡️.

11 🚐€ 9 + € 1,25/pp tourist tax 🚰 € 0,50/60liter Ch 🚿(12x) € 0,50/
kWh. **Surface:** grassy. 🚐 01/01-31/12.
**Distance:** 🚶on the spot ⊗100m 🍴2km 🚴500m 🚶1km 🚶on the spot.
**Remarks:** Trout pond, golf court 500m, playground.

### 🏕️S Schöppingen 🌿🏡 9F2
**Schulze Althoff**, Heven 48. **GPS:** n52,07361 e7,22361.⬆️.

30 🚐€ 20/night, 3p incl., +3p € 4/pp 🚰🚽Ch 🚿(12x),6Amp
WC included 🔌sanitary € 2/pp ⚡€ 5.🚽
**Location:** Rural, simple. **Surface:** grassy. 🚐 01/01-31/12.
**Distance:** 🚶2,5km 🏊on the spot 🎣on the spot 🍴2,5km 🚌on the spot.
**Remarks:** Swimming pool available.

### 🏕️S Senden 9G2
**Sportpark Senden**, Buldenerstrasse 13b. **GPS:** n51,85419 e7,47433.⬆️.

10 🚐free. **Location:** Simple, noisy. **Surface:** grasstiles.
🚐 01/01-31/12.
**Distance:** 🚶on the spot ⊗200m 🍴300m 🚌on the spot.
**Remarks:** Parking at sports park.

### 🏕️S Senden 9G2
**Wohnmobilstellplatz Steinhoff**, Gettrup 37.
**GPS:** n51,83305 e7,46878.⬆️.

DE

10 🕙 6 🚰 🗑Ch 🔌(6x)€ 0,50/kWh. **Location:** Rural, isolated.
**Surface:** grassy/metalled. 🕐 01/01-31/12.
**Distance:** 🚲Senden 4km ⊗2,5km 🚊2,5km.

### Sendenhorst 🛶 ⚓ — 9G2
Westor 31. **GPS:** n51,84286 e7,81849. ⬆➡

3 🕙free 🚰€ 0,50/40liter 🗑Ch 🔌€ 0,50.
**Location:** Urban, simple, central, noisy. **Surface:** metalled.
**Distance:** 🚲on the spot ⊗300m 🚲1km 🚊on the spot.
**Remarks:** At swimming pool, max. 3 nights.

### Siegen — 11H1
An der Alche, Freudenbergerstraße 67. **GPS:** n50,88073 e8,00764. ⬆
4 🕙free 🚰€ 0,50/40liter 🗑Ch 🔌(4x)€ 0,50/kWh.
🕐 01/01-31/12.
**Distance:** 🚲1km 🚴5km ⊗200m 🚊1km.
**Remarks:** Max. 3 days, outside environmental zone.

### Siegen — 11H1
Hallenbad Weidenau, Poststraße 27. **GPS:** n50,89463 e8,02405. ➡

3 🕙free 🚰€ 1/10minutes 🗑Ch 🔌(2x)€ 1/8h.
**Location:** Urban. **Surface:** metalled. 🕐 01/01-31/12.
**Distance:** 🚲200m ⊗200m 🚲200m 🚊250m 🚲on the spot
🚶on the spot.
**Remarks:** Max. 3 days, green zone: environmental badge obligatory.

### Simmerath — 11E2
Wohnmobilhafen Rurseezentrum, Seeufer 1, Rurberg.
**GPS:** n50,60658 e6,38177. ⬆

12 🕙 8/24h 🚰€ 2 🗑Ch 🛒 **Location:** Rural, comfortable.
**Surface:** grasstiles. 🕐 01/01-31/12.
**Distance:** ⛵100m 🚊50m.
**Remarks:** Canoe rental.

### Soest — 9H3
AquaFun, Ardeyweg 35. **GPS:** n51,56944 e8,07778.
9 🕙€ 9 🚰€ 1/5minutes 🗑Ch 🔌€ 1/2kWh. 🕐 01/01-31/12.
**Distance:** 🚲3,5km 🚴4km 🚲1km 🚊1,5km.
**Remarks:** At swimming pool, e-bike rental.

### Soest — 9H3
City Motel, Altes Stellwerk 9. **GPS:** n51,57503 e8,11478. ⬆

---

30 🕙 8 🚰🗑Ch 🔌(14x)€ 0,50/kWh WC🗑€ 2 🛒€ 3/3 📶included.
**Location:** Urban, comfortable, central, quiet. **Surface:** gravel.
🕐 01/01-31/12.
**Distance:** 🚲500m ⊗200m 🚊200m 🚌200m 🚲on the spot
🚶on the spot.
**Remarks:** Check in at reception.

### Solingen 🏺 — 11F1
Am Brandteich, Gräfrath. **GPS:** n51,21151 e7,07217. ⬆

10 🕙free. **Location:** Urban, simple, quiet. **Surface:** concrete.
🕐 01/01-31/12.
**Distance:** 🚲on the spot 🚴2,7km ⊗on the spot 🚊300m.
**Remarks:** Parking fire-station, max. 1 night, playground.

### Solingen 🏺 — 11F1
Technologiezentrum, Grünewalder Straße 29.
**GPS:** n51,16250 e7,07889.
4 🕙free. **Surface:** grasstiles. 🕐 01/01-31/12.
**Distance:** 🚲1km ⊗200m 🚊400m 🚌200m.

### Sonsbeck-Labbeck — 9E3
Campingpark Kerstgenshof, Marienbaumer Str. 158.
**GPS:** n51,66060 e6,37272.
10 🕙€ 9,50 🚰🗑Chincluded 🔌€ 0,50. **Surface:** grassy.
🕐 01/03-05/11.

### Stadtlohn 🛖 — 9F2
Freizeit- und Hallenbad, Uferstrasse 29.
**GPS:** n51,99792 e6,93019. ⬆➡

4 🕙free 🚰€ 0,50/100liter 🗑Ch 🔌(4x)€ 1/kWh WC🗑.
**Location:** Rural, simple, isolated. **Surface:** metalled.
🕐 01/01-31/12 🕐 water disconnected in winter.
**Distance:** 🚲800m 🚴1km 🚊800m.
**Remarks:** Parking swimming pool.

### Steinfurt ⚓ — 9G2
Wohnmobilstellplatz Steinfurt, Liederkerkerstrasse 70, Burgsteinfurt.
**GPS:** n52,14738 e7,34746. ⬆➡

25 🕙free 🚰€ 1/100liter 🗑Ch 🔌€ 1/2kWh. **Location:** Rural, simple.
**Surface:** gravel. 🕐 01/01-31/12.
**Distance:** 🚲1km 🚴500m 🚊200m.
**Remarks:** Parking behind police station, max. 3 nights, voluntary
contribution.

---

### Steinfurt ⚓ — 9G2
Am Rathaus, Emsdettener Straße 40. **GPS:** n52,12822 e7,39356.

6 🕙free. **Location:** Urban, simple. **Surface:** asphalted.
🕐 01/01-31/12.
**Distance:** 🚲400m 🚴200m ⊗400m 🚊400m 🚌200m.

### Steinhagen — 9H2
Am Cronsbach. **GPS:** n51,99998 e8,42351. ⬆➡

2 🕙free. **Location:** Urban, simple. **Surface:** metalled.
🕐 01/01-31/12.
**Distance:** 🚲100m ⊗100m 🚊100m.
**Remarks:** Max. 2 days.

### Stemwede 🐑 — 9H1
Reisemobil-Stellplatz Hollenmühle, Hinterm Teich 3, Levern.
**GPS:** n52,36783 e8,43833.

36 🕙 17 🚰🗑Ch 🔌 WC🗑 🛒 📶included. **Location:** Rural,
comfortable. **Surface:** grassy/gravel. 🕐 01/01-31/12.
**Distance:** ⊗on the spot 🚊3,2km.
**Remarks:** Bread-service.

### Stemwede 🐑 — 9H1
Park Stemwederberg, Stemwederbergstrasse/Freudeneck, Westrup.
**GPS:** n52,43246 e8,43973. ⬆➡

8 🕙free. **Location:** Rural, comfortable. **Surface:** grassy.
🕐 01/01-31/12.
**Distance:** 🚲2km ⊗2km 🚊2km 🚶on the spot.

### Stemwede 🐑 — 9H1
Hotel-Gasthof Moorhof, Wagenfelderstrasse 34, Oppenwehe.
**GPS:** n52,49979 e8,53507. ⬆

20 🕙€ 7, free with a meal 🚰🗑included 🔌€ 2,16Amp.
**Location:** Rural, quiet. **Surface:** grassy.

01/01-31/12 Mo, Thu.
**Distance:** on the spot.

### Straelen 9E3

**Fitnessbad Wasserstraelen**, Lingsforterstraße 100.
**GPS:** n51,45201 e6,25708.

27 €7 € 1/80liter Ch (30x)€0,50/kWh included.
**Surface:** asphalted. 01/01-31/12.
**Distance:** 1,2km 1km 1km.
**Remarks:** Max. 3 days.

### Tecklenburg 9G2

**Parkplatz Bismarckturm**, Am Weingarten.
**GPS:** n52,22129 e7,79905.

5 €4. **Location:** Simple, quiet. **Surface:** asphalted.
01/01-31/12.
**Distance:** 800m 200m.

### Tecklenburg 9G2

**Regenbogen-Camp**, Grafenstraße. **GPS:** n52,22941 e7,89052.
4 €10 Ch included. **Location:** Urban, simple, noisy.
**Surface:** asphalted. 01/01-31/12.
**Distance:** Tecklenburg 7km 50m 400m.

### Telgte 9G2

**Am Dümmert**, Emstor. **GPS:** n51,98497 e7,79151.
3 free € 1/100liter Ch €1/kWh. **Location:** Simple.
**Surface:** gravel. 01/01-31/12.
**Distance:** 600m 600m 600m on the spot.

### Telgte 9G2

**Waldschwimmbad Klatenberge**, Waldweg.
**GPS:** n51,99459 e7,78328.

20 free. **Location:** Rural, simple. **Surface:** asphalted.
01/01-31/12.
**Distance:** 1km 300m 900m on the spot.
**Remarks:** Parking swimming pool, recreation area.

### Telgte 9G2

**Altes Gasthus Lauheide**, Lauheide 3, K17.
**GPS:** n51,99862 e7,75319.

80 €10 Ch included WC. **Location:** Rural, quiet.
**Surface:** grassy. 01/01-31/12 Restaurant: Wed.
**Distance:** 4km on the spot bus 300m on the spot.

### Uedem 9E3

**Reisemobilstellplatz Uedem**, Bergstraße 99.
**GPS:** n51,66173 e6,28734.

26 €9 Ch WC included. **Location:** Rural, comfortable.
**Surface:** grassy. 01/01-31/12.
**Distance:** 1,5km 1,3km on the spot on the spot.

### Velbert 11F1

**Panoramabad**, Wiesenweg, Velbert-Neviges.
**GPS:** n51,30582 e7,08546.

4 free € 1/80liter Ch. **Location:** Urban, simple, quiet.
**Surface:** concrete. 01/01-31/12.
**Distance:** 800m nearby 500m.
**Remarks:** Parking swimming pool, max. 3 nights.

### Velbert 11F1

**Unter der Saubrücke**, Parkstraße, Velbert-Mitte.
**GPS:** n51,34097 e7,03050.

6 €5/24h € 1/100liter Ch €0,50/kWh.
**Location:** Urban, simple, quiet. **Surface:** gravel.
01/01-31/12.
**Distance:** 800m 1,6km 250m on the spot.
**Remarks:** Max. 3 nights.

### Velbert 11F1

**Domparkplatz**, Bernsaustrasse Schloss Hardenberg.
**GPS:** n51,31565 e7,08724.

4 free. **Location:** Urban. **Surface:** gravel. 01/01-31/12.
**Distance:** 600m on the spot.
**Remarks:** Max. 3 nights.

### Velbert 11F1

**Nizzabad**, Nizzatal 4, Langenberg. **GPS:** n51,34362 e7,13766.

3 free. **Location:** Simple, quiet. **Surface:** metalled.
01/01-31/12.
**Distance:** Langenberg 2,5km on the spot.
**Remarks:** Max. 3 nights.

### Velen 9F2

**Erholungsgebiet Waldvelen**, Klyer Damm 8-10.
**GPS:** n51,90167 e7,01167.

30 € 15-18, 2 pers. incl. Ch (50x)WC included
€ 1/4minutes € 4. **Location:** Rural, luxurious. **Surface:** grassy.
01/01-31/12.
**Distance:** 2km 8,5km on the spot on the spot.
**Remarks:** Bread-service (weekend).

### Velen 9F2

**Freibad Ramsdorf**, Velener Straße, Ramsdorf.
**GPS:** n51,88955 e6,92503.

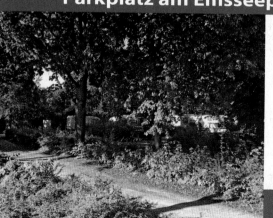

5 free. **Location:** Rural, simple, noisy. **Surface:** asphalted.
01/01-31/12.
**Distance:** Ramsdorf 300m 500m 200m on the spot on the spot.
**Remarks:** At swimming pool, max. 1 night.

### Viersen 11E1

**Am Familienbad Ransberg**, Heesstraße 80, Viersen-Dülken.
**GPS:** n51,25083 e6,35291.

9 € 10 € 0,50/100liter Ch (9x)included.
**Surface:** metalled. 01/01-31/12.
**Distance:** Dülken 400m, Viersen 3km 400m 2km 100m.
**Remarks:** Max. 3 days, to be paid at swimming pool.

### Vreden 9F2

**Wohnmobilpark Vreden**, Ottensteiner Strasse 59.
**GPS:** n52,03962 e6,84136.

50 € 8, 4 pers.incl Ch (14x)included WC € 2 € 3/h.
**Location:** Rural, simple, quiet. **Surface:** grassy.
01/01-31/12.
**Distance:** 500m on the spot.
**Remarks:** Breakfast-service, swimming pool € 2/pp.

### Vreden 9F2

**Zum Dornbusch**, Wüllener Straße 107. **GPS:** n52,03483 e6,84217.
10 free € 1/80liter WC. **Location:** Rural. **Surface:** metalled.
01/01-31/12.
**Distance:** 1,5km 650m 750m on the spot on the spot.

### Wachtendonk 9E3

**Bleiche P4**, Achter de Stadt. **GPS:** n51,40601 e6,33170.

24 € 7 € 0,50/60liter € 0,50 Ch (12x)€ 0,50/kWh.
**Surface:** gravel. 01/01-31/12.
**Distance:** 400m 100m 400m.
**Remarks:** Money in envelope in mail box.

### Wadersloh 9H3

Im Klostergarten 18, Liesborn. **GPS:** n51,71414 e8,25960.

4 free € 0,50/80liter Ch (4x)€ 0,50/12h.
**Location:** Rural. **Surface:** metalled. 01/01-31/12.
**Distance:** 400m 100m 400m on the spot on the spot.
**Remarks:** Behind gymnasium.

### Waldbröl 11G2

**Am Hallenbad**, Vennstrasse. **GPS:** n50,87511 e7,60987.

---

5 free. **Location:** Rural, simple, quiet. **Surface:** metalled.
01/01-31/12.
**Distance:** on the spot 350m 300m on the spot on the spot.
**Remarks:** Max. 2 days.

### Waldfeucht-Brüggelchen 11E1

**Reisemobilstellplatz Tilder Weg**, Tilderweg.
**GPS:** n51,07076 e5,99454.

8 € 5 € 1/80liter Ch (10x)€ 0,50/kWh.
**Location:** Rural, simple, quiet. **Surface:** metalled.
01/01-31/12.
**Distance:** 500m on the spot 500m 100m on the spot.
**Remarks:** Max. 4 nights, money in envelope in mail box.

### Waltrop 9G3

**Restaurant Zur Lohburg**, Lohburgerstrass 105, A2 Ausfahrt henreichenburg, Schiffshebewerk. **GPS:** n51,60613 e7,34882.

15 € 5 € 3 Ch € 3. **Surface:** grassy. 01/01-31/12.
**Distance:** 1km on the spot 1km.

### Warburg 10A3

**Schützenplatz**, Paderborner Tor 134. **GPS:** n51,48993 e9,13810.
5 € 5 Ch included. **Surface:** metalled.
01/01-31/12 15/09-15/10.
**Distance:** 500m 100m 200m.
**Remarks:** Max. 3 days.

### Warendorf 9G2

**Parkplatz am Emsseepark**, Sassenberger Strasse.
**GPS:** n51,95447 e7,99904.
14 free € 1/50liter Ch (14x)€ 1/kWh.
**Location:** Rural, simple, central, quiet. **Surface:** metalled.
01/01-31/12.
**Distance:** 500m on the spot 100m 800m 100m on the spot on the spot.

### Warendorf 9G2

**Parkplatz Zwischen den Emsbrücken**, Am Emswehr.
**GPS:** n51,95426 e7,99164.

---

2 free. 01/01-31/12.
**Distance:** 100m.

### Warstein 9H3

**Camperpark Zum Bayernstadl**, Enkerbruch 12a.
**GPS:** n51,43041 e8,37432.

40 € 8 € 1/100liter Ch (18x)€ 2/day.
**Surface:** gravel. 01/01-31/12.
**Distance:** 1,5km on the spot 1,5km 1,5km.
**Remarks:** Bread-service.

### Warstein 9H3

**Vans in Paradise**, Zu Hause im Waldpark. **GPS:** n51,42615 e8,35525.

30 € 15 Ch (76x),16Amp WC included € 2/2.
**Location:** Rural, isolated, quiet. **Surface:** grassy/gravel.
01/01-31/12.
**Distance:** 2km small menu 2km 2km.
**Remarks:** At Warstein brewery, bread-service + breakfast-service.

### Warstein 9H3

**Schützenhalle**, Schützenstraße 30, Hirschberg.
**GPS:** n51,43398 e8,27477.
3 free. **Location:** Rural. **Surface:** grassy.
01/01-31/12 Whitsuntide.
**Distance:** 500m, Warstein 12km 500m.

### Warstein 9H3

**Wohnmobilstellplatz**, Dammweg. **GPS:** n51,45103 e8,34750.

5 free.
**Location:** Simple. **Surface:** gravel/metalled.
01/01-31/12.
**Distance:** 2km 500m 1km 1km.
**Remarks:** At sports park.

**Tourist information Warstein:**
Warsteiner Brauerei, Zu Hause im Waldpark. Guided tour 1.45h, 2 drinks included. daily 12-17, Su 13-15h.

### Wassenberg 11E1

**Parkbad Wassenberg**, Auf dem Taubenkamp 2.
**GPS:** n51,09833 e6,14364.

DE

11 ⌇€ 5/day, € 20/week ⌇€ 1/100liter ⌇1 Ch ⌇€ 0,50/kWh.
**Location:** Rural, comfortable, quiet. **Surface:** metalled.
01/01-31/12.
**Distance:** 1,5km.
**Remarks:** To be paid at swimming pool.

**Reisemobilstellplatz am Tierpark**, L5 Fährsteg.
**GPS:** n51,63074 e6,20086.

13 ⌇€ 5/24h ⌇€ 0,50/kWh. **Location:** Rural, simple.
**Surface:** grassy. 01/01-31/12.
**Distance:** 500m 500m.

**Aral**, Industriestraße. **GPS:** n51,62029 e6,20972.
⌇€ 1 Ch. 01/01-31/12.

**Wegberger Reisemobilstellplatz, Schul- und Sportzentrum**,
Maaseiker Strasse 67. **GPS:** n51,13389 e6,28266.

10 ⌇€ 8 ⌇Ch ⌇included. **Surface:** grassy/gravel.
01/01-31/12.
**Distance:** 400m 400m 400m on the spot.
**Remarks:** To be paid at swimming pool, caution key € 20.

**Natur Solebad**, Am Hagen. **GPS:** n51,65910 e7,63414.

12 ⌇€ 5/24h ⌇€ 1/80liter ⌇Ch ⌇€ 0,50/kWh.
**Location:** Rural, simple. **Surface:** metalled.
01/01-31/12 15/10-31/10.
**Distance:** 400m 200m 400m on the spot.
**Remarks:** Tuesday and Friday market.

**Reisemobilstellplatz Römerwardt**, Rheinpromenade.
**GPS:** n51,66116 e6,59256.

---

45 ⌇€ 8, 01/04-31/10 € 10 ⌇€ 1/80liter ⌇Ch ⌇€ 1/kWh
⌇€ 1,50 included. **Location:** Rural, comfortable, quiet.
**Surface:** grassy/metalled. 01/01-31/12.
**Distance:** 1,5km 100m 1,5km on the spot on the spot.
**Remarks:** Check in on arrival, bread-service, bicycle rental, market
Wednesday and Saturday.

**Am Freibad**, Bullerteichstraße 12. **GPS:** n52,31556 e7,88070.

2 ⌇free. **Location:** Urban, simple. **Surface:** grasstiles.
01/01-31/12.
**Distance:** 600m 400m 750m 50m.

In Wickede. **GPS:** n51,49890 e7,88020.

4 ⌇free WC. **Location:** Urban. **Surface:** gravel. 01/01-31/12.
**Distance:** 1km.
**Remarks:** Max. 2 nights, use sanitary only during opening hours
swimming pool.

**Freizeitpark Wiehl**, Brücknerstrasse. **GPS:** n50,94716 e7,54585.

5 ⌇free ⌇€ 1/80liter ⌇Ch.
**Location:** Simple, central. **Surface:** metalled.
01/01-31/12.
**Distance:** 300m 5,4km 400m.
**Remarks:** Parking next to recreation park and disco, max. 3 nights.

**Sportplatz Eichhardt**, Friedhofstrasse.
**GPS:** n50,95110 e7,54482.

3 ⌇free.
**Location:** Urban. **Surface:** metalled.

---

01/01-31/12.
**Distance:** 1km 5,3km 1km 1km.
**Remarks:** Parking sports park, max. 3 nights.
**Tourist information Wiehl:**
www.wiehl.de. Small town in the green hills. 180 kilometres
marked hiking routes.
Wiehler Dahlienschau. 150 varieties of dahlias. 01/08-31/10
daily 9-19h. free.
Wiehler Trofsteinhöhle. Caves Temperature is approx. 8°C.
15/03-31/10 10-17h, 01/11-14/03 Sa-Su 11-16h.
Bergische Postkutsche, Nümrecht Post. Ride by mail-coach between
Wiehl and Nümbrecht. 01/05-30/09 Fri-Su 10-16h.

**Wielandshof**, Bauhofstraße 5. **GPS:** n50,80692 e8,10896.

6 ⌇€ 5 ⌇€ 0,50/60liter ⌇Ch ⌇(8x)€ 1/12h,10Amp.
**Surface:** gravel. 01/01-31/12.
**Distance:** 900m 900m 1km.
**Remarks:** Check in at farm.

**Gästehaus Wilgersdorf**, Kalkhain 23. **GPS:** n50,80889 e8,14722.
3 ⌇free. 01/01-31/12.
**Distance:** 4km on the spot 1km.

**Am Sportplatz**, Im Bungert, Herchen. **GPS:** n50,78025 e7,51308.

5 ⌇free ⌇(10x)€ 0,50/kWh. **Location:** Rural, simple, quiet.
**Surface:** gravel. 01/01-31/12.
**Distance:** 200m 8,5km 200m 200m on the spot
on the spot.
**Remarks:** Parking sports park.

**Hallenbad**, Bergische strasse 21, Dattenfeld.
**GPS:** n50,80754 e7,56105.

4 ⌇free ⌇€ 2 ⌇€ 2 Ch 2. **Location:** Rural, simple, quiet.
**Surface:** metalled. 01/01-31/12.
**Distance:** 8,5km on the spot on the spot.

**Auf dem Greent**, Dattenfeld. **GPS:** n50,80697 e7,55495.

50 ⌇free. **Location:** Rural, simple, quiet. **Surface:** asphalted/grassy.
01/01-31/12.

**Distance:** 🚶500m 🚴 8,5km ⊗500m 🛒500m.
**Remarks:** Fair ground.

| 🅿️🆂 | Windeck 👣 ⚿ | 11G2 |
|---|---|---|

Brunnenweg, Dattenfeld. **GPS**: n50,80486 e7,56087.⬆️➡️.

5 🅿️free. **Location:** Simple, quiet. **Surface:** grassy/gravel.
⚿ 01/01-31/12.
**Distance:** 🚶200m 🚴 8km ⊗200m 🛒150m 🚲 on the spot 🚶 on the spot.
**Remarks:** Recreation park.

| 🅿️🆂 | Windeck 👣 | 11G2 |
|---|---|---|

**Museumsdorf Altwindeck**, Im Thal Windeck 17, Alt-Windeck.
**GPS**: n50,81276 e7,57554.⬆️.

4 🅿️free. **Location:** Rural, simple, quiet. **Surface:** gravel.
⚿ 01/01-31/12.
**Distance:** 🚶2km 🚴 8,5km ⊗on the spot 🛒2km 🚲 on the spot 🚶 on the spot.
**Remarks:** Parking museum, max. 3 days.

| 🅿️🆂 | Winterberg 👣⚿❄️ | 11H1 |
|---|---|---|

**Wohnmobilpark Winterberg**, Neuastenberger Straße 4a, Neuasten-berg. **GPS**: n51,15974 e8,48383.⬆️.

70 🅿️€ 11,50, 15/12-15/03 € 15 + € 1,95/pp tourist tax
🔌€ 1/100liter 🔵Ch🚰 (72x)€ 0,60/kWh WC€ 1,50/6minutes
€ 2,50/2,50 🚿included. **Location:** Rural, simple, isolated, quiet.
**Surface:** grassy/gravel. ⚿ 01/01-31/12.
**Distance:** 🚶3km ⊗on the spot 🛒3km 🚲 on the spot 🚶 on the spot.
**Remarks:** Bread-service.

| 🅿️🆂 | Winterberg 👣⚿❄️ | 11H1 |
|---|---|---|

**Parkplatz Stadthalle**, Schulstrasse. **GPS**: n51,19163 e8,53810.⬆️➡️.

20 🅿️€ 18/24h 🔌€ 0,50/50liter 🔵Ch 🚰(10x)€ 0,50/3h.
**Surface:** grassy/gravel. ⚿ 01/01-31/12.
**Distance:** 🚶1km 🛒1km.

| 🅿️🆂 | Winterberg 👣⚿❄️ | 11H1 |
|---|---|---|

**Wohnmobil Winterberg**, Schneilstraße 6a.
**GPS**: n51,18807 e8,51359.⬆️➡️.
16 🅿️€ 12 + € 2,50/pp tourist tax 🔌€ 1/100liter 🔵€ 1
Ch 🚿WC🚰 🚿. 🔲 **Location:** Rural. ⚿ 01/01-31/12.
**Distance:** 🚶2,5km 🛒700m 🚏300m 🚶500m 🚲200m.

| 🅿️🆂 | Winterberg 👣⚿❄️ | 11H1 |
|---|---|---|

**Campingplatz Winterberg**. **GPS**: n51,18632 e8,50445.⬆️.

---

🅿️€ 20,50-22 🔌 🔵Ch 🚰(25x)€ 0,55/kWh WC€ 1 🔵€ 0,50.🚿
**Location:** Rural, luxurious. **Surface:** metalled. ⚿ 01/01-31/12.
**Distance:** 🚶2km ⊗on the spot 🛒2km 🚏20m 🚲on the spot
🚶on the spot 🚵on the spot 🚡on the spot.
**Remarks:** Parking at skipistes.

| 🅿️🆂 | Witten | 9G3 |
|---|---|---|

**Reisemobil-Center**, Pferdebachstrasse 150.
**GPS**: n51,45411 e7,35246.⬆️.

8 🅿️free 🔌€ 1/80liter 🔵Ch. **Surface:** gravel. ⚿ 01/01-31/12.
**Distance:** 🚶3km ⊗3km 🛒3km.

| 🅿️ | Wülfrath 👣 | 11F1 |
|---|---|---|

**Parkplatz**, Mettmanner Straße 42. **GPS**: n51,28188 e7,02741.⬆️.

6 🅿️free. **Location:** Urban, simple, quiet. **Surface:** concrete.
⚿ 01/01-31/12.
**Distance:** 🚶on the spot ⊗500m 🛒800m.

| 🅿️🆂 | Wuppertal | 11F1 |
|---|---|---|

**Wohnmobil-Oase Wuppertal**, Linderhauser Str. 70.
**GPS**: n51,29436 e7,24509.

10 🅿️€ 16 🔌€ 2 🔵Ch€ 3. **Surface:** gravel/metalled.
⚿ 01/01-31/12.
**Distance:** 🚶3km 🛒200m.
**Remarks:** Outside environmental zone.

| 🅿️🆂 | Xanten 🌿 | 9E3 |
|---|---|---|

**WomoPark-Xanten**, Fürstenberg 6. **GPS**: n51,65413 e6,46389.⬆️➡️.

70 🅿️€ 12 🔌€ 0,50/24h 🔵€ 0,50 Ch€ 1 🚰(70x)€ 3,50/24h WC€ 0,75
€ 1,75/pppd. 🚿 **Location:** Rural, comfortable, luxurious, quiet.
**Surface:** grassy. ⚿ 01/01-31/12.
**Distance:** 🚶700m 🚴10km 🏊1,4km 🚣1,4km ⊗800m 🛒300m
🚏300m 🚲on the spot 🚶on the spot.

---

**Remarks:** Check in on arrival.

| 🅿️🆂 | Zülpich | 11F2 |
|---|---|---|

**Wohnmobilpark Seepark**, Eichenallee.
**GPS**: n50,67660 e6,65867.⬆️➡️.

27 🅿️€ 9 🔌€ 1 🔵Ch🚰 included. 🔲 **Location:** Rural, simple,
isolated. **Surface:** grassy. ⚿ 01/01-31/12.
**Distance:** 🚶2km 🏊100m ⊗400m 🛒2km.
**Remarks:** Service nearby tenniscourt 100m.

# Rhineland-Palatinate/Saarland

| 🍇🆂 | Albersweiler | 16H2 |
|---|---|---|

**Weingut Hahn-Hof**, Löwensteinstraße 4. **GPS**: n49,22305 e8,04027.⬆️.

4 🅿️€ 10 🔌included. 🚿WC🚰. 🔲 **Location:** Rural, simple, isolated.
**Surface:** grassy. ⚿ 01/01-31/12.
**Distance:** 🚶500m 🚲on the spot 🚶on the spot.

| 🅿️🆂 | Albisheim | 16H1 |
|---|---|---|

Hauptstraße. **GPS**: n49,65061 e8,10066.⬆️.
3 🅿️free 🔌€ 1 🔵Ch. **Location:** Urban. **Surface:** metalled.
⚿ 01/01-31/12.
**Distance:** ⊗240m 🛒350m 🚏1km 🚶on the spot.

| 🔺🆂 | Alf 🌿🚤 | 11F3 |
|---|---|---|

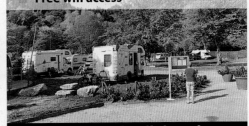
**Moselcamping Alf**, Am Mühlenteich. **GPS**: n50,05267 e7,11399.⬆️➡️.
100 🅿️€ 12, Jun € 14, Jul/Aug € 18 🔌🔵Ch🚰WC🚰against
payment 🚿included. 🔲 **Location:** Rural, comfortable, luxurious,
quiet. **Surface:** grassy. ⚿ 12/04-31/12.
**Distance:** 🚶100m 🏊on the spot 🚣on the spot ⊗200m 🛒2km
🚏100m 🚲on the spot 🚶on the spot.
**Remarks:** Bread-service, barbecue place.

| 🅿️🆂 | Alken ⚓ | 11G3 |
|---|---|---|

Moselstraße 1. **GPS**: n50,25090 e7,44590.⬆️.

DE

5 ⌂free. **Location:** Rural, simple. **Surface:** gravel.
⊙ 01/01-31/12.
**Distance:** 🚰200m ⊗100m 🛒200m on the spot.

| 🅿 | Altdorf | 16H2 |

**Gäuhalle**, Schulstraße. **GPS:** n49,28426 e8,22035. ⬆.

4 ⌂free. **Location:** Rural, simple, isolated, quiet. **Surface:** metalled.
⊙ 01/01-31/12.
**Distance:** 🚰300m ⊗300m on the spot 🅰 on the spot.

| 🅿 S | Altdorf | 16H2 |

**Spelzenhof**, Hauptstrasse 77. **GPS:** n49,28869 e8,22028. ⬆.

6 ⌂€ 10 🚰included 💧€ 2. **Location:** Simple. **Surface:** grassy.
⊙ 01/01-31/12 ⊙ Mon, Tue.
**Distance:** 🚰nearby 🚲7km ⊗150m ⛲400m 🛒nearby.

| 🅿 S | Altendiez | 11H3 |

**Gaststätte Lahnblickhalle**, Lahnblick 4.
**GPS:** n50,36610 e7,98040. ⬆➡.

6 ⌂€ 8 🚰💧included. **Location:** Simple. **Surface:** gravel.
⊙ 01/01-31/12 ⊙ Mo.
**Distance:** 🚰on the spot ⊗on the spot ⛲500m.
**Remarks:** At gymnasium, discount at restaurant € 5.

| 🅿 S | Altenglan 🚩 | 16G1 |

**Draisine**, Austrasse. **GPS:** n49,55001 e7,46465. ⬆.

4 ⌂free 🚰€ 1/100liter 🔌Ch 💧(6x)€ 1. **Location:** Rural, simple,
quiet. **Surface:** gravel. ⊙ 01/04-31/10.
**Distance:** ⊗100m 🛒100m on the spot 🅰 on the spot.

| 🅿 S | Alzey | 16H1 |

**Am Römerkastell**, Jean-Braun-Straße. **GPS:** n49,74412 e8,11804. ⬆.

---

4 ⌂free 🚰€ 1/100liter 🔌€ 1/time Ch€ 1/time 💧(4x)€ 0,50/kWh.
**Location:** Urban, simple, central. **Surface:** gravel.
⊙ 01/01-31/12. 💧
**Distance:** 🚰500m 🚲2km ⛲1km 🛒on the spot 🅰on the spot.

| 🅿 S | Andernach | 11G2 |

**Wohnmobilstellplatz Andernach**, Scheidsgasse/Uferstrasse.
**GPS:** n50,44176 e7,40796. ⬆.

110 ⌂€ 7 🚰€ 1/100liter 🔌Chincluded 💧(80x)€ 1/kWh WC€ 0,50.
🚿 **Surface:** metalled. ⊙ 01/01-31/12.
**Distance:** 🚰100m 🚲9km 🏊10m ⊗50m ⛲150m 🛒30m 🅰on the
spot 🅰 on the spot.
**Remarks:** Max. 3 nights.

| 🅿 S | Andernach | 11G2 |

**Wohnmobilstellplatz Monte Mare**, Klingelswiese 1.
**GPS:** n50,42633 e7,38492. ⬆.

14 ⌂€ 6 🚰€ 0,50/100liter 🔌Ch 💧(16x)€ 0,50/kWh WC💧🌐.
**Location:** Urban, comfortable, isolated, quiet. **Surface:** concrete.
⊙ 01/01-31/12.
**Distance:** 🚰2km 🏊Laach Lake 10km ⊗2km ⛲2km 🅰on the spot
🅰 on the spot.
**Remarks:** Bread-service, discount on access terme.

**Tourist information Andernach:**
🚩 ⊙ Sa 7-13h.

| 🅿 S | Annweiler | 16H2 |

**Am Kurpark**, Bindersbacherstrasse. **GPS:** n49,19624 e7,96817. ⬆➡.

10 ⌂free 🚰€ 1/80liter 🔌Ch. **Location:** Rural, quiet.
**Surface:** asphalted. ⊙ 01/01-31/12.
**Distance:** 🚰1km ⛲600m.
**Remarks:** Max. 3 days.

| 🅿 S | Bacharach 🚩 | 11G3 |

**Reisemobilplatz Sonnenstrand**, B9 Leinpfad.
**GPS:** n50,05487 e7,77123. ⬆➡.

---

30 ⌂€ 9 🚰€ 1 🔌Ch 💧(30x)€ 2,50/24h 🔌€ 1 🔌€ 3/3 🌐 🏠
**Location:** Comfortable, central, quiet. **Surface:** gravel.
⊙ 01/01-31/12 ⊙ high water.
**Distance:** 🚰on the spot 🏊Rhine river ⊗300m ⛲300m.
**Remarks:** Bread-service, dog € 1,50/night.

| 🅿 S | Bad Bergzabern | 16H2 |

**Schloßgärten**, Weinbergstrasse 7. **GPS:** n49,10322 e7,99737. ⬆➡.

10 ⌂€ 4 🚰€ 1/80liter 🔌€ 1 Ch 💧€ 1. 🏠
**Location:** Urban, simple, central, noisy. **Surface:** metalled.
⊙ 01/01-31/12 ⊙ water disconnected in winter.
**Distance:** 🚰on the spot ⊗on the spot ⛲200m 🛒on the spot.

| 🅿 S | Bad Bergzabern | 16H2 |

**Weingut Hitziger**, Liebrauenbergweg 3. **GPS:** n49,10667 e7,99611. ⬆.

8 ⌂€ 5 🚰Chincluded 💧€ 1/kWh. 🚿 **Location:** Rural, simple,
quiet. **Surface:** grassy. ⊙ 01/01-31/12.
**Distance:** 🚰1km ⊗2km ⛲2km.

| 🅿 S | Bad Dürkheim ♨ 🚩 | 16H1 |

**In der Silz**, Leistadterstrasse. **GPS:** n49,46944 e8,16722. ⬆➡.

170 ⌂€ 6 🚰€ 1/80liter 🔌Ch 💧(40x)€ 1/kWh. 🏠
**Location:** Urban, simple. **Surface:** grassy/gravel.
⊙ 01/01-31/12.
**Distance:** 🚰300m ⊗100m ⛲300m 🛒200m.
**Remarks:** Max. 3 days, servicepoint at Knaus Park.

| 🅿 S | Bad Dürkheim ♨ 🚩 | 16H1 |

**Katharinenhof**, In den Kornwiesen 1. **GPS:** n49,46633 e8,20144.

10 ⌂€ 10, € 18 service incl. + € 1/pp tourist tax 🚰🔌
Ch 💧WC 🌐included 🌐. 🏠 **Location:** Rural, quiet. **Surface:** gravel.
⊙ 01/01-31/12.
**Distance:** 🚰450m ⊗on the spot ⛲600m 🛒1km.

DE

**Remarks:** Bread-service.

### ⛺Ⓢ Bad Dürkheim 🚲🍴 16H1
**Knaus park,** In den Almen 3. **GPS:** n49,47472 e8,19167.⬆️.

16 🚐 € 10 🚰 € 1/70liter 🔌Ch.💧(8x)€ 0,70/kWh 🚿€ 3,30/pp 📶.🏠.
**Location:** Rural. **Surface:** gravel/metalled. 🔲 01/01-31/12.
**Remarks:** Sanitary at campsite.

### ⚓Ⓢ Bad Ems 🚤 11G3
**Yachthafen Kutscher's Marina,** Nievernerstrasse 20.
**GPS:** n50,33278 e7,70167.⬆️➡️.

16 🚐 € 10 🚰🔌Ch.💧(20x)€ 0,50/kWh WC🚿€ 1,2 x € 0,50.
**Location:** Urban, comfortable, noisy. **Surface:** gravel.
🔲 01/03-15/11.
**Distance:** 🚶500m 🚤on the spot ⊗1km 🛒300m.
**Remarks:** Barbecue place.

### 🚲Ⓢ Bad Kreuznach 🍴 16G1
**Wohnmobilstellplatz Salinental,** Karlshalle 11, Saline.
**GPS:** n49,82778 e7,85001.⬆️➡️.

40 🚐 € 13 🚰 € 0,50/60liter 🔌Ch.💧€ 3/night WC🚿€ 1.
**Location:** Rural. **Surface:** gravel. 🔲 01/01-31/12.
**Distance:** 🚶2km 🏊on the spot 🚤on the spot ⊗200m 🛒2km �In on the spot.

### 🍷Ⓢ Bad Kreuznach 🚲🍴 16G1
**Weingut Desoi,** Am Darmstädter Hof. **GPS:** n49,82803 e7,88934.⬆️.

3 🚐 € 5 🚰💧 included. **Location:** Rural, simple, quiet.
**Surface:** concrete. 🔲 01/01-31/12.
**Distance:** 🚶1,5km 🏊10km 🛒850m 🛒500m.

### 🍷Ⓢ Bad Kreuznach 🚲🍴 16G1
**Weingut Gut Neuhof,** Gut Neuhof. **GPS:** n49,86923 e7,85924.⬆️.

4 🚐 € 10 🚰💧included. **Location:** Rural, simple, quiet.

---

**Surface:** grassy. 🔲 01/01-31/12.
**Distance:** 🚶3km ⊗600m 🛒2,5km.

### 🚲Ⓢ Bad Marienberg 🍴🍴 11G2
**Marienbad,** Bismarckstrasse 65. **GPS:** n50,64321 e7,93515.➡️.

40 🚐 € 10 🚰 € 1/100liter 🔌Ch.💧(40x)€ 0,50/kWh 🚿included.
**Location:** Rural, luxurious, isolated, quiet. **Surface:** metalled.
🔲 01/01-31/12.
**Distance:** 🚶2km ⊗Bistro.
**Remarks:** 10 days € 78, bread-service, free use of sun beds and beach chairs.

### 🍷Ⓢ Bad Münster am Stein-Ebernburg 16G1
**Reisemobilstellplatz Weingut Rapp,** Schlossgartenstrasse 74.
**GPS:** n49,80800 e7,83208.⬆️.

3 🚐 € 10, dog € 1 🚰 € 1/100liter 🔌Ch.💧included.
**Location:** Rural, simple, quiet. **Surface:** gravel.
🔲 01/01-31/12.
**Distance:** 🚶500m 🚤15km ⊗500m 🚐2km.

### 🚲Ⓢ Bad Neuenahr 🍴 11F2
**Reisemobilhafen Am Ahrtor,** Kalvarienbergstrasse 1, Ahrweiler.
**GPS:** n50,53891 e7,09600.⬆️.

26 🚐 € 8, 2 pers.incl 🚰🔌Ch.💧€ 3 WCincluded 🚿€ 1 🔲€ 3 📶on demand. **Surface:** grassy. 🔲 01/03-31/12.
**Distance:** 🚶200m.

### ⛺Ⓢ Bad Neuenahr 🍴 11F2
**Apolinaris-Stadion,** Kreuzstrasse. **GPS:** n50,54456 e7,15132.➡️.

20 🚐 € 8/24h 🚰 € 1/80liter 🔌Ch.🚍 **Location:** Urban.
**Surface:** asphalted. 🔲 01/01-31/12.
**Distance:** 🚤3km.
**Remarks:** At sports park.

### 🚲Ⓢ Bad Neuenahr 🍴 11F2
**Wohnmobilstellplatz Bachem,** St.-Pius-Straße.
**GPS:** n50,54022 e7,10891.

---

20 🚐 € 8/24h. 🚍 **Location:** Urban, simple. **Surface:** asphalted.
🔲 01/01-31/12.
**Distance:** 🚶700m ⊗200m 🛒200m 🚐200m.
**Remarks:** Parking at the Ahr.

### 🚲Ⓢ Bad Sobernheim 🚲🍴 16G1
**Reisemobilstellplatz am Nohfels,** Hömigweg 1.
**GPS:** n49,77910 e7,65800.⬆️.

39 🚐 € 9 🚰 € 0,10/10liter 🔌Ch.💧(48x)€ 2,50/day,16Amp WC📶.
**Location:** Rural, comfortable, quiet. **Surface:** metalled.
🔲 01/01-31/12.
**Distance:** 🚶500m 🏊100m 🚤100m ⊗200m 🛒500m 🚐300m.
🚲on the spot 🚶on the spot.
**Remarks:** Bread-service.

### 🍴Ⓢ Battweiler 🍂 16G2
**Flugplatz Pottschütthöhe,** Pottschütthöhe.
**GPS:** n49,26761 e7,49096.⬆️.

10 🚐 € 15 🔌Ch.💧(10x)included. **Location:** Simple, isolated,
quiet. **Surface:** grassy/gravel. 🔲 01/01-31/12 🔲 Mo.
**Distance:** 🚶2km 🏊10km 🚤on the spot.
**Remarks:** At airfield.

### 🚲 Baumholder 🍂 16G1
**Freizeitzentrum Am Weiher,** Ringstrasse.
**GPS:** n49,61111 e7,33917.➡️.

3 🚐free. **Location:** Rural, simple. **Surface:** asphalted/grassy.
🔲 01/04-31/10.
**Distance:** 🚶2km 🏊on the spot ⊗McDonalds 250m 🛒250m.

### 🍴Ⓢ Becheln 🍴🍴 11G3
**Restaurant Zum Wolfsbusch,** Emser strasse 1.
**GPS:** n50,29609 e7,71503.⬆️.

5 ⛺ € 2, guests free ⇌ € 2. **Location:** Simple, quiet.
**Surface:** gravel/metalled. ◘ 01/01-31/12.
**Distance:** ⚓on the spot ⊗on the spot ⚑300m.

### ⛺S Beckingen 16F2

**Wohnmobilstellplatz Düppenweiler**, Brunnenstrasse 11, Düppenweiler. **GPS:** n49,41414 e6,76973. ⬆→.

30 ⛺ € 4 ⇌ € 1/100liter ⬛Ch ✎(6x)€ 1/8h. ⚒
**Location:** Rural, simple, quiet. **Surface:** metalled.
◘ 01/03-31/12.
**Distance:** ⚓on the spot ⊗300m.

### ⛺S Beckingen 16F2

**Landgasthaus Wilscheider Hof**, Zum Wilscheider Hof, Düppenweiler. **GPS:** n49,42562 e6,76422. ⬆→.

15 ⛺ € 5 ⬛Ch ✎(7x)€ 1/day WC ⬛€ 1,50. **Location:** Rural, comfortable, isolated, quiet. **Surface:** grassy. ◘ 01/01-31/12.
**Distance:** ⚓1,5km ⊗on the spot ⚑1,5km.

### ⛺S Bellheim 16H2

**Wohnmobilstellplatz Bellheim**, Auchtweide.
**GPS:** n49,19552 e8,27466. ⬆.

8 ⛺ € 5 ⇌ WCincluded ⬛€ 1/pp. ⚒ **Location:** Urban, simple, isolated, quiet. **Surface:** grassy/gravel. ◘ 01/05-31/10.
**Distance:** ⚓700m ⚲3km ⊗750m ⚑1km ▭200m ♣on the spot ♀on the spot.
**Remarks:** At tennis-courts, max. 24h, possibility for reservation.

### ⛺S Bendorf ⚓ 11G2

**Wohnmobilstellplatz In der Sayner Hütte**, Althansweg 2.
**GPS:** n50,44166 e7,57956. →.

6 ⛺free. **Location:** Urban, simple, quiet. **Surface:** gravel.
◘ 01/01-31/12.
**Distance:** ⚓2km ⚲4km ⊗100m ⚑2km.

### ⛺S Bernkastel ⚜☕🥐 11F3

**Weingut Studert-Prüm im Maximin Hof**, Hauptstrasse 150, Wehlen.
**GPS:** n49,93785 e7,04815. ⬆→.

43 ⛺ € 13 ⇌ Ch ⚲included ⚡€ 2/24h. 🚐🛢
**Location:** Rural, comfortable, isolated, quiet.
**Surface:** asphalted/gravel. ◘ 01/01-31/12.
**Distance:** ⚓500m ⚲on the spot ▭on the spot ⊗250m ⚑2km, bakery 300m ♀on the spot.

### P⛺S Bernkastel ⚜☕🥐 11F3

**Nikolausufer. GPS:** n49,91119 e7,06721. ⬆.

40 ⛺ € 1,20/h ⇌ ⬛Ch. 🅿 **Location:** Urban, simple.
**Surface:** asphalted/grassy. ◘ 01/01-31/12, 10-18h.
**Distance:** ⚓on the spot.
**Remarks:** Along the Moselle river, max. 6h.

### ⛺S Betzdorf 11G2

**Friedrichstrasse. GPS:** n50,78636 e7,87781. ⬆.

1 ⛺free. **Location:** Urban, simple, noisy. **Surface:** asphalted.
◘ 01/01-31/12.
**Distance:** ⚓500m ⊗200m.
**Remarks:** Max. 24h.

### ⛺S Betzdorf 11G2

**Schützenplatz**, Martin-Luther-Strasse. **GPS:** n50,79323 e7,86793. ⬆.

1 ⛺free. **Location:** Urban, simple. **Surface:** gravel.
◘ 01/01-31/12.
**Distance:** ⚓on the spot ⊗on the spot ⚑on the spot ▭1km.
**Remarks:** Max. 1 night.

### ⛺S Betzdorf 11G2

**Vor dem Stadion**, Eberhardystrasse. **GPS:** n50,78524 e7,86507. ⬆.

1 ⛺free. **Location:** Urban, simple, central. **Surface:** gravel.
◘ 01/01-31/12.
**Distance:** ⚓1km ⊗50m ▭1km ♣on the spot.
**Remarks:** Max. 1 night.

### ⛺S Bexbach ⚘☕⛲ 16G2

**Bexbacher Reisemobilhafen**, Im Blumengarten.
**GPS:** n49,34161 e7,25698. ⬆→.

35 ⛺ € 7 ⇌ € 1/80liter ⬛Ch ✎(36x)€ 2,50/night WC.
**Location:** Rural, luxurious, quiet. **Surface:** grassy. ◘ 01/01-31/12.
**Distance:** ⚓900m ⚲5km ⊗on the spot ⚑500m ▭200m ♣on the spot.
**Remarks:** Bread-service.

### ⚜S Biebernheim 11G3

**Reiterhof Pabst**, Auf dem Flürchen. **GPS:** n50,14127 e7,70828. ⬆→.

20 ⛺ € 7, 2 pers.incl. ⇌ ⬛Ch ✎(6x) 2. ⚒ **Location:** Rural, simple, isolated, quiet. **Surface:** grassy. ◘ 01/01-31/12.
**Distance:** ⚲10km.
**Remarks:** Bread-service.

### ©S Billigheim-Ingenheim 16H2

**Camping/Freibad im Klingbachtal**, Klingener Straße.
**GPS:** n49,13681 e8,07227. ⬆.

6 ⛺ € 12, dog € 3 ⬛Ch ✎(6x)€ 2,50/night WC ⬛against payment ⚡included. 🚐🛢 **Location:** Rural, comfortable, isolated, quiet. **Surface:** metalled. ◘ 01/04-31/10.
**Distance:** ⚓3km ⚲5km ♣on the spot ♀on the spot.
**Remarks:** Incl. access swimming pool.

### ⛺S Bingen/Rhein 11H3

**Wohnmobilpark Bingen**, Mainzer Straße, Bingen/Kempten.
**GPS:** n49,96860 e7,94417. ⬆→.

39 ⛺ € 7/night ⇌ ⬛Ch ✎€ 2,50/24h ⬛€ 3/3 ⚡included.
**Location:** Comfortable, quiet. **Surface:** grassy/metalled.
◘ 01/01-31/12.
**Distance:** ⚓2,5km ⚲1,5km ⊗800m ⚑2,7km.
**Remarks:** Bread-service, possibility for reservation.

### ⛺S Birgel ⚜ 11F3

**Historische Wassermühle**, Bahnhofstrasse 16.
**GPS:** n50,32033 e6,61764. ⬆.

DE

10 ⌂ € 15, free with a meal > € 15 ⚡💧 Ch 🚿(2x)included.
**Location:** Rural, simple, quiet. **Surface:** gravel.
🅿 01/01-31/12.
**Distance:** 🚶500m 🚲25km ⊗200m 🛒1km 🚌400m.

**Freizeitanlage Würzbacher Weiher**, Marxstraße, Niederwürzbach.
**GPS:** n49,24674 e7,19226.⬆➡.

10 ⌂ € 4,50 ⚡€ 1/10minutes 💧€ 1 Ch 🚿€ 1/4h.
**Location:** Rural, simple, quiet. **Surface:** grassy/gravel.
🅿 21/03-20/12 ❄ winter.
**Distance:** 🚶500m 🏊on the spot 🎣on the spot ⊗100m 🛒600m 🚌600m.
**Remarks:** At lake, Würzbacher Weiher.

**Hotel Restaurant Hubertushof**, Kirschendell 32.
**GPS:** n49,24456 e7,21573.⬆⬆.

8 ⌂ € 5 ⚡€ 1,50 🚿€ 2,50. **Location:** Rural, simple, quiet.
**Surface:** metalled. 🅿 01/01-31/12.
**Distance:** 🚶on the spot ⊗900m 🛒1km.
**Remarks:** Arrival < 19h, max. 2 nights, bread-service.

**Freizeitzentrum Blieskastel**, Bliesaue 1, Webenheim.
**GPS:** n49,23527 e7,26946.⬆.

3 ⌂ free ⚡. **Location:** Urban, simple, noisy. **Surface:** metalled.
🅿 01/01-31/12.
**Distance:** 🚶on the spot 🚲5km ⊗150m 🛒100m.

**Hotel-Restaurant St. Germanshof**, Hauptstrasse 10.
**GPS:** n49,04749 e7,89985.

4 ⌂ guests free. **Location:** Rural, simple, isolated, quiet.
**Surface:** metalled. 🅿 01/01-31/12 ◉ Mo.
**Distance:** 🚶5km ⊗350m 🛒7km.

**Weingut Benss**, Am Spiegelpfad 10. **GPS:** n49,59959 e8,17823.⬆.

6 ⌂ free ⚡(6x) WC 🚿Service € 5. **Location:** Rural, simple, quiet.
**Surface:** grassy. 🅿 01/01-31/12.
**Distance:** 🚲7km ⊗500m 🛒3km 🚌1,6km.

**Weingut W. Kohl**, Am Sonnenberg 3. **GPS:** n49,59902 e8,17925.⬆.

6 ⌂ € 10 ⚡🚿 WC included. 🏠 **Location:** Rural, simple.
**Surface:** grassy/metalled. 🅿 01/01-31/12.
**Distance:** 🚶500m ⊗500m 🛒3km 🚌2km.
**Remarks:** Check in on arrival.

**Braubacher Rheintreff**, Rheinuferstrasse, B42.
**GPS:** n50,26972 e7,64750.⬆➡.

30 ⌂ € 10 ⚡💧Ch 🚿 WCincluded 🗑€ 1 💩€ 3. 🚐
**Location:** Rural, comfortable, quiet. **Surface:** asphalted.
🅿 01/01-31/12.
**Distance:** 🚶300m 🏊on the spot 🎣on the spot ⊗300m 🛒300m 🚌300m.

**Wohnmobilplatz Juffer**, Moselweinstrasse 61.
**GPS:** n49,90518 e6,97760.➡.

25 ⌂ € 10 ⚡💧Ch 🚿 included. 💩 **Surface:** metalled.
🅿 01/01-31/12.
**Distance:** 🚶100m 🏊on the spot ⊗300m 🛒300m 🚌100m 🚲Mosel-Radweg 🚶on the spot.
**Remarks:** Bicycle rental at tourist office.

**Weingut Oster-Franzen**, Calmontstrasse 96.
**GPS:** n50,09593 e7,12383.⬆➡.

16 ⌂ € 14, 2 pers incl ⚡€ 0,50/60liter 💧Ch 🚿(16x) € 0,50/kWh
WC 🗑€ 1/6minutes, 2 x € 0,50 💩€ 3,50 🚿.
**Location:** Rural, comfortable. **Surface:** gravel. 🅿 01/03-30/11.
**Distance:** 🚶on the spot ⊗800m 🛒300m 🚲on the spot 🚶on the spot.

**Wohnmobilstellplatz Briedern**, Moselstrasse.
**GPS:** n50,11165 e7,20867.➡.

15 ⌂ € 6,50. 💩 **Location:** Rural, simple. **Surface:** grassy/gravel.
🅿 01/01-31/12.
**Distance:** 🚶on the spot ⊗300m 🛒200m 🚲on the spot.

**Moselufer. GPS:** n50,22471 e7,43930.⬆.

2 ⌂ free. **Location:** Urban, simple. **Surface:** metalled.
🅿 01/01-31/12.
**Distance:** 🚶500m ⊗500m 🚶on the spot.

**Salzwiese 9. GPS:** n50,22519 e7,44291.⬆➡.

4 ⌂ free. **Location:** Urban. **Surface:** concrete. 🅿 01/01-31/12.
**Distance:** 🚶400m 🏊Moselle river 200m ⊗400m 🚌3,5km.

**Hotel Schmause Mühle**, Baybachstrasse 50.
**GPS:** n50,20859 e7,39365.⬆.

20 ⌂ € 8 ⚡💧Ch 🚿€ 2,50/day WCincluded 🗑€ 1. 🚐
**Location:** Rural, simple, quiet. **Surface:** grassy/gravel.
🅿 01/01-31/12.
**Distance:** 🚶on the spot 🏊on the spot 🛒300m.

DE

### Burgen bei Bernkastel-Kues  16F1

**Weingut Bohn-Leimbrock**, Lindenstrasse 6.
**GPS:** n49,87986 e6,99967. ⬆.

4 ⊠ € 8 🚰 ⚡(3x) WC🚽. 🧺 **Location:** Rural. **Surface:** grassy/gravel. ⬛ 01/01-31/12.
**Distance:** 🚶150m ⚓20km ⊗200m 🍺4km 🚐50m 🚲on the spot 🚶on the spot.

### Burrweiler  16H2

**Wein- und Sektgut Hermann-Bruno Eberle**, Böchingerstrasse 1a.
**GPS:** n49,24649 e8,07989. ⬆.

3 ⊠ € 6 🚰 ⚡ WC included. 🧺 **Location:** Rural, simple, quiet.
**Surface:** metalled. ⬛ 01/01-31/12.
**Distance:** 🚶100m ⊗100m 🍺200m.
**Remarks:** Arrival <21h.

### Burrweiler  16H2

**Weingut Diether Bauer**, Weinstrasse 52. **GPS:** n49,24615 e8,07132. ⬆.

3 ⊠ € 5 🚰 ⚡ WC included. 🧺 **Location:** Rural, simple, quiet.
**Surface:** metalled. ⬛ 01/01-31/12.
**Distance:** 🚶on the spot ⊗100m 🍺300m.

### Burrweiler  16H2

**Weingut Hertel**, Raiffeisenstrasse 2. **GPS:** n49,24861 e8,07705. ⬆.

3 ⊠ € 5 🚰 ⚡ included WC on demand. **Location:** Rural, simple, quiet. **Surface:** metalled. ⬛ 01/04-31/10.
**Distance:** ⊗250m.

### Burrweiler  16H2

**Weingut Winzerhof**, Am Schlossberg 3. **GPS:** n49,25147 e8,07902. ⬆.

4 ⊠ € 8 🚰 ⚡ WC included. 🧺 **Location:** Rural, simple, quiet.
**Surface:** metalled. ⬛ 01/01-31/12.
**Distance:** 🚶1km ⊗500m 🍺300m.

### Cochem  11F3

Bergstrasse, K59. **GPS:** n50,15028 e7,17083.

4 ⊠ 9-19h € 2,50, overnight stay free. **Surface:** grasstiles/metalled. ⬛ 01/01-31/12.
**Distance:** 🚶300m ⊗300m.

### Cochem  11F3

Moselpromenade, B49. **GPS:** n50,14108 e7,16936. ⬆.

4 ⊠ 8-19h € 1/h, overnight stay free. **Surface:** metalled.
⬛ 01/01-31/12.
**Distance:** 🚶600m ⊗600m 🍺700m.
**Remarks:** Max. 11h.

### Cochem  11F3

**Wohnmobil-Stellplatz an der Nordbrücke**, Moselstrasse, B49.
**GPS:** n50,15329 e7,16828. ⬆.

16 ⊠ 8-19h € 1/h, overnight stay free. **Location:** Urban, simple.
**Surface:** metalled. ⬛ 01/01-31/12.
**Distance:** 🚶700m ⊗200m 🍺200m 🚐on the spot.
**Remarks:** Max. 11h.

### Cochem  11F3

**Wohnmobil-Stellplatz am Freizeitzentrum**, Stadionstrasse.
**GPS:** n50,16051 e7,17956. ⬆.

50 ⊠ € 0,50/h 🚰🍺🧺🚽
**Surface:** gravel/sand. ⬛ 01/01-31/12.
**Distance:** 🚶2,5km ⊗400m 🍺on the spot.
**Remarks:** Along the Moselle river, max. 24h, sanitary at campsite.

### Darscheid/Vulkaneifel  11F3

**Kucher's Landhotel**, Karl-Kaufmann-Strasse 2.
**GPS:** n50,21077 e6,88314. ⬆.

3 ⊠ € 15, guests free. 🏨🚲🧺 **Location:** Rural, simple.

**Surface:** asphalted. ⬛ 01/01-31/12.
**Distance:** 🚶650m ⚓450m ⊗on the spot 🚲on the spot 🚶on the spot.
**Remarks:** Breakfast-service.

### Deidesheim  16H2

**Weinhaus Villa Giessen**, Weinstrasse 3. **GPS:** n49,41210 e8,19105.

3 ⊠ € 8 🚰 ⚡ included. 🏨 **Location:** Rural, simple.
**Surface:** gravel/metalled. ⬛ 01/01-31/12.
**Distance:** 🚶on the spot ⚓5km ⊗500m 🍺1km 🚐900m.

### Deudesfeld  11F3

Meisburgerstrasse. **GPS:** n50,10084 e6,72932. ⬆➡.

8 ⊠ free 🚰 € 1/120liter 🚽 € 1 Ch ⚡ € 0,50/kWh.
**Location:** Rural, simple, isolated, quiet. **Surface:** grassy.
⬛ 01/01-31/12.
**Distance:** 🚶300m ⊗200m.

### Deudesfeld  11F3

**Leyendecker Platz**, Mandertscheider Strasse.
**GPS:** n50,10164 e6,73217. ⬆.

4 ⊠ free. **Location:** Rural, simple, isolated, quiet. **Surface:** gravel.
⬛ 01/01-31/12.
**Distance:** 🚶200m ⚡on the spot ⊗150m.

### Deuselbach  16F1

**Wohnmobilstellplatz Erbeskopf**, K130. **GPS:** n49,73589 e7,08327. ⬆.

50 ⊠ € 4 🚰🚐 Ch ⚡(5x) € 3/day WC included 🚽 € 0,50/5minutes.
**Location:** Rural, simple, isolated, quiet. **Surface:** metalled.
⬛ 01/01-31/12.
**Distance:** 🚶10km.

### Dexheim  16H1

**Weingut Bacchushof**, Wörrstädter Strasse 14.
**GPS:** n49,84812 e8,31144. ⬆.

5 🛏free. **Location:** Rural, simple. **Surface:** concrete. 🅾 01/01-31/12. **Distance:** 🚲 12km.

### ⛲Ⓢ Dierbach 16H2

Jahnstrasse. **GPS:** n49,08177 e8,06201.⬆.

10 🛏€5 🚰🚽Ch🚿(5x)included.🚾 **Location:** Simple, quiet. **Surface:** gravel. 🅾 01/01-31/12. **Distance:** 🚶700m 🚲12km 🚉1km 🍺3km 🚌50m. **Remarks:** At sports centre.

### ⛲Ⓢ Dierbach 16H2

Weingut Geiger, Hauptstrasse 21. **GPS:** n49,08344 e8,06673.⬆➡.

30 🛏€10 🚰🚽Ch🚿WCincluded 🧺€4 📶€2/day. **Location:** Rural, comfortable, quiet. **Surface:** grassy. 🅾 01/03-31/12. **Distance:** 🚶on the spot 🚲12km 🍺500m. **Remarks:** Bread-service, playground.

### ⛲Ⓢ Dolgesheim 16H1

Weingut Seck, Weinolsheimer Strasse 12. **GPS:** n49,79752 e8,26154.⬆.

3 🛏€5 🚰€2 🚽Ch🚿€2 WC🧺📶included.🚾 **Location:** Rural, simple, quiet. **Surface:** grassy. 🅾 01/01-31/12. **Distance:** 🚶200m 🚲13km ⊗300m 🍺2km.

### ⛲Ⓢ Dörrenbach 16H2

Übergasse. **GPS:** n49,08840 e7,96921.⬆.

10 🛏€6 🚰🚽Ch🚿included.🚾 **Location:** Rural, quiet. **Surface:** gravel/sand. 🅾 01/01-31/12. **Distance:** 🚶500m ⊗600m 🍺700m. **Remarks:** Next to sports fields.

### ⛲Ⓢ Eckersweiler 16G1

Am Sportplatz. **GPS:** n49,55646 e7,30577.⬆.

---

4 🛏free. **Location:** Rural, simple, isolated. **Surface:** grassy. 🅾 01/01-31/12. **Distance:** 🚶1,3km 🚲on the spot 🚶on the spot.

### ⛲Ⓢ Edenkoben 16H2

Wohnmobilstellplatz Kirchbergplatz, Bahnhofstraße. **GPS:** n49,28234 e8,13116.⬆.

40 🛏€5 🚰€1/100liter 🚽Ch🚿(8x)€1/kWh.🚾 **Location:** Urban. **Surface:** asphalted. 🅾 01/01-31/12. **Distance:** 🚶on the spot 🚲2km ⊗300m 🍺Aldi 800m. **Remarks:** Max. 3 nights.

### ⛲Ⓢ Edenkoben 16H2

Brennerei & Weinstube Göring, Blücherstrasse 45. **GPS:** n49,27792 e8,13487.

5 🛏€10 🚰🚽Ch🚿included WC 🚾 **Location:** Rural, simple, quiet. **Surface:** grassy. 🅾 01/01-31/12. **Distance:** 🚲3km.

### ⛲Ⓢ Edenkoben 16H2

Weingut Bernd und Herbert Schäfer, Rhodter Strasse 24. **GPS:** n49,27778 e8,12588.⬆.

3 🛏free 🚰free 🚿€5/night. **Location:** Rural, simple, quiet. **Surface:** grassy. 🅾 01/01-31/12. **Distance:** 🚲3,5km 🚶on the spot 🚶on the spot.

### ⛲Ⓢ Edenkoben 16H2

Weingut Edel Brauch, St.-Martiner-Strasse 30. **GPS:** n49,28906 e8,12290.⬆.

20 🛏€1/pp tourist tax 🚰€2/time 🚽Ch🚿€2/night. **Location:** Rural, simple, isolated, quiet. **Surface:** grassy. 🅾 01/01-31/12. **Distance:** 🚶1km 🚲3km ⊗1km 🍺1km 🚲on the spot.

---

### ⛲Ⓢ Edenkoben 16H2

Weingut Heinrichshof Fritz-Schneider, Klosterstraße 157a. **GPS:** n49,28313 e8,12368.⬆.

12 🛏€14, 2 pers incl 🚰🚽Ch🚿included.🚾 **Location:** Urban, simple, central. **Surface:** gravel. 🅾 01/03-30/11. **Distance:** 🚶1km ⊗700m.

### ⛲Ⓢ Edenkoben 16H2

Gasthof Ziegelhütte, Luitpoldstrasse 75-79. **GPS:** n49,28539 e8,13872.

3 🛏€5/night 🚿. **Surface:** metalled. 🅾 01/01-31/12. **Distance:** 🚶on the spot 🚲1km ⊗on the spot 🍺on the spot.

### ⛲Ⓢ Edesheim 16H2

Weingut Boos, Ludwigstrasse 150. **GPS:** n49,25785 e8,11673.⬆.

3 🛏€6 🚰🚽Ch🚿(3x)included. **Location:** Rural, simple, quiet. **Surface:** grassy. 🅾 01/01-31/12. **Distance:** 🚶500m ⊗300m 🍺1km. **Remarks:** Bread-service.

### ⛲Ⓢ Edesheim 16H2

Weingut Braun & Sohn, Ludwigsstrasse 151. **GPS:** n49,25761 e8,11587.⬆.

3 🛏€6 🚰🚽Ch🚿included.🚾 **Location:** Rural, simple, quiet. **Surface:** grassy. 🅾 01/01-31/12. **Distance:** 🚶300m ⊗300m 🚌2km.

### ⛲Ⓢ Edesheim 16H2

Weingut Erlenmühle, Erlenmühle 1. **GPS:** n49,25865 e8,11417.⬆.

5 🛏€5 🚰🚽Ch🚿included 🧺on demand.🚾 **Location:** Rural, simple, quiet. **Surface:** gravel. 🅾 01/01-31/12. **Distance:** 🚶500m ⊗on the spot 🍺1km. **Remarks:** Arrival <22h.

DE

## Edesheim    16H2

**Weingut Rehm**, Ludwigstrasse 36. **GPS**: n49,26015 e8,12734. ⬆.

6 🛏 € 12/night 🚰 🚿 (6x) WC 🛢 included. ♨
**Location:** Rural, simple, quiet. **Surface:** grassy.
◻ 01/01-31/12.
**Distance:** 🛒 on the spot ⊗800m 🚲1km.

## Ediger/Eller    11F3

**Stellplatz Ediger**, Moselweinstrasse. **GPS**: n50,09320 e7,15942. ⬆.

25 🛏 € 6 🚽 Ch included 🚿 € 2. **Location:** Rural, simple.
**Surface:** gravel/metalled. ◻ 01/04-30/11.
**Distance:** 🛒100m ⚓on the spot ➤on the spot ⊗on the spot ⚒on the spot ♨on the spot.
**Remarks:** Along the Moselle river in Ediger.

## Ediger/Eller    11F3

**Stellplatz Moselufer**, Eller. **GPS**: n50,09915 e7,14370. ⬆.

15 🛏 € 5. ♨ **Location:** Rural, simple. **Surface:** metalled.
◻ 01/04-30/11.
**Distance:** ⚓on the spot ➤on the spot ⊗on the spot 🍴200m ♨on the spot.
**Remarks:** Along the Moselle river in Eller.

## Eisenschmitt    11F3

**Hotel-Restaurant Molitors Mühle**, Eichelhütte.
**GPS**: n50,03681 e6,73766. ⬆.

5 🛏 guests free 🚰 🚿 WC 🛢 included. **Location:** Rural, simple.
**Surface:** gravel. ◻ 01/01-31/12.
**Distance:** 🛒1km 🚲6km ⚓on the spot ➤on the spot ⊗on the spot 🍴1km 300m ♨on the spot.
**Remarks:** Arrival <23h.

## Ellenz/Poltersdorf    11G3

**Weingut Loosen**, Im Goldbäumchen 4. **GPS**: n50,11389 e7,23528. ⬆➡.

14 🛏 € 7, 2 pers.incl 🚿 WC included 🛢 1/5minutes 📶.
**Location:** Rural, comfortable, quiet. **Surface:** gravel.
◻ 01/01-31/12.
**Distance:** 🛒on the spot ⚓150m ⊗500m 🍴1km 🚲on the spot ♨on the spot.
**Remarks:** Along Mosel.

**Tourist information Ellenz/Poltersdorf:**

☀ Strassenweinfest. Wine-growers and - houses open their doors, wine-tastery. ◻ end Sep.
☀ Wein- und Heimatfeste. Traditional wine celebration. ◻ last weekend Jul, 1st weekend Aug.

## Elmstein    16H2

**NaturFreundeHaus Elmstein**, Esthaler Strasse 63.
**GPS**: n49,36133 e7,95123. ⬆.

12 🛏 € 3 🚰 € 1 🚿 € 2 🛢 € 1/pp. ♨ **Location:** Rural, simple, central, quiet. **Surface:** gravel. ◻ 01/01-31/12.
**Distance:** 🛒3km ⊗on the spot ♨on the spot.
**Remarks:** Bread-service.

## Elmstein    16H2

**Stellplatz Elmstein**, Bahnhofstrasse 88. **GPS**: n49,34803 e7,94337. ⬆.

4 🛏 free 🚿 (4x) € 0,50/kWh. **Location:** Rural. **Surface:** gravel.
◻ 01/01-31/12.
**Distance:** 🛒500m ⊗100m 🍴500m.

## Elmstein    16H2

**Wohnmobilplatz Waldesruhe**, Schwarzbach 36.
**GPS**: n49,34037 e7,83397. ⬆.

10 🛏 € 5, free with a meal. **Location:** Rural, simple, isolated, quiet.
**Surface:** grassy. ◻ 01/01-31/12.
**Distance:** ⊗on the spot.
**Remarks:** To be paid at restaurant, breakfast-service.

## Elzweiler    16G1

**Stellplatz Elzweiler**, Hauptstraße 7. **GPS**: n49,58036 e7,51393. ⬆➡.

2 🛏 free 🚰 € 1 🚽 Ch free 🚿 € 1. **Location:** Rural. **Surface:** metalled.
◻ 01/01-31/12.
**Distance:** 🍴5km ♨on the spot ♨on the spot.
**Remarks:** Small pitches.

## Enkirch    11F3

**Wohnmobilplatz an der Mosel**, Moselvorgelände, B53.
**GPS**: n49,98396 e7,12157. ⬆➡.

200 🛏 € 7 🚰 € 1/80liter 🚽 Ch 🚿 (104x) € 1/2kWh WC 🛢 € 1
🔌 📶 € 1,50/30minutes ⚒ ♨ **Location:** Rural, comfortable, quiet. **Surface:** grassy. ◻ Easter-31/10.
**Distance:** 🛒300m ⚓on the spot ➤on the spot ⊗200m ♨on the spot.
**Remarks:** Along the Moselle river.

## Ensch    16F1

**Reisemobilplatz An den 2 Pappeln**, Am Moselufer/ B53.
**GPS**: n49,82760 e6,83549. ⬆➡.

45 🛏 € 5 🚰 € 2 🚽 Ch 🚿 (45x) € 2. ♨ **Location:** Rural.
**Surface:** grassy. ◻ 01/04-31/10.
**Distance:** 🛒200m ⚓on the spot ⊗300m 🍴500m 🚲100m.
**Remarks:** Bread-service.

## Eppelborn    16F2

**Wohnmobilstellplatz Finkenrech**, Tholeyer Straße 35.
**GPS**: n49,43258 e6,99672. ⬆➡.

3 🛏 € 5 🚿 (4x) € 0,50/kWh. 🚌 **Location:** Rural, simple, quiet.
**Surface:** gravel. ◻ 01/01-31/12.
**Distance:** 🚲3km ♨on the spot.
**Remarks:** Check in at reception.

## Eppenbrunn    16G2

Im Sportzentrum. **GPS**: n49,11179 e7,56512. ⬆.

DE

6 🛏free.
**Location:** Rural, simple, quiet. **Surface:** metalled.
⊙ 01/01-31/12.
**Distance:** 🚶500m ⊗on the spot 🚲1km 🚴on the spot 🧍on the spot.
**Remarks:** Parking sports centre in nature reserve Pfälzer Wald.

### Eppenbrunn 16G2
Neudorfstrasse. **GPS:** n49,11531 e7,55360.⬆.

5 🛏free. **Location:** Rural, simple, noisy. **Surface:** metalled.
⊙ 01/01-31/12.
**Distance:** 🚶on the spot 🚲800m 🚴800m 🚴100m 🚴on the spot 🧍on the spot.

### Erden 11F3
**Wohnmobilstellplatz Erden**, An Moselufer 1.
**GPS:** n49,97989 e7,02120.⬆.

21 🛏€ 10,50 + € 0,50/pp tourist tax 🚰Chincluded 🚿(21x)€ 3/day ⊒€ 0,30/minutes 🔌€ 2,50 🗑on demand. 🚽 **Location:** Rural, comfortable. **Surface:** grassy. ⊙ 01/04-31/10.
**Distance:** 🚲15km 🚴300m 🚴on the spot 🚴on the spot.
**Remarks:** Discount longer stays.

### Ernst 11G3
**Wohnmobilstellplatz im Weinberg**, Weingartenstrasse 106.
**GPS:** n50,14339 e7,23237.⬆➡.

30 🛏€ 9 🚰Ch 🚿included 🗑€ 5/10h. **Location:** Rural, comfortable. **Surface:** gravel. ⊙ 01/01-31/12.
**Distance:** 🚶300m ⊗on the spot 🚴200m 🚴100m 🚴on the spot 🧍on the spot.

### Ernst 11G3
**Mosella Schinkenstube**, Weingatenstrasse 97.
**GPS:** n50,14382 e7,23071.⬆.

18 🛏€ 10 🚰Ch 🚿 🗑included.
**Location:** Rural. **Surface:** grassy. ⊙ 01/01-31/12.
**Distance:** 🚴100m ⊗on the spot 🚴on the spot 🧍on the spot.
**Remarks:** Breakfest-service.

### Eschbach 16H2
**Weingut Wind**, Weinstrasse 3-5. **GPS:** n49,17594 e8,02171.⬆.

---

3 🛏€ 5, discount for clients 🚰€ 1/100liter 🚿€ 3 WCincluded. 🚽
**Location:** Rural, simple, quiet. **Surface:** gravel.
⊙ 01/01-31/12.
**Distance:** 🚶on the spot ⊗on the spot 🚴250m.
**Remarks:** Check in on arrival.

### Essingen 16H2
**Weingut Schweikart Dalberghof**, Kirchstrasse 16.
**GPS:** n49,23478 e8,17524.⬆.

3 🛏€ 5 🚰€ 1/100liter 🚿(3x)€ 1/night WC€ 1.
**Location:** Simple, quiet. **Surface:** grassy. ⊙ 01/01-31/12.
**Distance:** 🚶on the spot 🚴3km ⊗1km 🚴3km 🚴7km 🚴30m.
**Remarks:** Sale of wines.

### Eußerthal 16H2
**Wohnmobilstellplatz Eußerthal**, Haingeraidestraße 1.
**GPS:** n49,23865 e7,97597.⬆.

6 🛏€ 7,50 🚰🚿included. 🚽 **Location:** Rural, simple, isolated, quiet.
**Surface:** grassy. ⊙ 01/01-31/12.
**Distance:** 🚶1km 🚴on the spot 🧍on the spot.

### Fell 16F1
**Besucherbergwerk**, Auf den Schiefergruben, K82.
**GPS:** n49,75440 e6,79731.⬆.

30 🛏free, 01/04-30/11 € 4 🚿€ 2. **Location:** Isolated, quiet.
**Surface:** concrete. ⊙ 01/01-31/12.
**Distance:** 🚶2km ⊗on the spot 🚴on the spot 🧍on the spot.
**Remarks:** Bread-service.

### Fischbach 16G1
**Wohnmobilpark**, Marktstraße 1. **GPS:** n49,74046 e7,40444.⬆➡.

40 🛏€ 7 🚰Chincluded 🚿(40x)€ 2,. 🚽
**Location:** Rural, simple, central. **Surface:** grassy. ⊙ 01/01-31/12.

---

**Distance:** 🚶800m 🚴on the spot ⊗300m 🚴1,5km.
**Remarks:** Bread-service, service passerby € 3.

### Fischbach 16G1
**Historisches Kupferbergwerk**, Hosenbachstraße.
**GPS:** n49,75398 e7,38287.⬆.

10 🛏free. **Location:** Rural, simple, isolated, quiet. **Surface:** gravel.
⊙ 01/01-31/12.
**Distance:** 🚶1,7km ⊗on the spot.
**Remarks:** Visitors' center former copper mine.

### Fischbach bei Dahn 16G2
**Biosphärenhaus**, Am Königsbruch 2. **GPS:** n49,08690 e7,72478.⬆.
6 🛏€ 10 🚰€ 0,50/kWh WC. **Location:** Rural, isolated, quiet.
**Surface:** metalled. ⊙ 01/01-31/12.
**Distance:** 🚶1km ⊗1km 🚴1km.

### Flemlingen 16H2
**Weingut Eichhorn**, Maxstrasse 21. **GPS:** n49,24122 e8,09341.⬆.

8 🛏€ 5 🚰(10x)€ 3 WCincluded ⊒€ 2/pp. 🚽
**Location:** Rural, simple, quiet. **Surface:** grassy. ⊙ 01/01-31/12.
**Distance:** 🚶200m 🚴6km ⊗500m 🚴400m 🚴on the spot 🧍on the spot.

### Flonheim 16H1
**Weingut Meyerhof**, Aussiedlerhof. **GPS:** n49,78836 e8,04531.⬆.

4 🛏€ 8 🚰(4x)included. 🚽 **Location:** Rural, simple, quiet.
**Surface:** concrete. ⊙ 01/01-31/12.
**Distance:** 🚶700m 🚴4km ⊗100m 🚴100m.
**Remarks:** Bread-service.

### Föckelberg 16G1
**Wildpark Potzberg**, Auf dem Potzberg. **GPS:** n49,52240 e7,48079.⬆.

4 🛏free. **Location:** Rural, simple, quiet. **Surface:** asphalted/sand.
⊙ 01/01-31/12.
**Distance:** 🚶1km ⊗on the spot.

### Forst an der Weinstrasse 16H1
**Weingut Margarethenhof**, Wiesenweg 4. **GPS:** n49,42814 e8,19219.

**DE**

4 ⌷ € 10 🔌 WCincluded ⌷ € 4. 🏪 **Location:** Rural, simple.
**Surface:** grassy. 🅾 01/01-31/12. 🔵 15/06-17/06, 30/06-02/07.
**Distance:** 🚶1km 🚲7km ⊗1km 🛒 on the spot 🛝 on the spot.

| 🛟 S | **Freisen** | 16G1 |

**Weiselbergbad**, Zum Schwimmbad. **GPS:** n49,53324 e7,26048. ⬆️.

3 ⌷ € 5 🔌 € 2/day. **Location:** Rural, simple, noisy. **Surface:** metalled.
🅾 01/01-31/12.
**Distance:** 🚶1km 🚲3km ⊗800m 🛒 on the spot 🛝 on the spot.
**Remarks:** Check in at swimming pool.

| 🛟 S | **Gau-Algesheim** | 11H3 |

**Reimo Gau-Algesheim**, Bingerstrasse 8.
**GPS:** n49,96331 e8,01213. ⬆️➡️.

38 ⌷ € 6/night 🔌 🍺Chincluded 🔌(40x)€ 2/24h 📶.🚗
**Location:** Comfortable, quiet. **Surface:** metalled. 🅾 01/01-31/12.
**Distance:** 🚶800m 🚲2,5km ⊗500m 🛒200m.

| 🍷 S | **Gau-Bickelheim** | 16H1 |

**Winzerhof Schnabel**, Bahnhofstrasse 31.
**GPS:** n49,83941 e8,02116. ⬆️.

15 ⌷ € 5 🔌included 🔌(8x)€ 3/day 📶. **Location:** Rural.
**Surface:** grassy/gravel. 🅾 01/01-31/12.
**Distance:** 🚶400m 🚲3km ⊗5km 🛒1km 🛒200m.

| 🏕️ S | **Gau-Bickelheim** | 16H1 |

**Am Autohof**, B50. **GPS:** n49,83461 e7,99664. ⬆️.

15 ⌷ € 10 ⌷against payment. **Location:** Motorway, simple, noisy.
**Surface:** asphalted. 🅾 01/01-31/12.
**Distance:** 🚶5km 🚲 on the spot ⊗on the spot 🚐6km.

| 🍷 S | **Gau-Heppenheim** | 16H1 |

**Mohrenmühle**, Mohrenmühle 2. **GPS:** n49,75170 e8,16335. ⬆️.

3 ⌷ € 5 🔌 🍺Ch 🔌included. 🏪 **Location:** Rural, simple, quiet.
**Surface:** grassy. 🅾 01/01-31/12.
**Distance:** 🚶1,5km ⊗on the spot 🛒 on the spot 🛝 on the spot.
**Remarks:** Bread-service.

| 🍷 S | **Gau-Heppenheim** | 16H1 |

**Weingut Gustavshof**, Hauptstrasse 53. **GPS:** n49,74138 e8,17082. ⬆️.

3 ⌷ € 8 🔌 🔌(3x)included. 🔌 **Location:** Rural, simple, quiet.
**Surface:** concrete. 🅾 01/04-31/10.
**Distance:** 🚲4km ⊗2km 🛒3km.

| 🏕️ | **Gau-Odernheim** | 16H1 |

**Petersberghalle**, Mühlstraße. **GPS:** n49,78528 e8,19575. ⬆️➡️.

3 ⌷free. **Location:** Rural, simple. **Surface:** metalled.
🅾 01/01-31/12.
**Distance:** 🚶200m ⊗400m 🛒200m 🚐100m.
**Remarks:** Max. 3 days.

| 🏕️ | **Gebhardshain** | 11G2 |

**Festwiese**, Steinebacherstrasse. **GPS:** n50,74412 e7,82079. ⬆️.

5 ⌷free. **Location:** Urban, simple, central, quiet. **Surface:** asphalted.
🅾 01/01-31/12.
**Distance:** 🚶500m ⊗500m 🛒500m.

| 🏕️ | **Geiselberg** | 16G2 |

**Grillplatz Geiselberg**, Hauptstrasse, K31. **GPS:** n49,32381 e7,70957. ⬆️.

10 ⌷free. **Location:** Rural, simple, quiet. **Surface:** gravel.
🅾 01/01-31/12.
**Distance:** 🚶800m 🚲12km ⊗1km 🛒1km.
**Remarks:** Max. 3 days.

| 🏕️ S | **Germersheim** | 16H2 |

**An der Carnot'sche Mauer**, Rüdolf von Habsburgstrasse.
**GPS:** n49,21932 e8,37655. ⬆️➡️.

17 ⌷ € 5/24h 🔌 € 1/100liter 🍺Ch 🔌(8x)€ 0,50/kWh. ▣
**Location:** Urban, simple, central.
**Surface:** metalled.
🅾 01/01-31/12.
**Distance:** 🚶300m 🚲2km ⊗500m 🛒300m 🚐100m 🛝 on the spot.

| 🏕️ S | **Gerolstein** | 11F3 |

**Wohnmobilstellplatz Gerolstein**, Raderstraße 22.
**GPS:** n50,22096 e6,65387. ➡️.

25 ⌷ € 10/24h 🔌 € 1/100liter 🍺Ch 🔌(12x)included ⌷.🔌
**Location:** Urban, simple, quiet. **Surface:** grassy/metalled.
🅾 01/01-31/12. **Distance:** 🚶nearby 🚲25km ⊗500m 🛒1km.
**Remarks:** At swimming pool, use sanitary only during opening hours
swimming pool.

| 🏕️ | **Gevenich** | 11F3 |

**Am Sportplatz. GPS:** n50,14727 e7,08385. ➡️.

5 ⌷free. **Location:** Rural, simple, isolated. **Surface:** grassy.
🅾 01/01-31/12.
**Distance:** 🚶1km ⊗on the spot.

| 🏕️ S | **Gillenfeld** | 11F3 |

**Wohnmobilhafen Pulvermaar**, K14. **GPS:** n50,13294 e6,93218. ➡️.

30 ⌷ € 7, 2 pers. incl., dog € 1 🔌 € 1/50liter 🍺Ch 🔌 € 0,50/kWh
WC ⌷ € 2. **Location:** Rural, simple, isolated, quiet. **Surface:** gravel.
🅾 01/01-31/12.
**Distance:** 🚶3km 🏊on the spot 🛝on the spot ⊗200m 🛒200m
🚐300m.

| 🏕️ S | **Gillenfeld** | 11F3 |

**Feriendorf Pulvermaar**, Vulkanstrasse. **GPS:** n50,13000 e6,93194. ⬆️.

40 ⌷ € 7, 2 pers.incl. 🔌 € 1/50liter 🍺Ch 🔌 € 0,50/kWh WC ⌷ € 2/
stay. **Location:** Rural, comfortable, quiet. **Surface:** grassy/gravel.

DE

🗓 01/03-30/11.
**Distance:** 🏊3km ⚓7km ⚓on the spot ⛵on the spot ⊗150m 🍴150m 🛒200m.

### Gimbsheim　16H1
Schwimbadstrasse. **GPS:** n49,77806 e8,38278. ⬆.

8 🅿 € 4/night. **Location:** Rural, simple. **Surface:** asphalted/grassy. 🗓 15/05-15/09.
**Distance:** 🏊500m ⊗300m 🛒300m.

### Gimbsheim　16H1
**Weingut Falger-Baier**, Alsheimerstrasse 25.
**GPS:** n49,77733 e8,36959. ⬆.

3 🅿 € 5 💧included. 🍴 **Location:** Rural, simple.
**Surface:** concrete. 🗓 01/01-31/12.
**Distance:** 🏊300m 🍕Pizzeria 50m 🛒500m.

### Glan-Münchweiler　16G1
**Am Bahnhof**, Bahnhofstraße. **GPS:** n49,46935 e7,44420. ⬆.

3 🅿 free 🔌€ 1 Ch 💧(4x)€ 1/2h.
**Location:** Urban, simple, central, noisy. **Surface:** metalled.
🗓 01/01-31/12.
**Distance:** 🚲750m ⊗150m 🛒on the spot.

### Gleisweiler　16H2
**Weingut Kost**, Hainbachtalstrasse 3. **GPS:** n49,23862 e8,06737. ⬆.

3 🅿 free 🔌free 💧. **Location:** Rural, quiet. **Surface:** grassy.
🗓 01/01-31/12.
**Distance:** 🚲8km ⊗on the spot.

### Gleiszellen-Gleishorbach　16H2
B 48. **GPS:** n49,13083 e8,01139. ⬆.

20 🅿 free. **Location:** Rural, simple, isolated. **Surface:** grassy/gravel.
🗓 01/01-31/12.

---

**Distance:** 🏊300m ⊗300m ⚓on the spot 🚲on the spot ⛷on the spot.

### Gleiszellen-Gleishorbach　16H2
**Weingut Schönlaub**, Bergstrasse 14. **GPS:** n49,13131 e8,00465. ⬆.

2 🅿 free 🔌free 💧. **Location:** Rural, simple, quiet.
**Surface:** grassy. 🗓 01/01-31/12.
**Distance:** 🚲15km ⊗500m.
**Remarks:** Check in at Weingut.

### Graach/Mosel　11F3
**Wohnmobilpark Sun-Park**, Gestade 16a. **GPS:** n49,93322 e7,06249. ⬆.

140 🅿 € 10/day 🔌Ch 💧(132x)€ 3/day WCincluded 🚿€ 1,50/pp
⊙€ 2,50. **Location:** Rural, simple. **Surface:** grassy/gravel.
🗓 27/03-03/11.
**Distance:** 🏊200m ⚓on the spot ⊗200m 🛒2km ⚓on the spot 🚲on the spot ⛷on the spot.
**Remarks:** Bread-service, video surveillance.

### Grafschaft　11F2
**Panorama Sauna**, Panoramaweg 2. **GPS:** n50,56029 e7,05368. ⬆.

20 🅿 free. **Surface:** gravel. 🗓 01/01-31/12.
**Distance:** 🚲5km ⊗300m 🛒300m.

### Gries　16G2
**Seestube am Ohmbachsee**, Bahnhofstrasse 17b.
**GPS:** n49,41664 e7,40377. ⬆.

15 🅿 € 6/24h 🔌€ 1/80liter Ch 💧(6x)€ 0,60/kWh. 🚽
**Location:** Rural, simple, quiet. **Surface:** grassy/gravel.
🗓 01/01-31/12.
**Distance:** 🚲6km ⚓on the spot ⚓on the spot ⊗50m 🛒2km ⚓on the spot ⛷on the spot.
**Remarks:** Bread-service, possibility for reservation.

### Gundersheim　16H1
**Huppert's Wohnmobile Wingert**, Untere Grabenstraße 21.
**GPS:** n49,69499 e8,20465. ⬆➡.

---

12 🅿 € 5 🔌€ 3/day. 🚽 **Location:** Rural, simple.
**Surface:** gravel/sand. 🗓 01/01-31/12.
**Distance:** 🚲1km ⊗on the spot 🛒300m.
**Remarks:** Max. 3 nights.

### Guntersblum　16H1
**Am Sportanlage**, Alsheimerstrasse 85. **GPS:** n49,78974 e8,34373. ⬆.

16 🅿 € 5 🔌€ 1/80liter Ch 💧(12x)€ 0,50/kWh.
**Location:** Rural. **Surface:** gravel. 🗓 01/01-31/12.
**Distance:** 🏊500m ⊗500m 🛒500m.
**Remarks:** Max. 72h.

### Guntersblum　16H1
**Weingut Katharinenhof**, Alsheimerstrasse 95.
**GPS:** n49,78667 e8,34324. ⬆.

10 🅿 € 5 🔌included Ch 💧(7x)€ 2/24h. 🚽 **Location:** Rural,
simple, quiet. **Surface:** grassy. 🗓 01/01-31/12.
**Distance:** 🏊1km ⊗1km 🛒1km.

### Hachenburg　11G2
**P4 - Burggarten**, Alexanderring. **GPS:** n50,66250 e7,82694. ⬆.

8 🅿 free 🔌€ 1/70liter Ch 💧€ 1/3h WC. **Location:** Urban, simple,
quiet. **Surface:** grasstiles. 🗓 01/01-31/12.
**Distance:** 🏊300m ⊗300m 🛒300m ⚓on the spot 🚲on the spot.
**Remarks:** Historical centre.

### Hagenbach　16H2
**Stadtbrauhaus Hagenbach**, Stixwörthstrasse 2-4.
**GPS:** n49,00884 e8,25902.

10 🅿 free 💧. **Surface:** grassy/gravel. 🗓 01/01-31/12 ⊙ Mon, Tue.
**Distance:** 🏊1km ⚓5km ⊗on the spot 🛒750m 🛒1km.

### Hainfeld　16H2
Modenbach. **GPS:** n49,25730 e8,10328.

20 ⬛free. **Location:** Simple, quiet. **Surface:** gravel.
⬛ 01/01-31/12.
**Distance:** 🚶150m ⛽3km ⊗250m 🛒1km 🚲on the spot.

### Hainfeld 16H2

**Weingut Edgar und Andreas Lutz**, Weinstrasse 57.
**GPS:** n49,25756 e8,09928.⬆.
4 ⬛€ 6, € 8 service incl ⚡ WC 🛁. **Location:** Urban, simple.
**Surface:** metalled. ⬛ 01/01-31/12.
**Distance:** 🚶on the spot ⊗100m.
**Remarks:** Sale of wines.

### Hassloch 16H2

**Hotel Sägmühle**, Sägmühlweg 140. **GPS:** n49,34674 e8,25491.

2 ⬛€ 14, guests free ⚡(2x)WCincluded.🛁
**Location:** Simple, isolated, quiet. **Surface:** metalled.
⬛ 01/01-31/12.
**Distance:** 🚶2km ⛽10km ⊗300m 🛒1,5km 🚌4km.
**Remarks:** Bicycle rental.

### Hassloch 16H2

**Badepark Hassloch**, Lachener Weg 175. **GPS:** n49,34804 e8,24677.⬆.

9 ⬛free 🚰free. **Location:** Simple, quiet. **Surface:** metalled.
⬛ 01/01-31/12.
**Distance:** 🚶2km ⛽10km ⊗50m 🛒200m 🚌100m.
**Remarks:** Max. 24h.

### Hassloch 16H2

**Magin Reisemobile**, Hans-Böckler-Strasse 52.
**GPS:** n49,34968 e8,23935.⬆➡.

8 ⬛€ 12,50, 2 pers.incl 🚰Ch ⚡(8x)included.🛁
**Location:** Urban, simple, quiet.
**Surface:** gravel/metalled.
⬛ 01/01-31/12.
**Distance:** 🚶2km ⛽7km ⊗50m 🛒200m.

**Tourist information Hassloch:**
ℹ️ Holiday Park. Attractions park with shows. ⬛ 01/03-31/10 10-18h.

### Hauenstein 16G2

**Stellplatz am Deutschen Schumuseum Hauenstein**, Turnstrasse 5.
**GPS:** n49,18896 e7,85669.⬆.

16 ⬛€ 7 🚰Ch ⚡included. **Location:** Rural, simple, quiet.
**Surface:** gravel. ⬛ 01/01-31/12.
**Distance:** 🚶on the spot ⊗200m 🛒300m.
**Remarks:** Check in on arrival, pay at pay-desk of the museum.

### Heltersberg 16G2

**Am Bergbad**, Bergstrasse. **GPS:** n49,31654 e7,70380.⬆.

5 ⬛free. **Location:** Rural, simple, quiet. **Surface:** grassy/gravel.
⬛ 01/01-31/12.
**Distance:** 🚶900m ⊗850m.
**Remarks:** Parking swimming pool.

### Hemmelzen 11G2

**Hotel Im Heisterholz**, Heisterholzstrasse 10.
**GPS:** n50,69579 e7,58456.⬆.

4 ⬛€ 12 🚰⚡included. **Location:** Rural, quiet. **Surface:** gravel.
⬛ 01/01-31/12 🅿 Mo.
**Distance:** 🚶200m ⊗on the spot 🚌100m 🚲on the spot 🚶on the spot.
**Remarks:** € 2 reduction in restaurant.

### Herrstein 16G1

**Wohnmobilstellplatz Herrstein**, Brühlstrasse.
**GPS:** n49,77963 e7,33569.⬆.

3 ⬛free 🚰€ 1/80liter ⚡€ 0,50/kWh WC.
**Location:** Rural, simple. **Surface:** metalled.
⬛ 01/01-31/12.
**Distance:** 🚶300m ⊗on the spot.
**Remarks:** Max. 48h.

**Tourist information Herrstein:**
ℹ️ Touristinformation Deutsche Edelsteinstraße, Brühlstrasse 16. Renovated mall half-timbered city. ⬛ 01/05-01/10.

### Herxheim 16H2

**Festhalle**, Bonifatiusstraße. **GPS:** n49,14463 e8,21656.⬆➡.

8 ⬛free 🚰Chfree. **Location:** Simple, central. **Surface:** grasstiles.
⬛ 01/01-31/12.
**Distance:** 🚶on the spot ⛽4km ⊗150m 🛒200m 🚌75m 🚲on the spot.

### Heuchelheim-Klingen 16H2

**Gästehaus am Weingut Kuhn**, Hauptstrasse 2.
**GPS:** n49,14513 e8,05887.⬆.

3 ⬛€ 5 🚰Chincluded. 🚌 **Location:** Rural, simple, quiet.
**Surface:** metalled. ⬛ 01/01-31/12.
**Distance:** 🚶800m ⛽14km ⊗300m 🛒on the spot 🚶on the spot.

### Heuchelheim-Klingen 16H2

**Weingut Junghof**, Hauptstrasse 21. **GPS:** n49,14572 e8,05580.

4 ⬛€ 5, free with a meal 🚰€ 2/100liter ⚡€ 2/night.
**Location:** Simple. **Surface:** grassy/metalled. ⬛ 01/01-31/12.
**Distance:** 🚶on the spot ⛽14km ⊗500m 🛒2km 🚌500m.

### Heuchelheim-Klingen 16H2

**Mühlengrund**, Untermühle 1. **GPS:** n49,14734 e8,06406.⬆➡.

5 ⬛free. **Location:** Rural, simple, isolated. **Surface:** gravel.
⬛ 01/01-31/12.
**Distance:** 🚶1km ⛽9km ⊗on the spot.
**Remarks:** Restaurant closed on Monday and Tuesday.

### Hillesheim 11F3

**Markt- und Messeplatz**, Am Viehmarkt.
**GPS:** n50,28895 e6,67239.⬆➡.

6 ⬛€ 7 🚰Ch ⚡(6x)WCincluded. **Location:** Urban, simple,
central. **Surface:** gravel. ⬛ 01/01-31/12.
**Distance:** 🚶on the spot ⊗on the spot 🛒200m.

## Hillesheim — 11F3
**Wohnmobilstellplatz Birkenhof**, Birkenhof 1.
**GPS:** n50,28639 e6,69083.⬆.

8 🛏 € 10, 4 pers. incl. 🚰 🚮 (6x) 🛜included. **Location:** Rural, simple, quiet. **Surface:** gravel. 🕐 01/01-31/12.
**Distance:** 🚶1,5km ⊗1,5km 🛒1,5km 🚲300m 🧍300m.
**Remarks:** Bread-service, regional products.

## Hochspeyer — 16G1
**Am Schwimmbad**, Mühlhofstraße. **GPS:** n49,44108 e7,89333.⬆.

6 🛏 € 5/24h 🚰 € 1/80liter 🔌Ch 🔌(12x)€ 0,50/kWh.🚮
**Location:** Simple, central, quiet. **Surface:** asphalted.
🕐 01/01-31/12 🕐 01/08-15/08.
**Distance:** 🚶400m 🚲5km ⊗500m 🛒400m bakery 🚌1km.
**Remarks:** Max. 3 days.

## Höheinöd — 16G2
**Am Haus des Bürgers**, Hauptstrasse 24. **GPS:** n49,28691 e7,60468.⬆.

3 🛏free. **Location:** Rural, simple, quiet. **Surface:** metalled.
🕐 01/01-31/12.
**Distance:** 🚶on the spot 🚲8km.
**Remarks:** Max. 2 nights.

## Höhr-Grenzhausen — 11G2
**Wohnmobilstellplatz Grenzhausen**, Martin Lutherstrasse 5.
**GPS:** n50,43943 e7,65984.⬆➡.

5 🛏free 🚰 € 1/80liter 🔌Chfree 🔌(8x)€ 1/kWh.
**Location:** Urban, simple, central, quiet.
🕐 01/01-31/12.
**Distance:** 🚶1km 🚲600m ⊗1km 🛒1km 🚌on the spot 🚲on the spot 🧍on the spot.

## Höhr-Grenzhausen — 11G2
Ferbachstraße. **GPS:** n50,43330 e7,66833.⬆➡.

---

**Remarks:** Bread-service.

8 🛏free. **Location:** Urban. **Surface:** metalled. 🕐 01/01-31/12.
**Distance:** 🚶400m 🚲2km ⊗100m.
**Remarks:** Max. 72h.

## Höhr-Grenzhausen — 11G2
**Seiferwiesen-Parkplatz**, Seiferwiese. **GPS:** n50,44218 e7,65655.⬆➡.

2 🛏free. **Location:** Urban, simple, quiet. **Surface:** metalled.
🕐 01/01-31/12.
**Distance:** 🚶800m 🚲400m.

## Holzappel — 11G3
**Stellplatz am Herthasee**, Am Herthasee. **GPS:** n50,36135 e7,90274.➡.

12 🛏 € 6/24h, € 11/48h, € 15/72h 🚰 € 1/90liter 🔌Ch 🔌
(12x)€ 1/2kWh. 🚮
**Location:** Rural, comfortable, quiet. **Surface:** grassy.
🕐 01/01-31/12.
**Distance:** 🚶1km 🏊on the spot 🚲on the spot ⊗on the spot 🛒1km.

## Hornbach — 16G2
**Wohnmobilpark Hornbach**, Bahnhofstraße.
**GPS:** n49,18382 e7,36560.⬆➡.

26 🛏 € 8 🚰 € 1/60liter 🔌Ch 🔌(30x)€ 1/2kWh 🛜included. 🚮
**Location:** Rural, comfortable, quiet. **Surface:** gravel.
🕐 01/01-31/12.
**Distance:** 🚶on the spot 🚲8km ⊗on the spot 🚌300m 🧍on the spot.
**Remarks:** Barbecue place.

## Hörschhausen — 11F3
**Mechels Hof**, Dauner Straße 24. **GPS:** n50,24248 e6,92770.⬆.

3 🛏 € 5 + € 4/pp, dog € 1 🚰 🔌Chincluded 🔌(3x)€ 2/24h. 🚮
**Location:** Rural, simple. **Surface:** gravel. 🕐 01/01-31/12.
**Distance:** 🚲9km.

---

## Idar/Oberstein — 16G1
**Parking Börse**, Hauptstrasse 97. **GPS:** n49,71932 e7,30313.⬆.

12 🛏 € 6 🚰 € 1/100liter 🔌ChWC. 🏠 **Location:** Urban, simple.
**Surface:** asphalted. 🕐 01/01-31/12.
**Distance:** 🚶300m ⊗on the spot 🛒300m.
**Tourist information Idar/Oberstein**
👁 Edelsteinminen des Steinkaulenberges. Gem mine. 🕐 15/03-15/11 10-18h.
Ⓜ Deutsches Edelsteinmuseum. Gem museum. 🕐 01/05-31/10 9.30-17.30h, 01/11-30/04 10-17h 🕐 14/01-01/02.

## Ilbesheim — 16H2
**Weingut Erlenswein**, Wacholderhof. **GPS:** n49,18747 e8,03323.⬆.

6 🛏 € 10 🚰 🔌Ch 🔌included. 🚮 **Location:** Rural, simple, quiet.
**Surface:** grassy. 🕐 01/03-30/11.
**Distance:** 🚶1km.
**Remarks:** Check in at Weingut.

## Impflingen — 16H2
**Weingut Junker**, Sonnenberghof 1. **GPS:** n49,16242 e8,10728.⬆➡.

3 🛏 € 5 🚰included 🔌 🔌(4x)€ 2 WC. 🚮
**Location:** Simple, quiet. **Surface:** gravel. 🕐 01/01-31/12.
**Distance:** 🚶1km 🚲7km ⊗on the spot 🛒3km 🚌200m 🚲on the spot 🧍on the spot.
**Remarks:** Breakfest-service.

## Ingelheim am Rhein — 11H3
**Weingut Menk**, Außenliegend 143. **GPS:** n49,97190 e8,09295.⬆.

6 🛏 € 10 🚰 🔌Ch 🔌 WCincluded. **Location:** Rural, comfortable,
quiet. **Surface:** grassy. 🕐 01/01-31/12.
**Distance:** 🚶2km 🚲9km ⊗1,5km 🚌5,5km 🚲on the spot.

## Irmtraut — 11H2
Ober dem Dorfe 4. **GPS:** n50,55385 e8,06424.
3 🛏 € 5 🚰Ch 🔌 **Location:** Rural, simple, quiet.
**Surface:** metalled. 🕐 01/01-31/12.
**Distance:** ⊗300m.

## Jettenbach — 16G1
**Freizeitgelände Schwimmbad**, Austrasse.
**GPS:** n49,52919 e7,56453.⬆➡.

**DE**

6 🛏free 🔌🗑Ch🚿. **Location:** Simple, quiet. **Surface:** asphalted.
🅿 01/01-31/12.
**Distance:** 🚶500m 🚉800m.
**Remarks:** Service on demand.

### Jünkerath — 11F3

**Stellplatz Eifelland**, Glaadter Str. 16. **GPS:** n50,35013 e6,56522. ⬆.

8 🛏€6 🔌🗑Chincluded 🚿€ 2/night WC🚻. 🚲 **Location:** Rural,
simple, isolated, quiet. **Surface:** grassy. 🅿 01/01-31/12.
**Distance:** 🚶500m ⊗150m 🚉100m on the spot 🚶 on the spot.

### Kaisersesch — 11F3

Am Markt. **GPS:** n50,23284 e7,14059. ⬆.

3 🛏free. **Location:** Urban, simple, central, quiet. **Surface:** asphalted.
🅿 01/01-31/12.
**Distance:** 🚶on the spot 🚲1km ⊗300m 🚉500m 🚉1km.

### Kaiserslautern — 16G1

**Daennerplatz**, Mannheimer Straße 208.
**GPS:** n49,44300 e7,80230. ⬆➡.

11 🛏€ 10/24h 🔌€ 1/100liter 🗑Ch🚿(12x)€ 2/2kWh. 📷
**Location:** Urban. **Surface:** metalled. 🅿 01/01-31/12.
**Distance:** 🚶2,5km ⊗on the spot 🚉on the spot.
**Remarks:** Free bus to centre.

### Kaiserslautern — 16G1

**Gasthaus Licht Luft**, Entersweilerstraße 51.
**GPS:** n49,43828 e7,80338. ⬆.

14 🛏free 🔌🗑Chon demand. **Location:** Urban, central, quiet.
**Surface:** asphalted/gravel. 🅿 01/01-31/12.
**Distance:** 🚶2km 🚲5km ⊗on the spot 🚉on the spot 🚉3km on
the spot 🚶 on the spot.

### Kaiserslautern — 16G1

**Am Monte Mare**, Mailänder Straße 6. **GPS:** n49,45387 e7,81203. ⬆.

10 🛏free. **Location:** Rural, simple, quiet. **Surface:** metalled.
🅿 01/01-31/12.
**Distance:** 🚶4km 🚲1km ⊗300m.

### Kamp-Bornhofen — 11G3

**Bistro Rheinufer**, Rheinuferstrasse 66 A. **GPS:** n50,22292 e7,61966. ⬆.

7 🛏€ 8,50 🔌€ 1 🚿(4x)€ 2,50/night WC. 🗑 **Location:** Rural,
simple. **Surface:** grassy/metalled. 🅿 01/01-31/12.
**Distance:** 🚶on the spot ⊗on the spot 🚉300m 🚉on the spot
🚶 on the spot.
**Remarks:** Along the Rhine river, toilets only during opening hours
restaurant.

### Kandel — 16H2

**Adams Hof**, Rheinzaberner Strasse 1. **GPS:** n49,08902 e8,22194. ⬆.

30 🛏€ 10/night 🔌€ 2,50 🗑🚿(20x)€ 2,50/12h WC🚻.
**Location:** Rural, simple, quiet. **Surface:** grassy.
🅿 01/01-31/12.
**Distance:** 🚶1,5km 🚉on the spot ⊗on the spot 🚉1,5km 🚉1,5km.
**Remarks:** € 5 voucher Biergarten.

### Kapellen-Drusweiler — 16H2

**Weingut Manderschied**, Dorfstrasse 4. **GPS:** n49,10482 e8,03723. ⬆.

10 🛏free 🔌🚿(3x)free. **Location:** Rural, simple, quiet.
**Surface:** grassy. 🅿 01/01-31/12.
**Distance:** 🚶500m 🚉500m 🚉2km 🚉500m.

### Kelberg — 11F3

**Wohnmobilstellplatz am Schwimmbad**, Am Schwimmbad 3.
**GPS:** n50,28295 e6,91894. ⬆.

6 🛏free. **Location:** Rural, simple, central, quiet.

**Surface:** metalled. 🅿 01/01-31/12.
**Distance:** 🚶400m ⊗400m on the spot 🚴 on the spot 🚶 on the
spot.

### Kell am See — 16F1

**Am Camping Hochwald**, L 143. **GPS:** n49,63800 e6,80140. ⬆.

10 🛏€ 24, 2 pers.incl 🔌Ch🚿€ 0,50/kWh WC🚻.
**Location:** Rural, quiet. **Surface:** metalled. 🅿 01/05-30/08.
**Distance:** 🚶2km 🚉2km.
**Remarks:** Free entrance swimming pool.

### Kempenich — 11F2

**Eifel-Gasthof Kleefuß**, In der Hardt 1. **GPS:** n50,42209 e7,10951.

4 🛏guests free. **Location:** Rural. **Surface:** gravel.
🅿 01/01-31/12 🔒 Mon, Tue.
**Distance:** 🚶500m ⊗on the spot 🚉1km 🚉300m 🚶 Steinrausch
Erlebnispfad 200m.

### Kempfeld — 16G1

**An der Wildenburg**, Wildenburgstraße.
**GPS:** n49,77588 e7,25423. ⬆➡.

3 🛏free. **Location:** Rural. **Surface:** metalled. 🅿 01/01-31/12.
**Distance:** ⊗2km 🚉2km.

### Kesten — 16F1

**Wohnmobilpark Kesten/Mosel**, Urmetzgasse/K134.
**GPS:** n49,90306 e6,96232. ➡.

100 🛏€ 6/24h 🔌€ 0,50/50liter 🗑Chincluded 🚿(100x)€ 2/
24h,6Amp. 🚲
**Surface:** grassy/metalled. 🅿 01/04-31/10.
**Distance:** 🚶300m 🏊10m 🚉10m ⊗300m 🚉1km 🚉300m
🚴 on the spot 🚶 on the spot.
**Remarks:** Parking at the Moselle River, bread-service.

### Kinheim — 11F3

**Am Moselufer**, Moselweinstraße, B53. **GPS:** n49,97218 e7,05706. ⬆➡.

DE

50 ⬛€8 🚰Ch ✎€2/day 📶included. 🔧
**Location:** Rural, simple, quiet. **Surface:** grassy. ⬛ 01/01-31/12.
**Distance:** 🚶100m ⚓on the spot ⊗on the spot 🍽150m 🚲on the spot ⚘on the spot.
**Remarks:** Parking at the Moselle River.

**Tourist information Kinheim:**
🍷 Tag den offenen Weinkeller. Open wine-cellars. ⬛ 2nd Thu after Whitsuntide.
🍷 Wein- und Frülingsfest. Wine and spring celebration. ⬛ Whitsuntide.
🍷 Winzerfest. Wine festival. ⬛ 2nd weekend Sep.

### Kirchberg   11G3
**AMB-Reisemobile**, Herbert-Kühn-Straße 10.
**GPS:** n49,95400 e7,40829. ⬆️

15 ⬛€6 🚰Ch ✎included. **Location:** Rural, simple.
**Surface:** grassy. ⬛ 01/01-31/12.
**Distance:** 🚶700m ⊗700m 🍽700m 🚲600m ⚘on the spot.

### Kirchheimbolanden   16H1
**Festplatz Herrengarten**, Hitzfeldstrasse.
**GPS:** n49,66667 e8,01501. ⬆️➡️

8 ⬛free 🚰€1/70liter ⚡(8x)€0,50,16Amp 📶free.
**Location:** Urban, central, quiet. **Surface:** metalled.
⬛ 01/01-31/12 ☀ 2nd weekend May-Aug-Oct.
**Distance:** 🚶300m ⊗300m 🍽on the spot 🚲350m ⚘on the spot.
**Remarks:** Max. 2 nights.

### Kirkel   16G2
**Caravanplatz Mühlenweiher**, Unnerweg 5c.
**GPS:** n49,28184 e7,22900. ⬆️➡️

5 ⬛€5/night 🚰€1,50/time 🚰Ch ✎(5x)€3,50/day WC against payment 📶included. 🏪 **Location:** Rural, simple, quiet.
**Surface:** metalled. ⬛ 01/01-31/12.
**Distance:** 🚶600m ⚓3km 🍽1km 🚲on the spot ⚘on the spot.

### Kirn   16G1
**Wohnmobilstellplatz Auf der Kiesel**, Fontaine-les-Dijon-Strasse.
**GPS:** n49,78406 e7,45798.

3 ⬛€1,25/day. 🚐 **Location:** Urban, simple. **Surface:** concrete.
⬛ 01/01-31/12.
**Distance:** 🚶300m ⊗on the spot 🍽on the spot.
**Remarks:** Monday market.

### Klausen   16F1
**Zentralparkplatz**, Eberhardstrasse/ K51. **GPS:** n49,90550 e6,88104. ➡️

5 ⬛free. **Surface:** metalled. ⬛ 01/01-31/12.
**Distance:** 🚶on the spot ⚓2km ⊗400m 🍽400m.

### Kleinblittersdorf   16F2
**Wohnmobilpark Müller**, Zum Bergwald 8.
**GPS:** n49,12874 e7,05050. ⬆️
61 ⬛€18, 2 pers. incl 🚰€1/100liter 🚰Ch ✎€1/2kWh WC included 📶€2,50. **Location:** Urban, comfortable.
**Surface:** grassy/gravel. ⬛ 01/01-31/12.
**Distance:** ⚓50m ⊗1km 🍽1km 🚲on the spot.

### Kleinbundenbach   16G2
**Auf der Stampermühle**, Stampermühle 1.
**GPS:** n49,31778 e7,45694. ⬆️

10 ⬛€7 🚰 📶included. **Location:** Rural, simple, isolated.
**Surface:** gravel. ⬛ 01/01-31/12.
**Distance:** 🚶8km ⚓15km ⊗on the spot.

### Klüsserath   16F1
**Reisemobilpark Klüsserath**, B53. **GPS:** n49,84170 e6,85475. ⬆️

400 ⬛€7,20 🚰€1/90liter 🚰Ch ✎€1/2kWh 📶🔧
**Surface:** grassy. ⬛ Easter-31/10.
**Distance:** ⚓9km ⊗500m.
**Remarks:** Along the Moselle river, bread-service.

### Kobern   11G3
**Am Kalkofen B416**, Kobern-Gondorf. **GPS:** n50,30524 e7,46064. ⬆️

50 ⬛€5/24h ✎€1/80liter 🚰€0,10 Ch€0,10. 🚐
**Location:** Simple. **Surface:** metalled. ⬛ 01/01-31/12.
**Distance:** 🚶300m ⚓8km ⊗on the spot 🍽on the spot ⊗300m 🍽300m.

### Koblenz   11G3
**KNAUS Reisemobilstellplatz Koblenz**, Schartwiesenweg 6.
**GPS:** n50,36592 e7,60400. ⬆️

10 ⬛€18,50 🚰Ch ✎WC included 📶against payment. 🏪💳
**Location:** Urban, comfortable, central, quiet. **Surface:** metalled.
⬛ 01/01-31/12.
**Distance:** 🚶on the spot ⚓8km ⊗on the spot 🍽on the spot 🚲on the spot ⚘on the spot.
**Remarks:** Max. 3 days.

### Konz   16F1
**An der Saarmündung**, Am Moselufer 1.
**GPS:** n49,70553 e6,57574. ⬆️➡️

3 ⬛€8 🚰€2 🚰Ch WC against payment 📶. 🏪🚐
**Location:** Rural, simple, isolated, quiet. **Surface:** gravel/metalled.
⬛ 15/03-31/10.
**Distance:** 🚶1km ⚓on the spot 🍽on the spot ⊗100m 🍽1km 🚲400m ⚘on the spot ⚘on the spot.
**Remarks:** Check in at campsite, service 100m.

### Köwerich   16F1
**Weingut Hans Klären-Maringer 'Off'm Herrach'**, Beethovenstrasse 40. **GPS:** n49,84123 e6,86287. ⬆️➡️

20 ⬛€8 🚰Ch ✎according consumption WC €1 🍽€4. 🔧
**Location:** Rural. **Surface:** grassy. ⬛ 01/01-31/12.
**Distance:** 🚶500m ⚓500m 🍽500m ⊗on the spot 🍽2km 🚲100m ⚘on the spot.
**Remarks:** Check in at restaurant, bread-service.

### Kusel   16G1
**Parkplatz der Tuchfabriken**, Trierer Straße 61.
**GPS:** n49,54016 e7,39626. ⬆️➡️

3 ⬛free 🚰Ch ✎Service €5.
**Location:** Urban, simple, quiet. **Surface:** asphalted.
⬛ 01/01-31/12.
**Distance:** 🚶500m 🍽300m.
**Remarks:** Max. 3 days, key service at Touristinformation (300m).

DE

**DE**

### Lahnstein 11G3

**Wohnmobilstellplatz Kränchen**, Johannesstraße 44.
**GPS**: n50,30939 e7,59833. ➡.

60 € 11/24h € 1/100liter Ch € 0,50/kWh
WC € 1/3minutes. **Location**: Rural, simple. **Surface**: gravel.
01/01-31/12.
**Distance**: 1km 600m 600m 1,5km.

### Lambrecht 16H2

Blainviller-Straße 1. **GPS**: n49,37030 e8,07448. ⬆➡.

7 free € 1 Ch € 1/8h. **Location**: Rural, central, quiet.
**Surface**: gravel. 01/01-31/12.
**Distance**: on the spot on the spot 500m 900m on the
spot on the spot.
**Remarks**: Near sports fields.

### Landau 16H2

**La Ola Das Freizeitbad**, Horstring 2. **GPS**: n49,20230 e8,14270. ⬆➡.

5 € 10/24h € 4 Ch included.
**Location**: Urban, simple, quiet. **Surface**: metalled. 01/01-31/12.
**Distance**: 3km 1km 500m 100m.

### Landstuhl 16G2

Bahnstraße. **GPS**: n49,41595 e7,57092. ⬆➡.

2 free Chfree € 1/2kWh. **Location**: Urban, simple, noisy.
**Surface**: metalled. 01/01-31/12.
**Distance**: on the spot 1,3km 350m Aldi 100m.
**Remarks**: Max. 3 days.

### Langenlonsheim 16G1

**Weingut Im Zwölberich**, Schützenstrasse 14.
**GPS**: n49,89672 e7,89466. ⬆.

5 € 10 included. **Location**: Rural, simple, central, quiet.

---

**Surface**: asphalted/grassy. 01/01-31/12.
**Distance**: 500m 7km 500m 1km.

### Lauterecken 16G1

**Wohnmobilstellplatz Villa Toskana**, Friedhofweg 3a.
**GPS**: n49,65056 e7,58806. ⬆➡.

30 € 8 € 1/80liter Ch (18x)€ 1/8h WC € 3 € 1/5minutes.
**Location**: Urban, comfortable, luxurious, quiet. **Surface**: gravel.
01/01-31/12.
**Distance**: 300m on the spot 300m on the
spot on the spot.
**Remarks**: Bread-service.

### Leimersheim 16H2

**Sport- und Freizeithalle**, Rheinstraße 42.
**GPS**: n49,12534 e8,35457. ⬆.

5 free. **Location**: Rural, simple, quiet. **Surface**: gravel.
01/01-31/12.
**Distance**: 500m 4km 100m 100m on the spot 1km
on the spot on the spot.
**Remarks**: At tennis-courts.

### Leiwen 16F1

**Weingut Heinz Spieles**, Schulstrasse 20. **GPS**: n49,82331 e6,87524. ⬆.

4 € 8, 2 pers.incl € 1 Ch € 1 included.
**Surface**: grassy/gravel. 01/01-31/12.
**Distance**: 400m 400m 400m 700m 700m.
**Remarks**: Breakfast-service.

### Leiwen 16F1

**Moselblick**, Flurgartenstrasse 2/ Weinallee.
**GPS**: n49,82611 e6,88057. ⬆.

12 € 10 Ch WC € 1. **Location**: Rural.
**Surface**: grassy/gravel. 01/01-31/12.
**Distance**: 500m on the spot on the spot on the spot
300m 500m.

### Lemberg 16G2

**Lemberger Weiher**, Weiherstraße. **GPS**: n49,17284 e7,64731. ⬆.

---

5 free, service/electricity incl. € 7 Ch .
**Location**: Rural. **Surface**: grasstiles. 01/01-31/12.
**Distance**: 400m 100m 600m on the spot on the spot.
**Remarks**: Max. 3 days.

### Linz am Rhein 11G2

B42 Linzhausenstrasse. **GPS**: n50,56291 e7,27982. ⬆.

6 free. **Location**: Simple. **Surface**: asphalted. 01/01-31/12.
**Distance**: 500m on the spot 50m.
**Remarks**: Along the Rhine river, max. 3 days.

### Longuich/Mosel 16F1

**Feiten**, Rioler weg 2. **GPS**: n49,80417 e6,77899. ⬆➡.

40 € 8 € 0,50/70liter Ch € 2 WC € 1.
**Location**: Rural. **Surface**: grassy. 01/01-31/12.
**Distance**: 300m 2km on the spot on the spot on the
spot 1km.
**Remarks**: Along the Moselle river, playground.

### Longuich/Mosel 16F1

**WeinKulturgut Longen Schlöder**, Kirchenweg 9.
**GPS**: n49,81023 e6,76427. ⬆.

8 € 7 € 2 (3x)€ 2,50 WC € 3.
**Location**: Urban, simple, noisy. **Surface**: gravel/metalled.
01/01-31/12 Tue.
**Distance**: on the spot 1km 150m 150m on the spot
100m.

### Losheim am See 16F1

**Reisemobilplatz am Stausee**, Zum Stausee.
**GPS**: n49,51999 e6,74123. ⬆➡.

8 € 6 € 0,50/70liter Ch WC included.
**Location**: Rural, simple. **Surface**: grassy/gravel.

🔲 01/01-31/12.
**Distance:** 🚶1km ⛱200m ⛵200m ⊗100m 🛒1km 🚲on the spot 🎿on the spot.
**Remarks:** Parking at lake, in front of tourist office.

| 🅿🅢 | Lösnich 🌿🌊 | 11F3 |

**Stellplatz am Moselufer**, Gestade. **GPS:** n49,97560 e7,04276.⬆.

96 ⍓€7 🚰🚽Ch included. 🔌€ 2/day. 🚐 **Location:** Rural, simple, quiet. **Surface:** grassy. 🔲 01/03-01/11.
**Distance:** 🚶on the spot ⛵on the spot ⊗on the spot 🛒3km 🚲on the spot 🎿on the spot.
**Remarks:** Along the Moselle river, baker every morning.

| 🅿🅢 | Lutzerath 🧺 | 11F3 |

**Bürgerhaus zum Üssbachtal**, Trierer Strasse 2.
**GPS:** n50,13015 e7,01002.⬆.

10 ⍓€ 5/day 🚰€ 0,50 🚽Ch 🔌(6x)€ 0,50/kWh.
**Location:** Urban, simple. **Surface:** asphalted. 🔲 01/01-31/12.
**Distance:** 🚶on the spot ⊗on the spot 🛒on the spot.
**Remarks:** Check in at Hotel Restaurant Maas, Trierer Str. 30.

| 🅿🅢 | Maikammer | 16H2 |

**Sporthalle Kalmit**, Johannes Dammstrasse.
**GPS:** n49,30307 e8,13219.⬆➡.

3 ⍓€ 4/day 🚰🔌included. **Surface:** asphalted. 🔲 01/01-31/12.
**Distance:** 🚶500m ⊗nearby 🛒nearby.

| 🍇🅢 | Maikammer | 16H2 |

**Weingut Gerald Groß**, Bahnhofstraße 24.
**GPS:** n49,30578 e8,13809.⬆.

3 ⍓€ 13 🔌WC🚽included. 🚐 **Location:** Rural, simple, isolated, quiet. **Surface:** grassy. 🔲 01/01-31/12.
**Distance:** 🚶500m 🛒800m 🚲on the spot 🎿on the spot.

| 🍇🅢 | Maikammer | 16H2 |

**Weingut Hubert Müller**, Raiffeisenstrasse 59.
**GPS:** n49,30769 e8,13674.⬆➡.

3 ⍓€ 13 🚰🔌WC included. 🚐 **Location:** Rural, simple, isolated, quiet. **Surface:** gravel. 🔲 01/01-31/12.
**Distance:** 🚶on the spot ⛵7km 🎿on the spot 🎿on the spot.

| 🍇🅢 | Maikammer | 16H2 |

**Weingut Schädler**, Dieterwiesenstraße. **GPS:** n49,30848 e8,12530.

3 ⍓€ 7 🚰🔌WC included. **Location:** Simple, central.
🔲 01/01-31/12.
**Distance:** 🚶500m 🛒1km 🚲on the spot 🎿on the spot.

| 🅿🅢 | Mainz 🌊 | 11H3 |

**Wohnmobilstellplatz Mainz**, Dr.-Martin-Luther-King-Weg 21.
**GPS:** n49,99849 e8,24638.

56 ⍓€ 10 🚰€ 1/90liter 🚽Ch 🔌€ 0,50/kWh,16Amp 📶.
**Surface:** metalled. 🔲 01/01-31/12.
**Distance:** 🚶Old city centre 1,7km ⛵7km ⊗150m 🛒Aldi 200m 🚌bus 160m.
**Remarks:** Green zone: environmental badge obligatory.

| 🅿🅢 | Mandelbachtal 🌳 | 16F2 |

**Ommersheimer Weiher**, L107. **GPS:** n49,21899 e7,16766.⬆.

2 ⍓free 🚰€ 1 🔌(2x)€ 1/8h. **Location:** Rural, simple, isolated, quiet.
**Surface:** asphalted. 🔲 01/01-31/12.
**Distance:** ⛱on the spot 🛒on the spot.

| 🅿🅢 | Mandelbachtal 🌳 | 16F2 |

**Kloster Gräfinthal**, Gräfinthal. **GPS:** n49,15975 e7,11924.⬆.

2 ⍓free. **Location:** Rural, simple, noisy. **Surface:** metalled.
🔲 01/01-31/12.
**Distance:** ⊗100m.
**Remarks:** Nearby monastery.

| 🏕🅢 | Manderscheid 🚣 | 11F3 |

**Hotel Heidsmühle**, Mosenbergstrasse 22.
**GPS:** n50,08504 e6,80021.⬆.

20 ⍓free 🚰🔌(4x)€ 2,50/day. **Location:** Rural, simple, isolated, quiet. **Surface:** grassy/gravel. 🔲 01/01-31/12.
**Distance:** 🚶2km ⛵6km ⛵on the spot ⊗on the spot 🎿on the spot 🎿on the spot.

| 🅲🅢 | Manderscheid 🚣 | 11F3 |

**Campingplatz Vulkaneifel**, Herbstwiese.
**GPS:** n50,09713 e6,79969.➡.

8 ⍓€ 7,50/pp, dog € 1,50 🚰€ 0,50/100liter 🚽Ch 🔌€ 2,50
WC included 📶. **Location:** Rural, simple, quiet. **Surface:** metalled.
🔲 15/03-31/10.
**Distance:** 🚶800m ⊗800m 🛒800m 🎿on camp site 🎿on the spot 🎿on the spot.
**Remarks:** Bread-service.

| 🅿🅢 | Mayen | 11F3 |

**Wohnmobilstellplatz am Viehmarkt**, Polcherstrasse.
**GPS:** n50,32194 e7,22806.⬆.

6 ⍓free 🚰€ 1/80liter 🚽ChWC. **Location:** Simple. **Surface:** gravel.
🔲 01/01-31/12.
**Distance:** 🚶100m ⛵4km ⊗100m 🛒100m.
**Remarks:** Next to event ground, max. 3 nights.

| 🅿🅢 | Mayschoss 🚣🌊 | 11F2 |

**Ahruferplatz**, Ahr-Rotweinstraße 46. **GPS:** n50,51736 e7,01948.⬆.

75 ⍓€ 6 🚰€ 1/100liter 🚽Ch 🔌(15x)€ 2,50/day WC. 🚐
**Location:** Rural, central. **Surface:** asphalted/gravel.
🔲 01/01-31/12.
**Distance:** 🚶on the spot ⊗100m 🛒250m bakery 🚌50m.
**Remarks:** Along the Ahr river, parking at station.

| 🅿🅢 | Meckenheim | 16H2 |

**Sporthalle Meckenheim**, Rödersheimerstraße.
**GPS:** n49,41167 e8,24056.⬆.

10 ⌀free ⚡(6x)€ 0,50/kWh. **Location:** Rural, simple, quiet. **Surface:** gravel. ❑ 01/01-31/12.
**Distance:** ⛽1km ⚓6km ⊗200m 🛒800m 🚌4km ♨on the spot.
**Remarks:** At gymnasium.

### Meddersheim · 16G1

**Winzergenossenschaft**, Naheweinstrasse 63. **GPS:** n49,77988 e7,61347.
8 ⌀free ⚡free ⚡€ 3/day. **Location:** Rural, simple, quiet.
**Surface:** gravel. ❑ 01/01-31/12.
**Distance:** ⛽800m ⊗on the spot.
**Remarks:** Max. 2 nights, gate can be opened manually.

### Mehring · 16F1

**Weingut Zellerhof**, Zellerhof 1. **GPS:** n49,79369 e6,81944. ⬆️➡️

43 ⌀€ 6 ⚡€ 0,50/70liter ⚡Ch ⚡(43x)€ 0,50/kWh WC ⚡€ 1.
**Location:** Urban, comfortable, quiet. **Surface:** grassy/metalled.
❑ 01/01-31/12.
**Distance:** ⛽100m ⚓5km ⛱on the spot 🚐on the spot ⊗on the spot 🛒100m.

### Mehring · 16F1

**Wohnmobilstellplatz del Mosel**, Moselweinstrasse 2.
**GPS:** n49,79423 e6,81726. ⬆️

72 ⌀€ 8 ⚡€ 1/100liter ⚡Ch ⚡(60x)€ 2 WC ⚡€ 2. ♨
**Location:** Rural, comfortable, quiet. **Surface:** grassy.
❑ 01/01-31/12.
**Distance:** ⛽100m ⊗on the spot 🛒200m.
**Remarks:** Bread-service.

### Meisenheim · 16G1

**Schwimmbad Meisenheim**, In der Heimbach.
**GPS:** n49,71472 e7,65750. ⬆️

**DE**

12 ⌀€ 5 ⚡€ 1/100liter ⚡€ 1 Ch ⚡(12x)€ 1/kWh. 🏠
**Location:** Rural, simple, quiet. **Surface:** grassy/gravel.
❑ 01/01-31/12 ◐ 01/07-09/07.
**Distance:** ⛽1,6km ⊗on the spot 🛒500m.

### Mendig · 11G3

Brauerstraße. **GPS:** n50,37678 e7,28404. ⬆️

---

20 ⌀free ⚡€ 1/30liter ⚡Ch ⚡(12x)€ 0,50/kWh.
**Location:** Rural, quiet. **Surface:** gravel. ❑ 01/01-31/12.
**Distance:** ⛽200m ⊗Vulkanbrauhaus&Felsenkeller 🛒400m.
**Remarks:** In front of football ground, Vulkanmuseum Lava-Dome 100m.

### Merzig · 16F2

**Das Bad**, Saarwiesenring 3. **GPS:** n49,44541 e6,62418. ⬆️➡️

12 ⌀€ 7,50 ⚡€ 2/100liter ⚡Ch ⚡(12x)WC ⚡included.
**Location:** Rural, simple, quiet. **Surface:** grasstiles.
❑ 01/01-31/12.
**Distance:** ⛽2km ⚓5km ⊗on the spot 🛒2km 🚌bus 400m.
**Remarks:** Check in at swimming pool, caution key € 50, use sanitary only during opening hours swimming pool.

### Mettlach · 16F1

**Cloef-Atrium**, Alfred-Backer-strasse, Mettlach-Orscholz.
**GPS:** n49,50682 e6,53679. ⬆️➡️

10 ⌀€ 8 ⚡WC. 🏠 **Surface:** gravel. ❑ 01/01-31/12.
**Distance:** ⛽900m ⚓13km ⊗200m 🛒300m 🚌bus 300m ♨on the spot.
**Remarks:** Pay with SMS, max. 24h.

### Mettlach · 16F1

**Mettlacher Abtei-Bräu, P6**, Bahnhofstrasse 32.
**GPS:** n49,49847 e6,59612. ⬆️

10 ⌀€ 5 ⚡Chfree. **Surface:** gravel. ❑ 01/01-31/12.
**Distance:** ⛽500m ⚓7km ⛱on the spot 🚐on the spot ⊗on the spot 🛒aldi 1km 🛒700m.
**Remarks:** Along the Saar River, pay with SMS.

**Tourist information Mettlach:**
👁M Erlebniszentrum Villeroy&Boch. ❑ Mo-Fr: 9.30-19h, Sa 9.30-18h.
🛍 Villeroy&Boch Factory Outlet, Freiherr-vom-Stein-Strasse 4-6.
❑ Mo-Fr: 9.30-19h, Sa 9.30-18h.

### Minheim · 16F1

**Reisemobilpark Sonneninsel**, K53. **GPS:** n49,86500 e6,94111. ⬆️➡️

---

90 ⌀€ 7,20 ⚡€ 1/100liter ⚡Ch ⚡€ 1/2kWh. ♨
**Location:** Comfortable. **Surface:** grassy/gravel. ❑ 01/01-31/12.
**Distance:** ⚓10km ⊗400m 🛒3km.
**Remarks:** Along the Moselle river, next to football ground.

### Minheim · 16F1

**Weingut Thielen-Feilen**, Moselweinstraße 11.
**GPS:** n49,86421 e6,93857. ⬆️

3 ⌀€ 8,50 ⚡€ 2/night WC. ♨ **Location:** Rural, simple, isolated, quiet. **Surface:** grassy. ❑ 01/01-31/12.
**Distance:** ⛽on the spot ⛱300m 🛒300m.

### Minheim · 16F1

**Weinhaus Moselblick**, In der Olk 9. **GPS:** n49,86428 e6,93294. ⬆️

10 ⌀€ 9 ⚡Ch ⚡€ 1,50/day. ♨ **Surface:** grassy/gravel.
❑ 01/01-31/12.
**Distance:** ⛽200m ⛱200m 🚐200m 🛒100m ♨on the spot.
**Remarks:** Breakfast-service.

### Monreal · 11F3

**Parkplatz am Bahnhof**, Bahnhofstraße. **GPS:** n50,29678 e7,15407. ➡️

5 ⌀free. **Location:** Rural, simple, isolated, quiet.
**Surface:** gravel/metalled. ❑ 01/01-31/12.
**Distance:** ⛽500m ⊗on the spot ♨on the spot.

### Monzernheim · 16H1

**Weingut Helmut Geil**, Am Römer 26. **GPS:** n49,72376 e8,22715. ⬆️

3 ⌀€ 6 ⚡⚡(3x)included. ♨ **Location:** Rural, simple, quiet.
**Surface:** grassy. ❑ 01/01-31/12.
**Distance:** ⚓8km ⊗4km 🛒4km.
**Remarks:** Check in at Weingut.

## Monzingen 16G1

**Parkplatz Festhalle**, Rosengartenstrasse 11.
**GPS:** n49,79438 e7,59075.⬆️.

3 free. **Location:** Rural, simple, noisy. **Surface:** asphalted.
01/01-31/12.
**Distance:** on the spot ⊗on the spot 🚰1km 🚗350m.

## Monzingen 16G1

**Weingut Axel Schramm**, Soonwaldstrasse 49.
**GPS:** n49,81088 e7,48058.⬆️.

3 free free. **Location:** Rural, simple, isolated, quiet.
**Surface:** concrete. 01/01-31/12.
**Distance:** 1,2km ⊗1,5km

## Mörschied 16G1

**Wohnmobilstellplatz Mörschied**, Harfenmühle 2.
**GPS:** n49,80414 e7,26979.⬆️➡️.

11 € 12-16, 2 pers. incl Ch (10x)€ 2/night,6Amp € 0,50/
time € 5 included. **Location:** Rural, comfortable, isolated,
quiet. **Surface:** grassy/gravel. 01/01-31/12.
**Distance:** 6km ⊗on the spot on the spot on the spot.

## Mörsdorf 11G3

**Parkplatz Breitwies, P2**, Windorfer Straße.
**GPS:** n50,10465 e7,33760.⬆️➡️.

25 € 1/h, overnight stay free. **Location:** Rural, simple, isolated.
**Surface:** gravel/metalled. 01/01-31/12.
**Distance:** 500m ⊗500m on the spot.

## Münstermaifeld 11G3

**An der Stadthalle**, An den Gärten 6. **GPS:** n50,24583 e7,36778.⬆️.

2 free. **Location:** Urban, simple. **Surface:** metalled.
01/01-31/12.

---

**Distance:** 800m ⊗800m 🚰800m.

## Münstermaifeld 11G3

**Erlebnisbad Maifeld**, Pilligertorstrasse. **GPS:** n50,24522 e7,35831.

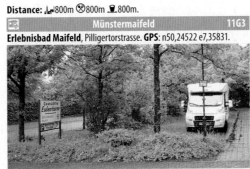

4. **Location:** Rural, simple. **Surface:** metalled.
01/09-15/05.
**Distance:** 700m ⊗700m 🚰700m.

## Nanzdietschweiler 16G2

Hauptstrasse. **GPS:** n49,44083 e7,43500.⬆️.

2 free € 1/100liter (4x)€ 1/8h. **Location:** Rural, simple,
isolated, quiet. **Surface:** metalled. 01/01-31/12.
**Distance:** 7km on the spot on the spot.

## Neef 11F3

**Wohnmobilstellplatz Zum Frauenberg**, Moseluferstraße.
**GPS:** n50,09455 e7,13730.⬆️➡️.

100 € 7 Chincluded (43x)€ 2/24h,10Amp.
**Location:** Rural, simple. **Surface:** grassy. 01/04-01/11.
**Distance:** on the spot on the spot ⊗200m 🚰500m on the
spot on the spot.
**Remarks:** Along the Moselle river, nearby sports fields, bread-service.

## Neumagen-Dhron 16F1

**Gaststatte Beim Ketsch**, In der Zeil. **GPS:** n49,86449 e6,90321.⬆️➡️.

100 € 6 Chincluded € 1,50/day WC € 2 € 3
against payment. **Location:** Urban, comfortable, quiet.
**Surface:** grassy/gravel. 01/01-31/12.
**Distance:** 200m ⊗on the spot 🚰500m on the spot on the
spot.
**Remarks:** Bread-service.

## Neumagen-Dhron 16F1

**Yachthafen Neumagen**, Moselstrasse 21.
**GPS:** n49,85188 e6,89232.⬆️➡️.

---

40 <9m € 6, >9m € 8 + € 2,50/pp, dog € 2 € 0,50/40liter
Ch € 0,60/kWh WC included € 3/24h.
**Location:** Rural. **Surface:** gravel. 01/01-31/12.
**Distance:** 100m on the spot on the spot ⊗on the spot
🚰1,3km.
**Remarks:** Check in at harbourmaster, boat rental, bicycle rental.

## Neustadt/Weinstrasse 16H2

Dammstrasse-Ost, Hambach. **GPS:** n49,33083 e8,13150.⬆️➡️.

10 free € 1/100liter € 1 Ch.
**Surface:** grassy. 01/01-31/12.
**Distance:** 200m ⊗200m 🚰200m 🚗4km.
**Remarks:** Next to swimming pool, service 500m.

## Neustadt/Weinstrasse 16H2

**Reisemobilstellplatz Martin-Luther-Kirche**, Martin-Luther-Strasse.
**GPS:** n49,35485 e8,15255.⬆️.

30 € 6/24h € 1/8minutes Ch (24x)€ 1/kWh.
**Surface:** metalled. 01/01-31/12.
**Distance:** 300m ⊗250m 🚰on the spot.

## Neustadt/Weinstrasse 16H2

**Festplatz Neustadt-Haardt**, Am Mandelring, Haardt.
**GPS:** n49,36719 e8,13945.⬆️.

2 free. **Location:** Rural, simple. **Surface:** asphalted.
01/01-31/12 Wine festivals.
**Distance:** 2km 5km ⊗100m.

## Neustadt/Weinstrasse 16H2

**Parkplatz am Rebenmeer**, Am Falltor, Duttweiler.
**GPS:** n49,30148 e8,21192.⬆️.

20 free. **Location:** Rural, simple, quiet. **Surface:** gravel/metalled.
01/01-31/12.

DE

**Distance:** 🚶300m 🚲5km ⊗300m 🍴250m bakery 🚴Kraut und Rüben-Radweg.

### Neustadt/Weinstrasse 16H2
**Wohnmobile Parkplatz Gimmeldinger Tal**, Peter-Koch-Strasse.
**GPS:** n49,37771 e8,15448. ⬆.

2🚐free. **Location:** Rural, simple, quiet. **Surface:** asphalted/metalled.
🔲 01/01-31/12.
**Distance:** 🚶500m 🚲5km ⊗on the spot 🍴on the spot 🚴on the spot 🚶on the spot.

### Neustadt/Weinstrasse 16H2
**Altes Weingut Steigelmann**, Lauterbachstrasse 33, Mussbach.
**GPS:** n49,37315 e8,17230. ⬆➡.

5🚐€7 🔌Ch🚿(5x)included. 🚲
**Location:** Rural, simple, quiet. **Surface:** grassy.
🔲 01/03-30/11.
**Distance:** 🚶500m 🚲3km ⊗400m 🍴700m 🚌450m 🚴on the spot.
**Remarks:** Check in at Weingut.

### Neustadt/Weinstrasse 16H2
**Rebenhof Wein- und Sektgut**, Andergasse 93, Hambach.
**GPS:** n49,32157 e8,12241. ⬆.

5🚐€8, 2 pers.incl 🔌🚿WC included. **Location:** Rural.
**Surface:** grasstiles/grassy. 🔲 01/01-31/12.
**Distance:** 🚲5km ⊗100m.

### Neustadt/Weinstrasse 16H2
**Weingut & Weinschenke Hans Abel**, Weinstrasse 103, Hambach.
**GPS:** n49,33788 e8,13171. ⬆.
3🚐free 🔌🚿€2,50. **Location:** Rural, simple. **Surface:** grassy
🔲 01/01-31/12 🔲 Thu.
**Distance:** 🚶Old city centre 3km 🚲4,5km ⊗300m 🍴bakery 200m 🚌bus on the spot 🚶on the spot.
**Remarks:** Reservation recommended.

### Neustadt/Weinstrasse 16H2
**Weingut Andres**, Langensteinstrasse 22, Lachen-Speyersdorf.
**GPS:** n49,33614 e8,20627. ⬆.
3🚐free 🚿. **Location:** Rural, simple, isolated. **Surface:** grassy.
🔲 01/01-31/12.
**Remarks:** Reservation recommended.

### Neustadt/Weinstrasse 16H2
**Weingut Carl Disson**, Andergasse 96, Hambach.
**GPS:** n49,32123 e8,12220. ⬆.

---

4🚐€7 🔌🚿WC included. **Location:** Rural. **Surface:** grassy.
🔲 01/01-31/12.
**Distance:** 🚲5km ⊗100m.
**Remarks:** Bread-service, wine tasting.

### Neustadt/Weinstrasse 16H2
**Weingut Hammer**, Zum Klausental 29, Diedesfeld.
**GPS:** n49,32041 e8,13248. ⬆.
3🚐€5 🔌🚿. **Location:** Rural, simple, isolated, quiet.
**Surface:** grassy. 🔲 01/01-31/12.
**Distance:** 🚲5km 🚴on the spot 🚶on the spot.

### Neustadt/Weinstrasse 16H2
**Weingut Klohr**, An der Eselshaut 67, Mussbach.
**GPS:** n49,37026 e8,17449. ⬆.
2🚐guests free 🔌🚿. **Location:** Rural. **Surface:** grassy.
🔲 01/01-31/12.
**Distance:** 🚶on the spot 🚲2km ⊗100m 🍴200m 🚌700m.
**Remarks:** Sale of wines.

### Neustadt/Weinstrasse 16H2
**Weingut Kreiselmaier**, Goethestrasse 77, Lachen.
**GPS:** n49,32255 e8,20061. ⬆.

3🚐€5 🔌€2/100liter 🚿€2/night.
**Location:** Rural, simple, quiet. **Surface:** grassy. 🔲 01/03-31/10.
**Distance:** 🚶on the spot 🚲4,5km ⊗250m 🍴3km 🚌150m 🚴Kraut-und-Rüben-Radweg.
**Remarks:** Sale of wines.

### Neustadt/Weinstrasse 16H2
**Weingut Müller-Kern**, Andergasse 38, Hambach.
**GPS:** n49,32266 e8,12681. ⬆.

3🚐€15, 2 pers.incl 🔌🚿(3x). **Location:** Urban, simple, quiet. **Surface:** grassy. 🔲 01/01-31/12.
**Distance:** 🚲4,5km ⊗300m 🚴on the spot 🚶on the spot.
**Remarks:** Adjacent walking and bicycle area.

### Neustadt/Weinstrasse 16H2
**Weingut Schäfer**, Schiessmauer 56, Mussbach.
**GPS:** n49,36335 e8,17111.

5🚐€15, 2 pers.incl 🔌Ch🚿WC included. 🚲
**Location:** Rural. **Surface:** grassy. 🔲 01/03-31/10.
**Distance:** 🚲2km.

---

### Neustadt/Weinstrasse 16H2
**Weinhaus Am Herzog**, Mandelring 195, Haardt.
**GPS:** n49,36982 e8,14499. ⬆.
2🚐€20 🔌🚿WC included. 🚲
**Location:** Rural, simple. **Surface:** metalled. 🔲 01/01-31/12.
**Distance:** 🚲4km ⊗500m 🚴on the spot 🚶on the spot.
**Remarks:** Motorhomes <6.5m, bicycle rental.

### Neustadt/Weinstrasse 16H2
**Weinhaus Kruppenbacher**, Andergasse 42, Hambach.
**GPS:** n49,32296 e8,12597. ⬆➡.

3🚐€10 🚿included WC €2,50. **Location:** Rural, comfortable, isolated. **Surface:** metalled. 🔲 01/01-31/12.
**Distance:** 🚴on the spot 🚶on the spot.

### Neustadt/Weinstrasse 16H2
**Weinland Königsbach-Neustadt**, Deidesheimer Strasse 12, Königsbach. **GPS:** n49,38712 e8,16239. ⬆➡.

5🚐€5 🔌🚿included. 🚲 **Location:** Rural, simple, quiet.
**Surface:** concrete. 🔲 01/01-31/12.
**Distance:** 🚲6,5km 🍴300m.

### Neustadt/Weinstrasse 16H2
**Weinland Meckenheim**, An der Eselshaut 76, Mussbach.
**GPS:** n49,37037 e8,17479. ⬆.

3🚐€5 🔌🚿included WC. 🚲 **Location:** Rural, simple, quiet.
**Surface:** grassy/gravel. 🔲 01/01-31/12.
**Distance:** 🚶400m 🚲2,3km ⊗300m 🍴200m 🚌650m 🚴on the spot.
**Remarks:** Check in on arrival.

### Neustadt/Weinstrasse 16H2
**Hambacher Schloss Kellerei**, Weinstrasse 110, Hambach.
**GPS:** n49,33724 e8,13135. ⬆.
2🚐free. **Location:** Urban, simple, quiet. **Surface:** asphalted.
🔲 01/01-31/12 🔲 01/10-31/10.
**Distance:** 🚲4,5km 🍴300m 🚌on the spot 🚴on the spot 🚶on the spot.
**Remarks:** Sale of wines.

### Neuwied 11G2
**Yachthafen Neuwied**, Rheinstrasse 180. **GPS:** n50,41413 e7,47946. ⬆.

40🚐€7, 2 pers.incl. 🔌Ch🚿€0,50/kWh WC included.
**Location:** Rural. **Surface:** metalled. 🔲 01/01-31/12.

DE

**Distance:** 2km 16km ⊗on the spot 2km 3km.
**Remarks:** Bread-service, cash payment.

### Nickenich · 11G3
**Wohnmobilstellplatz am Baggerado**, Auf dem Teich 1.
**GPS:** n50,40701 e7,33162.

8 €8 €1/100liter Ch (4x) 1/4h. **Location:** Rural, simple, quiet. **Surface:** metalled. 01/01-31/12.
**Distance:** 800m ⊗800m on the spot.

### Niederbreitbach · 11G2
**Campingplatz Neuerburg**, Im Freizeitparkt 1.
**GPS:** n50,52969 e7,41414.

8 €7, dog €1 80liter Ch €1,50/day €1 €4/3.
**Location:** Rural, comfortable. **Surface:** gravel.
01/01-31/12 sanitary 01/11-31/03.
**Distance:** 250m 13km on the spot ⊗on the spot on the spot on the spot.
**Remarks:** Bread-service.

### Niederkirchen bei Deidesheim · 16H2
**Wohnmobilstellplatz Niederkirchen**, An de Sportanlage 1.
**GPS:** n49,40891 e8,22141.

6 free €1/4h. **Location:** Rural, simple, quiet. **Surface:** gravel.
01/01-31/12.
**Distance:** 1km 4,5km ⊗1km.
**Remarks:** Service 300m.

### Nierstein · 16H1
**Weingut Gehring**, Ausserhalb 17. **GPS:** n49,85621 e8,32520.

30 €10 Ch (15x) €3/day WC €1/6minutes included.
**Location:** Rural, comfortable, quiet. **Surface:** grassy/metalled.
01/01-31/12.
**Distance:** 800m 17km 1,5km 1km ⊗10m 500m
1km 50m 10m.
**Remarks:** Bread-service.

### Nohfelden · 16F1
**Campingplatz Bostalsee, P6**, L325, Bosen.
**GPS:** n49,56039 e7,06113.

10 €12 €0,50/60liter Ch €0,50 €1/kWh included.
**Location:** Rural, simple, quiet. **Surface:** metalled.
01/01-31/12.
**Distance:** 500m 6km 200m €8/day ⊗on the spot
800m on the spot on the spot.

### Nonnweiler · 16F1
**Stellplatz Am Hallenbad**, Triererstrasse 2.
**GPS:** n49,60686 e6,97216.

5 free €1/100liter (4x) €0,50. **Location:** Rural, simple, quiet.
**Surface:** grassy/metalled. 01/01-31/12.
**Distance:** on the spot 1km ⊗on the spot 800m.
**Remarks:** Parking swimming pool, max. 48h.

### Nürburg · 11F3
**Wohnmobilpark Motorsporthotel**, Hauptstrasse 34.
**GPS:** n50,33963 e6,95095.

12 €10 included on demand.
**Location:** Rural, simple. **Surface:** grassy. 01/01-31/12.
**Distance:** 400m ⊗on the spot.
**Remarks:** At racing circuit, pay at hotel.

### Ober-Hilbersheim · 16H1
**Napoleonshöhe**, Sprendlingers Straße. **GPS:** n49,89785 e8,02421.

40 free €1/90liter Ch (6x) €1/8h. **Location:** Rural, simple,
noisy. **Surface:** grassy. 01/01-31/12.
**Distance:** 500m 300m.

### Oberbrombach · 16G1
**Wohnmobilstellplatz Höhenblick**, Sonnenberger Strasse.
**GPS:** n49,69481 e7,25960.

75 €7 Ch included (45x) €2/4kWh. **Location:** Rural,
comfortable, quiet. **Surface:** grassy/gravel. 01/01-31/12.

**Distance:** 400m ⊗4km 1,5km.

### Oberwesel/Rhein · 11G3
**Wohnmobilstellplatz Stadt Oberwesel**, Am Rhein / B9.
**GPS:** n50,10816 e7,72758.

20 €8/night. **Location:** Urban, simple, noisy.
**Surface:** metalled. 01/01-31/12.
**Distance:** 400m 10km on the spot on the spot ⊗200m
Lidl 1km 600m on the spot on the spot.
**Remarks:** Along the Rhine river.

### Oberwesel/Rhein · 11G3
**Camping Schönburgblick**, Am Hafendamm 1.
**GPS:** n50,10294 e7,73663.

20 €9 Ch included €0,60/kWh WC €2,50 €2.
**Location:** Urban, comfortable, quiet. **Surface:** grassy.
15/03-31/10.
**Distance:** 800m on the spot on the spot ⊗on the spot
200m 400m.
**Remarks:** Max. 8M, possibility for reservation.

### Ockenheim · 11H3
**Metzis Panoramablick**, Sporkenheimweg.
**GPS:** n49,94645 e7,97126.

30 €8 Ch €2/day €1/5minutes €3/3 included.
**Location:** Rural, comfortable, isolated, quiet. **Surface:** grassy/gravel.
01/01-31/12.
**Distance:** 1km ⊗400m 4km on the spot on the spot.
**Remarks:** Bread-service.

### Offenbach an der Queich · 16H2
**Am Queichtalzentrum**, Konrad-Lerch-Ring.
**GPS:** n49,20056 e8,19478.

2 free. **Location:** Simple. **Surface:** metalled.
01/01-31/12.
**Distance:** 100m 6km 500m 1km 400m.
**Remarks:** At sports centre, max. 3 days, outside environmental zone.

### Oppenheim · 16H1
**Womoland Oppenheim**, An der Festwiese.
**GPS:** n49,85673 e8,36502.

DE

20 🛏7 ⚡€ 1/50liter 🚱Ch ⚿3/24h.
**Location:** Rural, simple. **Surface:** grassy.
⬛ 01/01-31/12 ⬤ week before/after Whitsuntide.
**Distance:** 🛒500m ⊗500m 🚰500m.

### Osann-Monzel — 16F1
**Wohnmobilstellplatz Hotel Moselsteig**, Novianderweg 3.
**GPS:** n49,90865 e6,95776. ⬆.

8 🛏5 ⚿€ 2 📶against payment. 🚲
**Surface:** gravel. ⬛ 01/06-31/10.
**Distance:** ⚓9km ⊗on the spot 🚶on the spot ⚑on the spot.

### Osthofen — 16H1
**Festplatz Wonnegauhalle**, Herrnsheimer Strasse.
**GPS:** n49,69913 e8,32691. ⬆➡.

15 🛏free ⚡🚱Chfree ⚿(6x)€ 1/8h. **Location:** Rural, simple.
**Surface:** gravel. ⬛ 01/01-31/12.
**Distance:** 🛒500m 🚲7km 🚰500m.
**Remarks:** Max. 48h.

### Osthofen — 16H1
**Sommerried Stadion**, L439. **GPS:** n49,69222 e8,32805. ⬆.

10 🛏free. **Location:** Rural, simple. **Surface:** grassy/sand.
⬛ 01/01-31/12.
**Distance:** ⚓6km 🚰800m.
**Remarks:** Max. 48h.

### Osthofen — 16H1
**Weingut Borntaler Hof**, Alter Westhofer Weg.
**GPS:** n49,69985 e8,29860. ⬆➡.

40 🛏8 ⚡🚱WCincluded 📶. 🏠 **Location:** Rural, simple.
**Surface:** grassy/metalled. ⬛ 01/01-31/12.
**Distance:** ⚓9km.

---

### Ottweiler — 16F2
**Stellplatz am Wingertsweiher**, Am Wingertsweiher.
**GPS:** n49,41134 e7,18076. ⬆➡.

10 🛏€ 5/24h ⚡€ 1/150liter 🚱€ 1 Ch ⚿(6x)€ 3/8h.
**Location:** Rural, simple, isolated, quiet. **Surface:** grassy/metalled.
⬛ 01/01-31/12.
**Distance:** 🛒1,5km ⚓on the spot 🚶on the spot ⊗on the spot
🚰1,5km 🚲1km.
**Remarks:** Max. 7 days, money in envelope in mail box.

### Palzem — 16E1
**Weingut E. Pauly**, Obermoselstrasse 5.
**GPS:** n49,56402 e6,37581. ⬆➡.

5 🛏€ 7 ⚡🚱(5x)included WC. **Surface:** gravel/metalled.
⬛ 01/01-31/12.
**Distance:** ⚓on the spot 🚶on the spot ⊗50m 🚲4km 🚏450m.
**Remarks:** Not suitable for big motorhomes, beautiful view.

### Perl — 16E1
**Am Perlbad**, Auf dem Sabel 4. **GPS:** n49,47900 e6,38493. ⬆➡.

6 🛏€ 5 ⚡€ 1/6minutes 🚱Ch ⚿(8x)€ 1/8h. **Location:** Quiet.
**Surface:** metalled. ⬛ 01/01-31/12.
**Distance:** 🛒500m 🚲3,5km ⊗500m 🚰500m 🚌bus 500m.
**Remarks:** At swimming pool, to be paid at swimming pool.

### Pfaffen-Schwabenheim — 16H1
**Pferdepension am Sonnenhof**, Brühlstraße.
**GPS:** n49,85224 e7,95951. ⬆.

10 🛏€ 10 ⚡🚱⚿WCincluded. 🚲 **Location:** Rural, simple,
isolated, quiet. **Surface:** concrete. ⬛ 01/01-31/12.
**Distance:** ⚓7km ⊗on the spot 🚲aldi 700m.
**Remarks:** Breakfast-service.

### Piesport — 16F1
**Piesporter Goldtröpfchen**, Moselstrasse.
**GPS:** n49,87199 e6,92703. ➡.

---

30 🛏9 ⚡€ 1/80liter 🚱Ch ⚿3. 🚲 **Surface:** gravel.
⬛ 01/01-31/12.
**Distance:** 🛒100m 🚲11km ⚓on the spot 🚶on the spot ⊗on the
spot 🚰500m.
**Remarks:** Bread-service mo-sa.

### Piesport — 16F1
**Altes Kelterhaus**, St. Martinstrasse 33. **GPS:** n49,87872 e6,92590. ➡.

7 🛏€ 7,50, guests free ⚡€ 2,50 🚱Ch ⚿2,50. 🚲 **Surface:** gravel.
⬛ 01/01-31/12 ⬤ 01/11-28/02: Mo.
**Distance:** 🚲10km ⊗on the spot 🚰on the spot.
**Remarks:** Bicycle rental.

### Piesport — 16F1
**Weingut Heinz Kirsten**, In der Noo. **GPS:** n49,88017 e6,92597. ⬆.

6 🛏€ 6 ⚡🚱Ch ⚿€ 1. 🚲 **Location:** Rural. **Surface:** gravel.
⬛ 01/01-31/12.
**Distance:** 🛒on the spot 🚲7,5km 🏊Moselle river 600m 🚶Moselle
river 600m ⊗on the spot 🚰on the spot.
**Remarks:** Check in at Bahnhofstrasse 28.

### Piesport — 16F1
**Weingut Spang, Reisemobilplatz Rebengarten**, In den Dur 11.
**GPS:** n49,88287 e6,92781. ⬆➡.

3 🛏€ 10, 2 pers.incl ⚡included ⚿€ 0,70/kWh WC€ 2,50. 🚲
**Location:** Rural. **Surface:** gravel.
⬛ 01/03-30/11.
**Distance:** 🛒on the spot 🚲8km 🏊100m ⊗100m 🚰500m 🚏500m.
**Remarks:** Bread-service + breakfast-service.

### Piesport — 16F1
**Wohnmobilstellplatz Loreleyblick**, Loreleyblick 20.
**GPS:** n49,87323 e6,92535. ⬆.

5 ⛺ € 9 🚰 🔧Ch 💧(10x) 🛢€ 1. 🚽 **Location:** Rural. **Surface:** gravel.
📅 01/01-31/12.
**Distance:** 🚉on the spot 🚲11km ⊗1km 🍴300m.
**Remarks:** Bread-service.

### Pirmasens 16G2
**Am Messegelände**, Zeppelinstraße 11. **GPS:** n49,20446 e7,60885. ⬆️.

8 ⛺ € 5/24h 🚰 € 1/100liter 🔧Ch 💧€ 1/6h. 🚿
**Location:** Urban, simple, noisy. **Surface:** gravel.
📅 01/01-31/12.
**Distance:** 🚉450m 🚲6km ⊗450m 🍴450m 🚗1km.

### Pirmasens 16G2
**Forsthaus Beckenhof**, Beckenhofer Strasse.
**GPS:** n49,19604 e7,65635. ⬆️.

10 ⛺guests free. **Location:** Rural, simple, quiet. **Surface:** gravel.
📅 01/01-31/12.
**Distance:** 🚉6km ⊗on the spot.

### Plaidt 11G3
**Wohnmobilstellplatz am Vulkanpark**, Rauschermühle 6.
**GPS:** n50,38790 e7,40444. ⬆️.

10 ⛺free. **Location:** Rural. **Surface:** metalled.
📅 01/01-31/12.
**Distance:** 🚉1km 🚲5km ⊗1km 🍴3km 🚗2km 🎣on the spot 🎿on the spot.

### Polch 11G3
**Niesmann&Bisschof**, Clou-strasse 1. **GPS:** n50,30680 e7,30684. ⬆️.

25 ⛺free 🚰 € 0,50/80liter 🔧Ch 💧(12x)€ 0,50/kWh.
**Surface:** metalled. 📅 01/01-31/12.
**Distance:** ⊗on the spot 🚉on the spot.

### Pronsfeld 11E3
**Am Alten Bahnhof**, Bahnhofstrasse. **GPS:** n50,16343 e6,33669. ⬆️➡️.

50 ⛺ € 6 🚰 € 0,50/60liter 🔧Ch 💧(24x)€ 0,50/kWh.
**Location:** Rural, comfortable, quiet. **Surface:** grassy/gravel.
📅 01/01-31/12.
**Distance:** 🚉600m 🚲7,5km ⊗600m 🍴700m 🚗500m 🎿on the spot 🎣on the spot.

### Prüm 11E3
**Parking Prüm**, Bahnhofstraße. **GPS:** n50,19969 e6,41410. ⬆️.
15 ⛺ € 8 🚰 € 0,50 🔧Ch 💧€ 0,50/kWh 📶. **Location:** Rural.
**Surface:** gravel. 📅 01/01-31/12.
**Distance:** 🚉1km ⊗800m.

### Prüm 11E3
**Wohnmobilstellplatz Prüm**, Monthermeerstrasse 3.
**GPS:** n50,20956 e6,42715. ⬆️.

4 ⛺free. **Location:** Urban, simple. **Surface:** gravel.
📅 01/01-31/12.
**Distance:** 🚉600m 🚲2,2km ⊗500m 🍴500m 🚗200m.

### Pünderich 11F3
**Wohnmobilstellplatz Pünderich**, Moselallee.
**GPS:** n50,04355 e7,12548. ⬆️➡️.

80 ⛺ € 7 🚰 🔧Chincluded 💧(12x)€ 1,50/24h. 🚽
**Location:** Rural, simple, quiet. **Surface:** grassy.
📅 01/04-31/10.
**Distance:** 🚉on the spot 🚣on the spot 🚉on the spot ⊗300m 🍴500m.

### Ramstein-Miesenbach 16G1
**City Parkplatz**, Talstrasse. **GPS:** n49,45103 e7,55557. ⬆️➡️.

3 ⛺free. **Location:** Urban, simple, noisy. **Surface:** gravel.
📅 01/01-31/12.
**Distance:** 🚉on the spot 🚲3,7km ⊗800m 🍴aldi 1km 🚗300m.

### Ramstein-Miesenbach 16G1
**Freizeitbad Azur**, Schernauer Strasse 50. **GPS:** n49,44578 e7,56971. ⬆️.

30 ⛺free. **Location:** Rural, simple, noisy. **Surface:** metalled.
📅 01/01-31/12.
**Distance:** 🚉1km 🚲5,5km ⊗350m 🚗1km.

### Rech 11F2
**Wohnmobilstellplatz Burgwiese**, Im Bungert.
**GPS:** n50,51413 e7,03849.

15 ⛺ € 6. 🚽 **Location:** Rural. **Surface:** grassy. 📅 01/01-31/12.
**Distance:** 🚉500m 🚲11km 🚣on the spot 🚉on the spot ⊗300m
🚗350m.
**Remarks:** Along the Ahr river.

### Rech 11F2
Im Bungert. **GPS:** n50,51444 e7,03750. ⬆️.
10 ⛺ € 5. 🚽 **Location:** Rural. **Surface:** gravel.
📅 01/01-31/12.
**Distance:** 🚉on the spot ⊗on the spot 🚗on the spot 🎿on the spot.

### Reil/Mosel 11F3
**Am Moselufer**, Moselstrasse. **GPS:** n50,02566 e7,11493. ⬆️.

70 ⛺ € 10 🚰 🔧Ch 💧(48x)€ 2/day WC 📶included. 🚽
**Location:** Rural, comfortable, quiet. **Surface:** grassy.
📅 01/04-31/10.
**Distance:** 🚉500m 🚣on the spot ⊗450m.
**Remarks:** Along the Moselle river.

### Reipoltskirchen 16G1
**Wasserburg**, Kegelbahnstrasse. **GPS:** n49,63448 e7,66373. ⬆️➡️.

7 ⛺free 🚰 € 1/4minutes 🔧Ch 💧(4x)€ 1/12h.
**Location:** Rural, simple, central, quiet. **Surface:** metalled.
📅 01/01-31/12.
**Distance:** 🚉150m ⊗on the spot 🍞bakery 100m 🎿on the spot.

### Reipoltskirchen 16G1
**Stellplatz Ausbacherhof**, K42, Ausbacherhof.
**GPS:** n49,61307 e7,65667. ⬆️.

DE

4 🛏 free. **Location:** Rural, simple, isolated, quiet.
**Surface:** grassy/gravel. ⬛ 01/01-31/12.

| 🅖🅢 | **Remagen** | 11F2 |

**Wohnmobilhafen Goldene Meile**, Simrockweg 9–13.
**GPS:** n50,57667 e7,24750.➡️

30 🛏 € 12 🚰 € 1/90liter 🗑️Ch 🔌(18x)€ 1/6h. 🏠 **Surface:** grassy.
⬛ 01/04-31/10.
**Distance:** 🚲 10km ⛱️ on the spot 🚽 on the spot.

| 🅢 | **Rheinbreitbach** | 11F2 |

**Wohnmobilstellplatz Siebengebirgsblick**, Rolandsecker Weg 8.
**GPS:** n50,62193 e7,22812.⬆️

14 🛏 € 8 🚰 € 1/90liter 🗑️Ch 🔌(12x)€ 1/2kWh. **Location:** Simple.
**Surface:** grassy/gravel. ⬛ 01/01-31/12.
**Distance:** ⊗500m.
**Remarks:** To be paid at Rolandsecker Weg 8.

| 🅢 | **Rhodt unter Rietburg** | 16H2 |

Theresienstraße. **GPS:** n49,27464 e8,09917.⬆️

20 🛏 € 4. 🏠 **Location:** Rural, simple. **Surface:** gravel.
⬛ 01/01-31/12.
**Distance:** 🚲100m 🚲5km ⊗500m 🚽600m.

| 🅦🅢 | **Rhodt unter Rietburg** | 16H2 |

**Meyer Karl Herman**, Edesheimerstrasse 17.
**GPS:** n49,26883 e8,10868.⬆️

6 🛏 € 9 🚰 🔌(6x)included. 🛁 **Location:** Rural, simple, quiet.
**Surface:** gravel. ⬛ 01/01-31/12.
**Distance:** 🚲200m ⊗200m 🚽200m.

| 🅦🅢 | **Rhodt unter Rietburg** | 16H2 |

**Weingut Fader**, Traminerweg 1. **GPS:** n49,26972 e8,11057.⬆️➡️

---

12 🛏 € 15 🚰🗑️Ch 🔌(12x)included. 🛁 **Location:** Rural, simple,
quiet. **Surface:** gravel. ⬛ 01/04-31/10.
**Distance:** 🚲300m 🚲7km ⊗200m 🚽200m.

| 🅦🅢 | **Rhodt unter Rietburg** | 16H2 |

**Weingut Krieger**, Edesheimerstrasse 7. **GPS:** n49,26850 e8,10745.⬆️

2 🛏 € 5 🚰 free 🔌 on demand. 🏠 **Location:** Rural, simple, quiet.
**Surface:** grassy. ⬛ 01/01-31/12.
**Distance:** 🚲100m 🚲6km ⊗200m 🚽200m.

| 🅦🅢 | **Rhodt unter Rietburg** | 16H2 |

**Weingut Nichterlein**, Mühlgasse 15. **GPS:** n49,27349 e8,10802.⬆️

3 🛏 € 6 🚰 🔌WC included. 🛁 **Location:** Rural, quiet.
**Surface:** metalled. ⬛ 01/01-31/12.
**Distance:** 🚲300m 🚲5km ⊗200m 🚽400m.

| 🅦🅢 | **Rhodt unter Rietburg** | 16H2 |

**Weingut Jürgen Heußler**, Weyherer Strasse 34/35.
**GPS:** n49,27052 e8,10386.⬆️

3 🛏 € 3, guests free. 🛁 **Location:** Simple. **Surface:** gravel.
⬛ 01/01-31/12.
**Distance:** 🚲300m 🚲6km ⊗100m 🚽350m.

| 🅢 | **Rockenhausen** | 16G1 |

**Reisemobilhafen Rockenhausen**, Obermühle.
**GPS:** n49,62136 e7,82146.⬆️

5 🛏 free 🚰 € 1/80liter 🗑️Ch 🔌(6x)€ 1/6h. **Location:** Rural, simple.
**Surface:** gravel. ⬛ 01/01-31/12.
**Distance:** 🚲800m 🚽 on the spot.
**Remarks:** At swimming pool.

| 🅦 | **Rodalben** | 16G2 |

**Wohnmobilstellplatz Spielmannszug**, Am Entenstein 6.
**GPS:** n49,24476 e7,62101.⬆️➡️

---

20 🛏 free. **Location:** Rural, simple, isolated, quiet. **Surface:** grassy.
⬛ 01/01-31/12.
**Distance:** 🚲1km 🚽700m 1km.

| 🅦🅢 | **Roschbach** | 16H2 |

**Weingut Koch**, Am Rosenkränzel 13. **GPS:** n49,24736 e8,11532.➡️

3 🛏 € 5 🚰 included 🗑️ 🔌 € 2/night WC. 🛁
**Location:** Rural, quiet. **Surface:** grassy. ⬛ 01/01-31/12.
**Distance:** 🚲5km ⊗400m.

| 🅦🅢 | **Ruppertsberg** | 16H2 |

**Winzerhaus Im Linsenbusch**, Hauptstrasse 70.
**GPS:** n49,39944 e8,20044.⬆️

4 🛏 € 10 🚰 🔌 included WC 📶. 🏠 **Location:** Rural, comfortable.
**Surface:** grasstiles. ⬛ 01/01-31/12.
**Distance:** 🚲 on the spot 🚲3km ⊗ on the spot 🚽1km 1,5km.

| 🅢 | **Saarbrücken** 🛒 | 16F2 |

**Reisemobilhafen Calypso**, Deutschmühlental 7.
**GPS:** n49,23027 e6,96222.⬆️

20 🛏 € 7 + reduction swimming pool 🚰 🗑️Ch included 🔌
(4x)€ 1/24h. 🏠 **Location:** Simple, noisy. **Surface:** metalled.
⬛ 01/01-31/12.
**Distance:** 🚲700m ⛱️100m ⊗ on the spot 🚽500m 🚌 on the spot.
**Remarks:** To pay at swimming pool.

| 🅢 | **Saarburg** | 16F1 |

**Reisemobilpark Saarburg**, Am Saarufer.
**GPS:** n49,60158 e6,55442.⬆️➡️

100 🛏 € 8, 01/03-31/10 € 10 + € 0,25/pp tourist tax 🚰 € 1/100liter 🗑️
Ch 🔌(70x)€ 0,50/kWh WC 📶 € 1,50 🛁
**Location:** Urban, comfortable, quiet. **Surface:** grassy/metalled.
⬛ 01/01-31/12 ⬛ Service: winter.

DE

**Distance:** 850m on the spot on the spot 200m.
**Remarks:** Bread-service.

### Saarburg | 16F1

**Reisemobilstellplatz Leukbachtal**, Leukbachtal 1.
**GPS:** n49,59921 e6,54130.

20 € 19,50, 2 pers.incl Ch WC included.
**Location:** Rural, comfortable, quiet. **Surface:** grassy.
01/03-31/10.
**Distance:** 1km 150m 150m 700m.

### Saarlouis | 16F2

**In den Fliesen**, St.Nazairer Allee. **GPS:** n49,32146 e6,74267.

30 free € 1/80liter Ch. **Location:** Urban, simple, quiet.
**Surface:** metalled. 01/01-31/12.
**Distance:** 500m 1,5km on the spot on the spot 500m
300m.
**Remarks:** At sports centre, bread-service.

### Saarlouis | 16F2

**Hotellerie Waldesruh**, Siersburger Strasse 8, Wallerfangen.
**GPS:** n49,34440 e6,67614.

2 € 10, guests free. **Location:** Rural, simple, noisy.
**Surface:** metalled. 01/01-31/12 Su-Mo.
**Distance:** 10km on the spot.

### Sankt Aldegund | 11F3

**Am Moselstausee. GPS:** n50,07899 e7,13119.

40 € 7 Chincluded (28x)€ 2/24h. **Location:** Rural, simple.
**Surface:** grassy/metalled. 01/04-01/12.
**Distance:** 250m on the spot 250m.
**Remarks:** Bread-service.

### Sankt Goarshausen | 11G3

**Loreley Besucherzentrum**, Auf der Loreley 7.
**GPS:** n50,14191 e7,73303.

---

25 € 5. **Location:** Rural, simple, isolated. **Surface:** gravel.
01/01-31/12.
**Distance:** 600m 600m.

### Sankt Ingbert | 16F2

**Reisemobilplatz 'Das Blau'**, Spieser Landstraße.
**GPS:** n49,28652 e7,13194.

8 free € 1/80liter Ch. **Location:** Simple, central, quiet.
**Surface:** grassy. 01/01-31/12.
**Distance:** 1,5km 3,5km 100m 1,7km on the spot.
**Remarks:** Next to parking swimming pool, service 100m.

### Sankt Julian | 16G1

**An der Ölmühle**, Mühlstraße (K26). **GPS:** n49,60758 e7,51480.

10 € 5 € 1 Ch € 1/kWh. **Location:** Rural, simple, quiet.
**Surface:** grassy. 01/04-31/10.
**Distance:** on the spot 300m.

### Sankt Martin | 16H2

**Edenkoperstrasse. GPS:** n49,29702 e8,10838.

14 € 6/day. **Surface:** asphalted. 01/01-31/12.
**Distance:** 5km.
**Remarks:** Max. 1 night.

### Sankt Martin | 16H2

**Keltenweg. GPS:** n49,30064 e8,10742.

20 € 6. **Location:** Rural, simple, isolated, quiet.
**Surface:** metalled. 01/01-31/12.
**Distance:** 2km 1km on the spot on the spot.

### Sankt Martin | 16H2

**Weingut Schreieck**, Friedhofstrasse 8. **GPS:** n49,30060 e8,10565.

---

17 15 Ch WC included.
**Location:** Rural, comfortable, quiet. **Surface:** grasstiles.
01/01-31/12.
**Distance:** on the spot 5km 350m on the spot on the spot.
**Remarks:** Bread-service.

### Sankt Martin | 16H2

**Weinkellerei Ziegler**, Mühlstrasse 26. **GPS:** n49,29921 e8,10028.
3 € 10 . 01/01-31/12.
**Distance:** on the spot 5km 550m.
**Remarks:** Reservation recommended.

### Sankt Martin | 16H2

**Winzer Holger Schneider**, Riedweg. **GPS:** n49,29814 e8,10824.

10 free for clients, € 1/pp tourist tax. **Surface:** gravel.
01/01-31/12.
**Distance:** 300m on the spot.

### Sankt Martin | 16H2

**Consulat des Weins**, Maikammerer strasse 44.
**GPS:** n49,29830 e8,10845.

10 guests free, tourist tax € 1.
**Location:** Urban, simple, quiet. **Surface:** gravel.
01/01-31/12.
**Distance:** 4,5km on the spot 100m on the spot on the
spot.

### Sankt Martin | 16H2

Riedweg 13-9. **GPS:** n49,29814 e8,10824.
€ 1/8minutes ChWC. 01/01-31/12.

### Sankt Wendel | 16F1

**Am Wendelinuspark**, Tholeyer Straße. **GPS:** n49,46907 e7,14267.

12 € 5 Ch included. **Location:** Urban, simple.
**Surface:** metalled. 01/01-31/12.
**Distance:** 1km on the spot 100m on the spot.
**Remarks:** Caution key service € 10, tickets Wendelinusbad.

### Schiersfeld | 16G1

**Sulzbachtal**, Bismarkstraße. **GPS:** n49,69274 e7,76895.

DE

8 ⑅free 🚰€ 1 Ch ⚡(8x)€ 1/4kWh ⚹.
**Location:** Rural, simple, quiet. **Surface:** gravel. ⬛ 01/01-31/12.
**Distance:** 🚾500m ⊗4km 🛒bakery 500m 🚲Moscheltalradweg 🚶on the spot.

| | Schleich | 16F1 |

**Zum Moselufer**, Am Moselufer. **GPS:** n49,81335 e6,84228. ⬆➡.

6 ⑅€ 5 🚰🛢Ch⚡€ 2 WC. 🚿 **Surface:** grassy. ⬛ 01/01-31/12.
**Distance:** ⚓on the spot 🎣on the spot ⊗on the spot 🚾200m.
**Remarks:** Along the Moselle river.

| | Schwabenheim/Selz | 11H3 |

**Reisemobilstellplatz Schwabenheim**, Ingelheimer Straße.
**GPS:** n49,93284 e8,09430. ⬆➡.

10 ⑅free ⚡(12x)free. **Location:** Rural, comfortable, quiet.
**Surface:** grasstiles. ⬛ 01/01-31/12.
**Distance:** 🚾200m 🏍8,5km ⊗200m 🚲on the spot 🚶on the spot.
**Remarks:** Max. 96h free, then € 3/24h.

| | Schwabenheim/Selz | 11H3 |

**Weingut Schuck Sonnenhof**, Ausserhalb 6.
**GPS:** n49,93130 e8,09117. ⬆.

3 ⑅€ 5 ⚡(2x)included WC. **Location:** Rural, comfortable, quiet.
**Surface:** grassy/gravel. ⬛ 01/01-31/12.
**Distance:** 🚾500m 🏍9km ⊗50m.

| | Schweich/Mosel bei Trier | 16F1 |

**Wohnmobilpark zum Fahrturm**, Am Yachthafen.
**GPS:** n49,81455 e6,75038. ➡.

40 ⑅<7m € 12, 2 pers. incl., + € 1/m, dog € 2,10 🚰🛢Ch⚡€ 0,60/
kWh,+ € 1 🚿€ 0,50 ⊗€ 3 ⚹against payment. 🚿
**Surface:** grassy. ⬛ 01/04-31/10.
**Distance:** ⚓on the spot 🎣on the spot ⊗on the spot 🚾on the spot

---

🚾50m 🚲on the spot 🚶on the spot.
**Remarks:** Boat rental.

| | Selzen | 16H1 |

**Weingut Kapellenhof**, Kapellenstrasse 18.
**GPS:** n49,86484 e8,25528. ⬆.

4 ⑅€ 5 🚰⚡(4x)included. 🚿 **Location:** Rural, simple, quiet.
**Surface:** grasstiles. ⬛ 01/01-31/12.
**Distance:** 🚾on the spot 🏍10km ⊗100m 🚾2km.

| | Siefersheim | 16H1 |

**Weingut Sommer**, Mühlweg 19. **GPS:** n49,79850 e7,95245. ⬆.

6 ⑅€ 7 🚰🛢Ch⚡(6x)included WC. 🚿 **Location:** Rural, simple.
**Surface:** grassy. ⬛ 01/04-31/10.
**Distance:** 🏍8km ⊗2km 🚾2km 🚲on the spot.

| | Sinzig | 11F2 |

**Wohnmobilhafen am Sportplatz**, Bäderstrasse.
**GPS:** n50,55128 e7,21731. ⬆.

10 ⑅€ 6/24h 🚰€ 1 🛢Ch⚡(12x)€ 0,50/kWh WC🚿€ 1/1,at Freibad.
🚐 **Location:** Rural, simple. **Surface:** gravel.
⬛ 01/01-31/12.
**Distance:** 🏍7km ⊗800m 🚲on the spot 🚶on the spot.

| | Sinzig | 11F2 |

**Sinziger Schloß**, Jahnstrasse. **GPS:** n50,54684 e7,24844. ⬆.

20 ⑅free. **Location:** Urban, simple. **Surface:** metalled.
⬛ 01/01-31/12.
**Distance:** 🚾100m 🚾on the spot.

| | Sinzig | 11F2 |

**Wohnmobilhafen am Thermalfreibad**, Bäderstrasse.
**GPS:** n50,54912 e7,21749. ⬆.

50 ⑅€ 6/24h 🚰€ 1 🛢Ch⚡(18x)€ 0,50/kWh 🚿€ 1/pp. 🚐

---

**Location:** Rural, simple. **Surface:** metalled.
⬛ 01/01-31/12.
**Distance:** ⊗50m 🚲on the spot 🚶on the spot.

| | Speyer | 16H2 |

**Techniek Museum Speyer**, Geibstrasse. **GPS:** n49,31222 e8,45009. ⬆.

90 ⑅€ 22 🚰🛢Ch⚡WC🚿included. 🚿
**Location:** Urban, comfortable, central, noisy. **Surface:** grassy.
⬛ 01/01-31/12.
**Distance:** 🚾on the spot 🏍8,5km ⊗150m 🚾200m 🚲on the spot 🚶on the spot.
**Remarks:** Bread-service, discount museum and theater.
**Tourist information Speyer:**
Ⓜ Technik Museum Speyer/Imax Filmtheater, Geibstrasse. ⬛ Mo-Fr
9-18h, Sa-Su 9-17h.

| | Spirkelbach | 16G2 |

**Grillplatz Spirkelbach**. **GPS:** n49,19454 e7,88208. ⬆.

4 ⑅€ 7 🚰🛢Ch⚡WCincluded. 🚿 **Location:** Rural, simple, quiet.
**Surface:** gravel. ⬛ 01/01-31/12.
**Distance:** 🚾500m ⊗2km 🚾500m 🚾2km 🚲on the spot 🚶on the spot.
**Remarks:** Check in on arrival, tel: 0171 3355971, grill and picknic area,
nature reserve Pfalzer Wald.

| | Sprendlingen | 16H1 |

**Wiesbach**, Bachgasse/Bleichstrasse. **GPS:** n49,85424 e7,98538. ⬆➡.

24 ⑅€ 4 🚰€ 2/10minutes 🛢Ch⚡(24x)€ 2/day. 🚿
**Location:** Rural, comfortable, quiet. **Surface:** asphalted.
⬛ 01/01-31/12.
**Distance:** 🚾700m 🏍3,4km ⊗500m 🚾900m 🚶on the spot.
**Remarks:** Parking at swimming pool, bread-service, entrance
swimming pool € 2/day.

| | Sprendlingen | 16H1 |

**Weingut Annenhof**, Außerhalb 13. **GPS:** n49,85778 e7,99278. ⬆.

4 ⑅free 🚰⚡WC🚿free. **Location:** Rural, simple. **Surface:** concrete.
⬛ 01/01-31/12.
**Distance:** 🏍3km ⊗500m 🚾800m.

| | Sprendlingen | 16H1 |

**Weingut Hembd**, Karlstrasse 24a. **GPS:** n49,86422 e7,98811. ⬆.

10 ☐€ 10 ⌁⚡ included. ♨ **Location:** Rural, simple.
**Surface:** grassy. ☐ 01/01-31/12.
**Distance:** ⚓4km ⊗500m ⚑500m.

### Sprendlingen 16H1

**Eura Mobil Stellplatz**, Graf-von-Sponheimstrasse.
**GPS:** n49,86297 e7,97612.⬆.

38 ☐free ⌁€ 1/100liter ⊟Ch ⚡(38x)free. **Location:** Rural, simple,
quiet. **Surface:** asphalted/metalled. ☐ 01/01-31/12.
**Distance:** ⚓600m ⚓4,4km ⚑300m.
**Remarks:** Workdays from 9h guided tours (free).

### Stadecken-Elsheim 11H3

**Weingut Mengel-Eppelmann**, Mühlstrasse 16.
**GPS:** n49,91575 e8,12107.⬆.

5 ☐€ 5, free for clients ⌁⚡included. **Location:** Rural, comfortable,
quiet. **Surface:** asphalted. ☐ 01/01-31/12.
**Distance:** ⚓on the spot ⚓6km ⊗on the spot ⚑1km.
**Remarks:** Playground.

### Stadtkyll 11F3

Kurallee. **GPS:** n50,35290 e6,52820.⬆.

2 ☐free. **Location:** Urban, simple, central. **Surface:** metalled.
☐ 01/01-31/12.
**Distance:** ⚓300m ⊗100m.

### Stromberg 11G3

**Reisemobilplatz Michelsland**, Königsberger Straße 1e.
**GPS:** n49,94709 e7,78818.⬆➡.

6 ☐€ 5 ⌁⊟Chincluded ⚡(6x)€ 0,50/kWh.♨
**Location:** Comfortable, quiet. **Surface:** grassy. ☐ 01/01-31/12.
**Distance:** ⚓500m ⚓500m ⚑50m Lidl.

### Thalfang ⛷❄ 16F1

**Wohnmobilstellplatz Thalfang**, Talstrasse 2.
**GPS:** n49,75103 e6,99902.⬆➡.

25 ☐€ 10 ⌁⊟Ch ⚡(6x)included. **Location:** Urban, simple, quiet.
**Surface:** grassy/gravel. ☐ 01/01-31/12 ☐ 21/09-30/09.
**Distance:** ⚓200m ⊘on the spot ⟶on the spot ⊗on the spot
⚑200m ⚓200m ♨on the spot.
**Remarks:** Max. 4 nights, check in at swimming pool.

### Thalfang ⛷❄ 16F1

**Ferienpark Himmelberg**, Birkenweg 73. **GPS:** n49,74835 e6,98721.⬆.

2 ☐free. **Location:** Rural, simple. **Surface:** metalled.
☐ 01/01-31/12.
**Distance:** ⚓300m.

### Thallichtenberg ♨ 16G1

**Burg Lichtenberg**, K23. **GPS:** n49,55716 e7,35975.⬆➡.

4 ☐free. **Location:** Rural, simple, quiet. **Surface:** asphalted
☐ 01/01-31/12.
**Distance:** ⚓7km ⊗300m ⚑1km.
**Remarks:** Max. 3 days.

### Tholey 16F1

**Parkplatz Am Schaumburg**, Am Schaumberg.
**GPS:** n49,48965 e7,03804.⬆.

±20 ☐free. **Location:** Rural, simple, quiet. **Surface:** metalled.
☐ 01/01-31/12.
**Distance:** ⚓500m ⊗100m ♨on the spot ♨on the spot.

### Traben-Trarbach ♨⚓ 11F3

**Wohnmobilstellplatz am Mosel**, Rissbacherstraße 155.
**GPS:** n49,96583 e7,10583.⬆.
45 ☐€ 12 ⌁⊟Ch ⚡(45x),6Amp WC ⊟📶included. ⛽
**Location:** Rural, comfortable. **Surface:** grassy/gravel.
☐ 01/04-31/12.
**Distance:** ⚓500m ⊘on the spot ⟶on the spot ⊗500m ⚑200m
⚓100m ♣on the spot.
**Remarks:** Along the Moselle river.

### Trechtinghausen 11G3

**Camping Marienort**, Mainzer Straße. **GPS:** n50,00426 e7,85516.⬆➡.

20 ☐€ 15, 2 pers.incl ⌁⊟Chincluded ⚡€ 2/24h WC⊟€ 1.
**Location:** Rural, comfortable, quiet.
**Surface:** grassy.
☐ 01/01-31/12.
**Distance:** ⚓2km ⊘on the spot ⟶on the spot ⊗on the spot ⚑650m
♨on the spot ♣on the spot.
**Remarks:** Bread-service, sanitary at campsite, narrow entrance.

### Trier ⚓ 16F1

**Reisemobilpark Treviris**, In den Moselauen.
**GPS:** n49,74092 e6,62502.⬆➡.

110 ☐€ 0,20/h 10-18h, € 10,60/18-10h ⌁€ 1/100liter ⊟Ch ⚡
(62x)€ 0,70/kWh WC€ 0,40 ⊟€ 1/3minutes.⛽
**Location:** Urban. **Surface:** grasstiles.
☐ 01/01-31/12.
**Distance:** ⚓3km ⚓6km ⊗400m McDonald's ⚑1km ♨on the spot.
**Remarks:** Along the Moselle river, bread-service.

### Trier ⚓ 16F1

**Weingut Vonnell**, Im Tiergarten 12. **GPS:** n49,73840 e6,65914.⬆➡.

15 ☐€ 10 ⌁⚡included. **Surface:** grassy/gravel.

DE

◘ 01/01-31/12.
**Distance:** 🚶3km 🚲7km ⊗2km 🚊1,5km 🚌3km.
**Remarks:** Bread-service.
**Tourist information Trier:**
ℹ Tourist Information, An der Porta Nigra, www.trier.de. Old Roman city with the best kept and also largest Roman gate in Europe: Porta Nigra.
ℹ Triercard. Free city bus and discount at museums, boat trips, swimming pool etc. 🎫 € 9,90, family card € 21, 3 days.

**Moselpromenade Reisemobilplatz Trittenheim**, Moselstrasse. **GPS:** n49,82436 e6,90295. ⬆➡.

30 🚐 € 6,50 🚰 € 0,50/100liter 🗑Ch 🚿(30x)€ 3/24h. 🛵
**Location:** Rural. **Surface:** grassy/metalled. ◘ 01/01-31/12.
**Distance:** 🚶500m 🚲19km ⊼on the spot 🎣on the spot ⊗300m 🚊400m.
**Remarks:** Along the Moselle river, bread-service.

**P3, Parkplatz Hallenbad**, Kamenerstrasse. **GPS:** n50,59776 e7,21962. ⬆.

6 🚐free 🚰€ 1/80liter 🗑ChWC. **Location:** Urban.
**Surface:** asphalted. ◘ 01/01-31/12.
**Distance:** 🚶100m 🎣100m 🚊150m on the spot.

**Wohnmobilhafen am Rhein**, Kaltenengerser Straße 3. **GPS:** n50,41849 e7,52448. ⬆.

24 🚐€ 7,50 🚰€ 1/4minutes 🗑Ch 🚿(24x)€ 1/8h WC € 1,50 🚗.
**Surface:** metalled. ◘ 01/01-31/12.
**Distance:** 🚶on the spot 🚲5km ⊼on the spot 🎣on the spot ⊗350m 🚌300m.
**Remarks:** Along the Rhine river, bread-service.

**Panorama-Mobilstellplatz Ürzig**, Moselufer B53. **GPS:** n49,97837 e7,00700. ⬆.

25 🚐€ 9,50 🚰🗑Chincluded 🚿€ 1,50/day. 🛵
**Location:** Comfortable, quiet. **Surface:** grassy. ◘ 01/04-31/10.
**Distance:** 🚲9km ⊼on the spot 🚊bakery 150m 🚴on the spot 🚶on the spot.
**Remarks:** Along the Moselle river.

Raffeisenstrasse. **GPS:** n50,12740 e6,27170. ⬆.

15 🚐€ 5 🚰€ 0,50/80liter 🗑Ch 🚿(2x)€ 0,50/kWh WC.
**Location:** Rural, comfortable, isolated, quiet. **Surface:** gravel.
◘ 01/01-31/12.
**Distance:** ⊗6,5km 🚊6,5km on the spot.

Rheinufer. **GPS:** n50,39749 e7,61277. ⬆.

3 🚐free 🚰🗑. **Location:** Urban, simple.
**Surface:** asphalted/metalled. ◘ 01/01-31/12.
**Distance:** 🚶centre 500m 🚲3km ⊼on the spot ⊗200m 🚊Aldi 200m.
**Remarks:** Along railwayline, Max. ^3m.

Moselweinstrasse. **GPS:** n50,14271 e7,21292. ⬆.

10 🚐€ 6. 🛵 **Location:** Rural, simple. **Surface:** gravel.
◘ 01/01-31/12.
**Distance:** 🚶100m ⊼on the spot ⊗100m 🚴on the spot 🚶on the spot.

**Wohnmobilpark Veldenz**, Hauptstrasse, K88. **GPS:** n49,89222 e7,01944. ➡.

40 🚐€ 6 🚰🗑Ch 🚿(24x)included 🗑€ 2. 🛵 **Location:** Rural.
**Surface:** grassy. ◘ 01/01-31/12.
**Distance:** 🚶300m ⊗300m 🚊300m 🚌200m.

**Weltkulturerbe Völklinger Hütte**, Rathausstraße. **GPS:** n49,24730 e6,84492. ➡.

10 🚐free 🚰€ 1/80liter 🗑Ch 🚿(6x)€ 0,25/h.
**Location:** Urban, simple, central, noisy. **Surface:** asphalted.
◘ 01/01-31/12.
**Distance:** 🚶500m 🚲1,1km ⊗400m 🚊850m 🚌on the spot 🚴on the spot.
**Remarks:** Visitors centre Industrial Heritage.

**Weingut Rudolf Hein**, Hauptstrasse 38. **GPS:** n49,63860 e8,16832. ⬆.

8 🚐€ 6 🚰🗑included 🚿(6x)€ 2/24h. 🛵 **Location:** Rural, simple, quiet. **Surface:** grassy. ◘ 01/01-31/12.
**Distance:** 🚲10km ⊗1km 🚊3km 🚌1km.

**An der Stadthalle**, Franz-Haas-Straße. **GPS:** n49,54188 e6,89232. ⬆➡.

10 🚐free 🚰€ 0,50 🚿(8x)€ 1/day 📶free.
**Location:** Urban, simple, central, quiet. **Surface:** metalled.
◘ 01/01-31/12.
**Distance:** 🚶on the spot ⊼3km ⊗on the spot 🚊100m.
**Remarks:** Parking in centre.

**Noswendeler See**, Seestrasse. **GPS:** n49,52021 e6,86387. ⬆.

5 🚐free. **Location:** Rural, simple. **Surface:** grassy/metalled.
◘ 01/01-31/12.
**Distance:** ⊼on the spot 🎣on the spot 🚊3km.

**Zum Wiesental**, Nunkirchen. **GPS:** n49,48866 e6,83575. ⬆➡.

5 🚐free. **Location:** Rural, simple, quiet. **Surface:** metalled.
◘ 01/01-31/12.
**Distance:** 🚶on the spot ⊗on the spot 🚊on the spot.

**Hotel Pension Steil**, Schlossstrasse 2, Lockweiler. **GPS:** n49,52765 e6,90158.

DE

4 🛏 guests free. **Surface:** metalled. 🅾 01/01-31/12.
**Distance:** 🚶1km ⊗on the spot 🛒500m.

| 🍴 | **Wadern** | 16F1 |

**Hotel Restaurant Reidelbacher Hof**, Reidelbach 5, Reidelbach.
**GPS:** n49,57727 e6,86866. ⬆.

5 🛏 € 5, guests free. 🚐 **Location:** Rural, simple, isolated, quiet.
**Surface:** asphalted. 🅾 01/01-31/12.
**Distance:** 🚶3km ✈ 9km ⊗on the spot 🛒3km.

**Tourist information Wadern:**

ℹ Tourist Information, Marktplatz 13, www.wadern.de. Nature reserve
Saar Hunsrück, many signposted cycle and hiking routes.

| 🚐S | **Waldfischbach-Burgalben** 👥 🚳 | 16G2 |

**In den Bruchwiesen**, Carentaner Platz.
**GPS:** n49,28155 e7,64772. ⬆➡.

6 🛏 free 🚰€ 1/80liter 🔌Ch🚿€ 1/8h. **Location:** Simple, central,
quiet. **Surface:** asphalted. 🅾 01/01-31/12.
**Distance:** 🚶600m ⊗100m.
**Remarks:** Behind gymnasium.

| 🚐S | **Waldmohr** | 16G2 |

**Wohnmobilstellplatz am Freibad**, Badstraße 12.
**GPS:** n49,38958 e7,33886. ➡.

2 🛏 free 🚰 1/80liter 🔌Ch🚿(4x)€ 1/2kWh.
**Location:** Urban, simple, central, quiet. **Surface:** metalled.
🅾 01/01-31/12.
**Distance:** 🚶500m 🛒400m.
**Remarks:** At swimming pool.

| 🚐S | **Waxweiler** 🌿 | 11E3 |

**Wohnmobilplatz Waxweiler**, Bahnhofstrasse.
**GPS:** n50,09401 e6,35669. ➡.

15 🛏 € 7 🚰 € 1 🔌Ch🚿€ 2. **Location:** Rural, simple, quiet.
**Surface:** metalled. 🅾 01/01-31/12.
**Distance:** 🚶on the spot ⊗1km 🛒500m.

| 🚐S | **Weiskirchen** 👥 🚳 | 16F1 |

**Wohnmobil Oase Schwarzrinder Seen**, Schwarzrinder See 1A.
**GPS:** n49,52564 e6,83060. ⬆➡.

17 🛏 € 10 🚰🔌Ch🚿📶 included. 🚲
**Location:** Rural, comfortable, isolated, quiet. **Surface:** gravel/sand.
🅾 15/04-31/10.
**Distance:** 🏊on the spot 🚶on the spot ⊗on the spot 🚴 on the spot
🎣 on the spot.
**Remarks:** Bread-service.

| 🚐S | **Weiskirchen** 👥 🚳 | 16F1 |

**Am Kurpark**, Burgstrasse. **GPS:** n49,55868 e6,81810. ⬆.

6 🛏 € 1,40/pp 🚰€ 0,50/40liter 🔌€ 0,50 Ch🚿€ 0,50/kWh. 🚐
**Location:** Rural. **Surface:** metalled. 🅾 01/01-31/12.
**Distance:** 🚶on the spot ⊗500m 🛒300m.
**Remarks:** Parking at the health resort, max. 2-3 days, pay at tourist office.

| ⚓ | **Westerburg** | 11H2 |

**Am Segelhafen**, Seestrasse, Pottum. **GPS:** n50,59526 e7,99860. ⬆.

10 🛏 free. **Location:** Rural, simple, quiet. **Surface:** metalled.
🅾 01/01-31/12.
**Distance:** 🚶250m 🏊on the spot 🚶on the spot ⊗250m.

| 🚐S | **Westhofen** | 16H1 |

**Parkplatz Nickelgarten**, Am Nickelgarten.
**GPS:** n49,70559 e8,24672. ⬆.

15 🛏 free 🚿(12x)€ 1/8h. **Location:** Rural. **Surface:** gravel.
🅾 01/01-31/12.
**Distance:** 🚶100m ✈ 4km ⊗100m.
**Remarks:** Max. 3 days, service at petrol station.

| 🍇S | **Westhofen** | 16H1 |

**Weingut Dreihornmühle**, An der Brennerei.
**GPS:** n49,70375 e8,25288. ⬆.

3 🛏 € 5 🚿€ 1/day. 🚐 **Location:** Rural. **Surface:** grassy.
🅾 01/01-31/12.
**Distance:** 🚶600m ⊗600m 🛒150m.
**Remarks:** Max. 24h.

| S | **Westhofen** | 16H1 |

**Tankstelle Raiffeisen**. **GPS:** n49,70039 e8,24699. ⬆.

🚰🔌Ch. 🅾 01/01-31/12.
**Remarks:** Coins at petrol station.

| 🍇S | **Weyher** 🌿 | 16H2 |

**Weingut Möwes**, Hübühl 10. **GPS:** n49,26982 e8,08663. ⬆.

2 🛏 € 8 🚿included. **Location:** Rural, quiet. **Surface:** metalled.
🅾 01/01-31/12.
**Distance:** 🚶200m ✈ 7km ⊗400m.

| 🍇S | **Weyher** 🌿 | 16H2 |

**Weingut Valentin Ziegler Sohn**, Hübühl 9.
**GPS:** n49,26937 e8,08609. ⬆.

2 🛏 € 5 🚰included 🚿on demand WC. 🚲 **Location:** Rural, quiet.
**Surface:** grassy. 🅾 01/01-31/12.
**Distance:** 🚶200m ✈ 7km ⊗300m.

| 🚐S | **Wintrich** 🚳 | 16F1 |

**Mosel Stellplatz Wintrich**, Moselstrasse.
**GPS:** n49,88417 e6,94833. ⬆➡.

90 🛏 € 9 🚰 € 1/100liter 🔌Ch🚿(90x) WC€ 0,50 ⚡€ 1/5minutes
📶included. 🚐 **Location:** Rural, comfortable, quiet.
**Surface:** grassy/gravel. 🅾 01/04-31/10.
**Distance:** 🚶on the spot 🏊on the spot 🚶on the spot ⊗100m
🛒200m 🚏200m 🚴on the spot 🎣on the spot.
**Remarks:** Along the Moselle river.

| 🍇S | **Wintrich** 🚳 | 16F1 |

**Weingut Clemens**, Kurfürstenstrasse 11.
**GPS:** n49,89000 e6,95416. ⬆➡.

DE

20 🚐 € 6,50-8,50 🚰 € 2 🗑 Ch 🚿 € 2 WC. ⚡
**Surface:** gravel/metalled. 🕐 01/01-31/12.
**Distance:** 🚶on the spot ⛵800m 🚲800m ⊗on the spot 🛒1km 🚴Moselradweg 🏃on the spot.

### Wissen 🛈 🌲 11G2
**Hahnhof**, Nistertalstraße. **GPS:** n50,76106 e7,72083. ⬆.

25 🚐 € 5 🗑 Ch 🚿 € 1/kWh WC 🚽 € 1,50. **Location:** Rural, isolated, quiet. **Surface:** gravel. 🕐 01/01-31/12.
**Distance:** 🚶2,5km ⊗on the spot 🛒2,5km 🚴on the spot.

### Wittlich 🍺 11F3
**Zweibächen**, Hasenmühlenweg. **GPS:** n49,99470 e6,87595. ⬆➡.

30 🚐 € 5/24h 🚿 € 1/80liter 🗑Ch. **Location:** Rural, simple.
**Surface:** grassy. 🕐 01/01-31/12.
**Distance:** 🚶1,3km ⊗4km 🛒1km 🚴1km.
**Remarks:** Max. 3 days, to be paid at swimming pool, service 50m.

### Worms 16H1
**Wohnmobilhafen**, Kastanienallee. **GPS:** n49,63458 e8,37513. ⬆➡.

30 🚐 € 5/24h 🚰 € 1 🗑Ch 🚿 (12x)€ 1/8h WC. 🚗
**Surface:** gravel. 🕐 01/01-31/12.
**Distance:** 🚶15 min walking 🚲7km ⛵Rhine promenade ⊗300m 🛒500m 🚌on the spot.
**Remarks:** Along river, service at Gaststätte Hagenbräu 300m from the parking, playground.

### Wörrstadt 16H1
**Spargelhof Weinmann**, Rommersheimer Strasse 105.
**GPS:** n49,83446 e8,10673. ⬆.

3 🚐 € 6 🚰 (6x)included. ⚡ **Location:** Rural, simple, central, quiet.
**Surface:** gravel. 🕐 01/01-31/12.
**Distance:** 🚶300m 🚲4km ⊗300m 🛒300m 🚌1,5km.

### Wörth am Rhein 🛈 16H2
**Sporthalle**, Waldstrasse, Schaidt. **GPS:** n49,05220 e8,08533. ⬆.

10 🚐free 🚰 € 1/100liter Ch 🚿(4x)€ 1/4h. **Location:** Rural, simple, isolated, quiet. **Surface:** gravel. 🕐 01/01-31/12.
**Distance:** 🚶500m ⊗250m 🛒400m.

### Zell/Mosel 🌲 11F3
**Wohnmobilstellplatz Römerquelle**, Am Freizeitzentrum, Kaimt.
**GPS:** n50,01632 e7,17662. ⬆➡.

70 🚐 € 7 🚿 € 1/100liter 🗑Ch 🚿 € 1/2kWh. ⚡ **Location:** Rural, comfortable. **Surface:** grassy/metalled. 🕐 01/01-31/12.
**Distance:** 🚶1km ⛵on the spot 🚌on the spot ⊗500m 🛒1km.
**Remarks:** Along the Moselle river, bread-service.

### Zell/Mosel 🏖 🌲 11F3
**Am Fussgängerbrücke. GPS:** n50,02991 e7,17754. ⬆.

23 🚐 € 7 🚿 € 0,50/90liter 🗑Ch 🚽 € 2,at camp site. ⚡
**Location:** Simple, quiet. **Surface:** asphalted. 🕐 Easter-31/10.
**Distance:** 🚶300m ⛵on the spot 🚌on the spot ⊗200m 🛒300m.

### Zeltingen-Rachtig 🌲 11F3
**Wohnmobilstellplatz Zeltingen**, An der Brücke.
**GPS:** n49,95478 e7,00942. ⬆.

45 🚐 € 10 🚰 🗑Ch 🚿(34x) 📶included. 🚗 📹 🚴
**Location:** Rural, simple, quiet. **Surface:** grasstiles.
🕐 18/03-15/11 🔵 high water.
**Distance:** 🚶50m 🚲9km 🚌on the spot ⊗300m 🛒700m 🚌on the spot 🚴on the spot 🏃on the spot.

### Zweibrücken 🏖 🍺 16G2
**Wohnmobilplatz am Freizeitpark an der Schließ**, Geschwister-Scholl-Allee 11. **GPS:** n49,25370 e7,37632. ⬆.

23 🚐 € 10-13 🚰 € 1/100liter 🗑Ch 🚿 € 0,60/kWh WC🚽included

---

🔌 € 2/2. 🚗 🚴 **Location:** Urban, comfortable, central, quiet.
**Surface:** gravel. 🕐 01/01-31/12.
**Distance:** 🚶500m 🚌on the spot 🚌100m.
**Remarks:** Check in at hotel.

# Hesse

### Aarbergen 11H3
**Im Brühl**, Hauptstraße 58, Michelbach. **GPS:** n50,23099 e8,05988. ⬆➡.

10 🚐 € 5 🚰 🗑Ch 🚿included. **Location:** Rural, quiet.
**Surface:** asphalted. 🕐 01/01-31/12.
**Distance:** ⊗300m.
**Remarks:** Max. 5 days, dog on leads.

### Alsfeld 🌿 12A2
**Erlenstadion**, Fulder Weg. **GPS:** n50,74844 e9,27947. ⬆➡.

40 🚐 € 5 🚿 € 1 🚰 € 1 Ch 🚿 € 0,50/kWh WC🚽. 🚗
**Location:** Urban, simple. **Surface:** metalled. 🕐 01/01-31/12.
**Distance:** 🚶200m 🚲1,8km ⊗400m 🛒400m.

### Alsfeld 🍴🛈 🌿 12A2
**Hotel zum Schäferhof**, A20 dir Eudorf. **GPS:** n50,76742 e9,29048. ⬆.

5 🚐free 🚿 € 7. **Location:** Urban, simple, quiet. **Surface:** metalled.
🕐 01/01-31/12.
**Distance:** 🚶2km ⊗on the spot 🛒500m.
**Remarks:** Check in at hotel, use of a meal desired.

### Amöneburg 12A2
**In den Lückeäckern. GPS:** n50,79554 e8,93135. ⬆.

4 🚐free 🚽. **Location:** Rural, simple, quiet. 🕐 01/01-31/12.
**Distance:** 🚶Old city centre 1km ⊗500m 🛒500m.
**Remarks:** Parking tennishall.

## Bad Arolsen  10A3

### Reisemobilhafen Twistesee Bad Arolsen

- **Located directly at lake**
- **Located in a quiet area**
- **Dogs beach**

www.reisemobilhafen-twistesee.de
info@reisemobilhafen-twistesee.de

**Reisemobilhafen Twistesee**, Bericher Seeweg 1, Wetterburg. **GPS**: n51,38396 e9,06546. 
130 € 12, tourist tax incl € 1/100liter Ch (120x)€ 0,50/kWh,16Amp WC € 1. 
**Location:** Rural, comfortable, luxurious, isolated. 
**Surface:** grassy/gravel. 01/01-31/12. 
**Distance:** 500m 50m 50m 800m 800m on the spot on the spot. 
**Remarks:** Directly at lake, bread-service, dogs beach.

## Bad Camberg  11H3

Jahnstraße. **GPS**: n50,29650 e8,26660. 

8 free € 0,50/day € 1 Ch € 1/2kWh. **Location:** Urban. 
**Surface:** gravel. 01/01-31/12 water: 01/12-31/03. 
**Distance:** 350m 2,5km 250m 300m.

## Bad Emstal  12A1

**Wohnmobilstellplatz Bad Emstal**, Karlsbader Straße 4. 
**GPS**: n51,24858 e9,24952. 

8 € 5 + € 1/pp tourist tax € 1/100liter Ch (12x)€ 1/8h. 
**Location:** Rural, comfortable. **Surface:** gravel/metalled. 
01/01-31/12. 
**Distance:** 1km on the spot on the spot on the spot.

## Bad Emstal  12A1

**Erzeberg**, Birkenstraße, Balhorn 21. **GPS**: n51,26927 e9,25147. 

20 € 5-12 + € 5/pp, dog € 1 Ch WC € 1 included. 
**Location:** Rural, simple. 
**Surface:** metalled. 
01/01-31/12. 
**Distance:** 100m on the spot on the spot. 
**Remarks:** Check in at campsite (100m), bread-service, use pool incl.

## Bad Endbach  11H2

**Kultur-, Sport- und Freizeitzentrum**, Am Bewegungsbad 4. 
**GPS**: n50,75669 e8,47875. 

18 € 5 + € 1,20 tourist tax Ch WC included,sanitary at spa resort. **Location:** Rural, simple, quiet. **Surface:** grasstiles. 
01/01-31/12. 
**Distance:** 1km on the spot 100m. 
**Remarks:** Check in at Lahn-Dill-Bergland-Therme 200m.

## Bad Hersfeld  12B1

**Geistalbad**, Am Schwimmbad. **GPS**: n50,87485 e9,70025. 

6 € 5 € 0,50/80liter Ch (6x)€ 0,50/kWh. 
**Location:** Urban, simple. **Surface:** asphalted/metalled. 
01/01-31/12 Lullusfest (Oct). 
**Distance:** 50m 3,9km 1km.

## Bad Hersfeld  12B1

**Acqua-fit**, Kolpingstraße 6. **GPS**: n50,86771 e9,72951. 
5 free. **Location:** Rural, simple. **Surface:** asphalted. 
01/01-31/12. 
**Distance:** 2km. 
**Remarks:** At swimming pool.

## Bad Hersfeld  12B1

Auf der Unteraue. **GPS**: n50,85764 e9,69786. 

3 free. **Surface:** metalled. 01/01-31/12. 
**Remarks:** At tennis-court.

## Bad Hersfeld  12B1

**Schilde-Park**, Seilerweg. **GPS**: n50,87092 e9,71179. 
4 free. **Surface:** metalled. 01/01-31/12. 
**Distance:** 500m 500m 550m.

## Bad Hersfeld  12B1

**Waldhotel Glimmesmühle**, Hombergerstraße. 
**GPS**: n50,88420 e9,66984. 

5 free with a meal included € 5. **Location:** Rural, simple. 
**Surface:** metalled. 01/01-31/12. 
**Distance:** on the spot 2km. 
**Tourist information Bad Hersfeld:** 
Lullusfest. Traditional folk festival for the honour of the founder of the city. week 16/10.

## Bad Karlshafen  10A3

**Am Rechten Weserufer**, Am Rechten Weserufer 2. 
**GPS**: n51,64508 e9,44953. 

12 € 11, 2 pers.incl € 0,50/100liter Ch (12x)€ 1/2kWh. 
**Location:** Central. **Surface:** grasstiles/grassy. 
01/01-31/12. 
**Distance:** on the spot on the spot on the spot on the spot on the spot on the spot. 
**Remarks:** Max. 4 days, check in at reception campsite.

## Bad König  17A1

**P3**, Am Bahndamm. **GPS**: n49,74312 e9,00320. 

9 € 5, free with use of spa (9x)included. 
**Location:** Urban, simple, central, noisy. **Surface:** metalled. 
01/01-31/12. 
**Distance:** 100m 100m 400m on the spot on the spot on the spot.

## Bad Nauheim  12A3

**Usa-Wellenbad**, Friedberger Strasse 16-20. 
**GPS**: n50,35352 e8,74305. 

40 € 5 WC. **Location:** Rural, simple, isolated. **Surface:** metalled. 
01/01-31/12. 
**Distance:** 1km on the spot 300m on the spot. 
**Remarks:** Max. 3 nights, check in at Wellenbad, 8-20h.

## Bad Orb  12A3

**Am Busbahnhof**, Austraße. **GPS**: n50,23014 e9,34659. 

4 € 7, tourist tax incl Ch (4x)WC included. 
**Location:** Urban, simple, central, noisy. **Surface:** metalled. 
01/01-31/12. 
**Distance:** 400m 450m 300m. 
**Remarks:** Historical centre.

## Bad Orb  12A3

**Am Kurpark**, Spessartstraße. **GPS**: n50,21700 e9,35477. 

DE

9 �𝔖 € 12, tourist tax incl ⌁ € 1/90liter ⬚Ch ⌁ € 1/8h. 🏠
**Location:** Rural, simple, quiet. **Surface:** gravel.
☐ 01/01-31/12.
**Distance:** 🚏1km � 6km ⊗200m 🛒1km 🚶on the spot.

**S Bad Salzschlirf** ♈ **12B2**
Riedstraße. **GPS:** n50,62090 e9,50304. ⬆️

10 �𝔖 € 4 ⌁ € 1 ⬚Ch ⌁ € 1. **Location:** Simple. **Surface:** asphalted.
☐ 01/01-31/12.
**Distance:** 🚏100m ⊗100m 🛒800m 🚗200m.

**S Bad Schwalbach** **11H3**
**Wohnmobilstellplatz im Stahlbrunnental**, Reitallee 21.
**GPS:** n50,13988 e8,06362. ⬆️➡️

4 �𝔖 free ⌁ € 0,50/50liter ⬚Ch ⌁ € 0,50/kWh. **Location:** Rural,
simple. **Surface:** metalled. ☐ 01/01-31/12.
**Distance:** 🚏500m ⊗400m.

**S Bad Soden-Salmünster** ♈♈ **12A3**
**Wohnmobilstellplatz Mernes**, Jossastraße.
**GPS:** n50,24152 e9,47728. ⬆️

6 ⟋€ 6 ⌁ € 0,50 ⬚Ch ⌁ (6x)€ 1. **Location:** Rural.
**Surface:** gravel/metalled. ☐ 01/01-31/12.
**Distance:** 🚏100m ⊗10m ⊗300m 🛒200m 🚗200m 🚲on the spot
🚶on the spot.

**S Bad Soden-Salmünster** ♈♈♈ **12A3**
**Spessart Therme**, Parkstraße 12, Bad Soden.
**GPS:** n50,28544 e9,35917. ⬆️➡️

33 ⟋€ 6, tourist tax incl ⌁ € 1/100liter ⬚Ch ⌁ (33x)€ 1/2kWh.
**Location:** Rural, luxurious, quiet. **Surface:** metalled.
☐ 01/01-31/12.
**Distance:** 🚏1km ⊗300m 🛒850m.

**Remarks:** Pay and coins at Spessart Therme.

**S Bad Sooden-Allendorf** ❧ **12B1**
**Reisemobilhafen Franzrasen**, Am Alten Festplatz, Allendorf.
**GPS:** n51,27149 e9,97209. ⬆️➡️

100 ⟋€ 8 ⌁ € 1/5minutes ⬚€ 0,50 Ch ⌁ (40x)€ 0,50/kWh,16Amp
⬚€ 2,50/30minutes. 🏠 **Location:** Rural, simple, isolated, quiet.
**Surface:** grassy/metalled. ☐ 01/01-31/12.
**Distance:** 🚏200m ⊗200m 🛒600m on the spot 🚶on the spot.
**Remarks:** Price including tourist taxes and public transport.

**S Bad Wildungen** ♈ **12A1**
**Wohnmobilstellplatz Bad Wildungen**, Bahnhofstrasse.
**GPS:** n51,12008 e9,13631. ⬆️➡️

16 ⟋€ 5 ⌁ € 1/45liter ⬚Ch ⌁ (15x)€ 1/2kWh. **Location:** Urban,
comfortable. **Surface:** grasstiles. ☐ 01/01-31/12.
**Distance:** 🚏1,5km ⊗350m on the spot 🚲on the spot.
**Remarks:** Max. 3 days.

**S Bad Wildungen** ♈ **12A1**
**Wohnmobilstellplatz Frekot**, Wiesenweg 23.
**GPS:** n51,11134 e9,06677.

15 ⟋€ 7,50, 2 pers. incl ⌁ ⬚Ch ⌁ € 0,33/kWh ⬚included ⬚€ 2.
❧ ☐ 01/01-31/12.
**Distance:** ⊗300m 🛒300m 🚲on the spot 🚶on the spot.
**Remarks:** Bread-service.

**S Bad Zwesten** ♈ **12A1**
**Reisemobilstellplatz**, Hardtstrasse 7. **GPS:** n51,05849 e9,17613. ⬆️

10 ⟋€ 6 ⌁ € 1/100liter ⬚Ch ⌁ (8x)€ 1/kWh. 📹
**Location:** Rural, comfortable, isolated, quiet.
**Surface:** gravel/metalled. ☐ 01/01-31/12.
**Distance:** 🚏400m ⊗400m 🛒300m.
**Remarks:** Max. 3 days.

**S Battenberg** ❄ **11H1**
**Festhalle Battenberg**, Festplatzweg. **GPS:** n51,00915 e8,63643. ⬆️➡️

5 ⟋free ⌁ ⬚Ch. **Location:** Rural, simple. **Surface:** gravel/metalled.
☐ 01/01-31/12.
**Distance:** 🚏1km ⊗1km 🛒400m.
**Remarks:** At community centre, service: Esso-station, Battenfelderstr. 6.

**S Battenberg** ❄ **11H1**
**Hallen- und Freibad**, Senonchesstraße. **GPS:** n51,01233 e8,63532. ⬆️

3 ⟋free ⌁ ⬚Ch. **Location:** Rural, simple. **Surface:** asphalted.
☐ 01/01-31/12.
**Distance:** 🚏300m 🏊100m on the spot 🛒on the spot 🚲on the
spot.
**Remarks:** Parking swimming pool, service: Esso-station, Battenfelderstr. 6.

**Tourist information Battenberg:**
👁 Besucherbergwerk Burgbergstollen. 150 years old mine shaft, can be
reached from Marktplatz. ☐ 01/05-30/09 1st Su of the month 14-17h.

**S Baunatal** ♈♈♈ **12A1**
**Parkstadion**. **GPS:** n51,25769 e9,39851. ⬆️➡️

16 ⟋€ 5/24h ⌁ € 1/100liter ⬚Ch ⌁ (16x)€ 0,50/kWh WC € 0,10. 🚗
**Location:** Rural, simple, quiet. **Surface:** grassy/gravel.
☐ 01/01-31/12.
**Distance:** 🚏500m � 4km 🚲on the spot 🚶on the spot.
**Remarks:** Max. 3 days.

**S Bebra** ⚑ **12B1**
**Natur- und Freizeitpark Fuldaaue Breitenbacher Seen**, Hersfelder
Straße. **GPS:** n50,95899 e9,78764. ⬆️

30 ⟋€ 5, € 18/week ⌁ € 1/100liter ⬚Ch ⌁ (18x)€ 0,50/kWh.
**Location:** Rural, comfortable. **Surface:** grassy. ☐ 01/04-31/10.
**Distance:** 🚏1km 🏊on the spot 🛒on the spot 🛒1km 🚲on the spot
🚶on the spot.

**Bebra** ⚑ **12B1**
**Am Schwimmbad**, Annastrasse 17. **GPS:** n50,97464 e9,79836. ⬆️➡️

DE

4 ⌷free. **Location:** Rural, simple. **Surface:** asphalted.
⌷ 01/01-31/12.
**Distance:** ⌷400m ⊗650m ⌷650m ⌷800m.
**Remarks:** Parking swimming pool.

### Bebra 🏕🚃 12B1
**Mehrzweckparkplatz**, Bei der Laupfütze/Rathausstrasse.
**GPS:** n50,97000 e9,79000.⬆.

10 ⌷free. **Location:** Rural, simple. **Surface:** metalled.
⌷ 01/01-31/12.
**Distance:** ⌷on the spot ⚹on the spot.

### Beerfelden 🌳❄ 17A1
**Parkplatz NordicCenter**, Seeweg. **GPS:** n49,56034 e8,97557.⬆.

4 ⌷free ⛽€0,50/50liter ⌷Ch ⚡(4x)€0,50/kWh.
**Location:** Rural, simple, quiet. **Surface:** asphalted.
⌷ 01/01-31/12.
**Distance:** ⌷1km ⌷1,5km ⚹on the spot ⚹on the spot.
**Remarks:** At sports park.

### Berkatal 12B1
Am Sportplatz. **GPS:** n51,23763 e9,91504.⬆➡.

3 ⌷free. **Location:** Rural, simple, isolated, quiet. **Surface:** asphalted.
⌷ 01/01-31/12.
**Distance:** ⌷800m ⊗500m ⚹on the spot.

### Biedenkopf 🌿🏕🌳❄ 11H1
**Parkplatz Stadtwerke**, Mühlweg 6. **GPS:** n50,90925 e8,52687.⬆➡.

4 ⌷€5/24h. ⚡€1/12h. **Location:** Urban, simple, central.
**Surface:** asphalted. ⌷ 01/01-31/12.
**Distance:** ⌷200m ⊗on the spot ⌷200m ⌷on the spot.
**Remarks:** Max. 3 days.

### Biedenkopf 🌿🏕🌳❄ 11H1
**Freizeitzentrum Sackpfeife**, An der Berggaststätte.
**GPS:** n50,94735 e8,53317.➡.

4 ⌷€5/24h. ⛽ **Location:** Rural, isolated, quiet. **Surface:** concrete.
⌷ 01/01-31/12.
**Distance:** ⊗on the spot ⚹on the spot ⚓on the spot.
**Remarks:** Max. 3 days.

### Biedenkopf 🌿🏕🌳❄ 11H1
**Halbersbacher Parkhotel Biedenkopf**, Auf dem Radeköppel 2.
**GPS:** n50,91183 e8,53515.⬆.

5 ⌷free with a meal. **Location:** Urban, simple. **Surface:** asphalted.
⌷ 01/01-31/12.
**Distance:** ⌷on the spot ⊗200m ⌷500m ⚹12km ⚓12km.

### Bischoffen 12H2
**P Aartalsee**, Am See. **GPS:** n50,70172 e8,46726.⬆.

10 ⌷€3/day, €5,50/night. **Surface:** grassy/gravel. ⌷ 01/01-31/12.
**Distance:** ⌷1,5km.

### Borken 🌳 12A1
**Borkener See**, Westrandstrasse. **GPS:** n51,04447 e9,27392.⬆.

2 ⌷free. **Location:** Rural, simple. **Surface:** asphalted.
⌷ 01/01-31/12.
**Distance:** ⌷500m ⛵4,5km ⌷100m ⚲1km ⌷500m.
**Remarks:** At swimming pool.

### Borken 🌳 12A1
**Naturbadesee Stockelache**, Kleinengliser Straße.
**GPS:** n51,06682 e9,24531.⬆.
3 ⌷€3. **Surface:** metalled. ⌷ 01/01-31/12.
**Distance:** ⛵650m ⚲Sandy beach ⚲on the spot ⊗on the spot
⌷Lidl-ReWe 3,7km ⚹on the spot ⚹on the spot.

### Borken 🌳 12A1
**Singliser See**, Main-Weser-Straße 60. **GPS:** n51,05598 e9,31303.
5 ⌷€3. **Location:** Rural. **Surface:** metalled. ⌷ 01/01-31/12.
**Distance:** ⌷Borken 2,4km ⚲on the spot ⌷700m ⚹on the spot ⚹on the spot.

### Braunfels 🌿 11H2
**Wohnmobilstation Schloss Braunfels**, Jahnplatz.
**GPS:** n50,51478 e8,38609.

4 ⌷€5, €7,50 service incl ⛽⌷Ch ⚹. **Location:** Rural, simple,
quiet. **Surface:** metalled. ⌷ 01/01-31/12.
**Distance:** ⌷on the spot ⊗350m ⌷550m ⚹on the spot.
**Remarks:** Pay and key service: Gasthof am Turm, Marktplatz 11, caution
€15.

### Breuberg 17A1
Bahnhofstraße 4, Neustadt. **GPS:** n49,81576 e9,04063.⬆➡➡.

4 ⌷free ⛽€1/5minutes ⌷Ch €1 ⚡(4x)€0,50/kWh.
**Location:** Urban, simple, central. **Surface:** asphalted.
⌷ 01/01-31/12.
**Distance:** ⌷on the spot ⊗300m ⌷550m ⚹on the spot.

### Breuna 🏕 10A3
**Märchenlandtherme**, Schulstraße. **GPS:** n51,41875 e9,18612.⬆.

3 ⌷free ⚹€3. **Surface:** gravel. ⌷ 01/01-31/12.
**Distance:** ⌷500m ⊗50m.

### Büdingen 🌿 12A3
Hinter der Meisterei 20. **GPS:** n50,29094 e9,12587.⬆.

8 ⌷free ⌷against payment. **Location:** Rural, simple, quiet.
**Surface:** metalled. ⌷ 01/01-31/12. **Distance:** ⌷Old city centre
750m ⊗500m. **Remarks:** At swimming pool, use sanitary only during
opening hours swimming pool.

### Büdingen 🌿 12A3
**Mühltorbrücke**, Mühltorstraße. **GPS:** n50,29051 e9,11581.⬆.

2 ⌷€5/5h WC. ⛽ **Surface:** metalled. ⌷ 01/01-31/12.
**Distance:** ⌷Old city centre 50m ⊗on the spot ⌷1km.
**Remarks:** Max. 2 nights.

### Büdingen 🌿 12A3
**Hotel-Restaurant Sonnenberg**, Sudetenstrasse 4.
**GPS:** n50,29044 e9,10038.

2 ⌄free. ☐ 01/01-31/12.
**Distance:** centre 800m on the spot 350m.
**Remarks:** Breakfest-service.

### ⚄S Burghaun 12B2
Oberste Straße. **GPS:** n50,69179 e9,73203. ⬆.

3 ⌄free 🚰€ 1/100liter Chfree ⚡(4x)€ 0,50/kWh.
**Location:** Urban, simple. **Surface:** asphalted. ☐ 01/01-31/12.
**Distance:** 800m 50m 150m.

### Calden 10A3
Waldschwimmbad Calden, Zum Lindenrondell.
**GPS:** n51,39420 e9,40064. ⬆.

3 ⌄free. **Location:** Rural, simple, isolated. **Surface:** grassy.
☐ 01/01-31/12.
**Distance:** 1km 1,5km 2km.

### ⚄S Diemelsee 9H3
Terrassenparkplatz Hohes Rad, Hohes Rad 1.
**GPS:** n51,36470 e8,71935. ⬆.

30 ⌄€ 5,60 WC . **Location:** Rural, simple, isolated.
**Surface:** grassy/gravel. ☐ 01/01-31/12.
**Distance:** Diemelsee on the spot 500m.
**Remarks:** Bread-service.

### ©S Diemelsee 9H3
Campingpark Hohes Rad, Hohes Rad 1. **GPS:** n51,36355 e8,71830. ⬆.

5 ⌄€ 5 + € 1,50/pp Ch ⚡€ 0,53/kWh WC included € 1/day.
**Location:** Rural, simple. **Surface:** grassy/gravel.
☐ 01/01-31/12.
**Distance:** on the spot on the spot 6km.

### ⚄S Diemelstadt 10A3
Autohof, Kupferkuhle. **GPS:** n51,49034 e9,00885. ⬆.
10 ⌄free 🚰€ 1 Ch€ 1. **Location:** Motorway.
**Surface:** asphalted. ☐ 01/01-31/12.
**Distance:** 500m on the spot 600m.

### ⚄S Diemelstadt 10A3
Steinberg. **GPS:** n51,50619 e9,00590.

---

4 ⌄free. **Location:** Rural. **Surface:** metalled. ☐ 01/01-31/12.
**Distance:** 1km 800m 1km.
**Remarks:** At sports park, swimming pool.

### ⚄S Dillenburg 11H2
Aquarena-Bad, Stadionstrasse. **GPS:** n50,73994 e8,27815. ⬆➡.

8 ⌄free 🚰€ 1/90liter Ch ⚡(6x)€ 1/8h. **Location:** Urban, simple.
**Surface:** asphalted. ☐ 01/01-31/12.
**Distance:** 300m 200m.

### ⚄S Edermünde 12A1
Aueweg, Grifte. **GPS:** n51,21252 e9,44905. ⬆.

6 ⌄€ 5 🚰€ 1/100liter Ch ⚡(6x)included15h,then € 1/3h.
**Location:** Rural, simple. **Surface:** asphalted.
☐ 01/01-31/12.
**Distance:** 300m 1,7km 300m 100m Premium-Radweg
R1 on the spot.

### ⚄S Edertal 12A1
Wohnmobilstellplatz Hemfurth/Edersee, Kraftwerkstrasse.
**GPS:** n51,17022 e9,05096. ⬆➡.

30 ⌄<8m € 6, >8m € 10 🚰€ 1/100liter Ch€ 1.
**Location:** Rural, simple. **Surface:** metalled. ☐ 01/01-31/12.
**Distance:** 500m on the spot 100m 500m.

### ⚄S Edertal 12A1
Wohnmobilstellplatz Rehbach, Am Eschelberg.
**GPS:** n51,18394 e9,02618. ⬆.

20 ⌄<8m € 6, >8m € 10. **Location:** Rural, simple. **Surface:** gravel.
☐ 01/01-31/12.
**Distance:** beach 200m on the spot.

### ⚄S Eltville am Rhein 11H3
Parkplatz Weinhohle, Weinhohle. **GPS:** n50,02832 e8,12406. ⬆.

---

+20 ⌄€ 5 🚰€ 1/60liter €1 Ch. **Location:** Urban, simple,
central. **Surface:** metalled. ☐ 01/01-31/12.
**Distance:** 200m 400m 50m.

### ⚄S Eltville am Rhein 11H3
Weingut Offenstein Erben, Wiesweg 13. **GPS:** n50,02871 e8,11728.
2 ⌄€ 15 WC included. **Location:** Rural, simple.
**Surface:** metalled. ☐ 01/01-31/12.
**Distance:** 1km.

### ⚄S Eltville am Rhein 11H3
Weinhof Martin, Bachhöller Weg 4, Erbach im Rheingau.
**GPS:** n50,02365 e8,08815.

4 ⌄€ 10 🚰 Ch ⚡ WC included . **Location:** Rural,
comfortable, quiet. **Surface:** metalled. ☐ 01/03-23/12.
**Distance:** 600m 400m.

### ⚄S Erbach 17A1
Alexanderbad, In der Stadtwiese. **GPS:** n49,66349 e8,98863. ⬆.

10 ⌄free 🚰€ 1/70liter Ch ⚡(6x)€ 0,50/kWh.
**Location:** Urban, simple, quiet. **Surface:** metalled.
☐ 01/01-31/12.
**Distance:** 800m 500m 100m 100m on the spot.
**Remarks:** Max. 72h.

### ⚄S Eschwege ❄ 12B1
Reisemobilhafen Werratalsee, Am werratalsee 2.
**GPS:** n51,19196 e10,06728. ⬆➡.

20 ⌄€ 11-16 🚰€ 0,50/40liter Ch ⚡(18x)€ 0,50/kWh WC use
sanitary € 3,30/pp. **Location:** Rural, simple, central, noisy.
**Surface:** metalled. ☐ 01/01-31/12.
**Distance:** 2km on the spot on the spot.
**Remarks:** Pay at bistro, service passerby € 4.

**Tourist information Eschwege:**
👁 Besuchbergwerk Grube Gustav, Höllethal, Meissner, Abterode. Slate
mine. ☐ 15/03-31/10 Tue-Su/holidays 13-16h.

### ⚄S Flörsbachtal-Lohrhaupten 👥 12B3
Am Schwimbad. **GPS:** n50,12178 e9,47258. ⬆➡.

---

10 🛏 € 9 🚰 Ch 🚿 € 1,50/24h WC included 🗑 against payment. 🔧
**Location:** Rural, comfortable, quiet. **Surface:** grassy/gravel.
🅾 01/01-31/12 🅾 Service: winter.
**Distance:** 🚶1km ⊗100m 🛒1km 🚲 on the spot 🚶 on the spot.
**Remarks:** Check in at Gartenstrasse 10a.

### Frankenberg/Eder  12A1
**Ederberglandhalle**, Teichweg 3. **GPS:** n51,05613 e8,80195. ⬆➡

4 🛏 free 🚰 € 1/25liter 🗑 Ch 🚿 (4x) € 2 WC 🗑.
**Location:** Urban, central. **Surface:** grassy/gravel.
🅾 01/01-31/12 🅾 water disconnected in winter.
**Distance:** 🚶500m ⊗200m 🛒100m.
**Remarks:** Use sanitary only during opening hours swimming pool.

### Friedberg  12A3
**Engel Caravaning**, Dieselstraße 4. **GPS:** n50,34646 e8,75685. ⬆

2 🛏 voluntary contribution is appreciated 🚰 € 0,50 🗑 Ch 🚿 (2x).
**Location:** Urban, simple, central. **Surface:** metalled.
🅾 01/01-31/12.
**Distance:** 🚶800m ⊗100m 🛒800m.
**Remarks:** Motorhome dealer, accessory shop, closed at night.

### Frielendorf  12A1
**Wohnmobilpark Silbersee**, Zum Silbersee.
**GPS:** n50,98389 e9,34667. ⬆➡

50 🛏 € 10 🚰 🗑 Ch included 🚿 (50x) € 2 🗑 € 2. 🔧 **Location:** Rural,
simple, quiet. **Surface:** grassy/metalled. 🅾 01/04-01/11.
**Distance:** 🚶1km 🏊250m 🛒350m 🛒2km 🚲 on the spot 🚶 on the
spot.
**Remarks:** Bread-service, video surveillance.

### Fritzlar  12A1
**Am Grauen Turm. GPS:** n51,13221 e9,26974. ⬆➡

10 🛏 € 7 🚰 € 1/90liter 🗑 Ch 🚿 € 1/2kWh. 🅿 **Location:** Urban,
central. **Surface:** metalled. 🅾 01/01-31/12.
**Distance:** 🚶100m ⊗100m 🛒600m.
**Tourist information Fritzlar:**
✒ Stadtführingen. Guided tour around the historic city center.
🅾 15/03-31/10 Tue-Sa 10.30, Su/holidays 11h. T € 4.

### Fulda  12B2
**Weimarerstrasse. GPS:** n50,55685 e9,66663. ⬆

30 🛏 € 0,10/1h, € 5/24h 🚰 € 1 🗑 Ch 🚿 € 1/6h 🗑 🅿
**Location:** Urban, simple, central. **Surface:** asphalted.
🅾 01/01-31/12.
**Distance:** 🚶400m 🛒50m.
**Remarks:** Max. 24h.

### Geisenheim  11H3
**Rheingau-Bad**, Rüdesheimer Str. 1. **GPS:** n49,98184 e7,94721.
14 🛏 € 7. **Location:** Urban. **Surface:** asphalted. 🅾 01/01-31/12.
**Distance:** 🚶on the spot 🏊100m ⊗500m 🍺400m.

### Gelnhausen  12A3
**Am Hallenbad. GPS:** n50,20125 e9,17795. ⬆

4 🛏 free. **Location:** Urban, simple, noisy. **Surface:** asphalted.
🅾 01/01-31/12.
**Distance:** 🚶1km ⊗100m 🛒100m 🚌on the spot.
**Remarks:** Parking at swimming pool.

### Gießen  11H2
**Badezentrum Ringallee**, Gutfleischstraße.
**GPS:** n50,58947 e8,68406. ⬆

6 🛏 free, 8-18h € 0,25/h 🚿 (6x) € 0,50/kWh. 🅿 **Location:** Urban,
simple. **Surface:** metalled. 🅾 01/01-31/12.
**Distance:** 🚶600m 🛒1,5km.

### Gilserberg  12A1
**Landgasthof Steller**, Marburgerstrasse 3.
**GPS:** n50,95047 e9,06220. ⬆

4 🛏 € 7,50, guests € 2,50 🚰 € 2,50 🚿 € 2,50 WC. 🔧
**Location:** Urban, simple. **Surface:** asphalted.
🅾 01/01-31/12 🅾 Wed.
**Distance:** ⊗500m 🛒250m 🚲 on the spot 🚶 on the spot.

### Gladenbach  11H2
**Restaurant Rosengarten**, Hoherainstrasse 45.
**GPS:** n50,77462 e8,57952. ⬆➡

3 🛏 € 5,50 🚰 🗑 Ch 🚿 included. **Location:** Urban, simple.
**Surface:** grassy. 🅾 01/01-31/12.
**Distance:** 🚶600m ⊗on the spot 🛒1km.
**Remarks:** Pay and key at restaurant.

### Grebenau  12B2
**Borngasse 20. GPS:** n50,74134 e9,47212. ⬆➡

4 🛏 free 🚰 🗑 Ch 🚿 free. **Location:** Rural, simple.
**Surface:** metalled. 🅾 01/01-31/12.
**Distance:** 🚶on the spot ⊗200m 🛒200m.
**Remarks:** At fire-station.

### Grebenhain  12A2
**Reisemobilstellplatz am Kurpark**, Hindenburgstraße, Hochwaldhau-
sen. **GPS:** n50,51910 e9,31756. ⬆

10 🛏 € 6-7,50 🚰 🗑 Ch 🚿 WC included. **Location:** Rural, simple,
central. **Surface:** gravel. 🅾 01/01-31/12.
**Distance:** 🚶500m ⊗500m 🚌bike-bus 200m 🚲 Vulkanradweg 200m
🚶 on the spot.
**Remarks:** Pay in at kiosk.

### Grebenhain  12A2
**Gasthof Zum Felsenmeer**, Jean-Berlit-Straße 1.
**GPS:** n50,51926 e9,31424. ⬆

10 🛏 € 5 + € 1/pp tourist tax 🚰 🚿 (2x) € 0,50/kWh, + € 1.
**Location:** Rural. **Surface:** grassy. 🅾 01/01-31/12.
**Distance:** ⊗on the spot.

### Großalmerode  12B1
**Am Mühlgraben**, Oststraße. **GPS:** n51,25841 e9,79349. ⬆
20 🛏 free 🚰 🗑 Ch 🚿. **Location:** Rural, comfortable.
**Surface:** grassy. 🅾 01/01-31/12.
**Distance:** 🚶700m 🛒150m.

### Großalmerode  12B1
**Panoramabad**, Heinrich-Koch-Straße. **GPS:** n51,26603 e9,78452.
🛏 free. **Location:** Simple. **Surface:** gravel. 🅾 01/01-31/12.
**Distance:** 🚶500m ⊗500m 🛒500m.
**Remarks:** Next to swimming pool.

### Grünberg  12A2
**Gallusplatz**, Gerichtsstraße. **GPS:** n50,59517 e8,95593. ⬆➡

DE

10 free ⛽€ 0,50 Ch (10x)€ 0,50/10h. **Location:** Urban, simple, central. **Surface:** gravel. 🅾 01/01-31/12. **Distance:** Old city centre 300m ⊗100m 🛒Aldi 400m 🚲 on the spot 🚶on the spot.

**⚿S** Habichtswald 10A3

**Am Erlebnisbad**, Hasenbreite, Ehlen. **GPS:** n51,32291 e9,31961. ⬆➡.

6 free ⛽€ 2/24h WC. **Location:** Rural, simple, isolated, quiet. **Surface:** grassy/metalled. 🅾 01/01-31/12 🅾 service: 01/10-31/03. **Distance:** 400m 🚴2,5km ⊗400m 🛒400m. **Remarks:** Caution € 20, key electricity/toilet at swimming pool.

**⚿S** Habichtswald 10A3

**Festplatz Kressenborn**, Bergweg, Dörnberg. **GPS:** n51,34361 e9,34389. ⬆.

4 free ⛽(2x)€ 2/24h WC. **Location:** Simple, quiet. **Surface:** gravel. 🅾 01/01-31/12 🅾 service: 01/10-31/03. **Distance:** 200m 🚴5,5km ⊗200m 🛒500m 🚶on the spot. **Remarks:** Caution € 20, key electricity/toilet at petrol station.

**⚿** Hatzfeld 11H1

Edertalstrasse. **GPS:** n50,99144 e8,54817. ⬆

5 free. **Location:** Urban, simple, quiet. **Surface:** grassy/gravel. 🅾 01/01-31/12. **Distance:** on the spot 🚶on the spot 🛒200m 🚲on the spot. **Remarks:** Behind fire-station.

**⚿** Helsa 12B1

Sportplatzweg. **GPS:** n51,25444 e9,68638. ⬆➡.

**⚿S** Herborn 11H2

**Herborner Schießplatz**, Sinner Landstraße. **GPS:** n50,67950 e8,30672. ⬆➡.

4 free. **Surface:** metalled. 🅾 01/01-31/12. **Distance:** 800m ⊗800m 🛒700m 🚲400m.

6 free ⛽€ 1/90liter Ch (6x)€ 1/kWh. **Location:** Simple. **Surface:** metalled. 🅾 01/01-31/12. **Distance:** 200m 🚴1,8km ⊗300m.

**⚓** Herbstein 12A2

**VulkanTherme Herbstein**, Zum Thermalbad 1. **GPS:** n50,56883 e9,34647. ⬆➡.

11 € 6 + € 1,50/pp tourist tax ⛽€ 1/100liter Ch (11x)€ 1/2kWh WC 🚿€ 1,50. **Location:** Rural, comfortable, quiet. **Surface:** metalled. 🅾 01/01-31/12. **Distance:** 1,1km ⊗800m 🛒300m 🚲on the spot 🚶on the spot. **Remarks:** Coins available at pay-desk of theTherme.

**⚿S** Hessisch Lichtenau 12B1

**Alter Bahnhof/Western Rail Station**, Bahnhofstrasse 5, Warlburg. **GPS:** n51,20055 e9,77833. ⬆➡.

10 € 10 🚿WC 🔌included. **Location:** Rural, isolated, quiet. **Surface:** asphalted. 🅾 01/01-31/12. **Distance:** 5km ⊗600m 🛒500m 🚶on the spot 🚲on the spot.

**⚿S** Hessisch Lichtenau 12B1

**Sportcenter Fürstenhagen**, Breslauer strasse 18. **GPS:** n51,20672 e9,69443. ⬆➡.

10 € 5/24h ⛽€ 1/80liter Ch 🔌€ 0,50/kWh. **Location:** Rural, simple, quiet. **Surface:** metalled. 🅾 01/01-31/12. **Distance:** 3km ⊗1km 🛒2km. **Remarks:** Check in at sport centre.

**⚿** Hessisch Lichtenau 12B1

Hopfelderstrasse. **GPS:** n51,19417 e9,72389. ⬆➡.

14 free. **Location:** Urban, simple, isolated, quiet. **Surface:** metalled. 🅾 01/01-31/12. **Distance:** 500m ⊗400m 🛒500m.

**⚿** Hessisch Lichtenau 12B1

**Wohnmobilstellplatz am Hallenbad**, Freiherr-vom-Stein-Straße 12. **GPS:** n51,20445 e9,72655. ⬆.

6 free. **Location:** Rural, simple, isolated, quiet. **Surface:** metalled. 🅾 01/01-31/12. **Distance:** 600m. **Remarks:** Parking swimming pool.

**⚿S** Hessisch Lichtenau 12B1

**Berggasthof Hoher Meißner**, Hoher Meissner 1. **GPS:** n51,20376 e9,84852. ⬆.

10 free ⛽🚿WC. **Location:** Rural, simple, isolated, quiet. **Surface:** metalled. 🅾 01/01-31/12. **Distance:** 10km ⊗on the spot 🚐on the spot 🚲on the spot 🚶on the spot.

**⚿** Hilders 12B2

**Ulsterwelle**, Heideweg 19. **GPS:** n50,56909 e9,99351. ⬆.

5 free. **Location:** Rural. **Surface:** gravel. 🅾 01/01-31/12. **Distance:** 750m 🚴50m 🛒800m. **Remarks:** At swimming pool.

**⚿S** Hirschhorn 17A1

**Beim Ätsche**, Jahnstraße 2. **GPS:** n49,44214 e8,89804. ⬆.

25 € 7 ⛽€ 0,50/40liter Ch 🔌€ 2,50/day,6Amp. **Location:** Rural, comfortable, quiet. **Surface:** grassy. 🅾 01/01-31/12 🅾 high water. **Distance:** 500m ⊗on the spot 🛒850m 🚆train 400m 🚲on the spot.

**Remarks:** Along the Neckar river.

| 🏕 | **Hirzenhain** | 12A2 |

**Festplatz Hirzenhain**, Robert-Eichenauerweg.
**GPS:** n50,39259 e9,13593. ⬆️➡️.

6 🛏free. **Location:** Urban, simple, central. **Surface:** metalled.
🅾 01/01-31/12.
**Distance:** 🚰100m ⊗100m 🛒 on the spot 🚲 on the spot.

| 🏕 S | **Hirzenhain** | 12A2 |

**Müller-Mobil**, Junkernwiese 2. **GPS:** n50,40004 e9,14744. ⬆️.

6 🛏free 🚽€ 1/130liter 🔲Ch 💧(6x). **Location:** Rural, simple, quiet.
**Surface:** metalled. 🅾 01/01-31/12.
**Distance:** 🚰1,5km ⊗on the spot 🚲on the spot 🚶on the spot.

| 🏕 S | **Hofgeismar** | 10A3 |

**Wohnmobilstellplatz Hofgeismar**, Am Sälber Tor.
**GPS:** n51,49521 e9,37547. ⬆️.

100 🛏free 🚽€ 1/80liter 🔲Ch 💧(18x)€ 2/2kWh.
**Location:** Rural, comfortable, central, quiet. **Surface:** gravel.
🅾 01/01-31/12.
**Distance:** 🚰on the spot 🛒300m ⊗ on the spot 🚶on the spot.

| 🏕 S | **Homberg/Efze** | 12A1 |

Wassmuthshäuserstrasse, Dresdener Alee.
**GPS:** n51,02757 e9,41470. ⬆️➡️.

7 🛏free 🚽€ 1/80liter 🔲Ch 💧free. **Location:** Urban, simple.
**Surface:** gravel. 🅾 01/01-31/12.
**Distance:** 🚰on the spot ⊗1km 🛒500m.
**Remarks:** Max. 4 days.

| 🏕 S | **Homberg/Ohm** | 12A2 |

**An der Stadthalle**, Stadthallenweg 12.
**GPS:** n50,72626 e8,99439. ⬆️➡️.

4 🛏free 🚽€ 1/10minutes 🔲Ch 💧(4x)€ 0,50/kWh.
**Location:** Rural, simple. **Surface:** metalled. 🅾 01/01-31/12.
**Distance:** 🚰400m ⊗350m 🛒1km 🚶on the spot.

| 🏕 S | **Hünfeld** | 12B2 |

**Hessisches Kegelspiel**, Zu den Unaben.
**GPS:** n50,67626 e9,77622. ⬆️➡️.

18 🛏€ 5 🚽€ 1/120liter 🔲Ch 💧(12x)€ 1/2kWh.
**Location:** Urban, simple. **Surface:** gravel. 🅾 01/01-31/12.
**Distance:** 🚰500m ⊗250m 🛒500m.

| 🏕 S | **Hünfeld** | 12B2 |

**Knaus Campingplatz**, Dr.-Detlev-Rudelsdorff-Allee.
**GPS:** n50,65299 e9,72409.
5 🛏€ 11 🚽Chincluded 💧€ 3,50 WC€ 3,50 📶.
**Location:** Rural. **Surface:** grassy. 🅾 01/01-31/12.
**Distance:** 🚰4km ⊗200m.
**Remarks:** Golf court.

| 🏕 S | **Hungen** | 12A2 |

**Inheiden**, Am Köstgraben. **GPS:** n50,45509 e8,90049. ⬆️➡️.

6 🛏free 🚽€ 2/100liter Ch 💧€ 2/6h WC.
**Location:** Rural, comfortable, quiet. **Surface:** grasstiles.
🅾 01/01-31/12 💧 water: 01/11-31/03.
**Distance:** 🏊Trais-Horloffer See ⊗3km 🛒500m 🚲bike-bus 1km.

| 🏕 S | **Idstein** | 11H3 |

**Wohnmobilhafen Idstein**, Himmelsbornweg.
**GPS:** n50,21775 e8,27923. ⬆️➡️.

12 🛏€ 10 🚽€ 1/80liter 🔲Ch 💧 1/24h. 🚌 **Location:** Rural.
**Surface:** gravel/metalled. 🅾 01/01-31/12 💧 water disconnected in
winter. **Distance:** 🚰500m Altstadt 🚴3,3km.

| 🏕 S | **Kassel** | 12A1 |

**Wohnmobilplatz Kassel**, Am Sportzentrum/Giessenallee, Kassel-süd.
**GPS:** n51,29250 e9,48750. ⬆️➡️.

12 🛏€ 15/day 🚽€ 1/100liter 🔲€ 0,50 Ch€ 0,50 💧(8x)included.
**Location:** Rural, simple, isolated, quiet.
🅾 01/01-31/12.
**Distance:** 🚴1,4km ⊗500m 🛒50m ⊗on the spot 🚶on the spot.
**Remarks:** With parking ticket free public transport, max. 3 nights.

**Tourist information Kassel:**
👁🛍 Treppenstrasse, shopping promenade, modern architecture.

| 🏕 S | **Kaufungen** | 12B1 |

**Festplatz**, Am Steckkopf. **GPS:** n51,28525 e9,61956. ⬆️➡️.

4 🛏free 🚽€ 2/40liter 🔲Ch. **Location:** Rural, simple, quiet.
**Surface:** metalled. 🅾 01/01-31/12.
**Distance:** 🏊800m Steinersee ⊗300m 🛒500m.
**Remarks:** Max. 3 days.

| 🏕 S | **Kirchheim** | 12B2 |

**Campingplatz Seepark**, Brunnenstrasse 20.
**GPS:** n50,81400 e9,52000. ⬆️➡️.

50 🛏€ 13, dog € 2 🚽€ 1 🔲Ch 💧(30x)€ 3/day 🔲€ 1,50 📶.
**Location:** Rural, simple. **Surface:** metalled.
🅾 01/01-31/12.
**Distance:** 🚰5km 🚴4,9km 🏊20m 🛒on the spot ⊗20m.

| 🏕 S | **Kleinwallstadt** | 17A1 |

Fährstraße 14. **GPS:** n49,87571 e9,16378.
12 🛏€ 5 🚽€ 1/5minutes 🔲Chincluded 💧€ 1/6h. 🚐
**Location:** Simple. **Surface:** metalled.
🅾 01/01-31/12 💧 water: 01/11-31/03.
**Distance:** 🚰500m 🏊on the spot 🛒500m.

| 🏕 S | **Korbach** | 12A1 |

Westring. **GPS:** n51,27260 e8,85509. ➡️.

5 🛏free. **Location:** Urban, quiet. **Surface:** grasstiles/metalled.
🅾 01/01-31/12.
**Distance:** 🚰1km ⊗1km 🛒Lidl 200m.
**Remarks:** At tennis-court and swimming pool, max. 3 nights.

| 🏕 S | **Laubach** | 12A2 |

**Quick Camp Caravanpark Laubach**, Kurze Hohl.
**GPS:** n50,55021 e9,00806. ⬆️.

30 🛏€ 6, 2 pers.incl 🚽€ 2 🔲€ 2 ChWC€ 2 💧.
**Location:** Rural, simple, isolated, quiet. **Surface:** grasstiles/grassy.
🅾 01/01-31/12.
**Distance:** 🚰1,5km ⊗1,5km 🛒1,5km.

| 🏕 S | **Lauterbach** | 12A2 |

**Freizeitzentrum Steinigsgrund**, Am Sportfeld 9.
**GPS:** n50,62758 e9,39288. ⬆️➡️.

**DE**

8 �€5 ⚡€1 🚰€1 Ch ⚿€1 〰included. **Location:** Urban, simple.
**Surface:** metalled. 🅿 01/01-31/12.
**Distance:** 🚶800m ⊗50m on the spot 🅰on the spot.

### Lauterbach 12A2
**Auf der Bleiche**, Bleichstrasse. **GPS:** n50,63849 e9,40444. ⬆➡

5 ⌐free. **Location:** Rural, simple. **Surface:** metalled.
🅿 01/01-31/12.
**Distance:** 🚶100m ⊗150m on the spot.

### S Lauterbach 12A2
David-Eifertstrasse. **GPS:** n50,64288 e9,39393. ⬆
🚰€1/80liter ⚡Ch ⚿. **Location:** Urban. 🅿 01/01-31/12.

### S Leun 11H2
**Lahnwiese**, Limburger Straße. **GPS:** n50,55089 e8,35346. ⬆➡

8 ⌐€6 ⚿€2 WC. **Location:** Rural, simple. **Surface:** grassy.
🅿 01/01-31/12.
**Distance:** 🚶400m ⊗400m ⚡400m.
**Remarks:** Along the Lahn river, max. 4 days.

### Lich 12A2
**P6**, Ringstraße. **GPS:** n50,51816 e8,82257. ⬆➡

3 ⌐free. **Location:** Rural, simple, central, quiet.
**Surface:** grassy/metalled. 🅿 01/01-31/12.
**Distance:** 🚶300m ⊗400m 🛒Lidl 50m 🚌100m.
**Remarks:** Max. 3 days.

### S Limburg 11H2
**Freizeitfalzeuge Singhof**, Hoenbergstraße 2.
**GPS:** n50,40312 e8,07148.

3 ⌐free 🚰 ⚿€3 〰free. **Location:** Rural, simple.
**Surface:** metalled. 🅿 01/01-31/12.
**Distance:** ⚡1km.

---

### S Limburg 11H2
**Lahn Camping**, Schleusenweg 16. **GPS:** n50,38902 e8,07387. ⬆➡

8 ⌐€ 12-15/24h 🚰€0,50/50liter ⚡Ch ⚿€0,50/kWh 〰€2/day.
**Location:** Rural, simple, quiet. **Surface:** gravel.
🅿 01/01-31/12.
**Distance:** 🚶900m ⚡1,5km ⊗Gaststätte.
**Remarks:** Along the Lahn river, summer: bread-service, biergarten.

### S Lindenfels 🌿 17A1
Kappstraße. **GPS:** n49,68077 e8,78304. ⬆➡

10 ⌐€5 🚰€1/80liter ⚡Ch ⚿(4x)€0,50/6h WC. 🚽
**Location:** Rural, comfortable, quiet. **Surface:** grassy.
🅿 01/01-31/12.
**Distance:** 🚶on the spot ⊗on the spot 🍴on the spot.
**Remarks:** Max. 3 days.

### S Lorsch 🍞 16H1
**Wohnmobilstellplatz Karolingerstadt Lorsch**, Odenwaldallee.
**GPS:** n49,65206 e8,57855. ⬆

16 ⌐€10 🚰€1/80liter ⚡Ch ⚿(16x)€1/2kWh. 🚽
**Location:** Rural, comfortable, quiet. **Surface:** metalled.
🅿 01/01-31/12.
**Distance:** 🚶800m ⚡4,5km ⊗800m 🚽800m 🍴on the spot.
**Remarks:** Max. 5 days.

### S Marburg 🌿🍞 12A2
Jahnstraße. **GPS:** n50,80354 e8,77544. ⬆⬆➡

8 ⌐€10/24h 🚰€1/100liter ⚡Ch ⚿(4x)€1/4h. 🚽
**Location:** Urban, simple. **Surface:** gravel. 🅿 01/01-31/12.
**Distance:** 🚶300m 🍴500m.
**Remarks:** Green zone: environmental badge obligatory.

### S Meineringhausen 12A1
**Hobbywiese**, Walmenstrasse 25. **GPS:** n51,25945 e8,93807. ⬆➡

---

17 ⌐€8 🚰Ch ⚿€0,50/kWh,or €3/day WC 🚽€1 〰included. 🚿
**Location:** Rural, comfortable. **Surface:** grassy/gravel.
🅿 01/01-31/12.
**Distance:** 🚶2km Korbach ⊗800m 🚽2km 🍴on the spot 🅰on the
spot.
**Remarks:** Bread-service.

### Melsungen 12B1
**Schloßbrücke**, Sandstraße. **GPS:** n51,13280 e9,54502. ⬆

10 ⌐€0,30/h, overnight stay free. 🚐
**Location:** Urban, central. **Surface:** metalled.
🅿 01/01-31/12.
**Distance:** 🚶200m ⚡5km ⊗on the spot 🚽on the spot 🅰on the spot.
**Remarks:** Along the Fulda river, in front of police station.

### Melsungen 12B1
**Waldparkplatz**, Dreuxallee. **GPS:** n51,12352 e9,55169. ⬆

5 ⌐free. **Location:** Urban, simple. **Surface:** grassy/gravel.
🅿 01/01-31/12.
**Distance:** 🚶centre 1,1km ⚡5km ⊗on the spot.

### S Mernes 🌳 12B3
**Wohnmobilstellplatz Mernes**, Jossastraße, Mernes.
**GPS:** n50,24109 e9,47700. ➡

6 ⌐€5 🚰€0,50/80liter ⚡Ch ⚿€0,50/kWh.
**Location:** Rural, comfortable, quiet. **Surface:** grasstiles.
🅿 01/01-31/12.
**Distance:** 🚶200m ⊗250m 🚽200m 🍴on the spot.
**Remarks:** To be paid at Gasthaus Zum Jossatal, Salmünsterer Straße 15.

### S Michelstadt 🌿 17A1
**Parkplatz Altstadt**, Wiesenweg. **GPS:** n49,68038 e9,00143. ⬆⬆➡

9 ⌐free 🚰€1/90liter ⚡Ch ⚿€1/2kWh WC.

DE

**Location:** Urban, simple, central, noisy. **Surface:** gravel/metalled.
🅿 01/01-31/12.
**Distance:** 🚶200m ⊗200m 🍺50m on the spot 🚴 on the spot.

| 📷 S | Münzenberg | 12A2 |
| --- | --- | --- |

**Sporthallenparkplatz**, Am Viehtrieb. **GPS:** n50,45712 e8,77171. ⬆➡

5 🚐free. **Location:** Rural, simple, quiet. **Surface:** gravel.
🅿 01/01-31/12.
**Distance:** 🚶800m 🚲2,6km ⊗500m.
**Remarks:** Max. 3 days.

| 📷 S | Münzenberg | 12A2 |
| --- | --- | --- |

**Sportplatz**, Butzbacher Straße, Gambach. **GPS:** n50,45770 e8,73412. ⬆

15 🚐free. **Location:** Rural, simple, noisy. **Surface:** asphalted.
🅿 01/01-31/12.
**Distance:** 🚲2,4km ⊗400m 🍺on the spot.
**Remarks:** Max. 3 days.

| 📷 S | Neuental | 12A1 |
| --- | --- | --- |

**Neuenhainer See**, Seeblick 14, Neuenhain.
**GPS:** n50,99533 e9,26652. ➡

12 🚐€4 🔌€1 🚰Ch 💧€1/12h WC 🗑€0,50 💧.
**Location:** Rural, simple. **Surface:** asphalted. 🅿 01/01-31/12.
**Distance:** 🚶Neuental 6km 🛶on the spot ⊗250m.
**Remarks:** Use sanitary facilities at campsite.

| 📷 S | Neukirchen | 12A1 |
| --- | --- | --- |

**Reisemobilpark Urbachtal**, Urbachweg 1.
**GPS:** n50,87139 e9,34861. ⬆➡

49 🚐€11,50 + €1/pp tourist tax 🔌€0,10/10liter 🚰Ch 💧
(52x)€0,60/kWh WC 🗑€2,80 💡€1 💧. **Location:** Rural,
comfortable, luxurious, quiet. **Surface:** grassy/metalled.
🅿 01/01-31/12. **Distance:** 🚶300m 🚲2km ⊗300m 🍺200m Rewe
🛒300m 🚴700m on the spot.

| 📷 S | Neukirchen | 12A1 |
| --- | --- | --- |

**Birkenallee**, Knüllgebirge. **GPS:** n50,86567 e9,34478.

5 🚐free 🔌💧free. **Surface:** asphalted. 🅿 01/01-31/12.
**Distance:** 🚶500m ⊗200m.

| | Niedenstein | 12A1 |
| --- | --- | --- |

**Am Hallenbad**, Am Schwimmbad 2. **GPS:** n51,22739 e9,31657. ⬆➡

2 🚐free. **Location:** Rural, simple. **Surface:** gravel.
🅿 01/01-31/12.
**Distance:** 🚶300m 🍺300m.

| 📷 S | Niestetal | 10B3 |
| --- | --- | --- |

**Spiekershäuser Straße/Fuldablick**. **GPS:** n51,32686 e9,55490. ⬆
3 🚐free 🔌€1/100liter 🚰Ch 💧€1/2kWh. **Surface:** asphalted.
🅿 01/01-31/12.
**Distance:** 🚶1,1km 🚴on the spot 🚶on the spot.
**Remarks:** Along the Fulda river, Kassel centre 6km.

| 📷 S | Oberaula 👭 | 12B1 |
| --- | --- | --- |

**Sportplatz**, Schwimbadstraße. **GPS:** n50,85421 e9,45908. ⬆➡

10 🚐free 🔌🚰Chfree. **Location:** Rural, simple. **Surface:** asphalted.
🅿 01/01-31/12.
**Distance:** 🚶800m 🍺Rewe 100m 🍺on the spot.

| 📷 | Oberaula 👭 | 12B1 |
| --- | --- | --- |

**Golfplatz**, Am Golfplatz 1. **GPS:** n50,83590 e9,46211. ⬆➡

3 🚐free.
**Location:** Rural, simple, isolated, quiet. **Surface:** grassy.
🅿 01/01-31/12.
**Distance:** 🚶2,5km 🚲11km.
**Remarks:** Max. 4 days, follow the signs 'Golfplatz', 18-holes golf course.

| 📷 | Oberaula 👭 | 12B1 |
| --- | --- | --- |

**Tennishalle**, Teichstrasse. **GPS:** n50,86116 e9,47353. ⬆➡

10 🚐free. **Location:** Rural, simple, isolated, quiet. **Surface:** metalled.
🅿 01/01-31/12.

**Distance:** 🚶500m ⊗500m 🍺Edeka 500m.
**Remarks:** Parking tennis-court, max. 4 days.

| 📷 S | Oberaula 👭 | 12B1 |
| --- | --- | --- |

**Reiterhof Aumühle**, Aumühle 1. **GPS:** n50,85235 e9,47794. ⬆
6 🚐€10 🔌🚰Ch 💧 WC 🗑 💧included. **Location:** Rural,
comfortable. **Surface:** gravel/metalled. 🅿 01/01-31/12.
**Distance:** 🚶1km ⊗1km 🍺1,5km.
**Remarks:** Use of sauna against payment.

| | Oberursel | 11H3 |
| --- | --- | --- |

**Wanderparkplatz Taunus**, Alfred-Lechler-Straße.
**GPS:** n50,21533 e8,53606. ⬆

5 🚐€7. 🅿 **Location:** Rural, simple, quiet. **Surface:** metalled.
🅿 01/01-31/12.
**Distance:** 🚶4km 🍺on the spot 🚇metro 100m 🍺on the spot 🚶on
the spot.
**Remarks:** Max. 3 nights, e-bike rental.

| 📷 S | Oestrich-Winkel | 11H3 |
| --- | --- | --- |

**Am Sportzentrum**, Kirchstraße 125. **GPS:** n50,00470 e7,99904. ⬆➡

20 🚐free 💧(4x)€0,50/kWh. **Location:** Rural, simple, central.
**Surface:** metalled. 🅿 01/01-31/12.
**Distance:** 🚶1km.
**Remarks:** Max. 2 days.

| 📷 S | Ottrau | 12A2 |
| --- | --- | --- |

**Am Schwimmbad 10**. **GPS:** n50,80400 e9,38500. ⬆

4 🚐€6 🔌💧 WC 🗑. **Location:** Rural, simple. **Surface:** asphalted.
🅿 01/01-31/12.
**Distance:** 🚶on the spot.

| 📷 S | Poppenhausen 👭 | 12B2 |
| --- | --- | --- |

**Sport- und Freizeitgelände Lüttergrund**, Sebastian-Kneippweg,
Wasserkuppe. **GPS:** n50,49012 e9,87689. ⬆➡

10 🚐€6 🔌€1 🚰Ch 💧€1/6h. **Location:** Rural, simple.
**Surface:** metalled. 🅿 01/01-31/12.
**Distance:** 🚶300m ⊗300m 🍺300m on the spot 🚶on the spot.
**Remarks:** Max. 4 nights.

| 📷 S | Rasdorf | 12B2 |
| --- | --- | --- |

**Sport- und Freizeitgelände**, Setzelbacher Straße.
**GPS:** n50,71422 e9,90306. ⬆➡

DE

4 🚐 € 4 🚰 € 1/120liter 🔧Ch 🔌 € 1/10h. **Location:** Rural, simple.
**Surface:** metalled. ⏲ 01/01-31/12.
**Distance:** 🚿850m 🚽500m.
**Remarks:** Max. 3 days.

### 🏕🅂 Reichelsheim/Odenwald 🌼     17A1

**Reichenbergschule**, Beerfurhterstrasse.
**GPS:** n49,71507 e8,84234.⬆➡.

20 🚐free 🚰 € 1/100liter 🔧Ch 🔌(8x)€ 0,50/kWh.
**Location:** Urban, simple, central. **Surface:** asphalted.
⏲ 01/01-31/12.
**Distance:** 🚿on the spot ⊗100m 🚲on the spot 🚶on the spot.

### 🏕 Reinhardshagen 👬     10B3

**Freibad**, Klinkersweg. **GPS:** n51,48694 e9,59194.⬆.

4 🚐free. **Location:** Rural, simple, isolated. **Surface:** asphalted.
⏲ 01/01-31/12.
**Distance:** 🚿2km 🏊on the spot ⊗2km 🚽2km 🚌on the spot
🚲on the spot 🚶on the spot.
**Remarks:** Parking swimming pool, OT Veckerhagen, max. 3 days.

### 🏕🅂 Ringgau     12B1

**Am Festplatz**, In der Röste, Gandenborn. **GPS:** n51,08139 e10,04239.⬆.

20 🚐free, service/electricity incl. € 7 🚰🔧Ch 🔌WC.
**Location:** Rural, simple, quiet. **Surface:** gravel.
⏲ 01/01-31/12.
**Distance:** 🚿100m 🚽200m.

### 🏕🅂 Rodgau     12A3

**Rodgau Point**, Liebigstraße 18. **GPS:** n50,05510 e8,89715.

35 🚐 € 8 🚰 € 1 🚽 € 2 Ch 🔌🔧. ⏲ 01/01-31/12.
**Distance:** 🚿on the spot 🚲1,5km.

---

### 🏕🅂 Rosenthal     12A1

**Fischewosse**, Willershäuser Straße 2. **GPS:** n50,97561 e8,86884.⬆.

5 🚐free 🚰 🚽🔌€ 2/day. **Location:** Urban, comfortable.
**Surface:** metalled. ⏲ 01/01-31/12 ⊙ first 2 weeks of July.
**Distance:** 🚿400m ⊗on the spot 🚽800m.
**Remarks:** Max. 48h.

### 🏕🅂 Rotenburg a/d Fulda 🌼     12B1

**Wohnmobilpark Am Wittlich**, Braacher Straße 14.
**GPS:** n51,00049 e9,72074.

50 🚐 € 6,50 🚰 € 1 🔧Ch 🔌(3x)€ 0,50/kWh. 🚮
**Location:** Rural, simple, quiet. **Surface:** grassy. ⏲ 01/01-31/12.
**Distance:** 🚿Old city centre 650m 🚽200m 🚲on the spot 🚶on the
spot. **Remarks:** Along the Fulda river, at sports park.

### 🏕🅂 Rotenburg a/d Fulda 🌼     12B1

**Am Kuckucksmarktgelände**, Braach. **GPS:** n51,00583 e9,69361.➡.

15 🚐free 🚰 € 1/50liter 🔧Ch. **Location:** Rural. **Surface:** unpaved.
⏲ 01/01-31/12.
**Distance:** 🚿200m 🏊on the spot 🚮on the spot ⊗200m.
**Remarks:** Max. 72h.

### 🏕🅂 Rotenburg a/d Fulda 🌼     12B1

**Im Heienbach: GPS:** n51,00223 e9,74141.⬆➡.

5 🚐free. **Location:** Simple. **Surface:** metalled.
⏲ 01/01-31/12.
**Distance:** 🚿1km ⊗1km 🚌1km.
**Remarks:** Parking swimming pool.

### 🏕🅂 Rotenburg a/d Fulda 🌼     12B1

**Biergarten Hof Hafermas**, Rotenburgerstrasse 13, Braach.
**GPS:** n51,00316 e9,69085.

3 🚐free 🚰 € 1 🔧Ch. **Surface:** gravel. ⏲ 01/01-31/12.

---

**Distance:** 🚿on the spot ⊗on the spot.
**Tourist information Rotenburg a/d Fulda:**
⚒ Kuckucksmarkt, Braach. Farmers market. ⏲ 01/05-30/09 last
weekend of the month10-18h.

### 🏕🅂 Rüsselsheim     11H3

**Mainufer**, Dammgasse. **GPS:** n49,99619 e8,40956.⬆.

7 🚐free. **Location:** Urban. **Surface:** asphalted. ⏲ 01/01-31/12.
**Distance:** 🏊on the spot ⊗400m 🚽300m 🚌on the spot.

### 🏕🅂 Schlitz     12B2

**Damenweg: GPS:** n50,66909 e9,56908.➡.

10 🚐free 🚰 € 1 🔧Ch. **Location:** Rural, simple. **Surface:** gravel.
⏲ 01/01-31/12.
**Distance:** 🚿500m 🚮on the spot 🚶on the spot.
**Remarks:** At swimming pool.

### 🏕🅂 Schlüchtern     12B2

**Ludovica-von-Stumm-Straße. GPS:** n50,34935 e9,53023.⬆.

5 🚐free. **Location:** Urban, simple, noisy. **Surface:** asphalted.
⏲ 01/01-31/12.
**Distance:** 🚿300m 🚲4,3km ⊗on the spot 🚽400m.

### 🏕🅂 Schwalmstadt     12A1

**Altstad Schwalmstadt-Treysa**, Zwalmstraße. **GPS:** n50,91447 e9,19327.

10 🚐free 🚰🔧Ch. **Surface:** grassy. ⏲ 01/01-31/12.
**Distance:** 🚿100m ⊗1km 🚽1km.
**Remarks:** Service nearby, indicated.

### 🏕🅂 Schwalmstadt     12A1

**Fünftenweg**, Ziegenhain. **GPS:** n50,91753 e9,24633.⬆➡.

5 🚐free 🚰🔧Ch. **Location:** Rural, simple. **Surface:** metalled.
⏲ 01/01-31/12.

DE

**Distance:** ⬇️on the spot.
**Remarks:** Parking swimming pool, service nearby, indicated.

### 📷🅂 Schwalmtal — 12A2

**Reisemobilplatz**, Friedenstrasse, Storndorf.
**GPS:** n50,65579 e9,26935. ⬆️➡️.

15 🛏️€ 3 🚰€ 1/80liter 🔌Ch 🔌(6x)€ 0,50/kWh. 🚿
**Location:** Rural, simple, isolated, quiet. **Surface:** asphalted.
📅 01/01-31/12.
**Distance:** ⬇️300m 🏍️on the spot 🚶on the spot.
**Remarks:** Nearby sports park.

### 📷🅂 Sinntal — 12B3

**Am Naturbad**, Aspenweg, Altengronau.
**GPS:** n50,25453 e9,63316. ⬆️➡️.

7 🛏️free 🚰€ 0,50/50liter 🔌Ch 🔌(7x)€ 3/24h.
**Location:** Rural, simple, quiet. **Surface:** metalled.
📅 01/01-31/12.
**Distance:** ⬇️1,5km ⊗1,5km 🚎1,5km 🚶on the spot.

### 📷🅂 Sontra — 12B1

Langhelle/Jahnstrasse. **GPS:** n51,07227 e9,94673.

5 🛏️free 🚰€ 0,50/80liter 🔌Ch 🔌€ 1/12h WC.
**Location:** Rural, simple, isolated, quiet. **Surface:** asphalted/metalled.
📅 01/01-31/12.
**Distance:** ⬇️600m 🚎on the spot.
**Remarks:** Parking behind swimming pool.

### 📷🅂 Sontra — 12B1

Vimoutiersstrasse. **GPS:** n51,07139 e9,93306. ⬆️.
5 🛏️free 🚰€ 0,50/100liter 🚽€ 0,50 ♿€ 0,50 🔌(3x)€ 0,50.
**Location:** Urban, simple.
**Surface:** gravel/metalled.
📅 01/01-31/12.
**Distance:** ⬇️on the spot 🚲19km ⊗500m 🗑️50m 🚎50m 🏍️500m.

### 📷🅂 Steinau/Strasse — 12B3

**Am Steines.** **GPS:** n50,31605 e9,46029. ⬆️.

5 🛏️free 🚰€ 1 🔌Ch€ 1 🔌(4x)€ 1/kWh. **Location:** Rural, simple,
quiet. **Surface:** asphalted. 📅 01/01-31/12.
**Distance:** ⬇️1km ⊗350m.
**Remarks:** Parking near sports centre, max. 2 days.

### 📷🅂 Tann/Rhön — 12B2

**Festplatz Tann**, Am Unsbach. **GPS:** n50,64195 e10,01802. ⬆️➡️.

8 🛏️€ 5 🚰€ 1/120liter 🔌Ch 🔌(8x)€ 1/6h. **Location:** Rural, simple,
isolated. **Surface:** gravel. 📅 01/01-31/12.
**Distance:** ⬇️1km ⊗1km 🚎1km 🏍️on the spot 🚶on the spot.
**Remarks:** Max. 3 days, tickets available at tourist office, petrol station
or Schreib- und Spielwaren Krenzer.

### 📷🅂 Ulrichstein 🌳 — 12A2

**Reisemobilstellplatz Panoramablick**, Erlenweg.
**GPS:** n50,57588 e9,20619. ⬆️➡️.

12 🛏️€ 5 🚰€ 1/80liter 🔌Ch 🔌(6x)€ 0,50/kWh. 🚿
**Location:** Rural, comfortable, quiet. **Surface:** asphalted.
📅 01/01-31/12.
**Distance:** ⬇️1km ⊗1km 🚎1km 🏍️on the spot 🚶on the spot
🛶on the spot.
**Remarks:** Beautiful view.

### 📷 Villmar — 11H2

**P3**, König-Konrad-Straße. **GPS:** n50,39102 e8,18625. ⬆️➡️.

10 🛏️free. **Location:** Rural, simple. **Surface:** metalled.
📅 01/01-31/12.
**Distance:** ⊗on the spot 🚎1,5km.
**Remarks:** Parking at the river.

### 📷 Vöhl — 12A1

**Camping-und Ferienpark Teichmann**, Herzhausen.
**GPS:** n51,17472 e8,89103. ⬆️.

10 🛏️€ 15 🚰 🔌 Ch WC included 🔌€ 3 ♿€ 4,50. 🚿
**Location:** Rural, comfortable. **Surface:** metalled.
📅 01/01-31/12.
**Distance:** ⬇️1km 🛶on the spot 🎣fishing permit € 8/day ⊗on the
spot.
**Remarks:** Max. 1 night.

### 📷 Volkmarsen — 10A3

Schulstraße. **GPS:** n51,41249 e9,11058. ⬆️.
4 🛏️free. **Surface:** asphalted. 📅 01/01-31/12.
**Distance:** ⬇️200m 🚲7,8km 🚎Aldi 650m.

### 📷🅂 Wahlsburg — 10B3

**Landhotel "Zum Anker"**, Weserstrasse 14.
**GPS:** n51,62447 e9,55212. ⬆️➡️.

60 🛏️€ 10 🚰€ 0,50/50liter 🔌Ch 🔌(60x)€ 0,50/kWh WC 🔌 📶 📺
📅 01/01-31/12.
**Distance:** ⬇️200m 🚎on the spot ⊗on the spot 🚎500m 🏍️on the
spot 🚶on the spot.
**Remarks:** Along the Weser river, bread-service.

### 📷🅂 Waldeck — 12A1

**Edersee Alm**, Am Bettenhagen 2. **GPS:** n51,18861 e9,00944. ⬆️➡️.

85 🛏️€ 13 🚰€ 1/100liter 🔌Chincluded 🔌€ 0,50/kWh WC 🔌€ 1/
stay. **Location:** Rural, luxurious. **Surface:** gravel. 📅 01/03-31/10.
**Distance:** 🛶on the spot 🎣fishing permit obligatory ⊗on the spot.
**Remarks:** Bread-service.

### 📷🅂 Waldeck — 12A1

**Seeblick Wohnmobil**, Güldener Ort 12. **GPS:** n51,20309 e9,05004. ⬆️.

13 🛏️€ 11 2 pers.incl, dog € 1 🚰🔌Ch 🔌€ 3 WC included. 🚿
**Location:** Rural, simple. **Surface:** grasstiles.
📅 01/01-31/12.
**Distance:** 🛶50m ⊗on the spot 🚎2km.
**Remarks:** At Edersee, bread-service, waste dump € 2.

### 📷🅂 Waldkappel 🌳 — 12B1

**Am Sportplatz.** **GPS:** n51,14177 e9,87278. ⬆️➡️.

4 🛏️free 🚰€ 1/100liter. **Location:** Rural, simple, isolated, quiet.
**Surface:** gravel. 📅 01/03-31/10.
**Distance:** ⬇️400m ⊗400m 🚎400m bakery 🚶Waldpark 500m.
**Remarks:** At sports park.

### 📷🅂 Wanfried 🌳 — 12B1

**In der Werraaue**, Eschweger Straße. **GPS:** n51,18722 e10,16528. ⬆️➡️.

12 🛏️€ 5 🚰€ 2/100liter 🔌Ch 🔌(12x)€ 0,50/kWh. 🚿
**Location:** Rural, simple, quiet. **Surface:** metalled.

◻ 01/01-31/12.
**Distance:** 🚶50m 🚲50m ♿on the spot 🧍on the spot.

| 🅿🅂 | **Weilburg** | 11H2 |

**Wohnmobilstation**, Hainallee. **GPS:** n50,48385 e8,25848. ⬆➡.

80 🅿 € 8, 2 pers.incl 🚰🗑 ♨included WC10-17h. ♿
**Location:** Urban, simple. **Surface:** metalled.
◻ 01/01-31/12 ⦿ events.
**Distance:** 🚶on the spot ⊗on the spot.
**Remarks:** Caution key € 15.

| 🅿🅂 | **Weilmünster** | 11H2 |

**In der Au**, Am Froschgraben, L3054. **GPS:** n50,43345 e8,37343. ⬆➡.

12 🅿voluntary contribution 🚰🗑Chfree ♨€ 2/16h.
**Location:** Rural, simple. **Surface:** metalled. ◻ 01/01-31/12.
**Distance:** 🚶on the spot ⊗100m 🗑100m ♿on the spot 🧍on the spot.

| 🅿🅂 | **Weilrod** | 11H3 |

**Taunus Mobilcamp**, Hochtaunusstrasse. **GPS:** n50,31138 e8,42581. ⬆.

40 🅿 € 12 2 pers.incl, dog € 1 🚰🗑 ♨€ 1/80liter 🗑Ch ♨€ 0,50/kWh
WC ⬜included 🚿€ 3/3. **Location:** Rural, simple, isolated, noisy.
**Surface:** metalled. ◻ 01/01-31/12.
**Distance:** 🚶500m ⊗on the spot 🗑6km.

| 🅿🅂 | **Weilrod** | 11H3 |

**Golfclub Taunus**, Merzhäuser Straße 29. **GPS:** n50,32082 e8,42694. ⬆.
2 🅿free, only guest players ⬜. **Location:** Rural, noisy.
**Surface:** asphalted. ◻ 01/05-30/09.
**Distance:** 🚶800m ⊗on the spot.

| 🅿🅂 | **Wetzlar** | 11H2 |

**An der Dill**, Falkenstrasse. **GPS:** n50,55667 e8,49111. ⬆➡.

16 🅿 € 8 🚰🗑Ch ♨(16x)included. **Location:** Urban, simple.
**Surface:** gravel. ◻ 01/01-31/12.
**Distance:** 🚶800m 🚲3km 🗑500m ♿on the spot.
**Remarks:** At sports park.

| 🅿🅂 | **Wetzlar** | 11H2 |

**Parkplatz Lahninsel**, Lahninsel. **GPS:** n50,55488 e8,49756. ⬆.

5 🅿 € 8 (8-19h), overnight stay free 🚰🗑Ch ♨included WC. 🚗
**Location:** Urban. **Surface:** asphalted. ◻ 01/01-31/12.
**Distance:** 🚶800m 🚲1,5km ⊗250m 🗑350m.

| 🅿🅂 | **Wiesbaden** ♨ | 11H3 |

**Reisemobilhafen Wiesbaden**, Wörther-See-Strasse/Saarstrasse.
**GPS:** n50,05583 e8,20972. ⬆.

40 🅿 € 7, overnight stay 21-9h € 3,50 🚰 ♨€ 0,50/60liter 🗑Ch ♨
(40x)€ 0,50/kWh WC ⬜€ 1. ♿
**Location:** Urban, comfortable. **Surface:** gravel.
◻ 01/01-31/12.
**Distance:** 🚶150m ⊗800m 🗑800m 🗑150m. **Remarks:** Service
passerby € 2, green zone: environmental badge obligatory.

| 🅿🅂 | **Willingen** ⛷❄ | 11H1 |

**Wohnmobilpark Willingen**, Am Hagen.
**GPS:** n51,29050 e8,61278. ⬆➡.

55 🅿 € 14, 2 pers incl 🚰 ♨€ 1/100liter 🗑Ch ♨€ 1/2kWh
WC ⬜€ 1,50/30minutes, at swimming pool 🚿included. ♿
**Location:** Rural, comfortable. **Surface:** metalled.
◻ 01/01-31/12.
**Distance:** 🚶1km ⊗100m 🗑1km 🗑300m 🚲300m.
**Remarks:** Bread-service, discount at subtropical swimming pool and
indoor skating rink.

| 🅿🅂 | **Witzenhausen** ⛺🏕🌳 | 10B3 |

**Reisemobilplatz Diebesturm**, Oberburgstrasse.
**GPS:** n51,34110 e9,85435. ⬆➡.

4 🅿 € 5 🚰 ♨€ 0,50/100liter 🗑Ch ♨(4x)€ 0,50. 🚗
**Location:** Urban, simple, central, noisy. **Surface:** gravel.
◻ 01/01-31/12.
**Distance:** 🚶500m ⊗on the spot 🗑500m.

| 🅿🅂 | **Witzenhausen** ⛺🏕🌳 | 10B3 |

**Reisemobilplatz Josef-Pott-Platz**, Laubenweg.
**GPS:** n51,34477 e9,85503. ⬆.

10 🅿 € 5 🚰 ♨€ 1/100liter 🗑Ch ♨(10x)€ 0,50/6h. 🚗
**Location:** Rural, simple, quiet. **Surface:** metalled.
◻ 01/01-31/12.
**Distance:** 🚶800m 🚲9km ⊗800m 🗑Aldi 100m ♿on the spot 🧍on
the spot.

| 🅿🅂 | **Witzenhausen** ⛺🏕🌳 | 10B3 |

**Haus des Gastes**, Ringkopfstrasse, Dohrenbach.
**GPS:** n51,31061 e9,83372. ⬆➡.

8 🅿 € 4 🚰🗑Chincluded ♨€ 2/24h WC. ♿
**Location:** Rural, simple, isolated, quiet. **Surface:** metalled.
◻ 01/01-31/12.
**Distance:** 🚶on the spot ⊗on the spot 🗑300m 🧍on the spot.
**Tourist information Witzenhausen:**
☀ Kesperkirmes. Village fair. ◻ beginning Jul.

| 🅿🅂 | **Wolfhagen** | 10A3 |

**Freizeitanlange Bruchwiesen**, Siemensstrasse.
**GPS:** n51,32944 e9,17083. ⬆➡.

35 🅿 € 3/24h 🚰 ♨€ 1/80liter 🗑Ch ♨(12x)€ 1/8h. 🚗
**Location:** Rural, simple, isolated, quiet. **Surface:** grassy/gravel.
◻ 01/01-31/12.
**Distance:** 🚶on the spot ⊗500m 🗑200m ♿on the spot 🧍on the
spot.

| 🅿🅂 | **Ziegenhagen** 🌿 | 10B3 |

**Erlebnispark Ziegenhagen**, Ziegenberg 3.
**GPS:** n51,37191 e9,76472. ➡.

15 🅿 € 5 🚰 € 1 🗑Ch. ♿
**Location:** Simple, isolated, quiet. ◻ 01/03-31/10.
**Distance:** 🚶6km.

DE

# Thuringia

### ♨⬛ Asbach/Sickenberg    12B1

**Grenzmuseum Schifflersgrund**, Sickenberger Straße 1.
**GPS:** n51,28667 e10,01052.

4 ⬛ € 4 ⛽ € 1/50liter ⬛Ch ✂(4x)€ 1. **Location:** Simple.
**Surface:** gravel. ⬛ 01/01-31/12.
**Distance:** 🚂3km ⊗3km ⬛3,5km 🚲3km 🚶800m.

### ⬛⬛ Bad Berka ♨    12D1

**P2**, Bleichstrasse. **GPS:** n50,89969 e11,28528. ⬆➡.

3 ⬛free ⛽€ 1/3minutes ⬛€ 1 Ch ✂(3x)€ 1/3h.
**Surface:** asphalted. ⬛ 01/01-31/12.
**Distance:** 🚂200m ⊗on the spot ⬛200m ⬛200m.
**Remarks:** 10/7/10 during inspection service out of order.

### ⬛⬛ Bad Colberg/Heldburg    12C3

**Am Rainbrünnlein. GPS:** n50,27967 e10,73063. ⬆.

5 ⬛free ⛽€ 1/60liter ⬛Ch ✂€ 1/8h. **Location:** Simple.
**Surface:** grasstiles. ⬛ 01/01-31/12.
**Distance:** 🚂100m ⊗200m ⬛200m.
**Remarks:** At sports park.

### ⬛⬛ Bad Frankenhausen/Kyffhäuser ♨    10D3

**Bornstraße, B85. GPS:** n51,35550 e11,10333. ⬆➡.

15 ⬛€ 14 ⛽⬛Ch ✂included. **Location:** Rural. **Surface:** metalled.
⬛ 01/01-31/12.
**Distance:** 🚂500m ⊗200m ⬛300m.
**Remarks:** Check in at pay-desk of the Therme.

### ⬛⬛ Bad Klosterlausnitz    12E1

**Kristall Sauna-Wellnesspark/Soletherme**, Köstritzerstrasse 16.
**GPS:** n50,91190 e11,87242. ⬆➡.

---

15 ⬛€ 10 + € 1,30/pp tourist tax ⛽€ 1/80liter ⬛Ch ✂€ 1/2kWh
WC⬛. **Location:** Rural, simple. **Surface:** gravel.
⬛ 01/01-31/12.
**Distance:** 🚂800m ⬛2,8km ⊗on the spot.
**Remarks:** At swimming pool.

### ⬛⬛ Bad Langensalza ♨    12C1

**Friederiken Therme**, Böhmenstrasse.
**GPS:** n51,11535 e10,64440. ⬆➡.

16 ⬛€ 4 + € 1,70/pp tourist tax ⛽€ 1 ⬛Ch ✂(8x)€ 1/10h.
**Surface:** metalled. ⬛ 01/01-31/12.
**Distance:** 🚂1km ⊗on the spot ⬛200m.
**Remarks:** Parking spa resort, pay at pay-desk of the Therme.

### ⬛⬛ Bad Liebenstein ⬛⬛    12C1

**Villa Georg**, Friedensallee 12. **GPS:** n50,81876 e10,35517. ⬆.

6 ⬛€ 8 ⛽€ 1/100liter ⬛Ch ✂€ 3 WC. **Location:** Comfortable,
quiet. **Surface:** gravel. ⬛ 01/01-31/12 ⬛ Tuesday.
**Distance:** 🚂500m ⊗on the spot ⬛800m 🚶on the spot.

### ⬛⬛ Bad Lobenstein    12E2

**Ardesia Therme**, Parkstrasse 8. **GPS:** n50,44981 e11,64294. ⬆➡.

11 ⬛€ 2,50 + € 1,50/pp tourist tax, free with use of spa ⛽€ 2 ⬛
Ch ✂€ 0,50/kWh WC⬛€ 3 ⬛. **Location:** Urban. **Surface:** metalled.
⬛ 01/01-31/12.
**Distance:** 🚂200m ⊗on the spot ⬛200m ⬛on the spot.

### ⬛⬛ Bad Salzungen ⬛⬛    12C1

**ErlebisINSEL Flößrasen**, Flössrasen 1. **GPS:** n50,81541 e10,23748. ⬆.

88 ⬛€ 10 + € 1,50/pp tourist tax ⛽€ 1/60liter ✂(88x)€ 1/2kWh
⬛€ 2/30minutes. ⬛✂ **Location:** Urban, comfortable.
**Surface:** metalled. ⬛ 01/01-31/12.
**Distance:** 🚂500m ⊗400m ⬛400m ⬛on the spot 🚶on the spot.
**Remarks:** Discount on access sauna/wellness.

### ⬛ Bad Tennstedt    12C1

**Am Schwimmbad**, Zweifeldersporthalle. **GPS:** n51,15994 e10,83952.
5 ⬛free. **Location:** Urban, simple. **Surface:** metalled.
⬛ 01/01-31/12.
**Distance:** 🚂500m ⊗500m ⬛500m.

### ♨⬛ Breitungen    12C2

**Hotel Jagdhaus Seeblick**, Seeblick. **GPS:** n50,74250 e10,32306. ⬆➡.

---

15 ⬛€ 5 ⛽according consumption ✂€ 2/day WC.⬛
**Location:** Rural, simple, quiet. **Surface:** grassy. ⬛ 01/01-31/12
⬛ Mon. **Distance:** 🚂2km ⬛1km ⊗on the spot ⬛2km 🚶on the spot.

### ⬛⬛ Brotterode    12C1

**Inselbergbad**, Am Bad 1. **GPS:** n50,82290 e10,45302. ⬆.

10 ⬛€ 5. ⬛ **Location:** Rural, simple. **Surface:** gravel.
⬛ 01/01-31/12.
**Distance:** 🚂500m ⊗on the spot ⬛Edeka 250m ⬛50m.
**Remarks:** To be paid at swimming pool.

### ⬛⬛ Dorndorf    12B1

**Kultur- und Freizeitzentrum**, Hardtstraße 3a.
**GPS:** n50,83453 e10,09087. ⬆.

8 ⬛€ 4 ⛽€ 1/90liter ⬛€ 1 Ch ✂€ 0,50/kWh. ⬛
**Location:** Rural, simple, quiet. **Surface:** grasstiles.
⬛ 01/01-31/12.
**Distance:** 🚂1km ⊗50m ⬛1km.
**Remarks:** Next to Fahrradherberge.

### ⬛⬛ Eisenach ⬛⬛    12C1

**Karl-Marx-Straße. GPS:** n50,97861 e10,32083. ⬆.

10 ⬛€ 10 ⛽⬛Ch ✂⬛. **Location:** Urban, comfortable.
**Surface:** gravel. ⬛ 01/01-31/12.
**Distance:** 🚂500m ⊗100m ⬛100m.

### ⬛ Eisenach ⬛⬛    12C1

**Automobilmuseum**, Heinrich-Erhardt-Platz.
**GPS:** n50,98122 e10,32342. ⬆.

3 ⬛free. **Location:** Urban, simple. **Surface:** metalled.
⬛ 01/01-31/12.
**Distance:** 🚂city centre 1km ⊗400m ⬛100m ⬛500m.
**Remarks:** At museum.

DE

## Eisenach 12C1
**Burg Wartburg**, Auf der Wartburg 1. **GPS**: n50,96775 e10,30989. ↑

5 € 5. **Location**: Urban, simple. **Surface**: metalled.
01/01-31/12.
**Distance**: 1,5km.
**Remarks**: Nearby castle Wartburg.

## Eisenach 12C1
**Landhotel Alte Fliegerschule**, Am Weinberg 1.
**GPS**: n50,98737 e10,37180.
4 € 10 on demand WC included.
**Location**: Rural, simple. **Surface**: metalled.
01/01-31/12.
**Distance**: 3km on the spot 3km on the spot on the spot.
**Remarks**: Breakfest-service.

## Eisenach 12C1
**Wohnmobile A. Waldhelm**, Ringstrasse 27.
**GPS**: n51,00194 e10,32667. ↑

20 € 10 Chincluded € 3/day WC € 0,50.
**Location**: Urban, simple. **Surface**: grasstiles.
01/01-31/12.
**Distance**: 1km 1km 1km Shuttle bus.
**Remarks**: Motorhome dealer, accessory shop, check in on arrival, bread-service.

## Eisfeld 12D2
**Festplatz**, Am Volkshaus. **GPS**: n50,42615 e10,90992. →

5 free. **Location**: Simple. **Surface**: grasstiles.
01/01-31/12. Whitsuntide.
**Distance**: 200m 200m 300m on the spot.

## Eisfeld 12D2
**Waldhotel Hubertus**, Coburgerstrasse 501.
**GPS**: n50,39680 e10,92269. ↑

20 free, use of a meal desired free € 5. **Location**: Rural, simple. **Surface**: asphalted/grassy. 01/01-31/12.
**Distance**: 3km on the spot 2km on the spot.
**Remarks**: Bread-service + breakfast-service.

## Erfurt 12D1

# Wohnmobilpark Trautmann Erfurt

- **Comfortable motorhome stopover**
- **Open all year**
- **Reservations possible**

**www.caravan-erfurt.de**
**info@caravan-erfurt.de**

**Wohnmobilpark Trautmann**, Rottenbacherweg 11, Melchendorf.
**GPS**: n50,95404 e11,06654. ↑
22 € 12,90 € 1,50/150liter Ch (22x)€ 1,50/5kWh,16Amp
WC € 1,50 € 3,50/1,50 € 1. **Location**: Urban, simple, noisy.
**Surface**: gravel. 01/01-31/12.
**Distance**: on the spot 3km 400m 300m 200m 300m
900m.
**Remarks**: Discount on access sauna/wellness, video surveillance.

## Erfurt 12D1
**P&R**, Am Urbicher Kreuz. **GPS**: n50,94992 e11,09456. →

15 free Ch. **Surface**: asphalted.
01/01-31/12.
**Distance**: 7km Total-shop Tram till 24am.
**Remarks**: Service at petrol station, outside environmental zone.

## Erfurt 12D1
**Am kleinen Ring**, Juri-Gagarin-Ring. **GPS**: n50,98111 e11,03472. ↑

4 free. **Location**: Urban. **Surface**: asphalted. 01/01-31/12.
**Distance**: Old city centre 1km 500m 500m.
**Remarks**: Max. 48h, green zone: environmental badge obligatory.

## Erfurt 12D1
**Egapark Parkplatz**, Gothaer Straße 40. **GPS**: n50,96484 e10,99650. ↑
5 free. **Location**: Simple, isolated. **Surface**: metalled.
01/01-31/12.
**Distance**: city centre 5,5km 200m on the spot.
**Remarks**: Outside environmental zone.

## Erfurt 12D1
**Eichenstrasse**. **GPS**: n50,97327 e11,02737. ↑ →

4 € 12. **Location**: Urban. **Surface**: asphalted. 01/01-31/12.
**Distance**: 200m 200m 300m on the spot.

## Erfurt 12D1
**Remarks**: Max. 48h, green zone: environmental badge obligatory.

## Erfurt 12D1
**P&R Parkplatz Thüringerhalle**, Werner-Seelenbinderstrasse.
**GPS**: n50,95771 e11,03605. ↑

7 free. **Location**: Urban, noisy. **Surface**: gravel.
01/01-31/12.
**Distance**: 2,6km 400m 1km Tram till 23am.
**Remarks**: Nearby B4, south edge of the city, green zone: environmental badge obligatory.

**Tourist information Erfurt:**
ℹ️ Erfurt-Card. Card gives for free entrance on among other things public transport and city museums, and discount on a lot of curiosities, guided tours, swimming pools, theater, souvernirs. € 14,90.
Stadtführung, Tourist Information, Benediktsplatz 1. Guided tour around the historic city center. 01/04-31/12 Mo-Fri 13h, Sa-Su 11h, 13h, 01/01-31/03 Sa-Su 11h, 13h. € 11.

## Gotha 12C1
Parkallee 1. **GPS**: n50,94402 e10,70948. ↑
3 free. **Location**: Urban, simple. **Surface**: metalled.
01/01-31/12.
**Distance**: 800m 800m.

## Heiligenstadt 10B3
**Stadthalle**, Aegidienstrasse 20. **GPS**: n51,37407 e10,13715. ↑

6 free € 0,50 Ch€ 0,50 € 1/3kWh WC. **Location**: Urban, comfortable. **Surface**: asphalted. 01/01-31/12.
**Distance**: 150m 200m 500m.
**Remarks**: At swimming pool, in front of town hall.

**Tourist information Heiligenstadt:**
ℹ️ City of churches, health resort.
Ⓜ️ Literaturmuseum Theodor Storm. Museum of important German writer. Tue-Fri 9-12h, 13-16h, Sa-Su 14-16h.

## Ichtershausen 12D1
**Autohof**, Thöreyerstrasse. **GPS**: n50,88824 e10,93478. ↑

20 € 6,50/24h, first hour free € 0,50 Ch€ 0,50 WC.
**Location**: Motorway. **Surface**: asphalted. 01/01-31/12.
**Distance**: 4km on the spot Esso-shop.

## Ichtershausen 12D1
**Freizeitfahrzeuge Mobilease**, Feldstrasse 1.
**GPS**: n50,86907 e10,96563. ↑

DE

5 ⛺ € 7,50 🚰🚽Ch. ♨(4x)included WC during opening hours.
**Surface:** gravel. 🗓 01/01-31/12.
**Distance:** 🚶3km ⊗500m 🛒bakery 500m.

### Ilfeld 10C3

**Gasthof Brauner Hirsch,** Dorfstrasse 42, Sophienhof.
**GPS:** n51,63467 e10,79223.⬆.

15 ⛺ € 5 🚰🚽Ch. ♨(3x)€ 0,35/kWh WC 🚽€ 2. **Location:** Rural.
**Surface:** metalled. 🗓 01/01-31/12.
**Distance:** ⊗on the spot 🚶3km 🎣on the spot ⚓on the spot.

### Ilmenau 12D2

**Festhalle,** Naumannstraße. **GPS:** n50,68139 e10,90472.⬆.

4 ⛺ free 🚰€ 2/80liter 🚽Ch. **Location:** Urban. **Surface:** asphalted.
🗓 01/01-31/12.
**Distance:** 🚶1km ⊗100m 🛒500m.
**Remarks:** Max. 24h.

### Kühndorf 12C2

**Flugschule Dolmar,** Am Flugplatz 1. **GPS:** n50,61198 e10,47079.➡.

20 ⛺ € 6 🚰€ 1 🚽Ch € 1,50 ♨€ 2/day WC 🚽€ 2. 🚿
**Location:** Rural, isolated. **Surface:** grassy/gravel.
🗓 01/01-31/12.
**Distance:** 🚶2km ⊗on the spot ⚓on the spot.
**Remarks:** Bread-service, parking behind the hangar.

### Lauscha ❄ 12D2

**Wanderparadies,** Steinachtal 1. **GPS:** n50,47752 e11,13486.
4 ⛺ € 14, 2 pers.incl 🚰🚽Ch♨€ 2 🔌included 🚿. **Location:** Rural.
**Surface:** grassy. 🗓 01/04-30/09.
**Distance:** 🚶2km ⊗2,5km ⚓on the spot.
**Remarks:** Bread-service, playground.

### Lauscha ❄ 12D2

**Parkplatz P4,** Obermühle. **GPS:** n50,48026 e11,16795.⬆.

10 ⛺ free. **Location:** Simple. **Surface:** asphalted.
🗓 01/01-31/12 🚫 1st and 2nd Sunday of advent.
**Distance:** 🚶300m ⊗100m 🛒1km ⚓on the spot 🎣on the spot.
**Remarks:** Max. 24h.

### Lauscha ❄ 12D2

**Sommerrodelbahn,** Lauschaer Straße, Ernstthal.
**GPS:** n50,48726 e11,17243.⬆.

10 ⛺ free. **Location:** Simple. **Surface:** asphalted. 🗓 01/01-31/12.
**Distance:** 🚶650m ⊗1km 🛒2km 🍴50m 🎣50m.

### Linda 12E2

**Knappmühle,** Ortsstraße. **GPS:** n50,68473 e11,78324.⬆.

10 ⛺ € 6 🚰🚽Ch. ♨(6x)€ 1/kWh. **Location:** Rural.
**Surface:** grassy/gravel. 🗓 01/03-31/10.
**Distance:** 🚶300m 🚲5km 🛒3km 🍴5km 🚶on the spot ⚓on the spot.

### Lindewerra 10B3

**Stellplatz Lindewerra,** Straße zur Einheit. **GPS:** n51,31320 e9,94570.
12 ⛺ free 🎣. **Location:** Rural, simple, isolated, quiet.
**Surface:** grassy/metalled. 🗓 01/01-31/12.
**Distance:** 🎣on the spot 🚶on the spot ⊗100m.
**Remarks:** Along river.

### Meiningen 12C2

**Rohrer Stirn,** Frankental. **GPS:** n50,56976 e10,43477.⬆.

10 ⛺ free 🚰€ 5 🚽Ch. ♨(6x)€ 0,50/kWh 🔌. **Location:** Urban,
simple, quiet. **Surface:** asphalted. 🗓 01/01-31/12.
**Distance:** 🚶2km ⊗200m 🛒1km.
**Remarks:** Parking at swimming pool, service on campsite.

### Meiningen 12C2

**Grossmutterwiesen,** Werrastrasse. **GPS:** n50,56172 e10,41266.⬆➡.

5 ⛺ free. **Location:** Simple. **Surface:** concrete. 🗓 01/01-31/12.
**Distance:** 🚶on the spot ⊗200m 🛒100m.
**Remarks:** Service possible at Kläranlage.

### Meiningen 12C2

**Volkshausplatz,** Landsbergerstrasse. **GPS:** n50,57427 e10,41369.⬆➡.

5 ⛺ free. **Location:** Urban, simple. **Surface:** metalled.
🗓 01/01-31/12.
**Distance:** 🚶200m 🍴on the spot ⊗200m 🛒200m.
**Remarks:** Service possible at Kläranlage.

### Mihla 12C1

**Graues Schloss;** Thomas-Münztzer-Straße 4.
**GPS:** n51,07854 e10,33166.⬆➡.

15 ⛺ € 8, guests free 🚰€ 5 ♨€ 5. **Location:** Rural, simple, quiet.
**Surface:** unpaved. 🗓 01/01-31/12 🚫 Whitsuntide.
**Distance:** 🚶on the spot 🎣fishing permit obligatory ⊗on the spot
🛒500m ⚓on the spot ⚓on the spot.

### Neustadt/Orla 12E1

**Gaststätte & Pension Heinrichs-Ruhe,** Heinrichsruhe 1, Rodaer
Strasse. **GPS:** n50,75545 e11,75595.⬆.

DE

20 �▤€ 10 ⛽€ 1/100liter ▦Ch⚡(6x)€ 0,50/kWh 📶.
**Location:** Rural. **Surface:** grassy/gravel.
⬛ 01/01-31/12 ⬛ Restaurant: Mo.
**Distance:** 🚶2,5km 🚲12km ⊗on the spot 🛒2km 🛍on the spot 🍴on the spot.
**Remarks:** Bread-service, bike and e-bike rental.

| | Nimritz | 12E2 |

**Wohnmobilstellplatz Nimritz**, Ortsstrasse 29.
**GPS:** n50,70079 e11,64858. ⬆️➡️

10 ⌧voluntary contribution ⛽€ 0,50 ▦Ch⚡(7x)€ 0,50/kWh.
**Surface:** grasstiles. ⬛ 01/01-31/12.
**Distance:** 🚶300m ⊗300m.

| | Nordhausen | 10C3 |

**Am Badehaus**, Grimmelallee 40. **GPS:** n51,50450 e10,78508. ⬆️➡️

2 ⌧€ 5, € 10 service and swimming pool incl ⛽€ 2 ▦€ 1 Ch€ 1 ⚡€ 1 🚿€ 3. **Location:** Urban, simple. **Surface:** metalled.
⬛ 01/01-31/12.
**Distance:** 🚶800m ⊗500m 🛒300m.
**Remarks:** At swimming pool.

| | Nordhausen | 10C3 |

**Am Kuhberg**, Parkallee. **GPS:** n51,51502 e10,78492. ⬆️

10 ⌧free. **Location:** Rural, isolated. **Surface:** asphalted.
⬛ 01/01-31/12.
**Distance:** 🚶2km ⊗on the spot 🛒500m.

| | Oberhof | 12C2 |

**Wohnmobilstellplatz Oberhof**, Jahnstrasse 7.
**GPS:** n50,70278 e10,72694. ⬆️➡️

60 ⌧€ 10-14 + € 2/pp tourist tax ⛽€ 1/80liter ▦Ch⚡(48x)€ 0,60/kWh 📶. **Location:** Urban, simple. **Surface:** asphalted.
⬛ 01/01-31/12.
**Distance:** 🚶400m ⊗200m 🛒500m 🛍on the spot.
**Remarks:** Bread-service.

**Tourist information Oberhof:**
👁 Rennsteiggarten Oberhof. Botanical garden. ⬛ 01/05-30/09 9-18, 01/10-31/10 9-17h.

| | Rudolstadt | 12D2 |

**Freizeit- und Erlebnisbad Saalemaxx**, Hugo-Trinckler-Straße 6.
**GPS:** n50,70635 e11,31659.

9 ⌧€ 7/24h ⛽€ 1/80liter ▦€ 1 Ch⚡€ 0,50/kWh.
**Surface:** gravel. ⬛ 01/01-31/12.
**Distance:** 🚶2km 🚲100m.
**Remarks:** Discount at swimming pool.

| | Saalfeld | 12D2 |

Reschwitzerstrasse, B281. **GPS:** n50,63720 e11,36751. ⬆️➡️

5 ⌧free. **Surface:** gravel. ⬛ 01/01-31/12.
**Distance:** 🚶2,8km ⊗200m.
**Remarks:** Parking at swimming pool.

| | Saalfeld | 12D2 |

**Saalfelder Feengrotten**, Feengrottenweg 2.
**GPS:** n50,63468 e11,33982. ⬆️➡️

10 ⌧€ 10 ⛽€ 3/5minutes ▦€ 3 Ch⚡(6x)€ 0,50/kWh WC€ 1. 🚽
**Location:** Rural, comfortable, quiet. **Surface:** grassy.
⬛ 01/01-31/12.
**Distance:** 🚶2,3km ⊗on the spot 🛒bakery 500m 🚲500m.
**Remarks:** Max. 72h.

| | Schleiz | 12E2 |

**Spitzbergs Zollhaus**, Burgkerstrasse 25.
**GPS:** n50,55507 e11,73438. ⬆️➡️

5 ⌧€ 5, free with a meal ⛽▦Ch⚡(7x)€ 2/24h.
⬛ 01/01-31/12 ⬛ Tue.
**Distance:** 🚶7km 🚲5,4km ⊗on the spot 🛒7km.

| | Schleiz | 12E2 |

**HEM-Großtankstelle**, Saalburgerstrasse.
**GPS:** n50,55004 e11,78788. ⬆️

8 ⌧€ 2 WC. **Location:** Motorway. **Surface:** asphalted.
⬛ 01/01-31/12.

**Distance:** 🚶5km ⊗on the spot 🛒shop.
**Remarks:** Industrial area, max. 24h.

| | Schmalkalden | 12C2 |

**Reisemobilparkplatz Westendpark**, Westendstrasse 2-4.
**GPS:** n50,72118 e10,44071.
8 ⌧€ 10 ⛽€ 1/80liter ▦Ch⚡(8x)€ 1/6h,10Amp.
**Location:** Urban. **Surface:** asphalted. ⬛ 01/01-31/12.
**Distance:** 🚶600m 🚲100m ⊗150m 🛒300m 🚉station 100m 🛍10m 🍴10m. **Remarks:** On the Schmalkalde river.

| | Schmiedefeld | 12C2 |

**Sportplatz**, Sportplatzstraße. **GPS:** n50,60324 e10,81491. ⬆️

20 ⌧€ 3 + € 1,80/pp tourist tax. **Location:** Rural, simple, quiet.
**Surface:** grasstiles/metalled. ⬛ 01/01-31/12.
**Distance:** 🚶500m ⊗400m 🍴on the spot 🛍on the spot.
**Remarks:** Pay at tourist office or Gasthaus Thüringer Hof.

| | Sitzendorf | 12D2 |

**Sitzendorfer Porzellanmanufaktur**, Hauptstrasse 26.
**GPS:** n50,63174 e11,16788. ⬆️

5 ⌧free. **Surface:** asphalted. ⬛ 01/01-31/12.
**Distance:** 🚶on the spot ⊗200m 🛒200m.

| | Sondershausen | 10C3 |

**P7 zur Windleite**, Hospitalstrasse. **GPS:** n51,37824 e10,86234. ⬆️➡️

5 ⌧free ⛽€ 1/5minutes ▦Ch⚡(4x)€ 1/2h. **Surface:** metalled.
⬛ 01/01-31/12.
**Distance:** 🚶2,5km ⊗500m 🛒100m.

| | Sondershausen | 10C3 |

**Freizeitpark Possen**, Possen 1. **GPS:** n51,33800 e10,86265.

DE

10 ⊠ € 4/stay ⚡included. **Surface:** metalled. ☐ 01/01-31/12.
**Distance:** 🚶5km ⊗on the spot.
**Remarks:** Bread-service.

### Stadtlengsfeld — 12B2

**Am Schwimmbad**, Eisenacher Straße. **GPS:** n50,79065 e10,11373.

6 ⊠free 🚰 € 1/80liter ⚡ € 1/kWh. **Location:** Rural, simple.
**Surface:** asphalted. ☐ 01/01-31/12.
**Distance:** 🚶1,5km.

### Steinheid — 12D2

**Am Rennsteig**, Eisfelder Straße, Limbach.
**GPS:** n50,47568 e11,06937.

4 ⊠free. **Location:** Rural, simple, noisy. **Surface:** gravel.
☐ 01/01-31/12.
**Distance:** ⊗150m 🚶10km on the spot.

### Steinheid — 12D2

**Thüringer Baumschmuck**, Neuhäuser Strasse 8-10.
**GPS:** n50,47302 e11,08672.

8 ⊠ € 5, free for clients 🚰 € 2/90liter ⚡included.
**Location:** Simple. **Surface:** unpaved. ☐ 01/01-31/12.
**Distance:** 🚶1,5km 🛒3km, bakery 50m 🚶on the spot 🍴on the spot 🚲on the spot.
**Remarks:** At Christmas Balls manufacturer.

### Tabarz — 12C1

Karl-Kornhaß-Straße. **GPS:** n50,87782 e10,52038.

8 ⊠free, tourist tax € 2/pp. **Location:** Rural, simple, quiet.
**Surface:** metalled. ☐ 01/01-31/12.
**Distance:** 🚶on the spot ⊗200m 🛒Rewe 400m.
**Remarks:** To be paid at TABBS sports centre.

### Tambach-Dietharz — 12C1

**Festplatz**, Burgstallstraße. **GPS:** n50,78902 e10,60897.

4 ⊠free, tourist tax € 1/pp ⚡Ch ⚡service € 6.
**Location:** Urban, simple. **Surface:** gravel. ☐ 01/01-31/12.
**Distance:** 🚶on the spot ⊗on the spot.
**Remarks:** Key service at town hall.

### Tambach-Dietharz — 12C1

**Freigelande Lohmühle**, Lohmühle 1-5. **GPS:** n50,81056 e10,62778.

30 ⊠ € 6 + € 4/pp 🚰Ch ⚡ € 2 WC € 1 € 1.
**Location:** Rural, simple, quiet.
**Surface:** grassy.
☐ 01/01-31/12. ◉ Mon.
**Distance:** 🚶2km ⊗on the spot 🛒3km 🚲on the spot 🚶on the spot.
**Remarks:** Check in on arrival, barefoot park, museum.

### Themar — 12C2

**Am Hexenturm**, Mauerstrasse. **GPS:** n50,50512 e10,61194.

5 ⊠free 🚰 € 1/50liter ⚡ € 2 Ch ⚡ € 1/kWh. **Location:** Urban,
simple, quiet. **Surface:** grasstiles. ☐ 01/01-31/12.
**Distance:** 🚶100m ⊗300m 🛒400m 🚲on the spot 🚶on the spot.
**Remarks:** Along the Werra river, 01/11-31/03 water disconnected.

### Tiefenort — 12B1

**Freizeitanlage Heerstatt**, Auf der Heerstatt.
**GPS:** n50,83444 e10,16306.

6 ⊠free ⚡ € 2/day. **Location:** Rural, simple. **Surface:** concrete.
☐ 01/03-31/10.
**Distance:** 🚶on the spot ⊗50m 🛒bakery 900m 🚶on the spot.
**Remarks:** On island in the Werra river.

### Treffurt — 12C1

**Wohnmobilstellplatz Unter den Linden**.
**GPS:** n51,13398 e10,23659.

20 ⊠free 🚰 € 0,50/80liter ⚡Ch ⚡(8x)€ 1/kWh.
**Location:** Rural, simple, quiet. **Surface:** grasstiles/grassy.
☐ 01/01-31/12. ◉ 15/07-31/07.
**Distance:** 🚶300m ⊗on the spot ⊗50m 🛒500m 🚶on the spot
🚶on the spot.
**Remarks:** Along river, water closed during wintertime.

**Tourist information Treffurt:**
ℹ Small town with half-timbered houses and medival castle
Normannstein.

### Vacha — 12B1

Frankfurter Strasse. **GPS:** n50,81856 e10,01327.
5 ⊠free. **Location:** Simple. **Surface:** gravel. ☐ 01/01-31/12.
**Distance:** 🚶1km ⊗1km.
**Remarks:** At swimming pool.

### Weimar — 12D1

Hermann Brill-Platz. **GPS:** n50,98501 e11,31701.

20 ⊠ € 10/24h 🚰 € 1 ⚡Ch ⚡(6x)€ 1/6h. **Surface:** metalled.
☐ 01/01-31/12.
**Distance:** 🚶Weimar centre 1,2km ⊗on the spot 🛒500m.

### Zella-Mehlis — 12C2

**Toschis Station**, An der Quelle 5. **GPS:** n50,64375 e10,68436.

10 ⊠ € 8 🚰 € 1 ⚡Ch ⚡(20x)€ 0,50/kWh ⚡. **Location:** Simple,
central. **Surface:** grassy/gravel. ☐ 01/01-31/12.
**Distance:** ⊗on the spot 🛒300m 🚶on the spot.
**Remarks:** Check in at reception, grill and picknic area.

### Zeulenroda — 12E2

**Badewelt Waikiki**, Am Birkenwege 1. **GPS:** n50,66543 e11,99355.

6 ⊠ € 10 🚰 ⚡Ch ⚡included,water and electricity € 10/day.
**Surface:** metalled. ☐ 01/01-31/12.

### Zeulenroda — 12E2

**Wohnmobilhafen Zeulenrodaer Meer**, Bleichenweg 30.
**GPS:** n50,65778 e11,96556.

DE

18 ⬥€ 10 + € 2/pp ⬥Ch ⬥(28x)€ 0,50/kWh WC ⬥included.
**Location:** Rural. **Surface:** gravel. ⬥ 01/01-31/12.
**Distance:** ⬥1,5km ⬥on the spot ⬥on the spot ⬥1km ⬥on the spot.
**Remarks:** At tourist office, use sanitary only during opening hours swimming pool, playground.

# Baden Württemberg

### Aalen ⬥ 17C3
**Hirschbach**, Hirschbachstrasse 68. **GPS:** n48,84524 e10,10712.⬥⬥.

12 ⬥free ⬥€ 1/80liter ⬥Ch ⬥€ 1/2kWh. **Location:** Rural.
**Surface:** asphalted. ⬥ 01/01-31/12.
**Distance:** ⬥800m ⬥100m ⬥200m.
**Remarks:** At swimming pool, max. 3 days.

### Aalen 17C3
**Limes-Thermen, P1**, Osterbucher Steige.
**GPS:** n48,82047 e10,07918.⬥.

10 ⬥free. **Location:** Rural, simple. **Surface:** grasstiles.
⬥ 01/01-31/12.
**Distance:** ⬥100m.

### Achern ⬥ 16H3
**Wohnmobilstellplatz Achern**, Kapellenstrasse/Badstrasse.
**GPS:** n48,62436 e8,07359.⬥.

14 ⬥€ 8 ⬥€ 1/100liter ⬥Ch ⬥(12x)€ 1/6h. ⬥
**Location:** Urban, simple, quiet. **Surface:** gravel/metalled.
⬥ 01/01-31/12.
**Distance:** ⬥500m ⬥4,8km ⬥650m ⬥on the spot ⬥on the spot.
**Remarks:** Next to swimming pool, tuesday and Saturday market.

### Albstadt ⬥ 20A1
**Sonnencamping**, Beibruck 54. **GPS:** n48,21438 e8,97879.⬥.

16 ⬥€ 10 ⬥€ 1/100liter ⬥Ch ⬥€ 0,60/kWh WC ⬥€ 2 ⬥⬥.⬥
**Location:** Rural. **Surface:** grassy/gravel. ⬥ 01/01-31/12.
**Distance:** ⬥5km ⬥500m ⬥2km ⬥on the spot ⬥on the spot ⬥2km ⬥2km.
**Remarks:** Max. 4 days.

### Allensbach 20A2
**Landgasthaus Mindelsee**, Gemeinmärk 7.
**GPS:** n47,74279 e9,04411.⬥.

15 ⬥€ 8, guests free. **Location:** Rural. **Surface:** metalled.
⬥ 01/01-31/12 ⬥ Tue.
**Distance:** ⬥5km ⬥on the spot.
**Remarks:** Max. 1 night, max 3,5t, bread-service.

### Allmersbach im Tal ⬥ 17B2
**SportErlebnisPark**, Schorndorfer Straße 68.
**GPS:** n48,90210 e9,47539.⬥.

10 ⬥€ 12 ⬥€ 1/80liter ⬥Ch ⬥ 1 ⬥€ 1/2kWh WC ⬥€ 0,50 ⬥€ 2 ⬥included. **Location:** Rural, comfortable, quiet. **Surface:** gravel.
⬥ 01/01-31/12.
**Distance:** ⬥500m ⬥on the spot ⬥1km.

### Alpirsbach ⬥ 19H1
**Bahnhofstrasse. GPS:** n48,34279 e8,39708.⬥.
4 ⬥free. **Location:** Simple, noisy. **Surface:** gravel.
⬥ 01/01-31/12.
**Distance:** ⬥650m ⬥650m ⬥on the spot.

### Amtzell ⬥ 20B2
**Wohnmobilstellplatz Büchelweisen**, Büchel 3.
**GPS:** n47,70871 e9,76684.⬥⬥.

36 ⬥€ 10 ⬥€ 1/90liter ⬥Ch ⬥(36x)€ 0,50/kWh WC ⬥€ 1,50.
**Location:** Rural, comfortable, quiet. **Surface:** grasstiles.
⬥ 01/01-31/12.
**Distance:** ⬥1,5km ⬥1km ⬥1km ⬥on the spot ⬥1,5km.
**Remarks:** Bread-service.

### Aspach ⬥ 17B2
**Gemeindehallen**, Rübengasse. **GPS:** n48,96437 e9,39706.
⬥free. ⬥ 01/01-31/12.
**Distance:** ⬥100m.
**Remarks:** At gymnasium.

### Aspach ⬥ 17B2
**Wanderparkplatz Fautenhau**, Im Fautenhau, Hohrot.
**GPS:** n48,97823 e9,39483.⬥.

5 ⬥free. **Location:** Rural. **Surface:** metalled. ⬥ 01/01-31/12.
**Distance:** ⬥on the spot.
**Remarks:** Max. 1 night, parking P0.

### Aspach ⬥ 17B2
**Wanderparkplatz Heiligental**, Heiligentalstrasse, Rietenau.
**GPS:** n48,99158 e9,40519.⬥.

5 ⬥free. **Location:** Rural, quiet. **Surface:** asphalted/grassy.
⬥ 01/01-31/12.
**Distance:** ⬥on the spot.
**Remarks:** Max. 1 night.

### Aspach ⬥ 17B2
**Caravan-Service-Station**, L1124. **GPS:** n48,96375 e9,37582.⬥.
⬥Ch. ⬥ 01/01-31/12.

### Aulendorf 20B1
**Schwaben-Therme**, Ebisweilerstrasse 5. **GPS:** n47,95797 e9,63728.⬥.

20 (P3) ⬥free. **Location:** Rural. **Surface:** metalled.
⬥ 01/01-31/12.
**Distance:** ⬥500m ⬥on the spot ⬥500m.
**Remarks:** Parking swimming pool, max. 2 nights.

### Aulendorf ⬥ 20B1
**Carthago-City**, Carthago Ring 1. **GPS:** n47,93759 e9,65246.
100 ⬥free ⬥€ 0,50/50liter ⬥Ch ⬥€ 0,50/kWh. **Surface:** metalled.
⬥ 01/01 31/12.
**Distance:** ⬥2,5km ⬥950m.
**Remarks:** At motohome manufacturer.

### Backnang ⬥ 17B2
**Martin-Dietrich-Allee. GPS:** n48,95041 e9,45281.⬥.

4 ⬥free ⬥€ 1/90liter ⬥Ch. **Location:** Rural, simple.
**Surface:** gravel. ⬥ 01/01-31/12.
**Distance:** ⬥1km ⬥400m ⬥on the spot ⬥on the spot.

### Bad Bellingen ⬥ 19G2
**Balinea Thermen**, Badstrasse 14. **GPS:** n47,72963 e7,55233.⬥.

## Bad Buchau

31 🛌 € 14 + € 1,45-2,25 tourist tax 🚰📶Ch 🔌included WC 🚽€ 1,50.
**Location:** Urban, noisy. **Surface:** asphalted/metalled.
⏱ 01/01-31/12.
**Distance:** 🚶500m 🚲5,5km ⊗on the spot ⛽on the spot.
**Remarks:** No trailers allowed.

### Bad Buchau — 20B1
**Adelindis Therme**, Am Kurpark. **GPS:** n48,06865 e9,60653. ⬆️

21 🛌 € 9,50 XL-pitch € 11 🚰€ 1/80liter 📶Ch 🔌€ 0,50/kWh
WC € 1. 🚽🚐 **Location:** Rural, simple, quiet. **Surface:** metalled.
⏱ 01/01-31/12.
**Distance:** 🚶500m ⊗200m ⛽on the spot 🚶on the spot.

### Bad Buchau — 20B1
**Seegasse. GPS:** n48,06832 e9,60962.

17 🛌 € 9,50 🚰 1/80liter 📶Ch 🔌(17x)€ 0,50/kWh. 🚐
**Location:** Simple, central. **Surface:** metalled.
⏱ 01/01-31/12.
**Distance:** 🚶500m.
**Remarks:** Adelindis Therme 300m.

### Bad Buchau — 20B1
**Federseemuseum**, Wellerstraße. **GPS:** n48,07051 e9,60949. ➡️

12 🛌 € 9 🔌(12x)€ 0,50/kWh WC 🚽. 🚐 **Location:** Rural.
**Surface:** asphalted. ⏱ 01/01-31/12.
**Distance:** 🚶800m.
**Remarks:** Adelindis Therme 500m.

### Bad Buchau — 20B1
**Am Freibad**, Friedhofstrasse. **GPS:** n48,06292 e9,61714. ⬆️

10 🛌 € 9. **Location:** Rural. **Surface:** asphalted. ⏱ 15/05-01/09.
**Distance:** 🚶700m.

## Bad Ditzenbach — 17B3
**Vinzenz Therme**, Badstraße 20. **GPS:** n48,59003 e9,70553. ⬆️

10 🛌 € 5, winter € 6 🚰📶Ch 🔌🚐 **Location:** Rural.
**Surface:** asphalted. ⏱ 01/01-31/12.
**Distance:** ⊗750m ⛽750m.
**Remarks:** Caution key € 50.

## Bad Dürrheim — 20A1
**Reisemobilhafen Bad Dürrheim**, Huberstraße 34/2.
**GPS:** n48,01204 e8,53506. ⬆️➡️

300 🛌 € 8,50 + € 2,50/pp tourist tax 🚰€ 1/100liter 📶Ch 🔌€ 2,50/
night WC € 2 🚽. **Location:** Rural, comfortable. **Surface:** gravel.
⏱ 01/01-31/12.
**Distance:** ⊗on the spot.
**Remarks:** Pay at reception, bread-service, special health arrangement
possible.

## Bad Herrenalb — 16H3
**Wohnmobilstation Siebentäler Therme**, Schweizer Wiese.
**GPS:** n48,80334 e8,44067. ⬆️

9 🛌 € 5 + tourist tax € 2,50/pp 🚰€ 1 🚽€ 1 Ch€ 1 🔌(4x)€ 0,50/kWh.
**Location:** Rural, simple. **Surface:** asphalted.
⏱ 01/01-31/12.
**Distance:** 🚶500m ⊗100m ⛽200m 🚐200m 🚲on the spot 🚶on
the spot.
**Remarks:** Max. 2 nights, use sanitary only during opening hours,
discount on access terme, friday market.
**Tourist information Bad Herrenalb:**
🚶 Quellenerlebnispfad, Kurpark Herrenalb. Hiking trails past 60
fountains.

## Bad Krozingen — 19G2
**Wohnmobilstellplatz Vita Classica**, Thürachstraße.
**GPS:** n47,91763 e7,68821. ⬆️➡️

80 🛌 € 12, from 7th night € 10,50 🚰📶Ch 🔌€ 3,50/day,16Amp
WC 🚽€ 3 🚽included. ♿
**Location:** Rural, comfortable. **Surface:** gravel.
⏱ 01/01-31/12.
**Distance:** 🚶600m 🚲3km ⊗50m ⛽600m 🏪800m 🚌on the spot
🚲on the spot 🚶on the spot.
**Remarks:** Bread-service, trailer € 2,50/night, bike and e-bike rental.

## Bad Liebenzell — 17A3
**Campingpark Bad Liebenzell**, Pforzheimer strasse 34.
**GPS:** n48,77850 e8,73120. ⬆️

16 🛌 € 8, tourist tax € 2/pp 🚰📶Ch 🔌(16x)WC 🚽included 🚽€ 3
📶🚐 **Location:** Rural, simple, noisy. **Surface:** metalled/sand.
⏱ 01/01-31/12.
**Distance:** 🚶on the spot 🚲17km ⊗500m ⛽100m 🚌on the spot
🚲on the spot 🚶on the spot.

## Bad Mergentheim — 17B1
**Wohnmobilstellplatz an der Solymar Therme**, Erlenbachweg.
**GPS:** n49,49194 e9,79167. ⬆️➡️

20 🛌 € 5, tourist tax € 2,70/pp 🚰€ 1/80liter 📶Ch 🔌(8x)€ 1/8h. 🚐
**Location:** Rural, simple. **Surface:** gravel.
⏱ 01/01-31/12.
**Distance:** 🚶Old city centre 1km ⊗200m ⛽Lidl 800m 🚌100m.
**Remarks:** Max. 3 nights.

## Bad Niedernau — 17A3
**Wohnmobilparkplatz Bad Niedernau**, Blaue Brücke.
**GPS:** n48,45931 e8,89959. ⬆️➡️

5 🛌 free. **Location:** Rural, simple. **Surface:** gravel. ⏱ 01/01-31/12.
**Distance:** 🚶500m ⊗600m ⛽3km 🚌station 650m Roma-Viterbo
🚶on the spot.
**Remarks:** Along the Neckar river, max. 3 nights.

## Bad Peterstal-Griesbach — 19H1
**An den Heilquellen**, Schwarzwaldstraße 43. **GPS:** n48,43384 e8,21369.

10 🛌 € 9, 2 pers.incl, dog € 0,50 🚰€ 1/80liter 📶Ch 🔌€ 1/6h
🚽€ 1 📶included. **Location:** Urban, comfortable, noisy.
**Surface:** grassy/gravel. ⏱ 01/01-31/12.
**Distance:** ⊗100m ♨400m 🚲on the spot 🚶on the spot.

## Bad Rappenau — 17A2
**Salinenpark**, Weinbrennerstrasse. **GPS:** n49,23517 e9,11396. ⬆️➡️

30 ⌕ € 3/pp, child € 2 ⚡ € 1/3minutes ⌫Ch ✎ (24x)€ 1/kWh.
**Location:** Rural, comfortable. **Surface:** metalled.
⬛ 01/01-31/12.
**Distance:** ⛷1km ⊗50m ⚓1km.
**Remarks:** Check in at pay-desk of the Therme, therme 400m.

### Bad Rappenau 17A2
**Autohof Bad Rappenau**, A6, Wilhelm-Hauff-Straße 43, Fürfeld.
**GPS:** n49,21043 e9,06927.⬆
15 ⌕ € 12, free for clients ⚡⌫ChWC⬜◉ ✎ ⌂
**Location:** Motorway, simple. **Surface:** metalled. ⬛ 01/01-31/12.
**Distance:** ✎300m ⊗on the spot ⚓on the spot.
**Remarks:** Breakfast-service.

### Bad Säckingen 19H2
**Reisemobilplatz Am Rheinufer**, Ausstrasse.
**GPS:** n47,54903 e7,94765.⬆➡

40 ⌕ € 12/24h, >7,8m € 16/24h ⚡ € 0,50/100liter ⌫ € 0,20 Ch ✎
(39x)included WC. ▯
**Location:** Urban, comfortable, quiet. **Surface:** gravel.
⬛ 01/01-31/12 ◉ beginning Mar, end Oct.
**Distance:** ⛷300m ✎6km ⚓50m ✎on the spot 🚲on the spot.
**Remarks:** Along river, several offers, i.e. free public transport.

**Tourist information Bad Säckingen:**
✎ Nachtwächterführungen. Evening tour guided by night watch in historical cloths and with lantern. Information and booking: Kurverwaltung. ⊤ € 5.

### Bad Saulgau 20B1
**GolfPark Bad Saulgau**, Koppelweg 103. **GPS:** n47,97928 e9,48623.⬆

30 ⌕ € 10, golfers free ⚡ € 1/100liter ⌫Ch ✎ € 1/6h ✎🚲
**Location:** Rural, isolated, quiet. **Surface:** metalled.
⬛ 01/03-31/10.
**Distance:** ⛷4km ⊗on the spot ⚓4km.
**Remarks:** At golf court.

### Bad Saulgau 20B1
**Wonhmobilstellplatz Sonnenhof-Therme**, Am Schönen Moos.
**GPS:** n48,01703 e9,48838.⬆

53 ⌕ € 10 + € 1,50/pp tourist tax ⚡ € 0,50/50liter ⌫Ch ✎
(69x)€ 0,50/kWh ◉. ▯ **Location:** Rural. **Surface:** metalled.
⬛ 01/01-31/12.
**Distance:** ⛷on the spot ⊗on the spot ⚓on the spot.
**Remarks:** Bread-service, discount on access terme.

### Bad Schönborn 17A2
**Reisemobilhafen WellMobilPark**, Kraichgaustraße 16.
**GPS:** n49,21839 e8,67144.⬆➡

86 ⌕ € 9,50, >10m € 14 ⚡ € 1/100liter ⌫Ch ✎ (112x)€ 0,50/
kWh WC € 0,20 ⚡€ 2 ◉ ✎€ 1/h. **Location:** Rural, luxurious.
**Surface:** gravel. ⬛ 01/01-31/12.
**Distance:** ⛷800m ⊗on the spot ⚓1km ⚍200m.
**Remarks:** Bread-service, swimming pool available.

### Bad Schussenried 20B1
**Am Zellersee**, Zellerseeweg. **GPS:** n48,00160 e9,64724.⬆

10 ⌕ € 5 + € 1,20/pp tourist tax ⚡⌫Ch ✎🚲
**Location:** Rural, simple, quiet. **Surface:** asphalted.
⬛ 01/01-31/12.
**Distance:** ⛷900m ⚖on the spot ⊗900m ⚓900m.

### Bad Schussenried 20B1
**Bierkrugmuseum**, Wilhelm Schussenstrasse 12.
**GPS:** n48,00325 e9,65902.⬆

30 ⌕free ⚡⌫Ch ✎€ 5,reduction for guests WC.
**Location:** Rural, simple, quiet. **Surface:** metalled.
⬛ 01/01-31/12.
**Distance:** ⛷on the spot ⊗150m ⚓250m.
**Remarks:** Brewery and brewery museum.

**Tourist information Bad Schussenried:**
Ⓜ Kloster Schussenried. History of the monastary. ⬛ Easter-Oct 13.30-17.30h.

### Bad Teinach 17A3
**Untere talstasse 33. GPS:** n48,68090 e8,69440. ⬆

20 ⌕free. **Location:** Rural, simple, isolated. **Surface:** asphalted.
⬛ 01/01-31/12.
**Distance:** ⛷50m ⊗100m ⚓100m ✎on the spot 🚲on the spot
✎on the spot.
**Remarks:** Parking swimming pool, max. 24h.

### Bad Teinach 17A3
**Stellplatz am Wanderheim**, Fronwaldstraße 48.
**GPS:** n48,69916 e8,69500.
5 ⌕free. **Location:** Rural, isolated, quiet. **Surface:** metalled.
⬛ 01/01-31/12.
**Distance:** ⛷centre 1,2km ⊗on the spot ⚓1,3km ⚍1km 🚲on the spot ✎on the spot.
**Remarks:** Max. 8M.

### Bad Urach 17B3
**Wohnmobilstellplatz Bad Urach**, Bäderstraße.
**GPS:** n48,50060 e9,37713.⬆

26 ⌕ € 8 ⚡ € 0,50/60liter ⌫€ 0,50 Ch€ 0,50 ✎included. ▯
**Location:** Urban, simple. **Surface:** asphalted. ⬛ 01/01-31/12.
**Distance:** ⛷on the spot ⚍5km ⊗200m ⚓800m ⚍200m 🚲10km ✎10km.
**Remarks:** Bicycle rental.

### Bad Waldsee 20B1
**Bauernhof Lott**, Mattenhaus 4. **GPS:** n47,95113 e9,75838.

10 ⌕ € 16, 2 pers.incl ⚡ € 1 ⌫Ch ✎ (10x)€ 0,50/kWh WC▯€ 4.
**Location:** Rural, comfortable, quiet. **Surface:** grassy.
⬛ 01/04-31/10.
**Distance:** ⛷3,5km ⚖3km ⚍3km ⊗200m ⚓3km.
**Remarks:** Bread-service.

### Bad Waldsee 20B1
**Waldsee-Therme**, Unterurbacher weg. **GPS:** n47,91441 e9,76047.⬆➡

39 ⌕ € 2 + € 2/pp tourist tax ⚡ € 1/100liter ⌫€ 2 Ch ✎ € 1/2kWh.
▯ **Surface:** metalled. ⬛ 01/01-31/12.
**Distance:** ⛷1km ⚖1km ⚍1km ⊗500m ⚓1km ⚍500m.
**Remarks:** Bread-service.

### Bad Wildbad 16H3
**Kernerstrasse. GPS:** n48,74132 e8,54740.⬆

11 ⌕ € 10 ⚡ € 1/3minutes ⌫Ch ✎ (16x)€ 2/8h. ▯
**Location:** Rural, simple, noisy. **Surface:** asphalted.
⬛ 01/01-31/12.
**Distance:** ⛷500m ⊗500m ⚓300m ✎on the spot 🚲on the spot
✎on the spot.
**Remarks:** Max. 3 days, thursday market.

### Bad Wimpfen 17A2
**Wohnmobilstellplatz SRH Gesundheitszentrum**, An der Alten Saline 2. **GPS:** n49,23383 e9,15069.⬆➡

8 ⚑ € 8 + € 1,80/pp tourist tax 🚰 € 1/100liter 🔌Ch.⚡(8x)€ 1/12h WC. 🛒 **Location:** Rural, comfortable, quiet. **Surface:** grasstiles. ⭕ 01/01-31/12.
**Distance:** 🚶800m 🏃 on the spot.
**Remarks:** Parking at health resort.

🅰🅱S **Bad Wurzach** ♨ 20C2

**Wohnmobilstellplatz Vitalium**, Riedhalde, An der Thermalquelle 1.
**GPS:** n47,91437 e9,90363. ⬆➡.

17 ⚑ € 5,50 + € 1,50/pp tourist tax 🚰 € 0,50 🔌 € 0,50 Ch.⚡included WC ⬜. **Location:** Rural, quiet. **Surface:** asphalted.
⭕ 01/01-31/12.
**Distance:** 🚶500m ⊗300m 🚎500m.
**Remarks:** Check in at pay-desk of Vitalium.

🅰🅱S **Baden-Baden** ♨ 16H3

**Wohnmobilparkplatz**, Hubertusstraße 2, Badenscheuern.
**GPS:** n48,78193 e8,20388. ⬆➡.

28 ⚑ € 12 🚰 € 1/100liter 🔌Ch.⚡(28x) 0,50/kWh. 🚽
**Location:** Urban, comfortable, noisy. **Surface:** metalled.
⭕ 01/01-31/12.
**Distance:** 🚶Baden-Baden 4km ✈1km ⊗100m 🚎150m 🚌on the spot 🏃 on the spot.
**Remarks:** Max. 4 days, video surveillance.

🅰🅱S **Baiersbronn** ♨ 16H3

**Schelkewiesen**, Neumühleweg/Lochweg.
**GPS:** n48,51016 e8,37272. ⬆➡.

15 ⚑ € 8, tourist tax incl 🚰 € 1/80liter 🔌Ch.⚡(12x)€ 0,50/kWh. 🚍
**Location:** Rural, simple, quiet. **Surface:** metalled.
⭕ 01/01-31/12.
**Distance:** 🚶300m ⊗100m 🚎100m 🚌200m 🚲on the spot 🏃 on the spot.
**Remarks:** Max. 8M.

🅰🅱S **Balingen** 🌿♨🍺 20A1

**Wohnmobilstellplatz an der Eyach**, Heinzlerstrasse.
**GPS:** n48,27024 e8,85300. ⬆➡.

---

10 ⚑free 🚰 € 1/100liter 🔌 € 1 Ch € 1 ⚡(8x)€ 0,50/kWh WC.
**Location:** Urban, simple. **Surface:** asphalted. ⭕ 01/01-31/12.
**Distance:** 🚶on the spot ⛵500m ⊗300m 🚎300m 🏃 on the spot.
**Remarks:** At swimming pool, max. 4 days, green zone: environmental badge obligatory.

🅰🅱S **Benningen am Neckar** 17A2

**Parkplatz Gemeindehalle**, Max-Eyth Strasse.
**GPS:** n48,94574 e9,23363.

4 ⚑free. **Location:** Rural, simple, noisy. **Surface:** metalled.
⭕ 01/01-31/12.
**Distance:** 🚶on the spot ⊗50m 🚎1km 🚌750m.

🅰🅱S **Bernau im Schwarzwald** 🏔❄ 19H2

**Sportzentrum Spitzenberg**, Sportplatzstraße.
**GPS:** n47,80614 e8,02803. ⬆➡.

15 ⚑free, tourist tax € 2,20/pp 🚰 € 1/100liter 🔌Ch.⚡ € 1/8h
⬜. **Location:** Rural, simple, quiet. **Surface:** grassy/gravel.
⭕ 16/04-30/09.
**Distance:** 🚶500m ⊗1km 🚌500m.
**Remarks:** Pay at tourist office.

🅰🅱S **Besigheim** 🌿🍴🍺 17A2

**Wohnmobilstellplatz bei der Minigolfanlage**, Auf dem Kies 32.
**GPS:** n48,99771 e9,14863. ⬆➡.

15 ⚑ € 7,50 🚰 € 1/50liter 🔌Ch.⚡(6x)€ 0,50/kWh ⚡free.
**Location:** Rural, comfortable, quiet. **Surface:** metalled.
⭕ 01/01-31/12.
**Distance:** 🚶500m ✈10km ⛵500m ⊗200m 🚌500m 🚎100m 🚲 on the spot 🏃 on the spot.
**Remarks:** At sports park, max. 3 nights.

🅰🅱S **Beuren** ♨ 17B3

**Panorama Therme**, Goethestraße. **GPS:** n48,56621 e9,39944. ⬆.

---

4 ⚑ € 6 🚰⚡ € 1/3kWh. **Location:** Urban, simple. **Surface:** metalled.
⭕ 01/01-31/12.
**Distance:** 🚶500m ⊗on the spot 🚌500m 🚎100m.

🅰🅱S **Beuron** 20A1

**Kloster Beuron**, Abteistraße. **GPS:** n48,05306 e8,96704. ⬆.

20 ⚑free ⚡ € 1. **Location:** Rural, simple. **Surface:** gravel.
⭕ 01/01-31/12.
**Distance:** 🚎on the spot.
**Remarks:** Parking monastery.

🅰🅱S **Beuron** 20A1

**Besi-Kanu-Sport**, Bahnhofstrasse 29. **GPS:** n48,08597 e9,09559. ⬆.

10 ⚑ € 5 🚰🔌Ch.⚡WCincluded. 🚿 **Location:** Rural, simple.
**Surface:** gravel. ⭕ 01/01-31/12.
**Distance:** 🚶1km ⊗200m 🚌5km.
**Remarks:** Canoe rental.

🅰🅱S **Biberach/Riss** 20B1

Rißstraße. **GPS:** n48,10401 e9,79582. ⬆.

18 ⚑ € 5 🚰 🔌Chincluded ⚡€ 0,50/kWh. 🚍
**Location:** Urban, simple, central. **Surface:** gravel.
⭕ 01/01-31/12 🔵 service: 01/11-28/02.
**Distance:** 🚶700m ⊗300m 🚎on the spot 🚲 Donau-Bodensee-Radweg.
**Remarks:** Max. 3 days.

🅰🅱S **Bietigheim-Bissingen** 17A2

**Wohnmobilstellplatz an der Enz**, Mühlwiesenstrasse.
**GPS:** n48,96110 e9,13329. ⬆.

9 ⚑ € 5 🚰 € 0,50/80liter 🔌Ch.⚡(8x)€ 0,50/kWh. 🚍
**Location:** Urban, simple. **Surface:** metalled.
⭕ 01/01-31/12.

DE

**Distance:** 📍200m ⛱1km 🚂1km ⊗100m 🚰100m 🏪100m.
**Remarks:** Max. 4 days, max. 8M, check in at Lama Bar.

**S** | **Blaubeuren** | **17B3**

**Parkplatz P6**, Dodelweg. **GPS**: n48,41351 e9,79102. ➡️

20 💧€ 5 🚿€ 1/5minutes 🚽Ch€ 1. 🔌 **Surface:** metalled.
🌙 01/01-31/12.
**Distance:** 📍1km ⊗1km 🚰1km 🏪800m.
**Remarks:** Parking at swimming pool, max. 2 days.

⚓ | **Blaustein** | **17B3**

**Freizeitbad Bad Blau**, Boschstraße. **GPS**: n48,41757 e9,91630. ⬆️
3 💧free. **Location:** Simple. **Surface:** gravel. 🌙 01/01-31/12.
**Distance:** 🚲6,5km ⊗200m 🚰500m.

**S** | **Blumberg** | **19H2**

**P1, Festplatz**, Oberes Ried. **GPS**: n47,83943 e8,54226. ⬆️➡️

20 💧€ 7,50, 01/11-30/04 € 6,50 🚿€ 1/50liter 🚽Ch 🔌
(36x)€ 1/24h ⏻€ 1,50. 🔌 **Location:** Rural, comfortable, quiet.
**Surface:** gravel/metalled. 🌙 01/01-31/12.
**Distance:** 📍800m ⊗100m 🚰100m 🏪400m.
**Remarks:** With payment: KONUS guest card with many advantages, next to sports fields.

**S** | **Blumberg** | **19H2**

**P2, Parkplatz Bahnhof Zollhaus**, Achdorf.
**GPS**: n47,83767 e8,55777. ⬆️

5 💧€ 7,50, 01/11-30/04 € 6,50 🚿. **Location:** Urban, simple, noisy.
**Surface:** gravel. 🌙 01/01-31/12.
**Distance:** 📍1,5km 🏪80m.

**S** | **Blumberg** | **19H2**

**P3, Achdorfer Tal. GPS**: n47,83528 e8,49833. ⬆️

10 💧€ 7,50, 01/11-30/04 € 6,50 🚿€ 1 🚽Ch 🔌(12x)€ 1/night, winter
€ 1,50. 🔌 **Location:** Rural, simple, isolated, quiet. **Surface:** gravel.
🌙 01/01-31/12.
**Distance:** 📍4km ⊗450m 🏪600m.
**Remarks:** With payment: KONUS guest card with many advantages, caution key € 10 (connection electricity), service at Kläranlage 800m.

**S** | **Böblingen** | **17A3**

Im Zimmerschlag. **GPS**: n48,67000 e9,03272. ⬆️➡️

4 💧free 🚿 free. **Location:** Urban, simple.
**Surface:** grasstiles/metalled. 🌙 01/04-31/10.
**Distance:** 📍3km ⊗100m 🚰1,5km 🏪on the spot 🏃on the spot.
**Remarks:** At sports grounds.

**S** | **Bodman-Ludwigshafen** | **20A2**

**Wohnmobilhafen am Bodensee**, Am Sportplatz.
**GPS**: n47,82369 e9,05153. ⬆️

20 💧€ 11 🚿€ 1/100liter 🚽Ch 🔌(4x)€ 2.
**Location:** Simple. **Surface:** grassy/metalled. 🌙 01/01-31/12.
**Distance:** 📍1km 🚲3,2km 🏪1,4km.

**S** | **Bonndorf** | **19H2**

**Schwimmbad**, Ob dem Tal 1. **GPS**: n47,81644 e8,33969. ⬆️
5 💧€ 7,50 + 🚿 1/pp tourist tax 🚿 WC on demand.
**Location:** Urban, comfortable, central. **Surface:** asphalted/metalled.
🌙 01/01-31/12.
**Distance:** 📍400m 🏪450m 🚰500m.
**Remarks:** Check in at swimming pool.

**S** | **Bonndorf** | **19H2**

**Wohnmobilstellplatz Holzschlag**, Schulstraße/Bonndorfer Straße,
Bonndorf-Holzschlag. **GPS**: n47,84970 e8,26784. ⬆️

💧€ 5, tourist tax € 0,80/pp 🚿Ch included. **Location:** Simple,
noisy. 🌙 01/01-31/12.
**Distance:** ⊗100m.

**S** | **Bönnigheim** | **17A2**

**Mineralfreibad Bönnigheim**, Bachstrasse 40.
**GPS**: n49,03910 e9,08439. ⬆️➡️

6 💧free 🚿 🔌. **Location:** Rural, simple.
**Surface:** grasstiles/metalled. 🌙 01/01-31/12.
**Distance:** 📍500m 🏪500m 🚰1km.
**Remarks:** Max. 5 days, caution key € 10 (water).

**S** | **Bönnigheim** | **17A2**

**Weinkellerei Heinz Kölle**, Schmiedsberger Weg 38.
**GPS**: n49,04228 e9,10328. ⬆️➡️
2 💧€ 5 🔌. **Surface:** grasstiles. 🌙 01/01-31/12.
**Distance:** ⊗800m 🏪800m.

**S** | **Bopfingen** | **17C3**

**Gasthof zum Bären**, Nördlinger Straße 3.
**GPS**: n48,85715 e10,35508. ⬆️

6 💧€ 6 🚿€ 1 🔌€ 1 Ch 🔌€ 1. **Location:** Urban. **Surface:** asphalted.
🌙 01/01-31/12.
**Distance:** 📍on the spot 🚲16km 🏪on the spot 🚰100m.
**Remarks:** Free with a meal.

**S** | **Boxberg** | **17B1**

**Gasthof Hagenmühle**, Uiffinger strasse 74.
**GPS**: n49,48710 e9,61299. ⬆️

12 💧€ 5 🚿(12x)€ 2,50. **Location:** Rural, simple.
**Surface:** grassy/gravel. 🌙 01/01-31/12 🍽 Restaurant: Thu.
**Distance:** 📍2km 🎣trout pond 🏪on the spot 🚰1km 🏪200m.

**S** | **Brackenheim** | **17A2**

**Weingut und Besenwirtschaft 'Zum Alten Pflug'**, Seebergweg.
**GPS**: n49,10261 e9,04994. ⬆️

3 💧€ 10, free for clients 🚿 🚽Ch 🔌(3x)€ 2 WC€ 2.
**Location:** Rural, simple, quiet.
**Surface:** metalled.
🌙 01/01-31/12.
**Distance:** 📍3km 🏪3km.
**Remarks:** Sunday on demand, when buying wine 1 night free.

**S** | **Brackenheim** | **17A2**

**Weingut Winkler**, Stockheimer strasse 13.
**GPS**: n49,08001 e9,06270. ⬆️

4 💧€ 5 🚿Ch included 🔌. 🔌 **Location:** Rural, simple.
**Surface:** grassy/metalled. 🌙 01/01-31/12.
**Distance:** 📍on the spot ⛱10km 🚂10km ⊗300m 🏪500m
🏪300m.
**Remarks:** When buying wine 1 night free.

**S** | **Breisach/Rhein** | **19G1**

**Wohnmobil-Parkplatz**, Josef-Buebstrasse.
**GPS**: n48,02944 e7,57576. ⬆️➡️

DE

80 ⌷free 8-20h, € 6/night, 2 nights € 10, 3 nights € 13, winter free ⌷€ 1/100liter ⌷€ 1 Ch ⌷ 1. 
**Location:** Urban, simple. **Surface:** asphalted.
⌷ 01/01-31/12. ⌷ Other parking in case of festivities.
**Distance:** ⌷300m ⌷on the spot ⌷on the spot ⌷300m ⌷1,5km.
**Remarks:** Ground of wine festival, bread-service.

### Breisach/Rhein 19G1

**Restaurant Kläsles Gastronomie Am Rhein**, Hafenstrasse 11.
**GPS:** n48,04292 e7,57378.⌷.

5 ⌷free. **Location:** Simple. **Surface:** metalled.
⌷ 01/01-31/12.
**Distance:** ⌷2km ⌷on the spot ⌷500m.
**Remarks:** Along the Rhine river, guests only.
**Tourist information Breisach/Rhein:**
⌷ Weinfest Kaiserstuhl Tuniberg. Wine festivals. ⌷ end Aug.

### Bretten 17A2

**Reisemobil-Stellplatz Bretten**, Willi-Hesselbacher-Weg.
**GPS:** n49,02980 e8,71914.⌷⌷.

4 ⌷free ⌷€ 1/100liter ⌷€ 1/10h. **Location:** Urban, comfortable.
**Surface:** metalled. ⌷ 01/01-31/12.
**Distance:** ⌷city centre 1,5km ⌷100m.
**Remarks:** Sports centre, max. 2 days.

### Bruchsal 16H2

**Stellplatz am Sportzentrum**, Giesgrabenweg.
**GPS:** n49,13227 e8,58981.⌷.

2 ⌷free. **Location:** Urban, simple, central. **Surface:** metalled.
⌷ 01/01-31/12.
**Distance:** ⌷1km ⌷4km ⌷100m ⌷1km ⌷on the spot ⌷on the
spot ⌷on the spot.
**Remarks:** At sports centre, max. 2 days.

### Buchen/Odenwald 17A1

**Wohnmobilhafen Morretal**, Mühltalstraße 15.
**GPS:** n49,52888 e9,31020.⌷.

---

12 ⌷€ 5/24h, 3 days € 20 ⌷€ 1/100liter ⌷Ch ⌷ (12x) € 0,50/kWh
WC ⌷€ 0,20 ⌷€ 3/day. ⌷ **Location:** Rural, comfortable, quiet.
**Surface:** grassy. ⌷ 01/01-31/12. **Distance:** ⌷800m ⌷on the spot.
**Remarks:** Parking Waldbad, use sanitary only during opening hours
swimming pool.

### Buchenbach 19H2

**Wanglerhof**, Vogtweg 1. **GPS:** n47,96820 e7,99269.⌷.

10 ⌷€ 17 ⌷Ch ⌷ (10x)includedstay WC ⌷€ 2 ⌷. ⌷.
**Location:** Rural, simple, isolated, quiet. **Surface:** grassy.
⌷ 01/01-31/12.
**Distance:** ⌷1km ⌷100m ⌷1km ⌷700m.

### Bühl 16H3

**Wohnmobilstellplatz am SchwarzwaldbadS**, Ludwig-Jahn-strasse 8.
**GPS:** n48,68862 e8,12995.⌷⌷.

20 ⌷€ 5 ⌷€ 2/100liter ⌷Ch. ⌷ **Location:** Urban, simple, noisy.
**Surface:** gravel/metalled. ⌷ 01/01-31/12.
**Distance:** ⌷1km ⌷6km ⌷500m ⌷1km ⌷on the spot ⌷on the
spot.
**Remarks:** Bread-service.

### Burkheim 19G1

Am Kirchberg. **GPS:** n48,10226 e7,59656.⌷.

14 ⌷free ⌷free. **Location:** Rural, simple, quiet. **Surface:** grasstiles.
⌷ 01/01-31/12.
**Distance:** ⌷500m ⌷200m ⌷500m ⌷on the spot ⌷on the spot.

### Calw 17A3

**Wohnmobilstellplatz Am Alten Bahnhof**, Bahnhofstrasse.
**GPS:** n48,70592 e8,73808.⌷⌷.

6 ⌷free ⌷€ 1/80liter ⌷€ 1 Ch € 1 ⌷ (4x) € 0,50/7kWh.
**Location:** Rural, simple, isolated, noisy. **Surface:** asphalted.

---

⌷ 01/01-31/12.
**Distance:** ⌷1km ⌷100m ⌷200m ⌷on the spot ⌷on the spot.

### Cleebronn/Tripsdrill 17A2

**Erlebnispark Tripsdrill**. **GPS:** n49,03102 e9,05096.⌷⌷.

30 ⌷€ 5/pp WC ⌷included.
**Location:** Rural, isolated, quiet.
**Surface:** grassy.
⌷ 06/04-03/11.
**Distance:** ⌷4km ⌷1km ⌷4km ⌷400m.
**Remarks:** Max. 2 nights.
**Tourist information Cleebronn/Tripsdrill:**
⌷ Erlebnispark Tripsdrill. Amusement park. ⌷ 19/03-06/11 9-18h.

### Crailsheim 17C2

**Autohof Euro Rastpark**, Marco-Polo-Straße 1, Satteldorf.
**GPS:** n49,18146 e10,06889.
10 ⌷€ 10 ⌷⌷. **Location:** Motorway, simple. **Surface:** metalled.
⌷ 01/01-31/12.
**Distance:** ⌷600m ⌷on the spot ⌷100m ⌷900m.

### Dettenheim 16H2

**Kartbahn Liedolsheim**, Kartbahnring 1. **GPS:** n49,14326 e8,43118.

180 ⌷free ⌷Ch ⌷ (10x) € 5/day WC ⌷€ 2,50.
**Location:** Rural, simple, isolated. **Surface:** grassy/metalled.
⌷ 01/01-31/12.
**Distance:** ⌷3km ⌷2km ⌷2km ⌷on the spot ⌷5km ⌷1,5km.
**Remarks:** Parking at Karting.

### Dietingen 20A1

**Reisemobilpark Turm und Kristalle**, Fronstraße 7.
**GPS:** n48,20036 e8,64610.
48 ⌷€ 10 ⌷Ch ⌷ (48x),16Amp. **Location:** Rural.
**Surface:** gravel. ⌷ 01/01-31/12.
**Distance:** ⌷800m ⌷100m ⌷50m ⌷on the spot.
**Remarks:** At museum.

### Donaueschingen 20A2

**Am Schlosspark**, Prinz Fritz Allee. **GPS:** n47,94746 e8,51183.⌷⌷.

20 ⌷free ⌷€ 1/50liter ⌷ (14x) € 0,50/kWh. **Location:** Rural, simple,
quiet. **Surface:** grassy. ⌷ 01/01-31/12.
**Distance:** ⌷1,5km ⌷Danube Bike Trail ⌷on the spot.
**Remarks:** Max. 2 days, service 300m.

### Donaueschingen 20A2

**Kläranlage**, Haberfeld. **GPS:** n47,94931 e8,52209.⌷⌷.
⌷€ 1/50liter ⌷Ch.
⌷ 01/01-31/12.

**Tourist information Donaueschingen:**
⌷ Tourismus- und Sportamt, Karlstrasse 58, www.donaueschingen.de.
Horse city, named after the source of the River danube.
⌷ Der Donau Radweg. Signposted cycle route along the Donau.

### Durbach 16H3

**Grol/Festplatz**, Almstrasse. **GPS:** n48,49407 e8,01105.⌷⌷.

DE

15 🛏€ 8,40 🚰€ 1/100liter 🧹(8x)€ 1/8h. 🚽
**Location:** Rural, simple, quiet. **Surface:** gravel.
⬛ 01/01-31/12 🔵 festivities.
**Distance:** 🚶500m 🚲10km ⊗on the spot 🛒on the spot 🚌50m 🏊on the spot.

### Durbach � 16H3
**Wohnmobilstellplatz Ebersweier**, Wiesenstraße, Ebersweier.
**GPS:** n48,50122 e7,98940. ⬆️➡️

6 🛏€ 8,40 🚰€ 1/80liter 🧹Ch 🧹(6x)€ 1/4h. 🚽
**Location:** Rural, simple, isolated, quiet. **Surface:** gravel/metalled.
⬛ 01/01-31/12.
**Distance:** 🚶500m 🚲10km 🛒750m 🚌200m 🏊on the spot.

### Eberbach 🌿🚣🌾 17A1
**Wohnmobilstellplatz In der Au**, In der Au.
**GPS:** n49,46162 e8,97812. ⬆️

7 🛏free. 🧹(6x)€ 1/2kWh. **Location:** Rural, simple, isolated.
**Surface:** gravel. ⬛ 01/01-31/12.
**Distance:** 🚶1km 🛶on the spot.
**Remarks:** At swimming pool, max. 2 nights.

### Eberbach 🌿🚣🌾 17A1
**Wohnmobilstellplatz Neckarlauer**, B37, Uferstrasse.
**GPS:** n49,46012 e8,98652. ⬆️

3 🛏free. **Location:** Rural, simple, quiet. **Surface:** grasstiles.
⬛ 01/01-31/12.
**Distance:** 🚴7,6km 🛒on the spot.
**Remarks:** Max. 2 days, max. 6,5m.

### Ehingen 🌿🚣🌾 20B1
**Wohnmobilstellplatz Ehingen**, Am Stadion.
**GPS:** n48,28053 e9,73571. ⬆️

10 🛏free 🚰€ 0,50/50liter 🧹Ch 🧹(4x)€ 0,50/kWh 📶free.
**Surface:** metalled. ⬛ 01/01-31/12.
**Distance:** 🚶1km 🏊1km ⊗on the spot 🛒500m 🚌10m 🏊Danube Bike Trail.

### Eichstetten 🌿🚣 19G1
**Weingut Köbelin**, Altweg 131. **GPS:** n48,09510 e7,72057. ⬆️

5 🛏€ 13 🚰🧹Ch 🧹included. 🐕 **Location:** Rural, simple, isolated, quiet. **Surface:** gravel/sand. ⬛ 01/01-31/12.
**Distance:** 🚶city centre 1,5km ⊗1,5km 🛒1,4km 🚌900m 🏊on the spot 🚶on the spot.

### Eigeltingen 🌿🚣 20A2
**Landgasthof Mönchhof**, Tannenbergstraße 16.
**GPS:** n47,88094 e8,95278.

4 🛏guests free 🚰🧹Ch 🧹€ 2. **Surface:** metalled.
⬛ 01/01-31/12.
**Distance:** 🚶6km ⊗on the spot 🛒4km 🚌on the spot.

### Eisenbach 🏔❄ 19H2
**Reisemobilpark Höchstberg**. **GPS:** n47,94938 e8,25441. ⬆️

20 🛏€ 8, tourist tax € 1,60/pp 🚰€ 1/100liter 🧹Ch 🧹(20x)included, only in summer. 🐕 **Location:** Rural, comfortable, quiet. **Surface:** grassy/gravel. ⬛ 01/01-31/12.
**Distance:** ⊗on the spot 🚶on the spot.

**Remarks:** Altitude 1033m, at sports park.

### Ellwangen 🚣 17C2
**Maxi-Autohof Ellwangen**, Max-Eyth-Strasse 1.
**GPS:** n48,95628 e10,18319. ⬆️

15 🛏€ 7,50/24h 🚰🧹ChWC 🧹📶against payment.
**Location:** Motorway. **Surface:** asphalted. ⬛ 01/01-31/12.
**Distance:** 🚶3km ⊗on the spot 🛒1km.

### Emmendingen 🚣 19H1
**Wohnmobilstellplatz am Freibad**, Am Sportfeld.
**GPS:** n48,11869 e7,84154. ⬆️

30 🛏free 🚰€ 1/80liter 🧹ChWC 🧹📶. **Location:** Urban, simple.
**Surface:** asphalted. ⬛ 01/01-31/12.
**Distance:** 🚶1km ⊗400m 🛒600m.
**Remarks:** In front of swimmingpool, max. 3 days.

### Endingen am Kaiserstuhl 19G1
**P2 Stadthalle**, Freiburger Weg. **GPS:** n48,13830 e7,70321. ⬆️➡️

20 🛏free. **Location:** Urban, simple, central. **Surface:** concrete.
⬛ 01/01-31/12.
**Distance:** 🚶200m 🛒200m.

### Eppingen 🌿🚣 17A2
**Wohnmobilhalt am Freibad**, Am Altstadring.
**GPS:** n49,13793 e8,91402. ⬆️

4 🛏free 🚰€ 1/80liter 🧹€ 1 Ch🧹1 🧹(4x)€ 1. **Location:** Rural, comfortable. **Surface:** metalled. ⬛ 01/01-31/12.
**Distance:** 🚶500m ⊗on the spot 🛒300m 🚌500m 🏊on the spot 🚶on the spot.

### Esslingen am Neckar 🌿🚣🍺🎋 17B3
**Äußerer Burgplatz**, Mülbergerstraße. **GPS:** n48,74713 e9,31064. ⬆️

2 🛏free. **Location:** Urban, simple. **Surface:** asphalted.

### Ebringen 19G2
**An der Schönberghalle**, Schulstraße 8.
**GPS:** n47,95639 e7,77667. ⬆️➡️

### Eberbach 🌿🚣🌾 17A1
In der Au. **GPS:** n49,46217 e8,97351. ⬆️
🚰€ 1/60liter 🧹Ch. ⬛ 01/01-31/12.

**☐** 01/01-31/12.
**Distance:** 🚶1km 🚲1km ⊗on the spot 🚏1km 🚌300m.
**Remarks:** Max. 48h.

### 🏞🅂 Ettenheim 19G1

**Ernst Caravan und Freizeit Center**, Rudolf Hell Straße 32-44.
**GPS:** n48,27431 e7,78161. ⬆€.

30 🍳free 🚰€ 1 🗑€ 1 Ch€ 1 ⚡(12x)€ 0,50/kWh.
**Location:** Motorway, simple. **Surface:** concrete. **☐** 01/01-31/12.
**Distance:** ⚓500m.
**Remarks:** Motorhome dealer, accessory shop, repairs.

### 🅂 Ettlingen 16H3

**Wohnmobilstellplatz Am Freibad**, Schöllbronner strasse.
**GPS:** n48,93561 e8,41/47. ⬆➡.

8 🍳free 🚰€ 2/5minutes 🗑Ch 💧(4x)€ 2/8h.
**Location:** Urban, simple. **Surface:** asphalted. **☐** 01/01-31/12.
**Distance:** 🚶100m 🚲3,3km ⊗100m 🚏700m 🚌on the spot
🚗on the spot 🚶on the spot.
**Remarks:** Parking swimming pool, max. 48h, market Wednesday and
Saturday.

### 🅂 Feldberg 19H2

**Altglashütten**, Dreiseenbahnweg. **GPS:** n47,85857 e8,11537.

16 🍳€ 10 + € 2,60/pp tourist tax 🚰€ 1/100liter 🗑Ch 💧(16x)€ 1/8h.
🏠**Location:** Urban. **Surface:** gravel.
**☐** 01/01-31/12.
**Distance:** 🚶on the spot ⊗on the spot 🚏2,5km 🚌Skibus.

### 🅂 Filderstadt 17A3

**Parkplatz P2**, Tübinger Strasse 40. **GPS:** n48,67347 e9,21456. ⬆➡.

8 🍳€ 7/24h 🚰€ 1/80liter 🗑Ch 💧(8x)€ 0,50/kWh,16Amp. 🏠
**Location:** Urban. **Surface:** gravel. **☐** 01/01-31/12.
**Distance:** 🚶500m ⊗500m 🚏500m 🚌500m.

### 🅂 Freiburg 19H1

**Reisemobilplatz Freiburg**, Bissierstraße/Am Eschholzpark.
**GPS:** n47,99915 e7,82643. ⬆➡.

---

60 🍳€ 9, motorhome >7m + € 1/m 🚰🗑Chincluded 💧(20x)€ 1/
kWh 🔌€ 1.🛁
**Location:** Urban, comfortable, central. **Surface:** asphalted/gravel.
**☐** 01/01-31/12.
**Distance:** 🚶Old city centre 1,5km 🚲4,3km ⊗450m 🚌on the spot.
**Remarks:** Max. 72h, green zone: environmental badge obligatory.

### 🏞🅂 Freiburg ❄ 🌲 19H1

**WV-Südcaravan**, Hanferstrasse 30, Hochdorf.
**GPS:** n48,04146 e7,81473. ⬆.

6 🍳free 🚰€ 1/80liter 🗑Ch€ 2 💧€ 5/day. **Location:** Urban, simple.
**Surface:** asphalted/metalled. **☐** 01/01-31/12.
**Distance:** 🚶Old city centre 10km 🚲3km ⊗300m 🚌3km.
**Remarks:** During opening hours, outside environmental zone.

### 🅂 Freudenberg 17A1

**P. Freudenberg-Süd**, Hauptstrasse. **GPS:** n49,74001 e9,31938. ⬆.

10 🍳€ 6/night 🚰€ 1/15minutes 🗑Ch 💧(6x)€ 2/8h,16Amp 🛜free.
🛁**Location:** Rural, comfortable. **Surface:** metalled.
**☐** 01/01-31/12.
**Distance:** 🚶50m 🚲20m 🚤20m ⊗300m 🚏500m 🚌200m
🚗on the spot.

### 🅂 Friedrichshafen 20B2

**Stellplatz Friedrichshafen**, Lindauerstrasse 2.
**GPS:** n47,65025 e9,49597. ⬆⬆➡.

25 🍳free, 01/04-31/10 € 13,20 🚰€ 1/100liter 🗑Ch 💧WC 🗑.🏠
**Location:** Urban, simple, noisy. **Surface:** asphalted/metalled.
**☐** 01/01-31/12.
**Distance:** 🚲200m 🚤200m ⊗450m 🚌850m.
**Remarks:** Max. 3 nights, payment only with coins.

### 🅂 Gaggenau ♨ 🌲 16H3

Badstrasze 15. **GPS:** n48,80786 e8,30275. ⬆.

---

6 🍳free 🚰🗑Ch 💧**Location:** Rural, simple.
**Surface:** grasstiles/metalled. **☐** 01/01-31/12.
**Distance:** 🚶1,5km 🚏800m 🚗on the spot 🚶on the spot.
**Remarks:** Parking spa resort, market Saturday.

### 🅂 Gaildorf 17B2

**Wohnmobilstellplatz Gaildorf**, Bleichgärten.
**GPS:** n49,00224 e9,76587. ⬆➡.

7 🍳free 🚰🗑Ch 💧(4x)free,16Amp. **Location:** Simple.
**Surface:** gravel. **☐** 01/01-31/12.
**Distance:** 🚶500m ⊗600m 🚏1,2km 🚌500m 🚗on the spot 🚶500m
🚵1,6km.
**Remarks:** Max. 3 days, service closed during wintertime.

### 🅂 Gailingen am Hochrhein 〰 20A2

**Rheinuferpark**, Strandweg. **GPS:** n47,69051 e8,75621. ⬆➡.
20 🍳€ 15 🚰🗑🏠 **☐** 01/04-31/10.
**Distance:** 🚶1km 🚲on the spot ⊗900m.
**Remarks:** Service on demand.

### 🅂 Gammertingen 🍴 20A1

**Freizeitanlage an der Lauchert**, Reutlingerstrasse.
**GPS:** n48,25611 e9,21056. ➡.

8 🍳free 💧(6x)€ 1/4h WC. **Location:** Simple. **Surface:** grassy/gravel.
**☐** 01/01-31/12.
**Distance:** 🚶1km 🚲on the spot 🚤on the spot ⊗1km 🚏700m
🚗on the spot 🚶on the spot.

**DE**

## Reisemobilstellplatz Geisingen

- **Comfortable motorhome stopover**
- **37 Flat motorhome pitches, gravel**
- **Electricity at each pitch**
- **Open all year**
- **Located in a quiet area**
- **Restaurants and shops at 500m**
- **Nearby Arena Geisingen**
- **Ideal base for walking and cycling**

www.geisingen.de
info@geisingen.de

### Geisingen — 20A2

**Reisemobilstellplatz Geisingen**, Am Espen 8.
**GPS:** n47,92016 e8,65153. ↑ →.
37 🅿 € 9 ⚡ € 1/80liter 🚰Ch ♿ (37x)€ 2/4kWh 📶included.
**Surface:** gravel. 🅾 01/01-31/12.
**Distance:** 🛒200m 🛒1,5km ⚓200m ✕200m 🚻500m 🚆500m
🚲200m ✗200m.

### Gengenbach — 19H1

**Kinzigdamm**, Berghauptener Straße. **GPS:** n48,40174 e8,00776.
40 🅿 € 10/24h + € 1,50-2,20/pp tourist tax ⚡🚰Chincluded ♿.
**Surface:** gravel. 🅾 01/01-31/12.
**Distance:** 🛒1km ✕300m 🚻700m ⚓900m.

### Gengenbach — 19H1

**An der Brennerei**, Streuobstgarten 1. **GPS:** n48,38750 e8,02000.
10 🅿 € 10 ♿ (8x)WCincluded. **Surface:** grassy. 🅾 01/01-31/12.
**Distance:** 🛒2km ✕1km.
**Remarks:** Sale of wines.

### Gernsbach — 16H3

Am Schwimmbad 1, Oberstrot. **GPS:** n48,74239 e8,34186.

5 🅿free ♿(4x)€ 1/8h. **Location:** Rural, simple, quiet.
**Surface:** grassy. 🅾 01/01-31/12.
**Distance:** 🛒200m ✕200m 🚲on the spot ✗on the spot.
**Remarks:** At swimming pool.

### Gernsbach — 16H3

**Parkplatz Murginsel**, Schlossstrasse/Klingelstrasse.
**GPS:** n48,75934 e8,33900. ↑ →.

8 🅿 € 5 ⚡ € 1/100liter 🚰Ch ♿(8x)€ 1/12h WC 🚮.
**Location:** Rural, simple. **Surface:** asphalted. 🅾 01/01-31/12.
**Distance:** 🛒500m ⚓on the spot ✕500m 🚻1km ⚓on the spot

---

🚲on the spot ✗on the spot.
**Remarks:** Max. 7 days.

### Giengen — 17C3

**Reisemobilstation Charlottenhöhle**, Lonetalstrasse 60, Hürben.
**GPS:** n48,58412 e10,21203. ↑ →.

15 🅿 € 7/night ⚡🚰Ch ♿(6x)€ 2/12h,16Amp WC⚡included.
**Location:** Rural, quiet. **Surface:** gravel. 🅾 01/01-31/12.
**Remarks:** At prehistoric cave, coins at Hölenhaus.

### Giengen — 17C3

**Am Schießberg**, Auf dem Schießberg. **GPS:** n48,62975 e10,25159. ↑.

8 🅿free. **Location:** Simple. **Surface:** gravel. 🅾 01/01-31/12.
**Distance:** 🛒1,5km ⚓4,3km ✕1,5km 🚻1,5km.

**Tourist information Giengen:**
👁 Charlottenhöhle. Caves. 🅾 01/04-31/10 8.30-11.30 and 13.30-17h,
Su/holidays 9-16.30h.

### Göppingen — 17B3

**Parkplatz P1, An der FWS-Arena**, Lorcherstrasse.
**GPS:** n48,71176 e9,64816. ↑.

6 🅿free ⚡ € 1/60liter 🚰Ch. **Location:** Urban. **Surface:** asphalted.
🅾 01/01-31/12.
**Distance:** 🛒1km ✕1km 🚻1km.
**Remarks:** Max. 2 nights.

### Grossbottwar — 17B2

**Winzerhäuser Tal**, In den Frauengärten.
**GPS:** n49,00363 e9,28739. ↑ →.

---

5 🅿 € 10 ⚡ € 1/100liter 🚰Ch ♿ € 1/2kWh. **Surface:** metalled.
🅾 01/01-31/12.
**Distance:** 🛒400m ✕400m ⚓200m.
**Remarks:** At sports park, max. 5 days.

### Grünkraut — 20B2

Bodnegger Straße. **GPS:** n47,74076 e9,65515. ↑.
3 🅿free. **Surface:** metalled. 🅾 01/01-31/12.
**Distance:** 🛒1km ✕1km 🚻1km.
**Remarks:** Max. 3 nights.

### Gschwend — 17B2

**Naturbadesee**, Frickenhofer Strasse. **GPS:** n48,93603 e9,75143. ↑.

3 🅿free. **Location:** Rural, simple. **Surface:** forest soil.
🅾 01/01-31/12.
**Distance:** 🛒1,5km.
**Remarks:** Service 2km.

### Gschwend — 17B2

Joosenhofer Sägmühle. **GPS:** n48,92312 e9,77393. ↑ →.
⚡ € 1/80liter 🚰Ch. **Surface:** asphalted. 🅾 01/01-31/12.

### Güglingen — 17A2

Kreuzgärten. **GPS:** n49,06492 e8,99489. ↑ →.

10 🅿free ⚡ € 2 🚰Ch. **Location:** Rural, simple. **Surface:** gravel.
🅾 01/01-31/12.
**Distance:** 🛒700m ✕500m 🚻Aldi-Lidl 500m 🚲on the spot ✗on
the spot.
**Remarks:** At swimming pool, max. 5 nights.

### Haigerloch — 20A1

**Wohnmobilstellplatz Haigerloch**, Weildorfer Kreuz 1.
**GPS:** n48,36875 e8,79384. ↑ →.

10 🅿free ⚡ € 1/60liter 🚰Ch ♿(10x)€ 1/8h. **Location:** Urban,
simple. **Surface:** asphalted. 🅾 01/01-31/12.
**Distance:** 🛒300m ✕500m 🚻300m 🚲on the spot.
**Remarks:** Max. 4 days.

### Hardheim — 17B1

**Am Alten Bahnhof**, Bretzinger Straße. **GPS:** n49,60245 e9,47126. ↑ →.

DE

12 ⛺free ⛽€ 1/80liter 🚽Ch.💧(8x)€ 1/2kWh. **Location:** Rural, comfortable, noisy. **Surface:** gravel. ⏰ 01/01-31/12.
**Distance:** 🚶1km 🚲1km 🚃1km.

### Haslach/Kinzigtal 🏕 19H1
**Wanderparkplatz Klosterplatz**, Klosterstraße 1.
**GPS:** n48,27572 e8,08509.⬆

10 ⛺free WC. **Location:** Urban, simple. **Surface:** concrete.
⏰ 01/01-31/12.
**Distance:** 🚶50m ⊗150m 🚃500m 🚌100m 🚶on the spot.
**Remarks:** At tourist office.

### Haslach/Kinzigtal 🏕 19H1
**Eichenbachsporthalle**, Strickerweg. **GPS:** n48,27854 e8,07968.⬆

10 ⛺free. **Location:** Simple. **Surface:** metalled.
⏰ 01/01-31/12.
**Distance:** 🚶500m 🚃300m.
**Remarks:** At gymnasium, at swimming pool.

### Haslach/Kinzigtal 🏕 19H1
**Waldseeparkplatz**, Waldseeweg. **GPS:** n48,27161 e8,09148.⬆

10 ⛺free. **Location:** Rural, simple. **Surface:** asphalted.
⏰ 01/01-31/12.
**Distance:** 🚶1km ⊗200m 🚃1km.

### Hausach 🏘 19H1
**Waldstadion**, Waldstraße. **GPS:** n48,28058 e8,17829.⬆➡

4 ⛺free ⛽WC. **Location:** Rural, simple, quiet. **Surface:** gravel/sand.
⏰ 01/01-31/12.
**Distance:** 🚶500m ⊗100m 🚶on the spot.

### Hausach 🏘 19H1
**Badepark**, Schanze 3. **GPS:** n48,28620 e8,16589.⬆➡

---

6 ⛺free. **Location:** Rural, simple. **Surface:** concrete.
⏰ 01/01-31/12.
**Distance:** ⊗on the spot 🚃500m 🚌on the spot 🚶on the spot.
**Remarks:** Nearby swimming pool.

### Hechingen 🌿🏕 20A1
**Freizeitanlage Domäne Areal**, Brielhof 1.
**GPS:** n48,33773 e8,94966.⬆

18 ⛺€ 18 💧included. **Location:** Simple. **Surface:** metalled.
⏰ 01/01-31/12.
**Distance:** 🚶2km 🚲200m ⊗on the spot.
**Remarks:** Discount at restaurants and Golf Park.

### Hechingen 🌿🏕 20A1
**Burg Hohenzollern**, K 7110. **GPS:** n48,32579 e8,96404.⬆

3 ⛺€ 4. 🛁 **Location:** Rural, simple. **Surface:** asphalted.
⏰ 01/01-31/12.
**Distance:** ⊗Imbiss 🚶on the spot.

### Hechingen 🌿🏕 20A1
**Zollernalbcamping**, Niederhechingerstrasse.
**GPS:** n48,35797 e8,96093.⬆➡

20 ⛺€ 10 ⛽€ 1 🚽Ch€ 1 💧€ 1/kWh WC€ 3 ⛴€ 2,50.
**Location:** Urban, simple, quiet. **Surface:** metalled.
⏰ 01/01-31/12 🚿 sanitary building: 01/11-01/04.
**Distance:** 🚶2km 🚃500m 🚌on the spot 🚶on the spot.
**Remarks:** Waste dump € 2/day.

### Heidenheim 17C3
In den Seewiesen. **GPS:** n48,69455 e10,16410.⬆➡

22 ⛺€ 2/day ⛽€ 1/70liter 💧€ 1 Ch 💧(18x)€ 0,50/kWh,16Amp. 🚽
**Location:** Rural, simple. **Surface:** asphalted/gravel.
⏰ 01/01-31/12.

---

**Distance:** 🚶city centre 3km 🚲5km 🚃1km.
**Remarks:** Green zone: environmental badge obligatory.

### Heilbronn 🌿🏕🍺 17A2
**Wertwiesenpark**, Neckarhalde. **GPS:** n49,13047 e9,20469.⬆➡

20 ⛺free ⛽€ 1/100liter 🚽Ch.💧(12x)€ 0,50/kWh.
**Location:** Comfortable. **Surface:** metalled. ⏰ 01/01-31/12.
**Distance:** 🚶2km 🚲7km 🚃100m 🚌500m.
**Remarks:** Green zone: environmental badge obligatory.

### Heiligenberg 🌿 20B2
**Sennerei Schläge**, Betenbrunner strasse.
**GPS:** n47,81892 e9,31445.⬆➡

10 ⛺€ 5/16-09h 💧🚽Ch.🚽 **Location:** Simple.
**Surface:** grassy/metalled. ⏰ 01/04-31/10.
**Distance:** 🚶200m 🏊300m 🚌300m ⊗200m 🚩bakery 200m
🚶on the spot.
**Remarks:** Max. 2 nights.

### Herbrechtingen 🌿 17C3
**P7 Eselstalparkplatz**, Baumschulenweg.
**GPS:** n48,61758 e10,17411.⬆➡

15 ⛺€ 7 💧€ 2 🚽Ch.💧€ 2/24h. **Location:** Rural, quiet.
**Surface:** asphalted. ⏰ 01/01-31/12.
**Remarks:** Check in at Hölenhaus.

### Herbrechtingen 🌿 17C3
**Stellplatz an der Bibrishalle**, Baumschulenweg.
**GPS:** n48,61944 e10,17111.⬆
5 ⛺free. **Surface:** asphalted. ⏰ 01/01-31/12.
**Distance:** 🚶on the spot ⊗700m.

### Herrenberg 17A3
**P Stadthalle**, Stadthallenstrasse. **GPS:** n48,59832 e8,86943.⬆➡
5 ⛺free ⛽€ 1 💧€ 1. **Location:** Simple, noisy.
⏰ 01/01-31/12.
**Distance:** 🚶300m ⊗100m 🚃50m.
**Remarks:** Green zone: environmental badge obligatory.

### Hessigheim 17A2
**Fasanenhof**, Römerweg 1. **GPS:** n49,00939 e9,18877.⬆
15 ⛺€ 5 💧. **Location:** Rural, simple. ⏰ 01/01-31/12.
**Distance:** 🚲3,5km 🚌on the spot 🚩shop with farm products
🚶on the spot 🚶on the spot.
**Remarks:** Farm/restaurant/Biergarten/shop.

### Hessigheim 17A2
**Felsengarten Kellerei Besigheim e.G.**, Am Felsengarten 1.
**GPS:** n48,99612 e9,18068.⬆

DE

5 ⛺ free ⚡🚿. **Location:** Simple. **Surface:** asphalted.
🔲 01/01-31/12.
**Distance:** 🚶1km ⊗ on the spot 🛒1km.
**Remarks:** Max. 2 nights.

### Heubach 17B3

**Am Freibad**, Mögglinger Strasse. **GPS:** n48,79726 e9,93763.

6 ⛺ € 6 ⚡ € 1/90liter 🔵Ch € 0,50 🚿(6x)€ 1/2kWh.
**Location:** Simple. **Surface:** grasstiles. 🔲 01/01-31/12.
**Distance:** ⊗200m 🛒Lidl 400m.

### Hinterzarten 19H2

Bahnhofstraße. **GPS:** n47,90441 e8,10996.
⛺ free. **Location:** Urban, simple. **Surface:** grassy.
🔲 01/01-31/12.
**Distance:** 🚶300m ⊗300m.
**Remarks:** At fire-station, max. 1 night.

### Höchenschwand 19H2

Natursportzentrum. **GPS:** n47,73652 e8,15990.

12 ⛺ € 8 ⚡🔵Ch 🚿(12x) € 1/6h WC € 3. **Location:** Rural,
comfortable. **Surface:** gravel. 🔲 01/01-31/12.
**Distance:** 🚶400m ⊗100m 🛒600m 🏊 on the spot.

### Holzmaden 17B3

**Urwelt-Museum Hauff**, Aichelbergerstrasse 75/90.
**GPS:** n48,63482 e9,52771.
6 ⛺ free. **Surface:** metalled. 🔲 01/01-31/12.
**Distance:** 🚶3km 🚴2,2km ⊗1km 🛒2km 🚌170m.
**Remarks:** Max. 1 night.

### Hornberg 19H1

**Hotel Schöne Aussicht**, Schöne Aussicht 1, Niederwasser.
**GPS:** n48,19443 e8,18494.
4 ⛺ € 8 ⚡ included 🔲. 🔲 01/01-31/12.
**Distance:** ⊗ on the spot.

### Hüfingen 19H2

**Wohnmobil-Stellplatz an der Breg**, Bräunlinger Straße.
**GPS:** n47,92361 e8,48707.

22 ⛺ € 6, tourist tax € 1/pp ⚡ € 1,20/100liter 🔵Ch 🚿€ 1,20/10h
WC € 1,20 ⊙ € 3,50/3,50. 🔲
**Location:** Urban, comfortable, noisy. **Surface:** grassy.
🔲 01/01-31/12.
**Distance:** 🚶300m ⊗300m.

---

**Remarks:** Check in on arrival, bread-service, thursday market.

### Hülben 17B3

**Phoenix Wohnmobihafen**, Kaltentalstrasse.
**GPS:** n48,52620 e9,41227.

12 ⛺ free ⚡ € 0,50/80liter 🔵Ch 🚿(6x) € 0,50/kWh WC 🔲.
**Location:** Rural, simple. **Surface:** gravel. 🔲 01/01-31/12.
**Distance:** 🚶400m ⊗200m 🛒400m 🚌500m 🚴 Vordere-Alb-Rad-
weg 🏊 on the spot 🎣 on the spot.
**Remarks:** Max. 4 days.

### Ihringen 19G1

**Kaiserstuhl Camping**, Nachtwaid 5. **GPS:** n48,03083 e7,65778.

6 ⛺ € 14,60 + tourist tax ⚡🔵Ch 🚿 € 1,80/3kWh WC 🔲 📶 included.
🏕 **Location:** Rural, comfortable. **Surface:** asphalted/metalled.
🔲 31/03-30/10.
**Distance:** 🚶600m ⊗200m 🚴 on the spot.

### Isny 20C2

**Parkplatz An der Untere Mühle**, Seidenstrasse 43.
**GPS:** n47,69457 e10,03780.

16 ⛺ € 7,50 + € 1,50/pp tourist tax ⚡🔵Ch included 🚿(8x) € 0,50/
kWh WC. **Location:** Urban. **Surface:** asphalted/gravel.
🔲 01/01-31/12.
**Distance:** 🚶300m ⊗100m 🛒300m 🚌200m.
**Remarks:** Max. 2 nights.

### Kaisersbach 17B2

**Schwaben-Park**, Hofwiesen 11, Gmeinweiler.
**GPS:** n48,90304 e9,65484.

10 ⛺ free. **Location:** Rural, simple. **Surface:** grassy.
🔲 01/04-31/10.
**Distance:** 🏊1,5km 🚣1,5km.
**Remarks:** Inclining pitches.

**Tourist information Kaisersbach:**
   Schwaben-Park. Amusement park. 🔲 19/03-06/11 9-18.

### Kappelrodeck 16H3

**Wohnmobileck am Heidenhof**, Grüner Winkel.
**GPS:** n48,58370 e8,12650.

---

17 ⛺ € 8/day, 3 days € 21, 7 days € 42 ⚡ 1/100liter 🔵
Ch 🚿(8x)€ 1/2kWh. 🔲 **Location:** Rural, simple, quiet.
**Surface:** gravel/metalled. 🔲 01/01-31/12.
**Distance:** 🚶800m ⊗150m 🛒500m 🏊 on the spot 🚶 on the spot.
**Remarks:** Max. 7 nights.

### Karlsruhe 16H2

**Am Yachthafen Maxau**, Maxau am Rhein.
**GPS:** n49,03720 e8,30583.

12 ⛺ free. **Surface:** gravel. 🔲 01/01-31/12.
**Distance:** 🚶Karlsruhe 9km ⊗ on the spot 🛒2km.
**Remarks:** Along the Rhine river, max. 24h, outside environmental zone.

### Karlsruhe 16H2

Ettlinger Allee. **GPS:** n48,98761 e8,40412.

2 ⛺ free. **Surface:** asphalted. 🔲 01/01-31/12.
**Distance:** 🚶centre 2,5km ⊗400m 🚇metro 400m.
**Remarks:** Max. 24h, outside environmental zone, small pitches.

### Kehl 16G3

**Am Wasserturm**, Schwimbadstrasse. **GPS:** n48,56350 e7,81400.

40 ⛺ € 8 ⚡ € 1/80liter 🔵Ch 🚿(40x) € 0,50/kWh. **Location:** Urban,
comfortable, quiet. **Surface:** gravel. 🔲 01/01-31/12.
**Distance:** 🚶1km ⊗100m 🛒500m 🚌 on the spot 🏊 on the spot
🚶 on the spot.
**Remarks:** Max. 3 days, friday market.

### Kehl 16G3

**Reisemobilstellplatz Hurst**, An den Sportanlagen 1, Kehl-Auenheim.
**GPS:** n48,60653 e7,83146.

18 ⛺ € 7,50 ⚡ € 1 🔵Ch 🚿(12x) € 3 WC € 0,50 🔲 € 1,50.
**Location:** Rural, simple, quiet. **Surface:** asphalted/grassy.
🔲 01/01-31/12.

---

**274**

**Distance:** 🚶500m ⊗on the spot 🚰500m ♨on the spot 🧍on the spot.
**Remarks:** Check in on arrival.

### 🅿🆂 Kehl 🛥 16G3
**Bürstner-Service-Centrum**, Elsässer strasse 80, Kehl-Neumühl.
**GPS:** n48,57010 e7,84042.⬆.

6 🚐free 🚰€ 1/100liter ⚡(6x)€ 1/kWh. **Location:** Rural, simple.
**Surface:** asphalted. ☀ 01/01-31/12.
**Distance:** 🚶1km 🚲100m ⊗600m ♨on the spot 🧍on the spot.
**Remarks:** Tuesday and Friday market.

### 🅿🆂 Kenzingen 19G1
**Ritter's Weingut**, Rossleiteweg 1. **GPS:** n48,18739 e7,78343.⬆➡.

10 🚐€ 12,50 🚰€ 2 ⚡€ 2,50/day WCincluded. 🚿 **Location:** Rural,
simple. **Surface:** grassy/gravel. ☀ 01/01-31/12.
**Distance:** 🚶1km 🏊5km 🚲2km ⊗on the spot 🚰1km 🚌1km
♨on the spot 🧍on the spot.

### 🅿🆂 Kirchberg/Jagst 17B2
**Wanderparkplatz Kirchberg-Tal**, Hohen Loher Strasse.
**GPS:** n49,20367 e9,98344.⬆.

6 🚐free ⚡. **Surface:** gravel. ☀ 01/01-31/12.
**Distance:** ⊗300m.

### 🅿 Kirchheim unter Teck 17B3
**Ziegelwasen**, Schlierbacher Straße. **GPS:** n48,64998 e9,45919.⬆➡.

6 🚐free.
**Location:** Urban, simple. **Surface:** asphalted/metalled.
☀ 01/01-31/12.
**Distance:** 🚶500m Altstadt ⊗500m 🚰500m 🚌100m ♨on the spot.
**Remarks:** Max. 3 days.

### 🅿🆂 Kisslegg 20C2
**Wohnmobilhafen Kißlegg**, Strandbadweg.
**GPS:** n47,79602 e9,87950.⬆.
24 🚐€ 5, 01/04-31/10 € 7 🚰€ 1/100liter 🅲Ch ⚡(24x)€ 0,50/kWh
WC. **Location:** Rural, comfortable, noisy. **Surface:** metalled.
☀ 01/01-31/12.
**Distance:** 🚶800m 🏊100m 🚲100m ⊗100m 🚰1km 🚌400m.

### 🅿 Kisslegg 20C2
**Familiefreizeitgelände St Anna**, Le Pouliguenstrasse.
**GPS:** n47,79119 e9,87229.⬆➡.

---

3 🚐free. **Surface:** grassy/metalled. ☀ 01/01-31/12.
**Distance:** 🚶800m ⊗500m 🚰500m.
**Remarks:** Max. 2 nights.

### 🅿🆂 Königschaffhausen 19G1
**Wohnmobilgarten im Kirschenhof Schmidt**, Königsweg 5.
**GPS:** n48,14277 e7,66273.⬆➡.

28 🚐€ 14 + € 1,25/pp tourist tax 🚰 🅲Ch ⚡6Amp WCincluded
🚽€ 2 🚿. **Location:** Rural, comfortable. **Surface:** gravel/metalled.
☀ 01/01-31/12.
**Distance:** 🚶500m ♨on the spot ♨on the spot.
**Remarks:** Wifi in café.

### 🅿🆂 Königsfeld 19H1
**Reisemobilpark Bregnitzhof**, Buchenberger Strasse 34.
**GPS:** n48,14028 e8,40583.⬆➡.

21 🚐€ 10 🚰€ 0,10/10liter 🅲Ch ⚡€ 1/2kWh. 🚿 **Location:** Rural,
luxurious, quiet. **Surface:** gravel. ☀ 01/01-31/12.
**Distance:** 🚶1km ⊗10 min walking.
**Remarks:** Check in between 14-19h, 18-holes golf course, discount
longer stays, Saunalandschaft Bregnitzhof.

### 🅿🆂 Konstanz 20B2
**Parkplatz Döbele**, Döbeleplatz. **GPS:** n47,65794 e9,16933.⬆➡.

12 🚐€ 1,40/h, € 18/24h 🚰🅲ChWCincluded. 📷
**Location:** Urban. **Surface:** asphalted/metalled. ☀ 01/01-31/12.
**Distance:** 🚶1km 🏊800m 🚲800m ⊗200m 🚰800m 🚌500m.
**Remarks:** Max. 24h.

### 🅿🆂 Korb 17B3
**Reisemobilstellplatz Unterm Korber Kopf**, Brucknerstrasse 14.
**GPS:** n48,84597 e9,35544.⬆.

6 🚐€ 3 🚰€ 0,50/80liter 🅲Ch ⚡(6x)€ 0,50/kWh.

---

**Surface:** metalled. ☀ 01/01-31/12.
**Distance:** 🚶400m ⊗Gaststätte 🚰300m 🚌500m.
**Remarks:** Max. 3 nights, coins at restaurant.

### 🅿🆂 Kraichtal 🌿 17A2
**Gochsheim**, Immenstrasse, Gochsheim. **GPS:** n49,10056 e8,74084.⬆.

2 🚐free. **Location:** Simple. **Surface:** asphalted. ☀ 01/01-31/12.
**Distance:** 🚶500m.
**Remarks:** At sports park, small pitches.

### 🅲🆂 Krauchenwies 20B1
**Seencamping Krauchenwies**, Ablacher Str. 4.
**GPS:** n48,01851 e9,23590.

24 🚐€ 9 🚰€ 1/100liter 🅲Ch ⚡€ 0,60 WC 🚿.
**Location:** Rural. **Surface:** gravel. ☀ 01/01-31/12.
**Distance:** 🚶1km 🏊100m 🚲100m ⊗700m 🚰1km 🚌500m
🚴100m 🧍2km.

### 🅿🆂 Kressbronn 20B2
**Wohnmobilstellplatz Tunau**, Tunau 4.
**GPS:** n47,58999 e9,57512.⬆➡.

40 🚐€ 21 🚰🅲Ch ⚡(40x)WC 🚽€ 1,50/pp 🚿included. 📷
**Location:** Rural, comfortable, quiet. **Surface:** asphalted/grassy.
☀ 01/04-31/10.
**Distance:** 🚶1km 🏊1km 🚲1km ⊗on the spot 🚰1km.

### 🅲🆂 Kressbronn 20B2
**Gohren am See**. **GPS:** n47,58818 e9,56256.
16 🚐€ 15 🚰🅲Ch ⚡€ 3/12h WC 🚽€ 1/day. **Location:** Urban,
comfortable, noisy. **Surface:** grassy/gravel. ☀ 01/04-15/10.
**Distance:** 🏊250m.

### 🅿🆂 Külsheim 17B1
**Am Schloss Külsheim**, Kirchbergweg. **GPS:** n49,67123 e9,52255.⬆➡.

12 🚐free 🚰€ 0,50/80liter 🅲Ch ⚡(12x)€ 0,50/kWh 🚿free.
**Location:** Rural, simple. **Surface:** grasstiles.
☀ 01/01-31/12 ☀ 10/09-25/09.
**Distance:** 🚶300m.

### 🅿🆂 Ladenburg 🛥 17A1
**Wohnmobilstellplatz Ladenburg**, Heidelberger Straße.
**GPS:** n49,46596 e8,61460.⬆➡.

35 ⌷€ 10/24h ⌷€ 1/80liter ⌷Ch ⌷€ 1/2kWh ⌷€ 1/24h. ⌷
**Location:** Urban, comfortable, central, quiet. **Surface:** grassy.
☐ 01/01-31/12.
**Distance:** ⌷Altstadt 500m, Heidelberg 10km ⌷3km ⊗200m
⌷200m.

### Lahr/Scharzwald — 19H1
**Stellplatz Breitmatten**, Breitmatten. **GPS:** n48,33954 e7,89885.

14 ⌷€ 6 ⌷€ 1/100liter ⌷Ch ⌷€ 0,50/kWh. ⌷
**Location:** Urban, comfortable. **Surface:** metalled.
☐ 01/01-31/12.
**Distance:** ⌷city centre 1,5km ⊗100m ⌷1,2km ⌷on the spot
⌷on the spot.
**Remarks:** Max. 3 nights.

### Langenau — 17C3
**Wohnmobilstellplätze Langenau**, Karlstraße 27.
**GPS:** n48,50193 e10,12203.⬆
4 ⌷free ⌷€ 0,50/65liter ⌷Ch ⌷€ 0,50/kWh. **Location:** Simple.
**Surface:** metalled. ☐ 01/01-31/12.
**Distance:** ⌷500m ⌷3,2km ⊗300m ⌷1,2km.

### Langenbrettach — 17B2
**Freibad Langenbeutingen**, Schwabbacker Strasse 24, Langenbeutingen. **GPS:** n49,21227 e9,40767.⬆

3 ⌷free. **Location:** Rural, simple. **Surface:** asphalted.
☐ 01/01-31/12.
**Remarks:** Parking swimming pool.

### Langenburg — 17B2
**Am Freibad**, In der Strut 5. **GPS:** n49,24973 e9,86681.⬆
3 ⌷free ⌷. **Surface:** gravel. ☐ 01/01-31/12.
**Distance:** ⌷1km ⊗700m.
**Remarks:** Not accessible coming from the west.

### Lauchringen — 19H2
**An der Wutach**, Badstrasse. **GPS:** n47,62556 e8,31361.➡

19 ⌷€ 8 ⌷€ 0,50/80liter ⌷Ch ⌷(16x)€ 2/24h ⌷included.
**Location:** Rural, comfortable, quiet. **Surface:** gravel.
☐ 01/01-31/12 ⬤ service: 01/11-01/04.
**Distance:** ⌷on the spot ⌷on the spot ⌷on the spot.
**Remarks:** Pay at town hall or swimming pool, caution € 20, key
electricity at pool.

### Lauda-Königshofen — 17B1
Badstrasse. **GPS:** n49,55886 e9,70099.⬆

4 ⌷free. **Location:** Rural, simple. **Surface:** asphalted.
☐ 01/01-31/12.
**Distance:** ⌷1km ⊗1,5km ⌷500m.
**Remarks:** Parking at swimming pool, service at Kläranlage ma-do
7-16h.

### Lauda-Königshofen — 17B1
**Gasthaus Zur Lamm**, St. Josefstrasse 30-32, Marbach.
**GPS:** n46,56568 e9,72834.⬆➡

12 ⌷€ 7/24h ⌷(12x)included ⌷WC free, at restaurant.
**Location:** Rural, simple, quiet. **Surface:** asphalted.
☐ 01/01-31/12 ⬤ Restaurant: Mo.
**Distance:** ⊗on the spot ⌷on the spot.

### Laufenburg — 19H2
**Laufenburg Baden P6**, Andelsbachstraße.
**GPS:** n47,56585 e8,06677.⬆➡

6 ⌷€ 8 ⌷€ 2/5minutes ⌷Ch € 2 ⌷(6x)€ 0,50/kWh ⌷WC ⌷.
**Location:** Urban, quiet. **Surface:** concrete. ☐ 01/01-31/12.
**Distance:** ⌷on the spot ⌷500m ⌷400m.
**Remarks:** Along the Rhine river.

### Laupheim — 20B1
**Schloß Grosslaupheim**, Claus-Graf-Stauffenberg-Straße.
**GPS:** n48,23008 e9,88775.⬆➡

7 ⌷€ 8 ⌷€ 0,50 ⌷€ 0,50 Ch € 0,50 ⌷included.
**Location:** Rural, simple, noisy. **Surface:** grassy. ☐ 01/01-31/12.
**Distance:** ⌷on the spot.

### Lautenbach — 16H3
Waldstraße. **GPS:** n48,51830 e8,11644.⬆
8 ⌷€ 5/day ⌷€ 1/100liter ⌷Ch ⌷€ 0,50/kWh. ⌷
**Location:** Rural. **Surface:** metalled. ☐ 01/01-31/12.
**Distance:** ⌷350m ⊗350m ⌷350m.
**Remarks:** Next to football ground.

### Leonberg — 17A3
**Parkplatz Steinstrasse**, Steinstrasse 19. **GPS:** n48,79705 e9,01751.⬆

5 ⌷free, Mo-Fr 8-18h € 2,50 ⌷€ 0,50/kWh. ⌷
**Surface:** asphalted. ☐ 01/01-31/12 ⬤ Sa 5-13h.
**Distance:** ⌷400m ⊗150m ⌷300m ⌷on the spot.
**Remarks:** Max. 3 nights, green zone: environmental badge obligatory,
market Saturday.

### Leutkirch im Allgäu — 20C2
**Wohnmobilstellplatz Leutkirch**, Kemptener Straße 62.
**GPS:** n47,82228 e10,03939.⬆

14 ⌷€ 8 ⌷€ 1/100liter ⌷Ch ⌷(14x)€ 0,50/kWh.
**Surface:** grasstiles. ☐ 01/01-31/12.
**Distance:** ⌷800m ⌷200m ⊗150m ⌷on the spot ⌷on the spot.

### Löffingen — 19H2
**Waldbad Löffingen**, Am Waldbad. **GPS:** n47,90017 e8,33287.⬆➡

7 ⌷€ 8, tourist tax € 2/pp ⌷ ⌷(4x)included ⌷€ 0,50, At
swimming pool. **Location:** Comfortable. **Surface:** concrete.
☐ 01/01-31/12 ⬤ service 01/10-01/05.
**Distance:** ⌷Swimming pool ⊗on the spot.
**Remarks:** Check in at pay-desk of swimming pool.
**Tourist information Löffingen:**
   Schwarzwaldpark. Game preserve and summer toboggan slide
(€ 1.02 a time). ⬤ Easter-Oct 9-18h.

### Malsch — 16H3
**Gast Caravanning**, Daimlerstr. 20b. **GPS:** n48,89079 e8,30747.⬆

6 ⌷free ⌷€ 1/80liter ⌷Ch. **Location:** Urban, simple.
**Surface:** asphalted/metalled. ☐ 01/01-31/12.
**Distance:** ⌷7,6km.
**Remarks:** Motorhome dealer, accessory shop, friday market.

### Mannheim — 16H1
**Neuostheim**, Hans-Thoma-Straße 3. **GPS:** n49,47446 e8,52522.

DE

15 ☐ € 10/24h 🔌 € 1/100liter ⚡Ch ⚡(15x)€ 1/kWh.
**Location:** Urban. **Surface:** grasstiles/metalled. ⚪ 01/01-31/12.
**Distance:** 🚆4km ⚓900m ⊗200m 🛒500m 🚌100m 🚲400m
🚶400m.
**Remarks:** Outside environmental zone.

### Mannheim/Friedrichsfeld    16H1
**Güma Reisemobile**, Steinzeugstrasse 21. **GPS:** n49,44570 e8,56780.⬆️

4 ☐ free 🔌⚡Ch ⚡WCfree. **Location:** Rural, simple, noisy.
**Surface:** metalled. ⚪ 01/01-31/12.
**Distance:** 🚆10km ⊗1km 🛒1km 🚌300m.
**Remarks:** Max. 3 nights, sanitary use during shop opening hours,
outside environmental zone.

### Marbach am Neckar    17A2
**Parkplatz Bolzplatz**, Poppenweiler/Weimarstrasse.
**GPS:** n48,93389 e9,26278.⬆️➡️

5 ☐ € 5 🔌⚡Ch ⚡€ 1/2kWh. 🚿 **Location:** Rural, simple.
**Surface:** metalled. ⚪ 01/01-31/12.
**Distance:** 🚆1km ⚓6,2km ⊗100m 🛒600m 🚌500m.
**Remarks:** Max. 2 nights, service: Gruppenklärwerk Häldenmühle,
L1100.

### Markelsheim    17B1
Jahnstraße 6. **GPS:** n49,47629 e9,83278.⬆️

2 ☐ free. **Location:** Rural, simple. **Surface:** grasstiles.
⚪ 01/01-31/12.
**Distance:** 🚆100m ⊗200m.
**Remarks:** Max. 2 days.

### Marpingen    16F2
**Parking am Grubenstollen. GPS:** n49,44350 e7,05940.
5 ☐ free 🔌⚡Ch ⚡WCfree. **Surface:** gravel.
⚪ 01/01-31/12.
**Distance:** 🚆1km ⊗800m 🛒1km.

### Maulbronn    17A2
**Am Kloster**, Hilsenbeuerstrasse. **GPS:** n48,99872 e8,80501.⬆️
8 ☐ free 🔌€ 1/100liter ⚡Chfree ⚡€ 1/kWh. **Location:** Simple.
**Surface:** metalled. ⚪ 01/01-31/12.
**Distance:** 🚆on the spot ⊗50m 🛒250m.
**Remarks:** Motorhome max. 7m, max. 2 nights.

### Meckenbeuren    20B2
**Wohnmobilplatz Besenwirtschaft Georgshof**, Pfingstweiderstrasse
10-12/1, Reute. **GPS:** n47,68022 e9,55308.⬆️➡️

9 ☐ € 9 🔌⚡Ch ⚡(9x)€ 0,50/kWh WC ☐ € 1. **Location:** Urban,
simple, quiet. **Surface:** metalled. ⚪ 01/01-31/12.
**Distance:** 🚆on the spot ⚓Bodensee 5km ⊗200m 🛒100m.

### Meersburg/Bodensee    20B2
**Wohnmobilparkplatz Allmend 1**, Allmendweg.
**GPS:** n47,70207 e9,27001.⬆️
20 ☐ € 12 🔌€ 1/100liter ⚡Ch ⚡€ 0,50/kWh WC.🚗
**Location:** Rural, central, quiet. **Surface:** gravel.
⚪ 01/01-31/12.
**Distance:** 🚆1km ⊗400m 🛒700m.

### Meersburg/Bodensee    20B2
**Wohnmobilparkplatz Ergeten**, Daisendorfer Strasse.
**GPS:** n47,70160 e9,26898.⬆️

38 ☐ € 15/24h 🔌€ 1/100liter ⚡Ch ⚡€ 0,50/kWh WC☐.🚗
**Location:** Urban, comfortable, quiet. **Surface:** metalled.
⚪ 01/01-31/12.
**Distance:** 🚆1km ⊗100m 🛒50m 🚌shuttle to centre.
**Remarks:** At edge of city.

### Meersburg/Bodensee    20B2
**Wohnmobilparkplatz Allmend 2**, Allmendweg.
**GPS:** n47,70148 e9,27187.⬆️
30 ☐ € 10.🚗 **Surface:** grassy/gravel. ⚪ 01/01-31/12.
**Distance:** 🚆1,2km ⊗550m 🛒800m.

### Meißenheim    19G1
**Wohnmobilpark Ortenau**, Winkelstrasse 36.
**GPS:** n48,41616 e7,77736.⬆️➡️

24+30 ☐ € 8 🔌€ 1/100liter ⚡Ch ⚡(24x)€ 3,50/24h.🚿
**Location:** Rural, comfortable. **Surface:** gravel/metalled.
⚪ 01/01-31/12.
**Distance:** 🚆500m ⊗200m 🛒800m 🚌on the spot 🚶on the spot.

### Memmingen    20C1
**Wohnmobil-stellplatz Memmingen**, Colmarer Straße/Hemmerles-
traße. **GPS:** n47,99531 e10,18245.⬆️⬆️

20 ☐ € 1/2h, € 5/24h ⚡€ 0,50/100liter ⚡Ch ⚡(18x)€ 0,50/kWh.🚗
**Location:** Urban, simple. **Surface:** metalled.
⚪ 01/01-31/12.
**Distance:** 🚆900m ⚓2,2km ⊗700m 🛒Lidl 600m.
**Remarks:** Max. 2 nights.

### Mengen    20B1
**Reisemobilstellplatz Zielfinger Seen**, Uferweg 18.
**GPS:** n48,03117 e9,28265.⬆️➡️

50 ☐ € 12 🔌€ 1/80liter ⚡Ch ⚡(16x)€ 0,60/kWh WC ☐ 📶included.
**Location:** Rural, comfortable, quiet. **Surface:** asphalted.
⚪ 01/03-31/10.
**Distance:** 🚆1km ⚓on the spot 🚌on the spot ⊗200m 🛒25km
🚲on the spot 🚶on the spot.
**Remarks:** Incl. access Badesee.

### Messkirch    20A1
**Messplatz P2**, Am Stachus. **GPS:** n47,99381 e9,11514.⬆️

4 ☐ free 🔌€ 1/80liter ⚡Ch WC. **Location:** Urban, simple.
**Surface:** metalled. ⚪ 01/01-31/12, service 01/04-30/09.
**Distance:** 🚆500m ⊗400m 🛒200m 🚌500m.

### Metzingen    17B3
**Reisemobilplatz Outletcity Metzingen**, Stetterstrasse 4.
**GPS:** n48,53241 e9,27574.⬆️

20 ☐ € 12 🔌⚡Ch ⚡(6x)included,16Amp.
**Location:** Urban, simple. **Surface:** gravel. ⚪ 01/01-31/12.
**Distance:** 🚆800m ⚓800m ⊗800m 🛒800m 🚌shuttle every 15
min.
**Remarks:** Money in envelope in mail box, service passerby € 2.

### Michelbach an der Blitz    17B2
Hagenhofweg 8. **GPS:** n49,07133 e9,76993.
2 ☐ free 🔌€ 1/100liter ⚡€ 3/24h. **Location:** Rural, quiet.
**Surface:** metalled. ⚪ 01/01-31/12.
**Distance:** 🚆300m ⊗400m 🛒600m 🚌300m 🚲on the spot 🚶on
the spot.
**Remarks:** Max. 2 days.

### Molpertshaus    20B2
**Gasthof Zum Adler**, Eintürner Straße 38. **GPS:** n47,87000 e9,80611.
4 ☐ € 4 🔌⚡Chincluded ⚡€ 2. ⚪ 01/01-31/12.
**Distance:** ⊗200m.

### Mosbach    17A2
Wasemweg. **GPS:** n49,36025 e9,14727.⬆️

18 ☐ free 🔌€ 1/150liter ⚡Ch ⚡(8x)€ 1/12h.
**Location:** Rural, comfortable, quiet. **Surface:** concrete.
⚪ 01/01-31/12.
**Distance:** 🚆800m 🛒300m 🚌on the spot 🚲on the spot.

DE

**Remarks:** Max. 3 nights.

**⊞S** **Mössingen** 20A1

**Wohnmobilstellplatz Firstwald**, Firstwaldstraße, Kernstadt.
**GPS:** n48,41348 e9,06915.⬆

10 🅿€ 5 🚰€ 1/50liter 🚽€ 1 Ch.🚿(10x)€ 0,50/kWh,16Amp.
**Location:** Urban, simple. **Surface:** grasstiles.
⬜ 01/01-31/12.
**Distance:** 🚶1,5km ⊗500m 🛒1km 🚌100m.
**Remarks:** Max. 3 nights.

**♨S** **Mühlberg** 🏕 20C1

**Ferienhof Musch**, Unterer weg 7. **GPS:** n47,98534 e9,98697.⬆

4 🅿€ 15, 2 pers.incl 🚰🚽Ch.🚿(3x)included WC🗑€ 3
🚿€ 2,50/day. **Location:** Rural, comfortable, isolated, quiet.
**Surface:** grassy/metalled. ⬜ 01/01-31/12.
**Distance:** 🚶10km ⊘100m 🛒100m ⊗10km 🛒10km.
**Remarks:** Bread-service.

**⊞** **Müllheim** 🏕 19G2

**Am Friedhof**, Am Engelberg, Hügelheim.
**GPS:** n47,83282 e7,62320.⬆➡

2 🅿free. **Location:** Rural, simple, isolated, quiet. **Surface:** asphalted.
⬜ 01/01-31/12.
**Distance:** 🚶500m ⊗300m 🛒1,5km 🚌400m.
**Remarks:** At cemetery.

**⊞** **Müllheim** 🏕 19G2

**Am Nüsslegarten**, Am Nüsslegarten, Britzingen.
**GPS:** n47,82891 e7,67336.⬆

2 🅿free. **Location:** Rural, simple, quiet. **Surface:** asphalted.
⬜ 01/01-31/12.
**Distance:** 🚶centre 700m ⊗250m 🛒250m 🚴 on the spot 🚶 on the
spot.
**Remarks:** Next to swimming pool, max. 2 nights.

**⊞** **Müllheim** 🏕 19G2

**Freibad Müllheim**, Ziegleweg 7. **GPS:** n47,80237 e7,63403.⬆

3 🅿free. **Location:** Urban, simple. **Surface:** asphalted.
⬜ 01/01-31/12.
**Distance:** 🚶city centre 1km ⊗200m 🛒500m 🚌600m.
**Remarks:** Next to swimming pool, max. 2 nights.

**⊞** **Müllheim** 🏕 19G2

**Parkplatz Nußbaumallee**, Nußbaumallee.
**GPS:** n47,80942 e7,62985.⬆

3 🅿free. **Location:** Urban, simple. **Surface:** asphalted.
⬜ 01/01-31/12.
**Remarks:** Max. 2 days.

**🍴S** **Müllheim** 🏕 19G2

**Restaurant Kreuz**, Bundesstrasse 3 Nr. 7. **GPS:** n47,80934 e7,60778.
5 🅿free 🚰on demand 🚿€ 5. **Surface:** gravel. ⬜ 01/01-31/12.
**Distance:** ⊗on the spot 🛒on the spot.
**Remarks:** Breakfast-service.

**⊞** **Müllheim** 🏕 19G2

**Markgräfler Kräuterhof**, Im Käppeleacker 3, Hügelheim.
**GPS:** n47,83237 e7,62045.⬆

4 🅿free. **Location:** Urban, simple. **Surface:** grasstiles.
⬜ 01/01-31/12.
**Distance:** 🚶500m ⊗50m 🛒1km 🚌300m.
**Remarks:** Herbery, herb-stube.

**⊞S** **Münsingen** 20B1

**Wiesentalstadion**, Grafenecker Straße. **GPS:** n48,40939 e9,48580.⬆

18 🅿€ 5/24h, 3 days € 12 🚰€ 1/100liter 🚽Ch.🚿€ 1/6h.
**Location:** Urban, simple. **Surface:** gravel. ⬜ 01/01-31/12.
**Distance:** 🚶1km ⊗200m 🛒within walking distance 🚴on the spot
🚶on the spot 🏊on the spot.

**⊞S** **Murg** 🛶 19H2

**Am Freibad. GPS:** n47,55196 e8,02403.⬆➡

15 🅿€ 10 🚰€ 1/100liter 🚿€ 0,50/kWh 🚿. 🚗 **Location:** Rural,
comfortable, quiet. **Surface:** gravel. ⬜ 01/01-31/12.
**Distance:** 🚶500m ⛰on the spot ⊗650m 🛒1km 🚴on the spot.

**⊞S** **Murrhardt** 17B2

**Parkplatz Festhalle**, Kaiser-Ludwig-Straße 25.
**GPS:** n48,97960 e9,57461.⬆➡

3 🅿free 🚰€ 1/90liter 🚽Ch. **Location:** Rural, simple.
**Surface:** asphalted. ⬜ 01/01-31/12.
**Distance:** 🚶400m ⊗100m.

**⊞S** **Nagold** 🍴🛒 17A3

**Wohnmobilhafen am Nagoldtal-Radweg**, Am Glockenrain.
**GPS:** n48,56389 e8,72306.⬆➡

22 🅿€ 3 🚰€ 1/80liter 🚽€ 1 Ch€ 1 🚿(12x)€ 1/kWh.🚗
**Location:** Rural, simple, quiet. **Surface:** gravel/metalled.
⬜ 01/01-31/12.
**Distance:** 🚶1km 🛒25m 🛒900m 🚌400m on the spot 🚶on the
spot.
**Remarks:** Market Wednesday and Saturday.

**⊞** **Nagold** 🍴🛒 17A3

**Am Bahnhof**, Bahnhofstraße. **GPS:** n48,55791 e8,72748.⬆➡

4 🅿free. **Location:** Rural, simple, noisy. **Surface:** asphalted.
⬜ 01/01-31/12.
**Distance:** 🚶700m ⊗100m 🛒on the spot 🚴on the spot 🚶on the
spot.
**Remarks:** Max. 4 nights, market Wednesday and Saturday.

**⊞S** **Nattheim** 17C3

**Ramensteinbad**, Dieselstrasse 22. **GPS:** n48,70261 e10,23745.⬆➡

4 🅿free 🚰🚽Chfree 🚿€ 1/2kWh. **Location:** Urban, quiet.
**Surface:** metalled. ⬜ 01/01-31/12 ⬛ 25/04-07/05.

DE

**Distance:** 500m 300m 200m Lidl.
**Remarks:** Parking swimming pool, max. 3 days.

### Neckarsulm — 17A2

**Freizeitbad Aquatoll**, Reisachmühlweg. **GPS:** n49,18802 e9,24302.

25 free € 1/60liter Ch. **Location:** Rural, simple.
**Surface:** asphalted/gravel. 01/01-31/12.
**Distance:** 1km 4km 450m 400m.
**Remarks:** Parking swimming pool, max. 24h.

### Neckarwestheim — 17A2

**Wohnmobilstellplätze Im Bühl**, Liebensteiner Strasse.
**GPS:** n49,04186 e9,18797.

2 free € 2 Ch (4x)€ 2/8h. **Surface:** metalled.
01/01-31/12.
**Distance:** 500m 200m 500m.
**Remarks:** From 4th night € 25/night.

### Nehren — 17A3

**Wohnmobilstellplatz an der Steinlach. GPS:** n48,43795 e9,05384.
8 free € 1 (8x)€ 1/kWh.
**Location:** Rural. **Surface:** grassy.
01/01-31/12.
**Distance:** centre 500m 1km on the spot on the spot.

### Neresheim — 17C3

**Stellplatz Alter Bahnhof**, Dischinger Straße 11.
**GPS:** n48,75102 e10,33957.

5 free € 1 Ch (4x)€ 1/4h. **Location:** Noisy.
**Surface:** metalled. 01/01-31/12.
**Distance:** on the spot 12km on the spot 300m.
**Remarks:** Service during opening hours.

### Neuffen — 17B3

**Am Schützenhaus**, Schützenhausweg. **GPS:** n48,54726 e9,37057.

16 free € 2/8minutes Ch (15x)€ 2/8h.
**Location:** Rural, simple, quiet. **Surface:** metalled.
01/01-31/12.
**Distance:** 1km 500m 500m on the spot.

### Neuhausen ob Eck — 20A1

**Wohnmobilstellplatz Auf der Eck**, Beim Friedhof.
**GPS:** n47,97473 e8,92397.

8 voluntary contribution € 1 € 1 Ch 1 (9x).
**Location:** Urban, simple. **Surface:** metalled. 01/01-31/12.
**Distance:** 300m 500m 1km 300m 2km 2km.
**Remarks:** Max. 4 days.

### Neunkirchen — 17A2

**Festplatz**, Zwingenbergerstrasse. **GPS:** n49,38818 e9,01531.

8 free € 1/90liter Ch. **Location:** Rural, simple, quiet.
**Surface:** asphalted. 01/01-31/12.
**Distance:** 300m 500m.
**Remarks:** Service next to: Autohaus Weishaupt, Industriestrasse 3 (200m).

### Nordheim — 17A2

Lauffener Straße. **GPS:** n49,10461 e9,13552.

2 € 5 Ch included. **Location:** Simple. **Surface:** asphalted.
01/01-31/12.
**Distance:** on the spot on the spot.
**Remarks:** In front of swimmingpool, max. 3 days.

### Nordheim — 17A2

**Müllers Weingut und Weinstube**, Im Auerberg 3.
**GPS:** n49,10236 e9,13810.

2 € 5, with electricity and water € 8 Ch. **Location:** Rural.
01/01-31/12.
**Distance:** 800m on the spot on the spot on the spot
on the spot.

### Nordheim — 17A2

**Rolf Willy Privatkellerei**, Schafhohle 26. **GPS:** n49,11212 e9,12845.
4 € 10, guests free (2x). 01/01-31/12.
**Distance:** 350m.

### Nordrach — 19H1

**Schwarzwald-Panorama Wohnmobilstellplatz**, Im Dorf 29.
**GPS:** n48,39873 e8,07927.

8 free € 1/10liter Ch (8x)€ 1/6h.
**Location:** Rural, simple, central. **Surface:** metalled.
01/01-31/12.
**Distance:** 100m 100m.

### Nürtingen — 17B3

**Stellplatz Plätschwiesen**, B313, Plätschwiesen, Oberensingen.
**GPS:** n48,63645 e9,33051.

12 € 5/24h € 1 Ch (8x)€ 1. **Location:** Urban.
**Surface:** metalled. 01/01-31/12.
**Distance:** 1km 4,4km on the spot 500m on the spot.
**Remarks:** Max. 7 days.

### Oberderdingen — 17A2

Schillerstraße 61. **GPS:** n49,05833 e8,79490.
8 € 5 € 1/10minutes € 1/8h.
**Surface:** metalled. 01/01-31/12.
**Distance:** on the spot 400m 100m.

### Oberkirch — 16H3

**Am Renchtalstadion**, Renchallee. **GPS:** n48,52972 e8,07250.

37 € 5/day, 3 days € 10 + € 2 tourist tax € 1/80liter € 1 Ch
(40x)€ 1/2kWh.
**Location:** Rural, simple, quiet. **Surface:** grassy/gravel.
01/01-31/12 week before and week after 1st weekend Sep.
**Distance:** 100m 100m 100m on the spot on the spot.

### Oberkirch — 16H3

**Waldparkplatz Schauenburg**, Burgstraße 29.
**GPS:** n48,53812 e8,09452.

4 € 8 (4x)€ 2. **Location:** Simple, isolated, quiet.
**Surface:** grassy/sand. 01/01-31/12.
**Distance:** 500m.
**Remarks:** Max. 4 days, € 8 voucher restaurant.

### Oberndorf/Neckar — 20A1

**Neckarhalle**, Austrasse 12. **GPS:** n48,28222 e8,58472.

DE

8 ⌧free ⛽€ 1/70liter 🚽Ch ⚡(4x)€ 1/8h. **Location:** Rural, simple, noisy. **Surface:** asphalted. 🅾 01/01-31/12.
**Distance:** 🚉1,5km 🚋300m 🛒200m 🚲50m 🏍on the spot 🚶on the spot.
**Remarks:** Max. 3 days.

### Oberstenfeld    17B2
**Mineralfreibad Oberes Bottwartal**, Beilsteiner Strasse 100.
**GPS:** n49,03160 e9,31890.

4 ⌧€ 8 🚰🚽Chincluded ⚡€ 1/kWh. **Location:** Simple, quiet.
**Surface:** asphalted. 🅾 01/01-31/12.
**Distance:** 🚋900m

### Oberteuringen    20B2
**Ferienhof Kramer**, St. Georg strasse 8. **GPS:** n47,73948 e9,47278.

6 ⌧€ 18, 2 pers.incl 🚰🚽Ch ⚡(8x)€ 2,50 WC🚽€ 4.
**Surface:** gravel/metalled. 🅾 01/05-15/09.
**Distance:** 🚉2km ⛵on the spot 🚋300m 🛒300m.

### Offenburg    16H3
**Strandbad & Tiki Bar Gifizsee**, Platanenallee 15.
**GPS:** n48,45785 e7,93663.

11 ⌧€ 22, 2 pers.incl 🚰€ 1/5minutes 🚽Ch ⚡(11x)€ 1/kWh
WC🚽🚰included. **Location:** Rural, simple. **Surface:** grasstiles.
🅾 01/04-31/10.
**Distance:** 🚉2,5km ⛵3,8km 🛒100m 🚋on the spot 🛒150m.
**Remarks:** Bread-service.

### Offenburg    16H3
**Bürgerpark**, Stegermattstraße 26a. **GPS:** n48,46565 e7,94566.

2 ⌧€ 2. **Location:** Urban, simple, central, quiet.
**Surface:** asphalted/metalled. 🅾 01/01-31/12.
**Distance:** 🚉500m 🚋300m.

---

**Remarks:** In front of swimmingpool, small pitches.

### Offenburg    16H3
**Camping + Freizeit Kuhn**, Im Drachenacker 4.
**GPS:** n48,48039 e7,92776.

10 ⌧free 🚰€ 0,50/50liter 🚽Ch ⚡(8x)free. **Location:** Urban, simple. **Surface:** metalled. 🅾 01/01-31/12.
**Distance:** 🚉2km ⛵3,7km 🛒500m.
**Remarks:** Service during opening hours.

### Öhringen    17B2
**Wohnmobilhafen Heicamp**, Verrenberger Weg 33.
**GPS:** n49,19223 e9,48025.

60 ⌧€ 14, 2 pers incl 🚰🚽Ch ⚡€ 0,50/kWh WC🚽€ 2.
**Distance:** 🚋on the spot.
**Remarks:** Bread-service.

**Tourist information Öhringen:**
RADius. Cycle route, 18km.

### Öllingen    17C3
**Parking Rathaus**, Hauptstrasse. **GPS:** n48,52816 e10,14813.

4 ⌧free 🚰🚽Chfree. **Surface:** grasstiles. 🅾 01/01-31/12.
**Distance:** 🚋100m 🛒100m 🛒on the spot.

### Oppenau    16H3
**Wohnmobilstellplatz Oppenau**, Hauptstrasse.
**GPS:** n48,47639 e8,16972.

6 ⌧€ 5/day + tourist tax 🚰€ 1,50/100liter 🚽Ch ⚡(6x)€ 1/8h.
**Location:** Rural, simple, quiet. **Surface:** gravel.
🅾 01/01-31/12.
**Distance:** 🚉300m 🚋150m 🛒bakery 300m 🚲on the spot 🚶on the spot.
**Remarks:** Use sanitary only during opening hours swimming pool.

### Oppenweiler    17B2
**Caravanstation**, Murrwiesenstraße 15.
**GPS:** n48,97999 e9,45898.

---

2 ⌧free 🚰€ 1/80liter 🚽Ch. **Surface:** asphalted. 🅾 01/01-31/12.
**Distance:** 🚉600m.
**Remarks:** Max. 2 days.

### Ostrach    20B2
**Wohnmobilstellplatz Weites Ried**, Schulstraße 12.
**GPS:** n47,91722 e9,35438.

8 ⌧€ 4 ⚡(4x)€ 1/8h. **Location:** Rural, isolated, quiet.
**Surface:** gravel. 🅾 01/01-31/12.
**Distance:** 🚉200m ⛵6km ⊗1km 🛒5km.

### Pforzheim    17A3
**Reisemobilplatz Oststadt am Enzauenpark**, Wildersinnstraße.
**GPS:** n48,89784 e8,72232.

15 ⌧free ⚡(6x)€ 1/kWh. **Location:** Urban, simple, noisy.
**Surface:** metalled. 🅾 01/01-31/12.
**Distance:** 🚉1,5km ⊗200m 🛒100m 🚋on the spot 🚲on the spot 🚶on the spot.
**Remarks:** Max. 2 days, service 200m, outside environmental zone.

### Pforzheim    17A3
**Parkplatz 2&3 Wildpark**, Tiefenbronnerstraße.
**GPS:** n48,87651 e8,71749.
⌧€ 3-5. **Location:** Urban. 🅾 01/01-31/12.
**Remarks:** Max. 1 night, outside environmental zone.

### Pforzheim    17A3
Hohwiesenweg. **GPS:** n48,89750 e8,72674.
🚰€ 1/80liter 🚽Ch. 🅾 01/01-31/12.
**Remarks:** Outside environmental zone.

### Pfullendorf    20B2
**Seepark Linzgau, P-Ost**, Bannholzerweg 18. **GPS:** n47,93097 e9,23728.

20 ⌧€ 4/24h ⚡€ 0,50/kWh. **Surface:** unpaved.
🅾 01/01-31/12.
**Distance:** 🚉2km ⛵on the spot ⊗50m 🛒450m.

### Pfullingen    17A3
**Wohnmobilplatz Schönbergbad**, Klosterstraße.
**GPS:** n48,45537 e9,22812.

DE

8 🛏free 🚰€ 1/50liter 🔌€ 1 Ch 💧€ 1/2kWh. **Location:** Urban, simple. **Surface:** grassy. ⬛ 01/01-31/12.
**Distance:** 🚶1,5km ⊗nearby 🚲 on the spot.
**Remarks:** Max. 4 days.

### 🏕S Radolfzell 20A2
**Wohmobilstellplatz in den Herzen**, Zeppelinstraße.
**GPS:** n47,73888 e8,95331.⬆️.

15 🛏€ 17/24h, 2 pers.incl 🚰€ 1/50liter 🔌Ch 💧(12x)€ 0,50/kWh.
**Surface:** metalled. ⬛ 01/01-31/12.
**Distance:** 🚶750m 🚲3km ⛰500m ⛴500m ⊗500m 🍴750m
🚌500m 🚴BodenseeRadweg 🥾Bodensee-Rundwanderweg.
**Remarks:** Max. 72h.

### 🏕S Radolfzell 20A2
**Wohnmobilstellplatz Halbinsel Mettnau**, Strandbadstrasse.
**GPS:** n47,73784 e8,98007.⬆️.

12 🛏€ 17/24h, 2 pers.incl 🚰€ 1/50liter 🔌Ch 💧(6x)€ 0,50/kWh.🅿️
**Surface:** asphalted. ⬛ 01/01-31/12.
**Distance:** 🚶750m 🚲2km ⛰750m ⚓1km ⊗500m 🍴750m
🚌500m ⛴500m 🥾1km.
**Remarks:** Max. 3 days.

### 🏕S Radolfzell 20A2
**Campingplatz Böhringer See**, Hindenburgstrasse 64.
**GPS:** n47,76176 e8,93488.⬆️.

5 🛏€ 10 🚰🔌Ch 💧€ 3 WC 🔌€ 1. **Location:** Rural, comfortable, quiet. **Surface:** metalled. ⬛ 01/01-31/12.
**Distance:** 🚶1km ⊗on the spot 🥾1km.

### 🏕S Rastatt 16H3
**Stellplatz am Familienbad Alohra**, Leopoldring 8.
**GPS:** n48,85409 e8,19970.⬆️.

5 🛏€ 7 🚰€ 1,50/10minutes 🔌Ch 💧(8x)€ 1,50/6h.
**Location:** Urban, simple. **Surface:** metalled. ⬛ 01/01-31/12.
**Distance:** 🚶500m 🚲 3,8km.
**Remarks:** Check in at pay-desk of swimming pool, discount at swimming pool and sauna, tuesday, thursday and saturday market 7-13h.

### 🏕 Ratzenried 20C2
**Parkplatz Turnhalle. GPS:** n47,72199 e9,90430.
3 🛏free. **Location:** Urban. **Surface:** asphalted. ⬛ 01/01-31/12.
**Distance:** 🚶on the spot ⊗200m 🍴200m 🚲on the spot 🥾on the spot.

### 🏕S Ravensburg 20B2
**Wohnmobilstellplatz Ravensburg**, Mühlbruckstrasse.
**GPS:** n47,78196 e9,60001.⬆️➡️.

19 🛏€ 8,50 🚰€ 1/80liter 🔌Ch 💧€ 0,50/kWh.
**Surface:** metalled. ⬛ 01/01-31/12.
**Distance:** 🚶centre 800m ⊗500m 🍴200m 🚌250m Donau-Bodensee Radweg.
**Remarks:** Max. 3 nights.

### 🍴 Ravensburg 20B2
**Am Gasthaus Anker**, Schlegel 22. **GPS:** n47,78378 e9,53787.
10 🛏free. ⬛ 01/01-31/12.

**Tourist information Ravensburg:**
ℹ️ Bodensee-Erlebniskarte. Card gives free access to all boats, telpher carriers, beaches etc. Around the Lake Constance in Germany, Switzerland and Austria. 🎫 € 72/3 days.
ℹ️ Tourist Information, Kirchstrasse 16. City of the Tore und Turme, gates and towers.

### 🏕S Rechberghausen 17B3
**Sportpark Lindach**, Am Desenbach. **GPS:** n48,72405 e9,63594.⬆️➡️.

6 🛏free 🚰€ 0,50/80liter 🔌Ch 💧(6x)€ 0,50/kWh. **Location:** Rural, simple. **Surface:** grassy. ⬛ 01/04-01/11.
**Distance:** 🚶1km ⛰500m 🥾1km 🍴1km 🚌500m on the spot.

### 🏕S Reichenau 20A2
**Zum Sandseele. GPS:** n47,69887 e9,04711.⬆️.

12 🛏€ 12/24h 🚰€ 1/80liter 🔌Ch 💧(8x)€ 1/2kWh.
**Surface:** asphalted/metalled. ⬛ 01/01-31/12.
**Distance:** 🚶1,5km ⛰on the spot ⚓on the spot ⊗100m 🥾2km.
**Remarks:** Max. 1 night.

### 🏕S Reichental 16H3
Auwiesenstraze. **GPS:** n48,73166 e8,39616.⬆️.

10 🛏free 🚰Ch. **Location:** Simple, isolated, quiet. **Surface:** gravel.
⬛ 01/01-31/12.
**Distance:** 🚶1km 🥾on the spot.

### 🏕S Renchen 16H3
**Wohnmobilstellplatz Renchen-Ulm**, Ullenburgstrasse, Ulm.
**GPS:** n48,58088 e8,04556.⬆️➡️.

12 🛏€ 6 🚰€ 1/100liter 🔌Ch 💧€ 1/2kWh. 🅿️ **Location:** Rural, comfortable, quiet. ⬛ 01/01-31/12.
**Distance:** 🚶300m ⊗300m 🚲on the spot 🥾on the spot.
**Remarks:** Friday market.

### 🏕S Reutlingen 17A3
**P&R Parkplatz**, Am Südbahnhof/Marktstrasse.
**GPS:** n48,48280 e9,22982.⬆️➡️.

3 🛏free 🚰Chfree 💧€ 0,50/kWh. **Location:** Urban, simple, noisy. **Surface:** gravel. ⬛ 01/01-31/12.
**Distance:** 🚶3km ⊗on the spot 🚲on the spot.
**Remarks:** In front of motorhome dealer Berger, max. 48h, green zone: environmental badge obligatory.

### 🏕S Reutlingen 17A3
**Sportpark Markwasen**, Hermann-Hesse-Straße.
**GPS:** n48,47536 e9,19377.⬆️.

10 🛏€ 8 🚰€ 1/80liter 🔌€ 1 Ch 🔌 1 💧(8x)€ 0,50/kWh.🅿️
**Location:** Urban, simple. **Surface:** gravel. ⬛ 01/01-31/12.
**Distance:** 🚶3km ⊗500m.
**Remarks:** Green zone: environmental badge obligatory, public transport included.

### 🏕S Rheinmünster 16H3
**Freizeit Center Oberrhein**, Am Campingpark 1.
**GPS:** n48,77250 e8,04240.⬆️.

DE

20 ⬛€ 7-9,50/24h ⛽ € 1/80liter ♨Ch ⚡(20x)€ 0,50/kWh,+ € 3.
**Location:** Rural, comfortable, quiet. **Surface:** grassy.
⬛ 01/01-31/12.
**Distance:** ⛲on the spot ⊗200m 🚲 on the spot 🚶 on the spot.

## Riedlingen 20B1
**Stadthalle**, Hindenburgstraße. **GPS:** n48,15189 e9,47766.➡.

3 ⬛free ⛽ € 1/100liter ♨Ch ⚡€ 1/4h. **Location:** Urban.
**Surface:** asphalted. ⬛ 01/01-31/12.
**Distance:** ⛲300m ⛲200m ⛲100m.
**Remarks:** Max. 3 days.

## Rielasingen-Worblingen 20A2
**Naturbad Aachtal**, Herdweg. **GPS:** n47,72127 e8,66332.⬆.
16 ⬛free, 01/05-15/30 € 6 ⛽ € 1/100liter ♨Ch ⚡(16x)€ 0,50/kWh
⬛01/05-30/09. **Location:** Rural. **Surface:** gravel.
⬛ 01/01-31/12.
**Distance:** ⛲600m.
**Remarks:** At swimming pool.

## Rottenburg/Neckar 17A3
**Wohnmobilhafen Neckarufer**, Ulmenweg 4.
**GPS:** n48,47213 e8,95010.⬆➡.

12 ⬛€ 5 ⛽ € 1 ♨Ch ⚡(8x)€ 0,50/kWh. 
**Location:** Urban, simple. **Surface:** asphalted. ⬛ 01/01-31/12.
**Distance:** ⛲800m ⛲800m ⛲100m ⛲400m 🚲 on the spot.
**Remarks:** Max. 4 days.

## Rottweil 20A1
**Parkplatz**, Stadionstrasse. **GPS:** n48,15556 e8,62861.⬆➡.

20 ⬛€ 5 ⛽ € 1 ♨Ch ⚡(16x)€ 1/8h. **Location:** Urban, simple, quiet.
**Surface:** gravel. ⬛ 01/01-31/12.
**Distance:** ⛲1km ⊗1km ⛲1km ⛲500m.
**Remarks:** Parking stadium.

## Rudersberg 17B3
**Am Freibad**, Bronnwiesenweg. **GPS:** n48,88410 e9,51920.⬆.
4 ⬛free ⛽€ 0,10/10liter ⚡€ 0,50 Ch ⚡€ 1/kWh ♨€ 1.
**Location:** Rural, simple, quiet. **Surface:** gravel.
⬛ 01/01-31/12.
**Distance:** ⊗850m ⛲850m.

## Rust 19G1
**Europapark Rust**, Europa-Parkstrasse. **GPS:** n48,27189 e7,71745.⬆.

200 ⬛8-20h € 2/h (max. € 6), 20-8h € 2,50/h (max. € 25) ⛽➡.

---

Ch ♨WC 🚿included. 🚻
**Location:** Rural, simple, noisy. **Surface:** grasstiles.
⬛ 24/03-04/11, 24/11-06/01 9-18.
**Distance:** ⛲1km ⊗on the spot 🚲 on the spot.

**Tourist information Rust:**
Europa-park, Europa-Park-Straße 2. Large amusement and theme
park with Europe as theme. ⬛ 24/03-04/11 9-18, 24/11-06/01 11-19.

## Sankt Blasien 19H2
**Rehbach Skilift**, Rehbachweg, Menzenschwand.
**GPS:** n47,81306 e8,06933.⬆.

20 ⬛€ 7 ⛽ ♨Ch ⚡(16x)€ 3/24h. **Location:** Rural, simple, quiet.
**Surface:** grassy/gravel. ⬛ 01/04-31/10.
**Distance:** ⛲8km ⛲bakery 500m 🚲 on the spot 🚶 on the spot
🚶 on the spot.
**Remarks:** At ski-lift Rehbach.

## Sankt Blasien 19H2
**Am Dom**, Fürstabt-Gerbert-Straße. **GPS:** n47,76039 e8,12923.⬆.
5 ⬛free. **Surface:** metalled. ⬛ 01/01-31/12.
**Distance:** ⛲on the spot ⛲200m.

## Sasbachwalden 16H3
**Wohnmobilstellplatz Sasbachwalden**, Talstraße 2.
**GPS:** n48,61945 e8,12147.⬆➡.

30 ⬛€ 7/night ⛽ € 1/80liter ♨Ch ⚡(20x)€ 2/24h. 🚻
**Location:** Rural, comfortable, quiet. **Surface:** gravel/metalled.
⬛ 01/01-31/12.
**Distance:** ⛲centre 300m 🏊9km ⛲9km ⛲100m ⛲250m ⛲250m
⛲100m 🚲 on the spot 🚶 on the spot.
**Remarks:** Waterfall 1km, swimming pool 800m.

## Schiltach 19H1
**Stellplatz P1 Lehwiese**, Am Hirschen. **GPS:** n48,29111 e8,34250.⬆➡.

10 ⬛free ⚡(3x). **Location:** Urban, simple, quiet. **Surface:** gravel.
⬛ 01/01-31/12.
**Distance:** ⛲200m ⊗50m ⛲50m ⛲on the spot 🚲 on the spot
🚶 on the spot.
**Remarks:** Busy parking during the day.

## Schluchsee 19H2
**P Aqua Fun**, Faulenfürster Straße 18. **GPS:** n47,81569 e8,18113.⬆.

22 ⬛€ 10 + € 2,70/pp tourist tax ⛽ € 1/100liter ♨Ch ⚡€ 1/8h. 🚻
**Location:** Rural, comfortable, central, quiet. **Surface:** asphalted.

---

⬛ 01/01-31/12.
**Distance:** ⛲200m.
**Remarks:** Max. 1 night.

## Schonach im Schwarzwald 19H1
**Parkplatz Obertal**, Schwimmbadweg. **GPS:** n48,14573 e8,18872.⬆.

10 ⬛€ 7 ⛽ € 1 ♨€ 1 Ch ⚡(8x)€ 1/8h. **Location:** Rural, comfortable.
**Surface:** grasstiles. ⬛ 01/01-31/12.
**Distance:** ⛲1km ⛲650m ⛲on the spot 🚶 on the spot 🚶 on the spot
🚶 on the spot.
**Remarks:** Max. 3 nights, coins at tourist info, free entrance swimming
pool, ski-lift and public transport.

## Schönwald im Schwarzwald 19H1
**Lynx Camp**, Friedhofstr. 18. **GPS:** n48,10984 e8,20094.⬆➡.

10 ⬛€ 23,80, 01/05-31/10 € 26,80 ⛽ € 0,80 Ch ⚡€ 0,60/kWh,+
€ 2 WC 🚿🚻 **Location:** Rural, simple, isolated.
**Surface:** gravel/metalled. ⬛ 01/01-31/12.
**Distance:** ⊗800m ⛲300m ⛲on the spot 🚶 on the spot.

## Schorndorf 17B3
**Oskar Frech SeeBad**, Lortzingstraße 56. **GPS:** n48,79645 e9,51410.
5 ⬛free ⛽ € 1 ♨€ 1 Ch ⚡€ 1 ⚡€ 0,50/kWh. **Location:** Urban.
**Surface:** metalled. ⬛ 01/01-31/12.
**Distance:** ⛲on the spot.
**Remarks:** At swimming pool.

## Schorndorf 17B3
**Top-Mobile**, Gmünder Straße 84/1. **GPS:** n48,80539 e9,54187.⬆.

10 ⬛€ 5 + € 4/pp ⛽€ 2 ♨Ch € 2 ⚡€ 0,50/kWh,+ € 1 WC 🚿€ 2
🚻€ 2/2 🚿€ 1.🚻 **Location:** Urban, simple, quiet. **Surface:** metalled.
⬛ 01/01-31/12.
**Distance:** ⛲10min ⛲300m.

## Schramberg 19H1
Bahnhofstraße, B462. **GPS:** n48,23017 e8,38323.➡.

2 ⬛free ⛽ € 1/80liter ♨Ch. **Location:** Rural, simple, noisy.
**Surface:** concrete. ⬛ 01/01-31/12.
**Distance:** ⛲on the spot ⊗100m ⛲50m ⛲10m 🚲 on the spot
🚶 on the spot.
**Remarks:** Max. 7 days, green zone: environmental badge obligatory.

## Schwäbisch Gmünd 17B3
**Schießtalplatz**, Schiesstalstraße. **GPS:** n48,80543 e9,81308.⬆.

DE

8 ⌁free ⛽€ 1/50liter 🔌Ch 🔌(8x)€ 0,50/kWh. **Location:** Rural, simple. **Surface:** gravel. ⬛ 01/01-31/12.
**Distance:** 🚶1km ⊗50m 🚌500m.
**Remarks:** Motorhome < 7m, max. 5 days a month, green zone: environmental badge obligatory.

### Schwäbisch Hall 17B2

**Wohnmobilstellplatz Auwiese**, Spitalmühlenstraße.
**GPS:** n49,12218 e9,73473. ⬆️➡️.

7 ⌁free. **Surface:** gravel. ⬛ 01/01-31/12.
**Distance:** 🚶1,5km ⊗100m.
**Remarks:** Max. 48h.

### Schwaigern 17A2

**Wohnmobilstellplatz Schaigern**, Gemminger Straße 91.
**GPS:** n49,14576 e9,04529. ⬆️.

2 ⌁free ⛽€ 1/90liter 🔌Ch 🔌free. **Surface:** asphalted.
⬛ 01/01-31/12.
**Distance:** 🚶1km ⊗300m 🚌on the spot 🚶on the spot.

### Schwetzingen 🍴 16H2

Ketscher Landstrasse. **GPS:** n49,37803 e8,55820. ⬆️.

12 ⌁free ⛽€ 3/80liter 🔌Ch. **Location:** Rural, simple, noisy.
**Surface:** grasstiles/metalled. ⬛ 01/01-31/12.
**Distance:** 🚶500m ⊗on the spot 🍴on the spot 🚌100m 🚴on the spot 🚶on the spot.
**Remarks:** Max. 3 nights.

### Seelbach 19H1

**Reisemobil-Wellness-Stellplatz Schwarzwälder Hof**, Am Tretenbach.
**GPS:** n48,30042 e7,94497. ⬆️.

16 ⌁€ 20 ⛽€ 1/90liter 🔌Ch 🔌(16x)€ 1/kWh WC 📶included. 🚻
**Location:** Rural, comfortable, noisy. **Surface:** grassy.

---

⬛ 01/01-31/12.
**Distance:** 🚶600m ⊗100m.
**Remarks:** Including access to swimming pool, use sanitary facilities, entrance 1p wellness/sauna.

### Seewald 🏕️ ❄️ ⛄ ⚓ 16H3

P4, L362. **GPS:** n48,55131 e8,49522. ⬆️➡️.

17 ⌁free WCfree. **Location:** Rural, simple, quiet. **Surface:** asphalted.
⬛ 01/01-31/12 ⬛ service 01/11-31/03.
**Distance:** 🚶1,5km ⊗25m 🚌600m.

### Siggen 20C2

Siggener Höhe. **GPS:** n47,70676 e9,92568.
2 ⌁free. **Location:** Rural. **Surface:** asphalted. ⬛ 01/01-31/12.
**Distance:** 🚶1km ⛵1km.
**Remarks:** Max. 2 nights.

### Sigmaringen 🌿⚓🍴 20B1

**Wohnmobilplatz Sigmaringen**, Georg Zimmerer Straße 4.
**GPS:** n48,08545 e9,21029. ⬆️➡️.

20 ⌁€ 8 ⛽€ 1/80liter 🔌Ch 🔌(20x)€ 1/4h. 🚻
**Location:** Simple. **Surface:** metalled. ⬛ 01/01-31/12.
**Distance:** 🚶500m ⊗500m 🍴200m 🚌on the spot.

### Sindelfingen 17A3

**Badezentrum Sindelfingen**, Hohenzollernstrasse.
**GPS:** n48,71993 e9,01779. ⬆️.

10 ⌁free. **Location:** Urban, simple. **Surface:** asphalted.
⬛ 01/01-31/12.
**Distance:** ⊗on the spot 🚌on the spot 🚴on the spot 🚶on the spot.

### Singen 🍴 20A2

**Wohnmobil-Stellplätze Landesgartenschau**, Schaffhauser Straße 35.
**GPS:** n47,75992 e8,82766. ⬆️➡️.

20 ⌁€ 5 ⛽🔌Chincluded 🔌(16x)€ 2/12h. **Surface:** grassy/gravel.
⬛ 01/01-31/12, service 15/03-15/11.
**Distance:** 🚶1km ⊗on the spot 🚌200m.
**Remarks:** Max. 72h.

### Singen 🍴 20A2

**Hallenbad**, Waldeckstraße 4. **GPS:** n47,76472 e8,84781. ⬆️.
3 ⌁free. **Surface:** asphalted. ⬛ 01/01-31/12.
**Distance:** 🚶500m ⊗500m 🍴400m.
**Remarks:** At swimming pool.

---

### Sinsheim 🍴 17A2

**Wohnmobilpark Sinsheim**, Am Ilvesbach.
**GPS:** n49,25022 e8,88002. ⬆️.

32 ⌁€ 9 ⛽€ 1/100liter 🔌Ch 🔌€ 0,50/kWh. 📶included. 🚻
**Location:** Rural, simple, quiet. **Surface:** metalled.
⬛ 01/01-31/12.
**Distance:** 🚶500m ⊗500m 🍴700m 🚌300m.
**Remarks:** Discount at swimming pool.

### Sternenfels 17A2

Diefenbach, Burrainstrasse, Diefenbach. **GPS:** n49,02440 e8,85535. ⬆️.
3 ⌁free. **Location:** Urban, simple. **Surface:** asphalted.
⬛ 01/01-31/12.
**Distance:** 🚶100m ⊗on the spot.

### Stetten 🌿 20B2

Alte Brennerei, Riedetsweilerstrasse 5. **GPS:** n47,69326 e9,29788. ⬆️.

15 ⌁€ 9 ⛽€ 1 🔌€ 1 Ch 🔌(6x)€ 0,50/kWh WC.
**Surface:** grassy/gravel. ⬛ 01/01-31/12.
**Distance:** 🚶300m ⊗2km 🍴2km 🚌300m 🚴300m 🚌300m.

### Stockach/Bodensee 20A2

WoMo-Park Papiermühle, Johann-Glatt-strasse 3.
**GPS:** n47,84169 e8,99945. ⬆️.

85 ⌁€ 14, 2 pers incl ⛽€ 0,50/50liter 🔌Ch 🔌(118x)WC 📶included.
**Location:** Rural, comfortable, quiet. **Surface:** gravel/metalled.
⬛ 01/03-30/11.
**Distance:** 🚶1,5km ⊗on the spot 🚌700m.
**Remarks:** Bread-service in summer period.

### Sulz am Neckar 🍴❄️⚓ 20A1

Stellplatz Wöhrd, Ludwigstraße. **GPS:** n48,36427 e8,63681. ➡️.

6 ⌁free ⛽€ 1/80liter 🔌€ 1 Ch€ 1 🔌(6x)€ 0,50/kWh.
**Location:** Rural, simple, quiet. **Surface:** concrete.
⬛ 01/01-31/12.
**Distance:** 🚶300m ⛵10km ⊗100m 🍴100m 🚌on the spot 🚴on the spot 🚶on the spot.

### Sulzburg ⚓ 19G2

Camping Sulzbachtal, Sonnmatt 4. **GPS:** n47,84773 e7,69868. ⬆️.

DE

10 ⫶€ 18 + tourist and eco tax 🚰🔌Ch🚿(10x)€ 0,70/kWh
WC◻🔌📶included.🚲
**Location:** Comfortable. **Surface:** grassy/gravel. ⬛ 01/01-31/12.
**Distance:** 🚶500m ⊗on the spot.

## Tauberbisschofsheim  17B1

**P Freibad**, Vittryallee. **GPS:** n49,62155 e9,66632.⬆.

3 ⫶free 🚰🔌Ch WC free ◻€ 0,50,during opening hours.
**Location:** Rural, simple. **Surface:** asphalted. ⬛ 01/01-31/12.
**Distance:** 🚶500m ⊗300m 🚆100m 🚌500m.
**Remarks:** Service at Kläranlage ma-do 7-16 uur.

## Tettnang  20B2

Loretostrasse. **GPS:** n47,66425 e9,59175.⬆➡.

14 ⫶€5 🚰€1 🔌€1 Ch€1 🚿(8x)€ 1/8h.📶
**Surface:** grassy/metalled. ⬛ 01/01-31/12.
**Distance:** 🚶800m ⊗200m 🚆200m 🚌200m.
**Remarks:** Max. 72h, market Saturday.

## Tettnang  20B2

**Gutshof Camping Badhütten**, Badhütten, Laimnau.
**GPS:** n47,63370 e9,64668.⬆.

70 ⫶€ 20 🚰€1 🔌Ch🚿€ 1/3kWh WC◻€ 0,50. **Location:** Rural.
**Surface:** grassy. ⬛ 01/01-31/12.

## Titisee  19H2

**Camping Bankenhof**, Bruderhalde 31a, Hinterzarten.
**GPS:** n47,88643 e8,13046.⬆.

8 ⫶€ 15, 2 pers.incl 🚰🔌Ch🚿WC◻included 🔌€ 3/3 📶€ 1/4h.
**Location:** Rural, comfortable, quiet.
**Surface:** gravel/sand.
⬛ 01/01-31/12.
**Distance:** 🚶3km ⛵Titisee 600m ⊗on the spot ⛷on the spot 🚴3km.

---

**Remarks:** Pay at reception.

## Todtmoos  19H2

**Jägermatt**, Vordertodtmoos. **GPS:** n47,73390 e8,00285.⬆➡.

20 ⫶€5 🚰🔌Ch included 📶.🚆 **Location:** Rural, simple, noisy.
**Surface:** gravel/metalled. ⬛ 01/01-31/12.
**Distance:** 🚶1km 🚆50m.

## Triberg im Schwarzwald  19H1

Sommerauer Strasse, Nußberg. **GPS:** n48,13161 e8,25294.⬆➡.

20 ⫶free. **Location:** Rural, simple, noisy. **Surface:** gravel.
⬛ 01/01-31/12.
**Distance:** 🚶2km ⊗on the spot.

## Trochtelfingen  20B1

**Eberhard-von Werderberg-Halle**, Siemensstrasse.
**GPS:** n48,30811 e9,23546.➡.

20 ⫶€3 🚰€ 1/80liter 🔌Ch🚿(4x)included,16Amp.
**Location:** Urban, simple. **Surface:** gravel. ⬛ 01/01-31/12.
**Distance:** 🚶Old city centre ⊗300m 🚆500m 🚌500m ⛷on the spot.
**Remarks:** To be paid at town hall.

## Trochtelfingen  20B1

**Kräuter- und Erlebnisgarten Alb-Gold Nudelfabrik**, Grindel 1.
**GPS:** n48,32838 e9,24001.⬆.

4 ⫶free. **Location:** Rural, simple, noisy. **Surface:** metalled.
⬛ 01/01-31/12.
**Distance:** 🚶3km ⊗on the spot 🚆on the spot ⛷on the spot.

## Tuttlingen  20A1

**Stellplatz Donaupark**, Stuttgarter strasse.
**GPS:** n47,98490 e8,81316.⬆.

12 ⫶free 🚰€ 1/5minutes 🔌€ 1 Ch📶. **Location:** Urban, simple.
**Surface:** metalled. ⬛ 01/01-31/12.

---

**Distance:** 🚶500m ⊗500m 🚆500m 🚌500m 🚴Donauradweg.
**Remarks:** Max. 3 nights.

## Überlingen  20A2

**Reisemobilhafen Überlingen**, Kurt-Hahn-strasse.
**GPS:** n47,77617 e9,15046.

20 ⫶€ 6, 15/03-14/10 € 10 🚰€ 0,10/10liter 🔌€ 0,50 Ch🚿
(30x)€ 0,50/kWh WC.📶 **Surface:** asphalted/gravel. ⬛ 01/01-31/12.
**Distance:** 🚶1km ⛵1km ⛵1km 🚆200m 🚆1,5km 🚌200m.
**Remarks:** Max. 3 days, price incl. bus transport (max. 5 pers) to the
city centre.

## Uhldingen-Mühlhofen  20B2

**Stellplatz zum See**, Ehbachstrasse 1. **GPS:** n47,72535 e9,23649.⬆.

21 ⫶8-18h € 1,50/h, max. € 6, night € 10 WC.
**Surface:** grasstiles/metalled. ⬛ 01/03-31/10.
**Distance:** 🚶1km ⛵800m 🚆2km ⊗kiosk on the spot 🚆300m.
**Remarks:** Max. 24h.

## Ulm  17C3

**P+R Friedrichsau**, Wielandstraße 74. **GPS:** n48,40774 e10,00929.⬆➡.

50 ⫶free 🚰€1 🔌Ch. **Location:** Urban, simple, central.
**Surface:** metalled. ⬛ 01/01-31/12.
**Distance:** ⊗200m 🚆on the spot.
**Remarks:** Max. 3 days, green zone: environmental badge obligatory.

## Ummendorf  20B1

**Bräuhaus Ummendorf**, Bachstrasse 10.
**GPS:** n48,06340 e9,83252.⬆➡.

6 ⫶free 🚰🔌🚿(5x)€ 3/day WC◻€ 3 📶. **Location:** Urban,
comfortable, quiet. **Surface:** metalled. ⬛ 01/01-31/12.
**Distance:** 🚶300m ⊗on the spot 🚆800m 🚌100m.
**Remarks:** 3 days free stay.

## Unterkirnach  19H1

**Reisemobilhafen Unterkirnach**, Rathausplatz.
**GPS:** n48,07719 e8,36707.⬆➡.

19 � 13 ⛲🍽 Ch included ☕€ 1,6Amp.
**Location:** Urban, luxurious, quiet. **Surface:** gravel.
🚽 01/01-31/12.
**Distance:** 🛒200m ⚓400m ⊗200m 🍴300m 🚌200m 🚲200m
🚶500m 🚴3km 🚆1,5km.
**Remarks:** Pay at tourist office, alternative arrangement if full.

### Unterkirnach 🌿⛺🏞🍺 19H1
**Ackerloch-Grillschopf**, Unteres Ackerloch 2.
**GPS:** n48,08473 e8,36573.⬆.

20 ⌱€ 5, tourist tax € 2,10/pp ⛲🍽 Ch ☕ WC included. 🚻
**Location:** Rural, simple. **Surface:** unpaved.
🚽 01/01-31/12 🅿 Nov.
**Distance:** 🛒1,5km ⊗on the spot 🚶on the spot 🦅on the spot 🎿on the spot.

### Untermünkheim 17B2
**Wohnmobilpark Ostertag**, Kupfer Straße 20, Übrigshausen.
**GPS:** n49,17603 e9,71321.⬆.

10 ⌱€ 10 ⛲€ 0,50 Ch ☕€ 0,50 🚽€ 1. **Location:** Rural,
comfortable. **Surface:** grassy/gravel. 🚽 01/03-30/11.
**Distance:** ⊗50m.
**Remarks:** At manege.

### Unteröwisheim 🌿 17A2
Muhlweg. **GPS:** n49,14306 e8,67250.⬆.

2 ⌱free. **Location:** Simple, quiet. **Surface:** gravel.
🚽 01/01-31/12.
**Distance:** 🛒500m 🚲on the spot.

### Uttenweiler 20B1
**Naturfreibad**, Weiherstrasse. **GPS:** n48,13814 e9,61962.⬆.
6 ⌱€ 6 ⛲🍽 Ch free 🔌€ 0,50/kWh. **Location:** Rural.
**Surface:** grassy/gravel. 🚽 01/05-01/11.
**Distance:** 🛒600m ⚓on the spot ⊗600m.

### Villingen/Schwenningen 🌿🍺🏞❄ 20A1
**Messegelände**, Waldeckweg. **GPS:** n48,04771 e8,53869.⬆.

---

4 ⌱free ⛲€ 1 Ch. **Location:** Urban, simple, noisy.
**Surface:** asphalted. 🚽 01/01-31/12.
**Distance:** 🛒1km 🍴500m.

### Vogt 20B2
**Sirgensteinhalle**, Schützenweg. **GPS:** n47,77601 e9,77001.⬆.
3 ⌱free. **Location:** Urban. **Surface:** unpaved.
🚽 01/01-31/12.
**Distance:** 🛒on the spot ⊗200m 🍴300m.
**Remarks:** Max. 3 days.

### Vogtsburg im Kaiserstuhl 19G1
Hauptstraße/L115, Oberrotweil. **GPS:** n48,09000 e7,64361.⬆.

8 ⌱free. **Location:** Rural, simple, isolated, quiet.
🚽 01/01-31/12.
**Distance:** 🛒800m 🍴50m 🚲on the spot 🚶on the spot.
**Remarks:** At swimming pool.

### Waiblingen 🌿⛺🍺🏞 17B3
**Parkplatz Hallenbad**, An der Talaue. **GPS:** n48,83029 e9,32540.⬆.

20 ⌱€ 8/24h ⛲€ 1/80liter 🍽 Ch ☕(6x)€ 1/8h WC.
**Location:** Urban. **Surface:** gravel. 🚽 01/01-31/12.
**Distance:** 🛒500m ⚓500m ⊗50m 🍴300m 🚌600m.
**Remarks:** Parking swimming pool, max. 3 nights, during congresses special tariff.

### Waldburg 20B2
**Am Waldburger**, Amtzeller Straße. **GPS:** n47,75800 e9,71672.⬆.
3 ⌱free. **Surface:** unpaved. 🚽 01/01-31/12.
**Distance:** 🛒200m ⊗300m 🍴300m.
**Remarks:** Next to sports fields, max. 3 nights.

### Waldkirch 🍺🏞 19H1
**Wohnmobilstellplatz Waldkirch**, Am Stadtrain.
**GPS:** n48,09023 e7,95833.⬆.

10 ⌱free ⛲€ 1/80liter Ch. **Location:** Urban, simple, central.
**Surface:** concrete. 🚽 01/01-31/12.
**Distance:** 🛒500m 🚶on the spot.
**Remarks:** Max. 2 days.

### Waldshut-Tiengen 19H2
**Wohmobil-Park Waldshut-Tiengen**, Jahnweg 22, Waldshut.
**GPS:** n47,61121 e8,22513.⬆➡.

---

44 ⌱€ 12 ⛲€ 1/100liter Ch ☕€ 1/kWh 🚽€ 0,50 📶 📱
**Location:** Urban, luxurious, quiet. **Surface:** metalled.
🚽 01/01-31/12.
**Distance:** ⊗on the spot.
**Remarks:** Along the Rhine river, bread-service.

### Walldürn 17B1
**Basilikaplatz**, Hauptstrasse. **GPS:** n49,58637 e9,36726.⬆➡.

8 ⌱free ⛲€ 1/80liter Ch ☕(4x)€ 0,50/kWh. **Location:** Rural,
simple. **Surface:** gravel. 🚽 01/01-31/12.
**Distance:** 🛒250m ⊗400m.
**Remarks:** Pilgrimage site.

### Walldürn 17B1
**Goldschmitt Technik-Center**, Industrieparkstrasse.
**GPS:** n49,58977 e9,39339.⬆➡.

30 ⌱free ⛲€ 1/80liter 🍽 Ch ☕(18x)€ 0,50/kWh.
**Location:** Rural, comfortable. **Surface:** asphalted/gravel.
🚽 01/01-31/12.
**Distance:** 🛒2,6km ⊗100m.
**Remarks:** Baker every morning.

### Wangen im Allgäu ⛺🏔❄ 20B2
**P17**, Am Klösterle. **GPS:** n47,68160 e9,83401.⬆➡.

40 ⌱€ 7 + € 1,60/pp tourist tax ⛲€ 0,50/120liter 🍽€ 0,50 Ch€ 0,50
☕(46x) WC. 📱 **Surface:** metalled. 🚽 01/01-31/12.
**Distance:** 🛒on the spot ⚓500m 🍴500m ⊗on the spot 🍴on the spot 🚌on the spot.

### Wangen im Allgäu ⛺🏔❄ 20B2
**Wohnmobilstellplatz Leonhardt's Stall-Besen**, Humbrechts 1.
**GPS:** n47,68497 e9,79696.
5 ⌱free ⛲☕(3x) WC. **Location:** Rural. **Surface:** gravel.
🚽 01/01-31/12.
**Distance:** 🛒100m 🚴2km 🚆1km ⊗on the spot 🍴1,5km 🚌1,5km
🚲on the spot 🚶on the spot 🎿1,5km 🏞200m.

**Tourist information Wangen im Allgäu:**
ℹ Tourist Information, Parkplatz 1, Rathaus. Traditional small Bavarian town. Every Thursday city walk through historical city centre, 10.30-12h.
🎫 € 5.
🚶 🚽 Wed.

### Wehr 19H2
Ludingarten. **GPS:** n47,62515 e7,90582.⬆➡.

7 ⏻ € 10/24h 🚰 € 1/100liter 🔲Ch 🧹(8x)€ 1/8h WC.
**Location:** Simple, quiet. **Surface:** metalled. 🔲 01/01-31/12.
**Distance:** 🚆nearby.
**Remarks:** Pay at tourist office, Hauptstr. 14 or Bistro Gleis 13, Bahnhofplatz.

### Weikersheim 17B1
**Campingplatz Schwabenmühle**, Weikersheimer Strasse 21, Laudenbach. **GPS**: n49,45795 e9,92691. ⬆️➡️.

6 ⏻ 7 🚰 € 1/80liter 🔲Ch 🧹(6x)€ 1/6h 🌊. 🚗
**Location:** Rural, simple. **Surface:** gravel. 🔲 Easter-15/10.
**Distance:** 🚆300m 🚌200m.

### Weil der Stadt 17A3
**Festplatz**, Jahnstrasse. **GPS**: n48,75268 e8,87453. ⬆️➡️.

4 ⏻free 🚰 € 1 🔲€ 1 Ch 🧹(4x)€ 1/4h. **Location:** Urban, simple, noisy. **Surface:** asphalted. 🔲 01/01-31/12.
**Distance:** 🚆300m ⊗300m 🛒250m 🚲on the spot 🚶on the spot.
**Remarks:** Max. 3 days.

### Weilheim 19H2
**Gret-Stube**, Fohrenbachstraße 5, Nöggenschwiel.
**GPS**: n47,69252 e8,21349.

3 ⏻ € 12 🚰 🔲Ch 🧹included.
**Location:** Rural. **Surface:** gravel. 🔲 01/01-31/12.
**Distance:** ⊗on the spot 🍴on the spot.
**Remarks:** Breakfast-service.

### Weingarten 20B2
**Festplatz**, Abt Hyller Strasse 55. **GPS**: n47,81009 e9,63041. ⬆️.

8 ⏻ € 5 🚰 € 1 🔲€ 1 Ch 🧹€ 2. **Surface:** metalled.
🔲 01/01-31/12.
**Distance:** 🚆1km 🛒500m 🚲on the spot 🚶on the spot.

---

**Remarks:** Max. 3 nights.

### Weinheim 17A1
**Am Miramar**, Waidallee. **GPS**: n49,53378 e8,64473.
5 ⏻free. **Location:** Rural, simple, noisy. **Surface:** asphalted.
🔲 01/01-31/12.
**Distance:** ⊗350m.
**Remarks:** At paradise pool.

### Weinsberg 17A2
Eugen-Diez-Straße 2. **GPS**: n49,14846 e9,28464. ⬆️➡️.

13 ⏻free 🚰 € 1/100liter 🔲Ch 🧹(6x)€ 0,50/kWh 🌊free.
**Location:** Rural, quiet. **Surface:** grasstiles. 🔲 01/01-31/12.
**Distance:** 🚆500m 🚌2km 🛒50m 🚲on the spot 🚶on the spot.

### Welzheim 17B2
**Aichstruter Stausee**, Seiboldsweiler, Aichstrut.
**GPS**: n48,90020 e9,63719. ⬆️.

10 ⏻ 7 🚰 € 1/80liter 🔲Ch 🧹€ 1/2kWh WC.
**Surface:** gravel. 🔲 01/01-31/12.
**Distance:** 🚆5km 🚲on the spot 🚶on the spot 🏊on the spot.
**Remarks:** At artificial lake, max. 1 week.

### Welzheim 17B2
**Am Bahnhof**, Bahnhofstraße. **GPS**: n48,87256 e9,63053. ⬆️.
3 ⏻free 🧹€ 1/kWh. 🔲 01/01-31/12.
**Distance:** 🚆400m ⊗400m.
**Remarks:** Max. 3 days.

### Welzheim 17B2
**Am Stadtpark**, Tannwaldweg. **GPS**: n48,86780 e9,63183. ⬆️.
2 ⏻free. **Location:** Rural. **Surface:** gravel. 🔲 01/01-31/12.
**Distance:** 🚆700m ⊗on the spot.
**Remarks:** Max. 3 days.

### Wertheim 17B1
**Wohnmobilstellplatz An der Taubermündung**, Linke Tauberstrasse.
**GPS**: n49,76501 e9,51213. ⬆️➡️.

54 ⏻ € 7/24h 🚰 € 1/90liter 🔲Ch. 🚌
**Location:** Rural, simple, noisy. **Surface:** gravel.
🔲 01/01-31/12 🔴 2nd sa of the month + high water.
**Distance:** 🚆500m 🚲on the spot.
**Remarks:** Along the Tauber river, max. 3 days.

### Wertheim 17B1
**Erwin Hymer World**, Hymerring 1. **GPS**: n49,77368 e9,58034. ⬆️.

---

90 ⏻free 🚰 € 1/90liter 🔲Ch 🧹€ 1/3h WCduring opening hours.
**Location:** Rural, comfortable. **Surface:** asphalted.
🔲 01/01-31/12.
**Distance:** ⊗400m 🛒3,7km.
**Remarks:** Baker at 8am, Wertheim Outletcentrum 100m.
**Tourist information Wertheim:**
🏺 Wertheim Village, Almosenberg. Outlet-shopping.

### Wildberg 17A3
**Wohnmobilstellplatz Wildberg**, Klosterhof 4.
**GPS**: n48,62055 e8,74485. ⬆️➡️.

4 ⏻free 🚰 € 1/50liter 🔲Ch 🧹€ 1/kWh.
**Location:** Quiet. **Surface:** asphalted/metalled.
🔲 01/01-31/12 🔴 service: 01/11-01/03.
**Distance:** 🚆historical centre 500m ⊗700m 🛒1km 🚲on the spot.
**Remarks:** Along river, nearby monastery.

### Wolfach 19H1
**Ferienhof Bartleshof**, Ippichen 6, Ippichen.
**GPS**: n48,30183 e8,26264. ⬆️.

3 ⏻ € 15 🚰 🔲Ch 🧹(3x) 🔲€ 2. **Location:** Rural, simple, quiet.
**Surface:** grassy/gravel. 🔲 01/01-31/12.
**Distance:** ⊗on the spot 🚶on the spot.

### Wolfach 19H1
**Trendcamping Schwarzwald**, Schiltacher Straße 80, Halbmeil.
**GPS**: n48,29053 e8,27763. ⬆️.

6 ⏻ € 18, 2 pers.incl 🚰 🔲ChWC 🔲included 🔲€ 3 🌊€ 2 🚿 🧹
**Location:** Rural, simple, quiet. **Surface:** grassy/sand.
🔲 10/04-15/10.
**Distance:** ⊗on the spot.

### Wolfegg/Allgäu 20B2
**Reisemobilhafen Loretopark**, Rötenbacher Straße.
**GPS**: n47,81489 e9,79802. ⬆️.
12 ⏻ € 5 🚰 € 1/80liter 🔲Ch 🧹€ 0,50/kWh. 🔲 01/01-31/12.
**Distance:** 🚆500m ⊗700m.
**Remarks:** Max. 5 days.

### Wolfegg/Allgäu 20B2
**Hofgarten**, Alttaner strasse. **GPS**: n47,82105 e9,79487. ⬆️.

2 ⏻ € 5. **Surface:** gravel/metalled. 🔲 01/01-31/12.
**Distance:** 🚆on the spot.
**Remarks:** Max. 2 nights.

## Wolfegg/Allgäu    20B2

**Gasthof Post**, Röthenbacher Straße 5. **GPS:** n47,81994 e9,79420.
4 free.
01/01-31/12.
**Distance:** 400m 50m.

**Tourist information Wolfegg/Allgäu:**
Automobilmuseum. 200 oldtimers. 01/04-31/10 9.30-18h,
01/11-31/03 Su 10-17h.
Bauernhaus-museum. Open air museum. 01/04-31/10 Tue-Su
10-18/17h Mo Apr Oct.

## Wutöschingen    19H2

**Wohnmobilplatz Degernau**, Ofteringer Strasse 1, Degernau.
**GPS:** n47,66639 e8,37917.

9 € 8/day, 2 pers.incl € 1/100liter Ch € 2/kWh,16Amp
WC 1 € 3/3. **Location:** Rural, comfortable, quiet.
**Surface:** grassy/gravel. 01/04-31/10.
**Distance:** on the spot 200m 1km 500m on the spot
on the spot on the spot.
**Remarks:** Arrival <20h, sauna, solarium.

## Zaberfeld    17A2

**An der Ehmetsklinge**, Seestrasse. **GPS:** n49,05607 e8,91646.
3 free against payment Ch € 0,50/kWh. **Location:** Rural.
**Surface:** metalled. 01/01-31/12.
**Distance:** 250m on the spot on the spot on the spot
250m on the spot on the spot.

## Zell am Harmersbach    19H1

**Stellplatz Zell am Harmersbach**, Nordracher Strasse.
**GPS:** n48,35146 e8,05942.

14 € 5 € 1/10minutes Ch (8x)€ 2/12h.
**Location:** Rural, simple, quiet. **Surface:** gravel.
01/01-31/12.
**Distance:** 2km 2km.

# Bavaria

## Absberg    17D2

**Badehalbinsel Brombachsee**, Gunzenhausen-Pleinfeld Ausfart
Absberg. **GPS:** n49,13770 e10,87389.

500 € 12/24h € 1/80liter Ch (250x)€ 0,50/kWh WC € 1.
**Location:** Rural, comfortable, quiet. **Surface:** grassy.
01/04-01/10.
**Distance:** 1km on the spot on the spot 1km on the spot
on the spot.
**Remarks:** Bread-service.

## Ahorn    12D3

**Freizeitzentrum Wittmannsberg**, Badstrasse 20, Eicha.
**GPS:** n50,22537 e10,90252.

---

4 free. **Location:** Rural, simple. **Surface:** metalled.
01/01-31/12.
**Distance:** on the spot 600m 5km.

## Aichach    17D3

**Reisemobilplatz**, Franz-Beck-Strasse 2.
**GPS:** n48,45889 e11,12611.

4 € 5 Chincluded. **Location:** Urban, simple, quiet.
**Surface:** grassy/gravel. 01/01-31/12.
**Distance:** 500m 500m 100m.

## Albertshofen    17C1

**An der Fähre Mainstockheim-Albertshofen**, Mainstraße.
**GPS:** n49,77254 e10,15749.

10 € 7 Ch included. **Location:** Rural, simple, quiet.
**Surface:** gravel. 01/01-31/12.
**Distance:** on the spot on the spot on the spot 50m
on the spot on the spot.
**Remarks:** Along Main river, closed when high water.

## Altmannstein    17E2

**Gasthof Forster**, Schulstrasse 9. **GPS:** n48,90125 e11,69559.

20 guests free Ch (4x)€ 2/night.
**Surface:** asphalted. 01/01-31/12.
**Distance:** on the spot on the spot 3km.
**Remarks:** Bread-service, check in before 19h (Mo-Tue 16h).

## Altötting    20G1

**P2 Dultplatz**, Traunsteinerstrasse. **GPS:** n48,22287 e12,67921.

8 free € 1/10liter Ch (8x)€ 1/4h. **Location:** Urban, simple,
central. **Surface:** gravel. 01/01-31/12.
**Distance:** 700m 300m 300m 250m.
**Remarks:** Max. 3 days.

---

## Altötting    20G1

**Wohnmobilstellplatz am Parkplatz**, Griesstraße.
**GPS:** n48,22946 e12,67493.

8 free € 1/80liter Ch (8x)€ 1/4h WC.
**Location:** Urban, simple, noisy. **Surface:** grasstiles.
01/01-31/12.
**Distance:** 600m 200m on the spot.
**Remarks:** Max. 3 days.

## Altusried    20C2

**Am Freibad**, Im Tal 4. **GPS:** n47,79915 e10,21934.

10 € 10-5 € 1 Ch € 0,50/kWh. **Location:** Rural, simple,
quiet. **Surface:** grassy/gravel. 01/01-31/12.
**Distance:** 500m 700m.
**Remarks:** Parking at swimming pool, max. 3 days.

## Amberg    17E1

**Gasfabrikstraße**. **GPS:** n49,44043 e11,86198.

10 free (12x)€ 1/12h. **Location:** Urban, simple, central, quiet.
**Surface:** asphalted. 01/01-31/12.
**Distance:** 500m 50m 1km 1km 50m 50m.
**Remarks:** Max. 72h.

## Amorbach    17A1

**P Altstadt**, Dr.F.A.Freundt-Straße. **GPS:** n49,64683 e9,22115.

5 free.
**Location:** Urban, simple. **Surface:** asphalted.
01/01-31/12.
**Distance:** 500m 400m Lidl 300m on the spot on the spot.

## Andechs    20D1

**Wohnmobilstellplatz Kloster Andechs**, Seefelder Straße.
**GPS:** n47,97530 e11,18551.

DE

40 🛏 € 14 🚰 ⚡Chincluded ⚡€ 3. **Surface:** metalled.
⬛ 01/01-31/12.
**Distance:** ⊗on the spot ⚓on the spot.
**Remarks:** Nearby monastery, bread-service.

| 🏕 S | Ansbach 🌿 | 17C2 |
**Freizeitbad Aquella**, Am Stadion 2. **GPS:** n49,30459 e10,55852. ⬆➡

12 🛏 free 🚰 € 0,50/50liter ⚡Ch ⚡(12x)€ 0,50/kWh.
**Location:** Urban, simple, central. **Surface:** metalled.
⬛ 01/01-31/12.
**Distance:** 🚆1km 🚲7,7km ⊗on the spot ⚓1km 🚌on the spot
🚴on the spot.
**Remarks:** At swimming pool, max. 3 days.

| 🏕 S | Ansbach 🌿 | 17C2 |
**Freizeitwelt Nagel**, Faunstraße 7. **GPS:** n49,25444 e10,59306. ⬆

8 🛏 free 🚰 € 1/80liter ⚡Ch ⚡(8x)€ 1/2kWh.
**Location:** Motorway, simple, noisy. **Surface:** gravel.
⬛ 01/01-31/12.
**Distance:** 🚆500m ⚓2km.
**Remarks:** At motorhome dealer.

| 🏕 S | Arnbruck 🏡🌲❄ | 17G2 |
**Landhotel Rappenhof**, Rappendorf 5. **GPS:** n49,13517 e12,95069. ⬆

5 🛏 € 15 🚰 ⚡Ch ⚡WCincluded. **Location:** Rural, simple.
**Surface:** grassy. ⬛ 01/01-31/12.
**Distance:** 🚆2km ⊗on the spot ⚓2km ⛷10km ⛷8km.
**Remarks:** Use of sauna against payment.

| 🏕 S | Arnstein | 12B3 |
**Badesee**, Am Alten Schwimmbad. **GPS:** n49,97667 e9,95917. ⬆

12 🛏 free 🚰 € 1/80liter ⚡Ch ⚡(4x)€ 1/2kWh.
**Location:** Rural, simple, quiet. **Surface:** grassy/metalled.
⬛ 01/01-31/12, service 01/04-31/10.
**Distance:** 🚆500m ⚓100m 🚌100m ⊗snack 100m ⚓500m
🚴on the spot.
**Remarks:** At the old swimming pool.

| 🏕 | Arnstein | 12B3 |
**Cancale Platz. GPS:** n49,97637 e9,96725.

---

5 🛏 free. **Location:** Urban. **Surface:** metalled. ⬛ 01/01-31/12.
**Distance:** 🚆100m ⊗100m ⚓100m.
**Remarks:** Max. 1 night.

| 🏕 S | Arzberg 🍺 | 12E3 |
**Friedrich-Ebert-Straße 6. GPS:** n50,05528 e12,18870. ⬆🚶

2 🛏 free 🚰 ⚡Ch ⚡WC 📶. **Location:** Urban, simple, simple, quiet.
**Surface:** asphalted/metalled. ⬛ 01/01-31/12.
**Distance:** ⊗300m ⚓250m ⊗on the spot 🚶on the spot.

| 🏕 S | Aschaffenburg 🌿🏡🍺🥨 | 12A3 |
**Willigesbrücke**, Grossostheimerstrasse. **GPS:** n49,97139 e9,13722. ⬆

25 🛏 € 3/24h ⚡(18x)€ 0,50/kWh. 🚂 **Location:** Urban, simple, quiet.
**Surface:** grassy/gravel. ⬛ 01/01-31/12.
**Distance:** 🚆historical centre 500m 🚲8km 🚌on the spot 🚴on the
spot.
**Remarks:** Parking along the Main, near Altstadt, being indicated with
small signs, max. 3 days.

| 🏕 S | Aschheim | 20E1 |
**Gasthof Zur Post**, Ismaningerstrasse 11. **GPS:** n48,17433 e11,71490. ⬆

4 🛏 € 10 WC. **Location:** Simple. **Surface:** asphalted.
⬛ 01/01-31/12.
**Distance:** 🚆on the spot ⊗on the spot ⚓300m.

| 🏕 S | Auerbach in der Oberpfalz | 17E1 |
**Am Behälterweiher. GPS:** n49,69455 e11,63030. ⬆
8 🛏 € 5 🚰 € 1/100liter ⚡Ch ⚡(8x)included5kWh. 🚂
**Location:** Urban. **Surface:** metalled. ⬛ 01/01-31/12.
**Distance:** 🚆on the spot ⊗on the spot ⚓on the spot.
**Remarks:** Max. 3 days.

| 🏕 S | Auerbach in der Oberpfalz | 17E1 |
**Gaststätte Schlupfloch**, Hohe Tanne 4a. **GPS:** n49,66947 e11,61035. ⬆
30 🛏 € 7 🚰 € 1/80liter ⚡Ch ⚡€ 0,50/kWh 📶 ⚡€ 2/day.
**Location:** Rural, isolated, quiet. **Surface:** grassy/gravel.
⬛ 01/01-31/12.
**Distance:** 🚆3,5km ⊗on the spot.

| 🏕 S | Aufseß | 12D3 |
**Brauerei-Gasthof Reichold**, Hochstahl 24.
**GPS:** n49,88389 e11,26855. ⬆➡

---

38 🛏 € 8 🚰 € 1/90liter ⚡Ch ⚡(38x)€ 2 WC ⚡ 1/3minutes.
**Location:** Rural, comfortable, quiet. **Surface:** grassy/metalled.
⬛ 01/01-31/12.
**Distance:** 🚆on the spot ⊗on the spot 🚌on the spot 🚴on the spot
🚶Brauereienweg.
**Remarks:** Bread-service, breakfast buffet € 8/pp.

| 🏕 S | Aufseß | 12D3 |
**Brauerei Rothenbach**, Im Tal 70. **GPS:** n49,88413 e11,22781. ⬆

3 🛏 € 5 🚰 ⚡🚮 **Location:** Urban, simple, central.
**Surface:** metalled. ⬛ 01/03-31/10.
**Distance:** 🚆on the spot ⊗on the spot ⚓on the spot 🚴on the spot
🚶on the spot.

| 🏕 S | Augsburg 🏖 | 17D3 |
**Schillstraße 109**, Lechhausen. **GPS:** n48,38914 e10,90435. ⬆➡

4 🛏 € 7 🚰 € 1/4minutes ⚡Ch ⚡€ 1/2kWh WC ⚡ 🚂
**Location:** Urban, simple, central. **Surface:** gravel.
⬛ 01/01-31/12.
**Distance:** 🚲3,2km ⊗Sportgaststätte ⚓250m 🚌200m 🚴on the
spot 🚶on the spot.
**Remarks:** At sports centre, outside environmental zone.

| 🏕 S | Augsburg 🏖 | 17D3 |
**Wohnmobilstellplatz Wertach**, Bürgemeister Ackermann strasse 1.
**GPS:** n48,36944 e10,87750. ⬆➡

15 🛏 € 8 🚰 € 1/90liter ⚡Ch ⚡(6x)€ 2/kWh. 🚂
**Location:** Urban, simple, noisy. **Surface:** gravel. ⬛ 01/01-31/12.
**Distance:** 🚆on the spot 🚲4,5km ⛱on the spot 🚌on the spot
⊗500m ⚓500m 🚴on the spot 🚶on the spot.
**Remarks:** Outside environmental zone.

| 🏕 S | Bad Abbach ♨ | 17E2 |
**Kaiser-Therme**, Kurallee 4. **GPS:** n48,92712 e12,04044. ⬆

---

DE

34 ⛺ € 12 + € 1,80/pp tourist tax 🚰 € 1/4minutes 🔌Ch ✦(16x)
WC. **Location:** Rural. **Surface:** grasstiles/grassy.
🚻 01/01-31/12.
**Distance:** 🛒2km ⊗600m 🍴2km.
**Remarks:** Check in at pay-desk of the Therme.

| ⓒⓢ | Bad Aibling | 20F1 |

**Stellplatz an der Therme P13**, Lindenstrasse/Heubergstrasse.
**GPS:** n47,85639 e12,00583. ⬆➡

31 ⛺ € 10 🚰 € 0,50/80liter 🔌Ch ✦(20x)included. 🚗
**Location:** Rural, comfortable. **Surface:** grasstiles/metalled.
🚻 01/01-31/12.
**Distance:** 🛒500m 🏊400m ⊗500m 🍴600m 🍺100m.
**Remarks:** Max. 3 days, use sanitary only during opening hours.

| ⓒⓢ | Bad Alexandersbad | 12E3 |

**Gasthof Riedelbauch**, Kleinwendern 12.
**GPS:** n50,00033 e12,01758. ⬆.

4 ⛺ € 5 🚰 ✦ € 1,50 WC. 🚗 **Location:** Rural, simple.
**Surface:** asphalted/metalled. 🚻 01/01-31/10.
**Distance:** 🛒2km ⊗on the spot 🍺2km 🚲on the spot 🚶on the spot 🏊on the spot.

| ⓒⓢ | Bad Bayersoien | 20D2 |

**Wohnmobilstellplatz Bad Bayersoien**, Am Bahnhof 6.
**GPS:** n47,68798 e10,99820. ➡

8 ⛺ € 14 🚰 € 1/80liter 🔌Ch ✦(12x)€ 1/2kWh. **Location:** Rural,
simple, quiet. **Surface:** gravel. 🚻 01/01-31/12.
**Distance:** 🛒400m 🏊300m 🚲300m ⊗400m 🍺400m.

| ⓒⓢ | Bad Berneck | 12E3 |

Bahnhofstraße 77. **GPS:** n50,04141 e11,66610. ➡

4 ⛺free 🚰 € 1/80liter 🔌Ch ✦ € 1/6h.

---

**Location:** Urban, simple, central, quiet. **Surface:** asphalted.
🚻 01/01-31/12.
**Distance:** 🛒on the spot ⊗on the spot 🍺200m.

| ⓒⓢ | Bad Birnbach | 17G3 |

**Camping Arterhof**, Hauptstraße 3, Lengham.
**GPS:** n48,43512 e13,10939. ⬆

20 ⛺ € 10 🚰 🔌ChWC ✦included. **Location:** Rural, simple,
isolated, quiet. **Surface:** gravel. 🚻 01/01-31/12.
**Distance:** ⊗on the spot.
**Remarks:** Max. 1 day, bread-service, dog € 3,50.

| ⓒⓢ | Bad Bocklet | 12B3 |

**Kurgarten**, Aschacherstrasse. **GPS:** n50,26490 e10,07486. ⬆➡

13 ⛺ € 8, tourist tax incl 🚰 € 1/80liter 🔌Ch ✦(13x)€ 0,50/kWh 📶.
**Location:** Rural, comfortable, quiet. **Surface:** metalled.
🚻 01/01-31/12.
**Distance:** 🛒500m 🚌Free bus to Bad Kissingen.
**Remarks:** Pay at midgetgolf.

| ⓒⓢ | Bad Brückenau | 12B3 |

**Sinnflut**, Ancenisstrasse. **GPS:** n50,31212 e9,79607. ⬆➡

20 ⛺ € 3 + tourist tax € 2,50/pp 🚰 € 1/100liter 🔌Ch ✦(8x)€ 1/8h.
🚗 **Location:** Urban, simple, noisy. **Surface:** gravel.
🚻 01/01-31/12.
**Distance:** 🛒250m ⊗250m 🍺250m.
**Remarks:** Nearby swimming pool.

| ⓒⓢ | Bad Brückenau | 12B3 |

**Stellplatz Buchwaldstrasse**, Buchwaldstrasse.
**GPS:** n50,30667 e9,78556. ⬆

20 ⛺ € 3 + tourist tax € 2,50/pp ✦(10x)€ 1/8h. 🚗
**Location:** Urban, simple, noisy. **Surface:** metalled.
🚻 01/01-31/12.
**Distance:** 🛒300m ⊗100m 🍺on the spot 🚌150m 🚲on the spot 🚶on the spot.

| ⓒⓢ | Bad Brückenau | 12B3 |

**Schlosspark König Ludwig I**, Schlüchterner Straße.
**GPS:** n50,30556 e9,74861. ⬆➡

---

10 ⛺ € 8 + € 2,80/pp tourist tax 🚰 € 1/100liter 🔌Ch ✦(10x)€ 0,50/
kWh. 🚗 **Location:** Urban, comfortable, quiet. **Surface:** asphalted.
🚻 01/01-31/12.
**Distance:** 🛒4km 🍺50m.

| 🍴 | Bad Feilnbach | 20F2 |

**Gasthof Tiroler Hof**, Aiblinger strasse 95.
**GPS:** n47,76476 e12,03857. ⬆.

3 ⛺guests free. **Location:** Rural, simple, isolated. **Surface:** gravel.
🚻 01/01-31/12.
**Distance:** 🛒on the spot ⊗on the spot 🍺1km.

| ⓒⓢ | Bad Füssing | 17G3 |

**Campingplatz Holmerhof**, Am Tennispark 10.
**GPS:** n48,35798 e13,30658. ⬆.

9 ⛺ € 9,10 + € 2,90/pp tourist tax 🚰 € 1/80liter 🔌Ch ✦
(12x) € 1/2kWh WC ✦ 2. **Location:** Rural, simple, quiet.
**Surface:** metalled. 🚻 01/01-31/12.
**Distance:** 🛒1km ⊗on the spot 🍺1km.
**Remarks:** Max. 3 days, use sanitary € 5/motorhome, no camping activi-
ties, swimming pool available.

| ⓒⓢ | Bad Gögging | 17E2 |

**Limes-Therme**, Heiligenstädter Str. 34. **GPS:** n48,81857 e11,78868. ⬆.

50 ⛺ € 12 + € 1,80/pp tourist tax 🚰 € 0,50/50liter 🔌
Ch ✦ € 0,50/kWh WC included. **Location:** Rural, simple, quiet.
**Surface:** asphalted. 🚻 01/01-31/12.
**Distance:** 🛒150m ⊗150m 🍺150m.
**Remarks:** Check in at pay-desk of the Therme, use sanitary only during
opening hours swimming pool.

| ⓒⓢ | Bad Griesbach | 17G3 |

**Kur-& Feriencamping Holmerhof Dreiquellenbad**, Singham 40.
**GPS:** n48,42037 e13,19194. ⬆.

DE

29 ⬛€ 22,20 ⌁⬛Ch⬧(29x)€ 0,60/kWh,16Amp WC⬛⬛included
⬛ **Location:** Rural, simple, quiet. **Surface:** metalled.
⬛ 01/01-31/12.
**Distance:** ⬛2km ⬧10km ⬛500m ⊗on the spot ⬛on the spot
⬛500m ⬛500m.
**Remarks:** Max. 3 days, thermal-Vital-Oase incl.

⬛⬛ **Bad Hindelang** ⬛❄ **20C2**

**Wiesengrund Wohnmobilpark**, Parkplatz Wiesengrund 1.
**GPS:** n47,49931 e10,37218. ⬆➡.

30 ⬛€ 10-16, tourist tax € 2,10/pp, child 7><16 € 0,90 ⌁€ 1/100liter
⬛Ch⬧€ 0,50/kWh WC⬛⬛ 1 ⬛⬛
**Location:** Rural, luxurious, quiet. **Surface:** grassy/gravel.
⬛ 01/01-31/12.
**Distance:** ⬛centre 500m ⊗on the spot ⬛1km ⬛on the spot ⬛3km
⬛3km.

⬛⬛ **Bad Hindelang** ⬛❄ **20C2**

**Wohnmobilplatz Bergheimat**, Passstraße 60, Oberjoch.
**GPS:** n47,51791 e10,42142. ⬆.

4 ⬛€ 15 ⌁⬧. **Location:** Rural, simple, quiet. **Surface:** gravel.
⬛ 01/01-31/12.
**Distance:** ⬛1,5km ⬛900m ⬛1,5km ⬛1km ⬛1km.

ⓒⓈ **Bad Kohlgrub** **20D2**

**Campingoase Reindl**, Sonnen 93. **GPS:** n47,65789 e11,04393. ⬆.

16 ⬛€ 16,40, 2 pers. incl., dog € 1 ⌁⬛Ch⬧€ 0,40/kWh WC⬛
⬛€ 2,50 ⬛⬧. **Location:** Rural, comfortable, quiet. **Surface:** gravel.
⬛ 01/01-31/12.
**Distance:** ⬛1,5km ⬛1,5km.

ⓊⓈ **Bad Königshofen** ⬛ **12C3**

**Frankentherme**, Am Kurzentrum 1. **GPS:** n50,30174 e10,47654. ⬆➡.

96 ⬛€ 12 ⌁€ 1/70liter ⬛Ch⬧(96x)€ 0,50/kWh,16Amp
WC⬛€ 0,50 ⬛€ 3 ⬛included.⬛
**Location:** Urban, luxurious. **Surface:** grasstiles/metalled.
⬛ 01/01-31/12.
**Distance:** ⬛400m ⬧15km ⬛100m ⬛100m ⬛1km ⬛200m
⬛300m ⬛300m.
**Remarks:** Caution key sanitary € 20, if full 2 alternatives will be given, special health arrangement possible.

**Tourist information Bad Königshofen:**
⬛ Kurverwaltung Königshofen, Am Kurzentrum 1, www.bad-koenig-shofen.de. Traditional small town with half-timbered houses, cycle and hiking routes in the surroundings.

ⓊⓈ **Bad Kötztingen** ⬛⬛ **17G2**

**Aqacur**, Bgm. Seidl Platz. **GPS:** n49,17539 e12,86196. ⬆.

4 ⬛€ 8, tourist tax incl ⌁€ 1/80liter ⬛Ch⬧€ 1/8h.
**Location:** Urban, simple. **Surface:** metalled. ⬛ 01/01-31/12.
**Distance:** ⬛700m ⊗300m ⬛50m.
**Remarks:** Max. 3 days.

⬛Ⓢ **Bad Neustadt** ⬛ **12C2**

**Parkplatz An der Saale**, Mühlbacher Straße.
**GPS:** n50,31637 e10,22205. ⬆➡.

---

**DE**

10 ⬛€ 15, dog € 3,50 ⌁⬛Ch⬧€ 0,80/kWh WC⬛€ 1 ⬛.⬛
**Location:** Rural, simple, noisy. **Surface:** grassy/gravel.
⬛ 01/01-31/12.
**Distance:** ⬛on the spot ⬛on the spot.

ⓊⓈ **Bad Kissingen** ⬛⬛⬛ **12B3**

**KissSalis Therme**, Heiligenfelder Allee 16.
**GPS:** n50,18861 e10,06139. ⬆➡.

18 ⬛€ 4 + € 3,50/pp tourist tax ⌁€ 1/10minutes ⬛
Ch⬧(18x)€ 1/8h.⬛ **Location:** Rural, comfortable, quiet.
**Surface:** asphalted. ⬛ 01/01-31/12.
**Distance:** ⬛500m ⊗on the spot ⬛on the spot ⬛on the spot
⬛on the spot.
**Remarks:** Pay at pay-desk of the Therme.

ⓊⓈ **Bad Kohlgrub** **20D2**

**Kurhotel Lauter im Park**, Kurhausstrasse 81.
**GPS:** n47,66412 e11,04315. ⬆.

---

54 ⬛€ 8 ⌁€ 1/80liter ⬛Ch⬧(48x)included.⬛⬛
**Location:** Rural, comfortable, quiet. **Surface:** grasstiles.
⬛ 01/01-31/12.
**Distance:** ⬛500m ⊗on the spot ⬛on the spot.

ⓊⓈ **Bad Reichenhall** ⬛ **20G2**

**Wohnmobilpark an der RupertusTherme**, Hammerschmiedweg.
**GPS:** n47,73466 e12,87536. ⬆➡.

25 ⬛€ 14, 2 pers incl ⌁€ 1/80liter ⬛Ch⬧⬛included.⬛
**Location:** Urban, comfortable. **Surface:** asphalted. ⬛ 01/01-31/12.
**Distance:** ⬛500m ⬧5km ⊗600m ⬛800m ⬛1,5km ⬛on the spot
⬛on the spot.
**Remarks:** Bicycle rental.

ⓊⓈ **Bad Rodach** ⬛ **12C2**

**Wohnmobilstellplatz Thermenaue an der ThermeNatur**, Thermal-badstrasse 18. **GPS:** n50,33452 e10,77499. ⬆➡.

70 ⬛€ 10 ⌁€ 1/100liter ⬛Ch⬧(70x)€ 0,60/
kWh WC⬛€ 2/30minutes ⬛€ 2/2 ⬛included.⬛
**Location:** Urban, comfortable. **Surface:** gravel/metalled.
⬛ 01/01-31/12, water: 01/04-30/09.
**Distance:** ⬛500m ⊗100m ⬛100m ⬛300m ⬛on the spot
⬛on the spot ⬛on the spot.
**Remarks:** Bread-service, key service at swimming pool.

ⓊⓈ **Bad Staffelstein** ⬛ **12D3**

**Wohnmobil-Stellplatz Obermain Therme**, Am Kurpark 1.
**GPS:** n50,10901 e10,99054. ⬆.

27 ⬛€ 11 ⌁€ 0,50/40liter ⬛Ch⬧(8x)€ 0,50/kWh WC⬛included.
⬛ **Location:** Comfortable, quiet. **Surface:** asphalted.
⬛ 01/01-31/12.
**Distance:** ⬛on the spot ⬧1,5km ⬛900m ⊗50m ⬛1,5km ⬛50m
⬛on the spot ⬛on the spot.
**Remarks:** Max. 4 nights, bread-service.

ⓊⓈ **Bad Steben** ⬛ **12E2**

**An der Therme**, P3, Steinbacher Straße. **GPS:** n50,36250 e11,63239. ⬆.

24 🛏 € 6 + € 2,90/pp tourist tax ⛽€ 0,10/10liter 🔧Ch 🚿€ 0,60/kWh WC 🚽€ 3/30minutes 📶. **Location:** Rural, luxurious, quiet. **Surface:** metalled. 🅿 01-01-31/12. **Distance:** 🚶500m 🏊200m 🍽500m. **Remarks:** Bread-service.

### Bad Tölz 🚵🚡🚣❄ 20E2

Bürgermeister Stohlreiterpromenade. **GPS:** n47,76252 e11,55142. ⬆➡

30 🛏 € 8/24h ⛽€ 1/50liter 🔧Ch. 🏧 **Location:** Rural, simple. **Surface:** asphalted. 🅿 01-01-31/12. **Distance:** 🚶1km 🏊on the spot 🚲on the spot ⊗500m 🍽500m 🚰500m. **Remarks:** Along river, max. 48h, incl. Kurkarte.

**Tourist information Bad Tölz:**
Alpamare. Large swimming pool complex with wave machine, Alpa, slides, sauna etc. 🅿 Su-Thu 8-21h, Fri-Sa 8-22h, 24/12-01/01 8-16h.

### Bad Windsheim 🚵🏵 17C1

Phoenix Reisemobilhafen, Bad Windsheimer Strasse 7. **GPS:** n49,51361 e10,41722. ⬆➡

100 🛏 € 11 + € 2,30/pp tourist tax ⛽€ 1/80liter 🔧Ch 🚿(80x)€ 0,50/kWh WC 🚽€ 0,50/4minutes 📺€ 2,50/2,50 📶. **Location:** Rural, comfortable, quiet. **Surface:** gravel. 🅿 01-01-31/12. **Distance:** 🚶1km ⊗100m 🍽500m 🚰1km. **Remarks:** Bread-service.

### Bad Windsheim 🚵🏵 17C1

Fränkisches Freilandmuseum, Eisweiherweg. **GPS:** n49,49705 e10,41667. ⬆➡

40 🛏 € 5 + € 2/pp tourist tax. **Location:** Simple. **Surface:** grassy. 🅿 01-01-31/12. **Distance:** 🚶1km ⊗500m 🍽500m. **Remarks:** Open air museum.

### Bad Wörishofen 🏵 20D1

Therme Bad Wörishofen, Thermenallee 1. **GPS:** n48,02120 e10,59100. ⬆➡

---

25 🛏 € 9 ⛽€ 1/100liter 🔧Ch 🚿WCincluded. 🏧 **Location:** Urban, simple. **Surface:** asphalted. 🅿 01-01-31/12. **Distance:** 🚶1,5km 🚲4,3km ⊗on the spot 🍽500m 🚰on the spot. **Remarks:** Check in at pay-desk of the Therme, max. 3 nights, max. 8M, bread-service.

### Balderschwang 🏔❄ 20C2

Wohnmobilplatz Schwabenhof, Schwabenhof 23. **GPS:** n47,45745 e10,12963. ⬆

56 🛏 € 12-17 + € 1,10/pp tourist tax ⛽€ 0,50 🔧Ch 🚿€ 4/day WC 🚽€ 0,50/5minutes. 🏧 **Location:** Rural, comfortable. **Surface:** grassy/gravel. 🅿 01-01-31/12. **Distance:** 🚶3km ⊗on the spot 🍽3km 🚰100m 🚴100m 🚲100m. **Remarks:** Bread-service, drying room for skis.

### Bamberg 🚵🚡🧁 12D3

Wohnmobilplatz, Rhein-Main-Donau Damm. **GPS:** n49,88626 e10,90296. ⬆

25 🛏 € 15, 2 pers.incl ⛽€ 1/100liter 🔧Ch 🚿€ 0,50/kWh 📶included. 🏧 **Location:** Urban, simple, quiet. **Surface:** gravel. 🅿 01-01-31/12. **Distance:** 🚶10 min walking 🏊on the spot ⊗on the spot 🍽on the spot. **Remarks:** Max. 24h.

### Bärenthal 🏔🌳 20A1

Baera Lodge, Gnadenweilerstrasse 36. **GPS:** n48,07448 e8,93287. 5 🛏 € 10 ⛽🔧Ch.🚿€ 2 WC 🚽€ 1 📶included. 🏧 **Location:** Rural. **Surface:** grassy/metalled. 🅿 01-01-31/12. **Distance:** 🚶on the spot. **Remarks:** Video surveillance.

### Bärnau 🏔🌳❄ 12F3

Gasthof und Wald-Pension Blei, Altglashütte 4. **GPS:** n49,77222 e12,38880.

30 🛏 € 10, guests free ⛽🔧Ch 🚿WCincluded. **Surface:** asphalted/grassy. 🅿 01-01-31/12. **Distance:** 🚶6km ⊗on the spot 🍽6km 🚴100m.

### Baunach 🚵 12D3

Sportplatz-Festplatz, Bahnhofstrasse 14-4. **GPS:** n49,98750 e10,85444. ⬆➡

---

12 🛏 free ⛽€ 1/80liter 🔧Ch 🚿€ 1/6h. **Location:** Rural, central, quiet. **Surface:** grassy/metalled. 🅿 01-01-31/12. **Distance:** 🚶200m 🚴1km ⊗200m 🍽200m 🚰200m 🚲200m on the spot 🚶on the spot. **Remarks:** Parking at the edge of nature reserve Haßberge, in the old part of the city, max. 2 nights.

### Bayerbach 🏵 17G3

Wohnmobilhafen VITAL Camping Bayerbach, Huckenham 11. **GPS:** n48,41537 e13,13010. ⬆⬆

8 🛏 € 12,50 2 pers.incl, dog € 2,50 🔧Ch 🚿(8x)€ 0,60/kWh WC 📶included. 🏧 **Location:** Rural, simple, isolated, quiet. **Surface:** metalled. 🅿 01-01-31/12. **Distance:** 🚶500m 🚴1km 🍽1km 🚰on the spot. **Remarks:** Max. 3 nights, use sanitary facilities at campsite.

### Bayreuth 🏵🏵 12E3

Grünewaldstraße. **GPS:** n49,94484 e11,59300. ⬆ 5 🛏 free ⛽🔧Ch. **Location:** Urban. **Surface:** grasstiles. 🅿 01-01-31/12. **Distance:** 🚶centre 3,5km 🍞bakery 300m.

### Bayreuth 🏵🏵 12E3

Lohengrin Therme Bayreuth, Kurpormenade 5. **GPS:** n49,94204 e11,63493. ⬆➡

24 🛏 € 6 ⛽€ 1/50liter 🔧€ 1 Ch € 1 🚿€ 1/6h WC 🚽€ 1,50. 🏧 **Location:** Rural, comfortable, central, quiet. **Surface:** asphalted. 🅿 01-01-31/12. **Distance:** 🚶1,5km 🚲3,5km ⊗500m 🍽1km 🚰on the spot 🚲on the spot 🚶on the spot. **Remarks:** Bread-service.

### Bayrischzell 🏔🏵❄ 20F2

Wohnmobilstellplatz Bayrischzell, Seebergstraße. **GPS:** n47,67189 e12,01023. ⬆

20 🛏 € 10 ⛽€ 0,50/80liter 🔧Ch 🚿(12x)€ 0,50/kWh. 🏧🚲 **Location:** Rural, comfortable, central. **Surface:** gravel. 🅿 01-01-31/12 🅿 Su/holidays. **Distance:** 🚶400m ⊗400m 🍽400m 🚰400m 🚌bus 5min 🚲on the spot.

### Beilngries 🏵 17E2

Landgasthof Euringer, Dorfstrasse 23. **GPS:** n49,01054 e11,50261. ⬆

6 🔴guests free 🚰. **Location:** Rural, simple, central.
**Surface:** asphalted/metalled. 🔲 01/01-31/12.
**Distance:** 🛁4km ⊗on the spot 🛒4km 🚌on the spot 🚲on the spot
🧍on the spot.

An der Altmühl 24. **GPS:** n49,02649 e11,47079. ⬆.

20 🔴€ 12 🚰 🔵Ch 🔌WC 🗓included. **Location:** Urban.
**Surface:** grassy. 🔲 01/03-31/10.
**Distance:** ⊗1km 🛒1,2km 🚌500m.
**Remarks:** Check in at reception campsite.

**Wohnmobilstellplatz am Sportzentrum**, Schwimmbadstraße 37.
**GPS:** n47,69920 e11,41556. ⬆➡.

16 🔴€ 7 🚰€ 1 🔵€ 1 Ch 🔌€ 0,50/kWh. 🖨 **Location:** Rural,
comfortable, quiet. **Surface:** asphalted. 🔲 01/04-31/10.
**Distance:** 🛁1km ⊗1km.
**Remarks:** Max. 3 nights, Alpenwarmbad 01/05-01/09 (swimming pool).

**Landgasthof Friesenmühle**, Friesenmühle 1.
**GPS:** n49,08534 e11,81176. ⬆➡.

10 🔴€ 5 🚰(2x) WC. **Location:** Simple, quiet.
**Surface:** grassy/gravel. 🔲 01/01-31/12 🔵 Wed.
**Distance:** 🛁1km ⊗on the spot 🛒1km.
**Remarks:** Max. 1 night, bread-service, motorhome service: volutary
contribution, apply< 22h.

**Wohnmobilstellplatz an der Schiffsanlegestelle**, Uferpromenade.
**GPS:** n49,10972 e11,43910. ⬆➡.

25 🔴free, 01/04-31/10 € 5 🚰€ 1 🔵Ch 🔌(16x)€ 1/8h. 🖨🚐

**Location:** Rural, simple, quiet. **Surface:** grasstiles/metalled.
🔲 01/01-31/12.
**Distance:** 🛁200m 🚌50m ⊗on the spot 🛒300m 🚌100m
🚲on the spot.
**Remarks:** Along river, pay in at kiosk.

**Reisemobilstellplätze Allweglehen**, Allweggasse 4.
**GPS:** n47,64820 e13,03988. ⬆.
14 🔴€ 12-20 🚰🔵Ch 🗓included. 🏠
**Location:** Rural, isolated, quiet. **Surface:** metalled. 🔲 01/01-31/12.
**Distance:** 🛁5km.
**Remarks:** Check in on arrival.

**Parkplatz Hochfelln-Seilbahn**, Maria-Eck-Straße 8.
**GPS:** n47,79710 e12,59079. ⬆.

10 🔴€ 4. 🖨 **Location:** Simple. **Surface:** gravel/metalled.
🔲 01/01-31/12.
**Distance:** 🛁1,2km ⊗on the spot 🛒500m 🧍on the spot 🚲on the
spot.
**Remarks:** Parking ski-lift, max. 3 nights.

**Am Tenniszentrum**, Buchenstrasse 17.
**GPS:** n47,80944 e12,38222. ⬆➡.

30 🔴€ 13 + € 1/pp tourist tax 🚰€ 3 🔵Ch 🔌€ 1,50/day WC🗓🔵€ 4
🗓included. **Location:** Urban, comfortable. **Surface:** metalled.
🔲 01/01-31/12.
**Distance:** 🛁800m 🚲2km 🏊Chiemsee 3km ⊗on the spot 🛒400m
🚌350m 🚲on the spot 🧍on the spot 🚵5km 🚣5km.
**Remarks:** At sports park, pay at reception.

**Wohnmobilstellplatz im Chiemseepark Bernau-Felden**, Rasthaus-
straße 11. **GPS:** n47,83111 e12,38528. ⬆.

16 🔴€ 6 🚰🔵ChWC€ 0,50 🗓€ 1. 🖨 **Location:** Comfortable, noisy.
**Surface:** gravel/metalled. 🔲 01/04-31/10.
**Distance:** 🛁2,5km 🚲600m 🏊on the spot 🚌on the spot ⊗on the
spot 🚲on the spot.
**Remarks:** Canoe and bicycle rental, charging point for electric bicycles.

**Seiseralm & Hof**, Reit 4. **GPS:** n47,79722 e12,35972. ⬆➡.

10 🔴€ 10 🚰🔵Ch 🔌€ 5/night 🗓€ 2,50 🗓included.
**Location:** Rural, simple, quiet.
**Surface:** asphalted.
🔲 01/01-31/12.
**Distance:** 🛁3,5km 🚲5km ⊗on the spot 🚲on the spot 🧍on the spot.
**Remarks:** Sauna € 10.

**Altes Gasthaus Artmeier**, Innenstetten 45.
**GPS:** n48,89675 e12,90262. ⬆.

10 🔴€ 5 🚰€ 1/100liter 🔵🔌(4x)€ 1/day. **Location:** Rural, simple,
quiet. **Surface:** gravel/sand. 🔲 01/04-30/09.
**Distance:** 🛁3km ⊗on the spot.

**Brauerei Biberach**, Weißenhorner Straße 24, Roggenburg.
**GPS:** n48,28808 e10,22047. ⬆➡.

8 🔴€ 9 🚰€ 1/80liter 🔵Ch 🔌€ 1/2kWh. 🖨🚐
**Location:** Simple, quiet. **Surface:** gravel/metalled. 🔲 01/01-31/12.
**Distance:** 🛁400m 🚲8km ⊗on the spot 🛒400m 🚌250m 🚲on the
spot 🧍on the spot.
**Remarks:** Bike and e-bike rental.

**Gasthof Stegmühle**, Stegmühle 2. **GPS:** n47,82437 e10,64428. ⬆.

4 🔴€ 5, guests free 🚰🔵Ch 🔌WCincluded 🗓.🚣
**Location:** Rural, simple. **Surface:** gravel/metalled.
🔲 01/01-31/12 🔵 Wed-Thu (market).
**Distance:** 🛁1km 🚌1km ⊗on the spot 🛒1km.

Rangenweg. **GPS:** n50,05407 e11,79292. ⬆➡.

20 🔴tourist tax € 1,50 🚰€ 1/40liter 🔵Ch 🔌(6x)€ 1/12h WC.
**Location:** Rural, simple, quiet. **Surface:** metalled.
🔲 01/01-31/12.
**Distance:** 🛁250m ⊗300m 🛒300m 🚲on the spot 🧍on the spot
🚵500m 🚣nearby.
**Remarks:** Pay at tourist office.

**Hallenbad Haselbach**, Viehweg 1. **GPS:** n50,39506 e9,99593. ⬆➡.

DE

5 🚐€ 5 🔌€ 1/100liter ⚡Ch♨️€ 0,50/kWh. **Location:** Urban, simple, quiet. **Surface:** asphalted. 🅿️ 01/01-31/12. **Distance:** 🚶1km ⊗1km 🚲2km 🚶on the spot 🏃on the spot 🚤on the spot.
**Remarks:** Parking swimming pool in Haselbach, money in envelope in mail box.

### 🍴🛏️S Bischofsheim an der Rhön 🍴 12B2

**Gasthof Roth**, Kreuzberg 10. **GPS:** n50,38222 e9,97806.⬆️.

20 🚐€ 6 WC. 🚐 **Location:** Rural, simple. **Surface:** grassy. 🅿️ 01/01-31/12.
**Distance:** ⊗on the spot 🚐on the spot 🏃on the spot.

### 🛏️S Bischofswiesen 🏔️🍴❄️ 20G2

**Götschen Alm**, Kollertradte 21, Loipl. **GPS:** n47,64817 e12,93631.⬆️.

15 🚐€ 10 excl. tourist tax 🔌 WC 🚿€ 3. **Location:** Rural, simple.
**Surface:** gravel. 🅿️ 01/05-30/10.
**Distance:** 🚶2km ⊗on the spot 🚐2km 🚐on the spot 🏃on the spot 🏃on the spot 🐎on the spot 🚤on the spot.
**Remarks:** Guests free.

### 🛏️S Blaichach 🏔️ 20C2

**Alpen-Rundblick Mobil Camping**, Am Eichbichl 1.
**GPS:** n47,54615 e10,25917.⬆️➡️.

60 🚐€ 11,50-13,50 + tourist tax € 1,70/pp 🔌€ 1/80liter ⚡Ch♨️
(54x)€ 0,60/kWh WC 🚿€ 1,60/pp 💡€ 2,50. 🚐 **Location:** Urban, luxurious. **Surface:** grassy/gravel. 🅿️ 01/01-31/12.
**Distance:** 🚶300m 🚴3,3km 🏊on the spot 🚐on the spot ⊗500m 🚐500m 🐎5km 🚤1km.
**Remarks:** Playground.

### 🛏️S Bodenmais 🌿🏔️🍴❄️ 17G2

**Concorde-Reisemobil-Stellplatz**, Kötztinger Straße.
**GPS:** n49,07147 e13,09273.⬆️.

---

12 🚐€ 10 + € 2,50/pp tourist tax 🔌€ 0,50/100liter ⚡Ch♨️€ 0,50/kWh. **Location:** Simple.
**Surface:** asphalted.
🅿️ 01/01-31/12.
**Distance:** 🚶800m ⊗200m 🚐200m.
**Remarks:** Use swimming pool, sauna, fitness-studio incl.

### 🛏️S Bodenwöhr 17F1

**Gasthof zum Troidlwirt**, Bodenwöhrer strasse 6.
**GPS:** n49,28305 e12,26272.⬆️.

20 🚐€ 10 ⚡Ch♨️(12x)€ 1 WC 🚿€ 1/time. 🚐 **Location:** Rural.
**Surface:** grassy/gravel. 🅿️ 01/01-31/12 💡restaurant, shower: Sa.
**Distance:** 🚶on the spot ⊗on the spot 🚐bakery 300m.

### 🛏️S Bogen 17F2

**Wohnmobilstellplätze am Volksfestplatz**, Kotaustraße 12.
**GPS:** n48,90744 e12,68877.⬆️.

5 🚐€ 15/24h 🔌€ 1/400liter ⚡Ch♨️(4x)€ 1/4h. **Location:** Urban, simple. **Surface:** grassy/metalled. 🅿️ 01/01-31/12 💡09/07-18/07.
**Distance:** 🚶300m ⊗on the spot 🚐Edeka 100m 🚐550m.
**Remarks:** Check in at pay-desk of swiming pool, possibility for reservation.

### 🛏️S Burgbernheim 17C1

**Wohnmobilstellplatz im Gründlein**, Freibadstrasse.
**GPS:** n49,44627 e10,31869.⬆️➡️.

12 🚐free 🔌€ 1/80liter ⚡Ch♨️(10x)€ 0,50/kWh 💡€ 1,50.
**Location:** Rural, simple, quiet. **Surface:** grasstiles.
🅿️ 01/01-31/12. **Distance:** 🚶500m 🚐500m 🚐500m 🏃on the spot 🏃on the spot. **Remarks:** Entrance swimming pool € 2, at swimming pool, max. 7 nights.

### 🍴🛏️S Burghaslach 17C1

**Hotel-Restaurant Steigerwaldhaus**, Oberrimbach 2.
**GPS:** n49,72890 e10,54078.⬆️.

---

10 🚐€ 10 🔌€ 4 WC. **Location:** Rural, simple. **Surface:** grassy. 🅿️ 01/01-31/12.
**Distance:** 🚶500m ⊗on the spot 🚐5km.
**Remarks:** Breakfast-service.

### 🛏️S Burghausen 🌿 20G1

**Waldpark Lindach**, Berghamer Strasse 1.
**GPS:** n48,15443 e12,80859.⬆️➡️.

18 🚐€ 8/24h 🔌€ 1/70liter ⚡Ch♨️(14x)€ 0,50/kWh WC 🚿. **Location:** Rural, comfortable, quiet. **Surface:** gravel. 🅿️ 01/01-31/12 💡 sanitary 01/11-31/03.
**Distance:** 🚶1,5km ⊗500m 🚐1,5km 🚐800m.
**Remarks:** Check in at Bürgerhaus Marktlerstr. 15a, max. 7 days, caution key sanitary € 20.

### 🛏️S Burgkirchen 🌿 20G1

**Glöcklhofer**, Peterhof 24. **GPS:** n48,15096 e12,75025.⬆️.

3 🚐€ 15, 2 pers.incl 🔌♨️€ 0,50/kWh WC 🚿 included.
**Location:** Rural, simple, isolated, quiet. **Surface:** grassy/metalled.
🅿️ 01/01-31/12.
**Distance:** 🚶2km ⊗2km 🚐2km.

### 🛏️S Burgkunstadt 🌿 12D3

**Alter Postweg**. **GPS:** n50,13965 e11,25017.⬆️.

4 🚐free 🔌€ 1 Ch. **Location:** Rural, simple. **Surface:** gravel. 🅿️ 01/01-31/12.
**Distance:** 🚶100m 🚴15km 🏊100m ⊗100m 🚐300m 🚐300m 🏃on the spot 🏃on the spot.
**Remarks:** Near sports fields, max. 48h.

### 🛏️S Bürgstadt 🍷 17A1

**Winzerfestplatz**, Josef-Ullrich-Straße. **GPS:** n49,71356 e9,26405.⬆️➡️.

25 🚐free 🔌€ 1/80liter ⚡Ch♨️(12x)€ 1/6h. **Location:** Rural,

DE

comfortable, quiet. **Surface:** asphalted. ▯ 01/01-31/12.
**Distance:** 🚂500m ⊗200m ⛲200m 🚲 on the spot 🚶 on the spot.

## Cadolzburg � 17D1

**Wohnmobilstellplatz Am Höhbuck. GPS:** n49,46123 e10,85188.

8 ⛺free 🚰€ 1/80liter ♻Ch 🔌(8x)€ 1/kWh. **Location:** Rural,
simple, quiet. **Surface:** asphalted. ▯ 01/01-31/12.
**Distance:** 🚂500m ⊗500m ⛲1km 🚌1km 🚶 on the spot.
**Remarks:** Max. 3 days.

## Cham 17F1

**Pension Kaesbauer**, Forstamtstraße 7. **GPS:** n49,22119 e12,65992.⬆.
5 ⛺free 🚰€ 3/24h WC🚽. **Location:** Urban, simple, central, quiet.
**Surface:** gravel. ▯ 01/01-31/12.
**Distance:** 🚂on the spot ⛲400m.
**Remarks:** Max. 24h.

## Coburg 🪣 12D3

**Wohnmobilstellplatz Vesteblick**, Rosenauer Straße 32.
**GPS:** n50,26972 e10,97611.⬆➡.

21 ⛺€ 12 🚰€ 1/100liter ♻Ch 🔌(21x)€ 0,60/kWh 🚽📶included.
**Location:** Comfortable, quiet. **Surface:** metalled. ▯ 01/01-31/12.
**Distance:** 🚂800m 🚲3km ⊗400m ⛲1km 🚌100m.
**Remarks:** At swimming pool.

## Coburg 🪣 12D3

**Aral-station**, Bambergerstrasse. **GPS:** n50,24833 e10,96639.⬆.

9 ⛺€ 2,50 🚰€ 1/20liter ♻Ch.
**Location:** Simple, central.
**Surface:** metalled.
▯ 01/01-31/12.
**Distance:** 🚂on the spot ⊗700m ⛲200m.
**Tourist information Coburg**
Ⓜ Die Veste Coburg. Medieval fortress.
✠ Schloß Ehrenburg. ▯ guided tour Tue-Su.

## Dachau 20E1

**Wohnmobilstellplatz Dachau**, Ostenstrasse 10.
**GPS:** n48,26260 e11,44167.⬆.
6 ⛺free. **Location:** Noisy. **Surface:** asphalted. ▯ 01/01-31/12.
**Distance:** 🚂500m ⊗300m ⛲350m 🚌300m 🚲 on the spot 🚶 on
the spot.

## Deggendorf 17G2

Konstantin-Bader-Straße. **GPS:** n48,82656 e12,96367.⬆.

---

3 ⛺free. **Location:** Urban, simple. **Surface:** asphalted.
▯ 01/01-31/12.
**Distance:** 🚂centre 500m 🏊on the spot ⊗250m ⛲300m.

## Deggendorf 17G2

**Elypso**, Sandnerhofweg 4-6. **GPS:** n48,82029 e12,91098.⬆.
4 ⛺€ 6,50 🚰€ 0,50/60liter 🔌€ 0,50/kWh. **Location:** Rural, simple.
**Surface:** metalled. ▯ 01/01-31/12.
**Distance:** 🚂5,3km 🚲4km 🥐bakery 300m.
**Remarks:** At swimming pool, arrival 9><20h.

## Deiningen 17C2

**Cowabanga**, Am Sportpark. **GPS:** n48,86292 e10,58042.➡.

10 ⛺free 🚰🔌€ 2,50 WC🚽. **Location:** Urban, simple.
**Surface:** asphalted. ▯ 01/01-31/12.
**Distance:** 🚂2km ⊗on the spot.
**Remarks:** Parking sports centre.

## Denkendorf 17E2

**Gasthof Lindenwirt**, Hauptstrasse 43.
**GPS:** n48,92490 e11,45460.⬆➡.

10 ⛺€ 5 🚰🔌(10x)included.🛁 **Location:** Urban, simple.
**Surface:** gravel/sand. ▯ 01/01-31/12.
**Distance:** 🚂on the spot 🚲700m ⊗100m ⛲100m 🚲 on the spot
🚶 on the spot.

## Dettelbach 🚣 17C1

**Zur Mainfähre**, An der Mainlände. **GPS:** n49,80076 e10,16751.⬆➡.

35 ⛺€ 5 🚰€ 1/60liter ♻Ch 🔌(24x)€ 0,50/kWh. 🚌
**Location:** Rural, comfortable, quiet. **Surface:** grassy
▯ 01/01-31/12 ▯ Service: winter.
**Distance:** 🚂100m 🚂on the spot ⊗100m ⛲100m 🚲 on the spot
🚶 on the spot.

## Dettelbach 🚣 17C1

**Am Weingut Mangold**, Köhlerstaße 12. **GPS:** n49,82917 e10,17583.⬆.

4 ⛺€ 5 🚰€ 1 ♻🔌(4x)€ 1 🚽€ 1/time.🛁
**Location:** Rural, simple, quiet. **Surface:** grassy. ▯ 01/01-31/12.
**Distance:** 🚂300m ⊗300m 🚲 on the spot 🚶 on the spot.
**Remarks:** Free of charge when buying 12 bottles of wine.

## Dießen 🚣 20D1

Seestraße. **GPS:** n47,95220 e11,10598.⬆.
12 ⛺€ 8/24h 🚰€ 1 🚽🔌 1 Ch 🔌(12x)€ 1/4h WC🚽.🚌
**Location:** Urban, simple. **Surface:** gravel. ▯ 01/01-31/12.

---

**Distance:** 🏊200m 🚂200m ⊗150m ⛲150m 🚌200m.
**Remarks:** Max. 3 days.

## Dietfurt/Altmühl 🚣 17E2

**An der Schiffsanlegestelle**, Griesstetter Straße.
**GPS:** n49,02747 e11,58222.⬆.

5 ⛺free 🚰♻Ch. **Location:** Rural, isolated, quiet. **Surface:** grassy.
▯ 01/01-31/12.
**Distance:** 🚂1km ⊗800m 🚲 on the spot 🚶 on the spot.
**Remarks:** Max. 24h, service 500m.

## Dingolfing 17F3

**Wohnmobilstellplatz Dingolfing**, Wollanger/Prasserweg.
**GPS:** n48,62827 e12,50206.⬆➡.

12 ⛺free 🚰€ 1/80liter ♻Ch 🔌(12x)€ 1/12h,16Amp 📶included.
**Location:** Rural, comfortable, quiet. **Surface:** gravel.
▯ 01/01-31/12 ▯ 01/10-31/10.
**Distance:** 🚂400m 🚲5km 🏊900m ⊗200m ⛲500m 🚲900m.
**Remarks:** Nearby swimming pool, max. 3 days.

## Dinkelsbühl 🌾 17C2

**Park- & Campanlage**, Dürrwanger Straße.
**GPS:** n49,07812 e10,32906.⬆.

12 ⛺€ 12 🚰♻Ch 🔌included 🚽€ 1,50.
**Surface:** metalled. ▯ 01/01-31/12.
**Distance:** 🚂1,5km ⊗100m ⛲500m.
**Remarks:** To be paid at campsite (500m).

## Dinkelsbühl 🌾 17C2

**Wohnmobilstellplatz P2a**, Mönchsrother Straße.
**GPS:** n49,06377 e10,32721.

40 ⛺€ 6/24h 🚰♻Ch 🔌🚌
**Surface:** grasstiles. ▯ 01/01-31/12.
**Distance:** 🚂on the spot ⊗300m ⛲300m.
**Remarks:** Max. 7 days.

## Dittelbrunn 12C3

**Gasthaus Goldene Flasche**, Strohgasse 1, Hambach.
**GPS:** n50,09787 e10,20763.⬆.

3 ⚡ € 1. **Location:** Urban, simple. **Surface:** metalled.
⊙ 01/01-31/12.
**Distance:** on the spot ⊗on the spot ⚡200m.

### 🅿 Dollnstein 🌿      17D2
Papst-Viktor-Straße. **GPS:** n48,87793 e11,07472. ⬆.

10 ⚡free. **Location:** Rural, simple, quiet. **Surface:** grassy/gravel.
⊙ 01/01-31/12.
**Distance:** 500m ⊗400m ⚡800m 🚲on the spot 🚶on the spot.
**Remarks:** Max. 48h.

### 🅿🅢 Donauwörth 🌿      17D3
**Wohnmobilstellplatz am Festplatz**, Neue Obermayerstraße 2.
**GPS:** n48,71490 e10,77874. ⬆➡.

20 ⚡free 💧€ 1/95liter 🔧Ch 💧€ 1/kWh. **Location:** Urban, simple.
**Surface:** asphalted. ⊙ 01/01-31/12.
**Distance:** on the spot ⊗on the spot ⚡500m 🚲on the spot.
**Remarks:** Max. 5 days.

### 🅿 Dorfprozelten      17B1
Maingasse. **GPS:** n49,77825 e9,37769. ⬆.
5 ⚡free. **Surface:** grassy/gravel. ⊙ 01/01-31/12.
**Distance:** on the spot on the spot ⊗75m.

### 🅿 Ebermannstadt      17D1
P2, Oberes Tor. **GPS:** n49,78222 e11,18946. ⬆➡.

10 ⚡free. **Location:** Urban, simple. **Surface:** metalled.
⊙ 01/01-31/12.
**Distance:** 750m ⊗450m ⚡100m.
**Remarks:** Max. 1 night.

### 🅿🅢 Ebern 🌿      12C3
**Wohnmobilhafen Ebern**, Walk-Strasser-Anlage.
**GPS:** n50,09312 e10,79496. ⬆➡.

---

20 ⚡6 💧🔧Ch 💧(26x)€ 1/2kWh WC included ⊙€ 2 .
**Location:** Urban, comfortable, noisy.
**Surface:** metalled.
⊙ 01/01-31/12.
**Distance:** on the spot 1km 2km ⊗100m ⚡200m 100m.

### 🅿🅢 Ebern 🌿      12C3
**Dietz**, Bahnhofstrasse. **GPS:** n50,10167 e10,78917. ⬆.

10 ⚡€ 5 💧€ 1/100liter 🔧Ch 💧WC. **Location:** Urban, simple.
**Surface:** asphalted/grassy. ⊙ 01/01-31/12.
**Distance:** 1km ⊗400m 400m.

### 🅿🅢 Ebrach      12C3
**Naturbad**, Schwimmbadweg. **GPS:** n49,84639 e10,48306. ⬆➡.

5 ⚡free 💧€ 1/80liter 🔧Ch. **Location:** Rural, simple.
**Surface:** metalled. ⊙ 01/01-31/12.
**Distance:** 2km ⊗2km 2km 500m.
**Remarks:** Parking swimming pool.

### 🅿🅢 Eggenfelden      17G3
Öttingerstraße. **GPS:** n48,40054 e12,76456. ⬆.
5 ⚡free 🔧Ch. **Location:** Simple, noisy. **Surface:** asphalted.
⊙ 01/01-31/12.
**Distance:** 500m ⊗300m.
**Remarks:** Max. 3 days.

### 🅿🅢 Eggenfelden      17G3
P2, Birkenallee. **GPS:** n48,40185 e12,77579. ⬆.

5 ⚡free. **Location:** Simple, quiet. **Surface:** grasstiles.
⊙ 01/01-31/12.
**Distance:** 1km.
**Remarks:** Max. 3 days.

### 🅒🅢 Eging am See      17G2
**Bavaria Kur-Sport Camping Park**, Grafenauer Str. 31.
**GPS:** n48,72120 e13,26519. ⬆➡.

10 ⚡€ 15, 2 pers.incl 💧🔧Ch 💧(10x)included.
**Location:** Rural, simple, quiet. **Surface:** asphalted. ⊙ 01/01-31/12.
**Distance:** 1km ⚡800m.
**Remarks:** Max. 2 days, check in at reception campsite, use sanitary facilities at campsite.

### 🅿🅢 Eibelstadt 🌿      17B1
**Wassersportclub Eibelstadt**, Mainparkring.
**GPS:** n49,73146 e9,98701. ⬆➡.

---

90 ⚡€ 10, >7.5m € 15, trailer € 5 💧€ 1/5minutes 🔧Ch 💧(90x)
included,6Amp WC ⊙€ 1 ⊙€ 5/5. **Location:** Rural, comfortable,
quiet. **Surface:** grassy/gravel. ⊙ 01/01-31/12.
**Distance:** 2km 50m ⊗50m ⚡500m 1km 🚲on the spot.
**Remarks:** Along Main river, bread-service (weekend).

### 🅿🅢 Eichstätt 🌿      17D2
**Schottenwiese/Volkfestplatz**, Schottenau.
**GPS:** n48,88400 e11,19816. ⬆➡.

70 ⚡€ 10 💧€ 1/100liter 🔧Ch 💧(48x)€ 0,50/kWh WC ⊙€ 0,50.
**Location:** Urban, central, quiet. **Surface:** metalled.
⊙ 01/01-31/12. ⊙ Eichstätter Volksfest.
**Distance:** 500m ⚡500m on the spot 🚲on the spot 🚶on the spot.
**Remarks:** Baker at 8am.

**Tourist information Eichstätt:**
🎪 Volksfestplatz. Flea market. ⊙ 10/05, 14/06, 12/07, 13/09, 04/10.
✱ Altstadtfest, Innenstad. City celebration. ⊙ 28/08-06/09.
✱ Eichstätter Volksfest, Volksfestplatz. Folk festival. ⊙ 02/09-11/09.
🌿 Informationszentrum Naturpark Altmühltal, Notre Dame 1. Information centre nature reserve. ⊙ 01/04-31/10 Mo-Sa 9-17h, Su 10-17h, 01/11-31/03 Mo-Fr 9-12h. 🎟 free.

### 🅿🅢 Einsiedl 🏔🌳❄      20E2
**Wohnmobilstellplatz**, B11. **GPS:** n47,57000 e11,30389. ⬆➡.

80 ⚡€ 6 💧€ 1/70liter 💧€ 1/kWh. **Location:** Rural, comfortable,
quiet. **Surface:** asphalted/gravel. ⊙ 01/01-31/12.
**Distance:** 500m on the spot on the spot ⊗500m ⚡3,5km
1,5km 1,5km.
**Remarks:** Max. 3 nights.

### 🅿🅢 Eisenheim 🌿      12C3
**Weingut Herbert Schuler**, An der Mainaue, Obereisenheim.
**GPS:** n49,88883 e10,17942. ⬆.

60 ⚡€ 5 💧€ 1/80liter 🔧Ch 💧(48x)€ 0,50. **Location:** Rural,
comfortable, quiet. **Surface:** grassy/metalled. ⊙ 01/01-31/12.
**Distance:** on the spot on the spot ⊗on the spot 🚲on the spot.
**Remarks:** Along Main river, bread-service, sale of wines.

### 🅿🅢 Eltmann am Main 🌿      12C3
**Parkplatz**, Mainlände. **GPS:** n49,97306 e10,66250. ⬆➡.

**DE**

30 🛏free 🚰 € 1/80liter 🔧Ch. 💧 € 1/6h WC. **Location:** Rural, simple. **Surface:** metalled. ⏰ 01/01-31/12. **Distance:** 🚶500m 🏊on the spot 🛒on the spot ⊗100m 🚉300m 🚲on the spot 🚶on the spot.

🅿S **Enderndorf** 〰🏊⛵🍞🎣🎡 17D2

**Wohnmobilstellplatz Panorama**, Kreisstraße, Spalt-Enderndorf. **GPS:** n49,15028 e10,91083.⬆.

60 🛏 € 10 🚰 € 1/80liter 🔧Ch. 💧(60x)€ 1/kWh. 🔌 **Location:** Rural, simple, quiet. **Surface:** grassy. ⏰ 01/04-31/10. **Distance:** 🚶400m 🏊400m 🛒400m ⊗400m 🚉3km 🚐150m 🚲on the spot. **Remarks:** Service accross the street, bread-service.

🅿S **Enderndorf** 〰🏊⛵🍞🎣🎡 17D2

**Reisemobilstellplatz Enderndorf-West**, Zum Hafen. **GPS:** n49,14777 e10,91126.⬆.

60 🛏 € 12/24h 🚰 € 1/100liter 🔧Ch. 💧(60x)€ 0,50/kWh. 🔌 **Location:** Rural, simple, isolated, quiet. **Surface:** grasstiles. ⏰ 01/01-31/12. **Distance:** 🚶200m 🏊150m ⊗200m 🚉200m 🚲on the spot 🚶on the spot.

🅿S **Erbendorf** 12E3

**Am Stadtpark**, Bahnhofstraße 21. **GPS:** n49,84144 e12,04769.⬆➡.

8 🛏free 🚰 € 1 🔧Ch. **Location:** Simple. **Surface:** gravel. ⏰ 01/01-31/12. **Distance:** 🚶100m ⊗200m 🚉200m. **Remarks:** Max. 3 days.

🅿S **Erding** ♨ 20E1

**Wohnmobilpark Erding**, Thermenallee 1. **GPS:** n48,29332 e11,88707.⬆➡.

---

55 🛏€12/day 🚰 € 1/80liter 🔧Ch. 💧 € 1/2kWh WC🚿. **Location:** Rural, luxurious, quiet. **Surface:** grasstiles/metalled. ⏰ 01/01-31/12. **Distance:** 🚶2km ⊗2km 🚉2km 🚐50m. **Remarks:** Max. 7 nights.

🅲S **Escherndorf** ⛵ 12C3

**Campingplatz Escherndorf**, An der Güß 9a. **GPS:** n49,85996 e10,17632.⬆.

22 🛏€ 9 🚰🔧Ch. 💧(22x)€ 0,50 WC🚿sanitary € 4/pp 📶€ 2. **Location:** Rural, comfortable, quiet. **Surface:** grassy. ⏰ 01/04-31/10. **Distance:** 🚶300m 🚉300m 🚲on the spot 🚶on the spot. **Remarks:** Max. 7 days, sanitary at campsite.

🅿S **Eslarn** 17F1

Sportplatzstraße. **GPS:** n49,57849 e12,50993.⬆. 3 🛏free 🚰. **Location:** Simple, quiet. **Surface:** asphalted. ⏰ 01/01-31/12. **Distance:** 🚶500m ⊗600m. **Remarks:** At football ground, max. 72h.

🅿S **Ettenbeuren** 20C1

**Wohnmobilpark Kammelaue**, Zum Sportplatz 12. **GPS:** n48,37565 e10,36021.⬆➡.

40 🛏€ 9,50, € 15 service incl 🚰🔧Ch. 💧 € 3,50 WC🚿included 🔌📶€ 2/24h. 🏠 **Location:** Rural, comfortable, quiet. **Surface:** grasstiles/metalled. ⏰ 24/03-31/10. **Distance:** 🚶500m ⊗on the spot 🚉500m 🚲on the spot 🚶on the spot.

🅿S **Feucht** 🎡 17D1

**Am Freibad Feuchtasia**, Chormantelweg. **GPS:** n49,37848 e11,22495.⬆.

9 🛏€ 9 🚰 € 1/80liter 🔧Ch. 💧(8x)€ 1/2kWh 🔌.🏠 **Location:** Urban, simple, quiet. **Surface:** grasstiles. ⏰ 01/01-31/12. **Distance:** 🚶1km 🚉900m 🚐900m. **Remarks:** At swimming pool, max. 3 nights.

👪 **Fichtelberg** ❄ 12E3

**Automobilmuseum**, Eckert Naglerweg 9. **GPS:** n49,99760 e11,85820.⬆.

---

16 🛏free. **Location:** Rural, simple. **Surface:** asphalted/metalled. ⏰ 01/01-31/12. **Distance:** 🚶700m ⊗100m 🚉1km 🚲on the spot 🚶on the spot. **Remarks:** Parking museum.

🅿S **Fischbachau** 20F2

**Wohlschlagerhof**, Schreiern 10. **GPS:** n47,76157 e11,91687.⬆. 3 🛏€ 12 🚰WCincluded 🔌.🚿♿ **Location:** Rural, comfortable, isolated, quiet. **Surface:** grassy/metalled. ⏰ 01/04-31/10. **Distance:** 🚶1,5km 🚉1,5km.

🅿S **Fischen** 🏔🎡 20C2

**Wohnmobil-Stellplatz Fischen**, Mühlenstraße. **GPS:** n47,44950 e10,26946.⬆.

11 🛏€ 8 + tourist tax € 2,50/pp 🚰 € 1 🔧 € 1 Ch. 💧(12x)€ 1/12h. 🔌 **Location:** Rural, simple. **Surface:** asphalted. ⏰ 01/01-31/12. **Distance:** 🚶1,2km 🚉on the spot 🚲on the spot 🚶on the spot. **Remarks:** Pay at Sportpark, Mühlenstraße 55, incl. access swimming pool.

🅿S **Forchheim** 17D1

**Sportinsel**, An der Regnitzbrücke. **GPS:** n49,72120 e11,04939.⬆➡.

20 🛏€ 9 🚰 € 1/100liter 🔧Ch. 💧 € 0,50/kWh WC🚿€ 1,50. 🔌 **Location:** Rural, comfortable, noisy. **Surface:** grasstiles. ⏰ 01/01-31/12 ⭕ sanitary building: 01/11-28/02. **Distance:** 🚶600m 🚴5km ⊗on the spot 🚉on the spot 🚲on the spot 🚶on the spot.

🅿S **Freyung** 🍞🏔🎡⛵❄ 17I2

**Freizeitpark Solla**, Solla 2a. **GPS:** n48,80104 e13,54125.⬆➡.

12 🛏€ 5 🚰 € 1/50liter 🔧Ch. 💧(12x)€ 0,50/kWh. **Location:** Rural, simple, quiet. **Surface:** grasstiles. ⏰ 01/01-31/12. **Distance:** 🚶2km ⊗500m 🎿on the spot 🎣on the spot.

🅿S **Freyung** 🍞🏔🎡🎣❄ 17H2

**Am Freibad**, Zuppingerstraße 1. **GPS:** n48,80515 e13,54102.⬆.

DE

12 free. **Location:** Urban, simple, quiet. **Surface:** metalled.
01/01-31/12.
**Distance:** 1km 1km 1km.

### Friedberg 17D3
Seestraße. **GPS:** n48,36540 e10,96529.

4 free. **Location:** Rural, simple, quiet. **Surface:** asphalted.
01/01-31/12.
**Distance:** 1,8km 5km on the spot on the spot 400m
800m on the spot on the spot.
**Remarks:** Small pitches.

### Friedberg 17D3
**Wallfahrtskirche**, Herrgottsruhstrasse.
**GPS:** n48,35765 e10,99095.

3 free. **Location:** Simple. **Surface:** gravel. 01/01-31/12.
**Distance:** 600m 600m 600m.

### Friedberg 17D3
Marquardtstrasse 2/A. **GPS:** n48,34825 e10,99757.
Ch free. 01/01-31/12.
**Distance:** on the spot.

### Friedenfels 12E3
**Stellplatz Frauenreuther Weiher**, Weißensteiner Weg, Frauenreuth.
**GPS:** n49,29278 e12,08556.

5 € 3,50 Ch € 1/2h. **Location:** Rural, simple, isolated.
**Surface:** metalled. 01/01-31/12.
**Distance:** 1,5km Frauenreuther Weiher.
**Remarks:** Max. 3 days, to be paid at office de tourisme.

### Friedenfels 12E3
**Zentral**, Gemmingenstraße. **GPS:** n49,88102 e12,10297.

6 € 3,50 Ch € 1/2kWh. **Location:** Simple, quiet.

---

**Surface:** metalled. 01/01-31/12.
**Distance:** on the spot 200m 200m 25m.
**Remarks:** Max. 3 days, pay at tourist office, Café Am Steinwald, Gemmingenstr. 19.

### Fürstenzell 17G3
**Wohnmobilstellplatz bei der Waldschänke**, Altenmarkt 1.
**GPS:** n48,55136 e13,34118.
€ 6 € 1/100liter Ch € 1,50.
**Location:** Isolated. **Surface:** grassy. 01/01-31/12.
**Distance:** 4km 200m.

### Füssen 20D2
**Camper's Stop**, Abt Hafnerstrasse 9. **GPS:** n47,58186 e10,70080.

120 € 15, trailer € 5 Ch € 1/kWh WC € 1 included.
**Location:** Urban, comfortable, noisy. **Surface:** gravel/metalled.
01/01-31/12.
**Distance:** 1,5km 600m 600m terrace 50m 250m
4km 400m.

### Füssen 20D2
**Wohnmobilstellplatz Füssen**, Abt Hafnerstrasse 1.
**GPS:** n47,58224 e10,70355.

30 € 14 Ch included (6x)€ 2,50 WC € 0,50 € 2.
**Location:** Urban, simple, noisy. **Surface:** metalled.
01/01-31/12.
**Distance:** 1,8km 1km 200m 300m 500m on the spot
on the spot on the spot on the spot.
**Remarks:** Sauna, solarium.

### Garmisch-Partenkirchen 20D2
**Alpencamp am Wank**, Wankbahnstraße 2.
**GPS:** n47,50573 e11,10802.

110 € 12, tourist tax > 16 € 3/pp, € 1 Umwelttaxe € 1/80liter
Ch (110x)€ 1/kWh WC € 1 .
**Location:** Rural, comfortable, noisy. **Surface:** asphalted.
01/01-31/12.
**Distance:** 1km 2km 50m 700m 50m 2,5km
1,5km.
**Remarks:** Check in on arrival.

### Garstadt 12C3
**GPS:** n49,97096 e10,17449.

15 free. **Location:** Rural, simple, quiet. **Surface:** gravel.

---

01/01-31/12.
**Distance:** 200m on the spot on the spot 200m on the spot on the spot.
**Remarks:** Service 500m, service nearby, indicated.

### Geisenfeld 17E3
Jahnstrasse. **GPS:** n48,67966 e11,61135.

5 free € 0,50/50liter Ch (3x)€ 0,50/kWh.
**Location:** Urban, simple, quiet. **Surface:** grassy/gravel.
01/01-31/12.
**Distance:** 700m 200m 800m on the spot.
**Remarks:** At football ground.

### Gerolzhofen 12C3
**P3 Zur Volkach**, Schallfelderstrasse. **GPS:** n49,89841 e10,35104.

4 free € 1/80liter Ch (4x)€ 0,50/kWh WC.
**Location:** Urban, simple. **Surface:** metalled. 01/01-31/12.
**Distance:** 100m 500m 300m 200m on the spot.
**Remarks:** Max. 3 days.

### Gerolzhofen 12C3
**P1 Geomaris**, Dingolshäuser Straße 2. **GPS:** n49,89980 e10,36035.

6 free. **Location:** Urban, simple. **Surface:** asphalted.
01/01-31/12.
**Distance:** 750m 200m.
**Remarks:** Parking swimming pool.

### Geslau 17C2
**Bauernhof Mohrenhof**, Lauterbach 3.
**GPS:** n49,34630 e10,32500.

14 € 13,50 Ch € 0,60/kWh WC € 0,50 € 4 € 2,50/2h.
**Location:** Rural, simple. **Surface:** gravel.
Easter-31/10.
**Distance:** 500m on the spot on the spot 2km on the spot
on the spot.
**Remarks:** Bread-service.

### Goldkronach 12E3
**Festplatz**, Schulstrasse. **GPS:** n50,01255 e11,68244.

4 �free ⚡€ 1/80liter 🚰Ch 💧(4x)€ 1/8h. **Location:** Simple, quiet.
**Surface:** gravel. 📅 01/01-31/12.
**Distance:** 🚶50m ⊗on the spot 🏪500m 🚲on the spot
🚳2km.

### 🏕🚿S Gößweinstein 🌿🌳 17D1

**Alte Jugendherberge**, Etzdorfer Straße 6.
**GPS:** n49,76556 e11,33028.⬆.

6 �€7 ⚡€ 1/80liter 🚰Ch 💧€ 1/2kWh. 🔌**Location:** Urban,
simple. **Surface:** metalled. 📅 01/01-31/12.
**Distance:** 🚶600m ⊗600m 🏪600m 🚲300m 🏃600m.

### 🚿 Gößweinstein 🌿🌳 17D1

**Am Hallenbad**, Balthasar-Neumann-Straße 33.
**GPS:** n49,77156 e11,34129.➡.

5 �free. **Location:** Urban, simple. **Surface:** asphalted.
📅 01/01-31/12.
**Distance:** 🚶500m ⊗200m 🏪100m 🚲200m 🏃200m.
**Remarks:** Playground.

### 🏕🚿S Grafenau 17G2

**Wohnmobilstellplatz am Bäreal Kurerlebnispark**, Freyunger Straße.
**GPS:** n48,85605 e13,40456.⬆ ➡.

18 �€ 13,90 ⚡€ 0,10/8liter 🚰💧(18x)€ 0,50/kWh 📶included
📱🚐**Location:** Urban, simple, quiet. **Surface:** grasstiles.
📅 01/01-31/12.
**Distance:** 🚶500m ⊗500m 🏪550m ReWe 🏃on the spot.
**Remarks:** Wifi in Touristinformation + 1/2h free internet in Stadt-
bücherei.

### 🏕🚿S Gräfendorf 12B3

**Volkert an der Roßmühle**, Roßmühle, Weickersgrüben.
**GPS:** n50,10660 e9,78309.⬆.

---

5 �€5 ⚡€ 2/100liter 🚰Ch 💧(5x)📶included. **Location:** Rural.
**Surface:** asphalted. 📅 01/04-31/10.
**Distance:** 🚶on the spot ⚡on the spot ⊗on the spot 🏃on the spot.
**Remarks:** At motorhome dealer, accessory shop, max. 24h, check in
at shop.

### 🏕🚿S Grafenrheinfeld 🚣 12C3

**Wohnmobilstellplatz am Naturbadesee**, Hermasweg 2.
**GPS:** n50,00831 e10,20325.⬆ ➡.

12 �€6 ⚡€ 1/100liter 🚰Ch 💧€ 0,50/kWh. **Location:** Rural,
comfortable. **Surface:** gravel. 📅 01/01-31/12.
**Distance:** 🚶on the spot ⚡on the spot ⊗500m 🏪500m 🚲on the
spot.
**Remarks:** At gymnasium.

### 🏕🚿S Grainau 20D2

**Wohnmobilhafen Zugspitzblick**, Griesener Strasse.
**GPS:** n47,47982 e11,05380.

80 �€21 ⚡🚰Ch 💧€ 0,80 WC🚽🔌.
**Location:** Rural. **Surface:** grassy/gravel. 📅 01/01-31/12.
**Distance:** 🚶2km ⊗50m 🏪100m 🚌100m.

### 🏕🚿 Greding 🌳 17D2

**Am Hallenbad. GPS:** n49,04409 e11,35551.⬆.

20 �free.
**Location:** Urban, simple. **Surface:** metalled.
📅 01/01-31/12.
**Distance:** 🚶Old city centre 300m ⚔500m ⊗250m 🏪250m
🚌on the spot 🚲on the spot 🏃on the spot.
**Remarks:** Parking at city wall in front of swimming pool.
**Tourist information Greding:**
ℹ City wall and towers.

### 🏕🚿S Großheubach 17A1

**Weingut Gasthaus Zur Bretzel**, Kirchstraße 1.
**GPS:** n49,72620 e9,22083.⬆.

25 �€17 ⚡🚰Ch 💧(25x)WCincluded 🔌€ 1.🚐
**Location:** Rural, comfortable, quiet. **Surface:** grassy/gravel.
📅 01/01-31/12 🔴 Mo, 01/11-15/11.
**Distance:** 🚶100m ⊗on the spot 🚲on the spot 🏃on the spot.
**Remarks:** To be paid at Gasthaus, € 10 euro discount coupon (restau-
rant, wine).

---

### 🏕🚿S Großweil 🏰🌳 20E2

**Berggasthof Kreut-Alm**, Kreut 1. **GPS:** n47,66184 e11,28286.⬆.

40 �€ 10 ⚡€ 6/day. **Location:** Rural, simple, isolated, quiet.
**Surface:** asphalted. 📅 01/03-31/10.
**Distance:** ⚔3,2km ⊗on the spot.

### 🏕 Großweil 🏰🌳 20E2

**Freilichtmuseum Glentleiten**, An der Glentleiten 4.
**GPS:** n47,66495 e11,28506.⬆ ➡.

10 ⌣free. **Surface:** gravel. 📅 15/11-15/03.
**Distance:** 🚶2km ⚔3,5km ⊗Gaststätte - Biergarten 🏪1km.
**Remarks:** Open air museum, only overnight stays.

### 🏕🚿S Günzburg 🌳 17C3

**Waldbad**, Heidenheimer Straße. **GPS:** n48,46287 e10,26944.➡.

24 ⌣€ 5, 01/05-30/09 € 8 ⚡€ 1/100liter 🚰💧(24x)€ 0,50/kWh.🚗
🛏**Location:** Rural, simple. **Surface:** gravel.
📅 01/01-31/12.
**Distance:** 🚶1,2km 🏪2km 🚲Danube Bike Trail.
**Remarks:** Parking swimming pool.

### 🏕🚿S Gunzenhausen 17D2

**Surfzentrum Schlungenhof. GPS:** n49,12790 e10,74559.⬆.

85 ⌣€ 6-11 + € 1,50/pp tourist tax ⚡€ 1/80liter 🚰Ch 💧(40x)
included WC🚽€ 1 📶. 🛏**Location:** Rural, comfortable, quiet.
**Surface:** grassy/gravel. 📅 01/04-30/10.
**Distance:** 🏊100m ⊗on the spot 🏪1,8km 🚲on the spot 🏃on the
spot.

### 🏕🚿S Gunzenhausen 17D2

**Altmühlsee, Seezentrum Mühr**, Seezentrum Muhr am See.
**GPS:** n49,13145 e10,73534.⬆ ➡ ⬆.

20 ⌣€ 9/24h. 🛏**Location:** Rural, comfortable, isolated, quiet.

DE

**Surface:** grassy. 01/04-30/10.
**Distance:** on the spot 200m on the spot on the spot.
**Remarks:** Max. 3 days.

### S Hammelburg 12B3
**Am Bleichrasen, P2**, Am Weiher. **GPS:** n50,11390 e9,88820.

24 € 6/24h Chincluded (24x)€ 0,50/kWh. WC.
**Location:** Urban, simple, quiet. **Surface:** asphalted.
01/01-31/12.
**Distance:** on the spot on the spot 200m 300m.

### S Hammelburg 12B3
**Forellenhof Reuss**, Am Erlich 30, Diebach.
**GPS:** n50,13310 e9,81917.

64 € 10 Chincluded (64x)€ 3/24h WC € 2 € 2.
**Location:** Rural, comfortable, quiet. **Surface:** gravel.
01/01-31/12 service: 31/10-01/03.
**Distance:** Hammelburg 7km on the spot on the spot on the spot on the spot.
**Remarks:** Bread-service, weekend: Gaststätte/Biergarten.

### S Hammelburg 12B3
**Hotel Kaiser**, An der Walkmühle 11. **GPS:** n50,11563 e9,90159.

4 free € 1/100liter Ch € 2/day. **Location:** Urban,
simple, quiet. **Surface:** grassy/gravel. 01/01-31/12.
**Distance:** 800m on the spot on the spot on the spot.
**Remarks:** Bread-service.

### S Hammelburg 12B3
**Restaurant Nöth**, Morlesauer Strasse 3. **GPS:** n50,11707 e9,80313.

6 free. **Location:** Rural, simple, quiet. **Surface:** gravel.
01/01-31/12.
**Distance:** on the spot on the spot on the spot on the spot
on the spot.
**Remarks:** Check in at restaurant, use of a meal desired.

### S Hassfurt 12C3
**Festplatz am Gries**, Untere Fischergasse 9.
**GPS:** n50,03068 e10,50094.

22 € 8/24h € 1 Ch € 2/day WC € 1.
**Location:** Urban, simple. **Surface:** asphalted. 01/01-31/12.
**Distance:** 200m 10m 200m 200m 200m on the spot
on the spot.
**Remarks:** Along Main river.

### S Hassfurt 12C3
**Naturfreunde**, Am Hafen 4. **GPS:** n50,02622 e10,51664.

23 € 8 € 1/100liter Ch € 2/24h € 0,50.
**Location:** Rural, comfortable. **Surface:** grassy. 01/01-31/12.
**Distance:** 1,5km on the spot on the spot on the spot
1,5km.

### Herrieden 17C2
**Volksfestplatz an der Altmühl**, Staatsstrasse 2248.
**GPS:** n49,23191 e10,49588.

10 free. **Location:** Urban, simple, central, quiet. **Surface:** asphalted.
01/01-31/12.
**Distance:** 100m 200m 200m on the spot on the spot.
**Remarks:** Parking at the old mill bridge.

### S Hersbruck 17D1
**Fackelmann Therme Hersbruck**, Badestrasse.
**GPS:** n49,51142 e11,44267.

6 € 6 € 1/50liter Ch € 1/8h.
**Surface:** gravel. 01/01-31/12.
**Distance:** on the spot 200m 200m.
**Remarks:** Check in at pay-desk of the Therme.

### S Herzogenaurach 17D1
**Freizeitbad Atlantis**, Würzburger Straße 35.
**GPS:** n49,57315 e10,86543.

12 € 9/24h € 1/80liter Ch (12x)€ 0,50/kWh.

**Location:** Rural, simple. **Surface:** gravel. 01/01-31/12.
**Distance:** 1,5km on the spot.
**Remarks:** € 2 reduction swimming pool.

### S Hilpoltstein 17D2
**Seezentrum Heuberg am Rothsee**, Heuberg.
**GPS:** n49,20954 e11,18595.

46 € 8/24h Chincluded (30x)€ 0,50/kWh.
**Location:** Urban, simple. **Surface:** metalled.
01/01-31/12 Service: winter.
**Distance:** 200m 200m on the spot on the spot.

### Hilpoltstein 17D2
**Am Main-Donau-Kanal**. **GPS:** n49,20455 e11,18813.

40 € 6. **Location:** Rural, simple, quiet. **Surface:** grassy.
15/04-15/10.
**Distance:** 1,9km Canal 1,9km 1km on the spot
on the spot.
**Remarks:** Service 2km.
**Tourist information Hilpoltstein:**
Burgfeste. Festival with events. beginning Aug.

### S Hirschaid 12D3
**Regnitz-Arena**, Georg-Kügel-Ring 3. **GPS:** n49,81180 e10,98620.

8 free € 1/80liter Ch € 0,50/kWh.
**Location:** Rural, simple, quiet. **Surface:** metalled. 01/01-31/12.
**Distance:** 600m on the spot 700m 900m on the spot
on the spot.
**Remarks:** At tennis-court, at swimming pool.

### S Hof/Saale 12E2
**Park Theresienstein**, Plauener Straße 54.
**GPS:** n50,32956 e11,92041.

10 free. **Location:** Urban, simple. **Surface:** metalled.
01/01-31/12.
**Distance:** 2,5km on the spot 1km.
**Remarks:** Max. 48h.

### Hof/Saale 12E2
**Utreusee**, Schaumberggrund. **GPS:** n50,28296 e11,91849.

10 ⬛free. **Location:** Rural, simple, isolated.
**Surface:** asphalted/metalled. ⬛ 01/01-31/12.
**Distance:** 6km ⬛350m ⬛on the spot ⊗50m ⬛500m ⬛on the spot ⬛on the spot.
**Remarks:** Max. 96h.

### Hof/Saale ⬛ 12E2
**Clean Park**, Ernst Reuterstrasse. **GPS:** n50,32641 e11,89248.⬆.

8 ⬛€5 ⬛€1 ⬛Ch ⬛€2 WC ⬛.
**Surface:** metalled. ⬛ 01/01-31/12.
**Distance:** 2km ⬛800m ⬛300m ⬛50m.
**Remarks:** Max. 72h.

**Tourist information Hof/Saale:**
⬛ Bürgerpark Theresienstein. Landscape park according English example. ⬛ 9-18h, winter 9-16h.
Untreusee. Lake with water sports.

### Hofheim in Unterfranken ⬛ 12C3
**Wohnmobilplatz Hofheim**, Johannisstraße 28.
**GPS:** n50,14185 e10,51957.⬆➡.

30 ⬛€8 ⬛€1/80liter ⬛Ch ⬛€0,50/kWh WC ⬛€2,50. ⬛
**Location:** Urban, comfortable. **Surface:** grasstiles.
⬛ 01/01-31/12.
**Distance:** 750m ⬛750m ⬛on the spot.
**Remarks:** At swimming pool, bread-service.

### Hohenberg/Eger ❄ 12E3
**Wiesenfestplatz**, Selberstrasse. **GPS:** n50,09762 e12,22085.⬆.

10-20 ⬛voluntary contribution ⬛Ch ⬛free WC.
**Location:** Rural, simple, quiet. **Surface:** metalled.
⬛ 01/01-31/12.
**Distance:** 200m ⬛50m ⬛100m ⬛50m ⬛50m.
**Remarks:** Beautiful view, porcelain museum.

### Hohenburg 17E1
**Sportplatz**, Sportplatzweg 1. **GPS:** n49,29194 e11,80917.⬆.

---

6 ⬛€8 ⬛€2 WC. **Surface:** metalled. ⬛ 01/01-31/12.
**Distance:** 1km ⬛1km.
**Remarks:** Parking at sports park.

### Immenstadt 20C2
**P 3 Viehmarktplatz**, Badeweg. **GPS:** n47,56192 e10,20857.⬆➡.

6 ⬛€8/24h ⬛ChWCincluded. ⬛ **Location:** Urban, simple, comfortable. **Surface:** asphalted. ⬛ 01/01-31/12.
**Distance:** ⬛700m.

### Ingolstadt ⬛ 17E3
**Parkplatz Hallenbad**, Jahnstrasse 9. **GPS:** n48,76025 e11,42038.⬆➡.

13 ⬛€5/24h ⬛€1/80liter ⬛€1 ⬛Ch ⬛€1 ⬛included ⬛.⬛
**Location:** Urban, comfortable. **Surface:** metalled.
⬛ 01/01-31/12.
**Distance:** ⬛on the spot ⬛1,6km ⬛on the spot ⬛on the spot ⬛on the spot ⬛on the spot.
**Remarks:** Parking at sports park, max. 3 days.

### Ingolstadt ⬛ 17E3
**Ingolstadt Village**, Marie-Curie-Straße 1.
**GPS:** n48,78556 e11,47750.⬆.

20 ⬛free. **Location:** Urban, simple. **Surface:** gravel.
⬛ 01/01-31/12.
**Distance:** 6km ⬛300m.
**Remarks:** Motorhome parking at Outlet.

### Inzell ⬛ 20G1
**Hausernhof**, Bichlstraße 24. **GPS:** n47,75948 e12,75252.⬆.

4 ⬛€10 + €1/pp tourist tax ⬛Ch ⬛€2/24h WC ⬛€1.
**Location:** Rural, simple, quiet. **Surface:** grassy. ⬛ 01/01-31/12.
**Distance:** 600m ⊗200m ⬛200m.

---

### Inzell ⬛ 20G1
**Camping Lindlbauer**, Kreuzfeldstraße 44.
**GPS:** n47,76717 e12,75417.⬆➡.

12 ⬛€15 ⬛Ch ⬛€2 WC ⬛included. **Location:** Rural, simple, quiet. **Surface:** metalled. ⬛ 01/01-31/12.
**Distance:** 750m ⬛1km ⬛on the spot ⬛on the spot.
**Remarks:** Max. 1 night, health resort 500m.

### Iphofen ⬛ 17C1
**Einesheimer Tor**, Ecke Einersheimer Straße/Stadtgraben Ost.
**GPS:** n49,70260 e10,26459.⬆.

9 ⬛free ⬛€1 ⬛Ch ⬛(6x)€1/12h WC. **Location:** Urban, simple.
**Surface:** gravel. ⬛ 01/01-31/12.
**Distance:** 200m ⊗200m ⬛700m.
**Remarks:** Parking at city wall.

### Ippesheim 17C1
**Kempe's Autohof Gollhofen**, Industriestraße 1.
**GPS:** n49,58546 e10,17579.

25 ⬛free WC €0,50 ⬛. **Location:** Motorway, simple.
**Surface:** asphalted. ⬛ 01/01-31/12.
**Distance:** ⬛1km ⊗on the spot.

### Kastl/Oberpfalz ⬛ 17E1
**Wanderparkplatz Am Alten Bahnhof**, Amberger Straße.
**GPS:** n49,36657 e11,68388.⬆.

5 ⬛free ⬛ WCfree. **Location:** Rural, simple, quiet.
**Surface:** gravel. ⬛ 01/01-31/12.
**Distance:** 200m ⊗200m ⬛100m ⬛50m ⬛on the spot ⬛on the spot.

### Kaufbeuren 20D1
**Wohnmobilplatz Kaufbeuren**, Buronstraße.
**GPS:** n47,89885 e10,61650.⬆➡.

8 ☝free 🚰🔌⚡Chfree ⚡(6x)€ 1/kWh. **Location:** Urban.
**Surface:** gravel. 🅾 01/01-31/12.
**Distance:** 🚶historical centre 3km 🚲1km.
**Remarks:** Max. 3 days.

**▣S** **Kelheim** 🚣 **17E2**
**Wohnmobilstellplatz "Am Pflegerspitz".**
**GPS:** n48,91331 e11,87657.⬆➡.

50 ☝€ 8,50 🚰€ 1/80liter 🔌Ch ⚡(18x)€ 0,50/kWh WC.
**Surface:** metalled. 🅾 01/01-31/12 🅾 service 01/11-31/03.
**Distance:** 🚶500m ⊗500m 🛒900m 🚲on the spot 🚶on the spot.
**Remarks:** Max. 3 nights, hindmost part, playground.

**▣S** **Kemnath** **12E3**
**Wohnmobilstellplatz Kemnath**, Am Eisweier 8.
**GPS:** n49,87219 e11,88774.⬆.

5 ☝free 🚰€ 1/80liter 🔌Ch ⚡(6x)€ 1/6h WC. **Location:** Simple,
quiet. **Surface:** grasstiles. 🅾 01/01-31/12.
**Distance:** 🚶650m 🚲on the spot ⊗650m 🛒650m.
**Remarks:** Max. 3 days.

**▣S** **Kempten** **20C2**
**Illerstadion**, Illerdamm/Jahnstrasse. **GPS:** n47,72915 e10,31940.⬆➡.

9 ☝€ 5 🚰€ 1/10minutes 🔌Ch.🚐 **Location:** Urban, simple, noisy.
**Surface:** metalled. 🅾 01/01-31/12.
**Distance:** 🚶500m 🚲2,7km.
**Remarks:** Max. 3 days.

**▣S** **Kiefersfelden** 🏔🚣❄ **20F2**
**Beim Schaupenwirt**, Kaiser-Franz-Josef-Allee 26.
**GPS:** n47,61828 e12,18096.⬆.
2 ☝free ⚡€ 3 🛢€ 5. **Location:** Simple, quiet. **Surface:** asphalted.
🅾 01/01-31/12.
**Distance:** 🚶500m 🛒1km.
**Remarks:** Max. 48h.

**▣S** **Kiefersfelden** 🏔🚣❄ **20F2**
**Hödenauer See**, Guggenauerweg 2. **GPS:** n47,62881 e12,18949.⬆➡.

10 ☝€ 8 WC 🛢€ 0,50. **Location:** Rural, simple, quiet.
**Surface:** grassy/gravel. 🅾 01/01-31/12.
**Distance:** 🚶2km 🚲3km 🏊on the spot 🚶on the spot ⊗50m
🛒300m.
**Remarks:** Max. 3 days, pay at Wasserskilift Hödenauersee.

**▣S** **Kiefersfelden** 🏔🚣❄ **20F2**
Bahnhofstrasse. **GPS:** n47,61057 e12,19125.⬆.

20 ☝€ 10. **Location:** Simple. **Surface:** asphalted. 🅾 01/01-31/12.
**Distance:** 🚶on the spot 🚲2km ⊗100m.
**Remarks:** Max. 3 days.

**▣S** **Kirchenlamitz** **12E3**
**Anfahrtsskizze**, Weißenstädter Straße.
**GPS:** n50,14905 e11,94055.⬆➡.

12 ☝free 🚰🔌Chfree ⚡voluntary contribution.
**Location:** Simple, quiet. **Surface:** asphalted. 🅾 01/01-31/12.
**Distance:** 🚶500m 🛒10m.

**▥S** **Kirchham** **17G3**
**Erlebnispark Haslinger Hof**, Ed 1. **GPS:** n48,34947 e13,29115.⬆.

25-30 ☝Overnight stay € 17 (incl. € 9 voucher) 🚰€ 1 🔌Ch.
**Location:** Rural, simple, quiet. **Surface:** gravel.
🅾 01/01-31/12.
**Distance:** ⊗on the spot.

**▣S** **Kitzingen** 🚣 **17C1**
**Wohnmobilpark Am Main**, Bleichwasen, Etwashausen.
**GPS:** n49,74274 e10,16491.⬆.

70 ☝€ 9 🚰€ 1/80liter 🔌Ch ⚡€ 0,50/kWh WC.
**Location:** Simple. **Surface:** asphalted. 🅾 01/01-31/12.
**Distance:** 🚶300m 🏊on the spot 🚶on the spot ⊗300m 🛒300m
🚲on the spot.

**Remarks:** Between Alter Mainbrücke and Nordbrücke, max. 3 nights,
bread-service.

**▣S** **Klingenberg** ⚓🚣 **17A1**
**Sonja's Wohnmobilhafen**, Zur Einladung.
**GPS:** n49,78370 e9,17805.⬆.

55 ☝€ 7,50 🚰€ 1/80liter 🔌Ch ⚡(50x)€ 2/day.🚐
**Location:** Rural, comfortable, quiet. **Surface:** grassy/gravel.
🅾 01/03-29/10.
**Distance:** 🚶500m 🚲on the spot ⊗500m 🛒2km 🚲on the spot
🚶on the spot.
**Remarks:** Check in on arrival, service passerby € 2.

**▣S** **Königsberg** 🌿🌳 **12C3**
Buchweg. **GPS:** n50,08472 e10,57028.⬆➡.

6 ☝free 🚰🔌. **Location:** Rural, simple, quiet. **Surface:** metalled.
🅾 01/01-31/12.
**Distance:** 🚶300m ⊗300m 🛒300m 🚐400m 🚲on the spot 🚶on
the spot.
**Remarks:** Parking sports park.

**▣S** **Königsbrunn** **20D1**
**Am Thermengelände**, Königsallee. **GPS:** n48,27243 e10,88283.⬆➡.

12 ☝€ 6/24h 🚰€ 1/80liter 🔌Ch ⚡(12x)€ 0,50/kWh.
**Location:** Urban, simple, noisy. **Surface:** metalled.
🅾 01/01-31/12.
**Distance:** 🚶1km 🛒1km.

**▣S** **Kreuth** 🌳 **20E2**
**Wildbad Kreuth**, Bremerweg. **GPS:** n47,62597 e11,74681.⬆.

8 ☝€ 5. 🚐 **Location:** Rural, simple. **Surface:** gravel/sand.
🅾 01/01-31/12.
**Distance:** 🚶2km ⊗1,5km 🚐50m 🚲on the spot 🚶on the spot.
**Remarks:** Max. 1 day.

**▣S** **Kreuzwertheim** 🚣 **17B1**
**Am Mainufer**, Fährgasse. **GPS:** n49,76251 e9,51840.⬆.

**DE**

15 ⌂ € 8 ⌐ € 2/160liter ⊟ChWC. ⚿ **Location:** Urban, simple, quiet.
**Surface:** gravel. ▣ 01/01-31/12.
**Distance:** ⌂Wertheim centre 1,2km ⌂on the spot ⊗600m
⌂on the spot.
**Remarks:** Along Main river, max. 1 night.

| ⊞S | Kronach | 12D3 |
|---|---|---|

**Hammermühle**, Am Sand. **GPS:** n50,23096 e11,32828. ⬆➡.

10 ⌂ € 5/24h ⌐ € 1 ⊟Ch ⚡(12x)€ 0,50/kWh. ⌂
**Location:** Rural, simple. **Surface:** asphalted.
**Distance:** ⌂10min ⌂on the spot ⊗200m ⌂300m.

| ⊞S | Kronach | 12D3 |
|---|---|---|

**Lucky Stable Ranch**, Mostrach 1. **GPS:** n50,21840 e11,34012. ⬆➡.

5 ⌂ € 5, 2 pers.incl ⌐ ⊟ ⚿ WCincluded ⌂€ 1,50 ▣€ 1,50 ⟋ ⌂
**Location:** Rural, simple, isolated, quiet. **Surface:** grassy/metalled.
▣ 01/01-31/12.
**Distance:** ⌂2km ⌂on the spot ⊗on the spot ⌂2km.
**Remarks:** At manege.

| ⊞S | Krün ⚘ ⛰ ⌂ ❄ | 20E2 |
|---|---|---|

**Tennsee Reisemobilhafen**, Am Tennsee 1.
**GPS:** n47,49083 e11,25444. ⬆➡.

37 ⌂ € 15-24 + tourist tax € 2/pp, Umwelttaxe € 0,70/pp ⌐ ⚿
⊟Ch ⚡€ 0,75/kWh WC⌂included ▣€ 3 ⟋€ 3/h. ⌂
**Location:** Rural, luxurious, quiet. **Surface:** grassy/gravel.
▣ 01/01-31/12 ▣ 04/11-15/12.
**Distance:** ⌂2,5km ⌂800m ⌂3km ⊗on the spot ⌂on the spot
⌂100m ⌂on the spot ⌂on the spot ⟋5km ⟋300m.
**Remarks:** Dog € 4.

| ⊞S | Kulmbach ⚘ ⌂ | 12D3 |
|---|---|---|

**Wohnmobilstellplatz Kulmbach**, Am Schwedensteg.
**GPS:** n50,11130 e11,46118. ⬆➡.

25 ⌂ € 3 ⌐ € 1/100liter ⊟Ch ⚡(25x)€ 1/2kWh. ⌂
**Location:** Urban, simple. **Surface:** gravel.
▣ 01/01-31/12 ▣ water disconnected in winter.
**Distance:** ⌂on the spot ⌂50m ⊗200m ⌂500m ⌂on the spot
⌂on the spot ⌂200m.

| ⊞S | Kümmersbruck | 17E1 |
|---|---|---|

**Wohnmobilstellplatz Kümmersbruck**, Am Butzenweg 33.
**GPS:** n49,41978 e11,89651. ⬆.

8 ⌂free. **Location:** Rural, simple, quiet. **Surface:** metalled.
▣ 01/01-31/12.
**Distance:** ⌂1km ⊗on the spot ⌂1,5km ⌂400m.
**Remarks:** At sports centre.

| ⊞S | Laberweinting | 17F2 |
|---|---|---|

**Waldgasthof**, Hart 1. **GPS:** n48,77148 e12,34414. ⬆.
25 ⌂ € 5 ⌐ ⊟Ch ⚡⌂. **Location:** Simple, isolated.
**Surface:** asphalted. ▣ 01/01-31/12.
**Distance:** ⌂4km ⊗on the spot.

| ⊞S | Lalling | 17G2 |
|---|---|---|

**Lalling-Freizeitgelände**, Waldstrasse. **GPS:** n48,84139 e13,13778. ⬆.

2 ⌂free ⌐ € 1/80liter ⊟Ch ⚡€ 3/day. **Location:** Rural, simple,
quiet. **Surface:** metalled/sand. ▣ 01/01-31/12.
**Distance:** ⌂2km ⊗800m.
**Remarks:** At tennis-courts.

| ⊞S | Lalling | 17G2 |
|---|---|---|

**Wohnmobilstellplatz Weber**, Euschertsfurth 34.
**GPS:** n48,83222 e13,14444. ➡.

8 ⌂ € 10 ⌐ ⊟Ch ⚡(10x)€ 0,30/kWh WC⌂€ 1,50. ⌂
**Location:** Rural, comfortable, quiet. **Surface:** grassy/metalled.
▣ 01/04-30/11.
**Distance:** ⌂1,5km ⊗100m.
**Remarks:** Swimming pool incl.

| S | Lalling | 17G2 |
|---|---|---|

**Ferienbauernhof Sieglinde**, Obstgarten 13, Hunding.
**GPS:** n48,84502 e13,14939. ⬆.

3 ⌂ € 5 ⌐ ⊟Chincluded ⚡(2x)€ 2/day WC⌂.
**Location:** Rural, simple, quiet. **Surface:** grassy. ▣ 01/04-31/12.
**Distance:** ⊗700m.

| ⊞S | Lalling | 17G2 |
|---|---|---|

**Lallinger Hof**, Hauptstrasse 23. **GPS:** n48,84560 e13,13851. ⬆.

4 ⌂guests free, € 5 ⚿against payment.
**Location:** Rural, simple, quiet. ▣ 01/04-31/10.
**Distance:** ⌂250m ⊗250m ⌂500m.
**Remarks:** Check in at restaurant.

| ⊞S | Lalling | 17G2 |
|---|---|---|

**Feng Shui Kurpark**, Euschertsfurther Straße.
**GPS:** n48,84137 e13,13952. ⬆.

10 ⌂ € 1 ⌐ ⊟Ch. **Location:** Simple, quiet. **Surface:** gravel/sand.
▣ 01/01-31/12.
**Distance:** ⌂on the spot ⊗600m.
**Remarks:** Not indicated.

| ⊞S | Lalling | 17G2 |
|---|---|---|

**Erikas Wohlfühlplatz**, Kleinfeld 6, Hunding.
**GPS:** n48,84333 e13,17944. ⬆.

10 ⌂ € 5 + €0,50/pp ⌐ ⚡(10x)€ 1/day WC⌂€ 4. **Location:** Rural,
simple, quiet. **Surface:** grassy/sand. ▣ 01/04-31/10.
**Distance:** ⌂250m ⌂on the spot ⌂on the spot ⊗3km ⌂200m
⟋on the spot ⟋on the spot.
**Remarks:** Check in at Kleinfeld 6.

| ⊞S | Landau/Isar | 17F3 |
|---|---|---|

**Am Festplatz**, Harburger Straße 20/B20.
**GPS:** n48,67712 e12,68323. ⬆➡.

± 20 ⌂free ⌐ € 0,50/100liter ⊟Ch ⚡(6x)€ 0,50/kWh.
**Surface:** grassy/gravel. ▣ 01/01-31/12.

**Distance:** 🚐1,5km ✈2,3km ⊗McDonalds 200m 🛒bakery 200m.

### 🅂 Landau/Isar 17F3

**Vilstaler Hof**, Andreasstraße 2. **GPS:** n48,60972 e12,69528.⬆.
15 🚐€ 10, dog € 7 🚰€ 1/100liter 🔌Ch€ 5 ✎included WC 🚿€ 3 📶.
**Location:** Rural. **Surface:** gravel/metalled. ⬛ 01/01-31/12.
**Distance:** 🚐7km ⊗on the spot.
**Remarks:** Breakfast-service.

### 🅂 Landsberg am Lech 🍲 20D1

**Waitzinger Wiese**, Gottesackerangerweg.
**GPS:** n48,05534 e10,87371.⬆.

8 🚐€ 7/24h 🚰€ 1/50liter 🔌Ch ✎(8x)€ 1/6h WC€ 0,50. 🚐
**Location:** Urban, simple. **Surface:** metalled. ⬛ 01/01-31/12.
**Distance:** 🚐400m ⊗300m.

### 🅂 Lauingen 17C3

**E-Park-Eisenbahn-Erlebnispark**, Riedhauser Straße 60.
**GPS:** n48,57237 e10,42187.⬆.

29 🚐€ 5/24h 🚰€ 1/5minutes 🔌€ 1 Ch ✎(8x)€ 0,50/kWh
WC✎included. 🚿 **Location:** Simple. **Surface:** metalled.
⬛ 01/01-31/12.
**Distance:** 🚐750m.
**Remarks:** Railroad theme park.

### 🅂 Lechbruck am See 🏵⬆🍴❄ 20D2

**Wohnmobilpark via Claudia**, Via Claudia 6.
**GPS:** n47,71556 e10,82139.⬆➡.

52 🚐€ 11,50, 2 pers. incl., dog € 3-3,50 🚰Ch ✎included
WC€ 1,50 ⚡€ 2,50 📶€ 3/24h. 🚿🚲
**Location:** Rural, comfortable. **Surface:** gravel. ⬛ 01/01-31/12.
**Distance:** 🚐5km ⛱on the spot ➤on the spot ⊗on the spot 🛒on
the spot 🚌on the spot 🚵10km 🚶on the spot.

### 🅂 Lenggries 🏵❄ 20E2

Dürrachstrasse, Fall. **GPS:** n47,57039 e11,53380.⬆➡.

25 🚐€ 0,50/h, € 4/24h 🚰€ 2 🔌WC. 🚐
**Location:** Rural, isolated, quiet. **Surface:** metalled.
⬛ 01/01-31/12 ⚙ service: 01/11-01/04.
**Distance:** 🚐250m ⛱250m 🛒150m 🚌8km 🚵on the spot 🚶on
the spot.
**Remarks:** Max. 7 days.

### 🅂 Leupoldsgrün 12E2

**Am Anger**, Hauptstraße 48. **GPS:** n50,29389 e11,79961.⬆.

8 🚐free 🚰€ 0,50/50liter 🔌Ch ✎€ 0,50/kWh 📶.
**Location:** Urban, simple. **Surface:** metalled. ⬛ 01/01-31/12.
**Distance:** 🚐100m ✈1km ⊗150m 🛒bakery 50m.
**Remarks:** At fire-station, charging point for electric bicycles.

### 🅂 Lindau 🏖🚣 20B2

**Blauwiese, P1. GPS:** n47,55869 e9,70130.⬆➡.

30 🚐€ 1/h, € 20/24h 🚰€ 0,50 🔌€ 0,50 ChWC. 🚣
**Location:** Simple. **Surface:** metalled. ⬛ 01/01-31/12.
**Distance:** 🚐on the spot ⛱1km ➤1km 🛒500m 🚌500m 🚌on the
spot.
**Remarks:** Max. 24h.

### 🅒🅂 Lindau 🏖🚣 20B2

**Gitzenweiler Hof**, Gitzenweiler 88. **GPS:** n47,58475 e9,70673.
17 🚐€ 17,50 + tourist tax 🚰Ch ✎WC✎included 📶.
**Location:** Rural, comfortable, quiet. **Surface:** asphalted/metalled.
⬛ 01/01-31/12.
**Distance:** ⊗150m.
**Remarks:** Max. 1 night, free entrance swimming pool.

### 🅒🅂 Lindau 🏖🚣 20B2

**Park Camping**, Frauenhoferstrasse 20. **GPS:** n47,53764 e9,73148.

12 🚐€ 12/24h 🚰🔌ChWC✎included, on camp site 📶.
**Location:** Urban, comfortable, quiet. **Surface:** gravel.
⬛ 15/03-31/10.
**Distance:** ⊗600m ⛱2km 🚌on the spot.
**Remarks:** Max. 24h.

**Tourist information Lindau:**
👁 Lindau Insel. Promenade along the lake with Mangturm, 700 years
old lighthouse.

### 🅂 Litzendorf 12D3

**ASV Naisa**, Am Wetterkreuz. **GPS:** n49,91559 e11,00261.⬆.

8 🚐free. **Location:** Rural, simple, quiet. **Surface:** gravel.
⬛ 01/01-31/12.
**Distance:** 🚐on the spot ⊗on the spot 🛒1km 🚌200m 🚵on the spot
🚶on the spot.

### 🅂 Litzendorf 12D3

**Tiefenellern**, Ellerbergstrasse. **GPS:** n49,91927 e11,07006.

3 🚐free. **Location:** Rural, simple, isolated. **Surface:** gravel.
⬛ 01/01-31/12.
**Distance:** 🚵on the spot 🚶on the spot.

### 🅒🅂 Lohr/Main 🚵🚣 12B3

**Lohr am Main**, Osttangente. **GPS:** n49,99429 e9,58053.⬆.

21 🚐free, night € 5 🚰€ 1/100liter 🔌Ch ✎(22x)€ 2/8h
WC 📶€ 2/h. 🚐 **Location:** Urban, simple, noisy. **Surface:** metalled.
⬛ 01/04-31/10.
**Distance:** 🚐300m ➤on the spot 🛒Aldi 800m.
**Remarks:** Along Main river, max. 3 days.

### 🅒🅂 Mainbernheim 🏵 17C1

Goldgrubenweg. **GPS:** n49,71153 e10,22045.⬆➡.

10 🚐free 🚰€ 1,25/100liter 🔌Ch ✎€ 0,50/kWh.
**Location:** Urban, simple, quiet. **Surface:** metalled.
⬛ 01/01-31/12.
**Distance:** 🚐on the spot ⊗200m 🛒200m 🚵100m.

### 🅒🅂 Mainstockheim 🚣 17C1

**Wohnmobilhafen Mainstockheim**, Albertshöfer straße.
**GPS:** n49,77173 e10,15595.⬆➡.

37 🚐€ 7 🚰🔌Ch ✎included. 🚐 **Location:** Rural, simple, quiet.
**Surface:** gravel. ⬛ 01/01-31/12.
**Distance:** 🚐on the spot ⛱5km ⛱on the spot ⊗100m 🛒100m
🚵on the spot.
**Remarks:** Along Main river.

### 🅒🅂 Manching 17E3

**Am Braunweiher**, Am Keltenwall. **GPS:** n48,71078 e11,49602.⬆.

30 🚐free 🚰€ 1/100liter 🔌Ch. **Location:** Simple, noisy.
**Surface:** grasstiles/metalled. ⬛ 01/01-31/12.
**Distance:** 🚐1,5km ✈1,3km ⊗800m 🛒Edeka 1km.

DE

**Remarks:** Max. 2 days.

## Markt Wald · 20C1

**Wohnmobilpark Markt Wald**, Bürgle 1a.
**GPS**: n48,14602 e10,57517.

20 €8 € 1/100liter Ch (10x)€ 0,50/kWh WC € 2/pppd.
**Location:** Rural, comfortable, quiet. **Surface:** grassy/gravel.
01/01-31/12.
**Distance:** 1km on the spot on the spot 1km 200m on the spot on the spot.
**Remarks:** At small lake, bread-service, use sanitary facilities at campsite.

## Marktbreit · 17C1

**An den Mainwiesen**, Marktstefter Straße 1.
**GPS**: n49,67250 e10,15028.

18 €7,50 € 1/100liter Ch € 1/kWh included.
**Location:** Rural, comfortable, quiet.
**Surface:** grassy.
01/01-31/12.
**Distance:** 1km on the spot 900m on the spot on the spot.
**Remarks:** Along Main river, at restaurants, playground.

## Marktheidenfeld · 17B1

**Martinswiese**, Georg-Mayr-Straße. **GPS**: n49,84918 e9,59887.

30 €5/24h € 1/100liter Ch (18x)€ 1/4h WCincluded.
**Location:** Rural, comfortable, quiet. **Surface:** gravel.
01/01-31/12 during event.
**Distance:** 600m on the spot on the spot 200m Lidl 650m on the spot on the spot.
**Remarks:** Along Main river, max. 2 nights.

## Marktheidenfeld · 17B1

Georg-Mayr-Straße. **GPS**: n49,85364 e9,60025.

20 free. **Location:** Rural, simple, noisy. **Surface:** gravel.
01/01-31/12.
**Distance:** 1km 50m Lidl 50m.
**Remarks:** Max. 3 days.

## Marktheidenfeld · 17B1

**Landgasthof Baumhof-Tenne**, Baumhofstraße 147.
**GPS**: n49,84401 e9,63104.

10 €5, free with a meal € 1/100liter € 3/day WC free.
**Location:** Rural, comfortable, quiet. **Surface:** gravel.
01/01-31/12 Mon, Tue.
**Distance:** on the spot on the spot on the spot.
**Remarks:** Max. 3 days, bread-service + breakfast-service.

## Marktleuthen · 12E3

Am Angerparkplatz. **GPS**: n50,12946 e11,99483.

10 free Ch (10x)free WC € 0,50.
**Location:** Urban, simple, quiet. **Surface:** metalled. 01/01-31/12.
**Distance:** 250m 150m 200m.
**Remarks:** Max. 7 days, bread-service.

## Marktoberdorf · 20D2

**Parkplatz der Bayerischen Musikakademie**, Kurfürstenstraße 19.
**GPS**: n47,78013 e10,62284.

4 free € 1/50liter Ch € 0,50/kWh. **Surface:** grasstiles.
01/01-31/12.
**Distance:** on the spot 100m.

## Marktredwitz · 12E3

**Wohnmobilstellplatz am Auenpark**, Dörflaser Platz, Fabrikstraße.
**GPS**: n49,99500 e12,08150.

20 free € 0,50/150liter € 0,50 Ch€ 0,50 (6x)€ 0,50/kWh.
**Location:** Rural, simple. **Surface:** asphalted/gravel.
01/01-31/12.
**Distance:** 300m 50m 150m.
**Remarks:** At sports park, at tennis-court.

## Massing · 17F3

**Am Freilichtmuseum**, Spirknerstraße. **GPS**: n48,39528 e12,60056.
10 free on demand. **Location:** Simple.
**Surface:** grassy/metalled.
01/01-31/12.
**Distance:** 1km Museumstüberl 500m.
**Remarks:** Open air museum, max. 24h, busy parking during the day.

## Mehlmeisel · 12E3

**Parkplatz Am Park**, Am Park. **GPS**: n49,97615 e11,85471.

5 free. **Location:** Urban, simple. **Surface:** metalled.
01/01-31/12.
**Distance:** on the spot 250m bakery 100m on the spot on the spot.
**Remarks:** Max. 3 nights.

## Mellrichstadt · 12C2

Malbachweg. **GPS**: n50,43139 e10,30972.

7 free € 1/80liter Ch (7x)€ 0,50/kWh. **Location:** Urban, simple, quiet. **Surface:** asphalted. 01/01-31/12.
**Distance:** 500m 750m 750m on the spot on the spot.
**Remarks:** Max. 3 days.

## Memmelsdorf · 12D3

**Seehofblick**, Pödeldorferstrasse 20-A. **GPS**: n49,92906 e10,95594.

4 €5 € 1/80liter Chincluded € 1/8h.
**Location:** Urban, simple. **Surface:** asphalted.
01/04-31/10.
**Distance:** on the spot 1km 250m on the spot on the spot.
**Remarks:** At football ground.

## Memmelsdorf · 12D3

**Stocksee**, Stockseestrasse. **GPS**: n49,92556 e10,93417.

5 €5 € 1/80liter Chfree (4x)€ 1/8h. **Location:** Urban.
**Surface:** asphalted. 01/01-31/12.
**Distance:** 1,2km 500m 100m.

## Miltenberg · 17A1

**Busparkplatz Ecke**, Jahnstrasse/Luitpoldstrasse.
**GPS**: n49,70464 e9,25860.

10 free. **Location:** Urban, simple, central. **Surface:** asphalted.
01/01-31/12.
**Distance:** 200m 200m 200m.

**Remarks:** Only overnight stays 17-10h.

### 🏕 Miltenberg 🌿⛲🏖 17A1

**Hallenfreibad Miltenberg**, Jahnstraße 1.
**GPS:** n49,70694 e9,26027.⬆

20 🚐free. **Location:** Urban, simple, noisy. **Surface:** metalled.
◻ 01/01-31/12.
**Distance:** 🚶500m ⊗200m 🛒200m 🚲on the spot 🧍on the spot.
**Remarks:** At swimming pool.

### ⚓ Miltenberg 🌿⛲🏖 17A1

**Am Yachthafen**, Steingässerstrasse. **GPS:** n49,70446 e9,25435.⬆

20 🚐free. **Location:** Rural, simple. **Surface:** grassy/gravel.
◻ 01/01-31/12.
**Distance:** 🚶800m 🛍on the spot ⊗800m 🛒500m 🚲on the spot
🚲on the spot.
**Remarks:** Along Main river.

### 🏕S Mistelgau 🍽 12D3

**Therme Obernsees**, An der Therme 1, Obernsees.
**GPS:** n49,91630 e11,37831.⬆

40 🚐€ 10, dog € 1,50 🔌€ 1/50liter 🍴Ch 🚿€ 1/12h,10Amp WC 🚽 ⊡.
🐕 **Location:** Rural, luxurious, quiet. **Surface:** grasstiles/metalled.
◻ 01/01-31/12.
**Distance:** 🚶1km ⊗Therme-Bistro ⊡on the spot 🚃on the spot
🚲on the spot 🧍on the spot.
**Remarks:** Bread-service, discount on access terme.

### 🏕S Mittenwald 🍽 20E2

**Wohnmobil-Stellplatz Karwendel**, Albert-Schott-Straße.
**GPS:** n47,43792 e11,26411.⬆➡

30 🚐€ 8,40/24h, tourist tax € 4,60/pp 🔌€ 1/100liter 🍴Ch
🚿(30x)€ 0,80/kWh. 🚽 **Location:** Rural, simple, noisy.
**Surface:** asphalted/gravel. ◻ 01/01-31/12.
**Distance:** 🚶250m ⊗200m 🚃on the spot.
**Remarks:** Along railwayline.

### 🏕S Mittenwald 🍽 20E2

**Hotel Jägerhof**, Partenkirchner Straße 35. **GPS:** n47,44652 e11,26440.
3 🚐€ 5/night 🔌. **Surface:** asphalted. ◻ 01/01-31/12.
**Distance:** 🚶600m ⊗500m.
**Remarks:** Free with a meal in hotel.

---

### 🏕S Mitterteich 12E3

**Freizeithugl Großbüchlberg**, Großbüchlberg 32.
**GPS:** n49,97286 e12,22496.

24 🚐€ 14, 2 pers. incl., dog € 1,50 🔌Ch 🚿(16x)€ 0,50
WC 🚽included ⊡€ 2,50/2,50 💧€ 1/24h. **Location:** Rural, luxurious,
isolated. **Surface:** metalled. ◻ 01/01-31/12.
**Distance:** ⊗200m.
**Remarks:** Bread-service.

### 🏕S Monheim 🌿⛲🍽 17D2

**An der Stadthalle**, Schulstraße. **GPS:** n48,84503 e10,85329.⬆

7 🚐free 🔌€ 1/100liter 🍴Ch 🚿(8x)€ 1/10h.
**Location:** Simple, central, quiet. **Surface:** grasstiles.
◻ 01/01-31/12.
**Distance:** 🚶400m ⊗500m 🛒500m.

### 🏕 Moosbach ⛰🍽 17F1

**Am Natur-Waldbad Tröbes**, Tröbes 38. **GPS:** n49,55851 e12,44074.⬆
9 🚐€ 10 🔌Ch 🚿WC 🚽. 🚰 **Location:** Rural, comfortable, quiet.
**Surface:** grassy. ◻ 01/03-31/10.
**Distance:** 🚶700m 🛍on the spot ⊗500m.
**Remarks:** Bread-service.

### 🏕 Moosbach ⛰🍽 17F1

**Bei der Wieskirche**, Am Badeweiher Tröbes, Friedhofgasse.
**GPS:** n49,59076 e12,41193.⬆➡

6 🚐€ 5 🔌Ch 🚿included. **Location:** Simple, quiet.
**Surface:** gravel. ◻ 01/03-31/10.
**Distance:** 🚶250m ⊗250m 🛒250m.
**Remarks:** Check in at Gästeinformation.

### 🏕S Mörnsheim 17D2

**Wohnmobilstellplatz Hammermühle**, Altendorf.
**GPS:** n48,87455 e11,02948.⬆➡

21 🚐€ 10, dog € 1 🔌Chincluded 🚿(21x)€ 0,60/kWh WC 🚽€ 2.
🚰 **Location:** Rural, comfortable, quiet. **Surface:** unpaved.
◻ 01/04-31/10.
**Distance:** 🚶Altendorf 2km 🍴on the spot ⊗Imbiss, Biergarten
🚲on the spot 🧍on the spot.
**Remarks:** Nature reserve Altmühltal, caution € 5, bread-service.

### 🏕S Münchberg 12E3

Schützenstraße 26b. **GPS:** n50,19978 e11,79519.⬆➡

---

9 🚐free 🔌Ch 🚿(8x). **Location:** Urban, simple, quiet.
**Surface:** asphalted. ◻ 01/01-31/12.
**Distance:** 🚶1km ⊗100m 🛒500m on the spot 🧍on the spot
🚲on the spot 🐕on the spot.
**Remarks:** At sports grounds, at swimming pool.

### 🏕S München 20E1

**Allianz-Arena Wohnmobilstellplätze**, Werner-Heisenberg-Allee 25,
Munich (München). **GPS:** n48,22089 e11,62505.⬆

110 🚐€ 15 🔌€ 1/100liter 🚿(10x)€ 1/kWh.
**Location:** Simple. **Surface:** asphalted.
◻ 01/01-31/12 ⊡ during event.
**Distance:** 🚶13km ⊗Bistro-Biergarten 🚃on the spot 🚲on the spot.
**Remarks:** Outside environmental zone, FC Bayern Erlebniswelt
(Fanmuseum).

### 🏕S München 20E1

**Oktoberfest-Camping**, De-Gasperi-Bogen, München-Riem, Munich
(München). **GPS:** n48,13342 e11,70746.⬆.
1000 🚐€ 35, 2 pers.incl, extra pers € 15 🔌🍴Ch 🚿WC 🚽included.
**Location:** Urban, comfortable, central, noisy.
**Surface:** metalled.
◻ Oktoberfest.
**Distance:** 🚶11km ⊗on the spot 🛒on the spot 🚃metro 300m.
**Remarks:** Opened 2 days before Oktoberfest, outside environmental
zone.

**Tourist information Munich (München):**

ℹ München CityTourCard. Card gives for free entrance on among other
things public transport and 50% discounts on curiosities.
🎫 € 10,90/day, € 20,90/3 days.
👁 Agustinerbräu, Neuhauserstrasse 16. Brewery from 1644.
✖ Schloß Nymphenburg. Former summer residence of the Witelbacher
monarchs. 🕐 Tue-Su 9-12.30h, 13.30-17h. 🎫 € 6.
⌒ Neumarkt. Ruins of citadel dominating the city.
✳ Oktoberfest. Beer festival, special motorhome parking.

### 🏕S Münnerstadt 12C3

**An der Lache, P1**, Seminarstrasse. **GPS:** n50,25188 e10,19348.⬆➡

4 🚐free 🔌€ 1/90liter 🍴Ch 🚿(4x)€ 0,50/kWh,16Amp WC 🚽.
**Location:** Urban, simple, quiet. **Surface:** metalled.
◻ 01/01-31/12.
**Distance:** 🚶350m.
**Remarks:** Max. 3 days.

### 🏕 Münnerstadt 12C3

**Am Oberen Tor, P2**, Dr. Engelhardt Weg. **GPS:** n50,24914 e10,19145.

DE

2 ⬛free. **Location:** Urban, simple, noisy. **Surface:** metalled.
⬛ 01/01-31/12.
**Distance:** 🚰on the spot 🛒on the spot.

### Murnau am Staffelsee ⬛S 20D2
**Am P&R Bahnhof**, Am Bahnhof. **GPS:** n47,68005 e11,19447. ⬆➡.

6 ⬛€ 1/24h 🚰€ 1/100liter 🗑Ch 💧(6x)€ 1/2kWh.
**Location:** Rural, comfortable, central, noisy.
**Surface:** grasstiles/metalled. ⬛ 01/01-31/12.
**Distance:** 🚰500m 10km ✖400m 🛒300m 🚽on the spot.
**Remarks:** Max. 72h.

### Naila ⬛S 12E2
Christian-Schlicht-strasse. **GPS:** n50,33071 e11,71127. ⬆.

4 ⬛free 🚰€ 1 Ch€ 1. **Location:** Urban, simple. **Surface:** metalled.
⬛ 01/01-31/12.
**Distance:** 🚰100m 50m ✖300m 🛒300m 🚲on the spot 🚶on the spot.
**Remarks:** Parking left side of the station, thursday market.

### Naila ⬛S 12E2
Badstraße. **GPS:** n50,32965 e11,70108. ⬆.

10 ⬛free. **Location:** Urban, simple, isolated. **Surface:** asphalted.
⬛ 01/01-31/12.
**Distance:** 🚰650m ✖600m 🛒500m.
**Remarks:** Max. 2 days, thursday market.

### Nesselwang ⬛S 20C2
**An der Riese**, Altspitzbahn. **GPS:** n47,61995 e10,49830. ⬆➡.

70 ⬛€ 10 🚰Ch💧(62x)€ 1/kWh 📶included. 🚾
**Location:** Rural, comfortable.
**Surface:** gravel/metalled.
⬛ 01/01-31/12.

**Distance:** 🚰500m ✖3,8km 1km 3km ✖200m 🛒500m
🚐500m 🚶on the spot 200m 200m.
**Remarks:** Baker every morning, code internet at tourist office.

### Neualbenreuth ⬛S 12F3
**Reisemobilhafen Sibyllenbad**, Parkplatz P2, Kurallee.
**GPS:** n49,98099 e12,42406. ⬆.

21 ⬛€ 10 + € 1/pp tourist tax 🚰Ch💧(20x)€ 0,50/kWh WC.
**Location:** Rural, simple, isolated, quiet. **Surface:** metalled.
⬛ 01/01-31/12.
**Distance:** 🚰1,5km ✖1,5km.
**Remarks:** Bread-service.

### Neubeuern 20F2
**P2**, Am Sportplatz. **GPS:** n47,77573 e12,14298. ⬆.

3 ⬛free. **Location:** Rural, simple, quiet. **Surface:** gravel.
⬛ 01/01-31/12.
**Distance:** 🚰500m ✖500m.
**Remarks:** Max. 48h.

### Neuburg/Donau ⬛S 17D3
**Parkplatz P1, Schlösslwiese**, Zur Ringmeierbucht.
**GPS:** n48,74022 e11,18434. ⬆.

30 ⬛free 🚰€ 1/100liter 🗑Ch. **Location:** Urban, simple, central,
quiet. **Surface:** gravel/sand. ⬛ 01/01-31/12.
**Distance:** 🚰on the spot ✖100m 🛒400m on the spot 🚶on the
spot.
**Remarks:** On the Danube river.

### Neumarkt/Oberpfalz 17E1
**Volksfestplatz**, Woffenbacherstrasse 38. **GPS:** n49,28118 e11,44528. ⬆.

25 ⬛free. **Location:** Simple. **Surface:** grassy/gravel.
⬛ 01/01-31/12 ⬛ Jura-Volksfest.
**Distance:** 🚰600m ✖200m 🛒1km.
**Remarks:** At sports centre.

### Neumarkt/Oberpfalz ⬛S 17E1
**Fritz Berger**, Fritz-Berger-Str. 1. **GPS:** n49,30500 e11,48444. ⬆.

⬛free 🚰Ch💧free. **Surface:** grassy. ⬛ 01/01-31/12.
**Distance:** 🚰2km 🛒2km.

### Neuötting ⬛S 20G1
Landshuter Straße. **GPS:** n48,24023 e12,67521.
4 ⬛free 🚰Ch💧. **Location:** Rural. **Surface:** grassy/gravel.
⬛ 01/01-31/12.
**Distance:** 🚰800m ✖700m 🛒100m.
**Remarks:** Playground.

### Neusäß 17D3
**Titania-Therme**, Birkenallee 1. **GPS:** n48,40089 e10,82508. ⬆.

5 ⬛free. **Location:** Urban, simple, central, quiet. **Surface:** metalled.
⬛ 01/01-31/12.
**Distance:** 🚰1,2km 3km 🛒1,2km on the spot 🚶on the spot.

### Neustadt/Aisch ⬛S 17C1
**Am Festplatz**, Bei den Sommerkellern. **GPS:** n49,58187 e10,60271. ⬆.

16 ⬛free 🚰€ 1 Ch💧€ 1. **Surface:** gravel. ⬛ 01/01-31/12.
**Distance:** 🚰500m 500m ✖500m 🛒500m on the spot
🚶on the spot.

### Neustadt/Aisch ⬛S 17C1
**Am Sportzentrum**, Eilersweg 1. **GPS:** n49,57630 e10,63250. ⬆➡.

8 ⬛€ 8/night 🚰€ 1/100liter 🗑Ch€ 0,50 💧(12x)€ 2/night € 1.
**Location:** Rural, simple, quiet. **Surface:** gravel/metalled.
⬛ 01/04-15/10.
**Distance:** 🚰500m ✖700m 🛒750m 1km 🚶on the spot.
**Remarks:** Nearby sports complex.

### Neustadt/Aisch 17C1
**Am Waldwad**, Eilersweg 5. **GPS:** n49,57462 e10,62993. ⬆➡.

6 ⬛free. **Location:** Rural. **Surface:** grasstiles.
⬛ 01/01-31/12.

**Distance:** 🛒3,5km ⊗4km ⛽4km 🚄1km 🚶 on the spot.
**Remarks:** At sports centre, at swimming pool.

### 📷S Niederwerrn 12C3
Jahnstrasse. **GPS:** n50,06073 e10,17526. ⬆️

35 🚐 voluntary contribution 🔌€ 3 🚰Ch 🚿WC 🚽.
**Location:** Urban, simple. **Surface:** asphalted. 📅 01/01-31/12.
**Distance:** 🛒on the spot ⊗on the spot 🚲on the spot.
**Remarks:** Near sports fields, max. 3 nights.

### 📷S Nordheim am Main 🚤 12C3
Zehnthofstrasse. **GPS:** n49,85952 e10,17909. ⬆️

50 🚐€ 8/24h 🔌Ch included 🚿(24x)€ 0,50. 🚽
**Location:** Rural, simple, quiet. **Surface:** metalled.
📅 01/04-31/10.
**Distance:** 🛒200m 🚄on the spot 🚲on the spot 🚶on the spot.
**Remarks:** Along Main river, max. 3 days.

### 📷S Nördlingen 17C3
Wohnmobilstellplatz "Kaiserwiese/Am Schlössle", Kaiserwiese.
**GPS:** n48,85488 e10,48445. ⬆️➡️

30 🚐€ 3/24h 🔌€ 2/75liter 🚰€ 2 Ch 🚿€ 2/24h WC 🚽🧺
**Location:** Urban, simple, quiet. **Surface:** asphalted.
📅 01/01-31/12.
**Distance:** 🛒on the spot ⊗McDonalds.
**Remarks:** Max. 48h.

### 📷 Nürnberg 🏛️ 17D1
Volkspark Dutzendteich, Munchener Strasse.
**GPS:** n49,42403 e11,10586. ⬆️➡️

8 🚐free. **Location:** Urban, simple. **Surface:** asphalted.
📅 01/01-31/12.
**Distance:** 🛒4km 🚄700m 🚄on the spot.
**Remarks:** Max. 3 nights.

### 📷 Nürnberg 🏛️ 17D1
Volkspark Marienburg, Kilianstrasse 189.
**GPS:** n49,47495 e11,09606. ⬆️➡️

8 🚐free. **Location:** Urban, simple, quiet. **Surface:** grasstiles/metalled.
📅 01/01-31/12.
**Distance:** 🛒centre 4km ⊗800m 🚄800m 🚄on the spot.
**Remarks:** Max. 3 nights.

### 📷 Nürnberg 🏛️ 17D1
Wöhrder See, Rechenberganlage, Dr Gustav Heinemannstrasse 50.
**GPS:** n49,46041 e11,11548. ⬆️

8 🚐free.
**Location:** Urban, simple, noisy. **Surface:** metalled.
📅 01/01-31/12.
**Distance:** 🛒3km ⊗500m 🚄on the spot 🚲on the spot 🚶on the spot.
**Remarks:** Max. 3 nights.
**Tourist information Nürnberg:**
ℹ️ City walk through old city centre, daily from Tourist Information, Hauptmarkt. 📅 14.30h.
ℹ️ Nürnberg Card. Card gives for free entrance on among other things public transport and museums, discounts on purchases, boat trips, city walks etc.
Ⓜ️ Spielzeugmuseum, Karlstrasse 13-15. Toy museum. 📅 Tue-Su 10-17h.
✠ Kaiserburg Nürnberg, Burg 13. Palace. 📅 01/04-30/09 9-18h, 01/10-31/03 10-16h. 🎫 € 7.
Tiergarten. Zoo. 📅 8-19.30.

### 📷S Oberammergau 🏔️🌲🚤❄️ 20D2
Reisemobilhafen Oberammergau, Ettalerstrasse 56B.
**GPS:** n47,59040 e11,07157. ⬆️➡️

20 🚐€ 12, 2 pers.incl 🔌🚰Ch 🚿€ 0,80/kWh 🚽against payment. 🚽
**Location:** Simple. **Surface:** gravel. 📅 01/01-31/12.
**Distance:** 🛒1,2km 🚄400m ⊗100m 🚄1,2km 🎿1km.

### 📷S Oberaudorf 🏔️🚤 20F2
Pechler Hof, Tatzlwurmstrasse 7. **GPS:** n47,66132 e12,16890. ⬆️

5 🚐€ 9 🚄🚰🚿included. **Location:** Rural, simple, quiet.
**Surface:** grassy. 📅 01/01-31/12.
**Distance:** 🛒1km ⊗500m 🚄200m 🚄100m.

### 📷S Oberaudorf 🏔️🚤 20F2
Hotel Feuriger Tatzlwurm, Tatzlwurm, B307.
**GPS:** n47,67223 e12,08448. ⬆️

10 🚐guests free 🔌. **Location:** Rural, simple, isolated.
**Surface:** gravel/metalled. 📅 01/01-31/12.
**Distance:** 🏊on the spot ⊗on the spot 🚄on the spot.

### 📷S Oberelsbach 12B2
Wohnmobilstellplatz Oberelsbach, Gangolfstrasse.
**GPS:** n50,44234 e10,11412. ⬆️

6 🚐€ 5 🔌€ 1/80liter 🚰Ch 🚿(6x)€ 0,50/kWh.
**Location:** Rural, simple, quiet. **Surface:** metalled. 📅 01/01-31/12.
**Distance:** 🛒500m ⊗500m 🚲on the spot 🚶on the spot.
**Remarks:** Max. 3 days, to be paid at town hall.

### 📷S Oberkotzau 12E2
Wohnmobilstellplatz Am Summa-Park, Fabrikstraße.
**GPS:** n50,26344 e11,93849. ⬆️➡️

9 🚐€ 12 🔌€ 1/100liter 🚰Ch 🚿WC 🚽📶included. 🚽
**Location:** Rural, comfortable, central, quiet. **Surface:** metalled.
📅 01/01-31/12.
**Distance:** 🛒200m ⊗450m 🚄200m 🔵on the spot 🚄on the spot 🚲on the spot 🚶on the spot.
**Remarks:** Max. 5 days.

### 📷S Obermaiselstein 🏔️❄️ 20C2
Wohnmobilplatz Allgäu, Am Goldbach 3, Niederdorf.
**GPS:** n47,44422 e10,24288. ⬆️➡️

30 🚐€ 11-12 + € 1,80/pp tourist tax 🔌€ 0,50/50liter 🚰Ch 🚿
(25x)€ 4/day WC 🚽€ 1 🧺 **Location:** Rural, comfortable.
**Surface:** asphalted/gravel. 📅 01/01-31/12.
**Distance:** 🛒700m ⊗on the spot.

### 📷S Obernbreit 17C1
Wohnmobilstellplatz Obernbreit an der Pröschelwiese, Marktbreiter Straße. **GPS:** n49,65910 e10,16570. ⬆️

DE

10 €3 ⚡ (2x) WCincluded. **Location:** Rural, simple, quiet.
**Surface:** gravel. 01/01-31/12.
**Distance:** on the spot ⊗200m 300m on the spot on the spot.
**Remarks:** Money in envelope in mail box.

### Oberstdorf 20C3
**Rubi-Camp**, Rubinger Straße 34. **GPS:** n47,42340 e10,27772.

80 €23-27, tourist tax €2,60/pp, dog €3,50 ⚡ Ch €0,70/kWh WC €3/time €5/day.
**Location:** Urban, comfortable, quiet. **Surface:** grassy. 01/01-31/12.
**Distance:** 1km ⊗bistro mini market 150m (skibus) on the spot on the spot on the spot.
**Remarks:** Bread-service.

### Oberstdorf 20C3
**Wohnmobilstellplatz Oberstdorf**, Hermann-von-Barth-Straße 9. **GPS:** n47,40856 e10,28625.

150 €12 + €2,60/pp tourist tax ⚡ Chincluded €2,50/24h WC free. **Location:** Rural, luxurious.
**Surface:** grassy/metalled. 01/01-31/12.
**Distance:** on the spot ⊗250m 100m on the spot 500m 800m.

### Oberthulba 12B3
**Reisemobilstellplatz Thulbatal. GPS:** n50,17419 e9,92499.

25 €10, 2 pers.incl ⚡ Chincluded (20x) €2 WC €1 €2,50. **Location:** Rural, simple. **Surface:** grasstiles.
15/03-31/10.
**Distance:** 1km on the spot ⊗150m.

### Oberviechtach 17F1
**Am Freibad**, Im Wiesengrund 20. **GPS:** n49,45296 e12,42458.

6 free ⚡ Ch (3x)free €2. **Location:** Simple, isolated.
**Surface:** asphalted. 01/01-31/12.
**Distance:** 1km 600m 900m.
**Remarks:** At swimming pool, max. 3 days.

### Ochsenfurt 17C1
Mainuferstraße. **GPS:** n49,66655 e10,06156.
15 free. **Location:** Urban. **Surface:** gravel. 01/01-31/12.
**Distance:** on the spot on the spot ⊗250m 600m.

### Oettingen 17C2
Schießwasen. **GPS:** n48,95690 e10,60894.

---

4 free ⚡ €1/10minutes Ch (4x)€1/8h. **Location:** Simple, quiet. **Surface:** metalled. 01/01-31/12 last weekend Jul, 1st weekend Aug.
**Distance:** 10 min walking 500m.

### Ostheim 12C2
**Streuwiesenparkplatz**, Nordheimer Straße/Alexander Straße. **GPS:** n50,45820 e10,22656.

6 €3 ⚡ €1/80liter Ch (6x)€0,50 WCincluded.
**Location:** Urban, simple, quiet. **Surface:** metalled.
01/01-31/12.
**Distance:** 300m ⊗300m 300m on the spot on the spot.
**Remarks:** To be paid at AVIA petrol station, 200m.

### Ottobeuren 20C1
**Parking Sportwelt**, Galgenberg 4. **GPS:** n47,94907 e10,29649.

10 free ⚡ €1/100liter Ch (6x)€0,50/kWh.
**Location:** Urban, comfortable. **Surface:** metalled.
01/01-31/12.
**Distance:** 1km.
**Remarks:** Coins at Sportwelt (9-23h), village with noteworthy cathedral.

### Parkstein 17E1
**Gasthof Bergstüberl**, Basaltstrasse 16. **GPS:** n49,73179 e12,07127.

15 free ⚡ WC. **Surface:** metalled. 01/01-31/12.
**Distance:** 200m ⊗50m.
**Remarks:** Nearbij Gasthof Bergstüberl, beautiful view.

### Passau 17H3
**Am Parkdeck Ilzbrücke**, Halser Straße. **GPS:** n48,57818 e13,47366.

13 €1/h, max. €8/day ⚡ €1/100liter Ch €0,50/kWh WC.
**Location:** Urban, comfortable, central, noisy. **Surface:** metalled.

---

01/01-31/12 high water.
**Distance:** centre 500m ⊗500m 500m on the spot on the spot.
**Remarks:** Max. 24h.

### Passau 17H3
**Am Parkhaus**, Bahnhofstraße. **GPS:** n48,57406 e13,44495.

15 €3/h, max. €13/day ⚡ Chincluded. **Location:** Urban, simple, noisy. **Surface:** metalled. 01/01-31/12.
**Distance:** 500m ⊗500m 500m 100m.
**Remarks:** At station, price incl. bus transport to the city centre.

### Passau 17H3
**Winterhafen Racklau**, Regensburgerstrasse/Racklau. **GPS:** n48,57412 e13,42690.

30 free. **Location:** Simple. **Surface:** gravel.
01/01-31/12 high water.
**Distance:** 2km On the Danube river on the spot ⊗500m 500m 300m.
**Remarks:** Max. 24h.

### Peiting 20D2
**Wellenfreibad**, Ammergauer Strasse 22/A. **GPS:** n47,79317 e10,92227.

3 free. 01/01-31/12.
**Distance:** 100m ⊗500m 1km.
**Remarks:** Parking at swimming pool, max. 48h, use sanitary only during opening hours swimming pool.

### Petting 20G1
**Ferienhof Stubern**, Stubern 1. **GPS:** n47,88988 e12,78455.

3 €15, 2 pers.incl ⚡ €2/100liter Ch €0,50/kWh WC.
**Location:** Rural, simple, quiet. **Surface:** grassy.
01/05-30/10.
**Distance:** 4km 5km 5km ⊗3km 2km on the spot on the spot.

### Petting 20G1
**Stellplatz Schneiderhof**, Seestrasse 11a.
**GPS:** n47,91375 e12,81120.

4 🛏 € 15, 2 pers.incl 🚰 Ch 💧€ 0,50/kWh WC included.
**Location:** Rural, comfortable, quiet. **Surface:** grassy.
🕐 01/05-30/10.
**Distance:** 🚶300m 🏊1km ⊗300m 🛒300m 🚗500m.
**Remarks:** Dog € 4.

### Pfaffenhofen/Ilm 17E3
**Am freibad**, Ingolstädter Straße 61. **GPS:** n48,53653 e11,50875. ⬆️

12 🛏 € 5 🚰 € 1/70liter 🚰€ 1 Ch 💧(12x)€ 0,50/kWh. 🚗
**Location:** Urban, simple, quiet. **Surface:** asphalted/gravel.
🕐 01/01-31/12.
**Distance:** 🚶800m ⊗700m 🛒800m on the spot 🚲on the spot.
**Remarks:** At sports park.

### Pfronten ❄ 20D2
**Wohnmobilstellplatz Wohlfahrt**, Am Wiesele 7, Weißbach.
**GPS:** n47,59829 e10,55240. ⬆️➡️

44 🛏 € 12, 2 pers.incl 🚰 € 1/100liter 🚰 Ch 💧(44x)€ 0,50/kWh
WC € 0,50/3minutes 🔌€ 3/3 📶 🚗
**Location:** Rural, comfortable, quiet. **Surface:** gravel.
🕐 01/01-31/12.
**Distance:** 🚶400m 🛒100m 🛒400m Skibus 🎿5km on the spot.

### Plattling 17G2
**Freizeit- und Sportzentrum Plattling**, Georg-Eckl-Straße 22.
**GPS:** n48,77226 e12,87331. ⬆️➡️

30 🛏 free 🚰€ 1/100liter 🚰 Ch 💧(6x)€ 0,50/kWh 🛒€ 1,80.
**Location:** Rural, simple. **Surface:** grassy/metalled. 🕐 01/01-31/12.
**Distance:** 🚶500m ⊗300m 🛒500m.
**Remarks:** At swimming pool, use sanitary only during opening hours swimming pool.

### Pleinfeld 17D2
**Freizeitanlage Ramsberg**, Leitenbuckstraße.
**GPS:** n49,12103 e10,93275. ⬆️➡️

---

30 🛏 € 12/24h 🚰€ 1/80liter 🚰 Ch 💧(26x) 0,50/kWh WC 🚗
**Location:** Rural, comfortable, quiet. **Surface:** grassy.
🕐 01/01-31/12.
**Distance:** 🚶800m 🛶on the spot 🛒on the spot ⊗100m 🛒5km
🚗300m on the spot 🎣on the spot.

### Pleystein 17F1
**Reisemobilplatz Pleystein**, Vohenstraußer Straße/Galgenbergweg.
**GPS:** n49,64429 e12,40548. ⬆️

8 🛏 free 🚰 WC free. **Location:** Simple. **Surface:** gravel.
🕐 01/01-31/12.
**Distance:** 🚶350m ⊗200m.

### Poppenricht 17E1
**Wohnmobilstellplatz an der Vils**, Vilsstrasse.
**GPS:** n49,48184 e11,83119. ⬆️

20 🛏 free 🚗 **Location:** Rural, simple, quiet. **Surface:** gravel.
🕐 01/01-31/12.
**Distance:** 🚶1km 🛶on the spot ⊗2km 🛒1km 🚗on the spot 🎣on the spot 🎣on the spot.
**Remarks:** Along the historic "Goldenen Straße" from Nürnberg to Prague, at sports centre.

### Pottenstein 17D1
**Wohnmobilpark Pottenstein**, Am langen Berg.
**GPS:** n49,76294 e11,40826. ⬆️

25 🛏 € 8 🚰€ 1/80liter 🚰 Ch 1 💧(6x)€ 1/kWh.
**Location:** Rural, simple. **Surface:** grassy/metalled.
🕐 01/01-31/12 🔵 Service: winter.
**Distance:** 🚶1km 🛒1km 🛒1,5km 🚗450m.

### Pottenstein 17D1
**Bernerhof**, Prüllsbirkig 1. **GPS:** n49,77936 e11,44498. ➡️

---

8 🛏 € 10 🚰€ 1/80liter 🚰 Ch included 💧(2x)€ 1/2kWh. 🎣
**Location:** Rural, simple, quiet.
**Surface:** gravel.
🕐 01/01-31/12.
**Distance:** 🚶3km ⊗800m 🛒3km 🚲on the spot.
**Remarks:** Breakfast buffet € 8/pp.
**Tourist information Pottenstein:**
👁 Teufelshöhle. Caves, constant temperature 9ºC and atmospheric humidity 98%. 🕐 19/03-06/11 9-17.
🏰 Burg Pottenstein. 1000 Jaar oude burcht. 🕐 Tue-Su 10-17h.
Sommerrodelbahn. Toboggan slide 1km. 🕐 01/04-31/10 10-17h.

### Prichsenstadt 17C1
**Wohnmobilstellplatz Schützengesellschaft 1752**, Wiesentheider Straße 3. **GPS:** n49,81701 e10,35175. ⬆️➡️

5 🛏 € 5 🚰€ 1 💧€ 2,50. **Location:** Rural, simple. **Surface:** gravel.
🕐 01/01-31/12.
**Distance:** 🚶300m 🛒1,5km ⊗on the spot 🛒bakery 200m 🚲on the spot 🎣on the spot.
**Remarks:** Charging point for electric bicycles.

### Rain/Lech 17D3
**Wohnmobilstellplatz Rain**, Fasanenweg.
**GPS:** n48,69195 e10,90699. ⬆️➡️

8 🛏 free 🚰€ 1/day 🚰 Ch 💧€ 1/6h. **Location:** Rural, simple.
**Surface:** metalled. 🕐 01/01-31/12.
**Distance:** 🚶1km ⊗600m 🚲on the spot 🎣on the spot.

### Ramsthal 12B3
**Festplatz**, Hauptstrasse, K6-4. **GPS:** n50,13750 e10,06111. ⬆️

12 🛏 free 🚰€ 1/80liter 🚰 Ch 💧(12x)€ 0,50/kWh.
**Location:** Rural, simple, quiet. **Surface:** grassy/metalled.
🕐 01/01-31/12.
**Distance:** 🚶400m ⊗Gasthof Wahler, Gaststätte zum Beck 🎣on the spot.

### Rehau 12E2
**Am Siedlerfestplatz**, Birkenstraße / Harststraße.
**GPS:** n50,24046 e12,02382. ⬆️
12 🛏 € 7 🚰€ 0,50/40liter 🚰 Ch 💧€ 0,50/kWh WC against payment. **Location:** Rural, comfortable, quiet. **Surface:** asphalted.
🕐 01/01-31/12.
**Distance:** 🚶1,5km 🛒1km.
**Remarks:** Use sanitary only during opening hours swimming pool.

### Reit im Winkl ❄ 20F2
**Wohnmobilpark Reit im Winkl**, Am Waldbahnhof 7, Groissenbach.
**GPS:** n47,67013 e12,48358. ⬆️➡️

250 ☕ 12, 15/12-14/05 € 14 ⌁ € 0,20/10liter ⬛Ch ⚡ € 0,75/kWh ☐use sanitary € 4,50. **Location:** Rural, comfortable, quiet.
**Surface:** grassy/metalled. ☐ 01/01-31/12.
**Distance:** 🚶1km 🏊1,5km 🛒200m ➤on the spot 🚲on the spot ⚲on the spot ⛷on the spot.
**Remarks:** Shuttle bus to ski-piste.

### Ⓢ Reit im Winkl 🏔❄     20F2
**Wohnmobilpark Reit im Winkl**, Am Waldbahnhof 7.
**GPS:** n47,65898 e12,54213.

50 ☕ 12, 15/12-15/03 € 14, excl. tourist tax ⌁€ 2 ⬛Ch ⚡ € 0,75/kWh. **Location:** Rural, simple, quiet. **Surface:** grassy/gravel.
☐ 15/12-15/03, 15/05-15/10.
**Distance:** 🚶4km 🏊1,5km ⊗500m 🛒200m ➤on the spot 🚲on the spot ⚲on the spot ⛷150m ⛷on the spot.

### Ⓢ Riedenburg 🏰🌳     17E2
**Volksfestplatz**, Austraße. **GPS:** n48,96446 e11,68181.

40 ☕ 6 ⌁⬛Chincluded ⚡€ 1/8h. 🚗
**Location:** Central. **Surface:** gravel/metalled.
☐ 01/01-31/12 ☀ last week of Aug.
**Distance:** 🚶450m 🏊on the spot ⊗300m 🛒20m.
**Remarks:** At the Main-Danube Canal.

### Ⓢ Roding     17F2
**Volksfestplatz**, Jahnstraße 21. **GPS:** n49,19806 e12,51722.
4 ☕free ⌁€ 1/70liter ⬛€ 1 Ch ⚡€ 0,50/kWh. **Location:** Urban, simple. **Surface:** asphalted/metalled. ☐ 01/01-31/12.
**Distance:** 🚶150m ⊗150m 🛒500m.
**Remarks:** Max. 1 day.

### Ⓢ Roßhaupten 🏔🌳❄     20D2
**Wohnmobilstellplatz Miller**, Augsburger Strasse 23.
**GPS:** n47,65889 e10,71944.

20 ☕ 10, 4 pers. incl. ⌁€ 1,50 ⬛Ch € 2 ⚡(3x)€ 2/day WC☐€ 2.
**Location:** Rural, comfortable, quiet. **Surface:** metalled.
☐ 01/04-01/10.
**Distance:** 🚶50m 🏊1,2km 🚉1,2km ⊗200m 🛒150m 🚌150m ⛷1km 🛒500m.
**Remarks:** Next to Camping- und Freizeitmarkt, reparation work.

### Ⓢ Roth 🌳     17D2
**Steinerne Eiche**, Hilpoltsteiner Strasse. **GPS:** n49,24089 e11,10637.

---

50 ☕free ⌁⬛Chfree. **Location:** Urban, simple, noisy.
**Surface:** metalled. ☐ 01/01-31/12.
**Distance:** 🚶1km ⚓100m 🛒200m 🚲on the spot ⚲on the spot.
**Remarks:** Service closed during wintertime.

### Ⓢ Rothenbuch 🌳🌳     12B3
**Freizeitanlage**, Heigenbrücker Weg. **GPS:** n49,97460 e9,39475.

10 ☕ 7 ⌁€ 1/80liter ⬛Ch ⚡(10x) 0,50/kWh. 🚗
**Location:** Rural, simple, quiet. **Surface:** grasstiles.
☐ 01/01-31/12.
**Distance:** 🚶250m ⚲on the spot.

### Ⓢ Rothenburg ob der Tauber 🌿     17C1
**Parkplatz P2**, Nördlinger Strasse. **GPS:** n49,37048 e10,18324.

25 ☕ 10/24h, € 2/h ⌁€ 1/45liter ⬛Ch ⚡€ 0,50/kWh WC.
**Location:** Central. **Surface:** metalled. ☐ 01/01-31/12.
**Distance:** 🚶700m ⊗200m 🛒200m 🚌200m.

### Ⓢ Rothenburg ob der Tauber 🌿     17C1
**Parkplatz P3**, Schweinsdorfer Strasse. **GPS:** n49,38222 e10,18889.

30 ☕ 10/24h, € 2/h ⌁€ 1/45liter ⬛ChWC.
**Location:** Urban, noisy.
**Surface:** metalled.
☐ 01/01-31/12.
**Distance:** 🚶on the spot.
**Tourist information Rothenburg ob der Tauber:**
Ⓜ Mittelalterliches Kriminalmuseum, Burggasse 3. History of 1000 years of jurisdiction. ☐ 01/04-31/10 10-18h, 01/11-31/03 13-16h. ☀ Schäfertanz. Traditional celebration. ☐ 27/03, 15/05, 04/09.

### Ⓢ Rothenkirchen     12D2
**Waldschwimmbad**, Badstraße 69. **GPS:** n50,37389 e11,31583.

---

40 ☕ 6 ⌁€ 1 ⬛Ch € 1 ⚡(16x)WC☐included.
**Location:** Rural, simple, quiet. **Surface:** metalled. ☐ 01/04-31/10.
**Distance:** 🚶1,5km ⊗900m.
**Remarks:** Parking swimming pool.

### Ⓢ Röthlein     12C3
**Sportanlage TSV/Bundeskegelbahn**, Friedhofstrasse.
**GPS:** n49,98694 e10,21583.

6 ☕free. **Location:** Urban, simple, quiet. **Surface:** unpaved.
☐ 01/01-31/12.
**Distance:** 🚶on the spot 🚲on the spot.

### Ⓢ Röttingen 🍃     17B1
**Wohnmobilplatz an der Tauber**, Neubronner Straße.
**GPS:** n49,50724 e9,96995.

20 ☕ 5 ⌁€ 1/70liter ⬛Ch ⚡€ 2/24h WC € 0,20 ☐€ 1,20. 🚗
**Location:** Rural, comfortable. **Surface:** gravel.
☐ 01/04-31/10 ☀ last 2 weeks of August.
**Distance:** 🚶300m 🏊on the spot ➤on the spot ⊗500m 🚌500m 🚲on the spot ⚲on the spot.
**Remarks:** Along the Tauber river.

### 🍇 Ⓢ Röttingen 🍃     17B1
**Bach**, KlingerStrabe 1. **GPS:** n49,50731 e9,97368.

10 ☕free ⚡€ 2,50/day WC☐€ 2,50/day.
**Location:** Rural, simple, quiet. **Surface:** gravel. ☐ 01/01-31/12.
**Distance:** 🚶500m 🏊on the spot ➤on the spot ⊗on the spot 🛒2km.
**Remarks:** Fishing permit available at town hall.

### Ⓒ Ⓢ Ruhpolding     20G2
**Campingplatz Ortnerhof**, Ortsstraße 5.
**GPS:** n47,74260 e12,66303.

16 ☕ 9 ⌁⬛Ch ⚡€ 0,70/kWh WC☐included ☀€ 3 📶€ 3/24h.
**Location:** Rural, simple. **Surface:** gravel. ☐ 01/01-31/12.
**Distance:** 🚶3km ⊗on the spot 🛒2km 🚌on the spot 🚲on the spot ⚲on the spot ⛷on the spot.
**Remarks:** At golf court, max. 1 night.

### Ⓢ Saaldorf-Surheim     20G1
**Am Paulbauernhof**, Gausburg 47. **GPS:** n47,89308 e12,94499.
12 ☕ 7 ⌁⬛Ch ⚡€ 2/day WC € 4 ☐. 🐴 **Location:** Rural, comfortable, isolated, quiet. **Surface:** grassy. ☐ 01/01-31/12.
**Distance:** 🚶3km ⊗2km 🛒2,5km.

Remarks: Bread-service.

### Saulgrub 20D2
**Ammertaler Hof**, Alte Römerstraße 10. GPS: n47,64416 e11,02779.⬆
3 🏕 € 15 🚰 ✎ WC 🗑. **Location:** Rural, simple, quiet. **Surface:** gravel.
🅿 01/01-31/12.
**Distance:** 🚶1,5km ⊗on the spot.

### Scheidegg 20C2
**Wohnmobilpark am Kurhaus**, Am Hammerweiher 1.
GPS: n47,57351 e9,84545.⬆

20 🏕 € 13,50 🚰 Ch ✎ (16x)included 🗑 € 2 📶.
**Surface:** gravel/metalled. 🅿 01/01-31/12.
**Distance:** 🛒Minishop.
**Remarks:** Bread-service.

### Scheinfeld 17C1
**Freibad Scheinfeld**, Badstrasse 5. GPS: n49,67434 e10,46173.⬆➡

14 🏕 € 7 🚰 Ch ✎ € 1/2kWh WC 🗑.🔥
**Location:** Rural, comfortable. **Surface:** gravel. 🅿 01/01-31/12.
**Distance:** 🚴on the spot 🚶on the spot.
**Remarks:** At swimming pool, picnic tables available.

### Schliersee 20E2
**Am Spitzingsee**, Spitzingstraße. GPS: n47,66648 e11,88851.⬆

10 🏕 summer € 12, winter € 9 (no service) 🚰 Ch.
**Location:** Rural, simple, isolated, quiet. **Surface:** gravel.
🅿 01/01-31/12 🔵 Service: winter.
**Distance:** 🚶5,4km 🏊 on the spot ⊗500m 🚶 on the
spot 🎣 on the spot.
**Remarks:** Altitude 1085m, at lake.

### Schlüsselfeld 17C1
Bambergerstrasse. GPS: n49,75572 e10,62267.⬆⬆

5 🏕 free 🚰 € 1/80liter Ch. **Location:** Urban, simple, central.
**Surface:** asphalted. 🅿 01/01-31/12.
**Distance:** 🚶on the spot ⊗on the spot 🛒on the spot 🚴50m 🚶50m.

### Schlüsselfeld 17C1
Aschbacher Straße. GPS: n49,75750 e10,61667.
5 🏕 free. **Location:** Urban. **Surface:** metalled. 🅿 01/01-31/12.
**Distance:** 🚶100m ⊗100m 🛒300m 🚴 on the spot 🚶on the spot.

### Schlüsselfeld 17C1
**Concorde**, Concorde-Straße 2–4. GPS: n49,76745 e10,56478.⬆

20 🏕 free 🚰 € 1/100liter Ch ✎ € 0,50/kWh 📶.
**Location:** Rural, simple, quiet. **Surface:** metalled.
🅿 01/01-31/12.
**Distance:** 🚶1km ⊗1km 🛒1km.
**Remarks:** At motohome manufacturer, bread-service.

### Schnelldorf 17C2
**BP-Truckstop Feuchtwangen**, Rudolph Dieselstrasse 1.
GPS: n49,17149 e10,24124.⬆

15 🏕 € 7 🚰 € 1/80liter Ch ✎ (3x) WC 🗑 € 2,50.
**Location:** Rural, simple. **Surface:** metalled. 🅿 01/01-31/12.
**Distance:** 🚲300m 🚶on the spot 🛒on the spot.
**Remarks:** Discount at restaurant € 5, special part for motor homes.

### Schöllkrippen 12A3
**Naturerlebnisbad**, Häfner-Ohnhaus-Straße.
GPS: n50,08484 e9,25247.⬆➡

35 🏕 € 9/24h 🚰 € 1/80liter Ch ✎ (24x) € 0,50/kWh 📶free1h. 🔋
**Location:** Rural, comfortable, quiet. **Surface:** grassy.
🅿 01/01-31/12.
**Distance:** 🚶500m 🛒on the spot 🚴on the spot 🚶on the spot.
**Remarks:** Bread-service.

### Schongau 20D2
**Festplatz**, Lechuferstrasse. GPS: n47,80906 e10,89815.⬆

70 🏕 € 5/24h 🚰 € 1/50liter Ch WC.🔥
**Location:** Urban, simple.
**Surface:** asphalted.
🅿 service: 20/03-05/11 🔵 during event.
**Distance:** 🚶400m 🚲100m 🛒400m 🚶on the spot.
**Remarks:** Caution key sanitary € 30, guests free.

### Schönsee 17F1
**Moorbad**, Böhmerwaldstrasse. GPS: n49,51091 e12,55321.⬆
5 🏕 free. **Location:** Simple. **Surface:** grassy. 🅿 01/01-31/12.
**Distance:** ⊗300m 🛒550m.
**Remarks:** Recreation park, max. 3 days.

### Schönwald 12E3
**Freizeitland Schönwald**, Grünhaid 4.
GPS: n50,20958 e12,09570.⬆⬆.

10 🏕 € 17,70 🚰 Ch ✎ WC 🗑 📶included. 🔥
**Location:** Urban, simple. **Surface:** grassy. 🅿 01/10-01/04.
**Distance:** 🚶on the spot 🏊on the spot 🚲1km ⊗on the spot 🛒1km
🚶 on the spot.
**Remarks:** Nearby camp site, breakfast-service.

### Schrobenhausen 17D3
**Am Klostergarten**, Rot-Kreuz-Straße.
GPS: n48,55835 e11,26234.⬆➡

5 🏕 free. **Location:** Simple, quiet. **Surface:** asphalted/metalled.
🅿 01/01-31/12.
**Distance:** 🚶400m ⊗400m 🛒400m.
**Remarks:** Shady.

### Schrobenhausen 17D3
**Stadtwerke-Kläranlage**, Köningslachenerweg 12.
GPS: n48,57374 e11,27519.⬆
🚰 Ch Service € 5. 🅿 01/01-31/12.
**Remarks:** Mo-Thu 7-12h, 13-16h, Fr 7-12h.

### Schwandorf 17E1
**Festplatz**, Angerring, Krondorf. GPS: n49,33230 e12,10247.⬆

30 🏕 free 🚰 Ch free.
**Location:** Simple. **Surface:** asphalted/grassy.
🅿 01/01-31/12 🔵 week before/after Whitsuntide.
**Distance:** 🚶500m ⊗200m 🛒500m.
**Remarks:** Along the Naab river.

### Schwangau 20D2
**Wohnmobilpark Schwangau**, Münchenerstrasse 151.
GPS: n47,59167 e10,77250.⬆

24 🏕 € 16-21 + € 1,90/pp tourist tax, dog € 2,50 🚰 Ch ✎
(24x) € 3 WC 🗑 📶included. 🔥 ✎ **Location:** Urban, comfortable.
**Surface:** grassy/gravel. 🅿 01/01-31/12.
**Distance:** 🚶2km 🏊on the spot ⊗on the spot
🛒 on the spot 🚴1km 🚶 on the spot.
**Remarks:** Dog € 2/day.

### Schwarzenbach an der Saale 12E3
Fleischgasse. GPS: n50,22324 e11,93311.⬆

**DE**

2 ⌷free ⚡€ 1 🔲Ch.⚡€ 1 WC. **Location:** Urban, simple, central.
**Surface:** metalled. ◻ 01/01-31/12.
**Distance:** ⚡on the spot ⚓on the spot ⚡on the spot ⊗on the spot ⚡on the spot ⚡100m ⚡100m ⚡100m.

| 🏖️🄎 | **Schweinfurt** 🎪 | 12C3 |

**Wohnmobilpark Saumain**, Am Hutrasen.
**GPS:** n50,03868 e10,23499. ⬆➡.

20 ⌷€ 10 ⚡€ 1/80liter 🔲Ch ⚡€ 0,50/kWh. 🔲 **Location:** Rural,
comfortable, quiet. **Surface:** grassy/gravel. ◻ 01/01-31/12.
**Distance:** ⚡1,5km ⚓1km ⚓on the spot ⚡on the spot ⊗100m ⚡100m ⚡on the spot.

| 🄎🄢 | **Segnitz** 🍃🍂 | 17C1 |

Mainstraße 20. **GPS:** n49,67012 e10,14242. ⬆.

4 ⌷free. **Location:** Urban, simple. **Surface:** metalled.
◻ 01/01-31/12.
**Distance:** ⚡on the spot ⚓on the spot ⚡on the spot ⊗200m.
**Remarks:** Max. 1 day.

| 🄎🄢 | **Segnitz** 🍃🍂 | 17C1 |

**Gasthaus zum Goldenen Anker**, Mainstraße 8.
**GPS:** n49,67063 e10,14344. ⬆.

9 ⌷€ 5 ⚡€ 0,50/50liter 🔲Ch ⚡(18x)€ 0,50.
**Location:** Urban, simple. **Surface:** grassy/gravel.
◻ 01/01-31/12 ◻ Restaurant: Thu.
**Distance:** ⚡850m ⚓on the spot ⚡on the spot ⚡1km ⚡on the spot.
**Remarks:** Along Main river.

| 🄎🄢 | **Selb** | 12E3 |

Papiermühlweg 2. **GPS:** n50,16952 e12,12512. ⬆➡.

10 ⌷€ 6 ⚡€ 0,50/100liter 🔲Ch ⚡€ 0,50/kWh

---

WC ⌷€ 0,50/10minutes. 🔲 **Location:** Urban, comfortable, quiet.
**Surface:** metalled. ◻ 01/01-31/12.
**Distance:** ⚡500m ⊗200m ⚡400m.
**Remarks:** At museum.

| 🄎🄢 | **Selb** | 12E3 |

**Eissporthalle**, Hanns-Braun-Straße 27. **GPS:** n50,15601 e12,13489. ➡.

10 ⌷free. **Location:** Rural, simple, isolated. **Surface:** gravel.
◻ 01/01-31/12.
**Distance:** ⚡1km ⊗200m ⚡1km ⚡on the spot ⚡on the spot.
**Remarks:** Hiking trails.

| 🄸🄢 | **Siegsdorf** | 20G1 |

**Gasthof Hörterer der Hammerwirt**, Schmiedstrasse, B306, Hammer.
**GPS:** n47,80096 e12,70392. ⬆.

5 ⌷guests free WC ⚡. **Location:** Rural, simple. **Surface:** metalled.
◻ 01/01-31/12 ◻ Wed.
**Distance:** ⚡6km ⚓on the spot ⊗on the spot ⚡100m ⚡100m ⚡on the spot ⚡on the spot ⚡2,5km ⚡300m.
**Remarks:** Max. 3 nights.

| 🄢 | **Sonthofen** ⛰ | 20C2 |

**Erlebnisbad Wonnemar**, Stadionweg 5.
**GPS:** n47,50344 e10,27883. ⬆➡.

10 ⌷€ 3,50/night. **Location:** Urban, simple. **Surface:** gravel.
◻ 01/01-31/12.
**Distance:** ⚡1,5km ⚓2,5km ⊗on the spot ⚡on the spot ⚡on the spot.
**Remarks:** Max. 1 night.

| 🄎🄢 | **Spalt** 🎪 | 17D2 |

**Wohnmobilpark Rezattal**, Obeltshauserstraße 3.
**GPS:** n49,17512 e10,92937. ⬆.

15 ⌷€ 9,50 + € 1,50/pp tourist tax ⚡ 🔲Ch ⚡(15x)€ 2,50/4kWh
WC € 1,50 ⚡€ 2,50. **Location:** Rural, comfortable, central.
**Surface:** gravel. ◻ 01/04-30/10.
**Distance:** ⚡on the spot ⊗100m ⚡50m ⚡on the spot ⚡on the spot ⚡on the spot.

| 🄎🄢 | **Speichersdorf** 🎪 | 12E3 |

**Sportheim ASV**, Am Sportplatz. **GPS:** n49,89045 e11,82703. ⬆.

---

10 ⌷€ 5 ⚡Chincluded ⚡€ 1,50. ⚡ **Location:** Rural, simple,
isolated, quiet. **Surface:** grassy. ◻ 01/01-31/12.
**Distance:** ⚡800m ⊗600m.
**Remarks:** At sports park.

| 🏖️🄢 | **Steinach/Straubing** | 17F2 |

**Firma Hubert Brandl Caravantastic**, Gewerbering 11.
**GPS:** n48,95639 e12,62250. ⚡.

3 ⌷free ⚡€ 1 🔲 ⚡.
**Location:** Simple. **Surface:** grassy. ◻ 01/01-31/12.
**Distance:** ⚡1,5km ⊗2km ⚡1km.
**Remarks:** Connection electricity < 18h.

| 🄸🄢 | **Steinberg am See** ⚓🏖️🎪 | 17F1 |

**Movin'G'round**, Am Steinberger See. **GPS:** n49,28247 e12,17357. ⬆.

25 ⌷€ 8 ⚡service € 2 Ch ⚡€ 2 ⚡€ 0,50/2minutes ⚡.
**Location:** Rural, simple. **Surface:** grassy. ◻ 01/04-31/10.
**Distance:** ⚡500m ⚓on the spot ⊗on the spot.
**Remarks:** Check in at pay-desk.

| 🄎🄢 | **Strullendorf** | 12D3 |

Hauptsmoorstraße 2. **GPS:** n49,85356 e10,97207. ⬆.

6 ⌷free.
**Location:** Rural, simple, noisy.
**Surface:** asphalted.
**Distance:** ⚡1,2km ⊗on the spot ⚡1km ⚡on the spot ⚡on the spot.

| 🄎🄢 | **Sulzbach-Rosenberg** 🍃🍂🧺 | 17E1 |

**Großparkplatz**, Bayreuther Straße. **GPS:** n49,50583 e11,74500. ⬆➡.

4 ⌷free ⚡€ 1/80liter 🔲Ch ⚡(4x)€ 0,50/kWh. **Location:** Urban,
simple, quiet. **Surface:** gravel. ◻ 01/01-31/12.
**Distance:** ⚡300m ⚓500m ⚡500m ⚡on the spot.
**Remarks:** Max. 24h.

DE

### ⌂Ⓢ Sulzemoos — 20D1

**Der Freistaat Caravaning**, Ohmstrasse. **GPS:** n48,28267 e11,26084. ⬆.

40 ⓈfreeⲘ€ 1/80liter ⲤCh ✎(20x)€ 1/kWh WC ⤦.
**Location:** Simple. **Surface:** gravel.
◻ 01/01-31/12.
**Distance:** ⬛800m ◢ 800m McDonalds 800m Ⲓ800m ➤600m.
**Remarks:** Motorhome dealer.

### ⌂ Tauberrettersheim — 17B1

Brunnenstrasse. **GPS:** n49,49635 e9,93720. ⬆➡.

6 Ⓢfree. **Location:** Rural, simple, quiet. **Surface:** grassy.
◻ 01/01-31/12.
**Distance:** ⬛on the spot ⲒLon the spot ➤on the spot ⊗50m
Ⲓbakery 200m ⚲on the spot ⚹on the spot.
**Remarks:** Swimming pool 100m.

### ⌂ Taufkirchen — 20E1

**Auf dem Dulipphof**, Hochstrasse 11. **GPS:** n48,03969 e11,62167.
10 Ⓢ€ 11 ⲘⲤCh ✎€ 0,50/kWh. ✤ **Location:** Rural, comfortable,
quiet. **Surface:** grassy/gravel. ◻ 01/01-31/12.
**Distance:** ⬛1km ⊗500m Ⲓ1km.
**Remarks:** Bread-service.

### ⌂Ⓢ Thierstein ❄❄❄ — 12E3

**Kaiserstein**, Hirtweg. **GPS:** n50,10610 e12,10490. ⬆➡.

10 Ⓢ€ 5/24h ⲘⲤCh ✎included ⤦voluntary contribution. ⲙ
**Location:** Rural, comfortable. **Surface:** metalled.
◻ 01/01-31/12 ◻ 01/10-31/03 water disconnected.
**Distance:** ⬛500m ◢500m ➤500m on the spot ⚹on the spot.
**Remarks:** Max. 2 nights, beautiful view.

### ⌂Ⓢ Thüngersheim ⤦ — 12B3

**Parkplatz Main-Aue**, Am Schwimbad. **GPS:** n49,88084 e9,83717. ⬆➡.

20 Ⓢfree Ⲙ ⲤChfree ✎(16x)€ 0,50/kWh.
**Location:** Rural, comfortable, noisy. **Surface:** grassy. ◻ 01/04-31/10.
**Distance:** ⬛500m ➤on the spot ⚲on the spot.
**Remarks:** Along Main river.

### ⌂Ⓢ Tirschenreuth ⤦ — 12F3

**Wohnmobilstellplatz am ZOB**, Mühlbühlstraße.
**GPS:** n49,87920 e12,33350. ⬆.

5 ⲤfreeⲘ€ 1 ⲤChWC. **Location:** Urban, simple.
**Surface:** asphalted. ◻ 01/01-31/12.
**Distance:** ⬛on the spot ⊗200m Ⲓ100m ➤on the spot ⚹on the
spot.

### ⌂Ⓢ Tirschenreuth ⤦ — 12F3

**Wohnmobilstellplatz am Fischhofpark**, Am Fischhof.
**GPS:** n49,87900 e12,34490. ⬆➡.

25 Ⓢfree. **Location:** Rural, simple. **Surface:** asphalted.
◻ 01/01-31/12.
**Distance:** ⬗on the spot ➤on the spot ⊗500m Ⲓ1km.

### ⚿Ⓢ Traunstein — 20F1

**Gasthaus Jobst**, Balthasar Permoserstrasse 64, Rettenbach.
**GPS:** n47,91188 e12,64899. ⬆.

10 Ⓢ€ 3, guests free Ⲙ€ 1 ✎€ 2,50 WC. **Location:** Rural, simple.
**Surface:** metalled. ◻ 01/01-31/12 ◻ Wed.
**Distance:** ⬛on the spot ⊗on the spot ➤on the spot ⚲on the spot
⚹on the spot ⚸on the spot.

### ⌂Ⓢ Traunstein — 20F1

**Firma Grüaugl**, Schmidhamerstrasse 31. **GPS:** n47,88227 e12,59941. ⬆.

12 Ⓢ€ 5 Ⲙ€ 1/100liter ⲤCh ✎€ 0,50/kWh. ⲙ
**Location:** Isolated. **Surface:** metalled. ◻ 01/01-31/12.
**Distance:** ⬛2,5km.
**Remarks:** Camping equipment store.

### ⌂Ⓢ Treuchtlingen ❄⚘⚘ — 17D2

**Reisemobilstellplatz am Kurpark**, Kästleinmühlenstrasse 20.
**GPS:** n48,96028 e10,91778. ⬆➡.

56 Ⓢ€ 11 Ⲙ€ 1/100liter ⲤCh ✎(56x)€ 1/8h WC included
◻€ 2/time ⤦. **Location:** Urban, comfortable, luxurious, quiet.
**Surface:** grasstiles. ◻ 01/03-31/12.

---

**Distance:** ⬛800m ⊗400m on the spot ⚹on the spot.
**Remarks:** Check in on arrival, bread-service.

### ⌂Ⓢ Trostberg — 20F1

Jahnstraße. **GPS:** n48,02194 e12,54607.

8 Ⓢfree Ⲙ€ 1/50liter ✎(2x)€ 1. **Surface:** gravel.
◻ 01/01-31/12 ◻ 01/09-10/09.
**Distance:** ⬛800m ⊗300m Ⲓ300m ➤station 1km.

### ⌂Ⓢ Tüßling — 20F1

**Gasthaus Kiefering**, Kiefering 40. **GPS:** n48,19406 e12,62778. ⬆.
10 Ⓢ€ 8 Ⲙ ✎€ 1,50/day WC ⲙ **Location:** Rural, comfortable,
quiet. **Surface:** gravel. ◻ 01/01-31/12.
**Distance:** ⬛3km ⊗on the spot Ⲓ3,5km.
**Remarks:** Bread-service.

### ⚘Ⓢ Übersee/Chiemsee — 20F1

**Bauernhof Steiner**, Almfischer 11, Stegen.
**GPS:** n47,80963 e12,49136. ⬆➡.

25 Ⓢ€ 11, 2 pers.incl Ⲙ ⲤCh ✎€ 0,50/kWh WC ◻€ 0,50/2minutes.
**Location:** Rural, comfortable, quiet. **Surface:** gravel.
◻ 01/01-31/12.
**Distance:** ⬛Übersee 2km ◢ 4,6km ⌂Chiemsee 6km Ⲓ1km.

### ⚘Ⓢ Übersee/Chiemsee — 20F1

**Wohnmobilstellplatz Schmid**, Stegen 4. **GPS:** n47,81237 e12,48843. ⬆.

28 Ⓢ€ 11, 2 pers.incl Ⲙ ⲤCh ✎€ 0,50/kWh ◻€ 1.
**Location:** Rural, comfortable. **Surface:** grassy/gravel.
◻ 01/01-31/12.
**Distance:** ⬛Übersee 2km ◢4km ⌂Chiemsee 5km ➤2km ⊗2km
Ⲓ1,5km ⚲on the spot.
**Remarks:** Bread-service.

### ⌂Ⓢ Veitshöchheim ⤦ — 17B1

**Parkplatz am Fußgängersteg**, Am Güßgraben.
**GPS:** n49,83623 e9,86916. ⬆➡.

5 Ⓢfree. **Location:** Rural, simple, quiet. **Surface:** metalled.
◻ 01/01-31/12.
**Distance:** ⬛500m ➤on the spot ⚹on the spot.
**Remarks:** Along Main river, max. 24h.

### ⌂Ⓢ Viechtach ⚘❄❄❄ — 17G2

**P1, Stadtmitte**, Bierfeldstraße. **GPS:** n49,07876 e12,88235. ⬆.

6 🛏free. **Location:** Simple, central. **Surface:** metalled. 🚰 01/01-31/12.
**Distance:** 🚶400m ⊗150m 🚱50m.
**Remarks:** In front of supermarket Edeka, max. 3 nights.

| 🆔 | Viechtach 🏕🏔❄ | 17G2 |

**P2, Stadthalle**, Friedhofstrasse. **GPS:** n49,07722 e12,88528. ⬆.

3 🛏free. **Location:** Urban, simple. **Surface:** metalled. 🚰 01/01-31/12.
**Distance:** 🚶centre 300m ⊗200m 🚱400m.
**Remarks:** Max. 3 nights.

| 🆔 | Viechtach 🏕🏔❄ | 17G2 |

**P5, TÜV**, Karl-Gareis-Straße. **GPS:** n49,08222 e12,88306. ⬆.

3 🛏free. **Location:** Urban, simple, noisy. **Surface:** asphalted. 🚰 01/01-31/12.
**Distance:** 🚶500m ⊗400m 🚱500m.
**Remarks:** Max. 3 nights, small pitches.

| 🆔🅂 | Viechtach 🏕🏔❄ | 17G2 |

**Berghütte 'Zum Pröller'**, Hinterviechtach 3, Kollnburg.
**GPS:** n49,02939 e12,83892. ⬆.

3 🛏€ 5 🔌included ⚡€ 5. **Location:** Rural, simple, isolated.
**Surface:** gravel. 🚰 01/01-31/12.
**Distance:** 🚶Viechtach 7km ⊗on the spot 🅿on the spot 🚵20m.
**Remarks:** Parking at skipistes.

| 🅂 | Viechtach 🏕🏔❄ | 17G2 |

Am Regenufer 1. **GPS:** n49,08303 e12,88824. ⬆.
🔌€ 1 🛏€ 1 Ch. 🚰 01/01-31/12.

**Tourist information Viechtach:**
⛱ Stadtplatz. Week market. ⊡ Wed 7-17h.

| 🆔 | Vilsbiburg | 17F3 |

Färberanger. **GPS:** n48,44889 e12,35307. ⬆.
2 🛏free. **Location:** Urban, simple, central. **Surface:** asphalted.
🚰 01/01-31/12.
**Distance:** 🚶on the spot ⊗50m 🚱400m.

| 🆔🅂 | Vilseck 🌿 | 17E1 |

Ziegelanger. **GPS:** n49,61145 e11,80068. ⬆.

4 🛏free 🔌🛏Chfree. **Location:** Urban, simple, central, quiet.
**Surface:** asphalted/gravel. 🚰 01/01-31/12.
**Distance:** 🚶200m 🏊on the spot 🅿on the spot ⊗on the spot
🚱650m 🚵200m 🚶200m.
**Remarks:** Max. 3 days.

| 🆔 | Vilshofen 🏕🌿 | 17G3 |

**Stellplatz an der Donau**, Obere Donaulände.
**GPS:** n48,63833 e13,18000. ⬆➡.

12 🛏free. **Location:** Simple, noisy. **Surface:** asphalted.
🚰 01/01-31/12.
**Distance:** 🚶500m 🏊On the Danube river 🅿on the spot ⊗500m
🚱500m.
**Remarks:** On the Danube river, max. 1 night.

| 🆔🅂 | Vilshofen 🏕🌿 | 17G3 |

**Yachthafen Vilshofen**, Am Bootshafen 1.
**GPS:** n48,63870 e13,18785. ⬆➡.

10 🛏€ 15 🔌€ 1 🛏Ch ⚡(10x)€ 2/day WC🛏€ 1. **Location:** Rural,
comfortable, quiet. **Surface:** gravel. 🚰 01/04-30/11.
**Distance:** 🚶500m 🏊On the Danube river.

| 🆔🅂 | Vohenstrauß | 17F1 |

**Stadthalle**, Neuwirtshauser Weg 11. **GPS:** n49,61872 e12,34523. ⬆.

8 🛏free 🔌🛏Ch ⚡free WC🛏. **Location:** Rural, simple, noisy.
**Surface:** gravel. 🚰 01/01-31/12 🅿 Service: winter.
**Distance:** 🚶100m ⚓800m ⊗50m 🚱100m.
**Remarks:** Max. 2 days, caution key sanitary € 50.

| 🆔 | Volkach 🌿🏕🌿 | 12C3 |

**Am Mainufer**, Am Gries. **GPS:** n49,87457 e10,16418. ⬆.

10 🛏€ 5,50. 🅿 **Location:** Rural, simple, quiet. **Surface:** metalled.
🚰 01/04-31/10.

**Distance:** 🚶on the spot 🅿on the spot ⊗300m 🚱200m 🚵on the
spot.
**Remarks:** Max. 3 days.

| 🆔 | Volkach 🌿🏕🌿 | 12C3 |

An der Mainbrücke. **GPS:** n49,86389 e10,22139. ⬆➡.

30 🛏€ 5,50. 🅿 **Location:** Urban, simple, noisy. **Surface:** gravel.
🚰 01/04-31/10.
**Distance:** 🚶500m 🏊on the spot 🅿on the spot ⊗500m 🚱500m
🚵on the spot.
**Remarks:** Along Main river, max. 3 days.

| 🆔 | Volkach 🌿🏕🌿 | 12C3 |

**Unter der Mainbrücke**, Mainufer. **GPS:** n49,86455 e10,21874. ⬆.

8 🛏€ 5,50. 🅿 **Location:** Urban, simple, noisy. **Surface:** gravel.
🚰 01/04-31/10.
**Distance:** 🚶1km 🅿on the spot ⊗900m 🚱1km 🚵on the spot.
**Remarks:** Max. 3 days.

| 🆔🅂 | Waidhaus | 17F1 |

**Barbara Sonneschein**, Pfrentsch 20. **GPS:** n49,61823 e12,49040. ⬆➡.

6 🛏€ 5 🔌🛏Chincluded ⚡€ 0,35/kWh 🛏€ 1,50. 🚵
**Location:** Rural, simple, isolated, quiet. **Surface:** grassy.
🚰 01/01-31/12.
**Distance:** 🚶3km ⊗3km 🚶on the spot.

| 🆔🅂 | Wald | 20D2 |

**Walder Badeweiher**, Am Sportplatz. **GPS:** n47,72294 e10,56348. ⬆➡.

10 🛏€ 5 🔌🛏Ch.🚵
**Location:** Rural, simple, quiet. **Surface:** gravel. 🚰 01/01-31/12.
**Distance:** 🚶500m 🏊on the spot ⊗250m 🚵on the spot 🚶on the
spot.
**Remarks:** Service at fire-station, 200m.

| 🆔🅂 | Waldkirchen 🌳❄ | 17H2 |

**Karoli-Badepark**, VDK Heimstrasse 8. **GPS:** n48,72222 e13,60278. ⬆.

DE

16 ⊠free ⊟€ 1/80liter ⊞Ch ⊿(10x)€ 0,50/kWh WC⊟.
**Location:** Rural, simple, quiet. **Surface:** gravel.
⊡ 01/01-31/12.
**Distance:** ⊿1km ⊗25m ⊿2km ⊷on the spot ⊹on the spot.
**Remarks:** Parking skating rink-swimming pool, bread-service, use sanitary only during opening hours swimming pool, against payment.

⊞S **Waldsassen** ⚓⊕ **12F3**
**P2 Schwanenwiese**, Schwanengasse. **GPS:** n50,00526 e12,30739.⬆.

4 ⊠€ 5 ⊿(4x)€ 2/10h WC. **Location:** Simple. **Surface:** metalled.
⊡ 01/01-31/12.
**Distance:** ⊿500m ⊿500m ⊿500m.
**Remarks:** Max. 3 days, pay at tourist office.

⊞ **Waldsassen** ⚓⊕ **12F3**
**P1**, Joseph-Wiesnetstrasse. **GPS:** n50,00250 e12,30361.⬆.

2 ⊠free. **Location:** Simple. **Surface:** metalled.
⊡ 01/01-31/12.
**Distance:** ⊿100m ⊿100m ⊿100m.
**Remarks:** Max. 3 days.

⊞S **Warmensteinach** ❄ **12E3**
Fleckl 4. **GPS:** n50,01119 e11,80565.

10 ⊠€ 7 + € 1/pp tourist tax ⊟⊞Ch ⊿WCincluded ⊟€ 2.⊡
**Location:** Rural, simple, quiet.
**Surface:** grassy.
⊡ 01/01-31/12.
**Distance:** ⊿on the spot ⊗600m ⊿1km ⊹on the spot ⊿on the spot.

⊞S **Wassertrüdingen** **17C2**
**An der Wörnitz**, Entengraben. **GPS:** n49,03926 e10,59494.⬆⊳.

12 ⊠free ⊟€ 1/80liter ⊞Ch ⊿(6x)€ 2/8h ⊟€ 1.
**Location:** Urban, simple, quiet. **Surface:** metalled.

---

⊡ 01/01/2019-31/12/2019.
**Distance:** ⊿on the spot ⊿on the spot ⊷on the spot ⊿1km.

⊞ **Weidenberg** ⊕ **12E3**
**Am Sportpark**, In der Au. **GPS:** n49,93859 e11,73117.⚐⬆.

5 ⊠free. **Location:** Rural, simple. **Surface:** gravel.
⊡ 01/01-31/12.
**Distance:** ⊿750m ⊗Chinese restaurant 100m ⊿1,5km.

⊞S **Weilheim in Oberbayern** ❀⚓⊕ **20D2**
Lohgasse. **GPS:** n47,84012 e11,13583.⬆.

8 ⊠€ 6 ⊟€ 0,50/50liter ⊞Ch ⊿€ 0,50/kWh WC.⊟.
**Location:** Urban, simple, central. **Surface:** asphalted.
⊡ 01/01-31/12.
**Distance:** ⊿Old city centre 500m ⊷100m ⊿200m.
**Remarks:** Along the Ammer river, max. 5 days.

⊞S **Weismain** ❀⚓ **12D3**
**Bauhof**, Burgkunstadterstrasse. **GPS:** n50,08639 e11,23872.⬆⊳.

6 ⊠free ⊟€ 1/100liter ⊞€ 1 Ch€ 1 ⊿(6x)€ 0,50/kWh.
**Location:** Urban, simple, central. **Surface:** asphalted.
⊡ 01/01-31/12.
**Distance:** ⊿on the spot ⊿on the spot ⊿200m ⊿200m ⊷200m.
**Remarks:** Parking in centre.

⊞S **Weissenburg** ❀⚓ **17D2**
**Kirchweihplatz, Limesbad**, Badstrasse 5.
**GPS:** n49,02476 e10,97180.⬆⊳.

6 ⊠free ⊟€ 1/60liter ⊞Ch ⊿(6x)€ 0,50/kWh. **Location:** Urban, simple, noisy. **Surface:** metalled. ⊡ 01/04-31/10.
**Distance:** ⊿Old city centre 300m ⊗La Fattoria, Frauentorstrasse 11; Mai Tai, Bismarckanlage 16; Wittelsbacher Hof, Fr.Ebertstrasse 21 ⊿700m ⊷on the spot ⊿on the spot.
**Remarks:** Service closed during wintertime.

⊞ **Weissenburg** ❀⚓ **17D2**
**Parkplatz Seeweiher**, An der Hagenau. **GPS:** n49,02660 e10,97500.⬆.

---

25 ⊠free. **Location:** Urban, simple, quiet. **Surface:** metalled.
⊡ 01/01-31/12.
**Distance:** ⊿200m ⊿1,5km ⊷on the spot ⊿on the spot.

⊞S **Weissenburg** ❀⚓ **17D2**
**Vino y Tapa Restaurant**, Silbermühle 4. **GPS:** n49,04521 e10,96679.⊳.

9 ⊠free ⊟⊿against payment. **Location:** Rural, simple, quiet.
**Surface:** grassy/metalled. ⊡ 01/01-31/12.
**Distance:** ⊿city centre 2km ⊗on the spot ⊿on the spot ⊿on the spot.
**Remarks:** Restaurant closed on Tuesday, restaurant closed on Monday.

⊞S **Weissenstadt** **12E3**
**Siebenquell**, Schönlinder Weg 32. **GPS:** n50,09314 e11,87152.⬆.

15 ⊠€ 12 + € 1/pp tourist tax ⊟⊞Chincluded ⊟€ 1.⌂⊡
**Location:** Rural, comfortable. **Surface:** gravel. ⊡ 01/01-31/12.
**Distance:** ⊿1,5km ⊿100m ⊗on the spot ⊿1,5km ⊿on the spot ⊿on the spot.
**Remarks:** Breakfast-service.

⊞S **Wertach** ❀⚓⛰❀⊞❄❀ **20C2**
**Camping Grüntensee**, Grüntenseestraße 41.
**GPS:** n47,61003 e10,44704.⬆⊳.

10 ⊠€ 15 + € 1,50/pp tourist tax ⊟⊞Ch ⊿(12x)€ 0,60/kWh.⊡
**Location:** Rural, luxurious, quiet. **Surface:** gravel.
⊡ 01/01-31/12.
**Distance:** ⊿2,5km ⊿600m ⊿on the spot ⊷on the spot ⊗on the spot ⊿1,5km ⊷1,5km ⊿on the spot ⊿on the spot ⊿on the spot ⊿on the spot.

⊞S **Wertach** ❀⚓⛰❀⊞❄❀ **20C2**
**Buron-Kinderpark**, Grüntenseestraße 44. **GPS:** n47,61028 e10,44972.

36 ⊠€ 5 ⊟€ 1/100liter ⊞Ch ⊿(24x)€ 1,50/24h ⊿.

DE

**Surface:** gravel. ☐ 01/01-31/12.
**Distance:** 🚶3km ⛰200m ⊗on the spot ⚕on the spot.

### 🏪S | Wertingen | 17D3

**Wohnmobilpark Wertingen**, Am Bahnhof 4.
**GPS:** n48,55948 e10,69065.⬆➡

12 🏕€7 🚰€ 0,50/50liter 🚿Ch☐(12x)€ 2/day. ♨
**Location:** Urban, comfortable, central, quiet. **Surface:** grassy/gravel.
☐ 01/01-31/12.
**Distance:** 🚶800m 🚉100m.
**Remarks:** Money in envelope in mail box.

### 🏪S | Wiesenttal | 12D3

**Wohnmobilstellplatz Streitburg**, Bahnhofstrasse, B470.
**GPS:** n49,80782 e11,21636.⬆➡

8 🏕€2 🚰🚿Ch☐included. **Location:** Rural, simple, quiet.
**Surface:** gravel. ☐ 01/01-31/12.
**Distance:** 🚶500m 🚲500m ⊗500m 🚉500m 🚌300m.
**Remarks:** Along railwayline.

### 🏪S | Wipfeld | 12C3

**An der Mainlände**, Follinaplatz. **GPS:** n49,91954 e10,17899.⬆➡

20 🏕€5 🚰€ 1/100liter 🚿ChWC. 🏠**Location:** Rural, comfortable.
**Surface:** asphalted. ☐ 01/01-31/12.
**Distance:** 🚶on the spot ⛰on the spot 🚲on the spot ⊗50m 🚉50m
⚕on the spot ⚘on the spot.

### 🏪S | Wolnzach | 17E3

**Schwimm- & Erlebnisbad Wolnzach**, Hanslmühlweg 6.
**GPS:** n48,59718 e11,62792.⬆

4 🏕free 🚰€ 1/80liter 🚿Ch⚡(4x)€ 0,50/kWh. **Location:** Rural,
simple, quiet. **Surface:** metalled. ☐ 01/05-30/09.
**Distance:** 🚶600m 🚲500m 🚉600m.
**Remarks:** Max. 3 days, service 100m.

### 🏪S | Wonneberg | 20G1

**Gasthof Alpenblick**, Traunsteiner Straße 21, Weibhausen.
**GPS:** n47,89880 e12,69123.⬆

5 🏕free, use of a meal desired WC☐against payment.
**Location:** Rural, simple, isolated, quiet. **Surface:** gravel.
☐ 01/01-31/12.
**Distance:** 🚶5km 🚲10km ⛰5km ⊗on the spot ⚕on the spot ⚘on
the spot.

### 🏪S | Wunsiedel | 12E3

**Wohnmobilstellplatz Festspielstadt Wunsiedel**, Ludwigstraße.
**GPS:** n50,03638 e11,99351.⬆

6 🏕€ 5/24h 🚰🚿Ch⚡included. ♨
**Location:** Rural, simple. **Surface:** asphalted/gravel.
☐ 01/01-31/12 💧 water: Nov-March.
**Distance:** 🚶600m ⊗300m 🚉1km.
**Remarks:** Pay at tourist office.

### 🏪S | Würzburg 🍂⚓ | 17B1

**Viehmarktplatz**, Dreikronenstraße. **GPS:** n49,79782 e9,92319.⬆

25 🏕€ 12/24h. 🏠**Location:** Urban, simple, noisy. **Surface:** asphalted.
☐ 01/01-31/12.
**Distance:** 🚶800m ⛰on the spot ⊗50m.
**Remarks:** Max. 2 days.
**Tourist information Würzburg:**
👁 Würzburger Residenz, Residenzplatz. Baroque castle, Unesco World
Heritage Site. ☐ 01/04-31/10 9-18h, 01/11-31/03 10-16.30h. 🎟 € 7,50.

### 🏪 | Zeil am Main 🍂 | 12C3

**Altstadtparkplatz**, Mittelweg. **GPS:** n50,00667 e10,59583.⬆➡

10 🏕free.
**Location:** Urban, simple, noisy. **Surface:** metalled.
☐ 01/01-31/12.
**Distance:** 🚶on the spot ⊗350m 🚉550m 🚌400m ⚘400m ⚕400m.

### 🏪 | Zeil am Main 🍂 | 12C3

**Parkplatz Tuchanger**, Oskar Winkler strasse.
**GPS:** n50,01083 e10,59056.⬆➡

20 🏕free. **Location:** Urban, simple. **Surface:** metalled.
☐ 01/01-31/12.
**Distance:** 🚶1km ⊗1km 🚉1km 🚌1km ⚘1km ⚕1km.
**Remarks:** Parking gymnasium.
**Tourist information Zeil am Main:**
⊗ Brauereigasthof Göller "Zum alten Freyung". Brewery restaurant
with regional specialities and Göller-beer. ☐ Mo-Su 9.30-01h.
🌟 Altstadt Weinfest. Wine festivals. ☐ 06/08-08/08.
🚲 Wein-Wander-Weg. Hiking trail through wine region.

### 🏪 | Zellingen 🍂 | 12B3

**Am Freibad**, Badstraße. **GPS:** n49,89476 e9,82680.⬆

6 🏕free. **Location:** Rural, simple, quiet. **Surface:** grassy.
☐ 01/01-31/12.
**Distance:** ⚘on the spot.

# 🇩🇰 Denmark

Capital: Copenhagen
Government: Constitutional monarchy
Official Language: Danish
Population: 5,605,948 (2017)
Area: 44,000 km²

## General information

Dialling code: 0045
General emergency: 112
Currency: Danish Krone (DKK), 1 DKK= 100 øre,
DKK 1 = € 0,13, € 1 = DKK 7,45
DKK 1 = £0.12, £1 = DKK 8,53 (October 2018)
Payments by credit card are accepted at almost
every shop and restaurant.

### Regulations for overnight stays/campsites

Overnight parking is allowed: for 1 night, if there
is no local prohibition, but no "camping" activities
are allowed.

### Additional public holidays 2019

Mai 17 Great Prayer Day
June 5 Danisch Constitution Day
June 23 Sankt Hans Eve

### Time Zone

Winter (Standard Time) GMT+1
Summer (DST) GMT+2

Aalborg
Aarhus
Jutland
pages: 317-331
Copenhagen
Odense
Funen
pages:
331-334
Seeland, Lolland,
Møn and Falster
pages: 334-337

**DK**

# Jutland

### ⚜S Aabybro 5C3
**Birthe&Leif Brinkmann**, Kanalvej 164. **GPS**: n57,11947 e9,73156.⬆.

3 🗓DKK 50. ⛽ **Location**: Simple, isolated. **Surface**: grassy.
◻ 01/05-30/09.
**Distance**: 🚰5km.

### ⚼S Aalborg 5C3
**Aalborg**, Skydebanevej 50. **GPS**: n57,05379 e9,87233.⬆.
🗓DKK 126 🚰🔌Ch 🔧against payment. 🏪 **Location**: Rural.
**Surface**: asphalted. ◻ 01/01-31/12.
**Distance**: 🚰centre 1,8km 🅿on the spot.
**Remarks**: Quick-Stop: >20h - <10h.

### ⚼S Aalborg 5C3
**Strandparken**, Skydebanevej 20. **GPS**: n57,05502 e9,88499.⬆.

2 🗓DKK 36-220 🚰DKK 38 🔌Ch 🔧against payment. 🏪
**Location**: Rural. **Surface**: grassy/gravel.
◻ 02/01-15/12.
**Remarks**: Quick-Stop: >20h - <10h, special part for motor homes.

**Tourist information Aalborg:**
ℹ Aalborg Tourist & Convention Bureau, østeraagade 8, www.
visitaalborg.com.
Ⓜ Søfarts - og Marinemuseum, Vestre Fjordvej 81. Maritime museum.
◻ 01/05-31/12.
Aalborg Zoo, Mølleparkvej 63. Zoo. ◻ 01/05-30/12.

### 🏪S Aalbæk 5C2
**Galleri & Selskabslokal Gyllegaard**, Hirtshalsvej 48.
**GPS**: n57,60619 e10,41757.⬆➡.

5 🗓DKK 100. ⛽ **Location**: Simple, isolated, quiet. **Surface**: grassy.
◻ 01/01-31/12.
**Distance**: 🚰4km 🏊1km ⊗4km 🛒4km.

### ⚓S Aalbæk 5C2
**Aalbæk Havn**, Sønder Havnevej 69. **GPS**: n57,59306 e10,42686.⬆.

6 🗓DKK 190 🚰🔌Ch 🚿(6x)WC 🗑DKK 20/20 🚿included. ⛽
**Location**: Urban, simple, quiet. **Surface**: gravel.
◻ 01/01-31/12.
**Distance**: 🚰800m 🅿on the spot 🚐on the spot ⊗800m 🛒800m
🚏250m.
**Remarks**: Pay at harbourmaster.

### ⚜S Aalbæk 5C2
**Ålbæk Bed & Breakfast**, Hirtshalsvej 524.
**GPS**: n57,60570 e10,36010.⬆.

8 🗓DKK 125 🚰🔋🔌(11x),3Amp WC🗑included 🗑. ⛽
**Location**: Rural, comfortable, isolated, quiet. **Surface**: grassy.
◻ 01/01-31/12.
**Distance**: 🚰4km 🏊4,5km ⊗5km 🛒4km 🚿on the spot 🧗on the
spot.

### 🏪 Aalbæk 5C2
**Skiveren Camping**, Niels Skiverens Vej 5-7.
**GPS**: n57,61616 e10,27891.⬆.

🗓22-8h DKK 10/h, 8-22h DKK 20/h (min. DKK 100). 🏪
**Location**: Rural, isolated. **Surface**: grassy. ◻ 18/03-30/09.
**Distance**: 🅿on the spot ⊗on the spot 🚐on the spot.
**Remarks**: Quick-Stop: >20h - <10h.

### ⚼S Aarhus 6D1
**Marselisborg Havn**, Marselisborg Havnevej 54.
**GPS**: n56,13927 e10,21916.➡.

24 🗓DKK 150 🚰DKK 7/3minutes 🔌Ch 🔧DKK 2,15/kWh WC 🗑DKK 7/
time 🚿included. 🏪 **Location**: Urban. **Surface**: gravel/metalled.
◻ 01/05-30/09.
**Distance**: 🚰on the spot 🅿on the spot 🚐on the spot ⊗on the spot.

### 🏪S Aarhus 6D1
**Aarhus Camping**, Randersvej 400. **GPS**: n56,22672 e10,16335.➡.
9 🗓DKK 100 🚰🔌Chagainst payment 🔧DKK 3,75/kWh 🗑DKK 5.
**Surface**: grassy. ◻ 01/01-31/12.
**Remarks**: Quick-Stop.

### 🏪S Åbenrå 6D2
**Camperstop Aabenraa**, Sønderskovvej 104.
**GPS**: n55,02513 e9,41471.⬆.

34 🗓DKK 100 🚰DKK 20/120liter 🔌Ch 🔧DKK 4,50/kWh
WC🗑DKK 10/5minutes 🗑DKK 25 🚿. 🏪 **Location**: Rural, simple,
central, quiet. **Surface**: grassy/gravel. ◻ 01/01-31/12.
**Distance**: 🚰2km 🏊8km 🅿400m 🚐400m ⊗700m 🛒600m.
**Remarks**: Chip-card available at campsite.

### 🏪S Åbenrå 6D2
**Lystbådehavn**, Kystvej 55. **GPS**: n55,03434 e9,42352.➡.

48 �DKK 125 🚰🔧Ch.⚡DKK 1 WCincluded ⬜DKK 20 ◉DKK 30
📶.🏠 **Location:** Rural, simple, comfortable, central. **Surface:** gravel.
⬛ 01/01-31/12.
**Distance:** 🏊1km ⛵on the spot 🍴on the spot ⊗on the spot 🛒300m
�鉄200m 🚲 on the spot 🚶on the spot.
**Remarks:** Harbour Åbenrå.

| ⓒ | Åbenrå 🌿🍽️🏭🏖️ | 6D2 |

**Sandskaer Strandcamping,** Sandskaervej 592.
**GPS:** n55,11703 e9,49592.⬆️
1 ⌶DKK 100. 🏤 **Location:** Rural. **Surface:** asphalted.
⬛ 18/03-18/09.
**Distance:** 🏊100m.
**Remarks:** Quick-Stop: >20h - <10h.

| ⓒ S | Aså | 5C3 |

**Asaa Camping og Hytteferie,** Vodbindervej 13.
**GPS:** n57,14560 e10,40264.⬆️
4 ⌶DKK 145 🚰🔧Ch⚡DKK 35/day WCincluded ⬜DKK 5/5minutes.
**Location:** Rural. **Surface:** grassy/gravel. ⬛ 09/04-24/09.
**Distance:** 🏊300m ⊗300m 🛒250m 🚲on the spot 🚶on the spot.
**Remarks:** Quick-Stop.

| 🏕️ S | Augustenborg 🌿🍽️🏭🏖️ | 6D2 |

**Augustenborg Slot,** Ny Stavensbøl 1. **GPS:** n54,94703 e9,85427.

70 ⌶DKK 130 🚰🔧Ch⚡ WC⬜included. 🛵 **Location:** Rural,
comfortable. **Surface:** grassy. ⬛ 01/01-31/12.
**Distance:** 🏊1,5km 🍴on the spot 🚲on the spot.

| 🏕️ S | Augustenborg 🌿🍽️🏭🏖️ | 6D2 |

**Augustenborg Yachthavn,** Langdel 6. **GPS:** n54,94074 e9,86942.⬆️.

19 ⌶DKK 140 🚰🔧Ch⚡DKK 25 WCincluded ◉⬜DKK 10. 🛵
**Location:** Rural, comfortable, central. **Surface:** grassy/gravel.
⬛ 01/04-31/10.
**Distance:** 🏊700m 🍴1km 🚲on the spot.

| 🏕️ S | Billund | 6C1 |

**Camperpark Billund,** Grenevej 5, Billund. **GPS:** n55,70480 e9,12406.⬆️

10 ⌶€ 16 🚰🔧Chincluded ⚡€ 3 WC⬜€ 3 ◉€ 3 📶.
**Location:** Rural, comfortable. **Surface:** grassy. ⬛ 01/01-31/12.
**Distance:** 🏊3,5km ⊗3,5km 🛒3,5km.

| 🏕️ S | Bindslev | 5C3 |

**Tannisbugt Hallen,** Stadion alle 7. **GPS:** n57,54559 e10,19943.⬆️.

20 ⌶DKK 75 🚰🔧ChWC. 🛵 **Location:** Urban, simple, quiet.
**Surface:** asphalted. ⬛ 01/01-31/12. ◉ 15/07-07/08.
**Distance:** 🏊on the spot ⊗on the spot 🛒400m.
**Remarks:** At gymnasium.

| ⓒ S | Broager | 6D3 |

**Gammelmark Strand Camping,** Gammelmark 20.
**GPS:** n54,88586 e9,72926.⬆️
5 ⌶DKK 150 🚰🔧⚡(5x)included.
**Surface:** grassy. ⬛ 23/03-02/10.
**Distance:** 🏊100m.
**Remarks:** Quick-Stop: >20h - <10h.

| ⓒ | Broager | 6D3 |

**Broager Strand Camping,** Skeldebro 32. **GPS:** n54,86780 e9,74419.
⌶DKK 99. ⬛ 01/01-31/12.
**Distance:** 🏊100m.
**Remarks:** Quick-Stop: >20h - <10h.

| 🐴 S | Brovst | 5C3 |

**Vilsbæk Ridecenter,** Kanalvej 34. **GPS:** n57,11895 e9,53640.⬆️.

10 ⌶DKK 75 🚰🔧Ch⚡ WCincluded. 🛵 **Location:** Rural, simple,
isolated, quiet. **Surface:** grassy. ⬛ 01/01-31/12.
**Distance:** 🏊2km.
**Remarks:** At manege.

| ⓒ S | Brovst | 5C3 |

**Tranum Klit Camping,** Sandmosevej 525. **GPS:** n57,17097 e9,46312.⬆️.
5 ⌶DKK 100 🚰🔧ChWC⬜📶included. **Location:** Rural, isolated.
**Surface:** grassy/metalled. ⬛ 19/03-02/10.
**Distance:** 🏊5km ⊗5km.
**Remarks:** Quick-Stop: >20h - <10h.

| 🏛️ S | Brædstrup | 6D1 |

**Hunos Museum & Samlinger,** Hallevej 7.
**GPS:** n55,98548 e9,50352.⬆️
⌶DKK 100 ⚡DKK 20. **Location:** Rural. **Surface:** grassy/gravel.
**Distance:** 🏊8,5km.
**Remarks:** At museum.

| 🏕️ S | Brønderslev | 5C3 |

**Serritslev Fiskepark,** Agårdsvej 35. **GPS:** n57,29750 e9,99597.⬆️.

20 ⌶DKK 50 🚰free WC. 🛵 **Location:** Rural, simple, isolated, quiet.
**Surface:** grassy. ⬛ 01/01-31/12.
**Distance:** 🍴on the spot.
**Remarks:** Fishpond.

| 🏕️ S | Brønderslev | 5C3 |

**Stenberggade. GPS:** n57,27475 e9,95239.⬆️.

20 ⌶free 🚰🔧Chfree. **Location:** Urban, simple. **Surface:** gravel.
⬛ 01/01-31/12.
**Distance:** 🏊on the spot ⊗250m 🛒1km.
**Remarks:** At gymnasium, bowling.

| 🐴 S | Brønderslev | 5C3 |

**Ny Vestermark,** Hollenstedvej 247. **GPS:** n57,21578 e10,04992.⬆️.

2 ⌶DKK 100 🚰🔧ChWC⬜included ◉against payment. 🛵
**Location:** Rural, isolated, quiet. **Surface:** grassy.
⬛ 01/01-31/12.
**Distance:** 🏊5km.

| 🐴 S | Bylderup-Bov 🏭 | 6C2 |

**Boskov,** Kvænholtvej 15. **GPS:** n54,94488 e9,06078.⬆️🏕️.

10 ⌶DKK 55 🚰🔧Ch⚡included. 🛵 **Location:** Rural, simple,
isolated, quiet. **Surface:** grassy/gravel. ⬛ 01/01-31/12.
**Distance:** 🏊4km 🛒200m.

| 🏕️ S | Bylderup-Bov 🏭 | 6C2 |

**B&B Bredevad,** Bredevadvej 5. **GPS:** n54,96885 e9,12138.⬆️.

2 ⌶DKK 110 🚰⚡WC⬜📶included. 🛵 **Location:** Rural,
comfortable, isolated. **Surface:** grassy. ⬛ 01/01-31/12.
**Distance:** 🏊15km 🍴9km 🛒4km 🚲on the spot 🚶on the spot.

| △ S | Bylderup-Bov 🏭 | 6C2 |

**Kristianshåb Autocamper Park,** Kristianshåbvej 5.
**GPS:** n54,96189 e9,06950.➡️.
25 ⌶DKK 110, 2 pers.incl 🚰🔧Ch⚡DKK 15/kWh WC⬜DKK 25.
**Location:** Comfortable, isolated.
⬛ 01/01-31/12.
**Distance:** 🏊6km 🏊1km ⊗5km.

**Tourist information Bylderup-Bov:**
🏰 Schackenborg Slot, Schackenborg 2, Tønder. Visit the castle garden.

| 🐴 S | Bækmarksbro | 6C1 |

**Staudehaven-Granly,** Kræmmergårdvej 5.
**GPS:** n56,41032 e8,31595.⬆️.

DK

3 �⃗DKK 50 ⛽included. **Location:** Simple, quiet.
**Surface:** grassy/gravel. ◻ 01/01-31/12.

| 🚿S | **Bælum** | 5C3 |

**Bakgaarden**, Hælskovvej 2. **GPS:** n56,83815 e10,12007.⬆.

4 ⌃DKK 75 ⛽Ch⛽included.🚲
**Surface:** grassy. ◻ 01/01-31/12.
**Distance:** 1km 🛒1km.

| ⚓S | **Bønnerup** 🚣 | 5D3 |

**Bønnerup Lystbådehavn**, Vestre Mole 2, Glesborg.
**GPS:** n56,53139 e10,71139.⬆.

20 ⌃DKK 150 ⛽Ch⛽(12x)included WC ◻ against payment.
🚲 **Location:** Rural, comfortable, quiet. **Surface:** gravel.
◻ 01/01-31/12.
**Distance:** 500m ⚓on the spot 🛒on the spot ✕250m 🛒400m.
**Remarks:** Parking at marina.

| ⚓S | **Børkop** 🚣 | 6D1 |

**Brejning Lystbådehavn**, Brejning Strand.
**GPS:** n55,67431 e9,68920.⬆.

12 ⌃DKK 150 ⛽⛽(12x)WC ◻included 📶.🚐📦
**Location:** Rural, simple, isolated, quiet. **Surface:** gravel/metalled.
◻ 01/05-30/10.
**Distance:** Børkop 5km 🚲4,1km ⚓10m ✕10m.
**Remarks:** Restaurant only in summer.

| 🚿S | **Ebeltoft** | 6D1 |

**Skøvgarde**, Havmøllevej 5. **GPS:** n56,24475 e10,77902.⬆➡.

2 ⌃DKK 50 ⛽DKK 20.🚲 **Location:** Rural, simple, isolated, quiet.
**Surface:** grassy. ◻ 01/01-31/12.
**Distance:** on the spot ⚲ on the spot.
**Remarks:** Pay at Havmøllevej 5 or 20.

---

| 🚿 | **Ebeltoft** | 6D1 |

**Lystebadehaven**, Havneweg 15. **GPS:** n56,19448 e10,66834.⬆.

7 ⌃overnight stay free ⛽🚐Ch⛽WCfree ◻according consumption.
**Location:** Urban, comfortable, central. **Surface:** asphalted/metalled.
◻ 01/01-31/12.
**Distance:** 500m ✕500m 🛒on the spot.

| ⚓S | **Ebeltoft** | 6D1 |

**Ebeltoft Skudehavn**, Skudehavnen 61. **GPS:** n56,19025 e10,66999.⬆.

15 ⌃DKK 160 ⛽🚐Chincluded ⛽DKK 2,50/kWh WC ◻ 📦against
payment 📶.🚐📦
**Location:** Urban. **Surface:** gravel. ◻ 01/05-15/09.
**Distance:** 1,2km on the spot ✕500m.

| 🚿S | **Ebeltoft** | 6D1 |

**Dråby Strand**, Dråby Strandvej 13. **GPS:** n56,22172 e10,73778.➡.
⌃DKK 100 ⛽🚐Chincluded ⛽DKK 26. ◻ 19/03-14/09.
**Remarks:** Quick-Stop: >20h - <10h.

| 🚿S | **Ebeltoft** | 6D1 |

**Ebeltoft Strand Camping**, Ndr. Strandvej 23.
**GPS:** n56,20983 e10,67852.
5 ⌃DKK 120 ⛽🚐ChWC ◻ 📶included.
**Surface:** asphalted. ◻ 01/01-31/12.
**Distance:** ⚓100m ✕1km 🛒600m.
**Remarks:** Quick-Stop: >20h - <10h.

| 🚿S | **Ebeltoft** | 6D1 |

**Elsegårde**, Kristoffenvejen 1. **GPS:** n56,16843 e10,72278.
⌃DKK 140 ⛽🚐Ch⛽against payment. ◻ 01/01-31/12.
**Remarks:** Quick-Stop: >20h - <10h.

| 🚿S | **Egå** 🚣 | 6D1 |

**Egå Marina**, Egå Havnevej 35. **GPS:** n56,20960 e10,28659.⬆.

7 ⌃DKK 160 ⛽🚐Ch⛽(7x)WCincluded ◻DKK 5/5minutes
◻DKK 40/10 📶.🚐📦 **Location:** Rural, comfortable.
**Surface:** asphalted. ◻ 01/01-31/12.
**Distance:** 2km ⚓400m on the spot ✕on the spot 🛒600m
🚗600m.
**Remarks:** Tallycard: service, electricity, sanitary building, caution
DKK 50.

| ⚓S | **Ejerslev** 🚣 | 5C3 |

**Ejerslev Havn**, Utkærvej 11. **GPS:** n56,91855 e8,92096.⬆➡.

10 ⌃DKK 100 ⛽🚐Ch⛽(10x)DKK 20 WC ◻included ◻DKK 20/20.

---

🚲 **Location:** Rural, isolated, quiet. **Surface:** gravel.
◻ 01/01-31/12.
**Distance:** 4km ⚓on the spot ✕on the spot 🛒4km 🚲on the spot
⚲ on the spot.
**Remarks:** Bread-service, last 2km gravel road, borrow cycles for free.

| 🚿S | **Engesvan** | 6C1 |

**Pårup Autocamperplads**, Silkeborgvej 8. **GPS:** n56,13694 e9,35028.⬆.
4 ⌃DKK 50 ⛽Ch⛽included. 🚲 **Location:** Urban, simple,
central. **Surface:** gravel. ◻ 01/04-01/11.
**Distance:** on the spot.

| ⚓S | **Erslev** | 5C3 |

**Sundby Mors Havn**, Sundbyvej 236. **GPS:** n56,88440 e8,63886.

15 ⌃DKK 60 ⛽DKK 20 WCfree.
**Location:** Simple. **Surface:** gravel.
**Distance:** ⚓on the spot on the spot ✕800m.

| 🚿S | **Erslev** | 5C3 |

**Inger-Marie og Knud Erik Nielsen**, Bindeleddet 4.
**GPS:** n56,83881 e8,68060.⬆.

4 ⌃DKK 40 ⛽🚐.🚲 **Location:** Rural, simple, isolated, quiet.
**Surface:** gravel. ◻ 01/01-31/12.
**Distance:** 1km.

| 🚿S | **Esbjerg** 🚣 ⛲ | 6C2 |

**Nebel Sø**, Vestervadsvej 17, Vester Nebel.
**GPS:** n55,55000 e8,54361.⬆➡.

25 ⌃DKK 60, 2 pers.incl ⛽DKK 10 ⛽DKK 25.🚲
**Location:** Rural, simple, isolated, quiet.
**Surface:** grassy/gravel.
◻ 01/04-01/11.
**Distance:** 15km on the spot.
**Remarks:** Fishpond, fishing license DKK90 www.nebelsoe.dk.

| 🚿S | **Fanø** | 6C2 |

**Fanø Fiskesø**, Storetoft 30. **GPS:** n55,43401 e8,39294.
4 ⌃DKK 100 ⛽🚐Ch⛽WC ◻ 📶against payment.
**Surface:** gravel. ◻ 01/01-31/12.
**Distance:** on the spot.
**Remarks:** At fish pond.

| 🚿 | **Fanø** | 6C2 |

**Feldberg Familie Camping**, Kirkevejen 3-5, Rindby.
**GPS:** n55,42894 e8,39211.
5 ⌃DKK 100. ◻ 23/03-21/10.
**Remarks:** Quick-Stop: >20h - <10h.

| ⚓S | **Farsø** | 5C3 |

**Hvalpsund Autocamperplads**, Fjordvej 1, Hvalpsund.
**GPS:** n56,70584 e9,20565.⬆➡.

**DK**

10 �〽DKK 115 ⏚⏚Ch⌁⌁WC⏺DKK 10/5minutes ◉DKK 20/20 ⌁included.🚐🧰 **Location:** Rural, comfortable, quiet. **Surface:** grassy. ⏺ 01/01-31/12. **Distance:** ⌁on the spot ⌁on the spot ⊗on the spot.

**☖S Fjerritslev** 5C3
**Erna K Nielsen**, Holmsøvej 31, Haverslev. GPS: n57,04102 e9,39252.⬆.

6 ⌽DKK 50 ⏚⌁included.🚿 **Location:** Rural, simple, quiet. **Surface:** grassy. ⏺ 01/01-31/12. **Distance:** ⌁on the spot ⌁Limfjord 1,7km.

**☖S Fjerritslev** 5C3
**Niels Balle**, Hedegardsvej 19, Hjortdal. GPS: n57,12505 e9,33422.⬆.

4 ⌽DKK 75 ⌁(1x)included.🚿 **Location:** Rural, simple, isolated. **Surface:** grassy. ⏺ 01/01-31/12. **Distance:** ⌁7km ⌁4km.

**⚓S Fjerritslev** 5C3
**Haverslev Havn**, Havegade 72. GPS: n57,02956 e9,39971.⬆.

15 ⌽DKK 100 ⏚⌁(6x)WC⏺⌁included.🚿 **Location:** Rural, comfortable, isolated, quiet. **Surface:** grassy/gravel. ⏺ 01/01-31/12. **Distance:** ⌁on the spot ⌁on the spot.

**☖S Flauenskjold** 5C3
**Flauenskjold Autocamping**, Agertoften 4, Dronninglund. GPS: n57,24854 e10,28477.⬆➡.

10 ⌽DKK 50 ⏚⏚⌁DKK 25 WCincluded.🚿 **Location:** Rural, simple, quiet. **Surface:** grassy/gravel. ⏺ 01/01-31/12. **Distance:** ⌁5km. **Remarks:** Money in envelope in mail box, festival and market place.

**☖S Fredericia** 6D2
**Lystbådehavnen**, Strandvejen 115, Sanddalbakke. GPS: n55,55246 e9,72805.⬆.

8 ⌽DKK 100 ⏚⌁Ch⌁(8x)WC⏺⌁included.🚐🧰🔧. **Location:** Rural, simple, quiet. **Surface:** metalled. ⏺ 01/01-31/12. **Distance:** ⌁1km ⌁on the spot ⌁on the spot ⊗on the spot ⌁1km ⌁200m. **Remarks:** Tallycard: service, electricity, sanitary building, caution DKK 50.

**☖S Fredericia** 6D2
**Fredericia Havn**, Svovlsyrekaj. GPS: n55,55780 e9,75980.⬆.

10 ⌽free. **Location:** Urban, simple. **Surface:** metalled. ⏺ 01/01-31/12. **Distance:** ⌁2km ⌁on the spot ⊗400m ⌁1km.

**⚓S Frederikshavn** 5C3
**Frederikshavn Marina**, Søsportsvej 8. GPS: n57,42375 e10,52709.⬆.

20 ⌽DKK 160 ⏚⌁Ch⌁(10x)WC⏺DKK 25/25 ⌁included. 🚐🧰 **Location:** Urban, comfortable, central, quiet. **Surface:** grassy/gravel. ⏺ 01/01-31/12. **Distance:** ⌁800m ⌁on the spot ⌁on the spot ⊗on the spot ⌁700m. **Remarks:** Pay at harbourmaster.

**⚓S Frederikshavn** 5C3
**Rønnerhavnen**, Nordre Strandvej. GPS: n57,46277 e10,53729.⬆➡.

10 ⌽DKK 150 ⏚⌁Ch⌁DKK 30 WC⏺⌁.🚐🧰 **Location:** Rural, comfortable, quiet. **Surface:** grassy. ⏺ 01/01-31/12. **Distance:** ⌁on the spot ⌁on the spot ⊗on the spot. **Remarks:** Palmestranden 200m.

**☖S Frederikshavn** 5C3
**Svalereden**, Frederikshavnsvej 112B. GPS: n57,36001 e10,50927. ⌽DKK 100 ⏚⌁Ch⌁. **Location:** Isolated. ⏺ 01/01-31/12. **Remarks:** Quick-Stop: >20h - <10h.

**☖S Fur** 5C3
**Fur Camping**, Råkildevej 6. GPS: n56,83352 e8,97739.

⌁€1/h ⏚⌁Chservice €6 ⌁DKK 0,50/kWh ⌁DKK 3,50. **Location:** Isolated, quiet. ⏺ 18/03-05/09. **Distance:** ⌁650m. **Remarks:** Max. 1 night.

**☖S Gistrup** 5C3
**Kirsten og Karl Age**, Gunderupvej 164. GPS: n56,93476 e9,95844.⬆.

4 ⌽DKK 100 ⏚included ⌁DKK 50.🚿 **Location:** Rural, simple, isolated. **Surface:** gravel.

**☖S Give** 6C1
**Give Camping**, Skovbakken 34. GPS: n55,85051 e9,22953. ⌽DKK 160 ⌁DKK 35/10kWh. 🚐 **Location:** Rural, comfortable. **Surface:** asphalted/grassy. ⏺ 19/03-25/09. **Distance:** ⌁500m ⌁on the spot ⌁500m. **Remarks:** Quick-Stop: >20h - <10h.

**☖S Glejbjerg** 6C2
**Betina & Klaus Jørgensen**, Gammelgårdsvej 3, Bolding. GPS: n55,55052 e8,78705.⬆.

4 ⌽free ⏚⌁Ch⌁free WC⏺. **Location:** Rural, comfortable, isolated, quiet. **Surface:** grassy/metalled. ⏺ 01/01-31/12. **Distance:** ⌁3km ⌁3km. **Remarks:** Regional products.

**⚓S Grenaa** 5D3
**Grenaa Marina**, Skakkes Holm 62. GPS: n56,40570 e10,92440.➡.

9 ⌽DKK 150 ⌁DKK 15/24h. **Location:** Urban. **Surface:** metalled. ⏺ 01/01-31/12. **Distance:** ⌁1km ⌁on the spot ⊗600m.

**☖S Grenaa** 5D3
**Fornæs**, Stensmarkvej 36. GPS: n56,45398 e10,94009.➡. ⌽DKK 150-200 ⏚⌁Chagainst payment ⌁DKK 3,75/kWh. ⏺ 19/03-21/09. **Remarks:** Quick-Stop: >20h - <10h.

**☖S Grenaa** 5D3
**Grenaa Strand Camping**, Fuglsangvej 58. GPS: n56,38976 e10,91171.➡. 15 ⌽DKK 100 ⌁Ch⌁DKK 30 **Surface:** asphalted. ⏺ 23/03-04/09. **Distance:** ⌁300m. **Remarks:** Quick-Stop: >20h - <10h. **Tourist information Grenaa:**

Kattegatcentret, Færgevej 4. The underwater world and shark centre. ◻ 10-16/17h ◻ 13/12-26/12.

### 🅢 Haderslev ☙ 6D2
**CamperParken**, Landevej 63, Christiansfeld.
**GPS:** n55,27227 e9,49742.⬆️

12 🛏DKK 100 🚰⚡Chincluded ⚓DKK 30 WC⬜. **Location:** Rural, comfortable, central. **Surface:** gravel. ◻ 01/01-31/12.
**Distance:** 🚶100m.

### 🅢 Haderslev ☙ 6D2
**Fam. Nowak**, Fjelstrupvej 37. **GPS:** n55,25488 e9,52556.⬆️

2 🛏free 🚰DKK 5 ⚓DKK 5 📶.
**Location:** Rural. **Surface:** gravel. ◻ 01/01-31/12.
**Distance:** 🚶3km 🚶100m on the spot.

### ⚓🅢 Haderslev ☙ 6D2
**Årøsund Lystbådehavn**, Aarøsund Havn 28.
**GPS:** n55,26226 e9,70732.⬆️➡️

10 🛏DKK 130 🚰⚡Ch ⚓WC⬜ 📷 📶included. 🚮. **Location:** Rural, comfortable, quiet. **Surface:** gravel.
◻ 01/01-31/12.
**Distance:** 🚶Haderslev 16km 🛒on the spot 🚶on the spot ⊗on the spot.

### ⚓🅢 Haderslev ☙ 6D2
**Haderslev Sejl Club**, Sydhavnsvej 1F. **GPS:** n55,24806 e9,50028.⬆️

15 🛏DKK 130 🚰⚡ChWC⬜ 📶included. 🚮 **Location:** Urban, simple, quiet. **Surface:** gravel. ◻ 15/05-30/09.
**Distance:** 🚶500m on the spot.

### 🅒🅢 Haderslev ☙ 6D2
**Danhostel Haderslev**, Erlevvej 34. **GPS:** n55,24431 e9,47710.⬆️
2 🛏DKK 110, 2 pers.incl WC⬜included. 🚐
**Location:** Rural, simple. **Surface:** asphalted. ◻ 18/03-23/10.
**Distance:** 🛒on the spot.
**Remarks:** Quick-Stop: >20h - <10h.

### 🅒🅢 Haderslev ☙ 6D2
**Gåsevig Strand**, Gåsevig 19. **GPS:** n55,14222 e9,49903.
🛏DKK 109 🚰⚡Ch ⚓against payment.
**Location:** Rural. ◻ 19/03-18/09.
**Remarks:** Quick-Stop: >20h - <10h.

### 🅒🅢 Haderslev ☙ 6D2
**Halk**, Brunbjerg 105. **GPS:** n55,18599 e9,65374.

---

1 🛏DKK 75 🚰⚡Ch ⚓against payment. **Surface:** gravel.
◻ 24/03-18/09.
**Remarks:** Quick-Stop: >20h - <10h.

### 🅒 Haderslev ☙ 6D2
**Årø Camping**, Årø 260. **GPS:** n55,25942 e9,75240.
🛏DKK 100. ◻ 01/01-31/12.

### 🅒 Haderslev ☙ 6D2
**Sønderballe Strand Camping**, Diernæsvej 218.
**GPS:** n55,13243 e9,47610.⬆️
2 🛏DKK 130 ⚓DKK 30. 🏠
**Location:** Rural. **Surface:** gravel. ◻ 18/03-18/09.
**Distance:** 🛒on the spot.
**Remarks:** Quick-Stop: >20h - <10h.

### 🅒 Haderslev ☙ 6D2
**Vikær Strand Camping**, Dundelum 29. **GPS:** n55,15008 e9,49444.
6 🛏DKK 125 ⚓(6x)against payment.
**Surface:** gravel. ◻ 19/03-02/10.
**Distance:** 🛒on the spot.
**Remarks:** Quick-Stop: >20h - <10h.

**Tourist information Haderslev:**
👁 Sillerup Mølle, Sillerup Møllevej 35. Mill, bake bread yourself.
◻ 01/07-31/08 Su 13-17h.
⚑ Wachman's Tour. Excursion with the night watch in the old part of the city. ◻ 01/07-31/08 Thu 21h.

### 🅢 Hadsund ◳ 5C3
**Hvirvelkærgård**, Kystvejen 202, Als. **GPS:** n56,76414 e10,28565.⬆️

10 🛏DKK 90 🚰⚡ ⚓DKK 30 WC⬜included. 🚮
**Location:** Rural, simple, quiet. **Surface:** grassy. ◻ 01/01-31/12.
**Distance:** 🚶1km ⊗1km.

### ⚓🅢 Hadsund ◳ 5C3
**Hadsund Havn**, Thygeslundvej 3. **GPS:** n56,70988 e10,10428.⬆️

10 🛏DKK 130 🚰 ⚓WC⬜included. 🚮 **Location:** Rural, comfortable, quiet. **Surface:** grassy. ◻ 01/01-31/12.
**Distance:** 🚶2km 🛒on the spot 🚶on the spot ⊗2km 🚶2km.

### ⚓🅢 Hadsund ◳ 5C3
**Øster Hurup Havn**, Havnen 46. **GPS:** n56,80405 e10,27851.⬆️

10 🛏DKK 150 🚰⚡Ch ⚓WC⬜📷 📶included.
**Location:** Urban. **Surface:** gravel. ◻ 01/01-31/12.
**Distance:** 🚶500m 🛒on the spot ⊗500m 🚶500m.
**Remarks:** Tuesday market.

### 🅢 Hadsund ◳ 5C3
**Højvang Ferie**, Hobrovej 62-64. **GPS:** n56,70773 e10,07975.⬆️

---

4 🛏DKK 100 🚰⚓(2x)WC⬜included. 🚮 **Location:** Rural, simple.
**Surface:** grassy. ◻ 01/01-31/12.

### 🅒🅢 Hadsund ◳ 5C3
**Øster Hurup**, Kystvejen 70. **GPS:** n56,79990 e10,27324.⬆️➡️
🛏DKK 130 🚰⚡Chagainst payment ⚓DKK 35/day 🛏DKK 5/time.
◻ 19/03-25/09.
**Remarks:** Quick-Stop: >20h - <10h.

### 🅢 Hampen ☙ 6C1
**Karin en Thomas Schultz**, Frisbækvej 27.
**GPS:** n55,99840 e9,35122.⬆️➡️

10 🛏free 🚰⚡ChWC. **Location:** Rural, simple, isolated, quiet.
**Surface:** grassy. ◻ 01/01-31/12.
**Distance:** 🚶2km 🚶5km 🚶2km.

### 🅒🅢 Hanstholm ◳ 5C3
**THY Minicamping (Rær Autocamperplads)**, Bybakken 1a.
**GPS:** n57,08945 e8,67104.⬆️➡️

20 🛏DKK 100 🚰⚡Ch ⚓DKK 30 WCincluded ⬜DKK 10 📶. 🚮
**Location:** Rural, comfortable. **Surface:** grassy. ◻ 01/01-31/12.
**Distance:** 🚶Hanstholm 4km 🚶5km 🛒on the spot.

### 🅒🅢 Hanstholm ◳ 5C3
**Hanstholm**, Hamborgvej 95. **GPS:** n57,10909 e8,66724.⬆️
🛏DKK 170 🚰⚡Ch ⚓📶against payment. 🚐 **Location:** Rural.
**Surface:** gravel. ◻ 01/01-31/12.
**Remarks:** Quick-Stop: >20h - <10h.

### 🅢 Hanstholm ◳ 5C3
**Circle K Hanstholm**, Bødkervej 25. **GPS:** n57,11617 e8,62865.
free 🚰⚡Chfree. ◻ 01/01-31/12.
**Remarks:** At petrol station.

**Tourist information Hanstholm:**
👁 Frøstrup mini-village, Søndergade 36, Frøstrup. Miniature village.
◻ 01/05-15/10 Wed-Thu 10-12h, 01/07-31/08 daily 13.30-16.30h.

### 🅢 Havndal ◳ 5C3
**Udbyhøj Havn**, Havnevej 62 Udbyhøj. **GPS:** n56,61111 e10,30583.⬆️⬆️

30 🛏DKK 150 🚰⚡Chincluded ⚓against payment WC⬜📶.
🚐 🚮 **Location:** Rural, comfortable. **Surface:** asphalted.
◻ 01/01-31/12.
**Distance:** 🛒on the spot 🚶on the spot 🚶500m.

**DK**

## Havndal ⬛ 5C3

**Rethe og Hans Jørn Mogensen**, Klattrupgade 36, Klattrup.
**GPS:** n56,66397 e10,21208. ⬆.

4 ⬛DKK 50 🚰⬛Ch 💧included. 🚿 **Location:** Rural, simple, quiet.
**Surface:** grassy/gravel. ⬛ 01/01-31/12.
**Distance:** 🚶2km 🛒2km.

## Havndal ⬛ 5C3

**Randers Fjord**, Midtvasen 21. **GPS:** n56,60997 e10,29334. ➡.
2 ⬛DKK 125 🚰⬛Chincluded 💧against payment.
**Surface:** gravel. ⬛ 01/01-31/12.
**Remarks:** Quick-Stop: >20h - <10h.

## Hejls 6D2

**Hejlsminde Strand Camping**, Gendarmvej 3.
**GPS:** n55,36851 e9,60095. ⬆.
2 ⬛DKK 160 🚰⬛Ch 💧against payment. 🏠
**Location:** Rural. **Surface:** gravel. ⬛ 19/03-14/09.
**Remarks:** Quick-Stop: >20h - <10h.

## Hemmet 6C1

**Bork Havn**, Kirkehøjvej 9A. **GPS:** n55,84850 e8,28257.
⬛DKK 120 🚰⬛Ch 💧against payment. ⬛ 18/03-24/10.
**Remarks:** Quick-Stop: >20h - <10h.

## Herning 6C1

**Møllegade. GPS:** n56,13722 e8,96513. ⬆.

4 ⬛free. **Location:** Urban, simple, central. **Surface:** metalled.
⬛ 01/01-31/12.
**Distance:** 🚶on the spot ⊗100m 🛒200m.

## Hirtshals ⬛ 5C3

**Hirtshals Autocamperplads**, Doggerbanke.
**GPS:** n57,59027 e9,96449. ⬆.

20 ⬛DKK 75. ⬛ ⬛ **Location:** Urban, simple, central. **Surface:** grassy.
⬛ 01/01-31/12.
**Distance:** 🚶500m ⊗850m ⊗500m 🛒200m.

## Hirtshals ⬛ 5C3

**Willemoesvej. GPS:** n57,59097 e9,98601.

40 ⬛free. **Location:** Simple, quiet. **Surface:** unpaved.
⬛ 01/01-31/12.
**Distance:** 🚶1km ⛱Sandy beach ⊗1km.
**Remarks:** Parking ferry to Norway.

---

## Hirtshals ⬛ 5C3

**Bastholm**, Tverstedvej 1. **GPS:** n57,56550 e10,03920. ⬆.

10 ⬛DKK 50 🚰⬛💧included. **Location:** Rural, isolated, noisy.
**Surface:** grassy. ⬛ 01/01-31/12.
**Distance:** 🚶Hirtshals 5km ⊗700m.
**Remarks:** Not suitable for big motorhomes, narrow road.

## Hirtshals ⬛ 5C3

**Hirtshals Transport Center**, Dalsagervej 1.
**GPS:** n57,57645 e9,98480. ⬆.

7 ⬛DKK 75, 15/10-31/03 DKK 35 🚰⬛Ch 💧DKK 45,5Amp. 🏠
**Location:** Simple, isolated. **Surface:** asphalted. ⬛ 01/01-31/12.
**Distance:** ⊗on the spot.
**Remarks:** At petrol station, video surveillance.

## Hirtshals ⬛ 5C3

**Tornby Strand**, Strandvejen 13. **GPS:** n57,55540 e9,93264.
10 ⬛DKK 120-170, 2 pers incl. 🚰⬛Chagainst payment 💧DKK 40
. **Surface:** grassy/gravel. ⬛ 01/01-31/12.
**Distance:** ⊗on the spot.
**Remarks:** Quick-Stop: >20h - <10h.

## Hirtshals ⬛ 5C3

**Kjul Camping**, Kjulvej 12. **GPS:** n57,58279 e10,03132. ⬆.
2 ⬛DKK 130. 🏠 **Location:** Rural, isolated, quiet. **Surface:** grassy.
⬛ 18/03-30/09.
**Distance:** ⊗2,5km.
**Remarks:** Quick-Stop: >20h - <10h, golf court 1km.

**Tourist information Hirtshals:**
Ⓜ Nordsømuseet, Willemoesvej 2. Oceanarium, large aquarium.
⬛ 11/01-01/12 10-17.

## Hjallerup 5C3

**Peter Bastholm Galleri Retro**, Alborgvej 715.
**GPS:** n57,17919 e10,15856. ⬆.

5 ⬛DKK 100 💧DKK 25 ⬛. **Location:** Rural, isolated, quiet.
**Surface:** gravel. ⬛ 01/01-31/12.
**Distance:** 🎣fish pond.

## Hjørring 5C2

**Thomas Lindrup**, Tverstedvej 31. **GPS:** n57,57484 e10,12842. ⬆➡.

6 ⬛DKK 120 🚰⬛Ch 💧(6x)WC⬛included. 🚿 **Location:** Rural,
comfortable, isolated, quiet. **Surface:** grassy. ⬛ 01/01-31/12.

---

## Hjørring 5C2

**Martin Urban**, Tverstedvej 41, Uggerby.
**GPS:** n57,57523 e10,12868. ⬆➡.

6 ⬛DKK 120 🚰⬛Ch 💧included. 🚿 **Location:** Rural, isolated,
quiet. **Surface:** grassy. ⬛ 01/04-20/10.
**Distance:** 🚶3km ⊗3km 🛒3km.

## Hobro ⚓ 5C3

**Hobro Sejlklub**, Nedre Strandvej 75. **GPS:** n56,64382 e9,81092. ⬆.

3 ⬛DKK 130 🚰💧WC⬛📶included. **Location:** Urban.
**Surface:** grassy. ⬛ 01/04-31/10.
**Distance:** 🚶city centre 1km ⛽on the spot ⬛on the spot.
**Remarks:** Money in envelope in mail box.

## Hobro 5C3

**Hobro City Camping Gattenborg**, Skivevej 35.
**GPS:** n56,64015 e9,78265. ⬆➡.

3 ⬛DKK 172 🚰⬛Ch 💧DKK 30/1day WC⬛included. 🚿
**Location:** Urban. **Surface:** gravel. ⬛ 01/01-31/12.
**Distance:** 🚲on the spot 🚶on the spot.
**Remarks:** Quick-Stop.

## Holstebro ⬛ 6C1

**Viborgvej. GPS:** n56,35851 e8,63041. ⬆.

4 ⬛free. **Location:** Urban, simple. **Surface:** asphalted.
⬛ 01/01-31/12.
**Distance:** 🚶800m ⊗800m 🛒800m.

## Holsted 6C2

**Holsted Golfbanen**, Bergardsvej 4, Vejen-Esberg.
**GPS:** n55,52353 e8,93228.

15 ⬛€ 10 🚰💧WC. **Surface:** gravel. ⬛ 01/04-30/10.
**Distance:** 🚶1km.

## ⑤⑤ Horsens ♨♨ 6D1

**Lystbådehavn**, Jens Hjernøes Vej 35. **GPS:** n55,85764 e9,87417. ⬆➡

5 ⑤DKK 160 ⚡Ch ⚡WC⬜included ◻ ⬛.◻ ⬛
**Location:** Rural, comfortable, quiet.
**Surface:** gravel.
◻ 01/01-31/12.
**Distance:** ◻3km ⬛on the spot ◻on the spot ⊗on the spot.
**Remarks:** Harbour Horsen, special motorhome parking, Tallycard: service, electricity, sanitary building, caution DKK 50.
**Tourist information Horsens:**
👁 Dolmen "Jættestuen", åbjerg Skov. Dolmen. ◻ 01/01-31/12.

## ⑤ Hovborg 6C2

**Holme Å Camping**, Torpet 6. **GPS:** n55,60919 e8,93281. ➡

40 ⑤DKK 120, 15/06-19/08 DKK 145, dog DKK 10 ⚡ChWC ◻
DKK 30/30 ⬛included. ◻ ⬛ **Location:** Rural, comfortable, quiet.
**Surface:** grassy. ◻ 01/01-31/12.
**Distance:** ◻1km ⬛1km.
**Remarks:** Quick-Stop: >20h - <10h.

## ⑤ Hoven 6C1

**Kvindehojskole**, Bredgade 10, Tarm. **GPS:** n55,85065 e8,75938. ⬆

6 ⑤free WCfree. **Location:** Urban, simple. **Surface:** gravel.
◻ 01/01-31/12.
**Distance:** ◻on the spot.
**Remarks:** Parking and stay overnight possible at several places; Brugsen 2/3 campers; sport hall.

## ⑤⑤ Hurup Thy ♨♨ 5B3

**Hurup AutoCamper-plads**, Kløvermarken 15.
**GPS:** n56,75070 e8,42920. ⬆

6 ⑤DKK 50 ⬛. **Location:** Urban, simple, noisy. **Surface:** gravel.
◻ 01/01-31/12.
**Distance:** ◻on the spot ⊗750m ⬛750m.
**Remarks:** Money in envelope in mail box.

## ⑤⑤ Hurup Thy ♨♨ 5B3

**Nordisk Folkecenter**, Kammersgaardsvej 16.
**GPS:** n56,69358 e8,41306. ⬆

---

8 ⑤DKK 70 ⚡WCincluded ⬛. ◻ **Location:** Rural, simple, isolated, quiet. **Surface:** gravel. ◻ 01/01-31/12.
**Distance:** ◻on the spot ⬛4km.
**Remarks:** Check in at reception, access energy-park incl.

## ⑤ Husum-Ballum 6C2

# Ballum Camping Husum-Ballum

- Ideal base for walking and cycling
- Convenient for longer stays
- Located in nature reserve

## ballumcamping.eu
## info@ballumcamping.eu

**Ballum Camping**, Kystvej 37, Ballum. **GPS:** n55,06873 e8,66128.
16 ⑤DKK 110 or € 15 ⚡Ch ⚡(16x)DKK 3,50/kWh
WC⬜DKK 1,50/1minutes ◻DKK 25/25 ⬛included. ◻ ⬛
**Location:** Rural. **Surface:** grassy/gravel.
◻ 01/01-31/12 ◻ 14/01-28/02 and 01/11-13/12.
**Distance:** ◻500m ◻1,5km ◻5km ◻500m ⬛500m ⬛500m
⬛on the spot ⬛on the spot.
**Remarks:** Payment also in euros.

## ⑤⑤ Hvide Sande ⚓⬛ 6B1

**Autocamper Fabriksvej 31**, Fabriksvej 31.
**GPS:** n56,00262 e8,12024. ⬆

45 ⑤DKK 110. ◻ ⬛ **Location:** Rural, simple. **Surface:** gravel/sand.
◻ 01/01-31/12.
**Distance:** ◻800m ◻500m ⬛500m.

## ⑤⑤ Hvide Sande ⚓⬛ 6B1

**Autocamper Fabriksvej 42. GPS:** n56,00475 e8,11754. ⬆

20 ⑤DKK 110. ◻ ⬛ **Location:** Rural, simple, quiet.
**Surface:** gravel/sand. ◻ 01/01-31/12.
**Distance:** ◻200m ◻on the spot ⬛200m.
**Remarks:** Beach parking, beautiful view.

## ⑤⑤ Hvide Sande ⚓⬛ 6B1

**Autocamper P**, Tungevej 6. **GPS:** n55,99722 e8,12222. ⬆

---

40 ⑤DKK 90 WC ◻DKK 10. ◻ ⬛ **Location:** Rural, simple, quiet.
**Surface:** gravel/metalled. ◻ 01/01-31/12.
**Distance:** ◻200m ⬛on the spot ⊗200m ⬛300m ⬛on the spot.
**Remarks:** Beach parking, service Hvide Sande Camping, 1km, DKK 37,50.

## ⑤⑤ Hvide Sande ⚓⬛ 6B1

**Bjerregaard**, Sdr. Klitvej 185. **GPS:** n55,86775 e8,18094. ⬆
2 ⑤DKK 100 ⚡Ch ⚡against payment.
**Surface:** gravel. ◻ 15/04-01/10.
**Remarks:** Quick-Stop: >20h - <10h.

## ⑤⑤ Hvide Sande ⚓⬛ 6B1

**Hvide Sande Camping**, Karen Brands Vej 70.
**GPS:** n55,98689 e8,13478. ⬆
3 ⑤DKK 90 ⚡Ch ⚡against payment WC⬜included. ◻
**Location:** Rural, comfortable. **Surface:** grassy. ◻ 03/04-26/10.
**Distance:** ◻1,5km ◻100m ⊗1,5km.
**Remarks:** Quick-Stop: >20h - <10h.

## ⑤⑤ Højer 5C3

**Birgitte & Jørgen Pedersen**, Bredkærvej 89.
**GPS:** n57,44060 e10,05720. ⬆

10 ⑤DKK 50 ⚡Chincluded ⚡DKK 15,6Amp. ◻
**Location:** Rural, isolated, quiet. **Surface:** grassy.
◻ 01/01-31/12.
**Distance:** ◻3km ⊗3km ⬛3km.
**Remarks:** Money in envelope in mail box.

## ⑤⑤ Højslev ⬛ 5C3

**Virksund Lystbådehavn**, Sandkrogen 10. **GPS:** n56,61014 e9,29139. ⬆

12 ⑤DKK 125 ⚡WC ⬛included. ◻
**Location:** Rural, simple. **Surface:** gravel. ◻ 15/05-15/10.
**Distance:** ◻on the spot.

## ⑤⑤ Højslev ⬛ 5C3

**Lund Forsamlingshus**, Ørslevklostervej 229.
**GPS:** n56,60402 e9,24250. ⬆

10 ⑤DKK 50 ⚡ChWCincluded.
**Location:** Rural, simple. **Surface:** gravel.
**Distance:** ◻3km.

## ⑤⑤ Højslev ⬛ 5C3

**Virksund Camping**, Sundvej 14, Virksund. **GPS:** n56,60785 e9,28917.
⑤DKK 4/h, weekend DKK 8/h ⚡Chagainst payment ⚡

DK

⊡ 01/04-02/10.
**Remarks:** Quick-Stop: >20h - <10h.

### Jelling 🌿✈    6D1
**Kolleruplund**, Vongevej 25. **GPS:** n55,79270 e9,46830. ⬆

3 ⌁DKK 90 🚰DKK 10/time ᶜʰDKK 10/time 🚿DKK 40 📶included.
🧺 **Location:** Rural, comfortable, isolated, quiet. **Surface:** gravel.
⊡ 01/01-31/12.
**Distance:** ⟂8km ⊗8km ⚓8km.

### ⚓S   Juelsminde ⛵    6D1
**Havn & Marina**, Havnegade 15. **GPS:** n55,71457 e10,01509. ⬆

12 ⌁DKK 175 🚰🚻ᶜʰ 🚿(12x)DKK 2,50/kWh WC⬛📶included.
🚐🚿 **Location:** Rural, comfortable, central, quiet. **Surface:** gravel.
⊡ 01/05-01/11.
**Distance:** ⟂200m ⚓on the spot ▸on the spot ⊗on the spot ⚓200m.
**Remarks:** Tallycard: service, electricity, sanitary building, caution DKK 50.

### ©S   Juelsminde ⛵    6D1
**Strand Camping og Vandrerhjem**, Rousthøj Allé 1a.
**GPS:** n55,71243 e10,01444. ➡

20 ⌁DKK 125, 2 pers.incl 🚰🚻ᶜʰ 🚿DKK 3,10/kWh,+ DKK 10
WC⬛DKK 2/1minutes ◉DKK 35/time 📶included. 🚐🚿
**Location:** Urban, comfortable, noisy. **Surface:** metalled.
⊡ 23/03-21/10.
**Distance:** ▸on the spot ⚓on the spot ⊗200m ⚓550m 🚗on the spot.

### 🌿S   Karup    6C1
**2B Pack**, Ulvedalsvej 43. **GPS:** n56,31528 e9,27361. ⬆

4 ⌁DKK 75 🚰🚻ᶜʰincluded 🚿DKK 25.
**Location:** Isolated, quiet. ⊡ 01/05-31/10.
**Distance:** 🚶on the spot.

### ©S   Karup    6C1
**Hessellund Sø**, Hessellundvej 12. **GPS:** n56,32308 e9,11501.
⌁DKK 171 🚰🚻ᶜʰ 🚿against payment. ⊡ 27/03-29/09.
**Remarks:** Quick-Stop: >20h - <10h.

### 🏭S   Knebel    6D1
**August Art**, Havvej 21. **GPS:** n56,24560 e10,48820. ➡

---

15 ⌁DKK 100 🚰🚻ᶜʰ 🚿WC⬛📶included.
**Location:** Rural, simple, quiet. **Surface:** gravel. ⊡ 01/01-31/12.
**Distance:** ⚓800m ⚓500m.
**Remarks:** At art galery.

### 🏭   Knebel    6D1
**Sølyst Gaard Strand Camping**, Dragsmurvej 15, Fuglsø.
**GPS:** n56,17546 e10,53394. ⬆
⌁DKK 145 WC🚿DKK 5/time. **Surface:** grassy. ⊡ 19/03-18/09.
**Distance:** ⚓200m.
**Remarks:** Quick-Stop: >20h - <10h.

### ⚓S   Kolding 🍦⛵    6D2
**Kolding Marina**, Skamlingvejen 5. **GPS:** n55,48746 e9,50051. ⬆

15 ⌁DKK 160 🚰🚻ᶜʰ.🚿WC⬛📶against payment. 🚐🚿
**Location:** Rural, comfortable, quiet. **Surface:** grassy/gravel.
⊡ 01/05-01/10.
**Distance:** ⟂2,6km ⚓on the spot ⊗on the spot.
**Remarks:** Near marina, Tallycard: service, electricity, sanitary building, caution DKK 50.

### ©S   Kvissel    5C3
**Bondegård Hansen**, Mejlingvej 65. **GPS:** n57,46753 e10,39556. ⬆

10 ⌁DKK 75 🚰🚻ᶜʰ 🚿WCincluded ⬛DKK 10. 🚿
**Location:** Rural, comfortable, quiet. **Surface:** grassy.
⊡ 01/01-31/12.
**Distance:** ⟂1km ⚓5km.

### ©S   Langå    5C3
**Langå**, Skov Alle 16. **GPS:** n56,38780 e9,90439. ➡
⌁DKK 140 🚰🚻ᶜʰ 🚿DKK 3,50/kWh WCincluded ⬛DKK 2/time.
⊡ 01/01-31/12.
**Remarks:** Quick-Stop: >20h - <10h.

### 🏭S   Lemvig ⛵    5B3
**Aa Mølle**, Remmerstrandvej 188. **GPS:** n56,54199 e8,50310. ⬆

15 ⌁DKK 75 WCincluded. 🚿
**Location:** Rural, simple. **Surface:** grassy.
**Distance:** ⚓100m ▸100m.
**Remarks:** Near mill.

### 🏭S   Lemvig ⛵    5B3
**Lemvig Havn**, Havnen 11. **GPS:** n56,55395 e8,30956. ⬆

---

10 ⌁free. **Location:** Urban, simple, central. **Surface:** gravel.
⊡ 01/01-31/12.
**Distance:** ⊗250m ⚓250m.
**Remarks:** Max. 12h.

### ©S   Lemvig ⛵    5B3
**Lemvig Strand Camping**, Vinkelhagevej 6.
**GPS:** n56,56726 e8,29426. ⬆
5 ⌁DKK 100 🚿DKK 35. **Location:** Rural. **Surface:** grassy.
**Distance:** ⟂3km ⚓on the spot ▸on the spot ⊗800m.
**Tourist information Lemvig:**
👁 Bovbjerg Fyr, Fyrvej 27. Lighthouse.

### ©   Løgstrup    5C3
**Hjarbæk Fjord Camping**, Hulager 2. **GPS:** n56,53416 e9,33118.
⌁DKK 125. ⊡ 01/01-31/12.
**Remarks:** Quick-Stop: >20h - <10h.

### 🏭S   Løgstør ⛳🍦⛵    5C3
**Løgstør Golfklub**, Viborgvej 13, Ravnstrup.
**GPS:** n56,94689 e9,25390. ⬆

5 ⌁DKK 100 🚿(4x)included WC⬛. 🚿
**Location:** Rural, simple, isolated, quiet. **Surface:** gravel.
**Distance:** ⟂2km ⊗2km ⚓2km.
**Remarks:** At golf court.

### ⚓S   Løgstør ⛳🍦⛵    5C3
**Løgstør Lysbadehavn**, Kanalvejen 19. **GPS:** n56,96728 e9,24528. ⬆➡

15 ⌁DKK 135 🚰🚿(12x)WC⬛📶included.
**Location:** Urban, comfortable, central. **Surface:** grassy/metalled.
⊡ 01/01-31/12.
**Distance:** ⟂200m ⚓on the spot ▸on the spot ⊗on the spot ⚓200m.
**Remarks:** Pay at harbourmaster.

### 🌿S   Løgstør ⛳🍦⛵    5C3
**Skovsgaard**, Munksjørupvej 37, Overlade. **GPS:** n56,86660 e9,27150. ⬆

3 ⌁DKK 50 🚰🚿WC. 🚿 **Location:** Rural, isolated, quiet.
**Surface:** grassy. ⊡ 01/01-31/12.
**Distance:** ⟂1km ⚓1km.

### 🍴   Løgstør ⛳🍦⛵    5C3
**Café Bondestuen**, Over Aggersund 49. **GPS:** n57,00835 e9,28776. ⬆

**DK**

6 🛏 free. **Location:** Rural, simple. **Surface:** gravel.
⏰ 01/01-31/12.
**Distance:** ⊗on the spot.

---

### Løgumkloster 🌿 6C2

Møllegade. **GPS:** n55,06090 e8,94896. ⬆➡.

3 🛏 free 🚰DKK 20/100liter 🔌Ch. **Location:** Rural, simple, central.
**Surface:** gravel. ⏰ 01/01-31/12.
**Distance:** 300m ⊗300m 1km.
**Remarks:** Max 3,5t.

---

### Løkken 5C3

Galleri Munkens Klit, Munkensvej 11, Ingstrup.
**GPS:** n57,33871 e9,70522. ⬆➡.

6 🛏 DKK 150/ € 20 🚰 DKK 7/day WC 📶included. 🏠
**Location:** Rural, comfortable, isolated, quiet. **Surface:** grassy.
⏰ 01/04-31/12.
**Distance:** 3km 1,5km 1,5km ⊗3km 3,5km 100m
100m.

---

### Løkken 5C3

Løkkensvej 875. **GPS:** n57,38972 e9,77385. ⬆➡.

40 🛏 DKK 100 🚰DKK 35 WC DKK 10 📶DKK 25. **Location:** Rural,
simple, isolated. **Surface:** grassy. ⏰ 01/01-31/12.
**Distance:** 4,5km.

---

### Løkken 5C3

Hugo Ottesen, Kettrupvej 80. **GPS:** n57,31135 e9,67861. ⬆.

5 🛏 DKK 100 🚰 📶 **Location:** Rural, simple, isolated.
**Surface:** grassy. ⏰ 01/01-31/12.

---

### Løkken 5C3

Camping Rolighed, Grønhøj Strandvej 35.
**GPS:** n57,31786 e9,69601. ⬆.

---

10 🛏 DKK 100 🚰🔌Ch 🚿against payment. 🏠
**Location:** Rural. **Surface:** grassy. ⏰ 01/01-31/12.
**Distance:** 1,5km.
**Remarks:** Quick-Stop: >18h - <10h.

---

### Løkken 5C3

Gl.Klitgaard, Lyngbyvej 331. **GPS:** n57,41784 e9,76017.
10 🛏 DKK 148 🚰🔌Ch 🚿against payment. 🏠 **Surface:** grassy.
⏰ 15/04-23/10.
**Remarks:** Quick-Stop: >20h - <10h.

---

### Løkken 5C3

Grønhøj Strand, Kettrupvej 125. **GPS:** n57,32127 e9,67293.

4 🛏 DKK 100 🚰🔌Chincluded 🚿DKK 30 DKK 5 DKK 25/25.
**Surface:** grassy/gravel. ⏰ 12/04-22/09.
**Distance:** 8km 700m 4km ⊗1,5km 1,5km.
**Remarks:** Quick-Stop: >20h - <10h.

---

### Løkken 5C3

Løkken By Camping, Søndergarde 69. **GPS:** n57,36480 e9,70940. ⬆.
2 🛏 DKK 125 🚰🔌Ch 🚿 📶. **Surface:** asphalted. ⏰ 01/01-31/12.
**Remarks:** Quick-Stop: >20h - <10h.

---

### Løkken 5C3

Løkken Strand, Furreby Kirkevej 97. **GPS:** n57,38533 e9,72571.

10 🛏 DKK 100 🚰🔌Chincluded 🚿against payment WC 📶.
⏰ 29/04-04/09.
**Remarks:** Quick-Stop: >20h - <10h.

**Tourist information Løkken:**
ℹ Løkken Turistbureau, Jyllandsgade 15, www.loekken.dk. Bathing
resort.
Ⓜ Vendsyssel historiske museum "Jens Thomsens Gård", Strand-
fogedgården i Rubjerg, Langelinie 2. Cultural past of the coast area.
Hiking-trails. ⏰ 25/06-30/08 Thu-Su 11-17h.
    Familiy Farm Fun Park, Lyngbyvej 86, Vittrup. Animal park.
⏰ 14/05-24/10 10-18.

---

### Mariager 5C3

Kongsdal Bådelaug, Kongsdal Havn 8. **GPS:** n56,68383 e10,07023. ⬆.

24 🛏 DKK 120 🚰🔌Ch 🚿(24x)WCincluded DKK 5/3minutes 📶.
🏠 **Location:** Rural, comfortable, isolated, quiet. **Surface:** gravel.
⏰ 01/01-31/12 🅿 service 01/11-31/03.
**Distance:** 7km on the spot on the spot.
**Remarks:** Tallycard.

---

### Mariager 5C3

Mariager, Ny Havnevej 5A. **GPS:** n56,65399 e9,97640. ⬆➡.
2 🛏 DKK 100 🚰🔌Chagainst payment 🚿DKK 40 DKK 5/time.
⏰ 01/01-31/12.
**Remarks:** Quick-Stop: >20h - <10h.

---

### ⚓ Nibe 5C3

Lystbadehavn, Bryggen 52B. **GPS:** n56,98780 e9,63590. ⬆➡.

15 🛏 DKK 120 🚰🔌Ch DKK 20 WC DKK 10 DKK 30/30
📶included. 🚿 **Location:** Rural, comfortable, quiet.
**Surface:** grassy/gravel. ⏰ 01/01-31/12.
**Distance:** 500m on the spot on the spot ⊗100m 500m
500m.
**Remarks:** Beautiful view.

---

### Nibe 5C3

Sølyst Nibe Camping, Løgstørvej 2. **GPS:** n56,97248 e9,62460.
🛏 DKK 140 🚰🔌Ch 🚿against payment.
**Location:** Isolated. ⏰ 01/01-31/12.
**Remarks:** Quick-Stop: >20h - <10h.

---

### Nordborg 6D2

Autocamperplads Als, Købingsmarksvej 53. **GPS:** n55,07887 e9,72912.

25 🛏 DKK 100 🚰DKK 15/80liter 🔌Chincluded 🚿DKK 39
📶DKK 15/24h. **Surface:** metalled. ⏰ 01/04-25/10.
**Distance:** 3km on the spot on the spot ⊗3km 3km on
the spot on the spot on the spot.

---

### Nordborg 6D2

Kvickly, Gartnervænget. **GPS:** n55,05611 e9,74150. ⬆➡.

4 🛏 free. **Location:** Urban, simple. **Surface:** asphalted.
⏰ 01/01-31/12.
**Distance:** on the spot ⊗300m on the spot.
**Remarks:** At supermarket.

---

### Nordborg 6D2

Lone & Henning Carlsson, Kådnervej 7. **GPS:** n55,03194 e9,73111. ⬆.

5 🛏 DKK 100 🚰🔌 DKK 20 WC 📶. **Location:** Rural,
comfortable, quiet. **Surface:** gravel. ⏰ 01/01-31/12.
**Distance:** 5km.
**Remarks:** Narrow entrance.

---

### Nykøbing Mors 5C3

Morsø Sejlklub & Marina, Jernbanevej 3A.
**GPS:** n56,79282 e8,86370. ⬆➡.

18 ⬛DKK 130 ⛽🔌Ch.⚡DKK 3/kWh WC⬛DKK 10 ⬛DKK 60 📶included. 🚐🧺 **Location:** Urban, comfortable, quiet.
**Surface:** gravel. ⬛ 01/01-31/12.
**Distance:** 🏊150m ⚓on the spot 🍴on the spot ⊗on the spot 🚰200m.
**Remarks:** Tallycard: service, electricity, sanitary building, caution DKK 25.

### Nykøbing Mors 5C3
**Morsø Traktormuseum**, Kjeldgårdsvej 49, Outrup.
**GPS:** n56,78038 e8,66547. ⬆➡.

4 ⬛DKK 100 WC⬛included. 🚐🧺 **Location:** Rural, simple.
**Surface:** metalled. ⬛ 01/01-31/12.
**Remarks:** Use sanitary only during opening hours, 20% reduction museum.

### Nørager 5C3
**Stellplads E45 Autocamper**, Fyrkildevej 39, Ladelund.
**GPS:** n56,77505 e9,70986. ⬆.

15 ⬛DKK 50 ⛽included. ⚡DKK 25. 🚐 **Location:** Rural, simple, isolated, quiet. **Surface:** grassy. ⬛ 01/01-31/12.
**Distance:** 🛣E45 5km.

### Nørre Nebel 6B1
**Kløvergaardens**, Kollevej 50. **GPS:** n55,76496 e8,30281. ⬆➡.

20 ⬛DKK 100 ⛽🔌DKK 40 ⚡📶included. 🚐
**Location:** Rural, isolated, quiet. **Surface:** grassy.
**Distance:** 🏊2km ⊗2km 🚰2,5km 🚲2km.

### Nørre Nebel 6B1
**Nymindegab**, Lyngtoften 12. **GPS:** n55,81368 e8,19992.
3 ⬛DKK 75 ⛽🔌Ch.⚡against payment.
**Location:** Rural. **Surface:** asphalted. ⬛ 17/03-27/09.
**Remarks:** Quick-Stop: >20h - <10h.

### Odder 6D1
**Norsminde havn**, Gl Krovej. **GPS:** n56,02253 e10,26262. ⬆.
4 ⬛DKK 150 WC⬛included. **Location:** Rural, comfortable, quiet.
**Surface:** metalled. ⬛ 15/04-01/10.
**Distance:** 🏊Odder 11km ⚓on the spot 🍴on the spot ⊗on the spot 🚰4km 🚌500m.

### Odder 6D1
**Jørgen Petersen**, Aarhusvej 354. **GPS:** n56,01650 e10,18157. ⬆➡.

3 ⬛DKK 100 ⛽🔌Ch.⚡WC⬛included. 🚐 **Location:** Rural, luxurious, isolated, quiet. **Surface:** grassy/gravel. ⬛ 01/05-01/10.
**Distance:** 🏊4km ⊗4km 🚰4km 🚲on the spot.

### Odder 6D1
**Odder strand Camping**, Toldvejen 50. **GPS:** n55,93891 e10,25054. ➡.

⬛DKK 155 ⛽🔌Ch.⚡against payment WC⬛included.
**Location:** Comfortable, quiet. ⬛ 17/03-23/09.
**Remarks:** Quick-Stop: >20h - <10h.

### Outrup 6C1
**Autocamperplads Outrup**, Gartnervænget 18.
**GPS:** n55,71551 e8,34654. ⬆➡.

15 ⬛DKK 110, dog DKK 20 ⛽🔌Ch.⚡DKK 20 WC⬛📶included.
**Location:** Rural, comfortable, isolated, quiet. **Surface:** grassy/gravel.
⬛ 01/01-31/12.
**Distance:** 🏊500m ⊗300m 🚰500m 🚲on the spot.

### Pandrup 5C3
**Blokhus Klit Camping**, Kystvejen 52. **GPS:** n57,22048 e9,58479.
⬛DKK 100, 26/06-04/08 DKK 140 ⛽DKK 60. **Location:** Rural, isolated, quiet. **Surface:** metalled. ⬛ 23/03-18/09.
**Remarks:** Quick-Stop: >20h - <10h.

### Randers 5C3
**Mellerup Bådelaug**, Amtsvejen 153, Mellerup.
**GPS:** n56,52431 e10,22213. ⬆.

3 ⬛DKK 130 ⛽⚡WC📶included. 🚐 **Location:** Rural, simple, quiet. **Surface:** gravel. ⬛ 01/05-30/09.
**Distance:** 🏊Mellerup 1,2km ⚓on the spot 🍴on the spot.
**Remarks:** Pay at harbourmaster.

### Randers 5C3
**Randers havn**, Toldbodgade 16. **GPS:** n56,46280 e10,05262. ⬆.

10 ⬛DKK 150. **Location:** Urban, simple. **Surface:** gravel.
⬛ 01/01-31/12.
**Distance:** 🏊500m ⚓on the spot ⊗on the spot.
**Remarks:** Max. 24h.

### Ranum 5C3
**Livøvej**. **GPS:** n56,89110 e9,16608. ⬆.

10 ⬛free. **Location:** Rural, simple, quiet. **Surface:** grassy/gravel.
⬛ 01/01-31/12.
**Distance:** ⚓on the spot 🍴on the spot ⊗on the spot.
**Remarks:** Ferry boat to island Livø, at harbour.

### Redsted M. 5C3
**Thissinghus Havn**, Thissingvej. **GPS:** n56,71822 e8,62818. ⬆.

10 ⬛DKK 60 ⚡WC⬛included. 🚐 **Location:** Rural, simple, isolated.
**Surface:** grassy. ⬛ 01/01-31/12.
**Distance:** 🏊3km ⚓on the spot 🍴on the spot 🚰3km.
**Remarks:** Money in envelope in mail box.

### Ribe 6C2
**Stampemøllevej**. **GPS:** n55,32480 e8,75740. ⬆.

25 ⬛free ⛽🔌Ch WC free.
**Location:** Urban, simple, central. **Surface:** asphalted.
⬛ 01/01-31/12.
**Distance:** 🏊500m ⊗100m 🚰400m.
**Remarks:** Parking south of centre, max. 48h.

### Ribe 6C2
**Storkesøen**, Haulundvej 164. **GPS:** n55,31703 e8,76022. ⬆➡.

24 ⬛DKK 150 ⛽🔌Ch.⚡WC included ⬛DKK 5.
**Location:** Rural, comfortable, quiet. **Surface:** grassy. ⬛ 01/01-31/12.
**Distance:** 🏊1km 🍴on the spot.
**Remarks:** At fish pond.

### Ribe 6C2
**Saltgade**. **GPS:** n55,33258 e8,76830. ⬆.

DK

15 ⬛free. **Location:** Urban, noisy. **Surface:** asphalted.
⬛ 01/01-31/12.
**Distance:** 🚰on the spot 🛒200m 🛒200m.
**Remarks:** Max. 48h.

**⬛S Ribe 🌿⛴🛒 6C2**

**Maglegaard**, Toftlundvej 6. **GPS:** n55,31067 e8,79151.

3 ⬛DKK 100 🚰 DKK 20.
**Location:** Rural, simple, quiet. **Surface:** grassy.
**Distance:** 🚰3km.

**⬛S Ribe 🌿⛴🛒 6C2**

**Ribe camping**, Farupvej 2. **GPS:** n55,34059 e8,00000.

2 ⬛DKK 75 🚰DKK 20 DKK 20 ChDKK 50. 🚐
⬛ 01/01-31/12.
**Distance:** 🚰1km 🛒350m 🛒2km.
**Remarks:** Quick-Stop: >20h - <10h.

**Tourist information Ribe:**
ℹ️ Ribe Tourism Office, Torvet 3, http://www.visitribe.com/. Oldest city of Denmark to Ribeå River.
👁️ Vadehavscentret, Okholmvej 5. Wadden Sea centre. ⬛ 10-16/17h ⬛ 01/12-31/01.
🅜 Museet Ribes Vikinger, Odins Plads 1. Viking period in Denmark.
⬛ daily 10-16h, summer 10-18h ⬛ 01/11-31/03 Mo.
🅜 Ribe Vikingecenter. Open air museum. ⬛ 01/05-30/06, 01/09-15/10 Mo-Fri 10-15.30h, 01/07-31/08 daily 11-17h.
⊗ Weis Stue, Torvet 2. Oldest inn of Denmark with traditional Danish kitchen.

**⬛S Ringkøbing 🛒 6B1**

**Lystbadenhavn**, Fiskerstraede 60. **GPS:** n56,08611 e8,24056.⬆️

10 ⬛DKK 150 🚰Ch (6x)DKK 2,60/kWh WCincluded
DKK 10/3minutes. 🏪 **Location:** Urban, comfortable, central, quiet. **Surface:** grassy/gravel. ⬛ 01/01-31/12.
**Distance:** 🚰on the spot 🏊on the spot 🚶on the spot ⊗500m 🛒500m.
**Remarks:** Parking at pier, beautiful view.

**⬛S Ringkøbing 🛒 6B1**

**Annemette & Svend Erik Jensen**, Birkmosevej 6.
**GPS:** n56,08806 e8,26722.➡️

---

15 ⬛free. **Location:** Simple. **Surface:** grassy. ⬛ 01/01-31/12.
**Distance:** 🏊1km ⊗500m 🛒200m.

**⬛S Ringkøbing 🛒 6B1**

**Stellplatz Søndervig**, Solvej 2. **GPS:** n56,11186 e8,11760.

12 ⬛DKK 110 🚰Chincluded 🚰 DKK 36/kWh 📶.
**Surface:** grassy/gravel. ⬛ 01/01-31/12.
**Distance:** 🏊600m.
**Remarks:** Special part for motor homes.

**Tourist information Ringkøbing:**
Fishing and Family Park West, Hovervej 56. Recreation park with swimming pool. ⬛ 10h-sunset.

**⚓S Roslev ⚓ 5C3**

**Sallingsund Sejlklub**, Færgevej 7. **GPS:** n56,76333 e8,86667.➡️

12 ⬛DKK 120 🚰Ch 🚰 WC 📶included.
**Location:** Rural, comfortable, isolated. **Surface:** grassy.
⬛ 01/05-30/09.
**Distance:** 🏊on the spot 🚶on the spot ⊗200m 🛒200m.

**⚓S Roslev ⚓ 5C3**

**Sundsøre Lystbådehavn**, Sundsørevej 2B.
**GPS:** n56,70991 e9,17324.⬆️.

8 ⬛DKK 130 🚰 WC included. **Location:** Rural, isolated, quiet. **Surface:** grassy/gravel. ⬛ 01/01-31/12.
**Distance:** 🏊on the spot 🚶on the spot ⊗on the spot.
**Remarks:** At marina and ferry-boat.

**⬛S Rødding 6C2**

**JH ståldesign**, Timekær 11. **GPS:** n55,33044 e9,05417.⬆️.
3 ⬛DKK 75 🚰DKK 25 Ch 🚰 DKK 25/24h WC DKK 25/time
DKK 25/time 📶included. **Location:** Rural, simple, quiet.
**Surface:** gravel. ⬛ 01/01-31/12.
**Distance:** 🚰4km ⊗500m 🛒4km.

**🍇S Rødding 6C2**

**Inga & Ejnar Gejl**, Skodborgskovvej 25, Skodborgskov.
**GPS:** n55,40056 e9,15722.⬆️.

---

3 ⬛free. **Location:** Rural, simple, isolated, quiet. **Surface:** grassy.
⬛ 01/01-31/12.
**Distance:** 🚰5km ⊗3km.

**⬛S Rødding 6C2**

**Brændekilde**, Haderslevvej 59. **GPS:** n55,35750 e9,18833.⬆️.

13 ⬛free 🚰DKK 25 Ch 🚰 DKK 25 WC.
**Location:** Rural, simple, noisy. **Surface:** gravel. ⬛ 01/01-31/12.
**Distance:** 🚰1km.
**Remarks:** Max. 1 week.

**⬛S Rødding 6C2**

**FB Camping Service**, Industriparken 13. **GPS:** n55,42556 e9,16083.⬆️.

15 ⬛free 🚰DKK 10 Ch 🚰 DKK 40/day.
**Location:** Urban, simple. **Surface:** gravel. ⬛ 01/01-31/12.
**Distance:** 🚰500m ⊗500m 🛒500m.
**Remarks:** At motorhome dealer.

**⬛S Rødekro 🍴🍽 6C2**

**Rødekro Fiskepark**, østermarkvej 3-7. **GPS:** n55,08806 e9,30889.⬆️➡️.

25 ⬛DKK 150/pp 🚰Ch 🚰 DKK 35/24kWh,10Amp WCincluded
📶. **Location:** Rural, simple, quiet. **Surface:** grassy.
⬛ 01/01-31/12.
**Distance:** 🚰2km 🏊on the spot 🚶on the spot ⊗on the spot 🛒2km 🛒100m.
**Remarks:** At fish lake.

**⬛S Rømø ⛴ 6C2**

**Autocamperplads Oasen Rømø**, Rømersvej 9.
**GPS:** n55,09408 e8,54118.⬆️➡️.

180 ⬛DKK 125 🚰DKK 1/100liter Ch 🚰 DKK 7/3kWh
WC DKK 7/4minutes ⬛DKK 21/14 📶included. 🚐
**Location:** Rural, comfortable, luxurious, quiet. **Surface:** gravel.

DK

◻ 01/01-31/12. **Distance:** 🍴2km ⛱1km ⊗500m 🚰500m.

▣Ⓢ **Rømø** ⚓ **6C2**
**Kommandørgården Camping**, Havnebyvej 201.
**GPS:** n55,09854 e8,54292. ↑→
2 ⬛DKK 125 ≋included. 🚻🚮
**Location:** Rural, comfortable. **Surface:** grassy. ◻ 01/01-31/12.
**Distance:** 🍴1,5km ⊗on the spot 🚰300m.
**Remarks:** Quick-Stop: >20h - <10h.

▣Ⓢ **Rømø** ⚓ **6C2**
**Rømø Familie Camping**, Vestervej 13. **GPS:** n55,16254 e8,54518. ↑→

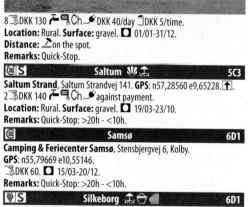

10 ⬛DKK 110, 14/10-23/03 DKK 70, 2 pers.incl 🚰🔌Ch🔌DKK 35/kWh ≋. 🚐🚮
**Location:** Rural, simple. **Surface:** gravel. ◻ 01/01-31/12.
**Distance:** 🍴1km ⊗3km.

⚓Ⓢ **Rønde** **6D1**
**Nappedam Bådelaug**, Molsvej 33. **GPS:** n56,27755 e10,49529. ↑

18 ⬛DKK 150 🔌Ch🔌WC🔌DKK 25 ≋included.
**Location:** Rural. **Surface:** gravel. ◻ 15/05-15/10.
**Distance:** 🍴3,5km ⛱on the spot ⊗1,3km 🚰3,5km.
**Remarks:** Max 3,5t, free bicycles available.

▣Ⓢ **Rønde** **6D1**
**Kaløvig Strandgård**, Strandvejen 150. **GPS:** n56,29330 e10,40399. →

8 ⬛DKK 130 🚰🔌Ch🔌DKK 40/day ⬛DKK 5/time.
**Location:** Rural. **Surface:** gravel. ◻ 01/01-31/12.
**Distance:** ⛱on the spot.
**Remarks:** Quick-Stop.

▣Ⓢ **Saltum** 🌿⚓ **5C3**
**Saltum Strand**, Saltum Strandvej 141. **GPS:** n57,28560 e9,65228. ↑
2 ⬛DKK 140 🚰🔌Ch🔌against payment.
**Location:** Rural. **Surface:** gravel. ◻ 19/03-23/10.
**Remarks:** Quick-Stop: >20h - <10h.

▣ **Samsø** **6D1**
**Camping & Feriecenter Samsø**, Stensbjergvej 6, Kolby.
**GPS:** n55,79669 e10,55146.
⬛DKK 60. ◻ 15/03-20/12.
**Remarks:** Quick-Stop: >20h - <10h.

▣Ⓢ **Silkeborg** ⚓🍴🔌 **6D1**
**Anne & Gert Lassen, Ellinglund**, Ellingvej 16, Funder Kirkeby.
**GPS:** n56,16546 e9,40954.
3 ⬛DKK 100 🚰🔌Ch🔌WC🔌≋.
**Location:** Rural, comfortable. **Surface:** grassy. ◻ 01/01-31/12.
**Distance:** 🍴2km.

▣Ⓢ **Silkeborg** ⚓🍴🔌 **6D1**
**Jørgen Engebjerg**, Lemmingvej 12. **GPS:** n56,22124 e9,53991. ↑

**DK**

---

3 ⬛DKK 75. **Location:** Rural, isolated. **Surface:** gravel.
◻ 01/01-31/12.
**Distance:** 🍴5km.

▲Ⓢ **Silkeborg** ⚓🍴🔌 **6D1**
**Sø-Camping**, Århusvej 51. **GPS:** n56,16984 e9,57657.
⬛DKK 94/pp 🚰🔌Ch🔌against payment.
◻ 18/03-23/10.
**Remarks:** Quick-Stop: >20h - <10h.
**Tourist information Silkeborg:**
👁 AQUA, Vejlsøvej 55. Aquarium. ◻ 01/09-31/05 Mo-Fri 10-16h,
Sa-Su 10-17h, 01/06-31/08 10-18h.

▣Ⓢ **Sindal** **5C3**
**A35 Sindal Camping Danmark & Kanoudlejning**, Hjørringvej 125.
**GPS:** n57,46849 e10,17945.

3 ⬛DKK 110 🚰🔌Chagainst payment 🔌DKK 30 WC🔌included. 🚐
**Location:** Rural, simple. **Surface:** grassy. ◻ 01/01-31/12.
**Distance:** 🍴1,5km 🚰1,5km.
**Remarks:** Quick-Stop: >20h - <10h.

▣ **Skagen** **5C2**
Fiskehuskajen. **GPS:** n57,71929 e10,58771. ↑

10 ⬛free, June-Aug DKK 150. 🚐🚮 **Location:** Urban, simple, central.
**Surface:** asphalted. ◻ 01/01-31/12.
**Distance:** 🍴on the spot ⛱on the spot ⊗on the spot.
**Remarks:** Grenen 3km, fish sales, in front of tourist office.

▣ **Skagen** **5C2**
**P-plads på Grenen i Skagen**, Akandevej.
**GPS:** n57,73895 e10,63283. ↑

20 ⬛free, June-Aug DKK 150. 🚐 **Location:** Rural, simple, isolated.
**Surface:** asphalted. ◻ 01/01-31/12.
**Distance:** 🍴4km ⛱on the spot 🚶on the spot ⊗100m 🚰3km 🚶on the spot.
**Remarks:** Parking at Grenen.

▣Ⓢ **Skagen** **5C2**
**Råbjerg Mile**, Kandestedvej 55. **GPS:** n57,65636 e10,45081. ↑
⬛22-8h DKK 10/h, 8-22h DKK 20/h (min. DKK 100) 🚰🔌Chincluded.
🔌against payment. **Location:** Rural. **Surface:** grassy/gravel.
◻ 20/03-30/09.
**Remarks:** Quick-Stop: >20h - <10h.

---

▣ **Skagen** **5C2**
**Skagen Camping**, Flagbakkevej 55. **GPS:** n57,71989 e10,53991. ↑→
⬛DKK 120. 🚻 **Location:** Rural, isolated, quiet. ◻ 18/03-01/09.
**Remarks:** Quick-Stop: >20h - <10h.

▣Ⓢ **Skals** **5C3**
**Ulbjerg**, Skråhedevej 6. **GPS:** n56,64495 e9,33915.
⬛€ 10,50 🚰🔌Ch🔌against payment. ◻ 01/01-31/12.
**Remarks:** Quick-Stop: >20h - <10h.

▣Ⓢ **Skjern** ⚓ **6C1**
**Stauning Havn**, Strandvejen, Stauning. **GPS:** n55,95488 e8,37352. ↑

6 ⬛DKK 150 🚰🔌Ch🔌WCincluded 🔌.🚐🚮
**Location:** Rural, simple. **Surface:** grasstiles. ◻ 01/01-31/12.
**Distance:** 🍴Skjern 8km ⛱on the spot 🚶on the spot ⊗on the spot.

▣Ⓢ **Skjern** **6C1**
**Skjern å Camping**, Birkvej 37. **GPS:** n55,93316 e8,49291.
⬛DKK 100 🚰🔌Ch🔌against payment. ◻ 01/01-31/12.
**Remarks:** Quick-Stop: >20h - <10h.

▣Ⓢ **Skærbæk** 🌿⚓ **6C2**
**Skærbæk**, Ullerupvej 76. **GPS:** n55,16768 e8,78508. →

70 ⬛DKK 50 🚰DKK 7 🔌Ch🔌DKK 4. 🚐🚮
**Location:** Rural, simple. **Surface:** grassy. ◻ 01/01-31/12.
**Distance:** 🍴1km ⛱1km 🚰1km.
**Remarks:** Quick-Stop: >20h - <10h.

▣ **Snedsted** **5B3**
**Krohavens Familiecamping**, Stenbjerg Kirkevej 21.
**GPS:** n56,91827 e8,36527.
⬛DKK 105 🔌. **Location:** Rural. **Surface:** gravel.
◻ 01/04-01/10.
**Remarks:** Quick-Stop: >20h - <10h.

▣Ⓢ **Spøttrup** ⚓ **5C3**
**Gyldendal hav**, Vester Hærup Strandvej 34.
**GPS:** n56,58107 e8,71066. ↑

15 ⬛DKK 120 🚰🔌Ch🔌(4x)WC🔌≋included. 🚿
**Location:** Rural, simple, quiet. **Surface:** gravel/sand.
◻ 01/01-31/12.
**Distance:** ⛱Sandy beach 🚶on the spot ⊗on the spot.

▣Ⓢ **Storvorde** **5C3**
**Egense Lystbådehavan**, Kystvej 1. **GPS:** n56,98270 e10,30451. ↑

---

6 🍽DKK 170 ⛲ 🔧(6x) WC🔲. 🚿 **Location:** Rural, simple, quiet.
**Surface:** metalled. 🅾 01/01-31/12.
**Distance:** ⚓on the spot ⛽on the spot 🚤1km.
**Remarks:** Pay at harbourmaster.

### Storvorde 5C3
**Nørkærvej ved Limfjorden**, Nørkærsvej 34.
**GPS:** n57,02564 e10,11224.⬆.

15 🍽free ⛲free. **Location:** Isolated, quiet. **Surface:** grassy/gravel.
🅾 01/01-31/12.
**Distance:** 🛒2,5km ⚓on the spot ⛽on the spot ⊗2,5km.

### Storvorde 5C3
**Egense**, Kystvej 6. **GPS:** n56,98071 e10,30086.⬆.

3 🍽DKK 100. **Surface:** gravel. 🅾 24/03-17/09.
**Remarks:** Quick-Stop: >17h - <10h.

### Stouby 6D1
**Rosenvoldvej. GPS:** n55,67563 e9,81477.⬆.

4 🍽DKK 110.
**Location:** Rural, simple, quiet. **Surface:** unpaved.
🅾 18/03-25/09.
**Distance:** 🛒4km ⚓on the spot ⛽on the spot ⊗on the spot 🚤4km.
**Remarks:** Money in envelope in mail box.

### Stouby 6D1
**Løgballe Camping**, Løgballevej 12. **GPS:** n55,70786 e9,84423.➡.

6 🍽DKK 75 ⛲DKK 30 🍽DKK 30 ChDKK 30 🔧DKK 35.🏠
**Location:** Rural, simple, quiet.
**Surface:** gravel.
🅾 18/03-25/09.
**Distance:** 🛒4km ⊗2km 🚤4km.
**Remarks:** Quick-Stop: >20h - <10h, money in envelope in mail box.

### Strandby 5C3
**Strandby havn**, Søndre Havnevej 27. **GPS:** n57,49249 e10,50245.⬆.

---

6 🍽DKK 120 ⛲🔧WCincluded. 🚿
**Location:** Urban, simple. **Surface:** metalled. 🅾 01/01-31/12.
**Distance:** ⚓on the spot ⚓on the spot ⛽on the spot ⊗on the spot
🚤on the spot.
**Remarks:** Pay at harbourmaster.

### Struer 5C3
**Holstebro-Struer Lystbådehavn**, Fjordvejen.
**GPS:** n56,49380 e8,59068.⬆➡.

6 🍽DKK 132 ⛲🔧WC🔲DKK 25 📶included. 🏠
**Location:** Urban, comfortable, quiet. **Surface:** gravel.
🅾 01/04-14/11 🅾 winter.
**Distance:** 🛒100m 🚤100m.
**Remarks:** Tallycard: service, electricity, sanitary building, caution DKK 50.

### Struer 5C3
**Venø Havn**, Venø. **GPS:** n56,55102 e8,61622.⬆.

4 🍽DKK 100 ⛲🍽Ch🔧WC🔲📶included. 🚿
**Location:** Rural, simple. **Surface:** gravel.
🅾 01/01-31/12.
**Distance:** ⚓on the spot ⊗on the spot 🚤on the spot.
**Remarks:** Ferry boat to island ± DKK 95 round trip.

**Tourist information Struer:**
👁 Gimsinghoved, Gimsinghoved 1. Former large Danish farm.

### Sydals 6D3
**Drejby**, Kregnæsvej 85. **GPS:** n54,86162 e9,99898.⬆.
🍽DKK 150 ⛲🍽Ch🔧. 🅾 18/03-02/10.
**Remarks:** Quick-Stop: >20h - <10h.

### Sydals 6D3
**Lysabildskov**, Skovforten 4. **GPS:** n54,89159 e10,05268.
🍽DKK 120 ⛲🍽Ch🔧against payment. 🅾 19/03-30/09.
**Remarks:** Quick-Stop: >20h - <10h.

### Sydals 6D3
**Mommark Marina Camping**, Mommarkvej 380.
**GPS:** n54,93157 e10,04392.
2 🍽DKK 120. **Surface:** asphalted. 🅾 19/03-30/09.
**Distance:** ⚓on the spot.
**Remarks:** Quick-Stop: >20h - <10h.

### Sydals 6D3
**Sønderby Strand Camping**, Sønderbygade 4-6, Kegnæs.
**GPS:** n54,86586 e9,89222.
🍽DKK 120. **Surface:** grassy. 🅾 18/03-03/10.
**Distance:** ⚓100m. **Remarks:** Quick-Stop: >20h - <10h.

**Tourist information Sydals:**
ℹ Sydals Turistbureau, Kegnæsvej 52.
👁 Kegnæs Fyr, Nørre Landevej 7. Lighthouse. 🅾 01/06-30/09 Mo-Su 9-19h.

### Sæby 5C3
**Sæby Havn**, Havnen 20. **GPS:** n57,33218 e10,53373.⬆➡.

---

20 🍽DKK 190 ⛲included 🔧(20x)DKK 2,50. 🚿 **Location:** Urban,
simple, central. **Surface:** asphalted. 🅾 01/01-31/12.
**Distance:** ⚓100m ⛽on the spot ⊗100m 🚤100m.

### Sæby 5C3
**Top Plads hos Ase en Helmer**, Understedvej 65, Understed.
**GPS:** n57,37249 e10,46447.⬆.

20 🍽DKK 100 ⛲🍽Ch🔧DKK 20 WC🔲DKK 15 🔲. 🚿
**Location:** Rural, comfortable, isolated, quiet. **Surface:** grassy.
🅾 01/01-31/12.

### Sæby 5C3
**Voerså Fiskerleje**, Havstokken 11, Voerså.
**GPS:** n57,20389 e10,49389.⬆➡.

20 🍽DKK 140 ⛲🍽Ch🔧(20x)WC🔲included. 🚿
**Location:** Rural, comfortable, isolated. **Surface:** gravel.
🅾 01/04-31/10.
**Distance:** 🛒3km ⚓on the spot ⛽on the spot ⊗3km 🚤3km.
**Remarks:** Money in envelope in mail box, canoe and boat rental.

### Sæby 5C3
**Dansbjerg**, Hjørringvej 160. **GPS:** n57,32544 e10,36967.⬆➡.

6 🍽DKK 50 🔧. **Location:** Rural, simple, isolated, quiet.
**Surface:** grassy/gravel. 🅾 01/01-31/12.
**Distance:** 🛒1km 🚤1km.
**Remarks:** At manege.

### Sæby 5C3
**Lene en Knut Holdensgård**, Holdenggårdvej 16, Sønder.
**GPS:** n57,21616 e10,45253.⬆.

3 🍽DKK 50 ⛲🔧🚿. **Location:** Rural, simple, isolated, quiet.
**Surface:** grassy. 🅾 01/01-31/12.

DK

## Tarm 6C1

**Erik Andersen**, Blåkildevej 41. **GPS:** n55,89825 e8,48057.⬆.

3 ⚏DKK 50 🚰included. 🛢 **Location:** Rural, simple, quiet.
**Surface:** grassy. ◻ 01/01-31/12.
**Distance:** 🚶3km 🏊500m 🛒500m ⊗3km 🛒3km.

## Tarm 6C1

**Par3Golf**, Grimlundvej 2. **GPS:** n55,83819 e8,71321.⬆.

⚏free. **Location:** Rural, simple, isolated, quiet. **Surface:** gravel/sand.
◻ 01/01-31/12.
**Distance:** 🚶Tarm 19km.
**Remarks:** At golf court.

## Tårs (Hjørring) 5C3

**Vendelbo Vans Autocampere**, Damhusvej 23.
**GPS:** n57,38972 e10,11500.⬆.

8 ⚏DKK 100 🚰🅟Ch🔌 (8x)WC☕included. 🛢🚿
**Location:** Urban, comfortable, central, quiet. **Surface:** grassy/gravel.
◻ 01/01-31/12.
**Distance:** 🚶100m 🏊500m 🛒500m ⊗300m 🛒300m 🚲200m.
**Remarks:** At motorhome dealer, max. 48h, sanitary 9-17h.

## Thisted 5C3

Thisted Kystvej. **GPS:** n56,95197 e8,68221.⬆.
5 ⚏free. **Location:** Rural, isolated. **Surface:** gravel.
◻ 01/01-31/12.
**Distance:** 🚶1,4km 🏊on the spot 🛒on the spot ⊗850m 🛒700m.
**Remarks:** Max. 24h, beautiful view.

## Thisted 5C3

**Vilsund Havn**, Gamle Færgevej 30. **GPS:** n56,88232 e8,62848.⬆.

6 ⚏DKK 120 🚰🔌WCincluded ☕DKK 10. 🛢🚿
**Location:** Rural, simple. **Surface:** gravel. ◻ 01/01-31/12.
**Distance:** 🚶Thisted 11km ⊗100m.
**Remarks:** To be paid at petrol station.

## Thisted 5C3

**Silstrupgård B&B**, Åsvej 5B, Silstrup. **GPS:** n56,93047 e8,64754.⬆.

4 ⚏DKK 100 🚰🅟Ch🔌WC☕included 🔊.
**Location:** Rural, simple. **Surface:** gravel. ◻ 01/01-31/12.
**Distance:** 🚶Thisted 5km.

## Thisted 5C3

**Thisted Camping**, Iversensvej 3. **GPS:** n56,95309 e8,71249.
⚏DKK 135 🚰🅟Ch🔌against payment ◻ 01/01-31/12.
**Remarks:** Quick-Stop: >20h - <10h.

## Thisted 5C3

**Nystrup Camping Klitmøller**, Trøjborgvej 22, Klitmøller.
**GPS:** n57,03302 e8,47927.⬆.
5 ⚏DKK 100. 🚉 **Location:** Rural. **Surface:** gravel. ◻ 01/03-30/10.
**Remarks:** In nature reserve, Quick-Stop: >20h - <10h.

**Tourist information Thisted:**
ℹ Thy Turistbureau i Thisted, Store Torv 6, www.visitthy.dk. Bathing resort.
👁 Thisted Bryghus, Bryggerivej 10. Brewery, information at Turistbureau. ◻ summer Wed 11h. 🎫 DKK 50.

## Thorsager 6D1

**Dagli Brugsen**, Thorsgade 26. **GPS:** n56,34305 e10,46286.⬆.

4 ⚏free. **Location:** Urban, simple. **Surface:** gravel/metalled.
◻ 01/01-31/12.
**Distance:** 🚶on the spot 🛒on the spot.
**Remarks:** Behind supermarket Brugsen, max. 24h.

## Thyborøn 5B3

**Thyborøn**, Idrætsvej 3. **GPS:** n56,69456 e8,20456.
⚏DKK 100 🚰🅟Ch🔌 ◻ 01/01-31/12.
**Remarks:** Quick-Stop: >20h - <10h.

## Thyholm 5C3

**Jegindø Havn**, Havnegade 26. **GPS:** n56,65219 e8,63575.⬆.

4 ⚏DKK 120 🚰🔌 (2x)WC☕🔊included. 🛢🚿
**Location:** Rural, simple, quiet. **Surface:** grassy. ◻ 01/01-31/12.
**Distance:** 🛒on the spot 🛒on the spot ⊗100m.
**Remarks:** At harbour.

## Tinglev 6C2

**Stefan Christiansen**, Oksevejen 13. **GPS:** n54,97365 e9,34601.➡.

8 ⚏DKK 100 🚰🅟Ch🔌 (6x)DKK 27/24h WC☕DKK 10 🔊included.
🛢 **Location:** Rural, luxurious, isolated, quiet. **Surface:** grassy.
◻ 01/01-31/12.
**Distance:** 🚶8km 🏊2km 🛒on the spot 🛒on the spot ⊗800m 🚲on

the spot 🚶on the spot.
**Remarks:** Golf court 1km, picnic tables available.

## Toftlund 6C2

**Dahl**, Lebækvej 2. **GPS:** n55,17839 e9,07768.⬆➡.

50 ⚏DKK 50, DKK 75 service incl 🚰🅟Ch🔌WC☕📷🔊included.
🛢 **Location:** Rural, simple, comfortable, isolated, quiet.
**Surface:** grassy. ◻ 01/01-31/12.
**Distance:** 🚶2km ⊗2km 🛒2km.

## Tønder 6C3

**Autocamperplads Tønder**, Sønderlandevej.
**GPS:** n54,93558 e8,87754.➡.

40 ⚏DKK 110, 01/07-30/09 DKK 125 🚰DKK 3/20liter 🅟Ch🔌WC
☕📷DKK 4/time 🔊included. 🚉🚿 **Location:** Rural, comfortable,
quiet. **Surface:** gravel. ◻ 04/01-19/12.
**Distance:** 🚶1km ⊗300m 🛒1,5km 🚲400m.
**Remarks:** Incl. access swimming pool.

## Tønder 6C3

**Kennel Roager**, Flensborg Landevej 25. **GPS:** n54,93190 e8,99793.⬆.

5 ⚏DKK 100 🚰🔌DKK 20/24h WCincluded ☕DKK 20 📷DKK 30 🔊.
🛢 **Location:** Rural, simple, isolated, noisy. **Surface:** grassy.
◻ 01/01-31/12.
**Distance:** 🚶10km 🛒4km.

## Ulfborg 6C1

Tingvej. **GPS:** n56,27297 e8,32253.⬆.

4 ⚏free. **Location:** Simple. **Surface:** gravel. ◻ 01/01-31/12.
**Distance:** 🚶on the spot ⊗on the spot 🛒300m.
**Remarks:** Nearby town hall.

## Ulfborg 6C1

**Thorsminde Havn**, Vesterhavsgade 1a. **GPS:** n56,36578 e8,12163.⬆➡.

DK

10 �了DKK 100 ⏚ DKK 30. 🚿 **Location:** Rural, simple.
**Surface:** asphalted. 🔲 01/01-31/12.
**Distance:** ⚓on the spot ⊗on the spot 200m.

### 🍴S Ulfborg 6C1
**Vestergaard**, Hugvej 5, Vedersø. **GPS:** n56,24961 e8,16796.⬆

15 �了DKK 50 ⏚included. 🚿
**Location:** Rural, simple, isolated. **Surface:** grassy.
🔲 01/01-31/12.
**Distance:** ⚓Ulfborg 14km ⚓North Sea 1,5km on the spot.
**Remarks:** Max. 48h, payment also in euros, breakfast-service.

### Ulfborg 6C1
**Tvind Skolecenter**, Skorkærvej 8. **GPS:** n56,25636 e8,28110.⬆

15 �I free. **Location:** Rural, simple, isolated.
🔲 01/01-31/12 ⊙ first 2 weeks of Aug.
**Distance:** ⚓8km ⊗8km 8km.

### ©S Ulfborg 6C1
**Rejkjær**, Ringkobingvej 24. **GPS:** n56,23319 e8,30966.
⌠DKK 100 ⏚Ch against payment. 🔲 03/04-18/10.
**Remarks:** Quick-Stop: >20h - <10h.

### ©S Ulfborg 6C1
**Vedersø Klit Camping**, Øhusevej 23. **GPS:** n56,25829 e8,14130.⬆
⌠DKK 70-130 ⏚Ch DKK 35 against payment DKK 25.
**Location:** Rural. **Surface:** gravel. 🔲 07/04-22/10.
**Distance:** ⊗on the spot on the spot.

### Vandel 6C1
**Dagli' Brugsen**, Hans Thomsens Vej 103. **GPS:** n55,71285 e9,21800.⬆

3 ⌠free.
**Location:** Simple. **Surface:** metalled.
🔲 01/01-31/12.
**Distance:** ⊗on the spot on the spot.
**Remarks:** At petrol station and supermarket, max. 11h, Legoland 6km.

### 🍴S Vemb 6C1
**Flamingo Naturpark**, Skalstrupvej 10. **GPS:** n56,35396 e8,31230.⬆
50 ⌠DKK 50 ⏚WC. 🚿 **Location:** Rural, simple, isolated.
**Surface:** grassy.
**Distance:** ⚓4,5km 2km 2km 4,5km.
**Remarks:** Including access park.

### ⚓S Vesløs 5C3
**Amtoft Havn**, Gårdbækvej 12. **GPS:** n57,00647 e8,94068.⬆

---

5 ⌠DKK 100 ⏚Ch (10x)DKK 25,6Amp WC DKK 10 ⊙
DKK 20 included. 🚿 **Location:** Rural, comfortable, quiet.
**Surface:** grassy/gravel. 🔲 01/01-31/12.
**Distance:** ⚓on the spot ⚓on the spot on the spot on the spot.

### 🍴 Vesløs 5C3
**Vejlernes Grill & Kiosk**, Aalborgvej 219B. **GPS:** n57,02518 e9,01585.

⌠free. **Surface:** gravel. 🔲 01/01-31/12.

### ©S Vestervig 5B3
**Krik-Vig**, Krikvej 112. **GPS:** n56,77800 e8,26210.⬆

20 ⌠DKK 110 ⏚Ch against payment. **Location:** Rural.
**Surface:** grassy. 🔲 19/03-23/10.
**Remarks:** Quick-Stop: >20h - <10h.

### 🌾S Viborg 5C3
**Hanne Mølgaard**, Jegstrupvej Vest 114. **GPS:** n56,46269 e9,34118.⬆

6 ⌠DKK 75 ⏚included. 🚿 **Location:** Rural, simple.
**Surface:** grassy.
**Distance:** ⚓5km.

### ⚓S Viborg 5C3
**Kjellerupvej 16. GPS:** n56,38420 e9,44058.⬆
5 ⌠DKK 100 ⏚Ch (2x),16Amp WC ⊙included.
**Location:** Rural, isolated, quiet. **Surface:** grassy.
🔲 01/01-31/12.
**Distance:** 1,5km.

### ⚓ Vinderup 5C3
**Sportsplads**, Nørgårdsvej. **GPS:** n56,48181 e8,78636.⬆➡

12 ⌠free. **Location:** Urban, simple. **Surface:** asphalted/metalled.
🔲 01/01-31/12.
**Distance:** ⚓500m ⊗500m 450m.

### ⚓S Vinderup 5C3
**Handbjerg Marina**, Strandvejen. **GPS:** n56,47568 e8,71337.➡

---

24 ⌠DKK 125 ⏚🚿against payment. 
**Location:** Rural, quiet. **Surface:** gravel. 🔲 01/01-31/12.
**Distance:** ⚓on the spot ⚓on the spot ⊗on the spot.

### © Vinderup 5C3
**Sevel Camping**, Halallé 6, Sevel. **GPS:** n56,45889 e8,86950.
⌠DKK 50.
**Surface:** gravel.
🔲 01/01-31/12.
**Remarks:** Quick-Stop: >20h - <10h.
**Tourist information Vinderup:**
M Hjerl Hedes Frilandsmuseum, Hjerl Hedevej 14. Open air museum.
🔲 01/05-30/09 10-16h, 01/07-31/07 10-17h.
Stubber Kloster, Stubbergård Sø. Ruins of former Benedictine
monastery. 🔲 01/01-31/12. T free.

### S Ørsted 5C3
Rougsøvej. **GPS:** n56,60599 e10,30269.⬆
5 ⌠DKK 90 ⏚included WC.
**Location:** Rural. **Surface:** gravel. 🔲 01/04-30/09.
**Distance:** ⚓on the spot on the spot.

### ©S Østbirk 6D1
**Elite Camp Vestbirk**, Møllehøjvej 4. **GPS:** n55,96396 e9,69972.➡

10 ⌠DKK 140 ⏚Ch DKK 3,50/kWh WCincluded.
**Location:** Rural, comfortable. **Surface:** grassy. 🔲 01/01-31/12.
**Remarks:** Quick-Stop: >18h - <10h.

### ⚓S Øster Assels 5C3
**Sillerslev Havn**, Havnevej 75. **GPS:** n56,68116 e8,72774.⬆

16 ⌠DKK 120 ⏚Ch WC included. 🚿 **Location:** Rural,
comfortable. **Surface:** gravel/sand. 🔲 01/01-31/12.
**Distance:** ⚓on the spot ⚓on the spot ⊗on the spot.

## Funen

### ⚓S Aarup 6D2
**Aalsbogaard Lystfiskersøer**, Store Landevej 125, Billesbølle.
**GPS:** n55,42686 e10,01935.
⌠DKK 50/pp ⏚DKK 20 DKK 10.
**Surface:** grassy. 🔲 01/01-31/12.
**Distance:** ⚓on the spot ⊗on the spot.
**Remarks:** At fish lake.

### ⚓S Aarup 6D2
**Meny Aarup**, Bredgade 44-46. **GPS:** n55,37975 e10,04714.⬆

**DK**

3 🛏free. **Location:** Urban, simple, central, quiet. **Surface:** concrete. 🅾 01/01-31/12.
**Distance:** 👟on the spot ⊗200m 🛒on the spot 🚲2km.
**Remarks:** At supermarket.

| 🍷S | Aarup 👫 | 6D2 |

**Annemette & Lars Mogensen**, Frøbjerg Vænge 31.
**GPS:** n55,34907 e10,08323.⬆

3 🛏free. **Location:** Rural, simple, isolated, quiet. **Surface:** gravel.
🅾 01/01-31/12.
**Distance:** 👟5km 🚐800m.
**Remarks:** Arrival <23h.

| 🍷S | Aarup 👫 | 6D2 |

**Jørgen Bjerring**, Magtenbøllevej 94. **GPS:** n55,37708 e10,17207.⬆

3 🛏DKK 75 🚰🔌Ch🔌(3x)DKK 30 🗑DKK 15.
**Location:** Rural, simple, comfortable, isolated, quiet. **Surface:** grassy.
🅾 01/01-31/12.
**Distance:** 👟5km ⊗4km 🛒4km 🏃on the spot.

| ⚓S | Assens | 6D2 |

**Assens Havn**, Nordre Havnevej 10. **GPS:** n55,27345 e9,88961.⬆

20 🛏DKK 160 🚰WC🗑.🛢 **Location:** Urban, simple, central, quiet.
**Surface:** grassy. 🅾 01/01-31/12.
**Distance:** 👟350m ⚓on the spot ⚓on the spot ⊗350m 🚐on the spot 🚲on the spot.
**Remarks:** Max. 24h, service at marina.

| ⚓S | Assens | 6D2 |

**Assens Marina**, Næsvej 29. **GPS:** n55,26811 e9,88809.⬆

12 🛏DKK 140 🚰Ch🔌(12x)WCincluded 🗑DKK 20/16minutes 🖥
DKK 30/time 🛢.🛢🛢 **Location:** Urban, comfortable, central,
quiet. **Surface:** grassy. 🅾 01/01-31/12.

**Distance:** 👟1,5km ⚓on the spot ⚓on the spot ⊗150m 🛒1km 🚲on the spot 🏃on the spot.

| 🍷S | Assens | 6D2 |

**Britta Bang**, Lilletoftevej 7, Gamtofte. **GPS:** n55,28165 e9,98850.

3 🛏DKK 100 🚰🔌Ch🔌(2x)included WC. **Location:** Rural,
comfortable, isolated, quiet. **Surface:** gravel. 🅾 01/01-31/12.
**Distance:** 👟7,5km ⊗7km 🛒7km 🚲on the spot.
**Remarks:** Check in at B&B <22h, max. 48h.

**Tourist information Assens:**
Ⓜ Vestfyns Hjemstavnsgård, Klaregade 23, Gummerup, Glamsbjerg.
Open air museum. 🅾 01/04-31/10 10-16h 🅾 Mo.

| Bagenkop 🌸🚊 | 6E3 |

**Bagenkop Lystbådehavn**, Færgevej. **GPS:** n54,75123 e10,67600.⬆➡

9 🛏DKK 130 🚰🔌(12x) WC 🛢.🛢🛢 **Location:** Urban,
simple, central. **Surface:** asphalted. 🅾 01/01-31/12.
**Distance:** 👟10km ⚓500m ⚓600m ⚓on the spot 🛒on the spot 🚲on the spot.

| 🚌S | Bogense 🚊 | 6D2 |

**Maria Nordgaard Pedersen**, Halsvej 52.
**GPS:** n55,60545 e10,26875.⬆

4 🛏DKK 80 🔌DKK 30. **Location:** Rural, simple, isolated, quiet.
**Surface:** grassy. 🅾 01/01-31/12.
**Distance:** 👟14km ⚓500m 🚲on the spot.
**Remarks:** Money in envelope in mail box.

| ⚓S | Bogense 🚊 | 6D2 |

**Bogense Havn**, Vestre Havnevej 29. **GPS:** n55,56806 e10,07833.⬆

8 🛏DKK 100 🚰🔌 WCincluded 🗑🖥🛢.
**Location:** Urban, simple, quiet. **Surface:** gravel. 🅾 01/01-31/12.
**Distance:** 👟200m ⚓300m 🛒300m ⊗on the spot 🚐200m.

| 🚌S | Faaborg 🌸🚊 | 6D2 |

**Faaborg Havn**, Kanalvej 19. **GPS:** n55,09641 e10,23389.⬆

6 🛏DKK 140 🚰DKK 5/10minutes 🔌(6x)DKK 3/kWh WC🗑🛢against
payment 🛢included 🛢.🛢🛢 **Location:** Urban, comfortable,
central, quiet. **Surface:** gravel. 🅾 01/06-30/09.
**Distance:** 👟200m ⚓on the spot ⚓on the spot ⊗on the spot 🛒500m 🚐200m.
**Remarks:** Check in at harbourmaster.

| ⚓S | Faaborg 🌸🚊 | 6D2 |

**Havnen Fjellebroen**, Fjellebrovejen 81. **GPS:** n55,06009 e10,38140.⬆

10 🛏DKK 100 🚰🔌DKK 12 WC🗑DKK 5 🛢included. 🚲
**Location:** Rural, simple, isolated, quiet. **Surface:** gravel.
🅾 01/01-31/12.
**Distance:** 👟10km ⚓on the spot ⚓on the spot 🛒3km 🚲on the spot.
**Remarks:** Money in envelope in mail box.

| 🚌S | Faaborg 🌸🚊 | 6D2 |

**Faaborg Camping**, Odensevej 140. **GPS:** n55,11667 e10,24477.⬆➡

3 🛏DKK 150 🚰🔌Ch🔌(3x)DKK 35/24h 🗑DKK 35 🛢included 🛢.
🏠🛢 **Location:** Rural, comfortable, isolated, noisy. **Surface:** grassy.
🅾 01/01-31/12.
**Distance:** 👟2,5km ⊗2km 🛒2km 🚲on the spot.

| 🚌S | Ferritslev 🌸 | 6D2 |

**Jørgen Christensen**, Rolfvej 45. **GPS:** n55,32321 e10,56940.⬆

4 🛏free. **Location:** Urban, simple, isolated, quiet. **Surface:** gravel.
🅾 01/01-31/12.
**Distance:** 👟1km 🚐2km.

| ⛺S | Frørup | 6E2 |

**Kongshøj**, Kongshøjvej 5. **GPS:** n55,22122 e10,80628.⬆
🛏DKK 105 🚰🔌Ch🔌.
**Location:** Simple, isolated, quiet. 🅾 01/01-31/12.
**Distance:** ⚓on the spot.
**Remarks:** Quick-Stop: >20h - <10h.

| 🚌S | Gram | 6C2 |

**Anholm Fiskesø**, Folevej 11. **GPS:** n55,30564 e8,99888.⬆

DK

15 ⌇DKK 150, dog DKK 10 ⛽🔌Ch included 🚿DKK 35. 🚮
**Location:** Rural, simple, isolated, quiet. 🗓 01/04-30/11.
**Distance:** 🚶5km 🛒on the spot ⊗1km 🍴5km.
**Remarks:** At fish pond.

### 🅢 Gram 6C2
**Gram Slot**, Slotsvej 54. **GPS:** n55,29722 e9,05946. ⬆
50 ⌇DKK 80/pp ⛽🔌WC included. **Location:** Rural, quiet.
**Surface:** grassy. 🗓 01/01-31/12.
**Distance:** 🛒200m 🍴1km.

### 🅢 Gram 6C2
**Annemettes bondegård**, Ribelandevej 18.
**GPS:** n55,28647 e9,00098. ⬆

3 ⌇DKK 100 ⛽🔌Ch 🚿DKK 25. 🚮
**Location:** Rural, simple, isolated, quiet. **Surface:** grassy/gravel.
🗓 03/01-01/11.
**Distance:** 🚶3km 🍴3km.

### 🅢 Humble 6E3
**Pilestræde**. **GPS:** n54,82833 e10,69888. ⬆

2 ⌇free. **Location:** Urban, simple, central, noisy. **Surface:** asphalted.
🗓 01/01-31/12.
**Distance:** 🚶on the spot ⊗on the spot 🍴on the spot 🚲on the spot.

### 🅢 Humble 6E3
**Ristinge**, Ristingevej 104. **GPS:** n54,81944 e10,63988. ➡
4 ⌇DKK 150, 2 pers.incl ⛽🔌Ch 🚿DKK 40/day WC included
🔌DKK 30/time 🔌DKK 30/time 🔌DKK 10/day 🚿. **Surface:** gravel.
🗓 03/06-28/08. **Distance:** 🏖300m 🛒500m ⊗on the spot 🍴on the
spot 🚲on the spot 🚶on the spot.
**Remarks:** Quick-Stop: >20h - <10h.

### 🅢 Kerteminde 6E2
**Kerteminde Marina**, Marinavejen 4. **GPS:** n55,45439 e10,66443. ⬆

17 ⌇DKK 140 ⛽🔌Ch 🚿WC against payment included 🚿.
🔌 **Location:** Rural, comfortable, central, quiet. **Surface:** gravel.
🗓 01/01-31/12.
**Distance:** 🚶500m 🏖on the spot 🛒on the spot ⊗250m 🍴150m
🚲500m 🚶on the spot.

### 🅢 Kerteminde 6E2
**Color Camp Kerteminde**, Hindsholmvej 80.
**GPS:** n55,46409 e10,67183. ⬆

---

15 ⌇DKK 150, 2 pers.incl ⛽🔌Ch 🚿(12x)DKK 40 WC included 🔌
DKK 40 🔌DKK 15/day 🚿 🚲 🚿 **Location:** Urban, comfortable, noisy.
**Surface:** grassy/metalled. 🗓 21/03-18/09.
**Distance:** 🚶on the spot 🏖50m 🛒50m ⊗800m 🍴2km 🚲on the
spot 🚶1km.

### 🅢 Middelfart ⚓ 6D2
**Lystbådehavn**, Østre Hougvej 112. **GPS:** n55,49250 e9,73028. ⬆

13 ⌇DKK 60-180 ⛽DKK 5/10minutes 🔌Ch 🔌(12x)DKK 2,50/kWh
WC 🔌DKK 2/1minutes 🔌 included. 🔌🚿
**Location:** Rural, luxurious, isolated, quiet.
**Surface:** asphalted/metalled. 🗓 01/03-21/10.
**Distance:** 🚶2km 🏖on the spot 🛒on the spot ⊗on the spot 🍴on
the spot. **Remarks:** Harbour Middelfahrt, Tallycard: service, electricity,
sanitary building, caution DKK 50.

### ⚓🅢 Middelfart ⚓ 6D2
**NyHavn 2**, Havnegade. **GPS:** n55,50503 e9,73787. ⬆

20 ⌇DKK 150 ⛽🔌16Amp WC 🔌included. 🔌🚿
**Location:** Urban, comfortable, central, quiet. **Surface:** gravel.
🗓 01/01-31/12.
**Distance:** 🚶on the spot 🏖on the spot 🛒on the spot ⊗100m
🍴400m 🚲500m 🚶on the spot.
**Remarks:** Max. 48h.

### ⚓🅢 Middelfart ⚓ 6D2
**Strib Bådehavn**, Strandvejen 271, Strib. **GPS:** n55,53829 e9,76387. ⬆

7 ⌇DKK 130 ⛽🔌Ch 🚿(7x)WC 🔌DKK 50/time 🔌included
🚿🔌🚿 **Location:** Rural, comfortable, central, quiet.
**Surface:** gravel/metalled. 🗓 01/01-31/12.
**Distance:** 🚶500m 🏖on the spot 🛒on the spot ⊗350m 🍴1km
🚲on the spot 🚶on the spot.

### ⚓🅢 Millinge 6D2
**Fasled Havn**, Fiskerstræde 1. **GPS:** n55,15347 e10,14431. ➡

---

20 ⌇DKK 125 ⛽🔌(16x)DKK 20/day WC 🔌🔌included 🚿🔌🚿
**Location:** Rural, comfortable, isolated, quiet, noisy.
**Surface:** grassy/gravel. 🗓 01/01-31/12.
**Distance:** 🚶5km 🏖on the spot ⊗200m 🍴500m 🚲on the spot 🚶on
the spot.
**Remarks:** Check in at harbourmaster, bread-service, wifi code:
havnen2.

### 🅢 Nyborg 🌳 6E2
**Hjejlevej 107**. **GPS:** n55,29734 e10,83963. ⬆

⌇free. **Location:** Simple, isolated. **Surface:** metalled.
**Distance:** 🚶2,5km 🍴2km.

### 🅢 Nyborg 🌳 6E2
**Sulkendrup Mølle**, Sulkendrupvej 1. **GPS:** n55,29384 e10,71287. ⬆

3 ⌇DKK 90 ⛽DKK 25 🔌Ch 🚿(3x)DKK 25 WC 🔌DKK 15 🔌DKK 30/
time 🔌included. 🚿
**Location:** Rural, simple, isolated. **Surface:** sand. 🗓 01/01-31/12.
**Distance:** 🚶5km ⊗5km 🍴5km 🚲on the spot.

**Tourist information Nyborg:**
🏛 Borgmestergården, Slotsgade 11. Local history. 🗓 01/05-31/10
10-15/16h.
⚔ Nyborg Fæstning, Slotsgade 1. Fortress.
⚔ Nyborg Slot / Danehofslottet, Slotsgade 34. Castle, end 12th
century. 🗓 01/04-31/10 10-15/16h.

### 🏕 Odense 6D2
**Tarup Campingcenter**, Agerhatten 31. **GPS:** n55,36539 e10,46603.

2 ⌇free. **Location:** Urban, simple, quiet. **Surface:** grasstiles.
🗓 01/01-31/12.
**Distance:** 🚶6km 🚴2km 🚲on the spot.

### 🅢 Rudkøbing 🌳⚓ 6E2
**Færgegårdens**, Spodsbjergvej 335. **GPS:** n54,93219 e10,82945.

**DK**

10 �~DKK 130, 2 pers.incl ⌐🔥Ⓒ⌐Ⓗincluded ⌐⌐DKK 30/day. 🚐 ⌐
**Location:** Urban, comfortable, central, quiet.
**Surface:** grasstiles/metalled. ☐ 01/01-31/12.
**Distance:** ⌐on the spot ⌐2km ⌐on the spot ⌐on the spot ⊗on the spot ⌐200m ⌐1km ⌐1km.
**Remarks:** Max. 6,5m.

### Simmerbølle 6E2
**Linkehøj**, Ndr. Landevej 71. **GPS:** n54,94658 e10,76556.⌐

10 ⌐DKK 100 ⌐included ⌐DKK 20/day �120 Ⓦ⌐DKK 12/time. 🚐
**Location:** Rural, simple, isolated, quiet. **Surface:** grassy.
☐ 01/01-31/12.
**Distance:** ⌐3km ⌐3,5km ⌐3,5km ⌐100m.

### Svendborg 6D2
**Svendborg Golfbane**, Tordensgårdevej 3.
**GPS:** n55,08771 e10,55490.⌐

10 ⌐DKK 120 ⌐DKK 15/time ⌐Ⓦ⌐included. ⌐
**Location:** Rural, comfortable. **Surface:** grassy/metalled.
☐ 01/01-31/12.
**Distance:** ⌐5km ⌐5km ⊗on the spot.
**Remarks:** Next to golf court, payment also in euros.

### Svendborg 6D2
**Carlsberg**, Sundbrovej 19. **GPS:** n55,03344 e10,61332.⌐⌐

20 ⌐DKK 130, 2 pers.incl ⌐🔥Ⓒ⌐⌐(10x)DKK 30/24h Ⓦ⌐DKK 3
⌐DKK 35/time ⌐included. 🚐 ⌐ **Location:** Rural, comfortable,
isolated, quiet. **Surface:** grassy. ☐ 17/03-02/10.
**Distance:** ⌐5km ⌐1,5km ⌐1,5km ⊗on the spot ⌐on the spot
⌐on the spot.
**Remarks:** Quick-Stop: >20h - <10h.

### Svendborg 6D2
**Idrætshallen**, Ryttervej 70. **GPS:** n55,05668 e10,57613.⌐
⌐Ⓒ⌐. **Location:** Simple.

**Tourist information Svendborg:**
ℹ️✖ Egeskov Slot, Kværndrup. Citadel with park and 6 museums.
☐ 01/05-31/10 10-17/20h.
✖ Valdemars Slot, Slotsalléen 100, Troense, Tåsinge. Castle on the island
Tåsinge, fully furnished. ☐ 01/05-31/10 10-17h ⌐ May, Sep, Oct: Mo.

### Søby, æro 6D2
**Søby Havn**, Havnen 6. **GPS:** n54,94140 e10,25943.⌐
3 ⌐DKK 120 ⌐⌐Ⓦ⌐included ⌐DKK 10. **Location:** Rural, simple,

---

quiet. **Surface:** metalled/sand. ☐ 01/01-31/12.
**Distance:** ⌐500m ⌐500m ⌐500m.

### Tranekær 6E2
**Dageløkke Havn**, Dageløkke Havn 7. **GPS:** n55,06229 e10,86265.⌐

2 ⌐DKK 140 ⌐⌐(4x)Ⓦ⌐included ⌐DKK 12/24h.
🚐 ⌐ **Location:** Rural, comfortable, isolated, quiet.
**Surface:** gravel/metalled. ☐ 01/01-31/12.
**Distance:** ⌐10km ⌐on the spot ⌐on the spot ⊗on the spot ⌐on
the spot ⌐on the spot ⌐on the spot.

### Tranekær 6E2
**Emmerbølle Strand Camping**, Emmerbøllevej 24.
**GPS:** n55,03619 e10,84855.⌐⌐

4 ⌐DKK 140 ⌐⌐Ⓒ⌐included ⌐(4x)DKK 40/day ⌐🚐
⌐ **Location:** Rural, comfortable, isolated. **Surface:** gravel.
☐ 18/03-18/09.
**Distance:** ⌐on the spot ⌐1,5km ⊗on the spot ⌐on the spot ⌐on
the spot ⌐on the spot.
**Remarks:** Quick-Stop: >20h - <10h.

### Varde 6C2
**Fritidscenter**, Lerpøtvej 55. **GPS:** n55,63649 e8,47655.⌐
10 ⌐DKK 50 ⌐⌐Ⓦ⌐. **Location:** Rural, simple, isolated, quiet.
**Surface:** grassy. ☐ 01/05-31/10.
**Distance:** ⌐500m ⌐700m.
**Remarks:** At sports centre, check in at swimming pool.

### Varde 6C2
**Jensen**, Ringkøbingvej 143. **GPS:** n55,65762 e8,48942.⌐

8 ⌐DKK 100 ⌐⌐DKK 30 Ⓦ⌐. ⌐ **Location:** Rural, comfortable,
isolated, quiet. **Surface:** grassy/metalled. ☐ 01/01-31/12.
**Distance:** ⌐5km ⊗5km ⌐5km.

### Varde 6C2
Stålværksvej. **GPS:** n55,62130 e8,47494.⌐

2 ⌐free. **Location:** Urban, simple, central. **Surface:** asphalted.
☐ 01/01-31/12.
**Distance:** ⌐on the spot ⊗200m ⌐200m.

### Varde 6C2
**Joan & Preben Christensen**, Ringkøbingvej 259, Hindsig.
**GPS:** n55,72077 e8,49345.⌐

---

5 ⌐DKK 150 ⌐⌐Ⓒ⌐. ⌐ **Location:** Rural, comfortable, quiet.
**Surface:** grassy. ☐ 01/01-31/12.
**Distance:** ⌐12km ⌐3km.

### Ærøskøbing 6D2
**Ærøskøbing Camping**, Sygehusvej 40. **GPS:** n54,89408 e10,40118.
⌐DKK 150 ⌐⌐included. ☐ 01/04-23/10.
**Distance:** ⌐on the spot.
**Remarks:** Quick-Stop: >20h - <10h.

# Seeland, Møn, Lolland and Falster

### Boeslunde 6E2
**Campinggaarden Boelunde**, Rennebjergvej 110.
**GPS:** n55,28463 e11,26837.
⌐DKK 140 ⌐⌐Ⓒ⌐against payment. ☐ 01/04-30/09.
**Remarks:** Quick-Stop: >20h - <10h.

### Bogø By 6F2
**Farø Parkplatz**, Grøsundvej. **GPS:** n54,94876 e11,98696.

25 ⌐free ⌐⌐ⒸⓌfree. **Location:** Rural, noisy. **Surface:** gravel.
☐ 01/01-31/12.
**Distance:** ⌐200m ⌐on the spot ⌐on the spot ⊗100m.

### Bogø By 6F2
**Café-Restaurant Stalden**, Hougårdsbanke 5.
**GPS:** n54,93000 e12,02806.
4 ⌐free for clients ⌐⌐Ⓒ⌐Ⓦ⌐against payment.
**Location:** Rural. **Surface:** grassy. ☐ 01/01-31/12.
**Distance:** ⌐1km ⊗on the spot.

### Borre 6F2
**Klintholm Havn**, Klintholm Havneby 24. **GPS:** n54,95418 e12,46695.⌐
10 ⌐DKK 140 Ⓦ⌐included. ⌐ **Location:** Rural, simple, noisy.
**Surface:** asphalted. ☐ 01/01-31/12.
**Distance:** ⌐on the spot ⌐on the spot ⊗on the spot.

### Dalby 6E2
**Camp Hverringe**, Blæsenborgvej 200. **GPS:** n55,50937 e10,71233.
⌐DKK 75. ☐ 18/03-23/10.
**Distance:** ⌐on the spot.
**Remarks:** Quick-Stop: >20h - <10h.

### Dannemare 6E3
**Hummingen**, Pumpehusvej 1. **GPS:** n54,71317 e11,24606.
⌐DKK 140 ⌐⌐Ⓒ⌐against payment. ☐ 18/03-23/10.
**Remarks:** Quick-Stop: >20h - <10h.

### Dronningsmølle 6F1
**Dronningmølle**, Strandkrogen 2b. **GPS:** n56,08393 e12,39112.
⌐DKK 160 ⌐⌐Ⓒ⌐. ☐ 15/03-14/09.
**Remarks:** Quick-Stop: >20h - <10h.

### Fakse 6F2
**Feddet**, Feddet 12. **GPS:** n55,17366 e12,10118.
⌐DKK 75, dog DKK 30 ⌐⌐Ⓒagainst payment ⌐included.
☐ 01/01-31/12.
**Remarks:** Quick-Stop: >20h - <10h.

**Tourist information Fakse:**
ℹ️ Faksekystens Turistinformation, Hovedgaden 29, Fakse Ladeplads,
www.faksekysten.dk. The municipality Fakse has 30 kilometres coast-
line, marked cycle and hiking routes.
✱ Fortællerfestival, Fakse Lime Beach. Festival for story tellers.
☐ last weekend Jun.
✱ Rivierafest, Fakse Ladeplads. Festival with free herring-table on
Sunday. ☐ Thu-Su of week 29.

## Farum  6F1
Hovedgade 32. **GPS**: n55,81222 e12,36917.

3 free. **Location**: Urban, simple, noisy. **Surface**: asphalted.
01/01-31/12.
**Distance**: 500m 100m on the spot 500m on the spot on the spot.

## Farum  6F1
Stavnsholt Renseanlæg. **GPS**: n55,81278 e12,40556.
Chfree. Mo-Thu 7-15.30h, Fr 7-11.30h.

## Frederikssund  6F1
**Marbæk Lystbådehavn**, Strandlystvej 26 D.
**GPS**: n55,82778 e12,06389.

6 DKK 125 Ch WCincluded against payment
DKK 20/20. **Location**: Rural, comfortable, quiet. **Surface**: gravel.
01/01-31/12.
**Distance**: 1,5km on the spot on the spot 1,5km 1,5km on the spot on the spot.

## Frederikssund  6F1
**B&B Bybjerggaard**, Sundbylillevej 42. **GPS**: n55,83579 e12,11622.
DKK 50/pp.
**Distance**: on the spot.

## Frederiksværk  6F1
**Frederiksværk Havn**, Havnelinien 23. **GPS**: n55,96673 e11,99986.

4 DKK 140 included. 01/01-31/12.
**Distance**: 2km on the spot on the spot.

## Føllenslev  6E1
**Vesterlyng**, Ravnholtvej 3. **GPS**: n55,74278 e11,30883.
DKK 130 Ch against payment. 31/03-22/10.
**Remarks**: Quick-Stop: >20h - <10h.

## Gedser  6F3
**Gedser Lystbådehavn**, Vestre Strand 1. **GPS**: n54,58194 e11,92361.
10 DKK 120 Ch DKK 10 WC DKK 10 DKK 38/38 included
**Location**: Rural, isolated, quiet. **Surface**: gravel.
01/01-31/12.
**Distance**: 100m 50m 50m 200m 800m on the spot on the spot on the spot.
**Remarks**: Check in at harbourmaster.

## Gilleleje  6F1
**Smidstrup Farmen**, Jydebjergvej 32. **GPS**: n56,10346 e12,22722.
DKK 100 . **Location**: Rural. **Surface**: grassy/gravel.
01/01-31/12.
**Distance**: 1,5km 2km 1,5km.
**Remarks**: Max. 3 days.

## Greve  6F1
**Copenhagen Motorhome Camp**, Hundige Strandvej 72.
**GPS**: n55,59399 e12,34247.

42 DKK 205, 15/06-31/08 DKK 215 Ch DKK 52 included.
**Surface**: grassy. 01/04-31/10.
**Distance**: Copenhagen 19km 1km 3km 800m.

## Gørlev  6E2
**Reersø Havn**, Strandvejen 101, Reersø. **GPS**: n55,51750 e11,11833.

5 DKK 100 WC included.
**Location**: Rural, simple, quiet. **Surface**: gravel. 01/04-01/11.
**Distance**: 300m on the spot on the spot on the spot on the spot on the spot.
**Remarks**: Money in envelope in mail box.

## Helsinge  6F1
**Anisse Vingård**, Præstevej 89, Annisse. **GPS**: n55,98114 e12,17474.
DKK 75 . 01/01-31/12.

## Hillerød  6F1
**JOHS**, Hestehavevej 24. **GPS**: n55,90221 e12,31155.

DKK 150 . **Surface**: grassy/gravel.
**Distance**: on the spot on the spot.

## Hundested  6E1
**Hundested Havn**, Havnegade 8. **GPS**: n55,96557 e11,84845.

5 DKK 150 Ch WC against payment.
**Location**: Urban, comfortable. **Surface**: metalled.
01/01-31/12.
**Distance**: 500m on the spot on the spot on the spot 200m 200m on the spot.

## Hundested  6E1
**Lynæs Havn**, Lynæs Havnevej 15 B, Lynæs.
**GPS**: n55,94407 e11,86507.

10 DKK 160 Ch WC included free.
**Location**: Rural, simple, quiet. **Surface**: metalled.

## 01/01-31/12.
**Distance**: 2km 500m on the spot 2km on the spot on the spot.

## Kalundborg  6E1
**Debbies Bed & Breakfast**, Hovvejen 114. **GPS**: n55,67564 e11,14552.
5 DKK 150 . **Location**: Rural, simple, isolated, noisy.
**Surface**: grassy. 01/01-31/12.
**Distance**: 4km on the spot.
**Remarks**: Breakfast-service.

## Kalvehave  6F2
**Lystbådehavn**, Kalvehave Havnevej 26. **GPS**: n54,99584 e12,16641.
2 DKK 140 WC included. **Location**: Rural, simple,
central. **Surface**: grassy/gravel. 01/01-31/12.
**Distance**: 150m on the spot on the spot 100m 150m.

## Karise  6F2
**Lægårdens**, Vemmetoftevej 2A. **GPS**: n55,27260 e12,22306.
DKK 105 Ch . 01/01-31/12.
**Remarks**: Quick-Stop: >20h - <10h.

## Karrebæksminde  6E2
**Naestved Sjelklub**, Ved Broen 29. **GPS**: n55,17706 e11,65018.

6 18 Ch WC DKK 50/50 included.
**Location**: Rural, simple, quiet. **Surface**: gravel.
15/04-15/09.
**Distance**: on the spot on the spot on the spot on the spot on the spot on the spot.

## Kirke Hyllinge  6F1
**Gershøj Havn**, Gershøj Havnevej 5, Gershøj.
**GPS**: n55,71667 e11,98000.

10 € 8 Ch against payment WC included.
**Location**: Rural, simple, quiet. **Surface**: gravel. 01/01-31/12.
**Distance**: 1,5km on the spot on the spot.

## Korsør  6E2
**Pit-Stop Storebælt**, Halskov Havn 2. **GPS**: n55,34769 e11,11463.

40 DKK 75 Chincluded.
**Location**: Rural, simple. **Surface**: grassy. 01/01-31/12.
**Distance**: 1km 500m on the spot on the spot 500m on the spot on the spot on the spot.
**Remarks**: Along busy through road, use camp-site facilities allowed, closed at night.

## Korsør  6E2
**Lystbådehavn**, Sylowsvej 10. **GPS**: n55,32664 e11,13190.

DK

20 ⚡DKK 160 🚿 included WC ▯🔌 📶 against payment. 🛏🚐 🧺
**Location:** Rural, simple, quiet. **Surface:** gravel.
🅿 01/01-31/12.
**Distance:** 🚲300m ⛵4km 🛒on the spot 🏪on the spot ⊗on the spot 🍴300m 🚶on the spot.

### ▣ Korsør ⚓🎣🌊 6E2
**Lystskov**, Korsør Lystskov 2. **GPS:** n55,32219 e11,18505.
⚡DKK 90. 🅿 19/03-25/09.
**Remarks:** Quick-Stop: >20h - <10h.
**Tourist information Korsør:**
🎯 Korsør Fæstning, Korsør Coastal Battery, The Fortress, Søbatteriet 7. Fortress. 🅿 01/05-30/09 Wed-Su 11-16h.

### 🍇Ⓢ Lynge 🌊 6F1
**Irene & Aage Andersen**, Stengårdsvej 12.
**GPS:** n55,81972 e12,27376.⬆.

3 ⚡free 🚿DKK 10/50liter. **Location:** Rural, simple, quiet.
**Surface:** grassy. 🅿 01/01-31/12.
**Distance:** 🚲1km 🛒on the spot 🏪on the spot.

### 🅿️Ⓢ Munke Bjergby 🍽 6E2
Dojringevej 40a. **GPS:** n55,49637 e11,55065.⬆.

10 ⚡free 🚿DKK 10/20liter 🪑DKK 10 🚿DKK 30.
**Location:** Rural, comfortable, quiet. **Surface:** grassy.
🅿 01/01-31/12.
**Distance:** 🚲8km 🛒on the spot 🚶on the spot.
**Remarks:** Max. 48h.

### 🅿️Ⓢ Nykøbing 🌿⚓🎣🌊 6E1
**Lystbådehavn**, Snekkevej 9. **GPS:** n55,91610 e11,67287.⬆.

10 ⚡DKK 110 🚿🪑Ch 🚿 WC ▯included 🔌DKK 25/20.🛏🚐 🧺
**Location:** Urban, simple, quiet. **Surface:** grassy.
🅿 01/01-31/12.
**Distance:** 🚲500m ⛵100m 🛒100m ⊗on the spot 🐟on the spot.

### ⚓Ⓢ Nykøbing F. 6F3
**Toreby Sejlklub**, Dæmningen 2, Sundby Lolland.
**GPS:** n54,76051 e11,86041.⬆.
5 ⚡DKK 120 🚿 WC ▯included. **Location:** Urban, simple, quiet.
**Surface:** gravel. 🅿 01/05-30/09.
**Distance:** ⊗on the spot 🍴on the spot 🚶on the spot.
**Remarks:** Money in envelope in mail box.

### ▣Ⓢ Nykøbing F. 6F3
**Falster City Camping**, Østre Alle 112. **GPS:** n54,76243 e11,89479.
⚡DKK 120 🚿🪑Ch 🚿against payment. 🅿 01/04-01/12.
**Remarks:** Quick-Stop: >20h - <10h.

### 🅿️Ⓢ Næstved ⚓🍴 6E2
**Rådmandshaven. GPS:** n55,23166 e11,75344.⬆🔚.

14 ⚡free. **Location:** Urban, simple, noisy. **Surface:** concrete.
🅿 01/01-31/12.
**Distance:** 🚲500m ⊗500m 🍴500m 🛒on the spot.
**Remarks:** Parking in front of town hall, special part for motor homes.

### ⚓Ⓢ Præstø ⚓🎣🌊 6F2
**Præstø Havn**, Fjordstien 1. **GPS:** n55,12444 e12,04333.⬆.

5 ⚡DKK 115 🚿🪑Ch 🚿 WC ▯🔌DKK 25/25 📶included. 🛏🚐 🧺
**Location:** Urban, simple, quiet. **Surface:** asphalted.
🅿 01/01-31/12.
**Distance:** 🚲500m ⛵7km 🛒on the spot 🏪on the spot ⊗on the spot 🍴on the spot.

### 🅿️Ⓢ Ringsted 🌿⚓ 6E2
**Autocamper P-plads Ringsted**, Delingen.
**GPS:** n55,45029 e11,80077.⬆.

6 ⚡free 🚿free. **Location:** Urban, simple. **Surface:** grasstiles.
🅿 01/01-31/12.
**Distance:** 🚲1km ⊗900m 🍴900m.
**Remarks:** Max. 48h.

### 🅿️Ⓢ Ringsted 🌿⚓ 6E2
**Mogens Madsen**, Vibevej 34. **GPS:** n55,44222 e11,80667.⬆.

3 ⚡free 🚿against payment. **Location:** Urban, simple, noisy.
**Surface:** metalled. 🅿 01/01-31/12.
**Distance:** ⛵4 km 🍴800m.

### ▣ Ringsted 🌿⚓ 6E2
**Skovly Camping**, Nebs Møllevej 65. **GPS:** n55,49615 e11,85768.
⚡DKK 150. 🅿 01/01-31/12.
**Remarks:** Quick-Stop: >20h - <10h.

### ▣Ⓢ Roskilde 6F1
**Camp Roskilde**, Baunehøjvej 7. **GPS:** n55,67374 e12,08209.
⚡DKK 150 🚿DKK 45. 🅿 18/03-02/10.
**Remarks:** Quick-Stop: >20h - <10h.

### ⚓Ⓢ Rødvig ⚓🌊 6F2
**Rødvig Fiskerihavn**, Fiskerihavnen 8. **GPS:** n55,25417 e12,37500.⬆.

4 ⚡€ 12 🚿🪑🚿 WCincluded 🔌DKK 5/4minutes. 🛏🚐 🧺
**Location:** Rural, simple, quiet. **Surface:** metalled.
🅿 01/01-31/12.
**Distance:** 🚲200m 🛒on the spot 🏪on the spot ⊗on the spot.
**Remarks:** Check in at harbourmaster.

### ▣ Rødvig ⚓🌊 6F2
**Rødvig Camping**, Højstrupvej 2 A. **GPS:** n55,25059 e12,34970.

5 ⚡DKK 100. 🚲🎣🚿🚶.
**Location:** Rural, simple, quiet. **Surface:** grassy. 🅿 01/04-28/09.
**Distance:** 🚲2km 🛒on the spot.
**Remarks:** Quick-Stop: >20h - <10h.

### ⚓Ⓢ Sakskøbing 6E3
**Sakskøbing Lystbådehavn**, Maltrup Vænge 38.
**GPS:** n54,81078 e11,61957.
5 ⚡DKK 125 🚿🚿 WCagainst payment 📶included.
**Location:** Rural, simple, quiet. **Surface:** gravel.
🅿 01/05-15/10.
**Distance:** 🚲900m ⊗500m.

### ⚓Ⓢ Sjællands Odde ⚓🎣🌊 6E1
**Sjællands Odde Havn**, Østre Havnevej 42.
**GPS:** n55,97139 e11,36956.⬆.

2 ⚡€ 16 🚿🚿 WCincluded 🔌DKK 5/5minutes. 🛏🚐 🧺
**Location:** Rural, simple, quiet. **Surface:** gravel.
🅿 01/01-31/12.
**Distance:** 🛒on the spot 🏪on the spot ⊗300m 🚶on the spot.

### ⚓Ⓢ Skælskør 🌿⚓🌊 6E2
**Skælskør Havn**, Havnevej 20. **GPS:** n55,25223 e11,28992.⬆.

15 ⚡€ 14 🚿🪑Ch 🚿(15x)DKK 25/kWh WCincluded 🔌DKK 5/5minutes 🔌DKK 25/25 📶free. 🛏🚐 🧺 **Location:** Urban, simple, central. **Surface:** metalled. 🅿 01/01-31/12.
**Distance:** 🚲on the spot 🛒on the spot 🏪on the spot ⊗on the spot 🐟on the spot 🚶on the spot.
**Remarks:** Free bicycles available.

### ▣Ⓢ Skælskør 🌿⚓🌊 6E2
**Skælskør Nor**, Kildehusvej 1. **GPS:** n55,25818 e11,28395.
⚡DKK 150 🚿🪑Ch 🚿. 🅿 01/01-31/12.
**Remarks:** Quick-Stop: >20h - <10h.

DK

### Store Fuglede — 6E2

**Bjerge Sydstrand Camping**, Osvejen 30. **GPS**: n55,56298 e11,16489. DKK 150. 01/01-31/12.
**Distance:** on the spot.
**Remarks:** Quick-Stop: >20h - <10h.

### Taastrup — 6F1

**Park Hotel**, Brorsonsvej 3. **GPS**: n55,65389 e12,30000.

10 DKK 200 (3x)DKK 25/day WC included on demand. **Location:** Urban, simple, quiet. **Surface:** metalled. 01/01-31/12.
**Distance:** 300m 1,5km on the spot 300m on the spot on the spot.
**Remarks:** Breakfast buffet DKK 75, code wifi in restaurant.

### Tårs (Harpelunde) — 6E2

**Tårs Havn Lolland**, Tårsvej 215, Harpelund Lolland. **GPS**: n54,87811 e11,02381.
2 DKK 125 WC included. **Location:** Rural, simple, isolated, quiet. **Surface:** asphalted. 01/01-31/12.
**Distance:** 5km.
**Remarks:** Harbour Tårs.

### Torrig — 6E2

**Kragenæs Havn**, Kragenæsvej 84. **GPS**: n54,91565 e11,35730. DKK 135 Ch against payment. 18/03-23/10.
**Remarks:** Quick-Stop: >20h - <10h.

### Ugerløse — 6E1

**Minnislyst**, Tølløsevej 294. **GPS**: n55,59730 e11,68250.

€ 10 Ch included.
**Location:** Rural. 01/01-31/12.
**Distance:** 2,2km 2,2km 2km.

### Vejby — 6F1

Åmosevejen 18. **GPS**: n56,06386 e12,17215. DKK 100. **Location:** Rural. 01/01-31/12.
**Distance:** 2km.
**Remarks:** Max. 3 days.

### Vig — 6E1

**Kongsøre Camping**, Egebjergvej 342. **GPS**: n55,82390 e11,66743. DKK 120. 01/04-30/09.
**Distance:** on the spot.
**Remarks:** Quick-Stop: >20h - <10h.

### Væggerløse — 6F3

**Marielyst Feriepark & Camping**, Godthåbs Allé 7, Marielyst. **GPS**: n54,67357 e11,94427. DKK 100.
**Remarks:** Quick-Stop: >20h - <10h.

### Værløse — 6F1

**Furesø Museer**, Skovgårds alle 37. **GPS**: n55,78528 e12,37722.

4 free. **Location:** Urban, simple, noisy. **Surface:** metalled. 01/01-31/12.
**Distance:** on the spot 250m 250m on the spot on the

spot.

### Værløse — 6F1

**Bryggeri Skovlyst**, Skovlystvej 2. **GPS**: n55,76317 e12,38365.

3 free WC. **Location:** Rural, simple, quiet. **Surface:** gravel. 01/01-31/12.
**Distance:** 5km on the spot on the spot on the spot.

DK

# 🏳️ Spain

Capital: Madrid
Government: Constitutional monarchy
Official Language: Spanish
Population: 48,958,000 (2017)
Area: 505,992 km²

## General information
Dialling code: 0034
General emergency: 112
Currency: Euro

## Regulations for overnight stays
Wild camping is allowed having gained permission from the municipality, police or property owner. Along the Mediterranean coast wild camping is almost always forbidden. Parking places (P) mentioned here can be considered as tolerated places to stay overnight.

## Additional public holidays 2019
January 6 Epiphany
April 19 Good Friday
May 1 Labor Day
June 20 Corpus Christi
August 15 Assumption of the Virgin Mary
October 12 National Holiday
November 1 All Saints' Day
December 6 Constitution Day
December 8 Immaculate Conception

## Time Zone
Winter (Standard Time) GMT+1
Summer (DST) GMT+2

ES

Green Spain
pages: 338-349

Navarre and Rioja
pages: 349-350

Zaragoza

Barcelona

Madrid

Mediterranean Sea
Communities
pages: 350-361

Spanish interior
pages: 361-366

Valencia

A Coruña

Sevilla

Andalusia
pages: 366-371

Murcia

prime meridian

# Green Spain

**🅿️S** A Coruña 🌀⚓🍴🧺 **29C1**
Puerto de San Pedro de Visma, Zona de O Portiño.
**GPS**: n43,37167 w8,44472.⬆️.

12 🅿️free 🚰🚽Ch free. **Surface**: metalled. ⏹️ 01/01-31/12.
**Distance**: 🚶3km ⚓on the spot ⊗50m 🛒1km Carrefour 🚌1km.
**Remarks**: Max. 48h.

**🅿️** A Coruña 🌀⚓🍴🧺 **29C1**
Tore de Hercules. **GPS**: n43,38378 w8,40228.⬆️.

20 🅿️free WC. **Location**: Rural, simple, quiet. **Surface**: asphalted.
⏹️ 01/01-31/12.
**Distance**: 🚶1km ⊗50m 🛒50m.
**Remarks**: Near sports fields, max. 48h.

**⚓S** A Coruña 🌀⚓🍴🧺 **29C1**
**Parking Marina Coruña**, Paseo Marítimo Francisco Vázquez s/n.
**GPS**: n43,36976 w8,38786.⬆️.

15 🅿️€ 1,50/h, € 22/24h 🚰🚽Ch ✎ WC 🗑️📶included. 🚐
**Location**: Urban, simple, quiet. **Surface**: metalled.
⏹️ 01/01-31/12.
**Distance**: 🚶centre 800m ⊗on the spot.
**Remarks**: Parking marina.

**🅿️S** A Coruña 🌀⚓🍴🧺 **29C1**
**Yakart**, Carretera de mesoiro, 63. **GPS**: n43,33228 w8,425.⬆️.

15 🅿️€ 10/24h 🚰🚽Ch ✎included. 🚐 **Location**: Urban, simple, noisy. **Surface**: metalled. ⏹️ 01/01-31/12.
**Distance**: 🚶centre 4,5km ⊗500m 🛒70m.
**Remarks**: At motorhome dealer, monitored parking.

**🅿️S** A Guarda 🧺 **29B2**
**GPS**: n41,89892 w8,87825.⬆️.

5 🅿️free.
**Location**: Urban, simple, central. **Surface**: asphalted.
**Distance**: 🚶1km ⊗300m 🛒500m.
**Remarks**: Parking harbour.

**🅿️S** A Laracha 🌀 **29C1**
**Area de O Regado**, AC-552. **GPS**: n43,24972 w8,61694.⬆️.
3 🅿️free 🚰🚽Ch free. **Surface**: asphalted.

**🅿️S** A Laracha 🌀 **29C1**
Av. Laracha, 39. **GPS**: n43,31616 w8,59483.⬆️➡️.

10 🅿️free 🚰🚽Ch free. **Location**: Rural, simple, quiet.
**Surface**: asphalted. ⏹️ 01/01-31/12.
**Distance**: 🚶A Laracha 11km ⊗1,3km.
**Remarks**: Max. 48h.

**🅿️S** A Pontenova **29D1**
Camiño do Antigo Ferrocarril. **GPS**: n43,35578 w7,18939.⬆️.
6 🅿️free 🚰🚽Ch free. **Surface**: asphalted. ⏹️ 01/01-31/12.
**Distance**: 🚶800m ⊗800m 🚲on the spot 🚶on the spot.

**Remarks:** Next to swimming pool, max. 48h.

⌖🅂 **A Pontenova** 29D1
Rua de la Estación. **GPS:** n43,34739 w7,19171. ⬆️➡️.

8 🌲free ⛽🚰Chfree. **Surface:** asphalted. 🕐 01/01-31/12.
**Distance:** ⊗200m ⚡100m.
**Remarks:** Max. 48h.

⌖🅂 **A Rúa** 29D2
**Área Recreativa O Aguillón. GPS:** n42,38800 w7,11459. ⬆️.
10 🌲free ⛽🚰Chfree. **Location:** Rural. **Surface:** asphalted/grassy.
🕐 01/01-31/12.
**Distance:** ⚾500m ⛱️on the spot ⊗500m ⚡500m 🚴on the spot
🚶on the spot.
**Remarks:** Next to football ground, max. 72h.

⌖🅂 **Agurain** 29H2
Bizkaia Kalea. **GPS:** n42,85324 w2,38495. ⬆️➡️.

7 🌲free ⛽🚰Chfree. **Location:** Rural, simple, quiet.
**Surface:** asphalted. 🕐 01/01-31/12.
**Distance:** ⚾500m ⊗500m ⚡350m.
**Remarks:** Max. 48h.

⌖🅂 **Amurrio** 29H2
Araba Kalea. **GPS:** n43,05528 w2,99806. ⬆️➡️.

10 🌲free ⛽🚰Chfree. **Location:** Urban, simple, noisy.
**Surface:** gravel. 🕐 01/01-31/12.
**Distance:** ⚾500m ⊗500m ⚡100m.
**Remarks:** Max. 48h, no camping activities.

⌖ **Añana** 29G2
Mercado Kalea. **GPS:** n42,80344 w2,98437. ⬆️.

3 🌲free. **Location:** Rural, simple, isolated. **Surface:** metalled.
🕐 01/01-31/12.
**Distance:** ⊗300M.

⌖🅂 **Arcade** 29C2
Rúa do Peirao. **GPS:** n42,33946 w8,61329. ⬆️.
7 🌲free ⛽🚰Chfree. **Location:** Rural, simple, quiet.
**Surface:** metalled. 🕐 01/01-31/12.
**Distance:** ⚾300m ⛱️on the spot ⛵on the spot ⊗100m ⚡200m.
**Remarks:** Max. 7 days.

⌖ **Arrigorriaga** 29H2
Carretera Buia Etorbidea. **GPS:** n43,23772 w2,91938. ⬆️.

🌲. **Location:** Urban, simple. **Surface:** asphalted.
🕐 01/01-31/12.

⌖🅂 **Artziniega** ⛰️ 29G2
**GPS:** n43,11854 w3,13136. ⬆️➡️.

6 🌲free ⛽🚰Chfree ⚡(6x)€ 3/12h. **Location:** Rural, simple, quiet.
**Surface:** grasstiles. 🕐 01/01-31/12.
**Distance:** ⚾on the spot ⊗on the spot ⚡300m.
**Remarks:** Next to sports fields, max. 72h.

⌖🅂 **As Neves** 29C2
Camino del Emenjeric. **GPS:** n42,08726 w8,41374. ⬆️➡️.

5 🌲free ⛽🚰Chfree. **Location:** Rural, simple, quiet.
**Surface:** asphalted/metalled. 🕐 01/01-31/12.
**Distance:** ⚾on the spot ⊗200m ⚡200m.
**Remarks:** Max. 48h, shady.

⌖🅂 **As Nogais** 29D2
Calle Rosalía de Castro. **GPS:** n42,81066 w7,1069. ⬆️➡️.
6 🌲free ⛽🚰Chfree. **Location:** Urban. **Surface:** asphalted.
🕐 01/01-31/12.
**Distance:** ⚾500m ⊗500m ⚡500m 🚶on the spot.
**Remarks:** Max. 48h, swimming pool and picnic area available.

⌖🅂 **As Pontes de García Rodríguez** 29D1
Rúa Juan Antonio Suanzes. **GPS:** n43,45103 w7,85445. ⬆️.
5 🌲free ⛽🚰free. **Location:** Simple, quiet. 🕐 01/01-31/12.
**Distance:** ⚾200m ⊗200m 🚴on the spot 🚶on the spot.
**Remarks:** Well situated for visiting Parque Natural de las Fragas do
Eume, max. 48h.

⌖ **Avilés** 29E1
Avenida de Gijón. **GPS:** n43,55159 w5,91282. ⬆️.

5 🌲free ⛽🚰Chfree. **Location:** Urban, simple, quiet.
**Surface:** asphalted. 🕐 01/01-31/12.
**Distance:** ⚾1km ⊗500m ⚡800m.
**Remarks:** Max. 72h.

⌖🅂 **Bakio** 🏄 29H2
**Parking**, BI 3101. **GPS:** n43,42783 w2,80442. ⬆️.

20 🌲free, weekend and 01/08-30/09 € 6 ⛽WCfree.
**Location:** Urban, simple. **Surface:** grasstiles.
🕐 01/01-31/12.
**Distance:** ⚾100m ⛱️200m ⚡100m 🚴on the spot.
**Remarks:** Behind tourist info.

⌖🅂 **Barrio Cosío** ⛰️🌳 29F2
**Área de Autocaravanas del Valle del Nansa**, Ctra. General CA-281.
**GPS:** n43,23349 w4,39892. ⬆️.

6 🌲first day free, then € 5 ⛽€ 3 🚰Ch 📶. **Location:** Rural, simple,
quiet. **Surface:** metalled. 🕐 01/01-31/12.
**Distance:** ⚾on the spot ⊗on the spot ⚡100m.
**Remarks:** Max. 24h.

⌖🅂 **Bárzana** ⛰️ 29E1
**Area de Bárzana-Quirós**, El Felguere. **GPS:** n43,15611 w5,97306.

15 🌲free ⛽🚰Chfree. **Location:** Rural, simple, quiet.
**Surface:** asphalted. 🕐 01/01-31/12 ⦿ holidays.
**Distance:** ⚾100m ⊗100m ⚡100m.
**Remarks:** Max. 48h.

⌖🅂 **Beasain** 29H2
Igartza Oleta Kalea. **GPS:** n43,04682 w2,21228. ⬆️➡️.

12 🌲free ⛽€ 3 🚰Ch ⚡(1x)€ 3. **Location:** Urban, simple, quiet.
**Surface:** asphalted. 🕐 01/01-31/12.
**Distance:** ⚾city centre 1km ⊗500m.
**Remarks:** Coins at bar and sports centre.

⌖🅂 **Becerreá** 29D2
Parque Empresarial. **GPS:** n42,85283 w7,15179. ⬆️.
16 🌲free ⛽🚰Chfree. **Surface:** asphalted. 🕐 01/01-31/12.
**Distance:** ⚾1,5km ⊗400m.
**Remarks:** Industrial area, max. 48h.

⌖🅂 **Beche** 29C1
Lugar Beche, 6. **GPS:** n43,18318 w8,3067. ⬆️.
5 🌲free ⛽🚰Chfree. **Location:** Rural, isolated, quiet.
**Surface:** gravel. 🕐 01/01-31/12.
**Distance:** ⛱️on the spot ⛵on the spot 🚴on the spot 🚶on the spot.
**Remarks:** Along river, max. 48h, narrow road.

⌖🅂 **Behobia** 🧺 27A2
N10, Calle de Aria Juncal. **GPS:** n43,34310 w1,7598. ⬆️.

**ES**

6 ⌗€ 3/2h < 19.30, overnight stay free. **Location:** Urban, simple, noisy. **Surface:** asphalted. ⬛ 01/01-31/12. **Distance:** on the spot ⚙500m ⊗200m ⚱500m ⊞on the spot.

### ⊞S Bergara 🌿 29H2
Telleria Kalea, Labegaraieta. **GPS:** n43,10481 w2,42265. ⬆.

20 ⌗free ⊯⊟Chfree. **Location:** Urban, simple, quiet. **Surface:** asphalted. ⬛ 01/01-31/12. **Distance:** 2km ⊗on the spot ⊞200m ⊞on the spot. **Remarks:** At sports centre, max. 48h.

### ⊞ Bergondo 29C1
Dp-0804, Aldea Mariñán. **GPS:** n43,32413 w8,20903. ⬆.

10 ⌗. **Location:** Rural, simple, quiet. **Surface:** grassy. ⬛ 01/01-31/12. **Distance:** 2,5km ⚱50m ⊗200m. **Remarks:** Max. 48h.

### ⊞S Bermeo 🌿 29H2
**Área de la Pérgola**, Matxitxako Bidea, 10. **GPS:** n43,42306 w2,72556. ⬆➡.

10 ⌗free ⊯⊟Chfree. **Location:** Urban, simple. **Surface:** asphalted. ⬛ 01/01-31/12. **Distance:** 500m ⊗500m ⚱500m ⊞300m. **Remarks:** Nearby football ground, max. 48h.

### ⊞S Bertamirans 🛒 29C1
Rúa das Pesqueiras, 6. **GPS:** n42,86009 w8,64838. ⬆.

12 ⌗free ⊯⊟Chfree. **Surface:** asphalted. ⬛ 01/01-31/12. **Distance:** Santiago 8km ⊗100m ⚱50m Carrefour ⊞dir. Santiago every 30 min. **Remarks:** At supermarket, max. 48h.

### ⊞S Bilbao 🌿🏖 29H2
**Kobetamendi**, Monte Kobeta, 31. **GPS:** n43,25961 w2,96355. ⬆➡.

72 ⌗€ 15/day ⊯⊟Ch ⚙included WC. **Location:** Urban, comfortable, quiet. **Surface:** grasstiles. ⬛ 01/01-31/12. **Distance:** centre 4,5km ⚙2,8km ⊞Bilbao-bus 58. **Remarks:** 16/10-14/05 free parking, asphalt, max. 72h, service passerby €6.

**Tourist information Bilbao:**
ℹ Bilbao. Capital of the Basque Country and previously centre of the iron industry.
✝ Basilica de Begoña, Virgen de Begoña, 38, Bilbao-Vizcaya. Basilica.

### ⊞S Boiro 👐🏖 29C2
**Playa Mañons**, S/n 15930 Chancelas–Abanqueiro. **GPS:** n42,63138 w8,85311. ⬆➡.

8 ⌗free ⊯⊟free. **Location:** Rural, simple, isolated, quiet. **Surface:** metalled. ⬛ 01/01-31/12. **Distance:** ⚱50m.

### ⊞S Boiro 👐🏖 29C2
**Praia Xardín de Barraña**, La, Av. de Compostela, 54. **GPS:** n42,64183 w8,89481. ⬆➡.

10 ⌗€ 6,07 ⊯⊟Chincluded. 🛏 **Surface:** asphalted. ⬛ 01/01-31/12. **Distance:** 500m ⚱20m ⊗200m Bistro Prima ⚱400m. **Remarks:** Max. 48h.

### ⊞S Boñar 29F2
**El Soto Park**, Polígono Parque Soto. **GPS:** n42,87255 w5,32592. ⬆.
13 ⌗ ⊯⊟Chfree. **Location:** Rural, simple, quiet. **Surface:** grassy/metalled. ⬛ 01/01-31/12. **Distance:** 800m ⊗on the spot ⚱600m. **Remarks:** Along river, at swimming pool, shady.

### ⊞ Bueu 29C2
PO315 dir Cabo Udra. **GPS:** n42,33460 w8,8248.
10 ⌗free. **Location:** Isolated, quiet. **Surface:** sand. ⬛ 01/01-31/12. **Distance:** ⚱200m. **Remarks:** Max. 48h.

### ⊞ Bueu 29C2
**Puerto**, Avda. de Montero Rios. **GPS:** n42,32732 w8,7838.

⌗. ⬛ 01/01-31/12.

### ⊞S Burela 29D1
**Area de Burela**, Rúa Rafael Vior, 65, parking Hospital de Burela. **GPS:** n43,65216 w7,35891. ⬆.

5 ⌗free ⊯⊟Chfree. **Location:** Urban, simple, quiet. **Surface:** asphalted. ⬛ 01/01-31/12. **Distance:** 1km ⊗300m ⚱200m. **Remarks:** Max. 48h.

### 🏠S Cabárceno 👐🏖 29G2
**Área Lago del Acebo**, Calle Coraliza, N634> dir Parque de la naturaleze de Cabárceno. **GPS:** n43,35802 w3,81959. ⬆.

30 ⌗free ⊯⊟Chfree. **Location:** Rural, isolated, quiet. **Surface:** asphalted. ⬛ 01/01-31/12. **Distance:** 100m ⚱50m ⊞50m ⊗200m ⚱200m. **Remarks:** Max. 48h.

### ⊞S Camariñas 🏖 29B1
Praia do Ariño, Cobadiña. **GPS:** n43,13090 w9,1583. ⬆➡.

5 ⌗free ⊯⊟Chfree. **Location:** Rural, simple, isolated, quiet. **Surface:** asphalted. ⬛ 01/01-31/12. **Distance:** 4km ⚱on the spot ⊗1,5km. **Remarks:** Max. 48h, max. 8M.

### ⚓ Camariñas 🏖 29B1
**Puerto Club Nautico**, Rúa Castelo. **GPS:** n43,12694 w9,18333. ⬆.

5 ⌗free. **Location:** Urban, simple, quiet. **Surface:** asphalted. ⬛ 01/01-31/12. **Distance:** city centre 1km ⊗100m.

### ⊞S Candás 29E1
**Area de La Fuente de los Angeles**, Calle Estacion. **GPS:** n43,58495 w5,77197. ⬆.

ES

6 🅿️free 🚰🗑️ChWCfree. **Location:** Urban, simple.
**Surface:** asphalted. 🅿️ 01/01-31/12.
**Distance:** 🛒500m 🏖️1km ⊗500m ⚓500m.
**Remarks:** Along railwayline.

### 🏕️S Cangas de Morrazo 29C2

**Camping Car Area Playa Arneles**, Ctra Viso- Vilanova s/n.
**GPS:** n42,27618 w8,83399.⬆️.

35 🅿️€ 12 🚰€ 3/time 🗑️Ch 🚿€ 3/day WC 🚽⊟€ 3/time 📶€ 1/day.
**Location:** Rural, luxurious, isolated, quiet. **Surface:** grassy.
🅿️ 01/04-01/11.
**Distance:** 🛒2km 🏖️350m ⊗300m ⚓300m on the spot
🏊 on the spot.
**Remarks:** Max. 9m.

### 🏕️S Cangas de Morrazo 29C2

Ruá Campo Morelo, Gatañal. **GPS:** n42,25546 w8,79758.⬆️.
5 🅿️free 🚰🗑️Chfree. **Surface:** asphalted. 🅿️ 01/01-31/12.
**Distance:** 🛒2km.
**Remarks:** Behind gymnasium.

### 🏕️S Cangas de Onís 29F1

**Parking Lanzadera Picos de Europa**, Calle del Llreau.
**GPS:** n43,35211 w5,12536.⬆️.

4 🅿️free 🚰🗑️Chfree. **Location:** Urban. **Surface:** asphalted.
**Distance:** ⊗100m.
**Remarks:** Max. 48h.

### 🏕️S Cangas del Narcea 29E1

Av. de Oviedo. **GPS:** n43,18068 w6,54848.⬆️➡️.

2 🅿️free 🚰🗑️Chfree. **Location:** Urban, simple, central.
**Surface:** asphalted. 🅿️ 01/01-31/12.
**Distance:** 🛒500m ⊗400m.
**Remarks:** Max. 72h, no camping activities.

### 🏕️S Cariño 29D1

Rúa Concepción Arenal. **GPS:** n43,73359 w7,87429.⬆️➡️.

---

15 🅿️free 🚰🗑️Chfree. **Location:** Rural, simple, quiet.
**Surface:** asphalted. 🅿️ 01/01-31/12.
**Distance:** 🛒300m 🏖️150m ⊗300m ⚓100m.
**Remarks:** At sports centre.

### 🏕️S Carnota 29B1

Playa de Lombans. **GPS:** n42,84092 w9,09667.⬆️.
5 🅿️free 🚰🗑️Chfree.
**Location:** Isolated, quiet. 🅿️ 01/01-31/12.
**Distance:** 🏖️400m.
**Remarks:** At football ground.

### 🏕️S Carnota 29B1

**Area de Mar de Lira**, Calle Miñarzo s/n. **GPS:** n42,80306 w9,12944.

4 🅿️free. **Surface:** sand.
**Distance:** 🛒Carnota 5km 🏖️10m ⊗on the spot.
**Remarks:** Parking next to hatchery.

### 🏕️S Cartelle 29C2

**Camperpark O Mundil**, Antigua Carretera OU-659.
**GPS:** n42,21444 w8,03306.⬆️.

12 🅿️€ 10 🚰🗑️Ch 🚿WC 🚽⊟📶free. **Location:** Rural, isolated,
quiet. **Surface:** gravel/metalled. 🅿️ 01/01-31/12.
**Distance:** 🏖️1km zona fluvial Río Arnoia ⊗10m 🏊 on the spot.
**Remarks:** At swimming pool, max. 72h.

### 🏕️S Castro Caldelas 29D2

Travesía da Devesa. **GPS:** n42,37479 w7,41832.⬆️.
8 🅿️free 🚰🗑️Chfree. 🅿️ 01/01-31/12.
**Distance:** 🛒850m ⊗850m ⚓850m.
**Remarks:** Max. 48h.

### 🏕️S Castro de Rei 29D1

Castro de Ribeiras de Lea. **GPS:** n43,14663 w7,49211.⬆️.
5 🅿️free 🚰🗑️Ch 🚿📶free. **Location:** Luxurious, quiet.
**Surface:** metalled. 🅿️ 01/01-31/12.
**Distance:** ⊗250m ⚓1km.
**Remarks:** Next to sports fields, max. 48h.

### 🏕️S Cenlle 29C2

**Thermas de Barbantes**, Lugar Barbantes.
**GPS:** n42,33252 w8,01296.⬆️.
50 🅿️free 🚰🗑️Ch 🚿WC 🚽. **Location:** Rural, isolated, quiet.
**Surface:** asphalted. 🅿️ 01/01-31/12.
**Distance:** 🛒Cenlle 10km 🏖️on the spot ⛵on the spot ⊗on the spot.
**Remarks:** Max. 48h, free entrance swimming pool, picnic area.

### 🏕️S Chantada 29C2

**Champ de Sangoñedo**, Estrada do Seixo. **GPS:** n42,60598 w7,77989.⬆️.
5 🅿️free 🚰🗑️ChWCfree. **Location:** Rural, simple, quiet.
**Surface:** gravel. 🅿️ 01/01-31/12.
**Distance:** 🛒500m ⛵on the spot ⊗600m 🚲on the spot 🏊on the
spot.
**Remarks:** At footballstadium, max. 48h.

---

### 🏕️S Coaña 29D1

**Area de Ortiguera**, Barrio Nueva Rasa.
**GPS:** n43,56082 w6,73352.⬆️➡️.

2 🅿️free 🚰🗑️Chfree. **Location:** Rural, simple, quiet.
**Surface:** asphalted. 🅿️ 01/01-31/12.
**Distance:** 🏖️50m ⊗on the spot ⚓on the spot.
**Remarks:** Max. 48h.

### 🏕️ Coaña 29D1

Barrio Nueva Rasa. **GPS:** n43,56267 w6,73391.⬆️➡️.

3 🅿️free. **Location:** Rural, simple, quiet. **Surface:** asphalted.
🅿️ 01/01-31/12.
**Distance:** 🏖️250m ⛵100m ⊗200m ⚓200m.
**Remarks:** At lighthouse.

### 🏕️S Cóbreces 29G1

**Área auto caravanas Las Hazas**, Bº. Los Corrales.
**GPS:** n43,38899 w4,21106.⬆️➡️.

25 🅿️€ 9 🚰€ 4 🗑️Ch 🚿(25x)€ 3 WC 🚽⊟time,€ 4/4 📶included.
**Location:** Rural, comfortable, isolated. **Surface:** gravel.
🅿️ 01/01-31/12.
**Distance:** 🛒300m ⛵1km ⊗500m ⚓600m 🚗700m.
**Remarks:** Max. 72h, video surveillance.

### 🏕️S Colombres 29F1

**Area de Casa Junco**, N-634. **GPS:** n43,38056 w4,55472.

15 🅿️free 🚰🗑️Chfree. **Surface:** asphalted.
**Distance:** ⊗on the spot.

### 🏕️S Colunga 29F1

**Area de Los Llanos**, Avda de Asturias N-632.
**GPS:** n43,48449 w5,26048.⬆️.

23 🅿️€ 4,50 🚰€ 3 🗑️WC 🚽€ 1. **Location:** Rural, simple.

ES

**Surface:** asphalted. ▯ 01/01-31/12.
**Distance:** 🚶500m 🚲2km ⊗200m.
**Remarks:** Next to petrol station, max. 48h, thursday market.

| 🅿️S | **Cospeito** | 29D1 |

Camiño da Lagoa. **GPS:** n43,23984 w7,55579.⬆️.
5 🚐free 🚰🚽Ch💧free. **Location:** Rural, simple, quiet.
**Surface:** asphalted. ▯ 01/01-31/12.
**Distance:** 🚶300m ⊗300m 🛒300m.
**Remarks:** Bird watching, max. 48h.

| 🅿️S | **Cudillero** | 29E1 |

Puerto. **GPS:** n43,56568 w6,1517.⬆️.

5 🚐. **Location:** Simple. **Surface:** asphalted.
**Remarks:** Parking in harbour.

| 🅿️S | **Cudillero** | 29E1 |

Hotel Rest. Casa Fernando II, N-632. **GPS:** n43,56028 w6,17722.⬆️.

5 🚐free 🚰🚽Ch€ 3.
**Location:** Simple, quiet. **Surface:** asphalted. ▯ 01/01-31/12.
**Distance:** ⊗on the spot.

| 🅿️S | **Elorrio** | 29H2 |

Calle San Jose. **GPS:** n43,12830 w2,5485.⬆️➡️.

10 🚐free 🚰🚽Ch💧.
**Location:** Urban. **Surface:** asphalted. ▯ 01/01-31/12.
**Distance:** 🚶500m ⊗500m.
**Remarks:** Max. 72h.

| 🅿️S | **Eltziego** | 29H3 |

Área de Barrihuelo, Carr. de Laguardia.
**GPS:** n42,51496 w2,61546. ⬆️➡️.

14 🚐free 🚰🚽Chfree 💧€ 2/12h. **Location:** Urban, simple, quiet.
**Surface:** asphalted/metalled. ▯ 01/01-31/12.
**Distance:** 🚶300m ⊗100m.
**Remarks:** Coins at tourist info and restaurant, max. 72h.

| 🅿️S | **Ferrol** | 29C1 |

Ctra. de la Malata. **GPS:** n43,49333 w8,23972.⬆️.

---

15 🚐free 🚰🚽Chfree. **Location:** Simple, quiet. **Surface:** asphalted.
▯ 01/01-31/12.
**Distance:** 🚶700m ⊗300m 🛒1km 🍴on the spot.
**Remarks:** Max. 48h.

| 🅿️S | **Finisterre** | 29B1 |

Area El Campo, Calle de La Coruña, 53. **GPS:** n42,91110 w9,2636.⬆️.

30 🚐€ 5 🚰€ 3/time 🚽Ch 💧🚿included.
**Location:** Rural, simple, quiet. **Surface:** gravel. ▯ 01/01-31/12.
**Distance:** 🚶700m 🏖️on the spot ⊗500m 🛒50m.
**Remarks:** Private beach.

| 🅿️S | **Finisterre** | 29B1 |

Praia de Langosteira. **GPS:** n42,92320 w9,26149.

5 🚐free 🚰 ▯ 01/01-31/12.
**Distance:** 🏖️on the spot ⊗1km 🛒1km.
**Remarks:** Beach parking, max. 48h.

| 🅿️S | **Foz** | 29D1 |

Atalaia Camper Park, Crta general Forxán.
**GPS:** n43,57945 w7,27392. ⬆️➡️.

62 🚐€ 10 🚰€ 3/time 🚽Ch 💧(20x)€ 3/day WC🧻€ 1/time 🚿€ 4
🚿included. 🚌 **Location:** Rural, luxurious, central. **Surface:** sand.
▯ 01/04-30/11.
**Distance:** 🚶700m 🏖️600m 🛒1km 🍴750m.
**Remarks:** Free bicycles available.

| 🅿️S | **Foz** | 29D1 |

Rua Dos Astilleiros 6. **GPS:** n43,56347 w7,25733. ⬆️➡️.

50 🚐free 🚰🚽Chfree. **Location:** Rural, simple, quiet.
**Surface:** grassy/metalled. ▯ 01/01-31/12.
**Distance:** 🚶500m 🏖️on the spot ⊗300m 🛒600m.
**Remarks:** Max. 48h.

---

| 🅿️S | **Fuente Dé** | 29F2 |

Picos de Europa, C621. **GPS:** n43,14433 w4,81274.
🚐free. **Location:** Isolated, quiet. **Surface:** grasstiles.
▯ 01/01-31/12.
**Remarks:** Parking funicular railway.

| 🅿️S | **Gedrez** | 29D2 |

Área de Casa Funsiquín, CN-9, 42. **GPS:** n43,01344 w6,6081.⬆️.
8 🚐guests free 🚰🚽Chfree 🧻🚿. **Location:** Rural, isolated, quiet.
**Surface:** grassy. ▯ 01/01-31/12.
**Distance:** 🚶200m 🍴on the spot.
**Remarks:** Max. 24h, max. 6m.

| 🅿️S | **Gijón** | 29E1 |

Área de El Arbeyal, Polígono Puerto Musel.
**GPS:** n43,54467 w5,69562.⬆️.

18 🚐free 🚰🚽free. **Location:** Urban, simple, noisy.
**Surface:** asphalted. ▯ 01/01-31/12.
**Distance:** 🚶3km 🏖️on the spot 🍴on the spot.
**Remarks:** Max. 48h.

| 🅿️S | **Gijón** | 29E1 |

Camino de las Mimosas, El Rinconin. **GPS:** n43,54708 w5,63648.

20 🚐free. **Location:** Urban, simple, central. **Surface:** asphalted.
▯ 01/01-31/12.
**Distance:** 🏖️300m.
**Remarks:** Baker every morning (Jul/Aug).

| 🅿️S | **Gorliz** | 29H2 |

Paseo de Astondo. **GPS:** n43,41220 w2,94194.⬆️.

🚐€ 8/day, overnight stay free. 🚌 **Location:** Urban, simple.
**Surface:** asphalted. ▯ 01/01-31/12.
**Distance:** 🚶500m 🏖️50m 🍴on the spot.
**Remarks:** Parking beach, no camping activities.

| 🅿️S | **Gozon** | 29E1 |

Area Autocaravanas El Molino, Ctr. Luanco-Cabo Peñas.
**GPS:** n43,62541 w5,81125.⬆️➡️.

25 🚐€ 10 🚰🚽Chincluded 💧€ 4,60. 🚌 **Location:** Rural,
comfortable, quiet. **Surface:** grassy. ▯ 01/01-31/12.
**Distance:** 🏖️500m ⊗on the spot 🍴on the spot 🍴on the spot.
**Remarks:** To be paid at campsite.

| 🅿️S | **Grado** | 29E1 |

Avenida de los Deportes. **GPS:** n43,38327 w6,07487.⬆️➡️.

ES

8 ⓢfree ⚡🚰Chfree. **Location:** Urban, simple, central.
**Surface:** asphalted. 🅾 01/01-31/12.
**Distance:** 🚶800m ⊗100m 🚆300m �
50m.
**Remarks:** At sports grounds, max. 72h.

| ♿S | Grandas de Salime ⛰ | 29D1 |

Calle Pedro de Pedre. **GPS:** n43,21592 w6,87576. ⬆➡.

2 ⓢfree ⚡🚰Chfree. **Location:** Rural, simple, quiet.
**Surface:** asphalted. 🅾 01/01-31/12.
**Distance:** 🚶200m ⊗100m 🚆200m.
**Remarks:** At swimming pool, max. 48h.

| ♿S | Guitiriz | 29C1 |

Rua do Voluntariado. **GPS:** n43,17727 w7,88062. ⬆.
5 ⓢfree ⚡🚰Ch▬free. **Location:** Rural, simple, quiet.
**Surface:** gravel. 🅾 01/01-31/12.
**Distance:** 🚶800m ⊗100m 🚆800m 🏍on the spot 🚶on the spot.
**Remarks:** Max. 48h.

| ♿S | Hernani | 29H2 |

Ibaiondo Industrialdea. **GPS:** n43,26922 w1,96242. ⬆.

10 ⓢfree ⚡🚰Chfree.
**Location:** Urban, simple. **Surface:** asphalted.
**Distance:** 🚶1,2km ⛵1,5km 🚆1,2km.
**Remarks:** Max. 5 nights, no camping activities.

| ♿S | Hornachuelos | 31E1 |

Valle Medio del Guadalquivir. **GPS:** n37,83186 w5,24808. ⬆.
ⓢfree ⚡🚰Chfree. **Location:** Simple, central, quiet.
**Surface:** unpaved. 🅾 01/01-31/12.
**Distance:** ⊗550m.

| ♿S | Illa de Arousa | 29C2 |

**Área de Surf Camp**, Playa de Xestelas. **GPS:** n42,53565 w8,86929. ⬆.
ⓢ€10 🚰€3. 🅾 01/06-30/09.
**Distance:** ⚓on the spot 🛥on the spot ⊗on the spot.
**Remarks:** Surf spot.

| ♿S | Illa de Arousa | 29C2 |

**Praia do Bao**, PO-307. **GPS:** n42,54687 w8,85872. ⬆.
15 ⓢfree. **Location:** Rural, simple, quiet. **Surface:** asphalted/grassy.
🅾 01/01-31/12.
**Distance:** 🚶1km ⛱50m ⊗on the spot 🚶on the spot.
**Remarks:** Max. 24h.

| ♿S | Illano ⛰ | 29D1 |

**Area de Folgueirou**, Area recreativa de Folgueirou.
**GPS:** n43,34252 w6,85433. ⬆.

30 ⓢfree ⚡🚰Chfree. **Location:** Rural, simple, quiet.
**Surface:** grassy/gravel. 🅾 01/01-31/12.
**Distance:** ⊗on the spot.

| ♿S | Infiesto | 29F1 |

**Area de Autocaravanas Infiesto**. **GPS:** n43,34542 w5,36507. ⬆.
5 ⓢfree ⚡🚰Chfree. **Location:** Rural. **Surface:** asphalted.
🅾 01/01-31/12.
**Distance:** 🚶300m ⊗300m 🚆300m.
**Remarks:** Max. 72h, no camping activities.

| ♿S | Labastida | 29H2 |

Fray Domingo Salazar Kalea, 21. **GPS:** n42,58794 w2,79588. ⬆➡.

3 ⓢfree ⚡🚰Chfree 🔌€1/30minutes. **Location:** Rural, simple,
isolated. **Surface:** asphalted. 🅾 01/01-31/12.
**Distance:** 🚶200m ⊗300m.
**Remarks:** At sports centre, max. 48h.

| ♿S | Lanestosa 🍴 | 29G2 |

**Area de Lanestosa**, Calle Mirabueno. **GPS:** n43,21789 w3,43878. ⬆.

22 ⓢfree, service €8/24h ⚡🚰Ch🚿WC🚽included.
**Location:** Rural, simple. **Surface:** gravel. 🅾 01/01-31/12.
**Distance:** 🚶200m ⊗400m 🚆6km 🏍on the spot 🚶on the spot.
**Remarks:** Max. 7 days.

| ♿S | Langreo 🌳 | 29E1 |

**Ecomuseo Minero Valle de Samuño**, Calle Puente Carbón.
**GPS:** n43,27835 w5,67433. ⬆.

11 ⓢfree ⚡🚰Chfree. **Location:** Rural, simple, quiet.
**Surface:** asphalted/metalled. 🅾 01/01-31/12.
**Distance:** ⊗on the spot.
**Remarks:** At Ecomuseum.

| ♿S | Legazpi | 29H2 |

**Parque Mirandaola de Legazpi**, Carretera Legazpia, GI 2630.
**GPS:** n43,03678 w2,33758. ⬆➡.

5 ⓢfree ⚡🚰Chfree. **Location:** Urban, simple, noisy.
**Surface:** asphalted. 🅾 01/01-31/12.
**Distance:** 🚶1,5km ⊗on the spot 🚶on the spot.
**Remarks:** Max. 48h.

| ♿S | Lekeitio 🌿⛵ | 29H2 |

Iñigo Artieta Etorbidea. **GPS:** n43,35849 w2,50743. ⬆➡.

14 ⓢfree ⚡€3/100liter 🚰Ch. **Location:** Urban, comfortable, quiet.
**Surface:** asphalted. 🅾 01/01-31/12.
**Distance:** 🚶500m ⛱500m ⊗500m 🚆300m.
**Remarks:** Coins at tourist info.

| ♿S | Liérganes ⛵ | 29G2 |

Calle de Puente Romano. **GPS:** n43,34479 w3,74183. ⬆.

10 ⓢfree ⚡🚰Chfree. **Location:** Urban, simple, central.
**Surface:** asphalted. 🅾 01/01-31/12.
**Distance:** 🚶200m ⊗250m 🚆350m.
**Remarks:** Parking nearby train station, max. 48h.

| ♿S | Llanes | 29F1 |

**La Talá**, Avenida la Paz. **GPS:** n43,42367 w4,76768. ⬆.

19 ⓢ€3/24h ⚡€1 🚰Ch 🚿€1. 🚅€1. **Location:** Rural, simple, central.
**Surface:** asphalted. 🅾 01/04-31/12.
**Distance:** 🚶1km ⛱1,3km ⊗1km 🚆300m.
**Remarks:** Video surveillance.

| ♿S | Lugo 🏺 | 29D1 |

**Pabellón Municipal de Deportes**, Avda. de Santiago.
**GPS:** n43,00452 w7,56144. ⬆.

15 ⓢfree ⚡🚰Chfree. **Surface:** asphalted. 🅾 01/01-31/12.
**Distance:** 🚶5 min ⛵5,2km 🚆10min.
**Remarks:** Parking gymnasium, max. 48h.

**ES**

**P S**     Lugo 🪣     29D1
**Plaza de Asturias**, Rúa Ánxel Fole. **GPS**: n43,01203 w7,55496.⬆
15 📷€ 14/24h 🚰🗑free. **Surface**: asphalted. ⬛ 01/01-31/12.

**S**     Lugones     29E1
**Area de Lugones**, Calle Conde de Santa Bárbara.
**GPS**: n43,40694 w5,81139.⬆.

4 📷free 🚰🗑Chfree. **Location**: Urban, simple.
**Surface**: asphalted/metalled. ⬛ 01/01-31/12.
**Distance**: 🚶9km Oviedo ⊗on the spot 🛒on the spot 🚌200m.
**Remarks**: Next to sports centre.

**S**     Luou     29C2
**Santiso**, Trasellas, 13. **GPS**: n42,79745 w8,58413.⬆.
10 📷free 🚰🗑Chfree. **Location**: Rural, isolated, quiet.
**Surface**: grassy/metalled. ⬛ 01/01-31/12.
**Distance**: ⊗on the spot 🚲on the spot 🚶on the spot.
**Remarks**: Max. 48h.

**S**     Marcilla     29H3
**Av. Complejo Deportivo. GPS**: n42,32134 w1,73195.⬆.
10 📷€3 🚰🗑Ch. **Location**: Rural, simple, isolated, quiet.
**Surface**: asphalted. ⬛ 01/01-31/12.
**Distance**: 🚶2km ⊗on the spot 🛒2,1km.
**Remarks**: Sports centre, to be paid at bar.

**S**     Mazaricos     29B1
**Calle Picota 13. GPS**: n42,93458 w8,9906.⬆.

6 📷free 🚰🗑Chfree. **Location**: Urban, simple, quiet.
**Surface**: asphalted/metalled. ⬛ 01/01-31/12.
**Distance**: 🚶500m ⊗200m 🛒800m ⚓on the spot 🚶on the spot.
**Remarks**: Max. 72h.

**S**     Mazaricos     29B1
**NaturMaZ**, Aeródromo da Fervenza. **GPS**: n42,98398 w9,00771.⬆.
6 📷€6 🚰🗑€4 🗑€3. **Location**: Isolated, quiet.
**Surface**: grassy/gravel. ⬛ 01/01-31/12.
**Distance**: 🚶10km 🏊on the spot ▶on the spot 🚲on the spot 🚶on the spot.
**Remarks**: At airfield, picnic and barbecue place.

**S**     Melide     29C2
**Rúa Ines de Castro. GPS**: n42,91089 w8,01182 ⬆

5 📷free. **Location**: Urban. **Surface**: asphalted. ⬛ 01/01-31/12.
**Distance**: 🚶centre 300m ⊗400m 🛒800m 🚌bus > Santiago
🚶Route of Santiago de Compostela.

**S**     Melide     29C2
**Casa Familia**, N-547, 43. **GPS**: n42,88685 w7,962.

3 📷€10 🚰🗑Ch🔌included. **Location**: Rural. **Surface**: grassy.
⬛ 01/01-31/12.
**Distance**: 🚶Melide 5km ⊗2km 🚌bus 400m.

**S**     Mieres     29E1
**Area de Mieres**, Calle Asturias. **GPS**: n43,25194 w5,78083.⬆.

6 📷free 🚰🗑Chfree. **Location**: Urban, simple. **Surface**: asphalted.
⬛ 01/01-31/12.
**Distance**: 🚶100m ⚓500m ⊗on the spot 🛒on the spot.
**Remarks**: Along railwayline.

**S**     Milladoiro     29C1
**Traversia do Porto, Ames. GPS**: n42,84512 w8,58079.⬆.

15 📷free 🚰🗑Chfree.
**Surface**: asphalted.
⬛ 01/01-31/12 ⬛ 1st week Aug.
**Distance**: ⊗200m 🛒200m 🚌dir. Santiago every 15 min.
**Remarks**: At swimming pool, max. 48h, monday market.

**S**     Miño     29C1
**AP-9 Coruña-Ferrol ><, km 15,5. GPS**: n43,37404 w8,18736.⬆.

12 📷free 🚰🗑ChWC🗑free. **Location**: Motorway, simple, noisy.
**Surface**: asphalted. ⬛ 01/01-31/12.
**Distance**: ⊗on the spot 🛒on the spot.
**Remarks**: Parking nearby motorway.

**S**     Miranda de Ebro     29G2
**Calle de Burgos. GPS**: n42,68880 w2,95403.⬆➡.

7 📷free 🚰🗑Chfree. **Location**: Urban, simple, noisy.
**Surface**: metalled. ⬛ 01/01-31/12.
**Distance**: 🚶1km 🛒3km 🚌river.

**Tourist information Miranda de Ebro:**
🎪 Medieval annual fair. ⬛ around May 1.

🎪 Week market. ⬛ Sa.

**S**     Mondariz     29C2
**Área recreativa da Praia do Val**, PO-252.
**GPS**: n42,23727 w8,45943.⬆.
10 📷free 🚰🗑Chfree. **Location**: Rural, simple, quiet.
**Surface**: gravel. ⬛ 01/01-31/12.
**Distance**: 🚶1,2km ▶on the spot ⊗750m 🛒1km 🚶on the spot.

**S**     Mondoñedo     29D1
**Calle de Vicedo. GPS**: n43,42778 w7,37028.⬆.
10 📷free 🚰🗑Chfree. **Location**: Urban, simple, quiet.
**Surface**: grasstiles. ⬛ 01/01-31/12.
**Distance**: 🚶500m ⊗500m 🛒1,5km.
**Remarks**: Max. 48h.

**S**     Monfero     29C1
**Área de Fragas do Eume**, Lugar Vilafail Nº 2.
**GPS**: n43,39643 w8,07621.⬆➡.

12 📷€8 🚰🗑Chincluded 🔌€2/day WC🗑.
**Location**: Rural, isolated, quiet. **Surface**: gravel.
⬛ 01/01-31/12.
**Distance**: 🚶8km ⊗2,5km 🚲on the spot 🚶on the spot.
**Remarks**: In nature reserve, baker every morning, narrow entrance.

**S**     Monforte de Lemos 🌿⚓     29D2
**Auditorio Multiusos de Monforte**, Calle de la Circuvalación / Calle de
Santa Clara. **GPS**: n42,52750 w7,5119.⬆.

20 📷free 🚰🗑Chfree. **Location**: Simple, quiet. **Surface**: asphalted.
⬛ 01/01-31/12.
**Distance**: 🚶700m ⊗500m 🛒550m 🚌300m.
**Remarks**: Beside river, max. 48h.

**S**     Muros de Nalón     29E1
**AS-317. GPS**: n43,55394 w6,11398.
20 📷free. **Location**: Rural, simple, quiet. **Surface**: asphalted
⬛ 01/01-31/12.
**Distance**: 🏊100m ⊗2km 🛒2km 🚌2km.

**S**     Muxia     29B1
**AC 440. GPS**: n43,09893 w9,21239.⬆.

4 📷free 🚰🗑Chfree. **Location**: Rural, simple, isolated, quiet.
**Surface**: asphalted/grassy. ⬛ 01/01-31/12.
**Distance**: 🚶500m 🏊200m ⊗100m 🛒800m.
**Remarks**: Max. 48h, max. 8M.

**S**     Nava     29E1
**Area de Nava**, Avda. de la Constitución. **GPS**: n43,35722 w5,49917.⬆.

4 ⛺free 🚐🚽Chfree.
**Surface:** asphalted/metalled.
🅿 01/01-31/12.
**Distance:** 🛒900m 🏊10km.
**Remarks:** At sports centre, max. 72h, no camping activities.

### 🅂 Navelgas 🏔 29E1
**Area de Navelgas**, Recinto Ferial. **GPS:** n43,40402 w6,54167. ⬆️

15 ⛺free 🚐🚽Chfree. **Location:** Urban, simple, quiet.
**Surface:** asphalted/metalled. 🅿 01/01-31/12.
**Distance:** 🛒100m ⊗100m.

### Navia 29D1
**Area de la Granja**, C/ Travesía de la Granja.
**GPS:** n43,54528 w6,72028. ⬆️➡️

10 ⛺free 🚐🚽Chfree 🏊.
**Location:** Urban, simple, quiet. **Surface:** gravel/metalled.
**Distance:** 🏊1,5km ⊗on the spot 🍴on the spot.

### 🅂 Negreira 29C1
Rua Castelao 17. **GPS:** n42,91212 w8,73357. ⬆️
5free 🚐🚽Chfree. **Location:** Urban, simple, noisy.
**Surface:** asphalted. 🅿 01/01-31/12.
**Distance:** 🛒on the spot ⊗200m 🍴400m.
**Remarks:** Max. 6m.

### 🅂 Nogueira de Ramuín 29C2
Camiño Grupo Escolar. **GPS:** n42,41003 w7,72161. ⬆️
20 ⛺free 🚐🚽Chfree. **Location:** Simple, quiet. **Surface:** metalled.
🅿 01/01-31/12.
**Distance:** 🛒400m ⊗400m 🍴on the spot 🚶on the spot.
**Remarks:** At swimming pool, max. 48h.

### Noia 🌊🏖 29C2
Paseo Poeta Avilés de Taramancos. **GPS:** n42,78783 w8,8906.

50 ⛺free.
**Location:** Simple. **Surface:** asphalted. 🅿 01/01-31/12.
**Distance:** 🛒on the spot ⊗50m 🍴50m Bus 20m.

### 🅂 Noia 🌊🏖 29C2
**Hipermercado Eroski**, Carretera Puerto Abarquiña.
**GPS:** n42,79799 w8,88836. ⬆️

20 ⛺free 🚐free. **Location:** Urban, simple, quiet. **Surface:** asphalted.
🅿 01/01-31/12.
**Distance:** 🛒city centre 1,7km ⊗on the spot 🍴on the spot.
**Remarks:** At supermarket, Quick-Stop: >20h - <10h.
**Tourist information Noia:**
👁 El Pendo, 5km S. Santander. Cave with petroglyphs.

### 🅂 O Barco 29D2
Ruá Malecón Campiño. **GPS:** n42,41063 w6,97493. ⬆️➡️

10 ⛺free 🚐🚽Chfree.
**Location:** Quiet. **Surface:** unpaved. 🅿 01/01-31/12.
**Distance:** 🛒400m ⊗250m 🍴250m.
**Remarks:** At sports centre, max. 48h, max. 7m.

### 🅂 Oleiros 29C1
Rúa Marcial del Adalid, Muíño do Vento.
**GPS:** n43,33936 w8,35474. ⬆️➡️

3 ⛺free 🚐🚽Chfree. **Location:** Urban, simple, noisy.
**Surface:** asphalted. 🅿 01/01-31/12.
**Distance:** 🏊650m 🚶on the spot.
**Remarks:** Max. 48h.

### 🅂 Oñati 29H2
**Area Autocaravanas Oñate**, Martzelino Zelaia Kalea.
**GPS:** n43,02743 w2,40531. ⬆️➡️

18 ⛺free 🚐🚽Chfree WC. **Location:** Rural, simple, quiet.
**Surface:** grasstiles. 🅿 01/01-31/12.
**Distance:** 🛒900m 🍴on the spot.
**Remarks:** Max. 72h.

### 🅂 Ortigueira 29D1
**Parking Barro Soto**, Calle Mourón Travesía Constitución.
**GPS:** n43,68691 w7,85776. ⬆️

10 ⛺free 🚐🚽Chfree. **Location:** Rural, simple, quiet.
**Surface:** asphalted. 🅿 01/01-31/12.
**Distance:** 🛒500m 🏊100m ⊗300m 🍴800m.
**Remarks:** At swimming pool.

### 🅂 Ourol 🏔 29D1
Rúa Ourol, 1. **GPS:** n43,56485 w7,64348. ⬆️➡️

8 ⛺free 🚐🚽Ch 🏊8 🏊free. **Location:** Rural, comfortable,
isolated, quiet. **Surface:** metalled. 🅿 01/01-31/12.
**Distance:** 🛒on the spot.
**Remarks:** At swimming pool, max. 48h.

### 🅂 Oviedo 29E1
Calle Daniel Moyano. **GPS:** n43,38266 w5,82396. ⬆️➡️

16 ⛺free 🚐🚽Chfree. **Location:** Rural, simple, quiet.
**Surface:** asphalted. 🅿 01/01-31/12.
**Distance:** 🛒Oviedo 10km 🏊1km ⊗150m 🍴50m 🚌200m.

### 🅂 Padrón 29C2
Rua Vila de Rianxo. **GPS:** n42,73258 w8,66091. ⬆️
10 ⛺free 🚐🚽Chfree. **Location:** Urban, simple, quiet.
**Surface:** asphalted. 🅿 01/01-31/12.
**Distance:** 🛒300m ⊗200m 🍴500m.
**Remarks:** Along river, max. 48h.

### 🅂 Pajares 🏔❄ 29E2
**Valgrande-Pajares**, Brañillín. **GPS:** n42,97889 w5,77194. ⬆️➡️

12 ⛺free 🚐🚽Chfree. **Location:** Rural. **Surface:** asphalted.
🅿 01/01-31/12.

### 🅂 Palas de Rey 29C2
Ctra. Centro de Salud, 4. **GPS:** n42,87448 w7,85965. ⬆️
5 ⛺free 🚐🚽Chfree. **Location:** Rural, simple, isolated, quiet.
**Surface:** gravel/metalled. 🅿 01/01-31/12.
**Distance:** 🛒800m ⊗on the spot 🍴700m 🚶on the spot.

### 🚻🅂 Parada do Sil 29D2
**Rural Pepe**, Campo da Feira 17. **GPS:** n42,38287 w7,57106. ⬆️
4 ⛺guests free 🚐🚽Ch 💶€ 2. 🅿 01/01-31/12.
**Distance:** ⊗on the spot 🍴on the spot.

### 🅂 Peñacerrada 29H2
Urizaharra Hiribidea 23. **GPS:** n42,64309 w2,71181. ⬆️

8 ⛺free 🚽. **Location:** Rural, isolated, quiet.
**Surface:** asphalted/grassy. 🅿 01/01-31/12.
**Distance:** 🍴bakery 100m.

**Remarks:** Max. 48h.

⊞S | **Pobladura de las Regueras** | 29E2
LE-460. **GPS:** n42,69502 w6,23049.⬆️
50 🛏free 💶€ 3,50 ⛽Ch 💶€ 3,50 🚿€ 5. **Location:** Simple, quiet.
**Surface:** asphalted. ⬛ 01/01-31/12.
**Distance:** 🚰500m ⊗250m.

⊞S | **Pobra do Brollòn** | 29D2
**Campo Municipal de Fut. GPS:** n42,56944 w7,39417.⬆️
8 🛏free 🚽⛽Chfree.
**Location:** Isolated, quiet. **Surface:** metalled. ⬛ 01/01-31/12.
**Distance:** 🚰1,3km ⊗1,3km.
**Remarks:** At football ground, max. 48h.

⊞S | **Poio** | 29C2
Parque de Seca, 4ª Travesia Seara. **GPS:** n42,43867 w8,69219.⬆️

20 🛏free 🚽⛽Chfree. **Location:** Urban. **Surface:** grasstiles.
⬛ 01/01-31/12.
**Distance:** 🚰2km ⊗300m 🚰200m.
**Remarks:** Max. 72h.

⊞S | **Pola de Laviana** | 29E1
**Area de Pola de Laviana,** Av. Real Titánico.
**GPS:** n43,25478 w5,56836.⬆️

8 🛏free 🚽⛽Chfree. **Location:** Rural, simple. **Surface:** grasstiles.
⬛ 01/01-31/12.
**Distance:** 🚰1,5km ⊗1,5km 🚰1,5km.

⊞S | **Pontedeva** | 29C2
Ctra. Trado-Armean. **GPS:** n42,17646 w8,15477.⬆️
7 🛏free 🚽⛽Chfree. **Location:** Rural, simple, quiet. **Surface:** sand.
⬛ 01/01-31/12.
**Distance:** 🚰600m ⊗500m 🚰800m.
**Remarks:** Max. 48h.

⊞S | **Pontevedra** | 29C2
Rua Vial 2. **GPS:** n42,43347 w8,63471.

20 🛏free 🚽⛽Chfree. **Location:** Urban. **Surface:** metalled.
⬛ 01/01-31/12.
**Distance:** 🚰centre 700m ⊗500m 🚰800m.
**Remarks:** Max. 72h.

⊞S | **Posada de Valdeón** | 29F2
Calle del General Mola. **GPS:** n43,15285 w4,91747.⬆️➡️

18 🛏€ 10 🚽⛽Ch🚿. **Location:** Rural. **Surface:** grassy.

---

⬛ 01/01-31/12.
**Distance:** ⊗on the spot 🚰on the spot.
**Remarks:** Max. 96h, in Parque Nacional de Los Picos de Europa.

⊞S | **Potes** 🌿⛰️ | 29F2
Poblado Mijares. **GPS:** n43,15531 w4,61894.

+5 🛏free. **Location:** Rural, central, quiet. **Surface:** gravel.
⬛ 01/01-31/12.
**Distance:** 🚰200m ⊗150m 🚰50m.

P | **Potes** 🌿⛰️ | 29F2
Santo Toribio de Liébana, CA885. **GPS:** n43,15028 w4,65389.

🛏free.
**Location:** Isolated, quiet. **Surface:** asphalted.
⬛ 01/01-31/12.
**Distance:** 🚰Potes 3km 🚶on the spot.
**Remarks:** Parking monastery.

**Tourist information Potes:**
🎪 Local products. ⬛ Mo.
☀️ Historical cattle market, since 1379. ⬛ 01/08-15/08.

⊞S | **Redondela** 🐚 | 29C2
Avda. de Mendiño. **GPS:** n42,28972 w8,61055.
15 🛏free 🚽⛽Ch. **Surface:** asphalted. ⬛ 01/01-31/12.
**Distance:** 🚰600m ⛵500m ⊗600m 🚰600m.
**Remarks:** Nearby police station.

⊞S | **Rentería** 💒 | 29H2
**Área Rural de Listorreta-Barrengoloia.**
**GPS:** n43,26800 w1,90135.⬆️

2 🛏free 🚽⛽Chfree. **Location:** Rural, simple, isolated, quiet.
**Surface:** asphalted. ⬛ 01/01-31/12.
**Distance:** 🚰Renteria 7km 🚶on the spot.
**Remarks:** Parking nature reserve.

⊞S | **Ribadavia** | 29C2
Rua Álvaro Cunqueiro. **GPS:** n42,28543 w8,14271.
80 🛏free 🚽⛽Chfree. **Location:** Rural. **Surface:** sand.
⬛ 01/01-31/12.
**Distance:** 🚰500m ⊗300m 🚰300m.

⊞S | **Ribadeo** | 29D1
**Eroski,** Camino de Vilar. **GPS:** n43,54000 w7,06055.⬆️

6 🛏free 🚽⛽Chfree. **Location:** Urban, simple, central.
**Surface:** asphalted. ⬛ 01/01-31/12.

---

**Distance:** 🚰500m ⟋1km 🚰on the spot.
**Remarks:** At supermarket.

⊞S | **Ribadeo** | 29D1
Rúa Daniel Cortezón. **GPS:** n43,53556 w7,04528.
5 🛏free. **Location:** Urban, central, noisy. **Surface:** asphalted.
⬛ 01/01-31/12.
**Distance:** 🚰300m ⊗300m 🚰300m.
**Remarks:** No camping activities.

⊞S | **Ribadesella** | 29F1
**Área de Autocaravanas Ribadesella.**
**GPS:** n43,46025 w5,05415.⬆️➡️

5 🛏free 🚽⛽Chfree. **Location:** Rural, simple, central, quiet.
**Surface:** metalled. ⬛ 01/01-31/12.
**Distance:** 🚰500m.

⊞S | **Ribamontán al Monte** | 29G1
A8 Bilbao > Santander. **GPS:** n43,40282 w3,62877.
10 🛏free 🚽⛽Chfree. **Location:** Motorway. ⬛ 01/01-31/12.
**Remarks:** Parking nearby motorway.

⊞S | **Ribamontán al Monte** | 29G1
A8 Santander > Bilbao. **GPS:** n43,40446 w3,62476.
10 🛏free 🚽⛽Chfree. **Location:** Motorway. **Surface:** asphalted.
⬛ 01/01-31/12.
**Remarks:** Parking nearby motorway.

⊞S | **Riós** | 29D3
**Repsol,** Autovía de las Rías Bajas. **GPS:** n41,98297 w7,28602.⬆️
10 🛏free 💶€ 1/100liter ⛽Ch 🚿€ 2/h WC. **Location:** Motorway, simple, noisy. **Surface:** asphalted.
⬛ 01/01-31/12.
**Distance:** 🚰500m.
**Remarks:** At petrol station.

⊞S | **Riosa** ⛰️ | 29E1
**Área de El Angliru,** Viapará s/n. **GPS:** n43,24806 w5,90667.⬆️

15 🛏€ 5 🚽⛽Chincluded 🌿. **Location:** Rural, simple, isolated, quiet. **Surface:** metalled. ⬛ 01/01-31/12.
**Distance:** ⊗on the spot.
**Remarks:** No camping activities.

⊞S | **Riu de Cerdanya** | 29F1
C 16. **GPS:** n42,34513 e1,83315.
5 🛏free WC.
**Location:** Rural, simple, noisy. **Surface:** metalled. ⬛ 01/01-31/12.
**Distance:** 🚰1km ⟋on the spot ⊗50m.

⊞S | **Sada** | 29C1
Avenida do Porto. **GPS:** n43,35484 w8,25381.⬆️

5 🛏 🚽⛽Chfree.
**Location:** Urban, simple, quiet. **Surface:** metalled. ⬛ 01/01-31/12.
**Distance:** 🚰300m ⛵100m 🚲100m ⊗200m 🚰400m.
**Remarks:** Max. 48h.

⊞S | **Salinas** | 29E1
Calle el Agüil. **GPS:** n43,57038 w5,95904.⬆️

ES

12 ⛺free. **Location:** Urban, simple, central. **Surface:** asphalted.
◯ 01/01-31/12.
**Distance:** 🚶200m 🚲1km 🛒500m.

### 🅟🅢 San Antolín de Ibias · 29D2
Barrio Torgoal. **GPS:** n43,04389 w6,86931.⬆.
5 ⛺free.
**Location:** Rural. **Surface:** unpaved. ◯ 01/01-31/12.
**Distance:** ⊗1km.
**Remarks:** Max. 72h.

### 🅢 San Antolín de Ibias · 29D2
Barrio el Fojo. **GPS:** n43,03887 w6,87202.
free 🚰🚽Ch. ◯ 01/01-31/12.

### 🅢 San Cibrao · 29D1
Rúa Manuel Antonio 13. **GPS:** n43,69409 w7,43831.⬆➡.

10 ⛺free 🚰🚽Chfree. **Location:** Rural, simple, quiet.
**Surface:** unpaved. ◯ 01/01-31/12.
**Distance:** 🚶400m 🚲600m ⊗150m 🛒300m 🏊on the spot.
**Remarks:** At sports park, max. 48h.

### 🅢 San Clodio · 29D2
**Parque de Pena da Mula**, Calle del Troque.
**GPS:** n42,46750 w7,28583.⬆.

3 ⛺free 🚰🚽Chfree. **Surface:** asphalted. ◯ 01/01-31/12.
**Distance:** 🚶200m 🏊Playa Fluvial 25m 🍴cafetaria.

### 🅢 San Leonardo de Yagüe · 29G3
N-234, km 402. **GPS:** n41,83310 w3,05295.⬆.
20 ⛺free 🚰🚽Chfree. **Location:** Rural, simple, isolated, quiet.
**Surface:** gravel. ◯ 01/01-31/12.
**Distance:** 🚶1km ⊗500m 🛒1,5km.
**Remarks:** Max. 48h.

### 🅢 San Martín del Rey Aurelio · 29E1
**Área del Pozo Entrego**, Avenida de la Vega, AS17.
**GPS:** n43,28639 w5,63889.⬆.

3 ⛺free 🚰🚽Chfree. **Location:** Urban, simple. **Surface:** asphalted.
◯ 01/01-31/12.
**Distance:** 🚶on the spot ⊗on the spot 🛒Alcampo 1km.
**Remarks:** Max. 48h.

### 🅢 San Sebastian · 29H2
Paseo de Berio nº 2. **GPS:** n43,30797 w2,01426.⬆.

44 ⛺€ 7,60, 01/10-31/05 € 4 🚰🚽Chincluded. 🔌🧺
**Location:** Urban, noisy.
**Surface:** grasstiles.
◯ 01/01-31/12.
**Distance:** 🚶city centre 3km 🚲2km ⊗50m 🚌100m bus city centre
33 and 5.
**Remarks:** Max. 48h, marked pitches, registration with licence plate
number.

#### Tourist information San Sebastian:
ℹ Centro de Atracción y Turismo (CAT), Boulevard Alameda, 8, www.
donostia.org. Old city with, Parte Vieja, historical city centre with
numerous cafés, restaurants and tapa bars.
Ⓜ Aquarium, Plaza de Carlos Blasco Imaz, 1. Museum for oceanogra-
fics. ◯ 10-19h, Sa/Su/holidays 10-20h, 01/07-31/12 10-21h.
✈ Su-morning.

### 🅢 Santa Eulalia de Oscos · 29D1
Calle Teresa de Francisco. **GPS:** n43,25770 w7,01861.

17 ⛺free 🚰🚽Chfree. **Surface:** metalled. ◯ 01/01-31/12.
**Distance:** 🚶on the spot 🚲on the spot 🛒100m 🚲on the spot
🏊on the spot.

### 🅢 Santander · 29G1
**Área de Las Llamas**, Calle Marino Fernández-Fontecha.
**GPS:** n43,47222 w3,80354.⬆➡.

25 ⛺free 🚰🚽Chfree. **Location:** Urban, comfortable, quiet.
**Surface:** metalled. ◯ 01/01-31/12.
**Distance:** 🚶1km ⊗550m 🛒1km 🍴on the spot.
**Remarks:** Max. 48h.

### 🅢 Santander · 29G1
**Calle César Llamazares**, Nueva Montaña. **GPS:** n43,44336 w3,83747.⬆.

10 ⛺free. **Location:** Urban, simple, isolated. **Surface:** asphalted.
◯ 01/01-31/12.
**Distance:** 🚶3,5km 🛒700m.
**Remarks:** Max. 48h.

### ✪🅢 Santander · 29G1
**Marina de Santander**, Calle Tramo de Unión, Camargo.
**GPS:** n43,42736 w3,80537.⬆.

6 ⛺€ 6 🚰🚽Chincluded 🚿(2x)€ 3/24h 🔌€ 5 〰€ 4/30minutes.
⚓ **Location:** Simple. **Surface:** metalled. ◯ 01/01-31/12.
**Distance:** ⊗100m 🛒3km.
**Remarks:** Service at marina.

### 🅟🅢 Santiago de Compostela · 29C1
Rúa Manuel María. **GPS:** n42,89560 w8,5317.⬆.
100 ⛺€ 3,50/8-20h 🚰€ 3 🚽Ch.
**Surface:** asphalted.
◯ 01/01-31/12.
**Distance:** 🚶centre 2,5km 🚲3km ⊗50m 🚌line 1 > centre.
**Remarks:** Ticket for overnight stay € 12.

#### Tourist information Santiago de Compostela:
ℹ Oficina de Turismo, Rúa del Villar, 43, www.santiagoturismo.com.
City known for the termination of the pilgrime route.
👁 Plaza de la Quintana. Impressive square.
🎆 Fiesta del Apóstol Santiago. Most important festival of Galicia.
◯ 15/07-31/07.

### Santillana del Mar · 29G1
Calle Castío. **GPS:** n43,38642 w4,10185.⬆.
10 ⛺free. **Location:** Rural, simple, isolated, quiet. **Surface:** gravel.
◯ 01/01-31/12.
**Distance:** 🚶700m ⊗700m.

### 🅢 Sanxenxo · 29B2
Playa Pragueira. **GPS:** n42,40967 w8,86157.⬆.

20 ⛺€ 10, Jul/Aug € 12 🚰🚽Ch🚿included 🔌€ 3.
**Location:** Simple, quiet. **Surface:** grassy. ◯ 01/01-31/12.
**Distance:** 🚶1,5km 🏊on the spot ⊗200m 🛒1km.
**Remarks:** Max. 7m, narrow road.

### 🅢 Sanxenxo · 29B2
**Área de Cachadelos**, PO-308. **GPS:** n42,41751 w8,86952.⬆➡.
65 ⛺€ 10 🚰🚽Ch🚿included 🔌. **Surface:** grassy.
**Distance:** 🏊200m 🚲2km 🛒on the spot.
**Remarks:** Service passerby € 3.

### 🅢 Sarria · 29D2
**Area Autocaravanas**, Rúa Castelao 4-14. **GPS:** n42,77194 w7,41028.⬆.

15 ⛺free 🚰🚽Chfree. **Location:** Rural, simple, quiet.
**Surface:** gravel. ◯ 01/01-31/12.
**Distance:** 🚶800m 🏊on the spot ⊗800m.
**Remarks:** At sports centre, max. 48h.

### 🅢 Sopela · 29H2
**Polideportivo de Urko**, Kalea Gatzarrine, 26D.
**GPS:** n43,37370 w2,9898.⬆➡.

24 🅿free ⟋€ 1/100liter ᴄᴄCh ⟍(8x)€ 1.
**Location:** Rural, comfortable, quiet. **Surface:** asphalted.
⦿ 01/01-31/12 ◉ service 01/10-31/05.
**Distance:** 🚶500m ⊗300m ➞450m metro > Bilbao.
**Remarks:** Max. 48h, coins at tourist info, service 50m, no camping activities.

### Suesa 29G1
**Area de Autocaravanas Suesa**, Mojante 25.
**GPS:** n43,44736 w3,72788.⬆

66 🅿€ 9 ⟋ᴄᴄChincluded ⟍(10x)€ 3 WC 🔲 🏠
**Location:** Comfortable. **Surface:** grasstiles. ⦿ 01/01-31/12.
**Distance:** 🚶1km ⟋1,8km ⟍1,5km ⊗1km ⊡1km.
**Remarks:** Max. 96h, pay at reception campsite.

### Tapia de Casariego 29D1
**Area de Playa Grande**, Av. San Esteban. **GPS:** n43,56667 w6,94639.⬆

15 🅿€ 4 ⟋ᴄᴄChfree.
**Location:** Rural. **Surface:** grasstiles. ⦿ 01/01-31/12.
**Distance:** 🚶500m ⊗500m ⊡500m.

### Taramundi 29D1
Barrio los Castros. **GPS:** n43,35955 w7,10698.
20 🅿free ⟋ᴄᴄChfree. **Surface:** asphalted. ⦿ 01/01-31/12.
**Distance:** 🚶150m ⊗150m ⊡150m.
**Remarks:** Beautiful view.

### Teverga 🏔 29E1
**La Plaza**, AS265. **GPS:** n43,15945 w6,10075.⬆

10 🅿free ⟋ᴄᴄChfree. **Location:** Rural, simple, quiet.
**Surface:** grasstiles. ⦿ 01/01-31/12.
**Distance:** 🚶300m, Teverga 1,5km ⊗300m.

### Teverga 🏔 29E1
**Parking Senda del Oso**, Entrago. **GPS:** n43,16954 w6,09755.⬆

---

20 🅿free ⟋ᴄᴄChfree ⦿€ 3. **Location:** Simple, noisy.
**Surface:** asphalted. ⦿ 01/01-31/12.
**Distance:** ⊗on the spot ⟍on the spot.
**Remarks:** Max. 48h.

### Tolosa 29H2
San Esteban Auzoa Auzoa, 26. **GPS:** n43,13348 w2,08315.⬆➞

12 🅿€ 1/24h ⟋ᴄᴄChincluded. 🚆 **Location:** Urban, simple, noisy.
**Surface:** asphalted. ⦿ 01/01-31/12.
**Distance:** 🚶700m ⊗700m ⊡500m.
**Remarks:** Along railwayline, max. 72h, max. 7m.

### Torquemada 29F3
Calle Barrio Nuevo 29. **GPS:** n42,03696 w4,31626.⬆
4 🅿free ⟋ᴄᴄChfree. **Location:** Simple, quiet.
**Surface:** asphalted/gravel. ⦿ 01/01-31/12.
**Distance:** 🚶500m ⊗300m ⟍on the spot ⚲on the spot.
**Remarks:** Max. 48h.

### Touro 29C2
**Praza do Luar**, Rúa de Castelao, Fonte Díaz. **GPS:** n42,87061 w8,31277.

5 🅿free ⟋ᴄᴄChfree.
**Location:** Rural. **Surface:** asphalted. ⦿ 01/01-31/12.
**Distance:** 🚶600m ⊗900m ⊡900m ⟍on the spot.
**Remarks:** At sports park, max. 48h.

### Tui 29C2
**Puente Tripes**, Avenida de Portual. **GPS:** n42,04333 w8,64656.⬆

3 🅿free.
**Location:** Urban, simple. **Surface:** asphalted. ⦿ 01/01-31/12.
**Distance:** ⟋1,3km ⊗500m ⊡Lidl 1,5km.
**Remarks:** Max. 48h.

### Vegadeo 29D1
**Area de Vegadeo**, Calle Emilio Cotarelo, s/n.
**GPS:** n43,46667 w7,05167.⬆➞

---

8 🅿free ⟋ᴄᴄChfree. **Location:** Urban, simple, quiet.
**Surface:** asphalted/metalled. ⦿ 01/01-31/12.
**Distance:** ⊗on the spot ⟍on the spot.
**Remarks:** Max. 72h.

### Venialbo 29E3
Calle Tajada. **GPS:** n41,39115 w5,53899.⬆
20 🅿free ⟋ᴄᴄChfree. **Location:** Simple, quiet. **Surface:** grassy.
⦿ 01/01-31/12.
**Distance:** 🚶on the spot ⊗200m.
**Remarks:** Max. 72h.

### Viana 29H3
Paraje le Vizcaína 19. **GPS:** n42,51947 w2,36017.⬆

19 🅿€ 2/24h ⟋ᴄᴄChincluded. **Location:** Rural, simple, quiet.
**Surface:** asphalted. ⦿ 01/01-31/12.
**Distance:** 🚶1,5km ⊗1km.
**Remarks:** At sports centre, max. 48h, to be paid at bar.

### Vila de Cruces 29C2
**A Carixa**, Estrada Merza-Bodaño. **GPS:** n42,76199 w8,25602.⬆
30 🅿free ⟋ᴄᴄWCfree 🔲. **Surface:** asphalted. ⦿ 01/01-31/12.
**Distance:** 🚶Vila de Cruces 10km ⊗on the spot.
**Remarks:** Picnic area, recreation area.

### Vila de Cruces 29C2
Travesía Besexos. **GPS:** n42,79153 w8,16479.⬆➞
30 🅿free ⟋ᴄᴄChfree. **Surface:** asphalted. ⦿ 01/01-31/12.
**Distance:** 🚶1km ⊗400m ⊡1,2km.
**Remarks:** Max. 48h.

### Vilalba 29D1
Rua da Feira. **GPS:** n43,29556 w7,67694.⬆
15 🅿free ⟋ᴄᴄChfree. **Location:** Urban, central, noisy.
**Surface:** asphalted. ⦿ 01/01-31/12.
**Distance:** 🚶500m ⊗300m ⊡300m.

### Villanueva de Oscos 29D1
**Area de Villanueva**, Lugar de Villanueva. **GPS:** n43,31056 w6,98583.⬆
2 🅿free ⟋ᴄᴄChfree. **Surface:** gravel. ⦿ 01/01-31/12.
**Remarks:** Max. 48h.

### Villaseco de los Reyes 30E1
SA CV 183. **GPS:** n41,15912 w6,18668.⬆
10 🅿free ⟋ᴄᴄChfree ⟍. **Location:** Rural, simple, isolated.
**Surface:** asphalted/gravel. ⦿ 01/01-31/12.
**Distance:** 🚶300m ⊗on the spot.
**Remarks:** Near sports fields, max. 48h.

### Vitoria Gasteiz 29H2
**Área de Lakua**, Portal de Foronde. **GPS:** n42,86684 w2,68539.⬆➞

10 🅿free ⟋ᴄᴄChfree. **Location:** Urban, comfortable, central, quiet.
**Surface:** asphalted. ⦿ 01/01-31/12.
**Distance:** 🚶2km ⟋5km ⊗100m ⊡bakery 50m ➞50m.
**Remarks:** Max. 72h, market Wednesday.

### Xinzo de Limia 29C2
Camiño da Cerámica. **GPS:** n42,06168 w7,71941.⬆

**ES**

20 ⛺free 🚰🗑Chfree. **Location:** Urban. **Surface:** asphalted.
📅 01/01-31/12.
**Distance:** 🛒200m ⊗200m 🚉200m.

| 🅿S | **Zegama** | 29H2 |

San Bartolome, 13. **GPS:** n42,97578 w2,29275. ⬆➡.

8 ⛺free 🚰Chfree 🅿€ 3/2h 💧(4x)€ 2. **Location:** Urban, simple,
quiet. **Surface:** asphalted. 📅 01/01-31/12.
**Distance:** 🛒300m ⊗300m 🚉300m 🚶on the spot.
**Remarks:** At museum.

| 🅿S | **Zumaia** 🌊 | 29H2 |

Calle de la Estación. **GPS:** n43,29279 w2,24684. ⬆➡.

25 ⛺free 🚰🗑Chfree. **Location:** Simple, noisy. **Surface:** asphalted.
📅 01/01-31/12.
**Distance:** 🛒2km 🏊4,4km 🚲on the spot 🚶on the spot.

# Navarre and Rioja

| 🅿 | **Aínsa** 🌿 | 32C1 |

Plaza del Castillo. **GPS:** n42,41916 e0,13515.
20 ⛺€ 0,50/h, € 5/day.
**Surface:** asphalted/grassy.
📅 01/01-31/12.
**Distance:** 🛒600m ⊗350m 🚉1,2km.
**Remarks:** Max. 24h.

**Tourist information Aínsa:**
ℹ The capital of a medieval kingdom by surrounded fortress walls.
🚶 📅 Tue.

| 🖼 | **Albarracín** 🌿 | 33A1 |

**Quesería Sierra de Albarracín,** Pol. Los Rubiales, 1.
**GPS:** n40,43286 w1,4405.

6 ⛺free. 📅 01/01-31/12.
**Distance:** 🛒1km 🚲200m ⊗1km 🚉1km.

| 🅿S | **Alcañiz** | 33A1 |

**Parking Alcañiz,** Av. Zaragoza. **GPS:** n41,05204 w0,13902. ⬆.
25 ⛺free 🚰🗑Chfree. **Location:** Urban, simple, central.
**Surface:** gravel/sand. 📅 01/01-31/12.
**Distance:** 🛒750m ⊗75m 🚉50m.

| 🏔S | **Alquézar** 🌿 | 32C1 |

**Alquézar,** Ctra.Barbastro,. **GPS:** n42,16456 e0,01499.
⛺€ 16,50-19,50 🚰🗑Ch 💧€ 5. 📅 01/01-31/12.

**Tourist information Alquézar:**
ℹ Historical city.

| 🏨S | **Aoiz** | 27A3 |

**Hotel Ekai. GPS:** n42,77624 w1,38536. ⬆.

---

10 ⛺free 🚰🗑🍴📶free. **Location:** Rural, simple.
**Surface:** gravel/metalled. 📅 01/01-31/12.
**Distance:** 🛒3km ⊗on the spot.

| 🅿S | **Arguedas** 🌿⛱ | 32A1 |

**Aparcamiento Municipal de Autocaravanas de Arguedas,** Calle Val.
**GPS:** n42,17370 w1,59159. ⬆➡.

9 ⛺free 🚰€ 2/100liter 🗑Ch. **Location:** Rural, simple, quiet.
**Surface:** gravel. 📅 01/01-31/12.
**Distance:** 🛒800m ⊗800m 🚉800m.
**Remarks:** At Parque de Bardenas Reales, max. 48h.

| 🅿 | **Arguedas** 🌿⛱ | 32A1 |

**Parking Entorno Virgen del Yugo,** Camino a la Hermita de la Virgen del
Yugo. **GPS:** n42,20550 w1,58591. ⬆.
30 ⛺free. **Location:** Isolated, quiet. **Surface:** asphalted.
📅 01/01-31/12.
**Distance:** 🛒4km 🚉4km.

| 🅿 | **Arguedas** 🌿⛱ | 32A1 |

**Parking Senda Viva. GPS:** n42,19018 w1,58494. ⬆.
14 ⛺free. **Location:** Isolated, quiet. **Surface:** asphalted.
📅 01/01-31/12.
**Distance:** 🛒3km ⊗3km 🚉3km.

| 🅿 | **Ariza** | 30H1 |

**Area de Servicios La Cadiera,** A2 Madrid > Zaragoza.
**GPS:** n41,31210 w2,00329.
5 ⛺.

| 🅿S | **Arnedillo** 🏔 | 29H3 |

Calle Miguel del Pozo. **GPS:** n42,21361 w2,23972. ⬆➡.

30 ⛺€ 10 🚰🗑Ch💧(40x)€ 1/4h 🚽🧻,cold shower 📶included.
🌿 **Location:** Rural, comfortable. **Surface:** asphalted.
📅 01/01-31/12.
**Distance:** 🛒200m ⊗200m 🚉200m 🚶on the spot.
**Remarks:** Follow the signs in the village.

| 🅿S | **Arróniz** | 29H2 |

Carretera Barbarin 38. **GPS:** n42,58911 w2,09575. ⬆.
6 ⛺free 🚰🗑Chfree. **Surface:** asphalted. 📅 01/01-31/12.
**Distance:** 🛒300m 🏊3km ⊗250m.
**Remarks:** Max. 48h, no camping activities.

| 🅿S | **Ayegui** | 29H2 |

Plaza San Pelayo. **GPS:** n42,65436 w2,0451. ⬆.
20 ⛺€ 4 🚰🗑Chincluded. 🗑 **Surface:** grasstiles.
**Distance:** 🛒700m ⊗700m 🚉700m.
**Remarks:** Next to swimming pool.

| 🅿S | **Berriozar** 🌿 | 27A3 |

Av. Berriozar. **GPS:** n42,84043 w1,66557. ⬆➡.

---

30 ⛺free 🚰€ 2/100liter 🗑Ch. **Location:** Urban, simple.
**Surface:** concrete. 📅 01/01-31/12.
**Distance:** 🛒4km Pamplona 🚉500m.
**Remarks:** Max. 72h, coins at sports centre (9-21h).

| 🅿S | **Calatayud** | 30H1 |

Calle Fernández Ardavín. **GPS:** n41,35030 w1,6457. ⬆➡.

4 ⛺free 🚰🗑Chfree. **Location:** Urban. **Surface:** metalled.
📅 01/01-31/12.
**Distance:** 🛒on the spot ⊗500m 🚉500m.
**Remarks:** Behind police station.

| 🅿S | **Cascante** | 29H3 |

Av. Fuentes Dutor Parking Termolúdico. **GPS:** n41,99372 w1,68669. ⬆.

40 ⛺free 🚰🗑free. **Location:** Urban, simple. **Surface:** asphalted.
📅 01/01-31/12.
**Distance:** 🛒750m ⊗800m 🚉600m.
**Remarks:** Playground.

| 🅿S | **Falces** | 29H3 |

Calle la Mota. **GPS:** n42,39295 w1,79574. ⬆.
6 ⛺free 🚰🗑Chfree. **Location:** Simple. **Surface:** metalled.
📅 01/01-31/12.
**Distance:** 🛒700m 🚉300m.

| 🖼S | **Fontellas** | 32A2 |

**Aceite Artajo,** Autovía A-68, Km 102, Finca Los Llanos.
**GPS:** n42,00068 w1,56067.

10 ⛺free 🚰🗑Chfree. **Location:** Rural. **Surface:** grassy.
📅 01/01-31/12.
**Distance:** 🛒3,5km 🏊3,5km ⊗5,5km 🚉5,5km 🚲on the spot.
**Remarks:** Max. 72h.

| 🅿S | **Haro** 🌿⛱ | 29H2 |

LR111. **GPS:** n42,57253 w2,86739. ⬆.

10 � free ⌐ free. **Location:** Rural, simple, quiet. **Surface:** gravel.
◻ 01/01-31/12.
**Distance:** ⌂1,5km ⊗1,3km ⌂1,5km.

### Haro 🌿🎣     29H2

**Parking centro deportivo**, Av de los Ingenieros del Ministerio Obras Públicas, LR-111. **GPS:** n42,57734 w2,85154. ⬆.

4 ⌂free ⌐ free.
**Location:** Urban, simple. **Surface:** asphalted.
◻ 01/01-31/12.
**Distance:** ⌂500m ◢14km ⌂on the spot.
**Remarks:** At sports park, Haro, Rioja Wine Capital, wine museum, wine cellars.

**Tourist information Haro:**
ⓘ Capital of Rioja wine.

### Irura     29H2

**Area del Frontón**, Calle Zilar. **GPS:** n43,16778 w2,0652. ⬆➡.

4 ⌂free ⌐⌐Chfree. **Location:** Urban, simple, noisy.
**Surface:** asphalted. ◻ 01/01-31/12.
**Distance:** ◢100m.

### Jaca     32B1

**Membrilleras**, Calle San Indalecio. **GPS:** n42,56806 w0,54503. ⬆.

15 ⌂free ⌐. **Surface:** asphalted. ◻ 01/01-31/12.
**Distance:** ⌂300m ⊗300m.

### Logroño     29H3

**Avenue de la Sonsierra**, LR132. **GPS:** n42,47916 w2,4571. ⬆.

3 ⌂free ⌐⌐Chfree. **Location:** Urban, simple, noisy.
**Surface:** asphalted. ◻ 01/01-31/12.
**Distance:** ⌂700m ⌂100m ⊗400m ⌂300m ⌂20m.

---

**Remarks:** Max. 48h.

### Logroño     29H3

**Emblase de la Grajera**, Pontano de la Grajera.
**GPS:** n42,44909 w2,50189. ⬆.

15 ⌂free. **Location:** Rural, simple. **Surface:** concrete.
◻ 01/01-31/12.
**Distance:** ⌂7km ◢1km ⌂on the spot.
**Remarks:** Parking at lake, golf court and park La Grajera.

### Maya     27A2

**Otsondo**, NA 4453. **GPS:** n43,23304 w1,49885. ⬆.
6 ⌂free ⌐WC free. **Location:** Rural, isolated, noisy. **Surface:** gravel.
◻ 01/01-31/12.
**Distance:** ⌂3km.

### Navarrete 🌿     29H3

**Calle de la Carretera. GPS:** n42,42458 w2,55584. ⬆.

⌂free. **Location:** Urban, simple. **Surface:** asphalted.
◻ 01/01-31/12.
**Distance:** ⌂1km ◢3km ⊗600m 🚌800m.
**Remarks:** Parking at sports park.

### Nuévalos     30H1

**GPS:** n41,22089 w1,79292.
10 ⌂free. **Location:** Rural, simple. **Surface:** metalled.
◻ 01/01-31/12.
**Distance:** ⌂1,1km ⌂on the spot ⊗400m ⌂1,3km ⚲on the spot.

### Ochagavía     27B3

**Aparcamiento. GPS:** n42,90603 w1,08773. ⬆.
10 ⌂free. **Location:** Urban, simple, quiet. **Surface:** asphalted.
◻ 01/01-31/12.
**Distance:** ⌂on the spot ⊗50m.

### Olite     32A1

**Calle Molinacho. GPS:** n42,48048 w1,64705. ⬆.
10 ⌂free ⌐⌐Chfree. **Location:** Rural, simple, quiet.
**Surface:** asphalted. ◻ 01/01-31/12.
**Distance:** ⌂800m ⊗300m ⌂700m.
**Remarks:** Next to church, max. 72h.

### Pamplona 🌿     27A3

**Calle Biurdana. GPS:** n42,82098 w1,65667. ⬆.
35 ⌂€ 10, 05/07-15/07 € 20/24h ⌐€ 2 ⌐Ch 🔧🚐💳
**Location:** Urban, simple, quiet. **Surface:** asphalted.
◻ 01/01-31/12.
**Distance:** ⌂2km ⊗500m ⚲on the spot ⚲on the spot.
**Remarks:** Max. 48h, video surveillance.

### Roncesvalles 🏔     27A3

**Calle Roncesvalles. GPS:** n43,00901 w1,31888. ⬆.
10 ⌂free. **Location:** Rural, isolated, quiet. **Surface:** asphalted.
◻ 01/01-31/12.
**Distance:** ⊗100m.

### Roncesvalles 🏔     27A3

**Paseo Ibaneta. GPS:** n43,02018 w1,32401. ⬆.

---

5 ⌂free. **Location:** Rural, simple. **Surface:** asphalted.
◻ 01/01-31/12.
**Distance:** ⌂1,5km.
**Remarks:** Beautiful view.

### Sabiñánigo     32C1

**Avda. Del Ejército 27. GPS:** n42,50624 w0,3567. ⬆.
20 ⌂€ 2/24h ⌐⌐Chfree. **Location:** Simple, quiet.
**Surface:** asphalted. ◻ 01/01-31/12 ◻ last weekend of June.
**Distance:** ⌂on the spot ⊗300m.

### Tudela     32A1

**Avenida de la Argentina 20. GPS:** n42,05853 w1,61197. ⬆.

10 ⌂free ⌐⌐Chfree. **Location:** Urban. **Surface:** metalled.
◻ 01/01-31/12.
**Distance:** ⌂500m ⊗500m ⌂on the spot.
**Remarks:** Max. 48h.

### Zaragoza     32B2

**Parque de Atracciones de Zaragoza. GPS:** n41,61994 w0,90122.
10 ⌂.
**Distance:** ◢4,5km.
**Remarks:** Parking amusement park.

# Mediterranean Sea Communities

### Águilas 🌊     31H2

**Autocaravanas Anibal**, Ctra. Nacional 332, KM 3,37.
**GPS:** n37,38893 w1,61554. ⬆.
60 ⌂€ 7 ⌐€ 3 WC ⌐€ € 1. ⌂📶 ⓘ € 1. 🚐
**Location:** Rural, isolated, quiet. **Surface:** gravel/metalled.
◻ 01/01-31/12.
**Distance:** ⌂1km ⌂1km ⊗1km ⚲on the spot ⚲on the spot.

### Águilas 🌊     31H2

**Playa de la Carolina. GPS:** n37,37614 w1,62903.
⌂free. **Location:** Isolated. ◻ 01/01-31/12.
**Remarks:** Beach parking.

### Albalate del Arzobispo     33A1

**Ronda del Pintor Gárate. GPS:** n41,12125 w0,50854. ⬆.
10 ⌂free ⌐⌐Ch. **Location:** Central, quiet.
**Surface:** gravel/metalled. ◻ 01/01-31/12.
**Distance:** ⌂300m ⚲on the spot.
**Remarks:** Max. 48h.

### Alcossebre 🌿     33B1

**Las Moreras AC**, Calle Na Violante de Hungría, 18.
**GPS:** n40,24530 e0,27162. ⬆➡.

24 ⌂€ 9, Aug € 15 ⌐⌐Chincluded 🔧€ 3 WC ⌐ ◻.
**Location:** Urban, comfortable, quiet. **Surface:** gravel.
◻ 01/01-31/12.
**Distance:** ⌂400m ⌂600m ⊗400m ⌂300m ⚲on the spot ⚲on the spot.

**Tourist information Alcossebre:**
🏰 Xivert Castillo. Castle, 13-14th century.

### Alcover     32E3

**Avinguda Catalunya 2. GPS:** n41,26315 e1,17324. ⬆.

ES

5 ⬜€ 5/24h 🚰♨️ Ch included. **Location:** Rural, simple, central, quiet.
**Surface:** concrete. ⏺ 01/01-31/12.
**Distance:** 🚶on the spot 🚲700m ⊗350m ⚓100m 🚆300m.
**Remarks:** Max. 48h.

| | | |
|---|---|---|
| 🏭S | **Alicante** | 33A3 |

**Playa de San Juan**, Avinguda de Costa Blanca 168.
**GPS:** n38,37868 w0,41134.⬆️
41 ⬜€ 8-10 🚰♨️ Ch WC included. **Location:** Urban.
**Surface:** metalled. ⏺ 01/01-31/12.
**Distance:** 🚶on the spot ⚓on the spot ⊗on the spot ⚓300m
🚆100m.
**Remarks:** Max. 2 days.

| | | |
|---|---|---|
| 🏭S | **Alicante** | 33A3 |

Vía Pista. **GPS:** n38,28923 w0,52072.⬆️
50 ⬜free. **Surface:** unpaved. ⏺ 01/01-31/12.
**Distance:** 🚶Alicante 7km ⚓on the spot ⚓on the spot ⊗600m.
**Remarks:** Beach parking, max 3,5t.

| | | |
|---|---|---|
| 🏭S | **Alicante** | 33A3 |

**Villafranqueza**, Av. Pintor Gastón Castelló 41.
**GPS:** n38,37808 w0,48822.⬆️

25 ⬜€ 7 🚰♨️ Ch WC ♨️ included. **Location:** Noisy.
⏺ 01/01-31/12.
**Distance:** 🚗1km ⊗50m 🚆50m.
**Remarks:** Next to petrol station.

| | | |
|---|---|---|
| 🏭S | **Altafulla** | 33B1 |

**Área de Servicio Mèdol**, AP-7 km 237, Barcelona > Taragona.
**GPS:** n41,14157 e1,34590.
10 ⬜free 🚰♨️ Ch free. **Location:** Motorway. **Surface:** asphalted.
⏺ 01/01-31/12.
**Distance:** ⊗on the spot ⚓on the spot.

| | | |
|---|---|---|
| 🏭S | **Altafulla** | 33B1 |

**Área de Servicio Mèdol**, AP-7 km 237, Taragona > Barcelona.
**GPS:** n41,14054 e1,34746.
10 ⬜free 🚰♨️ Ch free. **Location:** Motorway. **Surface:** asphalted.
⏺ 01/01-31/12.
**Distance:** ⊗on the spot ⚓on the spot.

| | | |
|---|---|---|
| 🏭S | **Altea** | 33A3 |

**San Antonio Camperpark**, Ctra. del Albir 5/6, CV7651.
**GPS:** n38,58544 w0,05989.⬆️

50 ⬜€ 17, 2 pers. incl 🚰♨️ Ch ♨️€ 0,50/kWh,10Amp WC ♨️€ 3/4
♨️ included. 🚿 **Location:** Rural, comfortable, noisy. **Surface:** gravel.
⏺ 25/09-12/05.
**Distance:** 🚶Altea > 1km < Albir ⚓100m ⊗500m ⚓500m
🚆200m, tram 1km.
**Remarks:** Bread-service, discount longer stays.

| | | |
|---|---|---|
| 🏭S | **Amposta** | 33B1 |

**Casa de Fusta**, Partida L'Encanyissada. **GPS:** n40,65851 e0,67475.⬆️➡️

---

70 ⬜free 🚰♨️€ 3 ♨️ Ch 🚿♨️. **Location:** Rural, comfortable, isolated,
quiet. **Surface:** gravel/sand. ⏺ 01/01-31/12.
**Distance:** ⚓on the spot ⊗on the spot ⚓on the spot 🚲on the spot
🚶on the spot.
**Remarks:** Bread-service.

| | | |
|---|---|---|
| 🏭S | **Arbúcies** | 32G2 |

**Área de Arbúcies**, Camí del Molí. **GPS:** n41,81437 e2,52076.⬆️

⬜free 🚰♨️ Ch free. **Location:** Urban, simple, central, quiet.
**Surface:** asphalted. ⏺ 01/01-31/12.
**Distance:** 🚶500m ⊗700m ⚓700m 🚆250m.
**Remarks:** Max. 48h.

| | | |
|---|---|---|
| 🏭S | **Archena** 🏔️ | 31H1 |

Avendia del Río Segura. **GPS:** n38,12214 w1,29427.⬆️
30 ⬜free 🚰♨️ Ch free. **Surface:** gravel. ⏺ 01/01-31/12.
**Distance:** ⊗150m ⚓Mercadona 1,5km.

| | | |
|---|---|---|
| 🏭S | **Ascó** 🌾 | 32D3 |

C/ Alcalde Tomas Biarnes Radua. **GPS:** n41,18673 e0,56802.⬆️➡️

25 ⬜free 🚰♨️ Ch WC free. **Location:** Urban, simple, central, noisy.
**Surface:** asphalted. ⏺ 01/01-31/12.
**Distance:** 🚶100m ⚓200m 🛒200m ⊗500m ⚓500m.
**Remarks:** Max. 48h, picnic area, playground.

| | | |
|---|---|---|
| 🏭S | **Avinyo** | 32F2 |

**Area Municipal de Avinyó**, Calle Industria.
**GPS:** n41,86556 e1,97472.⬆️➡️

10 ⬜free 🚰♨️€ 1/50liter ♨️ Ch. **Location:** Rural, simple, quiet.
**Surface:** gravel/sand. ⏺ 01/01-31/12.
**Distance:** 🚶300m 🚲3km ⚓300m ⚓300m 🚆250m.
**Remarks:** Nearby swimming pool, video surveillance.

| | | |
|---|---|---|
| 🍇S | **Avinyonet del Penedès** | 32F3 |

**Area Cellar Can Battle - Artcava**, Masia Can Batlle s/n, BV2411.
**GPS:** n41,36790 e1,77306.⬆️➡️

---

10 ⬜free 🚰♨️ Ch free. **Location:** Rural, simple, isolated, quiet.
**Surface:** gravel. ⏺ 01/01-31/12.
**Distance:** 🚶1km 🚲6km ⊗1km ⚓1km.
**Remarks:** Wine tasting.

| | | |
|---|---|---|
| 🏭S | **Ayora** | 33A2 |

**El Nogal**, Romeral 5. **GPS:** n39,05870 w1,0324.⬆️

20 ⬜€ 10 🚰♨️ Ch 🚿€ 2/day WC ♨️€ 1 ⊡€ 3/2 ♨️ included.
**Location:** Rural, comfortable, isolated, quiet.
**Surface:** grassy.
⏺ 01/01-31/12.
**Distance:** 🚶2km ⚓2km ⚓2km 🚆2km 🚲on the spot 🚶on the spot.
**Remarks:** Beautiful view.

| | | |
|---|---|---|
| 🏭S | **Ayora** | 33A2 |

**Calle Manuel Reig**, N-330. **GPS:** n39,05605 w1,0526.⬆️
⬜free 🚰♨️ Ch free. **Surface:** unpaved. ⏺ 01/01-31/12.
**Distance:** 🚶700m.

| | | |
|---|---|---|
| 🏭S | **Balsicas** | 33A3 |

**Calle Laguna de Cifuentes**, Torre-Pacheco. **GPS:** n37,82074 w0,97462.
20 ⬜€ 7 🚰♨️€ 3 ♨️ Ch 🚿€ 2 WC ⊡♨️€ 5 ♨️.
**Location:** Motorway. **Surface:** asphalted. ⏺ 01/01-31/12.
**Distance:** 🚶300m.
**Remarks:** Industrial area, motorhome washing place.

| | | |
|---|---|---|
| 🏭S | **Barberà de la Conca** | 32E3 |

**Area de la Cooperativa Barberá**, Calle Comercio 40.
**GPS:** n41,41025 e1,22734.⬆️

10 ⬜free 🚰♨️ Ch free. **Location:** Rural, simple, central, quiet.
**Surface:** gravel. ⏺ 01/11-31/08.
**Distance:** 🚶on the spot ⊗on the spot ⚓500m.

| | | |
|---|---|---|
| 🏭S | **Barcelona** 🌸🎡🍜🌾 | 32G3 |

**CityStop**, Rambla Guipúzcoa. **GPS:** n41,42433 e2,20748.⬆️

80 ⬜€ 35 🚰♨️ Ch 🚿€ 4/24h WC ♨️♨️.📷🚲 **Location:** Urban,
comfortable. **Surface:** asphalted. ⏺ 01/01-31/12.
**Distance:** 🚶1km 🚲2km ⚓1km ⊗400m ⚓500m 🚆200m.

| | | |
|---|---|---|
| 🏭S | **Barcelona** 🌸🎡🍜🌾 | 32G3 |

**Park & Ride del Besòs**, Carrer del Taulat, B10 > salida 24 / 25, Sant Adrià
del Besos. **GPS:** n41,41565 e2,22363.⬆️

ES

30 🗒€ 3/h, € 30/24h 🚰⬛Ch🖊WC 🔊included 🗑.
**Location:** Urban. **Surface:** metalled. ⬛ 01/01-31/12.
**Distance:** 🚶1km ⊗300m 🚉300m 🚋Tram 100m, metro 500m.
**Remarks:** Max. 72h, monitored parking.

| | Barcelona 🌿⛲🍽🏖 | 32G3 |

**Garcia Fària**, Carrer de Josep Pla. **GPS:** n41,40662 e2,21829.⬆.

10 🗒€ 20. 🛏 🗑
**Location:** Urban, simple, noisy. **Surface:** asphalted.
**Distance:** 🚶1km 🏊2km ⊗100m 🛒150m 🚉400m 🚌on the spot 🚲on the spot 🚶on the spot.
**Remarks:** Max. ⌃4.50m.

| | Barruera 🏔 | 32E1 |

Carrer de Riu. **GPS:** n42,50127 e0,79614.⬆.
🗒free. **Location:** Rural, isolated. **Surface:** unpaved.
⬛ 01/01-31/12.
**Distance:** 🚶800m ⊗800m 🛒800m 🚲on the spot 🚶on the spot.
**Remarks:** Along river.

| | Bellcaire d'Empordà 🌿 | 32H2 |

## Area Massis del Montgri
## Bellcaire d'Empordà

- **Located in nature reserve**
- **5km to the beach**
- **Electricity/water/drainage at each pitch**

**www.massisdelmontgri.cat**
**info@massisdelmontgri.cat**

**Àrea Massís del Montgrí**, Camí Vell d'Ullà, 21.
**GPS:** n42,07521 e3,09748.⬆➡.
36 🗒€ 9-13, 13/07-18/08 € 15 🚰⬛Ch🖊(14x)€ 4 WC 🔊 1/8minutes 🔘€ 4 🔊included.🚿
**Location:** Rural, comfortable. **Surface:** grassy. ⬛ 01/01-31/12.
**Distance:** 🚶500m 🏊5km ⊗500m 🛒250m 🚌100m 🚲on the spot 🚶on the spot.
**Remarks:** Video surveillance, swimming pool (summer).

| | Bellvei | 32F3 |

**Bellvei del Penedès**, Camino Plains. **GPS:** n41,24613 e1,56992.⬆➡.

30 🗒€ 6 🚰⬛Chincluded 🖊€ 3 🔊€ 1/day. **Location:** Comfortable, isolated, quiet. **Surface:** grassy/gravel. ⬛ 01/01-31/12.

---

**Distance:** 🚶1km 🚴6,5km 🏊5km ⊗1,2km 🚉1km on the spot.

| | Benagéber 🏔 | 33A2 |

Ctra. CV-3930. **GPS:** n39,70913 w1,10136.⬆➡.

70 🗒free 🚰⬛Chfree. **Location:** Rural, simple, isolated, quiet.
**Surface:** gravel/sand. ⬛ 01/01-31/12.
**Distance:** 🚶100m ⊗400m 🚲on the spot 🚶on the spot.
**Remarks:** Max. 72h, picnic and barbecue place.

| | Besalú | 32H2 |

Carrer del Pont, 6. **GPS:** n42,19891 e2,70406.⬆.

15 🗒free 🚰€ 3 ⬛ChWC. **Location:** Rural, simple, quiet.
**Surface:** gravel/metalled. ⬛ 01/01-31/12.
**Distance:** 🚶800m ⊗100m.

| | Bicorp | 33A2 |

Junto al Polideportivo. **GPS:** n39,13278 w0,79056.⬆.

20 🗒€ 7 🚰⬛Chincluded WC🗑. **Location:** Rural, isolated.
**Surface:** gravel. ⬛ 01/01-31/12.
**Distance:** 🚶200m 🛒850m.

| | Bigastro | 33A3 |

**Camper Area La Pedrera**, Calle Cañada de Andrea, 100.
**GPS:** n38,05116 w0,89863.⬆.
20 🗒€ 12 🚰⬛Ch🖊WC🔘🔊included.
**Location:** Rural. **Surface:** gravel. ⬛ 01/01-31/12.
**Distance:** 🚲on the spot 🚶on the spot.

| | Blanes 🌿⛲🏖 | 32H3 |

Carrer d'Antoni Gaudí. **GPS:** n41,66873 e2,78440.⬆.

🗒free, 15/06-15/09 € 10.
⬛ 01/01-31/12.
**Distance:** 🚶on the spot 🏊350m ⊗250m 🛒450m.
**Tourist information Blanes:**
ℹ Oficina de Turismo, Paseo de Catalunya, 2, www.blanes.net. Bathing resort.
👁 Jardín Botànic Mar i Murtra. Botanical garden.
🍴 Mas Enlaire. Local products. ⬛ Mo-Fri 8-14h.
🍴 Passeig de Mar. Clothing, souvenirs etc. ⬛ Mo-morning.

| | Bordils | 32H2 |

**Can Carreras del Mas**, Carrer Creu 34. **GPS:** n42,04580 e2,91320.⬆.

---

5 🗒€ 12 🚰🖊🔘€ 2 🔘€ 4 🔊included.
**Location:** Rural, quiet. **Surface:** grassy. ⬛ 01/01-31/12.
**Distance:** 🚶400m ⊗100m.
**Remarks:** Narrow entrance.

| | Bovera | 32D3 |

Carrer del Esport. **GPS:** n41,32496 e0,63774.⬆.
10 🗒free 🚰⬛Ch. **Location:** Rural, simple, quiet.
**Surface:** gravel/metalled. ⬛ 01/01-31/12.
**Distance:** 🚶200m ⊗300m 🛒450m.
**Remarks:** At swimming pool.

| | Cabanes | 32H1 |

**El Noguer**, Camí de la Creu. **GPS:** n42,30594 e2,97592.⬆.

30 🗒€ 10 🚰⬛Ch🖊(16x)WC 🔊included.🚿
**Location:** Rural, simple, quiet. **Surface:** grassy. ⬛ 01/01-31/12.
**Distance:** 🚶Figueres 4km ⊗400m 🛒450m 🚌300m 🚲on the spot 🚶on the spot.
**Remarks:** Video surveillance.

| | Cadaqués | 32H1 |

**Parking SABA**, Riera de Sant Vicenç. **GPS:** n42,28964 e3,27260.

🗒€ 20,20/24h WC. 🛏 🗑 **Surface:** asphalted.
**Distance:** 🚶100m 🏊1km 🚲1,5km ⊗100m 🛒100m.
**Tourist information Cadaqués:**
🍴 La Riera. Week market. ⬛ Mo 8-14h.

| | Calaf | 32F2 |

**Area Calaf Barcelona**, Calle Doctor Fleming, 6.
**GPS:** n41,72940 e1,52610.⬆.
10 🗒€ 10 🚰⬛Chincluded 🖊€ 3 🔊free.
**Location:** Rural, simple. **Surface:** asphalted. ⬛ 01/01-31/12.
**Distance:** 🚶500m ⊗300m 🛒1km.

| | Calaf | 32F2 |

**Area Municipal de Calaf**, Carrer Berlin. **GPS:** n41,73500 e1,51389.⬆.

4 🗒free 🚰⬛Chfree. **Location:** Urban, comfortable, quiet.
**Surface:** gravel/metalled. ⬛ 01/01-31/12.
**Distance:** 🚶300m ⊗400m 🛒300m 🚌400m.
**Remarks:** Max. 48h, market Saturday.

| | Calaf | 32F2 |

Calle de Leida-Girona. **GPS:** n41,73306 e1,52667.⬆.

5 🛏free 🚰🗑Chfree.
**Location:** Urban, simple. **Surface:** gravel. ⬛ 01/01-31/12.
**Distance:** 🚉800m 🚴1km 🛒800m 🏊700m 🚌600m.
**Remarks:** At petrol station, inclining pitches, video surveillance.

| 📷🛉S | **Caldes de Malavella** | 32H2 |

Carrer Solei. **GPS:** n41,83873 e2,81080.⬆️.

5 🛏free 🚰🗑Ch🔌 free. **Location:** Urban, comfortable, noisy.
**Surface:** gravel. ⬛ 01/01-31/12.
**Distance:** 🚉500m 🛒200m 🏊300m 🚌100m.
**Remarks:** Max. 3 days.

| 📷🛉S | **Callosa d'en Sarrià** 🌿🏔 | 33A3 |

**Fonts de l'Algar**, Partida Segarra s/n. **GPS:** n38,65430 w0,09289.⬆️.

40 🛏€ 14 🚰🗑Ch🔌€ 5 WC🗑€ 2 🛜included. 🎦📷
**Location:** Rural, comfortable, isolated. **Surface:** asphalted.
⬛ 01/01-31/12 ⬛ 2nd + 3rd week October.
**Distance:** 🏊700m ⊗700m.

| 📷🛉S | **Calnegre** | 31H2 |

**Puntas Calnegre**, Ctra. Puntas de Calnegre, nº 42.
**GPS:** n37,51179 w1,41198.⬆️.

17 🛏€ 6,50, 01/06-30/09 € 8 🚰🗑Ch🔌included.
**Surface:** metalled. ⬛ 01/01-31/12.
**Distance:** 🏊600m.

| 📷🛉S | **Calnegre** | 31H2 |

**Taray Camper Park**, RM-D21, Puntas de Calnegre.
**GPS:** n37,51520 w1,3985.⬆️.

50 🛏€ 6 🚰€ 1/100liter 🗑Ch🔌€ 4. **Location:** Rural, simple.
**Surface:** sand. ⬛ 01/01-31/12 ⬛ 01/06-30/09.
**Distance:** 🏊100m ⊗500m 🏊500m.
**Remarks:** Bread-service.

---

| 📷🛉S | **Calpe** 🏖🛥 | 33A3 |

**Camper Park Sol de Calpe Boreal**, Avenida Bulgaria 4.
**GPS:** n38,64969 e0,06792.

89 🛏€ 17-27 🚰🗑Ch🔌€ 0,40/kWh WC🛜 included. 🎦📷
**Location:** Urban, comfortable, luxurious, quiet. **Surface:** gravel.
⬛ 01/01-31/12.
**Distance:** 🚉on the spot 🏊700m ⊗on the spot 🏊on the spot.
**Remarks:** Swimming pool available.

| 🛉S | **Calpe** 🏖🛥 | 33A3 |

**Camperpark Sol de Calpe Austral**, Calle Estonia 3-5.
**GPS:** n38,64444 e0,05999.

160 🛏€ 15 🚰🗑Ch🔌 WCincluded 🗑🛜. **Location:** Urban,
luxurious. **Surface:** metalled. ⬛ 01/01-31/12.
**Distance:** 🚉on the spot 🏊200m ⊗on the spot 🏊on the spot
🚌100m.

| 📷🛉S | **Calpe** 🏖🛥 | 33A3 |

**Mediterráneo Camper**, Calle Partida Colari 7E.
**GPS:** n38,65126 e0,06942.⬆️.

75 🛏€ 12, Jul/Aug € 13 🚰🗑Ch🔌 WC🗑 included 🗑€ 3/3 🛜€ 2/
day. **Location:** Urban, central. **Surface:** gravel. ⬛ 01/01-31/12.
**Distance:** 🏊beach 750m 🏊75m 🛒Mercadona 300m.
**Remarks:** Discount longer stays.

---

| 📷🛉S | **Calpe** 🏖🛥 | 33A3 |

**Paraiso Camper**, Urbanización Los Almendros, 9A.
**GPS:** n38,64920 e0,06653.⬆️.

60 🛏€ 8-14 (discount longer stays) 🚰🗑Ch🔌(60x)5kWh WC🗑
🗑€ 4/3 🛜included. 🎦📷 **Location:** Urban, comfortable, luxurious,
central. **Surface:** gravel. ⬛ 01/01-31/12.
**Distance:** 🚉1,8km 🚴7km 🛒800m 🛒800m ⊗400m 🏊250m
🏊400m 🚌600m 🚲300m 🚶100m.
**Remarks:** Includes 5kWh/day, WIFI, showers with hot water and small
pool.

| 📷🛉S | **Calpe** 🏖🛥 | 33A3 |

**Euronautica caravanning**, Ctra. N233. **GPS:** n38,65578 e0,03660.

20 🛏€ 10 🚰€ 4 🗑€ 4 Ch🔌€ 4 🔌included WC€ 2 🗑€ 2 🛜. 🛴
**Location:** Urban, simple, central. **Surface:** asphalted.
-⬛ 01/01-31/12 ⬛ Sa-Su.
**Distance:** 🚉1,5km 🚴1km 🏊1km 🏊1,5km 🚌500m.
**Remarks:** Motorhome dealer, arrival during opening hours.

| 📷🛉S | **Cambrils** 🏖 | 33B1 |

**Camperpark Playa y Fiesta**, Carretera N-340, Km. 1138.
**GPS:** n41,04471 e0,99437.⬆️.

120 🛏€ 10,45 + € 4,40-8,80/pP 🚰🗑Ch🔌€ 3 WC🗑€ 4/3
🛜€ 1/h. **Location:** Rural, comfortable, isolated, quiet.
**Surface:** grassy/metalled. ⬛ 01/01-31/12.
**Distance:** 🚉4km 🏊on the spot 🛒on the spot ⊗on the spot 🏊4km
🚲on the spot 🚶on the spot.

| 📷🛉S | **Cambrils** 🏖 | 33B1 |

**Area de Cambrils**, A7. **GPS:** n41,08542 e1,03777.

**ES**

10 🚐free, 20-8h € 16 🚰⬛Ch🚿WC⬛included ⬛€ 4. 🔌♻
**Location:** Motorway, simple, central, noisy. **Surface:** asphalted.
⬛ 01/01-31/12.
**Distance:** 🚶 on the spot.
**Tourist information Cambrils:**
ℹ Oficina de Turismo, Paseo les Palmeres, nº 1, www.turcambrils.info.
Bathing resort in traditional Mediterranean style.

| 🏕🛏S | **Cantallops** | 32H1 |

**Restaurant Can Pau**, Carretera de Cantallops s/n.
**GPS:** n42,41863 e2,91386.
50 🚐guests free 🚰⬛Chfree. **Surface:** asphalted.
**Distance:** 🚶1km ☕100m.
**Remarks:** Swimming pool.

| 🏕🛏S | **Cantonigròs** | 32G2 |

**Collsacabra**, Carrer de Màrius Anglada. **GPS:** n42,04263 e2,40467.
8 🚐free 🚰⬛Ch⬛(4x) 🚿.
**Location:** Rural. **Surface:** unpaved. ⬛ 01/01-31/12.
**Distance:** 🚶300m ⊗500m ☕50m 🚐550m.
**Remarks:** Next to football ground, max. 48h.

| 🏕🛏S | **Carcaixent** | 33A2 |

**Hort de Soriano**, Font de la Parra. **GPS:** n39,07045 w0,40918.⬆

15 🚐free 🚰⬛Ch⬛free. **Location:** Rural, comfortable, quiet.
**Surface:** sand. ⬛ 01/01-31/12 ⬛ Mo, Aug.
**Distance:** 🚶7km 🚶on the spot.
**Remarks:** Max. 48h, picnic and barbecue place. At recreation area,
first drive into Carrer Julián Ribera (39°7'19'N 00°27'04'W) ± 5km, than
follow Hort de Soriano.

| 🏕🛏S | **Cartagena** 🌊⚓🏴🗑 | 33A3 |

**Area Autocaravanas Cartagena**, Molino Derribao s/n.
**GPS:** n37,65373 w1,00345.⬆

30 🚐€ 10 🚰⬛Ch🚿WC⬛⬛€ 4 🚿included. **Location:** Rural,
comfortable, quiet. **Surface:** gravel. ⬛ 01/01-31/12.
**Distance:** 🚶centre 5km, port 8km ⊗400m 🚐400m 🚐400m 🚲on
the spot 🚶on the spot.
**Remarks:** Bread-service, sunday market Bohio 500m, Thursday market
Dolores 1km.

| 🏕🛏S | **Cartagena** 🌊⚓🏴🗑 | 33A3 |

**Área Belmonte Plus**, Ctra. de Tentegorra, 1.
**GPS:** n37,61500 w1,00555.⬆

---

15 🚐€ 10 🚰⬛Ch🚿included. **Location:** Urban, noisy.
**Surface:** asphalted. ⬛ 01/01-31/12.
**Distance:** 🚶500m ⊗750m ☕on the spot 🚐on the spot.
**Remarks:** At petrol station.

| 🏕🛏S | **Cassà de la Selva** | 32H2 |

Passeig del Ferrocarril 119. **GPS:** n41,88216 e2,87758.⬆

9 🚐free 🚰⬛ChWC🚿. **Location:** Urban. **Surface:** metalled/sand.
⬛ 01/01-31/12.
**Distance:** 🚶700m.
**Remarks:** Max. 48h, discount at swimming pool.

| 🏕🛏S | **Cervera** 🌊 | 32E3 |

**Centre d'Accolida Turistica**, Av. Francesc Macià.
**GPS:** n41,67815 e1,28385.⬆

20 🚐free 🚰⬛Ch🚿free. **Location:** Urban, quiet. **Surface:** sand.
⬛ 01/01-31/12.
**Distance:** 🚶500m ⊗500m ☕500m.
**Remarks:** Near office de tourisme, friday market.

| 🏕🛏S | **Ceutí** | 31H2 |

**Ceutí**, Pz José Virgili 1. **GPS:** n38,08099 w1,26717.

20 🚐free 🚰⬛Ch🚿WCfree.
**Location:** Simple. **Surface:** asphalted. ⬛ 01/01-31/12.
**Distance:** 🚶300m 🚶4,5km ⊗170m ☕200m.

| 🏕🛏S | **Creixell** 🌊 | 33C1 |

**Area 340**, Carrer Aneto. **GPS:** n41,16663 e1,45707.⬆

25 🚐€ 10-20 🚰⬛Ch🚿⬛€ 1 🚿included. 🚿
**Location:** Comfortable, noisy. **Surface:** gravel. ⬛ 01/01-31/12.
**Distance:** 🚶650m ☕300m.
**Remarks:** Video surveillance.

| 🏕🛏S | **Daimús** | 33A2 |

**Area Camper Dunes**, Carrer Garbi 2a. **GPS:** n38,96981 w0,14509.⬆

---

65 🚐€ 9, 01/07-31/08 + Semana Santa € 10, trailer € 1 🚰
Ch🚿€ 4,50,10Amp WC⬛⬛€ 3/3 🚿included. **Location:** Urban,
comfortable. **Surface:** gravel/metalled. ⬛ 01/01-31/12.
**Distance:** 🚶350m ⊗50m ☕100m 🚐on the spot.
**Remarks:** Discount longer stays.

| 🏕🛏S | **Deltebre** | 33B1 |

**Agrobotiga del Delta**, Avda. Les Goles de l'Ebre, 2.
**GPS:** n40,72605 e0,72261.⬆➡

50 🚐free 🚰⬛Chfree. **Location:** Rural, simple, central.
**Surface:** concrete. ⬛ 01/01-31/12.
**Distance:** 🚶800m ⊗19km 🚶1,5km ⊗600m 🚐on the spot.

| 🏕🛏S | **Dolores** | 33A3 |

**Levantri**, Pustida de Cebadas 182. **GPS:** n38,14186 w0,78053.
8 🚐€ 13,50, 01/05-30/09 € 15 🚰⬛Ch🚿WC🚿⬛€ 15
**Location:** Rural, simple, quiet. **Surface:** grassy/gravel.
⬛ 10/09-31/12.
**Distance:** 🚶5km 🚶1,5km ☕1,6km 🚐1,4km 🚲on the spot 🚶on
the spot.
**Remarks:** Max. 8M, swimming pool available.

| 🏕🛏S | **El Campello** 🌊🍃 | 33A3 |

**Camper Area 7**, Avenida Fabraquer 14, Alicante.
**GPS:** n38,40500 w0,40968.⬆

49 🚐€ 15, 2 pers.incl 🚰⬛Ch🚿⬛€ 3/24h,6Amp WC⬛⬛€ 3/3
🚿included. 🚿 **Location:** Urban, luxurious, central.
**Surface:** gravel. ⬛ 01/01-31/12.
**Distance:** 🚶2,5km 🚶5km 🚶500m 🚐500m ⊗200m ☕250m 🚐on
the spot.
**Remarks:** Possibility for reservation.

| 🏕🛏S | **El Campello** 🌊🍃 | 33A3 |

**Camper Area Campello Beach**, Calle Juan de la Cierva.
**GPS:** n38,39479 w0,40985.

45 🚐€ 12, Jul-Aug € 14 🚰⬛Ch🚿€ 4/day WCincluded ⬛€ 3
⬛€ 4/3 🚿€ 2. 🚿
**Location:** Urban, luxurious, quiet. **Surface:** gravel/sand.
⬛ 01/01-31/12.
**Distance:** 🚶1km 🚶5km 🚶400m ⊗500m ☕500m 🚐on the spot.

| 🏕🛏S | **El Campello** 🌊🍃 | 33A3 |

**Restaurante O.V.N.I. Coveto Fuma**, N332.
**GPS:** n38,45746 w0,36129.⬆

---

5 🛏€7 ⚡🚰Ch🛠WC🚿included. **Location:** Rural, quiet.
**Surface:** sand. ⊙ 01/01-31/12.
**Distance:** ⚓1,3km ⊗on the spot.

| 📷🛒 | El Campello 🌿🍃 | 33A3 |

Disaminado Afueras 459. **GPS:** n38,41863 w0,39478.
20 🛏free. **Surface:** metalled. ⊙ 01/01-31/12.

| 📷🛒S | El Catllar | 33B1 |

**Area de El Catllar**, Cami de la Foni. **GPS:** n41,17658 e1,32685.⬆

10 🛏free ⚡🚰Chfree. **Location:** Simple, central, quiet.
**Surface:** metalled. ⊙ 01/01-31/12.
**Distance:** ⚓200m ⊗200m 🏍on the spot 🚶on the spot.
**Remarks:** Max. 72h.

| 📷🛒S | El Grao de Castellón | 33A1 |

**Autocaravanas El Grao de Castellón**, Calle Astrònom Francesc Aragó.
**GPS:** n39,97981 e0,02282.
50 🛏free ⚡🚰Ch🚿.
**Surface:** grasstiles/metalled. ⊙ 01/01-31/12.
**Distance:** ⚓2,5km ⚓100m 🛒100m 🛒600m 🏍on the spot 🚶on the spot.
**Remarks:** Max. 48h, no camping activities.

| 🌿🛒S | El Masroig | 33B1 |

**Celler El Masroig**, Passeig de Arbre 3. **GPS:** n41,12658 e0,73385.⬆➡

10 🛏free ⚡🚰ChWC. **Location:** Rural, simple. **Surface:** gravel.
⊙ 01/01-31/12.
**Distance:** ⚓on the spot ⊗200m 🛒200m.
**Remarks:** Sale of wines.

| 📷🛒S | El Palomar | 33A2 |

**Font de Sis**, Avenida Riuet. **GPS:** n38,85749 w0,5032.

17 🛏€5 ⚡🚰Ch🛠€3/day 🚿€2/day.
**Location:** Isolated. ⊙ 01/01-31/12.
**Distance:** ⚓200m ⊗on the spot 🛒200m.
**Remarks:** Picnic and barbecue place.

| 📷🛒S | Els Muntells | 33B1 |

Carrer Major. **GPS:** n40,66852 e0,75903.⬆

---

10 🛏€6, €3 without service 🚰⚡ChWCincluded.
**Location:** Rural, simple, isolated, quiet. **Surface:** asphalted/gravel.
⊙ 01/01-31/12.
**Distance:** ⚓500m ⚓1,2km ⊗400m 🛒600m 🏍on the spot 🚶on the spot.
**Remarks:** Max. 48h, picnic area, playground.

| 🛏🛒S | Felanitx | 33D2 |

Seguna Volta 77. **GPS:** n39,46993 e3,10529.
10 🛏€9,50 🚰⚡Ch🛠€3 WC🚿. **Location:** Rural, isolated, quiet.
**Surface:** asphalted. ⊙ 01/01-31/12.

| 📷🛒 | Figueres | 32H1 |

**Parking Supermercado Esclat**, Avda. de los Paisos Catalans, N260.
**GPS:** n42,26042 e2,95096.⬆⬆

5 🛏free. **Surface:** asphalted.
**Distance:** ⚓on the spot ⊗500m 🛒on the spot 🚗50m.
**Remarks:** Max. 48h.

**Tourist information Figueres:**
🏛 Rambla. Antiques market. ⊙ 3rd Sa of the month.
🏛 Plaza Catalunya en Plaza del Gra. ⊙ Tue-Thu-Sa 9-14h.

| 🛏🛒S | Garrigàs | 32H2 |

**Área del Empordà Norte**, A7 km-35. **GPS:** n42,17333 e2,93194.⬆
10 🛏free 🚰⚡WCfree. **Location:** Motorway. **Surface:** metalled.
⊙ 01/01-31/12.

| 🛏🛒S | Garrigàs | 32H2 |

**Área del Empordà Sur**, A7 km-35. **GPS:** n42,17456 e2,93074.⬆

10 🛏free 🚰⚡WCfree. **Location:** Motorway. **Surface:** metalled.
⊙ 01/01-31/12.

| 📷🛒S | Girona 🌿🍴🎁 | 32H2 |

**Vayreda la Devesa**, Placa de Mela Mutermilch.
**GPS:** n41,98392 e2,81384.⬆

28 🛏<6m €10, 6m><8m €12, >8m €15 🚰⚡Ch🛠€1/40minutes
WC🚿included. 🛠 **Location:** Urban, simple, central.
**Surface:** metalled. ⊙ 01/01-31/12.
**Distance:** ⚓1km ⊗100m 🛒100m 🚗200m 🏍100m.
**Remarks:** Registration via intercom or phone, arrival <20h, video surveillance.

| 🛏🛒S | Granollers | 32G3 |

Passeig Fluvial. **GPS:** n41,59857 e2,27833.⬆
13 🛏free 🚰⚡Chfree. **Surface:** asphalted. ⊙ 01/01-31/12.

---

**Distance:** ⚓city centre 1,5km ⊗500m 🛒500m.

| 📷🛒S | Gualta | 32H2 |

**Camping Car Park de Torroella**, C-31. **GPS:** n42,02456 e3,13490.⬆
60 🛏€12,45 🚰⚡Ch🛠(50x)included 📷🚗 📀
**Surface:** gravel.
⊙ 01/01-31/12.
**Distance:** ⚓8km ⊗400m 🛒400m.
**Remarks:** Mandatory, one-time fee Pass'Etapes € 4, bicycle rental.

| 📷🛒S | Ibi | 33A3 |

**Área Chambit**, Calle Pedro Valdivia. **GPS:** n38,62222 w0,56694.⬆

25 🛏free 🚰free.
**Location:** Urban, simple. **Surface:** sand. ⊙ 01/01-31/12.
**Distance:** ⚡2,3km ⊗750m 🛒1,4km.
**Remarks:** Max. 4 days.

| 📷🛒S | Jalance | 33A2 |

N330. **GPS:** n39,18740 w1,0761.⬆

10 🛏free 🚰⚡Chfree.
**Location:** Isolated. **Surface:** asphalted. ⊙ 01/01-31/12.
**Distance:** ⚓300m ⊗550m 🛒700m.
**Remarks:** Parking next to swimming pool, max. 48h.

| 📷🛒S | L'Alqueria de la Comtessa | 33A2 |

**Camperpark KM Zero**, Metge Panella nº 1.
**GPS:** n38,93878 w0,15276.⬆➡

35 🛏€10 🚰⚡Ch🛠(35x)€3,50/day,6Amp WC🛠📷€3/3
🚿included. **Location:** Urban, comfortable. **Surface:** asphalted.
⊙ 01/09-31/05.
**Distance:** ⚓100m ⚡1,5km ⚓4km ⊗200m 🛒200m 🚗150m
🏍300m 🚶500m.
**Remarks:** Car rental, discount longer stays.

| 📷🛒S | L'Olleria | 33A2 |

Carrer J Bautista Ferrere. **GPS:** n38,91572 w0,55402.

5 🛏free 🚰⚡Ch. **Location:** Urban. **Surface:** asphalted.
⊙ 01/01-31/12.
**Distance:** ⚓300m ⚡2km ⊗250m.
**Remarks:** Max. 48h.

| 📷🛒S | La Azohia 🌊 | 33A3 |

Carretera a La Azohía. **GPS:** n37,56332 w1,17393.

**ES**

50 ⌇free.
**Location:** Simple. **Surface:** unpaved. ⬛ 01/01-31/12.
**Distance:** ⌇50m ⊗100m 🍽100m.

| 🍴🚿S | **La Guàrdia dels Prats** �̃ | 32E3 |

**Heretat Masia Poblet**, Carretera d'Artesa.s/C-14.
**GPS:** n41,41468 e1,17487.⬆.

14 ⌇€ 10, guests free ⚡(14x)€ 3/night 📶included. 🚽
**Location:** Rural, simple, isolated, quiet. **Surface:** grassy/gravel.
⬛ 01/01-31/12 ◯ Tue.
**Distance:** ⊗on the spot 🍽5km 🛒5km 🚲on the spot 🚶on the spot.

| 🚐S | **La Marina** | 33A3 |

**Finca La Escuera**, Escuera 300. **GPS:** n38,14360 w0,66939.

11 ⌇€ 15 🚰🔌Ch⚡€ 0,40/kWh,10Amp WC◯▣€ 4 📶included.
**Location:** Rural, comfortable, quiet.
**Surface:** gravel.
⬛ 01/01-31/12.
**Distance:** ⌇300m 🏖3km ⊗300m 🍽300m 🚌300m 🚶on the spot.
**Remarks:** Dutch owners, bread-service.

| 🚐S | **La Pobla de Segur** | 32E1 |

**Avenida Camp de la Sala. GPS:** n42,24029 e0,96635.⬆.
12 ⌇free 🚰🔌Ch⚡free.
**Location:** Noisy. **Surface:** asphalted. ⬛ 01/01-31/12.
**Distance:** ⌇1km ⊗250m 🍽550m.

| 🚐S | **La Roca del Vallès** | 32F3 |

**Área de l'Alba**, C251, km3,5. **GPS:** n41,62470 e2,00000.⬆.
10 ⌇€ 10-15 🚰🔌Ch⚡included.
**Surface:** grassy. ⬛ 01/01-31/12.
**Remarks:** At motorhome dealer.

| 🚐S | **La Romana** | 33A3 |

**Finca EuroPeCa**, Cuevas de San Anton 2. **GPS:** n38,35662 w0,90378.

5 ⌇€ 11, 2 pers. incl, extra pers € 2,50 🚰🔌Ch⚡€ 0,30/kWh
WC◯€ 1 ◯€ 3,50 📶included.
**Location:** Rural, comfortable, isolated. **Surface:** gravel.
⬛ 15/09-15/06.
**Distance:** ⌇1,5km ⊗1,5km 🍽1,5km 🚶on the spot.
**Remarks:** Bread-service, possibility for reservation: 0034638278693,
discount longer stays, swimming pool (summer).

| 🚐S | **La Salzadella** | 33B1 |

**Av. Tomas Molins. GPS:** n40,41611 e0,17305.⬆➡.

6 ⌇free 🚰🔌Chfree. **Location:** Rural, simple, quiet.
**Surface:** asphalted. ⬛ 01/01-31/12.
**Distance:** ⌇250m ⊗250m 🍽250m.
**Remarks:** Village of cherries: cherry soap, cherry jam.

| 🚐S | **La Selva del Camp** | 32E3 |

**Plaça Catalunya. GPS:** n41,21002 e1,13944.
8 ⌇free 🚰🔌Ch⚡free. **Location:** Urban, comfortable, central.
**Surface:** asphalted. ⬛ 01/01-31/12.
**Distance:** ⊗400m 🍽100m.

| 🚐S | **La Sénia** | 33B1 |

**Carrer dels Domenges. GPS:** n40,63897 e0,28502.⬆➡.

10 ⌇free 🚰€ 2 🔌Ch. **Location:** Rural, simple, quiet.
**Surface:** gravel. ⬛ 01/01-31/12.
**Distance:** ⌇800m ⊗200m 🍽200m.

| 🚐S | **La Seu d'Urgell** | 32F1 |

**Parking Doctor Peiró**, Avinguda del Camí Ral de Cerdanya.
**GPS:** n42,35871 e1,46476.⬆.

10 ⌇free 🚰€ 2/100liter ▣€ 2/2h.
**Surface:** unpaved. ⬛ 01/01-31/12 ◯ during event.
**Distance:** ⌇500m ⊗350m.
**Remarks:** Max. 2 nights.

| 🚐S | **La Tallada d'Empordà** | 32H2 |

**L'Empordanet**, Carretera de Marenyà, 6. **GPS:** n42,08335 e3,05734.

⌇€ 12 🚰€ 3 🔌Ch ⚡📶included.
**Surface:** gravel/metalled. ⬛ 01/01-31/12.
**Distance:** ⌇1km ⊗on the spot 🍽on the spot.
**Remarks:** Max. 48h, swimming pool.

| 🚐S | **La Vilella Baixa** | 32D3 |

**Carrer Catalunya. GPS:** n41,21718 e0,76383.
4 ⌇free 🚰🔌ChWCfree.
**Location:** Rural. **Surface:** gravel. ⬛ 01/01-31/12.
**Distance:** ⌇250m 🍽250m.
**Remarks:** Max. 48h, barbecue place, picnic area.

| 🌁 | **Lavern** | 32F3 |

**Cava Guilera**, Masia Ca l'Artigas. **GPS:** n41,39848 e1,77038.⬆.

4 ⌇free. **Location:** Rural, simple, isolated, quiet. **Surface:** grassy.
⬛ 01/01-31/12.
**Distance:** ⊗1,5km 🍽5km 🚲on the spot 🚶on the spot.
**Remarks:** Max. 2-3 days.

| 🚐S | **Les Masies de Voltregà** | 32G2 |

**Voltreganès. GPS:** n42,01766 e2,24537.⬆.
7 ⌇free 🚰🔌Ch⚡. **Surface:** metalled. ⬛ 01/01-31/12.
**Distance:** ⌇1km ⊗350m.
**Remarks:** At swimming pool.

| 🏭S | **Lleida** | 32D3 |

**Autocaravanas Miguel**, Ctra. N-IIa 456. **GPS:** n41,58945 e0,57591.⬆.

40 ⌇€ 8 🚰🔌Ch⚡(4x)€ 2/night WC📶included. 🚽
**Location:** Rural, simple, isolated. **Surface:** grassy/gravel.
⬛ 01/01-31/12.
**Distance:** ⌇5km ⚒4,5km ⊗750m 🍽2km 🚌on the spot.

| 🚐S | **Lorca** | 31H2 |

**Camperstop Finca Lerna**, Las Canales. **GPS:** n37,70460 w1,76392.⬆.

20 ⌇€ 10 🚰🔌Ch⚡€ 3 WC◯€ 1 ◯€ 4 📶included.
**Location:** Rural, comfortable, isolated, quiet. **Surface:** gravel.
⬛ 01/01-31/12.
**Distance:** ⌇7km 🏖12km ⊗2km 🚲on the spot 🚶on the spot.
**Remarks:** At horse farm, discount longer stays.

| 🚐S | **Lorca** | 31H2 |

**Caravanas Lorca**, P.I. Saprelorca Buzón 233. **GPS:** n37,61205 w1,75993.
20 ⌇free 🚰€ 2 🔌€ 2 Ch⚡. **Surface:** gravel. ◯ Su.
**Distance:** ⌇7km ⚒300m 🏖20km ⊗50m.
**Remarks:** At motorhome dealer.

| 🚐S | **Lorquí** | 31H2 |

**Parque de la Constitución. GPS:** n38,07909 w1,25918.

15 ⌇free 🚰🔌Chfree. **Location:** Urban, simple, central.
**Surface:** asphalted/metalled. ◯ Mo 07-15h, market.
**Distance:** ⌇500m ⚒5km ⊗300m.

| 🚐S | **Los Alcázares** | 33A3 |

**Camping Car Área Narejos**, Calle Bergantín 6.
**GPS:** n37,76298 w0,83069.
90 ⌇€ 12,90 🚰🔌€ 3 WC📶included ◯€ 3/3.
**Location:** Urban, comfortable, noisy.
**Surface:** asphalted.
**Distance:** ⌇700m ⊗on the spot.

ES

## L'Arboç 32F3

**Área del Penedés Norte**, AP7 dir Barcelona. **GPS**: n41,28794 e1,59117.
10 free Chfree.
**Location:** Motorway. **Surface:** metalled. 01/01-31/12.
**Distance:** on the spot on the spot.

## L'Arboç 32F3

**Área del Penedés Sur**, AP7 dir Taragona. **GPS**: n41,29029 e1,59235.

10 free Chfree.
**Location:** Motorway. **Surface:** asphalted. 01/01-31/12.
**Distance:** on the spot on the spot.

## Manlleu 32G2

Passeig del Ter. **GPS**: n41,99774 e2,27740.
11 free Ch. **Surface:** asphalted. 01/01-31/12.
**Distance:** 500m 500m.
**Remarks:** At sports park.

## Mas de Barberans 33B1

**Finca Poc A Poc**. **GPS**: n40,71817 e0,37035.

5 € 8-10 ChWC included.
**Location:** Rural, comfortable, isolated, quiet. **Surface:** grassy/gravel.
01/01-31/12.
**Distance:** 2km 2km 2km on the spot on the spot.
**Remarks:** Beautiful view.

## Moncófar 33A2

Carrer Guipuzkoa. **GPS**: n39,79668 w0,14033.

100 free Chfree.
**Location:** Urban. **Surface:** metalled. 01/01-31/12.
**Distance:** on the spot 900m 1km.

## Montanejos 33A1

**Parquing Montanejos**. **GPS**: n40,07319 w0,52634.

7 free. **Location:** Rural, simple, quiet. **Surface:** asphalted.
01/01-31/12.
**Distance:** 600m on the spot on the spot 600m on the spot.
**Remarks:** Along river.

## Montblanc 32E3

**Restaurant Masia Poblet**, C14, La Guardia dels Prats.
**GPS**: n41,41464 e1,17479.

---

10 € 10, guests free Chincluded € 3,10Amp.
**Location:** Rural, comfortable, isolated, quiet.
**Surface:** grassy/metalled. 01/01-31/12.
**Distance:** 5km on the spot 5km on the spot on the spot.
**Remarks:** Max. 2 days, video surveillance.

## Montblanc 32E3

**Area de Autocaravanas Sam**, Avda. Lluis Companys.
**GPS**: n41,36933 e1,17180.

10 € 10 Ch WC included. **Location:** Urban, simple.
**Surface:** asphalted. 01/01-31/12.
**Distance:** 800m 350m 800m 400m.
**Remarks:** At motorhome dealer.

## Montseny 32G3

**Área de Montseny**, AP7-Nord km-117 > Francia.
**GPS**: n41,64700 e2,42586.

20 free free. **Location:** Motorway, simple, noisy.
**Surface:** metalled. 01/01-31/12.
**Distance:** on the spot on the spot.
**Remarks:** Parking nearby motorway.

## Montseny 32G3

**Área de Montseny**, AP7-Sur>Barcelona. **GPS**: n41,64803 e2,42661.

20 free free. **Surface:** metalled. 01/01-31/12.
**Distance:** on the spot on the spot.

## Moraira 33A3

**Moraira Park**, Av. Madrid. **GPS**: n38,69003 e0,13296.
60 free. **Location:** Urban, simple, central, quiet.
**Surface:** metalled/sand.
**Distance:** 200m 150m 150m on the spot on the spot.

## Morella 33A1

N232. **GPS**: n40,62398 w0,09141.

---

30 free Chfree. **Location:** Rural, simple, isolated, quiet.
**Surface:** grassy/metalled. 01/01-31/12.
**Distance:** 1,5km 1,5km 1,5km on the spot.
**Remarks:** Max. 72h.

## Mula 31H2

Camino de las Curtis. **GPS**: n38,03972 w1,48139.

5 free Chfree.
**Location:** Simple. **Surface:** asphalted. 01/01-31/12.
**Distance:** 500m 500m.

## Murcia 33A3

**Camperpark Casablanca**, F16. **GPS**: n38,00189 w1,01939.

120 € 10 Ch € 2/24h WC € 3/3 included.
**Location:** Rural, comfortable, central. **Surface:** gravel.
01/01-31/12.
**Distance:** Murcia 11km 500m 15km 500m 1km
on the spot on the spot on the spot.
**Remarks:** 24/24 surveillance.

## Murcia 33A3

**Camperpark Huerta de Murcia**, Carril los Cánovas, Rincón de
Almodóvar, Los Ramos. **GPS**: n38,00520 w1,04229.

32 € 13 Ch WC € 0,50 € 4/4 included.
**Location:** Rural, comfortable. **Surface:** gravel.
01/01-31/12.
**Distance:** Alquerías 1,7km 40km 1km 1km on the spot
on the spot.
**Remarks:** Bread-service, video surveillance, discount longer stays.

## Navarcles 32F2

**Area Municipal d'Autocaravanas**, Calle de la Font de la Cura.
**GPS**: n41,75661 e1,90833.

**ES**

6 ⵣfree ⛽🚰Chfree ♨. **Location:** Urban, isolated, quiet.
**Surface:** gravel. ⬛ 01/01-31/12.
**Distance:** 🚶500m 🏊3km ⛱100m ⊗600m 🗑200m 🚌700m
🚶50m.

### Navata 32H2
**Restaurante Can Janot**, Ctra. de Olot nº 2.
**GPS:** n42,22600 e2,86325.⬆.

20 ⵣguests free ⛽€5 ChWC at restaurant.
**Location:** Rural, simple, quiet. **Surface:** grassy.
⬛ 01/01-31/12.
**Distance:** 🚶100m ⊗on the spot 🗑100m 🚲150m on the spot
🚶on the spot.

### Nules 33A2
**Parking Autocaravanas L' Alquería**, Camí la Serratella 25.
**GPS:** n39,83580 w0,10442.⬆.

15 ⵣfree ⛽€3 Ch ♨€3 WC.
**Surface:** grassy/sand. ⬛ 01/01-31/12.
**Distance:** ⛱150m on the spot 🚶on the spot.

### Oliva 33A2
**Area Camper Kikopark**, C/ Assagador de Carro.
**GPS:** n38,93282 w0,09742.⬆.

15 ⵣ€ 18-26,50 ⛽Ch ♨ WCincluded.
**Surface:** gravel/sand. ⬛ 01/01-31/12.
**Distance:** 🚶2,3km ⛱on the spot ⊗on the spot 🗑on the spot.
**Remarks:** Stop & Go arrival >15h, departure <15h.

### Orihuela 33A3
**Bon Bini**, Los Quicos 12, La Matanza, **GPS:** n38,12596 w0,99001.⬆➡.
10 ⵣ€7 ⛽Chincluded ♨€ 0,40/kWh. **Location:** Rural,
isolated, quiet. **Surface:** gravel. ⬛ 01/01-31/12.
**Distance:** 🚶5km ⛱5km 🗑5km 🚲on the spot 🚶on the spot.
**Remarks:** Dutch owners, car rental.

### Palamós 32H2
**Autocaravanning Palamós**, Camí Vell de la Fosca, 18.
**GPS:** n41,85592 e3,13535.⬆.

96 ⵣ€ 13, 15/07-31/08 € 20 ⛽Ch ♨ WC ⬛€ 4 included.
**Location:** Urban, comfortable. **Surface:** gravel. ⬛ 01/01-31/12.
**Distance:** ⛱500m ⊗500m.
**Remarks:** Motorhome washing place.

### Palamós 32H2

**EmpordArea**, C/ Pui Gorgoll s/n - C/ Pla del Llop s/n.
**GPS:** n41,85740 e3,11467.⬆➡.
48 ⵣ€ 13, 14/07-01/09 € 20 ⛽Ch ♨(48x),8Amp WC ⬛€ 1 ⬛€ 4
included. **Location:** Urban, comfortable, luxurious, quiet.
**Surface:** gravel/metalled. ⬛ 01/01-31/12.
**Distance:** 🚶1km 🏊1,3km ⛱1km ⛵1km ⊗700m 🗑350m
🚌500m 🚲1,2km 🚶1,2km.
**Remarks:** Bread-service, video surveillance, rental of electric scooters
and bicycles.

### Peñíscola 33B1
**Area camper Vizmar**, Cami de la Volta.
**GPS:** n40,39357 e0,40778.⬆➡.

25 ⵣ€7 ⛽Ch ♨€ 4/day WC included € 3,95/day.
**Location:** Rural, comfortable, quiet. **Surface:** gravel.
⬛ 15/09-15/06 ⬛ Semana Santa.
**Distance:** 🚶3km ⛱500m ⊗300m 🗑300m 🚌300m.
**Remarks:** Discount longer stays.

### Peñíscola 33B1
**Camper Park Los Pinos**, C/ Abellers, 2.
**GPS:** n40,37912 e0,38827.⬆➡.

30 ⵣ€ 10, 16/06-14/09 tariff camp site ⛽Ch ♨,10Amp
WC ⬛€ 4,50/4,50 included. **Location:** Rural, luxurious, quiet.
**Surface:** gravel/metalled. ⬛ 01/01-31/12.
**Distance:** 🚶1,5km ⛱2km ⊗1,5km 🗑800m.

### Peñíscola 33B1
**Stop&Go La Volta**, Camino de la Volta 20.
**GPS:** n40,39793 e0,40316.⬆➡.

70 ⵣ€ 8, 01/07-31/08 € 10, 2 pers. incl, pers + € 1-2 ⛽
Ch ♨€ 3,6Amp WC ⬛€ 4/4 included.

**Location:** Rural, comfortable, isolated, quiet. **Surface:** grassy/gravel.
⬛ 01/01-31/12.
**Distance:** 🚶4km, Peñíscola 5km ⛱1km ⊗2km 🗑4km 🚌1km.

### Peñíscola 33B1
**Parking Els Daus**, Avenida Valencia, 93. **GPS:** n40,37831 e0,40640.⬆.
130 ⵣ€ 6,30-12,60 ⛽ChWCincluded. **Surface:** grassy.
⬛ 01/01-31/12.
**Distance:** 🚶2km ⛱100m ⊗100m 🚌30m.
**Remarks:** Beach parking.

### Peralada 32H1
C-252, 206. **GPS:** n42,30597 e3,00845.⬆.

6 ⵣfree ⛽🚰Chfree. **Location:** Urban. **Surface:** metalled.
⬛ 01/01-31/12.
**Distance:** 🚶200m ⊗200m 🗑300m.
**Remarks:** Max. 48h.

### Pineda de Mar 32G3
**Àrea Pineda de Mar**, Carrer Tarragona, 24.
**GPS:** n41,62199 e2,68941.⬆.

30 ⵣ€ 10, 01/07-27/08 € 15 ⛽Ch ♨€3 WC ⬛€ 1 included.
**Location:** Urban, quiet. **Surface:** grassy.
⬛ 01/01-31/12 9-21h.
**Distance:** 🚶on the spot ⛱100m ⊗100m.

### Platja d'Aro 32H2
Calle Roma. **GPS:** n41,81070 e3,05713.⬆.

30 ⵣfree ⛽🚰Chfree. **Surface:** asphalted. ⬛ 01/10-31/03.
**Distance:** ⛱750m.
**Remarks:** Max. 2 days.

### Ponts 32E2
Carr. de la Seu d'Urgell 95. **GPS:** n41,92069 e1,19076.⬆.

30 ⵣ€7 ⛽€3 Ch ♨€3.
**Location:** Rural. **Surface:** gravel. ⬛ 01/01-31/12.
**Distance:** 🚶600m ⛱500m 🗑600m 🚌800m.
**Remarks:** At petrol station.

### Prats de Lluçanès 32F2
B-432 2. **GPS:** n42,00442 e2,03410.
10 ⵣfree ⛽€ 0,50 Ch ♨€ 1/2h WC ⬛€ 1.
**Location:** Rural, simple, quiet. **Surface:** gravel. ⬛ 01/01-31/12.
**Distance:** 🚶700m ⛱900m 🗑700m 🚌850m.
**Remarks:** Max. 48h, picnic area.

**358**

**ES**

## Quart | 32H2
Avinguda de la Bóbila. **GPS:** n41,93944 e2,83917.⬆

4 ⊞free ⊞ ⊟Chfree. **Surface:** metalled. ⬛ 01/01-31/12.
**Distance:** on the spot 6,5km on the spot on the spot.
**Remarks:** Max. 48h, max. 8M.

## Ramonete | 31H2
**Wo-Mo Puerto Villa Brisa**, Los Curas, D21, Puntas de Calnegre.
**GPS:** n37,52589 w1,4336.⬆➡

50 ⊞€ 7 ⊞€ 0,10/10liter ⊟Ch ⊞€ 0,50/kWh ⊟€ 2 ⊞€ 4/4 ⊞⊞.
**Location:** Simple, isolated. **Surface:** gravel. ⬛ 19/09-30/05.
**Distance:** 5km 5km 5km 500m.
**Remarks:** Bread-service.

## Rialp | 32E1
Paseig del Pallars. **GPS:** n42,43925 e1,13384.

5 ⊞free ⊞ ⊟Ch ⊞€ 2,50. **Surface:** gravel. ⬛ 01/01-31/12.
**Distance:** 200m 200m 200m 100m.
**Remarks:** Next to football ground.

## Ricote | 31H1
**Huerta de Rivote**, Calle Alharbona. **GPS:** n38,15098 w1,36674.⬆➡
30 ⊞free ⊞ ⊟Chfree. **Surface:** gravel. ⬛ 01/01-31/12.

## Ripoll | 32G2
**Can Guetes**, Carretera C-26 Km.126. **GPS:** n42,20267 e2,19390.⬆

5 ⊞free ⊞ ⊟Chfree. **Location:** Urban, simple, central.
**Surface:** asphalted. ⬛ 01/01-31/12.
**Distance:** on the spot 500m 150m on the spot on the spot.
**Remarks:** Max. 24h.

## Ripoll | 32G2
**Calle Pla D'Ordina**, Raval de Barcelona. **GPS:** n42,20008 e2,18695.⬆

5 ⊞free. **Location:** Urban, simple, noisy. **Surface:** asphalted.
⬛ 01/01-31/12.
**Distance:** 300m 500m 500m.
**Remarks:** Parking next to police station, max. 24h.
**Tourist information Ripoll:**
⚐ Centrum. Week market. ⬛ Sa-morning.

## Rupit | 32G2
BV-5208. **GPS:** n42,02651 e2,46383.⬆

8 ⊞€ 5 ⊞€ 1/50liter ⊟Ch ⊞€ 1/h. **Location:** Simple, central.
**Surface:** asphalted. ⬛ 01/01-31/12.
**Distance:** 200m bakery.

## San Fulgencio | 33A3
**Camper Park San Fulgencio**, Mar Cartabrico 7, Centro Comercial las
Dunas. **GPS:** n38,12080 w0,66005.⬆

40 ⊞first day € 14, then € 12 ⊞ ⊟Ch ⊞,5,5Amp WC⊟€ 3/3
⊞included. **Location:** Rural, comfortable. **Surface:** gravel.
⬛ 01/01-31/12.
**Distance:** 1,5km 200m 150m 150m.
**Remarks:** Service passerby € 5.

## San Fulgencio | 33A3
**Ghol**, Calle Mar Cantabrico. **GPS:** n38,11896 w0,65614.⬆
14 ⊞6m € 8, 9m € 10, 11m € 13 ⊞ ⊟Ch ⊞,2kWh/day
WC⊟€ included.⊞⊞ **Location:** Urban, central. **Surface:** gravel.
⬛ 01/01-31/12.
**Distance:** on the spot 2km 400m Lidl 150m.
**Remarks:** Next to petrol station.

## San Fulgencio | 33A3
**Oasis**, Caminal del Convenio. **GPS:** n38,11972 w0,66194.⬆

14 ⊞€ 10, 15/06-15/09 € 14 ⊞ ⊟Ch ⊞€ 0,40/kWh,16Amp
WC⊟€ 3/2 ⊞included.
**Location:** Comfortable. **Surface:** gravel. ⬛ 01/01-31/12.
**Distance:** San Fulgencio 7km beach 1,5km 200m 200m
300m.

## San Javier | 33A3
**Camper Park La Ribera**, Avenida Romería de San Blas.
**GPS:** n37,80416 w0,81584.⬆

200 ⊞€ 9-14, 2 pers. incl ⊞ ⊟Ch ⊞€ 2 WC⊟ included ⊞€ 3/
time ⊞€ 1/24h. ⊞**Location:** Urban, comfortable, luxurious, quiet.
**Surface:** gravel. ⬛ 01/01-31/12.
**Distance:** 1,3km on the spot 800m.

## San Rafael del Río | 33B1
**Restaurante Spätzle-Fritz**, Planes del Reine, San Jorge, CV-11.
**GPS:** n40,57507 e0,39333.⬆

50 ⊞€ 8, guests free ⊞€ 2 ⊟€ 2 Ch ⊞€ 4 WC⊟€ 2 ⊞.
**Location:** Rural, comfortable, isolated, quiet. **Surface:** gravel.
⬛ 01/01-31/12.
**Distance:** 3,5km 7km 9km on the spot.

## Sant Feliu de Guíxols | 32H2
Carrer de la Via del Tren. **GPS:** n41,79036 e3,04414.⬆
15 ⊞€ 10 ⊞ ⊟Ch ⊞€ 3 ⊞. **Surface:** sand. ⬛ 01/01-31/12.
**Distance:** 2km 1km 800m.
**Remarks:** Video surveillance.

## Sant Feliu de Guíxols | 32H2
**Parking Narcis Massanas**, Ronda Narcis Massanas.
**GPS:** n41,78020 e3,02303.⬆

15 ⊞€ 5 ⊞ ⊟Chincluded. **Location:** Simple, quiet.
**Surface:** unpaved. ⬛ 01/01-31/12.
**Distance:** 200m 1,5km 200m 500m 50m.
**Remarks:** Max. 5 days.

## Sant Hilari Sacalm | 32G2
**Area Autocaravana**, Carretera de la Font Picant.
**GPS:** n41,88417 e2,50778.⬆

79 ⊞free ⊞ ⊟Chfree ⊞(2x)€ 1/8h WC⊟€ 2.
**Location:** Rural, simple, quiet. **Surface:** gravel/sand.
⬛ 01/01-31/12.
**Distance:** 300m 200m 200m 700m 10m 10m.
**Remarks:** Nearby swimming pool, max. 48h, key service at swimming
pool, no camping activities.

## Sant Joan de les Abadesses | 32G1
**Area Sant Joan de les Abadesses**, Passeig de l'Estació.
**GPS:** n42,23535 e2,28412.⬆

ES

15 ⊼free ⌁🔲Chfree.
**Location:** Urban, simple, central, quiet. **Surface:** unpaved.
🅾 01/01-31/12.
**Distance:** ⊗500m 🛋500m 🚏200m 🚲on the spot 🚶on the spot.
**Remarks:** 5 special pitches, all parking places permitted.

### 🅂 Sant Julià de Vilatorta | 32G2
**Guilleries - Savassona. GPS:** n41,92161 e2,32185.⬆
4 ⊼free ⌁Ch 🔲free. **Location:** Rural, simple, central, quiet.
**Surface:** metalled. 🅾 01/01-31/12.
**Distance:** ⊥300m ⊗200m 🛋200m.

### 🅂 Sant Llorenç de Morunys 🏔❄ | 32F2
**Plaça del Mur. GPS:** n42,13675 e1,59253.⬆

6 ⊼€4 ⌁🔲Ch 🚿included.
**Location:** Rural. **Surface:** metalled. 🅾 01/01-31/12.
**Distance:** ⊥on the spot ⊗150m.
**Remarks:** Max. 48h, pay at tourist office.

### 🅂 Sant Pere de Torelló | 32G2
**Bellmunt. GPS:** n42,06695 e2,28438.⬆
12 ⊼free ⌁🔲Ch. **Location:** Rural, simple, isolated.
**Surface:** unpaved. 🅾 01/01-31/12.
**Distance:** ⊥1,5km ⊗850m 🚲on the spot.

### 🅂 Santa Coloma de Cervelló | 32F3
**Santa Coloma de Cervelló**, Can Julià, s/n.
**GPS:** n41,36495 e2,02512.⬆➡

6 ⊼free ⌁🔲Chfree. **Location:** Simple, isolated, quiet.
**Surface:** asphalted. 🅾 01/01-31/12.
**Distance:** ⊥500m ⚓5km ⊗400m 🛋500m.

### 🅂 Santa Coloma de Queralt | 32E3
**Carrer Llorac. GPS:** n41,53686 e1,38181.⬆
10 ⊼free ⌁🔲Chfree ⚡€2.
**Location:** Rural. **Surface:** unpaved. 🅾 01/01-31/12.
**Distance:** ⊥100m ⊗500m 🛋600m.
**Remarks:** Max. 48h.

### 🅂 Segorbe 🌿⚓ | 33A2
**Area de Segorbe**, Escalera de la Estación.
**GPS:** n39,84805 w0,48166.⬆➡

12 ⊼free ⌁🔲Chfree. **Location:** Simple, central, quiet.
**Surface:** asphalted/metalled. 🅾 01/01-31/12.
**Distance:** ⊥1km ⚓2km ⊗800m 🛋800m 🚏on the spot.

---

**Remarks:** Max. 48h.

### 🅂 Sils | 32H2
**Area de Sils**, Carrer de l'Estany. **GPS:** n41,80751 e2,74572.⬆

10 ⊼free ⌁🔲Chfree. **Location:** Urban, simple, central.
**Surface:** gravel/sand. 🅾 01/01-31/12.
**Distance:** ⊥700m ⊗on the spot 🛋on the spot 🚏50m.
**Remarks:** Max. 48h.

### 🅂 Simat de la Valldigna | 33A2
**Carrer dels Brolls. GPS:** n39,04120 w0,308.⬆

20 ⊼free ⌁🔲Chfree. **Surface:** sand. 🅾 01/01-31/12.
**Distance:** ⊥500m ⊗450m 🛋500m.

### 🅂 Sitges | 32F3
**Avda. del Cami Pla. GPS:** n41,25083 e1,81838.⬆

10 ⊼€5, 01/04-31/10 €8 ⌁🔲Ch.
**Location:** Simple. **Surface:** asphalted. 🅾 01/01-31/12.
**Distance:** ⊥800m ⚓2,5km 🛋50m.
**Remarks:** Industrial area, max. 7 days, Barcelona 40km.

### 🅂 Sta.Pola | 33A3
**Camper Area Santa Pola**, C/ Electricistas, 14.
**GPS:** n38,20805 w0,57416.⬆➡

33 ⊼€9-12 ⌁🔲Ch ⚡€3 WC🔲🔲€4 🚿 🚌 **Location:** Rural,
comfortable, isolated. **Surface:** gravel/metalled. 🅾 01/01-31/12.
**Distance:** ⊥1,7km ⚓1,8km ⊗200m 🛋800m.
**Remarks:** Industrial area, bread-service, video surveillance.

### 🅂 Tavernes de la Valldigna | 33A2
**Area Camper La Finca**, Carrer del Carbi. **GPS:** n39,08178 w0,21245.⬆
60 ⊼€8 ⌁🔲Ch ⚡€3 WC🔲🔲€3 🚿included.
**Location:** Urban, comfortable, quiet. **Surface:** gravel/metalled.
🅾 01/01-31/12.
**Distance:** ⊥750m ⚓50m 🛋600m.
**Remarks:** Bread-service, video surveillance.

### 🅂 Tavertet | 32G2
**Carrer Jaume Balmes. GPS:** n41,99462 e2,41572.⬆
10 ⊼€10 ⌁🔲Ch 🚿included. **Surface:** gravel/sand.
🅾 01/01-31/12.
**Distance:** ⊥100m ⊗450m.

### 🅂 Torelló | 32G2
**Vall des Ges**, Carrer del Ter. **GPS:** n42,04988 e2,25029.⬆
12 ⊼free ⌁🔲Ch. **Surface:** metalled. 🅾 01/01-31/12.

---

**Distance:** ⊥700m ⊗400m.

### 🅂 Torroella de Montgrí | 32H2
**La Granja**, Carrer de la Santa Espina. **GPS:** n42,03803 e3,13612.
25 ⊼€ 15-20 ⌁Ch 🚿(25x),20Amp WC🔲🚿included.
**Location:** Urban, comfortable. **Surface:** metalled.
🅾 01/01-31/12.
**Distance:** ⊥100m ⚓5km 🚏300m ⊗100m 🛋100m 🚏500m
🚲on the spot 🚶on the spot.
**Tourist information Torroella de Montgrí:**
🎪 Traditional week market. 🅾 Mo.

### 🅂 Tortosa | 33B1
**Área de Tortosa**, Cami de la Toia. **GPS:** n40,80277 e0,51388.⬆➡

30 ⊼free ⌁🔲Chfree. **Location:** Simple, central, quiet.
**Surface:** asphalted. 🅾 01/01-31/12.
**Distance:** ⊥1,1km ⚓10km ⊗50m 🛋1km.

### 🅂 Totana | 31H2
**Camperstop Sierra Espuña**, Morti s/n Camino del Polideportivo.
**GPS:** n37,79380 w1,51139.⬆

25 ⊼€7 ⌁🔲Ch 🚿€3/day WC🔲€1 🔲€3 🚿included.
**Location:** Rural, comfortable. **Surface:** gravel. 🅾 01/01-31/12.
**Distance:** ⊥2,5km ⚓5km 🛋450m.

### 🅂 Tremp | 32E2
**Passeig de Conca de Tremp. GPS:** n42,16312 e0,89043.⬆

10 ⊼free ⌁🔲free 🚿€1/2h.
**Surface:** asphalted. 🅾 01/01-31/12.
**Distance:** ⊗200m 🛋200m.
**Remarks:** Max. 48h, no camping activities.

### 🅂 Turis | 33A2
**Carretera de Silla Tunis. GPS:** n39,38944 w0,69777.⬆

10 ⊼free ⌁🔲Chfree.
**Location:** Simple. **Surface:** unpaved. 🅾 01/01-31/12.
**Distance:** ⊥500m ⊗1,7km 🛋400m.

### 🅂 Ulldecona | 33B1
**Finca Mola de la Torre**, Partida Llacuna. **GPS:** n40,61786 e0,46010.
3 ⊼€8,50, 2 pers. incl ⌁🔲included.
**Location:** Rural. **Surface:** grassy. 🅾 01/01-31/12.
**Distance:** ⊥2,5km ⚓2,5km 🛋2,5km 🚲on the spot 🚶on the spot.
**Remarks:** At swimming pool.

## Valencia 🌾♨🍴 33A2

**Area Camping-car La Marina**, Carrer del Rio 556B, El Saler.
**GPS:** n39,38666 w0,3321. ⬆.

70 ⚡€ 11-15 🚰🔌Ch WC 🔌€ 1 📶included. 🚽
**Location:** Rural, isolated. **Surface:** gravel. ⭕ 01/01-31/12.
**Distance:** 🏙Valencia 6km ⛱beach 150m ⊗600m 🛒500m �on the spot 🚶on the spot ✝on the spot.
**Remarks:** Discount longer stays.

## Valencia 🌾♨🍴 33A2

### Valencia Camper Park
### Valencia

- Excellent location for city visit
- Open all year
- Wifi included

**www.valenciacamperpark.com**
**valcampark@gmail.com**

**Valencia Camper Park**, Calle Universo, Bétera.
**GPS:** n39,57958 w0,44494. ⬆.
78 ⚡€ 12-14, 2 pers. incl, extra pers € 3 🔌€ 0,50/40liter 🔌Ch 🔌
(52x)€ 3/24h,4Amp, 6Amp € 5 WC🔌€ 3 📶included. 📷🚽
**Location:** Urban, luxurious. **Surface:** gravel. ⭕ 01/01-31/12.
**Distance:** 🏙Valencia 12km 🛒1,5km 🚂train 300m.
**Remarks:** Possibility for reservation, discount longer stays, swimming pool (summer).

## Vallirana 32F3

Carrer Major, N340. **GPS:** n41,38239 e1,92719. ⬆➡.

6 ⚡free 🚰🔌Ch.
**Location:** Simple, noisy. **Surface:** asphalted. ⭕ 01/01-31/12.
**Distance:** 🏙800m ⊗300m 🛒800m.

## Vic 32G2

**Area Municipal de Vic**, Carrer de la Fura.
**GPS:** n41,93444 e2,24000. ⬆➡.

20 ⚡€ 5 🚰€ 2/100liter 🔌Ch 🔌€ 6/3h. 🚽
**Location:** Rural. **Surface:** grassy. ⭕ 01/01-31/12.
**Distance:** 🏙1,8km ⛱2km ⊗300m 🛒500m �mi400m.
**Remarks:** Max. 48h.

## Vic 32G2

**Área de pernocta ASM**, Carrer del Blat. **GPS:** n41,95688 e2,24765. ⬆.

6 ⚡free 🚰🔌Ch free.
**Location:** Rural, simple. **Surface:** asphalted. ⭕ 01/01-31/12.
**Distance:** 🏙3,5km 🚲500m ⊗3,5km 🛒3,5km.
**Remarks:** Video surveillance.

## Viladrau ⛰ 32G2

**Area de Viladrau**, Carrer Montseny s/n. **GPS:** n41,84544 e2,38732. ⬆.

16 ⚡€ 3-5 🚰🔌Ch 📶free. **Location:** Rural, simple, quiet.
**Surface:** gravel/sand. ⭕ 01/01-31/12.
**Distance:** 🏙500m ⊗500m 🛒500m.
**Remarks:** Max. 48h.

## Vilafranca del Penedès 32F3

**Vilafranca del Penedès**, Avda. Tarragona, N-340a.
**GPS:** n41,34001 e1,69147. ⬆➡.

10 ⚡free 🚰🔌Ch. **Location:** Rural, simple, central, quiet.
**Surface:** gravel/sand. ⭕ 01/01-31/12.
**Distance:** 🏙500m ⛱1,2km ⊗900m 🛒850m Lidl �mion the spot ✝on the spot.

## Yecla 33A2

**Finca Caravana**, Paraje Fuente del Pinar A-14.
**GPS:** n38,71443 w1,11948.

10 ⚡€ 8 🚰🔌Ch included. **Location:** Rural, simple, isolated.
**Surface:** gravel/sand. ⭕ 01/01-31/12.
**Remarks:** Discount longer stays.

# Spanish interior

## Aguilar de Campoo 29F2

N611, Ctra Palencia-Aguillar de Campoo.
**GPS:** n42,78631 w4,25757. ⬆➡.

10 ⚡free 🚰🔌Ch free.
**Location:** Urban, simple. **Surface:** asphalted. ⭕ 01/01-31/12.
**Distance:** 🏙1km 🚲3,1km ⊗1km 🛒1km.
**Remarks:** Max. 48h.

## Alcuéscar 30D3

**La Tierra Verde**, Cordel de Mérida s/n. **GPS:** n39,16121 w6,25227.

5 ⚡free 🚰€ 1 🔌€ 2,50 Ch€ 2,50 🔌€ 2,50 WC🔌€ 2,50 📶.
**Location:** Rural. **Surface:** grassy. ⭕ 01/01-31/12.
**Distance:** 🚲1,5km ⛱15km 🚶5km ⊗1km 🛒2,5km �mi1km.

## Alcuéscar 30D3

**Hostal Los Olivos. GPS:** n39,16461 w6,26425. ⬆.
5 ⚡guests free. **Surface:** gravel. ⭕ 01/01-31/12.
**Distance:** ⊗on the spot.

## Aldeadávila de la Ribera 30D1

**GPS:** n41,22028 w6,61333. ⬆.

5 ⚡free 🚰🔌Ch free. **Surface:** asphalted. ⭕ 01/01-31/12.
**Distance:** 🏙400m ⊗on the spot 🛒200m.
**Remarks:** Max. 48h.

## Aldeanueva de Barbarroya 30E2

Calle Aldeanueva. **GPS:** n39,75843 w5,01482. ⬆.
5 ⚡free 🚰🔌Ch free. ⭕ 01/01-31/12.
**Distance:** 🏙700m 🛒700m.
**Remarks:** Max. 72h.

## Algora 30H1

**Area 112**, Autovía A2 km 112. **GPS:** n40,95669 w2,66403. ⬆.
🚰🔌Ch 🚂 📶free.
**Surface:** gravel/metalled. ⭕ 01/01-31/12.
**Remarks:** At petrol station and supermarket, playground.

## Almazán 30H1

Camino Viejo del Cubo de la Solana. **GPS:** n41,49259 w2,53385.
10 ⚡free. **Surface:** asphalted.
**Remarks:** Parking at swimming pool.

## Ampudia 29F3

**Area de San Martín**, Glorieta. S. Martín.
**GPS:** n41,91130 w4,78082. ⬆➡.

6 ⚡free 🚰🔌Ch free. **Location:** Rural, simple.
**Surface:** gravel/metalled. ⭕ 01/01-31/12.
**Distance:** 🏙400m.
**Remarks:** Max. 72h, no camping activities.

ES

## Andorra `33A1`

**Area en Andorra. GPS:** n40,98384 w0,44724.

10 free € 0,20/130liter Ch.
**Surface:** asphalted. 01/01-31/12.
**Distance:** 1km 13km 1,2km.
**Remarks:** Coins at petrol station, playground.

## Astorga `29E2`

**Parking plaza de Toros. GPS:** n42,45138 w6,06593.

15 free Chfree. **Surface:** metalled.
**Distance:** 500m 1,4km 500m 500m.
**Remarks:** Max. 48h.

## Astudillo `29F3`

**Area de la Joya**, Urbanizacion de don Bosco. **GPS:** n42,18944 w4,3.

10 free Chfree.
**Location:** Rural, simple. **Surface:** gravel. 01/01-31/12.
**Distance:** 1km 300m.
**Remarks:** No camping activities.

## Avila `30F1`

**Parking del Palacio de Congresos**, Calle Molino dell Carril.
**GPS:** n40,66111 w4,70472.

10 free.
**Surface:** asphalted.
01/01-31/12.
**Distance:** centre 800m 2,2km 250m.
**Remarks:** Monitored parking.

**Tourist information Avila:**
Small medieval town surround by ramparts.
The San Vicenta basilica is a Roman building.

## Badajoz `30C3`

**La Codosera**, Ctra. de Alburquerque, BA 053. **GPS:** n39,23870 w7,20297.
free Chfree.
**Location:** Rural. **Surface:** unpaved. 01/01-31/12.
**Distance:** 2km on the spot.
**Remarks:** Swimming pool.

## Badajoz `30C3`

**Parque del Guadiana**, Camino Viejo de San Vicente.
**GPS:** n38,88481 w6,97845.

---

20 free Chfree. **Surface:** asphalted. 01/01-31/12.
**Distance:** 600m on the spot.

## Baltanàs `29F3`

**Area de la Ermita de Revilla**, Plaza Arrañales de Revilla.
**GPS:** n41,93472 w4,2475.

5 free Chfree.
**Location:** Rural, simple. **Surface:** concrete. 01/01-31/12.
**Distance:** on the spot 500m.
**Remarks:** No camping activities.

## Becerril de Campos `29F3`

**Carretera de Monzón. GPS:** n42,10997 w4,64315.
free Chfree. **Surface:** metalled. 01/01-31/12.
**Distance:** on the spot 14km 500m 500m.
**Remarks:** No camping activities.

## Bretocino `29E3`

**Area para Autocaravanes**, Cuesta de los Nogales.
**GPS:** n41,88654 w5,75517.

5 +25 € 7 Chincluded € 3,10Amp WC .
**Location:** Rural, comfortable, quiet. **Surface:** concrete.
20/03-20/10.
**Distance:** 300m 300m.
**Remarks:** Service passerby € 3, swimming pool.

## Burgo de Osma `30G1`

**Calle de Santos Iruela. GPS:** n41,58662 w3,07338.

10 free . **Location:** Rural, simple. **Surface:** metalled.
01/01-31/12.
**Distance:** 500m 200m 500m.

## Burgos `29G3`

**Calle Farmacéutico Obdulio Fernández. GPS:** n42,35012 w3,68068.

---

20 free Chfree.
**Location:** Urban. **Surface:** asphalted. 01/01-31/12.
**Distance:** city centre 1km 100m 100m on the spot on the spot.

## Burgos `29G3`

N120, Calle de Cartuja de Miraflores. **GPS:** n42,34037 w3,69361.

5 € 0,60/h, max. € 2,60, 20-10h free.
**Location:** Central, quiet. **Surface:** asphalted.
**Distance:** 2,6km.
**Remarks:** Parking beside river.

**Tourist information Burgos:**
City, 8th century, with a lot of curiosities such as the cathedral, the castle and Monasterio de las Huelgas.

## Cabrerizos `30E1`

**Don Quijote**, Ctra. Aldealengua km 4. **GPS:** n40,97500 w5,60306.
€ 17 Ch. 01/03-31/10.
**Remarks:** Formula Camper.

## Cáceres `30D2`

**Valhondo**, Calle Lope de Vega. **GPS:** n39,48021 w6,36844.

15 free Ch free.
**Location:** Simple, noisy. **Surface:** asphalted.
**Distance:** 600m 6,7km.
**Remarks:** Max. 24h, monitored parking.

**Tourist information Cáceres:**
Oficina de Turismo, Plaza Mayor, nº 3, www.inedito.com/caceres/.
City with historical centre.
PeroPalo. Traditional celebration. 21/02-24/02.

## Calaceite `33B1`

**Calle Font de la Vila 10. GPS:** n41,01866 e0,19027.
10 free Chfree. **Surface:** gravel. 01/01-31/12.
**Distance:** 400m 650m 350m.
**Remarks:** Max. 72h.

## Carinena `32A3`

**Calle del Carmen 40. GPS:** n41,33790 w1,23.
8 free Chfree.
**Location:** Urban. **Surface:** metalled. 01/01-31/12.
**Distance:** 600m 350m.

## Carrión de los Condes `29F3`

**Calle de Las Huertas. GPS:** n42,33875 w4,60808.

10 free Chfree.
**Location:** Rural, simple. **Surface:** metalled.
**Distance:** 200m 200m 200m.
**Remarks:** Max. 48h.

## Cervera de Pisuerga `29F2`

C/ El Maderao. **GPS:** n42,87139 w4,49972.

10 🅿free ⛽🚰Chfree. **Location:** Rural, simple, isolated.
**Surface:** sand. ⬛ 01/01-31/12.
**Distance:** ⬇500m ⊗500m 🚉500m.
**Remarks:** Along river, max. 48h.

| 🅿 | **Coca** ⚓ | 30F1 |

**GPS:** n41,21348 w4,52733. ⬆.

5 🅿free. **Location:** Urban, simple. **Surface:** metalled.
⬛ 01/01-31/12.
**Remarks:** Parking castle.

| 🅿 | **Consuegra** | 30G3 |

Calle Fuentecilla. **GPS:** n39,45339 w3,6106.
🅿free. **Location:** Isolated, quiet. **Surface:** sand.
⬛ 01/01-31/12.
**Remarks:** Isolated parking at foot of hill with windmills.

| 🅿 S | **Cuellar** ⚓ | 30F1 |

**Área El Castillo**, Calle del Alamillo, 40. **GPS:** n41,40083 w4,32028.⬆.

6 🅿free ⛽🚰Chfree.
**Location:** Rural, simple. **Surface:** metalled.
**Distance:** 🚿2km.
**Remarks:** At castle.

| 🅿 | **Cuenca** 🌿 | 30H2 |

**Parking del Auditorio**, Paseo del Huecar. **GPS:** n40,07639 w2,12917.
5 🅿€ 15/24h.
**Location:** Urban. **Surface:** metalled.
⬛ 01/01-31/12.
**Distance:** ⬇500m ⊗on the spot 🚉350m ⬛station 1km.

**Tourist information Cuenca:**
ℹ️ Historical centre with casas colgadas (hanging houses).
🎭 Processions of guilds with much pomp and splendour. ⬛ Easter.
🌿 Ciudad Encantada. Nature reserve.

| 🅿 S | **Cumbres Mayores** | 31D1 |

Calle Sevilla. **GPS:** n38,05937 w6,63797.➡.
8 🅿free ⛽🚰Chfree.
**Location:** Rural. **Surface:** metalled. ⬛ 01/01-31/12.
**Distance:** ⬇500m ⊗500m 🚉500m ☨on the spot.

| 🅿 S | **Daimiel** | 30F3 |

**Parque Nacional Las Tablas de Daimiel**, Carr. a las Tablas de Daimiel.
**GPS:** n39,13754 w3,69678.

10 🅿free WC.
**Location:** Rural. **Surface:** grassy/metalled. ⬛ 01/01-31/12.
**Distance:** ☨on the spot.

| 🅿 S | **Deleitosa** | 30E2 |

**Área PLA Deleitosa**, Calle Eras. **GPS:** n39,64041 w5,64599.⬆.
3 🅿free ⛽€ 3 🚰Ch⬛€ 1/h.
**Surface:** metalled. ⬛ 01/01-31/12.
**Distance:** ⊗500m 🚉500m.

| 🅿 S | **Don Benito** | 30D3 |

Avda. de los Deportes. **GPS:** n38,96250 w5,86305.⬆➡.
3 🅿free ⛽🚰Chfree.
**Location:** Central, noisy. **Surface:** metalled. ⬛ 01/01-31/12.
**Distance:** ⊗on the spot 🚉on the spot ⬛on the spot.

| 🅿 S | **Duruelo de la Sierra** | 29G3 |

Avenida del Duero. **GPS:** n41,95242 w2,92725.⬆.

16 🅿€ 4 🚰Ch. **Surface:** metalled. ⬛ 01/01-31/12.
**Distance:** ⬇400m ⊗250m.

| 🅿 S | **El Boalo** | 30F1 |

Calle del Cerro. **GPS:** n40,72109 w3,92273.⬆.
10 🅿free ⛽🚰Ch ⛽free. **Location:** Urban, comfortable.
**Surface:** grassy. ⬛ 01/01-31/12.
**Distance:** ⊗500m 🚉400m ☨on the spot.
**Remarks:** Max. 72h, playground.

| 🅿 S | **Espinosa de los Monteros** | 29G2 |

**Parking Las Cocinas**, BU-570 > Bárcenas. **GPS:** n43,08556 w3,5575.⬆.

10 🅿free ⛽🚰Chfree. **Location:** Simple, isolated.
**Surface:** asphalted. ⬛ 01/01-31/12.
**Distance:** ⬇1km ⊗1km 🚉1km ☨on the spot.
**Remarks:** Max. 48h, tuesday market.

| 🅿 S | **Foncastín** | 29F3 |

**Estación de Servicios La Loba**, A6, salida 175.
**GPS:** n41,44131 w4,97957.⬆.

5 🅿free ⛽🚰Chfree.
**Location:** Rural, simple. **Surface:** unpaved. ⬛ 01/01-31/12.
**Distance:** 🚿250m ⊗on the spot.

| 🅿 S | **Frómista** 🌿 | 29F3 |

Paseo de Julio Senador, P-980. **GPS:** n42,26494 w4,41198.⬆➡.

6 🅿free ⛽🚰Chfree.
**Location:** Urban, simple. **Surface:** metalled. ⬛ 01/01-31/12.
**Distance:** ⬇600m 🚿200m ⊗500m 🚉500m.
**Remarks:** At sports park, max. 48h, weigh bridge nearby € 0,50.

| 🅿 S | **Fuente de Cantos** | 31D1 |

Calle Real. **GPS:** n38,24900 w6,30079.⬆.
3 🅿free ⛽€ 3 🚰Ch. **Surface:** metalled. ⬛ 01/01-31/12.
**Distance:** ⬇on the spot ⊗on the spot.
**Remarks:** Max. 72h.

| 🅿 S | **Herrera de Pisuerga** | 29F2 |

**Fuente Los Caños**. **GPS:** n42,59011 w4,33225.⬆.
7 🅿free ⛽🚰Chfree.
**Location:** Rural. **Surface:** gravel. ⬛ 01/01-31/12.
**Remarks:** No camping activities.

| 🅿 S | **Hontoria del Pinar** | 29G3 |

**Cañón de Río Lobos**, C/ De la Cuesta Herrera.
**GPS:** n41,84379 w3,16514.⬆➡.

9+24 🅿free ⛽🚰Chfree. **Surface:** gravel. ⬛ 01/01-31/12.
**Distance:** ⬇500m ⊗450m.

| 🏠 S | **Huergas de Babia** | 29E2 |

**El Moriscal**, CL-626. **GPS:** n42,95651 w6,09335.⬆.
10 🅿€ 5 ⛽🚰Ch included.
**Location:** Rural. **Surface:** gravel. ⬛ 01/01-31/12.
**Distance:** ⬇on the spot ⊗on the spot.

| 🅿 S | **Jerez de los Caballeros** | 31D1 |

Calle Miguel Hermandez, Plaza de Toros. **GPS:** n38,32639 w6,7625.

8 🅿free ⛽🚰Ch 🚿free. **Location:** Urban, simple.
**Surface:** unpaved. ⬛ 01/01-31/12.
**Distance:** ⬇on the spot ⊗150m 🚉1km.
**Remarks:** Video surveillance.

| 🅿 S | **Jerte** | 30E2 |

**Area de Jerte**. **GPS:** n40,20976 w5,77284.
15 🅿free ⛽€ 3/150liter 🚰Ch ⛽(4x).
**Location:** Rural. **Surface:** asphalted/metalled. ⬛ 01/01-31/12.
**Distance:** ⬇city centre 2km ⊗400m 🚿on the spot ☨on the spot.
**Remarks:** Max. 72h, monitored parking.

| 🅿 S | **La Alberca** | 30D1 |

**Casa del Parque**. **GPS:** n40,48833 w6,11583.⬆.
10 🅿free ⛽🚰Chfree. **Surface:** metalled. ⬛ 01/01-31/12.
**Distance:** ⬇300m.
**Remarks:** Max. 48h, no camping activities.

| 🅿 S | **La Joyosa** | 32A2 |

**Área de Marlofa**, Calle Sobradiel. **GPS:** n41,73744 w1,06664.⬆➡.
free ⛽🚰Ch €3 WC⬛€ 3 🚿.
**Location:** Urban, simple, noisy. **Surface:** asphalted. ⬛ 01/01-31/12.
**Distance:** 🚿9km.

| 🅿 S | **Lagartera** | 30E2 |

Camino de la Estacion. **GPS:** n39,91151 w5,19978.⬆.

3 🅂free 🚰🅂free. **Surface:** asphalted. 🔲 01/01-31/12.
**Distance:** on the spot 🚲1,4km 🚊100m.
**Remarks:** Max. 48h.

### 🅂 León 29E2
Avenida los Peregrinos. **GPS:** n42,60471 w5,58525.⬆️

20 🅂free 🚰🅂Chfree. **Surface:** metalled. 🔲 01/01-31/12.
**Distance:** ⊗300m 🚊300m.
**Remarks:** Max. 48h, market on Sunday.

### 🅂 Logrosán 30E3
El Palomar, Carretera Villanueva-Seré. **GPS:** n39,33188 w5,48044.⬆️➡️
10 🅂free 🚰🅂Chfree. **Location:** Isolated. **Surface:** grassy.
🔲 01/01-31/12.
**Remarks:** Max. 48h.

### 🅂 Madrid 30G2
Valdebernando, Bulevar de Jose Prat. **GPS:** n40,39671 w3,62.
15 🅂free.
**Location:** Urban.
**Surface:** metalled.
🔲 01/01-31/12.
**Distance:** on the spot ⊗200m 🚐300m 🚲on the spot 🚶on the spot.
**Remarks:** Monitored parking.

**Tourist information Madrid:**
ℹ️ Oficina de Turismo, C/Duque de Medinaceli, 2, Madrid. Capital of the country with a lot of curiosities.
👁 Palacio Real, Madrid. Royal palace.
Ⓜ Museo de América, Madrid, Av de los Reyes Católicos.
Ⓜ Museo del Ejercito, Calle Mendez Nuñez 1, Madrid. Army museum.
Ⓜ Museo del Prado, Madrid. The largest art gallery of the world.
Ⓜ Museo Romántico, Calle de San Mateo 13, Madrid. Collection of the romanticism.
✝ Basílica de San Francisco el Grande, Madrid. Basilica.

### 🅂 Medellín 30D3
A.V. Guadiana. **GPS:** n38,96550 w5,96306.⬆️➡️

50 🅂free 🚰🅂Chfree. **Location:** Rural, simple, quiet.
**Surface:** gravel. 🔲 01/01-31/12.
**Distance:** 600m 🏊on the spot 🚣on the spot ⊗250m 🚊500m 🚲on the spot 🚶on the spot.
**Remarks:** Max. 48h.

### 🅂 Medinaceli 30H1
Area autocaravanas de Medinaceli, Calle Campo de San Nicolás 16.
**GPS:** n41,17129 w2,4313.
10 🅂free 🚰🅂Chfree. **Location:** Rural, quiet.
**Surface:** gravel/metalled. 🔲 01/01-31/12.
**Distance:** on the spot 🚲5km 🚲on the spot 🚶on the spot.
**Remarks:** Max. 72h.

### 🅂 Mérida 30D3
Área Teatro Romano de Mérida, C/ Cabo Verde, s/n.
**GPS:** n38,91903 w6,33611.⬆️

🅂<8m € 12/24h, >8m € 15/24h, trailer € 3 🚰🅂Ch 🔧€ 3 📶included.
**Location:** Urban. **Surface:** asphalted.
🔲 01/01-31/12.
**Distance:** 700m.
**Remarks:** Video surveillance.

**Tourist information Mérida:**
ℹ️ Oficina de Turismo, Calle Santa Eulalia, 64.
Also called Spanish Rome. Former stopover on the old silver trail.

### 🅂 Olmedo 30F1
Parque del Mudejar, N601, km 148,1. **GPS:** n41,29167 w4,68194.⬆️

9 🅂free 🚰🅂Chfree. **Location:** Rural, simple. **Surface:** metalled.
🔲 01/01-31/12.
**Distance:** ⊗100m 🚊200m.

### 🅂 Oropesa 30E2
Camino de Torralba. **GPS:** n39,92124 w5,16738.⬆️

4 🅂free 🚰🅂Chfree. **Surface:** metalled. 🔲 01/01-31/12.
**Distance:** 600m.
**Remarks:** Max. 48h, no camping activities.

### 🅂 Osorno 29F2
Los Chopos, N611 Osorno > Herrera de Pisuerga.
**GPS:** n42,41694 w4,35111.⬆️

30 🅂free 🚰🅂Chfree. **Surface:** asphalted. 🔲 01/01-31/12.
**Distance:** 700m 🚲2,2km ⊗on the spot.
**Remarks:** Max. 48h, monitored parking.

### 🅂 Palazuelos de Eresma 30F1
Calle Cordel. **GPS:** n40,92848 w4,05529.⬆️➡️
🚰€ 1 🅂Chfree. 🔲 01/01-31/12.
**Distance:** 🚲4km.

### 🅂 Palencia 29F3
Parque Isla Dos Aguas, Avda. Ponce de León, 12.
**GPS:** n42,00389 w4,53333.⬆️➡️

23 🅂free 🚰🅂Chfree. **Surface:** asphalted. 🔲 01/01-31/12.
**Distance:** on the spot 🚲4km ⊗on the spot 🚊El Arbol 50m 🚐100m.
**Remarks:** Max. 48h.

### Peñafiel 29F3
Calle de Los Destiladeros. **GPS:** n41,59440 w4,11582.⬆️

5 🅂free. **Location:** Rural, simple. **Surface:** asphalted.
🔲 01/01-31/12.
**Distance:** ⊗150m.
**Remarks:** Parking castle.

### 🅂 Peñaflor 32B2
Parking Surrecreo, Urbanizacion Los Rosales Peñaflor.
**GPS:** n41,72777 w0,79194.⬆️➡️
150 🅂€ 15 🚰🅂Ch 🚽WCincluded.
**Distance:** 🚲8km.

### 🅂 Pollos 29E3
Estación de Servicios La Loba 2000, A62, salida 169.
**GPS:** n41,41004 w5,13396.⬆️

10 🅂free 🚰🅂Chfree. **Location:** Motorway, simple.
**Surface:** metalled. 🔲 01/01-31/12.
**Distance:** 🚲200m ⊗on the spot 🚊on the spot.
**Remarks:** At petrol station.

### 🅂 Ponferrada 29D2
Calle Obispo Camilo Lorenzo 2. **GPS:** n42,54388 w6,58623.⬆️

40 🅂free 🚰🅂Ch. **Location:** Urban. **Surface:** asphalted.
🔲 01/01-31/12.
**Distance:** centre 500m ⊗on the spot 🚊on the spot 🚐600m.
**Remarks:** Monitored parking.

**Tourist information Ponferrada:**
ℹ️ Oficina de Turismo, C/ Gil Y Carrasco 4.

### 🅂 Ribaseca 29E2
Area de Léon, Carretera la Bañeza. **GPS:** n42,54439 w5,5882.

20 🛏 € 15-25 🚰 💧 Ch 🔧 WC 🚿 🔌 ≋ included. **Location:** Urban, isolated, noisy. **Surface:** asphalted. ⬛ 01/01-31/12.
**Distance:** 🚶8km ⊗2,3km 🚌800m.
**Remarks:** At motorhome dealer, car rental, motorhome washing place.

### Salamanca 🌿🍽 30E1
**Antiguo Campo De Rugbi. GPS:** n40,95917 w5,67464.
+10 🛏free. **Location:** Noisy. ⬛ 01/01-31/12.
**Distance:** 🚶1km 🛒100m Lidl/Mercadona.
**Remarks:** Next to sports fields.

### Saldaña 29F2
Calle de los Sauces. **GPS:** n42,51882 w4,74125.⬆

6 🛏free 🚰 💧 Chfree.
**Location:** Rural, simple. **Surface:** concrete. ⬛ 01/01-31/12.
**Distance:** 🚶1km ⊗1km.
**Remarks:** Next to sports fields, max. 48h.

### San Agustín ⛰ 33A1
**Alto Mijares**, TE-V-2001. **GPS:** n40,12680 w0,67667.⬆

10 🛏 € 3/pp 🚰 WC ≋included. **Location:** Rural, isolated, quiet.
**Surface:** unpaved. ⬛ 01/01-31/12.
**Remarks:** Max. 6m.

### Sancti-Spiritus 30D1
**Hostal-Restaurante La Ponderosa**, Carretera nacional 620 km303.
**GPS:** n40,73481 w6,36093.

🛏guests free 🚰 💧 ≋.
**Location:** Isolated, quiet. **Surface:** unpaved. ⬛ 01/01-31/12.
**Distance:** 🏍3km ⊗on the spot.

### Santelices 29G2
Diseminado Santelices 12A. **GPS:** n43,00397 w3,73891.⬆
32 🛏free 🚰 € 3 💧Ch 🔧(32x) WC 💧. **Location:** Urban.
**Surface:** metalled. ⬛ 01/01-31/12.
**Distance:** 🚶800m 🛒800m 🚌700m 🔄on the spot 🚶on the spot.

### Segovia 🌿 30F1
Plaza de Toros. **GPS:** n40,94083 w4,10778.⬆
10 🛏free 🚰 💧Chfree.
**Location:** Urban.
**Surface:** metalled.
⬛ 01/01-31/12 ⬛ Sa (market).
**Distance:** 🚶on the spot ⊗600m 🛒500m.
**Remarks:** Near arena, max. 72h.

---

**Tourist information Segovia:**
ℹ Oficina de Turismo, Plaza Mayor, 10. Old city, 800 years before Christ.
🏛🏰 Castillo Alcazar. Medieval castle, museum. 🕐 01/04-30/09 10-19h, 01/10-31/03 10-18h.

### Sepúlveda 🌿 30G1
Calle de el Postiguillo. **GPS:** n41,29897 w3,74479.

10 🛏free. **Surface:** asphalted. ⬛ 01/01-31/12.
**Distance:** 🚶300m 🚲12km ⊗100m.

### Soria 29H3
Monte de las Animas. **GPS:** n41,76769 w2,45391.

🛏free. **Surface:** gravel. ⬛ 01/01-31/12.

### Soria 29H3
**Hypermercado E. Leclerc**, Calle J, P 290. **GPS:** n41,77249 w2,48497.⬆
6 🛏free 🚰 € 2 💧Ch 🔧€ 2 ≋.
**Surface:** asphalted. ⬛ 01/01-31/12.
**Distance:** 🚶1,8km ⊗on the spot 🛒on the spot 🚌on the spot.
**Remarks:** Coins at petrol station.

### Terradillos 30E1
**Area del Encinar**, Paseo de Poniente. **GPS:** n40,88000 w5,58194.⬆
10 🛏free. **Location:** Simple, quiet. **Surface:** asphalted.
**Distance:** ⊗200m.

### Teruel 33A1
**Parking Cuartel**, Calle Tarazona de Aragon. **GPS:** n40,33170 w1,09243.
20 🛏free. **Surface:** asphalted. ⬛ 01/01-31/12.
**Distance:** 🚶110m ⊗300m 🛒50m 🚌on the spot.
**Remarks:** In front of police station.

### Toro 🌿 29E3
**Area de Rumbeolas**, Calle Santa María de la Vega.
**GPS:** n41,51489 w5,39301.
10 🛏 € 4 🚰 💧Chincluded 🔧 € 3.
**Location:** Rural. **Surface:** sand. ⬛ 01/01-31/12.
**Distance:** 🚶1,5km 🏍5,5km 🚶on the spot.

### Trujillo 🌿 30E3
Ronda de le Plaza de Toros. **GPS:** n39,45696 w5,87303.⬆
10 🛏free. **Surface:** asphalted. ⬛ 01/01-31/12.
**Distance:** 🚶centre 800m ⊗100m.

### Turégano 30F1
CL603. **GPS:** n41,15209 w4,0082.⬆

10 🛏free 🚰 💧Chfree.
**Location:** Rural, simple. **Surface:** asphalted. ⬛ 01/01-31/12.
**Distance:** ⊗200m.
**Remarks:** Behind former grain factory, max. 48h.

### Valencia de Alcántara 30C2
**Area de Puerto Roque**, N-521. **GPS:** n39,34104 w7,2775.⬆
10 🛏free 🚰 € 3 💧Ch.
**Location:** Rural. **Surface:** metalled. ⬛ 01/01-31/12.
**Distance:** 🚶9km ⊗on the spot.

---

### Valencia de Don Juan 29E2
**Area de Coyanza**, Calle Tres de Abril. **GPS:** n42,28750 w5,51333.⬆➡

12 🛏free 🚰 💧Chfree. **Location:** Urban, simple. **Surface:** concrete.
⬛ 01/01-31/12.
**Distance:** 🚶500m ⊗300m.
**Remarks:** Max. 48h.

### Valladolid 🌿🍽 29F3
**San Lorenzo**, Av. Ramón Pradera. **GPS:** n41,65583 w4,73722.⬆

15 🛏 € 5/24h 🚰 ≋included.
**Location:** Urban. **Surface:** asphalted. ⬛ 01/01-31/12.
**Distance:** 🚶city centre 1km 🏍3,2km ⊗400m.
**Remarks:** Max. 48h.

### Villacañas 30G3
Calle Juan Pablo II. **GPS:** n39,62101 w3,33188.⬆
2 🛏free. **Surface:** asphalted.
**Distance:** 🚶on the spot ⊗350m.
**Remarks:** Max. 48h.

### Villada 29F3
**C/ San Fructuoso**, Calle del Ferial Nuevo 10.
**GPS:** n42,25533 w4,9649.⬆➡

5 🛏free 🚰 💧Chfree. **Location:** Rural, simple, quiet.
**Surface:** gravel. ⬛ 01/01-31/12.
**Distance:** 🚶200m ⊗200m 🛒200m 🚌on the spot 🚶on the spot.
**Remarks:** Max. 48h, no camping activities.

### Villalpando 29E3
**Area de Servicios Villalpando**, A6, salida 236.
**GPS:** n41,85906 w5,41993.⬆
5 🛏free. **Location:** Motorway, simple, isolated, noisy.
**Surface:** asphalted. ⬛ 01/01-31/12.
**Distance:** 🏍200m ⊗on the spot 🛒on the spot.
**Remarks:** At petrol station.

### Villanueva de la Serena 30E3
Camino San Miguel. **GPS:** n38,97965 w5,78881.⬆
30 🛏free 🚰 💧Chfree.
**Location:** Urban, simple. **Surface:** asphalted. ⬛ 01/01-31/12.
**Distance:** 🚶city centre 1,5km ⊗450m 🛒800m.

### Villanueva del Fresno 31C1
Travesia Huertas 4. **GPS:** n38,37889 w7,16417.
10 🛏free 🚰 💧Ch ≋free.
**Location:** Urban. **Surface:** metalled. ⬛ 01/01-31/12.
**Distance:** 🚶on the spot ⊗200m 🛒600m.
**Remarks:** Max. 48h.

### Villaquirán de los Infantes 29G3
**Petrovicma**, N-620a. **GPS:** n42,22015 w3,99922.

ES

10 🏠free 🚰🔌ChWC 🚿. **Location:** Rural, quiet.
**Surface:** asphalted. ☐ 01/01-31/12.
**Distance:** ⊗100m 🏔100m 🚌300m.

### Viso del Marqués — 31F1

Calle Feria. **GPS:** n38,52709 w3,56287.
30 🏠free 🚰Ch..
**Location:** Urban. **Surface:** asphalted. ☐ 01/01-31/12.
**Distance:** 🚶400m ⊗650m.
**Remarks:** At sports grounds, max. 48h, tuesday market.

### Zafra — 31D1

Ctra. de los Santos de Maimona, Ex101. **GPS:** n38,42527 w6,41083. ⬆

30 🏠free 🚰🔋Chfree. **Location:** Urban, central, noisy.
**Surface:** asphalted. ☐ 01/01-31/12.
**Distance:** 🚶on the spot ⊗on the spot 🚌on the spot.

### Zamora — 29E3

Estadio Barrio 3 Arboles, Calle de los Pisones.
**GPS:** n41,50337 w5,75585.

18 🏠free. **Location:** Urban, simple, central. **Surface:** asphalted.
☐ 01/01-31/12.
**Distance:** 🚶1km ⊗1km.
**Remarks:** Playground.

# Andalusia

### Abla — 31G2

Area de Abla, A-92A. **GPS:** n37,14455 w2,77347. ⬆
7 🏠free 🚰🔋Chfree. **Surface:** asphalted. ☐ 01/01-31/12.
**Distance:** 🚶on the spot ⚓1,5km ⊗100m 🚌300m.
**Remarks:** Max. 48h.

### Abla — 31G2

Area de Montagón, Carretera ALP-503.
**GPS:** n37,15415 w2,77716. ⬆➡

13 🏠free 🚰🔋Chfree. **Location:** Rural, simple, quiet.
**Surface:** asphalted. ☐ 01/01-31/12.
**Distance:** 🚶1,5km ⚓2km ⊗1,5km 🚌1,5km.
**Remarks:** Next to football ground, max. 48h.

### Alanís — 31D1

Area de Alanís de la Sierra, Alameda del Parral.
**GPS:** n38,03729 w5,71057. ⬆
5 🏠free 🚰🔋Chfree.

---

**Location:** Urban, simple. **Surface:** metalled. ☐ 01/01-31/12.
**Distance:** 🚶on the spot ⊗200m 🚌280m.
**Remarks:** Max. 72h.

### Alcalá de Guadaíra — 31D2

Autocaravanas Hidalgo, A92 Sevilla><Malaga km 7.
**GPS:** n37,32856 w5,8056.

18 🏠€ 10 🚰€ 0,50 🔋Ch 🔌included 🚿. ☐ 01/01-31/12.
**Distance:** 🛣170m exit 15.
**Remarks:** Motorhome dealer, max. 24h.

### Alcázar de San Juan — 30G3

Area de Alcazar de San Juan. **GPS:** n39,38972 w3,21944.
10 🏠free 🚰🔋Ch. **Surface:** asphalted. ☐ 01/01-31/12.
**Distance:** 🚶on the spot ⊗150m 🚌300m.

### Algar — 31D3

Complejo Tajo del Aguila. **GPS:** n36,65111 w5,66555. ⬆
8 🏠€ 20 🚰🔋Ch 🔌 WC included.
**Location:** Rural. **Surface:** unpaved. ☐ 01/01-31/12.
**Distance:** ⊗1km 🚌on the spot 🚶on the spot.
**Remarks:** Max. 7 nights.

### Alicún de las Torres — 31G2

GR6104. **GPS:** n37,50836 w3,10802.

3 🏠free. **Surface:** metalled. ☐ 01/01-31/12.
**Distance:** 🚶100m ⊗100m.
**Remarks:** Next to the spa resort.

### Almayate — 31F3

Area AMG, Carretera Nacional 340, km 266,5.
**GPS:** n36,72372 w4,13999. ⬆

40 🏠€ 10 🚰🔋Ch 🔌🚿included. 🚻
**Location:** Rural, simple. **Surface:** gravel. ☐ 01/01-31/12.
**Distance:** 🚶700m 🏔100m ⊗100m 🚌2km 🚌200m.
**Remarks:** At motorhome dealer, max. 24h.

### Almensilla — 31D2

San Diego, A-8054. **GPS:** n37,31354 w6,09317.
15 🏠free 🚰🔋Chfree. ☐ 01/01-31/12.
**Distance:** ⊗on the spot.
**Remarks:** At petrol station BP and restaurant, restaurant visit
appreciated.

### Almerimar — 31G3

Parking Almerimar, Avenida del Mar. **GPS:** n36,70803 w2,80895.

---

136 🏠€ 8 🚰€ 1/100liter ..Ch 🔌🚿€ 3/24h WC 🗑🚿. 🚻
**Location:** Urban. **Surface:** metalled. ☐ 01/01-31/12.
**Distance:** 🚶city centre ± 1km 🏔100m ⊗50m 🚌1km.

### Almerimar — 31G3

Area del Puerto Deportivo Almerimar, Torre del puerto.
**GPS:** n36,69612 w2,79425. ⬆

20 🏠€ 12,69 🚰🔋Ch 🔌€ 3,15Amp WC included 🚿€ 3,50/24h.
**Location:** Urban, simple. **Surface:** metalled. ☐ 01/01-31/12.
**Distance:** 🏊on the spot ⊗100m 🚌300m 🏔100m 🚌100m.
**Remarks:** Check in at harbourmaster 9-14h, 16-21h.

### Antequera — 31E2

Area de Antequera, Calle Miguel de Cervantes.
**GPS:** n37,02139 w4,57191. ⬆

12 🏠free 🚰🔋Chfree. **Location:** Urban, simple, noisy.
**Surface:** asphalted. ☐ 01/01-31/12.
**Distance:** 🚶on the spot ⚓6,5km ⊗50m 🚌500m.
**Remarks:** Next to football ground.

### Archidona — 31E2

A7200. **GPS:** n37,09097 w4,38879. ⬆

12 🏠free 🔋Chfree. **Location:** Rural, simple, noisy.
**Surface:** concrete. ☐ 01/01-31/12.
**Distance:** 🚶250m 🏔1km 🚌500m 🚌1km 🚶on the spot.
**Remarks:** Max. 2 days.

### Arcos de la Frontera — 31D3

Hostal Rural Mesón la Plata. **GPS:** n36,75402 w5,78204. ⬆
10 🏠€ 10 🚰🔋Ch 🔌🚿€ 5 🚌€ 2 🚿included. 🚰
**Location:** Rural, comfortable, isolated, quiet, **Surface:** gravel.
☐ 01/01-31/12.
**Distance:** 🚶3km ⊗on the spot.
**Remarks:** Check in at reception, video surveillance.

**Tourist information Arcos de la Frontera:**
ℹ Oficina de Turismo, Plaza del Cabildo, 1, www.ayuntamientoarcos.
org. Old city with historical centre.

### Ayamonte — 31C2

Autocaravanas Puerto de Ayamonte, Calle Madrid.
**GPS:** n37,21082 w7,40541.
27 🏠€ 12,50 🚰€ 3 🔋Ch 🔌€ 2/24h WC 🗑🏠 **Location:** Urban,
comfortable. **Surface:** asphalted. ☐ 01/01-31/12.
**Distance:** 🚶on the spot 🏊on the spot ⊗200m 🚌400m 🚶on the
spot 🚶on the spot.

### Baena — 31F2

Área de Baena, Camino del Juncal. **GPS:** n37,62486 w4,32198.
8 🏠free 🔋Chfree. **Surface:** unpaved. ☐ 01/01-31/12.
**Distance:** 🚶historical centre 600m.
**Remarks:** No camping activities.

### Baeza — 31F1

Calle Manuel Acero. **GPS:** n37,99679 w3,45923. ⬆
30 🏠free 🚰🔋Chfree. **Surface:** sand. ☐ 01/01-31/12.
**Distance:** 🚶1km 🚌500m 🚌bakery.

**Remarks:** Max. 96h, no camping activities.

### Barbate — 31D3
**Autocaravanas Puerto de Barbate**, Avenida del Mar, s/n..
**GPS:** n36,18355 w5,93533.
36 ⬛€ 12,50 €3 Ch 2,50/24h WC
**Location:** Rural, comfortable, quiet. **Surface:** asphalted.
01/01-31/12.
**Distance:** 1,5km 1,5km on the spot on the spot.

### Benarrabá — 31E3
**Area Autocaravanas Benarrabá**, Carretera Comarcal MA-538.
**GPS:** n36,54935 w5,27901.
5 free Chfree. **Surface:** concrete. 01/01-31/12.
**Distance:** 500m 600m.

### Cabo de Gata — 31H3
**Cabo de Gata Camper Park**, Carrertera de San José.
**GPS:** n36,81639 w2,14918.

50 €7-10 (50x)€ 3/24h WC € 3,50/3,50 included.
**Location:** Rural, comfortable, isolated. **Surface:** gravel.
01/01-31/12.
**Distance:** 5km 7km 7km on the spot 5km on the spot
on the spot on the spot.
**Remarks:** Service passerby € 3, bicycle rental.

### Cabra — 31F2
**Area de Cabra II**, Calle de la Libertad. **GPS:** n37,47602 w4,44271.

8 free Chfree. **Location:** Urban. **Surface:** asphalted.
01/01-31/12 Mo 07-13h.
**Distance:** 600m 200m 150m 220m.

### Cabra — 31F2
**Auditorio Municipal Alcalde Juan Muños**, Juanita la Larga.
**GPS:** n37,46608 w4,42361.

4 free Chfree. **Location:** Urban, simple, quiet.
**Surface:** asphalted. 01/01-31/12.
**Distance:** 500m 300m 500m.
**Remarks:** Max. 48h.

### Cala de Mijas — 31E3
Av. del Mediterraneo. **GPS:** n36,50496 w4,68344.

50 free. **Location:** Urban, simple. **Surface:** sand.
01/01-31/12.
**Distance:** 500m 500m 800m 50m 100m 50m.

### Caleta de Vélez — 31F3
**Remarks:** Market Wednesday and Saturday.

**Autocaravanas Puerto de Caleta de Vélez**, Calle Miguel Ariza.
**GPS:** n36,74852 w4,06549.
33 €12,50 €3 Ch 0,50.
**Surface:** asphalted. 01/01-31/12.
**Distance:** on the spot on the spot 200m Aldi 1km.
**Remarks:** Golf court 2km.

### Canjáyar — 31G3
**Paraje de la Alcoholera**, A-348. **GPS:** n37,01400 w2,74523.

7 free Chfree. **Location:** Rural, simple, quiet.
**Surface:** asphalted/metalled. 01/01-31/12.
**Distance:** 1km 450m.
**Remarks:** At tennis-courts.

### Carboneras — 31H3
**El Rancho**, Paraje De La Hoyca, ALP-711. **GPS:** n37,00371 w1,91127.

40 €11 €5 Ch €3 WC € 1 € 3,50 included.
**Location:** Rural. **Surface:** grassy/gravel. 01/01-31/12.
**Distance:** 2km 2,4km Mercadona 2km.

### Casares — 31E3
Carretera M528. **GPS:** n36,44611 w5,27833.
10 free Chfree. **Location:** Rural.
**Surface:** gravel/metalled. 01/01-31/12.
**Distance:** 1,5km 1,5km 1km.
**Remarks:** Max. 48h.

### Castell de Ferro — 31F3
**Area Autocaravanas Tropic**, 2 Carretera de Malaga.
**GPS:** n36,72005 w3,36465.

60 €10 Ch WC € 1 included.
**Location:** Urban, comfortable, central, quiet.
**Surface:** unpaved.
01/01-31/12.
**Distance:** sea 1,5km on the spot 300m.
**Remarks:** Bread-service.

**Tourist information Castell de Ferro:**
Coastal town with former Arab fortress in the centre.
Week market. Sa.

### Chipiona — 31D2
**Autocaravanas Puerto de Chipiona**, Av. Rocío Jurado, s/n..
**GPS:** n36,74404 w6,42635.
63 €12,50 €3 Ch €2,50 WC
**Location:** Urban, central. **Surface:** gravel/sand. 01/01-31/12.
**Distance:** on the spot on the spot 300m 800m on the
spot on the spot.

### Conil de la Frontera — 31D3
Avda. del Rio. **GPS:** n36,27282 w6,08994.

20 free. **Surface:** asphalted. 01/01-31/12.
**Distance:** on the spot 500m 500m.
**Remarks:** Parking along coast road.

### Córdoba — 31E1
**Área del Centro Histórico**, Avda. de los Custodios.
**GPS:** n37,87528 w4,78778.
30 €11 Ch. **Location:** Noisy. **Surface:** asphalted/gravel.
01/01-31/12.
**Distance:** historical centre 300m 2,3km.
**Remarks:** In front of police station.

**Tourist information Córdoba:**
Museo Municipal Taurino, Plaza de las Bulas. Museum about bull-fighting. Tue-Fri 8.30-20.45h, Sa 8.30-16.30h, Su 8.30-14.30h Mo. € 4.
Torre de la Calahorra. Urban museum. 10-14, 16.30-20.30. € 4,50.
Oficina de Turismo, Torrijos, 10 (Plaza del Triunfo), www.cordoba-turismo.es. Historical and culturally rich city, city of the flamenco and bull-fighting.
Palacio del Marqués de Viana. Palace with collections of leather, silverware, porcelain etc. Mo-Sa 10-19h, Su 10-15h. € 8.
Mezquita. World-famous Moorish mosque. 10-18/19u.

### Cuevas de San Marcos — 31F2
**GPS:** n37,26059 w4,40237.

15 free free. **Location:** Rural, simple, isolated.
**Surface:** asphalted. 01/01-31/12.
**Distance:** 1km 500m 1km.
**Remarks:** Parking at swimming pool.

### Cuevas del Almanzora — 31H2
Barriada Palomares. **GPS:** n37,23241 w1,79701.
10 free. **Surface:** metalled. 01/01-31/12.
**Distance:** 1,8km on the spot on the spot.

### Cullar — 31G2
**Venta de Peral. GPS:** n37,55351 w2,60862.

20 free Ch WC free.
**Location:** Motorway. **Surface:** asphalted. 01/01-31/12.
**Distance:** 3km 300m.
**Remarks:** Video surveillance.

### Dólar — 31G2
**Area de Venta de Dólar**, A92. **GPS:** n37,19521 w2,98397.

ES

30 ⚏free 🚰🔌Chfree. **Location:** Motorway, simple.
**Surface:** metalled. 🅾 01/01-31/12.
**Distance:** 🚰2km 🚻50m ⊗on the spot.
**Remarks:** At petrol station.

**Doña Mencía** 🌿 `31F2`

**Área de Esparcimiento Dona Mencia**, Antigua Estación de Ferrocarril.
**GPS:** n37,54656 w4,35237.⬆

7⚏free 🚰free. **Location:** Rural, comfortable, quiet. **Surface:** gravel.
🅾 01/01-31/12.
**Distance:** 🚰500m ⊗La Cantina 🍴1,5km 🚲on the spot.
**Remarks:** Bicycle rental.

**Dos Hermanas** `31D2`

**Multiparking La Jabega**, Carretera SE 9024. **GPS:** n37,21278 w5,96389.

50 ⚏€10 🚰🔌Ch ⚡€3 WC▯◉€4 〰included.
**Location:** Rural, isolated, quiet. **Surface:** concrete.
🅾 01/01-31/12.
**Distance:** 🚰city centre Sevilla 18km ⊗2km.
**Remarks:** Video surveillance.

**Dos Hermanas** `31D2`

**Rubiales**, Calle Pasadilla de Barranco. **GPS:** n37,31030 w5,9584.⬆
20 ⚏€12 🚰🔌Chincluded ⚡€3.
**Surface:** gravel. 🅾 01/01-31/12.
**Distance:** 🚰Sevilla 10km 🚌> Sevilla 100m.

**El Bosque** `31D3`

Calle de Juan Ramón Jiménez. **GPS:** n36,75670 w5,51056.

5 ⚏free 🚰🔌Chfree. **Surface:** metalled. 🅾 01/01-31/12.
**Distance:** 🚰on the spot ⊗100m 🍴300m.

**El Higuerón** `31E1`

**Peter Pan**, Avenida Principal. **GPS:** n37,87107 w4,85465.⬆
10 ⚏€6 🚰€3 🔌Ch. **Surface:** concrete. 🅾 01/01-31/12.
**Distance:** 🚰Córdoba 7km ⊗on the spot 🍴450m, Mercadona 2km
🚌line 54 > Córdoba.

**El Puerto de Santa Maria** `31D3`

**Parking Pasarela**, Av. de Europa. **GPS:** n36,59840 w6,2212.⬆

---

50 ⚏€6. **Location:** Urban, simple. **Surface:** asphalted.
🅾 01/01-31/12.
**Distance:** 🚰500m ⊗200m Burgerking 🍴300m 🚌200m.

**El Real de la Jara** `31D1`

Avenida Aguablanca. **GPS:** n37,95089 w6.⬆
8 ⚏free 🚰🔌Ch ⚡. **Surface:** asphalted. 🅾 01/01-31/12.
**Distance:** 🚰on the spot ⊗300m.
**Remarks:** Max. 48h.

**Frailes** `31F2`

Calle Mecedero. **GPS:** n37,48848 w3,8308.⬆
10 ⚏free 🚰🔌Ch. **Surface:** metalled. 🅾 01/01-31/12.
**Distance:** 🚰500m ⊗500m.
**Remarks:** Max. 48h.

**Fuengirola** `31E3`

Calle Recinto Ferial. **GPS:** n36,54843 w4,61998.
+20 ⚏free. 🅾 01/01-31/12.
**Distance:** 🚰on the spot 🏊300m ⊗100m 🍴100m.

**Fuengirola** `31E3`

**Ristorante El Rengo**, Calle Tramo de Unión.
**GPS:** n36,53229 w4,63844.⬆
15 ⚏€4,50 🚰🔌Chincluded ⚡€5.
**Surface:** gravel/sand.
🅾 01/01-31/12.
**Distance:** 🚰2,5km 🏊1,6km ⊗on the spot 🍴Centro comercial 1km.

**Gelves** `31D2`

**Puerto Gelves**, Calle de Puerto Gelves. **GPS:** n37,33934 w6,02405.⬆

20 ⚏€ 12,10-16, >8,5m € 17,70-23 🚰🔌Ch ⚡€2,80
WC▯◉€3,50/time 〰included. 🚉 **Location:** Urban, comfortable.
**Surface:** asphalted. 🅾 01/01-31/12.
**Distance:** 🚰on the spot 🚲4,3km ⊗on the spot 🍴500m 🚌on the
spot.
**Remarks:** Monitored parking, Sevilla 10km, good bus connection.

**Granada** 🌿🚡 `31F2`

**Área de Geysepark-Cármenes**, Torre de Comares.
**GPS:** n37,15136 w3,59533.⬆

100 ⚏€18/day 🚰🔌ChService €5 ⚡€2/48h. 🚿
**Location:** Urban, simple. **Surface:** asphalted.
🅾 01/01-31/12.
**Distance:** 🚰200m 🚲2km ⊗200m 🍴200m 🚌200m.
**Remarks:** Covered parking, entrance motorhomes 2nd ramp, max.
^3.10m, advice: pre-order entrance tickets Alhambra.

**Granada** 🌿🚡 `31F2`

**Alhambra**, P5. **GPS:** n37,17168 w3,57974.⬆

---

50 ⚏€ 53/24h, 01/10-01/05 € 29/24h.
**Location:** Rural, simple. **Surface:** gravel.
🅾 01/01-31/12.
**Distance:** 🚰1,5km ⊗200m 🍴200m 🚌100m.

**Tourist information Granada:**

👁 Alhambra. Most important curiosity of the city, the best kept Arab
palace. 🅾 9-20h, winter, Sa 20-22h, Su 9-18h, summer Tue,Thu, Sa
22-24h.

👁 Cuevas del Sacromonte. Caves in Sacromonte mountain, gypsies
previously lived here. Now important tourist attraction and stage of
flamenco shows.

👁 El Albaicín. Moorish district facing the Alhambra.

**Grazalema** `31E3`

Calle Juan de la Rosa. **GPS:** n36,75807 w5,36365.

4 ⚏free. **Surface:** asphalted. 🅾 01/01-31/12.
**Distance:** 🚰300m ⊗200m 🍴500m.

**Huelva** 🚩 `31C2`

**Monumento a Colón**, Avenida Francesco Montenegro.
**GPS:** n37,21333 w6,93972.

15 ⚏free. **Surface:** asphalted. 🅾 01/01-31/12.
**Distance:** 🚰6km 🚻50m ⊗on the spot 🍴6km 🚌500m.

**Huércal-Overa** 🌿🏖 `31H2`

**Travesía de la Alameda. GPS:** n37,39823 w1,94672.⬆➡

10 ⚏free 🚰€ 0,50/100liter 🔌Ch. **Location:** Urban, simple.
**Surface:** metalled. 🅾 01/01-31/12 ◉ Mo 09-14h, market.
**Distance:** 🚰200m ⊗200m 🍴200m 🚲on the spot 🚶on the spot.
**Remarks:** Max. 72h, coins at El Pabellon Municipal.

**Isla Cristina** `31C2`

**Camper Park Playas de Luz**, Barriada la Estación s/n, Pozo del Camino.
**GPS:** n37,22190 w7,32336.⬆

---

70 ⬛€ 10 ⬛⬛Ch ✎€ 3,50/day WC ⬛€ 1/5minutes ⬛€ 4,50/3,50 ⬛included. ⬛⬛
**Location:** Comfortable. **Surface:** gravel. ⬛ 01/01-31/12.
**Distance:** ✈4km 🚂3km 🚏50m ⬛50m ⬛100m 🚌100m 🏊on the spot 🛒on the spot.

### ⬛S Jerez de la Frontera 31D3
**La Morada del Sur**, Avda. Tío Pepe, 21. **GPS:** n36,71298 w6,10965.
20 ⬛€ 15 ⬛⬛Ch ✎WC ⬛included ⬛⬛. **Location:** Urban.
**Surface:** metalled. ⬛ 01/01-31/12.
**Distance:** ⬛4km ⬛on the spot ⬛1km.

### ⬛S Júzcar 31E3
Av. Havaral. **GPS:** n36,62823 w5,172.
4 ⬛free ⬛⬛free. **Location:** Rural. **Surface:** grassy/metalled.
⬛ 01/01-31/12.
**Distance:** ⬛300m ⊗400m ⬛400m.

### ⬛ La Isleta 31H3
**Playa del Pénom blanca**, Carreta Noria. **GPS:** n36,81670 w2,05146. ⬆

15 ⬛free. **Location:** Rural, simple. **Surface:** gravel.
**Distance:** ⬛100m ⬛sandy beach 20m ⊗150m ⬛300m.
**Remarks:** Parking at sea.

### ⬛ La Línea de Concepción 31D3
Av. Principe de Asturias. **GPS:** n36,15583 w5,34553.

50 ⬛€ 1/h, € 15/24h. **Surface:** metalled. ⬛ 01/01-31/12.
**Distance:** ⬛500m ⬛1km ⬛200m ⬛1km.
**Remarks:** Market Wednesday.

### ⬛S La Línea de Concepción 31D3
**Area de Alcaidesa Marina**, Av. Principe de Asturias.
**GPS:** n36,15528 w5,35389. ⬆

60 ⬛€ 12 ⬛⬛Ch ⬛included. ⬛
**Surface:** metalled. ⬛ 01/01-31/12.
**Distance:** ⊗on the spot ⬛on the spot.
**Remarks:** Video surveillance.

### ⬛S Las Pajanosas 31D2
**Puerta de Sevilla**, C/Concepción Soto. **GPS:** n37,57683 w6,1058. ⬆

20 ⬛€ 3 ⬛⬛€ 3 Ch 3 ✎€ 3 WC ⬛included. ⬛
**Location:** Central, quiet. **Surface:** asphalted.
⬛ 01/01-31/12 ⬛ 01/08-01/09.
**Distance:** ⬛50m ⊗50m ⬛50m 🏊on the spot 🛒on the spot.

### ⬛S Lora del Río 31E2
Calle Olivo 2. **GPS:** n37,65858 w5,51909.
20 ⬛free ⬛⬛Chfree. **Surface:** asphalted. ⬛ 01/01-31/12.
**Distance:** ⬛700m ⬛200m.
**Remarks:** Max. 48h, playground.

### ⬛S Los Albaricoques 31H3
**Camper Park Olivares**, Cortijo Jurado. **GPS:** n36,84813 w2,118. ⬆
25 ⬛€ 10 ⬛⬛Ch ✎WC ⬛€ 3,50 ⬛included. ⬛⬛⬛
**Location:** Comfortable, isolated, quiet. **Surface:** gravel.
⬛ 01/01-31/12.
**Distance:** ⬛500m ⬛15km ⊗500m ⬛500m 🏊on the spot 🛒on the spot 🚲150m ⬛150m.

### ⬛S Málaga ⬛⬛⬛ 31F3
**Area Malaga Beach**, Crta.MA-24 Diseminado R 10,44 entrada Cala del Moral. **GPS:** n36,71320 w4,31691.

200 ⬛€ 10 ⬛⬛Chincluded ✎(46x)€ 3/24h WC ⬛€ 3/stay ⬛€ 1 ⬛free. **Location:** Rural, simple, quiet. **Surface:** grassy/gravel.
⬛ 01/01-31/12.
**Distance:** ⬛on the spot ⬛50m 🚏50m ⊗on the spot ⬛400m 🏊on the spot 🛒on the spot.
**Remarks:** 24/24 surveillance.

**Tourist information Málaga:**
⬛ Oficina de Turismo, Pasaje de Chinitas, 1, www.andalucia.org. Old sparkling port city with fine beaches.
⬛⬛ Alcazaba. Moorish castle complex with archeological museum.
⬛ Museo casa natal de Pablo Picasso, Plaza de la Merced. House where the painter was born. ⬛ Mo-Sa 10-20h ⬛ Su-afternoon.
⬛ Palacio de los Condes de Buena Vista, Calle San Agustin, 6. Art-historical museum.
⬛ ⬛ Su.

### ⬛S Marchena 31E2
Calle Sevilla s/n. **GPS:** n37,33083 w5,42416. ⬆

20 ⬛free ⬛⬛Chfree.
**Location:** Rural. **Surface:** metalled. ⬛ 01/01-31/12.
**Distance:** ⬛1km ⬛450m ⬛350m 🚉station 600m.

### ⬛S Montilla 31E2
**Área de El Coto**, Paseo de Cervantes, 8. **GPS:** n37,58763 w4,63432. ⬆
7 ⬛free ⬛⬛Chfree. **Surface:** asphalted. ⬛ 01/01-31/12.
**Distance:** ⬛500m ⬛450m.
**Remarks:** Max. 48h, no camping activities, beautiful view.

### ⬛S Olvera 31E2
Vía Verde de la Sierra. **GPS:** n36,94138 w5,25305. ⬆
4 ⬛€ 7 ⬛⬛Ch ✎ included. **Location:** Rural, isolated, quiet.
**Surface:** asphalted. ⬛ 01/01-31/12.
**Distance:** ⬛1km.

### ⬛S Palma del Río 31E2
Calle de la Bombilla s/n. **GPS:** n37,69222 w5,28361.
10 ⬛free ⬛⬛Chfree.
**Location:** Urban. **Surface:** unpaved. ⬛ 01/01-31/12.
**Distance:** ⬛500m.
**Remarks:** Max. 48h.

### ⬛S Peñarroya-Pueblonuevo 31E1
**El Pantano. GPS:** n38,27694 w5,27722. ⬆

20 ⬛€ 7 ⬛⬛ChService € 1,50 ✎€ 2 ⬛included.
**Location:** Comfortable, isolated, quiet.
⬛ 01/01-31/12.
**Distance:** ⬛4km ⬛lake 🚏on the spot 🏊on the spot 🛒on the spot.
**Remarks:** Direct access to the lake, motorhome washing place € 1, swimming pool.

### ⬛S Priego de Córdoba ⬛ 31F2
**Parque Niceto Alcalá - Zamora**, Calle del Carrusel s/n.
**GPS:** n37,44361 w4,21186. ⬆

10 ⬛free ⬛⬛Chfree. **Location:** Urban, simple. **Surface:** concrete.
⬛ 01/01-31/12.
**Distance:** ⬛500m ⊗500m ⬛500m.
**Remarks:** Max. 48h.

**Tourist information Priego de Córdoba:**
⬛ Iglesia de la Aurora.

### ⬛S Ronda ⬛ 31E3
Calle Torero Francisco Romero. **GPS:** n36,75188 w5,14793. ⬆

60 ⬛€ 10 ⬛⬛Ch ✎€ 4/24h.
**Location:** Urban, quiet. **Surface:** grassy.
⬛ 01/01-31/12.
**Distance:** ⊗100m.

**Tourist information Ronda:**
⬛ Oficina de Turismo, Plaza de España, 9, www.andalucia.org. Impressive historic town, inspiration of many famous writers.
⬛ El Mercadillo. Plaza de Toros, the cradle of the bull-fighting.

### ⬛S Rute 31F2
Calle de Jésus Obrero. **GPS:** n37,33113 w4,37323. ⬆➡

6 ⬛free ⬛⬛Chfree.
**Location:** Rural, simple. **Surface:** asphalted.
**Distance:** ⬛500m ⊗500m ⬛300m.
**Remarks:** Parking next to police station, max. 48h.

ES

## San Juan de los Terreros · 31H2

**Playa de Entrevista**, A332. **GPS**: n37,35083 w1,67972.

>20 free . **Surface**: gravel/sand. 01/01-31/12.
**Distance**: 500m 100m 2km 2,5km.
**Remarks**: Parking beach.

## Sancti Petri La Barrosa · 31D3

Carretera de la Barossa. **GPS**: n36,38612 w6,2053.

20 free. **Surface**: metalled. 01/01-31/12.
**Distance**: 2km 200m 1km 5km.
**Remarks**: Parking beach.

## Sanlúcar de Barrameda · 31D2

**Sanlúcar AC Parking**, Camino de la Reyerta, s/n.
**GPS**: n36,76195 w6,39617.

70 € 8, 01/05-30/06 € 10, 01/07-31/08 € 12 Ch (30x) € 3/day,5Amp WC € 3/3 included. **Location**: Rural, isolated.
**Surface**: grassy. 01/01-31/12.
**Distance**: 4km 100m 100m 300m 350m 400m 500m.
**Remarks**: Discount longer stays.

## Sanlúcar de Guadiana · 31C2

HU4401. **GPS**: n37,47009 w7,464.

15 free Ch. **Location**: Rural. **Surface**: metalled.
01/01-31/12.
**Distance**: 300m 600m 300m 500m on the spot on the spot.

## Sevilla · 31D2

**Area Ac Sevilla Centro**, Carretera de la Esclusa, Seville (Sevilla).
**GPS**: n37,36239 w5,99452.

100 € 12 Ch (40x) € 3 WC € 4,50/4,50 included.

---

**Location**: Urban, central, noisy.
**Surface**: asphalted.
01/01-31/12.
**Distance**: 2km 200m 300m on the spot 200m 200m.
**Remarks**: Possibility for reservation.

## Sevilla · 31D2

**Parking Caravane**, Calle Aeropuerto de San Pablo, Seville (Sevilla).
**GPS**: n37,41050 w5,94072.

50 € 12 Ch included € 3 € 1 .
**Surface**: unpaved. 01/01-31/12.
**Distance**: city centre 8km 2km.

## Sevilla · 31D2

**Parking Las Razas**, Avenida de Las Razas, 41, Seville (Sevilla).
**GPS**: n37,36336 w5,98921.
30 € 10 Ch included € 5 . **Location**: Urban, central, noisy. **Surface**: asphalted. 01/01-31/12.
**Distance**: city centre 3km 100m.

## Sevilla · 31D2

**Parking Puente de los Remedios**, Avenida Presidente Adolfo Suarez, Seville (Sevilla). **GPS**: n37,37235 w5,99444.
+10 € 10 € 5. **Location**: Urban. **Surface**: asphalted.
01/01-31/12.
**Distance**: on the spot 300m 400m 400m.

## Sevilla · 31D2

**Parking Santa Justa**, Avda. de Kansas City, Seville (Sevilla).
**GPS**: n37,39194 w5,97333.
30 € 22/24h.
**Surface**: asphalted. 01/01-31/12.

**Tourist information Seville (Sevilla):**
Alcazar, Plaza del Triumfo.
Italica. Roman ruins, 9 km at north of Sevilla on N630.
Almeda de Hercules. Su-morning.
Parque de los Descubrimientos. Theme park science, in pavilion of Expo 1992. Fri-Su, summer Tue-Thu from 18h 10/01-28/02.
Calle de las Sierpes. Famous shopping street.

## Taberno · 31H2

**Área El Rancho**, Los Llanos (La Carrasquilla), Santopetar.
**GPS**: n37,46028 w2,03833.

8 € 8 Ch (4x) WC included. **Location**: Rural, simple, quiet. **Surface**: gravel. 01/01-31/12 Mo.
**Distance**: 600m 13km on the spot.
**Remarks**: Entrance swimming pool € 2.

## Tarifa · 31D3

**Área de Tarifa**, C/El Lentiscal 29. **GPS**: n36,08776 w5,76566.

70 € 12 Ch included € 5/day .
**Surface**: grassy. 01/01-31/12.
**Distance**: 50m 200m 200m 50m 50m on the spot on the spot.
**Remarks**: Video surveillance.

---

## Tarifa · 31D3

Av. Pintor Guillermo Pérez Villalta. **GPS**: n36,01798 w5,61064.
40 € 8/24h Ch included. **Location**: Simple, central.
**Surface**: sand. 01/01-31/12.
**Distance**: 1km 300m 300m 200m.

## Tarifa · 31D3

**GPS**: n36,06804 w5,6856.

20 free. **Surface**: sand. 01/01-31/12.
**Distance**: 10km on the spot 50m 100m.
**Remarks**: Parking beach.

**Tourist information Tarifa:**
Tourist Office, Duke of Kent House, Cathedral Square, Gibraltar, www.gibraltar.gi. British colony at the northwest end of the Rock of Gibraltar.
Siege Tunnels, Gibraltar. Labyrinth of tunnels, ingenious defence system.

## Torre de Benagalbón · 31F3

**Camper Areas M&H El Rincón**, Cortijo Casillas De Los Rubios.
**GPS**: n36,71658 w4,23799.

35 € 10, Jul/Aug € 12 Ch included € 3/24h WC € 1 € 7,50 € 1/24h. **Location**: Rural, comfortable, quiet.
**Surface**: gravel. 01/01-31/12.
**Distance**: 1km 3km 700m 100m 700m 750m.
**Remarks**: Car rental.

## Úbeda · 31G1

Travesia Commendador Messias. **GPS**: n38,00649 w3,37953.
10 free Ch free. **Surface**: asphalted. 01/01-31/12.
**Distance**: centre 1km 1,8km 250m on the spot on the spot.
**Remarks**: Max. 48h.

## Ubrique · 31D3

Calle La Harana 27, Plaza de las Palmeras. **GPS**: n36,67056 w5,44972.
10 free Ch free.
**Location**: Urban. **Surface**: metalled/sand. 01/01-31/12.
**Distance**: centre 300m on the spot 400m.
**Remarks**: At swimming pool, max. 72h.

## Valverde del Camino · 31C1

Ctra. de Zalamea. **GPS**: n37,58111 w6,75138.

10 free Ch free.
**Surface**: asphalted/sand. 01/01-31/12.
**Distance**: 500m.

## Vejer de la Frontera · 31D3

**Área El Palmar**, Carril del pino. **GPS**: n36,23613 w6,06866.
100 <8m € 12/24h, >8m € 15/24h, trailer € 3 Ch € 3 WC . **Location**: Rural. **Surface**: unpaved.
01/01-31/12.
**Distance**: 500m 250m.

## Vélez-Rubio · 31H2

**Área Puerta Oriental de Andalucía**, Calle Granada.
**GPS**: n37,65194 w2,07555.

10 🛏free 🚰🗑Chfree. **Location:** Rural, simple, quiet.
**Surface:** gravel. 📷 01/01-31/12 ⊙ 1st week Aug.
**Distance:** 🚶500m 🛒 2,2km ⊗500m 🍴500m.
**Remarks:** Max. 48h.

| 🏕 S | Vera | 31H2 |

**Acvera Motorhome Park & Aire**, Camino de Los Pescadores s/n.
**GPS:** n37,26030 w1,85347.⬆

160 🛏€ 10 🚰🗑Ch 🔧(160x)€ 3 WC 📷 📶included.
**Location:** Rural, comfortable. **Surface:** metalled.
📷 01/01-31/12.
**Distance:** 🚶Vera 2km 🛒 4,7km 🏖beach 10km ⊗on the spot.
**Remarks:** Discount longer stays, tennis & padel lessons, 11 tennis
courts.

| 🏕 S | Vera | 31H2 |

**Oasis al Mar**, Avenida del Salar. **GPS:** n37,22731 w1,82819.⬆.

50 🛏€ 10, trailer € 1/day 🚰🗑Ch 🔧€ 3/day 📷€ 3 📶included.
**Location:** Rural, comfortable. **Surface:** gravel. 📷 01/11-01/05.
**Distance:** 🚶centre Vera 4,4km 🏊2km.
**Remarks:** Motorhome washing place € 4.

| 🏕 S | Villanueva de Algaidas 🏞 | 31E2 |

Calle de la Archidona, A-7201. **GPS:** n37,17810 w4,45021.⬆.
20 🛏free 🚰🗑Chfree. **Location:** Rural, simple. **Surface:** asphalted.
📷 01/01-31/12.
**Distance:** 🚶500m ⊗50m.
**Remarks:** Max. 48h.

ES

# Finland

Capital: Helsinki
Government: parliamentary constitutional republic
Official Language: Finnish and Swedish
Population: 5,518,371 (2017)
Area: 336,855 km²

## General information
Dialling code: 0358
General emergency: 112
Currency: Euro
Credit cards are accepted almost everywhere.

## Regulations for overnight stays
Wild camping is in general allowed in the National Parks, on private land with permission of the owner.

## Additional public holidays 2019
January 6 Epiphany
April 19 Good Friday
April 22 Easter Monday
May 1 Labour Day
June 21 Midsummer Eve
June 22 Midsummer
November 1 All Saints'Day
December 6 Independence Day

## Time Zone
Winter (Standard Time) GMT+2
Summer (DST) GMT+3

Lapland
page: 375

Rovaniemi

Oulu
pages: 374-375

Oulu

Eastern Finland
page: 374

Western Finland
pages: 373-374

Southern Finland
pages: 372-373

Helsinki

## Southern Finland

### Hamina 4F2
**Aallokko Caravan**, Helsingintie. **GPS:** n60,56039 e27,18280.

20 €10 + €2,50/pp Chincluded €3/24h.
**Location:** Rural, simple, quiet. **Surface:** gravel.
01/04-31/10.
**Distance:** 1km on the spot on the spot 1km.
**Remarks:** Use of sauna against payment.

### Helsinki 4F3
Mustikkanaantie / Blåbärslandsvägen. **GPS:** n60,18240 e24,99173.

10 free. **Location:** Rural, simple. **Surface:** asphalted.
01/01-31/12.
**Distance:** 5,5km 1km on the spot on the spot on the spot 100m.

### Imatra 4F2
**ABC Imatra**, Tiedonkatu 2. **GPS:** n61,18466 e28,73800.

20 €5 Ch included at restaurant.
**Location:** Simple, noisy. **Surface:** asphalted.
**Distance:** 3km on the spot on the spot on the spot.

### Jyväskylä 4E2
Vespuolentie 674. **GPS:** n61,99235 e25,67093.

10 free. **Location:** Rural, simple, quiet. **Surface:** asphalted.
01/01-31/12.
**Distance:** 10km on the spot on the spot.

### Karjaa 4E3
**ABC Karjaa**, Lepinpellonkatu 2. **GPS:** n60,05489 e23,64809.

4 €5 Ch included WC free.
**Location:** Rural, simple. **Surface:** asphalted.
01/01-31/12.
**Distance:** 2km on the spot on the spot on the spot 10km.

### Kortela 4E3
**ABC Rauma Kortela**, Unajantie 2. **GPS:** n61,09888 e21,50387.

10 €5 Chincluded €5/24h. **Location:** Motorway, simple, noisy. **Surface:** asphalted. 01/01-31/12.
**Distance:** 3,5km on the spot on the spot.

### Lepaa 4E2
**Kyläkauppa Pikkuakka**, Tyrvännöntie 576.
**GPS:** n61,11587 e24,34537.

12 €20 Ch WCincluded. **Location:** Rural, simple, quiet.
**Surface:** grassy. 01/01-31/12.
**Distance:** 7km 1km 1km on the spot on the spot.

### Liikkala 4F2
**Onnelan Tila**, Hakalantie 37. **GPS:** n60,70986 e27,01708.

2 ⌁€ 20 ⚡ ⚒ included. **Location:** Rural, simple, isolated, quiet.
**Surface:** grassy. ◻ 01/01-31/12.
**Distance:** ⚓2km ⚓2km.

### ⬛⬛S Parikkala 4F2
Tukkikuja. **GPS:** n61,55592 e29,49803.⬆.

6 ⌁free ⚒€ 10. **Location:** Urban, simple, quiet. **Surface:** asphalted.
◻ 01/01-31/12.
**Distance:** ⚓300m ⚓on the spot ⚓on the spot ⊗300m ⚓300m.
**Remarks:** At harbour.

### ⬛⬛S Särkisalmi 4F2
**Oronmyllyn Toimintakeskus**, Oronmyllyntie 250.
**GPS:** n61,62059 e29,37868.⬆➡.

12 ⌁€ 10 ⚒(4x)€ 10/24h WC⬛. ⚒ **Location:** Rural, simple,
isolated, quiet. **Surface:** grassy. ◻ 01/01-31/12.
**Distance:** ⚓7km ⚓100m ⚓100m.

### ⬛⬛S Savonlinna 4F2
Punkaharjuntie. **GPS:** n61,86686 e28,89861.⬆.
6 ⌁free ⚒. **Location:** Urban, simple, noisy. **Surface:** asphalted.
◻ 01/01-31/12.
**Distance:** ⚓on the spot ⊗100m ⚓1km.

### ⬛⬛S Ylämaa 4F2
**Korupirtti Oy Ravintola**, Kikikylantie 7. **GPS:** n60,79054 e28,01026.

5 ⌁free ⚒€ 1/time. **Location:** Rural, simple, quiet. **Surface:** gravel.
◻ 01/01-31/12.
**Distance:** ⚓1km ⚒on the spot ⊗on the spot.
**Remarks:** At museum.

# Western Finland

### ⬛⬛S Björköby 4D2
**Svedjehamn**, Björköntie 1014. **GPS:** n63,35974 e21,29995.⬆.
15 ⌁€ 4 WCincluded. **Location:** Rural, isolated, quiet.
**Surface:** unpaved. ◻ 01/05-31/10.
**Distance:** ⚓3km ⚓on the spot ⚓on the spot ⊗on the spot.

### ⬛⬛ Hanhikoski 4E2
**Maatilamatkailu Koivusalo**, Vanhatie 386.
**GPS:** n62,96175 e22,77427.➡.

3 ⌁€ 20 ⚓ ⚒ WCincluded. ⚒ **Location:** Rural, simple, quiet.
**Surface:** grassy/gravel. ◻ 01/01-31/12.
**Distance:** ⚓4km ⊗200m.

**Remarks:** Sauna € 10.

### ⬛⬛S Hattu 4G1
**Arhipan Pirtti**. **GPS:** n62,92948 e31,28065.⬆.
⌁€ 14 ⚓ ⚒€ 4 WC ⚒. **Location:** Rural, isolated.
**Distance:** ⚓300m ⚓on the spot.

### ⬛⬛S Huittinen 4E2
**ABC Huittinen**, Loimijoentie 89. **GPS:** n61,16713 e22,68061.⬆.

7 ⌁€ 5 ⚓ ⚒Ch. ⚒ ⚒included ⚒. ⚒ ⚒ **Location:** Urban, simple.
**Surface:** asphalted. ◻ 01/01-31/12.
**Distance:** ⚓1km ⚓1km ⊗on the spot ⚓on the spot.

### ⬛ Ikaalinen 4E2
**Ikaalisten Kylpylä Rantasipi**, Hämyläntie 2.
**GPS:** n61,77586 e23,01928.⬆.

20 ⌁€ 12 ⚒included WC. ⚒ ⚒ **Location:** Rural, simple, quiet.
**Surface:** asphalted. ◻ 01/01-31/12.
**Distance:** ⚓3km ⚓on the spot ⚓on the spot ⊗on the spot.

### ⬛⬛S Ilmarinen 4E3
**Ilmaristen Matkailutila**, Väänteläntie 45.
**GPS:** n60,49801 e22,37492.⬆➡.

6 ⌁€ 15 ⚓ ⚒(4x)€ 5/24h WC⬛€ 2 ⚒included. ⚒ ⚒
**Location:** Rural, simple, quiet. **Surface:** gravel.
◻ 01/01-31/12.
**Distance:** ⚓2km ⊗2km ⚓1,5km ⚓700m.

### ⬛⬛ Kangasala 4E2
**Mobilan Auto Kylä**, Kustaa Kolmannen tie 75.
**GPS:** n61,44124 e24,12997.⬆➡.

5 ⌁free. **Location:** Rural, simple, quiet. **Surface:** asphalted.
◻ 01/01-31/12.
**Distance:** ⚓6km ⚓100m ⚓100m.
**Remarks:** At museum.

### ⬛⬛S Keitele 4E1
**Matkailukeskus Lossisaari**, Sininentie 205.
**GPS:** n63,18941 e26,34270.⬆.

5 ⌁€ 23 ⚓ ⚒Ch. ⚒WC⬛included ⚒at restaurant.
**Location:** Rural, comfortable, quiet. **Surface:** grassy/gravel.
◻ 01/01-31/12.
**Distance:** ⚓1,5km ⚓on the spot ⚓on the spot ⊗on the spot
⚓1,5km.
**Remarks:** Behind petrol station, bread-service.

### ⬛ Killinkoski 4E2
**Killinkosken Kyläyhdistys**, Inkantie 60. **GPS:** n62,40382 e23,89105.⬆.

5 ⌁free ⚒free. **Location:** Rural, simple, quiet. **Surface:** grassy.
◻ 01/01-31/12.
**Distance:** ⚓on the spot ⚓on the spot ⚓400m.

### ⬛ Lempäälä 4E2
**Kärppälän Rustholli**, Kärppäläntie 50. **GPS:** n61,33448 e23,67716.➡.

8 ⌁€ 25 ⚒WC⬛included. ⚒ **Location:** Rural. **Surface:** grassy.
◻ 01/01-31/12.
**Distance:** ⚓6km ⚓100m ⚓100m.

### ⬛⬛S Mieto 4E2
**Hakunin kotieläintila**, Hakunintie 193.
**GPS:** n62,57169 e22,26394.⬆➡.

2 ⌁€ 10 ⚓ ⚒ ⚒included. ⚒ **Location:** Rural, simple, isolated,
quiet. **Surface:** grassy/gravel. ◻ 01/01-31/12.
**Distance:** ⚓2km.
**Remarks:** Sauna € 10.

### ⬛⬛S Nokia 4E2
**ABC Nokia Kolmenkulma**, Rounionkatu 140.
**GPS:** n61,50143 e23,56800.⬆➡.

10 ⌁€ 5 ⚓ ⚒Chincluded ⚒(10x)€ 5/24h ⚒. ⚒ ⚒
**Location:** Motorway, simple, noisy. **Surface:** asphalted.
◻ 01/01-31/12.

**Distance:** 2km on the spot on the spot on the spot.

## Pyhäjärvi  4E1
**Vaskikello Klokkenmuseum**, Vaskikellontie 420.
**GPS:** n63,71402 e25,91985.

5 free free WC. **Location:** Motorway, simple, quiet.
**Surface:** asphalted.
**Distance:** 4km on the spot 200m.

## Tuuri  4E2
**Kyläkaupan Onnela Karavaanarialue**, Onnelantie 45.
**GPS:** n62,60595 e23,71426.

243 € 20 Ch € 5 WC included. **Location:** Rural,
luxurious, quiet. **Surface:** asphalted. 01/01-31/12.
**Distance:** 300m 300m.
**Remarks:** Swimming pool and sauna on site.

## Vaajakoski  4E2
**ABC Vaajakoski**, Vaajakoskentie 850. **GPS:** n62,22871 e25,90290.

10 € 5 Ch included € 5/24h at restaurant
**Location:** Motorway, noisy. **Surface:** asphalted. 01/01-31/12.
**Distance:** on the spot on the spot on the spot.

## Vaasa  4D2
**ABC Kiitokaari Vaasa**, Kiitokaari 2. **GPS:** n63,05239 e21,71773.

20 € 5 Ch included € 5/24h at restaurant.
**Location:** Motorway, simple, noisy. **Surface:** asphalted.
01/01-31/12.
**Distance:** 8km on the spot on the spot on the spot.

## Viitasaari  4E1
**ABC Viitasaari**, Kokkosalmentie 78. **GPS:** n63,07527 e25,86618.

4 € 10 Ch (4x)included. **Location:** Motorway,
simple. **Surface:** asphalted. 01/01-31/12.

**374**

---

**Distance:** 1km on the spot on the spot on the spot on
the spot on the spot.

## Ylönkylä  4E3
**Katiskanmäki**, Särkisalontie 2. **GPS:** n60,16479 e22,99639.

30 € 6 + € 5/pp Ch € 5 WC included
**Location:** Rural, simple, quiet. **Surface:** gravel.
01/01-31/12.
**Distance:** 8km 5km 5km on the spot 8km.

# Eastern Finland

## Heinävesi  4F2
**Heinäveden satama**, Kermarannantie 48.
**GPS:** n62,43835 e28,63796.

4 € 10 included WC. **Location:** Rural, simple, quiet.
**Surface:** asphalted. 01/01-31/12.
**Distance:** 2km on the spot.

## Iisalmi  4F1
Untamonkatu 6. **GPS:** n63,56465 e27,19025.

10 free. **Location:** Urban. **Surface:** asphalted. 01/01-31/12.
**Distance:** on the spot 800m 250m 250m.
**Remarks:** At gymnasium.

## Iisalmi  4F1
Luuniemenkatu 11. **GPS:** n63,55102 e27,18841.

10 free. **Location:** Urban, simple, quiet. **Surface:** gravel.
01/01-31/12.
**Distance:** 2km 100m 100m 500m 500m.

## Ilomantsi  4F1
**Hyvinvointikeskus Toivonlahti**, Henrikintie 4.
**GPS:** n62,67684 e30,91145.
12 € 10.
**Distance:** on the spot on the spot 200m.

## Jongunjoki  4F1
**Eräkeskus Wilderness Lodge Oy**, Alakylä 15.
**GPS:** n63,52483 e30,03822.

---

5 € 8 + € 4/pp Ch included € 4/24h.
**Location:** Rural, simple, isolated, quiet. **Surface:** grassy/sand.
01/01-31/12.
**Distance:** 3km on the spot on the spot on the spot on
the spot.

## Karhunpää  4F1
**Laitalan Lomat**, Laitalantie 85. **GPS:** n63,61440 e28,86089.

10 € 12 € 2/day WC included. **Location:** Rural, quiet.
**Surface:** grassy/gravel. 01/01-31/12.
**Distance:** 9km on the spot on the spot on the spot.
**Remarks:** Sauna € 10.

## Lieksa  4F1
**ABC Lieksa**, Kalliokatu 8. **GPS:** n63,32240 e30,00854.
guests free Ch.
**Surface:** asphalted. 01/01-31/12.
**Distance:** on the spot.

## Rantasalmi  4F2
**Hotelli Rinssi-Eversti**, Ohitustie 5. **GPS:** n62,06390 e28,30890.

6 € 10 Ch included (6x)€ 5/24h WC at restaurant at
restaurant at restaurant. **Location:** Rural, simple, quiet.
**Surface:** asphalted. 01/01-31/12.
**Distance:** 300m 100m 100m on the spot 500m.
**Remarks:** Use of sauna against payment.

## Sulkava  4F2
Alanteentie. **GPS:** n61,78528 e28,37769.

5 € 14 Ch WC included. **Location:** Urban, quiet.
**Surface:** asphalted. 01/01-31/12.
**Distance:** 500m on the spot on the spot 100m 500m.

# Oulu

## Kontiomäki  4F1
**Neste Kontiomäki**, Viitostie 2. **GPS:** n64,31988 e28,04344.
20 € 6 WC included. **Location:** Motorway, isolated, quiet.
**Surface:** asphalted. 01/01-31/12.
**Distance:** on the spot on the spot on the spot.
**Remarks:** At petrol station.

## Puolanka  3D3
**Pororajan Majoitus**, Pudasjärventie 1. **GPS:** n64,87494 e27,64344.
8 € 15 € 5 WC. **Location:** Rural, simple, quiet.

**Surface:** asphalted. ⬛ 01/01-31/12.
**Distance:** 🚲1km ⊗1km 🛒1km ♒on the spot.

| 📷 S | **Sanginkylä** | | 4E1 |

**Valkeisen virkistysalueella**, Puolangantie 207.
**GPS:** n64,86477 e26,74733.
🎫€ 10 🔌€ 2 📶.
**Distance:** ⊘on the spot ♒on the spot.
**Remarks:** Fishing permit available.

| 📷 S | **Siikajoki** | | 4E1 |

**Ruokolahden lava**, Limingantie 197, Paavola.
**GPS:** n64,61267 e25,23947.⬆.
8 🎫free Ch 🔌€ 5 WC🚽€ 15.
**Location:** Rural. **Surface:** gravel. ⬛ 23/05-06/09.
**Distance:** 🚲2km ⊘on the spot ♒on the spot.
**Remarks:** Key at kiosk.

| 🍴 S | **Ylivieska** | | 4E1 |

**Hotelli Käenpesä**, Lintutie 1. **GPS:** n64,06782 e24,52621.
4🎫€ 20 🔌 WC🚽. **Location:** Urban, simple. **Surface:** asphalted.
⬛ 01/01-31/12.
**Distance:** 🚲800m ⊗on the spot.
**Remarks:** Check in at hotel.

# Lapland

| 🍴 S | **Anetjärvi** 🌳 | | 3D3 |

**Aneen Loma**, Anetjärventie 72A. **GPS:** n65,91851 e27,98786.
10 🎫€ 25 🔌 WC🚽📶included. **Location:** Rural, simple, isolated,
quiet. **Surface:** gravel. ⬛ 01/01-31/12.
**Distance:** ⊘on the spot ♒on the spot.
**Remarks:** At the beach, sauna incl..

| 📷 S | **Tanhua** | | 3C2 |

**Tanhuan Erämajat**, Pessijoentie 2. **GPS:** n67,52802 e27,53691.⬆.
10 🎫€ 5 🚰🚽WC🚽. **Location:** Rural, simple, isolated, quiet.
**Surface:** grassy.
**Distance:** ⊗300m 🛒600m.
**Remarks:** Use of sauna against payment.

FI

# 🇫🇷 France

Capital: Paris
Government: Unitary republic
Official Language: French
Population: 66,900,000 (2017)
Area: 551,500 km²

## General information
Dialling code: 0033
General emergency: 112
Currency: Euro
Payments by credit card are accepted almost everywhere, however chip and pin systems are non-compatible with British cards and fuel for example can only be bought at supermarkets during opening hours.

## Regulations for overnight stays
Wild camping is accepted almost everywhere throughout inland France. Special regulations for motor homes you can find on signs by entering the town. It is permitted to stopover at motorway services, be aware that toll roads often issue time constrained tickets.

## Additional public holidays 2019
April 19 Good Friday
May 1 Labor Day
May 8 Liberation Day
July 14 National Holiday
August 15 Assumption of the Virgin Mary
November 1 All Saints Day
November 11 Armistice Day 1918

## Time Zone
Winter (Standard Time) GMT+1
Summer (DST) GMT+2

FR

Lille
**Hauts-de-France**
pages: 376-383

**Normandie**
pages: 400-417

Metz

Paris

**Brittany**
pages: 417-441

**Ile-de-France**
page: 417

**Grand Est**
pages: 383-400

Rennes

**Pays de la Loire**
pages: 441-458

**Centre-Val de Loire**
pages: 458-469

Dijon

**Bourgogne-Franche-Comté**
pages: 469-477

Lyon

**Nouvelle-Aquitaine**
pages: 502-536

Bordeaux

**Auvergne-Rhône-Alpes**
pages: 477-502

**Occitanie**
pages: 536-564

**Provence-Alpes-Côte d'Azur**
pages: 564-575

Montpellier

Marseille

prime meridian

**Andorra**
page: 564

**Corsica**
page: 576

Ajaccio

# Hauts-de-France

### Ambleteuse · 13C2
D940 > Wimereux. **GPS:** n50,80638 e1,61484. ⬆.

15 🅢 € 5. 🚰 **Location:** Rural, simple, quiet. **Surface:** grassy. ⊙ 01/01-29/12.
**Distance:** 🚶750m ⛵1,2km.

### Amiens 🌿🛶 · 15H1
Boulevard Faidherbe. **GPS:** n49,89430 e2,28675. ⬆.
10 🅢free. **Location:** Urban, simple. **Surface:** asphalted.
⊙ 01/01-31/12.
**Distance:** 🚶centre 800m ⊗300m 🚌300m.
**Remarks:** Servicepoint at camping Parc des Cygnes GPS: n49,92103 e2,25973.

### Amiens 🌿🛶 · 15H1
**Parc Moulin Saint-Pierre**, Rue Massey. **GPS:** n49,90001 e2,31072. ⬆.
20 🅢free. **Location:** Urban, simple, quiet. **Surface:** asphalted.
⊙ 01/01-31/12.
**Distance:** 🚶city centre 2km 🚉500m.
**Remarks:** Servicepoint at camping Parc des Cygnes GPS: n49,92103 e2,25973.

### Amiens 🌿🛶 · 15H1
**Parc des Cygnes**, 111, Avenue des Cygnes. **GPS:** n49,92086 e2,25971.
5 🅢 € 13 🚰Chincluded WC 🍴🔌📶.🚰 **Location:** Rural, simple, isolated, quiet. **Surface:** asphalted. ⊙ 01/04-15/10.

**Distance:** 🚶city centre 5km ✈3km 🚌bus 50m.
**Remarks:** Max. 24h.

### Tourist information Amiens:
ℹ️ Office de Tourisme, 23 Place Notre Dame, www.amiens-tourisme.com. Capital of the department Somme.
👁 St.Leu. Picturesque district.
Ⓜ Musée Picardie, 48, rue de la République. Archeology, Middle Ages, Fine art. ⊙ Tue-Su 10-12h, 14-18h.
Zoo d'Amiens, 101, rue du Faubourg de Hem. City-zoo. ⊙ 10-17h, 01/04-30/09 10-18h ⊙ 16/11-31/01.

### Ⓒ🅢 Arques · 13D2
**Parking des 3 etangs**, Rue Michelet. **GPS:** n50,74551 e2,30459. ⬆➡.

30 🅢 € 3,50 🚰 € 1,50 🅢Ch🅣 € 1,50. 🚰 **Location:** Urban, simple, quiet. **Surface:** gravel. ⊙ 01/04-31/10.
**Distance:** 🚶2km 🚉100m.
**Remarks:** Behind camp site Beauséjour.

### Ⓒ🅢 Arras 🌿🚰🛒 · 13D3
Rue des Rosati. **GPS:** n50,29463 e2,78812. ⬆.

10 🅢free 🚰 € 2/100liter 🅢Ch🅣 € 2/h. **Location:** Urban, simple, quiet. **Surface:** asphalted. ⊙ 01/01-31/12.
**Distance:** 🚶700m ⊗500m.
**Remarks:** Max. 48h.

### Tourist information Arras:
👁 Hôtel de Ville. Town hall in Gothic style. Also guided tours of the subterranean passages of Arras.
⛲ ⊙ Wed, Sa.

### Ⓒ🅢 Avion · 13D3
Rue de la Cité Saint-Antoine. **GPS:** n50,41519 e2,83093. ⬆.
6 🅢free 🚰 € 3/30minutes 🅢Ch➕ € 3/30minutes 📶free.
**Location:** Urban, simple. **Surface:** metalled. ⊙ 01/01-31/12.
**Distance:** 🚶on the spot ⊗100m 🚉150m.
**Remarks:** Max. 48h.

### Bailleul · 13D2
Rue du Collège. **GPS:** n50,74010 e2,73170. ⬆.

20 ⛺free. **Location:** Urban, simple, quiet. **Surface:** asphalted.
◻ 01/01-31/12.
**Distance:** 700m 2,8km.
**Remarks:** At commemorative monument.

**S** | Banteux | 11A3

Rue du port. **GPS:** n50,06259 e3,20106. ⬆➡.

6 ⛺€ 5 ChWC (8x)included. **Location:** Rural, simple, quiet.
**Surface:** grassy/gravel.
◻ 01/01-31/12 ◻ service 01/11-31/03.
**Distance:** 500m 2,5km 20m on the spot on the spot.
**Remarks:** Baker every morning.

**S** | Bapaume | 13D3

Avenue Abel Guidet. **GPS:** n50,10133 e2,85045. ⬆➡.

2 ⛺free € 2 ChWC. **Location:** Urban, central.
**Surface:** metalled. ◻ 01/01-31/12.
**Distance:** 300m 300m.
**Remarks:** Coins at tourist info, town hall and bakery.

**S** | Bavay | 11B3

Chemin de Ronde. **GPS:** n50,30004 e3,79551. ➡.
10 ⛺free Chfree. **Location:** Urban, simple, quiet.
**Surface:** gravel. ◻ 01/01-31/12.
**Distance:** 200m 200m 100m.
**Remarks:** Max. 72h.

**S** | Beautor | 16A1

Rue du Port. **GPS:** n49,66083 e3,34927. ⬆.

3 ⛺free € 2 Ch € 2/h WC. **Location:** Urban, simple, quiet.
**Surface:** asphalted. ◻ 01/01-31/12.
**Distance:** 500m 50m 200m.
**Remarks:** Along river, max. 48h.

**S** | Beauvais | 15G2

**Parking St. Quentin**, Avenue Nelson Mandela.
**GPS:** n49,43160 e2,07038. ⬆.

20 ⛺free WC. **Location:** Urban, simple, noisy. **Surface:** asphalted.
◻ 01/01-31/12.
**Distance:** 1km 200m 100m.
**Remarks:** Max. 72h, video surveillance.

**S** | Bellicourt | 11A3

**Hameau de Riqueval**, D1044. **GPS:** n49,95156 e3,23519. ⬆➡.

4 ⛺free € 4 Ch € 4. **Location:** Rural, comfortable.
**Surface:** asphalted. ◻ 01/01-31/12 ◻ service: 01/10-31/03.
**Distance:** 300m on the spot on the spot.
**Remarks:** At museum, max. 48h, coins at tourist info.

**S** | Berck-sur-Mer | 13C3

**Les Sternes**, Chemin aux Raisins. **GPS:** n50,39701 e1,56431. ⬆➡.

80 ⛺€ 10 Chincluded. **Location:** Urban, simple, quiet.
**Surface:** gravel. ◻ 01/01-31/12.
**Distance:** 1,5km 100m 1,3km.
**Remarks:** Baker every morning.

**S** | Berck-sur-Mer | 13C3

**Parking Terminus**, Rue Dr. Calot, Berck-Nord.
**GPS:** n50,42361 e1,56750. ⬆.

40 ⛺€ 10 Chincluded. **Location:** Urban, simple, noisy.
**Surface:** gravel. ◻ 01/01-31/12.
**Distance:** 2,5km beach 200m 2,2km.
**Remarks:** Beach parking.

**S** | Berck-sur-Mer | 13C3

**Chez Mireille**, Chemin Genty. **GPS:** n50,41654 e1,57696. ⬆➡.

80 ⛺€ 9 € 1 Ch (4x)€ 2 WC free. **Location:** Rural,
simple, quiet. **Surface:** grassy. ◻ 01/04-31/10.
**Distance:** 600m 800m on the spot.
**Remarks:** To be paid at bar.

**S** | Bergues | 13D2

**Parking Stade J. Andries**, Rue Maurice Cornette.
**GPS:** n50,96543 e2,43596. ⬆➡.

49 ⛺free. **Location:** Urban, simple, quiet. **Surface:** gravel.
◻ 01/01-31/12.
**Distance:** 500m 2,2km.
**Remarks:** Behind football ground, max. 48h.

**S** | Bertry | 11A3

8 Rue Victor Hugo. **GPS:** n50,09092 e3,44829. ⬆.

5 ⛺free Ch. **Location:** Rural, simple, noisy. **Surface:** gravel.
◻ 01/01-31/12.
**Distance:** on the spot 500m 700m.
**Remarks:** At station, max. 72h.

**S** | Blérancourt | 16A1

Avenue de la Libération. **GPS:** n49,51285 e3,14996. ⬆.

6 ⛺free Chfree. **Location:** Rural, simple, quiet.
**Surface:** gravel. ◻ 01/01-31/12.
**Distance:** 500m 750m.

**S** | Boulogne-sur-Mer | 13C2

**Parking Moulin Wibert**, Boulevard Sainte Beuve, D940.
**GPS:** n50,74308 e1,59688. ⬆.

40 ⛺first 48h € 7, € 9/24h € 4/10minutes Ch. 
**Location:** Rural, simple, isolated, quiet. **Surface:** metalled.
◻ 01/01-31/12.
**Distance:** centre 2,5km 5,5km on the spot on the spot.

**S** | Boulogne-sur-Mer | 13C2

Boulevard Chanzy. **GPS:** n50,72194 e1,60027. ⬆.

FR

20 ⓩfree. **Location:** Simple. **Surface:** asphalted.
🅿 01/01-31/12.
**Distance:** 🚋500m ⛵4,5km 🛒300m 🚌300m.
**Remarks:** Nearby casino.
**Tourist information Boulogne-sur-Mer:**
🛈 Boulevard Clocheville. 🅿 Wed-morning.
🛈 place Dalton, centre. 🅿 Wed + Sa morning.
🛈 place Vignon. 🅿 Su-morning.

### Bourseville 13C3
Lotissement le Village. **GPS:** n50,10350 e1,52702. ⬆️➡️.

35 ⓩ€5 🚰€2/10minutes ⚡Ch 🔌€3 WC 🚽♿.
**Location:** Isolated, quiet. **Surface:** asphalted. 🅿 01/01-31/12.
**Distance:** 🚋500m ⛵3km ⊗500m 🛒500m.

### Boussois 11B3
Rue du Rivage. **GPS:** n50,28845 e4,04544.⬆️.

4 ⓩfree 🚰⚡Ch 🔌free2h. **Location:** Rural, simple, quiet.
**Surface:** gravel. 🅿 01/01-31/12.
**Distance:** 🚋1km ⊗50m 🛒50m 🛒500m 🚶on the spot.
**Remarks:** Along Sambre River.

### Bray-Dunes 13D2
Carrefour Market Bray Dunes, Rue Pierre Decock.
**GPS:** n51,06275 e2,52162.⬆️.

6 ⓩfree 🚰€2/10minutes ⚡Ch 🔌€2/h WC.
**Location:** Rural, simple, isolated, noisy. **Surface:** grasstiles.
🅿 01/01-31/12.
**Distance:** 🚋2km ⊗50m 🛒on the spot.
**Remarks:** At supermarket Carrefour, only overnight stays 20-8.30h.

### Bruyères-et-Montberault 16A1
Avenue de Verdun. **GPS:** n49,52538 e3,66080.⬆️.

4 ⓩfree. **Location:** Urban, simple, quiet. **Surface:** asphalted.
🅿 01/01-31/12.
**Distance:** 🚋100m ⊗100m 🛒200m.

### Calais 13C2
Flot Bleu Park, Rue d'Asfeld. **GPS:** n50,95961 e1,83277.⬆️.

100 ⓩ€10/24h 🔌€2,only 2-euro coins ⚡Ch 🚐 📦
**Location:** Urban, comfortable. **Surface:** asphalted. 🅿 01/01-31/12.
**Distance:** 🚋1,5km ⛵plage de Calais 600m.
**Tourist information Calais:**
Ⓜ Centre d'Information Eurotunnel. Exhibition about the Channel tunnel.
🛈 🅿 Wed, Thu, Sa.

### Cassel 13D2
Route d'Oxelaere, C301. **GPS:** n50,79328 e2,48852.⬆️➡️.

5 ⓩfree 🚰€2 ⚡Ch 🔌€2. **Location:** Rural, isolated, quiet.
**Surface:** gravel. 🅿 01/01-31/12.
**Distance:** 🚋1km.
**Remarks:** At sports park, coins at tourist info.

### Catillon-sur-Sambre 11A3
Avenue de la Groise, N43. **GPS:** n50,07624 e3,64615.⬆️.

4 ⓩ€5 🚰⚡Ch 🔌included. 🛒 **Location:** Rural.
**Surface:** asphalted. 🅿 01/01-31/12.
**Distance:** 🚋200m 🛒on the spot.
**Remarks:** At the canal, max. 72h.

### Catillon-sur-Sambre 11A3
Rue de la Gare. **GPS:** n50,07699 e3,64404.⬆️.

20 ⓩfree.
**Location:** Rural, simple. **Surface:** gravel. 🅿 01/01-31/12.
**Distance:** 🚋500m 🛒on the spot.
**Remarks:** At the canal, baker every morning.

### Caudry 11A3
Rue de Cambrai. **GPS:** n50,12471 e3,40322.
6 ⓩ€5 🚰🔌 . **Location:** Urban, simple. **Surface:** asphalted.
🅿 01/01-31/12.
**Distance:** ⊗700m.
**Remarks:** Max. 72h.

### Cayeux-sur-Mer 13C3
Aire de camping-cars Les Galets de la Mollière, Rue Faidherbe.
**GPS:** n50,20300 e1,52612.⬆️➡️.

30 ⓩ€7 🚰€3 ⚡Ch 🔌€3 . **Location:** Rural, simple, isolated.
**Surface:** gravel. 🅿 01/05-01/11.
**Distance:** 🚋2km ⛵At the sea, no beach ⊗2km 🛒2km.
**Remarks:** Max. 24h, to be paid at campsite.

### Cayeux-sur-Mer 13C3
Route blanche, Le Hourdel, D102. **GPS:** n50,21448 e1,55208.➡️.

30 ⓩfree. **Location:** Rural, simple, isolated, quiet. **Surface:** gravel.
🅿 01/01-31/12.
**Distance:** 🚋500m, Cayeux 6km ⛵sea 50m 🛒500m 🛒3km.

### Château-Thierry 16A2
Aire de Château, Avenue d'Essômes. **GPS:** n49,03657 e3,38365.⬆️➡️.

13 ⓩ€7,50 + €0,22/pp tourist tax 🚰⚡Ch 🔌€4/24h WC included
 🚐 📦 **Location:** Urban, comfortable. **Surface:** asphalted.
🅿 01/01-31/12.
**Distance:** 🚋city centre 2km ⛵on the spot 🛒on the spot ⊗on the spot 🛒on the spot 🛒on the spot 🚶on the spot.
**Remarks:** Along the Marne river.

### Chavignon 16A1
Le domaine de ZAZA, La Fontaine Dubois.
**GPS:** n49,47941 e3,53396.⬆️.

5 ⓩ€6 🚰⚡Ch 🔌included 💧 €3/48h. **Location:** Simple.
**Surface:** gravel. 🅿 01/01-31/12.
**Distance:** 🚋2km ⛵2km 🛒on the spot.
**Remarks:** Check in at museum.

### Comines 11A2
Ferme Hélicicole, Chemin de l'Apothicaire. **GPS:** n50,74190 e3,02322.

6 ⓩ€5 🚰€2/10minutes ⚡Ch 🔌€3/24h. 🛒 **Surface:** gravel.
🅿 01/01-31/12.
**Distance:** 🚋3,5km 🛒on the spot 🚶on the spot.

**Remarks:** Max. 48h.

### Conty 15G1
Rue du Marais. **GPS:** n49,74333 e2,15583. ⬆.

70 ⌇free ⛽€3/100liter ⬛Ch WC 🔧. **Location:** Urban, simple, quiet. **Surface:** grassy. ◯ 01/01-31/12.
**Distance:** 🚶200m. 🚲6,5km 🛒300m ⊗300m 🏪300m.
**Remarks:** Coins at tourist info, town hall and bakery.

### Coquelles 13C2
**Cité Europe**, Boulevard du Kent. **GPS:** n50,93250 e1,81110. ⬆.

20 ⌇free. **Location:** Urban, simple. **Surface:** asphalted.
◯ 01/01-31/12.
**Distance:** ⊗on the spot 🏪on the spot.

### Coucy-le-Château-Auffrique 🌿🌿 16A1
Chemin du Val Serain. **GPS:** n49,52037 e3,31150. ⬆➡.

6 ⌇€5 ⛽ ⬛Ch 🔧 WC included. 🏪 **Location:** Rural, comfortable.
**Surface:** gravel. ◯ 01/01-31/12.
**Distance:** 🚶500m ⊗on the spot 🏪500m.
**Remarks:** Castle 1km.

### Crespin 11B3
Rue du Vivier. **GPS:** n50,41950 e3,66274. ⬆➡.

3 ⌇free ⛽€2 ⬛Ch. **Location:** Urban, simple. **Surface:** asphalted.
◯ 01/01-31/12.
**Distance:** 🚲2km.
**Remarks:** At cemetery, coins at town hall.

### Doullens 13D3
Rue du Pont à l'Avoine, N25-Arras-Amiens. **GPS:** n50,15390 e2,34260. ⬆.

4 ⌇free ⛽€2 ⬛Ch. **Location:** Urban, simple, noisy.
**Surface:** asphalted. ◯ 01/01-31/12.
**Distance:** 🚶500m 🏪200m.

### Embry 13C2
**Les Salons de l'Embryenne**, D108. **GPS:** n50,49534 e1,96610. ⬆➡.

8 ⌇€7 ⛽€3 ⬛Ch 🔧€3/1h WC ⬛€3/12minutes 🔧🔧. **Location:** Rural, isolated, quiet. **Surface:** gravel.
◯ 01/01-31/12.
**Distance:** 🚶300m.
**Remarks:** Bread-service, video surveillance, picnic and barbecue place.

### Enquin-les-Mines 13D2
**La Ferme des Templiers de Flechinelle**, 2 Rue des Templiers, Fléchinelle. **GPS:** n50,58175 e2,30505.

4 ⌇€7 ⛽€2 ⬛Ch 🔧included 🔧. **Surface:** gravel.
◯ 01/01-31/12.
**Distance:** ⊗on the spot.

### Equihen-Plage 🏖 13C2
**Plage de la Crevasse**, Rue du Beurre Fondu.
**GPS:** n50,67993 e1,56830. ⬆➡.

20 ⌇€8/24h ⛽€3/10minutes ⬛Ch 🔧(8x)€3/4h 🔧🏪🔧. **Location:** Comfortable, quiet. **Surface:** grassy/gravel.
◯ 01/01-31/12.
**Distance:** 🚶100m 🏊100m 🏪100m 🏪100m.

### Esquelbecq 13D2
**Parking de la Chenaie**, Rue d'Arneke. **GPS:** n50,88395 e2,43119. ⬆.
8 ⌇free ⛽€3/100liter ⬛Ch 🔧€3/1h. **Surface:** asphalted.
◯ 01/01-31/12.
**Distance:** 🚶200m 🏪200m.

### Estaires 13D2
Rue Aimé Coupet. **GPS:** n50,64273 e2,72009.

3 ⌇free ⛽€2/10minutes ⬛Ch 🔧€2/1h 🔧(3x)€4/12h. **Location:** Urban, simple, quiet. **Surface:** grasstiles.
◯ 01/01-31/12.
**Distance:** 🚶200m ⊗150m.
**Remarks:** Cash payment.

### Fort Mahon Plage 13C3
**Plage Parking de la Dune**, Rue de la Bistouille.
**GPS:** n50,33833 e1,55611. ⬆.

60 ⌇€10/24h ⛽Ch included. 🏪 🔧 **Surface:** gravel.
◯ 01/01-31/12.
**Distance:** 🚶100m 🏊600m 🏪100m 🏪on the spot 🚶on the spot.
**Remarks:** Tuesday and Friday market.

### Grand-Fort-Philippe 13D2
Rue Maréchal Foch. **GPS:** n51,00249 e2,09718. ⬆➡.

5 ⌇free. **Location:** Rural, quiet. **Surface:** gravel.
◯ 01/01-31/12.
**Distance:** 🚶200m 🏊400m 🚶100m.
**Remarks:** In front of campsite, max. 72h, saturday-morning fishmarket.

### Grandvilliers 15G1
Place de la Censé. **GPS:** n49,66536 e1,93576. ⬆.
3 ⌇free ⛽€2/10minutes ⬛Ch 🔧€1/1h WC free.
**Surface:** asphalted. ◯ 01/01-31/12.
**Distance:** 🚶100m ⊗100m 🏪400m.

### Gravelines ⚓ 13D2
**Parking des Miaules**, Rue des Islandais/Rue du Port.
**GPS:** n50,98766 e2,12232. ⬆.

20 ⌇€7 🔧. 🏪 🔧 **Location:** Rural, simple, quiet. **Surface:** gravel.
◯ 01/01-31/12.
**Distance:** 🚶500m 🚶on the spot ⊗300m.

### Gravelines 13D2
Rue de la Gendarmerie. **GPS:** n50,99342 e2,13177. ⬆➡.
⛽€2/100liter ⬛Ch 🔧.

### Grenay 13D3
Parc Aragon. **GPS:** n50,44823 e2,73838. ⬆.

3 ⌇free ⛽⬛Ch 🔧(2x) 🔧free. **Surface:** gravel/metalled.
◯ 01/01-31/12.
**Distance:** 🚶on the spot 🏪bakery 100m.
**Remarks:** Max. 2 nights.

### Hautmont 11B3
**Yacht Club Hautmont**, Boulevard de l'Ecluse.
**GPS:** n50,25114 e3,91599. ⬆.

5 🏕 € 10 ⚡Ch 🔌 WC 🚿included. **Location:** Urban, comfortable, quiet. **Surface:** grassy. ⬛ 01/01-31/12. **Distance:** 🚂600m 🏊2km 🎣on the spot ⊗600m 🍺600m 🚌200m 🚲on the spot.
**Remarks:** Along Sambre River, check in at harbourmaster, caution key € 20.

| 🏞 S | **Hondschoote** 🌾 | **13D2** |

Impasse Spinnewyn. **GPS:** n50,97628 e2,58033. ⬆➡.

8 🏕free 🔌 € 2/100liter ⚡Ch 🔌 € 2/1h. **Location:** Urban, simple. **Surface:** asphalted. ⬛ 01/01-31/12. **Distance:** 🚂800m ⊗800m 🍺800m 🚌300m 🚲on the spot 🎣on the spot.
**Remarks:** Behind Moulin de la Victoire, coins available, addresses indicated on the spot.

| 🏞 S | **La Calotterie** | **13C2** |

Chemin des Bas Prés. **GPS:** n50,48885 e1,69489.
10 🏕 € 10 🔌 ⚡Ch 🔌included. 🚿 **Location:** Rural, comfortable, quiet. **Surface:** grassy. ⬛ 01/01-31/12. **Distance:** 🏊300m ⊗1km.

| 🏞 | **La Chapelle-Monthodon** | **16A2** |

Rue du Chemin de Chézy. **GPS:** n49,02904 e3,63616. ⬆.

5 🏕free. **Location:** Rural, simple, isolated, quiet. **Surface:** grassy/metalled. ⬛ 01/01-31/12.

| 🏞 | **Landrecies** | **11B3** |

Avenue Dumey. **GPS:** n50,12772 e3,69085. ⬆➡.

4 🏕free. **Location:** Rural, simple. **Surface:** asphalted/grassy. ⬛ 01/01-31/12. **Distance:** 🚂500m 🚲on the spot 🍺200m 🚌100m.
**Remarks:** At the canal.

| 🏞 | **Laôn** 🌾 | **16A1** |

Promenade de la Couloire. **GPS:** n49,56313 e3,62967. ⬆.

---

6 🏕free. **Location:** Urban, simple. **Surface:** asphalted. ⬛ 01/01-31/12. **Distance:** 🚂300m ⊗500m. **Remarks:** Near city wall.

| 🏞 | **Laôn** 🌾 | **16A1** |

Rue du Maréchal Alphonse Juin. **GPS:** n49,55665 e3,61411. ⬆.

6 🏕free. **Location:** Urban, simple. **Surface:** asphalted. ⬛ 01/01-31/12. **Distance:** 🚂2km 🎣on the spot. **Remarks:** Medieval village.

| 🏞 S | **Le Crotoy** ⛱ 🌊 | **13C3** |

**Camping-Car Park le Tarteron,** Route de Rue. **GPS:** n50,22972 e1,64128. ⬆.

25 🏕 € 8,80, 01/07-31/08 € 10 🔌 ⚡Ch 🔌 (4x) 🚿included. 🚐 🎫 **Location:** Noisy. **Surface:** gravel. ⬛ 01/01-31/12. **Distance:** 🚂2km 🏊2km 🎣2km. **Remarks:** Mandatory, one-time fee Pass'Etapes € 4.

| 🏞 S | **Le Crotoy** ⛱ 🌊 | **13C3** |

**Aire du Marais,** Chemin du Marais. **GPS:** n50,22855 e1,61222. ⬆.

35 🏕 € 7/24h 🔌 € 2/10minutes ⚡Ch 🔌 € 2/1h. 🚐 **Surface:** grassy/gravel. ⬛ 01/01-31/12. **Distance:** 🚂1,5km 🏊on the spot ⊗1,5km 🧺Laverie Crotelloise, 20, avenue du Gal de Gaulle 🚲on the spot 🎣on the spot. **Remarks:** Max. 24h.

| 🏞 S | **Le Crotoy** ⛱ 🌊 | **13C3** |

**Bassin des Chasses.** **GPS:** n50,21800 e1,63300. ⬆.

100 🏕 € 7/24h 🔌 € 2/100liter ⚡Ch 🔌 € 2/1h. 🚐 🎫 **Location:** Simple. **Surface:** sand. ⬛ 01/01-31/12. **Distance:** 🚂100m 🏊800m ⊗400m 🧺Laverie Crotelloise, 20, avenue

---

du Gal de Gaulle 🚲on the spot 🎣on the spot. **Remarks:** Steam train Baie de Somme.

| 🏞 S | **Le Nouvion-en-Thiérache** 🍴 | **11B3** |

Allée du S/l François d'Orléans. **GPS:** n50,00542 e3,78078. ⬆.

5 🏕free 🔌 € 3 ⚡Ch 🔌 € 3/h. **Location:** Rural, simple. **Surface:** asphalted. ⬛ 01/01-31/12. **Distance:** 🚂2km 🚲on the spot ⊗on the spot 🍺1km 🚲on the spot 🎣on the spot. **Remarks:** Max. 72h, coins at campsite.

| 🏞 S | **Le Portel** | **13C2** |

Rue des Champs. **GPS:** n50,71188 e1,57485. ⬆➡.

40 🏕 € 3, 01/06-30/09 € 5 🔌 € 2/10minutes ⚡Ch 🔌 € 2/4h 🎫 🚐 🚿 **Surface:** metalled. ⬛ 01/01-31/12. **Distance:** 🚂200m 🏊300m ⊗300m 🍺300m. **Remarks:** Next to sports fields, 300m from beach (stairs), friday market.

| 🏞 S | **Le Touquet-Paris Plage** ⛱ 🍦 🍴 🌊 | **13C2** |

**Parc International de la Canoke,** Boulevard de la Canche. **GPS:** n50,52648 e1,59869. ⬆➡.

200 🏕 € 10/24h 🔌 € 2/100liter ⚡Ch 🔌 € 2/55minutes. **Surface:** grassy/gravel. ⬛ 01/01-31/12. **Distance:** 🚂on the spot 🏊on the spot ⊗on the spot 🍺on the spot 🚌on the spot.

| 🏞 ⛪ S | **Le Touquet-Paris Plage** ⛱ 🍦 🍴 🌊 | **13C2** |

**Centre Nautique du Touquet Base Nord,** Avenue Jean Ruet. **GPS:** n50,53588 e1,59285. ⬆➡.

60 🏕 € 15/24h 🔌 € 2/100liter ⚡Ch 🔌 € 2/55minutes. 🚐 **Surface:** asphalted. ⬛ 01/01-31/12. **Distance:** 🚂on the spot 🏊on the spot ⊗on the spot 🍺on the spot 🚌on the spot.

**Tourist information Le Touquet-Paris Plage:**
Aqualud. Leisure pool park. ⬛ 15/02-30/11 10-18h.

| 🏞 S | **Le-Cateau-Cambrésis** 🌳 | **11A3** |

Avenue du Maréchal Leclerc, N43. **GPS:** n50,10197 e3,55491. ⬆.

5 ⛺free ⛽🚰Ch 🚿(4x)free. **Location:** Urban, simple, noisy.
**Surface:** asphalted. ⬛ 01/01-31/12.
**Distance:** 🚶1km 🛒250m.

### 🅿S Lens 13D3

**Stade Bollaert-Delelis P6**, Rue Maurice Fréchet.
**GPS:** n50,43192 e2,82057.⬆.

6 ⛺free ⛽€3 🚰Ch ▬ 🚿. **Location:** Simple. **Surface:** asphalted.
⬛ 01/01-31/12.
**Distance:** 🚶500m ⊗McDonalds 🛒1km 🚌on the spot.
**Remarks:** Max. 24h.

### 🅿S Long 13C3

**Camping Municipal La Peupleraie**, Rue de la Chasse à Vaches.
**GPS:** n50,03457 e1,98313.

8 ⛺€5 ⛽€2/150liter 🚰Ch 🚿€2/h WC🚽 📶. **Location:** Rural,
comfortable, quiet. **Surface:** grassy/gravel. ⬛ 01/01-31/12
🅿 service: 16/10-30/04.
**Distance:** ⛵on the spot 🚌on the spot.

### 🏕S Longfossé 13C2

**Ferme du Louvet**, 5, Route de Wierre, D52 Desvres > Samer.
**GPS:** n50,64667 e1,79062.⬆➡.

8 ⛺€14 ⛽🚰Ch🚿included. **Location:** Rural, isolated, quiet.
**Surface:** gravel. ⬛ 01/01-31/12.
**Remarks:** Narrow entrance.

### 🏕S Longpont 16A2

Rue Saint-Louis, D17. **GPS:** n49,27395 e3,22129.⬆.

3 ⛺free. **Location:** Rural, simple. **Surface:** gravel. ⬛ 01/01-31/12.
**Distance:** 🚶100m.
**Remarks:** Max. 3 days, abbey 150m.

### 🏕S Luzoir 16B1

**Triperie de Luzoir**, Place de l'Église. **GPS:** n49,92520 e3,96261.⬆🏕.

2 ⛺free. **Location:** Urban, simple. **Surface:** grassy.
⬛ 01/01-31/12.
**Distance:** 🚶100m 🚲8km 🚶Axe vert.
**Remarks:** At cemetery, max. 48h.

### 🏕S Maisnil-lès-Ruitz 🌳 13D3

**Parc d'Olhain**, Rue de Rebreuve. **GPS:** n50,43926 e2,57826.⬆➡.

25 ⛺€9,50 ⛽🚰Ch 🚿€2,10. 📶 🚿 **Location:** Comfortable,
isolated, quiet. **Surface:** gravel. ⬛ 01/01-31/12.
**Remarks:** Recreation park.

### 🏕S Malzy 16B1

**Étangs des Sources**, 16 rue des Marichoux.
**GPS:** n49,90602 e3,72153.⬆.

4 ⛺€5 ⛽€2 🚰€2 Ch€2 🚿€2 WCfree. 🚿 **Location:** Rural,
comfortable, isolated, quiet. **Surface:** gravel.
⬛ 15/03-01/11 🔵 Tue, Wed, Thu.
**Distance:** 🚶8km 🚌on the spot 🚲800m 🚶on the spot.
**Remarks:** Fishing lake (trout).

### 🏕S Marck 13C2

**La Ferme des Aigrettes**, Allée de la Découverte.
**GPS:** n50,95626 e1,92830.⬆➡.

5 ⛺€8 ⛽🚰Ch 🚿included. **Location:** Comfortable, quiet.
**Surface:** asphalted. ⬛ 01/01-31/12.
**Distance:** 🛒250m 🚶on the spot.
**Remarks:** Max. 48h, call for entrance code.

### 🏕S Marcoing 11A3

Place de la Gare. **GPS:** n50,12126 e3,18204.⬆.

6 ⛺free ⛽🚰Ch 🚿(4x). **Location:** Rural, simple.

### 🏕S Merlimont 13C3

Place de la Gare. **GPS:** n50,46026 e1,58053.⬆.

12 ⛺free Chfree. **Location:** Simple. **Surface:** gravel.
⬛ 01/01-31/12.
**Distance:** 🚶on the spot.

### 🏕S Mers-les-Bains 🌊 13C3

Chemin de la Petite Allée. **GPS:** n50,06175 e1,40150.⬆➡.

50 ⛺€7,50 ⛽€2 🚰Ch 🚿included. 📶 🚿 **Location:** Comfortable.
**Surface:** gravel. ⬛ 01/01-31/12.
**Distance:** 🚶1,3km ⛱sandy beach 1,5km 🛒Auchan 600m.

### 🏕S Montreuil-sur-Mer 🌿 13C3

Avenue des Garennes. **GPS:** n50,45944 e1,75939.⬆➡.

8 ⛺free ⛽€2/100liter 🚰Ch 🚿(2x)€2 WCfree.
**Location:** Comfortable. **Surface:** asphalted. ⬛ 01/01-31/12.
**Distance:** 🚶500m ⊗300m 🛒450m 🚲on the spot 🚶on the spot.
**Remarks:** Max. 48h, market Saturday.

### 🏕S Morienval 15H2

Route de Pierrefonds 32. **GPS:** n49,30352 e2,92309.⬆➡.

25 ⛺€8 ⛽€2/100liter 🚰Ch 🚿(21x)€2/day. 🚿 **Location:** Rural,
comfortable, quiet. **Surface:** grassy/gravel.
⬛ 05/04-15/11.
**Distance:** 🚶500m ⊗500m 🛒500m 🚲on the spot 🚶on the spot.
**Remarks:** In case of absence, money in an envelope in mail box.

### 🏕S Neufchâtel-Hardelot 🌊 13C2

Avenue Joseph Lesur. **GPS:** n50,62605 e1,58152.⬆.

10 ⛺free. **Location:** Rural, simple, isolated. **Surface:** gravel.
⬛ 01/01-31/12. **Distance:** ⛱300m ⊗1km 🛒850m.

## Neufchâtel-Hardelot 13C2

Place R.L. Peeters. **GPS:** n50,63500 e1,59888. 🔼.

15 free. **Location:** Simple. **Surface:** asphalted. 01/01-31/12.
**Distance:** 1,7km.

## Neuilly-Saint-Front 16A2

Chemin de la Chantraine. **GPS:** n49,16713 e3,26003. 🔼.

20 free € 3 Ch € 3/55minutes. **Location:** Rural, simple.
**Surface:** grassy. 01/01-31/12.
**Distance:** 600m.

## Nuncq-Hautecôte 13D3

La Pommeraie, 13, route nationale. **GPS:** n50,30516 e2,29375. 🔼➡.

5 € 6 € 2 Ch € 4 free. **Location:** Rural, comfortable,
quiet. **Surface:** gravel. 01/01-31/12.
**Distance:** 50m.
**Remarks:** Covered pool € 3.

## Oye-plage 13D2

Route du Pont d'Oye. **GPS:** n50,97703 e2,03915. 🔼➡.

5 free € 2 Ch. **Location:** Urban, simple. **Surface:** metalled.
01/01-31/12 service: 01/11-01/04.
**Distance:** on the spot 3km 200m 500m.
**Remarks:** At cemetery, max 3,5t.

## Oye-plage 13D2

**GPS:** n50,99703 e2,05412. 🔼➡.

3 free. **Location:** Isolated, quiet. **Surface:** gravel/sand.
01/01-31/12.
**Distance:** 3km 800m 100m.
**Remarks:** Nature reserve.

## Péronne 15H1

Boulevard du Fort Carabit. **GPS:** n49,92626 e2,92685.
5 free € 2 Ch free. **Location:** Rural, simple. **Surface:** gravel.
01/01-31/12.
**Distance:** on the spot 550m 1,5km.

## Picquigny 13D3

Rue de la Cavée d'Airaines. **GPS:** n49,94388 e2,13496. 🔼.

20 € 5 Ch € 2 WCincluded. **Location:** Rural.
**Surface:** grassy. 01/01-31/12.
**Distance:** 500m 500m on the spot.

## Quend 13C3

Ferme de la Grande Retz. **GPS:** n50,32893 e1,61811. 🔼➡.

10 € 8 Ch € 4 included. **Surface:** grassy.
01/01-31/12.
**Distance:** 3km 9km 9km 2km.

## Quend-plage-les-Pins 13C3

Plage des Pins. **GPS:** n50,32410 e1,55545. 🔼.

50 € 7/24h € 2/10minutes Ch € 2/15minutes.
**Location:** Comfortable. **Surface:** forest soil. 01/01-31/12.
**Distance:** 800m beach 900m on the spot on the spot.
**Remarks:** Only exact change.

## Richebourg 13D2

Rue de la Briqueterie. **GPS:** n50,58028 e2,74639. 🔼➡.

6 free € 2/100liter € 2/55minutes included.
**Location:** Rural, comfortable. **Surface:** grassy. 01/01-31/12.
**Distance:** 500m on the spot on the spot.
**Remarks:** Max. 48h.

## Rozoy-sur-Serre 16B1

Portes de la Thiérache, Rue de la Praille.
**GPS:** n49,71367 e4,12202. 🔼➡.

5 free € 2/120liter Ch. **Location:** Rural, comfortable,
quiet. **Surface:** gravel. 01/01-31/12.
**Distance:** 1km 1km on the spot on the spot.

## Saint-Omer 13D2

De Haut Pont, Rue de la Gaieté. **GPS:** n50,75654 e2,25943. 🔼➡.

13 € 5 € 2 Ch. **Location:** Simple, noisy.
**Surface:** asphalted/gravel. 01/01-31/12.
**Distance:** 900m 900m.
**Remarks:** Max. 72h.

## Saint-Simon 21D3

Rue du Puits. **GPS:** n45,65289 w0,08517. 🔼.

6 free € 2,50/100liter Ch € 2,50/10minutes.
**Location:** Rural, simple, quiet. **Surface:** asphalted.
01/01-31/12.
**Distance:** 1km.

## Saint-Valery-sur-Somme 13C3

Rue de la Croix l'Abbé. **GPS:** n50,18220 e1,62881. 🔼➡.

180 € 12/24h Ch (40x)included. **Location:** Rural,
central, quiet. **Surface:** gravel.
01/01-31/12.
**Distance:** 1km on the spot on the spot.
**Remarks:** Market on Sunday.

## Stella-plage 13C3

Cours des Champs Elysées. **GPS:** n50,47470 e1,57726. 🔼.

20 free. **Location:** Rural, simple, isolated. **Surface:** asphalted.
01/01-31/12.
**Distance:** 1km on the spot 650m on the spot on the spot.
**Remarks:** Parking at dune.

## Tardinghen 13C2

Le site des 2 caps, La Ferme d'Horloge, 1615 Route d'Ausques, D249. GPS: n50,86250 e1,64890. ⬆➡.

30 ⛺ €6/24h ⚡€4 Ch ⬆€4/24h 📶.
**Location:** Comfortable, isolated, quiet. **Surface:** metalled.
🅿 01/01-31/12.
**Distance:** 🛒1,6km.
**Remarks:** Swin-golf €5.

## Tardinghen 13C2

Le site des 2 caps, Le Fond de Sombre, Hervelinghen > Wissant. GPS: n50,89361 e1,68972. ⬆➡.

10 ⛺ €6/24h. **Location:** Simple, isolated, quiet. **Surface:** grassy.
🅿 01/01-31/12.
**Distance:** 🏊1km.

## Tergnier 16A1

Base de loisirs de La Frette, Rue de la Prairie. GPS: n49,64891 e3,31200. ⬆.

20 ⛺ €10 ⚡€3/100liter Ch ⬆€3/30minutes 📶€3. 🛢
**Location:** Rural, comfortable. **Surface:** gravel. 🅿 01/01-31/12.
**Distance:** 🛒1,5km 🏊on the spot 🍴on the spot ⊗on the spot.

## Villers-Côtterets 16A2

Rue Alfred Juneaux. GPS: n49,26052 e3,08713. ⬆➡.

6 ⛺free ⚡€3 Ch ⬆€3/h 🛢. **Location:** Urban, simple, quiet.
**Surface:** asphalted. 🅿 01/01-31/12.
**Distance:** 🛒on the spot ⊗600m 🍴600m.
**Remarks:** Max. 72h, service 50m.

## Watten 13D2

3 Rue Paul Mortier. GPS: n50,83101 e2,20887. ⬆➡.

3 ⛺free ⚡€4 Ch ⬆€4/55minutes. **Location:** Simple, quiet.

---

**Surface:** metalled.
🅿 01/01-31/12.
**Distance:** 🛒500m ⊗500m 🍴500m 🏃on the spot.
**Remarks:** Coins at tourist info, supermarket, tabac-press and cafe.

## Wissant 13C2

Parking Wissant, Avenue Georges Clémenceau. GPS: n50,88684 e1,67064. ⬆➡.

15 ⛺free Ch free. **Location:** Urban, simple, noisy.
**Surface:** metalled. 🅿 01/01-31/12.
**Distance:** 🛒700m 🏊1,1km.
**Remarks:** Max. 48h, bread-service.

# Grand Est

## Aix-en-Othe 19B1

Aire du Moulin à Tan. GPS: n48,22901 e3,72500. ⬆.

6 ⛺€6 ⚡Ch ⬆€2,50 WC included 🅿€3,50/1,50.
**Location:** Urban, comfortable, central. **Surface:** grassy.
🅿 01/04-15/10.
**Distance:** 🛒1km ⊗1km 🍴1,5km 🚲1km 🏃1km.

## Allarmont 19F1

Le Meix du Haut Regard, 21, rue du Haut Regard. GPS: n48,48070 e7,01381. ⬆.

2 ⛺€5 ⚡included Ch ⬆€5/24h 🅿€4 free.
**Location:** Simple. **Surface:** gravel. 🅿 01/01-31/12.
**Distance:** 🛒400m ⊗400m 🍴400m.
**Remarks:** Steep ramp, swimming pool.

## Amnéville 16E2

Rue de l'Europe. GPS: n49,24780 e6,13842. ⬆.

10 ⛺€12/24h ⚡Ch ⬆WC included. **Location:** Rural, simple,
quiet. **Surface:** asphalted/grassy. 🅿 01/01-31/12.
**Distance:** 🛒1,8km.
**Remarks:** Pay at tourist office, shady.

## Ancerville 16C3

Impasse des Pransons. GPS: n48,63641 e5,01582. ⬆.

---

2 ⛺free. **Location:** Urban, simple, quiet. **Surface:** asphalted/grassy.
🅿 01/01-31/12.
**Distance:** 🛒on the spot ⊗400m 🍴400m.
**Remarks:** Inclining pitches.

## Arc-en-Barrois 19C2

Camping municipal, D3/D159. GPS: n47,95056 e5,00528. ⬆➡.

25 ⛺€5 ⚡ Ch WC included,on camp site. **Location:** Urban,
simple. **Surface:** gravel.
🅿 01/04-30/09 📅 Whitsuntide.
**Distance:** 🛒500m ⊗on the spot 🍴500m.

## Avioth 16D1

Rue de l'Hôpital. GPS: n49,56561 e5,39067. ⬆.

2 ⛺free. **Location:** Urban, simple, central, quiet. **Surface:** asphalted.
🅿 01/01-31/12.
**Distance:** 🛒on the spot ⊗on the spot 🏃on the spot.

## Avize 16B3

Rue du Bourg Joli. GPS: n48,97175 e4,00999. ⬆.

5 ⛺free ⚡Ch free. **Location:** Urban, simple, central, quiet.
**Surface:** asphalted. 🅿 01/01-31/12.
**Distance:** 🛒on the spot ⊗200m 🍞bakery 50m.
**Remarks:** Next to town hall.

## Avocourt 16D2

Restaurant La Terrasse, Rue du Moulin. GPS: n49,20417 e5,14227. ⬆.

4 ⛺free. **Location:** Rural, simple. **Surface:** grassy.
🅿 01/01-31/12.
**Distance:** 🛒on the spot ⊗on the spot.

## Azannes-et-Soumazannes 16D2

Les Vieux Métiers, Domaine des Roises. GPS: n49,31096 e5,47714. ⬆.

2 free. **Location:** Rural, simple, isolated, quiet. **Surface:** gravel.
01/01-31/12.
**Distance:** 2,5km 2,6km.
**Remarks:** At museum.

**Baccarat** 19F1
Place du General Le'Clerc. **GPS:** n48,44667 e6,74000.

15 €4 €2,50 Ch €2,50/3h WC **Location:** Simple.
**Surface:** asphalted.
01/01-31/12, Fri-morning market.
**Distance:** 300m on the spot on the spot 300m 300m.
**Remarks:** Along river, max. 24h.
**Tourist information Baccarat:**
M Musée du Cristal. Crystal museum. Mo-Sa 10-18h.

**Bains-les-Bains** 19E2
Rue de la pavée. **GPS:** n47,99916 e6,26460.

19 €9 Ch included. **Location:** Simple, quiet.
01/01-31/12.
**Distance:** on the spot 100m.
**Remarks:** To be paid at town hall, service 500m.

**Bar-le-Duc** 16D3
Halte du port Fluvial, Rue du Débarcadère.
**GPS:** n48,77536 e5,16654.

7 free €2,10/100liter Ch €2,10/1h. **Location:** Urban, simple, noisy. **Surface:** asphalted.
01/01-31/12.
**Distance:** 75m on the spot 150m 150m 150m on the spot.
**Remarks:** At the canal, coins at tourist info, 7 rue Jeanne d'Arc.

**Bar-sur-Aube** 19C1
7, Rue des Varennes. **GPS:** n48,23451 e4,70115.

2 free €3,50/100liter Ch €3,50/1h. **Location:** Urban, simple, quiet. **Surface:** asphalted. 01/01-31/12.
**Distance:** 300m 500m 500m on the spot on the spot.
**Remarks:** Max. 24h, coins at tourist info.

**Beaulieu-en-Argonne** 16C2
Parking Mairie, Grande Rue, D2B. **GPS:** n49,03183 e5,06665.

6 free. **Location:** Urban, simple, central, quiet. **Surface:** grassy.
01/01-31/12.
**Distance:** on the spot 50m on the spot on the spot.
**Remarks:** In front of town hall.

**Beaulieu-en-Argonne** 16C2
Parking St. Rouin, D2. **GPS:** n49,03554 e5,02975.

4 free. **Location:** Rural, simple, isolated. **Surface:** grassy/gravel.
01/01-31/12.
**Distance:** Beaulieu 6km.
**Remarks:** Isolated parking.

**Beaunay** 16B3
Ferme De Bel Air, Rue Principale. **GPS:** n48,88177 e3,87475.

12 €8 Ch (6x)included. **Location:** Rural, simple, isolated, quiet. **Surface:** gravel. 01/01-31/12.
**Distance:** 2km 2km 2km.

**Bellefontaine** 22E2
Lotissement les Replats. **GPS:** n46,55960 e6,06865.

6 free €2 Ch €1/1h. **Location:** Rural, simple, quiet.
**Surface:** asphalted. 01/01-31/12.
**Distance:** 400m.

**Benfeld** 19G1
Concessionnaire CLC Alsace, 9, Rue de Hollande, RN83 dir Strasbourg-Colmar. **GPS:** n48,37772 e7,59778.

5 free Ch free. **Location:** Motorway, simple, noisy.
**Surface:** asphalted. 01/01-31/12.
**Distance:** 2km 2km 600m.
**Remarks:** At motorhome dealer.

**Biesheim** 19G1
Camping-Car Park Ile du Rhin, Ile du Rhin. **GPS:** n48,02964 e7,56937.
20 €7 + €1,50/pp tourist tax Ch (20x)included,6Amp. **Surface:** asphalted. 01/01-31/12.
**Distance:** centre 2,5km 2km.

**Bitche** 16G2
La Citadelle, Rue Bombelles. **GPS:** n49,05431 e7,43446.

5 free €2/10minutes Ch €2/55minutes WC.
**Location:** Rural, simple, quiet. **Surface:** gravel.
01/01-31/12.
**Distance:** 750m 750m 750m.

**Bogny-sur-Meuse** 16C1
Rue de la Meuse. **GPS:** n49,85780 e4,74225.

20 €3,40/24h €2/100liter Ch €2,80/24h,only 2-euro coins WC €1,50.
**Location:** Rural, comfortable, quiet. **Surface:** asphalted.
01/01-31/12. **Distance:** on the spot on the spot 250m 400m 500m on the spot on the spot.
**Remarks:** Along the Meuse river, service 75m.

**Bonzée** 16D2
Parking de la Base de Loisirs du Colvert, D21.
**GPS:** n49,09806 e5,61551.

6 €6,20 €4 Ch €5 WC. **Location:** Rural, comfortable, isolated, quiet. **Surface:** gravel. 01/04-31/10.
**Distance:** 1km on the spot on the spot.

**Bourbach-le-Haut** 19F2
Route Joffre. **GPS:** n47,79463 e7,02868.

10 🅿€5 🔌 Ch 🚿 included. 🚿 **Location:** Rural, simple, quiet.
**Surface:** asphalted. 📅 15/03-15/11.
**Distance:** 🚶50m ⊗100m 🚲5km.
**Remarks:** In front of fire-station.

### Brienne-le-Château 19C1
Rue de la Gare. **GPS:** n48,39617 e4,53130. ⬆➡.

5 🅿free 🔌€ 3/10minutes 🔋 Ch 🚿€ 3/55minutes. **Location:** Urban,
simple, noisy. **Surface:** asphalted. 📅 01/01-31/12 💧 water
disconnected in winter.
**Distance:** 🚶300m ⊗400m 🛒300m.
**Remarks:** At former station, coins at tourist info, supermarket
Champion.

### Bruley 16E3
D118, rue Saint-Martin. **GPS:** n48,70640 e5,85554. ⬆.

10 🅿free 🔌€ 3/10minutes 🔋 Ch 🚿(2x)€ 3/8h.
**Location:** Comfortable, quiet. **Surface:** gravel. 📅 01/01-31/12.
**Distance:** 🚶200m ⊗300m 🛒300m.
**Remarks:** Max. 48h.

### Bulgnéville 19E1
**Étang des Récollets**, Rue des Récollets.
**GPS:** n48,20733 e5,83899. ⬆➡.

10 🅿€ 3/24h 🔌 Ch WC included. **Location:** Rural, luxurious, quiet.
**Surface:** asphalted. 📅 15/04-31/12.
**Distance:** 🚶700m 🏊1,8km 🏊on the spot 🎣on the spot ⊗100m
🛒700m.

### Bulgnéville 19E1

**Camping Porte des Vosges**, ZA La Grande Tranchée, Route de Contrexe-
ville. **GPS:** n48,19901 e5,84463. ⬆.
50 🅿€ 17, 07/07-31/08 € 19 🔌 Ch 🚿 WC 📶 included.

---

🏠 🚿 **Location:** Rural, comfortable, luxurious, quiet.
**Surface:** grassy/metalled. 📅 01/04-31/10.
**Distance:** 🚶on the spot 🏊3km 🛒500m ⊗on the spot 🛒1km
🚗200m 🏊on the spot 🚶on the spot.
**Remarks:** Possibility for reservation.

### Burnhaupt-le-Haut 19G2
**Parking du Super U**, Rue du Pont d'Aspacht.
**GPS:** n47,74114 e7,14773. ⬆.
4 🅿free 🔌€ 2/10minutes 🔋 Ch 🚿€ 2/h. **Location:** Urban,
simple, quiet. **Surface:** asphalted. 📅 01/01-31/12.
**Distance:** 🚶2km ⊗100m 🛒on the spot.

### Certilleux 19D1
Rue de l'Église. **GPS:** n48,31193 e5,72679. ⬆.

8 🅿free 🔌free. **Location:** Rural, simple. **Surface:** asphalted.
📅 01/01-31/12.
**Distance:** 🚶on the spot.
**Remarks:** Beautiful view.

### Chamery 16B2
**Salle Polyvalente**, Rue du Château Rouge.
**GPS:** n49,17475 e3,95446. ⬆➡.

5 🅿free 🔌€ 2/100liter 🔋 Ch 🚿€ 2/2h. **Location:** Rural, simple,
quiet. **Surface:** gravel. 📅 01/01-31/12.
**Distance:** 🚶300m ⊗400m.
**Remarks:** In front of community centre, max. 48h.

### Champigny-lès-Langres 19D2
Rue du Port, D74. **GPS:** n47,88167 e5,33861. ⬆.

5 🅿free WC. **Location:** Rural, simple, noisy. **Surface:** gravel.
📅 01/01-31/12.
**Distance:** ⊗400m 🛒1,4km 🚗on the spot.

---

### Champlitte 19D2
140 Rue de la République. **GPS:** n47,60956 e5,52106.
2 🅿free 🔌 Ch free. **Location:** Simple, quiet. **Surface:** asphalted.
📅 01/01-31/12.
**Distance:** 🚶1km ⊗on the spot.

### Champougny 16D3
D145f. **GPS:** n48,54410 e5,69277. ⬆.

2 🅿free. **Location:** Rural, simple, quiet. **Surface:** grassy.
📅 01/01-31/12.
**Distance:** 🚶200m 🚲25m.

### Chaource 19B1
Chemin de Ronde/Rue des Roises. **GPS:** n48,05944 e4,13861. ⬆➡.

10 🅿free 🔌€ 2/100liter 🔋 Ch 🚿€ 2/1h. **Location:** Rural,
comfortable, quiet. **Surface:** grassy. 📅 01/01-31/12.
**Distance:** 🚶100m ⊗on the spot 🛒on the spot 🏊on the spot
🏊on the spot.
**Remarks:** Coins available at Office du Tourisme and bar, monday-
morning market.

### Charleville-Mézières 16C1
Rue des Pâquis. **GPS:** n49,78056 e4,72056. ⬆.

8 🅿free 🔌€ 2/100liter 🔋 Ch 🚿€ 2/55minutes 🎣€ 5,40 🚿free.
**Location:** Urban, simple, noisy. **Surface:** asphalted. 📅 01/01-31/12
💧 electricity: 01/11-31/03.
**Distance:** 🚶800m 🛒on the spot ⊗500m 🛒2km 🚗600m 🏊on the
spot 🏊on the spot.
**Remarks:** Service only with 2-euro coins, ask for electricity at campsite.
**Tourist information Charleville-Mézières:**
Ⓜ Musée Ardennes, Place Ducale. Regional museum. 📅 10-12, 14-18
🌙 Mo.
🛒 place Ducale. Regional products. 📅 Tue, Thu, Sa.

## ⚓S Charmes 〰 19E1

**Port de Plaisance. GPS:** n48,37334 e6,29542 ⬆.

60 ⌁ € 8 ⛽ 🚰Ch ⚡(80x)included WC ⚡€ 1,50 🚿€ 3/day.
**Location:** Urban, central. **Surface:** grassy/metalled.
◻ 01/01-31/12.
**Distance:** 🚶1km ⚓1,5km ⚓on the spot 🚉on the spot ▣on the spot.
**Remarks:** Service closed during wintertime.
**Tourist information Charmes:**
✈ ◻ Fri-morning.

## ⚓S Châtenois 19G1

**Allee des Bains 10. GPS:** n48,27476 e7,39853.

7 ⌁free ⛽€ 2 🚰ChWCfree. **Location:** Urban, simple, quiet.
**Surface:** asphalted/grassy. ◻ 01/04-15/11.
**Distance:** 🚶400m ⊗250m.
**Remarks:** Max. 24h.

## ⚓S Chaumont 〰 19D1

**Port de la Maladière**, RN74 Neufchâteau > Chaumont.
**GPS:** n48,11815 e5,15437 ⬆.

12 ⌁€ 7,40 + € 0,22/pp tourist tax ⛽🚰Ch ⚡WC ⚡€ 2,50
▣€ 2,50/3,50 🚿included. 🏊 **Location:** Rural, quiet. **Surface:** gravel.
◻ 01/04-31/10.
**Distance:** 🚶4km ⚓Canal de la Marne ⊗100m 🚉1km.
**Remarks:** Baker every morning.

## ⚓S Chavanges 〰 16C3

**Ruelle du Fief Berthaux. GPS:** n48,50691 e4,57627 ⬆➡.

8 ⌁free ⛽€ 3 🚰€ 3 Ch▣. **Location:** Simple, quiet.
**Surface:** asphalted/gravel. ◻ 01/01-31/12.
**Distance:** 🚶300m 🚉400m.
**Remarks:** Coins at the shops.

## ⚓S Chavannes-sur-l'Etang 🌿〰 19F2

**Aire pique-nique La Porte d'Alsace**, RD419, Rue d'Alsace.
**GPS:** n47,63325 e7,01858 ⬆➡.

15 ⌁€ 8 ⛽🚰Ch ⚡WCincluded. 🏊 **Location:** Rural, comfortable,
quiet. **Surface:** asphalted. ◻ 01/01-31/12.
**Distance:** 🚶900m ⚓on the spot ⊗900m 🚉1km 🚲on the spot
✿ on the spot.
**Remarks:** Parking picnic area.

## ⚓S Colmar 〰 19G1

**Port de Plaisance de Colmar**, 6 rue du Canal.
**GPS:** n48,08054 e7,37599 ⬆.

25 ⌁€ 11-15 + € 0,22/pp tourist tax ⛽🚰Ch ⚡WC ⚡▣€ 3/2
🚿included. **Location:** Rural, comfortable, quiet.
**Surface:** asphalted/grassy. ◻ 01/01-31/12.
**Distance:** 🚶1,3km 🚉200m 🚌on the spot 🚲on the spot
✿ on the spot.
**Remarks:** Baker 8.30-09.00.

## ⚓S Colmar 〰 19G1

**Domaine du Wolfloch**, 113 Route De Bâle. **GPS:** n48,06046 e7,36396.

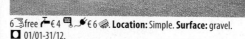

6 ⌁free ⛽€ 4 🚰 ⚡€ 6 🍴. **Location:** Simple. **Surface:** gravel.
◻ 01/01-31/12.

## P Colmar 〰 19G1

**Rue de la Cavalerie. GPS:** n48,08218 e7,35990 ⬆.
20 ⌁€ 3/h. 🚐🍴 **Location:** Urban, simple, central, noisy.
**Surface:** asphalted.
**Distance:** 🚶200m ⊗on the spot 🚉on the spot ▣on the spot.
**Remarks:** Max. 4h.

## P Colmar 〰 19G1

**Rue Henry Wilhelm. GPS:** n48,08366 e7,35527 ⬆.
16 ⌁€ 3/h. 🚐🍴 **Location:** Urban, simple, central.
**Surface:** asphalted. ◻ 01/01-31/12.
**Distance:** 🚶400m ⊗400m 🚉400m.
**Remarks:** Max. 4h.

## ⚓S Colombey-les-deux-Eglises 🌿✈ 19C1

**Rue de Général de Gaulle. GPS:** n48,22316 e4,88619 ⬆.

10 ⌁free ⛽🚰Ch WCfree. **Location:** Simple, quiet.
**Surface:** asphalted/gravel. ◻ 01/01-31/12.
**Distance:** 🚶on the spot ⊗50m 🚉50m.
**Remarks:** Museum and Memorial Général De Gaulle 800m.

## ⚓S Commercy 🌿✈🍴 16D3

**Parking de la Boîte à Madeleines**, Rue de la Louvière.
**GPS:** n48,75378 e5,59928 ⬆.

3 ⌁free ⛽🚰Ch ⚡free. **Location:** Comfortable, isolated, quiet.
**Surface:** asphalted. ◻ 01/01-31/12.
**Distance:** 🚶1km ⊗on the spot 🚉on the spot.

## ⚓S Commercy 🌿✈🍴 16D3

**Rue du Docteur Boyer. GPS:** n48,76374 e5,59616 ⬆➡.

4 ⌁free ⛽€ 3/15minutes 🚰Ch ⚡(4x)€ 3/4h 🚿free 🍴.
**Location:** Urban, comfortable, central, quiet. **Surface:** asphalted.
◻ 01/01-31/12.
**Distance:** 🚶800m ⚓on the spot ⚓on the spot ⊗600m 🚉100m
🚲on the spot ✿ on the spot.
**Remarks:** On the canal.

## ⚓S Consenvoye 16D2

**Gr la Grande Rue. GPS:** n49,28547 e5,28403 ⬆.

5 ⌁free ⛽🚰free. **Location:** Urban, simple, quiet. **Surface:** asphalted.
◻ 01/01-31/12.
**Distance:** 🚶100m 🚌on the spot ⊗50m.

## ⚓S Contrexéville ⛲♨ 19E1

**Camping de Contrexéville**, 660 Rue du 11 Septembre 1944.
**GPS:** n48,18069 e5,88527 ⬆.

10 ⌁€ 11 + € 0,33/pp tourist tax ⛽🚰Ch ⚡WC ⚡▣€ 5/
time 🚿included 🍴🚐🍴 **Location:** Rural, luxurious, quiet.
**Surface:** gravel/metalled. ◻ 30/03-31/10.
**Distance:** 🚶1km ⊗800m 🚉1km.
**Remarks:** Max. 72h.
**Tourist information Contrexéville:**
ℹ Office de Tourisme, 116 rue du Shah de Perse, www.contrex-min-
ceur.com. Health resort. ◻ 01/04-31/10.

## ⚓S Contrisson 〰 16C3

**Ballastière. GPS:** n48,80530 e4,94714 ⬆➡.

FR

10 🛏free WC. **Location:** Rural, simple, isolated, quiet.
**Surface:** grassy/sand. ▣ 01/01-31/12.
**Distance:** 🚰800m ⛱on the spot ⛽on the spot ⊗1km 🛒1km.
**Remarks:** At small lake.

| | | Corgirnon 🍴 | 19D2 |

Allée du Parc. **GPS:** n47,80681 e5,50308.⬆➡

8 🛏€ 6,50 🚰🗑Ch🚿 included. 🛁 **Location:** Rural, comfortable,
isolated, quiet. **Surface:** gravel. ▣ 01/01-31/12 ◉ water
disconnected in winter.
**Distance:** 🚰500m ⛱10km 🛒500m, baker on site (Tue-Su).
**Remarks:** Bread-service, service closed during wintertime.

| | | Cornimont | 19F2 |

Rue de la poste. **GPS:** n47,96087 e6,83358.⬆

6 🛏free 🚰€ 2/10minutes 🗑Ch🛒€ 2/1h. **Location:** Urban, simple,
quiet. **Surface:** asphalted. ▣ 01/01-31/12.
**Distance:** 🚰on the spot ⊗200m 🛒500m.

| | | Damvillers | 16D2 |

Rue de l'Isle d'Envie, D905. **GPS:** n49,33790 e5,39752.⬆

3 🛏free 🚰€ 2/100liter 🗑Ch🛒€ 2/60minutes. **Location:** Urban,
simple, central, noisy. **Surface:** asphalted.
▣ 01/01-31/12.
**Distance:** 🚰on the spot ⊗on the spot 🛒on the spot ⛽on the spot
🎣400m 🧍400m.
**Remarks:** Max. 6,5m.

| | | Damvillers | 16D2 |

Etang, D905. **GPS:** n49,34978 e5,39970.⬆

10 🛏free. **Location:** Rural, simple, isolated, quiet. **Surface:** grassy.
▣ 01/01-31/12.
**Distance:** 🚰Damvillers 1km ⛽on the spot 🛒500m 🧍700m.

| | | Darney | 19E1 |

Route de Vittel 6. **GPS:** n48,09395 e6,04324.⬆

4 🛏free 🚰€ 2 🗑Ch🚿€ 2/4h WC. 🚐 **Location:** Urban.
**Surface:** asphalted. ▣ 01/01-31/12.
**Distance:** 🚰on the spot 🛒on the spot.
**Remarks:** Picnic tables available.

| | | Dienville 🌿⛱⚓ | 19C1 |

**Parking Autobus**, Rue de Dienville. **GPS:** n48,34735 e4,52779.⬆

6 🛏free. **Location:** Urban, simple, isolated, quiet. **Surface:** asphalted.
▣ 01/01-31/12.
**Distance:** 🚰700m ⛱300m ⊗300m 🎣on the spot.

| | | Dieue-sur-Meuse ⚓ | 16D2 |

**Port de plaisance**, Route des Dames. **GPS:** n49,07110 e5,42634.⬆⬆

15 🛏free 🚰🗑Chfree. **Location:** Rural, simple, quiet.
**Surface:** grassy. ▣ 01/01-31/12.
**Distance:** 🚰200m ⛽on the spot ⊗200m 🛒200m.
**Remarks:** At the canal.

| | | Dolancourt ⚓ | 19C1 |

**Nigloland**, RN19. **GPS:** n48,26086 e4,60945.⬆

30 🛏€ 6/24h, free with a meal 🚰🗑Ch🚿 included.
**Location:** Simple, isolated. **Surface:** asphalted. ▣ 03/04-03/11.
**Distance:** ⊗on the spot.
**Remarks:** Parking amusement park, max. 24h.

| | | Dommartin-lès-Remiremont | 19F2 |

Place de l'Église. **GPS:** n47,99959 e6,64401.⬆

8 🛏free 🚰€ 3/10minutes 🗑Ch🚿€ 3/h 🗑. **Location:** Urban,
simple, quiet. **Surface:** asphalted. ▣ 01/01-31/12.
**Distance:** 🚰on the spot ⊗50m.
**Remarks:** Max. 72h.

| | | Donjeux ⚓ | 19D1 |

**Halte Nautique**, D67a. **GPS:** n48,36586 e5,14891.⬆

4 🛏free 🚰🗑Ch🚿(4x)free. **Location:** Comfortable, quiet.
**Surface:** gravel/metalled. ▣ 01/01-31/12.
**Distance:** 🚰1km ⛱Canal de la Marne ⛽on the spot ⊗1km 🛒800m
🎣on the spot.
**Remarks:** Baker every morning.

| | | Dun-sur-Meuse 🌿 | 16D2 |

Rue du Vieux Port. **GPS:** n49,38919 e5,17787.⬆

16 🛏€ 8 🚰🗑Ch🚿WC🚽📶included. 🛁 **Location:** Rural,
comfortable, central, quiet. **Surface:** gravel. ▣ 01/01-31/12
◉ sanitary building: 01/11-01/04.
**Distance:** 🚰600m ⛱on the spot ⛽on the spot ⊗400m 🛒600m.

| | | Épernay 🍷 | 16B2 |

Rue Dom Pérignon. **GPS:** n49,03602 e3,95130.⬆

3 🛏free.
**Location:** Urban, simple, central, noisy. **Surface:** asphalted.
▣ 01/01-31/12.
**Distance:** 🚰within walking distance 🚌Avenue Jean Jaurès.
**Remarks:** Behind church St.Pierre-St.Paul, coins at tourist info.

**Tourist information Épernay**
👁 Cave de Catellane, 154, avenue de Verdun.
👁 Mercier, 70, avenue de Champagne. ▣ Mo-Sa 9.30-11.30h, 14-
16.30h, Su/holidays 9.30-11.30h, 14-17.30h.

| | | Épinal | 19E1 |

**Camping-Car Park**, Chemin du Petit Chaperon Rouge.
**GPS:** n48,17969 e6,46865.⬆

50 🛏€ 10,70 🚰🗑Ch🚿(20x)📶included. 🚐🗑
**Location:** Comfortable, quiet. ▣ 01/01-31/12.
**Distance:** 🚰1,5km.
**Remarks:** Mandatory, one-time fee Pass'Etapes € 4.

| | | Épinal | 19E1 |

**Port d'Épinal**, Quai de Dogneville, D12. **GPS:** n48,18671 e6,44493.⬆

FR

5 ⬛summer € 5,50, winter € 8,50 🚰⬛Ch 🚿Service € 3/15min 🗑.
**Surface:** asphalted.
**Distance:** 🏪1km 🏖3,5km ⚓on the spot.
**Remarks:** Max. 48h.

### ⬛S Essoyes 🌿⚓ 19C1
Impasse de la Gare. **GPS:** n48,06067 e4,53444.⬆.

3 ⬛free 🚰€ 2/10minutes ⬛Ch🔌€ 2/1h. **Location:** Urban,
comfortable, central, quiet. **Surface:** asphalted.
⬛ 01/01-31/12.
**Distance:** 🏪600m ⊗600m 🍴200m 🚲300m 🚶300m.
**Remarks:** Coins at tourist info.

### ⬛S Esternay 16A3
Place des Tilleuls, D48, Rue de la Paix. **GPS:** n48,73245 e3,55698.⬆.

10 ⬛free 🚰⬛WC 📶free. **Location:** Urban, simple, central, quiet.
**Surface:** gravel.
⬛ 01/01-31/12 ⬛ water: 15/11-15/03.
**Distance:** 🏪within walking distance ⊗200m 🍴400m.
**Remarks:** Behind church, Wifi code: wifi-la-champagne.

### ⬛S Etival-Clairefontaine 19F1
Rue du général Haxo. **GPS:** n48,36355 e6,86504.⬆.

20 ⬛free 🚰⬛Chfree. **Location:** Simple, central, quiet.
**Surface:** gravel. ⬛ 01/01-31/12 ⬛ water disconnected in winter.
**Distance:** 🏪on the spot ⊗on the spot 🍴100m 🚶on the spot.
**Remarks:** Behind town hall, max. 7m.

### ⬛S Favières 19E1
Base de Loisirs. **GPS:** n48,46660 e5,96124.⬆.

8 ⬛free 🚰⬛Ch🔌WC 📶. **Location:** Rural, comfortable, central,
quiet. **Surface:** gravel/metalled. ⬛ 01/01-31/12.
**Distance:** 🏪200m 🏖13km ⚓on the spot 🚤on the spot ⊗on the

---

spot 🍴bakery 300m 🚵on the spot 🚶on the spot.

### ⬛S Ferrette 🔊 19G3
Rue de Lucelle. **GPS:** n47,48882 e7,31118.⬆.

5 ⬛free 🚰€ 2/10minutes ⬛Ch🔌€ 2/55minutes. **Location:** Rural,
simple, isolated, quiet. **Surface:** asphalted.
⬛ 01/01-31/12.
**Distance:** 🏪700m ⊗700m 🍴2km 🚐on the spot 🚶on the spot.

### ⬛S Fessenheim 19G2
Allée de la Guyane. **GPS:** n47,91833 e7,53139.⬆.

40 ⬛free 🚰€ 2 ⬛Ch🔌€ 2. **Location:** Rural, simple, quiet.
**Surface:** asphalted/gravel. ⬛ 01/01-31/12.
**Distance:** 🏪700m ⊗700m 🍴200m 🚐on the spot 🚵on the spot.
**Remarks:** Coins available at swimming pool, supermarket.

### ⬛S Forbach 16F2
Avenue Saint-Rémy. **GPS:** n49,18519 e6,89252.⬆.

4 ⬛free 🚰€ 2/100liter ⬛Ch 📖. **Location:** Urban, simple.
**Surface:** asphalted. ⬛ 01/01-31/12.
**Distance:** 🏪350m ⊗200m 🚐950m.

### ⬛S Fraize 19F1
Impasse de la Gare/ Place Jean Sonrel. **GPS:** n48,18188 e7,00360.➡.

7 ⬛free 🚰€ 3 ⬛Ch🔌€ 3 WC. **Location:** Noisy. **Surface:** asphalted.
⬛ 01/01-31/12.
**Distance:** 🏪100m ⊗100m 🍴100m.
**Remarks:** Behind tourist info.

### ⬛S Froncles 19D1
Halte Nautique. **GPS:** n48,29954 e5,15246.⬆.

10 ⬛€ 3 🚰€ 3/day ⬛Ch 🚿(8x)€ 3/day 🗑€ 2,50 🔌€ 3/3 📶. 🚣
**Location:** Comfortable. **Surface:** gravel. ⬛ 01/01-31/12.
**Distance:** 🏪500m ⚓river-beach on the spot ⊗on the spot

---

🍴1km 🚵on the spot.
**Remarks:** Baker on site (Tue-Su).

### ⬛S Fumay 11C3
Quai des Carmélites. **GPS:** n49,99736 e4,70986.⬆.

10 ⬛free. **Location:** Rural, simple, quiet. **Surface:** unpaved.
⬛ 01/01-31/12.
**Distance:** 🏪700m ⊗800m.
**Remarks:** Along the Meuse river.

### ⬛S Gérardmer ⚓🏖❄ 19F1
Chemin de la Rayée, La Mauselaine. **GPS:** n48,05846 e6,88862.⬆.

100 ⬛€ 6/24h 🚰€ 2/100liter ⬛Ch.🚌 **Surface:** asphalted.
⬛ 01/01-31/12.
**Distance:** 🏪Gérardmer 1,7km ⚓2km ⛷on the spot 🎿on the spot.
**Remarks:** Parking at skipistes, coins at tourist info.

### ⬛S Gérardmer 19F1
**Parking de la Prairie**, Boulevard d'Alsace.
**GPS:** n48,07199 e6,87333.⬆.

100 ⬛€ 6 🚰€ 2/100liter ⬛ChWC. 🚌 **Location:** Simple, central,
noisy. **Surface:** asphalted/gravel. ⬛ 01/01-31/12.
**Distance:** 🏪on the spot.
**Remarks:** Coins at tourist info.

**Tourist information Gérardmer:**
🚶 ⬛ Thu, Sa.

### ⬛S Giffaumont-Champaubert 🌿⚓🏖 16C3
**Site de Chantecoq**, Rue du Grand Der. **GPS:** n48,56809 e4,70096.⬆.

58 ⬛€ 4 20-8h, parking free 🚰€ 3,80/80liter ⬛Ch🔌€ 3,80/45minutes WC.
**Location:** Rural, simple. **Surface:** grassy.
⬛ 01/01-31/12.
**Distance:** ⚓on the spot ⊗900m.
**Remarks:** At lake Der de Chantecoq, coins at tourist info.

### ⬛S Giffaumont-Champaubert 🌿⚓🏖 16C3
**Station Nautique, P1**, Rue du Port. **GPS:** n48,55358 e4,76434.⬆.

48 🚐 € 6 20-8h, parking free 🚰 € 2,50/8minutes 🗑
Ch 💧 € 2,50/45minutes 📶included 🧺.📱🚮 **Location:** Rural,
quiet. 📅 01/01-31/12.
**Distance:** 🛒on the spot 🏊on the spot ⊗200m 🚉8km Montier-en-
Der 🚴on the spot 🚶on the spot.

### 🔲🅂 Giffaumont-Champaubert 〰🦆🌿 16C3
**Station Nautique, P5**, La Cachotte. **GPS:** n48,55071 e4,76829.⬆.

72 🚐 € 6 20-8h, parking free 🚰 € 2,50/8minutes 🗑
Ch 💧 € 2,50/45minutes 🧺.🚮 **Location:** Urban, comfortable,
central, quiet. **Surface:** grassy. 📅 01/01-31/12.
**Distance:** 🛒on the spot 🏊650m ⊗70m 🚉1km 🚴on the spot
🚶on the spot.

### Givet 11C3
Rue Jean Jaurès. **GPS:** n50,13593 e4,82138.⬆.

12 🚐free. **Location:** Urban, simple, central, quiet. **Surface:** asphalted.
📅 01/01-31/12.
**Distance:** 🛒on the spot 🛍on the spot ⊗on the spot 🚉on the spot
🍴on the spot 🚶on the spot.

### 🅲🅂 Givet 11C3
**Camping Municipal**, Rue Berthelot. **GPS:** n50,14291 e4,82611.⬆.

5 🚐free 🚰 € 3/100liter 🗑Ch 💧 € 3/h. **Location:** Rural, simple.
**Surface:** asphalted. 📅 01/01-31/12.
**Distance:** 🛒750m 🏊750m 🚉1km.
**Remarks:** Coins at campsite.

### 🔲🅂 Goncourt 🌿 19D1
Rue des Lottes, D74. **GPS:** n48,23685 e5,60998.⬆.

20 🚐 € 3 💧 € 3 🗑ChWC 📶. **Location:** Rural, comfortable.
**Surface:** asphalted/gravel. 📅 01/01-31/12.
**Distance:** 🛒100m 🏊on the spot ⊗100m 🚉100m.

---

**Remarks:** Along the Meuse river, max. 48h, baker at 8am.

### 🔲🅂 Gondrecourt-le-Château 16D3
Rue du Général Leclerc. **GPS:** n48,51373 e5,50386.⬆.

3 🚐free 🚰🗑Ch💧. **Location:** Urban, simple, central, quiet.
**Surface:** concrete. 📅 01/01-31/12.
**Distance:** 🛒200m ⊗100m 🚉on the spot.
**Remarks:** Coins at town hall.

### 🔲🅂 Gondrecourt-le-Château 16D3
**Parking Musée du Cheval**, Rue Saint Blaise.
**GPS:** n48,51390 e5,50975.⬆.

2 🚐free. **Location:** Urban, simple, quiet. **Surface:** gravel/metalled.
📅 01/01-31/12.
**Distance:** 🛒on the spot ⊗50m 🚉50m.

### 〰🅂 Gueberschwihr 19G1
**Marzolf**, Route de Rouffach. **GPS:** n48,00269 e7,28275.
2 🚐free 🚰💧. **Location:** Rural. 📅 01/01-31/12.
**Distance:** ⊗250m.

### 🔲 Guebwiller 🚂🛝🌿 19G2
Avenue Maréchal Foch. **GPS:** n47,90554 e7,21869.⬆.

20 🚐free. **Location:** Urban, simple, central, noisy. **Surface:** gravel.
📅 01/01-31/12.
**Distance:** 🛒300m 🏊on the spot 🛍on the spot ⊗300m 🚉300m
🛒300m 🚶on the spot 🎣5km.

### 🔲🅂 Haironville 🌱🌿 16D3
**GPS:** n48,68438 e5,08586.⬆➡.

5 🚐free 🚰 € 2/10minutes 🗑Ch💧 € 2/50minutes. **Location:** Rural,
simple, central, quiet. **Surface:** gravel.
📅 01/01-31/12.
**Distance:** 🛒200m 🚉200m.
**Remarks:** Coins at the shops in the village.

### ⚓🅂 Harskirchen 16F3
**Port de Plaisance**, Rue de Bissert. **GPS:** n48,93912 e7,02851.⬆➡.

---

2 🚐 € 5 💧 € 1/100liter 🗑Ch 💧 € 1/8h WC 📶included. 🚮
**Location:** Simple. **Surface:** gravel. 📅 15/03-11/11.
**Distance:** 🛒350m 🏊on the spot 🚴on the spot.
**Remarks:** At canal Houillères de la Sarre, max. 24h.

### 🔲🅂 Hartmannswiller 19G2
Grand Rue. **GPS:** n47,86311 e7,21494.⬆.

4 🚐free 🚰🗑Ch💧free. **Location:** Rural, simple, quiet.
**Surface:** asphalted. 📅 01/01-31/12.
**Distance:** 🛒200m.

### 🔲🅂 Haybes 〰 11C3
**Halte Fluviale**, Quai du Docteur Adolphe Hamai.
**GPS:** n50,01093 e4,70762.⬆.

4 🚐free 🚰🗑Ch € 2,05 💧 € 3,30/3,30. **Location:** Urban, simple,
quiet. **Surface:** metalled. 📅 01/01-31/12.
**Distance:** 🛒200m ⊗50m 🚉bakery 200m 🚴on the spot.
**Remarks:** Along the Meuse river, max. 2 nights, service at camping
municipal.

### 🔲 Heiligenstein 19G1
Lieu-dit Lindel, D35. **GPS:** n48,42780 e7,45147.⬆.

3 🚐free. **Location:** Rural, simple. **Surface:** gravel.
📅 01/01-31/12.
**Distance:** 🛒800m ⊗300m 🚉500m 🚶on the spot.
**Remarks:** Hiking trails and wine tasting.

### 🔲🅂 Heudicourt sous les Côtes 〰🚂🌿 16D3
Entrée 2, D133. **GPS:** n48,94035 e5,71741.⬆.

50 🚐 € 5 💧 € 3 🗑Ch 💧 € 4 WC 🚮. **Location:** Rural, simple,
quiet. **Surface:** grassy. 📅 01/04-31/10.
**Distance:** 🛒3km 🏊100m 🛍100m 🚴on the spot 🚶200m.
**Remarks:** Next to campsite.

### Heudicourt sous les Côtes 16D3

**Ste Nautique de Madine**. **GPS:** n48,93549 e5,71548.

60 €12 Ch (20x)WC included. **Location:** Rural, comfortable, quiet. **Surface:** grassy/gravel. 01/04-31/10. **Distance:** 3km on the spot on the spot on the spot on the spot.
**Remarks:** Service passerby € 5, view on Lac de Madine.

### Hirtzbach 19G2

Place de la Gare. **GPS:** n47,60061 e7,22542.

10 free Chfree. **Location:** Simple, quiet. **Surface:** asphalted. 01/01-31/12.
**Distance:** 300m 200m on the spot on the spot.

### Hombourg-Haut 16F2

Rue des Suédois. **GPS:** n49,12448 e6,77888.

6 free € 2/100liter Ch 2/4h. **Location:** Urban, simple, quiet. **Surface:** asphalted. 01/01-31/12.
**Distance:** 400m 200m on the spot.
**Remarks:** Max. 48h.

### Issoncourt 16D3

**Parking Relais de la Voie Sacrée**, Rue de la Voie Sacrée 1. **GPS:** n48,97070 e5,28776.

6 free. **Location:** Rural, simple, quiet. **Surface:** gravel. 01/01-31/12.
**Distance:** 50m on the spot.

### Javernant 19B1

Le Cheminot, N77. **GPS:** n48,14789 e4,01046.

5 free. **Location:** Simple. **Surface:** asphalted. 01/01-31/12.

---

### Joinville 19D1

**Halte Nautique**, Rue des Jardins. **GPS:** n48,44583 e5,15000.

16 free € 2/10minutes Ch 2/55minutes. **Location:** Urban, simple, quiet. **Surface:** gravel/metalled. 01/01-31/12.
**Distance:** 500m on the spot on the spot 800m 100m on the spot.

### Juzennecourt 19C1

Place de la Mairie. **GPS:** n48,18429 e4,97890.

4 free Ch WC. **Location:** Simple, quiet. **Surface:** metalled. 15/04-15/11.
**Distance:** on the spot bakery in the village on the spot.
**Remarks:** Parking townhall.

### Kaysersberg 19G1

**Aire Camping-car P1**, Place de l'Erlenbad. **GPS:** n48,13565 e7,26325.

80 € 20/24h Ch WC included. **Location:** Urban, simple, quiet. **Surface:** asphalted. 01/01-31/12.
**Distance:** 300m 300m 300m.
**Remarks:** Wifi at Office de Tourisme.
**Tourist information Kaysersberg:**
Musée Albert Schweitzer. The life of Albert Schweitzer.

### Kilstett 16G3

**Place de la Mairie**, Rue du Lieut de Bettignies. **GPS:** n48,67501 e7,85691.

7 free. **Location:** Urban, simple, quiet. **Surface:** asphalted. 01/01-31/12.
**Distance:** on the spot on the spot.

### Kilstett 16G3

Rue de l'Industrie. **GPS:** n48,67914 e7,84178.
Ch.

---

### La Bresse 19F2

**Camping du Haut des Bluches**, 5, route des Planches. **GPS:** n47,99889 e6,91762.
17 07/07-11/11 € 10-13,80, € 17,10 Ch WC € 5 included. **Location:** Rural, quiet. **Surface:** asphalted. 01/01-31/12 10/03-01/07.
**Distance:** 4km on the spot on camp site 4km on the spot on the spot 5km 8km.
**Remarks:** Website: www.hautdesbluches.com, zone camping-car, bread-service.

### La Bresse 19F2

Route de Niachamp. **GPS:** n47,99430 e6,85431.
€ 2/100liter Ch. 01/01-31/12.

### La Cheppe 16C2

**Champ d'Attila**, Rue de Champo d'Attila. **GPS:** n49,04892 e4,49377.

4 free € 2/100liter Ch 2/2h WC. **Location:** Rural, simple, quiet. **Surface:** asphalted. 01/01-31/12.
**Distance:** 500m 300m on the spot.
**Remarks:** Max. 7m.

### Lachaussée 16E2

**Domaine du Vieux Moulin**, Grande Rue. **GPS:** n49,03564 e5,81755.

4 free free. **Location:** Rural, simple, isolated. **Surface:** grassy. 01/01-31/12.
**Distance:** 100m 50m on the spot on the spot.
**Remarks:** Along Étang de Lachaussée, check in at restaurant, regional products.

### Laheycourt 16C3

5 Rue de la Gare. **GPS:** n48,88903 e5,02165.

3 free. **Location:** Rural, simple, quiet. **Surface:** grassy/gravel. 01/01-31/12.
**Distance:** on the spot 50m 50m.
**Remarks:** Along the Chée river, max. 7 days.

### Langres 19D2

**Place de Bel Air**, Avenue Jean Ernest Darbot. **GPS:** n47,85885 e5,33225.

---

FR

10 ⓩfree WC. **Location:** Urban, simple, noisy. **Surface:** asphalted. ◘ 01/01-31/12.
**Distance:** ⌷on the spot ⌷on the spot ⌷on the spot.
**Remarks:** Video surveillance.

| 🅢 | Langres 🌂 | 19D2 |

Ruelle de la Poterne. **GPS:** n47,85795 e5,32989.⬆➡.

6 ⓩfree ⌷Chfree. **Location:** Urban, simple, central, quiet.
**Surface:** asphalted. ◘ 01/01-31/12.
**Distance:** ⌷800m ⊗400m ▣600m.
**Remarks:** Max. 24h.

| 🅢 | Langres 🌂 | 19D2 |

**Parking Sous-Bie**, Allée des Marronniers. **GPS:** n47,86104 e5,33674.⬆.

20 ⓩfree. **Location:** Simple, quiet. **Surface:** asphalted.
◘ 01/01-31/12.
**Distance:** ⌷400m ⊗200m ⌷on the spot.
**Remarks:** Max. 8M, inclining pitches, video surveillance, free elevator to old town.

**Tourist information Langres:**
⌷ ◘ Fri.

| 🅢 | Launois-sur-Vence | 16C1 |

Avenue Louis Jolly. **GPS:** n49,65467 e4,54005.⬆.

10 ⓩfree. **Location:** Rural, simple, quiet. **Surface:** unpaved.
◘ 01/01-31/12.
**Distance:** ⌷on the spot ⊗50m.
**Remarks:** In front of tourist office, max. 48h.

| 🅢 | Launois-sur-Vence | 16C1 |

Rue du Thin. **GPS:** n49,65810 e4,53987.⬆⬆➡.
⌷€ 2/100liter ⌷Ch⌷€ 2/1h. ◘ water: frost.
**Distance:** ⊗150m.
**Remarks:** Coins at tourist info and restaurant.

**Tourist information Launois-sur-Vence:**
⌷ Relais de Poste. Monthly antiques and flea market. ◘ 3rd Su of the month 9-18h.

| | Le Bonhomme ❄ | 19F1 |

Col du Bonhomme, D148, route des Crètes.
**GPS:** n48,16495 e7,07971.⬆.

5 ⓩfree. **Location:** Rural, simple, isolated, quiet. **Surface:** gravel.
◘ 01/01-31/12.
**Distance:** ⌷5,5km ⊗on the spot ⌷on the spot ⌷on the spot ⌷on the spot ⌷6km.

| 🅢 | Le Gault-Soigny | 16A3 |

Rue de la Liberté, D373. **GPS:** n48,81758 e3,59072.⬆.

2 ⓩfree ⌷Chfree. **Location:** Rural, simple, quiet.
**Surface:** asphalted. ◘ 01/01-31/12.
**Distance:** ⌷on the spot.
**Remarks:** Near Salle des Fêtes, service 50m.

| 🅢 | Lepuix | 19F2 |

Route du Ballon d'Alsace. **GPS:** n47,81280 e6,84146.➡.

9 ⓩfree ⌷€ 3 ⌷Ch⌷€ 3 ◿. **Location:** Rural, simple, quiet.
**Surface:** grasstiles. ◘ 01/01-31/12.
**Distance:** ⌷500m.

| 🅢 | Les Islettes ⌷ | 16C2 |

Route du Lochères. **GPS:** n49,12122 e5,03684.⬆➡.

16 ⓩ€ 7 ⌷Ch◿ WC⌷ ◿included. ⌷ **Location:** Rural, comfortable, quiet. **Surface:** gravel. ◘ 01/01-31/12.
**Distance:** ⌷3km ◿0,5km ⊗3km ⌷3km.

| 🅢 | Les Riceys ⌷ | 19B2 |

D452. **GPS:** n47,99222 e4,36458.⬆➡.

40 ⓩfree ⌷€ 2 ⌷Ch⌷€ 2 ◿. **Location:** Simple, isolated, quiet.
**Surface:** asphalted. ◘ 01/01-31/12.
**Distance:** ⌷500m ⊗500m ⌷500m.

| 🅢 | Ligny-en-Barrois 🌂⌷ | 16D3 |

**Aire de Pilvetus**, Chemin des Pains de Seigle.
**GPS:** n48,69262 e5,33621.⬆.

10 ⓩfree ⌷Chfree. **Location:** Rural, simple, isolated.
**Surface:** gravel. ◘ 01/01-31/12.
**Distance:** ⌷1,2km ⌷1,3km ⌷1,5km.
**Remarks:** At cemetery, max. 7 days.

| 🅢 | Ligny-en-Barrois 🌂⌷⌷⌷ | 16D3 |

**Relais Nautique**, Rue Jean Willemert. **GPS:** n48,68787 e5,31943.⬆➡.

12 ⓩ€ 2 + € 0,20/pp tourist tax ⌷€ 2/10minutes ⌷ Ch⌷€ 2/55minutes WC⌷€ 2 ◉€ 4 ◿free. ⌷ **Location:** Urban, comfortable, central, quiet. **Surface:** asphalted.
◘ 01/01-31/12.
**Distance:** ⌷200m ⌷on the spot ⊗200m ⌷200m ⌷on the spot ⌷on the spot.
**Remarks:** Along Canal de la Marne au Rhin, small pitches.

| 🅢 | Linthal ⌷⌷ | 19F2 |

Rue du Markstein, D430. **GPS:** n47,94495 e7,12783.⬆.

4 ⓩfree ⌷Ch⌷free. **Location:** Simple, quiet.
**Surface:** asphalted. ◘ 01/01-31/12.
**Distance:** ⌷200m ⌷on the spot ⊗200m ⌷200m ⌷on the spot.

| | Longeville-en-Barrois ◿ | 16D3 |

Gr Grande Rue. **GPS:** n48,74201 e5,20645.⬆.

10 ⓩfree. **Location:** Urban, simple, quiet. **Surface:** asphalted.
◘ 01/01-31/12.
**Distance:** ⌷100m ⌷on the spot ⊗100m ⌷100m ⌷on the spot ⌷on the spot.
**Remarks:** Along the Ornain river.

| 🅢 | Longuyon ⌷⌷ | 16D2 |

**Parking Salvador Allende**, N18. **GPS:** n49,44802 e5,59973.⬆.

2 ⓩfree ⌷€ 2/100liter ⌷Ch⌷€ 2 WC ◿. **Location:** Urban, simple, central, noisy. **Surface:** asphalted.

◻ 01/01-31/12.
**Distance:** 🚰on the spot ⊗on the spot 🚽100m.
**Remarks:** Parking next to tourist info, not suitable for big motorhomes.

### 🅸🆂 Longwy 16D1

**Stade Municipal**, Avenue du 8 Mai 1945.
**GPS**: n49,52656 e5,76559.⬆️➡️.

7🏕free 🚰€ 2,50/20minutes 🗑Ch🚽€ 2,50/4h.
**Location:** Urban, simple, central, noisy. **Surface:** asphalted.
◻ 01/01-31/12.
**Distance:** 🚰on the spot ⊗400m 🚽350m.
**Remarks:** At football ground.

### 🅲🆂 Lunéville 🌿🎣🚣 16F3

**Les Bosquets**, Quai des Petits Bosquets. **GPS**: n48,59652 e6,49865.⬆️.

23🏕€ 5,50, 01/05-31/09 € 8 🚰🗑Ch🛒◻€ 2,90/2,90 🚿included.
🏠 **Location:** Comfortable, central, noisy.
◻ 01/01-31/12.
**Distance:** 🚰700m 🚣50m ⊗600m 🚽600m.
**Tourist information Lunéville:**
Ⓜ️✂️ Château Petit Versailles. Castle, 18th century and museum.
◻ 10-12h, 14-18h ◻ Tue. 🎟️ € 8.

### 🅸🆂 Lusigny-sur-Barse 19B1

**Route du Lac. GPS**: n48,26451 e4,29735.⬆️🎣.

10🏕free. **Location:** Rural, simple, isolated, quiet. **Surface:** asphalted.
◻ 01/01-31/12.
**Distance:** 🚰2,5km 🏊on the spot 🚣on the spot ⊗2,5km.
**Remarks:** At the lake, max 3,5t.

### 🅸🆂 Mailly-le-Camp 16B3

Rue Victor Hugo. **GPS**: n48,66820 e4,19494.⬆️.
8🏕free 🚰🗑Ch🛒. **Location:** Urban. **Surface:** gravel.
◻ 01/01-31/12.
**Distance:** 🚽400m.
**Remarks:** At tennis-courts.

### 🅸🆂 Marbotte 16D3

**Parking de la Mairie**, Rue Principale, D12.
**GPS**: n48,83445 e5,58142.⬆️.

2🏕free. **Location:** Simple, quiet. **Surface:** unpaved. ◻ 01/01-31/12.
**Distance:** 🚰on the spot.
**Remarks:** Motorhome max. 8m, max. 48h.

---

### 🅸🆂 Mareuil-sur-Ay 🚣 16B2

**Relais nautique**, Place Charles de Gaulle. **GPS**: n49,04522 e4,03490.⬆️.

8🏕free 🚰150liter 🗑Ch🚽3h,Service € 5. **Location:** Urban, comfortable, central, quiet. **Surface:** asphalted. ◻ 01/01-31/12
◻ water disconnected in winter.
**Distance:** 🚰on the spot 🚣on the spot ⊗on the spot 🚽on the spot 🚲on the spot.
**Remarks:** On the canal, in village, coins at supermarket.

### 🅸🆂 Martinvelle 19E2

**Martinvelle-jadis**, Le Champ le Moine. **GPS**: n47,97629 e5,99943.⬆️.

6🏕free 🚰€ 2 🗑Ch🛒€ 5 🛒(6x)€ 5/12h WC. **Location:** Isolated.
**Surface:** grassy/gravel. ◻ 01/03-30/10.
**Distance:** 🚰50m 🚣3km 🛒6km 🚲on the spot 🚶on the spot.

### 🅸🆂 Maxey-sur-Meuse 19D1

Sous la Voie, D19A. **GPS**: n48,44850 e5,69511.⬆️🎣.

4🏕free 🚰🚿(4x)WCfree. **Location:** Simple. **Surface:** gravel.
◻ 14/05-31/12.
**Distance:** 🚰500m 🚣2km 🛒500m.

### 🅸🆂 Maxey-sur-Vaise 🚣 16D3

Grande Rue. **GPS**: n48,53836 e5,66705.⬆️.

6🏕free. **Location:** Urban, simple, central, quiet. **Surface:** asphalted.
◻ 01/01-31/12.
**Distance:** 🚰on the spot.

### 🅸🆂 Mesnil-Saint-Père 19B1

Rue du Lac. **GPS**: n48,25524 e4,34090.⬆️.

50🏕free. **Location:** Simple, quiet. **Surface:** asphalted.
◻ 01/01-31/12.
**Distance:** 🏊beach 400m 🚣400m 🚽400m.
**Remarks:** Motorhome and Coach Parking, nearby lake Orient.

---

### 🅸🆂 Metz 16E2

**Allée Metz Plage. GPS**: n49,12371 e6,16887.⬆️.

8🏕free 🚰🗑Chfree.
**Location:** Urban, simple, noisy. **Surface:** asphalted.
◻ 01/01-31/12.
**Distance:** 🚰350m 🏊1,5km ⊗300m 🚶on the spot.
**Remarks:** At entrance campsite, max. 48h, inclining pitches.
**Tourist information Metz:**
✝ Place St Louis. Square surrounded by houses from the 14th century.
✝ Cathédrale St Etienne. Cathedral.

### 🅸🆂 Millery 16E3

Avenue de la Moselle, D40. **GPS**: n48,81507 e6,12716.⬆️.

5🏕free 🚰🗑Chfree. **Location:** Simple. **Surface:** asphalted.
◻ 01/04-31/10 ◻ water: 01/11-31/03.
**Distance:** 🚰on the spot 🏊3,5km 🚣on the spot 🚲on the spot 🚶on the spot.
**Remarks:** Along Mosel.

### 🅸🆂 Mirecourt 19E1

Place Thierry/RD 166. **GPS**: n48,29945 e6,13591.⬆️➡️.

20🏕€ 6/24h 🚰€ 2/10minutes 🗑Ch🛒€ 2/55minutes WC.
🏠🔌 **Location:** Rural, comfortable, central. **Surface:** gravel.
◻ 01/01-31/12.
**Distance:** 🚰on the spot 🚽500m.

### 🅸 Mittelbergheim 19G1

**Parking Zotzenberg**, Rue Ziegelscheuer. **GPS**: n48,39853 e7,44179.🎣.

4🏕free. **Location:** Rural, simple, quiet. **Surface:** asphalted.
◻ 01/01-31/12.
**Distance:** 🚰300m 🏊3km ⊗300m 🚽300m 🚶on the spot.
**Remarks:** At cemetery, wine tasting.

### 🅸🆂 Monthermé 16C1

Rue du Général de Gaulle. **GPS**: n49,88136 e4,73015.
3🏕free 🚰€ 3 🗑Ch. **Location:** Rural. **Surface:** metalled.
◻ 01/01-31/12.
**Distance:** 🚽750m.

### 🅸🆂 Monthermé 16C1

**Etape fluviale**, Quai A. Briand. **GPS**: n49,88608 e4,73593.⬆️.

± 20 🅿️ € 3 + € 0,20/pp tourist tax 🚰💧€ 2,80/day ⬜€ 1,50
💧€ 3,50/3,50. **Surface:** grasstiles. ⏰ 01/01-31/12.
**Distance:** 🛒300m.
**Remarks:** Along the Meuse river, check in at harbourmaster.

### Monthureux-sur-Saône | 19E1
D460. **GPS:** n48,03199 e5,97390. ⬆️➡️.

8 🅿️free 🚰💧Ch WC free 💧€ 3/48h, Wifi-Stop.
**Location:** Rural, simple, quiet. **Surface:** gravel/metalled.
⏰ 01/01-31/12.
**Distance:** 🛒on the spot 🍴on the spot ❌200m 🛒75m.
**Remarks:** At football ground.

### Montier-en-Der | 19C1
Rue de l'Isle. **GPS:** n48,47861 e4,76861. ⬆️.

6 🅿️free 🚰€ 2/8minutes 💧Ch 🚰€ 2,80/55minutes WC.
**Location:** Simple, central, noisy. **Surface:** gravel.
⏰ 01/01-31/12.
**Distance:** 🛒on the spot ❌50m 🛒500m 🍴200m.
**Remarks:** Coins at tourist info.

### Montigny-lès-Vaucouleurs | 16D3
Rue de la Côte. **GPS:** n48,58875 e5,63007. ⬆️.

10 🅿️free. **Location:** Rural, simple, quiet. **Surface:** gravel.
⏰ 01/01-31/12.
**Distance:** 🛒200m 🚐200m 🚲on the spot 🚶100m.

### Montplonne | 16D3
Rue du Four. **GPS:** n48,68630 e5,16934. ⬆️➡️.

5 🅿️free. **Location:** Rural, simple, quiet. **Surface:** gravel.
⏰ 01/01-31/12.
**Distance:** 🛒300m 🚶on the spot.
**Remarks:** At football ground, next to cemetery.

---

### Morley | 16D3
**Parking Lavoir**, D5A. **GPS:** n48,57848 e5,24878. ⬆️.

5 🅿️free. **Location:** Rural, simple, central, quiet. **Surface:** grassy.
⏰ 01/01-31/12.
**Distance:** 🛒on the spot.

### Mouzon | 16C1
**Halte fluviale**, Rue du Moulin Lavigne. **GPS:** n49,60689 e5,07695. ⬆️.

8 🅿️€ 8 + € 0,20/pp tourist tax, 01/11-31/03 free 🚰💧Ch 💧
(6x) WC ⬜💧〰️ included.
**Location:** Rural, comfortable, central, quiet. **Surface:** asphalted.
⏰ 01/01-31/12 ⏺ Service: winter.
**Distance:** 🛒100m 🚐on the spot ❌300m 🚲on the spot
🚶on the spot.
**Remarks:** Along the Meuse river, sanitary and wifi code at harbour master, felt museum 100m (May-Sep).

### Munster | 19F1
**Aire de camping-cars Munster**, Rue du Dr Heid.
**GPS:** n48,03779 e7,13471. ⬆️.

54 🅿️€ 8 🚰€ 3 💧Ch 💧€ 1,50/12h, 6Amp WC ⬜€ 1,50 〰️ included
📷⬜ **Location:** Rural, comfortable, quiet. **Surface:** gravel.
**Distance:** 🛒on the spot ❌on the spot 🍴on the spot 🚲on the spot
🚶on the spot.

### Murbach | 19G2
**Abbaye de Murbach**, Rue de Guebwiller.
**GPS:** n47,92321 e7,16059. ⬆️➡️.

20 🅿️free 🚰💧Ch 🍴free. **Location:** Rural, isolated, quiet.
**Surface:** gravel/metalled. ⏰ 01/01-31/12.
**Distance:** 🛒350m 🏊on the spot ❌on the spot 🍴5km 🚶on the spot
🚴5km.

### Mutigny | 16B2
**Aire des étangs**, Route de Montflambert.
**GPS:** n49,06894 e4,02669. ⬆️➡️.

---

8 🅿️free 🚰150liter 💧Ch ⏱3h, Service € 5 🧹.
**Location:** Rural, simple, isolated, quiet. **Surface:** asphalted.
⏰ 01/01-31/12.
**Distance:** 🛒1km ❌3km 🛒3km.

### Nancy | 16E3
**Parking Faubourg Des III Maisons**, Rue Charles Keller.
**GPS:** n48,70403 e6,17598. ⬆️.

10 🅿️€ 4,50. 🚐 🧹 **Location:** Central. **Surface:** asphalted.
⏰ 01/01-31/12.
**Distance:** 🛒city centre ± 1km.

### Nancy | 16E3
**Port Saint Georges**, N57, boulevard du 21ème Régiment d'Aviation.
**GPS:** n48,69221 e6,19318.

15 🅿️€ 15,50 + € 1,50/pp 💧Ch 💧included WC ⬜.
**Location:** Urban, central, noisy. **Surface:** asphalted.
⏰ 01/05-01/11.
**Distance:** 🛒500m 🏊on the spot 🚐on the spot ❌100m 🛒100m
🚐100m.
**Remarks:** Max. 5 nights, check in at harbourmaster.

**Tourist information Nancy:**
Ⓜ️ Musée Historique Lorraine, Palais Ducal. Regional museum.
⏰ 15/06-15/09 ⏺ Tue.
Zoo Haye, Velaine-en-Haye. Zoo with centre for
wild birds.

### Nant-le-Grand | 16D3
Grand Rue, D169A. **GPS:** n48,67530 e5,22382. ⬆️.

4 🅿️free. **Location:** Rural, simple, quiet. **Surface:** grassy/gravel.
⏰ 01/01-31/12.
**Distance:** 🛒on the spot.

### Natzwiller | 19G1
D130. **GPS:** n48,44883 e7,25582.
5 🅿️free. **Location:** Rural. **Surface:** forest soil.
⏰ 01/01-31/12.
**Distance:** 🏊on the spot 🚐on the spot 🚴on the spot 🚶on the spot.

### Neuf-Brisach | 19G1
Place de la Porte de Bâle. **GPS:** n48,01688 e7,53187. ⬆️.

**FR**

3 ⌁free. **Location:** Urban, simple. **Surface:** asphalted.
⬛ 01/01-31/12.
**Distance:** ⌁300m ⊗300m ⚑300m.

**Tourist information Neuf-Brisach:**
ℹ Point I Neuf-Brisach, 6, place d'Armes, www.tourisme-rhin.com/.
City worth a visit with defences of Vauban.

## Niderviller 16F3
**Marina Niderviller**, 1 Avenue de Lorraine. **GPS:** n48,71735 e7,09906.

14 ⌁€ 15 ⛽€ 2/stay ⚑€ 2,50/time Ch€ 2,50/time ⚡€ 3/1day
WC⌁€ 0,30/1minutes. **Location:** Rural, simple, quiet.
**Surface:** metalled. ⬛ 01/01-31/12.
**Distance:** ⌁200m ⛽on the spot.
**Remarks:** Motorhome max. 8m, boat rental.

## Nixéville-Blercourt 16D2
16 Rue de la Grand. **GPS:** n49,11118 e5,24007.

4 ⌁€ 6 ⛽Ch ⚡included. **Location:** Rural, simple, quiet.
**Surface:** concrete.
**Distance:** ⌁100m.

## Nogent-sur-Seine 16A3
**Parking Camping/Piscine**, Rue du Camping.
**GPS:** n48,50388 e3,50888.

5 ⌁€ 10,79/night ⛽Chfree ⚡€ 2/3h. **Location:** Urban,
simple, quiet. **Surface:** asphalted. ⬛ 01/01-31/12.
**Distance:** ⌁1,5km ⊾2km ⊗1,5km ⚑1,5km ⊾2km.
**Remarks:** Max. 48h.

## Nomexy 19E1
Rue de l'Estrey. **GPS:** n48,31131 e6,38535.

10 ⌁€ 6,60, € 8,60 service incl ⛽Ch ⚡. **Location:** Simple.
**Surface:** asphalted. ⬛ 01/01-31/12.

---

**Distance:** ⌁on the spot ⊗750m ⚑800m ⊾on the spot.
**Remarks:** Max. 72h.

## Nonsard Lamarche 16D3
**Base de Loisirs**, Base de Loisirs de Madine.
**GPS:** n48,93064 e5,74873.

30 ⌁€ 12 ⛽€ 3/15minutes Ch ⚡€ 3/15minutes.
⊾ **Location:** Rural, simple, comfortable, isolated, quiet.
**Surface:** grassy/metalled. ⬛ 01/04-31/10.
**Distance:** ⌁700m ⊾on the spot ⛽on the spot ⊗on the spot ⊾on
the spot ⋀on the spot.
**Remarks:** At lake Madine, coins at campsite.

## Nothalten 19G1
**Domaine Jean-Marie & Fabrice Wassler**, 22 route du Vin.
**GPS:** n48,35083 e7,41982.

8 ⌁€ 7 ⛽Ch ⚡included. ⊾ **Location:** Simple, quiet.
**Surface:** gravel. ⬛ 01/01-31/12.
**Distance:** ⌁600m ⊗100m ⊾on the spot.

## Nubécourt 16D2
Rue Raymond Poincaré/D151. **GPS:** n48,99704 e5,17256.

8 ⌁free. **Location:** Rural, simple, central, quiet. **Surface:** asphalted.
⬛ 01/01-31/12.
**Distance:** ⌁on the spot ⛽200m ⊾on the spot ⋀on the spot.

## Obernai 19G1
**Parking des Remparts**, Rue Poincaré. **GPS:** n48,45972 e7,48667.

50 ⌁free ⛽free. **Location:** Urban, simple. **Surface:** gravel.
⬛ 01/01-31/12.
**Distance:** ⌁300m ⚐2,7km ⊗300m ⚑300m ⊾200m.
**Remarks:** Large parking in centre, video surveillance.

## Obernai 19G1
**Parking de l'Altau**, Route d'Ottrott. **GPS:** n48,46239 e7,47369.

---

10 ⌁free. **Location:** Urban, simple, central. **Surface:** asphalted.
⬛ 01/01-31/12.
**Distance:** ⌁600m ⊗600m ⚑600m.
**Remarks:** Max. 24h, video surveillance.

## Oltingue 19G3
Place Saint Martin. **GPS:** n47,49158 e7,39068.

4 ⌁free ⛽€ 2/10minutes Ch ⚡€ 2/55minutes WCfree.
**Location:** Urban, simple, noisy. **Surface:** asphalted.
⬛ 01/01-31/12.
**Distance:** ⌁100m ⊾on the spot ⊗100m ⚑200m ⊾on the
spot ⋀on the spot.

## Orbey 19F1
**Hôtel Restaurant Les Terrasses du Lac Blanc**, Lac Blanc.
**GPS:** n48,13540 e7,08957.

8 ⌁€ 7 ⛽included Ch ⚡(8x)€ 2,50. ⊾ **Location:** Comfortable,
quiet. **Surface:** grassy/gravel.
**Distance:** ⊾500m ⛽500m ⊾on the spot.
**Remarks:** Guests free.

## Orchamps Vennes 19F3
**La ferme des Ravières**, 16 Les Ravières. **GPS:** n47,10692 e6,49251.

6 ⌁€ 7 ⛽Chincluded. ⊞ **Location:** Rural, simple, isolated, quiet.
**Surface:** grassy/gravel. ⬛ 01/01-31/12.
**Distance:** ⌁3km ⊗on the spot.

## Orschwihr 19G2
Rue de la Source. **GPS:** n47,93722 e7,23083.

5 ⌁free ⛽Service € 4,30 Ch. **Location:** Rural, simple, quiet.
**Surface:** asphalted. ⬛ 01/01-31/12.
**Distance:** ⌁200m ⊗200m ⚑5km ⊾on the spot ⋀on the spot.
**Remarks:** Max. 48h.

**⊞S Orschwiller 19G1**

**Aire de service du Haut-Koenigsbourg**, A35.
**GPS:** n48,23278 e7,40477.
30 ⌂free ⚡⚡ChWC ⚡. **Location:** Motorway, noisy.
**Surface:** asphalted. ⬛ 01/01-31/12.
**Distance:** ⚡on the spot ⊗on the spot.

**⊞S Peigney 19D2**

**Lac de la Liez**, D284, rue Côté de Recey.
**GPS:** n47,87272 e5,38077. ⬆➡.

8 ⌂€ 10,50 ⚡⚡Ch ⚡⚡€ 2. ⚡ **Location:** Simple.
**Surface:** asphalted. ⬛ 01/01-31/12.
**Distance:** ⚡500m ⚡on the spot ⚡on the spot ⊗on the spot ⚡on the spot.

**Pfaffenheim 19G2**

**Aire du Winzerhof**, 10 Rue de la Tuilerie. **GPS:** n47,98639 e7,29167. ⬆.

5 ⌂€ 5 ⚡⚡Ch ⚡⚡ (5x)WC included. ⚡ **Location:** Urban, simple, quiet. **Surface:** gravel/metalled. ⬛ 01/01-31/12.
**Distance:** ⚡400m ⊗400m ⚡3km ⚡on the spot ⚡on the spot.
**Remarks:** Guests free, sale of wines.

**⊞S Phalsbourg 16G3**

**Aire de camping car de Phalsbourg**, Rue du Commandant Taillant.
**GPS:** n48,76549 e7,25939. ⬆.

4 ⌂free ⚡€ 2/10minutes ⚡Ch ⚡⚡€ 2/1h ⚡. **Location:** Urban, simple. **Surface:** grasstiles.
⬛ 01/01-31/12.
**Distance:** ⚡on the spot ⊗150m ⚡800m.
**Remarks:** Max. 48h.

**⊞S Phalsbourg 16G3**

**TOTAL tankstation**, ZAC Louvois, Route du Luxembourg.
**GPS:** n48,76899 e7,24182. ➡.

10 ⌂free. **Location:** Simple, isolated, quiet. **Surface:** asphalted.
⬛ 01/01-31/12.
**Distance:** ⚡on the spot ⚡on the spot.
**Remarks:** Picnic area at artificial lake.

**⊞S Piney 19B1**

**Place des Anciens Combattants**, Rue du Général de Gaulle.
**GPS:** n48,35878 e4,33442. ⬆➡.

5 ⌂free ⚡€ 3/10minutes ⚡Ch ⚡⚡€ 3/1h. **Location:** Simple.
**Surface:** metalled. ⬛ 01/01-31/12 ⬛ water: frost.
**Distance:** ⚡500m ⊗500m ⚡500m.
**Remarks:** Coins at town hall and restaurant.

**⊞S Plainfaing ⚡ 19F1**

Rue de Gérardmer. **GPS:** n48,17167 e7,01255. ⬆➡.

12 ⌂€ 6 ⚡⚡Ch ⚡⚡ included. **Location:** Rural, simple, quiet.
**Surface:** asphalted. ⬛ 01/01-31/12.
**Distance:** ⚡200m ⊗200m ⚡on the spot.

**⊞S Plombières-les-Bains ⚡⚡ 19E2**

Allée Eugene Delacroix. **GPS:** n47,95822 e6,44966.

15 ⌂free ⚡⚡ (5x). **Location:** Simple, quiet. **Surface:** asphalted.
⬛ 01/01-31/12.
**Distance:** ⚡1km ⊗300m.

**⊞S Pompierre 19D1**

Chemin de la Corvée. **GPS:** n48,25691 e5,67188. ⬆➡.

3 ⌂free ⚡⚡free. **Location:** Urban, simple, noisy.
**Surface:** asphalted. ⬛ 01/01-31/12.
**Distance:** ⚡1km ⚡500m ⚡500m.

**⚡S Pont-à-Mousson ⚡⚡⚡ 16E3**

**Port de plaisance**, Avenue des Etas Unis, D910.
**GPS:** n48,90296 e6,06088. ⬆.

45 ⌂€ 10 ⚡⚡Ch ⚡⚡WC ⚡⚡ included. **Location:** Urban, luxurious. **Surface:** asphalted. ⬛ 01/04-31/10.
**Distance:** ⚡400m ⚡3,4km ⚡on the spot ⊗400m ⚡400m ⚡on the spot.
**Remarks:** Max. 15 days, check in at reception, bread-service.

**⊞S Rebeuville 19D1**

Rue du Cougnot. **GPS:** n48,33530 e5,70128. ⬆➡.

2 ⌂free ⚡⚡Ch ⚡free. **Location:** Rural, simple, isolated.
**Surface:** asphalted. ⬛ 01/04-31/10.
**Distance:** ⚡5km ⚡on the spot ⚡on the spot ⊗5km ⚡5km ⚡500m.
**Remarks:** Along river, max. 7 days.

**⊞S Reims 16B2**

**Parc du CIS de la Comédie**, Esplanade André Malraux, chaussée Bocquaine. **GPS:** n49,25000 e4,02160. ⬆➡.

9 ⌂free ⚡⚡Chfree. **Location:** Urban, simple, central, noisy.
**Surface:** metalled. ⬛ 01/01-31/12.
**Distance:** ⚡15 min walking ⚡1,4km ⊗350m ⚡100m.
**Remarks:** Max. 48h, call for entrance code, noisy place.

**⊞S Remiremont ⚡ 19F1**

Rue du Lit d'Eau. **GPS:** n48,01540 e6,60208. ⬆.

31 ⌂€ 6 ⚡⚡Ch included ⚡⚡€ 3/24h ⚡ ⚡ ⚡ **Location:** Urban, comfortable. **Surface:** gravel. ⬛ 01/01-31/12.
**Distance:** ⚡1km ⚡on the spot ⚡on the spot ⊗on the spot ⚡on the spot ⚡on the spot ⚡on the spot ⚡on the spot.
**Remarks:** At small lake, at station, video surveillance.

**⚡S Rennepont ⚡⚡ 19C1**

**Domaine Rennepont**, 31 Rue Principale. **GPS:** n48,14927 e4,85430. ⬆.

4 ⌂€ 22 ⚡⚡€ 3 ⚡included WC ⚡⚡€ 3 ⚡ ⚡ ⚡ ⚡ ⚡

**Pierre-Percée 19F1**

D182A. **GPS:** n48,46723 e6,92911. ⬆.

**Location:** Rural, simple, isolated, quiet. **Surface:** grassy/gravel.
🅿 15/03-31.10.
**Distance:** 🚰on the spot 🏊200m ⊗on the spot 🅇 on the spot.
**Remarks:** Baker every morning.

### Revigny-sur-Ornain    16C3
**Stade/Office de Tourisme**, Rue de l'Abattoir.
**GPS:** n48,82642 e4,88330.⬆️➡️.

2 🛌free 🚰€1 🚽Chfree ☕€1. **Location:** Urban, simple, central,
quiet. **Surface:** asphalted. 🅿 01/01-31/12.
**Distance:** 🚰500m 🛒100m ⊗on the spot 🍽on the spot
🍺on the spot.
**Remarks:** Coins at tourist info.

### Revin    16C1
Rue du Port. **GPS:** n49,93962 e4,63843.⬆️.
14 🛌free 🚰€2/100liter 🚽Ch☕€2/1h,16Amp ⚡.
**Surface:** metalled. 🅿 01/01-31/12.
**Distance:** 🚰on the spot ⊗on the spot 🍽on the spot.
**Remarks:** Max. 8M.

### Rhodes    16F3
**Port Municipal**, Rue Principale. **GPS:** n48,75784 e6,90053.⬆️.

30 🛌€18/24h 🚰🚽Ch☕WC included. **Location:** Rural,
comfortable, quiet. **Surface:** grassy. 🅿 01/04-30/09.
**Distance:** 🏊on the spot 🛒on the spot 🍽on the spot 🅇 on the spot.
**Remarks:** Along Etang du Stock.

### Ribeauvillé    19G1
Route de Guémar. **GPS:** n48,19273 e7,33393.⬆️.
🛌. **Location:** Urban, central, noisy. **Surface:** asphalted.
🅿 01/01-31/12.
**Distance:** 🚰1km 🛒1km 🍽1km 🚲on the spot 🅇 on the spot.
**Tourist information Ribeauvillé:**
🅇 🅿 Sa.

### Richardmenil    16E3
Rue du lac. **GPS:** n48,59457 e6,16078.⬆️.

5 🛌free 🚰🚽Ch☕(4x)free. **Location:** Isolated, quiet.
**Surface:** asphalted. 🅿 01/01-31/12.
**Distance:** 🚰1km 🏊on the spot 🛒on the spot ⊗500m 🍽1km
🍺1km 🅇 on the spot.
**Remarks:** At small lake.

### Riquewihr    19G1
Avenue Jacques Preiss. **GPS:** n48,16608 e7,30175.⬆️.

15 🛌€8/24h 🚰🚽Ch☕🍽2. 🍺 **Location:** Simple, noisy.
**Surface:** asphalted. 🅿 01/01-31/12.
**Distance:** 🚰200m ⊗200m 🍽200m.
**Remarks:** Motorhomes <7m, video surveillance.
**Tourist information Riquewihr:**
👁 Office de Tourisme, Rue de 1ère Armée. Picturesque street with
houses of the 16th century.

### Rollainville    19D1
23 Rue de la Cure. **GPS:** n48,36185 e5,73842.⬆️➡️.

1 🛌free 🚰☕free. **Location:** Urban, simple, central.
**Surface:** asphalted. 🅿 01/01-31/12.
**Distance:** 🚰on the spot.
**Remarks:** Baker at 8am.

### Rouffach    19G2
Place des Sports. **GPS:** n47,95539 e7,29558.⬆️➡️.

5 🛌free 🚰€5 ⚡. **Location:** Urban, simple, quiet.
**Surface:** asphalted. 🅿 01/01-31/12 🅾 Service: winter.
**Distance:** 🚰800m ⊗600m.
**Remarks:** Coins at tourist info.

### Rupt-sur-Moselle    19F2
Quai de la Parelle. **GPS:** n47,92061 e6,66194.⬆️.

8 🛌free 🚰€3/10minutes 🚽Ch☕(4x)€3/3h WC.
**Location:** Simple, quiet. **Surface:** asphalted.
🅿 01/01-31/12.
**Distance:** 🚰on the spot ⊗350m 🍽250m 🚲on the spot 🅇 Voie Verte.
**Remarks:** Max. 7 days, coins at the shops and town hall.

### Saint-Dié-des-Vosges    19F1
Avenue de la Vanne de Pierre. **GPS:** n48,28659 e6,96597.⬆️➡️.

42 🛌€6 🚰🚽Ch☕📶included. 🍺⚡ **Location:** Comfortable.

**Surface:** asphalted/gravel. 🅿 01/01-31/12.
**Distance:** 🚰500m ⊗500m 🍽700m.

### Saint-Dizier    16C3
**Centre Loisirs Caravanning**, Route de Villiers en Lieu.
**GPS:** n48,64255 e4,91035.⬆️➡️.

6 🛌free 🚰🚽Ch☕(4x)WCfree. **Location:** Rural, comfortable,
noisy. **Surface:** asphalted. 🅿 01/01-31/12.
**Distance:** 🚰1,5km 🍽400m.
**Remarks:** At motorhome dealer, coins during opening hours.

### Saint-Hippolyte    19G1
14 rue Kleinforst. **GPS:** n48,23084 e7,37681.⬆️.

3 🛌free 🚰€4 🚽Ch. **Location:** Urban, simple, quiet.
**Surface:** asphalted. 🅿 01/01-31/12.
**Distance:** 🚰on the spot ⊗300m 🚲on the spot 🅇 on the spot.
**Remarks:** Service 100m, 3 parking spaces Allée des Cygnes n48.23242,
o7.37239, 3 parking spaces Rue Windmuehl n48.23172, e.36443.

### Saint-Imoges    16B2
Rue de la Briquetrie. **GPS:** n49,10689 e3,97903.

8 🛌free 🚰150liter 🚽Ch🍽1h,service € 2. **Location:** Rural, quiet.
**Surface:** asphalted. 🅿 01/01-31/12.
**Distance:** 🚰500m 🛒300m 🚲on the spot 🅇 on the spot.

### Saint-Mihiel    16D3
Chemin Gué Rapeau. **GPS:** n48,90227 e5,53960.⬆️➡️.

4 🛌€3 🚰€3 🚽Chfree ☕€3/24h. **Location:** Rural, simple,
isolated, quiet. **Surface:** asphalted. 🅿 01/01-31/12.
**Distance:** 🚰1,5km ⊗1km 🍽1,5km.
**Remarks:** Directly at the river, nearby sluices, next to camping
municipal, max. 24h.

### Saint-Nabord    19F1
Rue de la Croix Saint Jacques. **GPS:** n48,04527 e6,58175.⬆️.

FR

7 ⛺free ⚡€ 3/80liter 🚰Ch🚽 € 3. **Location:** Simple, quiet.
**Surface:** asphalted. 🅾 01/01-31/12.
**Distance:** 🛒300m ⊗200m 💧50m.
**Remarks:** Coins at the shops.

### 🅿️S Saint-Nicolas-de-Port 16E3
Rue du Jeu de Paume. **GPS:** n48,63515 e6,30048. ⬆️➡️

10 ⛺free ⚡€4 🚰Ch🚽. **Location:** Urban, simple, central, quiet.
**Surface:** gravel. 🅾 01/01-31/12.
**Distance:** 🛒on the spot ⊗150m 💧200m 📷100m.

### 🅿️S Sainte-Livière 🌳 16C3
1 rue Sainte Libaire. **GPS:** n48,60133 e4,82139. ⬆️

19 ⛺€ 8 ⚡🚰Ch🔌 (19x)WC 🚿included. 🏧 **Location:** Urban,
comfortable, central, quiet. **Surface:** gravel.
🅾 01/01-31/12.
**Distance:** 🛒on the spot 🏊2km Lake Der-Chantecoq 🚣2km 🚲200m
🚶200m.
**Remarks:** Bread-service, service passerby € 3.

### 🅿️ Sainte-Marie-aux-Mines 🌳⛵🌳❄️ 19G1
Place des Tisserands. **GPS:** n48,24700 e7,18322. ⬆️⬆️

10 ⛺free. **Location:** Urban, simple, quiet. **Surface:** asphalted.
🅾 01/01-31/12.
**Distance:** 🛒100m ⊗100m 💧500m 📷300m.
**Remarks:** Max. 24h.
**Tourist information Sainte-Marie-aux-Mines:**
ℹ️ Office de Tourisme, 86, rue Wilson, www.tourisme.fr/office-de-tour-
isme/sainte-marie-aux-mines-68.htm. Mineral city with silvermine,
Mine d'Argent Sainte-Barthélemy.

### 🅿️S Sainte-Marie-du-Lac-Nuisement 🌳⛵🌊 16C3
Port de Nuisement, D13A. **GPS:** n48,60285 e4,74922. ⬆️⬆️

6 ⛺free ⚡€ 3/8minutes. 🚰Ch🚽 € 3/55minutes.
**Location:** Rural, comfortable, central, quiet. **Surface:** asphalted.
🅾 01/01-31/12.
**Distance:** 🛒4km ⊗on the spot ⊗800m 🚲1km 🚶on the spot.
**Remarks:** Coins at tourist info.

### 🅿️S Sapignicourt 🌳 16C3
Rue Deperthes à Larzicourt. **GPS:** n48,65111 e4,80583. ⬆️

4 ⛺free ⚡€ 2,50/10minutes 🚰Ch🚽 € 2,50/55minutes.
**Location:** Rural, simple, isolated, quiet. **Surface:** grassy.
🅾 01/01-31/12.
**Distance:** 🛒500m.
**Remarks:** Coins at town hall and Mr. Bauer, 14, grande rue.

### 🅿️ Sarralbe 16F2
**Parc François Mitterand**, Rue de la Sarre. **GPS:** n49,00171 e7,03240. ⬆️

4 ⛺free. **Location:** Simple. **Surface:** asphalted. 🅾 01/01-31/12.
**Distance:** 🛒350m ⊗350m.
**Remarks:** At sports centre.

### 🅿️S Saverne ⛴️ 16G3
Rue des Emouleurs. **GPS:** n48,74512 e7,36854. ➡️

40 ⛺€ 7 ⚡€ 2/10minutes 🔌€ 2/6h. 🏧♻️ **Location:** Simple,
central. **Surface:** gravel/sand. 🅾 01/01-31/12.
**Distance:** 🛒centre 650m ⊗500m 💧600m.
**Remarks:** At harbour.

### 🅿️S Saverne ⛴️ 16G3
**Camping Les Portes d'Alsace**, Rue du Père Liebermann.
**GPS:** n48,73131 e7,35504. ⬆️

12 ⛺€ 10-14 + € 0,90/pp tourist tax ⚡🚰Ch🔌 WCincluded
🏧€ 2,50 🔌€ 2,50 🚿. **Location:** Rural, comfortable, quiet.
**Surface:** gravel. 🅾 01/04-30/09.
**Distance:** 🛒2km ⊗2km 💧2km.
**Tourist information Saverne:**
🅼🏛️ Château de Rohan. Museum, former summer residence of the
bishops of Strasbourg.

### 🅿️ Sedan 🌳 16C1
**Château Fort**, Rue Hue Tanton. **GPS:** n49,70145 e4,95092. ⬆️⬆️
4 ⛺free. 🅾 01/01-31/12.
**Distance:** 🛒400m ⊗400m.
**Remarks:** Parking places around the castle of Sedan.

### 🅿️ Seuil-d'Argonne 16C3
Rue du Commandant Laflotte, D2/D20. **GPS:** n48,98294 e5,06215. ⬆️

5 ⛺free. **Location:** Rural, simple, quiet. **Surface:** gravel.
🅾 01/01-31/12.
**Distance:** 🛒700m ⊗650m 💧650m 🚲650m 🚶650m.
**Remarks:** In fron of sports fields.

### 🅿️S Sézanne 16B3
Place du Champ Benoist. **GPS:** n48,72222 e3,72125. ⬆️

7 ⛺free ⚡🚰Ch🔌free WC.
**Location:** Urban, simple, central, noisy. **Surface:** asphalted.
🅾 01/01-31/12 🔵 Fri-Sa market.
**Distance:** 🛒on the spot 💧50m 💧300m 📷50m.

### 🅿️ Sierck-les-Bains 16E2
Place de la Gro. **GPS:** n49,44424 e6,36217. ⬆️

8 ⛺free. **Location:** Simple. **Surface:** asphalted. 🅾 01/01-31/12.
**Distance:** 🛒200m ⊗200m 💧350m 🚲on the spot.
**Remarks:** Along the Moselle river, nearby police station.

### 🅿️S Soufflenheim ⛴️ 16H3
**Place de la Foire**, 1A Rue de Koenigsbruck.
**GPS:** n48,83233 e7,96045. ⬆️

13 ⛺free ⚡€ 2 🚰Ch🚽 € 2. **Location:** Urban, simple, quiet.
**Surface:** asphalted. 🅾 01/01-31/12.
**Distance:** 🛒300m ⊗200m 💧300m 🚐200m.
**Remarks:** Narrow road.

### 🅿️ Souilly 16D2
Route de St.André-en-Barrois, D159. **GPS:** n49,02730 e5,27985. ⬆️

6 ⛺free. **Location:** Rural, simple. **Surface:** gravel. 🅾 01/01-31/12.
**Distance:** 🛒600m ⊗600m 💧bakery 600m.
**Remarks:** Next to sports fields, max. 7 days.

FR

### Soultz  19G2

Rue de la Marne. **GPS**: n47,88806 e7,23139. ⬆.

3 free ⚡🅰Ch free. **Location**: Urban, simple, quiet.
**Surface**: asphalted. ⬜ 01/01-31/12.
**Distance**: 🚶200m ⊗200m 🚆500m 🚌500m on the spot.

### Stenay  16D1

D947. **GPS**: n49,48979 e5,18323. ⬆➡.

49 € 8, 01/10-31/03 € 9 + € 0,20/pp tourist tax ⚡🅰
Ch 🚿WC🚽🅰€ 4/4 included. 🏠 **Location**: Rural, comfortable,
quiet. **Surface**: metalled. ⬜ 01/01-31/12.
**Distance**: 🚶150m ⊗150m 🚆800m, bakery 300m.
**Remarks**: Pay and entrance code at harbourmaster, musée Européen
de la Bière, beer museum.

### Stenay  16D1

**Port de plaisance**, Rue du Port. **GPS**: n49,49096 e5,18312. ⬆➡.

6 € 8, 01/10-31/03 € 9 + € 0,20/pp tourist tax ⚡🅰
Ch 🚿WC🚽🅰€ 4/4 included. **Location**: Urban, comfortable,
central, quiet. **Surface**: asphalted. ⬜ 01/01-31/12.
**Distance**: 🚶on the spot ⊗200m 🚆500m.
**Remarks**: Pay at harbourmaster.

**Tourist information Stenay**:
Ⓜ Musée de la Bière. Beer museum.
Château, Louppy-sur-Loison. Renaissance castle, 17th century.

### Suippes  16C2

Rue de l'Abreuvoir. **GPS**: n49,13074 e4,53419. ⬆.

10 free ⚡🅰€ 2 Ch€ 2 🅰. **Location**: Urban, simple.
**Surface**: asphalted. ⬜ 01/01-31/12.
**Distance**: 🚶on the spot ⊗200m 🚆200m.

### Tannois  16D3

**Parking du Belvédère**, D169. **GPS**: n48,71977 e5,22967. ⬆.

---

10 free. **Location**: Rural, simple, isolated, quiet. **Surface**: gravel.
⬜ 01/01-31/12.
**Distance**: 🚶1,3km 🚤1,5km 🚲on the spot 🚶on the spot.
**Remarks**: Max. 7 days.

### Thann  19F2

**Parking du Centre**, Rue des Martyrs. **GPS**: n47,80889 e7,10460. ⬆➡.

30 free ⚡🅰€ 4/15minutes ChService € 4 🅰. **Location**: Urban,
simple, noisy. **Surface**: asphalted. ⬜ 01/01-31/12.
**Distance**: 🚶250m ⊗50m 🚆50m.
**Remarks**: Max. 7 days.

### Thann  19F2

**Place du Bungert**, Rue des Pélerins. **GPS**: n47,81159 e7,10450. ⬆.

14 free WCfree. **Location**: Urban, simple, central, quiet.
**Surface**: asphalted.
⬜ 01/01-31/12 ⬛ Sa-morning market.
**Distance**: 🚶200m 🏊on the spot ⊗200m 🚆500m 🚌on the spot
🚲on the spot 🚶on the spot.
**Remarks**: Max. 7 days, max. 7m.

### Thaon-les-Vosges  19E1

**Aire du Coignot**, Rue du Coignot. **GPS**: n48,24920 e6,42520. ⬆➡.

10 free ⚡€ 2,80 Ch. **Location**: Simple, quiet.
**Surface**: asphalted/gravel. ⬜ 01/04-30/11.
**Distance**: 🚤1,5km 🚆400m.
**Remarks**: Next to port fluvial, max. 9m.

### Thiaucourt-Regniéville  16E3

Rue du Stade. **GPS**: n48,95220 e5,86090. ⬆➡.

8 free ⚡€ 2/20minutes Ch🚿(4x)€ 3/6h.
**Location**: Rural, comfortable, isolated, quiet. **Surface**: grassy/gravel.
⬜ 01/01-31/12.

---

**Distance**: 🚶700m ⊗700m 🚶500m.
**Remarks**: At tennis-courts.

### Thierville-sur-Meuse  16D2

**Thierville sur-meuse**, Avenue de l,etangbleu.
**GPS**: n49,17499 e5,36357. ⬆.

6 free. **Location**: Rural, simple. **Surface**: asphalted.
⬜ 01/01-31/12.
**Distance**: 🚶100m 🚤50m ⊗50m 🚲on the spot 🚶on the spot.
**Remarks**: Along the Meuse river.

### Tilleux  19D1

Grande Rue. **GPS**: n48,29951 e5,72636. ⬆➡.

2 free.
**Location**: Simple, quiet. **Surface**: gravel. ⬜ 01/01-31/12.
**Distance**: 🚶100m.
**Remarks**: Near church, max. 7 days, inclining pitches, entrance road
max. 3,5t.

### Tonnoy  16E3

**Aire de d' accueil Camping Car du Grand Vanné**, RD 74.
**GPS**: n48,54934 e6,24337. ⬆.
32 € 8/24h ⚡🅰Ch 🚿included. 🏠 **Surface**: grassy.
⬜ 01/05-30/09.
**Distance**: 🚶1km 🏊on the spot 🚤on the spot 🚲on the spot.
**Remarks**: Along the Moselle river, former campsite.

### Toul  16E3

Chemin du Cimetière. **GPS**: n48,67670 e5,88549. ⬆➡.

8 € 7/24h ⚡🅰Ch 🚿(8x)included. **Location**: Urban, comfortable,
quiet. **Surface**: asphalted. ⬜ 01/01-31/12.
**Distance**: 🚶500m 🚤4km ⊗500m 🚆500m.
**Remarks**: Max. 72h.

### Trémont  18C3

**Domaine du Sablon**, La Montcellière. **GPS**: n47,16491 w0,44972. ⬆.
6 € 5 ⚡🅰Ch 🚿WC🚽included. 🏠 **Location**: Rural, comfortable,
isolated, quiet. **Surface**: grassy. ⬜ 01/01-31/12.
**Distance**: 🚶1km ⊗on the spot.
**Remarks**: Shady, sale of wines.

**FR**

## Trois Épis 19G1

**Aire municipale**, Place des Antonins. GPS: n48,10101 e7,22948. ↑ →.

10 free ⚡€2 ⚡€0,50/time Ch€0,50/time €3/1h WC€0,50 €1. **Location:** Urban, simple, quiet. **Surface:** asphalted.
01/01-31/12.
**Distance:** 150m 150m 150m on the spot.
**Remarks:** At cemetery, max. 7 days, max. 8M.

## Turckheim 19G1

Quai de la gare. **GPS:** n48,08555 e7,27739. ↑.

10 €5.
**Location:** Urban, simple, noisy. **Surface:** metalled.
01/01-31/12.
**Distance:** historical centre 250m 250m 300m on the spot.
**Remarks:** Max. 7 days.

## Ungersheim 19G2

**Ecomusée**, Grosswald. **GPS:** n47,85150 e7,28540. ↑ →.

20 €6 Ch included. **Location:** Rural, simple, quiet.
**Surface:** gravel/metalled. 01/01-31/12.
**Distance:** 6km 200m 7km.
**Remarks:** Check in at hotel, shady.

## Val-d'Ornain 16C3

D2. **GPS:** n48,80327 e5,07284. ↑.

6 free. **Location:** Rural, simple, isolated, noisy. **Surface:** gravel.
01/01-31/12.
**Distance:** 400m on the spot on the spot.

## Val-et-Châtillon 16F3

**Piémont Vosgien**, Grande Rue / D993a. **GPS:** n48,56039 e6,96525. ↑.

6 free ⚡€3 Ch €3/55minutes. **Location:** Comfortable, quiet. **Surface:** gravel. 01/01-31/12.

---

**Distance:** 100m 3,5km on the spot.
**Remarks:** Max. 4 days, bread-service.

## Valonne 19F3

2 rue des carrières. **GPS:** n47,34064 e6,65873. ↑.

6 €5 ⚡€2 Ch included. **Location:** Rural, simple, isolated, quiet. **Surface:** gravel. 01/01-31/12.
**Distance:** 500m.

## Vaucouleurs 16D3

Rue du Cardinal Lépicier. **GPS:** n48,60187 e5,66814. ↑ →.

3 €5 ⚡€2/100liter Ch €2. **Location:** Urban, simple, central, quiet. **Surface:** asphalted.
01/01-31/12.
**Distance:** on the spot 500m 500m 100m.
**Remarks:** Check in at town hall.

## Vauquois 16C2

**Parking municipal**, D212. **GPS:** n49,20405 e5,07398. ↑.

4 free. **Location:** Rural, simple, quiet. **Surface:** gravel.
01/01-31/12.
**Distance:** on the spot.
**Remarks:** Max. 7 days, max. 8M.

## Velaines 16D3

13 rue Nancois. **GPS:** n48,70589 e5,29804. ↑.

4 free. **Location:** Urban, simple, central, quiet. **Surface:** gravel.
01/01-31/12.
**Distance:** on the spot 200m 300m.
**Remarks:** Max. 7 days.

## Vendeuvre-sur-Barse 19C1

Place du 8 mai 1945, Rue du Pont Chevalier.
**GPS:** n48,23727 e4,46646. ↑ →.

---

5 free ⚡€3 Ch €3. **Location:** Urban, simple.
**Surface:** asphalted. 01/01-31/12. tue-evening, wed-morning (market).
**Distance:** 100m on the spot ATAC on the spot.

## Ventron 19F2

1 Chemin du Plain. **GPS:** n47,93906 e6,86900. ↑.

10 free ⚡€2/100liter Ch €2/55minutes.
**Location:** Simple, central, quiet. **Surface:** asphalted.
01/01-31/12.
**Distance:** 300m 300m 300m.
**Remarks:** Max. 7 days, max. 8M, coins at tourist info.

## Ventron 19F2

**Parking ski**, Route de Frère Joseph. **GPS:** n47,92514 e6,86223. ↑.

10 free. **Location:** Urban, simple, quiet. **Surface:** asphalted.
01/01-31/12.
**Distance:** Ventron 3,2km on the spot on the spot on the spot.
**Remarks:** Parking at skipistes, max. 7 days.

## Verdun 16D2

**Dragées Braquir**, Rue du Fort de Vaux, D112.
**GPS:** n49,15955 e5,39989. ↑.

10 free. **Location:** Urban, simple, central, quiet.
**Surface:** asphalted/metalled. 01/01-31/12.
**Distance:** on the spot.
**Remarks:** Max. 1 night.

## Viéville 19D1

**Halte Nautique La Licorne**, Place de Verdun.
**GPS:** n48,23825 e5,12988. ↑.

4 €3 ⚡€3/day (6x)€3/day. **Location:** Rural, simple, quiet.
**Surface:** gravel. 01/01-31/12.
**Distance:** on the spot on the spot 500m 500m on the spot on the spot.
**Remarks:** At the canal.

## Vigneulles-lès-Hattonchâtel 16D2

Rue Miss Skinner. **GPS:** n48,99200 e5,70122. ↑.

2 free. **Location:** Rural, isolated, quiet. **Surface:** gravel/metalled. 01/01-31/12.
**Distance:** 2km on the spot on the spot.
**Remarks:** At castle.

### ⚲S Villeneuve-Renneville-Chevigny 16B3
**Champagne Leclère-Massard**, 12, rue du Plessis. **GPS:** n48,91488 e4,05959.

6 €5 Ch included €2/day. **Location:** Comfortable.
**Surface:** asphalted. 01/01-31/12.
**Distance:** 3km 2km 3km 3km on the spot.
**Remarks:** Tu-Su fresh bread, champagne tastery.

### ⚲S Villers-sous-Châtillon 16B2
**Halte camping-cars**, Rue du Parc. **GPS:** n49,09642 e3,80078.

5 free €3/100liter Ch €3/1h. **Location:** Rural, simple,
quiet. **Surface:** asphalted. 01/01-31/12.
**Distance:** 1,2km 50m 1,2km 2km.
**Remarks:** Max. 6m, max. 7 days, coins at town hall and restaurant du Commerce.

### Void-Vacon 16D3
**Rue de la Gare. GPS:** n48,68240 e5,61960.

12 free €2/20minutes Ch €2/20minutes. **Location:** Rural,
simple, isolated, quiet. **Surface:** grassy/gravel.
01/01-31/12.
**Distance:** 700m 10m 10m 300m 100m.
**Remarks:** Coins at shop/town hall.

### ⚲S Vouziers 16C2
**Aire du Champ de Foire**, Rue de Condé 33. **GPS:** n49,40030 e4,70197.
9 free €2/100liter Ch €2/20minutes.
**Location:** Urban. **Surface:** grassy/metalled. 01/01-31/12.
**Distance:** 200m 350m.
**Remarks:** Max. 48h.

### ⚲S Wadelincourt 16C1
**Ferme du Chemin de Noyers**, Rue Hubert Desrousseaux.
**GPS:** n49,68075 e4,93553.

1 free free. **Location:** Rural, simple, isolated, quiet.
**Surface:** grassy/gravel. 01/01-31/12.
**Distance:** 2km 4km 2km 2km.
**Remarks:** Inclining pitches, regional products.

### ⚲S Walscheid 16F3
**Parking du plan d'eau de Walscheid**, Route d'Alsace.
**GPS:** n48,64558 e7,15664.

5 free Ch free. **Location:** Rural, simple, quiet.
**Surface:** asphalted. 01/01-31/12.
**Distance:** 1km on the spot.

### Wassy 19C1
**Lac des Leschères**, Réservoir Leschères Centre.
**GPS:** n48,48991 e4,94924.

2 free. **Location:** Rural, simple, quiet. **Surface:** asphalted.
01/01-31/12.
**Distance:** 1,5km on the spot on the spot 1,5km 1km
on the spot.

### ⚲S Westhalten 19G2
Rue St Blaise, D18, Vallée Noble, dir Soultzmatt..
**GPS:** n47,95626 e7,25135.

10 free €2 Ch. **Location:** Rural, simple, noisy.
**Surface:** asphalted. 01/03-30/11.
**Remarks:** Max. 48h.

### ⚲S Westhalten 19G2
**Domaine du Bollenberg. GPS:** n47,94459 e7,25652.

6 free (3x) free. **Location:** Rural, simple, quiet.
**Surface:** grassy/gravel. 01/01-31/12.
**Distance:** 5km on the spot 5km.
**Remarks:** Max 3,5t.

### ⚲S Willer-sur-Thur 19F2
Place de l'Eglise. **GPS:** n47,84315 e7,07292.

10 free ChWC free. **Location:** Urban, central, quiet.
**Surface:** asphalted. 01/01-31/12.
**Distance:** 250m 500m 500m, bakery 50m 500m on the
spot 500m.
**Remarks:** Max. 24h, max. 6m.

### ⚲S Wissembourg 16H2
**Parking de la Pépiniere**, Rue de la Scierie. **GPS:** n49,03209 e7,94657.

10 €5 Ch included. **Location:** Urban, simple.
**Surface:** asphalted/gravel. 01/01-31/12.
**Distance:** 1km 200m 200m 300m.

**Tourist information Wissembourg:**
Office de Tourisme, 9, place de la République, www.ot-wissembourg.fr.
Syndicat d'Intitiative, 2, rue de Kuhlendorf, Betschdorf. Many half-timbered houses and two half-timbered churches, rich potter's tradition with traditional blue-grey glaze.
M Musée de la poterie, Betschdorf. Potters' museum with work shop.
01/11-Easter.

## Normandie

### ⚲S Agon-Coutainville 15B2
Boulevard Louis Lebel-Jéhenne. **GPS:** n49,05176 w1,59123.

25 €7,50/24h Ch included. **Location:** Urban,
comfortable, quiet. **Surface:** grassy.
01/01-31/12.
**Distance:** 500m 400m 800m.
**Remarks:** Service passerby €2,70.

### ⚲S Allouville-Bellefosse 15E1
Place des Tilleuls. **GPS:** n49,59677 e0,67477.

6 free €2/100liter Ch €2/h. **Location:** Rural, simple.
**Surface:** asphalted. 01/01-31/12.
**Distance:** on the spot 5,5km 250m 500m on the spot
on the spot.

## Ardevon — 15B3

### La Bidonnière Ardevon

- **Paved and flat motorhome pitches**
- **Beautiful view**
- **Sanitary facilities**

www.labidonniere.fr
campingcar@ardevivre.fr

**La Bidonnière**, 5 route de la Rive. **GPS**: n48,60352 w1,47612. ⬆️.
50 🚐 € 10,90 🚰 € 3 💧 € 0,50/time Ch ⚡ (40x)€ 3/24h,10Amp
WC 🚽 € 3 🚿 € 4,50/time 📶 included.
**Location**: Rural, luxurious, quiet. **Surface**: grassy/gravel.
🅿️ 01/01-31/12.
**Distance**: 🛒 on the spot 🏊 3km ⊗1km 🚉 3km 🚌 1,5km
🚴 on the spot 🚶 on the spot.
**Remarks**: Bread-service, free bicycles available, view on Mt.St.Michel.

## Argentan — 15D3

**De La Dentelle**, Rue Charlotte Corday. **GPS**: n48,73984 w0,01664.

4 🚐 free 🚰 € 2,20/time 🍽️Ch 🔌 € 2,20/h. **Location**: Urban, simple.
**Surface**: asphalted. 🅿️ 01/01-31/12.
**Distance**: 🛒 500m 🏊 on the spot 🚴 on the spot ⊗550m 🚉 500m
🚶 on the spot.
**Remarks**: Coins at campsite and tourist info.

## Arromanches-les-Bains — 15C1

**Arromanches 360, Cinéma Circulaire**, Chemin du Calvaire / D514.
**GPS**: n49,33924 w0,61419. ⬆️.

20 🚐 € 6 🚰 € 2 Ch 🚴 **Location**: Rural, comfortable.
**Surface**: grassy/metalled. 🅿️ 01/01-31/12.
**Distance**: 🛒 400m 🏊 300m ⊗750m.
**Remarks**: Beautiful view.

## Arromanches-les-Bains — 15C1

Rue François Carpentier. **GPS**: n49,33904 w0,62553. ⬆️.

14 🚐 free 🚰 € 2/10minutes 🍽️Ch 🔌 € 2/1h 📶 free15minutes.
**Location**: Urban, simple, quiet. **Surface**: asphalted. 🅿️ 01/01-31/12.
**Distance**: 🛒 150m 🏊 100m 🚉 100m 🚶 250m.
**Remarks**: Next to camping municipal, max. 1 night.

## Auderville — 15B1

D901. **GPS**: n49,71431 w1,93481. ⬆️.

15 🚐 free. **Location**: Rural, simple, quiet. **Surface**: grassy/gravel.
🅿️ 01/01-31/12.
**Distance**: 🛒 300m 🏊 700m ⊗600m.

## Auffay — 15F1

Parking de la Gare. **GPS**: n49,71339 e1,09890. ⬆️.

4 🚐 free 🚰 € 3/100liter 🍽️Ch 🔌 € 3/1h 🛁. **Location**: Urban, simple,
quiet. **Surface**: gravel. 🅿️ 01/01-31/12.
**Distance**: 🛒 800m ⊗600m 🚉 600m 🚌 on the spot 🚴 on the spot
🚶 on the spot.

## Avranches — 15B3

**Centre Culturel**, Boulevard Jozeau Marigné.
**GPS**: n48,68585 w1,367. ⬆️➡️.

8 🚐 free 🚰 € 2/10minutes 🍽️Ch. **Location**: Urban, simple, quiet.
**Surface**: gravel/metalled. 🅿️ 01/01-31/12.
**Distance**: 🛒 200m 🏊 1,9km ⊗200m 🚉 200m.
**Remarks**: Behind community centre, max. 1 night, attractive medieval
centre.

**Tourist information Avranches:**
- 👁️ Jardins des Plantes. Garden with exotic plants.
- ⛪ Basilique St Germain. 🅿️ 9-12h, 14-16h.
- 🎭 place des Halles. 🅿️ Sa + Tue-morning.

## Bagnoles-de-l'Orne — 15D3

Avenue du Dr Paul Lemuet. **GPS**: n48,55558 w0,40973. ⬆️.

6 🚐 free. **Location**: Urban, simple, noisy. **Surface**: asphalted.
🅿️ 01/01-31/12.
**Distance**: 🛒 400m ⊗400m 🚉 900m 🚶 on the spot.
**Remarks**: Max. 48h.

## Bagnoles-de-l'Orne — 15D3

D235. **GPS**: n48,55821 w0,4129. ⬆️➡️.

6 🚐 free. **Location**: Urban, simple, quiet. **Surface**: gravel.
🅿️ 01/01-31/12.
**Distance**: 🛒 on the spot ⊗400m 🚉 400m 🚶 on the spot.
**Remarks**: Behind tourist info, Place du Marché.

## Bagnoles-de-l'Orne — 15D3

D916. **GPS**: n48,55034 w0,40202. ⬆️.

4 🚐 free 🚰 🍽️Ch. **Location**: Simple. **Surface**: asphalted.
🅿️ 01/01-31/12.
**Distance**: 🛒 900m 🚉 on the spot 🛒 on the spot 🚌 on the spot.

## Bardouville — 15F1

Allée de la Ligne des Hêtres. **GPS**: n49,43027 e0,92362. ⬆️➡️.

3 🚐 free 🚰 🍽️Ch. **Location**: Rural, comfortable, central, quiet.
**Surface**: asphalted. 🅿️ 01/01-31/12.
**Distance**: 🛒 300m 🚴 500m 🚉 500m.

## Barfleur — 15C1

Chemin de la Masse. **GPS**: n49,67368 w1,2641.

20 🚐 free 🚰 € 5,50 🍽️ChWC. **Location**: Urban, simple.
**Surface**: grassy/gravel. 🅿️ 01/01-31/12.
**Distance**: 🛒 200m 🏊 on the spot ⊗350m.
**Remarks**: Service at camping municipal.

## Barneville-Carteret — 15B1

Quai Émile Valmy, Rue du Port. **GPS**: n49,37223 w1,79042.

12 🚐 free. **Location**: Urban, simple, quiet. **Surface**: asphalted.
🅿️ 01/01-31/12.
**Distance**: 🛒 600m 🏊 on the spot 🚴 on the spot ⊗600m.
**Remarks**: In front of the Gare Maritime.

## Barneville-Carteret — 15B1

**Carrefour Market**, Route du Pont Rose. **GPS**: n49,38553 w1,75239.
🚰 € 2/100liter 🍽️Ch 🔌 € 2/1h. **Location**: Urban, simple.

FR

**Surface:** asphalted. 01/01-31/12.

### Baubigny 15B1
La Rue Bazin. **GPS:** n49,41479 w1,80041.

10 € 5 Ch included. **Location:** Rural, simple, quiet.
**Surface:** asphalted. 01/01-31/12.
**Distance:** on the spot 1,5km.
**Remarks:** Repair possibilities motorhome.

### Bayeux 15C2
Boulevard Fabian Ware. **GPS:** n49,27242 w0,71053.

10 overnight stay € 4. **Location:** Urban, simple, noisy.
**Surface:** gravel. 01/01-31/12.
**Distance:** 900m 700m 800m.
**Remarks:** At museum.

### Bayeux 15C2
Rue Pierre Trébucien. **GPS:** n49,27585 w0,71273.

28 € 4. **Location:** Urban, simple, quiet. **Surface:** asphalted.
01/01-31/12.
**Distance:** on the spot 750m.

### Bayeux 15C2
Voie de la Rivière. **GPS:** n49,28168 w0,69604.
€ 3/100liter Ch. **Location:** Rural. 01/01-31/12.
**Distance:** 850m.

**Tourist information Bayeux:**
Musée Mémorial de la Bataille de Normandie, Boulevard Fabian
Ware. Battle of Normandy, June 6 till August 22, 1944. 9.30-17h,
01/05-30/09 9-19h.
Cathédrale Nôtre Dame. Gothic cathedral.

### Beauvoir 15B3
Aire de camping-car du mont St Michel, Route du Mont Saint-Michel.
**GPS:** n48,59426 w1,5122.

122 € 15,50 Ch (122x) included.
**Location:** Rural, comfortable, quiet. **Surface:** grassy/gravel.
01/01-31/12.
**Distance:** 500m 500m on the spot.
**Remarks:** Service passerby € 4,50, le Mont Saint Michel 5km.

### Beauvoir 15B3
Le Mont-St-Michel, Rue Au Bis. **GPS:** n48,60841 w1,50756.

---

220 € 17,20/24h.
**Location:** Rural, simple, noisy. **Surface:** asphalted.
01/01-31/12.
**Distance:** 3,5km on the spot on the spot on the spot on the spot on the spot.
**Remarks:** Free shuttle to Le Mont-Saint-Michel 07.30-00.30h.

### Bernières-sur-Mer 15D2
Rue Victor Tesnière. **GPS:** n49,33472 w0,41984.

35 free. **Location:** Urban, simple, central. **Surface:** gravel.
01/01-31/12.
**Distance:** on the spot 100m 200m 50m 100m on the
spot on the spot on the spot.

### Bernières-sur-Seine 15F2
Parking du Stade, Rue de la Roseraie. **GPS:** n49,23135 e1,33778.

6 free. **Location:** Rural, simple, isolated. **Surface:** grassy/gravel.
01/01-31/12.
**Distance:** 200m 5km 5km.

### Beuvron-en-Auge 15D2
Parking de la Gare, Avenue de la Gare. **GPS:** n49,18560 w0,0495.

16 € 6 Ch included.
**Location:** Rural, comfortable, quiet. **Surface:** gravel.
01/01-31/12.
**Distance:** 200m on the spot on the spot.
**Remarks:** Max. 24h, pay and coins at Tabac-Presse 200m.

### Blangy-Sur-Bresle 13C3
Zone de Loisirs. **GPS:** n49,92338 e1,65535.
6 € 4 € 2/100liter Ch € 2/h. **Surface:** grassy.
01/04-31/10.
**Distance:** on the spot on the spot.

### Bretteville-sur-Odon 15D2
Auto Camping Car Service, 4-6 Avenue des Carrières.
**GPS:** n49,18449 w0,41465.

---

6 free Ch free. **Location:** Urban, simple. **Surface:** metalled.
01/01-31/12.
**Distance:** 1km 500m.

### Bréville-les-Monts 15D2
Rue des Dentellières. **GPS:** n49,24167 w0,228.

4 free € 2/10minutes Ch. **Location:** Rural, simple, quiet.
**Surface:** asphalted. 01/03-15/11.
**Distance:** 300m 1,3km.
**Remarks:** Max. 72h, (may-july-aug) 48h, coins at tourist info Merville
and harbour.

### Bricquebec 15B1
Bas de Cattigny, D900, route de Cherbourg.
**GPS:** n49,47402 w1,64674.

6 free € 5 Ch free (2x) € 5. **Location:** Comfortable, quiet.
**Surface:** gravel. 01/01-31/12.
**Distance:** 1km on the spot.

### Broglie 15E2
Parc de la bibliothèque. **GPS:** n49,00563 e0,52948.

8 € 5/24h € 2,50/100liter Ch € 2,50/1h.
**Location:** Rural, simple, quiet. **Surface:** grassy/metalled.
01/03-31/10.
**Distance:** 200m 200m 200m, 7.30-19h.
**Remarks:** Along river.

**Tourist information Broglie:**
Fri 7-13h.

### Buchy 15F1
D919, Route de Forges. **GPS:** n49,58538 e1,36417.

15 free € 2,50/100liter Ch € 2,50/h. **Location:** Urban,
comfortable. **Surface:** gravel/sand. 01/01-31/12.

**Distance:** 500m 500m 500m on the spot.
**Remarks:** Coins at town hall, monday-morning market.

| Cabourg | 15D2 |

Avenue Michel d'Ornano. **GPS:** n49,28225 w0,11994.

6 free 2/10minutes Ch. **Location:** Rural, comfortable, quiet. **Surface:** asphalted. 01/01-31/12.
**Distance:** centre 900m 7,5km 1,6km on the spot.
**Remarks:** Nearby Hippodrome.

| S Cabourg | 15D2 |

**Station Service Carrefour Market**, Avenue de la Divette.
**GPS:** n49,27774 w0,13469.
free 2 Ch. **Surface:** asphalted. 01/01-31/12.
**Distance:** 1km on the spot.

| S Cambremer | 15D2 |

Place de l'Europe/Avenue des Tilleuls. **GPS:** n49,14991 e0,04729.

10 free 3/100liter Ch 3/1h. **Location:** Rural, simple, central, quiet. **Surface:** gravel.
01/01-31/12 Service: winter.
**Distance:** 50m 100m bakery 100m.
**Remarks:** Coins at the shops and town hall.

| S Campigny | 15E2 |

Chemin de la Motte. **GPS:** n49,31139 e0,55223.

6 free Chfree. **Location:** Rural, simple, quiet.
**Surface:** grassy. 01/01-31/12.
**Distance:** 6,5km 200m.
**Remarks:** On inner court of old presbytery, max. 24h.

| S Canisy | 15C2 |

Rue Jean Follain. **GPS:** n49,07615 w1,1753.

3 free ChWC. **Location:** Simple. **Surface:** asphalted.
01/01-31/12.
**Distance:** on the spot on the spot.
**Remarks:** Coins at the shops.

| S Carentan | 15C1 |

**Camping-Car Park de Carentan**, Chemin du Grand Bas Pays.
**GPS:** n49,30937 w1,2392.

9 € 10,80 Ch included. **Location:** Urban, comfortable, quiet. **Surface:** gravel/metalled. 01/01-31/12.
**Distance:** 500m on the spot 500m 500m.
**Remarks:** Mandatory, one-time fee Pass'Etapes € 4.

| S Carolles | 15B3 |

Chemin des Pêcheurs. **GPS:** n48,75931 w1,57062.

15 € 8,50 3/100liter Ch € 3/55minutes.
**Location:** Rural, comfortable. **Surface:** grassy/gravel.
01/01-31/12.
**Distance:** 150m on the spot on the spot.
**Remarks:** Only exact change.

| S Caumont-l'Éventé | 15C2 |

**Souterroscope des Ardoisières**, Route de Saint Lô, D71.
**GPS:** n49,08868 w0,81645.

3 free € 2/10minutes Ch € 2/55minutes WC.
**Location:** Rural, simple, isolated. **Surface:** asphalted.
01/01-31/12, service 15/02-15/11.
**Distance:** 100m 50m on the spot.

| S Cérences | 15B2 |

Rue de l'hôtel au Roy. **GPS:** n48,91268 w1,43498.

6 free € 2 Ch. **Location:** Rural, simple, quiet. **Surface:** gravel.
01/01-31/12.
**Distance:** 400m 400m 500m on the spot.
**Remarks:** Coins at the shops.

| S Cerisy-la-Forêt | 15C2 |

**GPS:** n49,19788 w0,93209.

10 free € 2 Ch € 2. **Location:** Rural, simple, isolated.
**Surface:** gravel. 01/01-31/12.
**Distance:** 500m 800m 500m.

**Remarks:** Near abbey.

| Cherbourg | 15B1 |

**Musée Cité de la Mer**, Llée du President Menut.
**GPS:** n49,64740 w1,61782.

40 free. **Location:** Urban, simple. **Surface:** asphalted.
01/01-31/12.
**Distance:** 1km on the spot 1km on the spot.
**Remarks:** Max. 1 night.

**Tourist information Cherbourg:**
M Musée Fort du Roule. War museum. 9.30-12h, 14-17.30h.

| S Clecy | 15D2 |

Rue du Stade. **GPS:** n48,91886 w0,48114.

5 free € 2/20minutes Ch. **Location:** Simple, quiet.
**Surface:** gravel. 01/01-31/12.
**Distance:** 100m 100m 300m 200m.
**Remarks:** Coins at the shops in the village.

| S Clères | 15F1 |

Rue Edmond Spalikowski. **GPS:** n49,60228 e1,11667.

15 free € 5/120liter Ch € 5/6h. **Location:** Comfortable, quiet. **Surface:** gravel. 01/01-31/12 service: 01/11-28/02.
**Distance:** 500m 500m 500m on the spot.
**Remarks:** Nearby football ground, max. 72h, coins at shops and tourist office.

| S Colleville-Montgomery | 15D2 |

Rue de Saint-Aubin/Rue les Petites Rues.
**GPS:** n49,27166 w0,29891.

9 € 5 Chfree. **Location:** Rural, simple, quiet. **Surface:** grassy.
15/03-15/11.
**Distance:** 200m 450m.

**Tourist information Colleville-Montgomery:**
M Musée Omaha Beach, St.Laurent-sur-Mer. Collection of military vehicles, weapons and costumes.

| S Cormeilles | 15E2 |

Route du Château de Malou, D810. **GPS:** n49,24926 e0,37371.

FR

12 ⬛free ⬛€ 2/100liter ⬛Ch. **Location:** Rural, comfortable, quiet.
**Surface:** asphalted. ⬛ 01/01-31/12.
**Distance:** ⬛200m ⬛river ⬛200m ⬛400m.

### Coudeville-sur-Mer ⬛ 15B2

Avenue de la Mer D351. **GPS:** n48,88707 w1,56607. ⬛⬛.

30 ⬛€ 7 ⬛⬛Chincluded. ⬛⬛ **Location:** Rural, comfortable,
quiet. **Surface:** grassy/gravel. ⬛ 01/01-31/12.
**Distance:** ⬛500m ⬛200m ⬛200m ⬛500m ⬛500m.

### Courcy 15B2

**Ferme de la Pommeraie**, La Pommeraie. **GPS:** n49,05861 w1,4092. ⬛.

3 ⬛€ 6 ⬛€ 2 ⬛Ch⬛included ⬛€ 2 WC€ 1/day ⬛€ 1/day.
**Location:** Rural, simple, isolated, quiet. **Surface:** gravel/metalled.
⬛ 01/01-31/12.
**Distance:** ⬛3km ⬛on the spot ⬛3km.
**Remarks:** Service passerby € 2.

### Courseulles-sur-Mer ⬛⬛⬛ 15D2

Avenue de la Libération. **GPS:** n49,33440 w0,44551. ⬛.

12 ⬛€ 6,50 ⬛€ 2 ⬛Ch⬛. **Location:** Urban, comfortable, central.
**Surface:** asphalted. ⬛ 01/04-02/10.
**Distance:** ⬛50m ⬛200m ⬛pizzeria 50m.
**Remarks:** Nearby entrance campsite, max. 24h.

### Courseulles-sur-Mer ⬛⬛⬛ 15D2

**Juno Beach**, Voie des Français Libres. **GPS:** n49,33694 w0,46502. ⬛.

25 ⬛free. **Location:** Central, quiet. **Surface:** metalled.
⬛ 01/01-31/12.
**Distance:** ⬛100m ⬛50m.

### Couterne 15D3

Place de la Mairie. **GPS:** n48,51223 w0,41417. ⬛.

---

10 ⬛free ⬛⬛ChWCfree. **Location:** Urban, simple.
**Surface:** asphalted. ⬛ 01/01-31/12.
**Distance:** ⬛on the spot ⬛nearby ⬛nearby ⬛on the spot.
**Remarks:** Max. 1 night, closed when frosty.

### Criel-sur-Mer ⬛ 13C3

**Le Mont Joli-Bois**, 29 Rue de la Plage. **GPS:** n50,02566 e1,30860. ⬛.

19 ⬛€ 9,90 ⬛€ 5,40 ⬛Ch⬛⬛€ 5,40 ⬛⬛
**Surface:** asphalted. ⬛ 01/02-30/11.
**Distance:** ⬛1,2km ⬛900m ⬛900m ⬛1,2km.

### Deauville ⬛ 15D2

Boulevard des Sports. **GPS:** n49,35727 e0,08417. ⬛.

8 ⬛free ⬛⬛Ch⬛(6x)free. **Location:** Urban, simple, quiet.
**Surface:** gravel. ⬛ 01/01-31/12.
**Distance:** ⬛on the spot ⬛800m ⬛500m ⬛on the spot.
**Remarks:** Behind stadium, max. 24h.

### Dieppe ⬛⬛⬛⬛ 13B3

**Aire d'accueil Front de Mer**, Boulevard Maréchal-Foch.
**GPS:** n49,93188 e1,08433.

40 ⬛€ 12/24h ⬛⬛Ch⬛(8x)included1h. ⬛⬛
**Location:** Urban, simple, central. **Surface:** asphalted.
⬛ 01/01-31/12.
**Distance:** ⬛600m ⬛100m ⬛500m ⬛500m ⬛100m.
**Remarks:** Max. 48h, borrow cycles for free.

### Dieppe ⬛⬛⬛⬛ 13B3

Quai de la Marne. **GPS:** n49,93014 e1,08667. ⬛⬛.

48 ⬛€ 12/24h ⬛⬛Ch⬛(8x)included ⬛. ⬛⬛ **Location:** Urban,
simple, central. **Surface:** asphalted. ⬛ 01/01-31/12.
**Distance:** ⬛800m ⬛on the spot ⬛on the spot ⬛800m ⬛800m
⬛on the spot.

---

**Remarks:** Max. 48h, bread-service, borrow cycles for free.
**Tourist information Dieppe:**
⬛ Château Dieppe. Castle, 15th century, with maritime museum.
⬛ 10-12h, 14-18h ⬛ 01/10-31/05 Tue.
⬛ ⬛ Tue, Thu 8-14h.
⬛ Normandic market.
⬛ Sa 8-14h.

### Dives-sur-Mer ⬛ 15D2

Rue de l'Avenir. **GPS:** n49,29028 w0,10345. ⬛⬛.

10 ⬛free ⬛€ 2/10minutes ⬛Ch ⬛. **Location:** Rural, comfortable,
quiet. **Surface:** asphalted. ⬛ 01/01-31/12.
**Distance:** ⬛500m ⬛900m.
**Remarks:** Nearby Port Guillaume, max. 48h.

### Doudeville 15E1

Place du Mont Criquet, centre-ville. **GPS:** n49,72000 e0,78750. ⬛.

12 ⬛free ⬛€ 3,50/100liter ⬛Ch. **Location:** Urban, simple, central,
quiet. **Surface:** asphalted. ⬛ 01/01-31/12.
**Distance:** ⬛100m ⬛100m ⬛100m ⬛on the spot ⬛on the spot
⬛on the spot.
**Remarks:** Coins at town hall, market Saturday.

### Douville-en-Auge 15D2

La Maison Blanche. **GPS:** n49,27122 w0,03287. ⬛⬛.

5 ⬛€ 9 ⬛included. **Location:** Rural, simple, quiet.
**Surface:** grassy/gravel. ⬛ 01/01-31/12.
**Distance:** ⬛8km.

### Dragey-Ronthon 15B3

Route de la Plage. **GPS:** n48,70945 w1,5139. ⬛.

9 ⬛free. **Location:** Simple, isolated. **Surface:** grassy/sand.
⬛ 01/01-31/12.
**Distance:** ⬛2km ⬛on the spot ⬛on the spot ⬛on the spot.
**Remarks:** Max. 24h.

### Ducey ⬛⬛ 15B3

**P du Domaine**, Rue St Quentin. **GPS:** n48,62513 w1,294. ⬛⬛.

30 🅿free ⛽€ 2/100liter 🔧Ch 🚰€ 2 WC. **Location:** Simple, noisy. **Surface:** gravel/metalled. 🕐 01/01-31/12. **Distance:** 🛒500m ⊗500m 🚶500m 🧍on the spot. **Remarks:** Only exact change.

🅱🆂 **Ecouché** 15D3
Rue Racinet. **GPS:** n48,71527 w0,12775.⬆️

3 🅿free ⛽€ 2/10minutes 🔧Ch 🚰€ 2/h. **Location:** Rural, simple, quiet. **Surface:** grassy/gravel. 🕐 01/01-31/12. **Distance:** 🛒500m ⊗500m 🚶250m bakery. **Remarks:** Max. 5 days, picnic tables available.

🅱 **Elbeuf** 15F2
Allée du Front de Seine. **GPS:** n49,29262 e1,00807.⬆️
2 🅿free. **Location:** Urban, central, noisy. **Surface:** asphalted. 🕐 01/01-31/12. **Distance:** 🛒centre 500m ⊗200m 🚶200m.

🅱 **Elbeuf** 15F2
Rue de Maréchall Gallieni. **GPS:** n49,28478 e1,00677.⬆️
2 🅿free. **Location:** Urban, noisy. **Surface:** asphalted. 🕐 01/01-31/12. **Distance:** 🛒500m ⊗500m 🚶500m.

🅦🆂 **Englesqueville-la-Percée** 15C1
**Ferme de la Rouge Fossé**, D514. **GPS:** n49,38781 w0,94829.⬆️

6 🅿€ 5 ⛽€ 3 🔧Ch ✂️(6x)included. 🚿
**Location:** Rural, comfortable, isolated, quiet. **Surface:** grassy/gravel. 🕐 01/01-31/12. **Distance:** 🛒3km ⛱️500m 🚏100m.

🅱🆂 **Equeurdreville** 15B1
Rue Jean Bart. **GPS:** n49,65517 w1,65125.⬆️

4 🅿free ⛽€ 2,50 🔧Chfree. **Location:** Urban, simple. **Surface:** gravel/sand. 🕐 01/01-31/12. **Distance:** 🛒1km ⊗1km 🚶on the spot.

🆂 **Étoutteville** 15E1
**Espace du Beau Soleil**, Rue du Prieuré. **GPS:** n49,67609 e0,79073.⬆️

6 🅿free ⛽€ 2/140liter 🔧Ch 🚰€ 2/1h. **Location:** Rural, comfortable, isolated, quiet. **Surface:** concrete. 🕐 01/01-31/12. **Distance:** 🛒500m 🚏400m.

🅱🆂 **Etretat** 15E1
**Aire de stationnement Maupassant**, Rue Guy de Maupassant. **GPS:** n49,70009 e0,21579.⬆️➡️

30 🅿€ 8/24h ⛽€ 2/100liter 🔧Ch 🚰€ 3/55minutes 🚿.🚽
**Location:** Comfortable, central, quiet. **Surface:** grassy/metalled. 🕐 01/01-31/12. **Distance:** 🛒1km ⛱️1,2km ⊗1km 🚏1km 🚏350m 🚶on the spot. **Remarks:** Next to camping municipal, max. 24h.

🆂 **Etretat** 15E1
Pl. de la Gare. **GPS:** n49,70843 e0,21524.

10 🅿free. **Location:** Simple, quiet. **Surface:** metalled. 🕐 01/01-31/12. **Distance:** 🛒900m ⛱️1km ⊗900m 🚏900m. **Remarks:** Max. 7 days.

🅿 **Etretat** 15E1
Route du Havre. **GPS:** n49,70101 e0,19973.⬆️➡️
🅿€ 3,30-5.🚰 **Surface:** unpaved. 🕐 01/01-31/12. **Distance:** 🛒centre 750m ⛱️900m ⊗700m.

**Tourist information Etretat:**
ℹ️ Office de Tourisme, Place Maurice Guillard, www.etretat.net. The cliffs which have the shape of an arch are a well-known tourist attraction.

🅱🆂 **Evreux** 15F2
**Camping-Car Park Evreux le Cadran**, 64 boulevard de Normandie. **GPS:** n49,02302 e1,13839.⬆️

6 🅿€ 9,20 ⛽🔧Ch ✂️(6x)included. 🚿 **Location:** Urban, central, noisy. **Surface:** asphalted. 🕐 01/01-31/12. **Distance:** 🛒500m ⛱️2km ⊗150m 🚏150m. **Remarks:** Mandatory, one-time fee Pass'Etapes € 4.

🅱🆂 **Falaise** 15D2
**Parking Carrefour**, Rue Maurice Nicolas. **GPS:** n48,89752 w0,19035.⬆️

3 🅿free ⛽€ 1 🔧Ch. **Location:** Urban, simple. **Surface:** asphalted. 🕐 01/01-31/12. **Distance:** 🛒on the spot ⛱️1km ⊗1,5km 🚶on the spot. **Remarks:** Coins at campsite, coins at supermarket.

🅱🆂 **Fécamp** 15E1
**Parking de la Mâture**, Chaussée Gayant. **GPS:** n49,76024 e0,37412.⬆️➡️

64 🅿€ 5/night ⛽€ 3/100liter 🔧ChWC.🚽 **Location:** Urban, simple, central. **Surface:** asphalted. 🕐 01/01-31/12. **Distance:** 🛒on the spot ⊗200m 🚏200m 🚏200m. **Remarks:** Coins at tourist info(100m).

**Tourist information Fécamp:**
ℹ️ Office de Tourisme, Quai Sadi Carnot, www.fecamptourisme.com. City against the chalk-cliff of the Côte d'Albâtre, fishing-port is now mainly a marina.
Ⓜ️🅇 Palais Bénédictine, 110 rue Alexandre Le Grand. Museum with Bénédictine distillery and tasting-pub. 🕐 01/07-31/08 10-18.45h, 01/09-30/06 10.30-12.30h, 14.30-17.30h.

🍇 **Fermanville** 15B1
**Le Cap Lévi**, 17 route du Phare. **GPS:** n49,69002 w1,4673.⬆️➡️

6 🅿€ 5. 🔧 **Location:** Rural, simple, quiet. **Surface:** grassy. 🕐 01/01-31/12.

🅱🆂 **Fervaches** 15C2
La Vallée. **GPS:** n48,99550 w1,0826.⬆️➡️

8 🅿free ⛽€ 3 🔧Ch. **Location:** Rural, comfortable, quiet. **Surface:** grassy/gravel. 🕐 01/01-31/12. **Distance:** 🛒150m 🚏150m. **Remarks:** Wifi code at grocery.

🅲🆂 **Forges-les-Eaux** 15G1
**Aire de camping car de la Minière**, Boulevard Nicolas Thiessé. **GPS:** n49,60569 e1,54288.⬆️

🇫🇷 **FR**

35 🛏9 🔌⛽Ch 🚿(38x)included WC ⬛€2 📶 🚿
**Location:** Urban, comfortable, central, quiet. **Surface:** asphalted.
🅿 30/03-14/10.
**Distance:** 🚂2km ⊗1km 🛒900m 🚌300m 🚲2km.
**Remarks:** Max. 48h, to be paid at campsite, sanitary at campsite.

### 🚲S Formigny 15C1
**La Ferme du Lavoir,** Route de Saint Laurent sur mer.
**GPS:** n49,34041 w0,89654. ⬆.

10 🛏€ 10/night 🔌⛽Ch 🚿WC ⬛ 📶included. 🚐 🚿
**Location:** Rural, comfortable, quiet. **Surface:** grassy/gravel.
🅿 01/01-31/12.
**Distance:** 🚂200m 🚴1km 🚶4km ⊗500m 🍴4km.
**Remarks:** Organic orchards, cider production.

### 🚲S Gacé 🍃 15E3
Rue du Marché aux Bestiaux. **GPS:** n48,79500 e0,29583. ⬆.

30 🛏free 🔌⛽€2 Ch. **Location:** Urban, simple, central, quiet.
**Surface:** asphalted. 🅿 01/01-31/12.
**Distance:** 🚂on the spot 🚴2,5km ⊗50m.
**Remarks:** In front of tourist office, max. 24h.

### 🚲S Gavray 15B2
D38. **GPS:** n48,91113 w1,34641. ⬆.

8 🛏free 🔌⛽€4/10minutes 🔌Ch. **Location:** Urban, comfortable.
**Surface:** asphalted. 🅿 01/01-31/12.
**Distance:** 🚂400m ⊗200m 🍴600m 🎬100m.
**Remarks:** In front of police station.

### 🚲S Gisay-la-Coudre 15E2
D35. **GPS:** n48,95001 e0,62670. ➡.

6 🛏free 🔌⛽€2/100liter 🔌Ch. **Location:** Rural, simple, quiet.
**Surface:** asphalted. 🅿 01/01-31/12.

---

**Distance:** 🚂La Barre-en-Ouche 3km 🚌on the spot ⊗300m.
**Remarks:** Coins available at restaurant La Tortue.

### 🚲S Giverny 🍃⛵ 15F2
Chemin du Roy. **GPS:** n49,07329 e1,52979. ⬆➡.

30 🛏free.
**Location:** Urban, central. **Surface:** grassy. 🅿 01/04-01/11.
**Distance:** 🚂on the spot ⊗500m 🍴500m 🚌on the spot.
**Remarks:** Max. 1 night.

### 🚲S Gonzeville 15E1
La Ruette. **GPS:** n49,76590 e0,80738. ⬆.

4 🛏free 🔌⛽WC. **Location:** Rural, simple, isolated, quiet.
**Surface:** asphalted/gravel. 🅿 01/01-31/12.
**Distance:** 🚂on the spot ⊗7km 🍴7km 🚌100m 🚲on the spot.
🚶on the spot.

### 🚲S Gournay-en-Bray 15G1
Avenue Sadi Carnot. **GPS:** n49,48055 e1,72640. ⬆.

8 🛏free 🔌⛽Chfree. **Location:** Urban, simple, central, quiet.
**Surface:** asphalted. 🅿 01/01-31/12 🅿 Thu-morning closed because
of market + 2nd weekend Sep.
**Distance:** 🚂on the spot ⊗on the spot 🍴on the spot 🎬on the spot
🚲on the spot 🚶on the spot.
**Remarks:** Max. 48h.

### 🚲S Gournay-en-Bray 15G1
Route du Vieux Saint-Clair. **GPS:** n49,50106 e1,72245. ⬆➡.

10 🛏€6 🔌⛽€1 🚿€2. 🚿 **Location:** Rural, simple, isolated, quiet.
**Surface:** grassy/gravel. 🅿 01/01-31/12.
**Distance:** 🚂2,5km ⊗3km 🍴3km 🎬2,5km 🚲on the spot
🚶on the spot.

### 🚲S Gouvets 15C2
Le Bourg D454. **GPS:** n48,93133 w1,09492. ⬆.

---

20 🛏free 🔌⛽🚿WCfree. **Location:** Rural, simple, isolated, quiet.
**Surface:** grassy. 🅿 01/01-31/12.
**Distance:** 🚂on the spot ⊗6km 🚶on the spot.

### 🚲S Gouville-sur-Mer 🚿 15B2
Chemin du Beau Rivage. **GPS:** n49,09970 w1,60896. ⬆➡.

40 🛏€ 5,50/19-10h 🔌⛽🔌Ch 🚿WCincluded. 🚐 🚿
**Location:** Urban. **Surface:** gravel. 🅿 01/01-31/12.
**Distance:** 🚴on the spot ⊗on the spot 🚌50m.

### 🚲S Grainville-Langannerie 15D2
Rue de Lapford. **GPS:** n49,01438 w0,26805. ⬆➡.

6 🛏free 🔌⛽€2/10minutes 🔌Ch 🚻€2/55minutes 🚿.
**Location:** Rural, comfortable. **Surface:** metalled.
🅿 01/01-31/12.
**Distance:** 🚂100m.
**Remarks:** Near Salle des Fêtes.

### 🚲S Grandcamp-Maisy 15C1
Rue du Moulin d'Odo. **GPS:** n49,38620 w1,03782. ➡.

34 🛏€ 8, 01/04-30/09 € 10,50 🔌⛽🔌Ch 🚿included.
**Location:** Rural, comfortable, quiet. **Surface:** gravel.
🅿 01/01-31/12.
**Distance:** 🚂500m 🍴500m.

### 🚲S Granville 🍃⛵🍴🚿 15B2
Haute Ville, Rue du Roc. **GPS:** n48,83530 w1,6095. ⬆.

20 🛏€9 🔌⛽€3/10minutes 🔌Ch 🚻€3/55minutes 🚿.🚐
**Location:** Simple. **Surface:** asphalted/gravel. 🅿 01/01-31/12.
**Distance:** 🚂500m ⊗500m 🍴500m 🚌on the spot.
**Remarks:** Motorhome parking behind sea aquarium, upper city,
Atlantic Wall 50m, max. 24h.

FR

**Tourist information Granville:**
ℹ️ Office de Tourisme, 4, Cours Jonville, www.ville-granville.fr. The old centre, Haute-Ville, is surrounded by ramparts. The lower city is a bathing resort.
⛩️ 🅾️ Wed, Sa.

### Gréville-Hague — 15B1
D402. **GPS:** n49,67509 w1,80127. ⬆️.

10 🅿️free 🚰 € 2 💧Ch 🚽 € 2 WC. **Location:** Rural, comfortable.
**Surface:** metalled. 🅾️ 01/01-31/12.
**Distance:** 🚶on the spot 🛒100m.
**Remarks:** Next to sports fields.

### Grigneuseville — 15F1
La Plaine d'Hermesnil, 7 rue de la Plaine.
**GPS:** n49,64427 e1,19900. ⬆️.

7 🅿️ € 8 🚰💧Chincluded 🚿(4x)€ 3. 🛁 **Location:** Rural, comfortable, isolated, quiet. **Surface:** gravel. 🅾️ 01/01-31/12.
**Distance:** 🚶2,5km 🚲7km ⊗2,5km 🛒2,5km.
**Remarks:** Service passerby € 3, barbecue place, picnic area.

### Grosville — 15B1
Bar-Epicerie Caladjo, Rue des Touzés. **GPS:** n49,50659 w1,74311. ⬆️.

15 🅿️ € 6 🚰 € 2 💧Ch 🚿 € 2. **Location:** Rural, simple.
**Surface:** gravel. 🅾️ 01/01-31/12.
**Distance:** ⊗on the spot 🛒on the spot.

### Gruchet-Le-Valasse — 15E1
Route de l'Abbaye. **GPS:** n49,54058 e0,50149. ⬆️.

12 🅿️free 🚰 € 2/100liter 💧Ch 🚽 € 2/h. **Location:** Rural, simple, isolated. **Surface:** asphalted. 🅾️ 01/01-31/12.
**Distance:** 🚶2km 🚲7,5km ⊗2km 🛒2km 🐾on the spot.
**Remarks:** Service passerby € 2.

### Guilberville — 15C2
D159. **GPS:** n48,98871 w0,94844. ⬆️➡️.

---

8 🅿️free 🚰 € 2/100liter 💧Ch 🚽 € 2/1h. **Location:** Rural, simple, quiet. **Surface:** gravel. 🅾️ 01/03-01/11.
**Distance:** 🚶300m 🚲1,5km ⊗300m 🛒300m.
**Remarks:** Coins at tourist info, Bistro and bakery, playground.

### Hauteville-sur-Mer — 15B2
Avenue du Sud. **GPS:** n48,97026 w1,55514. ⬆️➡️.

20 🅿️ € 8 🚰💧Ch 🚿3Amp 📶included, Nearby campsite.
**Location:** Rural, simple, quiet. **Surface:** grassy.
🅾️ 01/01-31/12.
**Distance:** 🏊500m 🛶500m 🚲450m 🚶on the spot.
**Remarks:** Next to campsite.

### Hermanville-sur-Mer — 15D2
Rue Verte. **GPS:** n49,28592 w0,31243. ⬆️.

6 🅿️free 🚰💧Chfree. **Location:** Simple, central, quiet.
**Surface:** asphalted. 🅾️ 01/01-31/12.
**Distance:** 🚶on the spot 🛒bakery 🚌200m.
**Remarks:** Tuesday market.

**Tourist information Hermanville-sur-Mer:**
⛩️ 🅾️ Tue morning.

### Hérouvillette — 15D2
Place l'Aiguillon, Avenue de Caen, D 513A.
**GPS:** n49,21983 w0,24497. ⬆️➡️.

8 🅿️free 🚰💧Chfree. **Location:** Rural, comfortable.
**Surface:** asphalted. 🅾️ 01/01-31/12.
**Distance:** 🚶250m 🛒200m.

### Heurteauville — 15E1
Les Cerisiers, Rue de Village. **GPS:** n49,44777 e0,81333. ⬆️➡️.

12 🅿️ € 8 + € 0,50/pp tourist tax 🚰💧Chincluded 🚿(12x)€ 2. 🛁
**Location:** Rural, comfortable, isolated, quiet.

---

**Surface:** grassy/gravel.
🅾️ 01/04-31/10.
**Distance:** 🚶5km 🏊on the spot 🚲on the spot ⊗5km 🛒5km 🐾on the spot 🚶on the spot.
**Remarks:** Along the Seine river, max. 9m.

### Honfleur — 15E1
Bassin de l'Est, Quai de la cale. **GPS:** n49,41916 e0,24166. ⬆️.

240 🅿️ € 11/night 🚰💧Ch 🚿(60x)included. 🛒♻️
**Location:** Urban, simple, central. **Surface:** gravel. 🅾️ 01/01-31/12
⛽ Service: winter.
**Distance:** 🚶500m 🚲2,7km ⊗300m 🛒500m.
**Remarks:** At harbour.

### Incheville — 13C3
Rue Mozart. **GPS:** n50,01397 e1,50441.

12 🅿️ € 9,50/24h 🚰💧Chincluded. 🛒♻️ **Location:** Comfortable, isolated, quiet. **Surface:** asphalted. 🅾️ 01/01-31/12.
**Distance:** 🚶500m 🏊on the spot 🛶on the spot 🛒supermarket, bakery 600m 🐾on the spot 🚶on the spot.

### Isigny-sur-Mer — 15C1
Quai Neuf. **GPS:** n49,32150 w1,10456. ⬆️.

6 🅿️free 🚰 € 2/100liter 💧Ch. **Location:** Rural, simple, quiet.
**Surface:** asphalted. 🅾️ 01/01-31/12.
**Distance:** 🚶300m 🛶on the spot 🛒200m.

### Janville — 15D2
Route d'Argences. **GPS:** n49,15645 w0,16818. ⬆️.

5 🅿️ € 6 🚰 € 2 🚿 € 2. **Location:** Rural, simple, quiet. **Surface:** gravel.
🅾️ 01/01-31/12.
**Distance:** 🛒750m.

### Jobourg — 15B1
Nez de Jobourg, D202. **GPS:** n49,67722 w1,93806. ⬆️.

10 ⌷free ⌷WCfree. **Location:** Rural, simple, central, quiet.
**Surface:** metalled. ⌷ 01/01-31/12.
**Distance:** ⌷500m ⌷500m.

🏠S | **Jouy-sur-Eure** 🏝 | 15F2

**Des 3 Etangs**, Chemin des sources. **GPS:** n49,06059 e1,30743. ⬆.

40 ⌷€ 6 ⌷included ⌷6Amp. **Location:** Rural, isolated, quiet.
**Surface:** grassy. ⌷ 01/01-31/12. ⌷ Tue.
**Distance:** ⌷1,4km ⌷on the spot ⌷on the spot ⌷on the spot
⌷1,4km ⌷on the spot.
**Remarks:** Fishing permit available.

🏠S | **Jumièges** 🏝🏝 | 15E1

Rue Alphonse Callais. **GPS:** n49,43106 e0,81452. ⬆➡.

20 ⌷free ⌷€ 3/100liter ⌷Ch. **Location:** Rural, simple, central.
**Surface:** grassy/gravel. ⌷ 01/03-30/11.
**Distance:** ⌷1km ⌷500m ⌷200m ⌷200m ⌷on the spot ⌷on the
spot ⌷on the spot.
**Remarks:** Coins at Tourist Info and bakery.

🏠S | **L'Aigle** | 15E3

Avenue du Mont Saint Michel. **GPS:** n48,76010 e0,61462. ⬆➡.

12 ⌷free ⌷€ 4 ⌷Ch⌷. **Location:** Urban, simple. **Surface:** gravel.
⌷ 01/01-31/12.
**Distance:** ⌷500m ⌷1km ⌷700m ⌷200m.

🏠 | **La Bouille** 🏝🏝 | 15F2

**Parking du Bac**, D 67. **GPS:** n49,35103 e0,93330. ⬆.
10 ⌷free. **Location:** Rural, simple, noisy. **Surface:** asphalted.
⌷ 01/01-31/12.
**Distance:** ⌷300m ⌷2km ⌷on the spot ⌷on the spot ⌷300m
⌷300m.
**Remarks:** Along the Seine river, max. 24h.

🏠S | **La Ferrière-aux-Etangs** 🏝 | 15C3

Rue de l'Etang. **GPS:** n48,65931 w0,51706. ⬆➡.

20 ⌷free ⌷€ 2/10minutes ⌷Ch⌷⌷€ 2/h.
**Location:** Simple, quiet. **Surface:** grassy/gravel.
⌷ 01/01-31/12.
**Distance:** ⌷400m ⌷400m ⌷400m on the spot.
**Remarks:** At lake, former campsite, only exact change.

🏠S | **La Ferté-Macé** 🌼 | 15D3

**La Lande**, D908. **GPS:** n48,58670 w0,37154. ⬆.
16 ⌷€ 6, 01/07-31/08 € 8 ⌷Ch⌷(5x)included ⌷.⌷⌷
**Location:** Rural, isolated, quiet. **Surface:** gravel.
⌷ 01/01-31/12.
**Distance:** ⌷1,5km ⌷on the spot ⌷1km.
**Remarks:** At lake.

🏠S | **La Ferté-Macé** 🌼 | 15D3

Ruelle des Fournelles, D916. **GPS:** n48,59018 w0,35528. ⬆.

15 ⌷free ⌷⌷Ch WCfree. **Location:** Urban, simple.
**Surface:** asphalted. ⌷ 01/01-31/12.
**Distance:** ⌷on the spot ⌷on the spot ⌷on the spot.
**Remarks:** Parking at church.

🏠S | **La Haye-du-Puits** 🛒 | 15B1

Place du Champ de Foire. **GPS:** n49,29353 w1,54386. ⬆.

5 ⌷free ⌷⌷Chfree. **Location:** Urban, simple, central.
**Surface:** asphalted. ⌷ 01/01-31/12.
**Distance:** ⌷200m ⌷400m ⌷500m ⌷on the spot.
**Tourist information La Haye-du-Puits:**
🏛 Château, Pirou. Castle, 12th century.

🏠S | **La Lucerne-d'Outremer** | 15B3

D35. **GPS:** n48,78437 w1,42727. ⬆.

6 ⌷free, voluntary contribution ⌷⌷Ch⌷WCfree.
**Location:** Urban, simple. **Surface:** asphalted. ⌷ 01/01-31/12.
**Distance:** ⌷on the spot ⌷100m ⌷100m.
**Remarks:** Next to castle, max. 2 days.

🏠S | **La Mailleraye-sur-Seine** 🏝🏝 | 15E1

Quai Paul Girardeau. **GPS:** n49,48444 e0,77333. ⬆➡.

34 ⌷€ 5 + € 0,50/pp tourist tax, 01/11-31/03 free ⌷€ 3/10minutes ⌷
Ch⌷€ 3/1h. ⌷
**Location:** Urban, comfortable, central.
**Surface:** grassy.
⌷ 01/01-31/12 ⌷ 2nd weekend April/May.
**Distance:** ⌷200m ⌷on the spot ⌷on the spot ⌷on the spot
⌷200m ⌷on the spot ⌷on the spot.
**Remarks:** Along the Seine river, coins at town hall and shops.

🏠 | **La Poterie-Cap-d'Antifer** 🏝 | 15E1

**Parking Cap d'Antifer**, Route de la Côte. **GPS:** n49,68317 e0,16480. ⬆.

5 ⌷free. **Location:** Rural, simple, quiet. **Surface:** grassy/gravel.
⌷ 01/01-31/12.
**Distance:** ⌷2km ⌷on the spot.
**Remarks:** Max. 7 days.

🏠S | **La Roche-Mabile** | 15D3

Le Bourg. **GPS:** n48,48756 w0,05075. ⬆.
2 ⌷free ⌷€ 2 ⌷Ch⌷€ 2/1h. **Location:** Rural, simple, quiet.
**Surface:** gravel. ⌷ 01/01-31/12.
**Distance:** ⌷on the spot ⌷on the spot ⌷on the spot.
**Remarks:** Coins at supermarket in the village.

🏠S | **La Vespière** | 15E2

Chemin de la Grand Mare/Campaugé. **GPS:** n49,02763 e0,42221. ⬆.

2 ⌷free ⌷€ 2/100liter ⌷Ch⌷€ 2/1h. **Location:** Simple.
**Surface:** asphalted. ⌷ 01/01-31/12.
**Distance:** ⌷300m ⌷A28 2,2km ⌷Carrefour 200m.

🏠S | **La-Rivière-Saint-Sauveur** | 15E1

**Parking de l'Orange**, Chemin des Bancs, D580.
**GPS:** n49,40856 e0,26926. ⬆.

20 ⌷free ⌷€ 5/100liter ⌷Ch⌷€ 5/30minutes.
**Location:** Rural, simple, central, quiet. **Surface:** asphalted.
⌷ 01/01-31/12.
**Distance:** ⌷on the spot ⌷700m ⌷supermarket + bakery 100m.
**Remarks:** Coins at the shops in the village.

🏠 | **Langrune-sur-Mer** | 15D2

**Parking Harivel**, Rue du Colonel Pierre Harivel.
**GPS:** n49,32474 w0,36814. ⬆➡.

FR

3 free. **Location:** Urban, simple, central, noisy. **Surface:** asphalted/metalled. 01/01-31/12. **Distance:** on the spot beach 50m 50m. **Remarks:** Max. 48h, max. 7m.

### Lapenty 15C3
Rue du Plan d'Eau. **GPS:** n48,57859 w1,00929.

6 free Ch. **Location:** Rural, simple, quiet. **Surface:** gravel. 01/01-31/12. **Distance:** on the spot 50m 50m. **Remarks:** Max. 48h.

### Le Billot 15D2
D39. **GPS:** n48,96948 e0,07217.

15 free € 2,50 Ch € 2,50 WC. **Location:** Rural, simple, quiet. **Surface:** gravel/metalled. 01/01-31/12. **Distance:** 200m on the spot. **Remarks:** Coins at Relais du Billot 200m, beautiful view.

### Le Havre 15E1
Rue Andreï Sakharov. **GPS:** n49,50472 e0,17187.

13 € 6 Ch included. **Location:** Urban, simple, noisy. **Surface:** asphalted. 01/01-31/12. **Distance:** city centre 6km 3km 400m 300m on the spot.

**Tourist information Le Havre:**
Musée de l'Ancienne Havre, rue Jerome Bellarmato. History of the city. Wed-Su 14-18h.
Canyon Parc, CD34, Epretot. Family park in western style.

### Le Mesnil-Jumièges 15E1
Base de loisirs, Route de Mesnil. **GPS:** n49,41172 e0,84494.

15 € 5,20, Jul/Aug € 10,30 € 3,10/100liter Ch WC. **Location:** Rural, comfortable, isolated. **Surface:** grassy/metalled.

---

01/01-31/12. **Distance:** 1km 200m 200m 1km 1km on the spot on the spot on the spot. **Remarks:** Max. 3 days.

### Le Mont-Saint-Michel 15B3
Aire Camping-car du Mont-Saint-Michel. **GPS:** n48,61401 w1,50773.

€ 12,50-15,50/24h Ch included. **Location:** Rural. **Surface:** grassy/gravel. 23-06h. **Distance:** La Rotisserie on the spot.

### Le Mont-Saint-Michel 15B3
Parking Véolia, P8, La Jacotière Ardevon. **GPS:** n48,61388 w1,5058.

50 € 17,60/24h. **Location:** Rural. **Surface:** metalled. 01/01-31/12. **Distance:** 100m. **Remarks:** Max. 8M, free shuttle to Le Mont-Saint-Michel.

**Tourist information Le Mont-Saint-Michel:**
Office de Tourisme, Corps de Garde des Bourgeois, www.mont-saint-michel.net. Town with abbey on a cliff in the sea.

### Le Noyer-en-Ouche 15E2
Ferme Lesur, La Godinière, D140. **GPS:** n49,01017 e0,72444.

5 € 7,50 € 3 € 3. **Surface:** grassy. 01/01-31/12.

### Le Sap 15E2
Les Terriers, Rue Nicolas Lesieur, D12. **GPS:** n48,89525 e0,33249.

4 free Ch free. **Location:** Simple. **Surface:** gravel. 01/01-31/12. **Distance:** 500m on the spot 500m 500m. **Remarks:** Next to fire-station.

### Le Tréport 13C3
Du Funiculaire, Route Touristique, D126E. **GPS:** n50,05777 e1,36222.

---

40 € 6,40, 2 pers.incl € 2,30/100liter Ch € 2,30/55minutes. **Location:** Comfortable, isolated, quiet. **Surface:** grasstiles. 01/01-31/12. **Distance:** Le Tréport centre 2km 2km 100m. **Remarks:** Free cableway to city centre, max. 48h.

### Le Tréport 13C3
Parc Sainte Croix, Rue Pierre Mendès France. **GPS:** n50,05954 e1,38919.

61 € 10 Ch included € 1,80. **Location:** Comfortable, isolated, quiet. **Surface:** asphalted. 01/01-31/12. **Distance:** 700m 700m 500m Mr.Ed. **Remarks:** Industrial area, near camping municipal, max. 48h, baker every morning (Jul/Aug).

**Tourist information Le Tréport:**
Château d'Eu, Eu. Royal castle, 19th century. 15/03-01/11 Sa.

### Le Vaudreuil 15F2
Rue du Bout des Jardins. **GPS:** n49,25811 e1,20846.

2 free Ch (1x)free. **Location:** Urban, simple, noisy. **Surface:** asphalted. 01/01-31/12. **Distance:** on the spot 1km 600m 600m. **Remarks:** Max. 7 days.

### Les Aspres 15E3
Place de l'Ilton. **GPS:** n48,68947 e0,60193.

free Ch WC free. **Location:** Rural, simple. **Surface:** asphalted. 01/01-31/12. **Distance:** on the spot 100m 100m on the spot.

### Les Pieux 15B1
Plage Sciotot, Plage Sciotot. **GPS:** n49,50722 w1,84731.

FR

6 free.
**Location:** Rural, simple. **Surface:** metalled. 01/01-31/12.
**Distance:** on the spot beach 50m on the spot on the spot.
**Remarks:** Large parking, 50m from beach.

**S Les Pieux** 15B1
**Intermarché**, Route de Cherbourg. **GPS:** n49,51736 w1,79797.
€ 2/100liter Ch.

**S Lessay** 15B2
Place Saint Cloud. **GPS:** n49,21850 w1,53548.

6 free Ch WCfree. **Location:** Urban, simple.
**Surface:** asphalted. 01/01-31/12.
**Distance:** on the spot 150m 200m.
**Remarks:** Check in at town hall (service).

**Lion-sur-Mer** 15D2
**Parking de la Mairie**, Rue du General Gallieni.
**GPS:** n49,30174 w0,31316.

4 free.
**Location:** Urban, central, noisy. **Surface:** asphalted.
01/01-31/12.
**Distance:** on the spot on the spot 100m.
**Remarks:** At sea, parking townhall, only overnight stays 20-10h.

**Lisieux** 15E2
**Basilique de Lisieux**, Rue des Champs Rémouleux.
**GPS:** n49,14136 e0,23379.

12 free . **Location:** Urban, simple, noisy. **Surface:** asphalted.
01/01-31/12.
**Distance:** 500m 200m 750m on the spot.

**S Lisieux** 15E2
**Le Bowling de Lisieux**, Rue de Paris. **GPS:** n49,14644 e0,23826.

10 € 8-10 Ch . **Location:** Urban. **Surface:** grassy.
01/01-31/12.
**Distance:** 700m.
**Remarks:** Call if no one is present.

**S Lisieux** 15E2
**Parking du Carmel**, Rue d'Alençon. **GPS:** n49,14420 e0,22821.
3free € 2,80/100liter Ch € 2,80/1h WC. **Location:** Simple.
01/04-30/09.
**Distance:** on the spot river on the spot on the spot.
**Remarks:** Coins at tourist info.

**S Lison** 15C2
**Les Miniatures des Bois**, Route de Littry. **GPS:** n49,22770 w1,02733.

5 € 6 + € 0,50/pp € 2 € 3 Ch € 3 € 1. **Location:** Rural,
quiet. **Surface:** gravel. 01/01-31/12.
**Distance:** 2km 2,6km on the spot.

**S Longny-au-Perche** 15E3
**Le Monaco Parc**, Route de Chartres. **GPS:** n48,51503 e0,73958.
25 € 10,50 € 2 Ch included . . **Location:** Rural,
simple, isolated. **Surface:** asphalted. 01/01-31/12.
**Distance:** 1km 50m 1km 1km on the spot.

**Luc-sur-Mer** 15D2
Route de Lion-sur-Mer. **GPS:** n49,31430 w0,34346.

4 free. **Location:** Rural, simple. **Surface:** asphalted.
01/01-31/12.
**Distance:** 200m.

**Lyons-la-Fôret** 15F2
**Parking de Besguay**, La Cuette. **GPS:** n49,39908 e1,47912.

8 free. **Location:** Urban, simple, central, quiet.
**Surface:** gravel/metalled. 01/01-31/12.
**Distance:** 100m 100m 100m 200m on the spot.

**S Marigny** 15B2
Rue Auguste Eudeline, D53. **GPS:** n49,09911 w1,24776.

10 free € 2/10minutes Ch € 2/55minutes.
**Location:** Urban, simple. **Surface:** metalled. 01/01-31/12.
**Distance:** 700m 200m 700m 700m on the spot.

**S Merville Franceville** 15D2
Boulevard Wattier. **GPS:** n49,28483 w0,21071.

6 free € 2/10minutes Ch. **Location:** Rural, comfortable, quiet.
**Surface:** asphalted. 01/03-15/11.
**Distance:** 500m 75m.
**Remarks:** Max. 48h, coins at the shops in the village.

**S Mesnières-en-Bray** 15F1
Grand'rue. **GPS:** n49,76627 e1,38088.

10 free Chfree. **Location:** Rural, quiet. **Surface:** gravel.
01/01-31/12.
**Distance:** 5km 10km 350m 5km 300m on the spot
on the spot.

**S Montebourg** 15B1
**Parking Louis Lecacheux**. **GPS:** n49,48486 w1,37449.

10 free Chfree. **Location:** Simple. **Surface:** metalled.
01/01-31/12.

**S Montfiquet** 15C2
**Hotel-Restaurant Relais de la Fôret**, L'Embranchement, D572.
**GPS:** n49,19400 w0,863.

60 € 14 Chincluded WCuse sanitary € 2. **Surface:** asphalted.
01/01-31/12.
**Distance:** 1km 1km.
**Remarks:** Pay at reception, picnic tables available.

**S Montville** 15F1
Place de l'Abbé Kerebel. **GPS:** n49,54710 e1,07304.

15 free € 4,50/100liter Ch € 4,50/1h free,(8-22.30).
**Location:** Urban, comfortable, central, quiet. **Surface:** gravel.
01/01-31/12.
**Distance:** 400m 500m 600m 400m 300m.
**Remarks:** Coins at mairie, restauration Hexagone, museum, market
Saturday.

**Tourist information Montville:**
⚐ ▢ Mo-morning.

| 🅦🆂 | **Mortain** 🌿 | 15C3 |

Place du Château. **GPS**: n48,64887 w0,94489. ⬆️➡️.

6 🅿️free ⌁🔌Ch🚻WCfree. **Location:** Urban, simple.
**Surface:** asphalted. ▢ 01/01-31/12.
**Distance:** 🚉on the spot ⊗on the spot 🛒on the spot 🚶on the spot.
**Remarks:** Max. 48h.

**Tourist information Mortain:**
ℹ️ Office de Tourisme, Rue du Bourglopin, www.ville-mortain.fr. Hiking trail to the Grande and Petite Cascade, waterfalls.

| 🅦🆂 | **Moulins-la-Marche** | 15E3 |

Rue Jean Gabin. **GPS**: n48,65173 e0,47559. ⬆️.

10 🅿️free ⌁🔌Chfree. **Location:** Rural, simple. **Surface:** gravel.
▢ 01/01-31/12.
**Distance:** 🚉300m ⊗300m 🚶on the spot.

| 🅦🆂 | **Moutiers-au-Perche** | 15E3 |

Rue Ernest Boulay. **GPS**: n48,47635 e0,84636. ⬆️.

3 🅿️free ⌁🔌free. **Location:** Urban, simple. **Surface:** gravel.
▢ 01/01-31/12.
**Distance:** 🚉100m ⊗300m 🛒5km 🚶on the spot.
**Remarks:** Picnic area.

| 🅦🆂 | **Neufchâtel-en-Bray** 🌿🍽️ | 15F1 |

**Aire Camping Car Sainte Claire**, Rue la Grande Flandre.
**GPS**: n49,73725 e1,42938. ⬆️.

14 🅿️€12 🔌Ch🚻WC⌁€2,on camp site ▣ 📶included.
**Location:** Urban, comfortable, central, quiet. **Surface:** grassy/gravel.
▢ 01/01-31/12.
**Distance:** 🚉1,5km 🚲2,5km ⊗500m 🛒500m 🔌on camp site.
**Remarks:** Max. 8M.

| 🅦🆂 | **Nonancourt** | 15F3 |

D53, Rue Hippolyte Lozier. **GPS**: n48,77269 e1,19261. ⬆️.

---

▢ 01/01-31/12.
**Remarks:** Shady, gate opens automatically.

7 🅿️free ⌁🔌Ch🚿(2x)free. **Location:** Urban, simple, quiet.
**Surface:** asphalted. ▢ 01/01-31/12.
**Distance:** 🚉200m ⊗300m.

| 🅦🆂 | **Norville** 🌿 | 15E1 |

Clos Saint Martin. **GPS**: n49,47859 e0,64021. ⬆️➡️.

3 🅿️free ⌁€2/12minutes 🔌Ch🛒€2/3h. **Location:** Urban, comfortable, central, noisy. **Surface:** asphalted/grassy.
▢ 01/01-31/12.
**Distance:** 🚉on the spot ⊗500m.
**Remarks:** Max. 72h.

| 🅦🆂 | **Notre-Dame-de-Courson** 👐 | 15E2 |

La Gaillardière/D4. **GPS**: n48,99021 e0,25922. ⬆️.

5 🅿️free ⌁€2/20minutes 🔌Ch🛒€2/20minutes.
**Location:** Rural, comfortable, quiet. **Surface:** gravel.
▢ 01/01-31/12.
**Distance:** 🚉200m 🍴Le Tournebroche 200m 🚶on the spot.
**Remarks:** Service only with 1-euro coins.

| 🅦🆂 | **Oissel** 🌿🚣 | 15F2 |

Île du Bras Saint-Martin. **GPS**: n49,33783 e1,09183. ⬆️.

2 🅿️free ⌁€2/10minutes 🔌Ch🛒€2/55minutes.
**Location:** Urban, comfortable, central, quiet.
**Surface:** gravel.
▢ 01/01-31/12.
**Distance:** 🚉200m 🏊on the spot 🚲on the spot ⊗200m 🛒200m 🚣200m 🚶on the spot.
**Remarks:** <7m, coins at the bakery: 1, Rue du Maréchal Foch.

| 🅒🆂 | **Orbec** | 15E2 |

**Parc de Loisirs**, Rue St. Pierre, D915. **GPS**: n49,01758 e0,40506. ⬆️.

6 🅿️free. **Location:** Simple, quiet. **Surface:** unpaved.

---

| 🅦🆂 | **Ouistreham** | 15D2 |

Rue des Dunes/Boulevard Maritime. **GPS**: n49,28716 w0,24968. ⬆️.

45 🅿️€10 ⌁🔌Chincluded. 🚿🧺 **Location:** Urban, comfortable, noisy. **Surface:** asphalted/gravel. ▢ 01/01-31/12.
**Distance:** 🚉650m ⊗150m 🛒2km 🚶on the spot.
**Remarks:** Near car ferry.

| 🅦🆂 | **Picauville** | 15B1 |

Place du Général Leclerc. **GPS**: n49,37965 w1,42138.

5 🅿️free. **Location:** Urban, simple. **Surface:** asphalted.
▢ 01/01-31/12.
**Distance:** 🚉on the spot ⊗90m 🛒250m.

| 🅦🆂 | **Pirou-Plage** 🚣 | 15B2 |

Rue des Hublots. **GPS**: n49,16522 w1,58937. ⬆️➡️.

6 🅿️free ⌁€2/10minutes 🔌Ch🛒€2/55minutes. **Location:** Simple.
**Surface:** asphalted. ▢ 01/01-31/12.
**Distance:** 🚉500m 🏊500m ⊗500m 🛒500m.
**Remarks:** Coins at campsite Clos Marin and restaurant La Marée, market on Sunday.

| 🅦🆂 | **Pommeréval** | 15F1 |

**Centre équestre Lerat**, Route des Essarts.
**GPS**: n49,73825 e1,29796. ⬆️.

2 🅿️€7,50, 2 pers.incl. 🚿WC⌁included. **Location:** Rural, isolated, quiet. **Surface:** grassy. ▢ 01/01-31/12.
**Distance:** 🚉500m 🚲8km ⊗12km 🛒8km.

| 🅒🆂 | **Pont-de-l'Arche** 🌿 | 15F2 |

**Camp Eure**, Quai Maréchal Foch. **GPS**: n49,30594 e1,15605. ⬆️➡️.

10 🅿️free, 01/04-31/10 €5 ⌁€2,50/10minutes 🔌ChWC⌁included.

FR

🏠 📷 **Location:** Urban, comfortable, central. **Surface:** asphalted. 🔲 01/01-31/12 💧 water: 01/10-31/03. **Distance:** 🚰on the spot 🛒2km 🏊on the spot ⊗50m 🍴50m 🚉100m.

### 🅿️ S Pont-d'Ouilly 15D2
Rue de la Libération. **GPS:** n48,87794 w0,41304. ⬆️➡️.

43 🅿️€ 10/24h 🚰€2 🍽Ch 🧹(43x)included. 🚐 🧽 **Location:** Rural, comfortable, quiet. **Surface:** gravel. 🔲 01/01-31/12. **Distance:** 🚰550m 🛒on the spot ⊗550m 🍴550m. **Remarks:** Along the Orne river.

### 🅿️ S Port-en-Bessin-Huppain 15C1
**Super U**, Avenue du Général de Gaulle. **GPS:** n49,34307 w0,75212. ⬆️.

7 🅿️free 🚰€3 🍽Ch 🚿€3/24h. **Location:** Rural, simple. **Surface:** gravel/metalled. 🔲 01/01-31/12. **Distance:** 🚰200m 🏊400m ⊗100m 🍴100m.

### 🅿️ Port-en-Bessin-Huppain 15C1
Rue du 11 Novembre. **GPS:** n49,34583 w0,75861. ⬆️➡️.

17 🅿️€ 6/night. 🧹 **Location:** Rural, simple. **Surface:** gravel. 🔲 01/01-31/12. **Distance:** 🚰300m 🏊400m ⊗400m 🍴500m. **Remarks:** Max. 7 nights.

### 🅿️ Portbail 15B1
Rue Lechevalier. **GPS:** n49,33689 w1,70084. ⬆️.

30 🅿️free. **Location:** Simple, quiet. **Surface:** gravel. 🔲 01/01-31/12. **Distance:** 🚰300m 🏊on the spot 🛒on the spot ⊗300m 🚲on the spot 🚶on the spot. **Remarks:** Service 500m.

### S Portbail 15B1
Rue Gilles Poerier. **GPS:** n49,33776 w1,69273. ⬆️.

---

free 🚰€2 🍽Ch 🚿€2/1h. **Location:** Simple, quiet. **Surface:** asphalted. 🔲 01/01-31/12. **Distance:** 🚰200m. **Remarks:** At fire-station.

### 🅿️ Préaux-Saint-Sébastien 15E2
Le Bourg. **GPS:** n48,98679 e0,30732. ⬆️➡️.

2 🅿️free. **Location:** Isolated, quiet. **Surface:** asphalted. 🔲 01/01-31/12. **Distance:** 🛒on the spot.

### 🅿️ Quiberville 13B3
Avenue de la Plage. **GPS:** n49,51652 w1,28741. ⬆️.

10 🅿️free. **Location:** Simple. **Surface:** grassy. 🔲 01/01-31/12. **Distance:** 🚰200m 🏊on the spot ⊗100m 🍴150m 🛒on the spot. **Remarks:** At museum, max. 24h.

### 🅿️ S Quiberville 13B3
**Camping de la Plage de Quiberville**, Rue de la Saâne. **GPS:** n49,90504 e0,92725. ⬆️.

8 🅿️free 🚰€3,80. **Location:** Urban, simple, central, quiet. **Surface:** grassy/sand. 🔲 01/04-31/10. **Distance:** 🚰100m 🏊100m ⊗400m 🚲on the spot 🚶on the spot. **Remarks:** Max. 48h, coins at campsite.

### 🅿️ S Rauville-la-Bigot 15B1
Résidence de la Moinerie, D900. **GPS:** n49,51622 w1,68371. ⬆️.

10 🅿️free 🚰🍽Chfree 🚿. **Location:** Comfortable, quiet. **Surface:** asphalted. 🔲 01/01-31/12. **Distance:** 🚰500m.

### 🅿️ S Réville 15C1
**Ferme de la Froide Rue**, 165, Rue des Monts. **GPS:** n49,62583 w1,25278. ⬆️.

---

6 🅿️€ 7,50 🚰🍽Ch 🧹 **Location:** Rural, comfortable. **Surface:** grassy. 🔲 01/01-31/12. **Distance:** 🚰1km.

### Ri 🏘️ 15D3
**L'abeille de Ri**, Houay. **GPS:** n48,78553 w0,14713. ⬆️.

2 🅿️free. **Location:** Rural, simple, quiet. **Surface:** forest soil. 🔲 01/01-31/12. **Distance:** 🚰300m 🛒4km ⊗4km 🍴8km.

### 🅿️ S Rots 15D2
**Centre Commercial Cora**, Chemin de la Croix Vautier, N13. **GPS:** n49,19985 w0,46027. ⬆️.

5 🅿️free 🚰🍽Chfree 🚿. **Location:** Urban, simple, noisy. **Surface:** asphalted. 🔲 01/01-31/12. **Distance:** 🛒1km ⊗on the spot 🍴on the spot. **Remarks:** Terrain with video surveillance.

### 🅿️ Rouen 15F1
Quai Bas Jacques Anquetil. **GPS:** n49,43305 e1,09659. ⬆️.

14 🅿️free. **Location:** Urban, central, noisy. **Surface:** asphalted. 🔲 01/01-31/12. **Distance:** 🚰700m 🛒2km 🏊on the spot ⊗700m 🍴600m. **Remarks:** Along the Seine river.

**Tourist information Rouen:**
ℹ️ Office de Tourisme, 25, Place de la Cathedrale, www.rouentourisme.com. Large city with historical centre on theseine river, city of Jeanne d'Arc.
👁️ Église St.Maclou.
👁️ Place du Vieux-Marché. The square of the stake of Jeanne d'Arc.
Ⓜ️ Musée de la Céramique. Collection of international ceramics.
⛪ Vieux Marché. 🔲 daily 8-12h.

### 🅿️ S Rugles 15E3
Place de la Liberté. **GPS:** n48,82319 e0,71087. ⬆️.

20 �free 🚰🚽Ch📶free. **Location:** Urban, simple, central, quiet.
**Surface:** metalled. 🗓 01/01-31/12.
**Distance:** 🛒on the spot ⊗200m 🚉200m.
**Remarks:** Max. 48h.

### 📷S Ry 🌿 15F1
**Place Flaubert**, Rue Grand' Rue. **GPS:** n49,47244 e1,34465. ⬆

2 � free 🚰🚽free. **Location:** Rural, simple. **Surface:** asphalted.
🗓 01/01-31/12.
**Distance:** 🛒on the spot ⚓on the spot ⊗250m 🚉250m 🥾on the
spot 🚶on the spot.
**Remarks:** Along river.

### 📷S Saint Fromond 15C2
Rue des Gabariers, D8. **GPS:** n49,22202 w1,08956. ⬆

30 � free 🚰€2 🚽Ch📶€2. **Location:** Rural, simple.
**Surface:** asphalted/gravel. 🗓 01/01-31/12.
**Distance:** 🛒on the spot ⊗50m 🚌on the spot.

**Tourist information Saint Fromond:**
🛈 Office de Tourisme, Bd de Verdun, Carentan, www.ot-carentan.fr.
Old bishop city with Gothic cathedral.

### 📷📷S Saint-André-de-l'Eure 15F3
Boulevard Verdun. **GPS:** n48,90644 e1,26927. ⬆

10 � free 🚰🚽Chfree. **Location:** Urban, comfortable, noisy.
**Surface:** metalled. 🗓 01/01-31/12.
**Distance:** 🛒1km 🚽on the spot 🚉1km 🚌on the spot.
**Remarks:** Along railwayline.

### 📷S Saint-Aubin-sur-Gaillon 15F2
**Salle de Fêtes**, Rue des Brûlins. **GPS:** n49,14574 e1,32982. ⬆

12 � free. **Location:** Rural, simple. **Surface:** asphalted.
🗓 01/01-31/12.

---

**Distance:** 🛒on the spot ⚓2km ⊗50m 🚉1,5km 🚶on the spot.

### 📷S Saint-Aubin-sur-Mer 13B3
**Parking du Grand Sable. GPS:** n49,89372 e0,87425.

15 � €8 🚰€2/100liter Ch... **Surface:** gravel. 🗓 01/04-31/10.
**Distance:** ⚓on the spot 🚽on the spot.
**Remarks:** Beach parking, to be paid at campsite.

### 📷S Saint-Cyr-du-Ronceray 15E2
**Aire de campingcars de Valorbiquet**, Rue de Copplestone.
**GPS:** n49,05507 e0,29663. ⬆

6 � free 🚰🚽Ch📶free. **Location:** Rural, simple, central.
**Surface:** asphalted. 🗓 15/03-30/10.
**Distance:** 🛒on the spot ⊗200m 🚉8 km.
**Remarks:** Max. 48h, barbecue place.

### 📷S Saint-Hilaire-du-Harcouët 15C3
**Place de la Motte. GPS:** n48,57602 w1,09086. ⬆➡

3 � free 🚰€2 🚽Ch📶€2. **Location:** Urban, simple.
**Surface:** asphalted/metalled. 🗓 01/01-31/12.
**Distance:** 🛒on the spot 🚌300m ⊗on the spot 🚉on the spot.
**Remarks:** Behind church.

### 📷S Saint-Jean-le-Thomas 🌊 15B3
**Boulevard Stanislas. GPS:** n48,72567 w1,52296. ⬆➡

17 � €8, 15/11-15/03 free 🚰€2 🚽Ch📶€2 WC📶€1 ⚓🚐
🍽 **Location:** Rural, comfortable. **Surface:** asphalted/grassy.
🗓 01/01-31/12.
**Distance:** 🛒500m ⚓100m ⊗100m 🚉500m 🥾on the spot
🚶on the spot.

### 📷S Saint-Jouin-Bruneval 🌿🌊 15E1
**Rue des Pruniers. GPS:** n49,65099 e0,16322. ⬆➡

20 � free 🚰€2/100liter 🚽Ch📶€2/1h. **Location:** Rural, simple,

---

isolated, quiet. **Surface:** gravel. 🗓 01/01-31/12.
**Distance:** 🛒1km ⚓1km ⊗300m 🚉1km.
**Remarks:** Coins at the shops and restaurant.

### 📷S Saint-Jouin-Bruneval 🌿🌊 15E1
**Plage de Bruneval**, Saint Jouin plage. **GPS:** n49,64970 e0,15349. ⬆

20 � free **Location:** Simple, quiet. **Surface:** gravel/metalled.
🗓 01/01-31/12.
**Distance:** 🛒4km ⚓pebbled beach 🚽on the spot ⊗100m 🚉4km.

### 📷S Saint-Langis-lès-Mortagne 15E3
Chemin de la Folle Entreprise. **GPS:** n48,51835 e0,52968. ⬆

8 � free 🚰€2/100liter 🚽Ch📶 ⚓€2/h.
**Location:** Rural, simple, quiet. **Surface:** unpaved.
🗓 01/01-31/12.
**Distance:** 🛒1,5km 🚽on the spot ⊗on the spot 🚉1km 🚶on the spot.
**Remarks:** At lake.

### 📷S Saint-Lô 🌿⛲🍽 15C2
**Place de la Vaucelle. GPS:** n49,11351 w1,10309. ⬆➡

10 � free 🚰€2/10minutes 🚽Ch📶€2/h ⚓.
**Location:** Urban, comfortable, central, quiet. **Surface:** asphalted.
🗓 01/01-31/12.
**Distance:** 🛒100m ⊗180m 🚉100m 🚌on the spot.
**Remarks:** Along river.

**Tourist information Saint-Lô:**
👁 Haras National, Rue du Maréchal Juin. National Stud farm estab-
lished by Napoleon in 1806. 🗓 01/06-30/09 14-18.
Ⓜ Musée de la Libération, Place du Champ de Mars. Invasion in 1944.
🗓 10-19h, winter 14-19h 🗓 Tue. 🎟 € 4.
✝ Nôtre Dame. Renovated church 13th century.

### 📷S Saint-Martin de Bréhal ⛲🌊 15B2
Av. de l'Hippodrome. **GPS:** n48,89829 w1,56583. ⬆➡

20 � €6 + € 0,80/pp 🚰🚽Chincluded. ⚓ **Location:** Urban, simple,
central. **Surface:** asphalted. 🗓 01/01-31/12.
**Distance:** 🛒300m ⚓beach 150m ⊗300m 🚉400m.

### 📷S Saint-Nicolas-d'Aliermont 🌿 15F1
Place du 19 Mars 1962, Rue d'Arques 88. **GPS:** n49,88045 e1,22092. ⬆

FR

2 🛏free 🚰 € 2/10minutes 🗑Ch 🚽 € 2/1h.
**Location:** Urban, simple, central, quiet.
**Surface:** asphalted.
🅾 01/01-31/12.
**Distance:** 🛒200m 🏊12km ⊗200m 🍴200m � on the spot.
**Remarks:** Behind town hall, max. 48h, coins at town hall and library.

**Saint-Nicolas-de-Bliquetuit** 🌿⛵🌳 15E1
Route du Bac. **GPS:** n49,52083 e0,72777. ⬆➡

12 🛏free 🚰 € 2/10minutes 🗑Ch 🚽 € 2/1h. **Location:** Simple, quiet.
**Surface:** asphalted. 🅾 01/01-31/12.
**Distance:** 🛒1,4km 🏊on the spot 🚤on the spot ⊗2km 🍴2km
🚶on the spot.
**Remarks:** Along the Seine river, max. 48h, coins at town hall, bar and restaurant.

**Saint-Nicolas-de-la-Taille** 15E1
Voie Grout. **GPS:** n49,51250 e0,47414. ⬆➡

5 🛏free 🚰 € 3,50 🗑Ch 🚽 € 3,50. **Location:** Rural, simple.
**Surface:** asphalted. 🅾 01/01-31/12.
**Distance:** 🛒on the spot 🚲7km ⊗200m 🍴bakery 300m
🚶on the spot.
**Remarks:** Coins at townhall and bakery.

**Saint-Ouen-sur-Iton** 15E3
Rue du Clos de l'Iton. **GPS:** n48,73531 e0,69588. ⬆➡

6 🛏free 🚰Ch. **Location:** Rural, simple, quiet. **Surface:** gravel.
🅾 01/01-31/12.
**Distance:** 🛒150m 🍴150m ⊗5km.

**Saint-Pair-sur-Mer** 15B2
Avenue Léon Jozeau-Marigné. **GPS:** n48,81711 w1,56988. ⬆➡

30 🛏 € 9,50 🚰 € 2,50/10minutes 🗑Ch 🚽 € 2,50/55minutes 📶.🍴

---

**Location:** Urban, simple. **Surface:** asphalted/gravel.
🅾 01/01-31/12.
**Distance:** 🛒500m 🏊beach 500m ⊗500m 🍴on the spot.
**Remarks:** Parking at tennis-court, max. 48h.

**Saint-Pierre-Église** 15B1
Parking du 8 Mai 1945. **GPS:** n49,66897 w1,40387. ➡

6 🛏free 🚰 € 3/100liter 🗑Ch 🚽 € 3. **Location:** Urban, simple,
central, quiet. **Surface:** metalled. 🅾 01/01-31/12.
**Distance:** 🛒300m ⊗200m 🍴on the spot.
**Remarks:** Coins at supermarket.

**Saint-Pierre-le-Vieux** 🌿🌳 15F1
**Ferme du Moulin**, Route de la Vallée du Dun.
**GPS:** n49,85816 e0,88000. ⬆➡

5 🛏 € 5 + € 1/pp 🚰 € 2 🗑Ch 🚽 € 3. **Location:** Comfortable,
isolated, quiet. **Surface:** grassy/gravel. 🅾 01/01-31/12.
**Distance:** 🛒1km ⊗1km 🍴1km 🚶on the spot.

**Saint-Pierre-lès-Elbeuf** 15F2
Rue Galbois. **GPS:** n49,27121 e1,04862. ⬆➡

4 🛏free 🚰Ch free. **Location:** Rural, simple. **Surface:** grassy.
🅾 01/01-31/12.
**Distance:** 🛒500m 🚲on the spot ⊗300m 🍴650m.
**Remarks:** Service 2,5km GPS N49.28799 01.04589.

**Saint-Pierre-sur-Dives** 15D2
**Aire Camping-Cars de la Halle Médiévale**, Place du Marché.
**GPS:** n49,01713 w0,03047. ⬆

12 🛏 € 5/24h 🚰 € 3 🗑Ch. 🍴 🎫
**Location:** Urban, simple, central. **Surface:** gravel. 🅾 01/01-31/12
🔵 Mo-morning market.
**Distance:** 🛒on the spot ⊗50m 🍴150m.
**Remarks:** Service passerby € 3.

**Saint-Romain-de-Colbosc** 15E1
**Caux Estuaire**, Route d'Oudalle, Parc Éco-Normandie.
**GPS:** n49,52108 e0,34658. ⬆➡

---

13 🛏free 🚰Ch free. **Location:** Rural, isolated, quiet.
**Surface:** metalled. 🅾 01/01-31/12 🔵 service: 01/10-31/03.
**Distance:** 🛒1,5km ⊗1,5km 🍴1,5km 🚶on the spot.
**Remarks:** Next to castle, max. 3 days.

**Saint-Saire** 🌳 15F1
Rue de la Gare, D7. **GPS:** n49,69677 e1,49476. ⬆

8 🛏free 🚰 € 3/10minutes 🗑Ch 🚽 € 3/h. **Location:** Rural, simple,
isolated, quiet. **Surface:** grassy. 🅾 01/01-31/12.
**Distance:** 🛒300m ⊗on the spot 🚲on the spot 🚶on the spot.

**Saint-Sauveur-le-Vicomte** 🌿 15B1
Place Auguste Cousin. **GPS:** n49,38678 w1,52947.

3 🛏free 🚰Ch free. **Location:** Urban, central, noisy.
**Surface:** asphalted. 🅾 01/01-31/12.
**Distance:** 🛒on the spot ⊗300m 🍴300m.
**Remarks:** Next to town hall, max. 48h.

**Saint-Sever-Calvados** 15C2
Place de la Mairie. **GPS:** n48,84169 w1,04842. ⬆➡

15 🛏free 🚰Ch free. **Location:** Urban, simple, noisy.
**Surface:** gravel. 🅾 01/01-31/12.
**Distance:** 🛒100m 🚲15km 🍴100m.

**Saint-Vaast-la-Hougue** ⚓ 15C1
**Aire de la Gallouette**, Rue Galouette. **GPS:** n49,58400 w1,267. ⬆

27 🛏 € 8/night 🚰 € 2/10minutes 🗑Ch 🚽 € 2/1h. 🍴 🎫
**Location:** Urban, comfortable, quiet. **Surface:** metalled.
🅾 01/01-31/12.
**Distance:** 🛒300m 🏊on the spot 🍴300m.
**Remarks:** Near campsite Gallouette, max. 48h.

**Tourist information Saint-Vaast-la-Hougue:**
ℹ Office de Tourisme, 1, place Gen. de Gaulle, http://ot-pointedesaire.com

com. Important port for allied forces in 1944. Now large marina.
👁 Île de Tatihou, Port. Island in front of the coast, maritime museum and bird hide.
⭕ 01/04-30/09 10-18h.

### Saint-Valery-en-Caux 🌊⚓🍴 13B3
Quai d'Aval. **GPS:** n49,87220 e0,70898.⬆

40 🏕 € 6/24h 🚰 € 3,50/10minutes 📶Ch.🏭 ⚡ **Location:** Urban, comfortable, central, quiet. **Surface:** asphalted.
⭕ 01/01-31/12.
**Distance:** 🛒600m 🍴on the spot 🛒on the spot ⊗500m 🍞bakery 600m 🏊on the spot.
**Remarks:** Max. 48h, coins at tourist info.

### Saint-Vigor-le-Grand 15C2
**Les Peupliers**, Rue de Magny. **GPS:** n49,29949 w0,67436.⬆

7 🏕 € 10, € 12 service incl 🚰📶Ch.⚡included.🚾
**Location:** Rural, comfortable, isolated, quiet. **Surface:** gravel.
⭕ 01/01-31/12.
**Distance:** 🛒2km.
**Remarks:** Service passerby € 4, Bayeux centre 3,5km, Arromanches beaches 6,5km.

### Saint-Wandrille-Rançon 🍴 15E1
**Ferme de la Mare**. **GPS:** n49,54031 e0,76800.⬆➡

3 🏕 € 5 + € 1/pp 🚰📶Ch.⚡(3x)€ 2 WC🚾 ⚡ **Location:** Rural, comfortable, isolated, quiet. **Surface:** gravel. ⭕ 01/01-31/12.
**Distance:** 🛒3km ⊗3km.

### Sainte-Honorine-des-Pertes 15C1
**Garage Vally**, Route d'Omaha Beach, D514, dir Colleville-sur-Mer. **GPS:** n49,34868 w0,81635.⬆

32 🏕 € 9 🚰 € 1,50/100liter 📶Ch.⚡(32x)included.🚾
**Location:** Rural, comfortable, quiet. **Surface:** grassy.
⭕ 01/01-31/12.
**Distance:** 🛒200m 🍴800m ⊗100m.
**Remarks:** Service passerby € 2,50.

### Sainte-Marie-du-Mont 15C1
**Camping-Car Park Utah Beach**, La Madeleine, D913.
**GPS:** n49,41800 w1,18677.⬆

49 🏕 € 10,80 🚰Ch.(12x)📶included.🏭 ⚡ **Location:** Simple, quiet. **Surface:** grassy/gravel. ⭕ 01/01-31/12.
**Distance:** 🍴500m.
**Remarks:** Mandatory, one-time fee Pass'Etapes € 4, code wifi: f2d1941a5c.
**Tourist information Sainte-Marie-du-Mont:**
🅼 Musée du Débarquement, Utah-Beach. Landing museum.

### Sainte-Mère-Église 15B1
**Super U**, ZA les Crutelles. **GPS:** n49,40461 w1,32223.

10 🏕free 🚰 € 2 📶Ch.
**Location:** Urban, simple, quiet. **Surface:** asphalted.
⭕ 01/01-31/12.
**Distance:** 🛒1km 🍴on the spot.
**Remarks:** Motorhome washing place max. ^3.80m.
**Tourist information Sainte-Mère-Église:**
ℹ Borne 0 de la voie de la Liberté. Marker 0, start of the Libery Road.
ℹ Office de Tourisme, 2, Rue Eisenhower, www.sainte-mere-eglise. info. Village well-known for the paratrooper who landed on the church-tower.
🅼 Musée Airborne. Exhibition about the invasion at St.-Mère-Eglise.
⭕ 10-12h, 14-18h.

### Sallenelles 15D2
Boulevard Maritime D514. **GPS:** n49,26474 w0,22694.⬆

2 🏕free 🚰 € 2/10minutes 📶Ch. **Location:** Rural, simple, quiet.
**Surface:** asphalted. ⭕ 01/01-31/12.
**Distance:** 🛒100m 🍴on the spot 🍴300m.
**Remarks:** Behind town hall, max. 48h, max. 6m.

### Sassetot le Mauconduit 🍴 15E1
**Château de Sissi**, Rue Elisabeth d'Autriche.
**GPS:** n49,80522 e0,53091.⬆
10 🏕guests free 🚰📶Ch. ⭕ 11/02-31/12.
**Distance:** ⊗on the spot.

### Sideville-Lorimier 🍴 15B1
**Camping-car l'Orimier**, Route du Pont Roger, D152.
**GPS:** n49,58722 w1,69222.⬆

6 🏕 € 7/night 🚰📶Ch.⚡(6x)included. **Location:** Comfortable, quiet. **Surface:** asphalted/grassy. ⭕ 01/01-31/12.
**Remarks:** Regional products.

### Siouville-Hague 15B1
Avenue des Peupliers. **GPS:** n49,56356 w1,8442.

40 🏕 € 7/24h 🚰 € 4/100liter 📶Ch.➕ € 4/1h. **Surface:** grassy.
⭕ 01/01-31/12.
**Distance:** 🍴200m.

### Soligny-La-Trappe 15E3
Rue de Vaugelay. **GPS:** n48,61419 e0,53479.
🚰 € 2 📶Ch.➕ 2. **Surface:** metalled. ⭕ 01/01-31/12.
**Distance:** ⚡on the spot 🍴250m.

### Soumont-Saint-Quentin 15D2
Rue de la Mine. **GPS:** n48,97840 w0,25.⬆

20 🏕 € 8 + € 0,20/pp tourist tax 🚰📶Ch.⚡🚾 **Location:** Simple, quiet. **Surface:** grassy. ⭕ Easter-01/11.
**Distance:** 🛒1km ⊗500m 🍴500m.
**Remarks:** Former iron mine.

### Sourdeval 15C3
**Parc Saint-Lys**, Rue Jean Baptiste Janin.
**GPS:** n48,72603 w0,92308.⬆➡

8 🏕free 🚰📶Ch.⚡free. **Location:** Urban, simple.
**Surface:** gravel/metalled. ⭕ 01/01-31/12.
**Distance:** 🛒100m ⊗400m 🍴400m.
**Remarks:** Max. 72h.

### Surtainville 15B1
Rue des mielles. **GPS:** n49,46373 w1,82871.

10 🏕free 🚰 € 4,30/10minutes 📶Ch.➕ € 4,30/55minutes.
**Location:** Urban, simple, quiet. **Surface:** metalled.
⭕ 01/01-31/12.
**Distance:** 🍴100m ⊗500m.
**Remarks:** Coins at camping municipal.

### Tinchebray 15C3
Rue André Breton, D911. **GPS:** n48,76302 w0,73753.⬆➡

3 ⛺free 🚰🔌Ch♻free. **Location:** Urban, simple.
**Surface:** asphalted. 🅿 01/01-31/12.
**Distance:** 🛒on the spot ⊗300m.
**Remarks:** Max. 48h.

**ⓈTourlaville** 🌊 **15B1**
**Espace Loisirs Collignon**, Rue des Algues. **GPS:** n49,65398 w1,56606.

10 ⛺free 🚰€ 2 🔌Ch. **Location:** Simple. **Surface:** asphalted.
🅿 01/01-31/12.
**Remarks:** Coins at campsite or swimming pool.

**Tourlaville** 🌊 **15B1**
Quai Amiral Kniskern/Boulevard Maritime. **GPS:** n49,64549 w1,59976.

10 ⛺free. **Location:** Urban, simple, noisy. **Surface:** asphalted.
🅿 01/01-31/12.
**Remarks:** Parking at ferry-boat.

**ⓈTourouvre** 🌳 **15E3**
**La Sablonnière**, Rue de Saint-Gilles, D32.
**GPS:** n48,59203 e0,64473. ⬆➡.

9 ⛺€ / 🚰🔌Chincluded ♻(4x)€ 3/24h 🗑 . **Location:** Rural,
simple, quiet. **Surface:** asphalted.
🅿 01/01-31/12.
**Distance:** 🛒800m ⊗500m 🍴700m.

**ⓈTréauville** **15B1**
1, La Chaussee, D65. **GPS:** n49,54444 w1,83472. ⬆.

10 ⛺€ 6,50 🚰🔌Ch♻included. **Surface:** grassy/metalled.
**Distance:** ⛱2,5km.

**ⓈTroarn** **15D2**
Super U, Route de Rouen. **GPS:** n49,17907 w0,1907. ⬆.

---

Remarks: Service 100m.

⛺free 🚰€ 2 🔌Ch♻€ 2 WC. **Location:** Urban.
**Surface:** asphalted. 🅿 01/01-31/12.
**Distance:** 🛒on the spot ⊗150m 🍴on the spot.

**ⓈVal-de-Saâne** 🌳 **15F1**
Rue Moulin du Traversin. **GPS:** n49,70390 e0,96506. ⬆.

6 ⛺free 🚰€ 2/100liter 🔌Ch🍴€ 2/1h.
**Location:** Urban, comfortable, central, quiet. **Surface:** asphalted.
🅿 01/01-31/12.
**Distance:** 🛒300m ⊗300m 🍴300m on the spot 🏊on the spot.
**Remarks:** Coins at town hall, bakery and restaurant,
market on Sunday.

**ⓈValognes** **15B1**
Place Félix Buhot. **GPS:** n49,51159 w1,47813. ⬆.

7 ⛺free 🚰€ 2 🔌Ch🍴€ 2. **Location:** Simple. **Surface:** asphalted.
🅿 01/01-31/12.
**Distance:** 🛒1km 🍴on the spot.
**Remarks:** At supermarket Carrefour.

**ⓈValognes** **15B1**
Zone Artisanale d'Armanville, Chemin de la Brique.
**GPS:** n49,51433 w1,50004. ⬆.

⛺€ 5/24h 🚰€ 2 🔌Ch🍴€ 2 WC. **Location:** Simple.
**Surface:** asphalted. 🅿 01/01-31/12.
**Distance:** 🛒1km.
**Remarks:** Motorhome washing place.

**ⓈVassy** **15C2**
Rue du Moulin. **GPS:** n48,85830 w0,6705. ⬆.

8 ⛺free 🚰🔌Ch. **Location:** Rural, simple, isolated.
**Surface:** asphalted. 🅿 01/01-31/12.
**Distance:** ⊗350m.

---

**ⓈVeules-les-Roses** 🌿⛲ **13B3**
**Camping des Mouettes**, Avenue Jean Moulin 7.
**GPS:** n49,87596 e0,80289. ⬆➡.

15 ⛺€ 10/24h, summer € 15/24h, tourist tax € 0,40/pp 🚰
Ch WC ☐included,sanitary at campsite 🚿
**Location:** Rural, simple, isolated, quiet. **Surface:** gravel/metalled.
🅿 01/04-14/10.
**Distance:** 🛒300m ⛱500m 🌊500m ⊗300m 🍴300m 🚌on the
spot 🏊on the spot.
**Remarks:** Max. 48h.

**ⓈVeulettes-sur-Mer** 🌿🌊 **15E1**
Chemin des Courses. **GPS:** n49,85233 e0,60165. ⬆.

10 ⛺€ 5 🚰€ 3,50/100liter 🔌Ch🍴€ 3,50/1h ♻(16x).
**Location:** Rural, simple, central, quiet. **Surface:** asphalted.
🅿 01/01-31/12.
**Distance:** 🛒200m ⛱100m 🌊100m ⊗400m 🍴400m 🏊on the
spot 🏊on the spot.
**Remarks:** Behind Syndicat d'Initiative, coins at tourist info, campsite
and supermarket.

**ⓈVeulettes-sur-Mer** 🌿🌊 **15E1**
**Parking de la Plage**, Digue Jean Corruble.
**GPS:** n49,85488 e0,60702. ⬆.

50 ⛺€ 7 🚰€ 3,50/10minutes 🔌Ch🍴€ 3,50/1h WC.
**Location:** Rural, simple, quiet. **Surface:** grassy.
🅿 01/01-31/12.
**Distance:** 🛒500m ⛱pebbled beach 50m 🌊50m ⊗500m 🍴400m
🏊500m.
**Remarks:** Beach parking, seaview.

**ⓈVilledieu-les-Poêles** 🌿⛲🌊 **15B2**
Place des Quais. **GPS:** n48,84195 w1,22269. ⬆.
6 ⛺free 🚰€ 4 🔌Ch♻€ 4. **Location:** Urban. **Surface:** metalled.
🅿 01/01-31/12.
**Distance:** 🛒on the spot ⊗on the spot.

**ⓈVilledieu-les-Poêles** 🌿⛲🌊 **15B2**
**Parc de la Commanderie**, Rue Taillemarche.
**GPS:** n48,83682 w1,22436. ⬆.

5 ⛺free. **Location:** Urban, simple. **Surface:** asphalted.
🅿 01/01-31/12.

FR

**Distance:** ⬆on the spot 🚲2,4km ⊗100m 🛒100m.

### 🅢 Villers-Bocage — 15C2
Rue du Canada. **GPS:** n49,07973 w0,6609. ⬆➡.

5 🚐free 🚰€ 2/10minutes 🅲h 🔌€ 2/55minutes 🚿.
**Location:** Urban, simple, quiet. **Surface:** asphalted.
🅿 01/01-31/12.
**Distance:** 🚲1,5km ⊗on the spot 🛒400m 🎡on the spot.
**Remarks:** Max. 48h.

### 🅢 Villers-sur-Mer ⚓ — 15D2
**Paleospace l'Odyssée**, Rue des Martois.
**GPS:** n49,32910 e0,01273. ⬆➡.

14 🚐€ 12 🚰€ 2 🅲h 🚿included 📶€ 1 🚿.🗑 🚗
**Location:** Comfortable, quiet. **Surface:** gravel. 🅿 01/01-31/12.
**Distance:** ⬆1km 🏖beach 250m 🛒bakery 1,5km.
**Remarks:** Max. 48h.

### 🅢 Vimoutiers ⚓ — 15E2
D916, Avenue du Dr. Dentu. **GPS:** n48,93152 e0,19604. ⬆.

6 🚐free 🚰🅲h 🚿(2x)WCfree. **Location:** Urban, simple, central.
**Surface:** asphalted. 🅿 01/01-31/12.
**Distance:** ⬆400m 🛒500m 🛒Carrefour 200m.
**Remarks:** Major centre in the Camembert-region, Camembert museum.

### 🅢 Vire — 15C2
Place du champ de foire. **GPS:** n48,84084 w0,88862. ⬆➡.

25 🚐free 🚰🅲hfree. **Location:** Urban, simple, noisy.
**Surface:** asphalted. 🅿 01/01-31/12 🅿 Fri-Sa.
**Distance:** ⬆on the spot ⊗on the spot 🛒on the spot.
**Remarks:** Water closed during wintertime, friday-Saturday market.

### 🅢 Yvetot — 15E1
**Parking du square Pierre Bobée**, Rue de l'Étang.
**GPS:** n49,61617 e0,76216. ⬆.

7 🚐free 🚰€ 3/10minutes 🅲h 🔌€ 3/1h 🚿. **Location:** Urban,
simple. **Surface:** asphalted. 🅿 01/01-31/12.
**Distance:** ⬆600m 🚲4km ⊗600m 🛒600m.
**Remarks:** Max. 48h.

# Ile-de-France

### 🅢 Bray-sur-Seine — 19A1
Quai de l'Ile. **GPS:** n48,41713 e3,23745. ⬆.

30 🚐free 🚰🅲hfree 🔲. **Location:** Urban, simple, noisy.
**Surface:** asphalted. 🅿 01/01-31/12.
**Distance:** ⬆100m ⊗100m.
**Remarks:** Along the Seine river, max. 72h, max. 7m.

**Tourist information Bray-sur-Seine:**
🚶 🅿 Fri 8-13h.

### 🅢 Coupvray — 15H3
**Parking Disneyland Paris**, Boulevard du Parc.
**GPS:** n48,87500 e2,79700. ⬆.

🚐€ 40/day 🚰🅲hWC🚿included. 🗑 🚗 **Location:** Urban,
comfortable, noisy. **Surface:** asphalted. 🅿 01/01-31/12.
**Distance:** ⬆11km ⊗on the spot.
**Remarks:** Motorhome area at amusement park, water closed during wintertime, note: tariffs will be charged per day, even if you arrive in the evening.

**Tourist information Coupvray:**
Disneyland Paris, Marne-la-Vallée. Attractions and themepark.

### 🅢 Milly-la-Forêt — 18H1
Route de Nemours. **GPS:** n48,39798 e2,48021. ⬆.
6 🚐free 🚰🅲hfree. **Location:** Rural. **Surface:** asphalted.
🅿 01/01-31/12.
**Distance:** ⬆1km 🚲9,4km A6.
**Remarks:** In front of Conservatoire Nationale des Plantes, gate opens automatically.

### 🅢 Milly-la-Forêt — 18H1
**Total**, 49-51 Avenue de Ganay. **GPS:** n48,40720 e2,46782. ⬆.

10 🚐€ 3,50 🚰🅲h. **Surface:** grassy. 🅿 01/01-31/12.
**Distance:** ⬆centre 500m 🚲7,7km A6.
**Remarks:** Behind petrol station, gate open 6-21h.

### 🅢 Provins — 16A3
**Parking Office de Tourisme**, Chemin de Villecran.
**GPS:** n48,56189 e3,27993. ⬆➡.

30 🚐€ 8/24h 🚰€ 3,50 🅲h 🔌€ 3,50 🚿.🗑 🚗 **Surface:** gravel.
🅿 01/01-31/12 🔲 service: frost.
**Distance:** ⬆500m ⊗500m.
**Tourist information Provins:**
🚶 🅿 Sa 8-14h.

### 🅢 Saint-Cyr-sur-Morin — 16A3
Avenue Daniel Simon. **GPS:** n48,90627 e3,18516.
4 🚐free 🚰🅲hfree. **Location:** Urban, simple, central, quiet.
**Surface:** grassy. 🅿 01/01-31/12.
**Distance:** ⊗300m 🛒130m.
**Remarks:** Behind church.

### 🅢 Saint-Fargeau-Ponthierry — 15H3
**Base de loisirs Seine-Ecole**, Avenue Max Pierrou.
**GPS:** n48,53610 e2,55065. ⬆.
5 🚐€ 5,20 🚰🅲hincluded. **Surface:** grassy.
**Distance:** ⬆850m.
**Remarks:** Recreation park.

### 🅢 Souppes-sur-Loing — 18H1
**GPS:** n48,18083 e2,72343. ⬆➡.

5 🚐€ 5 🚰€ 1/120liter 🅲h 🚿included. 🚻 **Location:** Isolated,
quiet. **Surface:** asphalted. 🅿 01/01-31/12.
**Distance:** ⬆1km ⊗1km 🛒1km.
**Remarks:** On the canal, max. 72h.

# Brittany

### 🅢 Antrain ⛵ — 15B3
Route de Pontorson. **GPS:** n48,46307 w1,47938. ⬆.

2 🚐free 🚰🅲h 🔌WCfree. **Location:** Urban, simple, central, quiet.
**Surface:** asphalted. 🅿 01/01-31/12.
**Distance:** ⬆100m 🏊100m 🎣100m ⊗100m 🛒1km 🚴on the spot 🥾2km.

### 🅢 Arzal — 18A2
Barrage d'Arzal, D139. **GPS:** n47,50089 w2,38074. ⬆.

15 🚐free. **Location:** Rural, simple, quiet. **Surface:** asphalted.
🅿 01/01-31/12.
**Distance:** ⬆1,5km 🏖50m 🛶50m ⊗50m 🛒50m.
**Remarks:** Max. 24h.

**FR**

## Arzon 14D3

**Aire d'accueil des Camping-cars de Kermor**, Avenue de Kerlun, Kerjouanno. **GPS**: n47,53886 w2,88028. ↑→.

49 �图€ 7,60/24h ⌐€ 2,50/10minutes ⌐Ch ⌐(16x) ⌐included. ⌐ **Location:** Rural, comfortable, quiet. **Surface:** asphalted. ⌐ 01/01-31/12.
**Distance:** ⌐1km ⌐250m ⌐450m.
**Remarks:** Nearby Plage du Fageo, June/Sep max. 72h.

## Audierne 14B2

Rue Lamartine. **GPS**: n48,02733 w4,53721.↑.

15 ⌐€ 7/24h ⌐⌐Ch⌐ included. ⌐⌐ **Location:** Urban, simple, quiet. **Surface:** unpaved. ⌐ 01/01-31/12.
**Distance:** ⌐1,5km ⌐on the spot ⌐500m ⌐on the spot.

## Auray 14D3

Chemin de Bellevue. **GPS**: n47,66365 w2,97393. ↑→.

5 ⌐free ⌐⌐ChWCfree. **Location:** Urban, simple, quiet.
**Surface:** asphalted. ⌐ 01/01-31/12.
**Distance:** ⌐200m ⌐400m ⌐1km.
**Remarks:** Small pitches.

## Auray 14D3

Place du Golheres. **GPS**: n47,66524 w2,99036. ↑→.

3 ⌐free ⌐€ 2 ⌐Ch. **Location:** Urban, simple. **Surface:** asphalted. ⌐ 01/01-31/12.
**Distance:** ⌐500m ⌐600m ⌐on the spot.
**Remarks:** During inspection 2015 service out of order.

**Tourist information Auray:**
⌐ ⌐ Mo.

## Availles-sur-Seiche 18B1

D106. **GPS**: n47,96248 w1,19902.↑.
6 ⌐free ⌐⌐Chfree. **Location:** Rural, simple. **Surface:** unpaved.
⌐ 01/01-31/12.
**Distance:** ⌐400m ⌐100m ⌐300m.
**Remarks:** Max. 24h.

## Baden 14D3

**Aire des Iles**, Kerhilio. **GPS**: n47,60606 w2,87282.↑.
49 ⌐€ 8,50-12,80 ⌐€ 2/10minutes ⌐Ch⌐ WC⌐ ⌐included.
**Location:** Rural, comfortable. **Surface:** metalled/sand.
⌐ 01/01-31/12.
**Distance:** ⌐300m ⌐900m.

## Baud 14D2

Rue du Champ de Foire. **GPS**: n47,87375 w3,02008. ↑→.

5 ⌐free. **Location:** Urban, central, quiet. **Surface:** metalled.
⌐ 01/01-31/12.
**Distance:** ⌐on the spot ⌐1,5km ⌐200m ⌐on the spot.
**Remarks:** Max. 72h, service 500m.

## Baud 14D2

Rue de Pont Augan. **GPS**: n47,87580 w3,02518. ↑→.
⌐⌐Chfree. ⌐ 01/01-31/12.

## Bazouges-la-Pérouse 15B3

Boulevard de Castel Marie. **GPS**: n48,42416 w1,57408. ↑→.

7 ⌐free ⌐⌐Chfree. **Location:** Urban, simple, central, quiet.
**Surface:** asphalted.
⌐ 01/01-31/12 ⌐ Service: winter.
**Distance:** ⌐200m ⌐150m ⌐200m.
**Remarks:** Max. 48h.

## Bécherel 15A3

La Feronière. **GPS**: n48,29769 w1,93971.↑.

15 ⌐free. **Location:** Rural, simple. **Surface:** gravel.
⌐ 01/01-31/12.
**Distance:** ⌐700m ⌐700m ⌐on the spot ⌐200m.
**Remarks:** Max. 48h.

## Bédée 18A1

Place de l'Eglise. **GPS**: n48,18099 w1,94416. ↑→.

6 ⌐free ⌐⌐Chfree. **Location:** Urban, simple. **Surface:** asphalted.
⌐ 01/01-31/12.
**Distance:** ⌐1km ⌐200m ⌐50m.
**Remarks:** Nearby cemetery.

## Belle-Isle-en-Terre 14D1

**Les Jardins du Guer**, Rue Guerveur, D33.
**GPS**: n48,54425 w3,39472. ↑→.

6 ⌐€ 4,80, 15/06-15/09 € 5,20 ⌐⌐Ch ⌐included.
**Location:** Urban, comfortable, central, quiet. **Surface:** gravel.
⌐ 01/01-31/12 ⌐ service: 01/11-01/04.
**Distance:** ⌐100m ⌐on the spot ⌐50m ⌐350m ⌐mountainbike trail ⌐on the spot.
**Remarks:** Narrow entrance.

## Belz 14D3

**Parc de Loisirs**, Rue des Sports. **GPS**: n47,66940 w3,17744.↑→.

10 ⌐free. **Location:** Simple, quiet. **Surface:** gravel/metalled.
⌐ 01/01-31/12.
**Distance:** ⌐1km ⌐1km ⌐800m.

## Berric 14D3

Chemin de l'Étang. **GPS**: n47,63294 w2,52905. ↑→.

5 ⌐€ 5 ⌐€ 2/10minutes ⌐Ch⌐€ 2/55minutes.⌐
**Location:** Rural, comfortable, quiet. **Surface:** asphalted.
⌐ 01/01-31/12.
**Distance:** ⌐500m ⌐on the spot ⌐on the spot ⌐500m ⌐500m.
**Remarks:** Along river, coins at the shops in the village, access via Rue du Grand Pont.

## Berric 14D3

Rue du Grand Pont. **GPS**: n47,63304 w2,52888.→.

6 ⌐€ 5 ⌐€ 2/100liter ⌐ChWC.⌐ **Location:** Rural, simple, quiet.
**Surface:** asphalted/grassy. ⌐ 01/01-31/12.
**Distance:** ⌐300m ⌐on the spot ⌐on the spot ⌐400m.
**Remarks:** Coins at the shops.

## Bignan 14D2

Salle des Sports. **GPS**: n47,87760 w2,77342.↑.

3 ⌐free ⌐⌐Ch. **Location:** Urban, simple. **Surface:** asphalted.
⌐ 01/01-31/12.

FR

**Distance:** 🚶300m ⊗250m.
**Remarks:** At gymnasium.

| 🅢 | Binic ⚓🏖🌊 | 14D1 |

**Aire camping-car de l'Ic**, Rue de l'Ic. **GPS:** n48,60059 w2,83573. ⬆➡.

50 ⏳free 🚰🔌Chfree. **Location:** Urban, simple, central, quiet.
**Surface:** gravel. ⬛ 01/01-31/12.
**Distance:** 🚶500m ⊗700m 🛒700m 🚌500m 🚶500m.
**Remarks:** Water closed during wintertime.

**Tourist information Binic:**
🏖 ⬛ Thu.

| | Bohal | 18A1 |

Place de l'église. **GPS:** n47,78133 w2,43788.⬆.
⏳free. **Location:** Simple. **Surface:** metalled. ⬛ 01/01-31/12.
**Distance:** 🚶on the spot.
**Remarks:** Near church.

| 🅢 | Bourg-Blanc | 14B1 |

**Aire Centre Nautique**, Rue de Brest. **GPS:** n48,49188 w4,50312.⬆.

20 ⏳free 🚰🔌Chfree. **Location:** Rural, simple, quiet. **Surface:** sand.
⬛ 01/01-31/12.
**Distance:** 🚶900m 🎣fish pond 🛒100m 🚶on the spot 🚶on the spot.

| 🅢 | Bréal-sous-Montfort ⚓ | 18A1 |

**Les Jardins de Brocéliande**, Les Mesnils.
**GPS:** n48,05384 w1,88963. ⬆➡.

12 ⏳€6 🚰🔌Ch. 🔋 ⊘ **Location:** Rural, simple, quiet.
**Surface:** unpaved. ⬛ 01/01-31/12.
**Distance:** 🚶2,5km 🏄3,5km ⊗on the spot 🚴on the spot 🚶on the spot.

| 🅢 | Brech ⚓ | 14D3 |

Rue de Pont Douar/Avenue des Pins, D768.
**GPS:** n47,71917 w3,00111. ⬆➡.

6 ⏳free 🚰€3 🔌Ch. **Location:** Simple, noisy. **Surface:** grassy.
⬛ 01/01-31/12.
**Distance:** 🚶100m ⊗400m 🛒200m.
**Remarks:** Parking nearby small lake, plan d'eau, coins at the bakery.

| | Brest | 14B1 |

**Parking Océanopolis**, Rue du Cormoran. **GPS:** n48,38893 w4,43535.⬆.

24 ⏳free. **Location:** Urban, simple, quiet. **Surface:** asphalted.
⬛ 01/01-31/12.
**Distance:** 🚶5km 🏊on the spot 🚌on the spot 🚌300m.
**Remarks:** Max. 1 night, 01/06-30/08 only overnight stays (18.30-9h),
busy parking during the day, gate closes at 20h.

| 🅢 | Brest | 14B1 |

**Port du Moulin Blanc**, Rue Eugène Berest.
**GPS:** n48,39174 w4,43612.⬆.
⏳Chfree. ⬛ 01/01-31/12.

**Tourist information Brest:**
👁 Tour Tanguy. Diorama old Brest. ⬛ daily, 01/10-31/05 Wed, Su
afternoon.
Océanopolis. Sea-centre, penguin and seals. ⬛ 01/04-31/08 9-18h,
01/09-31/03 10-17h ⬤ Mo.

| | Brillac | 14D3 |

Rue Saint-Maur. **GPS:** n47,54143 w2,81748.⬆.

7 ⏳free. **Location:** Urban, simple, central, quiet. **Surface:** asphalted.
⬛ 01/01-31/12.
**Distance:** 🚶on the spot 🏊400m ⊗450m 🛒200m 🚌on the spot
🚶on the spot.

| 🅒🅢 | Callac (22) | 14C1 |

Av Ernest Renan. **GPS:** n48,40200 w3,43737.➡.

6 ⏳free 🚰🔌Chfree. 🔋€2. **Location:** Rural, simple, quiet.
**Surface:** gravel. ⬛ 01/01-31/12.
**Distance:** 🚶800m 🏊200m 🚌200m 🚶on the spot.
**Remarks:** Lac Verte Vallée.

| 🅢 | Camaret-sur-Mer 🌀 | 14B1 |

Rue Georges Ancey. **GPS:** n48,27513 w4,60793. ⬆➡.

75 ⏳free, 01/04-31/10 ⬛€6 🚰🔌Ch🔋€2/55minutes.🔋⊘
**Location:** Rural, comfortable, quiet. **Surface:** gravel.
⬛ 01/01-31/12.
**Distance:** 🚶1km 🏊500m ⊗500m 🛒500m 🚴on the spot
🚶on the spot.
**Remarks:** Max. 72h.

| 🅒🅢 | Campénéac | 18A1 |

Rue de l'Étang. **GPS:** n47,95736 w2,29039. ⬆➡.

30 ⏳free 🚰🔌€2 WC. **Location:** Rural, simple, quiet. **Surface:** grassy.
⬛ 01/01-31/12.
**Distance:** 🚶250m 🚌on the spot ⊗250m 🛒250m.
**Remarks:** Coins at Fauchoux, rue nationale 32.

| 🅢 | Campénéac | 18A1 |

Rue de la Fontaine. **GPS:** n47,95674 w2,29364. ⬆➡.
🚰€2 🔌ChWC. ⬛ 01/01-31/12.
**Distance:** 🚶on the spot ⊗on the spot 🛒on the spot.
**Remarks:** Coins at town hall and supermarket, overnight stay: 43.7911
12.4925.

| 🅒🅢 | Cancale ⚓🌊 | 15B3 |

**Aire camping-car Ville Ballet**, Rue des Français Libres.
**GPS:** n48,67004 w1,86583. ⬆➡.

30 ⏳€10, first hour free 🚰€3,50/10minutes 🔌Ch🔋€3,50/h. 🔋
📖 **Location:** Rural, simple, quiet. **Surface:** grassy.
⬛ 01/01-31/12.
**Distance:** 🏊300m 🛒1km 🛒800m 🚌100m.
**Remarks:** Max. 72h, bread-service.

**Tourist information Cancale:**
👁 La Ferme Marine. Guided tour oyster farm. ⬛ summer 11h,15h,17h
Français, 14h English, 16h Deutsch.

| 🅒🅢 | Carantec ⚓🌊 | 14C1 |

**Aire du Meneyer**, Rue Castel an Dour. **GPS:** n48,65967 w3,9138.⬆.

20 ⏳free 🚰€3/100liter 🔌Ch🔋€3/55minutes ⊘.
**Location:** Urban, comfortable, quiet. **Surface:** gravel/metalled.
⬛ 01/01-31/12.
**Distance:** 🚶1km 🏊500m ⊗700m 🛒700m.
**Remarks:** Max. 48h, service 50m.

| 🅒🅢 | Carantec ⚓🌊 | 14C1 |

Chemin du Roch Glaz. **GPS:** n48,65235 w3,90308. ⬆.

10 ⏳free. **Location:** Rural, simple, quiet. **Surface:** asphalted.
⬛ 01/01-31/12.
**Distance:** 🏊beach 300m ⊗500m 🚶on the spot.
**Remarks:** Max. 24h, seaview.

| 🅒🅢 | Carantec ⚓🌊 | 14C1 |

Rue Pen Al Lann. **GPS:** n48,66866 w3,89348. ⬆.

**FR**

15 🏕free. **Location:** Rural, simple, quiet. **Surface:** gravel.
⬛ 01/01-31/12.
**Distance:** 💧500m 🏊150m 🛒150m ⊗1km 🚰1km 🚶on the spot.
**Remarks:** At tennis-courts, max. 48h.

### Carantec 14C1
**Square du Grand Sacconex**, Rue du Kélenn.
**GPS:** n48,66892 w3,91085. 🔼.

10 🏕free. **Location:** Rural, simple, quiet. **Surface:** grassy.
⬛ 01/01-31/12.
**Distance:** 💧300m 🏊on the spot 🛒on the spot ⊗on the spot
🚰300m 🚶on the spot.
**Remarks:** At gymnasium.
**Tourist information Carantec:**
Ⓜ Musée Maritime. Navigation museum. ⬛ 15/05-15-09 ⬤ Thu.

### Carhaix-Plouguer 14C2
Rue de Bazeilles/Rue des Augustins. **GPS:** n48,27829 w3,57257. 🔼.

10 🏕free. 🚰🈳Ch🈺free. **Location:** Urban, simple, central.
**Surface:** asphalted. ⬛ 01/01-31/12.
**Distance:** 💧200m ⊗200m 🚰200m.

### Carnac 14D3
**Square d'Illertissen. GPS:** n47,58505 w3,08242. 🔼➡️.

20 🏕free. 🚰€ 2/10minutes 🈳Ch🈺€ 2/2h. **Location:** Urban, simple.
**Surface:** asphalted. ⬛ 01/01-31/12.
**Distance:** 💧50m 🏊1,5km ⊗50m 🚰50m.
**Remarks:** Max. 48h.
**Tourist information Carnac:**
ℹ Office de Tourisme, 74, avenue des Druides, http://www.ot-carnac.
fr/. Seaside resort and important place of finding of 30.000 prehistoric
menhirs.
Ⓜ Musée de Préhistoire. Prehistoric museum. ⬛ 10-12.30h and
14-18h ⬤ 01/12-01/04.

### Caro 18A1
**Parc des Sports. GPS:** n47,86421 w2,32582. 🔼.

---

3 🏕free. **Location:** Rural, simple, quiet. **Surface:** asphalted.
⬛ 01/01-31/12.
**Distance:** 💧600m ⊗600m.

### Caulnes 15A3
**Lavoir Fontaine**, Rue de Dinan. **GPS:** n48,28655 w2,15517. 🔼➡️.

5 🏕free. 🚰€ 2/10minutes 🈳ChWC. **Location:** Urban, simple, quiet.
**Surface:** gravel. ⬛ 01/01-31/12.
**Distance:** 💧500m ⊗100m 🚰100m 🚐200m.
**Remarks:** Max. 7 days.

### Cesson-Sévigné 18B1
**Route de La Valette. GPS:** n48,11802 w1,59121. 🔼.

6 🏕free. 🚰€ 2,60/10minutes 🈳Ch🈺€ 2,60/55minutes 🛢.
**Location:** Rural, simple, central, quiet. **Surface:** metalled.
⬛ 01/01-31/12.
**Distance:** 💧500m 🏊on the spot 🛒on the spot ⊗100m 🚰100m
🚐500m 🚶on the spot.

### Châteauneuf-du-Faou 14C2
**Penn ar Pont. GPS:** n48,18286 w3,81576. 🔼➡️.

10 🏕free.
**Location:** Simple, quiet. **Surface:** gravel. ⬛ 01/01-31/12.
**Distance:** 💧1,3km 🚲on the spot 🚶on the spot.

### Châtillon-en-Vendelais 18B1
D108. **GPS:** n48,23112 w1,17959.

10 🏕free. 🚰🈳Chfree. **Location:** Rural, simple, quiet.
**Surface:** asphalted. ⬛ 01/01-31/12.
**Distance:** 💧2km 🏊lake 🛒on the spot 🚶on the spot.
**Remarks:** At the lake, next to campsite.

---

### Cléden-Cap-Sizun 14B2
**Place du 19 mars 1962**, Rue de la ville d'ys.
**GPS:** n48,04803 w4,65008. 🔼.

20 🏕free 🚰€ 2/10minutes 🈳Ch. **Location:** Rural, simple, quiet.
**Surface:** asphalted/metalled. ⬛ 01/01-31/12.
**Distance:** 💧on the spot 🚲on the spot.

### Cléden-Cap-Sizun 14B2
**Pointe du Van**, D7. **GPS:** n48,05936 w4,70727. 🔼.

20 🏕free. **Location:** Rural, simple, quiet. **Surface:** grassy/gravel.
⬛ 01/01-31/12.
**Distance:** 💧5km 🏊on the spot 🚲on the spot 🚶on the spot.

### Cléden-Cap-Sizun 14B2
**Route de Kastel Koz**, Beuzec-Cap-Sizun. **GPS:** n48,08473 w4,51844. 🔼.

20 🏕free. **Location:** Rural, simple, isolated, quiet.
**Surface:** asphalted/gravel. ⬛ 01/01-31/12.
**Distance:** 🏊on the spot 🚶on the spot.

### Cléden-Poher 14C2
**Route du Stade. GPS:** n48,23686 w3,67165. 🔼➡️.

15 🏕free. 🚰🈳Ch🧺(4x)free. **Location:** Simple, quiet.
**Surface:** asphalted. ⬛ 01/01-31/12.
**Distance:** 💧300m 🏊50m 🚰bakery 200m 🚐400m.
**Remarks:** Voluntary contribution.

### Cléder 14C1
**Camping-Car Park Cléder**, Le Poulennou.
**GPS:** n48,69150 w4,12098. 🔼.

20 🏕€ 9,80, 01/05-30/09 € 12,20 🚰🈳Ch🧺(20x)included. 🚐
**Location:** Rural, comfortable, quiet. **Surface:** gravel.
⬛ 01/01-31/12.
**Distance:** 💧3km 🚲on the spot.

**Remarks:** Mandatory, one-time fee Pass'Etapes € 4.

**Cléder** `14C1`

**Espace Nature des Palujous**. **GPS:** n48,68636 w4,15212.
free. **Surface:** sand. 01/01-31/12.

**Cléguérec** `14D2`

**Etang du Portoir**, St-Jean. **GPS:** n48,11670 w3,05534.

4 free. **Location:** Rural, simple, isolated, quiet. **Surface:** asphalted. 01/01-31/12.
**Distance:** 2km on the spot 2km 2km.

**Clohars-Carnoët** `14C2`

**Place de NAVA**, Route de Quimperlé. **GPS:** n47,79790 w3,585.

10 free € 2/70liter Ch € 2/50minutes WC.
**Location:** Simple. **Surface:** asphalted. 01/01-31/12.
**Distance:** 200m 10km 4,5km bakery 200m.

**Combrit** `14B2`

**Place du 19 mars 1962**, Hent Ty Plouz. **GPS:** n47,88755 w4,1546.

10 free € 2/10minutes Ch € 2/60minutes.
**Location:** Urban, simple, quiet. **Surface:** metalled. 01/01-31/12.
**Distance:** on the spot 5km 200m 1,3km on the spot.
**Remarks:** Coins at the shops in the village.

**Commana** `14C1`

**Place du salles de Sports**, D11. **GPS:** n48,41611 w3,96139.

5 free free. **Location:** Rural, simple, isolated, quiet.
**Surface:** grassy. 01/01-31/12.
**Distance:** 200m 300m bakery 300m on the spot on the spot.

**Concarneau** `14C2`

**Le Porzou**, Allée Jean Bouin. **GPS:** n47,86320 w3,9051.

---

20 free, 01/04-30/09 20-8 uur € 6 € 4/10minutes
Ch € 4/55minutes WC. **Location:** Urban, simple.
**Surface:** asphalted. 01/01-31/12.
**Distance:** city centre 2km on the spot on the spot
on the spot.
**Remarks:** Foot ferry to centre.

**Concarneau** `14C2`

**Parking de la Gare**, Avenue de la Gare. **GPS:** n47,87864 w3,9202.

47 free, 01/04-30/09 20-8 uur € 6 € 4 Ch € 4/55minutes
**Location:** Urban, simple. **Surface:** asphalted. 01/01-31/12
01/11-30/11.
**Distance:** 500m beach 1,4km on the spot on the spot.
**Remarks:** Parking station.

**Tourist information Concarneau:**
Mo, Fri.

**Crac'h** `14D3`

**Intermarché**, AC Les Alizés. **GPS:** n47,60421 w2,99669.

8 free € 2/10minutes Ch € 2 € 4,50.
**Location:** Rural, simple, quiet. **Surface:** asphalted.
01/01-31/12.
**Distance:** on the spot on the spot.

**Crozon** `14B1`

**Le Fret**, Le Sillon, D55. **GPS:** n48,28457 w4,50934.

15 free € 2,40/10minutes Ch. **Location:** Rural, simple, quiet.
**Surface:** unpaved. 01/01-31/12.
**Distance:** 5,5km on the spot 50m 250m 5,5km on the spot.

**Crozon** `14B1`

**Parking du Loc'h**, Rue de l'Atlantique, Morgat.
**GPS:** n48,22523 w4,50851.

---

30 € 4,75/24h Ch included WC. **Location:** Urban,
simple. **Surface:** asphalted. 01/01-31/12.
**Distance:** 300m on the spot on the spot on the spot
100m on the spot.
**Remarks:** Max. 48h, market Wednesday.

**Crozon** `14B1`

**Parking Office de Tourisme**, Boulevard de Pralognan, D887.
**GPS:** n48,24770 w4,4934.

20 free € 2,30/100liter **Location:** Urban, simple.
**Surface:** asphalted. 01/01-31/12.
**Distance:** 50m on the spot on the spot.
**Remarks:** Nearby Office de Tourisme, max. 48h.

**Crozon** `14B1`

**E.Leclerc Express**, Route de Brest. **GPS:** n48,24896 w4,4144.
5 free Ch. **Location:** Urban. **Surface:** asphalted.
01/01-31/12.
**Distance:** 6km 150m on the spot.

**Damgan** `14D3`

**Parking de Kervoyal**. **GPS:** n47,51465 w2,56038.

70 € 7,50, 01/04-31/10 € 9,50 Ch included. **Location:** Rural,
comfortable, quiet. **Surface:** metalled/sand. 01/01-31/12.
**Distance:** 600m Sandy beach.
**Remarks:** Parking at the beach, max. 48h.

**Dinan** `15A3`

**Rue du Port**, D12. **GPS:** n48,45450 w2,0389.

10 € 5. **Location:** Urban, simple, central. **Surface:** asphalted.
01/01-31/12.
**Distance:** 800m 800m on the spot 500m on the spot.

**Dol-de-Bretagne** `15B3`

**Place Jean Hamelin**. **GPS:** n48,54736 w1,75442.

30 🛏free 🚰€ 2 🚽Ch🔲€ 2. **Location:** Urban, simple, noisy.
**Surface:** asphalted. ⬛ 01/04-31/10.
**Distance:** 🛒on the spot ⊗100m 🚉100m 🚌150m.

### Douarnenez 14B2
Rue Jean Barre. **GPS:** n48,09192 w4,3328.⬆.

4 🛏free.
**Location:** Urban, simple, noisy. **Surface:** asphalted.
⬛ 01/01-31/12.
**Distance:** 🛒on the spot ⊗200m 🚉200m.
**Remarks:** Max. 24h, narrow road, not suitable for motorhomes +7m.

### Elliant 14C2
Rue Saint Gilles. **GPS:** n47,99648 w3,89044.⬆.

15 🛏free 🚰€ 2,45 🚽Ch🔲€ 2,45. **Location:** Simple. **Surface:** sand.
⬛ 01/01-31/12.
**Distance:** 🛒on the spot ⊗150m.
**Remarks:** Coins at the shops.

### Elven 14D3
Avenue des Martyrs de la Résistance, Le Guého.
**GPS:** n47,73879 w2,58134.⬆➡.

26 🛏free 🚰€ 2 🚽Ch🔲✂(12x)€ 2/4h.
**Location:** Rural, simple, quiet. **Surface:** grassy/gravel.
⬛ parking 01/01-31/12 service 01/07-31/08.
**Distance:** 🛒1,5km ⊗800m 🚉800m.

### Erdeven 14D3
Chemin De Kerouriec. **GPS:** n47,62717 w3,17988.⬆.

10 🛏€ 7 🚰€ 2 Ch✂(10x)€ 2/night WC🔲. **Location:** Rural,
simple, isolated, quiet. **Surface:** grassy. ⬛ 01/01-31/12.
**Distance:** 🏖1,1km.

### Erdeven 14D3
Parc Kerhillio, Boulevard d'Atlantique. **GPS:** n47,61429 w3,15958.⬆➡.

30 🛏€ 9,20-11,40 🚰🚽Ch✂included. 🚻 **Location:** Rural,
simple. **Surface:** grassy. ⬛ 01/01-31/12.
**Distance:** 🏖500m ⊗200m 🚉200m 🚲on the spot 🚶on the spot.

### Erquy 15A3
Caroual Plage, Rue des Hirondelles. **GPS:** n48,62120 w2,4724.⬆➡.

41 🛏€ 6,50-7,50 + € 1/pp tourist tax 🚰€ 2/100liter 🚽
Ch🔲€ 2/1h. 🚻 **Location:** Urban, comfortable, central.
**Surface:** asphalted/metalled. ⬛ 01/01-31/12.
**Distance:** 🏖2,5km 🚲on the spot.
**Remarks:** Beach parking, max. 24h, baker at 8am.

### Étel 14D3
Camping municipal, Rue de la Barre. **GPS:** n47,65100 w3,202.⬆➡.

25 🛏€ 8, 01/11-31/03 € 10 🚰€ 2/100liter 🚽Ch✂(16x)included 🔲.
**Location:** Rural, simple. **Surface:** grassy. ⬛ 01/04-30/09.
**Distance:** 🛒500m 🏖200m ⊗800m 🚲on the spot 🚶on the spot.
**Remarks:** Baker every morning (Jul/Aug).

### Fouesnant 14C2
Plage Mousterlin, Chemin de Kerneuc. **GPS:** n47,85144 w4,04662.⬆.

15 🛏free. **Location:** Rural, simple, quiet. **Surface:** grassy/sand.
⬛ 01/01-31/12.
**Distance:** 🏖beach 50m ⊗400m 🚉500m 🚲on the spot
🚶on the spot.
**Remarks:** Beach parking, max. 48h.

### Fouesnant 14C2
Leclerc, D45, Route de Quimper. **GPS:** n47,90234 w4,02938.⬆.

12 🛏free 🚰€ 2/10minutes 🚽Ch🔲€ 2/55minutes.
**Location:** Simple, noisy. **Surface:** asphalted. ⬛ 01/01-31/12.

**Distance:** 🚉on the spot.

### Fougères 15B3
Allée des Fêtes. **GPS:** n48,35660 w1,20242.⬆.

25 🛏free 🚰🚽ChWCfree. **Location:** Urban, simple.
**Surface:** asphalted. ⬛ 01/01-31/12.
**Distance:** 🛒500m ⊗200m 🚉200m.

### Fougères 15B3
Parking de la Poterne, Boulevard de Rennes.
**GPS:** n48,35524 w1,2113.⬆➡.

16 🛏free 🚰🚽Chfree. **Location:** Urban, simple, central.
**Surface:** metalled. ⬛ 01/01-31/12.
**Distance:** 🛒on the spot ⊗250m 🚉300m 🚶on the spot.
**Remarks:** Castle of Fougères 500m.

### Fréhel 15A3
La Ville Oie, Rue des Sports, D117, Pléhérel-plage.
**GPS:** n48,65032 w2,35241.⬆➡.

40 🛏€ 6 🚰€ 4/80liter 🚽Ch🔲€ 4/1h 🚻
**Location:** Rural, simple, isolated. **Surface:** gravel/metalled.
⬛ 01/01-31/12.
**Distance:** 🛒1,1km 🏖beach 1,2km 🚲on the spot.

### Gâvres 14C3
Les Joncs, Rue des Filets Bleus. **GPS:** n47,69515 w3,35097.⬆.
40 🛏€ 5-7,60, 16/06-31/08 tariff camp site 🚰€ 2 🚽Ch✂included.
**Surface:** grassy. ⬛ 01/01-31/12.
**Distance:** 🛒100m 🏖100m.

### Glomel 14C2
Etang du Coronc, Rue du Lac. **GPS:** n48,22052 w3,38972.⬆➡.

6 🛏free 🚰€ 2/100liter 🚽Ch🔲€ 2/1h 🔲. **Location:** Rural, simple,
quiet. **Surface:** asphalted/gravel. ⬛ 01/01-31/12.
**Distance:** 🏖150m 🚉400m.
**Remarks:** At lake.

### Goulven 14B1
Aire Naturelle Ty Poas. **GPS:** n48,63109 w4,30833.⬆➡.

15 ⊞ € 6 + € 0,22/pp tourist tax ⛽🚰Ch🚿WC🗑included.♨ **Location:** Rural, comfortable, quiet. **Surface:** grassy/metalled. 🗓 15/06-30/09. **Distance:** 🚶500m ⚓beach 200m 🛒500m 🚲on the spot 🧍on the spot.

### Grand-Fougeray 18B2
Rue Camille de Jourdan. **GPS:** n47,72233 w1,7298.⬆

5 ⊞free ⛽€ 2/100liter 🚰Ch🗑 **Location:** Urban, simple. **Surface:** asphalted. 🗓 01/01-31/12. **Distance:** 🚶300m ⊗300m.

### Gueltas 14D2
Boju, Keriffe. **GPS:** n48,10406 w2,79064.⬆➡

16 ⊞free WCfree. **Location:** Rural, simple, quiet. **Surface:** gravel. 🗓 01/01-31/12. **Distance:** 🚶1km ▸on the spot. **Remarks:** At the Nantes-Brest Canal.

### Gueltas 14D2
Rue Maurice Maugain, D125. **GPS:** n48,09667 w2,80111.⬆➡

10 ⊞free ⛽free. **Location:** Rural, simple, isolated, quiet. **Surface:** gravel. 🗓 01/01-31/12. **Distance:** ⚓200m. **Remarks:** Nearby sports park.

### Guern 14D2
Kervazo, Rue de la Vallée, D1. **GPS:** n48,02815 w3,09215.⬆

8 ⊞free ⛽🚰Chfree. **Location:** Rural, simple, quiet. **Surface:** asphalted. 🗓 01/01-31/12. **Distance:** 🚶250m ⊗on the spot 🛒bakery 300m.

### Guern 14D2
Etang du Ponterre, D1. **GPS:** n48,03472 w3,0975.⬆

---

6 ⊞free. **Location:** Rural, simple, quiet. **Surface:** gravel. 🗓 01/01-31/12. **Distance:** 🚶700m ▸on the spot 🛒700m bakery. **Remarks:** Fishing permit available.

### Guichen 18B1
Le Boel, Pont Réan. **GPS:** n48,00221 w1,77336.⬆➡

5 ⊞ € 5,40 ⛽🚰ChWCfree. **Location:** Simple, quiet. **Surface:** metalled. 🗓 01/01-31/12. **Distance:** 🚶500m ⚓on the spot ▸on the spot ⊗on the spot 🛒bakery 150m. **Remarks:** Max. 24h.

### Guidel 14C2
D152, Guidel-Plage > Fort-Bloqué. **GPS:** n47,75035 w3,50574.⬆➡

15 ⊞free WC. **Location:** Rural, simple. **Surface:** gravel/sand. 🗓 01/01-31/12. **Distance:** 🚶1,5km ⚓100m ⊗1,5km 🚲on the spot 🧍on the spot. **Remarks:** Behind Résidence Maéva, beach parking, max. 24h.

### Guidel 14C2
La Falaise, Guidel plage. **GPS:** n47,76640 w3,5258.⬆

7 ⊞free. **Location:** Simple. **Surface:** metalled. 🗓 01/01-31/12. **Distance:** ⚓on the spot. **Remarks:** Behind yachting school, max. 24h.

### Guidel 14C2
Plage du Loc'h, D152. **GPS:** n47,75650 w3,5159.⬆➡

6 ⊞free. **Location:** Quiet. **Surface:** sand. 🗓 01/01-31/12. **Distance:** ⚓250m.

### Guidel 14C2
Arc-en-Ciel, ZA de Pen Mané. **GPS:** n47,80980 w3,4633.

---

⛽€ 2 🚰Ch⚡€ 2 WC. 🗓 01/01-31/12.

### Guimiliau 14C1
Parking Salle Polyvalente, Rue des Bruyeres. **GPS:** n48,48676 w3,99665.⬆➡

15 ⊞free ⛽🗑free. **Location:** Simple, central, noisy. **Surface:** metalled. 🗓 01/01-31/12. **Distance:** 🚶on the spot ⊗400m 🛒400m 🚲on the spot 🧍on the spot. **Remarks:** Max. 2 nights.

### Guingamp 14D1
Place du Vally. **GPS:** n48,56024 w3,1489.⬆➡

10 ⊞free ⛽🚰Chfree WC. **Location:** Urban, simple, central. **Surface:** asphalted. 🗓 01/01-31/12 ⏺ Fri market. **Distance:** 🚶on the spot ⊗100m. **Remarks:** Max. 24h.

### Guiscriff 14C2
La Gare de Guiscriff, Rue de la Gare. **GPS:** n48,05722 w3,65401.⬆⬆⬆

4 ⊞free ⛽🚰Ch🚿(4x). **Location:** Rural, simple, isolated, quiet. **Surface:** metalled. 🗓 01/01-31/12. **Distance:** 🚶1km 🛒bakery 1km 🚲on the spot 🧍on the spot.

### Guissény 14B1
Rue de Plouguerneau. **GPS:** n48,63299 w4,41127.⬆

8 ⊞free ⛽🚰Ch⚡. **Location:** Urban, simple, central. **Surface:** gravel. 🗓 01/01-31/12. **Distance:** 🚶on the spot ⚓beach 550m 🛒250m bakery. **Remarks:** Coins at the shops and town hall.

### Hédé-Bazouges 15B3
La Magdelaine. **GPS:** n48,30592 w1,79218.

FR

50 ☐free. **Location:** Rural, simple. **Surface:** grassy/gravel.
☐ 01/01-31/12.
**Distance:** 🚰1km 🏖on the spot 🎣on the spot ⊗50m 🚲 on the spot
🚶on the spot.

**Hillion** 14D1
Le Tertre Piquet, Lermot-plage. **GPS:** n48,53098 w2,66387. ⬆➡.

20 ☐free 🚰Ch WC free. **Location:** Simple, isolated. **Surface:** grassy.
☐ 01/01-31/12.
**Distance:** 🏖sandy beach 100m.
**Remarks:** Beach parking, max. 48h.

**Hillion** 14D1
Rue Olivier Provost. **GPS:** n48,51743 w2,66772. ⬆.

7 ☐free 🚰Ch free. **Location:** Simple, central, quiet. **Surface:** gravel.
☐ 01/01-31/12.
**Distance:** 🚰500m 💧100m 🚲on the spot.
**Remarks:** Max. 48h.

**Hirel** 15B3
D155. **GPS:** n48,60841 w1,82032. ⬆➡.

100 ☐€ 6/night 🚰€ 2/100liter 🚰Ch ⊞€ 2/50minutes. 🚿
**Location:** Rural, simple. **Surface:** grassy/gravel.
☐ 01/01-31/12.
**Distance:** 🚰700m 🏖200m 🎣200m.

**Huelgoat** 14C1
**Place du Camping-cars**, Route du Fao, D769a.
**GPS:** n48,36115 w3,75612. ⬆➡.

30 ☐free 🚰€ 5/10minutes 🚰Ch ⊞1h. **Location:** Rural, simple,
quiet. **Surface:** metalled. ☐ 01/01-31/12.
**Distance:** 🚰500m 🏖on the spot 🎣on the spot ⊗500m 💧500m
🖥500m 🚲500m 🚶500m.

---

**Remarks:** In front of campsite municipal, service 100m.

**Janzé** 18B1
Aire du Hardier, D41. **GPS:** n47,97258 w1,53825. ⬆.

5 ☐€ 10 🚰€ 2 🚰Ch WC free. 🚿 **Location:** Motorway, simple.
**Surface:** asphalted.
**Distance:** ✒on the spot.
**Remarks:** At petrol station.

**Josselin** 14D2
Place St.Martin. **GPS:** n47,95639 w2,55056. ⬆➡.

50 ☐free 🚰€ 2,50 🚰Ch WC 🧺 **Location:** Urban, central.
**Surface:** metalled. ☐ 01/01-31/12 ⏺ Sa 9-14h.
**Distance:** 🚰300m ⚡N24 900m ⊗300m 💧bakery 300m 🖥1km
🚲on the spot.
**Remarks:** Castle of Josselin 400m, market Saturday.

**Tourist information Josselin:**
ℹ Office de Tourisme, Place de la Congregation, www.paysdejosselin.
com. City is dominated by the castle of Rohan.

**Kergrist-Moëlou** 14D2
**Lotissement Hélène Le Chevalier. GPS:** n48,31016 w3,31876.

4 ☐free 🚰 🚰Ch free. **Location:** Rural, isolated, quiet.
**Surface:** gravel. ☐ 01/01-31/12.
**Distance:** 🚰100m ⊗500m 🚲on the spot.

**Kerlouan** 14B1
Aire de Camping-Car de Ménéham, Lestonquet.
**GPS:** n48,66952 w4,36161. ⬆.
50 ☐€ 7 🚰Ch 🚿WC € 3,50/24h ⏺€ 5/3 📶included. 🚌🧺 🚲
**Surface:** grassy. ☐ 01/01-31/12.
**Distance:** 🏖on the spot 🎣on the spot ⊗850m.
**Remarks:** Next to campsite, video surveillance.

**Kernascléden** 14C2
Domaine du Scroff, Canquisquelen. **GPS:** n47,99785 w3,31845. ⬆.

2 ☐€ 10 🚰🚰Ch 🚿WC 📶included. **Location:** Rural, comfortable,
quiet. **Surface:** grassy. ☐ 01/01-31/12.
**Distance:** 🚰1km ⊗on the spot 🚶on the spot.
**Remarks:** Heated pool.

**La Chèze** 14D2
Chemin d'Alénor, Allée du 19 mars 1962.
**GPS:** n48,13419 w2,65787. ⬆➡.

---

10 ☐€ 4,50, weekend/holidays free 🚰🚰Ch 🚿(6x)WC free. 🚿
**Location:** Simple, quiet. **Surface:** asphalted.
☐ 01/01-31/12.
**Distance:** 🚰200m 🎣on the spot 💧200m 🚲mountainbike trail.
**Remarks:** Parking at small lake.

**La Fontenelle** 15B3
Rue de la Quintaine. **GPS:** n48,46575 w1,50495. ⬆.

10 ☐free 🚰€ 2/10minutes 🚰Ch € 2/55minutes. **Location:** Rural,
simple, quiet. **Surface:** asphalted.
☐ 01/01-31/12.
**Distance:** 🚰on the spot ⊗350m 🚲on the spot 🚶on the spot.
**Remarks:** Next to cemetery, adjacent walking and bicycle area.

**La Martyre** 14C1
Route de Ploudiry, D35. **GPS:** n48,44861 w4,15694. ⬆.

10 ☐free 🚰🚰Ch 🚿WC free. **Location:** Rural, quiet.
**Surface:** gravel. ☐ 01/01-31/12.
**Distance:** 🚰100m ⊗100m 💧100m 🚲on the spot 🚶on the spot.
**Remarks:** Nearby Maison du Plateau.

**La Roche-Bernard** 18A2
Place du Dôme. **GPS:** n47,51753 w2,29733. ⬆.

10 ☐free. **Location:** Urban, simple, central. **Surface:** asphalted.
☐ 01/01-31/12.
**Distance:** 🚰50m ⊗100m 💧50m.

**La Roche-Bernard** 18A2
Halte Camping-car, Rue du Patis. **GPS:** n47,52012 w2,30466. ⬆➡.

15 ☐€ 7, 01/07-25/08 € 11,10 🚰🚰Ch 🚿€ 4,60 WC 🚰.
**Location:** Urban, comfortable, quiet. **Surface:** grassy.
☐ 02/04-16/09.
**Distance:** 🚰100m 🏖50m 🎣50m ⊗100m 💧100m.

**Remarks:** Next to campsite du Patis.
**Tourist information La Roche-Bernard:**
ℹ Small town especially known for the beautiful hanging bridge over the Vilaine river, 50m high and over 400m long.

### La Roche-Derrien 14D1

Rue du Jouet. **GPS:** n48,74696 w3,25976. ⬆.

12 free €4 €2 Ch (6x) €2 **Location:** Rural, simple, central, quiet. **Surface:** gravel.
01/01-31/12.
**Distance:** 100m 100m 100m.
**Remarks:** Coins at the shops and town hall.

### Lampaul-Guimiliau 14C1

Route du Saint-Jacques. **GPS:** n48,49408 w4,03857. ⬆ ➡.

15 free Ch. **Location:** Rural, simple, quiet.
**Surface:** grassy/sand. 01/01-31/12.
**Distance:** 250m 350m.

### Lampaul-Plouarzel 14B1

**Aire de Porspaul**, Rue de Beg ar Vir. **GPS:** n48,44667 w4,77722. ⬆ ➡.

50 free €7,20/24h €2/10minutes Ch €2/55minutes WC €2 €3,50. **Location:** Rural, comfortable. **Surface:** grassy.
01/01-31/12.
**Distance:** 150m 100m 200m 500m on the spot on the spot.
**Remarks:** Baker at 9am, shower and washing machine Jul/Aug.

### Landerneau 14B1

Rue du Calvaire. **GPS:** n48,44694 w4,25667. ⬆.

25 free €6,50 €2,55 Ch €2,55 **Location:** Rural, comfortable. **Surface:** grassy/gravel. 01/01-31/12.
**Distance:** 500m river 500m 500m on the spot.

### Landivisiau 14C1

**P de Keravel**, Rue du Manoir. **GPS:** n48,51015 w4,0758. ⬆ ➡.

---

15 free Ch free. **Location:** Urban, simple, quiet.
**Surface:** asphalted. 01/01-31/12.
**Distance:** on the spot on the spot 100m centre.

### Landudec 14B2

**Super U**, Rue des Écoles. **GPS:** n48,00143 w4,34088. ⬆.

5 free €2/10minutes Ch €2/55minutes. **Location:** Rural, simple. **Surface:** asphalted. 01/01-31/12.
**Distance:** 1km on the spot on the spot.
**Remarks:** Motorhome washing place.

### Lanfains 14D1

**Étang du Pas**, Le Pas, D7. **GPS:** n48,36466 w2,87938. ⬆.

6 free Ch WC free. **Location:** Simple, quiet.
**Surface:** asphalted/grassy. 01/05-01/10.
**Distance:** on the spot on the spot.
**Remarks:** Parking at small lake.

### Languidic 14D2

**Zone Lanveur**, Place du Bouilleur de Cru.
**GPS:** n47,83722 w3,16188. ⬆ ➡.

20 free Ch free. **Location:** Motorway, simple, noisy.
**Surface:** metalled. 01/01-31/12.
**Distance:** 700m N24 300m.

### Lanloup 14D1

**Parking du Bourg**, Rue de Saint-Roch. **GPS:** n48,71359 w2,96389. ⬆.

2 free WC free. **Location:** Rural, simple, quiet. **Surface:** gravel.
01/01-31/12.
**Distance:** on the spot 2km 2km.

### Lannilis 14B1

**Aire Fontaine Rouge**. **GPS:** n48,55667 w4,50528. ⬆ ➡.

---

20 free Ch WC free. **Location:** Rural, simple, noisy.
**Surface:** metalled. 01/01-31/12.
**Distance:** 1km 1,5km 1,5km.

### Lannilis 14B1

Rue Haie Blanche. **GPS:** n48,57125 w4,52151. ➡.

20 free Ch free. **Location:** Urban, simple, quiet.
**Surface:** asphalted. 01/01-31/12.
**Distance:** 100m bakery 150m.
**Remarks:** In front of cemetery.

### Lanvallay 15A3

Rue du terrain des sports. **GPS:** n48,45420 w2,03028. ⬆.

5 free €2/100liter Ch €2/h. **Location:** Urban, simple.
**Surface:** asphalted. 01/01-31/12.
**Distance:** 50m 50m 50m.

### Larmor-Baden 14D3

Route d'Auray. **GPS:** n47,58816 w2,89868. ⬆ ➡.

3 free free. **Location:** Simple. **Surface:** asphalted
01/01-31/12.
**Distance:** 50m 100m 100m.
**Remarks:** Max. 6,5m.

### Larmor-Plage 14C3

**Parking les Pins**, Rue des Pins. **GPS:** n47,70970 w3,3791. ⬆ ➡.

4 free Ch WC free. **Location:** Central. **Surface:** asphalted.
01/01-31/12.
**Distance:** on the spot 50m 100m 100m.
**Remarks:** Nearby plage de Toulhars, max. 72h.

### Le Conquet 14B1

**Parking Parklec'H**, Rue Général Leclerc. **GPS:** n48,36055 w4,7701. ⬆.

FR

+10 ⛌free ⛽€ 2,50/100liter 🚿Ch🚽 € 2,50/1h. **Location:** Urban, noisy. **Surface:** gravel. 🕐 01/01-31/12.
**Distance:** 🚏200m ⛱beach 800m ⊗400m 🏪bakery 300m 🚲on the spot.
**Remarks:** Coins at tourist info and town hall.

| 🅿S | Le Croisty | 14C2 |
|---|---|---|

**Aire de pique-nique**, D132, Kergoff. **GPS:** n48,06720 w3,38196.

8 ⛌free ⛽€ 2 🚿Ch🚽 € 2/55minutes WC🚽. **Location:** Rural, comfortable, isolated, quiet. **Surface:** asphalted. 🕐 01/01-31/12.
**Distance:** 🚏1,5km 🚶on the spot.

| 🅿S | Le Faou | 14C1 |
|---|---|---|

**Camping-Car Park**, Rue de la Grève. **GPS:** n48,29529 w4,18501.⬆

20 ⛌€ 10,26, 01/04-30/09 € 12,66 ⛽🚿Ch🚿(20x)📶included. 🖥🗑 **Location:** Urban, simple. **Surface:** grassy/metalled. 🕐 01/01-31/12.
**Distance:** 🚏500m ⊗600m 🏪1,5km.
**Remarks:** Mandatory, one-time fee Pass'Etapes € 4.

| 🍽S | Le Faouët | 14C2 |
|---|---|---|

**Restaurant Ty Blomen**, Le Grand Pont. **GPS:** n48,03575 w3,48125.⬆

15 ⛌free ⛽€ 2 🚿Ch. **Location:** Rural, simple. **Surface:** asphalted. 🕐 01/01-31/12.
**Distance:** ⊗on the spot.
**Remarks:** Inclining pitches.

| 🅿S | Le Folgoët | 14B1 |
|---|---|---|

**Parking Freppel**, Route de Gorrékear. **GPS:** n48,56002 w4,33507.⬆➡

30 ⛌free ⛽🚿Ch🚿free. **Location:** Rural, simple, central, quiet.
**Surface:** gravel/metalled. 🕐 01/01-31/12.
**Distance:** 🚏on the spot ⊗100m 🏪100m.
**Remarks:** Nearby basilica.

| 🅿S | Le Guilvinec 🦞 | 14B2 |
|---|---|---|

**Parking de la Petite Sole**, Rue Jean Baudry.
**GPS:** n47,79588 w4,27997.⬆

16 ⛌€ 4/24h ⛽€ 2/100liter 🚿Ch🚽 € 2/10minutes WC🗑.
**Location:** Urban, simple, noisy. **Surface:** asphalted. 🕐 01/01-31/12
🔵 Su market.
**Distance:** 🚏on the spot ⛱on the spot ⊗100m 🏪100m 🚲on the spot.
**Remarks:** Coins at tourist info.

| 🅿S | Le Guilvinec 🦞 | 14B2 |
|---|---|---|

**Le Malamok**, Rue Mejou Bihan. **GPS:** n47,79827 w4,27665.
20 ⛌free. **Location:** Urban. **Surface:** asphalted. 🕐 01/01-31/12.
**Distance:** 🚏500m ⊗300m.

| 🅿S | Le Trévoux | 14C2 |
|---|---|---|

**Parking du Plan d'Eau**, Rue des Sports. **GPS:** n47,89683 w3,64228.⬆

4 ⛌free ⛽🚿Ch🚽free. **Location:** Simple. **Surface:** gravel.
🕐 01/01-31/12.
**Distance:** 🚏on the spot.
**Remarks:** Nearby tennis-courts, max. 48h, crowdy during the day.

| 🅿 | Le Trévoux | 14C2 |
|---|---|---|

**Plan d'Eau**, Rue de Quimperlé. **GPS:** n47,89356 w3,6386.➡

10 ⛌free. **Location:** Simple. **Surface:** gravel. 🕐 01/01-31/12.
**Distance:** ⛱on the spot 🏪bakery.
**Remarks:** At lake.

| 🅿S | Le Vivier-sur-Mer 🦞 | 15B3 |
|---|---|---|

**Camping-Car Park**, Rue de l'Abri des Flots.
**GPS:** n48,60291 w1,77255.⬆

49 ⛌€ 9,60 ⛽🚿Ch🚿(40x),4Amp 📶included. 🖥🗑
**Location:** Rural, comfortable, quiet. **Surface:** grassy/gravel.
🕐 01/01-31/12.
**Distance:** 🚏on the spot ⛱100m 🚆100m ⊗150m 🏪150m 🚲on the spot.
**Remarks:** Mandatory, one-time fee Pass'Etapes € 4.

| 🅿 | Léhon 🦞🦀 | 15A3 |
|---|---|---|

**Parking Club de Tennis**, Lieu-dit Lehon.
**GPS:** n48,44177 w2,04233.⬆➡

6 ⛌free ⛽🚿Chfree. **Location:** Urban, simple, quiet.
**Surface:** asphalted. 🕐 01/01-31/12.
**Distance:** 🚏on the spot ⊗400m 🏪bakery 100m 🚶on the spot.
**Remarks:** At tennis-court.

| 🅿S | Les Forges | 14D2 |
|---|---|---|

**Place de l'Église**, D117. **GPS:** n48,01820 w2,6482.⬆

5 ⛌free ⛽🚿🚿WCfree. **Location:** Rural, simple.
**Surface:** metalled. 🕐 01/01-31/12.
**Distance:** 🚏100m 🏪100m.

| 🅿 | Lézardrieux | 14D1 |
|---|---|---|

**L'Île à Bois**, Rue de l'Île à Bois. **GPS:** n48,83002 w3,08165.⬆

5 ⛌free. **Location:** Simple, isolated, quiet. **Surface:** gravel/sand.
🕐 01/01-31/12.
**Distance:** 🚏Lézardrieux 6km ⛱50m 🚶on the spot.
**Remarks:** Max. 24h, servicepoint at campsite 1km.

| S | Lézardrieux | 14D1 |
|---|---|---|

**Camping Municipal**, Cité des Gardiens de Phare.
**GPS:** n48,78021 w3,1147.⬆➡
€ 5 ⛽🚿Chincluded. 🕐 01/01-31/12.
**Distance:** 🚶on the spot.

| 🅿S | Liffré | 18B1 |
|---|---|---|

**Intermarché**. **GPS:** n48,22459 w1,50165.⬆➡

10 ⛌free ⛽🚿Ch🚿free. **Location:** Urban, simple.
**Surface:** asphalted. 🕐 01/01-31/12.
**Distance:** 🛒300m 🏪on the spot.

| 🅿S | Lizio | 14D2 |
|---|---|---|

**Rue du Souvenir**. **GPS:** n47,86202 w2,5263.⬆

10 ⛌free ⛽🚿Chfree. **Location:** Rural, simple, quiet.
**Surface:** metalled. 🕐 01/01-31/12. **Distance:** 🚏150m.

**S** | **Locmaria-Plouzané** | 14B1

**Zône détente Ty Izella**, Rue de la Fontaine.
**GPS**: n48,37343 w4,64386.⬆.

6 free ⚡🚰Chfree. **Location**: Rural, quiet. **Surface**: gravel.
🗓 01/01-31/12.
**Distance**: 🛒100m ⊗250m 🚉250m.

**S** | **Locmaria-Plouzané** | 14B1

**Plage de Portez**, Rue de Portez, Porsmilin.
**GPS**: n48,35501 w4,67269.⬆➡.

8 🔲€5, tourist tax €0,60/pp ⚡🚰Chincluded ⚡€3.
**Location**: Rural, simple, quiet. **Surface**: gravel.
🗓 18/04-18/09.
**Distance**: 🛒3,5km 🏖beach 50m 🚌on the spot 🚶on the spot.
**Remarks**: To be paid at campsite.

**S** | **Locmariaquer** | 14D3

**Aire de Pierres Plates**, > Route des Plages.
**GPS**: n47,55720 w2,9486.⬆➡.

20 free. **Location**: Simple. **Surface**: metalled.
🗓 01/01-31/12.
**Distance**: 🏖beach 50m 🚌on the spot.
**Remarks**: Max. 24h, 500m from 'Les Pierres Plates'.

**S** | **Locmariaquer** | 14D3

**Résidence de Cresidui. GPS**: n47,57204 w2,95328.
⚡€2/100liter 🚰Ch.

**Tourist information Locmariaquer:**
ℹ Office de Tourisme, Rue de la Victoire,
www.ot-locmariaquer.com. Port city with many megalithics, signed dolmen.

**S** | **Locminé** | 14D2

**Rue Laennec / rue du Pont Person. GPS**: n47,88788 w2,83174.⬆.

5 free. **Location**: Simple. **Surface**: asphalted. 🗓 01/01-31/12.
**Distance**: 🛒on the spot 🏖on the spot ⊗on the spot.
**Remarks**: Parking at marina, max. 1 night.

**S** | **Locqueltas** | 14D3

**Rue de la Fontaine. GPS**: n47,75841 w2,76901.⬆.

6 free ⚡🚰Ch ⚡(4x)€3,50 WCfree. **Location**: Rural, simple, quiet. **Surface**: gravel.
🗓 01/01-31/12.
**Distance**: 🛒100m 🏖600m ⊗100m 🚉100m.
**Remarks**: Max. 24h, coins at Bar-Tabac, 18 Place de la Mairie, town hall.

**S** | **Locronan** | 14B2

**Parking de la Croix de Mission**, Rue du Prieuré.
**GPS**: n48,09811 w4,21245.⬆.

10 free, 01/06-15/10 €6/24h ⚡€2/10minutes 🚰Ch ⚡€2/2h.
**Location**: Urban, simple, quiet. **Surface**: grassy/sand.
🗓 01/01-31/12.
**Distance**: 🛒100m ⊗50m 🚲on the spot 🚶on the spot.

**S** | **Loctudy** | 14B2

**Camping-Car Park Plage de Langoz**, Rue des Mésanges.
**GPS**: n47,82813 w4,16563.
23 🔲€10,04, 01/04-30/09 €12,44 ⚡🚰Ch ⚡(20x)included. 🔲 ⚡
**Surface**: metalled. 🗓 01/01-31/12.
**Distance**: 🏖200m.
**Remarks**: Mandatory, one-time fee Pass'Etapes €4.

**S** | **Loctudy** | 14B2

**Plage des Sables Blancs**, Chemin de Toul Pesked.
**GPS**: n47,80110 w4,20044.

6 free. **Location**: Rural, simple. **Surface**: grassy/sand.
🗓 01/01-31/12.
**Distance**: 🛒4km 🏖beach 80m 🚌on the spot 🚶on the spot.
**Remarks**: Beach parking.

**S** | **Loudéac** | 14D2

**Parking de la Gare**, Boulevard de la Gare.
**GPS**: n48,18058 w2,76277.⬆➡.

3 free ⚡🚰Chfree. **Location**: Urban, simple. **Surface**: asphalted.
🗓 01/01-31/12.
**Distance**: 🛒600m ⊗50m 🚉200m 🏧200m 🚌on the spot.

**S** | **Maël-Carhaix** | 14C2

**Place de l'école**, Route de Rostrenen. **GPS**: n48,28344 w3,42148.⬆➡.

3 free ⚡€2,25 🚰Ch WC. **Location**: Urban, simple.
**Surface**: asphalted. 🗓 01/01-31/12.
**Distance**: 🛒100m ⊗100m 🚉100m.
**Remarks**: Coins at town hall.

**S** | **Malansac** | 18A2

**Rue Saint Fiacre. GPS**: n47,67820 w2,29942.⬆➡.

5 free ⚡🚰Chfree. **Location**: Rural, comfortable, quiet.
**Surface**: grassy. 🗓 01/01-31/12.
**Distance**: 🛒100m 🚉100m 🏧100m.

**S** | **Malestroit** | 18A1

**Chemin de l'Écluse. GPS**: n47,81250 w2,38197.⬆➡.

12 free 📶. **Location**: Rural, comfortable, quiet.
**Surface**: gravel/metalled. 🗓 01/01-31/12.
**Distance**: 🛒100m 🚌on the spot 🚉on the spot ⊗100m 🏧100m 🍽200m.
**Remarks**: Max. 48h.

**S** | **Malestroit** | 18A1

**Chemin des Tanneurs. GPS**: n47,80772 w2,37885.⬆➡.

12 free 📶. **Location**: Comfortable, quiet. **Surface**: gravel/metalled.
🗓 01/01-31/12.
**Distance**: 🛒500m 🏖on the spot ⊗350m.
**Remarks**: Max. 48h.

**S** | **Malestroit** | 18A1

**Rue de Narvik. GPS**: n47,80896 w2,37591.⬆➡.

**S** | **Locmiquelic** | 14C3

**Port de Ste. Catherine**, Quai Rallier du Baty.
**GPS**: n47,72364 w3,34958.⬆.

10 free ⚡🚰Chfree. **Location**: Simple. **Surface**: gravel.
🗓 01/01-31/12.
**Distance**: 🛒1km 🚲N24 1,4km 🚉600m.
**Remarks**: Max. 48h.

⊤⊒Chfree. **Surface:** asphalted. ▭ 01/01-31/12.
**Distance:** ⊿1,5km ⊿600m ⊿600m ⊗2km ⊒1km.

🅂 Marzan 🛥 18A2
Rue de la Source. **GPS:** n47,54023 w2,32383.⬆.

20 free ⊤⊒ChWCfree. **Location:** Urban, simple, quiet.
**Surface:** asphalted. ▭ 01/01-31/12.
**Distance:** ⊿50m ⊿20m.
**Remarks:** Max. 72h.

🅂 Maure-de-Bretagne 18A1
Rue de Campel, D65. **GPS:** n47,89230 w1,99031.⬆➡.

3 free ⊤⊒Chfree. **Location:** Urban, simple, central, quiet.
**Surface:** gravel. ▭ 01/01-31/12.
**Distance:** ⊿200m ⊿on the spot ⊗200m ⊒200m ⊿on the spot ⊿on the spot.

🅂 Mauron 18A1
Route du Plan D'eau. **GPS:** n48,07883 w2,27573.

10 free ⊤⊒Chfree. **Location:** Rural, simple, quiet.
**Surface:** gravel/metalled. ▭ 01/01-31/12.
**Distance:** ⊿500m ⊗500m.

🅂 Mauron 18A1
Rue de la Libération. **GPS:** n48,08024 w2,27677.⬆➡.

12 free ⊤€ 2,50/100liter ⊒ChWC. **Location:** Rural, simple, quiet.
**Surface:** asphalted. ▭ 01/01-31/12.
**Distance:** ⊿150m ⊿on the spot ⊿on the spot ⊗150m ⊒150m ⊿on the spot ⊿on the spot.

🅂 Mégrit 15A3
**Parking du Stade**, Rue des Granitiers. **GPS:** n48,37817 w2,24722.⬆.
free ⊤⊒Chfree. **Surface:** asphalted/gravel. ▭ 01/01-31/12.
**Distance:** ⊒on the spot.

🅂 Mellé 15B3
Rue Rouviel. **GPS:** n48,48919 w1,18814.⬆.

4 free ⊤⊒ChWCfree. **Location:** Simple, quiet.
**Surface:** metalled. ▭ 01/01-31/12.
**Distance:** ⊿200m ⊗100m ⊒200m.
**Remarks:** Nearby football ground, max. 48h.

🅂 Meslin 14D1
Allée des Loisirs, D28. **GPS:** n48,44363 w2,56994.⬆.

10 free ⊤⊒Chfree. **Location:** Urban, simple, central.
**Surface:** metalled. ▭ 01/01-31/12.
**Distance:** ⊿300m ⊗bar/crêperie 50m ⊒50m.

🅂 Moëlan-sur-Mer 14C2
Rue de Beg Tal Gward. **GPS:** n47,77749 w3,64404.⬆➡.

4 free. **Location:** Rural, isolated, quiet. **Surface:** asphalted.
▭ 01/01-31/12.
**Distance:** ⊿Moëlan 5km ⊿sea 50m.
**Remarks:** Along Mosel.

🅂 Moëlan-sur-Mer 14C2
Kerdoualen, Route de l'Île Percée. **GPS:** n47,79045 w3,70314.⬆.

4 free. **Location:** Rural, isolated, quiet. **Surface:** gravel.
▭ 01/01-31/12.
**Distance:** ⊿200m.

🅂 Mohon 14D2
Route de Josselin, D793. **GPS:** n48,04903 w2,52838.

10 free ⊤. **Location:** Rural, simple. **Surface:** grassy.
▭ 01/01-31/12.
**Distance:** ⊿1km ⊗150m ⊒250m.

🅂 Moncontour 14D2
**Camping la Tourelle**, Rue François Lorant.
**GPS:** n48,35271 w2,63719.⬆➡.

3 € 4 ⊤⊒Ch included. **Location:** Rural, simple, quiet.
**Surface:** gravel. ▭ 01/01-31/12.
**Distance:** ⊿1,5km ⊗1,5km ⊒1,5km.
**Remarks:** Max. 48h.

🅂 Monterrein 18A1
**Parking de la Mairie**, Rue de la Mairie. **GPS:** n47,88055 w2,35872.

2 free. **Location:** Simple, quiet. **Surface:** asphalted.
▭ 01/01-31/12.
**Distance:** ⊿on the spot ⊗200m.

🅂 Montertelot 🛥 18A1
Rue du Casset. **GPS:** n47,88306 w2,4225.

20 free. **Location:** Simple, quiet. **Surface:** grassy.
▭ 01/01-31/12.
**Distance:** ⊿200m ⊿100m ⊿100m ⊗300m.
**Remarks:** Near sports fields.

🅂 Morlaix 14C1
Rue de Brest. **GPS:** n48,57422 w3,8316.⬆➡.

9 free ⊤⊒Chfree. **Location:** Urban, simple, central, noisy.
**Surface:** asphalted. ▭ 01/01-31/12.
**Distance:** ⊿on the spot ⊿on the spot ⊗200m ⊒100m ⊿200m ⊿on the spot ⊿on the spot.

🅂 Mûr-de-Bretagne 14D2
**L'ancienne Gare**, Place de la Gare. **GPS:** n48,19814 w2,98961.⬆.

4 free ⊤⊒Chfree. **Location:** Urban, simple. **Surface:** metalled.
▭ 01/01-31/12.
**Distance:** ⊿700m ⊗500m ⊿on the spot.

🅂 Mûr-de-Bretagne 14D2
**Anse de Leandroanec**, Plage de Leandroanec.
**GPS:** n48,20969 w3,01309.⬆.

8 🚐free. **Location:** Rural, simple, isolated, quiet. **Surface:** gravel.
🅿 01/01-31/12.
**Distance:** 🚰2,5km 🏊on the spot.
**Remarks:** Inclining pitches.

---

### Mûr-de-Bretagne    14D2

**Chapelle Sainte-Suzanne**, Place Ste Suzanne.
**GPS:** n48,20260 w2,98835. ⬆➡

4 🚐free. **Location:** Urban, simple. **Surface:** metalled.
🅿 01/01-31/12.
**Distance:** 🚰300m ⊗100m.

---

### S    Neulliac    14D2

Rue des Deux Croix, D767. **GPS:** n48,12812 w2,98552. ⬆➡

4 🚐free ⛽€ 2 🔌Ch 🔲€ 2. **Location:** Urban, simple, isolated, quiet.
**Surface:** asphalted. 🅿 01/01-31/12.
**Distance:** 🚰300m ⊗300m.

---

### S    Névez    14C2

**Parking du Stade**, Rue de Port Manech, Impasse du Stade.
**GPS:** n47,81560 w3,7894. ⬆

20 🚐free ⛽€ 2/10minutes 🔌Ch 🔲€ 2/55minutes 🚽free.
**Location:** Urban, simple. **Surface:** asphalted. 🅿 01/01-31/12.
**Distance:** 🚰850m ⊗300m 🛒850m.
**Remarks:** Parking next to stadium, max. 24h, service only with 2-euro coins.

---

### S    Névez    14C2

**Plage de Tahiti**, Kerstalen. **GPS:** n47,79287 w3,79011. ⬆

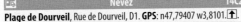

± 11 🚐free 🚽free. **Location:** Rural, simple, quiet.
**Surface:** grassy/sand. 🅿 01/01-31/12.
**Distance:** 🏊beach 150m.
**Remarks:** Beach parking, max. 24h.

---

### Névez    14C2

**Plage de Dourveil**, Rue de Dourveil, D1. **GPS:** n47,79407 w3,8101. ⬆

5 🚐free. **Location:** Simple. **Surface:** sand. 🅿 01/01-31/12.
**Distance:** 🏊on the spot 🚴on the spot.
**Remarks:** Max. 24h, no camping activities.

---

### Névez    14C2

Rue de la Plage. **GPS:** n47,80499 w3,74261. ⬆

5 🚐free. **Location:** Rural, simple. **Surface:** sand.
🅿 01/01-31/12.
**Distance:** 🏊50m 🚴on the spot 🚶on the spot.
**Remarks:** Max. 24h.

---

### Névez    14C2

Rue des Iles, Raguénez. **GPS:** n47,78908 w3,80174. ⬆

10 🚐free. **Location:** Rural, simple. **Surface:** asphalted.
🅿 01/01-31/12.
**Distance:** 🏊sea 10m, beach 150m ⊗100m.
**Remarks:** Max. 24h.

---

### S    Noyal-Pontivy    14D2

**Le Valvert**, Caudan. **GPS:** n48,07833 w2,91583. ⬆➡

20 🚐free ⛽🚽free. **Location:** Rural, comfortable, isolated, quiet.
**Surface:** asphalted. 🅿 01/01-31/12.
**Distance:** 🚰Noyal-Pontivy 4,5km 🏊on the spot 🚣on the spot ⊗50m.
**Remarks:** At small lake.

---

### Noyal-Pontivy    14D2

**Le Manoir**, Avenue de la Liberation. **GPS:** n48,06689 w2,87937.

10 🚐free. **Location:** Rural, simple. **Surface:** gravel. 🅿 01/01-31/12.
**Distance:** 🚰150m ⊗250m 🛒300m.

---

### Paimpol    14D1

**Parking de Goas Plat**, Rue de Goas Plat. **GPS:** n48,77535 w3,04009. ⬆

37 🚐€ 8. 🚐 ⊘ **Location:** Urban, simple, central, quiet.
**Surface:** asphalted.
**Distance:** 🚰centre 500m 🏊2km ⊗500m 🛒500m.
**Remarks:** Max. 24h.

---

### Paimpol    14D1

**Parking Pierre Loti**, Rue Pierre Loti. **GPS:** n48,78404 w3,0463.

37 🚐free, 01/06-30/09 € 5. 🏍 **Surface:** gravel/sand.
🅿 01/01-31/12.
**Distance:** 🏊on the spot 🏊1km 🚲400m 🚌100m 🚴on the spot 🚶on the spot.
**Remarks:** Service 100m.

---

### S    Paimpont 🌿    18A1

Rue de l'Enchanteur Merlin. **GPS:** n48,02286 w2,17128. ⬆

70 🚐€ 4 ⛽€ 3,70/10minutes 🔌ChWC 🔲 📶included. 🚐
**Location:** Urban, simple, quiet. **Surface:** gravel.
🅿 01/01-31/12.
**Distance:** 🚰200m 🏊200m 🚲200m ⊗200m 🛒200m 🚴on the spot 🚶100m.
**Remarks:** Coins at tourist info and supermarket.

---

### S    Péaule    18A2

Rue du Stade. **GPS:** n47,58043 w2,35128.
20 🚐free ⛽🔌Ch. **Location:** Simple. **Surface:** asphalted.
🅿 01/01-31/12.
**Distance:** ⊗450m 🛒400m.

---

### S    Pénestin 🌿⛱🌊    14D3

**Aire de camping-cars de la Mine d'Or**, 34 Allée des Coquelicots.
**GPS:** n47,47048 w2,48631. ⬆
24 🚐€ 10, 01/04-31/10 € 13, tourist tax incl ⛽🔌Chfree
📶included. 🚐 **Location:** Rural, isolated, quiet.
**Surface:** gravel. 🅿 01/01-31/12.
**Distance:** 🚰2km 🏊200m 🚲200m 🚴on the spot.

---

### S    Pénestin 🌿⛱🌊    14D3

Allée du Grand Pré. **GPS:** n47,48111 w2,47361. ⬆➡

7 🚐free, € 6/night + € 0,20/pp ⛽€ 2,50/100liter 🔌Ch 🔲€ 2,50/1h.
**Location:** Urban. **Surface:** asphalted.
🅿 01/01-31/12.
**Distance:** 🚰500m 🏊1,5km ⊗500m.

---

FR

**Remarks:** Check in all aires in Pénestin: Office de tourisme; Bar-PMU Le Narval, Rue Calvaire; Café O 20 100 O, Port de Tréhiguier, max. 48h, coins at tourist info.

### Pénestin 🌿⚓🐚 14D3

**Aire camping-car de la Pointe du Bile**, Route de l'Espernel. **GPS:** n47,44524 w2,48029. ⬆️.

10 🛢️free, € 6/night + € 0,20/pp. **Location:** Rural, simple, quiet. **Surface:** grassy/sand. ⭕ 01/01-31/12. **Distance:** 🏖️100m ⊗400m. **Remarks:** Max. 48h.

### Pénestin 🌿⚓🐚 14D3

**Allée de Poudrantais. GPS:** n47,46681 w2,48716. ⬆️.

4 🛢️free, € 6/night + € 0,20/pp. **Location:** Urban, simple, quiet. **Surface:** gravel/metalled. ⭕ 01/01-31/12. **Distance:** 🏖️50m. **Remarks:** Max. 48h.

### Pénestin 🌿⚓🐚 14D3

**Chemin de Camaret. GPS:** n47,49386 w2,49075. ⬆️.

4 🛢️free, € 6/night + € 0,20/pp. **Location:** Urban, simple, quiet. **Surface:** gravel. ⭕ 01/01-31/12. **Distance:** 🏖️100m. **Remarks:** Max. 48h.

### Pénestin 🌿⚓🐚 14D3

**Plage de la Source**, Allée du Maro. **GPS:** n47,48158 w2,49005. ⬆️.

10 🛢️gratis, overnachten € 6 + € 0,20/pp. **Location:** Rural, simple, quiet. **Surface:** grassy/metalled. ⭕ 01/01-31/12. **Distance:** 🏖️300m. **Remarks:** Max. 48h.

### Pénestin 🌿⚓🐚 14D3

**Plage du Palandrin**, L'Isle du Clos Parc, Kerséguin. **GPS:** n47,45000 w2,46417. ⬆️➡️.

---

6 🛢️free, € 6/night + € 0,20/pp tourist tax. **Location:** Rural, simple, isolated. **Surface:** grassy/sand. ⭕ 01/01-31/12. **Distance:** 🏖️Sandy beach ⊗1km. **Remarks:** Pay at tourist office.

### Pénestin 🌿⚓🐚 14D3

Route du Loguy. **GPS:** n47,49050 w2,49667. ⬆️.

20 🛢️free, € 6/night + € 0,20/pp. **Location:** Rural, simple, quiet. **Surface:** grassy/metalled. **Distance:** 🏖️150m. **Remarks:** Max. 48h.

### Penmarch 🐚 14B2

**Aire de Kérity**, Rue Victor Hugo. **GPS:** n47,79981 w4,34794. ⬆️.

10 🛢️free, 01/04-31/10 € 4/19-9h. 🚐 **Location:** Rural, simple, quiet. **Surface:** grassy/gravel. ⭕ 01/01-31/12. **Distance:** 🚿1,5km 🏖️50m ⊗1km 🛒5km 🚲on the spot 🚶on the spot.

### Penmarch 🐚 14B2

**Aire du Ster**, Rue de la Grande Grève. **GPS:** n47,80042 w4,31807. ⬆️.

30 🛢️free, 01/04-31/10 € 4/19-9h. **Surface:** sand. ⭕ 01/01-31/12. **Distance:** 🏖️Sandy beach 🛒2km 🚲on the spot 🚶on the spot. **Remarks:** Beach parking.

### Penmarch 🐚 14B2

**Aire du Viben**, Rue de la Plage. **GPS:** n47,82390 w4,3708. ⬆️.

30 🛢️free, 01/04-31/10 € 4/19-9h. 🚐 **Location:** Rural, simple, quiet. **Surface:** metalled. ⭕ 01/01-31/12. **Distance:** 🚿1km 🏖️50m 🛒900m 🚲on the spot 🚶on the spot. **Remarks:** Sandy beach.

---

### S Penmarch 🐚 14B2

**Aire de Kerameil**, Rue du Pont Nevez. **GPS:** n47,81369 w4,36077. ⬆️. 🚐 € 2/10minutes 🗑️Ch🚻WC. ⭕ 01/01-31/12. **Remarks:** Only overnight stays 19-9h.

### 🏕️ Penvins 14D3

**Camping La Gree Penvins**, Chemin du Marais 20. **GPS:** n47,49746 w2,68606. ⬆️➡️.

22 🛢️€ 7. **Location:** Urban, comfortable, quiet. **Surface:** grassy. ⭕ 01/01-31/12. **Distance:** 🏖️on the spot ⊗350m. **Remarks:** Max. 48h.

### S Penzé 14C1

Rue du Dossen. **GPS:** n48,59811 w3,93439. ⬆️.

5 🛢️free 🚐🗑️Ch🚻WCfree. **Location:** Urban, simple, quiet. **Surface:** asphalted. ⭕ 01/01-31/12. **Distance:** 🚿100m 🏖️on the spot 🚲on the spot ⊗50m 🛒250m 🚲on the spot 🚶on the spot. **Remarks:** Nearby port.

### S Piré-sur-Seiche 18B1

Rue de Boistrudan. **GPS:** n48,00719 w1,42871.

7 🛢️free 🚿🗑️Chfree. **Location:** Rural, simple. **Surface:** metalled. ⭕ 01/01-31/12. **Distance:** 🚿300m 🚲on the spot 🛒300m 🚲500m. **Remarks:** At fish lake.

### S Plabennec 14B1

Rue de l'Aber. **GPS:** n48,50155 w4,43374. ⬆️.

5 🛢️free 🚿🗑️Chfree. **Location:** Rural, simple. **Surface:** metalled. ⭕ 01/01-31/12. **Distance:** 🏖️on the spot 🚲on the spot 🚲on the spot 🚶on the spot. **Remarks:** Parking at small lake.

### ⚜️S Planguenoual 15A3

Bien y Vient. **GPS:** n48,53447 w2,54506. ⬆️.

6 🚐 €5 ⚡💧 €2/24h. **Location:** Rural, comfortable, isolated, quiet. **Surface:** grassy. 🕐 01/01-31/12. **Distance:** 🚶on the spot.

### Planguenoual 15A3
Ferme Gesbert, D786. **GPS:** n48,54883 w2,5556. ⬆➡

6 🚐 free ⚡ €2 Ch €2. **Location:** Rural, simple, isolated, quiet. **Surface:** grassy/gravel. 🕐 01/01-31/12. **Distance:** 💧1,5km ⊗1km 🍴1km. **Remarks:** Regional products.

### Plelauff 14D2
Le Bout du Pont. **GPS:** n48,22434 w3,18048. ⬆

12 🚐 free ⚡ Ch 🚽 free WC. **Location:** Rural, comfortable. **Surface:** asphalted. 🕐 01/01-31/12. **Distance:** 💧500m on the spot ⊗200m 🚶on the spot.

### Plémet 14D2
Rue de l'Étang, D16. **GPS:** n48,17897 w2,58918. ⬆➡

15 🚐 free ⚡ €3/100liter Ch 🚽 €3/55minutes WC. **Location:** Rural, simple, quiet. **Surface:** gravel. 🕐 01/01-31/12. **Distance:** 💧500m. **Remarks:** Parking at small lake, coins at town hall.

### Pléneuf-Val-André 15A3
Avenue du Général Leclerc. **GPS:** n48,58355 w2,55669. ⬆➡

30 🚐 €8 ⚡ €2 Ch. **Location:** Urban, simple, central, quiet. **Surface:** grassy/gravel. 🕐 01/01-31/12. **Distance:** 💧1km 450m. **Remarks:** Max. 72h.

### Plérin 14D1
Place François Guego. **GPS:** n48,53986 w2,7264. ⬆

---

9 🚐 free. **Location:** Urban. **Surface:** asphalted. 🕐 01/01-31/12. **Distance:** 💧200m ⊗200m 🍴200m.

### Plérin 14D1
Rue de Martin Plage. **GPS:** n48,55564 w2,72686. ⬆⬆
3 🚐 free. **Surface:** asphalted. 🕐 01/01-31/12. **Distance:** 💧on the spot on the spot.

### Plérin 14D1
Rue de Tournemine. **GPS:** n48,56835 w2,77075. ⬆
12 🚐 free. **Surface:** gravel. 🕐 01/01-31/12. **Distance:** 💧300m 300m.

### Pleslin-Trigavou 15A3
D28. **GPS:** n48,53631 w2,05009. ⬆

20 🚐 free ⚡ Ch WC free. **Location:** Urban, simple. **Surface:** asphalted. 🕐 01/01-31/12. **Distance:** 💧on the spot 🍴400m on the spot 🚶on the spot. **Remarks:** Cycle and hiking routes: voie verte, Circuit des Mégalithes.

### Plessala 14D2
Rue de l'Étang. **GPS:** n48,27394 w2,62427. ⬆➡

12 🚐 free ⚡ Ch free. **Location:** Urban, simple, quiet. **Surface:** gravel. 🕐 01/01-31/12. **Distance:** 💧200m on the spot ⊗500m. **Remarks:** At fish lake, max. 48h, fishing permit available.

### Plestin-les-Grèves 14C1
Voie Communale de l'Armorique. **GPS:** n48,68157 w3,63411. ⬆

6 🚐 free. **Location:** Rural, simple, quiet. **Surface:** unpaved. 🕐 01/01-31/12. **Distance:** 💧3km 50m ⊗2km 🚶on the spot. **Remarks:** Beach parking, max. 24h.

### Plestin-les-Grèves 14C1
Du Grand Rocher, Avenue de la Lieue de Grève. **GPS:** n48,66968 w3,5858.

10 🚐 free. **Location:** Rural, simple, isolated, quiet. **Surface:** gravel. 🕐 01/01-31/12. **Distance:** 💧1,3km 100m ⊗1,3km.

### Plestin-les-Grèves 14C1
Route de la Corniche. **GPS:** n48,67235 w3,63602. ⬆

---

**FR**

6 🚐 free. **Location:** Rural, simple, quiet. **Surface:** grassy/sand. 🕐 01/01-31/12. **Distance:** 💧1km on the spot ⊗300m 🍴Lidl 2km. **Remarks:** Max. 24h.

### Plestin-les-Grèves 14C1
Avenue des Frères Le Gall. **GPS:** n48,66232 w3,62562. ⚡ €2/10minutes Ch 🚽 €2/1h. **Remarks:** Motorhome washing place.

### Pleubian 14D1
Port Béni. **GPS:** n48,84834 w3,17053. ⬆

4 🚐 free. **Location:** Rural, simple, isolated, quiet. **Surface:** asphalted. 🕐 01/01-31/12. **Distance:** 💧Pleubian 2,5km on the spot ⊗2,5km 🚶on the spot. **Remarks:** Max. 24h.

### Pleubian 14D1
Rue de Kermagen, Kermagen. **GPS:** n48,85667 w3,14194. ⬆

4 🚐 free. **Location:** Simple, quiet. **Surface:** grassy. 🕐 01/01-31/12. **Distance:** 💧Pleubian 1,6km beach 100m 🚶on the spot. **Remarks:** Max. 24h.

### Pleubian 14D1
Rue de Pen Lan, Lanéros. **GPS:** n48,85760 w3,07883. ⬆

4 🚐 free. **Location:** Simple. **Surface:** asphalted. 🕐 01/01-31/12. **Distance:** 💧Pleubian 5,5km on the spot 🚶on the spot. **Remarks:** Max. 24h.

### Pleumeur-Bodou 14C1
Parking de Toul ar Stang, Rue de Toul ar Stang, Ile Grande. **GPS:** n48,79868 w3,58342. ⬆➡

6 🚐 €6/night ⚡ €2/10minutes Ch 🚽 €3/day. **Location:** Rural,

simple, quiet. **Surface:** grassy.
◻ 01/01-31/12.
**Distance:** 🚲Plemeur-Bodu 6km ⚓sandy beach 150m ⊗150m
🚰300m on the spot.

| 🏕S | **Pleumeur-Bodou** ⚓⚓ | 14C1 |

**Cosmopolis-Parc Scientifique**, Route du Radome.
**GPS:** n48,78297 w3,52587.⬆️.

20 🚐parking free, € 5/night 🚰🔌Ch 🧹WCincluded. 🚗🗑
**Surface:** gravel/sand. ◻ 01/01-31/12.
**Distance:** 🚲1km ⚓1km ⊗on the spot 🚶on the spot.

| 🅿S | **Plévenon** 🌿⚓ | 15A3 |

**Aire de la Roche aux Cygrons. GPS:** n48,65595 w2,32843.

8 🚐free 🚰€ 2,30 🔌Ch. **Surface:** grassy/gravel.
◻ 01/01-31/12.
**Distance:** 🚲350m ⊗450m.
**Remarks:** Max. 1 night, coins at shops and tourist office, bread-service.

| 🅿 | **Plévenon** 🌿⚓ | 15A3 |

**Parking Cap Fréhel. GPS:** n48,68174 w2,31811.

40 🚐free, 01/06-30/09 8-22h € 5. **Surface:** metalled.
**Distance:** ⚓50m.

| 🏕S | **Pleyben** ⚓ | 14C2 |

Pont Coblant/D785. **GPS:** n48,19337 w3,98182.➡️.

80 🚐€ 9 🚰🧹WC🗑. **Location:** Rural, simple, quiet. **Surface:** grassy.
◻ 15/06-15/09.
**Distance:** 🚲300m ⚓on the spot ⊗300m 🚰300m 🚴on the spot.
**Remarks:** On the canal, former campsite.

| 🏕S | **Ploemeur** | 14C2 |

**Aire de la Vraie Croix**, Route de Larmor. **GPS:** n47,72784 w3,41423.⬆️.

3 🚐free 🚰🔌Chfree. **Location:** Rural, simple, noisy.

---

**Surface:** concrete. ◻ 01/01-31/12.
**Distance:** 🚲1km.
**Remarks:** Industrial area, max. 48h.

| 🏕S | **Ploemeur** | 14C2 |

**Aire du Courégant**, RD 152. **GPS:** n47,70850 w3,46552.
4 🚐free. **Surface:** unpaved. ◻ 01/01-31/12.
**Distance:** 🚲Ploemeur 4,5km ⊗450m.

| 🏕S | **Ploemeur** | 14C2 |

**Aire du Fort-Bloqué**, Allée des Korrigans. **GPS:** n47,73698 w3,49756.
6 🚐free. **Location:** Urban. **Surface:** sand. ◻ 01/01-31/12.
**Distance:** 🚲Ploemeur 6km ⚓550m ⊗350m.

| 🏕S | **Ploemeur** | 14C2 |

**Aire du Pérello**, Chemin des Douves. **GPS:** n47,69891 w3,44684.
6 🚐free. **Surface:** unpaved. ◻ 01/01-31/12.
**Distance:** 🚲Ploemeur 5km ⚓180m.

| 🏕S | **Ploemeur** | 14C2 |

**Centre-ville**, Rue du Fort Bloqué, Rue Louis Lessart.
**GPS:** n47,73679 w3,42991.⬆️.

7 🚐free. **Location:** Simple, central, quiet. **Surface:** asphalted.
◻ 01/01-31/12.
**Distance:** 🚲on the spot ⊗100m 🚰400m.
**Remarks:** Parking centre, max. 24h.

| 🏕S | **Ploemeur** | 14C2 |

**Golf Ploemeur**, D152, Boulevard de l'Atlantique.
**GPS:** n47,72316 w3,48156.⬆️➡️.

9 🚐free. **Location:** Rural, isolated, quiet. **Surface:** gravel.
◻ 01/01-31/12.
**Distance:** 🚲Ploemeur 5km 🛣N165 10km ⚓beach 300m ⊗260m
🚰1,8km 🚶on the spot 🏃on the spot.

| 🏕S | **Ploemeur** | 14C2 |

**Kerroch**, Place Louis Kermabon. **GPS:** n47,70331 w3,45477.
4 🚐free. **Location:** Urban. **Surface:** asphalted. ◻ 01/01-31/12.
**Distance:** 🚲Ploemeur 4,5km ⚓400m ⊗140m.

| 🏕S | **Plogoff** ⚓ | 14B2 |

**Aire Naturelle Kerguidy Izella**, Rue Guillaume Pennamen.
**GPS:** n48,03694 w4,68139.⬆️.

30 🚐€ 12 🚰🔌Ch 🧹WC🗑🚿included. **Location:** Rural, luxurious,
quiet. **Surface:** grassy. ◻ 01/01-31/12.
**Distance:** 🚲2km ⚓4km 🚰1km 🚰2km 🚴on the spot.
**Remarks:** 9><20h.

| 🏕S | **Plogoff** ⚓ | 14B2 |

**Parking de l'Eglise**, Rue Bethany. **GPS:** n48,03727 w4,6652.⬆️➡️.

---

3 🚐free 🚰€ 2/10minutes 🔌Ch 🚗€ 2. **Location:** Rural, simple.
**Surface:** asphalted. ◻ 01/01-31/12.
**Distance:** 🚲centre.

| 🏕S | **Plogoff** ⚓ | 14B2 |

**Aire de la Pointe du Raz**, Route des Langoustiers.
**GPS:** n48,03651 w4,7173.⬆️.

40 🚐€ 5. 🚴 **Location:** Rural, simple, quiet. **Surface:** unpaved.
◻ 01/01-31/12.
**Distance:** 🚲3km ⊗50m 🚴on the spot 🚶on the spot.

| 🏕S | **Plogoff** ⚓ | 14B2 |

**Parking du Stade**, Rue du 19 Mars 1962. **GPS:** n48,03245 w4,66316.⬆️.

30 🚐free. **Location:** Rural, simple, quiet. **Surface:** grassy/metalled.
◻ 01/01-31/12.
**Distance:** 🚲on the spot ⚓500m ⊗450m 🚰450m bakery.

| 🏕S | **Plomelin** | 14B2 |

Rue Hent Keramer. **GPS:** n47,93410 w4,1515.⬆️.

4 🚐free 🚰€ 2/10minutes 🔌Ch 🚗€ 2/h. **Location:** Rural, simple,
quiet. **Surface:** asphalted. ◻ 01/01-31/12.
**Distance:** 🚲on the spot ⊗400m 🚰200m.
**Remarks:** Parking sports park, max. 24h, shady.

| 🏕S | **Plonévez-Porzay** | 14B2 |

Rue des Eglantines. **GPS:** n48,12469 w4,22414.⬆️.

15 🚐free 🚰€ 2/10minutes 🔌Ch 🚗€ 2/55minutes.
**Location:** Rural, comfortable, quiet. **Surface:** grassy.
◻ 01/01-31/12.
**Distance:** 🚲600m ⊗450m 🚰450m 🚴on the spot.

| 🏕S | **Plonévez-Porzay** | 14B2 |

Kervel Izella. **GPS:** n48,11570 w4,28065.⬆️.

10 🛏free. **Location:** Rural, simple. **Surface:** grassy/sand.
⬛ 01/01-31/12.
**Distance:** 🚶8km ⛱50m ⚲on the spot 🚲on the spot.
**Remarks:** Beach parking, max. 48h.

### ⬛S Plouarzel 14B1

**Aire de camping-car de Ruscumunoc**, Route de Ruscumunoc.
**GPS:** n48,42232 w4,78486. ⬆➡.

40 🛏free, 01/04-15/09 € 4,50 🚰€ 2/10minutes 🔌Ch 🚿€ 3 🚽€ 1
📶 🔧 **Location:** Rural, comfortable, quiet. **Surface:** grassy.
⬛ 01/01-31/12.
**Distance:** 🚶3km ⛱100m ⚲on the spot 🏃on the spot.

### ⬛S Ploubalay 15A3

Rue des Ormelets. **GPS:** n48,58057 w2,14524. ⬆.

3 🛏free 🚰🔌Chfree. **Location:** Urban, simple, central.
**Surface:** asphalted. ⬛ 01/01-31/12.
**Distance:** 🚶250m ⊗100m 🛒500m ⚲on the spot.

### ⬛S Ploubalay 15A3

Rue du Chaffaud. **GPS:** n48,57800 w2,14166.
70 🛏€ 10 WC . 🏠 **Location:** Rural, simple, quiet.
**Surface:** asphalted. ⬛ 01/01-31/12.
**Distance:** 🚶on the spot ⊗450m 🛒450m.

### ⬛ Ploubazlanec 14D1

**Park Nevez**, Cité de Lan ar Mendy. **GPS:** n48,80090 w3,0305. ⬆.
3 🛏free. **Location:** Urban, simple. **Surface:** asphalted.
⬛ 01/01-31/12.
**Distance:** 🛒bakery.
**Remarks:** Max. 24h.

### ⬛ Ploubazlanec 14D1

**Pointe de l'Arcouest**, Route de l'Embarcadère.
**GPS:** n48,82102 w3,01948. ⬆.

20 🛏free, 28/04-13/10 € 8/24h. **Location:** Simple, isolated, quiet.
**Surface:** grassy. ⬛ 01/01-31/12.
**Distance:** 🚶2km ⛱50m 🏃on the spot.

### ⬛ Ploubazlanec 14D1

Rue du Port Loguivy/D15. **GPS:** n48,82011 w3,06279. ⬆.

---

6 🛏free. **Location:** Simple. **Surface:** asphalted. ⬛ 01/01-31/12.
**Distance:** 🚶100m ⚲on the spot ⊗100m 🛒100m.

### ⬛S Ploudalmézeau 14B1

**Aire camping-cars Kerros**, Rue de Porsguen, Portsall.
**GPS:** n48,56583 w4,69944. ⬆➡.

37 🛏€ 5,30/24h 🚰€ 3 🔌Ch🚿included55minutes 🚽 🔧
**Location:** Rural, comfortable, quiet. **Surface:** grassy.
⬛ 01/01-31/12.
**Distance:** 🚶on the spot ⛱350m ⊗200m 🛒200m.
**Remarks:** Max. 3 days.

### ⬛ Plouescat 14C1

Rue de Pen an Théven. **GPS:** n48,65902 w4,21863. ⬆.

6 🛏free. **Location:** Rural, comfortable, quiet. **Surface:** metalled.
⬛ 01/01-31/12.
**Distance:** 🚶3,5km ⛱100m ⚲on the spot.

### 📷S Plouescat 14C1

**Intermarché**, La Rocade-Kerchapalain.
**GPS:** n48,65083 w4,18444. ⬆➡.

4 🛏free 🚰€ 2 🔌Ch🚽€ 2 ⬛€ 5/4. **Location:** Rural, simple, noisy.
**Surface:** asphalted. ⬛ 01/01-31/12.
**Distance:** 🚶500m ⊗600m ⚲on the spot 🛒on the spot.
**Remarks:** Parking supermarket.

### ⬛ Plouézec 14D1

Lein ar Lan. **GPS:** n48,74788 w2,9853. ⬆.

3 🛏free. **Location:** Simple, quiet. **Surface:** asphalted.
⬛ 01/01-31/12.
**Distance:** 🚶on the spot 🛒on the spot.
**Remarks:** Service at camping municipal.

---

### ⬛ Plouézec 14D1

**Parking A. Le Calvez**, Route de Paimpol. **GPS:** n48,75041 w2,98651. ⬆.

7 🛏free. **Location:** Simple, quiet. **Surface:** asphalted.
⬛ 01/01-31/12.
**Distance:** 🚶100m ⊗200m 🛒100m.
**Remarks:** Max. 24h.

### ⬛ Plouézec 14D1

**Parking de la Corniche**, Bréhec. **GPS:** n48,72875 w2,9455. ⬆.

5 🛏free. **Location:** Simple. **Surface:** asphalted. ⬛ 01/01-31/12.
**Distance:** ⛱on the spot.
**Remarks:** Beautiful view.

### ⬛ Plougasnou 🌿⛱🏖 14C1

**Parking de la Métairie**, Rue Charles de Gaulle.
**GPS:** n48,69404 w3,79209. ⬆.

7 🛏free 🚰€ 2,50/10minutes 🔌Ch🚽€ 2,50/1h WC .
**Location:** Rural, simple, quiet. **Surface:** gravel.
⬛ 01/01-31/12.
**Distance:** 🚶on the spot ⛱sandy beach 1,4km ⊗200m 🛒250m
bakery 🚲on the spot 🏃on the spot.
**Remarks:** Tuesday morning market.

### ⬛S Plougasnou 🌿⛱🏖 14C1

Rue des Grands Viviers, Le Diben. **GPS:** n48,70811 w3,82731. ⬆.

7 🛏free 🚰€ 2 🔌Ch🚽. **Location:** Rural, simple, isolated, quiet.
**Surface:** asphalted. ⬛ 01/01-31/12.
**Distance:** 🚶300m ⛱on the spot 🚲on the spot ⊗300m
🏃on the spot.
**Remarks:** Max. 48h, coins at town hall.

### ⬛S Plougastel-Daoulas 14B1

Rue de la Fontaine Blanche. **GPS:** n48,37111 w4,36428.

FR

15 ⌑free ⛽🚰Ch ⌑free. **Location:** Simple. **Surface:** asphalted. ⬛ 15/05-15/10.
**Distance:** 🚶450m ⊗450m 🍺450m.
**Remarks:** Parking at sports grounds.

**Plougonvelin**     14B1
Rue de Bertheaume. **GPS:** n48,33792 w4,70742. ⬆️➡️.

80 ⌑€ 8/24h ⛽🚰Ch ⚓WC⌑included. 🛏🧺
**Location:** Rural, comfortable, quiet. **Surface:** grassy/sand.
⬛ 01/01-31/12.
**Distance:** 🚶1km ⊿beach 650m.

**Plougonven**     14C1
Rond-Point de Kerivoas. **GPS:** n48,52633 w3,71836. ⬆️➡️.

2 ⌑free ⛽🚰Chfree. **Location:** Rural, simple, quiet.
**Surface:** asphalted. ⬛ 01/01-31/12.
**Distance:** 🚶400m.
**Remarks:** At sports centre.

**Plouguerneau**     14B1
Lilia. **GPS:** n48,61891 w4,55341. ⬆️➡️.

10 ⌑free ⛽€ 5/10minutes 🚰Ch🧺€ 5/55minutes. **Location:** Urban,
comfortable, quiet. **Surface:** asphalted.
⬛ 01/01-31/12.
**Distance:** 🚶400m ⊿850m 🍺450m.

**Plouha**     14D1
Plage de Palus, Route du Palus. **GPS:** n48,67667 w2,88556. ⬆️.

10 ⌑free. **Location:** Rural, simple, isolated, quiet. **Surface:** grassy.
⬛ 01/03-31/10.
**Distance:** 🚶3km ⊿sandy/pebbled beach 100m ⊿50m 🚶on the spot.
**Remarks:** Max. 3 days.

**Plouharnel**     14D3
Des Sables Blancs, Route de Quiberon. **GPS:** n47,56783 w3,12509.

---

40 ⌑€ 12/24h ⛽🚰Ch ⚓included. **Location:** Rural, simple.
**Surface:** grassy. ⬛ 01/01-31/12.
**Distance:** 🚶4km ⊿100m ↝100m.
**Remarks:** Max. 72h, service passerby € 4,50.

**Plouhinec**     14B2
Aire du Champion, Rue Brizeux. **GPS:** n48,01694 w4,50194.
5 ⌑free ⛽€ 2 🚰Ch. **Surface:** asphalted. ⬛ 01/01-31/12.
**Distance:** 🍺on the spot.
**Remarks:** At supermarket.

**Ploumoguer**     14B1
Rue Huon de Kermadec, D28. **GPS:** n48,40507 w4,72492. ⬆️➡️.

30 ⌑free, July-Aug € 4 ⛽€ 2/80liter 🚰Ch⚓€ 2 🧺€ 4/2,30.
**Location:** Rural, quiet. **Surface:** asphalted. ⬛ 01/04-30/11.
**Distance:** 🚶200m ⊗200m 🍺200m.
**Remarks:** Next to stadium, max. 48h, coins at town hall, supermarket,
bakery and Tabac.

**Plouneour**     14B1
Parking des Menhirs. **GPS:** n48,65090 w4,30573. ⬆️.

10 ⌑free. **Location:** Rural, simple, quiet. **Surface:** metalled.
⬛ 01/01-31/12.
**Distance:** 🚶1km ⊿50m ⊗50m.
**Remarks:** At sea.

**Plouvorn**     14C1
Plan d'Eau de Lanorgant. **GPS:** n48,57776 w4,03069. ⬆️➡️.

19 ⌑€ 6/24h ⛽🚰Ch ⚓included WC ⌑ 🛏 **Location:** Rural,
comfortable, quiet. **Surface:** metalled. ⬛ 01/01-31/12.
**Distance:** 🚶500m ⊿100m ↝100m ⊗500m 🍺500m.
**Remarks:** Parking at small lake.

**Pluméliau**     14D2
Allée du vieux Blavet. **GPS:** n47,98229 w3,04209. ⬆️.

---

15 ⌑free ⛽🚰Chfree. **Location:** Rural, simple. **Surface:** gravel.
⬛ 01/01-31/12.
**Distance:** 🚶500m ↝on the spot ⊗250m ⊿on the spot
🚶on the spot.
**Remarks:** Along the Blavet river, attention: max. ^3.1m.

**Pont-Aven**     14C2
Camping-Car Park Les Quatre, Rue Louis Lomenech.
**GPS:** n47,85401 w3,74333. ⬆️➡️.

39 ⌑€ 10,43, 01/05-30/09 € 10,83 ⛽🚰Ch ⚓⌑included. 🛏🧺
**Location:** Urban, simple, central. **Surface:** asphalted.
⬛ 01/01-31/12.
**Distance:** 🚶450m ⊗450m.
**Remarks:** Parking near stadium Sinquin, mandatory, one-time fee
Pass'Etapes € 4.

**Pont-Aven**     14C2
Parking de Bel Air du Cimitière, Rue des Abbès Tanguy.
**GPS:** n47,85646 w3,75203. ⬆️.

5 ⌑free WCfree. **Location:** Urban, simple. **Surface:** asphalted.
⬛ 01/01-31/12.
**Distance:** 🚶400m.
**Remarks:** Inclining pitches.

**Pont-Aven**     14C2
Parking du Bois Amour, Rue de la Belle Angèle.
**GPS:** n47,85930 w3,74402. ⬆️.

20 ⌑free.
**Location:** Urban, simple. **Surface:** gravel. ⬛ 01/01-31/12.
**Distance:** 🚶550m ⊗300m 🍺700m.

**Pont-Aven**     14C2
Parking du Parcours Sportif, Rue de Rustéphan.
**GPS:** n47,85865 w3,75296.

FR

30 ⧈free. **Location:** Comfortable. **Surface:** grassy/gravel.
▢ 01/01-31/12.
**Distance:** ⛟900m ⊗850m ⚓150m on the spot.

⛟S **Pont-l'Abbé** 14B2

**Terre plein de la Madeleine**, Rue du Pont Neuf.
**GPS:** n47,86754 w4,22591. ⬆.

20 ⧈free. **Location:** Urban, simple, quiet. **Surface:** unpaved.
▢ 01/01-31/12.
**Distance:** ⛟on the spot ⛟50m ⊗400m ⛟1km.

⛟S **Pont-l'Abbé** 14B2

**Leclerc**, Route de Saint Jean Trolimont. **GPS:** n47,86414 w4,23646. ⬆.

6 ⧈free ⚡€ 1/100liter ⚓Ch ⊞ € 1/2h ⟿. **Location:** Urban, simple.
**Surface:** asphalted. ▢ 01/01-31/12.
**Distance:** ⛟1,5km ⚓on the spot ⛟on the spot ⛟on the spot.
**Remarks:** At supermarket.

⛟S **Pontivy** ⛵⛲ 14D2

**Piscine Decouverte**, Rue de Cascade. **GPS:** n48,07458 w2,97778.
10 ⧈free ⚡⚓Chfree. **Location:** Rural, simple, isolated.
**Surface:** grassy. ▢ 01/01-31/12.
**Distance:** ⛟1km.
**Remarks:** At swimming pool.

⛟S **Pontivy** ⛵⛲⛲ 14D2

Rue de la Fontaine. **GPS:** n48,06758 w2,96941. ⬆.

6 ⧈free. **Location:** Urban, simple. **Surface:** asphalted.
▢ 01/01-31/12.
**Distance:** ⛟800m ⛟on the spot ⚓bakery 300m ⛟on the spot.
**Remarks:** Monday market.

⛟S **Port-Louis** ⚓ 14C3

**Aire de la Côte Rouge**, D781 Port-Louis > Riantec.
**GPS:** n47,70873 w3,34295. ⬆.

14 ⧈€ 11/24h ⚡⚓Ch ⚘(4x)included ⚎.⛟⛟ ▢ 01/01-31/12.
**Surface:** asphalted. ▢ 01/01-31/12.
**Distance:** ⛟on the spot ⚓on the spot.

⛟S **Port-Louis** ⚓ 14C3

**Aire des Remparts**, Promenade Henri François Buffet.
**GPS:** n47,70496 w3,35602. ⬆.

20 ⧈€ 11/24h ⚡⚓Ch ⚘included. ⛟ ⚎ **Location:** Urban.
▢ 01/01-31/12.
**Distance:** ⛟100m ⛟100m ⛟on the spot.
**Remarks:** In front of campsite.

⛟S **Poullaouen** ⛵ 14C1

D236, Rue de Ty Meur. **GPS:** n48,33672 w3,64218. ⬆➡.

5 ⧈free ⚡⚓Chfree.
**Location:** Rural, comfortable, quiet. **Surface:** gravel.
▢ 01/01-31/12.
**Distance:** ⛟200m ⊗150m ⚓Véloroute Roscoff-Nantes ⛟on the spot.

⛟S **Primelin** 14B2

**Camping Municipal de Kermaléro**, Route de l'Océan.
**GPS:** n48,02550 w4,61821. ⬆.

15 ⧈free, 13/06-13/09 € 3 ⚡⚓€ 2/100liter ⚓Ch ⊞ € 3/h.
**Location:** Rural, simple, quiet. **Surface:** metalled.
▢ 01/01-31/12.
**Distance:** ⛟1km ⛟1km.

⛟S **Priziac** 14C2

**Base de Loisirs du Lac du Bel Air**, Rue du Bel Air.
**GPS:** n48,06237 w3,41079. ⬆.

10 ⧈free ⚡€ 3 ⚓ChWC ⚎. **Location:** Rural, simple, quiet.
**Surface:** asphalted. ▢ 01/01-31/12.
**Distance:** ⛟200m ⊗300m.

**Remarks:** Service on campsite.

⛟S **Questembert** 14D3

Célac. **GPS:** n47,66253 w2,46943. ⬆➡.

27 ⧈€ 5, 01/05-30/09 € 7 ⚡⚓Chincluded. ⛟⚎
**Location:** Rural, simple, quiet. **Surface:** asphalted.
▢ 01/01-31/12.
**Distance:** ⛟200m.
**Remarks:** At fish pond, monday regional market.

⛟S **Quiberon** ⚓⛵ 14D3

Rue de Port Kerné. **GPS:** n47,49165 w3,13941. ⬆➡.

140 ⧈€ 6,40/24h ⚡€ 1/60liter ⚓Ch ⚎.⛟⚎
**Location:** Rural, simple. **Surface:** gravel.
▢ 01/01-31/12 ⚙ service: 15/10-01/04.
**Distance:** ⛟2km ⛟sea 250m ⊗2km ⚓2km ⛟on the spot ⛟on the spot ⛟on the spot.
**Remarks:** Next to camping municipal, max. 3 days, bread-service only in summer, seaview.

⛟S **Quimper** ⛵⛲ 14C2

Route de l'Innovation/D34. **GPS:** n47,97399 w4,09319. ⬆.

2 ⧈free ⚡€ 2/100liter ⚓Ch ⊞ € 2/10minutes.
**Location:** Urban, simple, noisy. **Surface:** asphalted.
▢ 01/01-31/12.
**Distance:** ⛟1km ⊗on the spot ⚓on the spot ⛟on the spot ⛟on the spot.
**Remarks:** Parking at centre commercial, special part for motor homes.

⛟S **Quimperlé** 14C2

**Aire Saint Nicolas**, Rue du Viaduc. **GPS:** n47,86640 w3,54334. ⬆➡.

3 ⧈free ⚡⚓Chfree. **Location:** Simple. **Surface:** metalled.
▢ 01/01-31/12.

⛟S **Quintin** ⛵ 14D1

Place du Champ de Foire. **GPS:** n48,40056 w2,90222. ⬆➡.

FR

7 ⌂free 🚐 🔧 Ch free. **Location:** Urban, simple, quiet.
**Surface:** asphalted. 🅾 01/01-31/12 🔧 Service: winter.
**Distance:** 🛒on the spot 🏊on the spot.
**Remarks:** Next to swimming pool, near the lake, tuesday market.

**Tourist information Quintin:**
🏛 🅾 Tue-morning.

**Quistinic** 🏛 14D2

De Poul Fetan. **GPS:** n47,89311 w3,15166. ⬆.

15 ⌂free WC. **Location:** Rural, simple. **Surface:** metalled/sand.
🅾 01/01-31/12.
**Remarks:** Max. 48h.

**Radenac** 🌊 14D2

**Sente Verte**, Les Gambris. **GPS:** n47,95778 w2,71333. ⬆.

5 ⌂free. **Location:** Rural, simple, quiet. **Surface:** gravel.
🅾 01/01-31/12.
**Distance:** 🛒700m 🚲on the spot 🚴on the spot 🏊on the spot.
**Remarks:** At small lake.

**Redon** 18A2

Quai Surcouf. **GPS:** n47,64510 w2,0897. ⬆➡.

6 ⌂free 🚐 🔧 Ch free.
**Location:** Simple, noisy. **Surface:** asphalted.
🅾 01/01-31/12.
**Distance:** 🛒500m 🏊on the spot 🚲100m 🚴140m 🍴200m.
**Remarks:** At harbour, in front of Bureau du Port de Plaisance, max. 24h.

**Tourist information Redon:**
👁 Manoir de l'Automobile de Loheac. Car collection: Ferrari, Lamborghini, Porsche, Maserati.

**Réguiny** 📻 14D2

**Base de Loisirs**, Rue de la Piscine. **GPS:** n47,96843 w2,73828. ⬆.

10 ⌂free 🚐 🔧 Ch free WC. **Location:** Rural, simple, quiet.
**Surface:** unpaved. 🅾 01/01-31/12.
**Distance:** 🛒1,3km 🥖bakery 1,3km 🚴on the spot 🏊on the spot.

**Rennes** 📻 18B1

Rue du Professeur Maurice Audin. **GPS:** n48,13531 w1,64542. ⬆.

5 🚐€ 11 + € 0,45/pp tourist tax 🚐€ 2/100liter 🔧Ch 🔌 🔧€ 3
📶€ 1/30minutes. **Location:** Rural, simple. **Surface:** asphalted.
🅾 01/01-31/12.
**Distance:** 🛒3km 🏊100m 🚲100m 🍴3km 🏊on the spot.
**Remarks:** In park, max. 48h.

**Tourist information Rennes:**
M Musée de Bretagne. Regional museum.
🏛 🅾 Tue-Sa.

**Riantec** 14C3

**Camping-car Park de Kerdurand**, Rue du Stade.
**GPS:** n47,71735 w3,31778. ⬆.
49 🚐€ 8, 01/06-30/09 € 10 🚐 🔧 Ch 🔧(40x)included. 🚗 📋
**Location:** Rural. **Surface:** grassy.
🅾 01/01-31/12.
**Distance:** 🏊800m 🍴1,5km.
**Remarks:** Mandatory, one-time fee Pass'Etapes € 4, video surveillance.

**Riantec** 14C3

**Leclerc**, Rond-point de Kersabiec. **GPS:** n47,72611 w3,32137. ⬆.

10 ⌂free 🚐€ 2 🔧Ch 🔌€ 2/55minutes 📋 **Location:** Simple.
**Surface:** asphalted. 🅾 01/01-31/12.
**Distance:** 🍴on the spot.

**Riantec** 14C3

Route de Plouhinec. **GPS:** n47,71163 w3,29858. ⬆➡.

4 ⌂free 🚐€ 2/10minutes 🔧Ch 🔌€ 2/55minutes 📋.
**Location:** Rural, simple. **Surface:** metalled. 🅾 01/01-31/12.
**Distance:** 🛒1,5km.
**Remarks:** Near old laundry place (still operational!), max. 24h.

**Rochefort-en-Terre** 🌴🏛🏞📻 18A2

**Parking des Grées**, Rue du Souvenir. **GPS:** n47,69975 w2,33384. ⬆.

>100 🚐€ 2/24h. 🚗 **Location:** Rural, simple, quiet. **Surface:** gravel.
🅾 01/01-31/12.
**Distance:** 🛒200m.

**Rohan** 🌊 14D2

**Port de Plaisance**, Rue Saint-Gouvry. **GPS:** n48,07187 w2,75559. ⬆➡.

20 ⌂free 🚐 🔧 Ch WC free. **Location:** Rural, comfortable, quiet.
**Surface:** asphalted. 🅾 01/01-31/12.
**Distance:** 🛒500m 🏊on the spot 🚲on the spot 🚴500m 🏊on the spot.
**Remarks:** At the Nantes-Brest Canal.

**Romagné** 15B3

Allée des Prunus, D812. **GPS:** n48,34409 w1,27415. ⬆.

5 ⌂free 🚐 🔧 Ch WC free. **Location:** Urban, simple, noisy.
**Surface:** metalled. 🅾 01/01-31/12.
**Distance:** 🛒100m 🚲1,7km 🍴200m 🚴50m.
**Remarks:** Max. 7 days.

**Roscoff** 🌿🏛🏞📻 14C1

Route du Laber. **GPS:** n48,71215 w3,99918. ⬆.

30 ⌂free 🚐 🔧 Ch free. **Location:** Rural, simple, isolated, noisy.
**Surface:** asphalted. 🅾 01/01-31/12.
**Distance:** 🛒2km 🏊on the spot 🚲on the spot 🚴on the spot 🏊on the spot.
**Remarks:** Service 200m.

**Tourist information Roscoff:**
ℹ Office de Tourisme, 46, rue Gambetta, www.roscoff-tourisme.com.
Seaside resort and former pirates town.
🏛 🅾 Wed.

**Rostrenen** 14D2

Rue Rosa l'Hénaff, D23. **GPS:** n48,23318 w3,32019. ⬆➡.

15 ⌂free 🚐€ 2/100liter 🔧Ch 🔌€ 2/1h.
**Location:** Urban, simple. **Surface:** gravel.
🅾 01/01-31/12.
**Distance:** 🛒400m 🍴100m.
**Remarks:** Coins at tourist info, town hall, maison de presse, tabac.

**Ruffiac** 18A1

Rue Biard. **GPS:** n47,81823 w2,28413. ⬆.

FR

3 🅿free. **Location:** Simple, central, quiet. **Surface:** metalled.
🅞 01/01-31/12.
**Distance:** 🚰on the spot ⊗150m ⛽400m.

| 🅢 | Sains | 15B3 |

Rue du Puits Rimoult. **GPS:** n48,55305 w1,58603. ⬆➡.

11 🅿€ 5 + € 0,50/pp tourist tax 🚰Ch. ♨
**Location:** Rural, simple, quiet. **Surface:** grassy/metalled.
🅞 01/01-31/12.
**Distance:** 🚰100m 🚲2km ⊗150m ⛽150m 🚌on the spot 🚴100m
🚶on the spot.
**Remarks:** Max. 7m.

| 🅢 | Saint Aignan | 14D2 |

15, Boulevard Valmy. **GPS:** n47,26600 e1,37790.
29 🅿€ 9,60, 01,32/05-30/09 € 10,80 + € 1,32/pp tourist tax
🚰♨,6Amp 📶included. **Surface:** metalled. 🅞 01/01-31/12.
**Distance:** 🚰400m ⚓500m ⊗400m.

| 🅢 | Saint Aignan | 14D2 |

Place de l'Église. **GPS:** n48,18306 w3,01361. ⬆➡.

20 🅿free. 🚰Ch WC free. **Location:** Comfortable, quiet.
**Surface:** asphalted. 🅞 01/01-31/12.
**Distance:** 🚰100m 🚴on the spot 🚶on the spot.
**Remarks:** Square behind the church.

| 🅢 | Saint Aignan | 14D2 |

**Anse de Sordan**, D15B. **GPS:** n48,19967 w3,07026. ⬆.

10 🅿free.
**Location:** Isolated, quiet. **Surface:** sand. 🅞 01/01-31/12.
**Distance:** ⚓200m ⛵200m ⊗500m 🚴on the spot 🚶on the spot.

| 🅢 | Saint Gérand | 14D2 |

Keroret, D322. **GPS:** n48,11333 w2,89028. ⬆.

12 🅿free 🚰 🗓Ch WC free. **Location:** Rural, comfortable, quiet.
**Surface:** asphalted. 🅞 01/01-31/12.
**Distance:** 🚰800m ⛵on the spot ⊗150m 🚴on the spot
🚶on the spot.
**Remarks:** At the Nantes-Brest Canal.

| 🅢 | Saint-Aubin-d'Aubigné 🧺 | 18B1 |

Rue de Rennes. **GPS:** n48,26147 w1,60621. ⬆.

5 🅿free 🚰 🗓Ch WC free. **Location:** Urban, simple.
**Surface:** asphalted. 🅞 01/01-31/12.
**Distance:** 🚰on the spot ⊗100m ⛽on the spot 🚌on the spot
🚶on the spot.

| 🅢 | Saint-Barnabé | 14D2 |

Place du Vieux Chêne, Rue Pierre Loti. **GPS:** n48,13672 w2,70146. ⬆.

10 🅿free 🚰 🗓Ch free. **Location:** Urban, simple, central.
**Surface:** gravel. 🅞 01/01-31/12.
**Distance:** 🚰200m ⛽bakery 50m.

| 🅢 | Saint-Benoît-des-Ondes 🦐 | 15B3 |

Rue Bord de Mer. **GPS:** n48,61681 w1,84714. ⬆➡.

10 🅿€ 6/24h 🚰€ 3/50liter 🗓Ch 🔌€ 3/15minutes. **Location:** Rural,
simple. **Surface:** asphalted.
**Distance:** 🚰400m ⚓on the spot ⛵on the spot ⊗100m ⛽400m
🚌on the spot 🚶on the spot.

| 🅢 | Saint-Brice-en-Coglès 🧺 | 15B3 |

**Espace Jules Verne**, Rue de Normandie, D102.
**GPS:** n48,41126 w1,36252. ⬆.

8 🅿free 🚰€ 2/10minutes 🗓Ch 🔌€ 2/55minutes WC.
**Location:** Urban, simple, central. **Surface:** asphalted/metalled.
🅞 01/01-31/12.
**Distance:** 🚰300m ⊗500m ⛽400m 🚌300m 🚴on the spot.

| 🅢 | Saint-Carreuc 🦐 | 14D1 |

Rue de la Lande, D27. **GPS:** n48,40219 w2,73917. ⬆.

12 🅿free 🚰€ 2/10minutes 🗓Ch 🔌€ 2/55minutes.
**Location:** Rural, simple, isolated, noisy. **Surface:** metalled.
🅞 01/01-31/12.
**Distance:** 🚰300m ⛵on the spot 🚶on the spot.
**Remarks:** At Etang-du-Plessis, max. 24h.

| 🅢 | Saint-Connan | 14D1 |

Etang Neuf. **GPS:** n48,41906 w3,10901. ⬆.

2 🅿free 🚰 🗓Ch 🔌 free. **Location:** Isolated, quiet.
**Surface:** metalled. 🅞 01/01-31/12.
**Distance:** ⚓on the spot ⛵50m ⊗50m.

| 🅢 | Saint-Derrien | 14C1 |

**GPS:** n48,54820 w4,1817. ⬆.

20 🅿free 🚰€ 3 🗓Ch 🔌€ 3 WC free. **Location:** Rural, simple, quiet.
**Surface:** gravel/metalled. 🅞 01/05-31/10.
**Distance:** 🚰100m ⚓on the spot ⛵on the spot ⊗300m ⛽300m.
**Remarks:** Nearby recreation area.

| 🅢 | Saint-Gelven 🌿 | 14D2 |

Rue de l'Ecole, D95. **GPS:** n48,22442 w3,09589. ⬆.

10 🅿free 🚰 🗓Ch free. **Location:** Urban, simple. **Surface:** gravel.
🅞 01/01-31/12.
**Remarks:** Service 100m.

| 🅢 | Saint-Gelven 🌿 | 14D2 |

Tregnanton, D117. **GPS:** n48,21153 w3,08457. ⬆.

8 🅿free. **Location:** Rural, isolated, quiet. **Surface:** grassy/metalled.
🅞 01/01-31/12.
**Distance:** 🚰2,5km ⚓on the spot ⛵on the spot 🚶on the spot.

| 🅢 | Saint-Gildas-de-Rhuys 🦐 | 14D3 |

**Camping municipal de Kerver**, Route du Rohu.
**GPS:** n47,52238 w2,85803. ⬆➡.

FR

35 ⌁ € 6,70 € 2 🔲Ch 🛁🚐 **Location:** Rural, simple, quiet.
**Surface:** asphalted. ☐ 15/03-04/11.
**Distance:** 4km 50m 400m 4km.

## 🔵S Saint-Guyomard 14D3

Route de Malestroit, D112. **GPS:** n47,78166 w2,51188. ⬆➡.

5 ⌁ € 5/night 🚰 3 🔲Ch 🚽 € 3. **Location:** Rural, simple, quiet.
**Surface:** asphalted. ☐ 01/01-31/12.
**Distance:** 300m 100m.
**Remarks:** Behind church, check in at town hall.

## 🔵S Saint-Jacut-de-la-Mer 15A3

Rue de la Manchette. **GPS:** n48,58969 w2,18947. ⬆➡.

26 € 7/24h 🚰 🔲Ch included. 🚽🛒 **Location:** Comfortable.
**Surface:** grassy/gravel. ☐ 01/01-31/12.
**Distance:** 1km 500m.
**Remarks:** Baker at 8am.

## 🔵S Saint-Malo 15A3

Aire des îlots, Avenue de la Guimorais.
**GPS:** n48,68109 w1,96348. ⬆➡.

150 ⌁ € 7, 25/06-04/09 € 12, 2 pers. incl 🚰 3 🔲Ch 🚿
(40x) 📶included. **Location:** Rural, comfortable. **Surface:** grassy.
☐ 01/01-31/12.
**Distance:** sandy beach 100m 100m 200m on the spot.

## 🔵S Saint-Malo 15A3

Parking Paul Féval, Rue Paul Féval. **GPS:** n48,64341 w1,99385. ⬆.

200 ⌁ € 7,50, overnight stay 19-9h free 🚰 € 3 🔲Ch 🚐
**Location:** Urban, simple. **Surface:** gravel. ☐ 01/01-31/12.
**Distance:** 800m 800m on the spot.
**Remarks:** Free bus to centre.

---

## 🔵S Saint-Malo ⬆ 15A3

**Parking du Grand Domaine. GPS:** n48,61568 w2,0117.
⌁free. **Surface:** grassy. ☐ 01/01-31/12.

## 🔵 Saint-Malo ⬆ 15A3

**Parking Le Davier**, Avenue J. Kennedy. **GPS:** n48,67356 w1,98098.
⌁free. ☐ 01/01-31/12.
**Distance:** 100m 400m.
**Remarks:** Max. 24h.

## 🔵 Saint-Malo 🖐 15A3

**Parking Marville**, Avenue de Marville. **GPS:** n48,64142 w2,00226.

20 ⌁free. **Location:** Urban, simple. **Surface:** asphalted.
☐ 01/01-31/12.
**Distance:** 300m 300m 100m.
**Remarks:** Max. 24h.

## 🔵 Saint-Malo ⬆🖐 15A3

Rue Henri Lemairié. **GPS:** n48,65467 w1,97374.

20 ⌁free.
**Location:** Urban, simple. **Surface:** metalled.
☐ 01/01-31/12.
**Distance:** on the spot 1km 1km.
**Remarks:** Max. 24h.

**Tourist information Saint-Malo:**
🅼🏰 Château. Castle, 14/15th century, historical museum.
☐ 10-12h, 14-18h.
🏰 Fort National. Fort designed by Vauban. At ebb accessible by foot.

## 🔵S Saint-Nicolas-du-Pélem 14D2

**Parking des Associations. GPS:** n48,31506 w3,16022. ⬆➡.

10 ⌁free. 🚰 🔲Ch 🚽free. **Location:** Urban, simple, noisy.
**Surface:** asphalted. ☐ 01/01-31/12.
**Distance:** 400m 200m.
**Remarks:** Service 1km GPS N48,306605 W-3,164207.

## Saint-Nicolas-du-Tertre 18A1

Terres du Bourg. **GPS:** n47,80047 w2,22383.
5 ⌁free. ☐ 01/01-31/12.
**Distance:** 300m on the spot on the spot on the spot.

## 🔵S Saint-Pierre-Quiberon 14D3

Rue du Stade. **GPS:** n47,51160 w3,13903. ⬆➡.

20 ⌁ € 9,50, 15/06-15/09 € 13,50 🚰 € 2/10minutes
🔲Ch 🚽 € 2/45minutes 📶included 🚿🚽 **Location:** Simple.

---

**Surface:** asphalted. ☐ 01/01-31/12.
**Distance:** 1km 1,5km on the spot on the spot.
**Remarks:** Max. 48h.

## 🔵S Saint-Pol-de-Léon 14C1

Quai de Pempoul. **GPS:** f48,68361 w3,97083. ⬆➡.

30 ⌁ € 6 € 2 🔲Ch 🚽 € 2 WCfree. **Location:** Rural, comfortable,
noisy. **Surface:** metalled. ☐ 01/01-31/12.
**Distance:** 800m on the spot on the spot 800m 800m.
**Remarks:** At sea.

## 🔵S Saint-Renan 14B1

Route de l'Aber. **GPS:** n48,43878 w4,63063. ⬆.

20 ⌁ € 4/day 🚰 🔲Chfree. 🚿 **Location:** Rural, quiet.
**Surface:** gravel. ☐ 01/01-31/12.
**Distance:** 1km on the spot.
**Remarks:** Nearby camp site, Jul/Aug max. 48h.

## 🔵S Saint-Rivoal 14C1

Saint-Rivoal, D42. **GPS:** n48,34930 w3,99782. ⬆.

6 ⌁free. 🚰 🔲Ch 🚿free. **Location:** Rural, simple, isolated, quiet.
**Surface:** grassy/metalled. ☐ 01/01-31/12.
**Distance:** 300m 500m on the spot on the spot.

## 🔵S Saint-Servais 14C1

Cité Yan d'Argent. **GPS:** n48,50984 w4,15434. ⬆.

10 ⌁free. 🚰 🔲Ch 🚿 WCfree. **Location:** Rural, simple, quiet.
**Surface:** gravel/metalled. ☐ 01/01-31/12.
**Distance:** 200m 200m 200m.

## 🔵S Saint-Thégonnec 14C1

Park an Iliz, D118. **GPS:** n48,52215 w3,94637. ⬆.

25 ⌁free 🚰 🔲Ch 🚿free. **Location:** Urban, comfortable, central,
quiet. **Surface:** gravel. ☐ 01/01-31/12.

**Distance:** 🚶on the spot ⊗150m 🛒150m 🚲on the spot 🧍on the spot.
**Remarks:** Free coins available at shops.

**Tourist information Saint-Thégonnec:**
🏥 ⓘ Fri.
⊗ Crêperie Steredenn, Rue de la Gare 6.

### Santec 14C1
**Le bistrot à Crêpes**, Rue de Méchouroux.
**GPS:** n48,70102 w4,03868. ⬆➡.

15 ⑤guests free 🚰€ 2 🗑Ch 🚿(14x)€ 2/24h WC ≋free.
**Location:** Rural, simple, quiet. **Surface:** grassy. ⓘ 01/01-31/12
⚫ Wed.
**Distance:** 🏖La plage du Staol 100m ⊗on the spot 🛒800m 🚲on the spot 🧍on the spot.
**Remarks:** Max. 24h, bread-service.

### Sarzeau 14D3
Rue du Stang, St.Colombier. **GPS:** n47,54665 w2,72151. ⬆➡.

5 ⑤€ 4,50 🚰🗑Chincluded. **Location:** Urban, simple, quiet.
**Surface:** asphalted.
**Distance:** 🚶St.Colombier 100m ⊗50m 🛒50m 🚌50m.
**Remarks:** Max. 48h.

### Sarzeau 14D3
Rue Closchebey, Saint Jacques. **GPS:** n47,48968 w2,79704. ⬆➡.
⑤. ⓘ 01/01-31/12.
**Distance:** 🚶on the spot 🏖450m ⊗on the spot 🛒on the spot.
**Remarks:** At supermarket.

### Scaër 14C2
Rue de la Gare. **GPS:** n48,02524 w3,7055.
20 ⑤free 🚰🗑Ch. **Location:** Urban. **Surface:** grassy/sand.
ⓘ 01/01-31/12.
**Distance:** ⊗450m 🛒200m.
**Remarks:** Coins at the shops and town hall.

### Scaër 14C2
Rue Louis Pasteur. **GPS:** n48,02774 w3,6951. ⬆.

60 ⑤free 🚰€ 2/10minutes 🗑Ch 🚿€ 2/55minutes WC free.
**Location:** Rural, simple, quiet. **Surface:** asphalted.
ⓘ 01/01-31/12.
**Distance:** 🚶500m 🛒bakery 200m 🚲on the spot 🧍on the spot.
**Remarks:** Max. 72h, coins at campsite and tourist info.

### Sérent 14D2
**Du Pont Salmon**, Rue du Général De Gaule.
**GPS:** n47,82445 w2,50194. ⬆➡.

10 ⑤free. **Location:** Urban, simple, quiet. **Surface:** asphalted.
ⓘ 01/01-31/12.
**Distance:** 🚶400m ⊗400m 🛒400m on the spot.

### Silfiac 14D2
**P Salle Polyvalente**, Rue du Résistant P. le Bourlay.
**GPS:** n48,14816 w3,15668. ⬆➡.

10 ⑤free 🚰🗑Chfree. **Location:** Rural, simple, quiet.
**Surface:** asphalted. ⓘ 01/01-31/12.
**Distance:** 🚶150m 🛒150m 🚲on the spot 🧍on the spot.

### Silfiac 14D2
**Etang de Pont Samuel**, Pont Samuel. **GPS:** n48,12847 w3,17109. ⬆➡.

5 ⑤free. **Location:** Rural, simple, isolated. **Surface:** unpaved.
ⓘ 01/01-31/12.
**Distance:** 🚲300m ⊗200m on the spot 🧍200m.

### Sizun 14C1
Rue de Cornouaille. **GPS:** n48,40018 w4,07905.
€ 2 🚰🗑Ch🛒. **Surface:** asphalted. ⓘ 01/01-31/12.
**Distance:** 🚲750m ⊗700m.

### Sougéal 15B3
Le Placis, D15. **GPS:** n48,50651 w1,52562. ⬆➡.

30 ⑤free 🚰🗑ChWC free. **Location:** Rural, simple, isolated, quiet.
**Surface:** grassy/gravel. ⓘ 01/01-31/12.
**Distance:** 🚶on the spot ⊗300m 🛒bakery 500m.

### Sulniac 14D3
**Salle des Fêtes**, Rue des Écoles. **GPS:** n47,67756 w2,56642. ⬆➡.

20 ⑤free 🚰🗑Chfree. **Location:** Rural, simple, quiet.
**Surface:** asphalted. ⓘ 01/01-31/12.
**Distance:** 🚶400m 🛒bakery 500m.

### Surzur 14D3
Allée du Petit Train. **GPS:** n47,58309 w2,63258. ⬆.
12 ⑤€ 7 🚰🗑Ch🚿🛒📷 **Location:** Rural. **Surface:** grassy.
ⓘ 01/01-31/12.
**Distance:** 🚶on the spot ⊗750m 🛒750m.

### Theix 14D3
Allée de Noyalo. **GPS:** n47,62726 w2,66183. ⬆➡.

10 ⑤free 🚰🗑Chfree. **Location:** Urban, simple, quiet.
**Surface:** asphalted. ⓘ 01/01-31/12 ⚫ **Service:** winter.
**Distance:** 🚶500m ⊗500m 🛒500m 🚲50m 🧍50m.
**Remarks:** Max. 24h.

### Tinténiac 15B3
Quai de la Donac. **GPS:** n48,33168 w1,83202. ⬆.

10 ⑤€ 3 🚰🗑Chfree. 📷 **Location:** Rural, simple.
**Surface:** grassy/gravel. ⓘ 01/04-31/10.
**Distance:** 🚶500m 🏖on the spot 🛶on the spot ⊗100m 🛒550m.

### Trébeurden 14C1
Route de Lannion, D65. **GPS:** n48,76711 w3,5514. ⬆.

5 ⑤parking free, € 7/night 🚰€ 4,30 🗑Ch🛒€ 4,30 📷.
**Location:** Rural, comfortable, central, quiet. **Surface:** asphalted.
ⓘ 01/01-31/12.
**Distance:** 🚶on the spot 🏖1,4km ⊗1,5km 🛒1km bakery, Intermarché 1,5km.
**Remarks:** Max. 72h, max. 8M.

### Trébeurden 14C1
**Corniche de Pors Mabo**. **GPS:** n48,76886 w3,57794. ⬆.

5 ⑤parking free, € 7/night. **Location:** Rural, simple, quiet.
**Surface:** gravel.
**Distance:** 🚶on the spot 🏖800m 🛶800m ⊗300m 🛒300m.

### Trébeurden 14C1
Impasse du Vieux Puits. **GPS:** n48,76999 w3,56849. ⬆.

5 🅿 parking free, € 7/night. **Location:** Urban, simple, quiet.
**Surface:** asphalted.
**Distance:** 🚰 on the spot 🏊 1,5km ⊗ on the spot 🍴 on the spot.

| 📷📷 | **Trébeurden** 🛶 🏖 | 14C1 |

Route de Pors Mabo. **GPS:** n48,76194 w3,56537. ⬆.

10 🅿 parking free, € 7/night. **Location:** Rural, simple, quiet.
**Surface:** metalled.
**Distance:** 🚰 1,5km 🏊 200m 🍴 200m.

| 📷📷 | **Trébeurden** 🛶 🏖 | 14C1 |

Rue Pierre Marzin. **GPS:** n48,76842 w3,56284. ⬆.

20 🅿 parking free, € 7/night. **Location:** Urban, simple, quiet.
**Surface:** metalled. 🔲 01/01-31/12.
**Distance:** 🚰 on the spot 🏊 1km ⊗ 300m 🍴 600m 🚲 on the spot
🚶 on the spot.

| 📷📷 S | **Trégastel** 🛶 | 14C1 |

Rue de Poul-Palud. **GPS:** n48,82437 w3,49874. ⬆.

56 🅿 8 🚰 Chincluded 🍴 📷 **Location:** Rural, comfortable,
isolated, quiet. **Surface:** asphalted. 🔲 01/01-31/12.
**Distance:** 🚰 1km ⊗ 1km 🍴 Super U 🚶 on the spot.
**Remarks:** Aug max. 3 nights, max. 5 nights.

| 📷📷 S | **Tréguier** | 14D1 |

**Bois du Poète,** Boulevard Anatole le Braz.
**GPS:** n48,78932 w3,23144. ⬆➡.

30 🅿 free 🔌 Chfree. **Location:** Simple, quiet. **Surface:** asphalted.
🔲 01/01-31/12.
**Distance:** 🚰 100m 🏊 20m 🛒 20m ⊗ 100m 🍴 100m.
**Remarks:** Along river, shady.

| S | **Tréguier** | 14D1 |

**Super U,** Boulevard Jean Guehenno. **GPS:** n48,77892 w3,23346. ⬆.

---

🚰 € 1/10minutes 🔌 Ch 🔌 € 1/55minutes. **Location:** Urban.
**Surface:** asphalted. 🔲 01/01-31/12.
**Distance:** 🚰 200m ⊗ 200m 🍴 on the spot.

| 📷📷 S | **Trégunc** 🏖 | 14C2 |

**Parking Quentel,** Place de la Mairie, Rue de Pont-Aven.
**GPS:** n47,85472 w3,85139. ⬆.

5 🅿 free 🚰 € 3/10minutes 🔌 Ch 🔌 € 3/55minutes WC 📷
**Location:** Urban, simple. **Surface:** asphalted. 🔲 01/01-31/12.
**Distance:** 🚰 100m.
**Remarks:** Behind town hall, max. 24h.

| 📷📷 | **Trégunc** 🏖 | 14C2 |

**Parking de Pouldohan,** Route de Pouldohan.
**GPS:** n47,84435 w3,88832. ⬆➡.

5 🅿 free. **Location:** Rural, simple, isolated. **Surface:** grassy.
🔲 01/01-31/12.
**Distance:** 🏊 400m 🛒 400m.

| 📷📷 | **Trégunc** 🏖 | 14C2 |

**Plage Ster Greich. GPS:** n47,84918 w3,88656. ⬆.

10 🅿 free. **Location:** Rural, simple, isolated, quiet. **Surface:** sand.
🔲 01/01-31/12.
**Distance:** 🏊 on the spot 🚲 on the spot.
**Remarks:** Max. 24h.

| 📷📷 | **Trégunc** 🏖 | 14C2 |

**Route de Kerlaëron. GPS:** n47,82964 w3,8872. ⬆.

6 🅿 free.
**Location:** Rural, simple. **Surface:** grassy. 🔲 01/01-31/12.
**Distance:** 🏊 200m.
**Remarks:** Max. 24h.

| 📷📷 | **Trégunc** 🏖 | 14C2 |

**Rue de Porzh Breign. GPS:** n47,84079 w3,89736. ⬆➡.

---

5 🅿 free. **Location:** Rural, simple, quiet. **Surface:** grassy.
🔲 01/01-31/12.
**Distance:** 🏊 200m.
**Remarks:** Max. 24h.

| 📷📷 S | **Trégunc** 🏖 | 14C2 |

**Supermarché Casino,** Route de Concarneau, D783.
**GPS:** n47,85633 w3,86343. ⬆.

4 🅿 free 🚰 € 2 🔌 Ch 🔌 € 2/55minutes 📷. **Location:** Simple.
**Surface:** asphalted. 🔲 01/01-31/12.
**Distance:** 🍴 on the spot 🛒 on the spot.

| 📷📷 S | **Tremblay** | 15B3 |

Route de Fougères. **GPS:** n48,42328 w1,47095. ⬆.

6 🅿 free 🚰 € 2/10minutes 🔌 Ch 🔌 € 2/55minutes. **Location:** Urban,
simple. **Surface:** asphalted. 🔲 01/01-31/12.
**Distance:** 🚰 400m 🍴 200m 🚌 on the spot.

| 📷📷 S | **Trémuson** | 14D1 |

**Aire du Buchon,** Rue de Brest, D712. **GPS:** n48,52250 w2,85278. ⬆➡.

5 🅿 free 🚰 🔌 Chfree. **Location:** Urban, simple. **Surface:** asphalted.
🔲 01/01-31/12 ⦿ service: frost.
**Distance:** 🚰 500m ⊗ 50m 🍴 200m.
**Remarks:** Max. 48h.

| 📷📷 S | **Trévou-Tréguignec** | 14D1 |

Rue de Trestel. **GPS:** n48,81902 w3,35432. ⬆.
20 🅿 8, 01/10-31/03 € 6 🚰 € 5 🔌 Ch 🚲 📷 📷 **Surface:** metalled.
🔲 01/01-31/12.
**Distance:** 🚰 200m 🏊 50m ⊗ 100m.

| 📷📷 S | **Val-d'Izé** | 18B1 |

Rue du Château. **GPS:** n48,17904 w1,30133. ⬆.

3 🅿 free 🚰 🔌 Ch 🚲 WCfree. **Location:** Urban, simple, quiet.

**Surface:** asphalted. ▢ 01/01-31/12.
**Distance:** 🚲100m 🚶on the spot ⊗100m 🛒100m 🏊 on the spot.
**Remarks:** Next to sports fields.

### Vannes 14D3
**Camping-Car Park**, Avenue du Maréchal Juin.
**GPS:** n47,63283 w2,77996.⬆.

34 🛏€ 11, Jul/Aug € 13,40 🚰🍳Ch 🧹(34x),10Amp WC 📶included.
🚿🔌 **Location:** Urban, comfortable, quiet. **Surface:** asphalted.
▢ 01/01-31/12.
**Distance:** 🚲Vannes 4km 🛒200m ⊗200m 🍴1km 🚌on the spot
🚴 on the spot 🏊 on the spot.
**Remarks:** Mandatory, one-time fee Pass'Etapes € 4, free shuttle (summer).

**Tourist information Vannes:**
ℹ Office de Tourisme, 1, rue Thiers, www.tourisme-vannes.com. The old district is surrounded by ramparts with gates and parks with historical wash places.
⛪ Cathédrale St Pierre.

### Vitré 18B1
**Camping Municipal de Vitré**, 109 Boulevard des Rochers.
**GPS:** n48,10974 w1,1986.
10 🛏free. **Location:** Urban. **Surface:** metalled.
▢ 01/01-31/12.
**Tourist information Vitré:**
ℹ Office de Tourisme, Place du Général de Gaulle, www.ot-vitre.fr. Small medieval town with large castle and ramparts. Marked city walk, information OT.
🚶 ▢ Mo.

# Pays de la Loire

### Angers 18C2
Boulevard Olivier-Couffon. **GPS:** n47,46616 w0,56549.⬆.

30 🛏€ 15/24h 🚰🍳Chincluded. 🚿 **Location:** Urban, noisy.
**Surface:** asphalted. ▢ 01/01-31/12.
**Distance:** 🚲1km 🚴3km ⊗on the spot 🍴on the spot.
**Remarks:** Max. 72h, monitored parking, Château d'Angers 600m.

**Tourist information Angers:**
👁 Haras National du Lion d'Angers. National stud-farm. ▢ 10-18h.
🎫 free.
🏛 Château d' Angers. Fortified castle, museum for contemporary art.
▢ 10-17.30h. 🎫 € 8,50.

### Angrie 18C2
Route du Vieux Bourg. **GPS:** n47,57176 w0,97312.⬆➡.

10 🛏free 🚰🍳ChWCfree. **Location:** Rural, simple, quiet.
**Surface:** gravel/metalled. ▢ 01/01-31/12 ▢ 1st weekend Aug.
**Distance:** 🚲400m 🚴on the spot.
**Remarks:** Max. 48h, picnic tables available, playground.

### Arnage 18D1
Rue du Port. **GPS:** n47,93035 e0,18418.⬆➡.

2 🛏free 🚰€ 2 🍳Ch🚿€ 2/15minutes 🧹. **Location:** Urban, simple, quiet. **Surface:** asphalted. ▢ 01/01-31/12.
**Distance:** 🚲250m 🚶on the spot ⊗250m 🍳500m 🏊 on the spot.
**Remarks:** Along Sarthe River.

### Asnières-sur-Vègre 18D2
D190. **GPS:** n47,88950 w0,23716.⬆➡.

5 🛏free 🚰WCfree. **Location:** Rural, simple, quiet. **Surface:** gravel.
▢ 01/01-31/12.
**Distance:** 🚲200m ⊗200m.

### Assérac 14D3
Pen-Bé. **GPS:** n47,42556 w2,45528.⬆.

5 🛏free WC. **Location:** Urban, simple, quiet. **Surface:** grassy.
▢ 01/01-31/12.
**Distance:** 🚲50m 🚴100m 🚶100m ⊗200m 🍴200m.

### Assérac 14D3
**Parking Marché aux Bœufs**, Chemin de la Marché aux Bœufs.
**GPS:** n47,43111 w2,45194.

15 🛏free. **Location:** Rural, simple. **Surface:** gravel/metalled.
▢ 01/01-31/12.
**Distance:** 🚲1km 🚴300m 🚶300m ⊗2km 🍴2km.

### Aubigné-sur-Layon 18C3
Rue de 17 mars 1962. **GPS:** n47,21167 w0,46383.⬆.

5 🛏free 🚰🍳Chfree. **Location:** Simple, quiet. **Surface:** grassy/sand.
▢ 01/01-31/12.
**Distance:** 🚲100m ⊗300m.

### Auvers-le-Hamon 18D1
Chemin du tour. **GPS:** n47,90115 w0,34654.⬆.

10 🛏free. **Location:** Rural, simple, quiet. **Surface:** gravel.
▢ 01/01-31/12.
**Distance:** 🚲500m 🚴on the spot ⊗500m.
**Remarks:** At small lake.

### Averton 18D1
**Étang des Perles**, Route de Étang des Perles.
**GPS:** n48,34744 w0,24468.➡.

10 🛏free 🚰€ 2,50/80liter 🍳Ch🚿€ 2,50/2h WCfree 🧹.
**Location:** Rural, comfortable, quiet. **Surface:** gravel.
▢ 01/01-31/12.
**Distance:** 🚴lake 🚶on the spot 🚴 on the spot 🏊 on the spot.
**Remarks:** Playground.

### Batz-sur-Mer 14D3
Route de la Govelle. **GPS:** n47,26747 w2,4537.⬆.

8 🛏€ 8 🚰€ 2 🍳Ch🚿€ 2 WC. 🚿 🧹
**Location:** Simple. **Surface:** metalled.
▢ 01/01-31/12.
**Distance:** 🚲1,5km 🚴100m ⊗100m 🍴1,5km 🚌50m.
**Remarks:** Max. 24h, coins at tourist info and town hall.

### Baugé-en-Anjou 18D2
Rue du Pont des Fées. **GPS:** n47,53886 w0,09637.⬆➡.

10 🛏free 🚰€ 3/15minutes 🍳Ch🚿€ 3/15minutes.
**Location:** Rural, comfortable, quiet. **Surface:** gravel.
▢ 01/01-31/12.
**Distance:** 🚲2km ⊗400m 🚴on the spot 🏊 on the spot.
**Remarks:** Max. 48h.

### Baugé-en-Anjou 18D2
**Super U**, Avenue d'Angers. **GPS:** n47,54570 w0,11296.⬆.
15 🛏free 🚰€ 2 🍳Ch🚿. **Location:** Urban, simple, noisy.
**Surface:** asphalted. ▢ 01/01-31/12.
**Distance:** 🚲500m ⊗300m 🍴on the spot.

### Bazouges-sur-le-Loir 18D2
**Camping-Car Park**, Pré de la Boisardière. **GPS:** n47,68691 w0,16985.
27 🛏€ 8,95/24h 🚰🍳Ch 🧹(36x)included. 🚿🧹
▢ 01/01-31/12.
**Remarks:** Mandatory, one-time fee Pass'Etapes € 4.

### Bazouges-sur-le-Loir 18D2
Voie de la Liberté. **GPS:** n47,68994 w0,16952.⬆.

FR

6 free. **Location:** Rural, simple, quiet. **Surface:** gravel. ◯ 01/01-31/12. **Distance:** 200m 200m on the spot on the spot.

🅱️S | **Beauvoir-sur-Mer** | 18A3

**Place des Paludier**, Rue de Nantes. **GPS:** n46,91685 w2,0465.➡️

24 free, night € 5 € 2,50/3minutes Ch € 2,50/15minutes WC . **Location:** Urban, simple. **Surface:** asphalted. ◯ 01/01-31/12. **Distance:** 400m 800m 800m. **Remarks:** Max. 48h.

🅱️ | **Belleville-sur-Vie** | 21B1

Rue des Écoliers. **GPS:** n46,78160 w1,42875.⬆️➡️

15 free. **Location:** Urban, simple, noisy. **Surface:** asphalted. ◯ 01/01-31/12. **Distance:** 500m 500m 200m. **Remarks:** Near Salle des Fêtes.

🅱️S | **Benet** | 21C2

Rue de la Gare. **GPS:** n46,36896 w0,59482.

10 free Ch WC free. **Location:** Urban, simple, quiet. **Surface:** asphalted. ◯ 01/01-31/12. **Distance:** 300m 300m on the spot 50m. **Remarks:** Monday market.

🅱️S | **Blain** | 18A2

Place Jollan de Clerville, Rue Victor Schoelcher. **GPS:** n47,47444 w1,76139.➡️⬆️

30 free Ch free WC. **Location:** Urban, simple, central, noisy. **Surface:** gravel. ◯ 01/01-31/12. **Distance:** on the spot 100m 100m.

🅱️ | **Blain** | 18A2

Rue de la Petite Arche. **GPS:** n47,46934 w1,76205.⬆️➡️

12 free. **Location:** Comfortable, quiet. **Surface:** clay soil. ◯ 01/01-31/12. **Distance:** 500m 500m on the spot.

🅱️ | **Blaison-Gohier** | 18C3

Rue de Thibaut de Blaison. **GPS:** n47,39923 w0,37515.⬆️➡️

5 free. **Location:** Simple. **Surface:** asphalted. ◯ 01/01-31/12. **Distance:** on the spot 200m 200m.

🅱️S | **Bouchemaine** | 18C2

25 rue Chevrière. **GPS:** n47,41913 w0,61117.⬆️➡️

45 € 9-15 Ch WC € 1,25 included. **Location:** Urban, comfortable, central. **Surface:** grassy/gravel. ◯ 01/01-31/12 ● 1st weekend Sep. **Distance:** 300m 200m 300m 50m. **Remarks:** Along the river Maine, former campsite, baker every morning (Jul/Aug).

🅱️S | **Bouère** | 18C2

Rue des Sencies. **GPS:** n47,86320 w0,47661.⬆️

16 free € 2/80liter Ch € 2/55minutes. **Location:** Rural, comfortable, quiet. **Surface:** grassy. ◯ 01/01-31/12. **Distance:** on the spot 50m bakery 100m.

🅱️S | **Bouin** | 18A3

**Port du Bec**, Rue du Port du Bec. **GPS:** n46,93871 w2,07318.⬆️

33 € 5 € 2,50/10minutes Ch € 2,50/4h WC. **Location:** Rural, simple, isolated, quiet. **Surface:** gravel. ◯ 01/01-31/12. **Distance:** 4km Beauvoir-sur-Mer on the spot on the spot.

🅱️ | **Bouin** | 18A3

Les Brochets. **GPS:** n46,99821 w2,03314.⬆️

10 free. **Location:** Rural, simple, isolated. **Surface:** metalled. ◯ 01/01-31/12. **Distance:** 4,5km Bouin on the spot.

🅱️S | **Bouin** | 18A3

**Parking de La Coupelasse**, La Bilaille. **GPS:** n47,00918 w2,02782.

10 free. **Location:** Rural, simple, isolated, quiet. **Surface:** grassy/gravel. ◯ 01/01-31/12. **Distance:** on the spot.

🅱️S | **Bourgneuf-en-Retz** | 18A3

D758. **GPS:** n47,04028 w1,95704.⬆️

12 free € 2 € 2 Ch € 2 WC free. **Location:** Simple. **Surface:** asphalted. ◯ 01/01-31/12 ● Service: winter. **Distance:** 300m 200m 300m 300m. **Remarks:** Parking tourist info, max. 48h.

🅱️S | **Boussay** | 18B3

Place des Marronniers. **GPS:** n47,04240 w1,18648.⬆️➡️

free € 2/100liter Ch € 2/60minutes. **Location:** Urban, simple, noisy. **Surface:** asphalted. ◯ 01/01-31/12. **Distance:** 200m 200m 200m on the spot. **Remarks:** Max. 48h, coins at town hall, poste.

🅱️S | **Brem-sur-Mer** | 21A1

**L'aire des Chenes Verts**, 24 Rue des Moulin. **GPS:** n46,60977 w1,82681.

28 € 8,50, July-Aug € 11 included. ◯ 01/01-31/12. **Distance:** 800m 850m 1km.

🅱️ | **Brétignolles-sur-Mer** | 21A1

**Parking de la Normandelière**, Rue de la Source. **GPS:** n46,61664 w1,85974.⬆️

25 ⓢfree. **Location:** Urban, simple, quiet. **Surface:** metalled.
🄳 01/01-31/12.
**Distance:** 🚰1,5km 🏖sandy beach 500m 🚉1,5km 🚲on the spot 🚶on the spot.
**Remarks:** Service: Super U D38, GPS 46,62537 -1,85787.
**Tourist information Brétignolles-sur-Mer:**
🚶 🄳 Thu, Su.

### Briollay 18C2

**Plage de Briollay**, Rue de Tierce. D52. **GPS:** n47,56766 w0,50733. ⬆➡.

20 ⓢfree 🚰 € 2/100liter 🚽Ch WC free. **Location:** Rural, comfortable, quiet. **Surface:** grassy/gravel. 🄳 01/01-31/12.
**Distance:** 🚰550m ✖450m.
**Remarks:** Along Sarthe River, coins at the shops, closed when frosty and high water.

### Brissac-Quincé 18C3

Rue de l'Aubance. **GPS:** n47,35465 w0,4463. ⬆➡.

10 ⓢ€ 4 🚰🚽Ch included. **Location:** Urban, simple, quiet.
**Surface:** asphalted. 🄳 01/01-31/12.
**Distance:** 🚰300m ✖300m 🚉300m on the spot 🚶on the spot.
**Remarks:** Max. 2 days.

### Brissac-Quincé 18C3

**Domaine de la Belle Etoile**, La Belle Étoile.
**GPS:** n47,33404 w0,43597. ⬆.

8 ⓢ€ 4 + € 0,20/pp tourist tax 🚰🚽Ch 🛁€ 3 WC €1 €3
included. **Location:** Rural, comfortable, quiet. **Surface:** grassy.
🄳 01/10-30/04.
**Distance:** 🚰1,5km 🚉2km.

### Brissac-Quincé 18C3

**Domaine de L'Etang**, Route de Saint-Mathurin.
**GPS:** n47,36103 w0,43529. ⬆.

6 ⓢ€ 12-15 🚰🚽Ch 🛁WC €5 included. 🚿
**Location:** Rural, comfortable, quiet. **Surface:** grassy.
🄳 01/01-31/12.
**Distance:** 🚰1,5km ✖500m 🚉2km 🚲on the spot 🚶on the spot.
**Remarks:** To be paid at campsite.

### Chailland 18C1

**Coccimarket. GPS:** n48,22139 w0,86583. ⬆➡.

4 ⓢfree 🚰🚽Ch free. **Location:** Rural, simple. **Surface:** asphalted.
🄳 01/01-31/12.
**Distance:** 🚰300m ✖300m 🚉on the spot.
**Remarks:** Max. 24h.

### Chaille-les-Marais 21B2

Rue du 8 Mai 1945. **GPS:** n46,39228 w1,02127. ⬆.

20 ⓢfree 🚰€ 3 WC free. **Location:** Rural, simple, quiet.
**Surface:** grassy. 🄳 01/01-31/12 Thu-morning.
**Distance:** 🚰100m ✖100m 🚉300m 🚉50m.
**Remarks:** At fire-station and sports park.

### Challans 18A3

**Parking du Viaud Marais. GPS:** n46,85027 w1,8742. ⬆➡.

20 ⓢfree 🚰🚽Ch free. **Location:** Urban, central, noisy.
**Surface:** asphalted. 🄳 01/01-31/12.
**Distance:** 🚰1km ✖500m 🚉500m 🚗100m.
**Remarks:** Max. 3 days.

### Chalonnes-sur-Loire 18C3

Le Champ du Bois, D751. **GPS:** n47,35105 w0,74466. ⬆.

20 ⓢ€ 9 🚰€ 2 🚽Ch included. **Location:** Rural, comfortable.
**Surface:** grassy. 🄳 01/01-31/12.
**Distance:** 🚰1km on the spot 🚉1km on the spot.
**Remarks:** Nearby camp site.

### Chambretaud 18C3

**Aire des Diamants**, Rue Notre Dame. **GPS:** n46,92300 w0,9717. ⬆➡.

5 ⓢfree 🚰€ 2/150liter 🚽ChWC. **Location:** Rural, simple.
**Surface:** asphalted. 🄳 27/03-01/10.
**Distance:** 🚰1km 🚲5km ✖on the spot 🚉1km.

### Champ-Sur-Layon 18C3

Rue du Soleil Levant. **GPS:** n47,26369 w0,57289. ⬆.

2 ⓢfree 🚰🚽Ch (1x)WC free. **Location:** Rural, simple, quiet.
**Surface:** asphalted/metalled. 🄳 01/01-31/12.
**Distance:** 🚰150m 🚲6km 🚉6km 🚲on the spot 🚶on the spot.

### Champtocé-sur-Loire 18C2

Rue de la Hutte. **GPS:** n47,41143 w0,86958. ⬆➡.

8 ⓢfree 🚰🚽Ch free. **Location:** Rural, simple. **Surface:** asphalted.
🄳 01/01-31/12.
**Distance:** 🚰300m 🚤5,7km ✖400m 🚉400m 🚗200m.
**Remarks:** At stadium.

### Champtoceaux 18B3

**Parking Champalud**, Place de Niederheimbach.
**GPS:** n47,33816 w1,2649. ⬆➡.

8 ⓢfree 🚰€ 4/24h 🚽Ch 🛁WC. **Location:** Urban, simple, quiet.
**Surface:** asphalted. 🄳 01/01-31/12.
**Distance:** 🚰150m ✖100m 🚉150m on the spot 🚲on the spot 🚶on the spot.
**Remarks:** Square behind the church, max. 48h, payment and wifi code at tourist office.

### Champtoceaux 18B3

**Le Port du Moulin**, Le Cul du Moulin, D751.
**GPS:** n47,33913 w1,27445. ⬆.

5 ⓢfree WC free. **Location:** Rural, simple, quiet.

**Surface:** gravel/metalled. ☐ 01/01-31/12.
**Distance:** 🚶1,5km 🛒on the spot 🍴on the spot ⊗on the spot 🚉1,5km.
**Remarks:** Along Loire river, max. 48h.

**Changé** 🍽🌳🌊 **18C1**
**Parking du plan d'eau du Port**, Rue du Bac.
**GPS:** n48,10047 w0,78584. ⬆➡.

10 🚐free 🚰🗑ChWCfree. **Location:** Urban, simple.
**Surface:** gravel/sand. ☐ 01/01-31/12.
**Distance:** 🚲5km 🛒on the spot 🚉800m.
**Remarks:** Along the Mayenne river.

**Chantenay-Villedieu** 🚻 **18D1**
Route du Plan d'Eau. **GPS:** n47,91668 w0,16849. ⬆➡.
5 🚐free 🚰🗑ChWCfree. **Location:** Rural, comfortable, quiet.
**Surface:** grassy/gravel. ☐ 01/04-31/10.
**Distance:** 🏊150m 🛒150m 🚉650m.
**Remarks:** At lake, next to campsite.

**Chantonnay** **21B1**
Rue de l'Arc en Ciel. **GPS:** n46,68754 w1,04104. ⬆➡.

5 🚐free 🚰€ 2/100liter 🗑Ch🍴€ 2/60minutes.
**Location:** Rural, simple, noisy. **Surface:** asphalted.
☐ 01/01-31/12.
**Distance:** 🚶1km ⊗500m 🚉1km.
**Remarks:** Next to sports fields, coins at tourist info.

**Chanzeaux** 🌊 **18C3**
**Aire de Ploizeau**, Rue de Bel Air a Chanzeaux D121.
**GPS:** n47,25548 w0,63848. ⬆.

5 🚐free 🚰€ 2/100liter 🗑ChWC🗑. **Location:** Rural, simple, quiet.
**Surface:** gravel. ☐ 01/05-31/10.
**Distance:** 🚶1km 🛒on the spot ⊗1km 🚉1km 🚴on the spot
🚶on the spot.
**Remarks:** Coins at town hall.

**Charcé-Saint-Ellier-sur-Aubance** **18C3**
Rue Saint Ellier. **GPS:** n47,35647 w0,41146. ⬆.

5 🚐free 🚰🗑ChWCfree. **Location:** Rural, simple, quiet.
**Surface:** metalled/sand. ☐ 01/01-31/12.
**Distance:** 🚶100m ⊗3km 🚉3km.

**Château-d'Olonne** **21A1**
**Les Plesses**, Rue des Plesses. **GPS:** n46,49132 w1,74293. ⬆➡.

---

20 🚐€ 7,50/night, € 12,50/2 nights 🚰€ 2,15/6minutes 🗑Ch.🗑.
**Location:** Urban, simple. **Surface:** asphalted.
☐ 01/01-31/12.
**Distance:** 🛒2km 🚉500m.

**Château-Gontier** 🌿🍽🌳 **18C2**
Quai-du-Docteur Lefevre. **GPS:** n47,82450 w0,70206. ⬆.

30 🚐free. **Location:** Urban, simple, central. **Surface:** asphalted.
☐ 01/01-31/12.
**Distance:** 🚶200m 🛒on the spot ⊗50m 🚉1km 🚲1,1km.
**Remarks:** Along the Mayenne river.

**Châteauneuf-sur-Sarthe** 🚻 **18C2**
**L'aire de repos**, Rue de la Gare. **GPS:** n47,67774 w0,4866. ⬆.

6 🚐€ 5,15 🚰€ 4 🗑Ch🗑🍴.
**Location:** Rural, comfortable, quiet. **Surface:** grassy/gravel.
☐ 01/01-31/12 ☐ service: 01/10-01/05.
**Distance:** 🚶400m 🛒400m 🚉500m.
**Remarks:** Along Sarthe River.

**Chauché** **21B1**
L'Oiselière. **GPS:** n46,84159 w1,30211.
11 🚐€ 8 🚰🗑Ch 🧺included. **Location:** Rural.
**Surface:** unpaved. ☐ 01/01-31/12.
**Distance:** 🚶3km ⊗3km.
**Remarks:** Service on campsite.

**Chavagne-en-Paillers** **18B3**
Place des Arcades. **GPS:** n46,89083 w1,24917. ⬆➡.

3 🚐free 🚰€ 2/10minutes 🗑Ch🍴€ 2/55minutes.
**Location:** Urban, simple, central, quiet.
**Surface:** asphalted.
☐ 01/01-31/12.
**Distance:** 🚶300m 🛒50m 🚉150m 🚲300m.
**Remarks:** Coins at tourist office/Rest. Le petit Marmiton/Boulanger de Quartier, 8 rue G de Gaulle/ Carrefour Express, 197 rue G de Gaulle.

**Chavagnes les Eaux** **18C3**
Rue de l'Église. **GPS:** n47,27024 w0,45437. ⬆⬆.

---

4 🚐free 🚰🗑Chfree. **Location:** Simple, quiet. **Surface:** metalled.
☐ 01/01-31/12.
**Distance:** 🚶on the spot 🚉150m.
**Remarks:** Behind church.

**Chemillé-Melay** 🚻 **18C3**
**La ferme Cabri d'Anjou**, La Chaperonnière.
**GPS:** n47,22275 w0,7524. ⬆.

2 🚐free. **Location:** Rural, simple, isolated, quiet. **Surface:** grassy.
☐ 01/01-31/12.
**Distance:** 🚶2km ⊗3km 🚉3km 🚴on the spot 🚶on the spot.
**Remarks:** Cheese farm.

**Chênehutte-Trèves-Cunault** 🌊 **18D3**
Rue Beauregard, D751, Cunault. **GPS:** n47,32685 w0,19459. ⬆➡.

20 🚐free 🚰€ 4/100liter 🗑Ch 🍴€ 4/6h 🗑. **Location:** Rural,
simple, quiet. **Surface:** grassy. ☐ 01/01-31/12.
**Distance:** 🚶800m 🛒on the spot ⊗800m 🚉800m 🚴on the spot
🚶on the spot.
**Remarks:** Max. 72h.

**Chenillé-Changé** 🌿🌊 **18C2**
Le Pin, D78. **GPS:** n47,69919 w0,66693. ⬆➡.

8 🚐€ 5 🚰🗑Chincluded 🍴€ 4. **Location:** Simple. **Surface:** gravel.
☐ 01/01-31/12.
**Distance:** 🛒on the spot ⊗100m.
**Remarks:** Along the Mayenne river.

**Cholet** **18C3**
**Ch'ti Père Eric**, 109 Avenue de Beaupréau. **GPS:** n47,08165 w0,9053. ⬆.

6 🚐€ 5 🚰€ 2 🧺included 🍴€ 3/24h. **Location:** Rural, simple,
isolated, quiet. **Surface:** grassy/metalled. ☐ 01/01-31/12.
**Distance:** 🚶4km ⊗on the spot 🚉4km 🚴on the spot 🚶on the spot.

### Clefs-Val d'Anjou — 18D2

D938. **GPS:** n47,62442 w0,07698. ⬆.

10 ⬛free. **Location:** Rural, simple, noisy. **Surface:** metalled.
⬛ 01/01-31/12.
**Distance:** ⬛500m ⊗500m ⬛500m.

### Coëx — 21A1

Rue des Goélettes. **GPS:** n46,69668 w1,76397. ⬆.

4 ⬛free ⬛€ 4/10minutes ⬛Ch ⬛€ 4/55minutes.
**Location:** Rural, central. **Surface:** asphalted.
⬛ 01/01-31/12.
**Distance:** ⬛200m ⊗500m ⬛500m.
**Remarks:** Max. 48h, coins at town hall.

### Combrée — 18C2

Rue de Bretagne, Bel-Air. **GPS:** n47,71281 w0,9989. ➡.

3 ⬛free ⬛Ch WC free. **Location:** Rural, simple.
**Surface:** asphalted/grassy. ⬛ 01/01-31/12.
**Distance:** ⬛100m.
**Remarks:** Picnic tables available.

### Combrée — 18C2

Aire du Plan d'Eau, D203. **GPS:** n47,70321 w1,02755. ⬆.

3 ⬛free. **Location:** Rural, simple, quiet. **Surface:** asphalted.
⬛ 01/01-31/12.
**Distance:** ⬛200m ⬛on the spot ⬛on the spot ⊗50m.
**Remarks:** Behind tennis-court, picnic tables available.

### Concourson-sur-Layon — 18C3

Place du Prieuré. **GPS:** n47,17372 w0,34199. ⬆➡.

10 ⬛free ⬛€ 3/100liter ⬛Ch WC. **Location:** Urban, simple, quiet.
**Surface:** asphalted. ⬛ 01/01-31/12.

---

**Distance:** ⬛400m ⊗400m ⬛400m on the spot ⬛on the spot
⬛ on the spot.
**Remarks:** Coins at the bakery and auberge du Haut Layon, service 200m.

### Dampierre-sur-Loire — 18D3

L'aire d'accueil de Dampierre-sur-Loire, Route de Montsoreau.
**GPS:** n47,24157 w0,0232. ⬆.

80 ⬛€ 6 + € 0,50/pp tourist tax ⬛Ch included WC free. ⬛
**Location:** Urban, simple, central, quiet. **Surface:** forest soil.
⬛ 01/04-31/10.
**Distance:** ⬛on the spot ⬛100m ⊗on the spot ⬛4,5km ⬛on the
spot ⬛ on the spot.
**Remarks:** On the river Loire, behind town hall.

### Damvix — 21C2

Camping-Car Park, Le Grand Port. **GPS:** n46,31159 w0,73249.
16 ⬛€ 8,40-10,80 ⬛Ch ⬛(16x),10Amp ⬛included.
**Location:** Rural. **Surface:** metalled. ⬛ 01/01-31/12.
**Distance:** ⬛on the spot.
**Remarks:** Mandatory, one-time fee Pass'Etapes € 4.

### Deux-Evailles — 18C1

Site de la Fenderie, Champ de Vigne, D129.
**GPS:** n48,20203 w0,52018. ⬆➡.

6 ⬛free ⬛€ 2 ⬛Ch ⬛€ 2 WC free.
**Location:** Rural, comfortable, quiet. **Surface:** grassy/gravel.
⬛ 01/01-31/12.
**Distance:** ⬛1km ⬛20m ⬛20m ⊗20m ⬛5km Montsurs
⬛ on the spot.
**Remarks:** Coins at Auberge, playground, fishing permit available.

### Doué-la-Fontaine — 18D3

Domaine des Sablonniéres, Rue Jean Gaschet.
**GPS:** n47,18280 w0,25742. ⬆.

3 ⬛free ⬛Ch free. **Location:** Urban, simple, quiet.
**Surface:** gravel/metalled. ⬛ 01/01-31/12.
**Distance:** ⬛500m ⊗300m ⬛500m ⬛on the spot ⬛on the spot.

### Doué-la-Fontaine — 18D3

Roseraie les Chemins, Route de Cholet. **GPS:** n47,18554 w0,31436. ⬆.

8 ⬛free. **Location:** Rural, simple, quiet. **Surface:** gravel.
⬛ 01/01-31/12.
**Distance:** ⬛2km ⊗2km ⬛3km ⬛on the spot ⬛on the spot.

---

**Remarks:** Rose grower.

### Durtal — 18D2

Place de la Poste. **GPS:** n47,67188 w0,2406.
5 ⬛free ⬛€ 2 ⬛Ch free ⬛€ 2. **Location:** Urban.
**Surface:** asphalted. ⬛ 01/01-31/12.
**Distance:** ⬛on the spot ⬛100m ⬛260m ⬛400m.

### Durtal — 18D2

Rue du Petit Port. **GPS:** n47,66842 w0,24172. ⬆.

5 ⬛free. **Location:** Rural, quiet. **Surface:** asphalted. ⬛ 01/01-31/12.
**Distance:** ⬛300m ⬛2,4km.

### Durtal — 18D2

Rue Beausite. **GPS:** n47,67139 w0,2406. ⬆.

2 ⬛free ⬛€ 2/10minutes ⬛€ 2 ⬛Ch ⬛€ 2/60minutes.
**Location:** Urban, simple, noisy. **Surface:** asphalted.
⬛ 01/01-31/12.
**Distance:** ⬛300m ⬛2,4km.
**Remarks:** Inclining pitches.

### Faye d'Anjou — 18C3

Chateau du Fresne, D55, Rue des Monts.
**GPS:** n47,29923 w0,53806. ⬆➡.

5 ⬛free ⬛Ch WC free. **Location:** Rural, simple, quiet.
**Surface:** gravel. ⬛ 01/01-31/12.
**Distance:** ⬛2km ⊗3km.

### Fégréac — 18A2

Le Bellion. **GPS:** n47,59995 w2,09109. ⬆.
10 ⬛free. **Location:** Rural, isolated. **Surface:** gravel/metalled.
⬛ 01/01-31/12.
**Remarks:** Max. 48h.

### Feneu — 18C2

Port Albert. **GPS:** n47,56560 w0,60994. ⬆.

6 ⬛free ⬛€ 2 ⬛Ch. **Location:** Rural, quiet. **Surface:** gravel.
⬛ 01/01-31/12.
**Distance:** ⬛1,5km.
**Remarks:** Along the Mayenne river, coins at the shops in the village.

### Fontaines — 21C2

Place du Champ de Foire. **GPS:** n46,42291 w0,81952.

**FR**

20 free ⌁ ◨ ChWCfree. **Location:** Rural, simple. **Surface:** gravel.
◘ 01/01-31/12.
**Distance:** 2km ⊗on the spot ⇌on the spot.

**Fontenay-le-Comte** ❀ **21C1**
Avenue du Général de Gaulle. **GPS:** n46,46203 w0,80544. ➡.

20 free €7 ⌁ €2/4minutes ◨Ch ✎included. **Location:** Simple,
isolated, noisy. **Surface:** asphalted. ◘ 01/01-31/12.
**Distance:** 500m ⊗500m ☘500m.
**Remarks:** In front of police station, max. 24h, centre.

**Fontevraud l'Abbaye** **18D3**
Allée des Jardins. **GPS:** n47,18444 e0,04917. ⬆➡.

8 free ⌁ ◨ChWCfree. **Location:** Urban, simple, central.
**Surface:** asphalted. ◘ 01/01-31/12.
**Distance:** 400m ⊗400m ☘400m ⇌300m.

**Foussais-Payré** **21C1**
Place du Prieuré. **GPS:** n46,53000 w0,68275. ⬆➡.

20 free ⌁ ◨Chfree. **Location:** Rural, simple. **Surface:** gravel
◘ 01/01-31/12 ◙ water: frost.
**Distance:** 500m ⊗500m ☘200m.

**Freigné** **18B2**
Aire du Plan d'Eau, D185. **GPS:** n47,55049 w1,12591.
free. **Surface:** grassy. ◘ 01/01-31/12.
**Distance:** ⇌on the spot ⊗400m ☘400m.

**Fresnay-sur-Sarthe** **18D1**
Rue de la Gare. **GPS:** n48,28171 e0,02978. ⬆➡.

8 free ⌁ ◨Chfree. **Location:** Rural, simple, quiet.
**Surface:** asphalted. ◘ 01/01-31/12.
**Distance:** 600m ⊗600m ☘50m.

---

**Gené** **18C2**
Escale du Haut Anjou, La Petite Fenouillère.
**GPS:** n47,63770 w0,79641. ⬆➡.

7 €14 ⌁ ◨Ch ✎included. **Location:** Rural, simple.
**Surface:** gravel. ◘ 01/01-31/12.
**Distance:** 1,2km ⇌fish pond.
**Remarks:** Cheese farm.

**Gorron** **15C3**
Route de Brecé, Rue du Maine. **GPS:** n48,40735 w0,80993. ⬆➡.

6 free ⌁ ◨Ch ✎(3x)free. **Location:** Simple, quiet.
**Surface:** gravel. ◘ 01/01-31/12.
**Distance:** on the spot ☘200m.
**Remarks:** Max. 2 nights.

**Grez-en-Bouère** **18C2**
Place A. Peigné. **GPS:** n47,87306 w0,52306. ⬆.

6 free ⌁ ◨ WC. **Location:** Rural, simple, quiet. **Surface:** asphalted.
◘ 01/01-31/12, service: 01/04-30/11.
**Distance:** 50m ⊗50m ☘100m.
**Remarks:** Max. 48h.

**Grez-Neuville** **18C2**
Rue du Port, D291. **GPS:** n47,60119 w0,68504. ⬆➡.

8 free ⌁ ◨Chfree. **Location:** Rural, simple. **Surface:** grassy.
◘ 01/01-31/12.
**Remarks:** Former campsite, max. 1 night.

**Guenrouet** **18A2**
Rue des Hauts du Port. **GPS:** n47,52198 w1,94978. ⬆➡.

2 free ⌁ €2 ◨Ch €2. **Location:** Simple, quiet.
**Surface:** asphalted/gravel. ◘ 01/04-31/10.
**Distance:** 200m ⊗50m ☘200m ⇌200m.

---

**Remarks:** Along canal of Nantes/Brest, next to campsite Saint Clair,
max. 24h.

**Guérande** ❀ **14D3**
Avenue de la Brière, D99E. **GPS:** n47,33389 w2,42083. ⬆➡.

20 free ⌁ €6,50/100liter ◨Ch €5/1h.
**Location:** Simple, noisy. **Surface:** asphalted/grassy. ◘
01/01-31/12.
**Distance:** 1km.

**Herbignac** **18A2**
Rue du Pré Grasseur. **GPS:** n47,44050 w2,32941. ⬆.
2 free ⌁ €2 ◨€2 Ch 2. **Location:** Rural, comfortable, quiet.
**Surface:** gravel. ◘ 01/01-31/12.
**Distance:** on the spot ⇌on the spot.

**Jans** **18B2**
Place de l'Église. **GPS:** n47,62222 w1,61222. ⬆➡.

6 free ⌁ ◨ChWCfree. **Location:** Simple, quiet. **Surface:** gravel.
◘ 01/01-31/12.
**Distance:** on the spot ⊗100m.
**Remarks:** Behind town hall.

**Jard-sur-Mer** **21A1**
Route des Goffineaux. **GPS:** n46,41074 w1,59358. ⬆➡.

16 free €6,10/24h, €10,20/48h ⌁ €2/10minutes ◨Ch.
**Location:** Rural, simple. **Surface:** asphalted. ◘ 01/01-31/12.
**Distance:** 1km ⇌50m ☘1,5km ⇌1,5km.

**Juigne-sur-Loire** **18C3**
Domaine des 2 moulins, Route de Martigneau.
**GPS:** n47,40374 w0,47702. ⬆.

5 €5 ⌁ ◨Ch ✎ WC ≈included. **Location:** Rural, comfortable,
quiet. **Surface:** gravel. ◘ 01/01-31/12.
**Distance:** 1km ⇌4km ☘2km ⇌1km ⇌500m ⇌on the spot
⚘on the spot.
**Remarks:** When buying wine 1 night free.

**Juvigné** **18C1**
Plan d'Eau de Saint Martin, Rue de la Croixille, D29.
**GPS:** n48,22806 w1,03806. ⬆.

20 🛏free 🚰🗑Ch WC free. **Location:** Urban, simple. **Surface:** gravel. ⬛ 01/01-31/12.
**Distance:** 🛒200m 🚲20m ⊗200m ⚓100m 🚶on the spot.
**Remarks:** Max. 72h.

**🅿🅂 La Baconnière** 18C1

Place de l'Eglise. **GPS:** n48,18361 w0,89139. ➡.

5 🛏free 🚰🗑Ch 🧹free.
**Location:** Urban, simple. **Surface:** asphalted.
⬛ 01/01-31/12.
**Distance:** 🛒on the spot ⚓100m.
**Remarks:** Inspection 2017: closed because of renovation, behind church, max. 1 night, service (winter) on demand (town hall).

**🅿🅂 La Barre-de-Monts** 18A3

**Camping-Car Park La Grande Côte**, Route de la Grande Côte.
**GPS:** n46,88528 w2,15196.
49 🛏€ 10,08-12,49 🚰🗑Ch 🧹(40x) 📶included. 🚐 📋
**Surface:** metalled/sand. ⬛ 01/01-31/12.
**Distance:** 🛒800m 🏖200m ⊗800m.
**Remarks:** Mandatory, one-time fee Pass'Etapes € 4.

**🅿🅂 La Baule** 14D3

Boulevard Guy de Champsavin, La Baule-Escoublac.
**GPS:** n47,28196 w2,42509. ⬆➡.

16 🛏€ 15 🚰€ 3 🗑Ch 🧹(20x)€ 3/55minutes 📋. **Location:** Urban, comfortable, quiet. **Surface:** metalled. ⬛ 01/01-31/12.
**Distance:** 🏖beach 700m.

**🅿🅂 La Bernerie-en-Retz** 18A3

**Parking Wilson**, Avenue de Jean d Arc. **GPS:** n47,07871 w2,03399. ⬆.

30 🛏€ 9,50-11,50 + € 0,60/pp tourist tax 🚰🗑Ch 🧹included WC
📋🚐📋
**Location:** Urban. **Surface:** asphalted. ⬛ 01/01-31/12.
**Distance:** 🛒300m 🏖100m ⊗300m ⚓300m 🚌on the spot.
**Remarks:** Max. 48h, coins at tourist info.

**🅿🅂 La Chapelle-Hermier** 21A1

**Camping Yelloh! Village Le Pin Parasol**, 6 Chateaulong.
**GPS:** n46,66716 w1,75618. ⬆.

20 🛏€ 10, 01/07-31/08 € 12 🚰🗑Ch 🧹WC included 📷 📶 🚐
📋 **Location:** Rural, comfortable, quiet. **Surface:** grassy/gravel.
⬛ 17/05-15/09.
**Distance:** 🛒5km 🏖12km 🚲1km ⊗on the spot ⚓12km 🚏on the spot 🚶on the spot.
**Remarks:** Swimming pool.

**🅿🅂 La Chapelle-Saint-Florent** 18B3

**Aire du Stade**, Rue de l'Evre. **GPS:** n47,33411 w1,05178. ⬆➡.

6 🛏free 🚰🗑Ch free. **Location:** Rural, simple, quiet.
**Surface:** gravel/metalled. ⬛ 01/01-31/12.
**Distance:** 🛒300m 🏖300m ⚓50m.
**Remarks:** Max. 9m.

**🅿🅂 La Daguenière** 18C2

Chemin de Beausse, Rue de Stade. **GPS:** n47,42222 w0,43936. ⬆.

12 🛏free 🚰€ 2/100liter 🗑Ch. **Location:** Rural, simple.
**Surface:** grassy/gravel. ⬛ 01/01-31/12.
**Distance:** 🛒200m 🏖300m ⚓300m.
**Remarks:** Next to sports fields.

**🅿🅂 La Daguenière** 18C2

**Port Maillard**. **GPS:** n47,41743 w0,43781. ⬆.

10 🛏free 🗑Ch WC. **Location:** Rural, comfortable. **Surface:** unpaved.
⬛ 01/01-31/12 📷 high water.
**Remarks:** Along Loire river.

**🅿🅂 La Faute-sur-Mer** 21B2

**Camping-Car Park Les Amourettes**, Route de la Point d'Arcay.
**GPS:** n46,31607 w1,30776.
32 🛏€ 9,29, 01/04-30/09 € 10,44 🚰🗑Ch 🧹(32x) 📶included. 🚐📋
📋 **Surface:** asphalted. ⬛ 01/01-31/12.
**Remarks:** Mandatory, one-time fee Pass'Etapes € 4.

**🅿🅂 La Faute-sur-Mer** 21B2

**Camping-Car Park Les Pins**, Rond Point Fleuri.
**GPS:** n46,33297 w1,32231. ⬆.

31 🛏€ 9,29, 01/04-30/09 € 10,44 🚰🗑Ch 🧹(31x) 📶included. 🚐
📋 **Surface:** asphalted.
⬛ 01/01-31/12.
**Distance:** 🛒on the spot 🏖850m ⊗100m.
**Remarks:** At tourist office, mandatory, one-time fee Pass'Etapes € 4.

**🅿🅂 La Flèche** 💈 18D2

Promenade du Maréchal Foch. **GPS:** n47,69767 w0,07875. ⬆.

10 🛏free 🚰🗑Ch free.
**Location:** Urban, simple, noisy. **Surface:** asphalted.
⬛ 01/01-31/12 📷 tue-evening, wed 06-16h (market).
**Distance:** 🛒100m ⊗100m ⚓100m.

**🅿🅂 La Fresnaye-sur-Chédouet** 👥 15E3

**La forêt de Perseigne**, Les Ventes du Four, D236.
**GPS:** n48,43469 e0,25972. ⬆➡.

20 🛏free 🚰🗑Ch free. **Location:** Rural, simple, quiet.
**Surface:** gravel. ⬛ 01/01-31/12.
**Distance:** 🛒La Fresnaye 1,5km 🚶on the spot.

**🅿🅂 La Meilleraie-Tillay** 21C1

**Zone de loisirs du Moulin Bonnet**, Rue des Ombrages.
**GPS:** n46,73923 w0,84578. ⬆➡.

10 🛏free 🚰€ 2/5minutes 🗑Ch WC 🗑€ 1. **Location:** Rural, simple, isolated, quiet. **Surface:** asphalted. ⬛ 01/04-31/10.
**Distance:** 🛒700m 🏖700m ⚓700m.
**Remarks:** Coins at town hall.

**🅿🅂 La Plaine-sur-Mer** 18A3

Boulevard des Nations Unies. **GPS:** n47,13994 w2,19057. ⬆➡.

8 🛏free 🚰🗑Ch free. **Location:** Simple, isolated.
**Surface:** asphalted. ⬛ 01/01-31/12.
**Distance:** 🛒300m ⊗800m ⚓500m. **Remarks:** Max. 24h.

## La Poitevinière — 18C3

**Aire de la Fontaine**, Place de la Fontaine, D15.
**GPS**: n47,22750 w0,897.⬆.

5 free 🚰🔌Ch🚻WCfree. **Location:** Urban, comfortable, quiet.
**Surface:** asphalted. ☀ 01/01-31/12.
**Distance:** 🛒50m 🛍on the spot 🚲on the spot ⚘on the spot.
**Remarks:** Coins available at bar.

## La Roche-sur-Yon — 21B1

Chemin des Amoureux. **GPS**: n46,66833 w1,41861.⬆.

20 free 🚰🔌Chfree. **Location:** Urban, central. **Surface:** metalled.
☀ 01/01-31/12.
**Distance:** 🛒500m ⊗500m 🚱500m 🚲on the spot ⚘on the spot.
**Remarks:** Max. 36h.

## La Roche-sur-Yon — 21B1

**Les Crins au Bord du Lac**, La Brunetière. **GPS**: n46,71104 w1,40663.

3 €5 🚰🔌⚫€4/4 🔌included. **Location:** Rural, comfortable,
isolated, quiet. **Surface:** grassy/gravel. ☀ 01/01-31/12.
**Distance:** 🛒6km ⊿on the spot 🛍on the spot ⊗2km 🚱1km
🚞300m 🚲1km ⚘on the spot.
**Remarks:** Bike/canoe rental.

## La Séguinière — 18C3

**Camping Car Park de la Séguinière**, Avenue de Nantes.
**GPS**: n47,06005 w0,93668.⬆➡.

20 €8,40, 01/04-30/09 €15,80 + €1,0/pp tourist tax 🚰🔌
Ch🔌included. 🚐 **Location:** Simple. **Surface:** asphalted.
☀ 01/01-31/12.
**Distance:** 🛒100m ⊗on the spot 🚱50m.
**Remarks:** Mandatory, one-time fee Pass'Etapes €4.

## La Selle-Craonnaise — 18C1

**Base de Loisirs**, La Rincerie. **GPS**: n47,86330 w1,06843.⬆➡.

+5 free 🚰€2 🔌Ch. **Location:** Simple, isolated, quiet.
**Surface:** gravel. ☀ 01/01-31/12.
**Distance:** ⊿on the spot 🚲on the spot ⚘on the spot.
**Remarks:** At lake, playground.

## La Suze-sur-Sarthe — 18D2

Rue du Camping. **GPS**: n47,88904 e0,03305.⬆➡.

73 €9, 01/04-15/05 €6 + €0,22/pp tourist tax 🚰€2/100liter 🔌
Ch🔌(36x)included WC🚻 🧺🚐
**Location:** Rural, comfortable, quiet. **Surface:** grassy/gravel.
☀ 01/01-31/12.
**Distance:** 🛒300m ⊿50m 🛍50m ⊗300m 🚲on the spot
⚘on the spot.

## La Tranche-sur-Mer — 21B2

Boulevard de la Petite Hollande. **GPS**: n46,34965 w1,44769.⬆➡.

16 €4,50 🚰€3,50/10minutes 🔌Ch🔌🧺⚓ **Location:** Simple,
quiet. ☀ 01/01-31/12.
**Remarks:** Max. 48h.

## La Tranche-sur-Mer — 21B2

**Parking du Stade**, Avenue du Général de Gaulle.
**GPS**: n46,35028 w1,43688.⬆➡.

80 free, 14/06-14/09 €10 🚰€3,50 🔌Ch⚓ **Location:** Rural.
**Surface:** asphalted. ☀ 01/01-31/12.
**Distance:** 🛒1km.
**Remarks:** Max. 15 days.

## La Turballe — 14D3

Boulevard de la Grande Falaise. **GPS**: n47,33106 w2,49919.⬆➡.

23 €8,50, July-Aug €11 🚰🔌Chincluded. 🚐🧺
**Location:** Comfortable, quiet. **Surface:** gravel. ☀ 01/01-31/12.
**Distance:** 🛒2km ⊿300m. **Remarks:** Max. 72h.

## La Turballe — 14D3

**Camping-Car Park**, Rue du clos Mora. **GPS**: n47,35150 w2,50558.
23 €10,20 🚰🔌Ch🔌(23x)🔌included. 🚐🧺
**Surface:** metalled. ☀ 01/01-31/12.
**Distance:** 🛒800m ⊿800m ⊗600m 🚱400m 🛍on the spot.
**Remarks:** Mandatory, one-time fee Pass'Etapes €4.

## La Turballe — 14D3

Rue Alphonse Daudet. **GPS**: n47,34870 w2,50804.⬆.

20 €8,50, July-Aug €11 🚰🔌Chincluded. 🚐🧺
**Location:** Urban, simple, quiet. **Surface:** gravel/metalled.
☀ 01/01-31/12.
**Distance:** 🛒800m ⊿500m 🚱100m 🚱100m.
**Remarks:** Max. 5 days.

## Lassay-les-Châteaux — 15C3

Allée du Haut Perrin. **GPS**: n48,43777 w0,49822.⬆.

8 free 🚰€1/80liter 🔌Ch🚻€1/2h. **Location:** Urban, simple,
central. **Surface:** asphalted. ☀ 01/01-31/12.
**Distance:** 🛒100m ⊗100m.
**Remarks:** Coins at Tourist Info and bakery.

## Laval — 18C1

**Parking de la Halte Fluviale**, Rue du Vieux Saint-Louis.
**GPS**: n48,07589 w0,77142.⬆.

10 free 🚰🔌free WC🚻. **Location:** Urban, simple, noisy.
**Surface:** asphalted. ☀ 01/01-31/12.
**Distance:** 🛒300m 🛍on the spot ⊗on the spot 🚱on the spot.
**Remarks:** Parking nearby viaduct.

**Tourist information Laval:**
Ⓜ✖ Vieux Château. Medieval castle, museum with collection of naive
art. ☀ 9.30-12h and 13.30-18.30h.

## Le Champ-Saint-Père — 21B1

48 Rue de la Nanté. **GPS**: n46,50551 w1,35036.⬆.

19 €9 🚰🔌Ch🔌(19x)included,3Amp. 🚐🧺 **Location:** Rural,
comfortable. **Surface:** asphalted/grassy. ☀ 01/01-31/12.
**Distance:** 🛒200m 🚱100m ⊗200m 🚱800m 🚲on the spot
⚘on the spot.
**Remarks:** Possibility for reservation, thursday market.

## Le Coudray Macouard — 18D3

Route de Bron. **GPS**: n47,18806 w0,11722.⬆➡.

5 ⟂free 🚰🚽Chfree. **Location:** Rural, simple, isolated, quiet.
**Surface:** grassy/sand. ⭘ 01/01-31/12.
**Distance:** 🚶800m ⚓800m.
**Remarks:** Near sports fields.

| 🚐S | Le Croisic 🏖⚓🪣🐚 | 14D3 |

**La Vigie**, Avenue de Pierre Longue, D45. **GPS:** n47,28917 w2,53667.⬆

9 ⟂€ 7 + € 0,75/pp tourist tax 🚰€ 5/150liter 🗑Ch.🚽🧹
**Location:** Rural, simple, noisy. **Surface:** asphalted.
⭘ 01/01-31/12.
**Distance:** 🚶3km ⚓50m ⊗3km 🛒3km.
**Remarks:** Max. 48h, no camping activities.

| 🚐S | Le Croisic 🏖⚓🪣🐚 | 14D3 |

**Le Lin Gorzé**, Rue du Lin Gorzé. **GPS:** n47,29917 w2,52194.⬆➡

9 ⟂€ 7 + € 0,75/pp tourist tax 🚰€ 5/150liter 🗑Ch 🧹
**Location:** Simple, quiet. **Surface:** asphalted. ⭘ 01/01-31/12.
**Distance:** 🚶500m ⚓500m ⊗500m 🛒800m.
**Remarks:** Max. 48h, no camping activities.

| 🚐S | Le Croisic 🏖⚓🪣🐚 | 14D3 |

**Les Courlis**, Rue des Courlis. **GPS:** n47,29000 w2,505.⬆➡

15 ⟂€ 7 + € 0,75/pp tourist tax 🚰€ 5/150liter 🗑Ch 🧹
**Location:** Simple, quiet. **Surface:** gravel. ⭘ 01/04-31/10.
**Distance:** 🚶500m ⚓500m ⊗500m 🛒500m.
**Remarks:** Max. 48h, no camping activities.

| 🚐S | Le Croisic 🏖⚓🪣🐚 | 14D3 |

**P1 Kerdavid**, 1 Rue Kerclavid. **GPS:** n47,29835 w2,51995.⬆

8 ⟂€ 7 + € 0,75/pp tourist tax 🚰€ 5/150liter 🗑Ch.🚽🧹
**Location:** Urban, simple, quiet. **Surface:** asphalted. ⭘ 01/01-31/12.
**Distance:** 🚶500m ⚓500m 🚲500m 🛒800m.
**Remarks:** Max. 48h, no camping activities.

---

**Tourist information Le Croisic:**
Océarium du Croisic. Sea aquarium.
⭘ 01/06-31/08 10-20h, 01/05-31/05, 01/09-30/09 10-13h, 14-19h,
01/10-30/04 14-19h.

| 🚐S | Le Fenouiller | 21A1 |

**Camping-Car Park**, 7 rue du Centre. **GPS:** n46,71491 w1,90777.
41 ⟂€ 10,50-12,90 🚰🗑Ch (41x) 📶included. 🚽🧹
**Surface:** gravel/metalled. ⭘ 01/01-31/12.
**Remarks:** Mandatory, one-time fee Pass'Etapes € 4.

| 🚐S | Le Guédéniau 🍴 | 18D2 |

**Plan d'eau**, Rue du Lavoir. **GPS:** n47,49405 w0,04488.⬆➡

25 ⟂free 🚰🗑ChWCfree. **Location:** Rural, comfortable, quiet.
**Surface:** metalled. ⭘ 01/01-31/12.
**Distance:** 🚶on the spot.
**Remarks:** Recreation area at lake.

| 🚐S | Le Mans 🏖⚓🪣🐚 | 18D1 |

**Rue Denfert Rochereau. GPS:** n48,01111 e0,19750.⬆

8 ⟂€ 8 🚰🗑Chincluded. **Location:** Urban, simple, noisy.
**Surface:** asphalted. ⭘ 01/01-31/12 ⭘ Su-morning (market).
**Distance:** 🚶500m ⊗500m 🛒500m.
**Remarks:** Max. 24h, sunday morning market.

**Tourist information Le Mans:**
Ⓜ Le Musée des 24 Heures - Circuit de la Sarthe, 9 Place Luigi Chinetti.
Motorcar museum.
⌂ Place des Jacobins. ⭘ Wed + Su-morning, Fri.

| 🚐S | Le Pallet 🍴 | 18B3 |

**Rue Pierre Abelard. GPS:** n47,13494 w1,3305.⬆

20 ⟂free 🚰€ 1 🗑Ch. **Location:** Rural, simple. **Surface:** asphalted.
⭘ 01/01-31/12.
**Distance:** 🚶500m ⊗500m 🛒500m 🚴on the spot 🚶on the spot.
**Remarks:** Wine museum, coins at the shops in the village.

| 🚐S | Le Poiré-sur-Vie | 21B1 |

**Rue de Roc. GPS:** n46,76773 w1,51162.⬆➡

5 ⟂€ 5/day, first 48h free 🚰🗑Chfree 🧹
**Location:** Central, quiet. **Surface:** gravel.
⭘ 01/01-31/12.
**Distance:** 🚶500m ⊗500m 🛒500m.

| 🚐S | Le Pouliguen | 14D3 |

**Avenue de l'Océan. GPS:** n47,27201 w2,43276.⬆

---

26 ⟂€ 10,50 🚰🗑Ch 📶included. 🚽🧹 **Location:** Simple, quiet.
**Surface:** grassy. ⭘ 01/01-31/12.
**Distance:** 🚶200m ⚓200m.
**Remarks:** Max. 72h.

| 🚐S | Le Puy-Notre-Dame | 18D3 |

**Place du Gâte Argent**, Rue du Parc. **GPS:** n47,12390 w0,23155.⬆➡

15 ⟂free 🚰🗑Chfree. **Location:** Urban, simple, quiet.
**Surface:** metalled. ⭘ 01/01-31/12.
**Distance:** 🚶100m ⊗200m 🛒200m.
**Remarks:** Next to cemetery, shady.

| 🍇S | Le Puy-Notre-Dame | 18D3 |

**Cave-Champignonnière St.Maur**, 1 Rue du Chateau, Sanziers.
**GPS:** n47,11755 w0,20526.⬆➡

8 ⟂free 🚰🧹(1x)on demand WCfree. **Location:** Simple, quiet.
**Surface:** metalled. ⭘ 01/03-31/10.
**Distance:** 🚶2km ⊗1km.
**Remarks:** At mushroom grower.

| 🍇S | Le Puy-Notre-Dame | 18D3 |

**Domaine de la Girardrie**, 1 Rue Fontaine de Cix.
**GPS:** n47,11616 w0,24127.⬆

5 ⟂free 🚰free. **Location:** Rural, simple, quiet. **Surface:** gravel.
⭘ 01/01-31/12.
**Distance:** 🚶1km ⊗1km 🛒1km.

| 🍇S | Le Puy-Notre-Dame | 18D3 |

**Domaine de la Renière**, Les Caves. **GPS:** n47,13429 w0,24256.⬆

5 ⟂€ 6 🚰included 🧹€ 5/24h. 🐕 **Location:** Rural, simple, quiet.
**Surface:** metalled. ⭘ 01/03-01/11.
**Distance:** 🚶700m.
**Remarks:** When buying wine 1 night free.

| 🍇S | Le Puy-Notre-Dame | 18D3 |

**Domaine du Vieux Tuffeau**, Les Caves. **GPS:** n47,13498 w0,24704.➡

FR

6 🛏free 🚰free ⚡€ 5/night. **Location:** Rural, simple, quiet. **Surface:** metalled. ⏰ 01/01-31/12. **Distance:** 🚶1km ⊗1km.

### Le Puy-Notre-Dame　18D3
**Domaine des Hauts Buards**, 17 Rue des Troglodytes. **GPS:** n47,11149 w0,22544.⬆️.

5 🛏free. **Location:** Rural, simple, isolated, quiet. **Surface:** gravel. ⏰ 01/01-31/12. **Distance:** 🚶7km ⊗7km 🍴7km 🚲on the spot 🧍on the spot.

### Le Vaudelnay　18D3
**Domaine du Vieux Pressoir**, 235, Rue Château d'Oiré. **GPS:** n47,14669 w0,25239.⬆️➡️.

2 🛏free.
**Location:** Rural, simple, quiet. **Surface:** grassy/metalled. ⏰ 01/01-31/12. **Distance:** 🚶3km ⊗3km 🍴3km 🚲on the spot 🧍on the spot. **Remarks:** No arrival on Sunday, opening hours shop 9-12 and 14-18h.

### Les Epesses　21C1
Le Puy du Fou, D27. **GPS:** n46,89425 w0,92506.⬆️➡️.
100 🛏€ 9 🚰€ 2/100liter 🚿Ch.🧺(36x)€ 2/12h WC.🛒.
**Location:** Simple, isolated, noisy.
**Surface:** grassy/gravel.
⏰ 31/03-25/09.
**Remarks:** Baker at 8am, free shuttle to Puy du Fou.

### Les Essarts　21B1
Rue de la piscine. **GPS:** n46,77380 w1,23499.⬆️➡️.

10 🛏free 🚰€ 2/10minutes 🚿Ch.🧺(2x)€ 2/55minutes.
**Location:** Rural, simple. **Surface:** asphalted. ⏰ 01/01-31/12.
**Distance:** 🚶600m 🚲5,6km ⊗600m 🍴600m.
**Remarks:** At swimmingpool and campsite.

### Les Herbiers　21B1
Rue Saint Exupéry. **GPS:** n46,87410 w1,01765.⬆️➡️.

8 🛏free 🚰🚿Chfree. **Location:** Simple. **Surface:** asphalted/gravel. ⏰ 01/01-31/12. **Distance:** 🚶600m ⊗600m 🍴600m. **Remarks:** Max. 24h.

### Les Sables-d'Olonne　🏖️　21A1
**Indigo Parking Plage**, Rue Printanière. **GPS:** n46,49646 w1,77493.⬆️.

150 🛏€ 15,10/24h, winter free 🚰🚿Ch.🧺WCincluded. 🛒⚡ **Location:** Urban, simple. **Surface:** gravel. ⏰ 01/01-31/12 🔘 service: 06/11-31/03.
**Distance:** 🚶on the spot 🏖️beach 600m ⊗600m 🍴400m.
**Tourist information Les Sables-d'Olonne:**
ℹ️ Cours Dupont. ⏰ Wed + Sa morning.
　Zoo d'Olonne. Zoo.

### Longeville-sur-Mer　21B1
**Camping-Car Park**, Avenue du Docteur Mathevet.
**GPS:** n46,40326 w1,50558.
33 🛏€ 9,50 🚰🚿Ch.🧺(34x)🧺included. 🛒⚡ **Location:** Rural.
**Surface:** forest soil. ⏰ 01/01-31/12.
**Remarks:** Mandatory, one-time fee Pass'Etapes € 4.

### Longeville-sur-Mer　21B1
**Camping-Car Park**, Boulevard du 8 mai. **GPS:** n46,42212 w1,49191.
15 🛏€ 9,50 🚰🚿Ch.🧺(15x)🧺included. 🛒⚡ **Surface:** grassy. ⏰ 01/01-31/12.
**Remarks:** Mandatory, one-time fee Pass'Etapes € 4.

### Longué-Jumelles　18D3
Boulevard Victor Hugo. **GPS:** n47,38097 w0,11236.⬆️➡️.

10 🛏free 🚰🚿ChWCfree. **Location:** Simple, quiet. **Surface:** gravel. ⏰ 01/01-31/12.
**Distance:** 🚶100m 🚲3,3km ⊗on the spot 🍴on the spot.
**Remarks:** Service 300m: N 47,38046 W -0,11488, attention: follow the signs.

### Luçon　🏰⚓　21B1
**Domaine des Guifettes**. **GPS:** n46,43339 w1,18189.⬆️➡️.

26 🛏€ 10,50 🚰🚿Ch.🧺included WC🧺. **Location:** Rural, comfortable, isolated, quiet. **Surface:** gravel/metalled.
**Distance:** 🏖️on the spot 🍴on the spot ⊗on the spot 🍴on the spot 🛒on the spot 🚲on the spot.
**Remarks:** Free entrance swimming pool, jacuzzi, sauna, midget golf.

**Tourist information Luçon:**
ℹ️ Centre Ville. ⏰ Wed + Sa morning.

### L'Aiguillon-sur-Mer　21B2
**Centre de Voile**, Avenue Amiral Coubert.
**GPS:** n46,33238 w1,30726.⬆️➡️.

40 🛏€ 5 + € 0,40/pp 🚰€ 2/100liter 🚿ChWC. **Location:** Rural, simple. **Surface:** asphalted. ⏰ 01/01-31/12.
**Distance:** 🚶300m 🏖️300m 🍴on the spot ⊗300m 🍴300m.
**Remarks:** At lake, yachting school.

### Maillé　⚓　21C2
La Petite Cabane. **GPS:** n46,34082 w0,79349.

5 🛏€ 8, tourist tax € 0,20/pp 🚰included 🚿€ 3 Ch 3 WC🧺🧺. 🛒⚡**Location:** Rural, simple, quiet. **Surface:** grassy/gravel. ⏰ 01/01-31/12.
**Distance:** 🚶500m 🚐200m.
**Remarks:** Check in at harbourmaster, service passerby € 3, bicycle rental 500m.

### Maillezais　21C2
Rue de l'Ecole. **GPS:** n46,37081 w0,74123.➡️.

20 🛏free 🚰€ 2/100liter 🚿Ch. **Location:** Simple.
**Surface:** asphalted. ⏰ 01/01-31/12.
**Distance:** 🚶500m ⊗500m 🍴200m.

### Maisdon-sur-Sèvre　18B3
**Domaine des Croix**, Les Croix. **GPS:** n47,10710 w1,38757.⬆️.

12 🛏free 🚰🚿Ch.🧺€ 4/24h WC🧺€ 1. **Location:** Rural, comfortable. **Surface:** gravel. ⏰ 01/01-31/12.
**Distance:** 🚶1km.
**Remarks:** Max. 72h, wine tasting.

### Mamers　18E1
Rue de la Piscine. **GPS:** n48,35523 e0,37187.⬆️➡️.

8 ⌁€ 7/night, € 18/3 nights ⌁⌁Ch ⌁included.
**Location:** Rural, comfortable, quiet. **Surface:** grassy/gravel.
⬛ 01/01-31/12.
**Distance:** ⌁1km ⌁500m ⌁500m ⊗1km ⌁1km.
**Remarks:** Entrance code available at campsite.

### Mansigné 18D2
**Camping de la Plage**, Route du Plessis.
**GPS:** n47,75130 e0,13233. ⬆➡.

10 ⌁€5 ⌁€ 2/80liter ⌁Ch⌁€ 2/2h ⬛€ 5/4. ⌁ **Location:** Rural,
comfortable, quiet. **Surface:** grassy/gravel.
**Distance:** ⌁700m ⌁on the spot.

### Martigné-Briand 18C3
**Jardin des Vieux Pressoirs**, Rue d'Anjou.
**GPS:** n47,23584 w0,42851. ⬆➡.

6 ⌁free ⌁⌁Chfree. **Location:** Comfortable. **Surface:** metalled.
⬛ 01/01-31/12.
**Distance:** ⌁200m ⊗200m ⌁100m.
**Remarks:** Closed when frosty.

### Martigné-Briand 18C3
**Domaine de la Touche Blanche**, La Touche Blanche.
**GPS:** n47,26977 w0,45274. ⬆.

6 ⌁free ⌁⌁€ 3/day. **Location:** Rural, simple, quiet.
**Surface:** gravel. ⬛ 01/01-31/12.
**Distance:** ⌁3km ⊗3km ⌁3km ⌁on the spot ⌁on the spot.

### Maulévrier 18C3
Route des Aubiers. **GPS:** n47,00652 w0,74014.

⌁free ⌁⌁Chfree. **Surface:** metalled.
**Distance:** ⌁500m ⊗500m ⌁600m.

---

### Mayenne 18C1
Quai Carnot. **GPS:** n48,30000 w0,62. ⬆➡.

2 ⌁free ⌁€ 2/100liter ⌁Ch. **Location:** Urban, simple, noisy.
**Surface:** asphalted. ⬛ 01/01-31/12.
**Distance:** ⌁1km ⌁10m.
**Remarks:** Nearby basilica, max. 24h, coins at tourist info.

### Mervent 21C1
**Parking du Chêne Tord**, Chemin du Chêne Tord.
**GPS:** n46,52385 w0,76432.

⌁€5 ⌁⌁Chincluded. **Location:** Rural, simple, isolated, quiet.
**Surface:** gravel. ⬛ 01/01-31/12.
**Distance:** ⌁1km.
**Remarks:** At cemetery.

### Mesnard-la-Barotière 21B1
Base de Loisirs de la Tricherie. **GPS:** n46,85280 w1,11764. ⬆.

10 ⌁free ⌁€ 3 ⌁ChWC ⌁ **Location:** Rural, simple, noisy.
**Surface:** grassy. ⬛ 01/01-31/12.
**Distance:** ⌁2km ⌁beach ⌁on the spot ⊗on the spot ⌁on the
spot.
**Remarks:** At lake of Tricherie.

### Mesquer 14D3
**Aire de la Bôle de Merquel**, Route de la Bôle de Merquel.
**GPS:** n47,41474 w2,46826. ⬆.

15 ⌁free ⌁⌁Ch ⌁free. **Location:** Quiet.
**Surface:** gravel/metalled. ⬛ 01/01-31/12.
**Distance:** ⌁1km ⌁300m.
**Remarks:** Max. 48h.

### Mesquer 14D3
**Aire du Parc de la Lande**, Route de Campzillon.
**GPS:** n47,39309 w2,46549. ⬆.
20 ⌁€ 5,50/night. **Surface:** grassy. ⬛ 01/04-31/10 ⬛ winter.
**Distance:** ⌁1,2km.
**Remarks:** Max. 72h.

### Mesquer 14D3
Avenue de Praderoi, Quimiac. **GPS:** n47,40564 w2,48739. ⬆.

---

5 ⌁free. **Location:** Quiet. **Surface:** forest soil. ⬛ 01/01-31/12.
**Distance:** ⌁400m ⌁sandy beach 300m.
**Remarks:** Picnic area, tuesday morning market.

### Mesquer 14D3
Route de Kerlagadec. **GPS:** n47,39567 w2,46752.
⌁⌁Chfree. ⬛ 01/01-31/12.
**Distance:** ⌁1km ⌁2km.
**Remarks:** Coins at town hall and supermarket.

### Mezeray 18D2
Rue de la Vezanne. **GPS:** n47,82300 w0,01485. ⬆➡.

4 ⌁free ⌁€ 2/100liter ⌁Ch⌁€ 2/h. **Location:** Rural, simple.
**Surface:** gravel. ⬛ 01/01-31/12 ⬛ frost.
**Distance:** ⌁500m.

### Montfort-le-Gesnois 18E1
**Parc des Sittelles. GPS:** n48,03763 e0,41375. ⬆➡.

16 ⌁€ 10 ⌁⌁Ch ⌁included. **Location:** Rural, simple, quiet.
**Surface:** forest soil. ⬛ 01/01-31/12.
**Distance:** ⊗50m.
**Remarks:** Inspection 2017: closed because of renovation.

### Montreuil-Bellay 18D3
**Place Dom Deschamps**, Rue Georges Girouy.
**GPS:** n47,13272 w0,15835. ⬆.

30 ⌁free ⌁€ 2,20/10minutes ⌁ChWC.
**Location:** Urban, simple. **Surface:** gravel/metalled.
⬛ 01/01-31/12 ⬛ 15/06-15/09 10-19h.
**Distance:** ⌁150m ⌁on the spot ⌁150m ⌁on the spot
⌁on the spot ⌁on the spot.
**Remarks:** Along river, nearby campisite Les Nobis, coins at the shops
and town hall.

### Montreuil-Bellay 18D3
**Caveau de la Prévoté**, Rue du Cohu 55, Méron.
**GPS:** n47,13522 w0,11121. ⬆.

3 ⅗free 🚰🗑Ch♿〰free. **Location:** Simple, quiet.
**Surface:** metalled. 🅾 01/01-31/12.
**Distance:** 🚶50m ⊗3km 🛒3km.

**Tourist information Montreuil-Bellay:**
ℹ️ Office de Tourisme, Place du Concorde, www.ville-montreuil-bellay.
fr. City with a fortress from 1025.

🚐Ⓢ **Montreuil-Juigné** 🌳 **18C2**
Rue Saint Jean Baptiste. **GPS:** n47,54132 w0,61526.⬆️➡️.

8 ⅗free 🚰€ 2/100liter 🗑Ch. **Location:** Rural, simple.
**Surface:** gravel/metalled. 🅾 01/01-31/12.
**Distance:** 🚶1km ⊗50m 🛒800m.
**Remarks:** Along the Mayenne river, max. 72h, coins at camping
municipal.

🚐Ⓢ **Moutiers-sur-le-Lay** **21B1**
Palias. **GPS:** n46,55375 w1,15483. ⬆️➡️.

6 ⅗free 🚰🗑Ch♿WC. **Location:** Simple.
**Surface:** grassy/metalled. 🅾 01/01-31/12.
**Distance:** 🚶400m ⊗400m 🛒400m⊗200m.
**Remarks:** At gymnasium.

🚐Ⓢ **Mouzillon** **18B3**
Route de la Vendée. **GPS:** n47,13944 w1,28194.⬆️➡️.

12 ⅗free 🚰€ 2 🗑Ch. **Location:** Simple. **Surface:** asphalted.
🅾 01/01-31/12.
**Distance:** 🚶200m ⊗200m 🛒200m 🎣on the spot.

🚐Ⓢ **Mouzillon** **18B3**
En Vignoble Nantais, La Tucauderie. **GPS:** n47,12697 w1,23695.⬆️.

6 ⅗€ 5 ♿WCincluded. **Surface:** gravel. 🅾 01/01-31/12.

---

🚐Ⓢ **Nantes** 🚃🍴🌳 **18B3**
**Camping-car park du Petit Port**, Boulevard du Petit Port.
**GPS:** n47,24252 w1,5568.⬆️➡️.

15 ⅗€ 10,90, 01/04-30/09 € 13,30 🚰🗑Ch〰included. 📷
🗑 **Location:** Urban, simple, central. **Surface:** grassy/metalled.
🅾 01/01-31/12.
**Distance:** 🚶on the spot 🚲3,5km ⊗on the spot 🛒300m
🚃tram 150m.
**Remarks:** Mandatory, one-time fee Pass'Etapes € 4, wifi code: 44-2207,
entrance code: 2207A.

**Tourist information Nantes:**
Ⓜ️ Musée Jules Verne.

🚐Ⓢ **Noirmoutier-en-l'Ile** 🚃🌳 **18A3**
**Aire de La Guérinière**, Rue de la Tresson. **GPS:** n46,96591 w2,21482.⬆️.

49 ⅗€ 9-11, 08/07-02/09 € 14,50 🚰🗑Ch♿〰included.
🚐🗑 **Location:** Comfortable, quiet. **Surface:** grassy/gravel.
🅾 01/01-31/12.
**Distance:** 🏖sandy beach 450m ⊗200m 🛒100m.
**Remarks:** Max. 48h, video surveillance.

🚐Ⓢ **Noirmoutier-en-l'Ile** 🚃🌳 **18A3**
La Place de l'ancien moulin à eau. **GPS:** n47,00139 w2,25167.⬆️.

150 ⅗€ 5, 01/04-31/10 € 8, parking free 🚰€ 2/100liter 🗑
Ch🚰€ 2/1h〰free.♿🗑 **Location:** Simple. **Surface:** asphalted.
🅾 01/01-31/12.
**Distance:** 🚶750m 🏖sandy beach 2,5km 🛒750m.
**Remarks:** Near pool park, max. 72h.

🚐Ⓢ **Noirmoutier-en-l'Ile** 🚃🌳 **18A3**
Place des Urmeaux/d95, L'Epine. **GPS:** n46,98060 w2,26404.⬆️.

62 ⅗€ 9/24h, € 16/48h, € 23/92h 🚰100liter 🗑Ch📷
included50minutes WC. 📷🗑 **Location:** Urban. **Surface:** metalled.
🅾 01/01-31/12.
**Distance:** 🚶100m 🏊1,3km 🎣on the spot ⊗200m 🛒300m 🎣on
the spot.
**Remarks:** Max. 72h.

🚐Ⓢ **Noirmoutier-en-l'Ile** 🚃🌳 **18A3**
Place R. Ganachaud, l'Herbaudière. **GPS:** n47,02016 w2,30061.⬆️.

---

18 ⅗€ 5, 01/04-31/10 € 8, parking free 🚰€ 2/100liter 🗑
Ch🚰€ 2/1h. **Location:** Simple. **Surface:** asphalted.
🅾 01/01-31/12.
**Distance:** 🚶on the spot 🏊on the spot ⊗350m.
**Remarks:** Parking behind town hall, max. 72h.

**Tourist information Noirmoutier-en-l'Ile:**
⚓ Place de la République. 🅾 Fri.
Sealand Aquarium, Le Vieux Port.

🚐Ⓢ **Notre-Dame-de-Monts** **18A3**
10 Route de la Taillée. **GPS:** n46,83125 w2,12092.⬆️.
12 ⅗€ 12 🚰🗑Ch♿€ 2 WC. **Location:** Urban. **Surface:** metalled.
🅾 01/01-31/12.
**Distance:** 🚶800m 🏖beach 2km ⊗on the spot 🛒750m.

🚐Ⓢ **Notre-Dame-de-Monts** **18A3**
**Aire de la Clairière**, Rue de la Clairière.
**GPS:** n46,83460 w2,14282.⬆️➡️.

35 ⅗€ 7/20-8h, 01/10-31/03 € 5/20-8h 🚰🗑Chincluded. 📷🚐
🗑 **Location:** Rural, simple, quiet. **Surface:** asphalted/gravel.
🅾 01/01-31/12 🅿 service: 01/12-01/04.
**Distance:** 🚶800m 🏖200m 🚲200m ⊗800m 🛒800m.
**Remarks:** Motorhome parking at the beach.

🚐Ⓢ **Notre-Dame-de-Monts** **18A3**
**Parking De Gaulle**, Rue des Maraichins. **GPS:** n46,83118 w2,13006.⬆️.

20 ⅗€ 7/20-8h, 01/10-31/03 € 5/20-8h 🚰🗑ChWCfree. 📷🌳
**Location:** Simple. **Surface:** asphalted.
🅾 01/01-31/12 🅿 service: 01/12-01/04.
**Distance:** 🚶300m ⊗500m 🛒300m.
**Remarks:** No camping activities.

🚐Ⓢ **Nozay** 🌳 **18B2**
Étang de Nozay. **GPS:** n47,57500 w1,62528.⬆️.

16 ⅗€ 8 🚰🗑Ch♿(16x)WCincluded. 📷🗑 **Location:** Simple.
**Surface:** gravel. 🅾 01/01-31/12 🅿 service: frost.
**Distance:** 🚶1,5km 🏊2km 🚲10m ⊗200m 🛒400m.
**Remarks:** Playground.

🚐Ⓢ **Olonne-sur-Mer** 👥 **21A1**
**Aire camping-cars OlonnEscale**, Rue des Anciens Combattants
d'Afrique du Nord. **GPS:** n46,53814 w1,77517.⬆️➡️.

21 ⌂€ 8/24h ⚡Ch✂ included. Location: Simple.
**Surface:** asphalted. ◘ 01/01-31/12.
**Distance:** 300m 6km 600m 300m.
**Remarks:** Jul/Aug max. 48h, max. 72h.

**S Olonne-sur-Mer 21A1**
**Port Olona**, Rue des Bossis. **GPS:** n46,50765 w1,78889.⬆➡.
38 ⌂€ 8/24h ⚡ included. Location: Rural, quiet.
**Surface:** asphalted. ◘ 01/01-31/12.
**Distance:** city centre 1,5km 1,5km 700m 650m.

**S Oudon 18B3**
**Aire de Camping-Car Oudon**, Rue de la Vieille Cour.
**GPS:** n47,34567 w1,28415.⬆.

8 ⌂free ⚡Ch. Location: Rural, simple, quiet.
**Surface:** grassy/gravel. ◘ 01/01-31/12.
**Distance:** 300m 500m 400m on the spot on the spot.
**Remarks:** Servicepoint at campsite 1km.

**S Pellouailles-les-Vignes 18C2**
Impasse de la Chapelle, D323. **GPS:** n47,52141 w0,43698.⬆.

3 ⌂free ⚡Chfree. Location: Rural, simple, quiet.
**Surface:** asphalted. ◘ 01/01-31/12.
**Distance:** on the spot 1,4km 100m bakery 50m.

**S Piacé 18D1**
**Fam. Michaud**, Rue de Vaugoust. **GPS:** n48,26031 e0,11567.

11 ⌂€ 6 €1 ⚡Ch✂(11x)€ 2/24h,6Amp WCincluded €2
€2. Location: Rural, comfortable. **Surface:** grassy/gravel.
◘ 01/01-31/12.
**Distance:** 200m 7km on the spot 5km 200m 300m.

**S Piriac-sur-Mer 14D3**
**Parking de Brambel**, Avenue du Général de Gaulle, D452.
**GPS:** n47,39647 w2,51292.⬆.

10 ⌂€ 6,50 €2/100liter ⚡ChWC. Location: Comfortable, quiet. **Surface:** metalled. ◘ 01/01-31/12.
**Distance:** 3km sandy beach 50m 2km 2km.
**Remarks:** Parking to sea.

**Piriac-sur-Mer 14D3**
**Parking de Lérat**, Route de Mesquêne, D99, Lieu-dit Lérat.
**GPS:** n47,36807 w2,53273.⬆.

30 ⌂€ 6,50 €2/100liter ⚡Ch. Location: Simple.
**Surface:** metalled. ◘ 01/01-31/12.
**Distance:** 2,5km 600m 600m 500m 500m.

**S Piriac-sur-Mer 14D3**
**Port de Piriac**, Rue de la Tranchée. **GPS:** n47,37861 w2,5422.⬆.

15 ⌂€ 6,50 €2/100liter ⚡Ch✂€2. Location: Simple, quiet. **Surface:** gravel. ◘ 01/01-31/12.
**Distance:** 500m 500m 500m.
**Tourist information Piriac-sur-Mer:**
⬆ 01/06-30/09 Mo + Wed + Sa-morning, 01/10-30/05 Tue.
Arts market. ◘ 01/07-31/08 Thu-evening.

**S Pontmain 15C3**
**Parking de la Mairie**, Le Bourg. **GPS:** n48,43796 w1,06042.⬆➡.

50 ⌂free ⚡Chfree. Location: Urban, simple, quiet.
**Surface:** gravel. ◘ 01/01-31/12.
**Distance:** on the spot 600m.
**Remarks:** Max. 1 night, picnic tables available.

**S Pornic 18A3**
Le Val Saint-Martin. **GPS:** n47,12053 w2,09162.⬆➡.

7 ⌂free €2/100liter ⚡Ch. Location: Comfortable, isolated.
**Surface:** asphalted. ◘ 01/01-31/12.
**Distance:** city centre 1,5km.

**Remarks:** Next to swimming pool.
**S Pouancé 18B2**
Rue de l'Hippodrome, Aubin. **GPS:** n47,75223 w1,18007.⬆➡.

5 ⌂€ 4,40 ⚡Ch✂(4x)WCfree. Location: Rural, simple, quiet. **Surface:** grassy. ◘ 01/01-31/12.
**Distance:** 500m small beach 20m 20m 1km 1km.
**Remarks:** Along étang de Saint-Aubin.

**S Pouzauges 21C1**
**Parking de la Vallée**, D49/D203. **GPS:** n46,77639 w0,82861.⬆➡.

20 ⌂free ⚡Chfree WC. Location: Simple. **Surface:** asphalted.
◘ 01/01-31/12.
**Distance:** 1km 1km 1km.

**S Préfailles 18A3**
**Camping-Car Park de La Pointe**, Chemin du Port aux Anes.
**GPS:** n47,13872 w2,22213.⬆.

49 ⌂€ 11,20 ⚡Ch✂(49x) included. Location: Comfortable. **Surface:** asphalted/gravel. ◘ 01/01-31/12.
**Distance:** 1,5km 800m 1,5km.
**Remarks:** Mandatory, one-time fee Pass'Etapes € 4.

**S Préfailles 18A3**
**Camping-Car Park Les Pinettes**, D313, chemin des Pinettes.
**GPS:** n47,13663 w2,23843.

39 ⌂€ 12 ⚡Ch included. Location: Rural, simple, quiet.
**Surface:** gravel/metalled. ◘ 01/01-31/12.
**Distance:** 3km 50m 200m 3km.
**Remarks:** Mandatory, one-time fee Pass'Etapes € 4, baker every morning.

**Préfailles 18A3**
**Aire de Biochon**, Chemin de Levertrie. **GPS:** n47,12973 w2,19028.

70 ☐€ 5-7,20 + € 0,40-1,20/pp tourist tax. **Location:** Rural, simple, quiet. **Surface:** gravel/sand. ☐ 01/01-31/12.
**Distance:** 3km 500m 500m 3km 3km.
**Remarks:** Max. 48h, baker every morning, service 300m.

### Préfailles 18A3
Rue de la Prée. **GPS:** n47,13439 w2,2117.
€ 2,50/100liter Ch. **Location:** Simple. ☐ 01/01-31/12.
**Remarks:** Coins at tourist info.

### Pruillé-l'Éguillé 18E2
**Berce Loisirs**, La Quellerie. **GPS:** n47,82509 e0,42632.

23 ☐€ 7 €2 Ch (23x)€ 2/24h WC 1.
**Location:** Rural, comfortable, quiet. **Surface:** grassy/gravel.
☐ 01/01-31/12.
**Distance:** 1,2km on the spot 1,2km on the spot on the spot.
**Remarks:** At fish pond, barbecue place.

### Rablay sur Layon 18C3
**Parking les Lavandières**, D54. **GPS:** n47,29772 w0,57767.

5 ☐free Ch WC free. **Location:** Rural, simple, quiet.
**Surface:** gravel/sand. ☐ 01/03-31/08.
**Distance:** 300m.

### Riaille 18B2
Rue de la Benate. **GPS:** n47,51412 w1,28803.

5 ☐free Ch WC free. **Location:** Rural, simple, quiet.
**Surface:** gravel. ☐ 01/01-31/12.
**Distance:** 700m 700m 700m.
**Remarks:** Max. 48h.

### Rouans 18A3
**Aire naturelle de Messan**, Route des Marais.
**GPS:** n47,19272 w1,85419.

8 ☐€ 4, tourist tax € 0,60/pp Ch WC free.
**Location:** Rural, simple. **Surface:** grassy/metalled.
☐ 01/01-31/12.
**Distance:** 1km on the spot on the spot 1km.
**Remarks:** To be paid at town hall.

### Saint-Aubin-de-Luigné 18C3
**Domaine La Biquerie**, Domaine viticole de la Biquerie D17.
**GPS:** n47,30843 w0,70211.

30 ☐free Ch free.
**Location:** Rural, simple, quiet. **Surface:** grassy.
☐ 01/01-31/12.
**Distance:** 5km 5km 5km 5km on the spot on the spot.

### Saint-Aubin-de-Luigné 18C3
**Camping du Layon**, Rue Jean de Pontoise.
**GPS:** n47,32796 w0,67112.

10 ☐€ 2,50 Ch included. **Location:** Urban, central, quiet.
**Surface:** asphalted. ☐ 01/05-30/09.
**Distance:** 50m 100m 250m 250m 250m on the spot on the spot.
**Remarks:** Max. 7 days, pay at campsite or town hall.

### Saint-Calais 18E2
**Boulevard du Docteur Gigon**. **GPS:** n47,92416 e0,74459.

7 ☐free Ch (2x)WC free. **Location:** Rural, simple, quiet.
**Surface:** asphalted. ☐ 01/01-31/12.
**Distance:** 400m on the spot.

### Saint-Calais 18E2
Le Champ Long, D249. **GPS:** n47,93375 e0,74568.

15 ☐free WC. **Location:** Rural, simple. **Surface:** asphalted.
☐ 01/01-31/12.
**Distance:** 1,6km lake on the spot on the spot.

### Saint-Clément-des-Levées 18D3
Rue de la Laiterie. **GPS:** n47,33064 w0,18042.

10 ☐free €2 Ch. **Location:** Simple. **Surface:** metalled.
☐ 01/01-31/12.
**Distance:** 300m.
**Remarks:** Coins at the shops and town hall.

### Saint-Cyr-en-Bourg 18D3
**Cave de Saumur**, Route de Saumoussay.
**GPS:** n47,19642 w0,07266.

15 ☐free Ch WC free. **Location:** Rural, simple, quiet.
**Surface:** asphalted. ☐ 15/03-15/09.
**Distance:** 3km 500m.
**Remarks:** Max. 48h, wine tasting 300m.

### Saint-Georges-sur-Loire 18C2
**Place Manche Real**, Rue de la Villette. **GPS:** n47,40610 w0,76301.

12 ☐free Ch free. **Location:** Rural, simple, quiet.
**Surface:** asphalted. ☐ 01/01-31/12.
**Distance:** 300m 100m 300m 300m.
**Remarks:** Next to the old abbey, max. 72h.

### Saint-Gervais 18A3
Route de St Urbain. **GPS:** n46,89999 w2,00134.
10 ☐free € 3/10minutes Ch € 3/55minutes.
☐ 01/01-31/12.
**Distance:** 300m 300m.

### Saint-Gilles-Croix-de-Vie 21A1
**La Rabalette**, Rue de la Rabalette. **GPS:** n46,70302 w1,94728.

35 ☐free, 15/03-15/11 € 6,50 €2,60/10minutes Ch.
**Location:** Urban, simple. **Surface:** asphalted. ☐ 01/01-31/12.
**Distance:** 500m 1km 500m 500m.
**Remarks:** Nearby lake Soudinière, coins at tourist info.

### Saint-Gilles-Croix-de-Vie 21A1
**Stade de la Chapelle**, Rue du Bois. **GPS:** n46,69449 w1,92716.

30 ☐free, 15/03-15/11 € 6,50 €2,60 Ch.
**Location:** Urban, simple, quiet. **Surface:** unpaved.
☐ 01/04-30/09 weekend and school holidays.
**Distance:** 500m.
**Remarks:** Max. 48h, coins at tourist info.
**Tourist information Saint-Gilles-Croix-de-Vie:**
☐ St.Gilles: Tue, Thu, Su; Croix de Vie; Wed, Sa.

### Saint-Hilaire-de-Chaléons 18A3
Rue Eloi Guitteny, D61. **GPS:** n47,10389 w1,86639.

2 ⌘free ⚡🔌ChWCfree. **Location:** Comfortable, central.
**Surface:** asphalted. 🅿 01/01-31/12.
**Distance:** 🚶100m 🏊500m 🚊100m.
**Remarks:** Next to campsite de l'Etoile, max. 24h.

### Saint-Hilaire-de-Riez 🏖🌊 21A1
**Base des vallées**, Chemin des Vallées. **GPS:** n46,73154 w1,91132.⬆

10 ⌘free ⚡€ 2,60/10minutes 🔌Ch 🧹 **Location:** Rural, simple.
**Surface:** asphalted. 🅿 01/01-31/12.
**Distance:** 🚶St.Hilaire 3,7km 🏊7km.

### Saint-Hilaire-de-Riez 🏖🌊 21A1
**Parking des Becs**, Avenue des Becs. **GPS:** n46,76040 w2,02656.⬆➡

20 ⌘€ 6/24h ⚡€ 2,60/10minutes 🔌Ch. 🚐 🧹
**Location:** Simple. **Surface:** asphalted.
🅿 01/01-31/12.
**Distance:** 🚶100m 🏊sandy beach 750m ⊗200m.
**Remarks:** Recreation park, max. 3 nights, lock-up parking, guarded.

### Saint-Hilaire-de-Riez 🏖🌊 21A1
**Allée de la Plage de la Parée Préneau. GPS:** n46,72865 w1,99167.⬆

48 ⌘free, night € 6. 🚐 **Location:** Rural. **Surface:** metalled.
🅿 01/01-31/12.
**Distance:** 🏊on the spot.
**Remarks:** Beach parking.

### Saint-Hilaire-de-Riez 🏖🌊 21A1
**Champ Gaillard**, Avenue de Baisse. **GPS:** n46,76903 w2,03337.⬆

28 ⌘free. **Location:** Rural, isolated. **Surface:** gravel. 🅿 01/01-31/12.
**Distance:** 🏊sandy beach 1km.

### Saint-Jean-de-Monts 21A1
**Le Repos des Tortues**, 38 rue de Notre Dame de Monts.
**GPS:** n46,79879 w2,07344.⬆

98 ⌘€ 9, 01/07-31/08 € 12 ⚡🔌Ch 🧹 (49x),4Amp WC 🔲€ 4,50
📶included. 🚐 🧹 **Location:** Rural, luxurious. **Surface:** grassy/gravel.
🅿 01/01-31/12.
**Distance:** 🚶800m 🏊1,5km ⊗50m 🚊2km 🛒400m.
**Remarks:** Video surveillance.

### Saint-Jean-de-Monts 21A1
**Aire de stationnement des Pimprenelles**, Rue des Pimprenelles.
**GPS:** n46,78837 w2,07986.⬆

20 ⌘€ 9-13,66, tourist tax incl ⚡🔌Ch 🧹included. 🚐 🧹
**Location:** Comfortable, noisy. **Surface:** asphalted.
🅿 01/04-01/11.
**Distance:** 🏊sandy beach 200m.

**Tourist information Saint-Jean-de-Monts:**
🏠 🅿 Wed, Sa.

### Saint-Jean-sur-Mayenne 🌊 18C1
**Les Marchanderies. GPS:** n48,12793 w0,75244.⬆➡

25 ⌘€ 9 ⚡🔌Ch 🧹 WC included. 🚿 **Location:** Rural, luxurious,
quiet. **Surface:** grassy/gravel. 🅿 01/03-30/11.
**Distance:** 🚶500m 🏊on the spot ⊗300m 🛒400m bakery
🚶on the spot.
**Remarks:** Along the Mayenne river.

### Saint-Léonard-des-Bois 🌲 18D1
**Aire Municipale**, Le Gué Plard. **GPS:** n48,35318 w0,08127.⬆

6 ⌘free ⚡🔌Chfree.
**Location:** Rural, simple, quiet. **Surface:** asphalted/grassy.
🅿 01/01-31/12.
**Distance:** 🚶350m.
**Remarks:** Max. 1 night, departure Vélorail, € 15 per bike for 4 pers.

### Saint-Mars-la-Jaille 🏖🌊 18B2
**Square de La Commune Libre du Bouffay**, Rue Neuve.
**GPS:** n47,52327 w1,18357.⬆➡

12 ⌘free ⚡🔌ChWCfree. **Location:** Rural, comfortable, quiet.
**Surface:** asphalted. 🅿 01/01-31/12.
**Distance:** 🚶200m 🏊on the spot 🚶on the spot.
**Remarks:** Parking at small lake, max. 48h, playground.

### Saint-Michel-Chef-Chef 18A3
**Camping-Car Park Le Thar-Cor La Plaine sur Mer**, Avenue Cormier.
**GPS:** n47,16017 w2,16881.⬆

24 ⌘€ 8,40-15,80 + € 1/pp tourist tax ⚡🔌Ch 🧹(4x) 📶included.
🚐 🧹 **Location:** Simple, isolated, quiet. **Surface:** gravel/metalled.
🅿 01/01-31/12.
**Distance:** 🏊sandy beach 400m 🚶400m 🚊400m.
**Remarks:** Mandatory, one-time fee Pass'Etapes € 4.

### Saint-Michel-Chef-Chef 18A3
**Mairie de Saint-Michel-Chef-Chef**, Rue du Chevecier.
**GPS:** n47,18209 w2,14664.⬆

30 ⌘€ 3,30, 20-8h € 9,30 ⚡🔌Chincluded.
**Location:** Simple. **Surface:** asphalted.
🅿 01/01-31/12.
**Distance:** 🚶300m ⊗300m 🚊300m.
**Remarks:** Parking townhall, coins at tourist info and town hall.

### Saint-Michel-Chef-Chef 18A3
**Camping Clos Mer et Nature**, Route de Tharon.
**GPS:** n47,17309 w2,15779.⬆

### Saint-Loup-du-Gast 15C3
**Zone d'Activité du Creusot. GPS:** n48,38750 w0,58548.⬆➡

10 ⌘free ⚡🔌ChWCfree. **Location:** Rural, simple, quiet.
**Surface:** asphalted. 🅿 01/01-31/12.
**Distance:** 🚶500m 🏊on the spot 🚶on the spot ⊗500m 🚶on the
spot 🚶on the spot 🚶on the spot.

🚰€6 🚽€2/100liter 🗑Ch🚻€2. **Location:** Simple, quiet.
**Surface:** grassy. ⏻ 01/01-31/12.
**Distance:** 🚶500m ⛱sandy beach 400m 🛒300m.
**Remarks:** Check in at reception campsite.

### Saint-Michel-en-l'Herm 21B2

1 Route de la Mer, D60. **GPS:** n46,35161 w1,24821.⬆.

4🚐free 🚽€2 🗑Ch. **Location:** Simple. **Surface:** asphalted/gravel.
⏻ 01/01-31/12.
**Distance:** 🚶200m ⊗200m 🛒200m.
**Remarks:** Max. 48h, max. 7m, coins at the shops.

### Saint-Michel-et-Chanveaux 18B2

**Aire de la Coulée Verte**, Rue de Bretagne.
**GPS:** n47,68034 w1,13252.⬆.

4🚐free 🚽🚿free. **Location:** Quiet. **Surface:** unpaved.
⏻ 01/01-31/12.
**Distance:** ⛱on the spot ⊗100m.

### Saint-Michel-Mont-Mercure 21C1

Place du Sommet. **GPS:** n46,83222 w0,88222.⬆➡.

20🚐free 🚽€2/100liter 🗑Ch. **Location:** Simple, isolated.
**Surface:** gravel. ⏻ 01/01-31/12.
**Distance:** 🚶500m ⊗on the spot 🛒500m.

### Saint-Nazaire 18A3

**Parking du Théâtre**, Boulevard Paul Leferme. **GPS:** n47,27895 w2.⬆.

28🚐€7,65 🚽€4/10minutes 🗑Ch🚿included. 🅿.
**Location:** Urban, simple, isolated. **Surface:** metalled. ⏻ 01/01-31/12.
**Distance:** 🚶on the spot 🛒500m 🚌50m.
**Remarks:** Free bus to centre.

### Saint-Nazaire 18A3

Route de l'Océan, D292, Saint-Marc-sur-Mer.
**GPS:** n47,23700 w2,30033.⬆.

15🚐free 🚽€4/100liter 🗑Ch🚻€4/1h 🚿. **Location:** Rural, simple,
quiet. **Surface:** gravel. ⏻ 01/01-31/12.
**Distance:** 🚶2km ⊗100m 🚌100m.

### Saint-Nazaire 18A3

Quai du Port de Méan. **GPS:** n47,29937 w2,18333.
3🚐free. **Surface:** metalled. ⏻ 01/01-31/12.
**Distance:** 🚶4km ⊗1km 🛒150m.

### Saint-Nazaire 18A3

Route du Bois Joalland. **GPS:** n47,27954 w2,26229.⬆.

5🚐free.
**Location:** Simple, central. **Surface:** gravel. ⏻ 01/01-31/12.
**Distance:** 🚶500m ⛱on the spot 🎣on the spot 🚲on the spot
🏊on the spot.

### Saint-Philbert-de-Grand-Lieu 18B3

Chemin de la Plage. **GPS:** n47,04500 w1,64172.⬆➡.

25🚐free 🚽🗑Chfree WC. **Location:** Central. **Surface:** gravel.
⏻ 01/01-31/12.
**Distance:** 🚶1km ⛱on the spot 🎣on the spot ⊗550m 🛒1km.

### Saint-Rémy-la-Varenne 18D3

Rue St Aubin-D132. **GPS:** n47,39805 w0,31612.⬆➡.

3🚐free 🚽🗑ChWCfree. **Location:** Urban, simple, quiet.
**Surface:** asphalted. ⏻ 01/01-31/12.
**Distance:** 🚶on the spot ⊗100m 🛒100m 🚌150m 🚲on the spot
🏊on the spot.
**Remarks:** Shady.

### Saint-Saturnin 18D1

**Camping-car Park**, Rue de l'Antonnière. **GPS:** n48,06236 e0,15603.
16🚐€10,80 🚽🗑Ch🚿(16x),6Amp 📶included. **Location:** Urban,
comfortable. ⏻ 01/01-31/12.
**Distance:** ⊗500m.
**Remarks:** Mandatory, one-time fee Pass'Etapes €4.

### Saint-Saturnin-sur-Loire 18C3

Route de Saumur, D751. **GPS:** n47,39245 w0,43285.⬆➡.

3🚐free 🚽🗑Chfree. **Location:** Urban, simple, quiet.
**Surface:** metalled. ⏻ 01/01-31/12.
**Distance:** 🚶on the spot ⊗100m 🛒100m 🚌100m 🚲on the spot
🏊on the spot.
**Remarks:** Nearby bus station, shady.

### Saint-Viaud 18A3

Rue de Couetard. **GPS:** n47,25911 w2,0198.
20🚐free. **Location:** Rural, simple, central, noisy. **Surface:** grassy.
⏻ 01/01-31/12.
**Distance:** 🚶on the spot ⊗300m 🛒650m 🚲on the spot.

### Saint-Vincent-sur-Jard 21B1

**Aire du Goulet**, Chemin des Roulettes, Le Goulet.
**GPS:** n46,41038 w1,5413.⬆➡.

30🚐€5,75, 01/04-15/11 €9,20 🚽1h 🗑Ch🚻included1h. 🅿
🚿 **Location:** Rural, simple. **Surface:** metalled. ⏻ 01/01-31/12
⏻ Service: winter. **Distance:** 🚶1km ⛱100m ⊗400m.

### Sainte-Foy 21A1

Rue Maurice Raimbaud. **GPS:** n46,54568 w1,67306.
3🚐free 🚽🗑Ch🚿free. **Location:** Simple, central.
**Surface:** asphalted. ⏻ 01/04-31/10.
**Distance:** 🚶on the spot ⊗on the spot 🎣on the spot 🏊on the spot.
**Remarks:** Behind church, max. 48h, max. 8M.

### Sainte-Suzanne 18D1

**Camping-Car Park**, 15 rue du Camp des Anglais.
**GPS:** n48,09933 w0,35044.
21🚐€10,20, 01/06-30/09 €12,60 🚽🗑Ch🚿(20x) 📶included. 🅿
🚿 **Location:** Rural, comfortable, quiet. **Surface:** gravel/metalled.
⏻ 01/01-31/12.
**Distance:** 🚶200m ⊗200m.
**Remarks:** Mandatory, one-time fee Pass'Etapes €4.

### Sallertaine 18A3

**Camping-Car Park**, Route de Saint Urbain. **GPS:** n46,86032 w1,9607.
30🚐€8,44-10,44 🚽🗑Chincluded. 🅿 🚿 ⏻ 01/01-31/12.
**Remarks:** Mandatory, one-time fee Pass'Etapes €4.

### Saulgé l'Hôpital 18C3

**Terrain de Loisirs**, 4 Chemin de la Planche.
**GPS:** n47,29853 w0,38344.⬆⬆.

15🚐free 🚽🗑Chfree. **Location:** Rural, simple, quiet.
**Surface:** gravel/metalled. ⏻ 01/01-31/12.
**Distance:** 🚶100m ⊗100m 🛒100m.
**Remarks:** Service 100m.

### Saumur 18D3

**Camping-car park Ile D'offard**, Rue de Verden.
**GPS:** n47,25993 w0,06489.⬆.
35🚐€13,50 🚽🗑Ch🚿(35x),6Amp 📶included. 🅿 🚿
**Location:** Rural. **Surface:** gravel. ⏻ 01/01-31/12.
**Distance:** ⊗1km.
**Remarks:** Mandatory, one-time fee Pass'Etapes €4.

**FR**

**Tourist information Saumur:**

ℹ Office de Tourisme, Place de la Bilange, www.saumur-tourisme.com. Historical city on the Loire river.
👁 Tuffeau. Wine-cellars in tuff.
Village Troglodyte, Rochemenier, Louresse. Cave dwelling village.
⏰ 01/04-31/10 9.30-19h, 01/11-30/11, 01/02-31/03 Sa-Su 14-18h.
🏛🏇 Château de Saumur. Castle, 13th century, with museum for decorative art and horse museum. ⏰ 9.30-23h, 14-17.30h. 🎫 € 6.

### Segré 18C2

**Aire de l'Europe**, D775. GPS: n47,68497 w0,85719. 🔼

4 🚐 free 🚰🚽 Ch WC free. **Location:** Rural, simple, noisy. **Surface:** asphalted. ⏰ 01/01-31/12. **Distance:** 🛒 1km 🍴 on the spot.

### Segré 18C2

**Place du Moulin sous la Tour**, Rue Emile Zola. GPS: n47,68409 w0,87436. ➡

10 🚐 free 🚰🚽 Ch WC free. **Location:** Urban, simple, quiet. **Surface:** asphalted/gravel. ⏰ 01/01-31/12 ⚙ Service: winter. **Distance:** 🛒 300m ➤ on the spot ⊗ 100m 🍴 on the spot. **Remarks:** Steep entrance road.

### Segré 18C2

**Place du Port.** GPS: n47,68643 w0,86445. 🔼➡

10 🚐 free 🚰🚽 Ch free WC 🗑. **Location:** Urban, simple, noisy. **Surface:** asphalted. ⏰ 01/01-31/12. **Distance:** 🛒 on the spot 🍴 on the spot ⊗ 600m 🏧 500m. **Remarks:** Picnic area.

### Sillé-le-Guillaume 18D1

2, Place de la Gare. GPS: n48,18167 w0,13111. 🔼➡

8 🚐 free 🚰 € 3/80liter 🚽 Ch 🔌 € 3/2h. **Location:** Urban, simple, noisy. **Surface:** asphalted. ⏰ 01/01-31/12. **Distance:** 🛒 300m ⊗ 300m 🏧 400m 🚆 train 50m. **Remarks:** Coins at tourist info.

### Souvigné-sur-Sarthe 18D2

**Le Val de Taude**, Rue de la Vallée. GPS: n47,82782 w0,38896. 🔼➡

5 🚐 free. **Location:** Rural, simple, isolated, quiet. **Surface:** gravel. ⏰ 01/01-31/12. **Distance:** 🛒 200m.

### Talmont-Saint-Hilaire 21A1

**Parking des Gâtines**, Rue des Gâtines. GPS: n46,46761 w1,61718. 🔼

16 🚐 € 6,60/24h 🚰 € 3/10minutes 🚽 Ch 🔌 € 3/50minutes. 🗑🧺 **Location:** Rural, simple, quiet. **Surface:** asphalted. ⏰ 01/01-31/12. **Distance:** 🛒 500m 🏊 Small lake (100m) ⊗ 300m 🏧 100m.

### Talmont-Saint-Hilaire 21A1

**Parking du Château Guibert**, Avenue de la Plage. GPS: n46,44098 w1,66351. 🔼➡

16 🚐 € 6,60/24h 🚰 € 3/10minutes 🚽 Ch 🔌 € 3/50minutes WC 🧺. 🗑🧺 **Location:** Rural, simple. **Surface:** metalled. ⏰ 01/01-31/12. **Distance:** 🛒 600m 🏊 1km ⊗ 300m 🏧 800m. **Remarks:** Max. 48h.

### Tennie 18D1 🍴🧺

Rue du Camping. GPS: n48,10636 w0,0786. 🔼

6 🚐 free. **Location:** Rural, simple, quiet. **Surface:** gravel. ⏰ 01/01-31/12. **Distance:** 🏊 on the spot ➤ on the spot ⊗ 250m 🍴 on the spot. **Remarks:** At lake.

### Thoiré-sur-Dinan 18E2

19 rue Gabriel Guyon. GPS: n47,75343 e0,44621. 🔼

4 🚐 € 5 🚰🚽 Ch 🔧 included. 🧺 **Location:** Rural, comfortable, quiet. **Surface:** gravel. ⏰ 01/01-31/12. **Remarks:** Picnic and barbecue place.

### Turquant 18D3

**Aire Municipal**, Rue des Ducs d'Anjou. GPS: n47,22393 e0,02858. 🔼➡

20 🚐 free 🚰 € 2,50 🚽 Ch WC. **Location:** Simple, central. **Surface:** metalled. ⏰ 01/01-31/12. **Distance:** 🛒 100m ⊗ 50m 🏧 50m 🍴 on the spot 🏍 on the spot 🍽 on the spot. **Remarks:** Behind church, coins at the shops in the village.

### Vaiges 18C1

Rue Robert Gletron, D57. GPS: n48,04189 w0,48285. 🔼

5 🚐 free 🚰 € 3 🚽 Ch. **Location:** Urban, simple, noisy. **Surface:** gravel. ⏰ 01/01-31/12. **Distance:** 🛒 500m 🥖 1,7km 🏧 20m 🏧 700m bakery.

### Valanjou 18C3

**Aire de Plaisance**, Rue de la Mairie. GPS: n47,21658 w0,60326. 🔼

6 🚐 free 🚰🚽 Ch WC free. **Location:** Rural, simple, quiet. **Surface:** metalled. ⏰ 01/03-31/10. **Distance:** 🛒 200m ➤ on the spot ⊗ 300m 🏧 300m 🍴 on the spot 🍽 on the spot. **Remarks:** Nearby town hall.

### Vauchrétien 18C3

**Domaine Dittiére**, Chemin de la Grouas Vauchrétien. GPS: n47,33273 w0,47231. 🔼

5 🚐 free 🚰 free. **Location:** Rural, simple, quiet. **Surface:** gravel. ⏰ 01/01-31/12. **Distance:** 🛒 500m ⊗ 500m.

### Venansault 21B1

Rue Pierre Nicolas Loué. GPS: n46,68250 w1,51472.

5 🚐 free. **Location:** Urban, noisy. **Surface:** sand. ⏰ 01/01-31/12. **Distance:** 🛒 500m 🏊 100m ⊗ 300m 🏧 500m.

FR

## Vendrennes 21B1

Route de l'Océan. **GPS:** n46,82690 w1,1217. ⬆.

10 🛢free 🚰€ 3/150liter 🗑ChWC. **Location:** Rural, simple, quiet.
**Surface:** metalled. ⬜ 01/01-31/12.
**Distance:** 🛒200m.
**Remarks:** Coins at the bakery.

## Vihiers 18C3

5 Rue Champ de Foire des Champs. **GPS:** n47,14355 w0,5358. ⬆➡.

10 🛢free 🚰🗑ChWCfree. **Location:** Urban, simple, quiet.
**Surface:** asphalted. ⬜ 01/01-31/12.
**Distance:** 🛒50m ⊗100m 🍴100m.

## Villebernier 18D3

**Camping-Car Park le Port Roux**, Le Port Roux.
**GPS:** n47,25395 w0,03454. ⬆➡.
40 🛢€ 9,15, 01/07-31/08 € 10,35 🚰🗑Ch 🧹 📶included. 📦🔌
**Location:** Rural. **Surface:** grassy.
⬜ 01/01-31/12.
**Remarks:** Along Loire river, mandatory, one-time fee Pass'Etapes € 4.

## Villeveque 18C2

Rue du Port. **GPS:** n47,56222 w0,42257. ⬆➡.

6 🛢free 🚰€ 2/100liter 🗑ChWCfree. **Location:** Rural, comfortable, quiet. **Surface:** gravel/metalled. ⬜ 01/01-31/12.
**Distance:** 🛒100m 🏊on the spot ⊗50m 🍴bakery 200m 🚲on the spot 🧍on the spot.
**Remarks:** Coins at town hall.

## Villiers-Charlemagne 18C1

**Village Vacances et Pêche**, Rue des Haies.
**GPS:** n47,92083 w0,68167. ⬆➡.

25 🛢€ 5/night 🚰🗑Chincluded. **Location:** Rural, comfortable, quiet.
**Surface:** grassy. ⬜ 01/01-31/12.
**Distance:** 🏊on the spot 🍴500m 🧍on the spot.
**Remarks:** Fishing permit available.

## Vouvant 21C1

Rue de Château Neuf. **GPS:** n46,57462 w0,77462. ⬆➡.

20 🛢€ 5/night 🚰🗑Chfree. **Surface:** gravel. ⬜ 01/01-31/12.
**Distance:** 🛒500m ⊗500m 🍴500m.

# Centre-Val de Loire

## Ainay-le-Vieil 21H1

La Tuilerie. **GPS:** n46,66159 e2,55582. ⬆➡.

6 🛢free 🚰🗑ChWCfree. **Location:** Rural, simple, quiet.
**Surface:** grassy. ⬜ 01/01-31/12.
**Distance:** 🛒850m ⊗800m.
**Remarks:** Castle 1km.

## Allogny 📶 18G3

D944. **GPS:** n47,21913 e2,32329. ⬆➡.

10 🛢free 🚰🗑ChWCfree. **Location:** Rural, simple, isolated, noisy.
**Surface:** asphalted. ⬜ 01/01-31/12.
**Distance:** 🛒800m 🏊50m 🍴50m.

## Amboise 🌿🏊🍴🎣 18E3

**Vinci Park**, Allée de la Chapelle Saint-Jean.
**GPS:** n47,41761 e0,98742. ⬆.

20 🛢€ 12/24h 🚰🗑Chincluded 🧹(20x)€ 2 🔌.
📦 **Location:** Rural, comfortable, central, quiet.
**Surface:** asphalted/grassy. ⬜ 01/01-31/12.
**Distance:** 🛒200m 🏊200m ⊗200m 🍴200m 🚲on the spot
🧍on the spot.
**Remarks:** Next to campsite, castle 500m.

## Amboise 🌿🏊🍴🎣 18E3

**Parking St. Jean**, Avenue Leonardo da Vinci 43, D61.
**GPS:** n47,40814 e0,98986. ⬆➡.

11 🛢free. **Location:** Urban, simple, quiet. **Surface:** asphalted.
⬜ 01/01-31/12.

**Distance:** 🛒on the spot ⊗1,5km 🍴1,5km 🚲on the spot.

## Angé 18F3

Place de la Mairie. **GPS:** n47,33239 e1,24450. ⬆➡.

20 🛢€ 8 🚰€ 3/100liter 🗑Ch 🧹 📶free.
**Location:** Urban, simple, central, quiet. **Surface:** gravel/sand.
⬜ 01/01-31/12.
**Distance:** 🛒on the spot ⊗50m.
**Remarks:** Coins at town hall and supermarket.

## Ardentes 21G1

Avenue de Verdun. **GPS:** n46,74682 e1,82826. ⬆.

4 🛢free 🚰€ 2,50/10minutes 🗑Ch 🧹€ 4/4h WC 🔌.
**Location:** Motorway, noisy. **Surface:** gravel. ⬜ 01/01-31/12.
**Distance:** 🛒on the spot 🍴on the spot.

## Argenton-sur-Creuse 21F1

Rue de la Grenouille. **GPS:** n46,58715 e1,52497. ⬆➡.

15 🛢free. **Location:** Urban, simple, noisy. **Surface:** sand.
⬜ 01/01-31/12.
**Distance:** 🛒50m 🚂3,4km 🍴500m.

## Argenton-sur-Creuse 21F1

Alleé du Champ de Foire. **GPS:** n46,58501 e1,52283. ⬆.
🚰🗑ChWCfree. **Location:** Rural, simple. ⬜ 01/01-31/12.
**Distance:** 🛒on the spot.

## Athée-sur-Cher 18E3

**Aire d'Athée-sur-Cher**, D83, Rue de Cigogné.
**GPS:** n47,31439 e0,91756. ⬆➡.

3 🛢free 🚰🗑Chfree. **Location:** Rural, simple, isolated, quiet.
**Surface:** metalled. ⬜ 01/01-31/12 🔲 service: frost.
**Distance:** 🛒800m 🚂11km 🍴1,5km 🚂1km 🚲on the spot.
**Remarks:** Max. 24h.

## Aubigny-sur-Nère 🌿🏊 18H3

Parc des Sports, D7. **GPS:** n47,48201 e2,44995. ⬆➡.

FR

9 ⌶free ⌷⌷Chfree. **Location:** Rural, simple, isolated, quiet.
**Surface:** asphalted. ⌷ 01/01-31/12.
**Distance:** ⌷1km ⌷1km ⌷2km on the spot ⌷on the spot.
**Remarks:** Playground.

| ⌷S | Aubigny-sur-Nère 🌿🏖 | 18H3 |

**Parking du Pré qui Danse**, Mail Guichard.
**GPS:** n47,49140 e2,43830.⌷.

10 ⌶free ⌷⌷Chfree. **Location:** Urban, simple, noisy.
**Surface:** asphalted. ⌷ 01/01-31/12.
**Distance:** ⌷200m ⌷200m ⌷200m ⌷100m.

| ⌷S | Avoine 🏖💦 | 18D3 |

Avenue de la République. **GPS:** n47,21287 e0,17706.⌷.

11 ⌶€ 5 ⌷€ 2/10minutes ⌷Ch ⌷(11x)€ 2/24h
⌷⌷ **Location:** Rural, comfortable, central, quiet.
**Surface:** asphalted/metalled. ⌷ 01/01-31/12.
**Distance:** ⌷1km ⌷Lac Mousseau 300m ⌷300m ⌷300m.
**Remarks:** Max. 3 nights.

| ⌷S | Azay-le-Rideau 🌿🏖🍽 | 18E3 |

**Camping-car Park**, Rue du Stade. **GPS:** n47,25925 e0,46992.⌷⌷.
48 ⌶€ 9,80, 01/06-30/09 € 11 ⌷⌷Ch ⌷(40x) ⌷included.
**Location:** Urban, comfortable, central, quiet. **Surface:** asphalted.
⌷ 01/01-31/12.
**Distance:** ⌷200m ⌷300m ⌷on the spot ⌷on the spot.
**Remarks:** Mandatory, one-time fee Pass'Etapes € 4.

| ⌷S | Azé | 18F2 |

**M et Mme Hersant**, Les Places, D957 Épuisay-Galette.
**GPS:** n47,86451 e0,97659.⌷⌷.

6 ⌶€ 10 ⌷⌷Ch ⌷included. ⌷ **Location:** Rural, comfortable,
isolated, quiet. **Surface:** grassy/gravel. ⌷ 01/01-31/12.
**Distance:** ⌷7km ⌷on the spot.

| ⌷S | Barlieu 🏖 | 18H3 |

Base de loisirs de Badineau. **GPS:** n47,47918 e2,63168.⌷.

15 ⌶€ 2, first night € 3,50 ⌷€ 2,50/100liter ⌷Ch ⌷€ 2,50/h
WC. ⌷ **Location:** Rural, simple, quiet. **Surface:** grassy/gravel.
⌷ 19/04-31/10.
**Distance:** ⌷1km ⌷on the spot ⌷on the spot.
**Remarks:** At small lake.

| ⌷ | Bauzy | 18F2 |

**L'étang communal**, Route de Neuvy. **GPS:** n47,53734 e1,60982.
3 ⌶free. **Location:** Rural. **Surface:** metalled. ⌷ 01/01-31/12.

| ⌷ | Benais | 18D3 |

Rue Saint-Vincent. **GPS:** n47,29875 e0,21598.⌷.

6 ⌶free. **Location:** Rural, simple, quiet. **Surface:** grassy.
⌷ 01/01-31/12.
**Distance:** ⌷350m ⌷350m ⌷on the spot ⌷on the spot.

| ⌷S | Bessais-le-Fromental | 21H1 |

**Base de loisirs de l'Étang de Goule**, Champ de la Croix.
**GPS:** n46,73402 e2,80034.⌷⌷.

50 ⌶free ⌷€ 2 ⌷Ch. **Location:** Rural, simple, isolated, quiet.
**Surface:** asphalted/grassy. ⌷ 01/01-31/12 ⌷ service: frost.
**Distance:** ⌷4km ⌷on the spot ⌷on the spot ⌷on camp site ⌷on
camp site.

| ⌷S | Blois 🌿🍽 | 18F2 |

**P2**, Rue Jean Moulin. **GPS:** n47,58653 e1,32641.⌷.

40 ⌶€ 8/24h ⌷⌷ChWC ⌷included. ⌷⌷ **Location:** Urban,
comfortable, central. **Surface:** asphalted. ⌷ 01/01-31/12.
**Distance:** ⌷on the spot ⌷7km ⌷100m ⌷100m ⌷on the spot.
**Tourist information Blois:**
⌷ Château de Blois.
⌷ Cathédrale St Louis.
⌷ Quatier Coty. ⌷ Wed 7-13h.

| ⌷S | Bonneval | 18F1 |

Rue de la Grève. **GPS:** n48,17980 e1,38840.⌷⌷.

8 ⌶free ⌷⌷ChWCfree. **Location:** Urban, simple, central, quiet.
**Surface:** asphalted. ⌷ 01/01-31/12.
**Distance:** ⌷200m ⌷200m ⌷350m.

| ⌷S | Bonny-sur-Loire 🌿💦 | 18H2 |

Chemin de la Cheuille. **GPS:** n47,55925 e2,83967.⌷.

3 ⌶free ⌷€ 2/100liter ⌷Ch ⌷€ 2/30minutes WC ⌷
⌷ **Location:** Rural, simple, central, quiet. **Surface:** gravel.
⌷ 01/05-30/09.
**Distance:** ⌷150m ⌷50m ⌷300m ⌷on the spot ⌷on the spot.
**Remarks:** Along La Cheuille river.

| ⌷S | Boulleret | 18H3 |

Place des Charmes. **GPS:** n47,42304 e2,87244.⌷⌷.

4 ⌶free ⌷€ 2/100liter ⌷Ch ⌷(1x)€ 2/6h WC ⌷free.
**Location:** Urban, simple, central. **Surface:** asphalted. ⌷ 01/01-31/12.
**Distance:** ⌷on the spot ⌷on the spot ⌷on the spot ⌷on the spot
⌷on the spot.
**Remarks:** Coins at the shops and restaurant, sanitary building: 01/05-
30/09.

| ⌷S | Bourges | 18G3 |

Rue du Pré Doulet. **GPS:** n47,08390 e2,38085.
15 ⌶free ⌷€ 2,50/100liter ⌷Ch ⌷€ 2,50/10minutes
⌷. **Location:** Urban, simple, central. **Surface:** gravel/sand.
⌷ 01/01-31/12.
**Distance:** ⌷1,5km ⌷700m ⌷on the spot ⌷on the spot.
**Tourist information Bourges:**
⌷ Ballades de Bourges. Festivities and market in the city centre.
⌷ 01/07-31/08.

| ⌷S | Bourgueil | 18D3 |

**Jardin de Tanneries**, Rue des Tanneries. **GPS:** n47,28014 e0,17058.⌷.

6 ⌶free. **Location:** Urban, simple, central, quiet. **Surface:** gravel/sand.
⌷ 01/01-31/12.
**Distance:** ⌷300m ⌷150m.
**Remarks:** Max. 1 night.

| ⌷ | Bourré 💦 | 18F3 |

**Domaine Deniau**, Route des Vaublins 18.
**GPS:** n47,35101 e1,24603.⌷⌷.

FR

6 ⌂free. **Location:** Rural, simple, isolated, quiet. **Surface:** forest soil. ◐ 01/01-31/12.
**Distance:** 2,5km 1km 1km.

### Brézolles 15F3

Rue de Verneuil, D939. **GPS:** n48,69083 e1,06972. ⬆.

10 ⌂free ⌐ Chfree. **Location:** Urban, simple, central, quiet.
**Surface:** gravel. ◐ 01/01-31/12.
**Distance:** 200m 200m.

### Briare-le-Canal 18H2

**Flot Bleu Park**, Val du Martinet. **GPS:** n47,64304 e2,72270. ⬆.

39 €9/24h ⌐ Chincluded. **Location:** Urban, comfortable, quiet. **Surface:** grassy. ◐ 01/01-31/12.
**Distance:** on the spot 4,5km on the spot on the spot 800m 800m 100m 500m.
**Remarks:** Max. 72h.

### Briare-le-Canal 18H2

7 Rue des Vignes. **GPS:** n47,63215 e2,73981. ⬆.

40 ⌂free ⌐ €2/100liter Ch €2. **Location:** Urban, simple, quiet. **Surface:** gravel. ◐ 01/01-31/12.
**Distance:** 300m 4,5km 50m 500m 800m on the spot on the spot.

### Céré-la-Ronde 18F3

**Camping-Car Park**, Rue du Stade. **GPS:** n47,25788 e1,18232. ⬆.

10 €8,40-10,80 Ch (10x) included. **Location:** Rural, simple, isolated. **Surface:** gravel. ◐ 01/01-31/12.
**Distance:** 500m.
**Remarks:** Mandatory, one-time fee Pass'Etapes €4.

### Chabris 18F3

Place du Champ de Foire. **GPS:** n47,25317 e1,65211. ⬆.

5 ⌂free ⌐ €2 Ch €2.
**Location:** Rural, central, quiet. **Surface:** gravel/metalled. ◐ 01/01-31/12.
**Distance:** on the spot 250m 250m.
**Remarks:** Coins at Tourist Info and Maison de la Presse (250m).

### Chaillac 21F2

**Camping-Car Park**, Les Vergnes. **GPS:** n46,43170 e1,28899.
15 €9,40-11,80 ⌐ Ch (15x) included. 
**Surface:** gravel/metalled. ◐ 01/01-31/12.
**Remarks:** Mandatory, one-time fee Pass'Etapes €4.

### Chambord 18F2

**Château de Chambord**, Place St.Louis. **GPS:** n47,61608 e1,51057.

100 €11/24h ⌐ €2/10minutes Ch €5/8h WC.
**Location:** Rural, simple, quiet. **Surface:** asphalted. ◐ 01/01-31/12.
**Distance:** 7km 300m 300m.
**Remarks:** Parking castle, max. 1 night.

### Champigny-sur-Veude 18D3

**Place du Chapeau Rouge**, Rue de la Bonne Dame.
**GPS:** n47,06499 e0,31773. ⬆ ➡.

8 ⌂free ⌐ Ch (2x)free. **Location:** Urban, simple, noisy.
**Surface:** asphalted. ◐ 01/01-31/12.
**Distance:** on the spot on the spot bakery 200m on the spot.
**Remarks:** At small lake.

### Chaon 18G2

**La Maison du Braconnage**, Rue des Genêts, D129.
**GPS:** n47,60942 e2,16611. ⬆ ➡.

10 ⌂free ⌐ Chfree. **Location:** Rural, simple, isolated, quiet.
**Surface:** grassy/metalled. ◐ 01/01-31/12.
**Distance:** 200m 200m bakery 50m.
**Remarks:** Video surveillance.

### Châteaudun 18F1

**Aire de Châteaudun**, 2 Rue des Fouleries.
**GPS:** n48,07172 e1,32421. ⬆ ➡.

7 ⌂free ⌐ €2/100liter Ch €2/20minutes WC.
**Location:** Urban, comfortable, central, quiet.
**Surface:** asphalted. ◐ 01/01-31/12.
**Distance:** 400m on the spot on the spot on the spot on the spot.
**Remarks:** Along Loir river, canoe rental, castel of Châteaudun 300m.

### Châteauroux 21F1

17, Avenue de Parc des Loisirs. **GPS:** n46,82278 e1,69507. ⬆.

5 ⌂free ⌐ €2,50/100liter Ch €2,50/h. **Location:** Urban, simple. **Surface:** asphalted. ◐ 01/05-31/10.
**Distance:** 3,6km 300m 2km 2km.
**Remarks:** Coins at campsite.

### Châtillon-Coligny 18H2

Rue du Loing. **GPS:** n47,81940 e2,84509.
⌂free ⌐ Ch WCfree. **Surface:** gravel. ◐ 01/01-31/12.
**Distance:** 250m 400m 450m.

### Châtillon-sur-Loire 18H2

Rue du Port. **GPS:** n47,59128 e2,76044. ⬆.

5 €9 ⌐ Ch €2 WCincluded. **Location:** Rural, comfortable, quiet. **Surface:** asphalted/gravel. ◐ 01/01-31/12.
**Distance:** 800m 9km A77 400m bakery 500m.
**Remarks:** At the canal.

### Chenonceaux 18F3

**Aire de Chenonceaux**, Chemin de la Varenne.
**GPS:** n47,33053 e1,06824. ⬆.

10 ⌂free. **Location:** Rural, simple, isolated, noisy. **Surface:** grassy. ◐ 01/01-31/12.
**Distance:** 500m 500m on the spot on the spot.
**Remarks:** Along railwayline.

### Chenonceaux 18F3

Rue du Château. **GPS:** n47,33020 e1,06648. ⬆.

**FR**

20 🛏free. **Location:** Rural, simple, isolated. **Surface:** metalled. 🗓 01/01-31/12.
**Distance:** 🚶500m ⊗500m 🚲 on the spot.
**Remarks:** Parking at castle of Chenonceaux, max. 24h.
**Tourist information Chenonceaux:**
✖ Castle.

| 🏕 S | **Cheverny** 🌿 | 18F2 |

**Château Cheverny P3**, D102. **GPS:** n47,49762 e1,46097. ⬆️➡️.

20 🛏free. **Location:** Rural, simple, quiet. **Surface:** grassy/metalled. 🗓 01/01-31/12.
**Distance:** 🚶250m ⊗250m 🛒250m bakery.
**Tourist information Cheverny:**
✖ Château Cheverny. Castle. 🗓 9.30-12h, 14.15-17h, Apr-Sep 9.30-18.15h.

| 🏕 S | **Chouzé-sur-Loire** | 18D3 |

**Aire de Chouzé-sur-Loire**, Rue de l'Eglise.
**GPS:** n47,23809 e0,12649. ⬆️➡️.

6 🛏free 🚰€2 🪠Ch. **Location:** Rural, comfortable, central, quiet.
**Surface:** gravel. 🗓 01/01-31/12.
**Distance:** 🚶on the spot ⊗250m 🛒on the spot 🚲on the spot 🚶on the spot.
**Remarks:** Coins at the shops and town hall.

| 🏕 S | **Civray-de-Touraine** 🏘 | 18F3 |

**Caves du Père Auguste**, 14 rue des Caves. **GPS:** n47,33497 e1,04718. ⬆️.

5 🛏free 🚰€2/120liter 🧺(4x)€4/24h WC🚿€3 🚿free.
**Location:** Rural, simple, quiet. **Surface:** asphalted.
🗓 01/01-31/12.
**Distance:** 🚶500m ⊗1,5km 🛒4km 🚶on the spot.

| 🏕 S | **Cloyes-sur-le-Loir** | 18F1 |

Rue du Colonel Boussa. **GPS:** n47,99171 e1,23216. ⬆️➡️.

5 🛏free 🚰€2 🪠Ch🔌€2/h. **Location:** Urban, simple.
**Surface:** asphalted. 🗓 01/01-31/12 💧 water: frost.
**Distance:** 🚶800m ⊗450m 🛒800m.

| 🏕 S | **Coullons** | 18H2 |

Place du Monument. **GPS:** n47,62012 e2,49319. ⬆️➡️.

10 🛏free 🚰🪠ChWCfree. **Location:** Urban, simple, quiet.
**Surface:** gravel. 🗓 01/01-31/12.
**Distance:** 🚶on the spot ⊗500m 🛒50m 🛒50m 🚶on the spot.

| 🏕 | **Courmemin** | 18F3 |

Rue des Tisserands. **GPS:** n47,47115 e1,62685.
3 🛏free. **Surface:** gravel. 🗓 01/01-31/12.
**Distance:** 🚶on the spot 🛒100m.
**Remarks:** Near church.

| 🏕 S | **Courville-sur-Eure** | 15F3 |

Avenue Thiers. **GPS:** n48,44600 e1,24166. ⬆️.
16 🛏free 🚰€2,50/100liter 🪠Ch🔌€2,50/55minutes.
**Surface:** asphalted. 🗓 01/01-31/12.
**Remarks:** Coins at campsite and shops.

| 🏕 S | **Culan** 🌿 | 21G2 |

Place du Champ de Foire. **GPS:** n46,54727 e2,34630. ⬆️.

20 🛏free 🚰€1,50/10minutes 🪠Ch🔌€1,50/h WC🚿.
**Location:** Urban, simple, noisy. **Surface:** asphalted.
🗓 01/01-31/12.
**Distance:** 🚶50m ⊗50m 🛒50m.
**Remarks:** Near office de tourisme, coins available at the shops.

| 🏕 | **Cuzion** 🌿🛥 | 21F2 |

**Base de Loisirs Pont des Piles**, Rue des Petites Côtes.
**GPS:** n46,45639 e1,61167. ⬆️➡️.

6 🛏free. **Location:** Isolated, quiet. **Surface:** grassy/metalled.
🗓 01/01-31/12.
**Remarks:** At castle, max. 1 night.

| 🏕 S | **Dampierre-en-Burly** 🌿🏘 | 18H2 |

**Etang du Bourg**, Rue nationale. **GPS:** n47,76250 e2,51413. ⬆️.

6 🛏free 🚰🪠Ch🔌WCfree. **Location:** Rural, simple, quiet.
**Surface:** gravel. 🗓 01/01-31/12.
**Distance:** 🚶1km 🏊on the spot 🛒on the spot ⊗1km 🛒1,5km 🛒500m 🚶on the spot.

| 🏕 S | **Dreux** | 15F3 |

**Camping-Car Park**, Rue Jean-Louis Chanoine. **GPS:** n48,74029 e1,33227.
9 🛏€11,25 🚰🪠(8x)included. 🧺 🚿 🗓 01/01-31/12.
**Distance:** 🚶2,5km ⊗on the spot 🛒2km.
**Remarks:** Mandatory, one-time fee Pass'Etapes €4.

| 🏕 S | **Dry** 🏘 | 18G2 |

Rue de Meung. **GPS:** n47,79824 e1,71419. ⬆️➡️.

10 🛏free 🚰€2/10minutes 🪠Ch🔌€2/1h WC. **Location:** Rural, simple. **Surface:** metalled. 🗓 01/01-31/12.
**Distance:** 🚶on the spot 🏊1km ⊗50m.
**Remarks:** Coins at town hall.

| 🏕 S | **Épineuil-le-Fleuriel** | 21H1 |

Le Bourg. **GPS:** n46,55690 e2,58265. ⬆️.

5 🛏free 🚰🪠Chfree. **Location:** Rural, simple, quiet.
**Surface:** gravel. 🗓 01/01-31/12.
**Distance:** 🚶500m 🛒500m.

| 🏕 S | **Esvres-sur-Indre** 🏘 | 18E3 |

**Salle des Fêtes**, Impasse Auguste Noyant. **GPS:** n47,28291 e0,78418. ⬆️.

7 🛏free 🚰🪠Chfree.
**Location:** Urban, simple, central, quiet. **Surface:** gravel.
🗓 01/01-31/12 💧 water disconnected in winter.
**Distance:** 🚶on the spot ⊗100m 🛒250m 🛒on the spot 🚲on the spot 🚶on the spot.

| 🏕 S | **Fontaines-en-Sologne** | 18F2 |

**Place du Champ de Foire**, Route de Bracieux. **GPS:** n47,51039 e1,55078.
4 🛏free. **Surface:** gravel. 🗓 01/01-31/12.
**Distance:** 🚶on the spot.
**Remarks:** Behind town hall.

| 🏕 S | **Genillé** 🏘 | 18F3 |

Rue de la Varenne. **GPS:** n47,18438 e1,09232. ⬆️➡️.

6 ⑤ € 5 🚰 € 2/100liter 🗑Ch 🚿 included. **Location:** Rural, simple.
**Surface:** gravel. 🅿 01/01-31/12.
**Distance:** 🛒500m ⊗500m 🚶on the spot.

### 📷S Germigny-des-Prés 18G2
21 Route de Saint-Benoît. **GPS:** n47,84430 e2,26798. ⬆.

5 ⑤free 🚰 🗑Chfree. **Location:** Rural, simple, quiet.
**Surface:** gravel/metalled. 🅿 01/01-31/12 💧 water disconnected in
winter. **Distance:** 🛒100m 🛒1,5km, bakery 600m.

### 📷S Gien 18H2
Quai de Nice. **GPS:** n47,67985 e2,64308. ⬆.

8 ⑤free 🚰 € 2 🗑Ch 📮 € 2. **Location:** Urban, noisy.
**Surface:** asphalted. 🅿 01/01-31/12.
**Distance:** 🛒2km 🛒on the spot.
**Remarks:** Max. 48h, coins at swimming pool.

### 📷S Gizeux 18D3
Aire de Gizeux, Route du Lavoir. **GPS:** n47,39275 e0,19689. ⬆➡.

10 ⑤free 🚰 € 2/100liter 🗑Ch.
**Location:** Rural, comfortable, central, quiet. **Surface:** gravel.
🅿 01/01-31/12.
**Distance:** 🛒200m 🛒500m ⊗200m 🛒on the spot 🏍 on the spot
🚶on the spot.
**Remarks:** Coins at the shops and town hall, Château de Gizeux 400m.

### 📷S Guilly 18G3
Le Prieuré Chambres d'Hôtes, Rue du Prieuré.
**GPS:** n47,07920 e1,72100. ⬆.

10 ⑤ € 5 🚰 € 3 🗑Ch 📮 🗑 **Location:** Rural, simple, quiet.
**Surface:** grassy/metalled. 🅿 01/01-31/12.
**Distance:** 🛒150m 🛒on the spot 🛒150m.

### 📷S Huisseau-sur-Cosson 18F2
Route de Chambord. **GPS:** n47,59375 e1,45974. ⬆.
4 ⑤free 🚰🗑Ch 🚿. **Location:** Urban. **Surface:** metalled.
🅿 01/01-31/12.
**Distance:** ⊗500m.

### 📷S Huisseau-sur-Cosson 18F2
Domaine des la grange, La Grange. **GPS:** n47,58758 e1,45916. ⬆.
6 ⑤free 🚰 € 3 🗑. **Location:** Rural, comfortable.
**Surface:** grassy/gravel. 🅿 01/01-31/12.
**Distance:** 🏊200m ⊗600m.

### 📷S Humbligny 18H3
Chemin des Faviots, D44. **GPS:** n47,25451 e2,65850. ⬆.

8 ⑤free 🚰 € 2/100liter 🗑Ch 📮 € 2/60minutes. **Location:** Rural,
simple. **Surface:** gravel. 🅿 01/01-31/12.
**Distance:** 🛒on the spot ⊗1km 🛒3km 🚗50m.
**Remarks:** Max. 24h, coins at town hall.

### 📷S La Chapelle-Saint-Mesmin 18G2
Chemin de Fourneaux. **GPS:** n47,88550 e1,83990. ⬆➡.

23 ⑤ € 6/24h, € 10/48h, € 13/72h 🚰🗑Ch 🚿 🛜included. 📮
🗑 **Location:** Urban, comfortable, quiet. **Surface:** grassy/gravel.
🅿 01/03-30/11.
**Distance:** 🛒500m 🚴2,7km 🏊50m 🛒50m ⊗500m 🛒500m 🏍on
the spot 🚶on the spot.
**Remarks:** Along Loire river, market Saturday.

### 📷S La Châtre 21G1
Rue du Champ de Foire. **GPS:** n46,58250 e1,98250. ⬆➡.

10 ⑤ € 2. 🛒 **Location:** Urban, simple, noisy. **Surface:** asphalted.
🅿 01/01-31/12.
**Distance:** 🛒50m ⊗50m 🛒50m.

### 📷S La Châtre 21G1
Supermarché Super U, Avenue d'Auvergne, D943.
**GPS:** n46,58278 e2,00139.
10 ⑤free 🚰 € 2/10minutes 🗑Ch 📮 € 2/1h. **Location:** Simple, quiet.
**Surface:** asphalted. 🅿 01/01-31/12.
**Distance:** 🛒800m 🛒50m.

### 📷S La Ferte-Beauharnais 18G2
D922. **GPS:** n47,54455 e1,84882. ⬆.

12 ⑤free 🚰 € 2/10minutes 🗑Ch 📮 € 2/55minutes WC.
**Location:** Simple, noisy. **Surface:** grassy/metalled. 🅿 01/01-31/12.

**Distance:** 🛒300m 🛒on the spot 🛒on the spot ⊗250m
🛒100m.
**Remarks:** At small lake, max. 24h.

### 📷S La Ferté-Saint-Cyr 18G2
D925, Rue Faubourg de Bretagne. **GPS:** n47,65623 e1,67249. ⬆➡.

4 ⑤free 🚰 € 2,50/100liter 🗑Ch € 2,50/1h. **Location:** Rural,
simple, quiet. **Surface:** metalled. 🅿 01/01-31/12.
**Distance:** 🛒200m ⊗200m.
**Remarks:** Max. 48h, coins at townhall and bakery.

### 📷S La Loupe 15F3
Place du 8 mai, Docteur Moenner St. **GPS:** n48,47262 e1,01768.
3 ⑤free 🚰 € 2,20 🗑Ch 🚿 € 2,20. **Surface:** asphalted.
🅿 01/01-31/12.
**Distance:** 🛒300m ⊗100m 🛒800m.
**Remarks:** Coins at tourist info.

### 📷S La Pérouille 21F1
Étang de la Roche, Le Champ Perrot. **GPS:** n46,70507 e1,52259. ⬆.

6 ⑤free 🚰 € 2/10minutes 🗑Ch 🚿 € 2 WC. **Location:** Rural,
isolated, quiet. **Surface:** grassy/gravel. 🅿 01/01-31/12.
**Distance:** 🛒750m 🚴5km A20 ⊗750m.
**Remarks:** At small lake, max. 8M, coins at town hall and restaurant
(750m).

### 📷S Lailly-en-Val 18G2
Camping-Car Park, Place de l'Église. **GPS:** n47,77023 e1,68544. ⬆➡.

21 ⑤ € 9,60/24h 🚰🗑Ch 🚿(20x)WC 🛜included. 📮 🗑
**Location:** Rural, comfortable, quiet. **Surface:** gravel.
🅿 01/01-31/12.
**Distance:** 🛒100m 🛒50m ⊗300m 🛒200m.
**Remarks:** Mandatory, one-time fee Pass'Etapes € 4.

### 📷S Lamotte-Beuvron 18G2
Aire municipale, Chemin de Maisonfort. **GPS:** n47,59795 e2,02524. ⬆.

10 ⑤ € 8 🚰🗑ChWC 🚿free. 🛒 **Location:** Urban, central.
**Surface:** metalled. 🅿 01/01-31/12 📷 Fri-morning, water
disconnected in winter.
**Distance:** 🛒200m 🚴4,5km 🏊on the spot 🛒on the spot ⊗200m
🛒300m 🛒100m 🏍on the spot 🚶on the spot.
**Remarks:** At the canal.

**Tourist information Lamotte-Beuvron:**
⛪ Avenue de la Republique. Market. 🅿 Fri-morning.

FR

### Langon (Loir-et-Cher) 18G3

**Parking Canal du Berry**, D976. **GPS:** n47,28253 e1,82862. ⬆.

7 ⬛free 🚰€ 2/10minutes 🅗Ch 🔌€ 2/1h. **Location:** Rural, quiet. **Surface:** asphalted. ⬛ 01/01-31/12 ⬛ Service: winter. **Distance:** 🛒50m 🚶on the spot ⊗100m 🍺100m. **Remarks:** Max. 7 days, coins at the shops and town hall.

### Le Blanc 🌾🌊 21E1

**Place du Général de Gaulle. GPS:** n46,63154 e1,06164. ⬆.

10 ⬛free 🚰€ 2/100liter 🅗Ch 🔌€ 2/h. **Location:** Urban, central, noisy. **Surface:** asphalted. ⬛ 01/01-31/12 ⬛ service: 01/11-01/04. **Distance:** 🛒on the spot ⊗250m. **Remarks:** Coins at tourist info.

### Le Châtelet 🌾 21G1

**Le Tivoli, Avenue de la Gare. GPS:** n46,64502 e2,27863. ⬆.

10 ⬛free 🚰€ 2 🅗Ch 🔌€ 2. **Location:** Rural, simple, isolated, quiet. **Surface:** asphalted. ⬛ 01/01-31/12. **Distance:** 🛒700m ⊗300m 🍺300m. **Remarks:** Shady.

### Léré 🌊 18H3

**Le Port, Rue du Champ des Noyers. GPS:** n47,47485 e2,87477. ⬆.

4 ⬛free 🚰€ 2 🅗Ch 🔌€ 2/h. **Location:** Rural, simple, quiet. **Surface:** asphalted. ⬛ 01/01-31/12. **Distance:** 🛒400m 🚶on the spot 🚲on the spot. **Remarks:** At the canal.

### Les Bordes 18H2

**Etang du Petit Moulin, Route de Gien. GPS:** n47,81041 e2,40729. ⬆➡.

6 ⬛free 🚰🅗Chfree. **Location:** Rural, simple, quiet.

**Surface:** gravel/metalled. ⬛ 01/01-31/12. **Distance:** 🛒400m 🏊100m ⊗150m 🍺2km 🍽500m 🚶on the spot 🚶on the spot.

### Les Choux 18H2

**Route de Dampierre 13. GPS:** n47,79716 e2,67276. ⬛free 🚰🅗Chfree. **Location:** Urban. **Surface:** metalled. **Remarks:** At sports park.

### Les Montils 🍴 18F2

**Camping-Car Park des Montils, Route de Seur. GPS:** n47,49308 e1,30571. ⬆.

45 ⬛€ 10,15 🚰🅗Ch 🔌(24x) 📶included. ♻. **Location:** Rural, simple, quiet. **Surface:** grassy. ⬛ 01/01-31/12. **Distance:** 🛒500m. **Remarks:** Mandatory, one-time fee Pass'Etapes € 4.

### Levet 🍺 21H1

**Chemin du Crot A Thibault. GPS:** n46,92306 e2,40639. ⬆.

3 ⬛free 🔌(3x) WC. **Location:** Rural, simple, isolated, quiet. **Surface:** gravel. ⬛ 01/03-31/10. **Distance:** 🛒250m ⊗250m 🍺250m. **Remarks:** Max. 24h.

### Loches 🌾🍴🍺 18E3

**Allée du Maquis Césario. GPS:** n47,12656 e1,00221. ⬆➡.

3 ⬛free. **Location:** Urban, simple, quiet. **Surface:** gravel. ⬛ 01/01-31/12. **Distance:** 🛒700m ⊗700m. **Remarks:** Max. 24h.

### Loches 🌾🍴🍺 18E3

**Espace Agnes Sorel, Avenue de bas Clos. GPS:** n47,12477 e0,99331. ⬆.

10 ⬛free. **Location:** Urban, simple, noisy. **Surface:** asphalted. ⬛ 01/01-31/12. **Distance:** 🛒on the spot ⊗on the spot 🍺on the spot. **Remarks:** Max. 24h.

### Loches 🌾🍴🍺 18E3

**P2, Avenue Louis XI. GPS:** n47,13315 e1,00023. ⬆.

5 ⬛free. **Location:** Urban, simple, quiet. **Surface:** asphalted. ⬛ 01/01-31/12. **Distance:** 🛒centre 500m ⊗500m 🍺500m. **Remarks:** Max. 24h.

### Loches 🌾🍴🍺 18E3

**Rue de l'Amiral de Pointis. GPS:** n47,13744 e1,00115. ⬆.

4 ⬛free. **Location:** Urban, simple, noisy. **Surface:** asphalted. ⬛ 01/01-31/12. **Distance:** 🛒1,4km ⊗1,4km.

### Loches 🌾🍴🍺 18E3

**Avenue Aristide Briand. GPS:** n47,12240 e1,00164. ⬆. 🚰🅗Chfree. ⬛ 01/01-31/12. **Remarks:** At entrance campsite.

### Louzouer 🍴 18H1

**Cidre Chivet, 323 Les Mussereaux. GPS:** n48,02833 e2,87062. ⬆➡.

12 ⬛€ 5 🚰€ 4 🅗Ch 🔌€ 5 WC€ 5 ♻. **Location:** Rural, comfortable, quiet. **Surface:** asphalted/metalled. ⬛ 01/01-31/12. **Distance:** 🛒4km ⊗13km 🍺13km 🚶on the spot 🚶on the spot.

### Luant 21F1

**L'Étang Duris. GPS:** n46,72222 e1,57338. ⬆.

10 ⬛free 🚰€ 2 🅗Ch 🔌€ 2. **Location:** Rural, isolated, quiet. **Surface:** gravel. ⬛ 01/01-31/12. **Distance:** 🛒3km 🏎3,3km A20 🚣lake ⊗bar/brasserie 🚶on the spot. **Remarks:** Coins at town hall and restaurant, fishing permit available.

### Marboué 🍴 18F1

**L'Espace Loisirs des Fontaines, Rue du Croc Marbot. GPS:** n48,11240 e1,32870. ⬆➡.

FR

10 ⬛free ⬛€ 2/10minutes ⬛Ch⬛€ 2/50minutes.
**Location:** Rural, comfortable, central, quiet. **Surface:** grassy/metalled.
⬛ 01/01-31/12.
**Distance:** ⬛on the spot ⬛500m ⬛150m ⬛on the spot
⬛on the spot

| ⬛S | **Marcilly-en-Villette** ⬛ | 18G2 |

Rue du Lavoir. **GPS:** n47,76197 e2,02448. ⬛⬛.

6 ⬛free ⬛⬛Chfree. **Location:** Rural, simple, quiet.
**Surface:** gravel. ⬛ 01/01-31/12.
**Distance:** ⬛200m ⬛400m ⬛500m ⬛on the spot.
**Remarks:** At tennis-court.

| ⬛S | **Martizay** | 21E1 |

**Aire de Loisirs**, Rue des Afrique du Nord.
**GPS:** n46,80528 e1,03806. ⬛⬛.

6 ⬛free ⬛⬛Ch⬛(4x)WCfree. **Location:** Rural, quiet.
**Surface:** metalled/sand. ⬛ 01/01-31/12.
**Distance:** ⬛on the spot ⬛bakery 500m.

| ⬛S | **Mehun-sur-Yèvre** | 18G3 |

Quai du Canal. **GPS:** n47,14409 e2,21010. ⬛.

6 ⬛€ 2,50 ⬛⬛Chincluded ⬛. **Location:** Rural, quiet.
**Surface:** asphalted. ⬛ 01/01-31/12.
**Distance:** ⬛500m ⬛400m.
**Remarks:** At the canal.

| ⬛S | **Menetou-Salon** | 18H3 |

Rue de la Liberté. **GPS:** n47,23162 e2,49002. ⬛⬛.

6 ⬛free ⬛⬛Ch⬛(6x)free. **Location:** Simple, central, quiet.
**Surface:** gravel/metalled. ⬛ 01/01-31/12.
**Distance:** ⬛on the spot ⬛50m ⬛100m ⬛100m.

| ⬛S | **Mennetou-sur-Cher** ⬛⬛ | 18G3 |

Place du 11 Novembre, N76. **GPS:** n47,26861 e1,86472. ⬛⬛.

---

8 ⬛free ⬛€ 2/10minutes ⬛Ch⬛€ 2/h. **Location:** Rural, quiet.
**Surface:** sand. ⬛ 01/01-31/12.
**Distance:** ⬛150m ⬛100m ⬛150m ⬛150m.
**Remarks:** Coins at shops and tourist office, small fortified town.

| ⬛S | **Méry-sur-Cher** | 18G3 |

Chemin Lucien Bonneau/N76. **GPS:** n47,24586 e1,98989. ⬛.

6 ⬛€ 7,55/24h ⬛€ 1/12minutes ⬛Ch⬛(7x)WCincluded. ⬛⬛
**Location:** Rural, quiet. **Surface:** metalled. ⬛ 01/01-31/12.
**Distance:** ⬛150m ⬛100m.
**Remarks:** Nights closed with barrier.

| ⬛S | **Meung-sur-Loire** ⬛⬛ | 18G2 |

Chemin des Grêves. **GPS:** n47,82327 e1,69814. ⬛⬛.

15 ⬛free ⬛€ 2 ⬛Ch⬛€ 2. **Location:** Rural, comfortable.
**Surface:** gravel. ⬛ 01/01-31/12.
**Distance:** ⬛400m ⬛300m ⬛250m bakery.
**Remarks:** At castle, at swimming pool.

| ⬛S | **Monthou-sur-Cher** | 18F3 |

17 Route du Plan d'Eau. **GPS:** n47,34980 e1,29375.
5 ⬛€ 10 ⬛⬛Ch⬛⬛included. **Location:** Rural.
**Surface:** grassy/metalled. ⬛ 01/01-31/12.
**Distance:** ⬛600m ⬛on the spot ⬛on the spot ⬛700m.
**Remarks:** Max. 48h.

| ⬛S | **Montigny** | 18H3 |

Le Vieux Château. **GPS:** n47,24283 e2,68627. ⬛⬛.

2 ⬛free ⬛€ 2/100liter ⬛€ 2/60minutes. **Location:** Rural, simple,
isolated, quiet. **Surface:** gravel. ⬛ 01/01-31/12.
**Distance:** ⬛800m ⬛850m.
**Remarks:** Coins at town hall, poste.

| ⬛S | **Montoire-sur-le-Loir** ⬛⬛ | 18E2 |

**Aire de Montoire-sur-le-Loir**, Boulevard des Alliés, Quartier Marescot.
**GPS:** n47,74990 e0,86317. ⬛⬛.

---

8 ⬛free. **Location:** Urban, simple, central, quiet. **Surface:** asphalted.
⬛ 01/01-31/12.
**Distance:** ⬛50m ⬛on the spot ⬛on the spot ⬛500m ⬛500m
⬛on the spot ⬛on the spot.

| ⬛S | **Montoire-sur-le-Loir** ⬛⬛ | 18E2 |

Avenue de la République. **GPS:** n47,75750 e0,86928. ⬛.

15 ⬛free. **Location:** Urban, comfortable, quiet. **Surface:** asphalted.
⬛ 01/01-31/12.
**Distance:** ⬛on the spot ⬛500m ⬛500m ⬛on the spot.
**Remarks:** At former station.

| ⬛S | **Montrésor** ⬛ | 18F3 |

Rue du 8 Mai. **GPS:** n47,15750 e1,20169. ⬛.

12 ⬛free ⬛⬛Chfree. **Location:** Rural, simple. **Surface:** asphalted.
⬛ 01/01-31/12 ⬛ water: frost.
**Distance:** ⬛500m ⬛500m ⬛bakery 500m.
**Remarks:** At castle.

| ⬛S | **Montrichard** ⬛ | 18F3 |

**Camping-Car Park**, Rue Frideloux. **GPS:** n47,33846 e1,17091. ⬛.
40 ⬛€ 10,26 ⬛⬛Ch⬛⬛included. **Location:** Comfortable.
**Surface:** gravel. ⬛ 01/01-31/12.
**Distance:** ⬛on the spot ⬛450m.
**Remarks:** Mandatory, one-time fee Pass'Etapes € 4.

| ⬛S | **Montrichard** | 18F3 |

**Camping-Car Park**, Rue Frideloux 33. **GPS:** n47,34016 e1,17045. ⬛⬛.

40 ⬛€ 10,92/24h ⬛⬛Ch⬛(40x)⬛included. ⬛⬛
**Location:** Rural, comfortable. **Surface:** grassy/gravel.
⬛ 01/01-31/12.
**Distance:** ⬛500m ⬛500m ⬛500m ⬛400m.
**Remarks:** Mandatory, one-time fee Pass'Etapes € 4.

| ⬛S | **Morogues** | 18H3 |

Route des Aix, D46. **GPS:** n47,23990 e2,59857. ⬛.

FR

4 ⏚free ⛽€ 2/100liter 🚽Ch🔌€ 2/60minutes.
**Location:** Rural, simple, isolated, quiet. **Surface:** gravel.
⬛ 01/01-31/12.
**Distance:** 🛒on the spot ⊗200m 🏊1km 🍴800m.
**Remarks:** Coins at tourist info Henrichemont (12km).

### Nazelles-Négron · 18E3
D5. **GPS:** n47,43130 e0,95396.
10 ⏚€ 6,80 🚽Chincluded WC🚽. **Location:** Urban, comfortable.
**Surface:** grassy/gravel. ⬛ 01/01-31/12.
**Distance:** 🛒on the spot ⊗80m.

### Neuillay-les-Bois · 21F1
Route de Buzançais, D1. **GPS:** n46,76917 e1,47333.⬆️

5 ⏚free ⛽🚽Ch🛠(2x)free. **Location:** Simple, quiet.
**Surface:** metalled. ⬛ 01/05-31/10.
**Distance:** 🛒50m 🍴50m ⊗50m 🏊50m.
**Remarks:** Max. 24h.

### Neuvy-Le-Barrois · 21H1
La Prairie, Le Pénisson, D45. **GPS:** n46,86159 e3,03930.⬆️➡️

6 ⏚€ 6 ⛽€ 4/100liter 🚽Ch🛠€ 4/24h,16Amp
🚽 2. **Location:** Rural, comfortable, isolated, quiet.
**Surface:** gravel/metalled. ⬛ 01/04-01/11.
**Distance:** 🛒200m ⊗200m.

### Neuvy-Pailloux · 21G1
Les Gloux, RN151. **GPS:** n46,88278 e1,83682.⬆️

15 ⏚free ⛽🚽Chfree. **Location:** Rural, simple, isolated.
**Surface:** asphalted. ⬛ 01/01-31/12.

### Nogent-le-Roi · 15F3
Rue du Pont des Demoiselles. **GPS:** n48,65059 e1,52894.⬆️
4 ⏚free ⛽🚽Chfree 🛠.
**Surface:** asphalted. ⬤ Service: winter.
**Distance:** 🛒400m ⊗400m 🏊400m.
**Remarks:** Next to sports fields, max. 72h.

### Nogent-sur-Vernisson · 18H2
Étang de la base Loisirs, Rue du Gué Mulet.
**GPS:** n47,84055 e2,73996.⬆️➡️

---

6 ⏚free.
**Location:** Simple, quiet. **Surface:** gravel. ⬛ 01/01-31/12.
**Distance:** 🛒1km 🏊on the spot 🍴on the spot 🏊1km.

### Nogent-sur-Vernisson · 18H2
Rue Georges Bannery. **GPS:** n47,85363 e2,74014.
⛽€ 2 🚽Ch🛠€ 2.
**Remarks:** Coins at tourist info, PMU Rue Bannery or bar in Rue A. Briand.

### Nouan-le-Fuzelier · 18G2
Rue des Peupliers. **GPS:** n47,53324 e2,03437.⬆️➡️

6 ⏚free. **Location:** Urban, simple. **Surface:** asphalted/metalled.
⬛ 01/01-31/12.
**Distance:** 🛒300m ⊗300m 🏊300m.
**Remarks:** Max. 72h.

### Orléans 🌼 · 18G2
Parc des expositions, Rue du Président Robert Schumann.
**GPS:** n47,87229 e1,91317.🅿️.

40 ⏚free ⛽free. **Location:** Urban, simple, isolated.
**Surface:** asphalted. ⬛ 01/01-31/12.
**Distance:** 🛒city centre 3km ⊗200m 🏊200m 🍴on the spot.
**Tourist information Orléans:**
ℹ️ Office de Tourisme, 6, rue Albert 1er, www.ville-orleans.fr. City with many old bldg. And monuments.
Ⓜ️ Maison Jeanne d'Arc. Museum about the life of Jeanne d'Arc.
⬛ 01/04-31/10 ⬤ Mo.
✝ Cathédrale Ste Croix. Gothic cathedral.
✝ Église Nôtre Dame de recouvrance. Church 16th century.
✝ Tour Saint Paul. Church 17th century.
🌳 Allée Pierre Chevallier. ⬤ Su morning.
🌳 Quai du Roi. ⬤ Sa-morning.
❄️ Fête de Jeanne d'Arc. Historical celebration. ⬛ 08/05.
Parc Floral. Flowers and zoo. ⬛ daily.

### Oulches · 21F1
Impasse de l'Étang. **GPS:** n46,61339 e1,29547.⬆️

5 ⏚free ⛽€ 2 🚽Ch🛠€ 2/1h. **Location:** Rural, simple, quiet.
**Surface:** gravel. ⬛ 01/01-31/12.
**Distance:** 🛒on the spot ⊗100m.
**Remarks:** Coins at town hall.

---

### Ouzouer-sur-Trézée · 18H2
Parking halte nautique, Rue Saint-Roche.
**GPS:** n47,67000 e2,80888.⬆️.

5 ⏚free ⛽🚽ChWC🚽free. **Location:** Urban, comfortable, quiet.
**Surface:** asphalted. ⬛ 01/04-31/10.
**Distance:** 🛒500m 🍴on the spot ⊗500m 🏊700m 🚗50m.
**Remarks:** At canal 'de Briare', max. 48h.

### Ouzouer-sur-Trézée · 18H2
Camping municipal, Chemin du Rochoir.
**GPS:** n47,66819 e2,80611.⬆️➡️

5 ⏚€ 5,20 ⛽🚽Ch🛠€ 2,60 WC🚽included ⬤. **Location:** Rural, simple, quiet. **Surface:** grassy/gravel. ⬛ 01/04-31/10.
**Distance:** 🛒800m ⊗600m.

### Paucourt · 18H1
Rue de l'Église. **GPS:** n48,03441 e2,79179.⬆️

20 ⏚€ 3 ⛽🚽included Chfree. 🚿 **Location:** Rural, simple.
**Surface:** asphalted. ⬛ 01/01-31/12 ⬤ water: frost.
**Distance:** 🛒on the spot 🎣4,5km ⊗4,5km 🏊4,5km 🚲on the spot 🥾on the spot.
**Remarks:** Behind church.

### Pont-de-Ruan · 18E3
D17. **GPS:** n47,26373 e0,57632.⬆️

6 ⏚free ⛽🚽Ch🛠. **Location:** Rural, simple, isolated.
**Surface:** gravel/sand. ⬛ 01/01-31/12.
**Distance:** 🛒300m 🍴100m.

### Pontlevoy 📻 · 18F3
4 rue de Coutant. **GPS:** n47,38619 e1,25905.⬆️➡️

10 ⏚free ⛽🚽Ch🛠free. **Location:** Rural, simple, quiet.
**Surface:** gravel. ⬛ 01/01-31/12. **Distance:** 🛒500m.

FR

## Pouligny-Saint-Pierre 🅴🅱🅂    21E1

Route du Blanc, D950, Bénavent. **GPS:** n46,65591 e1,02054. ⬆️➡️.

10 🛏️free 🚰€2 🚽€2 Ch€2 🔌€2. **Location:** Rural, simple, quiet.
**Surface:** gravel. ⭕ 01/01-31/12.
**Distance:** 🛒bakery 50m.
**Remarks:** Coins at the bakery.

## Prissac    21F2

Etang Rémy Louveau. **GPS:** n46,50492 e1,30752.
5 🛏️free 🚰€3/120liter 🚽Ch 🔌€3/55minutes 📶. **Location:** Rural,
comfortable. **Surface:** gravel. ⭕ 01/01-31/12.
**Distance:** 🚤on the spot 🚶on the spot.

## Reignac-sur-Indre 👫🌿    18E3

Rue Louis de Barberin, D58. **GPS:** n47,22922 e0,91585. ⬆️.

5 🛏️free 🚰€2/100liter 🚽Ch. **Location:** Rural, simple, central, noisy.
**Surface:** asphalted. ⭕ 01/01-31/12.
**Distance:** 🏊300m 🏖️20km 🚤on the spot 🚶on the spot
🚶on the spot.
**Remarks:** Max. 24h, coins at the shops in the village.

## Restigné    18D3

Rue Basse. **GPS:** n47,28041 e0,22614. ⬆️.
4 🛏️free 🚰€2/100liter 🚽Ch. **Location:** Urban, simple, central,
quiet. **Surface:** gravel. ⭕ 01/01-31/12.
**Distance:** 🚤on the spot ⊗on the spot 🚶on the spot 🚶on the spot.
**Remarks:** Coins at bakery, butcher and Bar-Tabac.

## Richelieu 🌿⛵👫    18D3

Avenue Pasteur. **GPS:** n47,01098 e0,32265. ⬆️➡️.

10 🛏️free 🚰€4 🚽WC. **Location:** Urban, simple, central.
**Surface:** gravel. ⭕ 01/01-31/12.
**Distance:** 🚤300m ⊗300m 🛒bakery 300m 🚶on the spot
🚶on the spot.
**Remarks:** Servicepoint at campsite 1km.

## Saint-Amand-Montrond 🌿    21H1

Base de Loisirs Virlay, Etangs de Goule.
**GPS:** n46,73362 e2,48851. ⬆️➡️.

21 🛏️free 🚰🚽Chfree. **Location:** Rural, simple, quiet.
**Surface:** asphalted/grassy. ⭕ 01/01-31/12.
**Distance:** 🚤1km ⛵5km ⊗500m 🛒500m 🚤on the spot
🚶on the spot.

## Saint-Amand-Montrond 🌿    21H1

Quai Lutin, via Avenue Maréchal Foch. **GPS:** n46,71818 e2,50480. ⬆️➡️.

4 🛏️free 🚰🚽Chfree. **Location:** Urban, simple.
**Surface:** asphalted/gravel. ⭕ 01/01-31/12.
**Distance:** 🚤200m 🏊on the spot 🚤on the spot ⊗200m 🛒200m.
**Remarks:** On the canal.

## Saint-Benoît-du-Sault 🌿    21F2

Place du Champ de Foire. **GPS:** n46,44117 e1,39249.

3 🛏️free 🚰€2/120liter 🚽Ch🔌€2/4h 📶📖. **Location:** Rural,
simple. **Surface:** asphalted. ⭕ 01/01-31/12.
**Distance:** 🚤300m 🛒300m.
**Remarks:** At tourist office.

## Saint-Brisson-sur-Loire    18H2

Rue des Ruets, route d'Autry, D52. **GPS:** n47,64680 e2,68028. ⬆️➡️.

6 🛏️free 🚰€1 🚽Ch🔌€1/1h. **Location:** Urban, simple, quiet.
**Surface:** asphalted. ⭕ 01/01-31/12.
**Distance:** 🚤100m ⊗100m 🛒100m 🚐50m 🚶on the spot.
**Remarks:** Parking nearby town hall.

## Saint-Claude-de-Diray    18F2

Rue du Moulin D98. **GPS:** n47,61356 e1,41402. ⬆️.

4 🛏️free. **Location:** Rural, simple, quiet. **Surface:** gravel.
⭕ 01/01-31/12.
**Distance:** 🚤500m.
**Remarks:** Next to cemetery.

## Saint-Denis-les-Ponts 👫    18F1

Aire de Saint Denis-les-Ponts, Rue Jean Moulin.
**GPS:** n48,06643 e1,28950. ⬆️➡️.

12 🛏️free 🚰€3/100liter 🚽Ch.
**Location:** Urban, comfortable, central, quiet. **Surface:** gravel.

⭕ 01/01-31/12 ⬛ Service: winter.
**Distance:** 🚤Châteaudun 3km 🏊on the spot 🚤on the spot ⊗100m
🛒on the spot 🚶on the spot.
**Remarks:** Max. 48h, coins at the shops in the village, Châteaudun (city
and castle) 4km.

## Saint-Dyé-sur-Loire 👫    18F2

Parking de la base nautique, val des chateaux.
**GPS:** n47,65454 e1,47852. ⬆️.

4 🛏️free. **Location:** Rural, simple, quiet, **Surface:** grassy.
⭕ 01/01-31/12.
**Distance:** 🚤800m 🏊on the spot 🚤on the spot ⊗800m 🛒800m
🚶on the spot 🚶on the spot.
**Remarks:** Along Loire river, max. 48h, canoe rental.

## Saint-Épain 🅴🅱🅂    18E3

Plan d'eau. **GPS:** n47,14415 e0,53958. ⬆️.

6 🛏️€5,10 🚰🚽Ch🔌€1,70 WC included. 🔌 **Location:** Rural,
comfortable, quiet. **Surface:** grassy. ⭕ 01/01-31/12.
**Distance:** 🚤300m 🚤on the spot ⊗300m.
**Remarks:** Pay at town hall, key service at town hall, fishing permit
available at Tabac and supermarket.

## Saint-Genouph 👫    18E3

Rue de l'Auberdière. **GPS:** n47,37702 e0,60200. ⬆️➡️.

3 🛏️free 🚰🚽Ch📶free. **Location:** Rural, simple. **Surface:** gravel.
⭕ 01/01-31/12.
**Distance:** 🚤350m ⊗350m.

## Saint-Georges-sur-Arnon 🅴🅱🅂    21G1

N151 **GPS:** n46,97740 e2,06908. ⬆️.

10 🛏️free 🚰🚽ChWCfree. **Location:** Simple, isolated.
**Surface:** asphalted. ⭕ 01/01-31/12.
**Distance:** 🚤4km 🛒4km.

## Saint-Georges-sur-Arnon 🅴🅱🅂    21G1

Rue de la Vallee. **GPS:** n46,99999 e2,09840.

FR

10 ⛺free ⚑🚰Chfree. **Location:** Rural, isolated, quiet.
**Surface:** gravel. ⬛ 01/01-31/12.
**Distance:** ⚓on the spot ⛵on the spot.
**Remarks:** At small lake, former campsite, max 3,5t.

**Saint-Georges-sur-Moulon** 18H3

Route de Ville. **GPS:** n47,18596 e2,41786.⬆➡.

2 ⛺free ⚑🚰Chfree WC. **Location:** Simple, isolated, quiet.
**Surface:** gravel. ⬛ 01/01-31/12.
**Distance:** ⚓1,5km ⊗1km ⛵1,5km.

**Saint-Gondon** 18H2

Rue de Sully. **GPS:** n47,69808 e2,53876.⬆.

2 ⛺free ⚑🚰Chfree. **Location:** Rural, simple, quiet.
**Surface:** asphalted. ⬛ 01/01-31/12.
**Distance:** ⚓300m ⛵300m ⛟200m.
**Remarks:** Max. 48h.

**Saint-Gondon** 18H2

Rue du Petit Clou. **GPS:** n47,69995 e2,54356.⬆.

5 ⛺free ⚑🚰Chfree. **Location:** Rural, simple. **Surface:** metalled.
⬛ 01/01-31/12.
**Distance:** ⚓100m.
**Remarks:** In front of cemetery.

**Saint-Jean-le-Blanc** 18G2

Base de loisirs de l'Ile Charlemagne, Levée de la Chevauchée.
**GPS:** n47,89437 e1,93870.⬆.

10 ⛺free ⚑€ 2/100liter 🚰Ch. **Location:** Urban, simple, isolated.
⬛ 01/01-31/12.
**Distance:** ⚓Orléans 3km ⚓on the spot ⚓on the spot ⚓on the spot.

**Saint-Lubin-en-Vergonnois** 18F2

Place Jacques Michaux. **GPS:** n47,61241 e1,23927.⬆.

---

4 ⛺free ⚑🚰Ch. **Location:** Urban, simple, noisy. **Surface:** gravel.
⬛ 01/01-31/12.
**Distance:** ⚓on the spot ⛵bakery 50m.

**Saint-Nicolas-de-Bourgueil** 18D3

Rue de la Treille. **GPS:** n47,28496 e0,12528.⬆➡.

5 ⛺free. **Location:** Rural, simple, quiet. **Surface:** gravel/sand.
⬛ 01/01-31/12.
**Distance:** ⚓150m ⊗150m ⛵250m.

**Saint-Saturnin** 21G2

Route de Perassay, D111E. **GPS:** n46,50565 e2,23585.⬆.

6 ⛺free ⚑€ 2/10minutes 🚰Ch ⚑€ 2 💳. **Location:** Rural, simple,
quiet. **Surface:** gravel. ⬛ 01/01-31/12.
**Distance:** ⚓300m ⛵bakery 200m.
**Remarks:** Barrier, near sports fields, max. 7 days, shady.

**Sainte-Maure-de-Touraine** 18E3

Aire du Bois Chaudron, D910, Le Bois Caudron.
**GPS:** n47,09315 e0,61275.⬆➡.

40 ⛺€ 4 ⚑€ 2 🚰Ch € 3 💦(4x)€ 2/24h WC ⚑€ 2 🔌€ 4/3
🚿included. 🍽 **Location:** Rural, comfortable, isolated, quiet.
**Surface:** grassy. ⬛ 01/01-31/12.
**Distance:** ⚓1,5km ⚓4,4km ⊗1,5km ⛵1,5km ⚓on the spot.
**Remarks:** Bread-service.

**Sainte-Maure-de-Touraine** 18E3

Parking Ronsard, Rue de la Métairie. **GPS:** n47,11096 e0,61640.⬆➡.

15 ⛺free ⚑🚰Chfree WC. **Location:** Urban, simple, central, quiet.
**Surface:** asphalted. ⬛ 01/01-31/12.
**Distance:** ⚓200m ⚓3km ⊗200m ⛵200m ⛟on the spot.

**Sainte-Sévère-sur-Indre** 21G2

Place du Champ de Foire, rue de Verdun. **GPS:** n46,48724 e2,07167.⬆.

---

30 ⛺free ⚑€ 2/time 🚰Ch🚿free. **Location:** Rural, simple, quiet.
**Surface:** gravel/sand. ⬛ 01/01-31/12.
**Distance:** ⚓100m ⊗on the spot ⛵200m.
**Remarks:** Max. 7 days.

**Sancoins** 21H1

Quai du Canal. **GPS:** n46,83356 e2,91568.⬆➡.

20 ⛺free ⚑€ 2/100liter 🚰ChWC. **Location:** Simple, quiet.
**Surface:** gravel/metalled. ⬛ 01/01-31/12.
**Distance:** ⚓200m ⚓on the spot ⛵on the spot ⛵200m ⛟150m
⚓on the spot ⚓on the spot.

**Saran** 18G2

Allée Claude Bernard. **GPS:** n47,95106 e1,87315.⬆.

10 ⛺free ⚑🚰Chfree. **Location:** Simple, central. **Surface:** gravel.
⬛ 01/01-31/12.
**Distance:** ⚓on the spot ⚓on the spot ⊗1,5km ⛵1km ⛟800m
⚓on the spot ⚓on the spot.

**Selles-sur-Cher** 18F3

Avenue Kleber-Loustau, D856. **GPS:** n47,27639 e1,55889.⬆.

15 ⛺€ 5-11,50 ⚑🚰Ch ⚓. **Location:** Rural, comfortable, quiet.
**Surface:** asphalted. ⬛ 01/04-30/09.
**Distance:** ⚓500m ⚓200m ⊗500m ⛵500m.
**Remarks:** To be paid at campsite, service on campsite.

**Sully-sur-Loire** 18H2

Espace Loisirs Georges Blareau, Chemin de la Salle Verte.
**GPS:** n47,77139 e2,38451.⬆➡.

35 ⛺free ⚑🚰Chfree. **Location:** Comfortable, quiet.
**Surface:** gravel/metalled. ⬛ 01/01-31/12. **Distance:** ⚓800m ⚓on
the spot ⛵on the spot ⊗800m ⛵800m. **Remarks:** Nearby castle of
Sully, not suitable for motorhomes +7m, narrow entrance.

FR

## Sury-prés-Léré — 18H3

Route de Savigny. **GPS**: n47,48301 e2,86527.

6 free € 2/100liter Ch € 2/60minutes.
**Location:** Rural, simple, quiet. **Surface:** asphalted.
01/01-31/12.
**Distance:** 1,5km 50m 1,5km on the spot.
**Remarks:** Coins at town hall and restaurant.

## Theillay — 18G3

Chemin du Ronaire. **GPS**: n47,31849 e2,03775.

5 free Chfree. **Location:** Rural, simple, quiet.
**Surface:** gravel/metalled. 01/01-31/12 water: 01/11-31/03.
**Distance:** 250m 250m.
**Remarks:** At cemetery, max. 9m.

## Thenay — 21F1

Rue de la Paix, D48. **GPS**: n46,63199 e1,43096.

3 free € 2/100liter Ch € 2/1h. **Location:** Rural, simple,
quiet. **Surface:** asphalted/gravel.
01/01-31/12.
**Distance:** 200m.
**Remarks:** Max. 24h, max. 8M, coins at the shops and town hall.

## Thiron-Gardais — 18F1

**Aire de Thiron-Gardais**, Avenue de la Gare.
**GPS**: n48,31194 e0,99583.

5 free free.
**Location:** Urban, simple, quiet. **Surface:** asphalted.
01/01-31/12.
**Distance:** 200m 300m 300m 300m on the spot 100m.

## Tour-en-Sologne — 18F2

Rue de la Mairie. **GPS**: n47,53786 e1,49973.

5 free € 2,50/100liter Ch € 2,50/h WC.
**Location:** Rural, comfortable, quiet. **Surface:** gravel.
01/01-31/12.
**Distance:** 100m 200m bakery 100m on the spot.
**Remarks:** Coins at townhall and bakery.

## Tours — 18E3

**Parking relais du Lac**, Avenue du Général Niessel.
**GPS**: n47,36700 e0,70007.

6 free € 2/10minutes Ch . **Location:** Urban, simple, noisy.
**Surface:** asphalted. 01/01-31/12.
**Distance:** 2,5km 300m 500m on the spot.

## Vailly-sur-Sauldre — 18H3

Rue du Pont. **GPS**: n47,45727 e2,64665.

10 € 7 € 2 ChWC. **Location:** Comfortable, central.
**Surface:** gravel/metalled. 01/01-31/12.
**Distance:** 300m on the spot on the spot on the spot.
**Remarks:** Along the Sauldre river.

**Tourist information Vailly-sur-Sauldre:**
Fri.

## Valençay — 18F3

Avenue de la Résistance. **GPS**: n47,16080 e1,56163.

10 free € 2 Ch € 4 . **Location:** Rural, quiet.
**Surface:** metalled. 01/01-31/12.
**Distance:** 100m 100m 100m.
**Remarks:** Nearby entrance castle.

**Tourist information Valençay:**
Château. Castle, 15th-18th century. 01/03-30/11.

## Vendôme — 18F2

**Aire de Vendôme**, Rue Geoffroy Martel. **GPS**: n47,79111 e1,07528.

5 free. **Location:** Urban, simple, central. **Surface:** asphalted.
01/01-31/12.
**Distance:** 500m.

## Villaines les Rochers — 18E3

**Aire de Villaines-les-Rochers**, Place de la Mairie/ Rue des Ecoles.
**GPS**: n47,22083 e0,49583.

7 free ChWCfree. **Location:** Urban, comfortable, central,
quiet. **Surface:** asphalted. 01/01-31/12.
**Distance:** on the spot 100m 100m on the spot
on the spot.
**Remarks:** Max. 24h.

## Villandry — 18E3

**Camping-Car Park**, 14 Rue Principale. **GPS**: n47,33930 e0,50762.
35 € 10,83, 01/04-31/10 € 12,83 Ch included.
**Location:** Isolated, quiet. **Surface:** asphalted. 01/01-31/12.
**Distance:** 400m 400m 400m.
**Remarks:** Mandatory, one-time fee Pass'Etapes € 4.

## Villedômer — 18E2

**Aire de Loisirs de Lavoir**, Rue du Lavoir.
**GPS**: n47,54465 e0,88727.

6 free, 15/06-15/09 € 5 € 2/100liter Ch € 4/1h.
**Location:** Rural, simple, central, quiet. **Surface:** metalled.
01/01-31/12.
**Distance:** 100m 8,1km 100m 200m 200m on the
spot on the spot.
**Remarks:** Max. 24h, coins at town hall (200m), bakery (200m) and
supermarket (50m).

## Villefranche-sur-Cher — 18G3

Avenue du Val de Cher. **GPS**: n47,29184 e1,76851.
5 free € 2 Ch. **Location:** Rural. **Surface:** gravel.
01/01-31/12.
**Distance:** 300m 200m.

## Villequiers — 18H3

**L'Étappe Berrichonne**, Le Petit Azillon.
**GPS**: n47,08828 e2,77429.

6 € 6,50 € 3 Ch . **Location:** Isolated, quiet.
**Surface:** gravel/metalled. 01/01-31/12.
**Distance:** 3km.

## Vitry-aux-Loges — 18G2

Rue des Érables. **GPS**: n47,93915 e2,27078.

5 free Chfree. **Location:** Rural, simple, quiet.
**Surface:** asphalted. 01/01-31/12.
**Distance:** 200m on the spot 200m on the spot
on the spot.
**Remarks:** At canal of Orléans.

FR

## S Vouvray 18E3

Parking Bec de Cisse, Rue Bec de Cisse.
GPS: n47,40929 e0,79735.

3 free € 3/100liter Ch € 3/1h WC. Location: Rural, comfortable, central, quiet. Surface: asphalted. 01/01-31/12 Service: winter.
Distance: on the spot 8,5km 500m 150m 150m on the spot on the spot.
Remarks: Max. 48h, coins at campsite and tourist info.

# Bourgogne-Franche-Comté

## S Anost 19B3

Place Centrale. GPS: n47,07738 e4,09869.

10 free Ch free. Location: Rural, simple, quiet. Surface: metalled. 01/01-31/12 01/08-28/08.
Distance: on the spot on the spot on the spot.

## S Arc-et-Senans 22E1

Grande Rue. GPS: n47,03343 e5,78120.

6 free € 2 Ch. Location: Rural, simple, quiet. Surface: gravel.
01/01-31/12 Service: winter.
Distance: 500m 500m.
Remarks: Coints at mairie, supermarket and campsite.

## S Arinthod 22D2

Rue de la Prélette. GPS: n46,39654 e5,57013.

5 € 6 Ch included. Location: Rural, simple, quiet.
Surface: gravel. 01/01-31/12.
Distance: 100m.
Remarks: Near sports fields.

## S Arnay-le-Duc 19C3

Rue de l'Arquebuse. GPS: n47,13028 e4,49112.
11 € 8/24h Ch € 3. Location: Central, quiet.
Surface: gravel. 01/01-31/12.
Distance: 600m 600m 200m.

## S Arsure-Arsurette 22E1

Châlet des Arches, Route de l'Aliance de vie blanc.
GPS: n46,72168 e6,08402.

10 free € 2. Location: Rural, simple, isolated. Surface: asphalted.
01/01-31/12.
Distance: on the spot on the spot on the spot.

## S Autun 22B1

Route de Chalon. GPS: n46,95548 e4,31667.

17 free € 4 Ch WC. Location: Urban, simple.
Surface: asphalted. 01/01-31/12.
Distance: city centre 2km 100m 100m 900m on the spot on the spot.
Remarks: Parking at small lake Le Vallon at N80, in front of McDonalds, coins at tourist info.

Tourist information Autun:
Musée Rolin. Roman and Medieval excavations.
Wed, Fri, Su.

## S Auxerre 19A2

Quai de l'Ancienne Abbaye. GPS: n47,79742 e3,57738.

10 free. Location: Urban, simple, central, quiet.
Surface: grassy/metalled. 01/01-31/12.
Distance: 300m 300m 300m.
Remarks: Along the Yonne river.

Tourist information Auxerre:
Tue, Fri.

## S Baume-les-Dames 19E3

Quai du Canal. GPS: n47,34023 e6,35778.

30 € 9,30 + € 0,20/pp tourist tax € 2 Ch WC included
€ 1,70. Location: Rural, comfortable, quiet.
Surface: asphalted/grassy. 01/01-31/12.
Distance: on the spot 5,3km on the spot on the spot on the spot.
Remarks: Bread-service.

Tourist information Baume-les-Dames:
Abbaye Nôtre Dame. Historical monument, 18th century.

## Baume-les-Messieurs 22D1

Cascade des Tufs, Rue des Moulins. GPS: n46,69124 e5,63946.

## S Beaune 22C1

Avenue Charles de Gaulle. GPS: n47,01731 e4,83628.

10 free. Location: Rural, simple, quiet. Surface: gravel/metalled.
01/01-31/12.
Distance: on the spot on the spot on the spot.

5 free € 4 Ch € 4/4h.
Location: Urban, simple, central. Surface: asphalted.
01/01-31/12.
Distance: 500m 2,6km 200m 300m.
Remarks: 5 special pitches, all parking places permitted.

Tourist information Beaune:
M Hôtel Dieu et Musée. Former hospital, 15th century, museum.
Château de Meursault, Meursault. Castle with vineyard and wine tastery.

## S Beine 19B2

Domaine Alain Geoffroy, Rue de l'Equerre à Beines.
GPS: n47,82093 e3,71886.
5 free free. Surface: gravel. 01/01-31/12.
Distance: on the spot 600m.

## S Belvoir 19F3

Chateaux Belvoir, Lieu-dit La Vierge. GPS: n47,32139 e6,61097.

3 free. Location: Rural, simple, isolated, quiet.
Surface: asphalted/gravel. 01/01-31/12.
Distance: 2km 2,2km.

## S Besançon 19E3

Parking du Crous, Cité Carnot, Quai Veil Picard.
GPS: n47,23702 e6,01644.

12 € 7 Ch included. Location: Urban, simple, quiet.
Surface: asphalted. 01/01-31/12.
Distance: on the spot 500m 500m on the spot.
Remarks: Max. 72h, max. 8M.

Tourist information Besançon:
Jardin Botanique, Avenue de la Paix. Botanical gardens. 7-19
Sa after11. free.
Château, Vaire-le-Grand. 15/08-18/09, 19/09-14/08 by agreement.
Tue, Fri, Su.
Parc Zoologique de la Citadelle, Citadelle. Zoo. 10-17/19h.

## Blanot 22C2

Grottes de Blanot. GPS: n46,48476 e4,74417.

5 🛏free. **Location:** Rural, simple, isolated, quiet. **Surface:** grassy/gravel. 🅾 01/01-31/12. **Distance:** 🚰1,7km.

## 🅿🆂 Bois-d'Amont 🌿⛵ 22E2
Impasse de l'Eglantine. **GPS:** n46,53771 e6,13934. ⬆➡.

10 🛏free 🚰€2 🚽Ch🚻€2. **Location:** Rural, comfortable, quiet. **Surface:** asphalted. 🅾 01/01-31/12 ● Service: winter. **Distance:** 🚰on the spot ⊗400m 🛒600m 🏃on the spot 🚴on the spot.

## 🅿🆂 Brognard ⛵ 19F2
**Base de Loisirs de la Savoureuse**, Rue de Paquis. **GPS:** n47,52834 e6,85652. ⬆.

3 🛏free 🚰🚽Chfree. **Location:** Rural, simple, noisy. **Surface:** asphalted. 🅾 01/01-31/12. **Distance:** 🚰2km ⚓200m 🛒50m 🛍1,3km. **Remarks:** Max. 48h.

## 🅿🆂 Broindon 19C3
**Aire Du Cerisier Chambertin**, Rue du cerisier. **GPS:** n47,19834 e5,04522. 🛏free 🚰🚴. **Location:** Rural. **Surface:** gravel/metalled. 🅾 01/04-30/11.

## 🅿🆂 Bucey-les-Gy 19E3
Chemin de Tranot 1. **GPS:** n47,42456 e5,83974. ⬆.

5 🛏free 🚰€2/20minutes 🚽€2 Chfree 🚿(5x)€0,50/4h. **Location:** Rural, simple. **Surface:** gravel. 🅾 01/01-31/12. **Distance:** 🛒100m. **Remarks:** Coins available at the shop.

## 🅿🆂 Bussy-le-Grand 19C2
**Château de Bussy**, Rue du Château. **GPS:** n47,56069 e4,52544. 5 🛏free. **Location:** Rural. **Surface:** gravel. 🅾 01/01-31/12. **Distance:** ⊗200m. **Remarks:** At castle.

## 🅿🆂 Chablis 19B2
Route d'Auxerre, D235. **GPS:** n47,81711 e3,78425. ⬆.

5 🛏free 🚰🚽free. **Location:** Urban, simple, quiet. **Surface:** asphalted. 🅾 01/01-31/12. **Distance:** 🚰centre 500m ⊗100m 🛒200m.

## 🅿🆂 Chalon-sur-Saône 🧺 22C1
**P Ville Historique**, Promenade Sainte Marie. **GPS:** n46,78365 e4,86046. ⬆.

2 🛏free 🚰🚽Chfree. **Location:** Urban, simple. **Surface:** asphalted/gravel. 🅾 01/01-31/12. **Distance:** 🚰500m ⊗50m. **Remarks:** Free shuttle to centre.

## 🅿🆂 Champagnole 22E1
20, Rue Georges Vallerey. **GPS:** n46,74633 e5,89918. ⬆.

5 🛏€6 🚰€4 🚽Ch🚻€3. **Location:** Urban, simple, quiet. **Surface:** gravel/sand. 🅾 24/03-23/09. **Distance:** 🚰500m 🛒250m. **Remarks:** Max. 1 night, coins at campsite.

## ©🆂 Charolles ⛵ 22B2
Route de Viry. **GPS:** n46,43956 e4,28203. ⬆.

8 🛏€3 🚰€2 🚽Ch🚻€3. **Location:** Rural, simple. **Surface:** gravel. 🅾 01/04-01/10. **Distance:** 🚰300m ⊗500m 🛒800m. **Remarks:** Max. 48h.

## 🅿🆂 Château-Chinon 19B3
Rue Jean Sallonnyer. **GPS:** n47,06304 e3,93627. ⬆.

4 🛏free 🚰🚽Chfree 🚻. **Location:** Simple. **Surface:** metalled. 🅾 01/05-30/10. **Distance:** 🚰200m ⊗250m 🛒250m. **Remarks:** Max. 1 night.

## 🅿🆂 Châtillon-en-Bazois 22A1
Place Pierre Saury. **GPS:** n47,05310 e3,65511. ⬆.

5 🛏free 🚰€2 🚽Ch. **Location:** Urban, simple, central, quiet. **Surface:** metalled. 🅾 01/04-31/10.

**Distance:** 🚰on the spot ⊗50m 🛒50m. **Remarks:** Coins at tourist info.

## 🅿🆂 Chaumot 19A3
**Le port**, Pré de la Vieille Echeintr. **GPS:** n47,25828 e3,64781. 3 🛏free 🚰€2 🚽Ch🚿€2 🚻€2. **Location:** Rural, simple, quiet. **Surface:** grassy/gravel. 🅾 01/01-31/12 ● service: 15/11-15/04. **Distance:** 🚰on the spot ⊗100m 🐟on the spot 🏃on the spot. **Remarks:** Coins at town hall.

## 🅿🆂 Chiddes 22B1
Le Bourg. **GPS:** n46,86108 e3,94091. ⬆➡.

4 🛏free 🚰🚽Chfree 🚻. **Location:** Simple. **Surface:** gravel. 🅾 01/01-31/12. **Distance:** 🚰on the spot ⊗on the spot. **Remarks:** Max. 48h, free coins available at restaurant.

## 🍇🆂 Chiddes 22B1
Augendre. **GPS:** n46,86781 e3,94364. 🛏€3 + €0,22/pp tourist tax 🚰€2 🚿€2,50. **Surface:** gravel.

## 🅿🆂 Clairvaux-les-Lacs 22E1
Route de Lons-le-Saunier, D678. **GPS:** n46,58246 e5,74660. ⬆.

6 🛏free 🚰🚽Chfree. **Location:** Urban, simple, quiet. **Surface:** gravel/metalled. 🅾 01/01-31/12. **Distance:** 🚰1km ⊗500m 🛒nearby. **Remarks:** On entering village, nearby police station.

## 🅿🆂 Clairvaux-les-Lacs 22E1
Chemin des Tilleuls. **GPS:** n46,57526 e5,74020. ⬆. 5 🛏free. **Surface:** grassy/gravel. 🅾 01/01-31/12. **Distance:** 🚰900m ⊗900m.

## 🏛 Clairvaux-les-Lacs 22E1
**Musée des Maquettes**, Route de Lons. **GPS:** n46,58489 e5,73849. 20 🛏free. **Location:** Isolated. 🅾 01/01-31/12.

## 🅿🆂 Cluny 22C2
Chemin Georges Malère. **GPS:** n46,43479 e4,66621. ⬆. 6 🛏free. **Location:** Rural. **Surface:** asphalted. 🅾 01/01-31/12. **Distance:** 🚰800m ⊗350m 🏃on the spot.

## 🆂 Cluny 22C2
Rue des Griottons. **GPS:** n46,43101 e4,66779. free 🚰🚽Ch. 🅾 01/01-31/12.

## 🅿🆂 Conliège 🌿⛵ 22D1
Rue du Saugeois. **GPS:** n46,65270 e5,59981. ⬆➡.

2 🛏free 🚰🚽Ch🚻free. **Location:** Urban, simple. **Surface:** asphalted. 🅾 01/01-31/12. **Distance:** ⊗100m.

## 🅿🆂 Consolation-Maisonnettes ⛵ 19F3
**Parc du Seminaire du Cirque de Consolation.**, D377. **GPS:** n47,15848 e6,60600. ⬆.

10 ⚡€ 10/24h 🚰🚻Ch🔧WCincluded 🗑. **Location:** Rural, simple.
**Surface:** asphalted. 🕐 01/01-31/12.
**Distance:** 🏊on the spot.
**Remarks:** Check in at shop.

### 🅿S Corravillers 19F2
Rue de la Mairie. **GPS:** n47,89431 e6,62162. ⬆➡.

2 ⚡free 🚰€ 2/23minutes 🚻Ch🔧€ 2/23minutes.
**Location:** Rural, simple. **Surface:** grassy/gravel.
🕐 01/01-31/12.
**Distance:** ⊗500m 🍽500m.

### 🅿S Corre 19E2
Fluvial Loisirs, Pré le Saônier. **GPS:** n47,91402 e5,99308. ⬆➡.

32 ⚡€ 10 🚰🚻Ch🔧🗑included 🔌€ 4/3 💧€ 3/day.
**Location:** Rural, comfortable, quiet. **Surface:** grassy.
🕐 01/01-31/12.
**Distance:** 🏊200m ➛50m ⊗50m 🍽bakery 300m, supermarket 500m 🛒100m.

### 🅿S Cousance 22D2
Grande Rue, Champs de foire. **GPS:** n46,52929 e5,39154. ⬆.

4 ⚡free 🚰🚻ChWCfree. **Location:** Simple, quiet.
**Surface:** asphalted. 🕐 01/01-31/12.
**Distance:** 🏊100m 🚲6,6km 🍽100m.

### 🅿S Crosey-le-Petit 19F3
Rue de Begein. **GPS:** n47,35039 e6,48913. ⬆➡.

1 ⚡free. **Location:** Rural, simple. **Surface:** asphalted/gravel.
🕐 01/01-31/12.
**Distance:** 🚴on the spot 🚶on the spot.

### 🅿S Digoin 22B2
D982. **GPS:** n46,47300 e4,00344.

---

5 ⚡free 🚰€ 3 🚻Ch🔧€ 3 🗑. **Location:** Motorway.
**Surface:** metalled. 🕐 01/01-31/12.
**Distance:** 🏊2km ⊗100m 🍽200m.

### 🅿S Digoin 22B2
Place de la Grève, Route de Vichy. **GPS:** n46,48102 e3,97288. ⬆➡.

10 ⚡free 🚰€ 2 🚻Ch🔧€ 2 WC. **Location:** Simple, central.
**Surface:** asphalted. 🕐 01/01-31/12.
**Distance:** 🏊on the spot ⊗on the spot 🍽on the spot 🛒on the spot.
**Remarks:** Next to office de tourisme, friday market.

### 🅲S Dijon 19C3
Aire de Dijon, 3, Boulevard Chainoine Kir. **GPS:** n47,32125 e5,01090. ⬆.

16 ⚡€ 11,60, 01/07-31/08 € 12,55 🚰🚻Ch🔧(17x)included.
🏨 **Location:** Urban, comfortable, noisy. **Surface:** asphalted.
🕐 01/04-31/10 💧 water: frost.
**Distance:** 🏊centre Dijon 1,5km 🚲10km 🍽300m ➛300m ⊗500m
🛒500m ➛Dijon 150m 🚶10m.
**Remarks:** Attention: motorhomes ^3m take access road from southerly direction.

**Tourist information Dijon:**
ℹ Office de Tourisme, 11 Rue des Forges, Place Darcy, www.destina-tiondijon.com. City worth a visit with a number of large mansions and streets with half-timbered houses.

### 🅿 Dôle 19D3
Parking de Lahr, Avenue de Lahr. **GPS:** n47,08983 e5,49641. ⬆➡.

20 ⚡free. **Location:** Urban, simple, central, noisy. **Surface:** asphalted.
🕐 01/01-31/12 🎪 Village fair: mid-May.
**Distance:** 🏊on the spot 🍽on the spot ⊗400m 🚶on the spot.
**Remarks:** At harbour.

**Tourist information Dôle:**
Ⓜ Maison natale de Louis Pasteur, 43 Rue Pasteur. Birth house Pasteur, museum. 🕐 1/4-31/10 10-12h, 14-18h, 01/11-31/03 Sa-Su 14-18h
🕐 Su-morning.

### 🅿S Ecuisses 22C1
Place Marcel Pagnol, Route du Bourg. **GPS:** n46,76019 e4,52283. ⬆.

20 ⚡free 🚰€ 2 🚻Ch🔧€ 2. **Location:** Simple. **Surface:** metalled.
🕐 01/01-31/12.
**Distance:** 🏊on the spot.
**Remarks:** Max. 48h, coins at townhall and bakery.

---

### 🅿S Esmoulières 19F2
D236. **GPS:** n47,85243 e6,61502. ⬆.

2 ⚡free. **Location:** Rural, simple. **Surface:** asphalted.
🕐 01/01-31/12.

### 🅿S Étang-sur-Arroux 22B1
Place du Mousseau. **GPS:** n46,86631 e4,18946. ⬆➡.

20 ⚡free 🚰🚻Chfree. **Location:** Simple, central, quiet.
**Surface:** asphalted. 🕐 01/01-31/12.
**Distance:** 🏊100m 🍽on the spot ⊗on the spot 🛒100m.
**Remarks:** Near post office, max. 24h, max. 8M.

### 🅿S Faucogney-et-la-Mer 19F2
Rue des Chars. **GPS:** n47,83735 e6,56003. ⬆➡.

6 ⚡free 🚰€ 2/23minutes 🚻Ch🔧€ 2/20minutes.
**Location:** Rural, simple. **Surface:** grassy/gravel.
🕐 01/01-31/12.
**Distance:** 🏊800m.

### 🅿S Fontaine-Française 19D3
Rue Berthault. **GPS:** n47,52487 e5,36768. ⬆➡.

5 ⚡free 🚰€ 3 🚻Ch. **Location:** Rural, simple.
**Surface:** asphalted/grassy. 🕐 01/01-31/12.
**Distance:** 🏊100m 🚲16km 🍽on the spot 🛒250m bakery.
**Remarks:** Along river and betwee 2 lakes, coins at shops in the village 08-21h.

### 🅿S Fours 22A1
Rue des Saules, D981. **GPS:** n46,81720 e3,71806. ⬆.

8 ⚡free 🚰🚻Ch🔧free. **Location:** Urban, simple.
**Surface:** gravel. 🕐 01/01-31/12.
**Distance:** 🏊200m ⊗200m 🍽200m.

FR

**⬛S** **Génelard** 🏖️⛵ 22B2
Place du Bassin, D974. **GPS:** n46,57750 e4,23500. ⬆️➡️

2 🏕️free 🚰♨️Ch✏️free. **Location:** Simple. **Surface:** asphalted.
⬛ 01/01-31/12.
**Distance:** 🛒on the spot.

**⬛S** **Gilly-sur-Loire** 22B2
Le Gatefer. **GPS:** n46,53768 e3,78218. ⬆️
10 🏕️free 🚰♨️Chfree. **Surface:** metalled. ⬛ 01/01-31/12.

**⬛S** **Givry** 22C1
**Relais camping-car**, Rue de la Gare. **GPS:** n46,78000 e4,74830. ⬆️

15 🏕️free 🚰✏️€ 2/100liter ♨️Ch➕€ 2/1h. **Location:** Comfortable.
**Surface:** asphalted. ⬛ 01/01-31/12.
**Distance:** 🛒on the spot ⊗300m 🥖bakery 300m ♿on the spot
🏃on the spot.
**Remarks:** Coins at restaurant.

**🍴S** **Givry** 22C1
**Moulin Madame**, Rue du Moulin Madame. **GPS:** n46,79266 e4,77251.
🏕️€ 15 🚰♨️Ch✏️📶🍴. ⬛ 01/01-31/12.
**Remarks:** Barbecue place.
**Tourist information Givry:**
⛪ Marché. Market. ⬛ Thu.
🚲 La Voie Verte de Givry à Cluny. Cycle route on former railway,.

**⬛S** **Gray** 19D3
Rue de la Plage. **GPS:** n47,45253 e5,60259. ⬆️➡️

12 🏕️€ 5 🚰♨️Ch✏️included. **Location:** Rural, comfortable.
**Surface:** gravel. ⬛ 01/01-31/12.
**Distance:** 🚲on the spot ⊗on the spot ♿on the spot 🏃on the spot.
**Remarks:** Near camping municipal.

**⬛S** **Gron** 19A1
Rue des Petits Prés. **GPS:** n48,16011 e3,25636. ⬆️
5 🏕️free 🚰♨️ChWC. **Location:** Simple, quiet. **Surface:** asphalted.
⬛ 01/01-31/12.

**⬛S** **Gurgy** 19A2
Quai des Fontaines. **GPS:** n47,86348 e3,55376. ⬆️➡️

20 🏕️€ 7/24h 🚰♨️Chincluded ✏️(12x). 🚤 **Surface:** grassy/gravel.
⬛ 15/03-31/10.
**Distance:** 🛒50m 🚲7km 🛥️on the spot ⊗500m 🛒300m.
**Remarks:** Along the Yonne river, coins at supermarket.

---

**⬛S** **Heuilley-sur-Saône** 19D3
Rue Condé. **GPS:** n47,32800 e5,45471. ⬆️

25 🏕️free 🚰€ 3 ♨️ChWC. **Location:** Rural, quiet.
**Surface:** gravel/sand. ⬛ 01/01-31/12.
**Distance:** 🛒on the spot 🚲100m ⊗100m.
**Remarks:** Coins at town hall.

**⬛S** **Jeurre** 22D2
35, Rue Principale. **GPS:** n46,36662 e5,70769. ⬆️➡️

15 🏕️€ 5-7 🚰♨️€ 2 ♨️Ch➕€ 2 ✏️€ 3/day. **Location:** Rural, simple.
**Surface:** grassy. ⬛ 01/04-31/10.

**⬛S** **La Chapelle des Bois** ❄️ 22E1
**Station de ski**, Chemin du Marais Blanc. **GPS:** n46,60307 e6,11317. ⬆️

40 🏕️free 🚰free. **Location:** Rural, simple. **Surface:** gravel.
⬛ 01/01-31/12.
**Distance:** ⊗on the spot 🎿on the spot 🚠on the spot.

**⬛S** **La Chapelle-de-Guinchay** 22C2
**Maison de Pays**, Le Clos Meziat. **GPS:** n46,21017 e4,76720. ⬆️

± 10 🏕️free 🚰♨️ChWCfree. **Location:** Rural, comfortable, quiet.
**Surface:** gravel/metalled. ⬛ 01/01-31/12.
**Distance:** 🛒centre 1,2km 🛣️A6 10km ⊗1,2km 🛒1,2km.

**⬛S** **La Charité-sur-Loire** 18H3
Quai de la Tête de l'Ourth. **GPS:** n47,17577 e3,01254.

3 🏕️free. **Location:** Simple, quiet. **Surface:** asphalted.
⬛ 01/01-31/12.
**Distance:** 🛒200m ⊗200m.
**Remarks:** Parking at river.

**⬛S** **La Charité-sur-Loire** 18H3
Quai Romain Mollot. **GPS:** n47,17483 e3,01123. ⬆️

---

5 🏕️free. **Location:** Urban, simple, quiet. **Surface:** asphalted.
⬛ 01/01-31/12.
**Distance:** 🛒250m 🛥️on the spot 🚲on the spot ⊗on the spot 🛒on
the spot.
**Remarks:** Parking at the river, max. 24h.

**⬛S** **La Montagne** 19F2
D136. **GPS:** n47,92581 e6,58710. ⬆️

2 🏕️free. **Location:** Rural, simple. **Surface:** asphalted.
⬛ 01/01-31/12.
**Distance:** 🎿on the spot.
**Remarks:** Parking at skipistes.

**⬛S** **La Pesse** 22E2
Rue de l'Epicéa, D25. **GPS:** n46,28400 e5,84764. ⬆️

15 🏕️free 🚰€ 2 ♨️ChWC.
**Location:** Rural, simple, quiet. **Surface:** unpaved.
⬛ 01/01-31/12.
**Distance:** 🛒on the spot 🏃on the spot 🎿on the spot.
**Remarks:** Coins at Tourist Info and bakery, at start of langlauf circuit.

**🍴S** **La Pesse** 22E2
**Ferme Auberge de La Combe aux Bisons**, Lieu-dit Pré Reverchon.
**GPS:** n46,29278 e5,86011.

3 🏕️guests free 🚰. **Location:** Simple, isolated. ⬛ 01/01-31/12
⬛ Mon, Tue.
**Distance:** ⊗on the spot.

**⬛S** **Laignes** 🌾 19B2
Chemin du Moulin Neuf, D965. **GPS:** n47,84850 e4,36132. ⬆️➡️

7 🏕️free 🚰♨️Chfree. **Location:** Simple, quiet. **Surface:** grassy.
⬛ 01/01-31/12.
**Distance:** 🛒1km 🛥️on the spot ⊗1km.

FR

**Remarks:** Parking at river, max. 24h, max. 7m.

🚐⚡ **Lamoura** ❄ `22E2`

**Porte de la Serra**, Route de Prémanon, D25.
**GPS:** n46,41107 e5,99458. ⬆.

20 🛏free 🚰⚡ Ch free WC. **Location:** Rural, simple.
**Surface:** asphalted. 🅿 01/01-31/12.
**Distance:** ⊗winter 🎿 on the spot ⛷ on the spot.
**Remarks:** Service sportcentre La Serra, only in winter time.

🚐⚡ **Lamoura** ❄ `22E2`

Route de Prémanon, D25. **GPS:** n46,40139 e5,98561. ⬆.

6 🛏free 🚰. **Location:** Rural, isolated, quiet. **Surface:** asphalted.
🅿 01/01-31/12.
**Distance:** 🎿 on the spot ⛷ on the spot.

🚐⚡ **Larochemillay** `22B1`

**Place de l'Église**, Centre Bourg. **GPS:** n46,87793 e4,00155. ⬆.
4 🛏free 🚰⚡ Ch free. **Location:** Simple. 🅿 01/01-31/12.
**Distance:** 🛒 on the spot ⊗ on the spot.
**Remarks:** Coins at town hall and restaurant, max. 48h.

🚐⚡ **Le Russey** `19F3`

Rue Foch. **GPS:** n47,16219 e6,72281. ⬆ ➡.

3 🛏free 🚰⚡ Ch. **Location:** Rural, quiet. **Surface:** gravel.
🅿 01/01-31/12.
**Distance:** ⊗500m 🛒1km.
**Remarks:** Near Salle des Fêtes, coins at town hall, poste.

🚐⚡ **Le Vernois** `22D1`

**Caveau des Byards**. **GPS:** n46,73342 e5,59405. ⬆.

2 🛏free 🚰 free. **Location:** Urban, simple. **Surface:** grassy/gravel.
🅿 01/01-31/12.

🚐⚡ **Les Fourgs** `22F1`

D6. **GPS:** n46,83337 e6,42505.
12 🛏free ⚡(12x) €3/10h. **Location:** Rural. 🅿 01/01-31/12.
**Distance:** ⊗2km 🛒2km.
**Remarks:** Parking at skipistes.

🚐⚡ **Les Rousses** 🌿🚵❄ `22E2`

**Parking du Balancier**, Route Blanche, N5.
**GPS:** n46,44852 e6,07591. ⬆.

20 🛏free, €4/Winter 🚰€3,50 Ch⊞WC.
**Surface:** asphalted.
🅿 01/01-31/12.
**Distance:** ⊗Restaurant 🛒5km.
**Remarks:** Coins at tourist info, ski station, ski rental, ski school.

🚐⚡ **Les Rousses** 🌿🚵❄ `22E2`

**Parking l'Aube**, Route du Lac. **GPS:** n46,48779 e6,06690. ⬆➡.

30 🛏free, €4/Winter 🚰€5/100liter Ch⊞€5/1h ⊘.
**Location:** Simple. **Surface:** asphalted. 🅿 01/01-31/12.
**Distance:** 🛒500m ⊗500m 🛒200m.

🚐⚡ **Loisia** `22D2`

Rue du Pont. **GPS:** n46,48376 e5,46536.
3 🛏free 🚰⚡ Ch free. **Location:** Simple, quiet.
**Surface:** grassy/gravel.
**Distance:** ⊗on the spot.

🚐⚡ **Louhans** `22D1`

**Halte nautique**, Rue du Port. **GPS:** n46,62952 e5,21302. ⬆.

25 🛏€4 + €0,20/pp tourist tax 🚰€2,20 Ch⊞WC.
**Location:** Comfortable, quiet. **Surface:** gravel. 🅿 01/01-31/12.
**Distance:** 🛒400m ⊗on the spot.
**Remarks:** To be paid at Halte Nautique, sanitary building: 01/05-30/09.

🚐⚡ **Luxeuil-les-Bains** 🌿🚵♨ `19E2`

**Place de l'Etang de la Poche**, Rue Gambetta.
**GPS:** n47,81679 e6,38659. ⬆.

20 🛏free 🚰€2/100liter ⚡Ch⊞€2/1h. **Location:** Simple, quiet.
**Surface:** gravel. 🅿 01/01-31/12 🔘 Service: winter.
**Distance:** 🛒1km ⛱100m ⊗1km 🛒Auchan/Aldi 500m 🛒1km.
**Remarks:** Max. 72h, coins at tourist info.

**Tourist information Luxeuil-les-Bains:**
ℹ Fougerolles. Since the 16th century the small town is the centre of distilleries (Kirsch and cherry brandy).

🚐⚡ **Luzy** `22B1`

Place du champ De Foire. **GPS:** n46,79028 e3,96840. ⬆➡.

---

4 🛏free 🚰⚡ Ch WC free. **Location:** Simple.
**Surface:** asphalted/metalled. 🅿 01/01-31/12.
**Distance:** 🛒centre 300m ⊗100m 🛒200m 🚂500m.
**Remarks:** Max. 48h, coins at the shops and restaurant.

🚐⚡ **Magny-Cours** `22A1`

**Avia**, Bardonnay. **GPS:** n46,87223 e3,16051. ⬆➡.
20 🛏free 🚰€2 ⚡€2 Ch€2 WC€2. **Location:** Motorway, simple, noisy. **Surface:** asphalted. 🅿 01/01-31/12.
**Distance:** ⚡on the spot ⊗500m.
**Remarks:** Coins at petrol station.

🚐⚡ **Mailly-le-Château** `19A2`

**L'espace naturel du Beauvais**, Rue du Beauvais.
**GPS:** n47,59308 e3,63059. ⬆.
🛏free 🚰€3 Ch⚡€3 ⊘. **Location:** Isolated, quiet.
**Surface:** grassy. 🅿 01/01-31/12.
**Distance:** 🛒650m.
**Remarks:** Coins at the shops.

🚐⚡ **Maisod** 🌿🚵🛶 `22D2`

**La Mercantine**. **GPS:** n46,46500 e5,68864. ⬆.

40 🛏€9 🚰€2 Ch. **Location:** Rural, simple, isolated, quiet.
**Surface:** gravel. 🅿 01/01-31/12.
**Distance:** ⛱100m 🛒200m.
**Remarks:** At lake Vouglans, max. 24h.

🚐 **Marigny-le-Cahouët** `19C3`

Chemin des Écluses. **GPS:** n47,46370 e4,45598. ⬆.
🛏free. **Surface:** gravel/metalled. 🅿 01/01-31/12.
**Distance:** 🛒200m 🛒on the spot 🥖bakery 200m ⊗on the spot 🍽on the spot.
**Remarks:** At the canal, picnic area.

🚐⚡ **Marsannay-la-Côte** `19C3`

**Espace du Rocher**, Rue du Rocher. **GPS:** n47,27099 e4,99224. ⬆➡.

5 🛏free 🚰⚡ Ch free. **Location:** Urban, simple, quiet.
**Surface:** asphalted. 🅿 01/01-31/12 🔘 service: 15/11-15/03.
**Distance:** 🛒500m ⚡3,5km 🛒750m.
**Remarks:** Max. 48h.

🚐⚡ **Marzy** `22A1`

**Allée des Vignes du Clos**. **GPS:** n46,97982 e3,09357. ⬆.

3 🛏free 🚰€2 Ch. **Location:** Simple, quiet. **Surface:** asphalted.
🅿 01/01-31/12.

FR

**Distance:** ⊗100m.
**Remarks:** Max. 72h.

🏕️S | **Mesnay** 🎏 | 22E1
Rue Vermot. **GPS:** n46,89834 e5,80036. ⬆️➡️.

20 🅿️free 🚰€ 2/20minutes 🔌Ch 💧€ 2/20minutes ♻️.
**Location:** Urban, simple, quiet. **Surface:** grassy.
🅿️ 01/01-31/12.
**Distance:** 🚰500m, 2,5km Arbois.

🚲S | **Métabief** | 22E1
Avenue des Crêts. **GPS:** n46,76396 e6,34481. ⬆️.

45 🅿️€ 9, 01/04-30/11 € 7 🚰€ 2/10minutes 🔌Ch 💧€ 2/4h. 🚐.
**Location:** Rural, simple. **Surface:** gravel/metalled.
🅿️ 01/01-31/12.
**Distance:** 🚰1km 🚴2km.
**Remarks:** Barrier.

🚲S | **Montbard** | 19B2
Place Gambetta, Rue Carnot. **GPS:** n47,62333 e4,33194.

5 🅿️free. **Location:** Simple. **Surface:** gravel. 🅿️ 01/01-31/12.
**Distance:** 🚰300m 🚴 on the spot 🚶 on the spot.
**Remarks:** Bicycle rental.

🏕️S | **Montbéliard** 🌿 | 19F3
Parking du Champ de Foire. **GPS:** n47,50663 e6,79128. ⬆️.

4 🅿️free 🚰€ 2/100liter 🔌Ch 💧€ 2/1h. **Location:** Urban, simple, quiet. **Surface:** asphalted. 🅿️ 01/01-31/12.
**Distance:** 🚰900m ⊗400m 🛒900m.
**Remarks:** Max. 48h.

🏕️S | **Montreux-Château** 〰️ | 19F2
D11. **GPS:** n47,60198 e7,00179. ⬆️.

7 🅿️€ 5/24h 🚰€ 5/10minutes 🔌Ch 💧(8x) WCincluded. 🚐

---

**Location:** Simple. **Surface:** gravel. 🅿️ 01/01-31/12.
**Distance:** 🏊on the spot 🚶on the spot ⊗on the spot.

🏕️S | **Moussières** 🌿🎏 | 22E2
Combe au Prost. **GPS:** n46,32111 e5,89778. ⬆️.

6 🅿️free 🚰€ 2 🔌Ch 💧€ 2. **Location:** Rural, simple. **Surface:** gravel.
🅿️ 01/01-31/12.
**Distance:** 🐄 on the spot.
**Remarks:** In front of cheese farm.

🚲S | **Mouthe** ⛰️ | 22E1
Place de l'Eglise. **GPS:** n46,71042 e6,19570. ⬆️➡️.

20 🅿️free 🚰€ 3,50 🔌Ch 💧€ 3,50. **Location:** Rural, simple.
**Surface:** asphalted. 🅿️ 01/01-31/12.
**Distance:** 🚰300m ⊗300m 🚶 on the spot.
**Remarks:** Coins at the bakery, supermarket, tourist office.

🚲S | **Nancray** | 19E3
Rue du Musée. **GPS:** n47,23933 e6,18588. ⬆️.
🅿️free 🚰€ 2 🔌Ch. **Location:** Rural, isolated, quiet.
**Surface:** grassy. 🅿️ 01/03-31/10.
**Distance:** 🚰1,3km ⊗1,3km.

🚲S | **Nolay** | 22C1
Avenue de la Liberté. **GPS:** n46,95016 e4,62828. ⬆️.

10 🅿️free 🚰€ 3 🔌Ch 💧€ 3. **Location:** Urban, simple, quiet.
**Surface:** gravel. 🅿️ 01/01-31/12.
**Distance:** 🚰100m ⊗300m 🛒300m.
**Remarks:** Coins at tourist info and town hall.

**Tourist information Nolay:**
🏞️ Site Champêtre du Bout du Monde, Vauchignon. Water falls.

🏕️S | **Nozeroy** | 22E1
Rue des Remparts. **GPS:** n46,77249 e6,03516. ⬆️➡️.

10 🅿️€ 8 🚰🔌Ch 💧included,2Amp. **Location:** Rural, isolated, quiet.
**Surface:** grassy/gravel. 🅿️ 01/01-31/12.
**Distance:** 🚰200m ⊗300m.

🏕️S | **Nuits-Saint-Georges** | 19C3
Rue de Cussigny. **GPS:** n47,13178 e4,95189. ⬆️⬆️➡️.

---

10 🅿️free 🚰🔌Chfree. **Location:** Urban, simple. **Surface:** asphalted.
🅿️ 01/01-31/12.
**Distance:** 🚰400m 🚴2,1km ⊗500m 🛒Intermarché 300m.

**Tourist information Nuits-Saint-Georges:**
🎏 🅿️ Fri.

🏕️S | **Orgelet** | 22D2
Place Ancien Champ de Foire, Rue du Faubourg de l'Orme.
**GPS:** n46,52232 e5,60860. ⬆️.

10 🅿️free 🚰🔌ChWCfree. **Location:** Simple.
**Surface:** grassy/metalled. 🅿️ 01/01-31/12.
**Distance:** 🚰300m.
**Remarks:** Closed when frosty.

🏕️S | **Pontigny** | 19B2
Rue Paul Desjardins, Pré Neuf. **GPS:** n47,91180 e3,71243.
13 🅿️€ 7 🚰€ 3/10minutes 🔌Ch 💧€ 2/2h ♻️ 🚐.
**Location:** Urban. **Surface:** gravel. 🅿️ 01/01-31/12.
**Distance:** 🚰on the spot ⊗on the spot.

🏕️S | **Pougues-les-Eaux** 🎏 | 19A3
D907. **GPS:** n47,08315 e3,09382. ⬆️.

5 🅿️free 🚰€ 2/10minutes 🔌Ch 💧€ 2/10minutes ♻️.
**Location:** Urban, simple, noisy. **Surface:** asphalted.
🅿️ 01/01-31/12.
**Distance:** 🚰250m 🚴1,4km ⊗100m.
**Remarks:** Coins at campsite and tourist info.

🏕️S | **Prissé** | 22C2
Vignerons des Terres Secrètes, Rue de l'Ancienne Gare.
**GPS:** n46,32226 e4,75257. ⬆️.

5 🅿️free 🚰€ 2 🔌ChWC. **Location:** Rural, simple. **Surface:** gravel.
🅿️ 01/03-30/11 ⬛ winter.
**Distance:** 🚰500m 🚴3km 🚶on the spot.
**Remarks:** Max. 24h.

🏕️S | **Pruzilly** | 22C2
La Croix Blanche, salle des Fêtes, La croix blanche/D469.
**GPS:** n46,25708 e4,69792. ⬆️.

6 �whfree ⌁⌁ChWCfree. **Location:** Rural, simple.
**Surface:** asphalted. ◯ 01/01-31/12.
**Distance:** ⌁on the spot ⊗on the spot.
**Remarks:** Max. 48h, vins de Côte de Beaujolais.

**⌁S Quarre-les-Tombes 19B3**
Rue des Ecoles. **GPS:** n47,36853 e3,99936.⤒.
6 ⌁free ⌁⌁free. **Surface:** metalled. ◯ 01/04-31/10.
**Distance:** ⌁100m ⊗100m ⌁100m.

**⌁S Raddon-et-Chapendu 19F2**
**GPS:** n47,84899 e6,47427.⤒➜.

6 ⌁free ⌁€ 2/23minutes ⌁€ 2/23minutes. **Location:** Rural, simple.
**Surface:** gravel. ◯ 01/01-31/12.
**Remarks:** Near sports fields.

**⌁S Randevillers 19F3**
Rue de la Cote. **GPS:** n47,30944 e6,52707.⤒➜.

3 ⌁free. **Location:** Rural, simple, isolated, quiet.
**Surface:** asphalted/gravel. ◯ 01/01-31/12.
**Distance:** ⌁5km ⊗5km.

**⌁S Rémilly 22B1**
Le Bourg/D3. **GPS:** n46,81995 e3,81171.⤒.
4 ⌁free ⌁⌁Chfree. **Location:** Quiet. **Surface:** grassy.
◯ 01/01-31/12.
**Distance:** ⌁200m ⊗200m.
**Remarks:** Coins at town hall and restaurant, max. 48h.

**⌁S Rogny-les-Sept-Écluses 18H2**
Quai Sully. **GPS:** n47,74673 e2,88104.⤒.

4 ⌁free ⌁⌁Chfree. **Location:** Simple, quiet. **Surface:** grassy.
◯ 01/01-31/12.
**Distance:** ⌁on the spot ⊗350m.
**Remarks:** At the canal.

**⌁S Rouvray 19B3**
Place du Champs de Foire, D906. **GPS:** n47,42271 e4,10412.⤒➜.

4 ⌁free ⌁⌁Chfree. **Location:** Rural, simple, quiet.
**Surface:** metalled. ◯ 01/01-31/12.
**Distance:** ⌁on the spot ⊗on the spot ⌁200m.
**Remarks:** Max. 48h.

**⌁S Saint-Amour 22D2**
Le Champ de Foire. **GPS:** n46,43303 e5,34207.
⌁free. **Surface:** unpaved. ◯ 01/01-31/12.
**Distance:** ⌁300m ⊗300m.

**⌁S Saint-Benin-d'Azy 22A1**
1 rue François Mitterrand. **GPS:** n47,00381 e3,40113.
3 ⌁free ⌁⌁Ch⌁free. **Location:** Simple, quiet.
◯ 01/01-31/12.
**Distance:** ⌁1km ⊗1km ⌁1km.

**⌁S Saint-Bresson 19F2**
La Rue Saint Bresson. **GPS:** n47,86999 e6,50226.⤒➜.

2 ⌁free. **Location:** Rural, simple. **Surface:** asphalted.
◯ 01/01-31/12.

**⌁S Saint-Claude 22E2**
Avenue de la Libération, D436. **GPS:** n46,38049 e5,85209.⤒➜.

3 ⌁free ⌁⌁Ch⌁free. **Location:** Urban, simple, noisy.
**Surface:** asphalted. ◯ 01/01-31/12.
**Distance:** ⌁1km ⌁on the spot.
**Tourist information Saint-Claude:**
ℹ Tourist town, production of pipes.
👁 Musée du Pipe et Diamant. Pipes and diamond exhibition.
◯ 01/06-30/09 9.30-12h, 14-18.30h, 01/10-31/05 14-18h ◯ Su.

**⌁S Saint-Fargeau 19A2**
Rue de Laveau, D18. **GPS:** n47,63968 e3,06999.⤒.

10 ⌁free ⌁⌁ChWCfree. **Location:** Urban, central, noisy.
**Surface:** asphalted. ◯ 01/01-31/12.
**Distance:** ⌁50m ⊗50m.

**⌁S Saint-Gengoux-le-National 22C1**
**GPS:** n46,60624 e4,66844.⤒.

16 ⌁free ⌁€ 3/15minutes ⌁Ch ⌁€ 3/50minutes WC ⌁.
**Location:** Simple, quiet. **Surface:** gravel. ◯ 01/01-31/12.
**Distance:** ⌁500m.
**Remarks:** At former station.
**Tourist information Saint-Gengoux-le-National:**
⌁ La Voie Verte. Cycle route on former railway,.

**⌁S Saint-Hippolyte 19F3**
Esplanade des Fetes. **GPS:** n47,31874 e6,81543.

9 ⌁free. **Location:** Urban, simple, quiet. **Surface:** grassy/metalled.
◯ 01/01-31/12.
**Distance:** ⌁300m ⌁on the spot ⌁on the spot ⌁on the spot
⌁ on the spot.

**⌁S Saint-Honoré-les-Bains 22B1**
Allée de la Cressonnière. **GPS:** n46,90471 e3,84059.⤒➜.

4 ⌁free ⌁€ 2 ⌁€ 2 Ch ⌁€ 2. **Location:** Rural, simple, central.
**Surface:** gravel. ◯ 01/01-31/12.
**Distance:** ⌁300m ⊗250m ⌁50m.
**Remarks:** Max. 48h, coins at town hall and supermarket.

**⌁S Saint-Julien-du-Sault⊗ 19A1**
Stade Jean Sax, Rue du Stade. **GPS:** n48,02906 e3,30116.⤒➜.
13 ⌁free ⌁⌁Chfree. **Surface:** gravel. ◯ 01/01-31/12.

**⌁S Saint-Léger-sur-Dheune 22C1**
Route de Saint-Bérain. **GPS:** n46,84648 e4,63248.⤒.

12 ⌁€ 7/24h + € 0,75/pp tourist tax ⌁⌁Chincluded. ⌁⌁
◯ 01/01-31/12.
**Distance:** ⌁on the spot.

**⌁S Saint-Loup-sur-Semouse 19E2**
Rue de Champ de Tir. **GPS:** n47,88643 e6,27051.

FR

4 🛏free 🚰€3 🅲Ch 🚽€1. **Location:** Simple, quiet.
**Surface:** asphalted. 🅾 01/03-30/11.
**Distance:** 🛒on the spot 🏊500m ⊗300m 🍴200m 🚌on the spot.
**Remarks:** Behind church, max. 24h.

### Saint-Pierre-le-Moûtier · 22A1
**Camping-Car Park**, 13 rue de Beaudrillon. **GPS:** n46,78576 e3,11953.⬆
48 🛏€10,04, 15/06-15/09 €12,44 🚰🅲Ch 🧹(16x)included. 📷🧺
**Location:** Rural. **Surface:** grassy. 🅾 01/01-31/12.
**Distance:** 🛒550m ⊗550m 🍴550m.
**Remarks:** Mandatory, one-time fee Pass'Etapes €4.

### Saint-Point-Lac · 22E1
Rue du Lac. **GPS:** n46,81268 e6,30375.

30 🛏€10/24h 🚰€1/100liter 🅲ChWC. 📷🧺 **Location:** Rural,
luxurious, quiet. **Surface:** gravel/sand. 🅾 15/03-15/11.
**Distance:** 🏊100m ⊗on the spot 🍴on the spot 🧍on the spot.
**Remarks:** Max. 3 nights.

### Sainte-Marie-en-Chanois · 19F2
Rue de la Lolonge. **GPS:** n47,83663 e6,51216.⬆➡

5 🛏free. **Location:** Rural, simple. **Surface:** asphalted.
🅾 01/01-31/12.

### Salins-les-Bains · 22E1
**Place Aubarède**, Rue de la République, D472.
**GPS:** n46,93254 e5,87899.⬆

6 🛏free 🚰🅲Ch 🚽free. **Location:** Simple. **Surface:** asphalted.
🅾 01/01-31/12.
**Distance:** 🛒50m.
**Remarks:** Permitted to park/stay overnight on all parkings.

### Sancey-le-Grand · 19F3
D31. **GPS:** n47,29040 e6,57742.⬆

2 🛏free.
**Location:** Rural, simple. **Surface:** gravel. 🅾 01/01-31/12.
**Distance:** 🛒500m.

### Sancey-le-Long · 19F3
D31/D464. **GPS:** n47,30513 e6,59477.⬆

---

2 🛏free 🚰€2 🅲Ch 🚽€2. **Location:** Rural, simple. **Surface:** gravel.
🅾 01/01-31/12.
**Distance:** 🍴on the spot.
**Remarks:** Coins at supermarket, cafe, centre commercial.

### Saulx · 19E2
Place de l'Eglise. **GPS:** n47,69620 e6,28030.⬆➡
🚰€2/100liter 🅲€2/2h WCfree. **Location:** Simple, central, quiet.
🅾 01/01-31/12.
**Distance:** 🛒on the spot ⊗300m 🍴300m.

### Savigny-le-Sec · 19C3
Rue de la Mare. **GPS:** n47,43365 e5,04607.⬆

10 🛏€5 🚰🅲Chincluded WC. **Location:** Rural, simple, isolated,
quiet. **Surface:** asphalted/gravel. 🅾 01/01-31/12.
**Distance:** 🛒1,3km 🍞bakery 1,3km.

### Savoyeux · 19D2
**Port de plaisance**, Rue des Chênes. **GPS:** n47,56270 e5,73971.⬆
4 🛏€5 🚰🅲Ch 🚽€2 WCincluded 🚿€2 💧€1/12h. 🗑
**Location:** Rural, simple, isolated. **Surface:** gravel/metalled.
🅾 01/01-31/12.
**Distance:** 🛒1,5km ⊗1km.
**Remarks:** Pay at harbourmaster.

### Scey-sur-Saône-et-Saint-Albin · 19E2
D3. **GPS:** n47,65366 e5,97379.⬆
7 🛏free 🚰€2 🅲Ch 🚽€2/1h 🌊. **Location:** Rural, isolated.
**Surface:** metalled. 🅾 01/01-31/12.
**Distance:** 🛒1km 🍴1,5km.
**Remarks:** Picnic tables available.

### Semur-en-Auxois · 19B3
Avenue Louis Pasteur. **GPS:** n47,49506 e4,34945.⬆

30 🛏free 🚰🅲Chfree. **Location:** Simple, quiet. **Surface:** asphalted.
🅾 01/01-31/12 💧 water: Nov-March.
**Distance:** 🛒historical centre 1,3km 🚲10km ⊗800m 🍴800m.
**Remarks:** Barrier, at football ground.

**Tourist information Semur-en-Auxois:**
🎭 Alise-Ste-Reine. Findings of Gallo-Roman city. 🅾 01/04-31/10
daily.

### Sens · 19A1
Avenue de Sénigallia. **GPS:** n48,18622 e3,28570.
25 🛏€10 + €0,20/pp tourist tax 🚰€2/10minutes 🅲Ch🔌
**Location:** Urban, comfortable. **Surface:** forest soil.
🅾 01/01-31/12.
**Distance:** 🛒250m 🍴200m.
**Remarks:** Possibility for reservation.

### Sermamagny · 19F2
Rue Alfred Lallemand. **GPS:** n47,68351 e6,81416.⬆

---

30 🛏free. **Location:** Rural, simple, isolated, quiet. **Surface:** grassy.
🅾 01/01-31/12.
**Distance:** 🛒2,5km ⊗300m 🍴2km.

### Seurre · 22D1
Rue de la Perche à l'Oiseau. **GPS:** n47,00405 e5,14318.⬆➡

7 🛏free 🚰🅲Ch 🚽Service €4/20min 🧹. **Location:** Rural, simple,
quiet. **Surface:** asphalted. 🅾 01/01-31/12.
**Distance:** 🛒800m 🏊100m 🍴100m ⊗700m 🍴700m.
**Remarks:** Camper service 8-20h.

### Thoirette · 22D2
Grande Rue. **GPS:** n46,26924 e5,53529.⬆

5 🛏€6 🚰🅲Ch 🧹included. 📷🔌 **Location:** Simple. **Surface:** gravel.
🅾 01/01-31/12.
**Distance:** 🛒25m 🏊50m 🍴25m 🧍on the spot.

### Tournus · 22C2
Quai de la Marine. **GPS:** n46,56757 e4,91118.⬆

8 🛏free 🚰🅲Ch 🧹. **Location:** Urban, simple, quiet.
**Surface:** metalled. 🅾 01/01-31/12.
**Distance:** 🛒300m ⊗300m 🍴500m 🚗300m.
**Remarks:** Market Saturday.

### Treigny · 19A2
Rue du Champ de Foire. **GPS:** n47,54982 e3,18159.⬆
2 🛏free 🚰🅲Ch. **Location:** Simple, quiet. **Surface:** asphalted.
🅾 01/01-31/12.
**Distance:** 🛒200m 🍴200m 🍴200m.

### Uchon · 22B1
**Auberge La Croix Messire Jean**. **GPS:** n46,80781 e4,26013.
6 🛏free. **Surface:** grassy. 🅾 01/01-31/12.

### Vaivre-et-Montoille · 19E2
20 avenue des Rives-du-Lac. **GPS:** n47,63718 e6,10752.⬆

FR

4 ᠍free 🚰€ 2 🚽Ch 🚻 € 2. **Location:** Rural, simple, quiet.
**Surface:** asphalted. 🅿 01/01-31/12.
**Distance:** ⛽on the spot ⊗100m 🚶on the spot 🚲on the spot.
**Remarks:** Directly at lake, coins at campsite.

| 📷S | **Vaivre-et-Montoille** 🛶〜 | **19E2** |

Avenue des Rives du Lac. **GPS:** n47,62938 e6,12701.⬆.

7 ᠍free 🚰€ 2,50 🚽Ch. **Location:** Rural, simple, quiet.
**Surface:** asphalted. 🅿 01/01-31/12.
**Distance:** ⛽1,5km 🏖beach 100m 〜100m ⊗25m 🚲on the spot
🚶on the spot.
**Remarks:** Swimming pool complex, lake.

| 📷 | **Vellevans** | **19F3** |

D464. **GPS:** n47,31042 e6,49139.⬆.

2 ᠍free. **Location:** Rural, simple, isolated, quiet. **Surface:** asphalted.
🅿 01/01-31/12.
**Distance:** ⛽5,2km ⊗5km.

| 📷S | **Verosvres** | **22C2** |

Le Bourg. **GPS:** n46,39954 e4,44419.⬆.
7 ᠍free 🚽Ch 🚿. **Location:** Comfortable. **Surface:** grassy/gravel.
🅿 01/01-31/12.
**Distance:** 🏊250m 🚰120m.

| 📷S | **Villers-le-Lac** 🌿〜 | **19F3** |

Vedettes Panoramiques, Rue du Clos Rondot.
**GPS:** n47,05948 e6,67195.⬆.

8 ᠍free 🚰€ 2 🚽Ch 🚿free 🚮. **Location:** Simple.
**Surface:** concrete. 🅿 01/01-31/12.
**Distance:** ⛽50m.
**Remarks:** Small pitches.

| 📷S | **Villers-le-Lac** 🌿〜 | **19F3** |

Bateaux du Saut du Doubs. **GPS:** n47,05611 e6,67034.⬆.

50 ᠍free 🚰€ 3,50 🚽Ch at office/shop.
**Location:** Simple, central. **Surface:** grassy/gravel.
🅿 01/04-31/10.
**Distance:** ⛽100m.
**Remarks:** Check in at Bateaux.

| 📷S | **Vinzelles** | **22C2** |

Clos Bonin. **GPS:** n46,27145 e4,77008.⬆.

10 ᠍free 🚰🚽Chfree. **Location:** Rural, simple. **Surface:** asphalted.
🅿 01/01-31/12.
**Distance:** ⛽200m 🛣A6 2,8km ⊗on the spot 🚰on the spot 🚂on
the spot.

# Auvergne-Rhône-Alpes

| 📷S | **Aiguebelle** | **25E1** |

Aiguebelle, Pré de foire. **GPS:** n45,54289 e6,30635.⬆.

18 ᠍free 🚰🚽Chfree. **Location:** Urban, simple, quiet.
**Surface:** asphalted/grassy. 🅿 01/01-31/12 ◻ Thu-morning closed
because of market. **Distance:** ⛽on the spot 🛣6,1km ⊗120m 🚰150m.
**Tourist information Aiguebelle:**
🏛 🅿 Tue-morning.

| 📷S | **Aigueperse** 🌿 | **22A3** |

Place du Foirail, Rue de la Porte aux Boeufs. **GPS:** n46,02634 e3,20313.⬆.

15 ᠍free 🚰€ 2/10minutes 🚽Ch 🚻€ 2/1h. **Location:** Urban, simple,
central, quiet. **Surface:** asphalted.
🅿 01/01-31/12 ◻ 17/08-28/08.
**Distance:** ⛽on the spot ⊗200m 🚰300m.
**Remarks:** Market square.

| 📷 | **Aiguilhe** 〜🍴 | **25B2** |

Avenue de Bonneville. **GPS:** n45,05063 e3,88356.⬆.

6 ᠍free. **Location:** Urban, simple, central. **Surface:** asphalted.
🅿 01/01-31/12.
**Distance:** ⛽on the spot 🚰350m.
**Remarks:** Max. 24h.

| 📷S | **Aix-les-Bains** 〜🍴🌄 | **22E3** |

Camping-Car Park, Rue des Goélands. **GPS:** n45,69627 e5,88926.
85 ᠍€ 13,36 🚰🚽Ch 🚿(52x)🔌€ 5/3 〜included.🚮🚮
**Location:** Urban, simple, noisy. **Surface:** grassy.
🅿 01/01-31/12.
**Distance:** ⛽500m 🚲on the spot ⊗200m 🚰500m 🚂200m.
**Remarks:** Mandatory, one-time fee Pass'Etapes € 4.

| 📷S | **Alba-la-Romaine** 🌿🌄 | **25C3** |

Bragigous. **GPS:** n44,55329 e4,59741.⬆.

35 ᠍€ 4 🚰🚽Ch 🚿 **Location:** Rural, quiet. **Surface:** grassy/gravel.
🅿 01/01-31/12.
**Distance:** ⛽on the spot ⊗200m 🚰200m.
**Remarks:** Service to be paid at retirement home.

| 📷S | **Albertville** | **22F3** |

Parking Conflans, Montée Adolphe Hugues, Conflans.
**GPS:** n45,67389 e6,39694.⬆.
4 ᠍free 🚰€ 5 🚽ChWC 🚮. **Surface:** asphalted. 🅿 01/01-31/12.
**Distance:** ⛽650m ⊗on the spot.
**Tourist information Albertville:**
🏛 Quai des Allobroges. 🅿 Thu 6-18h.

| 📷S | **Allanche** 〜🌄 | **24H1** |

Aire de la Gare, Chemin de la Roche Marchal.
**GPS:** n45,23000 e2,93139.⬆.

25 ᠍free 🚰€ 2 🚽Ch. **Location:** Rural, simple, quiet.
**Surface:** gravel/sand. 🅿 01/05-30/09, parking 01/01-31/12.
**Distance:** ⛽300m ⊗300m 🚰300m.
**Remarks:** Altitude 1000m, coins at camping, tourist info and town hall,
accessed via Allanche centre.

| 📷S | **Allevard** 🐑 | **25E1** |

Avenue des Bains. **GPS:** n45,38838 e6,07110.⬆➡.
24 ᠍€ 5 🚰🚽ChWC 〜included.🚮🚮 **Location:** Rural.
**Surface:** gravel. 🅿 01/01-31/12.
**Distance:** ⛽500m ⊗300m 🚲on the spot 🚶on the spot.
**Remarks:** Thursday market.

| 📷S | **Alpe d'Huez** | **25E2** |

Parking de Brandes, Quartier des Bergers, chemin de font morelle.
**GPS:** n45,08654 e6,07916.⬆➡.

65 ᠍€ 11/day + € 0,83/pp tourist tax 🚰🚽Ch 🚻WC.🚮🚮
**Surface:** asphalted.
**Distance:** ⛽1km ⊗350m 🚲on the spot.
**Remarks:** First buy a parking ticket at Palais des Sports et des
Congrès.

| 📷 | **Ambierle** | **22B2** |

Complexe sportif, Rue Sainte Claude. **GPS:** n46,10663 e3,89384.⬆➡.

FR

3 ⓈⒺfree 🚰♨Chfree. **Location:** Rural, simple, quiet.
**Surface:** asphalted. ⬛ 01/01-31/12.
**Distance:** 🚰on the spot ⊗200m 🛒300m.
**Remarks:** At sports park, narrow road.

🅿️Ⓢ **Annecy** 🌿⛵🏔🌲🏞 **22E3**
**Parking de Colmyr**, Rue des Marquisats, N1508.
**GPS:** n45,89070 e6,13915. ⬆➡.

10 ⓈⒺfree 🚰♨Chfree.
**Location:** Urban, simple, central, quiet. **Surface:** asphalted.
⬛ 01/01-31/12.
**Distance:** 🚰700m ⛱100m 🛒on the spot ⊗700m 🛒700m.
**Remarks:** Max. 24h, market days Tuesday, Friday, Sunday.

**Tourist information Annecy:**
ℹ Office de Tourisme, Bonlieu, 1 rue Jean Jaurès, www.lac-annecy.
com. Located on lake of the same name and surrounded by mountain
peaks. The old city centre exists of covered lanes, canals and bridges.
⛺ Place de Romains. ⬛ Tue 7-19h.

🅿️Ⓢ **Anse** **22C3**
**Cave Saint Cyr**, 31 chemin de Trechen - D70. **GPS:** n45,93169 e4,68623.

4 ⓈⒺfree, service € 5 🚰♨Ch✎. **Location:** Rural, simple, quiet.
**Surface:** gravel/metalled. ⬛ 01/01-31/12.
**Distance:** 🚰700m 🛒600m.
**Remarks:** At wine-grower.

🅿️Ⓢ **Anthy-sur-Léman** **22F2**
Rue du Lac. **GPS:** n46,35889 e6,42192. ⬆.

5 ⓈⒺfree 🚰♨free. **Location:** Rural, simple, quiet. **Surface:** gravel.
⬛ 01/01-31/12.
**Distance:** 🚰700m ⛱50m ⊗on the spot.
**Remarks:** Max. 48h, max. 7m.

🅿️Ⓢ **Archignat** **21H2**
Rue des Chalets. **GPS:** n46,37336 e2,42408. ⬆➡.

---

5 ⓈⒺ€ 8 + € 0,20/pp tourist tax 🚰♨€ 2 ♨Ch ✎€ 3 WC⬛included. ♨
**Location:** Rural, comfortable, quiet. **Surface:** grassy.
⬛ 01/01-31/12.
**Distance:** 🚰on the spot 🛒on the spot.

🅿️Ⓢ **Arçon** **22B3**
Le Bourg. **GPS:** n46,00977 e3,88793. ⬆➡.

3 ⓈⒺfree 🚰♨Chfree. **Location:** Rural, simple, quiet.
**Surface:** metalled/sand. ⬛ 01/01-31/12.
**Distance:** 🚰on the spot ⊗50m.

🅿️Ⓢ **Ardes** **25A1**
Avenue du Maréchal Leclerc. **GPS:** n45,40194 e3,12910. ⬆.
5 ⓈⒺfree 🚰♨Ch. **Location:** Urban, simple. **Surface:** gravel.
⬛ 01/01-31/12.
**Distance:** 🚰200m ⊗400m.

🅿️Ⓢ **Arlanc** **25A1**
Loumans. **GPS:** n45,41233 e3,71782. ⬆➡.

+10 ⓈⒺfree 🚰♨€ 2 ♨Ch. **Location:** Rural, simple, quiet.
**Surface:** asphalted/grassy. ⬛ 01/04-31/10.
**Distance:** 🚰500m 🛒on the spot ⊗100m 🛒1km 🚶on the spot.
**Remarks:** At swimming pool and small lake, coins at tourist info.

🅿️Ⓢ **Arlebosc** 🌿 **25C2**
Place du Marché aux Fruits. **GPS:** n45,03683 e4,65238. ⬆.

10 ⓈⒺfree 🚰♨Chfree. **Location:** Rural, simple, quiet.
**Surface:** gravel. ⬛ 01/01-31/12.
**Distance:** 🚰on the spot 🛒bakery 150m 🚶on the spot.

🅿️Ⓢ **Arnac (Cantal)** **24G2**
Lacan. **GPS:** n45,06056 e2,23389. ⬆.

2 ⓈⒺfree 🚰♨€ 2/100liter ♨Ch🛁€ 2/1h. **Location:** Rural, simple,
quiet. **Surface:** grassy/gravel. ⬛ 01/01-31/12.

---

**Distance:** 🚰50m ⊗150m 🛒150m.

🅿️Ⓢ **Aubignas** **25C3**
La Grangette/D363. **GPS:** n44,58732 e4,63177. ⬆.

10 ⓈⒺvoluntary contribution € 5 🚰♨€ 2/100liter ♨ChWC.
**Location:** Rural, simple, quiet. **Surface:** gravel.
⬛ 01/01-31/12.
**Distance:** 🚰350m.
**Remarks:** Beautiful view.

🅿️Ⓢ **Aubusson-d'Auvergne** 🍴❄ **22A3**
**Base de Loisirs-lac d'Aubusson**, Route du Lac d'Aubusson.
**GPS:** n45,75377 e3,61079. ⬆.

50 ⓈⒺ€ 3, 01/04-31/10 € 6 🚰♨ChWC 📶included. 🚌
**Location:** Rural, simple, isolated, quiet. **Surface:** metalled.
⬛ 01/01-31/12.
**Distance:** ⛱on the spot 🛒on the spot ⊗200m 🛒8km
🚶on the spot.

🅿️Ⓢ **Aurec-sur-Loire** **25B1**
Place de la Gare. **GPS:** n45,37164 e4,19919. ⬆.

3 ⓈⒺfree 🚰♨Chfree. **Location:** Urban, simple, central, quiet.
**Surface:** gravel/sand. ⬛ 01/01-31/12.
**Distance:** 🚰450m ⊗450m 🛒500m 🛒50m.
**Remarks:** At station, max. 48h.

🅿️Ⓢ **Aurillac** ⛲🍴 **24G2**
**Place du Champ de Foire**, Cours d'Angoulême.
**GPS:** n44,92944 e2,44963. ⬆➡.

10 ⓈⒺfree 🚰♨€ 3,50 ♨Ch🛁€ 3,50. **Location:** Urban, simple, noisy.
**Surface:** asphalted. ⬛ 01/01-31/12 ⬤ service: 31/10-01/05.
**Distance:** 🚰on the spot ⊗100m 🛒100m.
**Remarks:** Max. 24h, coins at tourist info.

**Tourist information Aurillac:**
☀ European street theatre and festival.
⬛ 3rd week Aug.

🅿️Ⓢ **Avermes** **22A1**
Avenue des Isles. **GPS:** n46,58587 e3,30509. ⬆.

---

**FR**

3 � free ⛽ € 2 Ch WC. **Location:** Urban, simple, quiet.
**Surface:** metalled. ⬛ 01/01-31/12.
**Distance:** 🚶200m 🚲20km.
**Remarks:** At sports centre.

**S | Aydat 🌊 | 21H3**
Rue du Stade. **GPS:** n45,66025 e2,97778. ⬆➡.

41 ⌐ € 9,50/24h ⛽ Ch 💧 (28x) WC 📶 included. 🛒 📋
**Location:** Rural, comfortable, quiet. **Surface:** grassy.
⬛ 01/01-31/12.
**Distance:** 🚶200m 🏊on the spot 🚲on the spot ⊗on the spot
🛒250m 🚶on the spot.
**Remarks:** Former campsite, max. 8,20m.

**Balazuc | 25B3**
**Parking Champsgelly**, La Croisette. **GPS:** n44,50601 e4,37366. ⬆➡.

5 ⌐ free. **Location:** Rural, noisy. **Surface:** gravel.
⬛ 01/01-31/12.
**Distance:** ⊗280m 🛒1km.

**S | Banne | 25B3**
Quartier l'Eglise, D251. **GPS:** n44,36539 e4,15691. ⬆.

25 ⌐ free ⛽ € 3/1h 🔵Ch 💧 € 3/1h. **Location:** Rural, simple, quiet.
**Surface:** gravel/metalled. ⬛ 01/01-31/12.
**Distance:** 🚶500m.
**Remarks:** Behind church, beautiful view.

**S | Barjac 🌿 | 25B3**
Rue Basse. **GPS:** n44,30589 e4,34343. ⬆.

20 ⌐ free ⛽ Ch 🔵 € 3,water 10 min + electricity 55min.
**Location:** Urban, simple. **Surface:** grassy/gravel. ⬛ 01/01-31/12.
**Distance:** 🚶100m ⊗100m 🛒on the spot.
**Remarks:** Coins at tourist info and town hall, friday market.

**S | Beaulieu | 25B2**
Lous Saux. **GPS:** n45,12662 e3,94799. ⬆➡.

5 ⌐ free ⛽ 🔵Ch 💧(2x)free. **Location:** Rural, simple, quiet.
**Surface:** gravel. ⬛ 01/04-31/10 ⬤ service 01/11-31/03.
**Distance:** 🚶800m ⊗300m 🚴on the spot 🚶on the spot.
**Remarks:** Max. 48h.

**S | Beaulon 🌊 | 22A1**
**Écluse de Beaulon**, La Curesse. **GPS:** n46,60443 e3,65840. ⬆➡.

+10 ⌐ free ⛽ 🔵Ch free 💧(4x)€ 2/6h. **Location:** Rural, simple,
isolated, quiet. **Surface:** gravel. ⬛ 01/01-31/12.
**Distance:** 🚶1,2km 🚣Canal 🚴on the spot ⊗1,2km 🛒1,2km 🚶on
the spot 🚶on the spot.

**S | Beausemblant 🎰 | 25C1**
**Drôme des Collines**, Rue des Glycines, D122.
**GPS:** n45,21826 e4,83282. ⬆➡.

4 ⌐ free ⛽ 🔵Ch free. **Location:** Urban, simple, quiet.
**Surface:** gravel. ⬛ 01/01-31/12.
**Distance:** 🚶100m ⊗100m 🛒300m 🚶on the spot.
**Remarks:** Max. 48h.

**Beauzac | 25B1**
**Espace La Dorlière**, D42. **GPS:** n45,26161 e4,10170. ⬆.

8 ⌐ free ⛽ 🔵Ch free WC. **Location:** Rural, simple, quiet.
**Surface:** gravel/sand. ⬛ 01/05-31/10.
**Distance:** 🚶250m ⊗300m.

**S | Bellerive-sur-Allier | 22A2**
**Riv'Air Camp**, Rue Claude Decloitre. **GPS:** n46,11514 e3,43114. ⬆.

39 ⌐ € 10 ⛽ 🔵Ch 💧(50x)WC 📶included 🔵. 🛒 **Location:** Urban,
comfortable, isolated, quiet. **Surface:** grassy/metalled.
⬛ 01/01-31/12.
**Distance:** 🚶2,5km 🚲17km 🏊on the spot 🚴on the spot ⊗350m
🛒800m.
**Remarks:** Along the Allier river.

**Belleville | 22C2**
Ancienne Avenue du Port. **GPS:** n46,10626 e4,75470. ⬆.

8 ⌐ free ⛽ 🔵Ch free. **Location:** Urban, simple, noisy.
**Surface:** asphalted. ⬛ 01/01-31/12.
**Distance:** 🚶centre 500m 🚲A6 900m ⊗500m 🛒500m.

**S | Belley 🍺 | 22D3**
Route de Saint-Germain, D41. **GPS:** n45,75535 e5,67790. ⬆.

20 ⌐ free ⛽ € 2 🔵Ch 🚌 € 2 WC. **Location:** Urban, comfortable,
noisy. **Surface:** asphalted. ⬛ 01/01-31/12.
**Distance:** 🚶city centre 1km ⊗1km 🛒1km 🚌1km.
**Remarks:** Near sports park, service only with 1-euro coins.

**S | Belleydoux | 22E2**
**Relais Flot Bleu**, Route Principale/D33. **GPS:** n46,25556 e5,77994. ⬆.
⌐ € 2 ⛽ 🔵Ch 💧 € 2/20minutes. **Location:** Rural, simple,
isolated. **Surface:** metalled/sand. ⬛ 01/01-31/12.
**Distance:** 🚶400m.

**S | Belmont-de-la-Loire | 22B2**
Place de l'Église. **GPS:** n46,16543 e4,34634. ⬆.

3 ⌐ free ⛽ 🔵Ch free. **Location:** Rural, simple, central, quiet.
**Surface:** metalled. ⬛ 03/03-19/07, 01/08-31/10.
**Distance:** 🚶50m ⊗100m 🛒100m 🚴on the spot.
**Remarks:** Shady.

**S | Bessay-sur-Allier | 22A2**
Rue Emile Guillaumin. **GPS:** n46,44093 e3,36431. ⬆.

10 ⌐ free ⛽ 🔵Ch free. **Location:** Rural, quiet. **Surface:** metalled.
⬛ 01/01-31/12.
**Distance:** ⊗on the spot 🛒bakery 200m.

**S | Bibost | 22C3**
D91. **GPS:** n45,79500 e4,55144. ⬆.
6 ⌐ free ⛽ 🔵Ch 💧free. **Location:** Rural, simple, noisy.
**Surface:** gravel. ⬛ 01/01-31/12.
**Distance:** 🚶500m ⊗on the spot.
**Remarks:** Beautiful view.

**FR**

### ⚏Ⓢ Billy 22A2
7 Rue de la Fontaine. **GPS:** n46,23586 e3,43044. ⬆⬆

3 🗑free 🚰🗑Chfree. **Location:** Urban, simple, quiet.
**Surface:** asphalted. ⬛ 01/01-31/12.
**Distance:** 🚶on the spot ⊗450m 🛒150m.
**Remarks:** Max. 48h.

### ⚏Ⓢ Blesle ⛰ 25A1
Route du Babory, D8. **GPS:** n45,31733 e3,17424. ⬆

6 🗑free. **Location:** Rural, simple, quiet. **Surface:** gravel/sand.
⬛ 01/01-31/12.
**Distance:** 🚶300m ⊗300m 🛒300m 🚲on the spot.
**Remarks:** Max. 2 nights, service at camping municipal.

### ⛆Ⓢ Blesle ⛰ 25A1
**Hôtel-Restaurant Le Scorpion**, Le Basbory, D909.
**GPS:** n45,31219 e3,18677. ⬆

25 🗑€ 12,50 🚰🗑Ch🛁(8x)WC🗑📶included. **Location:** Rural,
comfortable, quiet. **Surface:** grassy. ⬛ 01/01-31/12.
**Distance:** 🏊5,8km ⊗on the spot 🚲on the spot.

### ⚏Ⓢ Boën 🍽 22B3
Boulevard Moizieux. **GPS:** n45,74401 e4,00263. ⬆➡

8 🗑free 🚰🗑Chfree. **Location:** Urban, simple, central, quiet.
**Surface:** gravel. ⬛ 01/01-31/12.
**Distance:** 🚶200m 🏊900m ⊗200m 🛒300m.

### ⚏Ⓢ Bonlieu-sur-Roubion 25C3
330 chemin des chênes. **GPS:** n44,54735 e4,90558.
15 🗑€ 10 🗑ChWC. **Location:** Rural. **Surface:** gravel.
⬛ 01/04-30/09.
**Distance:** ⊗2,5km 🛒2,5km.

### ⚏Ⓢ Boulieu-lès-Annonay 🌿 25C1
Chemin du Lavoir. **GPS:** n45,26928 e4,66963. ⬆➡

---

6 🗑free 🚰🗑ChWCfree. **Location:** Rural, comfortable, quiet.
**Surface:** gravel. ⬛ 01/01-31/12.
**Distance:** 🚶400m ⊗400m 🛒400m.
**Remarks:** Voluntary contribution, market on Sunday.

### ⚏Ⓢ Bourg-en-Bresse 🌿🍰 22D2
Allée du centre nautique 5. **GPS:** n46,20944 e5,24157.
1 🗑free 🚰🗑Chfree. **Location:** Urban. **Surface:** metalled.
⬛ 01/01-31/12.
**Distance:** 🚶city centre 1km ⊗550m 🛒500m.

### ⚏ Bourg-en-Bresse 🌿🍰 22D2
**Parking V.L./Bus**, Allée Loys Van Boghem.
**GPS:** n46,19854 e5,23766. ⬆

10 🗑free WC100m. **Location:** Urban, simple, central, noisy.
**Surface:** asphalted. ⬛ 01/01-31/12 ⬤ Wed, Sa.
**Distance:** 🚶on the spot 🏊6km ⊗100m 🛒200m 🚌on the spot
🚲on the spot.

### ⚏ Bourg-Saint-Andéol 25C3
Chemin de la Barrière. **GPS:** n44,37520 e4,64327. ⬆

30 🗑free 🚰🗑Ch🛁free. **Location:** Noisy. **Surface:** asphalted
⬛ 01/01-31/12.
**Distance:** 🚶750m 🛒50m.
**Remarks:** Along railwayline, max. 48h.

### ⚏ Bourg-Saint-Maurice 🚠⛰❄ 22F3
Les Chapieux. **GPS:** n45,69532 e6,73364.
+20 🗑free. **Location:** Rural, isolated, quiet. **Surface:** grassy.
⬤ winter.

### ⛆Ⓢ Bourget du Lac 🚣⛰ 22E3
**International au l'Ile de Cygnes. GPS:** n45,65250 e5,86378. ⬆➡

29 🗑€ 6,20-12,50 🚰🗑ChWC🗑📶included. 🚐🗑
**Location:** Rural, comfortable, quiet. **Surface:** metalled.
⬛ 01/01-31/12.
**Distance:** 🚶500m 🏊500m 🏖beach 300m 🛒100m ⊗on the spot
🛒on the spot 🚌100m 🚲on the spot 🚶on the spot.

### ⚏Ⓢ Bourgneuf 25E1
D925. **GPS:** n45,55257 e6,21091. ⬆

---

30 🗑free 🚰€ 2 🗑Ch. **Location:** Simple, noisy. **Surface:** metalled.
⬛ 01/01-31/12.
**Distance:** 🚶400m 🏊5km 🍴Brasserie/Pizzeria 🥖bakery.
**Remarks:** Coins available at Pizzeria/Tabac.

### ⚏Ⓢ Bouvante ⛰❄ 25D2
**Village de Font d'Urle**, Font d'Urle. **GPS:** n44,89789 e5,32195. ⬆

10 🗑free 🚰€ 2/100liter 🗑Ch🛁(5x)€ 7/24h WC🗑€ 2.
**Location:** Rural, simple, quiet. **Surface:** gravel.
⬛ 15/05-30/09.
**Distance:** ⊗on the spot 🚶nordic walking 🐎on the spot.
**Remarks:** Altitude 1550m, coins at riding school.

### ⚏Ⓢ Brioude 🌿⚓ 25A1
**Parking Centre Historique**, Avenue de Lamothe, D588.
**GPS:** n45,29444 e3,38778. ⬆➡

30 🗑free 🚰€ 2 🗑Ch🚐€ 2. **Location:** Urban, simple, central, quiet.
**Surface:** asphalted/gravel. ⬛ 01/01-31/12.
**Distance:** 🚶100m ⊗100m 🛒100m 🚲on the spot.
**Remarks:** Coins at tourist info(100m).

**Tourist information Brioude:**
👁 L'aquarium-la Maison du Saumon et de la Rivière, Place de la
Résistance. Museum about the salmon. ⬛ 01/04-30/11.

### ⚏Ⓢ Calvinet 24G2
**Aire de Calvinet**, Le Puech D66. **GPS:** n44,71023 e2,35914. ⬆➡

6 🗑€ 2,50 🚰€ 2/100liter 🗑Ch🚐€ 2/55minutes WC🗑€ 1.
**Location:** Rural, comfortable, quiet. **Surface:** gravel. ⬛ 01/01-31/12
⬤ service 01/11-31/03.
**Distance:** 🚶1,5km ⊗1,5km 🛒1,5km.
**Remarks:** Nearby sports ground.

### ⚏Ⓢ Cassaniouze 24G2
Le Bourg N. **GPS:** n44,69347 e2,38233. ⬆➡

FR

6 ⛺free 🚰€ 2/80liter ⚡Ch 🔌€ 2/1h 🚿€ 1. **Location:** Rural, simple, quiet. **Surface:** gravel. ⬛ 01/01-31/12 ⬛ service 01/11-31/03. **Distance:** 🛒600m ⊗600m 🏊600m.

**⚅S Cayrols** 24G2

L'Étang, D51. **GPS:** n44,83000 e2,23278. ⬆➡.

10 ⛺free 🚰€ 3,80 ⚡Ch 🔌€ 3,80 WC. **Location:** Rural, comfortable, quiet. **Surface:** metalled. ⬛ 01/01-31/12 ⬛ service 01/11-31/03. **Distance:** 🛒100m 🏊200m. **Remarks:** Max. 1 week, coins at the shops in the village and petrol station.

**⚅S Chalmazel** ⛰❄ 22B3

Station de Chalmazel, Le Pont Ouest. **GPS:** n45,70149 e3,85459. ⬆.

8 ⛺€ 13 🚰⚡Ch🛠 included. **Location:** Comfortable. **Surface:** metalled. ⬛ 01/01-31/12. **Distance:** 🛒50m 🏊on the spot ⊗50m 🏪50m 🚌on the spot 🚶on the spot 🚵2km. **Remarks:** Along river, coins at tourist info.

**⚅S Chambéry** ⛰❄ 25E1

Rue Costa de Beauregard. **GPS:** n45,56289 e5,93302. ⬆. 6 ⛺free 🚰⚡Chfree. **Location:** Urban. **Surface:** asphalted. ⬛ 01/01-31/12 ⬛ water: 15/11-01/03. **Distance:** 🛒500m 🚲1,2km ⊗500m 🏊500m. **Remarks:** Water closed during wintertime.

**Tourist information Chambéry:**

👁 Vieux Cité. Historical centre with old mansions. 🏛 Château des Ducs de Savoie. Complex of buildings, 13-14th century.

**⚅S Chambon-sur-Lac** ⛰❄ 24H1

Camping Les Bombes, La Vergne. **GPS:** n45,56991 e2,90176. ⬆➡.

30 ⛺€ 7 🚰⚡Ch🛠 **Location:** Rural, simple, quiet. **Surface:** grassy/gravel. ⬛ 27/04-16/09. **Distance:** 🛒500m 🚲200m 🚣1km ⊗500m 🏊500m bakery 🚵on the spot 🚶on the spot. **Remarks:** Pay and coins at campsite.

**⚅S Chamonix-Mont-Blanc** ⛰❄ 22F3

Parking Grépon, Aiguille du Midi, D1506. **GPS:** n45,91578 e6,86970. ⬆.

50 ⛺€ 14/24h 🚰included WCfree. 🚿 **Location:** Urban, simple. **Surface:** asphalted. ⬛ 01/01-31/12, service only during summer period. **Distance:** 🛒1km 🚲350m 🏊600m 🚌on the spot 🚵on the spot.

**Tourist information Chamonix-Mont-Blanc:**

Aiguille du Midi. Telpher carrier from Chamonix (1036 m.) To Aiguille de Midi (3842m).

Montenvers et mer de Glace. Tramline from Montenvers to the ice lake, a glacier of 7 km long and 1.2 km broad.

**⚅S Champagnac** 24G1

D12. **GPS:** n45,35806 e2,39929. ⬆➡.

4 ⛺free 🚰⚡ChWCfree. **Location:** Simple, quiet. **Surface:** asphalted. ⬛ 01/05-31/10. **Distance:** 🛒on the spot ⊗on the spot.

**⚅S Champeix** 25A1

Champeix, Route de Montaigut, D996. **GPS:** n45,58845 e3,11568. ⬆➡.

20 ⛺free 🚰€ 2 ⚡Ch. **Location:** Rural, simple, isolated, quiet. **Surface:** grassy/gravel. ⬛ 01/04-31/10. **Distance:** 🛒1,3km ⊗1,3km 🏊500m. **Remarks:** Max. 48h.

**⚅S Champoly** 22B3

La Péniche, Chemin de la salle des fêtes. **GPS:** n45,85583 e3,83227. ⬆➡.

2 ⛺free 🚰€ 2 ⚡Ch🔌€ 2. **Location:** Rural, simple, quiet. **Surface:** asphalted. ⬛ 01/01-31/12. **Distance:** 🛒300m ⊗400m.

**⚅S Chamrousse** ❄ 25E2

Place des Niverolles, Rue de la Cembraie. **GPS:** n45,12666 e5,87356. ⬆.

12 ⛺€ 10 🚰⚡Ch🛠 included WC. **Location:** Rural, simple, isolated, quiet. **Surface:** asphalted. ⬛ 01/01-31/12. **Distance:** 🛒400m ⊗400m 🚌on the spot 🚵400m. **Remarks:** Max. 24h.

**⚅S Chanaleilles** ⛰ 25A2

Le Bourg. **GPS:** n44,85971 e3,49052. ⬆.

5 ⛺free 🚰⚡ChWCfree. **Location:** Rural, simple, isolated, quiet. **Surface:** asphalted/gravel. ⬛ 01/01-31/12. **Distance:** 🛒500m ⊗400m on the spot.

**⚅S Chanteuges** 🌿 25A2

Ancienne Gare. **GPS:** n45,07234 e3,53005. ⬆.

6 ⛺free 🚰⚡Chfree WC. **Location:** Rural, simple, isolated, quiet. **Surface:** gravel. ⬛ 01/01-31/12. **Distance:** 🛒200m ⊗300m. **Remarks:** Max. 8M.

**⚅S Charbonnières-les-Varennes** 21H3

Route de Saint-Georges, Paugnat. **GPS:** n45,88457 e2,97993. ⬆.

9 ⛺free 🚰€ 2/10minutes ⚡Ch🔌€ 2/55minutes. **Location:** Rural, comfortable, quiet. **Surface:** grassy. ⬛ 01/01-31/12. **Distance:** 🛒500m ⊗500m 🏊bakery 500m 🚶on the spot. **Remarks:** Coins at the shops in the village, trail to volcano crater.

**⚅S Charix** ⛰🌳 22D2

Auberge du Lac Genin. **GPS:** n46,21981 e5,69556. ⬆.

20 ⛺€ 5 + € 0,20/pp tourist tax, guests free 🚰⚡Chfree. 🚣 **Location:** Rural, simple, isolated, quiet. **Surface:** gravel. ⬛ 01/05-30/09. **Distance:** 🛒4,7km 🚲lake 🚶on the spot ⊗on the spot 🚵on the spot 🚶on the spot.

**⚅S Charlieu** 🌿 22B2

Place d'Eningen. **GPS:** n46,16031 e4,17813. ⬆.

**FR**

5 ⚏free ⚏🗑ChWCfree. **Location:** Rural, simple, quiet.
**Surface:** gravel/metalled. ⬜ 01/01-31/12.
**Distance:** 🏛historical centre 500m ⊗500m 🛒500m.
**Remarks:** In front of police station.

**⚏S Charols 25C3**
**Aire municipale**, D9. **GPS:** n44,59160 e4,95441.

10 ⚏free ⚏🗑free Ch. **Location:** Urban, simple, quiet.
**Surface:** asphalted. ⬜ 01/01-31/12.
**Distance:** 🏛200m ⊗200m 🛒50m.

**⚏S Chaspuzac 25A2**
**Aérodrome du Puy-en-Velay**, Rue du Vol à Voile.
**GPS:** n45,07491 e3,76131. ⬆➡.

4 ⚏free ⚏€2🗑ChWC. **Location:** Rural, simple, isolated, quiet.
**Surface:** asphalted. ⬜ 01/03-15/11 ⬤ service: 01/11-28/02.
**Distance:** ⊗50m ⚏on the spot.
**Remarks:** View on airport.

**⚏S Chastreix 24H1**
**Parking Station de Ski**, Chastreix Sancy. **GPS:** n45,53507 e2,77695. ⬆.

14 ⚏free ⚏🗑Ch ⚡€9,(winter) WC€2,(winter).
**Location:** Rural, simple, quiet. **Surface:** metalled.
⬜ 01/01-31/12.
**Distance:** 🏛Chastreix 6km ⚏on the spot.
**Remarks:** Check in between 9-17h.

**⚏S Château-sur-Allier 21H1**
Domaine Fessebois. **GPS:** n46,76391 e3,03058. ⬆➡.

4 ⚏free ⚏€3🗑Ch ⚡€3. **Location:** Rural, simple, isolated.
**Surface:** gravel. ⬜ 01/01-31/12.
**Distance:** 🏛200m 🚲10km ⊗1,5km 🛒1,5km ⚏on the spot.
**Remarks:** Picnic area.

**⚏S Châtel-Guyon 🎎 ♨ 21H3**
**Pré Morand**, Avenue de Russie. **GPS:** n45,91707 e3,05779. ⬆➡.

14 ⚏free, 01/04-31/10 €5 ⚏€2 🗑Ch 🚐€2/2h 🗑
**Location:** Simple. **Surface:** gravel. ⬜ 01/01-31/12.
**Distance:** 🏛on the spot 🚌> Riom >Clermont-Ferrand.
**Remarks:** Next to spa resort.

**⚏S Châtel-Guyon 🎎 ♨ 21H3**
**Parking des Roches**, Chemin de Bussane.
**GPS:** n45,91789 e3,06545. ⬆.

10 ⚏free. **Location:** Urban, simple, quiet. **Surface:** asphalted.
⬜ 01/01-31/12.
**Distance:** 🏛500m ⊗600m 🛒600m.

**⚏S Chaudes-Aigues 🎎 ♨ 24H2**
**Parking Beauredon**, Avenue Georges Pompidou, D921.
**GPS:** n44,84972 e3,00306. ⬆➡.

15 ⚏free ⚏€2 🗑Ch 🚐€2/55minutes. **Location:** Urban, simple,
quiet. **Surface:** gravel. ⬜ 15/04-15/10.
**Distance:** 🏛400m ⊗400m 🛒400m ⚏on the spot.

**Tourist information Chaudes-Aigues:**
ℹ Office de Tourisme, 1, avenue Georges Pompidou, www.chaude-
saigues.com. Small town with warm thermal sources (82°C).

**⚏S Chevagnes 22A1**
Route Nationale. **GPS:** n46,61028 e3,55219. ⬆➡.

4 ⚏free ⚏🗑Ch ⚡free. **Location:** Comfortable, isolated, quiet.
**Surface:** gravel. ⬜ 01/01-31/12.
**Distance:** 🏛on the spot ⊗200m.

**⚏S Chichilianne 25D2**
Passière. **GPS:** n44,81226 e5,57532. ⬆.

4 ⚏€5 ⚏€3 🗑Ch ⚡€3. **Location:** Rural, simple, quiet.

Surface: grassy. ⬜ 01/03-31/10 ⬤ water disconnected in winter.
**Distance:** 🏛on the spot ⊗on the spot 🛒250m bakery.
**Remarks:** Coins at town hall or Maison du Parc.

**⚏S Chomelix 🎎 25B1**
**Centre Multi Activités Chomelix**, Route d'Estables, D135.
**GPS:** n45,26219 e3,82573. ⬆⬆.

5 ⚏free ⚏€4 🗑Ch. **Location:** Rural, simple, quiet. **Surface:** gravel.
⬜ 01/01-31/12.
**Distance:** 🏛on the spot ⊗on the spot 🚲on the spot ⚏on the spot.

**⚏S Chonas-l'Amballan 25C1**
Chemin du Coussas. **GPS:** n45,45979 e4,81243. ⬆.
2 ⚏free. **Location:** Urban, quiet. **Surface:** gravel.
⬜ 01/01-31/12.
**Distance:** ⊗200m.

**⚏S Clansayes 🌿🏖🧁🌳🌾 25C3**
**Aire de Toronne**, Quartier Toronne RD133.
**GPS:** n44,36975 e4,79901. ⬆.

20 ⚏€10, 2 pers. incl., dog €1,50 ⚏🗑Chincluded ⚡€4/day,5Amp
WC€2 🗑.
**Location:** Rural, comfortable, isolated, quiet. **Surface:** grassy/gravel.
⬜ -03/01-23/12.
**Distance:** 🏛2km ⊗buvette-menu rapide-restauration 🛒3km.
**Remarks:** Bread-service, regional products, swimming pool (summer).

**⚏S Clermont Ferrand 22A3**
**P&R Les Pistes**, Rue de la Fontaine de la Ratte.
**GPS:** n45,79810 e3,11222. ⬆➡.

6 ⚏€8 🗑Chincluded. ⚏ **Location:** Urban, simple
**Surface:** asphalted. ⬜ 01/01-31/12.
**Distance:** 🏛historical centre 3km ⊗900m 🚌50m.
**Remarks:** Nearby Michelin museum, check in at parking attendant.

**⚏S Collanges 25A1**
Rue de Rompady. **GPS:** n45,43956 e3,21564. ⬆.
5 ⚏€6 ⚏€2 🗑Ch ⚡€2. **Location:** Rural, comfortable, quiet.
**Surface:** grassy/gravel. ⬜ 01/01-31/12.

**⚏S Colombier-le-Jeune 25C2**
Le Village. **GPS:** n45,01106 e4,70132. ⬆.

2 ⚏free ⚏🗑Chfree. **Location:** Rural, simple, quiet.
**Surface:** metalled. ⬜ 01/01-31/12 ⬤ water disconnected in winter.
**Distance:** 🏛on the spot ⊗150m 🛒200m ⚏on the spot.

## Coltines 24H2

D40. **GPS:** n45,09612 e2,98555. ⬆➡.

5 ⓢfree 🚰 € 2/100liter 🧺Ch € 2/60minutes.
**Location:** Rural, simple, quiet.
**Surface:** gravel.
⬜ 15/04-15/10.
**Distance:** 400m 400m 400m.
**Remarks:** Coins at Epicerie-Presse, Centre Chantarisa and town hall.

## Combloux 22F3

**Parking du Bouchet**, Route du Bouchet. **GPS:** n45,89896 e6,63275. ⬆.
6 ⓢfree. **Surface:** asphalted. ⬜ 01/01-31/12.
**Distance:** on the spot.
**Remarks:** At ski-lift.

## Condat 24H1

**Parking au Pont**, D678. **GPS:** n45,33889 e2,76250. ⬆.

4 ⓢfree 🚰 Service € 2,50 🧺Ch. **Location:** Simple.
**Surface:** asphalted. ⬜ 01/01-31/12. service: 01/10-01/05.
**Distance:** 50m 50m 50m.
**Remarks:** Coins at campsite La Borie Basse (500m).

## Cornas 25C2

**Impasse de Iris**, Grande Rue, D86. **GPS:** n44,96024 e4,84722. ⬆.

5 ⓢfree 🚰🧺Chfree. **Location:** Simple. **Surface:** gravel.
⬜ 01/01-31/12.
**Distance:** 200m 200m bakery 200m.
**Remarks:** Max. 48h, several 'Caves' with wine tasting.

## Coubon 25B2

Route du Plan d'Eau. **GPS:** n44,99735 e3,91742.

5 ⓢfree 🚰 € 3 🧺ChWC. **Location:** Simple, quiet.
**Surface:** asphalted. ⬜ 01/03-01/11 14/07 + last weekend of
September.
**Distance:** on the spot 100m 200m.
**Remarks:** Along Loire river, key service at supermarket Vival and bar/
tabac 75m.

## Coucouron 25B2

Les Eygades. **GPS:** n44,80168 e3,96148. ⬆.

33 ⓢ€ 9 🚰🧺Ch included. **Location:** Rural, simple.
**Surface:** gravel. ⬜ 01/05-31/10.
**Distance:** 1km on the spot on the spot on the spot 1km
on the spot.
**Remarks:** At Lac de Coucouron, max. 7 days, outside season free stay
on campsite municipal (no facilities).

## Cournon d'Auvergne 22A3

**Les Pres des Laveuses**, Rue de Laveuses.
**GPS:** n45,73994 e3,22225. ⬆➡.

10 ⓢ€ 4,20 🚰 € 2,50 🧺Ch. **Location:** Rural, simple.
**Surface:** gravel. ⬜ 01/01-31/12.
**Distance:** 2km on the spot on the spot on the spot.

## Cours-la-Ville 22B2

La Rivière. **GPS:** n46,10399 e4,32315. ⬆.

10 ⓢfree 🚰🧺Chfree. **Location:** Rural, simple.
**Surface:** grassy/gravel. ⬜ 01/01-31/12.
**Distance:** 300m 700m on the spot on the spot.
**Remarks:** Along the river Trambouze, to be reached from northern
direction, Boulevard Pierre de Coubertin.

## Courtenay 22D3

**Etang de Salette**, Courtenay. **GPS:** n45,72417 e5,37124. ⬆.

7 ⓢfree. **Location:** Rural, isolated, quiet. **Surface:** gravel.
⬜ 01/01-31/12.
**Distance:** 1km on the spot Pizzeria bread service 1,2km
on the spot.

## Crandelles 24G2

Lac des Genevrières. **GPS:** n44,95877 e2,34289.

10 ⓢfree 🚰 € 3,50 🧺Ch. **Location:** Comfortable, central, quiet.
**Surface:** gravel. ⬜ 01/04-31/10.

**Distance:** 300m 50m 50m 50m 300m.

## Craponne-sur-Arzon 25B1

Place de la Gare. **GPS:** n45,33381 e3,84996. ⬆.

+20 ⓢfree 🚰 € 2 🧺Ch € 2/h.
**Location:** Urban, simple, quiet. **Surface:** asphalted/gravel.
⬜ 01/01-31/12. service 01/11-31/03.
**Distance:** 150m 150m on the spot.

## Crémieu 22D3

Rue du 19 mars 1962. **GPS:** n45,72549 e5,24670. ⬆.

12 ⓢfree 🚰🧺Chfree. **Location:** Urban, simple, central.
**Surface:** asphalted. ⬜ 01/01-31/12.
**Distance:** 300m 250m 300m 100m.

## Crest 25C2

Place du Champ de Mars, Avenue Agirond. **GPS:** n44,72600 e5,02100. ⬆.

17 ⓢ€ 5/24h 🚰 € 2 🧺Ch € 2 free. **Location:** Urban, simple,
noisy. **Surface:** asphalted. ⬜ 01/01-31/12.
**Distance:** 200m pizzeria bakery 50m.
**Remarks:** Max. 8M.

## Creuzier-le-Vieux 22A2

Place des Guinards. **GPS:** n46,15443 e3,43128. ⬆.

6 ⓢfree 🚰 € 2 🧺Ch. **Location:** Urban, simple, quiet.
**Surface:** metalled. ⬜ 01/01-31/12.
**Distance:** on the spot 500m on the spot on the spot.
**Remarks:** Coins at the bakery, bakery 500m.

## Cros-de-Géorand 25B2

**Campng-Car Park Lac de la Palisse**, D160.
**GPS:** n44,78041 e4,10356. ⬆.
6 ⓢ€ 9,40 🚰🧺Ch (4x) included. **Location:** Rural.
**Surface:** gravel. ⬜ 01/01-31/12.
**Remarks:** Mandatory, one-time fee Pass'Etapes € 4.

## Die 25D2

**Aire de Meyrosse**, Avenue du Maréchal Leclerc, D238.
**GPS:** n44,75103 e5,37385. ⬆.

**FR**

30 ⌷ € 5-9/24h ⌷ Ch included WC free. **Surface:** grassy/gravel.
⬛ 01/01-31/12.
**Distance:** 300m ⊗300m 1km.
**Remarks:** Max. 1 night, pay at Police Municpale.

### S Diou 22B2
Chemin de la Procession. **GPS:** n46,53523 e3,74401. ⬆➡

3 ⌷ free ⌷ Ch ⌷ free. **Location:** Rural, simple. **Surface:** grassy.
⬛ 01/01-31/12.
**Distance:** ⊗900m.

### S Doizieux 25C1
**Au bon air des chirats**, Le Châtelard. **GPS:** n45,44239 e4,63307.
2 ⌷ free ⌷ € 2 ⌷ € 5. **Location:** Rural, isolated, quiet.
**Surface:** grassy. ⬛ 01/01-31/12.
**Distance:** 5km 350m on the spot.

### S Dompierre-sur-Besbre 22A2
**Les Gauffroux. GPS:** n46,51822 e3,68469. ⬆

7 ⌷ free ⌷ Ch ⌷ WC free. **Location:** Simple. **Surface:** gravel.
⬛ 01/01-31/12.
**Distance:** on the spot ⊗300m 200m.

### S Donzère 25C3
**Aire de respos de Combelonge**, RN 7.
**GPS:** n44,44060 e4,71899. ⬆➡

15 ⌷ free ⌷ Ch WC free. **Location:** Motorway, simple, noisy.
**Surface:** asphalted. ⬛ 01/01-31/12.
**Distance:** 500m 7km.
**Remarks:** Near RN7.

### S Drugeac 24G1
La Gare SNCF. **GPS:** n45,16694 e2,38667. ⬆➡

4 ⌷ free ⌷ € 2/100liter ⌷ Ch ⌷ € 2/1h.

---

**Location:** Rural, simple, quiet. **Surface:** asphalted. ⬛ 01/01-31/12
⬤ service: 01/11-01/05.
**Distance:** 100m ⊗100m 100m.
**Remarks:** At former station, now start Vélorail.

### S Ebreuil 21H2
**Parking du Stade**, D915. **GPS:** n46,10954 e3,07606. ⬆

10 ⌷ free. **Location:** Simple. **Surface:** gravel. ⬛ 01/01-31/12.
**Distance:** 6,5km ⊗2km.
**Remarks:** In front of campsite municipal, service 500m.

### S Ebreuil 21H2
Chemin des Nières. **GPS:** n46,11083 e3,08111. ⬆
⌷ Ch free. ⬛ 01/01-31/12.
**Remarks:** Overnight stay on Parking du Stade.

### S Estivareilles 21H2
**Salle Polyvalente**, Rue de la République.
**GPS:** n46,42471 e2,61529. ⬆➡

20 ⌷ free ⌷ Ch free. **Location:** Urban, simple. **Surface:** gravel.
⬛ 01/01-31/12.
**Distance:** on the spot 9km ⊗200m bakery 200m.

### S Eyzin-Pinet 25C1
Rue du Stade. **GPS:** n45,47463 e4,99965. ⬆

6 ⌷ free ⌷ Ch free. **Location:** Rural, simple, central, quiet.
**Surface:** gravel. ⬛ 01/01-31/12.
**Distance:** 50m 50m 20m on the spot on the spot.

### S Faverges 22E3
Route d'Annecy, D2508. **GPS:** n45,74943 e6,28626. ⬆➡

20 ⌷ free ⌷ Ch free. **Location:** Rural, simple, noisy.
**Surface:** gravel. ⬛ 01/01-31/12 ⬤ Service: winter.
**Distance:** 800m ⊗800m on the spot 100m 100m.
**Remarks:** Max. 48h, market Wednesday.

### S Faverolles 25A2
**Place de la mairie**, Le Bourg, D248. **GPS:** n44,93906 e3,14756. ⬆

---

4 ⌷ free ⌷ € 2/10minutes ⌷ Ch ⌷ € 2/55minutes.
**Location:** Urban, simple. **Surface:** gravel/metalled.
⬛ 01/01-31/12.
**Distance:** 200m ⊗200m on the spot.

### S Flaine 22F3
**Parking P1**, Flaine, 74300 Magland. **GPS:** n46,00377 e6,69083.

25 ⌷ € 5. **Surface:** gravel. ⬛ 01/01-31/12.
**Distance:** ⊗200m on the spot.
**Remarks:** Parking at skipistes.

### S Fontanes 25C1
Fontanès, 42140. **GPS:** n45,54681 e4,44027. ⬆

3 ⌷ free ⌷ Ch free. **Location:** Rural, simple, quiet.
**Surface:** asphalted. ⬛ 01/01-31/12.
**Distance:** 500m 13km 400m.
**Remarks:** At tennis-courts, inclining pitches.

### S Gervans 25C2
**Place des Amandiers**, Rue de l'école. **GPS:** n45,10932 e4,83031. ⬆➡

4 ⌷ free ⌷ Ch free. **Location:** Simple. **Surface:** gravel.
⬛ 01/01-31/12.
**Distance:** on the spot on the spot ⊗250m 250m
on the spot.
**Remarks:** Max. 24h, no camping activities.

### S Gipcy 21H2
Le Bourg. **GPS:** n46,50235 e3,05320. ⬆
8 ⌷ free ⌷ € 2 ⌷ Ch ⌷ € 2 WC. **Location:** Rural, simple, comfortable. **Surface:** gravel. ⬛ 01/01-31/12.

### S Grane 25C2
**Domaine Distaise**, 95 Distaise, 26400 Grane.
**GPS:** n44,75564 e4,86768. ⬆➡

15 🛏€4 🚰€1 〰included. **Surface:** grassy. ☐ 01/01-31/12.
**Distance:** 🏃on the spot.

### 🅿S Gresse-en-Vercors — 25D2

**Parking de la station**, Route du Grand Veymont.
**GPS:** n44,89184 e5,54766.

2 🛏free 🚰🔌Ch. **Location:** Simple. **Surface:** gravel.
☐ 01/01-31/12.
**Distance:** 🚶on the spot.
**Remarks:** Max. 24h, service on campsite.

### 🅿S Grignan — 25C3

900 route de Montélimar. **GPS:** n44,41980 e4,89365.⬆
15 🛏free 🚰€2 🔌Ch 🚿€2.
**Location:** Urban. **Surface:** asphalted.
**Distance:** 🚶1km ⊗on the spot.

**Tourist information Grignan:**
ℹ Office de Tourisme, Place du jeu de Ballon,
www.guideweb.com/grignan.
✗ Château de Grignan. Renaissance castle with collection of wall
tapestries. ☐ 9.30-11.30h, 14-17.30h ⭕ 01/11-31/03 Tue.
🎋 ☐ Tue.
🎋 Les Puces de la Tuilère. Flea market. ☐ 2nd Su of the month.

### 🅿S Hauteluce — 22F3

**Du Grand Tetras**, Les Saisies, 1634, route du Mont Bisanne.
**GPS:** n45,74782 e6,53491.⬆
50 🛏€ 16-19 + € 0,50/pp tourist tax 🚰🔌Ch 🚿included,10Amp
〰against payment. **Location:** Rural. **Surface:** metalled.
☐ 01/01-31/12.
**Distance:** 🚶Les Saisies 2km 🎿on the spot.

### 🅿S Hauteluce — 22F3

**Parking de la Fôret**, Tetras, D123. **GPS:** n45,74633 e6,53441.

5 🛏free 🚰€2 🔌Ch€2 🚿. **Location:** Rural, simple, isolated,
quiet. **Surface:** gravel. ☐ 01/01-31/12.
**Distance:** 🚶3km ⊗3km 🍺3km.

### 🅿S Hauteluce — 22F3

**Parking Du Col des Saisies**, Hauteluce 73620.
**GPS:** n45,76297 e6,53382.⬆➡

40 🛏€8 🚰€2/10minutes 🔌Ch€2 🔋€2 WC. **Location:** Rural.
**Surface:** asphalted. ☐ 01/01-31/12.
**Distance:** 🚶500m ⊗400m 🍺500m 🚌skibus (winter) 🎿200m
⛷200m.

### 🅿S Hauterives — 25C1

D538. **GPS:** n45,25497 e5,03022.

🛏€5 🚰50liter 🔌Chincluded WC. **Location:** Rural, simple.
**Surface:** gravel.
**Distance:** 🚶250m ⊗250m.

**Tourist information Hauterives:**
👁 Palais Idéal du Facteur Cheval.

### 🅿S Hotonnes — 22D3

Les Plans d'Hotonnes, D39B. **GPS:** n46,03857 e5,70023.
1 🛏free 🚰€1 🔌ChWC. **Location:** Rural. **Surface:** asphalted.
☐ 01/01-31/12.
**Distance:** ⊗200m.

### 🅿S Illiat — 22C2

**GPS:** n46,18495 e4,88802.⬆

4 🛏free 🚰🔌ChWCfree. **Location:** Rural, simple, quiet.
**Surface:** gravel. ☐ 01/01-31/12.
**Distance:** 🚶650m ⚓200m 🎣200m 🍺350m 🚴on the spot
🏃on the spot.
**Remarks:** At small lake.

### 🅿S Issoire — 25A1

Boulevard André Malraux. **GPS:** n45,54521 e3,24107.⬆➡

10 🛏free 🚰€2/100liter 🔌Ch. **Location:** Simple, quiet.
**Surface:** gravel/metalled. ☐ 01/01-31/12.
**Distance:** 🚶300m ⊗300m 🍺100m 🚶on the spot.
**Remarks:** Max. 7 days.

### 🅿S Izernore — 22D2

Rue de l'Oignin. **GPS:** n46,21847 e5,55041.⬆⬆

8 🛏free 🚰🔌Chfree.
**Location:** Rural, simple, central, quiet.
**Surface:** gravel.
☐ 01/01-31/12 ⭕ service 01/11-31/03.
**Distance:** 🚶on the spot 🚲6km ⊗500m 🍺500m 🚴500m 🏃500m.
**Remarks:** On the foot of the Monts Berthiand.

### 🅿S Jaligny-sur-Besbre — 22A2

Rue de la Chaume. **GPS:** n46,38155 e3,59147.⬆➡

5 🛏free 🚰🔌Ch 🚣(5x)free. **Location:** Rural, simple, quiet.
**Surface:** gravel. ☐ 01/01-31/12.
**Distance:** 🚶200m ⚓on the spot 🎣on the spot ⊗250m 🍺250m.
**Remarks:** Along the Besbre river.

### 🅿S Job — 22A3

25 Route de Chansert, D255. **GPS:** n45,62019 e3,74502.⬆➡

10 🛏free 🚰🔌Chfree. **Location:** Rural, simple, quiet.
**Surface:** gravel. ☐ 01/01-31/12.
**Distance:** 🚶500m ⊗500m 🚴on the spot 🏃on the spot.
**Remarks:** Playground.

### 🅿S Joux — 22B3

**Salle des Fêtes**, La Noirie, D79. **GPS:** n45,88869 e4,37587.⬆

10 🛏free 🚰🔌Chfree. **Location:** Rural, simple, quiet.
**Surface:** asphalted. ☐ 01/01-31/12 ⭕ water disconnected in winter.
**Distance:** 🚶200m 🚲3,2km ⊗200m 🍺200m.
**Remarks:** Nearby castle garden.

### 🅿S La Balme de Sillingy — 22E3

**Aire de Camping-cars Domaine du Tornet**.
**GPS:** n45,97124 e6,03135.⬆

20 🛏€6 🚰🔌Chincluded. 🚿 **Location:** Rural, simple, central,
noisy. **Surface:** gravel. ☐ 01/04-31/10.
**Distance:** 🚣100m (fishing permit available) ⊗100m 🏃on the spot.
**Remarks:** Recreation park, max. 48h.

### 🅿S La Bénisson-Dieu — 22B2

**Parking de l'école**, Rue des Comtes du Forez.
**GPS:** n46,15094 e4,04708.⬆➡

2 🛏free. **Location:** Rural, simple, central, quiet. **Surface:** gravel.
☐ 01/01-31/12.
**Distance:** 🚶on the spot ⊗200m.

### � S La Bourboule 🏔🌊♨ 24H1
Chemin de la Suchére. **GPS:** n45,58572 e2,73489.⬆

10 🚐free 🚰€5 🗲Ch 🧺. **Location:** Simple, quiet.
**Surface:** metalled. 🛢 01/01-31/12.
**Distance:** 🚶500m ⊗500m.
**Remarks:** Max. 48h.

### ⚎íp La Bourboule 🏔🌊♨ 24H1
Plateau de Charlannes. **GPS:** n45,57811 e2,73513.⬆

10 🚐free. **Location:** Rural, simple, quiet. **Surface:** asphalted.
🛢 01/01-31/12.
**Distance:** 🚶6,5km ⊗350m 🚲 on the spot ♀ on the spot.
**Remarks:** Parking at funicular railway.

### ⚎íp S La Chaise-Dieu 25A1
Esplanade de la Gare. **GPS:** n45,31682 e3,69694.⬆

8 🚐free 🚰€2/100liter 🗲Ch. **Location:** Urban, simple, quiet.
**Surface:** gravel/sand. 🛢 01/04-31/10.
**Distance:** 🚶500m ⊗on the spot.
**Remarks:** Coins at shops and tourist office.

### ⚎íp S La Chambre 25E1
Place du champ de foire. **GPS:** n45,36287 e6,29730.
9 🚐free 🚰🗲Ch 🧺 **Surface:** metalled. 🛢 01/01-31/12.
**Distance:** 🚶300m ⊗400m 🚰100m on the spot ♀ on the spot.
**Remarks:** Max. 72h.

### ⚎íp S La Chapelle-Laurent ❄ 25A1
D10. **GPS:** n45,18028 e3,24389.⬆

20 🚐free 🚰voluntary contribution 🗲Ch.
**Location:** Rural, simple, quiet. **Surface:** grassy. 🛢 01/01-31/12
🛢 service: 15/11-31/03.
**Distance:** 🚶50m 🚲nearby ⊗100m 🚰100m on the spot
♀ on the spot.

### íp La Clusaz 22F3
Route des Confins. **GPS:** n45,92298 e6,48380.
🚐free. 🛢 01/01-31/12.
**Distance:** ⊗800m ♀ on the spot.
**Remarks:** Parking at pistes.

### ⚎íp S La Féclaz 🌿🏔🌊♨❄ 22E3
Aire Camping-cars de la Féclaz, Les Déserts.
**GPS:** n45,64210 e5,98411.⬆

---

**Distance:** 🚶1km 150m.
**Remarks:** Max. 24h, theater, regional products.

40 🚐€4 🚰€1,50 🗲Ch🚻€1,50. **Surface:** asphalted.
🛢 01/01-31/12.
**Distance:** 🚶on the spot ⊗300m 🚰600m 🍴300m 🚲 on the spot.

### ⚎íp S La Mure 25E2
Sur les bords de Jonche, Boulevard Fréjus-Michon.
**GPS:** n44,90617 e5,78301.
7🚐€8 🚰🗲Ch🚻. 🚂 **Location:** Urban. **Surface:** asphalted.
🛢 15/04-15/11.
**Distance:** 🚶on the spot ⊗150m 🚰400m.
**Remarks:** Max. 72h, picnic area.

### 🍇 La Roche-Blanche 22A3
Les Trolières, La Pigné Sud, Route des Fours à Chaux.
**GPS:** n45,71567 e3,14790.⬆

100 🚐€6 🚰€2/100liter 🗲Ch 🧺(4x)€2/6h. 🚲
**Location:** Rural, simple, isolated, quiet. **Surface:** grassy.
🛢 01/03-30/11.
**Distance:** 🚣1,1km.
**Remarks:** Max. 48h.

### ⚎íp S La Roche-de-Glun 25C2
Camping-Car Park, Rue de Crussol. **GPS:** n45,00921 e4,84583.
41 🚐€10,60-11,80 🚰🗲Ch 🧺(20x)included.🎟
**Surface:** grassy/gravel. 🛢 01/01-31/12.
**Remarks:** Mandatory, one-time fee Pass'Etapes € 4.

### ⚎íp S La Tania 🏔❄ 25F1
D98. **GPS:** n45,43340 e6,57679.
7🚐free 🧺. **Location:** Rural, simple. **Surface:** gravel.
🛢 01/01-31/12.
**Distance:** ⊗2km 🚲 on the spot.

### ⚎íp S La Tour-d'Auvergne 🏔🌊 24H1
7 Route de Clermont. **GPS:** n45,53290 e2,68213.⬆

25 🚐free 🚰€2/100liter 🗲Ch🚻€2. **Location:** Simple, quiet.
**Surface:** metalled. 🛢 01/01-31/12.
**Distance:** 🚶on the spot ⊗650m bakery.

### 🍇 S Lablachère 25B3
La Ferme Théâtre, D104, Notre Dame. **GPS:** n44,45481 e4,22004.⬆

20 🚐€5 + € 0,70/pp tourist tax 🚰€2 🧺€3/12h. **Location:** Rural,
comfortable, quiet. **Surface:** gravel. 🛢 01/01-31/12.

---

### ⚎íp S Lacapelle-Viescamp 24G2
D18. **GPS:** n44,92167 e2,26361.🚲.

5 🚐free 🚰€3/100liter 🗲Ch🚻€3/1h. **Location:** Rural, simple.
**Surface:** metalled. 🛢 01/01-31/12.
**Distance:** 🚶100m ⊗100m 🚰 on the spot.
**Remarks:** Coins available at the shop.

### ⚎íp S Lachamp-Raphaël 🏔🌲 25B2
D122, Le Village. **GPS:** n44,81133 e4,28860.⬆

5 🚐free 🚰€2 🗲Ch.
**Location:** Rural, simple, quiet. **Surface:** gravel.
🛢 01/01-31/12.
**Distance:** 🚶300m ⊗300m 🍞Bread 300m ♀departure Nordic.
**Remarks:** Altitude 1330m, coins at bar/hotel, beautiful view.

### 🍴 Lagorce 25B3
Le Sainte Anne, Leyris. **GPS:** n44,49581 e4,42190.
2 🚐free. **Location:** Simple, isolated. 🛢 01/01-31/12.
**Distance:** ⊗on the spot.

### ⚎íp S Lalouvesc 🍴 25C2
Vallon d'Or, Sainte Agathe. **GPS:** n45,11947 e4,53384.⬆

3 🚐free 🚻. **Location:** Simple, central. **Surface:** asphalted.
🛢 01/01-31/12.
**Distance:** 🚶on the spot ⊗100m 🚰100m.

### S Lalouvesc 🍴 25C2
Place du Lac, La Fontaine. **GPS:** n45,12149 e4,53393.⬆
10free 🚰€2/15minutes 🗲Ch🧺. **Location:** Urban, simple, quiet.
**Surface:** asphalted. 🛢 15/05-15/10.
**Distance:** 🚶200m ⊗200m 🚰 on the spot.
**Remarks:** Coins at tourist info and town hall.

### ⚎íp S Lamastre 🌊 25C2
Parking Pont de Tain, Place Pradon. **GPS:** n44,98672 e4,58001.⬆

20 🚐free 🚰€2/100liter 🗲€2,50 Ch🚻€2/1h🧺.
**Location:** Rural, simple, quiet. **Surface:** grassy/gravel.
🛢 01/01-31/12.
**Distance:** 🚶on the spot ⊗on the spot 🚰 on the spot.
**Remarks:** Along river, max. 48h, coins at tourist info.

### ⚎íp S Lamure-sur-Azergues 22C3
Quartier Neuf. **GPS:** n46,06120 e4,49185.⬆➡

10 🚐free ⚡€2 🚰Ch🔌€2 WC.
**Location:** Rural, simple. **Surface:** asphalted.
⚪ 01/01-31/12.
**Distance:** 🚃on the spot ⊗100m 🚉100m 🚆train/bus 🚶on the spot.
**Remarks:** Near train station.

### ⬛S Lanarce 25B2
**Camping Municipal**, Jammes. **GPS**: n44,72578 e4,00403.
10 🚐free, 15/06-15/09 €12 🚰Ch🔌€3 WC🔌 included. 🚃
**Location:** Rural, comfortable, quiet. **Surface:** grassy.
⚪ 15/04-30/10.
**Distance:** 🚃700m 🏊on the spot 🚣on the spot ⊗700m.
**Remarks:** Beside river.

### ⬛S Lans-en-Vercors 25D2
La Sierre. **GPS**: n45,11628 e5,60966.
3 🚐free ⚡€4 🚰ChWC🔌. **Location:** Rural. **Surface:** asphalted.
⚪ 01/01-31/12.
**Distance:** 🚃5km ⊗on the spot 🎿on the spot.
**Remarks:** At ski-lift.

### ⬛S Lans-en-Vercors 25D2
Route de l'Aigle. **GPS**: n45,12418 e5,59125. ⬆➡.

50 🚐free ⚡€4 🚰ChWC. **Location:** Rural, simple, noisy.
**Surface:** gravel. ⚪ 01/01-31/12 ▪ Service: winter.
**Distance:** 🚃500m ⊗on the spot 🎿on the spot.
**Remarks:** Large parking, max. 7 days, tuesday and Saturday market.

### ⬛S Lapalisse ❄🌳❄ 22A2
Place Jean Moulin, RN7 dir Roanne. **GPS**: n46,25000 e3,63500.➡.

15 🚐free ⚡🚰Ch🔌WC free. **Location:** Urban, simple, central,
quiet. **Surface:** asphalted. ⚪ 01/01-31/12.
**Distance:** 🚃300m 🏊on the spot ⊗on the spot 🚉on the spot.
**Remarks:** Coins at tourist info.

### ⬛ Laprugne 22A3
Domaine La Bourbonnaise, D477. **GPS**: n45,98661 e3,74569.

10 🚐free. **Location:** Rural, simple. **Surface:** asphalted.
⚪ 01/01-31/12.
**Distance:** 🚃200m ⊗on the spot.

### ⬛S Lapte 25B1
Rue du Docteur Tassy, Chamdappe. **GPS**: n45,18419 e4,21363.
🚐free ⚡€2 🚰Ch. **Surface:** gravel. ⚪ 01/01-31/12.
**Distance:** 🚃150m. **Remarks:** Max. 48h.

---

### ⬛S Laqueuille 21H3
**Place de Foirail**, Le Bourg. **GPS**: n45,65008 e2,73289. 🚁.

2 🚐free ⚡€2/10minutes 🚰Ch🔌€4/8h 🔌. **Location:** Simple,
quiet. **Surface:** asphalted. ⚪ 01/01-31/12.
**Distance:** ⊗100m 🚉100m.

### ⬛S Lathuile 22E3
**Les Jardin du Tailleter**, 190 route de la Porte, Bout du lac, N 508.
**GPS**: n45,79480 e6,20796. ⬆➡.

24 🚐€8 ⚡🚰Chincluded 🔌(24x)€2 🔌. **Location:** Rural,
simple. **Surface:** grassy. ⚪ 01/06-31/08.
**Distance:** 🏊Lake of Annecy 750m.
**Remarks:** Max. 24h.

### ⬛ Lavaudieu 🌿⛱ 25A1
Le Bourg. **GPS**: n45,26297 e3,45606. 🚁.

10 🚐free. **Location:** Simple, isolated, quiet. **Surface:** grassy/gravel.
⚪ 01/01-31/12.
**Distance:** 🚃200m 🏊on the spot ⊗on the spot 🚶on the spot.

### ⬛S Le Bessat 🌳❄ 25C1
Croix de Chaubouret. **GPS**: n45,36812 e4,52768. 🚁.

4 🚐free ⚡€2,50/20minutes 🚰Ch🔌(4x)€2,50/6h.
**Location:** Rural, simple, quiet.
**Surface:** asphalted.
⚪ 01/01-31/12.
**Distance:** 🚃1km ⊗100m 🚴mountainbike trail 🚶on the spot
🎿on the spot.
**Remarks:** Altitude 1200m, coins at Chalet des Alpes and the shops.

### ⬛S Le Breuil-sur-Couze 25A1
Allée de Treize Vents. **GPS**: n45,46867 e3,26121. ⬆➡.

8 🚐free ⚡🚰Chfree. **Location:** Urban, simple. **Surface:** gravel.

---

⚪ 01/01-31/12.
**Distance:** 🚵900m 🚉800m.
**Remarks:** Along railwayline.

### ⬛S Le Cheix-sur-Morge 22A3
D425. **GPS**: n45,95138 e3,17812. ⬆➡.

6 🚐free ⚡🚰Chfree. **Location:** Rural, simple, isolated, quiet.
**Surface:** gravel. ⚪ 01/01-31/12 ▪ water disconnected in winter.
**Distance:** 🚃500m ⊗950m 🚶on the spot.
**Remarks:** Max. 48h.

### ⬛S Le Cheylard 25C2
**Super U**, Chemin du pre-jalla, ZI la Palisse.
**GPS**: n44,91143 e4,44162. 🚁.

20 🚐free ⚡€2 🚰🔌€2. **Location:** Rural, simple, noisy.
**Surface:** asphalted. ⚪ 01/01-31/12.
**Distance:** 🚃2km ⊗110m 🚉50m.
**Remarks:** Max. 24h.

### ⬛ Le Cheylas 25E1
Avenue de la Libération. **GPS**: n45,37170 e5,99014.
6 🚐free ⚡🚰ChWC free. **Surface:** asphalted/metalled.
⚪ 01/01-31/12 ▪ water: 01/11-31/03.
**Distance:** 🚃on the spot 🚉50m.

### ⬛S Le Crozet ⛱ 22B2
**Les Minières**, Le Bourg. **GPS**: n46,16934 e3,85727. ⬆➡.

2 🚐free ⚡€2/30minutes 🚰🔌€2/4h. **Location:** Rural, simple.
**Surface:** metalled. ⚪ 01/01-31/12.
**Distance:** ⊗150m.

### ⬛ Le Grand Bornand 22F3
164 Route de La Broderie. **GPS**: n45,94144 e6,43636.

10 🚐free. **Location:** Rural, simple, quiet. **Surface:** metalled.
⚪ 01/01-31/12.
**Distance:** 🚃600m ⊗250m 🚶on the spot 🎿on the spot.
**Remarks:** Max. 48h.

### ⬛S Le Lac d'Issarlès 🌳 25B2
Le village/D16. **GPS**: n44,81948 e4,06156. 🚁.

24 🅿️ € 11,40 🚰Ch🧹WC included. 🅿️ **Location:** Rural, simple, central. **Surface:** metalled. 🅿️ 01/04-01/11.
**Distance:** 🚶100m ⛵400m 🛒100m 🍴100m.
**Remarks:** Attention: this town is not Issarlès!.

### Le Monastier-sur-Gazeille 🌿 25B2
Rue Augustin Ollier. **GPS:** n44,93720 e3,99250.⬆️➡️.

20 🅿️free 🚰 € 2/5minutes 🚰Ch. **Location:** Rural, simple, quiet.
**Surface:** gravel. 🅿️ 01/03-31/10.
**Distance:** 🚶300m ⛵300m 🛒500m 🚴 on the spot.

### Le Monestier 🏔️ 25A1
D39. **GPS:** n45,56364 e3,66088.⬆️➡️.

10 🅿️free 🚰Chfree. **Location:** Rural, simple, quiet.
**Surface:** gravel. 🅿️ 01/01-31/12.
**Distance:** 🚶300m ⛵300m 🚴 on the spot 🚶 on the spot.

### Le Puy-en-Velay 25B2
**Camping-Car Park,** Place Maréchal Leclerc.
**GPS:** n45,04489 e3,89498.⬆️.

26 🅿️ € 11,90-31,10 🚰Ch🧹(26x)🛜included.📷📠
**Location:** Urban, comfortable, central, quiet. **Surface:** asphalted.
🅿️ 01/01-31/12.
**Distance:** 🚶1km ⛵1km 🛒2km 🚌300m.
**Remarks:** Mandatory, one-time fee Pass'Etapes € 4.

### Le Puy-en-Velay 25B2
**Boulevard de Cluny. GPS:** n45,04963 e3,88976.⬆️.
🚰 € 2 🚰Ch.

### Le Reposoir 22F3
Route Departementale D204. **GPS:** n46,01010 e6,53648.

10 🅿️free 🚰Chfree WC. **Location:** Urban, simple, quiet.
**Surface:** metalled. 🅿️ 01/01-31/12.

**Distance:** 🚶150m ⛵250m 🚶 on the spot.

### Le Teil 25C3
Alleé Paul Avon. **GPS:** n44,55138 e4,68972.⬆️.

6 🅿️free 🚰Chfree. **Location:** Rural, noisy.
**Surface:** grassy/metalled. 🅿️ 01/01-31/12.
**Distance:** 🚶600m ⛵on the spot ⛵on the spot 🛒500m.
**Remarks:** Nearby D86, max. 24h, shady.
**Tourist information Le Teil:**
🎪 Thu morning.

### Le Vernet 📶 25A2
**Place de l'étang,** D48. **GPS:** n45,03560 e3,66952.⬆️.

14 🅿️ € 3 🚰Chincluded 🧹(14x) € 3/night. 🅿️ **Location:** Rural, simple, isolated, quiet. **Surface:** grassy/sand. 🅿️ 01/01-31/12
🅿️ service: 01/11-30/04.
**Distance:** 🚶50m 🚴 on the spot 🚶 on the spot.
**Remarks:** Max. 72h.

### Lélex 22E2
Chemin Frênet. **GPS:** n46,29932 e5,93140.⬆️.
8 🅿️free 🚰 € 5 🚰Ch 🧹 € 8/24h 🧹 **Surface:** metalled.
🅿️ 01/01-31/12.
**Distance:** 🚶650m ⛵650m 🛒650m 🚴 on the spot 🚶 on the spot
🚴650m.
**Remarks:** At tennis-courts, max. 1 week.

### Les Carroz-Arâches 🏔️❄️ 22F3
**Télécabine Les Cluses,** 595 Route de la Télécabine.
**GPS:** n46,02500 e6,64361.

15 🅿️ € 4,50 🚰included 🚰Ch🧹. 🅿️ 01/06-30/11,
**Distance:** 🚶500m ⛵500m.
**Remarks:** Parking funicular railway.

### Les Deux-Alpes 25E2
Avenue de la Muzelle, D213. **GPS:** n45,02394 e6,12120.⬆️.
20 🅿️ € 12 🚰🚰Ch🧹included. 🅿️ winter.
**Remarks:** Beautiful view.

### Les Estables 🏔️❄️ 25B2
**Foirail de la Mézine,** Le Bourg/D36. **GPS:** n44,90231 e4,15679.⬆️.

8 🅿️free 🚰🚰ChWCfree. **Location:** Rural, simple, quiet.
**Surface:** asphalted. 🅿️ 01/01-31/12.
**Distance:** 🚶50m ⛵50m 🛒 on the spot 🚴500m 🚶 on the spot.
**Remarks:** Max. 7 days, service at petrol station, free wifi,

code at tourist info.

### Les Gets 🏔️🏔️❄️ 22F2
**Parking des Perrières,** Route du Front de Neige.
**GPS:** n46,14952 e6,65719.⬆️.

20 🅿️ € 0,90/pp tourist tax, winter € 17 🚰🚰Ch📷 📠
**Surface:** gravel. 🅿️ 11/06-11/09 and 17/12-15/04.
**Distance:** 🚶1km 🚴 on the spot.
**Remarks:** Max. 7 days, bus to centre every 30 minutes.
**Tourist information Les Gets:**
🎪 Week market. 🅿️ Thu-morning.

### Les Granges-Gontardes 25C3
**Domaine de la Tour d'Elyssas,** Quartier Combe d'Elissas.
**GPS:** n44,41811 e4,75465.⬆️.

8 🅿️free 🚰🚰Chfree 🧹 € 3. **Location:** Rural, simple, quiet.
**Surface:** grassy/gravel. 🅿️ 01/01-31/12.
**Distance:** 🚴9km.
**Remarks:** At wine-grower, max. 48h.

### Les Karellis 25F1
D81B. **GPS:** n45,22756 e6,40907.
🅿️free. **Surface:** asphalted. 🅿️ 01/01-31/12.
**Distance:** 🚶600m ⛵600m 🛒600m.
**Remarks:** Mountain station nearby St.Jean-de-Maurienne.

### Les Menuires 🏔️🏔️❄️ 25F1
**Les Bruyères,** Dir Val Thorens. **GPS:** n45,32557 e6,53414.⬆️➡️.
70 🅿️ € 10/24h + € 0,20/pp tourist tax 🚰🚰Ch🧹(7x) € 2/4h WC 🧹
**Surface:** asphalted.
🅿️ 10/12-22/04 and 08/07-01/09.
**Distance:** 🚶 on the spot ⛵on the spot 🛒 on the spot 🚴 on the spot.
**Remarks:** Near the pistes.

### Les Noës 22B3
Le Bourg, D47. **GPS:** n46,04083 e3,85206.⬆️.

5 🅿️free 🚰🚰ChWCfree. **Location:** Rural, simple, quiet.
**Surface:** gravel. 🅿️ 01/01-31/12.
**Distance:** 🚶 on the spot ⛵50m 🚶 on the spot.

### Les Salles 22B3
**Domaine de la Plagnette,** La Plagnette. **GPS:** n45,84395 e3,81967.⬆️.
🅿️free 🚰🚰Ch🧹. **Location:** Rural. **Surface:** gravel.
🅿️ 01/01-31/12.
**Distance:** ⛵on the spot.

### Les Sauvages 22B3
Les Sauvages, 69170. **GPS:** n45,92083 e4,37711.⬆️➡️.

5 ⌁free ⛽ ⚡Ch free. **Location:** Rural, simple, quiet.
**Surface:** gravel. ⬜ 01/01-31/12.
**Distance:** ⛲on the spot ⊗100m ⚑100m 🚶on the spot.

### Lezoux 22A3

**Parking Musée départemental de la Céramique**, Rue de la République. **GPS:** n45,82686 e3,38459. ⬆➡.

25 ⌁free ⛽ ⚡Ch WC free.
**Location:** Comfortable, central, quiet. **Surface:** gravel.
⬜ 01/01-31/12. ● water: 01/11-31/03.
**Distance:** ⛲500m 🚲3,5km ⊗500m ⚑500m.

### ⚏S Lurcy-Lévis 21H1

**Plan d'eau des Sézeaux**, Rue de Fontgroix.
**GPS:** n46,73797 e2,93863. ⬆➡.

6 ⌁free ⛽ € 3/100liter ⚡Ch 🔌 € 3/55minutes WC.
**Location:** Rural, comfortable, quiet. **Surface:** grassy/gravel.
⬜ 01/01-31/12.
**Distance:** ⛲800m ⛵Small lake ⛳on the spot ⊗800m ⚑800m.
**Remarks:** Coins at cafe, in front of the church.

### ⚏S Lus-la-Croix-Haute 🏔❄ 25D2

D 505. **GPS:** n44,66712 e5,70800.

3 ⌁free ⛽ ⚡Ch free. **Location:** Simple. **Surface:** metalled.
⬜ 01/01-31/12.
**Distance:** ⛲200m ⊗500m 🎾on the spot ♨on the spot.
**Remarks:** At fire-station, tenniscourt.

### ⚏S Mâcot-la-Plagne 🏔❄ 25F1

**Caravaneige de Plagne Villages. GPS:** n45,50510 e6,68870. ⬆.
40 ⌁€ 22 ⚡Ch 🎿included ☁. **Surface:** asphalted.
⬜ 01/01-31/12.
**Distance:** ⊗300m 🎾on the spot.
**Remarks:** Video surveillance.

### ⚏S Mandailles-Saint-Julien 🏔 24H2

Le Mas, D17. **GPS:** n45,06916 e2,65611. ➡.

5 ⌁free ⛽ € 3,50 ⚡Ch. **Location:** Rural, simple, quiet.
**Surface:** metalled. ⬜ 01/01-31/12 ● service: 30/09-01/04.
**Distance:** ⛲200m ⊗200m ⚑200m 🚶on the spot.
**Remarks:** Max. 24h, coins at restaurants.

### ⚏S Manzat 21H3

Place du 14 Juillet. **GPS:** n45,96180 e2,93883. ⬆.

20 ⌁free ⛽ ⚡Ch free. **Location:** Rural, simple, quiet.
**Surface:** unpaved. ⬜ 01/01-31/12.
**Distance:** ⛲on the spot 🚲5,6km ⊗250m ⚑200m.
**Remarks:** In front of police station.

### ⚏S Marcolès 24G2

D66. **GPS:** n44,78028 e2,35389. ⬆.

5 ⌁free ⛽ ⚡Ch free ⚒. **Location:** Rural, simple, quiet.
**Surface:** gravel. ⬜ 01/01-31/12 ● service 01/11-31/03.
**Distance:** ⛲100m ⊗100m ⚑100m.
**Remarks:** Artists village.

### ⚏S Marsanne 🌿 25C3

Avenue de Bailliencourt, D57. **GPS:** n44,64545 e4,87149. ⬆.

5 ⌁free ⛽ ⚡Ch free. **Location:** Rural, simple, quiet.
**Surface:** grassy. ⬜ 01/01-31/12.
**Distance:** ⛲300m ⚑300m 🚶nearby.
**Remarks:** Max. 48h, medieval village.

### ⚏S Massiac 🏔 25A1

**Aire de Massiac**, Rue Jacques Chaban Delmas.
**GPS:** n45,25250 e3,19433. ⬆➡.

8 ⌁free ⛽ € 2/80liter ⚡Ch. **Location:** Rural, simple, quiet.
**Surface:** grassy. ⬜ 01/01-31/12.
**Distance:** ⛲400m 🚲1,4km ♨on the spot ⛳on the spot ⊗400m
⚑400m 🚌200m 🚲on the spot.

### ⚏S Massiac 🏔 25A1

**Aire du Bouclier Arverne**, Rue Jacques Chaban Delmas.
**GPS:** n45,25364 e3,19376. ⬆.

8 ⌁free ⛽ ⚡Ch free. **Location:** Urban, simple, quiet.
**Surface:** asphalted. ⬜ 01/01-31/12.
**Distance:** ⛲350m ⊗400m ⚑400m 🚲on the spot.

### ⚏S Mauriac 🌊 24G1

Rue du Val Saint Jean. **GPS:** n45,21863 e2,32183. ⬆➡.

12 ⌁free ⛽ € 2/100liter ⚡Ch 🔌 € 2/1h ⚒. **Location:** Rural, simple, quiet. **Surface:** metalled. ⬜ 01/01-31/12.
**Distance:** ⛲1km ⛱beach 300m ⊗1,2km ⚑1,2km.

### ⚏S Maurs 24G2

**Maurs La Jolie**, Route de Quezac. **GPS:** n44,71442 e2,19615. ⬆➡.

5 ⌁free ⛽ € 2/100liter ⚡Ch free 🔌 € 2/1h.
**Location:** Urban, simple, central, quiet. **Surface:** asphalted.
⬜ 01/01-31/12.
**Distance:** ⛲300m ⊗300m ⚑300m 🚶300m.
**Remarks:** Coins at Papetterie and tourist office.

### ⚏ Megève 22F3

Chemin des Ânes. **GPS:** n45,86401 e6,62010.
⌁free. ⬜ 01/01-31/12.
**Remarks:** In front of parking Télécabine du Jaillet.

### ⚏S Messeix 21H3

28 Rue des Lilas. **GPS:** n45,61576 e2,55621. ⬆➡.

6 ⌁free ⛽ € 2/10minutes ⚡Ch 🔌 € 2/55minutes.
**Location:** Urban, simple, quiet. **Surface:** asphalted.
⬜ 01/01-31/12.
**Distance:** ⛲500m 🚲18km ⚑1,7km 🚌on the spot.
**Remarks:** Coins at the shops.

### ⚏S Mévouillon 25D3

**Domaine le Clos de Bruis**, Clos de Bruis. **GPS:** n44,22812 e5,50529.
5 ⌁€ 5 + € 0,50/pp tourist tax ⛽ ⚡Ch 🔌 € 3,50 Ch € 3,50 ⚒.
**Location:** Rural, comfortable. **Surface:** gravel. ⬜ 01/01-31/12.
**Distance:** 🚲on the spot 🚶on the spot.

### ⚏S Meyras 25B2

Rue de la Dame de Vantadour, D26. **GPS:** n44,67939 e4,26845. ⬆.

FR

15 ☰€ 4/48h ☞€ 4/100liter ☐Ch ⚡€ 4/5kWh. 🔧
**Location:** Rural, simple, quiet. **Surface:** gravel.
☐ 01/04-31/10.
**Distance:** ⚓200m ⊗200m 🛒200m.
**Remarks:** Max. 48h, coins at the shops in the village.

### Mijoux 〰️ ⛰️ ❄️ 22E2
D50, Route de la Combe-en-Haut. **GPS:** n46,36963 e6,00247. ⬆️ ➡️.

20 ☰free ☞€ 3,50 ☐Ch ⊞€ 3,50. **Location:** Rural, simple, quiet.
**Surface:** gravel. ☐ 01/01-31/12. ⊙ Service: winter.
**Distance:** ⚓500m ⊗500m 🛒500m ☞on the spot ⛷on the spot.
**Remarks:** Coins at town hall and supermarket.

### Mirabel-aux-Baronnies 25D3
Chemin des Grottes. **GPS:** n44,31260 e5,09968. ⬆️.

7+10 ☰voluntary contribution ☞☐Chfree. **Location:** Rural.
**Surface:** grassy/metalled. ☐ 01/01-31/12.
**Distance:** ⚓200m.

### Molinet 22B2
**Canal Lateral à la Loire**, D779. **GPS:** n46,47190 e3,93960.

12 ☰free ☞€ 2 ☐Ch€ 2 ⊞€ 2. **Location:** Rural, simple, quiet.
**Surface:** grasstiles. ☐ 01/01-31/12.
**Distance:** ⚓1km ☞on the spot.

### Montalieu-Vercieu 22D3
Chamboud. **GPS:** n45,82776 e5,42100. ⬆️.

6 ☰free ☞☐Chfree WC campsite. **Location:** Rural, simple, isolated,
quiet. **Surface:** asphalted. ☐ 01/01-31/12.
**Distance:** ⚓2km ⊗2km 🛒2km ☞1,5km.
**Remarks:** Next to campsite/Base de Loisirs de la Vallée Bleue, max. 2
nights.

### Montbrison-sur-Lez 25C3
**Place Publique**, D24. **GPS:** n44,43663 e5,01779. ⬆️.

6 ☰free ☞⚡free. **Location:** Simple, quiet. **Surface:** metalled.
☐ 01/01-31/12.
**Distance:** ⚓100m ⊗100m 🛒100m.

### Montbrison-sur-Lez 25C3
Quartier le Chatelard. **GPS:** n44,42751 e5,02438. ⬆️.

6 ☰€ 5 ☞€ 2/60liter ☐Ch ⊞€ 2. **Location:** Simple, isolated, quiet.
**Surface:** gravel/metalled. ☐ 01/01-31/12.
**Remarks:** At football ground, coins at bar and garage, vineyard.

### Montbrun-les-Bains 〰️ 🌿 28D1
Toscan. **GPS:** n44,17247 e5,43881. ⬆️ ➡️.

10 ☰free.
**Location:** Rural, quiet. **Surface:** grassy. ☐ 01/01-31/12.
**Distance:** ⚓500m ⊗300m 🛒400m ☞on the spot ☗400m Tour de
la Citadelle.

### Montbrun-les-Bains 〰️ 🌿 28D1
588 Condamine. **GPS:** n44,17413 e5,44071. ⬆️.
☞€ 2 ☐Chfree ⊞€ 2. ☐ 01/01-31/12.

### Montélimar 25C3
**Domaine du Bois de Laud**, Avenue des portes du soleil.
**GPS:** n44,56517 e4,75691. ⬆️ ➡️.

8 ☰free ☞☐Chfree. **Location:** Urban, simple.
**Surface:** grassy/metalled. ☐ 01/01-31/12.
**Distance:** ⚓500m 🛒100m.
**Remarks:** Near centre commercial Leclerc, max. 48h.

### Montluçon 21H2
Route de l'Etang de Sault, Prémilhat. **GPS:** n46,33469 e2,55855. ⬆️ ➡️.

8 ☰free ☞€ 5/150liter ☐Ch ⚡ (6x)€ 2,50/10h ⚼. **Location:** Rural,
comfortable. **Surface:** gravel. ☐ 01/01-31/12.
**Distance:** ⚓5km Montluçon ⚓2,6km ⛵150m ⊶150m ⊗500m
⚕on the spot.
**Remarks:** Max. 72h.

### Montluçon 21H2
**Place de la Fraternité**, 6 Place de la Fraternité.
**GPS:** n46,35535 e2,58686. ⬆️.

15 ☰free ☞€ 5/150liter ☐Ch ⊞€ 2,50/10minutes WC ⚼.
**Location:** Urban, simple, noisy. **Surface:** asphalted.
☐ 01/01-31/12. ⊙ water: Nov-March.
**Distance:** ⚓on the spot ⊗450m 🛒150m
⊶on the spot.
**Remarks:** Thu-morning closed because of market (6-15h).

### Montmurat 24G2
Le Bourg, D345. **GPS:** n44,62811 e2,19804. ⬆️.

10 ☰free ☞€ 1 ☐Ch. **Location:** Rural, simple, isolated, quiet.
**Surface:** gravel. ☐ 01/01-31/12.
**Distance:** ⚓on the spot.

### Montoldre 22A2
1851 D268, 03150 Montoldre. **GPS:** n46,33272 e3,44727. ⬆️ ➡️.

7 ☰free ☞€ 2/100liter ☐Ch. **Location:** Rural, simple, quiet.
**Surface:** asphalted. ☐ 01/01-31/12.
**Distance:** ⚓centre ⊗300m.
**Remarks:** In front of town hall.

### Montpeyroux 22A3
D797C, Rue De l'Hume. **GPS:** n45,62373 e3,19911. ⬆️.

+10 ☰free ☞€ 2,50 ☐Ch ⊞€ 2,50/1h. **Location:** Rural, simple,
quiet. **Surface:** gravel. ☐ 01/01-31/12.
**Distance:** ⚓100m ⛵200m ⊗200m ☞on the spot.
**Remarks:** Coins at the shops in the village.
**Tourist information Montpeyroux**
ℹ️ Small town with wine-cellar Cave de Montpeyroux. ☐ Mo/Sa
8.30-12.30h, 14-18/19h, Su 10.30-12h, 16-19h.

### Montsalvy 24G2
Avenue de lóeuvre L. Conlombant. **GPS:** n44,70778 e2,49667. ⬆️ ➡️.

11 🚐free 🚰€ 2/80liter 🔌Ch 🔲€ 2/1h WC. **Location:** Rural, comfortable, quiet. **Surface:** asphalted. 🅾 01/01-31/12. **Distance:** 🛒400m ⊗400m 🛒400m.

| 🅂 | **Morillon** 🔌🍴🌳❄ | 22F3 |

**GPS:** n46,08291 e6,68124. ⬆➡

20 🚐free 🔌ChWCfree. **Surface:** asphalted. 🅾 01/01-31/12. **Distance:** 🛒200m ⊗100m 🛒300m 🎿100m.

| 🅂 | **Moulins** 🔌🍴🌳 | 22A2 |

**Flot Bleu Park**, Chemin de Halage/n2009.
**GPS:** n46,55852 e3,32491. ⬆➡

92 🚐€ 0,10/h 🚰€ 2/20minutes 🔌Ch 🔲 2 🛁(12x)€ 2/4h 🔌🚐 **Location:** Urban, comfortable, central, quiet. **Surface:** grassy/metalled. 🅾 01/01-31/12. **Distance:** 🛒1km ⊗100m 🛒300m 🛒on the spot.

| 🅂 | **Murat** ❄ ⊗ | 24H2 |

Avenue du Dr Louis Mallet. **GPS:** n45,10912 e2,86728. ⬆

8 🚐free 🚰€ 2/10minutes 🔌Ch 🔲€ 2/1h WC.
**Location:** Urban, simple, central, noisy. **Surface:** asphalted. 🅾 01/01-31/12. **Distance:** 🛒300m ⊗100m 🛒1,5km 🛒100m 🛒on the spot. **Remarks:** Coins at tourist info, marked pitches in the back of de parking.

**Tourist information Murat:**
⌘ 🅾 Fri-morning.

| 🅂 | **Murat-le-Quaire** 🏔 | 21H3 |

**Camping-Car Park Les Rives du Lac**, Route de la Banne d'Ordanche. **GPS:** n45,60274 e2,73797. ⬆➡

37 🚐€ 10,70/24h 🔌Ch 🛁(32x)🔊included. 🚐🔌 **Location:** Rural, comfortable, quiet. **Surface:** grassy/metalled. 🅾 01/01-31/12. **Distance:** 🛒1,2km 🛒12km 🏊100m 🛒100m day pass available ⊗on the spot 🛒on the spot 🎿100m 🛒5km. **Remarks:** Mandatory, one-time fee Pass'Etapes € 4.

| 🅲🅂 | **Murol** 🔌🏔❄ | 24H1 |

**Domaine du lac Chambon**, Plage Est. **GPS:** n45,57149 e2,92943. ⬆
25 🚐€ 10 🛁(15x)included. **Location:** Rural, comfortable, quiet. **Surface:** grassy. 🅾 20/04-01/09. **Distance:** 🏊100m. **Remarks:** Entrance code available at campsite.

| 🅲🅂 | **Nantua** 🔌🏔🍴🔌 | 22D2 |

**Aire de service du Lac de Nantua**, Route de Port, D74. **GPS:** n46,15497 e5,59656. ⬆➡

13 🚐€ 8, tourist tax € 0,20/pp 🚰🔌Ch 🛁WCincluded. 🏊 **Location:** Urban, comfortable, central. **Surface:** gravel. 🅾 01/04-30/09. **Distance:** 🛒700m 🛒7km 🏊on the spot 🛒on the spot ⊗150m 🛒150m 🛒on the spot 🛒on the spot. **Remarks:** At Nantua lake.

| 🅂 | **Naucelles** | 24G2 |

Rue du Terrou. **GPS:** n44,95694 e2,41757. ⬆

5 🚐free 🚰€ 3,50/100liter 🔌Ch 🔲€ 3,50/1h. **Location:** Urban, simple, quiet. **Surface:** asphalted. 🅾 01/01-31/12. **Distance:** 🛒Spar 300m. **Remarks:** Coins at supermarket in the village.

| 🅲🅂 | **Néris-les-Bains** 🍴 | 21H2 |

**Camping du Lac**, Avenue Marrx Dormoy, D155. **GPS:** n46,28673 e2,65235. ⬆➡

6 🚐€ 8 🚰🔌Ch 🛁(6x)WCincluded 🔊€ 1,50/h. 🔌 **Location:** Urban, comfortable. **Surface:** gravel. 🅾 01/03-31/10. **Distance:** 🛒500m 🛒12km 🛒bakery 500m. **Remarks:** Max. 3 nights, to be paid at campsite.

| 🅲🅂 | **Neussargues-Moissac** | 24H1 |

Allée des Peupliers. **GPS:** n45,13438 e2,98130. ⬆➡

5 🚐free 🚰€ 2/100liter 🔌Ch 🔲€ 2/2h WC 🔊🔌 **Location:** Rural, comfortable, quiet. **Surface:** gravel. 🅾 01/01-31/12 🅾 water disconnected in winter. **Distance:** 🛒300m ⊗50m 🛒300m 🛒on the spot 🛒on the spot. **Remarks:** Coins at town hall and restaurant.

| 🅲🅂 | **Neuvéglise** | 24H2 |

Le Bourg. **GPS:** n44,92924 e2,98344. ⬆
3 🚐free 🔌Chfree. **Location:** Urban, simple, central. **Surface:** asphalted. 🅾 01/01-31/12. **Distance:** 🛒on the spot ⊗100m 🛒200m.

| 🅲🅂 | **Noailly** | 22B2 |

**Parking Maison du Temps Libre**. **GPS:** n46,13656 e4,01157. ⬆➡

3 🚐free. **Location:** Simple, quiet. **Surface:** asphalted. 🅾 01/01-31/12. **Distance:** 🛒on the spot 🛒200m.

| 🅲🅂🅂 | **Noirétable** 🔌🏔🌳🔌 | 22B3 |

Rue du plan d'Eau. **GPS:** n45,80739 e3,76935. ⬆➡

7 🚐free 🚰€ 3 🔌Ch 🔲€ 1/2h 🔌. **Location:** Rural, simple, quiet. **Surface:** metalled. 🅾 01/01-31/12. **Distance:** 🛒800m 🏊100m 🛒100m 🛒100m 🛒800m 🛒on the spot 🛒on the spot 🛒on the spot. **Remarks:** Next to campsite (50m), max. 48h, coins at campsite.

| 🅲🅂 | **Nyons** | 25D3 |

**Promenade de la Digue**. **GPS:** n44,35778 e5,13861. ⬆

20 🚐€ 10/24h 🚰🔌ChWC 🔊included. 🚐🔌 **Location:** Noisy. **Surface:** gravel. 🅾 01/01-31/12. **Distance:** 🛒250m ⊗250m 🛒250m 🛒250m. **Remarks:** Next to Parc loisirs aquatique, max. 48h.

| 🅂🅂 | **Nyons** 🔌🏔 | 25D3 |

**Domaine Rocheville**, 117 Route de Montélimar, RD538. **GPS:** n44,36884 e5,11809. ⬆

10 🚐€ 8,10 🚰🔌Ch 🛁€ 5/12h WC 🛁summer 🔊included. 🔌🔌 **Location:** Rural, isolated, quiet. **Surface:** grassy/gravel. 🅾 01/01-31/12. **Distance:** 🛒city centre 2km 🛒200m 🛒on the spot. **Remarks:** Regional products.

**Tourist information Nyons:**
ℹ Pavillon du Tourisme, Place de la Libération. Important Olive-city in the Provence.
Ⓜ Musée de l'Olivier, Espace Vignolis. Museum about the olive-tree and production of olive oil. 🅾 daily 🅾 01/11-28/02 Su.
⌘ Centre-ville. Regional market. 🅾 Thu-morning.

| 🅲🅂 | **Orcines** 🔌🏔 | 21H3 |

Route de Limoges, D941B. **GPS:** n45,78838 e3,01114. ⬆➡⬆

FR

51 ⌖€ 8, 01/10-30/04 € 6 ⛽€ 2/100liter 🔲Ch ▣€ 2/4h 〰.
🚐⬚ **Location:** Rural, simple, noisy. **Surface:** asphalted/grassy.
🔲 01/01-31/12.
**Distance:** ⊗on the spot.
**Remarks:** Next to sports fields.

### Orcines 🏖⛰ 21H3
Route du Puy de Dôme, D68. **GPS:** n45,76958 e2,98624. ⬆.

10 ⌖free ⛽🔲ChWCfree.
**Location:** Rural, simple, isolated, quiet. **Surface:** asphalted.
🔲 01/01-31/12 ◉ Service: winter.
**Distance:** ⅄ on the spot.

### Orcines 🏖⛰ 21H3
D941. **GPS:** n45,80394 e2,98726.

10 ⌖free. **Location:** Simple, noisy. **Surface:** metalled.
🔲 01/01-31/12.
**Distance:** ⅄ on the spot.

### Orgnac l'Aven 25B3
Le Fez, D217. **GPS:** n44,30419 e4,43240. ⬆.

5 ⌖free ⛽🔲Chfree. **Location:** Rural, simple, quiet.
**Surface:** gravel. 🔲 01/01-31/12.
**Distance:** ⚓200m ⊗50m 🍽300m.
**Remarks:** Caves of Aven d'Orgnac 2km.

### Panissières 22B3
**Ferme Seigne**, Rue des Lauriers. **GPS:** n45,78835 e4,34355. ⬆.

4 ⌖€ 7 ⛽🔲Ch ✎included4 WC ✎use sanitary € 3,60/pp.
**Location:** Rural, simple, quiet. **Surface:** metalled. 🔲 01/01-31/12
◉ Service: winter.
**Distance:** ⚓300m ⊗300m 🍽300m.

---

### Paray-le-Frésil 22A1
Le Bourg. **GPS:** n46,65472 e3,61294. ⬆.

3 ⌖free ⛽🔲Chfree ▣€ 2/55minutes ⬚ **Location:** Rural, simple,
quiet. **Surface:** gravel. 🔲 01/01-31/12.
**Distance:** ⚓on the spot ⊗200m ⅄ on the spot.

### Paulhac 24H2
Le Bourg. **GPS:** n45,00669 e2,90394. ⬆.

4 ⌖free ⛽€ 2 🔲Ch ✎€ 2,at townhall. **Location:** Rural, simple,
isolated, quiet. **Surface:** grassy. 🔲 01/01-31/12.
**Distance:** ⚓on the spot 🚲on the spot.

### Périgny 22A2
Rue de l'Église. **GPS:** n46,25208 e3,55422. ✈.

6 ⌖free 🔲ChWCfree. **Location:** Rural, simple, isolated, quiet.
**Surface:** gravel. 🔲 01/01-31/12.
**Distance:** ⚓on the spot ⊗400m.

### Pierrefort 24H2
Côte de Chabridet. **GPS:** n44,92172 e2,84199. ⬆➡.

40 ⌖free ⛽€ 2/100liter 🔲Ch ▣€ 2. **Location:** Rural, simple.
**Surface:** gravel. 🔲 01/01-31/12.
**Distance:** ⚓200m ⊗300m 🍽300m🚲on the spot.
**Remarks:** Coins at tourist info, service 100m.

### Planfoy 🍴 25C1
Chemin du Vignolet. **GPS:** n45,37445 e4,44910. ⬆➡.

10 ⌖free ⛽€ 2,50/15minutes 🔲Ch ✎(8x)€ 2,50/6h.
**Location:** Rural, simple, quiet. **Surface:** asphalted. 🔲 01/01-31/12.
**Distance:** ⚓1,3km ⚔7km 🍽1,3km ⅄on the spot.
**Remarks:** Coins at the shops in the village.

---

### Pleaux 24G1
**Parc des Auzerals**, Place d'Empeyssine.
**GPS:** n45,13556 e2,22833. ⬆➡.

10 ⌖free ⛽🔲Ch ✎WCfree. **Location:** Urban, simple, central,
quiet. **Surface:** asphalted/gravel. 🔲 01/01-31/12.
**Distance:** ⚓on the spot ⊗100m 🍽100m.
**Remarks:** Max. 7 days, max. 9m.

### Pont-de-Veyle 22C2
D933, Rue de la Poste. **GPS:** n46,26437 e4,88697. ✈.

20 ⌖free ⛽🔲. **Location:** Urban, simple, central, noisy.
**Surface:** gravel. 🔲 01/01-31/12.
**Distance:** ⚓on the spot ⚔3,5km ⚲on the spot ⚲on the spot
⊗50m 🍽150m.
**Remarks:** Monday-morning market.

### Pontcharra-sur-Turdine 22C3
Place A. Schweitzer. **GPS:** n45,87405 e4,49133. ⬆.

4 ⌖free ⛽🔲ChWCfree. **Location:** Urban, simple, quiet.
**Surface:** asphalted. 🔲 01/01-31/12.
**Distance:** ⚓50m ⚲on the spot ⊗50m 🍽50m 🚌on the spot.

### Pouilly-sous-Charlieu 22B2
**Place du Marché**, Rue de la République.
**GPS:** n46,14335 e4,10832. ⬆➡.

10 ⌖free ⛽🔲ChWCfree. **Location:** Urban, simple.
**Surface:** asphalted. 🔲 01/01-31/12 ◉ Su-morning (market).
**Distance:** ⚓on the spot ⚲on the spot 🍽on the spot.

### Pouilly-sous-Charlieu 22B2
Rue de la Berge. **GPS:** n46,14699 e4,10075. ⬆.
4 ⌖free.
**Location:** Rural, simple. **Surface:** gravel. 🔲 01/01-31/12.
**Distance:** ⚲on the spot ⚲on the spot ⊗on the spot.
**Remarks:** Parking at the Loire river.

### Pradelles 25B2
**Aire de la Salaison**, N88. **GPS:** n44,77540 e3,88752. ⬆➡.

40 ⛺free 🚰🚻Ch ⚡(8x)€ 2 🚿free. **Location:** Rural, comfortable. **Surface:** grassy/gravel. 🅾 01/01-31/12.
**Distance:** 🛒1km ⊗on the spot 🍽on the spot 🚲on the spot.
**Remarks:** Max. 24h, regional products and bread.

### Prapoutel-les-Sept-Laux 25E1

Les Adrets 38190. **GPS:** n45,25769 e5,99785.

15 ⛺free 🚰WC. **Location:** Rural, isolated. **Surface:** metalled.
🅾 01/01-31/12.
**Distance:** 🚶50m.
**Remarks:** Parking at pistes.

### Prunet 24G2

Le Bourg. **GPS:** n44,82049 e2,46398.➡

3 ⛺free 🚰🚻Ch🚐free. **Location:** Rural, simple, quiet.
**Surface:** gravel. 🅾 01/01-31/12 🔲 service 01/11-31/03.
**Distance:** 🛒300m ⊗300m.

### Puy-Saint-Martin 25C3

Champ de Mars. **GPS:** n44,62753 e4,97492.⬆➡

25 ⛺free 🚰🚻Ch. **Location:** Rural, comfortable. **Surface:** grassy.
🅾 01/01-31/12.
**Distance:** 🛒on the spot ⊗50m 🍽bakery 300m.
**Remarks:** Former campsite, max. 48h, voluntary contribution.

### Randan 22A3

Rue du Puy de Dôme. **GPS:** n46,01630 e3,35075.⬆➡

6 ⛺free 🚰€ 2/15minutes 🚻Ch🚐€ 2/15minutes. **Location:** Urban, simple, quiet. **Surface:** gravel. 🅾 01/01-31/12.
**Distance:** 🛒500m ⊗500m 🍽200m.
**Remarks:** Coins at Maison de la Presse, Rue de Commerce.

### Raucoules 25B1

Le Bourg. **GPS:** n45,18640 e4,29750.⬆➡

5 ⛺free 🚰€ 2/20minutes 🚻Ch⚡(4x)€ 2/4h.
**Location:** Rural, simple, central, quiet. **Surface:** asphalted.
🅾 01/01-31/12.
**Distance:** 🛒200m ⊗300m 🍽on the spot 🚶on the spot.
**Remarks:** Coins available at the shops.

### Renaison 22B3

La Rivière. **GPS:** n46,04749 e3,92121.⬆➡

6 ⛺free 🚰🚻Chfree. **Location:** Rural, simple, quiet.
**Surface:** grassy/gravel. 🅾 01/01-31/12.
**Distance:** 🛒400m 🍽on the spot 🍽700m.
**Remarks:** Along river.

### Retournac 25B1

**Aire de la Chaud**, Rue de la Loire. **GPS:** n45,20328 e4,04501.⬆➡

20 ⛺free 🚰🚻Chfree. **Location:** Rural, simple, isolated, quiet.
**Surface:** gravel. 🅾 01/01-31/12 🔲 Service: winter.
**Distance:** 🛒200m 🏊on the spot 🍽on the spot ⊗650m 🚲on the spot 🚶on the spot.
**Remarks:** Along Loire river.

### Reventin-Vaugris 25C1

Rue Mouret. **GPS:** n45,46821 e4,84239.⬆

10 ⛺free 🚰WC. **Location:** Rural, simple, central, quiet.
**Surface:** gravel/metalled. 🅾 01/01-31/12.
**Distance:** 🛒on the spot ⚓6km ⊗100m 🍽bakery 100m.
**Remarks:** Max. 7 days.

### Riom 22A3

Route d'Ennezat, D224. **GPS:** n45,89455 e3,12477.⬆➡

4 ⛺free 🚰€ 2/10minutes 🚻Ch🚐€ 2/1h.

---

**Location:** Urban, simple, central, noisy. **Surface:** gravel.
🅾 01/01-31/12.
**Distance:** 🛒700m ⚓2,5km ⊗nearby 🍽nearby.

### Riom-es-Montagnes 24H1

Rue du Champ de Foire. **GPS:** n45,28444 e2,65389.⬆➡
🚰€ 2/100liter 🚻Ch🚐€ 2/1h.
**Location:** Simple. 🅾 01/01-31/12.
**Distance:** 🛒on the spot ⊗100m 🍽100m.
**Remarks:** Overnight stay on Parking de la Piscine, GPS N 45,27902 E 2,66403.

### Roanne 22B3

**Port de Plaisance**, Quai Commandant de Fourcauld.
**GPS:** n46,03750 e4,08306.⬆➡

10 ⛺€ 6 🚰€ 2,50/15minutes 🚿€ 2,50 Ch€ 2,50 🚐€ 2,50/4h WC
🚿🚐 **Location:** Urban, comfortable, quiet. **Surface:** gravel.
🅾 01/01-31/12.
**Distance:** 🛒500m ⚓500m ⊗2km 🍽2km 🚐on the spot 🚲on the spot 🚶on the spot.
**Remarks:** Max. 6 days.

### Romans-sur-Isère 25C2

Avenue Gambetta. **GPS:** n45,04521 e5,05879.⬆

4 ⛺free. **Location:** Urban, simple. **Surface:** metalled.
🅾 01/01-31/12.
**Distance:** 🛒centre 700m ⊗50m 🍽300m.
**Remarks:** Parking in front of Marques Avenue, max. 48h.

### Ruoms 25B3

**Camping-Car Park La Grand Terre**, La Grand Terre.
**GPS:** n44,42381 e4,33253.⬆
15 ⛺€ 11,40-13,60 🚰🚻Ch⚡(12x)🚿included. 🚐🚲
**Location:** Rural. **Surface:** grassy/metalled. 🅾 01/01-31/12.
**Distance:** 🛒3km ⊗200m 🍽on the spot 🚶on the spot.
**Remarks:** Mandatory, one-time fee Pass'Etapes € 4.

### Ruynes-en-Margeride 25A2

Le Bourg. **GPS:** n45,00111 e3,22389.⬆➡

8 ⛺free 🚰€ 2/10minutes 🚻Ch🚐€ 2/55minutes.
**Location:** Urban, simple, quiet. **Surface:** gravel/sand.
🅾 01/01-31/12.
**Distance:** 🛒50m 🍽6km ⊗50m 🍽50m.

### Sagnes-et-Goudoulet 25B2

**Camping-Car Park**, Les Sagnes. **GPS:** n44,79030 e4,22606.⬆
6 ⛺€ 9,80 🚰🚻Ch⚡(12x)included. 🚐🚲 **Location:** Rural.
**Surface:** gravel. 🅾 01/01-31/12.
**Remarks:** Mandatory, one-time fee Pass'Etapes € 4.

### Saillans 25D2

**La Roche, Quartier Tourtoiron**, Montmartel.
**GPS:** n44,69549 e5,19350.⬆➡

20 ⌷free ⌷€3 ⌷€2 ⌷ChWC.
**Location:** Rural, simple, quiet. **Surface:** gravel.
◻ 01/01-31/12.
**Distance:** ⌷500m ⌷500m.
**Remarks:** Along the Drôme river, max. 24h, closed when high water.

**Saint-Agrève** 25B2
Coussac. **GPS:** n45,01042 e4,39339.⌷.

10 ⌷free ⌷€3 ⌷Ch ⌷€3,water 10 min + electricity 50min WC.
**Location:** Urban, simple, quiet. **Surface:** asphalted.
◻ 01/01-31/12.
**Distance:** ⌷500m ⌷500m ⌷500m.
**Remarks:** Coins at tourist info.

**Saint-Agrève** 25B2
Le Lac de Véron, Pré de Gardy, D120. **GPS:** n44,99981 e4,40164.⌷.

5 ⌷€5/24h ⌷on demand ⌷free. **Location:** Rural, comfortable,
quiet. **Surface:** unpaved. ◻ 01/04-31/10.
**Distance:** ⌷village 1km ⌷100m ⌷200m ⌷on the spot ⌷on the
spot ⌷on the spot.
**Remarks:** At fish lake.

**Saint-Alban-Auriolles** 25B3
Rue Marius Perbost. **GPS:** n44,42693 e4,30096.⌷.

35 ⌷free ⌷€3 ⌷Ch ⌷€3. **Location:** Urban, simple.
**Surface:** gravel. ◻ 01/01-31/12.
**Distance:** ⌷300m ⌷200m.

**Saint-André-d'Apchon** 22B3
La Prébande. **GPS:** n46,03385 e3,92705.⌷.

3 ⌷free ⌷Chfree. **Location:** Rural, simple, quiet.
**Surface:** gravel. ◻ 01/01-31/12.
**Distance:** ⌷300m ⌷100m ⌷200m.

---

**Remarks:** Shady.

**Saint-André-de-Chalencon** 25B1
Place des Droits de l'Homme. **GPS:** n45,27254 e3,97010.⌷.
2 ⌷free ⌷€2/10minutes ⌷Ch ⌷€2/1h.
**Location:** Urban, simple, central. **Surface:** gravel/sand.
◻ 01/01-31/12.
**Distance:** ⌷1,5km ⌷on the spot ⌷on the spot.

**Saint-Bon-Tarentaise** ❄ 25F1
D91A. **GPS:** n45,43036 e6,62600.⌷⌷.

30+ ⌷free ⌷€3 ⌷Ch ⌷. **Location:** Rural, simple.
**Surface:** asphalted. ◻ 01/01-31/12.
**Distance:** ⌷on the spot ⌷250m ⌷400m ⌷on the spot.

**Saint-Bonnet-le-Château** 25B1
Esplanade de la Boule. **GPS:** n45,42514 e4,06436.⌷.

50 ⌷free ⌷Ch WCfree. **Location:** Simple, central.
**Surface:** metalled. ◻ 01/01-31/12 ◻ Fri.
**Distance:** ⌷200m ⌷1km ⌷200m ⌷200m.

**Tourist information Saint-Bonnet-le-Château:**
Ⓜ Musée de la Pétanque et des Boules, Esplanade de la Boule. All
about the beloved French national sport. ◻ 01/04-31/10.
Ⓜ Musée International Pétanque et Boules, Boulevard des Chauchères.
⌷ ◻ Fri.

**Saint-Bonnet-le-Froid** 25C1
Chemin de Brard. **GPS:** n45,14136 e4,43454.⌷⌷.

6 ⌷€5 ⌷Ch ⌷included. ⌷ **Location:** Urban, simple, central,
quiet. **Surface:** gravel. ◻ 01/03-15/11.
**Distance:** ⌷150m ⌷150m ⌷150m ⌷on the spot.
**Remarks:** Access via D105.

**Saint-Bonnet-Tronçais** 21H1
**Parking du Stade**, Route de Tronçais, D39.
**GPS:** n46,66001 e2,69717.⌷.
10 ⌷free ⌷€2 ⌷Ch ⌷€2. **Location:** Simple, quiet.
**Surface:** gravel. ◻ 01/01-31/12 ◻ water disconnected in winter.
**Distance:** ⌷300m ⌷on the spot ⌷500m ⌷500m ⌷on the spot.
**Remarks:** Max. 48h, coins at the bakery and campsite.

**Saint-Bonnet-Tronçais** 21H1
Rue de l'Étang. **GPS:** n46,65896 e2,69228.⌷⌷.
10 ⌷free. **Location:** Simple, central, quiet. **Surface:** gravel.
◻ 01/01-31/12.
**Distance:** ⌷on the spot ⌷27km ⌷Lake 450m ⌷130m ⌷bakery
200m.

**Saint-Christophe-sur-Dolaison** 25B2
**Place des Jardins**, Le Bourg. **GPS:** n44,99802 e3,82158.⌷.

---

6 ⌷free ⌷€2 ⌷Ch ⌷€2. **Location:** Rural, simple, quiet.
**Surface:** asphalted. ◻ 01/01-31/12.
**Distance:** ⌷100m ⌷150m ⌷on the spot ⌷on the spot.
**Remarks:** Coins at town hall.

**Saint-Désirat** 25C1
Musée de l'Alambic, Distillerie Jean Gauthier, D291.
**GPS:** n45,25856 e4,79261.⌷.

5 ⌷free ⌷ ⌷WCfree. **Location:** Simple. **Surface:** asphalted.
◻ 01/01-31/12.
**Distance:** ⌷300m ⌷300m.
**Remarks:** Max. 1 night.

**Saint-Donat-sur-l'Herbasse** 25C2
Route de St.Bardoux. **GPS:** n45,11902 e4,98284.⌷.

50 ⌷free ⌷Chfree. **Location:** Rural, simple, central, quiet.
**Surface:** asphalted. ◻ 01/01-31/12.
**Distance:** ⌷400m ⌷400m ⌷1km.
**Remarks:** In front of gymnasium, max. 1 night.

**Saint-Éloy-les-Mines** 21H2
Rue du Puy-de-Dôme, RN144. **GPS:** n46,15559 e2,83615.⌷⌷.

30 ⌷free ⌷€2 ⌷Ch ⌷€2. **Location:** Rural, simple, quiet.
**Surface:** metalled. ◻ 01/01-31/12.
**Distance:** ⌷on the spot ⌷700m ⌷400m Carrefour Market.
**Remarks:** Max. 48h.

**Saint-Étienne-la-Varenne** 22C3
Le Bourg. **GPS:** n46,07731 e4,63024.⌷.

4 ⌷free ⌷Ch ⌷free. **Location:** Rural, simple, quiet.
**Surface:** gravel/metalled. ◻ 01/01-31/12.
**Distance:** ⌷on the spot ⌷50m ⌷on the spot ⌷on the spot.
**Remarks:** Next to church.

**S** Saint-Félicien 25C2

Place du Pré Lacour sud. **GPS:** n45,08453 e4,62848.

6 free € 2 Ch € 2. **Location:** Urban, simple, quiet.
**Surface:** asphalted/gravel. 01/01-31/12.
**Distance:** on the spot on the spot on the spot.
**Remarks:** Behind police station, max. 2 nights.

**S** Saint-Ferréol-Trente-Pas 25D3

**La Pisciculture l'Eau Claire**, La Condamine. **GPS:** n44,43781 e5,23862.
WC. **Surface:** gravel. 01/01-31/12.
**Remarks:** Trout pond, regional products.

**S** Saint-Flour 24H2

Cours Chazerat. **GPS:** n45,03389 e3,08750.

20 free € 2 Ch € 2/55minutes. **Location:** Urban, simple.
**Surface:** metalled. 01/04-31/10.
**Distance:** on the spot 4,6km 50m 50m on the spot
on the spot.
**Remarks:** Higher part of the city.

**S** Saint-Flour 24H2

Place de l'Ander, ville basse. **GPS:** n45,03556 e3,09750.

8 free € 2/100liter Ch € 2/55minutes. **Location:** Urban,
simple. **Surface:** asphalted. 01/01-31/12.
**Distance:** 300m 4km 300m 300m on the spot.
**Remarks:** Near campsite, lower part of the city.

**Tourist information Saint-Flour:**
Office de Tourisme, 17bis, place d'Armes, www.saint-flour.com. City
with car-free historical centre, Vieux Saint Flour.

**S** Saint-Forgeux 22C3

Le Tram. **GPS:** n45,85733 e4,47566.

free Ch free WC. **Location:** Rural, simple, quiet.
**Surface:** metalled. 01/01-31/12.
**Distance:** 300m 300m 300m on the spot.

**S** Saint-Genest-de-Beauzon 25B3

**Domaine la Pize**, La Pize. **GPS:** n44,43759 e4,19431.

---

€ 10 ChWCincluded . **Location:** Rural, isolated, quiet.
**Surface:** unpaved. 01/01-31/12.
**Distance:** 1,6km on the spot.

**S** Saint-Georges 25A2

**Aire du Cantal**, D909. **GPS:** n45,03167 e3,13500.

free € 2 Ch € 2 WC. **Location:** Motorway, simple, noisy.
**Surface:** asphalted. 01/01-31/12.
**Distance:** 3km 500m 200m 500m.
**Remarks:** At petrol station Esso.

**S** Saint-Georges-d'Espéranche 25C1

Chemin des Platières. **GPS:** n45,55560 e5,07478.

14 free Ch free. **Location:** Rural, simple, central, quiet.
**Surface:** metalled. 01/01-31/12.
**Distance:** on the spot 100m 500m.
**Remarks:** Max. 48h.

**S** Saint-Gérand-de-Vaux 22A2

**Etang du Moulin**, Les Gaillards. **GPS:** n46,38416 e3,39972.

30 free € 2/100liter Ch € 2/1h WC. **Location:** Rural,
comfortable, isolated, quiet. **Surface:** grassy. 01/01-31/12.
**Distance:** 600m on the spot 600m.
**Remarks:** Coins at restaurant.

**S** Saint-Germain-Lespinasse 22B2

Place du 8 mai 1945. **GPS:** n46,10510 e3,96229.

3 free Ch free. **Location:** Rural, simple, quiet.
**Surface:** gravel. 01/01-31/12.
**Distance:** 200m 50m 50m.

**S** Saint-Gérons 24G2

**Camping-Car Park Plage d'Espinet**. **GPS:** n44,93257 e2,23190.
26 free € 9,40-11,80 Ch included. 01/01-31/12.

---

**Distance:** 2km Snackbar.
**Remarks:** Mandatory, one-time fee Pass'Etapes € 4.

**S** Saint-Gervais-les-Bains 22F3

77, impasse Cascade. **GPS:** n45,88864 e6,71287.

20 free € 2 Ch € 2. **Location:** Rural, simple, quiet.
**Surface:** asphalted. 01/01-31/12.
**Distance:** 200m 200m 200m 300m.
**Remarks:** Parking skating rink.

**S** Saint-Haon-le-Châtel 22B3

**Fondanges**, Route de la Croix du Sud, D39.
**GPS:** n46,06362 e3,91313.

3 free Ch free. **Location:** Rural, quiet. **Surface:** metalled.
01/01-31/12.
**Distance:** 400m 400m 400m 400m.

**S** Saint-Hilaire-sous-Charlieu 22B2

**Le Grand Couvert**, Les Perches. **GPS:** n46,11054 e4,18827.

2 free. **Location:** Rural, simple, isolated, quiet. **Surface:** gravel.
01/01-31/12.

**S** Saint-Jean-d'Ardières 22C2

**Domaine de Grande Ferrière**, 831 route des Rochons.
**GPS:** n46,12954 e4,71581.

5 free Ch free € 5/4night WC. **Location:** Rural, simple.
**Surface:** gravel. 01/01-31/12.
**Distance:** 3km 6km 5km 500m 3km 3km.
**Remarks:** Max. 48h.

**S** Saint-Jean-de-Bournay 25D1

Place du Marche. **GPS:** n45,50130 e5,13845.

10 free free Ch. **Location:** Rural, simple, central, quiet.
**Surface:** asphalted. 01/01-31/12.

FR

**Distance:** 🚶on the spot ⊗100m 🚰 100m.

**🚐S Saint-Jean-de-Maurienne** 🏔🏕❄ **25E1**

Rue Louis Sibue. **GPS:** n45,27995 e6,34776.⬆.
10 🚐free 🚰€ 2 🧺Ch🚽€ 2 WC. **Location:** Urban, simple, quiet.
**Surface:** asphalted. 🅾 01/01-31/12.
**Distance:** 🚲2,5km ⊗100m 🚰120m.
**Remarks:** Max. 48h.

**🚐S Saint-Jean-en-Royans** 🏕🌳 **25D2**

Rue de la Gare. **GPS:** n45,02028 e5,29032.⬆➡.

10 🚐free 🚰🧺Chfree. **Location:** Simple, quiet. **Surface:** gravel.
🅾 01/01-31/12.
**Distance:** 🚶200m ⊗200m 🚰200m.
**Remarks:** Nearby amusement, max. 7 days, max. 8M.

**S Saint-Julien-Chapteuil** **25B2**

**L'Holme**, La Croix Blanche. **GPS:** n45,03917 e4,06305.⬆.
🚰🧺Ch. 🅾 01/01-31/12.
**Remarks:** Service in front of campsite.

**🅲S Saint-Just** **25A2**

**Camping Municipal**, Le Bourg. **GPS:** n44,88972 e3,20889.⬆.

10 🚐€ 8,25, 04/07-28/08 € 9,90 🚰🧺Ch🚽🧹(4x) WC.🧺🎥
**Location:** Rural, comfortable, quiet. **Surface:** grassy.
🅾 01/01-31/12.
**Distance:** 🚶50m ⊗100m 🚰100m 🍽on the spot.
**Remarks:** Incl. use camp-site facilities.

**🚐S Saint-Just-d'Ardèche** **25C3**

**Domaine La Favette**, D86, route des Gorges d'Ardèche.
**GPS:** n44,30134 e4,60649.

6 🚐€5 🚰€ 2 🧺Ch🚽€ 2. **Location:** Rural, isolated, quiet.
**Surface:** gravel. 🅾 01/01-31/12.
**Distance:** ⊗800m 🚰1,4km.
**Remarks:** At wine-grower, max. 24h.

**Tourist information Saint-Just-d'Ardèche:**
ℹ Good starting point to discover the Ardèche gorges.
🎪 🅾 Thu.

**🚐S Saint-Just-en-Chevalet** **22B3**

Boulevard de l'Astrée, D53. **GPS:** n45,91411 e3,84727.⬆.

5 🚐free 🚰€ 2 🧺ChWCfree.
**Location:** Rural, simple, noisy. **Surface:** asphalted/metalled.
🅾 01/01-31/12 🅾 Thu-morning.

**Distance:** 🚶on the spot ⊗on the spot 🚰on the spot 🍽on the spot
🚶on the spot.

**🚐S Saint-Mamet-la-Salvetat** **24G2**

D20. **GPS:** n44,85714 e2,30981.⬆➡.

3 🚐free 🚰€ 2/100liter 🧺Ch🚽€ 2/1h WC. **Location:** Rural, simple,
quiet. **Surface:** asphalted. 🅾 01/01-31/12.
**Distance:** 🚶400m ⊗500m 🚰350m.
**Remarks:** Coins at the shops and town hall.

**🚐S Saint-Marcel-d'Urfé** **22B3**

Le Bourg. **GPS:** n45,87361 e3,88391.⬆.

3 🚐free 🚰🧺ChWCfree. **Location:** Simple, quiet. **Surface:** gravel.
🅾 01/01-31/12.
**Distance:** 🚶on the spot ⊗on the spot.
**Remarks:** At tennis-court.

**🚐S Saint-Marcel-en-Murat** **21H2**

D243. **GPS:** n46,32184 e3,00837.⬆.

10 🚐free 🚰€ 2/100liter 🧺Ch🚽€ 2/1h. **Location:** Rural, simple,
isolated, quiet. **Surface:** gravel. 🅾 01/01-31/12.
**Distance:** 🚶4km Montmarault 🚲3,5km exit 11 A71 ⊗nearby.
**Remarks:** Coins at town hall and restaurant.

**🚐S Saint-Martin-d'Estréaux** **22B2**

Place des Gouttes. **GPS:** n46,20713 e3,79877.⬆.

3 🚐free 🚰🧺ChWCfree. **Location:** Simple, quiet.
**Surface:** asphalted. 🅾 01/01-31/12.
**Distance:** 🚶200m 🚰200m.

**🚐S Saint-Martin-en-Haut** 🌳 **22C3**

**Etang du Kaiser**, Lieu-dit-Jeangouttière. **GPS:** n45,64206 e4,53511.⬆.

4 🚐€ 8 🚰🧺ChWC. **Location:** Rural, comfortable, quiet.
**Surface:** gravel.

🅾 01/01-31/12.
**Distance:** 🚶St.Martin 4km 🚲on the spot 🚵on the spot 🚶on the spot.
**Remarks:** At small lake, max. 72h.

**🚐S Saint-Ours-les Roches** **21H3**

**Vulcania**, 2 route de Mazayes. **GPS:** n45,81221 e2,94877.⬆.

65 🚐€ 10 🚰€ 2/100liter 🧺Ch🧹(20x)€ 2/6h 🧺. **Location:** Rural,
simple, quiet. **Surface:** asphalted/gravel. 🅾 15/03-13/11.
**Remarks:** Max. 2 nights.

**🚐S Saint-Paul-des-Landes** **24G2**

Rue du Moinac. **GPS:** n44,94250 e2,31694.⬆➡.

3 🚐free 🚰€ 3,50 🧺Ch🚽€ 3,50. **Location:** Rural, simple, central,
quiet. **Surface:** asphalted. 🅾 01/01-31/12.
**Distance:** 🚶50m ⊗200m 🚰50m.
**Remarks:** Max. 24h, coins at petrol station.

**🚐S Saint-Paul-le-Jeune** **25B3**

Rue Louis Roux, D901. **GPS:** n44,33999 e4,15322.

12 🚐free 🚰€ 2 🧺Ch🚽€ 2. **Location:** Urban, central.
**Surface:** grassy. 🅾 01/01-31/12.
**Distance:** 🚶on the spot 🚰100m.
**Remarks:** Coins at the shops in the village.

**🚐S Saint-Paul-Trois-Châteaux** **25C3**

**Parking Office de Tourisme**, Le Courreau, Place Chausy.
**GPS:** n44,34786 e4,76995.

30 🚐free 🚰🧺Chfree WC. **Location:** Urban, simple, central, quiet.
**Surface:** asphalted. 🅾 01/01-31/12.
**Distance:** 🚶50m ⊗50m 🚰on the spot.
**Remarks:** At tourist office, max. 24h.

**Tourist information Saint-Paul-Trois-Châteaux:**
🎪 Marché. 🅾 Tue-morning.
🎪 Marché aux truffes du Tricastin. 🅾 Dec-Mar Su-morning.

**🚐S Saint-Pierre-en-Faucigny** **22E3**

Avenue de la Gare. **GPS:** n46,05884 e6,37450.⬆.

4 ⅍free 🚰🔧Ch🔧free. **Location:** Urban, simple, noisy.
**Surface:** asphalted. ⬜ 01/01-31/12.
**Distance:** 🚉on the spot ⊗60m on the spot 🚌on the spot.
**Remarks:** Nearby railway station.

**Saint-Pourçain-sur-Sioule** 🌊⛵🏖 22A2

**Aire Camping-car de la Moutte**, Rue de la Moutte.
**GPS:** n46,31262 e3,29656. ⬆➡.

73 ⅍free 🚰€ 4 🔧Ch🔧(8x)€ 4/4h.
**Location:** Urban, comfortable, central, quiet. **Surface:** grassy.
⬜ 01/01-31/12.
**Distance:** 🚉800m on the spot ⊗on the spot 🛒on the spot.
**Remarks:** Along the Sioule river, max. 7m.

**Saint-Rémèze** 25C3

**Les Chais du Vivarais**, D362. **GPS:** n44,39536 e4,50576. ⬆.

3 ⅍free 🚰🔧Ch🔧free. **Location:** Rural, simple, quiet.
**Surface:** asphalted. ⬜ 01/03-15/11.
**Distance:** 🚉500m ⊗200m.
**Remarks:** Max. 48h.

**Tourist information Saint-Rémèze:**
👁 Grotte Aven Marzal. Caves. ⬜ Sa/Su/Holidays, 01/04-30/09
10.30-18h.
👁 Grotte de la Madelaine. Caves. ⬜ Apr-Oct 10-18h.
Ⓜ Musée de la lavande. Museum and distillery with lavender fields.
⬜ 01/05-30/09 10-17h, Apr + Oct Sa-Su-holiday 10-17h.
  Zoo préhistorique, Route des Gorges. Prehistoric park. ⬜ 10.30-
17.30h.

**Saint-Rémy-de-Blot** 21H3

Place du Bourg. **GPS:** n46,07722 e2,93139. ⬆.

7 ⅍free WC. **Location:** Rural, simple, isolated, quiet.
**Surface:** grasstiles. ⬜ 01/01-31/12.
**Distance:** ⊗on the spot.

**Saint-Restitut** 25C3

Le Village. **GPS:** n44,33144 e4,79093. ⬆.

10 ⅍free 🚰🔧Chfree. **Location:** Urban, simple, noisy.
**Surface:** asphalted. ⬜ 01/01-31/12.
**Distance:** 🚉on the spot ⊗200m.
**Remarks:** Max. 7 days.

**Saint-Rirand** 🏔 22B3

Le Bourg. **GPS:** n46,07501 e3,85016. ⬆➡.

3 ⅍free 🚰🔧Chfree. **Location:** Rural, simple, isolated, quiet.
**Surface:** gravel. ⬜ 01/01-31/12.
**Distance:** 🚉on the spot 🚶on the spot.

**Saint-Romain-d'Ay** 🍴 25C1

Praperier, D6. **GPS:** n45,16430 e4,66339. ⬆.

8 ⅍free 🚰€ 2/20minutes 🔧Ch🔧(4x)€ 2/4h WC.
**Location:** Simple. **Surface:** asphalted. ⬜ 01/01-31/12 🔴 Service:
winter.
**Distance:** 🚉550m ⊗100m.
**Remarks:** Coins at town hall and superette.

**Saint-Romain-de-Lerps** 🍴 25C2

Le Village, D287. **GPS:** n44,98029 e4,79596. ⬆.

10 ⅍free 🚰🔧Ch🚐€ 4,100 liter water + 1h electricity
WC. **Location:** Rural, simple, isolated, quiet. **Surface:** gravel.
⬜ 01/01-31/12 🔴 01/10 and 01/04.
**Distance:** 🚉100m ⊗100m 🛒100m.
**Remarks:** Less suitable for motorhomes >6,5m, coins at bakery, bar/
resto 3duPic and town hall, panoramic view over the Rhône-valley
200m.

**Saint-Romain-Lachalm** 25B1

Rulière/D23. **GPS:** n45,26399 e4,33576. ⬆.

4 ⅍free 🚰€ 2/10minutes 🔧Ch€ 2 🔧(4x)€ 2/4h.
**Location:** Rural, simple, isolated. **Surface:** asphalted.

⬜ 01/01-31/12.
**Distance:** 🚉100m 🍴 400m 🛒bakery 200m.
**Remarks:** Max. 8M, coins at the shops and town hall.

**Saint-Sauves-d'Auvergne** 🏔 21H3

**Domaine de Lavaux**, D82. **GPS:** n45,61688 e2,68975. ⬆➡.

50 ⅍€ 8 🚰🔧Ch🔧(10x)€ 4/day WCincluded 🚿€ 1,25 ⚡€ 5.
🐕 **Location:** Rural, comfortable, isolated, quiet. **Surface:** grassy.
⬜ 15/04-15/09.
**Distance:** 🚉1km 🚶on the spot.

**Saint-Symphorien-sur-Coise** 22C3

Bois des Pinasses. **GPS:** n45,62578 e4,45837. ⬆.

5 ⅍free.
**Location:** Rural, simple. **Surface:** gravel. ⬜ 01/01-31/12.
**Distance:** 🚉1km 🏊50m.
**Remarks:** Next to sports fields.

**Saint-Symphorien-sur-Coise** 22C3

Rue des Rameaux. **GPS:** n45,63378 e4,45883. ⬆.
🚰🔧Chfree. **Location:** Simple. ⬜ 01/01-31/12.
**Remarks:** Free coins at Bar-Tabac and town hall.

**Saint-Théoffrey** 25E2

**Camping Ser-Sirant**, Chemin du Lavoir. **GPS:** n45,00034 e5,77819. ⬆.
4 ⅍€ 8-9,50 🚰€ 1,50 🔧Ch. **Location:** Rural. **Surface:** grassy.
**Distance:** 🏊beach Saint Théoffrey.
**Remarks:** At lake Laffrey, pay at reception campsite.

**Saint-Thomé** 25C3

N107, Les Crottes. **GPS:** n44,50059 e4,63445. ⬆.

1 ⅍free 🚰🔧Chfree. **Location:** Rural, isolated. **Surface:** asphalted.
⬜ 01/04-31/10.
**Distance:** 🚶on the spot.

**Saint-Victor-sur-Loire** 🍴🏖 25B1

**Base Nautique du lac de Grangent**, Rue de la plage.
**GPS:** n45,44787 e4,25626. ⬆➡.

12 ⅍free 🚰🔧Ch🔧(4x)€ 2,90/4h WC.
**Location:** Rural, comfortable. **Surface:** asphalted.
⬜ 01/01-31/12.
**Distance:** 🚉3km 🏊on the spot on the spot ⊗on the spot 🛒3km
🚶on the spot.
**Remarks:** On the river Loire, max. 72h, coins at the shops in the village.

FR

## Salers 24H1

**Le Mouriol**, Route du Puy Mary. **GPS:** n45,14718 e2,49900.⬆

15 🛏€ 12 + € 0,50/pp tourist tax ⚰€ 3 🚰ChWC included,on camp site.
**Location:** Rural. **Surface:** asphalted. 🔲 01/04-31/10.
**Distance:** 🚲1,2km ⊗50m.
**Remarks:** Next to camping municipal, coins at campsite and tourist info.

## Salers 24H1

D680. **GPS:** n45,14010 e2,49478.
12 🛏€ 3.🏠 **Location:** Rural. **Surface:** asphalted/metalled.
🔲 01/01-31/12.
**Distance:** 🚲500m.

## Salers 24H1

Rue Notre-Dame. **GPS:** n45,13898 e2,49583.
6 🛏€ 3.🏠 **Surface:** asphalted. 🔲 01/01-31/12.
**Distance:** 🚲250m.
**Remarks:** Max. 7 days.

## Sallanches 22F3

**Parking de Charousse**, 70 route du Fayet. **GPS:** n45,93210 e6,63337.⬆
3 🛏free ⚰€ 2/20minutes 🚰Ch. **Location:** Urban, central, noisy.
**Surface:** asphalted. 🔲 01/01-31/12.
**Distance:** 🚲400m ⊗100m.
**Remarks:** Max. 24h.

## Samoëns 22F3

**Aire d'accueil camping-car de Vercland**, Hameau de Vercland. **GPS:** n46,07228 e6,70189.⬆➡

10 🛏free ⚰€ 6 🚰Ch 6. **Location:** Rural, simple, quiet.
**Surface:** metalled. 🔲 01/01-31/12 🔲 Service: winter.
**Distance:** 🚲2km ⊗100m.🚱2km.

## Samoëns 22F3

**Parking du Giffre**. **GPS:** n46,07666 e6,71899.⬆

5 🛏€ 10 ⚰🚰Ch 🔧🧹 **Surface:** asphalted. 🔲 01/01-31/12
🔲 Service: winter.
**Distance:** 🚲100m ⊗100m 🚱100m 🚌Skibus to Samoëns 1600
⛷100m 🚶on the spot.
**Remarks:** Near campsite du Giffre, parking 150m.

## Sansac-de-Marmiesse 24G2

Rue de la Vidalie. **GPS:** n44,88389 e2,34639.⬆➡

4 🛏free ⚰€ 3,50. 🚰Ch € 3,50.
**Location:** Urban, simple, central. **Surface:** asphalted. 🔲 01/01-31/12
🔲 service: 01/10-30/04.
**Distance:** 🚲on the spot ⊗200m 🚶on the spot.
**Remarks:** Max. 7 days, coins at the bakery.

## Sassenage 25D1

Rue Pierre de Coubertin. **GPS:** n45,21346 e5,66858.⬆
9 🛏free ⚰🚰Chfree. **Surface:** asphalted. 🔲 01/01-31/12.
**Distance:** 🚲on the spot 🚶on the spot.
**Remarks:** At sports grounds, max. 48h.

## Sauges 25A2

Place du Brieul. **GPS:** n44,95940 e3,54395.⬆

10 🛏free ⚰🚰Chfree. **Location:** Simple, central.
**Surface:** asphalted. 🔲 01/01-31/12.
**Distance:** 🚲on the spot 🛵600m 🚱bakery 200m 🚶on the spot
⛷on the spot.

## Sauret-Besserve 21H3

D523. **GPS:** n45,99245 e2,80946.⬆

4 🛏free ⚰€ 2 🚰Ch. **Location:** Rural, simple, isolated.
**Surface:** gravel/metalled. 🔲 01/01-31/12.
**Distance:** 🚲on the spot ⊗300m 🚱on the spot.
**Remarks:** Near church.

## Ségur-les-Villas 24H1

Le Bourg. **GPS:** n45,22311 e2,81818.⬆➡

10 🛏free ⚰€ 3/100liter 🚰Ch 3/1h. **Location:** Rural, simple,
quiet. **Surface:** grassy. 🔲 01/05-30/10.
**Distance:** 🚲200m ⊗300m 🚱200m,
**Remarks:** Nearby football ground, coins at the shops in the village.

## Serrières-en-Chautagne 22E3

**GPS:** n45,87964 e5,84230.⬆

15 🛏free ⚰🚰ChWCfree. **Location:** Rural, central, quiet.
**Surface:** metalled. 🔲 01/01-31/12 🔲 Service: winter.
**Distance:** 🚲on the spot 🚤1km 🏖beach 50m 🛵on the spot ⊗200m
🚱100m 🚱100m.
**Remarks:** At little mountain stream, max. 72h.

## Seyssel 22E3

**Parking Base de Loisirs**, Quai du Rhône. **GPS:** n45,95146 e5,83343.

5 🛏free 🚰Chfree.
**Location:** Rural, simple, central, quiet. **Surface:** gravel.
🔲 01/01-31/12 🔲 Service: winter.
**Distance:** 🚲800m 🚤on the spot 🛵on the spot ⊗500m 🚱800m
⛷on the spot.
**Remarks:** At recreational lake and Rhone river.

## Seyssel 22E3

Quai du Rhône. **GPS:** n45,95001 e5,83406.

5 🛏free ⚰🚰Chfree.
**Location:** Rural, simple, central, quiet. **Surface:** grassy.
🔲 01/01-31/12 🔲 Service: winter.
**Distance:** 🚲400m 🚤on the spot 🛵on the spot ⊗400m 🚱400m
🚌400m 🚶on the spot.
**Remarks:** Along the Rhone river.

## Siaugues-Sainte-Marie 25A2

D590. **GPS:** n45,09303 e3,62784.⬆

4 🛏free ⚰€ 2/10minutes 🚰Ch 2/h. **Location:** Rural, simple,
quiet. **Surface:** asphalted. 🔲 01/01-31/12.
**Distance:** 🚲300m ⊗300m 🚱bakery 200m.

## Sixt-Fer-à-Cheval 22F3

Route du Cirque du Fer à Cheval. **GPS:** n46,05698 e6,78048.⬆

20 🛏free ⚰🚰Ch 🔧€ 4/12h. **Location:** Urban, simple, quiet.
**Surface:** asphalted. 🔲 01/01-31/12.
**Distance:** 🚲500m 🚤on the spot 🚱500m.

## Solignac-sur-Loire 25B2

Le Vis. **GPS:** n44,96471 e3,88001.⬆

20 🛏€ 12 ⚰🚰Ch 🔧WCincluded.🏠🧹 **Location:** Rural,
comfortable, isolated, quiet. **Surface:** grassy. 🔲 01/05-01/11.
**Distance:** 🚲800m ⊗800m 🚱800m.

FR

## Solignat 25A1

Route des Dauphins d'Auvergne, D32. **GPS:** n45,51701 e3,17074. ⬆.

5 free € 2/100liter Ch € 2/1h. **Location:** Rural, simple, quiet. **Surface:** grassy. 01/01-31/12.
**Distance:** 100m.
**Remarks:** Max. 48h.

## Sorbier 22A2

Route de varennes sur Tèche. **GPS:** n46,36275 e3,65906.
2 free Ch free. **Location:** Rural. **Surface:** gravel.
01/01-31/12.
**Remarks:** Picnic tables available, playground.

## St Anthème 25B1

Rambaud. **GPS:** n45,52354 e3,91464. ⬆➡.

30 € 5 Chincluded.
**Location:** Rural, simple, central, quiet. **Surface:** grassy/gravel.
01/01-31/12 water: frost.
**Distance:** 200m beach 250m 200m on the spot.
**Remarks:** Next to campsite Rambaud, water disconnected.

## Super Besse 24H1

La Binche, Ronde de Vassivière. **GPS:** n45,50644 e2,85342. ⬆➡.

172 € 9,90/24h € 1/20minutes Ch (100x) € 2,50/4h
. **Location:** Comfortable, quiet. **Surface:** asphalted.
01/01-31/12.
**Distance:** 300m 300m on the spot 300m.
**Remarks:** On ring-road around the lake, P5, P7 and P10, no camping activities.

## Super Lioran 24H2

Aire de Laveissière, Parking Font d'Alagnon.
**GPS:** n45,08856 e2,73819. ⬆.

25 free. **Location:** Rural, simple, quiet. **Surface:** asphalted.
01/01-31/12.
**Distance:** 200m 200m 50m 30m 30m.

## Super Lioran 24H2

P5. **GPS:** n45,08705 e2,74793. ⬆.
70 free. 01/01-31/12.
**Distance:** 400m 400m 400m.

## Suze-la-Rousse 25C3

Route de Bollène, D94. **GPS:** n44,28598 e4,83185.

15 free free. **Location:** Rural, simple. **Surface:** grassy/gravel.
01/01-31/12.
**Distance:** 850m on the spot on the spot.
**Remarks:** At sports grounds.

## Suze-la-Rousse 25C3

50 Impasse de la Zone Artisanale. **GPS:** n44,28965 e4,84783.
Chfree. **Location:** Simple. 01/01-31/12.
**Distance:** 1,5km.

## Talizat 24H2

Place du 19 mars 1962. **GPS:** n45,11417 e3,04583. ⬆.

2 free € 2 Ch € 2. **Location:** Rural, simple, central, quiet.
**Surface:** asphalted. 01/04-31/10.
**Distance:** on the spot 100m 100m on the spot.
**Remarks:** Coins at town hall and restaurant, behind town hall, max. 48h, max. 7m.

## Tence 25B2

Place du Fieu. **GPS:** n45,11580 e4,29220. ⬆.

6 free € 2/10minutes Ch. **Location:** Urban, simple, quiet.
**Surface:** gravel/metalled. 01/01-31/12.
**Distance:** 200m 200m 200m on the spot.
**Remarks:** Max. 24h.

## Thiel-sur-Acolin 22A2

Rue de la Motte. **GPS:** n46,52269 e3,58776. ⬆.

11 free Ch free. **Location:** Rural, isolated, quiet.
**Surface:** gravel. 01/01-31/12.
**Distance:** 650m.

## Thiel-sur-Acolin 22A2

Rue de la Motte. **GPS:** n46,52279 e3,58757. ⬆.
11 free € 2/10minutes Ch € 2/1h. **Location:** Urban, comfortable, quiet. **Surface:** metalled/sand.
**Distance:** 1km 500m 1km.
**Remarks:** Max. 9m.

## Thiers 22A3

Base de loisirs Iloa, D44 > Dorat. **GPS:** n45,87070 e3,48311. ⬆.

10 free free. **Location:** Rural, simple, isolated, quiet.
**Surface:** metalled. 01/01-31/12.
**Distance:** 2,6km on the spot.

## Thiézac 24H2

Aire de camping-car La Sapinière, D59.
**GPS:** n45,01583 e2,66278. ⬆➡.

8 free € 2 Ch € 2. **Location:** Rural, simple, isolated, quiet.
**Surface:** asphalted. 01/01-31/12.
**Distance:** 50m 100m 100m.
**Remarks:** Max. 24h, coins at petrol station.

## Thueyts 25B2

Chemin d'Echelle du Roi, via N102. **GPS:** n44,67274 e4,21917. ⬆➡.

10 free € 2/5minutes Ch € 2/30minutes,service
€ 2. **Location:** Rural, simple, quiet. **Surface:** grassy/gravel.
15/03-15/11.
**Distance:** 500m 200m on the spot.
**Remarks:** Near the Ardèche river and Pont du Diable, next to sports fields, max. 24h.

## Tiranges 25B1

Accueil Camping Car, La Nerceyre. **GPS:** n45,30702 e3,99107. ⬆➡.

10 free € 2 Ch € 2. **Location:** Rural, simple, quiet.
**Surface:** asphalted. 01/01-31/12.
**Distance:** 400m 400m 400m.
**Remarks:** Max. 7m.

## Tournon-sur-Rhône 25C2

Chemin de la Beaume/D86. **GPS:** n45,07337 e4,82150. ⬆➡.

10 € 5 Chfree. **Location:** Urban, simple, quiet.
**Surface:** asphalted. 01/01-31/12.
**Distance:** 1km 5km 1km 1km.

**Remarks:** Max. 24h.
**Tourist information Tournon-sur-Rhône:**
⌖ ❏ Wed, Sa.
✐ Route Panoramique, place Jean Jaurès. Starting point touristic route.

| 🅰 S | **Tourzel-Ronzières** | 25A1 |

Chemin du Clos, D23. **GPS:** n45,52989 e3,13504.⬆

12 🍴free ⛽Ch🚰 WCfree. **Location:** Rural, simple, isolated, quiet. **Surface:** grassy/gravel. ❏ 01/05-30/09.
**Distance:** 🚶500m ⊗500m.

| 🅰 S | **Treffort** 🏔🎡 | 25D2 |

Plage de la Salette, D110b. **GPS:** n44,90732 e5,67208.⬆

12 🍴€ 10/24h ⛽€ 2 🔌Ch🔲€ 2 📶.🚗 ✐ **Surface:** gravel. ❏ 01/05-30/09.
**Distance:** 🚶3km ⊿lake ⊷lake ⊗on the spot 🚴on the spot 🏊on the spot.
**Remarks:** At lake Monteynard.

| 🅰 S | **Treteau** ⊿ | 22A2 |

Rue du Rosier, D21. **GPS:** n46,36800 e3,51758.⬆➡

+10 🍴€ 3,50/night ⛽€ 2 🔌Ch🔲€ 2 WC. ✐ **Location:** Rural, simple, quiet. **Surface:** grassy/metalled. ❏ 05/03-30/10.
**Distance:** 🚶500m ⊿on the spot ⊷day pass available ⊗100m 🎣on the spot.
**Remarks:** At small lake.

| 🅲 S | **Trévoux** 🌿⚓🍰🍴 | 22C3 |

Chemin du Camping. **GPS:** n45,94017 e4,76694.⬆

4 🍴€ 5 ⛽€ 5 🔌Ch ✐€ 5 WC🔲€ 2.🚗
**Location:** Urban, simple, central, quiet. **Surface:** grassy/gravel.
❏ 01/01-31/12.
**Distance:** 🚶on the spot ✐7km ⊿100m ⊗1km 🏊1km 🎣1km.
**Remarks:** Along river, at entrance campsite, pay at campsite or town hall.

| 🅰 S | **Ugine** | 22F3 |

Place du 8 Mai 1945. **GPS:** n45,74634 e6,41774.⬆

3 🍴free ⛽€ 2 🔌🔲€ 2. **Location:** Urban, simple.
**Surface:** asphalted. ❏ 01/01-31/12.
**Remarks:** Next to office de tourisme, max. 24h.
**Tourist information Ugine:**
⌖ ❏ Wed, Sa-morning.

| 🅰 S | **Val d'Isère** | 25F1 |

Le Pont Saint-Charles, Route du Col de l'Iseran, D902.
**GPS:** n45,45432 e6,97005.⬆

50 🍴free ⛽🔌Chfree. **Location:** Rural, simple, quiet.
**Surface:** gravel. ❏ 01/01-31/12.
**Distance:** 🚶1km ⊗on the spot 🚴on the spot.
**Remarks:** Parking at skipistes.

| 🅰 S | **Valette** ⊿ | 24H1 |

D678. **GPS:** n45,27000 e2,60222.⬆➡

5 🍴free ⛽€ 2 🔌Ch🔲€ 2. **Location:** Rural, comfortable, quiet.
**Surface:** gravel. ❏ 01/01-31/12 ❏ service: 01/11-01/05.
**Distance:** 🚶50m ⊷100m ⊗150m.
**Remarks:** Max. 72h.

| 🅰 S | **Valloire** | 25F1 |

**Camping-Car Park Les Verneys**, Route du Galibier.
**GPS:** n45,14591 e6,42011.⬆
30 🍴€ 9,40-13 ⛽🔌Ch ✐(28x)WC 📶included.🚗 ✐
**Surface:** asphalted.
❏ 01/01-31/12.
**Distance:** ⊗on the spot 🚴250m.
**Remarks:** Mandatory, one-time fee Pass'Etapes € 4, free shuttle.

| 🅰 S | **Vallon-Pont-d'Arc** ⛵🏔⊿ | 25B3 |

Chemin du Chastelas. **GPS:** n44,40537 e4,39683.⬆

30 🍴€ 8,80/24h ⛽€ 2 🔌Ch🔲€ 2 WC.🚗 ❏ 01/01-31/12.
**Distance:** 🚶300m ⊗100m 🎣100m.
**Remarks:** Max. 48h, free shuttle to the Pont d'Arc, 2x per hour.

| 🅲 S | **Vallon-Pont-d'Arc** ⛵🏔⊿ | 25B3 |

**Domaine de l'Esquiras**, Chemin du Fez. **GPS:** n44,41583 e4,37738.⬆

5 🍴€ 8, peak season € 10 + € 0,60/pp tourist tax ⛽🔌Ch ✐€ 3 WC🔲free. **Location:** Rural, simple, quiet. **Surface:** gravel.
❏ 12/04-21/09.
**Distance:** 🚶800m ⊗800m 🏊1,5km.
**Remarks:** Use sanitary facilities + swimming pool € 4/pp.

**Tourist information Vallon-Pont-d'Arc:**
ℹ Office de Tourisme, 1 Place de l'Ancienne Gare, http://pontdarc-ardeche.fr. Small tourist town with the well-known Pont d'Arc, a natural arc over the Ardèche river.
👁 Grotte des Huguenots. Former shelter of the Huguenots. ❏ 15/06-31/08.
⌖ ❏ Thu-morning.

| 🅰 S | **Valuéjols** | 24H2 |

Place de 19 Mars 1962. **GPS:** n45,05349 e2,92927.⬆

15 🍴€ 3 ⛽🔌Chincluded. ✐ **Location:** Rural, simple, quiet.
**Surface:** asphalted. ❏ 01/01-31/12.
**Distance:** 🚶400m ⊗400m 🏊400m 🚴on the spot 🎣on the spot 🏊on the spot.
**Remarks:** Max. 7 days.

| 🅰 S | **Varennes-sur-Allier** | 22A2 |

**Place Hôtel de Ville**, Rue de Beaupuy. **GPS:** n46,31288 e3,40476.⬆➡

100 🍴free ⛽€ 2/100liter 🔌Ch🔲€ 2/h WC.
**Location:** Urban, simple, central, noisy. **Surface:** metalled.
❏ 01/01-31/12.
**Distance:** 🚶on the spot ⊗on the spot 🎣on the spot.
**Remarks:** Coins at town hall, tuesday market.

| 🅰 S | **Vassieux-en-Vercors** 🏔🎡❄ | 25D2 |

Avenue du Mémorial, D76. **GPS:** n44,89703 e5,36927.⬆

30 🍴free ⛽€ 2 🔌Chfree ✐€ 2. **Location:** Rural, simple.
**Surface:** metalled. ❏ 01/01-31/12 ❏ Service: winter.
**Distance:** 🚶200m ⊗200m 🏊200m 🎣on the spot 🚴7km Font D'Urle 🏊on the spot.
**Remarks:** Next to football ground.

| 🅰 S | **Vaujany** 🏔🎡❄ | 25E1 |

Télécabine. **GPS:** n45,15694 e6,08011.⬆➡

FR

10 ⌷free ⌷⌷Chfree ⌷€ 10/24h. **Location:** Urban, simple, quiet.
**Surface:** gravel. ⌷ 01/01-31/12.
**Distance:** ⌷300m ⌷300m ⌷300m ⌷300m.
**Remarks:** Coins at tourist info (electricity).

| ⌷⌷S | Védrines-Saint-Loup ⌷ | 25A2 |

Route du Plan d'Eau. **GPS:** n45,06758 e3,27565.⌷

5 ⌷free ⌷€ 3,50 ⌷Ch ⌷€ 2/55minutes. **Location:** Rural, simple, isolated, quiet. **Surface:** gravel/metalled.
⌷ 01/01-31/12.
**Distance:** ⌷400m ⌷on the spot ⌷on the spot ⌷on the spot.

| ⌷⌷S | Velzic ⌷ | 24H2 |

Lavernière, Rue de Fracort. **GPS:** n45,00166 e2,54638.⌷⌷

5 ⌷free ⌷€ 3,50 ⌷Ch. **Location:** Rural, simple, isolated.
**Surface:** asphalted. ⌷ 01/01-31/12 ⌷ service: 31/10-01/04.
**Distance:** ⌷1km ⌷1km ⌷1km ⌷on the spot.
**Remarks:** Max. 24h, coins at épicerie Pas de Peyrols.

| ⌷⌷S | Verclause | 25D3 |

D116. **GPS:** n44,37884 e5,42617.
10 ⌷free ⌷€ 2 ⌷Ch ⌷⌷free. **Location:** Simple. **Surface:** gravel.
⌷ 01/01-31/12.
**Distance:** ⌷250m ⌷on the spot ⌷on the spot.

| ⌷⌷S | Vernosc-lès-Annonay | 25C1 |

Rue de la Lié. **GPS:** n45,21914 e4,71409.⌷
6 ⌷free ⌷⌷Ch ⌷. **Location:** Rural. **Surface:** gravel.
⌷ 01/01-31/12.
**Distance:** ⌷200m ⌷200m ⌷200m.
**Remarks:** Next to town hall.

| ⌷⌷S | Vézac | 24H2 |

Route de Cavanière. **GPS:** n44,89059 e2,51779.⌷⌷

8 ⌷free ⌷€ 3,50 ⌷Ch. **Location:** Rural, simple. **Surface:** asphalted.
⌷ 01/01-31/12.
**Distance:** ⌷100m ⌷50m ⌷700m.
**Remarks:** At golf court, coins at bar/tabac, 50m.

| ⌷⌷S | Vic-sur-Cère | 24H2 |

Avenue des Tilleuls. **GPS:** n44,98194 e2,63111.⌷⌷

10 ⌷free ⌷€ 2 ⌷Ch ⌷€ 2. **Location:** Rural, comfortable, quiet.
**Surface:** asphalted. ⌷ 01/01-31/12.
**Distance:** ⌷200m ⌷200m ⌷150m.
**Remarks:** Coins at tourist info, Avenue Mercier.

| ⌷⌷S | Vieille-Brioude | 25A1 |

Rue de Combevignouse. **GPS:** n45,26540 e3,40557.⌷⌷

6 ⌷free ⌷€ 2/10minutes ⌷Ch ⌷€ 2/55minutes ⌷. **Location:** Urban, simple, central, quiet. **Surface:** asphalted.
⌷ 01/01-31/12.
**Distance:** ⌷150m ⌷200m.
**Remarks:** Service 200m.

| ⌷⌷S | Vieillevie ⌷ | 24G2 |

Aire de Vieillevie, Le Bourg. **GPS:** n44,64432 e2,41773.⌷⌷

5 ⌷free ⌷€ 2/100liter ⌷Ch ⌷€ 2/h. **Location:** Rural, comfortable, quiet. **Surface:** gravel. ⌷ 01/01-31/12.
**Distance:** ⌷50m ⌷100m ⌷50m ⌷50m.

| ⌷⌷S | Vienne ⌷⌷ | 25C1 |

Place Joseph Muray et Jean Tardy, N7. **GPS:** n45,53860 e4,87271.⌷⌷

6 ⌷free ⌷⌷Chfree.
**Location:** Urban, simple, central, noisy. **Surface:** asphalted
⌷ 01/01-31/12 ⌷ Fri market.
**Distance:** ⌷50m ⌷2km ⌷50m ⌷50m ⌷50m.
**Remarks:** Max. 7 days, friday market.

| ⌷⌷S | Villards-de-Lans | 25D2 |

Chemin des Bartavelles. **GPS:** n45,06619 e5,55609.⌷

15 ⌷free ⌷. **Location:** Rural, simple, quiet. **Surface:** asphalted
⌷ 01/01-31/12.
**Distance:** ⌷600m ⌷600m ⌷600m.
**Remarks:** Max. 48h.

| ⌷ | Villars-les-Dombes ⌷⌷ | 22C3 |

Parc des Oiseaux, RN83. **GPS:** n45,99126 e5,02582.⌷⌷

35 ⌷guests free. **Location:** Simple, quiet. **Surface:** asphalted/grassy.
⌷ 01/01-31/12 ⌷ sundays, holidays, winter.
**Distance:** ⌷2km ⌷1km ⌷1km ⌷2km ⌷2km on the spot.
**Remarks:** Parking bird park, max. 1 night, gate closed from 21-8h.
**Tourist information Villars-les-Dombes:**
Parc des Oiseaux. Bird park, 23ha. ⌷ 9.30-18.30h, winter 10-17.30h.

| ⌷⌷S | Villebois | 22D3 |

**Domaine des Cèdres**, 1180 route des Hauts Fourneaux.
**GPS:** n45,83999 e5,42647.⌷
10 ⌷€ 10 ⌷€ 5 ⌷€ 4 ⌷Ch ⌷ 4 ⌷€ 5,10Amp WC⌷.
**Location:** Rural, luxurious. **Surface:** grassy/gravel.
⌷ 01/01-31/12 ⌷ Sa.
**Distance:** ⌷200m ⌷1km.

| ⌷⌷S | Villefranche-d'Allier | 21H2 |

Avenue du 8 Mai 1945. **GPS:** n46,39565 e2,85672.⌷

4 ⌷free ⌷€ 2/10minutes ⌷Ch ⌷(4x)€ 2/2h WC. **Location:** Urban, simple. **Surface:** asphalted. ⌷ 01/01-31/12.
**Distance:** ⌷150m ⌷12km ⌷150m ⌷150m.
**Remarks:** Coins available at the shops.

| ⌷⌷S | Villefranche-sur-Saône | 22C3 |

**Camping-car Park**, Route de Riottier. **GPS:** n45,97278 e4,75135.⌷
128 ⌷€ 13,30 ⌷⌷Ch ⌷(128x)WC ⌷included.⌷⌷
**Location:** Urban, luxurious. **Surface:** grassy.
⌷ 01/01-31/12 ⌷ sanitary 16/09-14/05.
**Distance:** ⌷A6 1,3km ⌷Station > Lyon 3,4km.
**Remarks:** Mandatory, one-time fee Pass'Etapes € 4, wifi code: 692712.

| ⌷⌷S | Villerest ⌷ | 22B3 |

**Aire camping-car du Grezelon**, D18, Route de Seigne.
**GPS:** n45,98610 e4,04300.

15 ⌷€ 8 + € 0,25/pp tourist tax ⌷€ 4 ⌷Ch ⌷
**Location:** Simple, quiet. **Surface:** gravel.
⌷ 01/01-31/12 ⌷ service: 01/10-30/04.
**Distance:** ⌷1,5km ⌷1,5km ⌷1km ⌷on the spot.
**Remarks:** At Lac du Villerest and barrage, max. 48h.

| ⌷⌷S | Violay | 22B3 |

Place Giroud. **GPS:** n45,85268 e4,35564.⌷⌷

FR

3 ⌂free ⊤ ⊟€2 Ch€2. **Location:** Rural, simple, quiet. **Surface:** metalled. ⬛ 01/01-31/12. **Distance:** 100m ✦ A89 9km ⊗200m ⬯150m. **Remarks:** Beautiful view.

### Virieu  25D1
Rue du May, D17. **GPS:** n45,48166 e5,47746. ⬆➡.

4 ⌂free ⊤ ⊟ChWCfree. **Location:** Rural, simple, central, quiet. **Surface:** gravel. ⬛ 01/01-31/12. **Distance:** on the spot ⊗200m ⬯200m 人 on the spot. **Remarks:** Picnic area at edge of the village.

### Viverols  25B1
**Camping Le Pradoux**, Le Ruisseau. **GPS:** n45,43123 e3,88279.

6 ⌂free ⊤ ⊟€2 ⊟Ch⊟€2. **Location:** Simple, quiet. **Surface:** gravel. ⬛ 01/04-31/10. **Distance:** 500m ⊗500m.

### Vogüé  25B3
Chemin de Setras. **GPS:** n44,55163 e4,41308.

20 ⌂free ✦. **Location:** Simple, quiet. **Surface:** asphalted. ⬛ 01/01-31/12. **Distance:** 50m ⊿Ardèche 200m 人 on the spot. **Remarks:** At cemetery.

### Vorey-sur-Arzon  25B1
**Aire Les Moulettes**, Chemin de Félines. **GPS:** n45,18667 e3,90489. ⬆.

5 ⌂€2 ⊤€3 ⊟Ch⊟€4. **Location:** Rural, simple. **Surface:** gravel. ⬛ 01/01-31/12 ⬤ service: 15/09-30/04. **Distance:** 200m ↦ on the spot ⊗200m ⬯200m 人 on the spot. **Remarks:** Along river Arzon.

---

### Ytrac  24G2
Impasse Jean de la Fontaine. **GPS:** n44,91510 e2,36368. ⬆➡.

10 ⌂free ⊤€3,50 ⊟Ch⊟€3,50. **Location:** Rural, simple, central. **Surface:** asphalted. ⬛ 01/01-31/12. **Distance:** 150m ⊗100m ⬯150m. **Remarks:** Max. 7 days, coins at shops and tourist office.

# Nouvelle-Aquitaine

### Accous  27B3
La Nabe, D339. **GPS:** n42,91028 w0,61939. ⬆➡.

20 ⌂€12 ⊤⊟Ch⊟WC✦⬛⬛≋included. **Location:** Rural, comfortable, isolated, quiet. **Surface:** grassy/gravel. ⬛ 01/01-31/12. **Distance:** 7km 100m 人 on the spot.

### Adriers  21E2
Chemin du Bois Rivault. **GPS:** n46,25712 e0,80373. 15 ⌂free. **Surface:** gravel/sand. ⬛ 01/01-31/12. **Distance:** ⊗500m.

### Agris  21D3
**Aire municipale**, Le Pont d'Agris, D6. **GPS:** n45,78619 e0,33944. ⬆.

2 ⌂free ⊤€2/100liter ⊟Ch⊟€2/10minutes. **Location:** Rural, simple, noisy. **Surface:** asphalted. ⬛ 01/01-31/12. **Distance:** 2km ⊗on the spot ⬯on the spot ↦on the spot 人on the spot.

### Aigre  21D3
**Parc des Charmilles**, Rue des Charrières. **GPS:** n45,89341 e0,00578. ⬆.

5 ⌂€4 ⊤⊟Ch✦(4x)included. **Location:** Simple. **Surface:** metalled. ⬛ 01/04-31/10. **Distance:** 350m ⊗on the spot ⬯on the spot. **Remarks:** 4th night free.

### Aillas  24C3
**Plaine des Sports**, À Bourg. **GPS:** n44,47514 w0,07318. ⬆.

---

5 ⌂free ⊤ ⊟Chfree. **Location:** Rural, simple, quiet. **Surface:** gravel. ⬛ 01/01-31/12. **Distance:** 200m ⊗100m. **Remarks:** Next to sports fields.

### Aire-sur-l'Adour  27C1
Rue des Graviers. **GPS:** n43,70333 w0,25535. ⬆.

50 ⌂€5 ⊤€2 ⊟Ch. **Location:** Rural, simple, quiet. **Surface:** gravel. ⬛ 01/01-31/12 ⬤ 3rd week Jun. **Distance:** 200m ⊿on the spot ↦on the spot ⊗200m. **Remarks:** Near campsite, max. 72h.

### Airvault  21D1
Rue Faubourg des Cyprès. **GPS:** n46,82516 w0,14219. ⬆.

10 ⌂free ⊤ ⊟ChWCfree. **Location:** Urban, simple, central. **Surface:** asphalted. ⬛ 01/01-31/12. **Distance:** 250m ⊗250m ⬯250m.

### Allassac  24F1
Avenue du Saillant. **GPS:** n45,25897 e1,47358. ⬆.

4 ⌂free ⊤ ⊟Ch✦(2x)free. **Location:** Urban, simple, noisy. **Surface:** gravel/sand. ⬛ 01/01-31/12. **Distance:** 500m ✦5km ⊗500m ⬯500m. **Remarks:** Parking station.

### Andernos-les-Bains  24B2
**Port Ostréicole**, Avenue du Commandant Allègre. **GPS:** n44,74477 w1,10969. ⬆➡.

55 ⌂€14 ⊤€3,50/100liter ⊟Ch⊟€2,10 ✦⬛. **Location:** Urban, comfortable, quiet. **Surface:** grassy/metalled. ⬛ 01/01-31/12. **Distance:** 500m ⊿on the spot ↦on the spot ⊗50m. **Remarks:** In harbour, max. 48h.

## Anglet 27A1

**Aire de camping-car de La Barre**, Avenue de l'Adour, D405.
**GPS**: n43,52608 w1,51488.

50 € 6, Jul/Aug € 10 € 3 Ch. **Location**: Simple.
**Surface**: grassy/metalled. 13/04-11/11.
**Distance**: 1km 300m 50m 500m 500m 100m.
**Remarks**: Private property.

## Anglet 27A1

**Parking "Haut" - Plage des Corsaires**, Boulevard des Plages.
**GPS**: n43,50696 w1,53373.

80 € 6, Jul/Aug € 10 Ch included. **Location**: Urban,
simple, noisy. **Surface**: asphalted. 01/01-31/12.
**Distance**: 500m, Biarritz 2km 500m 500m 500m.
**Remarks**: Max. 24h, baker every morning.

## Angliers 18D3

**Aire de repos de la Briande**, D347. **GPS**: n46,95861 e0,10472.

8 free WC free. **Location**: Rural, comfortable, quiet.
**Surface**: asphalted. 01/01-31/12.
**Distance**: Angliers 1km 50m.

## Angoisse 24E1

**Le Pont du Jour**, L'Hépital, D704. **GPS**: n45,43296 e1,14413.

8 free € 2 € 1 Ch € 3. **Location**: Rural, comfortable,
quiet. **Surface**: grassy. 01/04-31/10.
**Distance**: 500m 1km 4,5km.

## Angoulins 21B2

**Parking de la plage de la Platère**, Rue du Chay.
**GPS**: n46,10623 w1,13565.

17 € 5. **Location**: Rural, simple, quiet. **Surface**: asphalted
01/05-30/09.

---

**Distance**: 1km on the spot on the spot.
**Remarks**: Bread-service.

## Angoulins 21B2

Chemin des Marais. **GPS**: n46,10602 e1,11710.
2€ 3/24h Ch included. **Surface**: asphalted. 01/01-31/12.

## Aramits 27B2

Rue Ripaude. **GPS**: n43,12140 w0,7312.
10 free Ch free. **Surface**: asphalted. 01/01-31/12.
**Distance**: 400m 650m.

## Arcachon 24B2

Boulevard Mestrézat, D650. **GPS**: n44,65142 w1,14864.

20 free Ch free.
**Location**: Urban, simple, noisy. **Surface**: asphalted/gravel.
01/01-31/12.
**Distance**: 1km 2km 50m.
**Remarks**: Max. 24h.

**Tourist information Arcachon:**
place du XI Novembre. Covered market. 01/06-31/08 daily 7-13h.

## Arçais 21C2

**Aire camping-cars du Coursault**, Rue du Marais.
**GPS**: n46,29643 w0,68782.

50 € 10/24h Ch WC included.
**Location**: Rural, simple, quiet. **Surface**: grassy.
01/01-31/12 water disconnected in winter.
**Distance**: 400m on the spot 150m nearby on the spot.

## Arette 27B2

**Aire de camping car d'Arette**, Place de la Mairie.
**GPS**: n43,09477 w0,71511.

10 free Ch WC. **Location**: Simple. **Surface**: asphalted.
01/01-31/12.
**Distance**: on the spot 200m 250m.

## Arzacq-Arraziguet 27C2

Place du Marcadieu. **GPS**: n43,53481 w0,41035.

10 free Ch WC free. **Location**: Urban, central.
**Surface**: asphalted. 01/01-31/12.
**Distance**: on the spot 500m 500m 100m 100m.

## Aubeterre-sur-Dronne 24D1

**Base de Loisirs**, D2, Route de Ribérac. **GPS**: n45,26934 e0,17586.

---

7 free Ch free. **Location**: Rural, comfortable, isolated, quiet.
**Surface**: gravel/metalled. 01/01-31/12.
**Distance**: 500m on the spot 300m 500m on the spot.
**Remarks**: At tennis-courts.

**Tourist information Aubeterre-sur-Dronne:**
Place de Village. Thu, Su.

## Aubusson 21G3

**Parking Champ de Foire**, Rue des Fusilles, D988.
**GPS**: n45,95694 e2,17528.

70 free Ch WC free. **Location**: Urban, simple, central.
**Surface**: asphalted. 01/01-31/12.
**Distance**: 500m 250m 500m.

## Aulnay 21C2

Place Charles de Gaulle, Rue Haute de l'Eglise.
**GPS**: n46,02306 w0,35444.

10 free WC free. **Location**: Urban, central. **Surface**: metalled.
01/01-31/12.
**Distance**: 200m 200m 200m.

## Aulnay 21C2

Rue de Salles. **GPS**: n46,02239 w0,34528.

10 free. **Location**: Urban, simple, quiet. **Surface**: gravel.
01/01-31/12.
**Distance**: 200m 200m 250m 200m.
**Remarks**: Max. 24h.

## Auriat 21F3

**Etang d'Auriat**. **GPS**: n45,87790 e1,64277.

3 free Ch free. **Location**: Rural, isolated, quiet.
**Surface**: metalled. 01/01-31/12.
**Distance**: on the spot on the spot.

FR

## Ayen — 24F1
Route de la Noix, Ayen Bas. **GPS:** n45,24964 e1,32343.

20 free Chfree. **Location:** Rural, simple, quiet.
**Surface:** grassy. 01/01-31/12.
**Distance:** 300m 400m 300m.
**Remarks:** Nearby D39, campsite and sports grounds.

## Azerat — 24E1
Le Bourg. **GPS:** n45,14954 e1,12496.

6 €3 €2 €3 Ch. **Location:** Rural, simple, quiet.
**Surface:** gravel. 01/01-31/12.
**Distance:** 50m 150m.
**Remarks:** Pay at town hall.

## Azur — 27A1
**Camping-Car Park**, Route du Lac. **GPS:** n43,78842 w1,3119.

31 € 9,60/24h Ch included.
**Location:** Rural, comfortable, quiet. **Surface:** gravel.
01/01-31/12.
**Distance:** 1,5km 150m 150m 200m on the spot
on the spot.
**Remarks:** Mandatory, one-time fee Pass'Etapes € 4.

## Badefols-sur-Dordogne — 24E2
Le Bourg. **GPS:** n44,84254 e0,79160.

10 free € 2/100liter ChWCfree.
**Location:** Rural, simple, quiet. **Surface:** asphalted.
01/01-31/12 Sa market.
**Distance:** on the spot bakery 50m.
**Remarks:** Coins at town hall.

## Bajamont — 24E3
**Association des Amis d'Euriope**, Pépelat bas.
**GPS:** n44,23917 e0,70057.
€7 €3 . **Location:** Rural, simple, quiet.
**Surface:** grassy. 01/01-31/12.
**Distance:** on the spot on the spot.
**Remarks:** Regional products.

## Barbezieux-Saint-Hilaire — 24C1
Avenue Aristide Briand 8. **GPS:** n45,47323 w0,14795.

4 free Chfree. **Location:** Urban, comfortable, quiet.
**Surface:** asphalted. 01/01-31/12.
**Distance:** 400m 600m.

## Barbezieux-Saint-Hilaire — 24C1
**E.Leclerc**, Rue du Commandant Foucaud. **GPS:** n45,47047 w0,16032.

8 free € 2/100liter Ch. **Location:** Urban, simple, central,
noisy. **Surface:** asphalted. 01/01-31/12.
**Distance:** 500m 400m on the spot.

## Bazas — 24C3
Rue de l'Eyrevieille. **GPS:** n44,43389 w0,21509.

5 free ChWCfree. **Location:** Urban, central, noisy.
**Surface:** metalled. 01/01-31/12 Service: winter.
**Distance:** on the spot.

## Beaumont du Périgord — 24E2
Avenue Rhinau, D660. **GPS:** n44,77469 e0,76559.

20 free Chfree. **Location:** Urban, simple, quiet.
**Surface:** asphalted. 01/01-31/12.
**Distance:** 800m.
**Tourist information Beaumont du Périgord:**
Bastide de Beaumont.

## Bellac — 21E2
**Aire d'accueil camping-car rives du Vincou**, Rue des Tanneries.
**GPS:** n46,11513 e1,05242.

4 free Chfree. **Location:** Rural, isolated, quiet.
**Surface:** asphalted. 01/01-31/12.
**Distance:** 1km 1km 1,2km.
**Remarks:** Service 100m.

## Bellac — 21E2
**Le Champ de foire**, Rue des Doctrinaires.
**GPS:** n46,12085 e1,05018.

4 free. **Location:** Urban, simple. **Surface:** asphalted.
01/01-31/12.
**Distance:** on the spot on the spot on the spot.
**Remarks:** >3,5t not allowed.

## Bellac — 21E2
**Parking de la Mairie**, Place de la République.
**GPS:** n46,12155 e1,04604.

2 free. **Location:** Urban, simple. **Surface:** asphalted.
01/01-31/12.
**Distance:** 300m.

## Bénéjacq — 27C2
**L'Esplanade du Lagoin**, Place de la Fontaine.
**GPS:** n43,19009 w0,20914.

6 free € 2/100liter Ch € 2/h . **Location:** Urban,
comfortable, quiet. **Surface:** asphalted. 01/01-31/12.
**Distance:** 500m 50m 500m.
**Remarks:** Max. 48h, coins at the bakery, restaurant and pharmacy.

## Bergerac — 24D2
**Aire de Pombonne**, Avenue Marceau Feyry.
**GPS:** n44,87104 e0,50408.

21 € 5,05/24h € 2/100liter Ch . **Location:** Simple.
**Surface:** metalled. 01/01-31/12.
**Distance:** city centre 3km 1km.
**Remarks:** Max. 3 days.
**Tourist information Bergerac:**
Musée du Tabac, Maison Peyrarède, Place du Feu. History of tobacco.
Mo-Fri 10-12h, 14-18, Sa 10-12h, 14-17h, Su 14.30-17.30h, Nov-Mar
Mo-Fr.
Église Notre Dame, Rue Saint Esprit. Wed, Sa 7-13h.

## Bernos-Beaulac — 24C3
La Grande Route, N524. **GPS:** n44,36949 w0,24257.

10 ⌷€4 ⚡€ 2/10minutes ⚐Ch.🛏🗑
**Location:** Rural, simple, quiet. **Surface:** gravel/metalled.
🔲 01/01-31/12 ◉ water: frost.
**Distance:** 〰river ⛽on the spot 🍞bakery 100m.
**Remarks:** Coins at petrol station.

| ⊞S | Bessines-sur-Gartempe | 21F2 |

**Place du Champ de Foire**, Rue d'Ingolsheim.
**GPS:** n46,10979 e1,37008. ⬆.

4 ⌷free ⚡⚐Ch🛏. **Location:** Urban, simple. **Surface:** asphalted.
🔲 01/01-31/12 ◉ 14/07, 29/09-10/10.
**Distance:** 〰on the spot 🚲900m ⊗100m 🚌50m.

| ⊞ | Beynac-et-Cazenac 🌴⛵🌾 | 24E2 |

Le Parc, D703. **GPS:** n44,84466 e1,14560. ➡.

20 ⌷free. **Location:** Rural, simple, quiet. **Surface:** gravel.
🔲 01/01-31/12.
**Distance:** 〰historical centre 500m ⊗500m.

| ⊞S | Biarritz 🍺 | 27A2 |

**Aire de camping-cars Gabrielle Dorziat**, Allée Gabrielle Dorziat.
**GPS:** n43,45974 w1,56893.

19 ⌷€ 12/24h ⚡⚐Ch🛁included. **Location:** Urban.
**Surface:** grassy/metalled. 🔲 01/01-31/12.
**Distance:** 🏊1km ⊗400m.
**Remarks:** Max. 48h.

| ⊞S | Biarritz 🍺 | 27A2 |

**Parking Milady**, Avenue de la Milady. **GPS:** n43,46536 w1,57162. ⬆.

32 ⌷€ 12 ⚡⚐Ch🛁included. 🛏🗑 **Location:** Urban, simple,
noisy. **Surface:** asphalted. 🔲 01/01-31/12.
**Distance:** 〰500m 🏊300m ⊗500m 🚌500m 🚎200m.
**Remarks:** Baker every morning.

⌂ Rue des Halles. 🔲 daily.

| ⊞S | Biron 🌱 | 24E2 |

Route de Vergt de Biron. **GPS:** n44,63080 e0,87055. ⬆.

10 ⌷free ⚡€ 2/100liter ⚐Ch🛏€ 2/1h. **Location:** Rural, simple,
quiet. **Surface:** grassy/metalled. 🔲 01/01-31/12 ◉ service 01/11-
31/03.
**Distance:** 〰250m ⊗250m on the spot.
**Remarks:** Coins at grocery.

| ⊞S | Biscarrosse 🌴🌾 | 24B3 |

**Port de Navarrosse**, 710 chemin de Navarrosse.
**GPS:** n44,43223 w1,16566. ⬆.

80 ⌷€ 12,50, 15/09-14/06 € 8, 15/07-31/08 € 16 ⚡🗑
Ch🛁WC🚿included. 🛏🗑 **Location:** Rural, comfortable.
**Surface:** metalled. 🔲 01/01-31/12.
**Distance:** 〰4km 🏊50m ⊗100m 🍺50m 🚲on the spot.
**Remarks:** Video surveillance.

| ⊞S | Biscarrosse 🌴🌾 | 24B3 |

Rue des Viviers, Biscarrosse-plage. **GPS:** n44,46027 w1,24627. ⬆.

180 ⌷€ 12,50, 15/09-14/06 € 8, 15/07-31/08 € 16 ⚡🚰🗑
Ch🚿WC🚿included. 🛏 **Location:** Rural, simple, quiet.
**Surface:** forest soil. 🔲 01/05-31/10.
**Distance:** 〰2,5km 🏊400m 🍺100m 🚲50m 🚶on the spot.
**Remarks:** Video surveillance.

| ⊞ | Blanquefort | 24C2 |

**Château Saint Ahon**, Rue de Saint-Ahon 57.
**GPS:** n44,92663 w0,63217. ⬆➡.

4 ⌷€ 3 ⚡free. 🛒
**Location:** Urban, comfortable, central, quiet.
**Surface:** gravel/metalled. 🔲 01/01-31/12 ◉ Su/holidays.
**Distance:** 〰300m 🚲12km ⊗300m 🚌on the spot 🚲on the spot.
**Remarks:** Arrival <18h, max. 48h.

| ⊞S | Blasimon | 24C2 |

Rue Abbé Greciet. **GPS:** n44,74836 w0,07537. ⬆.

4 ⌷free ⚡⚐Chfree. **Location:** Urban, simple, quiet.
**Surface:** gravel. 🔲 01/01-31/12.
**Distance:** 〰100m ⊗100m 🍺100m.

| ⊞ | Blasimon | 24C2 |

**Château la Peyraude**, Bleurette. **GPS:** n44,73463 w0,09942. ⬆➡.

15 ⌷€ 5 ⚡⚐Ch🚿WC🚿. 🛒 **Location:** Rural, comfortable,
isolated, quiet. **Surface:** grassy. 🔲 01/01-31/12.
**Distance:** 〰3km ⊗on the spot.
**Remarks:** Arrival <22h, regional products.

| ⊞ | Blaye 🌱⚓🌾 | 24C1 |

**Parking de la Citadelle**, Rue Pierre Semard.
**GPS:** n45,12549 w0,66535. ⬆.

30 ⌷€ 3. **Location:** Urban, simple, central, quiet.
**Surface:** gravel/metalled. 🔲 01/01-31/12.
**Distance:** 〰250m 🏊on the spot ⛽on the spot ⊗200m 🍺2km
🚲300m 🚶on the spot.

| 🏳S | Blaye 🌱⚓🌾 | 24C1 |

**Château le Cône**, Route des Cônes. **GPS:** n45,13742 w0,66507. ⬆➡.

25 ⌷free ⚡⚐Ch🛁(4x)free. **Location:** Rural, comfortable, quiet.
**Surface:** asphalted/gravel. 🔲 01/01-31/12.
**Distance:** 〰2km 🏊on the spot ⊗on the spot.

| ⊞S | Boismé 🌴🌾 | 21C1 |

Rue des Essarts. **GPS:** n46,77765 w0,43347. ⬆➡.

4 ⌷free ⚡⚐ChWCfree. **Location:** Rural, isolated, quiet.
**Surface:** metalled. 🔲 01/01-31/12.
**Distance:** 〰500m ⛽on the spot 🏊500m 🍺on the spot 🚲on the
spot 🚶on the spot.
**Remarks:** At small lake, playground.

FR

## Bordeaux — 24C2

**GPS:** n44,86948 w0,56446.
20+ free. **Location:** Urban, simple, noisy. **Surface:** asphalted.
01/01-31/12.
**Distance:** city centre 2km on the spot on the spot
on the spot 1,2km.

## Bort-les-Orgues — 24H1

Rue de la Fontaine Grande. **GPS:** n45,39913 e2,49710.

6 free Chfree. **Location:** Urban, simple, central, quiet.
**Surface:** asphalted. 01/01-31/12.
**Distance:** 200m river 200m 200m.

## Bosmoreau-les-Mines — 21F3

Le Bourg. **GPS:** n45,99936 e1,75194.

3 free Chfree. **Location:** Rural, simple, quiet.
**Surface:** gravel. 01/01-31/12.
**Distance:** 500m.

## Bouglon — 24D3

**Aire de Repos**, Le Clavier. **GPS:** n44,38599 e0,10271.

4 free WCfree. **Location:** Rural, simple, quiet.
**Surface:** asphalted. 01/01-31/12.
**Distance:** 500m 500m 500m.
**Remarks:** Picnic area.

## Bougon — 21D2

**Musée des Tumulus**, La Chapelle. **GPS:** n46,37845 w0,06825.

10 free free. **Location:** Rural, simple, isolated.
**Surface:** asphalted. 01/01-31/12.
**Distance:** 3km.
**Remarks:** Parking museum.

## Bourcefranc-le-Chapus — 21B3

Rue du Président Kennedy. **GPS:** n45,84546 w1,14929.

---

10 € 7,50 € 3 .
**Location:** Urban, simple, central. **Surface:** asphalted.
01/01-31/12.
**Distance:** 250m 750m 250m 250m.
**Remarks:** Max. 24h, coins at tourist info and town hall.

## Bourcefranc-le-Chapus — 21B3

**Le Bois du Pin**, Prise du Portail Rouge. **GPS:** n45,82611 w1,14278.

20 € 7,50. **Location:** Rural, simple, isolated, quiet.
**Surface:** gravel. 01/01-31/12.
**Distance:** 4km on the spot on the spot 3km.
**Remarks:** Bread-service only in summer.

## Bourdeilles — 24E1

**Plaine des Loisirs**, Le Bourg. **GPS:** n45,32270 e0,58260.

40+ € 4 + € 0,55/pp tourist tax € 2/100liter Ch.
**Location:** Comfortable, quiet. **Surface:** grassy. 01/01-31/12.
**Distance:** 500m on the spot on the spot 200m 200m.

## Bourg-sur-Gironde — 24C1

Quai Jean Bart. **GPS:** n45,03794 w0,55699.

10 € 5 € 3. **Location:** Urban, simple, central. **Surface:** asphalted.
01/01-31/12.
**Distance:** on the spot on the spot on the spot on the spot
on the spot.

## Bourganeuf — 21F3

Place de l'Etang, Avenue du Dr Butaud. **GPS:** n45,95444 e1,75750.

10 free Chfree. **Location:** Urban, central. **Surface:** gravel.
01/01-31/12 tue-evening, wed-morning (market).
**Distance:** on the spot 300m on the spot.
**Remarks:** Max. 48h.

---

## Branne — 24C2

Route de Cabara. **GPS:** n44,83191 w0,18448.

3 free € 2/100liter Ch € 2/1h. **Location:** Urban, simple,
noisy. **Surface:** metalled. 01/01-31/12.
**Distance:** 400m on the spot 300m 500m.

## Brantôme — 24E1

Chemin de Vert Galant. **GPS:** n45,36134 e0,64842.

80 € 7,50 € 2/12minutes Ch. **Location:** Comfortable,
quiet. **Surface:** grassy. 01/01-31/12.
**Distance:** 200m 100m 300m.

## Brantôme — 24E1

**Aire Camping-cars Font Vendôme**, Route de Nontron.
**GPS:** n45,37924 e0,64588.

7 € 3,50 € 2 Chfree € 1/night WC. **Location:** Simple,
noisy. **Surface:** asphalted. 01/01-31/12.
**Distance:** 3,5km 1km 1km.
**Remarks:** At motorhome dealer, money in envelope in mail box.
**Tourist information Brantôme:**
Fri-morning.

## Braud-et-Saint-Louis — 24C1

D136. **GPS:** n45,24285 w0,58006.

6 free € 2/time ChWC . **Location:** Rural, simple, isolated,
quiet. **Surface:** gravel/metalled. 01/01-31/12.
**Distance:** 100m 200m.
**Remarks:** Service passerby € 2.

## Bressuire — 21C1

Place Labâte. **GPS:** n46,84417 w0,49086.

5 free Chfree. **Location:** Urban, simple, noisy. **Surface:** sand.
01/01-31/12.

---

**Distance:** 400m ⊗400m 400m.

### Brive-la-Gaillarde  24F1
Rue des 3 Provinces. **GPS:** n45,16486 e1,54170.↑.

12 first night € 9, € 7 each additional night + tourist tax € 0,60/pp Ch (12x)€ 3/6h. **Location:** Urban, simple.
**Surface:** asphalted.
**Distance:** 1km ⊗150m 500m.
**Remarks:** Free bus to centre.

### Bujaleuf  21F3
Route du Champ de Foire. **GPS:** n45,80418 e1,63696.↑→.

5 free Chfree. **Location:** Rural, simple, quiet.
**Surface:** grassy/gravel. 01/01-31/12.
**Distance:** 1,5km on the spot 1,5km.
**Remarks:** Max. 24h, service 1,5km GPS N45,79747 E1,63141.

### Burie  21C3
**Place du Champ de Foire**, Avenue de la Republique.
**GPS:** n45,77185 w0,42487.↑.

5 free Chfree. **Location:** Urban, simple, central, quiet.
**Surface:** grassy. 01/01-31/12.
**Distance:** on the spot ⊗300m 300m.

### Bussière-Poitevine  21E2
**Croix de l'Hosanne**, Rue du Quatriéme Zouave.
**GPS:** n46,23670 e0,90173.→.

10 free € 2/100liter Ch WC. **Location:** Rural, simple, quiet. **Surface:** gravel. 15/03-14/11.
**Distance:** 450m.
**Remarks:** Coins at the shops.

### Buzet-sur-Baïse  24D3
**Port de Buzet-Val d'Albret. GPS:** n44,25799 e0,30569.↑.

20 7 Chfree € 2 WC€ 2 € 2 € 2/24h.
**Location:** Rural, comfortable, quiet. **Surface:** grassy.
01/01-31/12.
**Distance:** 6,5km on the spot ⊗350m 350m on the spot on the spot.

### Cadillac  24C2
Avenue du Parc. **GPS:** n44,63871 w0,31721.↑.

10 free Ch€ 2/3h WCfree. **Location:** Urban, simple, quiet.
**Surface:** asphalted. 01/01-31/12.
**Distance:** on the spot ⊗100m 100m 100m.
**Remarks:** Max. 3 nights, closed when frosty.

### Cambo-les-Bains  27A2
**Zone Artisanale**, Chemin Arroka. **GPS:** n43,35537 w1,41173.↑.
44 € 10 Ch included. **Location:** Urban, comfortable.
**Surface:** metalled. 01/01-31/12.
**Distance:** 500m ⊗100m 500m 200m.

### Cancon  24E3
Rue des Écoles. **GPS:** n44,53638 e0,62562.↑→.

10 free Ch WCfree. **Location:** Urban, simple.
**Surface:** metalled. 01/01-31/12.
**Distance:** 100m 100m 100m.
**Remarks:** Shady.

### Capbreton  27A1
**Plage l'Océanide, Parking des Ortolans**, Allée des Ortolans.
**GPS:** n43,63578 w1,44681.→.

135 € 10-18 Ch (120x) WCincluded.
**Surface:** asphalted. 15/11-31/03.
**Distance:** 1,5km on the spot on the spot ⊗1,5km 1,5km.
**Remarks:** Beach parking, 14/07-20/08: max. 2 nights.

### Capian  24C2
D13/Chemin de Lavergne. **GPS:** n44,71177 w0,33093.↑.

10 free € 2/10minutes Ch € 2/55minutes.
**Location:** Rural, simple, isolated, quiet. **Surface:** gravel.
01/01-31/12.
**Distance:** 500m ⊗300m 150m.

### Carcans  24B1
Route de Bombannes, Maubuisson. **GPS:** n45,08545 w1,14866.↑.

20 € 6,40 Chfree € 2. **Location:** Rural, simple, isolated, quiet. **Surface:** asphalted/gravel. 01/06-30/09.
**Distance:** 2km 400m ⊗2km 2km on the spot on the spot.

**Tourist information Carcans:**
Office de Tourisme, Maison de la Station, www.carcans-maubuisson.com. Touristic town between the ocean and a wine region, 120km signposted cycle routes.

### Casseneuil  24E3
Rue Grande, D225. **GPS:** n44,44667 e0,61861.↑.

20 free Chfree. **Location:** Rural, simple, quiet.
**Surface:** asphalted. 01/01-31/12.
**Distance:** 600m on the spot ⊗800m 600m on the spot on the spot.

### Castelculier  24E3
Rue du Champs de Baze. **GPS:** n44,17475 e0,69452.↑.

5 free € 2 Ch. **Location:** Urban, simple, quiet.
**Surface:** metalled. 01/01-31/12.
**Distance:** 200m ⊗350m 400m.

### Casteljaloux  24D3
Ste Castel Chalets, D933. **GPS:** n44,29230 e0,07361.↑→.

11 € 10, Jul/Aug € 15 + € 0,52/pp tourist tax Ch WC included. **Location:** Rural, comfortable, quiet.
**Surface:** gravel/sand. 01/04-31/10.
**Distance:** 2km Lac de Clarens.

### Casteljaloux  24D3
Impasse de la Fôret. **GPS:** n44,31068 e0,07933.↑→.

4 free Chfree. **Location:** Urban, simple, quiet.
**Surface:** asphalted/gravel. 01/01-31/12.

**Distance:** 🚶250m ⊗400m 🛒250m.
**Remarks:** Parking at swimming pool, max. 48h.

### Casteljaloux 21 24D3
**La Taillade**, Route de la Forge, La Réunion.
**GPS:** n44,26998 e0,08004. ⬆

4 ⬛€8 🚰Ch ✦included WC. **Location:** Rural, isolated, quiet.
**Surface:** forest soil. 📅 01/04-31/10.

### Caumont-sur-Garonne 🚣 24D3
**Bourg de Caumont. GPS:** n44,44202 e0,17887. ⬆

15 ⬛free 🚰€2/15minutes 🧺Ch 🚽€2/4h. **Location:** Rural, simple,
quiet. **Surface:** gravel. 📅 01/01-31/12.
**Distance:** ✦8km 🛒on the spot.

### Cellefrouin 21D3
**D739. GPS:** n45,89361 e0,38639. ⬆➡

20 ⬛free 🚰🧺ChWCfree. **Location:** Rural, simple, isolated, quiet.
**Surface:** gravel. 📅 01/01-31/12.
**Distance:** 🚶300m.

### Celles-sur-Belle 21D2
**Place de l'Aumônerie**, Rue des Halles.
**GPS:** n46,26278 w0,20806. ⬆➡

10 ⬛free 🚰🧺Chfree. **Location:** Urban, simple, quiet.
**Surface:** gravel. 📅 01/01-31/12.
**Distance:** 🚶100m 🏊100m 🛒100m.
**Remarks:** Max. 7 days.

### Chabanais 🚣 21E3
**Chemin des Tanneries, N141. GPS:** n45,87447 e0,72008.

4 ⬛free. **Location:** Urban, simple, central, noisy. **Surface:** asphalted.
📅 01/01-31/12 🔵 Thu.
**Distance:** 🚶on the spot 🏊on the spot ⊗100m 🛒100m.

---

**Remarks:** Along the river Vienne.

### Chaillevette 21B3
**Rue de l'Étang. GPS:** n45,72155 w1,05872. ⬆➡
6 ⬛€7 🚰🧺Ch ✦€2. **Location:** Rural, isolated, quiet.
📅 01/04-30/09.
**Distance:** 🚐on the spot 🏍on the spot 🅰on the spot.

### Chalus 21E3
**Aire des Energies**, Avenue Jean Jaurès. **GPS:** n45,66095 e0,98798. ⬆

10 ⬛free 🚰€2 🧺Ch 🚽€2. **Location:** Simple. **Surface:** gravel.
📅 01/01-31/12.
**Distance:** 🚶1,2km 🛒on the spot.
**Remarks:** Behind petrol station.

### Chamberet 21F3
**Ris Combeix. GPS:** n45,57926 e1,70843. ⬆

7 ⬛free 🚰🧺Ch ✦(1x). **Location:** Rural, comfortable, isolated,
quiet. **Surface:** grassy. 📅 01/01-31/12.
**Distance:** 🚶1,3km ⊗1,3km.

### Chamberet 21F3
**Route de St Dulcet. GPS:** n45,57961 e1,72051. ⬆

4 ⬛free 🚰🧺Ch ✦. **Location:** Urban, simple, quiet.
**Surface:** gravel. 📅 01/01-31/12.
**Distance:** 🚶900m ⊗400m 🛒400m.
**Remarks:** Next to football ground.

### Chambon-sur-Voueize 🌿🅰🍴 21H2
**Rue du Stade. GPS:** n46,18579 e2,43426. ⬆

4 ⬛free 🚰€2/10minutes 🧺Ch 🚽€2/1h. **Location:** Rural, quiet.
**Surface:** asphalted. 📅 01/01-31/12 🔵 service 01/11-31/03.
**Distance:** 🚶500m 🏊500m 🛒200m.
**Remarks:** Near camping municipal.

### Chamboulive 24F1
**GPS:** n45,42255 e1,71639.
10 ⬛free 🚰€2/10minutes 🧺Ch ✦€2/12h. 📅 01/03-30/11.
**Distance:** 🚶1,2km 🛒on the spot ⊗1,2km 🛒1,2km.
**Remarks:** Service closed during wintertime.

### Chasseneuil-sur-Bonnieure 21D3
**Rue de la Gare, Place du Champ de Mars.
GPS:** n45,82493 e0,45172. ⬆➡

---

3 ⬛free 🚰€2/100liter 🧺Ch 🚽€2/1h WCfree.
**Location:** Urban, simple, central, noisy. **Surface:** gravel.
📅 01/01-31/12.
**Distance:** 🚶on the spot ✦3km ⊗on the spot 🛒on the spot
🚐400m.
**Remarks:** At supermarket.

### Château-Larcher 21D2
**Val de Clouère. GPS:** n46,41444 e0,31556. ⬆➡

10 ⬛€5,50 🚰🧺Ch🚽WCincluded. 🐕
**Location:** Rural, comfortable, isolated, quiet. **Surface:** grassy/gravel.
📅 01/03-30/11.
**Distance:** 🚶300m 🏊100m ⊗300m 🛒300m.
**Remarks:** At small lake, former campsite, baker every morning.

### Château-l'Evêque 24E1
**Place de la Fontaine. GPS:** n45,24472 e0,68743. ⬆

8 ⬛free 🚰€2 🧺Ch🚽€2.
**Location:** Urban, comfortable. **Surface:** gravel. 📅 01/03-31/10
🔵 summer: Su (flea market).
**Distance:** 🚶50m 🏊100m 🛒on the spot 🚐on the spot.
**Remarks:** Max. 48h, coins at shops in the village 08-21h.

### Châteauneuf-sur-Charente 21D3
**Rue du Prieuré. GPS:** n45,59876 w0,05655. ⬆➡

4 ⬛free 🚰€2/10minutes 🧺Ch🚽€2/10minutes 📷.
**Location:** Urban, simple, central, quiet. **Surface:** asphalted.
📅 01/01-31/12.
**Distance:** 🚶on the spot ⊗100m 🛒300m.

### Châtelaillon-Plage 21B2
**Camping-Car Park**, 3 boulevard Georges Clémenceau.
**GPS:** n46,07253 w1,07886. ⬆

51 ⬛€ 9,23, 01/06-30/09 € 11,63 🚐🔧Ch🔌(48x)📶included.
🏠🧹 **Location:** Rural, simple. **Surface:** asphalted/grassy.
⬛ 01/01-31/12.
**Distance:** 700m 800m ⊗700m.
**Remarks:** Mandatory, one-time fee Pass'Etapes € 4.

### Châtelaillon-Plage — 21B2
**Les Boucholeurs**, Avenue de l'Abbé Guichard.
**GPS:** n46,05538 w1,08738.⬆️

7 ⬛free. **Location:** Urban, simple. **Surface:** asphalted.
⬛ 01/01-31/12.
**Distance:** 150m 150m ⊗150m.
**Remarks:** Max. 48h.

### Châtelus-le-Marcheix — 21F3
Rue du Tursaud. **GPS:** n45,99894 e1,60339.⬆️➡️

2 ⬛free 🚐€ 2 🔧Ch💡 2. **Location:** Rural, simple.
**Surface:** gravel/metalled. ⬛ 01/01-31/12.
**Distance:** 300m ⊗300m 300m.
**Remarks:** Next to camping municipal.

### Chef-Boutonne — 21D2
Chemin du Parc. **GPS:** n46,10982 w0,07869.⬆️➡️

20 ⬛free 🚐🔧ChWCfree. **Location:** Comfortable, quiet.
**Surface:** grassy/gravel. ⬛ 01/04-31/10.
**Distance:** 800m 300m ⊗800m 🚐on the spot.

### Chénérailles — 21G2
Route d'Aubusson, lotissement Marlaud, D990.
**GPS:** n46,11058 e2,17753.⬆️➡️

5 ⬛free 🚐€ 4 🔧Ch💡€ 4. **Location:** Simple. **Surface:** asphalted.
⬛ 01/01-31/12.
**Distance:** 200m 50m 100m.
**Remarks:** Coins available at restaurant le Coq d'Or (50m).

### Cherves-Richemont — 21C3
Allee des Coquelicots. **GPS:** n45,74030 w0,35607.⬆️➡️

5 ⬛free 🚐🔧Chfree. **Location:** Rural, simple, quiet.
**Surface:** asphalted. ⬛ 01/01-31/12 ⦿ service: 01/11-15/04.
**Distance:** 500m 100m 500m.
**Remarks:** Bread-service.

### Chey — 21D2
Place de la Liberté. **GPS:** n46,30412 w0,05002.⬆️➡️

5 ⬛free 🚐🔧ChWCfree. **Location:** Rural, comfortable, quiet.
**Surface:** asphalted. ⬛ 01/01-31/12.
**Distance:** 50m.

### Chirac — 21E3
Le bourg. **GPS:** n45,91397 e0,65723.
5 ⬛free 🚐🔧Ch🔌. **Location:** Rural, simple, quiet.
**Surface:** asphalted. ⬛ 01/01-31/12.
**Distance:** ⊗100m 🚐on the spot 🚶on the spot.
**Remarks:** Max. 48h.

### Cieux — 21E3
Avenue du Lac. **GPS:** n45,99173 e1,04939.⬆️

20 ⬛€ 8 🚐€ 2 🔧Ch🔌€ 1,50. 🚿 **Location:** Simple.
**Surface:** grassy. ⬛ 15/04-15/10.
**Distance:** 100m 100m ⊗450m.

### Civrac-en-Médoc — 24B1
**Route de Montignac**, Montignac. **GPS:** n45,33619 w0,922.⬆️

5 ⬛free. **Location:** Rural, simple, isolated, quiet. **Surface:** gravel.
⬛ 01/01-31/12.
**Distance:** 2km.

### Clérac — 24C1
**Étang des Prés de Réaux**, Route des Vignes.
**GPS:** n45,17906 w0,228.⬆️

8 ⬛free 🚐🔧Chfree. **Location:** Rural, simple, isolated, quiet.

**Surface:** gravel. ⬛ 01/01-31/12.
**Distance:** 200m 🚿on the spot ⊗100m 🚐100m 🚲on the spot
🚶on the spot.
**Remarks:** At small lake, max. 1 night.

### Cognac — 21C3
Place de la Levade, Quartier Saint-Jacques. **GPS:** n45,69847 w0,33265.⬆️

7 ⬛free 🚐€ 2/100liter 🔧Ch💡 2/h. **Location:** Urban, simple,
central. **Surface:** asphalted. ⬛ 01/01-31/12.
**Distance:** ⊗on the spot 🚐100m 500m 🚲on the spot
🚶on the spot.
**Remarks:** Along the Charente river.

**Tourist information Cognac:**
👁 Otard. Cognac distillery in 16th century castle. Guided tour and
tasting. ⬛ daily ⦿ 01/01-31/03 weekend.
Ⓜ Cognac-musée. Culture around the Cognac. ⦿ 01/10-31/05 14-
17.30h, 01/06-30/09 10-12h, 14-18h.

### Collonges-la-Rouge — 24F2
**Parking le Marchadial**. **GPS:** n45,05833 e1,65889.⬆️➡️

40 ⬛free, 01/03-31/10 € 8/24h 🚐🔧Ch🔌WCincluded.
**Location:** Rural, simple, quiet. **Surface:** gravel.
⬛ 01/01-31/12.
**Distance:** 500m ⊗500m 🚐500m 🏪1km.
**Remarks:** Closed when frosty.

### Concèze — 24F1
D56E. **GPS:** n45,35472 e1,34583.⬆️➡️

3 ⬛free 🚐🔧Chfree. **Location:** Rural, simple, quiet.
**Surface:** gravel. ⬛ 01/01-31/12.
**Distance:** on the spot.

### Confolens — 21E2
**Camping les Ribières**, Avenue de Sainte-Germain.
**GPS:** n46,01894 e0,67570.⬆️➡️

12 ⬛€ 8, July-Aug € 10 🚐🔧Ch💡€ 6 📶included. 🚐🧹
**Location:** Rural, simple, central, noisy. **Surface:** metalled.
⬛ 01/01-31/12 ⦿ service: 30/09-01/04.
**Distance:** 750m 🚿on the spot ⊗500m 🚐500m 🏪on the spot
🚲on the spot 🚶on the spot.
**Remarks:** Canoe rental.

**Tourist information Confolens:**
🏛 🛈 Wed, Sa.

**FR**

**⊞S Contis-Plage** `24A3`
Avenue du Phare. **GPS:** n44,09333 w1,31861. ⬆.

70 ⬛€ 9-13 ⛽€ 2 ⬛Ch⬛WC. ⬛ **Location:** Simple.
**Surface:** gravel. ⬛ 01/01-31/12.
**Distance:** ⬛200m ⬛ on the spot.
**Remarks:** Max. 72h.

**⊞S Couhé** `21D2`
Place du Marché. **GPS:** n46,29906 e0,17882. ⬆.

25 ⬛free ⛽⬛Ch WC free. **Location:** Urban, simple, central, quiet.
**Surface:** asphalted. ⬛ 01/01-31/12.
**Distance:** ⬛200m ⬛100m ⬛.

**⊞S Coulon** 🌿⬛ `21C2`
**Parking d'Autremont**, Rue André Cramois.
**GPS:** n46,32102 w0,59063. ⬆➡.

100 ⬛€ 10 ⛽⬛Ch ⬛ WC included. ⬛ ⬛
**Location:** Urban, comfortable, central, quiet. **Surface:** grassy/gravel.
⬛ 01/04-30/11.
**Distance:** ⬛350m ⬛350m ⬛350m ⬛ on the spot ⬛ on the spot.

**⊞S Coulonges-sur-l'Autize** `21C1`
Avenue de la Gare. **GPS:** n46,48011 w0,59393. ⬆.

2 ⬛free ⛽⬛Ch ⬛ WC free. **Location:** Urban, simple, quiet.
**Surface:** asphalted. ⬛ 01/01-31/12.
**Distance:** ⬛450m ⬛350m ⬛350m.
**Remarks:** Max. 24h, picnic area.

**⊞S Courcon** `21C2`
Rue du Stade. **GPS:** n46,24175 w0,80567. ⬆.

6 ⬛free ⛽⬛Ch. **Location:** Urban, comfortable, quiet.
**Surface:** metalled. ⬛ 01/01-31/12.
**Distance:** ⬛800m ⬛900m ⬛ on the spot.

**Remarks:** Max. 48h.

**⊞S Courpière** `22A3`
**Les Taillades**, Allée des Taillades. **GPS:** n45,75460 e3,54890.
38 ⬛€ 10,80-12,50 + € 0,50/pp tourist tax ⛽⬛Ch ⬛ ⬛.
**Location:** Urban. **Surface:** grassy. ⬛ 01/01-31/12.
**Distance:** ⬛450m ⬛450m ⬛800m.

**⊞S Coutras** `24D1`
**Aux Petits Rois**, Rue des Grands Champs 10.
**GPS:** n45,02509 w0,09662. ⬆.

8 ⬛voluntary contribution ⛽⬛Ch ⬛ free. **Location:** Rural, simple,
isolated, quiet. ⬛ 01/01-31/12.
**Distance:** ⬛2km ⬛2km ⬛2km.
**Remarks:** Friday-Saturday market.

**⊞S Créon** 🌿 `24C2`
**Vélo-centre**, Boulevard Victor Hugo, D20.
**GPS:** n44,77663 w0,34806. ⬆➡.

5 ⬛free ⛽€ 3 ⬛Ch⬛€ 1/4h. **Location:** Urban, simple, central.
**Surface:** asphalted. ⬛ 01/01-31/12 ⬛ tue-evening, wed-morning
(market).
**Distance:** ⬛500m ⬛100m ⬛600m ⬛ on the spot.
**Remarks:** Max. 5 days.

**⊞S Cressat** `21G2`
D990, Rue de la Prade. **GPS:** n46,13956 e2,11015. ⬆➡.

5 ⬛free ⛽€ 3/100liter ⬛Ch⬛€ 3/h. **Location:** Rural, simple,
quiet. **Surface:** asphalted. ⬛ 01/01-31/12.
**Distance:** ⬛100m ⬛500m.
**Remarks:** At fish lake, coins at superette 'la Montagne' (500m) and
town hall.

**⊞S Criteuil la Magdeleine** `21C3`
Le Bourg. **GPS:** n45,53836 w0,21551. ⬆➡.

3 ⬛free ⛽⬛Ch ⬛ WC free. **Location:** Rural, simple, quiet.
**Surface:** asphalted. ⬛ 01/01-31/12.
**Distance:** ⬛ on the spot ⬛100m.

**⊞S Cubzac-les-Ponts** 🌿 `24C2`
38 Rue du Port. **GPS:** n44,96564 w0,46002. ⬆➡.

2 ⬛free. **Location:** Rural, simple, quiet. **Surface:** gravel.
⬛ 01/01-31/12.
**Distance:** ⬛1km.

**⊞S Cussac** `21E3`
**Jardin de la Palène**, Rue du 8 Mai 1945.
**GPS:** n45,70519 e0,84936. ⬆➡.

4 ⬛free ⛽€ 2 ⬛Ch⬛ (2x)€ 2. **Location:** Rural, comfortable, quiet.
**Surface:** grassy/gravel. ⬛ 01/04-31/10.
**Distance:** ⬛200m ⬛200m ⬛100m.
**Remarks:** Coins at town hall, bar and restaurant.

**⊞S Damazan** `24D3`
**Gites La Vignerai**, Route Cap de Bosc. **GPS:** n44,28130 e0,26285. ⬆.

6 ⬛€ 8 ⛽€ 2 ⬛€ 2 Ch⬛ 2 ⬛€ 2/day WC⬛€ 5 ⬛. ⬛ ⬛
**Location:** Rural, simple, quiet. **Surface:** gravel/metalled.
⬛ 01/01-31/12.
**Distance:** ⬛500m ⬛1km.

**⊞S Dampniat** `24F1`
**Stade**, Le Mas. **GPS:** n45,16262 e1,63728. ⬆.

4 ⬛free ⛽100liter ⬛Ch⬛ (2x)1h. **Location:** Rural, simple, quiet.
**Surface:** gravel. ⬛ 01/01-31/12.
**Distance:** ⬛850m.
**Remarks:** At sports centre, max. 72h.

**⊞S Dax** 🐚 `27B1`
**Parking du Pont des Arènes**, Boulevard des Sports.
**GPS:** n43,71427 w1,04931. ⬆➡.

8 ⬛free ⛽⬛ free. **Location:** Urban, simple, noisy.
**Surface:** asphalted. ⬛ 01/01-31/12.
**Distance:** ⬛ on the spot ⬛ on the spot ⬛1km.
**Remarks:** Max. 72h, saturday market in the halls.

**Tourist information Dax:**
Office de Tourisme, 11, cours Foch, www.dax.fr. Health resort with warm water sources and medicinal mud.

### S — Dolus-d'Oléron — 21B3
Route du Stade. **GPS:** n45,91137 w1,25255.

40 €6 €4/100liter €4/1h. **Location:** Rural, simple.
**Surface:** grassy/metalled. 01/01-31/12.
**Distance:** 500m 1,2km Hypermarché.
**Remarks:** Coins at tourist info.

### S — Domme — 24F2
Le Pradal. **GPS:** n44,80053 e1,22156.

20 €9/24h €2/100liter Ch €2/1h.
**Location:** Simple, quiet. **Surface:** asphalted. 01/01-31/12
Service: winter.
**Distance:** 500m 500m.

**Tourist information Domme:**
Office de Tourisme, Place de la Halle, www.ot-domme.com. Fortified city worth seeing, parking for motorhomes outside of the town, being indicated.

### S — Dompierre-sur-Charente — 21C3
**Camping Municipal du Pré St Jean**, Rue de Saintonge.
**GPS:** n45,70099 w0,49438.

5 €2 water incl. €4 Ch. **Location:** Rural, simple, isolated.
**Surface:** gravel/metalled. 15/06-15/09.
**Distance:** on the spot 300m 100m 100m.
**Remarks:** Coins at the bakery and campsite.

### S — Donzenac — 24F1
Avenue Jean Chicou. **GPS:** n45,22773 e1,52561.
5 free ChWC. **Location:** Urban. **Surface:** asphalted.
01/01-31/12.
**Distance:** 100m 100m.
**Remarks:** Max. 1 day.

### S — Donzenac — 24F1
**Village de Vacance La Rivière**, Rue de la Rivière.
**GPS:** n45,21897 e1,51829.

Beauclair. **GPS:** n45,25145 e0,44335.

€5 €2/100liter Ch €2/1h. **Location:** Rural, simple, isolated. **Surface:** metalled. 01/01-31/12.
**Distance:** 1,5km Dronne river 1,5km.
**Remarks:** Pay and coins at Village Vacances Beauclair.

### S — Duras — 24D2
**Municipal du Château de Duras**, Le Bourg.
**GPS:** n44,67755 e0,17854.

5 free, July-Aug €2,60 + €3,15/pp Chfree €2,10 WC.
**Location:** Rural, simple, quiet. **Surface:** grassy.
01/01-31/12.
**Distance:** 350m 350m 350m.

### S — Eaux-Bonnes — 27C3
**Parking du Ley**, D918, Gourette. **GPS:** n42,96304 w0,33933.

70 €15 Ch €5 WC included. **Location:** Rural, simple.
**Surface:** asphalted. 01/01-31/12.
**Distance:** 1,4km 1,4km 1,4km 1,4km.

### S — Echillais — 21B3
Place de la Carrière. **GPS:** n45,89753 w0,95545.

15 €7,20 ChWC included. **Location:** Rural, simple.
**Surface:** asphalted. 01/01-31/12.
**Remarks:** Access via rue de l'église.

### S — Echiré — 21C2
Chemin du Marais. **GPS:** n46,39238 w0,41737.

4 free Ch. **Location:** Rural, comfortable, quiet.
**Surface:** gravel. 01/01-31/12.
**Distance:** on the spot 400m.

### S — Egletons — 24G1
**Parking Espace Ventadour**, Rue Henri Dignac.
**GPS:** n45,40406 e2,04791.

20 free €2/100liter Ch.
**Location:** Urban, simple, quiet. **Surface:** gravel. 01/01-31/12
Service: winter.
**Distance:** 300m 3,5km 300m 300m.

### S — Espés Undurein — 27B2
Etche Gochoki, D11. **GPS:** n43,26388 w0,88083.

6 €8 €2 Ch €2. **Surface:** grassy/metalled.
01/01-31/12.
**Distance:** 500m 500m 400m.

### S — Excideuil — 24E1
Rue Léon Barreau. **GPS:** n45,33614 e1,05269.

4 free Ch 3. **Location:** Urban, simple, central, noisy.
**Surface:** asphalted. 01/01-31/12.
**Distance:** on the spot 250m 100m.

### S — Felletin — 21G3
**Parking Lagrange**, Avenue Joffre. **GPS:** n45,88308 e2,17667.

10 free ChWCfree. **Location:** Urban, quiet. **Surface:** gravel.
01/01-31/12.
**Distance:** on the spot.

### S — Fontet — 24D2
**Base de Loisirs Fontet**. **GPS:** n44,56118 w0,02282.

20 €10 Ch WCincluded 1. **Location:** Rural, comfortable, quiet. **Surface:** grassy/gravel. 01/01-31/12.
**Distance:** on the spot bakery 500m, supermarket 4km.
**Remarks:** At lake, near marina.

10 free €5 Ch WCfree. **Location:** Rural, simple, quiet.
**Surface:** gravel. 01/01-31/12.
**Distance:** 4km 1,3km 4km 400m.
**Remarks:** Max. 48h.

FR

## Forgès 24G1

**Camping-Car Park**, Rue Pierre et Marie Curie.
**GPS**: n45,15403 e1,87089. ↑→.

33 ⬛ € 9,15 ⚰ ⬛Ch ⚡ (12x) 📶 included. 🛒 🧺 **Location**: Rural, comfortable, quiet. **Surface**: grassy. ⬛ 01/01-31/12.
**Distance**: ⚡on the spot 🎣 on the spot.
**Remarks**: Mandatory, one-time fee Pass'Etapes € 4.

## Fouras 21B2

**Plage Nord**, Avenue du Cadoret. **GPS**: n45,99194 w1,08694.

20 ⬛ € 8,20/24h ⚰ € 1/50liter. 🛒 **Location**: Urban, simple.
**Surface**: metalled. ⬛ 01/01-31/12.
**Distance**: ⚡on the spot ⊗on the spot 🎣on the spot.
**Remarks**: In front of campsite Cadoret, Fun golf, max. 48h, coins at campsite and tourist info.

## Fouras 21B2

**Prairie du Casino**, Avenue du Bois Vert. **GPS**: n45,99583 w1,10611.

30 ⬛ € 8,20/24h. **Location**: Rural, simple. **Surface**: metalled.
⬛ 01/01-31/12.
**Distance**: ⚡on the spot ⊗on the spot 🎣on the spot.
**Remarks**: Max. 48h.

## Fourques-sur-Garonne 24D3

**Halte Nautique d Pont des Sables**, Pont des Sables, D933.
**GPS**: n44,46081 e0,13932. ↑.

4 ⬛free ⚰ ⬛Chfree. **Location**: Urban, simple, noisy.
**Surface**: metalled. ⬛ 01/03-31/10.
**Distance**: ⚡Fourques 2,5km 🚣3km ⊗on the spot 🚲on the spot.

## Fromental 21F2

**Place Jean Theillaud**. **GPS**: n46,15950 e1,39643. ↑→.

4 ⬛free ⚰ ⬛Ch ⚡ (4x) WCfree. **Location**: Rural, quiet.

---

**Surface**: gravel. ⬛ 01/01-31/12.
**Distance**: ⚡on the spot 🎣on the spot.
**Remarks**: Near church.

## Frontenac 24C2

D236. **GPS**: n44,73781 w0,16308. →.

10 ⬛free ⚰ ⬛ChWC ⬛free. **Location**: Rural, simple.
**Surface**: grassy/gravel. ⬛ 01/01-31/12.
**Distance**: ⚡200m ⊗50m 🍞bakery 200m 🚲on the spot.
**Remarks**: Behind town hall, max. 48h.

## Fumel 24E3

Place Du Saulou, rue Massenet, D911. **GPS**: n44,49809 e0,97165. ↑→.

10 ⬛free ⚰ ⬛ChWCfree. **Location**: Urban, simple.
**Surface**: asphalted. ⬛ 01/01-31/12.
**Distance**: ⚡200m ⊗200m.
**Remarks**: Château de Bonaguil 7km.

## Gan 27C2

**Cave de Gan Jurançon**, Avenue Henri IV. **GPS**: n43,23670 w0,38979. ↑.

15 ⬛free ⚰ € 2/30minutes ⬛ChWC.
**Location**: Simple. **Surface**: asphalted.
⬛ 01/01-31/12.
**Distance**: ⚡900m ⊗on the spot 🎣bakery.
**Remarks**: Coins at Cave de Gan Jurançon, service accross the street.

## Gan 27C2

**Le Clos Husté**, Chemin de Cours-Husté. **GPS**: n43,19703 w0,41247. →.
5 ⬛free. **Location**: Simple.
**Distance**: ⚡5km.

## Garlin 27C2

Place du Marcadieu. **GPS**: n43,55854 w0,27533.
⬛free ⚰ ⬛Chfree. **Location**: Urban. **Surface**: metalled.
⬛ 01/01-31/12.
**Distance**: ⚡450m ⊗150m 🎣400m.

## Garos 27C2

**Le Moulin de Garos**, Quartier Moulin. **GPS**: n43,52684 w0,46819.
5 ⬛ € 3. ⬛ 01/01-31/12.

## Gastes 24B3

**Port de Gastes**, Avenue du Lac. **GPS**: n44,32880 w1,15068. ↑.

100 ⬛ € 2-4,50, 01/06-30/09 € 8 ⚰ ⬛ChWCincluded 📶. 🛒
**Location**: Comfortable. **Surface**: grassy. ⬛ 01/01-31/12 ⬛ **Service**: winter.

---

**Distance**: ⚡Parentis-en-Born 7km 🏊on the spot 🚣on the spot
⊗800m 🎣800m.
**Remarks**: Along lake, baker every morning.

## Gastes 24B3

**Camping Les Echasses**, 193 rue de Bernadon.
**GPS**: n44,31871 w1,13879. ↑.

6 ⬛ € 7-9 ⚰ € 3 ⬛Ch ⚡ included. **Location**: Simple.
**Surface**: grassy. ⬛ 01/01-31/12.
**Distance**: 🏊Gastes Lac 2km 🚲on the spot.
**Remarks**: Max. 1 night, no camping activities.

## Gencay 21D2

Place du Champs de Foire. **GPS**: n46,37315 e0,40638. ↑→.

10 ⬛free ⚰ € 2 ⬛Ch 🔌 € 2 WC.
**Location**: Urban, simple, central, noisy. **Surface**: grassy/metalled.
⬛ 01/01-31/12.
**Distance**: ⚡200m 🏊500m ⊗150m 🎣200m.
**Remarks**: Coins at the shops.

## Genté 21C3

Rue de l'Eglise. **GPS**: n45,62861 w0,315. ↑→.

6 ⬛free ⚰ ⬛Ch ⚡ (6x) WCfree. **Location**: Rural, comfortable,
quiet. **Surface**: asphalted. ⬛ 01/01-31/12.
**Distance**: ⚡on the spot.

## Gornac 24C2

**Aire Municipale**, Esplanade Fongave. **GPS**: n44,66020 w0,18129. ↑.

30 ⬛free ⚰ ⬛Chfree. **Location**: Rural, simple, isolated, quiet.
**Surface**: asphalted. ⬛ 01/01-31/12.
**Distance**: ⊗100m 🎣250m.

## Gouzon 21G2

Place du Champ de Foire, Rue d'Alcantera.
**GPS**: n46,19139 e2,24028. ↑→.

---

6 ⛺free ⛽🚰♻Ch WC free. **Location:** Rural, simple, quiet. **Surface:** metalled/sand. ⭕ 01/01-31/12. **Distance:** 🚶300m ⊗300m 🛒300m.

| 🚐S | Grayan-et-l'Hôpital | 24B1 |

Route de l'Océan. **GPS:** n45,43332 w1,1437. ⬆️➡️.

30 ⛺free ⛽€3,50 Ch 💧€3,50. **Location:** Rural, simple, isolated, quiet. **Surface:** grassy. ⭕ 01/06-16/09. **Distance:** 🚶5km 🏖200m ⊗100m 🚲on the spot 🚴on the spot 🚶on the spot. **Remarks:** Near campsite, coins at campsite.

| 🚐S | Grenade-sur-l'Adour | 27C1 |

Place du 19 mars 1962. **GPS:** n43,77500 w0,43472. ⬆️➡️.

10 ⛺free ⛽♻Ch WC free. **Location:** Rural, simple. **Surface:** asphalted/gravel. ⭕ 01/01-31/12. **Distance:** 🚶100m ⊗100m 🛒100m. **Remarks:** Next to cemetery, max. 1 night.

| 🚐 | Grézillac | 24C2 |

D11. **GPS:** n44,81727 w0,21692. ⬆️➡️.

5 ⛺free ⛽🚰Ch free. **Location:** Rural, quiet. **Surface:** asphalted. ⭕ 01/01-31/12. **Distance:** 🚶500m ⊗500m 🚲1,5km.

| 🚐S | Hautefort 🏖⛲ | 24E1 |

Route de Boisseuil. **GPS:** n45,26017 e1,14907. ⬆️.

3 ⛺free ⛽🚰Ch 🔌2 WC free. **Location:** Rural, simple, central. **Surface:** asphalted/grassy. ⭕ 01/01-31/12. **Distance:** 🚶50m ⊗100m 🛒100m. **Remarks:** Behind town hall.

**Tourist information Hautefort:**
🏰 Château Hautefort. Classified castle. ⭕ 01/04-30/09 daily, 01/10-31/03 afternoons ⭕ 12/11-29/02.
🛒 ⭕ Wed-morning.

| 🚐 | Hendaye | 27A2 |

**Gare des deux Jumeaux**, Rue d'Ansoenia.
**GPS:** n43,37019 w1,7648. ⬆️➡️.

25 ⛺€10 ⛽€2/100liter 🚰Ch 🔌€2/1h. 🚿 **Location:** Urban, simple. **Surface:** asphalted. ⭕ 01/01-31/12. **Distance:** 🚶on the spot 🏖800m ⊗450m 🛒450m 🚲on the spot. **Remarks:** Railway-station Hendaye-plage, max. 3 days, nights closed with barrier.

| 🚐 | Hiers-Brouage | 21B3 |

D3. **GPS:** n45,86242 w1,07799. ⬆️.

20 ⛺free. **Location:** Rural, isolated. **Surface:** grassy/gravel. ⭕ 01/01-31/12. **Distance:** 🚶250m ⊗250m 🛒250m. **Remarks:** Arrival >20h, departure <9h.

| S | Hiers-Brouage | 21B3 |

Rue Palissy, D3. **GPS:** n45,85284 w1,07745.
⛽€4 🚰Ch 🔌. **Surface:** metalled. ⭕ 01/01-31/12.

| 🚐S | Hiersac | 21D3 |

Route de Chateauneuf. **GPS:** n45,66603 w0,00095. ⬆️➡️.

3 ⛺free ⛽€2/10minutes 🚰Ch 🔌€2/h ♻. **Location:** Rural, simple, quiet. **Surface:** asphalted. ⭕ 01/01-31/12. **Distance:** 🚶500m ⊗500m 🛒500m. **Remarks:** Picnic tables available.

| 🚐S | Hostens 🎡 | 24C3 |

**Parking**, La Hourcade. **GPS:** n44,49718 w0,64867.
5 ⛺free WC. **Location:** Isolated. **Surface:** metalled/sand. **Distance:** 🚶1,2km ⊗1,2km 🚲on the spot 🚶on the spot. **Remarks:** At lake, picnic area.

| 🚐S | Houeillès | 24D3 |

**Aire de Repos**, Rue du 19 Mars 1962. **GPS:** n44,19611 e0,03250. ⬆️.

15 ⛺free ⛽WC free. **Location:** Rural, simple, quiet. **Surface:** grassy/gravel. ⭕ 01/01-31/12. **Distance:** 🚶100m 🛒250m. **Remarks:** Max. 24h.

| 🚐S | Hourtin 🏖⛲🌲🏖 | 24B1 |

**Aire de camping Car Hourtin**, 108, Avenue du Lac.
**GPS:** n45,18083 w1,08056. ⬆️➡️.

90 ⛺€7,90, 01/04-30/09 €11,90 ⛽🚰Ch 💧(40x)€2 WC included. 🚿♻ **Location:** Urban, comfortable, central, quiet. **Surface:** gravel/metalled. ⭕ 01/01-31/12. **Distance:** 🚶50m 🏖50m ⊗.

| 🚐S | Jarnages | 21G2 |

Route des Promenctes, D65. **GPS:** n46,18417 e2,08098. ⬆️➡️.

6 ⛺free ⛽€2 🚰Ch 🔌€2 ♻. **Location:** Rural, simple, quiet. **Surface:** asphalted. ⭕ 01/01-31/12. **Distance:** 🚶500m 🚲on the spot ⊗500m 🛒500m. **Remarks:** At tennis-courts.

| 🚐S | Javerdat | 21E3 |

Le Bourg. **GPS:** n45,95249 e0,98582. ⬆️.

| 🚐S | Guéret | 21G2 |

**Aire des Monts de Guéret**, RN145. **GPS:** n46,18189 e1,85837.
16 ⛺free ⛽€2/100liter 🚰Ch WC ♻free. **Location:** Rural, simple. **Surface:** asphalted. ⭕ 01/01-31/12. **Distance:** 🚶centre 4km 🚲500m. **Remarks:** Max. 48h.

| 🚐S | Gujan-Mestras | 24B2 |

**Aire des 3 Coccinelles**, Avenue des Loisirs. **GPS:** n44,61860 w1,0993.
76 ⛺€13,80, 01/07-31/08 €17,80 ⛽€4 Ch 💧(75x),6Amp ♻included. 🚿 **Location:** Urban. **Surface:** grassy/gravel. ⭕ 01/05-30/09. **Distance:** 🚶on the spot ⊗800m 🚶on the spot.

| 🚐S | Hagetmau | 27C1 |

Rue de Piquette. **GPS:** n43,65398 w0,5983. ⬆️.

4 ⬛free ⬛€ 2/100liter ⬛Ch⬛€ 2/55minutes WC. **Location:** Rural, quiet. **Surface:** gravel. ⬛ 01/01-31/12.
**Distance:** ⊗100m.
**Remarks:** Coins at Auberge Limousine (100m).

⬛⬛**S** | **Jonzac** ⬛⬛⬛⬛ | 24C1
Place du 8 Mai 1945. **GPS:** n45,44800 w0,433.⬛.

18 ⬛free ⬛€ 4,20/100liter ⬛Ch⬛€ 4,20/h. **Location:** Urban, simple, central. **Surface:** asphalted. ⬛ 01/01-31/12.
**Distance:** ⬛500m ⊗200m ⬛200m ⬛on the spot.
**Remarks:** Max. 24h, coins at tourist info.

⬛⬛**S** | **Jonzac** ⬛⬛⬛⬛ | 24C1
Place saint Exupéry. **GPS:** n45,44257 w0,43249.⬛⬛.

20 ⬛€ 9 ⬛⬛Ch⬛ included. **Location:** Rural, comfortable, quiet.
**Surface:** metalled. ⬛ 01/01-31/12.
**Distance:** ⬛800m ⊗900m ⬛on the spot.

⬛ | **Jonzac** ⬛⬛⬛⬛ | 24C1
**Chez M. Alex Beurg**, Chez Marchand. **GPS:** n45,44083 w0,40432. ⬛.

3 ⬛free. **Location:** Rural, simple, isolated, quiet. **Surface:** grassy.
⬛ 01/01-31/12.
**Remarks:** Max. 24h.

⬛⬛**S** | **Jumilhac-le-Grand** | 24E1
Boulevard du Pigeonnier, D78. **GPS:** n45,49219 e1,06092.⬛⬛.

2 ⬛free ⬛⬛Chfree. **Location:** Urban, simple.
**Surface:** asphalted/grassy.
**Distance:** ⬛on the spot ⊗200m ⬛bakery 200m ⬛on the spot.
**Remarks:** Near Château de Jumilhac.

⬛⬛**S** | **L'Hôpital-Saint-Blaise** ⬛ | 27B2
Parking l'Église, D25. **GPS:** n43,25088 w0,76925.⬛.

---

8 ⬛€ 10 ⬛⬛Chincluded ⬛€ 4. **Location:** Rural.
**Surface:** gravel/metalled. ⬛ 01/01-31/12.
**Distance:** ⬛on the spot ⊗2km.

⬛⬛**S** | **La Brée-les-Bains** | 21B2
Rue de la Baudette. **GPS:** n46,00810 w1,35764.⬛.

50 ⬛free ⬛€ 4,50 ⬛Ch. **Location:** Rural, simple, quiet.
**Surface:** asphalted. ⬛ 01/01-31/12.
**Distance:** ⬛200m.
**Remarks:** Coins at tourist info.

⬛⬛**S** | **La Coquille** | 24E1
N21, Place de l'église. **GPS:** n45,54268 e0,97785.⬛.

5 ⬛free ⬛⬛ChWCfree. **Location:** Urban, simple, central.
**Surface:** asphalted. ⬛ 01/01-31/12.
**Distance:** ⬛100m ⊗100m ⬛300m.

⬛⬛**S** | **La Couronne** | 21D3
Rue du Champs de Foire. **GPS:** n45,60619 e0,10015.⬛.

10 ⬛free ⬛⬛ChWCfree. **Location:** Urban, simple, central.
**Surface:** asphalted. ⬛ 01/01-31/12 ⬛ Wed-morning, Sa-morning market.
**Distance:** ⬛on the spot ⊗on the spot ⬛on the spot ⬛on the spot.

⬛⬛**S** | **La Courtine** | 21G3
Rue Impasse J Bayle. **GPS:** n45,70591 e2,25890.⬛⬛.

10 ⬛free ⬛€ 2/100liter ⬛Ch ⬛€ 2/1h. **Location:** Simple, quiet.
**Surface:** asphalted. ⬛ 01/01-31/12.
**Distance:** ⬛1km ⬛100m.
**Remarks:** Coins at the shops.

⬛⬛**S** | **La Croix-sur-Gartempe** | 21E2
La Maillerie. **GPS:** n46,14966 e1,01909.

---

⬛⬛**S** | **La Mothe-Saint-Héray** | 21D2
Rue du Pont l'Abbé. **GPS:** n46,35971 w0,11775.⬛⬛.

4 ⬛free ⬛€ 1/50liter ⬛ChWC. **Location:** Rural, comfortable.
**Surface:** gravel. ⬛ 01/01-31/12.
**Distance:** ⬛500m ⊗200m ⬛200m.

⬛⬛**S** | **La Pierre-Saint-Martin** ⬛⬛ | 27B3
**Aire de campingcar de la Pierre-Saint-Martin**, Braça de Guilhers.
**GPS:** n42,97918 w0,7487.⬛.

40 ⬛€ 10 ⬛⬛Ch ⬛(winter) ⬛. **Location:** Comfortable, isolated.
**Surface:** asphalted. ⬛ 01/01-31/12.
**Distance:** ⬛300m ⊗300m ⬛150m.

⬛⬛**S** | **La Réole** ⬛⬛⬛ | 24D2
**Les Justices**, Avenue Gabriel-Chaigne. **GPS:** n44,58059 w0,03036.⬛⬛.

10 ⬛€ 4 ⬛⬛Chfree. **Location:** Urban, simple, noisy.
**Surface:** grassy. ⬛ 15/04-01/10.
**Distance:** ⬛800m ⬛700m.
**Remarks:** Nearby Musée Automobile et Militaire.

⬛⬛**S** | **La Roche-Chalais** ⬛ | 24D1
**Halte Nautique des bords de Dronne**, D730.
**GPS:** n45,15701 e0,00419.⬛.

4 ⬛free ⬛€ 2/100liter ⬛Ch⬛€ 2/1h WCfree. **Location:** Rural, simple. **Surface:** metalled. ⬛ 01/01-31/12.
**Distance:** ⬛400m ⬛100m ⬛100m ⊗400m ⬛900m.
**Remarks:** Service at Intermarché, Av.d'Aquitaine, n45,14633 o0,00569.

## La Roche-Posay 21E1

**Super U**, ZA Les Chaumettes. **GPS:** n46,79361 e0,79750. ↑.

4 ⌁free ⌁ Chfree. **Location:** Simple, isolated, quiet.
**Surface:** asphalted. ☐ 01/01-31/12.
**Distance:** 1,5km 100m.

## La Rochefoucauld 21D3

Rue des Flots, Rivières, Place du Champ de Foire.
**GPS:** n45,74505 e0,38085. ↑.

5 ⌁free ⌁ Ch ⌁. **Location:** Rural, simple. **Surface:** asphalted.
☐ 01/01-31/12.
**Distance:** 1km 10m 200m 200m.
**Remarks:** Beside river Tardoire, next to campsite, Château de La
Rochefoucauld 1,3km.

## La Rochelle 21B2

**Port Neuf**, 6 Boulevard Aristide Rondeau.
**GPS:** n46,16046 w1,18453. ↑ →.

171 ⌁€ 12, tourist tax incl ⌁ Ch ⌁included. ⌁ ⌁
**Location:** Urban. **Surface:** gravel. ☐ 01/01-31/12.
**Distance:** centre 2,5km 1km on the spot.

## La Rochelle 21B2

**Parking Jean Moulin**, Avenue Jean Moulin.
**GPS:** n46,15234 w1,13999. ↑.

50 ⌁€ 13/24h, 01/04-30/09 € 15/24h ⌁ Ch ⌁ ⌁
**Location:** Simple, noisy. **Surface:** asphalted. ☐ 01/01-31/12.
**Distance:** 1,5km free.
**Remarks:** Shuttle bus to city centre.

**Tourist information La Rochelle:**
M La Maison Henri II, Rue de Augustins. Archeological museum.
☐ 15/5-30/9 Sa-Fr 10-19h Sa-Su 14-19h.
M Musée Maritime de la Rochelle, Bassin des Chautiers. Shipping
museum. ☐ daily 10-18.30h.
 Aquarium, Quai Louis Prunier. Sea aquarium. ☐ 01/07-31/08
9-23h, 01/09-30/06 10-20h.

## La Roque-Gageac 24E2

D703. **GPS:** n44,82428 e1,18376. ↑.

20 ⌁€ 7 ⌁€ 2/10minutes ⌁Ch ⌁€ 2/1h ⌁. **Location:** Simple.
**Surface:** metalled. ☐ 01/01-31/12.
**Distance:** 200m 100m 100m 200m 200m.
**Remarks:** Along the Dordogne river, canoe rental.

**Tourist information La Roque-Gageac:**
ℹ www.cc-perigord-noir.fr. Small town worth seeing, in the Dordogne
valley.

## La Sauvetat-du-Dropt 24D2

Route Départementale 19. **GPS:** n44,64759 e0,34127.

4 ⌁free ⌁. **Surface:** grassy/gravel. ☐ 01/01-31/12.
**Distance:** 100m 50m.

## La Teste-de-Buch 24B2

**Aire de Camping Car du Lac de Cazaux**, 66 Rue Guynemer.
**GPS:** n44,53158 w1,16025. ↑.

30 ⌁€ 12/24h ⌁ Ch ⌁included. ⌁ **Location:** Comfortable,
quiet. **Surface:** gravel/metalled. ☐ 01/01-31/12.
**Distance:** 450m 450m on the spot.

## La Teste-de-Buch 24B2

**Centre LeClerc**, Rue Pierre et Marie Curie. **GPS:** n44,61628 w1,11403. ↑.

15 ⌁free ⌁€ 2/10minutes ⌁Ch ⌁€ 2/30minutes.
**Location:** Urban, simple. **Surface:** asphalted. ☐ 01/01-31/12.
**Distance:** 4km on the spot on the spot.

## La Tremblade 21B3

85 Rue Marcel Gaillardon. **GPS:** n45,78268 w1,15228. ↑ →.

49 ⌁€ 12/24h ⌁ Ch ⌁,16Amp ⌁included. ⌁ ⌁
**Location:** Rural, comfortable, central, quiet. **Surface:** gravel/metalled.
☐ 01/01-31/12.
**Distance:** 2,2km on the spot 500m on the spot.
**Remarks:** Max. 72h, baker every morning.

## Labastide-d'Armagnac 27C1

Les Embarrats/D11. **GPS:** n43,97205 w0,18602. ↑ →.

20 ⌁free ⌁ Chfree. **Location:** Rural, simple, quiet.
**Surface:** grassy. ☐ 01/01-31/12.
**Distance:** 300m 300m.

## Labenne 27A1

**Camping-Car Park**, Route Océane. **GPS:** n43,59616 w1,45492. ↑.

80 ⌁€ 11,24, 01/04-31/10 € 13,64 ⌁ Ch ⌁ ⌁included. ⌁ ⌁
**Surface:** gravel. ☐ 01/01-31/12.
**Distance:** 1km 2km 2km 1km 1km.
**Remarks:** Mandatory, one-time fee Pass'Etapes € 4.

## Lacanau 24B1

**Le Huga**, Alleé des Sauviels. **GPS:** n45,00583 w1,16528. ↑ →.

125 ⌁€ 13,80/24h ⌁ Ch ⌁included. ⌁ ⌁
**Location:** Rural, comfortable, quiet. **Surface:** unpaved.
☐ 01/01-31/12.
**Distance:** 2km 2km 100m 2km on the spot
on the spot.
**Remarks:** In front of heliport, max. 48h.

## Ladaux 24C2

**Vignobles Lobre & Fils**, Le Bos. **GPS:** n44,69677 w0,24393. ↑ →.

5 ⌁free ⌁ Ch ⌁free ⌁. **Location:** Rural, simple, isolated,
quiet. **Surface:** grassy/metalled. ☐ 01/01-31/12.
**Distance:** 300m on the spot on the spot.

## Lalinde 24E2

Avenue Général Leclerc. **GPS:** n44,83938 e0,74302. ↑ →.

2 ⌁free ⌁ Chfree. **Location:** Simple. **Surface:** unpaved.
☐ 01/01-31/12.
**Distance:** 500m 500m 500m on the spot.

FR

**Remarks:** Near train station.

**⌖S Lanouaille** 24E1
Rue du Chemin Neuf. **GPS:** n45,39248 e1,14002.⬆.

6 ⌖free ⌷⌷Ch ⌷WCfree. **Location:** Rural, simple, central, quiet. **Surface:** asphalted/gravel. ◻ 01/01-31/12. **Distance:** ⌷50m ⊗100m ⌷100m ⌷ on the spot. **Remarks:** Max. 48h.

**⌖S Lanteuil** 24F1
Route du Doux. **GPS:** n45,12900 e1,66138.⬆.

5 ⌖free ⌷⌷Chfree. **Location:** Urban, simple, quiet. **Surface:** gravel. ◻ 01/01-31/12. **Distance:** ⌷100m ⊗100m.

**⌖S Lanton** 24B2
Allée Albert Pitres, Taussat. **GPS:** n44,71710 w1,06991.➡.

8 ⌖free ⌷⌷Chfree. **Location:** Urban, simple, isolated, quiet. **Surface:** asphalted. ◻ 01/01-31/12. **Distance:** ⌷2km ⌷sandy beach 100m ⌷on the spot ⊗100m ⌷4km.

**⌖S Laruns** 27C3
Artouste Fabrèges. **GPS:** n42,87914 w0,39693.⬆.

80 ⌖free ⌷€5/100liter ⌷Ch ⌷€5/1h ⌷WC. **Location:** Rural, simple. **Surface:** asphalted/grassy. ◻ 01/01-31/12. **Distance:** ⌷200m ⌷on the spot ⌷on the spot ⊗on the spot ⌷on the spot ⌷1km. **Remarks:** At lake, coins at tourist info.

**⌖S Laruns** 27C3
Parking du Cinéma, Avenue de la Gare. **GPS:** n42,98919 w0,42481.⬆.

30 ⌖free ⌷€6/24h ⌷⌷Ch ⌷WC. ⌷ **Location:** Urban, simple. **Surface:** asphalted. ◻ 01/01-31/12.

**Distance:** ⌷100m ⊗100m ⌷100m ⌷400m. **Remarks:** Max. 24h, coins at tourist info.

**⌖S Lauzun** 24D2
Rue Saint-Colomb. **GPS:** n44,62762 e0,45979.⬆.

2 ⌖free ⌷⌷WCfree. **Location:** Simple. **Surface:** gravel. ◻ 01/01-31/12. **Distance:** ⌷350m ⌷on the spot ⊗350m ⌷350m ⌷on the spot. **Remarks:** At small lake, max. 48h.

**⌖S Lavardac** 24D3
**GPS:** n44,18225 e0,29585. 5 ⌖free ⌷⌷WC. **Location:** Rural. **Surface:** gravel. ◻ 01/01-31/12. **Distance:** ⌷on the spot ⌷on the spot ⊗500m ⌷250m.

**⌖S Lavardac** 24D3
Rue de la Victoire - Place du Foirail. **GPS:** n44,17883 e0,29928.⬆.

3 ⌖free ⌷⌷Chfree. **Location:** Rural, simple. **Surface:** asphalted. ◻ 01/01-31/12. **Distance:** ⌷on the spot ⌷bakery 150m.

**⌖S Layrac** 24E3
Aire de Layrac, Rue du 19 Mars 1962. **GPS:** n44,13233 e0,65946.⬆➡.

4 ⌖free ⌷⌷Ch WCfree. **Location:** Urban, simple. **Surface:** asphalted. ◻ 01/01-31/12 ◻ 1st + 2nd weekend March, 1st weekend July. **Distance:** ⌷on the spot ⊗150m ⌷150m.

**⌖S Layrac** 24E3
Le Moulin, D129. **GPS:** n44,13640 e0,66441.⬆➡.

max. 4 ⌖€10/24h ⌷⌷Ch ⌷WCincluded. **Location:** Simple, noisy. **Surface:** gravel. ◻ 01/01-31/12. **Distance:** ⌷600m ⊗450m ⌷600m. **Remarks:** Call if no one is present, video surveillance.

**⌖S Le Bois-Plage-en-Ré** 21B2
Parking Municipal, Avenue du Pas des Boeufs. **GPS:** n46,17708 w1,38613.⬆. 15 ⌖free. **Location:** Simple. **Surface:** gravel/sand. **Distance:** ⌷150m.

**⌖ Le Bois-Plage-en-Ré** 21B2
Route du Petit Sergent. **GPS:** n46,18264 w1,40417. ⌖free. **Surface:** gravel. ◻ 01/01-31/12. **Distance:** ⌷200m ⌷200m.

**Remarks:** Max. 48h.

**⌖S Le Bois-Plage-en-Ré** 21B2
Aire Camping-Car Campéole, Avenue du Pas des Boeufs. **GPS:** n46,17741 w1,38674.⬆.

35 ⌖€16,95 ⌷€3 ⌷Ch ⌷€2/12h. ⌷ **Location:** Rural, simple. **Surface:** gravel/metalled. ◻ 01/01-31/12. **Distance:** ⌷150m. **Remarks:** Payment also possible at campsite.

**⌖S Le Bugue** 24E2
Place Léopold Salme. **GPS:** n44,91679 e0,92775.⬆.

60 ⌖€7/24h ⌷⌷Ch WCincluded. ⌷ **Location:** Simple, quiet. **Surface:** grassy. ◻ 01/04-01/10. **Distance:** ⌷200m ⌷20m ⊗100m ⌷Intermarché 100m. **Remarks:** Along the river Vézère, tuesday and Saturday market.

**⌖S Le Château d'Oléron** 21B3
Boulevard Philippe Dastre. **GPS:** n45,89641 w1,20236.⬆➡.

90 ⌖€12,50 ⌷⌷Ch ⌷WCincluded. ⌷ **Location:** Rural, comfortable. **Surface:** grassy. ◻ 01/01-31/12. **Distance:** ⌷on the spot. **Remarks:** Former campsite.

**⌖S Le Grand Village Plage** 21B3
Parking de l'épinette, Allée des Pins. **GPS:** n45,86222 w1,24111.⬆➡.

12 ⌖€6 ⌷⌷€4/100liter ⌷Ch ⌷€4. ⌷ **Location:** Rural, simple. **Surface:** asphalted. ◻ 01/01-31/12. **Distance:** ⌷1,5km. **Remarks:** 01/04-30/09 max. 24h.

**⌖S Le Mas-d'Agenais** 24D3
Grande Garesse. **GPS:** n44,40656 e0,22030.⬆➡.

8 ⌖free ⌷⌷Ch ⌷(8x)free. **Location:** Urban, comfortable.

**Surface:** gravel. ◻ 01/01-31/12.
**Distance:** ⚐600m ⚓800m ⊗600m 🍴500m.

### 🄲🄶🅂 Le Porge 🍴🍺 24B2
**La Grigne**, 35 avenue de l'Océan. **GPS:** n44,89425 w1,20154. ⬆.
30 🎫 € 9,20/24h 🚰 € 2 🚽Ch 🧺 € 4. 🚐 ⦾ **Location:** Rural.
◻ 01/03-26/11.

### 🅂 Le Porge 🍴🍺 24B2
**Intermarché**, D107. **GPS:** n44,87574 w1,07883. ⬆.
🚰 € 2/20minutes 🚽Ch. **Location:** Simple. ◻ 01/01-31/12.
**Distance:** ⚐on the spot ⚓150m.

### 🄲🄵🅂 Le Teich 24B2
**Parking de la Gare**, Rue de l'Industrie. **GPS:** n44,63303 w1,02643. ⬆.
🎫free 🚰 € 5/100liter 🚽Ch 🔌 € 5/h. **Location:** Simple.
◻ 01/01-31/12.
**Distance:** ⚐on the spot ⊗700m ⚓1km 🚲on the spot.

### 🄲🄵🅂 Le Temple-sur-Lot 24D3
**Avenue de Verdun**. **GPS:** n44,38000 e0,52639. ⬆ ➡.

4 🎫free 🚰🚽ChWCfree. **Location:** Urban, simple, quiet.
**Surface:** asphalted. ◻ 01/01-31/12.
**Distance:** ⚐on the spot ⊗100m ⚓100m 🚲on the spot.

### 🄲🄶🅂 Le Temple-sur-Lot 24D3
**Le Bosc**, D911. **GPS:** n44,38144 e0,53649.

16 🎫 € 6,50 🚰🚽Ch 🧺 📶included. 🚐 ⦾ **Location:** Rural.
**Surface:** grassy. ◻ 01/01-31/12.
**Distance:** ⚐800m ⊗800m 🚲800m 🚲on the spot.
**Remarks:** Picnic and barbecue place.

### 🄲🅂 Le Verdon-sur-Mer 🛥🍺 21B3
**Plage fluviale**, Allée des Baïnes. **GPS:** n45,54633 w1,0541. ⬆ ➡.

70 🎫 € 10,60 🚰 € 2/100liter 🚽Ch 🧺 ⦾ 🚐 📦 **Location:** Urban, comfortable, isolated, quiet.
**Surface:** gravel/metalled.
◻ 01/01-31/12.
**Distance:** ⚓50m ⊗500m ⚓2km 🚲on the spot.
**Remarks:** Coins at town hall, tourist info and the shops at the beach.

### 🄲🅂 Lège-Cap-Ferret 🌿🛥 24B2
**Route des Pastourelles**, Avenue Charles de Gaulle, D106, Claouey.
**GPS:** n44,75127 w1,18033. ⬆.

10 🎫free 🚰🚽Ch 🧺 (2x)free. **Location:** Urban, simple, noisy.
**Surface:** forest soil. ◻ 01/01-31/12.

---

**Distance:** ⚐on the spot ⚓1km ⚓600m ⊗600m 🚲on the spot.
**Remarks:** Coins at camping municipal, day parking also allowed, overnight stay on motorhome stopovers.

### 🄵🅁 Lège-Cap-Ferret 🌿🛥 24B2
**Avenue Edouard Branly**. **GPS:** n44,75203 w1,18809. ⬆.

15 🎫free.
**Location:** Rural, simple. **Surface:** forest soil.
◻ 01/01-31/12.
**Distance:** ⚐2km ⚓600m ⚓600m ⊗600m 🚽600m 🚲on the spot.
**Remarks:** Near campsite Les Embruns.

### 🄲🄵🅂 Lège-Cap-Ferret 🌿🛥 24B2
**D106**, Avenue de Bordeaux, L'Herbe. **GPS:** n44,68655 w1,2451. ⬆.

15 🎫free. **Location:** Rural, simple, quiet. **Surface:** asphalted/metalled.
◻ 01/01-31/12.
**Distance:** ⚐2km ⚓1km ⊗2km ⚓2km 🚲on the spot.
**Remarks:** At cemetery.

### 🄲🄵🅂 Léguillac-de-l'Auche 24E1
**Glenon**. **GPS:** n45,20319 e0,55876. ⬆ ➡.
6 🎫free 🚰 € 2 🧺 € 3/24h ⦾ **Location:** Rural, isolated, quiet.
**Surface:** grassy.
**Distance:** ⚐2km ⊗2km ⚓2km.

### 🄲🄵🅂 Lembras 24D2
**Aire de Caudeau**, Impasse de l'Anguillère.
**GPS:** n44,88300 e0,52522. ⬆ ➡.

10 🎫free 🚰🚽Chfree ⦾ (10x)€ 6/12h. **Location:** Rural, comfortable, central. **Surface:** gravel. ◻ 01/01-31/12.
**Distance:** ⚐200m ⚓200m 🚽200m 🚶2,5km.

### 🄲🅂 Léon 27A1
**Aire Municipale Berges du Lac**, Route de Puntaou.
**GPS:** n43,88444 w1,31861. ⬆.

80 🎫 € 11 🚰 🚽ChWCincluded. 🚐 ⦾ **Location:** Simple, noisy.
**Surface:** grassy/gravel. ◻ 01/01-31/12.
**Distance:** ⚐1km ⚓250m 🚽50m ⊗50m ⚓50m.
**Remarks:** Nearby lake, max. 48h.

### 🄲🄵🅂 Les Eyzies 🌿🛥 24E2
**Parking de la Vézère**, Promenade de la Vézère.
**GPS:** n44,93863 e1,00907. ⬆ ➡.

---

40 🎫 € 6/night 🚰 € 2/100liter 🚽Ch ⦾
**Location:** Urban, comfortable, quiet. **Surface:** grassy/sand.
◻ 01/01-31/12.
**Distance:** ⚐200m ⊗200m ⚓200m.
**Remarks:** Along the river Vézère, summer max. 48h, parking fee being collected at 9AM.

**Tourist information Les Eyzies:**
👁 Village Troglodytique de la Madeleine, Tursac. Troglodyte-village.
Ⓜ Le Village du Bournat, Le Bugue. Open air museum. ◻ 01/03-31/10 10-18/19h.

### 🄲🅂 Les Mathes/La Palmyre 🍴🍺 21B3
**Aire de la Garenne**, Rue de la Garenne, Les Mathes.
**GPS:** n45,71433 w1,14752. ⬆.

20 🎫01/02-30/11 € 10/24h 🚰 € 4/100liter 🚽ChWC. 📦
**Location:** Rural, simple, isolated. **Surface:** metalled.
◻ 01/01-31/12.
**Distance:** ⚐400m.
**Remarks:** Coins at town hall Mo-Fri 9-18h and tourist info La Palmyre daily 9-19h in July/Aug.

### 🄲🄵🅂 Les Mathes/La Palmyre 🛥🍺 21B3
**Aire du Corsaire**, Avenue de lAtlantique. **GPS:** n45,69193 w1,18896. ⬆.

90 🎫01/02-30/11 € 10/24h 🚰 € 4/100liter 🚽Ch 🔌 € 2/1h. 📦 ⦾
**Location:** Simple, central, quiet. **Surface:** asphalted.
◻ 01/01-31/12.
**Distance:** ⚐1km ⚓200m ⚓200m 🚲on the spot.
**Remarks:** Max. 7 days.

### 🄲🄵🅂 Les Mathes/La Palmyre 🛥🍴🍺 21B3
**Boulevard de la Plage**, La Palmyre. **GPS:** n45,68287 w1,17942. ⬆.

50 🎫01/02-30/11 € 10/24h. 📦
**Location:** Urban, simple, central, quiet. **Surface:** asphalted.
◻ 01/01-31/12 ◻ 01/07-31/08.
**Distance:** ⚐1,2km ⚓100m ⊗200m 🚲on the spot.

**Tourist information Les Mathes/La Palmyre:**
Zoo de la Palmyre. Zoo, 1600 animals, 14Ha.
◻ 01/04-30/09 9-20.30h, 01/10-31/03 9-12h, 14-18h.

### 🄲🄵🅂 Les Portes-en-Ré 21B2
**Parking de la Patache**, Route du Fier. **GPS:** n46,22925 w1,48315. ⬆.

**FR**

10 ⌕€ 10/24h ⌗≋ChWC included. 🚐 **Location:** Rural, simple. **Surface:** metalled. ⏱ 01/01-31/12. **Distance:** ⚓150m ⌗on the spot ⚐3,5km ♿on the spot. **Remarks:** Max. 24h, payment only with coins.

### Les Salles-Lavaugyon | 21E3
Le Tilleul, Route de St Mathieu. **GPS:** n45,73998 e0,70100. ⬆➡.

6 ⌕€ 5 ⌗≋⌗ (3x)included. **Location:** Rural, simple, isolated. **Surface:** gravel. ⏱ 01/04-01/11. **Distance:** ⚐800m ⊗800m ⚐on the spot. **Remarks:** Max. 8 days.

### Les Trois-Moutiers | 18D3
Rue des Deniers D49. **GPS:** n47,06333 e0,01826. ⬆.

5 ⌕free ⌗≋Ch free. **Location:** Rural, comfortable, central, quiet. **Surface:** asphalted. ⏱ 01/01-31/12. **Distance:** ⚐on the spot ⊗100m.

### Lescar | 27C2
Parking Jacques Monod, Chemin de Beneharnum. **GPS:** n43,33062 w0,43458.
5 ⌕free. **Location:** Simple, quiet. **Surface:** asphalted. ⏱ 01/01-31/12. **Distance:** ⚐on the spot ⊗on the spot ⚐on the spot ♿on the spot. **Remarks:** Max. 48h.

### Lescar | 27C2
Impasse du Vert Galant. **GPS:** n43,32669 w0,44373. ⬆. ⌗≋Ch free. **Location:** Rural, simple, quiet. **Surface:** asphalted. ⏱ 01/01-31/12. **Distance:** ⚐1,5km ⊗on the spot ⚐1km.

### Lesparre-Médoc | 24B1
Chemin de la Mouline. **GPS:** n45,30253 w0,91826.
6 ⌕€ 10 ⌗≋Ch ⌗€ 2 ▣€ 4/4 ≋included. **Surface:** grassy. ⏱ 01/01-31/12. **Distance:** ⚐1,5km ⊗350m.

### Lesparre-Médoc | 24B1
Rue Aristide Briand. **GPS:** n45,30539 w0,94012. ⌕free ⌗≋Ch free. **Location:** Urban. **Surface:** asphalted. ⏱ 01/01-31/12. **Distance:** ⚐250m ⊗250m ⚐200m.

### Lestelle-Bétharram | 27C2
Avenue de Bétharram/D937. **GPS:** n43,12522 w0,2074. ⬆.
10 ⌕free. **Location:** Urban, simple, noisy. **Surface:** asphalted. ⏱ 01/01-31/12. **Distance:** ⚐500m ⊗250m. **Remarks:** Nearby camping Le Saillet.

### Lezay | 21D2
Rue de Gâte Bourse. **GPS:** n46,26500 w0,01139. ⬆.

---

15 ⌕free ⌗≋Ch free. **Location:** Urban, simple, central. **Surface:** asphalted. ⏱ 01/01-31/12. **Distance:** ⊗170m ⚐350m.

### Libourne | 24C2
Camping-Car Park Lac des Dagueys, 3 rue de Schwandorf. **GPS:** n44,94787 w0,24356. ⬆⬆.

17 ⌕€ 11,26, 01/06-30/09 € 13,66 ⌗≋Ch ⌗(16x)included. 🚐 **Location:** Rural, comfortable, quiet. **Surface:** metalled. ⏱ 01/01-31/12. **Distance:** ⚐on the spot ⌗on the spot ⊗on the spot. **Remarks:** Mandatory, one-time fee Pass'Etapes € 4.

### Liginiac | 24G1
Le Maury-Liginiac. **GPS:** n45,39158 e2,30387. ⬆➡.

2 ⌕free ⌗≋Ch ⌗(1x)free. **Location:** Rural, simple, isolated, quiet. **Surface:** gravel. ⏱ 01/01-31/12 ▣ water disconnected in winter. **Distance:** ⚐4,5km ⚓Sandy beach ⊗on the spot. **Remarks:** At lake Neuvic. Follow restaurant Le Maury.

### Lignières-Sonneville | 21C3
Parc de la Charmille, Le Bourg. **GPS:** n45,55666 w0,18276. ⬆➡.

15 ⌕free ⌗≋Ch ⌗(1x)free. **Location:** Rural, simple, quiet. **Surface:** metalled. ⏱ 01/01-31/12. **Distance:** ⚐300m ⊗300m ⚐300m. **Remarks:** Near sports fields and castle.

### Limeuil | 24E2
D31. **GPS:** n44,88564 e0,89151. ⬆.

10 ⌕free. **Location:** Rural, simple, isolated. **Surface:** grassy/gravel. ⏱ 01/01-31/12. **Distance:** ⚓400m ⚐400m ⊗750m.

---

### Lissac-sur-Couze | 24F1
Parking du poste de secours. **GPS:** n45,09914 e1,46277. ⬆➡.

15 ⌕€ 4,75/stay ⌗€ 4,75/100liter ≋Ch ⌗(12x)€ 4,75/6h. 🚐≋ **Location:** Rural, comfortable. **Surface:** gravel. ⏱ 01/01-31/12. **Distance:** ⚓on the spot ⌗on the spot.

### Lit-et-Mixe | 24A3
Cap de l'Homy, 600, avenue Océan. **GPS:** n44,03730 w1,33419. ⬆.

36 ⌕€ 11,60-23,95 + € 0,61/pp tourist taks ⌗≋Ch ⌗WC. **Location:** Simple, quiet. **Surface:** forest soil. ⏱ 01/05-30/09. **Distance:** ⚓400m ⊗200m ⚐200m ♿on the spot. **Remarks:** Next to camping municipal.

### Lizant | 21D2
Aire de Loisirs, Rue du Bourrelier. **GPS:** n46,08614 e0,27834.
8 ⌕€ 4 ⌗≋Ch ⌗included WC. **Surface:** gravel. ⏱ 01/01-31/12. **Distance:** ⊗100m ⚐on the spot. **Remarks:** Playground.

### Londigny | 21D2
Place de l'Eglise. **GPS:** n46,08333 e0,13472.

5 ⌕free ⌗≋Ch ⌗WC free. **Location:** Isolated, quiet. **Surface:** gravel. ⏱ 01/01-31/12. **Remarks:** Max. 48h.

### Loudun | 18D3
Place de la Porte Saint Nicolas. **GPS:** n47,01357 e0,07833. ⬆➡.

3 ⌕free ⌗€ 2/10minutes ≋Ch ⌗€ 2/55minutes. **Location:** Urban, simple, noisy. **Surface:** asphalted. ⏱ 01/01-31/12. **Distance:** ⚐500m ⊗500m ⚐100m, bakery 10m. **Remarks:** Max 3,5t, max. 48h.

### Loulay | 21C2
Rue du 8 Mai. **GPS:** n46,04679 w0,50662. ⬆➡.

FR

6 🛏free 🚰🍽Chfree. **Location:** Rural, simple, central, quiet. **Surface:** gravel. ⬛ 01/01-31/12. **Distance:** 🏪400m 🍴500m.

| 🚐S | **Lussac** | 24D2 |

La Grange. **GPS:** n44,94628 w0,09541. ⬆➡.

8 🛏free 🚰🍽Ch 🧹 WCfree. **Location:** Rural, simple, quiet. **Surface:** gravel. ⬛ 01/01-31/12. **Distance:** 🏪800m.

| 🚐S | **Lussac-les-Châteaux** | 21E2 |

Place de l'Amitie. **GPS:** n46,40250 e0,72583. ⬆.

15 🛏free 🚰🍽ChWCfree. **Location:** Urban, simple, central, noisy. **Surface:** metalled. ⬛ 01/01-31/12 🛒 Wed, market. **Distance:** 🏪200m ⊗200m 🍴200m.

| 🚐 | **Marennes** 〰 | 21B3 |

1 Avenue William Bertrand. **GPS:** n45,82140 w1,13828. ⬆.

10 🛏€ 7,50. **Location:** Rural, simple, quiet. **Surface:** grassy/gravel. ⬛ 01/01-31/12. **Distance:** 🏪2,7km 🏊on the spot ⊗400m. **Remarks:** Max. 6,5m.

| 🚐S | **Marmande** | 24D3 |

La Filhole, Rue de la Filhole. **GPS:** n44,49667 e0,16412. ⬆.

30 🛏€ 9,20 🚰🍽Ch 🧹 included. 🛁 **Location:** Rural, simple, quiet. **Surface:** metalled/sand. ⬛ 01/01-09/06, 11/07-31/12 🛒 10/06-10/07. **Distance:** 🏪500m ⊗500m 🍴1km 🏃on the spot.

| 🚐S | **Marmande** | 24D3 |

Place du Moulin. **GPS:** n44,49833 e0,16028.

2 🛏free 🚰🍽Chfree. **Location:** Urban, noisy. **Surface:** asphalted. ⬛ 01/11-01/04. **Distance:** 🏪150m 🏊on the spot. **Remarks:** Max. 48h.

| 🚐S | **Marquay** | 24E2 |

D6. **GPS:** n44,94401 e1,13529. ⬆.

7 🛏free 🚰🍽Ch 🧹. **Location:** Isolated, quiet. **Surface:** gravel. ⬛ 01/01-31/12. **Distance:** ⊗100m.

| 🚐S | **Mauléon** | 18C3 |

Rue de la Bachelette. **GPS:** n46,91904 w0,75267. ⬆➡.

8 🛏free 🚰🍽Chfree. **Location:** Rural, simple, quiet. **Surface:** asphalted. ⬛ 01/01-31/12. **Distance:** 🏪500m ⊗500m 🍴500m. **Remarks:** Next to swimming pool.

| 🚐S | **Mauzé-sur-le-Mignon** | 21C2 |

**Le Port**, Rue du Port. **GPS:** n46,19989 w0,67952. ⬆.

10 🛏free 🚰€ 4 🍽Ch 🧹 WC. **Location:** Rural, simple. **Surface:** gravel. ⬛ 01/01-31/12. **Distance:** 🏪1km 🏊on the spot 🚲on the spot 🏃on the spot. **Remarks:** Coins at campsite and shops.

| 🚐S | **Médis** | 21B3 |

Rue Joseph Lelee. **GPS:** n45,63354 w0,97145. ⬆➡.

8 🛏€ 8 🚰🍽Ch 🧹 WC 🔌included. **Location:** Rural, comfortable, quiet. **Surface:** asphalted. ⬛ 01/01-31/12. **Distance:** 🍴1,8km. **Remarks:** At airfield.

| 🚐S | **Ménigoute** | 21D1 |

Rue des Vignes. **GPS:** n46,49790 w0,05795. ⬆.

20 🛏free 🚰🍽ChWCfree. **Location:** Rural, isolated, quiet.

4 🛏free 🚰🍽Chfree. **Location:** Urban, simple, quiet. **Surface:** gravel. ⬛ 01/01-31/12. **Distance:** 🏪200m ⊗on the spot 🍴100m.

| 🚐S | **Mensignac** | 24E1 |

Combecouyere-Sud. **GPS:** n45,22309 e0,56553.

3 🛏free 🚰€ 3 🍽Ch 🧹(2x)€ 3. **Location:** Rural, simple, quiet. **Surface:** metalled. ⬛ 01/03-31/10. **Distance:** 🏪200m ⊗400m 🍴400m.

| 🚐S | **Meschers-sur-Gironde** 〰 | 21B3 |

Rue du 19 Mars 1961. **GPS:** n45,55698 w0,94741. ⬆➡.

24 🛏€ 10 🚰🍽Ch 🧹 included. 🛁 **Location:** Rural, comfortable, quiet. **Surface:** concrete. ⬛ 01/01-31/12. **Distance:** 🏪on the spot ⊗500m.

| ⚓S | **Meschers-sur-Gironde** 〰 | 21B3 |

**Port de Plaisance**, Route des Salines. **GPS:** n45,55614 w0,9451. ⬆.

30 🛏€ 10/24h 🚰€ 2/80liter 🍽Ch 🧹(8x) 🍴€ 1,50 🔌€ 2/2 📶 🛁 **Location:** Rural, comfortable, isolated, quiet. **Surface:** asphalted. ⬛ 01/01-31/12. **Distance:** 🏪1km 🏊100m ⊗100m 🍴1km.

| 🚐S | **Messanges** | 27A1 |

**Camping-Car Park Plage Nord**, Avenue de la Plage. **GPS:** n43,81549 w1,40088. ⬆.

55 🛏€ 8,40, 01/05-30/09 € 10,80 🚰🍽ChWCincluded. 🛁📶 **Location:** Simple. **Surface:** metalled/sand. ⬛ 01/01-31/12. **Distance:** 🏪1,5km 🏊200m. **Remarks:** Mandatory, one-time fee Pass'Etapes € 4.

| 🚐S | **Messé** | 21D2 |

D114. **GPS:** n46,26306 e0,11203. ⬆.

FR

**Surface:** gravel. ☐ 01/01-31/12.
**Distance:** ⚓on the spot ⚑10km.

## 🅱️🅢 Meuzac 24F1

Étang de la Roche/D243. **GPS:** n45,54805 e1,44017. ⬆️➡️

15 ⊠free ⚑🍽️Chfree. **Location:** Rural, simple, quiet.
**Surface:** gravel. ☐ 01/01-31/12.
**Distance:** ⚑100m ⚡5km ⚓on the spot ⊗on the spot ⚑100m
⚑100m ♨️on the spot.
**Remarks:** Service 200m.

## 🅱️🅢 Meymac 24G1

**Parking Lac de Sechemailles**, Le Montbazet.
**GPS:** n45,52500 e2,12761. ⬆️➡️

20 ⊠free ⚑€2 🍽️Chfree ▣€2. **Location:** Rural, comfortable,
quiet. **Surface:** gravel. ☐ 01/01-31/12.
**Distance:** ⚑2km ⚑300m ⊗300m.
**Remarks:** Coins available at Office du Tourisme and bar.

## 🅒🅢 Meymac 24G1

Boulevard de la Garenne. **GPS:** n45,53973 e2,15381. ⬆️➡️
30 ⊠free ⚑€2 🍽️Ch ⚡(1x)€2. **Location:** Rural, simple, quiet.
**Surface:** gravel. ☐ 20/04-02/11.
**Remarks:** Coins at campsite and tourist info.

## 🅱️🅢 Mézières-sur-Issoire 21E2

Place de la République. **GPS:** n46,10726 e0,91014. ⬆️

4 ⊠free ⚑🍽️Chfree. **Location:** Rural, simple. **Surface:** asphalted.
☐ 01/01-31/12.
**Distance:** ⚑on the spot.

## 🅱️🅢 Mimizan 24D3

**Des Hournails**, Route du CEL. **GPS:** n44,21375 w1,28239. ⬆️

150 ⊠€14,50 ⚑€3/20minutes 🍽️Ch. **Location:** Simple.
**Surface:** gravel/sand. ☐ 01/06-30/09.
**Distance:** ⚓1,5km ♨️on the spot.

## 🅒🅢 Mimizan 24B3

**Camping du Lac**, Avenue de Woolsack, Mimizan-lac.
**GPS:** n44,21956 w1,22972. ⬆️

---

21 ⊠€11-18 + €0,22/pp tourist tax, dog €1,95 ⚑€2/15minutes
🍽️Ch ⚡🍽️WC ▣⚡€3 🔊. **Location:** Rural, comfortable.
**Surface:** grassy/gravel. ☐ 30/04-30/09.
**Distance:** ⚓6km ⊗on the spot ⚑on the spot.

## 🅱️🅢 Mirambeau 24C1

Rue du parc de loisirs. **GPS:** n45,37816 w0,56872. ⬆️➡️

20 ⊠€8 ⚑🍽️Ch ⚡included. 🏪🗑️ **Location:** Urban, luxurious,
central, quiet. **Surface:** grassy. ☐ 01/01-31/12.
**Distance:** ⚑500m ⚡3km ⊗50m ⚑150m.
**Remarks:** Former campsite.

## 🅱️🅢 Mirebeau 21D1

14 rue du Pas Martin. **GPS:** n46,78064 e0,19430. ⬆️➡️

⊠€7 ⚑€2/time 🍽️Ch ⚡€5/24h. **Location:** Rural, simple, quiet.
**Surface:** asphalted/gravel. ☐ 01/01-31/12.
**Distance:** ⚑2km ⚑1,5km.
**Remarks:** Barbecue place.

## 🅱️🅢 Moliets-et-Maa 27A1

Avenue de l'Océan, Moliets-Plage. **GPS:** n43,85091 w1,38188. ⬆️

120 ⊠€8, 01/05-30/08 €14 ⚑🍽️Ch ⚡WC. 🏪🗑️
**Location:** Comfortable, noisy. **Surface:** forest soil.
☐ 01/04-31/10.
**Distance:** ⚑200m ⚑750m ⊗200m ⚑200m.
**Remarks:** Max. 7 days, shady.

## 🅱️🅢 Monbahus 24D3

Rue du Château d'Eau. **GPS:** n44,54738 e0,53517. ⬆️➡️

3 ⊠free ⚑🍽️Ch ⚡(2x)free. **Location:** Rural, simple.
**Surface:** asphalted. ☐ 01/01-31/12 ▣ Service: winter.
**Distance:** ⚑300m ⊗200m ⚑300m.
**Remarks:** Beautiful view, steep entrance road.

---

## 🅥🅢 Monbazillac 24D2

**Château du Haut Pezaud**, Les Pezauds. **GPS:** n44,78471 e0,48687. ⬆️

10 ⊠€5, first night free ⚑€1,50 ⚡€3/day WC 🍽️€1/pppd 🔊€2/
day. **Location:** Rural, simple. **Surface:** grassy.
☐ 01/01-31/12.
**Distance:** ⊗table d'hôtes 🚶through the vineyards.
**Remarks:** Max. 7 nights, baker every morning, tasting of regional
products.

## 🅥🅢 Monbazillac 24D2

**Domaine La Lande**, Route de Ribagnac, D13.
**GPS:** n44,78822 e0,49587. ⬆️

10 ⊠free ⚑🍽️ChWCfree. **Location:** Rural, simple. **Surface:** grassy.
☐ 01/01-31/12.
**Distance:** ⚑800m ⊗200m ⚑on the spot.
**Remarks:** Baker every morning, sale of wines.

## 🅱️🅢 Monflanquin 24E3

**Chemin de la Source**, 3, Allée des Érables.
**GPS:** n44,52812 e0,75537. ⬆️

5 ⊠free ⚑🍽️Chfree.
**Location:** Simple. **Surface:** gravel.
☐ 01/03-01/11.
**Distance:** ⚑1,5km ⚓Lac de Coulon 150m ⊗1,3km ⚑250m.
**Remarks:** Service 500m n44,52477 o0,75642.

**Tourist information Monflanquin:**
ℹ️ Office de Tourisme, Place des Arcades, www.monflanquin-tourisme.
com. Medieval town.

## 🅱️🅢 Monpazier 24E2

La Duelle-Nord. **GPS:** n44,68499 e0,89362. ⬆️➡️

10 ⊠free ⚑🍽️Chfree. **Location:** Rural, simple, comfortable.
**Surface:** gravel. ☐ 01/01-31/12.
**Distance:** ⚑300m ⚑400m ⚑500m.

## 🅱️🅢 Monségur 24D2

Place du 8 mai. **GPS:** n44,65060 e0,08363. ⬆️➡️

FR

5 ⌇free 🚰 🔌free WC. **Location:** Simple, noisy. **Surface:** gravel.
⊡ 01/01-31/12.
**Distance:** 🛒on the spot ⊗300m 🚲400m.
**Remarks:** Max. 48h. No access via La Bastide.

**⊞S  Mont-de-Marsan  27C1**
**Aire ce camping-cars de Mont de Marsan**, 51 Avenue de Villeneuve.
**GPS:** n43,88992 w0,47559.⬆️

45 ⌇€ 5,10-7,50, 01/07-31/08 € 8,40 + tourist tax € 0,33/pp
🚰 € 1/5minutes 🔌Ch 💧(3x)€ 1/4h. 📶 🚮 **Location:** Rural, central,
quiet. **Surface:** asphalted/grassy. ⊡ 01/01-31/12.
**Distance:** 🛒2,3km 🚲500m.
**Remarks:** Max. 72h.

**⊞S  Montalivet-les-Bains  24B1**
**Camping-car Park de Vendays-Montalivet**, Avenue de l'Europe.
**GPS:** n45,37051 w1,14462.⬆️
40 ⌇€ 10 🚰 🔌Ch 💧(40x)included,6Amp. 📶 🚮 **Location:** Simple,
quiet. **Surface:** gravel. ⊡ 01/01-31/12.
**Distance:** 🛒800m 🏖350m ⊗nearby 🚲nearby.
**Remarks:** Mandatory, one-time fee Pass'Etapes € 4.

**⊞S  Montalivet-les-Bains  24B1**
**Camping-Car Park L'Océan**, Boulevard de Lattre de Tassigny.
**GPS:** n45,37625 w1,15664.⬆️

100 ⌇€ 9,20, 01/05-30/09 € 11,60 🚰 🔌Ch 💧 📶included. 📶 🚮
**Location:** Simple, quiet. **Surface:** grassy/metalled.
⊡ 01/01-31/12.
**Distance:** 🛒on the spot ⊗350m ⊗400m 🚲400m.
**Remarks:** Mandatory, one-time fee Pass'Etapes € 4.
**Tourist information Montalivet-les-Bains:**
🚶 ⊡ Fri.

**⊞S  Montboucher  21F3**
D36. **GPS:** n45,95152 e1,68069.⬆️➡️

10 ⌇free 🚰 🔌ChWCfree. **Location:** Rural, quiet.
**Surface:** grassy/gravel. ⊡ 01/01-31/12.
**Distance:** 🛒8km ⊗8km 🚲8km.

**⊞S  Montendre  24C1**
Place de la Paix. **GPS:** n45,28627 w0,41116.⬆️

---

15 ⌇free 🚰 🔌ChWCfree. **Location:** Urban, simple, central, quiet.
**Surface:** asphalted. ⊡ 01/01-31/12. ⊡ Thu 6-14h.
**Distance:** 🛒100m ⊗100m 🚲500m.

**⊞S  Monteton  24D2**
D423. **GPS:** n44,62249 e0,25745.⬆️➡️

20 ⌇free 🚰 🔌Chfree. **Location:** Rural, simple, quiet.
**Surface:** grassy. ⊡ 01/01-31/12.
**Distance:** 🛒on the spot 🚲150m.
**Remarks:** Beautiful view.

**⊞S  Montguyon  24C1**
**Plaine des Sports**, Rue de Vassiac. **GPS:** n45,21796 w0,18368.⬆️

15 ⌇free 🚰 🔌ChWCfree. **Location:** Urban, simple, central, quiet.
**Surface:** gravel. ⊡ 01/01-31/12.
**Distance:** 🛒500m ⊗500m 🚲500m 🚴on the spot.
**Remarks:** Max. 72h.

**⊞S  Montignac  24E1**
**P Vieux Quartiers**, Rue des Sagnes. **GPS:** n45,06800 e1,16547.⬆️➡️

35 ⌇€ 6/night 🚰 🔌Ch 💧included. 📶 🚮 **Location:** Urban,
comfortable, central. **Surface:** gravel. ⊡ 01/01-31/12.
**Distance:** 🛒200m ⊗200m 🚲200m.

**⊞S  Montignac  24E1**
**Ferme du Bois Bareirou**, Les Baraques, Montignac-Lascaux.
**GPS:** n45,09053 e1,11143.⬆️➡️

20 ⌇free 🚰 🔌€ 3 🔌Ch 🚽€ 3. **Location:** Rural, isolated, quiet.
**Surface:** grassy. ⊡ 01/01-31/12.
**Distance:** 🛒5km.
**Remarks:** Max. 3 days.

**⊞S  Montils  21C3**
Le Vignolet, D233. **GPS:** n45,65285 w0,50576.⬆️

---

20 ⌇free 🚰 🔌Ch 📶free. **Location:** Rural, simple, isolated.
**Surface:** gravel/metalled. ⊡ 01/01-31/12.
**Distance:** 🛒300m ⊗800m 🚲700m.

**⊞S  Montmorillon  21E2**
Rue Léon Dardant. **GPS:** n46,42326 e0,86788.⬆️

10 ⌇free 🚰 🔌€ 3/10minutes 🔌Ch 💧€ 2 🚮.
**Location:** Urban, simple, central, quiet. **Surface:** asphalted.
⊡ 01/01-31/12.
**Distance:** 🛒500m ⊗500m 🚲600m.
**Remarks:** Along the Gartempe river, max. 24h.

**⊞S  Morcenx  24B3**
Chemin de l'Abattoirs. **GPS:** n44,03811 w0,90914.⬆️

5 ⌇free 🚰 🔌Chfree. **Location:** Simple. **Surface:** grassy.
⊡ 01/01-31/12.
**Distance:** 🛒500m 🚲8,8km.
**Remarks:** Along railwayline.

**⊞S  Mortagne-sur-Gironde  21C3**
**Le Port de Mortagne**, Quai des Pêcheurs.
**GPS:** n45,47472 w0,79778.⬆️

50 ⌇€ 9 🚰 🔌Ch 💧WC 📶against payment 📶included.
🚮 **Location:** Rural, simple, isolated, quiet. **Surface:** grassy.
⊡ 01/01-31/12.
**Distance:** 🛒750m ⊗200m 🚲750m 🚴on the spot.
**Remarks:** In front of Capitainerie, max. 24h.

**⊞S  Moulismes  21E2**
RN147. **GPS:** n46,33306 e0,81000.⬆️

53 ⌇€ 8,40-9,60 🚰 🔌€ 4 🔌Ch 🚽€ 4 WC. **Location:** Rural, simple,
isolated, quiet. **Surface:** grassy/metalled.
⊡ 01/01-31/12.

FR

**Distance:** 🛒400m 🏊on the spot 🚰on the spot ⊗100m ☕400m.
**Remarks:** At small lake (plan d'eau).

**Mouthiers-sur-Boëme** 21D3
Chemin de la Chauveterie. **GPS:** n45,55424 e0,12488. ⬆➡.

10 🅿free 🚰🚽Chfree. **Location:** Urban, simple, central, quiet.
**Surface:** grassy/gravel. 📅 01/01-31/12.
**Distance:** 🛒on the spot ⊗on the spot ☕on the spot.
**Remarks:** Behind church.

**Mugron** 27B1
Avenue des Martyrs de la Résistance, D32e.
**GPS:** n43,74846 w0,75063. ⬆➡.

4 🅿free 🚰🚽Ch🛁(4x)free. **Location:** Rural, simple.
**Surface:** gravel. 📅 01/01-31/12.
**Distance:** 🛒300m 🚶on the spot.
**Remarks:** Max. 24h.

**Nailhac** 24E1
Lorserie, D62E3. **GPS:** n45,23276 e1,14214. ⬆➡.

6 🅿free 🚰🚽Chfree 🛁€ 3,50/24h 🚿. **Location:** Rural, simple,
isolated. **Surface:** metalled. 📅 01/01-31/12.
**Distance:** 🛒1,5km ⊗1,1km.

**Nantiat** 21F3
L'Étang des Haches, Route de Chamboret. **GPS:** n46,00484 e1,15332.
25 🅿€ 3,40 🛁€ 2/100liter 🚽Ch🛁€ 2/4h. **Location:** Simple, quiet.
📅 15/06-15/09.
**Distance:** 🛒1km.
**Remarks:** Coins at campsite and town hall.

**Naujan-et-Postiac** 24C2
Lafuge. **GPS:** n44,78715 w0,17928. ⬆➡.

5 🅿free. **Location:** Rural, simple. **Surface:** gravel.
📅 01/01-31/12.
**Distance:** 🛒200m.

**Nérac** 24D3
Place du Foirail. **GPS:** n44,13435 e0,33649. ⬆.

2 🅿free 🚰🚽Chfree. **Location:** Urban, simple. **Surface:** asphalted.
📅 01/01-31/12.
**Distance:** 🛒50m ⊗on the spot ☕on the spot.

**Nersac** 🌊 21D3
Aire municipal, 5 Rue de la Foucaudie. **GPS:** n45,62599 e0,05015. ⬆➡.

7 🅿free 🚰🚽Ch 🛁(4x)free. **Location:** Urban, simple, central, quiet.
**Surface:** asphalted. 📅 01/01-31/12.
**Distance:** 🛒on the spot ⊗100m ☕100m 🚮100m 🚲on the spot.
**Remarks:** Max. 48h, small pitches.

**Nespouls** 24F2
**GPS:** n45,05244 e1,49568. ⬆.

10 🅿free 🚰🚽Chfree. **Location:** Rural, comfortable.
**Surface:** gravel. 📅 01/01-31/12.
**Distance:** 🛒1km 🚲500m ⊗on the spot ☕on the spot.

**Nieuil-l'Espoir** 🌊 21E2
Allée du Champ de Foire. **GPS:** n46,48505 e0,45417. ⬆➡.

10 🅿free 🚰€ 2 🚽Ch🚌€ 2. **Location:** Rural, comfortable, quiet.
**Surface:** grassy/metalled. 📅 01/01-31/12.
**Distance:** 🛒200m 🚲500m ☕200m 🚮on the spot 🚶on the spot.
**Remarks:** At Base de Loisirs, coins at the shops.

**Nieul** 21F3
Place du 19 Mars 1962, D28. **GPS:** n45,92564 e1,17236. ⬆.

20 🅿free 🚰🚽ChWCfree. **Location:** Rural, central, quiet.
**Surface:** grassy/gravel. 📅 01/04-31/10.
**Distance:** 🛒400m 🚲400m ☕400m.
**Remarks:** Max. 72h.

**Nieulle-sur-Seudre** 21B3
Place de la Mairie. **GPS:** n45,75275 w1,00209. ⬆.

4 🅿free 🚰🚽Chfree 🚌€ 2. **Location:** Urban, simple, central, quiet.
**Surface:** asphalted. 📅 01/01-31/12.
**Distance:** 🛒on the spot ⊗250m ☕200m.
**Remarks:** Coins at town hall.

**Niort** 🌊🚲🍽 21C2
Aire des camping-cars du Pré Leroy, Rue de Bessac.
**GPS:** n46,32917 w0,46444. ⬆➡.

16 🅿€ 7,70/24h 🚰🚽Ch🚌included. 🚿
**Location:** Urban, comfortable, quiet. **Surface:** metalled.
📅 01/01-31/12.
**Distance:** 🛒1,2km ⊗150m ☕300m.
**Tourist information Niort:**
🏕 📅 Tue, Sa.
🚤 Marais Poitevin. Swamp area, possibility of making boat trips.

**Nonaville** 21D3
Pont à Brac. **GPS:** n45,52576 w0,09051. ⬆➡.

4 🅿free 🚰€ 2/100liter 🚽Ch🚌€ 2/10minutes 🚿.
**Location:** Rural, simple, quiet. **Surface:** gravel.
📅 01/01-31/12.
**Distance:** 🛒on the spot 🚲500m.

**Objat** 24F1
Parc Aquatique Espace Loisirs, Avenue Jules Ferry/D148E.
**GPS:** n45,27110 e1,41147. ⬆➡.

26 🅿€ 7,75, 01/11-31/03 € 9,75 🚰€ 2/100liter 🚽Ch🚿
included WC🚌€ 2 🚿🚲 **Location:** Rural, comfortable, quiet.
**Surface:** grassy/metalled. 📅 01/01-31/12.
**Distance:** 🛒500m 🚲500m.
**Remarks:** Max. 72h, coins at tourist info, baker on site: Tue-Sa, swimming
pool 200m.

**Ogeu-les-Bains** 27C2
Avenue de Pau. **GPS:** n43,15349 w0,5022.

4 ⌘free 🚐⚡Chfree. **Location:** Urban, simple.
**Surface:** asphalted/gravel. 🗓 01/01-31/12.
**Distance:** ⛽100m ☕500m.
**Remarks:** Max. 48h.

**ⓈⓈ Oloron-Sainte-Marie** 27B2
**Parking Tivoli**, Rue Adoue. **GPS:** n43,18399 w0,60854. ⬆➡.

7 ⌘free 🚐€ 4/55minutes ⚡Ch➕€ 4/55minutes.
**Location:** Urban, simple, comfortable. **Surface:** asphalted.
🗓 01/01-31/12.
**Distance:** ⛽100m ⚓on the spot ⛵on the spot ☕400m 🚌400m.
**Remarks:** Max. 48h, coins at tourist info.

**ⓈⓈ Ondres** 27A1
**P3**, Avenue de la Plage, Ondres-Plage. **GPS:** n43,57611 w1,48611. ⬆.

41 ⌘€ 8, Jul/Aug € 10 🚐⚡Ch🚿WCincluded. 🐕♿
**Surface:** asphalted. 🗓 15/04-01/11.
**Distance:** ⛽3km ⚓on the spot ⛵on the spot ⊗on the spot ☕on the spot 🚲 on the spot.
**Remarks:** Max. 48h.

**ⓈⓈ Oradour-sur-Glane** 21E3
Rue du Stade. **GPS:** n45,93570 e1,02471. ⬆.

30 ⌘free 🚐€ 2/100liter ⚡Ch➕€ 2 WC.
**Location:** Rural, simple, comfortable.
**Surface:** asphalted.
🗓 01/01-31/12 🅿 Service: winter.
**Distance:** ⛽800m ⊗800m ☕800m.
**Remarks:** Coins at tourist info, playground.
**Tourist information Oradour-sur-Glane:**
ℹ Office de Tourisme, Place du Champ de Foire. Martyre town, was attacked by 200 SS-soldiers on 10 June 1944. They assassinated the population. Afterwards the village was burned down. In commemoration a wall was built round the the city after the war. 🎫 free.

**ⓈⓈ Oradour-sur-Vayres** 21E3
Rue Jean Giraudoux. **GPS:** n45,73269 e0,86592. ⬆.

---

10 ⌘free 🚐⚡Chfree. **Location:** Urban, simple. **Surface:** gravel.
🗓 01/01-31/12.
**Distance:** ⛽200m ⊗200m.

**ⓈⓈ Orion** 27B2
**Labarraque**, 223 route de Narp. **GPS:** n43,41350 w0,85217.
9 ⌘€ 10 🚐⚡Ch🚿included,20Amp 📶. **Location:** Rural.
**Surface:** gravel. 🗓 01/01-31/12.
**Distance:** ⛽1km 🚶on the spot.
**Remarks:** Max. 24h, picnic and barbecue place.

**ⓈⓈ Pageas** 🎪 21E3
RN21. **GPS:** n45,67758 e1,00224. ⬆➡.

20 ⌘free 🚐€ 3 ⚡Ch➕€ 3 WC. **Location:** Rural, comfortable.
**Surface:** grassy/gravel. 🗓 01/01-31/12.
**Distance:** ⛽100m ⚓on the spot ⊗on the spot ☕on the spot.
**Remarks:** Near N21, coins at town hall.

**ⓈⓈ Pamproux** 21D2
Rue de la Cueille. **GPS:** n46,39625 w0,05874. ⬆➡.

3 ⌘free 🚐€ 2/20minutes ⚡Ch➕€ 2/20minutes.
**Location:** Rural, simple, quiet. **Surface:** asphalted.
🗓 01/01-31/12.
**Distance:** ⛽100m 🏊5,2km ☕100m.

**ⓈⓈ Parentis-en-Born** 🎪 24B3
**Site du Lac**, Route des Campings. **GPS:** n44,34432 w1,09879. ⬆.

25 ⌘€ 7 🚐⚡Ch🚿(4x)included. **Location:** Comfortable.
**Surface:** gravel. 🗓 01/01-31/12 🅿 Service: winter.
**Distance:** ⛽3km ⚓50m ⊗50m.

**ⓈⓈ Parthenay** 🌿⛺🌲🌾 21D1
**Aire base de loisirs Bois Vert**, Rue de Boisseau 14.
**GPS:** n46,64088 w0,26689. ⬆➡.

---

8 ⌘€ 9-10 🚐⚡Ch🚿included 🗑€ 3 🗑€ 2 📶€ 4/day.
**Location:** Urban. **Surface:** gravel. 🗓 05/04-31/10.
**Distance:** ⛽2,5km ⚓on the spot ⊗nearby ☕2km 🚌100m.
**Remarks:** Along the Thouet river, check in at campsite.
**Tourist information Parthenay:**
🎪 Les Halles. Weekly market in the halls and streets.
🗓 Wed.

**ⓈⓈ Pau** 27C2
**Place de Verdun**, Pont Lalanne. **GPS:** n43,29158 w0,36432. ⬆.

10 ⌘free 🚐. **Location:** Urban, noisy. **Surface:** asphalted.
🗓 01/01-31/12.
**Distance:** ⛽600m ⊗on the spot ☕200m.
**Remarks:** Max. 48h, free shuttle.

**ⓈⓈ Payzac** 24F1
Le Bourg. **GPS:** n45,40008 e1,21950. ⬆➡.

2 ⌘free 🚐⚡Ch➕free. **Location:** Rural, simple, quiet.
**Surface:** asphalted. 🗓 01/01-31/12.
**Distance:** ⛽on the spot ⊗200m ☕200m 🚶on the spot.

**ⓈⓈ Pellegrue** 24D2
**Le Touran**, Rue du Lavoir. **GPS:** n44,74514 e0,07416. ⬆➡.

3 ⌘free 🚐⚡Ch🚿free. **Location:** Urban, simple.
**Surface:** metalled. 🗓 01/01-31/12.
**Distance:** ⛽100m ⊗200m ☕700m.

**ⓈⓈ Pérignac** 21C3
Pla de l'Église. **GPS:** n45,62532 w0,46309. ⬆➡.

10 ⌘free 🚐⚡free. **Location:** Simple, central, quiet.
**Surface:** asphalted. 🗓 01/01-31/12.
**Distance:** ⛽on the spot ⊗on the spot ☕on the spot.
**Remarks:** Behind church.

**ⓈⓈ Périgueux** 🍵 24E1
**Espace des Prés**, Rue des Prés. **GPS:** n45,18770 e0,73081. ⬆➡.

FR

40 ⌷€ 6,50 ⌷⌷Ch included. ⌷⌷ **Location:** Urban, comfortable, central, quiet. **Surface:** asphalted. ⌷ 01/01-31/12 ⌷ water disconnected in winter.
**Distance:** ⌷800m ⌷800m ⌷200m.
**Remarks:** Max. 48h.

| | Pérols-sur-Vézère ⌷⌷ | 21G3 |
|---|---|---|

Le Bourg. **GPS:** n45,58665 e1,98460.⌷

10 ⌷free ⌷€ 5 ⌷Ch. **Location:** Rural, comfortable, quiet. **Surface:** grassy. ⌷ 01/01-31/12.
**Distance:** ⌷50m ⌷on the spot ⌷ on the spot ⌷ on the spot.
**Remarks:** Coins at tourist info.

| | Peyrat-le-Château | 21F3 |
|---|---|---|

Auphelle/D233. **GPS:** n45,80750 e1,84111.⌷⌷

100 ⌷€ 13, 07-07/24-08 € 18 ⌷€ 2,50/100liter ⌷€ 6/4h.
**Location:** Rural, quiet. **Surface:** grassy. ⌷ 12/04-07/11.
**Distance:** ⌷Lac de Vassière 300m.
**Remarks:** In front of campsite, bread-service in summer period.

| | Peyrat-le-Château | 21F3 |
|---|---|---|

**Parking Pré de l'Age. GPS:** n45,81468 e1,77085.
⌷€ 2 ⌷Ch.
**Remarks:** Coins at tourist info and town hall.

**Tourist information Peyrat-le-Château:**
⌷ Office de Tourisme, 1, Rue du Lac, www.peyrat-tourisme.com.
Tourist town close water sports lake, Lac de Vassière, marked cycle and hiking routes. ⌷ Sa-Su 15-17h.

| | Peyrehorade | 27B1 |
|---|---|---|

**Des Gaves**, Route de la Pêcherie. **GPS:** n43,54300 w1,1071.⌷
16 ⌷€ 9 ⌷Ch ⌷€ 2,50 WC ⌷. ⌷ **Location:** Rural, central, quiet. **Surface:** grassy. ⌷ 01/06-30/09.
**Distance:** ⌷150m ⌷on the spot ⌷on the spot ⌷150m ⌷150m ⌷200m.
**Remarks:** Bread-service.

| | Pissos | 24B3 |
|---|---|---|

Place de l'Église. **GPS:** n44,30817 w0,77598.
20 ⌷free.
**Location:** Urban. **Surface:** grassy/gravel. ⌷ 01/01-31/12.
**Distance:** ⌷230m.

| | Pomarez | 27B1 |
|---|---|---|

**Parking des Arènes**, Rue de la Mairie. **GPS:** n43,62853 w0,82895.
5 ⌷free ⌷⌷Ch ⌷ WC. **Location:** Urban, simple, noisy.
**Surface:** asphalted. ⌷ 01/01-31/12.
**Distance:** ⌷on the spot ⌷200m ⌷400m.
**Remarks:** At townhall, max. 72h.

| | Pomerol | 24C2 |
|---|---|---|

Rue de Tropchaud. **GPS:** n44,93192 w0,19951.⌷

---

4 ⌷free ⌷€ 2 ⌷€ 2. **Location:** Rural, simple, quiet.
**Surface:** asphalted. ⌷ 01/01-31/12.

| | Pons ⌷⌷ | 21C3 |
|---|---|---|

Place de l'Europe. **GPS:** n45,58086 w0,5528.⌷

10 ⌷free ⌷WC ⌷. **Location:** Urban, simple, central, noisy.
**Surface:** asphalted. ⌷ 01/01-31/12.
**Distance:** ⌷400m ⌷400m ⌷400m.
**Remarks:** Max. 24h.

| | Pons ⌷⌷ | 21C3 |
|---|---|---|

**Chateau Renaud**, D234E5, Bougneau. **GPS:** n45,60102 w0,5367.⌷

6 ⌷free. **Location:** Rural, simple, isolated. **Surface:** gravel.
⌷ 01/01-31/12.
**Distance:** ⌷on the spot ⌷1km.
**Remarks:** Along river.

| | Pons ⌷⌷ | 21C3 |
|---|---|---|

**Camping municipal Le Paradis**, Avenue du Poitou.
**GPS:** n45,57765 w0,55536.⌷

5 ⌷free ⌷€ 6 ⌷Ch ⌷€ 6/h. **Location:** Urban, simple.
**Surface:** asphalted. ⌷ 01/01-31/12.
**Distance:** ⌷300m.

| | Port-des-Barques | 21B2 |
|---|---|---|

**Pré des Mays**, Avenue des Sports. **GPS:** n45,94722 w1,09.⌷⌷

50 ⌷€ 8/24h ⌷€ 2/10minutes ⌷Ch ⌷€ 2/55minutes ⌷. ⌷ ⌷
**Location:** Rural, simple. **Surface:** grassy/gravel.
⌷ 01/01-31/12.
**Remarks:** In front of stadium.

| | Port-Sainte-Foy-et-Ponchapt | 24D2 |
|---|---|---|

Rue Jacques Jasmin. **GPS:** n44,84210 e0,20915.⌷⌷

---

4 ⌷free ⌷⌷Ch free. **Location:** Urban, simple, central, quiet.
**Surface:** asphalted. ⌷ 01/01-31/12.
**Distance:** ⌷on the spot ⌷600m ⌷600m.
**Remarks:** Along the Dordogne river, service 200m.

| | Prats-de-Carlux | 24F2 |
|---|---|---|

**Les Oies du Périgord Noir**, D47B. **GPS:** n44,89936 e1,31503.⌷

4 ⌷free. **Location:** Rural, simple, isolated, quiet. **Surface:** gravel.
⌷ 01/01-31/12.
**Distance:** ⌷3km ⌷3km ⌷3km.
**Remarks:** Max. 24h.

| | Rébénacq | 27C2 |
|---|---|---|

Chemin de Montés. **GPS:** n43,15690 w0,39733.⌷⌷

4 ⌷free ⌷⌷Ch ⌷free. **Location:** Rural, simple, quiet.
**Surface:** asphalted. ⌷ 01/01-31/12.
**Distance:** ⌷400m ⌷on the spot ⌷on the spot.
**Remarks:** At football ground, max. 48h.

| | Ribérac | 24D1 |
|---|---|---|

**Camping de la Dronne**, Route d'Angouleme, Aux Deux Ponts O.
**GPS:** n45,25704 e0,34255.⌷

10 ⌷free ⌷⌷Ch free. **Location:** Urban, simple. **Surface:** metalled.
⌷ 01/01-31/12 ⌷ water: frost.
**Distance:** ⌷1,3km ⌷50m ⌷900m.

| | Rivedoux-Plage ⌷ | 21B2 |
|---|---|---|

**Campéole Le Platin**, 125, Av Gustave Perreau.
**GPS:** n46,15889 w1,27139.⌷

20 ⌷€ 14-17 ⌷€ 3 ⌷Ch ⌷. **Location:** Urban, simple.
**Surface:** asphalted. ⌷ 01/01-31/12.
**Distance:** ⌷100m ⌷Plage Nord ⌷on the spot ⌷ on the spot.
**Remarks:** Next to campsite Le Platin, to be paid at campsite.

FR

## Rochefort 21B2
Rue de la Fosse aux Mâts. **GPS:** n45,92735 w0,95467. ↑→.

30 ⌃ € 4,10, tourist tax € 1,20/pp ⌐ ⌐ Ch included. ⌐ ⌐ **Location:** Urban, simple. **Surface:** asphalted. ◻ 01/01-31/12.

## Rochefort 21B2
Avenue Marcel Dassault. **GPS:** n45,94661 w0,96002. ↑.

25 ⌃ € 7,20 + € 1,20/pp tourist tax. ⌐ ⌐ **Location:** Urban, simple. **Surface:** asphalted. ◻ 01/01-31/12. **Distance:** ⌂ 1km.

## Rochefort 21B2
**Pont Transbordeur**, Chemin de Charente. **GPS:** n45,91792 w0,96388. ↑.

5 ⌃ free. **Location:** Urban, simple. **Surface:** grassy/gravel. ◻ 01/01-31/12.

## Rochefort 21B2
Rue de la Vieille Forme. **GPS:** n45,94448 w0,95554. ↑.

12 ⌃ € 7,20 + € 1,20/pp tourist tax. ⌐ **Location:** Urban, simple, quiet. **Surface:** gravel. ◻ 01/01-31/12. **Distance:** ⌂ 300m ⌐ 150m. **Remarks:** Near marina.

## Rochefort 21B2
**Port de Plaisance**, Quai Lemoigne de Sérigny. **GPS:** n45,94444 w0,95556. ↑.
⌐ ⌐ Ch free WC ⌐ € 2,50.
◻ 01/01-31/12.
**Tourist information Rochefort:**
👁 Corderie Royale. Old royal rope-walk.
⚓ ◻ Tue, Thu, Sa.

## Romagne 21D2
Rue du Vigneau. **GPS:** n46,26884 e0,30373. ↑→.

6 ⌃ free ⌐ ⌐ Ch WC free. **Location:** Rural, comfortable, quiet. **Surface:** gravel. ◻ 15/03-31/10. **Distance:** ⌂ 250m ⊗ 250m.

## Roquefort 24C3
Allée de Nauton. **GPS:** n44,04754 w0,32255. ↑.

6 ⌃ free ⌐ ⌐ Ch. **Location:** Rural, simple, quiet. **Surface:** grassy/gravel. ◻ 01/01-31/12. **Distance:** ⌂ 1,7km ⌐ 5km. **Remarks:** Next to camping municipal.

## Rouillac 21D3
**Super U**, Rue de Genac. **GPS:** n45,77650 w0,06133. ↑→.

4 ⌃ free ⌐ € 3/100liter ⌐ Ch ⌐ (2x) € 3/24h. **Location:** Urban, simple, central. **Surface:** gravel. ◻ 01/01-31/12. **Distance:** ⌂ 500m ⊗ 500m ⌐ 50m. **Remarks:** Coins available at supermarket.

## Roullet-Saint-Estèphe 21D3
**Aire de camping-car Roullet**, D210. **GPS:** n45,58086 e0,04461. ↑.

20 ⌃ free ⌐ ⌐ Ch free. **Location:** Rural, simple, quiet. **Surface:** asphalted. ◻ 01/01-31/12. **Distance:** ⌂ 300m ⌐ 150m ⌐ 350m.

## Roumazières-Loubert 21E3
**Aire de Détente de Ronmatiéres**, RN141. **GPS:** n45,88275 e0,57287. ↑→.

5 ⌃ free ⌐ ⌐ Ch ⌐ (2x) WC free. **Location:** Urban, simple, noisy. **Surface:** asphalted. ◻ 01/01-31/12. **Distance:** ⌂ 500m ⊗ 100m ⌐ 300m.

## Royan 21B3
**Camping-Car Park Royan**, Rue Bel-air. **GPS:** n45,62834 w1,01204. ↑.

40 ⌃ € 9,60, 01/07-31/08 € 12 + € 1,65/pp tourist tax ⌐ ⌐ Ch ⌐ (40x) ⌐ included. ⌐ ⌐ **Location:** Urban, comfortable, central, quiet. **Surface:** gravel/metalled. ◻ 01/01-31/12. **Distance:** ⌂ 500m ⊗ 500m ⌐ 500m. **Remarks:** Mandatory, one-time fee Pass'Etapes € 4.

## Royère-de-Vassivière 21G3
**Place du Docteur Perraud**, Rue de Vassivière, D3. **GPS:** n45,84012 e1,91122. ↑.

6 ⌃ free ⌐ ⌐ Ch WC free.
**Location:** Rural, simple, central. **Surface:** asphalted. ◻ 01/01-31/12 ◻ Thu>14h (market). **Distance:** ⌂ on the spot ⌐ 300m ⊗ 200m ⌐ on the spot. **Remarks:** Max. 48h.

## Ruffec 21D2
**SARL Remy Frères Camping-Cars**, Route de Montjean. **GPS:** n46,03316 e0,18366.

10 ⌃ free ⌐ ⌐ Ch free. **Location:** Urban, simple, quiet. **Surface:** asphalted. ◻ 01/01-31/12. **Distance:** ⌂ 1km. **Remarks:** At motorhome dealer.

## Sadroc 24F1
1 route de la Forge. **GPS:** n45,28325 e1,54854. ↑→.

6 ⌃ free ⌐ ⌐ Ch ⌐ free. **Location:** Urban, simple, central, quiet. **Surface:** asphalted. ◻ 01/01-31/12. **Distance:** ⌂ on the spot ⌐ 5,2km ⌐ 50m. **Remarks:** Max. 24h.

## Saint-Agnant 21B3
Place de Verdun. **GPS:** n45,86635 w0,9641. ↑.

10 ⌃ free ⌐ free. **Location:** Rural, simple. **Surface:** asphalted.

�***□*** 01/01-31/12.
**Distance:** ⊗1km.
**Remarks:** Next to town hall.

**⛽S** **Saint-Amand-sur-Sèvre** 🍴🌲 **21C1**
Boulevard de Maumusson. **GPS:** n46,86903 w0,8.⬆.

5 🍴free ⛽🔌Chfree. **Location:** Rural, simple, isolated, quiet.
**Surface:** grasstiles. □ 01/01-31/12.
**Distance:** 500m ⊗500m 🍷500m.

**🍴S** **Saint-Amand-sur-Sèvre** 🍴🌲 **21C1**
Le Moulin Chaligny. **GPS:** n46,88493 w0,82342.⬆.

10 🍴€ 10 ⛽🔌Ch 🔧WCincluded. **Location:** Rural, isolated, quiet.
**Surface:** grassy. □ 01/01-31/12.
**Distance:** 3km ⊗3km 🍷3km 🛁on the spot 🎣on the spot.
**Remarks:** Fruit-vegetables-wine-regional products for sale.

**⛽S** **Saint-Antoine-Cumond** **24D1**
Salle de Fête, Le Bourg, D43. **GPS:** n45,25537 e0,19988.⬆⬆.

10 🍴free ⛽🔌ChWCfree. **Location:** Rural, simple, quiet.
**Surface:** asphalted/gravel. □ 01/01-31/12.
**Distance:** 🍷on the spot ⊗on the spot 🍞bakery 100m.

**⛽S** **Saint-Antoine-de-Breuilh** **24D2**
Camping-Car Park, D936, Avenguda del Péirigord 89.
**GPS:** n44,84516 e0,15847.⬆➡.

26 🍴€ 8,84 ⛽🔌Ch 🔧(24x) 📶included. 🛏 📖 **Location:** Rural,
comfortable, quiet. **Surface:** concrete. □ 01/01-31/12.
**Distance:** 200m ⊗200m 🍷300m 🚌500m 🛁on the spot
🎣on the spot.
**Remarks:** Mandatory, one-time fee Pass'Etapes € 4.

**⛽S** **Saint-Avit-Sénieur** **24E2**
La Borie Neuve. **GPS:** n44,78417 e0,80486.
3 🍴€ 10 ⛽€ 5 🔧📶. **Location:** Rural. **Surface:** grassy.
□ 01/02-30/11.

**⛽S** **Saint-Caprais-de-Blaye** **24C1**
Aire de camping-car de Ferchaud, 169 Les Fermenteaux.
**GPS:** n45,29120 w0,5692.⬆➡.

8 🍴€ 7/24h ⛽🔌ChWCincluded. 🛏 **Location:** Rural, simple,
noisy. **Surface:** asphalted. □ 01/01-31/12.
**Distance:** 500m 🚲6,4km 🍷50m 🛁on the spot.
**Remarks:** Tourist information and picnic tables available.

**⛽S** **Saint-Césaire** 🏛🍴 **21C3**
Parking Paléosite, Rue de Groies. **GPS:** n45,75406 w0,50751.⬆➡.

20 🍴free ⛽🔌Chfree. **Location:** Rural, simple, isolated, quiet.
**Surface:** asphalted/metalled. □ 01/01-31/12.
**Distance:** 🍷on the spot ⊗500m 🛁100m 🚴on the spot.

**Tourist information Saint-Césaire:**
Paléosite, Route de la Montée Verte. Interactive park, in the foot-
steps of the Neanderthals. □ 10.30-18.30, Jul-Aug 10-20 ◐ January.

**⛽S** **Saint-Clément-des-Baleines** 🌿 **21B2**
Rue de la Forêt. **GPS:** n46,22756 w1,54644.⬆.

30 🍴€ 12,50/night ⛽🔌Ch 🔧included. 🛏 **Location:** Rural,
simple. **Surface:** grassy. □ 01/01-31/12.
**Distance:** 🏖250m 🍷500m 🚴on the spot 🎣on the spot.
**Remarks:** Next to campsite, payment only with coins.

**⛽S** **Saint-Cyprien** 🌿⛵ **24E2**
Parking de Carrefour Market, Place Mackenheim, Rue du Priolat.
**GPS:** n44,86828 e1,04435.⬆➡.

8 🍴€ 7 ⛽🔌Ch 🔧included. **Location:** Simple. **Surface:** asphalted.
□ 01/01-31/12.
**Distance:** 🍷50m 🍞bakery 50m, supermarket 100m.
**Remarks:** Max. 24h.

**Tourist information Saint-Cyprien:**
⊗ Marché repas gourmand. □ summer Thu-evening.

**⛽S** **Saint-Cyr** **21E1**
Camping-Car Park, Rue de la Bourdillière.
**GPS:** n46,72194 e0,45601.⬆.

36 🍴€ 9,90, 01/07-31/08 € 12,50 ⛽🔌Ch 🔧(36x) 📶included.
🛏 **Location:** Rural, comfortable, quiet. **Surface:** grassy.
□ 01/01-31/12.
**Distance:** 2km ⊗2km 🍷2km.
**Remarks:** Mandatory, one-time fee Pass'Etapes € 4.

**⛽S** **Saint-Denis-d'Oléron** **21B2**
Aire du Moulin, Route des Huttes. **GPS:** n46,02750 w1,38306.⬆.

170 🍴€ 12/24h ⛽🔌Ch 🔧WC included. 🛏 📖 **Location:** Rural,
simple. **Surface:** grassy. □ 01/01-31/12.
**Distance:** 1km.
**Remarks:** Max. 4 nights.

**⛽S** **Saint-Dizant-du-Gua** **24C1**
Les berges du Taillon, 6 Rue du Pérat. **GPS:** n45,43062 w0,707.⬆.

25 🍴free ⛽€ 2/100liter 🔌Ch 🔌€ 2/2h 📶free.
**Location:** Rural, simple, quiet. **Surface:** grassy.
□ 01/01-31/12.
**Distance:** 200m ⊗on the spot 🍷on the spot 🚴on the spot
🎣on the spot.
**Remarks:** Wifi code at shop.

**⛽S** **Saint-Estèphe** 🌿 **24C1**
Rue du Littoral. **GPS:** n45,26544 w0,7582.⬆.

10 🍴free ⛽🔌ChService € 5.
**Location:** Rural, simple, quiet. **Surface:** gravel/metalled.
□ 01/01-31/12.
**Distance:** 2km 🏖on the spot 🚶on the spot ⊗50m 🚴on the spot.
**Remarks:** Free, coins available at restaurant.

**⛽S** **Saint-Estèphe (24)** 🌿 **21E3**
Etang de Saint Estèphe, Route du Grand Etang.
**GPS:** n45,59458 e0,67437.⬆➡.

10 🛏 € 5 🚰 🅦 Ch included. 🛁 **Location:** Rural, comfortable.
**Surface:** forest soil. 🅾 01/01-31/12.
**Distance:** 🚶700m ⚓lake 🚣on the spot ⊗on the spot 🛒3km,
bakery 800m.
**Remarks:** Max. 48h, summer: beach, bar, restaurant.

### Saint-Front-la-Rivière — 24E1

Chez Boutau, D83. **GPS:** n45,46645 e0,72419. ⬆️.

10 🛏 free 🚰 🅦 Ch 🚿(2x)free. **Location:** Rural, comfortable,
isolated, quiet. **Surface:** metalled. 🅾 01/01-31/12.
**Remarks:** Max. 72h, picnic area.

### Saint-Genis-de-Saintonge — 21C3

Rue Fanny. **GPS:** n45,48330 w0,56569. ⬆️➡️.

20 🛏 € 7/24h 🚶10minutes 🅦Ch included. 🚿(20x)€ 3/24h. 🅿️
**Location:** Urban, comfortable, central, quiet. **Surface:** asphalted.
🅾 01/01-31/12.
**Distance:** 🚶400m ⊗on the spot 🛒on the spot.
**Remarks:** Behind cinema, max. 72h.

### Saint-Georges-de-Didonne — 21B3

**Parking Maudet**, Rue du Docteur Maudet.
**GPS:** n45,60408 w0,99964. ⬆️.

19 🛏 € 8/24h 🚰 🅦Ch included. 🅿️🗑 
**Location:** Urban, simple, central, quiet. **Surface:** asphalted.
🅾 01/01-31/12.
**Distance:** 🚶400m ⚓500m.
**Remarks:** Max. 72h.

### Saint-Georges-de-Didonne — 21B3

**Front de Mer**, Boulevard de la Côte de Beauté.
**GPS:** n45,59557 w0,99163. ⬆️.

20 🛏 € 8/24h. 🅿️🗑 **Location:** Urban, simple, quiet.
**Surface:** gravel/metalled. 🅾 01/01-31/12.
**Distance:** 🚶500m ⚓on the spot ⊗350m 🏊on the spot.
**Remarks:** Beach parking, max. 72h.

### Saint-Georges-de-Didonne — 21B3

**Parking Gillet**, Rue du Professeur Langevin.
**GPS:** n45,60324 w0,9921. ⬆️.

---

13 🛏 € 8/24h. 🅿️ **Location:** Urban, simple, central, quiet.
**Surface:** asphalted. 🅾 01/01-31/12.
**Distance:** 🚶on the spot ⚓800m ⊗on the spot 🛒on the spot.
**Remarks:** Max. 72h.

### Saint-Georges-de-Didonne 🏖 — 21B3

**Parking Miramar**, Rue du Port. **GPS:** n45,60031 w1,007. ⬆️.

18 🛏 € 8/24h. 🅿️ **Location:** Urban. **Surface:** gravel/metalled.
🅾 01/01-31/12.
**Distance:** 🚶1km ⚓100m 🚣on the spot ⊗200m 🛒1km.
**Remarks:** Max. 72h.

### Saint-Georges-Nigremont — 21G3

Le Bourg. **GPS:** n45,83649 e2,26448.
5 🛏 free 🚰 🅦Ch free. **Location:** Rural. 🅾 01/01-31/12.
**Distance:** ⊗650m.

### Saint-Germain-de-Marencennes — 21C2

Rue du Moulin Neuf. **GPS:** n46,07882 w0,78283. ⬆️.

10 🛏 € 7, 2 pers.incl 🚰 🅦Ch 🚽WC included. 🅿️ **Location:** Rural,
simple, quiet. **Surface:** asphalted. 🅾 01/01-31/12 ⚫ service 01/11-
31/03.
**Distance:** 🚶500m ⊗350m.

### Saint-Germain-et-Mons — 24E2

D21. **GPS:** n44,84795 e0,59294. ⬆️.

20 🛏 € 8 🚰 🅦Ch 🔌6Amp 🚿 🅿️ **Surface:** gravel.
🅾 01/01-31/12.
**Remarks:** Max. 72h.

### Saint-Gor — 27C1

Route de St Justin. **GPS:** n44,04370 w0,24218.
4 🛏 € 7 🚰 🚿 🚿 🅾 01/01-31/12.

### Saint-Hilaire-de-Lusignan — 24D3

D813. **GPS:** n44,22491 e0,51364. ⬆️.

---

3 🛏 free 🚰 € 3/10minutes 🅦Ch. **Location:** Rural, simple, noisy.
**Surface:** gravel. 🅾 01/01-31/12.
**Distance:** 🚶on the spot ⊗1km 🛒5km, bakery 500m.

### Saint-Hilaire-la-Palud — 21C2

Place de la Marie. **GPS:** n46,26444 w0,71306. ⬆️.

10 🛏 free. **Location:** Urban, simple, central. **Surface:** asphalted.
🅾 01/01-31/12.
**Distance:** 🚶on the spot ⊗500m 🛒500m.
**Remarks:** Parking in front of town hall, max. 2 nights.

### Saint-Jean-d'Angély — 21C3

**Aire de Boutonne**, Avenue de Marennes, D18.
**GPS:** n45,94537 w0,53735. ⬆️.

28 🛏 € 7/24h 🚰 🅦ChWC included. 🅿️🗑 **Surface:** gravel.
🅾 01/01-31/12.
**Distance:** 🚶1km ⚓100m 🚣100m ⊗200m 🛒1km 🚶on the spot.
**Remarks:** Max. 2 nights.

### Saint-Jean-de-Côle — 24E1

Le Bourg. **GPS:** n45,41984 e0,84048. ⬆️.

3 🛏 free 🚰 € 2 🅦Ch 🔌€ 2. **Location:** Rural, simple, quiet.
**Surface:** metalled. 🅾 01/01-31/12.
**Distance:** 🚶on the spot ⊗200m 🛒300m 🚌200m.
**Remarks:** At tennis-court, coins at tourist info.

### Saint-Jean-de-Luz — 27A2

Avenue Geneviève Antonios de Gaulle, D810.
**GPS:** n43,38527 w1,6629. ⬆️➡️.

17 🛏 € 4, 01/04-31/10 € 6 🚰 € 2/100liter 🅦 Ch 🔌€ 2/1h.
**Surface:** asphalted. 🅾 01/01-31/12.
**Distance:** 🚶200m 🚲2,2km ⚓300m 🚣300m ⊗100m 🛒100m.
**Remarks:** Max. 48h.

FR

**Tourist information Saint-Jean-de-Luz:**

ℹ️ Office de Tourisme, Place du Maréchal Foch, www.saint-jean-de-luz.com. Tourist town with beautiful shops. The local speciality is chipirones, octopus cooked in its own ink.

🏛️ Halles, Bd Victor Hugo. ⏰ morning.

**Saint-Jean-Pied-de-Port** 🟩 27A2

**Aire de camping-cars du fronton**, Chemin Chemin d'Olhonce. **GPS**: n43,15753 w1,23419.
50 🏕️ € 9 🔌 💧. **Location**: Rural. **Surface**: grassy/sand.
⏰ 31/03-01/11.
**Distance**: ⊗800m.

**Saint-Jean-Pied-de-Port** 🟩 27A2

**Parking du Jaï Alaï**, 5 Chemin de la Nasse.
**GPS**: n43,16519 w1,23208. ⬆️.

50 🏕️ € 7 🔌 💧Ch 🚿 included WC 🚽. 
**Location**: Urban, central. **Surface**: metalled.
⏰ 01/01-31/12.
**Distance**: ⏺350m ⛱️350m 🛒350m ⊗350m 🍴350m 🚶 on the spot.
**Remarks**: Nearby stadium, max. 48h.

**Tourist information Saint-Jean-Pied-de-Port:**

ℹ️ Office de Tourisme, 14, Place Charles de Gaulle, www.pyrenees-basques.com. Fortified city on the foot of the Roncesvallespass on the road to Santiago de Compostela.

🟩 Forêt d'Iraty. Nature reserve, hiking trails available at OT.

**Saint-Julien-le-Petit** 21F3

**Aire naturelle de camping**, Route de la Plage.
**GPS**: n45,82142 e1,70531. ⬆️.

12 🏕️ € 5, 2 pers.incl 🔌 💧Ch 🚿 WC 🚽. **Location**: Rural, quiet.
**Surface**: grassy. ⏰ 01/01-31/12.
**Distance**: 🚲 on the spot 🚶 on the spot.

**Saint-Junien-la-Bregère** 21F3

Rue du Chevalier de Châteauneuf. **GPS**: n45,88236 e1,75282. ⬆️.

3 🏕️free 🔌 💧Chfree. **Location**: Rural, quiet. **Surface**: asphalted.
⏰ 01/01-31/12.
**Distance**: ⏺500m on the spot 🚶 on the spot.

**Saint-Laurent** 21G2

Rue des Cerisiers, D4. **GPS**: n46,16639 e1,96167. ⬆️.

4 🏕️free 🔌 💧Ch 🚿free. **Location**: Rural, quiet. **Surface**: metalled.
⏰ 01/01-31/12.

---

**Distance**: ⏺on the spot ⊗on the spot.
**Remarks**: Behind church.

**Saint-Laurent-de-la-Prée** 21B2

**La Cabane**, Route de l'Océan. **GPS**: n45,99043 w1,04942. ⬆️.

10 🏕️€ 6 🔌 💧Chincluded. 🚽 **Location**: Rural, simple.
**Surface**: gravel. ⏰ 01/01-31/12.

**Saint-Laurent-Médoc** 24B1

Place du 8 mai 1945. **GPS**: n45,14903 w0,8215. ⬆️.

6 🏕️free 🔌 💧Ch 🚿. **Location**: Urban, simple.
**Surface**: gravel/metalled. ⏰ 01/01-31/12.
**Distance**: ⏺on the spot ⊗300m 🍴300m.

**Saint-Laurent-sur-Gorre** 21E3

**Les Chênes**, Allée des Primevères. **GPS**: n45,76528 e0,95639. ⬆️➡️.

20 🏕️€ 6 🔌 💧€ 2/100liter 💧Ch 🚿(7x)€ 2/4h WC 🚽 included.
**Location**: Rural, comfortable, quiet. **Surface**: grassy.
⏰ 01/01-31/12.
**Distance**: ⏺500m ⛱️on the spot 🛒on the spot ⊗300m 🍴300m.
**Remarks**: Shady.

**Saint-Leon-sur-l'Isle** 24D1

**Skate Park Bord de l'Isle**, D41E2. **GPS**: n45,12002 e0,49628.

6 🏕️free. **Location**: Rural, simple. **Surface**: metalled/sand.
⏰ 01/01-31/12.
**Distance**: ⏺2km 🚴5,3km 🛒on the spot ⊗2km 🍴2km.
**Remarks**: Service in village 750m, n45.11515 o0.5003400.

**Saint-Léon-sur-Vézère** 🟩 24E2

Le Bourg, C201. **GPS**: n45,01230 e1,08978. ⬆️.

15 🏕️€ 6 🔌 💧€ 2 WC. 🚽 **Location**: Rural, simple, isolated, quiet.
**Surface**: grassy/gravel. ⏰ 01/01-31/12.
**Distance**: ⏺100m ⊗200m 🍴150m.

---

**Remarks**: Coins at tourist info.

**Saint-Lon-les-Mines** 27B1

D6. **GPS**: n43,61458 w1,12617.
10 🏕️free 🔌 💧ChWC. **Surface**: grassy. ⏰ 01/01-31/12.
**Distance**: ⊗200m 🍴200m.
**Remarks**: Max. 48h, picnic tables available.

**Saint-Martin-de-Ré** 21B2

Rue de Rempart. **GPS**: n46,19925 w1,36514. ⬆️➡️.

17 🏕️€ 11 🔌 💧Chincluded. 🚽 **Location**: Rural. **Surface**: gravel.
⏰ 01/01-31/12.
**Distance**: ⏺500m ⛱️700m ⊗500m 🍴500m.
**Remarks**: 01/04-30/09 max. 72h.

**Saint-Mathieu** 🍴 21E3

Les Champs, D699. **GPS**: n45,71465 e0,78720. ⬆️➡️.

15 🏕️free 🔌 💧€ 2/100liter 💧Ch. **Location**: Rural, simple, quiet.
**Surface**: asphalted. ⏰ 01/01-31/12.
**Distance**: ⏺2km ⛱️on the spot ⊗on the spot.
**Remarks**: Nearby camp site.

**Saint-Médard-de-Guizières** 24D2

Place du 14 Juillet. **GPS**: n45,01526 w0,0579. ⬆️.

3 🏕️free 🔌 💧ChWCfree. **Location**: Urban, simple, central.
**Surface**: asphalted. ⏰ 01/01-31/12.
**Distance**: ⏺on the spot ⊗200m 🍴300m.

**Saint-Merd-les-Oussines** 21G3

D109. **GPS**: n45,63500 e2,03719. ⬆️➡️.

6 🏕️free 🔌 💧€ 2 💧Ch. **Location**: Rural, simple, isolated, quiet.
**Surface**: grassy/gravel. ⏰ 01/01-31/12.
**Distance**: ⏺400m 🍴400m.
**Remarks**: Coins at Auberge du Mont-Chauvet.

**Saint-Michel-de-Double** 24D1

D13. **GPS**: n45,08001 e0,28945.

6 ⌹free ⌁⌁Ch. **Location:** Rural, simple, isolated, quiet.
**Surface:** asphalted. ⬛ 01/01-31/12.
**Distance:** ⌁on the spot ⊗200m.

### Saint-Palais-sur-Mer 27B2

**Parking Place Ste. Elisabeth**, Rue Gaztelu Zena.
**GPS:** n43,32944 w1,0325. ⬆.

10 ⌹free ⌁⌁ChWCfree. **Location:** Simple, quiet.
**Surface:** asphalted. ⬛ 01/01-31/12.
**Distance:** ⌁200m ⊗250m ⌁250m.

### Saint-Pardoux 21C1

Place des Tulipiers. **GPS:** n46,57260 w0,3054. ⬆⮕.

5 ⌹free. **Location:** Urban, simple, quiet. **Surface:** asphalted.
⬛ 01/01-31/12.
**Distance:** ⌁50m ⌁200m.

### Saint-Paul-lès-Dax 27B1

Allée Salvador Allende. **GPS:** n43,73460 w1,07865. ⬆⮕.

7 ⌹free ⌁⌁Chfree. **Location:** Rural, simple, quiet.
**Surface:** gravel/sand. ⬛ 01/01-31/12.
**Distance:** ⌁1km ⌁500m ⌁500m ⌁2km.
**Remarks:** Max. 72h, shady.

### Saint-Pée-sur-Nivelle 27A2

**Flot bleu park St. Pée sur Nivelle**, Promenade du Parlement de
Navarre. **GPS:** n43,34945 w1,5215. ⬆⮕.

50 ⌹€ 18,50/24h ⌁€ 2,50/120liter ⌁Ch ⌁€ 2,50/4h. ⌁
**Location:** Comfortable, quiet. **Surface:** asphalted. ⬛ 01/01-31/12.
**Distance:** ⌁3km ⌁on the spot ⊗500m Restaurant Aintzira Le Lac
⌁on the spot.
**Remarks:** Parking at lake, max. 48h, bread-service.

### Saint-Pey-d'Armens 24C2

**Château Gerbaud**, 4 Gerbaud. **GPS:** n44,85310 w0,10699. ⬆.

40 ⌹€ 5 ⌁⌁Chincluded ⌁(8x)€ 3. **Location:** Rural, simple.
**Surface:** grassy. ⬛ 01/01-31/12.
**Distance:** ⊗1km ⌁bakery 1km, supermarket 2km.
**Remarks:** Max. 48h, vineyard.

### Saint-Pierre-d'Oléron 21B2

**La Faucheprère**, Avenue des Pins, La Cotinière.
**GPS:** n45,92393 w1,3427. ⬆.

8 ⌹€ 9 ⌁€ 4 ⌁Ch ⌁€ 4. **Location:** Rural, simple.
**Surface:** grassy/gravel. ⬛ 01/01-31/12.
**Remarks:** In front of campsite municipal, pay at reception.

### Saint-Porchaire 21C3

Place du Champ de Foire. **GPS:** n45,82063 w0,78215. ⬆.

10 ⌹free ⌁⌁ChWCfree. **Location:** Urban, simple, central, quiet.
**Surface:** gravel. ⬛ 01/01-31/12.
**Distance:** ⌁400m ⊗200m ⌁1km.
**Remarks:** Max. 48h.

### Saint-Privat 24G1

Rue des Chanaux. **GPS:** n45,14037 e2,09765. ⬆.

10 ⌹free ⌁€ 2 ⌁Ch⌁€ 2. **Location:** Urban, simple, central, quiet.
**Surface:** grassy/metalled. ⬛ 01/01-31/12.
**Distance:** ⌁200m ⊗200m ⌁200m.

### Saint-Quentin-sur-Charente 21E3

**Barrage du Lavaud**, Lieu-dit Versennes, D214.
**GPS:** n45,82714 e0,68813. ⬆⮕.

15 ⌹free ⌁⌁Ch ⌁(4x)WCfree. **Location:** Rural, comfortable,
isolated, quiet. **Surface:** gravel. ⬛ 01/01-31/12 ⬛ service: 01/10-
30/04.

**Distance:** ⌁4km ⌁no swimming ⊗4km ⌁4km ⌁on the spot
⌁on the spot.
**Remarks:** Max. 3 days.

### Saint-Romain-la-Virvée 24C2

Rue des Milonis. **GPS:** n44,96449 w0,40139. ⮕.

8 ⌹free ⌁⌁Chfree. **Location:** Rural, comfortable, isolated, quiet.
**Surface:** asphalted. ⬛ 01/01-31/12.
**Distance:** ⌁on the spot ⌁10km ⊗250m ⌁1km.
**Remarks:** Next to sports fields.

### Saint-Saud-Lacoussière 21E3

**Étang de la Gourgousse**, Route du Grand Etang.
**GPS:** n45,55780 e0,82237. ⬆.

4 ⌹free. **Location:** Rural, isolated, quiet. **Surface:** forest soil.
⬛ 01/01-31/12.
**Distance:** ⌁Sandy beach ⌁on the spot ⌁on the spot.
**Remarks:** Max. 72h.

### Saint-Saud-Lacoussière 21E3

**Domaine Sous Chardonnièras**, 4, Impasse Sous Chardonnièras.
**GPS:** n45,54053 e0,81909. ⬆.

4 ⌹€ 12,50 ⌁⌁ ⌁WC⌁included. ⌁ **Location:** Rural, simple,
quiet. **Surface:** grassy. ⬛ 01/01-31/12.
**Distance:** ⌁500m ⌁2km ⌁2km ⊗500m ⌁500m.

### Saint-Sauveur 24E2

Le Bourg, D21. **GPS:** n44,86850 e0,58834. ⬆⮕.

3 ⌹free ⌁⌁ChWCfree. **Location:** Simple. **Surface:** asphalted.
⬛ 01/01-31/12 ⬛ service 01/11-31/03.
**Distance:** ⌁100m ⊗100m ⌁100m.

### Saint-Savin 24C1

**Aire de Civrac-de-Blaye**, Parc de la Mairie, D36, Civrac-de-Blaye.
**GPS:** n45,11222 w0,44444. ⬆.

FR

1⃣free 🚰🔧Ch WC free. **Location:** Rural, isolated, quiet.
**Surface:** grassy. 📅 01/01-31/12.
**Distance:** 🚰50m ⊗160m 🛒100m.

**Saint-Savin** 24C1

**Aire de St.Girons d'Aiguevives**, St.Girons d'Aiguevives.
**GPS:** n45,13972 w0,5425.

2⃣free 🚰. **Location:** Simple, isolated. **Surface:** grassy/gravel.
📅 01/01-31/12.
**Distance:** 🚰on the spot ⊗4km 🛒10km.
**Remarks:** Parking in front of church.

**Saint-Savin** 24C1

**Aire des Lacs du Moulin Blanc**, St.Christoly-de-Blaye.
**GPS:** n45,15167 w0,47583.

2⃣free 🚰WC free. **Location:** Simple, quiet. **Surface:** gravel.
📅 01/01-31/12.
**Distance:** 🚰800m ⊿50m 🚰on the spot ⊗on the spot 🛒3km.
**Remarks:** Parking at lake.

**Saint-Savin** 24C1

**Aire des Lagunes**, St.Mariens. **GPS:** n45,11790 w0,40243.

2⃣free 🚰WC free. **Surface:** asphalted. 📅 01/01-31/12.
**Distance:** 🚰on the spot ⊿6km 🚰6km ⊗2km 🛒3km.

**Saint-Savin** 24C1

**Parking Centre Culturel. GPS:** n45,13800 w0,4465.

2⃣free WC. **Location:** Simple, central. **Surface:** gravel.
📅 01/01-31/12.
**Distance:** 🚰on the spot ⊿3km 🚰3km ⊗150m 🛒800m, bakery
50m.
**Remarks:** Max. 48h.

**Saint-Savin** 24C1

**Aire de l'Église**, Générac. **GPS:** n45,18055 w0,54862. ⬆️➡️

2⃣free. **Location:** Rural, simple, quiet. **Surface:** asphalted.
📅 01/01-31/12.
**Distance:** 🚰on the spot ⊗6km 🛒10km.

**Saint-Savin** 24C1

**Aire de Marcenais**, Marcenais. **GPS:** n45,05808 w0,33889.

2⃣free. **Location:** Rural, simple, quiet. **Surface:** gravel.
📅 01/01-31/12.
**Distance:** 🚰on the spot ⊗6km 🛒6km.
**Remarks:** Next to community centre.

**Saint-Savin** 24C1

**Aire de Saugon**, Saugon. **GPS:** n45,17778 w0,50428. ⬆️➡️

2⃣free. **Location:** Urban, simple, central, quiet.
📅 01/01-31/12.
**Distance:** 🚰on the spot ⊿6km 🚰6km ⊗3km 🛒6km.
**Remarks:** Behind town hall.

**Saint-Savin** 24C1

**Aire de St. Vivien**, RN137, St.Vivien-de-Blay. **GPS:** n45,09917 w0,51666.

2⃣free. **Location:** Rural, simple. **Surface:** gravel.
📅 01/01-31/12.
**Distance:** 🚰on the spot ⊿3km 🚰3km ⊗3km 🛒3km.
**Remarks:** Parking at church.

**Saint-Savin** 24C1

**Aire du Dojo**, Cézac. **GPS:** n45,09100 w0,42009.

1⃣free. **Location:** Urban, central, quiet. **Surface:** metalled.
📅 01/01-31/12.
**Distance:** 🚰on the spot ⊿6km 🚰6km ⊗3km 🛒3km.
**Remarks:** Nearby town hall.

**Saint-Savin** 24C1

**Aire Maison de la Forêt**, Donnezac. **GPS:** n45,24879 w0,44317.

2⃣free. **Location:** Rural, simple, quiet. **Surface:** grassy/gravel.
📅 01/01-31/12.
**Distance:** 🚰on the spot ⊗6km 🛒6km.
**Remarks:** Next to community centre.

**Saint-Savin** 24C1

**Parking communal Aire de Cavignac**, Rue de Paix, Cavignac.
**GPS:** n45,10019 w0,39192. ⬆️.

2⃣free. **Location:** Urban, central, quiet. **Surface:** asphalted.
📅 01/01-31/12.
**Distance:** 🚰on the spot 🚰8km ⊗50m 🛒300m.

**Saint-Savin** 24C1

**Parking communal Aire de Saint Yzan**, Parking de la Gare, St.Yzan-de-
Soudiac. **GPS:** n45,14006 w0,40996. ⬆️.
2⃣free.
**Location:** Urban, simple, central, quiet. 📅 01/01-31/12.
**Distance:** 🚰on the spot ⊿12km 🚰800m ⊗3km 🛒3km 🚌on the
spot.

**Saint-Savin** 24C1

**Parking de Marsas**, Rue Chaignaud, Marsas.
**GPS:** n45,06770 w0,3849. ⬆️.

5⃣free. **Location:** Urban, simple, quiet. **Surface:** asphalted.
📅 01/01-31/12.
**Distance:** 🚰on the spot ⊗4km 🛒4km.

**Saint-Savin** 24C1

**Parking Maison des Jeunes**, Cubnezais.
**GPS:** n45,07500 w0,40861. ⬆️➡️.

2⃣free. **Location:** Urban, simple, central. **Surface:** asphalted.
📅 01/01-31/12.
**Distance:** 🚰50m ⊗3km 🛒3km.

**Saint-Séverin** 24D1

Rue de la Pavancelle. **GPS:** n45,31269 e0,25527. ⬆️➡️.

**FR**

2 🛏free 🚰🗑Ch ♨WCfree. **Location:** Rural, simple, central.
**Surface:** asphalted. 🅟 01/01-31/12.
**Distance:** 🚶200m ⊗200m 🛒 Spar 100m.
**Remarks:** Max. 7m.

### 🅢 Saint-Sorlin-de-Conac 🛗 24C1
Pôle Nature de Vitrezay. **GPS:** n45,32780 w0,71053. 🔼.

20 🛏free. **Location:** Rural, simple, isolated, quiet. **Surface:** grassy.
🅟 01/01-31/12.
**Distance:** 🚶6km ⊗400m.
**Remarks:** Nature reserve.

### 🅢 Saint-Sulpice-le-Guérétois 21G2
Le Masgerot. **GPS:** n46,18265 e1,84714. 🔼.

16 🛏free 🚰€ 3/100liter 🗑Ch📶. **Location:** Isolated, noisy.
**Surface:** asphalted. 🅟 01/01-31/12.
**Distance:** 🛢on the spot ⊗on the spot.
**Remarks:** Next to petrol station.

### 🅢 Saint-Sylvestre-sur-Lot 24E3
Place du Lot, Avenue Jean Moulin. **GPS:** n44,39621 e0,80499. 🔼➡.

12 🛏free 🚰🗑Chfree. **Location:** Urban, simple, quiet.
**Surface:** asphalted. 🅟 01/01-31/12.
**Distance:** 🚶150m, Penne d'Agenais centre 1,8km 🏊on the spot
⊗100m 🛒50m 🍴on the spot.
**Remarks:** Max. 24h, service 100m.

### 🅢 Saint-Trojan-les-Bains 21B3
**Parking de la Liberté**, Rue Marie Curie. **GPS:** n45,84371 w1,20899. 🔼.

9 🛏free 🚰€ 4. **Location:** Urban, simple. **Surface:** asphalted.
🅟 01/01-31/12.
**Distance:** 🚶200m ⊗on the spot 🍴on the spot.
**Remarks:** Max. 72h.

---

### 🅢 Saint-Trojan-les-Bains 21B3
**Parking Patoizeau**, 26 Boulevard de la plage.
**GPS:** n45,84100 w1,20491.

10 🛏free. **Location:** Rural, simple. **Surface:** asphalted.
🅟 01/01-31/12.
**Distance:** 🚶600m 🏊100m.
**Remarks:** In front of fire-station, max. 72h.

**Tourist information Saint-Trojan-les-Bains:**
ℹ Bureau Municipal de Tourisme, Carrefour du Port, www.st-trojan-les-bains.fr. Seaside resort on the island of Oléron, well-known for the mimosa and oyster culture.
🍴 place de Filles de la Sagesse. Food and drugs market.
🅟 Thu + Sa-morning, summer daily.
🍴 Marche Nocturne, rue de la République. Evening market.
🅟 Thu from 17h.

### 🍴🅢 Saint-Vincent-de-Cosse 24E2
**Ferme d'Enveaux. GPS:** n44,82669 e1,09822. 🔼➡.

50 🛏guests free 🚰🗑Chfree. **Surface:** unpaved.
🅟 01/01-31/12.
**Distance:** 🏊pebbled beach 50m 🚲on the spot ⊗on the spot
🍴on the spot.
**Remarks:** Along the Dordogne river, max. 48h, key service at canoe rental.

### 🅢 Saint-Vincent-Jalmoutiers 24D1
Le Bourg. **GPS:** n45,20055 e0,19091. 🔼➡.

25 🛏free 🚰🗑ChWCfree. **Location:** Rural, simple, isolated, quiet.
**Surface:** grassy. 🅟 01/01-31/12.
**Distance:** 🚶350m 🛒350m.

### 🅢 Saint-Ybard 24F1
**Foyer Rural**, Rue des Fontaines. **GPS:** n45,44886 e1,52271. 🔼.

2 🛏free 🚰🗑Chfree. **Location:** Urban, simple, central, quiet.
**Surface:** metalled. 🅟 01/01-31/12.
**Distance:** 🚶300m 🍴on the spot ⊗200m 🛒on the spot
🍴on the spot.

### 🅢 Saint-Yrieix-la-Perche 🛗 24F1
**Parking J.P Fabrègue**, Avenue de Lattre de Tassigny, D901.
**GPS:** n45,51271 e1,20646. 🔼.

---

5 🛏free 🚰€ 3,50 🗑Ch. **Location:** Urban, simple, quiet.
**Surface:** asphalted. 🅟 01/01-31/12.
**Remarks:** Coins at Tourist Info and Maison de la Presse.

### 🅢 Saint-Yrieix-la-Perche 🌿🛗 24F1
**Ferme du Poumier**, Lieu-dit Poumier, Marcognac.
**GPS:** n45,52065 e1,26853. 🔼➡.

4 🛏€6 🚰🗑Ch ♨included. **Location:** Rural, simple, isolated, quiet.
**Surface:** gravel. 🅟 01/01-31/12.
**Distance:** 🚶St.Yrieix 5km ⊗3km 🛒5km.

### 🅢 Sainte-Alvère 24E2
Rue de la Fontaine Saint Jean. **GPS:** n44,94500 e0,80499. 🔼➡.

10 🛏free 🚰€ 2,50/100liter 🗑Ch🔌€ 2,50/h. **Location:** Rural,
simple, isolated, quiet. **Surface:** gravel. 🅟 01/01-31/12.
**Distance:** 🚶500m ⊗500m 🛒500m.
**Remarks:** At sports centre, coins at town hall.

### 🅢 Sainte-Colombe-en-Bruilhois 24D3
Lieu-dit Bécade. **GPS:** n44,17889 e0,51692. 🔼.

4 🛏free 🚰🗑ChWCfree. **Location:** Rural, simple, quiet.
**Surface:** gravel. 🅟 01/01-31/12.
**Distance:** 🚶on the spot ⊗200m 🛒200m.

### 🅢 Sainte-Eulalie-en-Born 🍴 24B3
Route du Port, D652. **GPS:** n44,30634 w1,18206. 🔼.

20 🛏free, 01/04-31/10 € 4,50-7,50 🚰🗑ChWC ⊟included 📶€ 3.
**Location:** Rural, comfortable, quiet. **Surface:** grassy. 🅟 01/01-31/12
🅟 service: 01/11-01/03.
**Distance:** 🏊50m ⊗50m 🛒on the spot 🍴on the spot.
**Remarks:** At marina, to be paid at campsite.

FR

## Sainte-Feyre  21G2

**Parc Animalier**, PARC ANIMALIER DES MONTS DE GUÉRET.
**GPS**: n46,12656 e1,89072.
free €2 €2 Ch€2. **Location**: Rural. **Surface**: gravel.
01/01-31/12.

## Sainte-Fortunade  24F1

Domaine du Moulin de Lachaud. **GPS**: n45,19625 e1,73572.
5 free Ch. **Location**: Rural. **Surface**: grassy.
01/01-31/12.
**Distance**: on the spot on the spot.

## Sainte-Fortunade  24F1

Plateforme du stade - Route du Château. **GPS**: n45,20672 e1,77366.
4 free €2/150liter Ch€1/24h. **Surface**: gravel.
01/01-31/12.

## Sainte-Livrade-sur-Lot  24E3

Avenue René Bouchon. **GPS**: n44,39588 e0,59179.

8 free Chfree. **Location**: Urban, simple, central.
**Surface**: asphalted. 01/01-31/12.
**Distance**: on the spot 400m 250m.
**Remarks**: At fire-station.

## Sainte-Nathalène  24F2

**Les Ch'tis**, Le Bourg, D47. **GPS**: n44,90409 e1,28765.

6 €10 Ch included. **Location**: Rural, simple.
**Surface**: gravel. 01/01-31/12.
**Distance**: Sarlat 7km 50m bread service 50m.
**Remarks**: Market Wednesday (July-August).

## Saintes  21C3

**Aire camping-cars Avenue de Saintonge**, Chemin de la Prairie.
**GPS**: n45,74047 w0,62696.

12 €5/24h €5 Ch Service €5 .
**Location**: Urban, simple, central. **Surface**: asphalted.
01/01-31/12.
**Distance**: 1km 200m 650m Leclerc 100m.
**Remarks**: Max. 7 days.

### Tourist information Saintes:
Les Arènes. Roman anfiteatro.
Place 11 November. Tue + Fri morning.
Grande Foire. Large regional market.
1st Mon of the month.

## Salies-de-Béarn  27B2

**Aire Camping-car du Herre**, Chemin du Herré.
**GPS**: n43,47270 w0,9339.

24 €7/24h + €0,60/pp tourist tax €2,60/45minutes
Ch. **Location**: Rural, simple, quiet. **Surface**: gravel.
01/01-31/12.
**Distance**: 500m on the spot on the spot 300m 300m
300m.

## Salignac-Eyvigues  24F2

Rue des Ecoles. **GPS**: n44,97257 e1,32061.

10 free Chfree. **Location**: Rural, simple, quiet.
**Surface**: grassy. 01/01-31/12.
**Distance**: 300m 300m 250m.

## Salignac-Eyvigues  24F2

**Les Jardins du Manoir d'Eyrignac**, Rte des Jardins du Manoir.
**GPS**: n44,93875 e1,31609.

40 free. **Location**: Rural, isolated, quiet. **Surface**: grassy/gravel.
01/01-31/12.
**Distance**: Sarlat 13km on the spot on the spot.
**Remarks**: Nearby castle garden.

## Sanguinet  24B2

**Aire Des Bardets**, 1131, Avenue de Losa. **GPS**: n44,48399 w1,09154.

15 free, 01/05-18/09 €9 Chfree. **Location**: Simple, quiet.
**Surface**: metalled/sand. 01/01-31/12.
**Distance**: 800m on the spot on the spot 50m on the
spot.
**Remarks**: At lake, max. 48h, shady.

## Sanguinet  24B2

**Parking du Pavillon**, 519, Avenue de Losa.
**GPS**: n44,48579 w1,08479.

30 free, 01/05-15/09 €9 ChWC. **Location**: Simple, quiet.
**Surface**: forest soil. 01/01-31/12.

**Distance**: 700m on the spot Le Pavillon 1km.
**Remarks**: Max. 48h, shady.

## Sare  27A2

Route des Platane. **GPS**: n43,31179 w1,5839.

23 free, night €8 Ch. **Location**: Simple. **Surface**: asphalted.
01/01-31/12.
**Distance**: 400m 400m on the spot.
**Remarks**: Nearby swimming pool, cash payment.

### Tourist information Sare:
Office de Tourisme, Bourg, www.sare.fr. Typical Basque village in
Labourd-region.
Le petit train de la Rhune, Col de Saint Ignace. The little train runs
through the mountains in the Basque Country on the Franco-Spanish
border. 15/03-15/11 from 9h.
Les Grottes de Sare. Caves, prehistoric park and museum. 01/02-
31/12.

## Sarlat-la-Canéda  24F2

Place Flandres Dunkerque. **GPS**: n44,89530 e1,21266.

30 €7/24h, €15/48h €2 Ch €2 .
**Location**: Urban, simple, noisy. **Surface**: asphalted.
01/01-31/12.
**Distance**: 1km 100m bakery 50m.

### Tourist information Sarlat-la-Canéda:
Centre ville. Centre of the French trade in foie grass.
Sa-morning.

## Saujon  21B3

Route des Ecluses. **GPS**: n45,67503 w0,932.

14 €10/24h liter includedh.
**Location**: Urban, comfortable, central, quiet. **Surface**: asphalted.
01/01-31/12.
**Distance**: 900m 800m 800m on the spot on the spot
on the spot.
**Remarks**: Max. 6 days, coins at town hall.

## Sauvagnon  27C2

**Centre festif**, Rue du Béarn. **GPS**: n43,40361 w0,38635.

7 free ChWCfree. **Location**: Rural, simple, noisy.
**Surface**: asphalted. 01/01-31/12.
**Distance**: on the spot on the spot on the spot on the spot.
**Remarks**: Max. 48h.

### Sauvagnon 27C2

Rue du Béarn. **GPS**: n43,40310 w0,3876. ⬆.

6 ⭐free. **Location**: Rural, simple, quiet. **Surface**: grasstiles.
◻ 01/01-31/12.
**Distance**: 🛒on the spot 🚰on the spot.

### ♿Ⓢ Sauveterre de Guyenne 〰 24C2

Boulevard de 11 Novembre. **GPS**: n44,69022 w0,08624. ⬆.

4 ⭐free 🚰€ 1,50/90minutes 🔌Ch🔲€ 1,50/90minutes.
**Location**: Urban, simple, quiet, noisy. **Surface**: metalled.
◻ 01/01-31/12.
**Distance**: 🛒350m ⊗600m 🚰500m, bakery 100m.
**Remarks**: Coins at tourist info, supermarket.

### ♿Ⓢ Sauzé-Vaussais 21D2

Place des Halles. **GPS**: n46,13540 e0,10660. ⬆.

10 ⭐free 🚰🔌Ch🔲WCfree. **Location**: Central. **Surface**: asphalted.
◻ 01/01-31/12 ◉ water: 01/11-31/03.
**Distance**: 🛒on the spot ⊗on the spot 🚰on the spot.
**Remarks**: Max. 7 days.

### ♿Ⓢ Savignac-de-Nontron 21E3

Cocoon de Mendet, Mendet. **GPS**: n45,54294 e0,71375.

6 ⭐€ 10 🚰✎ included 📶. **Location**: Rural, comfortable.
**Surface**: grassy/gravel. ◻ 01/01-31/12.
**Distance**: 🛒300m ⊿300m ⊙300m ⊗5km 🚰5km 🚌50m.
**Remarks**: Possibility for reservation.

### ♿Ⓢ Savignac-Lédrier 24F1

Route de Juillac. **GPS**: n45,36401 e1,22066. ➡.

15 ⭐free 🚰🔌Ch🔲free. **Location**: Rural, isolated.
**Surface**: asphalted/gravel. ◻ 01/01-31/12.
**Distance**: 🛒on the spot ⊗100m 🧍on the spot.

---

**Remarks**: Coins at restaurant des Forges.

### ♿Ⓢ Segonzac 〰 21C3

Jardin Public, Rue Gourry. **GPS**: n45,61456 w0,22113. ⬆➡.

4 ⭐free 🚰🔌Ch✎(4x)WCfree. **Location**: Urban, comfortable,
central, quiet. **Surface**: gravel. ◻ 01/01-31/12.
**Distance**: 🛒500m, Cognac 8km ⊗500m 🚰500m.
**Remarks**: Wine tasting.

### ♿Ⓢ Segonzac 〰 21C3

Cognac Forgeron, Chez Richon. **GPS**: n45,62545 w0,17514. ⬆.

10 ⭐free 🚰WCfree. **Location**: Rural, quiet. **Surface**: grassy.
◻ 01/01-31/12.
**Distance**: 🛒500m.
**Remarks**: Check in on arrival, wine tasting.

### ♿Ⓢ Seignosse 27A1

Camping-car Park, D79. **GPS**: n43,69089 w1,42539. ⬆➡.

110 ⭐€ 10,43, 01/07-31/08 € 11,83 🚰🔌Ch✎(48x)📶included. 🚐
🛏 **Surface**: grassy/gravel.
◻ 01/01-31/12.
**Distance**: 🛒500m ⊿1,6km ⊙1,6km ⊗500m 🚰500m.
**Remarks**: Mandatory, one-time fee Pass'Etapes € 4, video surveillance.

### ♿Ⓢ Séreilhac 21E3

Allée Catherine Tabaraud. **GPS**: n45,76751 e1,07903. ⬆➡.

10 ⭐free 🚰€ 2/10minutes 🔌Ch🔲€ 2/h. **Location**: Rural,
comfortable, quiet. **Surface**: gravel. ◻ 01/01-31/12.
**Distance**: 🛒200m ⊙on the spot ⊗400m 🧍on the spot.

### ♿Ⓢ Sers 21D3

Rue du Champ de Foire. **GPS**: n45,59653 e0,32177. ⬆➡.

8 ⭐free 🚰€ 1/100liter 🔌Ch🔲€ 1/1h. **Location**: Rural,
comfortable, quiet. **Surface**: grassy. ◻ 01/01-31/12.

---

**Distance**: 🛒on the spot ⊗on the spot 🚰on the spot 🚲on the spot
🧍on the spot.
**Remarks**: Max. 48h.

### ♿Ⓢ Servières-le-Château 🍴🇫🇷 24G1

Centre touristique du lac de Feyt, Jaliot.
**GPS**: n45,14415 e2,03665. ⬆➡.

15 ⭐free, 29/03-27/09 € 5 🚰€ 2/100liter 🔌
Ch🔲€ 2/1h. **Location**: Rural, comfortable, isolated, quiet.
**Surface**: grassy/metallic. ◻ 01/01-31/12.
**Distance**: 🛒5km ⊿Sandy beach ⊙on the spot ⊗on the spot
🚰5km.
**Remarks**: Next to campsite.

### ♿Ⓢ Sévignacq Méracq 27C2

Aire du gave d'Ossau, Quartier Raguette.
**GPS**: n43,10681 w0,42082. ⬆➡.

20 ⭐€ 10 🚰€ 3 🔌Ch✎€ 2 WC◉. **Location**: Simple, quiet.
**Surface**: grassy/gravel. ◻ 15/02-10/11.
**Distance**: 🛒1km ⊿on the spot ⊙on the spot ⊗1km 🚰1km.
**Remarks**: Shady.

### ♿Ⓢ Solignac 21F3

D32. **GPS**: n45,75710 e1,26863. ⬆.
5 ⭐free 🚰🔌Ch. **Location**: Rural, simple. **Surface**: gravel.
◻ 01/01-31/12.
**Distance**: 🛒600m ⊗600m.

### ♿Ⓢ Soorts-Hossegor 27A1

Route des Lacs. **GPS**: n43,67279 w1,42087. ⬆.

85 ⭐€ 6/24h, 01/06-30/09 € 12 🚰€ 2/30minutes 🔌ChWC🚮. 🚐📷
**Location**: Rural, quiet. **Surface**: gravel. ◻ 01/01-31/12.
**Distance**: ⊿550m.
**Remarks**: Max. 5 days, max. 8M, shady.

### ♿Ⓢ Sorges 24E1

Aire de repos Grangearias, Le Bourg, N21.
**GPS**: n45,30570 e0,87238. ⬆.

4 ⭐free 🚰🔌Chfree. **Location**: Urban, simple, isolated, quiet.
**Surface**: metalled. ◻ 01/01-31/12.
**Distance**: 🛒100m ⊗200m 🚰250m.
**Remarks**: Service 100m.

### ♿Ⓢ Soubise 21B3

Sur la Rivière. **GPS**: n45,92833 w1,00666. ⬆.

**FR**

17 🛏 € 8/24h 🚰 Ch ⚡ WC included. 🏠 📋
**Location:** Rural, simple. **Surface:** grassy/metalled.
📅 01/01-31/12.
**Distance:** 🚶 on the spot ⊗ 50m.
**Remarks:** Along river, max. 24h, incl. showers and warm water.

### Soubrebost — 21G3

**La Martinèche Maison Martin Nadaud Parking**, RD13.
**GPS:** n45,98489 e1,85317. ⬆️.

3 🛏 free 🚰 🚰 Ch free. **Location:** Rural, simple, isolated, quiet.
**Surface:** asphalted. 📅 01/01-31/12.
**Distance:** 🚶 4km ⊗ 4km 🚰 4km.
**Remarks:** At museum, max. 9m.

### Soulac-sur-Mer — 21B3

**Boulevard de L'Amélie. GPS:** n45,49938 w1,1373. ⬆️.

45 🛏 € 4, 15/06-15/09 € 8 🚰 € 3,70/10minutes 🚰 Ch ⚡ € 3,70/h
🧺 🏠 **Location:** Urban, comfortable. **Surface:** gravel/metalled.
📅 01/01-31/12.
**Distance:** 🚶 2km ⊗ 50m 🚴 2,5km 🚰 2,5km 🚲 on the spot
🏃 on the spot.

### Sourzac — 24D1

D6089. **GPS:** n45,05147 e0,39518. ⬆️.

8 🛏 free 🚰 € 2/100liter 🚰 Ch WC. **Location:** Rural, central.
**Surface:** gravel/metalled. 📅 01/01-31/12 💧 water disconnected in winter.
**Distance:** 🚶 600m ⊗ 100m.
**Remarks:** Coins at petrol station.

### Soustons — 27A1

**Parking du Lac Marin**, Avenue de la Pêtre, Soustons Plage.
**GPS:** n43,77525 w1,41076. ⬆️.

---

82 🛏 € 8, 01/05-30/09 € 14 🚰 Ch ⚡ WC included. 🏠
🧺 **Location:** Rural, simple, quiet. **Surface:** gravel/metalled.
📅 01/01-31/12.
**Distance:** 🚶 city centre 3km ⚓ lake 50m, ocean 300m ⊗ 50m 🚰 50m
🚲 on the spot.
**Remarks:** Max. 72h.

### Taillebourg — 21C3

**Camping-Car Park**, Rue des pres du Vivier.
**GPS:** n45,83287 w0,64659. ⬆️.

16 🛏 € 10,04, 01/06-30/09 € 12,44 🚰 🚰 Ch ⚡ (12x),6Amp
WC 🚰 included. 🏠 **Location:** Rural, comfortable, quiet.
**Surface:** grassy. 📅 01/01-31/12.
**Distance:** 🚶 100m ⊗ 350m 🚴 350m.
**Remarks:** Along river, mandatory, one-time fee Pass'Etapes € 4.

### Talais — 21B3

Rue du Bourg 6. **GPS:** n45,47218 w1,05718.
4 🛏 € 5 🚰 € 4 🚰 Ch. 📅 01/01-31/12.
**Distance:** ⊗ 100m.

### Terrasson-Lavilledieu — 24F1

**MCD Camping-cars**, Rue Alphonse Daudet.
**GPS:** n45,13389 e1,30832. ⬆️➡️.

25 🛏 € 6 🚰 € 2 🚰 Ch ⚡ € 3. ⚡ **Location:** Rural, comfortable, quiet.
**Surface:** grassy. 📅 01/03-30/11.
**Distance:** 🚶 1km ⊗ 600m 🚰 600m.

### Terrasson-Lavilledieu — 24F1

**Parking Jeanne d'Arc**, Rue Marcel Michel. **GPS:** n45,12648 e1,30240. ⬆️.
120 🛏 € 3. 🏠 🧺 **Location:** Urban, simple, central.
**Surface:** asphalted. 📅 01/01-31/12.
**Distance:** 🚶 on the spot ⊗ on the spot.
**Remarks:** Thursday market.

### Thollet — 21F2

**Parking de la salle des fêtes**, D 10. **GPS:** n46,42233 e1,12290.
10 🛏 free 🚰 🚰 Ch. **Location:** Rural. **Surface:** metalled.
📅 01/01-31/12.
**Distance:** 🚴 on the spot.

### Thouars — 18D3

Levée de la Magdelaine, **GPS:** n46.97380 w0,21088. ⬆️.
10 🛏 € 5,40 🚰 € 2 🚰 Ch 🚰 included. **Location:** Rural, comfortable.
**Surface:** gravel. 📅 01/01-31/12.
**Distance:** 🚶 800m ⊗ 600m.

**Tourist information Thouars:**
🚻 📅 Tue, Fri.

### Thurageau — 21D1

**Fam. Turpeau**, Agressais. **GPS:** n46,78388 e0,25644. ⬆️.

5 🛏 free 🚰 🚰 Ch free. **Location:** Rural, simple, quiet.
**Surface:** gravel. 📅 01/01-31/12.
**Distance:** 🚶 2,5km.
**Remarks:** Goat farm, farm products.

---

### Tocane-Saint-Apre — 24D1

**Pré Sec**, D103. **GPS:** n45,25712 e0,49471. ⬆️➡️.

8 🛏 free 🚰 € 2/100liter 🚰 Ch 🔌 € 2/1h 🚰 free. **Location:** Rural,
simple. **Surface:** metalled. 📅 01/01-31/12.
**Distance:** 🚶 300m 🚴 100m ⊗ 300m 🚰 300m.
**Remarks:** Coins at the shops in the village.

### Tonnay-Charente — 21B3

**Camping-Car Park**, Quai des Capucins.
**GPS:** n45,93921 w0,88171. ⬆️➡️.

26 🛏 € 8,40-15,80 + € 1/pp tourist tax 🚰 🚰 Ch WC 🚰 included. 🏠
**Location:** Urban. **Surface:** gravel.
📅 01/01-31/12.
**Distance:** 🚶 1km ⊗ 300m 🚰 500m 🏃 on the spot.
**Remarks:** Mandatory, one-time fee Pass'Etapes € 4.

### Tonneins — 24D3

**Aire de camping-car de tonneins**, Place Pisseraule.
**GPS:** n44,38410 e0,31650.
7 🛏 free 🚰 🚰 Ch ⚡ € 2/5h. **Location:** Urban. **Surface:** asphalted.
📅 01/01-31/12.
**Distance:** 🚶 on the spot ⚓ on the spot ⊗ on the spot 🚰 300m.
**Remarks:** Coins at tourist info and town hall.

### Tournon-d'Agenais — 24E3

**Base de Loisirs Camp Beau**, Pont Roumio, Route de Libos, D102.
**GPS:** n44,40444 e0,99833. ⬆️.
15 🛏 free 🚰 🚰 Ch free. **Location:** Rural, simple, isolated.
**Surface:** gravel. 📅 01/01-31/12.
**Distance:** 🚶 500m ⊗ 100m.

### Tournon-d'Agenais — 24E3

D656. **GPS:** n44,40178 e0,99959. ⬆️.
10 🛏 free 🚰 🚰 Ch free. **Location:** Urban. **Surface:** metalled.
📅 01/01-31/12.
**Distance:** 🚶 300m ⊗ 300m.
**Remarks:** Max. 48h.

### Touvre — 21D3

**Place Hotel de Ville**, Route de Pontil. **GPS:** n45,66085 e0,25834. ⬆️.

7 🛏 free 🚰 🚰 Ch 🚰 free. **Location:** Rural, comfortable, quiet.
**Surface:** gravel. 📅 01/01-31/12.
**Distance:** 🚶 1km ⊗ 1km 🚰 1km 🚲 on the spot.

### Treignac — 24F1

**Les rivières**, Route du lac, D940. **GPS:** n45,54341 e1,79950. ⬆️➡️.

25 ⛺ € 2 🚐 € 2,50 ChWC. **Location:** Rural, simple, quiet. **Surface:** grassy/gravel. ⏰ 01/04-01/10 ⊙ service: frost. **Distance:** 🚶2km ⚓on the spot. **Remarks:** Along river.

**Tourist information Treignac:**
ℹ️ Office de Tourisme, 1, Place de la République. Free itinerary city tour along all curiosities, available at OT.

| | | Trémolat | 24E2 |

D30. **GPS:** n44,87378 e0,83065. ⬆️

5 ⛺free 🚐 € 2/25minutes Ch. **Location:** Rural, simple. **Surface:** asphalted. ⏰ 01/01-31/12. **Distance:** 🚶300m ⊗300m 🍴300m ⚓on the spot. **Remarks:** Coins at town hall.

| | | Tulle | 24F1 |

Avenue du Lieutenant Colonel Faro. **GPS:** n45,27995 e1,78571. ⬆️
6 ⛺ € 12 🚐 Ch 🛒 included. 🚂 Location: Rural, comfortable, isolated, quiet. **Surface:** asphalted. ⏰ 01/01-31/12. **Distance:** 🚶2,2km ⚓on the spot.

| | | Turenne | 24F2 |

Avenue du Sénateur Labrousse, D8. **GPS:** n45,05391 e1,57988. ⬆️➡️

6 ⛺free 🚐 Ch 🚽 WCfree. **Location:** Rural, comfortable, central. **Surface:** gravel. ⏰ 01/01-31/12. **Distance:** 🚶on the spot ⊗100m 🍴100m. **Remarks:** Behind tourist info, coins at tourist info and supermarket, narrow road, not suitable for motorhomes +7m.

**Tourist information Turenne:**
⛪ Tour de Cesar. ⏰ Easter-Oct daily, winter Su.

| | | Uhart-Mixe | 27B2 |

**Parking de la salle polyvalente d'Airetik**, Route départementale 933. **GPS:** n43,27780 w1,02245. ⬆️

4 ⛺ € 5/24h 🚐 € 2 🛒 € 2 🔌. **Location:** Rural, simple, quiet. **Surface:** asphalted. **Distance:** 🚶1km. **Remarks:** Max. 24h.

| | | Ussel | 24G1 |

**Aire du lac de Ponty**, Route du Lac. **GPS:** n45,54762 e2,28330. ⬆️

---

10 ⛺free 🚐 € 2 Ch € 2 WC. **Location:** Rural, simple, quiet. **Surface:** grassy/gravel. ⏰ 01/01-31/12. **Distance:** 🚶Ussel 3km 🏊8,5km ⊗300m 🍴1,5km ⚓on the spot 🚶on the spot. **Remarks:** At lake, in front of campsite, shady.

| | | Uzerche | 24F1 |

Place de la Petite Gare, Rue Paul Langevin. **GPS:** n45,42477 e1,56696. ⬆️➡️

30 ⛺free 🚐 ChWCfree. **Location:** Urban, simple, central, quiet. **Surface:** asphalted. ⏰ 01/01-31/12 ⊙ every twentieth day of the month. **Distance:** 🚶300m 🏊4,4km 🏊little stream ⊗500m 🍴bakery 500m 🚶on the spot. **Remarks:** Shady.

| | | Valeyrac | 24B1 |

**Port de Goulée**, Route Castillonaise. **GPS:** n45,40500 w0,91028.

5 ⛺free. **Location:** Rural, simple, isolated, quiet. **Surface:** gravel/metalled. ⏰ 01/01-31/12. **Distance:** 🚶50m ⚓on the spot 🚤on the spot ⊗20m 🚌on the spot 🚶on the spot. **Remarks:** At harbour.

| | | Vännäs | 24B1 |

**GPS:** n45,37606 w1,1568. ⬆️
100 ⛺ € 8,40-10,80 🚐 Ch included. **Location:** Urban, comfortable. **Surface:** grassy/sand. ⏰ 01/01-31/12. **Distance:** ⚓200m ⊗250m 🍴500m.

| | | Vanxains | 24D1 |

**Le Petit Verteillac**, D708. **GPS:** n45,21204 e0,28399. ⬆️➡️

4 ⛺free 🚐 Ch 🚽 WCfree. **Location:** Rural, simple. **Surface:** asphalted. ⏰ 01/01-31/12. **Distance:** 🚶400m 🍴700m.

| | | Varès | 24D3 |

Place de l'Europe, As Picadis. **GPS:** n44,42838 e0,35544. 
10 ⛺free 🚐 Chfree. **Surface:** metalled. ⏰ 01/01-31/12. **Distance:** 🍴bakery.

| | | Vasles | 21D1 |

**Mouton Village**, Rue de la Cité. **GPS:** n46,57329 w0,02309. ⬆️➡️

---

10 ⛺free 🚐 ChWCfree. **Location:** Rural, simple, quiet. **Surface:** gravel. ⏰ 01/01-31/12. **Distance:** 🚶400m 🍴400m.

| | | Verrières | 21C3 |

Chez Coutard. **GPS:** n45,57092 w0,26714. ⬆️➡️

3 ⛺free 🚐 Ch ♿(2x)free. **Location:** Rural, simple, quiet. **Surface:** asphalted. ⏰ 01/01-31/12. **Distance:** 🚶on the spot 🍴200m.

| | | Vertheuil | 24B1 |

**Château Ferré**, 3 rue des Aubépines. **GPS:** n45,26225 w0,82798. ⬆️➡️

5 ⛺free 🚐 ChWC. **Location:** Rural, comfortable, isolated, quiet. **Surface:** grassy/gravel. ⏰ 01/01-31/12. **Distance:** 🚶2km ⊗2km 🍴2km 🚶2,5km.

| | | Veyrines-de-Domme | 24E2 |

**Boutique des Bois d'Envaux**, Route des Milandes, 6-102 Le Falgueyrat. **GPS:** n44,82090 e1,10394. ⬆️

30 ⛺free 🚐. **Location:** Simple, isolated. **Surface:** grassy. ⏰ 01/04-30/09. **Distance:** ⊗on the spot. **Remarks:** Sale of foie gras and wine, monday evening marché gourmand.

| | | Vézac | 24E2 |

**Camping-Car Park**, La Malartrie. **GPS:** n44,82440 e1,16950. ⬆️

17 ⛺ € 11,10-13,50 🚐 Ch ♿(17x) included. 🚂. **Surface:** grassy/gravel. ⏰ 01/01-31/12. **Remarks:** Mandatory, one-time fee Pass'Etapes € 4.

| | | Vicq-sur-Gartempe | 21E1 |

25, Route de la Roche Posay. **GPS:** n46,72414 e0,86189. ⬆️➡️

FR

10 🛏free 🚰🔌ChWCfree. **Location:** Rural, simple, isolated, quiet. **Surface:** gravel. ⏱ 01/01-31/12. **Distance:** 🚶500m 🛒bakery 300m.

### Vielle-Saint-Girons 🚲 27A1

**Les Tourterelles**, Saint Girons-Plage. **GPS:** n43,95278 w1,35778.⬆️

40 🛏€ 9,90, 02/07-27/08 € 15,50, 16/07-20/08 € 15,95 🚰🔌 Chincluded 🔌€ 4 WC🔔🔊. **Location:** Rural, comfortable. **Surface:** gravel/metalled. ⏱ 01/04-30/09. **Distance:** 🏊300m ⊗500m 🛒500m. **Remarks:** Sanitary at campsite.

### Vieux-Boucau-les-Bains 27A1

**Aire camping-cars Village**, Promenade Bire Plecq. **GPS:** n43,77971 w1,40041.⬆️

150 🛏€ 8, 01/04-30/09 € 14 🚰🔌Ch🔌included 🔊.📠🔌 **Location:** Comfortable. **Surface:** gravel/sand. ⏱ 01/01-31/12. **Distance:** 🚶500m 🏊200m ⊗500m 🛒500m on the spot. **Remarks:** >3,5t not allowed, max. 24h.

### Vigeois 24F1

D7, route de Brive. **GPS:** n45,36717 e1,53392.⬆️➡️

12 🛏free 🚰€ 3/150liter 🔌Ch🔌€ 3/1h. **Location:** Rural, simple, isolated, quiet. **Surface:** grassy/gravel. ⏱ 01/04-31/10. **Distance:** 🚶2km 🏊7,2km 🏖beach 150m. **Remarks:** Coins at town hall and bars in the village.

### Villars-les-Bois 🚲 21C3

**Maison Bernard Begaud**, La Barre. **GPS:** n45,80002 w0,44085.⬆️➡️

3 🛏free. **Location:** Rural, simple, quiet. **Surface:** grassy. ⏱ 01/01-31/12. **Distance:** 🚶500m.

**Remarks:** Swimming pool.

### Villefranche-du-Périgord 24E2

**Plan d'eau**, Le Bourg. **GPS:** n44,63104 e1,07728.⬆️➡️

15 🛏free 🚰€ 2,50 🔌Ch🔌€ 2,50 🔌 **Location:** Rural, central, quiet. **Surface:** metalled. ⏱ 01/01-31/12. **Distance:** 🚶300m ⊗200m 🛒100m. **Remarks:** Max. 48h, max. 8M.

### Villeneuve-de-Marsan 27C1

40 Avenue du Stade. **GPS:** n43,88737 w0,30595.⬆️➡️

7 🛏free 🚰🔌Ch🔌(2x)free,16Amp. **Location:** Rural, simple, quiet. **Surface:** asphalted. ⏱ 01/01-31/12. **Distance:** 🚶1km ⊗1km 🛒1km. **Remarks:** Max. 48h, max. 9m.

### Villeréal 24E2

**Aire de Jeux**, Boulevard Alphonse de Poitiers, D104. **GPS:** n44,63798 e0,74065.⬆️

🛏free 🚰🔌Ch. **Surface:** asphalted. ⏱ 01/01-31/12. **Distance:** 🚶300m ⊗300m 🛒300m.

### Villeton 24D3

D120. **GPS:** n44,36386 e0,27279.⬆️

4 🛏€ 4,60, 01/04-31/10 € 5,60 🚰🔌Ch📠WC.🔌 **Location:** Rural, comfortable, quiet. **Surface:** gravel. ⏱ 01/01-31/12 💧 water disconnected in winter. **Distance:** 🎣10,5km 🏊on the spot 🚤on the spot ⊗on the spot 🛒500m. **Remarks:** Next to town hall.

### Vitrac 🚲🏕 24F2

Montfort, D703. **GPS:** n44,83558 e1,24852.⬆️➡️

10 🛏free 🚰€ 3/100liter 🔌Ch📠€ 3/h WC. **Location:** Rural, simple, quiet. **Surface:** grassy/gravel. ⏱ 01/01-31/12. **Distance:** 🚶50m 🏊2km beach at Dordogne river ⊗200m. **Remarks:** Coins available at restaurant Le Point Vue (200m).

### Vœuil-et-Giget 21D3

Place du Lavoir. **GPS:** n45,58473 e0,15464.⬆️

4 🛏free 🚰€ 2/100liter 🔌Ch. **Location:** Urban, simple, central, quiet. **Surface:** gravel/sand. ⏱ 01/01-31/12. **Distance:** 🚶on the spot ⊗on the spot 🛒6km. **Remarks:** Not suitable for big motorhomes.

### Yvrac 24C2

**Vignobles Pestoury**, 14 Chemin de Tellas. **GPS:** n44,89581 w0,4596.⬆️

16 🛏€ 5 🚰included. **Location:** Rural, simple, isolated, quiet. **Surface:** grassy. ⏱ 01/01-31/12. **Remarks:** Max. 24h, when buying wine 1 night free, regional products.

# Occitanie

### Adé 🚲🏕 27C2

**Féerie-des-Eaux**, 70 Avenue des Pyrénées, N21. **GPS:** n43,12834 w0,0277.⬆️➡️

27 🛏€ 10 🚰🔌Ch🔌included. 🔌 **Location:** Rural, comfortable, noisy. **Surface:** asphalted/grassy. ⏱ Easter-31/10. **Distance:** 🚶Lourdes 3,7km ⊗500m 🛒200m.

### Agde 🚲🏕🍴🐚 28A2

**Les Canoës**, Route de la Tamarissière. **GPS:** n43,29871 e3,45391.⬆️

🛏€ 13, 01/07-31/08 € 15 + € 0,83/pp tourist tax, dog € 3 🚰🔌Ch🔌included 💧€ 4/4. 📠🔌 **Location:** Rural, simple, isolated, quiet. **Surface:** grassy. ⏱ 01/04-31/10. **Distance:** 🚶3km 🏊on the spot 🚤on the spot ⊗900m 🚲on the spot 🎣on the spot. **Remarks:** Former campsite.

### Agde 🚲🏕🍴🐚 28A2

**Les Peupliers**, Route de la Tamarissière. **GPS:** n43,29846 e3,45194.⬆️

15 🛏€ 10, Jul/Aug € 12 🚰🔌Ch🔌(30x)€ 2 🔊.🔌

FR

**Surface:** grassy/gravel. 01/04-30/09.
**Distance:** 2km 1,7km on the spot.
**Tourist information Agde:**
Cathédrale Ste Étienne. Romanesque fortified cathedral, 12th century.

**⊞S Agos-Vidalos 27C3**
**Camping-Car Park Le Pibeste**, Avenue du Lavedan.
**GPS:** n43,03552 w0,07069. ⬆➡

6 € 9,60, 01/07-31/08 € 10,80 Ch included.
**Location:** Rural, comfortable, quiet. **Surface:** grassy/gravel.
01/01-31/12.
**Distance:** on the spot 10km on the spot 3km on the spot on the spot.
**Remarks:** Mandatory, one-time fee Pass'Etapes € 4.

**⊞S Aigues-Mortes 28B2**
**Les Poissons d'Argent**, CD62. **GPS:** n43,56476 e4,16289. ⬆

120 € 10 Ch included. (32x)€ 4/24h,5Amp .
**Location:** Simple. **Surface:** gravel.
01/03-31/10.
**Distance:** 3km 3km on the spot on the spot 1,5km Lidl 500m 500m.
**Remarks:** At fish lake, fishing permit incl, bread-service.
**Tourist information Aigues-Mortes:**
Office de Tourisme, Place Saint Louis, ot-aiguesmortes.com. Medieval fortress, 13th century, in the swamp of the Camargue, tourist attraction.
La Tour Carbonnière, Place Saint Louis. Tower, guard-post for the defence of the city.

**⊞S Aiguèze 25C3**
**GPS:** n44,30530 e4,55250. ⬆

+20 free. **Location:** Rural, simple, quiet. **Surface:** grassy/gravel.
01/01-31/12.
**Distance:** 300m 300m.
**Remarks:** Max. 1 night.

**©S Albas 24F3**
**Pech del Gal. GPS:** n44,47480 e1,23275. ⬆➡

10 free. Ch free. **Location:** Simple, isolated, noisy.
**Surface:** gravel. 01/01-31/12 water disconnected in winter.
**Distance:** 4km 4km.
**Remarks:** At weir.

**⊞S Albi 27G1**
**Base de Loisirs Pratgraussals**, Rue de Lamothe.
**GPS:** n43,92951 e2,13480. ⬆➡

20 free. Ch free. **Location:** Rural, simple, isolated, quiet.
**Surface:** asphalted. 01/01-31/12.
**Distance:** 1,5km 500m.
**Remarks:** At cemetery, service 200m.

**⊞S Albi 27G1**
**Parking Cathédrale. GPS:** n43,92750 e2,14111. ⬆➡

9 free. **Location:** Urban, simple, noisy. **Surface:** asphalted.
01/01-31/12.
**Distance:** 50m 50m 100m.
**Remarks:** Parking nearby cathedral Sainte Cécile, max. 48h.

**⊞S Albi 27G1**
**Supermarkt Leclerc**, Les portes d'Albi. **GPS:** n43,91846 e2,10968. ⬆

5 free € 2/55minutes Ch € 2/55minutes .
**Location:** Urban, simple, noisy. **Surface:** asphalted.
01/01-31/12.
**Distance:** 4km on the spot on the spot on the spot.
**Remarks:** Parking supermarket.

**S Albi 27G1**
Rue Michelet. **GPS:** n43,94583 e2,15111. ⬆➡
Ch free. 01/01-31/12.

**⊞S Alès 28B1**
**Place du camping-car**, Avenue Jules Guesde.
**GPS:** n44,12013 e4,08207. ⬆➡

6 free Ch free. **Location:** Urban, comfortable, central, noisy.
**Surface:** asphalted. 01/01-31/12.
**Distance:** on the spot on the spot on the spot 400m 600m on the spot routes available at tourist office.

**⊞S Alvignac 24F2**
**Parc du Samayou**, Route de Padirac. **GPS:** n44,82504 e1,69711. ⬆

10 free Ch WC. **Location:** Urban, simple, quiet.
**Surface:** asphalted. 01/01-31/12.
**Distance:** 100m 200m 200m.

**⊞S Alzon 28A1**
**Aire Municipale**, D999. **GPS:** n43,96567 e3,43902.

20 free € 2/100liter Ch. **Surface:** gravel/metalled.
01/01-31/12.
**Distance:** 100m.
**Remarks:** Coins at restaurant.

**⊞S Amélie-les-Bains-Palalda 32G1**
Carrer de l'Oreneta. **GPS:** n42,48105 e2,67866. ⬆

40 € 7 Ch included. **Location:** Simple, noisy.
**Surface:** gravel. 01/01-31/12.
**Distance:** 2km 500m.
**Remarks:** Behind hotel du Lion D'Or, max. 7 days.

**©S Amélie-les-Bains-Palalda 32G1**
**Camping Amélie**, Avenue Beau Soleil, D115.
**GPS:** n42,47894 e2,67414. ⬆

8 € 6,50 € 4 Ch € 4. **Location:** Simple, noisy.
**Surface:** grassy/gravel. 01/01-31/12.
**Distance:** on the spot 1km 1km.
**Remarks:** Max. 48h, coins at campsite.

**⊞S Anduze 28B1**
Place de la Gare. **GPS:** n44,05000 e3,98444. ⬆

20 free € 2/100liter Ch € 2/55minutes. **Location:** Urban, simple, central, quiet. **Surface:** unpaved. 01/01-31/12.
**Distance:** on the spot 300m 400m on the spot on the spot.
**Remarks:** Max. 48h.

FR

**Tourist information Anduze:**

👁 Bambousserie de Prafrance, 552 rue de Montsauve. Bamboo garden laid out in 1835, with a large variety of bamboo species.
📅 01/02-15/11.
👁 Train Touristique, 38 Place de la Gare. Tourist train from Anduze to St. Jean-du-Gard.
📅 26/03-31/10.

### Anglès 27H2
Route de Saint-Pons. **GPS:** n43,56553 e2,56544. ⬆

4 free ⛲€2 Ch. **Location:** Rural, simple, quiet.
**Surface:** gravel.
**Distance:** 500m ⊗50m 🚶 on the spot.
**Remarks:** At petrol station.

### Aniane 28A2
**Le Pont du Diable**, D27. **GPS:** n43,70270 e3,55988. ⬆

€5/day, €18/24h ⛲€3 Ch.
**Location:** Rural, simple, isolated. **Surface:** gravel.
📅 01/01-31/12.
**Distance:** 9km.
**Remarks:** Max. 48h, Pont du Diable 600m, St.Guilhem-le-Désert 4km, free shuttlebus Mai-Sept: weekend (11-19h), July-Aug daily (10-23h).

### Aniane 28A2
Lotissement du Camp de Sauve. **GPS:** n43,68652 e3,58254. ⬆→

15 free.
**Location:** Urban, simple. **Surface:** gravel. 📅 01/01-31/12.
**Distance:** 300m ⇢nearby ⊗300m 🚶300m.

### Aragnouet 27D3
Piau Engaly. **GPS:** n42,78599 e0,15800. ⬆→

120 free, Winter €15 ⛲Chfree (120x)included WC.
**Location:** Comfortable, isolated, quiet. **Surface:** asphalted.
📅 01/12-31/08.
**Distance:** 300m 300m 300m.
**Remarks:** Service only during winter period.

### Arcambal 24F3
**Aire Municipal**, D911. **GPS:** n44,45685 e1,51605. ⬆→

7 free ⛲Chfree. **Location:** Rural, simple. **Surface:** asphalted.
📅 01/01-31/12.
**Distance:** ⊗on the spot.

### Arfons 27G2
Pierron-Les Escudiés. **GPS:** n43,43972 e2,19472.

4 €5 ⛲Ch. **Location:** Simple, isolated, quiet. **Surface:** grassy.
📅 01/01-31/12.
**Distance:** 4km 1km 4km 4km.

### Argelès-Gazost 27C3
**Carrefour Market**, Route du Stade 45. **GPS:** n43,00455 w0,08636. ⬆

26 free ⛲€2 Ch.
**Location:** Rural, comfortable, quiet. **Surface:** asphalted.
📅 01/01-31/12.
**Distance:** 2km ⊗on the spot 150m on the spot 🚶on the spot.

### Argelès-sur-Mer 32H1
**Camping-Car Park L'Aire du Soleil**, Route du Littoral.
**GPS:** n42,57542 e3,04244. ⬆

21 €11,46, 01/05-30/09 €12,66 ⛲Ch (21x)included.
**Location:** Rural, simple, isolated, quiet. **Surface:** asphalted.
📅 01/09-30/06.
**Distance:** 3km Sandy beach.
**Remarks:** Mandatory, one-time fee Pass'Etapes €4.

**Tourist information Argelès-sur-Mer:**

ℹ Office de Tourisme, Palais des Congrès, Place Armand Lanoux, Perpignan, www.perpignantourisme.com. In the old city of Perpignan the Spanish influence is well visible in the colours of the houses and the palm trees.
ℹ Office de Tourisme, Place de l'Europe, www.argeles-sur-mer.com. Big touristic seaside resort with boulevard, marina and a lot of campsites.
✖ Palais du Rois de Majorque, Perpignan. Fortified palace of the kings of Mallorca.
Elne. 📅 Mo, Wed, Fri.

### Arre 28A1
D999. **GPS:** n43,96771 e3,52139. ⬆→

6 free ⛲€2 Ch WC. **Location:** Rural, simple, central, quiet.
**Surface:** metalled. 📅 01/01-31/12.
**Distance:** on the spot on the spot on the spot ⊗on the spot bakery 200m 🚶on the spot.

### Arreau 27D3
Chemin de Fregel. **GPS:** n42,90708 e0,35912. ⬆

25 free, July-Aug €2 ⛲Chfree.
**Location:** Urban, simple, central, quiet. **Surface:** metalled.
📅 01/01-31/12.
**Distance:** 100m 100m ⊗200m 500m 200m on the spot 🚶on the spot.

### Arrens-Marsous 27C3
Route d'Azun. **GPS:** n42,95853 w0,20778. ⬆

10 free ⛲€2/100liter Ch €2. **Location:** Rural, simple, isolated, quiet. **Surface:** asphalted. 📅 01/01-31/12.
**Distance:** 600m ⊗550m 100m on the spot 🚶on the spot.

### Arvieu 24H3
**GPS:** n44,19246 e2,65916. ⬆→

6 free ⛲€2/80liter Ch WC.
**Location:** Urban, simple, quiet. **Surface:** gravel.
📅 01/01-31/12.
**Distance:** 100m on the spot ⊗100m 100m 🚶on the spot.
**Remarks:** At sports centre, max. 72h, coins at the shops and town hall.

### Aubrac 24H3
D533. **GPS:** n44,62026 e2,98705. ⬆

10 free. **Location:** Rural, simple, quiet. **Surface:** gravel.
📅 01/01-31/12.
**Distance:** ⊗on the spot on the spot on the spot on the spot.

## Aubrac 24H3
**GPS**: n44,68193 e2,85431.
€ 2 Ch. **Surface**: gravel/metalled.
**Distance**: 1km.

## Auch 27D1
**Aire de l'Ile de St Martin**, Rue des Cormorans.
**GPS**: n43,63654 e0,58854.

40 € 8 Chincluded € 4 1,50. **Location**: Urban,
comfortable, quiet. **Surface**: asphalted/grassy. 01/01-31/12.
**Distance**: 1,3km 500m 500m.

## Aulus-les-Bains 27E3
Jouges. **GPS**: n42,78924 e1,33600.

7 free € 4/100liter Ch.
**Location**: Rural, simple. **Surface**: gravel.
01/01-31/12.
**Distance**: on the spot on the spot on the spot on the spot
on the spot.
**Remarks**: Max. 72h, pay at tourist office, servicepoint at campsite 1km.

## Auterive 27F2
Rue des Docteurs Basset. **GPS**: n43,35182 e1,47641.

15 free ChWC. **Location**: Urban, simple, quiet.
**Surface**: asphalted. 01/01-31/12.
**Distance**: 200m 200m 200m.
**Remarks**: Along river, service 300m.

## Auterive 27F2
Grande Allée du Ramier. **GPS**: n43,35025 e1,47730.
ChWCfree. **Location**: Urban. **Surface**: asphalted.
01/01-31/12.
**Remarks**: At fire-station.

## Autoire 24F2
D38. **GPS**: n44,85572 e1,82196.

10 € 4/24h € 2/100liter Ch € 2/1h WCincluded.
**Location**: Rural, simple, quiet. **Surface**: gravel/metalled.
01/01-11/11.
**Distance**: 300m 300m.
**Remarks**: Water falls 800m.

## Auzas 27E2
Base de Loisirs d'Auzas, La Grangère. **GPS**: n43,17016 e0,88690.

10 € 5 Ch (4x)included. **Location**: Rural, comfortable,
quiet. **Surface**: asphalted. 01/01-31/12.
**Distance**: At lake, service 500m.
**Remarks**: 500m on the spot on the spot.

## Avèze 28A1
**Aire de Loisirs du Pont Vieux**, D999. **GPS**: n43,97517 e3,59899.

6 € 8 Ch. **Surface**: metalled. 01/01-31/12.
**Distance**: 500m on the spot on the spot 500m 1,3km
on the spot.
**Remarks**: Next to campsite municipal, max. 48h.

## Ax-les-Thermes 27F3
A Bonascre, Rue des Chalets. **GPS**: n42,70340 e1,81657.

25 free € 2/100liter Ch (8x)€ 6/24h.
**Location**: Rural, simple, isolated, quiet. **Surface**: gravel.
01/01-31/12.
**Distance**: 10km 100m 200m.
**Remarks**: At ski-lift.

## Ax-les-Thermes 27F3
Avenue de l'Ariege, Parc d'Espagne. **GPS**: n42,71432 e1,84188.

35 € 5 Chincluded. **Location**: Urban, simple, noisy.
**Surface**: asphalted. 01/01-31/12.
**Distance**: 500m 500m 500m.
**Remarks**: At swimming pool.

## Ax-les-Thermes 27F3
La Capelette, N20. **GPS**: n42,72565 e1,83154.

30 € 8 10minutes Chincluded1h. **Location**: Urban,
simple, noisy. **Surface**: asphalted. 01/01-31/12.
**Distance**: 1km 1km 1km 100m on the spot on the
spot.

## Bagnères-de-Bigorre 27D3
Rue René Cassin. **GPS**: n43,07319 e0,15256.

30 free ChWCfree. **Location**: Urban, simple, noisy.
**Surface**: gravel. 01/01-31/12.
**Distance**: 850m 15km 500m 650m.

## Bagnères-de-Bigorre 27D3
Avenue de Belgique. **GPS**: n43,06917 e0,14889.

10 free. **Location**: Urban, simple, central, noisy. **Surface**: asphalted.
01/01-31/12.
**Distance**: 200m on the spot 200m 200m on the spot
on the spot on the spot.
**Remarks**: At station.

## Bagnères-de-Luchon 27D3
Lac de Badech, Rue Jean Mermoz. **GPS**: n42,79540 e0,59875.

50 € 4/24h Service € 4 Ch.
**Location**: Rural, simple, quiet. **Surface**: asphalted. 01/01-31/12
service: 01/12-01/04.
**Distance**: 1km 400m 500m on the spot on the spot.
**Remarks**: Coins at tourist info.

## Bagnols-sur-Cèze 28C1
Av. de l Europe, D8086. **GPS**: n44,16820 e4,61958.

20 free Chfree. **Location**: Noisy. **Surface**: gravel.
01/01-31/12.
**Distance**: 200m 200m 200m.
**Remarks**: Max. 24h.

## Balaruc-les-Bains 28A2
Avenue des Hespérides 335. **GPS**: n43,44499 e3,67564.

6 € 8,50 € 2,50/4minutes Ch € 2,50/55minutes.
**Location**: Urban, quiet. **Surface**: asphalted/gravel. 01/01-31/12.

FR

**Distance:** ↳on the spot ⚓on the spot ⊗on the spot ⚲700m.
**Remarks:** Max. 72h.

### ♨S Balaruc-les-Bains ⚓ 🏖 ⚓ 28A2
**Thermes Hespérides**, Allée des Sources.
**GPS:** n43,44574 e3,67770.⬆➡

18 💶€8,50 🚰🚿Ch🔌55minutes WCincluded 📶.🔋
**Location:** Urban, simple, noisy. **Surface:** asphalted.
🅾 01/01-31/12.
**Distance:** ↳1km ⊗400m ⚲700m.
**Remarks:** Free bus to centre.

### 🚐♿ Baraqueville 24G3
Rue du Val de Lenne. **GPS:** n44,27850 e2,43407.⬆

10 💶free 🚰€3 🚿Ch🔌. **Location:** Simple, quiet.
**Surface:** asphalted. 🅾 01/01-31/12 ⬤ service 01/11-31/03.
**Distance:** ↳on the spot ⚓850m ⊗400m ⚲50m 🚲on the spot
🚶on the spot.
**Remarks:** Coins at the shops in the village, inclining pitches.

### 🚐♿ Barbotan-les-Thermes ⚓ 27C1
Avenue des Thermes. **GPS:** n43,94884 w0,04344.⬆➡

6 💶€6. **Location:** Urban, simple, noisy. **Surface:** asphalted.
🅾 01/01-31/12.
**Distance:** ↳500m ⊗50m ⚲500m.

### 🚐S Bardigues 🌿⚓🌳 27E1
Rue des Amandiers. **GPS:** n44,03869 e0,89271.⬆➡

4 💶free 🚰€2/100liter 🚿Ch. **Location:** Rural, simple, quiet.
**Surface:** gravel. 🅾 01/01-31/12.
**Distance:** ↳150m ⊗150m ⚲150m.

### 🚐S Barèges 🏔❄ 27D3
**Le Tournabou**, Route de Tourmalet, D918. **GPS:** n42,90329 e0,10151.⬆

15 💶free 🚰free. **Location:** Rural, isolated, quiet. **Surface:** asphalted.
🅾 01/01-31/12.
**Distance:** ↳2,5km ⊗on the spot ⚲3km 🚲on the spot 🚶on the spot
🚴on the spot 🛶on the spot.

### 🚐S Beaucaire 28C1
**Les Marguilliers**, Chemin des Marguilliers.
**GPS:** n43,81667 e4,64107.⬆

9 💶€15/24h 🚰🚿Ch🔌included. **Surface:** gravel.
🅾 01/01-31/12.
**Distance:** ↳1,5km ⚓300m ⊗500m ⚲500m.

### 🚐 Beaucaire 28C1
Quai de la Paix. **GPS:** n43,80615 e4,63739.⬆

10 💶free 🚰€2/100liter 🚿Ch🔌€2/1h. **Location:** Urban, simple.
**Surface:** asphalted. 🅾 01/01-31/12.
**Distance:** ↳300m ⊗300m ⚲bakery 300m.
**Remarks:** Coins at tourist info, service closed during wintertime.

### 🚐S Beaumont-de-Lomagne 27E1
Boulevard Georges Brassens. **GPS:** n43,88028 e0,99057.⬆

4 💶free 🚰🚿Chfree. **Location:** Urban, simple, noisy.
**Surface:** asphalted. 🅾 01/01-31/12.
**Distance:** ↳300m ⊗300m ⚲300m.
**Remarks:** Max. 1 night.

### 🚐 Bédarieux 🏔🌳 27H2
Avenue Jean Moulin. **GPS:** n43,61071 e3,15329.⬆➡

15 💶free 🚰🚿Chfree. **Location:** Urban, simple, central, quiet.
**Surface:** grassy. 🅾 01/01-31/12.
**Distance:** ↳500m ⚓on the spot 🛶on the spot ⊗800m.
**Remarks:** Along the Orb river.

### 🚐S Bélesta 🌿🏔 27H3
Rue des Loisirs. **GPS:** n42,71560 e2,60786.⬆➡

10 💶€5 + €0,55/pp tourist tax 🚰€2/20minutes 🚿(8x)€2/4h
🔌.🔋 **Location:** Rural, simple, quiet. **Surface:** grassy/gravel.
🅾 01/04-31/10.
**Distance:** ↳100m ⊗300m 🚶on the spot.

### 🚐S Bellas 🏔 24H3
**Aire Privee Bellas**, D995, Sévérac-le-Château.
**GPS:** n44,31256 e3,12689.⬆

10 💶€5 🚰🚿Chincluded 🔌€3.🔋 **Location:** Rural, simple,
isolated, quiet. **Surface:** grassy. 🅾 01/01-31/12.
**Distance:** ↳4km ⊗4km 🚲on the spot 🚶on the spot.

### ⚓S Bellegarde 🚤 28C1
**Port de plaisance**, Las Courrejos Est. **GPS:** n43,74422 e4,51890.⬆

15 💶free 🚰€2 🚿Ch🔌€2/1h. **Location:** Rural, simple.
**Surface:** gravel/sand. 🅾 01/01-31/12.
**Distance:** ↳city centre 1,5km.
**Remarks:** Max. 48h, coins at harbourmaster.

### 🚐S Belmont sur Rance 🏔🌳 27H1
**Place de la Mairie**, Route de Lacaune. **GPS:** n43,81630 e2,75269.⬆

3 💶free 🚰€2/100liter 🚿Ch🔌€2/20minutes. **Location:** Urban,
simple. **Surface:** asphalted. 🅾 01/01-31/12.
**Distance:** ↳on the spot.
**Remarks:** Bakery 500m.

### 🚐S Belpech 27F2
**Stade municipal**, Rue du Stade. **GPS:** n43,19864 e1,74472.⬆

7 💶free 🚰🚿Ch🔌🚿(2x) WC. **Location:** Rural, simple.
**Surface:** grassy. 🅾 01/01-31/12.
**Distance:** ↳500m ⊗500m ⚲500m.
**Remarks:** At football ground.

## 🚐S Boisse Penchot 24G3
Rue du Chateau Bas. **GPS**: n44,59201 e2,20567. ⬆️➡️

8 🚐free 🚰€3/100liter 🚿Ch➕€3/1h. **Location**: Rural, comfortable. **Surface**: asphalted. 📅 01/01-31/12. **Distance**: 🚶400m ⊗on the spot 🛒on the spot 🚉400m. **Remarks**: Coins at restaurant.

## 🚐S Boissières 24F3
Layrolle. **GPS**: n44,54303 e1,40218. ⬆️

4 🚐free 🚰🚿Chfree. **Location**: Rural, simple, quiet. **Surface**: grassy/gravel. 📅 01/03-31/12 🔵 Service: winter. **Distance**: 🚶500m ⊗500m 🚉500m. **Remarks**: Service 100m.

## 🚐S Bonac Irazein 27E3
Lac Bonac, D4. **GPS**: n42,87541 e0,97565. ⬆️

10 🚐€6,60, 01/07-30/09 €7,60 🚰🚿Ch 🧹WCincluded. **Location**: Urban, simple, quiet. **Surface**: grassy/gravel. 📅 01/03-30/11. **Distance**: 🚶200m ⊘on the spot ⊗300m. **Remarks**: At artificial lake of Bonac.

## 🚐S Bouillac 24G3
Aire de Bouillac, D840. **GPS**: n44,57333 e2,15750. ⬆️➡️

12 🚐free 🚰€3 🚿ChWC. **Location**: Rural, simple. **Surface**: metalled. 📅 01/03-30/11. **Distance**: 🚶600m ⊘on the spot ⊗on the spot ⊗600m 🚉600m. **Remarks**: Max. 24h, coins at the shops.

## 🚐S Bourret 27E1
Cambonis. **GPS**: n43,93569 e1,14320.

3 🚐€10 🚰🚿Ch 🧹WC 〰️included. 🏠**Location**: Rural, simple,

---

quiet. **Surface**: metalled. 📅 01/01-31/12. **Distance**: ⊗2km 🚉2km. **Remarks**: Barbecue place, use of sauna against payment, swimming pool.

## 🚐S Bouzies 24F3
Le Bourg. **GPS**: n44,48365 e1,64527. ⬆️

10 🚐€5,50 🚰€2/100liter 🚿Ch➕€2/1h. 🏠**Location**: Rural, simple, quiet. **Surface**: gravel. 📅 01/01-31/12. **Distance**: ⊗200m 🚉300m 🚶on the spot.

## 🚐S Bozouls 24H3
Parking de la Médiathèque. **GPS**: n44,47199 e2,72104. ⬆️

10 🚐free 🚰🚿Ch. **Location**: Urban, simple. **Surface**: gravel. 📅 01/01-31/12. **Distance**: 🚶500m ⊗150m 🚉350m.

## 🚐S Branoux-les-Taillades 25B3
Aire de la Placette, La placette. **GPS**: n44,22607 e4,01036. ⬆️
4 🚐€3 🚰🚿Ch. **Surface**: metalled. 📅 01/01-31/12. **Distance**: ⊗100m. **Remarks**: Picnic area.

## 🚐S Bréau-et-Salagosse 28A1
Le Rieumage, D272. **GPS**: n43,99338 e3,56716. ⬆️

6 🚐€2 🚰🚿Ch. 🏕️**Location**: Rural, simple, isolated, quiet. **Surface**: gravel. 📅 01/01-31/12. **Distance**: 🚶500m ⊘on the spot 🚶on the spot.

## 🚐S Broquies 27H1
Route de Mazies. **GPS**: n44,00498 e2,69371. ⬆️

15 🚐free 🚰🚿Ch 🧹WC. **Location**: Rural, simple, isolated, quiet. **Surface**: gravel. 📅 01/01-31/12. **Distance**: 🚶50m ⊗on the spot 🚉on the spot. **Remarks**: Coins at supermarket.

## 🚐S Cadours 27E1
Rue Malakoff. **GPS**: n43,72320 e1,04861. ⬆️➡️

---

5 🚐free 🚰🚿Chfree. **Location**: Rural, simple. **Surface**: grassy. 📅 01/01-31/12. **Distance**: 🚶1km ⊗1km. **Remarks**: At football ground.

## 🚐 Parking Chartreux 24F3
Parking Chartreux, Rue de la Chartreuse. **GPS**: n44,44016 e1,44119. ⬆️➡️

3 🚐free 🚰🚿Chfree. **Location**: Urban, simple, quiet. **Surface**: gravel. 📅 01/01-31/12. **Distance**: 🚶500m ⊘on the spot ⊗250m 🚉50m 🚶on the spot. **Remarks**: Along river.

## 🚐 Cahors 24F3
Parking Saint George, Rue Saint George. **GPS**: n44,43875 e1,44111. ⬆️➡️

20 🚐free. **Location**: Urban, simple. **Surface**: asphalted. 📅 01/01-31/12. **Distance**: 🚶1,2km ⊗100m 🚶on the spot. **Remarks**: Max. 72h, service 300m, shuttle bus to city centre.
**Tourist information Cahors:**
🚹 📅 Wed, Sa.

## 🚐S Cahuzac-sur-Vère 27G1
Place du Mercadial. **GPS**: n43,98194 e1,91111. ⬆️

5 🚐free 🚰🚿ChWCfree. **Location**: Rural, simple. **Surface**: gravel. 📅 01/01-31/12. **Distance**: 🚶200m ⊗200m 🚉200m 🚶on the spot. **Remarks**: At cemetery.

## 🚐S Cajarc 24F3
Place de la Gare. **GPS**: n44,48458 e1,84573. ⬆️➡️

8 🚐free 🚰€1/200liter 🚿Ch. **Location**: Urban, simple, quiet.

FR

**Surface:** grassy. ◐ 01/01-31/12 ◉ water disconnected in winter. **Distance:** 🚰100m ⊗200m. 🚱200m.

🅱️S **Cajarc** 〰️ **24F3**

Rue de Cuzoul. **GPS:** n44,48241 e1,83952. ⬆️.

5 🏁 € 5,50 🚰🚱Chincluded. 🚙 **Location:** Rural, simple, quiet. **Surface:** gravel. ◐ 01/01-31/12. **Distance:** 🚰400m ⊗400m. **Remarks:** 100m from campsite.

🅱️S **Camarès** 〰️ **27H1**

Chemin des Zizines. **GPS:** n43,81654 e2,87988. ⬆️➡️.

16 🏁free, night € 5 🚰🚱ChWC🏁free. 🚙 **Location:** Rural, simple, quiet. **Surface:** gravel. ◐ 01/01-31/12. **Distance:** 🚰100m ⊾on the spot ⊶on the spot ⊗1km 🚱1km ⊿on the spot 🏊on the spot. **Remarks:** Max. 72h, service closed during wintertime.

🅱️S **Campagnac** 〰️ **24H3**

**Aire Municipale,** La Sagne. **GPS:** n44,41885 e3,08875. ⬆️➡️.

5 🏁free, 13/06-13/09 € 3 🚰🚱Ch. **Location:** Rural, simple, isolated, quiet. **Surface:** asphalted. ◐ 01/01-31/12. **Distance:** 🚰400m ⊗400m. 🚱400m. **Remarks:** Coins at campsite and town hall.

🅱️S **Campan** 〰️❄️ **27D3**

Le Bourg. **GPS:** n43,01817 e0,17828. ⬆️➡️.

5 🏁free 🚱ChWC. **Location:** Rural, simple, quiet. **Surface:** gravel. ◐ 01/01-31/12. **Distance:** 🚰100m ⊶on the spot ⊗300m. **Remarks:** Max. 48h.

🅱️S **Campan** 〰️❄️ **27D3**

Serre Crampe, Payolle. **GPS:** n42,93711 e0,30259. ⬆️.

15 🏁free 🚰🚱ChWCfree. **Location:** Rural, isolated, quiet. **Surface:** gravel. ◐ 01/01-31/12. **Distance:** 🚰5km ⊾150m ⊗150m ⊿350m 🚱6km ⊿on the spot 🏊on the spot ⊸on the spot ⊾on the spot. **Remarks:** Max. 48h, service 100m.

🅱️S **Campuac** 〰️ **24H3**

Les Crozes. **GPS:** n44,57027 e2,59162. ⬆️.

10 🏁free 🚰🚱ChWCfree. **Location:** Rural, simple. **Surface:** gravel. ◐ 01/01-31/12. **Distance:** 🚰100m 🚱100m. **Remarks:** Max. 7 days, service 100m.

🅱️S **Canet-de-Salars** 〰️ **24H3**

Les Fontanelles. **GPS:** n44,23260 e2,74716. ⬆️➡️.

6 🏁€ 6, tourist tax € 0,60/pp 🚰€ 2/80liter 🚱€ 2 Ch 🔧 WCincluded. **Location:** Rural, simple, quiet. **Surface:** grassy/gravel. ◐ 01/04-30/10. **Distance:** 🚰750m ⊾5km ⊗750m 🏊on the spot. **Remarks:** Coins at bar and garage.

🅱️S **Capdenac-Gare** 〰️ **24G3**

**Camping-Car Park Les Portes du Pays de Figeac,** Boulevard Paul Ramadier. **GPS:** n44,57302 e2,07292. ⬆️➡️.

50 🏁€ 9,30, Jul/Aug € 11 🚰🚱Ch 🔧(50x) 📶included. 🚙 **Location:** Rural, simple, noisy. **Surface:** gravel. ◐ 12/02-15/11. **Distance:** 🚰1km ⊶on the spot. **Remarks:** Along through road, mandatory, one-time fee Pass'Etapes € 4.

🅲S **Carcassonne** 🌿🏺🍲 **27G2**

**Camping de la Cité,** Route de Saint-Hilaire. **GPS:** n43,19980 e2,35317. ⬆️.

38 🏁€ 14-16/24h, tourist tax € 0,20/pp 🚰🚱Chincluded. 🚙 **Location:** Urban, comfortable, quiet. **Surface:** gravel. ◐ 01/01-31/12. **Distance:** 🚰3,5km ⊶on the spot.

**Tourist information Carcassonne:**

ℹ️ Office de Tourisme, 15, Boulevard Camille Pelletan, www. carcassonne-tourisme.com. Medieval fortified city, museum city with many curiosities.

🛒 The new city has a modern shopping centre.

🅱️S **Cardaillac** **24G2**

**Le Pré del Prie. GPS:** n44,67868 e1,99805. ⬆️.

12 🏁free 🚰€ 2/100liter 🚱Ch 🔌€ 2/1h. **Location:** Isolated, quiet. **Surface:** gravel. ◐ 01/01-31/12. **Distance:** 🚰100m ⊗on the spot 🚱100m. **Remarks:** Behind church.

🅲S **Carnon** **28B2**

**Mille Pépites,** Avenue Grassion Cibrand, Carnon-plage. **GPS:** n43,55097 e3,99417. ⬆️.

18 🏁€ 11,50-23 🚰🚱Ch 🔧 WC🏁included, on camp site ◉€ 6. 🚙 📇 **Location:** Rural. **Surface:** asphalted. ◐ 01/04-30/09. **Distance:** 🚰1km ⊾80m 🚱50m.

🅱️S **Castanet** **24G3**

**GPS:** n44,27889 e2,28944. ⬆️➡️.

4 🏁€ 8 🚰🚱Ch 🔧included WC. **Location:** Rural, comfortable, quiet. **Surface:** gravel. ◐ 01/01-31/12. **Distance:** 🚰on the spot. **Remarks:** Money in envelope in mail box.

🅱️S **Casteil** 〰️ **32G1**

D116. **GPS:** n42,53324 e2,39230. ⬆️.

5 ⬛free 🚰 WC. **Location:** Rural, simple, isolated, quiet.
**Surface:** forest soil. ⬛ 01/04-31/10.
**Distance:** 🚶1km ⊠ on the spot 🍴 on the spot.

### 🅂 Castelnau-de-Montmiral 27F1

**Domaine Les Miquels. GPS:** n43,96667 e1,80278. ⬆➡.

6 ⬛€ 10 🚰 Ch 🔧 included. 🛁 **Location:** Rural, comfortable,
isolated, quiet. **Surface:** grassy. ⬛ 01/01-31/12.
**Distance:** 🚶2,5km ⊠ on the spot 🍴2,5km.

### 🅂 Castelnau-Durban 27F3

**Aire Municipale**, D117. **GPS:** n42,99994 e1,33976. ⬆.

10 ⬛free 🚰 € 2/100liter Ch WC. **Location:** Urban, simple, noisy.
**Surface:** metalled. ⬛ 01/01-31/12.
**Distance:** 🚶on the spot ⊠100m.
**Remarks:** Parking in front of church, max. 48h.

### 🅂 Castelnaudary 27G2

**Camping-Car Park Castelnaudary**, Passage des Lavandières.
**GPS:** n43,31427 e1,94899. ⬆.

14 ⬛€ 9,20 🚰 Ch (14x) 🔧 included. 🚐 **Location:** Urban,
comfortable. **Surface:** grassy/gravel. ⬛ 01/01-31/12.
**Distance:** 🚶on the spot ⊠on the spot 🍴250m 🚌200m.
**Remarks:** Mandatory, one-time fee Pass'Etapes € 4.

### 🅂 Castelsarrasin 27E1

Allée de la Source. **GPS:** n44,03861 e1,10221. ⬆➡.

60 ⬛€ 3/24h 🚰 € 2,50/100liter Ch 🔧 € 2,50/24h. 🚐
**Location:** Rural, simple. **Surface:** gravel. ⬛ 01/01-31/12.
**Distance:** 🚶500m ⊠500m 🍴500m.

### 🅂 Castres 27G2

**Place Gerard Philipe**, Chemin des Porches. **GPS:** n43,60168 e2,24939.

75 ⬛free. **Location:** Urban, central, noisy. **Surface:** asphalted.

---

⬛ 01/01-31/12.
**Distance:** 🚶2km ⊠2km 🍴2km.
**Remarks:** Max 3,5t, free bus to centre.

### 🅂 Castres 27G2

Route de l'Industrie Z.I. de Melou. **GPS:** n43,59069 e2,20648. ⬆➡.
🚰 Ch free.
**Location:** Urban. **Surface:** asphalted. ⬛ 01/01-31/12.
**Tourist information Castres:**

✝ Palais Episcopal. Episcopal palace.
☂ ⬛ Tue, Thu-Su.

### 🅂 Catus 24F3

Place de la Vernière. **GPS:** n44,55576 e1,33829. ⬆➡.

10 ⬛free 🚰 Ch free. **Location:** Rural, simple.
**Surface:** gravel/sand. ⬛ 01/01-31/12.
**Distance:** 🚶on the spot 🍴200m.

### 🅂 Cauterets 27C3

**Ancien Boulodrome**, Avenue Charles Thierry.
**GPS:** n42,88628 w0,11522. ⬆➡.

24 ⬛€ 10 🚰 Ch 🔧 included. 🚐 **Location:** Rural, simple, quiet.
**Surface:** asphalted. ⬛ 01/01-31/12.
**Distance:** 🚶300m 🚲20km ⊠300m 🍴350m 🛒 on the spot 🧍on the
spot 🚿 on the spot.

### 🅂 Cauterets 27C3

Place de la Patinoire, D920. **GPS:** n42,89325 w0,11318. ⬆➡.

30 ⬛€ 10/24h 🚰 Ch 🔧 included. 🚐 **Location:** Rural,
comfortable, quiet. **Surface:** asphalted. ⬛ 01/01-31/12.
**Distance:** 🚶300m 🚲20km ⊠300m 🍴300m 🛒 on the spot 🧍on the
spot 🚿 on the spot.
**Remarks:** Max. 7 days.

### 🅂 Caylus 24F3

**Base de loisirs Labarthe**, D19. **GPS:** n44,23363 e1,77225. ⬆.

6 ⬛free 🚰 Ch free. **Location:** Rural, simple.
**Surface:** grassy/gravel. ⬛ 01/01-31/12.
**Distance:** 🚶200m ⊠200m 🍴200m.
**Tourist information Caylus:**

ℹ St.Antonin. Small town with the oldest town hall of France.

### 🅂 Cazaubon 27C1

**Aire Municipale du Lac de l'Uby**, Aire de la Base de l'Uby.
**GPS:** n43,93344 w0,03165. ⬆.

---

49 ⬛€ 9,60 + € 0,55/pp tourist tax 🚰 Ch 🔧 WC.
**Location:** Rural, comfortable, quiet. **Surface:** gravel.
⬛ 24/02-01/12.
**Distance:** 🚶on the spot ⊠on the spot 🍴on the spot 🚿3,6km.
**Tourist information Cazaubon:**

ℹ Health resort with mineral mud bathes and warmwater sources.

### 🏛 Cazes-Mondenard 24E3

**Musée du Corbillard**, Lieu dit Minguet. **GPS:** n44,23047 e1,21157.

⬛free. **Location:** Rural. ⬛ 01/01-31/12.
**Distance:** ⊠on the spot.
**Remarks:** Narrow entrance, regional products.

### 🅂 Celles 28A2

**Le Mas de Riri**, RD148, Lac de Salagou. **GPS:** n43,65939 e3,33529. ⬆.

80 ⬛€ 15,50 🚰 Ch 🔧 (80x) € 3,50/24h WC 🔧 € 4/time
🔧 included. 🚐 🚲 **Location:** Rural, simple, isolated, quiet.
**Surface:** gravel/metalled. ⬛ 01/04-30/09.
**Distance:** 🚶4km ⊠on the spot 🍴on the spot ⊗on the spot 🚿on
the spot 🧍on the spot.
**Remarks:** Not suitable for big motorhomes.

### 🅂 Chusclan 28C1

**Cave Chusclan**, Route d'Orsan, D138. **GPS:** n44,14552 e4,67762. ⬆➡.

6 ⬛free 🚰 Ch free. **Location:** Comfortable, isolated.
**Surface:** gravel. ⬛ 01/01-31/12.
**Distance:** ⊠500m 🍴500m.

### 🅂 Clermont-l'Hérault 28A2

Lac du Salagou. **GPS:** n43,64677 e3,38915. ⬆➡.

8 ⬛€ 5-7 🚰 € 2/100liter Ch 🔧 (6x). **Location:** Rural, simple,
isolated, quiet. **Surface:** gravel. ⬛ 01/01-31/12.
**Distance:** 🚶7km ⊠on the spot 🍴on the spot ⊗on the spot 🚿7km
🧍on the spot.
**Remarks:** Coins at campsite.

### 🅂 Collioure 32H1

**Aire de Camping-Car Dourat**, Route de Madeloc/D914.
**GPS:** n42,52315 e3,06741. ⬆.

**FR**

50 🛏 10/24h 🚰 ♨Ch WC included. 🅿 **Location:** Rural, simple, isolated, quiet. **Surface:** asphalted. 🗓 01/01-31/12.
**Distance:** 🚶2,3km 🏊2,5km ⊗2km 🛒2km.
**Remarks:** Monitored parking, may-Sep free shuttle to Collioure.

### 🛏🅂 Comps 28C1
Place des Arènes. **GPS:** n43,85402 e4,60724. ⬆.

50 🛏 € 6 🚰♨Ch 💶 € 2/50minutes WC. 🛴 **Location:** Rural.
**Surface:** grassy/gravel. 🗓 01/01-31/12.
**Distance:** 🚶50m 🏊on the spot 🛒on the spot 50m 🏍on the spot 🚶on the spot.

### 🛏🅂 Comps 28C1
**GPS:** n43,85390 e4,60912.

30 🛏 € 5. 🛴
**Location:** Rural. **Surface:** unpaved. 🗓 01/01-31/12.
**Distance:** 🚶500m 🛒on the spot ⊗500m.
**Remarks:** Along river.

### 🚻🅂 Concots 24F3
**Le Vinagrou**, Mas de Vinagrou. **GPS:** n44,39850 e1,64355. ⬆➡.

5 🛏guests free, € 5 🚰 € 2/100liter. 🅿 **Location:** Simple.
**Surface:** asphalted/metalled. 🗓 01/01-31/12.
**Distance:** 🚶500m ⊗on the spot.

### 🛏🅂 Condom 🎪 27D1
Avenue des Mousquetaires. **GPS:** n43,94836 e0,36378. ⬆.

12 🛏 € 3 🚰♨Ch. 🅿 **Location:** Rural, comfortable, isolated, quiet.
**Surface:** grassy/metalled. 🗓 01/01-31/12.
**Distance:** 🚶2km 🛒400m.
**Remarks:** Max. 3 days, to be paid at campsite, market Wednesday.

### 🚻🅂 Condom 🎪 27D1
**Ferme de Parette**, Route de Nérac, RN930.
**GPS:** n43,98742 e0,34942. ⬆➡.

8 🛏 € 10 🚰♨Ch 💶 € 2/1day WC included 💶 € 4.
**Location:** Rural, comfortable, isolated, quiet. **Surface:** grassy.
🗓 01/01-31/12.
**Distance:** 🚶2km ⊗2km 🛒2km.
**Tourist information Condom:**
Ⓜ Musée de l'Armagnac. All about Armagnac.

### 🛏🅂 Cordes-sur-Ciel 🌿🏊🌲 27G1
**Parking les Tuileries. GPS:** n44,06453 e1,95802. ⬆➡.

40 🛏free, 01/04-31/10 € 6 🚰60liter ♨Ch 💶included3h. 🅿
**Location:** Rural, simple, isolated, quiet. **Surface:** grassy/gravel.
🗓 01/01-31/12.
**Distance:** 🚶500m ⊗500m.
**Remarks:** Service closed during wintertime.

### 🛏🅂 Coupiac 🏰 27H1
Route de Martin. **GPS:** n43,95174 e2,58464. ⬆.

15 🛏free 🚰♨Ch 💶free. **Location:** Rural, simple, quiet.
**Surface:** grassy. 🗓 01/01-31/12.
**Distance:** 🚶500m 🛒450m.
**Remarks:** Behind petrol station, max. 72h.

### 🛏🅂 Cransac 🎪♨ 24G3
**Aire de Camping-car Cransac**, Route de la Gare.
**GPS:** n44,52267 e2,27416. ⬆.

6 🛏free 🚰 € 3/100liter ♨Ch 💶 € 3/1h. **Location:** Rural, simple.
**Surface:** gravel. 🗓 01/03-28/11.
**Distance:** 🚶500m ⊗500m 🛒500m 🛒on the spot.
**Remarks:** Max. 48h.

### 🛏🅂 Cuxac-Cabardès 🏰🎪 27G2
**Aire de Camping-Cars Garage Meric**, La Cabasse.
**GPS:** n43,36126 e2,30185. ⬆➡.

20 🛏 € 5 🚰♨Ch included 🛴💶 € 3/24h 📶🛴 **Location:** Rural,
simple, isolated, quiet. **Surface:** metalled. 🗓 01/01-31/12.
**Distance:** 🏊on the spot 🛒on the spot 🏍on the spot 🚶on the spot.

### 🚻🅂 Donzac 🛶🌾 24E3
**Lac de Sources**, D30. **GPS:** n44,11308 e0,82044. ⬆.

10 🛏free 🚰♨Chfree. **Location:** Rural, simple. **Surface:** gravel.
🗓 01/01-31/12.
**Distance:** 🚶500m 🛒on the spot.
**Remarks:** Max. 48h, playground.

### 🚻🅂 Douelle 🎪🌾 24F3
**Domaine Marcilhac**, D8. **GPS:** n44,47927 e1,34947. ⬆➡.

10 🛏free 🚰 € 2 ♨Ch. **Location:** Rural, simple. **Surface:** gravel.
🗓 01/01-31/12.
**Distance:** 🚶1km ⊗1km 🛒1km 🛒1km.

### 🛏🅂 Duilhac-sous-Peyrepertuse 27G3
Route du château. **GPS:** n42,86160 e2,56527. ⬆.

25 🛏free 🚰♨Ch 💶WCfree. **Location:** Rural, simple, quiet.
**Surface:** asphalted. 🗓 01/04-31/10.
**Distance:** 🚶200m ⊗150m.

### 🛏🅂 Entraygues-sur-Truyère 🌿🛶🎪🌾 24H2
Route de Villecomtal, D904. **GPS:** n44,64020 e2,56925. ⬆➡.

10 🛏free 🚰♨Ch 💶free.
**Location:** Rural, simple. **Surface:** grassy.
🗓 01/04-31/10.
**Distance:** 🚶700m 🏊on the spot 🛒on the spot ⊗300m 🛒300m.
**Remarks:** Free coins at tourist info and town hall, service 300m.

### 🅂 Entraygues-sur-Truyère 🌿🛶🎪🌾 24H2
Rue du 16 Août 1944. **GPS:** n44,64269 e2,56577.
🚰 € 3 ♨Ch 🛴.

FR

**Distance:** ⊗150m ☎150m.
**Remarks:** Coins at tourist info.

| 🅿️🆂 | Espalion 🎣 | 24H3 |

**Camping-Car Park**, Avenue Pierre Monteil.
**GPS:** n44,52156 e2,76921. ⬆️➡️.

25 🚐€ 10,80, 01/07-31/08 € 12 🚰🗑️Ch🖍️(8x)📶included.
🅿️ **Location:** Urban, comfortable. **Surface:** gravel/metalled.
⭕ 01/01-31/12. ⭕ 01/08-09/08.
**Distance:** 🚶1km ⊗1km ☎1km.
**Remarks:** Barrier, mandatory, one-time fee Pass'Etapes € 4.

| 🅲🆂 | Espelette | 27A2 |

**Bibier Gorri**, Chemin de Lapitxague. **GPS:** n43,35325 w1,44997.
🚐€ 9,25-16,80 🚰🗑️€ 3 Ch🖍️📶. **Location:** Rural.
**Surface:** grassy. ⭕ 01/01-31/12.
**Remarks:** Possibility for reservation.

| 🅿️🆂 | Espéraza | 27G3 |

Promenade François Mitterand. **GPS:** n42,93370 e2,21589. ⬆️.

20 🚐free 🚰🗑️Chfree. **Location:** Rural, simple, quiet.
**Surface:** grassy. ⭕ 01/01-31/12.
**Distance:** 🚶500m ⛱️on the spot 🍴on the spot ⊗500m.

| 🅿️🆂 | Espezel 🏔️ | 27G3 |

**Relais du Pays de Soult**, Avenue de Stade, D120.
**GPS:** n42,82322 e2,02146. ⬆️➡️.

6 🚐free 🚰🗑️Chfree. **Location:** Rural, comfortable, quiet.
**Surface:** asphalted. ⭕ 01/01-31/12.
**Distance:** 🚶100m ⊗on the spot 🍴on the spot.
**Remarks:** Barbecue place.

| 🅿️🆂 | Fanjeaux 🌿 | 27G2 |

Chemin des Fontanelles. **GPS:** n43,18611 e2,03222. ⬆️➡️.

15 🚐free 🚰🗑️Chfree. **Location:** Rural, comfortable, quiet.
**Surface:** grassy/gravel. ⭕ 01/01-31/12.
**Distance:** 🚶100m ⊗100m ☎100m.
**Remarks:** Next to maison de retraite (home for the elderly), max. 48h.

| 🅿️🆂 | Félines-Termenès | 27H3 |

Av. de Termenès, dir Mouthoumet. **GPS:** n42,98691 e2,61285. ⬆️.

3 🚐free 🚰🗑️Chfree. **Location:** Rural, simple, quiet.
**Surface:** gravel. ⭕ 01/01-31/12.
**Distance:** 🚶50m.
**Remarks:** Closed when frosty.
**Tourist information Félines-Termenès:**
👁️ Cité Médiéval, Villerouge Termenes. Medieval village and castle
from 12-14th century. ⭕ 01/07-30/09.

| 🅿️🆂 | Figeac 🧺 | 24G3 |

**Parking le Foiral**, Boulevard Colonel Teulié.
**GPS:** n44,61089 e2,03674. ⬆️➡️.

5 🚐free 🚰€ 2 Ch🖍️€ 2. **Location:** Urban, simple, central, noisy.
**Surface:** asphalted. ⭕ 01/01-31/12.
**Distance:** 🚶100m ⛱️400m 🍴100m 🚌100m.
**Tourist information Figeac:**
🎪 Marché régional. Regional market. ⭕ Sa-morning.

| 🆆🆂 | Fitou | 27H3 |

**Aragon**, Route Nationale 9, Les Cabanes de Fitou.
**GPS:** n42,89275 e2,99672. ⬆️.

15 🚐€ 5/12h, € 7/24h 🚰🗑️Ch🖍️€ 2,50 📶included.
**Location:** Rural. **Surface:** gravel. ⭕ 01/01-31/12.
**Distance:** 🛣️A9 6,5km ⊗on the spot 🍴500m.
**Remarks:** Video surveillance.

| 🅿️🆂 | Fleurance | 27E1 |

Route de Toulouse. **GPS:** n43,84769 e0,67165.

40 🚐free 🚰€ 2 🗑️Ch🖍️€ 2/2h. **Location:** Comfortable.
**Surface:** grassy/metalled. ⭕ 01/01-31/12.
**Distance:** 🚶on the spot 🍴on the spot 🚶on the spot.
**Remarks:** Coins at tourist info.

| 🅿️🆂 | Fleury-d'Aude 🎣🚣 | 28A2 |

**Base de Loisirs Étang de Pissevache**, Saint-Pierre-la-Mer.
**GPS:** n43,18972 e3,19694. ⬆️.

100 🚐€ 5/24h, 01/04-31/10 € 8,75/24h 🚰🗑️Chincluded 🖍️€ 2/4h
🅿️📶🚐 **Surface:** unpaved. ⭕ 01/01-31/12.
**Distance:** ⛱️sandy beach 300m.
**Remarks:** Parking directly behind the beach, next to tennis park and
small surf lake, follow Base de Loisirs.

| 🅿️🆂 | Fleury-d'Aude 🎣🚣 | 28A2 |

Les-Cabanes-de-Fleury. **GPS:** n43,21529 e3,23315. ⬆️.

100 🚐€ 7, tourist tax € 1/pp 🚰€ 2 🗑️Ch🖍️🔌.
**Surface:** metalled/sand. ⭕ 01/04-31/10.
**Distance:** 🚶on the spot ⛱️on the spot ⊗200m.
**Remarks:** Next to campsite municipal Rive d'Aude, coins at capitainerie
(1km).

| 🅿️🆂 | Florac 🌿🏔️🍇 | 25A3 |

D16. **GPS:** n44,32582 e3,59032. ⬆️➡️.

10 🚐free 🚰€ 4/100liter 🗑️Ch🖍️€ 4/1h WCfree.
**Location:** Rural, comfortable, central, quiet. **Surface:** asphalted.
⭕ 01/01-31/12.
**Distance:** 🚶150m ⛱️300m 🚶300m ⊗150m 🍴150m 🚵mountain-
bike trail 🚶on the spot.
**Remarks:** Nearby cemetery.

| 🅿️🆂 | Florensac | 28A2 |

**Domaine de Veyrac**, Route de Bessan, D28.
**GPS:** n43,36221 e3,47671. ⬆️➡️.

10 🚐€ 7 🚰🗑️Chfree. **Location:** Rural, simple, isolated, quiet.
**Surface:** gravel. ⭕ 01/01-31/12.
**Distance:** 🚶2,2km ⊗3km 🍴3,6km 🚵on the spot.

| 🅿️🆂 | Foix 🌿 | 27F3 |

**Parking de la Vigne**, Boulevard François Mitterrand.
**GPS:** n42,96055 e1,61088. ⬆️➡️.

**FR**

15 ⛽free ⚡🚰 Chfree. **Location:** Urban, simple. **Surface:** gravel. ⏱ 01/01-31/12.
**Distance:** 🚰600m ⊗on the spot 🛒500m.

**Tourist information Foix:**
ℹ️ Office de Tourisme, 29, rue Delcassé, www.mairie-foix.fr. Medieval city.
✈ ⏱ 1st, 3th (5th) Mo of the month.

## Fraïsse-sur-Agout 27H2

Chemin de la Salvetat. **GPS:** n43,60446 e2,79560. ⬆➡

15 ⛽€ 7 ⚡🚰 Ch ✂(3x)included. **Location:** Rural, simple, quiet. **Surface:** gravel/metalled. ⏱ 01/04-30/11.
**Distance:** 🚰400m 🏊50m 🛒50m 400m 🛒400m.
**Remarks:** At the edge of village, on the Agout river.

## Frejairolles 27G1

Domaine du Grand Chêne, 387 route de Réalmont, D74.
**GPS:** n43,86043 e2,24799. ⬆

10 ⛽€ 10 ⚡🚰 Ch ✂ WC 🚿 € 5/3 📶included. 🚐 **Location:** Rural, comfortable. **Surface:** grassy/gravel.
⏱ 01/01-31/12.
**Distance:** 🏊on the spot 🛒on the spot.

## Frontignan 28A2

Avenue des vacances - Quartier de l'entrée.
**GPS:** n43,43244 e3,75919. ⬆➡
49 ⛽€ 10/24h ⚡€ 2 Ch 🚿 📶 **Location:** Rural, simple, quiet.
**Surface:** gravel. ⏱ 02/05-30/10.
**Distance:** 🚰900m 🏊on the spot 🛒on the spot ⊗900m 🛒900m.
**Remarks:** Max. 72h.

## Gaillac 27F1

Parking des Rives Thomas, Rue Claude Nougaro.
**GPS:** n43,89951 e1,89494. ⬆

4 ⛽free ⚡🚰 Chfree. **Location:** Urban, simple, noisy.
**Surface:** asphalted. ⏱ 01/01-31/12.
**Distance:** 🚰200m ⊗200m 🛒200m.

## Gavarnie 27C3

Parking Holle, Route de la station des Espécières, D923.
**GPS:** n42,73857 w0,01959. ⬆

25 ⛽free, May-Oct € 8/24h ⚡🚰 Chincluded. 🚐
**Location:** Rural, simple, isolated, quiet. **Surface:** metalled.
⏱ 01/01-31/12.

**Distance:** 🚰1,5km 🏊100m ⊗1,5km 🛒800m 800m 🚶on the spot 🚲100m ⛵1,5km.

## Gavarnie 27C3

Parking du Cirque, Baretge. **GPS:** n42,73549 w0,0116. ⬆

20 ⛽€ 7. 🚐 **Location:** Rural, simple. **Surface:** asphalted. ⏱ 01/07-31/08.
**Distance:** 🚰200m 🏊200m ⊗200m 🛒200m 🚶on the spot 🚲on the spot ⛵on the spot.

**Tourist information Gavarnie:**
👁 Cirque de Gavarnie. Can be reached with a donkey, a horse or by foot. A giant waterfalll, snow pillars and mountain slopes.

## Gèdre 27C3

Aire Naturelle Le Cairn, Harneau d'Heas.
**GPS:** n42,74916 e0,08935. ⬆

10 ⛽€ 12. **Location:** Rural, simple, isolated, quiet. **Surface:** grassy. ⏱ winter.
**Distance:** 🚰9km 🛒200m 🚶on the spot.
**Remarks:** At Chapelle de Héas.

## Gèdre 27C3

Place de la Bergère, Gedre Débat. **GPS:** n42,78860 e0,01967. ⬆

10 ⛽free. **Location:** Rural, simple, isolated. **Surface:** asphalted. ⏱ 01/01-31/12.
**Distance:** 🚰on the spot ⊗250m 🛒50m.

## Gèdre 27C3

Auberge La Munia, Héas, D922. **GPS:** n42,78826 e0,01982.
5 ⛽€ 14, 2 pers.incl. **Location:** Rural, isolated, quiet. **Surface:** grassy.
⏱ 01/01-31/12.
**Distance:** ⊗on the spot.

## Génolhac 25B3

Les Taillades, Place du 19 Mars 1962, D906.
**GPS:** n44,35388 e3,94844. ⬆➡

10 ⛽free ⚡🚰 Chfree. **Location:** Rural, simple, isolated, quiet.
**Surface:** metalled. ⏱ 01/01-31/12.
**Distance:** 🚰200m 🛒800m 🚶on the spot.
**Remarks:** Max. 48h.

## Gignac 24F2

Le Moulin, Place des Troubadours. **GPS:** n45,00624 e1,45687. ⬆

10 ⛽free ⚡🚰 Chfree. **Location:** Simple, isolated.
**Surface:** metalled. ⏱ 01/01-31/12.
**Distance:** 🚰50m ⊗150m 🛒150m.
**Remarks:** Festival and market place.

## Gimont 27E1

Avenue de Cahuzac, RN124. **GPS:** n43,62987 e0,87009. ⬆

12 ⛽free ⚡🚰 Chfree. **Location:** Rural, simple, noisy.
**Surface:** gravel. ⏱ 01/01-31/12.
**Distance:** 🚰300m 🏊on the spot 🛒on the spot ⊗300m 🛒300m 300m 🚶on the spot.
**Remarks:** At lake, max. 48h, market Wednesday and Sunday.

## Girac 24F2

Camping-Car Park, D803 Pont de Puybrun.
**GPS:** n44,91822 e1,80442. ⬆

18 ⛽€ 9,40, 15/06-31/08 € 13 ⚡🚰 Ch ✂included. 🚐
**Location:** Rural. **Surface:** grassy/gravel. ⏱ 01/01-31/12.
**Distance:** 🚰2km 🛒1km.
**Remarks:** Along the Dordogne river, mandatory, one-time fee Pass'Etapes € 4.

## Gourdon 24F2

Esplanade du foirail. **GPS:** n44,73423 e1,38523. ⬆➡

8 ⛽free ⚡€ 1/100liter Ch ✂(8x)€ 1/kWh. **Location:** Simple, quiet. **Surface:** gravel. ⏱ 01/01-31/12 ⏺ water disconnected in winter.
**Distance:** 🚰200m 🛒100m 🛒200m on the spot.

## Gramat 24F2

La Garenne, Avenue Paul Mezet. **GPS:** n44,77966 e1,72904. ⬆➡

10 ⛽free ⚡🚰 Ch 🚐free. **Location:** Simple. **Surface:** gravel.
⏱ 01/01-31/12.
**Distance:** 🚰400m ⊗400m 🛒400m.

**Remarks:** Max. 48h.

### Grenade-sur-Garonne  27F1

**Parking de la salle des fêtes**, Rue de l'Amiral Cabanié.
**GPS:** n43,76838 e1,29464. ⬆.

10 🚐 free. **Location:** Urban, simple, noisy. **Surface:** asphalted.
🅿 01/01-31/12.
**Distance:** 🚶on the spot ⊗500m 🍺600m.
**Remarks:** Playground.

### S  Grenade-sur-Garonne  27F1

Quai de Garonne. **GPS:** n43,77201 e1,29673. ⬆.
4free 🚰🚻Ch.
**Location:** Noisy. **Surface:** gravel. 🅿 01/01-31/12.
**Distance:** 🚶100m ⊗100m 🍺100m 🚌100m.
**Remarks:** Service: Allées Alsace Lorraine (100m).

### S  Gruissan  27H3

**Aire des 4 Vents**, Avenue des quatre vents.
**GPS:** n43,10444 e3,09944. ⬆➡.

120 🚐 free, 12/02-30/11 € 9,75 🚰🚻ChWC included. 🚿♻
**Location:** Rural, comfortable. **Surface:** gravel. 🅿 01/01-31/12.
**Distance:** 🚶on the spot 🚲on the spot ⊗on the spot 🍺on the spot.

### S  Gruissan  27H3

**Aire des Châlets**, Avenue de la Jetée, Gruissan-plage.
**GPS:** n43,09583 e3,11111. ⬆➡.

80 🚐 € 9,75 🚰🚻Chincluded. **Surface:** gravel. 🅿 01/04-30/09.
**Distance:** 🚶2km 🏊on the spot 🚲on the spot ⊗2km 🍺2km.

### S  Gruissan  27H3

**Étang de Mateille**, Gruissan dir Narbonne-Plage, base de voile, D332.
**GPS:** n43,12083 e3,11417. ⬆.

150 🚐 € 9 🚰🚻Ch 🚿(24x) € 1,50 WC included.
**Location:** Rural, simple, quiet. **Surface:** grassy/metalled.
🅿 01/07-31/08.
**Distance:** 🚶4km 🏊on the spot 🚲on the spot ⊗800m 🍺Lidl 2km.
**Tourist information Gruissan:**
👁 L'Hospitalet. Probably the largest wine-cellar of the world.
👁 Vieux Port. Old fishing-port.

### S  Guzet-Neige  27E3

**Station de ski de Guzet. GPS:** n42,78007 e1,29979.
🚐 free WC. **Location:** Rural, simple, isolated. **Surface:** asphalted.
🅿 01/01-31/12.

---

**Distance:** 🚶10km ⊗2km on the spot.

### S  Ille-sur-Têt  32G1

**Aire de Camping-Car Les Orgues**, Chemin de Régleilles.
**GPS:** n42,68168 e2,62247. ⬆.

20 🚐 free WC. **Location:** Rural, simple, isolated, quiet.
**Surface:** gravel/metalled. 🅿 01/01-31/12.
**Distance:** 🚶2km.
**Tourist information Ille-sur-Têt:**
👁 Les orgues d'Ille sur Têt. Cliff formation.

### S  La Bastide-de-Sérou  27F3

**Camping lArize**, Bargnac, D15. **GPS:** n43,00194 e1,44556. ⬆.

15 🚐 € 13-28,70, Jul/Aug € 28 🚰🚻Ch 🚿€ 3/day WC 📶 included.
🚿♻ **Location:** Rural, comfortable, isolated, quiet.
**Surface:** asphalted/gravel. 🅿 01/04-01/11.
**Distance:** 🚶1km.

### La Canourgue  25A3

Avenue du Lot, D998. **GPS:** n44,43325 e3,20775. ⬆.

20 🚐 free 🚰🚻Chfree. **Location:** Rural, simple, isolated, quiet.
**Surface:** metalled. 🅿 01/01-31/12 🅿 Jul/Aug: tue.
**Distance:** 🚶500m 🚲1,3km ⊗600m 🍺600m 🏊600m.
**Remarks:** Max. 24h.

### S  La Cavalerie  27H1

**Camping-Car Park**, Centre du village. **GPS:** n44,00876 e3,15228. ⬆.

32 🚐 € 10,20 🚰🚻Ch 🚿(32x) included. 🔌♻ **Location:** Simple,
noisy. **Surface:** gravel. 🅿 01/01-31/12.
**Distance:** 🚶200m ⊗200m.
**Remarks:** Mandatory, one-time fee Pass'Etapes € 4.

### S  La Couvertoirade  28A1

Rue Droite. **GPS:** n43,91012 e3,31276.

---

10 🚐 € 4 🚰€ 3/100liter WC. **Location:** Rural, simple, isolated, quiet.
**Surface:** gravel. 🅿 01/01-31/12.
**Distance:** 🚶50m ⊗500m 🏊on the spot.
**Remarks:** Large parking on edge from village.
**Tourist information La Couvertoirade:**
ℹ Citadelle de l'Ordre de Tempeliers. Fortified city in original state.
Now many old craft industries are exercised. There is a toll-house at the entrance of the village, entrance fee is charged.

### S  La Grande Motte  28B2

**Aire camping-car Les Cigales**, Avenue de la Petite Motte.
**GPS:** n43,56789 e4,07404. ⬆⬆.

50 🚐 € 11-13, Jul-Aug € 16 + € 1/pp tourist tax 🚰🚻Ch 🚿 included
WC 🔌♻. **Location:** Rural. **Surface:** gravel. 🅿 01/01-31/12.
**Distance:** 🚶2km 🏊1,2km ⊗2km 🍺2km.

### S  La Palme  27H3

**Camping-Car Park Les Salins de La Palme**, Route de Port la Nouvelle.
**GPS:** n42,98033 e3,01858. ⬆.

49 🚐 € 9,60 🚰🚻Ch 🚿(48x) included. 🔌
**Location:** Rural, comfortable, isolated, quiet. **Surface:** grassy.
🅿 01/01-31/12.
**Distance:** 🚶2,5km 🏊2km ⊗on the spot 🍺on the spot 🏊on the spot.
**Remarks:** Mandatory, one-time fee Pass'Etapes € 4.

### La Roque-sur-Cèze  25C3

**Camping-Car Park**, Route de St. Laurent de Carnols.
**GPS:** n44,19567 e4,52320. ⬆.
28 🚐 € 10,40, 01/06-31/08 € 12,80 🚰🚻Ch 🚿(24x) included. 🔌
♻ **Location:** Rural. **Surface:** grassy. 🅿 01/01-31/12.
**Remarks:** Mandatory, one-time fee Pass'Etapes € 4.

### S  La Salvetat-sur-Agout  27H2

Chemin du Redoundel. **GPS:** n43,60584 e2,69911. ⬆.

6 🚐 free 🚰🚻Chfree. **Location:** Rural, comfortable, quiet.
**Surface:** gravel. 🅿 01/01-31/12.
**Distance:** 🚶600m ⊗900m 🍺Spar 650m.
**Remarks:** Near sports fields, service closed during wintertime.

### Labastide-Marnhac  24F3

D7. **GPS:** n44,38595 e1,39771. ⬆➡.

FR

10 ⌷free 🚰🔧Chfree. **Location:** Rural, simple. **Surface:** gravel.
📅 01/01-31/12.
**Distance:** ⊗100m.

### Labastide-Murat 24F2

Route de Gramat. **GPS:** n44,64944 e1,57061. ⬆️

10 ⌷free 🚰🔧Ch⊡€ 8. **Location:** Rural, simple.
**Surface:** asphalted. 📅 01/01-31/12.
**Distance:** ⌷300m 🛒10m ⊡10m.
**Remarks:** At supermarket Carrefour.

### Labruguière 27G2

**Domaine d'en Laure**, Avenue Arthur Batut.
**GPS:** n43,53139 e2,25528. ⬆️➡️

10 ⌷€ 7/24h 🔧€ 2/10minutes 🔧Ch⊡€ 2/minutes.
**Location:** Rural, simple, isolated, quiet. **Surface:** grassy/metalled.
📅 01/01-31/12.
**Distance:** ⌷2km 🏊on the spot 🛒on the spot ⊗1,3km ⊡1,3km.

### Lacapelle Marival 24G2

**Place de Larroque. GPS:** n44,72806 e1,92944.

50 ⌷free 🚰🔧Ch⊡. **Location:** Urban, simple, central.
**Surface:** asphalted. 📅 service 15/05-30/09.
**Distance:** ⌷on the spot ⊗100m ⊡50m.

### Lacroix-Barrez 24H2

**Aire de Camping Car Municipale**, Le Ventoux.
**GPS:** n44,77793 e2,63086. ⬆️➡️

10 ⌷€ 3,50 + € 0,20/pp tourist tax 🚰🔧Ch⌀(6x)included.
**Location:** Rural, comfortable, quiet. **Surface:** grassy. 📅 01/01-31/12
📅 service: 01/11-17/04.
**Distance:** ⌷400m.
**Remarks:** To be paid at town hall.

---

### Lagrasse 27H3

**Parking de la Promenade, P2**, Les Condamines.
**GPS:** n43,09273 e2,62004. ⬆️

40 ⌷€ 4, 01/06-30/09 € 6 🔧Ch WC free. **Location:** Rural,
simple, quiet. **Surface:** grassy/gravel. 📅 01/01-31/12.
**Distance:** ⌷on the spot 🏊on the spot 🛒on the spot ⊗on the spot
⊡on the spot.

### Laguepie 24G3

Chemin de Saint Cambraire. **GPS:** n44,14578 e1,97298. ⬆️➡️

6 ⌷free 🚰🔧Chfree. **Location:** Rural, simple, quiet.
**Surface:** grassy/gravel. 📅 01/01-31/12.
**Distance:** ⌷600m ⊗600m ⊡500m.
**Remarks:** Max. 24h.

### Laguiole 24H2

**Du Bouyssou**, La Serre. **GPS:** n44,67199 e2,92451. ⬆️

25 ⌷€ 10/day, € 40/week ⌀(24x)€ 5. **Location:** Rural, simple.
**Surface:** asphalted. 📅 01/01-31/12.
**Distance:** ⌷7km 🚶on the spot 🎿on the spot.

### Laguiole 24H2

Rue de Lavernhe. **GPS:** n44,68408 e2,85048. ⬆️

10 ⌷free 🚰🔧Ch⌀(2x)free. **Location:** Urban, simple.
**Surface:** gravel. 📅 01/01-31/12.
**Distance:** ⌷500m ⊗130m ⊡300m.

### Laguiole 24H2

**La Montagnettte**, Les Clauzades. **GPS:** n44,70457 e2,84037. ⬆️⬆️

30 ⌷free 🔧⌀(20x)€ 3. **Location:** Rural, simple, comfortable,
isolated, quiet. **Surface:** gravel. 📅 01/01-31/12.
**Distance:** ⌷4km ⊗3km ⊡4km.

---

### Laissac 24H3

**Aire Municipale**, Chemin d'Ampiac. **GPS:** n44,38590 e2,82160. ⬆️➡️

6 ⌷voluntary contribution 🚰🔧Ch WC free. **Location:** Rural, simple,
noisy. **Surface:** asphalted. 📅 01/03-30/11 ❄ frost.
**Distance:** ⌷500m ⊗500m ⊡500m.
**Remarks:** Max. 24h, tuesday morning market.

### Langogne 25B2

**Camping-Car Park**, Route du lac. **GPS:** n44,73700 e3,83448. ⬆️➡️

40 ⌷€ 10,30, 01/11-28/02 € 9,60 🚰🔧Ch⌀(16x)📶included.
🔌✏ **Location:** Rural, comfortable, quiet. **Surface:** grassy.
📅 01/01-31/12.
**Distance:** ⌷2km 🏊beach 1km 🛒on the spot ⊗2km ⊡2km.
**Remarks:** At lake Naussac, mandatory, one-time fee Pass'Etapes € 4.

### Langogne 25B2

**Centre Polyvalent. GPS:** n44,72281 e3,85419. ⬆️

10 ⌷free 🚰€ 2/100liter 🔧Ch. **Location:** Central, quiet.
**Surface:** asphalted. 📅 01/01-31/12.
**Distance:** ⌷on the spot ⊗300m ⊡300m 🚶on the spot.
**Remarks:** Coins at tourist info.

### Langogne 25B2

Rue de la Ponteyre. **GPS:** n44,72534 e3,83841. ⬆️
5 ⌷free. **Surface:** gravel. 📅 01/01-31/12.
**Distance:** ⌷city centre 1,5km 🏊on the spot ⊗on the spot.
**Remarks:** At lake.

### Lannemezan 27D2

**L'Espace du Nébouzan**, Chemin du Carrérot de Blazy.
**GPS:** n43,12779 e0,38085. ⬆️➡️

20 ⌷free 🚰🔧Ch⊡free. **Location:** Rural, comfortable, noisy.
**Surface:** gravel. 📅 01/01-31/12.
**Distance:** ⌷450m ⊗200m ⊡250m.

### Lanuéjols 28A1

Impasse de l'Engarenne. **GPS:** n44,12937 e3,38298.

FR

5 ⬜free ⛽🚽Ch 🚿(1x)free. **Location:** Rural, simple.
**Surface:** asphalted. ⬛ 01/01-31/12.
**Distance:** ⊗100m 🚰100m.

### 🏕S Lanuéjouls 24G3

**Aire Campingcar Lanuéjouls**, Avenue du Rouergue, D1.
**GPS:** n44,42528 e2,16139. ⬆➡.

14 ⬜€5 ⛽🚽Ch 🚿WC⬜included. **Location:** Rural, comfortable.
**Surface:** gravel. ⬛ 01/01-31/12.
**Distance:** 🚶100m ⊗100m 🚰100m.
**Remarks:** Barrier, ticket for access at shops in the village.

### 🏕S Lanzac 24F2

**La Ferme de Grezelade. GPS:** n44,87686 e1,47902. ⬆➡.

50 ⬜€3 ⛽🚽Ch⬜included WC⬜against payment. **Location:** Rural,
simple. **Surface:** grassy/gravel. ⬛ 01/01-31/12.
**Distance:** 🚶3km ⊗800m.

### 🏕S Lapradelle Puilaurens 27G3

D117. **GPS:** n42,81003 e2,30854. ⬆.

6 ⬜free ⛽🚽Chfree. **Location:** Rural, simple, quiet.
**Surface:** metalled. ⬛ 01/01-31/12.
**Distance:** 🚶on the spot ⊗100m.
**Remarks:** At fire-station.

### 🏕S Latour-Bas-Elne 32H1

**Aire de Latour Bas Elne**, Route de la Mer.
**GPS:** n42,60017 e3,00667. ⬆➡.

40 ⬜€10, Jun-Aug €14, trailer €4 ⛽🚽Ch 🚿included 🔌€3/48h.
🔌 **Location:** Comfortable. **Surface:** grassy. ⬛ 01/01-31/12.
**Distance:** 🚶3km.
**Remarks:** Baker at 9am, monitored parking.

---

### 🏕S Latour-de-Carol 32F1

**Village Club Yravals**, 2 Rue de Saneja. **GPS:** n42,45829 e1,89460. ⬆.

5 ⬜€10 + €0,22/pp tourist tax ⛽🚽Ch 🚿WCincluded 🔌€2/day.
**Surface:** grassy. ⬛ 01/04-31/10.
**Distance:** 🚶2km.

### 🏕S Latronquière 24G2

Place du Foirail. **GPS:** n44,79917 e2,07917. ⬆.

4 ⬜free ⛽🚽Ch 🚿WCfree. **Location:** Urban, simple.
**Surface:** asphalted. ⬛ 01/01-31/12.
**Distance:** 🚶300m 🏊3km 🚲3km ⊗300m 🚰300m.

### 🏕S Laudun-l'Ardoise 28C1

Place de la Résistance. **GPS:** n44,10791 e4,65556. ⬆.

3 ⬜free ⛽€4 🚽Ch ⬛€4. **Location:** Simple, central, noisy.
**Surface:** asphalted. ⬛ 01/01-31/12.
**Distance:** 🚶300m ⊗300m 🚰300m.
**Remarks:** Max. 7m, narrow entrance.

### 🏕S Laudun-l'Ardoise 28C1

Route d'Avignon, N580. **GPS:** n44,09527 e4,70164. ⬆.

3 ⬜free ⛽🚽Chfree. **Location:** Urban, simple, central.
**Surface:** asphalted. ⬛ 01/01-31/12.
**Distance:** 🚶5,5km ⊗300m 🚰500m 🚌300m.
**Remarks:** Behind police station, at tennis-court.

### 🏕S Laudun-l'Ardoise 28C1

**Vignerons de Laudun**, Avenue du Général de Gaulle.
**GPS:** n44,10388 e4,66362. ⬆.

10 ⬜free ⛽🚽Ch. **Location:** Simple, quiet. **Surface:** grassy/gravel.
⬛ 01/01-31/12.
**Distance:** 🚶300m ⊗300m 🚰100m.
**Remarks:** Max. 3 days.

---

### 🏕S Lauzerte 24E3

D2, Vignals. **GPS:** n44,26750 e1,14083. ⬆.

10 ⬜free ⛽🚽ChWCfree. **Location:** Simple. **Surface:** grassy/gravel.
⬛ 01/01-31/12.
**Distance:** 🚶Lauzerte 1km ⊗on the spot 🚰2km.
**Tourist information Lauzerte:**
🏛 ⬛ Wed-morning.

### 🏕S Le Barcarès 27H3

**Camping-Car Park Barcarès le Port**, Quai des Tourettes.
**GPS:** n42,80165 e3,03277. ⬆.

200 ⬜€10,80-13 ⛽🚽Ch 🚿(110x) 🔌included. 🗑.
**Location:** Urban, simple, central, quiet. **Surface:** metalled.
⬛ 01/01-31/12.
**Distance:** 🚶1,5km 🏊2km 🏖on the spot 🚲on the spot 🚰1,5km
🎣on the spot 🚶on the spot.
**Remarks:** Mandatory, one-time fee Pass'Etapes €4.

### 🏕S Le Bosc 28A1

**Parc Activités Méridienne. GPS:** n43,68827 e3,35459. ⬆➡.

10 ⬜free ⛽€2/100liter 🚽Ch ⬛€2/1h. **Location:** Motorway,
simple, isolated. **Surface:** asphalted. ⬛ 01/01-31/12.
**Distance:** 🚲400m ⊗on the spot 🚰Intermarché 50m.
**Remarks:** Behind petrol station.

### 🏕S Le Boulou 32H1

Chemin du Moulin Nou. **GPS:** n42,52719 e2,83704. ⬆➡.

21 ⬜free ⛽€2 ChWC. **Location:** Rural, simple, quiet.
**Surface:** asphalted. ⬛ 01/01-31/12.
**Distance:** 🚶300m 🚲1km 🏖on the spot ⊗300m 🚰300m
🚶on the spot.
**Remarks:** In front of cemetery, max. 24h.

### 🏕S Le Cap d'Agde 28A2

Rue du Gouverneur. **GPS:** n43,28600 e3,51739. ⬆➡.

FR

43 🛏 € 5-10, Jul/Aug € 12,50 🚰 € 2/100liter 🔌Ch🏕.🚐
**Location:** Rural, comfortable, central. **Surface:** asphalted/metalled.
🅾 01/01-31/12.
**Distance:** 🛒200m ⛱500m ⊗500m 🍴500m 🚲 on the spot.
**Remarks:** Nearby Camping La Clape, video surveillance.

| 🍴S | Le Caylar ⛵🏊🍴 | 28A1 |

**Domaine des Templiers**, Route de la Couvertoirade, D609.
**GPS:** n43,86944 e3,31466.⬆.

30 🛏 € 10 🚰15minutes 🔌Ch.🚿(9x)included12h WC🚽 € 4/pp
📷. **Location:** Rural, comfortable, isolated, quiet. **Surface:** gravel.
🅾 01/04-31/10.
**Distance:** 🛒600m 🚲500m ⊗on the spot.

| ©S | Le Fossat | 27F2 |

**Aire des Lallières**, Place de la Mairie. **GPS:** n43,17201 e1,41170.⬆➡.

21 🛏 € 12 🚰🔌Ch.🚿WC🚽📶included. **Location:** Rural, luxurious,
quiet. **Surface:** gravel. 🅾 01/03-30/11.
**Distance:** 🛒400m 🚽600m.

| 🅿S | Le Grau du Roi | 28B2 |

**Parking de la plage**, Rue du Commandant Marceau.
**GPS:** n43,54061 e4,13349.⬆.

40 🛏 € 11,60, June-Aug € 26,70 🚰 € 2/100liter 🔌
Ch🏕 € 2/55minutes.📷🚐 **Surface:** asphalted. 🅾 01/01-31/12.
**Distance:** 🛒centre 550m ⛱sandy beach 20m ⊗on the spot 🚽on
the spot.
**Remarks:** Beach parking, video surveillance.

| 🍴S | Le Houga | 27D1 |

**Ferme aux Cerfs**, Route de Mont de Marsan, D6.
**GPS:** n43,78198 e0,20367.⬆.

10 🛏 € 5 🚰🔌Chincluded 🚿 € 2/1day 📶. **Location:** Rural, simple,

quiet. **Surface:** grassy. 🅾 01/01-31/12.
**Distance:** 🛒2,5km ⊗on the spot.

| 🅿S | Le Malzieu-Ville 🌿⛱🍴🌲🌾 | 25A2 |

Place Foirail. **GPS:** n44,85506 e3,33385.⬆➡.

10 🛏free 🚰🔌ChWCfree 📶. **Location:** Rural, simple, central, quiet.
**Surface:** asphalted. 🅾 01/01-31/12.
**Distance:** 🛒on the spot 🚲10km ⛱on the spot ⊗200m 🚽200m
🏕 on the spot.

| 🅿S | Le Monastier-Pin-Moriès 🏔 | 25A3 |

Avenue de la République. **GPS:** n44,50889 e3,25162.⬆➡.

4 🛏free 🚰 € 3 🔌ChWCfree. **Location:** Rural, simple, isolated, quiet.
**Surface:** asphalted. 🅾 01/01-31/12.
**Distance:** 🛒1km 🚲1,5km 🚽1km.
**Remarks:** Coins at petrol station (200m), picnic area.

| 🅿S | Le Ségala | 27F2 |

Esplanade du Canal. **GPS:** n43,34089 e1,83544.⬆.

5 🛏free 🚰🔌WC. **Location:** Rural, simple, noisy. **Surface:** gravel.
🅾 01/01-31/12.
**Distance:** 🛒on the spot 🚲1km ⛱on the spot 🎣on the spot ⊗on
the spot 🍴on the spot.
**Remarks:** No camping activities.

| 🅿S | Le Ségur 🍴 | 27G1 |

Place de Marie. **GPS:** n44,10889 e2,05861.⬆➡.

3 🛏free 🚰🔌ChWCfree. **Location:** Rural, simple, quiet.
**Surface:** metalled. 🅾 01/01-31/12.
**Distance:** 🛒50m ⊗100m 🚽100m.
**Remarks:** At townhall.

| 🅿S | Les Angles 🏔🍴❄ | 32G1 |

**Pla del Mir. GPS:** n42,56321 e2,06780.⬆➡.

100 🛏 € 6-11 🚰 € 3,50 🔌ChWC. **Location:** Rural, simple, quiet.
**Surface:** asphalted. 🅾 01/01-31/12.
**Distance:** 🛒2,6km 🚲on the spot.

| 🅿S | Les Cabannes ❄🏊🍴 | 27F3 |

Quartier la Bexane. **GPS:** n42,78493 e1,68301.⬆➡.

30 🛏 € 5 🚰 € 2/100liter 🔌ChWC. 🚐🚿
**Location:** Rural, comfortable, central, quiet. **Surface:** asphalted
🅾 01/01-31/12.
**Distance:** 🛒300m ⊗300m.
**Remarks:** Max. 24h.

| 🅿S | Les Mages | 25B3 |

**Serre Marine**, Avenue du moulin. **GPS:** n44,23442 e4,16967.⬆➡.

20 🛏free 🚰🔌 € 2/time Ch. **Location:** Rural, simple, isolated, noisy.
**Surface:** metalled. 🅾 01/01-31/12.
**Distance:** 🛒700m ⊗700m 🚽800m.
**Remarks:** Picnic area.

| 🅿S | Leucate ⛵🏖 | 27H3 |

Chemin des Coussoules, La Franqui. **GPS:** n42,94329 e3,02917.⬆.

70 🛏 € 6 🚰🔌Ch € 7 on campsite. **Surface:** unpaved. 🅾 01/02-30/11
◉ summer.
**Distance:** 🛒2km ⛱on the spot 🎣on the spot ⊗2km 🚽2km.
**Remarks:** Next to campsite Coussoules.

| 🅿S | Leucate ⛵🏖 | 27H3 |

Le Goulet, D627. **GPS:** n42,91251 e3,02012.⬆.

150 🛏 € 11,80, 01/06-30/09 € 14,80 🚰 € 2 🔌Ch🏕 € 2.🚐
🚿 **Location:** Rural, simple, isolated, quiet. **Surface:** unpaved.
🅾 01/01-31/12.
**Distance:** 🛒centre Leucate 850m ⛱on the spot 🎣on the spot
⊗700m 🚽700m.
**Remarks:** Terraces, at lake of Leucate,
baker on site (20/03-31/10).

| 🅿S | Leucate ⛵🏖 | 27H3 |

**Mouret**, Chemin du Mouret, Leucate Plage.
**GPS:** n42,90022 e3,05272.⬆.

236 ⚡€ 11,80, 01/06-30/09 € 14,80 🚰 🔌Chincluded 🗑️🚿
📍Location: Rural, simple, noisy. Surface: asphalted/gravel.
🕐 01/01-31/12.
Distance: 🚶300m 🏖️on the spot 🍴on the spot.
Remarks: Beach parking, baker on site (20/03-31/10).

### ⒼⓈ Limoux 27G3
Parking, Rue Louis Braille. GPS: n43,05741 e2,21490. ⬆️➡️

30 ⚡free 🚰 🔌Chfree. Location: Urban, simple, central, quiet.
Surface: metalled. 🕐 01/01-31/12.
Distance: 🚶200m 🍴on the spot ❌200m.

### Ⓢ Lisle-sur-Tarn 27F1
Aire de Bellevue, Rue des Aulnes. GPS: n43,86167 e1,81833. ⬆️➡️

12 ⚡free 🚰€ 2/100liter 🔌Ch. Location: Rural, simple, isolated,
quiet. Surface: sand. 🕐 01/01-31/12 💧 water disconnected in
winter.
Distance: 🚶1,5km 🏖️on the spot 🍴on the spot ❌1,5km 🛒1,5km.
Remarks: Coins at Tourist Info and Maison de la Presse.

### Ⓒ Lodève 28A2
Baie des Vailhés, Celles. GPS: n43,67087 e3,35565. ⬆️

5 ⚡€ 7, 06/07-25/08 € 9, 01/10-30/03 free + tourist tax € 0,50/
pp. 🚣 Location: Rural, simple, isolated. Surface: grassy/sand.
🕐 01/05-30/09.
Distance: 🏖️on the spot ❌260m.
Remarks: At lake.
#### Tourist information Lodève:
ℹ️ Maison de Tourisme, 7, Place de la République, www.lodeve.com.
Old city to the gate of the Mediteranean.

### ⒼⓈ Lombez 27E2
Parking de la Gendarmerie, Route de Toulouse, D632.
GPS: n43,47417 e0,91592. ⬆️➡️

20 ⚡free 🚰 🔌WCfree. Location: Urban, comfortable.
Surface: gravel. 🕐 01/01-31/12.
Distance: 🚶200m ❌150m 🛒200m.

### ⒼⓈ Loudenvielle 27D3
Aire de campingcar Les Seguettes, Chemin du Hourgade.
GPS: n42,80163 e0,41088.

30 ⚡free, 01/07-15/09 € 4 🚰€ 2,50/100liter 🔌Ch€ 2,50/h. 🚣
Location: Rural, isolated, quiet.
Surface: gravel. 🕐 01/01-31/12.
Distance: 🚶700m ❌700m 🛒800m.
Remarks: At lake, coins at Tourist Info and Maison de la Presse.

### Ⓢ Loudenvielle 27D3
La Ribère, D25 Génos. GPS: n42,79936 e0,40813. ⬆️

10 ⚡free, 01/07-15/09 € 3. 🚣 Location: Rural, simple, quiet.
Surface: gravel. 🕐 01/01-31/12.
Distance: 🚶500m 🍴on the spot ❌400m 🛒500m 🚴on the spot
🚶on the spot.
Remarks: Max. 3 days.

### ⒼⓈ Lourdes 27C3
Le Vieux Berger, Route de Julos. GPS: n43,10451 w0,0332. ⬆️➡️

27 ⚡€ 14,44 🚰🔌Ch 🚿WC 💧🗑️€ 3/3 🔌included. 🚾
📍Location: Rural, luxurious, noisy. Surface: grassy/gravel.
🕐 01/01-31/12.
Distance: 🚶1km 🚲2km ❌700m 🛒700m 🚌100m 🚶on the spot.
Remarks: Next to campsite.

### ⒼⓈ Lourdes 27C3
Parking Arrouza, Esplanade du Paradis.
GPS: n43,08834 w0,0528. ⬆️➡️

50 ⚡€ 10 🚰€ 5/100liter 🔌Ch. 🚾 📍Location: Simple, central,
quiet. Surface: asphalted. 🕐 01/03-31/10.
Distance: 🚶city centre 1km.
Remarks: Monitored parking.

### Lourdes 27C3
Lapacca, Boulevard du Lapacca. GPS: n43,09832 w0,04198. ⬆️➡️

16 ⚡free. Location: Urban, simple. Surface: asphalted.
🕐 01/01-31/12.
Distance: 🚶350m.
Remarks: Pilgrimage site.
#### Tourist information Lourdes:
ℹ️ Office de Tourisme, Place Peyramale, www.lourdes-infotourisme.
com. Lively place of pilgrimage.
✝️ Basilique St.Pius X. Underground basilica, of the largest sanctuaries
in the world, there is place for 25,000 people.

### ⒼⓈ Lunas 28A1
Base de Loisirs Prade, D35. GPS: n43,70555 e3,18555. ⬆️➡️

75 ⚡free 🚰 🔌Chfree. Location: Simple, isolated, quiet.
Surface: grassy/metalled. 🕐 01/01-31/12.
Distance: 🚶900m 🏖️on the spot 🍴on the spot ❌200m 🛒700m
🚶200m.

### ⒸⓈ Luzech 24F3
Les Berges de Caïx, D9. GPS: n44,49068 e1,29506. ⬆️

15 ⚡€ 8,50 + € 0,80/pp tourist tax 🚰🔌Ch 🚿WCincluded 💧€ 2,50.
Location: Rural, simple, quiet. Surface: gravel.
🕐 01/01-31/12.
Distance: 🚶2km.
Remarks: Along Lot river.

### ⒼⓈ L'Hospitalet-près-l'Andorre 32F1
N22. GPS: n42,58823 e1,79833. ⬆️

5 ⚡free 🚰€ 2 🔌Ch 🚿€ 6. Location: Rural, simple, noisy.
Surface: asphalted. 🕐 01/01-31/12.
Distance: ❌100m 🚶on the spot.

### ⒼⓈ Marbre 27D3
Lac de Payolle, D918, Campan > Col d'Aspin.
GPS: n42,93704 e0,29249. ⬆️

10 ⬛free. **Location:** Rural, simple, isolated, quiet. **Surface:** grassy/gravel. ⬛ 01/01-31/12. **Distance:** ⬛5km ⬛50m ⬛50m ⊗700m ⬛5km ⬛on the spot ⬛on the spot.

| 🅱S | Marseillan-Plage ⬛⬛⬛ | 28A2 |

1, Rue des Goélands. **GPS:** n43,31902 e3,54864. ⬆⬆➡.

140 ⬛€ 4-6, Jul/Aug € 12 ⬛€ 2/5minutes ⬛Ch ⬛⬛⬛ **Location:** Comfortable, quiet. **Surface:** gravel. ⬛ 01/01-31/12. **Distance:** ⬛on the spot ⬛sandy beach 600m ⊗on the spot ⬛on the spot. **Remarks:** Max. 48h.

| 🅱 | Martel ⬛⬛ | 24F2 |

**Parking Monti,** D23. **GPS:** n44,93957 e1,60827. ⬆➡.

25 ⬛free. **Location:** Rural, simple. **Surface:** asphalted. ⬛ 01/01-31/12. **Distance:** ⬛400m ⊗400m ⬛400m.

| 🅱S | Marvéjols ⬛⬛⬛⬛⬛ | 25A3 |

**Le Pré de Suzon. GPS:** n44,55406 e3,28753. ⬆.

10 ⬛free ⬛⬛ChWCfree. **Location:** Urban, central. **Surface:** asphalted. ⬛ 01/01-31/12. **Distance:** ⬛on the spot ⬛7,5km ⊗on the spot ⬛on the spot.

**Tourist information Marvéjols:**
ℹ Maison de Tourisme, Porte du Soubeyran, www.ville-marvejols.fr. Old fortress city, gates with battlements and towers.

| 🅱 | Matemale ⬛⬛⬛⬛❄ | 32G1 |

**Forêt de la Matte. GPS:** n42,57964 e2,10227. ⬆.

10 ⬛free ⬛€ 1 ⬛ChWC ⬛. **Location:** Rural, simple, isolated, quiet. **Surface:** asphalted. ⬛ 01/01-31/12. **Distance:** ⬛3km ⬛on the spot ⬛on the spot ⊗300m.

---

**Remarks:** Parking at lake.

| 🅱 | Matemale ⬛⬛⬛⬛❄❄ | 32G1 |

Rue de la Truite. **GPS:** n42,56559 e2,10433. ⬆.

10 ⬛free. **Location:** Rural, simple, isolated, quiet. **Surface:** gravel. ⬛ 01/01-31/12. **Distance:** ⬛1,5km ⬛20m ⊗1,5km ⬛1,5km ⬛on the spot ⬛on the spot. **Remarks:** Parking at lake.

| 🅱S | Mauléon-Barousse ⬛⬛⬛ | 27D3 |

**Plot Bleu,** D925. **GPS:** n42,96121 e0,56798. ⬆.

6 ⬛free ⬛€ 3/20minutes ⬛Ch ⬛(4x)€ 3/3h ⬛. **Location:** Rural, comfortable, quiet. **Surface:** asphalted. ⬛ 01/01-31/12. **Distance:** ⬛on the spot ⬛on the spot ⊗350m ⬛400m.

| ©S | Maureillas-Las-Illas | 32H1 |

**Camping Maureillas,** Route de las Illas, D13. **GPS:** n42,48711 e2,80748. ⬆.

20 ⬛€ 8,20-12,70 + € 0,22/pp tourist tax ⬛⬛Ch ⬛⬛ 4 WC ⬛⬛ time,€ 6,50/4,50 ⬛included. **Location:** Rural, comfortable, quiet. **Surface:** metalled. ⬛ 01/01-31/12. **Distance:** ⬛500m ⊗500m ⬛500m ⬛on the spot.

| 🅱S | Mazamet | 27G2 |

D118. **GPS:** n43,46278 e2,34609. ⬆➡.

9 ⬛free ⬛⬛Chfree. **Location:** Rural, isolated, quiet. **Surface:** grassy/gravel. ⬛ 01/01-31/12 ⬛ Service: autumn/winter. **Distance:** ⬛8km ⬛on the spot ⬛on the spot ⊗on the spot. **Remarks:** Max. 48h.

| 🅱S | Mazamet | 27G2 |

Rue Galibert-Ferret, Champ de la Ville. **GPS:** n43,49089 e2,37918. ⬆.

10 ⬛free ⬛⬛Chfree. **Location:** Urban, central. **Surface:** asphalted. ⬛ 01/01-31/12 ⬛ Fri-Sa market. **Distance:** ⬛on the spot ⊗on the spot. **Remarks:** At townhall, max. 24h.

| 🅱S | Mazères-sur-Salat ⬛ | 27E3 |

**Aire Municipale,** Rue du quai du salat. **GPS:** n43,13457 e0,97630. ⬆.

---

15 ⬛free ⬛⬛Ch. **Location:** Urban, simple, quiet. **Surface:** asphalted. ⬛ 01/01-31/12. **Distance:** ⬛on the spot ⬛4,5km ⬛river.

| 🅱S | Mende ⬛⬛⬛⬛ | 25A3 |

**Camping-car Park Aérodrome,** Aérodrome Mende-Brenoux. **GPS:** n44,50666 e3,52723. ⬆➡.

38 ⬛€ 9,60/24h ⬛⬛Ch ⬛(24x) ⬛included. ⬛⬛⬛ **Location:** Rural, comfortable, isolated. **Surface:** grassy/gravel. ⬛ 01/01-31/12. **Distance:** ⬛4,5km ⬛on the spot ⊗on the spot ⬛on the spot. **Remarks:** At airfield, mandatory, one-time fee Pass'Etapes € 4.

| 🅱S | Mende ⬛⬛⬛⬛ | 25A3 |

Rue du Faubourg Montbel. **GPS:** n44,52063 e3,49660. ⬆.

20 ⬛free ⬛€ 2/10minutes ⬛Ch ⬛⬛ 2/55minutes. **Location:** Urban, comfortable, central, quiet. **Surface:** asphalted. ⬛ 01/01-31/12. **Distance:** ⬛on the spot ⬛on the spot ⊗200m ⬛400m ⬛on the spot ⬛on the spot. **Remarks:** Along Lot river, max. 96h.

| 🅱S | Mèze ⬛⬛ | 28A2 |

**Camping-Car Park Escale de Thau,** Avenue du stade. **GPS:** n43,44135 e3,59436. ⬆.

44 ⬛€ 12,46, 01/04-31/10 € 13,66 ⬛⬛Ch ⬛(44x) ⬛included. ⬛⬛ **Location:** Rural, simple, noisy. **Surface:** gravel. ⬛ 01/01-31/12. **Distance:** ⬛2,5km ⬛10km. **Remarks:** Mandatory, one-time fee Pass'Etapes € 4.

| 🅱S | Miélan | 27D2 |

Rue du Cubet. **GPS:** n43,43319 e0,30900. ➡.

6 🛏free 🚰💧Chfree. **Location:** Rural, simple, quiet.
**Surface:** gravel. ⏺ 01/01-31/12.
**Distance:** 🛒350m ⊗350m 🚉350m.

🏕S **Millau** ⛰🏔 **27H1**
**Camping-car Park**, Rue de la Saunerie 19.
**GPS:** n44,09610 e3,08577.⬆➡.

41 🛏€ 10,50 🚰💧Ch 💧(30x) 💦included. 🗑🚿 **Location:** Urban,
comfortable. **Surface:** gravel. ⏺ 01/01-31/12.
**Distance:** 🛒500m 🏊200m.
**Remarks:** Mandatory, one-time fee Pass'Etapes € 4, motorhomes
<7.5m.
**Tourist information Millau:**
ℹ Office de Tourisme, 1, Place du Beffroi, www.ot-millau.fr. City tourist
in the Valley of the Tarn and the Dourbie. Important for the leather
trade.
🚶 Vieux Millau. Historical hiking route, info at Office de Tourisme.

🏕S **Mirandol-Bourgnounce** **24G3**
Place de Foirail. **GPS:** n44,14167 e2,16667.⬆.

8 🛏free 🚰💧Chfree. **Location:** Urban, simple, quiet.
**Surface:** asphalted. ⏺ 01/01-31/12.
**Distance:** 🛒on the spot ⊗on the spot 🚉50m 🚲on the spot.

🏕S **Mirepoix** ☘ **27F3**
**Parking des Capitouls**, Allée de Palafrugell.
**GPS:** n43,08491 e1,87399.⬆.

20 🛏free 🚰💧ChWC. **Location:** Rural, simple, quiet.
**Surface:** asphalted. ⏺ 01/01-31/12.
**Distance:** 🛒centre 500m ⊗200m 🚉400m.
**Remarks:** Next to community centre.
**Tourist information Mirepoix:**
🐂 Cattle market. ⏺ winter 2nd, 4th Mo of the month.
🐂 ⏺ Thu, Sa.

🏕S **Moissac** 🏔 **27E1**
**Les Berges du Tarn**, Chemin de la Rhode. **GPS:** n44,09803 e1,09304.

44 🛏€ 8, 01/10-31/03 € 6 🚰💧Ch 💦included. 🗑🚿 🚿
**Location:** Urban, comfortable. **Surface:** gravel/sand.
⏺ 01/01-31/12.
**Distance:** 🛒900m ⊗900m.
**Remarks:** Along the Tarn river.

🏕S **Moissac** 🏔 **27E1**
**Chez Pascal**, 360 Chemin de Rosières. **GPS:** n44,11867 e1,14604.
10 🛏€ 10 🚰 **Location:** Rural, simple, quiet. **Surface:** grassy.
⏺ 05/05-31/10.
**Distance:** ⊗3,5km 🚉2,3km 🚲on the spot 🚶on the spot.

🏕S **Monclar-de-Quercy** 🏔🏔 **27F1**
**Lotissement les Terrasses du Lac, Base de Loisiers**, Route de la
Gresigne. **GPS:** n43,96990 e1,58885.⬆➡.

6 🛏free, June-Sep € 3,90/pp 🚰💧Chfree. 🚍 **Location:** Simple.
**Surface:** gravel. ⏺ 01/01-31/10.
**Distance:** 🛒2km 🏊on the spot 🛒on the spot 🚉2km 🚶on the spot.

🏕S **Mont Roc** 🏔🌲 **27G1**
**Aire Municipale**, Salle de Fêtes. **GPS:** n43,80330 e2,37192.⬆.

8 🛏free 🚰€ 2 💧Ch💧€ 2 WC. **Location:** Rural, simple, quiet.
**Surface:** metalled. ⏺ 01/01-31/12.
**Distance:** 🛒50m ⊗on the spot 🚉on the spot.
**Remarks:** Coins.

🏕S **Mont-Louis** ☘🏔 **32G1**
**Parking des Remparts**, Rue Lieutenant Pruneta 3.
**GPS:** n42,50765 e2,12273.⬆.

20 🛏€ 7 🚰included. 🗑🚿 **Location:** Urban, simple, quiet.
**Surface:** asphalted.
**Distance:** 🛒200m ⊗200m 🚉200m.
**Remarks:** Parking at city wall, max. 48h.

🏕 **Montagnac** **28A2**
D613. **GPS:** n43,47520 e3,49129.⬆➡.

5 🛏free.
**Location:** Simple, quiet. **Surface:** gravel. ⏺ 01/01-31/12.
**Distance:** 🛒1km ⊗1km 🚉1km.

🏕S **Montauban** ☘🏔 **27F1**
**Mr. Lacaze**, 225, route de Corbarieu, D21. **GPS:** n43,99188 e1,35196.⬆.

15 🛏€ 7 🚰💧Ch 💦included WC💧€ 1. 🚿🚿 **Location:** Rural,
simple. **Surface:** gravel. ⏺ 01/01-31/12. **Distance:** 🛒Montauban
3km 🚉1km. **Remarks:** Max 3,5t.

🏕S **Montauban** ☘🏔 **27F1**
**Port Canal**, Rue des Oules 125. **GPS:** n44,00744 e1,34105.⬆.

10 🛏€ 8 🚰💧Ch 💦. **Location:** Comfortable, quiet.
**Surface:** grassy/gravel. ⏺ 01/01-31/12.
**Distance:** 🛒2,5km.
**Remarks:** At the canal.

🍇S **Montauban** ☘🏔 **27F1**
**La Ferme des Pibouls**, Route de Saint-Antonin.
**GPS:** n44,03488 e1,40649.⬆.

12 🛏€ 5 🚰💧Chfree. 🚍
**Location:** Rural, simple. **Surface:** grassy.
⏺ 01/01-31/12.
**Distance:** 🛒5km ⊗on the spot 🚉on the spot.
**Remarks:** At supermarket.
**Tourist information Montauban:**
ℹ Office de Tourisme, 2, rue du Collège, officetourisme.montauban.
com. City of roses.
🐂 ⏺ Sa.

🍇 **Montcalm** **28B2**
**Le Caveau du Chêne**, Route d'Aigues Mortes, D58.
**GPS:** n43,57322 e4,30505.⬆.

FR

40 ⬛free for clients. **Location:** Rural, isolated, quiet. **Surface:** grassy. ⬛ 01/01-31/12.

### Montcuq 🚲🏕️ 24E3
Route de Cahors, D653. **GPS:** n44,34082 e1,20242.

15 ⬛free 🚰 € 2/100liter ⬛Ch🚽 € 2/1h. **Location:** Simple. **Surface:** gravel. ⬛ 01/01-31/12. **Distance:** 🚶250m ⊗250m 🛒50m. **Remarks:** Coins at Tourist Info and petrol station.

### Montdardier 28A1
**Parking voor Camping de la Couronne**, Chemin de l'église. **GPS:** n43,92885 e3,59073.⬆️➡️

5 ⬛free. **Location:** Rural, quiet. **Surface:** gravel. **Distance:** ⊗350m 🚶on the spot. **Remarks:** Nearby camp site, max. 72h, shady.

### Monteils 🏕️ 24G3
D47. **GPS:** n44,26694 e1,99667.⬆️

4 ⬛free 🚰 ⬛Chfree. **Location:** Rural, simple, quiet. **Surface:** grassy/gravel. ⬛ 01/01-31/12. **Distance:** 🚶100m ⊗500m 🛒50m.

### Montézic 🏕️ 24H2
**Les Prades Sud. GPS:** n44,71054 e2,64413.⬆️➡️

10 ⬛tourist tax 🚰⬛. **Location:** Rural, simple, quiet. **Surface:** asphalted. ⬛ 01/03-31/10. **Distance:** 🚶500m ⊗500m 🛒500m. **Remarks:** Money in envelope in mail box.

### Montferrand 27F2
**Col de Naurouze**, Route du Ségala, N113> D218. **GPS:** n43,35238 e1,82390.⬆️

20 ⬛free. **Location:** Rural, simple, quiet. **Surface:** gravel. ⬛ 01/01-31/12. **Distance:** 🚶2km ⬛on the spot ⊗on the spot 🛒2km 🚲 on the spot 🚶on the spot.

### Ⓟ Montpellier 🌿🏕️🍰 28B2
**Parking Joffre**, Rue d'Argencour. **GPS:** n43,61316 e3,88608. 10 ⬛€ 1/h. **Location:** Urban, simple, central. **Surface:** asphalted. ⬛ 01/01-31/12. **Distance:** ⚓4km ⊗1km 🚶on the spot. **Remarks:** Overnight stay possible. Via avenue Jean Mermoz.

**Tourist information Montpellier:**
- 👁 Corum. Opera-complex.
- 👁 Place de la Comédie. Square with many cafés.

### Montréal (Gers) 🏕️ 27D1
**Stade André Daubin**, D29. **GPS:** n43,95375 e0,19730.⬆️

20 ⬛free 🚰⬛Chfree. **Location:** Rural, simple. **Surface:** gravel. ⬛ 01/01-31/12. **Distance:** 🚶200m ⊗500m 🛒500m. **Remarks:** Parking at rugby ground.

**Tourist information Montréal (Gers):**
ℹ️ Office de Tourisme, place de l'Hôtel de Ville, www.montrealdugers.com/. Fortified city with ramparts, square with arcades and picturesque alleys.

### Montréjeau 🌿🏔️ 27D3
**Grande Halle**, Place de Verdun. **GPS:** n43,08448 e0,57112.⬆️

4 ⬛free. **Location:** Urban, simple, central, noisy. **Surface:** asphalted. ⬛ 01/01-31/12. **Distance:** 🚶100m ⊗200m 🛒400m 🚶on the spot.

### Monze 27G3
La Bretonne. **GPS:** n43,15475 e2,45867.⬆️

2 ⬛free. **Location:** Rural, simple, isolated, quiet. **Surface:** asphalted. ⬛ 01/01-31/12. **Distance:** 🚶50m ⊗500m. **Remarks:** Max. 48h.

### Mourèze 🌿🏕️🏔️ 28A2
D8. **GPS:** n43,61728 e3,36111.⬆️

6 ⬛€ 6 🚰⬛Chincluded. 💧 **Location:** Rural, simple, isolated, quiet. **Surface:** gravel. ⬛ 01/01-31/12. **Distance:** 🚶on the spot ⊗300m 🚶on the spot.

### Ⓢ Mur de Barrez 🏔️🏕️ 24H2
**Parc de la Corette**, Place du Foirail. **GPS:** n44,84170 e2,65970.⬆️➡️

6 ⬛free 🚰⬛Ch🚽free. **Location:** Urban, simple. **Surface:** asphalted. ⬛ 01/04-30/11. **Distance:** 🚶100m ⊗100m 🛒50m 🚲on the spot. **Remarks:** Free coins at tourist info and town hall, max. 72h.

### Ⓢ Murviel-lès-Béziers 🏕️ 27H2
**Camping-Car Park**, Route de Réals, D36. **GPS:** n43,43953 e3,13420.⬆️

25 ⬛€ 11,90 🚰⬛Ch🔌(20x)WC 📶included. 🚗 🧹 **Location:** Rural, comfortable, isolated, quiet. **Surface:** unpaved. ⬛ 01/01-31/12. **Distance:** 🚶700m ⚓10km ⊗700m 🛒1,7km 🚶on the spot. **Remarks:** Mandatory, one-time fee Pass'Etapes € 4, historical centre.

### Ⓢ Nages 27H2
**Aire de camping car du Lac**, Lac du Laouzas, D162. **GPS:** n43,64694 e2,78194.⬆️

22 ⬛€ 7,50, peak season € 8,50 🚰⬛Ch🚽included. **Location:** Isolated, quiet. **Surface:** grassy/gravel. ⬛ 31/03-01/11. **Distance:** ⚓on the spot. **Remarks:** Nearby base nautique.

### Ⓢ Najac 🌿🏕️🏔️🏕️ 24G3
Roc du Pont. **GPS:** n44,22167 e1,96778.⬆️➡️

10 ⬛€ 6-8 🚰⬛Ch🚽(12x)WCincluded. 🚗 🧹 **Location:** Comfortable, quiet. **Surface:** asphalted. ⬛ 01/01-31/12. **Distance:** 🚶1,8km ⚓on the spot 🚣on the spot ⊗500m 🛒3km 🚲on the spot 🚶on the spot. **Remarks:** Historical centre.

### Ⓢ Narbonne-Plage 27H3
Les Joncasses. **GPS:** n43,14433 e3,14594.⬆️ 30 ⬛€ 10,40-13,40 🚰€ 2 ⬛Ch🚽€ 2/1h. 🚗 **Location:** Rural, isolated, quiet. **Surface:** gravel. ⬛ 01/01-31/12. **Distance:** ⚓on the spot 🚣on the spot. **Remarks:** Next to campsite.

### Ⓢ Naucelle 😊🏕️ 24G3
Place du Ségala. **GPS:** n44,19723 e2,34175.⬆️

FR

4 ⓈⓈfree 🚰🔌Chfree.
**Location:** Simple, noisy. **Surface:** asphalted.
🅿 01/01-31/12.
**Distance:** 🚰on the spot 🛒1km ⬛1km ⊗on the spot 🔌on the spot.

### ⓈⓈ Nègrepelisse 🛒 27F1
Avenue Jean Fleury. **GPS:** n44,07408 e1,52664.⬆.

7 ⓈⓈfree 🚰🔌Chfree. **Location:** Urban, simple, noisy.
**Surface:** grassy/gravel. 🅿 01/01-31/12 ⬛ service: 01/12-01/04.
**Distance:** 🚰1km ⊗1km 🔌100m.
**Remarks:** Along through road, near sports fields.

### ⓈⓈ Nîmes 🌿🛒🍴 28B1
**Domaine de Fontbespierre**, 3359, route d'Anduze/d907.
**GPS:** n43,87138 e4,27734.⬆.

50 ⓈⓈ€ 10 🚰€ 2 🔌Ch 🚿€ 2/day WC. **Location:** Rural, isolated, quiet. **Surface:** grassy. 🅿 01/01-31/12.
**Distance:** 🚰6km ⊗6km 🔌6km.
**Remarks:** Terrain with video surveillance.

### ⓈⓈ Octon ⛰ 28A2
Avenue de la Molière. **GPS:** n43,65390 e3,30378.⬆.

8 ⓈⓈfree.
**Location:** Rural, simple, isolated, quiet. **Surface:** asphalted.
🅿 01/01-31/12.
**Distance:** 🚰50m ⊗50m 🔌50m 🏊Lac du Salagou. 🎣Lac du Salagou.
**Remarks:** Parking behind 'Clamery', Lac du Salagou.

### ⓈⓈ Olargues ⛰ 27H2
**Camping-Car Park**, Chemin du Coulayro Bas.
**GPS:** n43,55655 e2,91879.⬆.

12 ⓈⓈ€ 10,05, 16/06-14/09 € 11,25 🚰🔌Ch 🚿(12x)included. ⬛🔧
**Location:** Simple, quiet. **Surface:** asphalted. 🅿 01/01-31/12.

---

**Distance:** 🚰500m ⊗500m 🔌500m.
**Remarks:** Mandatory, one-time fee Pass'Etapes € 4.

### ⒸⓈ Oust 27E3
Foute d'Aulus les Bains. **GPS:** n42,87167 e1,21833.➡.

10 ⓈⓈ€ 15,50, Jul/Aug € 18 🚰🔌Ch 🚿WC 🔌.
**Location:** Rural, simple, quiet. **Surface:** gravel.
🅿 01/01-31/12.
**Distance:** 🚰1km ⊗800m.
**Remarks:** Next to campsite Les 4 Saisons, arrival >14h departure <12h.

### ⓈⓈ Ouveillan 27H2
**Aire Municipale**, Place Cave Coopérative.
**GPS:** n43,29204 e2,97080.⬆.

5 ⓈⓈfree 🚰🔌Chfree. **Location:** Rural, simple, simple, quiet.
**Surface:** gravel/metalled. 🅿 01/01-31/12.
**Distance:** 🚰2km ⊗2km 🔌2km.

### ⓈⓈ Padirac 24F2
**GPS:** n44,84632 e1,74949.⬆.
15 ⓈⓈfree 🚰€ 2/100liter 🔌Ch 🚿€ 2/2h. **Location:** Rural, quiet.
**Surface:** asphalted. 🅿 01/01-31/12.
**Distance:** ⊗850m 🔌900m.

### ⓉⓈ Palavas-les-Flots 28B2
**Port Fluvial, Base Paul Riquet**, Avenue de Lattre Tassigny.
**GPS:** n43,53091 e3,92316.⬆.

135 ⓈⓈ€ 15, Jul-Aug € 18 + € 0,83/pp tourist tax, extra charge >8m and trailer 🚰€ 3 🔌Ch 🚿€ 3 WC🔌included 📶.
**Location:** Urban, simple, noisy. **Surface:** asphalted.
🅿 01/01-31/12.
**Distance:** 🚰1km 🏊on the spot ⊗500m 🔌1km.
**Remarks:** Bicycle rental.

### ⓈⓈ Perville 🍴 24E3
Centre du village. **GPS:** n44,18066 e0,88011.

2 ⓈⓈfree 🚰🔌Chfree. **Location:** Rural, simple. **Surface:** asphalted.
🅿 01/01-31/12.
**Distance:** 🚰10km ⊗10km 🔌10km.

### ⓈⓈ Peyragudes 🏔❄ 27D3
**Parking de Balestas**, Culas. **GPS:** n42,79629 e0,44015.⬆.

---

25 ⓈⓈfree 🚰€ 2/100liter ⬛€ 2/1h. **Location:** Rural, simple, isolated, quiet. **Surface:** gravel. 🅿 01/01-31/12.
**Distance:** 🚰10km ⊗150m 🔌850m 🎿on the spot ⛷on the spot 🏔 on the spot.
**Remarks:** Coins at Maison de Peyragudes.

### ⓈⓈ Peyriac-de-Mer 🌊 27H3
Route des Bages. **GPS:** n43,09372 e2,96205.⬆.

20 ⓈⓈ€ 5/24h 🚰🔌Ch 🔌 **Location:** Rural, simple.
**Surface:** grassy/metalled. 🅿 01/01-31/12.
**Distance:** 🚰1km 🏊on the spot ⊗1km 🔌1km 🏊 on the spot 🎣on the spot.
**Remarks:** Next to rugby ground.

### ⓈⓈ Peyrusse le Roc 24G3
Le Thérondet/D87. **GPS:** n44,49500 e2,13972.⬆➡.

12 ⓈⓈfree 🚰🔌Chfree. **Location:** Simple. **Surface:** grassy/sand.
🅿 01/01-31/12.
**Distance:** 🚰500m ⊗500m 🔌500m.

### ⓈⓈ Pierrefitte-Nestalas 🏔🍴 27C3
Chemin de la Portere. **GPS:** n42,96042 w0,07697.⬆➡.

15 ⓈⓈfree 🚰€ 1/50liter 🔌ChWC. **Location:** Rural, isolated, quiet.
**Surface:** asphalted. 🅿 01/01-31/12.
**Distance:** 🚰200m 🚲10km ⊗200m 🔌200m 🏊 on the spot 🏔 on the spot.
**Remarks:** Max. 8 days.

### ⓈⓈ Pinsac 24F2
**Parking Salle des Fêtes**, D43. **GPS:** n44,85500 e1,51222.

5 ⓈⓈfree 🚰€ 2 🔌Ch. **Location:** Simple, comfortable.
**Surface:** gravel. 🅿 01/01-31/12.
**Distance:** 🚰on the spot 🚲9,5km 🔌700m.

### Piquecos 〠 27F1
**Parking de la Salle des Fêtes. GPS:** n44,10144 e1,32093.

7 ⏚free ⌁ ⬚Chfree. **Location:** Rural, simple. **Surface:** gravel.
⬛ 01/01-31/12.
**Distance:** ⛲100m ⛽on the spot.

### Pont-de-Salars 24H3
Place de la Rivière. **GPS:** n44,27822 e2,72853.⬆.

5 ⏚free ⌁€5/80liter ⬚Ch. **Location:** Simple. **Surface:** asphalted.
⬛ 01/05-31/10.
**Distance:** ⛲100m 🏊2km ⛽2km ⊗on the spot ⛲100m
🧍on the spot.
**Remarks:** Along river, max. 3 days, coins at the shops.

### Port Vendres 〰 32H1
**L'Anse des Tamarins,** Route de la Jetée. **GPS:** n42,51778 e3,11375.⬆.

40 ⏚€6, May/Okt 10 ⌁€2/100liter ⬚ChWC.☗ **Location:** Rural,
simple. **Surface:** gravel. ⬛ 01/01-31/12.
**Distance:** ⛲1,3km 🏊100m ⊗on the spot.

### Port-la-Nouvelle ⛵ 27H3
**Camping-Car Park,** Chemin des Vignes.
**GPS:** n43,01366 e3,04077.⬆➡.

100 ⏚€10, 01/07-31/08 €12,40 ⌁⬚Ch⬚on camp site
🛜included. ⬛ **Location:** Rural, simple. **Surface:** grassy/gravel.
⬛ 01/01-31/12.
**Distance:** ⛲2km 🚲8,6km 🏊2km ⊗2km ⛲1km Huit-à-huit,
Passage de l'Abbé Gavanon.
**Remarks:** Mandatory, one-time fee Pass'Etapes €4.

### Portiragnes ⛵〰 28A2
Avenue de la Grande Maïre. **GPS:** n43,27558 e3,35156.⬆.

30 ⏚€5 ⌁⬚Chincluded. **Location:** Rural, simple, quiet.

**Surface:** unpaved. ⬛ 01/01-31/12.
**Distance:** 🏖sandy beach 200m.
**Remarks:** Max. 48h.

### Pradinas 24G3
Place de l'Eglise. **GPS:** n44,23855 e2,26583.⬆➡.

5 ⏚free ⌁⬚Chfree. **Location:** Rural, simple, quiet.
**Surface:** gravel. ⬛ 01/04-31/10.
**Distance:** ⛲on the spot.

### Prayssac 〠 24E3
Avenue Maréchal Bessières. **GPS:** n44,50352 e1,19197.⬆.

10 ⏚free ⌁⬚Chfree WC. **Location:** Simple. **Surface:** grassy/gravel.
⬛ 01/01-31/12 ⬛ Service: winter.
**Distance:** ⛲200m ⛲1,5km.

### Preignan 27D1
Rue Emile Zola. **GPS:** n43,71243 e0,63378.⬆➡.

5 ⏚free ⌁⬚Chfree. **Location:** Rural, simple. **Surface:** gravel.
⬛ 01/01-31/12.
**Distance:** ⛲1km.
**Remarks:** At sports park.

### Puy l'Eveque 24E3
Place de la Gendarmerie. **GPS:** n44,50699 e1,13560.⬆.

8 ⏚free ⌁⬚ChWCfree. **Location:** Urban, comfortable.
**Surface:** gravel. ⬛ 01/01-31/12 ⬛ 01/08-11/08, service: winter.
**Distance:** ⛲250m ⊗300m ⛲300m.
**Remarks:** In front of town hall, max. 24h, upper city.

### Puylaurens 27G2
Rue Albert Thorel. **GPS:** n43,56861 e2,01194.⬆➡.

17 ⏚free ⌁⬚Chfree 〰. **Location:** Quiet. **Surface:** gravel.
⬛ 01/01-31/12.

**Distance:** ⛲700m ⊗100m ⛲700m ⛲400m.
**Remarks:** Max. 48h, wifi at supermarket.

### Quillan 27G3
**Camping-Car Park,** 20 Rue Baptiste Marcet.
**GPS:** n42,85472 e2,18166.⬆.

29 ⏚€10,10, 01/06-30/09 €11,30 ⌁⬚Ch ☗(28x)included. ⬛
**Location:** Rural, comfortable, quiet. **Surface:** gravel.
⬛ 01/01-31/12.
**Distance:** ⛲on the spot 🚲on the spot 🧍on the spot.
**Remarks:** Mandatory, one-time fee Pass'Etapes €4.

### Remoulins 〰 28C1
N86. **GPS:** n43,93789 e4,55851.⬆.

10 ⏚free ⌁€5/20minutes ⬚Ch. **Location:** Urban, simple, quiet.
**Surface:** asphalted. ⬛ 01/01-31/12.
**Distance:** ⛲100m ⊗100m ⛲100m.
**Remarks:** Parking nearby river, service on the other side of the bridge:
Route du Pont du Gare.
**Tourist information Remoulins:**
⌂ Pont du Gard. Roman aqueduct.

### Rennes-les-Bains 〰 27G3
**Plateau Sport Nature,** Route des Corbières.
**GPS:** n42,91479 e2,31814.⬆.

7 ⏚€5/24h ⌁⬚Chfree. **Location:** Rural, simple, isolated, quiet.
**Surface:** asphalted. ⬛ 01/01-31/12.
**Distance:** ⛲500m ⛲100m ⊗200m.
**Remarks:** At sports park.

### Requista 〠 27H1
Place François Fablé. **GPS:** n44,03465 e2,53599.⬆.

6 ⏚free ⌁⬚ChWCfree. **Location:** Urban, simple, quiet.
**Surface:** gravel. ⬛ 01/01-31/12 ⬛ service 01/11-30/04.
**Distance:** ⛲200m.
**Remarks:** At sports centre.

### Revel 27G2
**Roy des Eaux,** Chemin de la Pergue. **GPS:** n43,45286 e2,01233.⬆➡.
28 ⏚€7, 01/06-31/08 €9, tourist tax excl ⌁⬚Ch ☗included. ⬛
◢ **Surface:** gravel. ⬛ 01/01-31/12.
**Distance:** ⛲1km ⊗1km ⛲1km.
**Remarks:** Max. 7 nights.

## Rieupeyroux    24G3

15 Rue de la Calquière. **GPS**: n44,30861 e2,23194. ⬆➡

3 ☕free 🚐🗑Ch🧹free. **Location**: Simple, quiet.
**Surface**: asphalted. ⬛ 01/04-01/11.
**Distance**: 🚶500m ⊗500m 🛒1,5km.
**Remarks**: Next to school.

## Rieutort-de-Randon    25A3

Lac de Charpal. **GPS**: n44,62491 e3,56046. ⬆

10 ☕free WC. **Location**: Rural, isolated, quiet. **Surface**: unpaved.
⬛ 01/01-31/12.
**Distance**: 🚶8km 🏊18km ⚓on the spot 🚣on the spot ⊗on the spot
🎣on the spot.
**Remarks**: At lake Charpal.

## Rignac    24G3

Hameau du Lac, La Peyrade. **GPS**: n44,40456 e2,28958. ⬆➡

12 ☕free, June-Aug € 5 🚐🗑Chfree. 🚿 **Location**: Rural, simple,
quiet. **Surface**: grassy. ⬛ 01/01-31/12.
**Distance**: 🚶1km ⚓on the spot ⊗1km 🛒1km 🎣on the spot.

## Rivières    27G1

Aire de Salta, La Courtade Haute. **GPS**: n43,91072 e1,98889. ⬆➡

6 ☕12 🚐🗑Ch🚿(6x)included. 🚿 **Location**: Rural, comfortable,
quiet. **Surface**: gravel. ⬛ 01/06-30/09.
**Distance**: 🚶2km ⚓on the spot 🚣on the spot 🛒3km.
**Remarks**: Along the Tarn river, bread-service in summer period.

## Rocamadour    24F2

Le Château, D673. **GPS**: n44,80000 e1,61528. ⬆

30 ☕free. **Location**: Rural, simple, quiet. **Surface**: gravel.
⬛ 01/01-31/12. ⬛ 15/06-15/09.
**Distance**: 🚶300m ⊗100m.

## Rodés    32G1

Route Neuf de Conquille 8. **GPS**: n42,65560 e2,56263. ⬆

6 ☕€5 🚐🗑Chincluded 🚿€ 3. 🚿 **Location**: Rural, simple, quiet.
**Surface**: grassy/metalled. ⬛ 01/01-31/12.
**Distance**: ⊗1,5km 🛒450m.

## Rodez    24H3

Route du Gué de Salelles. **GPS**: n44,35731 e2,59374. ⬆➡

6 ☕free 🚐🗑Chfree. **Location**: Urban, simple, noisy.
**Surface**: gravel. ⬛ 01/01-31/12.
**Distance**: 🚶2km 🚲1km 🛒1km 🚴on the spot 🎣on the spot.
**Remarks**: Max. 72h.

## Roquecor    24E3

Place du Foirail, D82. **GPS**: n44,32346 e0,94496. ⬆

6 ☕free 🚐🗑Chfree. **Location**: Simple. **Surface**: asphalted.
⬛ 01/01-31/12.
**Distance**: 🚶250m ⊗300m 🛒250m.
**Remarks**: Max. 48h.

## Roquefort-sur-Soulzon    27H1

Aire Municipale, D23 / Aveneu de Lauras. **GPS**: n43,98120 e2,98163. ⬆

10 ☕free 🚐🗑ChWCfree.
**Location**: Simple, noisy. **Surface**: asphalted.
⬛ 01/01-31/12 ⬛ Service: winter.
**Distance**: 🚶100m.
**Remarks**: Parking behind tourist info, max. 7 days, inclining pitches.

## Roques    27F2

Parking E.Leclerc, Allée de Fraixinet. **GPS**: n43,51192 e1,36920. ⬆

6 ☕free 🚐€ 2/100liter 🗑Ch🚿€ 2/4h.
**Location**: Urban, simple, central, noisy. **Surface**: asphalted.
⬛ 01/01-31/12.

**Distance**: 🚶1km ⊗200m.
**Remarks**: Coins.

## Routier    27G3

Sous la Serre. **GPS**: n43,10813 e2,12362. ⬆➡

7 ☕free 🚐🗑Chfree. **Location**: Rural, simple, quiet.
**Surface**: grassy/gravel. ⬛ 01/01-31/12 ⬤ water disconnected in
winter.
**Distance**: 🚶on the spot ⊗130m 🛒170m.

**Tourist information Routier:**
ℹ Corbières. Region is known for its wines and the Cathar citadels, the
castle of Queribus in Cucugan is one of the last bastions of the Cathars.

## Saillagousse    32F1

Rue des Sports. **GPS**: n42,45764 e2,03766. ⬆

7 ☕free 🚐€ 4 🗑Chfree WC. **Location**: Urban, simple, quiet.
**Surface**: asphalted. ⬛ 01/01-31/12.
**Distance**: 🚶on the spot ⊗on the spot 🛒on the spot.
**Remarks**: Coins at tourist info and town hall.

## Saint-Affrique    27H1

Aire Municipale, Place de la Vernière. **GPS**: n43,95587 e2,88145. ⬆

3 ☕free 🚐🗑Ch💧free. **Location**: Urban, simple, noisy.
**Surface**: metalled. ⬛ 01/01-31/12.
**Distance**: 🚶300m ⊗200m 🛒200m.
**Remarks**: Max. 48h.

## Saint-André    32H1

Parking de Taxo. **GPS**: n42,55248 e2,97303. ⬆➡

6 ☕€ 2,30 🚐€ 2 🗑Ch💧€ 2. **Surface**: asphalted. ⬛ 01/01-31/12.
**Distance**: 🚶on the spot.
**Remarks**: Max. 3 nights, coins at tourist info.

## Saint-Antoine    27E1

**GPS**: n44,03587 e0,84209. ⬆➡

FR

10 �}free ⌐–€ 2 ⊟Ch. **Location:** Rural, simple, quiet.
**Surface:** asphalted. ⬤ 01/01-31/12.
**Distance:** 200m 4,3km 200m 200m.

### Saint-Antonin-Noble-Val 〰️〰️ 🅂 24F3
Chemin de Roumégous. **GPS:** n44,15222 e1,75139.⬆️➡️

15 �}free ⌐–⊟Chfree. **Location:** Rural, simple, quiet.
**Surface:** asphalted/gravel. ⬤ 01/01-31/12.
**Distance:** 200m ⊗300m 100m on the spot.

### Saint-Céré 🅂 24G2
Rue du Stade. **GPS:** n44,86139 e1,88583.⬆️

3 �}free ⌐–⊟Chfree. **Location:** Simple, central. **Surface:** asphalted.
⬤ 01/01-31/12.
**Distance:** 200m ⊗200m 150m.
**Remarks:** Behind stadium, nearby cemetery.

### Saint-Chély-d'Apcher 🅂 25A2
**Parking du Péchaud,** Boulevard G. d'Apcher, N9.
**GPS:** n44,80084 e3,27296.⬆️➡️

2 �}free ⌐–€ 2/100liter ⊟Ch€ 2/10minutes.
**Location:** Simple, central, quiet. **Surface:** asphalted.
⬤ 01/01-31/12.
**Distance:** 200m 2,5km 200m 200m on the spot.
**Remarks:** Coins at tourist info.

### Saint-Cirq-Lapopie 〰️⛵️⛰️🌳 🅂 24F3
**Aire Camping-Car,** Porte Roques. **GPS:** n44,47068 e1,67982.⬆️

40 �}€ 7,50 ⌐–€ 2/100liter ⊟Ch€ 2 WC€ 2. 🚿 **Location:** Rural,
isolated, quiet. **Surface:** grassy/gravel. ⬤ 01/01-31/12.
**Distance:** 1,5km on the spot ⊗50m.
**Remarks:** Along Lot river, near campsite, max. 48h.

### Saint-Cirq-Lapopie 〰️☂️⛰️🌳🟩 🅂 24F3
P1, Porte Roques. **GPS:** n44,47029 e1,67891.⬆️

50 �}€ 7 ⌐–€ 2/100liter ⊟Ch €2/h. **Location:** Rural,
comfortable, isolated, quiet. **Surface:** grassy. ⬤ 01/01-31/10.
**Distance:** 900m on the spot ⊗800m 800m 🚶 on the spot.
**Remarks:** Max. 2 nights, service 100m.

**Tourist information Saint-Cirq-Lapopie:**
ℹ️ Village, entirely under preservation order, has been built on a rock above the river Lot.
⌒ Grotte de Pech-Merle, Cabrerets. Temple cave, monument from the Paleolithicum with images of mammoth, horses and bizons.

### Saint-Clar 🅂 27E1
**Aire de repos,** Avenue de la Garlepe. **GPS:** n43,89111 e0,77250.⬆️

10 ⌎free ⌐–⊟ChWC⌎free.
**Location:** Rural, simple, isolated, quiet. **Surface:** grassy/gravel.
⬤ 01/01-31/12 ⬤ sanitary building: winter.
**Distance:** 500m ⊗250m.

### Saint-Côme-d'Olt ⛰️🌳 🅂 24H3
Rue des Ginestes. **GPS:** n44,51647 e2,82072.⬆️➡️

9 ⌎free ⌐–€ 2/10minutes ⊟Ch. **Location:** Rural, simple, noisy.
**Surface:** asphalted. ⬤ 01/01-31/12.
**Distance:** 500m ⊗500m 500m.
**Remarks:** At cemetery, coins at tourist info and supermarket.

### Saint-Cyprien ⛵️ 🅂 32H1
**Aire du Théâtre de la Mer,** Quai Arthur Rimbaud.
**GPS:** n42,61776 e3,03512.⬆️

49 ⌎€ 8,20, Jul/Aug € 12 ⌐–⊟Ch⊞included. 🛒
**Location:** Comfortable. **Surface:** asphalted. ⬤ 01/01-31/12
⬤ service 15/10-31/03.
**Distance:** 450m marina ⊗300m.

### Saint-Cyprien-sur-Dourdou ⛰️🌳 🅂 24G3
**La Citarelle,** Route de Conques, D901. **GPS:** n44,55258 e2,40978.⬆️➡️

13 ⌎€ 5 ⌐–€ 2/20minutes ⊟Ch⊞€ 1/2h. 🚿 **Location:** Rural,
comfortable, quiet. **Surface:** grassy/gravel. ⬤ 01/01-31/12.
**Distance:** 300m ⊗300m 350m.

### Saint-Félix-Lauragais 🅂 27F2
**Lac de Lenclas,** D622. **GPS:** n43,42667 e1,89806.

10 ⌎free ⌐–⊟ChWC. **Location:** Rural, simple, isolated, quiet.
**Surface:** gravel. ⬤ 01/01-31/12.
**Distance:** 100m ⊗100m.
**Remarks:** Max. 24h.

### Saint-Gaudens 🅂 27E3
**Aire de camping-car Le Belvedere,** Rue Chanteurs du Comminges.
**GPS:** n43,10997 e0,70813.⬆️➡️

60 ⌎€ 8 ⌐–⊟Ch 🔧included. 🛒
**Location:** Rural, comfortable, central, quiet. **Surface:** grassy.
⬤ 01/01-31/12.
**Distance:** 1,5km.
**Remarks:** Former campsite, max. 7 days.

### Saint-Geniez-d'Olt 🅂 24H3
**Parking,** Avenue de la gare. **GPS:** n44,46305 e2,97563.⬆️

10 ⌎free ⌐–WCfree. **Location:** Urban, simple, central, noisy.
**Surface:** gravel. ⬤ 01/01-31/12.
**Distance:** on the spot 500m 500m ⊗500m 300m.
**Remarks:** Max. 24h.

### Saint-Géry 🅂 24F3
**Domaine du Porche,** D662. **GPS:** n44,47818 e1,58091.⬆️

15 ⌎€ 5,50 ⌐–€ 2/100liter ⊟Ch⊞€ 2/1h WC. **Location:** Simple.
**Surface:** gravel. ⬤ 01/01-31/12.
**Distance:** ⊗100m 100m.
**Remarks:** Market on Sunday.

### Saint-Gilles 28B2
Quai du Canal. **GPS:** n43,67154 e4,43281.

35 free. **Location:** Rural, simple, central, noisy. **Surface:** asphalted.
01/01-31/12.
**Distance:** 500m 300m 500m.
**Tourist information Saint-Gilles:**
 Abbay St.Gilles. Abbey with underground church.

### Saint-Girons 27E3
Rue Aristide Berges. **GPS:** n42,98865 e1,13916.

7 free € 2/150liter Ch € 2/15minutes.
**Location:** Urban, simple, central, quiet. **Surface:** asphalted.
01/01-31/12.
**Distance:** 100m 600m.
**Remarks:** Max. 48h.

### Saint-Jean-du-Gard 28B1
Château du Péras, 1 Grande Rue. **GPS:** n44,10210 e3,89059.
21 € 13 Ch included. **Location:** Simple.
**Surface:** gravel. 01/01-31/12.
**Distance:** 750m 600m 800m.
**Remarks:** Max. 48h.

### Saint-Jean-et-Saint-Paul 27H1
Parking, Saint Jean d'Alcas. **GPS:** n43,92646 e3,00887.

10 free ChWC free. **Location:** Rural, simple, isolated, quiet.
**Surface:** asphalted/gravel. 01/01-31/12.
**Distance:** on the spot.
**Remarks:** At cemetery.

### Saint-Just-sur-Viaur 27G1
Parking La Fabrie, D532. **GPS:** n44,12402 e2,37588.

4 free Ch WC free. **Location:** Rural, isolated, quiet.
**Surface:** gravel. 01/01-31/12 service 01/11-31/03.
**Distance:** 10km on the spot on the spot.

### Saint-Lary-Soulan 27D3
Parking du Stade, Route de Vieille Aure. **GPS:** n42,82248 e0,32329.

---

60 € 6,50/night € 2/100liter Ch € 2/h.
**Location:** Rural, simple, noisy. **Surface:** asphalted.
01/01-31/12.
**Distance:** 500m 500m 500m on the spot on the spot.
**Remarks:** Parking behind stadium.

### Saint-Laurent-de-Carnols 25C3
Cave Coopérative Vinicole, Route de Bagnols D166.
**GPS:** n44,21002 e4,53132.
5 free € 2/100liter Ch € 2/1h. **Location:** Simple.
**Surface:** asphalted. 01/01-31/12.
**Distance:** 300m 300m 300m 200m.

### Saint-Laurent-de-Cerdans 32G1
Parking Halle Polyvalente, Place du Syndicat.
**GPS:** n42,38336 e2,61572.

15 free Ch WC free. **Location:** Urban, simple, quiet.
**Surface:** gravel. 01/01-31/12.
**Distance:** 500m 100m 500m on the spot.
**Remarks:** Max. 48h.

### Saint-Mamert-du-Gard 28B1
Rue des Fraisses. **GPS:** n43,88965 e4,19039.

6 free. **Location:** Rural, simple, quiet. **Surface:** asphalted.
01/01-31/12.
**Distance:** 400m on the spot on the spot.
**Remarks:** Max. 48h.

### Saint-Mamert-du-Gard 28B1
Route du Stade. **GPS:** n43,88491 e4,19054.
Ch free. **Location:** Quiet. 01/01-31/12.
**Distance:** on the spot.

### Saint-Mamet 27D3
Rue Pierre Baysse, D27. **GPS:** n42,78399 e0,60393.

7 € 5 Ch free. **Location:** Rural, simple, quiet.
**Surface:** asphalted. 01/01-31/12.
**Distance:** 200m 850m 150m.
**Remarks:** Next to cemetery, max. 72h, to be paid at town hall.

### Saint-Marsal 32G1
Le Village. **GPS:** n42,53755 e2,62242.

---

25 € 3 free. **Location:** Rural, simple, isolated, quiet.
**Surface:** asphalted. 01/01-31/12.
**Distance:** on the spot on the spot 50m.

### Saint-Martin-de-Londres 28A1
Rue des Sapeurs. **GPS:** n43,79046 e3,73470.

6 € 4 € 4 included. **Location:** Simple, central, noisy.
01/01-31/12.
**Distance:** 150m 250m on the spot.

### Saint-Martory 27E2
Aire Municipale, Place Nationale, D52E, D117.
**GPS:** n43,14203 e0,92939.

7 € 4 Ch (4x)included WC.
**Location:** Urban, simple, central. **Surface:** asphalted.
01/01-31/12 Thu (market).
**Distance:** on the spot 3km on the spot.
**Remarks:** Along river, max. 1 night.

### Saint-Maurice-en-Quercy 24G2
Place de l'église. **GPS:** n44,74306 e1,94722.

10 free. **Location:** Rural, simple, isolated, quiet. **Surface:** gravel.
01/01-31/12.

### Saint-Médard-de-Presque 24G2
D30. **GPS:** n44,87114 e1,84434.

40 € 10/24h, € 5/night Ch € 5/time included.
**Location:** Rural, comfortable. **Surface:** gravel. 01/01-31/12.
**Distance:** 1km.
**Remarks:** Barrier.

### Saint-Nicolas-de-la-Grave 27E1
Rue de la Calle, Rue Bouchotte. **GPS:** n44,06379 e1,02471.

FR

10 ⬛free ⛽🚰Chfree. **Location:** Simple. **Surface:** asphalted/gravel. ◻ 01/01-31/12. **Distance:** 100m 50m 100m.

### Ⓒ Ⓢ Saint-Nicolas-de-la-Grave 🍲 27E1

**Camping Car Park Pass'Etapes**, Avenue du Plan d'Eau. **GPS:** n44,08616 e1,02745.⬆➡.

12 ⬛€ 12,30-13,50 🚰stay 🚰Ch 🚰stay 🚿 📶included. 🛒 ♻ **Location:** Rural. **Surface:** asphalted. ◻ 01/01-31/12. **Distance:** 2,8km 200m 200m. **Remarks:** Summertime on campsite, wintertime in front of campsite.

### Ⓢ Saint-Puy 27D1

Grande Rue, D654. **GPS:** n43,87611 e0,46250.⬆.

3 ⬛free 🚰Ch WC free. **Location:** Urban, simple, central. **Surface:** asphalted. ◻ 01/01-31/12. **Distance:** 20m 50m 20m.

### Ⓢ Saint-Sauveur-Camprieu ❄ 28A1

**Aire Municipale**, D710 Maison du Bois. **GPS:** n44,10843 e3,48304.⬆.

6 ⬛free 🚰€ 2/100liter 🚰Ch. **Location:** Rural, simple, isolated, quiet. **Surface:** gravel. ◻ 01/01-31/12. **Distance:** 1km 1km on the spot on the spot. **Remarks:** Altitude 1000m, max. 7 days.

### Ⓢ Saint-Thibéry 28A2

**Domaine de la Vière**, Chemin de la Vière. **GPS:** n43,38301 e3,40137.⬆➡.

26 ⬛€ 10 🚰Ch 🚿 WC 📶included. 🛒 **Location:** Rural, comfortable, isolated, quiet. **Surface:** unpaved. ◻ 01/01-31/12. **Distance:** 2km A9 3km 14km 50m 4km. **Remarks:** During the weekend possible inconvenience of motocross.

### Ⓢ Ⓢ Sainte-Croix-Volvestre 27E3

**Aire Municipale**, Lenclos. **GPS:** n43,12673 e1,17094.⬆➡.

10 ⬛free 🚰Chfree. **Location:** Rural, simple, isolated, quiet. **Surface:** grassy/gravel. ◻ 01/01-31/12. **Distance:** 200m 500m 500m. **Remarks:** At football ground.

### Ⓢ Sainte-Eulalie-d'Olt 🌿 24H3

La Grave. **GPS:** n44,46466 e2,94974.⬆.

10 ⬛€ 8, 15/05-15/09 € 9 🚰Ch 🚿 included WC € 2 🗑 € 2. 🛒 ♻ **Location:** Rural, simple, quiet. **Surface:** gravel. ◻ 01/01-31/12. **Distance:** 300m on the spot 250m 350m. **Remarks:** Along Lot river, next to campsite.

### Ⓢ Sainte-Eulalie-de-Cernon 🌿 ⚓ 🏰 27H1

## Aires de Camping cars Sainte-Eulalie-de-Cernon

- Sanitary facilities
- Comfortable motorhome stopover
- Medieval town

**www.sainte-eulalie.info secretariat@sainte-eulalie.info**

Chemin de Millau. **GPS:** n43,98349 e3,13733.⬆➡. 22 ⬛€ 9,50/24h 🚰Ch WC 📶included. 🛒 ♻ **Location:** Rural, comfortable, isolated. **Surface:** grassy/gravel. ◻ 01/01-31/12. **Distance:** 500m 200m 150m.

### Ⓢ Ⓢ Sainte-Geneviève-sur-Argence 24H2

Rue de l'Argence. **GPS:** n44,80194 e2,76222.⬆➡.

30 ⬛free 🚰€ 2/10minutes 🚰Ch 🚿(4x). **Location:** Urban, simple. **Surface:** gravel. ◻ 01/01-31/12. **Distance:** 500m 500m 500m 500m 200m.

### Ⓢ Ⓢ Sainte-Marie-de-Campan 🏔 🏰 27D3

**Place du 19 Mars 1962**, D918. **GPS:** n42,98234 e0,22821.⬆.

5 ⬛free 🚰Chfree. **Location:** Rural, simple, quiet. **Surface:** asphalted. ◻ 01/01-31/12. **Distance:** 100m 250m 200m 🚴 on the spot 🚶 on the spot. **Remarks:** Max. 48h.

### Ⓢ Sainte-Marie-la-Mer 🌿 24H3

**Night4campingcar**, Rue Gustave Eiffel. **GPS:** n42,73246 e3,02548.⬆.

120 ⬛€ 6, Jul/Aug € 9,50 🚰Ch 🚿€ 3/24h,16Amp 📶included. 🛒 ♻ **Location:** Rural, comfortable, central, noisy. **Surface:** gravel. ◻ 01/01-31/12. **Distance:** 800m 1,2km on the spot on the spot.

### Ⓢ Salasc 28A2

**Aire Municipale**, Route de la Gloriette, D148. **GPS:** n43,61746 e3,31709.⬆.

2 ⬛free. **Location:** Rural, simple, isolated, quiet. **Surface:** grassy/gravel. ◻ 01/01-31/12. **Distance:** 300m 300m on the spot. **Remarks:** Max. 48h.

### Ⓢ Ⓢ Salles-Curan 🍴 24H3

**Aire de camping-car des Vernhes**, Lac de Pareloup. **GPS:** n44,20002 e2,77573.⬆➡.

73 ⬛€ 11/24h 🚰€ 4 🚰Ch 🚿€ 4/1h WC 📶included. 🛒 ♻ **Location:** Rural, comfortable, quiet. **Surface:** grassy/gravel. ◻ 01/04-31/10. **Distance:** 4km on the spot on the spot 4km 4km on the spot. **Remarks:** At lake, former campsite.

### Ⓢ Ⓢ Salles-sur-l'Hers 27F2

Allée des Platanes. **GPS:** n43,29194 e1,78844.⬆.

10 ⬛free 🚰Ch 🚰free. **Location:** Rural, simple, isolated, quiet.

FR

**Surface:** gravel. ☐ 01/01-31/12.
**Distance:** ⬤on the spot ⊗100m ⬤100m.
**Remarks:** At football ground.

### ⊞S Samatan 🌿🏖️🍴🐚 27E2
**Les Rivages Base de Loisirs**, Avenue de Lombez, D39.
**GPS:** n43,48791 e0,92616.➡️

10 ⛺€3 + €0,40/pp tourist tax ⛽🗑Ch ♨WCincluded.
**Location:** Rural, simple, quiet. **Surface:** asphalted.
☐ 01/01-31/12.
**Distance:** ⬤500m ⛵on the spot ⬌on the spot ⊗250m ⬤250m ⬤250m.

### ⊞S Sarrant 🍴 27E1
Route de Solomiac. **GPS:** n43,77532 e0,92822.⬆️➡️

20 ⛺free ⛽🏖free. **Location:** Rural, simple, quiet.
**Surface:** grassy/gravel. ☐ 01/01-31/12.
**Distance:** ⬤150m ⬌300m ⊗100m ⬤150m 🚶on the spot.
**Remarks:** At small lake, in front of football stadium.

### ⊞S Sauve 🌿🏖️⛰️ 28B1
D999. **GPS:** n43,94017 e3,95218.⬆️➡️

5 ⛺free ⛽🗑Chfree. **Location:** Urban, simple, central, noisy.
**Surface:** metalled. ☐ 01/01-31/12.
**Distance:** ⬤50m ⊗50m 🚶on the spot.
**Remarks:** Max. 7m.

### ⊞S Sauveterre-de-Comminges ⛰️🍴 27D3
Hameau de Bruncan, D9. **GPS:** n43,03391 e0,66711.⬆️➡️

5 ⛺€6 ⛽🗑Ch ♨WCincluded. 🐕 **Location:** Rural, simple,
isolated, quiet. **Surface:** asphalted/grassy. ☐ 01/01-31/12.
**Distance:** ⬤on the spot ⊗on the spot ⬤10km 🚲on the spot
🚶on the spot.
**Remarks:** Check in at bar, service passerby €3.

### ⊞S Sauveterre-de-Rouergue 🌿⛰️🍴 24G3
Le Sardou, D997. **GPS:** n44,21613 e2,31700.⬆️

15 ⛺free ⛽🗑Chfree ♨€2/day WC🗑€1,50/12minutes.
**Location:** Rural, comfortable, quiet. **Surface:** gravel.
☐ 01/05-31/10.
**Distance:** ⬤500m ⊗500m ⬤500m.
**Remarks:** Max. 7m, coins at tourist info, shady.

### ⊞S Ségur 🍴 24H3
Impasse du Pré Amat. **GPS:** n44,29087 e2,83503.⬆️

3 ⛺free ⛽🗑ChWCfree 🗑€2/6minutes. **Location:** Rural, simple,
quiet. **Surface:** asphalted. ☐ 01/05-31/10.
**Distance:** ⬤500m ⬌on the spot ⊗500m ⬤500m 🚶on the spot.
**Remarks:** Coins at town hall and supermarket, small pitches, covered
picnic area with electricity.

### Seix ⛰️ 27E3
Place de l'Allée. **GPS:** n42,86239 e1,20239.⬆️➡️

4 ⛺free ⛽🗑Chfree. **Location:** Urban, simple, central, quiet.
**Surface:** gravel. ☐ 01/01-31/12.
**Distance:** ⬤on the spot ⊗on the spot ⬤on the spot.
**Remarks:** Service 500m, canoe rental, market on Sunday.

### 🌾S Senergues 🌿⛰️🍴 24G3
**La Ferme des Autruches**, La Besse. **GPS:** n44,58861 e2,48361.⬆️

5 ⛺€5 ⛽🗑Ch ♨WC. **Location:** Rural, simple, quiet.
**Surface:** grassy/gravel. ☐ 01/03-30/11.
**Distance:** ⬤2km.

### ⊞S Sérignan-Plage ⛰️🏖 28A2
**Camping-Car Park Serignan Plage**, D37. **GPS:** n43,26909 e3,33149.

49 ⛺€9,60, 01/07-31/08 €12 ⛽🗑Ch🗑included. 🖥
**Location:** Rural, simple, quiet. **Surface:** grassy. ☐ 01/01-31/12.
**Distance:** ⬤4km ⛵200m ⊗200m ⬤on the spot.

---

**Remarks:** Service accross the street, mandatory, one-time fee
Pass'Etapes €4.

### 🍴S Sérignan-Plage ⛰️🏖 28A2
**Mini Golf du Lion**, Avenue de la Plage, D37.
**GPS:** n43,26892 e3,33629.⬆️

20 ⛺€8, 01/05-30/09 €13 + tourist tax €2/pp ⛽🗑Ch ♨€4/24h
WC🗑included 🖥€4. **Location:** Rural, comfortable, quiet.
**Surface:** unpaved. ☐ 01/01-31/12.
**Distance:** ⛵150m ⊗on the spot ⬤150m.
**Remarks:** Behind restaurant, bread-service, swimming pool.

### ⊞S Serres-sur-Arget 27F3
D45. **GPS:** n42,96990 e1,51869.⬆️

10 ⛺free 🗑. **Location:** Rural, simple, isolated, quiet.
**Surface:** metalled. ☐ 01/01-31/12.
**Distance:** ⬤500m.
**Remarks:** Next to community centre.

### ⊞S Sète ⛰️🍴🐚 28A2
**Parking Les 3 Digues**. **GPS:** n43,36663 e3,61523.⬆️

70 ⛺€6,66-9,66, Jul/Aug €11,66 ⛽€1/10minutes 🗑Ch 🧺🖥📦
**Location:** Rural, simple. **Surface:** gravel. ☐ 01/01-31/12.
**Distance:** ⛵50m ⊗on the spot 🚶on the spot.
**Remarks:** Beach parking, max. 72h, 01/06-30/09 no dogs allowed on
the beach.

### ⊞S Sommières ⛰️ 28B1
Chemin de la Princesse. **GPS:** n43,78701 e4,08717.⬆️

25 ⛺free ⛽€3 🗑Ch. **Location:** Simple. **Surface:** gravel.
☐ 01/01-31/12.
**Distance:** ⬤500m ⬌100m ⊗300m.
**Remarks:** In front of campsite municipal.

### ⊞ Sommières ⛰️ 28B1
Chemin de la Royalette. **GPS:** n43,77989 e4,08437.
⛺€5. ☐ 01/01-31/12.
**Remarks:** Next to sports fields.

### ⊞S Souillac ⛰️🐚 24F2
**Parking de Baillot**, Chemin de Baillot. **GPS:** n44,89139 e1,47667.⬆️➡️

20 ⓢfree ⌐€ 4 Ch ✎. **Location:** Rural, simple, central.
**Surface:** asphalted. ◻ 01/01-31/12. ◉ water disconnected in winter.
**Distance:** ⌂400m ⚓4,5km ⊗400m ⛾500m.
**Remarks:** Max. 7 days.

**Tourist information Souillac:**
ⓘ Bd Louis-Jean Malvy. Monastery-city, 12th century, between the regions Périgord and Quercy.

| ⓢⓈ | Soulom 🌿🏔 | 27C3 |

Place des Fêtes, D921. **GPS:** n42,95611 w0,0725. ⬆.

15 ⓢfree ⌐free. **Location:** Rural, simple, central, quiet.
**Surface:** asphalted. ◻ 01/01-31/12.
**Distance:** ⌂200m ⚓500m ⊗200m ⛾200m ⅄ on the spot.

| ⓢⓈ | Sousceyrac 🌊❄ | 24G2 |

Place des Condamines. **GPS:** n44,87255 e2,03649. ⬆.

10 ⓢfree ⌐🗑Ch ✎ WCfree. **Location:** Simple, central, noisy.
**Surface:** asphalted. ◻ 01/04-30/10.
**Distance:** ⌂on the spot ⌁on the spot ⊗on the spot ⛾100m.
**Remarks:** In front of town hall, max. 1 night.

| ⓢⓈ | Tarbes 🏔 | 27D2 |

**Aire de Service Camping-car Ambulance Didier**, Avenue de la Libération. **GPS:** n43,24284 e0,06790. ⬆➡.

30 ⓢ€ 12 ⌐🗑Chincluded ⌁€ 2/night. 🔌 **Location:** Urban, quiet.
**Surface:** asphalted. ◻ 01/01-31/12.
**Distance:** ⌂1km ⚓1km ⊗800m ⛾1km ⌁on the spot.
**Remarks:** Service only: water € 2, water + electricity € 5, video surveillance.

| ⓢⓈ | Thémines 24F2 |

Place de L'église. **GPS:** n44,74083 e1,82972. ⬆➡.

3 ⓢfree ⌐🗑Ch ✎free. **Location:** Urban, simple.

---

**Surface:** asphalted. ◻ 01/01-31/12.
**Distance:** ⌁on the spot.
**Remarks:** Near church.

| ⓢⓈ | Therondels 🎣🏔🌲 | 24H2 |

La Cazournie. **GPS:** n44,89833 e2,75937. ⬆➡.

10 ⓢfree ⌐🗑Chfree. **Location:** Rural, simple. **Surface:** grassy.
◻ 01/04-15/11.
**Distance:** ⌂500m ⊗100m ▣100m ⅄ on the spot.

| ⓢⓈ | Theza | 32H1 |

**Palmeraie des Alberes**, Route Départementale 914.
**GPS:** n42,63763 e2,93675.
6 ⓢ€ 12 ⌐🗑Ch ✎ WCincluded. **Location:** Simple, noisy.
◻ 01/01-31/12.
**Distance:** ⌂2km ⊗2km ⛾2km.
**Remarks:** Service passerby € 6.

| ⓢⓈ | Thues-entre-Valls 🏔🌲 | 32G1 |

**Gorges de la Carança. GPS:** n42,52346 e2,22517. ⬆.

25 ⓢfirst 24h € 9, € 5/24h ⌐🗑Ch 📶included. 🚐
**Location:** Rural, simple, isolated, quiet. **Surface:** grassy/sand.
◻ 01/01-31/12 ◉ frost.
**Distance:** ⌂2km ⚓on the spot ⌁on the spot ⊗300m ⅄ on the spot.

| ⓢⓈ | Thuir | 32H1 |

**Camping-Car Park Cité du Byrrh**, Chemin du Salaou.
**GPS:** n42,63040 e2,76814. ⬆.

24 ⓢ€ 11,80-13 ⌐🗑Ch ✎(24x) 📶included. 🚐🔌 **Location:** Rural, simple, isolated, quiet. **Surface:** gravel. ◻ 01/01-31/12.
**Distance:** ⌂500m ⊗500m ⌁on the spot ⅄on the spot.
**Remarks:** Mandatory, one-time fee Pass'Etapes € 4.

| 🚐Ⓢ | Trouillas | 32H1 |

**Les Oliviers de la Canterrane**, Solt de las Moles, D612.
**GPS:** n42,61399 e2,81599. ⬆➡.

20 ⓢfree ⌐🗑ChWC 🌿€ 2/2 📶free. **Location:** Rural, simple, isolated, quiet. **Surface:** gravel. ◻ 01/01-31/12.
**Distance:** ⌂500m ⚓4km ⌁on the spot.

| ⓢⓈ | Vabre 🌊 | 27G1 |

**Parking bij sportcomplex**, Route de Castres.
**GPS:** n43,69401 e2,42595. ⬆.

---

5 ⓢfree ⌐🗑Chfree. **Location:** Rural, simple, quiet.
**Surface:** asphalted/grassy. ◻ 01/01-31/12.
**Distance:** ⌂500m ⚓on the spot ⌁on the spot ⊗500m ⛾500m
🚿 on the spot ⅄ on the spot.
**Remarks:** Tenniscourt, swimming pool (summer).

| ⓢⓈ | Vabres-l'Abbaye | 27H1 |

**Aire Municipale**, Rue de la Vigne. **GPS:** n43,94575 e2,83957. ⬆.

25 ⓢfree ⌐🗑Chfree. **Location:** Urban, simple. **Surface:** gravel.
◻ 01/01-31/12.
**Distance:** ⌂50m ⚓on the spot ⌁on the spot.

| ⓢⓈ | Vailhan 🏔👥 | 28A2 |

**Parking de l'Eglise. GPS:** n43,55527 e3,29882. ⬆➡.

6 ⓢ€ 5 ⌐🗑Chincluded. **Location:** Rural, simple, quiet.
**Surface:** gravel. ◻ 01/01-31/12.
**Distance:** ⌂1km ⚓200m ⊗50m ⅄ on the spot.

| ⓢⓈ | Val Lauron 🏔❄ | 27D3 |

**Aire de Val Louron**, Hameau de la Belle Savette.
**GPS:** n42,79317 e0,38645. ⬆.

10 ⓢfree ⌐€ 4/100liter 🗑Ch. **Location:** Rural, simple, isolated.
**Surface:** gravel. ◻ 01/01-31/12.
**Distance:** ⌂on the spot ⊗on the spot ⌁on the spot ⅄on the spot
🚵on the spot 🎿on the spot.
**Remarks:** Coins at grocery.

| ⓢⓈ | Valderiés | 27G1 |

**Place de la Mairie**, D91. **GPS:** n44,01167 e2,23333. ⬆.

5 ⓢfree ⌐🗑ChWCfree. **Location:** Urban, simple, quiet.
**Surface:** asphalted. ◻ 01/01-31/12.
**Distance:** ⌂on the spot ⊗on the spot ⌁on the spot 🚵on the spot.
**Remarks:** Max. 7 days, service 100m, weighbridge.

**S** **Valence (Tarn-et-Garonne)** 🌿⛱️👫 24E3
**Aire de camping-car à Valence d'Agen**, Rue Garonne.
**GPS:** n44,10547 e0,88608. ⬆️.

10 🚐 € 5 🔌 € 5/15minutes 🚰Ch 🔌 € 5/kWh WC included
💳🚿 **Location:** Rural, comfortable, quiet. **Surface:** asphalted.
⏰ 01/01-31/12.
**Distance:** 🛒600m ⊗600m 🍴600m 🚲on the spot 🏊on the spot.

**S** **Valence-sur-Baïse** 👫 27D1
Route d'Auch, D930. **GPS:** n43,87272 e0,38787. ⬆️➡️.

7 🚐free 🚰Ch WC free. **Location:** Rural, simple, noisy.
**Surface:** gravel. ⏰ 01/01-31/12.
**Distance:** 🛒500m ⊗500m 🍴500m 🚌on the spot.

**Vallabrègues** 28C1
Route d'Aramon, D183A. **GPS:** n43,85745 e4,62623. ⬆️.

6 🚐free 🔌€ 2 🚰Ch 📺€ 2/h. **Location:** Rural, simple, quiet.
**Surface:** gravel. ⏰ 01/01-31/12 ⏰ high water.
**Distance:** 🛒500m ⊗600m 🍴600m.
**Remarks:** At lake and along the Rhone river, max. 7 days, coins at shop/
town hall.

**S** **Valleraugue** 28A1
**Aire Municipale**, Avenue de l'Aigoual, D986.
**GPS:** n44,08054 e3,63613. ⬆️.

6 🚐free 🔌€ 2 🚰Ch WC 📶. **Location:** Rural, simple, isolated.
**Surface:** asphalted. ⏰ 01/01-31/12.
**Distance:** 🛒450m ⊗500m 🍴on the spot 🚌100m.
**Remarks:** Picnic area.

**S** **Valras-Plage** ⛱️🏖️ 28A2
Avenue du Casino. **GPS:** n43,24230 e3,28162. ⬆️.

30 🚐free 🔌€ 2 🚰Ch. **Location:** Simple, quiet.

---

**Surface:** asphalted/metalled. ⏰ 01/10-30/06 ⏰ summer.
**Distance:** 🛒on the spot 🏊200m 🚌on the spot ⊗on the spot 🍴on
the spot.
**Remarks:** Behind casino/disco, service: Boulevard Pierre Giraud 200m,
no camping activities.

**S** **Valras-Plage** 🏖️🌊 28A2
**Parking Privee**, 23 Boulevard de la Recanette.
**GPS:** n43,25310 e3,29623. ⬆️.

20 🚐€ 10, 01/07-31/08 € 12 🚰Ch 🔌(9x)included. 🚿
**Location:** Urban. **Surface:** gravel.
**Distance:** 🛒800m 🏊800m 🍴800m.

**S** **Vayrac** 👫 24F2
**Camping-Car Park la Palenquière**, Route de la Dordogne.
**GPS:** n44,94467 e1,70307. ⬆️.

25 🚐€ 9,28, 01/06-30/09 € 12,44 🚰Ch 🔌(26x) 📶included. 🚐
**Location:** Rural, comfortable. **Surface:** gravel. ⏰ 01/01-31/12.
**Distance:** 🛒1km ⊗1km 🍴1km.
**Remarks:** Mandatory, one-time fee Pass'Etapes € 4.

**S** **Vénerque** 👫🌊 27F2
**Aire Municipale**, Allée du Duc de Ventadour.
**GPS:** n43,43356 e1,44021. ⬆️➡️.

10 🚐free 🔌🚰Ch 📺. **Location:** Rural, simple, central, quiet.
**Surface:** gravel/metalled. ⏰ 01/01-31/12.
**Distance:** 🛒on the spot 🏊on the spot 🚌on the spot ⊗300m
🍴300m 🚲3km.

**S** **Vernet-les-Bains** 🌿🏖️🌊 32G1
Chemin de la Laiterie. **GPS:** n42,54268 e2,39092. ⬆️.

7 🚐free 🔌€ 2,50/20minutes 🚰Ch 📺€ 2,50/20minutes.
**Location:** Rural, simple, isolated, quiet. **Surface:** gravel.
⏰ 01/03-31/10.
**Distance:** 🛒600m 🏊on the spot ⊗100m.
**Remarks:** Coins at tourist info and town hall.

**S** **Vers** 🌿⛱️🏖️👫🌊 24F3
**Halte Nautique**, Le bourg. **GPS:** n44,48551 e1,55503. ⬆️➡️.

---

20 🚐€ 5,50 🔌🚰Ch WC included. 🚿 **Location:** Rural, simple,
quiet. **Surface:** grassy. ⏰ 01/05-30/09.
**Distance:** 🛒100m 🏊100m ⊗200m 🍴100m 🚲on the spot
🏊on the spot.
**Remarks:** Service 100m.

**S** **Vézénobres** 28B1
Parc Audibal. **GPS:** n44,03851 e4,14118.
3 🚐€ 7 🔌🚰Ch 🔌included. **Location:** Simple, isolated, quiet.
⏰ 01/01-31/12.
**Distance:** 🛒1,5km 🏊1km 🍴1,5km.

**Vézins-de-Lévézou** 24H3
**La Ferme du Lévézou**, Les Vialettes du Ram.
**GPS:** n44,26275 e2,92293. ⬆️➡️.

6 🚐free. **Location:** Rural, simple, isolated, quiet. **Surface:** gravel.
⏰ 01/01-31/12.
**Distance:** 🛒6km 🍴25km.
**Remarks:** Max. 24h, regional products.

**S** **Vias** ⛱️🏖️🌊 28A2
**Aire de l'Espagnac**, 2080 Chemin de Portiragnes.
**GPS:** n43,31013 e3,36226. ⬆️➡️.

27 🚐€ 5,50-10,50 🚰Ch 🔌€ 3/24h 📶included. 🚿
**Location:** Rural, comfortable, isolated, quiet. **Surface:** grassy/gravel.
⏰ 01/01-31/12.
**Distance:** 🛒6km 🏖️9km 🏊10km.

**S** **Vic-en-Bigorre** 27D2
Rue du Stade, Avenue de Pau D6. **GPS:** n43,38472 e0,04917. ⬆️➡️.

4 🚐free 🚰Ch free. **Location:** Rural, simple, central, noisy.
**Surface:** gravel. ⏰ 01/01-31/12.
**Distance:** 🛒500m ⊗300m 🍴50m 📺50m.

**S** **Vicdessos** 🌿👫🌊 27F3
Rue de l'Église, D708. **GPS:** n42,76823 e1,50156. ⬆️➡️.

20 ⬛€ 8 🚰Ch 🧹(16x)included.🛢

**Location:** Rural, comfortable, central, quiet. **Surface:** metalled.
🕒 16/03-31/10.
**Distance:** 🚶on the spot ⊗on the spot 🛒on the spot.
**Remarks:** Thursday market.

**Villasavary** 27G2

**Camping-Car Park**, D623 Lieu dit Pradel. **GPS:** n43,21881 e2,03242.⬆

11 ⬛€ 8,40, 01/07-31/08 € 9,60 🚰Ch 🧹(8x)🛜included.🛢
**Location:** Rural, comfortable, isolated, quiet. **Surface:** asphalted.
🕒 01/01-31/12.
**Distance:** 🚶650m 🏊10km 🎣on the spot.
**Remarks:** Mandatory, one-time fee Pass'Etapes € 4,
video surveillance.

**Villecomtal** 24H3

Le Foirail D904. **GPS:** n44,53573 e2,56494.⬆➡

30 ⬛free 🚰Ch 🧹free. **Location:** Rural, comfortable, quiet.
**Surface:** metalled. 🕒 01/03-18/10.
**Distance:** ⊗500m 🛒500m.

**Villecomtal-sur-Arros** 27D2

Rue de la Fontaine. **GPS:** n43,40286 e0,19852.⬆➡

15 ⬛free 🚰€ 1,50/100liter 🍳Ch🔌€ 1,50/h.
**Location:** Rural, simple, central, quiet. **Surface:** gravel.
🕒 01/01-31/12.
**Distance:** 🚶on the spot ⊗200m 🛒200m 🎣50m.
**Remarks:** Coins at townhall and bakery.

**Villefranche-de-Lauragais** 27F2

**Aire de Camping-car Chez Paul et Arlette**, Chemin des Magnauques
10. **GPS:** n43,39665 e1,70928.⬆

12 ⬛€ 13 🚰Ch 🧹WC🔌€ 3 🛜included.🛒♻

---

**Location:** Urban, comfortable, quiet. **Surface:** grassy/gravel.
🕒 01/03-30/11.
**Distance:** 🚶2km 🏊2km 🎣400m 🛒500m.
**Remarks:** Friday market.

**Villefranche-de-Rouergue** 24G3

**Parking des Ruelles**, Traverse des Ruelles.
**GPS:** n44,35111 e2,03333.⬆

3 ⬛free. **Location:** Urban, simple, noisy. **Surface:** asphalted.
🕒 01/01-31/12.
**Distance:** 🚶100m ⊗100m 🛒100m.

**Tourist information Villefranche-de-Rouergue:**
🏛 place Notre Dame. 🕒 Thu.

**Villeneuve (Aveyron)** 24G3

La Coustone. **GPS:** n44,44104 e2,03737.⬆

10 ⬛€ 5-10 🚰Ch 🧹(4x)WCincluded.♨🚿 **Location:** Rural, simple,
quiet. **Surface:** gravel. 🕒 12/04-01/11.
**Distance:** 🚶200m ⊗200m 🛒200m.

**Villeneuve-lès-Maguelone** 28B2

Avenue René Poitevin. **GPS:** n43,52980 e3,86584.⬆➡

40 ⬛€ 12,50-16,50/24h 🚰€ 2,50 🍳Ch 🧹🛢♻
**Location:** Rural, simple, quiet. **Surface:** asphalted.
🕒 01/01-31/12.
**Distance:** 🚶500m 🏊8km 🏊2,5km ⊗500m 🛒250m 🚆50m 🚲on
the spot.
**Remarks:** 26/04-30/09: also cash payment at office de tourisme
(200m).

**Villeneuve Minervois** 27G2

**Aire Municipale**, Avenue du Jeu de Mail. **GPS:** n43,31516 e2,46432.⬆

4 ⬛free 🚰Ch WC.
**Location:** Urban, simple, quiet. **Surface:** asphalted/metalled.
🕒 01/01-31/12.
**Distance:** 🚶on the spot ⊗on the spot 🛒on the spot.
**Remarks:** Next to sports centre, in front of town hall, max. 48h.

**Vinassan** 27H2

Rue de la Fond. **GPS:** n43,20460 e3,07413.⬆
10 ⬛€ 8 🚰Ch 🧹included.🛢♻ **Location:** Simple, central.
**Surface:** unpaved. 🕒 01/01-31/12.
**Distance:** 🚶200m ⊗200m 🛒200m.

---

**Vinça** 32G1

**Camping-Car Park Portes du Canigou**, Lac des Escoumes.
**GPS:** n42,64939 e2,53184.⬆

35 ⬛€ 10,80-12 🚰Ch 🧹(32x)🛜included.🛢♻
**Location:** Rural, simple, noisy. **Surface:** gravel.
🕒 01/01-31/12.
**Distance:** 🚶650m 🏊on the spot 🚣on the spot ⊗100m 🛒650m
🚆500m 🚲on the spot 🎣on the spot.
**Remarks:** At artificial lake, mandatory, one-time fee
Pass'Etapes € 4.

**Tourist information Vinça:**
ℹ Office de Tourisme, Place Bernard Alart, www.ville-vinca.fr.
Catalan city on a lake of 10ha.

# Andorra

**Pas de la Casa** 32F1

Avinguda del Consell General. **GPS:** n42,54468 e1,73525.⬆

⬛20-8h € 2,10 🚰. **Surface:** metalled. 🕒 01/01-31/12.
**Distance:** 🎣on the spot.

**Sant-Julia-de-Lòria** 32F1

Carretera de la Rabassa. **GPS:** n42,46573 e1,49462.⬆➡

4 ⬛€ 0,50/h, 20-8h free 🚰Ch 🧹(4x)included.🛢
**Surface:** asphalted. 🕒 01/01-31/12.
**Distance:** 🚶1km.

# Provence-Alpes-Côte d'Azur

**Aix-en-Provence** 28D2

Avenue Fortuné Ferrini. **GPS:** n43,50654 e5,43591.⬆
10 ⬛€ 15 🚰Ch 🧹€ 4 WC🛜. **Location:** Rural. **Surface:** grassy.
🕒 01/01-31/12.
**Distance:** 🚶city centre 3km.

**Allos** 25F3

La Foux d'Allos, D908. **GPS:** n44,29583 e6,56944.⬆➡

5 ⬛free 🚰Ch WCfree. **Location:** Urban, central.
**Surface:** asphalted. 🕒 01/01-31/12.
**Distance:** 🚶1km ⊗100m 🛒100m 🚌Skibus 50m 🎿50m.

FR

**S** Allos ❄ 25F3

**Parking Val d'Allos**, Les Prés. GPS: n44,24289 e6,62220. ⬆.

30 🛏€ 6 🚿€ 2/20minutes 🔧Ch (16x)€ 2/4h WC.
⬗ **Location:** Rural, comfortable, quiet. **Surface:** asphalted.
🔲 01/01-31/12.
**Distance:** 🚶500m 🏊200m ⊗500m 🛒500m ⛷200m 🎿200m.
**Remarks:** Max. 72h, coins at ski-lifts.

**S** Allos ❄ 25F3

**Parking de la Cluite**, D226. GPS: n44,24677 e6,66918. ⬆.

5 🛏free. **Location:** Rural, simple, isolated, quiet. **Surface:** gravel.
🔲 01/01-31/12.
**Distance:** 🚶Allos 6,5km ⚑ on the spot.
**Remarks:** Jul/Aug shuttle bus to Lac d'Allos.

**S** Annot 28F1

**Chemin de la Colle Basse.** GPS: n43,96351 e6,66386. ⬆➡.

25 🛏free 🚰🔧Chfree. **Location:** Rural, simple, noisy.
**Surface:** grassy/gravel. 🔲 15/02-15/11 ❖ Snow, Tuesday before/
after Whitsuntide.
**Distance:** 🚶400m ⊗400m 🛒400m ⚑ on the spot.
**Remarks:** Shady, tuesday market.

**S** Arles 28C2

**Quai Kalymnos**, Avenue de la Camargue. GPS: n43,67796 e4,61802.

**🛏€ 5 🚰🔧Ch. 🔲 ⬗ Location:** Urban, simple, quiet.
**Surface:** metalled/sand. 🔲 01/01-31/12.
**Distance:** 🚶city centre ± 1km 🛒300m.
**Remarks:** Along the Rhone river.

**Tourist information Arles:**
ℹ Office de Tourisme, Boulevard des Lices, www.tourisme.ville-arles.
fr. City on the border of the nature reserve Camargue with Roman ruin.
The painter Van Gogh lived in Arles, 1888-89.
✝ Église St.Trophine. Romanesque and Gothic construction.
⌂ Palais Constantin. Large Roman imperial palace of which only the
baths are left.

**S** Aspres-sur-Buëch 25E3

**Avenue de la Gare.** GPS: n44,52060 e5,75349. ⬆➡.

---

10 🛏free 🚰🔧Chfree. **Surface:** grassy/gravel. 🔲 01/01-31/12.
**Distance:** 🛒200m.
**Remarks:** Behind tourist info.

**S** Avignon 28C1

**Aire de camping-car Pont d'Avignon**, 10 chemin de la Barthelasse.
GPS: n43,95691 e4,80184.

35 🛏€ 11,50-18,50, tourist tax incl 🚿€ 2,50 🔧Ch 🚿€ 2,50. 🔲
**Location:** Rural. **Surface:** grassy. 🔲 01/03-01/11.
**Distance:** 🚶city centre 1,5km ⊗200m 🛒200m 🚲 on the spot
⚑ on the spot.

**Tourist information Avignon:**
ℹ Office de Tourisme, 41, cours Jean Jaurès, www.ot-avignon.fr.
Roman city dominated by the Palais du Papes. 🔲 01/04-31/08, 01/10-
31/10 9-17h, 01/09-30/09 9-20h, 01/11-31/03 9-12.45h, 14-18h.
👁 Place d'Horloge. Cosy square in the old centre of the city.
👁 Pont Saint Bénézet. Known as the Pont d'Avignon, bridge over the
river Rhône.
⚒ Petit Palais. Former residence of the archbishop.

**S** Bagnols-en-Fôret 28F2

**Parc de Notre-Dame Les Merles**, Route du Muy, D47.
GPS: n43,53590 e6,68893. ⬆➡.

15 🛏€ 5 🚰🚿€ 4 🔧. **Location:** Rural, comfortable, isolated, quiet.
**Surface:** grassy/gravel. 🔲 01/01-31/12.
**Distance:** 🚶1km ⊗1km 🛒1km 🚲 on the spot.

**S** Banon 28D1

**Avenue Dieudonné Collomp.** GPS: n44,03810 e5,63080.
10 🛏€ 4 🚰🔧ChWCincluded. **Surface:** asphalted. 🔲 01/01-31/12.
**Distance:** ⊗250m.
**Remarks:** Service closed during wintertime.

**S** Banon 28D1

**Espace de la Grand Fontaine**, Rue de la Grande Fontaine.
GPS: n44,03982 e5,63006. ⬆.

15 🛏€ 5 🚰🔧Chincluded WC. **Location:** Rural, simple, quiet.
**Surface:** gravel/metalled. 🔲 01/01-31/12.
**Distance:** 🚶250m ⊗250m 🛒100m 🚲 on the spot ⚑ on the spot.
**Remarks:** Max. 7 days, tuesday morning market.

**S** Banon 28D1

**Fontaine de Crême**, Route de La Rochegiron D112.
GPS: n44,05960 e5,66880. ⬆.

---

10 🛏€ 10 🚰included 🚿€ 3 🔧. **Location:** Rural, simple, isolated,
quiet. **Surface:** grassy. 🔲 01/01-31/12.
**Distance:** 🚶3km ⊗3km 🚲 on the spot ⚑ on the spot.
**Remarks:** Regional products.

**S** Barcelonnette 25F3

**Aire de Camping Car Jacques Villain**, Chemin des Alpages.
GPS: n44,38222 e6,65778. ⬆➡.

20 🛏€ 6 🚿€ 2/100liter 🔧Ch 🚿€ 2/day. 🔲
**Location:** Rural, simple, isolated, quiet. **Surface:** forest soil.
🔲 01/04-31/10.
**Distance:** 🚶1km 🏊200m ⊗1km 🛒1km 🚲 on the spot
⚑ on the spot.
**Remarks:** Next to sports fields, shady.

**S** Barcelonnette 25F3

**Boulevard de l'Adroit.** GPS: n44,39001 e6,65263. ⬆.

10 🛏free. **Location:** Rural, simple, quiet. **Surface:** asphalted.
🔲 01/01-31/12.
**Distance:** 🚶500m ⊗500m 🛒600m ⚑ on the spot.
**Remarks:** At swimming pool, max. 48h.

**S** Bargemon 28F2

**D19, 24 Route de Seillans.** GPS: n43,62457 e6,55054.
🛏free 🚰🔧Ch 🚿€ 5. **Location:** Simple, quiet.
**Surface:** gravel/sand. 🔲 01/01-31/12.
**Distance:** 🛒 on the spot.

**S** Bédoin 28D1

**Camping-Car Park Bedoin**, Chemin des Sablières.
GPS: n44,12472 e5,17167. ⬆➡.

58 🛏€ 10,30 🚰🔧Ch 🚿(58x) 📶included. 🔲
**Location:** Rural, comfortable, quiet.
**Surface:** grassy/metalled.
🔲 01/01-31/12.
**Distance:** 🚶600m ⊗600m 🛒600m 🚲 Mont-Ventoux ⚑ on the spot.
**Remarks:** At swimming pool, mandatory, one-time fee
Pass'Etapes € 4.

**S** Bollène 25C3

**Centre Leclerc**, Route de Saint Paul Trois Châteaux, D26.
GPS: n44,32222 e4,74306. ⬆.

FR

10 ⌂free ⚡€2 ⛽Ch 🚰€2. **Location:** Urban, simple.
**Surface:** asphalted. 🅿 01/01-31/12.
**Distance:** 🛒4,3km.
**Remarks:** Service only during opening hours shop.
**Tourist information Bollène:**
👁 Village Troglodyte. Cave dwelling village. 🅿 01/04-31/10 9.30-19h,
01/11-31/03 Sa-Su, holidays, vacation 14-18h 🅿 01/12-31/01.

### 🅿S Bormes-les-Mimosas    28F3
Route de Bénat. **GPS:** n43,13797 e6,35038. ⬆➡.

30 ⌂free. **Location:** Urban, simple. **Surface:** metalled.
🅿 01/01-31/12.
**Distance:** 🛒2km ⊗300m 🍴on the spot.

### 🅿S Briançon 🌿⚓🏔❄🌸    25F2
**Parc des Sports**, Rue Jean Moulin. **GPS:** n44,89028 e6,62883. ⬆.

30 ⌂free ⚡€2/100liter ⛽Ch 🚰€2/h.
**Location:** Urban, simple, quiet. **Surface:** asphalted.
🅿 01/01-31/12.
**Distance:** 🛒2km ⊗on the spot 🍴1km.
**Remarks:** At sports park, max. 24h.
**Tourist information Briançon:**
ℹ Office de Tourisme, 1, place du Temple, www.ot-briancon.fr. Highest
city of Europe, fortress is now a tourist centre, in winter as winter sports
resort and in summer parapente, rafting and biking.
🍃 Parc des Écrins. Nature reserve.

### 🅿S Caille 🏔    28F1
**Aire de Caille**, Chemin de la Plaine. **GPS:** n43,77893 e6,73331. ⬆➡.

3 ⌂free ⚡€4/15minutes ⛽Ch 🚰€4/15minutes.
**Location:** Rural, simple, quiet. **Surface:** asphalted/gravel.
🅿 01/01-31/12.
**Distance:** 🛒50m ⊗200m 🍴100m 🚵on the spot 🏔10km
⛷150m.

### 🅿S Carpentras ⚓    28C1
**Parking de Coubertin**, Avenue de Coubertin.
**GPS:** n44,04398 e5,05372. ⬆.

8 ⌂free ⛽Chfree. **Location:** Urban, simple. **Surface:** asphalted.
🅿 01/01-31/12.
**Distance:** 🛒1,5km ⊗600m 🍴600m.
**Remarks:** At sports centre P.de Coubertin, max. 24h, market Friday-
morning.
**Tourist information Carpentras:**
👁 Hôtel Dieu. Former hospital, 18th century.
⚓ Centre-ville. 🅿 Fri-morning.

### 🅿S Carro ⚓    28C2
Quai Jean Verandy. **GPS:** n43,32931 e5,04076.

80 ⌂€7, 01/04-30/06 €9,10, 01/07-31/08 €11,20 ⚡ ⛽Chincluded.
**Location:** Urban, comfortable, central, quiet. **Surface:** gravel.
🅿 01/01-31/12.
**Distance:** 🛒on the spot ⚓on the spot 🍴on the spot ⊗100m
🍴200m.
**Remarks:** At harbour, max. 72h, fish sales from 08h.

### 🅿S Carry-le-Rouet    28D2
Avenue Pierre Sémard. **GPS:** n43,33829 e5,15921. ⬆.

4 ⌂free ⚡free. **Location:** Rural, simple, noisy. **Surface:** asphalted.
🅿 01/01-31/12.
**Distance:** 🛒1km ⚓1km ⊗1km 🍴1km 🏔500m.
**Remarks:** Nearby police station, max. 48h.

### 🅿S Castellane ⚓🏔⚓    28F1
Ancienne Route de Grasse. **GPS:** n43,84600 e6,51471. ⬆.

30 ⌂€9 ⚡ ⛽Chincluded WC. 🚐 **Location:** Urban, simple.
**Surface:** asphalted. 🅿 01/01-31/12.
**Distance:** 🛒100m ⚓3km ⊗100m 🍴100m 🚵on the spot.
**Remarks:** Directly at the river, near Pont du Roc, max. 48h, water
closed during wintertime.

### 🅿S Castellane ⚓🏔⚓    28F1
**Castellane Camping-cars**, Carrefour RD 955 et RD 402.
**GPS:** n43,87170 e6,51140.
35 ⌂€7 ⛽Ch 🚰. **Location:** Rural, quiet. **Surface:** grassy/gravel.
🅿 01/03-31/10.
**Distance:** 🛒3,5km ⚓350m 🍴3,5km 🏔on the spot.

### 🅿S Castellane ⚓🏔⚓    28F1
D402. **GPS:** n43,87173 e6,51152. ⬆➡.

40 ⌂€7 ⚡ ⛽Chincluded 🚿€3/24h. 🛁
**Location:** Rural, simple, isolated, quiet. **Surface:** grassy.
🅿 01/01-31/12.
**Distance:** 🛒3km ⚓3km ⊗3km 🍴3km 🚵on the spot 🏔on the spot.
**Remarks:** Bread-service.

### 🅿S Castellane ⚓🏔⚓    28F1
**La Halte Napoléon**, Route de Digne. **GPS:** n43,85468 e6,50159. ⬆.

25 ⌂€5,50 ⚡ ⛽Chincluded 🚿€3 WC 🚰. **Location:** Rural, simple,
isolated. **Surface:** grassy/metalled. 🅿 01/01-31/12.
**Distance:** 🛒800m ⚓3km ⊗800m 🍴500m 🏔on the spot.
**Remarks:** At museum, video surveillance.

### 🅿S Castellane ⚓🏔⚓    28F1
**Supermarché Casino**. **GPS:** n43,85222 e6,50791.

6 ⌂free ⚡€2 ⛽Ch. **Location:** Rural, simple, isolated.
**Surface:** metalled. 🅿 01/01-31/12.
**Distance:** 🛒400m ⊗300m 🍴50m 🛒400m.
**Tourist information Castellane:**
⚓ 🅿 Sa-morning.

### 🅿S Cavaillon    28C1
Avenue Boscodomini. **GPS:** n43,82097 e5,03736.
22 ⌂€9,60, 01/05-30/09 €13,60 ⚡ ⛽Ch 🚿(17x) 🚰included.
🔌 🧺 **Location:** Rural, comfortable. **Surface:** grassy/gravel.
🅿 01/01-31/12.
**Remarks:** Former campsite, monday market.

### 🅿S Cavalière    28F3
Avenue du Cap Nègre, D559. **GPS:** n43,15228 e6,43078. ⬆.

50 ⌂€20 ⚡ ⛽Ch 🚿 🚰included. **Location:** Rural, simple.
**Surface:** sand. 🅿 01/01-31/12.
**Distance:** 🛒50m ⚓50m ⊗50m 🍴200m.

### 🅿S Château-Arnoux-Saint-Auban    28E1
Avenue Gén. de Gaulle, N85. **GPS:** n44,09543 e6,01022. ⬆➡.

+10 ⌂free ⌂ 🗑Chfree. **Location:** Urban, simple, central, noisy. **Surface:** asphalted. 🅾 01/01-31/12. **Distance:** 🚶on the spot ⊗400m 🛒2,3km 🚲400m. **Remarks:** Max. 48h, service 50m.

### 🅿S Chorges 🏔 25E3
Place du Champ de Foire. **GPS:** n44,54600 e6,28008. ⬆➡

10 ⌂€5 🗑Chincluded. **Location:** Urban, simple, quiet. **Surface:** gravel. 🅾 01/01-31/12. **Distance:** 🚶400m ⊗400m 🛒1km 🚲on the spot 🚶on the spot. **Remarks:** Max. 48h.

**Tourist information Chorges:**
ℹ Lac de Serre Ponçon, Serre Ponçon. Clear blue artificial lake, many water sports.

### 🅿S Colmars-les-Alpes 🏔 25F3
Parking de la Lance, La Bourgade. **GPS:** n44,17943 e6,62695. ⬆

10 ⌂free ⌂€2 🗑Ch⌂€2 🛢. **Location:** Rural, simple, quiet. **Surface:** asphalted. 🅾 01/01-31/12 🅾 Service: winter. **Distance:** 🚶300m 🏊50m 🚿50m ⊗300m 🛒300m 🚲on the spot 🚶on the spot. **Remarks:** Max. 24h, tuesday market.

### 🅿S Comps-sur-Artuby 🏔 28F1
La Grange du Roux, D955. **GPS:** n43,70652 e6,50678. ⬆

10 ⌂free ⌂€3 🗑ChWC. **Location:** Rural, comfortable, quiet. **Surface:** gravel. 🅾 01/01-31/12. **Distance:** 🚶350m ⊗pizzeria/crêperie 50m 🛒350m 🚶350m. **Remarks:** Coins at the shops, beautiful view, picnic tables available.

### 🅿S Crots 🏔 25F3
Camping-Car Park, Plage de Canterenne. **GPS:** n44,53830 e6,45489. ⬆

40 ⌂€9,60-10,80 ⌂ 🗑Ch ⌂(16x) 📡included. 🎫
**Location:** Rural, simple, isolated, quiet.
**Surface:** asphalted.
🅾 01/01-31/12.
**Distance:** 🚶1km 🏊100m ⊗100m 🛒500m 🚶on the spot.
**Remarks:** Mandatory, one-time fee Pass'Etapes € 4, historical centre.

### 🅿S Cuges-les-Pins 🐑🏔 28E2
Le Jardin de la Ville, Sainte-Madeleine.
**GPS:** n43,28150 e5,70558. ⬆➡

25 ⌂€ 4,50 ⌂ 🗑Chincluded. **Location:** Rural, comfortable, isolated, quiet. **Surface:** grassy/gravel. 🅾 01/01-31/12. **Distance:** 🚶500m ⊗500m 🛒500m. **Remarks:** Monitored parking.

**Tourist information Cuges-les-Pins:**
Ⓜ Musée Légion Etrangères, Aubagne. Museum about the French Foreign Legion.

### 🚐 Dauphin 🌿🏔 28E1
Route de la Rencontre. **GPS:** n43,90028 e5,78417. ⬆

4 ⌂free. **Location:** Rural, simple, quiet. **Surface:** metalled.
🅾 01/01-31/12.
**Distance:** 🚶300m ⊗300m 🚲on the spot 🚶on the spot.
**Remarks:** Near Salle des Fêtes.

### 🅿S Digne-les-Bains 🏔🌊♨ 28E1
La Halle des Sports, Avenue René Cassin. **GPS:** n44,08280 e6,22170. ⬆

20 ⌂free ⌂€ 2,50/10minutes 🗑Ch.
**Location:** Urban, simple, central. **Surface:** gravel. 🅾 01/01-31/12 🅾 during fair.
**Distance:** 🚶city centre 1,4km 🏊300m 🍴on the spot ⊗300m 🛒300m 🚶on the spot.
**Remarks:** Natural swimming pool.

### 🅿S Digne-les-Bains 🏔🌊♨ 28E1
Le Vallon des Sources, Avenue des Thermes.
**GPS:** n44,07998 e6,26091. ⬆

25 ⌂free ⌂€2 🗑Ch. **Location:** Rural, simple.
**Surface:** asphalted/metalled. 🅾 01/03-01/11.
**Distance:** 🚶2,5km 🏊750m 🛒2km 🚿100m 🚲on the spot 🚶on the spot.
**Remarks:** Coins available at pay-desk of theTherme.

### 🅿S Esparron de Verdon 🌿🏔🌊 28E1
D82. **GPS:** n43,74233 e5,97366. ⬆

7 ⌂free ⌂. **Location:** Rural, simple. **Surface:** gravel/sand.
🅾 01/01-31/12.
**Distance:** 🚶500m 🏊500m ⊗500m 🛒500m 🚶on the spot.

### 🅿S Fayence 🌿 28F2
Allée des Jardins. **GPS:** n43,62308 e6,68982. ⬆➡

2 ⌂free ⌂€ 4 🗑Ch. **Location:** Urban, simple, central, noisy.
**Surface:** asphalted. 🅾 01/01-31/12.
**Distance:** 🚶750m ⊗750m 🛒300m.
**Remarks:** At tennis-court and swimming pool, max. 48h.

### 🅿S Fayence 🌿 28F2
P3. **GPS:** n43,62479 e6,69661. ⬆

3 ⌂free WC. **Location:** Urban, quiet. **Surface:** asphalted
🅾 01/01-31/12.
**Distance:** 🚶200m ⊗500m 🛒200m 🚲on the spot 🚶on the spot.
**Remarks:** Max. 48h.

### 🅿 Fayence 🌿 28F2
Avenue Robert Fabre. **GPS:** n43,62168 e6,69302.

5 ⌂. **Location:** Urban, noisy. **Surface:** asphalted.
**Distance:** 🚶on the spot ⊗300m 🚲on the spot 🚶on the spot.

### 🅿S Fontaine-de-Vaucluse 🏔🌊 28D1
Camping-Car Park, Route de Cavaillon. **GPS:** n43,92024 e5,12452. ⬆

30 ⌂€ 10,20, 01/07-31/08 € 12,60 ⌂ 🗑Ch ⌂(10x) 📡included. 🎫
🛢 **Location:** Rural, comfortable, quiet. **Surface:** gravel/metalled.
🅾 01/01-31/12.
**Distance:** 🚶500m ⊗500m 🚲on the spot 🚶on the spot.
**Remarks:** Mandatory, one-time fee Pass'Etapes € 4.

**FR**

## Fontvieille 28C1

**Parking du Moulin de Daudet**, Allée des Pins.
**GPS:** n43,72000 e4,71200.

€ 6,50/24h € 2/100liter .Ch. **Location:** Rural, comfortable, quiet. **Surface:** gravel. 01/01-31/12.
**Distance:** 800m 800m.
**Remarks:** Market Friday-morning.

## Gap 25E3

Avenue de Traunstein. **GPS:** n44,54176 e6,06101.
6 free Chfree. **Location:** Urban. **Surface:** asphalted.
01/01-31/12.
**Distance:** on the spot 600m 300m.
**Remarks:** Max. 48h.

## Gap 25E3

**Parking Dumont**, Avenue Commandant Dumont, N85.
**GPS:** n44,56544 e6,08447.

3 free € 3 Ch € 3.
**Location:** Urban, simple, noisy. **Surface:** asphalted.
01/01-31/12.
**Distance:** 300m on the spot on the spot 200m.
**Remarks:** Stay overnight allowed at other pitches, max. 7 days.

## Gap 25E3

Avenue d'Embrun 93. **GPS:** n44,56958 e6,10249.

6 free Ch free. **Location:** Urban, simple, noisy.
**Surface:** asphalted. 01/01-31/12.
**Distance:** 800m 100m 100m 50m.
**Remarks:** Free bus to centre.

## Gémenos 28D2

Cours Sudre. **GPS:** n43,29772 e5,62953.

3 free Ch WC free. **Location:** Urban, central, quiet.
**Surface:** metalled. 01/01-31/12.
**Distance:** 100m 100m 100m 50m.
**Remarks:** Near office de tourisme, max. 24h.

## Gigondas 28C1

**Domaine des Florets**, Route des Dentelles, D80.
**GPS:** n44,16220 e5,01725.

3 free free. **Location:** Rural, simple, quiet. **Surface:** gravel.
01/01-31/12.
**Distance:** 1,7km 500m on the spot Des Dentelles.
**Remarks:** Check in at tasting room.

## Gordes 28D1

**Parking Village des Bories**, D2. **GPS:** n43,90056 e5,19306.

20 free.
**Location:** Rural, simple. **Surface:** gravel. 01/01-31/12.
**Distance:** 2km 2km 2km.
**Remarks:** Max. 7 days.

## Greasque 28D2

**Musée de la Mine**, Route de Puits Hely d'Oissel.
**GPS:** n43,43281 e5,53439.

30 € 5 Chincluded. **Surface:** gravel. 16/01-20/12.
**Distance:** 600m.
**Remarks:** Max. 72h.

## Gréoux-les-Bains 28E1

Chemin de la Barque. **GPS:** n43,75562 e5,88862.

80 € 10/24h Ch WCincluded. **Location:** Urban,
simple, noisy. **Surface:** gravel. 01/01-31/12.
**Distance:** 150m 150m 150m on the spot.
**Remarks:** Max 3,5t, max. 30 days.

## Grimaud 28F2

Saint Pons Les Mûres, D98. **GPS:** n43,28000 e6,57806.

12 € 15 € 2,20 Chincluded € 2,20 . **Location:** Urban,
simple, central, noisy. **Surface:** asphalted. 01/01-31/12.
**Distance:** 800m 800m 200m 500m on the spot.
**Remarks:** Max. 72h.

## Guillaumes 28F1

**Place de Provence**, Avenue du Lieutenant Colonelli.
**GPS:** n44,08861 e6,85285.

10 free € 2/100liter Ch € 2/h.
**Location:** Rural, simple, quiet. **Surface:** grassy/gravel.
01/01-31/12.
**Distance:** 50m on the spot on the spot 50m 50m on
the spot on the spot.
**Remarks:** Max. 7 days, coins at Bar-Tabac, tourist info, town hall.

## Hyères 28E3

**Parking des Îles**, Avenue des Arbannais. **GPS:** n43,02864 e6,15438.
4 . **Location:** Urban. 01/01-31/12.
**Distance:** 100m bakery 100m.
**Remarks:** At harbour.

## Isola 25G3

M2205. **GPS:** n44,18811 e7,04350.

15 free Ch free. **Location:** Urban, simple, quiet.
**Surface:** asphalted. 01/01-31/12.
**Distance:** 500m 100m 100m 500m 500m on the
spot on the spot.
**Remarks:** Next to sports fields.

## Istres 28C2

**Parking du Castellan**, Chemin du Castellan 18.
**GPS:** n43,51550 e4,99288.

12 € 8/24h Chincluded. **Location:** Urban, central,
quiet. **Surface:** asphalted/gravel. 01/01-31/12.
**Distance:** 700m on the spot on the spot 200m
on the spot.
**Remarks:** At lake, max. 48h.

## Jausiers 25F3

Route de Jausiers-Barcelonette, D900. **GPS:** n44,41266 e6,72936.

6 free € 3 Ch . **Location:** Rural, simple, noisy.
**Surface:** metalled. 01/01-31/12.
**Distance:** 600m 50m 100m 400m on the spot
on the spot.
**Remarks:** Max. 7 days.

## Jausiers 25F3

**Aire Municipale Pont de Barnuquel**, Sainte-Anne, Route des Nites.
**GPS:** n44,41278 e6,72996.

20 ⌷free. **Location:** Rural, simple, quiet. **Surface:** grassy/gravel.
☐ 01/01-31/12.
**Distance:** ⚕600m ⚓on the spot ⊗100m ⚑400m ⚞on the spot ⚐ on the spot.
**Remarks:** Along river, service 200m.

### Jausiers  25F3
**Mazagrand**, Les Esminjots, D900. **GPS:** n44,42445 e6,73679.
8 ⌷free. **Surface:** gravel. ☐ 01/01-31/12.

### Jausiers  25F3
**Parking d'Arnaudville**, Rue Principale. **GPS:** n44,41967 e6,73515.
20 ⌷free. **Surface:** asphalted. ☐ 01/01-31/12.
**Distance:** ⚕on the spot.

### Jausiers  25F3
**Salle Polyvalente**, Rue des Écoles. **GPS:** n44,41822 e6,73646.
10 ⌷free. **Surface:** asphalted. ☐ 01/01-31/12.
**Distance:** ⚕on the spot.

### Jouques  28D2
**Parking Saint Honorat**, D11. **GPS:** n43,63176 e5,64414.⬆
5 ⌷free. ⚑⚓Ch.⚐
**Location:** Rural, simple. **Surface:** asphalted.
☐ 01/01-31/12.
**Distance:** ⚕750m ⊗750m ⚑750m.
**Remarks:** Find more possibilities on the city plan.

### L'Isle-sur-la-Sorgue  28C1
**Parking de la Gare**, Avenue Julien Guigue.
**GPS:** n43,91768 e5,04686.⬆

6 ⌷free.
**Location:** Simple, noisy. **Surface:** gravel. ☐ 01/01-31/12.
**Distance:** ⚕500m ⊗150m ⚑700m ⚞on the spot.
**Remarks:** At station.

### La Bréole  25E3
Bourg La Bréole, D707. **GPS:** n44,45777 e6,29194.➡

8 ⌷free. ⚑⚓ChWCfree. **Location:** Urban, simple, quiet.
**Surface:** asphalted. ☐ 01/01-31/12.
**Distance:** ⚕on the spot ⚓2km ⚓2km Lac de Serre Ponçon ⊗100m ⚑100m.
**Remarks:** At petrol station, max. 7 days.

### La Crau  28E3
**Espace Lavage Auto Grand Bleu**, La Moutonne.
**GPS:** n43,12417 e6,07444.

3 ⌷free. ⚑€ 4 ⚓Ch. **Location:** Simple, noisy. **Surface:** concrete.
☐ 01/01-31/12.

### La Londe-les-Maures  28E3
Rond-point Ducourneau, chemin du Pansard.
**GPS:** n43,13185 e6,23053.⬆➡

4 ⌷free. ⚑€3 ⚓Ch€ 3 ⚐.
**Location:** Simple, isolated, quiet. **Surface:** asphalted.
☐ 01/01-31/12.
**Distance:** ⚕800m ⚓3km ⊗800m ⚑800m.
**Remarks:** 03/07/2015 during inspection service out of order, max. 24h.

### La Martre  28F1
Chemin de Fontvieillle. **GPS:** n43,77233 e6,60255.⬆

3 ⌷€5 ⚑⚓Ch⚐included. **Location:** Simple, isolated, quiet.
**Surface:** grassy/gravel. ☐ 01/01-31/12.
**Distance:** ⚕300m ⊗300m ⚑300m.

### La Motte  28F2
Chemin des Correns. **GPS:** n43,48860 e6,54212.⬆➡

10 ⌷free. ⚑€ 2 ⚓Ch. **Location:** Rural, simple, isolated, quiet.
**Surface:** gravel. ☐ 01/01-31/12.
**Distance:** ⚕800m ⊗300m ⚑800m.
**Remarks:** At tennis-courts, max. 24h, coins at the shops.

### La Roche-des-Arnauds  25E3
D994, Chemin des Digues. **GPS:** n44,56134 e5,95637.⬆

5 ⌷free. **Location:** Urban, simple, noisy. **Surface:** asphalted.
☐ 01/01-31/12.
**Distance:** ⚕100m ⚓1km ⚓on the spot ⚞on the spot ⊗100m ⚑100m ⚞on the spot ⚞100m.
**Remarks:** Max. 24h.

### La Roquebrussanne  28E2
**GPS:** n43,33614 e5,97950.
4 ⌷free ⚑€ 2 ⚓Ch⚐€ 2. **Location:** Urban, noisy. **Surface:** gravel.
☐ 01/01-31/12.
**Distance:** ⚕on the spot ⊗300m.

### La Salle-les-Alpes  25F2
**Aire camping car Pontillas**, Chemin des Charrières.
**GPS:** n44,94805 e6,55564.⬆

20 ⌷€ 8 ⚑⚓Ch ⚐included. ⛟ **Location:** Urban, simple.
**Surface:** metalled. ☐ 01/01-31/12.
**Distance:** ⚕400m ⊗400m ⚑400m ⚞on the spot ⚐on the spot ⚞20m.
**Remarks:** Pay at tourist office.

### La Salle-les-Alpes  25F2
**Parking Camping Car Le Bez**, Chemin de l'Oratoire, Villeneuve.
**GPS:** n44,94417 e6,55583.⬆

15 ⌷€ 9, winter € 18 ⚑⚓Ch ⚐included ⚞€ 9,50. ⛟
**Location:** Urban, simple, central. **Surface:** grassy/gravel.
☐ 01/01-31/12.
**Distance:** ⚕200m ⊗50m ⚞on the spot ⚐on the spot ⚞20m.
**Remarks:** Parking at skipistes.

### Laragne-Montéglin  25E3
**Parking de Véragne**, Avenue de Provence, D1075.
**GPS:** n44,31212 e5,82543.⬆

15 ⌷free ⚑⚓Ch⚐free WC100m. **Location:** Urban, simple.
**Surface:** asphalted. ☐ 01/01-31/12.
**Distance:** ⚕300m ⊗300m ⚑300m ⚞on the spot ⚞on the spot.

### Laragne-Montéglin  25E3
**Intermarché**, D1075, Rue de Souvenir. **GPS:** n44,30300 e5,83700.⬆

30 ⌷free. ⚑€ 2 ⚓Ch. **Location:** Urban, noisy. **Surface:** metalled.
☐ 01/01-31/12.
**Distance:** ⚕2km.

### Le Lauzet-Ubay  25F3
D900. **GPS:** n44,42833 e6,43389.⬆➡

6 ☐free WCfree. **Location:** Urban, simple, quiet. **Surface:** gravel.
☐ 01/01-31/12.
**Distance:** 50m 50m 50m on the spot.
**Remarks:** At small lake, max. 2 days.

| | | | | |
|---|---|---|---|---|
Le Monêtier-les-Bains | 25F2

**Aire camping car les Charmettes**, Route des Bains.
**GPS:** n44,97131 e6,51279.

40 ☐€ 4,80/day + tourist tax ☐Chfree.
**Location:** Rural, simple, quiet. **Surface:** asphalted.
☐ 01/01-31/12.
**Distance:** 300m on the spot on the spot on the spot.
**Remarks:** Along river, parking at skipistes, discount longer stays.

| | | | | |
|---|---|---|---|---|
Le Monêtier-les-Bains | 25F2

**Col du Lautaret**, D1091. **GPS:** n45,03301 e6,40696.
35 ☐free. **Surface:** metalled/sand. ☐ 01/01-31/12.
**Distance:** 200m 200m 200m on the spot.

| | | | |
|---|---|---|---|
Le Thoronet | 28E2

D17, boulevard du 17 aout 1944. **GPS:** n43,45097 e6,30411.

2 ☐free ☐€ 2 Ch. **Location:** Rural, simple, central, noisy.
**Surface:** asphalted. ☐ 01/01-31/12.
**Distance:** on the spot 50m.
**Remarks:** Max. 48h, coins at tourist info.

| | | | |
|---|---|---|---|
Les Issambres | 28F2

**Chez Marcel**, Plage La Gaillarde, N98. **GPS:** n43,36559 e6,71202.

40 ☐€ 12, peak season € 16 ☐Chincluded €3/day
☐€ 0,50 ☐€ 5/5 . **Surface:** Comfortable, isolated, quiet.
**Surface:** gravel/sand. ☐ 01/01-31/12.
**Distance:** 3km 50m 200m 200m 50m.

| | | | |
|---|---|---|---|
Les Salles-sur-Verdon | 28E1

**L'Ermitage**, D957. **GPS:** n43,77434 e6,21773.

10 ☐€ 7, Jul/Aug € 9 ☐Ch €4 included.
**Location:** Rural, simple, isolated, quiet. **Surface:** gravel/sand.
☐ 01/01-31/12.
**Distance:** 700m Lac de Ste Croix 1km on the spot on the spot on the spot.
**Remarks:** Service passerby € 5, swimming pool incl.

| | | | | |
|---|---|---|---|---|
Malaucène | 25D3

Avenue Charles de Gaulle. **GPS:** n44,17792 e5,12970.

40 ☐€ 3,60 + € 0,70/pp tourist tax ☐Chfree.
**Location:** Rural, simple, noisy. **Surface:** gravel.
☐ 01/01-31/12.
**Distance:** 150m 150m 150m Mont-Ventoux on the spot.
**Remarks:** Between sports fields and gendarmerie.
**Tourist information Malaucène:**
Marché Provencal. ☐ Wed-morning.

| | | | |
|---|---|---|---|
Malemort-du-Comtat | 28D1

Avenue Docteur Tondut, D5. **GPS:** n44,02175 e5,15714.

5 ☐free ☐Chfree. **Location:** Rural, simple. **Surface:** gravel.
☐ 01/01-31/12 ☐ Service: winter.
**Distance:** 200m on the spot.
**Remarks:** Near Salle des Fêtes, max. 24h.

| | | | |
|---|---|---|---|
Malijai | 28E1

Impasse des Bugadières. **GPS:** n44,04433 e6,02971.

10 ☐free ☐Chfree. **Location:** Rural, simple. **Surface:** asphalted.
☐ 01/01-31/12.
**Distance:** on the spot on the spot 50m 50m on the spot.
**Remarks:** Along river.

| | | | |
|---|---|---|---|
Marseille | 28D2

**Marlyparc**, Chemin de Morgiou 120. **GPS:** n43,24085 e5,40693.

40 ☐€ 12 ☐Chincluded €5 .
**Location:** Urban, simple, central, quiet. **Surface:** metalled.
☐ 01/01-31/12.
**Distance:** 7km Marseille 3km 1km on the spot.
**Remarks:** Coins at tourist info and town hall.

| | | | | |
|---|---|---|---|---|
Ménerbes | 28D1

Rue de la Fontaine. **GPS:** n43,83193 e5,20828.

20 ☐€ 5 ☐ChWC . **Location:** Rural, simple. **Surface:** gravel.
☐ 01/01-31/12.
**Distance:** 250m 100m on the spot.
**Remarks:** Max. 7 days.

| | | | |
|---|---|---|---|
Mison | 25E3

**Les Armands Sud**. **GPS:** n44,26551 e5,85728.

4 ☐free ☐ChWCfree. **Location:** Rural, simple.
**Surface:** asphalted. ☐ 01/01-31/12.
**Distance:** 50m 200m 200m 200m.
**Remarks:** Playground.

| | | | |
|---|---|---|---|
Montclar | 27H1

D60, route Montclar-Faveyrolles. **GPS:** n43,96756 e2,65137.
10 ☐free ☐Ch free. **Surface:** gravel. ☐ 01/01-31/12.
**Distance:** 500m.
**Remarks:** Picnic area, playground.

| | | | | |
|---|---|---|---|---|
Montgenèvre | 25F2

**Aire de Camping Car Du Collet**, Cros Lateron, N94.
**GPS:** n44,93417 e6,73317.

220 ☐€ 13 ☐Ch (80x)included . **Location:** Rural,
simple, isolated, quiet. **Surface:** metalled. ☐ 01/01-31/12.
**Distance:** 500m 500m on the spot on the spot on the spot.
**Remarks:** Service passerby € 8.

| | | | | |
|---|---|---|---|---|
Moustiers-Sainte-Marie | 28E1

**P5**, D952. **GPS:** n43,84361 e6,21874.

FR

25 🛏 € 7,50, 31/10-31/03 free 🚰 € 2/10minutes 🔌
Ch 🔌 € 2/10minutes. 🚐 **Location:** Rural, simple. **Surface:** gravel.
⬛ 01/01-31/12.
**Distance:** 🚶10 min walking ⊗200m 🚰200m 🚲 on the spot
🏊 on the spot.
**Remarks:** Max. 2 nights, beautiful view.

### 🅢 Névache 25F2
D994G. **GPS:** n45,01666 e6,64261.

🛏 € 8,50 WC included. **Location:** Simple, isolated, quiet.
**Surface:** grassy. ⬛ 01/01-31/12.
**Distance:** 🚶1km 🏊 on the spot 🚣 on the spot 🎣 on the spot
🏊 on the spot.

### Névache 25F2
D994G, Rue de Roubion. **GPS:** n45,01698 e6,63062. ⬆️

15 🛏 free. **Location:** Urban, simple, quiet. **Surface:** grassy.
⬛ 01/01-31/12.
**Distance:** 🚶200m 🏊 on the spot 🚣 on the spot ⊗200m 🚲 on the
spot 🏊 on the spot.

### 🅢 Ollioules 28E3
Route des Gorges, DN8. **GPS:** n43,13868 e5,85002.
8 🛏 € 5. **Location:** Urban. **Surface:** asphalted. ⬛ 01/04-30/09.
**Distance:** 🚶600m ⊗600m 🚰450m.
**Remarks:** Max. 48h.

### 🅢 Oppède-le-Vieux 28D1
Parking Oppéde-le-Vieux, Chemin de Sous Ville.
**GPS:** n43,83094 e5,15897. ⬆️

5 🛏 € 5/day 🚰 free WC. 🚿 **Location:** Rural, simple. **Surface:** gravel.
⬛ 01/01-31/12.
**Distance:** 🚶500m 🚰500m.
**Remarks:** Max. 7 days.
**Tourist information Oppède-le-Vieux:**
🚶 Hiking route through medieval top-hill village.

### 🅢 Orcières-Merlette 25E2
Camping-car Casse Blanche, Pra Palier, P2.
**GPS:** n44,69517 e6,32567. ⬆️

21 🛏 € 18, Jul/Aug € 10 🚰 Ch 🚿 included WC 🔌 € 9,50/24h.
🚐 **Location:** Rural, simple. **Surface:** asphalted.
⬛ 17/12-17/04, 01/07-02/09.
**Distance:** 🚶 on the spot 🚴 on the spot.
**Remarks:** Summer: pay at tourist office, caution € 5.

### 🅢 Pélissanne 28D2
Provenque, Chemin de la Prouvenque.
**GPS:** n43,62805 e5,15307. ⬆️➡️

15 🛏 free 🚰 Ch free. **Location:** Urban, simple, quiet.
**Surface:** asphalted. ⬛ 01/01-31/12.
**Distance:** 🚶500m 🚴8km.
**Remarks:** Parking stadium, video surveillance.

### 🅢 Piolenc 25C3
Aire de la Grappe, 85 route d'Orange. **GPS:** n44,18460 e4,79980.
5 🛏 € 10 🚰 Ch 🚿 free. **Location:** Rural. **Surface:** gravel.
⬛ 01/01-31/12.
**Distance:** 🚶3,2km.

### 🅢 Plan-de-la-Tour 28F2
Parking Foch. **GPS:** n43,33787 e6,54532.

8 🛏 free. **Location:** Simple, central, quiet. **Surface:** gravel.
⬛ 01/01-31/12.
**Distance:** 🚶 on the spot ⊗100m 🚰150m.
**Remarks:** Max. 48h.
**Tourist information Plan-de-la-Tour:**
🚶 Thu morning 6-12h.

### 🅢 Port Saint-Louis-du-Rhône 28C2
Camping-car park, 1233 quai de la Suisse.
**GPS:** n43,38424 e4,81909. ⬆️➡️

100 🛏 € 8,40, 01/08-30/09 € 9,60 🚰 Ch 🔌 included. 🚐 🧺
**Location:** Simple, isolated, quiet. **Surface:** asphalted/gravel.
⬛ 01/01-31/12.
**Distance:** 🚶1,5km 🏊2km 🚣 on the spot ⊗1km 🚰1,5km.
**Remarks:** Mandatory, one-time fee Pass'Etapes € 4, market Wednesday
and Saturday.

### 🅢 Pra-Loup 25F3
Parking des Choupettes, D109. **GPS:** n44,36806 e6,60611. ⬆️

35 🛏 free 🚰 € 3 🚰 Ch 🔌 € 3 🚿. **Location:** Urban, simple, quiet.
**Surface:** asphalted. ⬛ 01/01-31/12.
**Distance:** 🚶400m ⊗400m 🚰400m on the spot 🚴50m.
**Remarks:** Parking at skipistes, max. 72h.

### 🅢 Puget Theniers 28F1
Aire de la Condamine, Route des Grandes Alpes.
**GPS:** n43,95306 e6,89944. ⬆️➡️

10 🛏 € 4 🚰 Ch 🚿 included. **Surface:** asphalted. ⬛ 01/01-31/12.
**Distance:** 🚶300m 🏊20m ⊗300m 🚰300m.

### 🅢 Puimoisson 28E1
Les Lavandins, Basses Touires. **GPS:** n43,87006 e6,12979. ⬆️➡️

40 🛏 € 4,90/24h 🚰 € 1/100liter 🔌 € 1,05/1h. 🚐
**Location:** Rural, simple, isolated. **Surface:** grassy.
⬛ 01/04-31/10.
**Distance:** 🚶650m ⊗650m.

### 🅢 Puy-Saint-Vincent 25F2
Les Sagnes-Station 1400, D404. **GPS:** n44,82478 e6,49839. ⬆️➡️

5 🛏 € 6, tourist tax € 0,60/pp 🚰 Ch 🚿 included. 🚿
**Location:** Rural, simple, quiet. **Surface:** asphalted.
⬛ 01/01-31/12.
**Distance:** 🚶 on the spot ⊗ on the spot 🚴 on the spot 🏊 on the spot
🚴 on the spot.

### 🅢 Puy-Saint-Vincent 25F2
Station 1600, Clôt de Saint-Romain, D4. **GPS:** n44,83245 e6,48331. ⬆️

20 🛏 € 6 🚰 Ch 🚿 included. 🚿 **Location:** Rural, simple, quiet.
**Surface:** asphalted. ⬛ 18/12-25/04.
**Distance:** 🚶200m ⊗200m 🚰200m 🚴200m.
**Remarks:** Altitude 1600m, at ski-lift, max. 15 days, information at
cableway.

FR

### Puyvert ⚊S 28D1
**Super U**, D118. **GPS:** n43,74763 e5,33727.⬆.

5 🍴free 🚰🗑Ch 💧(2x)free 🔌€ 4. **Location:** Rural, isolated, noisy.
**Surface:** asphalted. 🅿 01/01-31/12.
**Distance:** 🚶1,5km 🛒on the spot.
**Remarks:** Parking near Super-U, max. 24h.

### Quinson ⚊S 28E1
**Les Prés du Verdon**, Allée des Prés du Verdon.
**GPS:** n43,69801 e6,03911.⬆.

5 🍴free 🗑Chfree WC. **Location:** Rural, simple, quiet.
**Surface:** gravel/sand. 🅿 01/01-31/12.
**Distance:** 🏊100m 🚲100m ⊗300m 🛒500m 🧍on the spot.
**Remarks:** Near the prehistoric museum of the gorges du Verdon.

### Ramatuelle ⚊S 28F2
**Parking de Tamaris, Plage de Pamplonne**, Route des Tamaris.
**GPS:** n43,23893 e6,66149.⬆.

60 🍴18 🚰2 🗑Ch 💧(20x)€ 7/day WC. **Location:** Rural.
**Surface:** grassy. 🅿 01/01-31/12.
**Distance:** 🏊on the spot ⊗on the spot 🛒on the spot.
**Remarks:** Beach parking.

### Ramatuelle ⚊S 28F2
**Parking Municipal, Plage de Pamplonne**, Route de Bonne-Terrasse.
**GPS:** n43,21126 e6,66217.⬆➡.

130 🍴€ 10, 01/11-14/03 € 6, tourist tax € 0,80/pp 🚰🗑ChWC 📶.
**Location:** Rural, comfortable, quiet, noisy. **Surface:** gravel.
🅿 01/04-31/10.
**Distance:** 🏊200m ⊗200m 🛒2km 🧍on the spot.
**Remarks:** Beach parking, max. 48h, bread-service.
**Tourist information Ramatuelle:**
🏛 La place de l'Ormeau. Provencal Market. 🅿 Thu, Su.

### Reillanne ⚊S 28D1
**Aire Camping Car Reillanne**, Boulevard de la Tuilière.
**GPS:** n43,88020 e5,66404.
3 🍴free 🚰🗑Ch 💧free. 🅿 01/01-31/12.
**Distance:** 🚶500m.
**Remarks:** Service closed during wintertime.

### Riez ⚊S 28E1
**P de l'Auvestre**, Chemin du Relais. **GPS:** n43,82180 e6,09197.⬆➡.

---

30 🍴€ 5/24h 🚰🗑Chincluded. 🚐 **Location:** Rural, comfortable, quiet. **Surface:** gravel. 🅿 01/01-31/12.
**Distance:** 🚶500m ⊗500m 🛒100m on the spot 🧍on the spot.
**Remarks:** Market Saturday.

### Rochefort-du-Gard 28C1
**Vignerons du Castelas**, 674 Av de Signargues.
**GPS:** n43,97462 e4,68424.
3 🍴free. **Surface:** gravel. 🅿 01/01-31/12.
**Remarks:** Max. 72h.

### Rosans 25D3
D25. **GPS:** n44,39307 e5,47395.⬆.
🍴free. **Surface:** unpaved. 🅿 01/01-31/12.
**Distance:** 🚶200m ⊗650m.

### Roubion ⚊S 28G1
**Les Buisses**. **GPS:** n44,08397 e7,04287.⬆.

14 🍴free 🚰🗑Chfree. **Location:** Rural, simple, isolated, quiet.
**Surface:** asphalted. 🅿 01/01-31/12.
**Distance:** ⊗on the spot 🧍on the spot 🎿on the spot.
**Remarks:** At ski-lift, narrow entrance.

### Roussillon ⚊S 28D1
**Parking Saint Joseph**, D149. **GPS:** n43,89660 e5,29593.⬆➡.

20 🍴€ 7/night. 🚐
**Location:** Rural, comfortable. **Surface:** gravel.
**Distance:** 🚶800m ⊗800m 🚲on the spot 🧍on the spot.
**Remarks:** Max. 48h.
**Tourist information Roussillon:**
🚶 Sentier des Ocres. Hiking trail, 45 min.

### Sablet 25C3
**Domaine du Parandou**, D977. **GPS:** n44,19325 e4,99522.⬆➡.

5 🍴1,50 🚰€ 3 🗑Ch 💧(2x)€ 3 WC. **Location:** Rural, simple.
**Surface:** gravel. 🅿 01/01-31/12.
**Distance:** 🚶2km.

### Saint-André-les-Alpes ⚊S 28F1
**Chez Julo**, Chemin de Neouille. **GPS:** n43,96394 e6,51185.⬆➡.

---

30 🍴€ 8 🚰🗑Chincluded. 💧€ 3/24h. **Location:** Rural, simple, quiet. **Surface:** grassy. 🅿 01/01-31/12.
**Distance:** 🚶800m ⊗800m 🛒800m on the spot 🧍on the spot.

### Saint-André-les-Alpes ⚊S 28F1
**Grand Rue**. **GPS:** n43,96525 e6,50735.⬆➡.

30 🍴free 🚰🗑Chfree. **Location:** Urban, comfortable, quiet.
**Surface:** asphalted. 🅿 01/01-31/12.
**Distance:** 🚶on the spot 🏊2km 🛒100m 🧍250m 🚲on the spot.

### Saint-Chamas ⚊S 28C2
**Avenue Marx Dormoy**. **GPS:** n43,54636 e5,03246.⬆.

10 🍴free 🚰🗑Ch. **Location:** Urban, simple. **Surface:** gravel.
🅿 01/01-31/12.
**Distance:** 🏊on the spot ⊗on the spot.
**Remarks:** Near marina.

### Saint-Crépin ⚊S 25F2
D138. **GPS:** n44,70562 e6,60196.⬆➡.

24 🍴€ 8, tourist tax € 0,60/pp 🚰🗑Ch 💧€ 3,80 WC included.
🚐. **Location:** Rural, simple, quiet. **Surface:** grassy.
🅿 01/05-30/09.
**Distance:** 🚶500m 🏊on the spot 🚲on the spot ⊗on the spot 🚴on the spot 🧍on the spot. **Remarks:** Service on the other side of the bridge, swimming pool available.

### Saint-Jean-Saint-Nicolas ⚊S 25E2
**Camping Car Park**, Le Châtelard. **GPS:** n44,66782 e6,23484.⬆➡.

49 🍴€ 10,20 🚰🗑Ch 💧(60x) 📶included. 🚐 **Location:** Rural, simple, isolated, quiet. **Surface:** forest soil.
🅿 01/04-15/11.
**Distance:** 🚶600m 🏊on the spot 🚲on the spot ⊗600m 🛒600m 🧍on the spot.

---

FR

**Remarks:** Mandatory, one-time fee Pass'Etapes € 4.

### S Saint-Laurent-du-Var 28G1
Route des Pugets. **GPS:** n43,68584 e7,18459. 🔼.

7 free 🚰🔌Chfree. **Location:** Simple, noisy. **Surface:** asphalted.
☐ 01/01-31/12.
**Distance:** 1,2km 4,5km ⊗1,2km 🛒1,2km on the spot.
**Remarks:** Max. 7 days.

### S Saint-Laurent-du-Var 28G1
Avenue Francis Teisseire. **GPS:** n43,66628 e7,19595. 🔼➡️.

5 free. **Location:** Urban, simple, central, noisy. **Surface:** asphalted.
☐ 01/01-31/12.
**Distance:** city centre 2km 200m 600m ⊗500m 🛒500m.
500m.
**Remarks:** Max. 8M.

### S Saint-Mandrier-sur-Mer 28E3
Pin Roland, Impasse de la Mer. **GPS:** n43,07771 e5,90444. 🔼.

6 free 🚰🔌Chfree. **Location:** Urban, simple, noisy.
**Surface:** asphalted. ☐ 01/01-31/12.
**Distance:** 500m ⊗500m.
**Remarks:** Max. 48h.

### S Saint-Martin-de-Crau 28C2
Place François Miterrand. **GPS:** n43,63859 e4,81454. 🔼.
3 free 🚰🔌ChWCfree. **Location:** Urban, simple, central, quiet.
**Surface:** metalled. ☐ 01/01-31/12.
**Distance:** 400m ⊗100m 🛒400m.
**Remarks:** In front of town hall, max. 48h.

### S Saint-Michel-l'Observatoire 28E1
Place du Serre. **GPS:** n43,90908 e5,71750. 🔼.

10 free 🚰.
**Location:** Simple. **Surface:** gravel. ☐ 01/03-15/11.
**Distance:** 200m ⊗200m on the spot.
**Remarks:** Beautiful panorama.

### S Saint-Paul-lès-Durance 28E2
Rue du Camping le Retour. **GPS:** n43,68700 e5,70588. 🔼➡️.

---

6 free 🚰🔌Chfree. **Location:** Rural, simple, quiet.
**Surface:** gravel. ☐ 01/01-31/12.
**Distance:** 500m 4km ⊗500m 🛒700m.
**Remarks:** Max. 48h.

### S Saint-Pons 25F3
D900. **GPS:** n44,38571 e6,60912.
6 free 🚰🔌Chfree. **Surface:** gravel. ☐ 01/04-31/10.
**Distance:** ⊗on the spot.

### S Saint-Vallier-de-Thiey 28F1
Chemin de Sainte-Anne 2600. **GPS:** n43,69318 e6,81460.
3 free 🚰€ 2 Ch. **Location:** Rural, isolated, quiet.
**Surface:** metalled/sand. ☐ 01/01-31/12.
**Distance:** on the spot.

### S Saint-Véran 25F2
Parking St. Marie Madeleine, D5. **GPS:** n44,70447 e6,86091. 🔼.

20 €5 🚰🔌ChWCincluded. **Location:** Rural, simple, isolated,
quiet. **Surface:** metalled. ☐ 01/01-31/12.
**Distance:** 100m 100m 🛒200m ⨉on the spot on the spot
200m.

### S Sainte-Croix-du-Verdon 28E1
Route du Lac. **GPS:** n43,76077 e6,15102. 🔼.

20 €8/24h 🔌€ 2/10minutes Ch 🚰€ 2 WC.
**Location:** Rural, simple, quiet. **Surface:** asphalted.
☐ 01/01-31/12.
**Distance:** 100m Lac de Ste Croix 1km ⊗100m 🛒200m on
the spot ⨉on the spot.
**Remarks:** Max. 3 nights, water closed during wintertime, beautiful
view.

### S Sainte-Maxime 28F2
D25, le Muy dir Ste.Maxime. **GPS:** n43,31730 e6,62999. 🔼.

50 €10/24h, 01/10-31/03 € 5 🚰🔌Chfree. **Location:** Urban,
comfortable, quiet. **Surface:** metalled. ☐ 01/01-31/12.
**Distance:** city centre 1km 1,2km ⊗McDonalds 50m 🛒Lidl
200m.
**Remarks:** Max. 48h.
**Tourist information Sainte-Maxime:**
⛺ Thu-morning.
⨉ Les Greniers du Golfe, Aire des Magnoti. Bric-a-brac.
☐ Wed 08-18h.

---

### S Sainte-Tulle 28E1
Avenue Léo Lagrange. **GPS:** n43,78500 e5,76395.
20 €5 🚰🔌Chincluded. (3x) WC. 01/01-31/12.
**Distance:** 400m 350m.

### S Saintes-Maries-de-la-Mer 28B2
Avenue d'Arles, D570. **GPS:** n43,45535 e4,42750. 🔼➡️.

60 €12,30 + € 0,70 tourist tax 🚰🔌ChWCincluded.
**Location:** Simple, central, quiet. **Surface:** asphalted.
☐ 01/01-31/12.
**Distance:** 200m beach 400m ⊗100m 🛒50m 🖥100m.
**Remarks:** Max. 48h, service: 8.30-11.30h, 16-19.30h.

### S Saintes-Maries-de-la-Mer 28B2
Plage Ouest, Route d'Aigues-Mortes, D38.
**GPS:** n43,44991 e4,40407. 🔼.

50 €12,30 + € 0,70 tourist tax 🚰🔌Chincluded.
**Location:** Isolated, quiet. **Surface:** asphalted/gravel.
☐ 01/01-31/12.
**Distance:** 1,5km 50m.
**Remarks:** Beach parking.

### S Saintes-Maries-de-la-Mer 28B2
Valée des Lys, Parking Plage Est, Avenue Cousteau.
**GPS:** n43,45364 e4,43695. 🔼➡️.

150 €12,30 + € 0,70 tourist tax 🚰🔌Chincluded.
**Surface:** asphalted. ☐ 01/01-31/12.
**Distance:** 250m beach 50m ⊗100m 🛒250m.

### P Saintes-Maries-de-la-Mer 28B2
Parking du Large, Avenue du Docteur Cambon.
**GPS:** n43,45430 e4,43326. 🔼.

20 free. **Location:** Simple, central, noisy. **Surface:** gravel.
☐ 01/01-31/12.
**Distance:** 250m 700m ⊗250m 🛒250m.

### P Saintes-Maries-de-la-Mer 28B2
Route de Cacharel. **GPS:** n43,45684 e4,43305. 🔼.

**FR**

10 ⚡free. **Location:** Simple, isolated, quiet. 🅾 01/01-31/12. **Distance:** 🚰700m ⛱750m 🛒700m.

🚐Ⓢ **Salernes** 🏔 28E2

**Aire Municipal,** Route des Quatre Chemins. **GPS:** n43,55923 e6,23381.➡.

35 ⚡free 🚰Chfree. **Location:** Rural, simple, quiet. **Surface:** grassy/gravel. 🅾 01/01-31/12. **Distance:** 🚰300m ⛱Lac de Ste Croix 1km 🏃on the spot. **Remarks:** Max. 24h.

🚐Ⓢ **Salin-de-Giraud** 28C2

Rue de la Bouvine. **GPS:** n43,41222 e4,73056.⬆➡.

20 ⚡free 🚰€ 2 🚰Ch🚽€ 0,80. **Location:** Urban, simple, quiet. **Surface:** gravel. 🅾 01/04-31/10. **Distance:** 🚰500m ⊗500m 🛒500m. **Remarks:** At fire-station, coins at town hall, showers only in july/aug.

🚐 **Salin-de-Giraud** 28C2

Rue Georges-Jo Maillis. **GPS:** n43,41236 e4,73621.⬆➡.

50 ⚡free. **Location:** Urban, simple. **Surface:** asphalted. 🅾 01/01-31/12. **Distance:** 🚰on the spot ⛱10km ⊗200m 🛒200m.

🚐Ⓢ **Sarrians** 28C1

Avenue de la Camargue. **GPS:** n44,07943 e4,97788.⬆.

10 ⚡€ 3/day 🚰Ch🚽included. **Location:** Rural, simple. **Surface:** gravel. 🅾 01/04-31/10. **Distance:** 🚰800m 🛒500m.

🚐Ⓢ **Sault** 🍴 28D1

P3, Route de Saint-Trinit. **GPS:** n44,09434 e5,41308.⬆.

15 ⚡free 🚰€ 2 🚰Ch🚽€ 2/h. **Location:** Rural, simple. **Surface:** gravel. 🅾 01/01-31/12. **Distance:** 🚰500m ⊗500m 🚲on the spot 🏃4km chemin des Lavandes.

🚐Ⓢ **Sausset-les-Pins** ⚓ 28D2

Avenue Pierre Matraja. **GPS:** n43,33890 e5,10916.⬆.

15 ⚡free 🚰€ 4/100liter 🚰Ch🚽€ 4/1h. **Location:** Simple, isolated, quiet. **Surface:** asphalted. 🅾 01/01-31/12. **Distance:** 🚰1,2km ⛱800m ⊗1,2km 🛒1,2km 🚏5m. **Remarks:** At stadium, max. 72h.

🚐Ⓢ **Savines-le-Lac** 🏔 25F3

**Parking du Barnafret,** Av. du Faubourg, D954. **GPS:** n44,52495 e6,40090.⬆.

19 ⚡€ 9,50 🚰€ 2/120liter 🚰Ch🛠(20x)included. 🚽 **Location:** Rural, simple, central. **Surface:** asphalted. 🅾 01/01-31/12. **Distance:** 🚰300m ⛱500m ⊗100m 🚲on the spot 🏃on the spot. **Remarks:** At lake Serre Ponçon.

🚐Ⓢ **Seillans** 28F2

Chemin Des Clos. **GPS:** n43,63230 e6,64860.

3 ⚡free 🚰€ 4 🚰Ch. **Location:** Rural, simple. **Surface:** asphalted/gravel. 🅾 01/01-31/12. **Distance:** 🚰500m ⊗500m 🚲on the spot 🏃on the spot.

🚐Ⓢ **Selonnet** 🏔 25E3

Quartier de Boulangère. **GPS:** n44,36862 e6,31525.⬆➡.

7 ⚡free 🚰€ 2/10minutes 🚰Ch🚽€ 2/55minutes 📶. **Location:** Rural, simple, quiet. **Surface:** gravel. 🅾 01/01-31/12. **Distance:** 🚰300m ⊗300m 🛒300m.

**Remarks:** Coins at town hall, supermarket, bakery and Tabac, free wifi at town hall.

🚐Ⓢ **Sénas** 28D1

Rue du Moulin. **GPS:** n43,74403 e5,08020.➡.

6 ⚡free 🚰€ 2/100liter 🚰Ch🚽€ 2/30minutes. **Location:** Urban, simple. **Surface:** asphalted. 🅾 01/01-31/12 🔘 last weekend of August. **Distance:** 🚰200m 🚲1,5km ⊗200m 🛒200m. **Remarks:** Coins at tourist info and maison de presse.

🚐Ⓢ **Seyne** 25F3

Le Grand Puy. **GPS:** n44,32226 e6,39287. 3 ⚡free 🚰WCfree. **Location:** Rural. **Surface:** gravel/metalled.

🚐Ⓢ **Sillans-la-Cascade** 28E2

Route de Salernes. **GPS:** n43,56692 e6,18277.⬆➡. 10 ⚡free 🚰€ 3. 🅾 01/01-31/12. **Distance:** 🚰500m ⊗500m. **Remarks:** Free entrance swimming pool.

🚐Ⓢ **Sisteron** 🌿⚓🏔 25E3

Avenue de la Libération. **GPS:** n44,19105 e5,94542.⬆.

12 ⚡€ 4 🚰€ 2/20minutes 🚰Ch🚽€ 2/4h 🚿🚽. **Location:** Urban, simple. **Surface:** asphalted. 🅾 01/01-31/12 🔘 Service: winter. **Distance:** 🚰800m ⊗800m 🛒800m. **Remarks:** Along railwayline.

🚐Ⓢ **Sisteron** 🌿⚓🏔 25E3

**Parking Melchior Donnet,** D4085. **GPS:** n44,20028 e5,94389.⬆.

10 ⚡free 🚰€ 2 🚰Ch🚿€ 2/10minutes. **Location:** Urban, simple. **Surface:** asphalted. 🅾 01/01-31/12. **Distance:** 🚰on the spot 🚲4,5km.

🚐Ⓢ **Six-Fours-les-Plages** ⚓ 28E3

Port de la Coudoulière. **GPS:** n43,09750 e5,81194.

5 ⚡€ 10 🚰WCincluded 🚽€ 2. **Location:** Urban, simple, central. **Surface:** asphalted. 🅾 01/10-30/04. **Distance:** 🚰100m ⛱on the spot ⊗100m 🛒100m. **Remarks:** At harbour, max. 24h.

Ⓢ **Six-Fours-les-Plages** ⚓ 28E3

Promenade Gén. Charles de Gaulle. **GPS:** n43,11252 e5,81172.⬆. 🚰€ 3 🚰Ch. 🅾 01/01-31/12.

FR

## ♿S Sospel ⛰ 28G1

**Stade E. Donato**, D2566. **GPS**: n43,87876 e7,44213.⬆.

4 🏕€5 🚰🗑Chincluded WC. **Surface**: asphalted. ⏹ 01/01-31/12.
**Distance**: 🚶300m ⊗300m 🛒300m.
**Remarks**: Pay at tourist office.

## ♿S Thorenc ⛰🍴🏊 28F1

**Lac de Thorenc**, D2. **GPS**: n43,79921 e6,80802.⬆.

10 🏕free 🚰€5 🗑Ch🚿WC. **Location**: Rural, simple, isolated, quiet.
**Surface**: metalled. ⏹ 01/01-31/12.
**Distance**: 🚶750m 🏊on the spot 🍴on the spot ⊗200m 🛒épicerie
750m 🚿on the spot.
**Remarks**: Along Lake Thorenc, max. 48h.

## ♿S Trigance 28F1

Quartier Saint Roch. **GPS**: n43,76060 e6,44255.⬆.

5 🏕€5, dog €3,50 🚰€1 🗑€1 Ch🚿€1.🏊 **Location**: Rural,
isolated, quiet. **Surface**: asphalted/gravel. ⏹ 01/01-31/12.
**Distance**: 🚶on the spot 🏊on the spot ⊗100m 🛒100m.
**Remarks**: Max. 2 days, inclining pitches, beautiful view.

## ♿S Vaison-la-Romaine 🌿⛲ 25D3

**Parking du Colombier**, Avenue André Coudray.
**GPS**: n44,24650 e5,07392.⬆➡.

30 🏕€8/24h, tourist tax €0,55/pp 🚰🗑Chfree.🏊
**Location**: Urban, comfortable. **Surface**: gravel.
⏹ 01/01-31/12 ⏹ Tue-morning.
**Distance**: 🚶800m ⊗800m 🛒1km.

**Tourist information Vaison-la-Romaine:**
👁 Le Pont Romain. Bridge from the Roman Empire.
⛰ Le Château. Ruins of the castle of the Counts of Toulouse.
⛲ ⏹ Tue.

## ♿S Valberg ⛲⛰❄ 28F1

**Le Lagopède**, Route de Rouya. **GPS**: n44,09615 e6,93675.⬆➡.

---

16 🏕€10 + €0,20/pp tourist tax 🚰🗑Ch🚿(21x)WCincluded. 🚐
**Location**: Rural, comfortable, isolated, quiet. **Surface**: asphalted.
⏹ 01/01-31/12.
**Distance**: 🚶500m 🍴on the spot ⊗500m 🛒500m 🚴on the spot
⛰on the spot 🚲600m.

## ♿S Valréas 25C3

Traverse Pierre de Coubertin. **GPS**: n44,38713 e4,99245.⬆➡.

5 🏕free. **Location**: Simple. **Surface**: asphalted. ⏹ 01/01-31/12.
**Distance**: 🚶400m ⊗250m.
**Remarks**: Behind tourist info, max 3,5t.

## 🍇S Valréas 25C3

**Domaine du Lumian**, Route de Montélimar, D941.
**GPS**: n44,39384 e4,96325.⬆➡.

6 🏕free 🚰🗑Ch🚿free. **Location**: Rural, isolated, quiet.
**Surface**: gravel. ⏹ 01/01-31/12.
**Distance**: 🚶2,5km.

## ♿S Vars ⛰ 25F3

**Parking P5**, Allee Trub. **GPS**: n44,57510 e6,67789.⬆.

44 🏕free 🚰🗑Ch🚿(6x)WCfree. **Location**: Rural, simple, isolated,
quiet. **Surface**: gravel. ⏹ 01/01-31/12.
**Distance**: 🚶500m ⊗500m 🛒500m 🚴on the spot ⛰on the spot.
**Remarks**: Coins at tourist info.

## ♿S Vauvenargues 28D2

Boulevard Moraliste. **GPS**: n43,55485 e5,59764.⬆.

3 🏕free. **Location**: Rural, simple, quiet, quiet. **Surface**: asphalted.
⏹ 01/01-31/12.
**Distance**: 🚶300m ⊗210m 🛒300m 🚴on the spot ⛰on the spot.
**Remarks**: At cemetery.

## ♿S Veynes 25E3

**Base de Loisirs Les Iscles**, Les Graviers, D994.
**GPS**: n44,51830 e5,79860.⬆.

---

30 🏕free, June-Sep €6 🏊🏊 **Location**: Rural, simple, quiet.
**Surface**: gravel. ⏹ 01/01-31/12.
**Distance**: 🚶2km 🏊on the spot ⊗on the spot 🛒3km ⛰on the spot.
**Remarks**: Natural swimming pool, max. 48h, wifi at restaurant.

## ♿S Veynes 25E3

**Place du 19 Mars**, D994. **GPS**: n44,53332 e5,82346.⬆.
🏕free 🚰🗑Ch WCfree. **Surface**: asphalted. ⏹ 01/03-30/11
⏹ Thu-morning closed because of market.
**Distance**: 🚶1,5km.

## ♿S Villeneuve 28E1

**GPS**: n43,89611 e5,86167.⬆➡.

12 🏕free 🚰🗑Chfree. **Location**: Rural, simple, quiet.
**Surface**: gravel. ⏹ 01/01-31/12 ⏹ service: 30/11-01/03.
**Distance**: 🚶200m 🚲5,5km 🚴on the spot ⛰on the spot.
**Remarks**: At cemetery, max. 48h.

## ♿S Vinon sur Verdon 28E1

Chemin du Plan. **GPS**: n43,72952 e5,80141.⬆.

20 🏕free 🚰€2/20minutes 🗑Ch. **Location**: Rural, simple.
**Surface**: asphalted. ⏹ 01/01-31/12.
**Distance**: 🚶3km ⊗on the spot 🛒on the spot.
**Remarks**: Parking Carrefour Market, coins at petrol station.

## 🍇S Visan 25C3

**Domaine de Lucena**, 1600 chemin du Rastelet.
**GPS**: n44,31576 e4,98406.⬆.
5 🏕€5 🗑Ch🚿. **Location**: Isolated, quiet. **Surface**: gravel.
⏹ 01/01-31/12.
**Distance**: 🚶4km ⛰on the spot.

## 🍇S Visan 25C3

**Domaine des Lauribert**, D976. **GPS**: n44,34833 e4,97276.⬆.

20 🏕free 🚰🗑Chfree 🚿(8x)€2 WC. **Location**: Rural, comfortable,
isolated. **Surface**: unpaved. ⏹ 01/01-31/12.
**Remarks**: At wine-grower, max. 72h.

FR

# Corsica

### 🖼️S — Aléria — 33G1

**Le Banana's**, Casaperta. **GPS**: n42,17353 e9,42103. 🔼.

16 💶€ 15 ⛽🚰Ch🚿€ 5 〰included. 🚿 **Location:** Rural, comfortable. **Surface:** asphalted/grassy. 🗓 01/01-31/12.
**Distance:** 🏊river 200m 🛒800m ⊗on the spot.
**Remarks:** Swimming pool available.

### P — Col de Bavella 🏔 — 33G1

**Parking du Col**, D268. **GPS**: n41,79567 e9,22470. 🔼.

20 💶€ 4. 🅿🚻 **Location:** Rural, simple, isolated, quiet.
**Surface:** gravel/sand. 🗓 01/01-31/12.
**Distance:** ⊗250m.
**Remarks:** Overnight stay allowed.

### 🖼️S — Col de Vergio 🏔 — 33G1

D84. **GPS**: n42,28647 e8,89441. 🔼.

20 💶€ 12 ⛽🚰Ch included. **Location:** Rural, simple, isolated.
**Surface:** gravel/sand. 🗓 01/01-31/12.
**Distance:** ⊗100m 🏃on the spot 🚲1km.

### 🖼️ — Galéria 〰 — 33G1

D351. **GPS**: n42,41661 e8,65660.

20 💶free, night € 20. 🚿 **Location:** Rural, simple, isolated.
**Surface:** gravel.
**Distance:** 🏊600m ⊗on the spot ⊗on the spot 🏃on the spot.
**Remarks:** Canoe safari ± 1 hour, € 6/pp.

### 🖼️S — Ogliastro 〰 — 33G1

**Parking de la Plage**, Marine d'Albo D80. **GPS**: n42,81041 e9,33592. 🔼.

20 💶free, July-Aug € 7 ⛽service € 2 🚰Ch.
**Location:** Simple. **Surface:** unpaved.

---

🗓 01/01-31/12.
**Distance:** 🏊2km 🏖100m ⊗100m.
**Remarks:** Max. 7 nights, max. 8M, coins at the shops and restaurant.

### 🖼️S — Porto Vecchio 〰 — 33G2

**Camperpark Guiseppe**, Route de Palombaggia.
**GPS**: n41,55015 e9,30636. 🔼.

25 💶€ 25 ⛽🚰Ch🚿WC included 🚻€ 0,50 〰at restaurant.
🚿 **Location:** Rural, comfortable, quiet. **Surface:** unpaved.
🗓 01/05-30/09.
**Distance:** 🏊Porto Vecchio 9km 🏖white sandy beach 150m ⊗150m.

### 🖼️S — Porto Vecchio 〰 — 33G2

**Parking de la Plage**, Rue de Palavesa. **GPS**: n41,56389 e9,33601. 🔼➡.

50 💶€ 14 ⛽€ 2 🚰€ 5 Ch🚻,cold shower 〰included. 🚿
**Location:** Comfortable, quiet. **Surface:** sand. 🗓 15/05-15/09.
**Distance:** 🏊Porto Vecchio 10km 🏖500m ⊗500m.
**Remarks:** Bread-service.

### 🖼️ — Rogliano — 33G1

**Parking de Tollare**, L'arena/D153. **GPS**: n43,00733 e9,38831. 🔼.

10 💶free, July-Aug € 10. **Location:** Simple, isolated.
**Surface:** grassy/sand. 🗓 01/01-31/12.
**Distance:** 🏖on the spot 🚣on the spot 🏃on the spot.
**Remarks:** Attention: narrow road, 5,5km.

### 🖼️S — Sari-Solenzara 〰 — 33G1

**L'Aire de la Mer**, T10. **GPS**: n41,84214 e9,40138. 🔼.

35 💶€ 11,40 ⛽€ 4/10minutes 🚰🚿(16x)€ 2/2h 🧺. **Location:** Rural, comfortable. **Surface:** grassy/sand. 🗓 01/01-31/12.
**Distance:** 🏊800m 🏖on the spot 🛒on the spot ⊗1km 🍴800m 🛍1km 🏃1km.

# Greece

Capital: Athens
Government: Parliamentary democracy
Official Language: Greek
Population: 10,768,477 (2017)
Area: 131,957 km²

### General information
Dialling code: 0030
General emergency: 112
Currency: Euro

### Regulations for overnight stays
Wild camping and overnight parking is not officially allowed. Overnight parking places mentioned here are not official motorhome stopovers but tolerated areas.

### Additional public holidays 2019
January 6 Epiphany
March 11 Ash Monday, 41 days before Easter
March 25 Independence Day
April 28-29 Orthodox Easter
May 1 Labor Day
August 15 Assumption of the Virgin Mary
October 28 National Holiday, Ochi day

### Time Zone
Winter (Standard Time) GMT+2
Summer (DST) GMT+3

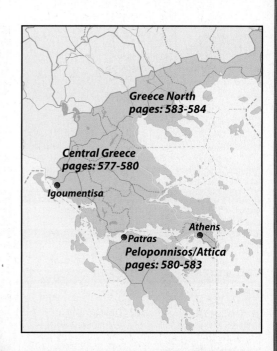

Greece North
pages: 583-584

Central Greece
pages: 577-580

Igoumentisa

Patras
Peloponnisos/Attica
pages: 580-583

Athens

## Central Greece

| | Achillio | 35G2 |
|---|---|---|

Epar. Od. Archilliou-Glifas. **GPS:** n39,00943 e22,95758.
**Distance:** on the spot on the spot on the spot.

| | Agios Nikolaos | 35F2 |
|---|---|---|

**GPS:** n38,34959 e22,15661.
01/10-30/04.
**Remarks:** Parking at harbour.

| S | Ammoudia | 35F2 |
|---|---|---|

**GPS:** n39,23636 e20,48073.

10 **Surface:** gravel/sand. 01/01-31/12.
**Distance:** on the spot 50m on the spot 100m 250m.
**Remarks:** At harbour.

| S | Ammoudia | 35F2 |
|---|---|---|

**Ammoudia Beach**, Paralias. **GPS:** n39,23989 e20,48116.

10 free **Location:** Rural, simple. **Surface:** sand.
01/01-31/12.
**Distance:** on the spot on the spot on the spot 200m 50m.
**Remarks:** Beach parking.

| | Arahova | 35G2 |
|---|---|---|

**GPS:** n38,47948 e22,58164.
01/01-31/12.

| S | Arillas | 35E2 |
|---|---|---|

**Restaurant Soukas**, Aglias-Platarias. **GPS:** n39,35278 e20,28861.

8 € 8, free for clients Ch WC .
**Location:** Rural, comfortable, quiet. **Surface:** grassy/sand.
01/05-01/10.
**Distance:** on the spot on the spot.

| | Armirichi Beach | 35H2 |
|---|---|---|

**GPS:** n38,26129 e24,25115.

2 free. **Location:** Isolated. **Surface:** gravel/sand.
01/01-31/12.
**Distance:** on the spot on the spot.
**Remarks:** Beach parking.

| S | Boukka | 35F2 |
|---|---|---|

**GPS:** n38,93125 e21,14200.

10 free. **Location:** Rural, simple, isolated, quiet. **Surface:** sand.
01/01-31/12.
**Distance:** on the spot 100m.
**Remarks:** Next to sports fields, beach parking.

| S | Chiliadou | 35F2 |
|---|---|---|

**GPS:** n38,39408 e21,92096.

**Surface:** gravel. 01/01-31/12.
**Distance:** Nafpaktos 7km on the spot 200m.
**Remarks:** Beach parking.

| | Chorefto | 35G1 |
|---|---|---|

**GPS:** n39,45168 e23,12364.

free. **Surface:** unpaved. 01/01-01/12.
**Distance:** Sandy beach.
**Remarks:** Parking at the beach.

| S | Corfu | 35E1 |
|---|---|---|

**Dionysus**, Dassia. **GPS:** n39,66472 e19,84440.
€ 18,20-21 Ch WC . 01/04-20/10.

| S | Corfu | 35E1 |
|---|---|---|

**Dolphin Camping**, Sidari. **GPS:** n39,78890 e19,72354.
€ 12-14,10 Ch WC . 01/07-10/09.

| S | Corfu | 35E1 |
|---|---|---|

**Karda Beach**, Dassia. **GPS:** n39,68611 e19,83861.
€ 22,30-23,60 Ch WC . 26/04-01/09.
**Distance:** on the spot.

**Tourist information Corfu:**
Esplanada, Kerkyra (Corfu). Meeting point for inhabitants and tourists.
Kerkyra (Corfu).
Frurion, Kerkyra (Corfu). Citadel, 1550.
Aqualand, Corfu Water Park, Ag.Ioannis. Leisure pool park.

| | Damasta | 35G2 |
|---|---|---|

**GPS:** n38,80436 e22,49485.

3 ⛺free. **Location:** Isolated. **Surface:** asphalted. ⬜ 01/01-31/12.
**Distance:** ⚓on the spot.
**Remarks:** Natural hot spring pond.

| △ S | **Delphi** 🌿 | 35G2 |

**Apollon. GPS:** n38,48388 e22,47550.
⛺🚰🛒Ch🗑🚿. ⬜ 01/01-31/12.

| △ S | **Delphi** 🌿 | 35G2 |

**Chrissa. GPS:** n38,47267 e22,46206.
55 ⛺€ 18,50-22,50 🚰🛒Ch🗑✏ WC🗑🚿. ⬜ 01/01-31/12.

| △ S | **Delphi** 🌿 | 35G2 |

**Delphi Camping. GPS:** n38,47833 e22,47450.
⛺€ 21,50-22,40 🚰🛒Ch🗑✏ WC🗑🚿.
**Location:** Rural. **Surface:** grassy/gravel. ⬜ 01/04-31/10.
**Distance:** ⚓on the spot ⊗on the spot 🏖on the spot 🚶‍♂on the spot
🚶‍♂on the spot.

**Tourist information Delphi:**
⌂ Site of Delphi. Archeological site. 🕐 7.30-17.30h ⊙ holiday. 🎟
€ 9.

| 🚐 S | **Dodoni** | 35F1 |

**Amphitheater. GPS:** n39,54606 e20,78466.⬆
15 ⛺€ 10 🚰. **Location:** Rural. **Surface:** grassy. ⬜ 01/01-31/12.
**Distance:** ✏ 2,1km ⊗500m 🚶‍♂on the spot.

| 🚐 | **Eratini** | 35F2 |

N48/E65 km 47. **GPS:** n38,33834 e22,19387.

⛺. **Surface:** grassy/sand. ⬜ 01/01-31/12.
**Distance:** ⚓on the spot ⛵on the spot.
**Remarks:** Beach parking, max 3,5t.

| △ S | **Erétria** ⛴ | 35G2 |

**Milos Camping. GPS:** n38,39139 e23,77556.
⛺€ 25-32 🚰🛒ChWC🗑⊙. ⬜ 15/04-30/09.

**Tourist information Erétria:**
⌂ Seaside resort and archological site Antique Eretria.

| 🍴 S | **Gliki** | 35F2 |

**Taverne Panorama,** Axerontas ipeiros. **GPS:** n39,32726 e20,61568.

5 ⛺guests free 🚰WC🗑. **Location:** Rural, simple, quiet.
**Surface:** grassy. ⬜ 01/01-31/12.
**Distance:** 🏖500m ⛲500m.
**Remarks:** Along the Acheron river.

| 🚐 | **Igoumenítsa** ⛴ | 35E2 |

**GPS:** n39,51540 e20,21087.

---

10 ⛺. **Surface:** sand. ⬜ 01/01-31/12.
**Distance:** ⚓on the spot ⊗100m.
**Remarks:** Beach parking.

| 🚐 | **Igoumenítsa** ⛴ | 35E2 |

**Grekou. GPS:** n39,51278 e20,25741.
⛺.
⬜ 01/01-31/12.
**Distance:** 🏖on the spot 🚙600m ⛲on the spot.
**Remarks:** Parking supermarket at the ring-road 6, dir Ioánnina.

**Tourist information Igoumenítsa:**
⌂ Goumani (titani). Archeological site.

| 🚐 | **Ioánnina** 🌿⛴ | 35F1 |

Sta Papagou 7. **GPS:** n39,67319 e20,85476.⬆

10 ⛺€ 12. **Surface:** metalled. ⬜ 01/01-31/12.
**Distance:** 🏖100m 🚌100m ⊗100m.
**Remarks:** Monitored parking.

| △ S | **Ioánnina** 🌿⛴ | 35F1 |

**Limnopoula. GPS:** n39,67770 e20,84280.
⛺€ 24 🚰🛒Ch✏.
⬜ 01/04-15/10.

**Tourist information Ioánnina:**
ℹ Capital of Epirus, important city in the Turkish time.
👁 Perama. Caves. ⬜ daily.

| △ S | **Itea** | 35G2 |

**Ayannis,** Kirra. **GPS:** n38,42440 e22,45880.
⛺€ 20-25 🚰🛒Ch✏. ⬜ 01/05-30/09.

**Tourist information Itea:**
Ⓜ Nautical Museum, Mouseio, 4, Galaxídi.

| 🚐 | **Kalpaki** | 35E1 |

**GPS:** n39,88539 e20,62385.⬆
10 ⛺free. **Location:** Rural. **Surface:** gravel. ⬜ 01/01-31/12.
**Distance:** 🏖200m ⊗200m.
**Remarks:** Next to school.

| 🍴 S | **Kanatadika** ⛴ | 35G2 |

**Bekatsas,** Paralia Kanatadika. **GPS:** n38,99389 e23,11551.

10 ⛺guests free 🚰WC🗑free,cold shower.
**Location:** Rural, comfortable, quiet. **Surface:** grassy.
⬜ 01/01-31/12.
**Distance:** 🏖5km ⚓Sandy beach ⊗on the spot ⛲5km.

| 🚐 S | **Kato Polidendri** ⛴ | 35G1 |

**GPS:** n39,65558 e22,89326.

---

10 ⛺free 🚰free. **Location:** Rural, isolated. **Surface:** unpaved.
⬜ 01/01-01/12.
**Distance:** 🏖1,5km ⚓Sandy beach.

| 🚐 S | **Kipi** | 35F1 |

**GPS:** n39,85738 e20,80483.⬆➡
25 ⛺free. **Location:** Isolated, quiet. **Surface:** grassy/gravel.
⬜ 01/01-31/12.
**Distance:** 🏖4km ⚓350m ⊗4km 🏖on the spot 🚶‍♂on the spot.

| 🚐 S | **Konitsa** | 35E1 |

**Kleidonia. GPS:** n39,96934 e20,66126.⬆➡
15 ⛺free 🚰. **Location:** Rural. **Surface:** grassy.
⬜ 01/01-31/12.
**Distance:** 🏖Konitsa 12km 🏖on the spot 🚶‍♂on the spot.

| 🚐 S | **Konitsa** | 35E1 |

**Epar.Od. Konitsas. GPS:** n40,05042 e20,75031.⬆➡
15 ⛺free. **Surface:** asphalted. ⬜ 01/01-31/12.
**Distance:** 🏖on the spot ⊗200m ⛲200m 🚶‍♂on the spot.

| 🍴 S | **Konitsa** | 35E1 |

**Bourazani Wild Life Resort,** Bourazani.
**GPS:** n40,05348 e20,62643.⬆➡
5 ⛺€ 10 🚰✏ WC🗑included.
**Location:** Rural, isolated, quiet. **Surface:** grassy/gravel.
⬜ 01/01-31/12.
**Distance:** 🏖Konitsa 14km ⊗on the spot 🏖on the spot 🚶‍♂on the spot.
**Remarks:** At mountainbike trail, discount at restaurant € 5.

| 🚐 | **Krioneri** | 35F2 |

**GPS:** n38,34397 e21,58823.

⛺. **Surface:** gravel. ⬜ 01/01-31/12.
**Distance:** ⚓on the spot ⛵on the spot ⊗300m.

| 🚐 | **Lazena** | 35F1 |

**GPS:** n39,51039 e20,97030.⬆➡
5 ⛺free. **Location:** Isolated, quiet. **Surface:** grassy/gravel.
⬜ 01/01-31/12.
**Distance:** 🏖2,5km.
**Remarks:** Less suitable for motorhomes >6,5m.

| 🚐 S | **Levkas** | 35F2 |

**L Camper Stop,** Epar. Od. Lefkadas, Apolpainas 225, Lefkada (Levkas).
**GPS:** n38,82579 e20,70007.⬆
3 ⛺€ 10-20 🚰🛒Ch🗑✏ WC🗑🚿. 🚲 **Location:** Urban,
comfortable. **Surface:** metalled. ⬜ 01/01-31/12.
**Distance:** 🏖1km ⚓1,8km ⊗1,5km.
**Remarks:** Monitored parking 24/24, scooter rental.

| 🚐 | **Levkas** | 35F2 |

**Vlycho. GPS:** n38,68318 e20,69819.
⛺. ⬜ 01/01-31/12.
**Distance:** ⛵on the spot.
**Remarks:** Parking on the quay.

| △ S | **Levkas** | 35F2 |

**Dessimi Beach,** Vlicho, Lefkada (Levkas). **GPS:** n38,67250 e20,71100.
⛺€ 28-35 🚰🛒Ch✏ WC🗑⊙. ⬜ 01/04-30/11.

| △ S | **Levkas** | 35F2 |

**Poros Beach,** Poros, Lefkada (Levkas). **GPS:** n38,64094 e20,69698.
⛺🚰🛒Ch🗑✏ WC🗑⊙. ⬜ 01/05-30/09.

| 🚐 S | **Ligkiades** 🌿 | 35F1 |

**GPS:** n39,69080 e20,88842.⬆
5 ⛺free 🚰✏. **Location:** Rural, isolated, quiet. **Surface:** gravel.
⬜ 01/01-31/12.
**Distance:** 🏖on the spot ⊗on the spot.
**Remarks:** Beautiful view.

---

GR

## Limnionas Beach 35G2

GPS: n38,71253 e23,75319.

2-3 free WC free,cold shower. **Location:** Rural, simple, isolated, quiet. **Surface:** metalled. 01/01-31/12.
**Distance:** on the spot 50m.

## Loggades 35F1

GPS: n39,66989 e20,92092.
10 free. **Location:** Rural, isolated, quiet. **Surface:** gravel.
01/01-31/12.
**Distance:** 2km on the spot on the spot on the spot.
**Remarks:** At lake.

## Melani Beach 35G1

GPS: n39,25963 e23,29588.

3. **Location:** Isolated. **Surface:** unpaved. 01/01-01/12.
**Distance:** Sandy beach.
**Remarks:** Beach parking.

## Mesolóngi 35F2

GPS: n38,36358 e21,42016.
. 01/01-31/12.
**Remarks:** Parking in harbour.

## Mesopotamou Beach 35H2

GPS: n38,24347 e24,24729.

. **Surface:** metalled.
**Distance:** on the spot on the spot.
**Remarks:** Parking at the beach.

## Metéora 35F1

Taverna Arsenis, East Street, Kalambaka. **GPS:** n39,70871 e21,65443.

20 guests free WC free. **Location:** Rural, isolated, quiet.
**Surface:** metalled. 01/01-31/12.

## Metéora 35F1

Camping International Rizos, Kalambaka. **GPS:** n39,69010 e21,64564.
Ch. 01/01-31/12.

## Metéora 35F1

Meteora Garden, Kalambaka. **GPS:** n39,70869 e21,60915.
Ch WC. 01/01-31/12.

## Metéora 35F1

Vrachos Kastraki, Kastraki. **GPS:** n39,71338 e21,61588.
€ 18 Ch. 01/01-31/12.

**Tourist information Metéora:**
✝ Important cultural inheritance, 24 monasteries built on enormous sandstone peaks, of which 6 can be visited.
9-13h, 15-17h.
against payment.

## Metochou Beach 35G2

GPS: n38,66093 e23,95309.

2-3 free. **Location:** Isolated. **Surface:** asphalted/sand.
01/01-31/12.
**Distance:** pebbled beach 100m.

## Métsovo 35F1

GPS: n39,83457 e21,06543.
10 free. **Location:** Rural, isolated, quiet. **Surface:** grassy/gravel.
01/01-31/12.
**Distance:** Métsovo 20km on the spot on the spot.
**Remarks:** Altitude 1350m, at lake.

## Métsovo 35F1

Country Cafe. **GPS:** n39,78073 e21,16253.
4 guests free on demand.
**Location:** Isolated, quiet.
**Surface:** gravel.
01/01-31/12.
**Distance:** Métsovo 3km on the spot on the spot on the spot on the spot.

**Tourist information Métsovo:**
Traditional mountain village.
Archotiko Tositsa. Restored 18th century mansion, museum or folk art. 8.30-13h, 16-18h. € 3.

## Molossi 35E1

O Lófos - Snack Bar Cafe Grill, Voutsaras, E92.
GPS: n39,66408 e20,58164.
5 guests free WC. **Surface:** grassy. 01/01-31/12.
**Distance:** on the spot.

## Mourteri 35G2

GPS: n38,56406 e24,16295.

. **Surface:** asphalted/sand. 01/01-31/12.
**Distance:** pebbled beach.
**Remarks:** Parking along coast road.

## Nafpaktos 35F2

Xiliadou, N48/E65 km 80,5. **GPS:** n38,38186 e21,81809.
.
**Surface:** gravel/sand.
01/01-31/12.
**Distance:** on the spot on the spot nearby.
**Remarks:** Parking at the beach.

**Tourist information Nafpaktos:**
Old city with Venetian Castle and circular walled harbor.

## Pades 35F1

GPS: n40,04007 e20,91068.
5 free € 5 WC. **Location:** Rural. **Surface:** grassy/gravel.
01/01-31/12.
**Distance:** on the spot on the spot on the spot.
**Remarks:** Panoramic view.

## Paltsi Beach 35G1

GPS: n39,23624 e23,31497.

± 12 free.
**Location:** Isolated. **Surface:** unpaved. 01/01-01/12.
**Distance:** Sandy beach 100m.
**Remarks:** Beach parking.

## Parga 35E2

Enjoy Lichnos. **GPS:** n39,28358 e20,43340.
€ 28-36 Ch WC. 01/05-15/10.

## Parga 35E2

Valtos Camping. **GPS:** n39,28556 e20,38972.
€ 20-21,50 Ch.
01/05-30/09.

**Tourist information Parga:**
Lively bathing resort.
Necromanteion of Ephyra. Oracle of death.

## Perama 35F1

EO Trikalon Ioanninon. **GPS:** n39,69069 e20,84734.
free. **Location:** Central, quiet. **Surface:** asphalted.
01/01-31/12.
**Distance:** on the spot 200m 200m on the spot.
**Remarks:** At lake, at mountainbike trail.

## Perdika 35E2

GPS: n39,38607 e20,27473.

free.
**Distance:** Perdika 7km on the spot.
**Remarks:** Beach parking.

## Pilion 35G1

Olizon, Milina. **GPS:** n39,16472 e23,21666.
€ 24-32 Ch WC. 01/05-15/10.

## Pilion 35G1

Sikia Fig Tree, Kato Gatzea. **GPS:** n39,31025 e23,10977.
€ 19-24,50 Ch WC. 01/04-31/10.

**Tourist information Pilion:**
Mythological peninsula, beautiful nature, authentic mountain villages and fishing towns.
Makrinitsa. Village worth seeing, car-free.
Miliés. Folk museum. 01/04-31/10 Tue-Su, 01/11-31/03 Wed-Su.
Archeological Museum, Athanasáki 1, Vólos. Tue-Su holiday.

## Plataria 35E2

Nautilos. **GPS:** n39,44389 e20,25806.
€ 21-23,50 Ch. 01/04-20/10.

## Potistika Beach 35G1

GPS: n39,26448 e23,29110.

5 free. **Location:** Isolated. **Surface:** unpaved. 01/01-01/12.
**Distance:** Sandy beach 100m.
**Remarks:** Beach parking.

GR

### 🅿️Ⓢ Pramanta — 35F1

Epar.Od. Ioanninon-Sirakou 13. **GPS**: n39,51332 e21,08711. ⬆️➡️
10 🏕️€ 10 🔌 WC⏢included. **Location:** Rural, simple, isolated, quiet.
**Surface:** gravel. ⬛ 01/01-31/12.
**Distance:** 🏪Pramanta 4km ⊗on the spot 🏍️on the spot 🏃on the spot.
**Remarks:** Parking at the caves.

### 🅿️Ⓢ Préveza 🚤🔱 — 35F2

**Mitikas,** Monolhiti Beach. **GPS**: n39,01719 e20,71555.

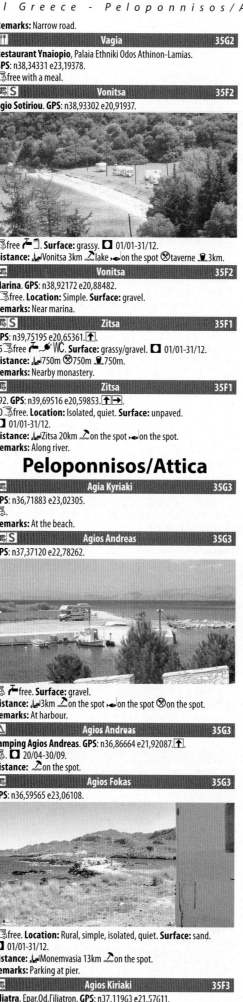

3 🏕️🚰⏢. **Location:** Rural, simple, quiet. **Surface:** asphalted/gravel.
⬛ 01/01-31/12.
**Distance:** 🏪Preveza 7km ⌇on the spot 🌊on the spot ⊗500m.
**Remarks:** Parking at the beach.

### 🅿️ Préveza 🚤🔱 — 35F2

**GPS**: n38,95008 e20,75498.
🏕️.

**Tourist information Préveza:**
⛰️ Kassópi, Kassópi. Archeological site.
⛰️ Nikopolis. Old Roman city.

### 🅿️ Psaropouli 🏔️🔱 — 35G2

**GPS**: n38,96778 e23,37853.

🏕️free. **Surface:** asphalted/sand. ⬛ 01/01-31/12.
**Distance:** 🏪on the spot ⌇pebbled beach.
**Remarks:** Parking along coast road.

### 🅿️ Sistrouni — 35F2

Lakka Souliou. **GPS**: n39,41586 e20,69796. ⬆️
10 🏕️free. **Location:** Isolated, quiet. **Surface:** grassy.
⬛ 01/01-31/12.
**Distance:** ⌇on the spot ⊗on the spot.
**Remarks:** Along the Acheron river, narrow road, picnic area.

### 🅿️ Sivota 🔱🔱 — 35E2

**Parking. GPS**: n39,40772 e20,24270.

± 4 🏕️free. **Surface:** unpaved.
**Distance:** 🏪200m ⌇harbour 200m ⊗200m 🚌50m.
**Remarks:** No beach.

### 🅿️ Spothi — 35F1

**GPS**: n39,67375 e20,93523. ⬆️
15 🏕️free. **Location:** Rural, isolated, quiet. **Surface:** gravel.
⬛ 01/01-31/12.
**Distance:** 🏪2km ⌇2km.
**Remarks:** Beautiful view.

### 🅿️ Tyria — 35F2

Epar.Od. Meliggon - Paramithias. **GPS**: n39,53351 e20,68794. ⬆️
12 🏕️free. **Location:** Rural. **Surface:** gravel. ⬛ 01/01-31/12.
**Distance:** 🏪350m ⌇500m ⊗100m.

### 🅿️ Tzoumerka — 35F1

Petrouni. **GPS**: n39,57899 e21,03291. ⬆️➡️
15 🏕️free.
**Location:** Isolated, quiet. **Surface:** grassy. ⬛ 01/01-31/12.

---

**Remarks:** Narrow road.

### 🅿️ Vagia — 35G2

**Restaurant Ynaiopio,** Palaia Ethniki Odos Athinon-Lamias.
**GPS**: n38,34331 e23,19378.
🏕️free with a meal.

### 🅿️ Vonitsa 🔱 — 35F2

**Agio Sotiriou. GPS**: n38,93302 e20,91937.

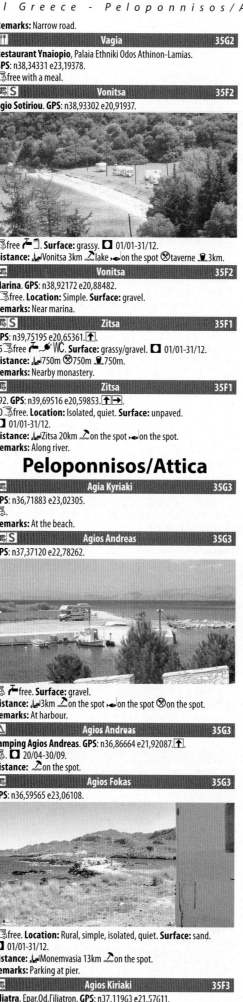

🏕️free 🚰⏢. **Surface:** grassy. ⬛ 01/01-31/12.
**Distance:** 🏪Vonitsa 3km ⌇lake ⌇on the spot ⊗taverne 🚌3km.

### 🅿️ Vonitsa — 35F2

**Marina. GPS**: n38,92172 e20,88482.
5 🏕️free. **Location:** Simple. **Surface:** gravel.
**Remarks:** Near marina.

### 🅿️Ⓢ Zitsa — 35F1

**GPS**: n39,75195 e20,65361. ⬆️
15 🏕️free 🚰🔌 WC. **Surface:** grassy/gravel. ⬛ 01/01-31/12.
**Distance:** 🏪750m ⌇750m 🚌750m.
**Remarks:** Nearby monastery.

### 🅿️ Zitsa — 35F1

E92. **GPS**: n39,69516 e20,59853. ⬆️➡️
10 🏕️free. **Location:** Isolated, quiet. **Surface:** unpaved.
⬛ 01/01-31/12.
**Distance:** 🏪Zitsa 20km ⌇on the spot ⌇on the spot.
**Remarks:** Along river.

# Peloponnisos/Attica

### 🅿️ Agia Kyriaki — 35G3

**GPS**: n36,71883 e23,02305.
🏕️.
**Remarks:** At the beach.

### 🅿️Ⓢ Agios Andreas — 35G3

**GPS**: n37,37120 e22,78262.

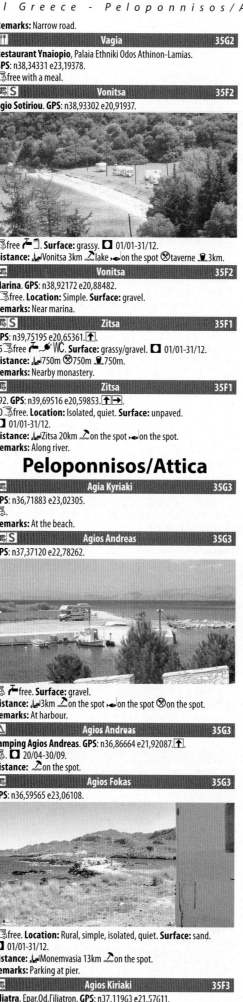

🏕️🚰free. **Surface:** gravel.
**Distance:** 🏪3km ⌇on the spot ⌇on the spot ⊗on the spot.
**Remarks:** At harbour.

### 🔺 Agios Andreas — 35G3

**Camping Agios Andreas. GPS**: n36,86664 e21,92087. ⬆️
🏕️. ⬛ 20/04-30/09.
**Distance:** ⌇on the spot.

### 🅿️ Agios Fokas — 35G3

**GPS**: n36,59565 e23,06108.

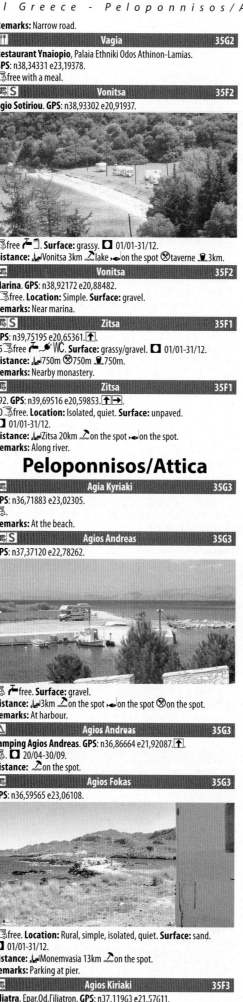

5 🏕️free. **Location:** Rural, simple, isolated, quiet. **Surface:** sand.
⬛ 01/01-31/12.
**Distance:** 🏪Monemvasia 13km ⌇on the spot.
**Remarks:** Parking at pier.

### 🅿️ Agios Kiriaki — 35F3

**Filiatra,** Epar.Od.Filiatron. **GPS**: n37,11963 e21,57611.
4 🏕️. ⬛ 01/01-31/12.

---

### 🅿️Ⓢ Aigio 🔱🔱 — 35F2

**En Plo Camperstop/beach cafe. GPS**: n38,22365 e22,14709.

10 🏕️€ 10, guests free 🚰🔌Ch.🔌€ 3 WC⏢included.
**Location:** Rural, simple, isolated, quiet. **Surface:** unpaved.
⬛ 01/01-01/12.
**Distance:** 🏪1,5km ⌇on the spot 🛒mini market 100m.

### 🔺Ⓢ Assini — 35G2

**Kastraki. GPS**: n37,52861 e22,87556.
🏕️€ 24,50-26,50 🔌Ch.🔌 WC⏢⏢. ⬛ 01/04-01/10.

### 🔺Ⓢ Athens 🏛️🔱🍽️ — 35G2

**Rovertou Galli. GPS**: n37,96987 e23,72263.
🏕️. ⬛ 01/01-31/12.
**Remarks:** Parking of the Acropolis, guarding after authorization Probably only outside the main season.

### 🔺Ⓢ Athens 🏛️🔱🍽️ — 35G2

**Athens camping,** Leoforis Athinon. **GPS**: n38,00889 e23,67222.
🏕️€ 29 🚰🔌Ch.🔌 WC⏢⏢🛒🔻.
⬛ 01/01-31/12.

**Tourist information Athens:**
👁️🚰🛒 Monasteraki. Old district with Athenian flea market.
⬛ Su 8-14h.
👁️ Panathenaic Stadium. Stadium of the first Olympic Games in 1896.
👁️🛒 Plaka. Old district around the Acropolis.
👁️ Tomb of the Unknown Soldier, Plateía Syntágmatos. Sunday 11h changing of the guard.
⛰️ Acropolis. Archeological site. ⬛ 01/05-31/10 Mo-Fri 8-18.30h, Sa-Su 8.30-14.30h, 01/11-30/04 8.30-16.30h
⬛ 01/05, 28/10, holiday.

### 🅿️Ⓢ Bozas 🔱 — 35G3

**GPS**: n36,70443 e22,82147.

20 🏕️free for clients 🚰Ch. **Location:** Isolated. **Surface:** sand.
⬛ 01/01-31/12.
**Distance:** ⌇on the spot ⊗on the spot.

### 🅿️ Diakofto 🔱🔱 — 35F2

**GPS**: n38,20176 e22,19282.

🏕️. **Surface:** asphalted. ⬛ 01/01-31/12.
**Distance:** ⌇pebbled beach ⌇on the spot ⊗on the spot 🚌500m.

### 🅿️ Diakofto 🔱🔱 — 35F2

Anapafseos. **GPS**: n38,19166 e22,19894.

GR

5 🛏free.
**Surface:** metalled.
🅿 01/01-31/12.
**Distance:** 🚉on the spot ⚓750m ⊗on the spot ⚡300m ➡on the spot.
**Remarks:** Nearby railway station, overnight stay allowed.
**Tourist information Diakofto:**
👁 Rack railway, Kalavryta. Train journey with rack-railway.

| 🛏 | Dimitsána | 35G3 |
|---|---|---|

**Kefalari tou Ai-Yanni. GPS:** n37,58320 e22,04719.
4🛏. 🅿 01/01-31/12.
**Remarks:** Parking water museum.

| 🍴 | Dimitsána | 35G3 |
|---|---|---|

**Taverna Koustenis**, Eparchiaki Odos Kato Davias.
**GPS:** n37,58650 e22,04459.⬆
5🛏free.
**Location:** Rural, simple. **Surface:** gravel.
🅿 01/01-31/12.
**Distance:** ✈9km ⊗on the spot ⚕on the spot.
**Remarks:** Beautiful view.
**Tourist information Dimitsána:**
🚶 Loúsios-kloof. 5km long and 300m deep, marked trails.

| 🛏S | Elea | 35F3 |
|---|---|---|

**GPS:** n37,36337 e21,69011.
15🛏free 🚰free. **Location:** Rural, simple, isolated. **Surface:** unpaved.
🅿 01/01-31/12.
**Distance:** ⚓on the spot ⊗1,5km.

| 🛏 | Elefsina 🌿🍵 | 35G2 |
|---|---|---|

**GPS:** n38,04235 e23,53942.
🛏free.
**Location:** Urban, noisy. **Surface:** asphalted. 🅿 01/01-31/12.
**Distance:** 🚉on the spot ➡150m.
**Remarks:** Parking in front of the ruins in the city center.

| 🛏S | Epidaurus | 35G2 |
|---|---|---|

**EO Isthmou Archaias Epidavrou. GPS:** n37,59675 e23,07444.

🛏🚰WCfree.
**Surface:** gravel. 🅿 01/01-31/12.
**Distance:** ⊗on the spot.
**Remarks:** Overnight stay on parking at the Ancient theater is generally tolerated.
**Tourist information Epidaurus:**
🏛 Ancient Epidaurus. Archeological site. 🅿 8-19h.

| 🛏 | Ermioni | 35G3 |
|---|---|---|

**Eparchiaki Ermionis Kranidiou. GPS:** n37,38833 e23,24776.

7🛏free. **Surface:** asphalted. 🅿 01/01-31/12.
**Distance:** 🚉on the spot ⚓on the spot ⊗800m ⚡200m 🚲on the spot 🏊on the spot.

| 🛏S | Ermioni | 35G3 |
|---|---|---|

**Hydras Wave. GPS:** n37,40583 e23,31556.

🛏 € 18 🚰🚽Ch 🚿WC🧺 📶. 🅿 15/04-15/10.

| 🛏 | Galatas | 35G2 |
|---|---|---|

Epar.Odos Ermionis. **GPS:** n37,49491 e23,45546.
20🛏. **Surface:** unpaved. 🅿 01/01-31/12.
**Distance:** 🚉on the spot ⚓on the spot ➡on the spot ⊗on the spot.
**Remarks:** At the quay.

| 🛏 | Gerolimenas | 35G3 |
|---|---|---|

**GPS:** n36,48230 e22,39969.

3🛏. **Surface:** asphalted. 🅿 01/01-31/12.
**Distance:** ⚓on the spot ➡on the spot ⊗50m ⚕on the spot.
**Remarks:** Parking at the beach.

| △S | Gialova Pylou | 35F3 |
|---|---|---|

**Navarino Beach. GPS:** n36,94770 e21,70620.
🛏 € 20-23 🚰🚽Ch 🚿WC🧺📶. 🅿 01/04-31/10.

| △S | Glifa Kyllini | 35F2 |
|---|---|---|

**Ionion. GPS:** n37,83640 e21,13340.
🛏 € 21-24,50 🚰🚽Ch 🚿🔌. 🅿 01/01-31/12.

| 🛏 | Gythion | 35G3 |
|---|---|---|

**Valtaki beach**, Valtaki. **GPS:** n36,78883 e22,58225.

🛏. **Surface:** sand. 🅿 01/01-31/12.
**Distance:** ⚓on the spot ⊗on the spot.
**Remarks:** At the beach, ± 5km from Gythion dir Skala.

| △S | Gythion | 35G3 |
|---|---|---|

**Gythion Bay. GPS:** n36,72942 e22,54535.
🛏 € 20,50-22 🚰🚽Ch 🚿🔌. 🅿 01/04-31/10.

| 🛏 | Kakovatos 🌊 | 35F3 |
|---|---|---|

**GPS:** n37,45721 e21,63869.
🛏. **Surface:** metalled. 🅿 01/01-31/12.
**Remarks:** Parking at the beach.

| 🛏 | Kalo Nero 🌊 | 35F3 |
|---|---|---|

**GPS:** n37,29786 e21,69525.

10🛏free. **Surface:** gravel.
**Distance:** 🚉100m ⚓Sandy beach ⊗100m.

| 🍴S | Kalogria | 35F2 |
|---|---|---|

**Camper Stop Kalogria**, Kalogria. **GPS:** n38,15986 e21,37162.⬆

40 🛏 € 19, 16/07-31/08 € 23 🚰🚽Ch 🚿(20x)€ 3,70/day WC🧺📶included.
**Location:** Rural. **Surface:** unpaved.

🅿 01/05-31/10.
**Distance:** ✈5km ✈11km ⚓500m ➡300m ⊗50m ⚡on the spot ➡on the spot 🚲on the spot ⚕on the spot.
**Tourist information Kalogria:**
🚶 Kotychi, Lapas. Visitors centre, swamp area.

| 🛏 | Kamares | 35G3 |
|---|---|---|

**Anatoliki Mani. GPS:** n36,68203 e22,52090.

🛏. **Surface:** sand. 🅿 01/01-31/12.
**Distance:** 🚉1km ⚓on the spot ➡on the spot ⊗350m.

| △S | Kameras Irion | 35F1 |
|---|---|---|

**Poseidon. GPS:** n40,01305 e22,59039.
🛏 € 30-38 🚰🚽Ch 🚿WC🧺. 🅿 01/04-31/10.

| 🛏 | Karathona 🚿🌊 | 35G2 |
|---|---|---|

**GPS:** n37,54389 e22,82278.

50🛏free. 🅿 01/01-31/12.
**Distance:** ⚓Sandy beach.

| 🍴 | Karavastasi 🌊 | 35G3 |
|---|---|---|

**Vasilis Taverne. GPS:** n36,68839 e22,82765.

🛏free.
**Distance:** ⚓Sandy beach ⊗on the spot.
**Remarks:** Free, use of a meal obligated.

| 🍴🍵S | Karavostasi 🌊 | 35G3 |
|---|---|---|

**Taverna O Faros**, Karavostasi. **GPS:** n36,69733 e22,38073.⬆➡

15🛏free 🚰. **Location:** Rural, simple. **Surface:** gravel.
**Distance:** ⚓on the spot ⊗on the spot.
**Remarks:** No beach.

| 🛏 | Kastro | 35F2 |
|---|---|---|

Killinis Beach. **GPS:** n37,87413 e21,10748.

**GR**

🔅free. **Surface**: grassy/sand.
**Distance**: 🚶2km 🏖on the spot 🛶on the spot ⊗Beach taverne.
**Remarks**: Beach parking.

**Tourist information Kastro:**
⚔ Chlemoutsi. Medieval castle.

| △S | Kato Alissos | 35F2 |

**Kato Allissos. GPS**: n38,14986 e21,57740.
🔅€ 18,30-19 🚰🔌Ch 🚿WC 🛒🕸. ◻ 30/06-01/09.

| △S | Kifisiá 🌿⚓🌊 | 35G2 |

**Dionissiotis. GPS**: n38,10535 e23,81355.
🔅€ 19 🚰🔌Ch 🚿WC 🛒🕸. ◻ 01/01-31/12.
**Remarks**: 18km north of Athens, route Athens dir Lamia.

**Tourist information Kifisiá:**
ℹ Holiday resort of the Athenian since the Roman time.
Ⓜ Goulándris, Levidou 13. History of nature.

| 🅿 | Killini | 35F2 |

Epar Od. Andravidas-Killinis. **GPS**: n37,92598 e21,16699.
🔅. ◻ 01/01-31/12.
**Distance**: 🚶2km.
**Remarks**: Parking at the beach.

| 🅿 | Kiveri 🌊 | 35G3 |

**GPS**: n37,52761 e22,73120.

10 🔅free. **Surface**: gravel.
**Distance**: 🚶200m 🏖pebbled beach 50m ⊗100m.
**Remarks**: At harbour.

| 🅿S | Kokkinia 🌊 | 35G3 |

**GPS**: n36,79762 e22,78485.

20 🔅free 🚰. **Surface**: metalled. ◻ 01/01-31/12.
**Distance**: 🏖Sandy beach ⊗400m.
**Remarks**: Beach parking.

| 🅿 | Korfos | 35G2 |

**GPS**: n37,76361 e23,13302.

🔅. **Surface**: gravel. ◻ 01/01-31/12.
**Remarks**: At fishing port.

| 🅿S | Korinthos 🌿⚓🌊 | 35G2 |

**Afrodites Waters**, Ancient Corinth. **GPS**: n37,91139 e22,87861. ⬆➡.

30 🔅€ 10 🚰🔌Ch 🚿WC 🛒included. **Location**: Urban,
comfortable, quiet. **Surface**: gravel. ◻ 01/01-31/12.

**Distance**: 🚶350m ⊗350m 🚌350m.
**Remarks**: Barbecue place.

| 🅿 | Korinthos 🌿⚓🌊 | 35G2 |

Ancient Corinth. **GPS**: n37,90750 e22,87806.

🔅. ◻ 01/01-31/12.

**Tourist information Korinthos:**
ℹ Important trade centre.
👁 Korinth Canal. Canal, 23m wide.
⌒ Acrocorinth. Fortress. ◻ 8-19h, winter 8-17h. 🎫 free.
⌒ Ancient Korinthos. Archeological site. ◻ 01/04-31/10 8-19h, 01/11-31/03 8-17h ◉ 25/12-26/12, 01/01, 25/03, Easter, 01/05.

| 🅿 | Koroni 🌿🌊 | 35G3 |

**GPS**: n36,79729 e21,96002.

🔅. ◻ 01/01-31/12.
**Remarks**: Parking at harbour.

| △S | Koroni 🌿🌊 | 35G3 |

**Camping Koroni. GPS**: n36,79942 e21,95068.
🔅€ 25 🚰🔌Ch 🚿WC 🛒🕸. ◻ 01/01-31/12.
**Distance**: 🚶600m 🏖on the spot ⊗on the spot.

**Tourist information Koroni:**
ℹ Port city with Venetian castle, 1206.

| 🅿 | Kosmas 🌿⚓🏔 | 35G3 |

Epar.Od.Leonidiou-Kosma. **GPS**: n37,09180 e22,74043.

🔅. **Surface**: metalled.
**Distance**: 🚶on the spot ⊗on the spot 🍺on the spot.
**Remarks**: Behind church.

| 🅿S | Kotronas | 35G3 |

Epar.Od. Chosiariou-Gerolimena. **GPS**: n36,61899 e22,49367. ⬆.

🔅free 🚰free. **Surface**: concrete. ◻ 01/01-31/12.
**Distance**: 🏖on the spot 🛶on the spot 🏖50m.
**Remarks**: Parking at pier.

| △S | Lambiri | 35F2 |

**Tsolis**, Old National Road. **GPS**: n38,32083 e21,97194.
🔅€ 17-20 🚰🔌Ch 🚿WC 🛒. ◻ 01/01-31/12.

| 🅿 | Legrena | 35G2 |

**GPS**: n37,66206 e23,99772.
🔅. ◻ 01/01-31/12.
**Remarks**: Parking at the beach.

| △S | Marathon 🌿 | 35G2 |

Ramnous. **GPS**: n38,13139 e24,00722.
🔅€ 27-35 🚰🔌Ch 🚿WC 🛒. ◻ 01/04-31/10.

**Tourist information Marathon:**
ℹ www.marathon.gr. The name marathon, course of 41 km, comes from this town.

| △S | Mayroyouni/Gythion | 35G3 |

**Meltemi. GPS**: n36,72986 e22,55360.
🔅€ 19 🚰🔌Ch 🚿WC 🛒. 

**Tourist information Mayroyouni/Gythion:**
ℹ Tourist Information Areópoli, Vasiléos Pávlou 21, Máni. Peninsula.
👁 Pýrgos Diroú, Máni. Caves.

| 🅿 | Monemvasía 🌿🌊 | 35G3 |

**GPS**: n36,68240 e23,03821.
🔅. **Surface**: metalled. ◻ 01/01-31/12.
**Distance**: 🚶500m 🏖on the spot 🛶on the spot.
**Remarks**: Parking harbour.

| 🅿 | Monemvasía 🌿🌊 | 35G3 |

**GPS**: n36,68745 e23,04257.
🔅. **Surface**: asphalted.
◻ 01/01-31/12.
**Distance**: ⊗on the spot 🍺on the spot 🚌shuttle to old town.

**Tourist information Monemvasía:**
ℹ Fortified city, lower town have been restored.
✝ Agía Sofia. Church 13th century.

| △S | Mycenae | 35G2 |

**Atreus. GPS**: n37,71911 e22,74114.
🔅€ 24-32 🚰🔌Ch 🚿WC 🛒.
◻ 01/01-31/12.

**Tourist information Mycenae:**
Ⓜ Archeological Museum, Argos. 🎫 € 12.
⌒ Archeological site. ◻ 1/4-31/10 8-19h, 1/11-31/3 8-17h ◉ holiday.
⌒ Agora Argos, Argos. Archeological site. ◻ summer 8.30-15h.

| 🅿 | Nafplio 🌿⚓🌊 | 35G2 |

**GPS**: n37,56823 e22,80170.

🔅free.
**Surface**: asphalted.
**Distance**: 🚶500m ⊗300m.
**Remarks**: Parking marina.

**Tourist information Nafplio:**
ℹ Tourist information, Ikostispémtis Martiou 2. First Greek capital.
Ⓜ Archeological Museum. ◻ Tue-Su 8.30-15h ◉ Mo.
⚔ Palamídi. Citadel 18th century.

| 🅿 | Neo Itylo | 35G3 |

**Black Pirate. GPS**: n36,69154 e22,38986. ⬆.

10 🔅free. **Surface**: grassy/gravel.
**Distance**: 🚶on the spot 🏖pebbled beach 🛶on the spot ⊗50m.

GR

## Olympia △S 35F3

**Alphios. GPS:** n37,64360 e21,61930.
€ 24-33 Ch WC. 01/04-31/10.
**Tourist information Olympia:**
Archeological Museum. Important Greek archeological museum.
Mo 11-19h, Tue-Su 8-19h.

## Paralia Platanou S 35G2

**GPS:** n38,17104 e22,26828.

**Location:** Rural, simple. **Surface:** gravel. 01/01-31/12.
**Distance:** on the spot.
**Remarks:** At the beach.

## Pátra △S 35F2

**Golden Sunset,** Old national Road km 19. **GPS:** n38,14389 e21,58778.
€ 32-39 Ch WC. 01/04-15/10.
**Tourist information Pátra:**
Archaïa Klauss. First commercial producer of wine of Greece.

## Perahóra 35G2

Limni Vouliagmenis. **GPS:** n38,03188 e22,87293.

**Distance:** on the spot on the spot.
**Remarks:** At the lake.

## Petalidi S 35G3

**GPS:** n36,95871 e21,93418.
**Surface:** asphalted.
**Remarks:** Nearby port.

## Petalidi 35G3

**GPS:** n36,95915 e21,92870.

**Surface:** asphalted.
**Distance:** on the spot.
**Remarks:** Parking in village, near the sea.

## Piraeus 35G2

Parkopolis, Fokionos 3. **GPS:** n37,94759 e23,64595.

± 10 € 13 included. **Location:** Urban. **Surface:** asphalted.
01/01-31/12.
**Distance:** on the spot metro > Athens 300m.

## Pírgos Dhiroú 35G3

Diros. **GPS:** n36,64206 e22,38357.

---

20. **Location:** Isolated. **Surface:** unpaved.
**Distance:** on the spot.

## Porto Kagio 35G3

Taverna Porto. **GPS:** n36,42811 e22,48697.
3 guests free. **Surface:** grassy.
**Distance:** on the spot on the spot on the spot mini market
on the spot.

## Rafina 35G2

**GPS:** n38,01835 e24,01227.
01/01-31/12.

## Salandi 35G3

**GPS:** n37,44748 e23,12474.

**Location:** Rural, isolated. **Surface:** gravel.
01/01-31/12.
**Distance:** Didyma 5km on the spot on the spot.
**Remarks:** At the beach.

## Savalia 35F2

Savalia Beach. **GPS:** n37,79685 e21,25578.

**Surface:** asphalted.
**Distance:** on the spot on the spot.

## Skoutari 35G3

**GPS:** n36,65921 e22,49962.

max. 3. **Surface:** concrete.
**Distance:** on the spot on the spot within walking distance.
**Remarks:** Near fishing-port.

## Sounion △S 35H2

Camping Bacchus. **GPS:** n37,67694 e24,04750.
€ 23 Ch WC.
01/01-31/12.
**Tourist information Sounion:**
Mineralogical Museum, Lavrió. Old mine shaft of the silvermines.
Wed, Sa-Su.
Archeological site.

## Tolo S 35G2

**GPS:** n37,51469 e22,85662.

---

WC. **Surface:** asphalted.
**Distance:** 500m 100m on the spot 200m.
**Remarks:** Near fishing-port.

## Tyrchu 35G3

Taverne Ostria. **GPS:** n37,31414 e22,82054.

3 guests free.
**Surface:** gravel. 15/05-30/09.
**Distance:** Tyros 10km on the spot on the spot on the spot.
**Remarks:** At the beach, attention: via steep path.

## Zacharo 35F3

**GPS:** n37,51917 e21,60248.

**Distance:** on the spot.

## Zacharo △S 35F3

Tholo Beach. **GPS:** n37,41160 e21,66830.
€ 18,50 Ch WC. 01/04-31/10.

# Greece North

## Ag.Mamas Moudania △S 35G1

Ouzoni Beach. **GPS:** n40,21611 e23,31833.
€ 17,60-23 Ch WC. 01/05-30/09.

## Akt Armenistis Sithonia △S 35G1

Armenistis. **GPS:** n40,15222 e23,91361.
€ 31-40 Ch WC. 01/05-15/09.

## Alexandroúpoli 39D5

Apollonias. **GPS:** n40,84342 e25,86477.
**Surface:** asphalted. 01/01-31/12.
**Remarks:** Parking near stadium.

## Alexandroúpoli 39D5

Commercial Port - TOL, Alexandroupolis. **GPS:** n40,84364 e25,87693.

01/01-31/12.
**Remarks:** Parking harbour.
**Tourist information Alexandroúpoli:**
Tourist Information, Mákris. Large holiday resort, beautiful beach.

## Gerakani △S 35G1

Kouyoni. **GPS:** n40,26464 e23,46347.
€ 22,25-24,50 Ch. 01/05-30/09.

## Kalamaria S 35G1

Zampetaz, Tessaloniki-Perea. **GPS:** n40,50239 e22,97138.

GR

10 ⓈfreeⒸ🗑Ch ⚊WC🔲 ⓦfree. **Location:** Urban, simple, noisy.
**Surface:** gravel. 🕐 9-17/20h 🅿 Su.
**Distance:** 🚶10km 🚲3km 🚆500m 🚌> Thessaloniki.
**Remarks:** At motorhome dealer.

22 Ⓢ€ 4 ⓒ⚊€ 3. **Location:** Urban, simple. **Surface:** asphalted.
🅿 01/01-31/12.
**Distance:** 🚶on the spot ⊗200m 🚆450m.
**Remarks:** Near archeological site and museum.

| ⓈS | Kastoriá 🍃 | 35F1 |
|---|---|---|

**GPS**: n40,50461 e21,27977.
Ⓢagainst payment ⓒ. 🅿 01/01-31/12.
**Remarks:** Voluntary contribution.

| Ⓒ S | Kastoriá 🍃 | 35F1 |
|---|---|---|

Meg. Alexandrou. **GPS**: n40,50461 e21,27970.
Ⓢfree. **Location:** Urban, central, noisy. **Surface:** asphalted.
🅿 01/01-31/12.
**Distance:** 🚶on the spot ⊗on the spot 🚆on the spot.

| ⚠S | Metamorphosi | 35G1 |
|---|---|---|

**Sunny Bay**. **GPS**: n40,22694 e23,58944.
Ⓢ€ 18,90-21,70 ⓒ🗑Ch ⚊WC🔲 ⓦ. 🅿 01/05-31/10.

| ⓈS | Moustheni | 39C5 |
|---|---|---|

**Moystheni Station**. **GPS**: n40,84413 e24,11506.⬆
10 ⓈfreeⒸ🗑ChWC🔲ⓦ. **Location:** Rural, comfortable.
**Surface:** asphalted. 🅿 01/01-31/12.
**Distance:** ⓐ100m ⊗on the spot 🚆mini market.
**Remarks:** Special part for motor homes, shop, restaurant, station 24/24.

| ⚠S | Ouranoupoli | 35G1 |
|---|---|---|

**Ouranoupoli**. **GPS**: n40,33944 e23,97056.
Ⓢ€ 28-31 ⓒ🗑Ch ⚊. 🅿 01/04-31/10.

| ⓒS | Porto Lagos | 39D5 |
|---|---|---|

**GPS**: n41,00633 e25,12028.

5 ⓈfreeⒸ. **Surface:** asphalted.
**Distance:** ⊗on the spot.
**Remarks:** Parking at pier.

| ⓒS | Thessaloníki 🍃🍴🍦🍽 | 35G1 |
|---|---|---|

**Camper Stop Sallonicco**, Voulgari 74. **GPS**: n40,59741 e22,96979.⬆

10 ⓈfreeⒸ🗑.
**Location:** Urban, simple, central, noisy. **Surface:** asphalted.
🅿 01/01-31/12.
**Distance:** 🚶on the spot 🚌150m.

**Tourist information Thessaloníki:**
ℹ Tourist Information, Plateia Aristolélous 8. Second city of Greece, busy port and many places of interest.
👁 Lefkos Pyrgos. White tower.
👁 Modiano. Turkish fair.
✝ Agios Dimitrios. Biggest church of Greece. 🅿 Tue-Sa.

| ⓒS | Vergina 🍃 | 35F1 |
|---|---|---|

**Parking**, Aristotelos 25. **GPS**: n40,48506 e22,31978.⬆➡

**GR**

# ⚑ Croatia

Capital: Zagreb
Government: parliamentarian democracy
Official Language: Croatian
Population: 4,300,000 (2017)
Area: 56,594 km²

## General information
Dialling code: 00385
General emergency: 112
Currency: Kuna, kn, 1 kuna = 100 lipa
1kn = € 0,13, € 1 = 7,41kn
10kn = £1.18, £1 = 8,48kn (October 2018)
Credit card are accepted almost everywhere.

## Regulations for overnight stays
Wild camping is forbidden.

### Additional public holidays 2019
January 6 Epiphany
May 1 Labor Day
June 20 Corpus Christi
June 22 Dan antifasisticke borbe, Anti-Fascist
Resistance Day
June 25 Dan drzavnosti, National Holiday
August 5 Victorie Day and National Thanksgiving
August 15 Assumption of the Virgin Mary
October 8 Independence Day

### Time Zone
Winter (Standard Time) GMT+1
Summer (DST) GMT+2

Inland page: 591
Istria/ Kvarner Bay pages: 585-587
Dalmatia pages: 587-591
Zagreb
Pula
Zadar
Split
Dubrovnik

---

# Istria/Kvarner Bay

### ⚠S Cres/Cres 37A2
**Kovačine**, Melin I, 20. **GPS:** n44,96278 e14,39694.
€ 19,20-41,10 Ch WC 19/03-16/10.
**Distance:** on the spot.
**Tourist information Cres/Cres:**
ℹ Turisticka zajednica, Riva Creskih Kapetana, www.tzg-cres.hr. Island can be reached with ferry service from Brestova, south of Rijeka and Valbiska, west Krk.

### ⚠S Cres/Martinščica 37A2
**Slatina. GPS:** n44,82091 e14,34238.
€ 16-28,20 Ch WC 19/03-31/10.

### ⚙S Cres/Nerezine 37A2
**Camping Lopari**, Nerezine. **GPS:** n44,68092 e14,39561.
3 € 11-21 Ch WC **Location:** Rural, comfortable, isolated, quiet. **Surface:** gravel. 25/03-10/10.
**Distance:** 1,5km 900m.

### ⚠S Cres/Nerezine 37A2
**Preko Mosta**, Osor 76, Nerezine. **GPS:** n44,69250 e14,39167.
€ 129-179 kn Ch WC 01/04-30/09.

### ⚠S Cres/Nerezine 37A2
**Rapoća**, Rapoća, Nerezine. **GPS:** n44,66357 e14,39756.
€ 20-28 Ch WC 22/04-10/10.

### ⚠S Crikvenica 37B2
**Kacjak**, Kacjak BB. **GPS:** n45,16703 e14,70511.
Ch WC 15/05-15/09.

### ⚙S Fažana 37A2
Ul.1.Maja. **GPS:** n44,92880 e13,80255.

€ 30 WC **Location:** Urban, simple, central.
**Surface:** grassy/sand. 01/01-31/12.
**Distance:** 100m on the spot 100m 100m on the spot on the spot.
**Remarks:** Max. 24h.

### ⚠S Fažana 37A2
**Bi Village**, Dragonja 115. **GPS:** n44,91750 e13,81111.
€ 21-46 Ch WC 21/04-30/09.

### ⚠S Fažana 37A2
**Pineta Fažana**, Perojska cesta bb. **GPS:** n44,93835 e13,79554.
€ 11,10-24,10 27/04-30/09.
**Tourist information Fažana:**
🌿 Nationaal Park Brijuni, Brijuni. Nature reserve, boat connection from Fažana. daily.

---

### 🅿 Grožnjan 37A2
**Parking bus. GPS:** n45,38163 e13,72375.

20 free. **Location:** Rural, simple, isolated, quiet. **Surface:** gravel.
01/01-31/12.
**Distance:** 200m 200m on the spot on the spot on the spot.
**Remarks:** Next to cemetery.

### ⚠S Ičiči 37A2
**Opatija. GPS:** n45,31083 e14,28472.
Ch WC 27/04-13/10.

### ⚠S Klenovica 37B2
**Klenovica**, Zidinice BB. **GPS:** n45,09788 e14,84393.
€ 19-26,60 Ch 01/05-30/09.
**Distance:** on the spot on the spot.

### ⚠S Koromačno 37A2
**Tunarica. GPS:** n44,96917 e14,09889.
€ 20,50-24,10 Ch WC 29/04-30/09.

### ⚠S Kraljevica 37A2
**Ostro. GPS:** n45,27109 e14,56402.
Ch 01/05-30/09.

### ⚙S Krk/Baška 37B2
**Kamp Mali**, Put Zablace 100. **GPS:** n44,96609 e14,74710.

33 € 13-25, dog € 3 Ch (30x),10Amp WC € 5 included. **Location:** Urban, comfortable, central, quiet.
**Surface:** grasstiles. 01/03-30/10.
**Distance:** 300m 150m on the spot on the spot 50m on the spot on the spot.

### ⚠S Krk/Baška 37B2
**Zablace**, Emila Geitslicha 34, Baška. **GPS:** n44,96694 e14,74528.
€ 38,50-47,30 Ch WC 01/05-01/10.

### ⚠S Krk/Klimno 37A2
**Slamni**, Klimno 8a. **GPS:** n45,15351 e14,61770.
€ 18-38 Ch 22/04-10/10.
**Remarks:** Mini-camp.

### ⚙S Krk/Krk 37A2
**Camperstop Krk**, Sv. Petar bb. **GPS:** n45,03574 e14,56819.
16 € 12,90-23,10 + tourist tax Ch included

---

WC € 2,80. **Location:** Urban. **Surface:** gravel.
01/01-31/12.
**Distance:** 1,2km 2km 100m Konzum.

### ⚙S Krk/Krk 37A2
**Camper Stop Felix**, Ulica Narodnog preporoda 51.
**GPS:** n45,02928 e14,58149.

12 € 30 Ch (12x),16Amp WC € 5 included.
**Location:** Urban, comfortable, central, quiet. **Surface:** grassy/gravel.
01/01-31/12.
**Distance:** 300m 300m 300m 50m 50m on the spot on the spot on the spot.

### ⚠S Krk/Krk 37A2
**Bor. GPS:** n45,02250 e14,56194.
€ 20,40-29 Ch WC 01/01-31/12.

### ⚠S Krk/Krk 37A2
**Jezevac**, Plavnička bb. **GPS:** n45,01963 e14,57000.
€ 26-38 Ch WC 25/03-01/10.

### ⚠S Krk/Krk 37A2
**Marta**, Škrbcici 29. **GPS:** n45,04930 e14,48940.
€ 12,30-17,10 Ch WC 01/05-30/09.
**Remarks:** Mini-camp.
**Tourist information Krk/Krk:**
ℹ Tourist Information, Vela placa 1/1, www.krk.hr. Krk accessible via toll-bridge south-east from Rijeka.
🎵 Jazz-festival, Kamplin. Aug.

### 🅿S Krk/Malinska 37A2
**Camp Mali Raj**, Brzac, Glavotok 10. **GPS:** n45,09080 e14,43720.

10 € 23-36, 15/07-19/08 € 50 Ch (10x)WC included.
**Location:** Rural. **Surface:** grassy/gravel. 01/05-31/10.
**Distance:** 2km 300m 300m 500m 2km on the spot on the spot.

### ⚠S Krk/Malinska 37A2
**Draga**, Palih Boraca 4. **GPS:** n45,12052 e14,52494.
€ 16,80-25,40 Ch WC 01/04-15/10.
**Remarks:** Mini-camp.

HR

## Krk/Malinska — 37A2

**Glavotok**, Glavokok 4. **GPS:** n45,09472 e14,44111.
€ 17,95-43,15 Ch WC. 22/04-02/10.
**Distance:** on the spot.

## Krk/Njivice — 37A2

**Njivice**, Primorska bb. **GPS:** n45,16963 e14,54740.
€ 20,80-40,20 Ch WC. 09/04-30/10.

## Krk/Omišalj — 37A2

**Pusca**, Pušča bb. **GPS:** n45,23613 e14,55108.
Ch WC. 01/06-30/09.

## Krk/Pinezici — 37A2

**Amar**, Njivine 8. **GPS:** n45,04351 e14,47985.
**Location:** Simple.
**Distance:** on the spot on the spot on the spot on the spot.
**Remarks:** Mini-camp.

## Krk/Punat — 37A2

**Maslinik**, Nikole Tesle 1. **GPS:** n45,01809 e14,63478.
€ 13,33-21,99 Ch WC. 01/04-04/10.
**Remarks:** Mini-camp.

## Krk/Punat — 37A2

**Pila**, Setalište Ivana Brusića. **GPS:** n45,01581 e14,62860.
250 € 15-20 Ch. 22/04-09/10.

## Krk/Punat — 37A2

**Škrila**, Stara Baška. **GPS:** n44,96611 e14,67389.
350 € 20,60-33,20 Ch.
01/04-01/10.
**Tourist information Krk/Punat:**
Otočić Košljun. Monastery.

## Krk/Šilo — 37A2

**Tiha Šilo**, Konjska bb. **GPS:** n45,14876 e14,67150.
€ 16,50-26 Ch WC. 01/04-15/10.
**Remarks:** Mini-camp.

## Labin — 37A2

**Kamp Tunarica**, Koromačno. **GPS:** n44,96933 e14,09979.
50 € 15, 01/07-31/08 € 19 Ch (50x) € 4/night,16Amp WC € 5 included. **Location:** Rural, simple, isolated, quiet.
**Surface:** forest soil. 01/05-30/09.
**Distance:** 15km on the spot on the spot on the spot on the spot 2km on the spot.

## Labin — 37A2

**Camping Romantik**, Kapelica 47b. **GPS:** n45,08167 e14,10188.
8 € 17-24 Ch WC € 5,30 included.
**Distance:** 2km on the spot on the spot.
**Remarks:** Mini-camp.

## Labin — 37A2

**Marina**. **GPS:** n45,03333 e14,15806.
€ 27,80-42,10 Ch WC. 25/03-30/10.

## Labin — 37A2

**Marina**, Sveta Marina. **GPS:** n45,03387 e14,15723.
€ 37-47 Ch WC.
25/03-30/10.
**Remarks:** Mini-camp.

**Tourist information Labin:**
Narodni muzej, N. Katunara 6. Ethnological museum. daily 10-13h, 17-19h.

## Lošinj/Mali Lošinj — 37A2

**Čikat**. **GPS:** n44,53750 e14,45056.
940 € 22,50-36,60 Ch WC. 01/01-31/12.

## Lošinj/Mali Lošinj — 37A2

**Poljana**. **GPS:** n44,55556 e14,44167.
€ 16,50-21 Ch WC. 17/03-17/10.
**Tourist information Lošinj/Mali Lošinj:**
Dolphins day, action day with possibility for adoption of a dolphin. 1st Sa Aug.

## Medulin — 37A2

**Indije**, Banjole. **GPS:** n44,82398 e13,85090.
Ch WC. 01/05-01/10.

## Medulin — 37A2

**Kazela**. **GPS:** n44,80695 e13,95015.
Ch WC. 01/04-15/10.

## Medulin — 37A2

**Kranjski Kamp**, Runke 52, Premantura. **GPS:** n44,80694 e13,91616.
€ 19,80-27,10 Ch WC. 01/06-18/09.
**Remarks:** Mini-camp.

## Medulin — 37A2

**Medulin**. **GPS:** n44,81417 e13,93194.
Ch WC. 03/04-09/10.

## Medulin — 37A2

**Piškera**, Indie 49, Banjole. **GPS:** n44,82332 e13,84855.
170-200kn Ch WC.
**Remarks:** Mini-camp.

## Medulin — 37A2

**Pomer**, Pomer. **GPS:** n44,82064 e13,90205.
Ch WC.
**Remarks:** Mini-camp.

## Medulin — 37A2

**Postolovic**, Bumbište 10. **GPS:** n44,82037 e13,85749.
Ch WC.
**Remarks:** Mini-camp.

## Medulin — 37A2

**Runke**, Premantura. **GPS:** n44,80742 e13,91632.
€ 28-37 Ch WC. 01/05-30/09.

## Medulin — 37A2

**Širola**, Rupice Bd. **GPS:** n44,82113 e13,85872.
10 Ch.
**Remarks:** Mini-camp.

## Medulin — 37A2

**Stupice**, Premantura. **GPS:** n44,79779 e13,91354.
Ch. 01/05-25/09.

## Medulin — 37A2

**Tasalera**, Premantura. **GPS:** n44,81425 e13,91275.
€ 27-35 Ch.
01/04-30/09.
**Tourist information Medulin:**
Premantura. Most Southern place of Istria.
Banjole. Fisherman's village with natural harbour.

## Moščenička Draga — 37A2

**Draga**. **GPS:** n45,24023 e14,25021.
131-186kn Ch. 15/04-01/10.
**Remarks:** Mini-camp.

## Moščenička Draga — 37A2

**Draga**. **GPS:** n45,24000 e14,25028.
165. 15/04-01/10.

## Motovun — 37A2

**Motovun Camping**, Rižanske Skupštine 1A.
**GPS:** n45,33446 e13,82523.

12 € 15-25 + tourist tax € 1/pp Ch WC included.
**Location:** Rural, comfortable. **Surface:** gravel.
01/01-31/12.
**Distance:** 50m on the spot 50m 50m 100m on the spot on the spot.
**Remarks:** Free entrance swimming pool, discount longer stays.

## Novi Vinodolski — 37B2

**Autocamp Sibinje**, Sibinj. **GPS:** n45,04405 e14,87751.
80 € 24 Ch WC. 01/04-30/09.
**Distance:** on the spot 50m 50m.
**Remarks:** Mini-camp.

## Novigrad (Istria) — 37A2

**Aminess Sirena camping**, Terre 6. **GPS:** n45,31528 e13,57556.
€ 32-52 Ch WC. 01/04-30/09.

## Novigrad (Istria) — 37A2

**Mareda**. **GPS:** n45,34149 e13,54610.
800 from € 17 Ch WC included. 15/04-30/09.
**Tourist information Novigrad (Istria):**
Hoofdstraat van de oude stad. Farmers market. daily.

Feest van de beschermheilige Pelegrinus, Umag. 23/05.

## Ogulin — 37B2

**Camperstop Sabljaci**, Sabljak Selo 65. **GPS:** n45,22998 e15,23396.
26 € 20,68, 01/07-31/08 € 23,42 Ch WC € 5/5 included. **Location:** Rural, comfortable, quiet.
**Surface:** grassy/metalled. 01/01-31/12.
**Distance:** 400m 400m 200m 400m 2km.
**Remarks:** Video surveillance, bicycle rental.

## Poreč — 37A2

30. Travinja/Karla Huguesa. **GPS:** n45,22104 e13,60742.

28 200kn, winter free. **Location:** Simple, central, noisy.
**Surface:** asphalted. 01/01-31/12.
**Distance:** 800m 2km 2km 400m 2km 500m on the spot on the spot.

## Poreč — 37A2

**Bijela Uvala**. **GPS:** n45,19139 e13,59667.
2000 € 35-52 Ch WC. 01/04-15/10.

## Poreč — 37A2

**Laternacamp**. **GPS:** n45,29639 e13,59444.
3000 from € 22,65 Ch WC. 01/04-15/10.
**Distance:** on the spot on the spot.

## Poreč — 37A2

**Puntica**, Funtana. **GPS:** n45,17749 e13,60406.
250 Ch WC. 11/04-13/10.

## Poreč — 37A2

**Zelena Laguna**. **GPS:** n45,19611 e13,58917.
1000 € 32,50-55 Ch WC. 01/04-15/10.

## Poreč — 37A2

**Materada**, Materada. **GPS:** n45,24628 e13,59600.
**Remarks:** Mini-camp.

**Tourist information Poreč:**
Turisticka zajednica, Zagrebacka 9, www.istra.com/porec. Old city, centre tourist and cultural.
Decumanus. Roman main street with palazzi from the Venetian time.
Zavicajnog muzeja poreštine. Native museum of Porec. daily 10-13h, 18-22h.
Eufrazijeva bazilika. Basilica, 6th century, in the centre. daily 7-19h.

## Pula — 37A2

**Puntižela**. **GPS:** n44,89806 e13,80722.
480 Ch WC included. 01/05-31/10.

## Pula — 37A2

**Stoja**. **GPS:** n44,86000 e13,81472.
750 € 32,50-45 Ch WC.
03/04-02/11.

**Tourist information Pula:**
Arheoloski Muzej Istre, Carrarina 3. Archeological museum. winter Mo-Fri 9-14h, summer Mo-Sa 9-19h.
Amfiteatar. Large anfiteatro from Roman time. daily 8-21h.
Ljetni klasicni Festival, Amfitheatar. Opera festival. Aug.

## Rab — 37B2

**Camperpark Lando Resort**, Kampor 321. **GPS:** n44,78404 e14,70682.
12 € 23,50-55 Ch WC € 7 included.
**Location:** Rural, comfortable. **Surface:** grassy/metalled.
01/01-31/12.
**Distance:** city centre 1,5km 50m 50m 1,5km on the spot on the spot.
**Remarks:** Heated pool.

## Rab — 37B2

**Mel**, Kampor 319. **GPS:** n44,79390 e14,70302.
**Remarks:** Mini-camp.

## Rab — 37B2

**Planka**, Kampor 326. **GPS:** n44,78049 e14,72048.
**Remarks:** Mini-camp.

**HR**

## △S Rabac — 37A2
**Oliva. GPS:** n45,07960 e14,14777.
300 ⬛Ch WC ◻. 15/03-30/09.
**Distance:** ⌇on the spot.

## △S Ribnik — 37B1
**Srce Prirode/Heart of Nature Camp,** Gorica Lipnička 8.
**GPS:** n45,56389 e15,39278.
30 € 29,40-35 ⬛Ch WC ◻. 01/04-31/10.
**Remarks:** Mini-camp.

## △S Rijeka — 37A2
**Preluk Katalinic,** Preluk 1. **GPS:** n45,35340 e14,33235.
90 ⬛Ch WC ◻.
**Remarks:** Mini-camp.

### Tourist information Rijeka:
Tourist Information, Kastav 47, Kastav. Walled city with rich history.
Pomorski i povijesni muzej, Muzejski trg 1. Navy museum. Mo-Fri 10-13h, 18-21h.
Velika trznica. Market opposite to Modello palace.
Carnaval van Rijeka. Feb.

## △S Rovinj — 37A2
**Aleja Ruera Boskovica. GPS:** n45,08898 e13,64537.

30 25kn/h 6-23h (± € 55), overnight stay free ⬛Ch WC included.
**Location:** Urban, simple, central, noisy. **Surface:** asphalted.
01/01-31/12.
**Distance:** 1km 300m 300m 300m 1km 300m on the spot on the spot.

## Rovinj — 37A2
**Camping Polari. GPS:** n45,06300 e13,67480.

40 € 12-32 ⬛Ch WC included 25kn 100kn.
**Location:** Rural, simple, quiet. **Surface:** grassy/metalled.
22/04-04/10.
**Distance:** 3km on the spot on the spot on the spot on the spot June/July/Aug on the spot on the spot.
**Remarks:** Camperstop max. 48h.

## △S Rovinj — 37A2
**Mon Paradiso,** Uvala Veštar. **GPS:** n45,04947 e13,69000.
40 € 36-50 ⬛Ch WC ◻. 01/06-30/09.
**Remarks:** Mini-camp.

## △S Rovinj — 37A2
**Polari. GPS:** n45,06258 e13,67477.
2150 € 18-44,80 ⬛Ch WC ◻. 22/04-02/10.

## △S Rovinj — 37A2
**Porton Biondi. GPS:** n45,09410 e13,64232.
396 114-226kn ⬛Ch WC ◻. 15/03-30/10.

## △S Rovinj — 37A2
**Vestar. GPS:** n45,05389 e13,68639.
800 € 15-52,40 ⬛Ch WC ◻. 22/04-25/09.

## △ Rovinj — 37A2
**Ulika,** Polari Bd. **GPS:** n45,06528 e13,67583.
◻. 01/04-01/10.
**Remarks:** Mini-camp.

### Tourist information Rovinj:
Turisticka zajednica, Budicin 12, www.istra.com/rovinj. City has been a cultural monument since 1963.
Aquarium, Obala G. Paliage 5. daily 9-21h.
Palazzo Califfi, Trg Marsala Tita 11. Tue-Su 10.30-14h, summer 18-20h.
Market.
Grisia, Grisia. Art festival. 2nd week Aug.

## △S Savudrija — 37A1
**Pineta. GPS:** n45,48667 e13,49250.
460 € 15,70-36,70 ⬛Ch WC. 22/04-25/09.

## △S Savudrija — 37A1
**Veli Jože,** Borozija. **GPS:** n45,49556 e13,50444.
⬛Ch WC ◻. 01/04-30/09.

## △S Savudrija — 37A1
**Ravna Dolina. GPS:** n45,49206 e13,50288.
◻. 01/05-30/09.

## △S Selce — 37B2
**Selce. GPS:** n45,15408 e14,72533.
€ 17,50-31,10 ⬛Ch ◻. 01/04-15/10.

## △S Selina — 37A2
**Camp Terre,** 79, Selina. **GPS:** n45,15770 e13,76765.

10 100-150kn ⬛Ch (14x),16Amp WC ◻ € 5 included.
**Location:** Rural, luxurious, isolated, quiet.
**Surface:** gravel.
01/01-31/12.
**Distance:** 3km 5km 3km 3km on the spot on the spot.

## △S Umag — 37A1
**Finida. GPS:** n45,39278 e13,54194.
204 € 15,70-36,30 ⬛Ch WC ◻. 22/04-25/09.

## △S Umag — 37A1
**Stella Maris. GPS:** n45,45056 e13,52278.
400 € 15,50-24,40 ⬛Ch ◻. 24/04-25/09.

## △S Vižinada — 37A2
**Agroturizam Jadruhi,** Jadruhi 11. **GPS:** n45,29978 e13,74819.

10 75kn ⬛Ch (6x)included,16Amp WC free.
**Location:** Rural, simple, isolated, quiet. **Surface:** gravel/metalled.
01/01-31/12.
**Distance:** 4km 6km on the spot 4km on the spot on the spot on the spot.
**Remarks:** Check in at restaurant.

## △S Vrsar — 37A2
**Dalmatinska ulica. GPS:** n45,14706 e13,60422.

30 100kn/day. **Location:** Urban, simple, central, noisy.
**Surface:** asphalted. 01/01-31/12.
**Distance:** 350m 350m 350m 350m 350m 350m on the spot on the spot.

## Vrsar — 37A2
**Camperstop Valkanela,** Fontana. **GPS:** n45,16501 e13,60804.

20 € 12-32 ⬛Ch WC included 100kn/24h.
**Location:** Urban, simple, central, quiet.
**Surface:** grassy.
20/04-29/09.
**Distance:** 500m on the spot on the spot on the spot 1km on the spot on the spot.
**Remarks:** Camperstop, max. 48h, use camp-site facilities incl.

## △S Vrsar — 37A2
**Porto Sole. GPS:** n45,14139 e13,60222.
15,40-38,60 ⬛Ch WC ◻. 01/03-01/11.

# Dalmatia

## △S Babino Polje — 34H1
**Mungos. GPS:** n42,73885 e17,53441.
€ 25-35 ⬛Ch ◻. 15/05-30/09.
**Remarks:** Mini-camp.

## △S Baška Voda — 37D3
**Basko Polje. GPS:** n43,34561 e16,96272.
€ 29-37 ⬛Ch WC ◻. 15/05-30/09.

## △S Bibinje — 37B3
**Andela. GPS:** n44,05557 e15,29263.
⬛Ch.
**Remarks:** Mini-camp.

## △S Bibinje — 37B3
**Dido,** Težački put. **GPS:** n44,05708 e15,29116.
€ 23, 2 pers.incl ⬛Ch WC ◻.
**Remarks:** Mini-camp.

## △S Bibinje — 37B3
**Kero,** Punta Bibinje. **GPS:** n44,05730 e15,28918.
€ 20 ⬛Ch WC ◻.
**Remarks:** Mini-camp.

## △ Bibinje — 37B3
**Kamp Punta,** Težački put. **GPS:** n44,05680 e15,29162.

**Remarks:** Mini-camp.

## △S Biograd na Moru — 37B3
**Dijana & Josip,** Put Solina 26. **GPS:** n43,93229 e15,45252.
€ 42-50 ⬛Ch WC ◻. 01/05-30/09.
**Remarks:** Mini-camp.

## △S Biograd na Moru — 37B3
**Ljutic,** Put Solina. **GPS:** n43,92654 e15,45353.
€ 26-36 ⬛Ch WC ◻. 01/05-01/10.
**Remarks:** Mini-camp.

## △S Biograd na Moru — 37B3
**Mia,** Put Solina 47. **GPS:** n43,93441 e15,44803.
€ 18-40 ⬛Ch WC ◻. 01/01-31/12.
**Remarks:** Mini-camp.

## △S Biograd na Moru — 37B3
**Soline,** Put Kumenta. **GPS:** n43,92756 e15,45595.
€ 21,90-39,20 ⬛Ch WC ◻. 22/04-30/09.

## △S Bol — 37C3
**Kito,** Ante Radića 1. **GPS:** n43,26407 e16,64820.
110-180 kn ⬛Ch WC ◻. 01/01-31/12.

## △S Dubrovnik — 39A5
**Solitudo,** Vatroslava Lisinskog 17. **GPS:** n42,66178 e18,07052.
24,20-51,60 ⬛Ch WC ◻. 01/04-31/10.

### Tourist information Dubrovnik:
Akvarij Dubrovnik, D. Jude 2. Sea aquarium. Mo-Sa 9-13h.
City Walls, Gunduličeva poljana 2. City wall surround the entire Old City. 10-12h, 01/04-31/10 10-18.30h. 90kn.
Place Stradun. Main street with Onofrio-fountain and Sveti Frane monastery.
Dubrovacki Muzej, Pred Dvorom 3. History of the city. Mo-Sa 9-14h.
Pomorski Muzej, Sveti Ivan. Shipping museum. Tue-Sa 9-16h.
Zomerfestival. 10/07-25/08.

## △S Dugi Rat — 37C3
**Ivo,** Duce Rogac. **GPS:** n43,44111 e16,65778.

HR

🏕€ 11-20 ⊐🔌WC⊐. ◻ 15/04-15/11.
**Remarks:** Mini-camp.

[A][S] **Dugi Rat** 🏖🏕⛰ 37C3
**Luka**, Duce Rogac. **GPS:** n43,44164 e16,65347.
🏕€ 12,50-21 ⊐🔌Ch⚲WC⊐. ◻ 30/06-01/09.
**Remarks:** Mini-camp.

[A] **Dugi Rat** 🏕⛰ 37C3
**Orij**, Orij, Duce Rogac. **GPS:** n43,44631 e16,63429.
**Remarks:** Mini-camp.

[A][S] **Grebaštica** 🌊 37C3
**Ante&Toni**, Brodarica. **GPS:** n43,63833 e15,95833.
25 🏕⊐🔌Ch⚲WC⊐◻. ◻ 01/05-01/10.
**Distance:** 100m ⛱on the spot.
**Remarks:** Mini-camp.

[A][S] **Grebaštica** 🌊 37C3
**Tomas**, D8. **GPS:** n43,63003 e15,93764.
30 🏕50kn + 25kn/pp, 01/07-01/09 70kn + 40kn/pp🔌
Ch⚲WC⊐. ◻ 01/05-01/11.
**Distance:** ⛱on the spot.
**Remarks:** Mini-camp.

[A] **Kaštel Kambelovac** 37C3
**U Dragama**, A. Starcevica 39. **GPS:** n43,54951 e16,37778.
🏕.
**Remarks:** Mini-camp.

[A] **Kaštel Štafilic** 37C3
**Koludrovac**, Resnik Bb. **GPS:** n43,54373 e16,31753.
**Remarks:** Mini-camp.

[A] **Kaštel Stari** 37C3
**Adria**. **GPS:** n43,55143 e16,35349.
🏕.
**Remarks:** Mini-camp.

[A][S] **Kolan** 🌊 37B2
**Sveti Duh**. **GPS:** n44,51518 e14,95525.
🏕120-150 kn ⊐🔌Ch⚲. ◻ 01/06-30/09.
**Remarks:** Mini-camp.

[A][S] **Korčula** 🐚🏕⛰🌊 34H1
**Kalac**. **GPS:** n42,95056 e17,14500.
🏕€ 40-50 ⊐🔌Ch⚲WC⊐. ◻ 01/06-01/10.

[A][S] **Korčula** 🐚🏕⛰🌊 34H1
**Oskorušica**, Oskorušica 27/ VI, Racišce. **GPS:** n42,96795 e17,07335.
🏕⊐🔌Ch⚲WC⊐.
**Remarks:** Mini-camp.

[A][S] **Korčula** 🐚🏕⛰🌊 34H1
**Vela Postrana**, Lumbardra 142. **GPS:** n42,92230 e17,17266.
🏕⊐🔌Ch⚲WC⊐◻.
**Remarks:** Mini-camp.

**Tourist information Korčula:**
[i] Turisticka zajednica, Obala Tudmana, www.korcula.net. City with historical centre, birth-place Marco Polo.
🎭 Marco Polo fest. ◻ 09/07-11/07.
🎭 Zwaarddansfestival. ◻ daily 04/07-23/08.

[Y][S] **Korenica** 🐚🏕⛰ 37B2
**Bistro Marina**, Zagrebačka 6. **GPS:** n44,74702 e15,70464.⬆➡.

12 🏕guests free ⚲€ 2/night,10Amp WC📶.
**Location:** Urban, simple, central, quiet. **Surface:** asphalted.
◻ 01/01-31/12 ◻ 06/01-30/01.
**Distance:** 100m ⊗on the spot 🚰10m 🚌100m 🛒on the spot ⚓on the spot.

[A][S] **Kornati/Murter** 🐚🏕⛰🌊 37B3
**Jazina**, Tisno. **GPS:** n43,80940 e15,62760.
🏕92-155kn ⊐🔌Ch⚲WC⊐. ◻ 01/04-15/10.

[A][S] **Kornati/Murter** 🐚🏕⛰🌊 37B3
**Jezera-Loviša**, Jezera. **GPS:** n43,79370 e15,62867.
🏕€ 16,55-36 ⊐🔌Ch⚲WC⊐. ◻ 28/04 10/10.

[A][S] **Kornati/Murter** 🐚🏕⛰🌊 37B3
**Kosirina**, Betina. **GPS:** n43,79727 e15,61004.
🏕⊐🔌Ch⚲WC⊐. ◻ 01/05-30/09.

[A][S] **Kornati/Murter** 🐚🏕⛰🌊 37B3
**Plitka Vala**, Betina. **GPS:** n43,80515 e15,61284.
🏕 14,50-23,60 ⊐🔌Ch⚲WC⊐. ◻ 01/04-31/10.

[A] **Kornati/Murter** 🏕⛰🌊 37B3
**Slanica**, Jurija Dalmatinca 17. **GPS:** n43,81682 e15,57733.
🏕109,40-173,40kn ⊐🔌Ch⚲WC⊐◻. ◻ 15/04-15/10.

[A] **Krvavica** 🌊 37D3
**Autocamp Krvavica**. **GPS:** n43,32375 e16,98559.
15 🏕€ 30. **Location:** Rural, isolated.
**Distance:** ⛱100m.

[A][S] **Kucište** 34H1
**Palme**. **GPS:** n42,97639 e17,12917.
🏕€ 16,50-26 ⊐🔌Ch⚲WC⊐◻. ◻ 01/06-01/10.

[A][S] **Kucište** 34H1
**Camp Ponta**, Viganj 5, Od Gaja. **GPS:** n42,97935 e17,10400.
🏕. ◻ 01/05-15/10.
**Remarks:** Mini-camp.

[A][S] **Lokva Rogoznica** 37C3
**Danijel**, Ruskamen bb. **GPS:** n43,40973 e16,74529.
🏕⊐🔌Ch⚲WC.
**Remarks:** Mini-camp.

[A][S] **Lokva Rogoznica** 37C3
**Linda**. **GPS:** n43,40834 e16,75683.
🏕⊐🔌Ch⚲WC.
**Remarks:** Mini-camp.

[A][S] **Lovište** 34H1
**Lupiš**. **GPS:** n43,02790 e17,03012.
🏕€ 20-30 ⊐🔌Ch⚲WC⊐◻. ◻ 01/03-01/11.
**Remarks:** Mini-camp.

[A][S] **Lukoran** 37B3
**Novi Kamp**, Punta 28. **GPS:** n44,10538 e15,15518.
🏕.
**Remarks:** Mini-camp.

[A][S] **Mlini** 39A5
**Kate**, Tupina 1. **GPS:** n42,62472 e18,20806.
🏕158-214kn ⊐🔌Ch⚲. ◻ 04/04-28/10.
**Remarks:** Mini-camp.

[A][S] **Mlini** 39A5
**Kupari**, Kupari bb. **GPS:** n42,62462 e18,18833.
🏕€ 11,50-15,20 ⊐🔌Ch⚲WC⊐📶. ◻ 01/04-30/09.
**Remarks:** Mini-camp.

[A][S] **Mlini** 39A5
**Matkovica**, Srebreno 8. **GPS:** n42,62450 e18,19295.
🏕€ 20-24 ⊐🔌Ch⚲WC.
**Remarks:** Mini-camp.

[A][S] **Mlini** 39A5
**Paradiso Laguna**, Za Gospom, Plat. **GPS:** n42,60759 e18,22838.
🏕109-130kn ⊐🔌Ch⚲.
**Remarks:** Mini-camp.

[A][S] **Mlini** 39A5
**Porto**, Srebreno. **GPS:** n42,62433 e18,19107.
🏕⊐🔌Ch⚲.
**Remarks:** Mini-camp.

[A][S] **Mljet** 34H1
**Marina**, Marina Matana,Ropa 11. **GPS:** n42,75260 e17,46000.
🏕€ 27,80-42,10 ⊐🔌Ch⚲WC⊐. ◻ 25/03-30/10.
**Remarks:** Mini-camp.

[C] **Mokalo** 34H1
**Adriatic**. **GPS:** n42,97694 e17,22500.
🏕100-270kn. ◻ 01/04-31/10.

[A] **Molunat** 39A5
**Adriatic I**, Višnjici 4, Ðurinici. **GPS:** n42,45341 e18,43554.
🏕⊐🔌Ch⚲.
**Remarks:** Mini-camp.

[A] **Molunat** 39A5
**Monika**, Molunat 10. **GPS:** n42,45284 e18,42871.
🏕80-180kn ⊐🔌Ch⚲. ◻ 01/01-31/12.
**Remarks:** Mini-camp.

[A] **Molunat** 39A5
**Adriatic II**. **GPS:** n42,45327 e18,43582.
**Remarks:** Mini-camp.

[Y][S] **Murvica** 37B3
**Camper stop Marni**, Kralja Tomislava 102.
**GPS:** n44,13305 e15,29338.⬆.

36 🏕150-190kn ⊐🔌Ch⚲WC⊐📶included. **Location:** Rural, comfortable, isolated, quiet. **Surface:** gravel. ◻ 01/01-31/12.
**Distance:** 5km ⛱on the spot ⊗1km 🚰2km.
**Remarks:** Video surveillance.

[A][S] **Nin** 🐚🏕⛰🌊 37B3
**Dišpet**, Put Ždrijaca 13. **GPS:** n44,24618 e15,18971.
🏕€ 26-35 ⊐🔌Ch⚲WC⊐📶. ◻ 01/04-15/10.
**Remarks:** Mini-camp.

[A][S] **Nin** 🐚🏕⛰🌊 37B3
**Nin**, Put Venere Anzotike 41. **GPS:** n44,24541 e15,17401.
🏕100-132kn ⊐🔌Ch⚲. ◻ 01/05-15/10.
**Remarks:** Mini-camp.

[A][S] **Nin** 🐚🏕⛰🌊 37B3
**Ninska Laguna**, Put blata 10. **GPS:** n44,24639 e15,17389.
🏕€ 10-20 ⊐🔌Ch⚲. ◻ 01/01-31/12.
**Remarks:** Mini-camp.

**Tourist information Nin:**
[M] Arheološka zbirka Nin, Trg Kraljevac 8. Archeological museum.
◻ 01/10-31/5 8-14h, 01/06-30/09 8-22h.

[A][S] **Novigrad (Dalmatia)** 37B3
**Adria-Sol Mulic**. **GPS:** n44,19019 e15,54703.
🏕€ 17,70-19,70 ⊐🔌Ch⚲WC⊐📶. ◻ 01/05-30/09.
**Remarks:** Mini-camp.

[A][S] **Obrovac** 37B3
**Zrmanja Camping Village**, Kruševo, Župani - Drage bb.
**GPS:** n44,18506 e15,69279.
🏕⊐🔌Ch⚲.
**Remarks:** Mini-camp.

[A][S] **Omiš** 37C3
**Galeb**. **GPS:** n43,44061 e16,68128.
🏕125-250kn ⊐🔌Ch⚲WC⊐. ◻ 13/05-01/11.

[A][S] **Omiš** 37C3
**Lisičina**, Lisičina 2. **GPS:** n43,44737 e16,69038.
🏕76-131kn ⊐🔌Ch⚲WC⊐. ◻ 01/01-31/12.
**Remarks:** Mini-camp.

[A][S] **Opuzen** 34H1
**Rio**, Put Zlatinovca 23. **GPS:** n43,01351 e17,46890.
🏕€ 18-25 ⊐🔌Ch⚲WC⊐. ◻ 01/04-30/10.

[A][S] **Orašac** 39A5
**Pod Maslinom**, Put prema moru b.b. **GPS:** n42,69907 e18,00592.
🏕KN 96-138 ⊐🔌Ch⚲WC⊐◻. ◻ 01/04-01/11.
**Remarks:** Mini-camp.

[A][S] **Pag** 🐚🏕⛰🌊 37B2
**Košljun**, Košljun B.B.. **GPS:** n44,39849 e15,07936.
🏕131-156kn ⊐🔌Ch⚲WC⊐. ◻ 01/06-01/10.
**Remarks:** Mini-camp.

[A][S] **Pag** 🐚🏕⛰🌊 37B2
**Pere**, Dinjiška. **GPS:** n44,35939 e15,18641.
🏕€ 15 ⊐🔌WC⊐. ◻ 01/05-15/10.
**Remarks:** Mini-camp.

[A][S] **Pag** 🐚🏕⛰🌊 37B2
**Porat**, Stjepana Radića bb., Povljana. **GPS:** n44,34914 e15,10547.
60 🏕€ 12,66-20,94 ⊐🔌Ch⚲WC⊐. ◻ 23/04-30/09.
**Remarks:** Mini-camp.

[A][S] **Pag** 🐚🏕⛰🌊 37B2
**Simuni**, V. Nazora b.b, Simuni. **GPS:** n44,45979 e14,97670.
🏕94-379kn ⊐🔌Ch⚲WC⊐◻. ◻ 01/01-31/12.

[A][S] **Pakoštane** 🏕🌊 37B3
**Blaž**. **GPS:** n43,90763 e15,50089.
🏕⊐🔌Ch⚲.
**Remarks:** Mini-camp.

[A][S] **Pakoštane** 🏕🌊 37B3
**Kozarica**. **GPS:** n43,90970 e15,49881.
🏕€ 16,90-48,90 ⊐🔌Ch⚲WC⊐. ◻ 15/04-15/10.

## Pakoštane · 37B3
**Marin. GPS:** n43,90442 e15,51866.
€ 13,50-32,50 Ch WC . 01/07-31/10.
**Remarks:** Mini-camp.

## Pakoštane · 37B3
**Nordsee. GPS:** n43,90525 e15,51617.
€ 14,40-27,50 Ch WC . 01/03-05/11.

## Pakoštane · 37B3
**Oaza Mira,** Dr. Franje Tuđmana bb, Drage. **GPS:** n43,88607 e15,53290.
150 € 23-56 Ch WC . 01/04-15/10.
**Remarks:** Mini-camp.

## Pakoštane · 37B3
**Oaza,** Drage. **GPS:** n43,87035 e15,55917.
€ 14-24 Ch WC . 01/04-15/10.
**Remarks:** Mini-camp.

## Pakoštane · 37B3
**Pakoštane. GPS:** n43,91120 e15,49983.
. 08/04-31/10.
**Remarks:** Mini-camp.

## Pašman · 37B3
**Camp Arboretum,** Barotul 8. **GPS:** n43,96283 e15,36082.
€ 20-22 Ch WC . 01/06-30/09.
**Remarks:** Mini-camp.

## Pelješac/Orebić · 34H1
**Camping Ponta,** Kvaternikova 3. **GPS:** n42,97722 e17,22444.
30 €65-85kn Ch WC . **Location:** Rural, comfortable, quiet. **Surface:** grassy/gravel. 01/01-31/12.
**Distance:** 4km on the spot on the spot.

## Pelješac/Orebić · 34H1
Ulica Bana Josipa Jelačića. **GPS:** n42,97499 e17,16929.
±10 €70kn. **Surface:** grassy/gravel. 01/01-31/12.
**Distance:** pebbled beach 500m.

## Pelješac/Orebić · 34H1
**Camping Adriatic,** Mokalo 6. **GPS:** n42,97672 e17,22489.
€ 14-35,50 Ch WC . 01/04-31/10.
**Remarks:** Mini-camp.

## Pelješac/Orebić · 34H1
**Glavna Plaža. GPS:** n42,97583 e17,18917.
€ 12-20,20 Ch WC . 15/05-15/10.

## Pelješac/Orebić · 34H1
**Paradiso. GPS:** n42,96750 e17,24293.
Ch .
**Remarks:** Mini-camp.

## Pelješac/Orebić · 34H1
**Perna. GPS:** n42,97638 e17,13272.
€ 13,50- 18,80 Ch . 16/04-14/10.

## Pelješac/Orebić · 34H1
**Trstenica,** Šetalište Kneza Domagoja 50. **GPS:** n42,97725 e17,18995.
25 Ch WC .
**Remarks:** Mini-camp.

## Pelješac/Orebić · 34H1
**Paradiso,** Obala Pomoraca 70 A. **GPS:** n42,96693 e17,24230.
.
**Remarks:** Mini-camp.

## Pelješac/Trpanj · 34H1
**Divna. GPS:** n43,00944 e17,26806.
100 Ch . 01/06-30/09.
**Remarks:** Mini-camp.

## Pelješac/Trpanj · 34H1
**Vrila. GPS:** n43,00360 e17,28467.
Ch WC . 20/05-10/10.

## Petrcane · 37B3
**Pineta,** Punta Radman 21. **GPS:** n44,17805 e15,16161.
€110-138kn Ch WC . 01/05-01/09.
**Remarks:** Mini-camp.

## Podgora · 37D3
**Sutikla. GPS:** n43,23455 e17,07759.
€99-198kn Ch WC . 22/06-15/09.

## Podstrana · 37C3
**Tamaris,** Sv.Martin 114. **GPS:** n43,47551 e16,56383.
50 € 18,70-21,37 Ch WC . 15/06-15/09.
**Distance:** on the spot.
**Remarks:** Mini-camp.

## Podstrana · 37C3
**Autocamp,** Cesta Svetog Martina. **GPS:** n43,47408 e16,56754.
.
**Remarks:** Mini-camp.

**Tourist information Podstrana:**
Sinjska alka, Sinj. Knight celebration. 5th August.

## Posedarje · 37B3
**Kristina. GPS:** n44,21288 e15,49820.
€ 12,80-15,80 Ch . 01/05-30/09.
**Remarks:** Mini-camp.

## Posedarje · 37B3
**Bristi. GPS:** n44,21231 e15,48038.

**Remarks:** Mini-camp.

## Povijana · 37B3
**Mali Dubrovnik,** Kralja P. Svacica 1. **GPS:** n44,34931 e15,10060.
Ch WC .
**Remarks:** Mini-camp.

## Povijana · 37B3
**Porat,** Ante Starcevica Bb. **GPS:** n44,14466 e15,08569.
30 €120-136kn Ch WC . 01/05-01/10.
**Remarks:** Mini-camp.

## Primošten · 37C3
Zagrebacka ul.. **GPS:** n43,58854 e15,92632.
10 € 7/24h.
**Distance:** 200m 200m 200m 200m.

## Primošten · 37C3
**Adriatic,** Huljerat b.b. **GPS:** n43,60645 e15,92193.
€ 16,80-30,90 Ch WC . 07/04-31/10.

## Privlaka · 37B3
**Dalmacija,** Ivana Pavla II 40. **GPS:** n44,25613 e15,12557.
€ 15,70-40,40 Ch WC. 01/05-15/10.

## Privlaka · 37B3
**Medanić,** Put Brtalica 47. **GPS:** n44,24887 e15,13379.
Ch WC .
**Remarks:** Mini-camp.

## Ražanac · 37B3
**Kamp Miočić,** Rtina I 139, Rtina. **GPS:** n44,29219 e15,30179.
Ch WC .

## Ražanac · 37B3
**Kamp Odmoree,** Rtina Stošići bb. **GPS:** n44,30040 e15,28881.
13 €345kn Ch .

## Ražanac · 37B3
**Planik. GPS:** n44,27778 e15,34472.
€ 14,94-19,33 Ch WC . 01/01-31/12.
**Remarks:** Mini-camp.

## Ražanac · 37B3
**Puntica,** Puntica 1. **GPS:** n44,28389 e15,34306.
€ 12-18,80 Ch WC . 01/05-15/10.
**Remarks:** Mini-camp.

## Rovanjska · 37B3
**Tamaris. GPS:** n44,25037 e15,53735.
30 €112-142kn Ch WC . 01/05-01/10.
**Remarks:** Mini-camp.

## Senj · 37B2
**Kamp Škver,** Filipa Vukasovica 5. **GPS:** n44,99385 e14,90012.

50 €69kn, Jun/Sep 89kn, Jul/Aug 106kn Ch night,20kn, 16Amp WC €35kn included **Location:** Urban, comfortable. **Surface:** gravel/metalled. 01/04-01/10.
**Distance:** 500m on the spot on the spot on the spot
150m 500m on the spot on the spot.
**Remarks:** Fishing permit available.

## Senj · 37B2
**Bunica,** Bunica 33. **GPS:** n45,02607 e14,88630.
Ch .
**Remarks:** Mini-camp.

## Senj · 37B2
**Ujca,** M. Cihlar Nehajeva, 4. **GPS:** n44,96833 e14,92167.
€100-150kn Ch WC . 01/05-01/10.
**Distance:** on the spot.
**Remarks:** Mini-camp.

## Šibenik · 37C3
**Slapovi Krke,** Lozovac-Gradina. **GPS:** n43,79207 e15,97042.

€ 12-17 Ch WC included.
**Surface:** unpaved. 01/04-30/10.
**Remarks:** 1km from Krka waterfalls.

## Šibenik · 37C3
**Solaris. GPS:** n43,69917 e15,87795.
€ 15-62 Ch WC . 24/03-20/10.

## Šibenik · 37C3
**Solaris-Zablaće,** Obala palih boraca 2a. **GPS:** n43,70524 e15,86850.
€ 30-32,50 Ch WC . 01/05-30/09.

**Tourist information Šibenik:**
Internationaal kinderfestival. 22/06-06/07.
Nacionalni Park Krka, Krka. Nature reserve.

## Skradin · 37C3
**Robeko Camping,** Piramatovci. Bilostanovi 12.
**GPS:** n43,89193 e15,82320.
Ch WC .
**Remarks:** Mini-camp.

## Slano · 39A5
**Baldo. GPS:** n42,79683 e17,84989.
€ 26-32 Ch . 19/04-09/10.
**Remarks:** Mini-camp.

## Slano · 39A5
**Bambo. GPS:** n42,77513 e17,88500.
Ch .
**Remarks:** Mini-camp.

## Slano · 39A5
**Banja,** Put Od Banje. **GPS:** n42,77414 e17,88405.
Ch .

## Slano · 39A5
**Rogac,** Grgurici. **GPS:** n42,78229 e17,87536.
€64-76kn Ch WC . 01/04-01/10.
**Remarks:** Mini-camp.

## Slano · 39A5
**Sladenovici,** Sladenovici 9. **GPS:** n42,78451 e17,85984.
€ 11 Ch .
**Remarks:** Mini-camp.

## Slatine · 37C3
**Domic,** Put Porta 71, Ciove. **GPS:** n43,49784 e16,34060.
.
**Remarks:** Mini-camp.

## Soline · 37B3
**Camping Mandarino. GPS:** n44,14148 e14,86495.
€ 20-48 Ch WC . 14/05-30/09.
**Remarks:** Mini-camp.

## Split · 37C3
**Stobreč. GPS:** n43,50401 e16,52644.

€ 20,80-45,90 Ch WC € 4,60/4,60 .
01/01-31/12.
**Distance:** centre 7km on the spot.
**Remarks:** Borrow cycles for free.

**Tourist information Split:**
Arheoloski Muzej, Zrinjsko-Frankopanska 25. Findings from Roman time and Middle Ages. Tue-Fri 9-14h, Sa-Su 9-13h, 01/06-30/09 Tue-Fri 9-12, 13-20h, Sa-Su 9-13h.
Galerija Ivana Mestrovica, Setaliste I. Mestrovica 46. Gallery.

**HR**

Mo-Sa 10-18h, Su 10-14h.
Ⓜ Muzej Hrvatskih Arheoloskih Spomenika, S. Gunjace bb. Archeological findings.
Mo-Sa 9-20h.
✕ Dioklecijanova palača. Roman palace.

### △S Starigrad/Paklenica — 37B3
**Camp National Park**, Paklenica. **GPS**: n44,28832 e15,44573.
🗒€35-50 ⌐█Ch ✎ WC ◫. ▢ 15/03-15/10.
**Remarks**: Mini-camp.

### △S Starigrad/Paklenica — 37B3
**Marko**, Paklenicka 7, Paklenica. **GPS**: n44,28643 e15,45247.
🗒€16-19 ⌐█Ch ✎ ▢ 01/01-31/12.
**Remarks**: Mini-camp.

### △S Starigrad/Paklenica — 37B3
**Pinus**, Ive Senjanina 5, Paklenica. **GPS**: n44,32242 e15,39288.
🗒€12,70-16,80 ⌐█Ch ✎ WC ◫. ▢ 01/05-01/09.
**Remarks**: Mini-camp.

### △S Starigrad/Paklenica — 37B3
**Pisak**, Paklenica. **GPS**: n44,27285 e15,47806.
🗒€124-146kn ⌐█Ch ✎ WC ◫. ▢ 01/05-01/10.
**Remarks**: Mini-camp.

### △S Starigrad/Paklenica — 37B3
**Plantaža**, Put Plantaže 2, Paklenica. **GPS**: n44,30056 e15,43211.
🗒€27-33 ⌐█Ch ✎ WC ▢ 01/01-31/12.
**Remarks**: Mini-camp.

### △S Starigrad/Paklenica — 37B3
**Vesna**, Paklenicka 103, Paklenica. **GPS**: n44,28610 e15,45243.
🗒 ⌐█Ch ✎ WC ◫. ▢ 01/01-31/12.
**Remarks**: Mini-camp.

### △ Starigrad/Paklenica — 37B3
**Jaz**, Seline, Paklenica. **GPS**: n44,28323 e15,46028.
🗒 ▢ 01/05-30/09.
**Remarks**: Mini-camp.

**Tourist information Starigrad/Paklenica:**
ℹ Nacionalni park "Paklenica". Nature reserve, 150 km biking ad hiking trails, bird observation, tunnels and caves.

### △S Ston — 34H1
**Prapratno. GPS**: n42,81778 e17,67611.
🗒€35-50 ⌐█Ch ✎ WC ▢ 01/05-30/09.

### △S Ston — 34H1
**Vrela**, Brijesta 10. **GPS**: n42,90397 e17,53266.
🗒€22-30 ⌐█Ch ✎ WC ◫. ▢ 01/04-30/10.
**Remarks**: Mini-camp.

### △S Sukošan — 37B3
**Brajde. GPS**: n44,04256 e15,30755.
🗒 ⌐█Ch ✎ WC.
**Remarks**: Mini-camp.

### △S Sukošan — 37B3
**Malenica**, Vl. Milan Gašparović. **GPS**: n44,03658 e15,32790.
50🗒 ⌐█ ✎ WC ◫. ▢ 01/05-01/10.
**Remarks**: Mini-camp.

### △S Sukošan — 37B3
**Oliva. GPS**: n44,04247 e15,30805.
🗒 ⌐█Ch ✎ WC ◫. ▢ 01/01-31/12.
**Remarks**: Mini-camp.

### △ Sukošan — 37B3
**Kamp Kaj**, Punta 15. **GPS**: n44,04278 e15,30655.
7🗒.
**Remarks**: Mini-camp.

### △S Supetar — 37C3
**Waterman Beach. GPS**: n43,38076 e16,56439.
🗒 ⌐█Ch ✎ WC ◫. ▢ 01/05-30/09.

### △ Sutivan — 37C3
**Mlin**, Brac. **GPS**: n43,38316 e16,47795.
🗒.
**Remarks**: Mini-camp.

### △ Sutivan — 37C3
**Sutivan**, Gorana Pavlova 12. **GPS**: n43,38523 e16,48460.
🗒. ▢ 01/01-31/12.

### △S Sv. Filip I Jakov — 37B3
**Antonio**, Turanj. **GPS**: n43,97488 e15,39990.
🗒 ⌐█Ch ✎ WC.
**Remarks**: Mini-camp.

### △S Sv. Filip I Jakov — 37B3
**Djardin**, Sveti Filip i Jakov bb. **GPS**: n43,96139 e15,42750.
🗒€14,60-26,20 ⌐█Ch ✎ WC ◫. ▢ 23/04-01/10.

---

### △S Sv. Filip I Jakov — 37B3
**Filip**, Put Primorja 10a. **GPS**: n43,96055 e15,42910.
🗒€9,73-26,66 ⌐█Ch ✎ WC ◫. ▢ 01/04-01/10.
**Remarks**: Mini-camp.

### △S Sv. Filip I Jakov — 37B3
**Maestral**, Turanj 90. **GPS**: n43,96611 e15,41162.
🗒€122-152kn ⌐█Ch ✎ WC ▢ 01/05-31/10.
**Remarks**: Mini-camp.

### △S Sv. Filip I Jakov — 37B3
**Moče**, Put Primorja 8. **GPS**: n43,95968 e15,42915.
🗒€14-27 ⌐█Ch ✎ WC ◫. ▢ 01/04-01/10.
**Remarks**: Mini-camp.

### △S Sv. Filip I Jakov — 37B3
**R & B**, Turanj. **GPS**: n43,96592 e15,41196.
6🗒.
**Distance**: ⚓on the spot ➤on the spot.
**Remarks**: Mini-camp.

### △S Sv. Filip I Jakov — 37B3
**Rio**, Put Primorja. **GPS**: n43,95583 e15,43500.
🗒€33-44 ⌐█Ch ✎ WC ◫.
**Remarks**: Mini-camp.

### △S Sv. Filip I Jakov — 37B3
**Bepo**, Turanj. **GPS**: n43,96562 e15,41254.
🗒.
**Distance**: ⚓on the spot ➤on the spot.
**Remarks**: Mini-camp.

### △S Sv. Filip I Jakov — 37B3
**Milan**, Sv. Petar. **GPS**: n44,00205 e15,36859.
3🗒.
**Remarks**: Mini-camp.

### △S Sveti Juraj — 37B2
**Camping Ujča**, Ujča 146/A. **GPS**: n44,96853 e14,92223.
🗒€100-110kn ⌐█Ch ✎ WC ◫. ▢ 01/05-01/10.
**Remarks**: Mini-camp.

### △S Sveti Petar na Moru — 37B3
**Autocamp Martin**, Jasminka en Neven Colic.
**GPS**: n44,00003 e15,36880.⬆
15🗒€15-30 ⌐█Ch ✎ WC ◫. **Location**: Rural, isolated, quiet.
**Surface**: grassy/gravel. ▢ 01/01-31/12.
**Distance**: ⚓on the spot ➤on the spot ⊗1km.

### △ Sveti Petar na Moru — 37B3
**Ante**, Turanj. **GPS**: n43,99637 e15,37915.
🗒.
**Remarks**: Mini-camp.

### △ Sveti Petar na Moru — 37B3
**Bozo. GPS**: n43,99688 e15,37838.
🗒.
**Remarks**: Mini-camp.

### △S Tkon — 37B3
**Brist. GPS**: n43,92312 e15,41493.
🗒 ⌐█Ch ✎.

### △ Tkon — 37B3
**Adriana. GPS**: n43,91734 e15,42596.
🗒.
**Remarks**: Mini-camp.

### △ Tribanj — 37B2
**Camp CTT**, D8. **GPS**: n44,34673 e15,32444.
7🗒€20. **Surface**: grassy/gravel. ▢ 01/01-31/12.
**Distance**: ⚓900m ⚓on the spot.
**Remarks**: Not suitable for motorhomes +7m.

### △ Tribanj — 37B2
**Punta Šibuljina**, Šibuljina. **GPS**: n44,33631 e15,34627.
150🗒€13,95-22 ⌐█Ch WC ◫. ▢ 23/04-08/10.
**Remarks**: Mini-camp.

### △ Tribanj — 37B2
**Ante**, Kopovine 9. **GPS**: n44,34469 e15,32842.
🗒.
**Remarks**: Mini-camp.

### △S Trogir — 37C3
**Seget**, Seget Donji. **GPS**: n43,51904 e16,22430.
50🗒from €21 ⌐█Ch ✎ WC ◫. ▢ 01/03-31/10.
**Distance**: ⚓800m ⚓on the spot.
**Remarks**: Mini-camp.

### △S Trogir — 37C3
**Vranjica Belvedere**, Seget Vranjica. **GPS**: n43,51196 e16,19159.
451🗒 ⌐█Ch ✎ WC ◫. ▢ 15/04-15/10.

**Tourist information Trogir:**

---

ℹ Tourist Information, Ivana Pavla II Square, www.trogir-online.com.
City with rich culture from Greek, Roman and Venetian time.
Ⓜ Town Museum, Fanfogna palace, Garagnin. History of the city.
16/09-14/06 by request 8-14h, 15/06-15/09 9-21h.
Ⓜ Zbirka Kairos. Ecclesiastical art collection. ▢ 15/6-15/9 8-13, 15-19h.
✕ Fortress Kamerlengo. Fortress. ▢ 15/6-15/9 9-20h.
✝ Katedrala St. Lawrence. Bell-tower of Cathedral of St. Lawrence, 47m. ▢ 15/6-15/9 9-12, 16-19h. ⊞ 5km.

### △S Vela Luka — 34H1
**Mindel**, Stani 193. **GPS**: n42,98369 e16,67060.
🗒€14 ⌐█Ch ✎ WC ◫. ▢ 01/01-31/12.

### △S Veli Rat — 37B3
**Camping Kargita**, Veli Rat 67. **GPS**: n44,15402 e14,82221.
30🗒€17,10-31 ⌐█Ch ✎ WC ◫. ▢ 23/04-01/10.
**Remarks**: Mini-camp.

### △S Viganj — 34H1
**Antony Boy. GPS**: n42,97889 e17,10752.
🗒€134-170kn ⌐█Ch ✎ WC ◫. ▢ 01/01-31/12.

### △S Vir — 37B3
**Sapavac**, Put Bunara 101. **GPS**: n44,29432 e15,07640.
🗒 WC.
**Distance**: ⚓on the spot ➤on the spot.
**Remarks**: Mini-camp.

### △ Vir — 37B3
**Auto Camp Luka. GPS**: n44,29721 e15,10256.
**Remarks**: Mini-camp.

### ⊞S Vodice — 37C3
**Camper stop Olivia**, Ulica Bribirskih knezova 16.
**GPS**: n43,76303 e15,77686. ⬆.

🗒70 kn ⌐█Ch ✎ WC ◫. ▢ 01/01-31/12.
**Distance**: ⚓300m.

### △S Vodice — 37C3
**Imperial**, Vatroslava Lisinskog 2/I. **GPS**: n43,75287 e15,78992.
145🗒€23-41 ⌐█Ch ✎ WC ◫. ▢ 21/03-11/11.

### △S Vransko Jezero — 37B3
**Crkvine. GPS**: n43,93035 e15,51012.
🗒€23-29 ⌐█Ch ✎ WC ◫. ▢ 15/04-15/10.

### △ Vrsi — 37B3
**Mulic**, Mulo. **GPS**: n44,26174 e15,21246.
🗒.
**Remarks**: Mini-camp.

### △S Zaboric — 37C3
**Jasenovo. GPS**: n43,65116 e15,95025.
50🗒€13-29 ⌐█Ch ✎ WC ◫. ▢ 01/05-01/10.
**Distance**: ⚓on the spot.
**Remarks**: Mini-camp.

### △S Zadar — 37B3
**Borik**, Radovana 7. **GPS**: n44,13528 e15,21528.
500🗒€19,20-30,10 ⌐█Ch ✎ WC ◫. ▢ 01/05-01/10.

**Tourist information Zadar:**
◉ Trg Pet Bunara. Square of the five fountains.
Ⓜ Arheoloski Muzej, Simuna Kozicica Benje bb. Archeological findings.
Mo-Sa 9-13h, 18-20h.
☀ Muziekavonden in de St. Donatius van Zadar. ▢ 01/07-15/08.

### △S Zaostrog — 34H1
**Uvala Borova**, Mkarska. **GPS**: n43,13123 e17,28750.
90🗒€21,80-32,60 ⌐█Ch ✎ WC ◫. ▢ 01/05-30/09.

### △S Zaton — 37B3
**Zaton. GPS**: n44,23385 e15,16671.
🗒€22,60-57,70 ⌐█Ch ✎ WC ◫. ▢ 30/04-30/09.

### △ Ždrelac — 37B3
**Ruža. GPS**: n44,00987 e15,27653.
40🗒 ⌐█ ✎ WC ◫.
**Remarks**: Mini-camp.

### △S Živogošče — 34H1
**Dole. GPS**: n43,17118 e17,19669.

�然€ 36-45 🚰🍴Ch🧹🚿WC⚡. ⬛ 01/05-30/09.

| △⛰ | | 34H1 |

**Vrbovica**, Vrbovica bb. **GPS:** n42,95882 e17,11394.

€120-160kn 🚰🍴Ch🧹🚿WC⚡🅿⬛. ⬛ 01/06-01/09.

**Remarks:** Mini-camp.

| △ | Žrnovo | 34H1 |

**Tri Žala**, Uvala Tri Žala 808. **GPS:** n42,96407 e17,09104.

�然. ⬛ 01/06-30/09.

**Distance:** 🏖on the spot 🚤on the spot ⚓1km 🍴1km.

**Remarks:** Mini-camp.

| △⛰ | Žuljana | 34H1 |

**Vucine. GPS:** n42,88257 e17,45135.

⌚🚰🍴Ch🧹🚿WC⚡.

**Remarks:** Mini-camp.

# Inland

| 🏕⛰ | **Kopačevo** 👫 | 39A3 |

**Autokamp Family Kopačevo**, Ferenca Kiša 7.
**GPS:** n45,59832 e18,78467.⬆.

20⌚€ 18 🚰🚿. **Location:** Rural. **Surface:** grassy.
⬛ 01/04-30/09.

| 🏕⛰ | **Koprivnica** | 36C3 |

**Cerine**, Miroslava Krleze 81. **GPS:** n46,15361 e16,84250.⬆.

11⌚first night 110kn, 75kn each additional night, 2 pers incl. + 7kn
tourist tax 🚰🍴Ch🧹🚿WC📶included. **Location:** Comfortable.
**Surface:** grasstiles. ⬛ 01/01-31/12.
**Distance:** 🏖1,5km ⊗300m 🍴1km.
**Remarks:** Parking spa resort, wifi code at swimming pool.

| △ | **Lipovac** | 39A3 |

**Spacva. GPS:** n45,04593 e18,99682.
6⌚⬛. ⬛ 01/05-01/10.

| 🏕⛰ | **Plitviča** 🌿⛲🏔🌲 | 37B2 |

**Bear**, Selište Drežničko 52. **GPS:** n44,94804 e15,63639.⬆➡.

30⌚132kn, 01/06-30/09 152kn, 01/07-31/08 172kn 🚰🍴Ch🧹
(30x),16Amp WC⚡🅿📶included. 🚿 **Location:** Rural, comfortable,
central, quiet. **Surface:** asphalted/gravel. ⬛ 01/04-15/10.
**Distance:** 🏖300m 🏊700m 🏖20km ⊗150m 🍴400m 🚤on the spot
🚣on the spot 🎣on the spot.
**Remarks:** Baker every morning, water falls Plitvica 5km.

| 🏕⛰ | **Plitviča** 🌿⛲🏔🌲 | 37B2 |

**Cvetkovic**, Jezerce 28. **GPS:** n44,86338 e15,63967.⬆.

20⌚€ 10/pp 🚰🍴Ch🧹🚿WC⚡📶included. 🚿
**Location:** Rural, comfortable, central, quiet. **Surface:** grassy/gravel.
⬛ 01/01-31/12.
**Distance:** 🏖800m ⊗10km 🍴800m 🚤800m 🎣on the spot 🚣on the
spot 🏄800m 🚴800m.
**Remarks:** Water falls Plitvica 2km.

| △⛰ | **Plitviča** 🌿⛲🏔🌲 | 37B2 |

**Korana. GPS:** n44,99260 e15,64916.

---

⌚€ 20-24 🚰🍴Ch🧹🚿. ⬛ 25/03-31/10.

**Tourist information Plitviča:**
🌿 Nacionalni Park Plitvička Jezera, www.np-plitvicka-jezera.hr.
National park Plitvice lakes. ⬛ 9-17h.

| △⛰ | **Racovica** | 37B2 |

**Turist**, Grabovac 102. **GPS:** n44,97222 e15,64750.
⌚€ 20-26,40 🚰🍴Ch🧹🚿WC⚡🅿🚿. ⬛ 30/04-01/10.

| 🏕⛰ | **Šimunčevec** | 37B1 |

**Val-travel**, Popovic Dure 9. **GPS:** n45,87839 e16,09302.

⌚€ 17,50 + tourist tax 🚰🧹🚿WCincluded. **Location:** Rural.
**Surface:** gravel. ⬛ 01/01-31/12.
**Distance:** 🚆Zagreb 18km 🚌100m.
**Remarks:** Dutch owners.

| 🏕⛰ | **Zagreb** 🌿🏛 | 37B1 |

**Camp-Zagreb**, Jezerska 6. **GPS:** n45,80253 e15,82622.⬆.

50⌚€ 23-35, 2 pers incl 🚰🍴Ch🧹🚿WC⚡included ⚡€ 3/3.
**Location:** Urban, luxurious. **Surface:** metalled. ⬛ 01/01-31/12.
**Distance:** 🚆on the spot 🚤on the spot ⊗on the spot 🚴on the spot
🎣on the spot.
**Remarks:** Bus to Zagreb € 8/round trip.

| 🏕⛰ | **Zagreb** 🌿🏛 | 37B1 |

**E Camper Zagreb**, Josipa Ressela. **GPS:** n45,78197 e15,97774.
20⌚150kn 🚰🍴Ch🧹included 📶. **Surface:** gravel/metalled.
⬛ 01/01-31/12.
**Distance:** 🚆2,5km ⊗600m 🍴on the spot 🚌400m 🎣on the spot
🚣on the spot.
**Remarks:** Max. 72h, water closed during wintertime.

| 🏕⛰ | **Zagreb** 🌿🏛 | 37B1 |

**Val-Travel Camp**, Ulica Popovic Dure 9. **GPS:** n45,88131 e16,08861.
⌚€ 14,50-17,50 🚰🧹🚿WCincluded. ⬛ 01/01-31/12.
**Distance:** 🚆18km.
**Remarks:** Max. 7m.

**Tourist information Zagreb:**
ℹ http://www.infozagreb.hr/. Capital, surface 64133 km$^2$, inhabitants
885,000, 11 theaters and 22 museums.
Ⓜ Archeological Museum, 19 Nikola Subic Zrinski Square. ⬛ Tue-Fri
10-17h, Sa-Su 10-13h.
Ⓜ Atelje Mestrovic, Mletacka 8. Former dwellinghouse of sculptor Ivan
Mestrovic. ⬛ Tue-Fri 10-18h, Sa-Su 10-13h.
Ⓜ Ethnographic Museum, Mazuranicev trg 14. ⬛ Tue-Thu 10-18h,
Fri-Su 10-13h.
Ⓜ Muzej Grada Zagreb, Opaticka 20. City museum. ⬛ Tue-Fri 10-18h,
Sa 11-19h, Su 10-14h.
Ⓜ Tehnicki Muzej, Savska cesta 18. Technical museum. ⬛ Tue-Fri
9-17h, Sa-Su 9-13h.
🎭 Medjunarodna Smotra Folklora. International folk festival.
⬛ 20/07/05-24/07/05.
🎭 Zomerfestival van Zagreb. ⬛ 01/07-15/08.
🌿 Park Prirode Kopacki Rit. Nature reserve, boat rental. ⬛ daily
8-16h.

# ▬ Hungary

Capital: Budapest
Government: parliamentary constitutional republic
Official Language: Hungarian
Population: 9,850,845 (2017)
Area: 93,024 km²

## General information

Dialling code: 0036
General emergency: 112
Currency: Forint (HUF)
€ 1 = 325 HUF, 100 HUF = € 0,31
£1 = 372 HUF, 100 HUF = £0.28 (October 2018)
Credit cards are accepted almost everywhere.

## Regulations for overnight stays

Free overnight stay is not allowed.

## Additional public holidays 2019

March 15 Revolution Memorial Day 1848
April 22 Easter Monday
August 20 Hungarian National Day
October 23 Revolution Memorial Day 1956
November 1 All Saints' Day

## Time Zone

Winter (Standard Time) GMT+1
Summer (DST) GMT+2

Northern Hungary
page: 592

Budapest

Transdanubia
page: 593

Central Hungary
page: 592

Great Hungarian
Plain
page: 592

Lake Balaton
pages: 592-593

# Northern Hungary

### ⛺ Bekölce                                    39A1

**Camping Bekölce**, Béke út 252. **GPS:** n48,08260 e20,24904.
10 🏕 € 15 🚰🔌Ch🧺included 🔥. **Location:** Rural, isolated, quiet.
**Surface:** metalled. 🅿 01/01-31/12.

### ⛺ Borsodbóta                                  39A1

**Camping Amedi**, Rákóczi út 181. **GPS:** n48,21329 e20,40569.
40 🏕 € 12,50, 01/07-31/08 € 16,50 🚰🔌Chincluded 🔥€ 4.
**Surface:** grassy. 🅿 01/05-30/09.

### ⛺ Budapest                                    36D2

**Arena Camping Budapest**, Pilisi u. 7/a. **GPS:** n47,50424 e19,15839.
🏕 € 21,35 🚰🔌Ch🧺WC🔥🏠
🅿 01/01-31/12.

### ⛺ Budapest                                    36D2

**Ave Natura**, Csermely u 3.
**GPS:** n47,51416 e18,97300.

12 🏕 € 18,50 🚰🔌Ch🧺(12x)€ 3,80 WC🔥📶included.
**Location:** Rural, isolated. **Surface:** grassy/sand.
🅿 01/04-31/10.
**Distance:** 🚲5km ⊗100m 🚊2km ▬on the spot 🚴on the spot 🧍on the spot.

### ⛺ Budapest                                    36D2

**Zugligeti Niche**, Zugligeti út 101. **GPS:** n47,51637 e18,97509.⬆
25 🏕 € 27, 2 pers.incl 🚰🔌Ch🧺WC🔥included.
**Surface:** grassy.
🅿 01/01-31/12.
**Distance:** 🚲5km ⊗on the spot 🖥on the spot ▬200m 🚴on the spot 🧍on the spot.
**Remarks:** Breakfast-service.

### ⛺ Hernádvécse                                  38D4

**Zonnebloempaleis**, Rákóczi út 96. **GPS:** n48,43360 e21,17230.
1 🏕 € 10, 04/06-31/08 € 12,50 🚰🔌Ch🔥included. **Location:** Rural.
**Surface:** grassy. 🅿 14/04-01/10.
**Distance:** 🚊2km.

**Remarks:** Max. 7m.

### ⛺ Pécs                                          36D3

**Família Camping**, Gyöngyösi utca 6. **GPS:** n46,08559 e18,26206.
15 🏕 € 10 🚰🔌Ch🔥included.
**Location:** Urban. **Surface:** metalled. 🅿 01/01-31/12.
**Distance:** 🚲2,5km ⊗200m 🚊100m ▬100m.

# Great Hungarian Plain

### ⛺ Püspökladány                                 39A2

**Árnyas Thermal Camping és Üdülőpark**, Petőfi Sándor Ut 62.
**GPS:** n47,32192 e21,10273.
50 🏕 € 10 🚰🔌Ch🔥included 📶free. **Location:** Rural, noisy.
**Surface:** grassy/metalled. 🅿 01/05-30/09.
**Distance:** 🏊on the spot.

### ⛺ Szentkirály                                  39A2

**Fantazia Tanya**, Felső Tanya 165. **GPS:** n46,94087 e19,93109.

20 🏕 € 13 🚰🔌Chincluded 🔥€ 4.
**Location:** Rural. **Surface:** grassy. 🅿 01/04-01/11.
**Distance:** 🧍on the spot.

### ⛺ Zsana                                        39A2

**Camping Oázis Tanya**, 1. Körzet 15. **GPS:** n46,41438 e19,61111.

20 🏕 € 15,30, 01/07-31/08 € 18,30 🚰Ch🔥(20x)€ 3 WC🖥🔥€ 3,75
📶included. **Location:** Rural. **Surface:** grassy. 🅿 15/04-30/09.

**Distance:** 🚲12km 🏊on the spot ▬5km ⊗on the spot 🚊12km
▬2km 🚴2km 🧍on the spot.

# Central Hungary

### ⛺ Csemő                                        39A2

**Békés Föld**, Bezzeg dülö. **GPS:** n47,13217 e19,73983.
4 🏕 € 12,50 🚰🔌Ch🔥included.
**Surface:** grassy/sand. 🅿 01/01-31/12.

# Lake Balaton

### ⛺ Balatonkeresztúr                            36C3

**Bertalan**, Ady Endre utca 51. **GPS:** n46,70333 e17,37047.⬆

6 🏕 € 12 🚰🔌Ch🧺WC🔥included. 🚿 **Location:** Urban, simple.
**Surface:** grassy. 🅿 01/01-31/12 🖥 service: Jul/Aug.
**Distance:** 🚲on the spot 🏊lake Balaton 300m ⊗200m 🚊150m
▬500m.

### ⛺ Cserszegtomaj                               36C3

**Camping Panorama**, Panoráma köz 1. **GPS:** n46,80667 e17,21306.
15 🏕 € 14 excl. tourist tax 🚰🔌Chincluded 🔥. **Surface:** grassy.
🅿 01/04-31/10.
**Distance:** 🚲5km 🏊5km ⊗2km 🚊2km.

### ⛺ Gyenesdiás                                   36C3

**Wellnes-Park**, Napfény utca 6. **GPS:** n46,76417 e17,30250.
🏕 € 14-17 + € 1,40/pp tourist tax 🚰🔌Ch🔥included.
**Surface:** grassy. 🅿 01/04-15/10.
**Distance:** 🚲2km 🏊lake Balaton 2km ⊗200m 🚊500m ▬2km.

### ⛺ Kisbárapáti                                  36D3

**Camping Jó Napot**, Ady Endre utca 46. **GPS:** n46,59827 e17,86750.

15 € 15,50 Chincluded € 3,50. **Location:** Rural.
**Surface:** grassy. 15/04-15/09.

### ⚠S | Koppányszántó | 36D3
**Tranquil Pines**, Dózsa György utca 334. **GPS:** n46,59027 e18,10344.

10 € 11,50 Ch included € 5,50. **Location:** Rural.
**Surface:** metalled. 01/01-31/12.
**Distance:** 1,5km.

### S | Somogyvár | 36D3
**Kimis Camp**, Bartók Béla utca 58. **GPS:** n46,58275 e17,62398.

36 € 10 Ch (24x)WC included € 1.
**Location:** Rural, comfortable. **Surface:** grassy. 15/04-20/09.
**Distance:** 500m on the spot.

# Transdanubia

### S | Bozsok | 36C2
**Nagy Vendégház**, Rákoczi út 105. **GPS:** n47,32059 e16,48590.

5 € 5 Ch WC. **Location:** Rural, comfortable.
**Surface:** grassy. 01/01-31/12.
**Distance:** 30m 400m.
**Remarks:** Arrival >14h departure <12h.

### ⚠S | Felsőszentmárton | 37D1
**Camping de-ommekeer**, Szent Lhászló Utca 38.
**GPS:** n45,85261 e17,69925.
15 € 19,50 Chincluded € 1,50. **Surface:** grassy.
01/04-30/09.
**Distance:** on the spot.

### ⚠S | Győr | 36C2
**Camping Pihenö**, Mártírok útja. **GPS:** n47,72515 e17,71406.

35 € 15,50 Ch included. **Location:** Urban, quiet.
**Surface:** grassy. 01/01-31/12.
**Distance:** 7km 9km on the spot.

### ⓘS | Halászi | 36C2
**Party Csárda**, Duna sétány. **GPS:** n47,88586 e17,32201.

5 € 15 + € 1,75/pp tourist tax Ch € 2 WC ,cold
included.
**Location:** Rural, simple. **Surface:** grasstiles. 01/01-31/12.
**Distance:** 300m on the spot on the spot on the spot
200m. **Remarks:** Wifi at restaurant.

### S | Lenti | 36C3
**Rudas**, Béke utca 32. **GPS:** n46,62582 e16,53266.

6 € 10 Ch on demand WCincluded .
**Location:** Rural, simple. **Surface:** grassy. 01/01-31/12.
**Distance:** 200m 800m 800m 30m 300m 600m.

### ⚠S | Magyaregregy | 36D3
**Camping Máré Vára**, Várvölgyi utca 2. **GPS:** n46,23407 e18,30913.

36 € 17,50 Ch (36x)WC included .
**Location:** Rural. **Surface:** grassy. 15/04-30/09.
**Distance:** 500m on the spot 1km 1km on the spot on
the spot. **Remarks:** Bread-service, swimming pool 200m.

### S | Mosonmagyaróvár | 36C2
**AquaThermalcamp**, Kigyo utca 1. **GPS:** n47,87715 e17,27948.

40 € 9 + 9/pp + € 1/pp tourist tax Ch € 3/24h
WC included . **Location:** Urban, comfortable.
**Surface:** grassy. 01/01-31/12.
**Distance:** 100m on the spot on the spot 100m.

### S | Mosonmagyaróvár | 36C2
**Kocisi Joseph**, Vízpart utca 59. **GPS:** n47,87335 e17,27851.

8 € 15 Ch included. **Location:** Rural, comfortable.
**Surface:** grassy/metalled. 01/01-31/12.
**Distance:** 300m 200m 200m.

### S | Nagysáp | 36D2
**Granárium Camper-port**, Granárium domb 3.
**GPS:** n47,68573 e18,60741.

7 € 15 Ch (4x),16Amp WC € 10 included .
**Location:** Rural, comfortable. **Surface:** gravel. 01/01-31/12.
**Distance:** 500m on the spot 500m 50m on the spot
on the spot.
**Remarks:** Possibility for reservation.

### ⒸS | Pápa | 36C2
**Thermalcamping Pápa**, Varkert Utca 7. **GPS:** n47,33781 e17,47359.

6 € 12 + € 1,60/pp tourist tax Ch WC included .
**Location:** Urban, simple. **Surface:** gravel.
01/01-31/12.
**Distance:** 500m on the spot 500m.
**Remarks:** Use sanitary facilities at campsite.

### ⚠S | Patosfa | 36D3
**Camping Farkas**, Petőfi utca 52-56. **GPS:** n46,12545 e17,65788.

9 € 19 Ch WC included.
**Location:** Rural. **Surface:** sand.
01/05-30/09.
**Remarks:** Natural swimming pool, bread-service, regional products.

### S | Sormás | 36C3
**István Parkhotel & Restaurant**, Külterület 28.
**GPS:** n46,46071 e16,90783.

16 € 7 Ch (16x)€ 3,50,10Amp WC € 3 included .
**Location:** Rural, comfortable, luxurious. **Surface:** grassy/metalled.
01/01-31/12.
**Distance:** 2km 1km on the spot on the spot on the spot
200m on the spot on the spot.

**HU**

# Ireland

Capital: Dublin
Government: parliamentary constitutional republic
Official Language: Irish and English
Population: 5,011,102 (2017)
Area: 69,825 km²

### General information
Dialling code: 00353
General emergency: 112
Currency: Euro
Credit cards are accepted almost everywhere.

### Regulations for overnight stays
Free overnight stay is allowed with consent of the landowner, and up to 24 hours on regular parking spaces.

### Additional public holidays 2019
March 17 Saint Patrick's Day
April 19 Good Friday
April 22 Easter Monday
May 6 Early Bank Holiday
June 3 June Bank Holiday
August 5 First Moday in August
October 28 October Bank Holiday
November 1 All Saints'Day

### Time Zone
Winter (Standard Time) GMT+0
Summer (DST)  GMT+1

Ulster page: 594
Connaught page: 594
Leinster page: 594
Dublin
Munster pages: 594-595

IE

## Ulster

### Buncrana · 1C1
R238. GPS: n55,12828 w7,45782. ↑.

10 ⚡free ⚡↯(3x)€ 5 🚿free. **Location:** Urban, simple, central.
**Surface:** metalled. ▢ 01/01-31/12.
**Distance:** ⊗on the spot ♨1km.
**Remarks:** Small pitches.

### Bundoran · 1C1
Campers Bundoran. GPS: n54,47619 w8,27427. ↑.

12 ⚡€ 15 ⚡WC 🚿included. **Location:** Urban.
**Surface:** grassy/metalled. ▢ 01/01-31/12.
**Distance:** ⚡on the spot ♨800m ⊗100m ♨100m.
**Remarks:** At shopping centre.

### Carndonagh · 1C1
The Diamond. GPS: n55,25178 w7,2623. ↑.

2 ⚡free ⚡€ 12 🗑Ch⚡. **Location:** Urban. **Surface:** asphalted.
▢ 01/01-31/12.
**Distance:** ⚡on the spot⊗on the spot ♨on the spot.
**Remarks:** Only overnight stays 18-9h.

### Crolly · 1C1
Camping Sleepy Hollows. GPS: n55,03002 w8,27087. ↑→.
⚡€ 22, 2 pers.incl ⚡€ 3 WC🚿included. **Location:** Rural, comfortable, isolated. **Surface:** grassy/metalled.

**Distance:** ⊗300m.

### Donegal · 1C1
Spierstown Camper Parking, National Road 15.
**GPS:** n54,66952 w8,06552. ↑.
6 ⚡€ 20 WC🚿included. **Location:** Rural, isolated, quiet.
**Surface:** metalled. ▢ 01/03-01/11.
**Distance:** ⚡3,5km.

### Donegal · 1C1
Parking 4 Port, Quaystreet. GPS: n54,65183 w8,1123.

10 ⚡€ 2,70/24h. **Location:** Urban. **Surface:** asphalted.
▢ 01/01-31/12.

### Dunfanaghy · 1C1
Corcreggan Mill, N56. GPS: n55,16689 w8,00437. ↑.
10 ⚡€ 25 ⚡Ch⚡against payment WC. **Location:** Rural, comfortable, isolated, quiet. **Surface:** gravel. ▢ 01/01-31/12.
**Distance:** ⚡3,5km ⊗2,5km.

## Connaught

### Achill Sound · 1B2
Hy Breasal B&B, St. Fionans Road. GPS: n53,92836 w9,93123.
10 ⚡€ 10, € 20 service incl ⚡↯Ch⚡WC 🚿. **Location:** Rural, comfortable, quiet. **Surface:** gravel.
**Distance:** ⚡on the spot ♨500m ⚡500m ⊗500m ♨750m ♨on the spot ♨on the spot.

### Cong · 1B2
Cong Motorhome Park, Quay Rd, Lisloughrey.
**GPS:** n53,53936 w9,27089.
5 ⚡€ 30, 2 pers.incl ⚡↯Ch⚡WC🚿included. 📮
⚡**Location:** Rural, comfortable, isolated. **Surface:** gravel.
▢ 01/01-31/12.
**Distance:** ⚡1,6km ⊗1,6km.

### Corraguan · 1B2
White Strand. GPS: n53,66904 w9,90211.
10 ⚡free. **Location:** Rural. ▢ 01/01-31/12.

### Crossmolina · 1B1
Gortnor Abbey Pier, Lake Rd. GPS: n54,09352 w9,2989. ↑.
5 ⚡free ⚡WCfree. **Location:** Simple, isolated, quiet.
**Surface:** concrete. ▢ 01/01-31/12.
**Distance:** ⚡2km ♨on the spot ♨on the spot ⊗2km.
**Remarks:** Max. 2 nights, video surveillance.

### Galway · 1B2
Galway Harbour, Dockstreet. GPS: n53,27004 w9,04885.
15 ⚡8-19h € 2/h, 19-8h € 4 ⚡↯€ 3/10kWh. 📮⚡**Location:** Urban, simple, quiet. **Surface:** asphalted.

▢ 01/01-31/12.
**Distance:** ⚡600m ♨on the spot ⊗600m.

### Oughterard · 1B2
Camp Street Cafe. GPS: n53,42912 w9,31955. ↑.
⚡guests free. **Location:** Central, noisy.
▢ 01/01-31/12.
**Distance:** ⚡on the spot ⊗on the spot ♨on the spot.

### Portumna · 1B2
Castle Avenue. GPS: n53,08388 w8,22038.
8 ⚡€ 10 ⚡WCincluded 🗑.📮⚡ **Location:** Rural, isolated, quiet.
**Surface:** asphalted. ▢ 01/01-31/12.
**Distance:** ⚡1,3km ♨on the spot ♨on the spot.

### Roosky · 1C2
Shannon River. GPS: n53,83192 w7,9197.
10 ⚡€ 10 ⚡Ch⚡€ 2. **Location:** Simple, central.
**Surface:** grassy/gravel. ▢ 01/01-31/12.
**Distance:** ♨on the spot ⊗100m ♨100m ♨on the spot ♨on the spot.
**Remarks:** Along river.

### Templeboy · 1B1
Beach Bar, Aughris head. GPS: n54,26908 w8,75696.
10 ⚡€ 20 ⚡Ch⚡included. **Location:** Rural. **Surface:** grassy.
▢ 01/01-31/12.
**Distance:** ♨on the spot ⊗on the spot.

## Leinster

### Carlingford · 1C2
Carlingford Marina, North Commons. GPS: n54,05228 w6,19314.
20 ⚡€ 10 ⚡Ch⚡WCincluded. 📮⚡**Location:** Rural, isolated, quiet. **Surface:** asphalted.
**Distance:** ⚡2km ♨on the spot ♨on the spot ⊗on the spot.

### Fethard-on-Sea · 1C3
Norman View Motorhome Park. GPS: n52,18342 w6,83659. ↑.
7 ⚡€ 12 ⚡included.
**Location:** Rural. **Surface:** grassy/gravel. ▢ 01/01-31/12.
**Distance:** ⚡1km ♨400m ♨1km.

### Glenmalure · 1C2
Glenmalure lodge, Wicklow Way. GPS: n52,95743 w6,35405.
4 ⚡guests free.
**Location:** Rural. **Surface:** metalled. ▢ 01/01-31/12.

### Rathdrum · 1C2
Derrybawn Farm Sanctuary. GPS: n52,99179 w6,32136.
7 ⚡€ 15. ⚡ **Location:** Rural, isolated, quiet. **Surface:** gravel.
▢ 01/04-01/11.

## Munster

### Ardmore · 1C3
Ardmore Seaview Motorhome Park. GPS: n51,95639 w7,72578. ↑.
30 ⚡€ 10 ⚡Ch⚡ **Surface:** grassy. ▢ 01/01-31/12.
**Distance:** ⚡500m ♨on the spot ♨on the spot ⊗500m.
**Remarks:** Money in envelope in mail box.

### Askeaton · 1B2
Askeaton Leisurecenter, The Quay. GPS: n52,60273 w8,97511. ↑.
5 ⚡free. **Location:** Urban. **Surface:** asphalted. ▢ 01/01-31/12.

## Ballinskellig 1A3
Cois Tra Lower. **GPS:** n51,82093 w10,27323.
10 free. **Location:** Rural. **Surface:** asphalted. 01/01-31/12.

## Ballydonegan 1A3
R575. **GPS:** n51,63334 w10,0625.
20 € 15. **Location:** Isolated, quiet. **Surface:** grassy.
01/01-31/12.
**Distance:** on the spot on the spot.

## Bandon 1B3
Cloghmacsimon. **GPS:** n51,74101 w8,74082.
15 € 7/24h Ch included.
**Surface:** asphalted. 01/01-31/12.
**Distance:** 500m 300m 500m.
**Remarks:** Next to petrol station, max. 2 days.

## Bantry 1B3
**Bantry Marina. GPS:** n51,67977 w9,46155.
€ 20/24h. **Location:** Isolated, quiet. **Surface:** asphalted.
01/01-31/12.
**Distance:** 600m on the spot on the spot 600m.
**Remarks:** Parking at pier.

## Bantry 1B3
**The West Lodge Hotel. GPS:** n51,67222 w9,47543.
€ 10. **Location:** Rural, isolated, quiet. **Surface:** gravel.
**Distance:** 2km on the spot.
**Remarks:** Breakfast-service.

## Castletownbere 1B3
**Berehaven Golf Club**, Filane West. **GPS:** n51,65417 w9,86125.
10 € 18, Jul/Aug € 20 Ch € 2 WC included.
**Location:** Rural. **Surface:** metalled. 01/01-31/12.
**Distance:** on the spot.

## Coarha Beg 1A3
**Bray Head Car park. GPS:** n51,89162 w10,39656.
5 € 2/day, € 10/night. **Location:** Simple, isolated, quiet.
**Surface:** asphalted. 01/01-31/12.
**Distance:** on the spot on the spot.
**Remarks:** Beautiful view.

## Cobh 1B3
**Whitepoint Moorings. GPS:** n51,84716 w8,30735.
30 € 10 Ch. **Location:** Urban, simple, quiet.
**Surface:** asphalted. 01/01-31/12.
**Distance:** 900m on the spot on the spot.
**Remarks:** Max. 48h.

## Eyeries 1B3
**Eyeries Motor Home Park. GPS:** n51,69319 w9,95386.

20 € 10 Ch € 5 included. **Location:** Rural.
**Surface:** gravel. 01/01-31/12.
**Distance:** 300m 1km 1km 300m 20m on the spot on the spot.
**Remarks:** Possibility for reservation.

## Kilfinnane 1B3
**Ballyhoura Camper Van Park. GPS:** n52,35872 w8,46656.
42 € 15 Ch included. **Location:** Rural.
**Surface:** metalled. 01/01-31/12.
**Distance:** on the spot on the spot on the spot on the spot on the spot.

## Kilrush 1B2
**Kilrush Marina**, Merchants Quay. **GPS:** n52,63520 w9,49518.
5 € 20 WC € 3. **Location:** Urban.
**Surface:** metalled. 01/01-31/12.
**Distance:** 800m on the spot 600m 500m.

## Kinsale 1B3
**Lidl Kinsale**, Barrack's Lane. **GPS:** n51,70796 w8,51726.
10 free. **Surface:** metalled. 01/01-31/12.
**Distance:** 750m 750m on the spot.
**Remarks:** Max. 1 night.

## Kinsale 1B3
**New Road Car Park. GPS:** n51,70969 w8,51945.
free. **Surface:** asphalted. 01/01-31/12.
**Distance:** 500m 500m.

**Remarks:** At fire-station.

## Liscanor 1B2
**Cliffs of Moher. GPS:** n52,97145 w9,42475.
€ 6/pp. **Location:** Rural. **Surface:** metalled. 01/01-31/12.
**Remarks:** Only for guest.

## Midleton 1B3
**Distillery Road Car Park. GPS:** n51,91344 w8,16981.
6 free € 0,25 € 0,25 Ch € 0,25. **Location:** Urban.
**Surface:** asphalted. 01/01-31/12.
**Remarks:** Max. 48h.

## Sneem 1B3
**Goosey Island Motor Home Park**, Inchinaleega East.
**GPS:** n51,83772 w9,89934.
26 € 10/24h Ch € 5. **Surface:** grassy/gravel.
01/01-31/12.
**Distance:** on the spot on the spot on the spot on the spot
on the spot on the spot.
**Remarks:** Along river, max. 48h, check in at bar.

## Sneem 1B3
**Sneem Hotel. GPS:** n51,83349 w9,89844.
€ 10. **Surface:** asphalted.
**Distance:** 500m 100m on the spot 500m.
**Remarks:** Max. 48h.

# Italy

Capital: Rome
Government: parliamentarian republic
Official Language: Italian
Population: 62,137,802 (2017)
Area: 301,339 km²

## General information
Dialling code: 0039
General emergency: 112
Currency: Euro
Credit cards are accepted almost everywhere.

## Regulations for overnight stays
Wild camping is allowed with permission of municipality, police or property owner when no problems occur.

## Additional public holidays 2019
January 6 Epiphany
April 25 Liberation Day
May 1 Labor Day
June 2 Festa della Republica, National Holiday
August 15 Assumption of the Virgin Mary
November 1 All Saints' Day
November 4 Armistice Day
December 8 Immaculate Conception

## Time Zone
Winter (Standard Time) GMT+1
Summer (DST) GMT+2

Map of Italy with regions:
Aosta Valley pages: 596-597
Piedmont pages: 597-607
Lombardy pages: 611-616
Trentino South Tyrol pages: 607-611
Friuli Venezia Giulia pages: 621-625
Veneto pages: 616-621
Liguria pages: 631-632
Emilia-Romagna pages: 625-631
San Marino page: 644
Tuscany pages: 632-644
Marche pages: 644-650
Umbria pages: 654-656
Abruzzo pages: 656-657
Molise page: 658
Lazio pages: 650-654
Campania pages: 660-661
Puglia pages: 658-660
Basilicata page: 662
Calabria pages: 662-663
Sardinia pages: 663-666
Sicily pages: 666-670

# Aosta Valley

**Antey-Saint-André** 22G3
Località Filey, SR46. **GPS:** n45,81246 e7,58898.⬆.
15 🚐 € 8, tourist tax € 0,20/pp ⛽🚰Ch.included.
**Surface:** metalled. ⬛ 01/01-31/12.
**Distance:** 🚶850m.
**Remarks:** To be paid at bar, service passerby € 5.

**Aosta** ⛰❄ 22G3
Via Cadutti del Lavoro. **GPS:** n45,73600 e7,33035.⬆.

30 🚐 € 12/24h 🚰🗑Ch.included 🔌 € 1/kWh.
**Location:** Urban, noisy. **Surface:** asphalted.
⬛ 01/01-31/12 ◑ Thu-morning closed because of market.
**Distance:** 🚶on the spot 🚴4,5km 🚉200m 🚌on the spot.
**Remarks:** Parking closes at 22h, video surveillance.

**Aymavilles** 22G3
Strada Comunale del Moulins. **GPS:** n45,70125 e7,23960.⬆.

20 🚐 € 6/24h 🚰🗑Ch. **Surface:** metalled. ⬛ 01/05-31/10.

**Bard** 22H3
SS 26 della Valle d'Aost. **GPS:** n45,61564 e7,74204.
6 🚐free. **Surface:** metalled. ⬛ 01/01-31/12.
**Distance:** 🚶on the spot.

**Bionaz** 22G3
Area Attrezzata Bosco di Lexert. **GPS:** n45,86380 e7,39615.
🚐€ 10/night 🚰🗑Ch. **Location:** Rural. **Surface:** grassy/gravel.
⬛ 01/01-31/12.
**Distance:** 🛒50m ⊗on the spot 🚉2,5km.
**Remarks:** Picnic area at small lake.

**Brusson** ⛰ 22H3
Foyer du Ski, Rue Vollon. **GPS:** n45,76617 e7,71117.

50 🚐 € 10,80/24h 🚰🗑Ch. 🔌included.
**Surface:** grassy/metalled. ⬛ 01/01-31/12.
**Distance:** 🎿on the spot.
**Remarks:** At lake.

**Cervinia/Breuil** ⛰❄ 22G3
Area Camper del Breuil, Strada Regionale 46.
**GPS:** n45,92614 e7,62026.⬆.
80 🚐 € 7,80/24h 🚰🗑Ch.
**Location:** Rural. **Surface:** asphalted. ⬛ 01/01-31/12.
**Distance:** 🚶1km 🏊Lago Blu 400m ⊗on the spot.
**Remarks:** Altitude 2000m, shuttle bus to city centre.

**Champorcher** ⛰❄ 22G3
Area pic-nic, Loc. Chardonney. **GPS:** n45,62141 e7,60992.⬆➡.
35 🚐 € 6 free. **Surface:** grassy.

**Distance:** ⊗300m 🚴300m.
**Remarks:** Nearby parking funicular railway.

**Chatillon** 22G3
Area Camper attrezzata Chatillon, Frazione Perolle.
**GPS:** n45,74889 e7,62388.⬆.

16 🚐 € 5/12h 🚰🗑Ch.🔌. **Surface:** metalled. ⬛ 01/01-31/12.
**Distance:** 🚶historical centre 🚴500m.

**Cogne** ⛰ 22G3
Fraz. Lillaz. **GPS:** n45,59602 e7,38815.⬆.

37 🚐 € 9,70, Jul/Aug and 24/12-06/01 € 11,70 🚰🗑Ch.🔌 € 2,50.
**Location:** Comfortable. **Surface:** asphalted. ⬛ 01/01-31/12.
**Distance:** 🚶100m 🛒on the spot ⊗100m 🚉100m 🚌on the spot
🎿1km.
**Remarks:** Altitude 1650m.

**Cogne** ⛰ 22G3
Fraz. Revettaz. **GPS:** n45,60840 e7,35830.⬆.

130 ⏚€ 9,70, Jul/Aug and 24/12-06/01 € 11,70 ⏚🔌Ch ⚡€ 2,50.
**Surface:** asphalted. ⬛ 01/01-31/12 ⬤ water disconnected in winter.
**Tourist information Cogne:**
🌿 Parco Nacionale Gran Paradiso, Vall d'Aosta. Nature reserve, information centres: Dégioz, Rhêmes-Notre-Dame and Cogne.

| 📷S | Courmayeur 🏔❄ | 22F3 |

**Funivia Val Veny. GPS:** n45,81428 e6,95612.⬆➡.
⏚free ⏚🔌. **Surface:** metalled. ⬛ 01/01-31/12.
**Distance:** 🚠3km ⊗on the spot.

| 📷S | Étroubles | 22G3 |

**Camping Tunnel**, Rue des Chevrières, 4. **GPS:** n45,81874 e7,22922.⬆.

6 ⏚€ 13, 15/07-26/08 € 18 ⏚🔌Ch ⚡(6x),6Amp 🔌included.
**Surface:** grassy/metalled. ⬛ 01/04-14/10.
**Distance:** 🚠on the spot ⚓16km 🚄100m ⊗100m 🍴300m 🚌200m
🚴100m 🚶100m ⚽3,5km 🏊100m.
**Remarks:** Max. 48h.

| 📷S | Fénis | 22G3 |

Località Chez Sapin. **GPS:** n45,73939 e7,48553.⬆.
5 ⏚free ⏚🔌Ch.
**Location:** Urban, simple. **Surface:** asphalted. ⬛ 01/01-31/12.
**Distance:** 🚠500m ⊗on the spot ⊗350m 🍴800m.
**Remarks:** At cemetery.

| 📷S | Fontainemore | 22H3 |

SR44. **GPS:** n45,64598 e7,85916.
2 ⏚free ⚡€ 3 WC ⬛€ 1,summer. **Location:** Rural, simple, isolated.
**Surface:** asphalted. ⬛ 01/01-31/12.
**Distance:** 🚠350m ⊗350m.
**Remarks:** To be paid at bar.

| 📷S | Gaby | 22H3 |

**Piazzale Vourry. GPS:** n45,70157 e7,87295.⬆.
9 ⏚free, 01/07-30/09 € 6 ⏚🔌WC. **Location:** Rural.
**Surface:** asphalted. ⬛ 01/01-31/12 ⬤ Service: winter.
**Distance:** 🚠1,5km ⚓50m ⊗700m.
**Remarks:** Altitude 1000m.

| 📷S | Gressoney-Saint-Jean 🏔❄ | 22H3 |

**P Weissmatten**, Via Bildschocke, Saint Jean.
**GPS:** n45,76028 e7,83556.⬆.

⏚€ 6/12h then € 0,50/h, 01/05-30/06 free ⏚🔌Ch ⚡included.
**Surface:** asphalted. ⬛ 01/01-31/12.
**Distance:** 🎿on the spot ⊗400m 🚠on the spot.
**Remarks:** Parking funicular railway.

| 📷S | Gressoney-Saint-Jean 🏔❄ | 22H3 |

**Tschaval**, La Trinité. **GPS:** n45,85657 e7,81362.⬆➡.

---

25 ⏚€ 8/24h ⏚🔌Ch ⚡🚐
**Surface:** grasstiles/metalled. ⬛ 01/01-31/12.
**Distance:** 🚶50m.

| 📷S | Valgrisenche 🏔 | 22G3 |

Localita' Mondanges. **GPS:** n45,62638 e7,06252.⬆.
20 ⏚free ⏚🔌
**Location:** Rural. **Surface:** asphalted. ⬛ 01/01-31/12.
**Distance:** 🚶on the spot.

| 📷S | Valsavarenche 🏔 | 25G1 |

Località Dégioz. **GPS:** n45,59404 e7,20721.⬆.
11 ⏚€ 5/12h, tourist tax € 0,80 ⏚🔌Ch.
**Location:** Rural, simple. **Surface:** grasstiles/metalled.
⬛ 01/04-31/10.
**Distance:** 🚠100m.
**Remarks:** Check in at town hall Tabaccheria or Bar Lo Fourquin, with registration number motorhome.

| 📷S | Verrès | 22G3 |

**Piazzale Grand Ronc**, Via Stazione. **GPS:** n45,66226 e7,69392.⬆.

6 ⏚€ 5 ⏚🔌free. **Location:** Urban, simple. **Surface:** asphalted.
⬛ 01/01-31/12.
**Distance:** 🚠200m ⚓1,5km.

# Piedmont

| 📷 | Acceglio 🏔 | 25F3 |

SP422. **GPS:** n44,47526 e6,98530.⬆➡.

6 ⏚free ⏚🔌Chfree. **Location:** Rural, simple, quiet.
**Surface:** grassy/gravel. ⬛ 01/01-31/12.
**Distance:** 🚠400m ⚓400m ⊗400m.
**Remarks:** At sports grounds, max. 24h.

| 📷S | Acqui Terme 🌿♨ | 26A2 |

**Area comunale**, SS456, Viale Einaudi. **GPS:** n44,66533 e8,47228.⬆.

100 ⏚€ 8 ⏚🔌Ch ⚡(16x)WCincluded. 🚐
**Location:** Urban, comfortable, central, noisy.
**Surface:** grasstiles/metalled. ⬛ 01/01-31/12.
**Distance:** 🚠1,5km ⚓25km 🏊on the spot ⊗50m 🍴250m
🚌1,5km.
**Remarks:** Parking beside river.

| 📷S | Aglié | 25H1 |

Via della Gula. **GPS:** n45,36662 e7,76381.⬆.

---

36 ⏚€ 12/24h + € 0,80/pp tourist tax ⏚🔌Chincluded ⚡€ 3
WC 🔌. **Location:** Rural. **Surface:** metalled.
⬛ 01/01-31/12.
**Distance:** ⊗2 restaurants 🍴300m ⬛on the spot 🚌on the spot
🚶on the spot ⚽200m.

| 📷S | Hône 🏔 | 22H3 |

Via Raffort. **GPS:** n45,61169 e7,73262.⬆.
11 ⏚€ 10 ⏚🔌Chincluded ⚡€ 1/6h. **Location:** Rural.
**Surface:** metalled. ⬛ 01/01-31/12.
**Distance:** 🚠350m ⚓7km ⊗on the spot ⊗250m.
**Remarks:** Max. 48h.

| 📷S | La Thuile 🏔((• ❄ ⬆ | 22F3 |

**Azzurra Camper. GPS:** n45,70823 e6,95335.⬆.

80 ⏚€ 13-20, tourist tax € 0,80/pp ⏚🔌Ch ⚡(45x)€ 3 ⬛€ 3 🔌€ 5.
**Location:** Rural. **Surface:** metalled.
⬛ 01/01-31/12.
**Distance:** 🚠500m 🚶500m ⚽100m.
**Remarks:** Bread-service, video surveillance.

| 📷S | Pont-Saint-Martin | 22H3 |

**Piazzale Palazzetto dello Sport**, Via C. Viola. **GPS:** n45,60025 e7,79338.
4 ⏚free. **Surface:** asphalted. ⬛ 01/01-31/12.
**Distance:** ⚓1km.

| 📷S | Rhêmes-Notre-Dame | 25G1 |

**Gipeto**, Loc. Chanavey. **GPS:** n45,57960 e7,12392.
30 ⏚€ 6/12h, >1 hour € 0,50/h ⚡included.
**Surface:** metalled. ⬛ 01/01-31/12.
**Distance:** 🚶on the spot.

| 📷S | Rhêmes-Notre-Dame | 25G1 |

Frazione Bruil. **GPS:** n45,57148 e7,11848.
20 ⏚free. **Surface:** asphalted.

| 📷S | Saint-Denis 🏔 | 22G3 |

Strada Regionale del Col Saint Pantaléon, Loc. Plaù.
**GPS:** n45,77129 e7,56092.

4 ⏚€ 7/24h ⏚🔌Ch ⚡WC. 🚐 **Location:** Quiet.
**Surface:** grasstiles/grassy. ⬛ 01/01-31/12.
**Distance:** ⚓16km.

| 📷S | Saint-Oyen 🏔 ❄ | 22G3 |

Rue de Flassin. **GPS:** n45,82133 e7,20822.⬆.
⏚€ 15/24h ⏚🔌Ch ⚡WCincluded ⬛€ 1.
**Location:** Rural, simple. **Surface:** grassy. ⬛ 01/01-31/12.
**Distance:** ⚓22km ⊗on the spot ⚽on the spot.

| 📷S | Saint-Pierre | 22G3 |

**Place des Valdôtains à l'étranger**, Località Pommier.
**GPS:** n45,70831 e7,22402.⬆.
8 ⏚free ⏚🔌. ⬛ 01/01-31/12.
**Distance:** 🚠300m ⊗300m ⬛on the spot.
**Remarks:** Parking next to police station.

| 📷S | Torgnon | 22G3 |

Plan Proriond. **GPS:** n45,80397 e7,55490.⬆➡.

40 ⛺free 🚐. **Location:** Urban, simple. **Surface:** metalled.
🅟 01/01-31/12.
**Distance:** 🚶on the spot ⊗500m 🍴1km 🚌400m.

**Alba Village**, Corso Piave 219, loc. San Cassiano.
**GPS:** n44,68553 e8,01095. ⬆➡.

10 ⛺€ 5 + € 0,50/pp tourist tax 🚐 € 2/30liter 🍴Ch 🧹 🏠
**Location:** Urban, simple, central. **Surface:** grassy.
🅟 01/01-31/12.
**Distance:** 🚶2,5km 🚲1km ⊗on the spot 🍴100m 🚌on the spot.
**Remarks:** Nearby Hotel&Camping Alba Village, max. 48h, check in at reception, monitored parking.

**Area comunale**, Viale Teresa Michel. **GPS:** n44,92075 e8,62722. ⬆.

25 ⛺free 🚐🍴Ch.
**Location:** Urban, simple. **Surface:** asphalted. 🅟 01/01-31/12.
**Distance:** 🚶2km 🚲2km ⊗on the spot 🍴500m 🚌on the spot.

Via Michelangelo Buonarrotti. **GPS:** n45,76879 e8,54495. ⬆.
20 ⛺free WCfree. **Location:** Rural, simple, quiet. **Surface:** metalled.
🅟 01/01-31/12.
**Distance:** 🚶2km ⊗200m 🍴2km 🚌on the spot 🚶on the spot.

Piazza Campo del Palio. **GPS:** n44,89712 e8,21057. ⬆.

>50 ⛺free 🚐. **Location:** Urban, simple, central, noisy.
**Surface:** asphalted. 🅟 01/01-31/12 ◉ Wed-Sa.
**Distance:** 🚶on the spot ⊗50m 🍴100m 🚌300m.

Via Giovanni Suppo. **GPS:** n45,07304 e7,39004. ⬆➡.

8 ⛺free 🚐🍴Chfree 📶. **Location:** Urban, simple, quiet.
**Surface:** asphalted. 🅟 01/01-31/12.
**Distance:** 🚶1km 🚲4,6km.
**Remarks:** Nearby sports complex.
**Tourist information Avigliana:**
🏕 🅟 Thu.

Via Carlo Alberto. **GPS:** n44,73108 e7,32000. ⬆.

---

4 ⛺free 🚐🍴Chfree. **Location:** Simple. **Surface:** asphalted.
🅟 01/01-31/12.
**Distance:** 🚶800m 🍴1km 🍴700m 🚌on the spot.

**Cian del Mondo**, Loc. Piano del Mondo.
**GPS:** n44,31994 e8,01858. ⬆➡.

20 ⛺€ 15 🚐🍴Ch 🔌(20x)€ 2,50/day WC 📶included.
**Location:** Rural, comfortable. **Surface:** gravel. 🅟 01/03-08/12.
**Distance:** 🚶700m 🍴500m 🚲on the spot 🚶on the spot.

**Area Comunale**, Via Brera. **GPS:** n45,91187 e8,50101. ⬆.

40 ⛺€ 12/24h 🚐🍴ChWCincluded. 🚐
**Location:** Urban, simple, noisy. **Surface:** metalled. 🅟 01/01-31/12.
**Distance:** 🚶500m 🚲2,8km ⛵Lago Maggiore 300m 🍴300m
🚌on the spot 🚶on the spot.
**Remarks:** Behind railway station, max. 72h, no camping activities, weekend: noisy.

Piazza 3° Alpini. **GPS:** n44,79581 e7,29366. ➡.

8 ⛺free 🚐🍴Chfree.
**Location:** Urban, simple. **Surface:** metalled. 🅟 01/03-01/11.
**Distance:** 🚶500m ⊗500m 🍴600m.

**Area Comunale**, Piazzale Sandro Pertini. **GPS:** n45,55559 e8,06760. ⬆.

30 ⛺free 🚐🍴free. **Location:** Urban. **Surface:** asphalted.
🅟 01/01-31/12.
**Distance:** 🚶on the spot ⊗100m 🚉station 100m.
**Remarks:** Square next to station F.S San Paolo.

---

**Piazzale 2**, Strada Statale 232. **GPS:** n45,66250 e8,08472.
8 ⛺€ 8/24h 🚐🍴Chincluded 🧹€ 3,50 🚐.
**Location:** Rural.
**Distance:** ⊗on the spot 🍴1,5km.

**P Area Camper**, Strada Communale Del Cimitero.
**GPS:** n44,32889 e7,49167. ⬆➡.

15 ⛺free 🚐🍴Chfree. **Location:** Urban, simple, quiet.
**Surface:** asphalted. 🅟 01/01-31/12.
**Distance:** 🚶100m ⊗450m 🍴900m 🚌200m.
**Remarks:** At sports park.

**Piazza Milanaccio**, Via Varallo. **GPS:** n45,72005 e8,27408. ⬆.

3 ⛺free 🚐🍴Chfree. **Location:** Urban. **Surface:** asphalted.
🅟 01/01-31/12 ◉ Jun.
**Distance:** 🚶300m.
**Remarks:** Market Saturday.

**Area Comunale**, Via Cesare Pavese. **GPS:** n45,54163 e8,11595. ⬆.

2 ⛺free 🚐🍴Chfree.
**Location:** Urban, quiet. **Surface:** asphalted. 🅟 01/01-31/12.
**Distance:** 🚶400m ⊗400m 🚌100m.
**Remarks:** Nearby sports center.

**Area Ricetto**, Via Mulino. **GPS:** n45,54624 e8,11573. ⬆.

25 ⛺free 🚐🍴Ch 🧹📶free. **Location:** Urban, comfortable.
**Surface:** metalled. 🅟 01/01-31/12.
**Distance:** 🚶400m ⊗400m.

Piazza Unione Europea. **GPS:** n44,72039 e8,29369. ⬆.

IT

>10 ⛽free. **Location:** Urban, simple, central, noisy.
**Surface:** asphalted. ● Tue, Fri 6-16h (market).
**Distance:** 🚶200m ✈4km ⊗100m 🛒250m �︎on the spot 🚌on the spot.

**S** | Casaleggio Boiro | 26A2
Via Castello. **GPS:** n44,63354 e8,73254. ⬆➡.

8 ⛽free 🚰🗑Ch ⚓(6x)free. **Location:** Rural, comfortable, quiet.
**Surface:** gravel. ● 01/01-31/12.
**Distance:** 🚶250m ✈10km ⊗150m 🛒250m 🚌200m.
**Remarks:** At sports park.

**S** | Castelletto Stura | 25G3
Via Cuneo. **GPS:** n44,44194 e7,63444. ⬆.

20 ⛽free 🚰🗑⚓free.
**Location:** Rural, simple. **Surface:** gravel.
**Remarks:** Nearby sports park.

**S** | Castiglione Falletto | 25H2
**Area comunale**, Piazzale Muntelier. **GPS:** n44,62379 e7,97486. ⬆.

4 ⛽free 🚰🗑Chfree. **Location:** Rural, comfortable, quiet.
**Surface:** metalled. ● 01/01-31/12.
**Distance:** 🚶100m ⊗100m 🛒100m 🚌on the spot 🏃on the spot.
**Remarks:** Playground.

**S** | Castiglione Tinella | 25H2
**Camperstop Ai Ciuvin, Agriturismo**, Strada Manzotti 3.
**GPS:** n44,73357 e8,18140. ⬆.

12 ⛽€ 20 🚰🗑Ch ⚓WC🗑included. **Location:** Rural,
comfortable, isolated, quiet. **Surface:** grassy. ● 01/01-31/12.
**Distance:** 🚶15km ✈20km ⊗on the spot 🛒15km.
**Remarks:** Max. 48h.

**S** | Cavour | 25G2
Via Vigone 3. **GPS:** n44,78766 e7,37660. ⬆.

---

15 ⛽free 🚰🗑Chfree. **Location:** Urban, simple, noisy.
**Surface:** asphalted. ● 01/01-31/12.
**Distance:** 🚶500m ⊗on the spot 🛒on the spot 🚌on the spot.

**S** | Cannobio | 23A2
**Area Comunale**, Via Al Fiume / Via San Rocco.
**GPS:** n46,06179 e8,69242. ⬆➡.

55 ⛽€ 15/24h 🚰🗑ChWCincluded. 🗑 **Location:** Rural,
comfortable, quiet. **Surface:** grasstiles. ● 01/01-31/12.
**Distance:** 🚶500m ⚓on the spot ⊗500m 🛒300m 🚲on the spot
🏃on the spot.
**Remarks:** Along river, max. 3 days.
**Tourist information Cannobio:**
🏛 ● Su.

**S** | Carcoforo | 22H3
**Le Giare**, SP11, Loc. Tetto Minocco. **GPS:** n45,90769 e8,05130. ⬆.

100 ⛽€ 12/day, € 18/weekend, € 50/week 🚰🗑Chincluded ⚓
(16x)€ 2 WC🗑€ 1. 🗑 **Location:** Rural, isolated, quiet. **Surface:** grassy.
● 01/01-31/12.
**Distance:** 🚶on the spot ⊗50m 🛒300m 🏃on the spot.
**Remarks:** Along the Egua river.

**S** | Casale Monferrato | 26A1
**Palazzetto dello Sport Paolo Ferraris**, Via Visconti.
**GPS:** n45,12556 e8,46194. ⬆.

15 ⛽free 🚰🗑Ch 📶in shopping centre. **Location:** Rural.
**Surface:** asphalted. ● 01/01-31/12.
**Distance:** 🚶1,5km ✈3,6km ⊗200m 🛒200m.
**Remarks:** At sports centre.

**S** | Casale Monferrato | 26A1
**Parcheggio Castello**, Piazza Castello. **GPS:** n45,13722 e8,44806. ⬆➡.

---

18 ⛽€ 5/24h 🚰🗑Chincluded ⚓. **Location:** Urban.
**Surface:** metalled. ● 01/01-31/12.
**Distance:** 🚶400m ⊗100m 🛒300m.

**S** | Ceresole Reale | 25G1
**Area sosta Camper Lungolago**, Strada Provinciale 50.
**GPS:** n45,43407 e7,22783.
⛽€ 10 🚰🗑Chincluded ⚓€ 3. **Location:** Simple, quiet.
● 01/01-31/12.
**Distance:** 🚶300m ⚓on the spot ⊗300m 🛒300m 🚲on the spot
🏃on the spot.

**S** | Ceresole Reale | 25G1
**Borgata Chiapili Inferiore**, SP50. **GPS:** n45,45049 e7,18765. ⬆.
⛽€ 8 🚰€ 4 ⚓€ 3. **Location:** Comfortable.
**Surface:** unpaved.
**Distance:** 🚶4km ⊗Ristorante Lo Sciatore 🛒2km.
**Remarks:** Along the Orco river, national Park 'Gran Paradiso'.

**S** | Cesana Torinese | 25F2
**Area Sosta Camper Casa Cesana**, Viale Sen. Bouvier.
**GPS:** n44,94782 e6,79516. ⬆.

12 ⛽€ 10/night 🚰🗑Chincluded ⚓(12x)€ 3/day,6Amp WC.
**Location:** Rural, simple. **Surface:** asphalted. ● 01/01-31/12.
**Distance:** 🚶300m ⊗50m 🛒100m.
**Remarks:** Check in at hotel.

**S** | Cherasco | 25H2
**Parking Area Camper**, Piazza Giovanni Paolo II.
**GPS:** n44,64946 e7,85529. ⬆.

8 ⛽free 🚰🗑Chfree ⚓(6x) WC. **Location:** Urban, simple, quiet.
**Surface:** asphalted. ● 01/01-31/12.
**Distance:** 🚶400m ✈3,7km ⊗200m 🛒300m 🚌300m.
**Remarks:** Max. 48h.

**S** | Chianocco | 25G1
**Area Camper Giraude**. **GPS:** n45,14110 e7,16592. ⬆➡.

20 ⛽€ 3-10 🚰🗑ChWCincluded. **Location:** Rural, simple.
**Surface:** grassy/gravel. ● 01/04-31/10.
**Distance:** 🚶1km.
**Remarks:** Max. 48h.

**S** | Chiaverano | 25H1
**Area Camper Lago Sirio**, Strada Provinciale 75.
**GPS:** n45,48585 e7,88815. ⬆.

60 ⌁€ 6-9/12h ⌁€ 5 Ch ⌁€ 3/24h WC⌐. **Location:** Rural.
**Surface:** grassy. ⌂ 01/01-31/12.
**Distance:** ⌁on the spot ⌁on the spot ⌁on the spot ⌁on the spot
⌁on the spot ⌁on the spot.
**Remarks:** At lake Sirio.

| | Chieri | 25H2 |

Strada San Silvestro. **GPS:** n45,01460 e7,83214.⬆.

10 ⌁free ⌁Chfree. **Location:** Urban, simple. **Surface:** asphalted.
⌂ 01/01-31/12.
**Distance:** ⌁on the spot ⌁50m ⌁50m ⌁50m.

| | Chieri | 25H2 |

Piazza Quarini, via Bernardo Vittone. **GPS:** n45,00391 e7,82744.

20 ⌁free. **Surface:** asphalted. ⌂ 01/01-31/12.
**Distance:** ⌁on the spot ⌁600m ⌁lidl 800m ⌁200m > Turin.
**Remarks:** Behind Barracks, tuesday market.

| | Chiusa di Pesio | 25H3 |

Via Provinciale (SP42). **GPS:** n44,27233 e7,66361.

8 ⌁€ 4 ⌁Ch.
**Distance:** ⌁on the spot ⌁300m ⌁700m ⌁on the spot ⌁on the
spot.

| | Chiusa di Pesio | 25H3 |

Cascina Veja, Fraz. Vigna 4. **GPS:** n44,29307 e7,67244.
⌁free WC. **Location:** Rural. **Surface:** grassy. ⌂ 01/01-31/12.
**Distance:** ⌁4km ⌁on the spot ⌁200m.

| | Chiusa di San Michele | 25G2 |

Via Pragallo. **GPS:** n45,10294 e7,33034.⬆→.

5 ⌁€ 7 ⌁ ⌁included.
**Location:** Rural, simple. **Surface:** gravel.
⌂ 01/04-31/10.

---

**Distance:** ⌁8km ⌁600m ⌁500m ⌁2km.
**Remarks:** Max. 48h, to be paid at Uffici Comunali, Piazza Bauchiero 2.

| | Chivasso | 25H1 |

Piazza Libertini, Via Gerbido. **GPS:** n45,18514 e7,89296.⬆.

20 ⌁free ⌁€ 2 ⌁. **Location:** Urban, simple. **Surface:** asphalted.
⌂ 01/01-31/12.
**Distance:** ⌁300m ⌁3km ⌁100m ⌁Carrefour 100m ⌁500m.
**Remarks:** Parking swimming pool.

| | Chivasso | 25H1 |

Via Ceresa 4. **GPS:** n45,19479 e7,89001.⬆.

20 ⌁€ 2,50 ⌁€ 2 ⌁Ch. ⌁ **Location:** Urban, simple.
**Surface:** metalled. ⌂ 01/01-31/12.
**Distance:** ⌁600m ⌁2km ⌁200m ⌁800m ⌁300m.

| | Collegno | 25G2 |

Collegno Area Sosta Camper, Corso Pastrengo angolo Viale Certosa.
**GPS:** n45,08070 e7,58313.⬆.

28 ⌁free ⌁€ 0,50 ⌁€ 0,50 Ch€ 1 ⌁€ 1/4h. **Location:** Urban,
quiet. **Surface:** asphalted. ⌂ 01/01-31/12.
**Distance:** ⌁500m ⌁4km ⌁1km ⌁on the spot.
**Remarks:** Coins at Autolavaggio Il Draghetto, video surveillance.

| | Cortemilia | 25H3 |

Strada San Roco. **GPS:** n44,57848 e8,18567.→.

10 ⌁free ⌁Chfree. **Location:** Rural, simple. **Surface:** gravel.
⌂ 01/01-31/12.
**Distance:** ⌁500m ⌁500m ⌁500m.
**Remarks:** Max. 48h.

| | Cravagliana | 22H3 |

Pian delle Fate, Loc. Brugarolo, SP di Valle Mastallone.
**GPS:** n45,85223 e8,22473.⬆.

---

30 ⌁€ 14 + € 1/pp ⌁Ch ⌁(4x)€ 2 WC⌐included.
**Location:** Rural, simple, quiet. **Surface:** grassy.
⌂ 15/03-15/10.
**Distance:** ⌁on the spot ⌁on the spot.

| | Crevoladossola | 22H2 |

Via Thomas Alva Edison. **GPS:** n46,15832 e8,30719.
8 ⌁free ⌁Chfree. **Location:** Rural. **Surface:** grasstiles.
⌂ 01/01-31/12.
**Distance:** ⌁1,5km.

| | Crissolo | 25G2 |

Baita della Polenta, Strada Provinciale 234.
**GPS:** n44,70075 e7,11686.⬆.

14 ⌁€ 12/24h ⌁Chincluded WC. **Location:** Rural.
**Surface:** grassy. ⌂ 01/01-31/12.
**Distance:** ⌁on the spot ⌁on the spot.
**Remarks:** Not suitable for big motorhomes, narrow entrance, entrance
road closed for motorhomes between 14-18h.

| | Crissolo | 25G2 |

Via Ruata. **GPS:** n44,69771 e7,15931.

20 ⌁free, 01/06-30/09 € 5 ⌁ChWCincluded. **Location:** Urban,
simple, quiet. **Surface:** asphalted. ⌂ 01/01-31/12.
**Distance:** ⌁on the spot ⌁on the spot ⌁on the spot.
**Remarks:** Near the chair-lift.

| | Cuceglio | 25H1 |

Area Camper Erbaluce, Via Porta Pia 69/71. **GPS:** n45,34724 e7,81168.

10 ⌁€ 12 ⌁Ch ⌁(10x) ⌁included. ⌁ **Location:** Rural,
comfortable. **Surface:** gravel. ⌂ 01/01 31/12.
**Distance:** ⌁2km ⌁on the spot ⌁1km ⌁500m.
**Remarks:** Wine tasting.

| | Cuneo | 25G3 |

Parco Fluviale, Piazzale Walther Cavallera.
**GPS:** n44,38563 e7,55154.⬆→.

8 ⌁free ⌁Ch ⌁free. **Location:** Urban, comfortable, quiet.
**Surface:** gravel. ⌂ 01/01-31/12.
**Distance:** ⌁300m ⌁on the spot ⌁850m ⌁600m ⌁on the spot.
**Remarks:** Max. 72h, video surveillance, elevator (free) to centre.

**Tourist information Cuneo:**
⌁ Piazza Galimberti. ⌂ Tue.

## Donato 25H1

**Area Camper Fabrizio de André**, Via S. Pertini, SP405.
**GPS**: n45,52774 e7,90944.⬆.

10 🅿 € 5 🚰🅱Ch WC included. **Location:** Rural. **Surface:** grasstiles.
🅾 01/01-31/12.
**Distance:** 🚶300m ⊗300m.
**Remarks:** Pay at Tabaccheria in the village.

## Druento 25G1

**Area Sosta Camper Il Vascello**, Viale Giacomo Medici del Vascello, 14.
**GPS**: n45,14291 e7,57091.⬆.
20 🅿 € 13 🚰🅱Ch included. **Location:** Comfortable.
**Surface:** grassy. 🅾 01/01-31/12.
**Distance:** 100m 500m.

## Entracque 25G3

**Area C'era una Volta**, SS22. **GPS**: n44,25151 e7,38975.⬆.

18 🅿 € 15 🚰🅱Ch (16x) WC € 5/day 🅱 € 1 included.
**Location:** Rural. **Surface:** unpaved. 🅾 01/01-31/12.
**Distance:** 🚶1km river-beach 500m 500m on the spot 1km
> Cuneo on the spot 🧍on the spot 1km.
**Remarks:** Monitored parking.

## Entracque 25G3

**Parcheggio Camper Real Park**, Ponterosso.
**GPS**: n44,26111 e7,37750.⬆.

66 🅿 € 6 🚰🅱Ch included. **Location:** Rural.
**Surface:** grassy/gravel. 🅾 01/01-31/12.
**Distance:** 🚶3km on the spot on the spot ⊗on the spot 400m
6km.
**Remarks:** Recreation park, max. 2 days.

## Entracque 25G3

Via del Mulino 1. **GPS**: n44,23389 e7,39723.⬆➡.

65 🅿 € 12/24h, € 20/48h 🚰🅱Ch (50x)included 🅱 € 2.
**Location:** Rural, simple. **Surface:** gravel. 🅾 01/01-31/12.
**Distance:** 🚶300m ⊗150m 500m 🧍on the spot on the spot.

## Fenestrelle 25G2

**Le Casermette**, Via Nazionale. **GPS**: n45,03671 e7,05090.⬆.

20 🅿 free, fri-su € 5-10, Jun-Aug € 10 🚰🅱Ch included.
**Location:** Rural. **Surface:** unpaved. 🅾 01/01-31/12.
**Distance:** ⊗100m.

## Fenestrelle 25G2

Via Nazionale, SS23. **GPS**: n45,03889 e7,04583.

9 🅿 free 🚰🅱Ch free. **Location:** Rural. **Surface:** asphalted.
🅾 01/01-31/12.
**Distance:** 500m ⊗400m on the spot.
**Remarks:** Next to cemetery.

## Formazza 23A2

**Area camping Punta Sabbioni**, Frazione Brendo.
**GPS**: n46,38277 e8,42389.⬆.
25 🅿 € 14/24h included WC 🅱 € 2.🅱 **Location:** Rural,
comfortable, isolated, quiet. **Surface:** grassy. 🅾 01/05-01/10.
**Distance:** ⊗1,2km on the spot 🧍on the spot.
**Remarks:** Video surveillance, barbecue place.

## Frabosa Soprana 25H3

Fontane. **GPS**: n44,23554 e7,83561.
🅿 free 🚰🅱Ch free. **Location:** Rural, isolated, quiet.
🅾 01/01-31/12.

## Frabosa Soprana 25H3

**Grotta di Bossea**, Loc.Bossea 10. **GPS**: n44,24077 e7,83939.⬆.
5 🅿 free 🚰🅱Ch free WC. **Location:** Rural, simple, isolated.
**Surface:** asphalted. 🅾 01/01-31/12.
**Distance:** 🚶12km on the spot ⊗on the spot 12km 🧍on the
spot.
**Remarks:** Parking at the caves.

## Garessio 25H3

**Area Comunale**, Str.Provinciale del Colle di San Bernardo (P582).
**GPS**: n44,19927 e8,02587.⬆.

30 🅿 free 🚰🅱Ch free. **Location:** Rural, simple. **Surface:** asphalted.
🅾 01/01-31/12.
**Distance:** 🚶1km 22km ⊗1km 🧍1km.

## Genola 25H3

**Grosso Vacanze**, Via Divisione Alpina Cuneense 2, SS20.
**GPS**: n44,59751 e7,65982.⬆.

4 🅿 free 🚰🅱Ch. **Location:** Rural. **Surface:** metalled.
🅾 01/01-31/12.
**Distance:** ⊗150m 🧍500m 350m.

**Remarks:** Motorhome dealer, accessory shop.

## Giaveno 25G2

SP187, via Torino. **GPS**: n45,04154 e7,36096.

🅿 free 🚰🅱free. **Surface:** asphalted. 🅾 01/01-31/12.
**Distance:** 🚶500m ⊗100m on the spot.

## Grinzane Cavour 25H2

**Piazza Ugo Genta**, Via Bricco 14. **GPS**: n44,65515 e7,98936.➡.

3 🅿 free 🚰🅱Ch free. **Location:** Rural, simple, isolated, noisy.
**Surface:** asphalted. 🅾 01/01-31/12.
**Distance:** 🚶500m ⊗500m 🧍2km on the spot 🧍on the spot.

## Ivrea 25H1

**La Dora d'Ivrea**, Via Dora Baltea. **GPS**: n45,46334 e7,87621.⬆.

10 🅿 € 5 🚰🅱 € 3 Ch included. **Location:** Rural, comfortable.
**Surface:** asphalted. 🅾 01/01-31/12.
**Distance:** 🚶500m 4,5km on the spot 300m Ipermercato
800m 350m.
**Remarks:** Beside river, playground.

## Locana 25G1

Via Nusiglie. **GPS**: n45,41361 e7,46278.
🅿 € 8/24h 🚰🅱Ch € 4/24h WC. **Location:** Rural.
**Surface:** grassy. 🅾 01/01-31/12.
**Distance:** 300m 🧍250m.

## Macugnaga 22H3

**Pecetto**, Di Iacchine Pierluigi Loc. Pecetto.
**GPS**: n45,97015 e7,95352.⬆➡.

28 🅿 € 10, 2 nights € 15 🚰🅱Ch included WC free.
**Location:** Rural, simple, quiet. **Surface:** concrete.
🅾 01/03-30/09.
**Distance:** 🚶1km ⊗100m 🧍500m 100m 🧍on the spot.
**Remarks:** At ski-lift.

## Madonna del Sasso 23A3

**Area Comunale**, Via Santuario, Fraz. Boleto.
**GPS**: n45,78974 e8,37222.⬆➡.

IT

8 ⛺free ⬒🚰Chfree. **Location:** Rural, simple, isolated, quiet. **Surface:** grasstiles. 🅿 01/01-31/12.
**Distance:** 🚶200m ⛱Lago d'Orta 700m ⊗100m 🚲50m 🛵 on the spot 🅿 on the spot.
**Remarks:** Narrow entrance, view at Lago d'Orta.

**⬛S** Maglione 🌿🏛 **25H1**
SP78, Via Cigliano. **GPS:** n45,34338 e8,01456.⬆.

20 ⛺free ⬒free. **Location:** Rural, simple, quiet. **Surface:** grassy.
🅿 01/01-31/12.
**Distance:** 🚶on the spot ⊗50m 🚲150m.
**Remarks:** Art city.

**⬛S** Marsaglia **25H3**
Agriturismo Cascina Zanot, Strada S. Rocco, 17.
**GPS:** n44,47120 e7,96010.⬆.

6 ⛺€25 ⬒🚰Ch 🔌 WC 🗑 included. 🛒 **Location:** Rural, comfortable, isolated, quiet. **Surface:** gravel. 🅿 01/01-31/12.
**Distance:** 🚶8km ⛱10km.
**Remarks:** Beautiful view, playground, sale of wines.

**⬛S** Melle **25G3**
SP8. **GPS:** n44,56245 e7,31739.⬆.

22 ⛺€3, 01/06-01/10 €7 ⬒🚰ChWCincluded. 🛒
**Location:** Rural, comfortable. **Surface:** metalled.
🅿 01/01-31/12.
**Distance:** 🚶100m ⛱200m ⊗250m 🍴300m 🚲100m.

**⬛S** Mergozzo 🏛🏞👫 **23A3**
Parcheggio Area Camper, Via Sempione 49.
**GPS:** n45,96204 e8,44320.⬆.

6 ⛺€10/24h ⬒🚰Chincluded 🔌(4x)€5/day. 🛒
**Location:** Rural, simple, noisy. **Surface:** asphalted.

---

🅿 01/01-31/12.
**Distance:** 🚶300m ⛱Lake Mergozzo 500m ⊗300m 🚲100m 🛵 on the spot 🅿 on the spot.
**Remarks:** To be paid at bar.

**⬛S** Mirabello Monferrato **26A2**
SS31. **GPS:** n45,02976 e8,52939.⬆.

8 ⛺free ⬒€2 🚰Ch€1. **Location:** Simple, isolated, quiet.
**Surface:** asphalted. 🅿 01/01-31/12.
**Distance:** 🚶900m ⛱10km ⊗800m 🍴50m 🚲50m.

**⬛S** Mombarcaro 🌿 **25H3**
SP103. **GPS:** n44,46900 e8,08352.⬆.

8 ⛺€5 ⬒🚰Ch 🔌included. 🛒 **Location:** Rural, comfortable, quiet. **Surface:** metalled. 🅿 01/01-31/12.
**Distance:** 🚶200m ⊗500m.
**Remarks:** Beautiful view.

**⬛S** Mondovì 🌿 **25H3**
Piazza della Republica. **GPS:** n44,38964 e7,81930.⬆.
18 ⛺free WC 🗑. **Location:** Urban, simple, central. **Surface:** asphalted
🅿 01/01-31/12.
**Distance:** 🚶400m 🔌5km ⊗50m 🍴100m 🚲on the spot.
**Remarks:** Nearby the old station.

**⬛S** Mondovì 🌿 **25H3**
Piazza le Giardini. **GPS:** n44,39430 e7,82370.⬆➡.

10 ⛺free ⬒🚰Chfree. **Location:** Urban, simple. **Surface:** asphalted.
🅿 01/01-31/12.
**Distance:** 🚶500m ⊗350m 🚲300m.
**Remarks:** Nearby bus station, parking under railway bridge.

**⬛S** Mondovì 🌿 **25H3**
Mondovicino Outlet Center, Via Tanaro.
**GPS:** n44,41889 e7,84966.⬆➡.

⛺free ⬒€1/100liter 🚰Ch. **Location:** Simple. **Surface:** asphalted.
🅿 01/01-31/12.
**Distance:** 🚶4km 🔌1,2km ⊗100m 🍴on the spot 🚲500m.
**Remarks:** Parking at Outlet Center and Centro Commercial.

**⬛S** Mongrando **25H1**
Area Comunale, Via dei Giovanni. **GPS:** n45,52543 e8,00595.⬆.

---

18 ⛺€10 ⬒🚰Ch 🔌(9x)€3,6Amp WC 📶included. 🛒🎦
**Location:** Urban, quiet. **Surface:** grassy. 🅿 01/01-31/12.
**Distance:** 🚶900m ⊗on the spot 🍴800m.
**Remarks:** At sports centre.

**⬛S** Montiglio Monferrato **25H2**
Via Padre Carpignano. **GPS:** n45,06230 e8,10390.

6 ⛺free. **Location:** Rural, simple, quiet. **Surface:** asphalted.
🅿 01/01-31/12.
**Distance:** 🚶200m ⊗600m.
**Remarks:** At cemetery.

**⬛S** Neive 🌿 **25H2**
Circolo Rosa Neive - Area Camper, Via Crocetta.
**GPS:** n44,72753 e8,11332.⬆.

8 ⛺€10/24h ⬒🚰Ch 🔌(6x)WC 🗑included. 🏠
**Location:** Rural, comfortable, quiet. **Surface:** grassy/gravel.
🅿 01/01-31/12.
**Distance:** 🚶100m ⊗100m.
**Remarks:** Check in at sport centre, playground.

**S** Niella Belbo **25H3**
Agriturismo Ca'd Tistu, Via Pian Lea, 2.
**GPS:** n44,49941 e8,07991.⬆➡.

6 ⛺€5 ⬒🚰Ch 🔌WCincluded. 🛒
**Location:** Rural, isolated, quiet. 🅿 01/01-31/12.
**Distance:** 🚶1,8km ⊗on the spot.
**Remarks:** Steep ramp.

**⬛S** Niella Tanaro **25H3**
Agriturismo I Fornelli, Via Fornello 1. **GPS:** n44,41418 e7,90988.⬆.

3 ⛺€5 ⬒€3,50 🚰Ch 🔌€2,50/24h WC 🗑.
**Location:** Rural, simple, isolated, quiet. **Surface:** grassy/gravel.

◻ 01/01-31/12.
**Distance:** ⚓4km 🚲2km ⊗1km 🚰10km.
**Remarks:** Farm products.

### Nizza Monferrato 26A2
**Parking Camper Piazzale S.Pertini**, Piazzale Sandro Pertini.
**GPS:** n44,77140 e8,35346.⬆.

13 🅿€5 🚰Ch 🔧Service, electricity incl. €3 🏪
**Location:** Urban, comfortable, central, quiet. **Surface:** grassy.
◻ 01/01-31/12.
**Distance:** ⚓200m ⊗500m 🚰500m.
**Remarks:** Max. 48h, gate closed, first call Motorhome Club Nicese between 9-20h.

### Novi Ligure 26A2
Viale Pinan Cichero, zona stadio comunale. **GPS:** n44,77041 e8,78181.⬆.

25 🅿free 🚰Chfree. **Location:** Urban, simple, noisy.
**Surface:** asphalted. ◻ 01/01-31/12.
**Distance:** ⚓1,5km 🚲2km ⊗on the spot 🚰600m.
**Remarks:** Parking gymnasium.

### Occimiano 26A2
Via Circonvallazione. **GPS:** n45,05834 e8,50940.⬆.

5 🅿€5 🚰Ch 🔧included. **Location:** Rural, comfortable.
**Surface:** asphalted. ◻ 01/01-31/12.
**Distance:** ⚓250m 🚲15km ⊗250m 🚰400m.
**Remarks:** To be paid at bar Concordia.

### Oggebbio 23A3
**Area Camper Oggebbio**, Via Martiri Oggebbiesi 6.
**GPS:** n45,99680 e8,65304.⬆.→.

22 🅿€18/24h 🚰Ch 🔧WCinclud.....24h. 🏠
**Location:** Rural, luxurious, isolated, quie....
**Surface:** gravel.
◻ 01/03-01/12.
**Distance:** ⚓1,2km ⊗700m 🚐on the spot 🚶o...
**Remarks:** Attention: narrow road, view on Lago M....
surveillance.

### Omegna 23A3
**Area Camper Lago d'Orta**, Via Caduti di Bologna 1.
**GPS:** n45,86340 e8,39840.⬆.→.

---

25 🅿€8-10/12h, 01/06-30/09 €14/12h 🚰
Ch🔧WC🗑included. 🅿️**Location:** Urban, comfortable, quiet.
**Surface:** metalled. ◻ 01/01-31/12.
**Distance:** ⚓1,8km 🏖beach ⊗800m 🚰800m 🚐on the spot
🚶on the spot.
**Remarks:** Caution key electricity €30, cash payment, video surveillance.

### Ormea 25H3
Via Orti della Rana. **GPS:** n44,14532 e7,90751.→.

10 🅿€10 🚰Ch. **Location:** Rural, comfortable, quiet.
**Surface:** grasstiles. ◻ 01/01-31/12.
**Distance:** ⚓1km ⊗500m 🚰1km.
**Remarks:** Pay at tourist office.

### Ormea 25H3
**Riserva la Regina**, Via Martinetto. **GPS:** n44,15162 e7,90929.⬆.
🅿€12,50/24h 🚰 🔧WC🗑1,50 🛜. **Location:** Rural, simple,
quiet. **Surface:** gravel. ◻ Easter-30/10.
**Distance:** ⚓500m 🎣fishing permit obligatory ⊗on the spot 🚰500m
🚶on the spot.
**Remarks:** Regional products.

### Oropa 22H3
**Area di Santuari**, Via Santuario di Oropa.
**GPS:** n45,62864 e7,97530.⬆.→.

31 🅿€10 🚰Ch 🔧WC🗑. **Location:** Rural. **Surface:** metalled.
◻ 01/05-31/10.
**Distance:** ⊗200m.

### Orta San Giulio 23A3
**Parco del Sacro Monte**, Via Sacro Monte. **GPS:** n45,79732 e8,41204.⬆.

10 🅿free 🚰WCfree. **Location:** Rural, simple, quiet. **Surface:** gravel.
◻ 01/01-31/12.
**Distance:** ⚓900m 🏊1km 🚲400m ⊗1km 🚴on the spot 🚶on the
spot.
**Remarks:** Nearby lake Orta, max. 48h.

### Orta San Giulio 23A3
**Panoramic**, Via Panoramica. **GPS:** n45,79729 e8,41527.⬆.→.

---

20 🅿€20/24h, 19/12-28/02 free. 🅿️**Location:** Rural, simple, noisy.
**Surface:** asphalted. ◻ 01/01-31/12.
**Distance:** ⚓500m 🏊Lago d'Orta 500m ⊗100m 🚐on the spot 🚴on
the spot 🚶on the spot.

### Ovada 26A2
Via Gramsci. **GPS:** n44,64084 e8,64920.→.

30 🅿free 🚰 🔧free. **Location:** Simple, central. **Surface:** grasstiles.
◻ 01/01-31/12.
**Distance:** ⚓300m 🚲3km ⊗100m 🚰500m.

### Piatto 22H3
**Area Comunale**, Fraz. Malina. **GPS:** n45,58908 e8,13630.⬆.

10 🅿free 🚰Ch. **Location:** Urban. **Surface:** asphalted.
◻ 01/01-31/12.
**Remarks:** At sports park.

### Pietraporzio 25G3
**Area Camper Pontebernardo**, Via Nazionale, SS21.
**GPS:** n44,34868 e7,01831.⬆.

21 🅿€5/24h 🚰Ch 🔧WCincluded. **Location:** Rural, comfortable.
**Surface:** gravel. ◻ 01/01-31/12.
**Distance:** ⊗450m 🚲450m 🚰600m.
**Remarks:** 3rd night free.

### Pinerolo 25G2
**Parco Olimpico**, Via Alpi Cozie. **GPS:** n44,88917 e7,35111.⬆.

80 🅿free 🚰Ch 🔧(10x)against payment. **Location:** Urban,
simple. **Surface:** unpaved. ◻ 01/03-01/11.
**Distance:** ⚓2km 🚲1,5km ⊗300m 🚰300m 🚐200m.
**Remarks:** Nearby sports park.

### Pinerolo 25G2
Via Vecchia di Buriasco. **GPS:** n44,88143 e7,34664.

⌐🍴Chfree. ⏰ 01/01-31/12.

**S** | **Pollone** ⌂ 🏕 | **22H3**

**Burcina di Pollone**, Via Felice Piacenza.
**GPS**: n45,58548 e8,00521. ⬆️➡️.

21 🅿€ 16/24h ⌐🍴Ch🚿WCincluded 🗑€ 2 🔌.📶
**Location**: Rural, comfortable. **Surface**: grasstiles.
⏰ 01/01-31/12.
**Distance**: 🛒600m ⊗on the spot.
**Remarks**: At parco Naturale Burcina, max. 48h.

**S** | **Pombia** 🎡 | **23A3**

**Safari Park**, Via Larino. **GPS**: n45,64167 e8,61740. ⬆️➡️.
50 🅿€ 20 ⌐🍴Ch🚿WC🗑included. 🏠 **Location**: Rural,
comfortable, quiet. **Surface**: grassy/gravel. ⏰ 16/03-01/10.
**Distance**: ⊗on the spot 🛒6km 🚲on the spot 🚶on the spot.
**Remarks**: Max. 2 days, check in at reception.

**S** | **Ponderano** | **25H1**

**Area Comunale**, Strada Vicinale al Cimitero.
**GPS**: n45,53683 e8,04949. ⬆️.

10 🅿free ⌐🍴Chfree. **Location**: Urban, simple. **Surface**: gravel.
⏰ 01/01-31/12.
**Distance**: 🛒400m.
**Remarks**: Nearby sports park.

**S** | **Pont Canavese** | **25G1**

**Feiteria**, Via Soana. **GPS**: n45,42153 e7,60020.
12 🅿€ 7,50 🚿€ 2,50 🍴Ch🚿€ 2,50. **Surface**: grassy.
⏰ 01/01-31/12.
**Distance**: ⊘on the spot.
**Remarks**: Max. 48h, video surveillance.

**S** | **Pontechianale** ⌂ ❄️ | **25G3**

**Chianale**, SP 251. **GPS**: n44,65055 e6,99280. ⬆️.

15 🅿free. **Location**: Rural, simple, isolated, noisy.
**Surface**: grassy/gravel. ⏰ 01/01-31/12.
**Distance**: 🛒400m ⊘500m.

**C S** | **Pontechianale** ⌂ ❄️ | **25G3**

**Area Camper**, Fraz Maddalena. **GPS**: n44,62158 e7,02776. ⬆️➡️.

30 🅿€ 7/24h ⌐🍴Ch. 🏠 **Location**: Rural, simple, central.
**Surface**: grassy. ⏰ 01/05-30/09.
**Distance**: 🛒200m ⊘200m 🏊200m 🚌200m.

---

**S** | **Pragelato** | **25F2**

**Villagio GoFree**, SS23. **GPS**: n45,02187 e6,94914.

18 🅿€ 16-21, 4 pers.incl ⌐🍴Ch🚿€ 1,50 WC🗑🔌.
**Location**: Rural. **Surface**: grassy. ⏰ 12/06-13/09.
**Distance**: ⊗on the spot 🚲on the spot 🚶on the spot 🚴on the spot
🚵on the spot.
**Remarks**: Spa, ski, tennis, golf.

**S** | **Prali** ❄️ | **25G2**

Fraz. Ghigo. **GPS**: n44,89176 e7,04956. ⬆️.

🅿free ⌐🍴Chfree. **Location**: Rural. **Surface**: grassy.
⏰ 01/01-31/12.
**Distance**: 🛒300m 🚣on the spot ⊗400m.
**Remarks**: Altitude 1450m, along river, at sports park.

**S** | **Prali** ❄️ | **25G2**

Piazza Garrou Emanuele 17. **GPS**: n44,89150 e7,04982. ⬆️.
🅿€ 5 ⌐🍴Chincluded. **Location**: Rural. **Surface**: grassy/gravel.
⏰ 01/01-31/12.
**Distance**: 🚣on the spot ⊗450m 🚵on the spot.
**Remarks**: Near the chair-lift, to be paid at Pro Loco.

**S** | **Prarostino** | **25G2**

**Porto di Montagne**, Via Piani. **GPS**: n44,86488 e7,26970. ⬆️.

12 🅿€ 7/24h ⌐🍴Ch🚿WCincluded. **Location**: Rural, comfortable.
**Surface**: grassy/gravel. ⏰ 01/01-31/12 💡 With snow.
**Distance**: ⊗300m 🚣200m 🚲on the spot 🚶on the spot.
**Remarks**: To be paid at bar.

**S** | **Prato Nevoso** 🏔️ ❄️ | **25H3**

**Area Stalle Lunghe**, Via Corona Boreale. **GPS**: n44,25200 e7,78192. ⬆️.

80 🅿€ 15-20 ⌐🍴Ch🚿included.
**Surface**: asphalted. ⏰ 01/01-31/12.
**Distance**: 🛒on the spot 🛣️A6 33km ⊗on the spot 🏊50m 🚵on the
spot.

**S** | **Prato Nevoso** 🏔️ ❄️ | **25H3**

Piazza G. Dodero. **GPS**: n44,25200 e7,78192. ⬆️➡️.

---

10 🅿free. **Location**: Rural, simple, central. **Surface**: asphalted.
⏰ 01/01-31/12.
**Distance**: 🛒on the spot ⊗on the spot 🚵on the spot 🚲on the spot.

**S** | **Premia** | **22H2**

**AleSte Area Camper**, Via Provinciale 33, Cadarese.
**GPS**: n46,29723 e8,36232. ⬆️.
15 🅿€ 15/24h ⌐🍴Chincluded 🔌€ 1/kWh. **Surface**: metalled.
⏰ 01/01-31/12.
**Distance**: ⊗on the spot 🚲on the spot 🚶on the spot.

**S** | **Rimasco** | **22H3**

**Il Laghetto**, Strada del Lago. **GPS**: n45,86109 e8,06450. ⬆️.

20 🅿€ 10/24h ⌐🍴Ch🔌€ 3/day WC🗑included.
**Location**: Rural, isolated, quiet. **Surface**: grassy.
⏰ 01/05-30/09 💡 Restaurant: Tue.
**Distance**: 🚣on the spot ⊗on the spot.
**Remarks**: At lake.

**S** | **Riva Valdobbia** 🏞️ | **22H3**

**Area Lo Chalet**, Via Circonvallazione. **GPS**: n45,83476 e7,95486. ⬆️.

48 🅿€ 13/24h ⌐🍴Ch🔌€ 2 WCincluded 🗑.📶
**Location**: Rural, simple. **Surface**: grassy/metalled.
⏰ 01/04-31/10.
**Distance**: 🚣on the spot ⊗on the spot 🚵on the spot.
**Remarks**: Along river.

**S** | **Roaschia** 🏔️ 🎡 | **25G3**

**Area camper I Funtanil**, Via Circonvallazione, SP 108.
**GPS**: n44,26758 e7,45860. ⬆️.

16 🅿€ 10/24h ⌐🍴Ch🚿(16x)WC🗑included.
**Location**: Rural, comfortable, quiet. **Surface**: gravel.
⏰ 01/01-31/12.
**Distance**: 🛒200m 🚴on the spot 🚌350m 🚶on the spot.
**Remarks**: Grill and picknic area.

**S** | **Romano Canavese** | **25H1**

Strada provinciale 56. **GPS**: n45,38644 e7,86177. ⬆️.

10 ⛺free ⛽🚿. **Location:** Rural, simple.
**Surface:** grasstiles/metalled. ⏲ 01/01-31/12.
**Distance:** 🚲2,2km ⊗on the spot 🚇1km 🚌400m.

| 🏕S | Rosta | 25G2 |

Via Buttigliera Alta 2, Via Piave. **GPS:** n45,07106 e7,46333.

5 ⛺free ⛽€ 2 🚿free Ch€ 2.
**Location:** Urban. **Surface:** asphalted. ⏲ 01/01-31/12.
**Distance:** 🚶on the spot 🚲12km ⊗300m 🚇on the spot 🚂train >
Turin 19min 🚴 on the spot.

| 🏕S | Saluzzo | 25G2 |

**Area Bodoni**, Via Olivero Matteo. **GPS:** n44,63886 e7,49192.⬆

19 ⛺free ⛽€ 0,50/60liter 🚿Ch€ 1 ⚡(12x) € 0,50/kWh.
**Location:** Urban, simple. **Surface:** grasstiles.
⏲ 01/01-31/12.
**Distance:** 🚶700m ⊗200m 🚇550m 🚌50m on the spot 🚴on the
spot.
**Remarks:** Max. 72h, small pitches.

| 🏕S | Saluzzo | 25G2 |

Via Cuneo 16. **GPS:** n44,63739 e7,49740.⬆.

±10 ⛺free ⛽🚿free. **Location:** Urban. **Surface:** asphalted.
⏲ 01/01-31/12.
**Distance:** 🚶1km ⊗650m 🚇100m 🚌150m.

| 🏕S | San Damiano d'Asti | 25H2 |

Via Monsignor Franco. **GPS:** n44,82659 e8,05921.⬆.

50 ⛺free ⛽🚿Ch. **Location:** Rural, simple. **Surface:** gravel.
⏲ 01/01-31/12.
**Distance:** 🚶1km ⊗1km 🚇1km.
**Remarks:** At cemetery.

---

| ⚜S | San Damiano d'Asti 🌿 | 25H2 |

**Agriturismo Gran Collina**, Borgata Stizza 38. **GPS:** n44,84036 e8,04951.
10 ⛺€ 12 🚿Ch⛽🚽WC🚿included 🍽.
**Surface:** grassy/gravel. ⏲ 01/03-01/11.
**Distance:** 🚶2km 🚲30km ⊗on the spot 🚇2km.
**Remarks:** Bicycle rental, regional products.

| ⚜S | San Damiano d'Asti 🌿 | 25H2 |

**Azienda Agricola Cascina Piana**, Fraz S.Grato.
**GPS:** n44,85136 e8,07417.⬆

25 ⛺€ 8 ⛽🚿Ch ⚡(8x)🚽WC🚿 included. **Location:** Rural,
comfortable, isolated, quiet. **Surface:** grassy.
⏲ 01/02-30/06 and 01/09-30/11.
**Distance:** 🚶1,5km ⊗1,5km 🚇700m.

| 🏕S | Sanfront | 25G2 |

Via Montebracco, SP26. **GPS:** n44,64944 e7,32056.⬆➡.

15 ⛺free ⛽🚿Chfree. **Location:** Urban, simple. **Surface:** unpaved.
⏲ 01/01-31/12.
**Distance:** 🚶on the spot 🏊Po 650m ⊗550m 🚇750m 🚌150m.
**Remarks:** At sports park, max. 24h.

| 🏕S | Santa Maria Maggiore ⛷ | 23A2 |

**Area Verde Attrezzata**, Via Alfredo Belcastro/via Pineta.
**GPS:** n46,13219 e8,45500.⬆➡🚿.

32 ⛺€ 20/24h ⛽🚿Ch ⚡🚐 **Location:** Rural.
**Surface:** grassy/gravel. ⏲ 01/01-31/12.
**Distance:** ⊗200m 🚴on the spot.
**Remarks:** Max. 48h.

| ⚜S | Santa Maria Maggiore ⛷ | 23A2 |

**Agriturismo Al Piano delle Lutte**, Via Domodossola 57.
**GPS:** n46,13569 e8,44753.

6 ⛺€ 10/24h ⛽🚿Ch ⚡according consumption WC🚿🚽
**Location:** Rural, simple. **Surface:** grassy/gravel.
⏲ 01/01-31/12.
**Distance:** ⊗1,5km 🚇1,4km 🚐on the spot 🚌on the spot.
**Remarks:** Regional products.

| 🏕S | Sant'Antonino di Susa | 25G2 |

**Area Sosta Il Sentiero Dei Franchi**, Borgo Cresto 16/1.
**GPS:** n45,09973 e7,27754.⬆.

---

20 ⛺€ 10 ⛽🚿Chincluded ⚡€ 2. **Location:** Rural, simple,
comfortable, quiet. **Surface:** grassy/gravel. ⏲ 01/01-31/12.
**Distance:** 🚶1km ⊗on the spot 🚇3km 🚌3km 🚴on the spot.
**Remarks:** Check in at restaurant.

| 🏕S | Sestriere ⛷❄ | 25F2 |

**Lago Losetta**, Strada Azzurri d'Italia. **GPS:** n44,96465 e6,88141.⬆.

60 ⛺€ 15/24h ⛽🚿Ch ⚡WC🚿 included. **Location:** Rural.
**Surface:** unpaved. ⏲ 01/01-31/12.
**Distance:** 🚶800m 🏔on the spot 🚡on the spot ⊗1km 🚌Shuttle
bus to ski-piste.
**Remarks:** Altitude 2046m, monitored parking.

| 🏕S | Sommariva Perno | 25H2 |

**Area comunale**, Loc.Piano, SP0. **GPS:** n44,75126 e7,89667.⬆.

10 ⛺free ⛽🚿Chfree. **Location:** Rural, simple, noisy.
**Surface:** gravel. ⏲ 01/01-31/12.
**Distance:** 🚶500m 🚲13km ⊗50m 🚇250m 🚌on the spot
🚴on the spot.
**Remarks:** Max. 48h.

| 🏕S | Susa 🌿 | 25G1 |

Piazza Repubblica. **GPS:** n45,13861 e7,05389.⬆.

12 ⛺€ 7/24h ⛽🚿Chincluded ⚡€ 1/kWh. **Location:** Urban, simple,
central. **Surface:** asphalted. ⏲ 01/01-31/12.
**Distance:** 🚶300m ⊗500m 🚇200m 🚌150m.

| 🏕S | Tagliolo Monferrato | 26A2 |

Str. del Varo. **GPS:** n44,63960 e8,67126.⬆➡.
21 ⛺€ 5/24h ⛽🚿Ch.
**Location:** Rural, simple, quiet. **Surface:** grassy/gravel.
⏲ 01/01-31/12.
**Distance:** 🚶250m 🚲2km ⊗200m 🚇400m.
**Remarks:** Max. 72h, keycard barrier at Bar/Tabac, caution € 10.

| 🏕S | Torino 🌿🍴 | 25H2 |

Corso Casale 327. **GPS:** n45,08084 e7,72993.⬆➡.

IT

10 ⚡free 🚰🔧Chfree. **Location:** Urban, noisy. **Surface:** asphalted.
🅿 01/01-31/12.
**Distance:** 🚶on the spot ⚓Po 700m ⊗100m 🚂150m.
**Remarks:** Parking funicular railway.

`🏕 S` **Torino** 🌿🍦 `25H2`
**Parco Ruffini**, Corso Lione/Corso Carlo Piaggia, Turin (Torino).
**GPS:** n45,05686 e7,63166.⬆.

20 ⚡free 🚰🔧Chfree. **Location:** Urban, simple, noisy.
**Surface:** asphalted. 🅿 01/01-31/12.
**Distance:** 🚶city centre 5km ⊗on the spot 🚂1km 🚋on the spot.

`🏕 S` **Torino** 🌿🍦 `25H2`
**Parking Caio Mario**, Corso Giovanni Agnelli, Turin (Torino).
**GPS:** n45,02888 e7,63924.⬆.

57 ⚡€ 18/24h 🚰€ 0,75 🔧€ 0,75 Ch€ 0,75 🚿€ 3/24h
WC€ 0,60/minutes 🚿free.🚐🧺 **Location:** Urban, comfortable.
**Surface:** grasstiles. 🅿 01/01-31/12.
**Distance:** 🚶4km 🚲4km ⊗100m 🚂100m 🚋Tram 4 centre.
**Remarks:** Max. 5 days, monitored parking 24/24.

**Tourist information Turin (Torino):**
Ⓜ Mole Antonelliana. National Film museum.
Ⓜ Museo Nazionale dell'Automobile, Corso Unità d'Italia 40. Museum
of motor-cars. 🅾 Tue-Sa, 10-18.30h, Su 10-20.30h 🅾 Mo.
Ⓜ Palazzo Madame. Historical art.
✚ Palazzo Reale. Royal palace.
✝ Cathedral, 1498.
✝ Basilica di Superga. Baroque basilica.

`🏕 S` **Usseaux** 🌿🌲🍽 `25G2`
**Magic Forest**, Strada Comunale dell'inverso 1.
**GPS:** n45,04170 e6,98518.⬆.

100 ⚡€ 15 🚰🔧Ch 🚿WC🚽€ 1 🅾€ 5 🚿included. **Location:** Rural,
comfortable. **Surface:** grassy. 🅾 01/06-01/09.
**Distance:** ⚓550m ⊗on the spot 🚂1km 🚶on the spot.
**Remarks:** Grill and picknic area.

`🏕 S` **Usseaux** 🌿🌲🍽 `25G2`
**Lago di Laux**, Via Lago 7. **GPS:** n45,04166 e7,02222.➡.

100 ⚡€ 15/24h 🚰€ 3 🔧€ 3 Ch🚿(54x)€ 2,50/24h 🚿.
**Location:** Rural, simple, isolated, quiet. **Surface:** grassy.
🅾 01/06-30/09 🅾 with mucht snowfall.
**Distance:** 🚶500m ⚓200m ⊗on the spot 🚂5km.
**Remarks:** Altitude 1450m, pay at restaurant, playground.

`🏕 S` **Valdieri** 🏔🐏 `25G3`
**Centro Alpino S.Anna**, Loc. S. Anna. **GPS:** n44,24513 e7,32548.⬆➡.

40 ⚡€ 12/24h 🚰🔧Chincluded 🚿€ 2.
**Location:** Rural. **Surface:** grassy/gravel. 🅾 01/05-30/09.
**Distance:** 🚶100m ⚓on the spot ⊗100m 🚂350m.
**Remarks:** At sports park, narrow entrance (bridge).

`🏕 S` **Valdieri** 🏔🐏 `25G3`
**Parco Alpi Marittime**, Terme di Valdieri. **GPS:** n44,20546 e7,26840.

⚡€ 12/night 🚰🔧Ch 🚿WC. **Location:** Rural. **Surface:** gravel.
🅾 01/01-31/12.
**Distance:** 🚋700m 🚶on the spot.

`🏕 S` **Valle Mosso** `22H3`
Piazza Alpini d'Italia. **GPS:** n45,63316 e8,14629.⬆.

3 ⚡free 🚰🔧Chfree.
**Location:** Urban, simple. **Surface:** asphalted. 🅾 01/01-31/12.
**Distance:** 🚶on the spot 🚂on the spot 🚋50m.

`🏕 S` **Varallo** `22H3`
**Area Comunale**, Via Sant'Antonio. **GPS:** n45,81797 e8,24857.⬆.

8 ⚡€ 10/24h 🚰🔧Ch 🚿(4x)included.
**Location:** Urban, quiet. **Surface:** gravel/sand. 🅾 01/01-31/12.
**Distance:** 🚶500m 🚂500m.
**Remarks:** To be paid at town hall.

`🏕 S` **Venaria Reale** `25G1`
**Relax and Go**, Via Scodeggio 15. **GPS:** n45,14108 e7,62404.➡.

15 ⚡€ 22/24h 🚰🔧Ch 🚿WC🚽included. **Location:** Rural, simple.
**Surface:** grassy. 🅾 01/01-31/12.
**Distance:** 🚶1km 🚲2km ⊗500m 🚂500m 🚌bus GTT, tram
72>Turin.
**Remarks:** Departure >8h, borrow cycles for free.

`🏕 S` **Venasca** `25G3`
SP8, Via Provinciale. **GPS:** n44,56620 e7,39328.⬆➡.

20 ⚡free 🚰🔧Chfree WC. **Location:** Rural, simple, noisy.
**Surface:** asphalted. 🅾 01/01-31/12.
**Distance:** 🚶600m ⚓on the spot ⊗750m 🚋650m.

`🏕 S` **Verbania** ⚓🧺 `23A3`
**Punto Sosta Camper**, Viale Giuseppe Azari, 97.
**GPS:** n45,93122 e8,55317.⬆.

34 ⚡€ 6/12h, € 12/24h 🚰🔧Ch 🚿(18x)included. 🚐
**Location:** Urban, simple, quiet. **Surface:** asphalted.
🅾 01/01-31/12.
**Distance:** 🚶900m ⚓1,2km ⊗200m 🚲on the spot 🚶on the spot.
**Remarks:** Max. 48h.

`🏕 S` **Verbania** ⚓🧺 `23A3`
Via Brigata Cesare Battisti. **GPS:** n45,94027 e8,57676.⬆➡.
10 ⚡free. **Location:** Urban, simple, noisy. **Surface:** asphalted.
🅾 01/01-31/12.
**Distance:** 🚶350m 🚲on the spot ⊗350m.
**Remarks:** Along river.

`S` **Verbania** ⚓🧺 `23A3`
Corso Europa 66. **GPS:** n45,92732 e8,56266.
🚰🔧Ch.

`🏕 S` **Vercelli** 🌿 `26A1`
Via Trento, c/o piazzale Pala-hockey. **GPS:** n45,33417 e8,41861.⬆.

10 ⚡free 🚰🔧free. **Location:** Urban, simple. **Surface:** asphalted.
🅾 01/01-31/12.
**Distance:** 🚶1,5km 🚲6km ⊗50m 🚂1,5km 🚋on the spot.

**Tourist information Vercelli:**
✝ Basilica di Sant'Andrea. Basilica, part of abbey.

`🏕 S` **Vernante** `25G3`
**Piazza Vermenagna**, E74. **GPS:** n44,24489 e7,53219.⬆.

**606**

IT

20 🛏 € 6,50 🚰 included. **Location:** Rural, simple. **Surface:** asphalted. ⬛ 01/01-31/12. **Distance:** 🛒200m ⊗200m 🚰300m on the spot 🏊 on the spot.

### ⬛S Vialfrè 25H1
Via Luigi Emanuel, SP55. **GPS:** n45,38298 e7,81754. ⬆

7 🛏 free 🚰 ⬛Ch free. **Location:** Rural, simple. **Surface:** grasstiles. ⬛ 01/01-31/12. **Distance:** 🛒 on the spot 🚲6km ⊗300m 🚰300m 🚰200m.

### ⬛S Vidracco 25H1
Damanhur Crea, Via Baldissero 21. **GPS:** n45,42884 e7,75327. ⬆

30 🛏 € 8/24h 🚰 ⬛Ch 🚿(24x)WC included. **Location:** Urban, simple, quiet. **Surface:** asphalted. ⬛ 01/01-31/12. **Distance:** 🛒200m 🚰650m ⊗cafetaria 🚰 on the spot 🚰500m. **Remarks:** Next to sports fields.

**Tourist information Vidracco:**
👁 Damanhur Crea, Via Baldissero 21. Extraordinary Italian artistic and spritual community.

### ⬛S Vignole Borbera 26A2
Via Circonvallazione. **GPS:** n44,70843 e8,88525. ⬆

10 🛏 free 🚰 ⬛Ch. **Location:** Urban, comfortable. **Surface:** asphalted. ⬛ 01/01-31/12. **Distance:** 🛒300m ⊗200m 🚰200m.

### ⬛S Villar Focchiardo 🏔🌲 25G2
Area Camper Villar Focchiardo, Via Fratta, SS24. **GPS:** n45,11336 e7,22408. ⬆➡

54 🛏 € 5-10, weekend € 15 🚰 ⬛Ch included. **Location:** Rural, comfortable, quiet. **Surface:** grassy. ⬛ 01/04-30/09. **Distance:** 🛒500m 🚲4,5km ⊗450m 🚰950m. **Remarks:** Max. 72h.

### ⬛S Villar Pellice 25G2
Parco Flissia, Via Cave del Fin. **GPS:** n44,80472 e7,15083. ⬆

20 🛏 € 8 🚰 ⬛ChWC included. **Location:** Rural, simple, isolated. **Surface:** grassy. ⬛ 01/04-01/10. **Distance:** 🛒500m 🚰 on the spot 🎣 fishing permit obligatory ⊗650m 🚰 agriturismo. **Remarks:** Max. 48h, service passerby € 3.

### ⬛S Vinadio ♒ 25G3
Area di Sosta Communale, Bagni di Vinadio, Fraz. Strapesi. **GPS:** n44,28747 e7,07534. ⬆

30 🛏 € 8/24h 🚰 ⬛Ch free. **Location:** Rural, simple. **Surface:** grassy/gravel. ⬛ 01/01-31/12. **Distance:** 🛒300m, Vinadio 10km 🚰 on the spot 🚲 on the spot. **Remarks:** Altitude 1350m, parking at the spa resort of Strapeis.

### ⬛S Vinadio ♒ 25G3
Campeggio dei Forti, Piazza d'Armi, SS21. **GPS:** n44,30667 e7,17083. ⬆

🛏 € 10-20 🚰 ⬛Ch 🚿 € 2/day ⬛ € 1,50 🚿 included. 🏪 **Surface:** grassy/gravel. ⬛ 01/01-31/12. **Distance:** 🛒400m 🚰 on the spot.

### ⬛S Volpedo 26B2
Lungo Curone Matteotti. **GPS:** n44,88512 e8,98707. ⬆➡

6 🛏 free 🚰 ⬛Ch free. **Location:** Rural. **Surface:** grassy/gravel. ⬛ 01/01-31/12. **Distance:** 🛒600m 🚰 on the spot ⊗400m 🚰500m. **Remarks:** At sports park.

# Trentino South Tyrol

### ⬛S Andalo 🏔🌲❄ 23D2
Via Rindole, 6, Loc. Rindole. **GPS:** n46,16113 e11,00647. ⬆➡

80 🛏 € 15-20, dog € 3 🚰 ⬛Ch included. 🚿(20x) € 5. **Location:** Rural, simple, quiet. **Surface:** asphalted. ⬛ summer. **Distance:** 🛒200m ⊗ on the spot 🚲 on the spot. **Remarks:** Service passerby € 10, beautiful view.

### ⬛S Arco ⛲ 23D3
Piazzale Carmellini, Viale Paolina Caproni. **GPS:** n45,92232 e10,89032. ⬆

14 🛏 € 1/4h, max. € 10/24h. 🏧 **Location:** Urban, simple. **Surface:** asphalted. ⬛ 01/01-31/12. **Distance:** 🛒200m ⊗200m 🚲 on the spot. **Remarks:** Max. 72h.

### S Arco ⛲ 23D3
Viale Rovereto. **GPS:** n45,91820 e10,89225. ⬆
🚰 ⬛Ch free. ⬛ water disconnected in winter.

### 🍴S Avio 🏔 23D3
Agriturismo Erta, Via Pozza, Località Erta 2. **GPS:** n45,74292 e10,96807. ⬆

25 🛏 € 15 🚰 ⬛Ch 🚿(16x)WC 🚿 included. **Location:** Rural. **Surface:** grassy. ⬛ 01/01-31/12. **Distance:** 🛒800m 🚲 200m 🚲300m ⊗ on the spot 🚰800m 🚰 on the spot 🚲 on the spot 🏊 on the spot 🏔20km.

### ⬛S Barbiano 🏔 23E1
Kollmann Stop, Frazione Colma, SS12. **GPS:** n46,58728 e11,52401. ⬆

10 🛏 € 12 🚰 € 5 ⬛Ch 🚿 included. **Location:** Simple, noisy. **Surface:** gravel. ⬛ 01/01-31/12. **Distance:** 🛒300m 🚲 9km ⊗300m 🚰300m 🚲 on the spot 🚲 on the spot. **Remarks:** Along through road, max. 48h, money in envelope in mail box.

### ⬛S Baselga di Pine ❄ 23E2
Ice Rink Piné, Via Dello Stadio. **GPS:** n46,12617 e11,25382. ⬆

10 🛏free.
**Location:** Rural, simple, quiet. **Surface:** metalled.
**Distance:** 🚰1km.
**Remarks:** >18.00h free.

---

### ⬛S **Bezzecca** 🎵 23D3

Via Peluca. **GPS:** n45,89861 e10,71833. ⬆️➡️.

22 🛏€ 10/24h 🚰🗑Chincluded. 🅿 **Location:** Rural, simple,
isolated, quiet. **Surface:** grasstiles. 📅 01/04-01/11.
**Distance:** 🚰450m 🏊2km ⊗300m.

---

### ⬛S **Bolzano/Bozen** 🌊🍲🏔 23E1

**Parking Fiera Messe**, Via Bruno Buozzi. **GPS:** n46,47417 e11,32617. ⬆️.

30 🛏free 🚰🗑Chfree. **Location:** Urban, simple, noisy.
**Surface:** asphalted. 📅 01/01-31/12.
**Distance:** 🚰centre 4km 🚲1,1km ⊗on the spot 🚱4km 🚮on the spot.
**Remarks:** Along railwayline.

---

### ⬛S **Bolzano/Bozen** 🌊🍲🏔 23E1

Via Maso della Pieve. **GPS:** n46,47327 e11,33693. ⬆️.

8 🛏€ 1/h 8-19h, Sa 8-13h, overnight stay free 🚰🗑Ch.🅿
**Location:** Urban, simple, noisy. **Surface:** asphalted.
📅 01/01-31/12.
**Distance:** 🚰city centre 3km 🚱100m 🚮on the spot.

---

### ⬛S **Borgo Valsugana** 🌊🍲🏔🎵 23E2

Via Tommaso Temanza. **GPS:** n46,05444 e11,46361. ⬆️➡️.

18 🛏€ 10/24h 🚰🗑Ch🧹included. **Location:** Urban, simple.
**Surface:** grasstiles.
**Distance:** 🚰100m 🏊20m 🚲20m ⊗100m 🚱100m 🚮on the spot.
**Remarks:** Max. 48h, service passerby € 5.

---

### ⬛S **Braies** 🏔🌊 23F1

**P2**, Lago di Braies, Fraz. San Vito. **GPS:** n46,70265 e12,08520. ➡️.

25 🛏€ 12 🚱€ 0,50. 🅿 **Location:** Rural, simple, quiet. **Surface:** gravel.
📅 30/05-31/10.
**Distance:** 🚰Braies 5km 🏊Lago di Braies 250m ⊗250m 🚱5km 🚮on
the spot 🚶on the spot.

---

### ⬛S **Braies** 🌊🏔🌊 23F1

**P1**, Lago di Braies, Fraz. San Vito. **GPS:** n46,70577 e12,08698. ⬆️.
🛏€ 9/day, € 7/night. **Surface:** gravel. 📅 01/01-31/12.
**Distance:** 🏊Lake Prags 850m.

---

### ⬛ **Brentonico** 🌊🏕🏔🎵 23D3

Via al Dosset. **GPS:** n45,81540 e10,95581. ⬆️➡️.

11 🛏€ 7 🚱€ 2/100liter 🗑Ch🧹€ 3/24h. **Location:** Rural,
comfortable, quiet. **Surface:** grasstiles. 📅 01/01-31/12.
**Distance:** 🚰400m 🚲10km ⊗250m 🚱300m.

---

### ⬛ **Brunico/Bruneck** 🌊🏕🏔❄ 23F1

**P2**, Piazza Mercato di Stegona. **GPS:** n46,79558 e11,93006. 🚶.

25 🛏€ 3. **Location:** Urban, simple, noisy. **Surface:** gravel.
📅 01/01-31/12.
**Distance:** 🚰800m ⊗500m 🚱500m 🚮on the spot 🚱on the spot
🚶on the spot.

**Tourist information Brunico/Bruneck:**
ℹ️ Associazione Turistica, Via Europa,24. Fortified city, 14th century.
Ⓜ️ Regional museum.
✳️ Annual fair. 📅 last week Oct.

---

### ⬛S **Caldaro** 🌊 23E2

**Camper Lago di Caldero**, San Giuseppe al Lago.
**GPS:** n46,38332 e11,25690. ⬆️➡️.

35 🛏€ 25, tourist tax incl 🚰🗑Ch🧹WC🚱€ 3,50/3,50
🛜included. 🅿 **Location:** Rural, comfortable, quiet. **Surface:** gravel.
📅 01/01-31/12.
**Distance:** 🚰5km Caldero 🏊Private beach ⊗50m 🚱Nearby campsite
🚮on the spot 🚱on the spot 🚶on the spot.
**Remarks:** Next to campsite, max. 4 days.

---

### ⬛S **Caldes** 23D2

**Rafting Val di Sole**, Loc. Contrè. **GPS:** n46,36139 e10,94528.

---

30 🛏€ 10, Jul € 13, Aug € 15 🚰🗑🧹(6x)€ 6 WC.
**Location:** Rural. **Surface:** asphalted. 📅 01/04-30/09.
**Distance:** 🚰2km ⊗200m 🚱2km 🚮900m.
**Remarks:** At sports centre, to be paid at bar.

---

### ⬛S **Caldonazzo** ⚓ 23E2

Via al Lago. **GPS:** n46,00501 e11,26307. ⬆️.

30 🛏€ 8/6-22h (01/04-30/9), € 10/night. 🅿 **Location:** Simple.
**Surface:** grassy/sand. 📅 01/01-31/12.
**Distance:** 🚰2km 🚱50m ⊗300m.
**Remarks:** Payment only with coins.

---

### ⬛S **Castelfondo** 23E1

**Belverde**, Via Alfonso Lamarmora. **GPS:** n46,45831 e11,13163. ⬆️.

16 🛏€ 15/24h 🚰🗑Ch🧹(16x). 🅿 **Location:** Rural, simple, quiet.
**Surface:** gravel.
**Distance:** ⊗800m 🚱800m 🚮300m 🚶on the spot.
**Remarks:** Max. 72h.

---

### ⬛S **Cavalese** ⚓ 23E2

**P Fondovalle**, SP232. **GPS:** n46,28438 e11,47256. ⬆️.

24 🛏€ 12, winter free 🚰🗑. **Location:** Simple.
**Surface:** grasstiles/metalled. 📅 01/01-31/12.
**Remarks:** Water closed during wintertime.

---

### ⬛S **Chiusa** 🌊🏔❄ 23E1

**Gamp**, Via Gries 10. **GPS:** n46,64128 e11,57244. ➡️.

20 🛏€ 14,50-16/24h 2 pers. + 2 children incl, dog € 2 🚰🗑Ch🧹
included. **Location:** Rural, simple. **Surface:** grassy. 📅 01/01-31/12.
**Distance:** 🚰300m 🚲800m ⊗on the spot 🚱mini market 🚮100m
🚱on the spot 🚶on the spot.
**Remarks:** Bread-service.

## Corvara in Badia · 23F1

**P Corvara**, Strada Planac SS244. **GPS:** n46,54105 e11,88388.

10 free. **Location:** Rural, simple, isolated. **Surface:** gravel. 01/01-31/12.
**Distance:** 3,5km on the spot 3,5km on the spot on the spot.

## Dimaro · 23D2

**Camper Solander**, Loc. Rovina. **GPS:** n46,32488 e10,86215.

10 € 20/24h, € 10/night Ch WC included € 1.
**Location:** Rural. **Surface:** gravel. 01/01-31/12.
**Distance:** 500m on the spot.
**Remarks:** Near campsite Dolomiti.

## Dimaro · 23D2

**Dolomiti**, Via Gole. **GPS:** n46,32507 e10,86267.
15 € 20-31 Ch included. **Location:** Rural.
**Surface:** asphalted. 01/01-31/12.
**Distance:** on the spot on the spot.
**Remarks:** Max. 48h.

## Folgaria · 23E3

**Area Sosta Bucaneve**, Via Negheli 87. **GPS:** n45,91849 e11,19255.

25 € 12.
**Location:** Simple. **Surface:** grasstiles.
01/01-31/12.
**Distance:** 300m on the spot 100m.
**Remarks:** Check in and pay at reception, golf court, shuttle bus.

## Folgaria · 23E3

SS3501. **GPS:** n45,91397 e11,17081.
€ 1 Ch.

## Folgarida · 23D2

**Hotel Belvedere**, Piazzale Belvedere 1. **GPS:** n46,29716 e10,86741.
10 € 20 € 5. **Surface:** asphalted. 01/01-31/12.
**Distance:** on the spot 200m 150m.

## Glorenza · 23D1

**Glurms Camping im Park**, > SS41. **GPS:** n46,67067 e10,54520.

40 € 12-16 + € 0,70/pp Ch included € 2 WC € 0,50.
**Location:** Rural. **Surface:** grassy. 01/01-31/12.
**Distance:** 500m on the spot 600m 1km 650m.
**Remarks:** Along the Adige river, water closed during wintertime.

## Glorenza · 23D1

**Camping Gloria Vallis**, Wiesenweg 5. **GPS:** n46,67322 e10,56942.
15 € 15, dog € 2 Ch included WC. **Location:** Rural.
**Surface:** grassy. 01/01-31/12.
**Distance:** 500m on the spot 700m 1km 1,5km on the spot.

## La Villa in Badia · 23F1

**Odlina**, Strada Ninz, 49. **GPS:** n46,58889 e11,90028.

45 summer € 25, winter € 30 Ch WC included € 5
€ 3. **Location:** Rural, luxurious, quiet. **Surface:** metalled.
01/01-31/12.
**Distance:** 400m 150m 150m on the spot on the spot
on the spot 300m.
**Remarks:** Reservation for Christmas holidays: info@odina.it, use of sauna against payment.

## Lago · 23E2

Via Tresselume, Tesero. **GPS:** n46,28291 e11,52557.

30 € 6 € 1 € 2 Ch € 1 (12x) € 2/8h.
**Location:** Rural, simple. **Surface:** metalled. 01/01-31/12.
**Distance:** 200m 200m 300m on the spot on the spot.
**Remarks:** Max. 48h, bicycle rental.

## Lavarone · 23E2

**Prà Grando**, Via Padova. **GPS:** n45,93602 e11,27099.

40 € 16,50 May/June/July, € 19 Aug, € 18 Dec-April Ch
(3x) € 1/3minutes included. **Location:** Rural, simple, quiet.
**Surface:** grassy/gravel. 01/05-30/09, 01/12-31/03.
**Distance:** 300m 32km Lago di Lavarone 1km 1km 300m
300m 300m 1km 1km.

## Lavarone · 23E2

SS 349, Loc Moar. **GPS:** n45,94575 e11,26397.

18 € 13/24h € 0,50 Ch. **Location:** Rural, simple, quiet.
**Surface:** metalled. 01/01-31/12.
**Distance:** 800m Lago di Lavarone 1,9km 500m.
**Remarks:** Next to sports fields, max. 72h.

## Levico Terme · 23E2

**Area Sosta Camper Valsugana**, Loc Pleina.
**GPS:** n46,00691 e11,28706.

50 € 19/24h Ch ,10Amp WC € 4 included.
**Location:** Rural, comfortable. **Surface:** grassy. 23/03-05/11.
**Distance:** 1,3km 200m, Lido di Levico 1,1km 50m 50m
on the spot on the spot on the spot.
**Remarks:** Max. 3 nights, check in at reception campsite.

## Levico Terme · 23E2

**Area 47**, SP1. **GPS:** n46,00415 e11,28880.

18 € 18-25, 14/07-18/08 € 30 Ch WC included.
**Location:** Rural, comfortable. **Surface:** asphalted.
27/04-09/09.
**Distance:** 1,3km on the spot.
**Remarks:** Including access to swimming pool and private beach.

## Mezzano · 23F2

Via del Pian. **GPS:** n46,15284 e11,81198.

20 € 14/24h Ch included € 1. **Location:** Urban, central,
noisy. **Surface:** grasstiles. 01/01-31/12.
**Distance:** 450m on the spot 350m.

## Moena · 23E2

**Bar Il Giardino**, SS 48 Forno di Moena. **GPS:** n46,35238 e11,63149.

40 € 13, 01/07-31/08, 25/12-08/01 € 15 € 5 Ch € 4/24h WC.
**Location:** Rural, comfortable, central. **Surface:** grassy/metalled.
01/01-31/12.
**Distance:** 3,5km 500m 2km 300m on the spot on the
spot on the spot.
**Remarks:** Max. 48h, skibus comes at parking.

## Molveno · 23D2

**Area attrezzata per camper Lago di Molveno**, Via Lungolago, 25, Loc.
Ischia. **GPS:** n46,14122 e10,95819.

54 € 8-15 Ch included. **Location:** Rural, simple, quiet.

IT

**Surface:** metalled. ▣ 01/01-31/12.
**Distance:** 🚶800m ⛵200m ⛱200m 🏊100m.
**Remarks:** Max. 48h.

### 🅿🆂 Pergine Valsugana 🛒 23E2
**Soleando Camperparking**, Via al lago 23/A.
**GPS:** n46,05121 e11,23593.⬆.

10 🛏 € 12 🚰🍽Ch🧹 included.
**Location:** Urban, simple, noisy. **Surface:** gravel. ▣ 01/01-31/12.
**Distance:** 🚶600m ⛱Lago di Caldonazzo 1km ⊗300m 🛒300m 🚌100m 🏊 on the spot.
**Tourist information Pergine Valsugana:**
ℹ www.apt.trento.it. City at the foot of the Dolomites with historical centre.
Ⓜ Palazzo Pretorio, Trento. Ecclesiastical museum.

### 🅿🆂 Ponte Arche 23D2
Via Lungo Sarca. **GPS:** n46,03707 e10,86585.
15 🛏 € 5/24h 🚰🍽Ch.
**Location:** Rural. **Surface:** grassy. ◉ winter.
**Distance:** 🚶1,5km ⛱on the spot ⊗400m 🛒800m 🚌350m.
**Remarks:** Along river.

### 🅿🆂 Predazzo 🏔❄ 23E2
**Latemar 2200**, SS48, dir Moena. **GPS:** n46,32582 e11,59970.⬆.

50 🛏free, peak season € 7-10/24h 🚰🍽Ch included.🚐
**Location:** Rural, simple, noisy. **Surface:** asphalted/gravel.
▣ 01/01-31/12.
**Distance:** 🚶2,5km 🛒2,5km 🚌on the spot 🚴on the spot 🚶on the spot 🚵on the spot 🎿on the spot.
**Remarks:** Parking ski-lifts.

### 🅿🆂 Rabbi 23D2
**Al Plan**, Loc. Plan, Bagni di Rabbi. **GPS:** n46,40768 e10,79559.⬆➡.

105 🛏 € 14-23, 2 pers. incl., dog € 2,50 🚰🍽Ch🧹WCincluded 🧺against payment ◉. **Location:** Rural, comfortable.
**Surface:** metalled. ▣ 30/04-14/10.
**Distance:** 🚶600m 🛒600m 🚌on the spot 🚴on the spot 🚶on the spot.
**Remarks:** Max. 48h.

### Racines 🏔 20E3
**Sportzone Ratschings**, Belprato, Stanghe.
**GPS:** n46,88254 e11,38383.⬆.

---

20 🛏free. **Location:** Rural, simple. **Surface:** gravel.
◉ 01/01-31/12.
**Distance:** 🚶400m 🚴5km ⊗400m 🛒400m 🚌400m 🚶Gilfenklam-mroute.

### 🅿🆂 Riva del Garda 🌿🍃 23D3
Via Monte Brione. **GPS:** n45,87986 e10,85872.⬆.

41 🛏 € 0,50/h, max. € 24/48h 🚰🍽Chincluded. 🚐
**Location:** Urban, simple. **Surface:** grasstiles.
◉ 01/11-07/12.
**Distance:** 🚶1,5km ⛱200m.
**Remarks:** Max. 48h.
**Tourist information Riva del Garda:**
Ⓜ Museo Civico, Piazza Battisti.

### 🅿🆂 Rovereto 🌿 23E3
**Area Camper Quercia**, Via Palestrina. **GPS:** n45,90232 e11,03704.⬆➡.

15 🛏 € 8/12h, € 16/24h 🚰🍽Ch🧹WC🧺included ◉.🚐🧹
**Location:** Urban, simple, noisy. **Surface:** grasstiles.
◉ 01/01-31/12.
**Distance:** 🚶1,5km 🚴2km.
**Remarks:** Caution € 5, bicycle rental, picnic tables available.
**Tourist information Rovereto:**
Ⓜ Museo Storico Italiano della Guerra, Via Castelbarco, 7. War museum.
◉ Mo-Fri 8.30-12.30h, 14-18h ◉ 01/01-28/02.
✠ Castel Beseno, Besenello. ▣ Tue-Su.

### 🅿🆂 San Candido 🏔❄ 23F1
**Area di Sosta Camper**, Via Prato alla Drava, 1/A.
**GPS:** n46,73924 e12,36559.➡.

90 🛏 € 20 🚰🍽Ch🧹WCincluded 🧺€ 2. 🔌 **Location:** Rural, comfortable, quiet. **Surface:** gravel. ▣ 01/01-31/12.
**Distance:** 🚶6km ⊗200m 🛒500m 🚌on the spot 🚴on the spot 🚶on the spot 🚵2km 🎿500m.
**Remarks:** Bicycle rental, shuttle bus San Candido and skipistes € 1/pp.

### 🅿🆂 San Martino di Castrozza 🏔❄ 23F2
**Area Sosta Tognola**, Loc.Tognola. **GPS:** n46,25373 e11,80158.⬆.

90 🛏 € 10-15 🚰🍽included Ch🔥€ 1/80minutes. 🚐
**Location:** Rural, comfortable, quiet. **Surface:** gravel. ▣ 01/01-31/12.
**Distance:** 🚶1,5km ⊗500m 🚌on the spot 🚶on the spot 🚵on the spot.
**Remarks:** Next to ski-lift, free shuttle.

---

### 🎿🅿🆂 San Vigilio di Marebbe 🏔❄ 23F1
**Restaurant Pizzeria Rittenkeller**, Str. Ras Costa, 2.
**GPS:** n46,70630 e11,92920.➡.

120 🛏01/04-30/11 € 25, 01/12-31/03 € 30 🚰🍽Ch🧹
included,4Amp. **Location:** Rural, simple, quiet. **Surface:** gravel.
▣ 01/01-31/12.
**Distance:** 🚶600m 🚴500m ⊗on the spot 🛒600m 🚌600m 🎿on the spot 🚵600m.
**Remarks:** Next to ski-lift, breakfast-service, reservation for Christmas holidays: info@ritterkeller.it.

### 🅿🆂 Santa Cristina Valgardena 🏔 23E1
**P1 Monte Pana**, Strada Pana. **GPS:** n46,55174 e11,71624.⬆.

50 🛏 € 15/24h. 🚐
**Location:** Simple, isolated, quiet. **Surface:** gravel. ▣ 01/01-31/12.
**Distance:** 🚶2,5km ⊗on the spot 🛒2,5km 🚶on the spot 🎿on the spot 🚵on the spot.
**Remarks:** Altitude 1650m, max. 7 days, narrow entrance.

### 🅿🆂 Selva di Val Gardena 🏔❄ 23F1
**Piz Sella**, Strada Plan de Gralba. **GPS:** n46,53204 e11,77230.⬆.

50 🛏 € 12/24h. **Location:** Rural, simple. **Surface:** gravel.
▣ 01/01-31/12.
**Distance:** 🚶4km ⊗150m 🚶on the spot 🎿on the spot.
**Remarks:** Inclining pitches.

### 🅲🆂 Sesto/Sexten 🏔❄♨ 23F1
**Caravanpark Sexten**, SS52 St Josefstrasse 54.
**GPS:** n46,66741 e12,39996.➡.

35 🛏 € 24-36 🚰🍽Ch🧹,4Amp WC🧺included ◉€ 4 🔥€ 2.
**Location:** Rural, luxurious, quiet. **Surface:** grasstiles.
▣ 01/01-31/12.
**Distance:** 🚶3km ⊗on the spot 🛒on the spot 🚌on the spot 🚴on the spot 🚶on the spot 🎿900m 🚵on the spot.
**Remarks:** Max. 72h, sauna and spa.

### 🅿🆂 Smarano ♨🏔🌳 23E2
**Area Sosta Ostaria del Filò**, Viale Merlonga 48/a.
**GPS:** n46,34962 e11,10956.⬆.

43 ⛺ € 10-13 🚰🔌Ch♨ WC🛒 € 1 💧€ 4. **Location:** Rural, isolated, quiet. **Surface:** grassy. 🅿 01/01-31/12.
**Distance:** 🚶1km ⊗on the spot.
**Remarks:** Check in at restaurant.

| 📷Ⓢ | **Solda** 🏔 | 23D1 |

Forststraße. **GPS:** n46,51448 e10,59578.
25 ⛺free. **Location:** Rural, simple. **Surface:** gravel.
🅿 01/01-31/12.
**Distance:** 🚶1km ⊗100m 🚶on the spot 🚲on the spot.

| 🍴Ⓢ | **Tirolo** | 23E1 |

**Camperstellplatz Schneeburghof**, Monte Benedetto 26.
**GPS:** n46,67780 e11,16490.⬆

55 ⛺ € 23 🚰🔌Ch♨ included. **Location:** Rural, comfortable.
**Surface:** gravel. 🅿 01/01-31/12.
**Distance:** ⚓on the spot.
**Remarks:** Bread-service, swimming pool (summer).

| 🍴Ⓢ | **Tonadico** 🏔❄ | 23F2 |

**Lanterna Verde**, Via Zocchet 10. **GPS:** n46,18216 e11,84318.➡

46 ⛺ € 16-20 🚰🔌Ch♨ WC included. **Location:** Rural, comfortable, quiet. **Surface:** grasstiles. 🅿 01/01-31/12.
**Distance:** 🚶1km ⊗100m 🚶1km ⚓on the spot 🚲on the spot 🚶on the spot 🛷15km 🎿15km.
**Remarks:** Max. 48h, check in at restaurant.

| 📷Ⓢ | **Trento** | 23E2 |

**P Zuffo**, Loc. Vela. **GPS:** n46,07650 e11,11050.⬆➡

20 ⛺ € 5 🚰€ 1 🔌Ch. **Location:** Simple, noisy. **Surface:** asphalted.
🅿 01/01-31/12.
**Distance:** 🚶1,8km ⛵150m 🚆200m.
**Remarks:** Max. 48h.

| 📷Ⓢ | **Trento** | 23E2 |

**Camper Trento Park**, Via Brennero, 181. **GPS:** n46,09438 e11,11335.
200 ⛺ € 15/24h 🚰🔌Ch♨ included WC🛒 € 1 📶.
**Location:** Urban, simple, noisy. **Surface:** asphalted.
🅿 01/03-31/10.
**Distance:** 🚶city centre 3km ⛵2km ⊗400m 🍺850m 🚆400m bus 3-11-17 > centre.

| 📷Ⓢ | **Trento** | 23E2 |

**GPS:** n46,04910 e11,12111.

---

30 ⛺ € 20 🚰🔌Ch♨€ 2 WC included. **Location:** Urban, comfortable, quiet. **Surface:** asphalted. 🅿 01/01-31/12.
**Distance:** 🚶on the spot ⊗1km 🚆1km.

| 📷Ⓢ | **Trento** | 23E2 |

**Parking Trentino**, Via Santi Cosma e Damiano 64.
**GPS:** n46,07674 e11,10411.⬆

20 ⛺ € 15 🚰🔌Ch♨ included. **Location:** Urban, simple, noisy.
**Surface:** grasstiles. 🅿 01/01-31/12.
**Distance:** 🚶1,8km ⊗300m ⊗300m 🚌bus > centre 15 min.
**Remarks:** Call for entrance code: 3389004343 Mr. Pisetta.

| 📷Ⓢ | **Trento** | 23E2 |

**P3 Giardino Botanico Fondo Viote**, SP85.
**GPS:** n46,02445 e11,03973.⬆

100 ⛺ € 4-10/10h, overnight stay free. **Location:** Rural, simple, isolated, quiet. **Surface:** asphalted. 🅿 01/01-31/12.
**Distance:** 🚶18km Trento ⊗150m 🚶on the spot 🚲on the spot 🚶on the spot 🚣on the spot.
**Remarks:** Altitude 1450m, max. 48h.

| 📷Ⓢ | **Tres** 🏔🍴 | 23E2 |

**Batuda**, SP della Predaia. **GPS:** n46,32040 e11,10202.⬆

15 ⛺ € 12/24h 🚰🔌Ch♨ WC included. **Location:** Rural.
**Surface:** grasstiles/metalled. 🅿 01/01-31/12.
**Distance:** 🚶800m ⊗1km.

| 🍴 | **Vezzano** | 23D2 |

**Vecchio Mulino**, Naran 1. **GPS:** n46,07684 e11,01980.⬆
10 ⛺ € 15.
**Location:** Rural, simple. **Surface:** grassy. 🅿 15/04-01/10.
**Distance:** ⊗on the spot.

# Lombardy

| 📷Ⓢ | **Biassono** | 23B3 |

Via al Parco/Via della Sciavatera. **GPS:** n45,63102 e9,28865.⬆➡

---

4 ⛺free 🚰🔌ChWCfree. **Location:** Rural, simple, isolated.
**Surface:** asphalted. 🅿 01/01-31/12.
**Distance:** 🚶500m ⊗300m 🛒Centro Commerciale Vilasanta 4km
🚆train > Milan 500m.

| 📷Ⓢ | **Borgofranco sul Po** | 26E1 |

Via Filipo Turati. **GPS:** n45,04775 e11,20524.⬆➡

4 ⛺free 🚰🔌Chfree. **Location:** Rural, simple, quiet.
**Surface:** grassy. 🅿 01/01-31/12 💧 water: frost.
**Distance:** 🚶600m ⚓1km ⊗200m ⊗300m 🚲200m 🚶200m.
**Remarks:** Playground.

| 📷Ⓢ | **Bormio** 🌼🏔❄ | 23C1 |

**Bormio 2000**, Via Battaglion Morbegno. **GPS:** n46,46260 e10,37190.⬆

80 ⛺ € 8/24h 🚰🔌Ch included. **Location:** Urban, comfortable.
**Surface:** gravel. 🅿 01/01-31/12.
**Distance:** 🚶500m ⊗500m 🚶on the spot.
**Remarks:** Parking funicular railway, service passerby € 5.

**Tourist information Bormio:**
ℹ Ufficio Informazioni e di Accoglienza Turistica, Via Roma, 131/b. Alps city, large winter sport area, also summer skiing.
⛷ Parco Nazionale dello Stelvio. Region with 50 glacier lakes and high mountain peaks. Access around Bormio.

| 📷Ⓢ | **Brescia** 🌼 | 23C3 |

**Agriturismo Cascina Maggi**, Via della Maggia 3.
**GPS:** n45,51232 e10,23634.

16 ⛺ € 15 🚰🔌Ch♨ included 📶. **Location:** Urban, comfortable.
**Surface:** metalled. 🅿 01/01-31/12.
**Distance:** 🚶2,5km ⊗on the spot 🍺500m 🚆on the spot.
**Remarks:** Max. 24h, check in at hotel, market Saturday.

| 📷Ⓢ | **Campione** | 23D3 |

**Area Camper Campione del Garda**, Via Verdi.
**GPS:** n45,75651 e10,74985.⬆

**IT**

30 ⌗€ 15/24h ⇌included. **Location:** Rural. **Surface:** unpaved. ◻ 01/04-31/10.
**Distance:** 500m ⚓on the spot ⊗200m 🚐100m.

### 🅿S Capo di Ponte 23C2
**Concarena**, Via Santo Stefano. **GPS:** n46,02447 e10,34325. ⬆➡.

12 ⌗€ 10/24h, 01/10-28/02 free ⇌🍴Ch ⚡(12x)WC⬚included.
**Location:** Rural. **Surface:** asphalted. ◻ 01/01-31/12.
**Distance:** 300m ⛽on the spot ⊗300m 🛒300m 🚐1km ♿on the spot.

### 🅿S Carenno 23B3
Via per il Colle. **GPS:** n45,79952 e9,46606. ⬆➡.
8 ⌗€ 5 ⇌🍴Ch ⚡WC⬚included. 🏠 **Location:** Simple, isolated, quiet. **Surface:** asphalted. ◻ 01/01-31/12.
**Distance:** 250m ⊗on the spot ♿on the spot ☂on the spot.
**Remarks:** Next to sports fields, max. 72h, pay at restaurant, steep entrance road.

### 🅿S Certosa di Pavia 🏛 26B1
**Parking Certosa**, Via di Vittorio, SP27. **GPS:** n45,25735 e9,14161. ⬆.

20 ⌗€ 15/24h ⇌🍴Ch ⚡WC⬚included. 🏠 **Location:** Simple. **Surface:** grassy/gravel. ◻ 01/01-31/12 ◻ water disconnected in winter. **Distance:** 1km ⊗200m ☂on the spot.
**Remarks:** Monastery Certosa di Pavia 450m.

### 🅿S Chiavenna 23B2
**Piazzale Leonardo da Vinci**, Via A. Moro, SS36.
**GPS:** n46,31424 e9,39631. ⬆➡.

20 ⌗free ⇌🍴Chfree. **Location:** Rural. **Surface:** asphalted. ◻ 01/01-31/12.
**Distance:** 800m ⊗500m 🛒200m.
**Remarks:** At sports park.

### 🅿S Chiesa in Valmalenco 23C2
Loc. Vassalini. **GPS:** n46,27020 e9,85670. ⬆.

---

20 ⌗free ⇌€ 3 🍴Ch. **Location:** Rural. **Surface:** gravel. ◻ 01/01-31/12.
**Distance:** 1km ⊗250m 🚲200m.
**Remarks:** Near sports fields.

### 🅿S Clusone 23C3
**Busgarina**, Via Vago 6, loc Fiorine. **GPS:** n45,87312 e9,91642. ⬆.

80 ⌗€ 15/24h ⇌🍴Chincluded ⚡(33x)€ 2 ⬚€ 1/7minutes 📶.
**Location:** Rural. **Surface:** unpaved. ◻ 01/01-31/12.
**Distance:** 3km ⛽on the spot ⊗on the spot ♿on the spot ☂on the spot.
**Remarks:** Barbecue place, picnic area, playground, swimming pool.

### 🅿S Clusone 23C3
Viale Vittorio Emanuele. **GPS:** n45,88926 e9,95812. ⬆.

5 ⌗free ⇌🍴Chfree 📶.
**Location:** Rural. **Surface:** asphalted. ◻ 01/01-31/12.
**Distance:** 600m ⊗200m 🛒on the spot 🚐200m.
**Remarks:** Max. 48h.

### 🍴S Colico 🏖🏔🏖 23B2
**L'Ontano**, Via Montecchio Nord. **GPS:** n46,14213 e9,37452. ⬆➡.

25 ⌗€ 20/24h ⇌🍴Ch ⚡WC⬚€ 1/3minutes 📶included. 🚻📹
**Location:** Rural, simple, quiet. **Surface:** metalled.
◻ 01/02-31/12.
**Distance:** 500m ⚓on the spot ⛽on the spot ⊗on the spot 🛒1km 🚐1km ♿on the spot ☂on the spot.
**Remarks:** Canoe rental, view on Lake Como.

### 🅿S Como 🌊🏖🍦🏖 23B3
**Area Camper Como**, Via Brennero 7, Tavernola.
**GPS:** n45,83518 e9,06140. ⬆.

10 ⌗€ 0,50/h, € 12/24h ⇌€ 1,50 🍴Ch€ 2,50 ⚡€ 1/kWh. 🚻🚲

---

**Location:** Comfortable. **Surface:** grasstiles. ◻ 01/01-31/12.
**Distance:** 🚶city centre Como 4,5km ⊗800m 🛒400m 🚐200m ♿on the spot ☂on the spot.

### 🅿S Como 🌊🏖🍦🏖 23B3
Via Aldo Moro. **GPS:** n45,80286 e9,09155. ⬆.

3 ⌗€ 0,50/h ⇌€ 1,50 🍴Ch€ 2,50 ⚡€ 0,50/kWh. 🚻🚲
**Location:** Urban, central, noisy. **Surface:** asphalted.
◻ 01/01-31/12.
**Distance:** 🚶city centre 1km ⊗150m 🚐100m ♿on the spot.

### 🅿S Costa Volpino 23C3
**Area camper Bersaglio**, Via Nazionale 24.
**GPS:** n45,82298 e10,08680. ⬆.
25 ⌗€ 14/24h ⇌🍴Ch ⚡included WC⬚€ 1. **Location:** Rural, simple, quiet. **Surface:** metalled. ◻ 01/01-31/12.
**Distance:** 900m ⚓on the spot ⊗100m ♿on the spot ☂on the spot.
**Remarks:** At lake, picnic and barbecue place, playground.

### 🅿S Crema 26C1
**Camper Club Crema**, Via Giacomo Crespi. **GPS:** n45,35442 e9,67577.
⌗free ⇌🍴Chfree. **Surface:** grasstiles/metalled.
◻ 01/01-31/12.
**Distance:** 1km 🛒200m.
**Remarks:** Max. 72h.

### 🅿S Cremona 🍞 26C1
**Piazzale della Croce Rossa**, Via Mantova.
**GPS:** n45,13744 e10,03464. ⬆.

20 ⌗free ⇌🍴Chfree.
**Location:** Urban, simple. **Surface:** asphalted. ◻ 01/01-31/12.
**Distance:** 🚶on the spot 🚲3km ⊗on the spot 🛒200m 🚐on the spot.
**Remarks:** Nearby stadium.

### 🅿S Desenzano del Garda 🏛🏖 23D3
**Area Sosta Camper La Spiaggia**, Via Vò, 19.
**GPS:** n45,48747 e10,52180. ⬆.

30 ⌗€ 15/24h ⇌🍴Ch ⚡included WC⬚🚲
**Location:** Rural, comfortable. **Surface:** gravel. ◻ 01/01-31/12.
**Distance:** 3,5km ⚓200m ⊗Pizzeria Stella Del Garda 🛒10m ♿on the spot.
**Remarks:** Video surveillance, barbecue place.

### 🍴S Esine 23C3
**Fontanelle on the Road**, Via Toroselle 12, SS42.
**GPS:** n45,90302 e10,21820.

---

IT

15 🛏️guests free 🔌💧Ch. **Surface:** grassy. ⬛ 01/01-31/12.
**Distance:** 🚶4km ⊗on the spot.

### 🅱️🅂 Gandino 23C3
Via Giovanni Pascoli. **GPS:** n45,81286 e9,90538. ⬆️➡️

2 🛏️free 🔌💧Chfree. **Surface:** grasstiles. ⬛ 01/01-31/12.
**Distance:** 🚶historical centre 250m.
**Remarks:** Max. 48h.

### 🅱️🅂 Gavirate 〰️ 23A3
Via Cavour. **GPS:** n45,83913 e8,72105. ⬆️➡️

30 🛏️€12/day 💧€ 1 💧€ 2 Ch€ 1 🔌€ 1/12h.🚰
**Location:** Rural, simple, quiet. **Surface:** grasstiles.
⬛ 01/01-31/12.
**Distance:** 🚶200m 🏊on the spot 🚤on the spot ⊗on the spot
🍴250m 🚴on the spot 🚶on the spot.
**Remarks:** At lake of Varese, friday market.

### 🅱️🅂 Germignaga ⛵〰️ 23A3
**Area Sosta Camper Germignaga**, Via Bodmer, 41/A.
**GPS:** n45,99170 e8,71923. ⬆️

10 🛏️€ 23, 15/07-20/08 € 28 💧🔌Ch 🔌€ 1/kWh 🔌€ 1/2minutes
📶€ 2,50. **Location:** Rural, simple, noisy. **Surface:** grassy.
⬛ 01/01-31/12.
**Distance:** 🚶1km 🏊on the spot 🚤on the spot ⊗1km 🍴500m
🚴300m 🚶on the spot.
**Remarks:** Video surveillance.

### 🅱️🅂 Germignaga ⛵〰️ 23A3
Via A. Bodmer. **GPS:** n45,99630 e8,72421. ⬆️

6 🛏️€ 1,50/h, € 15/24h 💧€ 1 💧€ 1 Ch.
**Location:** Urban, simple, central, quiet. S.
⬛ 01/01-31/12.

---

**Distance:** 🚶500m 🏊on the spot 🚤on the spot ⊗500m 🍴500m
🚴on the spot 🚶on the spot 🚶on the spot.
**Remarks:** Max. 48h, key electricity at pay-desk.

### 🅂 Iseo 23C3
Viale Europa. **GPS:** n45,65350 e10,04500.

5 🛏️free.
**Location:** Urban. **Surface:** unpaved. ⬛ 01/01-31/12.
**Distance:** 🚶1km 🏊250m ⊗600m 🚴300m.

**Tourist information Iseo:**
ℹ️ I.A.T. (Ufficio Informazioni e di Accoglienza Turistica), Lungolago
Marconi, 2. Old fishermen's village.
🛒 Week market. 📅 Fri.

### 🅱️🅂 Lanzada 〰️〽️ 23C2
Via Ganda 1. **GPS:** n46,26962 e9,87783. ⬆️
🛏️€ 15 💧🔌Ch 🔌included 🛏️€ 3.
**Location:** Rural, isolated, quiet. **Surface:** metalled. ⬛ 01/01-31/12.
**Distance:** 🚶7km.
**Remarks:** At sports centre.

### 🅱️🅂 Lecco 〰️ 23B3
Via Arturo Toscanini, Loc. Bione di Lecco. **GPS:** n45,83136 e9,40779. ⬆️

12 🛏️free 💧🔌Chfree. **Location:** Urban, simple, noisy.
**Surface:** asphalted. ⬛ 01/01-31/12.
**Distance:** 🚶2,8km 🏊on the spot ⊗500m 🍴1km 🚴650m 🚶on the
spot 🚶on the spot.
**Remarks:** At lake Garlate, at sports park, cycle routes.

### 🅱️ Lecco 〰️ 23B3
Via Prealpi 34. **GPS:** n45,86312 e9,42761. ⬆️
20 🛏️free, weekend € 10. 🚲 **Location:** Rural, simple, isolated, quiet.
**Surface:** gravel. ⬛ 01/01-31/12.
**Distance:** 🚶4,5km ⊗on the spot 🍴4,5km 🚴on the
spot 🚶on the spot 🚶on the spot.
**Remarks:** Pay at restaurant.

### 🅱️🅂 Livigno 〰️❄️ 23C1
**Aquafresca**, Via Palipert 374. **GPS:** n46,50713 e10,11952. ⬆️
🛏️€ 10-13 💧🔌Ch 🔌WC🚰🔌📷📶
**Location:** Rural. **Surface:** grassy. ⬛ 01/01-31/12.
**Distance:** ⊗100m 🚴on the spot 🚶on the spot 🛷on the spot.
**Remarks:** Free shuttle, playground.

### 🅱️🅂 Livigno 〰️❄️ 23C1
**Stella Alpina**, Via Palipert 570. **GPS:** n46,50515 e10,11958. ⬆️

28 🛏️€ 15/24h, 2 pers.incl 💧🔌Ch 🔌€ 3 WCincluded 🔌€ 2 📷📶
**Location:** Rural. **Surface:** gravel. ⬛ 01/01-31/12.
**Distance:** 🚶400m ⊗500m 🚌Free bus 🚶on the spot.
**Remarks:** Free shuttle to ski-lifts.

### 🅱️🅂 Livigno 〰️❄️ 23C1
**Trepalle**, SS301. **GPS:** n46,52655 e10,17578. ⬆️

---

50 🛏️€ 10 💧🔌Chincluded. **Location:** Rural. **Surface:** asphalted.
⬛ 01/01-31/12.
**Distance:** 🚶Livigno 6,6km 🏊200m 🍴200m 🚌bus to Livigno every
40 minutes 🚶on the spot.
**Remarks:** Altitude 2000m.

**Tourist information Livigno:**
👁️ Latteria di Livigno, Via Pemonte 911. Discover the secrets of dairy
products from Livigno. On Wednesday the possibility of preparing
meals, costs € 7, from 14h. 📅 summer Mo-Fr 8-20h.

### 🅱️🅂 Lodi 26B1
Via Generale Andrea Massena. **GPS:** n45,31295 e9,51731.
5 🛏️free 💧€ 0,50 💧€ 2 Ch€ 2 🔌€ 6/24h. **Location:** Urban.
**Surface:** metalled. ⬛ 01/01-31/12.
**Distance:** 🚶650m 🍴500m.

### 🅱️🅂 Lodrino 23C3
Via Kennedy, Localité Dade. **GPS:** n45,71450 e10,28107. ⬆️

3 🛏️free 💧🔌Ch 🔌free. **Location:** Comfortable.
**Surface:** asphalted. ⬛ 01/01-31/12.
**Distance:** 🚶500m.
**Remarks:** Max. 72h.

### 🅱️🅂 Luino ⛵〰️ 23A3
Via Gorizia. **GPS:** n45,97255 e8,75275. ⬆️➡️

16 🛏️€ 9 💧🔌Chincluded 🔌€ 3. 🚲 **Location:** Rural, isolated,
quiet. **Surface:** grasstiles/grassy. ⬛ 01/01-31/12.
**Distance:** 🚶Luino 5km ⊗on the spot 🍴3km 🚴on the spot 🚶on
the spot.
**Remarks:** At sports grounds, max. 72h, pay at restaurant.

### 🅱️🅂 Maccagno 🌿⛵〰️ 23A2
Via Virgilio Parisi. **GPS:** n46,04010 e8,73545. ⬆️➡️

18 🛏️free 💧free. **Location:** Rural, simple, central, noisy.
**Surface:** gravel. ⬛ 01/01-31/12.
**Distance:** 🚶300m 🏊200m 🚤200m ⊗300m 🍴300m 🚌300m
🚴on the spot 🚶on the spot.
**Remarks:** At sports centre, max. 72h, friday market.

### 🅱️ Maccagno 🌿⛵〰️ 23A2
Via Alberto Martinetti. **GPS:** n46,04130 e8,73857. ⬆️
6 🛏️free. **Location:** Urban, simple, quiet. **Surface:** grasstiles.
⬛ 01/01-31/12.
**Distance:** 🚶500m 🏊500m ⊗300m 🍴300m 🚌400m.

**Remarks:** Along railwayline.

### ⬛S Magnacavallo 26E1

Via Salvador Allende. **GPS:** n45,00587 e11,17906. ⬆➡.

15 🚐free ⛽🔧Chfree. **Location:** Simple. **Surface:** asphalted.
🔲 01/01-31/12.
**Distance:** 🚶200m ⊗200m 🚊200m 🚲50m.
**Remarks:** At sports park.

### ⬛S Mandello del Lario ⛱ 23B3

**Area Cima**, Via Giulio Cesare. **GPS:** n45,91830 e9,31589. ⬆➡.

12 🚐€ 10 ⛽🔧Chincluded. 🛒 **Location:** Urban, simple, central,
noisy. **Surface:** concrete. 🔲 01/01-31/12.
**Distance:** 🚶800m 🚢Lago di Lecco 400m ⊗on the spot 🚊200m
🚲200m 🚲on the spot 🏃on the spot.
**Remarks:** Check in at restaurant.

### ⬛S Mantova ⛱ 26D1

**Parco Paganini**, Via Fiera 11, Grazie di Curtatone.
**GPS:** n45,15333 e10,69111. ⬆➡.

108 🚐€ 12 ⛽🔧Ch🔧WC incluced.
**Location:** Rural, simple, central. **Surface:** asphalted/grassy.
🔲 01/03-13/11.
**Distance:** 🚶300m, Mantova 6km ⊗300m 🚊4km, bakery 300m.

### ⬛S Mantova ⛱ 26D1

**Sparafucile**, Via Legnago 1/a. **GPS:** n45,16336 e10,81244. ⬆➡.

54 🚐€ 15/12h, € 20/24h ⛽🔧Ch🔧WC included.
**Location:** Rural, comfortable, quiet. **Surface:** grassy/metalled.
🔲 01/01-31/12.
**Distance:** 🚶1km 🚴4km ⊗500m 🚊500m 🚲on the spot 🏃on the
spot.
**Remarks:** Thursday market.

### ⬛S Marmirolo 26D1

Via Ponte. **GPS:** n45,30459 e10,70838.
8 🚐€ 10 ⛽🔧Ch🔧included. **Location:** Rural. **Surface:** gravel.
🔲 01/01-31/12.
**Distance:** 🏊on the spot 🚊on the spot ⊗550m.

### ⬛S Menaggio 23B2

Via Armando Diaz 12. **GPS:** n46,02454 e9,23900.
20 🚐free ⛽free. **Location:** Rural. **Surface:** asphalted.
🔲 01/01-31/12.
**Distance:** 🚶550m 🏊on the spot ⊗200m 🚊200m 🚊on the spot.

### ⬛S Merate ⛱ 23B3

Via Papa Giovanni Paolo I, loc. Sartirana. **GPS:** n45,71326 e9,41865. ⬆.

10 🚐€ 15/24h ⛽🔧Ch 🔧included. 🏠 **Location:** Rural, simple,
quiet. **Surface:** grasstiles. 🔲 01/01-31/12.
**Distance:** 🚶300m ⊗400m 🚊800m 🚊200m 🚲on the spot.
**Remarks:** Max. 72h.

### ⬛S Milano ⛱ 26B1

**New Park**, Via L. Tukory 6, Milan (Milano).
**GPS:** n45,51167 e9,16019. ⬆.

50 🚐€ 25/24h ⛽🔧Ch 🔧WC included. 🏠
**Location:** Urban, central, quiet. **Surface:** asphalted.
🔲 01/01-31/12.
**Distance:** 🚶7km ⊗300m 🚊50m.
**Remarks:** Monitored parking.

### ⬛S Milano ⛱ 26B1

**Ripamonti SNC**, Via Ripamonti 481, Milan (Milano).
**GPS:** n45,40914 e9,20937. ⬆.

30 🚐€ 20/24h ⛽🔧Ch 🔧€ 5 WC included. 🏠
**Location:** Urban, simple, quiet. **Surface:** asphalted.
🔲 01/01-31/12.
**Distance:** 🚶centre 7km 🚴2km 📷on the spot 🚊Milan 40min
🚲on the spot.
**Remarks:** Check in at reception, monitored parking.

### ⬛S Milano ⛱ 26B1

**Camper Village Linate Parking**, Viale Enrico Forlanini, 123, Milan
(Milano). **GPS:** n45,46245 e9,27024. ⬆.
20 🚐€ 20/24h ⛽WC included. 🏠
**Location:** Urban, simple, noisy. **Surface:** grassy/metalled.
🔲 01/01-31/12.
**Distance:** 🚶centre 7km ⊗300m 🚊N 74 > centre 🚲on the spot.
**Remarks:** Monitored parking.

### ⬛S Milano ⛱ 26B1

**Leone Automobili**, Via Lainate 94, Rho, Milan (Milano).
**GPS:** n45,54232 e9,03328.
40 🚐€ 22-25 ⛽🔧Chincluded. 🔧€ 3/24h.
**Location:** Rural. **Surface:** grassy/gravel. 🔲 15/05-15/10.
**Distance:** 🚶Milan 16km 🚴3km 🚊650m.
**Remarks:** 24/24 surveillance.

**Tourist information Milan (Milano):**
🅼 Castello Sforzesco.
✝ Duomo. History of Gothic architecture. 🔲 Tue-Su.
⛪ Via Fauché. 🔲 Tue, Sa.
⛪ Mercatone del Naviglio Grande, Naviglio Grande. Antiques market,
400 stalls. 🔲 last Su of the month.
🍽 Galleria.

### ⬛S Moglia 26E2

Via Tazio Nuvolari. **GPS:** n44,93639 e10,91582. ⬆.

14 🚐free ⛽🔧Chfree. **Surface:** asphalted. 🔲 01/01-31/12.
**Distance:** 🚶300m 🚴A22 7km ⊗300m.
**Remarks:** At swimming pool.

### ⬛S Monte Marenzo ⛱ 23B3

Via Papa Gionvanni. **GPS:** n45,77639 e9,45222. ⬆➡.

8 🚐free ⛽🔧Chfree. 🔧€ 6/24h. **Location:** Rural, simple.
**Surface:** gravel/metalled. 🔲 01/01-31/12.
**Distance:** 🚶300m ⊗300m 🚊300m 🚊on the spot 🚲on the spot
🏃on the spot.
**Remarks:** Max. 72h, playground.

### ⬛S Monzambano 26D1

**Area attrezzata camper Comunale di Monzambano**, Via Degli Alpini
9/a. **GPS:** n45,38916 e10,69277. ⬆➡.

130 🚐€ 14/24h ⛽🔧Ch🔧(24x) € 1 included.
**Surface:** grassy. 🔲 01/01-31/12.
**Distance:** 🚶200m ⊗100m 🚊300m, bakery 100m 🚲on the spot
🏃on the spot.
**Remarks:** Max. 48h, market on Sunday.

### ⬛S Morbegno ⛱❄ 23B2

**Area Sosta Camper Morbegno**, Via del Foss.
**GPS:** n46,14419 e9,57500. ⬆.
22 🚐€ 12 ⛽🔧Ch🔧included. 🛒 **Location:** Rural, simple,
quiet. **Surface:** asphalted/grassy. 🔲 01/01-31/12.
**Distance:** 🚶historical centre 500m 🚴2km ⛷50m ⊗100m 🚊2km
🚊Skibus 🚲on the spot 🏃on the spot.
**Remarks:** At tennis-courts, money in envelope in mail box, monitored
parking 24/24, picnic and barbecue place.

### ⬛S Niardo 23C2

**Area di sosta Mr. Sanders**, Località Crist.
**GPS:** n45,97690 e10,31959. ⬆.

20 🚐€ 10 ⛽🔧Ch🔧€ 2. **Location:** Rural, simple, isolated, quiet.
**Surface:** grasstiles. 🔲 01/01-31/12.
**Distance:** 🚶Niardo 1,3km ⛷on the spot ⊗on the spot.
**Remarks:** Bread-service.

### ⬛S Nova Milanese ⛱ 23B3

Via G. Brodolini. **GPS:** n45,58298 e9,19668. ⬆➡.

4 🛏free 🚰🔌Chfree. **Location:** Urban, simple. **Surface:** asphalted. ⭕ 01/01-31/12.
**Distance:** 🚶500m ⚓1,6km ✖200m 🛒400m on the spot.
**Remarks:** At sports park, max. 48h, video surveillance.

### Novate Mezzola 〰 23B2
Via al Lido. **GPS:** n46,21083 e9,45000.⬆➡.

25 🛏free. **Location:** Rural. **Surface:** grassy/gravel.
⭕ 01/01-31/12.
**Distance:** 🚶800m ⚓on the spot ✖400m 🛒800m 🚲 on the spot.
**Remarks:** At lake Mezzola, signposted cycle routes.

### Olginate ⚓ 23B3
Via Cesare Cantù. **GPS:** n45,79523 e9,41610.⬆.

46 🛏€ 10/24h 🚰🔌Ch 🚿included. 🏪
**Location:** Simple, quiet.
**Surface:** metalled.
⭕ 01/01-31/12 ⭕ Thu>16h-Fri<16h (market).
**Distance:** 🚶200m ⚓on the spot ✖200m 🛒200m 🚲200m
🚲 on the spot 🏊 on the spot.
**Remarks:** At Olginate lake, to be paid at bar.

### Pizzighettone ⚓ 26C1
Via De Gasperi. **GPS:** n45,18538 e9,79402.⬆➡.

4 🛏free 🚰🔌Ch 🚿free. **Location:** Urban, simple. **Surface:** gravel.
⭕ 01/01-31/12.
**Distance:** 🚶400m ✖300m 🛒Lidl 100m 🚲350m.

### Quingentole 26E1
**GPS:** n45,04326 e11,09326.
8 🛏free 🚰🚿. **Location:** Rural, simple, isolated, quiet.
**Surface:** gravel. ⭕ 01/01-31/12.
**Distance:** ⚓on the spot 🚲on the spot ✖1,6km 🛒4,2km.

### Ruino 〰 ⚓ 🍇 26B2
**Agriturismo Adriana Tarantani**, Loc. Tre Venti.
**GPS:** n44,92833 e9,26311.⬆.

---

⭕ 01/01-31/12.
**Distance:** 🚶on the spot ⚓2km ✖300m 🛒Carrefour 200m 🚲400m.
**Remarks:** Max. 24h.

6 🛏guests free 🚰🔌Chfree 🚿€ 2,50. **Location:** Rural, simple.
**Surface:** grassy/gravel. ⭕ 01/01-31/12.
**Distance:** 🚶1km ✖on the spot 🛒1km 🚲100m.

### Sabbioneta ⚓ 26D2
Via Piccola Atene. **GPS:** n44,99459 e10,48849.⬆➡.

15 🛏free 🚰🔌Chfree. **Location:** Urban, simple, noisy.
**Surface:** metalled. ⭕ 01/01-31/12.
**Distance:** 🚶200m ✖400m 🛒500m on the spot.
**Remarks:** Max. 72h.

### San Benedetto Po 〰 26E1
Via Cardinal Ruffini. **GPS:** n45,04292 e10,93432.⬆.
8 🛏free 🚰🔌Chfree.
**Location:** Urban. **Surface:** asphalted. ⭕ 01/01-31/12.
**Distance:** 🚶500m ✖650m 🛒800m 🚲200m 🚲 on the spot.
**Remarks:** Behind swimming pool, nearby monastery.

### Santa Caterina Valfurva 23D2
**Agriturismo Zia Edda**, Via Forni, loc. Nassegno.
**GPS:** n46,40917 e10,50833.⬆➡.

25 🛏€ 12 🚰🔌Ch 🚿€ 3. **Surface:** grassy. ⭕ 01/01-31/12.
**Distance:** 🚶500m 🎿on the spot 🚠on the spot.

### Saronno 23B3
Via E.H.Griegh. **GPS:** n45,61265 e9,04274.⬆.

20 🛏free 🚰€ 0,20/100liter 🔌Ch. **Location:** Urban, simple.
**Surface:** asphalted. ⭕ 01/01-31/12.
**Distance:** 🚶1,5km ⚓3,5km 🛒500m 🚲200m.

### Saronno 23B3
Via Dalmazia 11. **GPS:** n45,62446 e9,02469.⬆.

3 🛏free.
**Location:** Urban, central. **Surface:** concrete.

---

### Sartirana Lomellina 26A1
Via Cavour. **GPS:** n45,11337 e8,66936.⬆➡.

3 🛏free 🚰€ 2/100liter 🔌Ch. **Location:** Urban, simple.
**Surface:** asphalted. ⭕ 01/01-31/12 ⭕ Sa-morning market.
**Distance:** 🚶100m ✖200m 🛒100m on the spot.

### Sirmione 〰 23D3
**Camper Park Sirmione**, Via Cantarane. **GPS:** n45,46083 e10,63333.⬆.

100 🛏€ 20/24h, € 11/20.30-9.30h 🚰🔌Ch 🚿€ 3 🔌€ 1 📶included.
**Location:** Rural. **Surface:** grassy/gravel.
⭕ 15/03-31/10.
**Distance:** 🚶4,5km 🏊Lake Garda 🛒100m 🚲1km 🚲100m.

### Sirmione 〰 23D3
Piazzale Montebaldo. **GPS:** n45,48694 e10,61028.⬆➡.

21 🛏from € 2,50 1/2h till-€ 21/24h 🚰🔌ChWC € 0,50.
**Surface:** asphalted. ⭕ 01/01-31/12.
**Distance:** 🚶200m 🏊no bathing ✖50m 🛒200m.

### Sondrio ⛰ ❄ 23C2
**Area Sportiva**, Via Vanoni. **GPS:** n46,16064 e9,86957.⬆.

6 🛏free 🚰🔌Chfree 🚿(2x).
**Location:** Urban. **Surface:** asphalted. ⭕ 01/01-31/12.
**Distance:** 🚶600m ✖on the spot 🛒200m 🚲1km.
**Remarks:** Parking sports park.

### Songavazzo 23C3
Via Pineta 71. **GPS:** n45,88104 e9,98940.

3 🛏free 🚰🔌Chfree. **Location:** Urban. **Surface:** asphalted.
⭕ 01/01-31/12.

IT

**Distance:** 🚰on the spot ⊗200m 🚽on the spot 🚿on the spot 🚶on the spot.

| 🚐🚽S | **Stezzano** | 23B3 |

Via Pietro Mascagni. **GPS:** n45,65594 e9,65301.⬆.

5 🚐free 🚰🚽Chfree.
**Location:** Urban. **Surface:** asphalted.
◻ 01/01-31/12.
**Distance:** 🚰500m 🚲6km ⊗350m 🛒Carrefour 850m 🚽on the spot.

| 🚐🚽S | **Sulzano** | 23C3 |

**Parking Gerolo**, Via Tassano 14. **GPS:** n45,68830 e10,10341.⬆➡.

30 🚐€ 17/24h, € 10/night 🚰🚽Ch 🚿WC📇€ 5.
**Location:** Rural, simple, quiet. **Surface:** grassy.
◻ 01/01-31/12.
**Distance:** 🚰300m 🏊Lago Iseo 400m ⊗500m 🚽300m 🚌400m.
**Remarks:** Picnic tables available.

| 🚐🚽S | **Ternate** 🚣 | 23A3 |

Via Roma. **GPS:** n45,78006 e8,69780.⬆➡.

17 🚐€ 10 🚰🚽Ch 🚿(4x)📶included. **Location:** Simple, central,
quiet. **Surface:** unpaved. ◻ 01/01-31/12.
**Distance:** 🚰200m 🏊on the spot 🚣on the spot ⊗100m 🚽200m
🚲on the spot 🚶on the spot.
**Remarks:** At Comabbio lake, pay at hotel.

| 🚐🚽S | **Tirano** 🚣 | 23C2 |

**Area Camper Tirano**, Via Polveriera/Via Sala Piero.
**GPS:** n46,21361 e10,15722.⬆➡.

20 🚐€ 15/24h 🚰🚽Ch 🚿included. 📇
**Location:** Comfortable. **Surface:** grasstiles. ◻ 01/01-31/12.
**Distance:** 🚰1km 🚌station 800m.

**Tourist information Tirano:**
ℹ Bernina Express. The highest-altitude trans-Alpine line in Europe,
with one of the steepest gradients in the world between Tirano (It) and
Chur (Ch). UNESCO's List of World Heritage. 🎫 ± € 100/pp return ticket
(Tirano-Chur), ± € 45/pp return ticket (Tirano-Pontresina).

| 🚐🚽S | **Torbole** 🏄🏊🚣 | 23D3 |

**Camperstop Torbole**, Via Al Cor. **GPS:** n45,87264 e10,87260.⬆➡.

---

120 🚐€ 20-34 🚰🚽Ch 🚿WC📇📶included. **Location:** Rural.
**Surface:** grassy. ◻ 01/01-31/12.
**Distance:** 🚰on the spot 🏊on the spot ⊗on the spot 🚽on the spot.
**Remarks:** Along Lake Garda.

| 🚐🚽S | **Treviglio** | 23B3 |

Via al Malgari. **GPS:** n45,53132 e9,60029.⬆.

25 🚐free 🚰🚽Chfree. **Location:** Urban. **Surface:** metalled.
◻ 01/01-31/12.
**Distance:** 🚰700m 🚽400m.
**Remarks:** At sports park.

| 🚐🚽S | **Valcanale** | 23C3 |

Via Alpe Corte. **GPS:** n45,94968 e9,85020.

5 🚐free. **Location:** Rural. **Surface:** gravel/sand.
◻ 01/01-31/12.
**Distance:** 🚰500m ⊗500m 🚣on the spot 🚶on the spot.

| 🚐🚽S | **Varzi** 🚣 | 26B2 |

Strada Circonvallazione. **GPS:** n44,82172 e9,19727.⬆➡.

30 🚐free, summer € 5 🚰🚽ChWCfree. 📇
**Location:** Rural, simple, central. **Surface:** asphalted/metalled.
◻ 01/01-31/12.
**Distance:** 🚰200m 🏊150m 🚽300m 🚌on the spot 🚣50m 🚶50m.
**Remarks:** Along the Staffora river, friday market.

| 🍴🚽S | **Varzi** 🚣 | 26B2 |

Via Generale Maretti 6. **GPS:** n44,81951 e9,19102.
5 🚐guests free 🚰free 🗑. **Location:** Rural. **Surface:** metalled.
◻ 01/01-31/12.
**Distance:** 🚰750m ⊗on the spot 🚽1km 🚌750m.

# Veneto

| 🍴🚽S | **Arquà Polesine** | 26F1 |

**Ostello Canalbianco**, SS 16, n15. **GPS:** n44,99665 e11,76243.
12 🚐€ 10 🚰🚽Ch 🚿WC📇. **Location:** Rural, simple, quiet.
**Surface:** metalled. ◻ 01/01-31/12.
**Distance:** 🚰city centre 3km ⊗on the spot 🚌station 3km.
**Remarks:** At youth hostel.

| 🚐🚽S | **Asiago** | 23E3 |

**P Verdi Mosele**, SS349, Via Giuseppe Verdi.
**GPS:** n45,87129 e11,50026.⬆.

---

20 🚐€ 1/h, € 4/day 🚰€ 5 🚽Ch. **Location:** Rural.
**Surface:** asphalted. ◻ 01/01-31/12.
**Distance:** 🚰300m ⊗on the spot 🚽500m.
**Remarks:** Bicycle rental.

| 🚐🚽S | **Asolo** 🏔 | 23F3 |

**Area Camper Communale**, Via Forestuzzo.
**GPS:** n45,79637 e11,91283.⬆➡.

20 🚐€ 7/24h 🚰🚽Ch 🚿(14x)included. 📇
**Location:** Rural, comfortable. **Surface:** grassy/sand.
◻ 01/01-31/12.
**Distance:** 🚰400m ⊗400m 🚽400m.
**Remarks:** Access 8-19.30h, barbecue place, picnic area.

| 🚐🚽S | **Auronzo di Cadore** 🏔🏔❄ | 23F1 |

**Taiarezze**, SR48, Via Reaneloc. **GPS:** n46,56217 e12,41640.⬆.

30 🚐€ 12-18 🚰🚽Chincluded. 📇 **Location:** Rural, simple, quiet.
**Surface:** asphalted. ◻ 01/01-31/12.
**Distance:** 🚰1,5km 🏊on the spot ⊗on the spot 🚽on the spot
🚌on the spot 🚣on the spot 🚶on the spot 🚴1,6km ⛷1,6km.
**Remarks:** Max. 48h, payment only with coins.

| 🚐🚽S | **Barbarano Vicentino** | 26E1 |

Viale Vittorio Veneto 66. **GPS:** n45,40725 e11,54654.⬆.

3 🚐free 🚰🚽free. **Location:** Urban. **Surface:** asphalted
◻ 01/01-31/12.
**Distance:** 🚰200m ⊗200m 🚽200m.
**Remarks:** Near sports fields.

| 🚐🚽S | **Bardolino** 🚣🏊 | 23D3 |

**Parking Serenella**, Via Gardesana dell'Acqua.
**GPS:** n45,56115 e10,71412.⬆➡.

10 🚐€ 12-15/24h 🚰🚽Chincluded. 📇 **Location:** Rural, simple,

IT

quiet. **Surface**: grasstiles. ☐ 01/01-31/12.
**Distance**: 🛒2km 🅿on the spot ⛽on the spot 🚿on the spot 🛒Lidl 2km 🚮on the spot 🛁on the spot 🏃on the spot.

### Bardolino 🍷Ⓢ 23D3
**Agricampeggio Terra e Sogni**, Via San Colombano 16A.
**GPS**: n45,55662 e10,72451.⬆
15 🚐 € 30-50 🚰🔌Ch🚿(15x)WC📶included. **Location**: Rural, comfortable, luxurious, quiet. **Surface**: grassy/gravel. ☐ 01/01-31/12.
**Distance**: 🛒centre 1,3km ⚡1km 🚮700m 🛁700m.
**Remarks**: Bicycle rental, playground, swimming pool available.

### Bardolino 🍷Ⓢ 23D3
**Agriturismo Tre Colline**, Località Palù, 26.
**GPS**: n45,50636 e10,77253.⬆
10 🚐 € 20-35,50 + € 1/pp tourist tax 🚰🔌Ch🚿WC📶included.
**Location**: Rural, comfortable, isolated, quiet. **Surface**: grassy.
☐ 01/03-31/12.
**Distance**: 🛒Bardolino 7km.
**Remarks**: Breakfast-service, barbecue place, swimming pool.

**Tourist information Bardolino:**
ℹ I.A.T. (Ufficio Informazioni e di Accoglienza Turistica), Piazzale Aldo Moro.

### Bassano del Grappa Ⓢ 23F3
**Parcheggio Gerosa**, Via Alcide de Gasperi.
**GPS**: n45,75831 e11,73091.⬆➡

20 🚐 € 12/24h 🚰🔌Ch🚿included WC. 🚐 **Location**: Urban.
**Surface**: asphalted. ☐ 01/01-31/12.
**Distance**: 🛒300m ⊗300m 🛁300m 🚮on the spot.
**Remarks**: Max. 48h.

### Bassano del Grappa Ⓢ 23F3
**Prato Santo Caterina**, Via Chini 6. **GPS**: n45,76009 e11,73413.
5 🚐free. **Location**: Urban. **Surface**: metalled. ☐ 01/01-31/12.
**Distance**: 🛒on the spot ⊗400m 🛁300m 🚮on the spot.

### Bassano del Grappa 🍴Ⓢ 23F3
**Fattoria Sociale Conca D'Oro**, Via Rivoltella Bassa, 22.
**GPS**: n45,78437 e11,73248.
10 🚐 € 10 🚰€ 2🔌Ch🚿€ 2 WC📶€ 2.
**Location**: Rural. **Surface**: grassy. ☐ 01/01-31/12.
**Distance**: 🛒3km 🚮on the spot.
**Remarks**: Bread-service.

### Belluno 🌿⛲🍦🌳Ⓢ 23F2
**Rio Cavalli**, Via Sagrogna 74. **GPS**: n46,15646 e12,26136.⬆

20 🚐 € 15 🚰🔌Ch🚿€ 5 WC📶included. **Location**: Comfortable, central, quiet. **Surface**: grassy/sand. ☐ 01/01-31/12.
**Distance**: 🛒3km ⛵6km 🅿on the spot ⊗on the spot 🛁3km 🚮on the spot.
**Remarks**: Arrival < 19h.

### Belluno 🌿⛲🍦🌳Ⓢ 23F2
Viale dei Dendrofori, loc. Lambioi. **GPS**: n46,13712 e12,21371.⬆➡

15 🚐8-18 € 0,80/h, overnight stay free 🚰🔌Chfree.

---

**Location**: Simple, central, noisy. **Surface**: grasstiles/metalled.
☐ 01/01-31/12.
**Distance**: 🛒100m ⊗100m 🛁100m.
**Remarks**: Nearby swimming pool and skating rink.

### Bibione 🌿Ⓢ 23H3
**Valle Vecchia**, Strada Brussa. **GPS**: n45,62458 e12,95866.⬆

100 🚐 € 10/08-18h, overnight stay free 🚰free WC📶🚿
**Location**: Rural, simple, isolated, quiet. **Surface**: grassy.
☐ 01/01-31/12.
**Distance**: 🛒12km ⚓sandy beach 250m ⊗12km 🛁12km 🚴on the spot 🏃on the spot.
**Remarks**: Guarded during the day, shower during opening hours, dog permitted on the beach.

### Borghetto di Valeggio sul Mincio 🌿Ⓢ 26D1
**Camper Parking Visconteo**, Strada provinciale 55.
**GPS**: n45,35537 e10,72017.⬆
60 🚐 € 10/24h 🚰€ 3🔌Ch🚿€ 2/24h 🔲.
**Location**: Rural, comfortable. **Surface**: gravel. ☐ 01/01-31/12.
**Distance**: 🛒on the spot ⚓Lake Garda 13km ⊗250m 🚴on the spot 🏃on the spot.
**Remarks**: Borghetto 200m.

### Castelguglielmo Ⓢ 26E1
Via Alessandro Volta. **GPS**: n45,02246 e11,53518.⬆➡

10 🚐free 🚰🔌Ch🚿free. **Location**: Urban. **Surface**: metalled.
☐ 01/01-31/12.
**Distance**: 🛒500m ⊗350m 🛁100m.

### Cavallino-Treporti 🍷Ⓢ 23G3
**Spiaggia di Cà Ballarin**, Via Gabrielle Berton.
**GPS**: n45,45998 e12,51659.⬆

4 🚐free. **Location**: Rural, simple, quiet. **Surface**: sand.
☐ 01/05-31/10.
**Distance**: 🛒1km ⚓on the spot 🅿on the spot ⊗on the spot 🛁1km 🚮300m.
**Remarks**: Beach parking.

**Tourist information Cavallino-Treporti:**
🎪 Week market. ☐ Tue-Thu morning.

### Chioggia Ⓢ 26G1
**2 Palme**, Lungomare Adriatica. **GPS**: n45,22122 e12,29624.⬆

100 🚐 € 15, peak season € 22 🚰🔌Ch🚿(100x),2Amp

---

WCincluded 📶€ 1/3minutes. 🚿 **Location**: Urban, simple, central.
**Surface**: grassy/gravel. ☐ 01/01-31/12.
**Distance**: 🛒city centre 1,5km ⚓200m ⊗on the spot 🛁1km 🚮on the spot.
**Remarks**: Chioggia: little Venice.

### Chioggia Ⓢ 26G1
**Parcheggio dal Padoan**, Via S. Felice, 10.
**GPS**: n45,22235 e12,29560.⬆
80 🚐 € 17, peak season € 20 🚰🔌Ch🚿WC📶€ 1 🔲.
**Location**: Urban, central.
**Surface**: grassy.
☐ 01/03-01/11.
**Distance**: 🛒on the spot ⚓300m ⊗15m 🚴on the spot 🏃on the spot.
**Remarks**: Monitored parking, Chioggia: little Venice.

### Cittadella Ⓢ 23F3
**Stazione Q8**, Via Cristofolo Colombo 1. **GPS**: n45,64377 e11,77432.
5 🚐free 🚰€ 1/60liter 🔌Ch🚿€ 2,50 🚿€ 1/h WC.
**Location**: Urban. **Surface**: metalled. ☐ 01/01-31/12.
**Distance**: 🛒on the spot.
**Remarks**: At petrol station.

### Cittadella Ⓢ 23F3
**Centro Sportivo**, Viale dello Sport. **GPS**: n45,64403 e11,77995.
20 🚐free. **Location**: Urban. **Surface**: asphalted. ☐ 01/01-31/12.
**Distance**: 🛒on the spot ⊗600m 🛁150m.
**Remarks**: At sports centre, swimming pool.

### Cittadella Ⓢ 23F3
**Villa Rina**, Via Riva del Grappa. **GPS**: n45,65035 e11,78778.

20 🚐free. **Location**: Urban. **Surface**: asphalted. ☐ 01/01-31/12.
**Distance**: 🛒on the spot ⊗200m 🛁Lidl 1,5km 🚮250m.

### Colà di Lazise ♨Ⓢ 23D3
**Villa dei Cedri**, Via Possoi. **GPS**: n45,46777 e10,74972.⬆➡

200 🚐 € 1/h, 5 hours min 🚰🔌Ch🚿📶included. 🚐
**Location**: Rural, comfortable, quiet. **Surface**: grasstiles.
☐ 01/01-31/12.
**Distance**: ⚓4km ⊗700m 🛁1,5km.
**Remarks**: Parco Termale 300m.

### Conegliano 🍺Ⓢ 23F2
**Area de Sosta Campeggio Club Conegliano**, Via San Giovanni Bosco, SS13. **GPS**: n45,87799 e12,30111.⬆➡

30 🚐 € 12/24h 🚰🔌Ch🚿(16x)included WC📶.
**Location**: Urban, simple, central, quiet. **Surface**: grassy.
☐ 01/01-31/12.
**Distance**: 🛒2km ⊗nearby 🛁on the spot.

### Domegge di Cadore Belluno 🏔❄☃♨Ⓢ 23F1
**Camping Cologna**, Vallesella di Cadore. **GPS**: n46,44605 e12,40658.⬆

IT

30 ⏟ € 10 🚐🔧Ch. **Location:** Rural, simple, quiet. **Surface:** grassy.
◻ 01/05-20/10.
**Distance:** 🚶1km ⛵At the lake 🚲on the spot ⊗on the spot 🍴1km
🚌1km 🐎on the spot 🏊on the spot.
**Remarks:** Max. 24h, narrow entrance.

| 📷S | Feltre | 23F2 |

**Area Camper Vincheto**, Via Casonetto 158C.
**GPS:** n46,03124 e11,95911.⬆
12 ⏟ € 15 🚐🔧Chincluded 🔌€ 3.
**Surface:** grassy/metalled. ◻ 01/01-31/12.
**Distance:** 🚶6km 🚲on the spot.

| 📷S | Feltre | 23F2 |

**Piazale Pra del Vescovo**, Viale A. Gaggia.
**GPS:** n46,02013 e11,90792.⬆

15 ⏟free 🚐🔧Chfree 🔌.
**Surface:** metalled. ◻ 01/01-31/12.
**Distance:** 🚶500m ⊗500m 🍴500m 🚌500m.
**Remarks:** Max. 48h.

| 📷S | Ferrara di Monte Baldo 🏔🎋 | 23D3 |

Via Chiesa. **GPS:** n45,67794 e10,85491.⬆

16 ⏟free 🚐🔧Chfree 🔌(16x)€ 5/day. **Location:** Rural, simple,
isolated, quiet. **Surface:** gravel. ◻ 01/01-31/12.
**Distance:** 🚶300m ⊗300m 🍴300m 🚌300m 🐎on the
spot 🏊on the spot.
**Remarks:** To be paid at bar, narrow road.

| 📷S | Garda 🚤 | 23D3 |

**P Centro**, SS249. **GPS:** n45,57501 e10,71019 ⬆

20 ⏟ € 17/24h 🚐🔧ChWCincluded.🚽 **Location:** Urban, simple.
**Surface:** metalled. ◻ 01/01-31/12.
**Distance:** 🚶200m ⊗on the spot 🍴on the spot.

| 📷S | Garda 🚤 | 23D3 |

Via Preite. **GPS:** n45,57620 e10,71404.⬆➡

---

30 ⏟ € 17/24h 🚐🔧Chincluded. 🚽◻
**Location:** Quiet. **Surface:** grasstiles. ◻ Easter-31/10.
**Distance:** 🚶300m ⛵Lake Garda 300m.

| 📷 | Grancona | 26E1 |

Strada di Grancona. **GPS:** n45,42403 e11,45221.⬆
30 ⏟free 🚐🔧Ch 🔌(2x)free.
**Location:** Rural. **Surface:** gravel. ◻ 01/01-31/12.
**Distance:** 🚶500m ⊗300m.

| 📷 | Lazise 🚤🍦🎋 | 23D3 |

**Parking Lazise Dardo**, Via San Martino, SP31.
**GPS:** n45,50623 e10,73584.

15 ⏟ € 17/24h. **Location:** Urban. **Surface:** grassy/gravel.
◻ 01/01-31/12.
**Distance:** 🚶200m 🚴5,8km ⛵200m 🍴200m 🚌200m.

| 📷 | Lazise 🚤🍦🎋 | 23D3 |

Via Mincio. **GPS:** n45,50028 e10,74045.⬆
15 ⏟free. **Location:** Urban, simple, central. **Surface:** asphalted.
◻ 01/01-31/12.
**Distance:** ⛵750m ⊗450m 🍴500m.

| ©S | Lazise 🚤🍦🎋 | 23D3 |

**Amici di Lazise**, Strada del Roccolo 8. **GPS:** n45,47910 e10,72632.⬆

3 ⏟ € 24-29 🚐🔧Ch 🔌WC ◻€ 4/4 🌊included. 🚲🛒
**Location:** Urban, comfortable, noisy. **Surface:** asphalted.
◻ 01/01-31/12.
**Distance:** 🚶3,5km 🚴5km ⛵400m 🚲400m ⊗on the spot 🍴on the
spot ◻on the spot 🍴100m 🐎400m 🏊400m.
**Remarks:** Swimming pool (summer).

| 📷S | Lido di Jesolo 🚤🌊 | 23G3 |

**Area camping Albatros**, Via Correr 102/A.
**GPS:** n45,52477 e12,68995.⬆➡

131 ⏟ € 15-32 🚐🔧Ch 🔌WC ◻🌊included. 🚲 **Location:** Rural,
comfortable, isolated, quiet. **Surface:** grassy. ◻ Easter-18/09.
**Distance:** 🚶500m ⛵700m ⊗100m 🍴100m ◻100m 🚌100m.

| 📷S | Lido di Jesolo 🚤🌊 | 23G3 |

**Boscopineta**, Via Vettor Pisani, 28. **GPS:** n45,52278 e12,69178.⬆

---

250 ⏟ € 11-26 🚐🔧Ch 🔌WC◻€ 1 ◻€ 5 🌊included.🚲
**Location:** Rural, comfortable, central. **Surface:** grassy.
◻ Easter-31/10.
**Distance:** 🚶100m ⛵400m ⊗250m 🚌on the spot.

| 📷S | Lido di Jesolo 🚤🌊 | 23G3 |

**Camping Park dei Dogi**, Viale Oriente 13.
**GPS:** n45,52146 e12,68828.⬆

200 ⏟ € 14-26, 4 pers.incl. 🚐🔧Ch 🔌WCincluded ◻€ 0,50 ◻€ 5
🌊€ 1/week. 🚲 **Location:** Rural, comfortable, central, quiet.
**Surface:** grassy. ◻ 01/01-31/12.
**Distance:** 🚶200m ⛵sandy beach 200m ⊗40m 🍴150m 🚌20m.

| 📷S | Lido di Jesolo 🚤🌊 | 23G3 |

**Jesolo Camper Don Bosco**, Via Oriente/via G.Don Bosco.
**GPS:** n45,52188 e12,68943.⬆➡

250 ⏟ € 11-20 🚐🔧Ch 🔌€ 3 WC ◻€ 1 ◻€ 5 🌊included. 🚲
**Location:** Rural, comfortable. **Surface:** grassy/gravel.
◻ 01/01-31/12.
**Distance:** 🚶100m ⛵100m ⊗on the spot 🍴100m 🚌on the spot.
**Remarks:** Bus to Venice stops in front of motorhome parking.

| 📷S | Livinallongo del Col di Lana 🏔🎋❄ | 23F1 |

**Sportbar del Ghiaccio**, Via Piagn,6 Arabba.
**GPS:** n46,49678 e11,87692.⬆

50 ⏟ € 17 🚐🔧Ch 🔌(17x)€ 3/24h WC ◻€ 3. **Location:** Rural,
comfortable, quiet. **Surface:** grassy/gravel. ◻ 01/01-31/12.
**Distance:** 🚶on the spot ⊗on the spot 🍴200m 🚌200m 🐎on the
spot 🏊on the spot 🎿200m.
**Remarks:** At the skating rink, check in at bar, service passerby € 6.

| ©S | Malcesine 🏔🎋 | 23D3 |

**Camping Lombardi**, Via Navene 141, loc. Campagnola.
**GPS:** n45,78429 e10,82187.⬆

20 🛏 € 18,40-24,40/24h + € 0,80/pp tourist tax 🚰🗑
Ch 🔌 € 2/24h,6Amp WC included 🛢 € 2 💧 🌊 according consumption. 🚌 **Location:** Rural, simple, quiet. **Surface:** grasstiles. 🗓 23/03-04/11.
**Distance:** 🚲 3km 🏖 Lake Garda 500m ⊗ 50m 🛒 on the spot 🚲 on the spot.
**Remarks:** Max. 48h.

🅿 **Marghera** 23F3
**Parcheggio Terminal Service**, Via dei Petroli 1/3 angolo via della Libertà. **GPS:** n45,46806 e12,26589.

🛏 € 10/24h.
**Location:** Simple, central, quiet. 🗓 01/01-31/12.
**Distance:** 🚌 > Venice.
**Remarks:** Monitored parking.

🚐🛏 S **Mirano** 23F3
**Camper Club Mirano**, Via viasana, 4. **GPS:** n45,49322 e12,08968. ⬆

🛏 € 15 🚰🗑 Ch 🔌 included. 🚲 **Location:** Rural, comfortable.
**Surface:** grasstiles. 🗓 01/01-31/12.
**Distance:** 🚲 historical centre 1,5km ⊗ 8km ⊗ 500m 🛒 600m 🚌 300m Padua-Venice.
**Remarks:** Max. 48h, for entrance email: camperclubmirano@libero.it or phone 3479831010.

🚐🛏 S **Misurina** 🌿🏖🏔🌲❄ 23F1
**Piazzale Loita**, Via Monte Piana. **GPS:** n46,58839 e12,25737. ⬆➡

50 🛏 € 2/h, € 18/day 🚰🗑 Ch included. 🚌
**Location:** Rural, simple, central, noisy. **Surface:** gravel.
🗓 01/01-31/12.
**Distance:** 🚲 300m ⛰ 500m ⊗ 50m 🛒 300m 🚌 on the spot 🚲 on the spot 🎿 3km.
**Remarks:** Max. 48h, cash payment.

🛏 **Misurina** 🌿🏖🏔🌲❄ 23F1
**P camper Rifugio Auronzo**, Rifugio Auronzo.
**GPS:** n46,61267 e12,29342. ➡

---

40 🛏 € 40 toll road incl., extra night € 25. 🚌 **Location:** Rural, simple, isolated. **Surface:** gravel. 🗓 01/05-30/10.
**Distance:** 🚲 Misurina 12km ⊗ on the spot 🛒 12km 🚌 on the spot 🏔 Tre Cime di Lavadero 🎿 15km.
**Remarks:** Beautiful view.

🚐🛏 S **Molina** 🏔🍴 23D3
**Camper el Crear**, Via Bartolomeo Bacilieri 145.
**GPS:** n45,61229 e10,90855. ⬆

20 🛏 € 5 🚰🗑 included. **Location:** Rural, simple, quiet.
**Surface:** grassy/gravel. 🗓 01/01-31/12.
**Distance:** ⊗ on the spot 🚶 on the spot.
**Remarks:** Max. 48h, pay at restaurant.

🛏 S **Montagnana** 🌿 26E1
Via Circonvallazione. **GPS:** n45,23528 e11,46639. ⬆➡

20 🛏 free 🚰🗑 Ch WC free. **Location:** Urban. **Surface:** asphalted.
🗓 01/01-31/12.
**Distance:** 🚲 200m ⊗ 200m 🛒 200m.
**Remarks:** At sports centre.

🚐🛏 S **Montebello Vicentino** 23E3
**Camper Park Fracanzana**, Loc. Fracanzana 3.
**GPS:** n45,44252 e11,37822.

44 🛏 € 18, 01/06-31/08 € 25 🚰🗑 Ch 🔌 (44x) WC 🛢 € 4/4 🌊 included. **Location:** Rural. **Surface:** grassy/metalled.
🗓 01/01-31/12.
**Distance:** 🚲 2km ⛰ 2km ⊗ 3km 🛒 2km 🚌 on the spot.
**Remarks:** Video surveillance.

🛏 S **Padova** 🌿 26F1
**Park Camper Pontevigordarzere**, Via Telemaco Signorini, Padua (Padova). **GPS:** n45,44267 e11,88926. ⬆
17 🛏 € 8/24h 🚰🗑 Ch 🔌 € 2/8h. 🚌 🛢 🗓 01/01-31/12.
**Distance:** 🚲 centre 4,5km ⊗ 300m 🛒 300m 🚌 on the spot.

🛏 **Padova** 🌿 26F1
**P1**, Piazza della Pace Ytzhak Rabbin, Via cinquantottesimo Fanteria, Padua (Padova). **GPS:** n45,39686 e11,87673. ⬆
🛏 8-20h € 10, 20-8h € 10, 18-10h € 20.
**Surface:** asphalted.
🗓 01/01-31/12.
**Distance:** 🚲 on the spot ⛰ 6km ⊗ on the spot 🛒 on the spot 🚌 on the spot.

---

**Tourist information Padua (Padova):**
👁 Caffe Pedrocchi, Via Oberdan. Café, meeting point for students.
👁 Capella degli Scrovegni. Chapel.

🚐🛏 S **Peschiera del Garda** 26D1
**Area Camper Frassino**, Via Frassino 11. **GPS:** n45,43115 e10,67500. ⬆

80 🛏 € 15 🚰🗑 Ch 🔌 WC 🌊 included. 🚌 ♻ **Location:** Rural, simple. **Surface:** gravel. 🗓 01/01-31/12.
**Distance:** 🚲 1,5km 🛒 300m.

🚐🛏 S **Peschiera del Garda** 26D1
**Area camper Peschiera**, Via Milano. **GPS:** n45,43995 e10,68474. ⬆

100 🛏 € 18/24h 🚰🗑 Ch 🔌 WC 🛢 € 1 🌊 included. 🚌
**Location:** Urban, simple, noisy. **Surface:** gravel.
🗓 01/01-31/12.
**Distance:** 🚲 200m 🚴 1km ⊗ 400m 🛒 400m 🚌 on the spot 🚲 on the spot 🚶 on the spot.
**Remarks:** Monday-morning market.

**Tourist information Peschiera del Garda:**
ℹ Tourist town at Lake Garda.
🚶 💧 Mo-morning.

🚐🛏 S **Pianiga** 23F3
**Il Graticolato**, Via Giulio Onesti. **GPS:** n45,45681 e12,03344. ⬆

15 🛏 € 6/24h 🚰🗑 Ch 🔌 included.
**Surface:** unpaved. 🗓 01/01-31/12.
**Distance:** 🚲 250m ⊗ 8km 🛒 200m 🛒 150m 💧 50m 🚌 250m 🚲 200m.

🛏 **Porto Tolle** 🌊 26G2
Via strada del Mare, loc. Barricata, SP38. **GPS:** n44,84997 e12,46342. ⬆

50 🛏 € 3,50. 🚲 **Location:** Rural, quiet. **Surface:** grassy/sand.
🗓 01/01-31/12.
**Distance:** ⛰ 50m.
**Remarks:** Beach parking.

🛏 S **Porto Tolle** 🌊 26G2
**Agriturismo La Ca del Delta Corte**, Via Mazzini, 1.
**GPS:** n44,96267 e12,40627.
8 🛏 € 15 🔌 € 2/day. **Location:** Isolated, quiet. **Surface:** gravel.
**Distance:** ⊗ on the spot.

🛏 S **Punta Sabbioni** 🏖🌊 23G3
**Parking Dante Alighieri**, Dante Alighieri 26.
**GPS:** n45,44132 e12,42131. ⬆

IT

36 ⏻ € 17-20 + € 3/pp 🚰 💻Ch ✎ € 3/24h WC⬜included 📷€ 3
📶free.🛁
**Location:** Urban, simple, central, quiet. **Surface:** grassy.
📅 01/03–01/11.
**Distance:** 🚉1,5km 🏖1,5km 🍴1,5km 🚌500m.
**Remarks:** Arrival <22h, monitored parking, ferry boat to Venice 500m.

| 📷S | Punta Sabbioni 🏖🌊 | 23G3 |

Lungomare Dante Alighieri. **GPS:** n45,44342 e12,42189.⬆️.

5 ⏻€ 1,60/h, € 9/12h, overnight stay free. **Location:** Simple, quiet.
**Surface:** gravel. 📅 01/01–31/12.
**Distance:** 🚉750m ⊗500m.
**Remarks:** Max. 24h.

| 🏕S | Punta Sabbioni 🏖🌊 | 23G3 |

**Agricamping da Scarpa**, Via Pealto 15.
**GPS:** n45,44279 e12,44055.⬆️➡️.

15 ⏻€ 15-21 + € 5-8/pp 🚰💻Ch ✎ WC⬜ € 3 📶included.🛁
**Location:** Rural, comfortable, quiet.
**Surface:** grassy.
📅 01/01–31/12.
**Distance:** ⛰500m ⊗on the spot 🍴500m 🚢ferry Venice 1,5km.
**Remarks:** Breakfast-service.

| 📷S | Recoaro Terme 🏖⛰🎪❄ | 23E3 |

**Area Communale**, Via Della Restistenza.
**GPS:** n45,70430 e11,22902.⬆️➡️.

16 ⏻€ 5/24h 🚰€ 0,10/10liter 💻Ch ✎(16x)€ 0,50/2h,6Amp.
**Location:** Rural. **Surface:** grassy/gravel. 📅 01/01–31/12.
**Distance:** 🚉on the spot ⊗on the spot 🍴on the spot 🚌on the spot
🚲on the spot.

| 📷S | San Salvaro | 26E1 |

**Monastero di San Salvaro**, Via Guglielmo Marconi.
**GPS:** n45,20485 e11,40877.
⏻free🚰💻Ch📅 01/01–31/12.

| 📷S | Santo Stefano di Cadore 🎪 | 23G1 |

**Albergo Gasperina**, Loc. Cima Canale, Val Visdende.
**GPS:** n46,60835 e12,63053.⬆️➡️.

---

49 ⏻€ 12/24h, Aug € 14 🚰💻Ch ✎(49x)€ 2,50/day WCincluded
⬜€ 2.🛁 **Location:** Rural, simple, isolated, quiet. **Surface:** gravel.
📅 01/06–01/10.
**Distance:** 🚉12km 🚏300m ⊗on the spot 🍴6km 🚲on the spot
🚶on the spot.
**Remarks:** Check in at restaurant, bread-service, 10% discount at
restaurant.

| 📷S | Sappada ⛰❄ | 23G1 |

Borgata Palù. **GPS:** n46,56254 e12,67991.⬆️➡️.

50 ⏻€ 12/24h 🚰💻Ch ✎(24x)included.🛁
**Location:** Rural, simple, quiet. **Surface:** gravel. 📅 01/01–31/12.
**Distance:** 🚉1,1km ⊗500m 🍴1km 🚲on the spot 🚶on the spot
🚲100m.
**Remarks:** Keycard at townhall, caution € 10.

| 📷S | Schio 🏖⛰🎪❄ | 23E3 |

**Camper Schio**, Via Cardatori. **GPS:** n45,71518 e11,34607.
15 ⏻€ 10 🚰💻Ch ✎. **Location:** Urban. **Surface:** metalled.
📅 01/01–31/12.
**Distance:** 🚉750m ⊗200m 🍴200m.
**Remarks:** On site of a former barracks complex, video surveillance.

| 📷S | Schio 🏖⛰🎪❄ | 23E3 |

**Parking Palasport**, Viale dell'Industria. **GPS:** n45,71389 e11,37599.⬆️.

4 ⏻free 🚰💻Chfree. **Location:** Urban. **Surface:** asphalted.
📅 01/01–31/12.
**Distance:** 🚉1km ⊗250m 🍴250m.

| 📷S | Sernaglia della Battaglia | 23F3 |

**Area attrezzata Le Grave**, Via Passo Barca, Falzè di Piave.
**GPS:** n45,85676 e12,16566.⬆️➡️.

26 ⏻€ 10 🚰💻Chincluded ✎€ 2/24h.🛁 **Location:** Rural, simple.
**Surface:** grassy. 📅 01/01–31/12.
**Distance:** 🚉500m ⛰on the spot ⊗100m 🍴500m 🚌300m.

| 📷S | Soave 🍷🌾 | 26E1 |

Via Invalidi del Lavoro. **GPS:** n45,42340 e11,24541.⬆️➡️.

---

16 ⏻€ 5. ✎Ch ✎(16x),16Amp WC📶included.🛁
**Surface:** grasstiles.
📅 01/01–31/12.
**Distance:** 🚉200m ✈3km 🚏on the spot ⊗200m 🍴200m 🚌300m.
**Remarks:** Nearby police station.

| 🏕S | Soave 🍷🌾 | 26E1 |

**Cantina Filippi**, Via Liberta 55. **GPS:** n45,46373 e11,23798.
12 ⏻€ 15 2 pers. incl., free for clients (>€ 30) 🚰💻Chincluded
✎WC⬜. **Location:** Rural. **Surface:** grassy. 📅 01/01–31/12.
**Distance:** ⊗on the spot.
**Remarks:** Barbecue place, playground.

| 📷S | Treviso 🌾 | 23F3 |

**Parking ex Foro Boario**, Via Castello d'Amore.
**GPS:** n45,67014 e12,25733.⬆️➡️.

13 ⏻free 🚰💻Chfree. **Location:** Rural, simple. **Surface:** metalled.
📅 01/01–31/12.
**Distance:** 🚉500m ✈11,5km ⊗500m 🍴500m 🚌200m.
**Remarks:** Max. 48h.

| 📷S | Treviso 🌾 | 23F3 |

Via Giovanni Boccaccio. **GPS:** n45,66769 e12,26361.⬆️➡️.

40 ⏻free 🚰💻Chfree. **Location:** Urban, simple, central, noisy.
**Surface:** asphalted. 📅 01/01–31/12.
**Distance:** 🚉1km ⊗500m 🍴500m 🚌300m.
**Remarks:** Along railwayline.

**Tourist information Treviso:**
🏛 Sile. Fish-market on island.

| 📷S | Venezia 🌾🏖🛥🌊 | 23G3 |

**Parcheggio Al Tronchetto**, Venice (Venezia).
**GPS:** n45,44146 e12,30514.⬆️.

40 ⏻€ 21/0–12h, 12–24h € 16 🚰✎included 🚢.🛁
**Location:** Urban, simple, central, quiet. **Surface:** asphalted.
📅 01/01–31/12.
**Distance:** 🚉2km ⛰on the spot ⊗2km 🍴2km 🚢ferry, train.

| 📷S | Venezia 🌾🏖🥘🌊 | 23G3 |

**Parco di San Giuliano**, Via San Giuliano 19, Venice (Venezia).
**GPS:** n45,46742 e12,27916.⬆️➡️.

100 ⛺ € 18/24h 🚰 Ch ✎ (30x)€ 4/24h WC included ⚡€ 5. 🚐
**Location:** Urban, comfortable, central, quiet. **Surface:** grassy.
⬛ 01/01-31/12.
**Distance:** 🚶4km 🚲5km ⊗200m 🍺1,5km 🚆ferry Venice 100m, bus
🚌 on the spot 🚶 on the spot.
**Tourist information Venice (Venezia):**
🏛 A.P.T. ( Azienda di Promozione Turistica), www.turismovenezia.it.
Historical city consits of 117 islands, 150 canals and 400 bridges.

### Verona — 26E1
**Area sosta camper Porta Palio**, Via dalla Bona.
**GPS:** n45,43354 e10,97879. ⬆

37 ⛺ € 5/4h, € 10/24h 🚰 Ch included. 🚐 ♻
**Location:** Urban, simple, central. **Surface:** asphalted.
⬛ 01/01-31/12.
**Distance:** 🚶500m ⊗Pizza (ordering service) 🚌bus 62 > centre.

### Verona — 26E1
**Agricamping Corte Finiletto**, Strada Bresciana, 41.
**GPS:** n45,44651 e10,91917. ⬆

15 ⛺ € 22, 2 pers.incl 🚰 Ch ✎ € 2 WC 📶 included.
**Location:** Rural, comfortable, isolated, quiet. **Surface:** grassy.
⬛ 01/01-31/12.
**Distance:** 🚶6km 🚲3km 🍺3km 🛒on the spot 🚴1,5km 🚶1,5km.
**Remarks:** 10% discount on presentation of the most recent guide.
**Tourist information Verona:**
👁 Arena. Large anfiteatro, in July/August opera performances.
👁 Via Capella. Known for the love drama of Romeo and Juliet.
🏛 Piazza dellen Erbe. ⬛ daily.

### Vicenza — 23E3
**Park Interscambio CentroBus**, Via Bassano, Zona sud-est.
**GPS:** n45,54321 e11,55886.

40 ⛺ € 10/24h 🚰 ✎ WC included. **Location:** Urban.
**Surface:** asphalted. ⬛ 01/01-31/12 ⚡ during event.
**Distance:** 🚶2km ⊗on the spot 🍺2km 🚌Free bus to centre, every 15
min 🚴 on the spot.
**Remarks:** At stadium, monitored parking 24/24, borrow cycles for free.

### Vicenza — 23E3
**Park Interscambio CentroBus**, Viale Cricoli, Zona nord.
**GPS:** n45,56418 e11,54903. ➡

18 ⛺ € 8,40/24h 🚰 Ch WC included.
**Location:** Urban. **Surface:** asphalted.
⬛ 01/01-31/12.
**Distance:** 🚶1,6km ⊗on the spot 🍺on the spot 🚌Free bus to centre.
**Tourist information Vicenza:**
👁 Quartiere delle Barche. District with palaces in Venetian style.

# Friuli Venezia Giulia

### Ampezzo — 23G1
Via Laucjit. **GPS:** n46,41170 e12,80073. ⬆➡

6 ⛺ € 7/24h 🚰 Ch ✎ WC included. **Location:** Rural, comfortable,
quiet. **Surface:** gravel. ⬛ 01/01-31/12.
**Distance:** 🚶500m 🍺650m 🛒on the spot.
**Remarks:** Next to sports fields.

### Andreis — 23G2
SP20. **GPS:** n46,19912 e12,61315. ⬆

20 ⛺ € 5/day 🚰 🍺. 🚐
**Location:** Simple, quiet. **Surface:** gravel.
**Distance:** 🚶200m ⏟little stream 🚶on the spot.

### Aquileia — 23H3
Via Achille Grandi. **GPS:** n45,76549 e13,36898. ⬆➡

20 ⛺ € 10/day 🚰 Ch WC included. 🚐
**Location:** Urban, quiet. **Surface:** grasstiles. ⬛ 01/01-31/12.
**Distance:** 🚶500m ⊗200m 🛒on the spot.
**Remarks:** Max. 48h.

### Arta Terme — 23G1
Terme di Arta. **GPS:** n46,47554 e13,01677. ⬆

7 ⛺ free 🚰 Ch free ✎.
**Surface:** grasstiles. ⬛ 01/01-31/12.

**Distance:** 🚶1km ⊗300m.
**Remarks:** Narrow entrance.

### Artegna — 23H2
Via Vicenza. **GPS:** n46,23465 e13,14919. ⬆➡

2 ⛺ free 🚰 Ch free. **Location:** Urban, simple, noisy.
**Surface:** concrete. ⬛ 01/01-31/12.
**Distance:** 🚶800m ⊗800m.
**Remarks:** Along railwayline.

### Barcis — 23G2
Loc. Portuz, SS251. **GPS:** n46,19055 e12,56507. ⬆

20 ⛺ € 12/24h 🚰 Ch ✎ included. 🚐 **Location:** Comfortable,
isolated, quiet. **Surface:** grasstiles/metalled. ⬛ 01/01-31/12.
**Distance:** 🚶400m 🚲on the spot ⊗500m 🍺500m 🛒on the spot
🚶 on the spot.
**Remarks:** At the lake of Barcis.

### Brugnera — 23G2
**Parco Di Villa Varda**, Via Villa Varda di S. Cassiano.
**GPS:** n45,88861 e12,52980. ⬆

40 ⛺ free 🚰 Ch free.
**Location:** Rural, quiet. **Surface:** gravel. ⬛ 01/01-31/12.
**Distance:** ⊗on the spot.
**Remarks:** Recreation park.

### Buttrio — 23H2
Via Cividale. **GPS:** n46,01583 e13,33674. ⬆

8 ⛺ free 🚰 Ch free.
**Surface:** grasstiles/metalled. ⬛ 01/01-31/12.
**Distance:** 🚶300m ⊗300m 🍺500m.
**Remarks:** Video surveillance.

### Capriva del Friuli — 23H2
Via degli Alpini. **GPS:** n45,94657 e13,51107. ⬆➡

IT

6 ⛟free ⛽🚰Ch 🔧free. **Location:** Rural, quiet. **Surface:** metalled.
◻ 01/01-31/12.
**Distance:** 🚃600m 🏍 on the spot 🚶 on the spot.

🅿S **Cavasso Nuovo** 23G2
Via Dante Alighieri. **GPS:** n46,19514 e12,77467.⬆.

4 ⛟free ⛽🚰Ch🔧free. **Location:** Noisy. **Surface:** asphalted.
◻ 01/01-31/12.
**Distance:** 🚃400m.

🅿S **Cividale del Friuli** 🌿 23H2
Via delle Mura. **GPS:** n46,09446 e13,43618. ⬆➡.

4 ⛟free ⛽🚰Chfree.
**Location:** Urban, quiet. **Surface:** asphalted.
**Distance:** 🚃500m ⊗500m 🏍 on the spot.
**Remarks:** Max. 72h.

🅿S **Clauzetto** 🍴 23G2
**Ambito delle Grotte di Pradis**, Via Pradis di sotto,76.
**GPS:** n46,24538 e12,88974.⬆.

10 ⛟free ⛽🚰Chfree. **Location:** Rural, isolated, quiet.
**Surface:** gravel. ◻ 01/01-31/12.
**Distance:** 🚃Clauzetto 3km ⊗150m 🏍 on the spot 🚶 on the spot.
**Remarks:** Parking at the caves.

🅿S **Codroipo** 🌿 23H2
Strada vicinale molino della sega, Passariano.
**GPS:** n45,94649 e13,00836.⬆.

8 ⛟free ⛽€ 3/1h 🚰Ch 🔧(8x)€ 3/6h. **Location:** Rural, quiet.
**Surface:** grasstiles. ◻ 01/01-31/12.
**Distance:** 🚃centre 3,5km ⊗300m 🚶 on the spot.
**Remarks:** Coins at tourist info.

---

🅿 **Colloredo di Monte Albano** 23H2
Strada Provinciale 49. **GPS:** n46,16556 e13,13932.⬆.

8 ⛟free. **Location:** Rural, simple, quiet. **Surface:** metalled.
◻ 01/01-31/12.
**Distance:** 🚃100m ⊗100m.
**Remarks:** Max. 7m.

🅿S **Cormons** 23H2
**P.le Luciano Zani**, Salita del Monte Quarin.
**GPS:** n45,96672 e13,47341.➡.

3 ⛟free ⛽🔧free. **Location:** Rural, isolated, quiet.
**Surface:** metalled. ◻ 01/01-31/12.
**Distance:** 🚃3,5km ⊗2km 🍺2,5km 🏍 on the spot 🚶 on the spot.

🅿S **Corno di Rosazzo** 23H2
Via dei Pini. **GPS:** n45,98955 e13,43917. ⬆➡.

8 ⛟free ⛽🚰Ch 🚿free. **Location:** Rural, simple, quiet.
**Surface:** asphalted. ◻ 01/01-31/12.
**Distance:** 🚃300m ⊗1,5km 🍺1km.
**Remarks:** Max. 48h.

🅿S **Forni di Sopra** ⛰🍴❄ 23G1
**Santa Viela**, SS52. **GPS:** n46,42500 e12,57036.⬆.

20 ⛟€7-9 ⛽🚰Chfree. 🛁 **Location:** Rural, simple, noisy.
**Surface:** asphalted. ◻ 01/01-31/12.
**Distance:** 🚃800m ⊗on the spot 🍺800m 🚌400m 🏍 on the spot
🚶 on the spot 🎿 on the spot 🛷 on the spot.
**Remarks:** No camping activities.

🅿S **Gemona del Friuli** 🌿⛰ 23H2
Piazzale Mons. Battista Monai. **GPS:** n46,27585 e13,13728. ⬆➡.

15 ⛟free ⛽🚰Chfree. **Location:** Rural, simple, central, noisy.
**Surface:** asphalted. ◻ 01/01-31/12.

---

**Distance:** 🚃on the spot ✈3,3km ⊗300m 🍺500m 🏍 on the spot.

🅿S **Gorizia** ⚓ 37A1
Viale Oriani. **GPS:** n45,94554 e13,61603. ⬆➡.

30 ⛟free ⛽🚰Chfree. **Location:** Urban, simple, quiet.
**Surface:** asphalted. ◻ 01/01-31/12.
**Distance:** 🚃centre 500m 🏍 on the spot.
**Remarks:** Max. 72h.

🅿S **Gradisca d'Isonzo** 23H2
Viale Trieste. **GPS:** n45,88577 e13,49582.⬆.

3 ⛟free ⛽🚰Chfree.
**Location:** Urban, central. **Surface:** asphalted. ◻ 01/01-31/12.
**Distance:** 🚃on the spot ✈2,3km ⊗on the spot 🍺on the spot.
**Remarks:** Max. 48h.

🅿 **Gradisca d'Isonzo** 23H2
**Agriturismo Ai Feudi di Marizza Monica e Villi**, Via Venuti, 11.
**GPS:** n45,89214 e13,46782. ⬆➡.
5 ⛟guests free. **Location:** Simple. ◻ 01/01-31/12.
**Distance:** ⊗on the spot.

🅿S **Grado** ⚓🏖 23H3
Viala Italia. **GPS:** n45,68218 e13,41230. ⬆➡.

41 ⛟€ 16/24h ⛽🚰Ch 🔧included. 🚐 **Location:** Simple.
**Surface:** asphalted. ◻ 01/01-31/12.
**Distance:** 🚃2km 🏊600m 🏍 on the spot.
**Remarks:** Video surveillance.

🅿S **Latisana** 23H3
Via Gasperi. **GPS:** n45,78163 e12,99325. ⬆➡.

10 ⛟free ⛽🚰Chfree. **Location:** Urban, simple. **Surface:** asphalted.
◻ 01/01-31/12.
**Distance:** 🚃500m ⊗on the spot 🍺on the spot.
**Remarks:** At supermarket.

🅿 **Malborghetto Valbruna** ⛰❄ 23H1
Malga Saisera. **GPS:** n46,45624 e13,46955.⬆.

---

10 🛏€ 0,60/h. 🚐
**Location:** Rural, isolated, quiet. **Surface:** gravel.
**Distance:** 5,5km ⊗5,5km 🚶on the spot.

**S** **Maniago** **23G2**
Via Colvera. **GPS:** n46,17632 e12,71149. ⬆➡.

5 🛏free 🚰🗑Ch 🧹free. **Location:** Urban, simple.
**Surface:** grasstiles. ⏹ 01/01-31/12.
**Distance:** 400m ⊗200m.

**S** **Monfalcone** **37A1**
Areacamper F.V.G, Via Consiglio d'Europa, 13.
**GPS:** n45,79754 e13,55867. ⬆.

36 🛏€ 15/24h 🚰🗑Ch 🧹 WC included. 🚐
**Location:** Urban, quiet. **Surface:** metalled. ⏹ 01/01-31/12.
**Distance:** city centre 3km ⊗100m.
**Remarks:** Nearby port, video surveillance.

**S** **Montereale Valcellina** **23G2**
Via dell'Omo. **GPS:** n46,15168 e12,66122. ⬆.

15 🛏€ 5 🚰🗑Ch 🧹included. **Location:** Urban, simple.
**Surface:** asphalted. ⏹ 01/01-31/12.
**Distance:** 500m 🍽300m.
**Remarks:** Service passerby € 2, key at petrol station/bar.

**S** **Mossa** **37A1**
Via delle Fornaci. **GPS:** n45,94563 e13,54536. ⬆➡.

4 🛏free. **Location:** Rural, quiet. **Surface:** metalled.
⏹ 01/01-31/12.
**Distance:** 1km ⊗on the spot 🚲on the spot 🚶on the spot.

**S** **Oleis** **23H2**
Via Rosazzo. **GPS:** n46,01634 e13,39311. ⬆.

10 🛏free 🚰🗑Ch 🧹free. **Location:** Quiet. **Surface:** metalled.
⏹ 01/01-31/12.
**Distance:** 100m.

**S** **Paluzza** **23G1**
Ponte di Sutrio, Via Nazionale. **GPS:** n46,51148 e13,00203. ⬆.

5 🛏free 🚰€ 3,50 🛏€ 3,50 Ch. **Location:** Simple, noisy.
**Surface:** gravel. ⏹ 01/01-31/12.
**Distance:** 150m 🍽150m.
**Remarks:** At petrol station.

**S** **Piancavallo** **23G2**
Via Barcis. **GPS:** n46,11141 e12,51411. ⬆➡.

70 🛏€ 13/24h 🚰🗑Ch 🧹 WC included. 🚗
**Location:** Quiet. **Surface:** metalled. ⏹ 01/01-31/12.
**Distance:** 600m 🚵on the spot.
**Remarks:** Max. 7 days, check in at hotel.

**S** **Pordenone** **23G2**
SS13, Pordenone. **GPS:** n45,97236 e12,64332. ⬆➡.

8 🛏free 🚰🗑Ch. **Location:** Urban, simple, noisy.
**Surface:** asphalted. ⏹ 01/01-31/12.
**Distance:** 1km 🚲3km ⊗200m 🍽on the spot.
**Remarks:** Max. 48h, to be paid at petrol station.

**S** **Preone** **23G1**
Strada Provinciale 12. **GPS:** n46,39736 e12,86561. ⬆.
10 🛏€ 13/24h 🚰🗑Ch 🧹included. **Surface:** grasstiles.
⏹ 01/01-31/12.
**Distance:** 500m ⊗350m 🍽350m.
**Remarks:** Inspection 2017: closed because of renovation.

**S** **Quinto di Trevisio** **23F3**
Camper Resort Quinto, Via Costamala 26.
**GPS:** n45,63901 e12,15728. ⬆➡.

28 🛏€ 20 🚰🗑Ch 🧹 WC included. 🚐
**Location:** Rural, luxurious. **Surface:** gravel. ⏹ 01/01-31/12.
**Distance:** 800m 🚵on the spot ⊗500m 🍽650m 🚶on the spot 🚲on the spot.
**Remarks:** Max. 5 days.

**S** **Ravascletto** **23G1**
Via Valcalda. **GPS:** n46,52348 e12,92790. ⬆.

10 🛏€ 6 🚰🗑Ch 🧹 (4x)included. **Location:** Simple.
**Surface:** asphalted. ⏹ 01/01-31/12.
**Distance:** 500m ⊗200m.
**Remarks:** Pay at tourist office.

**S** **Sacile** **23G2**
Viale Repubblica. **GPS:** n45,95662 e12,49667. ⬆.

7 🛏€ 9/24h 🚰🗑Ch included.
**Location:** Urban. **Surface:** metalled. ⏹ 01/01-31/12.
**Distance:** 600m ⊗300m 🍽on the spot.
**Remarks:** Max. 48h, video surveillance.

**S** **San Daniele del Friuli** **23G2**
Via Udine, SP16. **GPS:** n46,15610 e13,01368. ⬆➡.

20 🛏free 🚰🗑Ch free. **Location:** Rural, central, quiet.
**Surface:** grasstiles. ⏹ 01/01-31/12.
**Distance:** 300m ⊗300m 🍽300m 🚲200m.
**Remarks:** Parking sports park.

**S** **San Vito al Tagliamento** **23G2**
Area di sosta San Vito al Tagliamento, Via Pulet.
**GPS:** n45,91224 e12,86590. ⬆➡.

12 🛏€ 5/12h, € 8/24h, € 15/48h 🚰€ 1 🗑Ch 🧹included. 🚐
**Location:** Rural, simple, isolated, quiet. **Surface:** asphalted
⏹ 01/01-31/12.

**IT**

**Distance:** 500m 15km 500m 500m 500m.
**Remarks:** Max. 48h, gate can be opened manually.

**S** | **Sesto al Reghena** 23G2
Viale degli Olmi. **GPS:** n45,84615 e12,81273. ↑→.

6 €5/day €0,10/10liter €3 Ch€2 €1/12h.
**Surface:** asphalted. 01/01-31/12.
**Distance:** 500m 500m.

**S** | **Spilimbergo** 23G2
Via Udine. **GPS:** n46,10814 e12,90411. ↑→.

10 €5 Ch included. **Location:** Urban, simple, central.
**Surface:** grasstiles. 01/01-31/12.
**Distance:** 300m 300m 400m.
**Remarks:** Max. 48h.

**S** | **Tarcento** 23H2
Plein-air Torre, Via Sottocolleverzan. **GPS:** n46,21446 e13,22504. ↑→.

10 free Ch. **Location:** Urban, simple, quiet.
**Surface:** grasstiles.
01/01-31/12.
**Distance:** 200m 200m 200m.
**Remarks:** Nearby sports center, max. 72h, no camping activities.

**S** | **Tarvisio** 23H1
Localita Plezzut. **GPS:** n46,49633 e13,68937.
€15/24h Ch.
**Surface:** grasstiles. 01/01-31/12.
**Distance:** Tarvisio 10km on the spot on the spot.

**S** | **Tarvisio** 23H1
Parcheggio P3, Via Armando Diaz. **GPS:** n46,50426 e13,57157. ↑→.

16 €0,60/h Chfree WC. **Location:** Urban, simple, central.
**Surface:** metalled. 01/01-31/12.
**Distance:** 300m 100m 200m 200m.
**Remarks:** Max. 2 days.

**S** | **Tarvisio** 23H1
Monte lussari. **GPS:** n46,50737 e13,53421. ↑.

---

20 free. **Surface:** asphalted/metalled. 01/01-31/12.
**Distance:** on the spot 600m on the spot 100m.

**S** | **Timau** 23G1
Strada Statale 52bis. **GPS:** n46,58904 e12,97276. ↑→.

5 €5 Chincluded €5/day. **Location:** Rural, isolated,
quiet. **Surface:** grasstiles/grassy. 01/06-30/09.
**Distance:** 2,5km on the spot.
**Remarks:** At small lake, to be paid at bar.

**S** | **Tramonti di Sopra** 23G2
Area picnic Sot Trivea, Strada Da Lis Fornas.
**GPS:** n46,30133 e12,77974. ↑→.

4 €7 Ch included. **Location:** Rural, isolated, quiet.
**Surface:** grassy/gravel. 01/01-31/12.
**Distance:** 1,5km 1,5km.
**Remarks:** Beside river.

**S** | **Trieste** 37A1
Mamaca park, Via del Pane Bianco. **GPS:** n45,62539 e13,78707. ↑→.

6 €18 Chincluded €4/4h WC.
**Location:** Urban. **Surface:** gravel. 01/01-31/12.
**Distance:** 200m 100m.
**Remarks:** Call for entrance code, narrow entrance.

**S** | **Trieste** 37A1
Via Karl Ludwig Von Bruck. **GPS:** n45,63710 e13,76990. ↑→.

20 €4 Chincluded. **Location:** Urban, simple, noisy.
**Surface:** asphalted. 01/01-31/12.
**Distance:** 3km shuttle to centre.
**Remarks:** Max. 72h, pitches under motorway.

**P** | **Trieste** 37A1
Via Ottaviano Augusto. **GPS:** n45,64599 e13,75654.

---

€0,80/h 8-20h. **Location:** Urban, central, noisy.
**Surface:** asphalted. 01/01-31/12.
**Distance:** centre 500m 100m on the spot.
**Tourist information Trieste:**
Grotta del Giganta. Caves. Tue-Su, 01/07-31/08 Mo-Su.

**S** | **Udine** 23H2
Via Chiusaforte. **GPS:** n46,08115 e13,22317. ↑.

50 free Chfree. **Location:** Urban, simple, noisy.
**Surface:** grasstiles. 01/01-31/12.
**Distance:** city centre 2km 3,5km 160m 400m line 1 >
centre.

**S** | **Valvasone** 23G2
Via Pier Pasolini. **GPS:** n45,99819 e12,86031. ↑→.

8 free Ch free. **Location:** Rural, simple, quiet.
**Surface:** asphalted. 01/01-31/12.
**Distance:** 350m 350m 400m.
**Remarks:** Max. 48h.

**S** | **Villa Vicentina** 23H2
Via Duca d'Aosta. **GPS:** n45,81738 e13,39369. ↑.

5 free Chfree. **Location:** Simple. **Surface:** asphalted
01/01-31/12.
**Distance:** 200m on the spot.

**S** | **Vito d'Asio** 23G1
Via Gialinars, San Francesco. **GPS:** n46,31244 e12,93427. ↑→.

5 free Ch free.
**Location:** Rural, isolated, quiet. **Surface:** metalled.
01/01-31/12 With snow.
**Distance:** Vito d'Asio 15km 350m on the spot.
**Remarks:** Near sports fields.

IT

## Zoppola — 23G2

Via Manteghe. **GPS:** n45,96502 e12,78019. ↑→.

20 free ⌐🔲Ch free. **Location:** Rural, isolated, quiet.
**Surface:** metalled. ◻ 01/01-31/12.
**Distance:** centre 500m 850m 1,5km.
**Remarks:** At gymnasium, max. 48h.

# Emilia-Romagna

## Anita — 26F2

**Agriturismo Prato Pozzo**, Via Rotta Martinella 34/a.
**GPS:** n44,54892 e12,13322. ↑→.

20 € 6 + € 6/pp, guests free ⌐🔲Ch (12x)€ 2,60/day
WC included ▣. **Location:** Rural, comfortable, isolated, quiet.
**Surface:** grassy/metalled. ◻ 01/01-31/12.
**Distance:** 1km 500m 500m on the spot 1km 1km.

## Argenta — 26F2

**Area Golf Club**, Via Poderi. **GPS:** n44,63027 e11,81112. ↑.
5 € 5 ⌐🔲Ch included. **Location:** Rural.
**Surface:** gravel/metalled. ◻ 01/01-31/12.
**Distance:** 3km 1,5km 400m.
**Remarks:** Key at Golf Club.

## Argenta — 26F2

Via Galassi. **GPS:** n44,61265 e11,83972. ↑→.

10 free ⌐🔲free. **Location:** Urban. **Surface:** metalled.
◻ 01/01-31/12.
**Distance:** 200m 200m 200m 200m.
**Remarks:** At tennis-courts, max. 24h.

## Bagno di Romagna — 34C1

**Area camper Diga di Ridracoli**, SP112, Santa Sofia.
**GPS:** n43,88477 e11,83343.
13 € 21 ⌐🔲Ch WC included. **Location:** Rural, isolated.
**Surface:** grassy. ◻ 01/03-31/10.
**Distance:** on the spot on the spot.
**Remarks:** In nature reserve.

## Bagno di Romagna — 34C1

Via Lungo Savio 1. **GPS:** n43,84108 e11,96532.

10 free. **Surface:** metalled. ◻ 01/01-31/12.
**Distance:** 500m 1km 500m 500m on the spot.
**Remarks:** Parking swimming pool.

**Tourist information Bagno di Romagna:**
⌂ Week market. ◻ Fri 7.30-12.30h.

## Bellaria-Igea Marina — 26G3

**Parking delle Robinie**, Via Pinzon 260, Igea Marina, Zona sud.
**GPS:** n44,12783 e12,48873.

106 € 10-19 ⌐🔲Ch € 2,50/day,6Amp € 1.
**Location:** Rural, comfortable, central, quiet. **Surface:** grassy/gravel.
◻ 12/03-15/10, 8-22h.
**Distance:** 10m 200m 100m 50m.

## Bellaria-Igea Marina — 26G3

**Mare d'Inverno**, Via Murri, 13. **GPS:** n44,11639 e12,49972. ↑.

45 € 11, 21/06-31/08 € 17,50, holidays + € 2 ⌐🔲Ch € 2,50/day
€ 1. **Location:** Rural, comfortable, quiet. **Surface:** grassy.
◻ 15/03-30/09.
**Distance:** 800m 200m 800m 1,5km, bakery 800m
100m.

## Bellaria-Igea Marina — 26G3

**Area Sosta Rio Pircio**, Via Benivieni 6, Igea Marina.
**GPS:** n44,12688 e12,48849. ↑.

63 € 14, Jun € 16, Jul/Aug € 19 ⌐🔲Ch (63x)€ 2/day
WC € 1 included. **Location:** Rural, comfortable, central, quiet.
**Surface:** grasstiles/grassy. ◻ 01/01-31/12 ● 06/01-28/01.
**Distance:** 500m on the spot 300m 250m.

## Bellaria-Igea Marina — 26G3

**L'Adriatico Parking**, Via Benivieni, 12. **GPS:** n44,12644 e12,48740.

60 € 10, 21/06-31/08 € 19 ⌐🔲Ch € 2,50/day € 1 against
payment ⚡ € 1/24h,€ 5/week. **Location:** Rural, comfortable, quiet.
**Surface:** grassy. ◻ 15/03-31/12.
**Distance:** 250m.

## Bellaria-Igea Marina — 26G3

**Porto Mario Family Village**, Viale A. Pinzon 310.
**GPS:** n44,12308 e12,49416. ↑.
77 € 13-18 ⌐🔲Ch (77x)€ 2/24h WC ▣ ⚡ included.
**Location:** Rural, comfortable. **Surface:** metalled.
◻ 01/03-30/09.
**Distance:** 1km 100m on the spot.
**Remarks:** Bicycle rental.

## Berceto — 26C3

Via P. Salas. **GPS:** n44,51123 e9,98589. ↑→.

20 € 7 ⌐🔲Ch WC included.
**Surface:** asphalted. ◻ 01/01-31/12.
**Distance:** 200m 4km 200m 200m on the spot on the
spot.
**Remarks:** Caution € 20, key at kiosk in front of restaurant Rina.

## Bertinoro — 26G3

Via Superga, SP 83, Loc. Fratta Terme. **GPS:** n44,13749 e12,10313. ↑→.

free ⌐🔲Ch free.
**Location:** Rural. **Surface:** asphalted. ◻ 01/01-31/12.
**Distance:** 1km 1km 1km 300m.
**Remarks:** Near spa resort and sports centre.

## Bologna — 26E2

**Camper Stop Area Bottega del Camper Bologna**, Via della Beverara,
157. **GPS:** n44,52439 e11,33272. ↑.
€ 20/24h ⌐🔲Ch included.
**Surface:** gravel. ◻ 01/01-31/12.
**Distance:** city centre 1,5km on the spot.
**Remarks:** Motorhome dealer, arrival during opening hours.

**Tourist information Bologna:**
ℹ U.I.A.T. (Ufficio Informazioni e di Accoglienza Turistica), Piazza
Medaglie d'Oro, 2, urp.comune.bologna.it/IAT/IAT.nsf. City with histori-
cal centre.
Ⓜ Museum di Anatomia. Anatomy museum. ◻ Mo-Fri.
✝ Abbazia di Santo Stefano. Abbey with 4 churches.
✝ San Petronio. Church with gothic interior.

## Bomporto — 26E2

Piazza dello Sport, Via Verdi. **GPS:** n44,72886 e11,03585.

10 free ⌐🔲free. **Location:** Urban, simple. **Surface:** metalled.
◻ 01/01-31/12.
**Distance:** 500m 500m.
**Remarks:** Parking at sports park.

## Brisighella — 26F3

Piazzale Donatori di Sangue. **GPS:** n44,22168 e11,77883. ↑→.

18 € 8 ⌐🔲Ch free € 2/12h. **Location:** Urban.
**Surface:** asphalted. ◻ 01/01-31/12.
**Distance:** 1km 1km 1km 500m.
**Remarks:** Near spa resort.

IT

**IT**

⊞S **Carpi** 26D2

**Bruno Losi**, Piazzale delle Piscine. **GPS:** n44,78444 e10,86817. ⬆.

5 🅿free 🚰🗑Chfree. **Surface:** metalled. ☐ 01/01-31/12.
**Distance:** 🚶300m ⊗50m 🚌on the spot.
**Remarks:** Parking swimming pool, max. 72h.

⊞S **Casal Borsetti** 26G2

**Area Sosta Camper Mare e Parco**, Via Ortolani.
**GPS:** n44,55000 e12,27997. ⬆➡.

238 🅿€ 10, 01/06-01/09 € 12 🚰🗑Chincluded 🔌€ 3/24h WC🗑.
**Location:** Rural, comfortable, central, quiet. **Surface:** grassy/metalled.
☐ 01/01-31/12.
**Distance:** 🏖150m ⊗150m.
**Remarks:** Dogs beach.

⊞S **Casola Valsenio** 26F3

Via don Milani/Via Antonio Gramsci. **GPS:** n44,22597 e11,62953. ⬆➡.

3 🅿free 🚰free.
**Location:** Urban. **Surface:** asphalted. ☐ 01/01-31/12.
**Distance:** 🚶300m ⊗500m 🍴500m.
**Remarks:** At swimming pool.

⊞S **Casola Valsenio** 26F3

Viale Domenico Neri. **GPS:** n44,22483 e11,62392. ⬆.
4 🅿free 🚰free. **Location:** Urban. **Surface:** asphalted.
☐ 01/01-31/12.
**Distance:** 🚶100m ⊗500m 🍴100m 🚌250m.

⊞S **Castel San Pietro Terme** 26F3

Via Oriani. **GPS:** n44,39725 e11,59197. ⬆➡.

8 🅿free 🚰€ 1 🗑ChWC€ 0,20.
**Location:** Urban. **Surface:** asphalted. ☐ 01/01-31/12.
**Distance:** 🚶300m 🔌 4,2km 🍴200m ⊗250m 🍴250m 🚌250m.
**Remarks:** Nearby hospital.

⊞S **Castellarano** 26D2

**Parco Don Reverberi**, Via Don Reverberi.
**GPS:** n44,50777 e10,73419. ⬆➡.

5 🅿free 🚰🗑Chfree. **Location:** Rural, simple, noisy.
**Surface:** asphalted. ☐ 01/01-31/12.
**Distance:** 🚶500m 🏖500m 🍴500m ⊗500m 🍴500m.

⊞S **Castelnovo ne' Monti** ⛰ 26D3

**Impianti Sportivi**, Zona PEP, Via Fratelli Cervi, SS63.
**GPS:** n44,43277 e10,41133. ⬆.

4 🅿free 🚰🗑Chfree. **Location:** Rural, simple, quiet.
**Surface:** asphalted. ☐ 01/01-31/12.
**Distance:** 🚶500m ⊗100m 🍴on the spot 🚶200m 🚶on the spot.

⊞S **Cervia** ♨ 26G3

Via Aldo Ascione, Cervia-nord. **GPS:** n44,28151 e12,32459. ⬆.

50 🅿free 🚰🗑Chfree. **Location:** Simple, isolated, noisy.
**Surface:** asphalted. ☐ 01/01-31/12.
**Distance:** 🚶3km 🏖3km ⊗1,3km.
**Remarks:** No camping activities.

⊞S **Cervia** ♨ 26G3

Viale Tritone, Fraz. Pinarella. **GPS:** n44,23984 e12,35883. ⬆.

40 🅿free 🚰🗑Chfree. **Location:** Urban, simple, noisy.
**Surface:** asphalted/metalled. ☐ 01/01-31/12.
**Distance:** 🚶750m 🏖900m ⊗on the spot.
**Remarks:** No camping activities.

⊞S **Cervia** ♨ 26G3

Via Ravenna. **GPS:** n44,27597 e12,34107. ⬆.
🅿against payment. 🚐🔌 ☐ 01/01-31/12.
**Distance:** 🚶500m 🏖1km ⊗500m 🍴500m.
**Remarks:** No camping activities.

⊞S **Cervia** ♨ 26G3

**Terme di Cervia**, Viale C. Forlanini, Cervia-nord.
**GPS:** n44,27335 e12,32964. ⬆.

50 🅿€ 10/24h 🔌(6x)€ 2. **Location:** Rural, quiet.
**Surface:** grassy/gravel. ☐ 01/04-30/11.
**Distance:** 🚶3km 🏖3km ⊗50m.
**Remarks:** Parking spa resort.
**Tourist information Cervia:**
🏛 Week market. ☐ Thu.

⊞S **Cesena** 26G3

**Zona Ippodromo**, Via G. Ambrosini. **GPS:** n44,14549 e12,22865.
10 🅿free 🚰€ 1/100liter 🗑€ 2 ChWC. **Location:** Urban.
**Surface:** grasstiles. ☐ 01/01-31/12.
**Distance:** 🚶500m ⊗on the spot 🍴1km 🚌200m.
**Remarks:** At sports centre.

⊞S **Cesena** 26G3

**Agriturismo Macin**, Via San Mauro 5280. **GPS:** n44,13592 e12,16953. ⬆.

4 🅿€ 11, free for clients 🚰🗑Ch🔌WC🌿included.
**Location:** Rural. **Surface:** grassy/metalled. ☐ 01/01-31/12.
**Distance:** 🚶5km 🔌8,4km ⊗5km 🍴5km.

⊞S **Cesenatico** ♨ 26G3

**Area Camper Cesenatico**, Viale Camillo Benso Cavour 1/b.
**GPS:** n44,20620 e12,38875. ⬆.
160 🅿€ 15-28 🚰🗑Ch🔌WC🌿included. **Location:** Urban,
simple. **Surface:** grassy. ☐ 01/01-31/12.
**Distance:** 🏖500m ⊗on the spot.
**Remarks:** Check in on arrival, monitored parking 24/24.

⊞S **Cesenatico** ♨ 26G3

Piazzale della Rocca. **GPS:** n44,19855 e12,39086. ⬆.

35 🅿free 🚰€ 0,50/25liter 🗑Ch. **Location:** Simple.
**Surface:** metalled. ☐ 01/01-31/12.
**Distance:** 🚶500m 🏖2km ⊗200m 🍴500m 🚌200m.

⊞S **Cesenatico** ♨ 26G3

Via Mazzini, zona Ponente. **GPS:** n44,21408 e12,38008. ⬆.

21 🅿€ 12/24h 🚰🗑Ch🔌included. **Location:** Rural, simple.
**Surface:** grassy/gravel. ☐ 01/01-31/12.
**Distance:** 🚶centre 3,5km 🏖800m.
**Remarks:** At entrance campsite Cesenatico, max. 48h.

⊞S **Civitella di Romagna** 26F3

**Agriturismo Acero Rosseo**, Via Seggio.
**GPS:** n44,00200 e11,97539. ⬆➡.

20 🅿guests free 🚰free. **Location:** Rural. **Surface:** grassy.

01/01-31/12.
Distance: ⊗5km ⊗on the spot ⚑5km.

### ⑤S Collecchio 26C2
Via Spezia. GPS: n44,75178 e10,22265. ⬆➡.

③free ⌁⚑Ch. Location: Simple. Surface: asphalted.
01/01-31/12.
Distance: ⚑500m.

### ⑤S Comacchio 🌿 26F2
Area di sosta Cavallari, Via Villaggio San Carlo 9.
GPS: n44,70297 e12,16862. ⬆.

80 ③€ 18 ⌁⚑Ch ⚡included WC ⌁€ 2. Location: Rural, luxurious,
quiet. Surface: grassy. 16/02-30/11.
Distance: ⚑1km ⚘on the spot.
Remarks: Bicycle rental.

### ⑤S Comacchio 🌿 26F2
Via Fattibello. GPS: n44,69095 e12,18447. ⬆➡.

13 ③free. Location: Rural, central, quiet. Surface: metalled.
01/01-31/12.
Distance: ⚑300m ⚑100m.

### ⑨S Conselice 26F2
Agriturismo Massari, Via Coronella 110, Chiesanuova di Conselice.
GPS: n44,53167 e11,81856. ⬆➡.

10 ③€ 9/pp, guests free ⌁⚑Ch ⚡ WC ⌁⌁📶included.
Location: Rural. Surface: metalled.
01/01-31/12.
Distance: ⚑1,5km ⚑200m ⊗on the spot ⚑1,5km.

### ⑨S Faenza 26F3
Via Proventa. GPS: n44,31272 e11,89289. ⬆➡.

③free ⌁⚑Chfree. Surface: asphalted. 01/01-31/12.

---

Distance: ⚑4km ⚑2km.

### 🌿S Faenza 26F3
Agriturismo Trerè, Via Casale 19. GPS: n44,29968 e11,80368. ⬆➡.

5 ③€ 8 + € 5/pp, guests free ⌁⚑Chincluded ⚡€ 2 WC⌁.
Surface: metalled. 01/01-31/12.
Distance: ⚑7km ⚑on the spot ⚑200m ⊗on the spot.
Remarks: Dog € 4, swimming pool € 5.

### ⑤S Farini 26B2
Viale dei Sassi Neri. GPS: n44,70994 e9,56611. ⬆➡.

50 ③free ⌁⚑Chfree. Surface: grassy/gravel. 01/01-31/12.
Distance: ⚑400m ⚑on the spot.

### ⑤S Ferrara 🌿⛲⚱ 26F2
Via Rampari di San Paolo. GPS: n44,83544 e11,61090. ⬆➡.
31 ③€ 10/24h ⌁⚑€ 1/100liter ⌁€ 2 Ch € 1 ⚡€ 5/2h 📶📶.
Location: Central, noisy. Surface: metalled.
01/01-31/12.
Distance: ⚑800m ⚑6,5km ⊗250m ⚑500m ⚑50m.
Remarks: Max. 72h, video surveillance.

**Tourist information Ferrara:**
Ⓜ Museo della Cattedrale. Ⓣ € 6.
✠ Castello Estence.
✠ Palazzo Scifanoia.
⚐ Mo, Fri.

### ⑤S Fontanellato 🌿 26C2
Via XXIV Maggio. GPS: n44,87797 e10,16987. ⬆➡.

20 ③€ 10/24h ⌁⚑Ch ⚡(16x) WCincluded ⌁🚰.
Location: Urban, simple, noisy. Surface: asphalted.
01/01-31/12.
Distance: ⚑300m ⚑6km ⚑200m ⚑500m.
Remarks: Motorhome washing place.

### ⑤S Forlimpopoli 26G3
Via De Gasperi. GPS: n44,19044 e12,12608.

③free. Surface: asphalted. 01/01-31/12.
Distance: ⚑100m ⚑100m ⚑100m ⚑100m.
Remarks: Nearby railway station.

### S Forlimpopoli 26G3
Palazzetto dello Sport, Via del Tulipano. GPS: n44,18534 e12,11960.
⌁⚑Chfree. 01/01-31/12.

---

### ⑤S Gropparello 🌿⚑⛲ 26C2
Via D. Aligieri. GPS: n44,83521 e9,73051. ⬆➡.

10 ③free, weekend € 10 ⌁free ⌁🚰.
Location: Rural, simple, quiet. Surface: asphalted. 01/01-31/12.
Distance: ⚑100m ⚑500m.
Remarks: Castello di Gropparello 300m.

### ⑤S Guastalla 🌿🌾 26D2
Piazzale Ugo Foscolo. GPS: n44,92364 e10,65148. ⬆.

6 ③free ⌁⚑free ⚡(6x)€ 5.
Surface: asphalted. 01/01-31/12.
Distance: ⚑historical centre 300m ⚑1,5km ⊗600m ⚑100m
⚑on the spot.
Remarks: Cycle route along the Po river.

### ⑤S Imola 🌿⚑ 26F3
Via Pirandello. GPS: n44,34628 e11,70922.

30 ③free ⌁⚑Chfree. Surface: grassy/sand. 01/01-31/12.
Distance: ⚑700m ⚑50m ⊗80m ⚑50m supermercato Famila.
Remarks: In front of the Ferrari Circuit.

**Tourist information Imola:**
⚐ Piazza Gramsci. Mo-Thu, Sa 8-12.30h.

### 🏠⑤S Lagosanto 26F2
Locanda Il Varano, Via Valle Oppio 6, Marozzo di Lagosanto.
GPS: n44,78167 e12,12533. ⬆.

36 ③€ 15, guests free ⌁⚑Ch ⚡(36x) WC 📶.
Location: Rural, comfortable, quiet. Surface: gravel.
01/01-31/12.
Distance: ⚑3km ⚑12km ⊗on the spot ⚑500m.

### 🌿⑤S Langhirano 🌿⛰ 26D2
Salumificio La Perla, Quinzano. GPS: n44,58748 e10,23783. ⬆.

10 ⛟free ⛽🔌.
**Location:** Rural, simple, quiet. **Surface:** gravel.
◻ 01/01-31/12.
**Distance:** 🚉3km ⊗on the spot 🛒3km ⊀ on the spot.
**Remarks:** Producer Parma ham.

| 🏨S | Langhirano 🌱⛰ | 26D2 |
|---|---|---|

**La Fazenda**, Cascinapiano di Langhirano.
**GPS:** n44,63322 e10,27410. ⬆️➡️.

50 ⛟€ 10, guests € 5 ⛽🔌 🔧 ⬛Cincluded. **Location:** Simple, quiet.
**Surface:** grassy/gravel. ◻ 01/01-31/12.
**Distance:** 🚉1km 🚌on the spot ⊗on the spot 🛒500m.

| 📷S | Lido di Dante 🏖 | 26G3 |
|---|---|---|

Via Marabina 208. **GPS:** n44,38867 e12,31364.

30 ⛟€ 6-10 ⛽Chincluded. **Surface:** grassy. ◻ 01/04-30/09.
**Distance:** 🚉250m 🏖100m ⊗50m 🛒200m 🚏50m.

| 📷S | Maranello | 26E2 |
|---|---|---|

**Area Camper Maranello**, Via Fondo Val Tiepido 77, Torre Maina.
**GPS:** n44,51275 e10,87842. ⬆️.

10 ⛟€ 7 ⛽🔌€ 2 Ch 🔧 WC⬛ 📶. **Location:** Rural, quiet.
**Surface:** unpaved. ◻ 01/01-31/12.
**Distance:** ⊗on the spot 🚲on the spot.
**Remarks:** Entrance code available at bar.

| 📷S | Marzaglia | 26D2 |
|---|---|---|

**Area di sosta Marzaglia**, Strada Pomposiana 305.
**GPS:** n44,63514 e10,80733. ⬆️➡️.

30 ⛟€ 15, 2 pers.incl ⛽🔌 Ch 🔧€ 1,50/day WC⬛.🏠
**Location:** Rural, comfortable, quiet. **Surface:** gravel.
◻ 01/01-31/12.
**Distance:** 🚉Modena 10km 🚲7km.

| 📷S | Mesola | 26G2 |
|---|---|---|

**Oasi Park II**, Via Cristina 84, SP27, Bosco Mesola.
**GPS:** n44,86822 e12,24898. ➡️.

200 ⛟€ 8-15 ⛽🔌 Ch 🔧(100x)€ 2/day WC⬛ 📦against payment
📶included. **Location:** Rural, comfortable, quiet. **Surface:** grassy.
◻ 01/03-01/11.
**Distance:** ⊗400m 🛒1km.
**Remarks:** Free bicycles available.

| 📷S | Mesola | 26G2 |
|---|---|---|

Via Beatrice d'Este. **GPS:** n44,92331 e12,23469. ⬆️.

6 ⛟free ⛽Ch. **Location:** Rural, simple. **Surface:** asphalted.
◻ 01/01-31/12.
**Distance:** 🚉400m ⊗400m 🛒150m.
**Remarks:** Parking sports park.

| 🍇S | Mesola | 26G2 |
|---|---|---|

**Agriturismo Ca'Laura**, SP 27, Bosco Mesola.
**GPS:** n44,87122 e12,24444. ⬆️.

6 ⛟€ 25 ⛽Ch 🔧 WC⬛included. **Location:** Rural, luxurious,
quiet. **Surface:** metalled. ◻ 01/01-31/12.
**Distance:** 🏖10km ⊗on the spot 🛒1km 🚏1km.
**Remarks:** Bicycle rental, free entrance swimming pool, swimming
pool, training golf course.

| 📷S | Mirandola | 26E2 |
|---|---|---|

Via Luigi Galvani. **GPS:** n44,89812 e11,06199. ⬆️.
10 ⛟free ⛽Ch 🔧free. **Location:** Urban, simple, quiet.
**Surface:** gravel. ◻ 01/01-31/12.
**Distance:** 🚉500m ⊗1km 🛒1km 🚏500m.
**Remarks:** At cemetery.

| 📷S | Misano Adriatico | 26G3 |
|---|---|---|

**Centro Caravan Misano**, Via Taveleto 53. **GPS:** n43,96694 e12,67306.

12 ⛟€ 20 ⛽Ch 🔧(12x)€ 1,50,6Amp WC⬛€ 0,50 📦€ 1
📶included. **Location:** Urban, luxurious, quiet. **Surface:** grassy.
◻ 01/01-31/12.
**Distance:** 🚉500m 🚲5km 🏖2km ⊗500m 🛒500m.
**Remarks:** Arrival < 19h, caution key € 10, video surveillance.

| 📷S | Modena 🌱 | 26E2 |
|---|---|---|

**Camper Club Mutina**, Strada Collegarola 76/A, zona Vaciglio.
**GPS:** n44,61361 e10,94444. ⬆️.

32 ⛟€ 16/24h ⛽Ch 🔧 WC 📶included. **Location:** Rural,
luxurious, quiet. **Surface:** asphalted. ◻ 01/01-31/12.
**Distance:** 🚉600m 🚲3km 🛒3km 🚲600m ⊀on the spot.

| 🏨S | Modena 🌱 | 26E2 |
|---|---|---|

**Taverna Napoleone**, Via San Lorenzo 44, Castelnuovo Rangone.
**GPS:** n44,57766 e10,96552.

10 ⛟free ⛽free. **Location:** Rural. **Surface:** metalled.
◻ 01/01-31/12.
**Distance:** 🚉5km 🚲2,8km ⊗pizzeria 🛒5km.
**Remarks:** 10% discount at restaurant.

**Tourist information Modena:**
Ⓜ Galleria Ferrari, Via Dino Ferrari 43, Maranello. Museum of motor-cars.

| 📷S | Montese | 26E3 |
|---|---|---|

Via Campo del Sole. **GPS:** n44,26637 e10,94456. ⬆️.
8 ⛟€ 8 ⛽Ch 🔧(8x)free.
**Surface:** grasstiles.
**Distance:** 🚉500m 🏖550m 🛒550m 🚏400m.
**Remarks:** Max. 72h.

| 📷S | Monticelli d'Ongina | 26C1 |
|---|---|---|

Piazza Resistenza. **GPS:** n45,09050 e9,93537. ⬆️➡️.

10 ⛟free ⛽Chfree. **Location:** Simple, quiet. **Surface:** asphalted.
◻ 01/01-31/12.
**Distance:** 🚉centre 300m 🚲6,2km ⊗300m 🛒300m.

| 📷S | Parma 🌱🏖🍴 | 26D2 |
|---|---|---|

**Area Camper Parma**, Largo XXIV Agosto 1942, n° 21/a.
**GPS:** n44,80931 e10,28495. ⬆️➡️.

26 ⛟€ 20 ⛽Ch 🔧included WC⬛€ 1. **Location:** Urban,
comfortable. **Surface:** grasstiles. ◻ 01/01-31/12.
**Distance:** 🚉centre 3,5km 🚲7km 🛒Lidl 100m 🚏100m.
**Remarks:** Monitored parking, arrival <22h, service passerby € 4,
motorhome washing place 50m.

**Tourist information Parma:**
👁 Palazzo Pilotta. ◻ morning.
⛪ Via Verdi. Week market. ◻ Wed-Sa 7-14h.

| 📷S | Pavullo nel Frignano 🏕🏊 | 26D3 |
|---|---|---|

Via Marchiani. **GPS:** n44,34294 e10,83309. ⬆️.

IT

12 ⓈⒻfree 🚰🚽Chfree. **Location:** Comfortable, noisy.
**Surface:** gravel/sand. ⏲ 01/01-31/12.
**Distance:** 🚶700m ⊗600m 🛒600m 🚌600m.
**Remarks:** Picnic area.

| 🅘Ⓢ | Porto Corsini 🌊 | 26G2 |

**Ancora Blu**, Via G. Guizzetti. **GPS:** n44,49620 e12,27950. ⬆➡

163 ⒻⒻ€ 9, 01/06-31/08 € 11 🚰🚽Ch ⚡(20x)€ 3/day WC.
**Location:** Rural, comfortable, quiet. **Surface:** grassy.
⏲ 01/03-31/10.
**Distance:** 🚶500m ⊗200m 🚲300m ⊗300m 🛒300m.
**Remarks:** Video surveillance.

| 🅘ⓈⓈ | Portomaggiore 🌿 | 26F2 |

Via Giuseppe Mazzini. **GPS:** n44,69584 e11,81389. ⬆

10 ⒻⒻfree 🚰🚽Chfree.
**Location:** Urban. **Surface:** asphalted. ⏲ 01/01-31/12.
**Distance:** 🚶500m ⊗500m 🛒500m 🚌300m.
**Remarks:** Nearby cemetery.

**Tourist information Portomaggiore:**
🌿 Valli di Comacchio. Nature reserve, in winter whereabouts birds.

| 🅘Ⓢ | Premilcuore | 26F3 |

Via G. Matteotti 4. **GPS:** n43,97399 e11,77220.
5 ⒻⒻ€ 10 🚰🚽Ch ⚡ **Location:** Rural. **Surface:** grassy.
⏲ 15/05-15/09.
**Distance:** 🚶500m ⊗600m 🚌600m.
**Remarks:** Near the Rabbi river.

| 🅘Ⓢ | Premilcuore | 26F3 |

**Parcheggio Fluviale**, Loc. Fontanalba. **GPS:** n43,97618 e11,77615.

ⒻⒻ€ 1. **Surface:** metalled. ⏲ 01/01-31/12.
**Distance:** 🚶500m 🚲20m ⊗500m 🚌50m.
**Remarks:** Along river.

| 🅘Ⓢ | Ravenna 🌿⛵🍽 | 26G3 |

**Parking Bus-Camper**, Via E.Ferrari. Loc.Classe.
**GPS:** n44,37849 e12,23461. ⬆➡

---

50 ⒻⒻ€ 2,50/24h 🚰🚽Chincluded. **Location:** Urban, simple.
**Surface:** grasstiles. ⏲ 01/01-31/12.
**Distance:** 🚶Ravenna centre 6km.
**Remarks:** Nearby basilica.

| 🅘Ⓢ | Ravenna 🌿⛵🍽 | 26G3 |

Piazza della Resistenza. **GPS:** n44,41433 e12,18852. ⬆

10 ⒻⒻ€ 0,50/h, € 2,50/24h 🚰🚽Chincluded. 🏧
**Location:** Urban, simple, central.
**Surface:** grasstiles.
⏲ 01/01-31/12.
**Distance:** 🚶historical centre 500m 🚲5km ⊗150m 🛒500m 🚌50m.
**Remarks:** Max. 24h.

| 🅘Ⓢ | Ravenna 🌿⛵🍽 | 26G3 |

Via Pomposa. **GPS:** n44,43002 e12,20827. ⬆

40 ⒻⒻfree 🚰🚽Chfree. **Location:** Simple. **Surface:** asphalted.
⏲ 01/01-31/12.
**Distance:** 🚶city centre 2km 🚌100m 🛒on the spot.

| 🅘Ⓢ | Ravenna 🌿⛵🍽 | 26G3 |

Via Teodorico. **GPS:** n44,42317 e12,20981.

10 ⒻⒻfree 🚰🚽Chfree. **Location:** Urban, simple, quiet.
**Surface:** asphalted. ⏲ 01/01-31/12.
**Distance:** 🚶500m ⊗on the spot.
**Remarks:** In front of the Mausoleum.

| 🅘Ⓢ | Ravenna 🌿⛵🍽 | 26G3 |

Via Brancaleone/circonvallazione S. Gaetanino.
**GPS:** n44,42339 e12,20478. ⬆

25 ⒻⒻfree. **Location:** Urban, simple, noisy. **Surface:** metalled.
⏲ 01/01-31/12.
**Distance:** 🚶200m 🚲5km 🚲100m ⊗200m 🛒200m 🚌10m.

---

**Remarks:** Next to Rocca Brancaleone.

| 🅘Ⓢ | Ravenna 🌿⛵🍽 | 26G3 |

**Area Camper Atrezzata, Eurolandia**, SS16.
**GPS:** n44,33533 e12,26949. ⬆

72 ⒻⒻ€ 10/day, € 15/2 days 🚰🚽Chincluded 🔌€ 0,50/30minutes. 🏧
**Location:** Rural, simple. **Surface:** gravel.
⏲ 01/04-31/10.
**Remarks:** Video surveillance.

| 🅘Ⓢ | Ravenna 🌿⛵🍽 | 26G3 |

**Parco Divertimenti Mirabilandia**, SS16, via Romea Sud 463.
**GPS:** n44,33290 e12,26966. ⬆

400 ⒻⒻ€ 10 🚰🚽included. **Location:** Rural, simple, noisy.
**Surface:** gravel.
**Distance:** 🚶Ravenna centre 10km ⊗McDonalds.
**Remarks:** Max. 48h.

**Tourist information Ravenna:**
ℹ U.I.A.T. (Ufficio Informazioni e di Accoglienza Turistica), Piazza S.
Francesco, 7, http://www.turismo.ra.it/. City of the mosaics, historical
city with many curiosities.
🎪 Piazza Garibaldi. Antiques market. ⏲ 3rd weekend of the month.
  Parco Divertimenti Mirabilandia, SS16, via Romea Sud 463. Amusement park. ⏲ 01/04-15/09.

| 🅘Ⓢ | Reggio nell'Emilia | 26D2 |

**Parking Ex Foro Boario**, Via XX Settembre.
**GPS:** n44,70941 e10,62463. ⬆➡

6 ⒻⒻfree 🚰🚽Chfree.
**Location:** Urban, simple. **Surface:** grasstiles.
⏲ 01/01-31/12.
**Distance:** 🚶1km 🚲3,7km ⊗100m 🛒500m 🚌Free bus to centre.

| 🅘Ⓢ | Riccione 🌊 | 26G3 |

**La Baita degli Ulivi**, Via Ascoli Piceno. **GPS:** n43,98439 e12,64668. ⬆
ⒻⒻ€ 20 ⚓ **Location:** Noisy. **Surface:** gravel.
⏲ 01/01-31/12.
**Distance:** 🚲300m 🚲3,5km ⊗on the spot.
**Remarks:** Video surveillance.

| 🅘Ⓢ | Rimini 🌿⛵🌊 | 26G3 |

**La Valletta Sosta Verde**, Via Della Lama 47, SS 16.
**GPS:** n44,09889 e12,49867. ⬆➡

200 ⒻⒻ€ 11, >7,3m € 18, dog € 1 🚰🚽Chincluded ⚡(158x)€ 3,6Amp

IT

WC ⬛ € 1. **Location:** Rural, noisy. **Surface:** grassy/gravel.
⬛ 01/04-30/09.
**Distance:** Rimini 11km ∿ 3,8km ⚓ 2km ⊗ 800m ⛽ 800m.
**Remarks:** Shuttle bus to beach.

### Rimini 🌿⛺🏖 26G3
**Parking Settebello**, Via Roma 86. **GPS:** n44,05982 e12,57669. ⬆➡.

300 ⬛ € 10/24h ⬛ € 2 ⬛ Ch € 2 ✎(80x)€ 3/day.
**Location:** Urban, simple, central, noisy. **Surface:** metalled.
⬛ 01/01-31/12.
**Distance:** 200m ⚓ 500m.
**Remarks:** Next to cinema Settebello.

### Rimini 🌿⛺🏖 26G3
**P30 Chiabrera**, Via Chiabrera. **GPS:** n44,04803 e12,59548. ⬆.
⬛ 01/05-30/09 € 12,10. **Location:** Urban, simple, central, noisy.
**Surface:** asphalted.

### Rimini 🌿⛺🏖 26G3
**Camper Nautica**, Via Ortigara 78/80. **GPS:** n44,07461 e12,57005. ⬆.
20 ⬛ € 20-30/24h ⬛ ✎ € 1,50 ⬛ ∿. ⬛ 01/01-31/12.
**Distance:** ⚓ on the spot ⬛ on the spot ⊗ on the spot.
**Remarks:** Monitored parking 24/24.

**Tourist information Rimini:**
⊗ Casa Zanni, Via Casale, 205, Villa Verucchio. Restaurant with authentic Italian cuisine.

### Ro 🏖 26F1
**Mulino sul Po**, SP 14. **GPS:** n44,95498 e11,75668. ⬆.

4 ⬛ free ✎(4x)free WC ⬛. **Location:** Rural, simple, noisy.
**Surface:** metalled. ⬛ 01/01-31/12.
**Distance:** 1km ⬛ on the spot ⬛ on the spot.
**Remarks:** Along the Po river.

### Rocca San Casciano 💧 26F3
**Foro Boario**, Viale Dante Alighieri, SP23, 17.
**GPS:** n44,06173 e11,84604. ⬆.
4 ⬛ free ⬛ € 1/100liter ⬛ Ch ✎ € 1/4h.
**Location:** Rural. **Surface:** metalled. ⬛ 01/01-31/12.
**Distance:** 300m ⊗ 100m ⛽ 800m ⬛ 150m.

### Sala Baganza 26C2
Via Vittorio Emanuele, 42. **GPS:** n44,70856 e10,23070. ⬆.

50 ⬛ free ⬛ Ch ✎(4x)free. **Location:** Rural, simple, quiet.
**Surface:** asphalted. ⬛ 01/01-31/12.
**Distance:** 500m ⬛ 15km ⛽ 500m.

### Salsomaggiore Terme ⛱ 26C2
Via Antonio Gramsci. **GPS:** n44,82005 e9,98981. ⬆.

20 ⬛ free ⬛ ⬛ free. **Location:** Urban, simple, quiet. **Surface:** gravel.
⬛ 01/01-31/12.
**Distance:** 800m.
**Remarks:** Parking next to station.

### San Giuseppe 🌿🏖 26G2
**Ariaperta Sosta Camper**, Via Delle Nazioni 39.
**GPS:** n44,72578 e12,22528. ⬆.

99 ⬛ € 15 ⬛ Ch included ✎(32x)€ 3/24h,3Amp, € 6 6Amp
WC ⬛ € 2/4minutes. **Surface:** grassy. ⬛ 01/01-31/12.
**Distance:** 500m ⚓ 1,5km ⊗ 500m ⛽ 500m.

### San Piero in Bagno 34C1
Via G.Mazzini, Via Battistini. **GPS:** n43,86353 e11,97692. ⬆.

5 ⬛ free ⬛ Ch free.
**Location:** Rural. **Surface:** asphalted. ⬛ 01/01-31/12.
**Distance:** 500m ⬛ 1km ⊗ 500m ⛽ 500m ⬛ 200m.

### Santa Sofia 💧 34C1
Piazzale K. Marx. **GPS:** n43,94165 e11,90930. ⬆.

10 ⬛ free ⬛ Ch free. **Surface:** asphalted. ⬛ 01/01-31/12.
**Distance:** 200m ⊗ 650m ⛽ 650m ⬛ on the spot.

**Tourist information Santa Sofia:**
⬛ Foreste Casentinesi. National nature reserve.

### Serramazzoni 🌿⛺💧🌲❄ 26D3
Piazzale Largo Olimpico. **GPS:** n44,42223 e10,79402. ⬆➡.

20 ⬛ free ⬛ Ch free.
**Location:** Urban, noisy. **Surface:** asphalted. ⬛ 01/01-31/12.
**Distance:** 300m ⊗ 100m ⛽ 300m ⬛ 300m ⬛ 300m ⬛ 800m.

### Serramazzoni 🌿⛺🌲💧❄ 26D3
**Ristorante La Roccia**, Via Giardini Nord, Montagnana di Serramazzoni.
**GPS:** n44,47157 e10,82050. ⬆.

15 ⬛ free ⬛. **Location:** Rural, simple, quiet. **Surface:** gravel.
⬛ 01/01-31/12.
**Distance:** 8km Maranello ⊗ on the spot ⛽ 8km.
**Remarks:** Maranello: Ferrari factory and museum.

### Sestola 🌿⛺💧🌲 26D3
Via Guidellina. **GPS:** n44,22591 e10,77374. ⬆➡.
50 ⬛ free ⬛ Ch. **Surface:** asphalted. ⬛ 01/01-31/12.
**Distance:** 300m ⊗ 800m ⛽ 500m ⬛ on the spot.

### Soragna 🌿 26C2
Via Matteotti / via Gramsci. **GPS:** n44,92988 e10,12566. ⬆.

10 ⬛ free ⬛ Ch free. **Location:** Urban, simple, quiet.
**Surface:** asphalted. ⬛ 01/01-31/12.
**Distance:** 120m ⊗ 200m ⛽ 200m.

### Suviana 26E3
Via Lungo Lago. **GPS:** n44,12039 e11,04592.

60 ⬛ Free, hollidays € 9. ⬛ **Location:** Rural, simple, quiet.
**Surface:** asphalted. ⬛ 01/01-31/12.
**Distance:** ⚓ on the spot ⬛ on the spot ⊗ on the spot.
**Remarks:** At lake Suviana, canoe rental.

### Terenzo 🌿💧🌲 26C2
Loc. Bardone. **GPS:** n44,62528 e10,10083. ⬆.

8 ⬛ € 13 ⬛ Ch ✎ WC ⬛ included. ⬛ **Location:** Rural,
comfortable, quiet. **Surface:** metalled. ⬛ 01/01-31/12.
**Distance:** 200m ⬛ 12km ⛽ 12km ⬛ on the spot.
**Remarks:** Max. 2 nights.

### Tredozio 💧🌲 26F3
**Area Le Volte**, Via Salvo D'Acquisto. **GPS:** n44,07431 e11,73228. ⬆➡.

IT

40 🛏€ 5 🚰🔌Ch included 🚿€ 2,50. **Surface:** metalled.
🅿 01/01-31/12.
**Distance:** 🚶1,5km ⊗200m camping 🛒1,5km.
**Remarks:** Next to campsite Le Volte, max. 48h, discount at restaurant/ swimming-pool.

**Tresigallo** 26F2
Fraz. Finale di Rero. **GPS:** n44,81643 e11,90050.
5 🛏free 🚰🔌Chfree. **Surface:** metalled. 🅿 01/01-31/12.
**Distance:** ⊗600m 🛒750m 🚍on the spot.
**Remarks:** Nearby sports park.

**Vergato** 26E3
SS 64, Bologna-Pistoia. **GPS:** n44,28952 e11,11270.⬆

25 🛏free 🚰🔌Chfree. **Location:** Rural, simple. **Surface:** asphalted.
🅿 01/01-31/12.
**Distance:** 🚶400m ⊗400m 🛒500m 🚍500m.

**Vezzano Sul Crostolo** 26D2
Area Sosta Camper Matildica, SS63. **GPS:** n44,58960 e10,53608.
10 🛏free 🚰🔌Ch 🚿. **Surface:** asphalted. 🅿 01/01-31/12.
**Distance:** 🚶1,5km 🚍on the spot 🚴on the spot 🚶on the spot.
**Remarks:** Eco Parco di Vezzano, keycard at Bar Sport, Via Roma, SS63, n44,59963, o10,54542.

# Liguria

**Camporosso** 28H1
Camper Park Nervia, Via Primo Maggio. **GPS:** n43,79339 e7,63088.

60 🛏€ 13, 25/07-25/08 € 18-23, dog € 3 🚰🔌Ch 🚿€ 4/day,6Amp
WC🚽€ 1 🚿included. **Location:** Rural, comfortable.
**Surface:** metalled. 🅿 01/01-31/12.
**Distance:** 🚶500m 🛒700m 🚲700m ⊗on the spot 🚴on the spot 🚶on the spot.
**Remarks:** Video surveillance, bike/car rental, playground.

**Castelnuovo Magra** 26C3
Agriturismo Cascina dei Peri, Via Montefrancio 71.
**GPS:** n44,10355 e10,00734.⬆➡

3 🛏€ 10/pp, child € 3,50 🚰🔌Ch 🚿€ 3,50 WC🚽included 🔲€ 5.
**Location:** Rural, comfortable, isolated, quiet. **Surface:** grassy/gravel.
🅿 01/01-31/12.
**Distance:** 🚶2,4km.
**Remarks:** Dinner € 20/pp wine incl. (to order <16h), selling of wine and

olive oil, swimming pool from june.

**Celle Ligure** 26A3
Via Natta. **GPS:** n44,34888 e8,55674.⬆

25 🛏free 🚰Ch. **Surface:** asphalted. 🅿 01/01-31/12.
**Distance:** 🚶300m 🚲200m 🏊500m ⊗200m 🛒300m 🚍100m.

**Celle Ligure** 26A3
Agriturismo Cele, Via Sanda 30. **GPS:** n44,35007 e8,53901.
10 🛏€ 15 🚰🔌Ch 🚿WC🚽🚿included. **Location:** Rural.
**Surface:** metalled. 🅿 01/01-31/12.
**Distance:** 🚶1km 🏊1,5km ⊗on the spot.
**Remarks:** Playground.

**Cengio** 25H3
Area Attrezzata Cengio Isole, Via Isole.
**GPS:** n44,39083 e8,20194.⬆➡

10 🛏free 🚰🔌Chfree. **Location:** Urban. **Surface:** asphalted.
🅿 01/01-31/12.
**Distance:** 🚶600m 🏊on the spot ⊗on the spot 🛒1km 🚍800m.
**Remarks:** Nearby sports park.

**Cervo** 28H1
Camper Cervo, Via Steria. **GPS:** n43,92833 e8,10527.⬆➡

130 🛏€ 12-15/day 🚰🔌Ch included 🚿€ 3/24h WC🚽.
**Location:** Urban. **Surface:** gravel.
🅿 01/01-31/12.
**Distance:** 🚶on the spot 🚲2,5km 🏊1km ⊗900m 🛒600m.
**Remarks:** At tennis-courts, monitored parking, free bicycles available.

**Deiva Marina** 26B3
Via Aranella. **GPS:** n44,22543 e9,53288.⬆
10 🛏€ 15/24h 🚰included.
**Location:** Rural. **Surface:** unpaved.
🅿 15/03-15/11.
**Distance:** 🚶1,5km 🏊sea 2km 🛒on the spot 🚍150m 🚴on the spot.

**Diano Marina** 28H1
Oasi Camper, Via Sori 5. **GPS:** n43,90667 e8,07083.⬆➡

150 🛏€ 10-20/day 🚰🔌Ch included 🚿€ 3 WC🚽€ 1 🔲🚿.
**Location:** Rural, comfortable, quiet. **Surface:** grassy/gravel.
🅿 01/01-31/12.
**Distance:** 🚶600m 🚲6,8km 🏊800m ⊗600m 🛒600m 🚍600m
🚴mountainbike trail.
**Remarks:** Max. 72h, beachshuttle with bar/restaurant.

**Diano Marina** 28H1
Il bowling di Diano, Via Diano S. Pietro, 71 - Diano Castello.
**GPS:** n43,91683 e8,07576.⬆

100 🛏€ 15-30/night 🚰🔌Ch 🚿included 🔲🚿.
**Surface:** unpaved. 🅿 01/01-31/12.
**Distance:** 🚶1km 🚲5,5km 🏊1,2km ⊗on the spot 🛒50m.
**Remarks:** Narrow entrance, swimming pool, bar, bowling.

**Diano Marina** 28H1
Agriturismo Solo Blu, Via Gombi San Siro, 5.
**GPS:** n43,91743 e8,08510.⬆
24 🛏€ 14-30/24h, 2 pers.incl 🚰🔌Ch 🚿(24x)included WC🚽🚿.
**Location:** Rural, comfortable, quiet. **Surface:** gravel.
🅿 01/01-31/12.
**Distance:** 🚶1,2km 🏊500m 🛒750m 🚴on the spot.
**Remarks:** Shady, swimming pool.

**Finale Ligure** 26A3
Area Caprazoppa, Via Aurelia, SS1. **GPS:** n44,16549 e8,33750.⬆

40 🛏€ 18/24h 🚰🔌Ch included.
**Location:** Rural. **Surface:** gravel/sand.
🅿 01/01-31/12.
**Distance:** 🚶500m 🚲4km 🏊on the spot ⊗700m 🛒500m 🚍500m.
**Remarks:** At sea, max. 36h.

**Giusvalla** 26A3
Strada Comunale. **GPS:** n44,44885 e8,39329.

6 🛏free 🚰🔌Chfree. **Location:** Rural. **Surface:** grassy/sand.
🅿 01/01-31/12.
**Distance:** 🚶on the spot ⊗on the spot.

**Imperia** 28H1
Francy Park, Via dei Giardini. **GPS:** n43,86917 e8,00010.⬆

32 🛏€ 10, 01/06-30/09 € 13 🚰🔌Ch included 🔲.🚐
**Surface:** metalled. 🅿 01/01-31/12.
**Distance:** 🚶centre 4km 🏊sea 150m 🛒150m 🚍100m.

**La Spezia** 26C3
Viale San Bartolomeo. **GPS:** n44,10417 e9,85917.

IT

100 ⛺ € 6,50 🚰🔌 € 5 WC. **Surface:** grassy. ⬛ 01/01-31/12.
**Distance:** 🏖️4km 🚌on the spot ♨️on the spot.
**Remarks:** Monitored parking.
**Tourist information La Spezia:**
🛈 Lerici. Former fishing village, nowadays holiday resort.
🛈 Cinque Terre. Protected coast area.
⚔️ Castello di Lerici, Lerici. ⬛ 01/04-31/10.
⛪ Lerici. ⬛ Sa-morning.

### Levanto — 26C3
SP556, Loc. Moltedi. **GPS:** n44,17476 e9,61836. ⬆️➡️

16 ⛺ € 36/24h 🚰🗑Chincluded. ⬛ 01/01-31/12.
**Distance:** 🏖️500m 🏊1km 🚂train 100m.
**Remarks:** Behind railway station, well situated for visiting the Cinque Terre by train.

### Loano — 25H3
La Sosta, Via delle Fornaci, 31. **GPS:** n44,13115 e8,24111. ⬆️
41 ⛺ € 15 🚰🗑Ch🔌 WC 🔲 📶included. 🏠 **Location:** Rural,
isolated. **Surface:** gravel. ⬛ 01/01-31/12.
**Distance:** 🏖️2,5km 🏊2km ⊗400m 🚂1km.
**Remarks:** Video surveillance, picnic and barbecue place, shuttle bus.
**Tourist information Loano:**
👁 Grotta di Santa Lucia, Toirano. Stalactites and stalagmites.
👁 Grotta della Basura, Toirano. Man and beast from the stone age.

### Pietra Ligure — 26A3
Val Maremona, Via Crispi 43. **GPS:** n44,15484 e8,28397. ⬆️➡️

53 ⛺ € 13/24h, 01/06-30/09 € 16/24h 🚰🗑Ch🔌(53x)included
WC 🔲 € 0.70. **Location:** Urban, quiet. **Surface:** gravel
⬛ 01/01-31/12.
**Distance:** 🏖️2km 🏊200m 🚂600m.

### Pontinvrea — 26A3
Via Roma 15. **GPS:** n44,44309 e8,43739.

10 ⛺ € 5 🚰🗑Ch🔌(10x)included.
**Location:** Rural. **Surface:** gravel. ⬛ 31/03-30/09.
**Distance:** 🏖️150m 🚂150m 150m ♨️on the spot.

### San Lorenzo al Mare — 28H1
Area Camper Il Pozzo, Via Gaetano Salvemini.
**GPS:** n43,85512 e7,96083. ⬆️➡️

---

30 ⛺ € 15-31 🚰🗑Ch🔌 WC 🔲 € 4 📶included.
**Location:** Urban, luxurious. **Surface:** gravel. ⬛ 01/01-31/12.
**Distance:** 🏖️400m 🏊600m ⊗400m 🚂200m on the spot.
**Remarks:** Max. 7m.

### San Rocco — 26B3
Viale Franco Molfino, Camogli. **GPS:** n44,33472 e9,16084.

9 ⛺ € 15/24h.
**Location:** Rural. **Surface:** asphalted. ⬛ 01/01-31/12.
**Distance:** 🏖️300m 🏊700m ⊗150m 🚂350m on the spot ♨️on
the spot.
**Remarks:** Monitored parking, marked hiking trails in Parco di Portofino
(45min-2h).

### Santo Stefano al Mare — 28H1
Camper Village, Strada Porsani. **GPS:** n43,84378 e7,90824. ⬆️

60 ⛺ € 12-30/24h 🚰🗑Ch🔌 € 3 WC 🔲 € 1. **Location:** Rural, isolated.
**Surface:** gravel. ⬛ 01/01-31/12.
**Distance:** 🏖️2km 🎣10km 🏊800m 🚂on the spot.
**Remarks:** Free shuttle, swimming pool.

### Santo Stefano al Mare — 28H1
Marina degli Aregai, Via Gianni Cozzi. **GPS:** n43,83723 e7,90581.

± 30 ⛺ € 1,50/h, € 5-10/day. 🏠
**Location:** Urban. **Surface:** asphalted. ⬛ 01/01-31/12.
**Distance:** 🏖️on the spot 🏊Sandy beach ⊗on the spot 🚂800m
♨️on the spot.

### Sassello — 26A3
Piazza San Rocco. **GPS:** n44,48060 e8,48229.

5 ⛺free 🚰WC.
**Location:** Urban. **Surface:** metalled. ⬛ 01/01-31/12.
**Distance:** 🏖️on the spot ⊗50m 🚂50m on the spot ♨️on the spot

---

♨️on the spot.

### Sestri Levante — 26B3
Levante Camper, Via Liguria 39. **GPS:** n44,27848 e9,40209.
25 ⛺ € 18-28 🚰🗑Ch🔌,6Amp WC 🔲 € 0,50 📶included.
**Location:** Rural. **Surface:** grassy. ⬛ 01/01-31/12.
**Distance:** 🏖️1800m 🏊800m ⊗750m 🚂500m 🚂700m.

### Toirano — 28H1
Camper Paradise, Via Marici. **GPS:** n44,12491 e8,22498. ⬆️
15 ⛺ € 14-20 🚰🗑Ch🔌 WC 🔲📶included. **Location:** Rural,
comfortable, noisy. **Surface:** grassy/gravel. ⬛ 01/01-31/12.
**Distance:** 🏖️500m 🏊2km 🚂700m ♨️on the spot.
**Remarks:** Arrival <20h, video surveillance, free shuttle.

### Torriglia — 26B3
Area Comunale Piscina, Via degli Alpini. **GPS:** n44,51667 e9,16000. ➡️

10 ⛺free 🚰Chfree. **Surface:** grasstiles. ⬛ 01/01-31/12.
**Distance:** 🏖️200m ⊗300m 🚂250m 🚂350m.
**Remarks:** Next to swimming pool, market Saturday.

### Vado Ligure — 26A3
Area Sosta Camper, Via Aurelia 16, SS1. **GPS:** n44,27797 e8,44171. ⬆️

68 ⛺ € 8/12h, € 16/24h 🚰🗑Ch🔌included. 🏠
**Location:** Simple. **Surface:** metalled. ⬛ 01/01-31/12.
**Distance:** 🏖️600m 🏊50m ⊗50m.
**Remarks:** Ferry > Corsica 2km.

# Tuscany

### Alberese — 34B2
Parco Naturale della Maremma, Via del Bersagliere.
**GPS:** n42,66944 e11,10416. ⬆️➡️

50 ⛺free 🚰free.
**Location:** Rural. **Surface:** gravel/sand. ⬛ 01/04-30/09.
**Distance:** 🏖️100m 🏊7km ⊗on the spot 🚂100m 🚂200m ♨️on the
spot ♨️on the spot.

### Albinia — 34B2
Ai Delfini, Via Aurelia km 153. **GPS:** n42,50882 e11,19552. ⬆️➡️

24 ⛺ € 1/h, Aug € 1,50/h 4 pers incl. + tourist tax 🚰🗑
Ch🔌 WCincluded 🔲 € 1 📶5 incl., € 5 📶1h incl., € 10/15 days. 🚿
**Location:** Rural, comfortable, quiet. **Surface:** grassy/sand.
⬛ 24/04-31/10.
**Distance:** 🏖️2km 🏊50m ⊗on the spot 🚂2km.

**IT**

## Anghiari — 34C1

Via Campo della Fiera. **GPS:** n43,53904 e12,05291. ⬆.

8 ⓢfree ⚡🔧ChWC◻free. **Location:** Urban, simple, quiet.
**Surface:** asphalted. ◻ 01/01-31/12.
**Distance:** 🚶on the spot ⊗on the spot ⚡on the spot 🚰100m.

## Anghiari — 34C1

**Agriturismo Val della Pieve**, Via della Fossa 8.
**GPS:** n43,53657 e12,05131. ⬆➡.

10 ⓢ€ 15/24h, Jul/Aug € 20 🔧Ch 🔧 WC◻◻€ 3 〰included.
**Location:** Rural, comfortable, isolated, quiet. **Surface:** gravel.
◻ 01/01-31/12.
**Distance:** 🚶300m ⊗300m ⚡300m 🚰300m.
**Remarks:** Swimming pool € 3/pppd.

## Anghiari — 34C1

**Agriturismo La Taverna dei Sorci**, San Lorenzo.
**GPS:** n43,51467 e12,07799. ⬆.

20 ⓢfree ⚡free.
**Location:** Rural, simple, quiet. **Surface:** metalled. ◻ 01/01-31/12.
**Distance:** 🚶3km ⊗on the spot 🚰350m.

## Arcidosso — 34B2

**Parco Faunistico Monte Amiata**, Località Poderi.
**GPS:** n42,83740 e11,52922.

15 ⓢfree 🔧Ch. **Location:** Rural, isolated, quiet.
**Surface:** grassy/gravel. ◻ 01/01-31/12.
**Distance:** 🚶10km.
**Remarks:** Nature reserve.

## Arezzo — 34C1

Via Da Palestrina/Via Tarlati. **GPS:** n43,47213 e11,88773. ⬆.

30 ⓢ€ 0,80/h, € 8/24h ⚡€ 0,10/10liter 🔧Ch 〰. **Location:** Urban,

---

simple, quiet. **Surface:** asphalted.
◻ 01/01-31/12.
**Distance:** 🚶1km ⊗300m ⚡300m 🚰300m.
**Remarks:** Escalator to city centre.

## Arezzo — 34C1

**P Tarlati**, Via Guido Tarlati. **GPS:** n43,47237 e11,88362. ⬆.

50 ⓢfree. **Location:** Urban, simple, central. **Surface:** grasstiles.
◻ 01/01-31/12.
**Distance:** 🚶city centre 1km ⊗500m ⚡500m 🚰300m 🚲on the
spot.
**Remarks:** Escalator to city centre.

**Tourist information Arezzo:**
⚘ Week market.

## Barberino di Mugello — 26E3

**Lago di Bilancino**, Viale Antonio Gramsci.
**GPS:** n43,98911 e11,24145. ⬆➡.

100 ⓢ€ 16/night ⚡🔧Ch 🔧 WC◻〰included. **Location:** Rural,
comfortable, quiet. **Surface:** unpaved. ◻ 15/04-15/10.
**Distance:** 🚶1km ⚓100m ⊗on the spot 🚰800m 🚲on the spot
🚶on the spot.
**Remarks:** At lake Bilancino.

## Barberino di Mugello — 26E3

SS65, Fraz. Monte di Fó. **GPS:** n44,07613 e11,28062. ⬆.

10 ⓢfree ⚡🔧Chfree. **Location:** Rural, simple, quiet.
**Surface:** metalled. ◻ 01/01-31/12.
**Distance:** 🚶4km ⚓150m (camping) ⚡150m (camping).
**Remarks:** In front of campsite Il Sergente.

## Barga — 26D3

**Area San Cristoforo**, Via Hayange. **GPS:** n44,07234 e10,48131. ⬆➡.

30 ⓢ€ 10/24h ⚡🔧ChWC◻200m. ◻
**Location:** Urban, simple, central, quiet. **Surface:** gravel.
◻ 01/01-31/12.
**Distance:** 🚶centro storico within walking distance ⊗300m ⚡300m
🚰250m 🚶100m.

## Bibbiena — 34C1

**La Collina delle Stelle**, Loc. Casanova 63.
**GPS:** n43,71669 e11,85173. ⬆.

---

8 ⓢ€ 15-20, 2 pers.incl, extra pers € 5 ⚡🔧Ch 🔧€ 2/24h
WC◻◻€ 5, ironing services € 5 〰included.
**Location:** Rural, comfortable, quiet. **Surface:** gravel.
◻ 15/03-01/11, Christmas.
**Distance:** 🚶7km ⊗on the spot 🚰on the spot.
**Remarks:** Dog € 2/day, playground, swimming pool € 5/pp (free with
a meal).

## Borgo a Mozzano — 34A1

Via I° Maggio, SP2. **GPS:** n43,97612 e10,54113. ⬆.

4 ⓢfree ⚡🔧Ch 🔧(4x)free.
**Location:** Simple, noisy. **Surface:** gravel. ◻ 01/01-31/12.
**Distance:** 🚶200m 🚣Serchio river 🚲on the spot ⊗700m 🚰on the
spot.
**Remarks:** At tourist office, picnic tables available.

## Borgo San Lorenzo — 34B1

Via Caduti di Montelungo. **GPS:** n43,95112 e11,38518. ⬆.

10 ⓢfree ⚡🔧Chfree. **Location:** Urban, simple. **Surface:** asphalted.
◻ 01/01-31/12 ◻ Fri.
**Distance:** 🚶500m ⊗500m ⚡300m 🚰400m.
**Remarks:** Friday market.

## Buonconvento — 34B2

Viale della Liberta. **GPS:** n43,13854 e11,48109. ⬆.

25 ⓢfree.
**Location:** Simple. **Surface:** unpaved. ◻ 01/01-31/12.
**Distance:** 🚶50m ⊗50m.
**Remarks:** At the city walls.

## Buonconvento — 34B2

Viale Ferruccio Parri. **GPS:** n43,13065 e11,48349. ⬆➡.
⚡€ 1 🔧Ch. ◻ 01/01-31/12.

## Calci — 34A1

Via Brogiotti 35. **GPS:** n43,72769 e10,51722. ⬆➡.

IT

8 �▨ € 8/24h, € 0,50/h ⟶⬛ Ch included. ▦ **Location:** Urban, simple, noisy. **Surface:** asphalted. ◻ 01/01-31/12.
**Distance:** 🚰100m ⊗50m ▮200m 🚌50m.
**Remarks:** At sports park, payment only with coins.

### ▥S | Campiglia Marittima ꕔ ꔮ | 34B2

**Parcheggio La Pieve**, Via di Venturina.
**GPS:** n43,05672 e10,61439. ⬆➡.

4 ⌏free ⬛Ch. **Location:** Rural, simple, isolated, quiet.
**Surface:** asphalted. ◻ 01/01-31/12.
**Distance:** 🚰350m ⊗450m ▮500m.
**Remarks:** In front of cemetery, near gymnasium.

### ▥ | Capalbio | 34B2

Via Giacomo Leopardi, SP75. **GPS:** n42,45363 e11,42401.
10 ⌏free.
**Location:** Urban. **Surface:** metalled. ◻ 01/01-31/12.
**Distance:** 🚰100m ⊗200m ▮300m 🚌200m.

### ▥S | Capraia e Limite | 34B1

Via delle Ginestre, zona industriale, loc. Capraia Fiorentina.
**GPS:** n43,73660 e11,00442. ⬆.

20 ⌏free ⟶⬛Ch free. **Location:** Urban, simple, noisy.
**Surface:** metalled. ◻ 01/01-31/12.
**Distance:** 🚰500m ⛱200m 🚌100m.

### ▥S | Carmignano ꕔ ꔮ

## Agriturismo I Poderi Del Poggio Dei Colli

**Beautiful view**
**Electricity at each pitch**
**Restaurant on spot**

**Agriturismo I Poderi Del Poggio Dei Colli**, Via Poggio dei Colli, 5.
**GPS:** n43,79853 e11,01121. ⬆.
3 ⌏€ 20-25, Jul/Aug € 30 ⟶⬛Ch ✚WC included ▣.
**Location:** Comfortable, quiet. **Surface:** gravel.
◻ 01/01-31/12 ⊡ 01/10-30/11.
**Distance:** ⊗on the spot.
**Remarks:** Barbecue place, sale of wines.

---

### ▥S | Castagneto Carducci ꔮ | 34A2

**Camperesort**, Via Aurelia 373/B. **GPS:** n43,15630 e10,56097. ⬆➡.

50 ⌏€ 15 + € 5/pp, 15/06-15/09 € 15/Pp ⟶⬛Ch ✚WC ▯ 1
▣€ 3 ⤢included ⬛. 🍴 **Location:** Rural, luxurious, noisy.
**Surface:** grassy/gravel. ◻ 01/01-31/12.
**Distance:** 🚰1km ⛱1,2km ⊗on the spot ▮2km. **Remarks:** Parking nearby motorway, video surveillance, swimming pool incl.

### ▥S | Castagneto Carducci ꔮ | 34A2

**Parking Comune di Castagneto Carducci**, Viale delle Palme, Marina di Castagneto. **GPS:** n43,19323 e10,54152. ⬆➡.

20 ⌏€ 10/24h ⟶⬛Ch included. ▦
**Location:** Rural, simple, quiet. **Surface:** unpaved. ◻ 01/01-31/12.
**Distance:** ⛱100m.
**Remarks:** Max. 48h, dogs beach.

### ▥S | Castagneto Carducci ꔮ | 34A2

Via del Seggio, Marina di Castagneto. **GPS:** n43,18401 e10,54841. ⬆.

30 ⌏free ⟶. **Location:** Urban, simple, quiet. **Surface:** unpaved.
◻ 01/01-31/12.
**Distance:** 🚰2km ⛱500m ⊗2,5km ▮2,5km.

### ꕔS | Castagneto Carducci ꔮ | 34A2

**Agriturismo Eucaliptus**, Via Bolgherese, 275.
**GPS:** n43,20160 e10,61364.
5 ⌏€ 30 ⟶⬛Ch ✚WC ▯. **Location:** Rural, comfortable.
**Surface:** grassy. ◻ 01/01-31/12.
**Distance:** ⛱6,5km ▮4,5km.

### ▥S | Castel del Piano ꕔ ⛰ ꕿ | 34B2

Via Po. **GPS:** n42,888/2 e11,53733. ➡.

30 ⌏free ⟶⬛Ch free. **Location:** Rural, simple. **Surface:** asphalted.
◻ 01/01-31/12.
**Distance:** 🚰500m ⊗300m ▮500m 🚌200m.
**Remarks:** At footballstadium.

### ▥S | Castelfiorentino | 34B1

Via Che Guevara, circonvallazione Ovest. **GPS:** n43,60885 e10,96365. ⬆.

---

5 ⌏free ⟶⬛Ch free. **Location:** Simple, isolated.
**Surface:** asphalted. ◻ 01/01-31/12.
**Distance:** 🚰1,5km ⊗1,5km ▮1,5km.

### ▥S | Castellina in Chianti | 34B1

La Strada del Chianti, SR222. **GPS:** n43,47330 e11,28760. ⬆➡.

15 ⌏€ 10/24h ⟶⬛€ 0,20/10liter ⬛Ch ✚(8x)included WC€ 0,50. ▦
**Location:** Rural, comfortable. **Surface:** asphalted.
◻ 01/01-31/12.
**Distance:** 🚰200m.
**Tourist information Castellina in Chianti:**
✈ Via IV Novembre. Week market. ◻ Sa-morning.

### ▥S | Castelnuovo di Garfagnana ꕔ ⛰ ꕿ | 26D3

Via Valmaira. **GPS:** n44,11447 e10,40304. ⬆.

50 ⌏free ⟶⬛Ch free. **Location:** Urban, simple, noisy.
**Surface:** metalled. ◻ 01/01-31/12.
**Distance:** 🚰1km ⊗100m ▮800m 🚌200m.
**Remarks:** At sports park.

### ▥S | Castiglion Fiorentino | 34C1

Piazza Garibaldi, viale Marconi. **GPS:** n43,34465 e11,92278. ⬆.

20 ⌏free WC. **Location:** Rural, simple. **Surface:** asphalted
◻ 01/01-31/12 ⊡ Fri-morning market.
**Distance:** 🚰on the spot ⊗on the spot.

### ▥S | Castiglione della Pescaia ꕔ ⛰ ꕿ | 34B2

**Rocchette Serignano**, Via Rio Palma, Rocchette.
**GPS:** n42,77970 e10,79955. ⬆➡.

120 ⌏€ 20/day ⟶⬛€ 3 ⬛Ch € 5 ✚(18x)included ▯€ 1. 🍴
**Location:** Rural, comfortable. **Surface:** gravel. ◻ 01/04-15/09.
**Distance:** 🚰Castiglione della Pescaia 7km ⛱200m ⊗200m ▮200m
🚌100m ⛺on the spot.

IT

**Remarks:** Beach parking, unguarded.

### Castiglione della Pescaia 🌊⛱🌊 34B2
Via Andromeda. **GPS:** n42,76888 e10,89079. ⬆➡.

11 🚐free. **Location:** Urban, simple. **Surface:** asphalted.
🅾 01/01-31/12.
**Distance:** 🚶1km 🚰800m 🚌300m.

### Castiglione della Pescaia 🌊⛱🌊 34B2
Via Ponte Giorgini. **GPS:** n42,76515 e10,88545. ⬆➡.

5 🚐€ 1,50h, € 10/24h. **Location:** Urban, simple.
**Surface:** asphalted. 🅾 01/01-31/12 🅾 Sa.
**Distance:** 🚶on the spot ⊗100m 🚰500m 🚌on the spot.
**Remarks:** Market Saturday.

### Castiglione d'Orcia 🌊⛰ 34C2
**Area Pro Loco**, Viale Marconi. **GPS:** n43,00292 e11,61552. ⬆.

5 🚐free 🚰🗑Chfree. **Location:** Rural, simple. **Surface:** gravel/sand.
🅾 01/01-31/12.
**Distance:** 🚶200m 🚶on the spot.
**Tourist information Castiglione d'Orcia:**
✠ Rocco d'Orcia. Medieval citadel.

### Cecina 🌊⛱🌳 34A1
**Agricamper Impalancati**, Via Aurelia Nord, 108.
**GPS:** n43,33682 e10,49946. ⬆.

20 🚐€ 13, Jun/Sep € 18, Jul € 23, Aug € 28 🚰🗑Ch🛒included
🚽 1/1minutes 〰.🏖 **Location:** Rural, comfortable, isolated,
quiet. **Surface:** grassy/gravel. 🅾 01/01-31/12.
**Distance:** 🚶2,5km ⊗500m 🚰2km.
**Remarks:** Shuttle € 1/pp.

### Cecina 🌊⛱🌳 34A1
**Agricamper Gioia Selvaggia e Fabio**, Via Paratino Alto, 53.
**GPS:** n43,28780 e10,55314. ⬆.

18 🚐€ 15, Jul/Aug € 18 🚰🗑Ch🛒WC included. 🏖
**Location:** Rural, comfortable, quiet. **Surface:** grassy/gravel.
🅾 01/01-31/12.
**Distance:** 🚶3km 🏊7km ⊗3km 🚰3km.
**Remarks:** Swimming pool (summer).

### Certaldo 34B1
**Area Comunale**, Piazza dei Macelli. **GPS:** n43,54629 e11,04611. ⬆➡.

10 🚐free 🚰🗑Chfree. **Location:** Rural. **Surface:** metalled.
🅾 01/01-31/12.
**Distance:** 🚶medieval centre 150m (elevator) ⊗150m 🚰250m.

### Chianciano Terme 34C2
**20 Strada Provinciale 146 di Chianciano**. **GPS:** n43,04126 e11,81922.
20 🚐free 🚰€ 5 🗑Ch 🛒€ 6/24h. **Location:** Comfortable.
**Surface:** asphalted. 🅾 01/01-31/12.
**Distance:** ⊗600m 🚶on the spot.

### Chifenti ⛰🌊 34A1
**Area sosta Chifenti**, SS12. **GPS:** n44,00492 e10,56337.

10 🚐free 🚰🗑Ch 🛒free. **Location:** Rural, comfortable, central,
quiet. **Surface:** gravel. 🅾 01/01-31/12.
**Distance:** 🚶500m 🏊100m 🚶100m ⊗100m 🚰600m 🚌100m.

### Chiusdino 34B2
Abbazia San Galgano, SS441. **GPS:** n43,15283 e11,15137. ⬆.

15 🚐€ 1,50/h, € 10/8-20h, overnight stay free 🛒(9x)free.
**Location:** Rural, isolated, quiet. **Surface:** grasstiles.
🅾 01/01-31/12.
**Distance:** 🚶12km ⊗300m.
**Remarks:** Abbey of San Galgano 300m.

### Chiusi 34C2
Via Torri del Fornello. **GPS:** n43,01461 e11,94972. ⬆.

5 🚐free 🚰🗑Chfree. **Location:** Urban. **Surface:** asphalted.
**Distance:** 🚶100m 〰4,5km ⊗350m 🚰450m 🚌on the spot.
**Remarks:** Next to school.

### Cutigliano ⛰🌳🌊 26D3
Via di Risorgimento/Sp37. **GPS:** n44,09877 e10,75450. ⬆.

14 🚐€ 1,50/h, € 15/24h 🚰🗑Ch 🛒(14x)included. 🚌
**Location:** Rural, comfortable, quiet. **Surface:** metalled.
🅾 01/01-31/12.
**Distance:** 🚶200m 🏊300m 🚶300m ⊗350m 🚰350m 🚌100m.
**Remarks:** Max. 48h, picnic area.

### Dicomano ⛰🌳 34B1
SS67, Tosco Romagnola. **GPS:** n43,89407 e11,53715. ⬆.

4 🚐free 🚰🗑Chfree. **Location:** Rural, simple. **Surface:** asphalted.
🅾 01/01-31/12.
**Distance:** 🚶1km ⊗200m 🚌on the spot.

### Empoli 34B1
**Azienda Agricola Montaioncino**, Via Montaioncino 1.
**GPS:** n43,69103 e10,97624.

6 🚐€ 15 🚰🗑Ch 🛒WC included. **Location:** Rural, isolated, quiet.
**Surface:** grassy/gravel. 🅾 01/01-31/12.
**Distance:** 🚶5km.

### Equi Terme ⛰🌳🌊 26C3
Via della Stazione. **GPS:** n44,17009 e10,15513. ⬆➡.

40 🚐€ 10/night 🚰🗑Ch 🛒free. 🚌
**Location:** Rural, simple. **Surface:** gravel. 🅾 01/01-31/12.
**Distance:** 🚶300m 🏊on the spot ⊗300m 🚰300m 🚶300m.
**Remarks:** To be paid at caves, caves (500m) and marble quarry.

### Firenze 🌊⛱🍴 34B1
**FiPark**, Viale Europa, Fraz. Bagno a Ripoli, Florence (Firenze).
**GPS:** n43,75554 e11,30609. ⬆.

IT

40 🛏️7-19h € 2/h, 19-7h € 1/h, € 15/24h ⌐🚰♨️Chincluded. 🅿️
**Location:** Urban, simple.
**Surface:** metalled.
🔵 01/01-31/12.
**Distance:** 🚶centre 4km ⊗350m 🚉400m 🚌bus 23/33 > centre.

### 🅿️S    Firenze 🌿⛲🍽️    34B1

**Florence Park Scandicci**, Via di Scandicci 241, Florence (Firenze).
**GPS:** n43,76267 e11,20875.⬆️.

25 🛏️€ 15 ⌐included 🚿. **Location:** Urban, comfortable, central,
quiet. **Surface:** metalled. 🔵 01/01-31/12.
**Distance:** 🚶4km ⛵5km 🚉150m.
**Remarks:** Video surveillance.

### 🅿️S    Firenze 🌿⛲🍽️🧁    34B1

**Gelsomino SCAF**, Via del Gelsomino 11, Florence (Firenze).
**GPS:** n43,75173 e11,24388.⬆️.

150 🛏️€ 15/24h ⌐🚰♨️Chincluded. 🅿️
**Surface:** grasstiles.
🔵 01/01-31/12.
**Distance:** 🚶2km 🚌bus 37 > centre.
**Remarks:** Max. 7m.

**Tourist information Florence (Firenze):**
ℹ️ U.I.A.T. (Ufficio Informazioni e di Accoglienza Turistica), Piazza
Stazione, 4, www.firenze.turismo.toscana.it. Renaissance city with
many curiosities.
👁️ Ponte Vechio. Famous bridge with jeweller's shops.
✝️ Cappella Brancacci, Santa Maria del Carmine. Renovated frescoes.
🛍️ The Mall, le griffe, Via Europa 8, Leccio Reqqello. Factory outlet.

### 🅿️S    Firenzuola 🏔️🚤    26E3

**Area Picnic**, Loc. Badia a Moscheta. **GPS:** n44,07586 e11,42030.➡️.

10 🛏️free WC. **Location:** Rural, simple, isolated, quiet. **Surface:** grassy.
🔵 01/01-31/12.
**Distance:** 🚶Firenzuola 8km ⊗500m agriturismo Badia di Moscheta
🚶 on the spot.

### 🅿️S    Firenzuola 🏔️🚤    26E3

Loc. Pieve di Camaggiore. **GPS:** n44,14594 e11,45361.⬆️.

50 🛏️free ⌐ChWC. **Location:** Simple, quiet. **Surface:** grasstiles.
🔵 01/01-31/12.
**Distance:** 🚶Firenzuola 10km ⛵river 100m 🚉1km.
**Remarks:** Playground.

### 🅿️    Fivizzano 🏔️🚤    26C3

Piazza Libertà. **GPS:** n44,23914 e10,12735.⬆️.

6 🛏️free. **Location:** Urban, simple, quiet. **Surface:** asphalted.
🔵 01/01-31/12.
**Distance:** 🚶on the spot ⊗100m 🚉100m 🚌on the spot.

### 🍴S    Fivizzano 🏔️🚤    26C3

**Agriturismo Ristorante Al Vecchio Tino**, Loc. Germalla 1, Monte dei
Bianchi. **GPS:** n44,17380 e10,12603.⬆️.

6 🛏️€ 8/night ⌐♨️Ch🚿included. **Location:** Rural, luxurious.
**Surface:** gravel. 🔵 01/01-31/12.
**Distance:** ⊗on the spot 🚌3km.
**Remarks:** Swimming pool available.

### 🍇S    Foiano della Chiana    34C1

**Outlet Village Valdichiana**, Via Enzo Ferrari 5, loc. Farniole.
**GPS:** n43,22398 e11,80301.⬆️.

10 🛏️free. **Location:** Simple. **Surface:** asphalted. 🔵 01/01-31/12.
**Distance:** ⊗on the spot 🚉on the spot.
**Remarks:** Motorhome parking at Outlet.

### 🍇S    Follonica    34B2

**Agriturismo dal Pastore**, Via Cassarello, 342.
**GPS:** n42,92835 e10,78912.⬆️.

10 🛏️€ 10 + € 1/pp tourist tax ⌐♨️Ch🚿included.
**Location:** Rural, comfortable, noisy. **Surface:** grassy.
🔵 01/01-31/12.
**Distance:** 🚶city centre 2km ⛵2km ⊗100m 🚉1,5km.

---

**Remarks:** Barbecue place, regional products.

### 🅿️    Fonteblanda 🚤    34B2

**Talamone Wind Beach Parking**, Strada Provinciale Talamone.
**GPS:** n42,56334 e11,15659.⬆️➡️.

150 🛏️free, June-Sep € 15. **Location:** Rural, simple, isolated.
**Surface:** gravel.
🔵 01/01-31/12.
**Distance:** 🚶1,5km ⛵on the spot 🏖️on the spot ⊗1,5km 🚉1,5km.
**Remarks:** Beach parking, shuttle bus to village.

### 🅿️S    Gaiole in Chianti    34B1

Via Michelangelo Buonarroti. **GPS:** n43,46470 e11,43428.⬆️➡️.

5 🛏️free ⌐♨️Chfree. **Location:** Rural, simple. **Surface:** metalled.
🔵 01/01-31/12.
**Distance:** ⊗400m 🚉on the spot.
**Remarks:** At footballstadium.

### 🅿️S    Gallicano 🌿⛲🍽️🧁🚤    26D3

Via Maresciallo Guiliano Guazelli. **GPS:** n44,05827 e10,44565.⬆️➡️.

4 🛏️free ⌐♨️Ch🚿(2x)free. **Location:** Urban, simple, noisy.
**Surface:** metalled. 🔵 01/01-31/12.
**Distance:** 🚶500m ⊗450m 🚉100m.
**Remarks:** Grotta del Vento.

### 🅿️S    Greve in Chianti 🏛️    34B1

**Monte S. Michele**, Via Montebeni. **GPS:** n43,59066 e11,31355.⬆️➡️.

17 🛏️free ⌐♨️free. **Location:** Rural, comfortable, quiet.
**Surface:** metalled. 🔵 01/01-31/12.
**Distance:** 🚶500m 🚉500m.

**Tourist information Greve in Chianti:**
🏯 🔵 Sa-morning.

### 🅿️S    Isola dElba    34A2

**Area Camper Cavo**, San Bennato, Cavo, Elba (Isle) (Isola dElba).
**GPS:** n42,85459 e10,42267.⬆️.
30 🛏️€ 15-35, 4 pers.incl ⌐♨️Chincluded 🚿€ 3/24h 🗑️€ 1.
**Location:** Rural. **Surface:** gravel. 🔵 01/04-30/10.
**Distance:** 🚶600m ⛱️400m ⊗650m.

### 🅿️S    Isola dElba    34A2

**Area Camper La Perla**, Loc. Campo All'Aia, Procchio, Elba (Isle) (Isola
dElba). **GPS:** n42,78893 e10,24877.⬆️.
20 🛏️€ 20-46 ⌐♨️Ch🚿€ 2 WCincluded 🗑️🚿.
**Location:** Urban, comfortable. **Surface:** gravel. 🔵 01/01-31/12.
**Distance:** ⛱️on the spot ⊗150m 🚉400m.

IT

## Isola dElba — 34A2

Loc. Bocchetto, Porto Azzurro. **GPS:** n42,77114 e10,39985.
60 free, peak season € 10/24h Chfree. **Location:** Rural.
**Surface:** asphalted. 01/04-01/10.
**Distance:** city centre 1km 350m Coop 850m on the spot.
**Remarks:** Nearby cemetery.

## Isola dElba — 34A2

Sighello, area La Pila, Marina di Campo. **GPS:** n42,75357 e10,24228.
30 € 15 Ch € 3. **Surface:** unpaved. 01/05-30/09.
**Distance:** 400m 200m.
**Remarks:** At sports park.

## Larciano — 34B1

**Agriturismo Poggetto**, Via Stradella 1489.
**GPS:** n43,83319 e10,88042.

25 € 15/24h, free with a meal Ch € 3/day WC included
€ 1.
**Location:** Rural. **Surface:** grassy/gravel. 01/01-31/12.
**Distance:** 1km 1km 700m.
**Remarks:** Beautiful view.

## Livorno — 34A1

**Parco del Mulino**, Via Voltolino Fontani. **GPS:** n43,51394 e10,32503.

25 € 12, May/Sep € 15 Ch included.
**Location:** Comfortable, quiet. **Surface:** grassy/gravel.
01/01-31/12.
**Distance:** city centre 3km 200m 350m 550m 100m.
**Remarks:** Nearby beaches.

## Livorno — 34A1

Piazza Ordoardo Borrani, Viale d'Antignano.
**GPS:** n43,50465 e10,32144.

50 free. **Location:** Rural, simple, noisy. **Surface:** asphalted.
01/01-31/12.
**Distance:** 400m Antignano 100m 200m 300m 250m
150m.

## Livorno — 34A1

Calata Carrara. **GPS:** n43,55581 e10,30302.

30 free Ch free.
**Location:** Urban, simple, noisy. **Surface:** asphalted.
01/01-31/12.
**Distance:** on the spot 400m 600m.

## Tourist information Livorno:

Ufficio Informazioni, Piazza del Municipio. Medieval port city.

## Lucca — 34A1

**Il Serchio**, Via del Tiro a Segno 704, loc. Sant'Anna.
**GPS:** n43,85000 e10,48583.

50 € 25/24h, dog € 1 Ch (66x)WC € 5 included.
**Location:** Urban, comfortable, quiet. **Surface:** grasstiles.
01/03-31/01.
**Distance:** 1km 2km 200m 500m on the
spot on the spot on the spot.
**Remarks:** Waste dump € 2/day, shuttle € 1/pp, swimming pool € 5/pp.

## Lucca — 34A1

**Area Sosta Lucca**, Viale Gaetano Luporini.
**GPS:** n43,84028 e10,48878.

65 € 10/24h, peak season € 14/24h, € 3/h Ch included.
**Location:** Urban, simple, central, noisy. **Surface:** asphalted.
01/01-31/12.
**Distance:** 1km 2km 300m 500m 500m on the spot.

## Lucca — 34A1

Piazzale Don Franco Baroni. **GPS:** n43,85148 e10,50179.
250 free free. **Location:** Urban. **Surface:** gravel.
01/01-31/12.
**Distance:** 2km 600m 600m.

## Tourist information Lucca:

Casa di Puccini, Via di Poggio. Birth place of the composer. Tue-Su.
Wed, Sa, 3rd Su of the month antiques market.

## Lucignano — 34C1

SP19. **GPS:** n43,27664 e11,74512.

20 free Ch (9x)free. **Location:** Rural, simple.
**Surface:** grassy. 01/01-31/12.
**Distance:** 500m.
**Remarks:** At the edge of village.

## Marina di Bibbona — 34A2

**Area Sosta Barsotti**, Via dei Cipressi. **GPS:** n43,24899 e10,53396.

25 € 15/24h Ch € 2 WC included € 1/3minutes.
**Location:** Rural, comfortable, quiet. **Surface:** gravel.
01/01-31/12.
**Distance:** 500m 1km 500m 500m.

## Marina di Bibbona — 34A2

Piazza dei Ciclamini. **GPS:** n43,24348 e10,52978.
40 € 15/24h Chincluded € 2 WC. **Location:** Urban,
comfortable. **Surface:** metalled. 01/04-30/09.
**Distance:** 400m 240m 50m.

## Marina di Cecina — 34A1

**New Camping Le Tamerici**, Via della Cecinella, 5.
**GPS:** n43,29192 e10,51053.

40 € 25-44 Ch WC included.
**Location:** Rural, comfortable, quiet. **Surface:** asphalted.
15/04-30/09.
**Distance:** 1,5km 1km on the spot on the spot.
**Remarks:** Swimming pool.

## Marina di Cecina — 34A1

**Parcheggio Aqua Park**, Via Tevere. **GPS:** n43,30070 e10,49948.

100 € 8 Chincluded. **Location:** Rural, simple, quiet.
**Surface:** metalled. 01/03-15/11.
**Distance:** 2km 1km 200m 200m.

## Marina di Grosseto — 34B2

**Oasi di Maremma**, SP158 delle Collacchie Km 34,4.
**GPS:** n42,72611 e10,99055.

50 € 16, peak season € 20, 4 pers.incl Ch (100x)€ 2
WC € 1 € 4. **Location:** Rural, comfortable, quiet. **Surface:** grassy.
01/04-30/09.
**Distance:** 1km 1km 1km 1km on the spot.
**Remarks:** Water at each pitch, barbecue place, picnic area, shuttle € 1/pp.

## Marina di Grosseto — 34B2

**Area di sosta l'Oasi**, S332 > dir San Vincenzo d'Elba.
**GPS:** n42,73466 e10,97483.

50 € 14, Jun € 18, Jul/Aug € 23 Ch € 2 WC included
€ 2. **Location:** Rural, comfortable. **Surface:** grassy.
Easter-30/09.
**Distance:** Marina 1,5km 1,1km 400m nearby on the
spot on the spot.
**Remarks:** Monitored parking 24/24, grill and picnic area, playground.

## Marina di Grosseto — 34B2

Via Costiera, SP158. **GPS:** n42,73722 e10,96388.

IT

50 🛏free. **Location:** Rural, simple. **Surface:** gravel.
⏹ 01/01-31/12.
**Distance:** 🚆2km 🏊400m.

| 🚐S | **Marina di Grosseto** | 34B2 |

Via della Trappola/SP40. **GPS:** n42,72150 e10,99864.
10 🛏free. **Location:** Urban, noisy. **Surface:** metalled.
⏹ 01/01-31/12.
**Distance:** 🚆1,5km 🏊beach 2km ⊗100m 🚐on the spot.

| 🛢 | **Marina di Grosseto** | 34B2 |

Via Grossetana. **GPS:** n42,71552 e10,98646. ⬆➡.

8 🛏free. **Location:** Urban. **Surface:** sand. ⏹ 01/01-31/12.
**Distance:** 🚆on the spot 🏊400m ⊗400m 🍴on the spot 🚐on the
spot.
**Remarks:** At harbour.

**Tourist information Marina di Grosseto:**
🌿 Parco Naturale della Maremma. Nature reserve. ⏹ Wed, Sa, Su,
holidays 9h 01/06-30/09 guided walk 7h, 16h.

| 🚐S | **Marina di Pisa** 🌲🌊 | 34A1 |

**Parcheggio Camper Pisamo**, Viale Gabriela d'Annunzio.
**GPS:** n43,67909 e10,27887. ⬆.

130 🛏€ 1/h, night € 8 🚰🍳Ch🧹€ 2.🚿
**Location:** Rural, simple, noisy. **Surface:** gravel.
⏹ 01/01-31/12.
**Distance:** 🚆1km ✈8km 🏊sea 1km 🚣1km ⊗600m 🍴1,5km
🚐300m 🚲on the spot.

| 🚐S | **Marina di Pisa** 🌲🌊 | 34A1 |

**Area Sosta Camper Marina Di Pisa**, Via Litoranea, 1.
**GPS:** n43,65834 e10,28075. ⬆.

50 🛏€ 1/h, night € 8. **Location:** Comfortable, noisy.
**Surface:** asphalted. ⏹ 01/01-31/12.
**Distance:** 🏊on the spot 🚣on the spot ⊗150m 🍴1km.

| 🚐S | **Marradi** 🌿🏔🎡 | 26F3 |

**Area sosta Marradi**, Via San Benedetto. **GPS:** n44,07347 e11,61166. ⬆.

30 🛏free 🚰100liter 🍳Ch🧹8kWh,Service € 5. **Location:** Rural,
simple, quiet. **Surface:** asphalted. ⏹ 01/01-31/12.
**Distance:** 🚆50m 🌲on the spot ⊗100m 🍴200m 🚐on the spot.
**Remarks:** Caution key service € 7.

| 🚐S | **Massa Marittima** | 34B2 |

Viale del Risorgimento. **GPS:** n43,04530 e10,89050. ⬆➡.

10 🛏free 🚰🍳Chfree.
**Location:** Urban, simple, quiet. **Surface:** asphalted.
⏹ 01/01-31/12.
**Distance:** 🚆historical centre 650m ⊗600m 🍴500m 🚐on the spot.
**Remarks:** Near church.

| 🚐S | **Montalcino** 🌿🏔⛰ | 34B2 |

Via Osticcio. **GPS:** n43,04913 e11,48749. ⬆➡.

30 🛏€ 5/24h 🚰🍳Chfree. 🧳 **Location:** Rural, comfortable, quiet.
**Surface:** asphalted/metalled. ⏹ 01/01-31/12.
**Distance:** 🚆700m ⊗700m 🍴700m.

| 🌿 | **Montalcino** 🌿🏔⛰ | 34B2 |

**Agriturismo la Crociona**, La Croce 9. **GPS:** n43,03931 e11,50373. ⬆.
15 🛏€ 20, guests free. **Location:** Rural, isolated, quiet.
**Surface:** grassy. ⏹ 01/04-31/10.
**Distance:** 🚆3,5km ⊗on the spot.
**Remarks:** Regional products and wine.

| 🚐S | **Monte San Savino** | 34C1 |

Via del Casalino. **GPS:** n43,33177 e11,72204. ⬆.

20 🛏free 🚰🍳Chfree. **Location:** Rural, simple. **Surface:** gravel.
⏹ 01/01-31/12.
**Distance:** 🚆on the spot ✈4,2km ⊗200m 🚐150m.
**Remarks:** Near sports fields, steep ramp.

| 🚐S | **Montecatini Terme** 🏔🍷 | 34B1 |

Piazza Pietro Leopoldo, SS 436. **GPS:** n43,88286 e10,76386. ⬆.

40 🛏free 🚰free. **Location:** Urban, simple, central, noisy.
**Surface:** asphalted. ⏹ 01/01-31/12 ⏺ Thu (market).
**Distance:** 🚆100m ✈3km ⊗200m 🍴500m 🚐on the spot.
**Remarks:** In front of stadium, thursday market.

| 🚐S | **Montepulciano** 🌿 | 34C2 |

P5, Piazza Pietro Nenni. **GPS:** n43,09577 e11,78684. ⬆➡.

32 🛏€ 10/24h 🚰free. 🧳 **Location:** Rural, simple.
**Surface:** asphalted. ⏹ 01/01-31/12 ⏺ Wed morning, market.
**Distance:** 🚆200m ⊗100m 🍴400m.
**Remarks:** Cash payment.

| 🌿S | **Montepulciano** 🌿 | 34C2 |

**La Buca Vecchia**, Strada per Pienza, 38. **GPS:** n43,09903 e11,73939. ⬆.
7 🛏€ 20 + € 1/pp tourist tax 🚰🍳Ch🧹🌐included.
**Location:** Rural, comfortable, isolated, quiet. **Surface:** metalled.
⏹ 01/01-31/12.
**Distance:** 🚆5km.
**Remarks:** Check in on arrival, barbecue place.

| 🚐S | **Monteriggioni** 🌿 | 34B1 |

Via Cassia Nord 142. **GPS:** n43,38560 e11,22784.

30 🛏€ 16/24h 🚰🍳Ch🧹included WC🚾€ 0,50/3minutes.
**Location:** Rural, comfortable. **Surface:** grasstiles.
⏹ 01/01-31/12.
**Distance:** 🚆400m ⊗400m.
**Remarks:** Max. 72h, service passerby € 4.

| 🚐S | **Monteriggioni** 🌿 | 34B1 |

Strada di Monteriqqioni. **GPS:** n43,38801 e11,22511. ⬆.

5 🛏€ 3, 01/04-31/10 € 3,50. 🧳 **Location:** Rural, comfortable.
**Surface:** gravel. ⏹ 01/01-31/12.
**Distance:** 🚆300m ✈1,4km ⊗300m 🐾on the spot.

| 🌿S | **Monteriggioni** 🌿 | 34B1 |

**Agriturismo "Il Sambuco"**, Via Maestri del Lavoro 12, Uopini.
**GPS:** n43,35266 e11,29415.
8 🛏€ 15/24h 🚰free Ch🧹included WC🚾.
**Location:** Rural, comfortable, quiet. **Surface:** gravel.
⏹ 01/01-31/12.
**Distance:** 🚆1km ⊗350m 🚐300m.
**Remarks:** Regional products, swimming pool € 5.

| 🚐S | **Monteroni d'Arbia** | 34B1 |

Via San Giusto. **GPS:** n43,23048 e11,42371. ⬆➡.

20 🛏free ⛽🚰 Ch free. **Location:** Rural, simple. **Surface:** sand.
🅿 01/01-31/12.
**Distance:** 🚶50m.
**Remarks:** P centre.

### 🅿Ⓢ Montespertoli     34B1
**Molino del Ponte**, Via Volterrana Nord. **GPS:** n43,65606 e11,08445. ⬆.

5 🛏free ⛽€ 1/100liter 🚰€ 2 Ch. **Location:** Rural.
**Surface:** metalled. 🅿 01/01-31/12.
**Distance:** 🚶Montespertoli 2,3km 🛒on the spot 🏪400m.

### 🅿Ⓢ Montevarchi     34B1
Via B. Latini. **GPS:** n43,53052 e11,56784. ⬆.

20 🛏free ⛽🚰free. **Location:** Urban, simple. **Surface:** asphalted.
🅿 01/01-31/12.
**Distance:** 🚲7km 🛒Coop.
**Remarks:** Nearby stadium.

### 🅿Ⓢ Montopoli in Val d'Arno     34B1
**Camper di Alessio e Irene**, Piazza Amerigo Vespucci, Via di Masoria. **GPS:** n43,67333 e10,75222. ⬆.

31 🛏free ⛽🚰Ch free. **Location:** Urban, simple, central, quiet.
**Surface:** metalled. 🅿 01/01-31/12.
**Distance:** 🚶500m 🚲2km 🛒600m 🏪400m 🚌600m.
**Remarks:** Barbecue place, picnic area.

### 🅿Ⓢ Orbetello     34B3
**Lanino Parco Sosta**, Loc. Santa Liberata.
**GPS:** n42,43346 e11,15959. ⬆➡.

50 🛏€ 10/motorhome, € 8/pp, € 5/child ⛽🚰Ch 🚿(40x)included WC 📷. **Location:** Rural. **Surface:** grassy/gravel.
🅿 01/01-31/12.
**Distance:** 🚶Orbetello 5km 🏖50m 🛒200m 🏪alimentari.

---

**Remarks:** Max. 72h.

### 🅿Ⓢ Palazzuolo sul Senio 🌿⛰🪣⛰     26F3
**Parcheggio Casone**, Via Casone. **GPS:** n44,11073 e11,54968. ⬆➡.

50 🛏free ⛽🚰Ch free. **Location:** Rural, simple. **Surface:** asphalted.
🅿 01/01-31/12.
**Distance:** 🚶100m 🛒100m 🏪100m 🚌200m.
**Remarks:** Narrow entrance.

### 🅿Ⓢ Palazzuolo sul Senio 🌿⛰🪣⛰     26F3
Via Francesco Pagliazzi. **GPS:** n44,11551 e11,55000. ⬆.

6 🛏free. **Location:** Urban, isolated. **Surface:** metalled.
🅿 01/01-31/12.
**Distance:** 🚶on the spot 🛒600m 🏪350m 🚌200m.
**Remarks:** At swimming pool, next to cemetery, upper part of the parking.

### 🅿Ⓢ Pienza 🌿⛰     34C2
Via Mencattelli e Foro Boario. **GPS:** n43,07799 e11,68087. ⬆➡.

🛏8-22h first hour € 2, than € 1/h, overnight stay free ⛽🚰 Ch included WC. **Location:** Rural, simple. **Surface:** asphalted.
🅿 01/01-31/12 🛒 Fri-morning market.
**Distance:** 🚶100m.

### 🏆Ⓢ Pienza 🌿⛰     34C2
**Podere il Casale**, Via Podere II Casale 64. **GPS:** n43,08090 e11,71161.
8 🛏€ 25, 2 pers.incl ⛽🚿€ 3 WC 📶.
**Location:** Isolated, quiet. **Surface:** gravel. 🅿 01/01-31/12.
**Distance:** 🛒on the spot.
**Remarks:** Regional products.

### 🅿Ⓢ Pieve Santo Stefano     34C1
**Grey camper**, Via della Verna. **GPS:** n43,67058 e12,03729. ⬆➡.

20 🛏€ 10 ⛽🚰Ch 🚿WC included 🚿€ 1. **Location:** Urban, simple, noisy. **Surface:** metalled. 🅿 01/01-31/12.
**Distance:** 🚶on the spot 🚲1,7km 🛒300m 🏪350m 🚌200m.
**Remarks:** Nearby viaduct E45.

### 🏕Ⓢ Piombino     34A2
**Camperoasi**, Loc. Mortelliccio, Riotorto.
**GPS:** n42,95416 e10,66638. ⬆➡.

---

93 🛏Apr-Jun, Sep € 30, Jul/Aug € 40 ⛽🚰Ch 🚿WC 🚿€ 1 📷📶included. 🚻
**Location:** Rural, comfortable, quiet. **Surface:** grasstiles/grassy.
🅿 01/04-30/09 ⚫ 01/04-30/04 Mo-Thu.
**Distance:** 🏖200m 🛒50m 🏪50m.
**Remarks:** Water/drainage at each pitch, 10% discount on presentation of the most recent guide, reception open: 9.30-12.30 14-19.30.

### 🅿Ⓢ Piombino     34A2
**Area Sosta Camper Isolotto**, Loc. Mortelliccio, 7, Riotorto.
**GPS:** n42,95765 e10,67374. ⬆➡.

23 🛏€ 20, Jul/Aug € 28 ⛽🚰Ch 🚿included 🚿📷€ 4/time. 🚻📷
**Location:** Rural, comfortable, isolated. **Surface:** gravel.
🅿 01/01-31/12.
**Distance:** 🚶5km 🏖200m.
**Remarks:** Fruit-vegetables-wine-regional products for sale, swimming pool available.

### 🅿Ⓢ Piombino     34A2
**Area Sosta l'OrtiCillo**, Loc. Le Pinete, 3 Riotorto.
**GPS:** n42,98414 e10,68011. ⬆➡.

12 🛏€ 8-10, 01/07-31/08 € 14 + tourist tax € 0,50/pp ⛽🚰 Ch 🚿📶included.
**Location:** Rural, comfortable, quiet. **Surface:** gravel.
🅿 01/01-31/12.
**Distance:** 🚶300m.
**Remarks:** Barbecue place, borrow cycles for free, regional products.

### 🅿Ⓢ Piombino     34A2
**Carbonifera 1**, Loc. Torre Mozza. **GPS:** n42,94900 e10,69100. ⬆.

100 🛏€ 1,90-2,75/h, € 18-23/24h ⛽🚰Ch included. 🚌
**Location:** Rural. **Surface:** grassy/gravel. 🅿 01/01-31/12.
**Distance:** 🏖200m 🛒200m.
**Remarks:** Beach parking, no camping activities.

### 🅿Ⓢ Piombino     34A2
**Parcheggio Caldanelle**, Loc. Caldanelle. **GPS:** n43,00216 e10,52816. ⬆.

150 🛢 € 1,75-2,50/h, € 16,60-21,20/8-20h, overnight stay free 🚰Ch.🚐 **Location:** Rural, isolated, quiet. **Surface:** grassy.
🅿 01/01-31/12.
**Distance:** 🚉Piombino 9km ⛱1,5km.
**Remarks:** Beach parking, camper service 8-20h, no camping activities, shuttle bus.

## 🅂 Piombino 34A2
**Parcheggio di Alvin**, Piazzale Salvatore Allende.
**GPS:** n42,92578 e10,54219.⬆.

23 🛢 € 25/24h 🚰Chincluded. **Location:** Rural, simple, quiet.
**Surface:** gravel. 🅿 01/04-31/10.
**Distance:** 🚉1km ⛱200m ⊗300m 🍴300m.

## 🅂 Piombino 34A2
**Perelli 1-3**, Loc. Perelli. **GPS:** n42,95527 e10,61944.⬆.

50 🛢 € 2,20/h, € 18,70/8-20h, overnight stay free 🚰Chincluded.
🚐 **Location:** Rural, simple, quiet. **Surface:** grassy/sand.
🅿 01/06-30/09.
**Distance:** ⛱Sandy beach ⊗Perelli 1.
**Remarks:** Beach parking, service: Perelli 3, no camping activities, dogs beach.

## 🅂 Piombino 34A2
**Podere Mortelliccio**, Loc. Mortelliccio 8, Riotorto.
**GPS:** n42,95700 e10,67884.⬆.

8 🛢 € 20-25, Jul/Aug € 32 🚰Ch✂included 💻 3,50.
**Location:** Comfortable, noisy. **Surface:** gravel. 🅿 01/01-31/12.
**Distance:** 🚉4km ⛱400m ⊗500m 🍴1km.
**Remarks:** Regional products and wine, barbecue place.

## 🅂 Piombino 34A2
**Torremozza 2**, Loc. Torre Mozza. **GPS:** n42,94750 e10,69277.⬆➡.

90 🛢 € 1,90-2,75/h, € 18-23/24h 🚰Chincluded. 🚐
**Location:** Rural, simple, quiet. **Surface:** gravel.
🅿 01/01-31/12.
**Distance:** 🚉200m ⊗200m.
**Remarks:** Beach parking, no camping activities.

## 🅂 Piombino 34A2
Via della Pace. **GPS:** n42,93777 e10,52194.⬆.

150 🛢free 🚰 € 0,10/10liter 🅲Ch. **Location:** Urban, simple, noisy.
**Surface:** metalled. 🅿 01/01-31/12.
**Distance:** 🚉500m ⛱1km ⊗700m 🍴800m.
**Remarks:** Along busy road.

## 🅂 Piombino 34A2
**AgriCoccinella**, Loc. Scopicci, Riotorto. **GPS:** n42,94862 e10,70348.⬆.

23 🛢 € 20, Jul/Aug € 30 🚰Ch✂included. 🚐
**Location:** Rural, comfortable, quiet. **Surface:** grassy.
🅿 01/01-31/12.
**Distance:** ⛱500m ⊗300m 🍴2,5km 🍴50m.

## 🅂 Pisa 34A1
**Area Comunale**, Via di Pratale 78. **GPS:** n43,72240 e10,41550.
90 🛢 € 18 🚰included ✂ € 3. **Location:** Urban.
**Surface:** asphalted. 🅿 01/01-31/12.
**Distance:** 🚉on the spot.

## 🅂 Pisa 34A1
**Parcheggio camper**, Via di Pratale 78.
**GPS:** n43,72106 e10,42066.⬆➡.

100 🛢 € 12/night, € 1/h, € 5/6h 🚰 € 3 🅲Ch ✂ € 3.
**Location:** Urban, comfortable, quiet.
**Surface:** asphalted.
🅿 01/01-31/12.
**Distance:** 🚉800m ✈7km ⊗100m 🍴500m 🍴800m 🚐on the spot.
**Remarks:** Monitored parking.

## 🅂 Pisa 34A1
Via A. Paparelli. **GPS:** n43,72433 e10,41178.⬆.

100 🛢 € 1/h, overnight stay free.
**Location:** Urban, simple, noisy. **Surface:** asphalted/metalled.
🅿 01/01-31/12 🅿 Wed, Sa market.
**Distance:** 🚉on the spot ⊗100m 🍴200m 🚐on the spot.
**Remarks:** Max. 5 days.

## 🅂 Pistoia 34B1
Via Marino Marini/via della Quiete. **GPS:** n43,94389 e10,91556.⬆➡.

50 🛢free 🚰🅲Chfree. **Location:** Urban, simple, noisy.
**Surface:** asphalted. 🅿 01/01-31/12.
**Distance:** 🚉city centre 1km ✈6km ⊗300m 🍴500m 🚐on the spot.
**Remarks:** At sports park, max. 48h.

## 🅂 Pistoia 34B1
**Agricamper Podere Campofossato**, Via Calabbiana 2.
**GPS:** n43,99595 e10,89544.

8 🛢 € 20 🚰Ch ✂ 📶included. 🚐
**Location:** Rural, comfortable, quiet. **Surface:** grassy. 🅿 01/01-31/12.
**Distance:** 🚉10km ⛱on the spot ⊗on the spot 🚐100m 🍴on the spot.
**Remarks:** Regional products.

## 🅂 Poggibonsi 34B1
Via Fortezza Medicea, loc. Vallone. **GPS:** n43,46203 e11,14593.⬆➡.

± 15 🛢free 🚰 € 0,10/10liter 🅲Ch ✂ (6x)€ 1/12h.
**Location:** Rural. **Surface:** gravel. 🅿 01/01-31/12.
**Distance:** 🚉centre 500m ⊗400m 🍴500m.

**Tourist information Poggibonsi:**
ℹ Monteriggioni. Walled small town.

## 🅂 Pomarance 34B1
**Area Sosta Camper Attrezzata**, Viale della Costituzione.
**GPS:** n43,29966 e10,86974.⬆.

18 🛢 € 10/24h 🚰Ch ✂ WC 📶included. 🚐
**Location:** Urban, comfortable, noisy. **Surface:** metalled.
🅿 01/01-31/12.
**Distance:** 🚉on the spot ⊗100m 🍴200m 🍴100m 🚐50m.
**Remarks:** Max. 72h, video surveillance.

## 🅂 Pontassieve 34B1
Viale Hanoi/viale Lisbona. **GPS:** n43,77355 e11,42764.⬆.

free ⬚⬚Chfree. **Location:** Urban, simple. **Surface:** asphalted.
🅾 01/01-31/12.
**Distance:** 👟500m.

| 🏕S | Poppi | 34C1 |

**La Crocina**, Viale dei Pini. **GPS:** n43,71982 e11,76529. ⬆➡.

12 🅿free ⬚⬚Chfree. ⚡€ 3/5h.
**Location:** Urban, simple, quiet. **Surface:** asphalted.
🅾 01/01-31/12.
**Distance:** 👟historical centre 500m ✕300m 🚰700m 🚍on the spot.

| 🏕S | Porto Ercole | 34B3 |

**Le Miniere**, SP di Porto Ercole. **GPS:** n42,41749 e11,20386. ⬆➡.

130 🅿€ 20-25 ⬚⬚Ch ⚡WC 🚽€ 0,50 💡€ 5 📶included. 🚲
**Location:** Rural, comfortable, noisy. **Surface:** grassy.
🅾 Easter-30/09.
**Distance:** 👟Porto Ercole 2km ⛱800m ✕800m 🚰2km 🚍on the spot.
**Remarks:** Bread-service, borrow cycles for free, free shuttle to beach every 30 minutes.

| 🏕S | Porto Ercole | 34B3 |

**Parking Da Renzo**, SC della Feniglia. **GPS:** n42,41527 e11,20777. ⬆➡.

150 🅿€ 15-20/24h ⬚⬚Ch ⚡€ 3 WC 📶included. 🚲
**Location:** Rural, comfortable, quiet. **Surface:** grassy.
🅾 Easter-01/10.
**Distance:** 👟Porto Ercole 3km ⛱beach 1km ✕800m 🚍300m 🚲on the spot.
**Remarks:** Bike/car rental, picnic tables available, beach shuttle (August).

| 🏕S | Pratovecchio | 34C1 |

**Via Uffenheim. GPS:** n43,78666 e11,71952. ⬆➡.

---

12 🅿free ⬚⬚Ch ⚡free.
**Location:** Urban, simple, quiet. **Surface:** asphalted.
🅾 01/01-31/12.
**Distance:** 👟50m ⛱on the spot ✕100m 🚰100m 🚍100m.
**Remarks:** Along river, near sports fields, follow signs instead of GPS.

| 🏕S | Radda in Chianti | 34B1 |

**Via Degli Ulivi. GPS:** n43,48643 e11,37543. ⬆➡.

6 🅿€ 12/24h ⬚⬚WCfree. 🏠 **Location:** Rural, simple.
**Surface:** metalled. 🅾 01/01-31/12.
**Distance:** 👟200m (stairs).

| 🏕S | Radicofani | 34C2 |

**Via A. de Gasperi. GPS:** n42,89471 e11,77506. ⬆➡.

5 🅿free ⬚⬚Chfree. **Location:** Rural, simple.
**Surface:** grassy/gravel. 🅾 01/01-31/12.
**Distance:** 👟400m ✕800m.

| 🏕S | Radicondoli | 34B1 |

**Il Pianetto. GPS:** n43,25888 e11,04250. ⬆➡.

🅿free ⬚⬚Ch ⬚€ 1/h.
**Surface:** grassy/gravel. 🅾 01/01-31/12.
**Distance:** 👟medieval centre 300m ✕300m 🚰2km.

| 🏕S | Rapolano Terme | 34C1 |

**Area di sosta camper Il Pini**, Via Vittorio Veneto.
**GPS:** n43,29601 e11,60312.
50 🅿€ 10/24h, € 8/12h, € 6/6h ⬚€ 3 ⚡ 📶included.
**Surface:** gravel. 🅾 01/01-31/12.
**Distance:** 👟on the spot 🚤1km ✕300m.
**Remarks:** Terme Antica Querciolaia 200m.

| 🍴S | Rapolano Terme | 34C1 |

**Villa dei Boschi**, Loc. Villa dei Boschi 50, Fraz San Gimignanello, SP10.
**GPS:** n43,22829 e11,65429. ⬆.

20 🅿€ 20/24h, free with a meal ⬚⬚WC 📶included.
**Location:** Rural, simple, isolated. **Surface:** grassy. 🅾 01/01-31/12.
**Distance:** ✕on the spot.

| 🏕S | Rapolano Terme | 34C1 |

**Area di sosta Le Terme**, Via Trieste. **GPS:** n43,29268 e11,60781. ⬆.

---

64 🅿€ 5/6h, € 8/12h, € 12/24h ⬚⬚Ch ⚡WC 🚽included 📶€ 2.
🚲 ♨ **Location:** Rural, comfortable. **Surface:** gravel/metalled.
🅾 01/01-31/12.
**Distance:** 👟500m ✕50m 🚰200m.
**Remarks:** Terme Antica Querciolaia 50m.

| 🏕S | Rosignano Marittimo 🛝 | 34A1 |

**Molino a Fuoco**, Via dei Cavalleggeri Antica, Vada.
**GPS:** n43,32816 e10,46005. ⬆➡.

70 🅿01/07-31/08 € 10 ⬚⬚Chincluded. 🚲
**Location:** Rural, simple, quiet. **Surface:** grassy/gravel.
**Distance:** 👟400m ⛱500m ✕400m 🚰400m 🛝3km.
**Remarks:** Max. 72h.

| 🏕S | Rosignano Marittimo 🛝 | 34A1 |

**Il Fortullino**, Località il Fortullino. **GPS:** n43,43005 e10,39632. ⬆➡.

100 🅿€ 15/night, Jul-Aug € 20 ⬚⬚Ch ⚡ 🚽included.
**Location:** Comfortable, noisy. **Surface:** unpaved.
🅾 01/04-30/09.
**Distance:** 👟Castiglioncello 4km, Livorno 20km, Pisa 40km ⛱150m ✕Pizzeria 100m 🚰5km 🚲on the spot.
**Remarks:** Parking nearby motorway.

| 🏕S | Rosignano Marittimo 🛝 | 34A1 |

**SP39, Via Aurelia, Loc Caletta. GPS:** n43,39900 e10,42807. ⬆.

18 🅿€ 10 ⬚⬚ 🚲 **Location:** Urban, simple, noisy.
**Surface:** metalled.
**Distance:** 👟on the spot ⛱300m ✕100m 🚰100m 💡1km 🚍50m.
**Remarks:** Along busy road, max. 48h.

| 🏕 | Rosignano Marittimo 🛝 | 34A1 |

**Parcheggio del Lillatro**, Via Fratelli Gigli, loc Lillatro.
**GPS:** n43,38380 e10,43206. ⬆⬆.

40 ⛺ € 9. **Location:** Rural, simple, isolated, quiet. **Surface:** grassy/metalled. ☐ Easter-31/10. **Distance:** ⚓3km ⚓50m ⊗50m ⚓550m ⚓550m. **Remarks:** Nearby beaches.

### Rosignano Marittimo 34A1
**Sportiva Vada**, Via Mare Mediterraneo, Vada. **GPS:** n43,35208 e10,45183. ⬆➡.

75 ⛺ € 10/day. **Location:** Rural, quiet. **Surface:** unpaved. ☐ 01/06-31/08. **Distance:** ⚓400m ⚓200m ⊗200m ⚓400m.

### San Casciano dei Bagni 34C2
Via Della Pineta. **GPS:** n42,86530 e11,87383. ➡.

15 ⛺free. **Location:** Rural, simple. **Surface:** gravel/sand. ☐ 01/01-31/12. **Distance:** ⚓500m.

### San Casciano dei Bagni 34C2
Piazzale del Ponte. **GPS:** n42,87024 e11,87742. ⬆.

15 ⛺ € 6/12h, € 10/24h ⚓Ch. **Surface:** asphalted. ☐ 01/01-31/12. **Distance:** ⚓100m. **Remarks:** Near spa resort.

### San Casciano in Val di Pesa 34B1
**Parco del Poggione**, Piazza Dante Tacci. **GPS:** n43,65395 e11,18768. ⬆.

10 ⛺ € 8 ⚓ChWC⚓included. **Location:** Urban. **Surface:** gravel. ☐ 16/09-14/06. **Distance:** ⚓on the spot ⊗700m ⚓700m ⚓300m.

### San Gimignano 34B1
**Sosta Camper Santa Chiara**, Via di Castel San Gimignano, Loc. Fornace. **GPS:** n43,45572 e11,03476. ⬆➡.

30 ⛺ € 24/24h ⚓€ 2 ⚓Ch ⚓WC⚓included. **Location:** Rural, luxurious. **Surface:** gravel. ☐ 01/01-31/12. **Distance:** ⚓3km ⊗Osteria/bar ⚓1,5km ⚓shuttle. **Remarks:** Barbecue place, free shuttle bus to San Gimignano, tenniscourt.

### San Gimignano 34B1
**Park Santa Lucia**, Loc. Santa Lucia. **GPS:** n43,45205 e11,05586. ⬆➡.

50 ⛺ € 1/h, € 15/24h ⚓Chincluded ⚓(14x). **Location:** Rural, simple. **Surface:** gravel. ☐ 01/01-31/12. **Distance:** ⚓3km ⚓Citybus Linea 1. **Remarks:** Next to swimming pool, 24/24 video surveillance, shuttle bus to city centre.

### San Miniato Basso 34B1
**Area Camper Il Salice**, Via Pier delle Vigne 28/A, loc. La Catena. **GPS:** n43,68325 e10,82335. ⬆.

20 ⛺ € 20 ⚓Ch ⚓WCincluded. **Location:** Rural, comfortable, quiet. **Surface:** gravel. ☐ 01/01-31/12. **Distance:** ⚓2,5km ⊗400m ⚓300m ⚓300m. **Remarks:** Max. 3 days, monitored parking 24/24, shuttle bus to city centre.

### San Miniato Basso 34B1
**Piazza G. Impastato**, Via Pestalozzi/Via G. Pizzigoni, zona industriale. **GPS:** n43,69403 e10,83604. ⬆.

60 ⛺ € 0,50/h, overnight stay free ⚓free. **Location:** Urban, simple, noisy. **Surface:** asphalted. ☐ 01/01-31/12. **Distance:** ⚓3km ⚓800m ⊗50m ⚓100m ⚓100m.

### San Piero a Sieve 34B1
Via Giudici Falcone e Borsellino. **GPS:** n43,96260 e11,32732. ⬆➡.

20 ⛺free ⚓€ 2 ⚓Ch. **Location:** Urban, simple, quiet. **Surface:** metalled. ☐ 01/01-31/12. **Distance:** ⚓500m ⊗250m ⚓400m ⚓400m.

### San Quirico d'Orcia 34C2
Via delle Scuole. **GPS:** n43,05607 e11,60682. ⬆➡.

60 ⛺ € 10/24h ⚓free. **Location:** Rural, simple. **Surface:** asphalted. ☐ 01/01-31/12. **Distance:** ⚓200m. **Remarks:** Picnic area, playground.

### San Quirico d'Orcia 34C2
Strada di Bagno Vignoni, Bagno Vignoni. **GPS:** n43,02904 e11,62450. ⬆➡.

± 20 ⛺free. **Location:** Rural, simple, quiet. **Surface:** unpaved. ☐ 01/01-31/12. **Distance:** ⚓500m ⊗350m. **Remarks:** Parco dei Mulini: natural hot springs, free entrance, 400m.

### San Romano in Garfagnana 26D3
Via Campo Sportivo/via Prà di Lago. **GPS:** n44,17243 e10,34199. ⬆➡.

15 ⛺free ⚓Chfree. **Location:** Rural. **Surface:** grassy. ☐ 01/01-31/12. **Distance:** ⚓400m ⊗550m ⚓650m ⚓150m ⚓on the spot. **Remarks:** At sports park, Parco Avventura Selva del Buffardello 100m.

### San Vincenzo 34A2
**Area di Sosta - San Vincenzo**, Via Biserno. **GPS:** n43,08790 e10,54134. ⬆➡.

50 ⛺01/04-30/09 € 12/24h ⚓free. **Location:** Rural, simple, noisy. **Surface:** grassy/gravel. ☐ 01/01-31/12. **Distance:** ⚓1km ⚓beach 200m ⊗50m ⚓50m ⚓1km ⚓300m. **Remarks:** Beach parking, no camping activities, bicycle rental.

### San Vincenzo 34A2
**SS. Annunziata**, Via del Castelluccio, 142. **GPS:** n43,10086 e10,56001. ⬆.

IT

⌂€ 16-20, Jul/Aug € 35-45 🔌🗑Ch💧included 🗑€ 0,50 ▣€ 3 📶.
**Location:** Rural, comfortable, quiet. **Surface:** gravel.
☐ 01/01-31/12.
**Distance:** 🚂1km ⛟1km ⊗on the spot 🚌50m.
**Remarks:** 10% discount on presentation of the most recent guide, playground, swimming pool.

| 🏕S | Sansepolcro 〰🏔 | 34C1 |

Viale Alessandro Volta. **GPS:** n43,56976 e12,13727. 🔼.

20 ⌂free 🔌🗑Chfree. **Location:** Urban, simple. **Surface:** asphalted.
☐ 01/01-31/12.
**Distance:** 🚂200m ⊗200m 🚌100m.

| 🍴S | Sansepolcro 〰🏔 | 34C1 |

**Podere Violino**, Via del Tevere 1150, Gricignano.
**GPS:** n43,55539 e12,12312. 🔼➡.

8 ⌂€ 6 + € 5/pp 🔌🗑Ch💧WC 📶included. **Location:** Rural, comfortable, isolated, quiet. **Surface:** grassy. ☐ 15/02-31/12.
**Distance:** 🚂2km ⛟river ⊗on the spot 🚌1km.
**Remarks:** Arrival < 19h, restaurant closed on Sunday, swimming pool available.

| 🏕S | Santa Fiora | 34C2 |

Via Martiri della Niccioleta. **GPS:** n42,83531 e11,58397. 🔼➡.

20 ⌂free 🔌🗑Chfree 💧(6x)€ 1/2h. **Location:** Rural, simple.
**Surface:** gravel/sand. ☐ 01/01-31/12.
**Distance:** 🚂450m.

| 🏕S | Sasso Pisano 〰🏔🎭 | 34B2 |

**Buca San Rocco. GPS:** n43,16748 e10,86586. 🔼➡.

10 ⌂free 🔌€ 2 🗑Ch 💧€ 3/12h. **Location:** Rural, simple, quiet.
**Surface:** metalled. ☐ 01/01-31/12.
**Distance:** 🚂100m ⊗200m.

| 🏕S | Saturnia ♈ | 34B2 |

**L'Alveare dei Pinzi**, Strada della Peschiera, Saturnia.
**GPS:** n42,65597 e11,50368. 🔼➡.

400 ⌂€ 14/24h 🔌🗑Ch💧(120x)€ 2 WC🗑€ 0,50 ▣€ 6 📶included. 🚿 **Location:** Rural, comfortable, quiet. **Surface:** gravel.
☐ 01/01-31/12.
**Distance:** 🚂Saturnia 3km ⛟1,5km.
**Remarks:** Panoramic view, free shuttle to spa resort and Saturnia, bar/snack/fruit, terme di Saturnia (sulfur baths) 1,7km, Cascate del Mulino (water fall, free entry) 2,5km, friday market.

| 🏕S | Scandicci | 34B1 |

**Villa Constanza**, Via della Constitution.
**GPS:** n43,75474 e11,17510. 🔼➡.
⌂€ 10/24h. **Surface:** asphalted. ☐ 01/01-31/12.
**Distance:** ⊗on the spot 🚌on the spot.
**Remarks:** Video surveillance.

| ♉S | Scansano | 34B2 |

**Agricampeggio Gli Olmi**, Loc. La Poderina 41.
**GPS:** n42,68891 e11,32391. 🔼.
6 ⌂€ 15 🚰 💧WC🗑. **Location:** Rural, isolated, quiet.
**Surface:** gravel. ☐ 01/01-31/12.
**Distance:** 🚂1km ⛟1km.
**Remarks:** Swimming pool.

| 🍴S | Scarperia 🏔🎭 | 26E3 |

**Toscana Ranch**, Via di Galliano 21. **GPS:** n44,01189 e11,30681. 🔼.

20 ⌂€ 10 🔌🗑Ch💧WC💧included. **Location:** Rural, simple, quiet.
**Surface:** grassy. ☐ 01/01-31/12.
**Distance:** 🚂5km ⊗on the spot 🚩5km.
**Remarks:** Western style ranch.

| 🏕S | Sestino | 34C1 |

Via Travicello. **GPS:** n43,71223 e12,30356. 🔼➡.

12 ⌂free 🔌🗑💧free.
**Location:** Simple. **Surface:** grasstiles.
**Distance:** 🚂2km.
**Remarks:** Nearby sports park.

| 🏕S | Sesto Fiorentino | 34B1 |

**Area Antica Etruria**, Via Ferruccio Parri. **GPS:** n43,84150 e11,17667. 🔼.

50 ⌂€ 20/24h 🔌🗑Ch💧WC🗑included ▣📶€ 1,50/day 🚿.
**Location:** Rural, comfortable, noisy. **Surface:** grassy/gravel.

☐ 01/01-31/12.
**Distance:** 🔌1,5km ⊗400m 🚩400m 🚌50m > Florence.
**Remarks:** Monitored parking.

| 🏕S | Siena 〰🏔 | 34B1 |

**P1, Palasport**, Via Achille Sclavo. **GPS:** n43,33323 e11,31739. 🔼.

35 ⌂€ 20 🔌🗑ChWCincluded. **Location:** Urban, simple.
**Surface:** metalled. ☐ 01/01-31/12.
**Distance:** 🚂2,5km ⊗250m 🚌on the spot.

| 🏕S | Siena 〰🏔 | 34B1 |

**P2, Il Fagiolone**, Via di Pescaia. **GPS:** n43,31456 e11,31760. 🔼.

60 ⌂€ 20 🔌🗑WCfree. **Location:** Urban, simple, noisy.
**Surface:** metalled. ☐ 01/01-31/12.
**Distance:** 🚌on the spot.
**Remarks:** Along busy road.

| 🏕 | Siena 〰🏔 | 34B1 |

**Acqua Calda**, Via Fausto Coppi. **GPS:** n43,33627 e11,29695. 🔼.

⌂free. **Location:** Urban, simple. **Surface:** grasstiles.
☐ 01/01-31/12.
**Distance:** 🔌650m 🚌bus 10 centre Siena.

| 🏕 | Siena 〰🏔 | 34B1 |

Via delle Province/via Napoli. **GPS:** n43,34168 e11,30512. 🔼.

⌂free. **Location:** Urban, simple, noisy. **Surface:** asphalted.
☐ 01/01-31/12.
**Distance:** ⊗200m McDonalds 🚩200m 🚌on the spot.

**Tourist information Siena:**
👁 Palazzo Publico. Gothic town hall from 1342.
👁 Torre del Mangia. Bell tower. ☐ daily.
✝ Duomo. Romanesque Gothic cathedral.
🎪 La Lizza. Week market. ☐ Wed morning.
🎆 Palio, Piazza del Campo. Famous historical horse race. ☐ 02/07, 16/08.

| 🏕S | Stia | 34C1 |

**Parco comunale del Canto della Rana**, Via Londa, SP556.
**GPS:** n43,80417 e11,70326. 🔼➡.

IT

10 ⏚free 🚰🔧Ch ⚡free. **Location:** Rural, simple, quiet.
**Surface:** gravel. ⏰ 01/01-31/12.
**Distance:** 🍽500m ⊗600m 🛒700m.

| 🚐S | Suvereto 🌿🍴 | 34B2 |

Via dei Forni. **GPS:** n43,07572 e10,67802. ⬆.

12 ⏚free 🚰🔧. **Location:** Rural, simple, quiet. **Surface:** gravel.
⏰ 01/01-31/12.
**Distance:** 🍽medieval centre 200m ⊗300m 🛒300m.

| 🚐S | Torrita di Siena 🌿⚓ | 34C2 |

Via di Ciliano. **GPS:** n43,16475 e11,77173. ⬆.

6 ⏚free 🚰🔧Ch ⚡free. **Location:** Rural, comfortable, quiet.
**Surface:** metalled. ⏰ 01/01-31/12.
**Distance:** 🍽400m ⊗200m 🚲on the spot 🚶on the spot.

| 🚐S | Venturina ⚓♨ | 34B2 |

**Parco Termale Calidario**, Via di Caldana.
**GPS:** n43,03666 e10,60000. ➡.

49 ⏚free 🚰€ 1/100liter 🔧Ch. **Location:** Urban, quiet.
**Surface:** metalled. ⏰ 01/01-31/12.
**Distance:** 🍽800m 🚲50m 🛒800m 🚌300m.
**Remarks:** Thermal centre 50m.

| 🚐S | Vinci 🌿 | 34B1 |

Via Girolamo Calvi. **GPS:** n43,78080 e10,92830. ⬆.

15 ⏚€ 12/8-20h, overnight stay free 🚰🔧Chfree ⚡ 🚌
**Location:** Urban. **Surface:** gravel. ⏰ 01/01-31/12.
**Distance:** 🍽historical center 100m ⊗200m 🛒300m.

# San Marino

| 🚐S | San Marino | 26G3 |

**Camper Stop**, Via del Serrone 94. **GPS:** n43,92057 e12,45056. ⬆.
⏚free 🚰⚡free. **Surface:** grassy. ⏰ 01/01-31/12.
**Distance:** 🍽city centre 3km 🚌on the spot.

| 🚐S | San Marino | 26G3 |

**Gualdicciolo**, Via Fabrizio di Montebello. **GPS:** n43,94630 e12,40551.
20 ⏚free 🚰🔧ChWCfree.
**Surface:** metalled. ⏰ 01/01-31/12.
**Distance:** 🍽8km 🚲on the spot.

| 🚐S | San Marino | 26G3 |

**P10**, Via Napoleone Boneparte. **GPS:** n43,93567 e12,44362. ⬆.

20 ⏚€ 8/24h ⚡€ 2. **Location:** Urban. **Surface:** asphalted.
⏰ 01/01-31/12.
**Distance:** 🍽2km ⊗1,5km 🛒900m.
**Remarks:** Elevator to centre 50m.

| 🚐S | San Marino | 26G3 |

**P13, Baldasserona**, Borgo Maggiore. **GPS:** n43,94054 e12,44289. ⬆.

50 ⏚free 🚰🔧ChWCfree. **Location:** Rural. **Surface:** asphalted.
⏰ 01/01-31/12 ⏺ Service: winter.
**Distance:** 🍽300m ⊗650m.
**Remarks:** Service 300m, picnic tables available.

| 🚐S | San Marino | 26G3 |

**Strada Genghe di Atto**, Acquaviva. **GPS:** n43,94491 e12,42963. ⬆.

5 ⏚free 🚰🔧ChWCfree. **Surface:** asphalted. ⏰ 01/01-31/12.
**Distance:** 🍽6km.

**Tourist information San Marino:**
🎪 Borgo Maggiore. Week market. ⏰ Thu.

# Marche

| 🚐S | Amandola | 34D2 |

**Area Sosta Sibillini**, Piazzale Sandro Pertini. **GPS:** n42,97085 e13,35488.
52 ⏚€ 10 🚰🔧Ch ⚡€ 2 WC 🚿included. **Location:** Rural, simple,
quiet. **Surface:** asphalted. ⏰ 01/01-31/12.
**Distance:** 🍽800m ⊗850m.

**Remarks:** Picnic and barbecue place.

| 🚐S | Ancona 🌿⚓🏖 | 34D1 |

**Area di sosta Posatora**, Via Sanzio Blasi, Loc. Posatore.
**GPS:** n43,59964 e13,48530. ⬆➡.

30 ⏚€ 12 🚰🔧Ch ⚡(24x)included. 🚌
**Location:** Simple. **Surface:** metalled.
⏰ 01/01-31/12.
**Distance:** 🍽4,5km 🛒10m.
**Remarks:** Max. 72h, only exact change, entrance between 8-22h.

| 🚐S | Ancona 🌿⚓🍴 | 34D1 |

**Centro Commerciale Auchan**, Via Scataglini, Zona Industriale Baraccola,
SS16, Ancona-sud. **GPS:** n43,55133 e13,51506. ⬆➡.

25 ⏚free 🚰🔧Chfree.
**Location:** Simple. **Surface:** grasstiles. ⏰ 01/01-31/12.
**Distance:** 🍽8km 🚲3,6km ⊗on the spot 🛒on the spot.

**Tourist information Ancona:**
ℹ Riviera del Conera. Touristic peninsula with beaches and several
bathing resorts.

| 🚐S | Apecchio | 34C1 |

Via Isidoro Pazzaglia. **GPS:** n43,55938 e12,41969. ⬆➡.
30 ⏚free 🚰🔧Ch ⚡(6x)free.
**Location:** Urban. **Surface:** metalled. ⏰ 01/01-31/12.
**Distance:** 🍽100m ⊗100m 🛒50m 🚌100m.

**Tourist information Apecchio:**
🎪 Week market. ⏰ Fri-morning.

| 🚐S | Ascoli Piceno 🌿⚓🍴 | 34E2 |

**Ex Seminario**, Viale Alcide Gasperi. **GPS:** n42,85222 e13,58222. ⬆➡.

20 ⏚€ 3/night,20/h, night € 3 🚰included ⚡€ 2.
**Location:** Urban. **Surface:** asphalted. ⏰ 01/01-31/12.
**Distance:** 🍽centre 500m ⊗200m 🛒200m.
**Remarks:** Guarded parking.

| 🏠S | Ascoli Piceno 🌿⚓🍴 | 34E2 |

**Bed & Breakfast Chartaria**, Via Adriatico.
**GPS:** n42,84792 e13,57306. ⬆.
7 ⏚€ 15 🚰included ⚡€ 3. **Location:** Urban. **Surface:** grassy.
⏰ 01/01-31/12.
**Distance:** 🍽city centre 1km ⊗500m 🚲on the spot.
**Remarks:** Barbecue place.

**Tourist information Ascoli Piceno:**
ℹ City with many monumental bldg.
🎪 ⏰ Wed, Sa.

| 🚐S | Camerino 🌿 | 34D1 |

Via Macario Muzio, Viale Betti. **GPS:** n43,13677 e13,06718. ⬆.

IT

8 ⌗free ⌐🔲Chfree ⚡€ 1/4h WC🔲.
**Location:** Rural. **Surface:** asphalted. ◻ 01/01-31/12.
**Distance:** 🛒centre 500m ⊗350m.
**Remarks:** Beautiful view, picnic area, escalator to city centre.

### 🚿S Carpegna 34C1
Via Aldo Moro. **GPS:** n43,78083 e12,34040.⬆.

10 ⌗free ⌐€1 🔲Ch ⚡€ 0,60/h. **Location:** Urban.
**Surface:** concrete. ◻ 01/01-31/12.
**Distance:** 🛒300m ⊗300m 🍴300m 🚌400m.

### 🚿S Castelfidardo 34D1
**Croce Verde**, Via Lumumba/via Donato Bramonte.
**GPS:** n43,46603 e13,55563.⬆➡.

10 ⌗free ⌐🔲free. **Location:** Simple. **Surface:** asphalted.
◻ 01/01-31/12.
**Distance:** 🛒200m.
**Remarks:** Max. 48h.

### 🚿S Castelsantangelo sul Nera 34D2
Strada Provinciale 136. **GPS:** n42,89117 e13,15355.⬆.
8 ⌗free ⌐🔲Chfree. **Location:** Isolated, quiet. **Surface:** asphalted.
◻ 01/01-31/12.
**Distance:** 🛒200m ⊗500m.

### 🚿S Cerreto D'Esi 34D1
Via Dante Alighieri. **GPS:** n43,32714 e12,99114.➡.

10 ⌗free ⌐🔲Ch ⚡free. **Location:** Urban, simple.
**Surface:** metalled. ◻ 01/01-31/12.
**Distance:** 🛒1km ⊗500m 🚌200m.

### 🚿S Cingoli 34D1
**Area Balcone delle Marche**, Via San Esuperanzio.
**GPS:** n43,37643 e13,20943.
⌗€ 10 ⌐🔲Ch ⚡included. **Location:** Rural.
**Surface:** asphalted/gravel. ◻ 01/01-31/12.
**Distance:** 🛒200m ⊗200m 🍴100m 🚶on the spot.

### 🚿S Colmurano 34D1
Via Piero della Francesca, Contrada Peschiera.
**GPS:** n43,16260 e13,35828.⬆➡.

---

8 ⌗free ⌐🔲ChWCfree. **Location:** Rural. **Surface:** asphalted.
◻ 01/01-31/12.
**Distance:** 🛒400m ⊗550m 🚌850m.
**Remarks:** Near sports park and historical centre.

### 🚿S Corinaldo 〰 34D1
**CoriCamper**, Via Pecciameglio. **GPS:** n43,64688 e13,04850.⬆.
14 ⌗free ⌐🔲Ch ⚡free.
**Surface:** metalled. ◻ 01/01-31/12.
**Distance:** 🛒200m ⊗300m 🍴200m.
**Remarks:** Max. 48h.

### 🚿S Corinaldo 〰 34D1
Via Lepri 3. **GPS:** n43,64703 e13,04910.⬆.

8 ⌗free ⌐🔲Ch ⚡free. **Location:** Simple, comfortable.
**Surface:** asphalted. ◻ 01/01-31/12.
**Distance:** 🛒400m 🍴50m.

### 🚿S Corinaldo 〰 34D1
**Ristorante Camping Colverde**, Via per Montalboddo 52.
**GPS:** n43,63504 e13,09743.⬆➡.

10 ⌗€ 15, guests € 10 ⌐🔲Ch ⚡WC,on camp site 🔲included,on
camp site.🛁 **Location:** Rural, simple. **Surface:** grassy.
◻ 01/01-31/12.
**Distance:** 🛒5km ⊗on the spot.
**Remarks:** Max. 48h.

### 🚿S Cossignano 34E2
Via Gallo. **GPS:** n42,98050 e13,69213.⬆.
6 ⌗€ 6 ⌐€ 3 🔲Ch ⚡included. **Location:** Urban, simple.
**Surface:** metalled. ◻ 01/01-31/12.
**Distance:** 🛒on the spot ⊗500m 🚌400m.
**Remarks:** Max. 72h.

### 🚿S Cupramontana 34D1
**Verdicchio**, SP 11. **GPS:** n43,43934 e13,11837.⬆➡.

10 ⌗free ⌐🔲Chfree ⚡(10x). **Location:** Simple, noisy.
**Surface:** metalled. ◻ 01/01-31/12.
**Distance:** 🛒500m ⊗100m 🍴500m.
**Remarks:** Beautiful view of Monte San Vicino.

### 🚿S Fabriano 🏞🎪 34D1
Fraz. Poggio San Romualdo. **GPS:** n43,36473 e13,02534.⬆.

---

35 ⌗free ⌐🔲free. **Location:** Rural, simple, quiet. **Surface:** grassy.
◻ 01/01-31/12.
**Distance:** 🛒3,5km 🚶on the spot.

### 🚿S Fabriano 🏞🎪 34D1
Via Bruno Buozzi. **GPS:** n43,34650 e12,91645.➡.

16 ⌗free ⌐€ 2/100liter 🔲Ch ⚡(6x)€ 3/12h.
**Location:** Simple. **Surface:** grassy. ◻ 01/01-31/12.
**Distance:** 🛒3km.
**Remarks:** Next to sports centre.

### 🚿S Falerone 34D1
**Ex-stazione FS di Piane di Falerone**, Via Togliatti.
**GPS:** n43,09944 e13,49944.⬆.

15 ⌗free ⌐🔲Ch ⚡free.
**Surface:** metalled. ◉ 1st Su of the month.
**Distance:** 🛒100m ⊗200m 🍴200m 🚌100m.
**Remarks:** Nearby the old station and theatre Romano.

### 🚿S Fano 〰⛺🌊 34D1
**Lungomare Sassonia**, Via Ruggeri. **GPS:** n43,84238 e13,03197.⬆.

60 ⌗€ 5-8,50 ⚡(20x)€ 2 🔲.
**Surface:** grassy/gravel. ◻ 01/01-31/12.
**Distance:** 🛒1km 🚌2km 🍴50m ⊗50m 🍴600m.

### 🚿S Fano 〰⛺🌊 34D1
**Area di Sosta Adriatico**, SS16, Torrette di Fano.
**GPS:** n43,80789 e13,08198.⬆.

30 ⌗€ 10-23, camperstop 18-9h € 8-10 🔲Ch ⚡
(12x)WCincluded 🔲€ 0,50 🔲€ 3.🛁 **Location:** Rural, comfortable.
**Surface:** grassy/gravel. ◻ 22/04-11/09.
**Distance:** 🛒4km 🚌9km 🍴200m ⊗50m 🍴500m.
**Remarks:** Service passerby € 5.

## Fano — 34D1

Viale Kennedy. **GPS**: n43,84557 e13,01133. ➡.

16-20 free ⛲🔌Ch free. **Location**: Simple. **Surface**: asphalted.
📅 01/01-31/12.
**Distance**: 🚶200m 🏖2,7km ⛱800m.
**Remarks**: Nearby cemetery.

## Fano — 34D1

**Campo Nunzia**, SS Adriactica Sud-Loc. Torrette di Fano.
**GPS**: n43,80474 e13,08488. ⬆➡.

28 €10-15,50 ⛲🔌Ch 🔌€2,50/24h WC€1.
**Location**: Rural, comfortable. **Surface**: grassy/gravel.
📅 24/04-01/09.
**Distance**: 🚶7km 🏖10km ⛱150m.

## Fano — 34D1

**Ristorante La Tratta Maria Angela**, Via Fratelli Zuccari 37.
**GPS**: n43,83589 e13,04182. ⬆.

14 €7. **Location**: Simple, quiet. **Surface**: grassy.
📅 01/04-01/10.
**Distance**: 🚶2,5km ⛱50m 🛒on the spot ⊗on the spot.
**Remarks**: P camper.

**Tourist information Fano**:
ℹ 📅 Wed, Sa.

## Fermo — 34E1

**Area Camper 2004**, Lungomare Marina Palminese.
**GPS**: n43,15085 e13,81382. ⬆.

80 €12 ⛲🔌Ch 🔌(32x)included 🚿hot shower against payment
📶. **Surface**: grassy. 📅 01/04-30/09.
**Distance**: 🚶10km 🏖2,5km ⛱on the spot ⊗450m ⛽900m
🚌450m.
**Remarks**: Swimming pool.

## Fermo — 34E1

**Baia dei Gabbiani**, Viale A. de Gasperi, Lido S. Tomasso.
**GPS**: n43,22158 e13,78113. ⬆➡.

50 €13-20, Aug €25 ⛲🔌Ch 🔌included 🚿€0,50 📷.
**Location**: Urban, comfortable. **Surface**: grassy/gravel.
📅 01/01-31/12.
**Distance**: 🚶6,6km ⛱Private beach ⊗50m.

## Fermo — 34E1

**Onda Verde**, Via Usodimare, Lido di Fermo.
**GPS**: n43,20289 e13,78825. ⬆➡.

100 €10, 01/06-26/08 €15-20 ⛲🔌Ch 🔌2Amp
WC🚿included. **Location**: Rural, quiet. **Surface**: grassy.
📅 01/04-30/09. **Distance**: 🚶Fermo 10km 🏖10m ⊗500m ⛽200m.

## Fermo — 34E1

Via di Crollanza. **GPS**: n43,16176 e13,72318.

8 free ⛲🔌Ch WC. **Surface**: asphalted. 📅 01/01-31/12.
**Distance**: 🚶100m ⊗300m 🚌on the spot 🎣on the spot.

## Fossombrone — 34D1

Via Oberdan. **GPS**: n43,69301 e12,81835.

8 free ⛲🔌Ch free. **Location**: Urban. **Surface**: asphalted.
📅 01/01-31/12.
**Distance**: 🚶500m 🏖1,4km ⊗400m ⛽on the spot 🚌100m.

**Tourist information Fossombrone**:
ℹ Week market. 📅 Mo.

## Genga — 34D1

**Frasassi**, Fraz San Vittore. **GPS**: n43,40321 e12,97597. ⬆➡.

50 free ⛲🔌Ch WC 📶free. **Location**: Simple, quiet.
**Surface**: gravel. 📅 01/01-31/12.
**Distance**: 🚶7km ⊗on the spot.
**Remarks**: Nearby pay-desk Gole di Frasassi, free shuttle to the caves.

## Gradara — 26H3

**Parcheggio dei Cipressi**, Via Mancini. **GPS**: n43,94163 e12,77461. ⬆.
5 €5/3h, €24/24h ⛲🔌 🔌€3/6h. **Location**: Urban. **Surface**: grassy.
📅 01/01-31/12.
**Distance**: 🚶on the spot ⊗on the spot ⛽1,2km.

## Gradara — 26H3

**Parking P1**, Piazza Paolo e Francesca. **GPS**: n43,94083 e12,77083. ⬆.

14 €10/24h ⛲🔌Ch WC included. 🚰.
**Location**: Urban, simple, central. **Surface**: asphalted.
📅 01/01-31/12.
**Distance**: 🚶historical center 100m 🏖7,3km ⊗on the spot ⛽400m.
**Remarks**: Parking centre, castle 500m.

## Grottammare — 34E2

**Sosta Camper 43° Parallelo**, Via Carlo Alberto dalla Chiesa.
**GPS**: n42,96673 e13,87694. ⬆.
40 €15 ⛲🔌Ch 🔌 WC🚿📶.
**Location**: Urban. **Surface**: asphalted. 📅 01/03-30/11.
**Distance**: 🚶on the spot 🏖2,7km ⛱500m ⊗500m ⛽100m
🚌on the spot.
**Remarks**: Behind centro commerciale Cityper, along railwayline,
monitored parking.

## Grottammare — 34E2

**Briciola di Sole**, Contr. Granaro 19. **GPS**: n42,99045 e13,82536. ⬆.

14 €15, guests free ⛲🔌Ch 🔌included.
**Location**: Rural. **Surface**: gravel/metalled.
📅 01/04-31/10.
**Distance**: 🏖2,5km ⛱sea 5km ⊗on the spot ⛽2km.
**Remarks**: Restaurant with traditional kitchen, located on estate.

## Jesi — 34D1

Via Alfredo Zannoni. **GPS**: n43,51882 e13,24180. ⬆➡.

10 free ⛲🔌Ch free. **Location**: Urban, simple, quiet.
**Surface**: asphalted. 📅 01/01-31/12.
**Distance**: 🚶500m centro storico ⊗500m ⛽500m 🚌900m.

**Tourist information Jesi**:
ℹ Area with many vineyards.
👁 Grotte di Frasassi. Caves.

## Loreto — 34D1

**Area Camper Pro Loco**, Via Maccari. **GPS**: n43,44125 e13,61491. ⬆➡.

65 €12/24h ⛲🔌Ch included 🔌(20x)€3/day WC€1 🔌€2/8h.

Location: Rural, comfortable. **Surface:** grasstiles.
☐ 01/01-31/12.
**Distance:** 150m 15km.
**Remarks:** Max. 48h.

### Loreto 34D1

**Parking P1**, Via Benedetto XXV. **GPS:** n43,44129 e13,60756.⬆️.

6 € 6/day, overnight stay free WC. **Surface:** asphalted.
**Distance:** 300m 50m.
**Remarks:** Parking at city wall.

### Macerata 34D1

**Sferisterio**, Via Paladini. **GPS:** n43,29806 e13,45694.⬆️.
8 €5 Ch **Surface:** asphalted. ☐ 01/01-31/12.
**Distance:** 200m 200m.

### Macerata Feltria 34C1

Loc. San Gasparre. **GPS:** n43,80098 e12,42886.

4 free ChWC free.
**Location:** Rural. **Surface:** metalled. ☐ 01/01-31/12.
**Distance:** 1km on the spot Pizzeria 250m.
**Remarks:** Along Aspa river, at sports park.

**Tourist information Macerata Feltria:**
Week market. ☐ Tue.

### Marina di Montemarciano 37A3

Lungomare Alfredo Cappellini. **GPS:** n43,65936 e13,32780.⬆️.

40 € 0,70/h Ch (32x)€ 2.
**Location:** Simple, noisy. **Surface:** grassy. ☐ 15/05-15/09.
**Distance:** 4km 9km 50m pebbled beach 100m.
**Remarks:** To coast road and railwayline.

### Marotta 34D1

**Area di Sosta Marotta**, Lungomare Colombo 157, Mondolfo.
**GPS:** n43,76067 e13,15312.⬆️.

80 €8-14 Ch (80x)€ 2/24h WC included,cold shower.
**Location:** Rural, simple. **Surface:** grassy.
☐ 01/04-30/09.
**Distance:** 500m 1,5km 50m on the spot.
**Remarks:** Between coast road and railwayline.

### Matelica 34D1

**Porte Capamante**, Via Circonvallazione. **GPS:** n43,25917 e13,01083.➡️.

6-8 free free. **Location:** Urban, simple. **Surface:** asphalted.
☐ 01/01-31/12.

### Matelica 34D1

**Country House Salomone**, Località Salomone 437.
**GPS:** n43,29635 e13,00031.⬆️➡️.

40 € 7, free with a meal (16x)included WC at restaurant.
**Location:** Rural, simple. **Surface:** grassy/gravel.
☐ 01/01-31/12.
**Distance:** on the spot.
**Remarks:** Beautiful view.

### Mergo 34D1

**Area Sosta Comunale**, Via Colli. **GPS:** n43,47394 e13,03598.⬆️➡️.

10 free Ch free (8x).
**Location:** Simple. **Surface:** concrete. ☐ 01/01-31/12.
**Distance:** 300m.
**Remarks:** Nearby sports park.

### Mondavio 34D1

Via Cappuccini. **GPS:** n43,67744 e12,96165.⬆️➡️.
10 free Ch free. **Surface:** asphalted. ☐ 01/01-31/12.
**Distance:** 500m 700m.

**Tourist information Mondavio:**
Week market. ☐ Mo.

### Montalto delle Marche 34E2

Via Cuprense. **GPS:** n42,98726 e13,60870.⬆️.

6 free free. **Surface:** metalled. ☐ 01/01-31/12.
**Distance:** 100m.

### Monte San Giusto 34D1

**Campo Sportivo**, Via Magellano, Villa San Filippo.
**GPS:** n43,26343 e13,60070.⬆️➡️.

20 free Chfree. **Location:** Urban. **Surface:** asphalted.
☐ 01/01-31/12.
**Distance:** 1km.
**Remarks:** Near sports fields, outlet center leather and shoes.

### Monte Vidon Corrado 34D1

Viale Trento e Trieste. **GPS:** n43,12205 e13,48381.⬆️.

5 free Chfree. **Location:** Urban. **Surface:** metalled.
☐ 01/01-31/12.
**Distance:** 200m 200m 500m 450m.

### Montecosaro 34E1

Via Martiri della Libertà Ungherese. **GPS:** n43,31779 e13,63653.

30 free Chfree. **Location:** Urban. **Surface:** concrete.
☐ 01/01-31/12.
**Distance:** 100m 100m 100m 50m.

### Montefiore dell'Aso 34E1

Piazza Pietro Nenni. **GPS:** n43,04992 e13,75021.

10 free Ch free WC.
**Location:** Urban. **Surface:** sand. ☐ 01/01-31/12.
**Distance:** 200m 350m 100m on the spot.

### Montefiore dell'Aso 34E1

**Agricamper Il Poggio del Belvedere**, Contrada Aso no. 11.
**GPS:** n43,04611 e13,72500.⬆️.

6 € 8/pp Ch WC included.
**Location:** Rural. **Surface:** metalled. ☐ 01/01-31/12.
**Distance:** 3,5km.

### Montefortino 34D2

**Area Sosta Sibilla**, Via Tenna 3. **GPS:** n42,94490 e13,00000.
€ 19-26 . **Location:** Rural. **Surface:** gravel.
☐ 01/04-04/11.

**IT**

**Distance:** ⊗200m 🚐on the spot 🚲on the spot 🚶on the spot.

### Montelupone 34D1
Loc. San Firmano. **GPS:** n43,36383 e13,54950.⬆️.

20 🏕️free 🚰🚽free.
**Location:** Simple. **Surface:** asphalted. ⬛ 01/01-31/12.
**Distance:** 🚶500m.
**Remarks:** Parking sports park.

### Montelupone 34D1
Via Allesandro Manzoni. **GPS:** n43,34300 e13,57080.⬆️.

10 🏕️free 🚰🚽Chfree.
**Location:** Simple. **Surface:** asphalted. ⬛ 01/01-31/12.
**Remarks:** Parking city park.

### Morro d'Alba 37A3
**Area Comunale**, Via degli Orti. **GPS:** n43,60198 e13,21263.⬆️➡️.

30 🏕️free 🚰🚽free.
**Location:** Simple, quiet. **Surface:** asphalted.
⬛ 01/01-31/12.
**Distance:** 🚶500m.
**Remarks:** Access with electronic card, Bar Pro Loco or town hall.

### Offida 34E2
Via Tommaso Castelli. **GPS:** n42,93689 e13,69180.⬆️.

3 🏕️free 🚰🚽free. **Location:** Rural. **Surface:** unpaved.
⬛ 01/01-31/12.
**Distance:** 🚶400m ⊗350m 🚻350m.
**Remarks:** At the city walls.

### Pedaso 34E1
Via Martiri della Libertà. **GPS:** n43,09985 e13,84272.
🏕️free. **Surface:** asphalted. ⬛ 01/01-31/12.
**Distance:** 🚶on the spot ⚓on the spot ⊗150m.
**Remarks:** Parking at the beach.

### Pesaro 26H3
Via dell Aquedotto. **GPS:** n43,90842 e12,90097.⬆️.

---

12 🏕️free 🚰🚽Chfree 🔧(12x)€ 1. **Location:** Urban.
**Surface:** asphalted. ⬛ 01/01-31/12.
**Distance:** 🚶1km 🚲7,5km ⊗800m 🚻1km 🚌50m.

### Pesaro 26H3
**Waterfront Parking**, Via Calata Caio Duilio.
**GPS:** n43,92244 e12,90657.⬆️.
20 🏕️€ 12. **Location:** Urban. **Surface:** grassy. ⬛ 01/01-31/12.
**Distance:** 🚶300m ⚓on the spot ⊗on the spot 🚻1km 🚌400m.

### Pesaro 26H3
**Vallugola Parking**, Str. della Vallugola. **GPS:** n43,96227 e12,78689.
50 🏕️€ 13,50 🚰€ 3 🚽Ch 🔧€ 3/24h.
**Location:** Rural. **Surface:** grassy. ⬛ 01/01-31/12.
**Distance:** 🚶Pesaro 13,5km ⚓50m ⊗300m.
**Remarks:** Video surveillance.

**Tourist information Pesaro:**
🚶 Week market. ⬛ Tue.

### Petritoli 34E1
**Impianti Sportivi**, Via Calcinari. **GPS:** n43,07306 e13,65139.⬆️.

10 🏕️free 🚰🚽ChWCfree.
**Location:** Rural. **Surface:** sand. ⬛ 01/01-31/12.
**Distance:** 🚶1km ⊗900m 🚻900m 🚌900m.
**Remarks:** At sports park, picnic area, playground.

### Piandimeleto 34C1
Via Giacomo Leopardi. **GPS:** n43,72541 e12,41328.⬆️➡️.

9 🏕️free 🚰🚽Chfree.
**Location:** Urban. **Surface:** grassy. ⬛ 01/01-31/12.
**Distance:** 🚶100m ⊗on the spot 🚌200m

### Pietrarubbia 34C1
**Vulcangas**, Via Montefeltresca 107, Ponte Cappuccini.
**GPS:** n43,80278 e12,36667.⬆️.

2 🏕️free 🚰🚽WCfree. **Location:** Rural. **Surface:** metalled.
⬛ 01/01-31/12.
**Distance:** 🚶200m ⊗350m 🚌300m.

### Pievebovigliana 34D2
Via Rancia. **GPS:** n43,06583 e13,08526.⬆️.

---

10 🏕️free 🚰🚽Chincluded 🔧free 🔧€ 1.
**Location:** Rural. **Surface:** asphalted. ⬛ 01/01-31/12.
**Distance:** 🚶300m 🚻350m 🚌550m.

### Pioraco 34D1
Loc. Buchetto, SS361 km77. **GPS:** n43,18010 e12,97422.⬆️.

18 (+20) 🏕️€ 13 🚰🚽🔧(16x)WC🔧included. 🚿 **Location:** Rural,
comfortable, quiet. **Surface:** gravel. ⬛ 01/01-31/12.
**Distance:** 🚶700m 🚲on the spot ⊗summer 🚶on the spot.

### Pollenza 34D1
Contrada Morazzano. **GPS:** n43,26482 e13,34614.⬆️➡️.

8 🏕️free 🚰🚽Chfree. **Location:** Simple. **Surface:** asphalted.
⬛ 01/01-31/12.
**Distance:** 🚶500m.
**Remarks:** Nearby elevator to centre, max. 48h.

### Porto Recanati 34E1
**Area sosta camper Porto Recanati**, Viale Scarfiotti, loc. Scossicci.
**GPS:** n43,44605 e13,65639.⬆️.

35 🏕️€ 10-18 🚰🚽Chincluded 🔧(8x)€ 2 WC🔧€ 1.🚿
**Location:** Rural, simple. **Surface:** grassy. ⬛ 01/01-31/12.
**Distance:** 🚶500m 🚲3km 🔧50m 🚌200m 🚻1km.
**Remarks:** Max. 72h, video surveillance, dogs beach.

### Porto Recanati 34E1
**Karting Club Pista del Conero**, Viale Scarfiotti, loc. Scossicci.
**GPS:** n43,47067 e13,64246.⬆️.

80 🏕️€ 25/24h 🚰🚽Ch 🔧(80x)WCincluded 🔧€ 1 🚿free.🚿
**Location:** Rural, simple, noisy. **Surface:** gravel.
⬛ 01/04-30/09.
**Distance:** ⚓100m ⊗200m.

### Porto Recanati — 34E1
Via Lido delle Nazioni. **GPS**: n43,40918 e13,67679.
15 € 13. **Location**: Simple. **Surface**: sand.
01/01-31/12.
**Distance**: 2,5km on the spot on the spot on the spot.
**Remarks**: Beach parking.

### Porto Recanati — 34E1
**Campeggio Club Adriatico**, Via Scossicci, Scossicci.
**GPS**: n43,46393 e13,64642.
€ 17-30 Ch WC included. **Location**: Rural, comfortable, quiet. **Surface**: grassy. 09/04-29/09.
**Distance**: on the spot on the spot on the spot.

### Porto San Giorgio — 34E1
**La Perla dell'Adriatico**, Via San Martino 13.
**GPS**: n43,16400 e13,80836.
75 € 15, 16/07-26/08 € 20 Ch WC included, cold shower. **Location**: Rural, comfortable. **Surface**: unpaved.
01/04-30/09.
**Distance**: beach 200m 300m.
**Remarks**: Barbecue place, shuttle bus.

### Potenza Picena — 34E1
Via Togliatti, Porto Potenza Picena. **GPS**: n43,36167 e13,69306.

45 € 7/24h, € 10/48h, € 15/72h 2 Ch (12x) 2 WC against payment. **Location**: Urban. **Surface**: asphalted.
01/01-31/12.
**Distance**: 200m 600m 200m 200m.
**Remarks**: Thursday market.

### Recanati — 34D1
**Camperclub Recanati**, Viale Giovanni XXIII.
**GPS**: n43,40245 e13,55777.

25 free (22x)free. **Location**: Urban, simple.
**Surface**: asphalted. 01/01-31/12.
**Distance**: 500m.

### San Benedetto del Tronto — 34E2
**Sosta Camper 43° Parallelo**, Via Domenico Bruni.
**GPS**: n42,96677 e13,87670.
40 € 15 Ch. **Location**: Rural, simple.
**Surface**: asphalted. 01/01-31/12.
**Distance**: on the spot sandy beach 100m 80m.

### San Benedetto del Tronto — 34E2
Viale dello Sport. **GPS**: n42,92312 e13,89527.

70 € 7, Jul/Aug € 10 Ch included € 2. **Surface**: asphalted.
**Distance**: 4,3km 500m on the spot.
**Remarks**: Along railwayline, under viaduct.

### San Ginesio — 34D1
Via Ciarlatini. **GPS**: n43,10945 e13,31801.

---

8 free Ch free. **Surface**: gravel. 01/01-31/12.
**Distance**: 200m 200m 200m 1km.
**Remarks**: Swimming pool 100m.

### San Severino Marche — 34D1
**P7**, Viale Mazzini. **GPS**: n43,22757 e13,18836.

12 free free (12x) € 0,50/4h.
**Location**: Simple, quiet. **Surface**: asphalted. 01/01-31/12.
**Distance**: 800m.
**Remarks**: Parking sports park.

### Sant'Agata Feltria — 34C1
Piazzale Europa. **GPS**: n43,86386 e12,20549.

40 free, hollidays € 8/24h (6x)free.
**Location**: Rural. **Surface**: asphalted. 01/01-31/12.
**Distance**: 100m 300m 250m 300m.

### Sarnano — 34D2
Via Corridoni. **GPS**: n43,03444 e13,29972.

15 free Ch WC free. **Surface**: asphalted. 01/01-31/12.
**Distance**: 100m 100m 100m 50m.
**Remarks**: Thursday market.

### Sassoferrato — 34D1
Via Raffaello Sanzio. **GPS**: n43,43122 e12,85471.

8 free free (6x)€ 1/day. **Location**: Simple.
**Surface**: asphalted. 01/01-31/12.
**Distance**: 500m.

### Senigallia — 37A3
Via F. Podesti 234, SS16, Senigallia-sud. **GPS**: n43,70483 e13,23764.

---

14 € 10 free. **Location**: Simple, noisy. **Surface**: asphalted.
01/01-31/12.
**Distance**: 3km 3,3km 150m.
**Remarks**: Along busy road, next to petrol station, max. 48h.

### Tolentino — 34D1
Via Miguel Hernández Gilabert. **GPS**: n43,21046 e13,29613.
10 free Ch. **Location**: Urban. **Surface**: asphalted.
01/01-31/12.
**Distance**: 1km on the spot 550m 550m on the spot.

### Tolentino — 34D1
Viale Foro Boario. **GPS**: n43,20773 e13,28784.

15 free Ch free. **Location**: Urban. **Surface**: asphalted.
01/01-31/12.
**Distance**: 200m 200m 300m on the spot.
**Remarks**: At swimming pool.

### Urbania — 34C1
**Area camper Barco**, Loc. Barco Ducale Colonia.
**GPS**: n43,67916 e12,51277.
65 free Ch free. **Location**: Rural. **Surface**: gravel/sand.
01/01-31/12.
**Distance**: 1km 1km 1km 1km.
**Remarks**: Biking trail, behind former summer residence of dukes of Urbania.

### Urbania — 34C1
**Piazzale Fosso del Maltempo**, Viale Michelangelo.
**GPS**: n43,66482 e12,52191.

50 free Ch free.
**Location**: Urban, noisy. **Surface**: asphalted. 01/01-31/12.
**Distance**: 500m 700m 850m 250m.
**Remarks**: At sports park.
**Tourist information Urbania**:
Week market. Thu.

### Urbino — 34C1
Via Pablo Neruda. **GPS**: n43,73333 e12,62722.

10 free Ch free. **Location**: Rural. **Surface**: asphalted.
01/01-31/12.
**Distance**: historical centre 2,5km on the spot.
**Remarks**: At sports centre, shuttle bus to city centre.

IT

## Urbino 34C1
**Corte della Miniera**, Via Miniera, 10. **GPS**: n43,78336 e12,59091.
5 guests free Ch WC. **Location:** Rural.
**Surface:** grassy/gravel. 01/01-31/12.
**Distance:** Urbino 11km on the spot.
**Tourist information Urbino:**
Week market. Sa.

## Urbisaglia 34D1
**Abbadia di Fiastra**, P4. **GPS**: n43,22111 e13,40722.

50 € 15/24h Ch WC € 0,50 included.
**Location:** Rural. **Surface:** metalled. 01/01-31/12.
**Distance:** 4km 50m.
**Remarks:** Parking monastery, monitored parking, archaeological park Urbs Salvia 3km, hiking area.

## Visso 34D2
Largo Gregorio XIII. **GPS**: n42,93139 e13,09141.

15 free Ch € 0,80/h.
**Location:** Rural. **Surface:** asphalted. 01/01-31/12.
**Distance:** 800m 350m 350m.

# Lazio

## Acquapendente 34C2
**Agriturismo Buonomore**, SS Cassia Km 130.
**GPS**: n42,73367 e11,88361.

8 € 15-20, Aug € 25 Ch WC included.
**Location:** Rural, simple, quiet. **Surface:** grassy/gravel.
01/01-31/12.
**Distance:** 3km on the spot.
**Remarks:** Swimming pool incl.

## Acquapendente 34C2
Via Campo Boario. **GPS**: n42,74203 e11,86240.

20 free Chfree. **Location:** Urban.
**Surface:** asphalted/metalled. 01/01-31/12.
**Distance:** 250m 250m.
**Remarks:** At sports park.

## Albano Laziale 34D3
**Piazza Guerucci**, Via Riccardo Lombardi. **GPS**: n41,73206 e12,65213.

---

8 free Chfree. **Location:** Urban, simple, noisy.
**Surface:** asphalted. 01/01-31/12.
**Distance:** 1km 550m 700m train > Rome 55min.
**Remarks:** Next to post office and sports park.

## Amatrice 34D2
**AgriCamper Amatrice**, Località Retrosi. **GPS**: n42,62349 e13,31788.
20 € 10 Ch included. **Location:** Isolated. **Surface:** gravel.
01/01-31/12.
**Remarks:** Located in national nature reserve Gran Sasso.

## Bolsena 34C2
**Guadetto**, Via della Chiusa. **GPS**: n42,63604 e11,98695.

60 € 16/24h, dog € 1 Ch WC included.
**Location:** Rural. **Surface:** grassy/sand. 01/01-31/12.
**Distance:** 1km 10m 300m 1,5km on the spot on the spot.
**Remarks:** Bread-service, tuesday market.

## Bolsena 34C2
Via Santa Maria. **GPS**: n42,63898 e11,98562.

50 € 5/12h, € 10/24h. **Location:** Urban, simple.
**Surface:** asphalted. 01/01-31/12.
**Distance:** 800m 100m on the spot 400m 400m 100m on the spot on the spot.

## Bolsena 34C2
**Agricampeggio Le Calle**, Via Cassia km 111,200.
**GPS**: n42,63029 e11,99716.
20 € 15-19, incl. 2 pers, dog € 3 Ch WC included.
**Location:** Rural, comfortable, isolated, quiet. **Surface:** grassy.
01/04-01/11.
**Distance:** 2km on the spot 2km on the spot on the spot.
**Remarks:** Sale of wines.
**Tourist information Bolsena:**
Citadel and ramparts.

## Borgo San Pietro 34D3
**Area Sosta Camper "Il Ghiro"**, Via Cicolana.
**GPS**: n42,27060 e13,06277.
25 Ch WC. **Location:** Rural, isolated, quiet.
**Surface:** grassy. 01/01-31/12.
**Distance:** 500m 200m 200m.
**Remarks:** Video surveillance, barbecue place.

## Bracciano 34C3
**Le Mimose**, Via del Lago 25. **GPS**: n42,10856 e12,17893.

---

50 € 14/24h Chincluded (40x)€ 3/24h € 0,50.
**Location:** Rural, comfortable, quiet. **Surface:** gravel.
01/01-31/12.
**Distance:** 800m Lago di Bracciano 250m 150m 800m 200m.

## Capodimonte 34C2
**Temporanea**. **GPS**: n42,55979 e11,88714.

50 € 10-14/24h.
**Location:** Urban, simple, quiet. **Surface:** grassy. 01/01-31/12.
**Distance:** 2km on the spot 1,5km.
**Remarks:** At lake Bolsena, check in at bar.

## Cassino 35B1
**Parking Europa**, Via Agnone 5. **GPS**: n41,48289 e13,83750.

20 € 13,50-16,50, 2 pers.incl Service € 2,50 Ch € 3 WC € 1 € 4/day.
**Location:** Rural. **Surface:** grassy/gravel. 01/01-31/12.
**Distance:** 800m 4km 1km 1km 1,5km.
**Remarks:** Service passerby € 7.

## Castel di Tora 34D3
**Area Sosta**, Via Turano, SP34. **GPS**: n42,21362 e12,96888.
15 € 15/24h Ch WC included.
**Location:** Rural, quiet. **Surface:** gravel. 01/01-31/12.
**Distance:** 1km on the spot 250m.
**Remarks:** At Turano lake.

## Castel Gandolfo 34D3
**Parcheggio Bus Lago Albano**, Via Spiaggia del Lago.
**GPS**: n11,75797 c12,65359.

17 € 20/24h. **Location:** Rural, simple, noisy. **Surface:** metalled.
01/01-31/12.
**Distance:** on the spot on the spot 800m > Rome.
**Remarks:** At lake Albano.

## Civita Castellana 34C3
Via Terni. **GPS**: n42,29905 e12,41520.

---

+50 ⌁free ⌁🔧Chfree.
**Location:** Simple. **Surface:** asphalted. ▯ 01/01-31/12.
**Distance:** ⌁500m ⊗450m ⌁50m.
**Remarks:** At cemetery.
**Tourist information Civita Castellana:**
👁 Palazzo Farnese, Caprarola. Pentagonal country house, accessed by winding staircase.

### 🅢 Colle di Tora 🏖 34D3

Via Maria Letizia Giuliani. **GPS:** n42,20898 e12,94915. ⬆.

25 ⌁€ 10/24h ⌁🔧Ch 🔧WCincluded. **Location:** Rural, simple, quiet. **Surface:** gravel. ▯ 01/01-31/12.
**Distance:** ⌁on the spot ⌁on the spot ⊗on the spot.
**Remarks:** At Turano lake, pay at restaurant.

### 🅢 Colleferro 🌿 34D3

Viale Europa. **GPS:** n41,72540 e13,00989.
5 ⌁free ⌁🔧Chfree.
**Location:** Urban. **Surface:** metalled. ▯ 01/01-31/12.
**Distance:** ⌁on the spot 🚤5km ⊗on the spot ⌁500m 🚆train > Rome.
**Remarks:** Next to swimming pool.
**Tourist information Colleferro:**
ℹ Anagni. Region with number of old settlements.

### 🅢 Farfa in Sabina 34D3

**Abbazia di Santa Maria**, SP41A. **GPS:** n42,22166 e12,71603. ⬆.

20 ⌁free ⌁🔧Chfree. **Location:** Rural, simple, isolated.
**Surface:** gravel. ▯ 01/01-31/12.
**Distance:** ⌁4,7km.

### 🅢 Gaeta 🏖 35B1

**Playa Colorada**, Località S.Agostino, SS 213, Sperlonga>Gaeta.
**GPS:** n41,22812 e13,50281. ⬆.

60 ⌁€ 25-30, 2 pers.incl ⌁🔧Ch 🔧WCincluded ⌁€ 1 ⌁€ 0,50/h. ⌁ ⌁ **Location:** Rural, comfortable, central.
**Surface:** gravel. ▯ 01/04-30/09.
**Distance:** ⌁50m ⊗bar/restaurant ⌁200m.
**Remarks:** Picnic and barbecue place, shuttle to Gaeta, market Wednesday.

### 🅢 Gaeta 🏖 35B1

**Sosta Camper Internazionale**, Via Flacca km 20.500.
**GPS:** n41,23598 e13,49045.

---

30 ⌁€ 20-25 ⌁🔧Ch 🔧WCincluded ⌁€ 1. **Location:** Rural.
**Surface:** gravel. ▯ 01/01-31/12.
**Distance:** ⌁on the spot ⊗on the spot.
**Remarks:** Monitored parking.

### 🅢 Gaeta 🏖 35B1

**Copacabana Beach**, Via flacca Km 20.350, S.agostino Gaeta.
**GPS:** n41,23743 e13,48781. ⬆.

18 ⌁€ 25-30, 4 pers.incl ⌁€ 0,50 🔧Ch 🔧WC ⌁€ 0,50 ⌁€ 1. ⌁
**Location:** Rural, simple. **Surface:** gravel/sand.
▯ 01/04-30/09.
**Distance:** ⌁6km ⌁on the spot ⊗on the spot.
**Remarks:** Shuttle to Gaeta.

### 🅢 Gaeta 🏖 35B1

**Loremar**, Via Flacca, km 21,200. **GPS:** n41,23240 e13,49525.
6 ⌁€ 20-30 ⌁🔧Ch 🔧included WC 🔧. **Location:** Rural.
**Surface:** gravel. ▯ 01/01-31/12.
**Distance:** ⌁on the spot ⊗200m.
**Remarks:** Monitored parking 24/24.

### 🅢 Gaeta 🏖 35B1

**Oasi Camper Service**, Via Flacca km. 20,643, Loc. riviera di Ponente.
**GPS:** n41,23583 e13,49048. ⬆.

22 ⌁€ 25-35 ⌁🔧Ch 🔧WCincluded ⌁€ 1. ⌁
**Location:** Rural, simple. **Surface:** gravel. ▯ 01/04-01/10.
**Distance:** ⌁6km ⌁50m ⌁500m.

### 🅢 Gradoli 34C2

**Parcheggio camper San Magno**, Strada di Gradoli, SP114 km 6+137.
**GPS:** n42,59995 e11,86577. ⬆.

30 ⌁€ 15 ⌁🔧Ch 🔧included. ⌁
**Location:** Rural, comfortable, quiet. **Surface:** grassy.
▯ Easter-30/09.
**Distance:** ⌁7km ⌁on the spot 🔧on the spot ⌁on the spot 🔧on the spot 🔧on the spot.
**Remarks:** At lake Bolsena, closed at night, discount longer stays.

### 🅢 Latina 35A1

**Area Camper Alta Marea**, Strada Lungomare 3253, SP39, Loc. Foce Verde. **GPS:** n41,41043 e12,86008. ⬆.

---

91 ⌁€ 15 ⌁🔧Ch 🔧WC ⌁€ 0,50 🔧 included. ⌁ ⌁ ⌁
**Location:** Rural, comfortable, quiet. **Surface:** grassy.
▯ 01/04-30/09.
**Distance:** ⌁on the spot ⌁50m ⊗on the spot ⌁200m.

### 🅢 Latina 35A1

**Museo di Piana delle Orme**, Strada Migliara 43 Mezza.
**GPS:** n41,44452 e12,98479. ⬆.

25 ⌁free ⌁🔧Ch. **Location:** Rural, simple, quiet. **Surface:** gravel.
▯ 01/01-31/12.
**Distance:** ⌁Latina 10km ⊗2km ⌁500m.
**Remarks:** At museum.

### 🅢 Leonessa 34D2

Via Amor della Patria 21. **GPS:** n42,56436 e12,96172. ⬆.

50 ⌁free ⌁🔧Chfree. **Location:** Urban. **Surface:** asphalted.
▯ 01/01-31/12 ▯ Market day.
**Distance:** ⌁500m ⊗500m ⌁500m ⌁300m.

### 🅢 Lubriano 34C2

**Parco Paime**, Piazza Palme. **GPS:** n42,63500 e12,10512. ⬆.

17 ⌁€ 5/24h ⌁🔧Ch 🔧(36x)WC 🔧included. ⌁
**Location:** Comfortable, quiet. **Surface:** grasstiles.
▯ 01/01-31/12.
**Distance:** ⌁1km ⊗on the spot ⌁300m.
**Remarks:** Nights closed with barrier.

### 🅢 Lunghezza 🏖 34D3

**Camper Club Antichi Casali**, Via Lunghezzina 302/a.
**GPS:** n41,93039 e12,70454. ⬆.

40 ⌁€ 15/24h ⌁🔧Ch 🔧WC ⌁ 🔧included. ⌁ ⌁ ⌁
**Location:** Rural, comfortable, isolated, quiet. **Surface:** gravel.
▯ 01/01-31/12.

**Distance:** 🚶3km 🚲5km 🚌Rome 20min 🚶on the spot.
**Remarks:** Monitored parking 24/24, picnic and barbecue place, shuttle bus.

| 🏕️S | **Lunghezza** 〰️ | 34D3 |

**Camper Club Mira Lago Roma**, Via Lunghezzina 75.
**GPS:** n41,93159 e12,67642. ⬆️➡️.

60 🏕️€ 20/24h 🚰🔌Ch🔧 WC🚽€ 0,50 🚿€ 4 〰️included.
**Location:** Rural, comfortable, isolated, quiet. **Surface:** grassy.
📅 01/01-31/12.
**Distance:** 🏊700m 🎣on the spot 🛒on the spot ⊗on the spot 🍴on the spot 🚌on the spot.
**Remarks:** At 2 small lakes, service passerby € 5.

| 🏕️S | **Montalto di Castro** 〰️ | 34C3 |

**Area di Sosta La Pineta. GPS:** n42,36595 e11,49444.
🏕️ 15-28/24h, dog € 1 🚰🔌Ch🔧€ 3 WCincluded 🚽€ 1 🚿.
**Location:** Rural. **Surface:** grassy. 📅 01/04-30/09.
**Distance:** 🏖️sea 100m ⊗1km.
**Remarks:** Max. 72h, picnic and barbecue place, playground.

| 🏕️S | **Montalto di Castro** 〰️ | 34C3 |

**Il Pioppo**, Strada delle Murelle. **GPS:** n42,31271 e11,60526.⬆️.
🏕️ 12/24h 🚰🔌Ch🔧€ 2/24h WCincluded 🚽€ 1.
**Location:** Rural. **Surface:** grassy. 📅 01/01-31/12.
**Distance:** 🚶Montalto di Castro 5km ⊗400m.

| 🏕️S | **Montalto di Castro** 〰️ | 34C3 |

Via Arbea, Marina di Montalto di Castro.
**GPS:** n42,32981 e11,57699.⬆️➡️.

50 🏕️€ 7,50/day, overnight stay free 🚰🔌Chincluded. 🚐
**Location:** Rural, simple, quiet. **Surface:** grassy/gravel.
📅 01/01-31/12.
**Distance:** 🚶250m 🏊200m ⊗200m 🍴200m.
**Remarks:** Shady, thursday market.

| 🏕️S | **Montalto di Castro** 〰️ | 34C3 |

Via Torre Marina, Marina di Montalto di Castro.
**GPS:** n42,32137 e11,59015.⬆️➡️.

64 🏕️free, 01/06-15/09 8-20h € 7,50 🚰🔌Chincluded. 🚐
**Location:** Rural, simple. **Surface:** gravel. 📅 01/01-31/12.
**Distance:** 🚶500m 🏊200m ⊗400m 🍴300m.

| 🏕️S | **Montefiascone** | 34C2 |

**Cantina di Montefiascone**, Via Grilli 2. **GPS:** n42,53346 e12,04293.⬆️.

---

30 🏕️free 🚰🔌Ch🔧free. **Location:** Urban, comfortable, noisy.
**Surface:** metalled. 📅 01/01-31/12.
**Distance:** 🚶1km ⊗600m 🍴800m.

| 🏕️S | **Montefiascone** | 34C2 |

**Agricamper Bella Cima**, Strada Limitone.
**GPS:** n42,52241 e12,00767.⬆️➡️.

18 🏕️€ 15/24h 🚰🔌Ch🔧included.
**Location:** Rural. **Surface:** gravel. 📅 01/01-31/12.
**Distance:** 🚶4km ⊗4km 🍴4km.
**Remarks:** Swimming pool.

| 🏕️S | **Nettuno** | 35A1 |

**Area Sosta L'Ippocampo**, Via Palestrina 9.
**GPS:** n41,47354 e12,68916.⬆️.

50 🏕️€ 15 🚰🔌Ch🔧 WC🚽included. 🚐 **Location:** Rural, simple, quiet. **Surface:** gravel. 📅 01/01-31/12.
**Distance:** 🚶3km 🏊3km ⊗850m 🍴1km.

| 🏕️S | **Oriolo Romano** | 34C3 |

Viale degli Artigiani. **GPS:** n42,16699 e12,13902.➡️.

3 🏕️free 🚰🔌Chfree. **Location:** Simple. **Surface:** asphalted.
📅 01/01-31/12.
**Distance:** 🚶850m ⊗500m 🍴on the spot 🚉station 600m Roma-Viterbo.

| 🏕️S | **Pescia Romana** | 34B3 |

**Area La Pineta**, Loc. Marina di Pescia Romana.
**GPS:** n42,36552 e11,49389.⬆️➡️.

50 🏕️€ 15-25, dog € 1 🚰🔌Chincluded 🔧€ 3 WC🚽€ 1.
**Location:** Rural, comfortable, quiet. **Surface:** grassy.
📅 Easter-30/09.
**Distance:** 🚶Pescia Romana 5km 🏊100m 🍴100m.
**Remarks:** Bread-service, monday market.

| 🏕️S | **Rieti** | 34D2 |

Via Fonte Cottorella. **GPS:** n42,39548 e12,86463.⬆️➡️.

---

10 🏕️free 🚰🔌. **Location:** Urban, noisy. **Surface:** asphalted.
📅 01/01-31/12.
**Distance:** 🚶historical center 100m ⊗700m.

| 🏕️S | **Roma** 〰️🌴⛵🧺 | 34D3 |

**Area Attrezzata per Camper LGP Roma**, Via Casilina 700, Rome (Roma). **GPS:** n41,87595 e12,55515.⬆️.

200 🏕️€ 18/<8m, € 25/8><10m, € 35/10><18m + tourist tax € 2/pp 🚰🔌Ch🔧🚽against payment 〰️includedh. 🚐
**Location:** Urban, luxurious, central, quiet.
**Surface:** grassy.
📅 01/01-31/12.
**Distance:** ⊗100m 🍴100m 🚌bus service to city centre day and night.
**Remarks:** Accessory shop, trailer/additonal car € 15 on separate parking € 7, repairs. Exit 18 ring road (G.R.A.), follow Roma centro, ± 4km dir centre, company is on the left side of the road, turning after 2nd lights.

| 🏕️S | **Roma** 〰️🌴⛵🧺 | 34D3 |

**Prato Smeraldo**, Via Ardeatina/Via di Tor Pagnotta 424, Rome (Roma).
**GPS:** n41,80970 e12,52857.⬆️.

16 🏕️€ 16 🚰🔌Ch🔧€ 2/24h 〰️included. 🚐🚮
**Location:** Motorway, simple, noisy. **Surface:** grassy/metalled.
📅 01/01-31/12, 24/24h.
**Distance:** ⊗on the spot 🍴on the spot 🚌on the spot.
**Remarks:** Service passerby € 5. Exit 25 ring road (G.R.A.), second light to the right, Via di Tor Pagnotta.

| 🏕️S | **Roma** 〰️🌴⛵🧺 | 34D3 |

**Le Terrazze**, Via di Fioranello 170, Rome (Roma).
**GPS:** n41,79250 e12,54083.➡️.

40 🏕️€ 20, max. 4 pers.incl 🚰🔌Ch🔧(40x)included. 🚐
**Location:** Simple, quiet. **Surface:** metalled. 📅 01/01-31/12.
**Distance:** 🏊750m 🍴1km 🛒on the spot 🚌on the spot.
**Remarks:** Video surveillance, car rental, excursions. Exit 25 ring road (G.R.A.), dir Santuario Divino Amore.

| 🏕️S | **Roma** 〰️🌴⛵🧺 | 34D3 |

**Parcheggio IAT, Air terminal Ostiense**, Piazza G. da Verrazzano 9, Zone Mercati Generali, Rome (Roma). **GPS:** n41,86931 e12,48944.⬆️.

IT

70 �€ 6/2h, >1 hour € 1,50, € 20/24h ⌁ ⌂Ch ⌁ € 3,65/24h ⌁included. **Location:** Urban, simple, central, noisy.
**Surface:** asphalted. ⬛ 01/01-31/12.
**Distance:** ⊗70m ⬛300m ⟷metro 1km.
**Remarks:** Motorhome and Coach Parking, video surveillance.

### Roma — 34D3

**Area Sosta Camper Park Colombo**, Via C. Colombo 170, Rome (Roma).
**GPS:** n41,86236 e12,49713.
25 ⌁ 20 ⌁ ⌂Ch included. ⌁Service € 5.
**Surface:** asphalted. ⬛ 01/01-31/12.
**Distance:** ⬛100m.
**Remarks:** Monitored parking 24/24.

### Roma — 34D3

**Parkbus Roma**, Piazzale 12 Ottobre 1492, Rome (Roma).
**GPS:** n41,86931 e12,48944.
⌁€ 20 ⌁ ⌂Ch included. ⌁€ 3 WC.
**Location:** Urban. **Surface:** asphalted. ⬛ 01/01-31/12.
**Distance:** ⌁on the spot ⊗500m ⬛300m ⟷200m.
**Remarks:** Monitored parking, bicycle rental.

### Roma — 34D3

**Spazio Ardeatina**, Via Ardeatina, 933, Rome (Roma).
**GPS:** n41,79808 e12,53556.
⌁€ 20 ⌁ ⌂Ch ⌁included. **Surface:** asphalted.
**Distance:** ⌁Rome 11km ⌁on the spot ⊗on the spot ⌁450m ⟷on the spot.
**Remarks:** Monitored parking 24/24.

**Tourist information Rome (Roma):**
🛈 Città del Vaticano. Domicile of the pope. Independent state since 1929.
🛈 A.P.T. (Azienda di Promozione Turistica), Via Parigi, 11. Capital of the country, a lot of curiosities in the old town centre. Roma Archeologica Card: 7-days ticket € 27,50, free entrance to Roman National Museum, Colosseum, Palatine, Baths of Caracalla, Tomb of Cecilia Metella and Villa of the Quintili.
👁 Piazza del Campidoglio.
👁 Palatino, Via di S. Gregorio, 30. Archeological site. ⬛ 9h-sunset.
🎫 € 16, incl. Colosseum.
👁 Subiaco.
Ⓜ Musei Vaticani, Città del Vaticano. Paintings and art objects.
✝ Basilica di San Pietro. Basilica with Sistine Chapel.
◠ Colosseo, Piazza del Colosseo. Colosseum, anfiteatro, the most important monument of ancient Rome. ⬛ 9h-sunset. 🎫 € 12, entrance Palatine Hill incl.
◠ Forum Romanum, Via dei Fori Imperiali. Novel Forum, the political, economic, and religious centre of ancient Rome. ⬛ 9h-sunset.
◠ Pantheon, Piazza della Rotonda. Church of Santa Maria ad Martyres. ⬛ 9-19.30h, Su 9-18h, holidays 9-13h, Mass Sa 17, Su 10.30h, 16.30h.
🎫 free.
☀ Città del Vaticano. Pope blesses the mob for the window of the library. ⬛ Su 12h.
⌁ Piazza di Spagna.

### San Felice Circeo — 35B1

**Circeo Camper**, Viale Europa 1. **GPS:** n41,24095 e13,10426.

50 ⌁€ 23-33, 4 pers. incl ⌁ ⌂Ch ⌁€ 3/24h WC ⌁€ 1 ⬛€ 7 ⌁included. ⌁ **Location:** Rural, luxurious, central. **Surface:** grassy.
⬛ 01/04-20/09.
**Distance:** ⌁100m ⌁10m ⊗10m ⌁100m ⟷100m.

### San Felice Circeo — 35B1

**CirceMed**, Via Molella 2/A. **GPS:** n41,25684 e13,12089.

---

12 ⌁free ⌁ ⌂Ch ⌁free. **Location:** Urban, simple.
**Surface:** grasstiles/metalled. ⬛ 01/01-31/12.
**Distance:** ⌁250m ⊗250m ⌁250m.

### Velletri — 34D3

Via del Camelieto. **GPS:** n41,69314 e12,78264.
9 ⌁free ⌁ ⌂Ch. **Location:** Urban. **Surface:** metalled.
⬛ 01/01-31/12 ⬛ Thursday.
**Distance:** ⌁500m ⊗800m.

### Villa San Giovanni in Tuscia — 34C3

Viale Europa. **GPS:** n42,28160 e12,05282.

10 ⌁free ⌁free. **Location:** Rural, simple, quiet. **Surface:** asphalted.
⬛ 01/01-31/12.
**Distance:** ⌁200m ⊗550m.

### Viterbo — 34C2

**Agricampeggio Paliano**, Strada Pian di Tortora.
**GPS:** n42,39301 e12,08601.
100 ⌁€ 18, 2 pers.incl, extra pers € 5 ⌁ ⌂Ch ⌁WC ⌁ ⬛.
**Location:** Rural, simple, isolated. **Surface:** grassy.
**Distance:** ⌁city centre 2km.
**Remarks:** Video surveillance.

### Viterbo — 34C2

Piazza Mariano Romiti, loc. Belcolle. **GPS:** n42,40897 e12,11049.

50 ⌁free ⌁ ⌂Ch free.
**Location:** Urban, simple. **Surface:** asphalted.
⬛ 01/01-31/12.
**Distance:** ⌁Lazise centre 300m ⊗140m ⌁170m ⟷on the spot.
**Remarks:** At station.

### Viterbo — 34C2

**Bed&breakfast Axia**, Strada Procoio 2/C.
**GPS:** n42,41157 e12,05061.

5 ⌁€ 18 ⌁ ⌂Ch ⌁€ 3 ⌁included. ⌁
**Location:** Rural. **Surface:** grassy. ⬛ 01/01-31/12.
**Distance:** ⌁Viterbo 4km ⌁1,5km ⟷on the spot.
**Remarks:** 10% discount at entrance Terme dei Papi (900m), bus to Viterbo € 5.

### Viterbo — 34C2

**Agriturismo Monteparadiso**, Loc. Monterazzano.
**GPS:** n42,44161 e12,03062.

5 ⌁guests free. **Location:** Rural, simple, isolated. **Surface:** gravel.

---

60 ⌁€ 20-37 ⌁ ⌂Ch ⌁(50x)WC ⌁€ 1 ⬛€ 1 ⬛€ 3 ⌁included. ⌁
**Location:** Rural, comfortable, quiet. **Surface:** grassy.
⬛ 01/04-30/09.
**Distance:** ⌁500m ⊗200m ⌁200m ⟷on the spot.
**Remarks:** Video surveillance, barbecue place.

**Tourist information San Felice Circeo:**
✝ ⬛ Tue-morning.

### Terracina — 35B1

Via Amerigo Vespucci. **GPS:** n41,28528 e13,25450.

20 ⌁€ 8-12. ⌁ **Location:** Urban, simple. **Surface:** asphalted.
**Distance:** ⌁on the spot ⌁100m ⟷on the spot ⊗200m ⌁300m.

### Tivoli — 34D3

Via Aquaregna. **GPS:** n41,95841 e12,80465.

30 ⌁free ⌁ ⌂Ch free. **Location:** Urban, simple, central, quiet.
**Surface:** asphalted. ⬛ 01/01-31/12 ⬛ Wed, market.
**Distance:** ⌁400m ⊗350m ⌁350m.
**Remarks:** Along the Aniene river.

**Tourist information Tivoli:**
👁 Villa d'Este. Country house with gardens and fountains, 16th century.
◠ Villa Adriana. Roman villa.

### Trevignano Romano — 34C3

**Blue Lake Camper**, Via della Rena. **GPS:** n42,15877 e12,22411.

28 ⌁€ 15-20 ⌁ ⌂Ch ⌁WC ⌁. **Location:** Rural, comfortable, quiet.
**Surface:** gravel. ⬛ 01/01-31/12.
**Distance:** ⌁on the spot ⟷on the spot.
**Remarks:** At the lake.

### Tuscania — 34C2

Via Nazario Sauro. **GPS:** n42,42217 e11,87520.

IT

◨ 01/01-31/12.
**Distance:** 🚶7km ⊗on the spot.
**Remarks:** Near Termale Bullicame and Terme dei Papi.

| Viterbo | 34C2 |

**Terme dei Papi**, Strada Montarone. **GPS:** n42,41487 e12,06351.

57 🚐guests free. **Surface:** grassy/gravel. ◨ 01/01-31/12.
**Distance:** 🚶3km.
**Remarks:** At Terme dei Papi.

| Vitorchiano | 34C2 |

SP23 Via della Teverina. **GPS:** n42,47152 e12,17212. ⬆➡.

10 🚐free 🔌🗑Ch🔧. **Location:** Urban, simple. **Surface:** asphalted.
◨ 01/01-31/12.
**Distance:** 🚶500m.

## Umbria

| Amelia | 34C2 |

**Piazzale del Mercato**, Via Rimembranze.
**GPS:** n42,55200 e12,41880. ⬆.
10 🚐free 🔌🗑ChWCfree. **Location:** Urban. **Surface:** asphalted.
◨ 01/01-31/12 ◨ Mo-morning (market).
**Distance:** 🚶50m ⊗50m 🍴50m 🚲300m.

| Assisi | 34C2 |

Via Giosuè Borsi, loc. Santa Maria degli Angeli.
**GPS:** n43,05972 e12,58747. ⬆.

20 🚐€ 1,70/h, € 17/24h 🔌🗑Ch.🚐
**Surface:** asphalted. ◨ 01/01-31/12.
**Distance:** 🚶2km 🚌>Assisi 20min (retour € 1,80).

| Assisi | 34C2 |

**Area San Vittorino**, Via San vittorino. **GPS:** n43,07848 e12,60229. ⬆.

30 🚐€ 18/24h, € 1,80/h. **Surface:** asphalted. ◨ 01/01-31/12.
**Distance:** 🚶500m.
**Remarks:** Convento di San Francesco 1km.

| Assisi | 34C2 |

Viale Vittorio Emanuele II/SS147. **GPS:** n43,06864 e12,61420. ⬆.

10 🚐€ 20/24h. **Surface:** gravel. ◨ 01/01-31/12.
**Distance:** 🚶city centre 100m.

| Bevagna | 34D2 |

**Piazza dell'Accoglienza**, Via Raggiolo. **GPS:** n42,93417 e12,60639. ⬆.

50 🚐free 🔌🗑ChWC🗑free.
**Location:** Urban. **Surface:** gravel. ◨ 01/01-31/12.
**Distance:** 🚶100m ⊗100m 🍴100m 🚲on the spot.

| Borghetto | 34C1 |

Via Pontile. **GPS:** n43,18415 e12,02372.

4 🚐free 🔌🗑🔧free. **Surface:** asphalted. ◨ 01/01-31/12.
**Distance:** 🚤150m ⊗100m.
**Remarks:** At lake Trasimeno.

| Cannara | 34C2 |

Via Giaime Pintor, Loc. Casone. **GPS:** n42,99272 e12,57840.

20 🚐free 🔌🗑Chfree.
**Location:** Urban. **Surface:** asphalted. ◨ 01/01-31/12.
**Distance:** 🚶300m ⊗600m 🍴300m 🚌500m 🚲on the spot
**Remarks:** At sports park XXV Aprile, cycle routes.

**Tourist information Cannara:**
👁 Assisi. Historical city.

| Cascia | 34D2 |

**Piazzale Papa Leone XIII**, Via della Molinella.
**GPS:** n42,71968 e13,01605. ⬆➡.

14 🚐€ 8/24h 🔌🗑Chincluded 🔧(8x)€ 0,50/2h.
**Surface:** asphalted. ◨ 01/01-31/12 ◨ Service: winter.
**Distance:** 🚶300m ⊗300m 🍴300m 🚴100m 🛒100m.
**Remarks:** Escalator to city centre.

| Cascia | 34D2 |

SS Discascia. **GPS:** n42,72139 e13,01778.
20 🚐free 🔌🗑Ch🔧. **Surface:** gravel. ◨ 01/01-31/12.
**Distance:** 🚶1km.
**Remarks:** Next to petrol station.

| Castelluccio di Norcia | 34D2 |

**Pian Grande**, SP477. **GPS:** n42,80045 e13,18947.

25 🚐free. **Location:** Rural. **Surface:** grassy. ◨ 01/01-31/12.
**Distance:** 🚶Castelluccio 5km.
**Remarks:** Parco Nazionale dei Monti Sibillini.

| Castiglione del Lago | 34C2 |

Viale Divisione Partigiani Garibaldi. **GPS:** n43,12389 e12,05054. ⬆.

50 🚐€ 12 🔌🗑Ch🔧included. 🚐
**Location:** Rural. **Surface:** grassy. ◨ 01/01-31/12.
**Distance:** 🚶800m 🚤on the spot ⊗500m 🍴800m 🚌500m.
**Remarks:** At lake Trasimeno.

| Città di Castello | 34C1 |

**Piazzale E. Ferri**, Viale Nazario Sauro. **GPS:** n43,45892 e12,23465. ⬆➡.
25 🚐free 🔌€ 1/100liter 🗑Ch🔧.
**Location:** Urban. **Surface:** asphalted. ◨ 01/01-31/12.
**Distance:** 🚶300m 🚴1,5km ⊗on the spot 🍴1km 🚌200m.
**Remarks:** Escalator to city centre.

| Città di Castello | 34C1 |

**La Fontana del Boschetto**, Via Aretina 38. **GPS:** n43,45737 e12,22882.
20 🚐€ 15/24h 🔌🗑Ch🔧included WC🗑.
**Location:** Motorway. **Surface:** unpaved.
◨ 01/01-31/12.
**Distance:** 🚶2km 🚴on the spot ⊗on the spot 🍴2km 🚌on the spot.
**Remarks:** Free shuttle.

| Ferentillo | 34D2 |

Loc. Precetto, Via delle Macchie. **GPS:** n42,61802 e12,79347. ⬆.
5 🚐free 🔌🗑Chfree. **Location:** Urban. **Surface:** asphalted.
◨ 01/01-31/12.
**Distance:** 🚶200m ⊗350m 🍴700m 🚌on the spot.

| Ficulle | 34C2 |

**Parco Cittadino**, Via Orvieto SR 71. **GPS:** n42,83044 e12,06828. ⬆➡.

25 🚐free 🔌🗑Chfree WC. **Surface:** gravel.
◨ 01/01-31/12 ◨ events (01/07-31/08).
**Distance:** 🚶500m 🚴10km ⊗1km 🍴500m 🚌200m.

| Gualdo Cattaneo | 34C2 |

**Parco Acquarossa**, Via Bonifacio 6. **GPS:** n42,89168 e12,53591. ⬆.
50 🚐€ 8 🔌🗑Ch🗑WC🗑included. **Location:** Rural.
**Surface:** gravel. ◨ 01/01-31/12.
**Distance:** 🚶on the spot ⊗on the spot 🚌1km.
**Remarks:** Excursions, regional products.

| Gualdo Tadino | 34D1 |

Via Lucatonii. **GPS:** n43,23193 e12,78019.

20 free ⚡🚰Chfree. **Location:** Urban. **Surface:** asphalted. ⬛ 01/01-31/12. 🅿 Thu (market).
**Distance:** 🚶500m ⊗on the spot 🍽600m 🚌200m.
**Remarks:** Free shuttle.

| 🏕 S | Gubbio 〰 | 34C1 |
|---|---|---|

**Camperclub Gubbio**, Via del Bottagnone.
**GPS:** n43,35000 e12,56389.⬆.

80 ⚡€ 5 ⚡🚰Chincluded 🚿(8x)€ 1/2h. 🔌
**Surface:** asphalted. ⬛ 01/01-31/12.
**Distance:** 🚶historical centre 1,5km ⊗100m 🍽200m 🚌shuttle to centre 500m.
**Remarks:** Video surveillance, Teatro Romano 500m.

| 🏕 S | Monte Castello di Vibio 〰🌳🏛 | 34C2 |
|---|---|---|

Via Bartolomeo Jacopo della Rovere. **GPS:** n42,84168 e12,35055.➡.

10 free ⚡🚰Chfree. **Surface:** gravel. ⬛ 01/01-31/12.
**Distance:** 🚶350m ⊗50m.

| 🏕 S | Montefalco 〰🌳🍴 | 34D2 |
|---|---|---|

Via G. Pascoli. **GPS:** n42,89230 e12,64791.⬆.

25 ⚡€ 5,50/24h 🚰Ch 🚿WC. **Location:** Rural, simple, quiet.
**Surface:** grasstiles. ⬛ 01/01-31/12.
**Distance:** 🚶100m ⊗400m 🍽300m.

| 🏕 S | Montone | 34C1 |
|---|---|---|

Via Aldo Bologni. **GPS:** n43,36346 e12,32499.
⚡€ 10/24h 🚰Ch 🚿. **Surface:** asphalted. ⬛ 01/01-31/12.
**Distance:** 🚶200m ⊗250m.
**Remarks:** At sports park.

| 🏕 S | Norcia | 34D2 |
|---|---|---|

**Area Camper BackToCampi**, SP476. **GPS:** n42,84840 e13,09533.⬆.
30 free ⚡🚰Ch 🚿WC. **Location:** Rural, isolated, quiet.
**Surface:** grassy. ⬛ 01/01-31/12.

| 🏕 S | Orvieto 〰🌳🏛🍴 | 34C2 |
|---|---|---|

**Area Sosta Camper Battistelli Renzo**, Strada della Direttissima, Piazza delle Pace. **GPS:** n42,72562 e12,12736.⬆.

50 ⚡€ 18/day ⚡🚰Ch 🚿WC included 🅿. **Location:** Urban, noisy.
**Surface:** metalled. ⬛ 01/01-31/12.
**Distance:** 🚶funicular (retour € 1,60) 5 min 🍽2,4km ⊗50m pizzeria 🚌50m.
**Remarks:** Monitored parking.

**Tourist information Orvieto:**
ℹ U.I.A.T. (Ufficio Informazioni e di Accoglienza Turistica), Piazza Duomo, 24. City on volcanic plateau.
🎭 Del Crocifisso del Tufo. Ruins of Etruscan city.

| 🏕 S | Panicale 〰🏛 | 34C2 |
|---|---|---|

**Area Camper**, Viale della Repubblica. **GPS:** n43,02806 e12,10222.⬆➡.

8 ⚡€ 8/24h 🚰€ 0,50/180liter Ch 🚿€ 0,50/kWh.
**Surface:** grasstiles. ⬛ 01/01-31/12.
**Distance:** 🚶100m ⊗100m 🍽50m.
**Remarks:** Max. 72h.

| 🏕 S | Passignano sul Trasimeno | 34C1 |
|---|---|---|

**L'Airone Area Camper**, Lungolago Giappesi.
**GPS:** n43,18445 e12,14526.⬆.

18 ⚡€ 16-22/24h 2 pers. incl 🚰Ch 🚿WC € 0,50 📶included.
**Location:** Rural, comfortable. **Surface:** grassy.
⬛ 01/04-31/10.
**Distance:** 🚶500m 🏖beach 150m ⊗on the spot 🍽200m 🚌200m.
**Remarks:** At lake Trasimeno.

| 🏕 S | Passignano sul Trasimeno | 34C1 |
|---|---|---|

Via Europa, SS75bis, km 35,8. **GPS:** n43,18509 e12,14348.⬆.

12 ⚡€ 1,50/h, 20-8h free 🚰liter 🚿h WC. 🔌
**Location:** Urban, simple, noisy. **Surface:** asphalted.
⬛ 01/01-31/12.
**Distance:** 🚶400m 🍽200m ⊗100m 🚌150m 🚲on the spot.
**Remarks:** At lake Trasimeno.

| 🏕 S | Perugia 〰 | 34C2 |
|---|---|---|

**Il Bove**, Via Giovanni Ruggia. **GPS:** n43,09810 e12,38386.⬆➡.

50 ⚡€ 10/12h, € 18/24h ⚡🚰Chincluded 🚿WC 📶. 
**Location:** Urban. **Surface:** asphalted. ⬛ 01/01-31/12.
**Distance:** 🚶1,5km 🚲500m ⊗on the spot 🍽100m 🚌200m 🚲on the spot.
**Remarks:** Parking police station, video surveillance, playground.

**Tourist information Perugia:**
🏛 Palazzo dei Priori.
🎭 ⬛ Tue.

| 🏕 S | San Gemini | 34D2 |
|---|---|---|

Via della Libertà. **GPS:** n42,61200 e12,54372.

16 ⚡€ 10/24h 🚰Ch 🚿WC 📶. **Location:** Rural, simple, quiet.
**Surface:** metalled. ⬛ 01/01-31/12.
**Distance:** 🚶300m ⊗100m 🚌200m.

| 🏕 S | Sant'Anatolia di Narco | 34D2 |
|---|---|---|

**Purchetta**, SP209. **GPS:** n42,73599 e12,83598.
8 free ⚡🚰.
**Location:** Rural. **Surface:** grassy. ⬛ 01/01-31/12.
**Distance:** 🚶900m ⊗on the spot 🍽on the spot 🚌200m 🚲Spoleto/Norcia.

| 🏕 S | Scheggia e Pascelupo | 34D1 |
|---|---|---|

**Camper Scheggia**, Via Campo Sportivo. **GPS:** n43,40007 e12,66674.
⚡€ 12/24h 🚰Chincluded 🚿€ 2. **Location:** Urban, comfortable.
**Surface:** gravel. ⬛ 01/01-31/12.
**Distance:** 🚶450m ⊗500m.

| 🏕 S | Spello | 34D2 |
|---|---|---|

Via Centrale Umbra. **GPS:** n42,99371 e12,66730.⬆.

70 ⚡€ 8/24h 🚰Ch. 🔌 **Location:** Rural. **Surface:** asphalted.
⬛ 01/01-31/12.
**Distance:** 🚶500m 🚲1,1km ⊗500m 🍽500m 🚌on the spot.
**Remarks:** Parking sports park.

| 🏕 S | Spello | 34D2 |
|---|---|---|

**Terme Francescane Village**, Via Fonte Citerna.
**GPS:** n43,00619 e12,62116.⬆.
30 ⚡€ 18-35 ⚡🚰Ch 🚿€ 3 WCincluded.
**Location:** Rural. **Surface:** gravel. ⬛ 01/01-31/12.
**Distance:** 🚶Spello 6km ⊗2,5km.

| 🏕 | Spoleto 〰🏛🍴 | 34D2 |
|---|---|---|

**Parcheggio Ponciano**, Via del Tiro a Segno.
**GPS:** n42,73687 e12,74212.➡.

IT

25 ⬛€ 15.
**Location:** Simple, noisy. **Surface:** gravel. ⬛ 01/01-31/12.
**Distance:** 🚶500m ✕500m 🚰500m.

**⬛S** Spoleto 🚲⛵🏛 **34D2**
Via dei Filosofi. **GPS:** n42,74619 e12,73214. ⬆➡.

20 ⬛free 🚰⬛free. **Location:** Urban. **Surface:** gravel.
⬛ 01/01-31/12.
**Distance:** 🚶800m ✕300m 🚰300m on the spot.
**Tourist information Spoleto:**
👁 Montefalco. Village worth seeing, parking outside village, narrow streets.
👁 Ponte delle Torri. Aqueduct, 14th century.
⛺ ⬛ Tue, Fri.
✳ Art festival. ⬛ 01/06-31/07.

**⬛S** Terni 🚲⛵🏛 **34D2**
Piazzale Felice Fatati, SR209. **GPS:** n42,55690 e12,72006. ⬆.

⬛free Ch 3.
**Location:** Rural. **Surface:** unpaved. ⬛ 01/01-31/12.
**Distance:** 🚶Terni 7km ✕on the spot 🚰on the spot.
**Remarks:** Along river, nearby waterfalls.

**⬛S** Terni 🚲⛵🏛 **34D2**
Via Lombardo Radice. **GPS:** n42,56634 e12,63577. ⬆.

⬛€ 4/48h 🚰€ 0,50 ⬛Ch ✂included.
**Location:** Urban, noisy. **Surface:** asphalted. ⬛ 01/01-31/12.
**Distance:** 🚶50m ✕50m 🚰500m 🚰250m.
**Remarks:** At cemetery.

**⬛S** Todi 🚲⛵🏛 **34C2**
Area Porta Orvietana, Viale di Montesanto.
**GPS:** n42,78120 e12,40168. ⬆➡.

16 ⬛€ 15,40/24h, € 3/h 🚰⬛Ch 📶. **Location:** Simple.
**Surface:** asphalted. ⬛ 01/01-31/12 ⬛ Sa-morning market.
**Distance:** ✕450m 🚰500m.
**Remarks:** Elevator (free) to centre.

**⬛S** Torgiano **34C2**
Via Perugia. **GPS:** n43,02917 e12,43833. ⬆.

---

10 ⬛free 🚰€ 0,05/1liter ⬛Ch. **Location:** Urban.
**Surface:** asphalted. ⬛ 01/01-31/12.
**Distance:** 🚶200m ✈3,5km 🚰200m 🚰300m.
**Remarks:** Next to sports fields.

**⬛S** Trevi 🚲 **34D2**
Via Costa San Paolo. **GPS:** n42,87829 e12,75221. ⬆➡.

20 ⬛free 🚰⬛Chfree. **Surface:** grasstiles. ⬛ 01/01-31/12.
**Distance:** 🚶500m ✈5,1km ✕350m 🚰on the spot.
**Remarks:** At swimming pool.

# Abruzzo

**⬛S** Anversa degli Abruzzi **34E3**
Il Sagittario, Loc. Ponte delle Fornaci. **GPS:** n41,99995 e13,80960. ⬆.
10 ⬛€ 12 🚰⬛Ch ✂WC ⬛. **Location:** Rural. **Surface:** gravel.
⬛ 01/01-31/12.
**Distance:** 🚶1km ✕1km 🚰1km 🚲on the spot 🚶on the spot.

**⬛S** Anversa degli Abruzzi **34E3**
Bioagriturismo La Porta dei Parchi, Piazza Roma 3.
**GPS:** n42,00014 e13,79899. ⬆➡.

5 ⬛€ 10, free with a meal 🚰⬛Ch ✂WC ⬛€ 5 📶included.
**Location:** Rural. **Surface:** metalled. ⬛ 01/01-31/12.
**Distance:** 🚶1km ✕on the spot.

**⬛S** Barrea **34E3**

Barrea Sosta Camper, Strada Regionale 83.
**GPS:** n41,76129 e13,98768. ⬆.
23 ⬛€ 20-30 🚰⬛Ch ✂WC 📶included. 🚐🚗
**Location:** Rural, comfortable, quiet. **Surface:** grassy/gravel.
⬛ 01/01-31/12.
**Distance:** 🚶700m ✕on the spot 🚌shuttle to centre 🚲on the spot
🚶on the spot.
**Remarks:** At the lake, bicycle rental, picnic and barbecue place.

**⬛S** Campotosto **34D2**
Via Lago, SR557. **GPS:** n42,56208 e13,34805.
⬛€ 5 🚰. **Surface:** grassy. ⬛ 01/01-31/12.
**Distance:** 🚶Campotosto 3km 🚰on the spot.
**Remarks:** At lake Campotosto.

**⬛S** Casalbordino **34F3**
Via Alessandrini. **GPS:** n42,19952 e14,61800.
20 ⬛€ 5. **Location:** Rural. **Surface:** grassy/sand.

---

⬛ 01/01-31/12.
**Distance:** 🚶on the spot 🚰on the spot ✕on the spot.
**Remarks:** To be paid at bar in the village.

**⬛S** Casalbordino **34F3**
Area di sosta Ass Villa Sarda, Contr. Piana Sabelli.
**GPS:** n42,17773 e14,59994. ⬆.
20 ⬛⬛ 🚰⬛Ch ✂WC ⬛. **Location:** Rural. **Surface:** grassy. ⬛ 01/01-31/12.
**Distance:** 🚶1,5km 🚰1km ✕on the spot.

**⬛S** Fossacesia **34F2**
Area Camper, Via Lungomare Sud 168.
**GPS:** n42,24067 e14,52988. ⬆➡.

24 ⬛€ 10 🚰⬛Ch ✂included.
**Surface:** gravel/sand. ⬛ 01/03-30/11.
**Distance:** 🚶1km ✈6,5km 🚰on the spot ✕on the spot 🚰5km
🚰1,5km.
**Remarks:** Pebbled beach.

**⬛S** Isola del Gran Sasso **34E2**
S.Gabriele dell Addolorata. **GPS:** n42,51712 e13,65634. ⬆.

⬛free 🚰⬛Chfree.
**Location:** Urban. **Surface:** gravel/sand. ⬛ 01/01-31/12.
**Distance:** 🚶on the spot ✈4km ✕on the spot 🚰on the spot.
**Remarks:** Nearby basilica.

**⬛S** Lanciano **34E2**
Area Attrezzata, Strada provinciale Lanciano-Frisa, Lancianovecchia.
**GPS:** n42,23385 e14,39106. ⬆➡.

50 ⬛free 🚰⬛ChWCfree. **Location:** Urban. **Surface:** asphalted
⬛ 01/01-31/12 ⬛ Sa-morning market.
**Distance:** 🚶300m (stairs and elevator) ✕300m 🚰450m.
**Remarks:** At city walls, upper part of the parking, escalator to city centre.

**Tourist information Lanciano:**
ℹ Historical city with medieval Jewish district, Ripa Sacca.

**⬛S** L'Aquila 🚲❄ **34D2**
Via porta Napoli. **GPS:** n42,34175 e13,39510. ⬆.
10 ⬛free 🚰⬛Chfree. **Location:** Urban. **Surface:** gravel.
⬛ 01/01-31/12.
**Distance:** 🚶700m ✕500m 🚰2km.

**⬛S** L'Aquila 🚲❄ **34D2**
Via Strinella. **GPS:** n42,35323 e13,40708. ⬆.

10 ⌁free ⌁⌁Chfree. **Location:** Urban. **Surface:** asphalted.
▢ 01/01-31/12.
**Distance:** ⌁500m ⊗300m ⌁400m.
**Remarks:** In front of Hotel Federico II, adjacent Parco del Castello.

### Notaresco 34E2
Via Martiri della Libertà. **GPS:** n42,65527 e13,89578.⬆➡.
10 ⌁free ⌁⌁Chfree ⌁against payment. **Location:** Urban.
**Surface:** asphalted. ▢ 01/01-31/12.
**Distance:** ⌁on the spot ⊗on the spot ⌁500m.
**Remarks:** At tennis-courts.

### Ovindoli 34E3
Via Statale. **GPS:** n42,14143 e13,51740.⬆.

50 ⌁free ⌁⌁Chfree. **Location:** Simple. **Surface:** metalled.
▢ 01/01-31/12.
**Distance:** ⌁500m ⊗600m ⌁600m ⌁2km.

### Penne 34E2
**Agriturismo Il Portico**, Contrada Colle Serangelo 26.
**GPS:** n42,45592 e13,95165.➡.

15 ⌁€ 10, free with a meal ⌁⌁Ch⌁(7x)€ 3 WC⌁included.
**Location:** Rural. **Surface:** grassy.
▢ 01/01-31/12.
**Distance:** ⌁3km ⊗on the spot.
**Remarks:** Swimming pool (summer).

### Pescasseroli 34E3
**Area Camper S.Andrea**, Loc. Sant'Andrea, SS83.
**GPS:** n41,79888 e13,79222.⬆.

50 ⌁€ 17, 2 pers. incl ⌁⌁Ch⌁ WC⌁€ 0,50/5minutes ⌁included.
**Location:** Rural. **Surface:** unpaved.
▢ 8-13h, 14.30-20h.
**Distance:** ⌁1km ⊗1km ⌁on the spot.
**Remarks:** Free shuttle to centre.
**Tourist information Pescasseroli:**
⌁ Parco Nazionale d'Abruzzo. Nature reserve.

### Pineto 34E2
**Sand stone beach**, Via Tremiti, fraz. Scerne.
**GPS:** n42,64270 e14,04505.⬆.
3 ⌁free WC⌁. **Location:** Rural, simple, isolated. **Surface:** grassy.
▢ 01/05-31/10.
**Distance:** ⌁on the spot ⌁on the spot.

### Roccaraso 34E3
**Park Hotel Il Poggio**, SS17, C.da Poggio, 1, Loc Il Poggio.
**GPS:** n41,82638 e14,10111.⬆➡.

18 ⌁€ 20 ⌁⌁Ch⌁(18x)included ⌁. ▢ 01/01-31/12.
**Distance:** ⊗on the spot.
**Remarks:** Discount longer stays, shuttle bus to ski-piste.

### Roseto degli Abruzzi 34E2
**Agricamping Garden Beach**, Via degli Acquaviva, 45.
**GPS:** n42,72664 e13,98604.⬆.

30 ⌁€ 20-28, Jul/Aug € 33 ⌁⌁Ch⌁(20x)€ 0,50/kWh WC⌁€ 1
⌁included. **Location:** Rural, comfortable, central, quiet.
**Surface:** grassy. ▢ 01/03-01/10.
**Distance:** ⌁300m ⌁on the spot ⌁on the spot ⊗on the spot
⌁300m ⌁on the spot.
**Remarks:** Barbecue place, dog permitted on the beach, regional products.

### Roseto degli Abruzzi 34E2
**Area di Sosta Camper Romeo**, Via degli Orti 13, loc. Cologna Spiaggia.
**GPS:** n42,72287 e13,98076.⬆.

40 ⌁€ 20, 20/07-20/08 € 25 ⌁⌁Ch⌁(40x)WC⌁€ 1
⌁⌁included. **Location:** Rural. **Surface:** grassy.
▢ 01/01-31/12.
**Distance:** ⌁200m ⌁750m ⌁on the spot ⌁100m ⌁100m.
**Remarks:** Barbecue place.

### Roseto degli Abruzzi 34E2
**Sosta Camper Gulliver**, Via del Mare, snc - loc. Cologna Spiaggia.
**GPS:** n42,73559 e13,98024.⬆⬆.
50 ⌁€ 15-25 ⌁⌁Ch⌁ WC⌁⌁⌁included. ⌁
**Location:** Rural, comfortable, quiet. **Surface:** grassy.
▢ 01/04-30/09.
**Distance:** ⌁800m ⌁100m ⌁200m ⌁200m.
**Remarks:** Bicycle rental, picnic and barbecue place, playground.

### Roseto degli Abruzzi 34E2
**Area di sosta Isola del Sole**, Piana degli Ulivi.
**GPS:** n42,66902 e14,01189.⬆➡.

11 ⌁€ 20 ⌁⌁Ch⌁(11x)€ 2 WC⌁included.
**Location:** Rural. **Surface:** metalled. ▢ 01/01-31/12.
**Distance:** ⌁3km ⌁3km ⊗1km.
**Remarks:** Swimming pool (summer).

### Roseto degli Abruzzi 34E2
**Palazzo dello Sport**, Via Ticino. **GPS:** n42,66012 e14,02382.⬆➡.

10 ⌁free ⌁⌁Chfree. **Location:** Simple, isolated.
**Surface:** asphalted. ▢ 01/01-31/12 ▢ Tue.
**Distance:** ⌁200m ⌁1km ⊗300m ⌁300m.
**Remarks:** At gymnasium, tuesday market.

### San Salvo Marina 34F3
**Area Sosta Communale per Autocaravan**, SS16.
**GPS:** n42,07195 e14,76289.⬆.
30 ⌁€ 16/24h, € 20/48h, € 30/72h ⌁⌁Ch⌁⌁ 4 WCincluded
⌁cold shower. **Location:** Urban, comfortable, quiet. **Surface:** grassy.
▢ 01/05-15/09.
**Distance:** ⌁300m ⌁2,2km ⌁300m ⊗600m.

### Santo Stefano di Sessanio 34E2
**Ostello del Cavaliere**, Piazza Della Giudea.
**GPS:** n42,34429 e13,64314.⬆.
5 ⌁guests free ⌁. **Surface:** metalled. ▢ 01/01-31/12.
**Distance:** ⌁300m ⊗300m ⌁500m.

### Sant'Egidio alla Vibrata 34E2
Via Campania, Zona industriale. **GPS:** n42,81937 e13,69915.⬆➡.

10 ⌁free ⌁⌁Chfree. **Location:** Urban. **Surface:** asphalted.
▢ 01/01-31/12.
**Distance:** ⌁1km ⊗200m.
**Remarks:** Industrial area.

### Torino di Sangro 34F2
**Area camper Vitale**, Lido le Morgie. **GPS:** n42,20403 e14,60349.⬆.
100 ⌁€ 15/24h ⌁⌁Chincluded ⌁€ 2 WC⌁€ 0,50.
**Location:** Rural, simple. **Surface:** grassy/sand.
▢ 01/01-31/12.
**Distance:** ⌁8km ⌁beach 70m ⊗250m ⌁on the spot.

### Tortoreto Lido 34E2
**Frontemare Easy Park**, Via Napoli. **GPS:** n42,78425 e13,94966.⬆.
30 ⌁€ 15 ⌁⌁Ch⌁included WC⌁⌁.
**Surface:** asphalted. ▢ 01/04-01/10.
**Distance:** ⌁beach 200m.
**Remarks:** Max. 72h.

### Tortoreto Lido 34E2
Lungomare Sirena. **GPS:** n42,78863 e13,94989.⬆.

6 ⌁free. ▢ 01/01-31/12.
**Distance:** ⌁beach 100m.
**Remarks:** Max. 48h.

### Villalago 34E3
SP82b. **GPS:** n41,92255 e13,85621.⬆.

IT

13 🛏free 🚰🔌Chfree.
**Location:** Rural. **Surface:** asphalted. ⬛ 01/01-31/12.
**Distance:** 🏖on the spot.
**Remarks:** At lake Scanno, nearby beach and kosk.

# Molise

🚏S | **Campobasso** | 34F3

**Area di sosta Dominick Ferrante**, Contrada Macchie 1.
**GPS:** n41,56886 e14,65118.⬆⬆➡.

20 🛏€ 10/24h, € 15/48h 🚰🔌Ch✂included.
**Surface:** gravel.
**Distance:** 🚶800m.

🍴S | **Monteroduni** | 34E3

**Oasi San Nazzaro**, Vico 5 del Sole. **GPS:** n41,53448 e14,15924.

40 🛏€ 10, free with a meal 🚰🔌Ch ✂(6x)included.
**Surface:** grassy. ⬛ 01/01-31/12.
**Distance:** 🚶3,5km 🐟Fish lake ⊗on the spot.

🚏S | **Petacciato Marina** | 34F3

**Villagio la Torre**, SS16 Adriatica km535,5, Termoli ri Vasto.
**GPS:** n42,02432 e14,88739.⬆.

60 🛏€ 15-25 🚰🔌Ch✂(50x)included WC 🛁. **Location:** Rural,
isolated. **Surface:** gravel/sand. ⬛ 01/01-31/12.
**Distance:** 🚶4km ⌖on the spot ⊗on the spot 🏖on the spot.
**Remarks:** Access via gate next to tower ruins.

🚏S | **Petacciato Marina** | 34F3

**Parking spiaggia**, Via del Mare, SS16. **GPS:** n42,03543 e14,85337.⬆.

40 🛏8-20h € 6 🛁against payment. **Location:** Rural.
**Surface:** asphalted. ⬛ 01/01-31/12.
**Distance:** 🚶4,5km 🏊9,5km 🏖50m ⊗100m 🚌300m.

---

**Remarks:** Reserved place for motorhomes.

🚏S | **Petacciato Marina** | 34F3

**Parking Tolomei**, Via Marinelle, SS 16. **GPS:** n42,03219 e14,85844.⬆.
50 🛏€ 15 🚰🔌Chincluded ✂WC🛁€ 0,50 📶. **Location:** Rural.
**Surface:** gravel. ⬛ 01/01-31/12.
**Distance:** 🏖Direct access ⊗600m 🚌900m.
**Remarks:** Shuttle bus.

# Puglia

🚏S | **Alberobello** 🌿🏠 | 35D1

**Parcheggio Nel Verde**, Via Cadore. **GPS:** n40,78266 e17,23418.⬆.

60 🛏€ 18/24h, € 14/12h, € 10/6h 🚰🔌Ch ✂📶included.
**Surface:** grassy/gravel. ⬛ 01/01-31/12.
**Distance:** 🚶Trulli-centre 50m 🏖50m 🛁100m.
**Remarks:** No camping activities.

**Tourist information Alberobello:**
ℹ Centre of the Trulli-region. Trulli houses are curious houses built
without motar.
🏠 ⬛ Thu-morning.

🌿S | **Andria** | 35C1

**L'Altro Villaggio**, S.S.170. **GPS:** n41,08010 e16,27496.⬆.
🛏 18 🚰🔌Ch ✂included WC 🛁. **Location:** Rural, comfortable.
**Surface:** grassy/metalled. ⬛ 01/01-31/12.
**Distance:** ⊗900m 🏖350m 🏊on the spot.

🚏S | **Bari** | 35C1

**Area Hobby Park Wash**, Via Giovanni del Conte.
**GPS:** n41,11581 e16,88501.
🛏 € 15/24h 🚰🔌Ch ✂included 🛁📶.
**Location:** Urban. **Surface:** metalled. ⬛ 01/01-31/12.
**Distance:** 🚶centre 500m 🏖700m ⊗800m 🛁600m 🚌200m.
**Remarks:** Monitored parking.

🚏S | **Bari** | 35C1

**Gran Parcheggio Alberotanza**, Via Alberotaza, 43A.
**GPS:** n41,09520 e16,87868.

250 🛏€ 20 🚰€ 0,50/30liter 🔌€ 2,50 Ch ✂€ 0,50/kWh WC.
**Location:** Urban. **Surface:** asphalted. ⬛ 01/01-31/12.
**Distance:** 🚲7,8km ⊗500m 🛁500m 🚌400m.
**Remarks:** Monitored parking.

🚏S | **Brindisi** 🏖 | 35D1

**Freeland**, SS16 14. **GPS:** n40,60184 e17,95656.
15 🛏€ 13 🚰🔌Ch ✂included. **Location:** Urban. **Surface:** metalled.
⬛ 01/01-31/12.
**Distance:** 🚶5km.
**Remarks:** Video surveillance.

🏞S | **Brindisi** 🏖 | 35D1

**Garage Minnuta**, Strada Minnuta 6. **GPS:** n40,63517 e17,91824.

20 🛏€ 10 🚰€ 3 🔌€ 3 Ch 3 ✂€ 3 WC 🛁included.
**Location:** Urban. **Surface:** asphalted. ⬛ 01/01-31/12.
**Distance:** 🚶2km ⊗1km.

---

**Remarks:** 24/24 surveillance.

🚏S | **Castellana Grotte** 🌿 | 35D1

**Area Sapori & Sapori**, Via Turi. **GPS:** n40,88560 e17,15722.⬆.
10 🛏free 🚰🔌Chfree.
**Location:** Urban. **Surface:** asphalted. ⬛ 01/01-31/12.
**Distance:** 🚶1km ⊗on the spot 🛁1km 🚌1km.
**Remarks:** Caves 1,8km.

🚏S | **Castellana Grotte** 🌿 | 35D1

**Le Grotte di Castellana**, SS32. **GPS:** n40,87543 e17,14900.⬆.

10 🛏€ 5. **Location:** Rural.
**Surface:** grassy/gravel.
⬛ 01/01-31/12.
**Distance:** 🚶city centre 2km ⊗on the spot 🚌500m.
**Remarks:** Parking at the caves of Castellana, overnight stay allowed.

🍴S | **Castellana Grotte** 🌿 | 35D1

**Agriturismo Monte del Vento**, Via Alberobello 202.
**GPS:** n40,83457 e17,24166.
5 🛏€ 15/24h, free with a meal 🚰🔌Chincluded ✂WC🛁.
**Location:** Rural. **Surface:** unpaved. ⬛ 01/01 31/12.
**Distance:** ⊗on the spot.

🏞S | **Foggia** | 34G3

**Parking 92**. **GPS:** n41,43430 e15,48063.
🛏 10 🚰🔌Ch ✂included. **Location:** Rural. ⬛ 01/01-31/12.
**Distance:** 🚶6km ⊗1,3km.

🚏S | **Gallipoli** | 35D1

**Area Sosta Camper Nuovi Orizzonti**, Sp 221 Contrada L' Ariò.
**GPS:** n40,00286 e18,03374.⬆.
40 🛏€ 21, Aug € 26 🚰🔌Ch ✂WC🛁included. **Location:** Rural,
comfortable, quiet. **Surface:** forest soil. ⬛ 01/01-31/12.
**Distance:** 🚶Gallipoli 5km 🏖1,5km.
**Remarks:** Free shuttle to beach.

🚏S | **Gallipoli** | 35D1

**Autopark Spiaggia D'oro San Mauro**, Loc. Padula Bianca.
**GPS:** n40,09568 e18,01625.⬆➡.
50 🛏€ 20 🚰🔌Ch ✂🛁. **Location:** Quiet. ⬛ 01/06-30/09.
**Distance:** 🚶Gallipoli 4km 🏖100m.

🚏S | **Gallipoli** | 35D1

**CamperPark Baia Verde**, Via Rosa dei Venti, Loc. Baia Verde.
**GPS:** n40,03375 e18,02088.
70 🛏€ 20 🚰🔌Ch ✂included 🛁.
**Surface:** grassy. ⬛ 01/06-30/09.
**Distance:** 🚶Gallipoli 4km 🏖200m ⊗200m.

🚏S | **Gallipoli** | 35D1

**Campo delle Bandiere**, Loc. Padula Bianca. **GPS:** n40,09681 e18,01297.
🛏€ 15-25 🚰🔌ChWC🛁.
**Location:** Rural. **Surface:** sand. ⬛ 01/06-01/09.
**Distance:** 🏖Sandy beach.

🚏S | **Gallipoli** | 35D1

**La Sosta**, Via Beneficati Rossi, Loc. Padula Bianca.
**GPS:** n40,09454 e18,01572.⬆.
🛏€ 10-30 🚰🔌ChWC📶. **Surface:** sand. ⬛ 01/01-31/12.
**Distance:** 🏖50m ⊗on the spot.
**Remarks:** Video surveillance.

🚏 | **Gallipoli** | 35D1

**Via Cimitero**. **GPS:** n40,05479 e17,99689.⬆.
20 🛏€ 10/24h. **Surface:** asphalted. ⬛ 01/01-31/12.
**Distance:** 🚶centre 400m 🏊650m 🏖400m 🛁200m.

🚏S | **Lequile** | 35D1

**Salento Sosta Camper**, Via Preti di Campi 6. **GPS:** n40,28266 e18,13179.

**658**

18 🚐 € 15/24h 🚰🗑Ch🔌🚿. **Location:** Comfortable, quiet.
**Surface:** gravel. ☐ 01/01-31/12.
**Distance:** 🚶city centre Lecce 8km.
**Remarks:** Bike/car rental.

### Lesina 34F3
**Oasi**, Via Ludovica Ariosto. **GPS:** n41,86472 e15,35806.⬆.

15 🚐 € 12, Sept-Mar-Apr € 15, May/Aug € 18 🚰🗑
Ch🔌WC included. **Location:** Rural, comfortable, quiet.
**Surface:** asphalted. ☐ 01/01-31/12.
**Distance:** 🚶300m 🏊on the spot 🛒500m.

### Lucera 34G3
Via Montello. **GPS:** n41,49987 e15,33223.⬆.

100 🚐free 🚰🗑. **Location:** Urban. **Surface:** asphalted.
☐ 01/01-31/12.
**Distance:** 🚶900m ⊗300m 🛒500m.
**Remarks:** At station.

### Lucera 34G3
**Centro sportivo Casanova**, Strada Contrada Casanova.
**GPS:** n41,48849 e15,26008.⬆.
10 🚐€ 10 🚰🗑Ch included.
**Location:** Isolated. **Surface:** metalled. ☐ 01/01-31/12.
**Distance:** 🚶Lucera 9km.
**Remarks:** At sports centre.

### Margherita di Savoia 34G3
**Lido Baywatch**, Via Barletta. **GPS:** n41,36222 e16,17361.⬆➡.

12 🚐€ 20, 01/06-30/09 € 25 🚰🗑Ch🔌WC included.
**Location:** Rural, comfortable, quiet. **Surface:** gravel.
☐ 01/01-31/12.
**Distance:** 🚶2km 🏊on the spot ⊗on the spot.

### Marina di Felloniche 35D1
**Marcheddu Parking village**, SP214. **GPS:** n39,79729 e18,33392.
30 🚐€ 15-25 🚰🗑Ch🔌WC 🗑🔲🚿. **Location:** Rural.
**Surface:** unpaved. ☐ 01/04-15/10.
**Distance:** 🚶4km 🏊on the spot ⊗on the spot 🛒on the spot
🏊 on the spot.
**Remarks:** Barbecue place.

### Massafra 35D1
**Area di Sosta La Stella**, SS7, SS Appia km 633, Le Forche.
**GPS:** n40,59201 e17,09904.⬆.

20 🚐€ 16-20 🚰🗑€ 2,50 Ch🔌(18x)€ 3 WC🗑€ 1. **Location:** Rural.
**Surface:** grassy. ☐ 01/01-31/12.
**Distance:** 🚶1km ◢3km 🏊6km ⊗500m 🛒1km.
**Remarks:** Beachshuttle € 2.

### Mattinata 34G3
**Eden Park**, Porto di Mattinata, SP53. **GPS:** n41,70667 e16,06556.⬆.

30 🚐€ 14,60-26,60 🚰🗑ChWC included 🗑€ 0,50. **Location:** Rural,
comfortable. **Surface:** grassy/sand. ☐ 01/06-31/08.
**Distance:** 🚶1km 🏊pebbled beach 🛶on the spot ⊗1km 🛒1km.

### Melendugno 35D1
**Area Camper Salento I Faraglioni**, SP366 km 20.5, Sant'Andrea.
**GPS:** n40,25550 e18,43748.
15 🚐€ 15-32/24h, 4 pers.incl + tourist tax € 0,50 🚰🗑Ch🔌
included WC🗑€ 1 🔲. **Location:** Rural. **Surface:** unpaved.
☐ 01/01-31/12.
**Distance:** 🏊700m ⊗400m 🛒on the spot.
**Remarks:** Barbecue place, shuttle bus to beach, playground.

### Melendugno 35D1
**Gran Pasha**, Strada provinciale Lecce-Melendugno-San Foca, km.18.
**GPS:** n40,27724 e18,40510.
50 🚐€ 15 + € 0,50/pp tourist tax 🚰🗑Ch🔌€ 3 WC🗑included.
**Location:** Rural, comfortable, isolated. **Surface:** unpaved.
☐ 01/04-30/09.
**Distance:** 🚶1,5km 🏊1,5km.
**Remarks:** Bar, barbecue place, free shuttle.

### Monopoli 35D1
**Area du Sosta Camper Lido Millennium**, SP90, Loc. Capitolo, SS16
km850 Uscita Capitolo. **GPS:** n40,90374 e17,35261.⬆➡.

100 🚐€ 15-20 🚰🗑Ch🔌6Amp WC included 🗑€ 1.
**Location:** Rural, comfortable, central. **Surface:** gravel.
☐ Easter-30/09.
**Distance:** 🚶500m 🏊50m ⊗50m 🛒50m.
**Remarks:** Private beach.

### Otranto 35D1
**Oasy Park**, Via Renis. **GPS:** n40,13795 e18,48922.⬆➡.

50 🚐€ 18, Aug € 20, 2 pers. Incl 🚰🗑Ch🔌(70x),16Amp
WC included 🗑€ 1 🔲€ 4. **Location:** Rural, comfortable, quiet.
**Surface:** grassy/gravel. ☐ 01/01-31/12.
**Distance:** 🚶400m 🏊700m ⊗400m 🛒400m.

### Otranto 35D1
**Area Camper Fontanelle**, Sp366, km28. **GPS:** n40,19159 e18,45494.

20 🚐€ 15/24h, Jul-Aug € 25, 4 pers incl. + tourist tax 🚰🗑Ch🔌🚿€ 3
WC included 🗑€ 0,50. **Location:** Rural, comfortable, isolated, quiet.
**Surface:** grassy. ☐ 01/05-31/10.
**Distance:** 🚶Otranto 5km 🏊beach 400m.
**Remarks:** Shuttle bus to Otranto, regional products.

### Peschici 34G3
**Camper Marina Picola**, Loc. Pantanello, Baia di Peschici.
**GPS:** n41,94528 e16,00528.⬆.

45 🚐€ 13-27 🚰🗑Ch🔌🚿included WC🗑€ 0,50. **Location:** Rural,
comfortable. **Surface:** grassy/sand. ☐ 01/04-30/09.
**Distance:** 🚶2,5km, walking 800m (stairs) 🏊sandy beach 50m
⊗300m.

### Peschici 34G3
**AgriCamper Pane e Vino**, SS89 km 2,6. **GPS:** n41,92372 e16,01534.
20 🚐€ 10 🚰🗑Ch🔌🚿WC🗑.
**Location:** Rural, simple, isolated. **Surface:** sand.
**Distance:** 🚶3,5km ⊗on the spot 🏊on the spot.
**Remarks:** Borrow cycles for free.

### Peschici 34G3
**Area attrezzata per camper Dattoli**, Via Spiaggia, SS89.
**GPS:** n41,94522 e16,01138.
14 🚐€ 15-20 🚰🗑Ch🔌🚿WC included 🗑€ 0,50.
**Location:** Rural. **Surface:** unpaved.
☐ 01/01-31/12.
**Distance:** 🚶Old city 300m (stairs) 🏊100m ⊗100m 🛒1km.

### Putignano 35D1
**Grotte di Putignano**, SS172. **GPS:** n40,85706 e17,10944.
8 🚐free. ☐ 01/01-31/12.

### Rodi Garganico 34G3
**Area sosta camper Isola Bella**, Via delle More.
**GPS:** n41,92444 e15,84166.⬆➡.

30 🚐€ 15-20, Aug € 25 🚰🗑Ch🔌🚿WC🗑included.
**Location:** Rural, comfortable. **Surface:** grassy/sand.
☐ 01/06-15/09.
**Distance:** 🚶Lido del Sole 1,5km, Rodi Garganico 3,8km 🏊sandy beach
10m 🛶on the spot ⊗100m 🛒1,5km.

### San Giovanni Rotondo 34G3
**Coppa Cicuta**, Strada Comunale Pozzocavo-Tre Carrini.
**GPS:** n41,69599 e15,70423.⬆➡.

**IT**

IT

15 ⊟€ 12 🚰Ch💧(30x)€ 1,50/night WC included 📷€ 10.
**Location:** Rural, simple, quiet. **Surface:** gravel.
🗓 01/01-31/12.
**Distance:** 🚶3km 🛒on the spot.
**Remarks:** Shuttle € 2/pp.

| San Giovanni Rotondo | 34G3 |
|---|---|

**Lo Chalet**, Viale Padre Pio. **GPS:** n41,70658 e15,69799.
30 ⊟€ 15/24h 🚰Ch💧WC
**Location:** Rural, simple, quiet. **Surface:** metalled. 🗓 01/01-31/12.
**Distance:** 🚶1km 🛒on the spot.
**Remarks:** Free shuttle, santuario 300m.

| San Giovanni Rotondo | 34G3 |
|---|---|

**Di Cerbo**, Circonvallazione Sud, SP45bis. **GPS:** n41,69725 e15,73097.

20 ⊟€ 5,20/day, € 7,80/night 🚰Ch💧WC 1,50 📷€ 1.
**Location:** Rural, simple, noisy. **Surface:** asphalted.
🗓 01/01-31/12.
**Distance:** 🚶1km 🛒on the spot 🍽on the spot 🚐on the spot.
**Remarks:** Shuttle bus.

| P | San Giovanni Rotondo | 34G3 |
|---|---|---|

Viale Padre Pio. **GPS:** n41,70679 e15,69927.
150 ⊟€ 2,50, overnight stay free. **Surface:** asphalted.
**Remarks:** Shrine Padre Pio 200m.

| San Pietro in Bevagna | 35D1 |
|---|---|

**Holiday Area Camper**, Via Chidro di Specchiarica, Salento.
**GPS:** n40,30511 e17,69486.
50 ⊟€ 15-23 🚰Ch included 💧€ 2,50 WC
**Location:** Urban. **Surface:** unpaved. 🗓 01/06-30/09.
**Distance:** 🚶2km 🏖on the spot 🍽800m.
**Remarks:** Monitored parking 24/24.

| San Pietro in Bevagna | 35D1 |
|---|---|

**La Salina**, SP122, Manduria. **GPS:** n40,30121 e17,72630.
30 ⊟€ 14-21, 4 pers.incl 🚰Ch💧€ 2,50 WC included.
**Location:** Rural. **Surface:** gravel.
🗓 01/06-30/09.
**Distance:** 🚶1km 🏖on the spot 🛒450m 🏊on the spot.

| San Pietro in Bevagna | 35D1 |
|---|---|

**La Marina**, Via Favignana, Manduria. **GPS:** n40,30888 e17,67750.

80 ⊟€ 20/24h 🚰Ch included 💧€ 2 WC€ 0,50.
**Location:** Urban. **Surface:** unpaved. 🗓 01/06-01/09.
**Distance:** 🚶on the spot 🏖300m 🍽450m.
**Remarks:** Monitored parking.

| Santa Maria al Bagno | 35D1 |
|---|---|

**Area Camper Mondonuovo**, Via Torremozza.
**GPS:** n40,13494 e18,00166.
20 ⊟€ 15, Aug € 17 🚰Ch💧
**Surface:** gravel. 🗓 01/01-31/12.
**Distance:** 🏖beach 500m 🍽900m.

| Torre Canne di Fasano | 35D1 |
|---|---|

**Lido Tavernese**, SS379, uscita Torre Canne Sud.
**GPS:** n40,82023 e17,49875.

100 ⊟€ 15-22, Aug € 28 🚰Ch💧(80x)€ 2 WC included 🗑€ 1.
**Location:** Rural. **Surface:** grassy. 🗓 01/05-30/09.
**Distance:** 🚶3,5km 🛒on the spot 01/07-31/08.

| Torre dell'Orso | 35D1 |
|---|---|

**Camper Park Area La Torre. GPS:** n40,27824 e18,41413.
20 ⊟€ 10-35 🚰Ch💧🗑 **Location:** Urban, comfortable.
**Surface:** grassy. 🗓 01/06-30/09.
**Distance:** 🏖700m 🛒500m.
**Remarks:** Regional products.

| Troia | 34G3 |
|---|---|

**Campo della Fiera**, Via Sant'Antonio. **GPS:** n41,36158 e15,30616.

30 ⊟free 🚰Ch💧free.
**Location:** Urban. **Surface:** asphalted. 🗓 01/01-31/12.
**Distance:** 🚶200m 🛒300m 🍽350m.
**Remarks:** Near the cathedral.

| Vico del Gargano | 34G3 |
|---|---|

**Lido Azzurro**, Loc. Calenella. **GPS:** n41,94208 e15,98303.

50 ⊟€ 15, July € 20, Aug € 25 🚰Ch💧€ 3,(Aug) WC🗑📶included.
**Location:** Rural, comfortable, quiet. **Surface:** sand.
🗓 01/05-30/09.
**Distance:** 🚶2km 🏖Sandy beach 100m 🛒on the spot 🍽500m (camping) 🚐1km.

| Vieste | 34G3 |
|---|---|

**Fusilo Rosina**, Contrada S.Lucia. **GPS:** n41,91028 e16,12944.

70 ⊟Jun-Sep € 15, Jul € 20, Aug € 27,50 🚰Ch💧(70x)included WC🗑€ 0,50. **Location:** Rural. **Surface:** grassy. 🗓 01/06-15/09.
**Distance:** 🚶4km 🏖300m 🛒50m 🍽100m 🚐50m.
**Remarks:** Barbecue place, playground.

| Vieste | 34G3 |
|---|---|

**Parco Vacanze Eden Blu**, Lungomare Enrico Mattei 109.
**GPS:** n41,85985 e16,17396.
40 ⊟€ 13-32, 2 pers. incl 🚰Ch free 💧WC included.
**Location:** Rural. **Surface:** grassy. 🗓 01/04-31/10.
**Distance:** 🚶2km 🏖on the spot 🛒200m 🍽on the spot.
**Remarks:** Monitored parking 24/24.

**Tourist information Vieste:**
🏛 🗓 Mo.

| Zapponeta | 34G3 |
|---|---|

**Zapponeta Beach**, Via del Mare. **GPS:** n41,45694 e15,96083.

30 ⊟€ 13, 12/06-09/07, 21/08-10/09 € 15, 10/07-20/08 € 18, 2 pers. incl 🚰Ch💧€ 3 WC included 🗑€ 1. **Location:** Rural, comfortable, quiet. **Surface:** grassy/metalled. 🗓 01/04-30/09.
**Distance:** 🚶250m 🛒on the spot 🍽on the spot 🛒500m 🍽500m.
**Remarks:** Narrow entrance.

# Campania

| Agropoli | 35C1 |
|---|---|

**La Volpe Trentova**, Via Belvedere 133. **GPS:** n40,34133 e14,98026.
20 ⊟€ 12-27 🚰Ch💧WC🗑📷.
**Location:** Rural, comfortable. **Surface:** gravel. 🗓 01/01-31/12.
**Distance:** 🚶1,2km 🏖750m 🛒100m.

| Bacoli | 35B1 |
|---|---|

**Sea Oasi Village**, Via Spiaggia Romana. **GPS:** n40,82194 e14,04791.
100 ⊟€ 18-20, 4 pers.incl 🚰Ch included 💧€ 5 🗑€ 0,50.
**Location:** Rural. **Surface:** grassy. 🗓 01/01-31/12.
**Distance:** 🏖on the spot 🛒on the spot 🍽1km.

| Bacoli | 35B1 |
|---|---|

**Parco Naturale Agriturismo Fondi di Baia**, Via Fondi di Baia.
**GPS:** n40,81157 e14,07412.

20 ⊟€ 10 🚰Ch💧included.
**Surface:** asphalted. 🗓 01/01-31/12.
**Distance:** 🚶3km 🛒Baia 700m 🚐100m.

| Baia e Latina | 35B1 |
|---|---|

**Il Baglio Country Village**, Via Sturzo 13. **GPS:** n41,30386 e14,24754.
3 ⊟guests free 🚰Ch💧WC🗑📶. **Location:** Rural, simple, isolated, quiet. **Surface:** gravel. 🗓 01/01-31/12.
**Distance:** 🚶village 2km 🛒on the spot.
**Remarks:** Use of sauna against payment.

| Battipaglia | 35B1 |
|---|---|

**Camperstop Lagomare**, Via Andrea Doria 1, Fraz. Lago.
**GPS:** n40,55296 e14,90615.
40 ⊟€ 20/24h, max. 4 pers 🚰Ch💧3kWh WC🗑included.
**Location:** Rural, isolated. **Surface:** grasstiles.
🗓 01/01-31/12.
**Distance:** 🚶12km 🏖100m 🛒on the spot 🍽50m.

| Benevento | 35B1 |
|---|---|

**Sannio Camper Club**, Via Domenico Mustilli.
**GPS:** n41,13141 e14,78960.

50 ⊟€ 10/24h 🚰Ch💧included.
**Location:** Urban. **Surface:** metalled. 🗓 01/01-31/12.
**Distance:** 🚶500m 🚲1,8km 🍽300m.

**Tourist information Benevento:**
🏛 Piazza Risorgimento en Piazza Santa Maria. 🗓 Wed, Sa 8-13h.

| Casalbore | 35B1 |
|---|---|

**Agriturismo Le Mainarde**, Mainardi 16. **GPS:** n41,24516 e15,00242.
30 ⊟€ 15 🚰Ch💧included. **Location:** Rural. **Surface:** asphalted.
🗓 01/01-31/12.
**Distance:** 🚶1,5km 🛒on the spot.

## Case del Conte ⬛S 35C1

**Cilento Il Brigantino**, Case del Conte Baia Arena.
**GPS:** n40,23652 e14,95882.

30 🅿€ 10-21 🚰€ 1,50 ⬛Ch🚿€ 0,33/h. **Location:** Rural.
**Surface:** grassy. ⬛ 01/01-31/12.
**Distance:** ⊗2km 🚌600m.

## Caserta ⬛S 35B1

**Area Sosta Camper Feudo San Martino**, Via Feudo di San Martino, 5.
**GPS:** n41,06522 e14,32889.⬆
60 🅿€ 20 🚰⬛Ch🚿 included.
**Location:** Urban. **Surface:** gravel.
**Distance:** 🚶on the spot ⊗250m 🚆300m.

## Castro dei Volsci ⬛S 35B1

Piazza S. Sosio. **GPS:** n41,52706 e13,36989.
20 🅿free 🚰⬛Ch🚿free. **Location:** Rural, simple.
**Surface:** asphalted. ⬛ 01/01-31/12.
**Distance:** ⊗50m.

## Cava de' Tirreni ⬛S 35B1

Via Ido Longo, loc. Sant'Arcangelo. **GPS:** n40,69984 e14,69553.
20 🅿free 🚰⬛Ch🚿free. **Location:** Urban. **Surface:** grasstiles.
⬛ 01/01-31/12.
**Distance:** 🚶on the spot 🚲2,3km 🚆300m 🚌on the spot.

**Tourist information Cava de' Tirreni:**
ℹ Salerno. City with medieval centre.
Ⓜ Museo Civico, Amalfi. Museum with Tavole Amalfitane, the old Law of the Sea. ⬛ 8-14h, Sa 8-12h ⬛ holiday.

## Contursi Terme ⬛S 35C1

**Agriturismo Il Giardino**, Loc. Prato. **GPS:** n40,64891 e15,23002.
5 🅿€ 15 🚰⬛Ch🚿 included. **Location:** Rural.
**Surface:** metalled. ⬛ 01/01-31/12.
**Distance:** 🚶1km 🚲4,4km ⊗on the spot.
**Remarks:** Le Terme Vulpacchio 50m, swimming pool available.

## Marina di Camerota ⬛S 35C1

**Parcheggio Europa**, Via Sirene. **GPS:** n40,00302 e15,36493.⬆
🅿 18 🚰⬛Ch⬛ included. **Surface:** unpaved.
⬛ Easter-30/09.
**Distance:** 🚆300m ⊗on the spot 🚌on the spot.

## Mondragone ⬛S 35B1

**Dun Area Camper**, Via Domiziana, km 15.250.
**GPS:** n41,13159 e13,86150.⬆

50 🅿€ 10-20 🚰⬛Ch🚿. **Surface:** grassy/sand. ⬛ 01/01-31/12.
**Distance:** 🚶Mondragone 4km 🚆on the spot ⊗on the spot 🚊3km 🚌on the spot.
**Remarks:** Monitored parking 24/24.

## Napoli ⬛S 🌊🏖🍦🚤 35B1

**Parking IPM**, Via Colli Aminei 27, Naples (Napoli).
**GPS:** n40,87038 e14,24616.

50 🅿€ 22/24h 🚰⬛Chincluded 🚿€ 2/24h,3Amp. **Location:** Urban.
**Surface:** asphalted. ⬛ 01/01-31/12.

---

**Distance:** 🚶on the spot 🚲1,2km ⊗200m 🚆400m 🚌bus R4 centre Napoli 30m.
**Remarks:** Monitored parking.

## Napoli ⬛S 🌊🏖🍦🚤 35B1

**Parking Patry**, Via Nuova Poggioreale 120, Naples (Napoli).
**GPS:** n40,86788 e14,29436.⬆
25 🅿€ 24/24h 🚰⬛Ch🚿 included. **Location:** Urban.
**Surface:** metalled. ⬛ 01/01-31/12.
**Distance:** 🚶2km 🚆350m 🚊450m 🚌metro 300m.
**Remarks:** Monitored parking.

**Tourist information Naples (Napoli):**
ℹ A.A.C.S.T.(Azienda Autonoma di Cura Soggiorno e Turismo), Palazzo Reale, www.regione.campania.it. Capital of the province with many monuments and cultural treasures.
👁 Vesuvio. Volcano, observatorium on western edge of the crater. Visit with guide possible.
👁 Mergellina. Small peninsula with fishing-port and marina.
👁 Teatro San Carlo. Opera building.
Ⓜ Museo Nazionale Archeologico di Napoli, Piazza Museo Nazionale 19. Antique hellenic-roman civilisation. ⬛ Tue-Su 9-14h.
✠ Palazzo Reale. Royal palace. ⬛ 9-13.30h ⬛ Mo.
✝ Duomo San Gennaro. Cathedral with original interior.
⌂ Ercolano/Herculaneum. Ancient city buried together with Pompeii. ⬛ 9-14.45h, holidays 9-18.15h.
⌂ Mercato Corso Malta. ⬛ Mo, Fri.

## Nusco ⬛S 35C1

Via Donato Antonio Mottola. **GPS:** n40,88629 e15,09040.⬆➡
30 🚰⬛Ch🚿. ⬛ 01/01-31/12.

## Camper Village Maremirtilli 35C1

**Camper Village Maremirtilli**, Via Linora di Paestum, SP278.
**GPS:** n40,37607 e15,00119.
70 🅿€ 20 🚰⬛Ch🚿 WC⬛. **Location:** Rural, isolated, quiet.
**Surface:** grassy. ⬛ 01/01-31/12.
**Distance:** 🚶4km 🚊on the spot ⊗2km.
**Remarks:** At sea.

## Paestum ⬛S 🌊🚤 35C1

**Mediterranea Camper Village**, Via Linora di Paestum.
**GPS:** n40,39570 e14,99817.
30 🅿€ 13-20 + € 3/pp tourist tax 🚰⬛Ch🚿WCincluded ⬛€ 3 🚿.
**Location:** Rural. **Surface:** grassy. ⬛ 01/01-31/12.
**Distance:** 🚶Paestum 3,5km 🚊50m ⊗1,5km 🚊1,5km 🚌400m.
**Remarks:** Bread-service and meals, playground.

## Paestum ⬛S 🌊 35C1

**Camper Park Zone Archeologica**, Via Magna Grecia, Capaccio Paestum.
**GPS:** n40,41851 e15,00697.⬆
30 🅿€ 10 🚰⬛Ch🚿. **Location:** Rural. **Surface:** unpaved.
⬛ 01/01-31/12.
**Distance:** 🚶300m 🚊1,6km ⊗50m 🚌50m.
**Remarks:** Paestum Excavations 200m.

## Paestum ⬛S 🌊 35C1

**Gli Eucalipti Area di Sosta**, Via Linora, 76, Capaccio.
**GPS:** n40,38565 e15,00308.
25 🅿€ 13-18 + € 2,50/pp tourist tax 🚰⬛Ch🚿⬛ included.
**Location:** Rural, comfortable, quiet. **Surface:** grassy.
⬛ 01/05-01/10.
**Distance:** 🚶4km 🚊50m ⊗on the spot 🚌on the spot 🏍on the spot.
**Remarks:** Shuttle bus.

## Paestum ⬛S 🌊 35C1

**Fattoria del Casaro**, Via Licinella 5, Capaccio Paestum.
**GPS:** n40,41504 e15,00505.⬆
20 🅿€ 10/24h 🚰⬛Ch🚿⬛included.
⬛ 01/01-31/12.
**Distance:** 🚶600m 🚊beach 1,8km ⊗on the spot.
**Remarks:** Paestum Excavations 300m, regional products and bread.

## Paestum ⬛S 🌊 35C1

**Camper Park Mandetta**, Via Torre di Mare 2.
**GPS:** n40,41486 e14,98954.⬆
20 🅿€ 25 🚰⬛Ch🚿 WCincluded ⬛€ 1 ⬛. **Location:** Rural, comfortable. **Surface:** unpaved. ⬛ 01/01-31/12.
**Distance:** 🚶1km 🚊200m ⊗on the spot 🚊250m.

**Tourist information Paestum:**
ℹ A.A.C.S.T.(Azienda Autonoma di Cura Soggiorno e Turismo), Via Magna Grecia, 151. Old city, founded by the Greeks. In the surroundings many vestiges from that time. ⬛ 9h-sunset.

## Palinuro ⬛S 35C1

**Sosta Camper Palorcio**, Via San Sebastiano, 39.
**GPS:** n40,03831 e15,31236.
35 🅿€ 13-23, 05/08-26/08 € 30 🚰⬛Ch🚿 WC⬛ 🚿 included.
**Location:** Rural, comfortable. **Surface:** grassy. ⬛ 01/06-30/09.
**Distance:** 🚊1km ⊗900m.

---

## Palinuro ⬛S 35C1

Via Palorcio. **GPS:** n40,03722 e15,30944.
🅿€ 20/24h 🚰⬛ChWC⬛included. **Location:** Rural.
**Surface:** unpaved. ⬛ 01/01-31/12.
**Distance:** 🚶3,5km 🚊700m 🚊700m 🚶on the spot.

## Pontecagnano Faiano ⬛S 35B1

**Camper Stop Italy**, Via Dei Navigatori. **GPS:** n40,60304 e14,86387.⬆
45 🅿€ 12-20 🚰⬛Ch🚿 🚿. **Location:** Comfortable.
**Surface:** grassy. ⬛ 01/01-31/12.
**Distance:** 🚊50m 🚊50m 🚌on the spot 🚶on the spot.

## Pozzuoli ⬛S 35B1

**Castagnaro Park**, Via del Castagnaro 1. **GPS:** n40,86939 e14,12150.⬆
85 🅿€ 15 🚰⬛Ch🚿(80x)€ 3/24h WC⬛€ 1,50 🚿included.
**Location:** Rural, comfortable.
**Surface:** grassy/gravel.
⬛ 01/01-31/12.
**Distance:** 🚶300m 🚲4km ⊗300m 🚆300m 🚌200m.
**Remarks:** Monitored parking, reservation during Christmas period.

**Tourist information Pozzuoli:**
ℹ Cuma. Archeological site. ⬛ 9-14.45h, summer 18h.

## Sala Consilina ⬛S 35C1

Via Santa Maria della Misericordia. **GPS:** n40,41376 e15,56397.⬆
20 🅿€ 5/night 🚰⬛Ch🚿 included. **Surface:** metalled.
⬛ 01/01-31/12.
**Distance:** 🚶1,5km 🚲300m ⊗500m 🚊2,5km 🚌1,5km 🚵15km 🏊15km.
**Remarks:** Behind hotel Vallis Dea.

## Salerno ⬛S 35B1

Via Giovanni Paolo. **GPS:** n40,65965 e14,80463.⬆
45 🅿€ 10 🚰⬛Ch🚿€ 5,6Amp. **Location:** Urban, central, noisy.
**Surface:** asphalted. ⬛ 01/01-31/12.
**Distance:** 🚶on the spot 🚊1,5km.

## San Marco ⬛S 🚤 35C1

**L'Angolo Verde**, Via Pozzillo 10. **GPS:** n40,27303 e14,94049.
30 🅿€ 13-15 🚰⬛Chincluded 🚿 WC⬛free. **Location:** Urban, comfortable, luxurious. **Surface:** gravel. ⬛ 01/01-31/12.
**Distance:** 🚊150m.
**Remarks:** Possibility for reservation.

## Tramonti ⬛S 🏔🏔 35B1

**Agriturismo Costiera Amalfitana**, Via Falcone, 12 - Frazione Pietre.
**GPS:** n40,69929 e14,61811.⬆

22 🛏 € 22, 15/06-31/08 and 23/12-06/01 € 30 🚰🗑Ch⚡included
WC🚿. **Location:** Rural, comfortable. **Surface:** grassy/gravel.
🅿 01/01-31/12.
**Distance:** 🚶50m ⛵15km 🏖6km ⊗on the spot 🍴30m 🎯500m
�læ on the spot.
**Remarks:** Amalfi Coast, regional products.

# Basilicata

## 🌿S Grumento Nova 35C1
**Agriturismo Al Parco Verde**, Contrada Spineto, Moliterno-Grumento.
**GPS:** n40,28110 e15,90563.⬆➡.
20 🛏 € 20 🚰🗑Ch⚡WC🚿included. **Location:** Rural.
**Surface:** grassy. 🅿 01/06-01/10.
**Distance:** 🚶8km 🏖2km ⊗on the spot 🍴5km �train on the spot ⛽2km
🚠1km.
**Remarks:** Archeological site 200m.

## 🚐S Matera 🌿 35C1
**Area Camper Matera**, SS7, Via Appia. **GPS:** n40,67981 e16,62126.⬆.
25 🛏 € 14/24h 🚰🗑Ch⚡WC📶included. **Surface:** metalled.
🅿 01/01-31/12.
**Distance:** 🚶centre 3,5km.

## 🚐S Matera 🌿 35C1
**Parco Serra Venerdì**, Via dei Normanni. **GPS:** n40,66814 e16,58960.⬆.

12 🛏 € 18/24h 🚰⚡1 🗑Ch⚡2 WC🚿📶. **Location:** Rural,
comfortable, quiet. **Surface:** metalled. 🅿 01/01-31/12.
**Distance:** 🚶1,8km 🚠200m on the spot.

## 🚐S Metaponto 🌿 35C1
**Camper parking Nettuno**, Viale Magna Grecia, Metaponto Lido.
**GPS:** n40,35693 e16,83221.⬆.

50 🛏 € 13/24h, Jul/Aug € 18 🚰🗑Ch⚡WCincluded 🚿1.
**Location:** Rural. **Surface:** grassy/gravel. 🅿 01/01-31/12.
**Distance:** 🏖50m ⊗on the spot 🍴300m.
**Tourist information Metaponto:**
🏛 Archeological site. 🅿 9h-sunset.

## 🚐S Nova Siri 35C1
Via Tre Passi nel Delirio. **GPS:** n40,12801 e16,65424.⬆.
9 🛏 € 10 🚰🗑Chfree ⚡. **Location:** Rural. **Surface:** metalled.
🅿 01/01 31/12.
**Distance:** 🚶1,5km 🏖100m ⊗550m on the spot.
**Remarks:** Video surveillance.

## 🚐S Nuvolera 23D3
Via Scaiola. **GPS:** n45,52818 e10,36769.
4 🛏free. **Location:** Urban, simple. **Surface:** asphalted.
🅿 01/01-31/12.
**Distance:** 🏖10km ⊗75m 🍴100m.

# Calabria

## 🚐S Amantea 35C2
**Garden Park Caterina**, SS. 18, loc Coreca.
**GPS:** n39,09383 e16,08508.⬆.
10 🛏 € 20-25, 4 pers.incl 🚰🗑Ch⚡2,50 WCincluded 🚿1 🎯5.
**Location:** Rural, comfortable. **Surface:** grassy.
🅿 15/06-15/09.
**Distance:** 🚶on the spot 🏖on the spot 🚠on the spot ⊗nearby.

## 🚐S Bova Marina 35C3
**Mafalda's Camper Park**, Via Sotto Ferrovia, loc. San Pasquale.
**GPS:** n37,92422 e15,94800.⬆➡.
20 🛏 € 10-20 🚰🗑Ch⚡included 🚿. **Location:** Rural, comfortable,
isolated. **Surface:** gravel/sand. 🅿 01/01-31/12.
**Distance:** 🚶3km 🏖on the spot ⊗200m 🍴500m.

---

**Remarks:** Accessible via unpaved road, video surveillance.

## 🍴S Camigliatello Silano 35C2
**Rifugio dei Peccatori di Gola**, Strada per il Lago Cecita, SS17.
**GPS:** n39,35852 e16,48655.⬆.
20 🛏 € 15-19 🚰🗑Ch⚡WC. **Location:** Rural. **Surface:** grassy.
🅿 01/01-31/12.
**Distance:** 🚶4,5km 🏖1km ⊗on the spot.

## 🍴S Catanzaro Marina 🏖 35D2
**Il Chioschetto**, Via Carlo Pisacane 24. **GPS:** n38,83321 e16,64862.

10 🛏free 🚰⚡. **Location:** Simple. **Surface:** sand.
**Distance:** 🏖Sandy beach.

## 🚐S Cirella 35C1
**Area Camper Ulisse**, SS 18 km 270, Diamante.
**GPS:** n39,72500 e15,80930.

130 🛏 € 10-25, 4 pers.incl 🚰🗑Ch⚡WC🚿included 🎯📶.
**Location:** Rural. **Surface:** grassy/sand. 🅿 01/04-31/10.
**Distance:** 🚶800m 🏖on the spot 🚠on the spot ⊗on the spot
🍴on the spot 🎯on the spot.

## 🚐S Cirella 35C1
**Lido Alexander**, SS 18, Diamante. **GPS:** n39,72168 e15,81097.⬆.

50 🛏 € 8-17, 2 pers. incl. 🚰🗑Ch⚡3 WCincluded 🚿1 📶3.
**Location:** Rural. **Surface:** grassy/gravel. 🅿 01/01-31/12.
**Distance:** 🚶1,5km 🏖on the spot 🚠on the spot ⊗on the spot
🍴on the spot.

## 🚐S Cirella 35C1
**Lido delle Sirene**, SS 18, Contr. Riviere. **GPS:** n39,71822 e15,81137.➡.

100 🛏 € 13 🚰🗑Chincluded ⚡2 WC🚿.
**Location:** Rural. **Surface:** grassy.
🅿 01/01-31/12.
**Distance:** 🚶1km 🏖on the spot 🚠on the spot ⊗on the spot 🍴1km.

## 🚐S Cirella 35C1
**Lido Tropical**, Viale Glauco, 9, Diamante. **GPS:** n39,69222 e15,81556.⬆.

---

200 🛏 € 8-30, 4 pers.incl, dog € 2 🚰🗑Ch⚡included,4Amp
WC🚿. **Location:** Urban. **Surface:** grassy/sand.
🅿 01/01-31/12.
**Distance:** 🚶1,5km 🏖on the spot 🚠on the spot ⊗200m 🍴200m
�læ shuttle to town.
**Remarks:** Swimming pool available.

## 🚐S Cirò Marina 35D2
Via Maddalena. **GPS:** n39,35998 e17,12910.
25 🛏 € 6, 01/06-31/08 € 12 🚰⚡.
**Surface:** unpaved. 🅿 01/01-31/12.
**Distance:** 🚶1,2km 🏖50m.

## 🚐S Cirò Marina 35D2
**Village "Le Casette"**, Località Difesa Piana. **GPS:** n39,39815 e17,13625.
25 🛏 € 15-25 🚰🗑Ch⚡included.
**Location:** Rural. **Surface:** grassy/sand. 🅿 01/01-31/12.
**Distance:** 🚶4km 🏖300m ⊗on the spot 🚠.

## 🚐S Cittadella del Capo 35C2
**Torre Parise**, Via Parise. **GPS:** n39,56580 e15,87399.⬆.
16 🛏 € 15, Jul/Aug € 18, 3 pers. incl 🚰🗑Chincluded ⚡WC🚿.
**Location:** Rural. **Surface:** grassy. 🅿 01/01-31/12.
**Distance:** 🚶1,5km 🏖200m 🍴500m 🚠1km �train900m.
**Remarks:** Breakfast-service, swimming pool.

## 🌿S Condofuri Marina 35C3
**Agriturismo Antonino Gemelli**, Via Salinella 37.
**GPS:** n37,92372 e15,85150.⬆.
20 🛏 € 18-24 🚰🗑Ch⚡WC🚿🎯📶. **Location:** Rural.
**Surface:** gravel/sand. 🅿 01/01-31/12.
**Distance:** 🚶500m 🏖100m 🚠2km 🍴1km �train2,5km.

## 🍴S Corigliano Calabro 35C1
**B&B Club Tepee**, Contrada Sant'Agata 42, SS106bis > Cantinella.
**GPS:** n39,64528 e16,39909.
20 🛏 € 10 🗑Chincluded ⚡WC🚿.
**Location:** Rural. 🅿 01/01-31/12.
**Distance:** 🚶Corigliano 14km ⊗on the spot.

## 🚐S Cropani Marina 🏖 35D2
**Sena Park**, Viale Venezia 34. **GPS:** n38,91143 e16,80963.⬆➡.

25 🛏 € 12-28, 2 pers.incl 🚰🗑Ch⚡🚿3 WC🚿0,50 🎯📶included.
**Location:** Rural. **Surface:** grassy/sand. 🅿 01/01-31/12.
**Distance:** 🚶500m 🏖400m 🚠400m ⊗ristorante/pizzeria 🍴500m
�train station 2km.
**Remarks:** Playground, washing motorhome € 20.

## 🚐S Crotone 35D2
**Hera Lacinia Mare**, Via Filippo, 47, Campione III.
**GPS:** n39,00311 e17,16984.⬆.
10 🛏 € 20 🚰🗑Chincluded ⚡5 🚿.
**Surface:** gravel/metalled. 🅿 20/06-01/09.
**Distance:** 🚶on the spot 🏖on the spot 🚠on the spot ⊗100m 🍴200m.

## 🚐S Fuscaldo 35C2
**Tropical**, Via Lago Sotto Strada. **GPS:** n39,44123 e15,99678.⬆.

45 🗓€ 23 🚿⚡Ch🔌 WC🚽📶. **Location:** Comfortable.
**Surface:** gravel. ⏰ 01/01-31/12.
**Distance:** 🏖on the spot 🛒600m.

**📷S** Morano Calabro 🏖 **35C1**
Via Gaetano Scorza. **GPS:** n39,84098 e16,13731. ⬆➡.

10 🗓free 🚿⚡. **Location:** Urban, simple. **Surface:** asphalted.
⏰ 01/01-31/12.
**Distance:** 🏖200m 🚲7km ⊗200m 🛒200m.
**Remarks:** Next to church of San Bernardino, panoramic view.

**📷S** Palmi 🏖 **35C2**
Sosta Camper Prajola, Lungomare Donna Canfora.
**GPS:** n38,39333 e15,86277. ⬆➡.

25 🗓€ 15/24h 🚿⚡Ch🔌 included 📶. **Location:** Simple.
**Surface:** gravel. ⏰ 01/01-31/12.
**Distance:** 🏖on the spot.

**📷S** Praia a Mare 🏖 **35C1**
Nuova Playa, Contr. Fiucci. **GPS:** n39,86885 e15,78943. ⬆.

15 🗓€ 25, peak season € 35 🚿⚡Ch🔌 WC🚽included.
**Location:** Rural. **Surface:** grassy. ⏰ 01/01-31/12.

---

**Distance:** 🏖2km 🏖on the spot 🎣on the spot ⊗100m 🛒2km.
**Remarks:** Black sandy beach, in front of Dino island, barbecue place,
playground.

**📷S** Rossano 🏖 **35C1**
Sosta Camper Il Faro, C. da Foresta Faro Campo Trionto.
**GPS:** n39,62148 e16,75146. ⬆.

12 🗓€ 18-25, 2 pers. incl. 🚿⚡Ch🔌 WC🚽included.
**Location:** Rural, comfortable, isolated. **Surface:** grassy.
⏰ 01/03-31/10.
**Distance:** 🏖2km, Rossano 12km 🏖Sandy beach ⊗on the spot.
**Remarks:** Regional products.

**📷S** Santa Maria del Cedro 🏖 **35C1**
Sosta Camper Manuel, Via Lipari ss18. **GPS:** n39,75428 e15,80431.

50 🗓€ 15 🚿⚡Ch🔌 WC🚽included. **Location:** Urban, central,
noisy. **Surface:** grassy. ⏰ 01/01-31/12.
**Distance:** 🏖1km 🏖on the spot ⊗on the spot 🛒on the spot 🚶on
the spot 🚶on the spot.

**📷S** Scalea 🏖 **35C1**
Dolce Vita, Via Fiume Lao 7. **GPS:** n39,79667 e15,79265. ⬆.

100 🗓€ 16-21 🚿⚡Ch🔌€ 5 WC🚽€ 0,50 📶. **Location:** Rural.
**Surface:** grassy. ⏰ 01/05-30/09.
**Distance:** 🏖on the spot 🏖on the spot 🎣on the spot ⊗on the spot
🛒800m 🚶on the spot.

**📷S** Scalea 🏖 **35C1**
Lido Zio Tom, Corso Mediterraneo km 261,7.
**GPS:** n39,81306 e15,78917. ⬆.

---

140 🗓€ 10-20 🚿⚡Ch🔌 included,4Amp WC🚽€ 1.
**Location:** Rural. **Surface:** grassy/gravel.
⏰ 15/04-15/10.
**Distance:** 🏖600m 🏖on the spot ⊗300m 🛒400m 🚉station 1,5km.
**Remarks:** Bar, barbecue place, shuttle bus to city centre.

**📷S** Scalea 🏖 **35C1**
Area Lido Zio Tom, Corso Mediterraneo 94.
**GPS:** n39,80092 e15,79087. ⬆.
40 🗓€ 20/24h 🚿⚡Ch🔌 WC🚽€ 0,50. **Location:** Rural, simple,
isolated. **Surface:** grassy/gravel. ⏰ 01/01-31/12.
**Distance:** 🏖2km 🏖on the spot ⊗400m 🛒950m 🚶on the spot.

**📷S** Trebisacce 🏖 **35C1**
Blue Marine, Via Lungomare. **GPS:** n39,87512 e16,54189.
30 🗓€ 12,50 🚿⚡Ch🔌 included. **Location:** Rural.
**Surface:** unpaved. ⏰ 01/01-31/12.
**Distance:** 🏖1km 🏖on the spot ⊗500m 🛒850m.

# Sardinia

**📷S** Aglientu 🏖 **33G2**
Oasi Gallura, Localita'Vignola Mare 19, SP 90 km 53.
**GPS:** n41,12556 e9,06167.

95 🗓€ 20-24, 2 pers.incl 🚿⚡Ch🔌€ 3 WC🚽€ 6 📶included. 🐕
🧺 **Location:** Rural, comfortable, quiet. **Surface:** grassy/sand.
**Distance:** 🏖on the spot 🏖sandy beach 50m ⊗100m 🛒100m.

**📷S** Alghero 🏖 **33G2**

I Platani Area Camper Alghero, Strada vicinale Arenosu 2.
**GPS:** n40,60699 e8,27463.
🗓€ 15-30 🚿⚡Ch🔌 WC🚽€ 0,50/2minutes 🔌€ 5 📶included.
**Location:** Comfortable. **Surface:** grassy. ⏰ 01/01-31/12.
**Distance:** 🏖Alghero 7km 🏖1,5km.
**Remarks:** Monitored parking 24/24, free shuttle to beach and super-
market, dogs beach.

**📷S** Alghero 🏖 **33G2**
Paradise Park, Loc. Le Bombarde. **GPS:** n40,59180 e8,25610. ⬆➡.

150 🗓€ 18-25 🚿⚡Ch🔌 WC🚽€ 0,50/2minutes 🔌€ 5 📶included.
**Location:** Rural, comfortable, quiet. **Surface:** grassy/gravel.
⏰ 01/05-01/10.
**Distance:** 🏖2km 🏖1km ⊗on the spot 🛒on the spot 🚌50m.
**Remarks:** Free shuttle to beach and supermarket.

---

IT

## Arborea — 33G3

**Corsaro Beach**, Str. 26 Ovest. **GPS**: n39,80187 e8,54956.⬆.

10 🚐€ 5-10. **Surface:** forest soil. 🅿 15/06-15/09.
**Distance:** ⛱sandy beach 100m ⊗400m.
**Remarks:** To be paid at bar.

## Arbus — 33G3

**Spiaggia Scivu**, SC Scivu. **GPS**: n39,49426 e8,41444.⬆.

+50 🚐free, summer € 10/day, overnight stay free 🚐1.
**Location:** Isolated. **Surface:** gravel/sand. 🅿 01/01-31/12.
**Distance:** ⛱sandy beach 100m, stairs ⊗on the spot.
**Remarks:** Bar.

## Baradili — 33G3

**Area sosta camper Baradili**, Via Bia Genuri 1.
**GPS**: n39,72260 e8,89860.
10 🚐free 🚰€ 1 🚿€ 6/24h.
**Location:** Rural. **Surface:** grassy. 🅿 01/01-31/12.
**Distance:** ⊗100m.

## Bosa — 33G2

**S'Abba Drucche Spiagge**, SP49 Alghero-Bosa km 38+800.
**GPS**: n40,31641 e8,47352.⬆.

100 🚐€ 20 🚰🔌Ch🚿(96x),6Amp WCincluded 🚐1 🔌€ 5 📶 2.
**Location:** Rural, simple, isolated, quiet. **Surface:** unpaved.
🅿 15/03-30/10.
**Distance:** 🚶7km ⛱on the spot ⊗on the spot.
**Remarks:** Discount longer stays.

## Bosa — 33G2

**Parcheggio Nassiriya**, Via Sas Conzas. **GPS**: n40,29472 e8,49922.⬆➡.

10 🚐free. **Location:** Urban, simple. **Surface:** asphalted.
🅿 01/01-31/12.
**Distance:** 🚶300m ⊗150m.
**Remarks:** Along river.

## Bosa — 33G2

**Casa del Vento**, SP49. **GPS**: n40,32886 e8,43628.⬆.

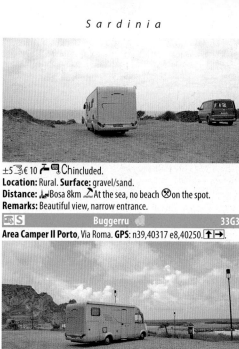

±5 🚐€ 10 🚰🔌Chincluded.
**Location:** Rural. **Surface:** gravel/sand.
**Distance:** 🚶Bosa 8km ⛱At the sea, no beach ⊗on the spot.
**Remarks:** Beautiful view, narrow entrance.

## Buggerru — 33G3

**Area Camper Il Porto**, Via Roma. **GPS**: n39,40317 e8,40250.⬆➡.

50 🚐€ 5-15, Jul/Aug € 20 🚰🔌Ch🚿€ 5. 🚮
**Surface:** sand. 🅿 01/04-31/10.
**Distance:** 🚶800m ⛱on the spot ⊗400m 🏖800m.
**Remarks:** Beach parking.

## Buggerru — 33G3

**Punta Sosta San Nicolao**, Loc. Cala Domestica.
**GPS**: n39,41757 e8,41147.⬆.

20 🚐€ 10 🚰Chincluded 🚿cold shower.
**Surface:** grassy/sand. 🅿 01/05-30/10.
**Distance:** 🚶4km ⛱sandy beach 50m ⊗50m.
**Remarks:** Beach parking.

## Cabras — 33G3

**Tanca Is Muras**, Località Mari Ermi. **GPS**: n39,96226 e8,40324.⬆.

🚐€ 12 🚿included. **Location:** Isolated. 🅿 01/05-01/10.
**Distance:** ⛱Sandy beach.

## Cagliari — 33G3

**Campernow**, Via Gerolamo Cardano. **GPS**: n39,23580 e9,13832.⬆.

10 🚐€ 17, 2 pers. incl 🚰🔌Ch🚿WC🔌€ 4 📶included.
**Location:** Urban, central, noisy. **Surface:** metalled.
🅿 20/04-15/10.
**Distance:** 🚶city centre 3km ⊗150m 🏪Lidl 100m 🚌100m.
**Remarks:** Barbecue place.

## Cagliari — 33G3

**Camper Cagliari Park**, Via Stanislao Caboni. **GPS**: n39,21024 e9,12772.

150 🚐€ 20 🚰🔌Ch🚿€ 5 WC🔌€ 0,50 📶included.
**Location:** Urban, comfortable, central. **Surface:** asphalted.
🅿 01/01-31/12.
**Distance:** 🚶city centre 1,5km 🚌300m.
**Remarks:** Monitored parking.

## Cala Gonone — 33G2

**Palmasera**, Viale Bue Marino. **GPS**: n40,27954 e9,62993.⬆.

100 🚐€ 20, Jul/Aug € 25-30 🚰🔌Ch🚿WC🔌€ 0,50
🔌€ 5 📶included. 🚮 **Location:** Rural, comfortable, quiet.
**Surface:** unpaved. 🅿 01/04-31/10.
**Distance:** 🚶800m ⛱500m 🍴ristoro 🏖200m 🚌on the spot.
**Remarks:** Shuttle bus to beach.

## Cala Sinzias — 33G3

SP18. **GPS**: n39,18912 e9,56273.

10 🚐free, summer € 10.
**Location:** Simple. **Surface:** sand. 🅿 01/01-31/12.
**Distance:** ⛱sandy beach 50m ⊗on the spot.
**Remarks:** Beach parking, pay in at kiosk.

## Cardedu — 33G3

**Cucamonga**, Marina di Gairo. **GPS**: n39,75397 e9,67130.⬆.

±20 🚐€ 10 🚰🔌Chincluded WC🚿. **Location:** Rural, isolated, quiet.
**Surface:** sand. 🅿 01/01-31/12.
**Distance:** ⛱pebbled beach 🏖7km.

## Cardedu — 33G3

**Motorpark I Ginepri**, Località Baccu e Ludu.
**GPS**: n39,77181 e9,63886.⬆.
🚐€ 20 🚰🔌Ch🚿€ 3 WC🚿included 📶.
**Location:** Rural, simple, isolated, quiet. **Surface:** grassy/gravel.
🅿 01/01-31/12.
**Distance:** ⛱1,8km.
**Remarks:** Monitored parking 24/24, free shuttle.

## Domus de Maria — 33G3

**Area Camper Chia**, Su Giudeu, Capo Spartivento, Chia.
**GPS**: n38,89128 e8,86264.⬆➡.

IT

100 ⬛€ 16-20 🚰 Ch 💧 WC included 🚿 € 0,50. ♨️
**Location:** Rural, comfortable. **Surface:** sand. 📅 Easter-01/11.
**Distance:** 🏖on the spot ⊗400m 🍴900m.

### Dorgali 33G2
**Argiturismo S'Ozzastra. GPS:** n40,33899 e9,60767.

15 ⬛€ 25-35 🚰€ 5 ⬛€ 8 Ch € 8 💧(12x)WC 📶 included ♨️.
**Location:** Rural, isolated, quiet. **Surface:** gravel.
📅 01/04-31/10.
**Distance:** 🏖5km ⚓5km 🚤5km ⊗2km 🍴5km.
**Remarks:** Dog on leads.

### Golfo Aranci 33G2
**Playa Vistas Chulas,** Via Cala Moresca. **GPS:** n40,98826 e9,63589.

±20 ⬛free. **Location:** Isolated. **Surface:** gravel/sand.
📅 01/01-31/12.
**Distance:** 🏖2km ⚓on the spot 🏃on the spot.
**Remarks:** 1km unpaved road, max. ^3.2m, beach parking, no camping activities.

### Gonnosnò 33G3
**Area sosta camper Gonnosnò,** Via Enrico Fermi.
**GPS:** n39,75870 e8,87540.
5 ⬛free 🚰€ 1 Ch 💧€ 6/24h. **Location:** Urban.
**Surface:** grassy/gravel. 📅 01/01-31/12.
**Distance:** 🏖on the spot ⊗250m.

### Masua 33G3
**La Nuova Colonia,** Masua Porto Flavia. **GPS:** n39,33409 e8,42052.

50 ⬛€ 18 🚰Ch included 💧€ 3 🍴free,at restaurant.
**Location:** Rural, isolated, quiet. **Surface:** unpaved.
📅 01/04-31/10.
**Distance:** ⚓sandy beach 50m, stairs ⊗on the spot.
**Remarks:** Former mineral mines, tour Porto Flavia.

### Nuoro 33G2
P.le Anfiteatro cittadino, Piazza Veneto. **GPS:** n40,31447 e9,32807.

5 ⬛free 🚰Ch free. **Surface:** asphalted. 📅 01/01-31/12.
**Distance:** 🏖1,2km.

### Olbia 33G2
**Camper service Marina di Cugnana,** Località Marina di Cugnana, SP73.
**GPS:** n41,02042 e9,51441.

30 ⬛€ 1,50/h, € 25/24h 🚰Ch 📶 included.
**Location:** Rural, isolated, noisy. **Surface:** grassy/gravel.
📅 01/05-30/09.
**Distance:** 🏖Olbia 12km ⚓on the spot ⊗on the spot.
**Remarks:** Shuttle bus to beach, swimming pool.

### Oristano 33G3
**Stadio Tharros,** Via Dorando Petri. **GPS:** n39,89710 e8,58927.
🚰Ch free. 📅 01/01-31/12.

### Orosei 33G2
**Osalla Beach Garden,** Osalla di Orosei. **GPS:** n40,34474 e9,68619.

34 ⬛€ 15-20 🚰Ch 💧WC included 🚿€ 0,50. **Location:** Rural, comfortable, quiet. **Surface:** gravel/sand. 📅 Easter-15/10.
**Distance:** ⚓300m ⊗on the spot 🍴3,5km.

### Quartu Sant'Elena 33G3
**Is Canaleddus,** Viale L. da vinci, SP17. **GPS:** n39,17957 e9,36489.

⬛€ 10 ♨️. **Surface:** unpaved. 📅 01/05-01/10.
**Distance:** ⚓pebbeled beach 150m ⊗on the spot.
**Remarks:** Beach parking.

### San Nicolò d'Arcidano 33G3
Viale Dei Giardini. **GPS:** n39,68530 e8,64570.

4 ⬛€ 5 🚰€ 4 ⬛€ 4 Ch € 4 💧€ 4.
**Surface:** asphalted. 📅 01/01-31/12.
**Distance:** 🏖on the spot.

### San Teodoro 33G2
Via Donat Cattin. **GPS:** n40,76658 e9,66884.

30 ⬛€ 8. 🚐
**Location:** Simple, noisy. **Surface:** asphalted. 📅 01/01-31/12.
**Distance:** 🏖800m ⚓1,8km ⊗100m.

### Sant'Anna Arresi 33G3
**Sosta camper Il Ruscello,** Via del Cormorano, loc. Is Pillonis.
**GPS:** n38,97772 e8,62317.

80 ⬛€ 17-22 🚰Ch 💧WC 📅€ 4 📶 included. **Location:** Rural,
comfortable, isolated. **Surface:** grassy/gravel. 📅 01/01-31/12.
**Distance:** ⚓3,5km ⊗on the spot.
**Remarks:** Shuttle bus to beach.

### Semestene 33G2
SP8. **GPS:** n40,39777 e8,72926.
15 ⬛free 🚰Ch 💧.
**Location:** Rural, noisy. **Surface:** gravel. 📅 01/01-31/12.
**Distance:** ⊗400m.

### Sini 33G3
**Area sosta camper Sini,** Via Argiolas. **GPS:** n39,74980 e8,90280.
5 ⬛free 🚰€ 1 Ch 💧€ 6/24h. **Location:** Rural. **Surface:** gravel.
📅 01/01-31/12.
**Distance:** ⊗500m 🍴4km.

### Siniscola 33G2
**Spiaggia di Berchida. GPS:** n40,48064 e9,80680.

+50 ⬛€ 12/day 🚰. **Location:** Rural, isolated. **Surface:** unpaved.
📅 01/01-31/12.
**Distance:** 🏖on the spot.

### Solanas 33G3
Via al Mare. **GPS:** n39,13333 e9,43254.

10 ⬛free. **Surface:** sand.
**Distance:** 🏖300m ⚓Sandy beach ⊗300m.
**Remarks:** Beach parking.

### Sorso 33G2
**Camp Site International,** Via degli Oleandri, SP 81 km 13, Platamona Lido. **GPS:** n40,81566 e8,46563.

IT

120 ⌇€ 20-26 🚰🔌Ch🚿WC🚽🔌€ 5 📶included. ♿
**Location:** Comfortable, quiet. **Surface:** unpaved.
🅿 01/04-30/09.
**Distance:** ⚓350m 🛒2km 🚌on the spot.

| | Stintino | | 33G2 |
|---|---|---|---|

**La Pineta**, Loc. Pozzo S.Nicola, SP34. **GPS:** n40,86843 e8,23610.⬆.

40 ⌇€ 19-21 🚰🔌Ch🚿 WCincluded 🚽€ 1,hot shower € 1 🔌€ 5.
**Location:** Rural. **Surface:** grassy/sand. 🅿 01/01-31/12.
**Distance:** ⚓3,5km ⊗on the spot.

| | Tancau sul Mare | | 33G3 |
|---|---|---|---|

**Area attrezzata Costa Orientale**, Viale Mare.
**GPS:** n39,98321 e9,68608.⬆➡.

55 ⌇€ 10-25, Jul/Aug electricity € 3,50 🚰🔌Ch🚿 WC🚽included
🔌€ 4. ♿ **Location:** Rural, comfortable. **Surface:** asphalted/sand.
🅿 Easter-31/10.
**Distance:** ⚓Santa Maria Navarese 900m 🏊sandy beach 50m ⊗50m
🛒250m.
**Remarks:** Shady.

| | Tonara | | 33G3 |
|---|---|---|---|

**Ostello delle Gioventù**, Via Muggianeddu, 2. **GPS:** n40,02855 e9,17542.
5 ⌇€ 10/24h 🚰🔌Ch🚿included.
**Surface:** metalled. 🅿 01/01-31/12.
**Distance:** ⚓500m ⊗on the spot.
**Remarks:** Steep ramp.

| | Tortolì | | 33G3 |
|---|---|---|---|

**Baia Cea**, Via del Muflone. **GPS:** n39,86874 e9,68034.⬆.

80 ⌇€ 16-20 🚰🔌Ch🚿€ 2,2Amp WC🚽included,cold shower.
**Location:** Rural, comfortable. **Surface:** unpaved.
🅿 01/01-31/12.
**Distance:** ⚓Tortolì 5km 🏖sandy beach 50m ⊗100m.

| | Tortolì | | 33G3 |
|---|---|---|---|

**Area Camper Rocce Rosse**, Via del Muflone. **GPS:** n39,86865 e9,67924.

70 ⌇€ 15-25, Aug € 35 🔌€ 4.
**Location:** Rural. **Surface:** sand. 🅿 01/06-30/09.
**Distance:** ⚓Tortolì 9km 🏖sandy beach 250m ⊗on the spot 🛒mini
market.
**Remarks:** Shady.

| | Tuili | 33G3 |
|---|---|---|

**GPS:** n39,73182 e8,97453.
3 ⌇free. **Location:** Rural, simple, isolated. **Surface:** gravel.
🅿 01/01-31/12.
**Distance:** ⚓5km 🚶on the spot.

| | Valledoria | | 33G2 |
|---|---|---|---|

**Punto Maragnani**, Via La Ciaccia, Loc. Maragnani.
**GPS:** n40,92021 e8,79240.⬆.

90 ⌇€ 20/24h 🚰🔌Ch🚿 WC🚽 📶included. ♿
**Location:** Rural, comfortable, quiet. **Surface:** metalled/sand.
🅿 01/01-31/12.
**Distance:** ⚓50m 🛒200m.
**Remarks:** Motorhome washing place.

| | Villaputzu | | 33G3 |
|---|---|---|---|

**Bella Vista Camper Service**, Località Prumari, Porto corallo.
**GPS:** n39,43820 e9,63243.

50 ⌇€ 12-25 🚰🔌Ch🚿 WC🚽€ 0,50 🔌€ 5 📶included.
**Location:** Rural, comfortable. **Surface:** gravel. 🅿 01/01-31/12.
**Distance:** ⚓Villaputzu 6km 🏖50m ⊗500m 🛒7km.

| | Villasimius | | 33G3 |
|---|---|---|---|

**Gli Aranci**, Viale dei Carrubi, loc. Pranu Zinnigas.
**GPS:** n39,15977 e9,50865.⬆➡.

100 ⌇€ 22 🚰🔌Ch🚿 WC🚽included. **Location:** Rural, comfortable,
quiet. **Surface:** unpaved. 🅿 01/01-31/12.
**Distance:** ⚓2km ⚓4km ⊗100m 🛒Eurospin 1km.
**Remarks:** Shuttle bus to beach.

# Sicily

| | Agrigento | | 35B3 |
|---|---|---|---|

**Albachiara**, Viale delle Dune 89, San Leone.
**GPS:** n37,24824 e13,60837.⬆.

40 ⌇€ 15-30 🚰🔌Ch🚿 WC🚽included 📶. 🍴♿ **Location:** Rural,
luxurious, quiet. **Surface:** grassy. 🅿 01/01-31/12.
**Distance:** ⚓2,5km ⚓on the spot ⊗on the spot 🚌on the spot.

| | Agrigento | | 35B3 |
|---|---|---|---|

**Il Pepe Rosa**, Strada Statale Occidentale. **GPS:** n37,23082 e13,68551.⬆.
20 ⌇€ 15 🚰🔌Ch🚿 WC🚽🔌.
**Location:** Rural. **Surface:** gravel. 🅿 01/01-31/12.
**Distance:** ⊗4km.
**Remarks:** Barbecue place.

| | Agrigento | | 35B3 |
|---|---|---|---|

**Valle dei Templi**, Viale Caduti di Marzabotto. **GPS:** n37,28881 e13,58181.
50 ⌇€ 5. **Location:** Simple. **Surface:** sand. 🅿 01/01-31/12.
**Distance:** ⊗450m 🚌on the spot.
**Remarks:** Near entrance and pay-desk of Valle dei Templi.

| | Augusta | 35C3 |
|---|---|---|

**Area Attrezzata Camper Nelly**, SS114 - Km 118,5, Contrada Agnone
Bagni. **GPS:** n37,31148 e15,09260.
⌇€ 15-18 🚰🔌Ch🚿 WCincluded 🚽€ 1 🔌€ 3. **Location:** Rural,
simple, isolated, quiet. **Surface:** gravel. 🅿 15/05-15/09.
**Distance:** 🚣6km ⚓1,5km ⊗180m.

| | Caccamo | 35B3 |
|---|---|---|

SS 285, Via Termitana. **GPS:** n37,93410 e13,66115.⬆.
10 ⌇free 🚰🔌Ch🚿 free. **Location:** Urban, simple.
**Surface:** gravel/metalled. 🅿 01/01-31/12.
**Distance:** ⚓900m ⊗300m 🛒650m.
**Remarks:** At castle.

| | Caltagirone | 35C3 |
|---|---|---|

**Piazzale San Giovanni**, Loc. San Giovanni.
**GPS:** n37,23949 e14,50717.⬆.
10 ⌇€ 4, overnight stay free 🚰🔌Chincluded.
**Location:** Urban. **Surface:** asphalted. 🅿 01/01-31/12.
**Distance:** ⚓historical centre 700m ⊗250m.

| | Caltanissetta | 35B3 |
|---|---|---|

Via Guastaferro. **GPS:** n37,48959 e14,04515.⬆➡.
25 ⌇free 🚰🔌Ch free. **Location:** Urban, simple, noisy.
**Surface:** asphalted. 🅿 01/01-31/12.
**Distance:** ⚓2km ⊗on the spot 🛒on the spot.
**Remarks:** Near post office.

| | Tortolì | | 33G3 |
|---|---|---|---|

**Tanca Orrì**, Lido Orrì. **GPS:** n39,90364 e9,68204.⬆.

60 ⌇€ 10-35 🚰🔌Ch🚿 WC🚽included. **Location:** Rural,
comfortable. **Surface:** sand. 🅿 01/05-30/09.
**Distance:** ⚓Tortolì 9km 🏊on the spot ⊗on the spot.

IT

## Camporotondo Etneo — 35C3

**Camperlot**
**Catania - Camporotondo Etneo**

- Open all year
- Comfortable motorhome stopover
- Excellent location

www.camperlot.it
camperlot.it@gmail.com

**Camperlot**, Via A. Tripoli. **GPS**: n37,53593 e14,99321.
25 € 10-16 Ch WC. **Location**: Rural. **Surface**: grassy/metalled. 01/01-31/12.
**Distance**: 12km 650m 650m.
**Remarks**: 20km from Etna, phone +39 3925919944 / +39 3208862973, barbecue place, playground.

## Castelbuono — 35B3
Via Guiseppe Mazzini. **GPS**: n37,93694 e14,09296.
10 free Ch. **Location**: Urban, simple, quiet.
**Surface**: asphalted. 01/01-31/12.
**Distance**: 700m 700m.

## Castellammare del Golfo — 35B3
**Playtime**, Viale Leonardo da Vinci, SS187.
**GPS**: n38,02494 e12,89086.
20 € 16/24h Ch included € 2 € 4.
**Location**: Rural. **Surface**: grassy. 01/01-31/12.
**Distance**: 200m 1km.
**Remarks**: Monitored parking 24/24, swimming pool available.

## Castelluzzo — 35B3
SP16. **GPS**: n38,12220 e12,72524.

free. **Location**: Simple. **Surface**: gravel.
**Distance**: on the spot.
**Remarks**: Beach parking, beach train.

## Castelluzzo — 35B3
**Parking Macari**, SP16. **GPS**: n38,13564 e12,73638.

free. **Location**: Rural, simple. **Surface**: sand.
**Distance**: on the spot 900m.

## Enna — 35B3
**Ennacamper**, C/da S.Giuseppe, Pergusa. **GPS**: n37,52277 e14,29000.
30 € 20/24h € 5 ChService € 5 € 4. **Location**: Rural, simple. **Surface**: sand. 01/01-31/12.
**Distance**: Enna 10km.
**Remarks**: Bicycle rental, free shuttle, cleaning motorhome € 5.

## Francavilla di Sicilia — 35C3
**Maremonti**, Via Cappuccini. **GPS**: n37,90855 e15,14347.

±50 gift. **Location**: Rural, simple. **Surface**: unpaved. 01/01-31/12.
**Distance**: 400m Riverbed 1,1km.
**Remarks**: Gole dell'Alcantara 6km.

## Furnari — 35C2
**Sosta Camper Tonnarella**, Corso Palermo 6.
**GPS**: n38,13218 e15,12469.

44 € 15-25 Ch WC included € 0,50 € 4.
**Location**: Urban, simple. **Surface**: gravel. 01/01-31/12.
**Distance**: on the spot on the spot 150m 250m.
**Remarks**: Monitored parking, excursion to the Eolie-islands.

## Gangi — 35B3
SP14. **GPS**: n37,79203 e14,21079.
15 € 15 Ch included.
**Surface**: gravel/sand. 01/01-31/12.
**Distance**: 750m 750m.
**Remarks**: Monitored parking.

## Giardini Naxos — 35C3
**Parking Lagani**, Via Stralcina 22, zona Recanati.
**GPS**: n37,82092 e15,26753.

30 € 15-30 Ch WC included € 1,(summer) € 5.
**Location**: Urban. **Surface**: metalled. 01/01-31/12.
**Distance**: on the spot 200m 50m 200m Bus to Taormina 300m.
**Remarks**: Special tariff for long stay during the winter, bar, view on Etna and Taormina.

## Giardini Naxos — 35C3
**Eden Parking**, Via Stracina. **GPS**: n37,82188 e15,26701.

30 € 7-25 Ch € 0,35/kWh WC € 1.
**Location**: Urban, central. **Surface**: grassy. 01/01-31/12.
**Distance**: on the spot 500m on the spot > Taormina.

## Giardini Naxos — 35C3
**Holiday Sun**, Viale Stracina 20. **GPS**: n37,82109 e15,26784.
30 € 7-25 Ch (30x),16Amp WC included against payment. **Location**: Urban. **Surface**: grassy/gravel. 01/01-31/12.
**Distance**: 500m beach 500m on the spot > Taormina.
**Tourist information Giardini Naxos:**
Sa-morning.

## Ispica — 35C3
**Associazione Camper Club Porto Ulisse**.
**GPS**: n36,69761 e14,98647.
30 € 16/24h Ch. **Surface**: grassy. Easter-30/09.
**Distance**: 100m.

## Licata — 35B3
**Giummarella**, Via Salvo D'Acquisto. **GPS**: n37,09943 e13,94267.
30 € 10-20 Ch included.
**Surface**: gravel. 01/01-31/12.
**Distance**: 600m.

## Licata — 35B3
**Ristorante La Sorgente**, Loc. Pisciotto.
**GPS**: n37,12666 e13,85194.

80 Jun € 15, Jul € 20, Aug € 25 Ch WC included.
**Location**: Rural. **Surface**: gravel. 01/01-31/12.
**Distance**: Licata 9km on the spot on the spot.
**Remarks**: Stairs to sandy beach.

## Linguaglossa — 35C3
Via Marneve. **GPS**: n37,83338 e15,10897.
4 free. **Location**: Rural, simple, quiet. **Surface**: asphalted. 01/01-31/12.
**Distance**: on the spot.

## Marina di Ragusa — 35C3
**Marina Caravan**, Via Portovenere 57. **GPS**: n36,78472 e14,56486.

60 € 15-20 Ch WC € 4 included.
**Location**: Urban, central. **Surface**: grassy. 01/01-31/12.
**Distance**: 500m 300m 100m 100m 200m.
**Remarks**: Water/drainage at each pitch, bicycle rental.

## Marina di Ragusa — 35C3
Via Falconara. **GPS**: n36,78821 e14,54697.
40 free Chfree WC. **Location**: Urban. **Surface**: asphalted. 01/01-31/12.
**Distance**: 1km 1km.

## Marsala — 35A3
**Sibiliana Beach Village**, Contrada Fossarunza 205/z 14.
**GPS**: n37,73520 e12,47497.
100 € 20/24h Ch WC included. **Location**: Rural, comfortable, quiet. **Surface**: unpaved.
**Distance**: 50m.

## Marsala — 35A3
**Nautisub Club S. Teodoro**, Contrada Birgi.
**GPS**: n37,91046 e12,46178.

±50 € 15-20 Ch € 2,50. **Location**: Rural.
**Surface**: grassy. 01/05-30/09.
**Distance**: 5km Sandy beach on the spot.

## Marsala — 35A3
Via Colonnello Maltese. **GPS**: n37,79497 e12,43270.
free Chfree. **Location**: Urban. **Surface**: asphalted.

IT

🅾 01/01-31/12 ⦿ Su-morning (market).
**Distance:** 🚲500m 🏊on the spot ⊗450m 🚏200m.

### ♨S | Mineo ⛰ | 35C3

**Le Bave di Bacco**, Strada Provinciale 86. **GPS:** n37,24137 e14,72239.⬆.
🛏guests free 🚰🖦. **Location:** Rural, simple, isolated.
**Surface:** grassy. 🅾 01/01-31/12.
**Distance:** 🚲5km.

### 🏕S | Montallegro | 35B3

**Vizzi Parking**, Via Lungomare, SP87. **GPS:** n37,38206 e13,30932.
🛏€ 15 🚰€ 3 🖦Ch🖦€ 2. **Surface:** gravel. 🅾 01/06-01/10.
**Distance:** 🏊100m.

### ♨S | Montallegro | 35B3

**Agriturismo Torre Salsa**, Bove Marina.
**GPS:** n37,37583 e13,32222.⬆➡.

20 🛏€ 17-24, 2 pers incl., 1 pers + € 5 🚰€ 4 🖦Ch🖦according
consumption WC🖦€ 1 ⦿€ 6 🖦€ 1,50/h. **Location:** Rural.
**Surface:** grassy. 🅾 01/01-31/12.
**Distance:** 🏊700m 🚶on the spot.
**Remarks:** Also pitches on the beach without service, estate 300 acres,
hiking and mountain bike trails.

### ♨S | Montevago | 35B3

**Agricamper Villa dei Pini**, Via Piersanti Mattarella.
**GPS:** n37,70083 e12,98000.
🛏€ 15 🚰🖦Ch🖦included. 🅾 01/01-31/12.
**Distance:** 🚲200m.

### ⛲S | Montevago | 35B3

**Centro Terme Acqua Pia**, Loc. Acque Calde. **GPS:** n37,70161 e12,93814.
20 🛏€ 20 + € 15/pp 🚰€ 3. 🅾 01/04-31/10.
**Remarks:** Including access spa resort.

**IT**

### 🏕 | Motta Camastra 🌿 | 35C3

S185, fraz. Ficarazzi. **GPS:** n37,87887 e15,17630.⬆.

10 🛏€ 15 🚰🖦Ch🖦WC🖦included. **Location:** Rural.
**Surface:** grassy/gravel. 🅾 01/01-31/12.
**Distance:** ⊗300m 🚲1km.
**Remarks:** In front of entrance of Gole dell'Alcantara.

### ♨S | Motta Camastra 🌿 | 35C3

**Agripark Gole dell'Alcantara**. **GPS:** n37,87692 e15,17759.⬆.
🛏€ 15, Aug € 20 🚰🖦Ch🖦WC🖦.
**Location:** Rural, isolated, quiet. **Surface:** gravel.
🅾 01/01-31/12.
**Distance:** 🚲1,5km ⊗250m.
**Remarks:** Regional products, swimming pool (summer).

### 🏕 | Nizza di Sicilia | 35C3

Via Marina. **GPS:** n37,99358 e15,41447.
5 🛏free. **Location:** Urban. **Surface:** asphalted. 🅾 01/01-31/12.
**Distance:** ⊗100m 🏊on the spot 🚏on the spot.
**Remarks:** At sea.

### 🏕S | Noto | 35C3

**Il Canneto**, Viale Lido di Noto, Lido di Noto.
**GPS:** n36,86083 e15,11944.⬆➡.

55 🛏€ 10-18 🚰🖦Chincluded 🖦€ 2 WC🖦.
**Location:** Urban. **Surface:** grassy/sand.
🅾 01/01-31/12.
**Distance:** 🏊on the spot ⊗200m 🚲1,2km.
**Remarks:** Bread-service and meals, direct access to the sandy beach.

### 🏕S | Noto | 35C3

**NotoParking**, Contrada Faldino, Noto. **GPS:** n36,88353 e15,08595.⬆➡.

40 🛏€ 18 🚰🖦Ch🖦€ 3 WC🖦€ 2 🖦included. **Location:** Rural,
comfortable, luxurious, quiet. **Surface:** grassy/gravel. 🅾 01/01-31/12.
**Distance:** 🚲3km 🏊5km ⊗200m 🚏200m 🚏150m.
**Remarks:** Bread-service, organised excursions in the surroundings, free
shuttle bus to Noto.

### 🏕S | Noto | 35C3

**Oasi Park Falconara**, Viale Ionio, Lido di Noto.
**GPS:** n36,87001 e15,12872.⬆.
50 🛏€ 15, 01/06-31/10 € 17-25 🚰🖦Ch🖦WC 🖦included.
**Surface:** gravel. 🅾 01/01-31/12.
**Distance:** 🚲Noto 4km 🏊beach 700m ⊗pizzeria 50m.
**Remarks:** Shuttle bus to Noto and beach.

### ♨S | Noto | 35C3

**Parcheggio Calamosche**, Oasi di Vendicari.
**GPS:** n36,81611 e15,09888.⬆➡.

40-50 🛏€ 16, Aug € 20 🚰🖦🖦€ 3 WC🖦included. **Location:** Rural,
simple. **Surface:** grassy. 🅾 01/06-30/09.
**Distance:** 🚲Noto 10km 🏊20 min walking ⊗bar/restaurant.

### 🏕S | Oliveri ⚓ | 35C2

**Azimut Sosta Camper**, Corso Cristoforo Colombo.
**GPS:** n38,12840 e15,05833.⬆.
100 🛏€ 12-22 🚰🖦Ch🖦(100x),6Amp WC🖦🖦included.
**Location:** Rural, comfortable. **Surface:** grassy/gravel.
🅾 01/03-31/10.
**Distance:** 🚲500m, Tindari 1,2km 🚴2,5km 🏊beach 50m 🚏50m
⊗50m 🚏200m ⦿10m 🚏100m ⛴100m 🚶200m.
**Remarks:** Monitored parking, barbecue place.

### 🏕S | Pachino | 35C3

**Area camper Venere**, Contrada Granelli. **GPS:** n36,70100 e15,02790.⬆.
🛏€ 20-26, 5 pers incl 🚰🖦Ch🖦WC🖦included. **Location:** Rural,
comfortable. **Surface:** unpaved. 🅾 01/06-30/09.
**Distance:** 🏊Sandy beach.

### 🏕S | Pachino | 35C3

**Dragomar**, Strada Marzamemi Portopalo di Capo Passero, Marzamemi.
**GPS:** n36,72732 e15,12083.⬆➡.

---

30 🛏€ 15-21 🚰🖦Ch🖦€ 3 WC🖦included. **Location:** Rural, simple,
quiet. **Surface:** gravel. 🅾 01/01-31/12.
**Distance:** 🏊on the spot ⊗400m 🚏600m.
**Remarks:** Seaview, no beach.

### 🏕S | Palermo 🌿⚓ | 35B3

**Area Attrezzata Camper Palermo**, Molo Santa Lucia.
**GPS:** n38,12980 e13,36160.⬆.
15 🛏€ 15 🚰🖦included. **Location:** Simple, central.
**Surface:** asphalted. 🅾 01/01-31/12.
**Distance:** 🚲on the spot ⊗on the spot 🚏on the spot.
**Remarks:** Monitored parking.

### 🏕S | Palermo 🌿⚓ | 35B3

**Green Car Palermo**, Via Quarto dei Mille 11b.
**GPS:** n38,11016 e13,34307.⬆.
25 🛏€ 20/24h 🚰🖦Ch🖦🖦included. **Location:** Rural, simple.
**Surface:** asphalted. 🅾 01/01-31/12.
**Distance:** 🚲piazza Indipendenza 300m ⊗50m 🚏50m 🚏200m.
**Remarks:** Monitored parking 24/24.

### 🏕S | Palermo 🌿⚓ | 35B3

**Parcheggio Saiwash**, Via Gaetano Costa 25. **GPS:** n38,09137 e13,33543.
🛏€ 15/24h 🚰🖦Ch🖦🖦included.
**Location:** Urban. **Surface:** metalled.
🅾 01/01-31/12.
**Distance:** 🚲historical centre 3km 🚴2km ⊗750m 🚏750m 🚏100m.
**Remarks:** Monitored parking 24/24.

### 🏕S | Palermo 🌿⚓ | 35B3

**Parking Giotto**, Piazzale John Lennon. **GPS:** n38,13240 e13,33148.
36 🛏€ 20/24h 🚰🖦Ch🖦included 🖦free. **Location:** Central.
**Surface:** asphalted. 🅾 01/01-31/12.
**Remarks:** 3 nights stay 10% discount.

### 🏕S | Palermo 🌿⚓ | 35B3

**Parking Ospedale Cervello**, Via Trabucco. **GPS:** n38,15619 e13,31354.
🛏free 🚰🖦. **Location:** Urban, simple, isolated. **Surface:** metalled.
🅾 01/01-31/12.
**Distance:** 🚲on the spot ⊗1,5km 🚏2km 🚏400m.
**Remarks:** Nearby hospital.

### 🏕S | Palermo 🌿⚓ | 35B3

**Parking Pippo Uscè**, Via Giuseppe Paratore 40.
**GPS:** n38,09588 e13,37198.
40 🛏€ 15/24h 🚰🖦Ch🖦included. **Location:** Urban.
**Surface:** metalled. 🅾 01/01-31/12.
**Distance:** 🚲city centre 3km ⊗400m 🚏300m 🚏100m.

### 🏕S | Palermo 🌿⚓ | 35B3

Via Uditore 17. **GPS:** n38,13140 e13,32515.⬆.
20 🛏€ 18 🚰🖦Chincluded 🖦WC🖦🖦.
**Location:** Urban. **Surface:** gravel. 🅾 01/01-31/12.
**Distance:** 🚲4km ⊗200m 🚏150m 🚏bus 110 > centre.
**Remarks:** Monitored parking, barbecue place, shuttle bus to city
centre.

### 🏕 | Palermo 🌿⚓ | 35B3

Piazza Alcide De Gasperi. **GPS:** n38,15170 e13,33944.
🛏free. **Location:** Urban. **Surface:** asphalted.
🅾 01/01-31/12.
**Distance:** 🚲3,5km ⊗on the spot 🚏350m 🚏bus 101/106 > centre.
**Remarks:** Nearby stadium.

### 🏕S | Palermo 🌿⚓ | 35B3

**Freesbee Parking**, Via Imperatore Federico 116.
**GPS:** n38,14722 e13,35277.
100 🛏€ 15-18 🚰🖦Chincluded 🖦€ 3/24h WC🖦€ 1.
**Location:** Urban. **Surface:** asphalted. 🅾 01/01-31/12.
**Distance:** 🚲Cathedral Palermo 400m 🏊2km ⊗50m 🚏1km
🚏150m.
**Remarks:** At motorhome dealer, 24/24 surveillance.

**Tourist information Palermo:**
ℹ U.I.A.T. (Ufficio Informazioni e di Accoglienza Turistica), Piazza
Castelnuovo, 34, www.regione.sicilia.it/turismo. Capital of Sicily, port
and economical heart of the Island.
👁 San Giovanni degli Eremiti.
👁 Santa Catarina.
🏛 Vucciria, Via Cassari-Argenteria. Palermo's most famous, pictur-

esque and historic market.

| **S** | **Piano San Paolo** | 35C3 |

**Terra Nostra**, Via Piano San Paolo 27. **GPS**: n37,16016 e14,52840.
20 € 20 Ch included . **Location**: Rural. **Surface**: sand.
01/01-31/12.
**Distance**: on the spot on the spot on the spot.

| | **Piazza Armerina** | 35B3 |

Via G. Lo Giudice. **GPS**: n37,38711 e14,37041.
free. **Location**: Urban, simple. **Surface**: asphalted.
01/01-31/12.
**Distance**: 200m 50m 50m.

| **S** | **Piazza Armerina** | 35B3 |

**Agricamper Valle Dell'Elsa**, SS65. **GPS**: n37,30173 e14,39605.
12 € 15/24h Ch WC included. **Location**: Rural,
comfortable, isolated, quiet. **Surface**: metalled. 01/01-31/12.
**Distance**: Piazza Armerina 20km on the spot.
**Remarks**: At swimming pool.

| | **Piazza Armerina** | 35B3 |

**Agriturismo Agricasale**, Contrada Ciavarina.
**GPS**: n37,34032 e14,38840.
40 € 15 Ch included WC.
**Location**: Rural, comfortable, isolated, quiet. **Surface**: unpaved.
01/01-31/12.
**Distance**: Piazza Armerina 13km bar/restaurant.
**Remarks**: Swimming pool € 3/pppd.

| | **Piazza Armerina** | 35B3 |

**Agriturismo Gigliotto**, SS 117bis km60. **GPS**: n37,29051 e14,38721.
20 € 20, 01/04-31/10 € 30 Ch WC included.
**Location**: Rural, comfortable, quiet. **Surface**: gravel.
01/01-31/12.
**Distance**: Piazza Armerina 13km.
**Remarks**: Swimming pool incl.

| **S** | **Piazza Armerina** | 35B3 |

SP90. **GPS**: n37,36805 e14,33421.
20 € 3-15/24h Ch included. **Location**: Rural, simple.
**Surface**: unpaved. 01/01-31/12.
**Distance**: Piazza Armerina 4,5km 400m.
**Remarks**: Villa Romana del Casale 400m.

| **S** | **Porto Empedocle** | 35B3 |

**Punta Piccola Park**, Scala dei Turchi, SP68.
**GPS**: n37,28916 e13,49250.

99 € 15-20, 01/07-31/08 € 25 Ch (65x)WC € 1
included. **Location**: Rural. **Surface**: gravel. 01/01-31/12.
**Distance**: 2,5km on the spot 200m 1km.
**Remarks**: Shopping service, direct access to the sandy beach.
**Tourist information Porto Empedocle**:
Valle dei Templi, Agrigento. The Valley of The Temples, archeology.

| **S** | **Portopalo di Capo Passero** | 35C3 |

**Cicogna**, Via Carlo Alberto, 2. **GPS**: n36,68333 e15,13638.
20 € 19 Ch (20x)included. **Location**: Rural, luxurious,
quiet. **Surface**: gravel. 01/06-30/09.
**Distance**: 50m sandy beach 300m.

| **S** | **Pozzallo** | 35C3 |

**Salvamar**, Zona Porto di Pozzallo. **GPS**: n36,71541 e14,82240.

30 € 15, 01/06-10/09 € 20, 2 pers. incl Ch included.
**Surface**: grassy. 01/01-31/12.
**Distance**: 200m 500m 1km.

| | **Pozzallo** | 35C3 |

**Il Giardino di Epicuro**, SP67. **GPS**: n36,73128 e14,86240.

---

50 € 10-20 Ch (22x)€ 3 cold shower.
**Surface**: grassy/sand. 01/05-30/09.
**Distance**: 500m on the spot 50m 300m.
**Remarks**: Sandy beach.

| **S** | **Realmonte** | 35B3 |

**Sosta camper Zanzibar**, C/o Capo Rossello.
**GPS**: n37,29495 e13,45438.

100 Jul € 10/24h, Aug € 22/24h Ch WC included € 1,hot
shower € 1. **Location**: Rural. **Surface**: gravel.
summer.
**Distance**: sandy beach on the spot 150m.
**Remarks**: Bus to Valle dei Templi (€ 7/pp, min. 4 pers).

| **S** | **Reitano** | 35B3 |

Via Lungomare Colonna. **GPS**: n38,01407 e14,33081.
20 € 10 Ch € 0,50,cold shower.
**Location**: Rural, simple. **Surface**: grassy. 15/07-18/09.
**Distance**: 500m .

| **S** | **Ribera** | 35B3 |

**Kamemi**, SS115, Secca Grande. **GPS**: n37,43840 e13,24469.
Camperstop € 10 Ch. 01/01-31/12 01/08-24/08 No
Camperstop.

| **S** | **Roccalumera** | 35C3 |

**Park Jonio**, Via Collegio, SS114 Roccalumera > Nizza di Sicilia.
**GPS**: n37,98027 e15,39606.

60 € 11-17, Jul/Aug € 15-20, 3 pers. incl Ch (60x).
**Location**: Rural, simple. **Surface**: gravel. 01/01-31/12.
**Distance**: within walking distance 250m Bar/snack on the
spot. **Remarks**: In front of Centro Sportivo.

| **S** | **San Giovanni La Punta** | 35C3 |

**Entertainmentcity Isivillage**, Via Fisichelli 63.
**GPS**: n37,58929 e15,08612.
guests free WC. **Location**: Rural. **Surface**: asphalted.
01/01-31/12.
**Distance**: 1,5km on the spot 550m.

| **S** | **San Vito Lo Capo** | 35B3 |

**Al Faro**, Via Faro 36. **GPS**: n38,18472 e12,73277.

30 € 18-30 Ch included hot shower € 1.
**Surface**: asphalted/grassy. 01/05-01/10.
**Distance**: 1km on the spot 300m 1km.

---

**Remarks**: Terrace on the sea, no beach, sandy beach 400m.

| **S** | **San Vito Lo Capo** | 35B3 |

**Area Sosta Camper Giovanni**, Via Savoia 13.
**GPS**: n38,16222 e12,73666.

90 € 13-20 Ch (90x) WC € 0,50 € 5 included.
**Location**: Rural. **Surface**: gravel. 01/01-31/12.
**Distance**: 300m 1,4km 1km 300m.
**Remarks**: Free shuttle to beach.

| **S** | **San Vito Lo Capo** | 35B3 |

**Emme Parking**, Via Savoia. **GPS**: n38,16644 e12,73568.
20 € 10-20 Ch WC included . **Location**: Rural.
**Surface**: gravel. 01/05-30/09.
**Distance**: 1km 2km on the spot on the spot.
**Remarks**: Video surveillance.

| **S** | **San Vito Lo Capo** | 35B3 |

**Monte Monaco**, Via del Secco, 80. **GPS**: n38,17438 e12,74552.
€ 15, July € 20, Aug € 25 Ch WC € 1. **Location**: Rural,
comfortable, quiet. **Surface**: gravel. 01/04-31/10.
**Distance**: 850m 300m 300m 850m.

| | **San Vito Lo Capo** | 35B3 |

Via la Piana. **GPS**: n38,16886 e12,74307.

free. **Surface**: unpaved. 01/01-31/12.
**Distance**: 800m 800m.
**Remarks**: Free shuttle to centre.

| **S** | **Scicli** | 35C3 |

**Club Piccadilly**, Via Mare Adriatico, Donnalucata.
**GPS**: n36,74750 e14,66306.
20 € 12-23 € 3 WC € 1/3minutes € 5 .
**Location**: Rural, luxurious, isolated, quiet. **Surface**: grassy.
01/01-31/12.
**Distance**: 1,5km sandy beach 100m.

| **S** | **Scopello** | 35B3 |

**Fontana Andrea**, Contrada Ciauli, SS 187.
**GPS**: n38,05492 e12,84290.
50 € 12/24h € 4 Ch € 2.
**Location**: Rural. **Surface**: grassy. 01/04-01/10.
**Distance**: 3,5km beach 300m 500m.

| **S** | **Scopello** | 35B3 |

**Agricampeggio Scopello**, Via Finanzierè Vincenzo Mazzarell.
**GPS**: n38,06777 e12,81777.

50 € 25-30 + € 0,50/pp tourist tax Ch included € 1.
**Surface**: gravel. 01/05-30/09.
**Distance**: historical centre 200m 1,5km 100m 400m.
**Remarks**: Farm products, shuttle to beach and Riserva dello Zingaro
€ 2,50/pp.

| **S** | **Siracusa** | 35C3 |

**Area di sosta camper Claud Car**, Via per Floridia 43.
**GPS**: n37,07243 e15,23293.
20 € 15-20 Ch included.

IT

**Location:** Urban, comfortable. **Surface:** metalled. ◻ 01/01-31/12.
**Distance:** ⛱10km ✖1km.

| 🅿️🅢 | Siracusa | 35C3 |

**Ippocamper**, Via Necropoli del Fusco 18. **GPS:** n37,09855 e15,18905.
20 🕳€ 13-18 🚰🔌Ch included 🚿WC 🗑€ 1 ◉ € 3. **Location:** Rural.
**Surface:** grassy. ◻ 01/03-31/10.
**Distance:** 🏊8km ✖1,5km.
**Remarks:** Barbecue place.

| 🅿️🅢 | Siracusa | 35C3 |

**Parcheggio Von Platen**, Via Augusto Von Platen 38.
**GPS:** n37,07692 e15,28738.
🕳€ 0,90/h, € 22/24h 🚰🔌Ch 🚿(5x)included WC 🗑.
**Location:** Urban. **Surface:** metalled.
◻ 01/01-31/12.
**Distance:** 🏊on the spot ✖700m 🛒500m 🚌on the spot.
**Remarks:** Near archeological site and museum, shuttle € 1/pp.

| 🅿️🅢 | Siracusa | 35C3 |

**Parking Paradise**, Via Giuseppe Agnello 1.
**GPS:** n37,07323 e15,27633.⬆
🕳from € 5 🚰🔌Ch 🚿included.
**Surface:** grassy/metalled. ◻ 01/01-31/12.
**Distance:** 🚌500m ✖50m 🛒500m.

| 🅿️🅢 | Siracusa | 35C3 |

Via Necropoli del Fusco. **GPS:** n99,99999 e99,99999.⬆
15 🕳€ 15-20 🚰🔌Ch 🚿included WC 🗑◉. **Location:** Urban,
comfortable. **Surface:** asphalted. ◻ 01/01-31/12.
**Distance:** 🚌2km ⛱1,5km.

| 🅿️🅢 | Siracusa | 35C3 |

Via Procione 6, zona Golfetto, Fontane Bianche.
**GPS:** n36,96361 e15,22027.⬆
15 🕳€ 20/24h 🚰🔌Ch 🚿WC 🗑included. **Location:** Rural,
comfortable, quiet. **Surface:** unpaved. ◻ 01/01-31/12.
**Distance:** 🚌Siracusa 15km ⛱on the spot ✖800m 🛒600m
🚌on the spot.
**Remarks:** Bus to Siracusa, natural swimming pool in sea.

| 🅿️ | Siracusa | 35C3 |

**Area sosta Siracusa**, Via Rodi 15. **GPS:** n37,06436 e15,28710.
🕳€ 0,60/h, night € 1. **Surface:** asphalted. ◻ 01/01-31/12.
**Distance:** 🚌Ortigia 500m ✖50m.

| 🍽️🅢 | Siracusa | 35C3 |

**Agriturismo Terrauzza sul Mare**, Via Blanco 8.
**GPS:** n37,01169 e15,28736.
15 🕳€ 15/24h 🚰🔌Ch 🚿included. **Location:** Rural. **Surface:** sand.
◻ 01/01-31/12.
**Distance:** ⛱100m 🛒1,5km.
**Remarks:** Regional products.

| 🅿️🅢 | Sutera | 35B3 |

Piazza Rettore Carruba. **GPS:** n37,52450 e13,72960.⬆
🕳free 🚰🔌Ch. **Location:** Urban. **Surface:** asphalted.
◻ 01/01-31/12.
**Distance:** 🚌on the spot ✖on the spot 🛒300m.

| 🅿️🅢 | Taormina 🌿 | 35C3 |

**Sosta Camper Pier Giovanni**, Trappitello, Via Spagnuolo.
**GPS:** n37,82196 e15,24502.⬆

15 🕳€ 10-20 🚰🔌Ch 🚿WC 🗑included. **Location:** Urban, simple,
noisy. **Surface:** grassy/metalled. ◻ 01/01-31/12.
**Distance:** 🚌500m ⛱4km 🛒300m 🚌300m.
**Remarks:** Shuttle bus to city centre.

| 🅿️🅢 | Terme Vigliatore 〰️ | 35C2 |

**Area Trinacria**, Via Lungomare Marchesana.
**GPS:** n38,14018 e15,14596.⬆⬆

120 🕳€ 15, Aug € 18 🚰🔌Ch 🚿included,cold shower ◉.
**Location:** Comfortable, quiet. **Surface:** grassy/gravel.
◻ 01/01-31/12.
**Distance:** ⛱50m ✖pizzeria 200m 🛒200m.
**Remarks:** Bread-service, excursion to the Eolie-islands, playground,
tuesday market.

| 🍽️🅢 | Trapani | 35A3 |

**Hotel Le Saline**, SP21 km4, contrada Nubia-Paceco.
**GPS:** n37,98304 e12,53106.⬆
20 🕳€ 15-25 🚰🔌Ch 🚿included 🗑€ 4 ◉€ 7,50 📶.
**Surface:** metalled. ◻ 01/01-31/12.

IT

# Luxembourg

Capital: Luxembourg
Government: Grand duchy
Official Language: French, German, Luxembourgish
Population: 594,130 (2017)
Area: 2,586 km²

## General information
Calling code: 00352
General emergency: 112
Currency: Euro

## Regulations for overnight stays
Parking overnight and camping by public road is forbidden. Motorhome-service only on campsites.

## Additional public holidays 2019
April 22 Easter Monday
May 1 Labor day
June 23 National Holiday
August 15 Assumption of the Virgin Mary
November 1 All Saints' Day

## Time Zone
Winter (Standard Time) GMT+1
Summer (DST) GMT+2

Luxembourg pages: 671-672

Luxembourg

---

### ⒼⓈ Berdorf — 16E1
**Camperhafen Martbusch**, 3, Beim Martbusch.
**GPS:** n49,82660 e6,34599. ⬆️➡️.

9 🅿️ € 10-15, dog € 2,50 🚰 € 1/100liter 🔧Ch 🔌€ 0,50/kWh 🚽🚿€ 3 🚿included. **Location:** Rural, comfortable, quiet. **Surface:** asphalted. 📅 01/01-31/12.
**Distance:** 🛒500m ⊗on the spot 🏥7km 🚉500m 🚲on the spot 🚶on the spot.
**Remarks:** Max. 2 nights, check in at reception campsite.

### ⒼⓈ Bleesbrück — 16E1
**Camping Bleesbrück**, 1, Bleesbreck. **GPS:** n49,87270 e6,18940.

4 🅿️€ 15 🚰🔧Ch 🔌WC 🚿included.
**Location:** Rural, simple, noisy. **Surface:** grassy/metalled.
📅 01/04-15/10.
**Distance:** 🛒2,5km ⊗on the spot 🏥2,5km.
**Remarks:** Arrival >18h departure <9h, if not camping tariff.

### ⒼⓈ Diekirch 🌿 — 16E1
**Camping de la Sûre**, Route de Gilsdorf.
**GPS:** n49,86597 e6,16489. ⬆️➡️.

9 🅿️€ 16 + € 1,50/pp tourist tax, dog € 2,50 🚰🔧Ch 🔌WC included 🚿sanitary only summer 🚽€ 3 🚿free.
**Location:** Rural, comfortable, central. **Surface:** grasstiles/grassy.
📅 01/01-31/12.
**Distance:** 🛒100m 🏊100m 🚲100m (permit € 4/month) ⊗100m 🏥100m.
**Remarks:** Max. 2 days, water closed during wintertime.

---

**Tourist information Diekirch:**
Ⓜ Conservatoire National de véhicules historique, 20-22, rue de Stavelot. Exhibition of historical vehicles. 📅 10-18h ⊙ Mo.
Ⓜ Musée National de l'histoire militaire, 10, Bamertal. War museum. 📅 Tue-Su 10-18h ⊙ Mo.
🍴 Rue de Marché. 📅 Tue 8-12h.
🎪 Al Dikkirch. Folk festival. 📅 2nd week Jul.

### ⒼⓈ Dudelange — 16E1
**Parking Gare-Usines. GPS:** n49,47176 e6,07772. ⬆️➡️.

8 🅿️free 🚰🔧Chfree 🔌. **Location:** Simple, noisy.
**Surface:** grasstiles/grassy. 📅 01/01-31/12.
**Distance:** 🛒1km 🏥1,1km 🚉near train station.
**Remarks:** Well situated for visiting Luxembourg city, 20min by train, max. 48h.

**Tourist information Dudelange:**
Ⓜ Musée National des Mines de Fer, Carreau de la Mine, Rumelange. History of the mines.

### △Ⓢ Ermsdorf 👥 — 16E1
**Neumühle. GPS:** n49,83917 e6,22503.
🅿️€ 16-20,50 🚰🔧Ch 🔌WC 🚽🚿€ 4 🚿included. **Location:** Rural, comfortable, isolated, quiet. **Surface:** grassy.
📅 15/03-31/10.
**Distance:** 🛒1km ⊗on the spot 🏥6km.

### ⒼⓈ Heiderscheid — 16E1

**Camperhafen Fuussekaul Heiderscheid**
- Electricity at each pitch
- Open all year
- Restaurant on the spot

www.fuussekaul.lu
info@fuussekaul.lu

**Camperhafen Fuussekaul**, Fuussekaul 4.
**GPS:** n49,87806 e5,99278. ⬆️➡️.
35 🅿️€ 12, Jul/Aug € 18 🚰🔧Ch 🔌(35x),16Amp WC included 🚽€ 1/5minutes 🚿€ 4/2,50 🔌€ 4,90/day. **Location:** Rural, luxurious, isolated, quiet. **Surface:** grasstiles/metalled. 📅 01/01-31/12.
**Distance:** 🛒1km 🏊8km 🚲8km 🏥5km ⊗on the spot 🏪on the spot

---

🚉on the spot 🚶on the spot.

**Tourist information Heiderscheid:**
🎪 Heischter Mart. Traditional market. 📅 end Jul.

### ⒼⓈ Heiderscheidergrund — 16E1
**Camping Bissen**, 11, Millewee. **GPS:** n49,90495 e5,95595.
3 🅿️€ 11, 18/07-18/08 € 16 🚰🔧Ch 🔌🚿included. **Surface:** gravel.
📅 01/01-31/12.
**Distance:** ⊗on the spot 🚉on the spot.
**Remarks:** Quick-Stop: >17h - <10h, along river.

### 🍴Ⓢ Hoscheid ⛰️ — 11E3
**Hotel-Restaurant Des Ardennes**, Haaptstrooss.
**GPS:** n49,94675 e6,08084. ✈️.

4 🅿️free with a meal 🚰🔌WC 🚿included. **Location:** Simple, quiet.
**Surface:** asphalted. 📅 01/02-15/12.
**Distance:** 🛒on the spot ⊗on the spot 🚉on the spot.
**Remarks:** Parking behind hotel.

### ⒼⓈ Junglinster — 16E1
Rue Emile Nilles. **GPS:** n49,70421 e6,25123. ⬆️➡️.

3 🅿️free 🚰€ 0,10/10liter 🔧Ch 🔌(4x)€ 0,50/kWh. **Location:** Simple.
**Surface:** asphalted. 📅 01/01-31/12.
**Distance:** 🛒200m.

### ⒼⓈ Koerich — 16E1
Chemin de la Source. **GPS:** n49,67070 e5,94229. ⬆️.
4 🅿️free 🚰€ 2/160liter 🔧Ch 🔌. **Location:** Urban, noisy.
**Surface:** metalled. 📅 01/01-31/12.
**Distance:** ⊗550m 🏥800m.

### ⒼⓈ Larochette 🌿♨️👥 — 16E1
**Camping Auf Kengert. GPS:** n49,80021 e6,19788.
2 🅿️€ 17,25-26,25 🔧Chincluded. 📅 01/03-08/11.
**Remarks:** Quick-Stop: >19h - <9h.

**Tourist information Larochette:**
👁️ Schiessentümpel. Waterfall with three cascades.
🏰 Château. 📅 Easter-Oct, 10-18h, daily.

### ⒼⓈ Liefrange — 16E1
**Camperhafen Leifreg**, 14, Haaptstrooss. **GPS:** n49,91136 e5,87438. ⬆️.

**Distance:** 🚂200m ⊗on the spot 🍴on the spot 🚌200m 🚲on the spot 🚶on the spot.
**Remarks:** Recreation park, near campsite.

23 ⌇€ 10, Jul/Aug € 15 ⌐🔌Ch✎✓ WC⌐€ 1 📶included. 🚐
**Location:** Rural, isolated, quiet. **Surface:** grasstiles/metalled.
⬜ 01/01-31/12.
**Distance:** 🚂on the spot ⚓Obersauer Stausee 500m ⊗on the spot.

12 ⌇free ⌐🔌Ch✎ (5x)free. **Location:** Rural, simple, quiet.
**Surface:** asphalted. ⬜ 01/01-31/12.
**Distance:** 🚂800m 🍴on the spot.
**Remarks:** At swimming pool, max. 48h.

| ⊞P | **Luxemburg** 🐚 | 16E1 |

**Glacis**, Boulevard de la Foire /Av. de la Faiencerie.
**GPS:** n49,61602 e6,12246.

| 🏕⊞S | **Schwebsange** 📧 | 16E1 |

**Camport**, Rue du Port. **GPS:** n49,51163 e6,36249. ⬆.

20 ⌇Mo-Fr € 1/h. **Location:** Urban, simple, noisy.
**Surface:** asphalted.
⬜ 01/01-31/12.
**Distance:** 🚂centre 650m 🚌on the spot.
**Remarks:** Overnight stay allowed.

**Tourist information Luxemburg:**
ℹ Luxembourg City Tourist Office, Place d'Armes, www.lcto.lu. Citadel
and fortifications have been changed in parks and walks, especially in
the lower city.
⬜ 01/04-31/10 Mo-Sa 9-19h, Su 10-18h, 01/11-31/03 Mo-Sa 9-18h.
👁 Casemates du Bock, Montée de Clausen. Casemates, 21km.
⬜ 01/03-31/10 10-20.30h.
Ⓜ Musée National d'histoire et d'art, Marché-aux-Poissons. Archeological findings. ⬜ Tue-Su 10-18h.
♞ Palais Grand Ducal, 17, rue du Marché-aux-Herbes. Ducal palace.
⬜ 01/07-31/08.
✝ Cathédrale Notre-Dame, Rue Notre Dame.
⬜ daily 10-12h, 14-17.30h.
⌂ Crypte Archéologique, Montée de Clausen.
⬜ 01/03-31/10 10-17h. ⊤ free.
⚘ Marché-aux-puces, place d'Armes. Bric-a-brac.
⬜ 2nd + 4th Sa of the month.
⚘ Markt, place Guillaume.
⬜ Wed + Sa morning.
✺ Schueberfouer. Folk festival.
⬜ 30/08-15/09.

18 ⌇€ 12,50, 2 pers.incl ⌐🔌Ch✎✓€ 2,50 WC⌐🔌€ 2
📶included,at restaurant. **Location:** Rural, comfortable, quiet.
**Surface:** grasstiles. ⬜ 01/04-31/10.
**Distance:** 🚂500m ✎fishing permit obligatory ⊗on the spot 🍴on
the spot 🚌500m.

**Tourist information Schwebsange:**
Ⓜ A Possen, 1 rue Aloyse Sandt, Bech-Kleinmacher. Folkore and wine
museum. ⬜ 01/05-31/10 14-19h, 01/03-30/04, 01/11-31/12 Fri-Su
14-19h ⊙ Mo.

| 🏕⊞S | **Vianden** ⛺🛒🌳👥 | 16E1 |

**Camperpark Vianden**, Rue Neugarten. **GPS:** n49,93164 e6,21551. ⬆.
16 ⌇€ 10, 01/04-15/10 € 15 ⌐€ 2/100liter 🔌Ch✎€ 1/2kWh.
🚐**Location:** Rural, comfortable, quiet. **Surface:** grasstiles/grassy.
⬜ 01/01-31/12.
**Distance:** 🚂850m ⚓on the spot ⊗850m 🚶on the spot.
**Remarks:** Along river.

| 🏕⊞S | **Vianden** ⛺🛒🌳👥 | 16E1 |

39, rue du Sanatorium. **GPS:** n49,93717 e6,20556. ⬆.

| ⊞S | **Nommern** 🐚🏔👥 | 16E1 |

**Europacamping Nommerlayen**, Rue Nommerlayen.
**GPS:** n49,78450 e6,16414. ⬆➡.

⌇free. **Location:** Simple, central, quiet. **Surface:** asphalted.
⬜ 01/01-31/12.
**Distance:** 🚂500m ✎100m ⊗500m 🍴500m 🚌on the spot 🚲on
the spot 🚶on the spot.
**Remarks:** At the chair-lifts (télésiege).

**Tourist information Vianden:**
👁 SEO. Large hydro-electric power-station. ⬜ Easter-Sep 10-20h.
⊤ free.
Ⓜ Bakkerij museum, 96-98, Grand-Rue. ⬜ Easter-Oct 11-17h ⊙ Mo.
♞ Château de Vianden. ⬜ 10-16 ⊙ 02/11, 25/12, 01/01.
⚘ Nessmoort. Nuts market. ⬜ 2nd Su Oct.
Télésiège. Chair-lift. ⬜ Easter-Oct.

13 ⌇€ 10-25 ⌐🔌Ch✎✓€ 2/2kWh WC⌐🔌€ 5,25/4,75 📶included.
**Location:** Rural, comfortable, isolated, quiet.
**Surface:** grasstiles.
⬜ 01/03-06/11.
**Distance:** 🚂1km ⊗on the spot 🍴on the spot 🚌1,5km 🚶on the spot.
**Remarks:** Quick-Stop: >17h - <10h.

| ⊞S | **Redange/Attert** | 16E1 |

Rue de la Piscine 24. **GPS:** n49,76918 e5,89459. ⬆➡.

| ⊞S | **Wiltz** 👥 | 11E3 |

**Camping-Parc Kaul**, 60 Campingstrooss. **GPS:** n49,97173 e5,93433. ⬆.

3 ⌇free ⌐€ 1 🔌Ch✎. **Location:** Rural, simple, isolated, quiet.
**Surface:** gravel. ⬜ 01/01-31/12.

# △S Montenegro

Capital: Podgorica
Government: parliamentary republic
Official Language: Montenegrin
Population: 644,000 (2017)
Area: 13,812 km²

## General information
Dialling code: 0382
General emergency: 112
Currency: Euro
Credit cards are accepted almost everywhere.

## Regulations for overnight stays
Free overnight stay is not allowed.

## Additional public holidays 2019
January 7-8 Christmas (Orthodox)
May 1 Labour Day
May 21 Independence Day
July 13 Statehood Day

## Time Zone
Winter (Standard Time) GMT+1
Summer (DST)  GMT+2

Montenegro
page: 673

Podgorica

ME

---

### △S Bijela — 39A4
Zlokovic. GPS: n42,45768 e18,66873.
50 ⛺ € 21 🚐🖥 Ch included 📶. Location: Urban, isolated.
Surface: grassy/sand. 🅾 01/03-01/11.
Distance: 🚴2km 🏊on the spot 🛒on the spot 🍽on the spot.

### △S Dobrilovina — 39A4
Kamp Eco Oaza. GPS: n43,01780 e19,40936.
25 ⛺ € 15 🚐🖥 Ch 🚿 included. Location: Rural, isolated, quiet.
Surface: grassy. 🅾 01/01-31/12.
Distance: 🏊200m 🥾on the spot.

### ⛔ Gusinje — 39A4
Restaurant Krojet, Vusanje. GPS: n42,55053 e19,82502.⬆
15 ⛺ € 15. Location: Rural. Surface: grassy. 🅾 01/04-30/10.
Distance: 🍽on the spot.

### ⛔S Kotor — 39A4
E65. GPS: n42,42761 e18,76881.⬆
20 ⛺ € 3/h, € 20/24h Ch free.
Location: Urban. Surface: gravel. 🅾 01/01-31/12.
Distance: 🚴500m 🏊on the spot 🛒on the spot 🍽200m 🍺200m.

### △S Morinj — 39A4
Naluka. GPS: n42,48694 e18,65214.
40 ⛺ € 20 🚐🖥 Ch 🚿 included. Location: Urban, quiet.
Surface: grassy/sand. 🅾 01/05-01/10.
Distance: 🏊on the spot 🛒on the spot 🍽600m.

### △S Petnjica — 39A4
Jatak. GPS: n42,97815 e19,07510.
40 ⛺ € 10 🚐🖥 Ch included 🚿 € 2 WC 🚿 € 2.
Location: Rural, isolated. Surface: grassy. 🅾 01/06-01/09.
Distance: 🍽on the spot.

### △S Petrovac — 39A4
Maslina, Buljarica bb 300. GPS: n42,19833 e18,96583.
100 ⛺ € 15,60 🚐🖥 Ch included 🚿 € 3 WC 📶. Location: Urban, central. Surface: grassy. 🅾 01/01-31/12.
Distance: 🚴2km 🏊400m 🛒300m 🍺200m.

### ⛔S Podgorica — 39A4

**Auto Camp Izvor Podgorica**
- Located directly at the river
- Beautiful view
- Paved and flat motorhome pitches

www.hostelizvor.me
campingizvor@gmail.com

Auto Camp Izvor. GPS: n42,48363 e19,30621.⬆
15 ⛺ € 5 + € 5/pp 🖥 Ch 📶 included.
Surface: concrete. 🅾 01/01-31/12.
Distance: 🍽on the spot.

### △S Rasova — 39A4
Miro Tara-Regata, Djrdjevica Tara. GPS: n43,14862 e19,29217.
20 ⛺ € 15 🚐🖥 Ch 🚿 included. Location: Rural, isolated.
Surface: grassy/gravel. 🅾 01/04-30/10.

### △S Ulcinj — 39A4
Miami beach. GPS: n41,90870 e19,24978.
30 ⛺ € 20 🚐🖥 Ch 🚿 included WC 🚿. Surface: grassy/sand.
🅾 01/05-01/10.
Distance: 🏊on the spot 🛒on the spot 🍽on the spot.

### △S Ulcinj — 39A4
Safari beach. GPS: n41,90466 e19,26533.

130 ⛺ € 15, 15/06-15/09 € 30 🚐🖥 Ch 🚿 included 🔌 € 3 📶.
Surface: grassy. 🅾 01/01-31/12.
Distance: 🚴7km 🏊100m 🛒on the spot 🍽on the spot.

### △S Utjeha-Bušat — 39A4
Oliva, Uvala Maslina-Utjeha. GPS: n42,01028 e19,15111.
25 ⛺ € 15 🚐🖥 Ch 🚿 included WC 🚿. Location: Urban.
Surface: grassy. 🅾 01/04-30/11.
Distance: 🏊on the spot 🛒on the spot 🍽on the spot.

### △S Utjeha-Bušat — 39A4
Utjeha, Uvala Maslina-Utjeha. GPS: n42,01012 e19,15095.⬆

25 ⛺ € 14, 20/06-01/09 € 16 🚐🖥 Ch 🚿 included 🔌 against payment 📶. Location: Urban, comfortable. Surface: grassy.
🅾 15/04-01/11.
Distance: 🏊on the spot 🛒on the spot 🍽on the spot 🍺100m.

### △S Žabljak — 39A4
Kod Boce. GPS: n43,14352 e19,11580.
30 ⛺ € 6 🚐🖥 Ch included 🚿 € 2 🚿. Location: Rural, comfortable, isolated, quiet. Surface: grassy/gravel.
🅾 15/04-30/10.
Distance: 🏊4km.

### △S Žabljak — 39A4
Razvrsje. GPS: n43,14443 e19,11510.
20 ⛺ € 10 🚐🖥 Ch 🚿 included. Location: Rural, isolated, quiet.
Surface: grassy/gravel. 🅾 01/01-31/12.
Distance: 🚴900m 🥾on the spot.

# The Netherlands

Capital: Amsterdam
Government: Constitutional monarchy
Official Language: Dutch
Population: 17,084,719 (2017)
Area: 41,543 km²

### General information
Country dial code: 0031
General emergency: 112
Currency: Euro

### Regulations for overnight stays
Wild camping is forbidden in the Netherlands. Several motorhome-friendly municipalities have regulated facilities where overnight parking is allowed.

### Additional public holidays 2019
April 22 Easter Monday
April 27 King's day
May 5 Liberation day
May 21 Pentecost Monday
December 26 Boxing day

### Time Zone
Winter (Standard Time) GMT+1
Summer (DST) GMT+2

Groningen pages: 681-684
Friesland pages: 676-681
Drenthe pages: 684-685
North Holland pages: 674-676
Flevoland page: 690
Overijssel pages: 685-689
Amsterdam
South Holland pages: 698-701
Utrecht pages: 697-698
Gelderland pages: 690-697
Rotterdam
Zealand pages: 701-703
North Brabant pages: 703-707
Limburg pages: 707-710
Maastricht

NL

## North Holland

### Aalsmeer — 9C2
**Jachthaven 't Drijfhuis**, Uiterweg 27. **GPS:** n52,26494 e4,74496.

4 € 20 Ch WC Included. **Location:** Rural, comfortable. **Surface:** metalled. 01/01-31/12.
**Distance:** 300m 1,5km 20m 50m 400m on the spot on the spot.

### Abbenes — 9C2
**Camperplaats 't Groene Hart**, Kaagweg 50. **GPS:** n52,22630 e4,61911.

25 € 14 Ch (6x) € 2/24h,10Amp WC € 0,20 € 1 € 5 included. **Location:** Rural, comfortable, quiet. **Surface:** grassy/gravel. 15/03-01/11.
**Distance:** 4km 900m 1,5km 1,5km 1,5km 4km Leiden <> Amsterdam on the spot on the spot.
**Remarks:** Keukenhof 7km, bicycle rental.

### Amsterdam — 9C1
**Amsterdam City Camp**, Papaverweg 50 Noord 4. **GPS:** n52,39847 e4,90010.

95 € 18, 01/08-31/08 € 21 + tourist tax € 2,50/pp, dog € 1 Ch (30x) € 4,10Amp included. **Location:** Urban, comfortable. **Surface:** metalled. 01/01-31/12.
**Distance:** 2km 20m 100m 1km 1,5km 500m.
**Remarks:** Video surveillance, free ferry to city centre.

### Amsterdam — 9C1
**Fam. Ackermann**, Lutkemeerweg 149, Amsterdam-Osdorp. **GPS:** n52,36358 e4,77240.

16 € 15, tourist tax incl € 4 Ch € 4/day.
**Surface:** metalled. 01/01-31/12.
**Distance:** 10km city centre 2km Tram > Amsterdam 1,2km.
**Remarks:** Arrival <18h. Via Osdorperweg, special license.

**Tourist information Amsterdam:**
VVV, Stationsplein 10 en Leidseplein 1, www.iamsterdam.com. City Card gives entrance to museums, public transport, boattrip on the canals etc., 24h/ € 55, 48h/€65, 72h/ € 75, available at VVV.
Canalbus. Boat trip on the canals. € 21.
Stelling van Amsterdam. Forts built to protect Amsterdam.
Albert Cuyp, Albert Cuyp. Market with over 260 stalls.
daily 9-17h Su.
Antiek, Noordermarkt.
Sa 9-17h.
Artis, Plantage Kerklaan 38-40. City-zoo. 9-17/18h.
Villa Arena, Arena boulevard. Furniture mall, 50 shops.
Tue-Sa 10-18h, Mo 13-18h.

### Andijk — 9D1
**Jachthaven Andijk**, Nieuwe Haven 1. **GPS:** n52,74521 e5,18443.

3 € 12,50 Ch WC **Location:** Rural, simple, quiet. **Surface:** asphalted. 01/05-31/10.
**Distance:** on the spot on the spot on the spot on the spot on the spot.

### De Rijp — 9C1
**Bloembolbedrijf Stoop**, Zuiddijk 34. **GPS:** n52,54813 e4,83416.

4 🛏 € 7 ⛽ € 1/100liter 🚿 (4x) € 2/day. 📷 **Location:** Rural, simple, quiet. **Surface:** concrete. 📅 01/01-31/12. **Distance:** 🚲3km 🏊200m 🛒200m ⊗3km 🚆3km.

⚓🅂 **Den Helder** 🏴 7C3
**Willemsoord**, Willemsoord 47. **GPS:** n52,96134 e4,76856.⬆️.

40 🛏 € 12,50, tourist tax incl ⛽🚽Ch🚿(3x) € 1/2kWh WC 🚿included. 📷 **Location:** Simple, central, quiet. **Surface:** metalled. 📅 01/01-31/12. **Distance:** 🚲400m 🏊300m 🛒300m ⊗400m 🚆1km 🚐600m. **Remarks:** Max. 48h, ferry boat to Texel 500m.

⚓🅂 **Den Oever** 🏴 7C3
**Haventerrein Oostkade**, Oostkade 3. **GPS:** n52,93395 e5,03974.⬆️.

10 🛏 € 10 ⛽ € 0,50/100liter 🚽 € 0,50 Ch 🚿(8x) WC 🚿included. 📷 **Location:** Motorway, simple, isolated, noisy. **Surface:** metalled. 📅 01/01-31/12. **Distance:** 🚲500m 🏊1,4km 🏊200m 🛒offshore fishing ⊗500m 🚆500m 🚐on the spot. **Remarks:** At old harbour, max. 3 days, saturday-morning fishmarket.

⚓🅂 **Enkhuizen** 🌿⛵🏴 9D1
**Gependam**, Dirck Chinaplein. **GPS:** n52,69806 e5,29005.⬆️.

6 🛏 € 10,85 Ch included WC € 0,20 🚽 € 1.📷 **Location:** Urban, simple, central. **Surface:** asphalted. 📅 01/01-31/12. **Distance:** 🚲1km 🏊on the spot 🛒on the spot ⊗100m 🚆1km 🚐100m. **Remarks:** Max. 48h.

**Tourist information Enkhuizen:**
Ⓜ Zuiderzeemuseum. Historical little town.
📅 01/04-31/10 10-17h.

⚓🅂 **Heerhugowaard** 🏴 9C1
**Recreatiehaven Broekhorn**, Ooster Vlaerdinge.
**GPS:** n52,67234 e4,81503.⬆️.
6 🛏 € 10 ⛽ € 0,50/50liter 🚽Ch🚿 € 0,50/kWh,16Amp 🔌🚿included. **Location:** Comfortable. **Surface:** metalled. 📅 01/01-31/12. **Distance:** 🚲1km 🛒on the spot ⊗1km 🚆on the spot 🚐850m.

⚓🅂 **Hoorn** 🌿🏴 9C1
**Jachthaven De Grashaven**, Visserseiland 221.
**GPS:** n52,63467 e5,05676.⬆️.

27 🛏 € 15 ⛽🚽Ch🚿WC🚿 € 1 🔌 € 5 🚿included. 📷🎥 **Location:** Urban, quiet. **Surface:** metalled. 📅 01/04-31/10. **Distance:** 🚲500m 🏊2,8km 🏊on the spot 🛒on the spot ⊗100m 🚆on the spot. **Remarks:** Check in at harbourmaster.

⚓🅂 **Huizen** 🏴 9D2
**Recreatieterrein Wolskamer**, IJsselmeerstraat.
**GPS:** n52,30860 e5,24046.⬆️.

8 🛏free Ch. **Location:** Simple, quiet. **Surface:** grassy. 📅 01/01-31/12. **Distance:** 🚲1km 🏊200m 🏊200m ⊗1km 🛒Lidl 300m 🚴on the spot 🚶on the spot. **Remarks:** Max. 48h, service at harbourmaster.

**Tourist information Huizen:**
🚶✝ Sa.

🅂 **Katwoude** 9C1
**De Simonehoeve**, Wagenweg 2. **GPS:** n52,48620 e5,03196.⬆️.

SIMONEHOEVE

10 🛏free. **Location:** Simple. **Surface:** asphalted. 📅 01/01-31/12. **Distance:** 🚲2km 🏊2km 🏊2km ⊗on the spot 🚆2km 🚐100m. **Remarks:** Cheese farm, nearby Hotel Volendam, free guided tour.

⚓🅂 **Laren** 🏴 9D2
**Sportcomplex De Biezem**, Schapendrift 64. **GPS:** n52,25717 e5,23884.

2 🛏free ⛽🚽ChWC🚿. **Location:** Urban, simple, noisy. **Surface:** metalled. 📅 01/01-31/12. **Distance:** 🚲1km 🏊1km. **Remarks:** Max. 1 night.

⚓🅂 **Medemblik** 🌿🏴 9D1
**Haven Medemblik**, Pekelharinghaven 50. **GPS:** n52,77139 e5,11361.⬆️.

5 🛏 € 10 + € 1,11/pp tourist tax ⛽🚽Ch🚿WC🚿🔌 € 4/3

🚿included. 🚆 **Location:** Urban, simple, quiet. **Surface:** metalled. 📅 01/01-31/12. **Distance:** 🚲1km 🏊200m 🚆on the spot ⊗50m 🚆1km 🚴50m 🚶on the spot. **Remarks:** Max. 48h, check in at harbourmaster.

**Tourist information Medemblik:**
Ⓜ Museum Stoomtram. Steam tram museum: Hoorn-Medemblik.

⚓🅂 **Middenmeer** 🏴 9C1
**Jachthaven Middenmeer**, Havenstraat. **GPS:** n52,81236 e4,99112.⬆️.

12 🛏 € 13,50 ⛽🚽Ch🚿WCincluded 🔌 € 5/2 🚿 € 2. **Location:** Rural, comfortable. **Surface:** metalled. 📅 01/01-31/12. **Distance:** 🚲500m 🚴1,7km 🏊50m 🛒50m ⊗500m 🚐150m 🚴on the spot. **Remarks:** Max. 48h, check in at harbourmaster.

⚓🅂 **Naarden** 🌿⚓🏴 9D2
**Jachthaven Naarden**, Onderwal 4. **GPS:** n52,30874 e5,14703.⬆️.

10 🛏 € 18 + € 2/pp tourist tax ⛽🚽Ch🚿WC🔌 € 5/3 🚿included. 📷🚲 **Location:** Rural, comfortable, quiet. **Surface:** grassy/metalled. 📅 01/01-31/12. **Distance:** 🚲Naarden-vesting (fortress) 2,3km 🚴600m 🏊500m lake Gooi ⊗on the spot 🚆on the spot 🚴on the spot.

**Tourist information Naarden:**
Ⓜ Vestingmuseum. Fortress museum.
📅 Tue-Fri 10.30-17h, Sa/Su/holidays 12-17h.

🌿🅂 **Nieuw Vennep** 9C2
**December hoeve**, IJweg 1391. **GPS:** n52,28705 e4,62614.⬆️.

15 🛏 € 12 ⛽🚽Ch🚿included. **Location:** Rural, simple, quiet. **Surface:** metalled. 📅 01/04-01/10. **Distance:** 🚲1,5km 🏊1,5km ⊗1,5km. **Remarks:** Only cash payment.

⚓🅂 **Opperdoes** 9C1
**Imkerij de Bijenstal**, Zwarte pad. **GPS:** n52,76255 e5,08027.

3 🛏 € 11,10, 2 pers.incl ⛽🚽(2x) € 3,50 🚿. 📷 **Location:** Rural, simple, isolated, quiet. **Surface:** gravel. 📅 01/01-31/12. **Distance:** 🚲500m 🚴2km 🛒300m 🚆500m. **Remarks:** Boat rental.

**Tourist information Opperdoes:**
Ⓜ Museum stoomtram, Van Dedemstraat 8, Medemblik. Steam tram

museum: Hoorn-Medemblik.

## Oudendijk 9C1

**Bruin Eetcafé Les Deux Ponts**, Slimdijk 2.
**GPS:** n52,60462 e4,95983.

10 free, use of a meal obligated. **Location:** Rural, simple, quiet.
**Surface:** gravel. 01/01-31/12.
**Distance:** 2km on the spot on the spot on the spot.

## Purmerend 9C1

**Het Bolwerk**, Nieuwstraat. **GPS:** n52,50681 e4,95049.

5 € 6,90 € 1 € 0,15/h free.
**Location:** Urban, simple, quiet. **Surface:** metalled.
01/01-31/12. water: 01/11-01/04.
**Distance:** 200m 200m.
**Remarks:** Max. 72h, tuesday morning market.
**Tourist information Purmerend:**
Centrum. Tue.

## Schagen 9C1

**Jachthaven Schagen**, Lagedijkerweg 2B. **GPS:** n52,79088 e4,78746.

21 € 12,50 + € 1,15/pp tourist tax € 0,50/100liter Ch
included WC € 0,50 € 4/4 € 1. **Location:** Urban, simple, quiet.
**Surface:** metalled. 01/01-31/12.
**Distance:** 500m on the spot 400m 500m.
**Remarks:** Check in at harbourmaster, caution key sanitary
building € 15.
**Tourist information Schagen:**
West Friese Folkloremarkt. Folkore market. Jun-Jul-Aug: Thu.

## Slootdorp 7C3

**De Tulpentuin**, Wierweg 7. **GPS:** n52,85627 e5,01010.

8 € 9 + € 1,25/pp Ch (8x)WC included.
**Location:** Rural, isolated, quiet. **Surface:** metalled.
01/01-31/12.
**Distance:** Wieringerwerf 2km 2km 500m 2km 2km
on the spot on the spot.
**Remarks:** At tulip grower, regional products.

## Stompetoren 9C1

**Het Schermer Wapen**, Oterlekerweg 3. **GPS:** n52,61285 e4,82096.

4 free, use of a meal obligated. **Location:** Urban, simple.
**Surface:** gravel. 01/01-31/12 Wed.
**Distance:** 500m on the spot 500m.

## Texel/De Cocksdorp 7C3

**De Krim**, Roggeslootweg 6. **GPS:** n53,15110 e4,85996.

10 € 16-37,50 Ch included. **Surface:** grassy/metalled.
01/01-31/12.

## Vijfhuizen 9C2

**Camperpark N205**, Floriadepark. **GPS:** n52,34190 e4,67972.

100 € 12,50 Ch (20x) € 2,50 WC € 1 € 4 included.

**Location:** Rural, comfortable. **Surface:** grassy. 01/01-31/12.
**Distance:** 750m on the spot on the spot on the spot.
**Remarks:** Next to MH17-monument, bread-service, 24/24 surveillance,
bicycle rental.

## Volendam 9C1

**Marinapark Volendam**, De Pieterman 1.
**GPS:** n52,48944 e5,05972.

36 € 14 10-17h, € 20/24h Ch included € 5 .
**Location:** Comfortable, quiet.
**Surface:** grasstiles/metalled.
01/01-31/12.
**Distance:** 1,5km 50m 50m 300m 300m 300m.
**Tourist information Volendam:**
VVV, Zeestraat 37, www.vvv-volendam.nl.
Old fishermen's village.
Volendams Museum, Zeestraat 41.
Life and Work in Volendam, 1800-1900. 01/03-30/11 10-17h.

## Weesp 9C2

**Vecht & Weide**, Dammerweg 5c. **GPS:** n52,28729 e5,07152.

13 € 14 tourist tax incl Ch (8x),10Amp WC € 3,50
included.
**Location:** Rural. **Surface:** metalled. 01/01-31/12.
**Distance:** 4km 400m 400m 3,5km bus 300m on the
spot on the spot.
**Remarks:** Max. 9m, only cash payment.

## Wormerveer 9C1

Wandelweg. **GPS:** n52,48936 e4,79485.
5 € 12 Ch **Location:** Urban. **Surface:** metalled.
01/01-31/12.
**Distance:** 1km 100m 100m.

## Zaandijk 9C1

**Parking Zaanse Schans**, Wezelstraat. **GPS:** n52,46901 e4,80363.
15 free. **Location:** Urban, simple. **Surface:** asphalted.
01/01-31/12.
**Distance:** 100m.
**Remarks:** Max. 48h.

## Zandvoort 9C1

Boulevard Barnaart. **GPS:** n52,38752 e4,53479.
13 € 22. **Location:** Rural. **Surface:** metalled. 01/01-31/12.
**Distance:** on the spot on the spot 350m bus on the spot
on the spot.

## 't Zand 7C3

**Camperplaats Molen de Hoop**, Parallelweg 33.
**GPS:** n52,83628 e4,74931.

14 € 15 Ch WC included. **Location:** Rural.
**Surface:** grasstiles/grassy. 01/01-31/12.
**Distance:** centre 300m 4km 300m 350m 300m 150m
on the spot on the spot.
**Remarks:** Near mill, money in envelope in mail box, call for entrance
code.

# Friesland

## Akkrum 7D3

**Tusken de Marren**, Ulbe Twijnstrawei 31. **GPS:** n53,04853 e5,82577.

20 € 17 € 0,50/100liter Ch € 2,50/night WC
€ 4/2 included. **Location:** Rural, comfortable, quiet.
**Surface:** grassy/metalled. 15/03-01/11.
**Distance:** 200m on the spot on the spot 700m 500m
on the spot.
**Remarks:** Information at harbourmaster, boat rental.

## Anjum 7E2

**Camperplaats Tún-Hûs**, Bantswei 1a. **GPS:** n53,37751 e6,12999.

15 🛏 € 12 🚰 🔲Ch 🧹 (20x)WC 🔲 € 1 🔌included. **Location:** Rural. **Surface:** grassy/metalled. ☐ 01/04-31/10. **Distance:** 🚶400m 🏊2km ⊗350m 🍴550m 🛒500m 🦽on the spot 🎣 on the spot.

| 🏕 S | Appelscha 🏴 | 7E3 |
|---|---|---|

**De Compagnonshoeve**, Vaart Noordzijde 104. **GPS:** n52,95222 e6,36278.⬆.

10 🛏 € 8 🚰 🔲Ch 🧹 € 1,50 🔌included. 🦽 **Location:** Rural, simple, quiet. **Surface:** grassy. ☐ 01/01-31/12. **Distance:** 🚶on the spot 🏊3km 🍴on the spot ⊗200m 🍴400m 🍴400m 🛒50m.

| 🏕 S | Appelscha 🏴 | 7E3 |
|---|---|---|

**Camperplaats Appelscha**, Noorder Es. **GPS:** n52,95459 e6,33619.⬆.

10 🛏 € 10 🚰 🔲Ch 🧹 (10x) € 2/night WC 🔲 € 0,50 🔌included. 🦽 **Location:** Rural, luxurious, quiet. **Surface:** grassy/metalled. ☐ 01/01-31/12. **Distance:** 🚶on the spot 🏊5km 🍴900m ⊗on the spot 🍴1km 🛒500m 🦽on the spot 🎣 on the spot.

| | Balk 🏴 | 7D3 |
|---|---|---|

**Jachthaven Lutsmond**, Sleatemar 1a. **GPS:** n52,90389 e5,59694.⬆.

10 🛏 € 7,50-12,50 + € 1/pp tourist tax 🚰🔲Ch 🧹 € 3 WC 🔲🔌. **Location:** Rural, comfortable. **Surface:** grassy. ☐ 01/01-31/12. **Distance:** 🚶1km 🏊on the spot 🍴on the spot ⊗nearby 🍴1km 🦽on the spot 🎣 on the spot.

| 🏕 S | Bergum 🌿🏴🏴 | 7E3 |
|---|---|---|

**Camperterrein Prinses Margriet Kanaal**, Opperdijk van Veenweg 22. **GPS:** n53,18643 e6,00176.⬆➡.

20 🛏 € 10/night 🚰🔲Chincluded 🧹(20x) € 2/night 🔌1h

---

free, 1 day € 7,50. 🦽 **Location:** Urban, comfortable, quiet. **Surface:** grassy/metalled. ☐ 01/01-31/12. **Distance:** 🚶2km 🏊2km 🍴on the spot ⊗2km 🍴200m 🛒on the spot 🦽on the spot 🎣 on the spot.

| 🏕 S | Bergum 🌿🏴🏴 | 7E3 |
|---|---|---|

**W.S.V. Bergumermeer**, Bergumerdaam 51. **GPS:** n53,18705 e5,99299.⬆.

10 🛏 € 11 + € 1/pp tourist tax 🚰 € 0,50/100liter 🔲Ch 🧹 € 0,50/kWh WC 🔲 € 0,50/time 🍴 € 3,50/3,50 🔌included. 🦽 **Location:** Urban, comfortable, central, quiet. **Surface:** metalled. ☐ 01/04-31/10. **Distance:** 🚶500m 🏊2,5km 🏊5km 🍴on the spot ⊗900m 🍴500m 🛒500m 🦽on the spot 🎣 on the spot. **Remarks:** Max. 72h.

| | Blesdijke | 7E3 |
|---|---|---|

**Stoutenburght**, Markeweg 35a. **GPS:** n52,83850 e6,03339.⬆.

12 🛏 € 10 🚰🔲Ch 🧹(12x),6Amp WC 🔲🔌included. **Location:** Rural. **Surface:** grassy. ☐ 01/01-31/12. **Distance:** 🚶5km 🏊2km 🍴2km 🦽on the spot 🎣 on the spot.

| 🏕 S | Bolsward 🌿 | 7D3 |
|---|---|---|

**Camperplaats Half-Hichtum**, Hichtumerweg 14. **GPS:** n53,07365 e5,52253.⬆.

5 🛏 € 16 🚰🔲Ch 🧹 WC 🔲🔲 € 3,50 🔌included. 🦽 **Location:** Rural, comfortable, quiet. **Surface:** grassy/metalled. ☐ 01/04-15/10. **Distance:** 🚶1km 🏊1,3km 🏊6km 🍴500m ⊗1km 🍴1km 🛒200m 🦽on the spot 🎣 on the spot.

| | Brantgum | 7E2 |
|---|---|---|

**Camperplaats Veldzicht**, Veldbuursterweg 9. **GPS:** n53,35556 e5,93632.⬆.

20 🛏 € 12 🚰🔲Ch 🧹 🔌included. 🦽 **Location:** Rural, comfortable, isolated, quiet. **Surface:** grassy/metalled. ☐ 01/01-31/12. **Distance:** 🚶Dokkum 7km 🏊2km ⊗3km 🍴3km 🦽on the spot 🎣 on the spot. **Remarks:** Ferry boat to Ameland 3km.

| 🏕 S | Burdaard 🏴 | 7E3 |
|---|---|---|

**Jachthaven Mounehiem**, Mounewei 17. **GPS:** n53,29711 e5,88261.⬆.

---

12 🛏 € 12 🚰🔲Ch 🧹 € 1/night,10Amp WC 🔲 € 0,50/5minutes 🍴 € 4,50/2,50 🔌included. 🦽 **Location:** Rural, comfortable, quiet. **Surface:** grassy/gravel. ☐ 01/01-31/12. **Distance:** 🚶on the spot 🏊2km 🏊on the spot 🍴on the spot ⊗100m 🍴500m 🛒2km 🦽on the spot 🎣 on the spot. **Remarks:** Passerby € 1/100l.

| 🏕 S | Damwoude | 7E3 |
|---|---|---|

**Camperplaats Prikkebosk**, Dammeloane 46. **GPS:** n53,28238 e6,01201.

2 🛏 € 12,50 🚰🔲🧹 WC 🔲🔌included. 🏠 **Location:** Rural, isolated, quiet. **Surface:** metalled. ☐ 01/01-31/12. **Distance:** 🚶1km 🍴on the spot ⊗5km 🍴1km 🦽on the spot 🎣 on the spot.

| 🏕 S | De Westereen 🏴 | 7E3 |
|---|---|---|

**Camperpark Kuikhorne**, Kûkhernsterwei 31. **GPS:** n53,24124 e6,01875.⬆➡.

50 🛏 € 10, 2 pers.incl 🚰 € 1/100liter 🔲Ch 🧹 € 2 WC 🔲 € 0,50 🍴 € 4/3 🔌included. 🦽 **Location:** Rural, comfortable, quiet. **Surface:** asphalted/grassy. ☐ 01/01-31/12. **Distance:** 🚶2km 🍴on the spot ⊗2km 🏊2km 🍴1,5km 🦽on the spot 🎣 on the spot. **Remarks:** Free FryslanCard at reception, max. 72h, boat rental.

| 🏕 S | Dokkum 🌿 | 7E2 |
|---|---|---|

Van Kleffenstraat 8. **GPS:** n53,32496 e5,99254. 5 🛏 € 12, 2 pers.incl 🚰 € 0,50 🔲Ch 🧹 € 0,50 WC 🔲🔌free. 🦽 **Location:** Urban, central. **Surface:** grassy/metalled. ☐ 01/01-31/12. **Distance:** 🚶on the spot 🍴on the spot ⊗400m 🍴200m 🛒400m 🦽on the spot 🎣 on the spot. **Remarks:** Max. 72h.

| 🏕 S | Drachten | 7E3 |
|---|---|---|

**VV Drachten**, Gauke Boelensstraat. **GPS:** n53,10289 e6,08832.⬆.

5 🛏free. **Surface:** asphalted. ☐ 01/01-31/12. **Distance:** 🚶500m 🍴on the spot 🍴500m 🦽on the spot 🎣 on the spot.

| 🏕 S | Drachten | 7E3 |
|---|---|---|

**Jachthaven De Drait**, Biskopswei 27, De Wilgen. **GPS:** n53,10244 e6,04549.⬆.

NL

15 �85 € 10 ⚡☕Ch 🚿 € 2 WC⊐🔲 € 3,50/3,50 📶included. 🏠
**Location:** Rural, isolated, quiet. **Surface:** metalled.
🔵 01/01-31/12.
**Distance:** 🚲centre 4km ⊗2,5km 🚰2,5km.
**Remarks:** Check in at harbourmaster, wifi code at harbour master, boat rental.

### Earnewâld 7E3
Eilansgrien. **GPS:** n53,12958 e5,93630. ⬆➡.

5 ⌂5 € 7,40 + € 1/pp tourist tax ⚡☕Ch 🚿included WC⊐ € 0,50 🔲
€ 3,50/3,50 📶. **Location:** Rural, simple, quiet. **Surface:** asphalted.
🔵 01/01-31/12.
**Distance:** 🚲200m ⊗500m 🚰200m.
**Remarks:** Max. 72h, sanitary/washing machine at tourist office (Summer season).

### Elsloo 7E3
**Camperplaats Kale Duinen**, Kloosterweg 5. **GPS:** n52,94360 e6,27313.
9 ⌂5 € 12,50 ⚡☕Ch 🚿included WC⊐ 📶. **Location:** Rural,
isolated, noisy. **Surface:** asphalted. 🔵 01/01-31/12.
**Distance:** 🚲2,5km ⊗2,5km 🏊on the spot 🚶on the spot.

### Harlingen 7D3
**P2, de Ried**, Harlingerstraatweg 92. **GPS:** n53,18148 e5,42945.
20 ⌂5 ⚡☕Ch 🚿WC. 🔵 01/01-31/12.
**Distance:** 🚲on the spot 🚏on the spot ⊗1,5km 🚰1,5km.

### Harlingen 7D3
**Tsjerk Hiddesluizen**, Nieuwe Vissershaven 17.
**GPS:** n53,17938 e5,41731. ⬆.

14 ⌂5 € 7,70 ⚡ € 1 ☕Ch 🚿 (16x) € 1/2kWh WC⊐🔲. 🔌
**Location:** Urban, comfortable, quiet. **Surface:** asphalted.
🔵 01/01-31/12.
**Distance:** 🚲500m ⊗500m 🚰500m 🚏100m.
**Remarks:** Max. 72h, laundromat/toilets/shower 500m.

### Heerenveen 7E3
**Thialf**, Pim Mulierlaan 1. **GPS:** n52,93843 e5,94495. ⬆.

4 ⌂5free. **Surface:** metalled.
🔵 01/01-31/12 🔲 during event.
**Distance:** 🚲2km ⊗2km 🚰2km.
**Remarks:** On parking ground of skating rink, max. 72h.

### Heerenveen 7E3
**De Koningshof**, Prinsenweg 1. **GPS:** n52,94759 e5,94438. ⬆.

---

4 ⌂5free. **Surface:** asphalted. 🔵 01/01-31/12.
**Distance:** 🚲1km ⊗on the spot 🚰4km 🚏500m.
**Remarks:** Large parking near A32, max. 72h.

### Heerenveen 7E3
**Gemeentewerf**, Venus 4. **GPS:** n52,96663 e5,93502.
🚰free. 🔵 Mon-Fri 9-15u.

### Hogebeintum 7D2
**Bezoekerscentrum Terp Hegebeintum**, Pypkedyk 4.
**GPS:** n53,33612 e5,85266. ⬆.

4 ⌂5free. **Location:** Simple, isolated. **Surface:** asphalted.
🔵 01/01-31/12.
**Distance:** 🚲4km.
**Remarks:** Parking information centre/VVV, highest mound in the Netherlands, max. 2 days, ferry boat to Ameland 3km.

### IJlst 7D3
**De Tsjalk**, De Tsjalk. **GPS:** n53,00846 e5,62741. ⬆.

4 ⌂5 € 9,50 🚿 WCfree ⊐ € 0,50/5minutes.
**Location:** Urban, simple, central, quiet. **Surface:** metalled.
🔵 01/01-31/12.
**Distance:** 🚲200m 🚏on the spot ⊗200m 🚰200m 🚏200m 🏊on the spot 🚶on the spot.

### Jelsum 7D3
**Camperplaats Tjem Tjoeg**, Aldlansdyk 28. **GPS:** n53,23041 e5,81765.

3 ⌂5 € 5 🚿included. **Location:** Rural. **Surface:** grassy.
🔵 01/04-30/09.
**Distance:** 🚲Leeuwarden 5km.

### Joure 7D3
**Passantenhaven Joure**, Grienedyk. **GPS:** n52,97210 e5,78836. ⬆.

4 ⌂5 € 10 + € 1/pp tourist tax ⚡ € 0,50/70liter ☕Ch 🚿 € 3 ⊐ € 1

---

🔲 € 7,50. **Surface:** metalled. 🔵 01/03-01/11.
**Distance:** 🚲500m ⊗50m.
**Remarks:** Max. 72h.

### Kollum 7E3
**Yn't Paradyske**, Paradyske. **GPS:** n53,26295 e6,14533.
⌂5 € 8 ⚡☕ € 2/24h 📶. **Location:** Rural, comfortable.
**Surface:** grassy. 🔵 01/01-31/12.
**Distance:** 🚲2km.

### Kollum 7E3
**Jachthaven de Rijd**, Cantecleer 2. **GPS:** n53,28727 e6,15139. ⬆➡.

12 ⌂5 € 10 ⚡☕Ch 🚿,10Amp WC⊐🔲 📶included. 🔌
**Location:** Urban, simple, central, quiet. **Surface:** metalled.
🔵 01/05-01/10.
**Distance:** 🚲on the spot 🚏on the spot ⊗500m 🚰500m 🚏500m 🏊on the spot 🚶on the spot.
**Remarks:** Max. 72h.

### Koudum 7D3
**De Kuilart**, De Kuilart 1. **GPS:** n52,90305 e5,46706. ⬆➡.

10 + 2 ⌂5 € 8 ⚡☕Chincluded 🚿 € 1/night,6Amp
WC⊐ € 0,35/5minutes 🔲 € 4,40/2,35 📶. 🔌
**Location:** Rural, luxurious, noisy. **Surface:** grassy/metalled.
🔵 01/01-07/05, 22/05-05/07, 25/08-31/12 🔲 holidays.
**Distance:** 🚲1,5km 🏊on the spot 🚏on the spot ⊗on the spot 🚰1km 🚏1km 🏊on the spot 🚶on the spot.
**Remarks:** Quick-Stop: >17h - <10h, check in at reception.

### Langweer 7D3
**Brandweerkazerne**, Pontdyk. **GPS:** n52,96000 e5,71972. ⬆.

4 ⌂5free 📶free. **Location:** Simple. **Surface:** metalled.
🔵 01/01-31/12.
**Distance:** 🚲500m 🏊500m ⊗500m 🚰500m.
**Remarks:** Max. 72h.

### Langweer 7D3
**Passantenhaven Langweer**, Pontdijk 2. **GPS:** n52,96091 e5,72240. ⬆.

3 ⌂5 € 7,50 + € 1/pp tourist tax ⚡ € 0,50 ☕Ch 🚿 € 2 WC⊐ € 0,50
🔲 € 5/3 📶 € 1. **Location:** Rural, comfortable, quiet. **Surface:** grassy.
🔵 01/04-31/10.
**Distance:** 🚲500m 🏊on the spot 🚏on the spot ⊗500m 🚰500m 🚏500m.

NL

## Leeuwarden 7D3

**Prinsentuin**, Wissesdwinger 1. **GPS**: n53,20528 e5,79659.⬆️.

2🚐 € 6,50 🚰🗑️Ch🚿6Amp WC🚽 € 4,31/3 📶included.♻️
**Location**: Urban, comfortable, central, quiet. **Surface**: metalled.
🅾️ 01/01-31/12.🚻 sanitary building: 01/11-01/04.
**Distance**: 🚶500m 🚲2km 🏊on the spot ⛽on the spot ⊗on the spot
🚂400m 🚉on the spot 🚌on the spot 🚶on the spot.
**Remarks**: Max. 48h.

## Leeuwarden 7D3

**Camperplaats Leeuwarden**, De Zwemmer 3.
**GPS**: n53,18445 e5,83748.

12🚐 € 10 + € 1/pp tourist tax 🚰 € 1 🗑️Ch🚿 € 2,50/
night WC📶included. **Location**: Urban, comfortable, quiet.
**Surface**: metalled. 🅾️ 01/01-31/12.
**Distance**: 🚶5km 🚲2km 🏊on the spot ⛽on the spot ⊗1km 🚂1km
🅿️5km 🚉300m 🚌on the spot 🚶on the spot.
**Remarks**: 4th night free, free bus to centre, discount at shops, discount museum and theater.

## Leeuwarden 7D3

**Leeuwarder Jachthaven**, Jachthavenlaan 3.
**GPS**: n53,19886 e5,83019.⬆️➡️.

10🚐 € 12,50 + € 1/pp tourist tax 🚰🗑️Ch🚿(10x) € 2,10Amp 🚽 € 1/
time 📶included.♻️ **Location**: Urban, comfortable, isolated, quiet.
**Surface**: grassy/gravel. 🅾️ 01/04-31/10.
**Distance**: 🚶2,5km 🚲1km 🏊on the spot ⛽on the spot ⊗500m
🚂500m 🚉400m 🚌on the spot 🚶on the spot.
**Remarks**: Call if no one is present, 058 2125759, check in at harbourmaster, bicycle rental.

## Leeuwarden 7D3

**Taniaburg**, Vierhuisterweg 72. **GPS**: n53,21955 e5,79286.⬆️➡️.

8🚐 € 14, 2 pers. incl., dog € 1,50 🚰🗑️Ch🚿 € 2/night,6Amp
WC🚽 € 2,50/3 📶included. **Location**: Rural, comfortable, quiet.
**Surface**: grassy/gravel. 🅾️ 01/04-01/11.
**Distance**: 🚶3km 🚲1km 🏊on the spot ⛽on the spot 🚂500m
🚉500m 🚌on the spot 🚶on the spot.
**Remarks**: Canoe and bicycle rental.

## Lekkum 7D3

**Camperplaats Lekkum**, Mearsterpaed 6. **GPS**: n53,22360 e5,81660.

---

15🚐 € 17 🚰🗑️Ch🚿10Amp WC🚽📶included.♻️
**Location**: Rural, luxurious, isolated, quiet. **Surface**: grassy/metalled.
🅾️ 01/01-31/12.
**Distance**: 🚶750m 🚲7km 🚉500m 🚂950m.

## Lemmer 7D3

**Jachthaven Lemmer**, Plattedijk 4-12. **GPS**: n52,84708 e5,69696.⬆️.

25🚐 € 14,50 + € 1/pp tourist tax 🚰 € 0,50 🗑️Ch🚿 € 0,50 WC🚽
€ 0,50 📶. **Location**: Urban, comfortable, quiet. **Surface**: metalled.
🅾️ 01/01-31/12.
**Distance**: 🚶1km 🚲2,7km 🏊on the spot 🚂1km.

## Lemmer 7D3

**Watersportcentrum Tacozijl**, Plattedijk 20. **GPS**: n52,85122 e5,68102.

25🚐 € 15,50-23 🚰🗑️Ch🚿 € 0,50/kWh WC🚽included 🚽
€ 4/time 📶 € 2,50/day. **Location**: Rural, comfortable, quiet.
**Surface**: grassy/metalled. 🅾️ 01/01-31/12.
**Distance**: 🚶2km 🏊on the spot 🚂2km 🚉200m 🚌on the spot
🚶on the spot.

**Tourist information Lemmer:**
👁️ Ir. D.F. Woudagemaal. The biggest steam pumpingstation of Europe.
🅾️ Tue-Sa 10-17h, Su 13-17h.

## Lollum 7D3

**Camperplaats Landgoed Hizzard**, Hizzaarderlaan 16.
**GPS**: n53,11913 e5,51428.⬆️.
4🚐 € 14,50, tourist tax incl 🚰🗑️Chincluded 🚿 € 2,50/24h
WC🚽 € 2,50 📶. **Location**: Rural, comfortable, isolated, quiet.
**Surface**: grassy. 🅾️ 01/01-31/12.
**Distance**: 🚶city centre Winsum 3,8km ⊗on the spot 🚂3,8km
🚉1,4km 🚌on the spot 🚶on the spot.
**Remarks**: Regional products.

## Makkum 7D3

**Gemeentehaven Makkum**, Workumerdijk 2.
**GPS**: n53,05329 e5,40317.⬆️.

2🚐 € 10 ChWC🚽included 🚽 € 2/2.♻️ **Location**: Urban, simple,
central, noisy. **Surface**: metalled. 🅾️ 01/04-31/10 🅾️ service: 01/11-01/04.
**Distance**: 🚶100m 🚉on the spot ⊗400m 🚂950m 🚉950m 🚌on
the spot 🚶on the spot.
**Remarks**: Max. 72h.

---

## Mirns 7D3

**De Braamberg**, Murnserdyk. **GPS**: n52,85249 e5,48190.⬆️.

10🚐 € 10 + € 1/pp tourist tax 🚰🗑️Chincluded 🚿 € 2/day
WC🚽. **Location**: Rural. **Surface**: gravel. 🅾️ 01/01-31/12.
**Distance**: 🚉beach 250m.

## Molkwerum 7D3

**Campercamping 't Seleantsje**, 't Seleantsje 2.
**GPS**: n52,90419 e5,39493.⬆️.

18🚐 € 10-12 + € 1,25/pp tourist tax, dog € 2 🚰🗑️
Ch🚿WCincluded 🚽 € 0,50/6minutes 🚽 € 4/2,50 📶 € 5/
day.🚿 **Location**: Rural, comfortable, quiet. **Surface**: grasstiles.
🅾️ 01/01-31/12.
**Distance**: 🚶300m 🏊on the spot ⛽on the spot ⊗on the spot 🚂4km
🚉1km 🚌on the spot 🚶on the spot.
**Remarks**: Check in at campsite, bread-service.

## Nes 7E3

**Manege Nes**, Burdineweg 2. **GPS**: n53,05468 e5,85558.⬆️➡️.

10🚐 € 5 🚰🗑️Ch🚿 € 2/night,16Amp WC🚽📶included.
♻️ **Location**: Rural, simple, quiet. **Surface**: grassy/metalled.
🅾️ 01/01-31/12.
**Distance**: 🚶700m 🚲1km 🏊10km ⛽50m ⊗700m 🚂700m
🚉700m 🚌on the spot 🚶on the spot.
**Remarks**: At manege.

## Nijetrijne 7E3

**Paviljoen Driewegsluis**, Lindedijk 2a. **GPS**: n52,83261 e5,92467.⬆️.

6🚐 € 10 + € 1/pp tourist tax 🚰 € 0,50 🗑️Ch🚿 € 1/kWh.
**Location**: Simple, quiet. **Surface**: metalled. 🅾️ 01/01-31/12.
**Distance**: ⛽on the spot ⊗on the spot 🚌on the spot 🚶on the spot.

## Oude Bildtzijl 7D3

**Hoeve Noordveld**, Oudebildtdijk 6. **GPS**: n53,30236 e5,71276.⬆️.

NL

5 🛏 € 15 🚰🔌Ch 🚿(5x)WC 🗑included. **Location:** Rural, comfortable, isolated. **Surface:** gravel. 📅 01/01-31/12. **Distance:** 🚶600m ⊗600m 🚲 on the spot.

## ⚓S Oudega 🛶 7E3

**Jachthaven Oudega**, Roundeel. **GPS**: n53,12315 e5,99961. ⬆️.

5 🛏 € 10 🚰 € 1/100liter 🚿 € 1 🗑 € 1. **Location:** Simple. **Surface:** grassy. 📅 01/04-01/11. **Distance:** 🚶200m ⊗200m 🚆200m. **Remarks:** Max. 48h.

## ⚓S Oudemirdum 🌳 7D3

**Landgoed de Syme**, Jan Schotanuswei 106a, via Oude Balksterweg. **GPS**: n52,85746 e5,51115. ⬆️➡️.

2 🛏 € 7,50 🚰included 🚿 € 2,50/night. 🚮 **Location:** Rural, simple, isolated, quiet. **Surface:** grassy/metalled. 📅 01/01-31/12. **Distance:** 🚶4km 🚴6km 🚆6km ⊗4km 🚆4km on the spot 🏊 on the spot. **Remarks:** Possibility for reservation.

## ⚓S Oudeschoot 🛶 7E3

**Minicamping 't Woutersbergje**, Van Bienemalaan 15-17. **GPS**: n52,93544 e5,96009. ⬆️➡️.

7 🛏 € 12,90 🚰🔌Ch 🚿 € 2,50/night,6Amp WC 🗑📷 € 3/2 🗑included. 🚮 **Location:** Rural, comfortable, central, quiet. **Surface:** metalled. 📅 01/01-31/12. **Distance:** 🚶3,5km 🚆300m 🚲 on the spot 🏊 on the spot.

## ⚓S Ried 🛶 7D3

**Jachthaven it Kattegat**, Berlikumerweg 13. **GPS**: n53,22416 e5,59330.

3 + 4 🛏 € 9,50 🚿🚮 **Location:** Rural, simple, quiet. **Surface:** grassy/metalled. 📅 01/04-01/10.

---

**Distance:** 🚶on the spot 🚴500m 🚆on the spot 🚆on the spot 🚆500m 🚲 on the spot 🏊 on the spot.

## 🌿S Rohel 7D3

**Aktiviteitenboerderij**, Vierhuisterweg 29. **GPS**: n52,90337 e5,84540. ⬆️.

5 🛏 € 15 + € 1/pp tourist tax 🚰🔌Ch 🚿 WC 🗑included. **Location:** Rural, isolated, quiet. **Surface:** metalled. 📅 01/01-31/12. **Distance:** 🚆on the spot 🚆on the spot ⊗on the spot 🚆on the spot.

## ⚓S Sint Jacobiparochie 7D3

# Camperpark Zwarte Haan Sint Jacobiparochie

## Located in nature reserve Located directly at sea Restaurant with regional specialties

## www.zwartehaan.nl info@dezwartehaan.nl

**Camperpark Zwarte Haan**, Nieuwebildtdijk 428. **GPS**: n53,30915 e5,63051. ⬆️. 20 🛏 € 12,50 🚰🔌Ch 🚿(20x),10Amp WC 🗑included. **Location:** Comfortable, isolated, quiet. **Surface:** grassy/metalled. 📅 01/01-31/12. **Distance:** 🚶50m, Sint Jacobiparochie 8km 🚴8km 🚆Wadden Sea 🚆100m ⊗on the spot 🚆5km 🚲 on the spot 🏊 on the spot.

## ⚓S Sint Nicolaasga 7D3

Westend 23. **GPS**: n52,91450 e5,73725.

20 🛏 € 10 🚰🔌Ch 🚿(20x) WC 🗑 € 0,50 📷included. **Location:** Rural, comfortable. **Surface:** gravel. 📅 01/04-01/10. **Distance:** 🚶1,2km 🚆20m 🚆20m 🚆1,2km. **Remarks:** Near marina.

## ⚓S Sloten 🌿🛶 7D3

**Jachthaven Lemsterpoort**, Jachthaven 7. **GPS**: n52,89265 e5,64486. ⬆️➡️.

10 🛏 € 12 🚰 € 0,50/100liter 🔌Ch 🚿 € 2,50/24h,6Amp WC 🗑 € 1/5minutes 🗑included. 🚮 **Location:** Urban, comfortable, quiet. **Surface:** grassy/metalled. 📅 01/01-31/12. **Distance:** 🚶100m 🚴2km 🚆on the spot 🚆on the spot ⊗100m

---

🚆100m 🚆500m 🚲 on the spot 🏊 on the spot.

## ⚓S Sneek 🛶 7D3

**Camperplaats Aquanaut**, Selfhelpweg 7. **GPS**: n53,02725 e5,66302.

12 🛏 € 15 🚰🔌Ch 🚿(12x) WC 🗑 € 0,50 📷 € 2,50 🗑. **Location:** Urban. **Surface:** metalled. 📅 01/01-31/12. **Distance:** 🚶500m 🚴500m 🚆100m 🚆500m 🚆500m 📷50m 🚆500m 🚲 on the spot 🏊 on the spot. **Remarks:** Water closed during wintertime.

## 🏨S Sneek 🛶 7D3

**Amicitia Hotel Sneek**, Graaf Adolfstraat. **GPS**: n53,02378 e5,67595. ⬆️➡️.

10 🛏 € 10, free with a meal 🚰🔌Ch 🚿 🗑 € 2,50 📷 € 10 🗑included. 🍴 **Surface:** metalled. 📅 01/01-31/12. **Distance:** 🚶1,5km 🚴400m 🚆8km ⊗on the spot. **Remarks:** Reservation during Sneek sailing week: info@amicitiahotel. nl, 1st week of August.

## ⚓S Stavoren 🌿⛵🛶 7D3

**Marina Stavoren Buitenhaven**, Suderstrand 2. **GPS**: n52,87360 e5,36715. ⬆️.

25 🛏 € 14,50, tourist tax incl 🚰🔌Ch 🚿 € 2,16Amp WC 🗑📷 € 4,50/2,50 🗑included 🚿. **Location:** Rural, comfortable, quiet. **Surface:** asphalted. 📅 01/04-31/10. **Distance:** 🚶Stavoren 500m 🚆on the spot 🚆on the spot ⊗on the spot 🚆500m 🚆500m 🚲 on the spot 🏊 on the spot. **Remarks:** Max. 3 nights, check in at harbourmaster.

## ⚓S Sumar 7E3

**Recreatiecentrum Bergumermeer**, Solcamastraat 30. **GPS**: n53,19044 e6,02316. ⬆️➡️.

10 🛏 € 20 🚰🔌Ch 🚿 WC 🗑included. 🚮 **Location:** Rural, luxurious, quiet. **Surface:** grassy/metalled. 📅 01/04-31/10. **Distance:** 🚶5km.

## ⚓S Sumar 7E3

**Recreatiecentrum Bergumermeer**, Solcamastraat-30. **GPS**: n53,19044 e6,02316.

1 🛏 € 8 17-10h. ☐ 01/04-31/10.
**Remarks:** Quick-Stop: >17h - <10h.

🚲S **Surhuisterveen** 7E3
**Zwembad Wettervlecke**, Badlaan 3. **GPS:** n53,17987 e6,16124.⬆️

5 🛏 € 5 🚰 € 1 💧 € 1 WCuse sanitary facilities at swimming pool
☐included. **Location:** Urban, simple, central. **Surface:** grassy.
☐ 01/05-12/09.
**Distance:** 🚉500m 🛒500m.

🚲S **Tersoal** 7D3
**Watersportbedrijf Lege Geaen**, Buorren 2.
**GPS:** n53,07729 e5,74360.⬆️➡️

6 🛏 € 10 + € 1,25/pp tourist tax 🚰 Ch 💧 € 2,50/night
WC 🌊included. **Location:** Rural, comfortable, quiet.
**Surface:** grassy/gravel. ☐ 01/04-31/10.
**Distance:** 🚉8km 🏖1,5km 🛍on the spot 🛒on the spot ⊗1,5km
🛒8km 🚲on the spot 🚶on the spot.

🚲S **Wartena** 7E3
**Jachthaven Wartena**, Stukenwei. **GPS:** n53,15145 e5,90532.

10 🛏 € 10 💧 € 0,50/100liter Ch 💧 WC 🌊 € 1 🔌 € 6 🌊.
**Location:** Rural, comfortable, central, quiet. **Surface:** grassy/metalled.
☐ 01/01-30/11.
**Distance:** 🚉200m 🛍on the spot 🛒on the spot ⊗500m 🛒500m.
🛒on the spot 🚲on the spot.
**Remarks:** Bicycle rental.

🚲S **Wijnjewoude** 7E3
**Op Het Eind**, Opper Haudmare 2. **GPS:** n53,05441 e6,17790.
2 🛏 € 8 🚰 € 1 💧 € 2 🌊. **Surface:** metalled.
☐ 01/01-31/12.
**Distance:** 🚉2km 🚲on the spot 🚶on the spot.

🚲S **Winsum** 7D3
**Camperplaats Winsum**, Skans 12. **GPS:** n53,15177 e5,63111.⬆️

---

4 🛏 € 10 🚰 Ch 💧included WC 🌊 🔌 🚿 🛁
**Location:** Urban, simple, central, quiet. **Surface:** metalled.
☐ 01/01-31/12.
**Distance:** 🚉on the spot ⊗200m 🛒500m.

🚲S **Wjelsryp** 7D3
**De Slypstien**, Westerein 31. **GPS:** n53,16431 e5,58775.
10 🛏 € 13 🚰 💧 WC 🌊included. **Location:** Rural. **Surface:** grassy.
☐ 01/01-31/12.

⚓S **Wommels** 7D3
**Jachthaven Wommels**, Terp 14. **GPS:** n53,10957 e5,58765.⬆️

8 🛏 € 11 🚰 💧 💧 WCincluded 🌊 € 0,50. 🛁 **Location:** Rural, simple,
quiet. **Surface:** grassy/metalled. ☐ 01/04-01/10.
**Distance:** 🚉300m 🛍on the spot 🛒100m.
**Remarks:** Market 100m, museum 200m.

**Tourist information Wommels:**
🏛 ☐ Tue-morning.

🚲S **Workum** 🌾🏕☕🍦 7D3
**Jachthaven Bouwsma**, Moleburren 11. **GPS:** n52,98230 e5,45518.⬆️

10 🛏 € 10-12,50 + € 1/pp tourist tax 🚰 Ch 💧 € 2,50/night,6Amp
WC € 2 🌊 € 1/7minutes 🔌 € 8/0 🌊included. 🛁
**Location:** Urban, central, quiet.
**Surface:** grassy/metalled.
☐ 01/04-31/10.
**Distance:** 🚉750m 🏖1,5km 🛍on the spot ⊗500m 🛒500m
🛒200m 🚲on the spot 🚶on the spot.
**Remarks:** Bicycle rental.

**Tourist information Workum:**
Ⓜ Jopie Huisman Museum, Noard 6.
Autodidact, paintings and drawings. 🎫 € 8,50.

🚲S **Woudsend** 🏕🍦 7D3
**Recreatiecentrum De Rakken**, Lynbaen 10.
**GPS:** n52,94649 e5,62732.⬆️➡️

15 🛏 € 17 + € 1/pp tourist tax 🚰 Ch 💧 WC 🌊included
🌊 € 4,50/2,50 🌊. **Location:** Rural, simple, quiet.
**Surface:** grassy/metalled. ☐ 15/03-15/10.
**Distance:** 🚉200m 🏖2,5km 🛍200m ⊗200m 🛒200m.

🚲S **Ypecolsga** 🎏🍦 7D3
**Camperplaats Waterloo**, Nr. 19. **GPS:** n52,92758 e5,59549.⬆️

---

13 🛏 € 10, 2 pers.incl 🚰 Ch 💧 € 2,50/24h 🌊included.
**Location:** Rural. **Surface:** grasstiles. ☐ 01/03-01/11.
**Distance:** 🚉3km 🏖1km 🛍1km ⊗3,5km 🛒3,5km 🛒nearby
🚲on the spot.

🚲S **Zurich** 7D3
**Camperplaats Zurich**, Caspar di Roblesdijk 3.
**GPS:** n53,11235 e5,39335.⬆️

3 🛏 € 3 + € 1,25/pp tourist tax. 🛁
**Location:** Urban, simple, central, noisy. **Surface:** metalled.
☐ 01/01-31/12.
**Distance:** 🚉on the spot 🏖1,5km 🛍on the spot 🛒on the spot 🚲on
the spot 🚶on the spot.
**Remarks:** Max. 72h.

# Groningen

🚲S **Appingedam** 🌾🏕☕🍦 7F2
**Camperplaats Appingedam**, Farmsumerweg 21.
**GPS:** n53,32062 e6,86689.⬆️

10 🛏free 🚰 Chfree 💧 € 1/kWh,10Amp.
**Location:** Urban, simple, central, noisy. **Surface:** metalled.
☐ 01/01-31/12.
**Distance:** 🚉750m 🛒Damsterdiep ⊗500m 🛒500m 🛒on the spot
🚲on the spot 🚶on the spot.
**Remarks:** Max. 72h.

**Tourist information Appingedam:**
🏛 Solwerderstraat. ☐ Sa 09-16h.

🚲S **Blauwestad** 🍦 7F3
**Havenkwartier Blauwestad**, Elfenbank. **GPS:** n53,16506 e7,03867.⬆️
10 🛏 € 8 + € 0,95/pp tourist tax 🚰 💧 € 1/kWh WC 🌊included. 🏠
**Location:** Simple, quiet. **Surface:** metalled.
☐ 01/01-31/12.
**Distance:** 🏖on the spot 🛒on the spot ⊗300m.

🚲S **Blijham** 7F3
**Camperpark Turfstee**, Turfweg 28. **GPS:** n53,11118 e7,02912.⬆️

55 🛏 € 10 + € 0,75 tourist tax 🚰 Ch 💧 WC 🌊 € 0,50/5minutes
🌊 € 7,50/0 🌊included. **Location:** Rural, comfortable, isolated.
**Surface:** grassy/gravel. ☐ 01/01-31/12.
**Distance:** 🚉3km 🏖3km 🛒3km 🛒on the spot 🚲on the spot.

NL

## Delfzijl 7F2

Zeebadweg. **GPS:** n53,33582 e6,92650.

8 free Chfree € 1. **Location:** Urban, simple.
**Surface:** asphalted/metalled. 01/01-31/12.
**Distance:** 500m on the spot on the spot 100m 300m.
**Remarks:** Max. 48h.

## Doezum 7E3

**Landgoed Jonker**, Provincialeweg 133a.
**GPS:** n53,20411 e6,26018.

60 € 10, 2 pers.incl Ch (20x) € 2/day,4Amp
WC included.
**Location:** Rural, luxurious, quiet. **Surface:** grassy/metalled.
25/03-01/10.
**Distance:** 1,5km on the spot on the spot on the spot.

**Tourist information Doezum:**
Abel Tasman Kabinet, Kompasstraat 1, Grootegast.
Local archaeological museum seafarer Abel Tasman.
Thu-Sa 13.30-16.30h.

## Finsterwolde 7F3

**Minicamping B&B Kostverloren 11**, Kostverloren 11.
**GPS:** n53,21356 e7,16193.

2 € 11 € 2 € 2,50/day WC included.
**Location:** Rural, comfortable, isolated, quiet. **Surface:** gravel.
01/04-01/11.
**Distance:** 4km 4km 4km 4km on the spot on the spot.

## Groningen 7E3

**Sportcentrum Kardinge**, Bieskemaar. **GPS:** n53,23946 e6,59680.

15 tourist tax. **Location:** Rural, simple, quiet. **Surface:** grassy.
01/01-31/12.
**Distance:** 3km 1km on the spot.
**Remarks:** Max. 72h.

**Tourist information Groningen:**
Prinsenhof en prinsenhoftuin. 15/03-15/10.

## Haren 7E3

**De Lijste**, Meerweg. **GPS:** n53,16298 e6,57878.
6 free. **Surface:** grassy. 01/01-31/12.
**Distance:** 1,3km no bathing 250m.
**Remarks:** Max. 72h.

## Lauwersoog 7E2

**Lauwersmeerplezier**, Kustweg 30. **GPS:** n53,40625 e6,20044.

23 € 17, 2 pers. incl WC € 3 included.
**Location:** Rural, comfortable, quiet. **Surface:** grassy/metalled.
01/01-31/12.
**Distance:** 500m on the spot on the spot 500m 500m.
**Remarks:** Service closed during wintertime.

## Lauwersoog 7E2

**Havenkantoor Lauwersoog**, Haven 2.
**GPS:** n53,40819 e6,19768.

2 € 2/m Ch WC included. **Location:** Urban, simple,
quiet. **Surface:** metalled. 01/01-31/12.
**Distance:** on the spot on the spot on the spot on the spot
on the spot.
**Remarks:** Motorhomes <7m.

## Lauwersoog 7E2

**Jachthaven Noordergat**, Noordergat 1.
**GPS:** n53,40493 e6,20311.

30 € 15 + € 1,15/pp tourist tax Ch included WC
€ 0,50/5minutes € 3/2,50. **Location:** Rural, simple, quiet.
**Surface:** concrete. 01/01-31/12.
**Distance:** on the spot on the spot on the spot on the spot.
**Remarks:** Max. 72h.

**Tourist information Lauwersoog:**
Lauwersmeergebied. Breeding area for birds and recreation area.
01/04-31/10 Tue-Su 11-17h.

## Leek 7E3

**Landgoed Nienoord**, Midwolderweg 19. **GPS:** n53,17137 e6,38138.

10 € 18 Ch included WC. **Location:** Comfortable.
**Surface:** metalled. 01/01-31/12.
**Distance:** 5km on the spot 1,5km.

**Tourist information Leek:**
Nationaal Rijtuig Museum, In Borg Nienoord.
Tue-Fri 10-17h, Sa-Su 13-17h.

## Leens 7E2

**Leenstertillen**, Leenstertillen 2. **GPS:** n53,35066 e6,37002.

15 € 12,50 Chservice € 3 included WC € 1.
**Location:** Rural, simple, quiet. **Surface:** grassy/gravel.
01/01-31/12.
**Distance:** 1,5km 50m 50m 1,5km 1,6km.
**Remarks:** Dog € 1,50/night, barbecue place.

## Losdorp 7F2

**Restaurant Eemshaven**, Schafferweg 29.
**GPS:** n53,37214 e6,84411.

4 consuming is appreciated Ch € 5,customersWC free.
**Location:** Rural, simple, quiet. **Surface:** metalled. 01/01-31/12
Mo.
**Distance:** 2km 2km 1km on the spot on the spot.
**Remarks:** Code wifi in restaurant.

## Lutjegast 7E3

**'t Kompas**, Kompasstraat 1. **GPS:** n53,23498 e6,25972.

5 free. **Surface:** metalled. 01/01-31/12.
**Distance:** 200m on the spot 200m on the spot.
**Remarks:** Behind the club-building.

## Midwolda 7F3

**Blauwestadhoeve**, Hoofdweg 156. **GPS:** n53,19424 e7,00751.

6 € 10 + € 0,95/pp tourist tax € 2,25 € 1,50 Ch € 1,50
(6x) € 1,45 WC € 1 € 1 € 1,45. **Location:** Rural.
**Surface:** grassy/metalled. 01/01-31/12.
**Distance:** 250m 2km 900m 500m 100m 250m
100m on the spot on the spot.

NL

## Midwolda — 7F3

### Jachthaven Midwolda

- **Located near marina**
- **Located directly at lake**
- **Beautiful view**

**www.jachthavenmidwolda.nl**
**info@watersporthuningas.nl**

**Jachthaven Midwolda**, Strandweg 1. **GPS**: n53,19634 e7,03068.
5 ☒ € 11,90, 2 pers. incl ⚡ € 0,50/100liter Ch ✎ € 2/day WC 🚿 included. **Location:** Rural, comfortable, quiet.
**Surface:** grassy. 📅 01/04-31/10.
**Distance:** 🚶 city centre 1km 🛒 on the spot ⊗ on the spot ⚡ 1km 🚰 500m ♨ on the spot.
**Remarks:** View at Lake Oldambt.

## Musselkanaal — 7F3

**Jachthaven Spoordok**, Havenkade 1. **GPS**: n52,92694 e7,01389.

35 ☒ € 14,20 + € 0,90/pp tourist tax ⚡ € 0,50/100liter Ch ✎ (35x) WC 🚿 included. **Location:** Rural, comfortable, quiet.
**Surface:** grassy/metalled. 📅 01/04-01/11.
**Distance:** 🚶 200m 🛒 on the spot ⚡ on the spot ⊗ on the spot ⚡ nearby 🚰 on the spot ♨ on the spot.
**Remarks:** Max. 72h.

## Nuis — 7E3

### Camperplaatsen "Het Knooppunt" Nuis

- **Beautiful view**
- **Walking and bicycle area**
- **Free wifi access**

**camperplaatsenhetknooppunt.nl**
**croffel@ziggo.nl**

**Het Knooppunt**, Oudeweg 47. **GPS**: n53,15061 e6,31021.
12 ☒ € 10, 2 pers. incl, extra pers € 2,50 ⚡ Ch ✎ € 2 WC 🚿 included. **Location:** Rural. **Surface:** grassy/metalled.
📅 01/04-01/10.
**Distance:** 🚶 on the spot ✎ 3km 🛒 5km ⚡ 2km ⊗ 200m ⚡ 3,5km 🚰 on the spot ♨ on the spot ♿ on the spot.
**Remarks:** Breakfast-service, charging point for electric bicycles.

## Onderdendam — 7E2

**Watersportvereniging Onderdendam**, Warffumerweg 12.
**GPS**: n53,33652 e6,58600.

---

6 ☒ € 10 + € 1/pp ⚡ € 0,50 Ch ✎ (6x) € 2,50 WC included
🚿 € 0,50 ⊞ € 3,50/time. **Location:** Rural, simple, quiet.
**Surface:** grassy/metalled. 📅 01/01-31/12.
**Distance:** 🚶 500m 🛒 on the spot ⚡ on the spot ⊗ 500m ⚡ 500m.

## Onstwedde — 7F3

Holte 9. **GPS**: n53,05021 e7,04459.

5 ☒ € 3 ⚡ Ch included ✎ € 2,4Amp. ♿ **Location:** Rural, simple.
**Surface:** grassy. 📅 01/01-31/12.
**Distance:** 🚶 1km ⊗ 1km ⚡ 1km 🚰 1km ♨ on the spot.

## Onstwedde — 7F3

**Camperplaats Op Streek**, Streekweg 4. **GPS**: n53,05615 e7,05517.
30 ☒ € 8,50 ⚡ Ch included ✎ € 1/24h 🚿. **Location:** Rural, isolated, quiet. **Surface:** grassy. 📅 01/01-31/12.
**Distance:** 🚶 2,8km ⚡ 2,8km ♨ on the spot ☀ on the spot.

## Onstwedde — 7F3

**Ooldershoeve**, Veenhuizen 6. **GPS**: n53,02214 e7,01250.
10 ☒ € 8, 2 pers. incl + tourist tax € 0,90/pp ⚡ € 1 Ch ✎ € 2 🚿 included.
**Location:** Rural. **Surface:** grassy. 📅 01/01-31/12.
**Distance:** 🚶 2km ⚡ 2,5km ♨ on the spot ☀ on the spot.

## Slochteren — 7F3

**Camperplek Duurswoldje**, Duwolaan 2.
**GPS**: n53,20051 e6,79020.

7 ☒ € 7 ⚡ Ch ✎ included 🚿 € 1/24h. **Location:** Rural, simple, quiet. **Surface:** grassy. 📅 01/01-31/12.
**Distance:** 🚶 500m 🛒 on the spot ⊗ on the spot ⚡ 1km 🚰 on the spot.
**Remarks:** Covered picnic area, small stock accommodation.

## Stadskanaal — 7F3

**De Roo Campers**, Unikenkade 1. **GPS**: n53,03556 e6,87617.

10 ☒ € 5 ⚡ Ch WC included 🚿.
**Location:** Rural, simple, quiet. **Surface:** grassy.
📅 01/01-31/12.
**Distance:** 🚶 8km ✎ 4km 🛒 on the spot ⚡ on the spot ⊗ 8km ⚡ 8km.

**Tourist information Stadskanaal:**
ℹ Pagedal, www.stadskanaal.nl. Daytime recreation.

## Ter Apel — 7F3

**Jachthaven De Runde**, Oosterkade 5. **GPS**: n52,87179 e7,07329.

---

14 ☒ € 7,50 + € 0,75/pp tourist tax ⚡ € 0,50/100liter Ch ✎
€ 1/2kWh WC 🚿 € 0,50 ⊞ € 4/2 🚿 included.
**Location:** Rural, comfortable, quiet. **Surface:** metalled.
📅 01/01-31/12.
**Distance:** 🚶 1km 🛒 on the spot ⚡ on the spot ⊗ on the spot ⚡ 1km 🚰 500m ♨ on the spot.
**Remarks:** Wifi 5h free.

## Termunterzijl — 7F2

**Zeestrand**, Schepperbuurt 4a. **GPS**: n53,30173 e7,03085.

15 ☒ € 10 + € 1,45/pp tourist tax ⚡ Ch ✎ € 3,10 WC included 🚿
€ 1/6minutes ⊞ € 4/2 🚿 € 2,50 ♿ 🚰 ♨
**Location:** Rural, comfortable, quiet. **Surface:** metalled.
📅 29/03-01/11.
**Distance:** 🚶 100m 🛒 100m ⚡ 100m ⊗ 300m ⚡ 4km 🚰 100m ♨ 100m ☀ 100m.
**Remarks:** Registration via intercom or phone.

## Veendam — 7F3

**Borgerswold**, Flora 2. **GPS**: n53,10637 e6,84826.

60 ☒ € 5 + € 3/pp ⚡ Ch ✎ 6Amp WC 🚿 included. ♿
**Location:** Rural, simple, quiet.
**Surface:** grassy.
📅 01/01-31/12.
**Distance:** 🚶 2km 🛒 beach 50m 🛒 on the spot ⊗ on the spot ⚡ 1km ⚡ 1,5km ♨ on the spot.
**Remarks:** Canoe rental.

**Tourist information Veendam:**
🅜 ✎ Museumspoorlijn STAR, Parallelweg 4, Veendam.
Museum railway line, tickets available at railwaystation.
🎫 round trip € 15.
🅜 Veenkoloniaalmuseum, Museumplein 5.
History of the peat, shipping and industry.
🕐 Tue-Thu 11-17h, Fri-Mo 13-17h 📅 01/09-30/06 Mo.
🎫 € 7,50.

## Winschoten — 7F3

**Jachthaven de Rensel**, Hellingbaan 4. **GPS**: n53,14405 e7,04760.

10 ☒ € 11, 2 pers. incl ⚡ € 0,50 Ch ✎ WC included.
**Location:** Simple, quiet. **Surface:** concrete. 📅 01/01-31/12.
**Distance:** 🚶 800m ⊗ 200m McDonalds ⚡ 200m AH.

NL

## Winschoten 7F3

**Hotel Café Restaurant Bowling In den Stallen**, Oostereinde 10. **GPS**: n53,15371 e7,06528.⬆.

10 🍴 consuming is appreciated 🚰 on demand 🔌.
**Location**: Rural, simple, quiet.
**Surface**: asphalted/metalled.
**Distance**: 🚲1km 🛒600m ➦600m ⊗on the spot 🍺1km 🚌600m.

**Tourist information Winschoten:**
👁 Stoomgemaal, Winschoter Oostereinde. Steam-engine 1895.

## Winsum 7E2

**Jachthaven/Camping Marenland**, Winsumerstraatweg. **GPS**: n53,33177 e6,51015.⬆➡.

10 🍴 € 14,50, 2 pers.incl. 🚰🔌Ch🔌WC⬜🔌 € 6,50/0 🔌included,at restaurant. 🚲 **Location**: Urban, comfortable, quiet.
**Surface**: grassy/metalled. 🕐 01/04-01/10.
**Distance**: 🚲300m ⟂200m ➦on the spot ⊗on the spot 🍺500m 🚌200m 🚲on the spot 🚶Pieterpad.

## Zeerijp 7F2

**Johanna Hoeve**, Groeveweg 1. **GPS**: n53,35058 e6,73776.

16 🍴 € 7,50 🚰🔌Chaccording consumption 🔌🔌included.
**Location**: Comfortable, quiet. **Surface**: grassy. 🕐 01/01-31/12.
**Distance**: 🚲2km.

## Zoutkamp 7E2

**Jachthaven Hunzegat**, Strandweg 17. **GPS**: n53,34114 e6,29406.⬆.

11 🍴 € 16,30 🚰🔌Ch,dump chem.toilet only with biodegradable liquid 🔌(10x)WCincluded 🔌 € 0,50 ⬜ € 7,50/0 🔌.🚐
**Location**: Rural, comfortable, quiet. **Surface**: grassy/metalled.
🕐 01/01-31/12.
**Distance**: 🚲500m 🚲 25km ⟂500m ➦on the spot ⊗500m 🍺500m 🚌200m 🚲on the spot.
**Remarks**: Bread-service.

**Tourist information Zoutkamp:**
👁 Zeehondencrèche, Hoofdstraat 94a, Pieterburen. Sanctory to cure sick seals. 🕐 Mo-Fr 9-17h, Sa-Su 10-17h. 🎫 € 10,50.

## Zuidbroek 7F3

**De Broeckhof**, W.A. Scholtenweg 18. **GPS**: n53,16118 e6,86054.⬆.

5 🍴 free 🚰🔌Ch🔌WC🔌 € 0,50 ⬜ € 1 🔌free.
**Location**: Rural, simple, central, quiet. **Surface**: metalled.
🕐 01/01-31/12.
**Distance**: 🚲500m ➦on the spot ⊗on the spot 🍺1km ⬜on the spot 🚌on the spot 🚲on the spot.
**Remarks**: Max. 72h.

# Drenthe

## Assen 7E3

Havenkade. **GPS**: n53,00054 e6,57742.⬆.
🍴 € 10 🚰 € 0,50 Ch🔌 € 1/kWh. **Location**: Simple, quiet.
**Surface**: metalled. 🕐 01/01-31/12.
**Distance**: 🚲city centre 1,5km ⟂on the spot ➦on the spot ⊗1km 🍺400m.

## Borger 7F3

**Nuuverstee**, Rolderstraat 4. **GPS**: n52,92633 e6,77447.⬆➡.

9 🍴 € 15 🚰🔌Ch🔌(9x),10Amp WC🔌🔌included. 🚲
**Location**: Rural, luxurious. **Surface**: grassy/metalled. 🕐 01/01-31/12.
**Distance**: 🚲800m 🛒600m ⟂2km ➦500m ⊗600m 🍺1km 🚌500m 🚲on the spot 🚶on the spot.
**Remarks**: Bread-service, charging point for electric bicycles, use of sauna against payment.

## Dwingeloo 9E1

**Torentjeshoek**, Leeuweriksveldweg 1. **GPS**: n52,81927 e6,36077.⬆➡.

6 🍴 € 10-19 + € 1,10/pp tourist tax 🚰🔌Ch🔌,10Amp WC🔌🔌included,on camp site. 🚲 **Location**: Rural, luxurious, quiet.
**Surface**: grassy/metalled 🕐 01/01-31/12.
**Distance**: 🚲2km 🚲 2km ⟂200m ➦200m ⊗2km 🍺2km 🚌1km 🚲on the spot 🚶on the spot.
**Remarks**: Arrival >16h, departure <11h.

## Eelderwolde 7E3

**Scandinavisch Dorp**, Oude Badweg 1. **GPS**: n53,16984 e6,55391.⬆.

5 🍴 free.
**Location**: Rural, simple, quiet. **Surface**: asphalted/grassy.
🕐 01/01-31/12 🍽 Restaurant: Tue, 01/10-01/04 Mo-Tue.
**Distance**: 🚲2km 🚲 5km ⟂500m ➦on the spot ⊗on the spot 🍺2km 🚌200m 🚲on the spot 🚶on the spot.
**Remarks**: Use of a meal desired.

## Eext 7F3

**Schaopvolte**, Stationsstraat 60a. **GPS**: n53,00007 e6,72862.⬆.

10 🍴 € 9,50 excl. tourist tax 🚰 € 1 🔌Ch🔌(6x) € 1/4kWh WC🔌 € 0,50 🚰 € 4,50 🔌 € 2/day. **Location**: Rural, simple, quiet.
**Surface**: grassy/gravel. 🕐 01/04-01/11.
**Distance**: 🚲2km.

## Elim 9E1

**De Barswieke**, Barsweg 9. **GPS**: n52,67144 e6,57821.⬆.

10 🍴 € 8 + € 1,10/pp tourist tax 🚰🔌Chincluded 🔌 € 1,50 WC🔌 € 0,50 🔌. **Location**: Rural, comfortable, quiet. **Surface**: grassy.
🕐 01/01-31/12.
**Distance**: 🚲1km 🚌1km.

## Emmen 9F1

Kerkhoflaan/Emmalaan. **GPS**: n52,78091 e6,90330.⬆➡.

10 🍴free.
**Location**: Urban, simple. **Surface**: grassy.
🕐 01/01-31/12.
**Distance**: 🚲1km 🍺Albert Heijn 600m.
**Remarks**: Behind hotel Eden, max. 72h, zoo Emmen 900m.

**Tourist information Emmen:**
Wildlands Adventure Zoo, Raadhuisplein 99. Zoo.
🕐 10-17h.

## Erica 9F1

**Achter op Erica**, Verlengde Herendijk. **GPS**: n52,73006 e6,92256.⬆.

15 🍴 € 8 🚰🔌Chincluded 🔌(15x) € 3 🔌 € 1. **Location**: Rural.
**Surface**: grassy. 🕐 01/01-31/12.
**Distance**: 🚲3,5km 🚌on the spot 🚶on the spot.
**Remarks**: Closed when frosty, possibility for reservation.

## Het Haantje 9F1

**Camperplaats 't Haantje**, Haantje 8. **GPS**: n52,81539 e6,83443.

30 🛏 € 15 + € 1,15/pp tourist tax 🚰🔌Ch 🚿,6Amp WC 🚽🚻 against payment 📶 included. **Location:** Rural. **Surface:** grassy. ⬛ 30/03-14/10.
**Distance:** 🚉Emmen 7km 🚲on the spot.

**Hoogersmilde** 7E3

**De Reeënwissel**, Bosweg 23. **GPS:** n52,90450 e6,38490.

🛏 € 12 🚰🔌Ch included 🚿 € 1 WC 📶. **Location:** Rural.
**Surface:** grassy/gravel. ⬛ 01/01-31/12.
**Distance:** ⊗on the spot 🚻1,3km 🚲on the spot 🚶on the spot.

**Hoogeveen** 9E1

Markt. **GPS:** n52,72821 e6,47966.
4 🛏 € 7,50 🚿 € 1/kWh.🔌🚰
**Location:** Urban, central, noisy. **Surface:** metalled.
⬛ 01/01-31/12.
**Distance:** 🚉on the spot ⊗100m 🚻50m 🚲on the spot 🚶on the spot.
**Remarks:** Max. 72h.

**Hoogeveen** 9E1

Terpweg 3. **GPS:** n52,72639 e6,50040.

3 🛏 free. **Location:** Rural, simple, isolated. **Surface:** metalled.
⬛ 01/01-31/12.
**Distance:** 🚉2km 🚴2,2km ⊗100m 🚻1km 🚌1km.
**Remarks:** At sports park, max. 72h.

**Matsloot** 🌊 7E3

**Camping Pool**, Matsloot 1a. **GPS:** n53,19354 e6,44980.⬆

10 🛏 € 10 🚰🔌Ch 🚿 WC 🚽🚻 📶 included.🚿 **Location:** Rural, simple, isolated, quiet. **Surface:** metalled. ⬛ 01/01-31/12.
**Distance:** 🚉5km 🏊on the spot 🚏on the spot ⊗on the spot.
**Remarks:** On Leekster lake.

**Meppel** 🍴 9E1

**Jachthaven**, Westeinde 32. **GPS:** n52,69615 e6,18096.⬆

---

15 🛏 € 8,10, 2 pers.incl 🚰 € 0,50 🔌Ch 🚿 WC 🚽🚻 € 3/3 📶.🚿
**Location:** Urban, comfortable, central, quiet. **Surface:** grassy.
⬛ 01/01-31/12.
**Distance:** 🚉500m 🏊on the spot 🚏on the spot ⊗on the spot 🚻400m.

**Nieuwlande** 9F1

**Bonenstee**, Brugstraat 87. **GPS:** n52,67889 e6,61194.⬆

20 🛏 € 7,50, 01/11-31/03 € 6 🚰🔌Ch 🚿(6x) € 1,50 WC 🚽
€ 1 📶 included. **Location:** Rural. **Surface:** grassy/metalled.
⬛ 01/01-31/12 ⬛ service 01/11-31/03.
**Distance:** 🚉2km 🏊4km 🚏4km ⊗2km 🚻2km 🚌100m 🚴bike junction 🚶on the spot.
**Remarks:** Max. 72h.

**Noord-Sleen** 🐑 9F1

**De Kalverweide**, Zweeloërstraat 1. **GPS:** n52,79330 e6,79475.⬆

10 🛏 € 12 🚰🔌Ch 🚿,6Amp WC 🚽 📶 included. **Location:** Rural, comfortable, quiet. **Surface:** grassy. ⬛ 01/01-31/12.
**Distance:** 🚉500m 🚌on the spot 🚲on the spot.
**Remarks:** Use of sauna against payment.

**Oosterhesselen** 9F1

**Sauna Hesselerbrug**, Verlengde Hoogeveensevaart 32.
**GPS:** n52,73535 e6,72029.

🛏 € 12,50, use of sauna obligatory. **Surface:** metalled.
**Distance:** 🚉4km 🏊4km.

**Ruinen** 9E1

**De Wiltzangh**, Witteveen 2. **GPS:** n52,78140 e6,36581.

10 🛏 € 12,50, tourist tax incl 🚰🔌Ch 🚿 € 0,50/kWh WC 🚽🚻
€ 4,50 📶 included. **Location:** Rural, comfortable, quiet.
**Surface:** grassy/sand. ⬛ 01/01-31/12.

---

**Distance:** 🚉2km ⊗2km 🚻on the spot 🚌2km 🚲on the spot 🚶on the spot.

**Ufelte** 9E1

**De Blauwe Haan**, Weg achter de es 11.
**GPS:** n52,80220 e6,27264.⬆➡

6 🛏 € 10 excl. tourist tax 🚰🔌Ch 🚿 € 2,50/night,10Amp WC 🚽 included 📶.🚿 **Location:** Rural, luxurious, quiet.
**Surface:** grassy/metalled. ⬛ 01/04-31/10.
**Distance:** 🚉5km 🚴2km 🏊3km 🚏3km ⊗2,5km 🚻5km 🚌2km 🚲on the spot 🚶on the spot.

**Westerbork** 7F3

**Vakantiepark het Timmerholt**, Gagelmaat 4.
**GPS:** n52,86923 e6,61806.⬆➡

4 🛏 € 11,90, 12/07-17/08 € 14,95 + € 1,70/pp tourist tax 🚰🔌 Ch 🚿 WC 🚽🚻 € 4/3 📶 included. 🍞🏪 **Location:** Rural, luxurious, quiet. **Surface:** grassy/metalled. ⬛ 01/01-31/12.
**Distance:** 🚉2km 🚴3km 🏊200m 🚏200m ⊗30m 🚻2km 🚌2km 🚲on the spot 🚶on the spot.
**Remarks:** Bread-service, water closed during wintertime.

**Tourist information Westerbork:**
🅜 Herinneringscentrum Kamp Westerbork, Oosthalen 8, Hooghalen.
⬛ Mo-Fri 10-17h, Sa-Su 11-17h, 01/07-31/08 and holidays 11-17h.

**Wijster** 9E1

**Grondsels**, Grondselweg 7. **GPS:** n52,80143 e6,49025.⬆

10 🛏 € 5 🚰🔌Ch 🚿 € 2 WC 🚽🚻 📶 included.
**Location:** Rural, simple, isolated, quiet. **Surface:** grassy/metalled.
⬛ 15/03-31/10.
**Distance:** 🚉3km 🏊on the spot ⊗3km 🚻5km 🚲on the spot.

# Overijssel

**Almelo** 9F1

Stationsstraat. **GPS:** n52,35827 e6,65589.
6 🛏 free 🚿.
**Location:** Urban. **Surface:** metalled. ⬛ 01/01-31/12.
**Distance:** 🚉600m.
**Remarks:** Max. 72h.

**Tourist information Almelo:**
ⓘ Markt- en Centrumplein. ⬛ Thu 8.30-14h, Sa 8.30-17h.

**Bathmen** 🐑 9E2

Prinses Margrietlaan. **GPS:** n52,25025 e6,29927.⬆

NL

2 ☐free. **Location:** Urban, simple, central, quiet. **Surface:** metalled. ☐ 01/01-31/12.
**Distance:** ⊿1km ⚓2,5km ⊗1km 🍺1km 🚲 on the spot 🚶 on the spot.
**Remarks:** Parking gymnasium, max. 2 nights.

| 🏛 | **Belt Schutsloot** | 9E1 |
|---|---|---|

**Café-Restaurant de Belt**, Havezatheweg 4. **GPS:** n52,66774 e6,05189.

10 ☐free for clients.
**Surface:** asphalted. ☐ 01/01-31/12.
**Distance:** ⊿3km ⚓1km ⊗1km 🍺 on the spot 🍺3km.
**Remarks:** North of Zwartsluis, at Belter- and Beulakerwijde.

| 🏕S | **Bentelo** 👥 | 9F2 |
|---|---|---|

**CamperCamping De Bentelose Esch**, Eschweg 2.
**GPS:** n52,21250 e6,67010. ⬆➡.

25 ☐ € 15, 2 pers.incl ⛽🔌Ch💧(25x)WC🚮 € 4 ≋included.
🚿 **Location:** Rural, luxurious, quiet. **Surface:** grassy/gravel.
☐ 15/03-01/11.
**Distance:** ⊿2km ⚓5km ⊗2km 🍺2km ⚌400m 🚲 on the spot 🚶 on the spot.

| 🏕S | **Beuningen** | 9F1 |
|---|---|---|

**De Nijenhaer**, Nijenhaerweg 25. **GPS:** n52,34471 e6,99325. ⬆.

15 ☐ € 12,50 ⛽🔌Ch💧WC🚮 ≋included. **Location:** Rural.
**Surface:** grassy. ☐ 01/01-31/12.
**Distance:** ⊿3km 🚲 on the spot 🚶 on the spot.

| 🏕 | **Borne** | 9F2 |
|---|---|---|

**De Aak. GPS:** n52,30197 e6,75906. ⬆.
1 ☐free. **Location:** Urban. **Surface:** metalled. ☐ 01/01-31/12.
**Distance:** ⊿200m ⊗200m 🍺500m.

| 🏕 | **Dalfsen** 🐑🎣🍴👥 | 9E1 |
|---|---|---|

Stationsweg 4. **GPS:** n52,49944 e6,25949. ⬆.

5 ☐free. **Location:** Rural, simple, central, quiet. **Surface:** grasstiles.
☐ 01/01-31/12.
**Distance:** ⊿500m ⊗500m 🍺800m ⚌ on the spot 🚲 on the spot 🚶 on the spot.
**Remarks:** Max. 48h.

| 🏕S | **Dalfsen** 🐑🎣🍴👥 | 9E1 |
|---|---|---|

**Starnbosch**, Sterrebosweg 4. **GPS:** n52,47538 e6,26336. ⬆➡.

7 ☐ € 10 + € 0,85/pp tourist tax ⛽🔌Ch💧(8x),10Amp WCincluded
🚮 € 0,40/5minutes ≋ € 5/0,50 ≋ € 1/1h.
**Location:** Rural, comfortable, quiet. **Surface:** grassy/sand.
☐ 01/01-31/12.
**Distance:** ⊿4km ⊗ on the spot 🍺4km ⚌3,3km 🚲 on the spot 🚶 on the spot.
**Remarks:** Max. 2 nights.

| 🏕S | **De Lutte** 👥 | 9F2 |
|---|---|---|

**Erve Velpen**, Beuningerstraat 25. **GPS:** n52,33224 e7,01197. ⬆.

20 ☐ € 7, tourist tax € 1/pp ⛽🔌Ch💧 € 2/day,6Amp 🚮
€ 1/8minutes ≋included. 🚿 **Location:** Rural, comfortable, isolated,
quiet. **Surface:** grassy. ☐ 01/01-31/12.
**Distance:** ⊿4km ⚌300m 🚲 bike junction 🚶 on the spot.

| 🏛 | **De Lutte** 👥 | 9F2 |
|---|---|---|

**De Twentse Nar**, Bentheimerstraat 80. **GPS:** n52,30990 e7,02370.
6 ☐free. ☐ 01/01-31/12.
**Distance:** ⊗ on the spot.

| 🏕S | **Den Ham** | 9E1 |
|---|---|---|

**De Linderbeek**, Zomerweg 56. **GPS:** n52,44526 e6,49870. ⬆.

4 ☐ € 12,50 ⛽🔌Ch💧WC🚮 € 5 ≋included. 🚐🚲
**Location:** Rural, comfortable, isolated, quiet.
**Surface:** asphalted/metalled. ☐ 01/04-01/10.
**Distance:** ⊿2,5km ⊗2km 🚲 on the spot 🚶 on the spot.
**Remarks:** Max. 7 nights, € 2,50 discount on presentation of the the most recent guide.

| 🏕S | **Diepenheim** 🎣🐑 | 9E2 |
|---|---|---|

**Camperpark Diepenheim**, Esweg 6. **GPS:** n52,18307 e6,57872. ⬆➡.

40 ☐ € 12,50, 2 pers.incl, tourist tax € 2,10 ⛽🔌Ch💧(30x),6Amp
WC🚮 € 1 ≋included. 🚿 **Location:** Rural, luxurious, quiet.
**Surface:** grassy/metalled. ☐ 15/03-01/11.
**Distance:** ⊿2km ⛵ on the spot ⚌ on the spot ⊗2km 🍺2km 🚲 on the spot 🚶 on the spot.
**Remarks:** Money in envelope in mail box.

| 🏛S | **Diepenheim** 🐑 | 9E2 |
|---|---|---|

**'t Holt**, Hengevelderweg 1A. **GPS:** n52,19500 e6,59186. ⬆.

3 ☐ € 5, free for clients ⛽🔌Chfree.
**Surface:** metalled.
☐ 01/01-31/12.
**Distance:** ⊿3km ⚌ on the spot ⊗ on the spot 🍺3km 🚲 on the spot.
**Remarks:** Golf court (pitch+putt).

| 🏛 | **Diepenheim** 🎣🐑 | 9E2 |
|---|---|---|

**In de Kokkerieje**, Grotestraat 94. **GPS:** n52,19923 e6,55452. ⬆.

☐free with a meal. ☐ Mo-Tue.
**Distance:** ⊿ on the spot ⚌1km 🍺500m.
**Remarks:** Parking behind restaurant.

| 🏕S | **Enschede** ⚓🍴 | 9F2 |
|---|---|---|

**De Loeks**, Moorvenweg 2a. **GPS:** n52,17757 e6,86599. ⬆➡.

15 ☐ € 18,50, dog € 1 ⛽🔌Ch💧(15x)WC🚮 € 2 ≋included. 🚿
**Location:** Rural, luxurious, isolated, quiet. **Surface:** grassy/metalled.
☐ 01/01-31/12 ☐ sanitary 01/11-31/03.
**Distance:** ⊿3km ⊗2km 🍺2km 🚲 on the spot 🚶 on the spot.

| 🏕 | **Enschede** ⚓🍴 | 9F2 |
|---|---|---|

**Diekmanterrein**, Weggelhorstweg. **GPS:** n52,20543 e6,90096. ⬆.

5 ☐ € 3,50 + € 0,20/pp tourist tax. **Location:** Urban, simple, isolated,
noisy. **Surface:** asphalted. ☐ 01/01-31/12.
**Distance:** ⊿2km ⚓1,4km ⚌ on the spot.

NL

## Enter 🏕 9E2

Werfstraat. **GPS**: n52,29808 e6,58271.⬆.

3 🚐 free. **Location**: Urban, simple. **Surface**: grassy/gravel.
🗓 01/01-31/12.
**Distance**: 600m on the spot on the spot ⊗600m 🚉700m 🚲 on the spot 🚶 on the spot.
**Remarks**: Max. 72h.

## Geesteren 9F1

**Camperplaats Het Witteven**, Witteveensweg 3.
**GPS**: n52,41755 e6,69116.⬆.

25 🚐 € 12,50 🔌Ch 🚿 WC 🚽 € 0,50 🛜 included. 🚽
**Location**: Rural. **Surface**: grassy. 🗓 01/03-01/11.
**Distance**: 3km 1,5km 🚉5km ⊗ 3km 🚲 on the spot 🚶 on the spot.

## Geesteren 9F1

**Zalencentrum Spalink**, Koelenbeekweg 10. **GPS**: n52,44060 e6,69555.

15 🚐 € 8,50 🔌Ch 🚿 WC. **Surface**: grassy/gravel.
🗓 01/01-31/12.
**Distance**: 3,5km ⊗ on the spot 🚉3,5km 🚲 on the spot 🚶 on the spot.
**Remarks**: Guests free.

## Geesteren 9F1

**Land van Maas en Webbink**, Vinckenweg 83.
**GPS**: n52,43513 e6,67557.
8 🚐 € 5. **Location**: Rural, quiet. **Surface**: gravel.
🗓 01/01-31/12.
**Distance**: 5km 🚉7km 1km ⊗50m 🚉500m 🚲 on the spot 🚶 on the spot.

## Genemuiden 9E1

Koppel. **GPS**: n52,62355 e6,03678.
2 🚐 free. **Location**: Urban. **Surface**: metalled. 🗓 01/01-31/12.
**Distance**: 200m ⊗250m 🚉800m.

## Giethoorn 9E1

**Camperplaats Haamstede**, Kanaaldijk 17.
**GPS**: n52,72828 e6,07570.⬆➡.

40 🚐 € 10, 2 pers.incl 🔌 € 0,50 🔌Ch 🚿 € 3 WC 🚽 € 0,50 🛜 included. 🚽 **Location**: Rural, comfortable, central, quiet.
**Surface**: grassy. 🗓 01/04-31/10.
**Distance**: 2km 🚉1km 20m ⊗1km 🚉1km 🚲 on the spot 🚶 on the spot.
**Remarks**: Arrival <21h.

## Giethoorn 9E1

**Camperresort Bodelaeke**, Vosjacht 10A. **GPS**: n52,71703 e6,07668.⬆.

99 🚐 € 15, 2 pers.incl 🔌 € 0,50/100liter 🔥 € 5 Ch € 5 🚿,16Amp WC 🚽 € 0,20 🔌 € 6/4 🛜 included. 🚐 **Location**: Rural, comfortable.
**Surface**: grassy/metalled. 🗓 15/03-28/10.
**Distance**: 1km on the spot on the spot ⊗ on the spot.
**Remarks**: Bike/boat rental.

## Giethoorn 9E1

**Passantenhaven de Zuiderkluft**, Vosjacht 1G.
**GPS**: n52,72134 e6,07449.

30 🚐 € 10 + € 1/pp 🔌 € 0,50/80liter 🔌Ch 🚿 € 1/2kWh WC 🚽 € 0,50 🔌 € 4/4 🛜.
**Location**: Comfortable. **Surface**: grassy/gravel.
🗓 01/01-31/12 🔌 service: 01/11-01/04.
**Distance**: 1km on the spot on the spot ⊗600m.
**Remarks**: Check in at harbourmaster.

**Tourist information Giethoorn:**
ℹ VVV, Eendrachtsplein 1, www.kopvanoverijssel.nl.
Village in nature reserve De Weerribben, Dutch Venice, boat trips possible.

## Gramsbergen 9F1

**Jachthaven 't Hooge Holt**, Kanaaldijk West 2b.
**GPS**: n52,60563 e6,67462.
10 🚐 € 10 🔌 € 1 🔌Ch 🚿 € 1/24h. **Location**: Simple, quiet.
**Surface**: grassy. 🗓 01/04-01/10.
**Distance**: 1km on the spot on the spot ⊗1km 🚉900m 900m 🚲 on the spot 🚶 on the spot.
**Remarks**: Max. 72h.

## Haaksbergen 🏕 9F2

**Henk Pen Caravans en Kampeerauto's**, Westsingel 2.
**GPS**: n52,14917 e6,71167.🚶.

2 🚐 free 🚿 free. **Location**: Simple, noisy. **Surface**: asphalted.
🗓 01/01-31/12.
**Distance**: 1km on the spot ⊗ on the spot 🚉1km.
**Remarks**: Motorhome dealer.

## Haaksbergen 🏕 9F2

**Camping Scholtenhagen**, Scholtenhagenweg 30.
**GPS**: n52,14820 e6,72467.⬆➡.

## — 9E1

24 🚐 € 10 🔌Ch 🚿 (24x) WC 🚽 € 0,90 🔌 € 5,25 🛜 included. 🚐
**Location**: Rural, luxurious, quiet. **Surface**: grassy. 🗓 01/01-31/12.
**Distance**: 2km 🚉7km ⊗3km 🚲 on the spot 🚉2,5km 1km 🚲 on the spot 🚶 on the spot.
**Remarks**: Max. 72h, bread-service, excl use swimming pool.

## Hardenberg 9E1

**De Kuserbrink**, Parkweg. **GPS**: n52,57746 e6,62927.⬆.

4 🚐 € 10 🔌 € 0,50/100liter 🔌Ch 🚿 (4x) € 1/kWh. 🚐
**Location**: Rural, comfortable, central, quiet. **Surface**: grasstiles.
🗓 01/01-31/12.
**Distance**: centre 500m 🚲 on the spot 🚶 on the spot.
**Remarks**: Max. 72h.

## Hardenberg 9E1

**Camperplaats Collendoorn**, Allemansweg 1a, Collendoorn.
**GPS**: n52,58845 e6,59146.⬆.

25 🚐 € 12 🔌Ch 🚿 WC 🚽 🛜 included. 🚐
**Location**: Rural, comfortable, isolated, quiet.
**Surface**: grassy/metalled. 🗓 01/01-31/12.
**Distance**: 3km 🚉2km 🚉2km 100m 🚲 bike junction 🚶 on the spot.
**Remarks**: Dog on leads.

## Hasselt 9E1

**Jachthaven de Molenwaard**, Van Nahuysweg 151.
**GPS**: n52,59367 e6,08741.⬆➡.

10 🚐 € 9 + € 0,70/pp tourist tax 🔌Ch 🚿 (10x) € 2,50/night WC 🚽 € 0,50/6minutes 🔌 € 3,75/3,75 🛜 included. 🚐
**Location**: Urban, luxurious, quiet. **Surface**: metalled.
🗓 01/01-31/12.
**Distance**: 500m on the spot on the spot ⊗500m 🚉500m 500m 🚲 on the spot 🚶 on the spot.
**Remarks**: Check in at harbourmaster.

## Heeten 9E1

**De Baanbreker**, Speelmansweg 8. **GPS**: n52,36026 e6,31190.⬆➡.

NL

10 🛏 € 4 🚻 € 1 🚿 € 0,50 Ch € 0,50 🔌 € 1,50. **Surface:** metalled.
🅿 01/01-31/12.
**Distance:** 🛒2km 🏊2km 🚲2km on the spot 🚶on the spot.
**Remarks:** Max. 48h.

### Hellendoorn
**Camperplaats Hancate**, Ommerweg 150a.
**GPS:** n52,43418 e6,44060. ⬆️➡️.

10 🛏 € 10 🚻 Ch 🚿 (4x) 🔌 included. 🚮 **Location:** Rural, simple,
quiet. **Surface:** grassy. 🅿 01/01-31/12.
**Distance:** 🛒5km on the spot ✖️100m 🚈200m on the spot
🚶on the spot.
**Remarks:** Money in envelope in mail box.

### Hengelo 9F2
**Jachthaven Hengelo**, Kanaalweg 8. **GPS:** n52,25123 e6,76216.

6 🛏 € 10 + € 1/pp tourist tax 🚻 Ch 🚿 included.
**Location:** Rural. **Surface:** grassy/metalled. 🅿 01/05-01/10.
**Distance:** 🛒3km on the spot ✖️on the spot 🚈3km on the spot
🚶on the spot.
**Remarks:** Max. 72h, max. 7m.

### Hengelo 9F2
**Camperplaats Eulerhook**, Vöckersweg 19.
**GPS:** n52,24652 e6,75365. ⬆️.

15 🛏 € 10 🚻 Ch 🚿 (15x) WC 🔌 included. 🚮 **Location:** Rural,
comfortable, noisy. **Surface:** metalled. 🅿 01/01-31/12.
**Distance:** 🛒4km 🏊2km ✖️500m ✖️4km 🚈3km 🚈1km on the
spot 🚶on the spot.
**Remarks:** Nearby motorway.

### Hertme 9F2
**Camperpark Rabo Scheele**, Hertmerweg 37.
**GPS:** n52,32663 e6,74691. ⬆️➡️.

25 🛏 € 12, 2 pers.incl 🚻 Ch 🚿 WC 🔌 included. 🚮
**Location:** Rural, comfortable, quiet. **Surface:** grassy/metalled.
🅿 01/01-31/12.
**Distance:** 🛒Hertme 500m, Borne 2km ✖️100m ✖️500m 🚈2km
🚈2km on the spot 🚶on the spot.

### Hoge Hexel 9E1
**Recreatiepark de Bonte Specht**, Piksenweg 23.
**GPS:** n52,39507 e6,52838. ⬆️.

16 🛏 € 12,50 🚻 Ch 🚿 WC 🔌 included. 🚌 **Location:** Rural,
luxurious. **Surface:** grassy. 🅿 01/01-31/12.
**Distance:** 🛒4km 🏊400m on the spot ✖️2km 🚈4km 🚈on the
spot 🚶on the spot.
**Remarks:** At fish pond.

### Holten 9E2
**Camperplaats Holten**, Schreursweg 5. **GPS:** n52,27862 e6,44847. ⬆️.
25 🛏 € 12 🚻 Ch 🚿,10Amp WC 🔌 included. 🚮
**Location:** Rural, comfortable, luxurious, quiet. **Surface:** grassy.
🅿 01/04-31/10.
**Distance:** 🛒1,5km 🏊2km ✖️500m 🚈on the spot 🚶on the spot.

### Holten 9E2
**Camperplaats Lookerland**, Rijssenseweg 34A.
**GPS:** n52,28515 e6,43866.

25 🛏 € 10 🚻 Ch € 2/day 🚿 (10x),10Amp WC 🔌 € 0,50
🔌 included. **Location:** Rural, quiet. **Surface:** grassy/metalled.
🅿 01/01-31/12.
**Distance:** 🛒1,3km 🏊3km ✖️1,3km 🚈1,3km 🚈100m 🚈on the spot
🚶Pieterpad.
**Remarks:** Max. 7 nights, money in envelope in mail box.

**Tourist information Holten:**
ℹ️ VVV, Dorpsstraat 27, www.vvvholten.nl.

### Kampen 9E1
Burgemeester Berghuisplein 1. **GPS:** n52,55268 e5,91356. ⬆️.

25 🛏 € 7,80 🚻 Ch WC included 🔌 € 0,50/6minutes. 🔌
**Location:** Urban, comfortable, central, quiet. **Surface:** metalled.
🅿 01/01-31/12.
**Distance:** 🛒historical centre 500m 🏊1,5km ✖️1,5km ✖️900m
🚈1km on the spot 🚶on the spot.
**Remarks:** Max. 72h, entrance code sanitary building at town hall.

**Tourist information Kampen:**
ℹ️ VVV, Oudestraat 151,
www.vvvkampen.nl.
Former Hanseatic town on the IJssel.

### Losser 9F2
**Brilmansdennen**, Bookholtlaan. **GPS:** n52,26927 e7,01378. ⬆️➡️.

3 🛏 free. **Surface:** metalled. 🅿 01/01-31/12.
**Distance:** 🛒1km.
**Remarks:** At sports park, max. 72h.

### Nieuwleusen 9E1
**Camperplaats Vechtdal**, Den Hulst 20. **GPS:** n52,59193 e6,29324. ⬆️.

12 🛏 € 6 + € 5/pp 🚻 Ch 🚿 WC 🔌 included. 🚌 🚿
**Location:** Rural, comfortable, quiet. **Surface:** grassy.
🅿 01/01-31/12.
**Distance:** 🛒800m 🚈800m on the spot 🚶on the spot.
**Remarks:** Bread-service, sauna and spa.

### Nieuwleusen 9E1
Koninging Julianalaan. **GPS:** n52,58213 e6,28076. ⬆️.

3 🛏 free. **Location:** Urban, simple. **Surface:** metalled.
🅿 01/01-31/12.
**Distance:** 🛒300m 🚈on the spot 🚶on the spot.
**Remarks:** Max. 48h.

### Nijverdal 9E1
**De Wilgenweard**, Sportlaan 6. **GPS:** n52,37118 e6,46538. ⬆️➡️.

3 🛏 € 5 + € 0,75/pp tourist tax. 🚮 **Surface:** metalled.
🅿 01/01-31/12.
**Distance:** 🛒500m 🏊on the spot ✖️on the spot ✖️on the spot
🚈500m 🚈200m on the spot 🚶on the spot.

### Oldemarkt 9E1
**VanWijk Jachthaven**, Dwarsveld 7. **GPS:** n52,82600 e5,96750.

10 ☕ € 11 🔌Ch✂(1x),4Amp WC🚰 € 0,50 📶included 📷.
**Location:** Rural. **Surface:** metalled. 📅 01/01-31/12.
**Distance:** 🚂900m 🚌750m ⛵20m 🚃50m ⊗900m 🍴900m
🚆750m.
**Remarks:** Nature reserve.

### 🅃🅢 Ommen 〰️🌸 9E1
**Landgoed De Stekkenkamp**, Beerzerweg 3.
**GPS:** n52,51128 e6,43933.⬆️➡️

8 ☕ € 7,50 + € 0,80/pp tourist tax 🔌 € 0,50/4minutes 🔌Ch✂(8x)
included. 📷 **Location:** Rural, simple, quiet. **Surface:** grasstiles/grassy.
📅 01/01-31/12.
**Distance:** 🚂1,2km ⛵1,2km 🚃1,2km ⊗1,2km 🍴1,2km 🚆1,2km
🚆 on the spot 🚶 on the spot.
**Remarks:** At historical farmhouse, max. 72h, money in envelope in
mail box.

### Overdinkel 🌸 9F2
**Camperplaats Skop'nboer**, Schaapskooiweg 2.
**GPS:** n52,24692 e7,03581.⬆️➡️

25 ☕ € 15, dog € 1 🔌Ch✂ WC🚰 📶included. 📷
**Location:** Rural, luxurious, quiet. **Surface:** grasstiles/grassy.
📅 01/01-31/12.
**Distance:** 🚂3km 🍴3km 🚆 on the spot 🚶 on the spot.

### 🅃🅢 Steenwijk 〰️ 9E1
**Camperplaats Passantenhaven Steenwijk**, Steenwijkerdiep 129.
**GPS:** n52,78667 e6,10082.⬆️➡️

10 ☕ € 10 + € 1/pp tourist tax 🔌 € 0,50/80liter 🔌Ch✂
€ 1/2kWh WC🚰 € 1/time 📷 € 4/4 📶included. **Location:** Urban.
**Surface:** grassy/metalled. 📅 01/04-31/10.
**Distance:** 🚂500m 🚲1km 🚃on the spot ⊗500m 🍴300m 📷200m
🚆500m.
**Remarks:** Check in at harbourmaster.

### 🅃🅢 Tubbergen 9F1
**De Vlaskoel**, Sportlaan 3. **GPS:** n52,41043 e6,78316.⬆️

---

**Remarks:** At swimming pool.

2 ☕free 🔌free. **Location:** Simple. **Surface:** metalled.
📅 01/01-31/12.
**Distance:** 🚂500m ⊗600m 🍴600m 🚆 on the spot 🚶 on the spot.
**Remarks:** At swimming pool.

### 🅃🅢 Vollenhove 〰️⚓ 9E1
De Haven. **GPS:** n52,68277 e5,94862.⬆️

6 ☕ € 12 🔌Ch✂ € 1 WC🚰 € 0,50. **Location:** Urban, simple,
central. **Surface:** metalled. 📅 01/01-31/12.
**Distance:** 🚂100m ⊗100m 🍴1km.
**Remarks:** Check in at harbourmaster.

### 🅒🅢 Vollenhove 〰️⚓ 9E1
**Recreatiecentrum 't Akkertien, Op de Voorst**, Noordwal 3.
**GPS:** n52,67609 e5,93914.

20 ☕ € 8 🔌Ch✂included 📷 € 4. 📅 01/01-31/12.
**Distance:** 🚂900m ⛵on the spot 🚃on the spot 🍴400m 🚆peak
season.

### 🅃🅢 Wierden 〰️⚓🍴🌸 9E1
**De Huurne**, Zandinksweg 22. **GPS:** n52,35003 e6,57474.

10 ☕ € 10 🔌Ch✂ 📶included. 📅 01/01-31/12.
**Distance:** 🚂2km ⛵3km 🍴2km 🚆700m 🚆 on the spot
🚶 on the spot.
**Remarks:** Max. 3 nights, max 3,5t.

### 🌸🅢 Wierden 〰️⚓🍴🌸 9E1
**Wijngaard Baan**, Kloosterhoeksweg 15. **GPS:** n52,32172 e6,56709.⬆️

14 ☕ € 12,50/24h 🔌Ch✂ WC🚰 📶included.
**Location:** Rural, comfortable, quiet. **Surface:** metalled.
📅 01/01-31/12.
**Distance:** 🚂3km 🚃on the spot ⊗on the spot 🍴3km 🚆on the spot
🚶 on the spot.

---

**Remarks:** Vineyard.

### 🅃🅢 Wijhe 〰️⚓🍴📷 9E1
**Passantenhaven Loswal**, Veerweg. **GPS:** n52,38639 e6,12830.⬆️

20 ☕ € 8,50 + € 0,50/pp tourist tax 🔌Ch WC included 🚰.📷
**Location:** Urban, simple, central. **Surface:** asphalted/metalled.
📅 24/04-02/11.
**Distance:** 🚂500m 🚃on the spot 🚃on the spot ⊗500m 🍴500m
🚆 on the spot 🚶 on the spot.
**Remarks:** Max. 3 nights.

**Tourist information Wijhe:**
🏛 Marktplein. 📅 Tue-morning.

### 🅃🅢 Zwartsluis 9E1
**Recreatiecentrum Zwartewater**, De Vleugel.
**GPS:** n52,63850 e6,07536.

15 ☕ € 10, 2 pers.incl 🔌Ch. **Surface:** gravel.
**Distance:** 🚂400m.
**Remarks:** Service at marina.

**Tourist information Zwartsluis:**
👁 Stoomgemaal Mastenbroek, Kamperzeedijk 5, Genemuiden.
Pumping-engine, 1856.

### 🅃🅢 Zwolle 〰️⚓🍴📷 9E1
Turfmarkt. **GPS:** n52,51326 e6,10380.⬆️

7 ☕mo-sa 8-18h € 5/day, free overnight stay. 🚉 **Location:** Urban,
simple, central. **Surface:** metalled. 📅 01/01-31/12.
**Distance:** 🚂800m ⊗1km 🍴650m 🚆 on the spot 🚶 on the spot.
**Remarks:** Max. 72h.

### 🅃🅢 Zwolle 〰️⚓🍴 9E1
**Jachthaven de Hanze**, Holtenbroekerdijk 44.
**GPS:** n52,53122 e6,07345.⬆️➡️

15 ☕ € 10, tourist tax incl 🔌Ch✂(15x) € 0,50/kWh WC🚰
€ 1/7minutes 📶included. 📷 **Location:** Rural, comfortable, central,
quiet. **Surface:** grassy/metalled. 📅 01/01-31/12.
**Distance:** 🚂2,5km 🚲2km ⛵on the spot 🚃on the spot ⊗1km
🍴1km 🚆500m 🚆 on the spot 🚶 on the spot.
**Remarks:** Max. 72h.

### 🅒🅢 Zwolle 〰️⚓🍴 9E1
**Agnietenplas**, Haersterveerweg 29A. **GPS:** n52,53779 e6,13169.⬆️
80 ☕ € 16,50, 2 pers.incl + tourist tax € 0,60/pp ✂ € 1/kWh 🚰📷
**Location:** Rural. **Surface:** grassy. 📅 01/01-31/12.

NL

**Distance:** 🚲3km ⛵on the spot ⛽on the spot.
**Remarks:** Caution sepkey € 20.
**Tourist information Zwolle:**
👁 Sassenpoort, Koestraat 46. Medieval gate building. ◻ Wed-Fri 14-17h, Sa/Su/holidays 12-17h.

# Flevoland

**⛊S Almere 🌱⚓ 9D2**

**Marina Muiderzand**, IJmeerdijk 4. **GPS**: n52,34155 e5,13493. ⬆➡.

20 (01/10-30/04 2 pl 🛏 € 16 ⛽🍽Ch ⚡ WC🚿◻ € 5/3 📶included.
**Location:** Rural, simple, quiet. **Surface:** asphalted.
◻ 01/01-31/12.
**Distance:** 🚲8km ⛵on the spot ⛽on the spot ⊗on the spot 🛒on the spot 🚌1km.
**Remarks:** Check in at harbourmaster, boat rental.
**Tourist information Almere:**
ℹ VVV, De Diagonaal 199, www.vvvalmere.nl.
🎪 Stadhuisplein. ◻ Wed, Sa 9-16h.
🎪 Biologische Boerenmarkt, Kempenhaanpad 14, www.stadsboerderijalmere.nl. ◻ Sa 9.30-13h.

**⛊S Almere-Haven 🏞⚓ 9D2**

**WSV Almere**, Sluiskade 11. **GPS**: n52,33257 e5,21715. ⬆.

40 🛏 € 15,50, 2 pers. incl ⛽🍽Ch ⚡(12x) € 0,50/2kWh WC🚿◻ € 5 📶included. 🚿 **Location:** Urban, simple. **Surface:** grassy.
◻ 01/03-01/11.
**Distance:** ⛵on the spot ⊗on the spot 🛒200m 🚲on the spot.

**⛊S Almere-Haven 🏞⚓ 9D2**

**Haven**, Sluiskade 3. **GPS**: n52,33366 e5,22170. ⬆.

2🛏 € 7 ⛽🍽ChWC🚿 € 0,50.
**Location:** Urban, comfortable, noisy. **Surface:** metalled.
◻ 02/05-04/09.
**Distance:** 🚲on the spot ⛵1km ⛽on the spot ⊗on the spot 🛒1km.
**Remarks:** Max. 72h, check in at harbourmaster.
**Tourist information Almere-Haven:**
🎪 De Brink. ◻ Fri 9-16h.

**⛊S Emmeloord 9D1**

**Camperplaats Emmeloord**, Casteleynsweg 1.
**GPS**: n52,73981 e5,77235. ⬆.
12🛏 € 9 ⛽🍽Ch ⚡ € 2/day 📶included. **Location:** Rural.
**Surface:** grassy. ◻ 01/01-31/12.
**Distance:** 🚲4,9km ⛽150m.
**Remarks:** Max. 7m, 2 bicylcles available.

**⛊S Ens 9D1**

**Camperplaats Schokland**, Redeweg 8. **GPS**: n52,62804 e5,79335.

18🛏 € 13,50 ⛽🍽Ch ⚡ € 0,50/kWh 🚿📶included.
**Location:** Rural, comfortable. **Surface:** grassy/gravel.
◻ 01/01-31/12.
**Distance:** 🚲3km ⛵2,5km 🚶on the spot.

**⛊S Lelystad 🏞☀⚓ 9D1**

**P Houtribhoek**, Houtribslag. **GPS**: n52,54762 e5,45666. ⬆➡.

4🛏free.
**Surface:** metalled.
◻ 01/01-31/12.
**Distance:** 🚲2km ⛵on the spot ⛽on the spot ⊗on the spot 🛒2km.
**Remarks:** Max. 48h.
**Tourist information Lelystad:**
🚶 Oostvaardersplassen.
6000 acres of lakes, mud fields, reed swamps, hiking route 5km and cycle route 35km.
🛒 Batavia Stad, Bataviaplein 60. Outlet-shopping.
◻ daily 10-18h. 🅿 free, parking € 3.

**⛊S Luttelgeest 9D1**

**Camping Craneburcht**, Kuinderweg 52. **GPS**: n52,78304 e5,84331.

10🛏 € 13,50 + € 0,75/pp tourist tax ⚡ € 2 WC. **Surface:** metalled.
◻ 01/03-30/11 ❄ winter: Mo-Tue.
**Distance:** 🚲200m ⊗on the spot 🛒7km.
**Remarks:** Arrival >17h, departure <10h.

**⛊S Nagele 9D1**

**Afslag Nagele**, Han Stijkelweg 11. **GPS**: n52,65034 e5,68610. ⬆.

20🛏 € 12, 2 pers.incl ⛽🍽Ch ⚡ € 2/night WC🚿📶included.
🚿 **Location:** Rural, comfortable, isolated, quiet.
**Surface:** grassy/metalled. ◻ 01/01-31/12.
**Distance:** 🚲3km.
**Remarks:** Max. 5 days.

**⛊S Urk 🌱 9D1**

**Haven**, Burgemeester Schipperkade. **GPS**: n52,66040 e5,59975. ⬆.

20🛏 € 16 ⛽🍽Ch ⚡(18x)WC🚿◻ 📶included. 🚿
**Location:** Rural, simple, noisy.
**Surface:** metalled.
◻ 01/01-31/12.
**Distance:** 🚲200m ⊗100m 🛒100m, bakery 300m.
**Remarks:** Max. 24h.
**Tourist information Urk:**
ℹ VVV, Wijk 2 2, www.vvvflevoland.nl.
Old fishermen's village, former island.
Ⓜ Het Oude Raadhuis, Wijk 2 2. Regional museum.
◻ 01/04-31/10 Mo-Fr 10-17h, Sa 10-16h, 01/03-30/11 Mo-Sa 10-16h.
🎪 Urkerhard. ◻ Sa 8.30-13h.
⚓ Stegentocht/Ginkiestocht.
Guided walk, reservation at Touristinfo Urk.

**⛊S Zeewolde 9D2**

**Camperpark De Wielewaal**, Wielseweg 9. **GPS**: n52,25981 e5,43727.

75🛏 € 20,50, 2 pers.incl, tourist tax € 1/pp, dog € 1 ⛽🍽Ch ⚡ € 2 WC🚿included. **Location:** Rural, comfortable, isolated, quiet.
**Surface:** metalled. ◻ 01/01-31/12.
**Distance:** 🚲7km ⛵on the spot ⛽on the spot 🛒7km.

# Gelderland

**⛊S Aalten 9F2**

**'t Noorden**, Lichtenvoordsestraatweg 44.
**GPS**: n51,93402 e6,58206. ⬆➡.

4🛏 € 10 ⚡ € 1/80liter 🍽Ch ⚡(4x)included. 🚿
**Location:** Rural, simple, noisy. **Surface:** gravel.
◻ 01/01-31/12.
**Distance:** 🚲700m ⊗on the spot 🚲on the spot.
**Tourist information Aalten:**
👁 Wijngoed De Hennepe, Romienendiek 3, www.wijngoeddehennepe.nl. Guided tour and tastery. ◻ shop Tue-Fr 13.30h-sunset, Sa 10h, guided tour/tasting Jul/Aug We 15h.
🎪 Hoge Blik. ◻ Thu 8-12h.

**⛊S Almen 🏞🍴 9E2**

**De Nieuwe Aanleg**, Scheggertdijk 10. **GPS**: n52,16711 e6,29744. ⬆➡.

12🛏 € 12,50 ⛽ € 0,75/100liter 🍽Ch ⚡(12x)included WC🚿 € 1/5minutes 📶. 🚿⚡ **Location:** Rural, comfortable, quiet.
**Surface:** metalled. ◻ 01/01-31/12.

**Distance:** 🚶2km 🏊on the spot 🛒on the spot ⊗on the spot 🍴2km 🚲on the spot 🚌on the spot 🚶on the spot.
**Remarks:** At the Twentekanaal.
**Tourist information Almen:**
🎯 Dorpsstraat. Small week market. 🕐 Tue 11-13h.

### Apeldoorn 9E2

**Malkander**, Dubbelbeek 38. **GPS:** n52,18305 e5,96673.⬆️.

4 🚐free. **Location:** Simple, isolated. **Surface:** metalled.
🕐 01/01-31/12, 15-09h.
**Distance:** 🚶2km ⊗150m 🍴1km 🚲on the spot.
**Remarks:** At swimming pool, max. 72h.

### Apeldoorn 9E2

**Willem Alexanderlaan** 651. **GPS:** n52,20974 e5,95899.⬆️.
8 🚐 € 8,80/24h. 🔌 **Location:** Urban. **Surface:** metalled.
🕐 01/01-31/12.
**Distance:** 🚶400m 🚴4,5km ⊗700m 🍴900m 🚌300m 🚲on the spot 🚶on the spot.
**Remarks:** Max. 72h.
**Tourist information Apeldoorn:**
🎯 Marktplein. Wed 8-13h, Sa 8-17h.

### Appeltern 9D3

**Strand Maaslanden**, Hamsestraat 2. **GPS:** n51,83107 e5,56193.⬆️.

10 🚐 € 10 🚰🔌Ch included WC 🚿 € 1. **Location:** Rural.
**Surface:** grassy/metalled. 🕐 01/04-30/09.
**Distance:** 🚶2km 🏊on the spot 🛒on the spot 🚲on the spot 🚶on the spot.
**Remarks:** Boat rental, bicycle rental, show-garden Appeltern 3km.

### Appeltern 9D3

**Herberg 't Mun**, Molenstraat 10, Blauwe Sluis.
**GPS:** n51,84048 e5,56360.

60 🚐 € 9,50 🚰🔌Ch (12x) € 3,6Amp WC 🚿included.
**Location:** Rural, simple, isolated, quiet. **Surface:** grassy/metalled.
🕐 01/01-31/12.
**Distance:** 🚶2km 🏊300m 🛒Trout farm ⊗on the spot 🍴2km 🚌on the spot 🚲on the spot 🚶on the spot.
**Remarks:** Show-garden Appeltern 3km.

### Arnhem 9E2

**Nieuwe Kade. GPS:** n51,97327 e5,91593.⬆️.

4 🚐 € 9 🚰 € 2,50 🔌Ch 🚿(4x) € 0,50/kWh WC 🧹.

---

**Location:** Urban, simple, central, quiet. **Surface:** metalled.
🕐 01/01-31/12.
**Distance:** 🚶1km 🚴4,7km ⊗200m 🍴1km 🚌1km 🚲on the spot 🚶on the spot.
**Remarks:** Along the Rhine river, payment with mobile phone, max. 48h, service at petrol station n51,970749 e5,94796.
**Tourist information Arnhem:**
🎯 Jansplaats. Small week market. 🕐 Tue 7.30-15h.

### Barneveld 9D2

**De Grote Glind**, Scherpenzeelseweg 158. **GPS:** n52,11540 e5,53775.

7 🚐 € 15, 2 pers.incl 🚰🔌Ch 🚿included WC 🚿. **Location:** Rural.
**Surface:** grassy. 🕐 01/05-30/09.
**Distance:** 🚶Barneveld 5km 🚌600m.
**Remarks:** At museum.

### Bemmel 9E2

**Dijkstraat/Wardstraat. GPS:** n51,88972 e5,90972.⬆️➡️.

3 🚐free. **Location:** Urban, simple, central, quiet. **Surface:** metalled.
🕐 01/01-31/12.
**Distance:** 🚶400m ⊗400m 🍴400m 🚌400m 🚲on the spot 🚶on the spot.
**Remarks:** Max. 72h.

### Borculo 9E2

**Hambroekplas/Berkelpalace**, Hambroekweg 10.
**GPS:** n52,11573 e6,53758.⬆️.

4 🚐 € 10 🚰 € 1/80liter 🔌Ch 🚿(4x)included. 🔌 **Location:** Rural, simple, noisy. **Surface:** grassy/gravel. 🕐 01/03-31/10.
**Distance:** 🚶500m 🏊150m ⊗50m 🍴500m 🚲on the spot 🚶on the spot.

### Borculo 9E2

**Bruggink Campers**, Kamerlingh Onnesstraat 19.
**GPS:** n52,12281 e6,52682.⬆️.

3 🚐free 🚿on demand. **Location:** Urban, simple, noisy.
**Surface:** metalled. 🕐 01/01-31/12, 18-9h.
**Distance:** 🚶1,5km 🏊2km 🛒500m ⊗1,5km 🍴1,5km 🚲on the spot.

### Bredevoort 9F2

**P2, recreatieplas Slingeplas**, Kruittorenstraat 10b.
**GPS:** n51,94722 e6,62318.⬆️➡️.

---

8 🚐 € 6-10 🚰 € 1/80liter 🔌Chincluded 🚿(8x) € 4/24h. 🔌🚿
**Location:** Rural, simple, quiet.
**Surface:** metalled.
🕐 01/04-01/10.
**Distance:** 🚶500m 🏊100m ⊗400m 🍴500m 🚲on the spot.
**Remarks:** Max. 72h, closed when frosty.
**Tourist information Bredevoort:**
ℹ️ VVV, Markt 8. City with half-timbered houses.
🎯 Book market. 🕐 3rd Sa of the month 10-17.

### Culemborg 9D2

**Jachthaven de Helling**, Beusichemsedijk.
**GPS:** n51,96117 e5,22148.⬆️➡️.

20 🚐 € 16,50 + tourist tax 🚰 € 0,50/100liter 🔌Ch 🚿 € 0,50/kWh WC 🚿 € 0,50/5minutes 🚿 € 4/4 🚿included.
**Location:** Urban, comfortable. **Surface:** grassy/sand.
🕐 01/04-01/11.
**Distance:** 🚶500m 🏊on the spot 🛒on the spot ⊗100m 🍴500m 🚌1,5km.
**Remarks:** Check in at harbourmaster.

### De Heurne 9E2

**De Haar**, Caspersstraat 14. **GPS:** n51,89802 e6,50035.⬆️➡️.

18 🚐 € 10 🚰 € 1/80liter 🔌Ch 🚿(15x),6Amp 🚿included. 🔌
**Location:** Rural, comfortable, quiet. **Surface:** grassy.
🕐 01/01-31/12.
**Distance:** 🚶1km 🚴8km 🍴1km 🚲on the spot 🚶on the spot.
**Remarks:** Filling station gas bottles 300m.

### Doesburg 9E2

**Jachthaven Doesburg**, Turfhaven. **GPS:** n52,01109 e6,13368.⬆️➡️.

6 🚐 € 5 + € 1,25/pp tourist tax 🚰 € 0,50/100liter 🔌Ch 🚿(6x) € 1/2kWh WC 🚿 € 0,18/1minutes. 🔌 **Location:** Urban, comfortable, central, quiet. **Surface:** concrete. 🕐 01/01-31/12 🔘 service: 16/10-01/04.
**Distance:** 🚶500m 🚴4km 🛒on the spot ⊗500m 🍴1km 🚌500m 🚲on the spot 🚶on the spot.
**Remarks:** Check in at harbourmaster.

### Doornenburg 9E2

**Kerkstraat. GPS:** n51,89416 e6,00129.⬆️.

NL

3 ⛺free. **Location:** Rural, quiet. **Surface:** metalled.
◻ 01/01-31/12.
**Distance:** 🚲400m ⊗200m cafetaria 🍴200m 🚌400m
🚴on the spot.
**Remarks:** Max. 3 days, view on castle Doornenburg.

| Duiven | 9E2 |

Oecumenpad. **GPS:** n51,94783 e6,02510.⬆️.

2 ⛺free. **Location:** Urban, simple, quiet. **Surface:** metalled.
◻ 01/01-31/12.
**Distance:** 🚲100m.

| Elst | 9E2 |

**Landgoed Welderen**, Grote Molenstraat 173.
**GPS:** n51,94221 e5,83054.⬆️.
10 ⛺ € 12 ⚡included. **Location:** Rural. ◻ 01/01-31/12.
**Distance:** ⊗on the spot 🚴on the spot 🚶on the spot.
**Remarks:** At golf court.

| Emst | 9E2 |

**Recreatiepark 't Smallert**, Smallertsweg 8.
**GPS:** n52,30910 e5,98126.⬆️.

20 ⛺ € 5 ⚡on demand. **Surface:** metalled. ◻ 01/01-31/12.
**Distance:** 🚲2km ⛱200m 🚤200m ⊗on the spot 🚴on the spot
🚶on the spot.
**Remarks:** Check in on arrival.

| Ermelo | 9D2 |

**Camperpark Strand Horst**, Buitenbrinkweg 82.
**GPS:** n52,31181 e5,56643.⬆️.

40 ⛺first night € 12, then € 10 🔌🗑Ch⚡(50x),4Amp WC🚽
€ 0,50/6minutes 📶included. 🚮 **Location:** Rural, comfortable, noisy.
**Surface:** grassy/metalled. ◻ 01/03-01/11.
**Distance:** 🚲4km 🏊50m ⛱200m 🚤200m ⊗500m 🛒4km.

| Garderen | 9D2 |

**Gasterij Zondag**, Apeldoornsestraat 163.
**GPS:** n52,21443 e5,70696.⬆️⬆️.

---

10 ⛺ € 15 🔌🗑Ch⚡.
**Location:** Rural. **Surface:** grassy.
◻ 01/01-31/12 ◻ Restaurant: Tue.
**Distance:** 🚲2km 🚤3,5km ⊗on the spot 🚴on the spot 🚶on the spot.
**Remarks:** Max. 48h, entrance next to restaurant, restaurant visit
appreciated.

| Geldermalsen | 9D2 |

Kostverlorenkade. **GPS:** n51,88507 e5,29030.

1 ⛺free. **Location:** Urban. **Surface:** metalled. ◻ 01/01-31/12.
**Distance:** 🚲100m 🚤3,6km ⛱on the spot 🚤on the spot
⊗on the spot.
**Remarks:** Parking at departure excursion boat.

| Gendringen | 9E2 |

Willem Alexanderplein. **GPS:** n51,86999 e6,37948.⬆️.

2 ⛺free. **Location:** Urban, simple, central. **Surface:** asphalted.
◻ 01/01-31/12.
**Distance:** 🚲200m ⊗100m 🛒500m.
**Remarks:** Max. 72h.

| Gendringen | 9E2 |

**Diekshuus**, Ulftseweg 4a. **GPS:** n51,87412 e6,38586.⬆️.

8 ⛺ € 10 🔌 € 1/80liter 🗑Ch⚡(4x)included. 🏪 **Location:** Rural,
simple, quiet. **Surface:** gravel. ◻ 01/01-31/12.
**Distance:** 🚲600m ⊗600m 🚴on the spot 🚶on the spot.
**Remarks:** At manege.

| Gendt | 9E2 |

**Camperpark Lingewaard**, Zandvoort 64. **GPS:** n51,88619 e5,95021.⬆️.

20 ⛺ € 14, 2 pers incl 🔌 € 1/100liter 🗑Ch⚡(20x) € 0,50/kWh
WC🚽📶included. **Location:** Rural. **Surface:** grassy/gravel.
◻ 01/01-31/12.

---

**Distance:** 🚲2km 🚤5km ⛱1,2km 🚤200m ⊗100m 🛒2km ◻on
the spot 🚌300m 🚴on the spot 🚶on the spot.

| Groenlo | 9F2 |

**Camping Marveld**, Elshofweg 6. **GPS:** n52,03604 e6,63134.⬆️.
6 ⛺ € 10 🔌 € 1/80liter 🗑Ch⚡(4x)included. 🏪 **Location:** Urban,
simple. **Surface:** metalled. ◻ 01/01-31/12.
**Distance:** 🚲1km ⊗500m.

| Groessen | 9E2 |

**Wellinghoeve**, Rijnstrangenweg 15. **GPS:** n51,92240 e6,02452.⬆️➡️.

25 ⛺ € 13,50 🔌🗑Ch⚡WC🚽📶included. 🚮 **Location:** Rural,
comfortable, quiet. **Surface:** grasstiles/grassy. ◻ 01/01-30/11.
**Distance:** 🚲4km 🚴on the spot 🚶on the spot.
**Remarks:** Bread-service (weekend).

| Harderwijk | 9D2 |

**P2 Lelykade**, Havendijk. **GPS:** n52,35211 e5,62497.⬆️.
4 ⛺ € 8,50 WC🚽. **Location:** Urban, simple. **Surface:** asphalted.
◻ 01/01-31/12.
**Distance:** ⛱on the spot ⊗130m 🛒500m.
**Remarks:** Max. 2 nights.

| Harderwijk | 9D2 |

**P Parkweg**, Parkweg. **GPS:** n52,34088 e5,62977.⬆️.

3 ⛺free. **Location:** Urban, simple. **Surface:** metalled.
◻ 01/01-31/12.
**Distance:** 🚲1,2km 🚤3km ⛱1,3km 🛒800m.
**Remarks:** Max. 48h, max. 8M.

| Harderwijk | 9D2 |

**Servicepunt Stijkel Campers**, Noorderbreedte 10.
**GPS:** n52,32804 e5,61269.
🔌🗑Ch. ◻ 01/01-31/12.

| Hattem | 9E1 |

**Jachthaven Hattem**, Geldersedijk 20. **GPS:** n52,47699 e6,06945.⬆️.

22 ⛺ € 10 + € 1,25/pp tourist tax 🔌Ch⚡(4x) € 2/24h WC🚽 € 0,50
◻ € 4/4 📶included.
**Location:** Urban, comfortable, central, quiet.
**Surface:** grasstiles/grassy. ◻ 01/01-31/12.
**Distance:** 🚲200m ⛱on the spot 🚤on the spot ⊗200m 🛒200m
🚌50m 🚴on the spot 🚶on the spot.
**Remarks:** Max. 72h, check in at harbourmaster, bread-service.

| Heerde | 9E1 |

**Brasserie Meet & Eat**, Eperweg 55. **GPS:** n52,37084 e6,02079.

---

**NL**

10 🛏free, use of a meal desired 🚰⚡(2x)included WC 📶. **Surface:** grassy/gravel.
🅿 Su (01/10-30/04).
**Distance:** 🚶3km 🏊1,5km 🛒1,5km ⊗on the spot 🍺2km 🚌100m.

### Hengelo 9E2
Elderinkweg 1-9. **GPS:** n52,04457 e6,30377.⬆.

2 🛏free. **Location:** Rural, simple. **Surface:** asphalted.
🅿 01/01-31/12.
**Distance:** 🚶500m 🚌100m.
**Remarks:** Next to sports fields, max. 24h.

### Heteren 9D2
Steenkuil, N837. **GPS:** n51,95456 e5,73094.⬆.

3 🛏free.
**Location:** Rural, simple, isolated, quiet. **Surface:** gravel/metalled.
🅿 01/01-31/12.
**Distance:** 🚶2km ⊗2km 🍺2km 🚌2km 🚲on the spot 🚶on the spot.
**Remarks:** Max. 72h.

### Huissen 9E2
Looveer. **GPS:** n51,93578 e5,94467.⬆➡.

3 🛏free. **Location:** Simple, central. **Surface:** grasstiles/metalled.
🅿 01/01-31/12.
**Distance:** 🚶200m 🏊200m 🛒200m ⊗200m 🍺on the spot 🚌500m
🚲on the spot 🚶on the spot.
**Remarks:** Max. 72h.

### Hurwenen 9D3
Het Uilennest, Groenestraat 2a. **GPS:** n51,81367 e5,31880.⬆.

16 🛏 € 12,50 🚰🍾Ch⚡WC 📶included. **Surface:** grassy/metalled.
🅿 01/01-31/12. **Distance:** 🏊600m 🍺on the spot ⊗600m 🚲on the
spot 🚶on the spot.

---

**Remarks:** Reservation in winter peak season, charging point for electric bicycles.

### Kerkwijk 9D3
Hippisch Centrum Bommelerwaard, Jan Stuversdreef 1-3.
**GPS:** n51,78876 e5,19929.⬆.

5 🛏 € 10 🚰⚡WC 📶included. **Location:** Rural. **Surface:** metalled.
🅿 01/01-31/12.
**Distance:** 🚶2km ⊗1,5km 🍺1,5km 🚌1,5km 🚲on the spot
🚶on the spot.

### Lathum 9E2
Jachthaven 't Eiland, De Muggenwaard 16.
**GPS:** n51,98819 e6,04462.⬆➡.

15 🛏 € 15, 2 pers.incl 🚰🍾Ch⚡(20x)WC 📶included.🚿
**Location:** Rural, comfortable, quiet. **Surface:** grassy/metalled.
🅿 01/01-31/12.
**Distance:** 🚶1km 🏊5km 🏊on the spot 🍺on the spot ⊗on the spot
🍺1km 🚲500m 🚶on the spot.
**Remarks:** Max. 48h.

### Lichtenvoorde 9E2
Zieuwentseweg. **GPS:** n51,99067 e6,55990.⬆.

4 🛏 € 10 🚰 € 1/80liter 🍾Ch⚡(4x)included. 🚐
**Location:** Urban, simple, central. **Surface:** gravel/sand.
🅿 01/01-31/12.
**Distance:** 🚶500m ⊗on the spot 🍺500m 🚌100m.
**Remarks:** Next to sports centre.

### Maasbommel 9D3
Eeterij 't Pont, Veerweg 1. **GPS:** n51,81963 e5,54507.⬆.

20 🛏 € 12 🚰Ch⚡🚿 **Location:** Rural. **Surface:** grassy/gravel.
🅿 01/01-31/12.
**Distance:** 🚶750m 🍺on the spot ⊗on the spot.
**Remarks:** Along the Meuse river, beautiful view.

### Megchelen 9E3
Theetuin, B&B Vita Verde, Nieuweweg 10. **GPS:** n51,83895 e6,38022.

---

3 🛏 € 10 ⚡included. **Surface:** grassy/gravel. 🅿 01/01-31/12.
**Distance:** 🚶500m 🚲5km ⊗500m 🍺4km 🚲on the spot
🚶on the spot.
**Remarks:** Bread-service.

### Meteren 9D3
Restaurant 3 Zussen, Rijksstraatweg 80. **GPS:** n51,85722 e5,28033.

5 🛏free. ⊗on the spot.
**Distance:** ⊗on the spot.
**Remarks:** Use of a meal desired.

### Millingen a/d Rijn 9E3
't Crumpse Hoekje, Crumpsestraat 28.
**GPS:** n51,85624 e6,03145.⬆➡.

12 🛏 € 8, 2 pers.incl 🚰 € 1/90liter 🍾Ch⚡(12x) € 2/day WC 🚽
€ 1/6minutes 📶included. 🚿 **Location:** Rural, luxurious, isolated,
quiet. **Surface:** gravel.
🅿 01/01-31/12.
**Distance:** 🚶1,4km 🏊4km 🛒2km ⊗1,4km 🍺1,4km 🚌800m 🚲on
the spot 🚶on the spot.

### Neede 9F2
Café restaurant De Olde Mölle, Diepenheimseweg 21.
**GPS:** n52,14153 e6,61035.

8 🛏 € 10 🚰 € 1/80liter 🍾Ch⚡. **Surface:** metalled.
🅿 01/01-31/12.
**Distance:** 🚶1km ⊗on the spot.
**Remarks:** Max. 72h.

### Neede 9F2
Camperpark Achterhoek, Diepenheimseweg 44.
**GPS:** n52,18023 e6,58588.⬆➡.

24 🛏 € 14,50, 04/07-23/08 € 16, 2 pers.incl 🚰🍾Ch⚡(24x)WC 🚽
€ 0,12/minutes 🅿 € 5,50/3,50 📶included. 🚿 **Location:** Rural,

NL

comfortable, noisy. **Surface:** grassy. ☐ 25/03-25/09.
**Distance:** 🚲4,5km 🛒on the spot ⊗on the spot 🍴4,5km 🚮on the spot 🚶on the spot.
**Remarks:** To be paid at campsite, bread-service, bicycle rental.

### Nijkerk    9D2
**Camperplaats Nijkerk**, Watergoorweg 44.
**GPS:** n52,22641 e5,47711.⬆️

4🏕free Chfree. **Location:** Urban, simple, noisy. **Surface:** metalled.
☐ 01/01-31/12.
**Distance:** 🚲500m ⚓2km ⛵2km 🛒500m ⊗300m 🍴500m 🚮200m 🚮on the spot 🚶on the spot.
**Remarks:** At sports centre.

### Nunspeet 🌿⚓🏊🍴    9D1
**Camperplaats De Zwaan**, Hardenbrinkweg 46.
**GPS:** n52,37901 e5,75363.⬆️➡️

60🏕 € 14 🚰🔌Ch🚿(45x)WC☐ € 0,50 💧 € 3/3 📶included.
🚮 **Location:** Rural, luxurious, quiet. **Surface:** grasstiles/grassy.
☐ 01/01-31/12.
**Distance:** 🚲2,5km ⚓3,5km ⛵2,5km 🛒2,5km ⊗1km 🍴2km 🚮900m 🚮Zwanenroute 🚶on the spot.
**Remarks:** No arrival on Sunday.
**Tourist information Nunspeet:**
⛺ ☐ Thu-morning.

### Otterlo ⚓🍴    9D2
**De Wije Werelt**, Arnhemseweg 100-102. **GPS:** n52,08592 e5,77319.

50🏕 € 20-35 🚰🔌Ch🚿(10x),6Amp WC☐included 💧 € 5/2 📶 € 3,50/day 🚮
**Location:** Rural, simple. **Surface:** grassy.
☐ 01/01-31/12.
**Distance:** 🚲500m 🛒500m ⊗on the spot 🍴campsite supermarket 🚮on the spot 🚮on the spot 🚶on the spot.
**Tourist information Otterlo:**
Ⓜ Kröller Müller Museum. Collection.

### Poederoijen 🌿🌱    9C3
**Slot Loevestein**, Loevestein 1. **GPS:** n51,81443 e5,02750.⬆️

4🏕free. **Location:** Rural, isolated, quiet. **Surface:** grasstiles.
☐ 01/01-31/12.
**Distance:** 🚲6km ⚓6km 🍴6km 🚮on the spot 🚶on the spot.

---

### Putten 🍴🌿    9D2
Brinkstraat. **GPS:** n52,26244 e5,60756.⬆️

2🏕free. **Location:** Urban, simple, central. **Surface:** metalled.
☐ 01/01-31/12.
**Distance:** 🚲200m ⊗300m 🍴300m 🚌250m 🚮on the spot 🚶on the spot.
**Remarks:** Max. 48h.

### Putten ⚓🍴🌿    9D2
**Camperplaats De Driest**, Driestweg 10. **GPS:** n52,23386 e5,61533.

15🏕voluntary contribution. **Surface:** grassy. ☐ 01/01-31/12.
**Distance:** 🚲2,5km 🚮on the spot 🚶on the spot.
**Remarks:** Max. 72h.
**Tourist information Putten:**
⛺ ☐ Wed.

### Rekken    9F2
**Grensovergang**, Oldenkotseweg. **GPS:** n52,09783 e6,75568.⬆️

5🏕 € 5. **Surface:** metalled. ☐ 01/01-31/12.
**Distance:** 🚲on the spot ⊗on the spot 🍴on the spot.
**Remarks:** Max. 72h, cycle and hiking routes.

### Ressen    9E2
**De Woerdt**, Woerdsestraat 4. **GPS:** n51,88867 e5,87215.

15🏕 € 9 + € 1/pp tourist tax 🚿(10x) € 1. 🚮 **Location:** Rural.
**Surface:** grassy/metalled. ☐ 01/01-31/12.
**Distance:** 🚲2km ⚓3,6km 🍴2km.
**Remarks:** Possibility for reservation, regional products, pitches in the orchard.

### Ruurlo 🍴    9E2
**Camping Tamaring**, Wildpad 3. **GPS:** n52,10239 e6,44257.➡️

2🏕 € 10 🚰 € 1/80liter 🔌Ch🚿(4x)included. 🏳️ **Location:** Rural,

---

simple, quiet. **Surface:** gravel/metalled. ☐ 01/01-31/12.
**Distance:** 🚲2km 🚮on the spot 🚶on the spot.
**Remarks:** Max. 8M.

### Silvolde    9E2
**Parking de Paasberg**, Terborgseveld. **GPS:** n51,91633 e6,37194.⬆️

4🏕free. **Location:** Urban, simple, quiet. **Surface:** metalled.
☐ 01/01-31/12.
**Distance:** 🚲city centre 1km ⊗300m.
**Remarks:** Parking at swimming pool, max. 72h.

### Sinderen    9E2
**NatuurlijkBUITEN**, Toldijk 11. **GPS:** n51,91297 e6,42384.⬆️

2🏕 € 12 🚰 € 1/80liter 🔌🚿(2x)📶included. 🚮
**Location:** Rural, comfortable, isolated, quiet. **Surface:** grassy/gravel.
☐ 01/01-31/12.
**Distance:** 🚲3km ⚓3km ⛵on the spot ⊗3km 🍴3km 🚌2km 🚮on the spot 🚶on the spot.
**Remarks:** Bread-service + breakfast-service, bicycle rental.

### Sinderen    9E2
**Biezenhof**, Kapelweg 42a. **GPS:** n51,90424 e6,45180.⬆️

4🏕 € 10 🚰 € 1/80liter 🔌Ch🚿included,6Amp. 🏳️
**Location:** Rural, simple, quiet. **Surface:** gravel.
☐ 01/01-31/12.
**Distance:** 🚲4km ⊗4km 🍴4km 🚮on the spot.

### Steenderen    9E2
**Camperplaats Landlust**, Landlustweg 2.
**GPS:** n52,06086 e6,18866.⬆️➡️

12🏕 € 12,50, 2 pers.incl 🚰🔌Ch🚿(12x)WC☐📶included. 🚮📷
**Location:** Rural, luxurious, central, quiet. **Surface:** grassy/metalled.
☐ 01/01-31/12.
**Distance:** 🚲on the spot 🛒1,5km ⊗300m 🍴150m 🚌150m 🚮on the spot 🚶on the spot.

### Stokkum 🍴    9E2
**Camping Brockhausen**, Eltenseweg 20. **GPS:** n51,87778 e6,21167.⬆️

---

NL

4 🛏 € 10 ⛽ € 1/80liter 🔧Ch 💧(4x)included 📶 € 2,50/day. 🚮
**Location:** Rural, simple. **Surface:** gravel. ⏱ 01/01-31/12.
**Distance:** 🛒800m ⊗500m 🚲2,5km 🚉2km 🚴on the spot
🚶on the spot.
**Remarks:** Bread-service.

### Terschuur 9D2

**Camperplaats Groot Westerveld**, Leemweg 2.
**GPS:** n52,16819 e5,53239. ⬆

8 🛏 € 7,50 ⛽ 🔧Ch 🔌 💧 € 2,50/night,10Amp WC 📶included.
🚿 **Location:** Rural, simple, quiet. **Surface:** grassy/metalled.
⏱ 01/03-30/09.
**Distance:** 🛒1,5km ⚓4km ⛴2km ⊗3km 🚲2km 🚉1km
🚴on the spot 🚶on the spot.

### Terwolde 9E2

**Brasserie Kriebelz**, Dorpsstraat 53, N792.
**GPS:** n52,28173 e6,09962. ⬆

2 🛏free. **Location:** Simple, central, quiet. **Surface:** metalled.
⏱ 01/01-31/12.
**Distance:** 🛒100m ⊗on the spot 🚉on the spot 🚴on the spot
🚶on the spot.

### Tiel 9D2

**Parking Waalkade**, Waalkade. **GPS:** n51,88518 e5,44079. ⬆

4 🛏 € 8,30. 🚮 **Surface:** asphalted. ⏱ 01/01-31/12.
**Distance:** 🛒500m ⚓on the spot ⛴on the spot ⊗on the spot
🚲500m on the spot.
**Remarks:** Max. 2 nights, cash payment.

### Tiel 9D2

**Restaurant de Betuwe**, Hoog Kellenseweg 7.
**GPS:** n51,90391 e5,44286.

---

10 🛏 € 8 ⛽. **Surface:** asphalted. ⏱ 01/01-31/12.
**Distance:** 🛒2km ⊗on the spot.

### Tolkamer 9E3

## Camperplaatsen Europakade Tolkamer

- ▪ Located directly at the river
- ▪ Electricity at each pitch
- ▪ Paved and flat motorhome pitches

**www.gelderseiland.nl**
**info@gelderseiland.nl**

**Europakade**, Europakade. **GPS:** n51,85122 e6,09938. ⬆➡
15 🛏 € 9 + € 0,90/pp tourist tax 💧(12x) € 1/kWh 📶included. 🚿
**Location:** Simple, central, quiet. **Surface:** metalled.
⏱ 01/01-31/12. ⏺ high water.
**Distance:** 🛒100m ⚓2,5km ⊗150m 🚉200m 📍2,5km 🚉200m
🚴100m 🚶100m.
**Remarks:** Max. 48h.

### Tolkamer 9E3

**Jachthaven de Bijland**, Zwarteweg 2. **GPS:** n51,85923 e6,09775.

20 🛏 € 8,20 ⛽ 🔧Ch 💧4kWh WC € 1/4minutes 📶included.
**Location:** Rural, comfortable, central. **Surface:** grassy.
⏱ 15/04-15/10.
**Distance:** 🛒200m 🚉200m 🚴on the spot 🚶on the spot.

### Tolkamer 9E3

**De Swaenebloem**, Bijland 3. **GPS:** n51,86235 e6,07937. ⬆➡

12 🛏 € 10 + € 0,90/pp tourist taks, guests free ⛽🔧Ch 💧(12x)
€ 1,50/day WC 📶included. 🚿 **Location:** Rural, comfortable, quiet.
**Surface:** grassy/metalled. ⏱ 01/01-31/12.
**Distance:** 🛒3,5km ⚓100m ⛴on the spot ⊗on the spot 🚲3,5km
🚉3km 🚴on the spot 🚶on the spot.
**Remarks:** Charging point for electric bicycles.

### Twello 9E2

Jachtlustplein 7. **GPS:** n52,23439 e6,09847. ⬆

1 🛏free. **Location:** Urban, simple, central, quiet. **Surface:** metalled.
⏱ 01/01-31/12.
**Distance:** 🛒100m ⊗100m 🚉100m 🚉on the spot 🚴on the spot
🚶on the spot.

---

### Uddel 9D2

**Camperplaats Ouwediek**, Oudedijk 31. **GPS:** n52,26464 e5,75480. ⬆

8 🛏 € 15 ⛽🔧Ch 💧included WC 🔌. **Location:** Rural,
comfortable, isolated, quiet. **Surface:** grassy. ⏱ 01/01-31/12.
**Distance:** 🚴on the spot 🚶on the spot.

### Varik 9D3

**Pleisterplaats Bol Varik**, Waalbandijk 8. **GPS:** n51,82589 e5,37829. ⬆

5 🛏 € 8, tourist tax incl ⛽free. ⏱ 01/01-31/12.
**Distance:** ⊗50m 🚉500m 🚉100m.
**Remarks:** Max. 48h, check in at restaurant.

### Varsseveld 9E2

**Pallandtbad**, Grutterinkpad. **GPS:** n51,94345 e6,46691. ⬆

3 🛏free. **Location:** Urban, simple, central. **Surface:** metalled.
⏱ 01/01-31/12.
**Distance:** 🛒200m ⊗200m 🚉200m 🚉200m.
**Remarks:** Behind swimming pool, max. 24h.

### Veessen 9E1

**Kozakkenhaven**, Veesser enkweg 16. **GPS:** n52,37540 e6,09252. ⬆
10 🛏 € 10 + € 1/pp tourist tax ⛽ 💧 € 2 📶included.
**Location:** Quiet. **Surface:** metalled. ⏱ 01/01-31/12.
**Distance:** ⛴on the spot ⊗100m.

### Vierakker 9E2

**Hanzestadcampers**, Vierakkersestraatweg 19.
**GPS:** n52,10659 e6,24122. ⬆

3 🛏 € 7,50 ⛽🔧Ch 💧(3x) 📶included. 🚿 **Location:** Rural, simple,
quiet. **Surface:** gravel. ⏱ 01/01-31/12.
**Distance:** 🛒500m ⊗1km 🚉500m 🚉500m 🚴on the spot
🚶on the spot.

### Voorst 9E2

**Boerderij de Kolke**, Klarenbeekseweg 30. **GPS:** n52,17355 e6,13318. ⬆

16 🛏 € 7,80 🚰 🔌Ch ⚡ (16x) € 1/kWh 📶included. 🚿
**Location:** Rural, comfortable, central, quiet. **Surface:** grassy/metalled.
🗓 01/01-31/12.
**Distance:** 🚉1km ⊗500m 🚴 on the spot 🚶 on the spot.
**Remarks:** Regional products.

## Voorst  9E2

**De Adelaar**, Rijksstraatweg 49. **GPS:** n52,17760 e6,14150. ⬆.

12 🛏 € 13, 01/04-31/10 € 14 🚰 🔌Ch ⚡ (12x) € 2,50 WC ⬜
€ 0,50 ⬛ € 4/4 📶included. 🚿 **Location:** Rural, luxurious, quiet.
**Surface:** grassy/metalled. 🗓 01/01-31/12.
**Distance:** 🚉1km ⚓7km 🏊200m 🚤200m ⊗150m ⬛1km 🚴 on
the spot.
**Remarks:** Incl. use camp-site facilities, playground.

## Voorthuizen  9D2

**Ackersate**, Harremaatweg 26. **GPS:** n52,18683 e5,62547. ⬆.

5 🛏 € 23 🚰 🔌Ch ⚡ WCincluded ⬜ € 1 ⬛ € 5,50,on camp site 📶.
🚿🔌
**Location:** Rural, simple. **Surface:** metalled. 🗓 01/04-27/10.
**Distance:** 🚉1,3km ⚓4,2km ⊗on the spot ⬛on the spot
🚴 on the spot 🚶 on the spot.

## Wageningen  9D2

Pabstendam. **GPS:** n51,96107 e5,65923. ⬆.

3 🛏free. **Location:** Rural, simple, quiet. **Surface:** grasstiles.
🗓 01/01-31/12.
**Distance:** 🚉650m ⊗650m.
**Remarks:** Nearby port.

## Westendorp  9E2

**Recreatieoord Hippique**, Doetinchemseweg 141.
**GPS:** n51,94964 e6,42084. ⬆➡.

10 🛏 € 10 🚰 € 1/80liter 🔌Ch ⚡(8x)WC ⬜ € 5/day ⬛ € 5
📶included. 🖥 **Location:** Rural, luxurious. **Surface:** grasstiles.
🗓 01/01-31/12.
**Distance:** 🚉500m 🏊2km 🚤3km ⊗1,5km ⬛3km 🚌1,5km 🚴 on
the spot 🚶 on the spot.
**Remarks:** Arrival 9><20h.

## Westervoort  9E2

Brouwerslaan. **GPS:** n51,96505 e5,97195. ⬆.

4 🛏free. **Location:** Simple. **Surface:** asphalted. 🗓 01/01-31/12
⬛ events.
**Distance:** 🚉500m ⊗250m ⬛AH 750m.
**Remarks:** At football ground, max. 72h.

## Wijchen  9D3

Oude Klapstraat 80. **GPS:** n51,80868 e5,72071. ⬆.

2 🛏free. **Location:** Urban. **Surface:** metalled. 🗓 01/01-31/12.
**Distance:** 🚉200m ⊗250m ⬛600m.
**Remarks:** Max. 48h.

## Wilp  9E2

**Kampeerhoeve Bussloo**, Grotenhuisweg 50. **GPS:** n52,20883 e6,10961.

2 🛏 € 10 🚰 € 1/80liter 🔌Ch ⚡included 📶against payment.
🖥 **Location:** Rural, simple, isolated, quiet. **Surface:** metalled.
🗓 01/03-31/10.
**Distance:** 🚉Breedevoort 4,5km 🚶Located on estate.

## Winterswijk  9F2

**Camping Ten Hagen**, Waliënsestraat 139A.
**GPS:** n51,99131 e6,71898. ⬆➡.

4 🛏 € 10 🚰 € 1/80liter 🔌Ch ⚡(4x)included 📶 € 3/24h 🔌
🖥🔌 **Location:** Rural, simple, isolated, quiet. **Surface:** grassy.
🗓 01/01-31/12.
**Distance:** 🚉city centre 3km ⚓on the spot ⊗3km 🚴2km 🚶 on the
spot 🚶 on the spot.
**Remarks:** Max. 24h, manufacturer of wooden clogs.

## Winterswijk  9F2

**Het Winkel**, De Slingeweg 20. **GPS:** n51,95176 e6,73621. ⬆➡.

4 🛏 € 10 🚰 € 1/80liter 🔌Ch ⚡(4x)included. **Location:** Rural,
simple, quiet. **Surface:** gravel/sand. 🗓 01/01-31/12.
**Distance:** 🚉4,5km ⊗on the spot 🚴 on the spot 🚶 on the spot.

## Winterswijk  9F2

**Vreehorst**, Vreehorstweg 43. **GPS:** n51,95028 e6,69251. ⬆➡.

4 🛏 € 10 🚰 € 1/80liter 🔌Ch ⚡(4x)included. 🖥 **Location:** Rural,
simple, quiet. **Surface:** sand. 🗓 01/01-31/12.
**Distance:** 🚉3,6km 🚴 on the spot 🚶 on the spot.

## Zaltbommel  9D3

**De Beersteeg**, Beersteeg. **GPS:** n51,81040 e5,24083. ⬆.

6 🛏free. **Surface:** metalled. 🗓 01/01-31/12.
**Distance:** 🚉centre 600m ⚓2,5km ⊗250m.

## Zelhem  9E2

**Carpoolplaats**, Stikkenweg/N330. **GPS:** n51,99893 e6,34541. ⬆.

## Camperplek Winterswijk Centrum, Stationsstraat 33.
**GPS:** n51,96843 e6,71616. ⬆.

6 🛏 € 10 🚰 € 0,50/100liter 🔌Ch ⚡ € 0,50/kWh,16Amp WC € 0,50/
time. 🖥🔌 **Location:** Urban, central, noisy. **Surface:** metalled.
🗓 01/01-31/12.
**Distance:** 🚉500m ⊗500m 🚌100m 🚴 on the spot.

## Winterswijk  9F2

**Landgoed Kreil**, Heenkamppieperweg 1.
**GPS:** n51,93734 e6,67493. ⬆➡.

2 ⬛free. **Location:** Rural, simple, noisy. **Surface:** asphalted. ◻ 01/01-31/12.
**Distance:** 1km.
**Remarks:** Max. 24h.

### Zevenaar 9E2
Bastion. **GPS:** n51,93127 e6,07923.⬆.

5 ⬛ € 8.▯ **Location:** Urban, simple, central, noisy.
**Surface:** metalled. ◻ 01/01-31/12.
**Distance:** 150m 50m.
**Remarks:** Max. 48h.

### Zutphen 9E2
De Heicohoeve, Lansinkweg 2. **GPS:** n52,11724 e6,22792.⬆.

20 ⬛ € 10 + € 1,55/pp tourist tax ⬛Ch⬛included,6Amp
WC⬛.⬛ **Surface:** grassy/gravel. ◻ 01/01-31/12.
**Distance:** 2,5km 900m 250m 1km 2,5km 800m
250m 50m.
**Remarks:** Dog on leads.

### Zutphen 9E2
Houtwal. **GPS:** n52,13609 e6,19747.⬆⬅.

8 ⬛ € 2, overnight stay free ⬛ € 1/80liter ⬛ (8x) € 1/kWh.
**Location:** Urban, simple, quiet. **Surface:** metalled.
◻ 01/01-31/12.
**Distance:** 1km.
**Remarks:** Nearby police station, max. 48h, beautiful view.

**Tourist information Zutphen:**
⬛ Groenmarkt-Houtmarkt-Zaadmarkt. ◻ Thu 8-12h, Sa 8-17h.
⬛ Lange Hofstraat. Farmers market. ◻ Thu 8-13h.

# Utrecht

### Amersfoort 9D2
Aan de Eem, Kleine Koppel. **GPS:** n52,16198 e5,37848.⬆.

3 ⬛ € 1,10/meter, 01/11-01/04 € 0,55/meter ⬛⬛WC⬛included.
▯▯⬛ **Location:** Urban, noisy. **Surface:** metalled. ◻ 01/01-31/12
⬛ **Service:** winter.
**Distance:** 600m 500m 500m on the spot.
**Remarks:** In front of fire-station, max. 24h.

**Tourist information Amersfoort:**
⬛ VVV, Breestraat 1, www.vvvamersfoort.nl.

### Baarn 9D2
De Zeven Linden, Zevenlindenweg 4. **GPS:** n52,19721 e5,24838.⬆.

3 ⬛ € 19 ⬛ € 2,50 ⬛Ch⬛.⬛ **Location:** Simple.
**Surface:** metalled. ◻ 01/04-01/11.
**Distance:** 2km 1km 2km 300m on the spot
on the spot.
**Remarks:** Only overnight stays 17-10h.

**Tourist information Baarn:**
⬛ Brink. ◻ Tue 8.30-14h.

### Benschop 9C2
Campererf Recreatie Landschap Rosenboom, Benedeneind Zuidzijde
283A. **GPS:** n52,00374 e4,95191.⬆.

4 ⬛ € 16,50 ⬛⬛Ch⬛WC⬛⬛included. **Location:** Rural,
isolated, quiet. **Surface:** metalled. ◻ 01/01-31/12.
**Distance:** 2km on the spot on the spot.
**Remarks:** Canoe and boat rental.

### Bunnik 9D2
Buitengoed de Boomgaard, Parallelweg 9.
**GPS:** n52,06065 e5,19943.⬆.

16 ⬛ € 21-24 ⬛Ch⬛WC⬛⬛ € 2.
**Location:** Rural, comfortable. **Surface:** metalled.
◻ 26/03-15/10.
**Distance:** 3km 800m.
**Remarks:** Arrival >17h departure <10h check in at reception next
morning, use camp-site facilities allowed.

### Bunschoten-Spakenburg 9D2
Jachthaven Nieuwboer, Westdijk 36. **GPS:** n52,26070 e5,37238.⬆.

8 ⬛ € 15-20, 2 pers.incl ⬛⬛Ch⬛WC⬛⬛ € 3,50/3,50
⬛included.⬛ **Location:** Rural, comfortable, quiet. **Surface:** grassy.
◻ 01/01-31/12.
**Distance:** 800m 6km 100m 700m 700m 700m on
the spot on the spot.

### Harmelen 9C2
H20 Recreatiecentrum, De Uithof 1. **GPS:** n52,08343 e4,96100.⬆.

3 ⬛free.
**Location:** Simple, quiet. **Surface:** metalled. ◻ 01/01-31/12.
**Distance:** 500m 500m 400m.
**Remarks:** Max. 72h.

### IJsselstein 9C2
Jachthaven Marnemoende, Noord IJsseldijk 107b.
**GPS:** n52,04583 e5,01861.⬆.

3 ⬛ € 15 ⬛⬛Ch⬛WC⬛⬛ € 4/2 ⬛included.⬛
**Location:** Rural, luxurious, quiet. **Surface:** gravel. ◻ 01/01-31/12.
**Distance:** 2km on the spot on the spot on the spot 2km
2km on the spot.

### Leusden 9D2
De Mof, Arnhemseweg 95. **GPS:** n52,10654 e5,41445.⬆.

10 ⬛free, use of a meal desired.
**Location:** Rural, simple. **Surface:** gravel.
◻ 01/01-31/12 ⬛ Mon, Tue.
**Distance:** 4km 4km on the spot on the spot on the spot.
**Remarks:** First check in at restaurant.

### Lopik 9C2
De Willige Waard, Lekdijk West 76, Willige Langerak.
**GPS:** n51,94254 e4,89331.⬆.

11 ⬛ € 14,50, 2 pers. incl., dog € 1 ⬛⬛Ch⬛WC⬛⬛included.⬛

NL

**Location:** Rural, quiet. **Surface:** metalled. 01/01-31/12.
**Distance:** 3km 1km 3,5km 1km 1km.

| 9C2 | Lopikerkapel |

**Camperplaats Biezenhoeve**, Biezendijk 2A.
**GPS:** n51,99950 e5,05010.

5 € 14 Ch 3/6/16Amp WC included.
**Location:** Rural, isolated, quiet. **Surface:** grassy/metalled.
01/01-31/12.
**Distance:** 1km 1km on the spot on the spot.

| 9C2 | Mijdrecht |

Rondweg. **GPS:** n52,20804 e4,86879.

4 free. **Location:** Urban, simple, noisy. **Surface:** metalled.
01/01-31/12.
**Distance:** 500m 500m 500m 500m.
**Remarks:** Max. 48h.

| 9D2 | Rhenen |

**Restaurant 3 Zussen**, Kerkewijk-zuid 115. **GPS:** n52,00682 e5,54006.

5 free. **Location:** Rural, simple. **Surface:** asphalted.
01/01-31/12.
**Distance:** 1km Veenendaal on the spot 1km on the spot
on the spot on the spot.
**Remarks:** Use of a meal desired.

| 9D2 | Vianen |

**P1 Evenemententerrein**, Kanaalweg, P1. **GPS:** n51,99549 e5,09620.

20 free. **Location:** Urban. **Surface:** metalled. 01/01-31/12
events.
**Distance:** 500m.
**Remarks:** During events: Hazelaarplein, max. 3 nights.

| 9D2 | Vianen |

**P2 Sluiseiland**, Aime Bonnestraat-Sluiseiland.
**GPS:** n51,99063 e5,09701.

---

10 free.
**Location:** Urban, simple. **Surface:** sand. 01/01-31/12.
**Distance:** on the spot on the spot 400m 400m.
**Remarks:** Max. 72h.

| 9D2 | Vianen |

**Ponthoeve**, Buitenstad 58. **GPS:** n51,99829 e5,09035.

6 free.
**Location:** Rural, simple. **Surface:** metalled.
01/01-31/12.
**Distance:** centre 400m 300m 800m 900m on the spot
on the spot.
**Remarks:** Max. 6m, max. 72h, inclining pitches.

**Tourist information Vianen:**
VVV, Voorstraat 97, www.vvv-vianen.nl. Historical centre.
Voorstraat (zuid). Wed 10-16h.

| 9D2 | Werkhoven |

**Camperplaats aan het Dorp**, Herenstraat 98.
**GPS:** n52,01759 e5,24344.

7 € 15 Ch (7x) WC included. **Location:** Rural.
**Surface:** gravel. 01/01-31/12.
**Distance:** 800m 500m, bakery 200m on the spot on the
spot on the spot.

| 9D2 | Wijk bij Duurstede |

**P2**, Inudatiekanaal. **GPS:** n51,97100 e5,35100.

3 € 10, 2 pers.incl WC . **Location:** Rural, simple, quiet.
**Surface:** asphalted. 01/01-31/12.
**Distance:** 200m 200m 500m on the spot on the spot.
**Remarks:** At harbour.

# South Holland

| 9C3 | Alblasserdam |

**Camperpark Kinderdijk**, Marineweg 3a.
**GPS:** n51,85971 e4,65816.

---

44 € 17, tourist tax incl Ch WC € 1 included.
**Location:** Urban, simple, central. **Surface:** metalled.
01/02-27/12.
**Distance:** on the spot 2km on the spot on the spot 300m
200m on the spot on the spot.
**Remarks:** World Heritage site Kinderdijk, 19 mills, 5km, waterbus ferry
300m.

**Tourist information Alblasserdam:**
Werelderfgoed Kinderdijk, Nederwaard 1, Kinderdijk.
World famous mill-area.
12/03-30/10 9-17.30, 31/10-30/12 11-16.
Wilgenplein. Mo-afternoon.

| 9C2 | Bleiswijk |

Jan van de Heidenstraat. **GPS:** n52,01415 e4,53411.

2 free. **Location:** Urban. **Surface:** metalled. 01/01-31/12.
**Distance:** 300m 5km 500m Jumbo 400m.
**Remarks:** Next to fire-station, max. 48h.

| 9C3 | Bleskensgraaf |

**Farm Nescio**, Elzenweg 19. **GPS:** n51,85674 e4,75266.

8 € 14 Ch WC included. **Location:** Rural,
comfortable, isolated, quiet. **Surface:** metalled. 01/01-31/12.
**Distance:** 2,5km 1,5km 1,5km 1km 2,5km.
**Remarks:** Possibility of guided tour.

| 9C2 | Delft |

**Delftse Hout**, Korftlaan 5. **GPS:** n52,01772 e4,37945.

20 € 24-28 Ch (20x) € 3,50/24h WC € 6,50
included. **Location:** Urban, comfortable, central.
**Surface:** grassy. 26/03-01.11.
**Distance:** 2km 1,2km 1km 1km 1km 1km sum-
mer > centre on the spot on the spot.
**Remarks:** Check in at reception campsite.

**Tourist information Delft:**
VVV, Hippolytusbuurt 4, www.delft.nl. Historical centre with canals
and merchant houses. church 01/03-31/10 Mo-Sa 9-18h, 01/11-
28/02 Mo-Sa 11-16h.

| 9C2 | Den Haag |

**Camperpark Den Haag**, Valutapad, The Hague (Den Haag).
**GPS:** n52,05282 e4,38013.

NL

55 ⌷ € 15,95 + tourist tax € 2,05/pp ⛽🚰Ch🚿(30x) € 3,75/24h,6Amp WC⌷included.
**Location:** Urban, comfortable. **Surface:** grassy/metalled.
☐ 01/01-31/12.
**Distance:** 🚶7km ⛵1,7km ⛴12km ⊗1km 🚉1km 🚌500m.
**Remarks:** Bread-service.

**Tourist information The Hague (Den Haag):**
ℹ️ VVV, Spui 68, www.denhaag.com. Government city and royal residence.
👁 Bezoekerscentrum Binnenhof, Binnenhof 8a. Guided tours in government buildings. ☐ Mo-Sa 10-16h. 🎫 € 5-10.
Madurodam, George Maduroplein 1. Miniature Holland.

### Dordrecht 9C3
**Vlijkade. GPS:** n51,81523 e4,68302.⬆️.

8 ⌷free.
**Location:** Urban, simple, central. **Surface:** metalled.
**Distance:** 🚶centre 1,2km.
**Remarks:** At the canal, max. 72h, temporary stopover.

### Dordrecht 9C3
Weeskinderendijk 5. **GPS:** n51,80861 e4,65611.⬆️.

2 ⌷ € 1/4h, first 24h free. **Location:** Urban, simple, noisy.
**Surface:** metalled. ☐ 01/01-31/12.
**Distance:** 🚶500m ⊗500m 🚉500m 🚌100m.
**Remarks:** Max. 72h.

### Dordrecht 9C3
**Jachthaven Westergoot,** Baanhoekweg 1.
**GPS:** n51,81453 e4,72473.⬆️.

11 ⌷ € 12 Ch🚿 € 2 WC⌷ € 0,50/7minutes ☐ € 5.
**Location:** Urban, quiet. **Surface:** asphalted.
☐ 01/01-31/12 ☐ during event.
**Distance:** 🚶city centre 5km 🚉on the spot 🚌on the spot.

### Giessenburg 9C3
**Boerenterras De Groot,** A.M.A. Langeraadweg 9.
**GPS:** n51,85327 e4,92205.

---

6 ⌷ € 10 ⛽🚰Ch🚿WC⌷📶included. 🚲 **Location:** Rural, simple, isolated, quiet. **Surface:** concrete. ☐ 01/01-31/12.
**Distance:** 🚶1,5km ⛵3km 🛒on the spot ⊗1,5km 🚉3,5km 🚲on the spot.

### Giessenburg 9C3
**Halfomhoeve,** Bovenkerkseweg 76/78. **GPS:** n51,84628 e4,87548.

3 ⌷ € 10 ⛽🚰Ch🚿WC⌷📶included. 🚲 **Location:** Rural, simple, isolated, quiet. **Surface:** concrete. ☐ 01/05-15/10.
**Distance:** 🚶2km ⛵3km 🛒on the spot ⊗1,5km 🚉1,5km 🚌on the spot 🚲on the spot.

### Giessenburg 9C3
**Landscheiding Giessenburg,** Landscheiding 1.
**GPS:** n51,84753 e4,92294.⬆️.

10 ⌷ € 10 ⛽🚰Ch🚿WC⌷📶included. 🚲 **Location:** Rural, comfortable, isolated, quiet. **Surface:** grassy/metalled.
☐ 01/01-31/12.
**Distance:** 🚶2km ⊗2km 🚉2km 🚲on the spot 🏊on the spot.

### Gorinchem 9C3
**Camperplaats De Punt,** Buiten de Waterpoort 8.
**GPS:** n51,82697 e4,96477.⬆️➡️.

24 ⌷ € 12,50 ⛽🚰Ch🚿 € 0,50 ☐ € 5/4 📶included.
**Location:** Comfortable, isolated, quiet.
**Surface:** gravel/metalled.
☐ 01/01-31/12.
**Distance:** 🚶500m ⛴on the spot 🛒on the spot ⊗300m 🚉1km 🚲on the spot.
**Remarks:** Max. 72h, check in at harbourmaster.

**Tourist information Gorinchem:**
ℹ️ VVV, Grote Markt 17, www.gorinchem.nl.
Historical centre with city walls.
🍴⊗ Slot Loevestein, Loevestein 1, Poederoijen.
Castle, 14th century.
🛒 Grote Markt. ☐ Mo 8.30-12.30h.

### Gouda 9C2
**Parking Klein Amerika,** Klein Amerika 30.
**GPS:** n52,01185 e4,71576.⬆️.

---

30 ⌷ € 8 ⛽🚰Ch🚿(12x)WC⌷included. 🚐 **Location:** Urban, simple, quiet. **Surface:** metalled. ☐ 01/01-31/12.
**Distance:** 🚶300m.
**Remarks:** Max. 3 days.

### Gouda 9C2
**Golfbaan IJsselweide,** Sluisdijk 15. **GPS:** n51,99718 e4,68821.⬆️.

5 ⌷ € 10,50, guests free.
**Surface:** asphalted. ☐ 01/01-31/12.
**Distance:** ⊗on the spot.
**Remarks:** At golf court.

**Tourist information Gouda:**
ℹ️ VVV, Markt 35, www.vvvgouda.nl. Historical centre with 300 monuments, famous for its Gouda-cheese.
👁 Kaaswaag, Markt. History of the Gouda cheese, cheesetasting.
☐ 01/04-30/09 13-17h, Thu 10-17h. 🎫 € 7,50.
🛒 Markt. ☐ Thu 8.30-13h, Sa 8.30-17h.
🛒 Montmartre, Markt. Antiques and flea market.
☐ 01/05-30/09 We 9-17h.

### Goudriaan 9C2
**Boerderij de Verwondering,** De Hoogt 14.
**GPS:** n51,89150 e4,90741.⬆️.

2 ⌷ € 10 ⛽🚰Ch🚿📶included. 🚲 **Location:** Rural, simple, isolated. **Surface:** concrete.
**Distance:** 🚶2,5km 🚉7km.

### Hillegom 9C2
**De Vosse,** Vosselaan. **GPS:** n52,29541 e4,59122.⬆️.

3 ⌷free. **Location:** Urban, simple. **Surface:** metalled.
☐ 01/01-31/12.
**Distance:** 🚶centre 1,3km ⊗1km 🚉1km.
**Remarks:** At swimming pool, max. 3 days.

### Hoek van Holland 9B2
Koningin Emmaboulevard. **GPS:** n51,97822 e4,12091.⬆️.

5 ⛺free. **Surface:** asphalted. ⬛ 01/01-31/12.
**Distance:** ⬛on the spot ⊗150m ⬛750m.

### Hoogblokland      9C2

**Landwinkel De Bikkerhoeve**, Bazeldijk 66. **GPS:** n51,89716 e4,99563.

4 ⛺ € 10 ⬛Ch ⬛ € 2 WCincluded ⬛. ⬛ **Location:** Rural,
simple, isolated, quiet. **Surface:** concrete. ⬛ 01/04-31/10.
**Distance:** ⬛2km ⬛ 1,4km ⊗2km ⬛2km ⬛on the spot
⬛ on the spot.

### Langerak      9C2

**Camperplaats Langerak**, Melkweg 3. **GPS:** n51,92069 e4,89975.
3 ⛺ € 15 ⬛⬛⬛WC⬛⬛.
**Location:** Rural. **Surface:** metalled.
**Distance:** ⬛on the spot ⬛on the spot.
**Remarks:** Max. 8M, bicycle rental.

### Leerdam      9C2

**De Galgenwaard**, Lingedijk 8a, Oosterwijk.
**GPS:** n51,87451 e5,07311.⬛.

3 ⛺ € 8 ⬛included ⬛ € 2 WC. ⬛ **Location:** Rural, simple, quiet.
**Surface:** metalled. ⬛ 01/04-01/10.
**Distance:** ⬛Leerdam 2km ⬛on the spot ⬛on the spot ⊗300m
⬛ Along the river Linge.
**Remarks:** Opening hours 7-22h, passenger ferry across the Linge.

### Leerdam      9C2

**Groenzoom**, Lingedijk. **GPS:** n51,88288 e5,08670.⬛.

3 ⛺free. **Location:** Urban, simple. **Surface:** metalled.
⬛ 01/01-31/12.
**Distance:** ⬛2,5km ⊗2,5km ⬛2,5km ⬛ on the spot.
**Remarks:** In front of Lingedijk 27, max. 72h, small pitches.

### Leerdam      9C2

**Parking Glasmuseum**, Lingedijk. **GPS:** n51,88676 e5,08699.⬛.

---

2 ⛺free. **Location:** Rural, simple. **Surface:** asphalted.
⬛ 01/01-31/12.
**Distance:** ⬛1km ⬛on the spot ⊗1km ⬛ on the spot.

### Leerdam      9C2

**Jachthaven Oude Horn**, Sundsvall 1. **GPS:** n51,88984 e5,09532.⬛.

3 ⛺free.
**Location:** Urban, simple. **Surface:** gravel. ⬛ 01/01-31/12.
**Distance:** ⬛300m ⊗300m ⬛300m.
**Remarks:** Max. 72h.

### Leiden      9C2

**P Haagweg**, Haagweg 6. **GPS:** n52,15963 e4,47852.⬛.

15 ⛺ € 12,50/24h. ⬛ ⬛ **Location:** Urban. **Surface:** metalled.
⬛ 01/01-31/12.
**Distance:** ⬛800m ⊗800m ⬛800m ⬛ Free bus to centre.
**Remarks:** Along railwayline, video surveillance, bicycle rental, free
shuttle (till 2am).

### Lexmond      9C2

**De Fruithof**, Achthoven 39. **GPS:** n51,97414 e5,00254.
2 ⛺ € 12 ⬛⬛included. **Location:** Rural. **Surface:** metalled.
**Distance:** ⬛150m ⬛on the spot ⬛on the spot ⬛ on the spot.
**Remarks:** Max. 7m.

### Maassluis      9B2

**Camperplaats Maassluis**, Govert van Wijnkade 50.
**GPS:** n51,91628 e4,24535.⬛.

3 ⛺free ⬛free. **Surface:** asphalted. ⬛ 01/01-31/12.
**Distance:** ⬛city centre 1km ⊗500m ⬛1,2km ⬛450m ⬛ on the
spot ⬛ on the spot.
**Remarks:** Max. 48h.

### Maassluis      9B2

**Veerstoep**, Deltaweg. **GPS:** n51,91509 e4,25037.
8 ⛺free. **Location:** Urban, simple. **Surface:** asphalted.
⬛ 01/01-31/12.
**Distance:** ⬛on the spot ⊗500m ⬛1,3km.

### Middelharnis      9B3

**Oosterdijkhaven**. **GPS:** n51,76138 e4,16902.
5 ⛺ € 10 WC⬛ **Location:** Urban. **Surface:** metalled.
⬛ 01/01-31/12.
**Distance:** ⬛3km ⊗250m ⬛400m.

---

### Nieuwland      9C2

**De Grienduil**, Geer 25. **GPS:** n51,90106 e5,02622.⬛.

4 ⛺ € 13-14,50, 4 pers.incl. + tourist tax € 1/pp ⬛⬛
Ch ⬛ WC⬛included ⬛ € 3,50. ⬛ **Location:** Rural, simple, quiet.
**Surface:** gravel. ⬛ 01/01-31/12.
**Distance:** ⬛on the spot ⊗2km ⬛4km ⬛ on the spot ⬛ on the spot.
**Remarks:** In winter limited services.

### Noordeloos      9C2

**Huis den Dool**, Botersloot 67. **GPS:** n51,91170 e4,95995.
3 ⛺ € 12,50 ⬛⬛Ch ⬛included ⬛. **Location:** Rural.
⬛ 01/01-31/12.
**Distance:** ⬛on the spot ⬛ on the spot.
**Remarks:** Charging point for electric bicycles.

### Noordwijk      9C2

**De Guldenroede**, Kraaierslaan. **GPS:** n52,27277 e4,47940.⬛.
15 ⛺ € 15 ⬛⬛Ch ⬛. **Location:** Rural, comfortable.
**Surface:** grassy. ⬛ 01/01-31/12.
**Distance:** ⬛1,7km ⊗800m.

**Tourist information Noordwijk:**
⬛ Space Expo, Keplerlaan 3. Space travel exhibition, visitor centre
Estec. ⬛ Tue-Su 10-17h, holidays Mo.

### Numansdorp      9C3

**Fort Buitensluis**, Fortlaan 10. **GPS:** n51,71727 e4,43866.

5 ⛺ € 20 ⬛⬛Ch ⬛ € 2/night WC⬛ € 0,50 ⬛ € 1 ⬛included. ⬛
**Location:** Comfortable, quiet. **Surface:** unpaved.
⬛ 01/04-01/11.
**Distance:** ⬛1,5km ⬛ 5km ⬛on the spot ⬛on the spot ⊗1,5km
⬛1,5km ⬛2,5km ⬛ on the spot ⬛ on the spot.
**Remarks:** At Hollands Diep, golf court 3km.

### Oostvoorne      9B2

**Jachthaven Geijsman**, Zanddijk 5. **GPS:** n51,92438 e4,10811.⬛.
10 ⛺ € 15 ⬛⬛Ch ⬛included,10Amp WC⬛⬛.⬛
**Location:** Urban, comfortable, quiet. **Surface:** metalled.
⬛ 01/04-01/10.
**Distance:** ⬛3km ⬛500m ⬛on the spot ⊗on the spot.

### Oud Beijerland      9C3

**De Oude Tol**, Randweg 31a. **GPS:** n51,82933 e4,39585.⬛.

4 ⛺free.
**Location:** Rural, simple, isolated, quiet. **Surface:** asphalted.
⬛ 01/01-31/12.
**Distance:** ⬛2km ⬛on the spot ⊗100m ⬛ on the spot ⬛ on the spot.
**Remarks:** Arrival >16h, max. 24h.

### Ouddorp      9B3

**Drive-in Camperpark Klepperduinen**, Vrijheidsweg 1.
**GPS:** n51,81724 e3,89850.⬛⬛.

---

NL

51 🚐 € 8,50-10,65/12h, € 15-21,50/24h + tourist tax € 0,95/pp, dog € 2,50/day 🚰Ch 🔌(51x) € 4/24h WC 🚿included 🗑.🔋. **Location:** Rural, luxurious, isolated, quiet. **Surface:** grassy/metalled. ◻ 01/01-31/12. **Distance:** 🚆500m ⚓1km ⊗on the spot 🍴on the spot 🚲on the spot.

### Poeldijk 🛥 9B2
**Booma Recreatie**, Vredebestlaan 14b. **GPS:** n52,02464 e4,21242.⬆️

10 🚐 € 6 🚰Ch included 🔌(10x) € 2/day. 🚲 **Location:** Rural, simple, quiet. **Surface:** gravel. ◻ 01/01-31/12. **Distance:** 🚆800m 🛒50m ⊗800m 🍴800m 🚌800m 🚲on the spot 🚶on the spot.

### Roelofarendsveen 9C2
**Groencentrum De Veense Bukker**, Hazenpad 1. **GPS:** n52,19336 e4,61475.⬆️

10 🚐 € 12,50, 2 pers.incl 🔌included 🔌 € 2,16Amp. **Location:** Rural, isolated, quiet. **Surface:** unpaved. ◻ 01/01-31/12. **Distance:** 🚆2km 🛒1km ⊗2km 🍴2km.

### Sassenheim 🛥 9C2
**Jachthaven Jonkman**, Jonkman 1. **GPS:** n52,22074 e4,54476.⬆️

6 🚐 € 15 🚰 € 0,50 Ch 🔌 € 1 WC 🚿 € 0,50 🚿included. 🚲 **Location:** Rural, simple, quiet. **Surface:** grassy/gravel. ◻ 15/03-01/11. **Distance:** 🚆2km 🔌1km ⚓on the spot 🛒on the spot ⊗on the spot 🍴2km 🚲on the spot. **Remarks:** Check in at harbourmaster.

### Schelluinen 9C3
**Campererf Kweetal**, Landscheiding 4. **GPS:** n51,84672 e4,91957.⬆️

---

10 🚐 € 10 🚰Ch WC 🚿 € 5/5 🚿included. **Location:** Rural, isolated, quiet. **Surface:** grassy/metalled. ◻ 01/01-31/12. **Distance:** 🚆6,5km Gorinchem 🔌3km 🛒400m ⊗1km 🍴4km 🚌500m 🚲100m 🚶100m. **Remarks:** Bread-service.

### Schiedam 🛥 9C2
Doeleplein 1. **GPS:** n51,91972 e4,40111.⬆️

2 🚐 € 7. 🚐 **Location:** Urban, simple, central, quiet. **Surface:** metalled. ◻ 01/01-31/12. **Distance:** 🚆500m 🔌1,5km ⚓on the spot 🛒on the spot ⊗500m 🍴500m 🚌500m. **Remarks:** Max. 72h.

### Schiedam 🛥 9C2
Noordvest 40. **GPS:** n51,91926 e4,39372.⬆️

6 🚐 € 7. 🚐 **Location:** Urban, simple, central, quiet. **Surface:** metalled. ◻ 01/01-31/12. **Distance:** 🚆city centre 100m. **Remarks:** Max. 72h.

**Tourist information Schiedam:**
Ⓜ Het Jenever Museum, Lange Haven 74-76. Making distilled spirits.
◻ Tue-Su 12-17h.
🏛 Lange Kerkstraat. ◻ Fri 9-16h.

### Streefkerk 9C2
**Camperplaats Streefkerk**, Middenpolderweg 2a. **GPS:** n51,91266 e4,81287.
5 🚐 € 12,50 🚰Ch 🔌 WC 🚿included 📷. **Location:** Rural, isolated. **Surface:** metalled. ◻ 01/01-31/12. **Distance:** 🚆6km ⊗3km.

### Strijensas 🛥 9C3
**Jachthaven Strijensas**, Sassendijk 6. **GPS:** n51,71472 e4,58735.⬆️➡️

6 🚐 € 8 🔌 € 0,50/100liter 🚰Ch 🔌 € 2,50 WC 🚿 € 1/7minutes 🚿included. **Location:** Rural, quiet. **Surface:** asphalted. ◻ 15/01-15/12. **Distance:** 🚆500m 🍴on the spot 🚲on the spot 🚶on the spot. **Remarks:** Max. 72h.

### Vlaardingen 🛥 9C2
**Parking Deltabrug**, Oosthavenkade 81. **GPS:** n51,90364 e4,34769.⬆️

4 🚐free. **Location:** Urban, noisy. **Surface:** metalled. ◻ 01/01-31/12.

---

**Distance:** 🚆1km ⚓on the spot ⊗50m 🍴100m 🚌500m. **Remarks:** Along railwayline, max. 48h.

### Wijngaarden 9C3
**'t Koeiestalletje**, Westeinde 26. **GPS:** n51,84378 e4,74631.

5 🚐 € 8 🚰Ch 🔌service € 2 WC 🚿. **Location:** Rural. **Surface:** metalled. ◻ 01/01-31/12 ◻ Sa-Su. **Distance:** 🚆5km 🔌5km ⊗5km 🚲on the spot 🚶on the spot. **Remarks:** Charging point for electric bicycles, regional products.

### Zevenhoven 🛥 9C2
**Camperplaats Zevenhoven**, Noordeinde 36. **GPS:** n52,19475 e4,77305.⬆️

5 🚐 € 10 🚰Ch 🔌 € 2,50 🚿included. 🚲 **Location:** Rural, comfortable. **Surface:** grassy/metalled. ◻ 01/01-31/12. **Distance:** 🚆1km 🔌1km 🚲on the spot 🚶on the spot.

### Zuid-Beijerland 🛥 9C3
**WSV de Hitsert**, Hitsertse Kade 8. **GPS:** n51,73826 e4,36529.

6 🚐 € 15,50 + € 0,75/pp tourist tax 🚰Ch 🔌 WC included 🚿 € 0,50 🚿. 🚲 **Location:** Rural, quiet. **Surface:** grassy/metalled. ◻ 01/05-01/11. **Distance:** 🚆800m 🔌1,5km ⚓on the spot 🛒on the spot ⊗on the spot 🍴800m 🚲on the spot 🚶on the spot. **Remarks:** Max. 72h, max. 8M.

# Zealand

### Axel 🛥 11B1
**P Watertoren**, Kinderdijk 4. **GPS:** n51,25972 e3,91028.⬆️

2 🚐free. **Location:** Urban, simple, noisy. **Surface:** metalled. ◻ 01/01-31/12. **Distance:** 🚆800m 🍴on the spot ⊗on the spot 🍴500m 🚲on the spot 🚶on the spot. **Remarks:** Max. 24h.

**Tourist information Axel:**
🏛 Noordstraat. ◻ Sa 8-16h.

### Breskens 🛥 9A3
**Vakantiepark Zeebad**, Nieuwe Sluisweg. **GPS:** n51,40193 e3,54420.⬆️

NL

10 🛏 € 14 WC 🔌 📶 🚰 ♿ **Location:** Rural, comfortable, quiet.
**Surface:** metalled. 🕐 01/01-31/12.
**Distance:** 🛒500m ⚓400m 🏊100m 🍴100m 🚴 on the spot
🚶 on the spot.
**Remarks:** Servicepoint at camping Zeebad, ferry to Vlissingen 500m
(pedestrian/bicycles).

| 🅿️🅂 | **Graauw** | 11B1 |

Zandbergsestraat. **GPS:** n51,32519 e4,10420.⬆️

7 🛏 free. **Location:** Rural, simple, quiet. **Surface:** gravel/sand.
🕐 01/01-31/12.
**Distance:** 🛒400m ⊗400m 🚴 on the spot.
**Remarks:** Max. 72h.

| 🅲🅂 | **Groede** 🌿🏖🏄 | 11A1 |

**De Ploeg, Parking Zuid,** Voorstraat 47. **GPS:** n51,38232 e3,51268.⬆️

40 🛏 € 12,50-20 + € 1,20/pp tourist tax 🚰 🔌Ch 🚿(35x) € 2,50
WC 🔌 📶included. 🛁 **Location:** Rural, comfortable, central, quiet.
**Surface:** metalled. 🕐 01/03-01/11 🌙 22-7h.
**Distance:** 🛒100m ⚓3km ⊗100m 🍴100m 🚌100m > Terneuzen
🚴 on the spot 🚶 on the spot.
**Remarks:** Caution € 10, dog € 4, sanitary/washing machine at
campsite.

| 🅲 | **Groede** 🌿🏖🏄 | 11A1 |

**Strandcamping Groede,** Zeeweg 1. **GPS:** n51,39632 e3,48719.⬆️

50 🛏 € 1/h. 🚪 ♿ **Location:** Rural, simple, quiet. **Surface:** gravel.
🕐 01/01-31/12.
**Distance:** 🛒Groede 3km ⚓sandy beach 200m ⊗60m 🍴on the
spot 🚴 on the spot 🚶 on the spot.
**Remarks:** Max. 1 night.

| 🅿️🅂 | **Hansweert** 🌿🏖 | 9B3 |

Westhavendijk. **GPS:** n51,44483 e4,00629.⬆️

---

5 🛏 free. **Location:** Rural, simple, isolated, quiet. **Surface:** asphalted.
🕐 01/01-31/12.
**Distance:** 🛒250m 🚤4km ⚓on the spot 🍴200m 🚴 on the spot
🚶 on the spot.
**Remarks:** Max. 6m, max. 72h.

| 🅿️🅂 | **Hulst** 🌿🏖🏄🍦 | 11B1 |

**Parkeerterrein Havenfort,** Havenfort. **GPS:** n51,27700 e4,04912.

15 🛏 € 0,80/h, mo-sa 9-17h, su 12-18h. 🚪 **Surface:** metalled.
🕐 01/01-31/12.
**Distance:** 🛒on the spot 🚿25m ⊗150m 🍴150m 🚌200m 🚴 on the
spot 🚶 on the spot.
**Remarks:** Max. 72h, shops open on Sunday.

**Tourist information Hulst:**

ℹ️ VVV, Grote Markt 19, www.bezoekhulst.nl. Fortified city with city
walls, shops open on Sunday.

| 🅿️🅂 | **Kamperland** 🏖🏄 | 9B3 |

**Camperpark Zeeland,** Campensweg 5.
**GPS:** n51,57495 e3,65236.⬆️➡️

102 🛏 € 15,50-19,50, 2 pers. incl. 🚰 € 0,20/min 🔌Ch 🚿(75x)
€ 4/24h,16Amp WC 🔌 € 0,25/min 🍴 € 6/4 📶included ♿ 🚪
♿ **Location:** Rural, luxurious, quiet. **Surface:** grassy/gravel.
🕐 01/01-31/12.
**Distance:** 🛒3km 🚤2km ⚓50m 🚿50m ⊗100m 🍴4km 🚌2km
🚴 on the spot 🚶 on the spot.

| 🅲🅂 | **Kamperland** 🏖🏄 | 9B3 |

**Roompot Beach Resort,** Mariapolderseweg 1.
**GPS:** n51,58972 e3,71666.

20 🛏 € 6 10-17h, € 14 17-10h 🚰 🔌Ch 🚿 WC 🔌 € 4,50/1,20 📶.
**Location:** Rural, isolated, noisy. **Surface:** asphalted.
🕐 01/01-31/12.
**Distance:** 🛒3km ⚓500m 🚿500m ⊗500m 🍴500m 🚌1km.

| 🅿️🅂 | **Kloosterzande** | 11B1 |

Hulsterweg. **GPS:** n51,36555 e4,02121.⬆️

---

2 🛏 free. **Location:** Rural, simple, central, quiet. **Surface:** metalled.
🕐 01/01-31/12.
**Distance:** 🛒500m ⊗80m 🍴700m 🚴 on the spot 🚶 on the spot.

| 🅿️🅂 | **Kruiningen** | 9B3 |

**Landwinkel de Plantage,** Kaasgat 4a. **GPS:** n51,46865 e4,04445.⬆️

15 🛏 € 13,50 🚰 🔌Ch 🔌 € 2,50/night,10Amp WC 🔌 📶included.
**Location:** Rural, comfortable, quiet. **Surface:** grassy.
🕐 01/01-31/12.
**Distance:** 🛒3km ⚓3km ⊗3km 🍴3km 🚿on the spot 🚌1km 🚴 on
the spot 🚶 on the spot.

| 🅲🅂 | **Middelburg** 🌿🏖🏄🍦🛍 | 9A3 |

**Stadscamping Zeeland,** Koninginnelaan 55.
**GPS:** n51,49686 e3,59739.⬆️
60 🛏 € 20-32,50, Jul/Aug € 25-37,50 🚰 🔌Ch 🚿 WC 🔌 📶included.
**Location:** Urban, comfortable, luxurious, quiet. **Surface:** unpaved.
🕐 01/01-31/12.
**Distance:** 🛒1,5km ⚓9km ⊗800m 🍴900m 🚿on the spot
🚶 on the spot.

| 🍴 | **Oosterland** 🌿 | 9B3 |

**Wok van Zeeland,** Rijksweg 6. **GPS:** n51,65767 e4,05336.⬆️

3 🛏 free. **Location:** Simple, isolated, noisy. **Surface:** asphalted.
🕐 01/01-31/12.
**Distance:** 🛒2km ⊗on the spot.
**Remarks:** Only overnight stays.

| 🅲🅂 | **Oostkapelle** | 9A3 |

**De Pekelinge,** Landmetersweg 1. **GPS:** n51,55725 e3,55139.⬆️
20 🛏 € 22,50-30,50 🚰 🔌Ch 📶included. ♿ ♿
**Location:** Simple, isolated, quiet. **Surface:** gravel/sand.
🕐 27/03-01/11.
**Distance:** 🛒nearby ⚓nearby ⊗on the spot 🍴on the spot.
**Remarks:** Arrival >20h departure <10h, max. 1 night.

| 🅿️🅂 | **Paal** 🏄 | 11B1 |

**Jachthaven,** Zeedijk van de van Alsteinpolder.
**GPS:** n51,35331 e4,10937.⬆️

4 🛏 free. **Location:** Rural. **Surface:** asphalted/metalled.
🕐 01/01-31/12.
**Distance:** 🛒100m 🍴on the spot 🚿on the spot ⊗on the spot 🚴 on
the spot 🚶 on the spot.
**Remarks:** Max. 72h.

NL

## Renesse 9B3

**Camping International**, Scharendijkseweg 8.
**GPS:** n51,74030 e3,78967. ⬆➡.

20 🛏 € 20, 11/07-22/09 € 35 ⛽🔌Ch🚿(16x)WC🚽included ⊡
€ 5/3,50 🚿 € 2.
**Location:** Rural. **Surface:** metalled. ⬛ 09/03-04/11.
**Distance:** 🚶1,5km 🚲2,5km ⛱on the spot ⊗on the spot ⚓on the spot 🚆1,5km 🚴on the spot 🧍on the spot.

## Sas van Gent 🌿🍴 11B1

**Kanaaleiland**, Oostkade. **GPS:** n51,22527 e3,80246. ⬆.

10 🛏free. **Surface:** metalled. ⬛ 01/01-31/12.
**Distance:** 🚶100m ⊗100m ⚓100m.
**Remarks:** Max. 24h.
**Tourist information Sas van Gent:**
🧍 Keizer Karelplein. ⬛ Tue 9-16h.

## Terneuzen 🌿🎣🍴 11B1

Rooseveltlaan. **GPS:** n51,32840 e3,85391. ⬆.

4 🛏free. **Location:** Rural. **Surface:** asphalted. ⬛ 01/01-31/12.
**Distance:** 🚶2,1km ⛱on the spot 🚊on the spot.
**Remarks:** Max. 24h.
**Tourist information Terneuzen:**
👁 Portaal van Vlaanderen, Zeevaartweg 11. Interactive Visitors Centre at the Terneuzen Locks, guided tour and boat excursions.
🧍 Markt. ⬛ Sa 9-16h.

## Tholen 🎣🍴 9B3

**Jachthaven**, Contre Escarpe 4. **GPS:** n51,53112 e4,22390. ⬆.

4 🛏 € 10,50 + € 1/pp tourist tax ⛽🔌Ch🚿 € 2/24h WC🚽⊡
€ 5 🚿included. **Location:** Urban, comfortable. **Surface:** metalled.
⬛ 01/01-31/12.
**Distance:** 🚶100m ⊗100m ⚓100m.
**Remarks:** Max. 72h.

## Vogelwaarde 11B1

Populierenstraat. **GPS:** n51,32562 e3,97758. ⬆.

---

2 🛏free. **Location:** Urban, simple, quiet. **Surface:** metalled.
⬛ 01/01-31/12.
**Distance:** 🚶1km ⚓400m 🚴on the spot 🧍on the spot.
**Remarks:** Max. 72h.

## Westdorpe 11B1

**De Baeckermat**, Bernhardstraat. **GPS:** n51,22917 e3,82167. ⬆.

2 🛏free. **Location:** Rural, simple, quiet. **Surface:** metalled.
⬛ 01/01-31/12.
**Distance:** 🚶500m 🚊on the spot ⊗100m ⚓500m 🚆on the spot 🚴on the spot 🧍on the spot.
**Remarks:** Max. 24h.

## Wolphaartsdijk 🌿🎣🍴 9B3

**Camping 't Veerse Meer**, Veerweg. **GPS:** n51,54325 e3,81253. ⬆.

7 🛏 € 17/24 ⛽🔌Ch🚿(5x)WC🚽on camp site ⊡on camp site 🚿included. 🚴 **Location:** Rural, comfortable, isolated, quiet.
**Surface:** metalled. ⬛ 01/01-31/12.
**Distance:** 🚶1,5km ⛱100m 🚊100m ⚓100m 🚆on the spot 🚴on the spot 🧍on the spot.

## Yerseke 🌿 9B3

**Zaetepolder**, Molenpolderweg 5. **GPS:** n51,49067 e4,05395.
12 🛏 € 10.
**Location:** Rural. **Surface:** asphalted. ⬛ 01/01-31/12.
**Distance:** ⛱on the spot 🚊on the spot ⊗900m ⚓600m.
**Tourist information Yerseke:**
ℹ VVV, Kerkplein 1, www.vvvzuidbevelandentholen.nl. Oyster and mussel culture.

## Zaamslag 🎣🍴 11B1

**Campererf de Feijter**, Zaamslagsedijk 6. **GPS:** n51,31953 e3,93574. ⬆.
🛏 € 10,50 ⛽🔌Chon demand 🔌16Amp 🚿included.
**Location:** Rural, isolated, quiet. **Surface:** grassy.
⬛ 01/01-31/12.
**Distance:** 🚶3km ⊗3km ⚓3km.

## Zierikzee 🌿🎣🍴 9B3

**De Zandweg**, Zandweg 30. **GPS:** n51,65691 e3,91210. ⬆.

12 🛏 € 12,50 ⛽🔌Ch🚿(12x),10Amp 🚿included. 🚴
**Location:** Rural, comfortable, central, noisy. **Surface:** asphalted.
⬛ 01/01-31/12. **Distance:** 🚶800m ⛱on the spot 🚊on the spot ⊗350m ⚓1km ⚓350m 🚴on the spot.
**Remarks:** Max. 72h, service passerby € 3.

---

# North Brabant

## Asten 11E1

**Camperplaats Wetland**, Tureluurweg 7.
**GPS:** n51,36687 e5,84214. ⬆.

50 🛏 € 9 + € 1,35/pp tourist tax ⛽🔌Ch🚿(37x) € 2 WC🚽⊡
€ 2/2 🚿included. **Location:** Rural, comfortable, isolated, quiet.
**Surface:** grassy/metalled. ⬛ 01/01-31/12.
**Distance:** 🚶2km 🚲4km ⛱9km ⊗2km ⚓1,5km 🚴on the spot 🧍on the spot.
**Remarks:** Located in nature reserve De Groote Peel, charging point for electric bicycles.

## Bakel 9D3

**Sporthal de Beek**, De Beekakker 13a. **GPS:** n51,50061 e5,74377. ⬆.

2 🛏free. **Location:** Urban, simple. **Surface:** metalled.
⬛ 01/01-31/12.
**Distance:** 🚶500m 🚴on the spot 🧍on the spot.
**Remarks:** At gymnasium.

## Bergen op Zoom 🌿 9B3

De Boulevard. **GPS:** n51,48405 e4,27941.

8 🛏free. ⬛ 01/01-31/12.
**Remarks:** Max. 72h.

## Bergen op Zoom 🌿 9B3

De Boulevard Noord. **GPS:** n51,48735 e4,27708. ⬆.

5 🛏free. **Surface:** metalled. ⬛ 01/01-31/12.
**Distance:** 🚶1km 🚲3,8km ⛱on the spot ⊗on the spot.
**Remarks:** Max. 72h. On the level of restaurant 'La Playa'.
**Tourist information Bergen op Zoom:**
Ⓜ❌ De Markiezenhof, Steenbergsestraat 8. Medieval palace built in the late 15th century. ⬛ Tue-Su 11-17h.

## Best 9D3

Carpoolplaats De Wilg. **GPS:** n51,52106 e5,39423. ⬆.

3 free. **Location:** Motorway, isolated. **Surface:** metalled. ◻ 01/01-31/12.
**Distance:** 500m 150m on the spot on the spot.
**Remarks:** Max. 24h.

### Bladel 11D1

## Recreatiepark De Achterste Hoef Bladel

- **Beautiful view**
- **Free wifi access**
- **Electricity/water/drainage at each pitch**

**www.achterstehoef.nl**
**info@achterstehoef.nl**

**Recreatiepark De Achterste Hoef \*\*\*\*\***, Toprijt 10.
**GPS:** n51,34398 e5,22753.
600 € 20-41 excl. tourist tax Ch WC
€ 6/0 included. **Location:** Rural. **Surface:** grassy.
◻ 05/04-29/09.
**Distance:** 3km on the spot 2km on the spot on the spot on the spot on the spot.
**Remarks:** Golf court, swimming pool available.

### Boxtel 9D3

**Dennenoord**, Dennendreef 5. **GPS:** n51,59770 e5,28661.

4 € 12,50 + € 1/pp tourist tax Ch WC € 4
included. **Location:** Rural, simple, isolated. **Surface:** metalled.
◻ 01/01-31/12.
**Distance:** 4km 4km,
**Remarks:** Max. 3 nights.

### Breda 9C3

Nijverheidssingel 391. **GPS:** n51,58793 e4,76366.
6 € 4.
**Surface:** metalled. ◻ 01/01-31/12.
**Distance:** 900m 800m 900m 200m.
**Tourist information Breda:**
VVV, Willemstraat 17-19, www.vvvbreda.nl. Many historical bldg. And castles.

### Budel 11D1

**Camperplaats Budel**, Heikantstraat 16. **GPS:** n51,26163 e5,59007.

25 € 9,50 Ch € 2,50/day,4Amp WC included.
**Location:** Urban. **Surface:** grasstiles/grassy. ◻ 01/01-31/12.
**Distance:** 800m 2km 600m 800m 800m 600m on the spot on the spot.
**Remarks:** Max. 72h, video surveillance, barbecue place, charging point for electric bicycles.

### De Heen 9B3

**Akkermans leisure & golf**, Heensemolenweg 23.
**GPS:** n51,60654 e4,24547.

5 € 12,50 Ch (16x) WC included.
**Location:** Rural, comfortable, isolated, quiet.
**Surface:** asphalted/metalled. ◻ 01/01-31/12.
**Distance:** 6km 3km on the spot 6km on the spot on the spot.

### Dorst 9C3

**Recreatiepark 't Haasje**, Klein Oosterhout 1A.
**GPS:** n51,60945 e4,88918.

7 € 22,10-26,50 Ch (10x) € 0,24 € 3,80/1,80
included. **Location:** Rural. **Surface:** grassy/metalled.
◻ 01/01-31/12.
**Distance:** 4km on the spot 100m on the spot on the spot on the spot on the spot.

### Drimmelen 9C3

## Camperpark Jachthaven Biesbosch Drimmelen

- **Located near marina**
- **Luxurious motorhome stopover**
- **Ideal base for walking and cycling**

**www.jachthavenbiesbosch.nl**
**info@jachthavenbiesbosch.nl**

**Camperpark Jachthaven Biesbosch**, Nieuwe Jachthaven 5.
**GPS:** n51,70750 e4,81008.
18 € 14,50, 15/06-15/09 € 17,50 Ch € 3/24h WC
€ 5/1,50 included. **Location:** Rural, comfortable.
**Surface:** asphalted/grassy. ◻ 01/01-31/12.
**Distance:** 1km on the spot 200m on the spot on the spot on the spot.
**Remarks:** Barbecue place, playground.

### Eindhoven 9D3

**P+R Meerhoven**, Sliffertsestraat 304. **GPS:** n51,43507 e5,42444.

10 first 24h € 3, € 5/24h Ch WC free. **Location:** Simple.
**Surface:** metalled. ◻ 01/01-31/12.
**Distance:** 4km on the spot 200m 500m on the spot
on the spot on the spot.
**Remarks:** Free bicycles available.

### Escharen 9D3

Burgemeester de Bourbonplein. **GPS:** n51,74390 e5,74496.

1 free.
**Location:** Central, noisy. **Surface:** metalled. ◻ 01/01-31/12.
**Distance:** on the spot.
**Remarks:** Near church.

### Escharen 9D3

**Bar Bistro De Brouwketel**, Hoogeweg 9.
**GPS:** n51,74152 e5,73376.

15 free. **Surface:** grassy/metalled. ◻ 01/01-31/12.

### Etten-Leur 9C3

**Jachthaven Turfvaart**, Westpolderpad 6. **GPS:** n51,59512 e4,65102.

10 € 15 € 0,50/100liter Ch WC included.
**Location:** Rural, comfortable, quiet. **Surface:** grassy/metalled.
◻ 01/01-31/12.
**Distance:** 1,5km on the spot 500m.
**Tourist information Etten-Leur:**
Mo-morning.

### Geertruidenberg 9C3

**WSV Geertruidenberg**, Statenlaan 15. **GPS:** n51,70362 e4,86311.

16 € 12 Ch WC € 0,50 € 3,50/1,50 included.
**Location:** Urban, comfortable, central, quiet. **Surface:** gravel.
◻ 01/01-31/12.
**Distance:** 500m 3km on the spot on the spot 500m.

NL

**Remarks:** Max. 3 days, max. 9m, check in at harbourmaster.

### Gemert 9D3

St.Gerardusplein. **GPS:** n51,55354 e5,69109.⬆.

2 🛏free.
**Location:** Urban, simple. **Surface:** gravel. ⬛ 01/01-31/12.
**Distance:** 🚶on the spot ⊗300m 🍺200m 🚗100m 🚲 on the spot 🚶on the spot.
**Remarks:** Max. 24h.

### Gemert 9D3

De Kokse hoeve, Koksedijk 25. **GPS:** n51,57380 e5,65846.

10 🛏free, use of a meal obligated. **Location:** Rural, simple, isolated, quiet. **Surface:** metalled. ⬛ 01/01-31/12.
**Distance:** 🚶2km.

### Grave 9D3

Het Arsenaal, Trompetterstraat. **GPS:** n51,75900 e5,73759.⬆.

1 🛏free 🚿free. **Location:** Urban, quiet. **Surface:** metalled. ⬛ 01/01-31/12.
**Distance:** 🚶100m ⊗200m 🍺50m 🚗200m.

### Grave 9D3

Gemaal van Sasse/Kazematten, Mars en Wijthdijk.
**GPS:** n51,76859 e5,73085.⬆.

2 🛏free.
**Location:** Rural. **Surface:** grasstiles. ⬛ 01/01-31/12.
**Distance:** 🚶500m 🚴200m ⊗500m 🍺500m 🚗400m 🚲 on the spot 🚶on the spot.

### Heeswijk-Dinther 9D3

Hotel-Restaurant de Leygraaf, Meerstraat 45A.
**GPS:** n51,66445 e5,47511.⬆.

4 🛏 € 11,20 🚿 WCincluded.

---

**Location:** Rural, comfortable. **Surface:** grassy.
⬛ 01/01-31/12.
**Distance:** 🚶1,5km 🚴6km ⊗ on the spot 🚲 on the spot 🚶on the spot.
**Remarks:** Check in on arrival, use sanitary only during opening hours.

### Helenaveen 9E3

Oude Hoeven, Soemeersingel 99. **GPS:** n51,40951 e5,90594.⬆.

5 🛏 € 8,50, 2 pers. incl 🚰 Ch 🚿 € 1,50 🔌. **Location:** Quiet.
**Surface:** grassy. ⬛ 01/04-01/11.
**Distance:** 🚲 on the spot 🚶on the spot.
**Remarks:** Max. 72h, money in envelope in mail box.

### Helmond 🚤 9D3

Parking Beatrixlaan, Beatrixlaan. **GPS:** n51,48100 e5,64870.⬆.

6 🛏 € 3/24h. 🔌 **Location:** Urban, simple, quiet. **Surface:** metalled.
⬛ 01/01-31/12.
**Distance:** 🚶300m 🚴500m ⊗300m 🍺500m 🚗on the spot 🚲 on the spot 🚶on the spot.
**Remarks:** Castle 500m.

### Hoogerheide 9B3

METO parking, Huijbergseweg. **GPS:** n51,42318 e4,33452.
5 🛏free.
**Location:** Simple. **Surface:** metalled. ⬛ 01/01-31/12.
**Distance:** 🚶800m ⊗800m 🍺800m.
**Remarks:** Max. 2 nights.

### Hoogerheide 9B3

Fam. Broos, Buitendreef 4, De Kooi. **GPS:** n51,42522 e4,34656.⬆.

5 🛏free 🚰 🚿(3x)free.
**Location:** Rural, simple, isolated. **Surface:** metalled.
⬛ 01/01-31/12.
**Distance:** 🚶3km 🚴3km ⊗3km 🍺3km 🚲 on the spot 🚶on the spot.

### Hulten 9C3

Restaurant Stad Parijs, Rijksweg 6. **GPS:** n51,56996 e4,96446.

15 🛏free 🍺 € 0,75. **Location:** Rural, simple, quiet. **Surface:** asphalted.
⬛ 01/01-31/12.
**Distance:** ⊗on the spot.
**Remarks:** Free, use of a meal obligated.

### Lage Zwaluwe 9C3

Jachthaven Crezée, Kwistgeldweg 1. **GPS:** n51,71520 e4,70124.

---

13 🛏 € 15 + tourist tax € 1/pp 🚰 Ch 🚿 € 3 WC 🚽 € 4/2 🔌included. 🚮 🗑 **Location:** Rural. **Surface:** asphalted/grassy.
⬛ 01/01-31/12.
**Distance:** 🚶300m 🚴700m ⊗200m 🍺1,5km 🚲 on the spot 🚶on the spot.

### Leende 11D1

Camperplaats Leenderstrijp, Strijperdijk 13.
**GPS:** n51,32721 e5,55518.⬆.

10 🛏 € 12,50 🚰 Ch 🚿 🔌included. **Location:** Rural, comfortable, quiet. **Surface:** grassy. ⬛ 01/01-31/12.
**Distance:** 🚶Eindhoven 10km ⊗1km 🍺1km 🚲 on the spot 🚶on the spot.

### Linden 9E3

Camperplaats De Kleine Geest, De Geest 3.
**GPS:** n51,74121 e5,80367.⬆.

25 🛏 € 10, 2 pers. incl, extra pers. € 1,50 🚰 Ch 🚿 € 2/day WC 🚽 € 0,50 🔌included. 🚮 **Location:** Rural, comfortable, isolated, quiet.
**Surface:** grassy/metalled. ⬛ 01/01-31/12.
**Distance:** 🚶5km 🚴2km 🚲 on the spot 🚶on the spot.
**Remarks:** Video surveillance.

### Linden 9E3

Jachthaven 't Loo, Hardweg 15. **GPS:** n51,75182 e5,82740.⬆.

30 🛏 € 12,50-15 🚰 Ch 🚿 € 2,50/day WC 🚽 € 1 🗑 € 4/3 🔌included. **Location:** Rural, comfortable, quiet. **Surface:** grassy.
⬛ 01/01-31/12.
**Distance:** 🚴on the spot 🚴on the spot ⊗on the spot 🍺on the spot 🚲 on the spot 🚶on the spot.
**Remarks:** Check in at harbourmaster 9-12h, 15-18h, caution key sanitary building € 20.

### Molenschot 9C3

Camperplaats De Trekvogel, Broekstraat 72.
**GPS:** n51,57277 e4,89423.⬆.

NL

12 ⊠ € 16 ⌂⚡Ch⚡(12x)WC⚡included. **Location:** Rural.
**Surface:** grassy/metalled. ○ 01/01-31/12.
**Distance:** ⌖200m ⚡on the spot ⚡on the spot.

### Nuenen 9D3

**Sportpark RKSV Nuenen**, Pastoorsmast 12.
**GPS:** n51,46317 e5,56277.⬆

5 ⊠free ⚡Ch. **Location:** Rural, simple, isolated. **Surface:** grassy.
○ 01/01-31/12 ○ July.
**Distance:** ⌖1,7km ⚡800m ⚡900m.
**Remarks:** Max. 5 days a month.

### Oijen 9D3

**Speciaalbierbrouwerij Oijen**, Oijensebovendijk.
**GPS:** n51,81049 e5,53126.

3 ⊠ € 10, free with a meal ⌂⚡included. **Location:** Rural, simple,
quiet. **Surface:** grassy/gravel. ○ 01/01-31/12.
**Distance:** ⚡on the spot ⚡on the spot ⚡on the spot ⚡on the spot
⚡on the spot.

### Oirschot 9D3

**Camperplaats Oirschot**, De Rijt. **GPS:** n51,50064 e5,32366.⬆➡

59 ⊠ € 13 ⌂⚡Ch⚡(28x) € 2 ⚡included.
**Surface:** gravel.
○ 01/01-31/12.
**Distance:** ⌖1km ⚡on the spot ⚡1km ⚡900m.
**Remarks:** Max. 72h.

**Tourist information Oirschot:**
🛈 VVV, Sint Odulphusstraat 11, www.vvvoirschot.nl.
City with 100 monumental buildings, hiking and biking routes.
○ 01/01-31/12.
Ⓜ Museum de Vier Quartieren, Sint Odulphusstraat 11.
Regional museum. ○ Tue-Su 13-16.30h.

### Oosteind 9C3

**Camperplaats Oosteind**, Ter Horst 19. **GPS:** n51,64705 e4,88326.⬆

---

4 ⊠ € 8 ⌂⚡Ch⚡included. **Location:** Rural, comfortable, isolated.
**Surface:** grassy. ○ 01/01-31/12.
**Distance:** ⌖2km ⚡1km ⚡500m.

### Oss 9D3

**Niesmann+Bischoff Campers Nederland**, Galliërsweg 39.
**GPS:** n51,75981 e5,55642.⬆

2 ⊠free ⌂⚡free. **Surface:** metalled. ○ 01/01-31/12.

### Oss 9D3

**Sportpark Rusheuvel. GPS:** n51,77743 e5,52295.⬆

⊠free. **Surface:** metalled. ○ 01/01-31/12.
**Distance:** ⌖750m ⚡750m ⚡AH 500m.
**Remarks:** Max. 3 nights.

### Oudenbosch 9C3

**Het Oude Bossche veld**, Moerdijksestraat 1.
**GPS:** n51,59558 e4,54117.⬆

15 ⊠ € 13 + € 1/pp tourist tax ⌂⚡Ch⚡⚡included.⚡
**Location:** Rural. **Surface:** grassy/metalled. ○ 01/01-31/12.
**Distance:** ⌖city centre 1km ⚡600m ⚡1km ⚡1km ⚡on the spot
⚡on the spot.
**Remarks:** Max. 72h, possibility for reservation.

### Overloon 9E3

**Van Well**, Roosendaalseweg 1. **GPS:** n51,56377 e5,91995.

15 ⊠ € 6,50 ⌂⚡Ch⚡ € 2 ⚡included. **Location:** Quiet.
**Surface:** grassy. ○ 01/01-31/12.
**Distance:** ⌖2,5km ⚡4km ⚡2km ⚡2,5km ⚡2,5km ⚡2,5km
⚡on the spot ⚡on the spot.

### Raamsdonksveer 9C3

**Jachthaven Dok12**, Kartuizerstraat 12. **GPS:** n51,69275 e4,86033.⬆
4 ⊠ € 10 ⌂⚡Ch⚡ € 2. **Location:** Rural. **Surface:** metalled.

---

○ 01/01-31/12.
**Distance:** ⚡on the spot ⚡on the spot ⚡on the spot ⚡500m ⚡on
the spot ⚡on the spot.

### Reusel 11D1

**De Wekker**, Wilhelminalaan 97. **GPS:** n51,36187 e5,17339.

5 ⊠Free, use of a meal obligated ⌂⚡⚡. **Location:** Simple, quiet.
**Surface:** sand. ○ 01/01-31/12 ○ Tue.
**Distance:** ⚡on the spot.

### Roosendaal 9C3

**Mobildrôme**, Argon 31-33, Oud Gastel. **GPS:** n51,56333 e4,46278.

8 ⊠free ⌂ € 0,50 ⚡Ch⚡ € 0,50/kWh.
**Surface:** metalled.
○ 01/01-31/12.
**Distance:** ⌖2km ⚡1,1km ⚡2km.
**Remarks:** Max. 48h.

**Tourist information Roosendaal:**
⚡ Rosada, A17, afrit 19. Factory outlet.

### Schijndel 9D3

**De Schootse Hoeve**, Schootsehoef 2. **GPS:** n51,60668 e5,42324.⬆

15 ⊠ € 15, 2 pers.incl ⌂⚡Ch⚡(4x)WC⚡included.
**Location:** Rural. **Surface:** grassy/metalled. ○ 01/01-31/12.
**Distance:** ⌖2km ⚡500m ⚡on the spot ⚡on the spot.

**Tourist information Schijndel:**
⚡ ⚡ Sa 10-14h.

### Sint Oedenrode 9D3

**Parking De Neul**, Dommelpark. **GPS:** n51,56720 e5,45832.⬆

3 ⊠ € 5. ⚡ **Location:** Simple, central, quiet. **Surface:** metalled.
○ 01/01-31/12 ○ during event.
**Distance:** ⌖historical centre 500m ⚡500m ⚡500m ⚡on the
spot ⚡on the spot.
**Remarks:** Max. 3x24h, to be paid at swimming pool.

### Steenbergen 9B3

**Jachthaven Steenbergen**, Havenpad 1. **GPS:** n51,58739 e4,31390.⬆

## Eurocamping Vessem

- Ideal base for walking and cycling
- Wifi
- Open all year
- Comfortable motorhome stopover
- Flat motorhome pitches
- Located in nature reserve
- Swimming pool, midgetgolf and playground

www.eurocampingvessem.nl
info@eurocampingvessem.nl

4 🛏 € 14,50 🚰Ch 🔌 included,6Amp WC. **Location:** Urban. **Surface:** metalled. 🅾 01/04-31/10. **Distance:** 🚶on the spot 🏊on the spot ⊗100m 🍺on the spot. **Remarks:** Max. 72h.

### Tilburg 9C3
**Hotel Ibis,** Doctor Hub. van Doorneweg 105. **GPS:** n51,54173 e5,05059.

15 🛏 € 7,50. 🚰 Location: Urban, simple. **Surface:** asphalted. 🅾 01/01-31/12. **Distance:** 🚶3km ⊗on the spot.

### Veghel 9D3
Hoogstraat. **GPS:** n51,61504 e5,53854. ⬆.

2 🛏 € 5. **Location:** Urban, simple, central, noisy. **Surface:** metalled. 🅾 01/01-31/12. **Distance:** 🚶250m ⊗100m 🍺100m. **Remarks:** Max. 72h, to be paid at town hall.

### Velp 9D3
**Mariëndaal,** Beukenlaan. **GPS:** n51,74687 e5,71181. ⬆.

2 🛏free 🚰Chfree. **Location:** Rural, simple, quiet. **Surface:** metalled. 🅾 01/01-31/12.

---

**Distance:** 🚶500m ⊗on the spot 🏃on the spot.

### Vessem 9D3

**Eurocamping Vessem,** Zwembadweg 1. **GPS:** n51,41197 e5,27490. ⬆. 40 🛏 € 13,50 🚰 € 1/80liter 🔌Ch 🔌 € 0,60/kWh 🍺 € 0,50 📶 € 1/day. **Location:** Rural. **Surface:** grassy. 🅾 01/01-31/12. **Distance:** 🚶1,5km 🚲7km ⛵5km 🛒on the spot ⊗1,5km 🍺on the spot 🚌300m 🏃on the spot 🏃on the spot.

### Vianen 9E3
**Ons Plekske,** Berkenkamp 59. **GPS:** n51,71602 e5,84489. ⬆.

25 🛏 € 13, 2 pers.incl 🚰Ch 🔌WC 📶 € 3/3 📶included. **Location:** Rural, luxurious, quiet. **Surface:** grassy. 🅾 01/01-31/12. **Distance:** 🚶on the spot 🚲3,5km ⛵2,6km 🛒2,6km 🏃on the spot 🏃on the spot. **Remarks:** Monitored parking 24/24.

### Wijk en Aalburg 9D3
**Bakkerij Hardeman,** Torenstraat 4. **GPS:** n51,75976 e5,13123. ⬆.

3 🛏 € 3 🚰Ch 🔌 € 2 WC 📶 € 7,50 📶included. 🚰 **Location:** Urban, comfortable, quiet. **Surface:** asphalted/metalled. 🅾 01/01-31/12. **Distance:** 🚶on the spot ⊗on the spot 🍺400m 🏃on the spot. **Remarks:** Check in on arrival.

### Zeeland 9D3
Vlasroot 35. **GPS:** n51,69682 e5,67543. ⬆. 4 🛏 € 5. **Location:** Urban, simple. **Surface:** metalled. 🅾 01/01-31/12. **Distance:** 🚶on the spot ⊗150m 🍺150m.

### Zeeland 9D3
**De Heische Tip,** Straatsven 4. **GPS:** n51,69623 e5,65841. ➡.

---

3 🛏 € 5. **Location:** Rural, simple, quiet. **Surface:** forest soil. 🅾 01/01-31/12. **Distance:** 🚶1,5km ⛵100m ⊗100m 🍺1,5km 🏃on the spot 🏃on the spot.

### Zundert 9C3
**Museum de Scooter,** Heischoorstraat 4. **GPS:** n51,49025 e4,64532.

10 🛏 € 14 🚰🔌Ch 🔌WC 📶included. **Location:** Rural, comfortable, isolated, quiet. **Surface:** grassy/metalled. 🅾 01/01-31/12. **Distance:** 🚶2,8km 🚲A17km 🏃on the spot 🏃on the spot. **Remarks:** Reservation during flower parade: museum@lambretta-nl.net.

# Limburg

### Afferden 9E3

## Camperpark Roland Afferden

- Located in nature reserve
- Comfortable motorhome stopover
- Ideal base for walking and cycling

www.campingroland.nl
info@campingroland.nl

**Camperpark Roland,** Rimpelt 17. **GPS:** n51,63747 e6,03037. ⬆➡. 38 🛏 € 10,10, 2 pers. incl, extra pers € 3,50 🚰🔌Ch 🔌(24x) € 2/day,6Amp WC 🔌 € 0,50 🔌 € 4,50/2,50 📶included. 🚰 **Location:** Rural. **Surface:** grassy. 🅾 01/04-31/10. **Distance:** 🚶1,5km 🚲6km ⛵1,6km 🛒300m 🍺1,5km 🚌1,5km 🏃on the spot 🏃on the spot. **Remarks:** Max. 72h, dog € 3,25, sanitary/washing machine at campsite, bicycle rental.

### Brunssum 11E1
**Schutterspark P1,** Heidestraat 20. **GPS:** n50,94582 e5,98385. ⬆.

10 🛏free. **Surface:** metalled. 🅾 01/01-31/12. **Distance:** 🚶1,5km ⊗100m Schuttershuuske. **Remarks:** Max. 72h, barefoot path.

### Gennep 9E3
Martinusplein. **GPS:** n51,69985 e5,97206. ⬆.

NL

5 🛏 € 5,50 + tourist tax. **Location:** Urban, simple, quiet. **Surface:** metalled. 🅿 01/01-31/12. **Distance:** 100m 4,6km 200m 150m bakery 100m, supermarket 250m on the spot on the spot. **Remarks:** Max. 72h.

### Grathem 11E1

## Camperplaats Twins Grathem

**Comfortable motorhome stopover**
**Ideal base for walking and cycling**
**Point of interest**

**mtshendriksvdburg@gmail.com**

**Camperplaats Twins**, Hunselerdijk 8. **GPS:** n51,22052 e5,86561. 10 🛏 € 10 Ch € 2,50/day WC included € 0,50 € 1. **Location:** Rural, comfortable, isolated, quiet. **Surface:** grassy. 🅿 01/04-31/10. **Distance:** 3km 3km 3km 500m on the spot.

### Grubbenvorst 9E3

**Het Kompas**, Meerlosebaan 7. **GPS:** n51,42861 e6,12889.

30 🛏 € 12, 2 pers. incl, extra pers € 2 Ch (30x),6Amp included. **Location:** Rural, comfortable, quiet. **Surface:** grassy/metalled. 🅿 01/03-01/12. **Distance:** 2km 500m 2km 2km 1km on the spot on the spot. **Remarks:** Max. 2 dogs, playground 100m, money in envelope in mail box.

### Heel 11E1

**De Tump**, Heelderweg 13. **GPS:** n51,17698 e5,88315.

5 🛏 € 7. **Location:** Rural. **Surface:** grassy. 🅿 01/05-31/10. **Distance:** 1km on the spot. **Remarks:** Max. 48h.

### Ittervoort 11E1

**Camperplaats Ittervoort**, Brigittastraat 31. **GPS:** n51,17565 e5,82228.

15 🛏 € 11, 2 pers. incl Ch € 2,50,6Amp WC included. **Location:** Rural, simple. **Surface:** grassy. 🅿 01/01-31/12. **Distance:** Ittervoort 500m, Thorn 2km 2,6km on the spot Jan Linders 750m on the spot on the spot. **Remarks:** Vineyard Thorn 600m.

### Kessel 11E1

**Camperplaats Kessel**, Hazenakkerweg 1. **GPS:** n51,29856 e6,05009.

18 🛏 € 12, 2 pers.incl Ch (18x) € 2,50/24h WC included. **Location:** Rural. **Surface:** asphalted/grassy. 🅿 01/01-31/12. **Distance:** city centre 200m 10km 100m 200m 500m 300m on the spot on the spot. **Remarks:** Max. 8M.

### Landgraaf 11E1

## Camperplaats Landgraaf Landgraaf

**Alpine skiing**
**Point of interest**
**Free wifi access**

**www.camperplaatsnederland.nl**
**info@camperplaatsnederland.nl**

**Camperplaats Landgraaf**, Tunnelweg 1a. **GPS:** n50,87217 e6,02288. 28 🛏 € 10 € 0,50/50liter Ch (18x) € 0,50/kWh included **Location:** Rural. **Surface:** grassy/gravel. 🅿 01/01-31/12. **Distance:** 300m 3km 3km 3km 300m 300m 1,6km 150m 50m 50m 250m.

### Landgraaf 11E1

**Camping de Watertoren**, Kerkveldweg 1. **GPS:** n50,91016 e6,07300.

6 🛏 € 10, peak season € 15 + € 1/pp tourist tax € 1/90liter Ch included. **Location:** Simple, isolated, quiet. **Surface:** grassy/gravel. 🅿 01/01-31/12. **Distance:** 2km.

### Lottum 9E3

**Camperstop IndeVerte**, Horsterdijk 97. **GPS:** n51,45130 e6,13144.

54 🛏 € 15 Ch WC € 1 € 4/4 included. **Location:** Rural, comfortable, isolated, quiet. **Surface:** grassy. 🅿 01/01-31/12. **Distance:** 3km. **Remarks:** Adults only, bread-service.

### Maasbree 11E1

**Camperplaats Rooth**, Rooth. **GPS:** n51,36820 e6,08374.

15 🛏 € 12 Ch (18x) WC . **Location:** Rural, comfortable. **Surface:** grassy/sand. 🅿 01/04-01/11. **Distance:** 3km 4km 2km 500m 3km 700m on the spot on the spot. **Remarks:** Max. 72h.

### Maasbree 11E1

**Restaurant Boszicht**, Provincialeweg 2. **GPS:** n51,36395 e6,07980.

3 🛏 free, use of a meal desired. **Location:** Simple, noisy. **Surface:** gravel. **Distance:** 2km 2km on the spot.

### Maastricht 11D2

## Camperplaats Maastricht Maastricht

**Excellent location for city visit**
**Free wifi access**
**Open all year**

**www.camperplaatsnederland.nl**
**info@camperplaatsnederland.nl**

**Camperplaats Maastricht**, Bosscherweg 35. **GPS:** n50,87489 e5,68024. 100 🛏 € 16 € 0,50/50liter Ch (67x) € 0,50/kWh,16Amp included. **Location:** Isolated, quiet. **Surface:** grassy/gravel. 🅿 01/01-31/12. **Distance:** 2,9km 100m 800m 600m 50m on the spot on the spot.

### Maastricht 11D2

**Maastricht Marina**, Hoge Weerd 20. **GPS:** n50,82270 e5,70077.

24 ⌂ € 19,50, 2 pers.incl, >8m + € 4,50 ⌐⊒Ch ⚡(20x),6Amp WC⊒◉ € 3,50/2,50 📶included. 🚐🚲 **Location:** Urban, comfortable, quiet. **Surface:** gravel/metalled. ☐ 01/02-03/01. **Distance:** 🛒1,5km 🚲2,8km 🏊50m 🚏50m ⊗50m ⚓1,5km 🚌800m 🚶on the spot 🎣on the spot. **Remarks:** Arrival 13><19h, max. 9m, reservation recommended.

### Meijel  11E1
**Nieuwehof**, Vieruitersten 25. **GPS:** n51,35261 e5,89561.⬆⬇➡.

29 ⌂ € 10 + € 1/pp tourist tax ⌐⊒Ch ⚡WCincluded ⊒📶on demand. 🚲 **Location:** Rural, comfortable, isolated, quiet. **Surface:** grassy/sand. ☐ 01/01-31/12. **Distance:** 🛒1,8km 🚲14km ⚓2km 🎣on the spot 🚶on the spot.

### Milsbeek  9E3
**De Diepen**, Zwarteweg 60. **GPS:** n51,73788 e5,95510.⬆⬆🚲.

3 ⌂ € 5,50 + € 1/pp tourist tax. **Surface:** grassy. ☐ 01/01-31/12. **Distance:** ⊗on the spot 🚲on the spot 🎣on the spot. **Remarks:** Next to Eethuis de Diepen.

### Neer  11E1
**Jachthaven Hanssum**, Hanssum 40b. **GPS:** n51,25778 e6,00361.⬆.

12 ⌂ € 12,50 ⌐Ch ⚡WC⊒ € 0,50/time. **Location:** Rural, comfortable, quiet. **Surface:** grassy/metalled. ☐ 01/01-31/12. **Distance:** 🛒3km 🚲on the spot ⊗200m. **Remarks:** Max. 48h, service near marina.

### Neer  11E1
**Café Restaurant Boothuis de Troost**, Hanssum 47. **GPS:** n51,25964 e6,00380.

4 ⌂ € 7,50, guests free ⚡. **Surface:** metalled.

### Nieuw Bergen  9E3
**Camperplaats Bos&Heide**, Op de Paal 4. **GPS:** n51,59008 e6,07269.⬆➡.

25 ⌂ € 7, tourist tax € 1/pp ⌐⊒Ch ⚡(25x) € 2 WCincluded. **Location:** Comfortable, quiet. **Surface:** grassy. ☐ 01/03-31/10. **Distance:** 🛒1,5km 🚲2km ⊗1,5km ⚓1,5km on the spot 🎣on the spot. **Remarks:** Located in nature reserve Maasduinen, regional products.

### Nuth  11E1
**Landgoed De Dael**, Dealderpad 1. **GPS:** n50,92268 e5,89007. 10 ⌂ € 15 ⚡. **Surface:** gravel. ☐ 01/01-31/12. **Distance:** ⊗500m ⚓1,3km.

### Ospel  11D1
**De Peeldijk**, Plattepeeldijk 19. **GPS:** n51,30504 e5,79827. 8 ⌂ € 10 ⌐Ch ⚡included,16Amp. **Location:** Rural. **Surface:** metalled. ☐ 01/01-31/12. **Distance:** 🛒city centre 1,5km. **Remarks:** Max. 72h.

### Ottersum  9E3
**Bier-Café Restaurant Old Inn**, Siebengewaldseweg 13. **GPS:** n51,68935 e6,00728.

20 ⌂free. **Surface:** metalled. ☐ 01/01-31/12. **Distance:** 🛒3km 🚗500m.

### Plasmolen  9E3
**Eldorado**, Witteweg 18. **GPS:** n51,73284 e5,91639.

13 ⌂ € 14,50-17 + € 1/pp tourist tax ⌐ € 0,50/100liter ⚡Ch ⚡(13x) € 0,50/kWh WC⊒ € 1 ◉ € 3 📶 € 5/24h. **Location:** Rural, comfortable, quiet. **Surface:** grassy. ☐ 01/01-31/12 ◉ **Service:** winter. **Distance:** 🛒200m 🚲8km 🏊on the spot 🚏on the spot ⊗200m ⚓200m 🎣on the spot 🚶on the spot. **Remarks:** Check in at Eldorado Boatshop Witteweg 9, max. 72h.

### Roermond  11E1
**Helenawerf Watersport**, De Ster 13. **GPS:** n51,19356 e5,98039.⬆⬆.

20 ⌂ € 12,50 ⌐Ch ⚡ € 1 WC⊒◉ € 3,50/3,50 📶🚐🚲. **Location:** Urban, central, quiet. **Surface:** gravel.

☐ 01/02-01/12. **Distance:** 🛒250m 🚲1km 🏊1,2km 🚏50m ⊗150m ⚓300m 🚌300m 🎣100m 🚶50m. **Remarks:** Max. 48h, check in at harbourmaster, possibility for reservation.

### Sittard  11E1
**De Nieuwe Hateboer**, Sportcentrumlaan. **GPS:** n51,00794 e5,88150.⬆.

10 ⌂free ⌐⊒ChWCuse sanitary facilities at swimming pool ⊒. **Location:** Urban, simple. **Surface:** asphalted. ☐ 01/01-31/12. **Distance:** 🛒2km 🚲6,2km 🏊2km ⚓2km 🎣100m 🚶on the spot. **Remarks:** At swimming pool, register via SMS (licence plate number) +31 6 27 82 55 82, max. 48h.

### Thorn  11E1
Waterstraat. **GPS:** n51,15860 e5,84403.⬆.

3 ⌂ € 2,50/9-18h. 🚗 **Surface:** gravel. ☐ 01/01-31/12. **Distance:** 🛒150m ⊗150m. **Remarks:** Max. 24h.

**Tourist information Thorn:**
ℹ VVV, Wijngaard 14, www.lekker-genieten.nl. The white village, with historical centre and Gothic collegiate church.

### Valkenburg  11E2

**Camperplaats Valkenburg aan de Geul**, Heunsbergerweg 1. **GPS:** n50,86037 e5,83148. 40 ⌂ € 15-25 + € 1/100liter ⚡Ch ⚡(30x) € 0,60/kWh,16Amp WCincluded ⊒ € 0,70 ◉ € 4,75/2,25 📶 € 2,50/24h 🚐📷. **Location:** Rural, comfortable, quiet. **Surface:** grassy/metalled. ☐ 01/01-31/12. **Distance:** 🛒500m 🚲2km 🏊1,5km 🚏1,5km ⊗on the spot ⚓500m 🚌500m 🎣on the spot 🚶on the spot. **Remarks:** Possibility for reservation, Maastricht 15km.

### Valkenburg  11E2
Burgemeester Henssingel. **GPS:** n50,86361 e5,83725.

6 🛏 € 1,70/h, max. € 8.
**Surface:** metalled.
🅾 01/01-31/12.
**Distance:** 🚶300m.
**Tourist information Valkenburg:**
ℹ VVV, Th.Dorrenplein 5, www.vvvzuidlimburg.nl.
Popular holiday resort.
👁 Gemeentegrot, Cauberg 4. Marl caves.
Ⓜ Steenkolenmijn, Daalhemerweg 31. Visiting a gallery of a mine.
🅾 01/04-30/11 10-17, 01/11-07/01 + weekend, guided tour 12h, 13h, 14h and 15h.

| 🆔S | Venlo 🌿 | 9E3 |

# Camperplaats De Boswesels Venlo

■ **Located in nature reserve**
■ **Free wifi access**
■ **Electricity/water/drainage at each pitch**

**www.camperkampeerplaatsvenlo.nl**
**info@camperkampeerplaatsvenlo.nl**

**Camperplaats de Boswesels**, Weselseweg/Kikvorstraat.
**GPS:** n51,39270 e6,19990. ⬆➡
16 🛏 € 12, tourist tax incl 🚰🗑Ch 🔌(16x),6Amp 📶included. 🚲
**Location:** Rural, simple. **Surface:** grassy.
🅾 01/04-01/11.
**Distance:** 🚶1km 🚣500m ✖1,5km 🚉1,5km 🚴on the spot 🚶on the spot.
**Remarks:** Charging point for electric bicycles.

| 🆔S | Venlo 🌿 | 9E3 |

**WSV De Maas**, Jachthavenweg 50. **GPS:** n51,39245 e6,14854. ⬆

20 🛏 € 14 🚰🗑Ch 🔌(20x)WC🗑📶 € 3/2 📶included.
**Location:** Urban, comfortable, quiet. **Surface:** metalled.
🅾 01/03-30/11.
**Distance:** 🚶Venlo centre 4km 🚣3,5km ✖on the spot 🚉500m.
**Remarks:** Max. 48h, check in at harbourmaster, free bicycles available, free ferry to city centre.

| 🆔S | Weert 🌿 | 11D1 |

**Camperplaats Weert**, Suffolkweg Zuid 30.
**GPS:** n51,25435 e5,69283. ⬆

28 🛏 € 12 🚰🗑Chincluded 🔌 € 2 WC🗑📶.
**Location:** Rural. **Surface:** grassy/gravel. 🅾 01/01-31/12.
**Distance:** 🚶on the spot 🚴on the spot.
**Remarks:** Max. 72h.

| 🆔S | Well 🌿🌳 | 9E3 |

**Camperplaats Seurenheide**, 't Leuken 3b.
**GPS:** n51,56721 e6,07919. ⬆➡

100 🛏 € 8/24h 2 pers incl 🚰🗑Ch 🔌 € 2/24h WCincluded. 🚲🧺
**Surface:** grassy. 🅾 01/01-31/12.
**Distance:** 🚶100m 🚣10km 🏊on the spot 🚉100m ✖30m 🍺100m 🍽150m 🚌100m 🚴on the spot 🚶on the spot.
**Remarks:** Check in at pay-desk.

| 🆔S | Well 🌿🌳 | 9E3 |

**Jachthaven 't Leuken**, De Kamp 7a. **GPS:** n51,56361 e6,06360. ⬆

60 🛏 € 12,50 🚰🗑Ch 🔌 WC🗑included. **Location:** Rural, comfortable, quiet. **Surface:** grassy. 🅾 01/04-01/11.
**Distance:** 🚶Well 2km 🚣11km 🏊on the spot 🚉on the spot ✖on the spot 🚴on the spot 🚶on the spot.
**Remarks:** Walking and bicycle area, acquatic sports area.

# Norway

Capital: Oslo
Government: parliamentary constitutional monarchy
Official Language: Norwegian
Population: 5,290,000 (2017)
Area: 323,787 km²

## General information
Dialling code: 0047
General emergency: 112
Currency: Norwegian krone (NOK),
€ 1 = NOK 9,50, NOK 1 = € 0,10
£1 = NOK 10,80, NOK 1 = £0.09 (October 2018)
Credit cards are accepted almost everywhere.

## Regulations for overnight stays
In general wild camping is allowed, you must hold at least 150 metres from the nearest house or cabin.

## Additional public holidays 2019
April 19 Good Friday
April 22 Easter Monday
May 17 Constitution Day
June 10 Pentecost Monday
July 29 St. Olaf's Day

## Time Zone
Winter (Standard Time) GMT+1
Summer (DST) GMT+2

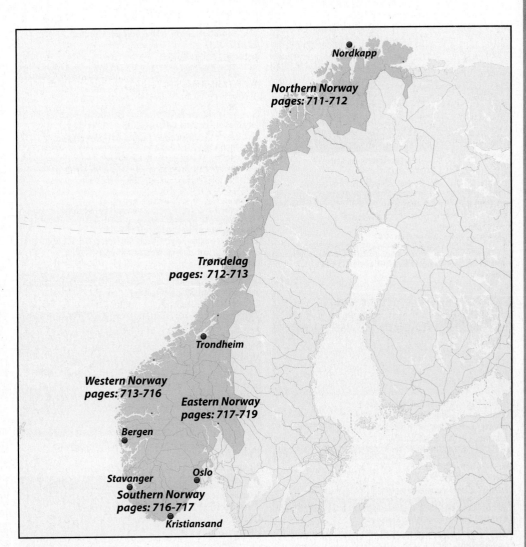

Nordkapp

**Northern Norway**
pages: 711-712

**Trøndelag**
pages: 712-713

Trondheim

**Western Norway**
pages: 713-716

**Eastern Norway**
pages: 717-719

Bergen

Stavanger · Oslo
**Southern Norway**
pages: 716-717

Kristiansand

# Northern Norway

### ⬛S Båstad 3A2
Eggumsveien. **GPS:** n68,30729 e13,65160.
30 NOK 100 ⛽WC. **Location:** Rural, isolated, quiet.
**Surface:** asphalted.
**Distance:** on the spot on the spot.
**Remarks:** Check in at cafe.

### ⬛S Bodø 3A3
Bobilparkering Sentrum, Hålogalandsgata 11.
**GPS:** n67,27866 e14,41026.
4 NOK 10/h, overnight stay free ⛽Chfree.
01/01-31/12.
**Distance:** 500m.

### ⚓S Botnhamn 3A2
Sjark- Og Småbåtforening. **GPS:** n69,50743 e17,90753.
5 NOK 75 Ch NOK 50. **Surface:** concrete.
**Distance:** on the spot on the spot on the spot on the spot.

### ⚓S Brønnøysund 4B1
Brønnøy havn, Havnegata. **GPS:** n65,47089 e12,20317.
NOK 225 ⛽Ch WC. 
**Location:** Rural. **Surface:** gravel. 01/01-31/12 snow.
**Distance:** on the spot on the spot on the spot.
**Remarks:** At shopping centre.

### ⚓S Brønnøysund 4B1
Fv54 45, Tofte. **GPS:** n65,47046 e12,13420.
5 NOK 150 WC NOK 20 NOK 100/100. **Location:** Rural, isolated,
quiet. **Surface:** asphalted. 01/01-31/12.
**Distance:** 6km on the spot on the spot.

### ⬛S Brønnøysund 4B1
Statiol, Valveien 48. **GPS:** n65,47919 e12,21634.
NOK 130 ⛽Ch.
**Distance:** on the spot on the spot 200m.
**Remarks:** Behind petrol station.

### ⬛S Evenes 3A2
Evenes Lofoten, Nerveien 654. **GPS:** n68,45810 e16,70223.

10 NOK 170 ⛽Chincluded (10x)NOK 30/day WC.
**Location:** Rural, simple. **Surface:** gravel. 01/01-31/12.
**Distance:** on the spot on the spot on the spot.
**Remarks:** Money in envelope in mail box, use of sauna against payment.

### ⬛S Fauske 3A3
Fauske Parkering AS. **GPS:** n67,25741 e15,38421.

NOK 150 ⛽Ch included. **Surface:** asphalted.
water disconnected in winter.
**Distance:** 700m on the spot on the spot on the spot.
**Remarks:** Max. 24h, money in envelope in mail box.

### ⬛S Fiskåbygd 4A3
Statoil, Van ylven. **GPS:** n62,08607 e5,57917.

6 free ⛽Ch. **Location:** Rural, simple, simple.
**Surface:** asphalted. 01/01-31/12.
**Distance:** on the spot on the spot on the spot ⊗300m
100m.
**Remarks:** At petrol station, max. 3 days.

### ⬛S Hammerfest 3B1
Jernbanetrasken. **GPS:** n70,66290 e23,67571.
10 NOK 200 ⛽Ch included. **Surface:** asphalted.
01/05-30/09.
**Distance:** on the spot on the spot ⊗300m.
**Remarks:** Behind the hotel.

### ⬛S Hattfjelldal 4C1
RV 73. **GPS:** n65,59578 e13,99090.
60 free ⛽Chfree. **Surface:** asphalted. 01/01-31/12.
**Distance:** ⊗100m.

### ⬛S Havøysund 3B1
Strandgata. **GPS:** n70,99502 e24,67328.
8 NOK 150 ⛽Chincluded NOK 5/kWh,16Amp.
**Location:** Isolated. **Surface:** asphalted. 01/01-31/12.
**Distance:** on the spot.

### ⬛S Hovden 3A3
Hovden-Halsa, E 17. **GPS:** n66,72466 e13,69884.

≋free. **Location:** Simple, central. **Surface:** asphalted. ◻ 01/01-31/12. **Distance:** 500m ⊗500m.

## Oksfjordhamn · 3B1
**Oksfjord Båtforening. GPS:** n69,90620 e21,32404.
≋NOK 100 🚰Ch NOK 50 WC. **Surface:** gravel.

## Skaland · 3A2
**Senjatrollet,** Finnsæter. **GPS:** n69,41020 e17,26334.
20 ≋free 🚰Ch. **Location:** Isolated. **Surface:** metalled.
◻ 26/05-04/09.

## Skutvik · 3A3
**Skutvik Båtforening. GPS:** n68,01368 e15,33414.
≋NOK 100. **Surface:** grassy.
**Distance:** on the spot on the spot.

## Sommarøy · 3A2
**Skipsholmvegen. GPS:** n69,63335 e17,99490.
voluntary contribution 🚰Ch. **Surface:** gravel. ◻ 01/01-31/12.
**Distance:** 1km on the spot on the spot ⊗800m.
**Remarks:** At the beach.

## Stokkvägen · 3A3
**Grønsvik Kystfort,** Aldesundveien, Fv17.
**GPS:** n66,34991 e13,00156.

8 ≋free WC. **Location:** Rural, simple. **Surface:** asphalted.
◻ 01/01-31/12.
**Distance:** on the spot 300m on the spot.

## Storforshei · 3A3
**Polarsirkel-Senteret,** Saltfjellet. **GPS:** n66,55175 e15,32134.
≋free. **Location:** Isolated, quiet. **Surface:** asphalted.
◻ 01/01-31/12.
**Distance:** on the spot.

## Stø · 3A2
**Stø Bobilcamp. GPS:** n69,01984 e15,10762.
13 ≋NOK 180 ChWC NOK 10. **Location:** Rural, simple,
isolated, quiet. **Surface:** gravel. ◻ 01/05-15/09.
**Distance:** on the spot on the spot ⊗on the spot on the spot.

## Svolvær · 3A2
**Bobilcamp Svolvær,** Purkholmen. **GPS:** n68,22733 e14,56016.

10 ≋free 🚰ChWC ≋free. **Location:** Rural, simple.
**Surface:** asphalted. ◻ 01/01-31/12.
**Distance:** 10km on the spot on the spot on the spot.

## Husøy i Senja · 3A2
**Fylkesveg. GPS:** n69,54522 e17,67056.
6 ≋NOK 100.
**Distance:** on the spot on the spot.

## Innhavet · 3A3
**Innhavet bobilparkering. GPS:** n67,96367 e15,92576.

≋NOK 200 🚰Ch included. **Surface:** gravel. ◻ 01/01-31/12.
**Distance:** on the spot on the spot on the spot 150m.
**Remarks:** To be paid at petrol station.

## Jøkelfjord · 3B1
**Jøkelfjord Bobilcamping. GPS:** n70,06207 e21,92987.
10 ≋NOK 100 Ch NOK 50.
**Distance:** on the spot on the spot.

## Kabelvåg · 3A2
**Kabelvåg Feriehus & Camping,** Mølnosveien.
**GPS:** n68,21747 e14,44541.
25 ≋NOK 240 🚰Ch NOK 40 NOK 50.
**Surface:** gravel/metalled. ◻ 01/01-31/12.
**Distance:** 2,5km on the spot on the spot.
**Remarks:** Canoe rental.

## Kirkenes · 3C1
**Havneveien. GPS:** n69,72754 e30,07291.

≋free 🚰Ch. **Surface:** asphalted.
**Distance:** 1km on the spot on the spot 100m.

## Kleppstad · 3A2
**Lofoten Bobilcamping,** Lyngvær. **GPS:** n68,22915 e14,21571.
30 ≋NOK 230 🚰Ch NOK 50 WC NOK 10.
**Location:** Rural, comfortable, isolated. **Surface:** grassy.
◻ 01/05-15/09.
**Distance:** on the spot.

## Lødingen · 3A2
**Båtforeningen. GPS:** n68,41249 e16,00871.
≋NOK 120 (18x)NOK 30 WCNOK 20. **Surface:** grassy/gravel.
**Distance:** on the spot on the spot ⊗1km 1km.
**Remarks:** Money in envelope in mail box.

## Melbu · 3A2
**Melbu Båtforenings,** Neptunveien. **GPS:** n68,49493 e14,81248.
≋NOK 150 included. **Surface:** gravel.
**Distance:** on the spot on the spot 900m.

## Mo i Rana · 3A3
E6. **GPS:** n66,30462 e14,12296.
🚰Ch.

## Narvik · 3A2
**Turist Parking,** Brugata. **GPS:** n68,44172 e17,41705.

## Utskarpen · 3A3
**Flostrandveien. GPS:** n66,31917 e13,31009.

7 ≋free. **Location:** Rural. **Surface:** asphalted/grassy.
**Distance:** on the spot on the spot on the spot.

## Utskarpen · 3A3
**Flostrandveien. GPS:** n66,31387 e13,28420.

## Vestpollen · 3A2
**Vestpollen,** E10. **GPS:** n68,31583 e14,71576.

8 ≋free. **Location:** Rural, simple. **Surface:** asphalted.
◻ 01/01-31/12.
**Distance:** 3km on the spot on the spot.

## Vevelstad · 4B1
**Steinmo Bobilparkering,** Fv17. **GPS:** n65,60550 e12,36637.
≋NOK 100. **Location:** Isolated, quiet. **Surface:** grassy/gravel.
**Distance:** on the spot on the spot.

## Øvergård · 3B2
**Hatteng,** E6, Oteren. **GPS:** n69,27228 e19,93653.

12 ≋free ChWC. **Location:** Rural, simple. **Surface:** metalled.
◻ 01/01-31/12.
**Distance:** 4km on the spot on the spot 4km.

# Trøndelag

## Flagvegen · 4B2
**GPS:** n63,85476 e11,32890.
2 ≋free. **Location:** Rural, simple, isolated. **Surface:** gravel.
◻ 01/01-31/12.
**Distance:** 550m 550m.

## Grong · 4B1
Fv391. **GPS:** n64,46587 e12,31143.

5 ≋free. **Surface:** asphalted.
**Distance:** 100m 100m 400m.
**Remarks:** Picnic area.

## Heimdal · 4B2
**Sandmoen Bobilparkering,** Sandmoflata 6.
**GPS:** n63,33155 e10,35678.

---

≋free. **Location:** Rural, simple. **Surface:** asphalted.
30 ≋NOK 250 🚰Ch WC included. **Location:** Urban,
simple. **Surface:** gravel/metalled. ◻ 01/01-31/12.
**Distance:** 200m on the spot ⊗200m 200m 200m
on the spot on the spot.

## Svolvær · 3A2
**Vestfjord Hotell Lofoten,** Fiskergata 46. **GPS:** n68,22949 e14,56492.

40 ≋NOK 300 🚰 (34x)WCincluded NOK 5.
**Location:** Rural, simple, quiet. **Surface:** metalled/sand.
◻ 01/01-31/12.
**Distance:** 500m on the spot ⊗on the spot 400m 250m
2km 2km.

NO

26 NOK 100-200 Ch (13x)NOK 100 WCincluded
NOK 20 NOK 50/24h. **Location:** Urban, simple, noisy.
**Surface:** asphalted. 01/01-31/12.
**Distance:** on the spot on the spot.
**Remarks:** Check in at reception, breakfast-service.

**S** Inderøy 4B2
**Inderøy Bobilcamp,** Sakshangvegen. **GPS:** n63,87790 e11,26847.

14 NOK 100 free. **Location:** Rural, simple, isolated, quiet.
**Surface:** gravel. 01/01-31/12.
**Distance:** 1,5km 300m on the spot.
**Remarks:** Pay at restaurant.

**S** Inderøy 4B2
**Kjerknesvågen Kai,** Vågavegen 650. **GPS:** n63,91311 e11,19049.

10 NOK 200 Ch WCincluded NOK 20.
**Location:** Rural, simple, isolated, quiet. **Surface:** gravel.
01/01-31/12 1st and 3rd weekend July.
**Distance:** on the spot on the spot on the spot.

**S** Leksvik 4B2
Hammerbergvegen. **GPS:** n63,66747 e10,61449.

14 NOK 150 included. **Location:** Urban, simple.
**Surface:** asphalted. 01/01-31/12.
**Distance:** 500m on the spot on the spot
1km.
**Remarks:** Pay at restaurant.

**S** Oppdal 4B2
**Trollheimsporten Turistsenter,** Festa. **GPS:** n62,61610 e9,47695.

8 NOK 150 Ch WCincluded NOK 10/4minutes.
**Location:** Rural, comfortable, quiet. **Surface:** asphalted.
01/01-31/12.

---

**Distance:** 12km on the spot on the spot on the spot.
**Remarks:** Sauna incl..

**S** Rennebu 4B2
**Berkåk Veikro,** Mjukliveien 1. **GPS:** n62,83215 e10,01117.

8 NOK 200 Ch WCincluded NOK 50. **Location:** Urban,
simple, noisy. **Surface:** gravel. 01/01-31/12.
**Distance:** on the spot on the spot 100m.

**S** Rinnan 4B2
**Rinnleirets Bobilcamp,** E6. **GPS:** n63,76421 e11,43589.

50 NOK 165 Ch (16x)included WC NOK 20.
**Location:** Rural, simple, noisy. **Surface:** gravel.
01/01-31/12.
**Distance:** on the spot on the spot on the spot.
**Remarks:** Money in envelope in mail box.

**S** Singsås 4B2
Fv30. **GPS:** n62,94926 e10,76208.
10 free Chfree. **Location:** Rural, simple, quiet.
**Surface:** grassy/gravel. 01/01-31/12.
**Distance:** 100m 100m on the spot.

**S** Trofors 4B1
**Store Svenningvatn.** **GPS:** n65,32528 e13,37714.
NOK 80. **Location:** Rural, isolated, quiet. **Surface:** gravel.
**Distance:** Trofors 25km on the spot on the spot.
**Remarks:** Money in envelope in mail box.

**S** Trondheim 4B2
**Nyhavna,** Maskinistgata 2. **GPS:** n63,43836 e10,42034.

50 NOK 250/day Ch (32x)included. **Location:** Urban,
simple, central. **Surface:** asphalted. 01/01-31/12.
**Distance:** on the spot 190m on the spot on the spot.
**Remarks:** Max. 5 days.

# Western Norway

**S** Ålesund 4A2
**Hjelsetgaarden Motorhome,** Sorenskriver Bullsgate.
**GPS:** n62,47670 e6,16110.

45 NOK 250 (30x)WC included. **Location:** Urban,
comfortable. **Surface:** asphalted. 01/01-31/12.
**Distance:** on the spot on the spot on the spot 50m
150m 200m.

---

**S** Åndalsnes 4A2
**Rauma,** Isfjordsvegen. **GPS:** n62,56659 e7,69109.

20 free . **Location:** Urban, simple. **Surface:** asphalted.
01/01-31/12.
**Distance:** 300m 100m 100m 200m 300m.
**Remarks:** Whale safari.

**S** Askvoll 4A3
**Askvoll Småbåtlag,** Rv608. **GPS:** n61,34679 e5,06360.

15 NOK 125 Ch NOK 35 WCincluded NOK 10 NOK 50.
**Location:** Rural, simple, quiet. **Surface:** gravel.
01/01-31/12.
**Distance:** 300m on the spot on the spot on the spot
300m.

**S** Austrheim 4A3
**Åvika,** Njøtevegen 292. **GPS:** n60,75028 e5,00472.
20 Ch WC. **Location:** Rural. 01/01-31/12.

**S** Austrheim 4A3
**Mastrevikane.** **GPS:** n60,78828 e4,94098.
NOK 120 . **Surface:** asphalted. 01/01-31/12.
**Distance:** 1km on the spot on the spot.

**S** Austrheim 4A3
**Kjelstraumen vertshus,** Austrheimsvegen. **GPS:** n60,79825 e4,93908.
20 NOK 150 (15x) WC . **Location:** Rural, isolated, quiet.
**Surface:** asphalted. 01/01-31/12.
**Distance:** on the spot on the spot 300m.

**S** Averøy 4A2
**Atlanterhavsveien.** **GPS:** n63,01209 e7,42823.

15 NOK 230 NOK 20 Ch NOK 30 WC NOK 20/20 .
**Location:** Rural, comfortable. **Surface:** gravel. 01/01-31/12.
**Distance:** on the spot on the spot on the spot on the spot.
**Remarks:** Boat rental.

**S** Bergen 4A3
**Bergenshallen,** Vilhelm Bjerknes vei 24. **GPS:** n60,35421 e5,35876.

28 NOK 150/24h Chincluded .
**Location:** Urban, simple. **Surface:** asphalted. 01/05-31/08.
**Distance:** 5km 500m on the spot.
**Remarks:** Max. 48h.

NO

## Bokn 5A1

**Langtid**, Langtid. **GPS:** n59,16978 e5,45382. 🔼.

25 🅵free. **Location:** Rural, simple. **Surface:** metalled.
🔲 01/01-31/12.
**Distance:** ⚓100m ⛽100m.
**Remarks:** Parking at ferry-boat.

## Bokn 5A1

**Føresvikvegen 580. GPS:** n59,23255 e5,43919. 🔼.
4 🅵NOK 50 💧(2x)NOK 50. 🏪 **Location:** Rural, simple.
**Surface:** asphalted. 🔲 01/01-31/12.
**Distance:** 🔌on the spot ⚓on the spot 🛒on the spot ⊗on the spot 🍴on the spot.
**Remarks:** To be paid at supermarket.

## Bremanger 4A3

**Iglandsvik Marina. GPS:** n61,83631 e4,93487. 🔼➡️.

20 🅵NOK 200 💧included ⚡NOK 30/40. 🚿
**Location:** Simple, quiet. **Surface:** gravel. 🔲 01/01-31/12.
**Distance:** ⚓on the spot 🛒on the spot ⊗500m 🛒300m 🍴on the spot.

## Bru 5A1

**Sokn Marina**, Åmøyveien. **GPS:** n59,05210 e5,67691.
30 🅵NOK 200 🔌🔧Ch ⚡WC 🚿🚿🚽 **Location:** Rural, comfortable, quiet. **Surface:** gravel/metalled. 🔲 01/01-31/12.
**Distance:** ⚓on the spot 🛒on the spot ⊗on the spot.

## Bryne 5A2

**Abobil.no**, Vesthagen 11. **GPS:** n58,72057 e5,64894.

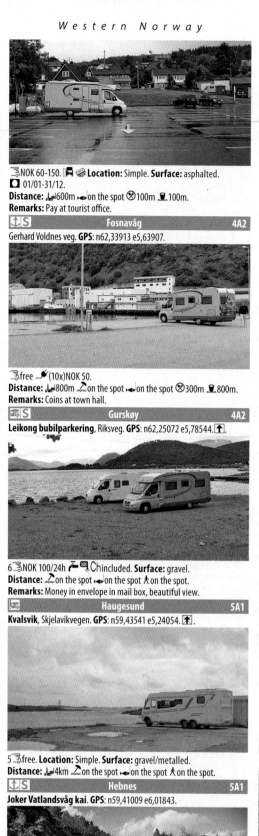

25 🅵free 🔌🔧Ch (25x)🚿free. **Location:** Rural.
**Surface:** asphalted. 🔲 01/01-31/12.
**Distance:** 🔌1km ⊗800m 🛒800m 🏃1km.
**Remarks:** At motorhome dealer.

## Egersund 5A2

**Nordre Eigerøy**, Ytstebrødveien. **GPS:** n58,45522 e5,90852. 🔼.
🅵NOK 150 🔌💧included. **Location:** Isolated. **Surface:** grassy.
🔲 01/01-31/12.
**Distance:** 🔌5,5km ⚓on the spot 🛒on the spot 🛒5,5km 🏃on the spot.

## Egersund 5A2

**Ved taxi-stasjon**, Jernbaneveien. **GPS:** n58,45373 e6,00243.
10 🅵NOK 60. 🔋 **Surface:** asphalted.
**Distance:** 🔌300m ⚓on the spot 🛒on the spot ⊗300m.

## Erfjord 5A1

**Hålandsosen**, Riksveg. **GPS:** n59,34806 e6,23703.
🅵free. **Location:** Isolated, quiet. **Surface:** gravel.
🔲 01/01-31/12.
**Distance:** ⚓on the spot 🛒on the spot 🛒200m.
**Remarks:** Beautiful view.

## Florø 4A3

**Bobilparkering Florø**, Strandavegen 19. **GPS:** n61,60061 e5,02252. 🔼.

---

🅵NOK 60-150. 🔋🚿 **Location:** Simple. **Surface:** asphalted.
🔲 01/01-31/12.
**Distance:** 🔌600m 🛒on the spot ⊗100m 🛒100m.
**Remarks:** Pay at tourist office.

## Fosnavåg 4A2

**Gerhard Voldnes veg. GPS:** n62,33913 e5,63907.

🅵free 💧(10x)NOK 50.
**Distance:** 🔌800m ⚓on the spot 🛒on the spot ⊗300m 🛒800m.
**Remarks:** Coins at town hall.

## Gurskøy 4A2

**Leikong bubilparkering**, Riksveg. **GPS:** n62,25072 e5,78544. 🔼.

6 🅵NOK 100/24h 🔌🔧Chincluded. **Surface:** gravel.
**Distance:** ⚓on the spot 🛒on the spot 🏃on the spot.
**Remarks:** Money in envelope in mail box, beautiful view.

## Haugesund 5A1

**Kvalsvik**, Skjelavikvegen. **GPS:** n59,43541 e5,24054. 🔼.

5 🅵free. **Location:** Simple. **Surface:** gravel/metalled.
**Distance:** 🔌4km ⚓on the spot 🛒on the spot 🏃on the spot.

## Hebnes 5A1

**Joker Vatlandsvåg kai. GPS:** n59,41009 e6,01843.

🅵NOK 100 🔌🔧. 🔲 01/01-31/12.
**Distance:** ⚓on the spot 🛒on the spot ⊗takeaway restaurant 🛒on the spot.

## Husnes 5A1

**Husnes Båtlag**, Onarheimsvegen. **GPS:** n59,87187 e5,76195. 🔼.

---

4 🅵NOK 150 🔌🔧Chincluded 💧NOK 50 WC 🚽NOK 10 ⚡NOK 40
🚿free. 🔋🚿 **Location:** Rural, simple, quiet. **Surface:** metalled.
🔲 01/01-31/12.
**Distance:** 🔌1,5km ⚓on the spot 🛒on the spot 🛒1,5km.
**Remarks:** Max. 48h, golf court 300m.

## Isfjorden 4A2

**Parking Romsdalsfjorden Rv64**, Rv64. **GPS:** n62,56819 e7,75412.
15 🅵free. **Location:** Rural. **Surface:** gravel. 🔲 01/01-31/12.
**Distance:** 🔌4,5km ⚓on the spot 🛒on the spot.

## Isfjorden 4A2

**Gjerdset Turistsenter**, Gjerdsetbygda. **GPS:** n62,57868 e7,56713. 🔼.

5 🅵NOK 100 🔌💧 WC 🚿included. 🚿
**Location:** Rural, comfortable. **Surface:** gravel.
**Distance:** 🔌13km ⚓200m 🛒200m 🚐100m.

## Jørpeland 5A1

**Jørpeland Bobilparkering. GPS:** n59,01757 e6,04377. 🔼.
10 🅵NOK 150 💧NOK 50 WC 🚽NOK 10/5minutes. **Location:** Urban, simple, quiet. **Surface:** asphalted. 🔲 01/01-31/12.
**Distance:** 🔌500m ⚓on the spot 🛒on the spot ⊗450m.

## Klokkarvik 4A3

**Kleppe Båtlag**, Kleppholmen. **GPS:** n60,18462 e5,15163. ➡️.

30 🅵NOK 150 🔌🔧Ch 💧(10x)WC 🚽NOK 10 🚿included. 🚿
**Location:** Rural, simple, isolated, quiet. **Surface:** asphalted.
🔲 01/01-31/12.
**Distance:** 🔌6km ⚓on the spot 🛒on the spot.

## Kristiansund 4A2

**Freiveien. GPS:** n63,12188 e7,72856.

10 🅵free. **Location:** Rural, simple. **Surface:** gravel.
🔲 01/01-31/12.
**Distance:** 🔌on the spot ⚓on the spot 🛒on the spot ⊗on the spot.

## Kristiansund 4A2

**Kristiansund Småbåtlag**, Freiveien 50. **GPS:** n63,11713 e7,73168. 🔼.

NO

5 ⌁NOK 7-35, overnight stay free. ⏸🅿 **Location:** Urban, simple. **Surface:** asphalted. 🅾 01/01-31/12.
**Distance:** ⚓1km ⚓on the spot ⛽on the spot ⊗on the spot.

| ⏏🅂 | **Kulleseid** | 5A1 |

**Kulleseidkanalen. GPS:** n59,74194 e5,23481.⬆.
10 ⌁NOK 100 ⚓NOK 50 🚿. 🅾 01/01-31/12.
**Distance:** ⚓on the spot 🚰300m.

| ⏏🅂 | **Måløy** 🏕🏔 | 4A3 |

**Småbåthavn,** Gate 1 vagsoy. **GPS:** n61,93236 e5,11212.⬆.

10 ⌁NOK 200 ⚓WC🚿included 🅾.⏸🅿
**Location:** Urban, central. **Surface:** asphalted. 🅾 01/01-31/12.
**Distance:** ⚓on the spot ⚓on the spot ⚓on the spot ⊗on the spot 🚰on the spot.
**Remarks:** Behind Aldi-süd.

| ⏏🅂 | **Matre** | 5A1 |

**Matre Havn,** Matre Havn. **GPS:** n59,84352 e5,98434.⬆.

6 ⌁NOK 100 ⚓included 🚿NOK 50 WC. **Location:** Rural, isolated, quiet. **Surface:** asphalted. 🅾 01/01-31/12.
**Distance:** ⚓on the spot ⚓on the spot.
**Remarks:** Money in envelope in mail box.

| 🅂 | **Nesflaten** | 5B1 |

**Fylkesveg. GPS:** n59,64471 e6,80223.⬆.
3 ⌁NOK 100. **Surface:** asphalted. 🅾 01/01-31/12.
**Distance:** ⚓on the spot ⚓on the spot.
**Remarks:** At the quay.

| 🅂 | **Norheimsund** 🌿 | 4A3 |

**Rosselandsvegen. GPS:** n60,37007 e6,10616.⬆.

8 ⌁free WC🚿. **Location:** Rural, simple. **Surface:** asphalted. 🅾 01/01-31/12.
**Distance:** ⚓2,5km ⚓on the spot ⚓on the spot ⊗100m ⚓on the spot ⚓on the spot.
**Remarks:** Nearby waterfalls.

| 🅂 | **Norheimsund** 🌿 | 4A3 |

**Norheimsund Badstrand,** Sandvegen 36.
**GPS:** n60,36869 e6,14811.⬆.

20 ⌁free WC. **Location:** Urban, simple. **Surface:** gravel.
🅾 01/01-31/12.
**Distance:** ⚓200m ⚓on the spot ⚓on the spot ⊗200m 🚰200m ⚓on the spot ⚓on the spot.

| 🅂 | **Odda** | 4A3 |

**Odda bobilcamp,** Røldalsvegen. **GPS:** n60,07144 e6,54865.
40 ⌁NOK 200 ⚓🚿included. **Surface:** asphalted.
**Distance:** ⚓on the spot ⚓on the spot.
**Remarks:** Max. 3 days, canoe and boat rental.

| 🅂 | **Rennesøy** | 5A1 |

**GPS:** n59,13787 e5,59161.
⌁free. **Surface:** asphalted. 🅾 01/01-31/12.
**Distance:** ⚓on the spot ⚓on the spot.

| 🅂 | **Rognaldsvåg** | 4A3 |

**Rognaldsvåg Bobilparkering,** Fv552 99-65. **GPS:** n61,56494 e4,79580.
8 ⌁NOK 150 ⚓WC🚿. **Location:** Rural, isolated. **Surface:** gravel.
🅾 01/01-31/12.
**Distance:** ⚓150m ⚓150m ⚓on the spot.

| 🅂 | **Rong** 🏖 | 4A3 |

**Ternholmvegen. GPS:** n60,51520 e4,91355.
8 ⌁free ⚓🚿Ch🚿. **Location:** Rural, simple, quiet.
**Surface:** asphalted. 🅾 01/01-31/12.
**Distance:** ⚓on the spot ⚓on the spot 🚰300m.

| 🅂 | **Rosendal** | 5A1 |

**Skåla Vika,** Skålafjæro. **GPS:** n59,98528 e6,00708.⬆➡.

80 ⌁NOK 175 ⚓🚿Ch🚿NOK 25 🚿included.
**Location:** Rural, simple. **Surface:** gravel. 🅾 01/01-31/12.
**Distance:** ⚓200m ⚓on the spot 🚰200m.
**Remarks:** Money in envelope in mail box.

| 🅂 | **Sand** | 5A1 |

**Hydrokaien,** Nordenden. **GPS:** n59,48516 e6,24756.

6 ⌁free WC. **Surface:** asphalted.
**Distance:** ⚓300m ⚓on the spot ⚓on the spot ⊗800m 🚰300m ⚓on the spot.
**Remarks:** At museum.

| 🅂 | **Sand** | 5A1 |

**Stasjon XY. GPS:** n59,47590 e6,28913.
🚰Ch.
**Remarks:** At petrol station.

| 🅂 | **Sandeid** | 5A1 |

**Kai. GPS:** n59,54198 e5,86770.⬆.

5 ⌁NOK 100 ⚓NOK 25 ⌁NOK 10. **Location:** Rural, simple.
**Surface:** asphalted. 🅾 01/01-31/12.
**Distance:** ⚓on the spot ⚓on the spot 🚰on the spot.
**Remarks:** Money in envelope in mail box.

| ⚓🅂 | **Sauda** | 5A1 |

**Bobil Havn,** Treaskjæret. **GPS:** n59,64480 e6,33716.⬆.
15 ⌁NOK 100 ⚓🚿ChWC🚿. 🚿 **Location:** Rural, comfortable, quiet. **Surface:** asphalted. 🅾 01/01-31/12.
**Distance:** ⚓1,2km ⚓on the spot ⚓on the spot ⊗1,2km 🚰1,2km ⚓100m.
**Remarks:** At the quay.

| ⚓🅂 | **Skånevik** | 5A1 |

**Fylkesveg. GPS:** n59,73385 e5,92672.⬆.

8 ⌁NOK 150 ⚓🚿Ch🚿included WC. 🚿 **Location:** Urban, simple.
**Surface:** gravel. 🅾 01/01-31/12.
**Distance:** ⚓500m ⚓on the spot ⚓on the spot ⊗400m.

| 🅂 | **Skare** 🏔 | 5B1 |

**Skare Kommune Odda,** Riksveg 13 144 langs E 134.
**GPS:** n59,88666 e6,65612.⬆.

50 ⌁NOK 100 ⚓🚿Chincluded. **Location:** Motorway, simple.
**Surface:** gravel. 🅾 01/01-31/12.
**Distance:** ⚓6km ⚓on the spot ⚓on the spot ⚓on the spot.
**Remarks:** Money in envelope in mail box, service 2km.

| 🅂 | **Sveio** | 5A1 |

**Victors Bobil camping,** Fylkesveg. **GPS:** n59,53016 e5,44353.⬆➡.

5 ⌁NOK 250-300 ⚓Ch🚿WC🚿🚿included.🚿
**Location:** Rural, isolated. **Surface:** grassy/gravel. 🅾 01/04-31/10.
**Distance:** ⚓9km ⚓on the spot ⚓on the spot 🚰9km.
**Remarks:** Small pitches.

| ⏏ | **Svelgen** 🏖 | 4A3 |

**Svelgen Hotell,** Granden. **GPS:** n61,76978 e5,29393.⬆.

NO

7 ⛺free. **Location:** Simple. **Surface:** asphalted. ⬛ 01/01-31/12.
**Distance:** 💧on the spot 🚽on the spot 🛒on the spot ⊗200m
⚡on the spot.

| 🚻S | Sykkylven | 4A2 |
|---|---|---|

**Sykkylven Småbåthamn**, Ullavikvegen. **GPS:** n62,39679 e6,58192.⬆.
10 ⛺NOK 100 🚽NOK 30 WC🛒♨️ 📶.
**Location:** Urban, simple, quiet. **Surface:** asphalted. ⬛ 01/01-31/12.
**Distance:** 💧500m 🚽on the spot 🛒on the spot ⊗500m ⚡500m.

| 🍴S | Sæbøvik | 5A1 |
|---|---|---|

**Halsnøy Samfunnshus**, Riksveg. **GPS:** n59,79431 e5,71196.⬆.

12 ⛺NOK 100 🚽♨️Chincluded 🚽NOK 50 WC🛒NOK 30. 🚿
**Location:** Rural, simple. **Surface:** asphalted.
⬛ 01/01-31/12 ⬤ water disconnected in winter.
**Distance:** 🚽on the spot 🛒on the spot ⊗on the spot ⚡200m.

| | Tau | 5A1 |
|---|---|---|

**Tau Båtforening**, Kvernvegen. **GPS:** n59,06086 e5,91343.⬆.
8 ⛺NOK 150 🚽ChWC🛒📶included. 🚿 **Location:** Rural,
comfortable, quiet. **Surface:** asphalted. ⬛ 01/01-31/12.
**Distance:** 🚽on the spot 🛒on the spot ⊗1km ⚡1km.

| ⚓S | Tjøvåg | 4A2 |
|---|---|---|

**Laternen Marina. GPS:** n62,31388 e5,70805.⬆➡.

⛺NOK 100 🚽(4x)NOK 25 🛒NOK 20 ⬤NOK 30. 🚿
**Location:** Comfortable. **Surface:** gravel. ⬛ 01/01-31/12.
**Distance:** 💧5km 🚽on the spot 🛒on the spot ⊗on the spot.
**Remarks:** Boat rental.

| ⚓S | Tresfjord | 4A2 |
|---|---|---|

**Småbåthavn. GPS:** n62,52520 e7,13085.⬆➡.

4 ⛺NOK 150 🚽NOK 30 🛒NOK 30 ChNOK 30 🚽WC. 🚿
**Location:** Rural, simple, quiet. **Surface:** gravel.
**Distance:** 💧100m 🚽on the spot 🛒on the spot ⚡100m.
**Remarks:** At petrol station.

| 🚻S | Urangsvåg | 5A1 |
|---|---|---|

Fylkesveg. **GPS:** n59,84002 e5,15190.
6 ⛺NOK 180 🚽♨️ChWC🛒included. **Surface:** asphalted.
**Distance:** 🚽on the spot 🛒on the spot.

| ⚓S | Vikedal | 5A1 |
|---|---|---|

**Vikedal Båthavn**, Riksveg. **GPS:** n59,49632 e5,89837.⬆➡.

---

30 ⛺NOK 100 🚽♨️Ch🚽NOK 50 WC🛒included ⬤NOK 30.
**Location:** Rural, simple. **Surface:** metalled. ⬛ 01/01-31/12.
**Distance:** 💧200m 🚽on the spot 🛒on the spot ⊗200m ⚡200m.
**Remarks:** Money in envelope in mail box.

| 🌾S | Viksdalen | 4A3 |
|---|---|---|

**GPS:** n61,39096 e6,26945.⬆.

6 ⛺NOK 150 🚽♨️Ch🚽included. **Location:** Rural, simple, isolated,
quiet. **Surface:** gravel. ⬛ 01/01-31/12.
**Distance:** 💧12km 🚽on the spot 🛒on the spot ⚡12km.
**Remarks:** Dead end street, narrow road, boat rental.

| ⚓S | Ølen | 5A1 |
|---|---|---|

**Fjellstøl Skianlegg**, Helgaland. **GPS:** n59,58853 e5,88857.⬆.

30 ⛺NOK 40. **Location:** Rural, simple. **Surface:** gravel.
⬛ 01/01-31/12.
**Distance:** 💧6km 🚶on the spot 🎿on the spot.
**Remarks:** Money in envelope in mail box.

| ⚓S | Ølen | 5A1 |
|---|---|---|

**Båtlag**, Fylkesveg. **GPS:** n59,60748 e5,81448.⬆.

10 ⛺NOK 140 💧🚽included WC🛒 ⬤NOK 30.
**Location:** Rural, simple. **Surface:** gravel. ⬛ 01/01-31/12.
**Distance:** 💧150m 🚽on the spot 🛒on the spot ⊗300m ⚡600m.
**Remarks:** Money in envelope in mail box.

| 🚻S | Ølensvåg | 5A1 |
|---|---|---|

**Ask Bobilparkering**, Gjerdevikvegen 46.
**GPS:** n59,59728 e5,75857.⬆➡.

30 ⛺NOK 100 🚽♨️Ch🚽(12x)NOK 30 📶included.
**Location:** Rural, luxurious. **Surface:** gravel. ⬛ 01/01-31/12.
**Distance:** 💧1km 🚽on the spot 🚶on the spot.
**Remarks:** Money in envelope in mail box, barbecue place.

---

| 🚻S | Øydegard 🏔 | 4A2 |
|---|---|---|

Riksvei, E39 70. **GPS:** n62,98958 e7,88272.⬆.

10 ⛺free 🚽WCfree. **Location:** Rural, simple, isolated, quiet.
**Surface:** asphalted.
**Distance:** 🚽on the spot 🛒on the spot.

# Southern Norway

| 🚻S | Åmli | 5B2 |
|---|---|---|

Dølemo 66. **GPS:** n58,71102 e8,34497.⬆.
30 ⛺NOK 150 🚽♨️Ch🚽WC🛒📶♨️ **Location:** Urban, isolated,
quiet. **Surface:** grassy. ⬛ 01/01-31/12.
**Distance:** ⚡on the spot 🐾on the spot.

| 🍴S | Åmli | 5B2 |
|---|---|---|

**Pan Garden**, Tveit 38. **GPS:** n58,74697 e8,50946.
10 ⛺NOK 100 🚽NOK 50 🛒NOK 40. **Location:** Rural, isolated, quiet.
**Surface:** grassy/gravel. ⬛ 01/01-31/12.
**Distance:** 🚽on the spot 🛒on the spot ⊗on the spot.

| 🚻 | Borhaug | 5B2 |
|---|---|---|

**Lista Fyr**, Toppveien 10. **GPS:** n58,10943 e6,56863.
10 ⛺free. **Location:** Rural. **Surface:** asphalted. ⬛ 01/01-31/12.
**Distance:** 💧1,5km ⚡100m.
**Remarks:** At lighthouse, max. 2 nights.

| ⚓S | Borhaug | 5B2 |
|---|---|---|

**Borshavn. GPS:** n58,10081 e6,58335.⬆.
⛺NOK 200 🚽♨️Ch🚽WC📶. **Surface:** asphalted.
**Distance:** 🚽on the spot 🛒on the spot.
**Remarks:** Max. 1 day.

| 🔺S | Byglandsfjord 🏔 | 5B2 |
|---|---|---|

**Neset Camping**, Setesdalsvegen 2035. **GPS:** n58,68735 e7,80419.⬆.
50 ⛺NOK 250 🚽♨️Ch🚽WC🛒NOK 40/40 📶.
**Surface:** grassy/metalled. ⬛ 01/01-31/12.
**Distance:** 💧Evje 13km 🚽on the spot 🛒on the spot.
**Remarks:** Boat rental.

| 🚻 | Edland | 5B1 |
|---|---|---|

Rv9. **GPS:** n59,71125 e7,57274.
4 ⛺free. **Location:** Rural, isolated, quiet. **Surface:** gravel.
⬛ 01/01-31/12.
**Distance:** 🚽on the spot 🛒on the spot.

| 🚻S | Eidstod ⛄ | 5B1 |
|---|---|---|

**Eidstod Kommune Vrådal**, Vråliosvegen.
**GPS:** n59,32570 e8,48630.⬆.

20 ⛺free 🚽♨️Chfree. **Location:** Rural, simple.
**Surface:** gravel/sand. ⬛ 01/01-31/12.
**Distance:** 💧on the spot ✏on the spot 🚽on the spot ⚡on the spot
🚶on the spot.

| 🚻S | Farsund | 5B2 |
|---|---|---|

**Farsund Bobil Camp**, Ferjeveien. **GPS:** n58,09439 e6,81278.
⛺NOK 175 💧🚽📶. **Surface:** metalled.
⬛ 01/01-31/12 ⬤ Service: winter.
**Distance:** 💧500m 🚽on the spot 🛒on the spot ⊗500m ⚡1,5km.

| 🚻S | Flekkefjord | 5B2 |
|---|---|---|

**Flekkefjord Bobilcamp**, Tollbodbrygga. **GPS:** n58,29267 e6,66296.⬆.

NO

25 ⭐NOK 255 🔧🔌Ch 🔥(16x)included WC🚿.🛒
**Location:** Rural, simple, quiet. **Surface:** asphalted.
🗓 01/01-31/12.
**Distance:** 🚶850m 🛒on the spot ⊗850m 🚰200m.
**Remarks:** Pay at shop.

**Sørlandets Caravansenter**, Grøm Næringspark 2.
**GPS:** n58,34011 e8,56658.
3 ⭐free 🔧🔌Chfree. **Location:** Simple.
**Distance:** 🚶1km 🏊 200m 🛒1km 🚰1km.
**Remarks:** At motorhome dealer, max. 24h.

| ⚓S | Hidrasund | 5B2 |
**Kirkehavn. GPS:** n58,22896 e6,52919.
⭐NOK 150 🔧🔌Ch. **Location:** Isolated, quiet. **Surface:** asphalted.
🗓 01/01-31/12.
**Distance:** 🚶2km 🛒on the spot ⊗2km 🚰1km 🚶on the spot.

| ⚓S | Hornes | 5B2 |
**Mineralparken Bobilcamp**, Mineralvegen 1.
**GPS:** n58,54993 e7,77542.⬆
40 ⭐NOK 250 🔧🔌Ch 🔥NOK 20 🔌NOK 40/40 📶included.
**Location:** Rural, comfortable, quiet. **Surface:** grassy.
🗓 01/01-31/12.
**Distance:** 🚶700m 🛒on the spot 🛒on the spot.
**Remarks:** Bread-service in summer period.

| ⚓S | Kviteseid 🏴 | 5B1 |
**Kviteseid**, Garverivegen. **GPS:** n59,40275 e8,48675.⬆.

5 ⭐free. **Location:** Rural, simple. **Surface:** gravel.
🗓 01/01-31/12.
**Distance:** 🚶on the spot 🛒on the spot 🛒on the spot ⊗on the spot 🚰on the spot 🚇on the spot 🚶on the spot.

| ⚓S | Lillesand | 5B2 |
**Lillesand gjesthavn**, Kokkenes. **GPS:** n58,24745 e8,38349.⬆.
25 ⭐NOK 200, 01/05-31/08 NOK 275 🔧🔌Ch 🔥included WC🚿.
**Location:** Rural, simple, quiet. **Surface:** asphalted.
🗓 01/01-31/12 🔌 Service: winter.
**Distance:** 🚶500m 🛒on the spot 🛒on the spot ⊗200m 🚰500m.

| ⚓S | Lindesnes | 5B2 |
**Spangereidveien. GPS:** n58,03998 e7,15014.⬆.

2 ⭐NOK 150 WC🚿 🔥NOK 20 🔌NOK 45/45. **Location:** Rural, simple, quiet. **Surface:** asphalted.
**Distance:** 🚶900m 🛒on the spot 🛒on the spot ⊗on the spot.
**Remarks:** Boat rental.

| ⚓S | Mandal | 5B2 |
**Mandal Havn**, Havnegata. **GPS:** n58,02440 e7,45566.⬆.
10 ⭐NOK 180 🔥.🛒 **Surface:** asphalted.
**Distance:** 🚶400m 🛒on the spot ⊗400m 🚰1km.

| ⚓S | Mysen | 5D1 |
Jernbanegaten 17. **GPS:** n59,55266 e11,32510.

---

8 ⭐free 🔧🔌Ch 🔥free.
**Location:** Urban. **Surface:** metalled. 🗓 01/01-31/12.
**Distance:** 🚶on the spot ⊗500m 🚰500m.
**Remarks:** Max. 48h.

| ⚓S | Risør | 5C2 |
Tjenngata. **GPS:** n58,72093 e9,22567.⬆➡.

⭐NOK 20/h, NOK 100/day 🔧🔌🔥included 🔌NOK 10 🔌NOK 30/30.
🛒 **Surface:** grassy. 🗓 01/01-31/12 🔌 Service: winter.
**Distance:** 🚶600m 🛒500m ⊗500m 🚰600m.

| ⚓S | Snig | 5B2 |
Stegganskogen, R460. **GPS:** n58,05313 e7,27103.⬆.

6 ⭐free 🔧WC. **Location:** Rural, simple. **Surface:** gravel.
🗓 01/01-31/12.
**Distance:** 🚶4,5km 🏊 on the spot 🛒on the spot 🛒on the spot 🚶on the spot.

| ⚓ | Tonstad | 5B2 |
**GPS:** n58,65957 e6,71582.⬆.
5 ⭐free. **Location:** Rural, simple, quiet. **Surface:** grassy/gravel.
🗓 01/01-31/12.
**Distance:** 🛒on the spot.

| ⚓S | Valle | 5B1 |
**Sanden Såre. GPS:** n59,27128 e7,46221.⬆➡.
⭐NOK 150-200 🔌Ch 🔥. **Location:** Rural, isolated, quiet.
**Surface:** grassy.
**Distance:** 🚶10km 🛒on the spot 🛒on the spot.
**Remarks:** Nearby waterfalls.

# Eastern Norway

| ⚓S | Brandbu | 4B3 |
**Tegneseriemuseet**, Rosendalsvegen. **GPS:** n60,41719 e10,50940.
4 ⭐NOK 100 🔥NOK 50 📶. **Surface:** asphalted. 🗓 01/03-01/10.
**Distance:** 🚶500m 🛒400m 🚰300m.
**Remarks:** At museum.

| ⚓S | Bøverdalen | 4A3 |
**Leirvassbu**, Leirdalsvegen. **GPS:** n61,54917 e8,24694.
⭐NOK 180 🔧WC🚿. **Location:** Rural, simple, isolated, quiet.
**Surface:** metalled. 🗓 20/06-30/09.
**Remarks:** Accessible via toll road (NOK 60).

| ⚓S | Dalen | 5B1 |
**Bobilparkering Dalen Bryggje**, Storvegen 4.
**GPS:** n59,44515 e8,02292.

---

15 ⭐NOK 200-280 🔌Ch 🔥WC🚿🔌 📶included. 🛒🔒
**Location:** Rural, comfortable. **Surface:** metalled.
🗓 01/01-31/12.
**Distance:** 🚶900m 🛒on the spot 🛒on the spot ⊗on the spot.
**Remarks:** Money in envelope in mail box.

| ⚓S | Dovre | 4B2 |
Krymsdalhyte. **GPS:** n62,08557 e9,64947.

⭐free. **Location:** Isolated. **Surface:** grassy.
🗓 01/01-31/12.
**Distance:** 🛒on the spot ⊗300m 🚶on the spot.
**Remarks:** Accessible via toll road (NOK 80), national Park 'Rondane'.

| ⚓S | Etnedal | 4B3 |
**Sebu Røssjøen**, Lenningsvegen. **GPS:** n61,12502 e9,71475.
⭐free.
**Distance:** 🛒on the spot.

| ⚓S | Flatdal | 5B1 |
**Kvåle Din gard**, Kvålevegen. **GPS:** n59,56042 e8,56248.⬆.

5 ⭐NOK 200 🔧🔌Ch 🔥WC🚿. **Location:** Rural, quiet. **Surface:** grassy.
🗓 01/01-31/12.
**Distance:** ⊗on the spot 🚰on the spot.

| ⚓S | Fredrikstad 🏴🔥 | 5C1 |
**Gjestehavn**, Frederikstad Dokka 1c. **GPS:** n59,21423 e10,92512.⬆.

15 ⭐NOK 250 🔌Ch 🔥WC🚿🔌NOK 40 📶included.🛒
**Location:** Urban, simple, central, quiet. **Surface:** asphalted.
🗓 01/04-01/10.
**Distance:** 🚶300m 🛒on the spot 🛒on the spot ⊗300m 🚰150m 🚇on the spot 🚶on the spot.

| ⚓S | Gjøvik | 4B3 |
**Gjøvik Marina**, Bryggevegen. **GPS:** n60,79555 e10,70116.
25 ⭐NOK 50 🔧🔌Ch. **Surface:** gravel. 🗓 15/06-13/09.
**Distance:** 🛒on the spot 🛒on the spot ⊗McDonalds 300m.
**Remarks:** To be paid at petrol station.

| ⚓S | Halden 🏴🔥 | 5D1 |
**Slippen Brygge**, Kiellands gate 22. **GPS:** n59,11539 e11,38128.⬆.

20 🛏NOK 150 ⚡✂ included. 🎣 **Location:** Urban, simple, quiet.
**Surface:** asphalted/gravel. 📅 01/01-31/12.
**Distance:** 🚶historical centre 500m 🏊on the spot 🛒on the spot
⊗500m 🍴800m 🚲on the spot 🚶on the spot.
**Remarks:** Money in envelope in mail box.

### ⚓S Hamar  4B3
**Hamar båtforening,** Brygga. **GPS:** n60,78846 e11,07138.⬆.
20 🛏NOK 120 ⚡🔌Ch ✂(6x). **Surface:** asphalted.
📅 01/06-30/09.
**Distance:** 🚶300m 🛒on the spot ⊗on the spot 🍴1km 🚗400m.

### Holmestrand 🍺〰  5C1
Hagemannsveien. **GPS:** n59,48048 e10,32933.
🛏free. **Location:** Isolated, quiet. **Surface:** asphalted.
📅 01/01-31/12.
**Distance:** 🏊on the spot 🛒on the spot.
**Remarks:** At harbour, playground.

### ⚓S Holmestrand 🍺〰  5C1
**Hakan Bobilhavn,** Weidemannsgate 13.
**GPS:** n59,48921 e10,32294.⬆➡.

40 🛏NOK 150 ⚡🔌Ch ✂NOK 2,80/kWh WC included. 🏪
**Location:** Urban, simple, quiet. **Surface:** asphalted.
📅 01/06-15/09.
**Distance:** 🚶200m 🏊on the spot 🛒on the spot ⊗on the spot
🍴300m.

### ⚓S Horten 🍺〰  5C1
**Horten Gjestehavn,** Tollbugata 2. **GPS:** n59,41302 e10,48695.⬆➡.

14 🛏NOK 200 ⚡✂ WC included. 🏪
**Location:** Urban, simple, central, quiet. **Surface:** asphalted.
📅 01/01-31/12 🔧 service: 16/09-31/03.
**Distance:** 🚶on the spot 🏊on the spot 🛒on the spot ⊗100m
🍴600m 🚲on the spot.

### ⚓S Hov  4B3
Fjordvegen 27. **GPS:** n60,69915 e10,33972.
2 🛏NOK 100 ⚡🔌Ch ✂. **Surface:** grassy.
**Distance:** 🏊on the spot 🛒on the spot.

### 🍴🛏S Høvringen  4B3
**Rondane Haukliseter Fjellhotell.** **GPS:** n61,88853 e9,48745.
15 🛏NOK 200 ⚡🔌Ch ✂WC. 🏪〰
**Location:** Rural, comfortable, quiet. **Surface:** grassy. 📅 01/01-31/12.
**Distance:** 🚶1km 🍴1km.
**Remarks:** Max. 72h, use of sauna against payment.

### Kongsberg  5C1
Glabak. **GPS:** n59,67205 e9,64166.
5 🛏NOK 170. **Surface:** asphalted. 📅 01/01-31/12.
**Distance:** 🛒on the spot ⊗400m 🍴550m 🚲on the spot.
**Remarks:** At swimming pool.

### ⚓S Kragerø  5C1
Allemannsveien. **GPS:** n58,87553 e9,41766.⬆.
🛏NOK 150. 🏪 **Surface:** unpaved.

---

**Distance:** 🚶on the spot 🛒100m.

### ⚓🏔〰 Kvelde  5C1
**Roppestad,** Farrisveien 863. **GPS:** n59,15310 e9,90844. ⬆.

10 🛏free ⚡🔌ChWCfree. **Location:** Rural, simple, isolated, quiet.
**Surface:** grassy. 📅 15/05-15/09.
**Distance:** 🚶18km 🏊50m 🛒50m 🚶on the spot.
**Remarks:** Max. 2 days.

### ⚓〰 Langesund  5C1
**Bobilparkering Smietangen,** Cudrios gate 17.
**GPS:** n59,00220 e9,74905.⬆.

8 🛏free. **Location:** Simple, central. **Surface:** concrete.
📅 01/01-31/12.
**Distance:** 🚶200m 🏊on the spot 🍴200m.
**Remarks:** Temporary stopover.

### ⚓S Larvik 🌿🚿🍺〰  5C1
**Indre Havn,** Strandpromenaden. **GPS:** n59,04892 e10,03361.⬆.

17 🛏NOK 150 or € 15 ⚡🔌Ch ✂ included. 🏪🏪
**Location:** Urban, simple, central, quiet. **Surface:** asphalted.
📅 01/01-31/12.
**Distance:** 🚶200m 🏊on the spot 🛒on the spot ⊗500m 🍴500m
🚗500m 🚲on the spot.
**Remarks:** Money in envelope in mail box.

### ⚓S Lillehammer  4B3
**Lysgårdsbakkene,** Lysgårdsvegen 55. **GPS:** n61,12431 e10,48914.
🛏NOK 70/24h. **Surface:** metalled.
**Distance:** 🚶250m.

### ⚓S Lunde  5C1
**Hogga Sluser,** Gamle Strengenvegen. **GPS:** n59,30216 e9,04331.⬆.
12 🛏NOK 150 ⚡🔌Ch ✂ included 🍴NOK 10. **Location:** Rural,
isolated, quiet. **Surface:** gravel/metalled. 📅 01/01-31/12.
**Distance:** 🏊on the spot 🛒on the spot.

### ⚓S Moss 🌿🚿🍺〰  5C1
**Bobilhavn,** Værftsgata 3. **GPS:** n59,43486 e10,65141.⬆.

14 🛏NOK 150 ⚡🔌Ch ✂ WC included. 🏪〰
**Location:** Urban, comfortable, central, quiet. **Surface:** asphalted.
📅 01/01-31/12.
**Distance:** 🚶500m 🚗3km 🏊on the spot 🛒on the spot ⊗300m
🍴100m 🚲on the spot.
**Remarks:** Max. 3 days.

---

### ⚓S Mysusæter  4B3
**Mysuseter Fjellstue. GPS:** n61,81161 e9,68463.
🛏NOK 40. **Surface:** metalled.

### ⚓S Notodden  5C1
**Notodden Bobilcamp,** Heddalsvegen. **GPS:** n59,55876 e9,24851.⬆.
13 🛏NOK 150 ⚡🔌Ch ✂(13x)included WCNOK 10 🍴NOK 20. 🏪
**Location:** Rural, comfortable, quiet. **Surface:** metalled.
📅 01/01-31/12.
**Distance:** 🚶1km 🏊on the spot 🛒on the spot ⊗on the spot
🍴250m.

### S Notodden  5C1
Heddalsvegen. **GPS:** n59,55981 e9,24834.
⚡NOK 20 🔌ChWCNOK 10 🍴NOK 20. 📅 01/01-31/12.

### ⚓S Os  4A3
**Steinneset Bobilparkering,** Hamnevegen 67.
**GPS:** n60,18161 e5,47372.
8 🛏NOK 150 ⚡✂. **Surface:** asphalted. 📅 01/01-31/12.
**Distance:** 🏊on the spot 🛒on the spot ⊗800m 🍴450m.

### ⚓ Oslo 🌿🚿🍺  4B3
Øvreseterveien. **GPS:** n59,98130 e10,67166.

15 🛏. **Location:** Rural. **Surface:** gravel.
**Distance:** 🚶3km 🏊on the spot 🛒on the spot ⊗3km 🍴200m 🚶on
the spot.

### ⚓S Oslo 🌿🚿〰  4B3
**Sjølyst Marina,** Drammensveien 164. **GPS:** n59,92026 e10,67506.⬆.

200 🛏NOK 300 ⚡🔌Ch ✂WC 〰included. 🎣〰
**Location:** Urban, simple, central, noisy. **Surface:** asphalted.
📅 01/06-20/09.
**Distance:** 🚶4km 🏊100m 🛒100m ⊗100m 🍴200m 🚗100m
🚲100m 🚶100m.
**Remarks:** Closed at night.

### ⚓S Oslo 🌿🚿🍺  4B3
**Bogstad Camp,** Ankerveien 117. **GPS:** n59,96293 e10,64203.⬆➡.

38 🛏NOK 320-360, 4 pers.incl ⚡🔌Ch ✂NOK 60/day WC 🍴NOK 15
◉NOK 40/40 〰included. 🏪🏪 **Location:** Rural, comfortable, quiet.
**Surface:** grassy/gravel. 📅 01/01-31/12.
**Distance:** 🚶city centre 6km 🏊700m 🛒700m ⊗on the spot 🍴on
the spot 🚲on the spot 🚶on the spot.

### ⚓S Rauland  5B1
**Raulandsfjell,** Fv362 4. **GPS:** n59,72005 e8,00510.
14 🛏NOK 180-250 ⚡✂WC🍴. **Location:** Rural, isolated.
**Surface:** metalled. 📅 01/01-31/12.
**Distance:** 🚶5km ⊗on the spot 🎿on the spot 🛷on the spot.
**Remarks:** At ski-lift.

### ⚓S Sandefjord 🌿🚿🍺〰  5C1
**Sandefjord Bobil havn,** Sandefjordsveien 5.
**GPS:** n59,12506 e10,22108.⬆➡.

16 🏕NOK 260 🔧🍽Ch 🛠 📶included. 🗑 ♨ **Location:** Urban, simple, quiet. **Surface:** asphalted. 🅿 01/01-31/12. **Distance:** 🏊700m ⚓on the spot 🚣on the spot ⊗700m 🚲1km 🚶on the spot 🧗on the spot. **Remarks:** Max. 72h.

| 🏕 | **Sarpsborg** 🧺 | 5D1 |

**Tindlund bobilparkering**, Neie Tidlundsveien. **GPS:** n59,27326 e11,04667.⬆.

6 🏕NOK 100 🛠(4x). **Location:** Urban, simple. **Surface:** gravel. **Distance:** 🏊1,3km.

| 🏕S | **Sarpsborg** 🧺 | 5D1 |

**Stamsaas Fritid**, Vogtsvei 40. **GPS:** n59,28532 e11,08414. 🧗.

10 🏕free 🔧free. **Location:** Urban, simple, noisy. **Surface:** asphalted. 🅿 01/01-31/12. **Distance:** 🏊1km 🚱350m. **Remarks:** Service during opening hours.

| 🏕S | **Seljord** | 5B1 |

**Flatin Gard**, Flatingrendi 3. **GPS:** n59,50725 e8,63964. 40 🏕NOK 100, NOK 200 service incl 🛠 WC 🍽NOK 30 📶. **Location:** Rural, isolated, quiet. **Surface:** grassy. 🅿 01/01-31/12. **Distance:** ⚓100m 🚣100m.

| 🏕 | **Siljan** | 5C1 |

**Sporevann. GPS:** n59,38476 e9,69584. 10 🏕free. **Location:** Rural, simple, isolated. **Surface:** unpaved. 🅿 01/01-31/12. **Distance:** 🏊11km ⚓on the spot 🚣on the spot.

| 🏕S | **Skien** 🚲🏕🍽 | 5C1 |

**Fritidspark**, Moflatveien 59. **GPS:** n59,18510 e9,59698. ⬆➡.

14 🏕NOK 200 🔧🍽Ch 🛠 WC 🍽NOK 20 📶included. ♨ **Location:** Rural, simple, central, quiet. **Surface:** asphalted. 🅿 01/04-01/10. **Distance:** 🏊historical centre 500m ⊗on the spot 🚱500m 🚲on the spot. **Remarks:** Check in at hotel, breakfast-service.

| 🏕 | **Skien** 🚲🏕🍽 | 5C1 |

**Teg Seil**, Bøleveien 4. **GPS:** n59,19634 e9,62039.⬆.

---

10 🏕NOK 150. ♨ **Location:** Urban, simple, quiet. **Surface:** asphalted. 🅿 01/05-30/09. **Distance:** 🏊700m ⚓on the spot 🚣on the spot 🚱400m 🚲on the spot. **Remarks:** At sailmaker.

| 🏕 | **Skreia** | 4B3 |

**Hersjøen. GPS:** n60,54498 e11,03309. 🏕NOK 45. **Location:** Isolated, quiet. **Surface:** grassy. **Distance:** ⚓on the spot 🚣on the spot 🚱6,5km.

| 🍇 | **Tyristrand** | 4B3 |

**Stall Myhre**, Holleiaveien 263. **GPS:** n60,11111 e10,07194. 🏕NOK 100. **Location:** Isolated, quiet. **Surface:** grassy. 🅿 01/03-01/10. **Distance:** 🏊3,5km. **Remarks:** At horse farm.

| 🏕S | **Tønsberg** 🚲🏕🧺♨ | 5C1 |

**Fjordgaten**, Fjordgatan 15. **GPS:** n59,27390 e10,40009. ⬆➡.

23 🏕NOK 150 🔧🛠included. 🗑 ♨ **Location:** Rural, simple, quiet. **Surface:** gravel. 🅿 01/01-31/12. **Distance:** 🏊1km ⚓50m 🚣50m 🚲on the spot 🧗on the spot.

| 🏕S | **Tønsberg** 🚲🏕🧺♨ | 5C1 |

**Storgaten**, Storgatan 1. **GPS:** n59,26323 e10,41569. ⬆➡.

8 🏕NOK 150 🔧Ch 🛠 WCincluded. 🗑 ♨ **Location:** Urban, simple, noisy. **Surface:** asphalted. 🅿 01/01-31/12. **Distance:** 🏊on the spot 🚣100m ⊗300m 🚱on the spot. **Remarks:** Max. 2 days.

| 🏕 | **Tønsberg** 🚲🏕🧺♨ | 5C1 |

**Messeområdet**, Stenmalveien 32. **GPS:** n59,28069 e10,41015.⬆.

12 🏕free. **Location:** Rural, simple, quiet. **Surface:** asphalted. 🅿 01/01-31/12. **Distance:** 🏊2km ⊗2km 🚱2km 🚲on the spot 🧗on the spot. **Remarks:** At the skating rink, picnic area.

| S | **Tønsberg** 🚲🏕🧺♨ | 5C1 |

**Shell**, Kjelleveien 28. **GPS:** n59,27879 e10,40092. 🔧🍽Ch. 🅿 01/01-31/12.

| 🏕 | **Ulefoss** | 5C1 |

**Norsjø Golfpark**, Romnesvegen 98. **GPS:** n59,30248 e9,26511. 🏕NOK 50. **Distance:** 🏊4km.

---

**Remarks:** At golf court.

| 🏕 | **Uvdal** | 4B3 |

**Uvdal resort. GPS:** n60,26515 e8,78849.⬆. 🏕NOK 150. **Surface:** grassy. **Distance:** ⚓on the spot 🚣on the spot.

| 🏕 | **Vågå** | 4B3 |

**Steinhole fjellcamp. GPS:** n61,62293 e8,99682. 🏕NOK 50. **Location:** Isolated, quiet. **Surface:** grassy.

| 🏕S | **Voll** 🍽♨ | 5C1 |

**Ole"s Kios og gatekjøkken**, Svanvikveien 653. **GPS:** n59,12797 e9,51008.⬆.

12 🏕NOK 150 🔧🍽Ch 🛠 WCincluded. ♨ 🅿 01/01-31/12. **Location:** Rural, simple, quiet. **Surface:** gravel. 🅿 01/01-31/12. **Distance:** 🏊1km ⚓on the spot 🚣on the spot ⊗on the spot 🚱on the spot 🚲on the spot 🧗on the spot. **Remarks:** Check in on arrival, regional products.

**NO**

# Poland

Capital: Warsaw
Government: parliamentary republic
Official Language: Polish
Population: 38,476,269 (2017)
Area: 311,888 km²

## General information
Dialling code: 0048
General emergency: 112
Currency: Zloty (PLN)
€ 1 = 4,32 PLN, 1 PLN = € 0,23
£1 = 4,92 PLN, 1PLN = £0.20 (October 2018)
Credit cards are accepted almost everywhere.

## Regulations for overnight stays
Free overnight stay is not allowed. On private property with permission of the owner.

## Additional public holidays 2019
January 6 Epiphany
May 3 Constitution Day
June 20 Corpus Christi
August 15 Assumption of Mary
November 1 All Saints' Day
November 11 Independence Day

## Time Zone
Winter (Standard Time) GMT+1
Summer (DST) GMT+2

Gdańsk

Pomeranian
pages: 720-721

Warmian-Masurian
page: 721

West Pomeranian
page: 720

Podlaskie
page: 721

Kuyavian-Pomeranian
page: 721

Mazovian
pages: 722

Warsaw

Greater Poland
page: 721

Lubusz
page: 721

Łódź
page: 722

Lublin

Lower Silesian
page: 722

Świętokrzyskie

Opole
page: 722

Silesian
page: 722

Subcarpathian
page: 722

Lesser Poland
page: 722

PL

## West Pomeranian

### Czaplinek 38A1
**Drawtur**, Ul. Pieciu Pomostów 1. **GPS:** n53,57671 e16,21984.

50 € 12 Ch € 2,50 WC 3,50 included.
**Location:** Rural, noisy. **Surface:** grassy.
**Distance:** 2km 50m on the spot on the spot 2km.
**Remarks:** Dog € 2/day.

### Miedzywodzie 6H3
**Narcyz**, Armii Krajowej 33. **GPS:** n54,00376 e14,69290.

8 € 20 Ch WC on demand included.
**Location:** Rural, central, noisy. **Surface:** grassy.
01/05-01/10.
**Distance:** 100m 800m 600m 100m 100m 50m.
**Remarks:** Breakfast-service.

### Miroslawiec 38A2
**Hotel Park Reduta Napoleona**, Lowicz Walecki 60.
**GPS:** n53,33081 e16,02333.

30 € 8,50 € 2,25 Ch € 7,50 WC € 2,50 included.
**Location:** Rural, isolated, quiet. **Surface:** grassy.
01/01-31/12.
**Distance:** 5km 100m 500m 50m 700m.

### Szczecin 8H2
**Hotel Panorama**, Ul.Radosna 60. **GPS:** n53,36420 e14,61550.

10 € 17 on demand included WC .
**Location:** Urban, simple. **Surface:** metalled. 01/01-31/12.
**Distance:** 10km 1km on the spot 1km on the spot.

### Wolin 8H1
**Fam. Lafrentz**, Gogolice 20, Gogolice. **GPS:** n53,83300 e14,62262.

13 € 12 Ch included. **Location:** Rural, quiet.
**Surface:** gravel. 01/01-31/12.
**Distance:** 1,4km 500m 50m 1,4km 1,4km 1,4km.

## Pomeranian

### Gdańsk 38B1
**Akademia Muzycna**, Lakowa 1-2. **GPS:** n54,34561 e18,66357.

15 € 1-1,50/h. **Location:** Urban, central.
**Surface:** grassy/metalled. 01/01-31/12.
**Distance:** 100m 100m 100m.

### Malbork 38B1
**Camping Nogat 197**, Ul. Parkowa 3. **GPS:** n54,04653 e19,03877.
30 € 19 Ch WC included . **Location:** Rural.
**Surface:** grassy/metalled. 01/05-30/09.
**Distance:** 1,5km on the spot on the spot on the spot on the spot.

## Malbork · 38B1

**Nad Stawem**, Ul. Solskiego 10. **GPS**: n54,04285 e19,02536.

30 € 12 Ch € 2,50 WC included. **Location**: Urban, central. **Surface**: grassy. 01/03-01/11. **Distance**: 200m 50m 200m.

## Parchowo · 38A1

**Kalex**, Jamnowski Mlyn 15. **GPS**: n54,22644 e17,63750.

10 € 14 Ch WC € 2 € 2 included. **Location**: Rural, isolated, quiet. **Surface**: grassy/sand. 01/04-01/11. **Distance**: 5km on the spot on the spot 5km.

## Wierzbna · 38A2

**De Vuijle vaetdoek "carpe Diem"**, 66-340 Przytoczna. **GPS**: n52,56639 e15,81722.

70 € 17,50 Ch WC included. **Location**: Rural, simple, isolated. **Surface**: grassy. 01/05-01/09.

## Zagaje · 38A1

**Gosciniec Zagaje**, Zagaje 1. **GPS**: n54,00583 e17,12778.
6 € 20 WC included. **Location**: Rural. **Surface**: grassy. 01/01-31/12. **Distance**: 4km 200m on the spot 4km on the spot on the spot.

# Warmian-Masurian

## Dobre Miasto · 38B1

Garnizonowa 16. **GPS**: n53,98594 e20,41430.
3 free. **Location**: Simple. **Surface**: metalled. 01/01-31/12. **Distance**: 1km. **Remarks**: At swimming pool.

## Gierloz · 38C1

**Wolf's Liar - Wilczy Szaniec**, 11-400 Kętrzyn. **GPS**: n54,07925 e21,49309.

10 € 12,50 included WC. **Location**: Rural, simple, comfortable. 01/01-31/12. **Distance**: on the spot. **Remarks**: Former headquarters of Hitler.

## Mikolajki · 38C1

**Hotelik Caligula**, Ul.Jana Pawla II. **GPS**: n53,80278 e21,57444.
20 € 16 Ch on demand included. **Surface**: gravel. 01/01-31/12. **Distance**: 100m 200m 500m 200m 200m.

## Milolyn · 38B1

**Mazur**, Ul Twarda 28a, Milomlyn. **GPS**: n53,76583 e19,84639.

4 € 7,50 € 1 € 1 Ch € 1 € 1. **Location**: Rural, quiet. **Surface**: grassy. 01/01-31/12. **Distance**: 500m 500m 1km 1km 400m 200m 500m 100m 100m.

## Mrągowo · 38C1

**Camping Seeblick**, Ruska Wieś 1. **GPS**: n53,94226 e21,32047.

30 € 15 Ch WC included. **Surface**: grassy. 01/01-31/12. **Distance**: on the spot on the spot on the spot on the spot. **Remarks**: Bread-service.

## Paslek · 38B1

**Kemping Bezplatny**, 526. **GPS**: n53,98052 e19,62524.

100 € 12,50 included WC. **Location**: Rural, simple, isolated. **Surface**: grassy. 01/01-31/12. **Distance**: 10km 10km on the spot 10km on the spot on the spot.

## Piecki · 38C1

**Restaurant Krutynska**, Krutyn 72. **GPS**: n53,68491 e21,43021.
20 € 13 Ch included. **Location**: Rural. **Surface**: grasstiles. 01/01-31/12. **Distance**: 300m 300m.

## Pieniezno · 38B1

**Caravanparc Pieniezno**, 14-520. **GPS**: n54,23454 e20,13697.

20 € 10 Ch WC included on demand. **Location**: Rural, quiet. **Surface**: grassy. 01/01-31/12. **Distance**: 1km 800m 800m 500m.

## Sorkwity · 38C1

**Haus am see**, Janowo 1. **GPS**: n53,83495 e21,20284.

5 € 10, >7m € 15 Ch included. **Location**: Rural. **Surface**: grassy. 01/01-31/12. **Distance**: 500m 50m 1km.

## Tolkmicko · 38B1

Swietokanska. **GPS**: n54,32367 e19,52264.

10 € 5 included WC € 0,50 € 2. **Location**: Rural, noisy. **Surface**: metalled. 01/01-31/12. **Distance**: 100m 50m on the spot 100m 100m.

## Łukta · 38B1

Plichta 9. **GPS**: n53,75989 e20,05300.
20 € 5 € 1. **Location**: Rural. **Surface**: grassy. 01/04-01/11.

# Podlaskie

## Białystok · 38D1

**Wodnych "Dojlidy"**, Plażowa 15-502. **GPS**: n53,10838 e23,21923.
14 PLN 15 + PLN 10/pp Ch (14x) € 1/kWh WC included. **Location**: Rural. **Surface**: grasstiles. 01/03-31/10. **Distance**: 1,5km on the spot on the spot on the spot on the spot. **Remarks**: Canoe and boat rental, playground.

# Lubusz

## Ownice · 8H3

**Fisch Camp**, Wolności 40. **GPS**: n52,53517 e14,89269.

30 € 12 Ch WC included € 1/1day. **Location**: Rural. **Surface**: grassy. 01/01-31/12.

# Greater Poland

## Biskupice · 38A2

**WojciechSzczepanski**, Jankowo-Mlyn 23. **GPS**: n52,44965 e17,16442.
20 € 20 Ch included. **Location**: Rural. **Surface**: grassy. 01/01-31/12.

## Poznań · 38A2

**Hotel-Camping Malta**, Ul. Krańcowa 98. **GPS**: n52,40331 e16,98434.
40 € 18-22,50 Ch WC included. **Surface**: grassy/metalled. 01/01-31/12. **Distance**: on the spot on the spot 1km on the spot on the spot. **Remarks**: Video surveillance.

# Kuyavian-Pomeranian

## Toruń · 38B2

**Camping Tramp**, Kujawska 14. **GPS**: n52,99925 e18,60755.
40 € 16 Ch € 4,50 WC included. **Location**: Rural, noisy. **Surface**: grassy/metalled. 01/05-01/10. **Distance**: 200m 2,5km on the spot on the spot.

PL

## Mazovian

**Ⓢ Warszawa 38C2**
**Parking**, 1 Sierpinia, Warsaw (Warszawa). **GPS**: n52,19189 e20,98069.
10 € 12 € 2 € 2 Ch € 3 € 5. **Location**: Urban.
**Surface**: metalled. 01/01-31/12.
**Distance**: city centre 5,5km 2km 100m 500m 300m.

**Ⓢ Warszawa 38C2**
**Parking**, Wybrzeze Gdanskie, Warsaw (Warszawa).
**GPS**: n52,25133 e21,01469.↑
15 € 1,50/h, € 30/24h. **Location**: Urban. **Surface**: metalled.
01/01-31/12.
**Distance**: city centre 3km 5km on the spot on the spot
250m.

## Lower Silesian

**Ⓢ Karpacz 38A3**
**Rezydencja Holandia**, Ul.Konstytucji 3-go Maja 67.
**GPS**: n50,77345 e15,74734.
15 € 5 € 1 Chfree € 1. **Location**: Rural.
**Surface**: metalled. 01/01-31/12.
**Distance**: 1km 900m.

**△Ⓢ Uciechów 38A3**
**Camping Forteca**, Ul.Wroclawska 12. **GPS**: n50,75572 e16,69438.
50 € 17 Ch € 3,50,16Amp included. **Surface**: grassy.
01/04-01/10.
**Distance**: 4km 100m.
**Remarks**: Bread-service.

## Opole

**Ⓢ Gora Swietej Anny 38B3**
**P Najem Pokoi**, Ul.Strzelecka 2A. **GPS**: n50,45785 e18,16895.↑→
5 € 10 Ch included. **Location**: Rural. **Surface**: grassy.
01/01-31/12.
**Distance**: 600m 100m.

**Ⓢ Naklo 38B3**
**Fam Urban**, Ul Strzelecka 91. **GPS**: n50,57790 e18,12715.
10 € 12 Ch WCincluded. **Location**: Rural, isolated, quiet.
**Surface**: grassy. 01/01-31/12.
**Distance**: 400m 100m.

## Łódź

**Ⓢ Lipce Reymontowskie 38C2**
**Bumerang**, Chlebow 3. **GPS**: n51,92795 e19,92847.
8 € 12 Chincluded € 3. **Location**: Rural. **Surface**: grassy.
01/01-31/12.

## Silesian

**Ⓢ Częstochowa 38B3**
**GPS**: n50,81242 e19,09076.↑
50 free. **Location**: Urban, simple. **Surface**: asphalted.
01/01-31/12.
**Distance**: on the spot 400m 2,5km.

## Lesser Poland

**△Ⓢ Gaj 38C4**
**Camping Korona**, Ul. Myslenicka 32. **GPS**: n49,96229 e19,89294.
30 € 15 Ch WCincluded. **Location**: Rural.
**Surface**: grassy/metalled. 01/01-31/12.
**Remarks**: Bread-service, video surveillance.

**Ⓢ Kraków 38C4**
**Camper ParkingA4**, Kryspinów 399, Liszki.
**GPS**: n50,04120 e19,80540.↑
50 € 5 € 1,20. **Location**: Simple, isolated. **Surface**: metalled.
01/01-31/12.
**Distance**: city centre 10km 1,5km.

**Ⓢ Kraków 38C4**
**Guesthaus Apis**, Ul.Podgorki 60. **GPS**: n49,98885 e19,96210.
5 € 20 WCincluded.
**Location**: Rural, simple, noisy. **Surface**: grassy/metalled.
01/01-31/12.
**Distance**: 10km Krakau 50m 400m on the spot.

**Ⓢ Kraków 38C4**
**Elcamp**, Ul.Tyniecka 118e. **GPS**: n50,03418 e19,87658.

10 € 7,50 € 0,50/40liter Ch included .
**Surface**: grassy/gravel. 01/01-31/12.
**Distance**: Kraków 5km 100m on the spot.

**ⓅⓈ Oswiecim 38B4**
**Auschwitz Parking**, Stanislaw-Leszezynskiej 11.
**GPS**: n50,02867 e19,20111.
10 € 10 € 2,50. **Surface**: metalled. 01/01-31/12.
**Remarks**: Near Auswitz-Birkenau memorial and museum.

**Ⓢ Sękowa 38C4**
DW977. **GPS**: n49,62666 e21,19565.↑
5 free free. **Location**: Isolated. **Surface**: grasstiles.
01/01-31/12.
**Distance**: 1,5km 1,5km.
**Remarks**: Next to sports fields.

**Wieliczka 38C4**
**Salt Mine**, Edwarda Dembowskiego 22. **GPS**: n49,98542 e20,05338.
20 € 7,50. **Location**: Urban. **Surface**: gravel/sand.
01/01-31/12.
**Distance**: 1,5km 400m 50m 500m.

## Subcarpathian

**△Ⓢ Wetlina 38D4**
**Camping Górna Wetlinka**. **GPS**: n49,14740 e22,52028.
15 € 18 Chincluded € 3. **Location**: Rural. **Surface**: grassy.
01/04-01/10.
**Distance**: 200m on the spot on the spot.

# Portugal

Capital: Lisbon
Government: Parliamentary democracy
Official Language: Portuguese
Population: 10,840,000 (2017)
Area: 92,212 km²

## General information
Dialling code: 00351
General emergency: 112
Currency: Euro
Payments by credit card are accepted almost everywhere.

## Regulations for overnight stays
If there is no local prohibition  wild camping is allowed, max. 48h, exept in the Algarve, in urban areas and drinking water protection areas.

## Additional public holidays 2019
January 6 Epiphany
April 19 Good Friday
April 25 Liberationday
May 1 Labor Day
June 10 National Holiday
June 20 Corpus Christi
August 15 Assumption of the Virgin Mary
October 5 Republic day
November 1 All Saints' Day
December 8 Immaculate Conception

## Time Zone
Winter (Standard Time) GMT+0
Summer (DST) GMT+1

Braga

Portugal North
pages: 723-727

Porto

Beira
pages: 727-731

Coimbra

Portugal Central
and Lisbon
pages: 731-735

Lisbon

Alentejo
pages: 735-738

Algarve
pages: 738-741

Faro

PT

# Portugal North

### Aguaçadoura — 29B3
Aguaçadoura Futebol Clube. GPS: n41,44389 w8,77722.

5 free. Location: Rural, simple. Surface: gravel/sand.
01/01-31/12.
Distance: 500m 50m 500m 500m.
Remarks: Parking at the beach.

### Amarante — 29C3
Av. Alexandre Herculano. GPS: n41,27286 w8,07178.

free. Surface: metalled.
Distance: 800m on the spot on the spot 50m on the spot.
Remarks: Parking near sports centre.

### Amarante — 29C3
GPS: n41,27020 w8,07708.

Surface: metalled. Wed.
Distance: on the spot on the spot.
Remarks: Market square along the river.

### Amarante — 29C3
Penedo da Rainha, São Gonçalo. GPS: n41,28031 w8,06925.
€ 10,90-22 Ch 04/01-30/11.
Distance: 1km on the spot on the spot 1km.
Tourist information Amarante:
Museu Municipal Amadeu de Souza Cardoso, Alameda Teixeira Pascoaes. Modern art.

### Arcos de Valdevez — 29C3
N202. GPS: n41,84749 w8,41524.

10 free. Location: Rural, simple, noisy. Surface: metalled.
01/01-31/12.
Distance: 300m on the spot.
Remarks: Along the Vez river.

### Avintes — 29B3
Parque Biológico de Gaia, Rue da Cunha.
GPS: n41,09730 w8,55414.

9 € 4 + € 4 /pp, entrance park incl Ch included WC
free, at reception. Location: Luxurious, quiet.
Surface: grasstiles. 01/01-31/12.
Distance: 10km 800m 100m > Porto.
Remarks: Check in at reception.

### Barcelos — 29C3
R.Rosa Ramalho. GPS: n41,52829 w8,61547.

12 free. Location: Rural, simple. Surface: metalled.
01/01-31/12.
Distance: centre 800m 3,5km on the spot.
Remarks: Parking swimming pool, thursday market.
Tourist information Barcelos:
Museu de Olaria de Barcelos, R. Cónego Joaquim Gaiolas. Ceramics and archeology. Tue-Su 10-12.30h, 14-18h, Thu 10-18h.

## Bico 30B1
R. Vasco da Gama. **GPS:** n40,73016 w8,64747.

30 free. **Location:** Rural, simple, isolated, quiet.
**Surface:** metalled. 01/01-31/12.
**Distance:** 300m on the spot on the spot on the spot.
**Remarks:** In fishing port.

## Braga 29C3
Bom Jesus do Monte. **GPS:** n41,55278 w8,38137.

25 free ChWCfree. **Location:** Urban, simple, noisy.
**Surface:** concrete. 01/01-31/12.
**Distance:** 6km 20m 100m.
**Remarks:** Parking at funicular railway.

## Braga 29C3
Sameiro. **GPS:** n41,53928 w8,36743.

10 free.
**Location:** Simple.
**Surface:** gravel/sand.
01/01-31/12.
**Remarks:** Parking at place of pilgrimage.

**Tourist information Braga:**
Semana Santa. Procession.
week before Easter.
Parque Nacional da Peneda-Gerês. Hiking routes.

## Bragança 29D3
Parque de Merendas, Rue Miguel Torga. **GPS:** n41,80417 w6,74611.

30 free Chfree.
**Location:** Rural, comfortable, quiet.
**Surface:** metalled.
01/01-31/12.
**Distance:** 200m 200m 200m.
**Remarks:** P below the castle, 01/07-15/09, max. 24h, beautiful view.

**Tourist information Bragança:**
Medival upper city and castle.
Museu Militar.
9-11.45h, 14-18.15h.
Parque Natural de Montesinho. Nature reserve.

## Caminha 29B3
Largo da Feira. **GPS:** n41,87490 w8,84113.

---

10 free. **Location:** Urban, simple. **Surface:** metalled.
01/01-31/12.
**Distance:** 500m 100m.

## Carregal do Sal 30C1
Quinta de Cabriz Loja. **GPS:** n40,42465 w8,01856.
free. **Surface:** unpaved. 01/01-31/12.
**Distance:** on the spot.
**Remarks:** Portugal Tradicional, max. 24h.

## Carregal do Sal 30C1
Luzio, Arruamento Urbano a Sul da Vila. **GPS:** n40,43116 w7,99471.

3 free Chfree. **Location:** Simple. **Surface:** grassy.
01/01-31/12.
**Distance:** 1km.
**Remarks:** Behind petrol station.

## Chaves 29D3
Alameda do Trajano. **GPS:** n41,73694 w7,46917.

6 free. **Location:** Urban, simple. **Surface:** metalled.
01/01-31/12.
**Distance:** historical centre 300m 8,6km 100m 100m.
**Remarks:** Along the Tâmega river.

## Chaves 29D3
Guest House Chaves, Rua da Solidão 46. **GPS:** n41,73498 w7,47272.
10 €12-15 €3 Ch €3 WC. **Surface:** grassy.
01/01-31/12.
**Distance:** on the spot.

**Tourist information Chaves:**
Torre de Mengem. Military museum.

## Covas 29C3
Parque Campismo de Covas, Lugar de Pereiras.
**GPS:** n41,88758 w8,69497.
€ 5,30-8 Ch WC. 01/01-31/12.

## Covas 29C3
Quinta do Retiro, Lugar Quinta do Retiro s/n. **GPS:** n40,35230 w7,91583.
5 € 15-20 Ch (5x),10Amp WC € 4,50 included.
**Surface:** grassy. 01/01-31/12.
**Distance:** 800m 3km 3km 3km 8km on the spot.

## Entre-os-Rios 29C3
**GPS:** n41,08357 w8,29322.

---

4 WC Lunchroom & co. **Location:** Simple, central, noisy.
01/01-31/12.
**Distance:** 100m on the spot on the spot 100m 100m.
**Remarks:** Parking along the Douro river.

## Espinho 29B3
**GPS:** n40,98916 w8,6452.

+10 free free,beach. **Location:** Rural, simple, isolated, quiet.
**Surface:** gravel/sand. 01/01-31/12.
**Distance:** 1km 25m 1km 1km.
**Remarks:** Beach parking.

## Espinho 29B3
Municipal de Espinho, Zona da Ribeira dos Mochos.
**GPS:** n41,01402 w8,63743.
€ 18,90-23,30 Ch WC. 01/01-31/12.

## Esposende 29B3
Forte de S.João Baptiste, Rue do Farol. **GPS:** n41,54222 w8,79111.

5 free Ch free. **Location:** Urban, simple.
**Surface:** asphalted. 01/01-31/12.
**Distance:** 1,5km on the spot on the spot
1,5km.
**Remarks:** Parking at lighthouse, free wifi for clients restaurant.

## Esposende 29B3
Parque de Campismo de Fão, Lírios - Fão. **GPS:** n41,50778 w8,77833.
Ch WC. 01/01-31/12.
**Distance:** 500m 500m on the spot 500m.

## Freixo de Espada a Cinta 30D1
Espaço Multiusos, R. do Samiteiro de Cima.
**GPS:** n41,08826 w6,81751.

12 free Ch (12x)free.
**Surface:** metalled. 01/01-31/12.
**Distance:** 900m 900m 900m.
**Remarks:** Arrival <18h.

## Freixo de Numão 30D1
Area de autocaravanas Jean Pierre Rossi, Av Dr Francisco Sa Carneiro.
**GPS:** n41,06000 w7,22111.

30 € 5 Ch WC included. **Location:** Rural, simple.
**Surface:** metalled. 01/01-31/12.
**Distance:** 900m 500m 500m.

### 🅂 Gerês ⬆ 29C3
Vila do Gerês. GPS: n41,73538 w8,15969. ⬆.

4 ⌦free ⛽free. **Location:** Rural, simple, isolated, quiet.
**Surface:** asphalted. ◻ 01/01-31/12.
**Distance:** ⌇1km ⊗on the spot.

### △🅂 Gondomar 29C3
Medas, Gavinho - Medas. GPS: n41,03917 w8,42694.
⌦€ 26-32 ⛽🔲Ch🔲✦WC🔲. ◻ 01/01-31/12.

### ♈ Gosende 30C1
**Cooperativa Capuchinhas CRL**, Campo Benfeito.
GPS: n41,00017 w7,92603.
⌦free. **Surface:** unpaved.
◻ 01/01-31/12.
**Distance:** ⬙ 5,1km.
**Remarks:** Portugal Tradicional.

### 🅂 Guilhufe 29C3
€M594. GPS: n41,19541 w8,31605. ⬆➡.

8 ⌦free ⛽🔲Chfree. **Location:** Simple, noisy. **Surface:** metalled.
◻ 01/01-31/12.
**Distance:** ⌇1km ⬙ 1,6km ⌇1km ⛽1km.

### 🅂 Izeda 29D3
Largo do Toural. GPS: n41,56750 w6,72333. ⬆➡.

30 ⌦free ⛽🔲Chfree. **Location:** Rural, simple, central, quiet.
**Surface:** metalled. ◻ 01/01-31/12.
**Distance:** ⌇centre ⊗200m ⛽200m.

### 🅂 Lamego ♈🍴 30C1
**Parque Lamego**, N2, Lugar da Raposeira.
GPS: n41,09016 w7,82214. ⬆➡.

15 ⌦€ 15, 01/06-15/09 € 18, 2 pers. incl ⛽🔲Ch🔲€ 4/day WC🔲.
🏠 **Location:** Rural, luxurious, isolated, quiet. **Surface:** unpaved.
◻ 01/01-31/12.
**Distance:** ⌇1,2km ⬙ 4,5km ⊗500m ⛽2km ⛽on the spot.
**Remarks:** Baker every morning, beautiful view, near Caves da Rapo-
seira, sale of wines.
**Tourist information Lamego:**
👁 Bodega Raposeira. Ⓣ free.
⚘ Nossa Senhora dos Remédios. Pilgrimage in Portugal, most impor-
tant festivity of the country. ◻ end Aug-beginning Sep.

### 🅂 Lordelo 29C3
R. da Igreja 350. GPS: n41,23472 w8,41139. ⬆➡.

20 ⌦free ⛽🔲Chfree. **Location:** Simple, quiet.
**Surface:** gravel/sand. ◻ 01/01-31/12.
**Distance:** ⌇400m ⛽400m ⛽400m.

### 🅂 Macedo de Cavaleiros 🌿 29D3
Rua das Piscinas. GPS: n41,53756 w6,95715. ⬆➡.

8 ⌦free ⛽€ 2/100liter 🔲Ch🔲€ 2/1h. **Location:** Urban, simple,
central, quiet. **Surface:** asphalted.
◻ 01/01-31/12.
**Distance:** ⌇200m ⊗200m ⛽300m ⛽on the spot.

### 🅂 Macedo de Cavaleiros 🌿 29D3
**Barragem do Azibo**, Frada da Pegada. GPS: n41,58333 w6,89944. ⬆.

10 ⌦free. **Location:** Rural, simple, quiet. **Surface:** metalled.
◻ 01/01-31/12.
**Distance:** ⌇2km ⬙ Sandy beach ⊗on the spot.
**Remarks:** At barrage, guarded during summer period.

### 🅂 Matosinhos 29B3
Av. de Praia. GPS: n41,26044 w8,72434. ⬆.

10 ⌦free. **Location:** Simple, noisy. **Surface:** metalled.
◻ 01/01-31/12.
**Distance:** ⌇200m ⊗200m ⛽600m ⛽on the spot.
**Remarks:** Beach parking.

### △🅂 Matosinhos 29B3
**Municipal de Angeiras**. GPS: n41,26722 w8,71972.
⌦€ 18,50-29 ⛽🔲Ch. ◻ 01/01-31/12.
**Remarks:** Service only € 3,15-5,40.

### 🅂 Melgaço 29C2
**Porta de Lamas de Mouro**, Lamas de Mouro.
GPS: n42,03979 w8,19588.
⌦free. **Location:** Rural, isolated, quiet. **Surface:** metalled.
◻ 01/01-31/12.
**Distance:** ⊗400m.

### 🅂 Melgaço 29C2
Rua do Mercado. GPS: n42,11549 w8,26095. ⬆.

---

6 ⌦free. **Location:** Rural, simple. ◻ 01/01-31/12.
**Distance:** ⊗on the spot.
**Remarks:** At shopping centre.

### 🅂 Miranda do Douro 🌿🏛🍴 29E3
Av. Eduardo Quero. GPS: n41,49167 w6,27333.

⌦free. **Location:** Rural. **Surface:** metalled.
**Distance:** ⌇25m ⛽200m.
**Remarks:** Near city wall.

### 🅂 Miranda do Douro 🏛🍴 29E3
Largo do Cestelo. GPS: n41,49611 w6,275.

⌦free. **Surface:** metalled. ◻ 01/01-31/12.
**Distance:** ⌇on the spot ⊗50m ⛽50m.
**Remarks:** Parking near ruins of castle.

### 🅂 Mirandela 🌿 29D3
Largo Cardal. GPS: n41,48685 w7,18391. ⬆.

15 ⌦free ⚡Fon. **Location:** Rural, simple, central, noisy.
**Surface:** asphalted. ◻ 01/01-31/12.
**Distance:** ⌇centre ⊗on the spot ⛽on the spot ⛽on the spot 🚲on
the spot 🚶on the spot.
**Remarks:** Large parking along the river.

### △🅂 Mirandela 🌿 29D3
Três Rios-Maravilha. GPS: n41,50683 w7,19716.
⌦€ 16,50-21,50 ⛽🔲Ch🔲✦WC🔲.
◻ 02/02-01/12.

**Tourist information Mirandela:**
Ⓜ Museu municipal. Modern Portuguese painting art.
Ⓣ free.
Ⓜ Villa Flôr. Village museum. Ⓣ free.

### △🅂 Mogadouro 29D3
**Mogadouro**, Complexo Desportivo Municipal. GPS: n41,33528 w6,71861.
⌦€ 13-15 ⛽🔲Ch🔲✦WC🔲. ◻ 01/04-30/09.
**Distance:** ⊗500m ⛽on the spot ⛽500m.

### 🅂 Mondim de Basto 29C3
**Area Mondim de Basto**. GPS: n41,41199 w7,95137. ⬆.

PT

30 🛏free 🚰 ♻Chfree. **Location:** Urban, simple, central.
**Surface:** metalled. 🅿 01/01-31/12.
**Distance:** 🚶300m ⊗300m 🚊300m.
**Remarks:** Friday market.

### 🅿S Montalegre 29C3
Rua João Rodrigues Cabrilho. **GPS:** n41,82280 w7,78684.⬆
🛏free 🚰 ♻Chfree. **Surface:** metalled. 🅿 01/01-31/12.
**Distance:** 🚶500m.

### 🅿 Murça 29C3
**Murça-Estádio**, Variante à N15. **GPS:** n41,40421 w7,44994.⬆

10 🛏free. **Surface:** asphalted. 🅿 01/01-31/12.
**Distance:** 🚶500m ⊗300m.
**Remarks:** At footballstadium.

### 🍴 Nelas 30C1
**Paço Dos Cunhas De Santar**, Largo do Paço, Santar.
**GPS:** n40,57273 w7,8925.
🛏free. 🅿 01/01-31/12.
**Remarks:** Portugal Tradicional, max. 24h, vineyard/restaurant, awning and generator prohibited.

### 🅿S Paredes de Coura 29C3
**AC Parking Areas Lda**, R. Bombeiros Voluntários 1.
**GPS:** n41,91060 w8,55826.⬆

46 🛏€ 12/24h, € 21/48h 🚰 ♻Ch 🧹(21x)WC🗑 📶included.
**Location:** Rural. **Surface:** metalled. 🅿 01/01-31/12.
**Distance:** 🚶150m 🏄13km 🏊500m 🛒150m 🚏30m 🚉50m.
**Remarks:** Video surveillance.

### 🅿S Peso da Régua 29C3
**Parque de pernoita de autocaravanas.**
**GPS:** n41,15570 w7,78058.⬆
16 🛏€ 3 🚰 ♻Ch 🧹free. **Surface:** metalled. 🅿 01/01-31/12.
**Distance:** 🚶1km ⊗100m.

### 🅿S Peso da Régua 29C3
**Parque Ovar**, Av. de Ovar. **GPS:** n41,16278 w7,79222.⬆

4 🛏free 🧹(4x)WCfree,150m. **Location:** Urban, simple, central, noisy.
**Surface:** asphalted. 🅿 01/01-31/12.
**Distance:** 🚶on the spot 🏄4km 🏊on the spot ⊗on the spot 🚉on the spot.

### 🅿 Ponte de Lima 29C3
Alameda de São João. **GPS:** n41,77052 w8,5847.⬆

---

15 🛏free. **Location:** Urban, simple. **Surface:** metalled.
🅿 01/01-31/12.
**Distance:** 🚶300m 🏊on the spot.
**Remarks:** Along river.

### ⛺S Póvoa de Varzim 29B3
**Rio Alto**, Estela. **GPS:** n41,46277 w8,77369.
🛏€ 19-32 🚰 ♻Ch 🧹WC🗑 🅿 01/01-31/12.
**Remarks:** Service passerby € 3,50-6.

### ⛺S Queimadela 29C3
**Parque de Campismo do Baragem. GPS:** n41,50379 w8,16216.
🛏 🚰 ♻Ch 🧹🗑. **Surface:** grassy/metalled 🅿 01/01-31/12.
**Distance:** 🏊100m 🚶100m 🏊on the spot.

### 🅿 Santa Maria da Feira 30B1
**GPS:** n40,91972 w8,54306.⬆

5 🛏free. **Location:** Rural, simple, quiet. **Surface:** gravel/sand.
🅿 01/01-31/12.
**Distance:** 🚶600m ⊗600m.
**Remarks:** Parking at castle.

### 🅿S São Romão do Coronado 29C3
R. Horizonte. **GPS:** n41,27841 w8,54962.⬆
4 🛏€ 2 ♻Chincluded 🧹€ 2. **Location:** Urban, simple, central, quiet. **Surface:** grassy/gravel. 🅿 01/01-31/12.
**Distance:** 🚶500m ⊗500m.

### 🅿S Soajo 29C3
M530. **GPS:** n41,87197 w8,2633.⬆

5 🛏free 🚰 ♻ChWCfree. **Location:** Rural, simple. **Surface:** metalled.
🅿 01/01-31/12.
**Distance:** 🚶100m 🏊100m.
**Remarks:** Parking near school.

### 🅿S Torre de Moncorvo 30D1
**Moncorvão. GPS:** n41,18083 w7,04167.⬆
9 🛏free 🚰 ♻Chfree 🗑. **Surface:** metalled. 🅿 01/01-31/12.
**Distance:** 🚶1,5KM.
**Remarks:** At sports park.

### 🍇 Valadares-SP do Sul 30C1
**Cooperativa Mimos**, Largo do Cruzeiro 1. **GPS:** n40,75704 w8,19997.⬆

3 🛏free. **Location:** Simple. **Surface:** grassy. 🅿 01/01-31/12.
**Distance:** 🚶on the spot.
**Remarks:** Portugal Tradicional.

---

### ⛺S Valpaços 29D3
**Do Rabaçal**, Rua Gago Coutinho. **GPS:** n41,63222 w7,24778.
🛏€ 15-19 🚰 ♻Ch 🧹WC🗑. 🅿 01/01-31/12.

### 🅿S Venda Nova 29C3
Av. Prof. Dr. Anibal Cavaco Silva, Rio Tinto. **GPS:** n41,17530 w8,54159.
3 🛏free 🚰 ♻Chfree. **Location:** Urban. **Surface:** asphalted.
🅿 01/01-31/12.
**Distance:** 🚶on the spot 🚇metro F.

### 🅿S Viana do Castelo 29B3
**Praia do Cabadelo**, Av. do Cabedelo. **GPS:** n41,68388 w8,83333.⬆
20 🛏free 🚰 ♻Chfree. **Surface:** metalled. 🅿 01/01-31/12.
**Distance:** 🚶400m 🏊on the spot ⊗100m.

### 🅿 Viana do Castelo 29B3
Rua de Lima. **GPS:** n41,69534 w8,81875.⬆

15 🛏free.
**Location:** Urban, simple. **Surface:** metalled/sand.
**Distance:** 🚶centre 700m.
**Remarks:** Large parking along the Limia river.

**Tourist information Viana do Castelo:**
⛪ Campo do Costelo. Market. 🅿 Fri.
🎉 Romaria da Nossa Senhora da Agonia.
Procession with Gigantes (giants). 🅿 3rd week Aug.

### ⛺S Vila Chã 29B3
**Sol de Vila Chã**, Rua do Sol, Facho. **GPS:** n41,29825 w8,73263.⬆
🛏 🚰 ♻Ch. 🅿 01/01-31/12.
**Distance:** 🏊300m 🚶10m 🚉on the spot 🚏100m.

### 🅿 Vila do Conde 29B3
Av. Júlio Graça. **GPS:** n41,34476 w8,74541.⬆

20 🛏free. **Location:** Urban, simple, central, noisy. **Surface:** metalled.
🅿 01/01-31/12.
**Distance:** 🚶400m 🏊150m 🚏150m ⊗200m 🚉400m.
**Remarks:** Along the Este river.

### 🅿 Vila do Conde 29B3
Av. Marques de Sa Bandiera. **GPS:** n41,34270 w8,74587.⬆

20 🛏free. **Location:** Urban, simple, central. **Surface:** gravel/sand.
🅿 01/01-31/12.
**Distance:** 🚶500m 🚏on the spot ⊗200m 🚉400m.
**Remarks:** Parking at sea.

### 🅿S Vila Nova de Cerveira 29B2
Av. dos Pescadores. **GPS:** n41,93823 w8,74685.⬆

# Beira

4 ⬜free 🚰🔧Ch📶free. **Location:** Rural, simple, quiet.
**Surface:** asphalted. ⏹ 01/01-31/12.
**Distance:** 🚶historical center 150m 🏖river-beach.
**Remarks:** Near Minho river and public pool park.

### Vila Nova de Cerveira    29B2
**Braseirão do Minho**, Rua da Tomada. **GPS:** n41,97490 w8,68456.⬆️
20 ⬜free 🚰🔧Ch🔧. **Location:** Rural, simple, quiet.
**Surface:** asphalted. ⏹ 01/01-31/12.
**Distance:** ⊗on the spot.
**Remarks:** Check in at restaurant.

### Vila Nova de Foz Côa    30D1
Rua Engenheiro Eugénio Nobre. **GPS:** n41,08028 w7,14806.⬆️➡️
10 ⬜free 🔧Chfree. **Location:** Rural, simple, quiet.
**Surface:** metalled. ⏹ 01/01-31/12.
**Distance:** 🚶500m ⊗500m.

### Vila Nova de Gaia    29B3
**Madalena**, Rua de Cerro, Praia de Madalena. **GPS:** n41,10750 w8,65556.
⬜€ 18,30-28,80 🚰🔧Ch🔧WC🔧.
⏹ 01/01-31/12.
**Remarks:** Service only € 3,15-5,40.
**Tourist information Vila Nova de Gaia:**
ℹ️ City of the port wine, at the left bank of the river Douro, Port houses can be visited daily.

### Vila Real 🌿    29C3
**Municipal de Vila Real**, Rua Dr. Manuel Cardona, Quinta da Carreira.
**GPS:** n41,30333 w7,73667.
⬜€ 13,20-20,90 🚰🔧Ch🔧WC🔧.
⏹ 01/01-31/12.
**Tourist information Vila Real:**
👁 Solar de Mateus. Baroque country house, 18th century, known from label of the Matheus wine.

### Vilartão    29D3
**Parque de campismo o tempo parou**, Rua da Bandera.
**GPS:** n41,76445 w7,21006.
12 ⬜€ 10 🚰🔧Ch🔧WC🔧. **Location:** Rural. **Surface:** unpaved.
⏹ 01/01-31/12.
**Remarks:** Swimming pool.

### Vinhais    29D3
**GPS:** n41,83381 w7,00271.⬆️

6 ⬜free 🚰🔧Chfree. **Location:** Urban, simple. **Surface:** gravel.
⏹ 01/01-31/12.
**Distance:** 🚶200m ⊗100m.
**Remarks:** Nearby swimming pool, tuesday market.

### Vizela    29C3
**B&B Casa do Monte Vizela**, Rua São Paio 872.
**GPS:** n41,38248 w8,26458.⬆️

3 ⬜€ 26 🚰🔧WC🔧 🔧€ 3/3 📶. 🏠 **Location:** Comfortable.
**Surface:** metalled. ⏹ 01/01/2019-31/12/2019.
**Distance:** 🚶1km 🚴2,5km 🚲1km 🚌1km ⚓150m 🏖300m.
**Remarks:** Breakfest-service.

### Aldeia da Ponte    30D1
Caminho do Freguil. **GPS:** n40,41092 w6,87159. 🔲

4 ⬜free 🚰🔧Chfree. **Location:** Rural, simple. **Surface:** metalled.
⏹ 01/01-31/12.
**Distance:** 🚶300m.
**Remarks:** Near old Roman bridge.

### Almeida 🌿    30D1
Rua da Guerreira. **GPS:** n40,72753 w6,90402.

⬜free 🔧WC. **Surface:** metalled. ⏹ 01/01-31/12.
**Remarks:** At fort-castle.

### Anadia    30B1
Rua Seabras de Castro. **GPS:** n40,44056 w8,4375. 🔲

⬜free. **Surface:** asphalted.
**Distance:** ⊗100m ⚐100m.

### Aveiro 🌿🏖    30B1
**Parque de S João**, Canal São Roque. **GPS:** n40,64328 w8,65859.⬆️

10 ⬜free 🚰free. **Surface:** grasstiles. ⏹ 01/01-31/12.
**Distance:** 🚶200m 🚴25m ⊗200m ⚐200m.
**Remarks:** Parking at the Canal and A25.
**Tourist information Aveiro:**
Ⓜ Ecomuseu da Troncalhada, Canal das Pirâmides. Salt-making.
⏹ summer.
Ⓜ Museu de Aveiro, Av. Sta. Joana Princesa. Collection baroque art.
⏹ Tue-Su 10-17.30h.

### Barril de Alva 🏖👣    30C1
EM517-1. **GPS:** n40,28611 w7,96167.⬆️

50 ⬜free 🚰🔧Ch🔧€ 1 WCfree. **Location:** Rural, simple, quiet.
**Surface:** unpaved. ⏹ 01/01-31/12.
**Distance:** 🚶500m 🏖river-beach ⊗on the spot.

### Barriosa    30C1
**Poço da Broca. GPS:** n40,29366 w7,75376.

⬜free. **Location:** Rural. ⏹ 01/01-31/12.
**Distance:** 🏊on the spot ⊗on the spot.
**Remarks:** Portugal Tradicional, restaurant and regional products for sale.

### Belmonte    30C1
**Parque de Santiago**, N345. **GPS:** n40,36380 w7,3411.⬆️

4 ⬜free 🚰🔧ChWC🔧free. **Location:** Urban, simple, noisy.
**Surface:** metalled. ⏹ 01/01-31/12.
**Distance:** 🚶500m ⊗on the spot ⚐150m ⊗on the spot.

### Castelo Bom 🏰    30D1
Avenida Santa Maria, N16. **GPS:** n40,61261 w6,83398.🔲

3 ⬜free. **Location:** Rural, simple. **Surface:** metalled.
⏹ 01/01-31/12.
**Distance:** 🚶on the spot.
**Remarks:** Less suitable for motorhomes >6,5m, typical village nearby spanish border.

### Castelo Branco 🌿    30C2
**Municipal de Castel Branco**, N18. **GPS:** n39,85815 w7,49351.
⬜🚰🔧ChWC🔧. ⏹ 02/01-15/11.
**Tourist information Castelo Branco:**
⛰ Castelo. Ruins of castle of the Templars.
🌳 Alameda da Liberdade. ⏹ Mo.

### Castelo de Paiva    29C3
R. Emidio Navarro. **GPS:** n41,03955 w8,27406.🔲

50 ⬜free 🚰🔧ChWCfree. **Location:** Simple, central, quiet.
**Surface:** metalled. ⏹ 01/01-31/12 🔲 Sa.
**Distance:** 🚶on the spot ⊗on the spot ⚐on the spot.
**Remarks:** Market square, market Saturday.

### Castelo Mendo 🌿🏰    30D1
P5, N16. **GPS:** n40,59444 w6,94833.🔲

3△free ⊨free. **Location:** Rural, simple, quiet. **Surface:** grassy/sand. ◻ 01/01-31/12.
**Distance:** ⌂on the spot ⚓6,8km.
**Remarks:** Beautiful view.

### Castelo Rodrigo 🌿 30D1
**GPS:** n40,87778 w6,96611.

△free. **Surface:** sand. ◻ 01/01-31/12.
**Remarks:** At the entrance of fort.

### Celorico da Beira 30C1
Maximiano António da Costa. **GPS:** n40,63944 w7,38909.⬆
2△free ⊨Ch⚒free. **Location:** Simple, central, quiet.
**Surface:** metalled. ◻ 01/01-31/12.
**Distance:** ⌂on the spot.

### Celorico da Beira 30C1
**GPS:** n40,63389 w7,40472.

10△. **Location:** Isolated, quiet. **Surface:** metalled.
◻ 01/01-31/12.
**Distance:** ⌂2km.
**Remarks:** Parking sports park.

### Cinfães 29C3
**GPS:** n41,07167 w8,08719.⬆.

10△free. **Surface:** metalled. ◻ 01/01-31/12.
**Distance:** ⌂100m ⊗100m ⚓100m.

### Coimbra 🌿🍽 30B1
**Parque do Choupalinho**, Av. Inês de Castro.
**GPS:** n40,19970 w8,42905.⬆.

20△free ⊨Ch free. **Surface:** metalled. ◻ 01/01-31/12.
**Remarks:** Max. 24h.

---

**Tourist information Coimbra:**
👁 Portugal dos Pequeninos. Miniature Portugal.
◻ 9-19h.

### Coimbrão 30B2
**Praia do Pedrógão. GPS:** n39,91500 w8,95.
△ € 15,60-18,20 ⊨Ch ⚒WC . ◻ 16/02-15/12.
**Distance:** ⌂50m ⊗on the spot ⚓on the spot ⚓10m.

### Condeixa 30B1
Av. Bombeiros Voluntarios de Condeixa. **GPS:** n40,11291 w8,49336.⬆➡.

6△free ⊨Ch free. **Surface:** asphalted. ◻ 01/01-31/12.
**Distance:** ⌂500m ⊗on the spot ⚓300m.
**Remarks:** Max. 48h, market Friday-morning.

### Condeixa 30B1
**Conímbriga**, Praça da Republiça Condeixa.
**GPS:** n40,09895 w8,4894.⬆.

5△free. **Location:** Simple. **Surface:** grassy/metalled.
◻ 01/01-31/12.
**Remarks:** Parking next to archaeological site.

### Estarreja 🍽 30B1
R. Dr. Antonio Madureira. **GPS:** n40,75417 w8,56611.⬆➡.

6△ € 2/48h ⊨Ch ⚒included. **Location:** Urban, simple, central.
**Surface:** metalled. ◻ 01/01-31/12.
**Distance:** ⌂on the spot ⊗on the spot ⚓on the spot.
**Remarks:** Check in Cafe Piscina, Ag. Seguros Rebelo, tuesday market 100m.

### Estarreja 🍽 30B1
Ribeira do Maurao. **GPS:** n40,81328 w8,61588.⬆➡.

6△free € 2 ⊨Ch. **Location:** Rural, simple, isolated, quiet.
**Surface:** metalled. ◻ 01/01-31/12.
**Distance:** ⌂on the spot 🏃on the spot.
**Remarks:** Nature reserve.

### Figueira da Foz ⚓ 30B1
Av. de Espanha. **GPS:** n40,14856 w8,86791.⬆.

---

30△ € 0,80/h, overnight stay free ⊨ChWC. 🚐
**Surface:** asphalted. ◻ 01/01-31/12.
**Distance:** ⌂on the spot ⌂on the spot ⊗100m.

### Figueira da Foz ⚓ 30B1
R.do Cabedelo. **GPS:** n40,14403 w8,86395.

10△. **Location:** Simple. **Surface:** sand. ◻ 01/01-31/12.
**Distance:** ⌂on the spot ⊗on the spot.
**Remarks:** Beach parking.

### Figueira da Foz ⚓ 30B1
**Jumbo**, Av. Francisco de Sá Carneiro. **GPS:** n40,16413 w8,8413.⬆.
⊨Ch free. ◻ 01/01-31/12.
**Remarks:** At petrol station.

### Fratel 30C2
Vila Velha de Ródão. **GPS:** n39,63250 w7,74694.⬆➡.

10△free ⊨Ch free. **Surface:** grassy. ◻ 01/01-31/12.
**Distance:** ⌂200m ⚓1km ⊗300m ⚓300m.

### Fundão 30C2
**Quinta do Convento. GPS:** n40,13276 w7,51205.
150△ € 13-17 ⊨Ch ⚒WC 🔌📶. ◻ 01/01-31/12.

### Furadouro 30B1
**Praia do Furadouro. GPS:** n40,87645 w8,67381.⬆.

30△free WC50m. **Location:** Rural, simple, quiet. **Surface:** asphalted.
◻ 01/01-31/12.
**Distance:** ⌂on the spot ⊗300m ⚓300m.
**Remarks:** Beach parking.

### Guarda 🌿🍽 30C1
**Parque Pólis**, Rua da Direcção Geral de Viação.
**GPS:** n40,54935 w7,24282.⬆➡.

PT

20 🗄free 🚰🔌Chfree. **Location:** Urban, simple, central.
**Surface:** metalled. 🅾 01/01-31/12.
**Distance:** 🚶historical centre 4km 🚲2,4km 🚗700m.
**Remarks:** Recreation park.

### △S Guarda 🥾🍽 30C1
**Rossio de Valhelhas**. GPS: n40,40333 w7,40528.
🗄🚰🔌Ch🔌. 🅾 01/05-30/09.
**Distance:** 🏊50m ⊗300m 🛒150m 🚗100m.
**Tourist information Guarda:**
🏛🍴 Medieval city.

### △S Idanha-a-Nova 30C2
**Municipal de Idanha-a-Nova**, Albufeira da Barragem Marechel
Carmona. **GPS:** n39,95056 w7,18722.
🔌€ 11-14 🔌Ch 🔌 WC🔌. 🅾 01/01-31/12.
**Distance:** 🏊50m ⊗on the spot 🛒on the spot 🚗8km.
**Remarks:** Service only € 2,60-4,40.

### 🅿 Idanha-a-Velha 30C2
N332. **GPS:** n39,99767 w7,14353.
🗄. **Surface:** metalled. 🅾 01/01-31/12.
**Tourist information Idanha-a-Velha:**
⌂ Archeological tour.

### 🅿 Ilhavo 🏖 30B1
Av. Infante Dom Henrique, Praia da Barra. **GPS:** n40,64375 w8,74456.⬆.

30 🗄free. **Surface:** metalled. 🅾 01/01-31/12.
**Distance:** 🚶300m 🏊300m.

### 🅿 Ilhavo 🏖 30B1
Costa Nova do Prado. **GPS:** n40,61222 w8,74917.⬆.

7 🗄free. **Surface:** metalled. 🅾 01/01-31/12.
**Distance:** 🚶on the spot 🏊on the spot ⊗on the spot 🛒on the spot.
**Remarks:** Beach parking.

### S Ilhavo 🏖 30B1
Av Ns.da Saude. **GPS:** n40,61417 w8,75222.⬆.
🚰ChWC. 🅾 01/01-31/12.
**Tourist information Ilhavo:**
Ⓜ Museu Histórico da Vista Alegre, Fábrica de Porcelanas da Vista
Alegre. Collection of porcelain. 🅾 Tue-Fri 9-18h, Sa-Su 9-12.30h, 14-17h.
Ⓜ Museu Marítimo de Ílhavo, Av. Dr. Rocha Madahil. Shipping mu-
seum. 🅾 Tue-Fri 10-12.30h, 14.30-18h, Sa-Su 14.30-17.30h.

### 🅿S Lorvão 30C1
Rua do Malhao. **GPS:** n40,25896 w8,31468.⬆➡.

10 🗄free 🚰🔌Chfree. **Location:** Central, quiet. **Surface:** metalled.
🅾 01/01-31/12.
**Distance:** 🚶on the spot.

### 🅿S Lousã 30C2
**VW Holiday**, Estrada da Telhada. **GPS:** n40,11877 w8,2536.⬆.

---

5 🗄voluntary contribution 🔌€ 2/day WC🔌.
**Location:** Rural, quiet. **Surface:** grassy. 🅾 01/01-31/12.
**Distance:** ⊗800m 🛒500m.

### △S Mira 🏖 30B1
**Praia de Mira**. **GPS:** n40,44472 w8,79806.
🗄🚰🔌ChWC🔌🔌. 🅾 16/01-15/11.
**Remarks:** Service only € 3,15-5,40.

### 🅿S Miranda do Corvo 🏔 30B2
Rua Porto Mourisco. **GPS:** n40,08803 w8,33232.⬆➡.

8 🗄free 🚰🔌Chfree. **Location:** Rural. **Surface:** asphalted.
🅾 01/01-31/12.
**Distance:** 🚶700m.

### 🅿S Oleiros 30C2
R. Dr. Barata Relvas. **GPS:** n39,92056 w7,91389.⬆.
🗄free 🚰🔌Chfree. **Surface:** metalled. 🅾 01/01-31/12.

### 🅿S Pardilhó 🥾🏖 30B1
**Parque de Merendas**, R. Joaquim Maria Resende.
**GPS:** n40,80111 w8,63472.⬆➡.

15 🗄€ 2/48h 🚰🔌Ch 🔌included. **Location:** Rural, comfortable,
isolated, quiet. **Surface:** metalled. 🅾 01/01-31/12.
**Distance:** 🚶600m 🏊on the spot 🛒on the spot.
**Remarks:** Max. 48h, check in at bar (service).

### 🅿S Penacova 30C1
Bairro de Carrazedos. **GPS:** n40,26722 w8,28306.⬆➡.

10 🗄free 🚰🔌ChWCfree. **Location:** Rural, simple, quiet.
**Surface:** metalled. 🅾 01/01-31/12.
**Distance:** 🚶400m 🚲3km 🏊800m ⊗400m.

### 🅿S Penamacor 🏔 30C2
**Lazer de Benquerença**, Benquerença. **GPS:** n40,22938 w7,22136.⬆.

---

10 🗄free 🚰🔌Chfree. **Location:** Rural, simple, quiet.
**Surface:** gravel/sand. 🅾 01/01-31/12.
**Distance:** 🚶2km 🏊on the spot.

### 🅿 Pinhel 30D1
**GPS:** n40,77360 w7,06206.

🗄. **Location:** Simple, central. **Surface:** metalled.
🅾 01/01-31/12.
**Distance:** ⊗on the spot 🛒on the spot.
**Remarks:** At townhall.

### 🅿S Praia de Mira 🏖 30B1
Praia da Mira. **GPS:** n40,45800 w8,8025.

6 🗄 🚰free. **Location:** Simple. **Surface:** metalled.
🅾 01/01-31/12.
**Distance:** 🚶on the spot.
**Remarks:** Beach parking.

### 🅿 Praia de Mira 🏖 30B1
**GPS:** n40,44620 w8,80447.

20 🗄free. **Surface:** sand.
**Distance:** 🚶500m 🏊100m 🛒1km.
**Remarks:** Beach parking.

### 🅿S Praia de Quiaos 🏖 30B1
Praia de Quiaos. **GPS:** n40,22034 w8,89116.

15 🗄 🚰free. **Location:** Simple. **Surface:** metalled.
🅾 01/01-31/12.
**Remarks:** Beach parking.

### 🅿S Sabugal 30D1
Rua do Cemitério. **GPS:** n40,34843 w7,08653.⬆➡.

**PT**

6 ⊠free ⚡🔌Chfree. **Location:** Simple. **Surface:** metalled.
🅾 01/01-31/12.
**Distance:** 🚶500m ⊗400m.
**Remarks:** At cemetery.

### 🅿️S Sangalhos 30B1
R. Mercado 150. **GPS:** n40,48639 w8,47528. ⬆➡.

20 ⊠free ⚡🔌Chfree. **Location:** Simple. **Surface:** metalled.
🅾 01/01-31/12.
**Remarks:** At sports centre.

### △S Santa Ovaia 30C1
**Ponte das Três Entradas**, Avô. **GPS:** n40,30667 w7,87139.
⊠€ 13-14,50 ⚡🚰 WC🔌⊙🔊. **Surface:** grassy.
🅾 01/01-31/12.
**Distance:** ⚓10m 🚶on the spot ⊗on the spot 🍴on the spot
�Ⅰ10m.

### 🍴S São João da Pesqueira 29C3
**Restaurant Carocha**, N222. **GPS:** n41,15120 w7,42378.
50 ⊠free ⚡🔌Chfree.
**Location:** Isolated. **Surface:** unpaved. 🅾 01/01-31/12.
**Distance:** 🚶1km ⊗on the spot.
**Remarks:** Next to restaurant and Port wine cellar Cave Cadão.

### ♨S Sao Joao de Areias 30C1
**Terra de Iguanas**, Estrada principal 76, Vila Dianteira.
**GPS:** n40,39045 w8,08574. ⬆.

4 ⊠€ 10 ⚡🔌Ch 🚰 WC🔌⊙🔊included. **Location:** Rural,
comfortable, quiet. **Surface:** sand. 🅾 01/01-31/12.
**Distance:** 🚶2km 🚲1km ⊗1,2km 🍴2km 🚏400m 🚌2km 🚶on
the spot.
**Remarks:** Max. 3 nights, swimming pool incl., vegetables and fruit
from the garden.

### ♨S São Pedro do Sul 🏔 30C1
**Termas São Pedro do Sul**, N46. **GPS:** n40,74056 w8,08639. ⬆➡.

6 ⊠free ⚡🔌Chfree. **Location:** Simple. **Surface:** asphalted.
🅾 01/01-31/12.
**Distance:** 🚶1km.
**Remarks:** Max. 48h.

### 🅿️S Sertã 🌿 30C2
R. Amaro Vicente Martins. **GPS:** n39,79729 w8,09588. ⬆.

4 ⊠free ⚡🔌Chfree. **Location:** Simple. **Surface:** asphalted.
🅾 01/01-31/12.
**Distance:** 🚶500m ⊗3km 🍴50m.
**Remarks:** At sports park.

### 🅿️S Sertã 🌿 30C2
**Palácio da Justiça**, R. Baden Powell. **GPS:** n39,80028 w8,09944. ⬆.

⊠free. **Location:** Simple. **Surface:** gravel/sand.
🅾 01/01-23/12.
**Distance:** 🚶100m 🚲3km ⊗50m 🍴100m.

### ♨S Sertã 🌿 30C2
**Albergue do Bonjardim**, Quinta da Portela, Nesperal.
**GPS:** n39,81306 w8,16278.

6 ⊠€6 ⚡🔌Ch 🚰(4x)€ 4 WC🔌⊙€ 5 🔊included.
**Location:** Rural, luxurious, isolated. **Surface:** grassy/gravel.
🅾 01/04-01/11.
**Distance:** 🚶500m 🚲2km ⊗2,5km 🍴500m 🚌50m 🚶on the spot.
**Remarks:** Sauna, steam bath and covered pool € 7,50, breakfast € 7,50,
wine tasting.

### 🅿️S Tabua 30C1
**Piscina**. **GPS:** n40,36306 w8,03.

3 ⊠free. **Surface:** metalled. 🅾 01/01-31/12.

### 🅿️S Tabua 30C1
Rua Aurora Jesus Goncalves. **GPS:** n40,36419 w8,02469.

10 ⊠free. **Surface:** metalled. 🅾 01/01-31/12.
**Distance:** 🍴on the spot.
**Remarks:** At supermarket.

### 🅿️S Trancoso 30C1
**Parque Sportivo**. **GPS:** n40,77160 w7,35621.

3 ⊠free. **Surface:** metalled.

### 🅿️S Trancoso 30C1
Av. Heróis de São Marcos. **GPS:** n40,77583 w7,35056.

10 ⊠. **Surface:** metalled.
**Distance:** ⊗50m.
**Remarks:** Note: Friday market day.

### 🅿️S Vagos 30B1
**Praia da Vagueira**. **GPS:** n40,54944 w8,77056. ⬆.
20 ⊠€ 7,50, 01/10-31/05 € 5 ⚡🔌Ch 🚰€ 2 🔌€ 0,50. **Surface:** sand.
🅾 01/01-31/12.
**Distance:** ⚓on the spot.
**Remarks:** Service passerby € 2,50.

### △S Vagos 30B1
**Vagueira**, Gafanha da Boa Hora. **GPS:** n40,55806 w8,74528.
⊠€ 16-25 ⚡🔌Ch 🚰 WC🔌. 🅾 01/01-31/12.
**Distance:** ⚓1km ⊗on the spot 🍴1km 🚌500m.
**Remarks:** Service only € 2,60-4,40.

### 🅿️S Vagueira 30B1
Rua Arménio, Praia da Vagueira. **GPS:** n40,56506 w8,76697. ⬆➡.

20 ⊠free. **Surface:** metalled. 🅾 01/01-31/12.
**Distance:** 🚶200m ⚓sandy beach 50m.
**Remarks:** Beach parking.

### 🅿️S Vila Nova de Oliveirinha 🌿⛲🍽🏕🌳 30C1
**Quinta do Tapadinho**, Rua dos Brandões. **GPS:** n40,36520 w7,92195.

3 ⊠€ 13,50 ⚡🔌Ch 🚰(5x)€ 3,50/24h,10Amp WC🔌⊙€ 5
🔊included. ⛲🍽 **Location:** Rural, comfortable, quiet.
**Surface:** grassy/sand. 🅾 01/01-31/12.
**Distance:** 🚶8km 🚲6km ⊗8km 🍴8km 🚌1km 🚶on the spot.
**Remarks:** Bread-service, swimming pool.

### 🅿️S Vilar Formoso 30D1
**Zaza**, Avenida das Tilia's, N332. **GPS:** n40,61528 w6,83833. ⬆.

PT

2 ⯐€ 5/24h ⯐€ 2 ⬡Ch ⯐(12x)€ 3/day. ⯐
**Location:** Simple. **Surface:** asphalted/gravel. ◻ 01/01-31/12.
**Distance:** ⯐500m ⯐baker on site.

| ⬛S | Viseu ⯐⯐ | 30C1 |

Av. Europa. **GPS:** n40,66533 w7,91681.⯐.
3 ⯐free ⯐⬡Chfree.
**Location:** Simple, central, quiet. **Surface:** asphalted.
◻ 01/01-31/12.
**Distance:** ⯐on the spot ⯐6km.

**Tourist information Viseu:**
⬛ Centre of Vinho do Dão.
⬛ Museu municipal, Castro Daire. Etnographical collection.

# Portugal Central and Lisbon

| ⬛S | A-dos-Cunhados | 30A2 |

R. Monsenhor José Fialho. **GPS:** n39,15222 w9,30083.⯐.

10 ⯐free ⯐⬡Chfree. **Location:** Simple, quiet. **Surface:** asphalted.
◻ 01/01-31/12.
**Distance:** ⯐100m ⯐6km ⯐beach 7km ⯐200m.

| ⬛S | Abrantes | 30B2 |

**Aquapolis**, São Joao. **GPS:** n39,45489 w8,18977.⯐.

10 ⯐free ⯐⬡Chfree. **Location:** Rural, simple. **Surface:** metalled.
◻ 01/01-31/12.
**Distance:** ⯐3km ⯐4,7km ⯐on the spot ⯐100m ⯐6km.
**Remarks:** Service 100m.

| ⬛S | Abrantes | 30B2 |

**Aquapolis**, São Joao. **GPS:** n39,45347 w8,19072.⯐.

2 ⯐free ⯐⬡Ch⯐free. **Surface:** metalled.
**Distance:** ⯐3km ⯐4,8km ⯐Sandy beach.
**Remarks:** Along the Tagus river.

| ⬛ | Abrantes | 30B2 |

Largo do Pralvo. **GPS:** n39,44956 w8,18968.⯐.

10 ⯐free. **Location:** Urban, simple, quiet. **Surface:** metalled.
◻ 01/01-31/12.
**Distance:** ⯐1km ⯐6,5km ⯐on the spot ⯐1km ⯐1km.
**Remarks:** Along the Tagus river.

| ⬛ | Abrantes | 30B2 |

**Parque Urbano de São Lourenço**, São Vincente.
**GPS:** n39,47530 w8,21541.⯐.

10 ⯐free. **Location:** Rural, simple, quiet. **Surface:** grassy/gravel.
◻ 01/01-31/12.
**Distance:** ⯐centre 2,4km ⯐4,4km ⯐50m ⯐1,8km.
**Remarks:** Max. 48h.

**Tourist information Abrantes:**
⯐ Posto de Turismo, Esplanada 1º de Maio, www.cm-abrantes.pt. City with historical centre.

| ⬛S | Alenquer | 30B3 |

**Alenquer camping**, Casal das Pedras. **GPS:** n39,05917 w9,02833.
4 ⯐€ 13-15,50 ⯐⬡Ch ⯐€ 2,50 ⯐. ◻ 01/01-31/12.
**Distance:** ⯐on the spot ⯐on the spot.

| ⬛ | Almada ⯐ | 30A3 |

**Costa de Caparicia**, R. Eduardo Luis. **GPS:** n38,56691 w9,19308.

10 ⯐free. **Location:** Simple. **Surface:** sand.
**Distance:** ⯐on the spot ⯐on the spot ⯐on the spot.

| ⬛ | Almourol | 30B2 |

**Castelo de Almourol**, Praia do Ribatejo. **GPS:** n39,46295 w8,38297.

10 ⯐free. **Location:** Simple. **Surface:** metalled.
◻ 01/01-31/12.
**Distance:** ⯐2km ⯐4km ⯐on the spot ⯐2km.
**Remarks:** On the banks of the Tejo river, parking castle.

| ⬛ | Arruda dos Vinhos | 30B3 |

**Casal da Pevide. GPS:** n38,99861 w9,08417.⯐.

3 ⯐free. **Location:** Urban, simple, noisy. **Surface:** asphalted.
◻ 01/01-31/12.
**Distance:** ⯐2km ⯐on the spot ⯐on the spot.
**Remarks:** Parking Intermarché.

| ⬛ | Assafora | 30A3 |

Estr. de São Julião. **GPS:** n38,91167 w9,41138.⯐.

4 ⯐free. **Location:** Rural, simple, quiet. **Surface:** metalled.
◻ 01/01-31/12.
**Distance:** ⯐800m ⯐on the spot.
**Remarks:** Picnic area.

| ⬛S | Baleal ⯐ | 30A2 |

Estrada do Baleal. **GPS:** n39,37240 w9,33702.⯐.

30 ⯐free ⯐free. **Location:** Rural, simple, quiet. **Surface:** asphalted.
◻ 01/01-31/12.
**Distance:** ⯐2km ⯐on the spot ⯐on the spot ⯐on the spot ⯐2km ⯐on the spot.
**Remarks:** Parking next to bar restaurant in village square, not recommended at the weekend.

| ⬛S | Batalha ⯐⯐ | 30B2 |

**Parque Cónego M. Simões Inácio**, Rua Cerca Conventual.
**GPS:** n39,66134 w8,82516.⯐.

15 ⯐free ⯐⬡Ch ⯐⯐free. **Location:** Urban, simple, quiet.
**Surface:** asphalted. ◻ 01/01-31/12 ⬛ Mo.
**Distance:** ⯐100m ⯐on the spot.
**Remarks:** At football ground/tennis, max. 48h.

| ⬛S | Bombarral | 30B2 |

R. Júlio César Machado. **GPS:** n39,27157 w9,16346.⯐.
⯐free ⯐⬡Chfree. **Location:** Simple, quiet. **Surface:** asphalted.
◻ 01/01-31/12.
**Distance:** ⯐750m ⯐300m ⯐750m.
**Remarks:** Nearby sports complex.

| ⬛ | Cabo Espichel ⯐⯐ | 30A3 |

**P Cabo Espichel. GPS:** n38,42031 w9,21353.

🚐free. **Location:** Rural, isolated, quiet. **Surface:** sand.
📷 01/01-31/12.
**Distance:** 🚌Sesimbra 13km ⛵At the sea.
**Remarks:** Beautiful view.

### Cascais 30A3
**Cap Raso. GPS:** n38,71134 w9,48498.

🚐free. **Location:** Rural, simple, quiet. **Surface:** sand.
📷 01/01-31/12.
**Distance:** 🚌6km ⊗on the spot 🛒6km 🚶on the spot 🏃on the spot.

### Cascais 30A3
**Ponta da Gate,** Estrada do Guincho. **GPS:** n38,72769 w9,47555. ⬆.

10 🚐free. **Location:** Simple, quiet. **Surface:** gravel.
📷 01/01-31/12.
**Distance:** 🚌8km ⛵on the spot ⛽on the spot ⊗on the spot 🛒8km
🚶on the spot.

### Cascais 30A3
**Guincho,** Areia, Guincho. **GPS:** n38,72167 w9,46639.
🚐 € 19,50-42,30 ⛽Ch🚿WC📷. 📷 01/01-31/12.
**Remarks:** Service only € 3,15-5,40.

### Castanheira de Pera 30C2
**Variante à Nacional 236. GPS:** n40,00847 w8,20467. ⬆.
20 🚐free ⛽Ch. 📷 01/01-31/12.
**Distance:** 🚌900m ⊗700m 🛒900m.
**Remarks:** Service 700m GPS N40,002978 W-8,206685.

### Cerradas 30A3
Estrada À-dos-Serrados. **GPS:** n38,91798 w9,38292. ⬆.

20 🚐free ⛽Chfree. **Location:** Rural, simple, quiet.
**Surface:** gravel. 📷 01/01-31/12.
**Distance:** 🚌on the spot ⛵5km ⊗on the spot.
**Remarks:** At gymnasium, max. 48h.

### Constância 30B2
Estrada National. **GPS:** n39,47670 w8,34365. ➡.

---

**Distance:** 🚌1km ⛵3,2km ⊗100m 🛒1km.
**Remarks:** May 12-13 festivities.

### Corroios 30A3
Avenida Amélia Rey Colaço. **GPS:** n38,63155 w9,1562. ⬆.
20 🚐free ⛽Chfree. **Location:** Urban. **Surface:** metalled.
📷 01/01-31/12.
**Distance:** 🚌on the spot ⊗1km 🛒800m 🚇station 1,5km.

### Coruche 30B3
**Area De Autocaravanas,** Rua 5 de Outubro.
**GPS:** n38,96139 w8,51944. ⬆.

100 🚐free ⛽Chfree. **Surface:** metalled.
📷 01/01-31/12 ◉ last Sa of the month.
**Distance:** 🛒on the spot 🚇on the spot.

### Costa da Caparica 30A3
**Caravanismo da Costa da Caparica,** Santo António da Caparica.
**GPS:** n38,65389 w9,23833.
🚐 € 18,89-36 ⛽Ch🚿WC📷. 📷 01/01-31/12.
**Distance:** ⛵500m ⊗on the spot 🛒on the spot 🚇100m.
**Remarks:** Service only € 3,15-5,40.

### Dois Portos 30A3
R. da Azenha. **GPS:** n39,03689 w9,18098. ⬆.

4 🚐free ⛽free. **Location:** Simple, quiet. **Surface:** metalled.
📷 01/01-31/12.
**Distance:** 🚌on the spot.

### Ericeira 30A3
**Municipal de Mil Regos,** N247, Casal do Moinho Velho.
**GPS:** n38,97778 w9,41861.
🚐 € 13-17 ⛽Ch🚿WC📷. 📷 01/01-31/12.
**Remarks:** Service in front of campsite.

**Tourist information Ericeira:**
⛲ Aldeia Museu de José Franco, Sobreiro. Miniature village. 📷 9-19h.
🎫 free.

### Fátima 30B2
Rua de Sao Vicente de Paulo. **GPS:** n39,63389 w8,67111. ⬆.

6 🚐free ⛽WCfree. **Location:** Urban, simple, quiet.
**Surface:** asphalted. 📷 01/01-31/12.

---

### Foz do Arelho 30B2
Av. do Mar. **GPS:** n39,42828 w9,22055. ⬆➡.

120 🚐€ 4 ⛽Ch🚿€ 2 WC📷€ 1 📶included.🚿
**Location:** Rural, simple, quiet. **Surface:** unpaved.
📷 01/01-31/12.
**Distance:** 🚌1km ⛵50m ⛽50m ⊗🛒1,5km 🚶on the spot
🏃on the spot.
**Remarks:** Beach parking.

### Lisbon 30A3
**Municipal de Lisboa-Monsanto,** Monsanto,
Estrada da Circunvalação. **GPS:** n38,72472 w9,20805.
🚐€ 24-30 ⛽Ch🚿WC📷. 
📷 01/01-31/12.
**Distance:** ⛵3km ⛽on the spot 🛒on the spot
🚇50m.

**Tourist information Lisbon:**
ℹ Lisboa Card. Card gives entrance to museums, public transport,
available at: Rua Jardim do Regedor 50 (10-18), Mosteiros do Jeronimos,
Museu dos Coches. 🎫 € 18,50/24h, € 31,50/48h, € 39/72h.
🎪 Market. 📷 Tue, Sa.
🎪 32 Covered markets, most important market: Av. 24 de Julho.
📷 6-14h ◉ Su.
🎪 Campo de Sta Clara. Flea market.
🎪 Rua de São Bento. Antiques market.
　　Arena near metro Campo Pequeno. 📷 01/05-30/09 Thu.
　　Feira Popular. Fairground, opposite the Entrecampos metro.
📷 01/05-30/09.
　　Oceanário, Parque das Nações. Aquarium. 📷 10-19h. 🎫 € 15,30.
🛍 Chiado. Elegant shopping district. ◉ elevator 7-24h.

### Mação 30C2
**Campo de Feiras,** Av. Vicente Mirrado. **GPS:** n39,55723 w7,99303. ⬆.

10 🚐free ⛽Ch🚿WCfree. **Location:** Urban, simple.
**Surface:** metalled. 📷 01/01-31/12.
**Distance:** 🚌500m ⊗6km ⊗500m 🛒500m.
**Remarks:** Max. 48h.

### Mafra 30A3
R. Arieiro. **GPS:** n38,95451 w9,33555. ⬆.

4 🚐free ⛽€ 1/80liter 🚿Ch. **Location:** Urban, simple, central, quiet.
**Surface:** asphalted. 📷 01/01-31/12.
**Distance:** 🚌1,5km ⛵2km 🛒on the spot.
**Remarks:** Max. 24h.

**Tourist information Mafra:**
❌ Posto do turismo, Palácio Nacional de Mafra - Torreão Sul, Terreiro D.
João V, www.cm-mafra.pt/turismo.
　　Parque Tapada Nacional, Portão do Codeçal. Safaripark. 📷 10-19h.

### Marinha Grande 30B2
**Praia Velha,** São Pedro de Moel. **GPS:** n39,76974 w9,02752. ⬆.

10 🅿free. **Location:** Rural, simple, quiet. **Surface:** metalled.
⬛ 01/01-31/12.
**Distance:** 🏖5km 🏔100m 🚉100m ⊗50m.
**Remarks:** Beach parking.

⚠️Ⓢ **Marinha Grande** 〰️ **30B2**
**ORBITUR São Pedro de Moel**, São Pedro de Moel.
**GPS:** n39,75806 w9,02583.
🚰🚽Ch🕳️. **Location:** Rural. **Surface:** grassy/sand.
⬛ 01/01-31/12.
**Remarks:** Service only € 3,15-5,40.

Ⓢ **Mira de Aire** 🌿 **30B2**
Av. Mota Pinto. **GPS:** n39,54240 w8,70347.⬆️.

12 🅿free 🚽Ch🕳️free. **Location:** Simple, quiet.
**Surface:** asphalted. ⬛ 01/01-31/12.
**Distance:** 🏖500m ⊗500m.
**Remarks:** Steep entrance road, caves 1,8km.

Ⓢ **Montalvo** **30B2**
**Horta Do Casinha**, Rua Circulação de Montalvinho.
**GPS:** n39,48550 w8,30765.⬆️.
6 🅿free 🚽Ch🕳️. **Location:** Rural, simple, quiet.
**Surface:** grassy. ⬛ 16/12-01/01.
**Distance:** 🏖on the spot.
**Remarks:** Narrow entrance.

**Montijo** **30B3**
**GPS:** n38,70286 w8,97665.

50 🅿free. **Surface:** metalled. ⬛ 01/01-31/12.
**Distance:** 🏖800m 🏔200m ⊗100m 🍽200m 🛒2km.
**Remarks:** Parking at ferry-boat to Lisbon.

Ⓢ **Nazaré** 🏖〰️ **30B2**
Rua Nossa Senhora da Vitória. **GPS:** n39,64696 w9,06936.⬆️.

20 🅿€ 10 🚽€ 3 Ch. **Location:** Rural, isolated, quiet.
**Surface:** metalled. ⬛ 01/01-31/12.
**Distance:** 🏔on the spot ⊗on the spot.
**Remarks:** Max. 24h.

**Nazaré** 🏖〰️ **30B2**
Avenue do Municipio. **GPS:** n39,59741 w9,0696.⬆️.

---

20 🅿free. **Location:** Urban. **Surface:** asphalted. ⬛ 01/01-31/12.
**Distance:** 🏖200m 🏔250m 🚉250m ⊗250m 🍽750m.

Ⓢ **Obidos** 🌿 **30B2**
**Casa Azzurra**, Rua do's Cumeiras 10. **GPS:** n39,39250 w9,16947.⬆️.

14 🅿€ 8 🚽€ 2/100liter Ch 🕳️€ 2/night WC🚽€ 1 ⬛€ 4/4
🕳️€ 1/day. **Location:** Rural, comfortable, isolated.
**Surface:** grassy/metalled. ⬛ 01/01-31/12.
**Distance:** 🏖4km 🚉on the spot ⊗4km 🍽4km 🚴on the spot 🚶on the spot.
**Remarks:** Service passerby € 5, barbecue place, swimming pool available.

Ⓢ **Obidos** 🌿 **30B2**
Rue do Ginasio. **GPS:** n39,35628 w9,15672.⬆️.

20 🅿€ 6/24h Ch🕳️included. **Location:** Rural, simple, quiet.
**Surface:** gravel/sand. ⬛ 01/01-31/12.
**Distance:** 🏖500m 🏔1km ⊗500m 🍽500m.
**Remarks:** Service passerby € 2.

Ⓢ **Odrinhas** **30A3**
**Parque Autocaravanas Odrinhas**, Rua do Castanhal 9.
**GPS:** n38,88312 w9,37491.⬆️➡️.

40 🅿€ 8 🚽Ch🕳️€ 3,50/day WC🚽€ 1 ⬛€ 4,50 🕳️included.
**Location:** Rural, comfortable, quiet. **Surface:** gravel/sand.
⬛ 01/01-31/12.
**Distance:** 🏖on the spot ⊗on the spot 🍽on the spot 🚉on the spot.
**Remarks:** Repair possibilities motorhome, swimming pool available.

Ⓢ **Outeiro da Cabeça** 🌿 **30B2**
Rua do Pavilhão Gimnodesportivo. **GPS:** n39,19306 w9,1825.⬆️.

5 🅿free 🚽Chfree. **Location:** Rural, simple, isolated.
**Surface:** gravel. ⬛ 01/01-31/12.

---

**Distance:** 🏖300m 🏔2,5km ⊗300m 🍽300m.

**Palmela** 🌿🏖 **30B3**
Av. dos Cavaleiros de Santiago e Espada. **GPS:** n38,56664 w8,90032.🚶.

6 🅿free. **Location:** Urban, simple, quiet. **Surface:** sand.
⬛ 01/01-31/12.
**Remarks:** Parking at castle.

Ⓢ **Pataias** **30B2**
**Intermarché. GPS:** n39,66041 w9,0151.⬆️.

10 🅿free 🚽Chfree ⬛ 🕳️. **Location:** Rural, simple, quiet.
**Surface:** asphalted. ⬛ 01/01-31/12.
**Distance:** 🏖200m ⊗on the spot 🍽on the spot ⬛on the spot.
**Remarks:** Parking Intermarché, max. 48h.

Ⓢ **Peniche** **30A2**
**ASA Peniche - Motorhome Park**, Rua da Liberdade 12.
**GPS:** n39,36622 w9,37917.⬆️.

60 🅿€ 5 🚽Ch🕳️ (60x)€ 3,4Amp, € 5 6Amp WC€ 0,50 🚽€ 1
⬛€ 4,50/2,50 🕳️included. 🚲 **Location:** Urban, luxurious, central.
**Surface:** asphalted. ⬛ 01/01-31/12.
**Distance:** 🏖centre 300m 🏔3,1km 🍽600m 🚉200m ⊗300m
🍽200m 🛒1,2km 🚴1,6km 🚶1,6km.
**Remarks:** Arrival <19.30h, bread-service, video surveillance, picnic and barbecue place.

**Peniche** **30A2**
Av. Porto De Pesca. **GPS:** n39,35852 w9,37752.⬆️🚶.

50 🅿free. **Location:** Urban, simple, central. **Surface:** asphalted
⬛ 01/01-31/12.
**Distance:** 🏖500m 🏔900m 🏊1km ⊗500m 🍽500m ⬛500m.
**Remarks:** At fire-station and marina.

**Peniche** **30A2**
**Farol do Cabo Cavoeiro**, Caminho do Farol.
**GPS:** n39,35989 w9,4082.🚶.

5 🅿free. **Location:** Rural, simple, isolated. **Surface:** metalled.
⬛ 01/01-31/12.
**Distance:** 🏔5km 🏊300m ⊗on the spot 🍽3km.
**Remarks:** At lighthouse.

**Peniche** **30A2**
R. de Liberdade. **GPS:** n39,36577 w9,37417.🚶.

PT

10 ⌛free. **Location:** Rural, simple. **Surface:** sand.
☐ 01/01-31/12.
**Distance:** 🚶1,7km 🏊50m ⊗200m 🛒200m.

**S** | **Peniche** | 30A2

**Peniche Praia**, Estrada Marginal Norte. **GPS:** n39,36959 w9,392.⬆.

23 ⌛€ 9, Jul/Aug € 15 🚰🔌Ch🔧WC☐included ☐€ 6,20/4,50 📶. **Location:** Rural, comfortable, quiet. **Surface:** grassy.
☐ 01/01-31/12.
**Distance:** 🚶1,5km 🏊At the sea 🎣on the spot ⊗on the spot 🛒1,5km 🏪on the spot 🚌1,5km.

**Tourist information Peniche:**
Ⓜ✕ Fortaleza de Peniche. Bathing resort.
Ⓜ✕ Posto de Turismo, Rua Alexandre Herculano, www.cm-peniche.pt. Bathing resort.

**Póvoa e Meadas** 🏕🌊 | 30C2

**Barragem de Nisa**, M1007. **GPS:** n39,48394 w7,5476.⬆.

10 ⌛free 🚰🔌Ch WC☐free. **Location:** Rural, simple, isolated, quiet.
**Surface:** grasstiles/grassy. ☐ 01/01-31/12.
**Distance:** 🚶4km ⊗4km.

🍇**S** | **Póvoa e Meadas** 🏕🌊 | 30C2

**Casa Carita**, Rua de Santo Antonio. **GPS:** n39,50532 w7,53139.⬆.

4 ⌛€ 5 🚰🔌🔧included. 🛁 **Location:** Rural, simple, isolated.
**Surface:** grassy/sand. ☐ 01/01-31/12.
**Distance:** 🚶500m ⊗500m.

🍇**S** | **Praia de Santa Cruz** 🌊 | 30A2

**GPS:** n39,14418 w9,37482.⬆.

50 ⌛free 🚰WCfree. **Location:** Rural, simple. **Surface:** asphalted.
☐ 01/01-31/12.
**Distance:** 🚶300m 🏊20m ⊗on the spot 🛒300m.

---

**Remarks:** Parking at the beach or near the cliffs.

**S** | **Ribamar** 🌊 | 30A3

R. do Cacho Longo, São Lourenço. **GPS:** n39,01120 w9,42078.⬆.

10 ⌛free. **Location:** Rural, simple, isolated. **Surface:** gravel.
☐ 01/01-31/12.
**Distance:** 🚶2km 🏊Sandy beach ⊗on the spot 🛒6km.

🍇**S** | **Salir do Porto** | 30B2

**Casa da Duna**, Rua Dom Fernando 50. **GPS:** n39,49939 w9,1517.⬆.
50 ⌛€ 5 🚰🔌Ch 🔧€ 2 WC☐€ 5 📶. **Location:** Rural, simple, noisy.
**Surface:** grassy. ☐ 01/05-31/12.
**Distance:** 🚶1,5km 🏊200m ⊗on the spot 🚲on the spot 🚶on the spot.

🍇**S** | **Salvaterra de Magos** | 30B3

**Parque d'Escaroupim**, RN 118. **GPS:** n39,02378 w8,79209.
16 ⌛free 🚰🔌Ch🔧. **Location:** Urban. **Surface:** metalled.
☐ 01/01-31/12.
**Distance:** 🚶on the spot ⊗500m 🛒200m.

🍇**S** | **São Mamede** | 30B2

Rua de São Martinho. **GPS:** n39,62238 w8,71536.⬆.

10 ⌛free 🚰🔌Ch free. **Location:** Urban, simple, quiet.
**Surface:** metalled.
**Distance:** 🚶on the spot ⊗200m 🛒200m.

**São Martinho do Porto** 🏖🌊 | 30B2

Av. Marigal. **GPS:** n39,50176 w9,14132.⬆.

15 ⌛free. **Location:** Rural, simple, noisy. **Surface:** metalled.
☐ 01/01-31/12.
**Distance:** 🚶1,4km ⛵5,5km 🏊sandy beach 50m 🎣50m ⊗850m 🚶on the spot.

🍇**S** | **Setúbal** | 30B3

**Ecoparque Do Outão**, N10-4. **GPS:** n38,50328 w8,92858.⬆.
60 ⌛€ 6, 2 pers.incl 🚰🔌Chincluded WC. **Location:** Rural.
**Surface:** grassy. ☐ 01/01-31/12.
**Distance:** 🚶4km 🏊on the spot ⊗3km.
**Remarks:** Monitored parking.

**Tourist information Setúbal:**
ℹ Posto Municipal de Turismo, Rua de Santa Maria, Apartado 80, www.mun-setubal.pt. Bathing resort.
☀ Festas Bocageanas. Local celebration. ☐ 15/09.

🍇**S** | **Sintra** 🌿🏛 | 30A3

Avenida Conde Sucena, São Pedro de Penaferrim.
**GPS:** n38,78883 w9,37473.⬆.

---

10 ⌛€ 7 🚰🔌Chincluded. 🛁 **Location:** Rural, simple, quiet.
**Surface:** asphalted. ☐ 01/01-31/12.
**Distance:** 🚶2km ⊗on the spot.
**Remarks:** At footballstadium.

**S** | **Tomar** | 30B2

Av. Gen. Bernardo Faria. **GPS:** n39,59972 w8,41306.

⌛free WC. **Location:** Simple. **Surface:** gravel/sand.
☐ 01/01-31/12.
**Distance:** 🚶200m ⊗200m 🛒300m.
**Remarks:** Nearby railway station.

🍇**S** | **Tomar** | 30B2

**Parque de Campismo de Tomar**, Rua Centro Republicano.
**GPS:** n39,60698 w8,41021.
50 ⌛free 🚰🔌Chfree WC☐.
**Location:** Urban. **Surface:** grassy/sand.
☐ 01/01-31/12.
**Distance:** 🚶on the spot 🚲on the spot 🚶on the spot.

**Tourist information Tomar:**
Ⓜ Sinagoga de Tomar, Museu Luso-Hebraico, Rua Dr. Joaquim Jacinto, 75. Synagogue and Jewish Portuguese history.
ℹ free.
✝ Convento de Cristo. Fortified monastery.
☀ Festa dos Tabuleiros. ☐ Whitsuntide.
Barragem de Castelo de Bode. Artificial lake, 15km east of the city.

△**S** | **Torres Vedras** | 30A2

**Municipal da Praia de Santa Cruz. GPS:** n39,13444 w9,37472.
⌛🚰🔌Ch 🔧WC☐. ☐ 01/01-31/12.

🍇**S** | **Turcifal** 🌿 | 30A3

Largo Brigadeiro França Borges. **GPS:** n39,04288 w9,26581.⬆➡.

5 ⌛free 🚰🔌Chfree. **Location:** Urban, central, quiet.
**Surface:** metalled. ☐ 01/01-31/12.
**Distance:** 🚶on the spot ⊗on the spot 🛒on the spot.

🍇**S** | **Vermoil** | 30B2

R. Vale de Fojo, Pombal. **GPS:** n39,85080 w8,66125.⬆.

5 ⌛free 🚰🔌Chfree. **Surface:** gravel/sand. ☐ 01/01-31/12.
**Distance:** 🚶200m ⊗300m 🛒300m.
**Remarks:** At cemetery.

## Vila Nova da Barquinha | 30B2

**Parque De Pernoita**, Largo do Primeiro de Dezembro.
**GPS:** n39,45763 w8,43297.

10 free ChWC free.
**Location:** Rural, simple, quiet. **Surface:** metalled.
**Distance:** 100m on the spot on the spot on the spot
150m on the spot on the spot on the spot.
**Remarks:** Along the Tagus river.

# Alentejo

## Alcácer do Sal | 30B3

**Barragem Pego do Altar**, Alcácer do Sal > N253 > Montemoro o Novo
> N380. **GPS:** n38,42055 w8,39384.

15 free ChWC free. **Location:** Rural. **Surface:** sand.
01/01-31/12.
**Distance:** Alcácer do Sal 13km on the spot 100m.

## Alcácer do Sal | 30B3

Rua do Cabo da Vila. **GPS:** n38,36903 w8,50276.
free.
01/01-31/12.
**Distance:** Old city 600m 5,6km 400m.
**Remarks:** Near arena.

**Tourist information Alcácer do Sal:**
Little town on the Rio Sado.

## Almograve | 31B1

Avenida da Praia. **GPS:** n37,65303 w8,80059.

30 free free. **Location:** Simple. **Surface:** grasstiles.
01/01-31/12.
**Distance:** on the spot.
**Remarks:** Beautiful view.

## Almograve | 31B1

**GPS:** n37,64830 w8,805.
10 free. **Surface:** gravel/metalled. 01/01-31/12.
**Distance:** 1,4km on the spot on the spot.
**Remarks:** Seaview.

## Alvito | 31B1

Rua de Tapadinha. **GPS:** n38,25917 w7,99222.
free. **Location:** Rural. **Surface:** metalled. 01/01-31/12.
**Remarks:** At swimming pool, small pitches, picnic area.

## Avis | 30C3

**Municipal Albufeira do Maranhão**, Barragam Albufeira do Maranhão.
**GPS:** n39,05682 w7,91145.
€ 8-12 Ch WC .
**Distance:** on the spot.
**Remarks:** Service only € 1,90.

## Beja | 31B1

**Parque da Cidade**, Rua de Lisboa. **GPS:** n38,02204 w7,87371.

3 free. **Location:** Urban. **Surface:** gravel/metalled.
01/01-31/12.
**Distance:** 900m 100m 250m 250m 100m on the spot
on the spot.
**Tourist information Beja:**
Villa Romana de Pisões. Roman ruins.
Festa de S. Lourenço e Sta. Maria. Annual fair. 2nd week Aug.

## Campo Maior | 30C3

**Barragem do Caia. GPS:** n39,00445 w7,14018.

. 01/01-31/12.

## Castelo de Vide | 30C2

**Estr. de São Vincente. GPS:** n39,41028 w7,44917.

free. **Location:** Rural, quiet. **Surface:** metalled.
01/01-31/12.
**Distance:** 1km 300m.
**Remarks:** At stadium.

## Castelo de Vide | 30C2

**Rua Luís de Camões. GPS:** n39,41583 w7,45778.

free. **Location:** Urban, simple, central.
**Surface:** concrete.
01/01-31/12.
**Remarks:** Near city wall.

**Tourist information Castelo de Vide:**
www.cm-castelo-vide.pt. Historical centre with medieval citadel.

## Cavaleiro | 31B1

**Cabo Sardano. GPS:** n37,59762 w8,81722.

30 free. **Location:** Simple. **Surface:** sand. 01/01-31/12.
**Distance:** on the spot.
**Remarks:** At lighthouse.

## Comporta | 30B3

**GPS:** n38,37849 w8,78544.

40 free Chfree. **Location:** Urban, simple, quiet.
**Surface:** grassy/sand. 01/01-31/12.
**Distance:** 250m 1km 250m 250m.
**Remarks:** Nearby police station.

## Comporta | 30B3

R. da Escola. **GPS:** n38,38308 w8,78712.

± 6 free. **Location:** Urban, simple, quiet. **Surface:** gravel/sand.
01/01-31/12.
**Distance:** 250m 1km 300m 500m.
**Remarks:** Near church.

## Elvas | 30C3

**Intermarché**, Rue Paco Bandera. **GPS:** n38,87458 w7,18429.

15 free Chfree. **Surface:** asphalted. 01/01-31/12.
**Distance:** historical centre 1,7km on the spot.
**Remarks:** At petrol station and supermarket, max. 48h.

## Elvas | 30C3

**GPS:** n38,87819 w7,17273.

.
**Surface:** metalled.
**Remarks:** Parking at aqueduct.

**Tourist information Elvas:**
Fortified city.

## Estrela | 31C1

**Aldeia de Estrela**, Cais. **GPS:** n38,26637 w7,38906.
5 free. **Location:** Rural, simple, quiet. **Surface:** gravel/sand.
01/01-31/12.
**Distance:** on the spot 300m.

## Estremoz | 30C3

Rossio Marquês de Pombal. **GPS:** n38,84320 w7,58672.

10 ⛵free 📶. **Location:** Urban, simple, central. **Surface:** metalled.
⭕ 01/01-31/12.
**Distance:** ♿on the spot ⊗50m ⚷50m.
**Tourist information Estremoz:**
⛺ Market. ⭕ Sa.

### S — Evora 〰️⛲ — 30C3
Av. Sanches de Miranda. **GPS:** n38,56325 w7,91672.⬆️.
2 ⛵free 🚰 ⚙Ch. **Surface:** asphalted. ⭕ 01/01-31/12.
**Distance:** ♿1,5km ⊗500m ⚷500m.

### Evora 〰️⛲ — 30C3
**GPS:** n38,57529 w7,90519.⬆️.

⛵free. **Location:** Urban, simple, noisy. **Surface:** gravel/metalled.
⭕ 01/01-31/12.
**Distance:** ♿1km ⊗500m ⚷500m.
**Remarks:** Parking university, illuminated.

### Evora 〰️⛲ — 30C3
Avenida Condas De Vilalva. **GPS:** n38,57592 w7,91491.⬆️.

⛵. **Location:** Urban, noisy. **Surface:** metalled.
⭕ 01/01-31/12.
**Distance:** ♿1km.

### Evora 〰️⛲ — 30C3
Lago da Porta de Avis. **GPS:** n38,57672 w7,91096.⬆️.

⛵free. **Location:** Urban, simple, noisy. **Surface:** gravel/metalled.
⭕ 01/01-31/12.
**Distance:** ♿1,5km.
**Remarks:** Parking at aqueduct.

### S — Evora 〰️⛲ — 30C3
Intermarche. **GPS:** n38,55188 w7,91345.⬆️.
⛵free 🚰 ⚙Ch. **Location:** Noisy.
**Surface:** asphalted.
⭕ 01/01-31/12.
**Distance:** ⚷on the spot.
**Tourist information Evora:**
ℹ️ Posto de Turismo, Praça do Geraldo, www.cm-evora.pt. City with historical centre.

---

⛪ Igreja de S. Francisco, Capela dos Ossos. Chapel of the bones.
⭕ 8-18h ◉ 12-14h.
⛺ ⭕ Tue.

### S — Ferreira do Alentejo — 31B1
**GPS:** n38,05675 w8,11955.

⛵free 🚰. **Surface:** asphalted. ⭕ 01/01-31/12.
**Distance:** ♿500m ⊗100m ⚷1km ⚷1,5km.
**Remarks:** Parking sports park.

### S — Grândola — 31B1
Parque de Grândola. **GPS:** n38,18525 w8,564.⬆️➡️.

7 ⛵free 🚰⚙Ch. **Location:** Urban, simple, central.
**Surface:** asphalted. ⭕ 01/01-31/12.
**Distance:** ♿1km 🚲7,4km ⊗600m ⚷500m 🚌1,4km.
**Remarks:** At sports grounds.

### S — Lousal — 31B1
Rua 25 Abril. **GPS:** n38,03591 w8,42908.⬆️➡️.

6 ⛵free 🚰⚙Chfree. **Surface:** gravel. ⭕ 01/01-31/12.
**Distance:** 🚲15km ⊗250m ⚷400m bakery ⚷on the spot.
**Remarks:** At the site of the old mines of Lousal.

### S — Luz — 31C1
R. de Mourão. **GPS:** n38,34297 w7,37395.⬆️➡️.

⛵free 🚰⚙Chfree. **Location:** Rural, simple, quiet.
**Surface:** metalled. ⭕ 01/01-31/12.
**Distance:** ⊗250m.

### S — Marvão 〰️⛲ — 30C2
N359-6. **GPS:** n39,39434 w7,3736.⬆️.

12 ⛵free 🚰⚙Chfree. **Location:** Rural, simple, quiet.
**Surface:** grassy/gravel. ⭕ 01/01-31/12.
**Distance:** ♿on the spot ⊗500m.

---

### Melides — 31B1
Praia de Melides. **GPS:** n38,12822 w8,78863.

⛵. **Surface:** metalled. ⭕ 01/01-31/12.
**Distance:** ♿Melides 6,2km ⚖Sandy beach ⊗on the spot.

### Mértola — 31C1
N122/IC27. **GPS:** n37,64250 w7,65833.

10 ⛵free. ⭕ 01/01-31/12.
**Distance:** ⊗200m ⚷200m.

### Mértola — 31C1
Rua dos Bombeiros Voluntários. **GPS:** n37,64110 w7,66352.
10 ⛵free.
**Surface:** gravel/sand.
⭕ 01/01-31/12.
**Distance:** ♿200m ⊗200m.
**Remarks:** At fire-station.
**Tourist information Mértola:**
⛪ Convento São Francisco. Former convent, exposition room and atelier. ⭕ 10-17h.

### S — Messejana — 31B1
**GPS:** n37,83167 w8,24694.⬆️.

50 ⛵€7 🚰€2 ⚙Ch 🚿 WC. **Location:** Rural. **Surface:** metalled.
⭕ 01/01-31/12.
**Distance:** ♿on the spot 🚲10km ⊗400m.
**Remarks:** Barbecue place, swimming pool.

### S — Mina de São Domingos 〰️ — 31C1
Rua Catarina Eufémia. **GPS:** n37,67052 w7,50194.⬆️.
⛵free 🚰€2 ⚙Ch. **Location:** Rural. ⭕ 01/01-31/12.

### Mina de São Domingos 〰️ — 31C1
Praia Fluvial, R265. **GPS:** n37,67228 w7,50418.⬆️.

20 ⛵free. **Location:** Rural, simple, noisy. **Surface:** metalled/sand.
⭕ 01/01-31/12.
**Distance:** ♿750m ⚖50m.
**Remarks:** At recreation area, marked pitches.

### Monsaraz 〰️ — 30C3
**GPS:** n38,44250 w7,38003.⬆️.

PT

±15 ⚠free. **Location:** Quiet. **Surface:** metalled. 🅾 01/01-31/12.
**Distance:** 🚶100m ⊗100m.
**Remarks:** Near city wall, beautiful view.

| S | Monsaraz | 30C3 |

Rue da Fonte. **GPS:** n38,45317 w7,38117.
€ 3,50 Ch.
🅾 Mo-Fr 8-21h, Sa-Su 8-12h.
**Remarks:** Call for the key.
**Tourist information Monsaraz:**
ℹ www.monsaraz.com.pt/.
Small medieval town.

| △ S | Montargil | 30B3 |

Ponte de Sôr. **GPS:** n39,09972 w8,145.
70 ⚠€ 30-37 🔧 Ch WC 🅾 01/01-31/12.
**Remarks:** Service only € 3-5.

| | Montemor-o-Novo | 30B3 |

A6-IP7. **GPS:** n38,61856 w8,07924. ↑.

2 ⚠free. **Location:** Motorway, simple, quiet.
**Surface:** asphalted/metalled. 🅾 01/01-31/12.
**Remarks:** Note: toll ticket is valid for 12 hours!.

| | Odeceixe | 31B1 |

**GPS:** n37,43750 w8,79833.

30 ⚠free. **Location:** Simple. **Surface:** sand. 🅾 01/01-31/12.
**Distance:** 🚶6km 🏖on the spot.
**Remarks:** Beach parking, no camping activities.

| S | Pedrogão do Alentejo | 31C1 |

**Alqueva Camping-Car Park**, Estrada nacional 258, Km38,5.
**GPS:** n38,11705 w7,63571. ↑.

25 ⚠first night € 7,50, € 6 each additional night 🔧Ch.
**Location:** Rural. **Surface:** gravel. 🅾 01/01-31/12.
**Distance:** 🚶1km 🏖1km 🚲1km ⊗1km 🏍on the spot 🏊on the spot ⚓on the spot.

| | Ponte de Sôr | 30C2 |

Avenida da Liberdade. **GPS:** n39,24996 w8,00824. ↑.

---

10 ⚠free. **Location:** Rural, simple, central, noisy. **Surface:** concrete.
🅾 01/01-31/12.
**Distance:** 🚶on the spot ⊗100m 🚰100m.

| S | Porto Covo | 31B1 |

Rua Carlos Tê. **GPS:** n37,85437 w8,78959. ↑→.
30 ⚠€ 3 Ch WC included 🚰 1. **Location:** Urban.
**Surface:** metalled. 🅾 01/01-31/12.
**Distance:** 🚶centre 250m 🏖750m 🚰500m.

| S | Redondo | 30C3 |

R. de Monsaraz. **GPS:** n38,64521 w7,54266. ↑.

50 ⚠free 🔧Ch free. **Location:** Urban, simple, quiet.
**Surface:** gravel/sand. 🅾 01/01-31/12.
**Distance:** 🚶400m ⊗400m 🚰100m.
**Remarks:** Market Saturday.

| | Reguengos de Monsaraz | 30C3 |

N255. **GPS:** n38,43077 w7,53315. ↑.

⚠free. **Surface:** asphalted.
**Remarks:** Parking at swimming pool.

| S | Reguengos de Monsaraz | 30C3 |

Campo 25 de Abril. **GPS:** n38,42150 w7,53534. ↑→.
🔧€ 3,50 Ch.
**Remarks:** Next to fire-station.

| | Santa Clara-e-Velha | 31B1 |

**Barragem de Santa Clara. GPS:** n37,51303 w8,44024.

⚠free. **Location:** Isolated. **Surface:** metalled/sand.
**Distance:** 🏖on the spot.
**Remarks:** Follow 'Pousada/Zona recreativa balnear'.

| S | Santiago do Cacém | 31B1 |

Rua das Nogueiras. **GPS:** n38,01276 w8,69453. ↑→.

---

7 ⚠free 🔧Ch free. **Surface:** grasstiles.
**Distance:** 🚶600m ⊗100m 🚰600m.
**Remarks:** At swimming pool.

| △ S | Santo António das Areias | 30C2 |

**Camping Asseiceira**, Asseiceira. **GPS:** n39,41012 w7,34062.
10 ⚠€ 16-20 🔧Ch WC 📶. **Surface:** grassy.
🅾 01/01-31/10.

| | São Martinho das Amoreiras | 31B1 |

N503. **GPS:** n37,56250 w8,34139.

⚠free. **Location:** Isolated, quiet. **Surface:** metalled.
🅾 01/01-31/12.
**Distance:** 🚶15km.
**Remarks:** At barrage.

| S | Terrugem | 30C3 |

Largo Joaquim Codero Vinaigre. **GPS:** n38,84556 w7,34861. ↑↑.

10 ⚠free 🔧Ch free. **Location:** Rural, simple, quiet.
**Surface:** asphalted.
**Distance:** ⊗300m.

| S | Vila Nova de Santo André | 31B1 |

Intermarché. **GPS:** n38,06521 w8,77951.
5 ⚠free 🔧Ch free 🅾€ 4/2. **Surface:** metalled.
🅾 01/01-23/12.
**Distance:** 🚰on the spot.
**Remarks:** At petrol station.

| S | Vila Nova de Santo André | 31B1 |

**Praia de Santo André**, Lagoa de Santo Andre.
**GPS:** n38,11396 w8,79552.

±15 ⚠free 🔧. **Location:** Simple. **Surface:** sand.
🅾 01/01-23/12.
**Distance:** 🚶5km 🏖on the spot ⊗on the spot ⚓bakery 1km.
**Remarks:** Beach parking.

| S | Vila Viçosa | 30C3 |

Avenida do Alandroal. **GPS:** n38,76988 w7,4154. ↑.

PT

10 ⌁€3 ⛽€2 ♨Ch. ⚓ **Location:** Rural, simple, quiet.
**Surface:** asphalted. ⏰ 01/01-31/12.
**Distance:** 🚶1km ⊗100m.
**Remarks:** At fire-station, monitored parking.

| 🏕 | Vila Viçosa 🌿✈️ | 30C3 |

Largo Gago Coutinho. **GPS:** n38,77661 w7,42034. ✈️.

10 ⌁free. **Location:** Urban, simple, central. **Surface:** sand.
⏰ 01/01-31/12.
**Distance:** 🚶250m ⊗25m 🛒100m.

# Algarve

| 🏕S | Albufeira ✈️🏖 | 31B2 |

**Motorhome Park Açoteias. GPS:** n37,08908 w8,15889.⬆️
50 ⌁€7,50, Jul €10,50, Aug €11,50 ♨Ch ⛽€3,50
WC ⚡€1 🔌 ⎈included. **Location:** Rural, comfortable, quiet.
**Surface:** unpaved. ⏰ 01/01-31/12.
**Distance:** 🚶city centre 10km 🏊650m ⊗200m 🛒200m.

| 🏕S | Albufeira ✈️🏖 | 31B2 |

**Motorhome Park Falésia,** Estrada do Alfarmar.
**GPS:** n37,09036 w8,16044.⬆️

30 ⌁€7-10 ⛽♨Ch ⚓ ⎈€0,50 🔌€4,50/3 ⎈included. 🏠 ✎
**Location:** Rural, comfortable, quiet. **Surface:** gravel.
⏰ 01/01-31/12.
**Distance:** 🚶4km 🏊400m ⊗1km 🛒500m ➤200m.
**Remarks:** Video surveillance.

| 🏕S | Albufeira ✈️🏖 | 31B2 |

**Parque da Galé,** Rua do Barranco Vale Rabelho, Guia.
**GPS:** n37,09347 w8,31125.⬆️

28 ⌁€9 ⛽♨Ch ⚓(28x) ⎈included. **Location:** Comfortable.
**Surface:** unpaved. ⏰ 01/01-31/12.
**Distance:** 🚶600m 🏊1,8km ⊗200m 🛒500m.

| 🏕S | Albufeira | 31B2 |

**Parque da Palmeira,** Rua da Palmeira. **GPS:** n37,09829 w8,24339.⬆️

---

90 ⌁€9 ⛽♨Ch 🚽WC ⎈€4,50 ⎈included.
**Location:** Urban. **Surface:** gravel. ⏰ 01/01-31/12.
**Distance:** 🚶Old city 1,7km ⛽7km 🏊1,5km 🛒800m Lidl 🚌bus terminal 300m.

**Tourist information Albufeira:**
ℹ️ Posto de Turismo, R. 5 de Outubro 4, www.cm-albufeira.pt. ⏰ 10-20h.
ZooMarine, N125. Attractions park, dolphinarium, aquarium.
⏰ 10-20h.

| 🏕S | Alcoutim | 31C2 |

Estrada da Pousada da Juventude. **GPS:** n37,47500 w7,47472.⬆️
⌁free ♨Chfree. **Surface:** sand.
⏰ 01/01-31/12.
**Distance:** 🚶500m ⊗200m.
**Remarks:** Next to 'Centro de Saude'.

**Tourist information Alcoutim:**
ℹ️ Fortified city. ⏰ 9-17.30h.

| 🏕S | Alferce | 31B2 |

**Povo de Baixo,** Rue de Sao Romao. **GPS:** n37,33467 w8,48914.
12 ⌁ ⛽♨Chfree. **Surface:** metalled. ⏰ 01/01-31/12.
**Distance:** 🛒400m.

| 🏕S | Algoz | 31B2 |

**Rancho Belchior. GPS:** n37,19528 w8,32246.⬆️
20 ⌁€8 ⛽♨Ch 🚽WC ⎈€3/1 ⎈included. 🏠
**Location:** Rural. **Surface:** unpaved. ⏰ 01/01-31/12.
**Distance:** 🚶4km ⊗1,6km.
**Remarks:** Discount longer stays.

| 🏕S | Aljezur 🌿🏔 | 31A1 |

Largo do Mercado. **GPS:** n37,31611 w8,80278. ✈️.

10 ⌁free WCfree. **Location:** Simple. **Surface:** metalled.
⏰ 01/01-31/12.
**Distance:** ⊗200m 🛒500m.

| 🏕S | Altura 🏖 | 31C2 |

Av. 24 de Junho. **GPS:** n37,17456 w7,49373.
20 ⌁free. **Location:** Urban. **Surface:** grassy/sand.
⏰ 01/01-31/12.
**Distance:** 🚶600m 🏊1,5km ⊗1km 🛒1km.

| 🏕S | Alvor 🏖 | 31B2 |

**Zona para autocaravanas,** Praia de Alvor.
**GPS:** n37,12482 w8,59506.⬆️

150 ⌁€4,50, June-Sep €7 ⛽♨Chincluded. ⚓
**Location:** Central. **Surface:** sand. ⏰ 01/01-31/12.
**Distance:** 🚶centre 400m 🏊100m ⊗on the spot.

| 🏕S | Ameixial | 31B2 |

**Estacionamento de Autocaravannas. GPS:** n37,36539 w7,97165.⬆️
10 ⌁free ⛽♨Chfree. **Location:** Rural, isolated, quiet.
**Surface:** unpaved. ⏰ 01/01-31/12.

| 🏕S | Budens | 31A2 |

**Figueira Caravan Park,** R. da Fonte. **GPS:** n37,07300 w8,84519.⬆️
35 ⌁€7,50-10 ⛽♨Ch ⎈10Amp ⎈included. **Location:** Rural,

---

comfortable. **Surface:** gravel.
⏰ 01/01-23/12.
**Distance:** 🚶Budens 2,5km 🏊1,8km ⊗250m 🏪Intermarché Budens.
**Remarks:** Discount longer stays.

| 🏕 | Budens | 31A2 |

**Praia Boca do Rio. GPS:** n37,06563 w8,82434. ✈️.

20 ⌁free. **Location:** Simple. **Surface:** sand. ⏰ 01/01-31/12.
**Distance:** 🚶2,2km 🏊50m.
**Remarks:** Forbidden during Summer period.

| 🏕 | Cabo de São Vicente 🌿🏖 | 31A2 |

N268. **GPS:** n37,02361 w8,995.

8 ⌁free. **Location:** Isolated, quiet. **Surface:** metalled.
⏰ 01/01-31/12.
**Distance:** 🚶Sagres 6km.
**Remarks:** Parking at lighthouse, beautiful view.

| 🏕S | Caldas de Monchique 🏔 | 31B2 |

**Parque Rural Autocaravanas Vale da Carrasqueira,** Barracão 190.
**GPS:** n37,27667 w8,54333.⬆️

14 ⌁€12,50-15,50 ⛽♨Ch ⚓WC ⎈included 🔌 ⎈.
**Location:** Rural, comfortable, isolated, quiet. **Surface:** gravel.
⏰ 01/01-31/12.
**Distance:** 🚶9km 🚶on the spot.
**Remarks:** Bread-service, barbecue place, swimming pool.

| 🏕 | Carrapateira 🏖 | 31A2 |

**Praia de Amado. GPS:** n37,19269 w8,90245. ✈️.

30 ⌁free. **Location:** Simple. **Surface:** gravel. ⏰ 01/01-31/12.
**Distance:** 🚶Carrapateira 2km ⊗100m 🚶on the spot.
**Remarks:** Beach parking, no camping activities.

| 🏕 | Carrapateira 🏖 | 31A2 |

**Praia de Bordeira. GPS:** n37,19735 w8,90726. ✈️.

10 ⛺free. **Location:** Simple. **Surface:** metalled.
◯ 01/01-31/12.
**Distance:** Carrapateira 2,5km.
**Remarks:** Parking near the cliffs.

| ⬛S | **Carvoeiro** | 31B2 |

Vale das Gramezines. **GPS:** n37,11205 w8,46701.
10 ⛺€ 4,50-12 ⬛Ch € 2,50 WC € 1 € 3
**Location:** Rural, comfortable, isolated, quiet. **Surface:** unpaved.
◯ 01/01-31/12.
**Distance:** 2km 1km.
**Remarks:** Swimming pool available.

| ⬛ | **Carvoeiro** | 31B2 |

Estr. do Farol. **GPS:** n37,08774 w8,44285.

8 ⛺. **Location:** Isolated. **Surface:** sand. ◯ 01/01-31/12.
**Distance:** 500m on the spot.
**Remarks:** Parking at lighthouse.

| ⬛ | **Carvoeiro** | 31B2 |

Praia Marinha. **GPS:** n37,09026 w8,41254.

⛺free. **Location:** Isolated. **Surface:** unpaved.
◯ 04/01-31/12.
**Distance:** 4km on the spot.
**Remarks:** Beach parking, beautiful view.

| ⬛S | **Castro Marim** | 31C2 |

Av. Dr. José Afonso Gomes. **GPS:** n37,21984 w7,44434.

± 20 ⛺free € 2,50/100liter ⬛Ch.
**Location:** Central, noisy. **Surface:** gravel.
◯ 01/01-31/12 ◯ 2rd Sa of the month.
**Distance:** 1,3km 50m.
**Remarks:** Coins at the shops in the village.

| ⬛S | **Consiguinte** | 31B2 |

**Vilamoura Rustic Motorhome Aire**, 436A, N125, Vale Judeu.
**GPS:** n37,11236 w8,1064.

---

20 ⛺8-12 € 1/50liter ⬛Ch € 0,50/kWh WC € 1 € 5/1
**Location:** Rural, comfortable, quiet. **Surface:** gravel.
◯ 01/01-31/12.
**Distance:** 750m 5km 400m 1,4km 200m on the spot
100m.
**Remarks:** Adults only.

| ⬛S | **Faro** | 31B2 |

**Faro Campervan Park**, Rua Aquilino Ribeiro Lote 2, Montenegro.
**GPS:** n37,02981 w7,97035.

⛺€ 10 ⬛Ch € 4,50/3 included.
**Location:** Rural, comfortable, isolated, quiet. **Surface:** gravel.
◯ 01/01-31/12.

| ⬛ | **Faro** | 31B2 |

**Parking Largo de São Francisco. GPS:** n37,01132 w7,93184.

6 ⛺free. **Surface:** metalled. ◯ 01/01-31/12.
**Distance:** centre 400m 300m.

| ⬛ | **Faro** | 31B2 |

**Parque Ribeirinho de Faro**, Doca de Faro.
**GPS:** n37,02551 w7,94657.

15 ⛺free. **Location:** Urban, simple. **Surface:** metalled.
◯ 01/01-31/12.
**Distance:** 600m.

| ⬛ | **Faro** | 31B2 |

**Lidl**, R. do Bom Joao. **GPS:** n37,01403 w7,91926.
5 ⛺free. **Location:** Simple, noisy. **Surface:** asphalted.
◯ 01/01-31/12.
**Distance:** city centre 1,5km on the spot.

| ⬛S | **Fuseta** | 31B2 |

**Casa Da Avo Nina**, Rua da Ponte Grande. **GPS:** n37,05544 w7,74975.
6 ⛺€ 10 Chincluded. **Location:** Urban. **Surface:** grassy.
◯ 01/01-31/12.
**Distance:** on the spot 300m 650m station 300m.

| ⬛S | **Lagos** | 31B2 |

**Area de servico**, Junto ao Estadio Municipal de Lagos.
**GPS:** n37,11563 w8,678.

---

20 ⛺€ 3, from 4th night € 2,50 € 2/100liter ⬛ChWC free.
**Surface:** gravel. ◯ 01/01-31/12.
**Distance:** city centre 2km 7,3km 2,3km McDonalds 450m.
**Remarks:** Check in and pay at reception stadio, market 1st Saturday
each month.
**Tourist information Lagos:**
Ⓜ Museu Municipal, Rua General Alberto da Silveira. Regional
museum. ◯ 9.30-12.30h, 14-17h ◯ holiday.

| ⬛S | **Manta Rota** | 31C2 |

**Praia de Manta Rota**, Quinta Manta Rota 15.
**GPS:** n37,16513 w7,52096.

80 ⛺€ 4,50 ⬛Ch € 5/12h included.
**Surface:** metalled. ◯ 16/09-30/06.
**Distance:** on the spot 6,5km 100m 100m 500m.

| ⬛S | **Moncarapacho** | 31B2 |

**Route 66. GPS:** n37,08313 w7,76494.
40 ⛺8-12 ⬛Ch WC € 3 included.
**Location:** Rural, comfortable, isolated. **Surface:** gravel/sand.
◯ 01/01-31/12.
**Distance:** 2,5km 3km on the spot.

| ⬛S | **Moncarapacho** | 31B2 |

**Área de Repouso Furnalha**, EM 516. **GPS:** n37,08003 w7,81165.

12 ⛺€ 8-12 ⬛Ch WC € 3. **Location:** Rural, isolated, noisy.
**Surface:** gravel. ◯ 01/01-31/12.
**Distance:** 2km 1,5km.

| ⬛S | **Moncarapacho** | 31B2 |

**Caravanas Algarve**, Sitio da Cabeca. **GPS:** n37,09502 w7,77427.

20 ⛺€ 12 ⬛Ch WC
**Location:** Rural, comfortable, quiet. **Surface:** gravel.
◯ 01/01-31/12.
**Distance:** 1km beach 6km 1km on the spot on the spot.

| ⬛S | **Odeleite** | 31C2 |

**Almada D´Ouro Club-Algarve**, M1063, Alcarias-Odeleite.
**GPS:** n37,33187 w7,46865.

**PT**

10 + 20 ⊠ € 4,50 ⟲ € 2,50 ⌁Ch ⚡ € 2,50 WC ☐ € 5 📶included. ♨
**Location:** Isolated, quiet. **Surface:** gravel. ☐ 01/01-31/12.
**Distance:** 🚶Odeleite 2,3km 🏃on the spot.
**Remarks:** At hunting club, discount longer stays.

### Paderne — 31B2
**Motorhome Friends,** Centieira. GPS: n37,15643 w8,20972. ⬆

21 ⊠ € 5 ⟲ ⌁Ch ⚡ (9x) € 3,50 WC ☐ ☐ € 5 📶included.
**Location:** Rural. **Surface:** grassy/gravel. ☐ 01/11-31/03.
**Distance:** 🚶1km ⛱10km 🏃on the spot.
**Remarks:** Max. 48h, bicycle rental € 5, car rental € 15.

### Paderne — 31B2
Cm 1177 920N. GPS: n37,16801 w8,20897.

12 ⊠free ⟲ ⌁Chfree. **Location:** Isolated, quiet. **Surface:** metalled.
☐ 01/01-31/12.
**Distance:** 🚶1km ⊗1km.

### Pêra — 31B2
**Mikki's Place,** Sitio das Arreias. GPS: n37,12781 w8,32305. ⬆➡

100 ⊠ € 8-11 ⟲ ⌁Ch ⚡ € 2,50/day WC ☐ ☐ on demand
📶included. **Location:** Rural, comfortable, isolated, quiet.
**Surface:** gravel/metalled. ☐ 01/01-31/12.
**Distance:** 🚶2km ⛱3km ⊗on the spot 🛒2km.

### Pereiro — 31C2
**Parque de autocaravanismo do Pereiro,** Pereiro.
GPS: n37,44695 w7,5924. ⬆
16 ⊠free ⟲ ⌁Chfree WC. **Surface:** unpaved.
☐ 01/01-31/12.
**Distance:** 🚶500m 🏃on the spot.
**Remarks:** Baker every morning.

### Quarteira — 31B2
Estrada Fonte Santa, M527-2. GPS: n37,07322 w8,07716. ⬆➡

---

100 ⊠ € 2/24h ⟲ € 2 ⌁Ch ⚡ € 2. ♨
**Surface:** gravel.
☐ 01/01-31/12.
**Distance:** 🚶2km ⛱6,8km ⛱sandy beach 2,5km ⊗50m
🛒150m Lidl �- on the spot.
**Remarks:** Tue 17h-Wed 17h adjacent parking because of Gypsy Market.

### Sagres — 31A2
**Fortaleze de Sagres.** GPS: n37,00523 w8,94545. ⬆

50 ⊠free. **Location:** Rural, simple, quiet. **Surface:** metalled.
☐ 01/01-31/12.
**Distance:** 🚶500m ⛱500m.
**Remarks:** At fort-castle.

### Sagres — 31A2
**Intermarché,** Cercas Velhas. GPS: n37,01466 w8,94135. ⬆
⟲ € 2/100liter ⌁Ch. ☐ 01/01-31/12.

### São Bartolomeu de Messines — 31B2
**Camperstop Messines,** Rua de Pául. GPS: n37,27979 w8,24133. ⬆➡

40 ⊠ € 6,50, 01/07-31/08 € 7,50 ⟲ ⌁ChWC ☐ ☐ € 4/4 📶included.
♨ **Location:** Rural, comfortable, quiet. **Surface:** gravel.
☐ 01/01-31/12.
**Distance:** 🚶6,5km ⛱6,4km ⊗1,2km.
**Remarks:** Shopping service.

### São Bartolomeu de Messines — 31B2
**Redstone Park,** En270 Boicas. GPS: n37,23734 w8,24629. ⬆
15 ⊠ € 7 ⟲ ⚡ included WC ☐ ☐ € 3. **Location:** Rural, simple, isolated,
quiet. **Surface:** grassy/gravel. ☐ 01/01-31/12.
**Distance:** 🚶5km ⊗50m ⛱5,3km.

### São Bartolomeu de Messines — 31B2
Rua António Aleixo. GPS: n37,25514 w8,2847. ⬆

4 ⊠free ⟲ ⌁Chfree. **Location:** Rural. **Surface:** gravel.
☐ 01/01-31/12.
**Distance:** 🚶centre 150m ⛱2,7km.
**Remarks:** Monday regional market.

### Silves — 31B2
**Algarve Motorhome Park Silves,** Estrada Nacional 124.
GPS: n37,18722 w8,45158. ⬆

---

50 ⊠ € 5-8,50/24h ⟲ ⌁Ch ⚡ ☐ 📶included. 🚐 
**Location:** Comfortable, quiet. ☐ 01/01-31/12.
**Distance:** 🚶1km ⊗800m ⛱200m.
**Remarks:** Video surveillance.

### Silves — 31B2
**Club Autocaravana Vacaria,** N124. GPS: n37,21834 w8,36924. ⬆➡

15 ⊠ € 6 ⟲ ⌁Ch ⚡ WC ☐ ☐ € 2 📶included. **Location:** Rural,
comfortable, isolated. **Surface:** gravel/metalled. ☐ 01/01-31/12.
**Distance:** 🚶9km �- 100m.
**Remarks:** Swimming pool.

### Silves — 31B2
**Parque do Castelo,** Rua do Encalhe. GPS: n37,19388 w8,43614. ⬆
40 ⊠first night € 5,50, € 4,50 each additional night, >10m + € 1 ⟲ ⌁
Ch ⚡ € 3/24h,6Amp WC ☐ € 0,50 📶included. 🚐
**Location:** Urban, simple, central. **Surface:** gravel.
☐ 01/09-29/04.
**Distance:** 🚶centre 500m ⊗500m ⛱Lidl 550m �- on the spot.

### Silves — 31B2
**Parque Ribeirinho de Silves.** GPS: n37,18527 w8,44551. ⬆
50 ⊠ € 6 ⟲ € 2 ⌁Ch ⚡ € 3/day ☐ € 0,50 ☐ € 4 🚐
**Location:** Rural. **Surface:** gravel. ☐ 15/09-30/06.
**Distance:** 🚶centre 650m ⊗650m ⛱450m 🚲on the spot
🏃on the spot.

### Silves — 31B2
**Barregem do Arade,** N124-3. GPS: n37,23960 w8,37699.

10 ⊠free.
**Location:** Isolated. **Surface:** sand.
**Distance:** 🚶Silves 10km.

**Tourist information Silves:**
Ⓜ Museu Municipal de Arqueologia. Archeological findings.
☀ Castello. ☐ 9-18h.
🎆 Festival da cerveja. Beer festival. ☐ July.

### Tavira — 31B2
**Parque de Autocaravanes.** GPS: n37,13637 w7,64013. ⬆

20 ⊠ € 9,90 ⟲ ⌁Ch ⚡ WC ☐ ☐ € 2 📶included. ♨
**Location:** Urban, central. **Surface:** grassy/gravel. ☐ 01/09-01/06
☐ summer.
**Distance:** 🚶1km.
**Remarks:** Swimming pool.

**PT**

**Tourist information Tavira:**
♜ Castello. ⏰ Mo-Fri 8-17.30h.

| 🅿 | **Vila do Bispo** | 31A2 |

**Praia da Barriga,** N1265. **GPS:** n37,09970 w8,94445.

⌂free. **Location:** Isolated, quiet. **Surface:** asphalted.
**Distance:** 🚶Vila do Bispo 3,8km ⛱on the spot ⊗on the spot.
**Remarks:** Beach parking.

| △S | **Vila do Bispo** | 31A2 |

**Sagres,** Cerro da Moita. **GPS:** n37,02278 w8,94583.
550 ⌂€ 30-38 🔌Ch ⚡ WC ▯ ⏰ 01/01-31/12.
**Distance:** ⛱2km ⊗on the spot 🍴on the spot 🚌500m.

| 🅿S | **Vila Real de Santo António** 〰 | 31C2 |

**Avenida de República. GPS:** n37,19955 w7,4153.⬆.

70 ⌂€ 4,50 🔌Ch ⚡€ 5/24h 📶included.
**Surface:** metalled/sand. ⏰ 01/01-31/12.
**Distance:** 🚶500m ⊗on the spot.

PT

# ■■■ Romania

Capital: Bucharest
Government: semi presidential republic
Official Language: Romanian
Population: 21,599,000 (2017)
Area: 238,391 km²

## General information
Dialling code: 0040
General emergency: 112
Currency: Leu (RON)
€ 1 = 4,66 RON, 1 RON = € 0,22
£1 = 5,33 RON, 1 RON = £0.19 (October 2018)
Credit card are mostly accepted in the main cities.

## Regulations for overnight stays
Wild camping is allowed with permission from
land owner/manager or local government.

## Additional public holidays 2019
April 28-29 Orhodox Easter
May 1 Labour Day
August 15 Assumption of Mary
November 1 All Saints' Day
November 30 Saint Andrew's Day
December 1 National Holiday

## Time Zone
Winter (Standard Time) GMT+2
Summer (DST) GMT+3

Transylvania
pages: 742-743

Moldavia
page: 743

Banat
page: 743

Wallachia
page: 743

Dobruja
page: 743

Bucharest

RO

# Transylvania

### △S  Aurel Vlaicu  39B2
**Camping Aurel Vlaicu**, Str. Pricipala 155. **GPS**: n45,91424 e23,27938.

⌂€ 12,50 🚰🔌Ch 🚿€ 2,50 WC⌐included.
**Location**: Rural. **Surface**: grassy. ◻ 15/04-30/09.
**Distance**: 🛁250m 🏊250m ⛰100m ⊗300m 🚋250m.

### △S  Baile Felix  39B1
**Camping Apollo. GPS**: n46,99608 e21,98056.
⌂€ 14 🚰🔌Ch 🚿 WC⌐included.
**Location**: Urban. **Surface**: metalled. ◻ 01/01-31/12.
**Distance**: 🛁100m ⊗1km 🚋100m.

### △S  Blǎjel  39C2
**Camping Doua Lumi**, Strada Tudor Vladimirescu 87-89.
**GPS**: n46,21032 e24,32478.

15 ⌂€13 🚰🔌Ch 🚿€ 3 WC⌐🔵included.
**Surface**: grassy. ◻ 01/04-15/10.

---

**Distance**: 🛁10km.

### 🔲S  Borşa  39B1
Strada Victoriei. **GPS**: n47,64958 e24,68838.
10 ⌂€4 🚰🔌Chincluded 🚿€ 2 WC⌐🔵.
**Location**: Rural, simple. **Surface**: grassy. ◻ 01/01-31/12.

### △S  Borşa  39B1
**Camping Borşa Turism**, Strada Pietroasa 9. **GPS**: n47,64769 e24,66889.
4 ⌂€3,50 + € 3,50/pp 🚰🔌Ch 🚿 WC⌐🔵€ 3,50 🔵included.
**Location**: Urban. **Surface**: gravel. ◻ 01/01-31/12.
**Distance**: 🛁1km ⊗1,5km 🚋900m 🏃on the spot.

### △S  Bran  39C2
**Vampire camping**, Soholstr. **GPS**: n45,52787 e25,37183.

⌂€ 15 🚰🔌Ch 🚿€ 3,50 WC⌐included.
**Location**: Rural. **Surface**: grassy. ◻ 01/04-01/11.
**Distance**: ⊗650m.

### △S  Cârţa  39C2
**Camping de Oude Wilg**, Str. Prundului 311. **GPS**: n45,78332 e24,56700.

---

⌂€ 11 🚰🔌€ 2,50 Ch 🚿€ 2,50 WC⌐included 🔵€ 3,50/3,50.
**Location**: Rural. **Surface**: grassy.
**Distance**: 🛁500m 🏊500m 🚴on the spot 🏃on the spot.

### △S  Gârbova  39B2
**Poarta Oilor**, Str. Eminescu 573. **GPS**: n45,85933 e23,72019.
⌂€ 17 🚰🔌Ch 🚿 WC⌐included.
**Location**: Rural. **Surface**: grassy. ◻ 01/05-30/09.

### △S  Gilǎu  39B2
**Camping Eldorado. GPS**: n46,76748 e23,35381.

⌂€ 13 🚰🔌Ch 🚿€ 2,50 WC⌐🔵included.
**Surface**: grassy. ◻ 15/04-15/10.
**Distance**: 🛁15km 🏊50m ⊗750m.

### △S  Miniş  39B2
**Camping Route Roemenië**, Minis 298. **GPS**: n46,13356 e21,59788.

38 ⌂€ 14 🚰€ 1,50 🔌€ 2,50 Ch 🚿€ 2,75 WC⌐included 🔵€ 4.
**Location**: Rural. **Surface**: grassy. ◻ 15/04-15/09.
**Distance**: 🛁1km.

**RO**

## Mureș △S 39C1

**Camping Mustang**, Câmpu Cetății 16/A. **GPS:** n46,66750 e25,00361.
40 € 11,50 Ch WC € 2,50 included.
**Location:** Rural, isolated, quiet. **Surface:** grassy.
01/04-31/10.
**Distance:** 3km 500m 400m.

## Nireș △S 39B1

**Camping Zwaluwnest**, Com. Mica 42A. **GPS:** n47,11918 e23,96788.

€ 11 Ch € 2,50 WC included € 4/4.
**Location:** Rural. **Surface:** grassy. 01/04-15/10.

## Ocna Sibiului ⊟S 39B2

Strada Mihai Viteazul 90. **GPS:** n45,88040 e24,04437.
3 € 5 € 1 € 2. **Surface:** grassy. 01/04-01/10.
**Distance:** 800m.

## Remetea △S 39B2

**Camping Turul**, Bihor 8. **GPS:** n46,73443 e22,34436.

€ 11,50 Ch € 2,50 WC included.
**Location:** Rural. **Surface:** grassy.
**Distance:** 100m 700m 900m.

## Richiș △S 39C2

**Camping La Curtea Richvini. GPS:** n46,09797 e24,48066.
€ 10 Ch € 3 WC included € 4. **Location:** Rural.
**Surface:** grassy.
**Distance:** on the spot.

## Vișeu de Sus ▨S 39B1

**Gara CFF Mocanita**, Strada Cerbului 5. **GPS:** n47,71461 e24,44282.

15 € 9 Ch WC according consumption included.
**Location:** Rural, simple, isolated. **Surface:** metalled.
01/01-31/12.
**Distance:** 1,5km 1km 1,5km.

## Zărnești △S 39C2

**Alpin Ranch**, Strada Pinului 13. **GPS:** n45,57861 e25,34389.

20 € 12 Ch WC included.
**Location:** Rural. **Surface:** grassy.
**Distance:** 800m.

# Moldavia

## Dărmănești ▨S 39C1

**Camperland**, Calea Trotusului 272. **GPS:** n46,40150 e26,48267.

25 € 15 Ch WC € 3,25 included.
**Location:** Rural, comfortable. **Surface:** grassy. 15/04-15/10.
**Distance:** 3km 400m 3,3km.
**Remarks:** Bread-service.

## Fundu Moldovei △S 39C1

**Camping de Vuurplaats**, Strada Principale 130.
**GPS:** n47,53417 e25,41528.

24 € 14,75 Ch € 2,75 WC € 4 included.
**Location:** Rural. **Surface:** grassy. 01/04-01/10.
**Distance:** on the spot on the spot.
**Remarks:** Barbecue place.

# Dobruja

## Jupiter △S 39D2

**Camping Popas Zodiac**, Gala Galaction str 49.
**GPS:** n43,85860 e28,59960.
€ 15,45-18,25 Ch included WC.
**Location:** Urban, comfortable. **Surface:** grassy. 15/04-31/10.
**Distance:** 200m 200m 100m.

## Murighiol ▥S 39D2

**Pension Laguna Albastra**, Strada Lagunei, 1.
**GPS:** n45,03824 e29,18161.
25 € 12 Ch included. **Location:** Simple, quiet.
**Surface:** grassy. 01/04-15/10.
**Distance:** on the spot on the spot on the spot.
**Remarks:** Swimming pool available.

## Navodari △S 39D2

**GPM Camping Holiday. GPS:** n44,27467 e28,61774.

30 € 16 Ch included. 25/04-30/09.
**Distance:** on the spot on the spot on the spot.

# Banat

## Mehadia △S 39B2

**Camping Hercules**, DN6. **GPS:** n44,86918 e22,38774.
5 € 15 Ch WC. **Location:** Rural, noisy.
**Surface:** metalled. 01/01-31/12.
**Distance:** on the spot 500m on the spot on the spot.

# Wallachia

## Bucharest ⊟S 39C2

**Casa Albă**, Padurea Baneasa, pe Aleea Privighetorilor 31 - 35.
**GPS:** n44,51734 e26,09249.

40 RON 80-90 Ch WC. **Location:** Urban, isolated, quiet. **Surface:** asphalted. 01/01-31/12.
**Distance:** 10km 5km 800m on the spot.

## Paclele Mici △S 39C2

**Popasul La Hangar**, 108. **GPS:** n45,34711 e26,70928.
15 € 7 Ch included. **Location:** Rural, simple, isolated, quiet. **Surface:** gravel/sand. 01/01-31/12.
**Distance:** on the spot.

# 🇸🇪 Sweden

Capital: Stockholm
Government: parliamentary constitutional monarchy
Official Language: Swedish
Population: 9,960,487 (2017)
Area: 450,295 km²

## General information
Dialling code: 0046
General emergency: 112
Currency: Swedish Krona (SEK)
€ 1 = SEK 10,45, SEK 10 = € 0,95
£1 = SEK 11,90, SEK 10 = £0.84 (October 2018)
Credit cards are accepted almost everywhere.

## Regulations for overnight stays
In general wild camping is allowed, not in private gardens and agricultural land.

## Additional public holidays 2019
April 19 Good Friday
April 22 Easter Monday
May 1 Labour Day
June 6 National day
June 21-22 Midsummer
December 13 Saint Lucy's Day

## Time Zone
Winter (Standard Time) GMT+1
Summer (DST) GMT+2

| Stockholm | AB | page: 744 |
|---|---|---|
| Västerbotten | AC | page: 744 |
| Norrbotten | BD | pages: 744-745 |
| Uppsala | C | page: 745 |
| Södermanland | D | page: 745 |
| Östergötland | E | pages: 745-746 |
| Jönköping | F | page: 747 |
| Kronoberg | G | page: 747 |
| Kalmar | H | pages: 748-750 |
| Gotland | I | page: 750 |
| Blekinge | K | pages: 750-751 |
| Skåne | M | pages: 751-754 |
| Halland | N | page: 754 |
| Västra Götaland | O | pages: 754-756 |
| Värmland | S | pages: 756-757 |
| Örebro | T | page: 757 |
| Västmanland | U | page: 757 |
| Dalarna | W | page: 757 |
| Gävleborg | X | page: 757 |
| Västernorrland | Y | pages: 757-758 |
| Jämtland | Z | page: 758 |

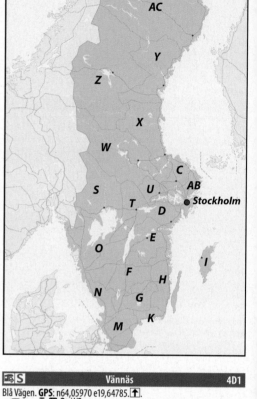

SE

## Stockholm

### Norrtälje    4D3
Nässelgrundet 7. **GPS:** n59,68147 e18,81752.⬆.
3 🏕SEK 200 ✂. **Surface:** grassy.
**Distance:** 🚶Norrtälje 19km ⛵on the spot ⛵on the spot.
**Remarks:** Canoe and boat rental.

### Skarpnäck    5G1
Ställplatsstockholm, Flatens Skogsväg 30.
**GPS:** n59,24822 e18,16159.⬆.
48 🏕SEK 220-270 🚐Ch ✂SEK 40 🪣.🚰 **Location:** Rural, comfortable, isolated. **Surface:** asphalted/grassy. ⬛ 01/01-01/11.
**Distance:** 🚶Stockholm 15km ⊗800m.

### Stockholm    5G1
Långholmens Husbilscamping Stockholm, Skutskepparvägen 1.
**GPS:** n59,32021 e18,03200.⬆.
75 🏕SEK 340 🚐Ch included ✂SEK 30 WC SEK 5 🔲SEK 70/70.
**Location:** Urban. **Surface:** metalled. ⬛ 15/05-28/09.
**Distance:** 🚶2,5km ⛵650m ⊗600m 💧750m 🚗500m 🚲on the spot.

### Stockholm    5G1
Tantolundens Husbilscamping Stockholm, Ringvägen 24.
**GPS:** n59,31241 e18,05299.⬆➡.
14 🏕SEK 250, 19/06-30/08 SEK 280 🚐Ch WC included.
**Location:** Urban. **Surface:** grassy/gravel. ⬛ 01/01-31/12.
**Distance:** 🚶2km ⛵500m ⊗600m.

### Stockholm    5G1
Strandvägen. **GPS:** n59,33124 e18,08595.
🏕SEK 15/h, overnight stay free. **Surface:** asphalted.
**Distance:** 🚶1km ⛵on the spot ⊗300m.
**Remarks:** At the quay.

## Västerbotten

### Byske    4D1
E45. **GPS:** n64,94809 e21,18009.⬆.
🏕free. **Location:** Motorway, simple, isolated, noisy.
**Surface:** asphalted. ⬛ 01/01-31/12.

**Distance:** 🚶1,7km ⊗1,5km 💧1,7km.

### Klimpfjäll 🏔    4C1
Stekenjokk. **GPS:** n65,09030 e14,45897.⛰.
10 🏕free. **Location:** Rural, isolated, quiet. **Surface:** unpaved.
⬛ 01/01-31/12 🔘 With snow.
**Distance:** ⛵on the spot ⛵on the spot 🚶on the spot.
**Remarks:** Beautiful view.

### Marsfjäll    4C1
Trappstegsforsen. **GPS:** n64,95526 e15,46639.⛰.
🏕free. **Location:** Rural, isolated, quiet. **Surface:** gravel.
⬛ 01/+01-31/12.
**Distance:** 🚶7km ⊗on the spot.

### Sävar    4D1
Sävar Rastplats, Skomakarvägen. **GPS:** n63,89191 e20,53027.⬆.

🏕free 🚐Ch free. **Surface:** asphalted.
**Distance:** 🚶2km ✂100m 💧1,7km.

### Skellefteå    4D1
Ställplats Campus, Laboratorgränd. **GPS:** n64,74601 e20,95595.⬆.
10 🏕SEK 100 🚐WC included. 🚰
**Location:** Urban. **Surface:** metalled.
⬛ 20/06-14/08.
**Distance:** 🚶1km ⛵on the spot ⛵on the spot ⊗100m 🚶on the spot.

### Tärnaby    4C1
Joeström. **GPS:** n65,74384 e15,08882.⬆.
🏕SEK 50 🚐. **Location:** Rural. **Surface:** grassy.
**Distance:** 🚶10km ⛵on the spot ⛵on the spot.
**Remarks:** Money in envelope in mail box.

### Vännäs    4D1
Blå Vägen. **GPS:** n64,05970 e19,64785.⬆.
20 🏕free 🚐🚿Ch WC.
**Location:** Rural, isolated. **Surface:** metalled. ⬛ 01/01-31/12.
**Distance:** ⛵150m 💧4km.

### Vilhelmina    4C1
Rastplats Meselefors, E45. **GPS:** n64,43398 e16,78733.⬆.
2 🏕free 🚐🚿Ch free. **Location:** Motorway, isolated, noisy.
**Surface:** asphalted. ⬛ 01/01-31/12.
**Distance:** ⛵on the spot ⛵on the spot.
**Remarks:** Max. 12h, picnic area.

### Vormsele    4C1
Blåviksjöns, Blå vägen. **GPS:** n64,82994 e18,03335.⬆.
🏕free. **Location:** Isolated, quiet. **Surface:** asphalted.
⬛ 01/01-31/12.
**Distance:** 🚶Vormsele 47km ⛵on the spot ⛵on the spot.

## Norrbotten

### Gällivare    3B3
Lappeasuando. **GPS:** n67,49093 e21,12025.

🏕free 🚐Ch WC free. **Location:** Isolated, quiet.
**Surface:** asphalted.
**Distance:** 🚶Gällivare 56km ⛵200m ⛵200m.

### Jävrebyn    4D1
Jävrefyrens väg. **GPS:** n65,14339 e21,50862.⬆.

20 � free ⌐−⌐🔌Ch. **Location:** Rural. **Surface:** grassy/gravel.
⭘ 01/06-30/09.
**Distance:** ⌂on the spot ⌐on the spot 🛒500m.

| 🅂 | Jokkmokk | 3B3 |

**Polcirkeln. GPS:** n66,55058 e19,76375.⬆.
⌐SEK 100 ⌐−⌐🔌Ch ⌐SEK 40 WCincluded. 🛁 **Location:** Rural.
**Surface:** asphalted/grassy.
**Distance:** ⌐2km ⊗on the spot.

| 🅂 | Jokkmokk | 3B3 |

**Laponia Rastplats,** E45. **GPS:** n66,64258 e19,82465.

⌐free. **Surface:** grassy/gravel.
**Distance:** ⌐5km 🛒100m.

| 🅂 | Kiruna | 3B2 |

Lastvägen 9. **GPS:** n67,84603 e20,25687.
⌐€ 24 🔌. **Location:** Urban, simple, central. **Surface:** asphalted.
⭘ 01/01-31/12.
**Distance:** ⊗100m 🛒100m ⌐100m.

| 🅂 | Moskosel | 3B3 |

E45. **GPS:** n65,95231 e19,51979.

⌐free ⌐−⌐🔌Chfree.
**Distance:** ⌐10km ⌂on the spot ⌐on the spot.
**Remarks:** Along river.

| 🅂 | Nikkala | 3C3 |

**Båtklubben Bothnia,** Haparandahamn 65.
**GPS:** n65,77154 e23,90442.⬆.
⌐SEK 100 ⌐SEK 40 🔌. **Location:** Rural, comfortable, quiet.
**Surface:** asphalted/grassy. ⭘ 01/05-01/11.
**Distance:** ⌂on the spot ⌐on the spot.
**Remarks:** Borrow cycles for free, use of sauna against payment.

| 🅂 | Övre Soppero | 3B2 |

**Ryssäjoki Naturrastplats. GPS:** n68,15435 e21,78256.

⌐. **Location:** Rural, isolated. **Surface:** unpaved.
**Distance:** ⌐8km ⌂on the spot ⌐on the spot.

| 🅂 | Porjus | 3B3 |

Strömgatan. **GPS:** n66,95671 e19,80798.
⌐free. **Surface:** asphalted. ⭘ 01/01-31/12.
**Distance:** ⌐500m.
**Remarks:** In front of fire-station.

---

| 🅂 | Vittangi | 3B2 |

**Rastplats Suptallen. GPS:** n67,66938 e21,40521.
⌐free ChWCfree. **Location:** Motorway. **Surface:** asphalted.
⭘ 01/01-31/12.
**Distance:** ⌐15km.

# Uppsala

| 🅂 | Älvkarleby | 4D3 |

**Älvkarleby Turist & Konferenshotell,** Västanåvägen 54.
**GPS:** n60,56518 e17,43796.
20 ⌐SEK 100 ⌐−WC 🔌.
**Distance:** ⌐100m ⊗on the spot.
**Remarks:** Pay at reception.

| 🅂 | Öregrund | 4D3 |

Kyrkogatan. **GPS:** n60,33958 e18,43672.⬆.
5 ⌐SEK 120. **Surface:** asphalted. ⭘ 01/01-31/12.
**Distance:** ⌐200m ⌂on the spot ⌐on the spot ⊗350m 🛒200m.

| 🅂 | Öregrund | 4D3 |

**Tullbacken,** Tullbacken. **GPS:** n60,34091 e18,44107.⬆.
3 ⌐SEK 120 WC⌐. **Location:** Urban, simple. **Surface:** asphalted.
⭘ 01/01-31/12.
**Distance:** ⌐on the spot ⌂on the spot ⌐on the spot ⊗100m
🛒200m.

| 🅂 | Uppsala | 4D3 |

Stallängsgatan. **GPS:** n59,84446 e17,65698.⬆.
10 ⌐SEK 180 ⌐(10x)WCincluded. **Surface:** gravel.
⭘ 01/01-31/12.
**Distance:** ⌐2km ⊗600m.

# Södermanland

| 🅂 | Eskilstuna | 5F1 |

**Sundbyholms Gästhamn,** Sundbyholm. **GPS:** n59,44749 e16,62593.⬆.
6 ⌐SEK 150 ⌐SEK 40.
**Distance:** ⌂on the spot ⌐on the spot ⊗on the spot 🧍on the spot.
**Remarks:** Next to castle.

| 🅂 | Mariefred | 5F1 |

**Mariefreds gästhamnen,** Gripsholmsvägen.
**GPS:** n59,25793 e17,22160.⬆.
4 ⌐SEK 260 WC⌐. **Location:** Urban, simple. **Surface:** asphalted.
⭘ 01/01-31/12.
**Distance:** ⌐on the spot ⊗200m 🛒200m.

| 🅂 | Mariefred | 5F1 |

**Statoil,** Storgatan 18. **GPS:** n59,25944 e17,21805.⬆.
2 ⌐free ⌐. **Surface:** asphalted. ⭘ 01/01-31/12.

| 🅂 | Nyköping | 5F1 |

**Nyköpings hamn,** Spelhagsvägen. **GPS:** n58,74460 e17,01524.⬆.
10 ⌐free ⌐−⌐Ch.
**Distance:** ⊗1km.
**Remarks:** Max. 2 days, service 100m.

| 🅂 | Oxelösund | 5F1 |

**Femöre Marina,** Fiskehamnsvägen 12. **GPS:** n58,65830 e17,11123.⬆.
15 ⌐SEK 150 ⌐Ch ⌐(10x)SEK 50. **Surface:** gravel.
**Distance:** ⌐3km ⌂on the spot ⌐on the spot ⊗on the spot.

| 🅂 | Strängnäs | 5F1 |

**Strängnäs Gästhamn,** Storgatan 38. **GPS:** n59,37860 e17,02599.⬆.
13 ⌐SEK 150, 01/05-31/08 SEK 200 ⌐(13x)WCincluded ⌐.
**Location:** Urban, simple, noisy. **Surface:** asphalted.
⭘ 01/01-31/12.
**Distance:** ⌂on the spot ⌐on the spot ⊗on the spot 🛒200m.
**Remarks:** Max. 48h.

| 🅂 | Trosa | 5G1 |

**Trosa Gästhamn,** Uddbergagatan 1. **GPS:** n58,89090 e17,55360.⬆.
19 ⌐SEK 100 ⌐−Ch ⌐SEK 80 WC⌐🔌. **Location:** Rural,
simple, noisy. **Surface:** gravel/metalled. ⭘ 01/01-31/12.
**Distance:** ⌐1km ⌂on the spot ⌐on the spot ⊗200m 🛒1km.
**Remarks:** Use of sauna against payment.

# Östergötland

| 🅂 | Borensberg | 5F1 |

**Kaffeteriet,** Magasinsgatan 7. **GPS:** n58,55885 e15,27995.⬆.

---

35 ⌐SEK 195 ⌐−⌐🔌Ch ⌐(19x) WCincluded ⌐ 🛒 📷 ⌐
**Location:** Rural, simple, isolated, quiet. **Surface:** gravel.
⭘ 01/04-15/10.
**Distance:** ⌐550m ⌂on the spot ⌐on the spot ⊗on the spot
🛒550m.
**Remarks:** At Göta Canal.

| 🅂 | Borensberg | 5F1 |

**Glasbruket,** Kanalvägen 17. **GPS:** n58,55909 e15,30322.⬆.

5 ⌐SEK 185 ⌐(8x)SEK 30 WC⌐. 📷 **Location:** Rural, simple,
isolated, quiet. **Surface:** grassy. ⭘ 01/05-30/09.
**Distance:** ⌐1,5km 🛒1,5km.
**Remarks:** At Göta Canal.

| 🅂 | Linköping | 5F2 |

**Flygvapenmuseum,** Carl Cederströms gata 2.
**GPS:** n58,41107 e15,52588.⬆.

20 ⌐free. **Location:** Rural, simple, isolated, quiet. **Surface:** grassy.
⭘ 01/01-31/12.
**Distance:** ⌐1km 🛒1km 🚲on the spot.
**Remarks:** Parking museum.

| 🅂 | Ljungsbro | 5F1 |

**Vetra Kloster Golfklubb,** Veda gård 2. **GPS:** n58,52862 e15,51955.⬆.

6 ⌐SEK 150 ⌐(6x)WC⌐included. 📷 **Location:** Rural, isolated,
quiet. **Surface:** gravel. ⭘ 01/04-31/10.
**Distance:** ⌐3km ⊗on the spot.
**Remarks:** At golf court.

| 🅂 | Mantorp | 5F2 |

**Östgöta Camping-Gruppen,** Möllersbrunnsvägen 3.
**GPS:** n58,36089 e15,28313.⬆.

24 ⌐SEK 100 ⌐−WC⌐. 🛁 **Location:** Rural, simple, isolated, quiet.

SE

**Surface:** gravel. 01/01-31/12.
**Distance:** 1km 800m 800m.
**Remarks:** At motorhome dealer.

| ⛺ S | Mjölby | 5E2 |

**Mjölby Golfklubb**, Blixberg Miskarp. **GPS:** n58,30753 e15,10125.

5 SEK 100 WC . **Location:** Rural, isolated, quiet.
**Surface:** gravel. 01/04-31/10.
**Distance:** on the spot on the spot.
**Remarks:** At golf court.

| ⚓ S | Motala | 5E1 |

**Södra Hamnen**, Fabriksgatan 12 H. **GPS:** n58,52979 e15,03811.

20 SEK 200 Ch WC included.
**Location:** Urban, simple, central, quiet. **Surface:** grassy.
01/01-31/12.
**Distance:** 1km on the spot on the spot 500m on the spot.

| 🍴 S | Motala | 5E1 |

**Borenshults slussar**, Verkstadsvägen 114.
**GPS:** n58,55550 e15,07820.

6 SEK 150 (6x)SEK 50/night WC included.
**Location:** Rural, simple, quiet. **Surface:** gravel. 01/05-31/08.
**Distance:** on the spot on the spot.
**Remarks:** Nearby sluices, at Göta Canal.

| 🍴 S | Motala | 5E1 |

**Café Mallboden**, Varvsgatan 17. **GPS:** n58,54829 e15,06689.

5 SEK 200 (4x)WC included. **Location:** Urban, simple,
quiet. **Surface:** grassy. 01/05-30/09.
**Distance:** 2km on the spot 500m.
**Remarks:** At Göta Canal.

| ⛺ S | Norrköping | 5F1 |

**Bråvikens Golfklubb**, Drurövägen. **GPS:** n58,60259 e16,32305.

6 SEK 100 WC . **Location:** Rural. **Surface:** asphalted.
01/04-31/10.
**Distance:** on the spot on the spot on the spot.

| ⛺ S | Norrköping | 5F1 |

**Söderköping Golfklubb**, Alsätersvägen 40.
**GPS:** n58,49662 e16,16989.

8 SEK 150 WC . **Location:** Rural, simple, isolated, quiet.
**Surface:** asphalted. 01/04-31/10.
**Distance:** on the spot on the spot.
**Remarks:** Golf court.

| ⛺ S | Norrköping | 5F1 |

**Park and Stay Norrköping City**, Generalsgatan 70.
**GPS:** n58,58663 e16,19624.
6 SEK 169/24h. **Location:** Central. **Surface:** asphalted.
**Distance:** on the spot on the spot on the spot.

| 🍴 S | Norsholm | 5F1 |

**Kapten Bille´s**, Slussvägen. **GPS:** n58,50818 e15,97840.

14 SEK 185 WC included. **Location:** Rural, simple, isolated,
quiet. **Surface:** gravel/metalled. 01/05-30/09.
**Distance:** on the spot on the spot 100m on the spot.
**Remarks:** At Göta Canal.

| | Ödeshög | 5E2 |

**Hästholmens hamn**, Hamngatan. **GPS:** n58,27904 e14,63522.

5 SEK 120 SEK 50/day WC included.
**Location:** Urban, simple, quiet. **Surface:** asphalted.
**Distance:** 500m on the spot on the spot on the spot 1km
on the spot.

| ⛺ S | Skänninge | 5E2 |

**Gripenbergs gårdsbutik**, Gripenberg 1. **GPS:** n58,40659 e15,08026.

10 SEK 175 SEK 25/night WC included. . **Location:** Rural,
simple, isolated. **Surface:** grassy.
01/01-31/12.
**Distance:** 1,5km 2km 1,5km on the spot.

| ⛺ S | Söderköping | 5F1 |

**Bergaskolan**, Skepparvägen. **GPS:** n58,48097 e16,33524.

22 SEK 185 Ch WC included. . **Location:** Rural, simple,
isolated, quiet. **Surface:** gravel. 12/04-29/09.
**Distance:** 500m on the spot on the spot 500m on the
spot.
**Remarks:** At former school, service on campsite.

| ⛺ | Söderköping | 5F1 |

**Kanalmagasinet AB**, Mem. **GPS:** n58,47923 e16,41422.

4 SEK 185 WC included. **Location:** Rural, simple, isolated,
quiet. **Surface:** grassy. 01/05-30/09.
**Distance:** on the spot on the spot on the spot on the spot.
**Remarks:** Pay at Kanalmagasinet.

| ⛺ S | Vadstena | 5E2 |

**Vadstena Golfklubb**, Kungs Starby 801. **GPS:** n58,42509 e14,89430.

20 SEK 200 (8x)WC included. **Location:** Rural, isolated,
quiet. **Surface:** gravel. 01/04-31/10.
**Distance:** 3,2km on the spot on the spot.
**Remarks:** At golf court.

| ⛺ S | Vadstena | 5E2 |

**Vadstena Ställplats**, Krönangsgatan 7.
**GPS:** n58,44496 e14,87933.

30 SEK 150, May-Sep SEK 195 Ch SEK 30/night WC .
**Location:** Urban, simple, central, quiet. **Surface:** grassy.
01/01-31/12 Service: winter.
**Distance:** 400m on the spot on the spot on the spot
500m on the spot.

| 🍴 S | Vreta Kloster | 5F1 |

**Bergs Slussar Vandrarhem**, Oscars Slussar 2.
**GPS:** n58,48524 e15,52970.

SE

25 ⬛SEK 185 ⚪⬛ChWC⬛included ⬛.⬛⬛ **Location:** Rural, simple, isolated, quiet. **Surface:** grassy. ⬛ 01/04-30/09. **Distance:** ⬛500m ⬛100m ⬛500m ⬛on the spot. **Remarks:** At Göta Canal.

# Jönköping

⬛⬛ **Aneby** 5E2
**Wiredaholm Golf & Konferens**, Nobyvägen. **GPS:** n57,91294 e14,64571.⬛

6 ⬛SEK 100 ⬛WC⬛included. **Location:** Rural, isolated, quiet. **Surface:** grassy. ⬛ 01/04-30/09. **Distance:** ⬛on the spot ⬛on the spot. **Remarks:** At golf court.

⬛⬛ **Bredaryd** 5E3
**Pelles**, Sunnaryd Solbacka. **GPS:** n57,01704 e13,69058.
2 ⬛SEK 200 ⬛⬛WC⬛SEK 50. ⬛⬛ **Location:** Rural, simple, isolated. **Surface:** grassy/gravel. ⬛ 01/01-31/12. **Distance:** ⬛on the spot. **Remarks:** Breakfast-service.

⬛⬛ **Gränna** 5E2
**Gränna Hamn**, Hamnvägen. **GPS:** n58,02728 e14,46070.⬛

30 ⬛SEK 200 ⚪⬛Ch⬛(20x),10Amp WCincluded ⬛.⬛⬛ **Location:** Rural, comfortable, isolated, quiet. **Surface:** asphalted. ⬛ 01/01-31/12. **Distance:** ⬛800m ⬛100m ⬛100m ⬛400m ⬛on the spot ⬛on the spot.

⬛ **Gränna** 5E2
**Gränna Hamn**, Amiralsvägen. **GPS:** n58,02868 e14,45960.⬛

20 ⬛SEK 120. ⬛⬛ **Location:** Rural, simple, isolated, quiet. **Surface:** asphalted. ⬛ 01/01-31/12. **Distance:** ⬛600m ⬛100m ⬛100m ⬛100m ⬛on the spot ⬛on the spot.

⬛⬛ **Gränna** 5E2
**BauerGårdens**, Bunn. **GPS:** n57,93629 e14,49227.⬛

100 ⬛SEK 250 ⚪⬛Ch⬛(70x)WC⬛⬛⬛included.⬛⬛ **Location:** Rural, simple, isolated, quiet. **Surface:** gravel. ⬛ 10/04-01/12. **Distance:** ⬛on the spot ⬛on the spot ⬛on the spot.

⬛⬛ **Hult** 5F2
**Ställplats Lyckarps**, RV 40. **GPS:** n57,63577 e15,09830.⬛➡.

19 ⬛€ 10 ⚪⬛Chincluded ⬛(10x)SEK 3. **Location:** Rural, simple, isolated, quiet. **Surface:** gravel. ⬛ 01/05-31/10. **Distance:** ⬛8km ⬛200m ⬛on the spot.

⬛⬛ **Jönköping** 5E2
**Hyltena Natt-Camp**, Hyltena 50. **GPS:** n57,66595 e14,18246.⬛

10 ⬛SEK 125 ⬛included WC⬛. ⬛⬛ **Location:** Rural, simple, noisy. **Surface:** asphalted. ⬛ 01/01-31/12. **Distance:** ⬛Jönköping 15km ⬛500m ⬛500m ⬛500m ⬛on the spot. **Remarks:** Quick-Stop.

⬛⬛ **Mullsjö** 5E2
**Ryfors Golf Club**, Tunarpsvägen. **GPS:** n57,90524 e13,82475.⬛
5 ⬛SEK 150 ⚪⬛WC⬛. ⬛⬛ **Location:** Rural, isolated, quiet. **Surface:** grassy. ⬛ 01/01-31/12. **Distance:** ⬛4,5km ⬛on the spot. **Remarks:** At golf court.

⬛⬛ **Rydaholm** 5E3
**Skeda Strand**, Skeda gård 1. **GPS:** n57,03727 e14,18147.⬛

30 ⬛SEK 120 ⚪⬛Ch⬛(6x)SEK 30/night,10Amp WC⬛included. ⬛⬛ **Location:** Rural, simple, isolated, quiet. **Surface:** grassy/gravel. ⬛ 01/04-31/10. **Distance:** ⬛12km ⬛on the spot ⬛on the spot ⬛12km ⬛12km ⬛on the spot ⬛on the spot. **Remarks:** Boat rental.

⬛⬛ **Rydaholm** 5E3
**Lady & Lufsen Ställplats Husbil**, Krusebacken. **GPS:** n56,98089 e14,22967.⬛

10 ⬛SEK 100 ⚪⬛Ch ⬛SEK 15/night ⬛.⬛ **Location:** Rural, simple, isolated, quiet. **Surface:** grassy. ⬛ 15/05-15/09. **Distance:** ⬛5km ⬛on the spot ⬛5km ⬛on the spot. **Remarks:** Max. 2 nights.

⬛⬛ **Sandhem** ⬛⬛ 5E2
**Kyrkekvarn Sörgården**, Kyrkekvarn 2. **GPS:** n57,99581 e13,84571.⬛

10 ⬛SEK 180 ⚪⬛Ch⬛WC⬛included. ⬛⬛ **Location:** Rural, isolated, quiet. **Surface:** grassy/gravel. ⬛ 01/04-31/10. **Distance:** ⬛6km. **Remarks:** Canoe rental.

⬛⬛ **Sandhem** ⬛⬛ 5E2
**Kohagens Badplats**. **GPS:** n57,98724 e13,77696.
3 ⬛free ⚪⬛Ch⬛free. **Location:** Rural. **Surface:** gravel. ⬛ 01/01-31/12. **Distance:** ⬛on the spot ⬛on the spot. **Remarks:** At lake.

⬛⬛ **Tenhult** 5E2
**Ställplats Bogla**, Bogla 29. **GPS:** n57,74284 e14,28935.⬛

30 ⬛SEK 100 ⚪Chincluded ⬛(20x)SEK 20. **Location:** Rural, isolated, quiet. **Surface:** gravel. ⬛ 01/01-31/12. **Distance:** ⬛Jönköping 5km.

⬛⬛ **Vrigstad** ⬛⬛ 5E3
**Timjan Café & Restaurang**, Flahult 2. **GPS:** n57,31552 e14,29112.⬛

6 ⬛SEK 100 ⬛SEK 50. ⬛ **Location:** Rural, simple, isolated, quiet. **Surface:** gravel. **Distance:** ⬛on the spot ⬛on the spot.

# Kronoberg

⬛⬛ **Diö** 5E3
**Sutareboda**. **GPS:** n56,60767 e14,23700.⬛
⬛SEK 100. ⬛ **Location:** Rural. **Distance:** ⬛Diö 5km.

⬛⬛ **Växjö** ⬛ 5E3
**Askelövsgatan Parkering**, Askelövsgatan. **GPS:** n56,87743 e14,79634.⬛

**SE**

5 ⬛9-18h SEK 5/h, overnight stay free. 🅿 **Location:** Urban, simple, central, quiet. **Surface:** asphalted.
⬛ 01/01-31/12.
**Distance:** 🚿500m ⊗350m 🛒300m 🚌500m 🚲 on the spot.

# Kalmar

| ⚓ | **Bläsinge** 〰🏖 | 5F3 |

**Bläsinge Hamn. GPS:** n56,62015 e16,70076.⬆.

15 ⬛SEK 100 🔌🚿(14x) WCincluded 🚿🚻
**Location:** Rural, simple, isolated, quiet. **Surface:** grassy/gravel.
⬛ 01/01-31/12.
**Distance:** ⚓on the spot 🚤on the spot ⊗on the spot 🛒15km.
**Remarks:** Money in envelope in mail box.

| 🎣S | **Borgholm** 〰🏖 | 5F3 |

**Stug o Fiske,** Verkstadsgatan 5. **GPS:** n56,86841 e16,66309.⬆➡.

29 ⬛SEK 150 🔌free Ch🚿(20x)WC⊐included.
**Location:** Rural, comfortable, quiet. **Surface:** grassy/gravel.
⬛ 24/03-10/10.
**Distance:** 🚿2km 🚤on the spot ⊗on the spot 🛒2km.
**Remarks:** Pay at restaurant.

| 🎣S | **Borgholm** 〰🏖 | 5F3 |

**Lindby Boden,** Lindby Bygata 23. **GPS:** n56,81571 e16,70548.➡.

50 ⬛SEK 70 🔌included 🚿(5x)SEK 30/day. **Location:** Rural, simple, isolated, quiet. **Surface:** grassy. ⬛ 01/01-31/12.
**Distance:** 🚿Borgholm 10km ⊗10km 🛒10km 🚲 on the spot 🚶on the spot.
**Remarks:** Money in envelope in mail box.

| 🎣S | **Borgholm** 〰🏖 | 5F3 |

**Slot Borgholm,** Sollidenvägen 5. **GPS:** n56,86975 e16,64785.⬆.

---

20 ⬛SEK 100.🅿 🛥 **Location:** Rural, simple, isolated, quiet.
**Surface:** gravel. ⬛ 01/01-31/12.
**Distance:** 🚿2km ⊗2km 🛒2km.
**Remarks:** Service 2,5km GPS N56,88224 E16,66190.

| ⚓S | **Borgholm** 〰🏖 | 5F3 |

**Hamnvägen. GPS:** n56,88301 e16,64790.⬆.

40 ⬛SEK 140 🔌🚿ChWC⊐included.🅿 🛥
**Location:** Urban, simple, central, quiet. **Surface:** grassy.
⬛ 01/01-31/12.
**Distance:** 🚿on the spot 🚤on the spot 🛥on the spot ⊗200m 🛒200m.
**Remarks:** Service 500m.

| 🎣S | **Byxelkrok** 〰 | 5F2 |

**Byxelkrok,** Neptunivägen. **GPS:** n57,34969 e17,03601.⬆.

15 ⬛SEK 100. **Location:** Rural, simple, isolated, quiet.
**Surface:** forest soil.
**Distance:** 🚿4km 🚤100m 🚤100m ⊗4km 🛒4km.
**Remarks:** Money in envelope in mail box.

| ⚓S | **Byxelkrok** 〰 | 5F2 |

**Oskarshamn,** Neptunivägen. **GPS:** n57,32767 e17,00812.⬆.

8 ⬛SEK 140 🔌🚿ChWC⊐📶included.
**Location:** Rural, simple, noisy. **Surface:** gravel. ⬛ 15/05-30/09.
**Distance:** 🚿500m 🚤on the spot 🚤on the spot ⊗on the spot 🛒500m.
**Remarks:** Check in at harbourmaster.

| ⚓S | **Degerhamn** | 5F3 |

**Gräsgårds hamn. GPS:** n56,31722 e16,53167.⬆.

25 ⬛SEK 80 🔌included 🚿(20x)SEK 30.🚻 **Location:** Rural, simple, isolated, quiet. **Surface:** grassy. ⬛ 01/01-31/12.
**Distance:** 🚿15km ⚓on the spot ⊗15km 🛒15km.
**Remarks:** Pay in at kiosk.

| ⚓ | **Degerhamn** | 5F3 |

**Degerhamns Ställplats & Hamn. GPS:** n56,35723 e16,40734.⬆.

---

40 ⬛free. **Location:** Rural, simple, isolated, quiet. **Surface:** grassy.
⬛ 15/04-18/10.
**Distance:** 🚿1,5km 🚤on the spot 🚤on the spot ⊗300m 🛒1,5km.

| 🎣S | **Färjestaden** 🚲 | 5F3 |

**Köpsenter,** Brovägen. **GPS:** n56,65293 e16,47138.⬆.

17 ⬛free. **Location:** Urban, simple, central, noisy. **Surface:** asphalted.
⬛ 01/01-31/12.
**Distance:** 🚿500m 🚤50m ⊗50m 🛒50m 🚌on the spot.
**Remarks:** At shopping centre, max. 1 night.

| 🎣S | **Fliseryd** 🎡 | 5F3 |

**Ställplats Jungnerholmarna,** Jungnerholmarna.
**GPS:** n57,13000 e16,25587.⬆.

10 ⬛SEK 90 🔌🚿Ch🚿(6x) WC⊐included.
**Location:** Rural, comfortable, central, quiet. **Surface:** grassy.
⬛ 01/01-31/12.
**Distance:** 🚿500m 🚤on the spot 🚤on the spot 🛒1,5km 🚶on the spot.
**Remarks:** Check in and key electricity at supermarket.

| 🎣S | **Grönhögen** | 5F3 |

**Ventlinge Stellplats,** Ventlinge 118. **GPS:** n56,28372 e16,40681.⬆➡.

20 ⬛SEK 120 🔌🚿Ch🚿(8x) WC⊐📶included.🚻
**Location:** Rural, comfortable, quiet. **Surface:** grassy.
⬛ 01/04-01/11.
**Distance:** 🚿1,5km 🚤300m 🚤300m ⊗1,5km 🛒1,5km.
**Remarks:** At golf court, farm products.

| ⚓S | **Grönhögen** | 5F3 |

**Grönhögens hamn,** Fiskaregränd. **GPS:** n56,26652 e16,39722.⬆.

30 ⬛SEK 150 🔌🚿Ch🚿(28x)WCincluded ⊐📶SEK 15.
**Location:** Rural, comfortable, quiet. **Surface:** grassy.

---

SE

**◘** 01/01-31/12.
**Distance:** on the spot 50m on the spot 500m 500m on the spot on the spot.
**Remarks:** Golf court 1km.

### ⚓ Hjorted 5F2

Vattencafé "Vattenfronten", Blankaholm.
**GPS:** n57,59028 e16,52972. ↑➡.

8 SEK 140 included SEK 40/24h WC □ ◉. **Location:** Rural.
**Surface:** grassy/gravel. **◘** 01/01-31/12.
**Distance:** 300m on the spot on the spot 300m.
**Remarks:** To be paid at bar.

### Hultsfred 5F2

Björnnäsets naturreservat. **GPS:** n57,45635 e15,72525. ↑.
10 SEK 50. **Location:** Rural, isolated, quiet. **Surface:** forest soil.
**◘** 01/01-31/12.
**Distance:** 8km on the spot on the spot on the spot.

### S Kalmar 5F3

Ölandskajen, ölandskajen 1. **GPS:** n56,66030 e16,36130. ↑.

18 SEK 160 SEK 40/24h WC □ ◉ included.
**Location:** Urban, simple, central, noisy.
**Surface:** asphalted.
**◘** 01/01-31/12 ◉ water disconnected in winter.
**Distance:** 200m 1km on the spot 200m 200m on the spot.
**Remarks:** Pay and coins at tourist office, historical centre.

### S Kalmar 5F3

Svinö. **GPS:** n56,68111 e16,38079. ↑.

20 free Ch WC free. **Location:** Rural, simple, isolated, noisy.
**Surface:** gravel. **◘** 01/01-31/12 ◉ Service: winter.
**Distance:** 4km 200m on the spot on the spot 4km
4km 5km on the spot.
**Remarks:** Dogs beach.

### Kalmar 5F3

Elevatorkajen, Skeppsbrogatan 49. **GPS:** n56,66360 e16,37060. ↑.

6 SEK 5/h, overnight stay free.
**Location:** Urban, simple, central, quiet.
**Surface:** asphalted.
**◘** 01/01-31/12.
**Distance:** 100m 1km on the spot 200m 200m 400m.

---

**Remarks:** Service 4km GPS N56,68111 E16,38079,
historical centre.

### S Köpingsvik 5F3

Kårehamns Fiskaffär. **GPS:** n56,95623 e16,88755. ↑➡.

40 SEK 100-190 Ch (25x)SEK 40 WC included □.
**Location:** Rural, comfortable, isolated, quiet. **Surface:** gravel.
**◘** 01/01-31/12.
**Distance:** 500m 100m on the spot on the spot 15km.
**Remarks:** Service 200m.

### ⚓ Löttorp 5G2

Böda, Bödahamnsvägen. **GPS:** n57,24052 e17,07503. ↑.

50 SEK 140 Ch (10x)SEK 20/24h WC □ included.
**Location:** Rural, comfortable, quiet. **Surface:** grassy/gravel.
**◘** 01/01-31/12.
**Distance:** 1km on the spot on the spot 1km.

### S Mönsterås 5F3

Hamnen Mönsterås, Hamngatan. **GPS:** n57,04151 e16,44874. ↑.

13 SEK 125 Ch (8x) WC □ ◉ included.
**Location:** Urban, comfortable, quiet. **Surface:** asphalted.
**◘** 01/01-31/12.
**Distance:** 100m on the spot on the spot 100m.
**Remarks:** At the quay, code internet at tourist office.

### S Nabelund 5G2

Nabelundsvägen 1. **GPS:** n57,34882 e17,08904. ↑➡.

40 SEK 140 Ch (4x) WC included.
**Location:** Rural, simple, isolated, quiet. **Surface:** grassy/gravel.
**◘** 01/01-31/12.
**Distance:** 7km on the spot on the spot 7km 7km.
**Remarks:** Pay at harbourmaster.

### ⚓ Oskarshamn 5F2

Oskarshamns gästhamn, Norra Strandgatan.
**GPS:** n57,26768 e16,45516. ↑.

---

10 SEK 100-150 Ch WC □ included ◉.
**Location:** Urban, simple, central, noisy.
**Surface:** asphalted.
**◘** 01/01-31/12.
**Distance:** 500m on the spot on the spot 500m 500m
400m.
**Remarks:** Pay at harbourmaster, service 2km GPS N57,27830 E16,47543.

### S Sandvik 5F3

Gästhamnen Sandvik, Stenhuggarvägen.
**GPS:** n57,07143 e16,85335. ↑.

40 SEK 100-190 Ch (30x)SEK 40 WC □ included.
**Location:** Rural, comfortable, quiet. **Surface:** gravel.
**◘** 01/01-31/12.
**Distance:** 100m on the spot on the spot on the spot
50m.

### ⚓ S Stora Rör 5F3

Stora Rörs Hamn, Stora Rörsvägen. **GPS:** n56,75654 e16,52817. ↑➡.

8 SEK 160 (6x) WC included. **Location:** Rural, simple, quiet.
**Surface:** asphalted. **◘** 01/01-31/12.
**Distance:** on the spot on the spot on the spot on the spot
100m.
**Remarks:** Pay at shop.

### S Storebrö 5F2

Stellplats Storbro Sportclub, Ulvekarrsvägen.
**GPS:** n57,59367 e15,83992. ↑➡.

20 SEK 150 (4x) WC included. **Location:** Rural, simple, quiet.
**Surface:** gravel. **◘** 01/01-31/12.
**Distance:** 300m.
**Remarks:** Money in envelope in mail box.

### S Storebrö 5F2

Tobo Golgklubb camping, Fredensborg 133.
**GPS:** n57,57566 e15,81154. ↑➡.

10 ⬛SEK 100 🔌Ch🚿(10x)WC⬛included. **Location:** Rural, simple, isolated, quiet. **Surface:** gravel. 🔲 01/01-31/12.
**Distance:** 🚶7km ⛱50m 🚊7km.
**Remarks:** Payment and sanitary facilities at Golfclub.

| 🅿 | Timmernabben 🍴 | 5F3 |

**Festplatsen Timmernabben**, Botsmansvägen.
**GPS**: n56,97350 e16,44028.⬆➡.

30 ⬛SEK 150 🔌🚿(20x)WC⬛included. 🛁 **Location:** Rural, simple, quiet. **Surface:** grassy/gravel. 🔲 01/01-31/12.
**Distance:** 🚶100m ⛱on the spot 🛶on the spot ⊗1km 🚊1km.

| 🅿S | Torngärd | 5F3 |

**Parkeerterrein Natuurreservaat**, Fagelvägen.
**GPS**: n56,33169 e16,54289.⬆.

6 ⬛SEK 40 🔌WCincluded. **Location:** Rural, simple, quiet.
**Surface:** gravel. 🔲 01/01-31/12.
**Distance:** 🚶15km ⛱on the spot 🛶15km ⊗15km 🚊15km.
**Remarks:** Bird reserve, money in envelope in mail box.

| 🅿S | Tuna ⚓ 🎣 | 5F2 |

**Ställplats Tuna**, Lillgatan. **GPS**: n57,57716 e16,10351.⬆➡.

12 ⬛SEK 100 🔌🚐Chincluded 🚿(4x)SEK 40 WC⬛.
**Location:** Rural, simple, central, quiet. **Surface:** gravel.
🔲 01/01-31/12.
**Distance:** 🚶2,5km ⊗100m 🚊on the spot.
**Remarks:** Money in envelope in mail box, moose park 9km, tourist train.

| 🅿S | Västervik 🍴 | 5F2 |

**Ställplats Sågen**, Värmeverksgatan. **GPS**: n57,75138 e16,65541.⬆➡.

45 ⬛SEK 100 🔌🚐Chincluded 🚿(15x)SEK 40. **Location:** Urban, simple, central, quiet. **Surface:** gravel.

---

🔲 01/01-31/12.
**Distance:** 🚶1,5km ⛱on the spot 🛶on the spot ⊗800m.
**Remarks:** Money in envelope in mail box, service 1,5km
GPS N57.74120 E16.66293.

| ⚓S | Västervik 🍴 | 5F2 |

**Barlastsudden Sea Port**, Barlastgatan 11.
**GPS**: n57,75464 e16,65149.⬆.
19 ⬛SEK 100 🔌🚿SEK 50. **Surface:** gravel. 🔲 22/06-30/09.
**Distance:** 🚶1km ⛱on the spot 🛶on the spot.

| 🏕 | Vimmerby 🌿🎡 | 5F2 |

**Astrid Lindgrens Värld**, Fabriksgatan 8.
**GPS**: n57,67514 e15,84151.⬆➡.

200 ⬛SEK 200. 🛁 🍴 **Location:** Urban, simple, central.
**Surface:** asphalted. 🔲 01/01-31/12.
**Distance:** 🚶1km ⊗1km 🚊1,3km.
**Remarks:** Quick-Stop: >19h - <8h.

# Gotland

| 🅿S | Burgsvik | 5G2 |

**Ställplats Sandkvie**, Öja Sandkvie 173. **GPS**: n57,01533 e18,31373.⬆.
35 ⬛SEK 120 🔌Ch🚿SEK 30 WC⬛📶. **Location:** Rural, comfortable, isolated, quiet. **Surface:** grassy. 🔲 01/01-31/12.
**Distance:** 🚶4km ⛱2km 🚶on the spot.

| 🅿S | Fårö | 5G2 |

**Lauterhorns**. **GPS**: n57,95249 e19,07995.
15 ⬛SEK 100, 01/06-31/08 SEK 120 🚰SEK 10/20liter 🚿(8x)SEK 30.
**Surface:** gravel.
**Distance:** 🚶on the spot.

| 🅿 | Gotlands Tofta | 5G2 |

**Tofta Beach**, Malvavägen 17. **GPS**: n57,49233 e18,13133.⬆➡.
250 ⬛SEK 130/24h. 🚐 🔲 15/04-18/10.
**Distance:** ⛱200m 🛶200m.

| 🅿S | Visby | 5G2 |

**Park and Stay**, Gutevägen. **GPS**: n57,62855 e18,28034.⬆.
35 ⬛SEK 169 🔌Ch. **Surface:** gravel. 🔲 15/04-18/10.
**Distance:** ⊗700m.

# Blekinge

| ⚓S | Hasslö 🍴 | 5F3 |

**Garpahamnen Hasslö**, Hamnvägen. **GPS**: n56,09990 e15,47368.⬆.
⬛SEK 130 WC⬛.
**Distance:** ⛱on the spot 🛶on the spot.

| ⚓S | Hasslö | 5F3 |

**Hasslö Stugby**, Fiskaregårdsvägen 2. **GPS**: n56,10227 e15,47770.⬆.

6 ⬛SEK 200 🔌🚿included ⬛SEK 10 🔲SEK 40. 🚐
**Location:** Rural, simple, isolated, quiet. **Surface:** grassy/gravel.
🔲 01/01-31/12.
**Distance:** ⛱on the spot 🛶on the spot ⊗on the spot 🚊300m
🚋on the spot.

| 🅿 | Karlshamn | 5F3 |

**Hamnplan**, Hamngatan 2A. **GPS**: n56,16520 e14,86522.⬆.

---

6 ⬛free. **Location:** Urban, simple, central, quiet. **Surface:** asphalted.
🔲 01/01-31/12 🔴 during event.
**Distance:** 🚶500m 🛶on the spot ⊗500m 🚊500m.
**Remarks:** Max. 24h.

| 🅿 | Karlshamn | 5F3 |

Saltsjöbadsvägen. **GPS**: n56,15835 e14,87974.⬆.

⬛free. **Location:** Rural, isolated. **Surface:** gravel.
**Distance:** 🚶2,5km.

| 🅿 | Karlshamn | 5F3 |

Stationsvägen. **GPS**: n56,17563 e14,86610.⬆.
⬛free. **Surface:** asphalted. 🔲 01/01-31/12.
**Distance:** 🚶800m ⊗800m 🚊800m 🛶on the spot.
**Remarks:** Near train station.

| ⚓S | Karlshamn | 5F3 |

**Ställplats Väggaviken**, Saltsjöbadsvägen.
**GPS**: n56,15840 e14,88486.⬆.

30 ⬛SEK 180 🔌🚐Ch🚿included WC⬛. 🛁 **Location:** Rural, simple, isolated, quiet. **Surface:** gravel. 🔲 01/06-31/08.
**Distance:** 🚶2km ⛱on the spot 🚊2km 🚲 on the spot.

| ⚓S | Karlshamn | 5F3 |

**Svaneviks småbåtshamn**, Idrottsvägen.
**GPS**: n56,15692 e14,88850.⬆.

12 ⬛SEK 180 🔌🚐Ch🚿WC⬛included. 🛁 **Location:** Rural, simple, isolated, quiet. **Surface:** gravel. 🔲 01/06-31/08.
**Distance:** 🚶3km ⛱on the spot 🛶on the spot ⊗on the spot.
**Remarks:** Pay at harbourmaster.

| 🅿 | Karlshamn | 5F3 |

**Kreativum Science Center**, Strömmavägen 28.
**GPS**: n56,19288 e14,85211.⬆.

5 🛏free. **Location:** Rural, simple, isolated, quiet. **Surface:** asphalted. ◻ 01/01-31/12.
**Distance:** 🛁4km 🏊800m.
**Remarks:** At museum, check in on arrival.

⚓S **Karlskrona** 🚐 5F3

**Karlskrona Stadsmarina**, Östra Hamngatan.
**GPS:** n56,16548 e15,59390.⬆.

24 🛏SEK 180 🔌🔥,10Amp WC⬛included 🔲.🏠
**Location:** Urban, simple, central, quiet. **Surface:** asphalted. ◻ 01/01-31/12.
**Distance:** 🛁1km 🏊on the spot 🛒on the spot ⊗200m 🍴1km.
**Remarks:** Pay at harbourmaster, out of season less pitches.

S **Karlskrona** 🚐 5F3

Argongatan. **GPS:** n56,16988 e15,59426.⬆➡.
🔌🏠Chfree. ◻ 01/01-31/12.

🏠S **Ramdala** 5F3

**Brofästet Senoren gårdsbutik**, Svartnabbsvägen.
**GPS:** n56,13769 e15,74035.⬆.

28 🛏SEK 100 🔌🏠Chincluded 🔥SEK 50/night WC.🏠
**Location:** Rural, simple, isolated, quiet. **Surface:** grassy.
◻ 01/04-30/09.
**Distance:** 🛁7km 🏊on the spot 🛒on the spot 🍴1,5km 🚲on the spot.
**Remarks:** Next to The viking village.

🏕 **Ronneby** 🚐 5F3

**Ronneby Golfklubb**, Reddvägen 14. **GPS:** n56,18962 e15,29355.⬆.

21 🛏SEK 75 🔌🏠Ch🔥(6x)SEK 75/night WC⬛.🏠🚲
**Location:** Rural, simple, isolated, quiet. **Surface:** gravel.
◻ 01/01-31/12.
**Distance:** 🛁2km ⊗on the spot 🚲on the spot.
**Remarks:** At golf court.

🏕 **Ronneby** 🚐 5F3

**Ställplats-Fridhemsvägen**, Fridhemsvägen.
**GPS:** n56,20776 e15,28109.⬆.

5 🛏free. **Location:** Urban, central. **Surface:** asphalted.
◻ 01/01-31/12.
**Distance:** 🛁300m ⊗100m 🍴400m 🚐300m 🚲on the spot 🧍on the spot.

⚓ **Ronneby** 🚐 5F3

**Ronneby Hamn**, Östra Piren. **GPS:** n56,17527 e15,30177.⬆.

20 🛏SEK 150 🔌🔥included. 🚽 **Location:** Rural, simple, isolated, quiet. **Surface:** metalled. ◻ 01/01-31/12.
**Distance:** 🛁3km 🏊on the spot 🛒on the spot ⊗1,5km 🚲on the spot.
**Remarks:** Service at Ronneby Rönninge.

⚓S **Sölvesborg** 🚐 6H1

**Hörviks gästhamn**, Kustvägen, Hörvik. **GPS:** n56,04139 e14,76556.⬆.

33 🛏SEK 150 🏠ChWC⬛. 🏠 **Location:** Rural, simple, isolated.
**Surface:** gravel. ◻ 01/04-15/10.
**Distance:** 🛁12km 🏊on the spot 🛒on the spot ⊗300m 🚐200m 🚲on the spot.

⚓S **Sölvesborg** 🚐 6H1

**Torsö hamn**, Oastensvägen, Västra Torsö. **GPS:** n55,99952 e14,64871.⬆.

6 🛏SEK 160 🔌🔥WC⬛included. 🚽 **Location:** Rural, simple, isolated, quiet. **Surface:** grassy. ◻ 01/01-31/12.
**Distance:** 🛁7km 🏊on the spot 🛒on the spot 🚲on the spot.

⚓ **Sölvesborg** 🚐 6H1

**Krokås gästhamn**, Krokåsvägen 1. **GPS:** n56,04890 e14,75669.⬆.

8 🛏SEK 100 🔌🔥(8x)SEK 20/night. 🚽
**Location:** Urban, simple, isolated, quiet. **Surface:** grassy/gravel.
◻ 01/05-31/08.
**Distance:** 🛁15km 🏊on the spot 🛒on the spot ⊗1,5km 🚲on the spot.

⚓ **Sölvesborg** 🚐 6H1

**Nogersunds gästhamn**, Östra Hamnvägen, Nogersunds.
**GPS:** n56,00509 e14,73863.⬆.

30 🛏SEK 160 🏠Ch🔥included WC⬛ 🚲.🏠 🚲 **Location:** Rural,

simple, isolated, quiet. **Surface:** grassy. ◻ 01/01-31/12.
**Distance:** 🛁11km 🏊on the spot 🛒on the spot 🚲on the spot.

🏠S **Sölvesborg** 🚐 6H1

**Sölveborgs golfbana**, Ljunganabbevägen.
**GPS:** n56,04428 e14,59946.⬆.

10 🛏SEK 200 🔌🔥WC⬛included 🚿.🏠 🚲 **Location:** Rural, simple, isolated, quiet. **Surface:** grassy. ◻ 01/01-31/12.
**Distance:** 🛁7km ⊗on the spot 🚲on the spot.
**Remarks:** At golf court.

⚓S **Sturkö** 🚐 5F3

**Ekenabben**. **GPS:** n56,10142 e15,63803.⬆.
8 🛏SEK 135 🔥SEK 30/night. 🚽 **Location:** Rural, simple, isolated, quiet. **Surface:** asphalted. ◻ 01/04-30/09.
**Distance:** 🛁7km 🏊on the spot 🛒on the spot ⊗on the spot 🚲on the spot.

⚓S **Sturkö** 🚐 5F3

**Ställplats Sanda**, Strandvägen. **GPS:** n56,11966 e15,65123.⬆.
6 🛏SEK 135 🔥SEK 30/night. 🚽 **Location:** Rural, simple, isolated, quiet. **Surface:** asphalted. ◻ 01/04-30/09.
**Distance:** 🏊on the spot 🛒on the spot ⊗1,5km 🚲on the spot.

⚓S **Torhamn** 🚐 5F3

**Sandhamn Marine**, Brändaskärsvägen 4.
**GPS:** n56,09351 e15,85479.⬆.

50 🛏SEK 100, 01/05-30/09 SEK 175 🔌🏠Ch🔥(30x)WC⬛🔲SEK 50 🚿included. 🏠 🚲 **Location:** Rural, comfortable, isolated, quiet.
**Surface:** gravel. ◻ 01/01-31/12.
**Distance:** 🛁1km 🏊on the spot 🛒on the spot ⊗on the spot.
**Remarks:** Borrow cycles for free.

🏕S **Trensum** 5F3

**GPS:** n56,20522 e15,00627.
10 🛏free 🔌🏠ChWC. **Location:** Rural, simple, isolated.
**Surface:** metalled. ◻ 01/01-31/12.

# Skåne

🏕S **Åhus** 6G1

**Strandvillan**, Kolonivägen 62. **GPS:** n55,94443 e14,32109.⬆.

16 🛏SEK 150 🔌🔥WC⬛included 🚿. **Location:** Rural, simple, isolated, quiet. **Surface:** grassy. ◻ 01/01-31/12.
**Distance:** 🛁2km ⊗700m.
**Remarks:** Max. 1 day.

🏕 **Åhus** 6G1

**Åhus husbilsparkering**, Kantarellvägen 3.
**GPS:** n55,93721 e14,31622.⬆.

30 ⌇SEK 150. 🚿 **Location:** Urban. **Surface:** forest soil.
⊙ 01/01-31/12.
**Distance:** 🛒1,5km ⚓400m 💧200m 🚲1,5km.

### Anderslöv 6G2

**Lady's Hage**, Sörbyvägen 100. **GPS:** n55,44392 e13,32986.⬆.

20 ⌇SEK 100. 🚿 **Location:** Rural, simple, isolated, quiet.
**Surface:** grassy. ⊙ 01/01-31/12.
**Distance:** 🛒900m ⊗1km 💧900m 🚲on the spot.

### Ängelholm 5E3

Sibirienvägen. **GPS:** n56,23618 e12,81852.

8 ⌇ 🚰WCfree. **Surface:** grassy.
**Distance:** 🛒4km ⚓100m ⊗4km 🚲on the spot 🚶on the spot.
**Remarks:** Nature reserve.

### Ängelholm 5E3

**Ängelholms Föreningshamn**, Segelvägen 9.
**GPS:** n56,26704 e12,84138.
30 ⌇SEK 150 ⚡(16x)included.
⊙ 01/06-06/12.
**Distance:** 🛒5km ⚓on the spot ⛽on the spot ⊗on the spot 💧5km.
**Remarks:** Max. 48h, pay at harbourmaster.

### Båstad 5E3

Italienska vägen. **GPS:** n56,43383 e12,83132.⬆.
⌇SEK 50. 🛒 **Surface:** grassy. ⊙ 01/01-31/12.
**Distance:** 🛒1km ⊗400m 💧500m.

### Borrby 6G1

**Catrinegården**, Borrby 1223. **GPS:** n55,46673 e14,21090.⬆.

4 ⌇SEK 120 🚰⌷Ch⚡(4x)SEK 30/night WC. 🚿
**Location:** Rural, simple, isolated, quiet. **Surface:** grassy.
⊙ 01/01-31/12.
**Distance:** 🛒2,5km ⊗on the spot 💧2,5km �委on the spot 🚲on the spot.
**Remarks:** Nature reserve.

### Bromölla 6H1

**Skåneporten Bromölla**, Kristianstadsvägen.
**GPS:** n56,06414 e14,49689.⬆.

---

20 ⌇free 🚰WC. **Location:** Rural, simple, isolated, noisy.
**Surface:** asphalted. ⊙ 01/01-31/12.
**Distance:** ⚡200m ⊗on the spot 💧1km 🚲on the spot.
**Remarks:** Service to be paid at campsite.

### Fjälkinge 6G1

**Tosteberga Ångar**, Tostebergavägen. **GPS:** n56,01567 e14,45466.⬆.

6 ⌇free. **Location:** Rural, simple, isolated, quiet. **Surface:** forest soil.
⊙ 01/01-31/12.
**Distance:** 🛒2km.
**Remarks:** Nature reserve.

### Fjälkinge 6G1

**Tosteberga Hamn**, Bodavägen 185. **GPS:** n55,99759 e14,44539.⬆.

15 ⌇SEK 150 🚰⚡WCincluded. 🚿 **Location:** Rural, comfortable,
isolated, quiet. **Surface:** grassy/gravel. ⊙ 01/01-31/12.
**Distance:** ⚓on the spot ⛽on the spot.

### Gärsnäs 6G1

**Ekogården**, Skräddaröd 126. **GPS:** n55,60681 e14,23481.⬆➡.

35 ⌇SEK 200 🚰⌷Ch⚡(16x)SEK 50 WC⌷▣📶included. 🚿
**Location:** Rural, luxurious, isolated, quiet. **Surface:** grassy.
⊙ 01/04-30/09.
**Distance:** 🛒Gärsnäs 10km.

### Höllviken 6F2

**Falsterbokanalens Båtklubb**, Västra hamnplan 1.
**GPS:** n55,41011 e12,93200.⬆.

8 ⌇SEK 200 🚰⌷Ch⚡(8x)included WC⌷.📦⚡
**Location:** Rural, isolated, quiet. **Surface:** asphalted.
⊙ 01/05-30/09.
**Distance:** ⚓on the spot ⊗on the spot 🚲on the spot.

---

### Höllviken 6F2

**Ställplats Foteviken**, Museivägen 27. **GPS:** n55,42774 e12,95213.⬆.

15 ⌇SEK 200, SEK 100 without service 🚰⌷Ch⚡(4x) WC⌷.📦⚡
**Location:** Rural, simple, isolated, quiet. **Surface:** grassy.
⊙ 01/02-30/11.
**Distance:** 🛒1km ⛽on the spot ⊗1km 💧1km 🚲on the spot.
**Remarks:** At museum.

### Jonstorp 5E3

**Bläsinge Gård**, Gamla Södåkravägen 127. **GPS:** n56,23770 e12,65567.
20 ⌇SEK 150 ⚡SEK 50. **Surface:** gravel. ⊙ 01/01-31/12.

### Kristianstad 6G1

**Sommarlust Ishall**, Kanalgatan 100. **GPS:** n56,04442 e14,16646.🚲.

30 ⌇free. **Location:** Urban, simple. **Surface:** asphalted.
⊙ 01/01-31/12.
**Distance:** 🛒2km ⊗400m 💧300m ⛽on the spot 🚲on the spot.
**Remarks:** Max. 24h.

### Landskrona 6F1

**Lundåkrahamnen**, Stuverigatan 43. **GPS:** n55,86171 e12,85009.⬆.

48 ⌇SEK 180 🚰⌷Ch⚡WC⌷▣📶included.📦⚡
**Location:** Rural, simple, quiet. **Surface:** grassy.
⊙ 01/01-31/12.
**Distance:** 🛒2km ⚓on the spot ⛽on the spot ⊗300m 🚶on the spot
🚲on the spot.
**Remarks:** Arrival <22h, monitored parking.

### Landskrona 6F1

**Gammeleksgården**, Rosenhällsvägen 40.
**GPS:** n55,92197 e12,84515.⬆➡.

6 ⌇SEK 150 🚰⌷Ch⚡WC⌷included ▣on demand. 🚿
**Location:** Rural, noisy. **Surface:** gravel. ⊙ 01/01-31/12.
**Distance:** 🚲on the spot 🚶on the spot.
**Remarks:** Arrival >18h, departure <10h, check in at B&B <22h,
breakfast € 6.

### Limhamn 6F1

**Lagunen**, Vakgatan 9. **GPS:** n55,59593 e12,93305.⬆.

SE

25 🗲€ 20 🚽🍴Ch🚿WC🔌📶included. 🛒 🧽
**Location:** Rural, simple, quiet. **Surface:** gravel.
🗓 01/01-31/12.
**Distance:** 🚲3km ⚓200m 🏊1km 🏪1km 🚌500m on the spot
🧍on the spot.

### ⚓🅂 Limhamn 🌿🎋🦪 6F1
**Limhamns Småbåtshamn**, Bryggövägen.
**GPS:** n55,58358 e12,91824.⬆️.

40 🗲SEK 220 🚽🍴Ch🚿WC🔌included 🔌.🚮 🧽
**Location:** Rural, simple, quiet. **Surface:** grasstiles.
🗓 01/01-31/12 🔌 Service: winter.
**Distance:** 🚲700m, Malmö 6km ⚓on the spot 🏪on the spot
🏊on the spot 🚴on the spot 🧍on the spot.

### 🅂🅂 Löderup 6G2
**Kåseberga Ställplats**, Ales väg 2. **GPS:** n55,38863 e14,06322.⬆️.

48 🗲SEK 120. 🚮 **Location:** Rural, isolated, quiet. **Surface:** grassy.
🗓 01/04-31/10.
**Distance:** 🏊on the spot ⚓300m 🚴on the spot.

### ⚓🅂 Malmö 6F1
**Andelshamnen Lagunen**, Vaktgatan 9. **GPS:** n55,59611 e12,93278.
10 🗲SEK 180/night 🚽🍴Ch🚿WC🔌📶.🏠 **Location:** Urban.
**Surface:** grassy/sand. 🗓 01/01-31/12.
**Distance:** 🚲centre 4km ⚓on the spot.
**Remarks:** Borrow cycles for free.

### 🅂🅂 Näsum 5E3
**Ställplats Axeltorp**, Olofströmsvägen 177-11.
**GPS:** n56,14389 e14,52012.⬆️.

22 🗲SEK 100 🚽🚿(10x)SEK 20 📶included.🚮
**Location:** Rural. **Surface:** grassy. 🗓 01/01-31/12.
**Distance:** 🚲4km 🏊on the spot 🏪on the spot 🚴on the spot 🧍on
the spot.
**Remarks:** At the lake, boat rental.

### 🅂🅂 Örkelljunga 5E3
**Bengt i Örkelljunga**, Skåneporten 2. **GPS:** n56,28548 e13,33957.

---

20 🗲SEK 50 🚽SEK 15 🍴Ch🚿SEK 50.
**Surface:** grassy. 🗓 01/01-31/12.
**Distance:** 🚲4km 🧽 on the spot 🏊1km.
**Remarks:** At motorhome dealer, max. 24h, pay at reception.

### 🅂🅂 Osby 5E3
**Spegeldammen**, Hässleholmsvägen. **GPS:** n56,36871 e13,98441.⬆️.
🗲free.
**Distance:** 🚲1,6km 🏪on the spot.
**Remarks:** Max. 2 nights.

### 🅂🅂 Simrishamn 🌊 6G1
**Österlens GK**, Williams väg 20, Djupadal. **GPS:** n55,61208 e14,28146.⬆️.

8 🗲SEK 250 🚿WC🔌📶included. 🏠 **Location:** Rural, isolated,
quiet. **Surface:** gravel. 🗓 01/04-31/10.
**Distance:** 🚲400m ⚓500m 🏊on the spot 🚴on the spot.
**Remarks:** At golf court.

### 🅂🅂 Simrishamn 🌊 6G1
**Parking Hammarlunda**, Gislövshammar.
**GPS:** n55,49015 e14,30745.⬆️.

30 🗲SEK 120 🚽🍴Ch🚿included WC.🚮 **Location:** Rural, simple,
isolated, quiet. **Surface:** grassy. 🗓 01/01-31/12.
**Distance:** 🚲8km ⚓700m 🏪700m 🏊2,5km 🚌on the spot 🚴on
the spot.

### ⚓🅂 Simrishamn 🌊 6G1
**Småbåtshamnen**. **GPS:** n55,56035 e14,34906.⬆️.

7 🗲SEK 205 🚽🍴Ch🚿(5x)SEK 2/kWh WC🔌📶.🏠 🧽
**Location:** Rural, simple, central, quiet. **Surface:** asphalted.
🗓 01/01-31/12.
**Distance:** 🚲500m ⚓on the spot 🏪on the spot 🏊on the spot 🏪on
the spot 🚴on the spot.
**Remarks:** Tallycard.

### 🅂🅂 Simrishamn 🌊 6G1
**Tobisviks Camping**, Tobisvägen 1. **GPS:** n55,56792 e14,33708.⬆️.

---

50 🗲SEK 120-200 🚽🍴Ch🚿WC🔌. 🏠 **Location:** Rural,
comfortable, isolated, quiet. **Surface:** grassy. 🗓 01/01-31/12.
**Distance:** 🚲3km ⚓on the spot 🏪on the spot 🚴on the spot.

### ⚓ Skanör 🌊 6F2
**Skanör hamn**, Hamnvägen 1. **GPS:** n55,41608 e12,83168.⬆️➡️.

10 🗲SEK 220 🚽🚿(10x),10Amp WC🔌included.🏠 🎥
**Location:** Rural, simple, isolated, quiet. **Surface:** gravel.
🗓 22/04-01/10.
**Distance:** ⚓on the spot 🏪on the spot 🏊on the spot 🏪1km
🚴on the spot.
**Remarks:** Discount longer stays.

### 🅂🅂 Smygehamn 🌊 6G2
**Köpmansmagasinet**, Smyge strandväg. **GPS:** n55,33978 e13,36172.⬆️.

40 🗲free. **Location:** Rural, simple, isolated, quiet. **Surface:** grassy.
🗓 01/01-31/12.
**Distance:** ⚓on the spot 🏪on the spot 🏊200m 🚌on the spot 🚴on
the spot.

### 🅂🅂 Trelleborg 🌊 6G2
**Trelleborgs turist Parkering**, Strandridaregatan.
**GPS:** n55,37536 e13,12004.⬆️.

🗲free, night SEK 100 🚽Ch WC (summer).🚮
**Location:** Rural, simple, isolated. **Surface:** gravel.
🗓 01/01-31/12.
**Distance:** 🚲2km ⚓on the spot 🏪on the spot 🏊1,5km 🏪800m
🚴on the spot.

### 🅂🅂 Yngsjö 6G1
**Gamla Skolan**, Yngsjövägen 1065. **GPS:** n55,84441 e14,20019.⬆️.

5 🗲SEK 200 🚽🚿WCincluded 🔌SEK 25.🚮 **Location:** Simple,
isolated. **Surface:** gravel. 🗓 01/05-30/09.

**Distance:** ⌖1,5km ⊗on the spot.
**Remarks:** Breakfast-service.

| ⚓S | Ystad 🍽 🕮 | 6G2 |

Västerleden 129. **GPS:** n55,42472 e13,78694.⬆.

10 🛏free. **Location:** Rural, isolated, quiet. **Surface:** grassy.
◯ 01/01-31/12.
**Distance:** ⌖on the spot ⊷on the spot 🚲on the spot.
**Remarks:** Max. 24h.

| ⚓S | Ystad 🍽 🕮 | 6G2 |

Ystads Marina, Segelgatan 1. **GPS:** n55,42666 e13,81730.⬆.

28 🛏free, night SEK 150 ⛽🔌Ch🚰(16x)SEK 10/2kWh WC
🚿SEK 10/4minutes 📷SEK 10 📶.🚍🚲
**Location:** Urban, simple, central, quiet. **Surface:** gravel.
◯ 01/06-15/09.
**Distance:** ⌖1km ⌖on the spot ⊷on the spot ⊗on the spot 📷on the
spot 🚌on the spot 🚲on the spot.
**Remarks:** Caution SEK 100.

# Halland

| ⚓S | Falkenberg | 5D3 |

Rastplats Skrea Backe. **GPS:** n56,90280 e12,57557.⬆➡.
20 🛏free ⛽🚰Ch🚰. **Location:** Rural, simple.
**Surface:** grassy/metalled. ◯ 01/01-31/12.
**Distance:** ⌖4,7km 🏊250m.

| ⚓S | Falkenberg | 5D3 |

Falkenbergs Båtsällskap, Gröningevägen 3.
**GPS:** n56,89360 e12,49318.
25 🛏€ 18 ⛽🚰Ch🚿included. **Location:** Urban. **Surface:** metalled.
◯ 01/05-01/09.
**Distance:** ⌖city centre 1,5km ⌖on the spot ⊷on the spot ⊗1km
🚲on the spot.

| ⚓S | Falkenberg | 5D3 |

Lövstavikens Båtförening, Sanddynevägen 58.
**GPS:** n56,89329 e12,46795.
20 🛏SEK 160 ⛽🚰Ch🚿WC🚰included. 🚍 **Location:** Rural,
simple, quiet. **Surface:** grassy/gravel.
**Distance:** ⌖3km ⌖on the spot.

| S | Fjärås | 5D3 |

Tjolöholms Slott, Tjolöholms byväg. **GPS:** n57,40173 e12,10161.⬆.
🛏SEK 100. **Surface:** grassy/gravel. ◯ 01/01-31/12.
**Distance:** ⊗on the spot.
**Remarks:** At castle, max. 2 days.

| 🌿 | Fjärås | 5D3 |

Skårs Gård, Förlandavägen. **GPS:** n57,40081 e12,26869.⬆.
6 🛏SEK 140 🚿WC🚰included. **Location:** Rural.
**Distance:** ⌖11km.

| 🚐 | Frillesås | 5D3 |

Espenäsvägen. **GPS:** n57,31674 e12,15298.
5 🛏SEK 100 WC🚰. **Surface:** grassy. ◯ 01/04-01/10.
**Distance:** ⌖1,5km ⌖on the spot.
**Remarks:** No dogs allowed on the beach, money in envelope in mail
box.

| ©S | Gullbrandstorp | 5E3 |

Strandgården, Skarviksvägen 2. **GPS:** n56,69518 e12,68550.
8 🛏SEK 250 🚿included.
**Distance:** ⌖on the spot ⊷on the spot.
**Remarks:** Max. 3 days, golf court 300m.

| 🚐 | Halmstad | 5E3 |

Citycamp Halmstad, Styrmansgatan. **GPS:** n56,66682 e12,86145.

---

50 🛏SEK 120, 01/06-31/08 SEK 140.
**Distance:** ⌖on the spot.

| ⚓S | Halmstad | 5E3 |

Halmstad Segelsällskap, Grötviksvägen. **GPS:** n56,64191 e12,77782.
10 🛏SEK 150 🚿included.

| 🍴 | Heberg | 5D3 |

E6. **GPS:** n56,88532 e12,60220.
5 🛏free. **Location:** Isolated, quiet. **Surface:** asphalted.
◯ 01/31-31/12.
**Distance:** ⊗on the spot.
**Remarks:** Max. 24h.

| 🚐 | Ullared | 5D3 |

Ställplats Ullared, Värnamovägen. **GPS:** n57,13232 e12,73472.⬆.
100 🛏free, night SEK 90. 🚍 🚿 **Surface:** gravel.
**Distance:** ⌖1km.
**Remarks:** Max. 48h.

| 🌿S | Unnaryd | 5E3 |

Tiraholms Fisk. **GPS:** n56,94263 e13,64560.
🛏SEK 100 🚣. **Surface:** grassy.
**Distance:** ⌖on the spot ⊗on the spot.
**Remarks:** At small lake, check in on arrival.

| ⚓S | Vallda | 5D3 |

Lerkilsvägen. **GPS:** n57,45602 e11,91516.
10 🛏DKK 150 🚿(4x)included WC🚰. **Location:** Comfortable.
**Surface:** unpaved. ◯ 01/01-31/12.
**Distance:** ⌖on the spot ⊗on the spot.

| ⚓S | Varberg | 5D3 |

Apelvik Strand, Tångkörarvägen, Apelviken.
**GPS:** n57,08157 e12,26156.⬆.

22 🛏SEK 150 WC🚰.🚲 **Location:** Urban, simple, noisy.
**Surface:** gravel/metalled. ◯ 20/04-03/09.
**Distance:** ⌖3km ⌖on the spot ⊗300m.
**Remarks:** Beach parking.

| ⚓S | Varberg | 5D3 |

Naturum Getterön, Lassavägen 1. **GPS:** n57,12627 e12,25332.

24 🛏SEK 125, 01/06-31/08 SEK 200 🚿included. 🚍 🚿
**Surface:** gravel.
**Distance:** 🚲on the spot.
**Remarks:** Nature reserve.

| ⚓S | Varberg | 5D3 |

Getterön Marina, Änggärdev. 1. **GPS:** n57,11399 e12,22588.⬆.
21 🛏SEK 170-200 🚿📷included. 🚍 🚿
**Surface:** metalled. ◯ 01/01-31/12.
**Distance:** ⌖on the spot ⊷on the spot.
**Remarks:** Monitored parking.

| ⚓S | Varberg | 5D3 |

Otto Torells gata 24. **GPS:** n57,11000 e12,24250.
14 🛏SEK 360 ⛽🚰Ch🚿WC🚰included. **Location:** Urban.
**Surface:** concrete. ◯ 01/01-31/12.
**Distance:** ⌖500m ⊗400m 🚌800m.

| ⚓S | Värobacka | 5D3 |

Bua hamn, Hamnvägen. **GPS:** n57,23926 e12,11410.⬆.
38 🛏SEK 180, 15/06-15/08 SEK 200 ⛽🚰Chincluded 🚿WC🚰SEK
10 📷. 🚍 **Location:** Urban, comfortable. **Surface:** asphalted.
◯ 01/01-31/12.
**Distance:** ⌖1km ⌖on the spot ⊗200m 🚌500m.

---

# Västra Götaland

| ⚓S | Åmål 🕮 | 5D1 |

Måkebergsvägen 4. **GPS:** n59,05615 e12,70862.⬆.

80 🛏SEK 100 ⛽Ch WC🚰📶included.🚲 **Location:** Rural, simple,
quiet. **Surface:** grassy/gravel. ◯ 01/04-15/10.
**Distance:** ⌖600m ⌖on the spot ⊷on the spot ⊗600m 🚌600m
🚲on the spot 🏊on the spot.
**Remarks:** Pay at harbourmaster, servicepoint at Camping Örnäs.

| 🚐S | Bengtsfors 🕮 | 5D1 |

Ekagatan. **GPS:** n59,02510 e12,23380.
10 🛏SEK 100-150 ⛽🚰Chincluded WC🚰📷. **Location:** Urban.
**Surface:** asphalted. ◯ 01/01-31/12.
**Distance:** ⌖750m ⌖on the spot ⊗750m 🚌1km.

| ⚓S | Bohus-björkö | 5D2 |

Björkö Hamn, Ljungblomsvägen 7. **GPS:** n57,72812 e11,67751.
🛏SEK 250 🚿included 🚰SEK 10 ⊗SEK 50. **Surface:** gravel.
◯ 01/01-31/12.
**Distance:** ⌖on the spot ⊷on the spot ⊗on the spot 🚌500m.

| PS | Broddetorp | 5E2 |

Naturum Hornborgasjön, Hornborgasjön. **GPS:** n58,32380 e13,58970.
10 🛏SEK 130 WC🚰.
**Location:** Rural. **Surface:** gravel. ◯ 01/01-31/12.
**Distance:** ⌖20km 🏊12km ⌖on the spot ⊷on the spot.

| ⚓ | Dals Långed 🕮 🕮 | 5D1 |

Ställplats Dals Långed, Christian Aarsruds väg 2.
**GPS:** n58,92272 e12,30742.⬆.

8 🛏SEK 150 ⛽🚰Ch🚿WC🚰📶included.🚲 **Location:** Rural,
comfortable, quiet. **Surface:** gravel. ◯ 01/05-25/10.
**Distance:** ⌖250m ⌖3km ⌖on the spot ⊷on the spot ⊗400m
🚌200m 🚲on the spot 🏊on the spot.

| 🚐S | Fiskebäckskil | 5D2 |

Skaftö Golfklubb, Stockeviksvägen 2. **GPS:** n58,23213 e11,45394.
5 🛏SEK 200 🚿included.
**Distance:** ⊗on the spot.
**Remarks:** At golf court.

| 🚐 | Floda | 5D2 |

Öjared Golf, Öjaredsvägen. **GPS:** n57,85467 e12,39777 ⬆.
🛏. **Surface:** asphalted.
**Remarks:** At golf court.

| 🚐S | Forsvik 🕮 | 5E1 |

Ställplats Forsvik Göta kanal, Baltzar von Platens väg 18.
**GPS:** n58,57525 e14,43557.

15 🛏SEK 150 WC🚰included. 🚍 **Location:** Rural, simple, quiet.
**Surface:** gravel. ◯ 01/05-30/09.
**Distance:** ⌖2km ⌖on the spot ⊷on the spot ⊗on the spot 🚲on
the spot.
**Remarks:** At Göta Canal.

**SE**

## ⊟S Göteborg 5D2
**Lisebergs Ställplats Skatås**, Skatåsvägen 25.
**GPS**: n57,70303 e12,03513.⬆.

37 SEK 240/24h 🔌🔲Ch🧹included. 🛒
**Location:** Quiet. **Surface:** asphalted. 📅 01/05-04/11.
**Distance:** 🚶3km ⊗750m ⚓750m 🚲 on the spot 🏊 on the spot.

## ⊟S Grebbestad 5D2
**SportShopen**, Rörvik 1. **GPS**: n58,67683 e11,27572.⬆.
50 SEK 150-200 🔌Ch included. 🧹SEK 50.
**Location:** Rural. **Surface:** gravel. 📅 01/01-31/12.
**Distance:** 🚶2km ⊗1,5km ⚓ on the spot.

## ⚓S Hälsö 5D2
Tjolmenvägen. **GPS**: n57,73152 e11,65794.
15 SEK 180 🔌🧹WC🔲included. 🛒
**Distance:** ⚓on the spot 🐟on the spot.

## ⚓S Henän ⛵ 5D2
**Henåns ställplats**, Ängsvägen 16. **GPS**: n58,23925 e11,67493.
30 SEK 150 🔌🔲Ch🧹WC🔲included. 🏠 **Location:** Rural,
comfortable. **Surface:** gravel/metalled. 📅 01/01-31/12.
**Distance:** ⚓on the spot ⊗400m ⚓400m.
**Remarks:** Pay at reception.

## ⊟S Hjo ☕🍴 5E2
**Tupp och höna Ställplats**, Svebråta Sörgården 3.
**GPS**: n58,34658 e14,14127.⬆.

20 SEK 70 🔌🔲Ch🧹SEK 30 WC🔲.🛒 **Location:** Rural, isolated,
quiet. **Surface:** gravel. 📅 01/05-30/09.
**Distance:** ⚓on the spot 🏊on the spot.

## ⊟S Hjo ☕🍴 5E2
Viktoriagatan. **GPS**: n58,30359 e14,28919.⬆➡.

6 free. **Location:** Urban, simple, central, quiet. **Surface:** asphalted.
📅 01/01-31/12.
**Distance:** 🚶500m ⚓500m 🐟500m ⊗400m ⚓300m 🏊on the
spot 🏊on the spot.

## ⊟S Hjo ☕🍴 5E2
**Bisonfarmen i Gate**, Mobolet Mohem.
**GPS**: n58,17747 e14,16246.⬆➡.

15 SEK 150 🔌🔲Ch🧹(10x) WC🔲.🛒 **Location:** Rural.
**Surface:** gravel. 📅 01/05-30/09.
**Distance:** ⊗on the spot 🏊on the spot.

---

**Remarks:** Beautiful view.

## 🍴⊟S Hjo ☕🍴 5E2
**Restaurang Stampens Kvarn**, Stampens kvarn 1.
**GPS**: n58,30745 e14,25516.⬆.

6 SEK 140 🔌🔲Ch🧹SEK 30 WC🔲🔲.🛒 **Location:** Rural,
comfortable, isolated, quiet. **Surface:** grassy. 📅 Easter-30/09.
**Distance:** 🚶1,5km ⊗on the spot 🏊on the spot.

## ⚓S Hönö 5D2
**Hönö Kläva Fiskehamn ek förening**, Öckerövägen 1.
**GPS**: n57,68343 e11,65040.⬆.
23-38 SEK 170-200 🔌Ch🧹included WC🔲🔲.🛒
**Location:** Comfortable. **Surface:** asphalted. 📅 01/01-31/12.
**Distance:** 🚶on the spot ⚓on the spot ⊗100m.

## 🏛 Hunnebostrand 5D2
**Nordens Ark**, Åby säteri. **GPS**: n58,44347 e11,43661.⬆.
10 SEK 200. 🏠 **Location:** Rural, isolated, quiet. **Surface:** unpaved.
📅 01/01-31/12.
**Remarks:** Parking zoo.

## ⚓S Karlsborg ⛵ 5E1
**Carlsborg Segelsällskap**, Västra Varvsgatan 6.
**GPS**: n58,53998 e14,50208.⬆.

40 SEK 180 🔌🔲Ch🧹WC🔲🔲included. 🛒🧹
**Location:** Rural, simple, quiet. **Surface:** grassy/gravel.
📅 29/04-31/10 🔲 during event.
**Distance:** 🚶300m ⚓on the spot ⊗400m ⚓300m 🏊on the spot.
**Remarks:** At the canal.

## ⊟S Kungshamn 5D2
**Smögenbrons Rum**, Dinglevägen 27. **GPS**: n58,36903 e11,24984.
SEK 200 🔌🔲Ch included. 📅 01/06-31/08.
**Distance:** 🚶1km ⚓on the spot 🐟on the spot ⊗1km.

## Lidköping 5E1
**Camp Active Studios**, Lovene, Kållands Åsaka 1.
**GPS**: n58,45263 e13,04888.
20 SEK 150 🔌🔲Ch🧹(20x)included WC🔲.🧹
**Location:** Rural. **Surface:** asphalted/gravel. 📅 01/04-30/09.
**Distance:** 🚶10km ⊗on the spot ⚓1,5km.
**Remarks:** Sports centre, swimming pool.

## ⚓S Lidköping 5E1
**Spikens Båtsällskap**. **GPS**: n58,68952 e13,20174.
SEK 120 🔌🔲Ch🧹SEK 30 🔲SEK 5/3minutes. 📅 01/05-30/09.
**Distance:** 🚶Lidköping 25km ⚓on the spot 🐟on the spot ⊗on the spot.

## ⊟S Lyrestad ⛵ 5E1
**Lyrestad Gästhamn**, Kanalvägen 9. **GPS**: n58,80324 e14,05703.⬆.

25 SEK 150, 17/06-07/08 SEK 175 🔌🔲Ch WC🔲🔲.🛒
**Location:** Rural, simple, quiet. **Surface:** grassy.
📅 01/06-31/08.
**Distance:** ⚓on the spot 🐟on the spot ⊗200m ⚓200m ⚓500m
🏊on the spot.

---

**Remarks:** At Göta Canal, next to midget golf, caution SEK 100.

## 🍴⊟S Lyrestad ⛵ 5E1
**Norrqvarn Hotell & Konferens**, Norrqvarns Slussområde.
**GPS**: n58,78655 e14,08360.⬆.

15 SEK 150 🧹(5x)SEK 25/night WC🔲.🛒🧹 **Location:** Rural,
simple, isolated, quiet. **Surface:** gravel. 📅 01/01-31/12.
**Distance:** 🚶3km ⚓on the spot 🐟on the spot ⊗on the spot 🏊on
the spot.
**Remarks:** At Göta Canal, check in on arrival, canoe and bicycle rental,
restaurant only in summer.

## ⚓S Lysekil 5D2
**Fiskhamnens**, Bangårdsgatan 2. **GPS**: n58,27445 e11,43972.⬆.
21 SEK 200 🔌WC🔲included. **Location:** Rural, isolated, quiet.
📅 01/01-31/12.
**Distance:** 🚶centre 700m ⚓on the spot ⊗200m.

## ⚓S Lysekil 5D2
**Kolholmarnas**, Bangårdsgatan 18. **GPS**: n58,27629 e11,44745.⬆.
36 SEK 200 🔌🧹WC🔲included. 📅 01/01-31/12.
**Distance:** 🚶600m ⚓600m ⚓600m.

## ⚓S Lysekil 5D2
**Valbodalens**, Valbogatan 37. **GPS**: n58,28905 e11,43849.⬆.
35 SEK 200 🔌(20x)WC included. 📅 16/06-14/09.
**Distance:** 🚶2km ⚓on the spot 🐟on the spot.

## ⊟S Mariestad ⛵ 5E1
Kajgatan 1. **GPS**: n58,71311 e13,81893.⬆.

14 SEK 140 🧹SEK 25 WC🔲🔲SEK 30. 🏠 **Location:** Rural, central,
quiet. **Surface:** asphalted. 📅 01/01-31/12.
**Distance:** 🚶300m ⚓on the spot 🐟on the spot ⊗150m ⚓1km
⚓800m 🏊on the spot 🏊on the spot.
**Remarks:** Max. 3 days.

## ⚓S Mariestad ⛵ 5E1
**Mariestads Hamnområde**, Hamngatan 58.
**GPS**: n58,71601 e13,82033.⬆.

46 SEK 140 🔌🔲Ch🧹SEK 25/night,6Amp🔲SEK 30.🛒🧹
**Location:** Urban, simple, central, quiet. **Surface:** asphalted.
📅 01/01-31/12.
**Distance:** 🚶800m ⚓on the spot 🐟on the spot ⊗500m ⚓1km
⚓1km 🏊on the spot.
**Remarks:** Max. 3 days.

## ⚓S Öckerö 5D2
**Hönö Röd**, Rödvägen. **GPS**: n57,69933 e11,63954.
30 SEK 150 🔌🔲Ch🧹WC🔲included. **Location:** Urban,
comfortable, quiet. **Surface:** asphalted. 📅 01/06-01/10.
**Distance:** ⚓300m 🐟300m ⚓500m.

## ⚓S Öckerö 5D2
**Hönö Kläva Hamn**, Öckerövägen. **GPS**: n57,68345 e11,65156.⬆.
SEK 170, 15/06-15/08 SEK 200 🧹included. 📅 01/01-31/12.
**Distance:** 🐟on the spot ⊗500m.

## Rävlanda ⟨S⟩ 5D2

Route 514. **GPS:** n57,67094 e12,49270.
⟨free⟩ Ch. **Location:** Isolated. **Surface:** asphalted.
01/01-31/12.
**Distance:** ⊗3km 900m.
**Remarks:** At lake.

## Sjötorp ⟨S⟩ 5E1

**Sjötorps Gästhamn**, Stenbordsvägen. **GPS:** n58,83716 e13,97865.

30 SEK 185 WC included.
**Location:** Urban, simple, quiet. **Surface:** gravel. 01/05-30/09.
**Distance:** 400m on the spot on the spot ⊗on the spot on the spot on the spot.
**Remarks:** At Göta Canal, caution SEK 200.

## Skärhamn ⟨S⟩ 5D2

**Hav & Logi Skärhamn**, Rövallen 1. **GPS:** n57,97059 e11,55519.
6 SEK 200-300 WC. **Location:** Rural, comfortable, quiet. **Surface:** asphalted. 10/04-16/10.
**Distance:** 2,5km ⊗on the spot 100m.

## Strömstad ⟨S⟩ 5D1

**Bojarparkering**, Kebalvägen. **GPS:** n58,95115 e11,17330.

30 SEK 100/24h ChWC included.
**Location:** Rural, simple, quiet. **Surface:** gravel. 01/01-31/12.
**Distance:** 3km 1km 200m ⊗300m 3km on the spot on the spot on the spot.
**Remarks:** Free bus to centre.

## Tanumshede ⟨S⟩ 5D1

Brehogsvägen 8. **GPS:** n58,72129 e11,34524.
10 free Ch WCfree.
**Location:** Urban. **Surface:** asphalted. 01/01-31/12.
**Distance:** 2km ⊗on the spot on the spot 300m.
**Remarks:** At shopping centre.

## Tidaholm 5E2

Smedjegatan. **GPS:** n58,18130 e13,96792.

2 free. **Location:** Urban, central, quiet. **Surface:** asphalted.
01/01-31/12.
**Distance:** 300m ⊗400m 400m.
**Remarks:** Max. 48h.

## Tidaholm 5E2

Södra Kungsvägen. **GPS:** n58,17838 e13,96083.
2 free. **Location:** Urban, simple, central, quiet. **Surface:** asphalted.
01/01-31/12.
**Distance:** 300m ⊗50m.
**Remarks:** Max. 48h.

## Töreboda ⟨S⟩ 5E1

**Hajstorp Slusscafé & Vandrarhem**, Brovaktarstugan 5, Hajstorp.
**GPS:** n58,74745 e14,10776.

16 SEK 200 Ch WC included. **Location:** Rural, isolated, quiet. **Surface:** gravel. 01/04-30/09.
**Distance:** 200m on the spot ⊗on the spot 400m on the spot.
**Remarks:** At Göta Canal, max. 3t.

## Trollhättan ⟨S⟩ 5D2

**Ställplatser Trollhättan**, Åkerssjövägen. **GPS:** n58,26531 e12,26549.
16 SEK 150 Ch.
**Distance:** 2,8km.

# Värmland

## Årjäng ⟨S⟩ 5D1

**Sandaholm Restaurang & Camping**, Sanda Sjövik.
**GPS:** n59,36078 e12,27807.

15 SEK 100 Ch (8x)SEK 40/24h WCincluded SEK 25/24h.
**Location:** Rural, simple, quiet. **Surface:** metalled.
01/04-01/10.
**Distance:** 6km on the spot on the spot ⊗on the spot 6km on the spot on the spot.

## Filipstad 5E1

**Asphyttans Slussar**, Konsul Lundströms väg. **GPS:** n59,61839 e14,18147.
SEK 120 included.
**Distance:** 12km.
**Remarks:** Canoe and boat rental.

## Hammarö 5E1

**Getingbergets Badplats**, Sättersvägen 569. **GPS:** n59,29690 e13,56170.
6 SEK 100. **Location:** Rural, isolated, quiet. **Surface:** gravel.
01/01-31/12.
**Distance:** on the spot on the spot.
**Remarks:** To be paid at golf court GPS N59,30313, E13,542056.

## Karlstad 5E1

Sävegatan 2. **GPS:** n59,39329 e13,51467.

25 free. **Location:** Urban, simple, central, noisy. **Surface:** asphalted.
01/01-31/12.
**Distance:** 500m 100m ⊗100m on the spot.

## Karlstad 5E1

Trädgårdsgatan. **GPS:** n59,37726 e13,50376.

4 SEK 5/h, SEK 25/day. **Location:** Urban, simple, central, noisy.
**Surface:** asphalted. 15/04-15/10.

---

**Distance:** 500m 1km ⊗500m 500m on the spot on the spot on the spot.
**Remarks:** Along railwayline, small pitches.

## Kil 5E1

**Fryksta**, Sjöleden. **GPS:** n59,52045 e13,32507.

6 free. **Location:** Rural, simple, isolated, quiet. **Surface:** gravel.
01/01-31/12.
**Distance:** 3km 2km on the spot on the spot ⊗on the spot on the spot on the spot.
**Remarks:** Only overnight stays 18-10h.

## Kristinehamn ⟨S⟩ 5E1

**Kristinehamns Gästhamn och Ställplats**, Hamnvägen 9.
**GPS:** n59,31138 e14,09558.
37 SEK 185 Ch (20x)SEK 30 WC included.
**Location:** Urban, comfortable, quiet. **Surface:** gravel.
01/01-31/12.
**Distance:** 700m ⊗50m 300m.
**Remarks:** Next to midget golf.

## Morokulien ⟨S⟩ 4B3

Kungsvägen. **GPS:** n59,93089 e12,24181.
10 free ChWC. **Location:** Isolated, quiet.
**Surface:** asphalted/metalled. 01/01-31/12.
**Distance:** ⊗on the spot.
**Remarks:** Next to petrol station.

## Nysäter ⟨S⟩ 5D1

**Nysäters gästhamn**, Marknadsvägen.
**GPS:** n59,28417 e12,78242.

20 SEK 100 SEK 20 WC included.
**Location:** Rural, comfortable, isolated, quiet. **Surface:** grassy/gravel.
15/05-15/09.
**Distance:** 500m on the spot on the spot ⊗500m 500m 500m on the spot on the spot.

## Säffle ⟨S⟩ 5D1

Karlsborgsgatan. **GPS:** n59,12405 e12,92426.

10 SEK 100 WC included.
**Location:** Rural, simple, quiet. **Surface:** gravel. 15/05-15/10.
**Distance:** 1km 2km on the spot on the spot 1km 900m on the spot on the spot.
**Remarks:** Check in at harbourmaster.

## Säffle 5D1

**Medborgarhusets**, Magasinsgatan 2. **GPS:** n59,13499 e12,92178.

SE

8 ⌧SEK 150 ⚡included. 🔌 ♨Location: Urban, simple, noisy.
**Surface:** asphalted. ⬛ 15/05-15/10.
**Distance:** 🚶700m ⚓300m ⬛on the spot 🚌on the spot ⊗500m
⬛on the spot 🚲on the spot 🧍on the spot.
**Remarks:** Pay at harbourmaster.

| 🏕 | Torsby | 4C3 |

Bangårdsgatan 10. **GPS:** n60,13623 e13,00304.⬆.
10 ⌧free. **Location:** Simple, noisy. **Surface:** metalled.
⬛ 01/01-31/12.
**Distance:** ⊗100m 🚌on the spot.
**Remarks:** At station, max. 48h.

# Örebro

| 🏕S | Askersund ⛵ | 5E1 |

**Askersund Citycamp & Gästhamn**, Sundsbrogatan 1.
**GPS:** n58,87879 e14,89928.⬆.

20 ⌧SEK 230 🔌🍴Ch⚡(20x)included WC⬛.🔥♨
**Location:** Urban, simple, central, quiet. **Surface:** gravel.
⬛ 01/04-01/11.
**Distance:** 🚶350m ⬛on the spot 🚌2km ⊗350m 🍺400m 🚗150m
🚲on the spot.

| S | Askersund ⛵ | 5E1 |

Hagavägen. **GPS:** n58,88079 e14,91382.
5free 🔌🍴Chfree. **Location:** Urban. **Surface:** metalled.
⬛ 01/01-31/12.
**Distance:** 🚶850m ⊗700m 🍺800m.

| ⚓S | Aspabruk | 5E1 |

**Aspa Båtklubb**, Norrviksvägen 4. **GPS:** n58,75961 e14,80499.

10 ⌧SEK 150 🔌ChWC⬛included. 🔌♨
**Location:** Rural. **Surface:** gravel. ⬛ 01/04-30/09.
**Distance:** 🚶1km ⚓on the spot 🚌on the spot ⊗on the spot 🚲on
the spot.

| 🏕S | Hällefors | 4C3 |

**Lantliv Hjulsjö**, Hjulsjö 108. **GPS:** n59,77813 e14,77634.⬆.
10 ⌧SEK 150 WC⬛included. **Location:** Rural, simple, isolated, quiet.
**Surface:** grassy. ⬛ 15/05-16/09.
**Distance:** ⚓on the spot 🚌on the spot.
**Remarks:** At lake, use of sauna against payment.

# Västmanland

| 🏕S | Arboga | 5F1 |

**Hjälmare Docka. GPS:** n59,38186 e15,94347.⬆.
10 ⌧SEK 150 ⚡included. **Surface:** grassy. ⬛ 01/04-15/10.
**Distance:** ⚓on the spot 🚌on the spot ⊗on the spot.
**Remarks:** At the canal.

| 🏕S | Lindesberg | 5E1 |

Fotbollsgatan. **GPS:** n59,60157 e15,18676.
10 ⌧free 🔌🍴Chfree. **Surface:** asphalted. ⬛ 01/01-31/12.
**Distance:** 🚶centre 2,5km ⊗2,5km 🍺2,5km.

**Remarks:** Max. 24h.

| 🏕S | Lindesberg | 5E1 |

**Lindesberg Stugby Ställplats**, Jungfruhagsvägen 1.
**GPS:** n59,58600 e15,23852.⬆.
10 ⌧SEK 200 🔌ChWC⬛. **Location:** Isolated, quiet.
**Surface:** grassy/gravel. ⬛ 01/01-31/12.
**Distance:** 🚶1,5km 🚌1,5km 🍺1,5km.

| ⚓S | Västerås | 4D3 |

**Västerås Gästhamn**, Lögarängsvägen 3. **GPS:** n59,60190 e16,54648.⬆.
15 ⌧SEK 200 🔌ChWC⬛included. 🔥**Location:** Rural,
comfortable, quiet. **Surface:** gravel. ⬛ 01/01-31/12.
**Distance:** 🚶500m ⚓on the spot 🚌on the spot ⊗500m.
**Remarks:** Max. 72h, pay at harbourmaster.

# Dalarna

| 🏕S | Borlänge | 4C3 |

**GPS:** n60,30070 e15,28120.
5 ⌧free 🔌🍴Chfree. **Location:** Rural, simple. **Surface:** asphalted.
⬛ 01/01-31/12.
**Distance:** ⚓on the spot 🚌on the spot ⊗on the spot.

| 🏕 | Falun | 4C3 |

Krongårdsvägen. **GPS:** n60,60171 e15,61502.⬆.
22 ⌧SEK 195 WC⬛included. 🔥**Location:** Central, quiet.
**Surface:** gravel. ⬛ 01/01-31/12.
**Distance:** 🚶900m ⚓900m 🍺1,1km.

| 🏕 | Ludvika | 4C3 |

Eriksgatan. **GPS:** n60,15020 e15,18936.
⌧free. **Location:** Urban. **Surface:** asphalted. ⬛ 01/01-31/12.
**Distance:** 🚶on the spot ⊗200m.
**Remarks:** Max. 24h.

| 🏕 | Särna | 4C3 |

**Lägerplats**, Byvägen. **GPS:** n61,80383 e12,90931.⬆➡.
6 ⌧SEK 60. **Location:** Rural. **Surface:** grassy.
**Distance:** ⚓on the spot 🚌on the spot.
**Remarks:** Along river.

| 🏖 | Säter | 4C3 |

**Säterdalens Folkpark. GPS:** n60,34854 e15,75439.
⌧free. ⬛ 01/01-31/12.
**Distance:** 🚶650m ⚓650m 🍺850m.

| 🏕S | Smedjebacken | 4C3 |

**Smedjebackens. GPS:** n60,13828 e15,41647.
5 ⌧SEK 100 🔌🍴Ch⚡⬛. **Surface:** gravel. ⬛ 01/05-01/10.
**Distance:** 🚶500m 🚌on the spot ⊗200m 🍺500m 🚲on the spot
🧍on the spot.

| 🏕S | Sollerön | 4C3 |

**Sollerö camping**, Levsnäs. **GPS:** n60,90048 e14,58318.⬆.
18 ⌧SEK 80-100 ⚡(8x)SEK 30. **Surface:** asphalted.
**Distance:** 🚲on the spot 🧍on the spot.
**Remarks:** Quick-Stop: >18h - <9h.

| 🏖S | Stjärnsund | 4C3 |

**Villa Solhem**, Bruksallén 17. **GPS:** n60,43421 e16,20744.⬆.
11 ⌧SEK 200 🔌🍴⚡(4x)SEK 20 WC⬛included 🔥against payment.
🔥**Location:** Urban, simple, central. **Surface:** asphalted/metalled.
⬛ 01/01-31/12.
**Distance:** 🚶on the spot ⚓300m 🚌300m.

# Gävleborg

| 🏕S | Axmar | 4D3 |

**Axmarbrygga Havskrog**, Boskär. **GPS:** n61,04877 e17,15774.⬆.
50 ⌧SEK 90 🔌🍴Ch⚡SEK 50 WCincluded ⬛SEK 10.
**Location:** Rural, isolated, quiet. **Surface:** gravel.
⬛ 07/04-05/11.
**Distance:** ⚓on the spot 🚌on the spot ⊗on the spot.
**Remarks:** Bread-service.

| 🏕 | Färila 🚻⛵ | 4C2 |

Laforsenvägen. **GPS:** n61,96147 e15,49969.⬆.
10 ⌧SEK 50. **Location:** Rural, simple, quiet. **Surface:** forest soil.
⬛ 01/01-31/12.
**Distance:** ⚓on the spot 🚌on the spot 🚲on the spot 🧍on the spot.

| 🏕S | Gävle | 4D3 |

**Hemlingbystugan**, Hemlingbyvägen 93. **GPS:** n60,65005 e17,16996.
⌧free 🔌WC. **Surface:** asphalted.
**Distance:** 🚶2km ⚓2km 🍺1,8km.
**Remarks:** Max. 3 days.

| 🏕S | Gävle | 4D3 |

**Södra Skeppsbron. GPS:** n60,67670 e17,15985.⬆.

9 ⌧SEK 150 ⚡WC⬛. **Location:** Urban. **Surface:** asphalted.
⬛ 01/01-31/12.
**Distance:** 🚶on the spot ⚓on the spot 🚌on the spot ⊗on the spot
⬛on the spot.
**Remarks:** Payment with mobile phone, max. 48h.

| 🏕S | Gävle | 4D3 |

**Culinarparkeringen**, Drottningsgatan 47, Anderholmen.
**GPS:** n60,67810 e17,15493.⬆.

12 ⌧SEK 2/h, overnight stay and weekend free. **Surface:** gravel.

| 🏕 | Ockelbo | 4C3 |

**Wij Trädgårdar**, Vigatan 4. **GPS:** n60,88722 e16,70139.
⌧free. ⬛ 23/05-06/09.
**Distance:** 🚶1km ⊗on the spot.
**Remarks:** Near mill, max. 3 days.

# Västernorrland

| 🏕S | Docksta | 4D2 |

**Skuleberget Havscamping**, Veåsand 211.
**GPS:** n63,06659 e18,36723.⬆.

42 ⌧SEK 250 🔌⚡(42x),10Amp WC⬛🔔included. 🔥♨
**Location:** Rural, comfortable, isolated, quiet. **Surface:** gravel.
⬛ 01/01-31/12.
**Distance:** 🚶3km ⚓50m 🚌50m 🧍on the spot.

| 🏕S | Kvissleby | 4D2 |

Svartvik. **GPS:** n62,31935 e17,36955.

20 ⌧free. **Location:** Noisy. **Surface:** grassy/gravel.
⬛ 01/01-31/12.
**Distance:** ⚓on the spot 🚌on the spot ⊗500m.

| 🍴 | Sandöverken | 4D2 |

**Hotell Höga Kusten AB**, Hornöberget. **GPS:** n62,80468 e17,95136.⬆.

≋free. **Surface:** asphalted.
**Distance:** ⊗on the spot ⋏on the spot.

**Skatan** 4D2
Galströmsvägen. **GPS:** n62,19896 e17,49645.
≋free ⌁≋ChWC. ◻ 01/01-31/12.
**Distance:** ⊗500m 🚐200m.

# Jämtland

**Bispgården** 4C2
**123 Holliday Sweden**, Sörböle 230. **GPS:** n62,99040 e16,62163.⬆.

25 ≋SEK 150 ⌁≋Ch ⚡SEK 25 WC ≋included. **Location:** Rural,
comfortable, isolated, quiet. **Surface:** grassy.
◻ 01/05-01/09.
**Distance:** ⊿8km.
**Remarks:** Dutch owners.

**Gällö** 4C2
**Alma Ångbåt**. **GPS:** n62,82794 e15,30652.
≋SEK 150. **Surface:** grassy.
**Distance:** ⊿on the spot ➤on the spot 🚐300m.

**Hammarstrand** 4C2
**Zorbcenter**, Dödviken 145. **GPS:** n63,14690 e16,17890.

11 ≋SEK 150 ⌁⚡(5x)SEK 20 WC included 🧺. **Location:** Rural,
simple, isolated, quiet. **Surface:** grassy. ◻ 01/05-30/09.
**Distance:** ⊿15km ➤on the spot 🚐1km.
**Remarks:** Along river, canoe and boat rental.

**Mattmar** 4C2
**Ångaren Östersund**, Södra Arvesund 516. **GPS:** n63,23573 e14,06810.
≋SEK 60 ⌁⚡SEK 60 ☐SEK 20. **Surface:** grassy/metalled.
◻ 01/01-31/12.
**Distance:** ⊿on the spot ➤on the spot ⊗on the spot.

**Svenstavik** 4C2
Centrumvägen. **GPS:** n62,76731 e14,43496.⬆.
≋SEK 100 ⌁≋Chfree ⚡WC. **Location:** Urban.
**Surface:** asphalted.
**Distance:** ⊿on the spot ⊗on the spot 🍴on the spot.

# ⬛ Slovakia

Capital: Bratislava
Government: parliamentary republic
Official Language: Slovak
Population: 5,445,829 (2017)
Area: 49,036 km²

## General information
Dialling code: 0421
General emergency: 112
Currency: Euro
Credit cards are accepted almost everywhere.

## Regulations for overnight stays
Wild camping is not allowed.

## Additional public holidays 2019
January 1 Republic Day
January 6 Epiphany
May 1 Labour Day
May 8 End of World War II
July 5 St. Cyril & St. Methodius Day
August 29 National Uprising Day
September 1 Constitution Day
September 15 Day of Lady Sorrows
November 1 All Saints' Day
November 17 Freedom and Democracy Day

## Time Zone
Winter (Standard Time) GMT+1
Summer (DST) GMT+2

*Slovakia
page: 759*

*Bratislava*

**SK**

## Bratislava

| △S | Bratislava | 36C1 |
|---|---|---|

**Camping Zlate Piesky**, Senecká cesta 2. **GPS**: n48,18836 e17,18557.⬆.
⌧ € 15,80, 2 pers.incl 🚰 ▣Ch ✎ € 3,50 WC included ⌧.
**Location:** Urban, central. **Surface:** grassy.
⬛ 01/05-15/10.
**Distance:** �foot8km 🍴100m ⊗on the spot 🚐200m.

## Trnava

| △S | Banka | 36C1 |
|---|---|---|

**Camping Pullmann Piestany**, Cesta Janka Alexyho 921.
**GPS**: n48,57609 e17,83444.
⌧ € 8 🚰 ▣ChWCincluded ⌧. **Location:** Urban. **Surface:** grassy.
**Distance:** �foot2km 🏊on the spot.

| △S | Dunajská Streda | 36C1 |
|---|---|---|

**CaravanCamp DS**, Kúpelná ulica 21. **GPS**: n47,98689 e17,61150.
15 ⌧ € 12 🚰▣Ch ✎ WC⌧ 📶included.
**Location:** Urban, central. **Surface:** grassy. ⬛ 01/04-01/11.
**Distance:** �foot1km 🍴350m 🍺900m.

| △S | Šamorín | 36C1 |
|---|---|---|

**Stellplatz Čilistov**, Čilistov. **GPS**: n48,01364 e17,30850.⬆.

25 ⌧ € 7 🚰 ▣Ch ✎ € 3 WC 📶included. ⌧ 🚗
**Location:** Rural, simple. **Surface:** grassy/gravel. ⬛ 01/04-31/10.
**Distance:** �foot Bratislava 20km 🏊50m 🍺500m 🚲200m.
**Remarks:** Dog € 4, golf court 2km.

## Žilina

| 🏨 | Liptovský Ján | 38C4 |
|---|---|---|

**Pension Horec**, Starojanka. **GPS**: n49,03709 e19,67526.
15 ⌧free. **Location:** Rural. **Surface:** metalled.
⬛ 01/01-31/12.

**Distance:** ⊗100m 🎿on the spot 🎿on the spot.
**Remarks:** At ski-lift.

| △S | Varín | 38B4 |
|---|---|---|

**Autocamp Varin**, Doktor Jozefa Tisu 13. **GPS**: n49,20833 e18,87861.⬆.
⌧ € 12 🚰 ▣Ch ✎ € 3,30 WC⌧ included 📶. **Location:** Rural, quiet.
**Surface:** grassy. ⬛ 01/05-11/10.
**Distance:** �foot on the spot.

## Banská Bystric

| △S | Brezno | 38C4 |
|---|---|---|

**Sedliacky Dvor**, Hliník 7, Rohozná. **GPS**: n48,79535 e19,72869.⬆.

20 ⌧ € 17,25 🚰 ▣Ch ✎ WC⌧ 💡 € 3,25 📶included.
**Location:** Rural. **Surface:** grassy. ⬛ 15/04-31/10.
**Distance:** �foot7km ⊗1,2km 🍺1,2km 🚐700m 🏊on the spot 🚶on the spot.
**Remarks:** Bread-service.

## Prešov

| △S | Haligovce | 38C4 |
|---|---|---|

**Camping Goralsky Dvor. GPS**: n49,37984 e20,43972.⬆.
⌧ € 10,50 🚰 ▣Ch ✎ € 3,50 WC⌧ 📶included.
**Location:** Rural. **Surface:** grassy.
**Distance:** ⊗on the spot.

| △S | Snina | 38D4 |
|---|---|---|

**Camping Snina**, Rybnícka 4483. **GPS**: n48,97384 e22,18919.
25 ⌧ € 9 🚰 ▣Chincluded ✎ € 2,50 ⌧ € 0,50 📶. **Location:** Rural,
isolated. ⬛ 15/05-15/09.
**Distance:** �foot3km 🏊50m 🍴50m 🏊on the spot 🚶on the spot.

| 🏨S | Vysoké Tatry | 38C4 |
|---|---|---|

**Camp Tatranec**, Tatranská Lomnica 202. **GPS**: n49,15826 e20,30944.⬆.
30 ⌧ € 12, 2 pers.incl 🚰 ▣Ch ✎ WC⌧. **Location:** Rural.

**Surface:** grassy. ⬛ 01/01-31/12.
**Distance:** �foot2,5km ⊗on the spot.
**Remarks:** Beautiful view.

| 🏨S | Vysoké Tatry | 38C4 |
|---|---|---|

**Pension Slnecny Dom**, Tatranská Lomnica 287.
**GPS**: n49,16664 e20,28169.⬆.
4 ⌧ € 10 🚰 ▣Ch ✎ included.
**Location:** Rural. **Surface:** metalled. ⬛ 01/01-31/12.
**Distance:** �foot on the spot ⊗on the spot 🎿on the spot 🎿on the spot.

## Košice

| △S | Vyšný Medzev | 38C4 |
|---|---|---|

**Camping Sokol**, Hrdinov SNP 64 - 68. **GPS**: n48,71472 e20,90222.
25 ⌧ € 17,50 🚰 ▣Ch ✎ € 2,50 WC⌧included.
**Location:** Rural. **Surface:** grassy. ⬛ 01/04-01/10.
**Distance:** ⊗on the spot.

# 🇸🇮 Slovenia

Capital: Ljubljana
Government: parliamentarian republic
Official Language: Slovenian
Population: 1,978,000 (2017)
Area: 20,373 km²

## General information
Dialling code: 00386
General emergency: 112
Currency: Euro
Credit card are accepted almost everywhere.

## Regulations for overnight stays
There is no regulation against overnight camping, but it is not yet generally accepted. In the National Park Triglav wild camping is forbidden.

## Additional public holidays 2019
February 8 Prešern Day - Slovenian cultural festival
April 27 Uprising against the Occupation Day
May 1-2 Labour Day
June 25 National Holiday
August 15 Assumption of the Virgin Mary
October 31 Reformation Day
November 1 All Saints' Day
December 26 Independence Day

## Time Zone
Winter (Standard Time) GMT+1
Summer (DST) GMT+2

Slovenia East pages: 763-768
Ljubljana
Slovenia West pages: 760-763

SL

# Slovenia West

**Ajdovščina** | 37A1
Avtodome Žonta, Predmeja 18. GPS: n45,95058 e13,87614.
10 € 20 WC ⚡ Location: Rural, comfortable, isolated, quiet.
Surface: grassy. 01/01-31/12.
Distance: 10km on the spot on the spot.
Remarks: Max. 8M.

**Ajdovščina** | 37A1
Avtokamp Ajdovščina, Cesta 5 Maja 14. GPS: n45,89134 e13,90141.
50 € 17,28 Ch WC included. Location: Rural.
Surface: grassy. 01/04-31/10.
Distance: 700m on the spot on the spot.

**Bled** | 36A3
Ljubljanska cesta. GPS: n46,36957 e14,11700.
20 € 20. Surface: unpaved.
Distance: city centre 1km 300m 100m.

**Bled** | 36A3
Camping Bled, Kidričeva 10 c. GPS: n46,36162 e14,08221.
€ 28,50-31,50 Ch WC 🏠
Surface: grassy.
01/04-15/10.
Distance: 2km on the spot on the spot on the spot on the spot.

**Tourist information Bled:**
Bled Castle. Exhibition about the history of Bled, during the summer also open-air concerts. 8-17h.
Soteska Vintgar Gorge, TD Gorje, Podhom 0, Gorje. Trail over bridges and galleries along a river.

**Bohinj** | 37A1
Bohinjska Bistrica. GPS: n46,27423 e13,95912.

22 € 15 Ch WC included. Location: Simple.
Surface: asphalted. 01/01-31/12.
Distance: 300m 7km 300m 300m on the spot on the spot.

**Bohinj** | 37A1
Srednja Vas v Bohinju 96. GPS: n46,29119 e13,93000.

20 € 15 Ch WC included. Location: Rural, simple, isolated, quiet. Surface: gravel. 01/01-31/12.
Distance: 3km lake 5km 3km 3km on the spot on the spot on the spot.

**Bohinjsko jezero** | 37A1
Kamp Zlatorog, Ukanc 2. GPS: n46,27887 e13,83739.
€ 20-35, 2 pers.incl Ch € 3,50 WC € 3 included.
25/04-30/09.
Distance: on the spot on the spot 150m.

**Tourist information Bohinjsko jezero:**
Savica Falls. Water falls.

**Bovec** | 23H1
Alpski turistični center Kanin Bovec, Dvor 43.
GPS: n46,33306 e13,53944.

14 € 20/24h, € 30/36h Ch included.
Location: Rural, isolated, quiet.
Surface: asphalted.
01/01-31/12 service: 01/11-15/03.
Distance: 1km on the spot on the spot on the spot.
Remarks: Max. 36h, payment only with coins.

**Tourist information Bovec:**
Triglav National Park, Dom Trenta, Soča. Information centre.
Kluže Fortress, Trg golobarskih žrtev 8. Fort above gorge.
Soča Trail, Soča. Hiking trail along the Soca river.

**Cerknica** | 37A1
Turistična Kmetija Logar, Žerovnica 16, Grahovo.
GPS: n45,75899 e14,42571.
4 free. Location: Rural, isolated, quiet. 01/01-31/12.
Distance: 7km 200m on the spot on the spot on the spot.

**Cerknica** | 37A1
Gostilna En Krajcar, Podskrajnik 24. GPS: n45,79418 e14,33869.
6 free Ch. Location: Isolated, noisy. Surface: metalled.
01/01-31/12.
Distance: on the spot.
Remarks: Bicycle rental.

**Cerkno** | 37A1
Kmetija Želinc, Straža 8. GPS: n46,10259 e13,94670.
5 € 12. 01/01-31/12.
Distance: on the spot on the spot.

**Domžale** | 37A1
ACG Autocenter Glavan, Češminova ulica 1a.
GPS: n46,14637 e14,60047.

2 free Ch (2x)free,16Amp. Location: Urban, simple, central, noisy. Surface: asphalted/gravel.
01/01-31/12.
Distance: 100m 3km 500m 300m 150m 150m 500m on the spot on the spot 20km 20km.

**Dornberk** | 37A1
Saksida, Zalošče 12a. GPS: n45,88963 e13,74751.

15 € 5+ € 10/pp Ch (15x)€ 3,16Amp WC included.
Location: Rural, comfortable, isolated.
Surface: gravel/metalled.
01/01-31/12.
Distance: 1km 350m 350m on the spot 1km 300m on the spot on the spot.
Remarks: Dog € 2/day, covered picnic area, swimming pool available.

**Gradac** | 37B1
Kamp Bela Krajina, Škrilje 11, Podzemelj.
GPS: n45,60463 e15,27619.

12 € 10/pp, winter € 5/pp Ch € 4 WC included.
Location: Rural, comfortable. Surface: grassy/gravel.
01/01-31/12.
Distance: 200m 200m on the spot on the spot 200m.
Remarks: Along river, special part for motor homes, playground.

**Idrija** | 37A1
Veri Krajnik, Carl Jakoba ulica 9. GPS: n45,99879 e14,02595.

3 🛏️ € 10 🚰🗑️Ch 💧included. ♨️ **Location:** Rural, simple, isolated, quiet. **Surface:** grassy/gravel. ⏱️ 01/01-31/12.
**Distance:** 🚶1,5km ⊗1,5km 🍺1,5km 🛒1,5km 🚲on the spot 🏊on the spot.
**Remarks:** Narrow entrance.

| 🚐S | **Ilirska Bistrica** | 37A1 |

**Motorhome Grill Danilo**, Bazoviška cesta 46.
**GPS:** n45,55846 e14,24340. ⬆️➡️.

6 🛏️ € 13 + tourist tax € 1,04pp 🚰🗑️Ch 💧(6x),16Amp WC 📶included 🍽️♨️ **Location:** Rural, comfortable, central, quiet. **Surface:** asphalted. ⏱️ 01/01-31/12.
**Distance:** 🚶500m 🚲10km 🍺100m ⊗on the spot 🍽️200m 🎦100m 🛒500m 🚲on the spot 🏊on the spot 🎿20km ⛷️20km.
**Remarks:** Breakfast-service.

| 🚐 | **Izola** 🌴⛵🍽️🎪 ⬆️ | 37A1 |

Tomažičeva ulica. **GPS:** n45,53230 e13,64861. ⬆️.
10 🛏️ € 15/24h. **Surface:** asphalted. ⏱️ 01/01-31/12.
**Distance:** 🚶500m 🍺200m 🛒100m.

| 🚐S | **Izola** 🌴⛵🍽️🎪 | 37A1 |

Cankarjev Drevored. **GPS:** n45,53808 e13,66397. ⬆️➡️.

5 🛏️ € 15/24h 🗑️Ch 💧(4x)included,16Amp. 🏠 **Location:** Urban, comfortable, quiet. **Surface:** asphalted/gravel.
⏱️ 01/01-31/12.
**Distance:** 🚶500m 🚲500m 🍺on the spot ⊗500m 🍽️500m 🛒on the spot 🚲on the spot 🏊on the spot.

| ⛰️S | **Kamniška Bistrica** 🏔️ | 36A3 |

**Kamp Alpe. GPS:** n46,30543 e14,60794.
10 🛏️ € 25 🚰🗑️Ch 💧WC. ⏱️ 01/05-01/10.

| ⛰️S | **Kobarid** 🔥🏔️ | 23H1 |

**Koren**, Drezneske Ravne 333. **GPS:** n46,25083 e13,58667.

🛏️ € 25-30 🚰🗑️Ch 💧WC 📶. ⏱️ 01/01-31/12.
**Distance:** 🚶500m 🍽️on the spot 🚲on the spot 🍺on the spot.

| ⛰️S | **Kobarid** 🔥🏔️ | 23H1 |

**Lazar**, Gregorciceva 63. **GPS:** n46,25530 e13,58720.
🛏️ € 26 🚰🗑️Ch 💧WC. ⏱️ 01/04-31/10.
**Distance:** ⊗on the spot 🍽️on the spot.
**Tourist information Kobarid:**
Ⓜ️ Kobariski muzej, Gregorciceva 1. Museum about the first World War.
⏱️ 01/04-30/09 9-18h, 01/10-31/03 10-17h.

---

⛵ Tolmin Chutes, LTO Sotočje, Petra Skalarja 4, Tolmin. Touristic route along the rapid to the thermal source of the river.

| 🚐S | **Koper** | 37A1 |

Ljubljanska cesta 13. **GPS:** n45,53790 e13,73780. ⬆️.
39 🛏️ € 10/24h 🚰🗑️Ch 💧WC 📶included. **Location:** Urban, simple, noisy. **Surface:** asphalted. ⏱️ 01/01-31/12.
**Remarks:** Nearby bus station.

| | **Kranj** 🍽️ | 37A1 |

**Stara Sava**, Gregorčičeva ulica. **GPS:** n46,24307 e14,35771. ⬆️➡️.

6 🛏️ € 10/24h 🗑️€ 0,50/40liter 🗑️Ch 💧€ 0,20/kWh.
**Location:** Urban, simple. **Surface:** gravel. ⏱️ 01/01-31/12.
**Distance:** 🚶200m ⊗200m 🍺100m.

| 🚐S | **Kranjska Gora** 🏔️⛰️❄️🚡 | 36A3 |

Borovška cesta. **GPS:** n46,48746 e13,77510. ⬆️➡️.

20 🛏️ € 15/24h 🚰🗑️Ch 💧WC 📶included. ♨️ **Location:** Rural, quiet. **Surface:** gravel. ⏱️ 01/01-31/12.
**Distance:** 🚶500m 🚲2km 🍺2km ⊗200m 🍽️500m 🚲on the spot 🏊on the spot 🎿on the spot ⛷️on the spot.
**Remarks:** To be paid at bar.

| ⛰️S | **Laze v Tuhinju** | 37A1 |

**Terme Snovik**, Snovik 7. **GPS:** n46,22661 e14,70440.
20 🛏️ € 25 🚰🗑️Ch 💧(3x)included. **Surface:** grassy.
⏱️ 01/01-31/12.
**Distance:** 🚲on the spot 🏊on the spot.

| 🚐S | **Ljubljana** 🌴⛵🍽️🎪 | 37A1 |

**Alo Camp**, Peruzzijeva ulica 105.
**GPS:** n46,02151 e14,52303. ⬆️.

12 🛏️ € 20-25 🚰🗑️Ch 💧(13x)WC 📶included. ♨️
**Location:** Simple, isolated, quiet. **Surface:** asphalted
⏱️ 01/01-31/12.
**Distance:** 🚶3km ⊗on the spot 🍽️500m 🛒50m 🚲on the spot 🏊on the spot.
**Remarks:** Check in at hotel, borrow cycles for free.

| 🚐S | **Ljubljana** 🌴⛵🍽️🎪 | 37A1 |

**Pri Kovaču**, Cesta II. grupe odredov 82, Dobrunje.
**GPS:** n46,03162 e14,60386. ⬆️.

8 🛏️ € 10/night, guests free 🚰🗑️Ch 💧(20x)€ 2/night,16Amp WC 📶€ 0,80 📶included 🍽️♨️🚲

---

**Location:** Rural, comfortable, central, quiet. **Surface:** gravel.
⏱️ 01/01-31/12 🍽️ Restaurant: Tue.
**Distance:** 🚶8km 🚲2,5km 🍺5km 🛒4km ⊗on the spot 🍽️100m, bakery 200m 🛒20m 🚲on the spot 🏊on the spot 🎿400m.

| 🚐S | **Ljubljana** 🌴⛵🍽️🎪 | 37A1 |

**Campark**, Na Produ 2, Črnuče.
**GPS:** n46,09974 e14,51672. ⬆️.

36 🛏️ € 10 🚰🗑️Ch included 💧🍽️€ 4 WC. **Location:** Urban, comfortable. **Surface:** metalled. ⏱️ 01/01-31/12.
**Distance:** 🚶2km ⊗200m 🍽️500m 🛒100m 🏊on the spot.
**Remarks:** Canoe rental.

| 🚐S | **Ljubljana** 🌴⛵🍽️🎪 | 37A1 |

**Camperstop Colonial**, Parmova 51.
**GPS:** n46,06461 e14,50203. ⬆️.

5 🛏️ € 12 🚰🗑️Ch 💧included. 🏠 **Location:** Urban, simple.
**Surface:** asphalted. ⏱️ 01/01-31/12.
**Distance:** 🚶2km 🍺100m 🍽️on the spot 🛒200m 🚲on the spot 🏊on the spot.
**Remarks:** At supermarket, max. 3 nights.

| 🚐S | **Ljubljana** 🌴⛵🍽️🎪 | 37A1 |

**P+R Dolgi most**, Ljubljana.
**GPS:** n46,03721 e14,46526. ⬆️.

10 🛏️free 🚰🗑️Ch 💧. **Location:** Urban, simple, noisy.
**Surface:** asphalted. ⏱️ 01/01-31/12.
**Distance:** 🚶centre 4km ⊗4km 🍽️4km 🛒1,2km.
**Remarks:** Special part for motor homes, free bus to centre.

| 🚐S | **Ljubljana** 🌴⛵🍽️🎪 | 37A1 |

**Sraka**, Masarykova 23a.
**GPS:** n46,05740 e14,51870.

15 🛏️ € 15, park € 10 🚰🗑️Ch 💧📶included. ♨️ **Location:** Urban.
**Surface:** gravel. ⏱️ 01/01-31/12.
**Distance:** 🚶1km ⊗on the spot 🍽️100m 🛒on the spot 🚲on the spot 🏊on the spot.
**Remarks:** Motorhome washing place.

| 🍽️ | **Ljubljana** 🌴⛵🍽️🎪 | 37A1 |

**Gostilna Livada**, Hladnikova 15. **GPS:** n46,03513 e14,50967. ⬆️.

9 guests free. **Location:** Rural, simple.
01/01-31/12.
**Distance:** 1km on the spot 500m.
**Remarks:** Free with a meal.

**Tourist information Ljubljana:**

Ljubljana Tourist Card. Card offers among other things free public transport, free access at museums and discount in restaurants, shops etc. Available at Tourist Office, railway station and several hotels. T € 20,70/24h.

Ljubljana Tourist Information Center, Krekov trg 10, www.visitljubljana.com. Capital, historical city with a lot of annual events.

National museum, Muzjeska 1. Archeological and historical museum. 10-18h, Thu 10-20h Mo.

Plecnik museum, Kurunova 4. Architectonic museum in the house of Joze Plecnik. Tue, Thu 10-14h.

Slovene Natural History Museum, Muzjeska 1. Zoological and botanic museum.
daily 10-18h, Thu 10-20h Mo.

Ljubljana Castle. Medieval fortress, tourist train at town centre.
01/10-30/04 10-21h, 01/05-30/09 9-22h.

Vodnikov trg. daily, summer 6-18h, winter 6-16h.
Zoo Ljubljana, Večna pot 70. Zoo.
summer 9-19h, winter 9-16h.

### Logatec — 37A1

Počivališče Lom. **GPS:** n45,89817 e14,25486.
6 free. **Location:** Motorway. **Surface:** asphalted. 01/01-31/12.
**Distance:** on the spot on the spot on the spot.
**Remarks:** At petrol station.

### Luče — 36A3

Camp Smica, Luče 4. **GPS:** n46,36117 e14,73626.
€ 12-16 Ch WC. 01/05-30/10.
**Distance:** on the spot on the spot 900m.

### Lukovica — 37A1

Gostilna Furman, Stari trg 19. **GPS:** n46,17026 e14,69233.

10 € 10, € 15 service incl Ch (10x) WC
**Location:** Urban, simple, central, quiet. **Surface:** gravel.
01/01-31/12.
**Distance:** on the spot 3km 3km on the spot 200m
100m on the spot on the spot.

### Lukovica — 37A1

OMV Istrabenz. **GPS:** n46,16690 e14,69380.
2 free Chfree. **Location:** Motorway, noisy.
01/01-31/12.
**Distance:** on the spot on the spot.
**Remarks:** Parking petrol station OMV Istrabenz.

### Mojstrana — 36A3

Camping Kamne, Dovje 9. **GPS:** n46,46444 e13,95778.
€ 20-28 Ch WC. 01/01-31/12.
**Distance:** 1km 1km.

### Podgrad — 37A1

Pension Patrik, Hrušica 100. **GPS:** n45,53257 e14,12055.

8 € 10-15, tourist tax incl Ch WC € 2,50 € 3,50/3,50
included. **Location:** Rural, isolated, quiet. **Surface:** gravel.
01/01-31/12.
**Distance:** 2,8km 40km 10km 2,8km 2,8km 50m
on the spot on the spot.
**Remarks:** Breakfast-service.

### Portorož — 37A1

Marina Portorož, Cesta solinarjev 8. **GPS:** n45,50505 e13,59847.

60 € 26, 01/04-15/11 € 34 + tourist tax € 0,63/pp Ch
(64x),16Amp included. **Location:** Urban, simple, quiet.
**Surface:** gravel. 01/01-31/12.
**Distance:** 1km on the spot on the spot on the spot on the spot 500m on the spot on the spot.
**Remarks:** Monitored parking 24/24, swimming pool available.

**Tourist information Portorož:**

Turistična organizacija Koper, Verdijeva 10, Koper. City with a Venetian past and a lot of curiosities.

Pomorski muzej Sergej Mašera, Cankarjevo nabrežje 3, Piran. Maritime museum. 9-12h, 15-18h, 01/07-31/08 9-12h, 18-21h Mo.

### Postojna — 37A1

Park Postojnska Jama, Veliki Otok. **GPS:** n45,78066 e14,20322.

20 € 20/24h Ch (20x)included,16Amp.
**Location:** Rural, simple, quiet.
**Surface:** concrete.
01/04-30/09.
**Distance:** 1km 3km 100m 1km on the spot
on the spot on the spot.
**Remarks:** Postojna caves 300m

**Tourist information Postojna:**

Križna jama, Bloška polica 7, Grahovo.
Largest water caves of Slovenia.

Perdjama Grad.
Castle, 16th century and caves.
01/05-30/09 9-18, 01/10-30/04 10-16h.

Postojnska Jama, Jamska cesta 30. Postojna caves.
01/05-30/09 9-18, 01/10-30/04 10-16h.

### Rateče — 36A3

Nordijski center Planica. **GPS:** n46,47708 e13,72418.

6 € 12 Ch WCincluded. **Location:** Rural, comfortable, quiet. **Surface:** metalled. 01/01-31/12.

**Distance:** 2km on the spot on the spot on the spot on the spot on the spot.

### Razdrto — 37A1

Penzion & Camp Mirjam, Razdrto 19. **GPS:** n45,75690 e14,06126.

9 € 12, 2 pers.incl Ch included WCon demand € 1
**Location:** Urban, simple, central, quiet. **Surface:** gravel.
01/05-31/10.
**Distance:** on the spot 1km 10km 10km on the spot
50m on the spot on the spot.
**Remarks:** Bread-service.

### Šempas — 37A1

Lepa Vida, Osek 4b. **GPS:** n45,92311 e13,75824.
5 € 20 Ch € 0,20 included. **Location:** Rural, comfortable, quiet. **Surface:** gravel. 01/01-31/12.
**Distance:** 500m 1km 3km 500m 500m.
**Remarks:** Wine tasting, sale of wines.

### Šenčur — 37A1

Camper Stop Cubis, Poslovna cona A 2.
**GPS:** n46,23855 e14,40769.

14 € 12 Ch (12x)included. **Surface:** gravel.
01/01-31/12.
**Distance:** 1km 150m 1km on the spot.
**Remarks:** Video surveillance.

### Senožeče — 37A1

Domačija Lojtrnik. **GPS:** n45,73408 e14,07007.
free € 5 5. **Location:** Rural, isolated, quiet.
**Surface:** unpaved. 01/01-31/12 15/06-15/07.
**Distance:** 6km 6km.
**Remarks:** At manege.

### Senožeče — 37A1

Gostišče Stari grad, Senožeče 5. **GPS:** n45,72364 e14,04709.
free. **Location:** Rural. **Surface:** asphalted. 01/01-31/12
Mon, Tue.
**Distance:** on the spot on the spot on the spot.

### Sežana — 37A1

Partizanska cesta 1. **GPS:** n45,70980 e13,87669.
5 € 8/24h € 2/160liter Ch € 0,50/kWh.
**Location:** Simple, noisy. **Surface:** metalled.
01/01-31/12.
**Distance:** 200m 200m 200m.

SL

**Remarks:** Along railwayline.

**|⊞|S** Sežana 37A1

**Brajda**, Štorje 5. **GPS:** n45,73730 e13,92679.⬆️
20 🚐€ 16, 01/07-31/08 € 20, 2 pers. incl., dog € 2 🚰🔌Ch 🛠️
(17x)€ 3 WC🚽🔌📶included. **Location:** Rural. **Surface:** grassy.
⬛ 01/05-30/09.
**Distance:** ⊗100m.
**Remarks:** Bicycle rental.

**|⊞|S** Škofja Loka 37A1

Škofja Loka- Gorenja vas. **GPS:** n46,16694 e14,30907.⬆️

5 🚐€ 0,50/h. 🅿️ **Location:** Urban, simple, central, quiet.
**Surface:** asphalted. ⬛ 01/01-31/12.
**Distance:** 🚶on the spot ⌅on the spot 🛒on the spot ⊗200m
🍽️200m.

**|⊞|S** Šmarje 37A1

**Garni Mimosa**, Srgaši 38a. **GPS:** n45,50843 e13,70560.⬆️➡️

5 🚐€ 10 🚰🔌€ 8/100liter 🛠️(1x)included,16Amp WC🔌on demand
📶🛒 **Location:** Urban, simple, central, quiet. **Surface:** gravel.
⬛ 01/01-31/12.
**Distance:** 🚶6km ⊗50m 🍽️50m 🚐100m 🛒on the spot
🛍️on the spot.

**|⊞|S** Smlednik 37A1

**Hotel Kanu**, Valburga 7. **GPS:** n46,16927 e14,42228.⬆️

20 🚐€ 10 🔌Ch 🛠️(4x),16Amp WC🔌🗑️€ 5 📶included 🍽️🛒🚮
**Location:** Rural, isolated, quiet. **Surface:** grasstiles. ⬛ 01/01-31/12
🔌 water disconnected in winter.
**Distance:** 🚶300m ⌅5km ⌅on the spot 🛒on the spot ⊗on the spot
🍽️300m 🚐300m 🛒on the spot 🛍️on the spot 🚵20km 🚲7km.

**|△|S** Tolmin 37A1

**Kamp Siber**, Klanec 8. **GPS:** n46,18082 e13,73792.

20 🚐€ 8/pp 🚰🔌Ch 🛠️€ 3 WC🔌📶 **Location:** Rural.
**Surface:** grassy/gravel. ⬛ 01/01-01/11.
**Distance:** 🚶1km ⌅on the spot 🛒on the spot 🍽️1km.

**|⊞|S** Tržič 36A3

**Gorenjska plaža**, Bistrica. **GPS:** n46,35448 e14,29447.⬆️

6 🚐free 🚰🔌Ch 🛠️free. **Location:** Urban, simple.
**Surface:** asphalted. ⬛ 01/01-31/12.
**Distance:** ⊗300m 🍽️300m 🛒on the spot 🛍️on the spot.
**Remarks:** At swimming pool.

# Slovenia East

**|⊞|S** Apače 36B3

**Ribiški dom Zgornje Konjišče**, Zgornje Konjišče 16.
**GPS:** n46,71510 e15,82372.
3 🚐free. **Location:** Rural, isolated, quiet. **Surface:** grassy.
⬛ 01/01-31/12.
**Distance:** 🚶on the spot ⊗on the spot 🛒on the spot 🛍️on the spot.

**|⊞|S** Braslovče 36B3

**Najem & Kamping**, Preserje 16b. **GPS:** n46,28915 e15,05524.⬆️

20 🚐€ 5 🚰🔌Ch 🛠️(2x)€ 5/day,16Amp 📶included. 🛒
**Location:** Rural, comfortable, isolated, quiet. **Surface:** gravel.
⬛ 01/01-31/12.
**Distance:** 🚶1km ⌅on the spot 🛒on the spot ⊗400m 🍽️1km
🚐1km 🛒on the spot 🛍️on the spot 🚵10km 🚲10km.
**Remarks:** Opening hours 7-22h.

**|⊞|S** Brestanica 37B1

**Bazen Brestanica**, Jetrno selo 2. **GPS:** n46,00124 e15,47492.⬆️

4 🚐€ 10 🚰🔌Ch 🛠️📶. **Surface:** gravel. ⬛ 01/01-31/12.
**Remarks:** At swimming pool.

**|⊞|S** Brestanica 37B1

**Ribiška družina Brestanica**, Raztez 1a. **GPS:** n46,00504 e15,49751.⬆️

10 🚐€ 10 🚰🔌Ch 🛠️WC📶included. 🛒 **Location:** Rural, isolated,
quiet. **Surface:** gravel. ⬛ 01/01-31/12.
**Distance:** 🛒on the spot ⊗on the spot 🛍️on the spot 🛍️on the spot.
**Remarks:** Fishpond, check in at restaurant.

**|⊞|S** Brežice 37B1

Pod obzidjem. **GPS:** n45,90487 e15,59394.
3 🚐free. **Location:** Urban, simple, central. **Surface:** asphalted.
⬛ 01/01-31/12.
**Distance:** 🚶on the spot ⊗200m 🍽️200m.

**|⊞|S** Cankova 36B3

**Turistična kmetija Ferencovi**, Krašči 23a. **GPS:** n46,75602 e16,04803.
3 🚐€ 5 🚰🛠️📶. **Location:** Rural, isolated, quiet.
**Surface:** gravel. ⬛ 01/01-31/12.

**Distance:** ⊗on the spot 🛒on the spot 🛍️on the spot.

**|⊞|S** Celje 36B3

**Mestini Park Celje**, Partizanska Cesta. **GPS:** n46,22550 e15,26082.⬆️

6 🚐free 🚰€ 0,50/40liter 🔌Ch 🛠️€ 0,50/kWh WC. **Location:** Rural,
simple. **Surface:** asphalted. ⬛ 01/01-31/12.
**Distance:** 🚶1km ⌅500m 🛒500m ⊗on the spot 🍽️1km 🛍️on the
spot 🛍️on the spot.

**|⊞|S** Celje 36B3

**Parking Glazija**, Ljubljanska cesta 20. **GPS:** n46,23319 e15,25904.

2 🚐€ 10 🚰🔌🛠️included. 🅿️ **Location:** Urban, simple.
**Surface:** metalled. ⬛ 01/01-31/12.
**Distance:** 🛒on the spot.
**Remarks:** At supermarket.

**|⊞|S** Celje 36B3

**Turistična kmetija Mirnik**, Leskovec 9, Ljubečna.
**GPS:** n46,25484 e15,30373.⬆️
10 🚐€ 10 🛠️included. **Location:** Rural, isolated, quiet.
**Surface:** unpaved. ⬛ 01/01-31/12.
**Distance:** 🛒on the spot 🛍️on the spot.

**|⊞|S** Celje 36B3

**Glavan Center Karavaninga**, Gaji 45. **GPS:** n46,24406 e15,30217.⬆️➡️

6 🚐€ 5 🚰€ 1/100liter 🔌Ch 🛠️(2x)€ 0,50/kWh,16Amp 📶.🅿️
**Location:** Rural, simple, isolated, quiet.
**Surface:** gravel.
⬛ 01/01-31/12.
**Distance:** 🚶3km ⌅4km 🛒4km ⊗200m 🍽️2km 🚐on the spot
🛒on the spot 🛍️on the spot.
**Remarks:** At motorhome dealer.

**Tourist information Celje:**
👁️ Jama Pekel, Šempeter. Caves.
🏰 Stari Grad Castle. Remainders of castle.
⛩️ Rimska Nekropola, Šempeter. Roman Necropolis,
archeological park.

**|⊞|S** Cirkulane 36B3

**Herman Lederhaus**, Dolane 8. **GPS:** n46,37114 e15,99682.⬆️

10 🚐€ 10 🚰🔌Ch 🛠️WC included. **Location:** Rural, simple.
**Surface:** grassy/gravel. ⬛ 01/01-31/12.
**Distance:** ⌅on the spot 🛒on the spot ⊗on the spot 🍽️50m.
**Remarks:** Restaurant and leather factory.

SL

## Dobrovnik 36C3

**Bukovniško Jezero. GPS:** n46,66903 e16,33928.⬆.
14 🅕free 🚰 💧 WC 📶. **Location:** Rural. **Surface:** gravel.
⬛ 01/01-31/12.
**Distance:** ⛱500m ⛟500m ⊗on the spot.
**Remarks:** Near the lake.

## Dolenjske Toplice 37B1

**Dolenjske Toplice**, Podhosta 48. **GPS:** n45,76739 e15,05151.⬆.
10 🅕€ 8-22 + € 0,64/pp tourist tax 🚰 Ch 🔌€ 3,50 WC included.
⚕ **Location:** Rural, simple, isolated, quiet. **Surface:** grassy/gravel.
⬛ 01/04-15/10.
**Distance:** 🚶800m ⛱on the spot ⛟on the spot ⊗800m ⛱800m
🚲 on the spot 🚶on the spot.
**Remarks:** Along the Krka river, terme Dolenjske Toplice 800m.

## Dolenjske Toplice 37B1

**Kamp Polje**, Meniška vas 47. **GPS:** n45,76735 e15,05150.

20 🅕€ 12, 22/06-16/09 € 16-18 + € 0,63/pp tourist tax 🚰 Ch 🔌€
2,75 WC 📶included. **Location:** Rural. **Surface:** grassy/gravel.
⬛ 01/04-15/10.
**Distance:** ⛱200m ⛟200m ⊗500m 🚲 on the spot 🚶on the spot.
**Remarks:** Dog € 2/day.

## Dolsko 37A1

**Domačija Pr Krač**, Dolsko 19. **GPS:** n46,09195 e14,67522.

10 🅕free 🚰 Ch 🔌 WC 📶. **Location:** Rural, simple, quiet.
**Surface:** grassy. ⬛ 01/01-31/12.
**Distance:** 🚶200m ⛱on the spot ⛟on the spot ⊗on the spot
⛱550m on the spot 🚶on the spot.
**Remarks:** Regional products.

## Grosuplje 37A1

**Parking Kongo**, Ljubljanska cesta. **GPS:** n45,96796 e14,65860.⬆.

30 🅕€ 12 🚰 Ch included 🔌.📶 **Location:** Rural, simple, noisy.
**Surface:** grassy/gravel. ⬛ 01/01-31/12.
**Distance:** 🚶1,7km 🚲100m ⛱50m ⛟100m 🚲 on the spot
🚶on the spot.
**Remarks:** Parking nearby motorway.

## Ivančna Gorica 37A1

**Turistična vas Pristava**, Pristava nad Stično 4.
**GPS:** n45,98999 e14,82394.⬆.

8 🅕€ 15 🚰🔌 included WC 📶. ⚕ **Location:** Rural, simple, isolated,

---

quiet. **Surface:** gravel. ⬛ 01/01-31/12.
**Distance:** 🚶1km ⊗500m ⛱5km 🚲on the spot 🚶on the spot.

## Ivanjkovci 36B3

**Vinoteka Svetinjska Klet**, Svetinje 5.
**GPS:** n46,46220 e16,16990.⬆.➡.

10 🅕free. **Surface:** metalled.
**Remarks:** Sale of wines.

## Jesenice na Dolenjskem 37B1

**Gostinstvo Strnisa**, Jesenice na Dolenjskem 7c.
**GPS:** n45,85869 e15,68979.⬆.

5 🅕€ 6 🚰€ 2 Ch 🔌€ 2,50 WC 📶.
**Location:** Urban. **Surface:** concrete.
**Distance:** ⊗on the spot.

## Kamnica 36B3

**Gostilna Koblarjev Zaliv**, Na Otok 20.
**GPS:** n46,56558 e15,61942.⬆.⬆.

20 🅕free, use of a meal desired 🔌 WC 📶included. **Location:** Simple,
quiet. **Surface:** grassy. ⬛ 01/01-31/12.
**Distance:** 🚶Maribor 2km 🚲5km ⛱on the spot ⛟on the spot ⊗on
the spot ⛱300m ⛟300m 🚞5km.
**Remarks:** Toilets only during opening hours restaurant, walking and
bicycle area along the Drava river to Maribor centre.

## Kocevje 37B1

**Turistični Komplex Jezero**, Trdnjava 3. **GPS:** n45,64421 e14,87140.⬆.

3 🅕€ 12 🚰 Ch 🔌(4x)included WC 📶. **Location:** Urban, simple,
isolated, quiet. **Surface:** asphalted. ⬛ 01/01-31/12.
**Distance:** 🚶1km ⛱200m ⛟200m ⊗on the spot ⛱1km ⛟1km
🚲 on the spot 🚶on the spot.
**Remarks:** Max. 48h, check in at tourist office, nature reserve.

## Kostanjevica na Krki 37B1

**Krška cesta. GPS:** n45,84891 e15,41795.⬆.

---

5 🅕free. **Location:** Rural, simple, quiet. **Surface:** grassy/metalled.
⬛ 01/01-31/12.
**Distance:** 🚶300m ⛱on the spot ⛟on the spot ⊗300m ⛱300m
🚲 on the spot 🚶on the spot.
**Remarks:** Along river.

## Kovor 36A3

**Glavna cesta. GPS:** n46,34010 e14,28201.⬆.

3 🅕free 🚰 Ch 🔌free. **Location:** Simple, central.
⬛ 01/01-31/12.
**Remarks:** At fire-station.

## Krško 37B1

**Raceland**, Pesje 30. **GPS:** n45,92977 e15,53500.⬆.

50 🅕€ 12 🚰 🔌 WC 📶included. ⚕ **Location:** Rural, isolated,
noisy. **Surface:** asphalted. ⬛ 01/01-31/12.
**Distance:** ⊗on the spot.
**Remarks:** Parking at Karting.

## Krško 37B1

**Parkirišče pri igrišču Šajspoh**, Cesta krških žrtev 14.
**GPS:** n45,96590 e15,48370.⬆.
🅕free. **Surface:** gravel. ⬛ 01/01-31/12.
**Distance:** 🚶250m ⊗250m 🚲 on the spot 🚶on the spot.

## Krško 37B1

**Stadium Matija Gubec**, Cesta krških žrtev 130a.
**GPS:** n45,94691 e15,48832.⬆.

30 🅕free. **Surface:** grassy/gravel. ⬛ 01/01-31/12.

## Krško 37B1

**Gostilna Stanislava Pečnik**, Gunte 8. **GPS:** n45,98645 e15,46572.⬆.

2 🅕free. ⬛ Su.
**Distance:** ⛱on the spot ⛟on the spot ⊗on the spot.

SL

## Laško | 37B1

**Thermana Park Laško**, Zdraviliška cesta 6.
**GPS:** n46,16188 e15,23132.

16 € 7-10/pp, dog € 4 Ch included (16x)€ 4/day,16Amp WC **Location:** Urban, simple, central, noisy.
**Surface:** grasstiles/metalled. 01/01-31/12.
**Distance:** 700m on the spot 700m on the spot on the spot on the spot on the spot 10km 10km.
**Remarks:** Max. 24h, check in at reception.

## Laško | 37B1

**Zdraviliške Laško**, Zdraviliška cesta 4. **GPS:** n46,15761 e15,23224.

4 € 7-10/pp, dog € 4 Ch included (4x)€ 4/day,16Amp WC **Location:** Urban, simple, central, noisy.
**Surface:** asphalted. 01/01-31/12.
**Distance:** 500m on the spot 500m on the spot on the spot on the spot on the spot 10km 10km.
**Remarks:** Discount on access terme.

## Lendava | 36C3

**Terme Lendava**, Tomsiceve 21A. **GPS:** n46,55396 e16,45813.

90 € 14/pp, dog € 3 Ch € 4 WC € 1/30minutes.
**Location:** Rural, isolated, quiet. **Surface:** asphalted/grassy.
01/01-31/12.
**Distance:** 2,5km 2km 1,2km.
**Remarks:** Including access spa resort.

## Ljutomer | 36B3

**Gostilna Trnek**, Mota 76. **GPS:** n46,55516 e16,21929.

25 guests free Ch included € 3 WC.
**Location:** Rural, isolated, quiet. **Surface:** grassy/gravel.
01/01-31/12.
**Distance:** on the spot on the spot on the spot 1km.
**Remarks:** Use sanitary only during opening hours.

## Mala Nedelja | 36B3

**Bioterme**, Moravci v Slovenskih Goricah 34 b.
**GPS:** n46,51437 e16,05109.

---

50 € 8 + € 0,64/pp tourist tax € 2/160liter Ch € 0,50/kWh included. **Location:** Rural, simple. **Surface:** grasstiles/grassy.
01/01-31/12.
**Distance:** 1,5km on the spot on the spot on the spot on the spot.
**Remarks:** Discount on access terme.

## Maribor | 36B3

**Avtobusna postaja Maribor**, Mlinska ulica 1.
**GPS:** n46,55852 e15,65573.

4 € 10 Ch included. **Location:** Noisy. **Surface:** asphalted.
01/01-31/12.
**Distance:** on the spot fast food on the spot on the spot.
**Remarks:** Nearby bus station P4, check in at tourist office.

## Maribor | 36B3

**Drava Center**, Limbuško nabrežje 2, Limbuš.
**GPS:** n46,56350 e15,58930.

8 € 10 WC. **Location:** Rural, simple, quiet.
**Surface:** gravel/metalled. 01/01-31/12.
**Distance:** 5km on the spot on the spot on the spot 5km on the spot on the spot.
**Remarks:** Boat rental, playground.

## Maribor | 36B3

Partizanska cesta 50. **GPS:** n46,56315 e15,65819.

4 8-17h € 0,50/h, overnight stay and weekend free.
**Location:** Urban, noisy. **Surface:** asphalted. 01/01-31/12.
**Distance:** city centre 1km 200m 300m.
**Remarks:** At station.

## Maribor | 36B3

Ulica Heroja Staneta. **GPS:** n46,56557 e15,64992.

---

2 € 16. **Location:** Urban, simple. **Surface:** asphalted.
01/01-31/12.
**Distance:** on the spot 200m 200m.
**Remarks:** Parking in centre.

## Metlika | 37B1

**Dependansa sobe Metlika**, Cesta bratstra in enotnosti 77.
**GPS:** n45,64663 e15,31778.

3 € 15 + € 0,64/pp tourist tax Ch included.
**Location:** Urban, simple, central, quiet. **Surface:** asphalted.
01/01-31/12.
**Distance:** 100m 1km 1km 100m 100m 100m on the spot on the spot.

## Moravske Toplice | 36B3

**Kamp Moravske Toplice**, Kranjčeva ulica 12 .
**GPS:** n46,67862 e16,22151.

200 € 32-60 2 pers. Incl., dog € 3 Ch € 4.
**Surface:** grassy/gravel. 01/01-31/12.
**Distance:** 400m 100m 200m on the spot on the spot.
**Remarks:** Including access spa resort 3000.

**Tourist information Moravske Toplice:**
Goričko Regional Park, Ulica ob igrišču 3, www.park-goricko.org.
Information centre.

## Murska Sobota | 36B3

**Lovenjak**, Polana 40. **GPS:** n46,68233 e16,13836.

10 € 6/pp + tourist tax Ch WC included.
**Location:** Comfortable. **Surface:** metalled. 01/01-31/12.
**Distance:** 3,5km on the spot on the spot on the spot.
**Remarks:** Breakfast-service, barbecue place, swimming pool € 4/pp.

## Novo Mesto | 37B1

**Old Gardening**, Skalickega 3. **GPS:** n45,79536 e15,17039.

10 € 15 + € 0,64/pp tourist tax Ch (10x)WC included.
**Location:** Urban, comfortable, quiet. **Surface:** grassy/gravel.
01/01-31/12 with mucht snowfall.
**Distance:** 400m 400m 300m 400m on the spot on the spot.

## Novo Mesto | 37B1

**Pri Belokranjucu**, Kandijska cesta 63. **GPS:** n45,79947 e15,17865.

3 🛏️€ 15 🔌Ch ⚡,16Amp 📶included 🅿️ 🚿

**Location:** Urban, simple, central, noisy. **Surface:** asphalted.

📅 01/01-31/12.

**Distance:** 🛒400m 🏊5km 🚆400m ⊗on the spot ⚡200m 🔆on the spot 🚌200m 🚶on the spot ⛪on the spot.

| 🏕️ | Obrežje Jug | 37B1 |
|---|---|---|

**OMV Istrabenz. GPS:** n45,85517 e15,68513.

2 🛏️free. **Location:** Motorway, noisy.

**Distance:** ⚡on the spot.

**Remarks:** Parking petrol station OMV Istrabenz.

| 🏕️S | Ormož | 36B3 |
|---|---|---|

**Bar Ribnik**, Ob ribniku 1. **GPS:** n46,40588 e16,15963.

3 🛏️free 🚆⚡free. **Location:** Rural. **Surface:** asphalted.

📅 01/01-31/12.

**Distance:** 🏊on the spot 🚆on the spot.

| 🏕️S | Otočec 🏞️🌲 | 37B1 |
|---|---|---|

**Kamp Otočec. GPS:** n45,83794 e15,23821.⬆️

30 🛏️€ 11/pp 🔌Ch ⚡€ 3,50 📶included 🚐 **Location:** Rural, comfortable. **Surface:** grassy/gravel. 📅 01/04-30/09.

**Distance:** 🛒500m 🏊on the spot 🚆on the spot ⊗500m ⚡500m.

**Remarks:** Along river.

| 🏕️S | Pesnica pri Mariboru | 36B3 |
|---|---|---|

**Naturasort**, Dolnja Počehova 34b. **GPS:** n46,59869 e15,65316.⬆️➡️

6 🛏️€ 15-22 🔌Ch ⚡WC 📶included. **Location:** Rural, comfortable, luxurious, isolated, quiet. **Surface:** grasstiles.

📅 01/01-31/12.

**Remarks:** At tennis-court, discount longer stays, use of sauna against payment.

| 🏕️S | Pivka | 37A1 |
|---|---|---|

**Park of Military History Pivka**, Kolodvorska cesta.

**GPS:** n45,66812 e14,18779.⬆️

8 🛏️€ 10 🔌Ch ⚡ 📶included,at restaurant. **Surface:** asphalted.

📅 01/01-31/12.

**Distance:** 🛒2km ⊗on the spot.

**Remarks:** At museum, video surveillance.

| 🏕️ | Podbočje | 37B1 |
|---|---|---|

**Turistična kmetija Hribar**, Podbočje 36. **GPS:** n45,86190 e15,47110.⬆️

5 🛏️free. **Surface:** gravel. 📅 01/01-31/12.

**Distance:** 🛒400m 🚆on the spot ⊗on the spot 🚴on the spot ⛪on the spot.

| 🏕️S | Podčetrtek | 37B1 |
|---|---|---|

**Golf Klub a Podčetrtek Amon**, Olimje 24. **GPS:** n46,14400 e15,56493.

20 🛏️€ 10 + € 1,25/pp tourist tax WC 📶included. **Location:** Rural, isolated, quiet. **Surface:** asphalted/gravel.

📅 01/01-31/12 🔆 With snow.

**Distance:** 🛒3km ⊗on the spot 🚴on the spot 🚶on the spot.

**Remarks:** At golf court, bicycle rental.

| 🏕️S | Podčetrtek | 37B1 |
|---|---|---|

**Terme Olimia Kamp Natura**, Zdravillška cesta 24.

**GPS:** n46,16529 e15,60522.

60 🛏️€ 16,50-21/pp, dog € 3 🔌Ch ⚡€ 4,20 WC 📶🔌 € 3 🚿 🚐

**Location:** Rural, comfortable, quiet. **Surface:** grasstiles/metalled.

📅 21/04-30/09.

**Distance:** ⊗on the spot ⚡on the spot.

**Remarks:** Including access spa resort.

### Tourist information Podčetrtek:

👁️ Sedovška Homestead, Aškercev trg 24, Šmarje pri Jelšah. Traditional farmstead.

Ⓜ️ Rogatec Open-air Museum, Ptujska cesta 23, Rogatec. Open air museum, 18-20th century. 📅 01/04-31/10 🔆 Mo.

⛪ Božjepotna Marijina cerkev, Sladka Gora, Šmarje pri Jelšah. Pilgrimage church.

⛪ Olimje Monastery and Pharmacy, Olimje 82. Monastery and one of the oldest pharmacies in the world.

| 🏕️S | Podsmreka | 37A1 |
|---|---|---|

A2. **GPS:** n45,94805 e14,77065.

5 🛏️free 🚆free. **Location:** Motorway. 📅 01/01-31/12.

**Distance:** ⚡100m.

**Remarks:** Guarded parking petrol station Petrol Podsmereka, highway Novo Mesto-Ljubljana.

| 🏔️S | Prebold | 37B1 |
|---|---|---|

**Dolina**, Dolenja Vas 147. **GPS:** n46,24015 e15,08771.

🛏️€ 15,50 🔌Ch ⚡WC. 📅 01/01-31/12.

**Distance:** ⊗200m ⚡200m.

| 🏕️S | Ptuj 🏞️🎣🍦 | 36B3 |
|---|---|---|

**Terme Ptuj**, Pot v toplice 9. **GPS:** n46,42109 e15,85585.⬆️

20 🛏️€ 22-24 🔌Ch ⚡(2x),16Amp WC 🔌against payment,€ 5/5 📶included 🚿 🚐

**Location:** Rural, simple. **Surface:** gravel.

📅 01/01-31/12.

**Distance:** 🛒1,5km ⚡4km 🚆500m ⊗200m ⚡800m 🚌1,5km 🚴on the spot 🏊25km.

### Tourist information Ptuj:

ℹ️ Maribor Tourist Board, Partizanska 47, Maribor, www.maribor-tourism.si. Old city with historical centre.

Ⓜ️✖️ Mariborski Grad, Maribor. Castle, 15th century, regional museum. 📅 01/04-31/12 Tue-Sa 9-17h, Su 9-14h 🔆 Mo.

Ⓜ️✖️ Ptujski Grad. Castle, 11th century with regional museum. 📅 01/05-31/10 9-18h.

| 🏕️S | Rečica ob Savinji 🏞️ | 36B3 |
|---|---|---|

**Gostisce Atelsek. GPS:** n46,34407 e14,91684.⬆️

5 🛏️free 🚆⚡€ 5 WC. **Location:** Rural, isolated, quiet.

**Surface:** gravel. ◻ 01/01-31/12.
**Distance:** ⚂2km ⊗on the spot ⚑2km 🏍on the spot 🚶on the spot 🏇2km 🏊on the spot.
**Remarks:** At restaurants.

### △S Rečica ob Savinji 🏔 36B3

**Menina. GPS:** n46,31167 e14,90917.
🚐€ 18-22 ⛽🗑Ch 🧺 WC🚿🛒📶 ◻ 01/01-31/12.
**Distance:** 🏊on the spot ⊗on the spot ⚑300m.
**Tourist information Rečica ob Savinji:**
👁 Mozirski gaj, Hribernikova 1, Mozirje. Botanical garden. ◻ 01/04-31/10 9-19h.
Ⓜ Musej Premogovništva, Stari jašek - Koroška cesta, Velenje. Coal mining museum.

### 🚐S Rogaška Slatina 36B3

**Eco vila Mila,** Kamence 19. **GPS:** n46,20169 e15,62350.
🚐€ 5, 01/04-31/10 € 10 + tourist tax € 1,27 🔌€ 0,50/kWh.
**Surface:** asphalted. ◻ 01/01-31/12.
**Distance:** ⊗on the spot.

### 🚐S Rogla 36B3

Rogla. **GPS:** n46,45259 e15,33117.⬆

8 🚐€ 12 ⛽🗑Ch 🧺📶included. **Surface:** gravel.
◻ 01/01-31/12.
**Distance:** ⚂Zreče 10km ⚑200m 🏍on the spot 🚶on the spot 🏇on the spot 🏊on the spot.
**Remarks:** Altitude 1517m.

### 🍴 Senovo 37B1

**Gostišče Senica,** Titova cesta 89. **GPS:** n46,01856 e15,47526.⬆
🚐guests free. ◻ 01/01-31/12.
**Distance:** ⚂1km ⊗on the spot.

### Sevnica 🌿 37B1

Cesta na Grad. **GPS:** n46,00862 e15,31527.⬆

5 🚐free ⛽🗑Ch 🧺. **Location:** Rural, simple. **Surface:** gravel.
◻ 01/01-31/12.
**Distance:** ⚂500m ⊗500m ⚑500m 🏍on the spot.
**Remarks:** Next to castle.

### 🚐S Slovenj Gradec 36B3

**Camperstop Slovenj Gradec,** Ozare 18.
**GPS:** n46,51418 e15,07678.⬆➡

6 🚐€ 5 ⛽🗑Ch 🧺(4x)📶included. **Location:** Comfortable, quiet.
**Surface:** gravel. ◻ 01/01-31/12.
**Distance:** ⚂500m ⊗500m ⚑500m 🏍on the spot.
**Remarks:** At youth hostel.

### 🍴S Slovenj Gradec 36B3

Razborca 66. **GPS:** n46,50230 e15,21017.⬆

---

18 🚐€ 10 ⛽🗑Ch 🧺📶included. 🛁 **Location:** Rural, simple, isolated, quiet. **Surface:** forest soil. ◻ 01/01-31/12.
**Distance:** ⊗on the spot 🏍on the spot 🚶on the spot 🏇on the spot 🏊on the spot.

### 🚐S Solcava ⛰🏔🌲 36A3

**Camper Stop Logarska Valley,** Solčava 53. **GPS:** n46,41939 e14,67387.
5 🚐€ 15 ⛽🗑🧺 WC📶included. **Location:** Rural.
**Surface:** grassy. ◻ 01/01-31/12.
**Distance:** ⚂3km 🏍on the spot 🚶on the spot.

### 🍇S Stahovica 🏘🌲 36A3

**Pri Jurju,** Kamniska Bistrica 5. **GPS:** n46,32685 e14,58706.⬆

20 🚐€ 5 ⛽🗑Ch 🧺(20x)€ 2/day,16Amp WCincluded 📶€ 5/day. 🛁 **Location:** Rural, simple, isolated, quiet. **Surface:** grassy.
◻ 01/01-31/12.
**Distance:** ⚂8km ⚂6km ⊗on the spot ⚑8km 🚌300m 🏍on the spot 🚶on the spot 🏇3km 🏊3km.

### 🚐S Straža 🏔🌾 37B1

**Avto Bradac Mali Raj,** Dolenje Polje 7a. **GPS:** n45,77128 e15,05124.⬆

20 🚐€ 15 ⛽🗑Ch 🧺 WC📶included. 🛁 **Location:** Rural, comfortable, quiet. **Surface:** grassy. ◻ 01/01-31/12.
**Distance:** ⚂2km 🏊on the spot ⛽on the spot ⊗1km ⚑2km 🚌800m 🏍on the spot 🚶on the spot 🏇15km 🏊15km.

### Tepanje 36B3

A1. **GPS:** n46,34776 e15,48695.
5 🚐free ⛽free. **Location:** Motorway, noisy.
**Distance:** ⚑on the spot.
**Remarks:** Guarded parking petrol station Petrol Tepanje I, on both sides of the highway Maribor-Ljubljana.

### 🍴S Vinica 🌾 37B1

**Farm Benetič,** Vinica 17. **GPS:** n45,46017 e15,25854.⬆
10 🚐€ 10 🗑Ch 🧺. **Location:** Isolated, quiet. **Surface:** gravel.
◻ 01/01-31/12.
**Distance:** 🏊on the spot ⛽on the spot ⊗on the spot.

### 🚐S Visnja Gora 🏔🌲 37A1

**Mestno kopališče,** Kopaliska Ulica 25.
**GPS:** n45,95268 e14,75097.⬆➡

20 🚐free ⛽🧺(1x)WC📶free. **Location:** Rural, simple, isolated, quiet. **Surface:** asphalted/gravel. ◻ 01/01-31/12.
**Distance:** ⚂on the spot ⚓1,7km ⚑1km 🚌200m 🏍on the spot

---

🚶on the spot 🏇10km 🏊10km.
**Remarks:** Check in at swimming pool, service during opening hours.

### 🚐S Visnja Gora 🏔🌲 37A1

**PrinceSport&Fun Center,** Kopališka ulica 27.
**GPS:** n45,95207 e14,75201.⬆➡

10 🚐free ⛽🧺WC. **Location:** Rural, simple, comfortable, quiet.
**Surface:** grassy/gravel. ◻ 01/01-31/12.
**Distance:** ⚂500m 🏊on the spot ⊗on the spot ⚑500m.

### 🚐S Vransko 37B1

**Kamp Podgrad Vransko,** Prapreče 30. **GPS:** n46,24409 e14,94310.⬆

12 🚐€ 10 + € 0,58/pp tourist tax ⛽€ 0,50/40liter 🗑Ch 🧺€ 0,50/kWh,16Amp WC🛒📶€ 4 🚿. **Location:** Rural, luxurious.
**Surface:** grassy/metalled. ◻ 01/01-31/12.
**Distance:** ⛽on the spot ⊗750m 🚶on the spot.

### 🚐S Žalec 🌿🍺 36B3

**Camperstop Žalec,** Mestni trg. **GPS:** n46,25418 e15,16274.⬆➡

4 🚐free ⛽€ 0,50/40liter 🗑Ch 🧺(4x)€ 0,50/kWh,16Amp.
**Location:** Urban, simple, central, quiet. **Surface:** metalled.
◻ 01/01-31/12.
**Distance:** ⚂500m ⊗100m ⚑500m 🚌500m 🏍on the spot 🚶on the spot.
**Remarks:** At sports park, caution key service € 20 at hotel.

### 🚐S Žalec 🌿🍺 36B3

Vrbje 83a. **GPS:** n46,24062 e15,15402.⬆

5 🚐free ⛽€ 2/140liter 🗑Ch 🧺€ 0,50/kWh. **Location:** Rural, isolated, quiet. **Surface:** gravel. ◻ 01/01-31/12.
**Distance:** ⚂2km 🏊500m ⛽500m ⊗2km ⚑2km 🏍on the spot 🚶on the spot.

### 🍴S Zdole 37B1

**Etnoart tourism Špiler,** Kostanjek 18. **GPS:** n46,01018 e15,54409.⬆

5 🗲€ 10 🛁🔧. **Surface:** grassy. ▣ 01/01-31/12.
**Distance:** ⊗on the spot.

**ⅢⅢS**     **Zdole**     **37B1**
**Gostilna pri Dularju**, Kostanjek 20. **GPS:** n46,00975 e15,54155.⬆.

10 🗲guests free 🛁🔧Ch🔧(3x). **Location:** Rural, quiet.
▣ 01/01-31/12.

**🗺S**    **Zgornje Jezersko** ⛵🏔🌳    **36A3**
**Camperstop Stara Pošta**, Zgornje Jezersko 124.
**GPS:** n46,40240 e14,50673.⬆.

9 🗲€ 10/pp 🛁🔧Ch🔧(16x)€ 3/24h WC⬜📷€ 4 📶included. 🧺
**Location:** Rural, luxurious, quiet. **Surface:** grassy. ▣ 01/04-30/09.
**Distance:** 🚲1km ⛱1km 🛒1km ⊗1km 🍴1km 🚌100m on the
spot 🚶on the spot.

**ⅤⅢS**    **Zgornje Jezersko** ⛵🏔🌳    **36A3**
**Camperstop Šenkova Domačija**, Zgornje Jezersko 140.
**GPS:** n46,40792 e14,51769.

5 🗲€ 10/pp, Jul/Aug € 12/pp 🛁🔧Ch🔧(5x)€ 3/night WC⬜📷€ 3
📶included. 🧺 **Location:** Rural, quiet. **Surface:** gravel/metalled.
▣ 01/01-31/12.
**Distance:** 🚲2km ⛱300m 🛒300m ⊗300m 🍴2km 🚌100m 🐴on
the spot 🚶on the spot 🎣on the spot.

**ⅠⅢS**    **Zreče**    **36B3**
**Thermal Spa**, Cesta na Roglo 15. **GPS:** n46,37096 e15,39021.⬆.

4 🗲€ 10 + € 1,30/pp tourist tax 🛁🔧Ch🔧📶included.
**Surface:** asphalted. ▣ 01/01-31/12.
**Distance:** 🚲300m 🛒300m ⊗on the spot 🍴300m.
**Remarks:** Check in at hotel, 20% reduction swimming pool.

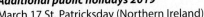

# United Kingdom

Capital: London
Government: Constitutional monarchy
Official Language: English
Population: 64,769,000 (2017)
Area: 242,495 km²

## General information

Dialing code: 0044
General emergency: 112
Currency: Pound sterling (GBP)
£1 = € 1,14, € 1 = £0.88 (October 2018)

## Regulations for overnight stays

Wild camping is forbidden in the UK. Motorway service stations allow overnight parking.

## Additional public holidays 2019

March 17 St. Patricksday (Northern Ireland)
April 19 Good Friday
April 22 Easter monday
May 1 Labour Day
May 6 Early May Bank Holiday
May 27 Spring Bank Holiday
July 12 Orangemens' Day (Northern Ireland)
August 5 Summer Bank Holiday
October 31 Halloween
November 5 Guy Fawkes Day
December 26 Boxing Day

## Time Zone

Winter (Standard Time) GMT+0
Summer (DST) GMT+1

Scotland pages: 770-773
Aberdeen
Edinburgh
Glasgow
prime meridian
Northern Ireland page: 769
Belfast
Leeds
Hull
Liverpool
Manchester
Wales pages: 773-775
England pages: 775-779
Cardiff
London
Portsmouth
Plymouth
Jersey page: 779

UK

# Northern Ireland

### Aghadowey — 1C1

**Golf Car Park, Brown Trout Golf and Country Inn**, 209 Agivey Road, A54. **GPS:** n55,03757 w6,60235.
⚡free. ⬜ 01/01-31/12.
**Remarks:** Max. 48h.

### Annalong — 1D2

Glasdrumman Road. **GPS:** n54,10953 w5,8971. ⬆️.
4 ⚡free 🚰£ 2/100liter ⚡£ 2/10kWh.
**Location:** Rural. **Surface:** gravel. ⬜ 01/01-31/12.
**Distance:** 🚶800m 🏊on the spot ⊗800m.
**Remarks:** Coins at restaurant.

### Antrim — 1D1

**McLarnon's Ramble Inn**, 236 Lisnevenagh Road.
**GPS:** n54,76198 w6,24265.
⚡free.
**Distance:** 🚶Antrim 7km.

### Ballinamallard — 1C1

**Ballinamallard Football Club**, Ferney Park. **GPS:** n54,41474 w7,60092.

⚡free. **Surface:** gravel. ⬜ 01/01-31/12.
**Distance:** 🚶1,5km.
**Tourist information Ballinamallard:**
🎣 Ballinamallard River, Kilgortnaleague Bridge, A35 Enniskillen > Irvinestown. Wild Salmon and Trout River.

### Broughshane — 1D1

**Houston Mills**, Buckna road. **GPS:** n54,89352 w6,20076. ⬆️.

⚡£5 🚰Ch 🚿(4x)£ 2/10h. 🚲
**Location:** Central, noisy. **Surface:** asphalted.
**Distance:** 🚶on the spot ⊗on the spot.
**Remarks:** Coins at supermarket.

### Carrickfergus — 1D1

**Carrickfergus Harbour Car Park**, Rodgers Quay.
**GPS:** n54,71330 w5,80902. ⬆️.
⚡free 🚰£ 1 🚰Ch 🚿£ 1. **Surface:** asphalted. ⬜ 01/01-31/12.
**Distance:** 🚶on the spot ⊗on the spot.
**Remarks:** Coins at harbourmaster and tourist office.

### Donaghadee — 1D1

**The Commons Parks**, Millisle Road. **GPS:** n54,63475 w5,5312. ⬆️➡️.
⚡free 🚰£ 2/100liter 🚿£ 2/1h.
**Surface:** asphalted. ⬜ 01/01-31/12.
**Distance:** 🚶on the spot 🏊on the spot 🍴on the spot ⊗on the spot 🏊on the spot.
**Remarks:** Coins at restaurant.

### Larne — 1D1

**Carnfunnock Country Park**, Coast Road. **GPS:** n54,89066 w5,84302.
31 ⚡£22.50-25.50 🚰Ch WC. **Location:** Urban, quiet.
**Surface:** grassy/metalled. ⬜ 10/03-26/11.
**Distance:** 🚶Larne 6km 🏊500m ⊗500m.

### Larne — 1D1

**Curran Caravan Park**, 131 Curran Rd. **GPS:** n54,85063 w5,80386.
⚡£16 ⚡£ 4. **Surface:** grassy. ⬜ 01/04-01/10.
**Distance:** ⊗1km 🏊1km.

### Newtownards — 1D1

**Daft Eddys**, Sketrick Island. **GPS:** n54,48812 w5,64807.

⚡free.
**Distance:** 🚶Newtownards 17km.
**Tourist information Newtownards:**
Ⓜ Somme Heritage Centre, 233 Bangor Road, Conlig, A21. The centre examines Ireland's role in the 1st World War.
  Castle Espie Wildfowl And Wetlands Centre, 78 Ballydrain Road, Comber. ⬜ 01/01-31/12 10-17 🔘 23-25/12.

### Portglenone — 1C1

**Portglenone Marina**, Gortgole Road. **GPS:** n54,87432 w6,47979. ⬆️.
5 ⚡£10 WC 🔘 🚿. **Location:** Urban, simple, quiet.
**Surface:** asphalted. ⬜ 01/01-31/12.
**Distance:** 🚶500m 🏊on the spot 🍴on the spot ⊗on the spot 🏊400m.

### Portrush — 1C1

**Sandhill Drive Motorhome Parking**. **GPS:** n55,20107 w6,65253. ⬆️.
10 ⚡£0.50/h 🚰£ 1,25/100liter 🚰Ch 🚿£ 1,25/kWh. 🚲 ♻️
**Location:** Simple, central. **Surface:** asphalted.
⬜ 01/01-31/12.
**Distance:** 🚶on the spot 🏊600m.
**Remarks:** Max. 72h.

### Whitehead — 1D1

**Bentra Golf Club**, Slaughterford Road. **GPS:** n54,75908 w5,72012. ⬆️.
⚡free 🚰£ 1 🚰Ch. **Surface:** asphalted.
**Distance:** 🚶1km 🏊1,5km ⊗150m.
**Remarks:** Coins at harbourmaster and tourist office.

# Scotland

### Aberdeen 2C2

**Aberdeen Lighthouse**, Greyhope Road. **GPS:** n57,14219 w2,05728.

8 free. **Location:** Rural, simple, quiet. **Surface:** asphalted.
01/01-31/12.
**Distance:** 3km 2,5km 1,5km on the spot.
**Remarks:** Whale and dolphin spotting.

### Aberdeen 2C2

**Hazlehead Park**, Hazledene Road. **GPS:** n57,13987 w2,17956.

20 free. **Location:** Simple, noisy. **Surface:** asphalted.
01/01-31/12.
**Distance:** 6km 2km 2km on the spot.

### Aberlour 2B1

**GPS:** n57,47020 w3,22929.

20 free. **Location:** Rural, simple, quiet. **Surface:** asphalted.
01/01-31/12.
**Distance:** 500m 100m 100m 500m 500m 250m
on the spot.

### Appin 2A2

**Creagan Station Tourers**, Creaganlea. **GPS:** n56,55130 w5,30619.
7 £15-20, 4 pers.incl Ch included.
**Surface:** grassy/gravel. 01/01-31/12.
**Distance:** Appin 3,5km on the spot on the spot 200m.

### Ardfern 2A2

**Ardfern Motorhome Park**, Lochgilphead.
**GPS:** n56,17402 w5,54799.

10 £15, 01/06-15/08 £20 Ch WC included.
**Location:** Rural, comfortable, isolated, quiet. **Surface:** gravel.
01/01-31/12.
**Distance:** 1km on the spot on the spot 1km 1km.

### Ardmair 2B1

**Ardmair Point Campsite**, A835. **GPS:** n57,93506 w5,19662.

---

50 £21 Ch WC included £ 4.
**Location:** Rural, comfortable, isolated, quiet.
**Surface:** grassy/metalled.
01/04-01/10.
**Distance:** 6km on the spot on the spot on the spot.

### Auchtertyre 2A1

A890. **GPS:** n57,28867 w5,57118.

8 free. **Location:** Rural, simple, quiet. **Surface:** asphalted.
01/01-31/12.
**Distance:** 2km.

### Balchrick 2B1

Lairg. **GPS:** n58,48394 w5,11249.

5 free. **Location:** Rural, simple, quiet. **Surface:** asphalted.
01/01-31/12.
**Distance:** on the spot 1km.

### Ballachulish 2B2

**Glencoe Mountain Resort Campsite**, Glencoe, A82 Ballachulish >
Achallader. **GPS:** n56,63295 w4,82744.

6 £15 Ch WC £ 1 included.
**Location:** Rural, comfortable, isolated, quiet.
**Surface:** asphalted/gravel. 01/01-31/12.
**Distance:** 15km on the spot on the spot on the spot.
**Remarks:** Parking ski-lifts.

### Ballater 2B2

**Balmoral Visitor Centre**, Crathie. **GPS:** n57,04022 w3,2161.
overnight stay free. **Location:** Isolated, quiet. **Surface:** asphalted.
01/01-31/12.
**Distance:** 1,5km.
**Remarks:** At castle.

### Balmacara 2A1

Reraig, Kyle Of Lochalsh. **GPS:** n57,28290 w5,62608.

---

40 £16.80 Ch £ 1,50/day,10Amp WC 3/h.
**Location:** Rural, comfortable, quiet.
**Surface:** grassy/gravel.
01/05-30/09.
**Distance:** 8km on the spot on the spot 8km on the spot.

### Banff 2C1

**Gamrie Bay**, Easter Cushnie, Gardenstown.
**GPS:** n57,65139 w2,33382.

6 £14 Ch included. **Location:** Rural, luxurious,
isolated, quiet. **Surface:** gravel. 01/01-31/12.
**Distance:** 2,5km 2,5km 2,5km 1km.

### Banff 2C1

Quayside. **GPS:** n57,67092 w2,52462.

10 free WC free. **Location:** Urban, simple, quiet. **Surface:** concrete.
01/01-31/12.
**Distance:** 300m on the spot on the spot 700m 700m
400m.

### Banff 2C1

Temple View. **GPS:** n57,66366 w2,51905.

25 free. **Location:** Urban, simple, quiet. **Surface:** concrete.
01/01-31/12.
**Distance:** 1km 300m 300m 200m 200m 400m.
**Remarks:** At football ground.

### Boat of Garten 2B2

**Loch Garten Nature Reserve**. **GPS:** n57,24382 w3,69541.
10 free.
**Location:** Rural. **Surface:** metalled. 03/04-03/09.
**Distance:** on the spot on the spot on the spot on the spot.
**Remarks:** Max. 2 nights.

### Callander 2B2

**Loch Katrine**, Trossachs Pier. **GPS:** n56,23368 w4,42897.

---

12 ⛺£18 🔌🚰Ch🔧💧included. 🚐♻ **Location:** Rural, isolated, quiet. **Surface:** asphalted. 📅 01/03-31/12. **Remarks:** At lake.

### 🅲🆂 Callander 🏔🍴♻ 2B2
**The Cabin at Loch Lubnaig**, A84. **GPS:** n56,27765 w4,2834. ⬆.

2 ⛺£7/pp Ch£ 2 💧£ 1. 🚐 **Location:** Rural, simple, isolated, noisy. **Surface:** asphalted. 📅 01/01-31/12. **Distance:** 🛒7,5km ⛱on the spot 🚰on the spot ⊗7,5km 💧7,5km on the spot 🚶1km **Remarks:** Max. 3 nights, gate closes at 20h.

### 🅸🆃🆂 Cruden Bay 🏔♻ 2C1
**Port Errol**, Harbour Street. **GPS:** n57,41130 w1,84546. ⬆.

⛺voluntary contribution (£10) 🚰free. **Location:** Rural, simple, quiet. **Surface:** metalled. 📅 01/01-31/12. **Distance:** 🛒on the spot ⛱on the spot 🚰on the spot ⊗850m 🚶on the spot. **Remarks:** Max. 3 days.

### 🅸🆂 Cullen 🏔♻ 2B1
**Port Long Road.** **GPS:** n57,69408 w2,81992. ⬆.

6 ⛺free 💧free. **Location:** Rural, simple, quiet. **Surface:** gravel. 📅 01/01-31/12. **Distance:** 🛒400m ⛱on the spot 🚰on the spot ⊗400m 💧400m 🚶on the spot.

### 🅸🆃 Dufftown 2B1
**Castle Road.** **GPS:** n57,45325 w3,12912.

20 ⛺free. **Surface:** asphalted. 📅 01/01-31/12. **Distance:** 🛒400m ⊗400m 💧400m.

---

### 🅸🆃 Dumfries ♻ 2B3
**P Long Stay**, White Sands. **GPS:** n55,06722 w3,6125. ⬆.

10 ⛺free. **Location:** Simple, noisy. **Surface:** asphalted. 📅 01/01-31/12. **Distance:** 🛒100m ⛱on the spot 🚰on the spot ⊗on the spot 💧on the spot on the spot 🚰on the spot.

### 🅸🆃 Dundonnell 🏔🏔♻ 2B1
**A832.** **GPS:** n57,75898 w5,03397. ⬆.

8 ⛺free. **Location:** Rural, simple, quiet. **Surface:** asphalted. 📅 01/01-31/12. **Distance:** 🛒5km 🚶300m.

### 🅸🆂 Dunnet 2B1
**Dunnet Bay Club Site.** **GPS:** n58,61485 w3,345. 54 ⛺£21.20 🔌🚰Ch🔧💧included 💧£4/1. 🚐 **Location:** Rural. **Surface:** grassy. 📅 23-03/09-10. **Distance:** ⛱on the spot 🚰on the spot ⊗4km 💧4km. **Remarks:** Beautiful view.

### 🅸🆂 Dunthulm 🏔🏔🏔♻ 2A1
**Camus More Campsite.** **GPS:** n57,65020 w6,40459. ⬆.

7 ⛺£8 🚰💧included. 🐾 **Location:** Rural, simple, isolated, quiet. **Surface:** grassy. 📅 15/05-07/09. **Distance:** 🛒10km ⛱on the spot ⊗10km 💧10km. **Remarks:** Nearby Dunthulm Castle.

### 🅸🆂 Durness 🏔🏔♻ 2B1
**Sango Sands Oasis**, A838, Sango Bay. **GPS:** n58,57013 w4,74269. ⬆➡.

60 ⛺£18 🔌🚰Ch🔧£ 4 💧included 💧£2/2 💧£ 5/day. 🐾 **Location:** Rural, comfortable, quiet. **Surface:** grassy/metalled. 📅 01/01-31/12. **Distance:** ⛱on the spot ⊗100m 💧200m 🚶on the spot.

### 🅸🆂 Easdale 🏔🏔🏔♻ 2A2
**Highland Arts Exhibition.** **GPS:** n56,29521 w5,64926. ⬆.

---

10 ⛺£10 🚰💧. 🐾 **Location:** Rural, simple, quiet. **Surface:** metalled. 📅 01/01-31/12. **Distance:** 🛒on the spot ⛱on the spot 🚰on the spot ⊗on the spot 💧4,5km on the spot 🚶on the spot.

### 🅸🆂 Falkirk 🏔🏔♻ 2B2
**The Falkirk Wheel**, Lime Road. **GPS:** n56,00031 w3,83982. ⬆.

30 ⛺£15 💧🗑💧. 🐾 **Location:** Rural, simple, quiet. **Surface:** asphalted. 📅 01/01-31/12. **Distance:** 🛒4km ⛱on the spot ⊗on the spot 💧4km on the spot 🚰on the spot 🚶on the spot. **Remarks:** Check in during opening hours or call: 01324676912, caution key sanitary £20.

### 🅸🆃 Fettercairn 🏔♻ 2B2
**Car Park Bowling Club**, Fettercairn, Laurencekirk. **GPS:** n56,84971 w2,57306. ⬆.

10 ⛺free. **Location:** Rural, simple, noisy. **Surface:** asphalted. 📅 01/01-31/12. **Distance:** 🛒100m ⊗100m 💧250m 100m.

**Tourist information Fettercairn:**
👁 Fettercairn Distillery Visitor Centre Information, Distillery Road. One of Scotland's oldest malt whiskey distilleries. 📅 01/05-30/09, Mon-Sa 10-14.30h. 🎫 £5.

### 🅸🆃 Fort William 🏔🏔🍴♻ 2A2
**West End Car Park**, Achintore Road. **GPS:** n56,81522 w5,11686. ⬆.

10 ⛺£2. 🚐 **Location:** Urban, simple, noisy. **Surface:** asphalted. 📅 01/01-31/12. **Distance:** 🛒200m ⛱200m 🚰200m ⊗200m 💧200m 🚲10km.

### 🅸🆃 Girvan ♻ 1D1
**Harbour street- Henriettastreet.** **GPS:** n55,24324 w4,85869. ⬆.

50 ⬛free WC. **Location:** Rural, simple, quiet. **Surface:** asphalted.
⬛ 01/01-31/12.
**Distance:** 🚲100m 🏖sandy beach 50m ⊗50m 🍴500m ▣600m
50m 🚶on the spot.

### Glenbrittle 🏔🌲🌊 2A1

**Glenbrittle Campsite**, Carbost. **GPS:** n57,20251 w6,29021.⬆.

33 ⬛£9/pp 🚿🍽Ch 🔌£6 WC⬛included ▣£6,50. 🚲
**Location:** Rural, comfortable, isolated, quiet.
**Surface:** grassy/metalled. ⬛ 01/04-01/10.
**Distance:** 🚲10km 🌲on the spot 🍴on the spot 🚶on the spot 🚣on the spot.

### Glennfinnan 🍴 2A2

**GPS:** n56,85773 w5,40607.
2 ⬛free. **Location:** Rural, simple, quiet. **Surface:** grassy/gravel.
⬛ 01/01-31/12.
**Distance:** 🚲on the spot 🚶on the spot.

### Hawick 🌿🏔🍴🌊 2B3

**Common Haugh**, Victoria Road. **GPS:** n55,42310 w2,79114.⬆.

50 ⬛free WC. **Location:** Urban, simple, central. **Surface:** asphalted.
⬛ 01/01-31/12.
**Distance:** 🚲800m ⊗800m 🍴on the spot 🚴on the spot
🚶on the spot.
**Remarks:** Max. 24h, special part for motor homes.

### Helensburgh 🌊 2B2

W Clyde St. **GPS:** n56,00198 w4,73503.⬆.

20 ⬛£1.20/h 9-18h WCfree. 🚽**Location:** Urban, simple, central,
noisy. **Surface:** asphalted. ⬛ 01/01-31/12.
**Distance:** 🚲200m 🌲on the spot 🚲on the spot ⊗200m 🍴250m
▣300m 🚴on the spot 🚶on the spot.

### Helmsdale 2B1

**Helmsdale Harbour**, Shore Street. **GPS:** n58,11522 w3,65113.

7 ⬛free. **Surface:** metalled. ⬛ 01/01-31/12.
**Distance:** 🚲200m 🌲on the spot 🚲50m ⊗200m 🍴on the spot
🚴on the spot 🚶on the spot.

### Irvine 🌿🏔🌊 1D1

Beach Drive. **GPS:** n55,60628 w4,69263.⬆.

---

100 ⬛free WCfree. **Location:** Rural, simple, quiet. **Surface:** asphalted.
⬛ 01/01-31/12.
**Distance:** 🚲1,5km 🏊4km 🌲on the spot 🚲on the spot 🍴1,2km
▣850m 🚴400m 🚶on the spot.
**Remarks:** At sea, historical centre.

### Jedburgh 🌿🏔 2B3

**Canongate**, 7 Queen Street. **GPS:** n55,47761 w2,55313.⬆.

15 ⬛free WC 🚿free. **Location:** Urban, simple, central, noisy.
**Surface:** concrete. ⬛ 01/01-31/12.
**Distance:** 🚲on the spot ⊗on the spot 🍴100m 🚴on the spot
🚴on the spot 🚶on the spot.
**Remarks:** At tourist office.

### Kalnakill 🌿🏔🌊 2A1

**GPS:** n57,54182 w5,84807.⬆.

4 ⬛free. **Location:** Rural, simple, isolated, quiet. **Surface:** asphalted.
⬛ 01/01-31/12.
**Distance:** 🚲2,2km.

### Kilchoan 🌊 2A2

**Far View Campsite**, Pier Road. **GPS:** n56,69409 w6,09621.⬆➡.

2 ⬛£15 🚿🍽Ch 🔌included. 🚲 **Location:** Rural, comfortable,
isolated, quiet. **Surface:** grassy/gravel. ⬛ 01/01-31/12.
**Distance:** 🚲1,5km 🌲500m 🚲500m ⊗500m 🚴on the spot
🚶on the spot.
**Remarks:** Ferry boat to Isle of Mull 400m.

### Kilchoan 🌊 2A2

**Kilchoan Ferry Terminal**, Pier Road. **GPS:** n56,69008 w6,09603.⬆.

15 ⬛free. **Location:** Rural, simple, isolated, quiet. **Surface:** asphalted.
⬛ 01/01-31/12.
**Distance:** 🚲2km 🌲on the spot 🚲on the spot ⊗1km.

---

### Kirkcudbright 🌿🏔🌊 1D1

Beaconsfield Place. **GPS:** n54,83707 w4,05045.⬆.

5 ⬛free WCfree. **Location:** Simple, central, noisy. **Surface:** asphalted.
⬛ 01/01-31/12.
**Distance:** 🚲on the spot 🌲on the spot ⊗on the spot 🍴on the spot
🚴on the spot 🚴on the spot 🚶on the spot.

### Kylesku 🌿🏔🌊 2B1

A894. **GPS:** n58,25756 w5,02726.⬆.

10 ⬛free. **Location:** Rural, simple, isolated, quiet. **Surface:** asphalted.
⬛ 01/01-31/12.
**Distance:** 🚲1Km 🌲on the spot 🚲on the spot ⊗1km.

### Lendalfoot 🌊 1D1

8 A77 Girvan. **GPS:** n55,16301 w4,94904.⬆.

4 ⬛free. **Location:** Rural, simple, noisy. **Surface:** concrete.
⬛ 01/01-31/12.
**Distance:** 🚲500m 🌲on the spot.

### Lochgelly 2B2

**Lochore Meadows Country Park**. **GPS:** n56,15061 w3,33675.⬆.
⬛£10 🚿Ch. **Location:** Isolated, quiet.
**Distance:** 🚲1,6km 🌲on the spot 🚲on the spot ⊗1,6km 🚴on the
spot 🚶on the spot.
**Remarks:** Arrival <17h.

### Lochwinnoch 🌊 1D1

**Castle Semple Country Park**, Lochlip Road.
**GPS:** n55,79569 w4,62302.⬆.

10 ⬛free WCfree. **Location:** Rural, simple, quiet. **Surface:** asphalted.
⬛ 01/01-31/12.
**Distance:** 🚲500m 🌲on the spot ⊗on the spot 🍴on the spot
🚴300m 🚴on the spot 🚶on the spot.

### Luskentyre 🌿🏔🌊 2A1

A859. **GPS:** n57,86673 w6,91537.⬆.

UK

3 �£5. **Location:** Rural, simple, isolated, noisy.
**Surface:** asphalted/metalled. ◯ 01/01-31/12.
**Distance:** ⮐on the spot ⮐on the spot.
**Remarks:** Online payment with PayPal.

| **Moffat** 🌱⛰🌊 | 2B3 |

**Grey Mare's Tail Nature reserve**, A708, Moffat Water Valley.
**GPS:** n55,41779 w3,28646. ⬆.

10 ⌚£2. 🚰 **Location:** Rural, simple, isolated, quiet. **Surface:** gravel.
◯ 01/01-31/12.
**Distance:** ⮐on the spot ⮑on the spot.

| S **New Abbey** 🌱⛵ | 2B3 |

**Parking Sweetheart Abbey**, A710, Main Street.
**GPS:** n54,98070 w3,61966. ⬆.

6 ⌚free WC. **Location:** Simple, quiet. **Surface:** asphalted/metalled.
◯ 01/01-31/12.
**Distance:** 🚶200m ⊗on the spot ⛽200m 🚶200m ⮑on the spot.

| **Newton Steward** 🍴🌊 | 1D1 |

**Galloway Forrest Park. GPS:** n54,97358 w4,43804. ⬆.

3 ⌚free. **Location:** Rural, simple, isolated, quiet.
**Surface:** asphalted/gravel. ◯ 01/01-31/12.
**Distance:** 🚶6km ⛽500m 🚶on the spot.

| **Oban** ⛵ | 2A2 |

**Lochavullin road. GPS:** n56,40948 w5,47142. ⬆.

4 ⌚£10. 🚰 **Location:** Urban, simple, noisy. **Surface:** asphalted.
◯ 01/01-31/12.
**Distance:** 🚶400m ⊗400m ⮐on the spot 🚶400m.
**Remarks:** At tourist office.

| S **Pairc Niseaboist** | 2A1 |

**Talla na Mara**, Island of Harris, A859. **GPS:** n57,85948 w6,99296.

---

3 ⌚£24 ⮐Ch⮑WC⮑. **Location:** Rural. **Surface:** unpaved.
◯ 01/04-31/10.
**Distance:** ⊗on the spot.
**Remarks:** Beautiful panorama.

| **Pitlochry** 🌱🍴 | 2B2 |

**Queen's View. GPS:** n56,71675 w3,85734. ⬆.

2 ⌚£2/24h. 🚌 **Location:** Rural, simple, isolated, quiet.
**Surface:** asphalted. ◯ 01/01-31/12.

| S **Scourie** 🌱🌊 | 2B1 |

**Scourie Campsite**, A894. **GPS:** n58,35157 w5,15523. ⬆⮑.

50 ⌚£20 🚰Ch⮑WC⮑included ⬚£2/1. ⛟
**Location:** Rural, comfortable, isolated, quiet.
**Surface:** grassy/metalled. ◯ 01/04-30/09.
**Distance:** 🚶200m ⮐on the spot ⮑on the spot ⊗on the spot
⛽200m.

| S **Seilebost** ⛰ | 2A1 |

**Seilebost School**, Isle of Harris, A859 11. **GPS:** n57,86873 w6,95357.
4 ⌚£21 🚰. 
**Location:** Rural. **Surface:** metalled. ◯ 01/04-31/10.
**Distance:** ⮐200m.
**Remarks:** Playground.

| S **Seilebost** ⛰ | 2A1 |

A859. **GPS:** n57,86615 w6,88152. ⬆.

10 ⌚£5. **Location:** Rural, simple, quiet. **Surface:** gravel/metalled.
◯ 01/01-31/12.
**Distance:** 🚶6km ⮐2km.
**Remarks:** Online payment with PayPal.

| S **Shawbost** | 2A1 |

**Eilean Fraoich Camp Site. GPS:** n58,31989 w6,68753. ⬆⮑.

25 ⌚£14-18 🚰Ch⮑£4 WC⮑included ⬚£4/3 ⮑£5/day. ⛟
**Location:** Rural, comfortable, isolated, quiet.
**Surface:** gravel/metalled. ◯ Easter-01/10.
**Distance:** 🚶500m ⮐1km ⊗500m.

| 🍴S **Sligachan** 🌊 | 2A1 |

**Sligachan Campsite**, A87. **GPS:** n57,29146 w6,17696. ⬆⮑.

---

100 ⌚£7.50/pp 🚰Ch⮑£5 WC⮑⬚£3 ⮑included. ⛟
**Location:** Rural, simple, isolated, quiet.
**Surface:** grassy/gravel.
◯ 01/04-15/10.
**Distance:** 🚶10km ⮐on the spot ⊗100m ⛽10km 🚶100m.

| S **Tomintoul** 🌱⛰❄🍴❄ | 2B2 |

**Tomintoul Bowlingclub Campsite**, 10 Tomnabat Lane.
**GPS:** n57,25073 w3,37636. ⬆.

5 ⌚£7 🚰⮑£3 WCincluded. ⛟ **Location:** Urban, simple, central,
quiet. **Surface:** gravel. ◯ 01/01-31/12.
**Distance:** 🚶300m ⊗300m ⛽300m 🚗300m 🚴300m 🚶300m
🚲12km.
**Remarks:** Money in envelope in mail box.
**Tourist information Tomintoul:**
ℹ Tourist Information Centre, The Square.
Ⓜ Tomintoul Museum, Tomnabat Lane. Historical regional museum.
◯ Easter-31/10, mon-sa 9.30-12h, 14-16h.

| S **Uig** | 2A1 |

**Uig Bay Campsite**, A87. **GPS:** n57,58559 w6,37971. ⬆⮑.

15 ⌚£7.50/pp 🚰Ch⮑£4 WC⮑⬚£3 ⮑included. ⛟
**Location:** Rural, simple, isolated, quiet. **Surface:** gravel/metalled.
◯ 01/01-31/12.
**Distance:** 🚶200m ⮐on the spot ⊗100m ⛽200m.

# Wales

| 🍴S **Abergynolwyn** | 1D3 |

**Riverside Guest House**, Llanegryn Street.
**GPS:** n52,64584 w3,95856. ⬆.

5 ⌚£10/night 🚰Chincluded ⮑£6/night. ⛟
**Location:** Rural, comfortable, central, quiet. **Surface:** grassy/metalled.
◯ 01/01-31/12.
**Remarks:** Arrival <18h, narrow entrance (2.6m), Snowdonia National
Park.

| S **Brecon** | 1D3 |

**The Watton Car Park**, Heol Gouesnou. **GPS:** n51,94609 w3,38531. ⬆.

UK

25 ⌁£0.70/h, max. £3.20 8-18h, overnight stay free WCfree,150m. ⌁
**Location:** Urban, simple, quiet. **Surface:** asphalted.
⌂ 01/01-31/12.
**Distance:** ⌁on the spot ⌁on the spot.
**Remarks:** 1 night per 7 nights.

| | Brecon | 1D3 |
|---|---|---|

**Coach-Lorry Park**, Canal Road. **GPS:** n51,94486 w3,38993. ⬆

10 ⌁£0.70/h, max. £3.20 8-18h, overnight stay free. ⌁
**Location:** Urban, simple, central, quiet. **Surface:** asphalted.
⌂ 01/01-31/12.
**Distance:** ⌁100m ⌁100m.
**Remarks:** 1 night per 7 nights.

| | Brecon | 1D3 |
|---|---|---|

**The Promenade Car Park**, Fenni-Fach Rd. **GPS:** n51,95089 w3,4036. ⬆

25 ⌁£0.70/h, max. £3.20 8-18h, overnight stay free. ⌁
**Location:** Urban, simple, isolated, quiet. **Surface:** asphalted.
⌂ 01/01-31/12.
**Distance:** ⌁600m ⌁on the spot ⌁700m.
**Remarks:** 1 night per 7 nights.

| | Builth Wells | 1F2 |
|---|---|---|

**The Groe Car Park**, The Strand. **GPS:** n52,14969 w3,40252. ⬆

20 ⌁£0.70/h, max. £3.20 8-18h, overnight stay free. WC. ⌁
**Location:** Urban, simple, quiet. **Surface:** asphalted.
⌂ 01/01-31/12.
**Distance:** ⌁on the spot ⌁on the spot ⌁on the spot.
**Remarks:** 1 night per 7 nights.

| | Builth Wells | 1F2 |
|---|---|---|

**Smithfield Car Park**, Brecon Rd. **GPS:** n52,14714 w3,40261. ⬆

50 ⌁£0.70/h, max. £3.20 8-18h, overnight stay free. ⌁

---

**Location:** Urban, simple, central. **Surface:** asphalted.
⌂ 01/01-31/12.
**Distance:** ⌁200m.
**Remarks:** 1 night per 7 nights.

| | Crickhowell | 1F2 |
|---|---|---|

**Beaufort Street Car Park**, Greenhill Way. **GPS:** n51,85838 w3,13557. ⬆

8 ⌁£0.70/h, max. £3.20 8-18h, overnight stay free. ⌁
**Location:** Urban, simple, central, quiet. **Surface:** asphalted.
⌂ 01/01-31/12.
**Distance:** ⌁50m.
**Remarks:** 1 night per 7 nights.

| | Hay-on-Wye | 1F2 |
|---|---|---|

**Oxford Road Car Park**, Oxford Road. **GPS:** n52,07316 w3,12592. ⬆

25 ⌁£0.70/h, max. £3.20 8-18h, overnight stay free WCfree. ⌁
**Location:** Urban, simple, central, quiet. **Surface:** asphalted.
⌂ 01/01-31/12.
**Distance:** ⌁150m ⌁150m ⌁150m ⌁on the spot.
**Remarks:** 1 night per 7 nights.

| | Knighton | 1F2 |
|---|---|---|

**Bowling Green Lane Car Park**, Bowling Green Lane.
**GPS:** n52,34324 w3,04553. ⬆

30 ⌁£0.70/h, max. £3.20 8-18h, overnight stay free WCfree. ⌁
**Location:** Rural, simple, central, quiet. **Surface:** asphalted.
⌂ 01/01-31/12.
**Distance:** ⌁200m ⌁300m ⌁on the spot.
**Remarks:** 1 night per 7 nights.

| | Llandrindod Wells | 1F2 |
|---|---|---|

**High Street Car Park**, High Street. **GPS:** n52,21151 w3,38042. ⬆

30 ⌁£0.70/h, max. £3.20 8-18h, overnight stay free. ⌁
**Location:** Urban, simple, central. **Surface:** asphalted.
⌂ 01/01-31/12.
**Distance:** ⌁150m ⌁on the spot.
**Remarks:** 1 night per 7 nights, max. 6m.

| | Llandudno Junction | 1D2 |
|---|---|---|

**Conwy Motorhome Stopover**, 40 Conway Rd.
**GPS:** n53,28441 w3,81271. ⬆
8 ⌁£10 ⌁Ch. ⌁
**Location:** Urban, central, quiet. ⌂ 01/01-31/12.
**Distance:** ⌁on the spot ⌁500m ⌁on the spot.

---

**Remarks:** Arrival <17h, at motorhome dealer.

| | Llandysul | 1D3 |
|---|---|---|

**Penrhiwgaled Arms**, Cross Inn. **GPS:** n52,18959 w4,35595. ⬆
5 ⌁£5.
**Distance:** ⌁on the spot.

| | Llanidloes | 1D3 |
|---|---|---|

**Mount Street Car Park**, Mount Lane. **GPS:** n52,44750 w3,53938. ⬆

12 ⌁£0.70/h, max. £3.20 8-18h, night £5. ⌁
**Location:** Urban, simple, central, quiet. **Surface:** asphalted.
⌂ 01/01-31/12.
**Distance:** ⌁on the spot ⌁100m ⌁100m ⌁100m.
**Remarks:** 1 night per 7 nights.

| | Moelfre | 1D2 |
|---|---|---|

**Lligwy Bay. GPS:** n53,35910 w4,26132.
⌁£10/night. **Location:** Rural. **Surface:** gravel/sand.
**Remarks:** Beach parking, max. 2 nights, max. 7m.

| | Nantgaredig | 1D3 |
|---|---|---|

**Railway Hotel**, B4310. **GPS:** n51,86533 w4,18976. ⬆
5 ⌁£5 WC. ⌂ 01/01-31/12.

| | New Quay | 1D3 |
|---|---|---|

**Parking Far Field**, Towyn Rd. **GPS:** n52,21181 w4,36087. ⬆

⌁£6/day £8/night. **Surface:** unpaved. ⌂ 01/01-31/12.
**Distance:** ⌁on the spot ⌁300m ⌁150m.

| | Newton | 1F2 |
|---|---|---|

**Back Lane Car Park**, Back Lane. **GPS:** n52,51534 w3,31735. ⬆

40 ⌁£0.70/h, max. £3.20 8-18h, night £5 WCfree. ⌁
**Location:** Urban, simple, central, quiet. **Surface:** asphalted.
⌂ 01/01-31/12.
**Distance:** ⌁150m ⌁on the spot ⌁on the spot.
**Remarks:** 1 night per 7 nights.

| | Newton | 1F2 |
|---|---|---|

**The Gravel Car Park**, Heol Les Herbiers. **GPS:** n52,51421 w3,31167. ⬆

25 ⌁£0.70/h, max. £3.20 8-18h, night £5. ⌁
**Location:** Urban, simple, central. **Surface:** asphalted.
⌂ 01/01-31/12.
**Distance:** ⌁250m ⌁50m ⌁250m.
**Remarks:** 1 night per 7 nights.

UK

## ⬜S Presteigne 1F2
**Hereford Street Car Park**, Hereford Street.
**GPS**: n52,27245 w3,00488. ⬆.

10 🅿£0.70/h, max. £3.20 8-18h, overnight stay free WCfree. 🚐.
**Location**: Urban, simple, central, quiet. **Surface**: asphalted.
🅾 01/01-31/12.
**Distance**: 🚰100m 🚄on the spot.
**Remarks**: 1 night per 7 nights, max. 6m.

## ⬜S Tenby 1D3
**Carew Airfield & Pavilion**, Sageston. **GPS**: n51,69362 w4,80973. ⬆.

5 🅿£15-20/night 🚰Ch WCincluded. 
**Location**: Comfortable, quiet. **Surface**: concrete. 🅾 01/01-31/12.
**Distance**: 150m 8km ⊗500m 🍴1,5km 1,5km.

## ⬜S Welshpool 1F2
**Berriew Street Car Park**, Berriew Rd. **GPS**: n52,65875 w3,14806. ⬆.

30 🅿£0.70/h, max. £3.20 8-18h, night £5 WCfree. 🚐.
**Location**: Urban, simple, central, quiet. **Surface**: asphalted.
🅾 01/01-31/12.
**Distance**: 🚰200m 🍴500m.
**Remarks**: 1 night per 7 nights.

## ⬜S Welshpool 1F2
**Church Street Car Park**, Church Street. **GPS**: n52,66031 w3,1438. ⬆.

25 🅿£0.70/h, max. £3.20 8-18h, night £5 WCfree. 🚐.
**Location**: Urban, simple, central, quiet. **Surface**: asphalted.
🅾 01/01-31/12.
**Distance**: 🚰150m 🍴300m.
**Remarks**: 1 night per 7 nights.

# England

## ⬜S Abingdon 1G2
**Rye Farm Pay & Display car park**, Bridge Street, A415.
**GPS**: n51,66746 w1,27799. ⬆.

8 🅿£7.30/24h WC. 🚐 **Location**: Urban, simple. **Surface**: asphalted.
🅾 01/01-31/12.
**Distance**: 🚰500m ⊗500m 🍴800m.
**Remarks**: Max. 24h, first call or mail, carparks.southandvale.uk@
parkindigo.com, 01235 470118.

## 🅿 Aldershot 1G3
**Parsons Barracks Car park**, Ordnance Road.
**GPS**: n51,24979 w0,75731. ⬆.

10 🅿£0.50/h. 🚐 **Location**: Urban, simple. **Surface**: asphalted.
🅾 01/01-31/12.
**Distance**: 🚰550m ⊗550m.

## ⬜S Appledore 1E3
**Churchfields Car Park**, The Quay. **GPS**: n51,05464 w4,19135. ⬆.

25 🅿£5 18-10h, £3 day WCfree. 🚐 **Location**: Urban, simple, quiet.
**Surface**: asphalted. 🅾 01/01-31/12.
**Distance**: 🚰150m 50m ⊗200m.
**Remarks**: Max. 2 nights, min. 6m space between motorhomes.

## ⬜S Arundel 1G3
**Mill Road Car Park**, Mill Road. **GPS**: n50,85392 w0,55067. ⬆.

50 🅿£10. 🚐
**Location**: Simple, quiet. **Surface**: grassy. 🅾 Sa-Su.
**Distance**: 🚰100m ⊗100m 🍴200m.
**Remarks**: At castle, arrival 8><16h.

## 🍴S Berwick-upon-Tweed 2C3
**The Barn at Beal**. **GPS**: n55,67754 w1,89434. ⬆ ⬆.

14 🅿£25 🚰Ch WCincluded. **Location**: Rural,
comfortable, quiet. **Surface**: gravel/metalled. 🅾 01/01-31/12.
**Distance**: 2km ⊗on the spot on the spot on the spot.
**Remarks**: Beautiful view, possibility for reservation.

## ⬜S Bideford 1E3
**Riverbank (long stay) Car Park**, Kingsley road.
**GPS**: n51,02086 w4,20386. ⬆.

20 🅿£5 18-10h, £3 day. 🚐 **Location**: Urban, simple, quiet.
**Surface**: asphalted. 🅾 01/01-31/12.
**Distance**: 🚰1,5km 50m ⊗500m 🍴1km 500m.
**Remarks**: Max. 2 nights, min. 6m space between motorhomes.

## ⬜S Bourton-on-the-Water 1G2
**Bourton Rovers**, Rissington Road. **GPS**: n51,87995 w1,7513. ⬆.

5 🅿£10 🚰ChWC free,Password at the bar.
**Location**: Rural, simple, central, quiet. **Surface**: grassy.
🅾 01/01-31/12.
**Distance**: 🚰500m ⊗500m 🍴500m.

## ⬜S Bourton-on-the-Water 1G2
**Bourton Vale Car & Coach Park**, Station Rd.
**GPS**: n51,88512 w1,75471. ⬆.

10 🅿9-18h parking rate, overnight stay £8 WCfree. 🚐.
**Location**: Urban, simple, central, quiet. **Surface**: asphalted.
🅾 01/01-31/12.
**Distance**: 🚰200m ⊗on the spot 🍴on the spot.

## 🍴S Brampton 2B3
**Blenkinsopp Castle Inn**. **GPS**: n54,97334 w2,52267. ⬆.
5 🅿£10 🚰. **Surface**: gravel.
**Distance**: ⊗on the spot.

## ⬜S Bridport 1F3
**Bridport rest area**, DT6 6AS. **GPS**: n50,72630 w2,7778.
15 🅿free WC. **Location**: Motorway. **Surface**: metalled.
🅾 01/01-31/12.
**Distance**: 🚰2km 🍴1,5km.
**Remarks**: Max. 1 day.

## ⬜S Bude 1E3
**Bude Town Football Club**, Broadclose Hill.
**GPS**: n50,83000 w4,5359. ⬆.

20 🅿£8 WC. **Location**: Simple. **Surface**: grassy.
🅾 01/01-31/12.
**Distance**: 🚰500m.
**Remarks**: At football ground.

## ⬜S Bude 1E3
**Sandparks Campsite**. **GPS**: n50,79655 w4,55533.

🛏£15 💧£ 4,50/night WC 🚽. 🚿 **Location:** Rural. **Surface:** grassy.
🅿 21/07-01/09.
**Distance:** ⛵on the spot 🚾50m.

### 🏢S Bury St Edmunds ⛵ 1H2
**Ram Meadow Carpark Annexe**, Cotton Lane.
**GPS:** n52,24775 e0,71893. ⬆.

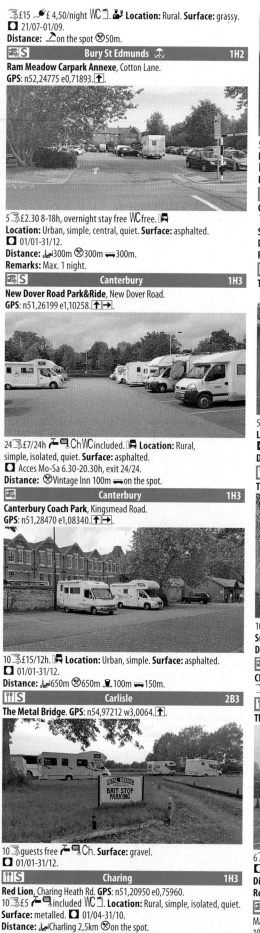

5 🛏£2.30 8-18h, overnight stay free WC free. 🏪
**Location:** Urban, simple, central, quiet. **Surface:** asphalted.
🅿 01/01-31/12.
**Distance:** 🚶300m 🚾300m 🚌300m.
**Remarks:** Max. 1 night.

### 🏢S Canterbury 1H3
**New Dover Road Park&Ride**, New Dover Road.
**GPS:** n51,26199 e1,10258. ⬆➡.

24 🛏£7/24h 🚻ChWC included. 🏪 **Location:** Rural, simple, isolated, quiet. **Surface:** asphalted.
🅿 Acces Mo-Sa 6.30-20.30h, exit 24/24.
**Distance:** 🚾Vintage Inn 100m 🚌on the spot.

### 🏢 Canterbury 1H3
**Canterbury Coach Park**, Kingsmead Road.
**GPS:** n51,28470 e1,08340. ⬆➡.

10 🛏£15/12h. 🏪 **Location:** Urban, simple. **Surface:** asphalted.
🅿 01/01-31/12.
**Distance:** 🚶650m 🚾650m 🚂100m 🚌150m.

### 🏢S Carlisle 2B3
**The Metal Bridge. GPS:** n54,97212 w3,0064. ⬆.

10 🛏guests free 🚻🍴Ch. **Surface:** gravel.
🅿 01/01-31/12.

### 🏢S Charing 1H3
**Red Lion**, Charing Heath Rd. **GPS:** n51,20950 e0,75960.
10 🛏£5 🚻🍴included WC 🚽. **Location:** Rural, simple, isolated, quiet.
**Surface:** metalled. 🅿 01/04-31/10.
**Distance:** 🚶Charling 2,5km 🚾on the spot.

### 🏢S Cheltenham 1F2
**The Gloucester Old Spot**, Tewkesbury Road, A4109.
**GPS:** n51,93325 w2,14881. ⬆.

5 🛏free, use of a meal obligated 🚻WC included, during opening hours.
**Location:** Rural, simple, isolated. **Surface:** gravel/sand.
🅿 01/01-31/12.
**Distance:** 🚤500m 🚾on the spot.

### 🏢S Chester 〰🏖⛲🛒 1F1
**Car Park, Little Roodee**, Castle Road. **GPS:** n53,18447 w2,89245.
🛏£5.80, overnight stay £1.50 🚻WC. **Location:** Urban, noisy.
**Surface:** asphalted. 🅿 01/01-31/12 ⭕ 01/05-13/05.
**Distance:** 🚤3,5km 🚾300m 🚂500m 🚌on the spot.
**Remarks:** Along the Dee river, gate closed from 22.30-6h.

### 🏢S Cirencester 1F2
**The Crown Inn**, High Street, Cerny Wick. **GPS:** n51,66264 w1,88933. ⬆.

5 🛏£10 🚻🍴Ch 💧WC during opening hours. 🚿
**Location:** Rural, simple. **Surface:** grassy/metalled.
🅿 01/01-31/12.
**Distance:** 🚾on the spot.

### 🏢S Cirencester 1F2
**The Thames Head Inn. GPS:** n51,68633 w2,02959. ⬆.

10 🛏£20 WC 🚽📶. **Location:** Rural, isolated, quiet.
**Surface:** grassy/gravel.
**Distance:** 🚶5km 🚾on the spot.

### 🏢 Clovelly 〰⛵🌊 1E3
**Clovelly Visitors Centre. GPS:** n50,99867 w4,40386.
🛏£7.25/pp, child £4.40. **Surface:** gravel.

### 🏢S Crediton 1F3
**Thelbridge Cross Inn**, Thelbridge Hill. **GPS:** n50,89530 w3,72228. ⬆.

6 🛏£5 💧(2x)£ 3,50. **Location:** Isolated, quiet. **Surface:** asphalted.
🅿 01/01-31/12.
**Distance:** 🚶14km 🚾on the spot.
**Remarks:** Discount at restaurant.

### 🏢S Dover 1H3
**Maison Dieu Road. GPS:** n51,12902 e1,31222.
10 🛏£1.10/h, max. £8.25, overnight stay free. 🏪
**Location:** Urban, simple. **Surface:** asphalted. 🅿 01/01-31/12.
**Distance:** ⛵1km 🚾500m 🚌800m.

### 🏢 Dover 1H3
**Marine Parade. GPS:** n51,12350 e1,31710.

10 🛏£1.10/h, max. £8.25, overnight stay free. 🏪
**Surface:** asphalted. 🅿 01/01-31/12.
**Distance:** ⛵on the spot 🚾100m.
**Remarks:** Max. 24h, max 3,5t.

### 🏢S Great Missenden 1G2
**The Black Horse**, Aylesbury Road. **GPS:** n51,71019 w0,71215.
5 🛏guests free 🚻WC.
**Location:** Rural, isolated. **Surface:** metalled.
**Distance:** 🚶800m 🚾on the spot.

### 🌿S Haughton 1F2
**Red Lion Farm**, Haughton, Stafford. **GPS:** n52,77790 w2,20244.
30 🛏£13 🚻WC 🚽. **Location:** Rural. **Surface:** grassy.
🅿 01/01-31/12.
**Distance:** 🚶Stafford 7km 🚾on the spot.

### 🏢 Helmsley 〰🌊 1G1
**Cleveland Way. GPS:** n54,24619 w1,06617. ⬆.

6 🛏9-18.30h parking rate £6, overnight stay free.
**Location:** Urban, central. **Surface:** asphalted.
🅿 01/01-31/12.
**Distance:** 🚶500m 🚾500m 🚂500m.

### 🏢 Holsworthy 1E3
**The Manor Car Park**, Western Road. **GPS:** n50,81133 w4,35282. ⬆.

6 🛏£5 18-10h, £3 day. 🏪 **Location:** Urban, simple, quiet.
**Surface:** asphalted. 🅿 01/01-31/12.
**Distance:** 🚶on the spot 🚾150m 🚂150m.
**Remarks:** Max. 2 nights, min. 6m space between motorhomes.

### 🏭S Huntingdon 1G2
**Wellsbridge Motorhomes Sales**, Ramsey Forty Foot, Ramsey.
**GPS:** n52,47540 w0,08834. ⬆.

5 🛏£5 💧WC. 🚿 **Location:** Rural, simple, isolated, quiet.
**Surface:** asphalted. 🅿 02/01-23/12.
**Distance:** 🚌on the spot.

### 🌿S Ipswich 1H2
**Burnt House Farm**, Wash Lane, Witnesham.
**GPS:** n52,11418 e1,20094. ⬆➡.

**UK**

5 🛏️ £9 🚰 Ch. 🚿 WC included. 📷 **Location:** Rural, comfortable, isolated, quiet. **Surface:** grassy/metalled. 🅿 01/01-31/12. **Distance:** 🚶2km ⊗2km.

### 🍴 Ipswich — 1H2

**Orwell Crossing Lorry Park**, A14 Eastbound, Nacton. **GPS:** n52,02473 e1,22678. ⬆.

20 🛏️ £18/18h. 📷 **Location:** Motorway, simple, noisy. **Surface:** asphalted. 🅿 01/01-31/12. **Distance:** ⊗on the spot.

### 🍴S Ivybridge — 1E3

**Lee Mill Services**, A38. **GPS:** n50,38493 w3,97041. ⬆➡.

10 🛏️ £17.50/night WC included. 📷 **Location:** Rural, simple, noisy. **Surface:** asphalted. 🅿 01/01-31/12. **Distance:** ⊗on the spot 🍽️500m. **Remarks:** Behind petrol station, discount at restaurant £5.

### ⛴S Liverpool — 1F1

**Liverpool Marina**, Coburg Wharf. **GPS:** n53,39051 w2,9864. 10 🛏️ £18/24h WC 📷 🚿 📶 🚌. **Location:** Urban. **Surface:** metalled. 🅿 01/01-31/12. **Distance:** 🚶1,5km 🏊on the spot ⊗100m 🚌400m.

### 🍴 Lydford — 1E3

**The Castle Inn. GPS:** n50,64359 w4,10893. 4 🛏️ guests free. **Location:** Simple, quiet. 🅿 01/01-31/12. **Distance:** ⊗on the spot.

### ⛴S Maidstone — 1H3

**Maidstone Services**, M20. **GPS:** n51,26687 e0,61502. ⬆.

8 🛏️ £20/24h, first 2 hours free WC 📷 📶 against payment. 🚌 🚐 **Location:** Motorway, simple, noisy. **Surface:** asphalted. 🅿 01/01-31/12. **Distance:** 🛒200m ⊗on the spot 🚌150m. **Remarks:** Payment with mobile phone.

**Tourist information Maidstone:** Ⓜ Museum of Kent Life, Lock Lane, Sandling. History and traditions of Kent. 🕐 10-17h.

### 🍴S Meppershall — 1G2

**The Airman Hotel**, Hitchin Road 16. **GPS:** n52,02526 w0,31787. 🛏️ £10 🚰 **Location:** Rural. **Surface:** gravel. 🅿 01/01-31/12. **Distance:** ⊗1,5km 🍽️1km.

### 🍴S Mevagissey — 1E3

**Willow Car & Coach Park**, Valley Road. **GPS:** n50,27155 w4,79044. ⬆➡.

10 🛏️10-18h £2/h, overnight stay £8 🚰on demand. 📷 **Location:** Simple, central. **Surface:** metalled. 🅿 01/01-31/12. **Distance:** 🚶150m 🏊1km ⊗300m.

### 🛁S New Milton — 1F3

**Orchard Lakes**, New Lane, Bashley. **GPS:** n50,77182 w1,6645. ⬆.

15 🛏️ £15 🚰 🍽️ Ch included 🚿 £5. 📷 **Location:** Rural, comfortable, isolated, quiet. **Surface:** grassy/metalled. 🅿 01/01-31/12. **Distance:** 🚶400m 🏊6,5km 🚶‍♀️on the spot 🚶 New Forest. **Remarks:** Arrival >18h.

### 🚐 Newhaven — 1G3

**West Side Promenade. GPS:** n50,78189 e0,05530. ⬆.

30 🛏️ £3. **Location:** Rural. **Surface:** grassy/metalled. 🅿 Easter-30/09. **Distance:** 🚶2km 🏊on the spot 🚶‍♀️on the spot ⊗400m 🍽️850m 🚌2km. **Remarks:** Arrival 8><17h.

### 🛁S Newnham on Severn — 1F2

**Elton Farm**, Elton Road A4151. **GPS:** n51,82355 w2,44753. ⬆. 5 🛏️ £5 🚰 🍽️ Ch. 📷 **Location:** Rural, simple, isolated. **Surface:** grassy. 🅿 01/01-31/12. **Distance:** 🚶‍♀️on the spot 🚌on the spot.

### 🍴S Oldham — 1F1

**The Hawthorn**, 365 Roundthorn Road. **GPS:** n53,53352 w2,08637. ⬆. 5 🛏️ £15 🚿 £2,50/night WC 📶 **Location:** Urban, simple, quiet. **Surface:** grassy/gravel. 🅿 01/01-31/12. **Distance:** 🚶3km ⊗on the spot.

### ⛴S Pickering — 1G1

**Antiques Centre**, Southgate. **GPS:** n54,24413 w0,78026.

5 🛏️ £10 🚰 Ch. 📷 **Location:** Simple. **Surface:** asphalted. 🅿 01/01-31/12. **Distance:** ⊗500m.

### 🚐 Praa Sands — 1E3

**Sydney Cove Car Park**, Castle Drive. **GPS:** n50,10440 w5,3919.

10 🛏️ £8/24h. 🚌 **Location:** Simple. **Distance:** 🏊100m ⊗100m.

### 🍴S Rake — 1G3

**The Flying Bull**, London Road. **GPS:** n51,04419 w0,85418.

5 🛏️ £5, guests free 🚰 🍽️ included WC 📶 at restaurant. **Location:** Rural, isolated, quiet. **Surface:** grassy. 🅿 01/01-31/12. **Distance:** 🚶3km ⊗on the spot. **Remarks:** Max. 1 night.

### 🍴 Rye — 1H3

**River Haven Hotel**, Winchelsea Road. **GPS:** n50,94880 e0,72990. ⬆.

5 🛏️ £10. **Surface:** gravel. 🅿 01/01-31/12. **Distance:** 🚶400m ⊗on the spot 🚌100m. **Remarks:** Pay at hotel.

### 🛁S Scarborough — 1G1

**South Moor Farm**, Dalby Forest Drive. **GPS:** n54,30049 w0,61169. ⬆. 5 🛏️ £10 🚰 Ch. 📶 included. 🚐 🚐 **Location:** Rural, simple, isolated. **Surface:** grassy. 🅿 01/01-31/12. **Distance:** 🚶19km 🏊6km ⊗200m 🚶200m.

### ⛴ Settle — 1F1

**Lower Greenfoot. GPS:** n54,06644 w2,27563. ⬆. 3 🛏️ day: parking rate, overnight stay £5. 🚌 **Surface:** asphalted. 🅿 01/01-31/12. **Distance:** 🚶500m ⊗500m 🍽️500m.

### 🍴 Settle — 1F1

**Helwith Bridge Inn**, Austwick Road, Helwith Bridge. **GPS:** n54,12127 w2,29113. ⬆. 5 🛏️ guests free. **Location:** Rural. **Surface:** gravel. 🅿 01/01-31/12. **Distance:** ⊗on the spot 🚲on the spot 🚶on the spot.

### 🍴S Sewerby — 1G1

**The Ship Inn**, Cliff Road. **GPS:** n54,10167 w0,16411. 5 🛏️ £15 🚰 Ch. **Surface:** unpaved. **Distance:** ⊗on the spot.

### 🍴S Shrewsbury — 1F2

**Halfway House**, Main Rd. **GPS:** n52,69799 w2,97851. 🛏️ guests free 🚿 **Surface:** asphalted/metalled. **Remarks:** Free, use of a meal obligated.

### 🍴 Shrewsbury — 1F2

**The Red Barn Inn**, Longden Road. **GPS:** n52,69786 w2,76066. 3 🛏️ guests free. **Surface:** asphalted/metalled. 🅿 01/01-31/12. **Distance:** 🚶1km. **Remarks:** Free, use of a meal obligated.

### ⛴ Skipton — 1G1

**Coach Street car park. GPS:** n53,96130 w2,01981. ⬆. 3 🛏️ 10-18h parking rate, overnight stay £5. **Location:** Urban, central, noisy. **Surface:** asphalted. 🅿 01/01-31/12. **Distance:** 🚶on the spot ⊗on the spot 🍽️on the spot.

**UK**

## Southampton 1G3

**Long Stay Car Park**, West Quay Road. **GPS**: n50,90090 w1,4083.⬆.

�配day max. £8, night £2. 🚗
**Location:** Urban. **Surface:** asphalted. ◻ 01/01-31/12.
**Distance:** 🚶800m ⊗800m 🚉800m.
**Remarks:** Max 3,5t.

## St Austell 1E3

**Edgemoor**, Enniscaven, St.Dennis. **GPS**: n50,39636 w4,8676.⬆.

5⌐£5/night ⌐🗑WCincluded. ♿ **Location:** Comfortable, quiet.
**Surface:** grassy/metalled. ◻ 01/01-31/12.
**Distance:** 🚶St.Austell 14,5km ♿ on the spot 🅿 on the spot.

## St Ives 1G2

**The Seven Wives**, Ramsey road. **GPS**: n52,33193 w0,07634.⬆.

5⌐£5 ⌐🗑Ch ♿£6/night WC. ♿ **Location:** Urban, simple,
central. **Surface:** metalled. ◻ 01/01-31/12.
**Distance:** 🚶1,4km ⊗on the spot.

## Staple Fitzpaine 1F3

**Home Mead**, New Road. **GPS**: n50,95970 w3,0489.⬆.

5⌐£5 ⌐included. ♿ **Location:** Rural, isolated, quiet.
**Surface:** grassy. ◻ 01/01-31/12.
**Distance:** ⊗on the spot.

## Stoke St Gregory 1F3

**The Royal Oak**, The Square. **GPS**: n51,04050 w2,9318.

5⌐guests free ⌐🗑Chfree ♿£5.
**Surface:** asphalted. ◻ 01/01-31/12.
**Distance:** ⊗on the spot 🅿50m 🚉50m.
**Remarks:** Parking in front of church.

## Stratford-upon-Avon 1G2

**Stratford Marina Car Park**, Bridgeway. **GPS**: n52,19280 w1,70154.⬆.

10⌐9-18h £8, overnight stay £15. 🚗 📹 **Location:** Urban, simple,
central. **Surface:** asphalted. ◻ 01/01-31/12.
**Distance:** 🚶200m ⊗200m 🚉200m.

## Stratford-upon-Avon 1G2

**The New Inn Hotel**, Clifford Chambers. **GPS**: n52,16929 w1,7168.⬆.

5⌐£8 ⌐♿£4,80. ♿ 🚿
**Location:** Rural, simple. **Surface:** grassy. ◻ 01/01-31/12.
**Distance:** ⊗on the spot 🚉on the spot.

**Tourist information Stratford-upon-Avon:**
🛈 Birthplace of William Shakespeare.

## Tallington 1G2

**The Whistle Stop**, Main Road. **GPS**: n52,66387 w0,38038.⬆.

⌐guests free. **Location:** Rural, simple, isolated, noisy.
**Surface:** gravel. ◻ 01/01-31/12.
**Distance:** 🚶8km ⊗on the spot 🅿8km.

## Tarrington 1F2

**The Tarrington Arms**, Ledbury road. **GPS**: n52,06473 w2,5604.

5⌐free WCfree.
**Location:** Rural, simple. **Surface:** metalled.
**Distance:** 🚶200m ⊗on the spot.

## Thaxted 1G2

**Margaret Street Car Park**, Margaret Street.
**GPS**: n51,95530 e0,34328.⬆.

2⌐free WCfree. **Location:** Urban, simple, central, quiet.
**Surface:** concrete. ◻ 01/01-31/12.
**Distance:** 🚶150m 🚉150m.
**Remarks:** Max. 48h in fortnight.

## Tintagel 1E3

**King Arthur's Car Park**, Fore Street. **GPS**: n50,66441 w4,75119.⬆.

50⌐£3.90 10-16h, £3 16-10h. WC. 🚗 **Location:** Simple.
**Surface:** asphalted.
**Distance:** 🚶on the spot ⊗on the spot 🚉100m.
**Remarks:** Opposite Tintagel Old Post Office.

## Tintagel 1E3

**Mayfair Car Park**, Fore Street. **GPS**: n50,66386 w4,75061.⬆.

30⌐£2 8.00-20h, £3.50 20-08h. 🚗 **Location:** Urban, simple, central.
**Surface:** grassy. ◻ 01/01-31/12.
**Distance:** 🚶on the spot ⊗100m 🚉on the spot.
**Remarks:** Next to King Arthur's Car Park.

## Tintagel 1E3

**Sword in Stone Car Park**, Bossiney Road. **GPS**: n50,66257 w4,74763.⬆.

20⌐£5.50/24h. 🚗
**Location:** Urban, simple. **Surface:** asphalted. ◻ 01/01-31/12.
**Distance:** 🚶150m ⊗250m.

**Tourist information Tintagel:**
👁 Tintagel Old Post Office, Fore Street. 600 year-old traditional Cornish Longhouse.
🏰 King Arthur's Castle, Castle Road. ◻ 25/03-30/10.

## Torrington 1E3

**Sydney House Car Park**, South Street. **GPS**: n50,95121 w4,14438.⬆.

20⌐£5 18-10h, £3 day. 🚗 **Location:** Urban, simple, quiet.
**Surface:** asphalted. ◻ 01/01-31/12.
**Distance:** 🚶300m ⊗250m 🚉250m.
**Remarks:** Max. 2 nights, min. 6m space between motorhomes.

## Westward Ho! 1E3

**Main Car Park**, Golf Links Rd. **GPS**: n51,04069 w4,23728.⬆.

UK

8 ⊠£7, 01/11-14/03 £3, night £5. 🚐 **Location:** Urban, simple, central, quiet. **Surface:** asphalted. ⬜ 01/01-31/12.
**Distance:** 🚲on the spot ⛽200m ⊗200m 🍴on the spot.
**Remarks:** Max. 2 nights, max. 5000kg, min. 6m space between motorhomes.

### Whaplode St Catherines    1G2

**The Bleu Bell Inn**, Cranesgate S. **GPS:** n52,75956 w0,0155.⬆.
5 ⊠£5, free with a meal 🚰Ch 🔧(2x)£ 2,50/night.🚿
**Location:** Simple. ⬜ 01/01-31/12 ⬤ Mo.
**Distance:** ⊗on the spot.

### Winchester    1G3

**Coach Park**, Worthy Lane, B3044. **GPS:** n51,06931 w1,31628.

10 ⊠£7, overnight stay free. 🚐
**Location:** Urban, simple. **Surface:** asphalted.
**Distance:** 🚲850m ⊗500m 🚌50m.
**Remarks:** Max. 24h.

### Yeovil    1F3

**Cartgate and Picnic Area**, A303/A3088 roundabout.
**GPS:** n50,96926 w2,74087.⬆.

20 ⊠free WC 📶Password at the restaurant. **Location:** Motorway, simple, noisy. **Surface:** asphalted. ⬜ 01/01-31/12.
**Distance:** 🚲15km ⊗on the spot.

### York    1G1

**Bleak House Farm**, 138 Mitchel's Ln. **GPS:** n53,93928 w1,05883.

5 ⊠£8 🚰Chincluded. **Location:** Rural. **Surface:** grassy.
⬜ 01/01-31/12.
**Distance:** 🚲3km 🚌1km 🚌200m 🚲 on the spot 🚶 on the spot.

# Jersey

### Saint Peter    15A2

**Hideaway Motorhome Stopover**, Beaumont Hill.
**GPS:** n49,20084 w2,16652.
5 ⊠€ 16 🚰Ch 🔧(5x)included.
**Surface:** gravel/sand. ⬜ 01/01-31/12.
**Distance:** ⛱900m 🚲900m ⊗800m 🚌900m 🚌800m 🚲800m
🚶800m.
**Remarks:** Adults only.

UK

INDEX